PREFACE TO THE SEVENTH EDITION

It gives us great pleasure and satisfaction to present this thoroughly revised and enlarged edition before the readers. An attempt has been made to correct all errors and omissions. While revising the book, due consideration has been given to the valuable suggestions made by the students and teachers of the subject. Almost every chapter has been updated by adding to/replacing the material in the previous edition. The chapter on Statistical Quality Control has been thoroughly revised. Many new exercises from the latest examination papers of various Indian Universities/Engineering. Institutions have been included. The book now covers question papers up to 2013 examinations.

We are indebted to the publishers, S. Chand & Company Pvt. Ltd., New Delhi for their sincere efforts, unfailing courtsey and cooperation in bringing out the book in this elegant form.

We hope the readers will find this book even more valuable and interesting than its earlier versions. Any constructive suggestions for further improvement of the book will be highly appreciated and thankfully acknowledged.

Prem Kumar Gupta
D.S. Hira

PREFACE TO THE FIRST EDITION

For more than thirty years, a new branch of science called Operations Research has been fast developing. The essence of Operations Research are models which help us arrive at optimum decisions. It is these models which constitute the subject matter of this book.

While writing on Operations Research a particular problem may be approached in many different ways. Thus, the exposition may be intended for mathematicians, economists, engineers, sociologists, etc. This book is written primarily for engineering graduates.

This book is simply an introduction to the vast subject of Operations Research. Efforts have been made to simplify the technical material without distorting it. The book does not require a high level of mathematical knowledge on the part of the reader. An elementary knowledge of differential and integral calculus is all that is required to understand the subject.

Each chapter begins with a number of important and interesting examples taken from a variety of fields. Almost every problem presents a new idea. The authors feel that knowing the various fields in which a model can help, the reader will gather more interest and incentive to know its theoretical and mathematical background and method of application. Additional examples at the end of each chapter are provided to test the reader's understanding of the subject matter.

Every effort has been made to present the subject in a easy, clear, lucid and systematic manner References at the end of each chapter are given to cover more advanced extension of the topics presented.

The authors express their deep gratitude and thanks to Shri T.K. Kundra, Design Engineer, I.D.D.C., I.I.T., New Delhi for his inspiration, valuable suggestions, guidance and help every moment they sought.

The authors also deeply appreciate Shri Pritam Singh and Shri Bau Singh for the time, effort, excellent work and most of all, patience in typing the manuscript and preparing tracings respectively.

Suggestions for further improvement of the book will be gratefully accepted.

Prem Kumar Gupta
D.S. Hira

OPERATIONS RESEARCH

For Engineering, Computer Science, Commerce & Management, Economics, Statistics, Mathematics, CA, ICWA and CS. Also Useful for IAS and Other Competitive Examinations.

PREM KUMAR GUPTA

B Sc (Hons.)-Mech. Engg., M Sc-Mech. Engg. (Distinction), M.I.E. (India)
Formerly Assistant Professor
P.E.C. Institute of Engineering and Technology (Deemed University)
Chandigarh

D S HIRA

B Sc -Mech. Engg., M Sc -Mech. Engg., Ph.D. (Roorkee)
Director General
Swami Vivekanand Group of Institutes, Banur, Distt. Patiala, Punjab

S Chand And Company Limited

(ISO 9001 Certified Company)

S Chand And Company Limited

(ISO 9001 Certified Company)

Head Office: Block B-1, House No. D-1, Ground Floor, Mohan Co-operative Industrial Estate, New Delhi – 110 044 | Phone: 011-66672000

Registered Office: A-27, 2nd Floor, Mohan Co-operative Industrial Estate, New Delhi – 110 044 Phone: 011-49731800

www.**schandpublishing.com**; e-mail: **info@schandpublishing.com**

Branches

Chennai : Ph: 23632120; chennai@schandpublishing.com
Guwahati : Ph: 2738811, 2735640; guwahati@schandpublishing.com
Hyderabad : Ph: 40186018; hyderabad@schandpublishing.com
Jalandhar : Ph: 4645630; jalandhar@schandpublishing.com
Kolkata : Ph: 23357458, 23353914; kolkata@schandpublishing.com
Lucknow : Ph: 4003633; lucknow@schandpublishing.com
Mumbai : Ph: 25000297; mumbai@schandpublishing.com
Patna : Ph: 2260011; patna@schandpublishing.com

First Edition 1976
Subsequent Editions and Reprints 1983, 86, 87, 89, 90, 92, 93, 95, 96, 97, 98, 99, 2000, 2001, 2002, 2003, 2004, 2005, 2006, 2007, 2008, 2009 (Twice), 2010, 2011, 2012 (Twice), 2013 (Twice), 2014 (Twice), 2016, 2018, 2019, 2020

Reprint 2021 (Twice)

ISBN: 978-81-219-0281-6 **Product Code:** H3OPR62ORSR10ENAG0XO

PRINTED IN INDIA

By Vikas Publishing House Private Limited, Plot 20/4, Site-IV, Industrial Area Sahibabad, Ghaziabad – 201 010 and Published by S Chand And Company Limited, A-27, 2nd Floor, Mohan Co-operative Industrial Estate, New Delhi – 110 044.

CONTENTS

Basics of Operations Research

The main purpose of this book is to provide the reader with basic concepts of operations research (abbreviated to OR). The subject is so vast that in any introductory text, such as this, the discussion of various topics has got to be limited. Complete volumes have b2een written on some of the topics discussed here. Attempt has been made to present a variety of material within a limited structure. References are indicated at the end to provide the reader with exhaustive treatment of the different topics.

This chapter provides an overall view of the subject of operations research. It covers some general ideas on the subject, thus providing a perspective. The remaining chapters deal with specific ideas and specific methods of solving OR problems.

1.1 DEVELOPMENT OF OPERATIONS RESEARCH

(*i*) *Pre-World War II:* No science has ever been born on a specific day. Operations research is no exception. Its roots are as old as science and society. Though the roots of OR extend to even early 1800s, it was in 1885 when Ferderick W. Taylor emphasised the application of scientific analysis to methods of production, that the real start took place. Taylor conducted experiments in connection with a simple shovel. His aim was to find that weight load of ore moved by shovel which would result in maximum of ore moved with minimum of fatigue. After many experiments with varying weights, he obtained the optimum weight load, which though much lighter than that commonly used, provided maximum movement of ore during a day. For a "first-class man" the proper load turned out to be 20 pounds. Since the density of ores differs greatly, a shovel was designed for each ore so as to assume the proper weight when the shovel was correctly filled. Productivity rose substantially after this change.

Another man of early scientific management era was Henry L. Gantt. Most job-scheduling methods at that time were rather haphazard. A job, for instance, may be processed on a machine without trouble but then wait for days for acceptance by the next machine. Gantt mapped each job from machine to machine, minimizing every delay. Now, with the Gantt procedure it is possible to plan machine loadings months in advance and still quote delivery dates accurately.

The well-known economic lot size model is attributed to F.W. Harris, who published his work on the area of inventory control in 1915.

In 1917, A.K. Erlang, a Danish mathematician, published his work on the problem of congestion of telephone traffic. The difficulty was that during busy periods, telephone operators were unable to handle the calls the moment they were made, resulting in delayed calls. A few years after its appearance, his work was accepted by the British Post Office as the basis for calculating circuit facilities. The formulae he developed on waiting time are of fundamental importance to the theory of telephone traffic.

During the 1930s, H.C. Levinson, an American astronomer, applied scientific analysis to the problems of merchandising. His work included scientific study of customers' buying habits, response to advertising and relation of environment to the type of article sold.

However, it was the First Industrial Revolution which contributed mainly towards the development of OR. Before this revolution, most of the industries were small scale, employing only a handful of men. The advent of machine tools — the replacement of man by machine as a *source of power* and improved means of transportation and communication resulted in fast flourishing industry. It became increasingly difficult for a single man to perform all the managerial functions (or planning, sale, purchase, production, etc.). Consequently, *a division of management function took place.* Managers of production, marketing, finance, personnel, research and development etc., began to appear. With further industrial growth, further subdivisions of management functions took place. For example, production department was subdivided into sections like maintenance, quality control, procurement, production planning, etc.

This industrial development, brought with it, a new type of problems called executive-type problems. These problems are a direct consequence of functional division of labour in an organization. In an organization, each functional unit (department or section) performs a part of the whole job and for its successful working, develops its own objectives. These objectives, though in the best interest of the individual department, may not be in the best interest of the organization as a whole. In fact, these objectives of individual departments may be inconsistent and clashing with each other. Consider, for example, the attitudes of the various departments of a business organization towards the inventory policy. The production department wants to have maximum production, associated with the lowest possible cost. This can be achieved by producing only one item continuously. Thus it is interested in long, uninterrupted production runs, because such runs minimise set-up and clean-up costs. Thus it prefers to have a large inventory in relatively few product lines.

The marketing department also wants a large but diverse inventory so that a customer may be provided immediate delivery over a wide variety of products. It would also like to have a flexible production policy so as to meet special demands at a short notice.

The finance department wants to minimize inventory so as to minimize the unproductive capital investments 'tied up' in it. Funds could be used elsewhere for better returns. It also believes that inventories should rise and fall with rise and fall in company's sales.

The personnel department wants to hire good labour and to retain it. This is possible only when goods are produced continuously for inventory during slack periods also. In other words, it is interested in maintaining a constant production level, resulting in large inventory.

To set an inventory policy which serves the interest of the organization as a whole and not that of any individual department is an executive-type problem, which can be satisfactorily solved by the application of OR techniques. The decision which is in the best interest of the organization as a whole is called *optimal* (*optimum or global optimum*) *decision* and the one in the best interest of an individual department is called *sub-optimal decision.*

(*ii*) *World War II:* During World War II, the military management in England called on a team of scientists to study the strategic and tactical problems of air and land defence. This team was under the direction of Professor P.M.S. Blackett of Univ. of Manchester and a former naval officer. "Blackett's circus", as the group was called, included three physiologists, two mathematical physicists, one astrophysicist, one army officer, one surveyor, one general physicist and two mathematicians. Many of these problems were of executive-type. The objective was to find out the most effective allocation of limited military resources to the various military operations and to the activities within each operation. The application included the effective use of newly invented radar, allocation of British Air Force Planes to missions and the determination of best patterns for searching submarines. This group of scientists formed the *first OR team.*

The name *operations research* (*or operational research*) was apparently coined in 1940 because the team was carrying out research on (military) operations. The encouraging results of these efforts led to the formation of more such teams in British Armed Services and the use of such scientific teams soon spread to Western Allies — the United States, Canada and France. Thus though this science of operations research originated in England, the United States soon took the lead. In United States these OR teams helped in developing strategies for mining operations, inventing new flight patterns and planning of sea mines.

(*iii*) *Post-World War II:* Immediately after the war, the success of military teams attracted the attention of industrial managers who were seeking solutions to their problems. Industrial operations research in U.K. and U.S.A. developed along different lines. In U.K. the critical economic situation required drastic increase in production efficiency and creation of new markets. Nationalisation of a few key industries further increased the potential field for OR. Consequently OR soon spread from military to government, industrial, social and economic planning.

In U.S.A. the situation was different. Impressed by its dramatic success in U.K., defence operations research in U.S.A. was increased. Most of the war-experienced OR workers remained in military services. Industrial executives did not call for much help because they were returning to the peace-time situation and many of them believed that it was merely a new application of an old technique. Operations research has been known by a variety of names in that country such as operational analysis, operations evaluation, systems analysis, systems evaluation, systems research, decision analysis, quantitative analysis, decision science and management science.

The progress of industrial operations research in U.S.A. was due to the advent of Second Industrial Revolution which resulted in *automation — the replacement of man by machine as a source of control.* The new revolution began around 1940s when electronic computers became commercially available. These electronic brains possessed tremendous computational speed and information storage. But for these digital computers, operations research with its complex computational problems could not have achieved its promising place in all kinds of operational environments.

In 1950, OR was introduced as a subject for academic study in American Universities. They were generally schools of engineering, public administration, business management, applied mathematics, economics, computer science, etc. Since then this subject has been gaining ever increasing importance for the students of Mathematics, Statistics, Commerce, Economics, Management and Engineering. To increase the impact of operations research, the Operations Research Society of America (ORSA) was formed in 1950. In 1953, the Institute of Management Sciences (IMS) was established. Other countries followed suit and in 1959 International Federation of OR Societies was established and in many countries International Journals on OR began to appear. Some of them (in English) are:

1. Operations Research, 2. Opsearch, 3. Operational Research Quarterly, 4. Management Science, 5. Transportation Science, 6. Mathematics of Operations Research, 7. International Journal of Game Theory, 8. Decision Science, etc.

Today, the impact of operations research can be felt in many areas. This is shown by the ever increasing number of educational institutions offering this subject at degree level. The fast increasing number of management consulting firms speaks of the pouplarity of the subject. Of late, OR activities have spread to diverse fields such as hospitals, libraries, city planning, transportation systems, crime investigation, energy conservation, environmental pollution, etc. Some of the Indian organisations using OR techniques are: Indian Airlines, Railways, Defence Organizations, Fertilizer Corporation of India, Delhi Cloth Mills, Tata Iron and Steel Co., etc.

Operations Research in India

In India, operations research came into existence with the opening of an OR unit in 1949 at the Regional Research Laboratory in Hyderabad. At the same time another OR unit was set up at the then Defence Science Laboratory to tackle the problems of stores, purchase and weapon evaluation. An OR unit under Professor P.C. Mahalonobis was established in 1953 in the Indian Statistical Institute, Kolkata to apply OR methods in national planning and survey. Operations Research Society of India (ORSI) was formed in 1957 and its first conference was held in Delhi in 1959. It was felt that there existed the need of producing well-trained operations researchers who could tackle practical problems. It was also decided to bring out a journal on operations research, the first volume of which came out in 1963 with the name 'Opsearch'. Some other Indian journals promoting the cause of operations research are 'Industrial Engineering and Management', 'Materials Management Journal of India', 'Defence Science Journal', 'Journal of the Indian Society of Statistics and Operations Research' (ISSOR), 'Pure and Applied Mathematika Sciences' (PAMS), etc.

Professor Mahalonobis made the first important application of OR in India in preparing the draft of the Second Five Year Plan. The Draft Plan frame is still the most scientifically formulated plan bearing programmes of massive economic development of India. It was estimated that India could become self-sufficient in food merely by reducing its wastage by 15%.

For academic studies, the first M.Sc. Course on OR was started by Delhi University in 1963. At the same time, Indian Institutes of Management at Kolkata and Ahmedabad introduced OR in their MBA courses. At present, this subject has been introduced in almost all Institutes and Universities for the students of Mathematics, Statistics, Commerce, Economics, Management and Engineering. Realising the importance of OR in Accounts and Administration, the government has introduced this subject for CA, ICWA and IAS examinations.

In the Industrial Sector, organised industries in India are becoming conscious of the role of operations research and a good number of them have well-trained OR teams. Some of Indian organisations, using OR techniques are: Indian Airlines, Railways, Defence Organisations, Fertiliser Corporation of India, Hindustan Steel Ltd., Tata Iron and Steel Co., TELCO, DCM, CSIR, STC, BHEL, SAIL, ONGC, etc. Assignment models have been used by Kirloskar company for allocation of their salesmen to different areas so as to maximize the profit. The company has also used linear programming models to assemble various diesel engines at the lowest possible cost. D.C.M., Calico and Binnys' have been using linear programming techniques for cotton blending. Many organisations are making use of PERT/CPM techniques for effective management and control of their construction projects. A number of organisations are utilising OR techniques for solving problems relating to staffing, production planning, blending, product mix, maintenance, inspection, advertising, capital budgeting, investment and the like.

1.2 DEFINITION OF OPERATIONS RESEARCH

Operations research, rather simply defined, is the research of operations. An operation may be called a set of acts required for the achievement of a desired outcome. Such complex, inter-related acts can be performed by four types of systems: Man, Machine, Man-Machine unit and any organisation of men, machines, and man-machine units. OR is concerned with the operations of the last type of system.

Many definitions of OR have been suggested from time to time. On the other hand are put forward a number of arguments as to why it cannot be defined. Perhaps the subject has too wide scope of applications to be defined in a precise manner. Also it is not easy to define operations research as it is not a science representing any well-defined social, biological or physical phenomenon. Some of the different definitions suggested are:

(1) OR is a *scientific method* of providing executive departments with a *quantitative basis* for decisions regarding the operations under their control. —Morse & Kimball

(2) OR, in the most general sense, can be characterised as the application of *scientific methods, tools and techniques* to problems involving the *operations of systems* so as to provide those in control of the operations with optimum solutions to the problems.

—Churchman, Ackoff, Arnoff

(3) Operations research is applied *decision theory*. It uses any *scientific, mathematical or logical means* to attempt to cope with the problems that confront the executive when he tries to achieve a thorough going rationality in dealing with his decision problems.

—Miller and Starr

(4) Operations research is a *scientific approach* to problem solving for executive management.

—H.M.Wagner

(5) Operations research is the art of giving *bad answers* to problems, to which, otherwise, *worse answers* are given.

—Thomas L. Saaty

(6) Operations research is the *art of winning wars without actually fighting them.*

—Auther Clark

(7) Operations research is an aid for the executive in making his decisions by providing him with the needed *quantitative information* based on the *scientific method of analysis.*

—C.Kittel

(8) Operations research is the *systematic, method-oriented* study of the basic structure, characteristics, functions and relationships of an organization to provide the executive with a *sound, scientific and quantitative basis* for decision-making.

—E.L. Arnoff & M.J. Netzorg

(9) Operations research is the application of *scientific methods* to problems arising from operations involving *integrated systems of men, machines and materials.* It normally utilizes the knowkedge and skill of an *interdisciplinary research team* to provide the managers of such systems with *optimum operating solutions.* —Fabrycky & Torgersen

(10) Operations research is an experimental and applied science devoted to observing, understanding and predicting the behaviour of purposeful man-machine systems; and operations research workers are actively engaged in applying this knowledge to practical problems in business, government and society.

—Operations Research Society of America

(11) Operations research is the application of *scientific method* by *interdisciplinary teams* to problems involving the control of organized (man-machine) systems so as to provide solutions which *best serve the purpose of the organization as a whole.*

—Ackoff & Sasieni

(12) Operations research utilizes the planned approach (*updated scientific method*) and an *interdisciplinary team* in order to represent complex functional relationships as mathematical models for the purpose of providing a *quantitative basis* fo decision-making and *uncovering new problems* for quantitative analysis.

—Thierauf & Klekamp

The most comprehensive and modern definition of operations research can be summarised as below:

(13) O.R. is the application of modern methods of *mathematical science* to *complex problems* involving *management* of large systems of men, machines, materials and money in industry, business, government and defence. The distinctive approach is to develop a *scientific model* of the system incorporating measurement of factors such as *chance and risk* to predict and compare the outcomes of *alternative decisions, strategies or controls.*

—J.O.R. Society, U.K.

It may be noted that most of the above definitions are not satisfactory because of the following reasons:

(*i*) They have been suggested at different times of development of operations research and hence emphasize only its one or the other aspect.

(*ii*) The interdisciplinary approach which is an important characteristic of operations research is not included in most of its definitions.

(*iii*) It is not easy to define operations research precisely as it is not a science repesenting any well-defined social, biological or physical phenomenon.

1.3 CHARACTERISTICS OF OPERATIONS RESEARCH

The various definitions of operations research presented in section 1.2 bring out the essential characteristics of operations research. They are

(*i*) its system (or executive) orientation,

(*ii*) the use of interdisciplinary teams,

(*iii*) application of scientific method,

(*iv*) uncovering of new problems,

(*v*) improvement in the quality of decisions,

(*vi*) use of computer,

(*vii*) quantitative solutions, and

(*viii*) human factors.

Let us consider each of these in some detail.

1.3-1 System (or Executive) Orientation of OR

One of the most important characteristics of OR study is its concern with problems as a whole or its system orientation. This means that an activity by any part of an organization has some effect on the activity of every other part. The optimum operation of one part of a system may not be the optimum operation for some other part. Therefore, to evaluate any decision, one must identify all possible interactions and determine their impact on the organization as a whole.

Many problems that appear simple on the surface may not be really so. Take, for example, the inventory policy of an organization, already considered in section 1.1. Production department is interested in long, uninterrupted production runs since they reduce the set-up and clean-up costs. To solve the porblem with this viewpoint is simple. However, these long runs will result in large raw material, in-process and finished product inventories in relatively few product lines. This will result in bitter conflict with finance, marketing and personnel departments. As already discussed finance department wants to have the minimum possible inventory; marketing department, a large but diversified inventory, while personnel department wants continuous production during slack periods also, resulting in large inventories.

In view of the above difficulties, it is necessary that the problem be analysed with painstaking care and all parts of the organization affected be thoroughly examined. When all factors affecting the system (organization) are known, a *mathematical model* can be prepared. A solution to this model will optimize the profits to the system as a whole. Such a solution is called an *optimal* (*optimum or global optimum*) *solution.*

1.3-2 The Use of Interdisciplinary Teams

The second characteristic of OR study is that it is performed by a team of scientists whose individual members have been drawn from different scientific and engineering disciplines. For example, one may find a mathematician, statistician, physicist, psychologist, economist and an engineer working together on an OR problem.

It has been recognised beyond doubt that people from different disciplines can produce more unique solutions with greater probability of success, than could be expected from the same number of persons from a single discipline. For example, when confronted with the problem of increasing production in a plant, the personnel psychologist will try to select better workers or improve their training; the mechanical engineer will try to improve the machines; the industrial engineer will try to simplify the operations or offer incentives; while the systems analyst will try to improve the flow of information through the plant. Thus the OR team can look at the problem from many different angles in order to determine which one (or which combination) of approaches is the best.

Another reason for the existence of OR teams is that knowledge is increasing at a very fast rate. No single person can collect all the useful scientific information from all disciplines. Different members of the OR team bring the latest scientific know-how in different disciplines to analyse the problem and help in providing better results.

1.3-3 Application of Scientific Method

The third distinguishing feature of OR is the use of scientific method to solve the problem under study. Most scientific research, such as chemistry and physics can be carried out well in the laboratories, under controlled conditions, without much interference from the outside world. However, the same is not true for the systems under study by OR teams. For example, no company can risk its failure in order to conduct a successful experiment. Though, experimentation on subsystems is sometimes resorted to, by and large, a research approach that does not involve experimentation on the total system is preferred.

An operations research worker is in the same position as the astronomer, since the latter can observe the system that he studies, but cannot manipulate it. Therefore, he constructs *representations of the systems and its operations* (*models*) on which he conducts his research. An OR worker also does the same. The construction of a model is described in section 1.12-2 and the reader may refer it for further details.

1.3-4 Uncovering of New Problems

The fourth characteristic of operations research, which is often overlooked, is that solution of an OR problem may uncover a number of new problems. Of course, all these uncovered problems need not be solved at the same time. However, in order to derive maximum benefit, each one of them must be solved. It must be remembered that OR is not effectively used if it is restricted to one-shot problems only. In order to derive full benefits, continuity of research must be maintained. Of course, the results of OR study pertaining to a particular problem need not wait until all the connected problems are solved.

1.3-5 Improvement in the Quality of Decisions

OR gives bad answers to problems, to which, otherwise, worse answers are given. It implies that by applying its scientific approach, it can only improve the quality of solution but it may not be able to give perfect solution.

1.3-6 Use of Computer

Another characteristic of OR is that it often requires a computer to solve the complex mathematical model or to manipulate a large amount of data or to perform a large number of computations that are involved.

1.3-7 Quantitative Solutions

OR approach provides the management with a quantitative basis for decision-making. For example it will give answer like, "the cost to the company, if decision A is taken is X; if decision B is taken is Y, etc."

1.3-8 Human Factors

In deriving quantitative solutions we do not consider human factors, which doubtlessly play a great role in the problems posed. Definitely an OR study is incomplete without a study of human factors.

1.4 SCIENTIFIC METHOD IN OPERATIONS RESEARCH

The scientific method in operations research consists of the following three phases:

(*i*) the judgement phase,

(*ii*) the research phase, and

(*iii*) the action phase.

Out of these, the research phase is the longest. However, the other two phases are also equally important as they provide the basis of the research phase. We shall now consider these phases in a little more detail.

1.4-1 The Judgement Phase

It consists of:

(*a*) *Determination of the operation:* An operation is a combination of different actions dealing with resources (*e.g.*, men and machines) which form a structure from which an action with regard to broader objectives is attained. For example, the act of assembling an engine is an operation. It consists of many actions which contribute towards the completed assembly. Any conceivable operation will always be associated with problems of its successful completion.

(*b*) *Determination of objectives and values associated with the operation:* In the judgement phase, due care must be given to define correctly the frame of references of the operation. Efforts should be made to find the type of situation, *e.g.*, manufacturing, engineering, tactical, strategic, etc. The amount of risk involved, other areas affected by the solution, etc., must be determined. Objectives and values, whether economic, social or aesthetic should be carefully determined so as to have a clear approach to the solution of the problem. Further, one must determine the time limits for finding the solution, degree of accuracy desired in the results as well as necessity of feedback of the obtained information into the operation.

(*c*) *Determination of effectiveness measures:* Effectiveness measure (or measure of effectiveness) is a measure of success of a model in representing a problem and providing a solution. It is the connecting link between the objectives and the analysis required for corrective action. It tests the success of a solution and determines if there is need for improving the method of attack or even of altering the solution. Measure of effectiveness may be expressed as ratio or rate. For example, in traffic studies it may be expressed in terms of cars per hour, cars per accident or delay per car; in bombing of ships it may be expressed as the number of hits per bomb, number of ships sunk per bomb, etc. Effectiveness measure must be chosen properly, since an improper choice may result in completely wrong conclusions about the problem.

(*d*) *Formulation of the problem relative to the objectives:* Since every operation is study with problems, the operations analyst must determine the type of problem, its origin and causes. Problems are of many types:

1. *Remedial type* with its origin in actual or threatened accidents, *e.g.*, airplane crashes, job performance hazards.
2. *Optimization type, e.g.*, performing a job more efficiently.
3. *Transference type* consisting of applying the new advances, improvements and inventions in one field to other fields. For example, use of isotopes in medicines on one hand (to determine the rate of absorption of substances in certain parts of human body) and in machinery on the other (for testing wearing qualities in automobile tyres).

4. *Prediction type, e.g.*, forecasting the problems associated with future developments and inventions.

Before selecting a problem for investigation, careful thought must be given to find whether the problem really exists. Hasty selection of problems often leads to wastage of time (devoted by the analyst) and wrong results.

1.4-2 The Research Phase

It includes

(*a*) *Observation and data collection for better understanding of the problem:* Many a time, actual observations by trained observers at the scene of operation may be difficult and dangerous too. If time permits, operational experiments simulating the actual problem should be set up. Where the information regarding the problem cannot be obtained, the analyst, with the incomplete data at hand, should try to find the missing parts of the problem.

(*b*) *Formulation of relevant hypotheses and models:* Tentative explanations, when formulated as propositions are called *hypotheses.* It is very important to state the hypothesis and its anticipated consequences before starting its verification. The formulation of a good hypothesis depends upon the sound knowledge of subjectmatter. A hypothesis must provide an answer to the problem in question. It must be capable of verification, otherwise, it may be refuted by empirical evidence.

An essential feature of OR is that it considers a problem as an entity rather than a collection of disconnected suboperations. *Model* is the device which treats the problem as a whole; it is essentially a hypothesis. Formulation of models may be based on pure theoretical considerations or on hypothesis derived from known facts and data. The time available for the development of a model is an important factor. For instance, when urgent answers are needed, little will be gained by developing elaborate models. Similarly, for rough estimates, a detailed development of model is only a wastage.

(*c*) *Analysis of available information and verification of hypothesis:* Most of the time that a scientist spends in training is devoted to learning how to analyse and interpret information. Qualitative as well as quantitative methods may be used for this purpose. For example, when it is required to find out work done by a force, a hypothesis is made. It is based on the knowledge of mechanics, giving $W = F \times S$, where S is the distance through which the point of application of the force F moves.

A hypothesis need not be proved for every possibility in order to be acceptable. Sampling methods are usually sufficient to verify it.

(*d*) *Prediction and generalization of results and consideration of alternative methods:* Once a model has been verified, a theory is developed from the model to obtain a complete description of the problem. This is done by studying the effects of changes in the parameters of the model. The theory so developed may be used to extrapolate into the future.

Lastly, the analyst determines the alternative methods of solving the problem and recommends a new research based on revised hypothesis. The advantages of this approach are obvious and need little justification if economic and time factors do not stand in the way.

1.4-3 The Action Phase

The action phase consists of making recommendations for remedial action to those who first posed the problem and who control the operations directly. These recommendations consist of a clear statement of the assumptions made, scope and limitations of the information presented about the situation, alternative courses of action, effects of each alternative as well as the preferred course of action.

A primary function of OR group is to provide an administrator with better understanding of the implications of the decisions he makes. The scientific method supplements his ideas and experiences and helps him to attain his goals more fully.

1.5 NECESSITY OF OPERATIONS RESEARCH IN INDUSTRY

After having studied as to what is operations research, we shall now try to answer as to why study OR or what is its importance or why its need has been felt by the industry.

As already pointed out, science of OR came into existence in connection with the war operations, to decide the strategy by which enemy could be harmed to the maximum possible extent with the help of the available warfare. War situation required reliable decision-making. But its need has been equally felt by the industry due to the following reasons:

(*a*) *Complexity:* In a big industry, the number of factors influencing a decision have increased. Situation has become big and complex because these factors interact with each other in complicated fashion. There is, thus, great uncertainty about the outcome of interaction of factors like technological, environmental, competitive, etc. For instance, consider a factory production schedule which has to take into account

(*i*) customer demand,
(*ii*) requirements of raw materials,
(*iii*) equipment capacity and possibility of equipment failure, and
(*iv*) restrictions on manufacturing processes.

Evidently, it is not easy to prepare a schedule which is both economical and realistic. This needs mathematical models, which, in addition to optimization, help to analyse the complex situation. With such models, complex problems can be split up into simpler parts, each part can be analysed separately and then the results can be synthesized to give insights into the problem.

(*b*) *Scattered responsibility and authority:* In a big industry, responsibility and authority of decision-making is scattered throughout the organization and thus the organization, if it is not conscious, may be following inconsistent goals. *Mathematical quantification* of OR overcomes this difficulty also to a great extent.

(*c*) *Uncertainty:* There is a great uncertainty about economic and general environment. With economic growth, uncertainty is also increasing. This makes each decision costlier and time-consuming. OR is, thus, quite essential from reliability point of view.

(*d*) *Knowledge explosion:* Knowledge is increasing at a very fast rate. Majority of the industries are not up to date with the latest knowledge and are, therefore, at a disadvantage. OR teams collect the latest information for analysis purposes which is quite useful for the industries.

1.6 SCOPE OF OPERATIONS RESEARCH

Having known the definition of OR, it is easy to visualize the scope of operations research. When we broaden the scope of OR, we find that it has really been practised for hundreds of years even before World War II. Whenever there is a problem of optimization, there is scope for the application of OR. Its techniques have been used in a wide range of situations:

1. *In Industry*

In the field of *industrial management,* there is a chain of problems starting from the purchase of raw materials to the dispatch of finished goods. The management is interested in having an overall view of the method of optimizing profits. In order to take decision on scientific basis, OR team will have to consider various alternative methods of producing the goods and the return in each case. OR study should also point out the possible changes in the overall structure like installation of a new machine, introduction of more automation, etc. OR has been successfully applied in *industry* in the fields of production, blending, product mix, inventory control, demand forecast, sale and purchase, transportation, repair and maintenance, scheduling and sequencing, planning, scheduling and control of projects and scores of other associated areas.

2. *In Defence*

OR has a wide scope for application in *defence operations.* In modern warfare the defence operations are carried out by a number of different agencies, namely airforce, army and navy. The activities performed by each of them can be further divided into sub-activities *viz.* operations, intelligence, administration, training and the like. There is thus a need to coordinate the various activities involved in order to arrive at optimum strategy and to achieve consistent goals. Operations research, conducted by team of experts from all the associated fields, can be quite helpful to achieve the desired results.

3. *Planning*

In both *developing and developed economies,* OR approach is equally applicable. In developing economies, there is a great scope of developing an OR approach towards *planning.* The basic problem is to orient the planning so that there is maximum growth of per capita income in the shortest possible time, by taking into consideration the national goals and restrictions imposed by the country. The basic problem in most of the countries in Asia and Africa is to remove poverty and hunger as quickly as possible. There is, therefore, a great scope for economists, statisticians, administrators, technicians, politicians and agriculture experts working together to solve this problem with an OR approach.

4. *Agriculture*

OR approach needs to be equally developed in *agriculture sector* on national or international basis. With population explosion and consequent shortage of food, every country is facing the problem of optimum allocation of land to various crops in accordance with climatic conditions and available facilities. The problem of *optimal distribution of water from the various water resources* is faced by each developing country and a good amount of scientific work can be done in this direction.

5. *Public Utilities*

OR methods can also be applied in big *hospitals* to reduce waiting time of out-door patients and to solve the administrative problems.

Monte Carlo methods can be applied in the area of *transport* to regulate train arrivals and their running times. Queuing theory can be applied to minimize congestion and passengers' waiting time.

OR is directly applicable to *business and society.* For instance, it is increasingly being applied in *L.I.C. offices* to decide the premium rates of various policies. It has also been extensively used in petroleum, paper, chemical, metal processing, aircraft, rubber, transport and distribution, mining and textile industries.

OR approach is equally applicable to big and small *organizations.* For example, whenever a department store faces a problem like employing additional salesgirls, purchasing an additional van, etc., techniques of OR can be applied to minimize cost and maximize benefit for each such decision.

Thus we find that OR has a diversified and wide scope in the social, economic and industrial problems of today.

1.7 OPERATIONS RESEARCH AND DECISION-MAKING

Operations research or management science, as the name suggests, is the science of managing. As is known, management is most of the time making decisions. It is thus a decision science which helps management to make better decisions. Decision is, in fact, a pivotal word in managing. It is not only the headache of management, rather all of us make decisions. We daily decide about minor to major issues. We choose to be engineers, doctors, lawyers, managers, etc.— a vital decision which is going to affect us throughout our lives. We choose to purchase at a particular shop—a decision of relatively minor importance.

Decision-making can be improved and, in fact, there is a scope of large scale improvement. The essential characteristics of all decisions are

(*i*) objectives,

(*ii*) alternatives,

(*iii*) influencing factors (constraints).

Once these characteristics are known, one can think of improving the characteristics so as to improve upon the decision itself.

Let us consider a situation in which a decision has been taken to see a particular movie and the problem is to decide the conveyance. Three alternatives are available: rickshaw, autorickshaw and a local bus.

In the first level of decision-making, autorickshaw is chosen as the mode of conveyance just by intuition, *i.e.*, it is decided at random. Evidently, it is a highly emotional and qualitative way of decision-making.

In the second level of decision-making, the three conveyances are compared and it is decided qualitatively that autorickshaw will be preferred since, though a little costlier, it is time-saving and more comfortable.

In the third level of decision-making, the three alternatives are compared and it is suggested that autorickshaw will be chosen, as it will be taking only 1/3rd time than an ordinary rickshaw and shall be only 10% costlier while more comfortable. The local bus is rejected since it would not reach the theatre in time at all.

Though outcome of all these decisions is the same, still we can judge the quality of each decision. We may brand the first decision as 'bad' since it is highly emotional, while we may call the second decision as 'good' since it is scientific though qualitative. The third decision is doubtlessly the best as it is scientific and quantitative.

It is the *scientific quantification* used in OR, which helps management to make better decisions. Thus in OR, the essential features of decisions, namely, objectives, alternatives and influencing factors are expressed in terms of scientific quantifications or mathematical equations. This gives rise to certain mathematical relations, termed as a whole as *mathematical model.* Thus the essence of OR is such mathematical models. For different situations different models are used and this process is continuing since World War II when the term OR was coined. However, with the advance of science and technology, decision-making in business and industry has become highly complex and extremely difficult. The decision-maker is not only faced with a large number of interacting variables, which at times do not lend themselves to neat quantitative treatment but also finds them too numerous and dynamic. Above all he has to take into consideration the actions of the competitors over which he has no control. This complexity of decision-making made the decision-makers look for various aids in decision-making. It is in these situations that operations research comes to our help. The managers today make full use of the OR techniques in various functional areas. It has been realised beyond doubt that intuition alone has no place in decision-making since such a decision becomes highly questionable when it involves the choice among several alternatives. OR provides the management much needed tools for improving the various decisions.

1.8 SCOPE OF OPERATIONS RESEARCH IN MANAGEMENT

Operations research is a problem-solving and decision-making science. It is a kit of scientific and programmable rules providing the management a 'quantitative basis' for decisions regarding the operations under its control. Some of the areas of management where OR techniques have been successfully applied are:

1. *Allocation and Distribution*

(*a*) Optimal allocation of limited resources such as men, machines, materials, time and money.

(*b*) Location and size of warehouses, distribution centres, retail depots, etc.

(*c*) Distribution policy.

2. *Production and Facility Planning*

(*a*) Selection, location and design of production plants, distribution centres and retail outlets.

(*b*) Project scheduling and allocation of resources.

(*c*) Preparation of forecasts for the various inventory items and computing economic order quantities and reorder levels.

(*d*) Determination of the number and size of the items to be produced.

(*e*) Maintenance policy and preventive maintenance.

(*f*) Scheduling and sequencing of production runs by proper allocation of machines.

3. *Procurement*

(*a*) What, how and when to purchase at the minimum procurement cost.

(*b*) Bidding and replacement policies.

(*c*) Transportation planning and vendor analysis.

4. *Marketing*

(*a*) Product selection, timing and competitive actions.

(*b*) Selection of advertising media.

(*c*) Demand forecasts and stock levels.

(*d*) Customer's preference for size, colour and packaging of various products.

(*e*) Best time to launch a new product.

5. *Finance*

(*a*) Capital requirements, cash-flow analysis.

(*b*) Credit policies, credit risks, etc.

(*c*) Profit plan for the company.

(*d*) Determination of optimum replacement polices.

(*e*) Financial planning, dividend policies, investment and portfolio management, auditing, etc.

6. *Personnel*

(*a*) Selection of personnel, determination of retirement age and skills.

(*b*) Recruitment policies and assignment of jobs.

(*c*) Wage/salary administration.

7. *Research and Development*

(*a*) Determination of areas for research and development.

(*b*) Reliability and control of development projects.

(*c*) Selection of projects and preparation of their budgets.

From all the above areas of applications, it can be concluded that OR can be widely used in taking timely management decisions and can be also used as a corrective measure.

1.9 SCOPE OF OPERATIONS RESEARCH IN FINANCIAL MANAGEMENT

Operations research has wide scope and has been successfully applied in the following areas of financial management:

1. *Cash Management*

A financial manager is responsible for adequate supply of funds to all the sections, departments and units of the organisation as adequate funds are essential for their proper function throughout the year. Linear programming techniques are helpful to determine the allocation of funds to each section. L.P. techniques have also been applied to identify sections having excess funds; these funds may be diverted to the sections that need them.

2. *Inventory Control*

In big organisations the amount invested in inventories can run into millions of rupees. Inventory control techniques of OR can help management to develop better inventory policies and bring down the investment in inventories. These techniques help to achieve optimum balance between inventory carrying costs, ordering costs and shortage costs. They help to determine which items to hold, how much to hold, when to order and how much to order.

3. *Simulation Technique*

Simulation considers various factors that affect the present and projected cost of borrowing money from commercial banks, and tax rates, etc. and provides an optimum combination of financing (debt, equity or retained earnings) for the desired amount of capital. Simulation replaces subjective estimates, judgement and hunches of the management by providing reliable information.

4. *Capital Budgeting*

It involves evaluation of various investment proposals (*viz.* market introduction of a new product or replacement of an equipment by a new one). Often the decisions have been made by considering internal rate of return or net present values. These methods, however, do not consider the risk factor in the venture. Risk factors can be calculated if the probability distributions of cash flows can be ascertained, say from past data. Hiller's and Hertz's models (simulation) and decision trees in conjunction with EMV (Expected Monetary Value) can be usefully employed to evaluate the various investment proposals/projects. OR techniques of linear programming, integer programming and dynamic programming have also been useful in selection of optimal investment portfolios (with or without estimates of risk).

1.10 APPLICATIONS OF VARIOUS OR TECHNIQUES

Operations research at present finds extensive application in industry, business, government, military and agriculture. Wide variety of industries–namely, airlines, automobiles, transportation, petroleum, coal, chemical, mining, paper, communication, computer, electronics, etc. have made extensive use of OR techniques. Some of the problems to which OR techniques have been successfully applied are:

1. **Linear programming** has been used to solve problems involving assignment of jobs to machines, blending, product mix, advertising media selection, least cost diet, distribution, transportation, investment portfolio selection and many others.
2. **Dynamic programming** has been applied to capital budgeting, selection of advertising media, employment smoothening, cargo loading and optimal routing problems.
3. **Inventory control** models have been used to determine economic order quantities, safety stocks, reorder levels, minimum and maximum stock levels.
4. **Queuing theory** has been helpful to solve problems of traffic congestion, repair and maintenance of broken-down machines, number of service facilities, scheduling and control of air traffic, hospital operations, counters in banks and railway booking agencies.

5. **Decision theory** has been helpful in controlling hurricanes, water pollution, medicine, space exploration, research and development projects.
6. **Network techniques of PERT and CPM** have been used in planning, scheduling and controlling construction of dams, bridges, roads, highways and development and production of aircrafts, ships, computers, etc.
7. **Simulation** has been helpful in a wide variety of probabilistic marketing situations. It has been, for example, used to find NPV (Net Present Value) distribution for the venture of market introduction of a new product.
8. **Replacement theory** has been extensively employed to determine the optimum replacement interval for three types of replacement problems:
   (*a*) replacement of items that deteriorate with time.
   (*b*) replacement of items that do not deteriorate with time but fail suddenly.
   (*c*) staff replacement and recruitment.

Other techniques extensively employed are game theory, statistical quality control, investment analysis, goal programming, etc.

1.11 OBJECTIVES OF OPERATIONS RESEARCH

The industrial growth has brought with it the need for *division of management function* within an organisation. Thus every organisation has in it a number of functional units or departments, each performing a part of the whole job and for its successful working, developing its own policies and objectives. These objectives, though in the best interest of the individual department, may not be in the best interest of the organisation as a whole. In fact, these objectives of the individual departments may be inconsistent and even clashing with each other. In this context reference was made in section 1.1 with regard to the attitudes of the various departments of a business organisation towards its inventory policy. Numerous examples of similar conflicts can be cited. Consider, for instance, the case of economic order quantity where there is a conflict between the acquisition cost and the inventory carrying cost with regard to the batch size with the former decreasing and the latter increasing with the batch size (Fig. 1.1). The total cost curve is cup-shaped. This cup shape as such or reversed is bound to occur whenever there are conflicting costs or conflicting gains. The objective of OR is to minimize the total cost *i.e.*, find the minimum of the cup-shaped cost curve or maxima of the reversed cup-shaped gain curve.

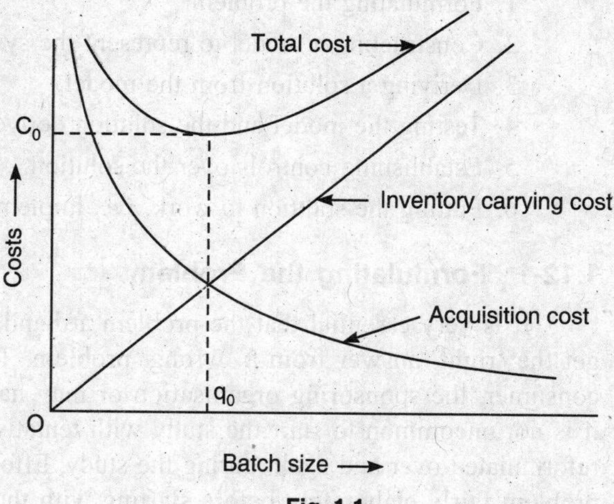

Fig. 1.1

With economic growth uncertainty is also growing. This makes each decision costlier and time-consuming. However, in the competitive world today, one has to take a quick decision because any delay or postponement may only help the competitors. The decision has to be quick as well as scund and this requires a rigorous and scientific approach to the problem. The application of OR methods helps in making decisions in such complex situations. OR combines the knowledge of various disciplines such as mathematics, statistics, economics, psychology and engineering and the combined effort of all these disciplines helps in analysing the problem in finer details.

Two business realities a manager has to face are 'change' and 'uncertainty'. The market demand fluctuates, raw materials and spares become scarce; production equipment fails or the change in Govt.'s policy may affect the company's resources drastically or impose restrictions on the current manufacturing processes. Under such situations past experience can be a (though only a rough) guide. A knowledge of the past data and future trends can help the manager to assess the risk and accordingly make his decisions. OR can help him here. The statistician will analyse the past data and extrapolate it for near future. The accountant will be able to estimate the cost associated with any decision while the engineer will assess the effect of changes in technology, quality of material, and availability of new types of machines.

To summarise, the objective of OR is to provide a scientific basis to the managers of an organisation for solving problems involving interaction of the components of the system, by employing a systems approach by a team of scientists drawn from different disciplines, for finding a solution which is in the best interest of the organisation as a whole.

1.12 PHASES OF OR OR METHODOLOGY OF OR or OR APPROACH or HOW OR WORKS

Operations research, like all scientific research, is based on scientific methodology, which proceeds along the following lines:

1. Formulating the problem.
2. Constructing a model to represent the system under study.
3. Deriving a solution from the model.
4. Testing the model and the solution derived from it.
5. Establishing controls over the solution.
6. Putting the solution to work, *i.e.*, implementation.

1.12-1 Formulating the Problem

It is very essential that the problem at hand be clearly defined. It is almost impossible to get the 'right' answer from a 'wrong' problem. The problem may be set out explicitly by the consumer, the sponsoring organisation or may have to be formulated by the OR team. In OR it is not uncommon to start the study with tentative formulation of the problem, which may be reformulated over and again during the study. Efforts should, however, be made to formulate the problem fairly elaborately before starting with the research. The problem formulation phase is generally lengthy, requiring considerable time and effort; but it is quite justified since, unlike other researches, OR is a search into the operations of a man-machine organisation and must take into consideration the economics of the operations.

In formulating a problem for OR study, analysis must be made of the four major components:

(*a*) the environment,

(*b*) the decision maker,

(*c*) the objectives,

(*d*) alternative courses of action and constraints.

Out of the four components, *environment* is most comprehensive since it embraces and provides a setting for the other three. In general, environment is the framework within which a system of organised activity is directed to attain the prescribed objectives or goals. It involves physical, social and economic factors which may affect the problem under consideration. OR team must study the environment or the organisation content involving men, machines, materials, suppliers, consumers, competitors, the government and the public. Obviously all the contents may not be equally important for a particular problem. For instance, in a price setting problem competitors will be most important, while in a production scheduling problem they may be ignored.

Decision-maker is the second component of the problem. Decision-maker or research consumer or system operator is the person who is in actual control of the operations (system) under study but is not satisfied with the existing state of affairs. Before OR approach can be successful, the operations researcher (operations analyst) must study the decision-maker and his relationship to the problem at hand.

Objectives are the third component of the problem to which analysis must be made. Objectives should be defined by taking into account the system (problem) as a whole. A common error is to identify the objectives, considering only a portion of the entire system. Under such conditions, what is considered best for this portion of the system, may actually prove harmful for the entire system. OR tries to take into account as broad a scope of objectives as possible.

Direct questioning of the decision-maker may not bring out all the objectives. Management, for example, may like to shift the plant in order to avoid an area of strong union influence. Often probing becomes necessary since the decision-maker is normally vague about the objectives and outcomes.

Alternatives are the final components of the problem. The research problem is to determine which alternative course of action is most effective to achieve a certain set of objectives. Others affected by the decisions under study should also be identified.

Further still, counteractions may be listed down *i.e.*, the expected reactions of the competitors to a particular course of action of the decision-maker must be noted. It may be easy to know them by interviews of the workers and public, if involved; but may be pretty difficult in the case of competitors.

The above list of objectives, courses of actions and alternatives may be too lengthy and may require *editing*. Firstly, the intermediate objectives *i.e.*, objectives which are not end in themselves but means to others already in the list, may be dropped from further consideration. For example, for maximising profits, reduction in production cost is a pre-requisite and may, therefore, be dropped out. Secondly, the objectives which remain unaffected by changing the courses of action are not important for further study and may be omitted. Thirdly, any duplication of the objectives must be carefully avoided.

Similar screening may be carried out for the courses of action. Technical feasibility, past experience, legal and social obligations may dictate the exclusion of some courses of action.

Once the modified list of objectives, alternative courses of actions and counteractions is ready, and the OR team has studied the environment (organisational content and structure) and identified the decision-maker, the problem can be taken up for further research.

There must be complete agreement on these points between the persons initiating the OR study (oprations researchers) and the persons performing these operations (system operators). In addition, a measure of effectiveness must be agreed upon by the parties involved.

1.12-2 Constructing a Model for the Problem Under Study

After formulating the problem, the next step is to construct a model for the system under study. In OR study, it is usually a mathematical model. A mathematical model consists of a set of equations which describe the system or problem. These equations represent : (*i*) the *effectiveness function* and (*ii*) *constraints*. The effectiveness function, usually called the *objective function* is a mathematical expression of the objectives, *i.e.*, mathematical expression of the cost or profit of the operation. *Constraints* or *restrictions* are mathematical expressions of the limitations on the fulfillment of the objectives. They are caused by the limited resources such as manpower, materials, money, equipment, space, etc.

The objective function and constraints are functions of two types of variables, *controllable* (also called *decision*) variables and *uncontrollable* variables. A variable that is directly under the control of the operations analyst is called controllable variable; the values of these variables are to be determined from the solution of the problem. For example in inventory control problems, the controllable (decision) variables are the order (batch) size and the interval between orders. A variable that is a function of the external environment and over which the operations analyst has no control, is called uncontrollable variable or *state of nature.* For instance in transportation problems, the per unit transportation cost is an uncontrollable variable. The general form of a mathematical model is

Optimize (maximize or minimize) $Z = f(x_1, x_2, ..., x_n)$,

subject to the constraints $g_i\,(x_1, x_2, ..., x_n) \leq, =, \geq b_i$,

and $x_1, x_2, ..., x_n \geq 0$,

where $x_1, x_2, ..., x_n$ = controllable or decision variables,

$f(x_1, x_2, ... x_n)$ = effectiveness function to be optimized,

$g_i\,(x_1, x_2, ..., x_n)$ = the ith constraint,

b_i = amount of the ith resource (which is uncontróllable),

and i = 1, 2, ..., m.

It must not be forgotten that a model is only an *approximation* of the reality (real situation). Hence it may not include all the variables. This is often misunderstood by those who are not familiar with the OR approach.

A model helps to analyse a system without the inerruption of the latter. It makes the problem more meaningful and clarifies important relationships among the variables. It also tells as to which of the variables are more important than the others. Once a model is formulated, it is possible to analyse the problem.

The next thing after the model has been constructed is to collect the data required by that model *i.e.*, to select the inputs. This information may be obtained from well-kept records, from current tests and experiments or even from hunches based on experience. Data collection is not a trivial step in decision-making process. It can affect the model's output significantly. Never assume that a problem is solved once the objectives are defined and the model is prepared. A medium-sized linear programming model with 50 decision variables and 25 constraints will have over 1300 data elements which must be defined! It requires painstaking effort and time to collect these data if the data collection errors are to be kept minimum.

1.12-3 Deriving Solution from the Model

A solution may be extracted from a model either by conducting experiments on it, *i.e.*, by *simulation* or by *mathematical analysis.* Some cases may require the use of a combination of simulation and mathematical analysis. This depends upon the nature and complexity of the system under study.

Mathematical analysis for deriving an *optimum* solution from a model consists of two types of procedures: *analytic* and *numerical.*

1. *Analytic procedures (solutions)*

They make use of the various branches of mathematics such as calculus or matrix algebra. For example, optimal solution to the E.O.Q. model can be obtained by simple application of differential calculus. Finite differences are helpful to solve replacement problems. Quite often some constraints (such as availability of storage space in case of E.O.Q. models) complicate the solution procedure. Nevertheless, the method of Lagrangian multipliers can be used to solve such problems too. In fact, the range of solution techniques is as wide as that of the problems. However, numerical solutions in some cases may be simpler than the strictly analytic procedures.

2. *Numerical procedures (solutions)*

A numerical procedure consists of trying various values of controllable variables in the model, comparing the results obtained and selecting that set of values of these variables which gives the best solution. These procedures vary from simple trial and error to complex *iteration.* During an iteration, successive trials of controllable variables tend to approach an optimum solution.

The algorithm starts with a trial (initial) solution and continues following a set of rules that improve it towards optimality. The trial solution is replaced by the improved one and the procedure is repeated till either no further improvement is possible or the cost of further computations is too high to justify.

3. *Monte Carlo methods (Simulation methods)*

Simulation is a quantitative procedure which describes a process by developing a model of that process and then conducting a series of organised trial and error experiments to predict the behaviour of the process over time. To find how the real process will react to certain changes, we introduce these changes in the model and simulate the reaction of the real process to them. For example, in designing an aircraft, its scale model is prepared and its behaviour is observed by testing it in a wind tunnel.

The Monte Carlo method is the earliest method of simulation; the method employs random numbers and is used to solve problems that involve probability wherein physical experimentation is not possible and mathematical formulation is too difficult. It is a method of simulation by sampling technique. That is, first of all, the probability distribution of the variable under consideration is determined; then a set of random numbers is used to generate a set of values of that variable that have the same distribution characteristics as the actual process. The steps involved in carrying out Monte Carlo simulation are:

(*i*) Select the measure of effectiveness of the problem. This is the element one wants to maximize or minimize. For example, this might be waiting time of customers in a queuing problem or number of items short in an inventory control problem.

(*ii*) Identify the variables that influence the measure of effectiveness significantly. These may be the number of service facilities in the queuing problem or minimum stock level in the inventory control problem.

(*iii*) Determine the probability distribution of each of the variable of interest.

(*iv*) Convert the probability distributions to cumulative probability distributions.

(*v*) Get a set of random numbers from random number table.

(*vi*) With the above random numbers, determine the sequence of values of the variables of interest.

(*vii*) Substitute the values of the variables in the formula chosen for the measure of effectiveness and calculate its value.

(*viii*) Repeat steps (*vi*) and (*vii*) until sample is large enough for the satisfaction of the decision-maker.

Since a model is an approximation of the real system or problem, the optimum solution for the model does not guarantee an optimum solution for the real problem. However, if the model is well formulated and tested, solution from the model will provide a good approximation to the solution of the real problem. This book is mainly devoted to the study of the various methods for finding these solutions.

1.12-4 Testing the Model and the Solution Derived from it

As already discussed, a model is never a perfect representation of reality. But, if properly formulated and correctly manipulated, it may be useful in predicting the effect of changes in control variables on the overall system effectiveness. The usefulness of a model is tested by determining how well it predicts the effect of these changes. Such an analysis is usually called *sensitivity analysis*. The utility or validity of the solution can be checked by comparing the results obtained without applying the solution with the results obtained when it is used.

The testing may be performed retrospectively. In a forecasting model, forecasts of the (say) immediately preceding 6 months may be compared with the actual demand that had materialised during that period.

Sometimes, considerable time may elapse before the data for testing accumulates. For a new product the forecasts may be made on the basis of demand of another item having similar characteristics. But one would have to wait for the future demand to materialise so that it can be compared with the forecasts. It may be noted that collection and editing of the past data for comparison may sometimes be quite painstaking.

1.12-5 Establishing Controls over the Solution

Life is not static, it is subjected to continuous, unceasing change. A solution which we felt was optimum today, may not be so tomorrow, since the values of the variables (parameters) may change, new parameters may emerge and the structural relationship between the variables may undergo a change.

A solution derived from a model remains a solution only so long as the uncontrolled (uncontrollable) variables retain their values and the relationship between the variables does not change. The solution itself goes 'out of control' if the values of one or more uncontrolled variables vary or relationship between variables undergoes a change. Therefore, controls must be established to indicate the limits within which the model and its solution can be considered as reliable. Also tools must be developed to indicate as to how and when the model or its solution will have to be modified to take the changes into account.

1.12-6 Putting the Solution to work (or Implementation)

Finally, because the objective of OR is not merely to produce reports but to improve the system performance, the results of the research must be implemented. For this, solution obtained above should be translated into operating procedures which can be easily understood and applied by those who control the operations. Changes necessary in existing procedures and resources must be clearly indicated and should be implemented. After the solution has been applied to the system, OR group must study the response of the system to the changes made. Actual performance of the system may indicate some additional changes or modifications to be made on the part of OR group because many a time solutions which look feasible on paper may conflict drastically with the capabilities and ideas of persons involved in the system. Many OR recommendations, though theoretically sound, do not get implemented because they turn out to be practically unworkable.

The success of an OR study depends upon the cooperation received from the management at the implementation stage. One way of getting this cooperation is to make management an active participant in all phases of OR study. The importance of this phase cannot be overemphasized since it is from this phase that the benefits of an OR study will be realized.

Finally, since no system is completely static, it is necessary to monitor the environment within which a system operates to ensure that the changing conditions do not render the solution 'useless' for future reference. Quite often products may become obsolete, new technology may come up, 'shortages' may change to 'surplus' and new raw materials may find place in the market. The solution obtained should, therefore, be continuously *reviewed, modified* and *updated* in the light of changing environment.

These phases of OR study are not rigid rules; they are seldom conducted in the order presented. In many projects, for instance, the formulation of the problem is not complete until the project itself is virtually completed. Obviously, there is a considerable interplay between the different phases.

1.13 MODELS IN OR

A model, as used in operations research, is defined as an idealized representation of the real life situation. It represents *one* or *a few* aspects of reality. Diverse items such as a map, a multiple activity chart, an autobiography, PERT network, break-even equation, balance sheet, etc. are all models because each one of them represents *a few aspects* of the real life situation. A map, for instance, represents the physical boundaries but normally ignores the heights of the various places, above the sea level. The objective of the model is to provide a means for analysing the behaviour of the system for the purpose of improving its performance.

1.14 CLASSIFICATION SCHEMES OF MODELS

The various schemes by which models can be classified are

1. By degree of abstraction
2. By function
3. By structure
4. By nature of the environment
5. By the extent of generality
6. By the time horizon.

1. By Degree of Abstraction

Mathematical models (*viz.* linear programming formulation of the blending problem or transportation problem) are the most abstract type since it requires not only mathematical knowledge but also great concentration to get the idea of the real-life situation they represent.

Language models (cricket or hockey match commentary) are also abstract type. *Concrete models* (model of earth, dam, building or plane) are the least abstract since they instantaneously suggest the shape or characteristics of the modelled entity.

2. By Function

Descriptive models explain the various operations in non-mathematical language and try to define the functional relationships and interactions between various operations. They simply describe some aspects of the system on the basis of observation, survey or questionnaire, etc. but do not predict its behaviour. The organisational chart, pie diagram and layout plan describe the features of their respective systems.

Predictive models explain or predict the behaviour of the system. Exponential smoothing forecast model, for instance, predicts the future demand.

Normative or prescriptive models develop decision rules or criteria for optimal solutions. They are applicable to repetitive problems, the solution process of which can be programmed without managerial involvement. Linear programming is a prescriptive or normative model as it prescribes what the managers must follow.

3. By Structure

(a) Iconic or Physical Models

In iconic or physical models, properties of the real system are represented by the properties themselves, frequently with a change of scale. Thus, iconic models resemble the system they represent but differ in size; they are *images*. For example, globes are used to represent the orientation and shape of various continents, oceans and other geographical features of the earth. A model of the solar system, likewise, represents the sun and planets in space. Iconic models of atoms and molecules are commonly used in physics, chemistry and other sciences. However, these models are usually scaled up or down. For example, in a globe, the diameter of the earth is scaled down, but its shape, relative sizes of continents, oceans, etc., are approximately correct. On the other hand, a model of the atom is scaled up so as to make it visible to the naked eye. Iconic models may be two-dimensional (photographs, maps, blue prints, paintings, sketches of insects, etc.) or three-dimensional (globes, automobiles, airplanes, etc.). Ordinarily it is easier to work with the model of a building, earth, sun, atom, etc., than with the modelled entity itself. Iconic models are quite specific and concrete but difficult to manipulate for experimental purposes. They represent a static event. Characteristics that are not relevant are not included. For instance, in the models used for the study of atomic structure, the colour of the model is irrelevant since it contributes no help in the study of the atom. Another limitation of iconic model is that it is either two-dimensional or three-dimensional. If a situation involves more than three dimensions, it cannot be represented by an iconic model.

(b) Analogue or Schematic Models

Analogue models can represent dynamic situations and are used more often than iconic models since they are analogous to the characteristics of the system under study. They use one set of properties to represent some other set of properties which the system under study possesses. After the model is solved, the solution is re-interpreted in terms of the original system.

For example, graphs are very simple analogues. They represent properties like force, speed age, time, etc. in terms of distance. A graph is well suited for representing quantitative relationship between any two properties and predicts how a change in one property affects the other.

An *organizational chart* is a common schematic model. It represents the relationships existing between the various members of the organization. *A man-machine chart* is also a schematic model. It represents a time varying interaction of men and machines over a complete work cycle. *A flow process chart* is another schematic model which represents the order of occurrence of various events to make a product. Contour lines on a map are analogous of elevation. Flow of water through pipes may be taken as an analogue of the 'flow' of electricity through wires. Similarly, demand curves and frequency distribution curves used in statistics are examples of analogue models. In analogue computers, quantities are represented by voltages and they are, therefore, aptly termed analogue.

Transformation of properties into analogous properties increases our ability to make changes. Usually it is easier to change an analogue than to change an iconic model and also lesser number of changes are required to get the same results. For example, it is easier to change the contour lines on a two-dimensional chart than to change the relief on a three-dimensional one. In general, schematic models are less specific and concrete but easier to manipulate than iconic models. They can represent dynamic situations and are more commonly used than the iconic models.

(c) Symbolic or Mathematical Models

Symbolic models employ a set of mathematical symbols (letters, numbers, etc.) to represent the decision variables of the system under study. These variables are related together by mathematical equation(s)/inequality(inequalities) which describe the properties of the system. A solution from the model is, then, obtained by applying well developed mathematical techniques. The relationship between velocity, acceleration and distance is an example of mathematical model. Similarly, cost-volume-profit relation is a mathematical model used in investment analysis. Allocation, sequencing, replacement models are all mathematical models.

In many research projects, all the three types of models are used in sequence; iconic and analogue models are used as initial approximations, which are, then, refined into symbolic model.

Mathematical models differ from those traditionally used in physical sciences in two ways:

1. Since OR systems involve social and economic factors, these models use probabilistic elements.
2. They consist of two types of variables: controllable and uncontrollable. The objective is to select those values for controllable variables which optimize some measure of effectiveness. Therefore, these models are used in decision situations rather than in physical phenomena.

In OR, symbolic models are used wherever possible, not only because they are easier to manipulate but also because they yield more accurate results. Most of this text, therefore, is devoted to the formulation and solution of these mathematical models.

4. By Nature of the Environment

(*a*) Deterministic Models

In deterministic models variables are completely defined and the outcomes are certain. Certainty is the state of nature assumed in these models. They represent completely closed systems and the parameters of the system have a single value that does not change with time. For any given set of input variables, the same output variables always result. E.O.Q. model is deterministic; here the effect of changes in the batch sizes on the total cost is known. Similarly linear programming, transportation and assignment models are deterministic models.

(*b*) Probabilistic Models

They are the products of an environment of risk and uncertainty. The input and/or output variables take the form of probability distributions. They are semi-closed models and represent the likelihood of occurrence of an event. Thus they represent, to an extent, the complexity of the real world and the uncertainty prevailing in it. As an example, the exponential smoothing model for forecasting demand is a probabilistic model. Similarly, game theory is a probabilistic model.

5. By the Extent of Generality

(*a*) General Models

Linear programming model is known as a general model since it can be used for a number of functions (*viz.* product mix, production scheduling, marketing, etc.) of an organisation.

(*b*) Specific Models

Sales response curve or equation as a function of advertising is applicable in the marketing function alone.

6. By the Time Horizon

(*a*) Static Models

They are one-time decision models. They represent the system at a specified time and do not take into account the changes over time. In these models cause and effect occur almost simultaneously and time lag between the two is zero. They are easier to formulate, manipulate and solve. Economic order quantity model is a static model.

(b) Dynamic Models

They are the models for situations in which time often plays an important role. They are used for optimization of multistage decision problems which require a series of decisions with the outcome of each depending upon the results of the previous decisions in the series. Dynamic programming is a dynamic model.

1.15 CHARACTERISTICS OF A GOOD MODEL

1. The number of simplifying assumptions should be as few as possible.
2. The number of relevant variables should be as few as possible. This means the model should be simple yet close to reality.
3. It should assimilate the system environmental changes without change in its framework.
4. It should be adaptable to parametric type of treatment.
5. It should be easy and economical to construct.

1.16 ADVANTAGES OF A MODEL

1. It provides a logical and systematic approach to the problem.
2. It indicates the scope as well as limitations of a problem.
3. It helps in finding avenues for new research and improvements in a system.
4. It makes the overall structure of the problem more comprehensible and helps in dealing with the problem in its entirety.
5. It permits experimentation and analysis of a complex system without directly interfering in the working and environment of the system.

1.17 LIMITATIONS OF A MODEL

1. Models are only idealised representation of reality and should not be regarded as absolute in any case.
2. The validity of a model for a particular situation can be ascertanied only by conducting experiments on it.

1.18 CONSTRUCTING THE MODEL

It was pointed out in previous sections that formulation of the problem requires analysis of the system under study. This analysis shows the various phases of the system and the way it can be controlled With the formulation of the problem, the first stage in model construction is over. The next step is to define a measure of effectiveness, *i.e.*, the next step is to construct a model in which effectiveness of the system is expressed as a function of the variables defining the system. The general form of OR model is

$$E = f(x_i, y_j),$$

where
E = effectiveness of the system,
x_i = variables of the system that can be controlled,
y_j = variables of the system that cannot be controlled but do affect E.

Deriving of solution from such a model consists of determining those values of control variables x_i, for which the measure of effectiveness is optimized. Optimization includes both maximization (in case of profits, production capacity, etc.) and minimization (in case of losses, cost of production, etc.).

Various steps in the construction of a model are

1. Selecting components of the system
2. Pertinence of components
3. Combining the components
4. Substituting symbols

1.18-1 Selecting Components of the System

All the components of the system which contribute towards the effectiveness measure of the system should be listed.

1.18-2 Pertinence of Components

Once a complete list of components is prepared, the next step is to find whether or not to take each of these components into account. This is determined by finding the effect of various alternative courses of action on each of these components. Generally, one or more components (*e.g.*, fixed costs) are independent of the changes made among the various alternative courses of action. Such components may be temporarily dropped from consideration.

1.18-3 Combining the Components

It may be convenient to group certain components of the system. For example, the purchase price, freight charges and receiving cost of a raw material can be combined together and called 'raw material acquisition cost'. The next step is to determine, for each component remaining on the modified list, whether its value is fixed or variable. If a component is variable, various aspects of the system affecting its value must be determined. For instance manufacturing cost usually consists of

(*i*) the number of units manufactured, and

(*ii*) the cost of manufacturing a unit.

1.18-4 Substituting Symbols

Once each variable component in the modified list has been broken down like this, symbols may be assigned to each of these subcomponents.

The foregoing steps will be clear from the example considered below:

A newsboy wants to decide the number of newspapers he should order to maximize his expected profit. He purchases a certain number of newspapers everyday and is able to sell some or all of them. He earns a profit on each paper sold. He can return the unsold papers, but at a loss. The number of persons who buy newspapers varies from day to day.

To construct the model for this problem, we identify the various relevant components (variables) and then assign symbols to them.

Let N = number of newspapers ordered per day,

A = profit earned on each newspaper sold,

B = loss on each newpaper returned,

D = demand *i.e.* number of newspapers sold per day,

p(D) = probability that the demand will be equal to D on any randomly selected day,

P = net profit per day.

If D > N *i.e.*, demand is more than the number of newspapers ordered, the profit to the newsboy is

$$P(D > N) = NA.$$

If on the other hand, demand is less than the number ordered, the profit is

$$P(D \leq N) = DA - (N - D)B.$$

∴ Net expected profit per day, P can be expressed as

$$P = \sum_{D=0}^{D=N} p(D)[DA - (N - D)B] + \sum_{D=N+1}^{\infty} p(D) \cdot NA.$$

This is a decision model of the risk type. Here, P is the measure of performance, N is the controlled variable, D is an uncontrollable variable, while A and B are uncontrollable constants. Solution of this model consists of finding that value of N which maximizes P.

1.19 APPROXIMATIONS (SIMPLIFICATIONS) IN OR MODELS

While constructing a model one comes across two conflicting objectives:

(*i*) the model should be as easy to solve as possible,

(*ii*) it should be as accurate as possible.

Moreover, the management must be able to understand the solution of the model and must be capable of using it. Obviously, one must pay due care to the mathematical complexity of the solution. Therefore, while constructing the model, the reality (problem under study) should be simplified but only to the point that there is no significant loss of accuracy. Some of the common simplifications include

1. Omitting certain variables
2. Aggregating variables
3. Changing the nature of variables
4. Changing the relationship between variables, and
5. Modifying constraints

1.19-1 Omitting Certain Variables

Clearly, variables having a large effect on system's performance cannot be omitted. It requires a lot of study to decide which variables have and which do not have large effects. For instance, in production and inventory control models, the effect of production-run sizes on in-process inventory costs is usually negligible as compared to effect of other variables and is, therefore, neglected.

1.19-2 Aggregating Variables

Most problems involve a large number of decision variables. For instance, some inventory problems involve the purchase of more than a million items. For solving such problems, the controlled variables are grouped into 'families'. A family is, then, supposed to consist of all identical members. One principle of 'family' formation is

1. Low usage, low cost
2. Low usage, high cost
3. High usage, low cost
4. High usage, high cost

1.19-3 Changing the Nature of Variables

The nature of variables may be changed in three ways:

(*i*) by treating a variable as constant,

(*ii*) by treating a discrete variable as continuous, and

(*iii*) by treating a continuous variable as discrete.

A variable may be treated as constant with its value equal to the mean of the variable's distribution. For example, in most production quantity models setup cost is treated as constant.

From both analytical and computational viewpoints it is easier to treat a discrete variable as continuous. Most of OR techniques deal with continuous variables. Even if the discrete variables are few in number, the computational difficulties become quite large. For instance, in inventory control models, withdrawals of items from stock that are actually discrete are assumed as continuous at a constant rate, over a planning period.

However, for processes in which time between events is a relevant variable, considerable simplification may be obtained by assuming that events occurring within a certain period occur instantaneously at the beginning or end of the period.

1.19-4 Changing the Relationship between Variables

Models can be simplified by modifying the functional form of the model. Non-linear functions require a complex solution method. The most powerful computational techniques are applicable only to models having linear functions. Therefore, non-linear functions are usually approximated to linear functions (*e.g.*, in linear programming). Many times, a curve is approximated to a series of straight lines (*e.g.*, in non-linear programming). Quadratic functions are used as approximations since their derivatives are linear (*e.g.*, in quadratic programming). Discrete functions (*e.g.*, binomial and Poisson) are sometimes approximated to continuous normal functions.

1.19-5 Modifying Constraints

Constraints can be deleted, added or modified to simplify the model. If it is not possible to solve a model with all the constraints, some of them may be temporarily ignored and a 'solution' obtained. If this 'solution' happens to satisfy these constraints too, it is accepted. If it does not, constraints are added, one at a time, with increasing complexity, until a solution satisfying these constraints is obtained. A general rule regarding constraints is that when they are dropped the solution derived from the model becomes optimistic (it gives better performance than the 'true' solution). On the other hand, adding of constraints makes the solution pessimistic.

1.20 TYPES OF MATHEMATICAL MODELS

Many OR models have been developed and applied to problems in business and industry. Some of these models are:

1. Mathematical techniques
2. Statistical techniques
3. Inventory models
4. Allocation models
5. Sequencing models
6. Project scheduling by PERT and CPM
7. Routing models
8. Competitive models
9. Queuing models
10. Simulation techniques
11. Decision theory
12. Replacement models
13. Reliability theory
14. Markov analysis
15. Advanced OR models
16. Combined methods.

1.20-1 Mathematical Techniques

In principle, any mathematical technique can become a useful tool for operations analyst. Mathematical techniques most commonly employed are: differential equations, linear difference equations, integral equations, operator theory, vector and matrix theory. Detailed description of these techniques is beyond the scope of this book. For details, the reader is referred to any standard text on calculus.

1.20-2 Statistical Techniques

Some of the most commonly applied techniques come from *probability theory* and *statistics.* Since in the world we live, the course of future events cannot be predicted with absolute certainty, probabilities are associated with these events to analyse the uncertainties and supply data with reasonable accuracy for decision-making. Probabilities are of the type—*objective* and *subjective.* The former has associated with it definite historical evidence and common experience *i.e.*, there is objective evidence to support the assignment of probabilities *e.g.*, in the game of tossing a fair coin, the probability of the coin lying with its head or tail up is each 0.5. In subjective probability, on the other hand, there is no historical evidence available and one has to rely on one's own estimation and the possible outcomes.

Statistical techniques also include discrete and continuous probability, renewal theory, Markov processes and stochastic processes. All these techniques are useful when dealing with uncertainty, errors, sampling, estimation and prediction.

1.20-3 Inventory Models

Inventory models deal with idle resources such as raw materials, spare parts, semi-finished and finished products. These models are concerned with two decisions:

(*i*) *how much to order* (produce or purchase) to replenish the inventory of an item and

(*ii*) *when to order* so as to minimize the total cost.

For the first decision–how much to order, there are two basic inventory costs taken into consideration: *ordering costs* and *carrying costs.* Ordering costs are basically the costs of getting the item into firm's inventory and consist of cost of sending the requisition to the purchase office, cost of issuing the purchase order, follow-up cost, receiving (the item) cost, cost of stationery, etc. The inventory carrying costs (also referred to as holding costs) include interest on capital invested in inventory, obsolescence cost, storage space cost, stores operation cost, taxes, insurance and pilferage cost and are expressed as a percentage of average inventory value (say 20 percent per year to hold inventory) or as cost per unit per unit time period (say Rs. 1.50 per unit per month to hold inventory). It can be seen that while the ordering costs decrease, the carrying costs increase with the quantity ordered at a time. *Economic Order Quantity* (E.O.Q.) is then calculated by balancing the two costs.

For the second decision—when to order, it is sufficient to fix the reorder level, which is the level of stock at which replenishment order is placed and is equal to the lead time multiplied with the demand during the lead time, where lead time is the time period (in days, weeks, etc.) between the placement of order and receipt of the goods. The reorder level is calculated by balancing the two costs—the inventory carrying costs and the cost of disservice to the customers in case of stockout (shortages) when the orders are not met in time. Besides E.O.Q. equations, linear, dynamic and quadratic programming are used to solve inventory models.

There are two basic inventory procedures namely, continuous time review system and fixed time review system. In continuous time review system, the stock position is continuously reviewed and as soon as the stock level reaches a predetermined level (reorder level), a fixed quantity is ordered. This procedure is suitable for items which are expensive and critical.

In the fixed time (periodic) review system, the inventory position is reviewed periodically. There is a pre–determined level known as replenishment level up to which the stock is replenished at every review period. This procedure is suitable for items which are less expensive and non-critical. Chapter 12 deals with these models.

1.20-4 Allocation Models

Allocation models are used to solve problems in which (*a*) there are a number of jobs to be performed and there are alternative ways of doing them and (*b*) resources or facilities are limited.

In such situations, the objective is to allot the resources to the jobs so as to optimize the overall effectiveness (*i.e.* minimize the total cost or maximize the total profit). This is called *mathematical programming.* When the objective function can be expressed as a linear function of the variables and the constraints are expressed as linear equalities/inequalities, this is called linear programming. Chapter 2 is devoted to this topic.

The simplest type of allocation model involves the association of a number of jobs to the same number of resources (men). This is called *assignment model.* The assignment problem becomes more complex if some of the jobs require more than one resource or if the resource can be used for more than one job. Such a problem is called *transportation problem.* The transportation and assignment models are discussed in Chapter 3 and Chapter 4 respectively.

1.20-5 Sequencing Models

These are applicable in situations in which the effectiveness measure (time, cost or distance) is a function of the order or sequence of performing a series of jobs (tasks). The selection of the appropriate order in which waiting customers (jobs) may be served is called sequencing. In these problems, generally there are n jobs to be performed, where each job requires processing on some or all of m different machines. The order in which these machines are to be used for processing each job as well as the processing time of each job on each machine is known and the problem is to select the sequence that minimizes the total elapsed time from the start of the first job to the completion of the last job as well as idle time of machines.

Only simple problems of this kind have been solved analytically. For others, simulation and heuristic methods have been used. Solution of sequencing models by analytical methods is taken up in Chapter 5.

1.20-6 Project Scheduling by PERT and CPM

In a large and complex project involving a number of interrelated activities, requiring a number of men, machines and materials, it is not possible for the management to make and execute an optimum schedule just by intution. Managements are, thus, always on the look out for some methods and techniques which may help in planning, scheduling and controlling the project. PERT and CPM are two of the many project management techniques used for these purposes. The project is diagrammatically represented with the help of network made of arrows representing different activities and interrelationships among them. This representation is used for identifying critical activities and critical path. CPM is used when the times required for the activities are known for sure and PERT is used when their times are not known for sure – only probabilistic estimates of times are known. Construction of network and identification of critical path further helps in guiding the transfer of resources from slack (non-critical) areas to critical areas in order to meet scheduling requirements. These techniques help to achieve project coordination and efficient use of resources. They are also used to determine time-cost trade-off, resource allocation and updating of networks. Chapter 14 deals with these techniques.

1.20-7 Routing Models

Routing problems in networks are the problems which are related to sequencing. There are two important routing problems:

(*a*) the travelling salesman problem

(*b*) the minimal path problem

In the travelling salesman problem, there are a number of cities a salesman has to visit. The distance (or time or cost) between every pair of cities is known. The salesman is to start from his home city, visit each city only once and return to his home city, and the problem is to find the shortest route in distance (or time or cost). These problems are discussed in Chapter 4.

In the minimal path problem, there are many routes available between one city (origin) and the other (destination) and the problem is to find the shortest route. These problems have been dealt with in Chapter 5.

1.20-8 Competitive Models (Game Theory)

These models are used when two or more individuals or organizations with conflicting objectives try to make decisions. In such situations a decision made by one decision-maker affects the decision made by one or more of the remaining decision-makers. Competitive models are applicable to a wide variety of situations such as two players struggling to win at chess, candidates fighting an election, two enemies planning war tactics, firms struggling to maintain their market shares, situations of collective bargaining, etc. The contending individuals or organisations may not always be at cross purposes. As an example, an equipment dealer and customer may be at cross purposes with regard to the price but would like to strike a bargain to their mutual benefit. Likewise, in a collective bargaining process, the trade union and management strive to strike a mutually advantageous deal and keep the company operations going.

Bidding problems involving bidding for contracts, rights, concession, license, etc. are quite common in industries. In bidding problems, as the bids are increased, the chance of winning increases but the expected profits decrease. The problem, then, is to decide the optimal bid that will balance the chances of winning and associated profits. Chapter 9 is devoted to competitive models.

1.20-9 Queuing Models

Queuing models involve the arrival of units to be serviced at one or more service facilities. These units (or customers) may be trucks arriving a loading station, customers entering a departmental store, patients arriving a doctor's clinic, ships arriving a port, letters arriving a typist's desk, etc. The arriving units may form one line and get serviced, as in a doctor's clinic. This will occur when the system has a single service channel. The system may have a number of service channels, which may be arranged in parallel or in series or a complex combination of both. In case of parallel channels, several customers may be serviced simultaneously, as in a barbar's shop. For series channels, a customer must pass successively through all the channels before service is completed *e.g.*, a product undergoing different processes over different machines. In queuing systems there is either too much or too less demand on the facilities so that either the units or the facilities have to wait. Costs are associated with both types of waiting times. In either case, the problem is to either schedule arriving units or provide extra facilities or both so as to obtain an optimum balance between the costs associated with waiting time and idle time. Queuing models are discussed in Chapter 10.

1.20-10 Simulation Techniques

Someties it may be very risky, cumbersome or time consuming to conduct real study or experiment to know more about a situation or problem. Also, sometimes due to a large number of variables or large number of interrelationships between variables, and the complexity of relationships, it may not be possible to develop an analytical model representing the situation. Even if a model is constructed, it may not be possible to solve it. Simulation may be helpful in such situations. It may be noted that simulation does not solve a problem; it only generates information or data needed for decision-making. Thus, simulation is a data generation technique and is used when actual experimentation is not feasible and analytical methods of building models and solving them are not helpful.

For example, to design an aeroplane, the designer can solve the various equations describing the aerodynamics of the plane. However, if these equations are too difficult to solve, a scale model of the aeroplane can be prepared and tested in a wind tunnel.

Simulation is a very powerful tool and is one of the most widely used operations research techniques. Many important managerial decision-making problems are too intricate to be solved by mathematical analysis and the experimentation with the actual system, even if possible, is too costly and risky. Simulation offers the solution by allowing experimentation with a model of the system without interfering with the real system. Simulation is thus, often, a bypass for complex mathematical analysis.

Simulation methods have been used in production lines, public transport system, warehouse management, queuing situations, inventory control problems, etc. The essence of simulation is to produce a model which imitates a real system, so that the model may be used as a basis for testing the policies.

1.20-11 Decision Theory

Decision-making is an every day process, it is a major part of a manager's job. As wrong decisions can be disastrous for the companies, the importance of right decisions cannot be overemphasized. Decisions may be classified into two categories: tactical decisions and strategic decisions. Tactical decisions are those that affect the organisation in the short run. Decisions regarding number of shifts to operate or number of salesmen to appoint are tactical decisions. Strategic decisions, on the other hand, have a far-reaching effect as they usually involve long-term commitment of resources. Launching of a new product, entering into new regions for business, diversification of products, automation, etc. form strategic decision of the company.

In the process of decision-making, the manager tries to identify the various alternative courses of action available to him and the risk associated with each. Modern statistical theory can be very useful in this context. Decision theory tries to quantify the outcome of each decision. While uncertainties are taken care of by estimating the probabilities of various outcomes, the outcomes are quantified in the form of monetary payoffs and the decision resulting in highest payoff is taken.

As an example consider a television manufacturing company that has to select the best among several alternative methods of expanding its production to meet the increased market demand. There could be the following three viable alternatives:

(*i*) expand the existing plant,

(*ii*) build a new plant,

(*iii*) subcontract extra production to other television manufacturing company.

Having identified the viable alternatives, the next step is to list the future events (called *states of nature*) that may occur. In the problem under discussion, the greatest uncertainty is about the future demand of the televisions. The various future events related to demand can be

(*i*) high demand,

(*ii*) moderate demand,

(*iii*) low demand,

(*iv*) no demand.

The expected return or *payoff* in rupees associated with each state of nature is then found out and the decision resulting in the highest payoff is taken.

Decision theory covers three categories of decision-making:

1. *Decision-making under conditions of certainty:* Here, only one state of nature exists *i.e.*, there is complete certainty about the future. Very few business situations will ever fall in this category.
2. *Decision-making under conditions of risk:* Here, more than one states of nature exist and there is enough information available to assign probability to each of the possible states.
3. *Decision-making under conditions of uncertainty:* Here, more than one states of nature exist but there is no information about the various states, not even sufficient knowledge to assign probabilities to them.

Decision theory is covered in Chapter 9.

1.20-12 Replacement Models

The replacement theory deals with industrial, military and other equipment that gets worn with usage and time and thereby functions with decreasing efficiency. For example, a machine requires higher operating cost, a transport vehicle requires more and more maintenance cost, a railway timetable becomes more and more out of date with time. The ever increasing repair and maintenance cost necessitates the replacement of equipment. However, there is no sharp, clearly defined time which indicates the need for this replacement. The replacement policy, in this case, consists of calculating the increased operating cost, maintenance cost, scarp value and cost of equipment to determine the optimal replacement interval.

Another category of replacement problem involves items such as electric bulbs, radio tubes, etc. which do not deteriorate with time but suddenly fail. The problem, here, is of finding which items to replace and whether or not to replace them in a group and, if so, when. The objective is to minimize the sum of the cost of the item, cost of replacing the item and the cost associated with failure of the item.

There is still another situation in which replacement becomes necessary. This is obsolescence due to new discoveries and better design of equipment. The equipment needs replacement not because it no longer performs to the design standards, but because more modern equipment performs to the higher standards. Chapter 11 is denoted to these problems.

1.20-13 Reliability Theory

Reliability is the capability of an equipment to work without any break down or failure for a specified period of time under given environmental conditions. The equipment may be simple device like a switch, a fan, an electric heater or a large and complex one such as a computer, a radar or an aeroplane. Reliability of the complex equipment depends upon the reliability of its components. It is essential that an equipment should well perform the function for which it is designed. Failure could result in great hazard and high costs. For instance, large downtime cannot be permitted in a computer, malfuntioning of parts is unthinkable in an aircraft.

The quantitative measure of reliability can be obtained for individual components by appropriate statistical procedures such as life testing. The reliability of the equipment can then by ascertained by using the reliability of the individual components and the design of the equipment which indicates the interconnection of the components.

Assessment of reliability is extremely useful in designing a complex, sophisticated equipment containing a large number of components.

1.20-14 Markov Analysis

Markov analysis for decision-making is used in situations where various states are defined. The probability of going from one state to another is known and depends on the present state but independent of how that state was reached. Morkov analysis is used to determine the long-run probability of being in a particular state (steady-state probability). This steady-state probability is used in decision-making.

Markov analysis analyzes the *current* behaviour of some variable in order to predict the future behaviour of that variable. This was first used by the Russian mathematician A. Markov to describe and predict the behaviour of gas particles in a closed container. In operations research, it has been successfully applied to a wide variety of situations. It has been used in examining and predicting the behaviour of customers in terms of their *brand loyalty* and their changing from one brand to another. It has also been used to study the life of *newspaper subscriptions.* Recently it has been used to study the customers' accounts behaviour *i.e.*, to study the customers as they change from 'current account' through 'one month overdue' to 'two months overdue' to 'bad debt'. In all these applications, future behaviour has been predicted by analysing the present one.

1.20-15 Advanced OR Models

(*i*) Non-Linear Programming

Non-linear programming is used to solve problems in which either the objective function and/or one or more of the constraints are non-linear in nature. Factors such as price discounts on bulk purchases, graduated income tax, etc. may cause non-linearity in the model. The non-linearity of the functions makes the solution of the problem much more involved as compared to linear programming problems, and there is no single algorithm like simplex method, which can be employed for solution of the problem. Though a number of algorithms have been developed, each is applicable to a specific type of non-linear programming problem only.

(*ii*) Dynamic Programming

Dynamic programming models are used to make a *series of interrelated decisions* for multi-stage problems that extend over a number of time periods. For example, a company may wish to make a series of marketing decisions over time which will result in highest possible sales. The underlying principle of this model is that regardless of what the previous decisions are, it tries to determine the optimum decision for the periods that still lie ahead. The dynamic programming approach divides the problem into a number of subproblems or stages. The decision made at each stage influences not only the next stage but also every stage to the end of the problem. Though dynamic programming has been used to solve problems in which time plays an essential role, yet in many dynamic programming problems time is not a relevant variable. For instance, suppose a company has marked capital C to be spent on advertising its products through three different media—newspaper, radio and television. In each medium the advertisement can appear a number of times per week. Each appearance has associated with it certain costs and returns and the problem is to determine the number of times the product be advertised in each medium so that the returns are maximum and the total cost is within the prescribed limit. In this situation time is not a variable, but the problem can be divided into stages and solved by dynamic programming.

Whereas linear programming has standard ways to formulate the problems and solve them, there is no such 'standard approach' in dynamic programming. It is, on the other hand, a general way of solving large, complex problems by splitting them into smaller problems which are more easily solved. It requires, however, a good bit of ingenuity to decide when a problem might be solved by using dynamic programming and how that solution should be approached. Dynamic programming involves manipulation of a large amount of data and requires electronic computers.

(*iii*) Integer Programming

It is used to solve problems in which some or all varialbles must have non-negative integer values. When all the variables are constrained to be intergers, the problem is called *all (pure) integer programming problem* and in case only some of the variables are restricted to have integer values, the problem is said to be *a mixed integer programming problem.* In some situations each variable can take on the values of either zero or one as in 'do' or 'not do' type of decisions. Such problems are referred to as *zero-one programming problems.*

Examples on integer programming are: number of trucks in a fleet, number of generators in a power house, etc. Approximate solutions can be obtained without using integer programming methods, but the approximation generally becomes poorer as the values of the variables become smaller. There are techniques like Gomory's cutting-plane algorithm, branch-and-bound algorithm and Bala's additive algorithm to solve these problems.

(*iv*) Goal Programming

Goal programming is quite similar to linear programming but is applied for situations which have multiple goals or objectives. For a company manufacturing lathes and milling machines, there can be the following objectives:

(*i*) maximize profit in rupees,
(*ii*) maximize number of lathes to be manufactured,
(*iii*) maximize number of milling machines to be manufactured.

It is obvious that the three goals cannot be added, since their units are different. Moreover goals (*ii*) and (*iii*) are conflicting. Goal programming asks the management to set some targets for each of the goals and rank them in the order of importance. Having received this information, goal programming tries to minimize the deviations from the targets. It starts with the most important goal and continues till the achievement of a less important goal would cause management to fail to achieve a more important one.

(*v*) Heuristic Programming

According to Thierauf and Klekamp, heuristic programming uses rules of thumb or intuitive rules and guidelines (generally under computer control) to explore the most likely paths and to make educated guesses in arriving at a problem's solution. Thus, checking all the alternatives, so as to obtain the optimum one, is not required. Heuristic models seem to be quite promising for future OR work. They bridge the gap between strictly analytical formulations and the operating principles which managers are habitual of using. They involve step-by-step search towards the optimal solution when a problem cannot be expressed in mathematical programming form. The search procedure examines successively a number of combinations that lead to stepwise improvement in the solution and the search stops when a near-optimal solution has been obtained.

(*vi*) Quadratic Programming

Quadratic programming refers to problems in which objective function is quadratic in form (contains squared terms) while the constraints are linear. A number of efficient algorithms have been developed for such problems.

(*vii*) Sensitivity Analysis

Once the optimal solution to a linear programming problem has been attained, it may be desirable to study how the current solution changes when the parameters of the problem get changed. The study of the effect of *discrete* changes in the values of the parameters on the optimal solution is called *sensitivity analysis or postoptimality analysis*. The objective is to determine how *sensitive* is the optimal solution to the changes in the values of these parameters.

(*viii*) Parametric Programming

The study of the effect of *continuous* changes in the values of the parameters on the optimal solution to a linear programming problem is called *parametric programming*. It is an extension of sensitivity analysis and aims at finding the various basic solutions that become optimal, one after the other, as the parameters of the problem change continuously their values.

(*ix*) Stochastic Programming

Also called *probabilistic programming,* it refers to linear programming that includes an evaluation of relative risks and uncertainties in various alternatives or choices available for management decisions.

1.20-16 Combined Methods

Real systems may not involve only one of the models discussed above. A production control problem, for example, normally consists of a combination of inventory, allocation and queuing models.

The usual method of solving such combined models consists of 'solving' them one at a time in some logical sequence. However, OR combines these models and constructs some type of *master model,* which takes into account the interaction of individual models.

Lastly, it must be emphasized that the above classification does not cover all OR problems. However, it does cover most of them. It is expected that in the days to come more and more of new processes will be revealed and subjected to mathematical analysis.

1.21 ROLE OF COMPUTERS IN OPERATIONS RESERACH

It was said in section 1.1 that the computer played a vital role in the development of OR. But for the computer, OR would not have achieved its present position. It is because in most OR techniques, computations are so complex and involved that these techniques would be of no real use in the absence of the computer. Most large-scale applications of OR techniques which require only a few minutes on the computer, may take weeks, months and even years to yield the same results manually.

Most of linear programming models for even small scale industries usually involve hundreds of decision variables and constraints. Likewise, most of the business problems, such as blending problems of oil refineries, may involve thousands of variables and constraints. It is simply impossible to solve such large problems manually; they are solved using sophisticated software packages. Many computer manufacturing companies have developed software packages for problems to be solved by the application of OR techniques. Companies such as IBM, ICL, UNIVAC, CDC have done so for solving scheduling, inventory, simulation, queuing, networking (PERT/CPM) and many other OR problems.

No doubt, the computer is an essential and integral part of OR. Today, OR methodology and computer methodology are growing in parallel. It appears that in the coming years the line dividing the two methodologies will disappear and the two sciences will combine to form a more general and comprehensive science.

1.22 DIFFICULTIES IN OPERATIONS RESEARCH

The previous sections have brought out the positive side of OR only. However, there is also the need to point out the negative side. Certain common traps and pitfalls can and have, ruined the otherwise good work. Some of these pitfalls are quite obvious while others are so subtle and hidden that extreme care is required to locate their presence.

In the very first phase of OR—the problem formulation phase—a number of pitfalls can and do arise. It is necessary that the right problem be selected and it must be completely and accurately defined. Is the right problem being solved? Is the scope considered wide and proper? Will it result in optimization or only sub-optimization? Will the solution properly reflect the objectives as well as the imposed constraints? Are proper effectiveness measures being used? This phase of problem formulation is perhaps the most important and toughest part of OR study.

Secondly, data collection may also consume a very large portion of time and money spent on OR study.

Thirdly, the whole study by operations analyst is based on his observations in the past. Strictly speaking, these observations can only be related to the laws that operated in the past, as there is no evidence that the laws will continue to operate in future also. If the laws are applied to the future, it clearly amounts to extrapolation in time.

Fourthly, the operations researcher, while making observations, may affect the behaviour of the system he is studying. Moreover, however comprehensive his experiments may be, his observations can never be more than a sample of the whole. These difficulties present special hazards to operations researcher. His aim is to find out what happens in a working organization. He can get the information in two ways: by direct observations or from the previous records. The behaviour of an organization depends upon the activities of the persons in it and the very fact that they are being observed is bound to affect their behaviour. On the other hand, accuracy of previous records is always doubtful and they seldom provide the complete information in all the points sought.

Perhaps the greatest difficulty in OR, however, is created by the time factor. The managers have to make decisions one way or the other, and a fairly good solution to the problem at the right time may be much more useful than the perfect solution too late. Further, the cost involved is also an important factor. Sometimes, some simple application of OR may yield a good solution quickly and it may be unwise to spend a lot of money and effort to produce a slightly better solution much later.

Other pitfalls in problem solving include

(*i*) warping the problem to fit a standard model, tool or technique,

(*ii*) failure to test the model and solution before implementation, and

(*iii*) failure to establish proper controls.

It is the responsibility of OR scientist to translate his highly specialised and technical thoughts, ideas and concepts into simple operational procedures capable of being easily understood by the management and workers alike. He must also ascertain that the new proposals are properly implemented. But for the proper implementation, the whole OR study becomes useless.

Lastly, what may appear to be a pitfall is the fact that OR study may raise more questions than it answers. However, this may ultimately result in more deep insight into the system, yielding further benefits and improvements.

1.23 LIMITATIONS OF OPERATIONS RESEARCH

1. Mathematical models, which are essence of OR, do not take into account qualitative factors or emotional factors which are quite real. All influencing factors which cannot be quantified find no place in mathematical models.
2. Mathematical models are applicable to only specific categories of problems.
3. OR tries to find optimal solution taking all the factors of the problem into account. Present day problems involve numerous such factors; expressing them in quantity and establishing relations among them requires huge calculations.

4. Being a new field, generally there is a resistance from the employees to the new proposals.
5. Management, who has to implement the advised proposals, may itself offer a lot of resistance due to conventional thinking.
6. Young enthusiasts, overtaken by its advantages and exactness, generally forget that OR is meant for men and not that men are meant for it.

Thus at the implementation stage, the decision cannot be governed by quantitative considerations alone. It must take into account the delicacies of human relationships. That is, in addition to being a pure scientist, one has to be tactful and learn the art of getting the decisions implemented. This art can be achieved by experience as well as by getting training in social sciences, particularly psychology.

In fact, many managers may make a joke of OR as they think that the decisions made otherwise may be better. But being aware of its limitations, they need to be convinced of its utility, which doubtlessly forms the essential guideline for making better decisions.

EXERCISES

1. Discuss the origin and development of OR. What are the limitations of OR? How computer has helped in popularising OR?
[*H.P.U. B.Tech. (May, 2013; V.T.U. Karnataka, 2012; P.T.U. B.E. (MBA and Mech.) 2011; MBA, 2005; P.U. M.Sc.(I.T.), 2003*]
2. What is OR? What are the characteristics and limitations of OR techniques?
[*G.N.D.U. B.Com. Nov., 2014; April, 2012; H.P.U. B.Tech. (Mech.) 2015; 2013; 12; J.N.T.U. MBA June, 2012; P.T.U. B.Tech. (Mech.) Dec., 2011; May, 2011; 2010; R.T.M. Nagpur U.B. Tech. Dec., 2006; Dec., 2003; H.P.U. B.E. (Mech.) 2009; Nagpur U. B.E. 2003; P.U. B.E.(Mech.) Nov., 2002; May, 2002; B.E. (E. & Ec.) 2002*]
3. Describe the various objectives of OR. Write any two merits of OR.
[*G.N.D.U. B.Com. April, 2014; P.T.U. B.Tech. (Mech.) April, 2013; 2010*]
4. What are the main characteristics of OR? Explain with suitable examples.
[*H.P.U. B.Tech. Nov., 2015; V.T.U. Karnataka, 2012; P.T.U. B.E. May, 2012; Madras U. MBA Nov., 2012; R.T.M. Nagpur U.B.E. (Mech.) 2011; Chennai U.B.C.A. Nov., 2010; P.T.U. MBA Nov., 2012; MCA, 2010; H.P.U. B.Tech. (Mech.) 2007; P.U.B.E.(E.&Ec.) April, 2002; MBA August, 2006; B. Com. 2006*]
5. Describe some methods of OR. [*P.U.B.Com. 2002*]
6. Operations research. What, where, why and how? [*P.U.B.E.(Elect.) 2001*]
7. Define operations research. Give features of OR. Briefly discuss techniques and tools of OR.
[*H.P.U. B.Tech. June, 2015; Chennai U.B.C.A. Nov., 2010; P.U.BBA 2008, 2001; B.Com. Sept., 2006; Sept., 2005; G.N.D.U. Sept., 2002*]
8. (*a*) What is the role of decision-making in OR? Define scientific decision-making and explain how it affects OR decisions. [*H.P.U.B.Tech. 7th Semester (Mech.) 2009; Nov., 2007; G.N.D.U., 2010, 2009; P.U.B.E. (Mech.) Nov., 2006; M.D.U. Rohtak B.E. (Mech.) Dec., 2006*]

   (*b*) Discuss the scope and limitations of OR.
   [*H.P.U. B.Tech. (Mech.) Nov., 2014; P.T.U. MBA May, 2015; Dec., 2014; M.Tech. Nov., 2012; R.U. MBA June, 2011; G.N.D.U., 2006; P.T.U. BCA, 2010; Gujarat Tech. U.B.E. Dec., 2012; U.P.U. MBA, 2010; V.T.U. Karnataka B.E. June, 2010; R.T.M. Nagpur U.B.Tech. June, 2006; P.U.B.E. 2001, 2000; B.Com. 2006, 03, 02, 00; B.E.(E.&Ec.) April, 2008, 2006; Pbi. U. MCA, 2001; Jammu U.B.E.(Mech.) 2004*]
9. "OR is the application of scientific methods, techniques and tools to problems involving the operations of a system so as to provide those in control of the system with optimum solutions to the problems." Discuss. [*G.N.D.U., 2005; R.T.M. Nagpur, U. B.Tech. Dec., 2005*]

10. What is OR? Describe briefly its applications.
[*P.T.U. B.Tech. (Mech.) Nov., 2012; R.U. MBA June, 2011; P.U. MBA, 2010; R.T.M. Nagpur U.B.Tech., 2009; J.N.T. U. Hyderabad MBA April, 2012; August, 2010; B.Tech. May, 2011, Nov., 2010; Chennai Univ. B.B.A. Nov., 2010; P.T.U. B.E. (Mech.) 2011; MCA, 2010; M.D.U. Rohtak B.E. (Mech.) Dec., 2006; Jammu U. B.E.(Mech.) 2004; P.U. B.Com., 2007, 2004, 2000; B.E.(T.I.T.) Nov., 2004; BBA 2010, 07, 01*]
11. Discuss the significance and scope of OR in modern management.
[*J.N.T.U. Hyderabad MBA April, 2012; B.Tech. August, 2011, 2010; R.U. MBA Dec., 2011; P.U. BBA, 2010, 08; R.T.M. Nagpur, B.Tech. June, 2007; H.P.U. B.Tech. (Mech.) 2007; P.U.B.E.(Mech.) 2002; B.Com. April, 2007; Sept., 2004; Jammu U. B.E. (Mech.) 2004; P.U.B. Com. Jan., 2005*]
12. Explain how and why OR methods have been valuable in aiding executive decisions.
[*J.N.T.U. Hyderabad B.Tech. August, 2013*]
13. "Mathematics of OR is mathematics of optimization." Discuss. [*Pbi.U. MCA, 2001*]
14. Discuss the various phases in solving an OR problem. [*J.N.T.U. Hyderabad MCA Feb., 2012;*]
[*G.N.D.U. B.Com. April, 2013; Madras U.MBA Nov., 2012; V.T.U. Karnataka B.E. June, 2012; U.P.U. MBA, 2010; Mumbai U. MBA, 2010; P.T.U. MBA Nov., 2013; Feb., 2011; R.U. MBA June, 2011; Dec., 2011; M.Tech. Dec., 2011; R.T. M. Nagpur U. B.Tech., 2010,09,06,04,03; SVSM PGDM, 2009; H.P.U.B.E. (Mech.) 2010, 2008; IGNOU MCA, 2003; Nagpur U. B.E.(Mech.) 2003; P.U.B.E. (E. & Ec.) April, 2008; 2006; 2000; B.Com., 2003*]
15. (*a*) Discuss scientific method in OR. [*V.T.U. Karnataka, 2012; Pbi.U. MCA, 2001*]
(*b*) Explain the role of operations research in business. [*Chennai U. B.B.A. Nov., 2010*]
(*c*) Explain methodology of OR [*P.T.U. MBA, 2009*]
16. What is the role of OR in decision-making ?
[*M.G.U. Keralal M.Com. June, 2010; H.P.U.B. Tech. (Mech.) Nov., 2010; P.U. B.Com. April, 2007; MBA Feb., 2009; August, 2006; Pondicherry U.M.B.A. August, 2006; P.T.U. B.Tech. (Mech.) May, 2011; May, 2007; MBA, 2006; B.Com., 2007; R.U. B.E.(Mech.) 2002; G.N.D.U. B.Com., 2010, 09, 04*]
17. "OR is an aid for the executive in making his decisions by providing him with the needed quantitative information, based on the scientific method analysis". Discuss this statement in detail, illustrating it with OR methods that you know. [*G.N.D.U. 2007*]
18. State three properties and three advantages of OR models.
19. Discuss briefly the components of a problem and mention the three major types of problems in decision-making under different environments.
20. Write short notes on the following:
(*i*) Areas of application of OR. [*P.U. B.E.(E.&Ec.) 2000; B.Com. March, 2006*]
(*ii*) Role of constraints and objectives in the construction of mathematical models.
(*iii*) Statistician's role as a member of the OR team.
(*iv*) Application of OR Techniques in areas of production, planning, financial management, etc.
(*v*) Scope of OR in public utilities and in Industry. [*H.P.U.B.Tech.(Mech.) June, 2010*]
21. What are the situations where OR techniques will be applicable?
[*M.G.U. Kerala M.Com. June, 2012; G.N.D.U. April, 2004; Mumbai U. MBA, 2010*]
22. Comment on the following statements:
(*i*) OR is the art of winning wars without actually fighting them. [*G.N.D.U. Sept., 2004*]
(*ii*) OR is the art of finding bad answers where otherwise worse exist.
[*J.N.T.U. Hyderabad B.Tech. June, 2009;* G.N.D.U. April, 2008; *P.T.U. MBA June, 2003*]
(*iii*) OR replaces management by personality.
[*G.N.D.U. April, 2005; Nellore MBA, 2002*]
23. Define a scientific model. Discuss in detail three types of models with special emphasis on the important logical properties and the relationships the three types bear to each other and to modelled entities. [*H.P.U. B.Tech. (Mech.) Nov., 2014; P.T.U. MBA Feb., 2011; J.N.T.U. Hyderabad B.Tech. April, 2011; H.P.U. B.Tech. (Mech.) Sept.,2009; Nov., 2007*]
24. Explain the different types of models used in OR. Explain briefly the general methods for solving these OR models. [*Madras U.MBA. Nov., 2012; P.T.U. B.Tech. (Mech.) April, 2013; MBA, 2012;*

M.Tech. Dec., 2011; B. Tech. (C.Sc.) 2009; R.U. MBA June, 2011; P.U.B.Com. Sept., 2006; Nagpur U. B.E.(Comp. Tech.) 2003; Nellore MBA, 2002; Pbi.U. MCA, 2001, P.T.U. MBA, 2003]

25. "Model building is the essence of OR approach". Discuss.
[*R.T.M. Nagpur U. B.Tech. (Mech.) June, 2007; Nellore MBA, 2002*]
26. Discuss in brief the role of OR models in decision-making.
[*H.P.U. B.Tech. Nov., 2015; R.T.M. Nagpur U. B.E.(Mech.) 2011; G.N.D.U. Sept., 2004; Jammu U. B.E.(Mech.) 2004*]
27. Give the essential characteristics of the following types of processes:
(*a*) Allocation (*b*) Competitive (*c*) Inventory (*d*) Waiting Line
(*e*) Replacement [*H.P.U. B.Tech. (Mech.) 2013; 12; June, 2010; Dec., 2009; 2007; R.T.M. Nagpur U. B.Tech., Sept., 2008; P.U. B.E.(Mech.) 2002*]
28. Give an account of the information requirements, assumptions and applications of the following models:
(*a*) Iconic (*b*) Analogue (*c*) Sequencing (*d*) Dynamic programming
(*e*) Replacement (*f*) Simulation
[*H.P.U.B. Tech. (Mech.) 2013; 12; 2010;R.U. MBA June, 2011; J.NT.U. Hyderabad B.Tech. May, 2009*]
29. Describe the classification schemes of OR models.
[*H.P.U. B.Tech. June, 2015, 2010; P.T.U. M.Tech. Nov., 2012; V.T.U. Karnataka, 2012; R.U. MBA June, 2011; Dec. 2011; J.N.T.U. Hyderabad B.Tech. Nov., 2010; R.T.M. MBA, 2006; Nagpur U. B.E.(Mech.) 2003; P.U.B.E.(Mech.) 2002*]
30. What do you understand by deterministic and probabilistic models?
[*P.T.U. B.E. (Mech.) May, 2011; Nagpur U. B.E.(Mech.) 2003*]
31. Explain approximations in OR models. What are advantages and characteristics of a good model?
[*H.P.U. B.Tech. (Mech.) June, 2015, 2013; P.U.B.E.(Mech.) Nov., 2012; Nov. 2006; Nov. 2002*]
32. Give two definitions of a model. What are OR models? What is the role of approximations in OR models? How OR models are classified and constructed?
[*H.P.U. B.E. (Mech.) 2008, P.U.B.E.(Mech.) 2001*]
33. What is an OR model? Give the main advantages of an OR model. Describe its limitations.
[*P.U. UIAMS MBA May, 2015; P.T.U. BE, (Mech.) May, 2011; J.N.T.U. Hyderabad B. Tech. May, 2011; P.U.B.E.(E.&Ec.) 2001*]
34. (*a*) Give any four comprehensive definitions of OR.
[*R.U. MBA June, 2011; P.U.B.E.(Mech.) 2000; B.Com. Sept., 2005, 04*]
(*b*) Classify a few models used in OR. Elaborate L.P. model and given an application of it.
[*P.U.B.E.(Mech.) Dec., 2012*]
(*c*) Discuss the scope of OR in business.
[*G.N.D.U. B.Com. April, 2014; Madras U.MBA April, 2012*]
35. (*a*) What are the essential characteristics of OR? Enumerate various types of models. Give a brief account of methods used in model formulations. [*P.U.B.E.(Mech.) 1997*]
(*b*) What are limitations of OR?
[*P.T.U.B. Tech. (Mech.) May, 2007; H.P.U. B.Tech. Nov., 2007; Pondicherry U.M.B.A. June, 2007; 2006*]
36. Discuss the advantages and disadvantages of the following models :
(*a*) Verbal (*b*) Schematic (*c*) Iconic (*d*) Mathematical
[*Dayalbagh Edu. Inst. Agra M. Tech. Dec., 2007*]
37. Explain the role of computers in OR. [*P.T.U. MCA, 2010*]
38. Discuss the role of OR in real life Problems. [*P.T.U. B.Tech. (C.Sc.) 2009*]
39. What are the advantages of using results from a mathematical model to make decision about operations? [*P.T.U. B.Tech. (Mech.) 2009*]
40. What are the limitations of using results from a mathematical model to make decision about operations? [*H.P.U. B.Tech. (Mech.) 2015, 13, 12; P.U. B.E. (Mech.) 2012; J.N.T.U. Hyderabad MCA Feb., 2012; R.U. MBA June, 2010; V.T.U. Karnataka B.E. Dec., 2010; R.T.M. Nagpur U.B.Tech., 2011; P.T.U. B.Tech. (Mech.) 2008*]
41. (*a*) "Operations research is more than just mathematics". Justify the statement, with an example.
[*G.N.D.U. B.Com. Nov., 2014*]
(*b*) List and explain the steps in conducting an 'operations research' study.
[*V.T.U. Karnataka B.E. June, 2011*]
42. Write a detailed note on the use of models for decision-marking. The answer should specifically cover the following:

(*a*) Need for model building.
(*b*) Type of model appropriate to the situation.
(*c*) Steps involved in the construction of the model.

[*H.P.U. B.Tech. (Mech.) June, 2015*; *Kuru. U. B.E.(Mech.) June, 2012*]

43. Explain the role of operations research in solving industrial problems.

[*P.T.U. B.Tech. (Mech.) Dec., 2011; June, 2011*]

44. Discuss briefly the scope of OR in financial management.

[*J.N.T.U. Hyderabad B.Tech. August, 2011*]

45. Is OR a discipline or a profession or set of techniques or a philosophy or a new name of an old thing? Justify your answer. [*J.N.T.U. Hyderabad B.Tech. Nov., 2010*]

46. Define OR. Give reasons why most definitions of OR are not satisfactory.

[*R.T.M. Nagpur U. B.Tech. June, 2005*]

47. (*a*) Explain the role of OR in solving industrial problems. [*P.T.U. B.Tech. (Mech.) Dec., 2011*]
(*b*) Explain the interdisciplinary approach of OR. [*J.N.T.U. MBA June, 2012*]

48. Suggest a suitable OR model, giving reasons if any, for each of the following OR problems:
(*a*) Stockpiling of crackers prior to Divali.
(*b*) Decision to replace police jeeps after 10 years of running even though some of them may be in working condition.
(*c*) Reinforcing the strength of maintenance staff at the ship dock in Bombay.
(*d*) A newspaper boy deciding the no. of copies of a daily paper he should order per day.
(*e*) A scooter, its driver and his companion riding towards their office.
(*f*) Statistical forecasting of the sales of ice-cream.
(*g*) Establishing dependency relationships among the activities involved in the manufacture and marketing of a new product.
(*h*) Modification in the design of a new product.
(*i*) Improving means of verbal communication to provide better feedback for control of a jobbing workshop.

[**Hint.** (*a*) It is an OR problem. Objective is to maximize the profit. Alternative courses of actions are the various quantities of crackers that may be stockpiled. Overstocking would result in wastage of unsold crackers left over after the end of Divali; while understocking would cause regret or opportunity loss. An empirical sales distribution may be compiled from the past historical data. Time of purchasing the crackers is also significant. Too early purchase will be associated with tie-up of capital as well as enhanced risk of deterioration of crackers while too late marketing may result in regret later. (*b*) Replacement (*c*) Queuing (*d*) Inventory (*e*) Although the driver and his companion are driving with a purpose in view, there is hardly any conflict amongst the three. There is no other alternative course of action but to drive. It is, therefore, not an OR problem. (*f*) Forecasting inventory (*g*) Network (*h*) Not an OR problem (*i*) Production scheduling/control.]

49. Suggest a suitable OR model, if any, for the following situations:
(*i*) Deciding the quantities of the three products to be produced per week by the company.
(*ii*) Opening another reservation counter at the railway station.
(*iii*) Setting minimum stock level of bicycles in a cycle store.
(*iv*) Deciding the optimal lot size of a product for placing order by a trading company.
(*v*) Adapting the exponential smoothing forecast model for fluctuations in demand.
(*vi*) Deciding the recruitment policy of salesmen in a state on the expansion of business.
(*vii*) Determination of the number of bomb hits to destroy enemy's nuclear plant.

[**Ans.** (*i*) Allocation (*ii*) Queuing (*iii*) Inventory (*iv*) Inventory (*v*) Inventory control (*vi*) Replacement (*vii*) Simulation]

50. Suggest the suitable model (whether iconic, analogue or symbolic) for the following:
(*a*) microfilmed documents,
(*b*) flow process chart in an organisation,
(*c*) exponential smoothing forecast (empirical) model,
(*d*) monogram for computing economic order quantity,
(*e*) motion film,
(*f*) normal distribution curve,
(*g*) templates used for manipulation towards best layout,
(*h*) histogram of the rainfall at a place,
(*i*) economic order quantity formula.

[**Hint.** Iconic: (*a*), (*e*); analogue: (*b*), (*d*), (*f*), (*g*), (*h*); symbolic: (*c*), (i)]

Linear Programming

2.1 INTRODUCTION

Linear programming is perhaps the most widely applied mathematical technique that helps managers in decision-making and planning for the optimal allocation of limited resources. It deals with the optimization (maximization or minimization) of a function of variables known as *objective function*, subject to a set of linear equations and/or inequalities known as *constraints.* The objective function may be profit, cost, production capacity or any other measure of effectiveness, which is to be obtained in the best possible or optimal manner. The constraints may be imposed by different resources such as raw material availability, market demand, production process and equipment, storage capacity, etc. By linearity is meant a mathematical expression in which the expressions among the variables are linear *e.g.*, the expression $a_1x_1 + a_2x_2 + a_3x_3 + ... + a_nx_n$ is linear. Higher powers of the variables or their products donot appear in the expressions for the objective function as well as the constraints (they do not have expressions like x_1^3, $x_2^{3/2}$, x_1x_2, $a_1x_1 + a_2 \log x_2$, etc.). The variables obey the properties of *proportionality* (*e.g.*, if a product requires 3 hours of machining time, 5 units of it will require 15 hours) and *additivity* (*e.g.*, amount of a resource required for a certain number of products is equal to the sum of the resource required for each).

It was in 1947 that George Dantzig and his associates found out a technique for solving military planning problems while they were working on a project for U.S. Air Force. This technique consisted of representing the various activities of an organization as a linear programming (L.P.) model and arriving at the optimal programme by minimizing a linear objective function. Afterwards, Dantzig suggested this approach for solving business and industrial problems. He also developed the most powerful mathematical tool known as "simplex method" to solve linear programming problems.

2.2 REQUIREMENTS FOR A LINEAR PROGRAMMING PROBLEM

All organizations, big or small, have at their disposal, men, machines, money and materials, the supply of which may be limited. If the supply of these resources were unlimited, the need for management tools like linear programming would not arise at all. Supply of resources being limited, the management must find the best allocation of its resources in order to maximize the profit or minimize the cost/loss or utilize the production capacity to the maximum extent. However, this involves a number of problems which can be overcome by quantitative methods, particularly the linear programming.

Generally speaking, linear programming can be used for optimization problems if the following conditions are satisfied:

1. There must be a well defined objective function (profit, cost or quantities produced) which is to be either maximized or minimized and which can be expressed as a linear function of decision variables.

2. There must be constraints on the amount or extent of attainment of the objective and these constraints must be capable of being expressed as linear equations or inequalities in terms of variables.

3. There must be alternative courses of action. For example, a given product may be processed by two different machines and problem may be as to how much of the product to allocate to which machine.

4. Another necessary requirement is that decision variables should be interrelated and non-negative. The non-negativity condition shows that linear programming deals with real life situations for which negative quantities are generally illogical.

5. As stated earlier, the resources must be in limited supply. For example, if a firm starts producing greater number of a particular product, it must make smaller number of other products as the total production capacity is limited.

2.3 ASSUMPTIONS IN LINEAR PROGRAMMING MODELS

A linear programming model is based on the following assumptions:

1. **Proportionality:** A basic assumption of linear programming is that proportionality exists in the objective function and the constraints. This assumption implies that if a product yields a profit of ₹ 10, the profit earned from the sale of 12 such products will be ₹ (10 × 12) = ₹ 120. This may not always be true because of quantity discounts. Further, even if the sale price is constant, the manufacturing cost may vary with the number of units produced and so may vary the profit per unit. Likewise, it is assumed that if one product requires processing time of 5 hours, then ten such products will require processing time of 5 × 10 = 50 hours. This may also not be true as the processing time per unit often decreases with increase in number of units produced. The real world situations may not be strictly linear. However, assumed linearity represents their close approximations and provides very useful answers.

2. **Additivity:** It means that if we use t_1 hours on machine A to make product 1 and t_2 hours to make product 2, the total time required to make products 1 and 2 on machine A is $t_1 + t_2$ hours. This, however, is true only if the change-over time from product 1 to product 2 is negligible. Some processes may not behave in this way. For example, when several liquids of different chemical compositions are mixed, the resulting volume may not be equal to the sum of the volumes of the individual liquids.

3. **Continuity:** Another assumption underlying the linear programming model is that the decision variables are continuous *i.e.*, they are permitted to take any non-negative values that satisfy the constraints. However, there are problems wherein variables are restricted to have integral values only. Though such problems, strictly speaking, are not linear programming problems, they are frequently solved by linear programming techniques and the values are then rounded off to nearest integers to satisfy the constraints. This approximation, however, is valid only if the variables have large optimal values. Further, it must be ascertained whether the solution represented by the rounded values is a feasible solution and also whether the solution is the *best* integer solution.

4. **Certainty:** Another assumption underlying a linear programming model is that the various parameters, namely, the objective function coefficients, R.H.S. coefficients of the constraints and resource values in the constraints are certainly and precisely known and that their values do not change with time. Thus the profit or cost per unit of the product, labour and materials required per unit, availability of labour and materials, market demand of the product produced, etc. are assumed to be known with certainty. The linear programming problem is, therefore, assumed to be *deterministic* in nature.

5. **Finite Choices:** A linear programming model also assumes that a finite (limited) number of choices (alternatives) are available to the decision-maker and that the decision variables are

interrelated and non-negative. The non-negativity condition shows that linear programming deals with real-life situations as it is not possible to produce/use negative quantities.

Mathematically these non-negativity conditions do not differ from other constraints. However, since while solving the problems they are handled differently from the other constraints, they are termed as *non-negativity restrictions* and the term *constraints* is used to represent constraints other than non-negativity restrictions and this terminology has been followed throughout the book.

2.4 APPLICATIONS OF LINEAR PROGRAMMING METHOD

Though, in the world we live, most of the events are non-linear, yet there are many instances of linear events that occur in day-to-day life. Therefore, an understanding of linear programming and its application in solving problems is utmost essential for today's managers.

Linear programming techniques are widely used to solve a number of business, industrial, military, economic, marketing, distribution and advertising problems. Three primary reasons for its wide use are:

1. A large number of problems from different fields can be represented or at least approximated to linear programming problems.
2. Powerful and efficient techniques for solving L.P. problems are available.
3. L.P. models can handle data variation (sensitivity analysis) easily.

However, solution procedures are generally iterative and even medium size problems require manipulation of large amount of data. But with the development of digital computers, this disadvantage has been completely overcome as these computers can handle even large L.P. problems in comparatively very little time at a low cost.

2.5 AREAS OF APPLICATION OF LINEAR PROGRAMMING

Linear programming is one of the most widely applied techniques of operations research in business, industry and numerous other fields. A few areas of its application are given below.

1. INDUSTRIAL APPLICATIONS

(*a*) **Product mix problems:** An industrial organisation has available a certain production capacity (men, machines, money, materials, market, etc.) on various manufacturing processes to manufacture various products. Typically, differents products will have different selling prices, will require different amounts of production capacity at the several processes and will therefore, have different unit profits; there may also be stipulations (conditions) on maximum and/or minimum product levels. The problem is to determine the product mix that will maximize the total profit.

(*b*) **Blending problems:** These problems are likely to arise when a product can be made from a variety of available raw materials of various compositions and prices. The manufacturing process involves blending (mixing) some of these materials in varying quantities to make a product of the desired specifications.

For instance, different grades of gasoline are required for aviation purposes. Prices and specifications such as octane ratings, tetra ethyl lead concentrations, maximum vapour pressure, etc. of input ingredients are given and the problem is to decide the proportions of these ingredients to make the desired grades of gasoline so that (*i*) maximum output is obtained and (*ii*) storage capacity restrictions are satisfied. Many similar situations such as preparation of different kinds of whisky, chemicals, fertilisers and alloys, etc. have been handled by this technique of linear programming.

(*c*) **Production scheduling problems:** They involve the determination of optimum production schedule to meet fluctuating demand. The objective is to meet demand, keeping inventory and employment at reasonable minimum levels, while minimizing the total cost of production and inventory.

(*d*) **Trim loss problems:** They are applicable to paper, sheet metal and glass manufacturing industries where items of standard sizes have to be cut to smaller sizes as per customer requirements with the objective of minimizing the waste produced.

(*e*) **Assembly-line balancing:** It relates to a category of problems wherein the final product has a number of different components assembled together. These components are to be assembled in a specific sequence or set of sequences. Each assembly operator is to be assigned the task / combination of tasks so that his task time is less than or equal to the cycle time.

(*f*) **Make-or-buy (sub-contracting) problems:** They arise in an organisation in the face of production capacity limitations and sudden spurt in demand of its products. The manufacturer, not being sure of the demand pattern, is usually reluctant to add additional capacity and has to make a decision regarding the products to be manufacured with his own resources and the products to be subcontracted so that the total cost is minimized.

2. MANAGEMENT APPLICATIONS

(*a*) **Media selection problems:** They involve the selection of advertising mix among different advertising media such as T.V., radio, magazines and newspapers that will maximize public exposure to company's product. The constraints may be on the total advertising budget, maximum expenditure in each media, maximum number of insertions in each media and the like.

(*b*) **Portfolio selection problems:** They are frequently encountered by banks, financial companies, insurance companies, investment services, etc. A given amount is to be allocated among several investment alternatives such as bonds, saving certificates, common stock, mutual fund, real estate, etc. to maximize the expected return or minimize the expected risk.

(*c*) **Profit planning problems:** They involve planning profits on fiscal year basis to maximize profit margin from investment in plant facilities, machinery, inventory and cash on hand.

(*d*) **Transportation problems:** They involve transportation of products from, say, *n* sources situated at different locations to, say, *m* different destinations. Supply position at the sources, demand at destinations, freight charges and storage costs, etc. are known and the problem is to design the optimum transportation plan that minimizes the total transportation cost (or distance or time).

(*e*) **Assignment problems:** They are concerned with allocation of facilities (men or machines) to jobs. Time required by each facility to perform each job is given and the problem is to find the optimum allocation (one job to one facility) so that the total time to perform the jobs is minimized.

(*f*) **Manpower scheduling problems:** They are faced by big hospitals, restaurants and companies operating in a number of shifts. The problem is to allocate optimum manpower in each shift so that the overtime cost is minimized.

3. MISCELLANEOUS APPLICATIONS

(a) **Diet problems:** They form another important category to which linear programming has been applied. Nutrient contents such as vitamins, proteins, fats, carbohydrates, starch, etc. in each of a number of food stuffs is known. Also the minimum daily requirement of each nutrient in the diet as well as the cost of each type of food stuff is given and the problem is to determine the minimum cost diet that satisfies the minimum daily requirement of nutrients.

(*b*) **Agriculture problems:** These problems are concerned with the allocation of input resources such as acreage of land, water, labour, fertilisers and capital to various crops so as to maximize net revenue.

(*c*) **Flight scheduling problems:** They are devoted to the determination of the most economical patterns and timings of flights that result in the most efficient use of aircrafts and crews.

(*d*) **Environment protection:** They involve analysis of different alternatives for efficient waste disposal, paper recycling and energy policies.

(*e*) **Facilities location:** These problems are concerned with the determination of best location of public parks, libraries and recreation areas, hospital ambulance depots, telephone exchanges, nuclear power plants, etc.

Oil refineries have used linear programming with considerable success. Similar trends are developing in chemical industries, iron and steel industries, aluminium industry, food processing industry, wood products manufacture and many others. Other areas where linear programming has been applied include quality control inspection, determination of optimal bombing patterns, searching of submarines, design of war weapons, vendor quotation analysis, structural design, scheduling military tanker fleet, fabrication scheduling, steel production scheduling, balancing of assembly lines and computations of maximum flows in networks.

In fact linear programming may be used for any general situation where a linear objective function has to be optimised subject to constraints expressed as linear equations/inequalities.

2.6 FORMULATION OF LINEAR PROGRAMMING PROBLEMS

First, the given problem must be presented in linear programming form. This requires defining the variables of the problem, establishing interrelationships between them and formulating the objective function and constraints. A model, which approximates as closely as possible to the given problem, is then to be developed. If some constraints happen to be non-linear, they are approximated to appropriate linear functions to fit the linear programming format. In case it is not possible, other techniques may be used to formulate and then solve the model.

EXAMPLE 2.6-1 (Production Allocation Problem)

A firm produces three products. These products are processed on three different machines. The time required to manufacture one unit of each of the three products and the daily capacity of the three machines are given in the table below.

TABLE 2.1

Machine	*Time per unit (minutes)*			*Machine capacity (minutes/day)*
	Product 1	*Product 2*	*Product 3*	
M_1	2	3	2	440
M_2	4	—	3	470
M_3	2	5	—	430

It is required to determine the daily number of units to be manufactured for each product. The profit per unit for product 1, 2 and 3 is ₹ 4, ₹ 3 and ₹ 6 respectively. It is assumed that all the amounts produced are consumed in the market. Formulate the mathematical (L.P.) model that will maximize the daily profit. *[G.N.D.U. BBA Sept., 1998; H.P.U. MCA, 1999]*

Formulation of Linear Programming Model

Step 1:

From the study of the situation find the *key decision* to be made. It this connection, looking for variables helps considerably. In the given situation key decision is to decide the number of units of products 1, 2 and 3 to be produced daily.

Step 2:

Assume symbols for variable quantities noticed in step 1. Let the number of units of products, 1, 2 and 3 manufactured daily be x_1, x_2 and x_3.

Step 3:

Express the *feasible alternatives* mathematically in terms of variables. Feasible alternatives are those which are physically, economically and financially possible. In the given situation feasible alternatives are sets of values of x_1, x_2 and x_3, where $x_1, x_2, x_3 \geq 0$,

since negative production has no meaning and is not feasible.

Step 4:

Mention the *objective* quantitatively and express it as a linear function of variables. In the present situation, objective is to maximize the profit.

i.e., maximize $Z = 4x_1 + 3x_2 + 6x_3$.

Step 5:

Put into words the *influencing factors* or *constraints*. These occur generally because of constraints on availability (resources) or requirements (demands). Express these constraints also as linear equations/inequalities in terms of variables.

Here, constraints are on the machine capacities and can be mathematically expressed as

$$2x_1 + 3x_2 + 2x_3 \leq 440,$$
$$4x_1 + 0x_2 + 3x_3 \leq 470,$$
$$2x_1 + 5x_2 + 0x_3 \leq 430.$$

Therefore, the complete mathematical (L.P.) model for the problem can be written as

maximize $Z = 4x_1 + 3x_2 + 6x_3$,

subject to constraints, $2x_1 + 3x_2 + 2x_3 \leq 440$,

$4x_1 + 3x_3 \leq 470$,

$2x_1 + 5x_2 \leq 430$,

where $x_1, x_2, x_3 \geq 0$.

EXAMPLE 2.6-2 (Diet Problem)

A person wants to decide the constituents of a diet which will fulfill his daily requirements of proteins, fats and carbohydrates at the minimum cost. The choice is to be made from four different types of foods. The yields per unit of these foods are given in table 2.2.

TABLE 2.2

Food type	*Yield per unit*			*Cost per unit*
	Proteins	*Fats*	*Carbohydrates*	*(₹)*
1	*3*	*2*	*6*	*45*
2	*4*	*2*	*4*	*40*
3	*8*	*7*	*7*	*85*
4	*6*	*5*	*4*	*65*
Minimum requirement	800	200	700	

Formulate linear programming model for the problem.

Formulation of L.P. Model

Let x_1, x_2, x_3 and x_4 denote the number of units of food of type 1, 2, 3 and 4 respectively.

Objective is to minimize the cost *i.e.*,

$$\text{Minimize } Z = ₹\,(45x_1 + 40x_2 + 85x_3 + 65x_4).$$

Constraints are on the fulfilment of the daily requirements of the various constituents.

i.e., for proteins, $3x_1 + 4x_2 + 8x_3 + 6x_4 \geq 800$,

for fats, $2x_1 + 2x_2 + 7x_3 + 5x_4 \geq 200$,

and for carbohydrates, $6x_1 + 4x_2 + 7x_3 + 4x_4 \geq 700$,

where x_1, x_2, x_3, x_4, each ≥ 0.

EXAMPLE 2.6-3 (Blending Problem)

A firm produces an alloy having the following specifications:

(i) *specific gravity* ≤ 0.98,

(ii) *chromium* $\geq 8\%$,

(iii) *melting point* $\geq 450°C$.

Raw materials A, B and C having the properties shown in the table can be used to make the alloy.

TABLE 2.3

Property	*Properties of raw material*		
	A	*B*	*C*
Specific gravity	0.92	0.97	1.04
Chromium	7%	13%	16%
Melting point	440°C	490°C	480°C

Costs of the various raw materials per ton are: ₹ 90 for A, ₹ 280 for B and ₹ 40 for C. Formulate the L.P. model to find the proportions in which A, B and C be used to obtain an alloy of desired properties while the cost of raw materials is minimum.

[*P.U. B.E. (E. & Comm.) De., 2011; G.N.D.U. BBA April, 2006*]

Formulation of Linear Programming Model

Let the *proportions* of raw materials A, B and C to be used for making the alloy be x_1, x_2 and x_3 respectively.

Objective is to minimize the cost

i.e., $\quad$ minimize $Z = 90x_1 + 280x_2 + 40x_3$.

Constraints are imposed by the specifications required for the alloy.

They are

$$0.92x_1 + 0.97x_2 + 1.04x_3 \leq 0.98,$$
$$7x_1 + 13x_2 + 16x_3 \geq 8,$$
$$440x_1 + 490x_2 + 480x_3 \geq 450,$$

and $\quad x_1 + x_2 + x_3 = 1,$

as x_1, x_2 and x_3 are the proportions of materials A, B and C in making the alloy.

Also $\quad x_1, x_2, x_3$, each ≥ 0.

EXAMPLE 2.6-4 (Advertising Media Selection Problem)

An advertising company wishes to plan its advertising strategy in three different media—television, radio and magazines. The purpose of advertising is to reach as large a number of potential customers as possible. Following data have been obtained from market survey:

TABLE 2.4

	Television	*Radio*	*Magazine I*	*Magazine II*
Cost of an advertising unit	*₹ 30,000*	*₹ 20,000*	*₹ 15,000*	*₹ 10,000*
No. of potential customers reached per unit	*2,00,000*	*6,00,000*	*1,50,000*	*1,00,000*
No. of female customers reached per unit	*1,50,000*	*4,00,000*	*70,000*	*50,000*

The company wants to spend not more than ₹ 4,50,000 on advertising. Following are the further requirements that must be met:

(*i*) *at least 1 million exposures take place among female customers,*
(*ii*) *advertising on magazines be limited to ₹ 1,50,000,*
(*iii*) *at least 3 advertising units be bought on magazine I and 2 units on magazine II,*
(*iv*) *the number of advertising units on television and radio should each be between 5 and 10.*

Formulate an L.P. model for the problem.

[*H.P.U.B. Tech. (Mech.) June, 2010; P.T.U. MBA May, 2002*]

Formulation of Linear Programming Model

Let x_1, x_2, x_3 and x_4 denote the number of advertising units to be bought on television, radio, magazine I and magazine II respectively.

The *objective* is to maximize the total number of potential customers reached.

i.e., maximize $Z = 10^5 (2x_1 + 6x_2 + 1.5x_3 + x_4)$.

Constraints are

on the advertising budget: $30{,}000x_1 + 20{,}000x_2 + 15{,}000x_3 + 10{,}000x_4 \le 4{,}50{,}000$
or $30x_1 + 20x_2 + 15x_3 + 10x_4 \le 450$,

on number of female customers reached by the advertising campaign: $1{,}50{,}000x_1 + 4{,}00{,}000x_2 + 70{,}000x_3 + 50{,}000x_4 \ge 10{,}00{,}000$
or $15x_1 + 40x_2 + 7x_3 + 5x_4 \ge 100$,

on expenses on magazine advertising: $15{,}000x_3 + 10{,}000x_4 \le 1{,}50{,}000$
or $15x_3 + 10x_4 \le 150$,

on no. of units on magazines: $x_3 \ge 3$,
$x_4 \ge 2$,

on no. of units on television: $5 \le x_1 \le 10$ or $x_1 \ge 5$, $x_1 \le 10$,

on no. of units on radio: $5 \le x_2 \le 10$ or $x_2 \ge 5$, $x_2 \le 10$,

where x_1, x_2, x_3 x_4, each ≥ 0.

EXAMPLE 2.6-5 (Inspection Problem)

A company has two grades of inspectors, I and II to undertake quality control inspection. At least 1,500 pieces must be inspected in an 8-hour day. Grade I inspector can check 20 pieces in an hour with an accuracy of 96%. Grade II inspector checks 14 pieces an hour with an accuracy of 92%.

Wages of grade I inspector are ₹ 5 per hour while those of grade II inspector are ₹ 4 per hour. Any error made by an inspector costs ₹ 3 to the company. If there are, in all, 10 grade I inspectors and 15 grade II inspectors in the company, find the optimal assignment of inspectors that minimizes the daily inspection cost. [*P.U. B.Com. April, 2008; D.U. MBA, 2003, 02, 00; NIIFT Mohali, 2000*]

Formulation of L.P. Model

Let x_1 and x_2 denote the number of grade I and grade II inspectors that may be assigned the job of quality control inspection.

The *objective* is to minimize the daily cost of inspection. Now the company has to incur two types of costs: wages paid to the inspectors and the cost of their inspection errors. The cost of a grade I inspector/hour is

₹ $(5 + 3 \times 0.04 \times 20)$ = ₹ 7.40.

Similarly, cost of a grade II inspector/hour is

₹ $(4 + 3 \times 0.08 \times 14)$ = ₹ 7.36.

∴ The objective function is

minimize $Z = 8(7.40x_1 + 7.36x_2) = 59.20x_1 + 58.88x_2$.

Constraints are
on the number of grade I inspectors : $x_1 \leq 10$,
on the number of grade II inspectors : $x_2 \leq 15$,
on the number of pieces to be inspected daily: $20 \times 8x_1 + 14 \times 8x_2 \geq 1,500$
or $160x_1 + 112x_2 \geq 1,500$,
where $x_1, x_2 \geq 0$.

EXAMPLE 2.6-6 (Product Mix Problem)

A chemical company produces two products, X and Y. Each unit of product X requires 3 hours on operation I and 4 hours on operation II, while each unit of product Y requires 4 hours on operation I and 5 hours on operation II. Total available time for operations I and II is 20 hours and 26 hours respectively. The production of each unit of product Y also results in two units of a by-product Z at no extra cost.

Product X sells at profit of ₹ 10/unit, while Y sells at profit of ₹ 20/unit. By-product Z brings a unit profit of ₹ 6 if sold; in case it cannot be sold, the destruction cost is ₹ 4/unit. Forecasts indicate that not more than 5 units of Z can be sold. Formulate the L.P. model to determine the quantities of X and Y to be produced, keeping Z in mind, so that the profit earned is maximum.

[B.P.U.T., 2012; P.U.B. Com. April, 2006; Jammu U.B.E. (Mech.) 2004; P.T.U.B.Tech., 2000]

Formulation of L.P. Model

Let the number of units of products X, Y and Z produced be x_1, x_2, x_z, where

x_z = number of units of Z produced
= number of units of Z sold + number of units of Z destroyed
= $x_3 + x_4$ (say).

Objective is to maximize the profit. Objective function (profit function) for products X and Y is linear because their profits (₹ 10/unit and ₹ 20/unit) are constants irrespective of the number of units produced. A graph between the total profit and quantity produced will be a straight line. However, a similar graph for product Z is non-linear since it has slope +6 for first part, while a slope of –4 for the second. However, it is piecewise linear, since it is linear in the regions (0 to 5) and (5 to 2Y). Thus splitting x_z into two parts, *viz.* the number of units of Z sold (x_3) and number of units of Z destroyed (x_4) makes the objective function for product Z also linear.

Thus the objective function is

$$\text{maximize } Z = 10x_1 + 20x_2 + 6x_3 - 4x_4.$$

Constraints are
on the time available on operation I: $3x_1 + 4x_2 \leq 20$,
on the time available on operation II: $4x_1 + 5x_2 \leq 26$,
on the number of units of product Z sold: $x_3 \leq 5$,
on the number of units of product Z produced: 2Y = Z
or $2x_2 = x_3 + x_4$ or $-2x_2 + x_3 + x_4 = 0$,
where x_1, x_2, x_3, x_4, each ≥ 0.

EXAMPLE 2.6-7 (Product Mix Problem)

A firm manufactures three products A, B and C. Time to manufacture product A is twice that for B and thrice that for C and if the entire labour is engaged in making product A, 1,600 units of this product can be produced. These products are to be produced in the ratio 3 : 4 : 5. There is demand for at least 300, 250 and 200 units of products A, B and C and the profit earned per unit is ₹ 90, ₹ 40 and ₹ 30 respectively.

Formulate the problem as a linear programming problem.

TABLE 2.5

Raw material	*Requirement per unit of product (kg)*			*Total availability (kg)*
	A	*B*	*C*	
P	6	5	2	5,000
Q	4	7	3	6,000

[*R.T.M. Nagpur U. B.Tech. Dec., 2003; H.P.U. B.Tech. (Mech.) Nov. 2010; P.T.U.B.E., 2001*]

Formulation of L.P. Model

Let x_1, x_2 and x_3 denote the number of units of products A, B and C to be manufactured.

Objective is to maximize the profit.

i.e., maximize $Z = 90x_1 + 40x_2 + 30x_3$.

Constraints can be formulated as follows:

For raw material P, $6x_1 + 5x_2 + 2x_3 \leq 5{,}000$,

and for raw material Q, $4x_1 + 7x_2 + 3x_3 \leq 6{,}000$.

Product B requires 1/2 and product C requires 1/3rd the time required for product A.

Let t hours be the time to produce A. Then $t/_2$ and $t/_3$ are the times in hours to produce B and C and since 1,600 units of A will need time 1,600t hours, we get the constraint,

$$tx_1 + \frac{t}{2}x_2 + \frac{t}{3}x_3 \leq 1{,}600t \quad \text{or} \quad x_1 + \frac{x_2}{2} + \frac{x_3}{3} \leq 1{,}600,$$

or

$$6x_1 + 3x_2 + 2x_3 \leq 9{,}600.$$

Market demand requires

$$x_1 \geq 300,$$
$$x_2 \geq 250,$$

and

$$x_3 \geq 200.$$

Finally, since products A, B and C are to be produced in the ratio 3: 4: 5,

$x_1 : x_2 : x_3 :: 3 : 4 : 5$

or

$$\frac{x_1}{3} = \frac{x_2}{4},$$

and

$$\frac{x_2}{4} = \frac{x_3}{5}.$$

Thus there are two additional constraints

$$4x_1 - 3x_2 = 0,$$

and

$$5x_2 - 4x_3 = 0,$$

where

$$x_1, x_2, x_3 \geq 0.$$

EXAMPLE 2.6-8 (Trim-Loss Problem)

A paper mill produces rolls of paper used in making cash registers. Each roll of paper is 100m in length and can be used in widths of 3, 4, 6 and 10cm. The company's production process results in rolls that are 24 cm in width. Thus the company must cut its 24 cm roll to the desired widths. It has six basic cutting alternatives as follows:

Cutting alternatives	*Width of rolls (cm)*				*Waste (cm)*
	3	*4*	*6*	*10*	
1	*4*	*3*	—	—	—
2	—	*3*	*2*	—	—
3	*1*	*1*	*1*	*1*	*1*
4	—	—	*2*	*1*	*2*
5	—	*4*	*1*	—	*2*
6	*3*	*2*	*1*	—	*1*

The minimum demand for the four rolls is as follows:

Roll width (cm)	*Demand*
2	2,000
4	3,600
6	1,600
10	500

The paper mill wishes to minimize the waste resulting from trimming to size. Formulate the L.P. model. *[P.U. B.Com. April, 2006]*

Formulation of L.P. Model

Key decision is to determine how the paper rolls be cut to the required widths so that trim losses (wastage) are minimum.

Let x_j (j = 1, 2, ..., 6) represent the number of times each cutting alternative is to be used. These alternatives result/do not result in certain trim loss.

Objective is to minimize the trim losses.

i.e., minimize $Z = x_3 + 2x_4 + 2x_5 + x_6$.

Constraints are on the market demand for each type of roll width:

For roll width of 3cm, $4x_1 + x_3 + 3x_6 \geq 2{,}000$,

for roll width of 4 cm, $3x_1 + 3x_2 + x_3 + 4x_5 + 2x_6 \geq 3{,}600$,

for roll width of 6cm, $2x_2 + x_3 + 2x_4 + x_5 + x_6 \geq 1{,}600$,

and for roll width of 10cm, $x_3 + x_4 \geq 500$.

Since the variables represent the number of times each alternative is to be used, they can not have negative values.

$\therefore x_1, x_2, x_3, x_4, x_5, x_6$, each ≥ 0.

EXAMPLE 2.6-9 (Production Planning Problem)

A factory manufactures a product each unit of which consists of 5 units of part A and 4 units of part B. The two parts A and B require different raw materials of which 120 units and 240 units respectively are available. These parts can be manufactured by three different methods. Raw material requirements per production run and the number of units for each part produced are given below.

TABLE 2.6

Method	*Input per run (units)*		*Output per run (units)*	
	Raw material 1	*Raw material 2*	*Part A*	*Part B*
1	7	5	6	4
2	4	7	5	8
3	2	9	7	3

Formulate the L.P. model to determine the number of production runs for each method so as to maximize the total number of complete units of the final product.

[H.P.U. B.Tech. (Mech.) June, 2008]

Formulation of Linear Programming Model

Let x_1, x_2, x_3 represent the number of production runs for method 1, 2 and 3 respectively.

The *objective* is to maximize the total number of units of the final product. Now, the total number of units of part A produced by different methods is $6x_1 + 5x_2 + 7x_3$ and for part B is $4x_1 + 8x_2 + 3x_3$. Since each unit of the final product requires 5 units of part A and 4 units of part B, it is evident that the maximum number of units of the final product cannot exceed the smaller value of

$$\frac{6x_1 + 5x_2 + 7x_3}{5} \quad \text{and} \quad \frac{4x_1 + 8x_2 + 3x_3}{4}.$$

Thus the objective is to maximize

$$Z = \text{Minimum of } \left(\frac{6x_1 + 5x_2 + 7x_3}{5}, \frac{4x_1 + 8x_2 + 3x_3}{4} \right).$$

Constraints are on the availability of raw materials. They are, for

raw material 1, $\quad 7x_1 + 4x_2 + 2x_3 \le 120,$

and raw material 2, $\quad 5x_1 + 7x_2 + 9x_3 \le 240.$

The above formulation violates the linear programming properties since the objective function is non-linear. (Linear relationship between two or more variables is the one in which the variables are directly and precisely proportional). However, the above model can be easily reduced to the generally acceptable linear programming format.

Let $y = \text{Min} \left(\frac{6x_1 + 5x_2 + 7x_3}{5}, \frac{4x_1 + 8x_2 + 3x_3}{4} \right).$

It follows that $\frac{6x_1 + 5x_2 + 7x_3}{5} \ge y$ and $\frac{4x_1 + 8x_2 + 3x_3}{4} \ge y.$

i.e., $\quad 6x_1 + 5x_2 + 7x_3 - 5y \ge 0,\quad$ and $\quad 4x_1 + 8x_2 + 3x_3 - 4y \ge 0.$

Thus the mathematical model for the problem is

$$\text{Maximize } Z = y,$$

subject to constraints

$$7x_1 + 4x_2 + 2x_3 \le 120,$$
$$5x_1 + 7x_2 + 9x_3 \le 240,$$
$$6x_1 + 5x_2 + 7x_3 - 5y \ge 0,$$
$$4x_1 + 8x_2 + 3x_3 - 4y \ge 0,$$

where $\quad x_1, x_2, x_3, y \ge 0.$

EXAMPLE 2.6-10 (Fluid Blending Problem)

An oil company produces two grades of gasoline P and Q which it sells at ₹ 30 and ₹ 40 per litre. The company can buy four different crude oils with the following constituents and costs:

TABLE 2.7

Crude oil	*Constituents*			*Price/litre*
	A	*B*	*C*	*(₹)*
1	*0.75*	*0.15*	*0.10*	*20.00*
2	*0.20*	*0.30*	*0.50*	*22.50*
3	*0.70*	*0.10*	*0.20*	*25.00*
4	*0.40*	*0.10*	*0.50*	*27.50*

Gasoline P must have at least 55 per cent of constituent A and not more than 40 per cent of C. Gasoline Q must not have more than 25 per cent of C. Determine how the crudes should be used to maximize the profit. [P.U. B.E. (Mech.) Dec., 1978]

Formulation of Mathematical Model

Key decision to be made is how much of each crude oil be used in making each of the two grades of gasoline. Let these quantities in litres be represented by x_{ij}, where i = crude oil 1, 2, 3, 4 and j = gasoline of grades P and Q respectively. Thus

x_{1p} = amount in litres of crude oil 1 used in gasoline of grade P,
x_{2p} = amount in litres of crude oil 2 used in gasoline of grade P,
... ...
... ...
x_{1q} = amount in litres of crude oil 1 used in gasoline of grade Q,
x_{2q} = amount in litres of crude oil 2 used in gasoline of grade Q,
... ...
... ...

Objective is to maximize the net profit.

i.e., maximize Z = ₹ $[30(x_{1p} + x_{2p} + x_{3p} + x_{4p}) + 40(x_{1q} + x_{2q} + x_{3q} + x_{4q}) - 20(x_{1p} + x_{1q}) - 22.50\,(x_{2p} + x_{2q}) - 25\,(x_{3p} + x_{3q}) - 27.50\,(x_{4p} + x_{4q})]$

or maximize Z = ₹ $[10x_{1p} + 7.50x_{2p} + 5x_{3p} + 2.50x_{4p} + 20x_{1q} + 17.50x_{2q} + 15x_{3q} + 12.50x_{4q}]$.

Constraints are on the quantities of constituents A and C to be allowed in the two grades of gasoline.

i.e., $0.75x_{1p} + 0.20x_{2p} + 0.70x_{3p} + 0.40x_{4p} \geq 0.55\,(x_{1p} + x_{2p} + x_{3p} + x_{4p})$,
$0.10x_{1p} + 0.50x_{2p} + 0.20x_{3p} + 0.50x_{4p} \leq 0.40\,(x_{1p} + x_{2p} + x_{3p} + x_{4p})$,
and $0.10x_{1q} + 0.50x_{2q} + 0.20x_{3q} + 0.50x_{4q} \leq 0.25\,(x_{1q} + x_{2q} + x_{3q} + x_{4q})$,
where $x_{1p}, x_{2p}, x_{3p}, x_{4p}, x_{1q}, x_{2q}, x_{3q}, x_{4q}$, each ≥ 0.

EXAMPLE 2.6-11 (Production Planning Problem)

A company manufacturing air coolers has, at present, firm orders for the next 6 months. The company can schedule its production over the next 6 months to meet orders on either regular or overtime basis. The order size and production costs over the next six months are as follows:

Month	:	*1*	*2*	*3*	*4*	*5*	*6*
Orders	:	*640*	*660*	*700*	*750*	*550*	*650*
Cost/unit (₹) for regular production	:	*40*	*42*	*41*	*45*	*39*	*40*
Cost/unit (₹) for overtime production	:	*52*	*50*	*53*	*50*	*45*	*43*

With 100 air coolers in stock at present, the company wishes to have at least 150 air coolers in stock at the end of 6 months. The regular and overtime production in each month is not to exceed 600 and 400 units respectively. The inventory carrying cost for air coolers is ₹ 12 per unit per month. Formulate the L.P. model to minimize the total cost.

Formulation of L.P. Model

Key decision is to determine the number of units of air coolers to be produced on regular as well as overtime basis together with the number of units of ending inventory in each of the six months.

Let x_{ij} be the number of units produced in month j (j = 1, 2, ..., 6), on a regular or overtime basis (i = 1, 2). Further let y_j represent the number of units of ending inventory in month j (j = 1, 2, ..., 6).

Objective is to minimize the total cost (of production and inventory carrying).

i.e., minimize Z = $(40x_{11} + 42x_{12} + 41x_{13} + 45x_{14} + 39x_{15} + 40x_{16}) + (52x_{21} + 50x_{22} + 53x_{23} + 50x_{24} + 45x_{25} + 43x_{26}) + 12(y_1 + y_2 + y_3 + y_4 + y_5 + y_6)$.

Constraints are

	for the first month,	$100 + x_{11} + x_{21} - 640$	$= y_1$,
	for the second month,	$y_1 + x_{12} + x_{22} - 660$	$= y_2$,
	for the third month,	$y_2 + x_{13} + x_{23} - 700$	$= y_3$,
	for the fourth month,	$y_3 + x_{14} + x_{24} - 750$	$= y_4$,
	for the fifth month,	$y_4 + x_{15} + x_{25} - 550$	$= y_5$,
and	for the sixth month,	$y_5 + x_{16} + x_{26} - 650$	$= y_6$.

Also, the ending inventory constraint is

$$y_6 \geq 150.$$

Further, since regular and overtime production each month is not to exceed 600 and 400 units respectively,

$x_{11}, x_{12}, x_{13}, x_{14}, x_{15}, x_{16}$, each ≤ 600,

and $x_{21}, x_{22}, x_{23}, x_{24}, x_{25}, x_{26}$, each ≤ 400.

Also $x_{ij} \geq 0$ $(i = 1, 2;\ j = 1, 2, ..., 6)$, $y_j \geq 0$.

EXAMPLE 2.6-12 (Transportation Problem)

A dairy firm has two milk plants with daily milk production of 6 million litres and 9 million litres respectively. Each day the firm must fulfil the needs of its three distribution centres which have milk requirement of 7, 5 and 3 million litres respectively. Cost of shipping one million litres of milk from each plant to each distribution centre is given, in hundreds of rupees below. Formulate the L.P. model to minimize the transportation cost.

	Distribution Centres 1	2	3	*Supply*
Plants 1	2	3	11	6
Plants 2	1	9	6	9
Demand	7	5	3	

Formulation of L.P. Model

Key decision is to determine the quantity of milk to be transported from either plant to each distribution centre.

Let x_1, x_2 be the quantity of milk (in million litres) transported from plant 1 to distribution centre no. 1 and 2 respectively. The resulting table representing transportation of milk is shown below.

	Distribution Centres 1	2	3	*Supply*
Plants 1	x_1	x_2	$6 - x_1 - x_2$	6
Plants 2	$7 - x_1$	$5 - x_2$	$9 - (7 - x_1) - (5 - x_2)$	9
Demand	7	5	3	

Objective is to minimize the transportation cost.

i.e., minimize $Z = 2x_1 + 3x_2 + 11(6 - x_1 - x_2) + (7 - x_1) + 9(5 - x_2) + 6[9 - (7 - x_1) - (5 - x_2)] = 100 - 4x_1 - 11x_2$.

Constraints are

$$6 - x_1 - x_2 \geq 0 \quad \text{or} \quad x_1 + x_2 \leq 6,$$

$$7 - x_1 \geq 0 \quad \text{or} \quad x_1 \leq 7,$$

$$5 - x_2 \geq 0 \quad \text{or} \quad x_2 \leq 5,$$

and $9 - (7 - x_1) - (5 - x_2) \geq 0$ or $x_1 + x_2 \geq 3$,

where $x_1, x_2 \geq 0$.

EXAMPLE 2.6-13 (Product Mix Problem)

A plant manufactures washing machines and dryers. The major manufacturing departments are the stamping deptt., motor and transmission deptt. and assembly deptt. The first two departments produce parts for both the products while the assembly lines are different for the two products. The monthly deptt. capacities are

Stamping deptt.	*: 1,000 washers or 1,000 dryers*
Motor and transmission deptt.	*: 1,600 washers or 7,000 dryers*
Washer assembly line	*: 9,000 washers only*
Dryer assembly line	*: 5,000 dryers only.*

Profits per piece of washers and dryers are ₹ 2,700 and ₹ 3,000 respectively. Formulate the L.P. model. [V.T.U. Karnataka B.Tech. Dec., 2011; Dec., 2010; P.U. B.Com. Jan., 2005]

Formulation of Linear Programming Model

Let x_1 and x_2 represent the number of washing machines and dryers to be manufactured each month.

The *objective* is to maximize the total profit each month.

$$\text{i.e. maximize } Z = 2{,}700x_1 + 3{,}000x_2.$$

Constraints are on the monthly capacities of the various departments.

For the stamping deptt., $\quad \dfrac{x_1}{1{,}000} + \dfrac{x_2}{1{,}000} \le 1$, or $x_1 + x_2 \le 1{,}000$,

for the motor and transmission deptt.,

$$\frac{x_1}{1{,}600} + \frac{x_2}{7{,}000} \le 1, \text{ or } 70x_1 + 16x_2 \le 1{,}12{,}000,$$

for the washer assembly deptt., $\quad x_1 \le 9{,}000$,
and for the dryer assembly deptt., $\quad x_2 \le 5{,}000$,
where $x_1 \ge 0$, $x_2 \ge 0$.

EXAMPLE 2.6-14 (Agriculture Problem)

A certain farming organization operates three farms of comparable productivity. The output of each farm is limited both by the usable acreage and by the amount of water available for irrigation. Following are the data for the upcoming season:

Farm	*Usable acreage*	*Water available in acre feet*
1	*400*	*1,500*
2	*600*	*2,000*
3	*300*	*900*

The organization is considering three crops for planting which differ primarily in their expected profit per acre and in their consumption of water. Furthermore, the total acreage that can be devoted to each of the crops is limited by the amount of appropriate harvesting equipment available.

Crop	*Minimum acreage*	*Water consumption in acre feet per acre*	*Expected profit per acre*
A	*400*	*5*	*₹ 400*
B	*300*	*4*	*₹ 300*
C	*300*	*3*	*₹ 100*

In order to maintain a uniform work load among the farms, it is the policy of the organization that the percentage of the usable acreage planted must be the same at each farm. However, any combination of the crops may be grown at any of the farms. The organization wishes to know how much of each crop should be planted at the respective farms in order to maximize expected profit. Formulate this as a linear programming problem.

[*Delhi U. M.B.A., 1975*]

Formulation of Linear Programming Model

The *key decision* is to determine the number of acres of each farm to be allotted to each crop.

Let x_{ij} (i = farm 1, 2, 3; j = crop A, B, C) represent the number of acres of the ith farm to be allotted to the jth crop.

The *objective* is to maximize the total profit.

i.e., $$\text{maximize } Z = ₹\left[400\sum_{i=1}^{3} x_{iA} + 300\sum_{i=1}^{3} x_{iB} + 100\sum_{i=1}^{3} x_{iC}\right].$$

Constraints are formulated as follows:

For availability of water in acre feet,

$$5x_{1A} + 4x_{1B} + 3x_{1C} \le 1{,}500,$$
$$5x_{2A} + 4x_{2B} + 3x_{2C} \le 2{,}000,$$
$$5x_{3A} + 4x_{3B} + 3x_{3C} \le 900.$$

For availability of usable acreage in each farm,

$$x_{1A} + x_{1B} + x_{1C} \le 400,$$
$$x_{2A} + x_{2B} + x_{2C} \le 600,$$
$$x_{3A} + x_{3B} + x_{3C} \le 300.$$

For availability of acreage for each crop,

$$x_{1A} + x_{2A} + x_{3A} \ge 400,$$
$$x_{1B} + x_{2B} + x_{3B} \ge 300,$$
$$x_{1C} + x_{2C} + x_{3C} \ge 300.$$

To ensure that the percentage of usable acreage is same in each farm,

$$\frac{x_{1A} + x_{1B} + x_{1C}}{400} \times 100 = \frac{x_{2A} + x_{2B} + x_{2C}}{600} \times 100 = \frac{x_{3A} + x_{3B} + x_{3C}}{300} \times 100$$

or $\quad 3(x_{1A} + x_{1B} + x_{1C}) = 2(x_{2A} + x_{2B} + x_{2C}),$

and $\quad (x_{2A} + x_{2B} + x_{2C}) = 2(x_{3A} + x_{3B} + x_{3C}),$

where $x_{1A}, x_{1B}, x_{1C}, x_{2A}, x_{2B}, x_{2C}, x_{3A}, x_{3B}, x_{3C}$, each ≥ 0.

The above relations, therefore, constitute the L.P. model.

EXAMPLE 2.6-15 (Product Mix Problem)

Consider the following problem faced by a production planner in a soft drink plant. He has two bottling machines A and B. A is designed for 8-ounce bottles and B for 16-ounce bottles. However, each can be used on both types of bottles with some loss of efficiency. The following data are available :

Machine	*8-ounce bottles*	*16-ounce bottles*
A	*100/minute*	*40/minute*
B	*60/minute*	*75/minute*

The machines can be run for 8 hours per day, 5 days a week. Profit on 8-ounce bottle is 15 paise and on 16-ounce bottle is 25 paise. Weekly production of the drink cannot exceed 3,00,000 ounces and the market can absorb 25,000 eight-ounce bottles and 7,000 sixteen-ounce bottles per week. The planner wishes to maximize his profit subject, of course, to all the production and marketing constraints. Formulate this as L.P. problem.

[*V.T.U. Karnataka B.E. Jan., 2010*]

Formulation of Linear Programming Model

Key decision is to determine the number of 8-ounce bottles and 16-ounce bottles to be produced on either of machines A and B per week. Let x_{A1}, x_{B1} be the number of 8-ounce bottles and x_{A2}, x_{B2} be the number of 16-ounce bottles to be produced per week on machines A and B respectively.

Objective is to maximize the weekly profit.

i.e., maximize Z = ₹ $[0.15\,(x_{A1} + x_{B1}) + 0.25(x_{A2} + x_{B2})]$.

Constraints can be formulated as follows:

Since an 8-ounce bottle takes $\frac{1}{100}$ minute and a 16-ounce bottle takes $\frac{1}{40}$ minute on machine A and the machine can be run for 8 hours a day and 5 days a week, the time constraint on machine A can be written as

$$\frac{x_{A1}}{100} + \frac{x_{A2}}{40} \le 5 \times 8 \times 60$$

$$\le 2{,}400, \text{ or } 2x_{A1} + 5x_{A2} \le 4{,}80{,}000.$$

Similarly, time constraint on machine B can be written as

$$\frac{x_{B1}}{60} + \frac{x_{B2}}{75} \le 2{,}400, \text{ or } 5x_{B1} + 4x_{B2} \le 7{,}20{,}000.$$

Since the total weekly production cannot exceed 3,00,000 ounces,

$$8(x_{A1} + x_{B1}) + 16(x_{A2} + x_{B2}) \le 3{,}00{,}000.$$

The constraints on market demand yield

$$x_{A1} + x_{B1} \ge 25{,}000,$$

$$x_{A2} + x_{B2} \ge 7{,}000,$$

where x_{A1}, x_{B1}, x_{A2}, x_{B2}, each ≥ 0.

EXAMPLE 2.6-16 (Product Mix Problem)

A manufacturer of biscuits is considering four types of gift packs containing three types of biscuits: orange cream (o.c.), chocolate cream (c.c.) and wafers (w.). Market research conducted to assess the preferences of the consumers shows the following types of assortments to be in good demand:

Assortment	*Contents*	*Selling price/kg (₹)*
A	*Not Less than 40% of o.c.* *Not more than 20% of c.c.*	*200*
B	*Not less than 20% of o.c.* *Not more than 40% of c.c.*	*250*
C	*Not less than 50% of o.c.* *Not more than 10% of c.c.*	*220*
D	*No restrictions*	*120*

For the biscuits the manufacturing capacity and costs are given below.

Biscuit variety	*Plant capacity (kg/day)*	*Manufacturing cost (₹/kg)*
o.c.	*200*	*80*
c.c.	*200*	*90*
W.	*150*	*70*

Formulate the L.P. model to find the production schedule which maximizes the profit assuming that there are no market restrictions. [*P.U.B.E. (Elect.) May, 1994; B.E. (Mech.) 1982; Delhi M.B.A., 1999, 1982*]

Formulation of L.P. Model

The *key decision* is to determine the quantities in kg of o.c., c.c. biscuits and wafers to be produced per day for gift packs A, B, C and D respectively.

Let x_{ij} (i = 1, 2, 3; j = A, B, C, D) be the quantities produced.

The *objective* is to maximize the profit.

i.e.,

$$\begin{aligned}\text{maximize } Z &= ₹\ 10[\{20(x_{1A} + x_{2A} + x_{3A}) - 8x_{1A} - 9x_{2A} - 7x_{3A}\}\\ &\quad + \{25(x_{1B} + x_{2B} + x_{3B}) - 8x_{1B} - 9x_{2B} - 7x_{3B}\}\\ &\quad + \{22(x_{1C} + x_{2C} + x_{3C}) - 8x_{1C} - 9x_{2C} - 7x_{3C}\}\\ &\quad + \{12(x_{1D} + x_{2D} + x_{3D}) - 8x_{1D} - 9x_{2D} - 7x_{3D}\}]\\ &= ₹\ 10[(12x_{1A} + 11x_{2A} + 13x_{3A}) + (17x_{1B} + 16x_{2B} + 18x_{3B})\\ &\quad + (14x_{1C} + 13x_{2C} + 15x_{3C}) + (4x_{1D} + 3x_{2D} + 5x_{3D})].\end{aligned}$$

The constraints can be formulated as follows:

(*i*) on the capacities of the plants:

$$x_{1A} + x_{1B} + x_{1C} + x_{1D} \leq 200,$$
$$x_{2A} + x_{2B} + x_{2C} + x_{2D} \leq 200,$$
$$x_{3A} + x_{3B} + x_{3C} + x_{3D} \leq 150.$$

(*ii*) on specifications of gift pack A :

$$x_{1A} \geq 0.4\ (x_{1A} + x_{2A} + x_{3A}) \quad \text{or} \quad 0.6x_{1A} - 0.4x_{2A} - 0.4x_{3A} \geq 0,$$
$$x_{2A} \leq 0.2\ (x_{1A} + x_{2A} + x_{3A}) \quad \text{or} \quad -\ 0.2x_{1A} + 0.8x_{2A} - 0.2x_{3A} \leq 0.$$

(*iii*) on specifications of gift pack B :

$$x_{1B} \geq 0.2\ (x_{1B} + x_{2B} + x_{3B}) \quad \text{or} \quad 0.8x_{1B} - 0.2x_{2B} - 0.2x_{3B} \geq 0,$$
$$x_{2B} \leq 0.4\ (x_{1B} + x_{2B} + x_{3B}) \quad \text{or} \quad -\ 0.4x_{1B} + 0.6x_{2B} - 0.4x_{3B} \leq 0.$$

(*iv*) on specifications of gift pack C:

$$x_{1C} \geq 0.5\ (x_{1C} + x_{2C} + x_{3C}) \quad \text{or} \quad 0.5x_{1C} - 0.5x_{2C} - 0.5x_{3C} \geq 0,$$
$$x_{2C} \leq 0.1\ (x_{1C} + x_{2C} + x_{3C}) \quad \text{or} \quad -\ 0.1x_{1C} + 0.9x_{2C} - 0.1x_{3C} \leq 0,$$

where x_{ij} (i = 1, 2, 3; j = A, B, C, D) ≥ 0.

EXAMPLE 2.6-17 (Product Mix Problem)

A manufacturer has five lathes and three milling machines in his workshop and produces an assembly that consists of 2 units of part A and 3 units of part B. The processing time for each part on the two types of machines is given below.

TABLE 2.8

Part	*Processing time in minutes on a*	
	Lathe	*Milling machine*
A	*10*	*18*
B	*25*	*12*

In order to maintain a uniform work-load on the two types of machines, the manufacturer has framed a policy that no type of machine should run more than 40 minutes per day longer than the other machine. Formulate the problem as L.P. problem if the objective is to produce the maximum number of assemblies in any 8-hour working day.

[P.T.U.B. Tech. 2001; P.U.B.E. (Mech.) 2006]

Formulation of L.P. Model

The *key decision* is to determine the number of units of part A and B to be produced each day that make the assembly. Let they be represented by x_1 and x_2 respectively.

The *objective* is to maximize the number of units of the final assembly.

i.e., maximize Z = minimum of $\left(\frac{x_1}{2}, \frac{x_2}{3}\right)$ [Refer example 2.6-9]

or maximize Z = y,

where $$y \leq \frac{x_1}{2} \quad \text{or} \quad x_1 - 2y \geq 0,$$

and $$y \leq \frac{x_2}{3} \quad \text{or} \quad x_2 - 3y \geq 0.$$

Further *constraints* can be formulated as follows:

There are five lathes and three milling machines that produce x_1 units of part A and x_2 units of part B each day.

∴ Constraint on time for lathes yields

$$10x_1 + 25x_2 \leq 5 \times 8 \times 60$$

or $$2x_1 + 5x_2 \leq 480,$$

and constraint on time for milling machines gives

$$18x_1 + 12x_2 \leq 3 \times 8 \times 60$$

or $$3x_1 + 2x_2 \leq 240.$$

The uniform work load constraint can be expressed as

$$\left| \left(\frac{10x_1 + 25x_2}{5} \right) - \left(\frac{18x_1 + 12x_2}{3} \right) \right| \leq 40$$

or $$|(2x_1 + 5x_2) - (6x_1 + 4x_2)| \leq 40$$

or $$|-4x_1 + x_2| \leq 40,$$

which may be expressed as a combination of two constraints

$$-4x_1 + x_2 \leq 40,$$

and $$4x_1 - x_2 \leq 40,$$

where $x_1 \geq 0$, $x_2 \geq 0$, $y \geq 0$.

EXAMPLE 2.6-18 (Product Mix Problem)

A firm produces three different products, 1, 2 and 3. Each product needs to be processed through two departments, A and B. Department A has two machines A_1 and A_2, while B has three machines, B_1, B_2 and B_3. Product 1 can be manufactured on any type of A and B machines. Product 2 can be manufactured on any of type A machines and only on B_1 of type B machines. Product 3 can be manufactured on machines A_2 of type A and B_3 of type B. Time taken to manufacture one unit of each of product on each type of machine is given in table below. The table also shows total available machine time per week, cost of running each machine at full capacity in a week, cost of raw material required per unit product and sale price per unit product. How many of each type of product be manufactured on which machine so as to maximize the net profit? Formulate the L.P. model for the problem.

TABLE 2.9

Machine	Product			Time available per week (minutes)	Cost/week at full capacity (₹)
	1	2	3		
A_1	4	6	—	5,000	250
A_2	5	7	11	10,000	500
B_1	7	8	—	8,000	400
B_2	8	—	—	4,000	200
B_3	3	—	7	5,600	280
Material cost (₹)	0.30	0.40	0.50		
Sale price (₹)	1.50	1.80	2.40		

Formulation as an L.P. Problem

Key decision is to determine the number of units of products 1, 2 and 3 to be manufactured on each of the machines, A_1, A_2, B_1, B_2 and B_3 per week.

Product 1 can be manufactured on six different combinations of machines: (A_1, B_1), (A_1, B_2), (A_1, B_3), (A_2, B_1), (A_2, B_2) and (A_2, B_3). Let $x_1, x_2, ..., x_6$ be the number of units of product 1 manufactured per week by these six different combinations.

Product 2 can be made by two different combinations of machines: (A_1, B_1) and (A_2, B_1). Let x_7 and x_8 be the number of units of product 2 made per week by these combinations.

Product 3 can be produced in only one way, *i.e.* by the combination of machines (A_2, B_3). Let x_9 be the number of units of this product produced per week by this combination.

Objective is to maximize the net profit. This profit function can be obtained as follows:

Product 1 can be manufactured by six different combinations of machines. The first one is (A_1, B_1). We shall find the cost of manufacturing one unit of this product on A_1 as well as B_1. To this we shall add material cost and subtract this sum from the sale price of the item. This will give the net profit per unit for product 1 if manufactured by a combination (A_1, B_1) of the machines.

Similarly, we shall find net profit/unit of the three products when made by different combinations of machines.

Unit manufacturing cost on A_1 for product 1

$$= ₹\ \frac{250}{5,000} \times 4 = ₹\ 0.20.$$

Unit manufacturing cost on B_1 for product 1

$$= ₹\ \frac{400}{8,000} \times 7 = ₹\ 0.35.$$

$\therefore$ Unit manufacturing cost on (A_1, B_1) for product 1= ₹ 0.55.
Material cost/unit for product 1 = ₹ 0.30.
$\therefore$ Total cost incurred on product 1 = ₹ 0.85.
Sale price/unit of product 1 = ₹ 1.50.
$\therefore$ Net profit/unit of product 1 = ₹ 0.65.

Similarly, unit profit of product 1 by (A_1, B_2)

$$= ₹\left[1.50 - \left(\frac{250}{5,000} \times 4 + \frac{200}{4,000} \times 8\right) - 0.30\right] = ₹\ 0.60.$$

Unite profit of product 1 by (A_1, B_3)

$$= ₹\left[1.50 - \left(\frac{250}{5,000} \times 4 + \frac{280}{5,600} \times 3\right) - 0.30\right] = ₹\ 0.85.$$

Unit profit of product 1 by (A_2, B_1)

$$= ₹\left[1.50 - \left(\frac{500}{10,000} \times 5 + \frac{400}{8,000} \times 7\right) - 0.30\right] = ₹\ 0.60.$$

Unit profit of product 1 by (A_2, B_2)

$$= ₹\left[1.50 - \left(\frac{500}{10,000} \times 5 + \frac{200}{4,000} \times 8\right) - 0.30\right] = ₹\ 0.55.$$

Unit profit of product 1 by (A_2, B_3)

$$= ₹\left[1.50 - \left(\frac{500}{10,000} \times 5 + \frac{280}{5,600} \times 3\right) - 0.30\right] = ₹\ 0.80.$$

Unit profit of product 2 by (A_1, B_1)

$$= ₹\left[1.80-\left(\frac{250}{5,000}\times 6+\frac{400}{8,000}\times 8\right)-0.40\right]= ₹\ 0.70.$$

Unit profit of product 2 by (A_2, B_1)

$$= ₹\left[1.80-\left(\frac{500}{10,000}\times 7+\frac{400}{8,000}\times 8\right)-0.40\right]= ₹\ 0.65.$$

Unit profit of product 3 by (A_2, B_3)

$$= ₹\left[2.40-\left(\frac{500}{10,000}\times 11+\frac{280}{5,600}\times 7\right)-0.50\right]= ₹\ 1.00.$$

∴ Objective function is to

$$\text{maximize } Z = ₹\ [0.65x_1 + 0.60x_2 + 0.85x_3 + 0.60x_4 + 0.55x_5 + 0.80x_6 + 0.70x_7 + 0.65x_8 + 1.00x_9].$$

Constraints are on machine capacities. They can be expressed as follows:

Machine A_1 is used to manufacture product 1 through combinations (A_1, B_1), (A_1, B_2), (A_1, B_3) with associated variables x_1, x_2 and x_3 and to manufacture product 2 through (A_1, B_1) with associated variable x_7. The total time demand on A_1 is $4x_1 + 4x_2 + 4x_3 + 6x_7$ per week and this should not exceed 5,000 minutes. Similarly, A_2 is used to manufacture product 1 through combinations (A_2, B_1), (A_2, B_2) and (A_2, B_3) with associated variables x_4, x_5 and x_6, product 2 through combination (A_2, B_1) with associated variable x_8 and product 3 through combination (A_2, B_3) with associated variable x_9. Thus the total weekly time demand on A_2 is $5x_4 + 5x_5 + 5x_6 + 7x_8 + 11x_9$ per week and this should not exceed 10,000 minutes. Likewise, total time demand on B_1 is $7x_1 + 7x_4 + 8x_7 + 8x_8$, on B_2 is $8x_2 + 8x_5$ and on B_3 is $3x_3 + 3x_6 + 7x_9$ which should not exceed 8,000, 4,000 and 5,600 minutes per week respectively. Thus the various constraints can we written as

$$\begin{aligned}
4x_1 + 4x_2 + 4x_3 + 6x_7 &\le 5,000,\\
5x_4 + 5x_5 + 5x_6 + 7x_8 + 11x_9 &\le 10,000,\\
7x_1 + 7x_4 + 8x_7 + 8x_8 &\le 8,000,\\
8x_2 + 8x_5 &\le 4,000,\\
3x_3 + 3x_6 + 7x_9 &\le 5,600,
\end{aligned}$$

where $x_1, x_2, ..., x_9$, each ≥ 0.

EXAMPLE 2.6-19 (Product Mix Problem)

A firm manufactures two items. It purchases castings which are then machined, bored and polished. Castings for items A and B cost ₹ 2 and ₹ 3 respectively and are sold at ₹ 5 and ₹ 6 each respectively. Running costs of the three machines are ₹ 20, ₹ 14 and ₹ 17.50 per hour respectively. Capacities of the machines are

	Part A	*Part B*
Machining capacity	*25/hr*	*40/hr*
Boring capacity	*28/hr*	*35/hr*
Polishing capacity	*35/hr*	*25/hr*

Formulate the L.P. model to determine the product mix that maximizes the profit.

[H.P.U.B. Tech. (Mech.) Nov., 2007; P.U. B.Com. 2012; April, 2007; Sept., 2006; Delhi U. MBA, 2002]

Formulation of L.P. Model

Let x_1 and x_2 represent the number of units of items A and B to be manufactured *per hour.*

The *objective* is to maximize the profit. Profit per part for items A and B is calculated in the table below.

TABLE 2.10

Cost and profit per part

	Part A (₹)	*Part B* (₹)
Machining cost	$\frac{20}{25} = 0.80$	$\frac{20}{40} = 0.50$
Boring cost	$\frac{14}{28} = 0.50$	$\frac{14}{35} = 0.40$
Polishing cost	$\frac{17.50}{35} = 0.50$	$\frac{17.50}{25} = 0.70$
Casting cost	2.00	3.00
∴ Total cost	3.80	4.60
Selling price	5.00	6.00
∴ Profit	1.20	1.40

Therefore, objective is to

$$\text{maximize } Z = 1.2x_1 + 1.4x_2.$$

Constraints are on the capacities of the machines. For *one hour running of each machine,* they are

$$\frac{1}{25}x_1 + \frac{1}{40}x_2 \le 1, \text{ or } 40x_1 + 25x_2 \le 1{,}000,$$

$$\frac{1}{28}x_1 + \frac{1}{35}x_2 \le 1, \text{ or } 35x_1 + 28x_2 \le 980,$$

$$\frac{1}{35}x_1 + \frac{1}{25}x_2 \le 1, \text{ or } 25x_1 + 35x_2 \le 875,$$

or

$$8x_1 + 5x_2 \le 200,$$
$$5x_1 + 4x_2 \le 140,$$
$$5x_1 + 7x_2 \le 175,$$

where $x_1 \ge 0$, $x_2 \ge 0$.

EXAMPLE 2.6-20 (Network Problem)

Given below is a network in which the figures written against the arrows (links) indicate the cost of travelling in rupees from the preceding to the following node.

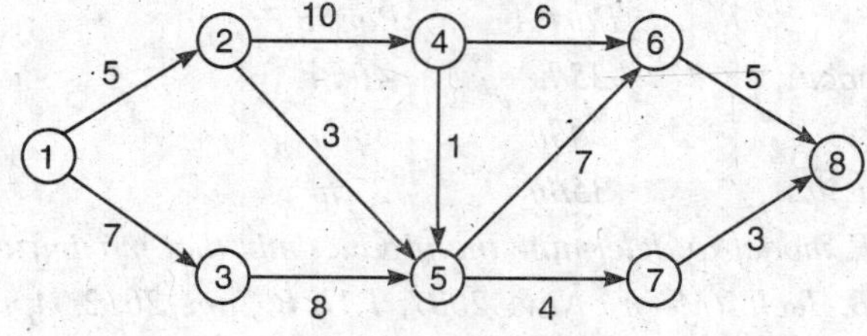

Fig. 2.1

Formulate the linear programming model to find the least cost route from node 1 to node 8.

Formulation of L.P. Model

Let us imagine that the person travels from node 1 to 8 along a succession of links. Let x_{ij} represent the link joining node i to j. If the person uses link x_{ij}, then x_{ij} will be given a value 1; if not, a value zero. The person reaches a node, say, j via one of the links, say, x_{ij} and leaves it by another link, say, x_{jk}. So, if a node j has several arrows, such as ij, hj, gj pointing towards it and several arrows, such as jk, jl, jm pointing away from it, then the equation for node j can be written as

$$x_{gj} + x_{hj} + x_{ij} - x_{jk} - x_{jl} - x_{jm} = 0.$$

This is because, for each of the links x_{ij} and x_{jk}, the value is 1 (the person uses this link) and for each of the links x_{gj}, x_{hj}, x_{jl} and x_{jm} the value is zero (the person does not use these links).

For the network shown in Fig. 2.1, we get for

node 2, $\quad x_{12} - x_{24} - x_{25} = 0,$
node 3, $\quad x_{13} - x_{35} = 0,$
node 4, $\quad x_{24} - x_{45} - x_{46} = 0,$
node 5, $\quad x_{25} + x_{35} + x_{45} - x_{56} - x_{57} = 0,$
node 6, $\quad x_{46} + x_{56} - x_{68} = 0,$
and node 7, $\quad x_{57} - x_{78} = 0.$

Further, since the person has to start from node 1, along one of the paths (links) starting from it, we have

$$- x_{12} - x_{13} = - 1.$$

Similarly, as the person has to reach node 8 along one of the paths, we get

$$x_{68} + x_{78} = 1.$$

The above eight are, then, the constraints (equality type) that must be satisfied. The objective is to minimize the total cost of travelling from node 1 to 8, given by

Minimize $Z = 5x_{12} + 7x_{13} + 10x_{24} + 3x_{25} + 8x_{35} + x_{45} + 6x_{46} + 7x_{56} + 4x_{57} + 5x_{68} + 3x_{78}$.

This is, then, the linear programming model for the network problem wherein every variable has a value 1 or 0.

EXAMPLE 2.6-21 (Product Mix Problem)

The Delhi Florist Company is planning to make up floral arrangements for the upcoming festival. The company has available the following supply of flowers at the costs shown:

Type	*Number available*	*Cost per flower* (₹)
Red roses	*800*	*0.20*
Gardenias	*456*	*0.25*
Carnations	*4,000*	*0.15*
White roses	*920*	*0.20*
Yellow roses	*422*	*0.22*

These flowers can be used in any of the four popular arrangements whose make up and selling prices are as follows:

Arrangement	*Requirements*	*Selling price*
Economy	*4 red roses*	₹ *6*
	2 gardenias	
	8 carnations	
Maytime	*8 white roses*	₹ *8*
	5 gardenias	
	10 carnations	
	4 yellow roses	
Spring-colour	*9 red roses*	₹ *10*

	10 carnations	
	9 white roses	
	6 yellow roses	
Deluxe-rose	*12 red roses*	*₹ 12*
	12 white roses	
	12 yellow roses	

Formulate a linear programming problem which allows the florist company to determine how many units of each arrangement should be made up in order to maximize profits assuming all arrangements can be sold. [*C.A. Dec., 1990*]

Formulation of L.P. Model

Let x_1, x_2, x_3 and x_4 be the number of units of each arrangement that should be made up to maximize the profits.

Profit by selling one unit of Economy arrangement

$$= ₹[6–(4×.20+2×.25+8×.15)] = ₹3.50,$$

profit by selling one unit of Maytime arrangement

$$= ₹[8–(8×.20+5×.25+10×.15+4×.22)] = ₹2.77,$$

profit by selling one unit of Spring-colour arrangement

$$= ₹[10–(9×.20+10×.15+9×.20+6×.22)] = ₹3.58,$$

and profit by selling one unit of Deluxe-rose arrangement

$$= ₹[12–(12×.20+12×.20+12×.22)] = ₹4.56.$$

Thus the *objective* is to

maximize $\quad Z = ₹\ [3.50x_1 + 2.77x_2 + 3.58x_3 + 4.56x_4]$.

The *constraints* are on the total number available for each type of flower:

For red roses, $\quad 4x_1 + 9x_3 + 12x_4 \leq 800$,

for gardenias, $\quad 2x_1 + 5x_2 \leq 456$,

for carnations, $\quad 8x_1 + 10x_2 + 10x_3 \leq 4{,}000$,

for white roses, $\quad 8x_2 + 9x_3 + 12x_4 \leq 920$,

and $\quad$ for yellow roses, $\quad 4x_2 + 6x_3 + 12x_4 \leq 422$,

where x_1, x_2, x_3, x_4, each ≥ 0.

EXAMPLE 2.6-22 (Flight Scheduling Problem)

An aircraft company, which operates out of a central terminal has 8 aircrafts of Type 1, 15 aircrafts of Type II and 12 aircrafts of Type III available for today's flights. The tonnage capacities (in thousands of tons) are 4.5 for Type 1,7 for type IInd 4 for Type III.

The company dispatches its planes to cities A and B. Tonnage requirements (in thousands of tons) are 20 at city A and 30 at city B; excess tonnage capacity supplied to a city has no value. A plane can fly once only during the day.

The cost of sending a plane from the terminal to each city is given by the following table:

	Type I	*Type II*	*Type III*
City A	*23*	*5*	*1.4*
City B	*58*	*10*	*3.8*

Formulate the L.P. model to minimize the air transportation cost.

[*H.P.U. B.Tech. (Mech.) Sept., 2013*]

Formulation of L.P. Model

The data given in the problem is shown in the table below. The *key decision* is to determine the number of each type of plane to be dispatched to either of cities *A* and *B*. Let x_{A1}, x_{A2}, x_{A3} and x_{B1}, x_{B2}, x_{B3} denote the number of planes of type I, II and III to be dispatched to cities *A* and *B* respectively.

Aircraft type:	*I*	*II*	*III*
Number:	8	15	12
Tonnage capacity: (*thousands of tons*)	4.5	7	4

City				*Requirement* (*thousands of tons*)
A	23 x_{A1}	5 x_{A2}	1.4 x_{A3}	20
B	58 x_{B1}	10 x_{B2}	3.8 x_{B3}	30

Cost matrix

Objective is to minimize the total cost of dispatching the planes.

i.e., minimize $Z = 23x_{A1} + 5x_{A2} + 1.4x_{A3} + 58x_{B1} + 10x_{B2} + 3.8x_{B3}$.

Constraints are

on the number of planes of type I available that can be dispatched to cities *A* and *B*,

$$x_{A1} + x_{B1} \le 8.$$

Similarly,

$$x_{A2} + x_{B2} \le 15,$$
$$x_{A3} + x_{B3} \le 12.$$

Since tonnage requirements (in thousands of tons) are 20 at city *A* and 30 at city *B*, supply cannot be less than these values. As excess tonnage capacity supplied to a city has no value, exactly 20 and 30 (thousands of tons) will be supplied to them. Therefore, the constraints are

$$4.5x_{A1} + 7x_{A2} + 4x_{A3} = 20,$$
$$4.5x_{B1} + 7x_{B2} + 4x_{B3} = 30,$$

where $x_{A1}, x_{A2}, x_{A3}, x_{B1}, x_{B2}, x_{B3}$, each ≥ 0.

EXAMPLE 2.6-23 (Portfolio Selection Problem)

The Agro Promotion Bank is trying to select investment portfolio for a cotton farmer. The bank has chosen a set of five investment alternatives, with subjective estimates of rates of return and risk, as follows:

Investment	*Annual rate of return (%)*	*Risk*
Tax-free municipal bonds	*6.0*	*1.3*
Corporate bonds	*8.0*	*1.5*
High grade common stock	*5.0*	*1.9*
Mutual fund	*7.0*	*1.7*
Real estate	*15.0*	*2.7*

The bank officer in charge of the portfolio would like to maximize the average annual rate of return on the portfolio. However, the wealthy investor has specified that the average risk of the portfolio should not exceed 2.0; and does not want more than 20% of the investment to be put into real estate. Formulate an L.P. model for the problem.

Formulation of L.P. Model

Let x_1, x_2, x_3, x_4, x_5 be the *proportion* (*fraction*) of portfolio allocated to investment of type 1, 2, 3, 4 and 5 respectively.

Objective is to maximize the annual rate of return on the portfolio.

i.e., maximize $Z = 0.06x_1 + 0.08x_2 + 0.05x_3 + 0.07x_4 + 0.15x_5$.

Constraints are

on the average risk: $$\frac{1.3x_1 + 1.5x_2 + 1.9x_3 + 1.7x_4 + 2.7x_5}{1} \le 2.0$$

or $$1.3x_1 + 1.5x_2 + 1.9x_3 + 1.7x_4 + 2.7x_5 \le 2,$$

on investment in real estate: $$\frac{x_5}{1} \le \frac{20}{100} \quad \text{or} \quad x_5 \le 0.2,$$

on the total amount of investment: $x_1 + x_2 + x_3 + x_4 + x_5 = 1$,
where x_1, x_2, x_3, x_4, x_5, each ≥ 0.

EXAMPLE 2.6-24 (Investment Problem)

Mr. Krishnamurty, a retired Govt. officer, has recently received his retirement benefits, viz., provident fund, gratuity, etc. He is contemplating as to how much funds he should invest in various alternatives open to him so as to maximize return on investment. The investment alternatives are: government securities, fixed deposits of a public limited company, equity shares, time deposits in banks, national saving certificates and real estate. He has made a subjective estimate of the risk involved. The data on the return on investment, the number of years for which the funds will be blocked to earn this return on investment and the subjective risk involved are as follows:

Investment alternatives	*Return*	*No. of years*	*Risk*
Govt. securities	6%	15	1
Company deposits	15%	3	3
Equity shares	20%	6	7
Time deposits	10%	3	1
N.S.C.	12%	6	1
Real estate	25%	10	2

He was wondering what percentage of funds he should invest in each alternative so as to maximize the return on investment. He decided that average risk should not be more than 4, and funds should not be locked up for more than 15 years. Formulate an L.P. model for the problem if he does not want more than 30% of the investment to be put in the real estate.

[*Bombay MMS, 1980*]

Formulation of L.P. Model

Let $x_1, x_2, x_3, x_4, x_5, x_6$ be the *percentage* of funds to be invested in alternative 1, 2, 3, 4, 5 and 6 respectively.

Objective is to maximize the return on investment.

i.e., maximize $Z = 0.06x_1 + 0.15x_2 + 0.20x_3 + 0.10x_4 + 0.12x_5 + 0.25x_6$.

Constraints are

on the average risk $x_1 + 3x_2 + 7x_3 + x_4 + x_5 + 2x_6 \leq 4$,
on the lock-up period $15x_1 + 3x_2 + 6x_3 + 3x_4 + 6x_5 + 10x_6 \leq 15$,
on investment in real estate $x_6 \leq 0.3$,
on the total amount invested $x_1 + x_2 + x_3 + x_4 + x_5 + x_6 = 1$,
where $x_1, x_2, ..., x_6$, each ≥ 0.

EXAMPLE 2.6-25 (Investment Problem)

A Mutual Fund Company has ₹ 20 lakhs available for investment in government bonds, blue chip stocks, speculative stocks and short-term deposits. The annual expected return and risk factor are given below:

Type of investment	*Annual expected return (%)*	*Risk factor (0 to 100)*
Government Bonds	14	12
Blue Chip Stocks	19	24
Speculative Stocks	23	48
Short-term Deposits	12	6

Mutual Fund is required to keep at least ₹ 2 lakhs in short-term deposits and not to exceed average risk factor of 42. Speculative stocks must be at most 20 per cent of the total amount invested. How should Mutual Fund invest the funds so as to maximize its total expected annual return? Formulate this as a linear programming problem. [*H.P.U.B. Tech. (Mech.) Nov., 2006*]

Formulation of L.P. Model

Let x_1, x_2, x_3 and x_4 denote the *amount* of funds to be invested in government bonds, blue chip stocks, speculative stocks and short-term deposits respectively. Let Z denote the total expected return.

Since the the company Company has ₹ 20 lakhs available for investment,

$$x_1 + x_2 + x_3 + x_4 \le 20{,}00{,}000.$$

Also, the company is required to keep at least ₹ 2 lakhs in short-term deposits.

Hence $x_4 \ge 2{,}00{,}000.$

The average risk factor is given by

$$\frac{12x_1 + 24x_2 + 48x_3 + 6x_4}{x_1 + x_2 + x_3 + x_4}.$$

Since the average risk factor for Mutual Fund Company should not exceed 42, we get the following constraint:

$$\frac{12x_1 + 24x_2 + 48x_3 + 6x_4}{x_1 + x_2 + x_3 + x_4} \le 42$$

or $\quad 12x_1 + 24x_2 + 48x_3 + 6x_4 \le 42\,(x_1 + x_2 + x_3 + x_4)$

or $\quad -30x_1 - 18x_2 + 6x_3 - 36x_4 \le 0.$

Further, speculative stocks must be at most 20 per cent of the total amount invested, hence

$$x_3 \le 0.20\,(x_1 + x_2 + x_3 + x_4)$$

or $\quad -0.2x_1 - 0.2x_2 + 0.8x_3 - 0.2x_4 \le 0.$

Finally, since the objective is to maximize the total expected annual return, the objective function for Mutual Fund Company can be expressed as

$$\text{maximize } Z = 0.14x_1 + 0.19x_2 + 0.23x_3 + 0.12x_4.$$

Thus the linear programming model for the Mutual Fund Company is formulated as below:

$$\text{maximize } Z = 0.14x_1 + 0.19x_2 + 0.23x_3 + 0.12x_4,$$

subject to the constraints

$$x_1 + x_2 + x_3 + x_4 \le 20{,}00{,}000,$$
$$x_4 \ge 2{,}00{,}000,$$
$$-30x_1 - 18x_2 + 6x_3 - 36x_4 \le 0 \quad \text{or} \quad 30x_1 + 18x_2 - 6x_3 + 36x_4 \ge 0 \text{ and}$$
$$-0.2x_1 - 0.2x_2 + 0.8x_3 - 0.2x_4 \le 0 \quad \text{or} \quad 0.2x_1 + 0.2x_2 - 0.8x_3 + 0.2x_4 \ge 0,$$

where $x_1 \ge 0$, $x_2 \ge 0$, $x_3 \ge 0$ and $x_4 \ge 0$.

EXAMPLE 2.6-26 (Portfolio Selection Problem)

A leading Charted Accountant is attempting to determine the 'best' investment portfolio and is considering six alternative investment proposals. The following table indicates point estimates for the price per share, the annual growth rate in the price per share, the annual dividend per share and a measure of the risk associated with each investment.

Portfolio data

	Shares under consideration					
	A	*B*	*C*	*D*	*E*	*F*
Current price/share (₹)	*80*	*100*	*160*	*120*	*150*	*200*
Projected annual growth rate	*0.08*	*0.07*	*0.10*	*0.12*	*0.09*	*0.15*
Projected annual dividend per share (₹)	*4.00*	*4.50*	*7.50*	*5.50*	*5.75*	*0.00*
Projected risk in return	*0.05*	*0.03*	*0.10*	*0.20*	*0.06*	*0.08*

The total amount available for investment is ₹ 25 lakhs and the following conditions are required to be satisfied.:

(*i*) *The maximum rupee amount to be invested in alternative F is ₹ 2,50,000.*

(*ii*) *No more than ₹ 5,00,000 should be invested in alternatives A and B combined.*

(*iii*) *Total weighted risk should not be greater than 0.10, where*

$$\text{total weighted risk} = \frac{\text{(Amount invested in alternative } j\text{) (risk of alternative } j\text{)}}{\text{Total amount invested in all the alternatives}}.$$

(*iv*) *For the sake of diversity, at least 100 shares of each stock should be purchased.*

(*v*) *At least 10% of the total investment should be in alternatives A and B combined.*

(*vi*) *Dividends for the year should be at least ₹ 10,000.*

Rupees return per share of stock is defined as price per share one year hence less current price per share plus dividend per share. If the objective is to maximize total rupee return, formulate the linear programming model for determining the optimal number of shares to be purchased in each of the shares under consideration. You may assume that the time horizon for the investment is one year. The formulated L.P. problem is not required to be solved. [*C.A. Nov., 1991*]

Formulation of L.P. Model

Let x_A, x_B, x_C, x_D, x_E and x_F be the number of shares to be purchased in each of the six alternative investment proposals. The objective is to maximize the total rupee return *i.e.*,

$$\begin{aligned}\text{maximize } Z &= (80 \times 1.08 - 80 + 4)\, x_A + (100 \times 1.07 - 100 + 4.50)\, x_B \\ &\quad + (160 \times 1.1 - 160 + 7.50)\, x_C + (120 \times 1.12 - 120 + 5.50)\, x_D \\ &\quad + (150 \times 1.09 - 150 + 5.75)\, x_E + (200 \times 1.15 - 200 + 0.00)\, x_F \\ &= 10.4x_A + 11.5x_B + 23.5x_C + 19.9x_D + 19.25x_E + 30x_F.\end{aligned}$$

Constraints can be formulated follows:

(*i*) $200x_F \le 2,50,000$ or $x_F \le 1,250$.

(*ii*) $80x_A + 100x_B \le 5,00,000$ or $0.8x_A + x_B \le 5,000$.

(*iii*) $80x_A \times 0.05 + 100x_B \times 0.03 + 160x_C \times 0.10 + 120x_D \times 0.20 + 150x_E \times 0.06$
$+ 200x_F \times 0.08 \le 0.10 \times (80x_A + 100x_B + 160x_C + 120x_D + 150x_E + 200x_F)$

or $4x_A + 3x_B + 16x_C + 24x_D + 9x_E + 16x_F \le 8x_A + 10x_B + 16x_C + 12x_D + 15x_E$
$+ 20x_F$

or $-4x_A - 7x_B + 0x_C + 12x_D - 6x_E - 4x_F \le 0$

or $4x_A + 7x_B - 12x_D + 6x_E + 4x_F \ge 0$.

(*iv*) $80x_A + 100x_B \ge 0.1\,(80x_A + 100x_B + 160x_C + 120x_D + 150x_E + 200x_F)$

or $72x_A + 90x_B - 16x_C - 12x_D - 15x_E - 20x_F \ge 0$.

(*v*) $4x_A + 4.5x_B + 7.5x_C + 5.5x_D + 5.75x_E + 0x_F \ge 10,000$.

Also $80x_A + 100x_B + 160x_C + 120x_D + 150x_E + 200x_F \le 25,00,000$,

Since at least 100 shares of each stock have to be purchased,

$x_A, x_B, x_C, x_D, x_E, x_F$, each ≥ 100.

EXAMPLE 2.6-27 (Product Mix Problem)

Consider a company that must produce two products over a production period of three months of duration. The company can pay for materials and labour from two sources: company funds and borrowed funds. The firm faces three decisions:

1. *How many units should it produce of product 1 ?*
2. *How many units should it produce of product 2 ?*
3. *How much money should it borrow to support the production of the two products?*

In making these decisions the firm wishes to maximize the profit contribution subject to the conditions stated below:

(i) Since the company's products are enjoying a seller's market, it can sell as many units as it can produce. The company would, therefore, like to produce as many units as possible subject to production capacity and financial constraints. The capacity constraints, together with cost and price data, are given in the table below:

Product	*Selling price (₹/unit)*	*Cost of production (₹/ unit)*	*Required hours per unit in deptt.*		
			A	*B*	*C*
1	*14*	*10*	*0.5*	*0.3*	*0.2*
2	*11*	*8*	*0.3*	*0.4*	*0.1*
	Available hours per production period of three months		*500*	*400*	*200*

(ii) The available company funds during the production period will be ₹ 3 lakhs.

(iii) A bank will give loans upto ₹ 2 lakhs per production period at an interest rate of 20 per cent per annum provided the company's acid (quick) test ratio is at least 1 to 1 while the loan is outstanding.

Take a simplified acid test ratio given by

$$\frac{\textit{Surplus cash on hand after production + Accounts receivable}}{\textit{Bank borrowings + Interest accrued thereon}}.$$

(iv) Also make sure that the needed funds are made available for meeting the production costs.

Formulate the above as linear programming problem. [C.A. Nov., 1992]

Formulation of L.P. Model

Let x_1 and x_2 be the number of units of products 1 and 2 to be produced and x_3 be the amount in rupees to be borrowed.

Objective is to maximize the net profit.

i.e., maximize Z = ₹ [$(14 - 10)x_1 + (11 - 8)\,x_2$ – cost associated with borrowed funds]

$$= ₹\left[4x_1 + 3x_2 - \frac{20}{100} \times \frac{3}{12}x_3\right]$$

$$= ₹\,(4x_1 + 3x_2 - 0.05x_3).$$

Constraints can be formulated as follows:

On production capacity of deptt. A : $0.5x_1 + 0.3x_2 \le 500,$

on production capacity of deptt. B : $0.3x_1 + 0.4x_2 \le 400,$

and on production capacity of deptt. C : $0.2x_1 + 0.1x_2 \le 200.$

As bank will give loans upto ₹ 2 lakhs,

$$x_3 \le ₹\ 2,00,000.$$

Now funds available with the company = ₹ $(3,00,000 + x_3)$.

Funds required for production = ₹ $(10x_1 + 8x_2)$.

Now funds required for production are ≤ funds available.

$\therefore \quad 10x_1 + 8x_2 \le 3,00,000 + x_3$

or $\quad 10x_1 + 8x_2 - x_3 \le 3,00,000.$

The constraint based on acid test ratio can be written as

$$\frac{\text{Surplus cash on hand after production + Accounts receivable}}{\text{Bank borrowings + Interest accrued thereon}} \ge \frac{1}{1}$$

or $$\frac{[(3,00,000 + x_3) - (10x_1 + 8x_2)] + (14x_1 + 11x_2)}{x_3 + 0.05x_3} \geq \frac{1}{1}$$

or $$4x_1 + 3x_2 + 3,00,000 \geq 0.05x_3$$

or $$4x_1 + 3x_2 - 0.05x_3 \geq - 3,00,000$$

or $$- 4x_1 - 3x_2 + 0.05x_3 \leq 3,00,000.$$

Thus, the L.P.P. is given by

Maximize $Z = 4x_1 + 3x_2 - 0.05x_3,$

subject to constraints

$$0.5x_1 + 0.3x_2 \leq 500,$$
$$0.3x_1 + 0.4x_2 \leq 400,$$
$$0.2x_1 + 0.1x_2 \leq 200,$$
$$x_3 \leq ₹\, 2,00,000,$$
$$10x_1 + 8x_2 - x_3 \leq ₹\, 3,00,000,$$
$$- 4x_1 - 3x_2 + 0.05x_3 \leq ₹\, 3,00,000,$$

where $x_1, x_2, x_3 \geq 0.$

EXAMPLE 2.6-28 (Product Mix Problem)

PQR Feed Company markets two mixes for cattle. The first mix, Fertilex, requires at least twice as much wheat as barley. The second mix, Multiplex, requires at least twice as much barley as wheat. Wheat costs ₹ 1.50 per kg and 1,000 kg are available this month. Barley costs ₹ 1.25 per kg and 1,200 kg are available. Fertilex sells for ₹ 1.80 per kg upto 99 kg and each additional kg over 99 sells for ₹ 1.65. Multiplex sells at ₹ 1.70 per kg upto 99 kg and each additional kg over 99 sells for ₹ 1.55. Bharat farms will buy any and all amounts of both mixes of PQR Feed Company. Formulate the mathematical model for the problem. [*C.S. June, 1994*]

Formulation of Mathematical Model

The data can be represented in the form of the table below:

Feed mixes	*Ingredients*			*Selling price/kg*
	Wheat		*Barley*	
Fertilex	2	:	1	₹ 1.80 upto 99 kg
				₹ 1.65 above 99 kg
Multiplex	1	:	2	₹ 1.70 upto 99 kg
				₹ 1.55 above 99 kg
Cost/kg	₹ 1.50		₹ 1.25	
Available quantity	1.000 kg		1,200 kg	

Let x_1 and x_2 be the quantities in kg of Feedmixes Fertilex and Multiplex to be marketed by the company. The *objective* is to maximize the monthly profit, which can be expressed as

$$\text{maximize } Z = ₹\, [\{99 \times 1.80 + 1.65\,(x_1 - 99) + 99 \times 1.70 + 1.55\,(x_2 - 99)\}$$
$$- \left\{1.50\left(\frac{2}{3}x_1 + \frac{1}{3}x_2\right) + 1.25\left(\frac{1}{3}x_1 + \frac{2}{3}x_2\right)\right\}]$$

$$= ₹\, [(1.65x_1 + 0.15 \times 99 + 1.55x_2 + 0.15 \times 99)$$
$$- \frac{1}{3}\,(3x_1 + 1.5x_2 + 1.25x_1 + 2.5x_2)]$$

$$= ₹ \left[(1.65x_1 + 1.55x_2 + 29.7) - \frac{1}{3}(4.25x_1 + 4x_2)\right]$$

$$= ₹ (0.23x_1 + 0.22x_2 + 29.7).$$

The constraint for availability of wheat can be written as

$$\frac{2}{3}x_1 + \frac{1}{3}x_2 \leq 1{,}000 \quad \text{or} \quad 2x_1 + x_2 \leq 3{,}000.$$

Similarly, constraint for availability of barley can be written as

$$\frac{1}{3}x_1 + \frac{2}{3}x_2 \leq 1{,}200 \quad \text{or} \quad x_1 + 2x_2 \leq 3600,$$

where $x_1, x_2 \geq 0$.

EXAMPLE 2.6-29 (Capital Budgeting Problem)

Renco Foundries is in the process of drawing up a Capital Budget for the next three years. It has funds to the tune of ₹ 1,00,000 which can be allocated across the projects A, B, C, D, and E. The net cash flows associated with an investment of ₹ 1 in each project are provided in the following table:

	Cash flow at time			
	0	*1*	*2*	*3*
From inv. A	– ₹ 1	+ ₹ 0.5	+ ₹ 1	₹ 0
From inv. B	₹ 0	– ₹ 1	+ ₹ 0.5	+ ₹ 1
From inv. C	– ₹ 1	+ ₹ 1.2	₹ 0	₹ 0
From inv. D	– ₹ 1	₹ 0	₹ 0	+ ₹ 1.9
From inv. E	₹ 0	₹ 0	– ₹ 1	+ ₹ 1.5

Note: *Time 0 = present, time 1 = 1 year from now, time 2 = 2 years from now, time 3 = 3 years from now.*

For example, ₹ 1 invested in investment B requires a ₹ 1 cash outflow at time 1 and returns ₹ 0.50 at time 2 and ₹ 1 at time 3. To ensure that the firm remains reasonably diversified, the firm will not commit an investment exceeding ₹ 75,000 in any project. The firm cannot borrow funds; therefore the cash available for investment at any time is limited to cash on hand. The firm will earn interest at 8% per annum by parking the uninvested funds in money market instruments. Assume that the returns from investments can be immediately reinvested. For example, the positive cash flow received from project C at time 1 can immediately be reinvested in project B.

Required: Formulate the L.P. model that will maximize cash on hand at time 3.

[Delhi U. MBA, 1999; C.A. Nov., 1995]

Formulation of L.P. Model

The company wants to decide the optimum allocation of funds to projects *A, B, C, D, E* and money market investments.

Let x_A, x_B, x_C, x_D and x_E be the amount in rupees invested in investments *A, B, C, D* and *E* and S_0, S_1, S_2 be the amount surplus at year 0, 1, 2 which is the amount invested in money market investments.

The *objective* is to maximize cash on hand at time 3.

At time 0

Funds available = ₹ 1,00,000.

Amount invested = ₹ $(x_A + x_C + x_D)$.

∴ S_0 = ₹ $[1{,}00{,}000 - (x_A + x_C + x_D)]$.

At time 1

Funds available = ₹ $(0.5x_A + 1.2x_C + 1.08S_0)$.

Amount invested = ₹ x_B.

∴ Constraint is $x_B \leq 0.5x_A + 1.2x_C + 1.08S_0$.

∴ Surplus is $S_1 = (0.5x_A + 1.2x_C + 1.08S_0) - x_B$.

At time 2

Funds available = ₹ $(x_A + 0.5x_B + 1.08S_1)$.

Amount invested = ₹ x_E.

∴ Constraint is $x_E \leq x_A + 0.5x_B + 1.08S_1$.

∴ Surplus is $S_2 = (x_A + 0.5x_B + 1.08S_1) - x_E$.

At time 3

Funds available = ₹ $(x_B + 1.9x_D + 1.5x_E + 1.08S_2)$.

Therefore, the objective function can be written as

maximize Z = ₹ $(x_B + 1.9x_D + 1.5x_E + 1.08S_2)$.

Also, since the company will not commit an investment exceeding ₹ 75,000 in any project,

x_A, x_B, x_C, x_D, x_E, each ≤ ₹ 75,000.

Thus the L.P. model can be written as

maximize Z = ₹ $(x_B + 1.9x_D + 1.5x_E + 1.08S_2)$,

subject to constraints

$$S_0 = 1,00,000 - (x_A + x_C + x_D),$$
$$S_1 = (0.5x_A + 1.2x_C + 1.08S_0) - x_B,$$
$$S_2 = (x_A + 0.5x_B + 1.08S_1) - x_E,$$

x_A, x_B, x_C, x_D, x_E, each ≤ ₹ 75,000,

where $x_A, x_B, x_C, x_D, x_E, S_0, S_1, S_2$, each ≥ 0.

EXAMPLE 2.6-30 (Capital Budgeting Problem)

A company has six independent projects available. The cash flows are given in the table below, wherein values within parenthesis are cash outflows and without parenthesis are cash inflows.

Project cash flows (₹'000)

Year	*A*	*B*	*C*	*D*	*E*	*F*
0	*(100)*	—	—	*(40)*	—	*(30)*
1	*(50)*	*(60)*	—	*(60)*	*(120)*	*(10)*
2	*(10)*	*(70)*	*(40)*	*50*	*100*	*20*
3	*70*	*10*	*(80)*	*10*	*(10)*	*10*
NPV (₹'000)	*20*	*15*	*10*	*30*	*10*	*5*

New capital for these projects is limted to

Year 0	*₹ 1,20,000*
Year 1	*₹ 2,00,000*
Year 2	*Nil*
Year 3	*Nil*

Cash generated from these investments can be reinvested in other projects in the same year. Express the problem in a linear programming format if the objective of the company is to maximize NPV and the projects are divisible.

Formulation of L.P. Model

Let x_1, x_2, x_3, x_4, x_5 and x_6 denote the *proportion* of projects *A*, *B*, *C*, *D*, *E* and *F* undertaken. The L.P. model can be written as maximize $Z = 20x_1 + 15x_2 + 10x_3 + 30x_4 + 10x_5 + 5x_6$,

subejct to constraints

$$100x_1 + 40x_4 + 30x_6 \le 120,$$
$$50x_1 + 60x_2 + 60x_4 + 120x_5 + 10x_6 \le 200,$$
$$10x_1 + 70x_2 + 40x_3 \le 50x_4 + 100x_5 + 20x_6,$$
$$80x_3 + 10x_5 \le 70x_1 + 10x_2 + 10x_4 + 10x_6,$$

where $x_1, x_2, x_3, x_4, x_5, x_6$, each ≥ 0.

EXAMPLE 2.6-31 (Blending Problem)

A manufacturing company making castings uses electric furnace to melt iron which must have the following specifications:

	Minimum	*Maximum*
Carbon	*3.10%*	*3.30%*
Silicon	*2.15%*	*2.25%*

Specifications and costs of various raw materials used for this purpose are given in table 2.11.

TABLE 2.11

Material	*Carbon %*	*Silicon %*	*Cost (₹)*
Steel scrap	*0.42*	*0.12*	*850/tonne*
Cast iron scrap	*3.80*	*2.40*	*900/tonne*
Remelt from foundry	*3.40*	*2.30*	*500/tonne*
Carbon briquettes	*100*	*0*	*7/kg*
Silicon briquettes	*0*	*100*	*10/kg*

If the total charge of iron metal required is 4 tonnes, find the weight in kg of each raw material that must be used in the optimal mix at minimum cost.

Formulation as L.P. Problem

Key descision is to determine the amount in kg of each of the five different raw materials to be mixed to make 4 tonnes of iron melt. Let x_1, x_2, x_3, x_4 and x_5 denote there amount.

Objective is to minimize the cost, *i.e.*,

$$\text{minimize } Z = \frac{850}{1,000}x_1 + \frac{900}{1,000}x_2 + \frac{500}{1,000}x_3 + 7x_4 + 10x_5$$
$$= 0.85x_1 + 0.9x_2 + 0.5x_3 + 7x_4 + 10x_5.$$

Constraints are on the specifications of iron melt.

For iron melt to have a minimum of 3.10% carbon,

$$0.42x_1 + 3.80x_2 + 3.40x_3 + 100x_4 \ge 3.10 \times 4,000$$
$$\ge 12,400,$$

for iron melt to have a maximum of 3.30% carbon,

$$0.42x_1 + 3.80x_2 + 3.40x_3 + 100x_4 \le 3.30 \times 4,000$$
$$\le 13,200,$$

for iron melt to have a minimum of 2.15% silicon,

$$0.12x_1 + 2.40x_2 + 2.30x_3 + 100x_5 \ge 2.15 \times 4,000$$
$$\ge 8,600,$$

for iron melt to have a maximum of 2.25% silicon,

$$0.12x_1 + 2.40x_2 + 2.30x_3 + 100x_5 \le 2.25 \times 4,000$$
$$\le 9,000.$$

Also, since the materials added must make up the full charge weight,

$$x_1 + x_2 + x_3 + x_4 + x_5 = 4{,}000,$$

where $x_1, x_2, ..., x_5$, each ≥ 0.

EXAMPLE 2.6-32 (Product Mix Problem)

A truck company has ₹ 50 lakh to invest and is to choose among three types of trucks A, B and C. Truck A has 12 tonne payload and is expected to average 50 km per hour. It costs ₹ 80,000. Truck B has a 20 tonne payload, is expected to average 45 km per hour and costs ₹ 1,00,000. Truck C is a modified form of B. It has sleeping space for the driver, which reduces its payload capacity to 17 tonne, while raising the cost to ₹ 1,20,000.

Truck A requires a crew of one man, and if driven on three shifts per day, could run for an average of 20 hours a day. Trucks B and C require a crew of two men each and if driven on three shifts per day, could be run for an average of 19 hours and 22 hours respectively. The company has a fleet of 120 crewmen available to it. If the total number of trucks are not to exceed 40, how many trucks of each type should be purchased if the company wants to maximize its capacity in tonne km per day ? Formulate the problem as L.P. problem.

Formulation as an L.P. Problem

Key decision is to determine the number of trucks of type *A*, *B* and *C* to be purchased.
Let the number of trucks of type *A*, *B* and *C* to be purchased be x_1, x_2 and x_3 respectively.
Constraints are
on the number of crews:

$$x_1 + 2x_2 + 2x_3 \leq 120,$$

on the number of trucks:

$$x_1 + x_2 + x_3 \leq 40,$$

and on the money to be invested:

$$80{,}000x_1 + 1{,}00{,}000x_2 + 1{,}20{,}000x_3 \leq 50{,}00{,}000$$

or

$$8x_1 + 10x_2 + 12x_3 \leq 500.$$

Objective is to maximize the tonne km/per day. For objective function equation, we are given the following data:

TABLE 2.12

Truck type	*Payload (tonnes)*	*km/hour*	*Average run (hours/day)*
A	12	50	20
B	20	45	19
C	17	45	22

For truck *A*, tonne km per day

$$= \text{Payload in tonne} \times \text{km/hour} \times \text{hours/day}$$

$$= 12 \times 50 \times 20 = 12{,}000.$$

Similarly, for truck *B*, tonne km per day

$$= 20 \times 45 \times 19 = 17{,}100,$$

and for truck *C*, tonne km per day

$$= 17 \times 45 \times 22 = 16{,}830.$$

Therefore, the objective function is

$$\text{maximize } Z = 12{,}000x_1 + 17{,}100x_2 + 16{,}830x_3,$$

where $x_1, x_2, x_3 \geq 0$.

EXAMPLE 2.6-33 (Trim Loss Problem)

A manufacturer of cylindrical containers receives tin sheets in widths of 30 cm and 60 cm respectively. For these containers the sheets are to be cut to three different widths of 15 cm, 21 cm and 27 cm respectively. The number of containers to be manufactured from these three widths are 400, 200 and 300 respectively. The bottom plates and top covers of the containers are purchased directly from the market. There is no limit on the lengths of standard tin sheets. Formulate the L.P. model for the production schedule that minimizes the trim losses.

[*H.P.U. B.Tech. (Mech.) Nov., 2014*]

Formulation as an L.P. Problem

Key decision is to determine how each of the two standard widths of tin sheets be cut to the required widths so that trim losses are minimum.

From the available widths of 30 cm and 60 cm, several combinations of the three required widths of 15 cm, 21 cm and 27 cm are possible. Let x_{ij} represent these combinations. Each combination results in certain trim loss.

Constraints can be formulated as follows:

The possible cutting combinations (plans) for both types of sheets are shown in the table below.

Width (cm)	*i = 1 (30cm)*			*i = 2 (60 cm)*					
	x_{11}	x_{12}	x_{13}	x_{21}	x_{22}	x_{23}	x_{24}	x_{25}	x_{26}
15	2	0	0	4	2	2	1	0	0
21	0	1	0	0	1	0	2	1	0
27	0	0	1	0	0	1	0	1	2
Trim loss (cm)	0	9	3	0	9	3	3	12	6

Thus the constraints are

$$2x_{11} + 4x_{21} + 2x_{22} + 2x_{23} + x_{24} \geq 400,$$

$$x_{12} + x_{22} + 2x_{24} + x_{25} \geq 200,$$

and $$x_{13} + x_{23} + x_{25} + 2x_{26} \geq 300.$$

Objective is to minimize the trim losses.

i.e., minimize $Z = 9x_{12} + 3x_{13} + 9x_{22} + 3x_{23} + 3x_{24} + 12x_{25} + 6x_{26}$,

where $x_{11}, x_{12}, x_{13}, x_{21}, x_{22}, x_{23}, x_{24}, x_{25}, x_{26} \geq 0$.

EXAMPLE 2.6-34 (War Strategy Problem)

The strategic bomber command receives instructions to interrupt the enemy tank production. The enemy has four key plants located in separate cities, and destruction of any one plant will effectively halt the production of tanks. There is an acute shortage of fuel, which limits the supply to 45,000 litres for this particular mission. Any bomber sent to any particular city must have at least enough fuel for the round trip plus 100 litres.

The number of bombers available to the commander and their descriptions are as follows:

TABLE 2.13

Bomber type	*Description*	*km/litre*	*Number available*
A	*Heavy*	*2*	*40*
B	*Medium*	*2.5*	*30*

Information about the location of the plants and their probability of being attacked by a medium bomber and a heavy bomber is given below.

TABLE 2.14

Plant	*Distance from base (km)*	*Probability of destruction by*	
		a heavy bomber	*a medium bomber*
1	*400*	*0.10*	*0.08*
2	*450*	*0.20*	*0.16*
3	*500*	*0.15*	*0.12*
4	*600*	*0.25*	*0.20*

How many of each type of bombers should be despatched, and how should they be allocated among the four targets in order to maximize the probability of success ? Formulate the L.P. model.

Formulation of L.P. Model

Key decision to be made is how many of either type of bombers be sent to each plant.

Let the bombers sent be x_{ij}, where i = type A, B and j = plant 1, 2, 3, 4.

Objective is to maximize the probability of success in destroying at least one plant and this is equivalent to minimizing the probability of not destroying any plant. Let Q denote this probability.

Then,
$$Q = (1-0.1)^{x_{A1}} \cdot (1-0.2)^{x_{A2}} \cdot (1-0.15)^{x_{A3}} \cdot (1-0.25)^{x_{A4}} \cdot$$
$$(1-0.08)^{x_{B1}} \cdot (1-0.16)^{x_{B2}} \cdot (1-0.12)^{x_{B3}} \cdot (1-0.20)^{x_{B4}}$$

Here the objective function is non-linear but it can be reduced to the linear form.

Now minimizing Q is equivalent to minimizing log Q and log Q is linear. Moreover, minimizing log Q is equivalent to maximizing – log Q or maximizing log $1/Q$. Taking base of log as 10,

$$\log 1/Q = -(x_{A1} \log 0.9 + x_{A2} \log 0.8 + x_{A3} \cdot \log 0.85 + x_{A4} \log 0.75$$
$$+ x_{B1} \log 0.92 + x_{B2} \log 0.84 + x_{B3} \log 0.88 + x_{B4} \log 0.80).$$

Therefore, the objective is to maximize

$$\log 1/Q = 0.0457x_{A1} + 0.09691x_{A2} + 0.07058x_{A3} + 0.12493x_{A4} + 0.03623x_{B1}$$
$$+ 0.07572x_{B2} + 0.05552x_{B3} + 0.09691x_{B4}.$$

Constraints are

(*a*) due to limited supply of fuel

$$\left(2 \times \frac{400}{2} + 100\right)x_{A1} + \left(2 \times \frac{450}{2} + 100\right)x_{A2} + \left(2 \times \frac{500}{2} + 100\right)x_{A3} + \left(2 \times \frac{600}{2} + 100\right)x_{A4}$$
$$+ \left(2 \times \frac{400}{2.5} + 100\right)x_{B1} + \left(2 \times \frac{450}{2.5} + 100\right)x_{B2} + \left(2 \times \frac{500}{2.5} + 100\right)x_{B3}$$
$$+ \left(2 \times \frac{600}{2.5} + 100\right)x_{B4} \le 45{,}000$$

i.e., $500x_{A1} + 550x_{A2} + 600x_{A3} + 700x_{A4} + 420x_{B1} + 460x_{B2} + 500x_{B3} + 580x_{B4} \leq 45{,}000.$

(*b*) due to limited number of aircrafts

$$x_{A1} + x_{A2} + x_{A3} + x_{A4} \leq 40,$$
$$x_{B1} + x_{B2} + x_{B3} + x_{B4} \leq 30,$$

where $x_{A1}, x_{A2}, x_{A3}, x_{A4}; x_{B1}, x_{B2}, x_{B3}, x_{B4}$, each ≥ 0.

EXAMPLE 2.6-35 (Production Scheduling Problem)

A company wants to plan the next week's production of its three products A, B nd C. These products are made on three machines—lathes, drills and grinders. Time available on lathes, drills and grinders for the next week is 200 hr., 250 hr. and 300 hr. respectively. The products can be made through different alternative routes shown in the table below. The products sell in the market at ₹ 20, ₹ 15 and ₹ 25 per unit respectively.

(*a*) *Formulate the L.P. model assuming unlimited market demand for the products.*

(*b*) *There is a fixed order (that has to be satisfied) of 250 units of A, 200 units of B and 150 units of C.*

The customer pays ₹ 20, ₹ 15 and ₹ 25 per unit of products A, B and C in the fixed order and is willing to pay ₹ 15, ₹ 10 and ₹ 20 per unit for the extra units of A, B and C respectively. Construct the model that maximizes the sales revenue.

(*c*) *If not more than 200 units of C can be sold in the market, what modifications would be required in the model ?*

(*d*) *If there is possibility of using overtime for making product A, how can it be taken into consideration ?*

TABLE 2.15

Machine	*Product A*			*Product B*		*Product C*			*Machine hours available*
	Route			*Route*		*Route*			
	1	*2*	*3*	*1*	*2*	*1*	*2*	*3*	
Lathes	*0.5*	*0.7*	*0.3*	—	*0.5*	*0.6*	*0.5*	*0.3*	*200*
Drills	*0.5*	*0.3*	*0.2*	*0.4*	*0.3*	*0.7*	*0.4*	*0.1*	*250*
Grinders	*0.6*	*0.4*	*0.6*	*0.7*	*0.5*	*0.4*	*0.3*	—	*300*

Formulation of L.P. Model

(*a*) *Key decision* to be made is to determine the number of units of products *A*, *B* and *C* to be manufactured through first, second and third routes.

Let the number of units of products *A*, *B* and *C* to be manufactured through first, second and third routes be $x_{A1}, x_{A2}, x_{A3}; x_{B1}, x_{B2}$ and x_{C1}, x_{C2}, x_{C3} respectively, where each is ≥ 0.

Objective is to maximize the sales revenue.

i.e., maximize $Z = 20(x_{A1} + x_{A2} + x_{A3}) + 15(x_{B1} + x_{B2}) + 25(x_{C1} + x_{C2} + x_{C3})$.

Constraints are on the machine hours available for each machine. They are

for lathes: $0.5x_{A1} + 0.7x_{A2} + 0.3x_{A3} + 0.5x_{B2} + 0.6x_{C1} + 0.5x_{C2} + 0.3x_{C3} \leq 200,$

for drills: $0.5x_{A1} + 0.3x_{A2} + 0.2x_{A3} + 0.4x_{B1} + 0.3x_{B2} + 0.7x_{C1} + 0.4x_{C2} + 0.1x_{C3} \leq 250$, and

for grinders: $0.6x_{A1} + 0.4x_{A2} + 0.6x_{A3} + 0.7x_{B1} + 0.5x_{B2} + 0.4x_{C1} + 0.3x_{C2} \leq 300.$

Thus the L.P. model is to maximize Z subject to the constraints and non-negativity restrictions mentioned above.

(*b*) The fixed order is for 250 units of A, 200 units of B and 150 units of C. The total number of units of product A produced are $x_{A1} + x_{A2} + x_{A3}$ and in order to satisfy the fixed order it must be ≥ 250.

i.e., for lathes: $x_{A1} + x_{A2} + x_{A3} \geq 250,$

for drills: $x_{B1} + x_{B2} \geq 200,$

for grinders: $x_{C1} + x_{C2} + x_{C3} \geq 150.$

These are, then, the additional constaints to be satisfied (along with the three earlier constraints).

The new objective function is slightly more involved and may be written as

$$\text{maximize } Z_1 = 250 \times 20 + 15\,(x_{A1} + x_{A2} + x_{A3} - 250) + 200 \times 15 + 10(x_{B1} + x_{B2} - 200) + 150 \times 25 + 20\,(x_{C1} + x_{C2} + x_{C3} - 150).$$

The problem is, thus, to maximize Z_1 subject to the above six constraints while satisfying the non-negativity conditions.

(*c*) This market limitation results in a new constraint

$$x_{C1} + x_{C2} + x_{C3} \leq 200,$$

and the problem is to maximize Z_1 while satisfying this 7th (additional) constraint also.

(*d*) Let x_{A10}, x_{A20} and x_{A30} represent the number of units of product A manufactured during overtime through routes 1, 2 and 3 respectively. The overtime machine hours available need to be given in the problem, which will result in three more constraints. The objective function representing sales revenue will have to be replaced by profit function as production during overtime is less profitable than regular production. Though the objective function becomes more complex and number of constraints becomes large, yet the problem remains a linear programming problem.

EXAMPLE 2.6-36 (Warehouse Problem)

A person running a warehouse purchases and sells identical items. The warehouse can accommodate 1,000 such items. Each month, the person can sell any quantity he has in stock. Each month, he can buy as much as he likes to have in stock for delivery at the end of the month, subject to a maximum of 1,000 items. The forecast of purchase and sale prices for the next six months is given below.

Month i	*1*	*2*	*3*	*4*	*5*	*6*
Purchase price c_i *(₹)*	*12*	*14*	*17*	*19*	*20*	*21*
Sale price s_i *(₹)*	*13*	*15*	*16*	*20*	*21*	*23*

If at present he has a stock of 200 items, what should be his policy ?

Formulation of L.P. Model

Key decision is to determine the number of items to be purchased and sold for each of the six months.

Let x_j and y_j (j = 1, 2, ..., 6) be the number of items purchased and sold for each of the six months, where $x_j, y_j \geq 0$.

Objective is to maximize the profit *i.e.*,

$$\text{maximize } Z = 13y_1 + 15y_2 + 16y_3 + 20y_4 + 21y_5 + 23y_6 - (12x_1 + 14x_2 + 17x_3 + 19x_4 + 20x_5 + 21x_6).$$

Constraints can be formulated as follows:

The person cannot sell anything that is not in stock. Therefore, for each month n = 1, 2, ..., 6,

$$200 + \sum_{j=1}^{n-1} (x_j - y_j) \geq y_n$$

or $$200+\sum_{j=1}^{n-1} x_j \geq \sum_{j=1}^{n-1} y_j + y_n$$

or $$200+\sum_{j=1}^{n-1} x_j \geq \sum_{j=1}^{n} y_j$$

or $$\sum_{j=1}^{n} y_j - \sum_{j=1}^{n-1} x_j \leq 200$$

or $$\sum_{j=1}^{6} y_j - \sum_{j=1}^{5} x_j \leq 200.$$

Further, since he cannot overstock beyond 1,000 items,

$$200+\sum_{j=1}^{n} (x_j - y_j) \leq 1,000$$

or $$\sum_{j=1}^{n} x_j - \sum_{j=1}^{n} y_j \leq 800$$

or $$\sum_{j=1}^{6} x_j - \sum_{j=1}^{6} y_j \leq 800.$$

The above relations, therefore, constitute the L.P. model.

EXAMPLE 2.6-37 (Caterer Problem)

A caterer is to organise garden parties for a week. He needs a total of 160, 120, 60, 90, 110, 100 and 120 fresh napkins during the seven days of the week. Each new napkin costs ₹ 3. He can use soiled napkins after getting them washed from a laundry. Ordinarily, washing charges are ₹ 0.60 per napkin and they are returned after four days. However, the laundry also provides express service at a cost of ₹ 1 per napkin, in which case they are returned after two days. Formulate the L.P. model to determine the planning schedule the caterer should adopt to buy or send napkins to the laundry so as to minimize the cost.

Formulation of L.P. Model

Key decision is to determine the number of napkins to be bought, to be sent for express laundry service, for ordinary laundry service or not to be sent at all, each day of the week.

Let x_j = number of napkins bought on jth day,

y_j = number of napkins sent for express laundry service on jth day,

z_j = number of napkins sent for ordinary laundry service on jth day,

and v_j = number of napkins soiled on jth day but not sent to laundry on jth day,

where $x_j, y_j, z_j, v_j \geq 0$.

Constraints can be formulated as follows:

On the first day, the caterer, obviously, has to start with new napkins. After use, if he sends napkins for washing, the earliest he can get washed napkins (by express service) is by the beginning of the 4th day. Therefore, he has to buy napkins for the first three days, which means,

$$x_1 = 160,$$

$$x_2 = 120,$$

and $$x_3 = 60.$$

At the end of first day, he will send y_1 and z_1 number of napkins for 2 days' and 4 days' service and v_1 will be the number kept in stock of soiled napkins: y_1 and z_1 will be received from the laundry for use at the beginning of 4th and 6th day respectively. Similarly, y_2 and z_2 sent to the laundry on the second day will be received for use at the beginning of 5th and 7th day. Likewise, y_3 and z_3 sent to the laundry on the third day will be received for use at the beginning of 6th and 8th day. Since 8th day is beyond the planning period, $z_3 = 0$. In the same manner, y_4 sent to the laundry for express service on 4th day will be received for use at the beginning of 7th day, while $z_4 = 0$.

Thus the schedule of supply of napkins during the 7 days is as shown below.

Type \ *Day*	1	2	3	4	5	6	7
New napkins	x_1	x_2	x_3	x_4	x_5	x_6	x_7
Express service	—	—	—	y_1	y_2	y_3	y_4
Ordinary service	—	—	—	—	—	z_1	z_2
Total required	160	120	60	90	110	100	120

Therefore, requirement constraints are

$$x_1 = 160,$$
$$x_2 = 120,$$
$$x_3 = 60,$$
$$x_4 + y_1 = 90,$$
$$x_5 + y_2 = 110,$$
$$x_6 + y_3 + z_1 = 100,$$

and $$x_7 + y_4 + z_2 = 120.$$

There is need to form another set of constraints on the total number of soiled napkins. The total number of soiled napkins on the jth day must be equal to the number of napkins sent to laundry plus those left in stock of soiled napkins.

However, the number of soiled napkins on the jth day = number used on jth day + number left on $(j - 1)$th day. These constraints are thus given by

$$y_1 + z_1 + v_1 = 160,$$
$$y_2 + z_2 + v_2 = 120 + v_1,$$
$$y_3 + z_3 + v_3 = 60 + v_2,$$
$$y_4 + z_4 + v_4 = 90 + v_3,$$
$$y_5 + z_5 + v_5 = 110 + v_4,$$
$$y_6 + z_6 + v_6 = 100 + v_5,$$

and $$y_7 + z_7 + v_7 = 120 + v_6.$$

Further as already discussed,

$$y_5 = y_6 = y_7 = 0,$$

and $$z_3 = z_4 = z_5 = z_6 = z_7 = 0.$$

This reduces the above set of constraints to

$$y_1 + z_1 + v_1 = 160,$$
$$y_2 + z_2 + v_2 = 120 + v_1,$$
$$y_3 + v_3 = 60 + v_2,$$
$$y_4 + v_4 = 90 + v_3,$$
$$v_5 = 110 + v_4,$$
$$v_6 = 100 + v_5,$$

and $$v_7 = 120 + v_6.$$

Objective is to minimize the cost of napkins.

i.e., minimize $= ₹\ [3(x_1 + x_2 + x_3 + x_4 + x_5 + x_6 + x_7) + 1(y_1 + y_2 + y_3 + y_4) + 0.6(z_1 + z_2)]$

$= ₹\ [3(x_1 + x_2 + x_3 + x_4 + x_5 + x_6 + x_7) + (y_1 + y_2 + y_3 + y_4) + 0.6(z_1 + z_2)]$.

The above relations, therefore, form the L.P. model.

EXAMPLE 2.6-38 (Product Mix Problem)

WELLTYPE manufacturing company produces three types of typewriters. All the three models are required to be machined first and then assembled. The time required for various models is as follows:

Type	*Manual typewriter*	*Electronic typewriter*	*Deluxe electronic typewriter*
Machine time (hours)	*15*	*12*	*14*
Assembly time (hours)	*4*	*3*	*5*

The total available machine time and assembly time is 3,000 hours and 1,200 hours respectively. The data regarding the selling price and variable costs for the three types are:

Type	*Manual*	*Electronic*	*Deluxe electronic*
Selling price (₹)	4,100	7,500	14,600
Labour, material and other variable costs (₹)	2,500	4,500	9,000

The company sells all the three types on credit basis, but will collect the amounts on the first of next month. The labour, material and other variable expenses will have to be paid in cash. This company has taken a loan of ₹ 40,000 from a Cooperative Bank and this company will have to repay it to the bank on 1st April, 1993. The TNC Bank from whom this company has borrowed ₹ 60,000 has expressed its approval to renew the loan. The balance sheet of this company as on 31.3.1993 is as follows:

Liabilities	₹	*Assets*	₹
Equity share capital	*1,50,000*	*Land*	*90,000*
Capital reserve	*15,000*	*Building*	*70,000*
General reserve	*1,10,000*	*Plant and machinery*	*1,00,000*
Profit and loss account	*25,000*	*Furniture and fixures*	*15,000*
Long term loan	*1,00,000*	*Vehicles*	*30,000*
Loan from TNC Bank	*60,000*	*Inventory*	*5,000*
Loan from Cooperative Bank	*40,000*	*Receivables*	*50,000*
		Cash	*1,40,000*
Total	*5,00,000*	*Total*	*5,00,000*

The company will have to pay a sum of ₹ 10,000 towards the salary of top management executives and other fixed overheads for the month. Interest on long-term loans is to be paid every month at 24% per annum. Interest on loans from TNC and Cooperative Banks may be taken to be ₹ 1,200 for the month. Also this company has promised to deliver 2 manual typewriters and 8 deluxe-electronic typewriters to one of its valued customers next month.

Also make sure that the level of operations in this company is subject to the availability of cash next month.

This company will also be able to sell all the types of typewriters in the market. The senior manager of this company desires to know as to how many units of each typewriter must be manufactured in the factory next month so as to maximize the profits of the company. Formulate this as L.P. model. [*C.A. May, 1993*]

Formulation of L.P. Model

Let x_1, x_2 and x_3 denote the number of manual, electronic and deluxe-electronic typewriters respectively to be manufactured in the factory next month *i.e.*, in the month of April, 1993.

Objective is to maximize the net profit.

i.e., maximize $Z = ₹\,[(4{,}100 - 2{,}500)\,x_1 + (7{,}500 - 4{,}500)\,x_2 + (14{,}600 - 9{,}000)\,x_3 - (10{,}000 + 2{,}000 + 1{,}200)]$

$= ₹\,[1{,}600x_1 + 3{,}000x_2 + 5{,}600x_3 - 13{,}200]$.

Constraints can be formulated as follows:

on machine time: $15x_1 + 12x_2 + 14x_3 \le 3{,}000$,

on assembly time: $4x_1 + 3x_2 + 5x_3 \le 1{,}200$.

The level of operations in the company is subject to the availability of cash next month *i.e.*, the cash required for manufacturing the three models can not exceed the cash available next month.

Now cash required $= ₹\,(2{,}500x_1 + 4{,}500x_2 + 9{,}000x_3)$.

The availability of cash next month from balance sheet can be calculated as follows:

Cash availability = Cash balance + receivables – loan to be repaid to cooperative bank – interest on loan from TNC and cooperative banks – interest on long term loans – top management salary and fixed overheads

$$= ₹\left[1{,}40{,}000 + 50{,}000 - (40{,}000 + 1{,}200 + \frac{1{,}00{,}000}{12} \times \frac{24}{100} + 10{,}000)\right]$$

$= ₹\,[1{,}90{,}000 - (40{,}000 + 1{,}200 + 2{,}000 + 10{,}000)]$

$= ₹\,1{,}36{,}800$.

$\therefore$ We get the constraint

$2{,}500x_1 + 4{,}500x_2 + 9{,}000x_3 \le 1{,}36{,}800$.

Further, the company has promised to deliver 2 manual typewriters and 8 deluxe-electronic typewriters to one of its customers.

$\therefore\ x_1 \ge 2,\ x_3 \ge 8$.

Also $x_2 \ge 0$.

These relations, therefore, represent the L.P. model.

EXAMPLE 2.6-39 (Product Mix Problem)

A manufacturing company has two plants, which produce and supply two products X and Y. Each plant can work up to 15 hours a day. In plant A, it takes 3 hours to prepare and pack 1,000 litres of X and 2 hours to prepare and pack 1 ton of Y. In plant B, it takes 2 hours to prepare and pack 1,000 litres of X and 2.5 hours to prepare and pack 1 ton of Y. In plant A, it costs ₹ 20,000 to prepare and pack 1,000 litres of X and ₹ 25,000 to prepare and pack 1 ton of Y, whereas these costs are ₹ 22,000 and ₹ 23,000 respectively in plant B. The company wants to produce 12,000 litres of X and 10 tons of Y and wants to organize the production so as to produce the products at minimum cost. Formulate this problem as an L.P. model.

[*H.P.U. B.Tech. (Mech.) 2013*]

Formulation of L.P. Model

Key decision is to determine the quantity of products X and Y in each of the plants A and B.

Let x_1, x_2 = quantity of product X (in '000 litres) to be produced and packed in plants A and B respectively,

x_3, x_4 = quantity of product Y (in tons) to be produced and packed in plants A and B respectively.

Objective is to minimize the total cost.

i.e., minimize Z = ₹ (20,000 x_1 + 22,000 x_2 + 25,000 x_3 + 23,000 x_4).

Constraints are

(*a*) On the preparation time : $3x_1 + 2x_3 \leq 15$,
$2x_2 + 2.5x_4 \leq 15$.

(*b*) On the daily production requirement : $x_1 + x_2 \geq 12$,
$x_3 + x_4 \geq 10$,

where x_1, x_2, x_3, x_4, each ≥ 0.

EXAMPLE 2.6-40 (Product Mix Problem)

A company produces two parts P_1 and P_2 used in television sets. A unit of P_1 costs the company ₹ 5 in wages and ₹ 6 in material, while a unit of P_2 costs the company ₹ 20 in wages and ₹ 10 in material. The company sells both parts on one-period credit terms, but the company's labour and material expenses must be paid in cash. The selling price of P_1 is ₹ 25/ unit and P_2 is ₹ 60/ unit. The company's production capacity is limited by two considerations. First, at the beginning of period 1, the company has an initial balance of ₹ 35,000 (cash + bank credit + collections from past credit sales). Second, the company has available in each period 1,600 hours of machine time and 1,400 hours of assembly time. The production of each P_1 requires 2 hours of machine time and 1.5 hours of assembly time, while production of each P_2 requires 2 hours of machine time and 3 hours of assembly time. Formulate the problem as L.P. model to maximize the total profit to the company.

[H.P.U. B.Tech. (Mech.) June, 2015; P.U. B.E. (T.I.T.) Dec., 2008]

Formulation of L.P. Model

The data of the problem can be expressed in the form of a table shown below.

Resources	*Parts*		*Total*
	P_1	P_2	*availability*
Budget	₹ (5 + 6)/unit	₹ (20+10)/unit	₹ 35,000
Machine time	2 hours/unit	2 hours/unit	1,600
Assembly time	1.5 hours/unit	3 hours/unit	1,400
Cost price (wages + material)	₹ 11/unit	₹ 30/unit	
Selling price	₹ 25/unit	₹ 60/unit	

Key decision is to determine the number of parts P_1 and P_2 to be produced. Let x_1 and x_2 denote the number of these parts.

Objective is to maximize the total profit.

i.e., maximize Z = Selling price – Cost price
= ₹ [(25 – 11) x_1 + (60 – 30) x_2]
= ₹ (14 x_1 + 30 x_2).

Constraints are

(*a*) on the total budget available : $11x_1 + 30x_2 \leq 35{,}000$, (*b*) on the machine time available : $2x_1 + 2x_2 \leq 1{,}600$,

(*c*) on the assembly time available: $1.5\, x_1 + 3x_2 \leq 1{,}400$.
where $x_1, x_2 \geq 0$.

EXAMPLE 2.6-41 (Personnel Problem)

A company, engaged in producing tinned food, has 300 trained employees on the rolls, each of whom can produce one can of food in a week. Due to developing taste of the public for this kind of food, the company plans to add to the existing labour force by employing 150 persons, in a phased manner, over the next 5 weeks. The newcomers would have to undergo a two-week training programme before being put to work. The training is to be given by employees from among the existing ones and it is known that one employee can train three trainees. Assume that there would be no production from the trainers and the trainees during training period as the training is off-the-job. However, the trainees would be remunerated at the rate of ₹ 300 per week, the same rate as for the trainers. The company has booked the following orders to supply during the next 5 weeks :

Week	:	*1*	*2*	*3*	*4*	*5*
No. of cans	:	*280*	*298*	*305*	*360*	*400*

Assume that the production in any week would not be more than the number of cans booked in the order so that every delivery of the food will be 'fresh'.

Formulate this problem as an L.P. model to develop a training schedule that minimizes the labour cost over the five-week period. [*Delhi U.M.B.A., 2000*]

Formulation of L.P. Model

Key decision is to determine the number of trainees to be recruited in the beginning of week 1, 2, 3, 4 and 5 respectively. Let x_1, x_2, x_3 , x_4 and x_5 denote their number.

Now trainees recruited in the beginning of week 1 would get salary for all the five weeks; those recruited in the beginning of week 2 would get salary for four weeks and so on.

Objective is to minimize the labour cost

i.e., minimize $Z = ₹\ 300\ [5x_1 + 4x_2 + 3x_3 + 2x_4 + x_5]$.

Constraints can be formulated as follows :

Week 1 : There are 300 trained empolyees available. Out of them, $\frac{x_1}{3}$ will be required to train the x_1 trainees recruited in the beginning of the week. As each trained employee can produce one can/week, we have the relation :

$$300 - \frac{x_1}{3} \geq 280.$$

Week 2 : On Similar reasoning,

$$300 - \frac{x_1}{3} - \frac{x_2}{3} \geq 298.$$

Week 3 : As the training period is 2 weeks, x_1 workers recruited in the beginning of week 1, would complete the training and become the trained employees and therefore,

$$300 + x_1 - \frac{x_2}{3} - \frac{x_3}{3} \geq 305.$$

In the same manner we have the following relations for week 4 and 5 :

Week 4 : $300 + x_1 + x_2 - \frac{x_3}{3} - \frac{x_4}{3} \geq 360.$

Week 5 : $300 + x_1 + x_2 + x_3 - \frac{x_4}{3} - \frac{x_5}{3} \geq 400.$

As 150 new persons, in all, are to be added during the five-week period,

$$x_1 + x_2 + x_3 + x_4 + x_5 = 150,$$

where $x_1, x_2, x_3, x_4, x_5 \geq 0.$

EXAMPLE 2.6-42 (Advertising Media Selection Problem)

An advertising agency is preparing an advertising campaign for a group of agencies. These agencies have decided that their target customers should have the following characteristics with importance (weightage) as given below.

	Characteristics	*Weightage (%)*
Age	*25–45 years*	*20*
Annual income	*Above ₹ 80,000*	*40*
Female	*Married*	*40*

The agency has made a careful analysis of three media and has compiled the following data:

Data item	*Media*		
	Magazine	*Radio*	*Television*
Audience size ('000)	*800*	*1,000*	*1,500*
Cost per advertisement (₹)	*10,000*	*30,000*	*1,00,000*
Min. no. of advertisements allowed	*15*	*10*	*10*
Max. no. of advertisements allowed	*25*	*15*	*15*
Reader characteristics			
(i) Age 25-45 years	*70%*	*60%*	*50%*
(ii) Annual income above ₹ 80,000	*60%*	*50%*	*40%*
(iii) Females married	*45%*	*40%*	*30%*

The advertising agency has earmarked a budget of ₹ 10,00,000 for this purpose. Formulate the L.P. model for the problem to maximize the total expected effective exposure.

Formulation of L.P. Model

Key decision is to determine the number of advertisements in each of the media. Let x_1, x_2 and x_3 denote the number of advertisements in magazine, radio and television respectively.

Objective is to maximize the total expected effective exposure. For this, first, effectiveness coefficient for each advertising media is calculated as follows :

Media	*Effectiveness coefficient*
Magazine	0.70(0.20)+0.60(0.40)+0.45(0.40) = 0.56
Radio	0.60(0.20)+0.50(0.40)+0.40 (0.40) = 0.48
Television	0.50(0.20)+0.40 (0.40)+0.30(0.40) = 0.38

Now effective exposure of each media = Effectiveness coefficient × Audience size.

Thus effective exposure of

magazine = 0.56 × 8,00,000 = 4,48,000,

radio = 0.48 × 10,00,000 = 4,80,000,

television $= 0.38 \times 15,00,000 = 5,70,000$.

$\therefore$ The objective function can be expressed as

maximize $Z = 4,48,000x_1 + 4,80,000x_2 + 5,70,000x_3$.

Constraints can be formulated as follows :

(*a*) budget constraint : $10,000x_1 + 30,000x_2 + 1,00,000x_3 \leq 10,00,000$

or $x_1 + 3x_2 + 10x_3 \leq 100$.

(*b*) minimum no. of advertisements allowed

constraints : $x_1 \geq 15, x_2 \geq 10, x_3 \geq 10$.

(*c*) maximum no. of advertisements allowed

constraints : $x_1 \leq 25, x_2 \leq 15, x_3 \leq 15$,

where $x_1, x_2, x_3 \geq 0$.

EXAMPLE 2.6-43 (Product Mix Problem)

A paper mill produces paper for books as well as for magazines. Each kg of paper for books requires 2 kg of material A and 3 kg of material B. For magazines the proportion is 2 kg of A and 2 kg of B for each kg of paper. The mill needs 15,000 kg paper for books and 6,000 kg for magazines. Materials A and B are availables as 3 and 5 lakh kg respectively. Requirement for books is twice that for magazines. Selling price per book paper is ₹ 14/kg and for magazines it is ₹ 10/kg. Cost of material A is ₹ 2/kg and that for mateiral B is ₹ 2.50/kg. It is required to find the product manufacturing plan and the optimum total profit. Formulate L.P. model for the problem.

[P.T.U. MBA, 2009]

Formulation of L.P. Model

Let the mill purchase (and then sell) x_1 kg of paper for books and x_2 kg of paper for magazines. The data given in the problem can be expressed in the form of a table shown below:

	Material A (kg)	*Material B (kg)*	*Requirement of paper (kg)*	*Sale price (₹ / kg)*
Paper for books (kg)	2	3	15,000	14/-
Paper for magazines (kg)	2	2	6,000	10/-
Available materials (kg)	3 lakhs	5 lakhs		
Cost (₹ / kg)	2/-	2.50/-		

Profit is the difference between the total sales received from paper for books and magazines and the total cost of the two materials. Thus the objective functions can be wirtten as

Maximize $Z = ₹ [(14x_1 + 10x_2) - 2(2x_1 + 2x_2) - 2.50(3x_1 + 2x_2)]$

$= ₹ (2.50x_1 + x_2)$.

Constraints can be formulated as follows:

On the requirement of paper for books : $2x_1 + 3x_1 \geq 15,000$ or $x_1 \geq 3,000$,

on the requirement of paper for magazines : $2x_2 + 2x_2 \geq 6,000$ or $x_2 \geq 1,500$,

on the availability of material A : $2x_1 + 2x_2 \leq 3,00,000$,

on the availability of material B : $3x_1 + 2x_2 \leq 5,00,000$,

as requirement of paper for books is twice that for magazines,

$x_1 = 2x_2$ or $x_1 - 2x_2 = 0$,

where $x_1, x_2 \geq 0$.

EXERCISES 2.1

1. What are the essential characteristics of a linear programming model?
[*H.P.U. B.Tech. (Mech.) 2012; P.T.U.B. Tech., 2010; D.U. M. com., 2000; IGNOU MCA, 2003*]
2. Explain the terms: key decision, objective, alternatives and constraints in the context of linear optimization models by assuming a suitable industrial situation.
[*J.N.T.U. Hyderabad B.Tech. (Mech.) May, 2012; G.N.D.U. B.Com., Sept. 2011; April, 2011; P.T.U. B. Tech., 2010, 2009,*]
3. Explain important characteristics of the industrial situations to which L.P. method can be successfully applied. Illustrate application of this technique with a suitable example. [*P.U.B.E. (Mech.) 2012*]
4. What is linear programming? Discuss the application of linear programming to managerial decision making. [*G.N.D.U. B.Com., 2014; M.G.U. Kerala M.Com., June, 2012; R.U. MBA June, 2011; J.N.T.U. Hyderabad B. Tech. August, 2011; Osmania U. MBA, 2010; B.E. (Elect.) 1997; M.Com., 2002*]
5. Discuss in detail the role of linear programming in managerial decision-making, bringing out limitations if any. [*R.U. MBA June, 2011; P.U.M. Com., 2003, 2001*]
6. Discuss the assumptions of proportionality, additivity, continuity, certainty and finite choices in the context of linear programming problems.
[*P.T.U. MBA Dec., 2014; Mumbai U. B.Com. April, 2013; H.P.U. B.Tech. (Mech.) 2012; R.U. MBA Dec., 2011; P.T.U. B.Tech. ((Mech., 2012; May, 2011; V.T.U. Karnataka B.E. Jan., 2010; Gujarat T.U. MBA Jan., 2011; Osmania U.MBA, 2010; R.T.M. Nagpur U.B.Tech., 2003; P.T.U. B.Tech. (Mech.) 2010; MBA, 2008; P.U. B.E. (T.I.T.) Dec., 2008; M.Com., 2001; P.U.B.Com. Jan., 2005; Sept., 2005; Sept., 2006; April, 2008*]
7. Explain the meaning of a linear programming problem stating its uses and give its limitations.
[*Chennai U.BBA Nov., 2010; Podicherry Univ. M.B.A. August, 2006; P.U. M.B.A. August, 2006*]
8. Write at least five application areas of linear programming.
[*J.N.T.U. MBA June, 2012; P.T.U. B.Tech., 2010, 2009; B. Tech. (Mech.) 2009; P.U.B.E. (Mech.) Nov., 2006; B.Com. Jan, 2005; P.T.U. B.Tech. (Mech.) 2010; Dec.,2006; C.A. (Final) Nov., 2000*]
9. Give some important applications of L.P. [*P.T.U. MBA Nov., 2012; Madras U.MBA Nov., 2012*]
10. A small manufacturer employs 5 skilled men and 10 semi-skilled men and makes an article in two qualities, a deluxe model and an ordinary model. The making of a deluxe model requires 2 hours work by a skilled man and 2 hours work by a semi-skilled man. The ordinary model requires 1 hour work by a skilled man and 3 hours work by a semi-skilled man. By union rules no man can work more than 8 hours per day. The manufacturer's clear profit of the deluxe model is ₹ 10 and of the ordinary model ₹ 8. Formulate the L.P. model of the problem.[*R.T.M. Nagpur; U.B.E. 2009; NIIFT Mohali, 2000, 01*]
(*Ans.* Maximize $Z = 10x_1 + 8x_2$, subject to $2x_1 + x_2 \leq 40$, $2x_1 + 3x_2 \leq 80$, $x_1, x_2 \geq 0$.)
11. Old hens can be bought for ₹ 2 each but young ones cost ₹ 5 each. The old hens lay 3 eggs per week and young ones 5 eggs per week, each egg being worth 30 paise. A hen costs ₹ 1 per week to feed. If a person has only ₹ 80 to spend on the hens, how many of each kind should he buy to get a profit of more than ₹ 6 per week assuming that he cannot house more than 20 hens ?
[*G.N.D.U. B.Com., Sept., 2010; April, 2006; J.N.T.U. Hyderabad B.Tech. (E.Sc.) Dec., 2011; P.U.B.Com. April, 2006; April, 2003*]
(*Ans.* Maximize $Z = 0.3\,(3x_1 + 5x_2) - (x_1 + x_2) = 0.5x_2 - 0.1x_1$, subject to $x_1 + x_2 \leq 20$, $2x_1 + 5x_2 \leq 80$, $-0.1x_1 + 0.5x_2 \geq 6$ and $x_1, x_2 \geq 0$; $x_1 = 0$, $x_2 = 16$, Z_{max} = ₹ 8).
12. A firm plans to purchase at least 200 quintals of scrap containing high quality metal X and low quality metal Y. Scrap can be purchased from two suppliers A and B. Scrap must contain 100 quintals of metal X and no more than 35 quintals of metal Y. The percentages of X and Y metals in terms of weight in the scrap supplied by A and B are given as

Metal	*Supplier A*	*Supplier B*
X	25%	75%
Y	10%	20%

The price of A's scrap is ₹ 200 per quintal and that of B's is ₹ 400 per quintal. Formulate as an L.P.P. to determine the quantity to be purchased from each supplier so that the cost is minimum.
[*P.T.U. B. Tech. (C.Sc.) 2009; D.U. MBA, 2001, 1998*]
(*Ans.* Minimize $Z = 200x_A + 400x_B$, subject to $x_A + x_B \geq 200$,

$0.25x_A + 0.75x_B \geq 100,$
$0.1x_A + 0.2x_B \leq 35,$
$x_A, x_B \geq 0.)$

13. A firm manufactures pain relieving pills in two sizes A and B. Size A contains 4 grains of element X, 7 grains of element Y and 2 grains of element Z. Size B contains 2 grains of element X, 10 grains of element Y and 8 grains of element Z. It is found by users that it requires at least 12 grains of element X, 74 grains of element Y and 24 grains of element Z to provide immediate relief. It is required to determine the least number of pills a patient should take to get immediate relief. Formulate the problem as standard L.P.P. *[P.T.U. B. Tech., (Mech.) 2009, 2008]*

(*Ans.* Minimize $Z = x_A + x_B$,
subject to $4x_A + 2x_B \geq 12,$
$7x_A + 8x_B \geq 24,$
$2x_A + 8x_B \geq 24,$
$x_A + x_B \geq 0.)$

14. A company sells two different products A and B. The company makes a profit of ₹ 40 and ₹ 30 per unit respectively on the two products. The products are produced by a common production process and are sold in two different markets. The production process has a capacity of 30,000 man-hours. It takes 3 hours to produce a unit of product A and 1 hour to produce a unit of product B. The market has been surveyed and company officials found out that the maximum units that can be sold for product A and B are 8,000 and 12,000 respectively. Formulate the above as a linear programming problem.

[Chennai U.B.B.A. Nov., 2010]

[*Ans.* Maximize $Z = 40x_1 + 3x_2$,
subject to $= 3x_1 + x_2 \leq 30{,}000,$
$x_1 \leq 8{,}000,$
$x_2 \leq 12{,}000,$
where $x_1, x_2 \geq 0.)$

15. A firm manufactures headache pills in two sizes A and B. Size A contains 2 grains of aspirin, 5 grains of bicarbonate and 1 grain of codeine. Size B contains 1 grain of aspirin, 8 grains of bicarbonate and 6 grains of codeine. It is found by users that it requires at least 12 grains of aspirin, 74 grains of bicarbonate and 24 grains of codeine for providing immediate relief. Formulate the problem as standard L.P.P. It is required to determine the minimum number of pills a patient should take to get immediate relief.

[P.T.U. MCA, 2010]

(*Ans.* Find x_1 and x_2,
subject to $2x_1 + x_2 \geq 12,$
$5x_1 + 8x_2 \geq 74,$
$x_1 + 6x_2 \geq 24,$
$x_1, x_2 \geq 0$

16. A paper mill produces paper for books as well as for magazines. Each kg of paper for book requires 2 kg of material A and 3 kg of material B. For magazines the proportion is 2 kg of A and 2 kg of B for each kg of paper. The mill needs 15,000 kg of paper for books and 60,000 kg for magazines. Materials A and B are available as 3 lakh kg and 5 lakh kg respectively. Requirement for books is twice that of magazines. Selling price of book paper is ₹ 7 and of magazine paper is ₹ 5. Cost of material A is ₹ 2 and that of material B is ₹ 2.50. Objective is to find the product manufacturing plan and the optimum annual profit. Formulate the problem as L.P.P. *[P.T.U. B.Tech. (Mech.) 2010; MBA, 2008]*

(*Ans.* Maximize $Z = 7(x_{1A} + x_{1B}) + (x_{2A} + x_{2B})$
$-2(x_{1A} + x_{2A}) - 2.50(x_{1B} + x_{2B})$
$= 5x_{1A} + 4.50_{1B} + 3x_{2A} + 2.50x_{2B},$
subject to $x_{1A} + x_{1B} \geq 15{,}000,$
$x_{2A} + x2B \geq 60{,}000,$
$x_{1A} + x_{2A} \leq 3{,}00{,}000,$
$x_{1B} + x_{2B} \leq 5{,}00{,}000,$
$x_{1A} + x_{1B} - 2x_{2A} - 2x_{2B} = 0,$
$x_{1A}, x_{1B}, x_{2A}, x_{2B} \geq 0.$

17. A firm manufactures three products A, B and C. The profits per unit product are ₹ 3, ₹ 2 and ₹ 4 respectively. The firm has two machines and the required processing time in minutes for each machine on each product is given below.

		Product		
		A	B	C
Machine	X	4	3	5
	Y	2	2	4

Machines X and Y have 2,000 and 1,500 machine-minutes respectively. The firm must manufacture 100 A's, 200 B's and 50 C's but no more than 150 A's. Set up an L.P. model to maximize the profit.

[*P.U. B.E. (Ec. & Comm.) Nov., 2011; B.Com. April, 2008; P.T.U. BCA, 2011*]

(*Ans.* Maximize $Z = 3x_A + 2x_B + 4x_C$,

subject to $4x_A + 3x_B + 5x_C \le 2{,}000$,

$2x_A + 2x_B + 4x_C \le 1{,}500$,

$x_A \ge 100$,

$x_A \le 150$,

$x_B \ge 200$,

$x_C \ge 50$.)

18. The manager of an oil refinery has to decide upon the optimal mix of two possible blending processes, of which the inputs and outputs per production run are as follows:

	Input		*Output*	
Process	*Crude A*	*Crude B*	*Gasoline X*	*Gasoline Y*
1	5	3	5	8
2	4	5	4	4

The maximum amount available of crude A and B is 200 units and 150 units respectively. Market requirements show that at least 100 units of gasoline X and 80 units of gasoline Y must be produced. The profits per production run from process 1 and process 2 are ₹ 3 and ₹ 4 respectively. Formulate the problem as a linear programming problem.

[*P.U. MBA, 2000; P.U.B.E. (Mech.) 1995; B.Com. Sept., 2005*]

(*Ans.* Maximize $Z = 3x_1 + 4x_2$,

subject to $5x_1 + 4x_2 \le 200$,

$3x_1 + 5x_2 \le 150$,

$5x_1 + 4x_2 \ge 100$,

$8x_1 + 4x_2 \ge 80$,

$x_1, x_2 \ge 0$.)

19. A company sells two different products A and B. The company makes a profit of ₹ 40 and ₹ 30 on the two products respectively. They are produced by a common production process and are sold in two different markets. The production process has a capacity of 30,000 man-hours. It takes 3 hours to produce a unit of A and 1 hour to produce a unit of B. The maximum number of units of A and B that can be sold in the market are 8,000 and 12,000 respectively. Formulate the above as a linear programming problem.

[*Chennai U.BBA, Nov., 2010*]

(*Ans.* Maximize $Z = 40x_1 + 30x_2$,

subject to $3x_1 + x_2 \le 30{,}000$,

$x_1 \le 8{,}000$,

$x_2 \le 12{,}000$,

$x_1, x_2 \ge 0$.)

20. A firm manufactures headache pills in two sizes A and B. Size A contains 3 grains of aspirin, 5 grains of bicarbonate and 4 grains of codeine. Size B contains 4 grains of aspirin, 8 grains of bicarbonate and 6 grains of codeine. It is found by users that it requires at least 62 grains of aspirin, 74 grains of bicarbonate and 64 grains of codeine for providing immediate relief. Formulate the problem as standard L.P.P. It is required to determine the minimum number of pills a patient should take to get immediate relief.

[*P.T.U. MCA, 2010*]

(*Ans.* Minimize $Z = x_1 + x_2$,

subject to $3x_1 + 4x_2 \ge 62$,

$$5x_1 + 8x_2 \geq 74,$$
$$4x_1 + 6x_2 \geq 64,$$
$$x_1, x_2 \geq 0.)$$

21. A firm plans to purchase at least 200 quintals of scrap containing high quality metal X and low quality metal Y. Scrap can be purchased from two suppliers A and B. Scrap must contain 100 quintals of metal X and no more than 35 quintals of metal Y. The percentage of X and Y in metals in terms of weight in the scrap supplied by A and B is given as

Metal	*Supplier A*	*Supplier B*
X	25%	75%
Y	10%	20%

The price of A's scrap is ₹ 200 per quintal and that of B's is ₹ 400 per quintal. Formulate the L.P.P. to determine the quantity to be purchased from each supplier so that the cost is minimum.

[*P.T.U. B. tech., 2010; Delhi U. MBA, 2001, 1998*]

(*Ans.* Minimize $Z = 200x_1 + 400\,x_2$,
subject to $x_1 + x_2 \geq 200$,
$0.25x_1 + 0.75x_2 \geq 100$,
$0.10x_1 + 0.20x_2 \leq 35$,
$x_1, x_2 \geq 0$.)

22. A firm manufactures pain relieving pills in two sizes A and B. Size A contains 4 grains of element X, 7 grains of element Y and 2 grains of element Z. Size B contains 2 grains of element X, 10 grains of element Y and 8 grains of element Z. It is found by users that it requires at least 12 grains of element X, 74 grains of element Y and 24 grains of element Z to provide immediate relief. It is required to determine the least number of pills a patient should take to get immediate relief. Formulate the problem as standard L.P.P.

[*P.T.U.B. Tech., 2009*]

(*Ans.* Minimize $Z = x_1 + x_2$,
subject to $4x_1 + 2x_2 \geq 12$,
$7x_1 + 10x_2 \geq 74$,
$2x_1 + 8x_2 \geq 24$,
$x_1, x_2 \geq 0$.)

23. A company produces two types of leather belts, type A and B. Belt A is of superior quality and B is of lower quality. Profits on the two types of belts are 40 paise and 30 paise per belt respectively. Each belt of type A requires twice as much time as required by a belt of type B. If all belts were of type B, the company would produce 1,000 belts per day. Belt A requires a fancy buckle and 400 fancy buckles are available for this per day. For belt of type B, only 700 buckles are available per day. Formulate L.P.P. model to determine the number of belts of the two types to be manufactured to get maximum profit. [*J.N.T.U. Hyderabad B. Tech. April, 2011; P.T.U. B. Tech., 2008*]

(*Ans.* Maximize $Z = 0.40\,x_1 + 0.30x_2$,
subject to $x_1 + x_2 \leq 800$,
$2x_1 + x_2 \leq 1{,}000$,
$x_1 \leq 400$,
$x_2 \leq 700$,
$x_1, x_2 \geq 0$.)

24. A firm makes products X and Y and has total production capacity of 9 tons per day. X and Y require same production capacity. The firm has permanent contract to supply at least 2 tons of X and at least 3 tons of Y to another company. Each ton of X requires 20 machine-hours of production time and each ton of Y requires 50 machine-hours of production time. Maximum possible machine-hours per day are 360. All the firm's output can be sold and profit made is ₹ 80 per ton of X and ₹ 120 per ton of Y. Determine the production schedule for maximum profit.

[*R.T.M. Nagpur B.E. (Mech.) Sept, 2010; 2008; 2007*]

(*Ans.* Maximize $Z = 80x + 120y$,
subject to $x_1 \geq 2$,
$x_2 \geq 3$,
$x_1 + x_2 \leq 9$,
$20x_1 + 50x_2 \leq 360$,
$x_1, x_2 \geq 0$.)

25. A firm makes two products X and Y and has a total production capacity of 9 tonnes per day, X and Y requiring the same production capacity. The firm has a permanent contract to supply at least 2 tonnes at X and at least 3 tonnes of Y per day to another company. Each tonne of X requires 20 machine-hours of production time and each tonne of Y requires 50 machine-hours of production time. The daily maximum possible number of machine-hours is 360. All the firm's output can be sold, and the profit made is ₹ 80 per tonne of X and ₹ 120 per tonne of Y. It is required to determine the production schedule for maximum profit and to calculate this profit.

[R.T.M. Nagpur U.B.Com. (Mech.) June, 2007; Dec., 2004]

26. A plant manufactures two products A and B: The profit contribution per unit has been estimated to be ₹ 20 and ₹ 24 for products A and B respectively. Each product passes through two departments of the plant. Time required for each product and the total time available in each department are as follows:

Department	*Time (hrs.) required/unit of*		*Available time (hr) per month*
	Product – A	*Product – B*	
1	2	2	1,500
2	3	2	1,500

The plant has to supply the products to market where the maximum demand for product B is 450 units/month. Formulate the problem as an LP model and find graphically, the number of products A and B to maximize the total profit per month. *[V.T.U. Karnataka B.E. June, 2011]*

27. Evening shift resident doctors in a government hospital work five consecutive days and have two consecutive days off. Their five days of work can start on any day of the week and the schedule rotates indefinitely. The hospital requires the following minimum no. of doctors working :

Days	*Doctors*
Sunday	35
Monday	55
Tuesday	60
Wednesday	50
Thursday	60
Friday	50
Saturday	45

Not more than 40 doctors can start their five working days on the same day. Formulate a general linear programming model to minimize the number of doctors employed by the Hospital.

[R.T.M. Nagpur B.E. (I.T.) 2009]

28. A pregnant woman is advised to take Iron, Zinc and Folic acid at least in the quantities 100mg, 150 mg and 100mg per day respectively. There are two types of medicines available in the form of a 500mg tablet and 250mg capsule. Each tablet is composed of 30mg of Iron, 45mg of Zinc and 40mg of Folic acid while a capsule contains the three ingredients as 20, 15 and 25mg respectively. The cost of each tablet is ₹ 3 and that of each capsule is ₹ 2. Determine the number of tablets and capsules to be purchased so that the total cost of medicines is minimum. *[J.N.T.U. Hyderabad B. Tech. (C.Sc.) Dec., 2011]*

29. A firm can produce three types of cloth, say, A, B and C. Three kinds of wool are required for it, say, red wool, green wool and blue wool. One unit length of type A cloth needs 2 yards of red wool and 3 yards of blue wool; one unit length of type B cloth needs 3 yards of red wool, 2 yards of green wool and 2 yards of the blue wool; and one unit length of type C cloth needs 5 yards of green wool and 4 yards of blue wool. The firm has a stock of only 8 yards of red wool, 10 yards of green wool and 15 yards of blue wool. It is assumed that the income obtained from one unit length of type A cloth is ₹ 3, of type B cloth is ₹ 5 and that of type C cloth is ₹ 4. Formulate the problem as linear programming problem. *[Madras U. M.Com. Nov., 2012; NIIFT Mohali, 2000]*

(*Ans.* Maximize $Z = 3x_A + 5x_B + 4x_C$,

subject to $2x_A + 3x_B \leq 8$,

$2x_B + 5x_C \leq 10$,

$3x_A + 2x_B + 4x_C \leq 15$,

$x_A, x_B, x_C \geq 0$.)

30. A dairy feed company may purchase and mix one or more of the three types of grains containing different amounts of nutritional elements. The data are given in the table below.
The production manager specifies that any feed mix for his livestock must meet at least minimal nutritional requirements, and seeks the least costly among all such mixes.

	Item	*One unit weight of* *Grain 1*	*Grain 2*	*Grain 3*	*Minimal requirement*
	A	2	3	7	1,250
Nutritional	B	1	1	0	250
ingredients	C	5	3	0	900
	D	6	25	1	232.5
Cost/unit weight (₹)		41	35	96	

Analyse the situation to recognize the key decision, objective, alternatives and restrictions. Formulate linear programming model for the problem.
[*P.U.B.E. (Mech.) 1978*]

(*Ans.* Minimize $Z = 41x_1 + 35x_2 + 96x_3$,
subject to $2x_1 + 3x_2 + 7x_3 \geq 1{,}250$,
$x_1 + x_2 \geq 250$,
$5x_1 + 3x_2 \geq 900$,
$6x_1 + 25x_2 + x_3 \geq 232.5$,
$x_1, x_2, x_3 \geq 0$.)

31. A farmer has a 100-acre farm. He can sell all the tomatoes, lettuce or radishes he can raise. The price he can obtain is ₹ 1 per kg for tomatoes, ₹ 0.75 a head for lettuce and ₹ 2 per kg for radishes. The average yield per acre is 2,000 kg of tomatoes, 3,000 heads of lettuce and 1,000 kg of radishes. Fertilizer is available at ₹ 0.50 per kg and the amount required per acre is 100 kg each for tomatoes and lettuce and 50 kg for radishes. Labour required for sowing, cultivating and harvesting per acre is 5 man-days for tomatoes and radishes and 6 man-days for lettuce. A total of 400 man-days of labour are available at ₹ 20 per man-day.

Formulate the L.P. model for this problem in order to maximize the farmer's total profit.
[*Dayalbagh Edu. Inst. Agra MBA Dec., 2014; Dec., 2011; J.N.T.U. Hyderabad B.Tech. April, 2011; V.T.U. Karnataka B.E. June, 2010; Nagpur U.B.E., 2003; Jammu U.B.E. (Mech.) 2004; P.U. B.E. (Mech.) Nov., 2002*]

(*Ans.* Maximize $Z = (2{,}000 - 50 - 100)x_1 + (2{,}250 - 50 - 120)x_2 + (2{,}000 - 25 - 100)x_3$
$= 1{,}850x_1 + 2{,}080x_2 + 1{,}875x_3$,
subject to $x_1 + x_2 + x_3 \leq 100$,
$5x_1 + 6x_2 + 5x_3 \leq 400$,
$x_1, x_2, x_3 \geq 0$.)

32. A manufacturer of metal office equipment makes desks, chairs, cabinets and bookcases. The work is carried out in three major departments: metal stamping, assembly and finishing. The exhibits A, B and C give requisite data of the problem.

Exhibit A

Department	*Time required in hours per unit of product* *Desk*	*Chair*	*Cabinet*	*Bookcase*	*Hours available per week*
Stamping	4	2	3	3	800
Assembly	10	6	8	7	1,200
Finishing	10	8	8	8	800

Exhibit B

	Cost (₹) of operation per unit of product			
Department	*Desk*	*Chair*	*Cabinet*	*Bookcase*
Stamping	15	8	12	12
Assembly	30	18	24	21
Finishing	35	28	25	21

Exhibit C

Selling price (₹) per unit of product	
Desk: 175	Chair: 95
Cabinet: 145	Bookcase: 130

In order to maximize weekly profits what should be the production programme ? Assume that the items produced can be sold. Which department needs to be expanded for increasing profits ?

[*Gujarat U. April, 1976*]

(*Ans.* Maximize $Z = [175 - (15 + 30 + 35)]x_1 + [95 - (8 + 18 + 28)]x_2 + [145 - (12 + 24 + 25)]x_3 + [130 - (12 + 21 + 21)]x_4$
$= 95x_1 + 41x_2 + 84x_3 + 76x_4$,
subject to $4x_1 + 2x_2 + 3x_3 + 3x_4 \le 800$,
$10x_1 + 6x_2 + 8x_3 + 7x_4 \le 1{,}200$,
$10x_1 + 8x_2 + 8x_3 + 8x_4 \le 800$,
$x_1, x_2, x_3, x_4 \ge 0$.)

33. The financial secretary of a firm wants to invest a sum of ₹ 10,000 so as to maximize its yield. He has the following alternatives :

Investment type	A_1	A_2	B_1	B_2	C_1	C_2
Yield	3%	2.5%	3.5%	4%	5%	4.5%

It is the firm's policy that at least 40% of the whole amount be invested in units of type A and not more than 35% in any of the other two types. Make a model for the investment plan if the whole of ₹ 10,000 is to be invested. [*P.T.U. MBA May, 2002; P.U.B.E. (Mech.) 2001*]

(*Ans.* Maximize $Z = 0.03x_{A_1} + 0.025x_{A_2} + 0.035x_{B_1} + 0.04x_{B_2} + 0.05x_{C_1} + 0.045x_{C_2}$,

subject to $x_{A_1} + x_{A_2} + x_{B_1} + x_{B_2} + x_{C_1} + x_{C_2} = 10{,}000$,

$x_{A_1} + x_{A_2} \ge 4{,}000$,

$x_{B_1} + x_{B_2} \le 3{,}500$,

$x_{C_1} + x_{C_2} \le 3{,}500$,

$x_{A_1}, x_{A_2}, x_{B_1}, x_{B_2}, x_{C_1}, x_{C_2} \ge 0$.)

34. A truck company requires the following number of drivers for its trucks during 24 hours:

Time	*No. required*
00 - 04 hr	5
04 - 08 hr	10
08 - 12 hr	20
12 - 16 hr	12
16 - 20 hr	22
20 - 24 hr	8

According to the shift schedule a driver may join for duty at midnight, 04, 08, 12, 16, 20 hours and work continuously for 8 hours. Formulate the problem as L.P. problem for optimal shift plan.

[*J.N.T.U. Hyderabad B. Tech. August, 2011; P.U.B.E. (Mech.) 2002*]

[**Hint:** Let x_1, x_2, x_3, x_4, x_5 and x_6 denote the number of drivers joining duty at 00, 04, 08, 12, 16 and 20 hours respectively. The objective is to minimize the number of drivers required *i.e.*, minimize $Z = x_1 + x_2 + x_3 + x_4 + x_5 + x_6$.

Drivers who join duty at 00 hours and 04 hours shall be available between 04 and 08 hours. As the number of drivers required during this interval is 10, we have the constraint

$$x_1 + x_2 \geq 10.$$

Likewise, $x_2 + x_3 \geq 20,$

$x_3 + x_4 \geq 12,$

$x_4 + x_5 \geq 22,$

$x_5 + x_6 \geq 8,$

and $x_6 + x_1 \geq 5,$

where $x_1, x_2, ..., x_6$, each ≥ 0.

35. A foundry is faced with a problem of scheduling production and subcontracting for three products, each requiring casting, machining and assembly operations. Casting operation for products 1 and 2 could be subcontracted but the castings for product 3 require special equipment and hence cannot be subcontracted. In foundry each unit of product 1 requires 6 minutes of casting time, product 2 requires 10 minutes and product 3 requires 8 minutes of casting time. Machining times per unit of products 1, 2 and 3 are 6, 3 and 8 minutes while assembly times are 3, 2 and 2 minutes respectively. The time available per week for casting, machining and assembly is 8,000, 12,000 and 10,000 minutes respectively. The overall profits obtained per unit of product 1, 2 and 3 are ₹ 7, ₹ 10 and ₹ 11 respectively with castings produced in foundry. With castings obtained from subcontractor the profit per unit for products 1 and 2 are ₹ 5 and ₹ 9 respectively. How should the foundry schedule its production and subcontracting so as to maximize the profit ? Formulate mathematical model only. [*P.U.B.E. (Prod.), 2001*]

[**Hint:** Let x_1, x_2, x_3 be the number of units of products 1, 2 and 3 respectively to be produced and x_4, x_5 be the number of units of products 1 and 2 to be subcontracted for casting only per week. Then the mathematical model for the problem will be

Maximize $Z = 7x_1 + 10x_2 + 11x_3 + 5x_4 + 9x_5,$

subject to $6x_1 + 10x_2 + 8x_3 \leq 8,000,$

$6(x_1 + x_4) + 3(x_2 + x_5) + 8x_3 \leq 12,000,$

and $3(x_1 + x_4) + 2(x_2 + x_5) + 2x_3 \leq 10,000,$

where $x_1, x_2, x_3, x_4, x_5 \geq 0$.]

36. A city hospital has the following minimal daily requirement of nurses:

Period 24 hr	*Clock time (24-hr day)*	*Minimal number of nurses required*
1	6 A.M. to 10 A.M.	2
2	10 A.M. to 2 P.M.	7
3	2 P.M. to 6 P.M.	15
4	6 P.M. to 10 P.M.	8
5	10 P.M. to 2 A.M.	20
6	2 A.M. to 6 A.M.	6

Nurses report to the hospital at the beginning of each period and work for 8 consecutive hours. The hospital wants to determine the minimal number of nurses to be employed so that there is sufficient number of nurses available for each period. Formulate this as linear programming problem.

[*Karn. U.B.E. (Mech.) 1997; P.U.B.E. (Mech.) 1997*]

(*Ans.* Min $Z = x_1 + x_2 + x_3 + x_4 + x_5 + x_6$,
subject to $x_1 + x_2 \geq 7$, $x_2 + x_3 \geq 15$, $x_3 + x_4 \geq 8$, $x_4 + x_5 \geq 20$, $x_5 + x_6 \geq 6$ and $x_6 + x_1 \geq 2$,
$x_1, x_2, ..., x_6$, each ≥ 0.)

37. A manufacturing firm closed down the production of a certain unprofitable product line. This necessitated the rational utilization of released excess production capacity. Management has been contemplating to devote this excess capacity to the manufacture of one or more of three products *A*, *B* and *C*. The details about available excess machine capacity and machine requirements for the various products are given in I and II.

I. *Machine type* — *Available excess machine time*

Machine type	Available excess machine time
Milling machine	250 hours/week
Lathe	150 hours/week
Grinder	50 hours/week

II. *Machine type* — *Machine hour requirements per unit of product*

Machine type	*A*	*B*	*C*
Milling machine	8	2	3
Lathe	4	3	—
Grinder	2	—	1

It is assumed that the unit profit would be ₹ 20, ₹ 6 and ₹ 8 respectively, for products *A*, *B*, and *C*. Formulate the L.P. problem. [*Indian Statistical Institute May, 1974*]

(*Ans.* Maximize $Z = 20x_1 + 6x_2 + 8x_3$,
subject to $8x_1 + 2x_2 + 3x_3 \leq 250$,
$4x_1 + 3x_2 \leq 150$,
$2x_1 + x_3 \leq 50$,
$x_1, x_2, x_3 \geq 0$.)

38. A farmer has 1,000 acres of land on which he can grow corn, wheat or soyabeans. Each acre of corn costs ₹ 100 for preparation, requires 7 man-days of work and yields a profit of ₹ 30. An acre of wheat costs ₹ 120 to prepare, requires 10 man-days of work and yields a profit of ₹ 40. An acre of soyabeans costs ₹ 70 to prepare, requires 8 man-days of work and yields a profit of ₹ 20. If the farmer has ₹ 1,00,000 for preparation and can count on 8,000 man-days of work, formulate the L.P. model to allocate the number of acres to each crop to maximize the total profit.

[*P.T.U. MBA Dec., 2013; Univ. of Madras BBA April, 2012; R.T.M. Nagpur U.B. Tech. June, 2003*]

(*Ans.* Maximize $Z = 30x_1 + 40x_2 + 20x_3$,
subject to $100x_1 + 120x_2 + 70x_3 \leq 1{,}00{,}000$,
$7x_1 + 10x_2 + 8x_3 \leq 8{,}000$,
$x_1 + x_2 + x_3 \leq 1{,}000$,
$x_1, x_2, x_3 \geq 0$.)

39. A manufacturer of a line of patent medicines is preparing a production plan on medicines *A* and *B*. There are sufficient ingredients available to make 20,000 bottles of *A* and 40,000 bottles of *B* but there are only 45,000 bottles into which both the medicines can be put. Furthermore, it takes 3 hours to prepare enough material to fill 1,000 bottles of *A*, it takes 1 hour to prepare enough material to fill 1,000 bottles of *B* and there are 66 hours available for this operation. The profit is ₹ 8 per bottle for *A* and ₹ 7 per bottle for *B*. Formulate the problem as a linear programming problem.

[*H.P.U. B.E. (Mech.) 2008*]

(*Ans.* Maximize $Z = 8x_A + 7x_B$,
subject to $x_A \leq 20{,}000$,
$x_B \leq 40{,}000$,
$x_A + x_B \leq 45{,}000$,
$$\frac{3}{1{,}000}x_A + \frac{1}{1{,}000}x_B \leq 66$$
or $3x_A + x_B \leq 66{,}000$,
$x_A, x_B \geq 0$.)

40. A farm is engaged in breeding pigs. The pigs are fed on various products grown on the farm. Because of the need to ensure certain nutrient constituents, it is necessary to buy additionally one or two products, which we shall call *A* and *B*. The nutrient constituents (vitamins and proteins) in each unit of the products are given below.

Nutrient	Nutrient contents in the products		Minimum amount of nutrients
	A	*B*	
1	36	6	108
2	3	12	36
3	20	10	100

Product *A* costs ₹ 20 per unit and product *B* costs ₹ 40 per unit. Formulate the L.P. model for products *A* and *B* to be purchased at the lowest possible cost so as to provide the pigs, nutrients not less than that given in the table. [*CA 2002, 2001*]

(*Ans.* Minimize $Z = 20x_A + 40x_B$,
subject to $36x_A + 6x_B \geq 108$,
$3x_A + 12x_B \geq 36$,
$20x_A + 10x_B \geq 100$,
$x_A, x_B \geq 0$.)

41. The *ABC* Electrical Appliance Company produces two products: refrigerators and ranges. Production takes place in two separate departments. Refrigerators are produced in deptt. I and ranges are produced in deptt. II. The weekly production cannot exceed 25 refrigerators in deptt. I and 35 ranges in deptt. II, because of limited available facilities in the two deptts. The company regularly employs a total of 60 workers in the two deptts. A refrigerator requires 2 man-weeks of labour while a range requires 1 man-week of labour. A refrigerator contributes a profit of ₹ 600 and a range contributes a profit of ₹ 400. Formulate the problem as the L.P. problem to determine the number of units of refrigerators and ranges that the company should produce to realize maximum profit.

[*Delhi M.B.A., 1975, 1977*]

(*Ans.* Maximize $Z = 600x_1 + 400x_2$
subject to $x_1 \leq 25$,
$x_2 \leq 35$,
$2x_1 + x_2 \leq 60$,
$x_1, x_2 \geq 0$.)

42. A plant manufactures two products *A* and *B*. The profit contribution of each product has been estimated as ₹ 20 for product *A* and ₹ 24 for product *B*. Each product passes through three departments of the plant. The time required for each product and total time available in each department are as follows:

Department	Hours required		Available hours during the month
	Product A	Product B	
1	2	3	1,500
2	3	2	1,500
3	1	1	600

The company has a contract to supply at least 250 units of product *B* per month. Formulate the problem as a linear programming model. [*P.U.B.E. (Mech.) 1978*]

(*Ans.* Maximize $Z = 20x_A + 24x_B$,
subject to $2x_A + 3x_B \leq 1{,}500$,
$3x_A + 2x_B \leq 1{,}500$,
$x_A + x_B \leq 600$,
$x_B \geq 250$,
$x_A, x_B \geq 0$.)

43. The salesmanager of a company has budgeted ₹ 1,20,000 for an advertising programme for one of the firm's products. The selected advertising programme consists of running advertisements in two different magazines. The advertisement for magazine 1 costs ₹ 2,000 per run while the advertisement for magazine 2 costs ₹ 5,000 per run. Past experience has indicated that at least 20 runs in magazine

1 and at least 10 runs in magazine 2 are necessary to penetrate market with any appreciable effect. Also experience has indicated that there is no reason to make more than 50 runs in either of the two magazines. Formulate the L.P. model to determine the number of runs in magazine 1 and magazine 2 to be made.

(*Ans.* Find ranges of x_1 and x_2,

subject to $20 \le x_1 \le 50,$

$10 \le x_2 \le 50,$

$2{,}000x_1 + 5{,}000x_2 \le 1{,}20{,}000,$

$x_1, x_2 \ge 0.$)

44. The *ABC* company wishes to plan its advertising strategy. There are two media under consideration, call them magazines I and II respectively. Magazine I has a reach of 2,000 potential customers and magazine II has a reach of 3,000 potential customers. The cost per page of advertising is ₹ 400 and ₹ 600 in magazines I and II respectively. The firm has a monthly budget of ₹ 6,000. There is an important requirement that the total reach for the income group under ₹ 20,000 per annum should not exceed 4,000 potential customers. The reach in magazines I and II for this income group is 400 and 200 potential customers. How many pages should be bought in the two magazines to maximize the total reach ? [*Delhi Dip. Mkt. and Sales Man., 1975*]

(*Ans.* Maximize $Z = 2{,}000x_{I} + 3{,}000x_{II},$

subject to $400x_{I} + 600x_{II} \le 6{,}000,$

$400x_{I} + 200x_{II} \le 4{,}000,$

$x_{I}, x_{II} \ge 0.$)

45. A firm produces three products. These products are processed on three different machines. The time required to manufacture one unit of each of the products and the daily capacity of the three machines is given in the table below.

Machine	*Time per unit (minutes)*			*Machine capacity (minutes/day)*
	Product 1	*Product 2*	*Product 3*	
M_1	2	8	2	940
M_2	4	—	8	970
M_3	2	5	—	430

It is required to determine the daily number of units to be manufactured for each product. The profit per unit for product 1, 2 and 3 is ₹ 4, ₹ 8 and ₹ 6 respectively. It is assumed that all the amounts produced are consumed in the market. Formulate an L.P. model for the problem.

(*Ans.* Maximize $Z = 4x_1 + 8x_2 + 6x_3,$

subject to $2x_1 + 8x_2 + 2x_3 \le 940,$

$4x_1 + 8x_3 \le 970,$

$2x_1 + 5x_2 \le 430,$

$x_1, x_2, x_3 \ge 0.$)

46. A firm manufactures three products P_1, P_2 and P_3. The minimum number of units of P_1, P_2 and P_3 that must be produced are 100, 200 and 150 respectively. These products require two types of raw materials M_1 and M_2 which the firm can purchase upto a maximum of 500 and 400 units respectively. Design a production plan so as to maximize the profit if the respective individual profits of P_1, P_2 and P_3 are ₹ 2, ₹ 5 and ₹ 4 respectively. Consumption of raw materials is shown in the table below.

Raw material	*Consumption of raw material per unit product*		
	P_1	P_2	P_3
M_1	$\frac{1}{2}$	1	1
M_2	2	$\frac{1}{2}$	$\frac{1}{5}$

(*Ans.* Maximize $Z = 2x_1 + 5x_2 + 4x_3,$

subject to $\frac{x_1}{2} + x_2 + x_3 \le 500,$

$$2x_1 + \frac{x_2}{2} + \frac{x_3}{5} \le 400,$$
$$x_1 \ge 100,$$
$$x_2 \ge 200,$$
$$x_3 \ge 150,$$
$$x_1, x_2, x_3 \ge 0.)$$

47. Formulate the L.P. model for the following problem:

A farm owner wants to know how many acres of three different crops to plant on three different plots in order to maximize profit. The farmer's tract of land consists of 2,000 acres. The farmer has subdivided the tract into three plots and has contracted with three local farm families to operate the plots. The farm owner has instructed each share cropper to plant three crops: corn, peas and soyabeans. The size of each plot has been determined by the capabilities of each local farmer. Plot sizes, crop restrictions and profit per acre are given in the following tables:

Table 1

Plot	*Acreage*	*Min.area to be planted (acres)*
1	500	300
2	800	480
3	700	420

Table 2

Crop	*Maximum acreage*	*Profit/acre (₹)*
Corn	900	600
Peas	700	450
Soyabeans	1,000	300

Any of the three crops may be planted on any of the plots. However, the farm owner has placed the following restrictions on the farming operation:

At least 60% of each plot must be under cultivation. To ensure that each share cropper works according to his potential and resources, the owner wants the same proportion of each plot to be under cultivation. The owner's objective is to determine how much of each crop to plant on each plot in order to maximize profit. [*Nellore M.B.A., 2002*]

[**Hint:** Let $x_{C_1}, x_{C_2}, x_{C_3}; x_{P_1}, x_{P_2}, x_{P_3}$ and $x_{S_1}, x_{S_2}, x_{S_3}$ denote the land in acres of plots 1, 2 and 3 on which corn, peas and soyabeans be planted. Then objective is to

$$\text{maximize Z} = ₹\left[600\,(x_{C_1} + x_{C_2} + x_{C_3}) + 450\,(x_{P_1} + x_{P_2} + x_{P_3}) + 300\,(x_{S_1} + x_{S_2} + x_{S_3})\right].$$

Constraints are

on size of plot: $x_{C_1} + x_{P_1} + x_{S_1} \le 500,$

$x_{C_2} + x_{P_2} + x_{S_2} \le 800,$

$x_{C_3} + x_{P_3} + x_{S_3} \le 700,$

on min. area to be planted: $x_{C_1} + x_{P_1} + x_{S_1} \ge 300,$

$x_{C_2} + x_{P_2} + x_{S_2} \ge 480,$

$x_{C_3} + x_{P_3} + x_{S_3} \ge 420,$

on max. acreage for each crop: $x_{C_1} + x_{C_2} + x_{C_3} \le 900,$

$x_{P_1} + x_{P_2} + x_{P_3} \le 700,$

$x_{S_1} + x_{S_2} + x_{S_3} \le 1{,}000,$

on proportion of each plot for cultivation to be same:

$$\frac{x_{C_1} + x_{P_1} + x_{S_1}}{500} = \frac{x_{C_2} + x_{P_2} + x_{S_2}}{800} = \frac{x_{C_3} + x_{P_3} + x_{S_3}}{700},$$

where $x_{C_1}, x_{C_2}, x_{C_3}; x_{P_1}, x_{P_2}, x_{P_3}; x_{S_1}, x_{S_2}$ and $x_{S_3} \ge 0.$]

48. A cosmetic manufacturing company is interested in selecting the advertising media for its product and the frequency of advertising in each media. The data collected over the past two years regarding the frequency of advertising in three media *i.e.*, newspaper, radio and television and the related sales of the product give the following results:

Frequency/week	*Television*	*Radio*	*Newspaper*
1	220	150	100
2	275	250	175
3	325	300	225
4	350	320	250

The cost of advertising in newspaper is ₹ 500 per appearance, while in radio and television it is ₹ 1,000 and ₹ 2,000 respectively. The budget provides ₹ 4,500 per week for advertisement. The problem is of determining the optimal combination of advertising media and advertising frequency.

[*DOEACC, 1999*]

49. A manufacturing company produces a final product that is assembled from three different parts. The parts are produced within the company by two different departments. Because of the specific setup of the machines, each department produces the three parts at different rates. The following table provides the production rates together with the maximum number of hours the two departments can allocate weekly to manufacture the three parts.

Department	*Maximum weekly capacity (hr)*	*Production rate (units/hr)*		
		Part 1	*Part 2*	*Part 3*
1	100	8	5	10
2	80	6	12	4

It would be ideal if the two departments could adjust their production facilities to produce equal quantities of the three parts, as this would result in perfect matches in terms of the final assembly. Formulate the problem as the L.P. model. [*P.T.U. M. Tech. April, 2012*]

(*Ans.* Max $Z = y$,

subject to

$$x_{11} + x_{21} - y \geq 0,$$
$$x_{12} + x_{22} - y \geq 0,$$
$$x_{13} + x_{23} - y \geq 0,$$
$$\frac{x_{11}}{8} + \frac{x_{12}}{5} + \frac{x_{13}}{10} \leq 100,$$
$$\frac{x_{21}}{6} + \frac{x_{22}}{12} + \frac{x_{23}}{4} \leq 80,$$
$$x_{11} + x_{21} = x_{12} + x_{22} = x_{13} + x_{23},$$
$$x_{11}, x_{12}, x_{13}, x_{21}, x_{22}, x_{23} \geq 0.)$$

50. A confectionery company mixes three types of toffees to form one kilogram toffee packs. The pack is sold at ₹ 17. The three types of toffees cost ₹ 20, ₹ 10 and ₹ 5 per kg respectively. The mixture must contain at least 0.3kg of the first type of toffees and the weight of the first two types of toffees must at least be equal to the weight of the third type. Determine the optimal mix for maximum profit.

[*P.U.B.E. (Mech.) Nov., 1994*]

(*Ans.* Max $Z = 17 - (20x_1 + 10x_2 + 5x_3)$,

subject to

$$x_1 + x_2 + x_3 = 1,$$
$$x_1 \geq 0.3,$$
$$x_1 + x_2 \geq x_3,$$
$$x_1, x_2, x_3 \geq 0.)$$

51. A company has three branch plants with excess capacity. All the three plants have the capability to produce a certain product. This product can be made in three sizes — large, medium and small that yield a net profit of ₹ 35, ₹ 30 and ₹ 25 per unit respectively. Plants 1, 2 and 3 have the excess capacity to produce 750, 900 and 450 units of the products respectively irrespective of the sizes involved. Plants 1, 2 and 3 have 13,000, 12,000 and 5,000 square feet of the storage space available per day. Each unit of the large, medium and small sizes produced per day requires 20, 15 and 12 square feet respectively. Sales forecasts indicate that 900, 1,200 and 750 units of large, medium and small sizes respectively can be sold per day.

To maintain a uniform work load among the plants and to retain some flexibility, the management has decided that the additional production assigned to each plant must use the same percentage of the excess capacity. How much of each of the sizes be produced by each plant to maximize the profit ? Formulate the problem as L.P. model. [*H.P.U. B.Tech. June, 2015*]

(*Ans.* Max $Z = 35(x_{l_1} + x_{l_2} + x_{l_3}) + 30(x_{m_1} + x_{m_2} + x_{m_3}) + 25(x_{s_1} + x_{s_2} + x_{s_3})$,

subject to

$$x_{l_1} + x_{m_1} + x_{s_1} \le 750,$$
$$x_{l_2} + x_{m_2} + x_{s_2} \le 900,$$
$$x_{l_3} + x_{m_3} + x_{s_3} \le 450;$$
$$20x_{l_1} + 15x_{m_1} + 12x_{s_1} \le 13{,}000,$$
$$20x_{l_2} + 15x_{m_2} + 12x_{s_2} \le 12{,}000,$$
$$20x_{l_3} + 15x_{m_3} + 12x_{s_3} \le 5{,}000,$$
$$x_{l_1} + x_{l_2} + x_{l_3} \ge 900,$$
$$x_{m_1} + x_{m_2} + x_{m_3} \ge 1{,}200,$$
$$x_{s_1} + x_{s_2} + x_{s_3} \ge 750;$$
$$\frac{x_{l_1} + x_{m_1} + x_{s_1}}{750} = \frac{x_{l_2} + x_{m_2} + x_{s_2}}{900} = \frac{x_{l_3} + x_{m_3} + x_{s_3}}{450},$$

where $x_{l_1}, x_{l_2}, x_{l_3}; x_{m_1}, x_{m_2}, x_{m_3}; x_{s_1}, x_{s_2}, x_{s_3} \ge 0$).

52. A plant has four machines, each capable of producing three variations of a single product. The profit/hour when producing the three variations on the respective machines is given in the table below:

	Profit/hour (₹) on machine			
Variation	1	2	3	4
1	5	6	4	3
2	5	4	5	4
3	6	7	2	8

The production rates per hour of the four machines when producing the three variations of the product are given below:

	Production (no./hr) on machine			
Variation	1	2	3	4
1	8	2	4	9
2	7	6	6	3
3	4	8	5	2

The demand for the three variations during the next month is expected to be 700, 500 and 400 units of variations 1, 2 and 3 respectively. The maximum available hours to produce the three variations during the next production period on the four machines are 90, 75, 90 and 85 respectively. Formulate the above problem for optimal shcedule of machines.

[**Hint:** Let $x_{11}, x_{12}, x_{13}, x_{14}; x_{21}, x_{22}, x_{23}, x_{24}; x_{31}, x_{32}, x_{33}$ and x_{34} denote the number of hours for which each variation is produced on each machine. The mathematical model for the problem can be expressed as

$$\text{Maximize } Z = 5x_{11} + 6x_{12} + 4x_{13} + 3x_{14} + 5x_{21} + 4x_{22} + 5x_{23} + 4x_{24} + 6x_{31} + 7x_{32} + 2x_{33} + 8x_{34},$$

subject to

$$8x_{11} + 2x_{12} + 4x_{13} + 9x_{14} \ge 700,$$
$$7x_{21} + 6x_{22} + 6x_{23} + 3x_{24} \ge 500,$$
$$4x_{31} + 8x_{32} + 5x_{33} + 2x_{34} \ge 400;$$
$$x_{11} + x_{21} + x_{31} \le 90,$$
$$x_{12} + x_{22} + x_{32} \le 75,$$

$x_{13} + x_{23} + x_{33} \leq 90,$
$x_{14} + x_{24} + x_{34} \leq 85;$
where $x_{11}, x_{12}, ..., x_{34}$, each ≥ 0.]

53. Consider the problem of scheduling the weekly production of a certain item for the next 4 weeks. The production cost of the item is ₹ 10 for the first two weeks and ₹ 15 for the last 2 weeks. The weekly demands are 300, 700, 900 and 800 units, which must be met. The plant can produce a maximum of 700 units each week. In addition the company can employ overtime during the second and third weeks. This increases the weekly production by an additional 200 units, but the cost of production increases by ₹ 5 per item. Excess production can be stored at a cost of ₹ 3 an item. How should the production be scheduled so as to minimize the total cost ? Formulate this as a linear programming problem.
[P.T.U. B.Tech. (Mech.) April, 2012; H.P.U.B. Tech. (Mech.) Dec., 2009]

[**Hint:**

Week	:	1	2	3	4
Demand	:	300	700	900	800
Regular production	:	x_{11}	x_{12}	x_{13}	x_{14}
Regular cost/unit (₹)	:	10	10	15	15
Overtime production	:	–	x_{22}	x_{23}	–
Overtime cost/unit (₹)	:	–	15	20	–
Units in inventory	:	y_1	y_2	y_3	y_4

The L.P. model is:

$$\text{Min } Z = [10x_{11} + 10x_{12} + 15x_{13} + 15x_{14} + 15x_{22} + 20x_{23} + 3(y_1 + y_2 + y_3 + y_4)],$$

subject to

$$x_{11} - 300 = y_1,$$
$$y_1 + x_{12} + x_{22} - 700 = y_2,$$
$$y_2 + x_{13} + x_{23} - 900 = y_3,$$
$$y_3 + x_{14} - 800 = y_4,$$
$$x_{11}, x_{12}, x_{13}, x_{14}, \text{ each } \leq 700,$$
$$x_{22}, x_{23}, \text{ each } \leq 200,$$
$$x_{11}, x_{12}, x_{13}, x_{14}, x_{22}, x_{23}, y_1, y_2, y_3, y_4 \geq 0.]$$

54. Two alloys A and B are made from four different metals I, II, III and IV according to the following specifications:

A	*B*
At most 80% of I,	Between 40% and 60% of II,
at most 30% of II,	at least 30% of III,
at least 50% of III.	at most 70% of IV.

The four metals are extracted from three different ores whose constituent percentage of these metals, maximum available quantity and cost per ton are tabulated below:

Ore	*Maximum quantity (tons)*	*Constituents %*					*Price (₹/ton)*
		I	*II*	*III*	*IV*	*others*	
1	1,000	20	10	30	30	10	300
2	2,000	10	20	30	30	10	400
3	3,000	5	5	70	20	0	500

Assuming the selling prices of alloys *A* and *B* as ₹ 2,000 and ₹ 3,000 per ton respectively, formulate the L.P. model for the problem. *[I.C.W.A. Dec., 1998]*

[**Hint:** Let x_{1A}; x_{2A}, x_{3A}; x_{1B}, x_{2B}, x_{3B} be the quantities in tons of ores 1, 2, 3 in making alloys A and B respectively. The L.P. model is:

$$\text{Max } Z = [\{2,000(x_{1A} + x_{2A} + x_{3A}) + 3,000(x_{1B} + x_{2B} + x_{3B})\} - \{300(x_{1A} + x_{1B}) + 400(x_{2A} + x_{2B}) + 500(x_{3A} + x_{3B})\}]$$

subject to

$$.2x_{1A} + .1x_{2A} + .05x_{3A} \leq 0.8(x_{1A} + x_{2A} + x_{3A}),$$
$$.1x_{1A} + .2x_{2A} + .05x_{3A} \leq 0.3(x_{1A} + x_{2A} + x_{3A});$$
$$.3x_{1A} + .3x_{2A} + .7x_{3A} \geq 0.5(x_{1A} + x_{2A} + x_{3A});$$
$$.1x_{1B} + .2x_{2B} + .05x_{3B} \geq 0.4(x_{1B} + x_{2B} + x_{3B}),$$
$$.1x_{1B} + .2x_{2B} + .05x_{3B} \leq 0.6(x_{1B} + x_{2B} + x_{3B}),$$

$.3x_{1B} + .3x_{2B} + .7x_{3B} \geq 0.3\ (x_{1B} + x_{2B} + x_{3B}),$

$.3x_{1B} + .3x_{2B} + .2x_{3B} \leq 0.7\ (x_{1B} + x_{2B} + x_{3B});$

$x_{1A}, x_{2A}, ..., x_{3B}$, each $\geq 0.$]

55. A bank is in the process of formulating its loan policy involving a maximum of ₹ 600 million. Table below gives the relevant types of loans. Bad debts are not recoverable and produce no interest revenue. To meet compitition from other banks, the following policy guidelines have been set: At least 40% of the funds must be allocated to the Agricultural and Commercial loans. Funds allocated to Housing must be at least 50% of all loans given to Personal, Car and Housing. The overall bad debts on all loans may not exceed 0.06.

Type of loan	*Interest rate (%)*	*Bad debt (Probability)*
Personal	17	0.10
Car	14	0.07
Housing	11	0.05
Agriculture	10	0.08
Commercial	13	0.06

Formulate the L.P. model to determine optimal loan allocations.

[P.T.U.B. Tech. April, 2012; MBA Dec., 2011; C.A. (Final) June, 2003]

(*Ans.* Max $Z = 0.17x_1 + 0.14x_2 + 0.11x_3 + 0.10x_4 + 0.13x_5$,

subject to $x_4 + x_5 \geq 0.4\ (x_1 + x_2 + x_3 + x_4 + x_5)$,

$x_3 \geq 0.5\ (x_1 + x_2 + x_3)$,

$0.10x_1 + 0.07x_2 + 0.05x_3 + 0.08x_4 + 0.06x_5 \leq 0.06\ (x_1 + x_2 + x_3 + x_4 + x_5)$,

$x_1 + x_2 + x_3 + x_4 + x_5 \leq 600;$

x_1, x_2, x_3, x_4, x_5, each ≥ 0.)

56. A security dealer recommends two types of investments A and B to his client. Investment A returns 6% and B 8%. The client has almost ₹ 1,00,000 to invest. The client wants the total annual return to be at least ₹ 7,000 and at least 2/5th of the amount to be invested in investment B. The security dealer gets 5% of the income from investment A and 4% of the income from investment B. Construct mathematical model for the problem to maximize the total fee of the security dealer.

(*Ans.* Max $Z = .06 \times .05x_1 + .08 \times .04x_2 = 0.003x_1 + 0.0032x_2$,

subject to $x_1 + x_2 \leq 1,00,000$,

$0.06x_1 + 0.08x_2 \geq 7,000$,

$x_2 \geq 0.4\ (x_1 + x_2)$,

$x_1, x_2 \geq 0$.)

57. An electronics company is engaged in the production of two components P_1 and P_2 that are used in T.V. sets. Each unit of P_1 costs the company ₹ 25 in wages and ₹ 25 in material, while each unit of P_2 costs ₹ 125 in wages and ₹ 75 in material. The company sells both products on one-period credit terms, but the company's labour and material expenses must be paid in cash. The selling price of P_1 is ₹ 150/unit and of P_2 is ₹ 350/unit. The company can sell as many units as it can produce. Its production capacity is, however, limited by two considerations: First, at the beginning of period 1, the company has an initial balance of ₹ 20,000. Second, the company has available in each period 4,000 hours of machine time and 2,800 hours of assembly time. The production of each P_1 requires 6 hours of machine time and 4 hours of assembly time, whereas the production of each P_2 requires 4 hours of machine time and 6 hours of assembly time. Formulate the problem as the L.P. model so as to maximize the total profit to the company.

[**Hint:** The data of the problem can be expressed in the form of table below:

Decision variables	*Components*	*Cost/unit (₹)*	*Sale price/unit (₹)*	*Machine time/unit*	*Assembly time/unit*
x_1	P_1	50	150	6 hr	4 hr
x_2	P_2	200	350	4 hr	6 hr
Total availability: 20,000		2,800 hr		4,000 hr	2,800 hr

Thus the L.P. model is

$$\text{maximize } Z = (150 - 50)\,x_1 + (350 - 200)\,x_2 = 100x_1 + 150x_2,$$

subject to
$$50x_1 + 200x_2 \le 20{,}000,$$
$$6x_1 + 4x_2 \le 4{,}000,$$
$$4x_1 + 6x_2 \le 2{,}800,$$
$$x_1, x_2 \ge 0.]$$

58. A computer manufacturing company purchases component parts and makes two models of monitors A and B. The components are assembled by the company to produce model A and model B of the monitors and each unit produced is then thoroughly inspected for quality and performance. The company then sells the two models under its own brand name. Information about the resources required to produce the two models has been obtained from both the production department and the accounts department. Model A requires 28 hours of labour to assemble from component parts, while model B requires 42 hours. After assembly, each monitor is tested in the inspection deptt. to ensure it is working satisfactorily. Because of the technical complexity of the product and the firm's desire to maintain good quality control, the inspection test is time-consuming. Model A requires 12 hours of inspection time while B requires only 6 hours as more time and care is taken at the assembly stage. The company employs 400 people in the assembly department, each working 7 hours a day, 6 days a week. 100 people are presently employed in the inspection department, each working 8 hours a day, 6 days a week. Current wage rates are ₹ 20 per hour in assembly and ₹ 15 per hour in inspection. The accounts deptt. has calculated that in terms of components and parts, model A costs ₹ 385 and model B costs ₹ 625 to produce. Currently the two models sell for ₹ 1,350 and ₹ 1,800 respectively. Each model requires a particular component — a microchip that forms part of the monitor's memory. The supplier of these chips can provide no more than 660 in any one working week.

Formulate the mathematical model that allows the production manager to determine the number of units of model A and B to produce weekly so as to maximize profits.

[**Hint:** The data regarding cost/profit can be expressed as follows:

		Model A	*Model B*
Component cost	:	₹ 385	₹ 625
Assembly time cost (*Hours needed × ₹ 20*)	:	₹ 560	₹ 840
Inspection time cost (*Hours needed × ₹ 15*)	:	₹ 180	₹ 90
Total cost/unit	:	₹ 1,125	₹ 1,555
Sale price/unit	:	₹ 1,350	₹ 1,800
∴ *Profit/unit*	:	₹ 225	₹ 245

The data regarding resource requirement can be expressed as

	Requirement/unit of Model A	*Model B*	*Total available*
Assembly time:	28 hr	42 hr	400 × 7 × 6 = 16,800 hr
Inspection time:	12 hr	6 hr	100 × 8 × 6 = 4,800 hr
Microchip components:	1 chip	1 chip	660 chips

∴ The L.P. model can be written as

$$\text{maximize } Z = ₹\,(225x_1 + 245x_2),$$

subject to
$$28x_1 + 42x_2 \le 16{,}800,$$
$$12x_1 + 6x_2 \le 4{,}800,$$
$$x_1 + x_2 \le 660,$$
$$x_1, x_2 \ge 0.]$$

59. An agriculturist has a 125 acre farm. He produces radish, mutter and potato. Whatever he raises can be fully sold in the market. He gets ₹ 5/kg for radish, ₹ 4/kg for mutter and ₹ 5/kg for potato. The average yield is 1,500 kg/acre of radish, 1,800 kg/acre of mutter and 1,200 kg/acre of potato. To produce each 100 kg of radish and mutter and to produce each 80 kg of potato, a sum of ₹ 12.50 has to be used for manure. Labour required for each acre to raise the crop is 6 man-days for radish and potato each and 5 man-days for mutter. A total of 500 man-days of labour at a rate of ₹ 40 per man-day are available. Formulate this as a linear programming model to maximize the agriculturist's total profit.

[*R.U. MBA June, 2011*; *H.P.U.B. Tech. (Mech.) Sept., 2009*]

(*Ans.* Maximize $Z = ₹ \left[(5 \times 1{,}500 - \frac{12.50}{100} \times 1{,}500 - 6 \times 40)\, x_1 + \left(4 \times 1{,}800 - \frac{12.50}{100} \times 1{,}800 - 5 \times 40\right) x_2 + \left(5 \times 1{,}200 - \frac{12.50}{100} \times 1{,}200 - 6 \times 40\right) x_3 \right]$

or maximize $Z = ₹\ (7{,}072.50x_1 + 6{,}775x_2 + 5{,}610x_3)$,

subject to $x_1 + x_2 + x_3 \leq 125$,

$6x_1 + 5x_2 + 6x_3 \leq 500$,

$x_1, x_2, x_3 \geq 0$.)

60. A company has three operational departments (weaving, processing and packing) with capacity to produce three different types of clothes namely, suitings, shirtings and woollens yielding the profit of ₹ 2, ₹ 4 and ₹ 3 per metre respectively. One metre suiting requires 3 minutes in weaving, 2 minutes in processing and 1 minute in packing. One metre of shirting requires 4 minutes in weaving, 1 minute in processing and 3 minutes in packing, while one metre woollen requires 3 minutes in each department. In a week, total run time of each department is 60, 40 and 80 hours of weaving, processing and packing respectively. Formulate the L.P. problem to find the product mix to maximize the profit.

[*C.A. Nov., 1998*]

(*Ans.* Maximize $Z = ₹\ (2x_1 + 4x_2 + 3x_3)$,

subject to $3x_1 + 4x_2 + 3x_3 \leq 3{,}600$,

$2x_1 + x_2 + 3x_3 \leq 2{,}400$,

$x_1 + 3x_2 + 3x_3 \leq 4{,}800$,

$x_1, x_2, x_3 \geq 0$.)

61. The owner of a fancy goods shop is interested to determine how many advertisements to release in the selected three magazines, A, B and C. His main purpose is to advertise in such a way that total exposure to principal buyers of his goods is maximized. Percentages of readers for each magazine are known. Exposure in any particular magazine is the number of advertisements released multiplied by the number of pricipal buyers. The following data are available:

Particulars	*Magazines*		
	A	*B*	*C*
Readers	1 lakh	0.6 lakh	0.4 lakh
Principal buyers	20%	15%	8%
Cost/advt.	₹ 8,000	₹ 6,000	₹ 5,000

The budgeted amount is at most ₹ 1.0 lakh for the advertisements. The owner has already decided that magazine A should have no more than 15 advertisements and that B and C each gets at least 8 advertisements. Formulate L.P. model for this problem.

[*C.A. Nov., 1996*]

(*Ans.* Maximize $Z = \left(\frac{20}{100} \times 1{,}00{,}000\right).x_1 + \left(\frac{15}{100} \times 60{,}000\right).x_2 + \left(\frac{8}{100} \times 40{,}000\right).x_3$

$= 20{,}000x_1 + 9{,}000x_2 + 3{,}200x_3,$

subject to $8{,}000x_1 + 6{,}000x_2 + 5{,}000x_3 \leq 1{,}00{,}000,$

$x_1 \leq 15,\ x_2 \geq 8,\ x_3 \geq 8,$

$x_1, x_2, x_3 \geq 0.$)

62. A company produces four products A, B, C and D. Raw material requirements, storage space needed, production rates and profits are given in the table below. The total amount of raw material available per day for all the four products is 180 kg. Total space available for storage is 230 square metre and 7 hours/day is used for production.

	A	B	C	D
Raw material (kg/piece)	2	2	1.5	4
Space (metre²/piece)	2	2.5	2	1.5
Production rate (piece/hr)	15	30	10	15
Profit (₹/piece)	5	6.5	5	5.5

Formulate the problem as the L.P. problem to maximize total profit.

[*P.T.U. B.Tech. (Prod.) Nov., 2012; J.N.T.U. Hyderabad MBA April, 2012*]

(*Ans.* Maximize $Z = 5x_A + 6.5x_B + 5x_C + 5.5x_D,$

subject to $2x_A + 2x_B + 1.5x_C + 4x_D \leq 180,$

$2x_A + 2.5x_B + 2x_C + 1.5x_D \leq 230,$

$\frac{x_A}{15} + \frac{x_B}{30} + \frac{x_C}{10} + \frac{x_D}{15} \leq 7$

or $2x_A + x_B + 3x_C + 2x_D \leq 210,$

$x_A, x_B, x_C, x_D \geq 0.$)

63. A manufacturer produces three products A, B and C. Each product requires processing on two machines M_1 and M_2. The time required to produce one unit of each product on a machine is given in the table below:

Product	*Time to produce one unit (hours)*	
	Machine M_1	*Machine M_2*
A	0.5	0.6
B	0.7	0.8
C	0.9	1.05

There are 85 hours available on each machine; the operating cost is ₹ 5/hour for machine M_1 and ₹ 4/hour for machine M_2. The product requirements are at least 90 units of A, at least 80 units of B and at least 60 units of C. The manufacturer wishes to meet the requirements at minimum cost. Formulate the problem as L.P. problem.

[*Delhi M.B.A., 1975*]

(*Ans.* Minimize $Z = (0.5 \times 5 + 0.6 \times 4)\, x_A + (0.7 \times 5 + 0.8 \times 4)\, x_B + (0.9 \times 5 + 1.05 \times 4)\, x_C$

$= 4.9x_A + 6.7x_B + 8.7x_C,$

subject to $0.5x_A + 0.7x_B + 0.9x_C \leq 85,$

$0.6x_A + 0.8x_B + 1.05x_C \leq 85,$

$x_A \geq 90,$

$x_B \geq 80,$

$x_C \geq 60,$

$x_A, x_B, x_C \geq 0$).

64. A fruit seller mixes pears, apples and grapes to make three different types of baskets. Pears are purchased at a cost of ₹ 40 a kg, apples at ₹ 60 a kg and grapes at ₹ 100 a kg. The specifications for the three types of baskets are as follows:

Type I must have at least 40% pears and at the most 25% grapes.

Type II must have at least 30% pears and at the most 40% grapes, and

Type III offers no restrictions on the constituents.

The sale price of type I is ₹ 70 per kg, of type II is ₹ 100 per kg and of type III is ₹ 60 per kg. The daily supply of fruit is limited to 80 kg of pears, 120 kg of apples and 40 kg of grapes. Formulate the model to represent how the fruit be mixed to maximize profit.

[**Hint:** Let ${}^xP_I, {}^xP_{II}, {}^xP_{III}$ be the quantity of pears in kg in basket of type I, II and III respectively. Similarly, let ${}^xA_I, {}^xA_{II}, {}^xA_{III}$ be the quantity of apples in kg in baskets of type I, II, and III respectively, and ${}^xG_I, {}^xG_{II}, {}^xG_{III}$ be the quantity of grapes in kg in baskets of type I, II and III respectively.

Then ${}^xP_j$, ${}^xA_j$ and ${}^xG_j$, all ≥ 0, where j = I, II, III.

Constraints are

for basket of type I: ${}^xP_I \geq 0.40\ ({}^xP_I + {}^xA_I + {}^xG_I)$, and

${}^xG_I \leq 0.25\ ({}^xP_I + {}^xA_I + {}^xG_I)$,

for basket of type II: ${}^xP_{II} \geq 0.30\ ({}^xP_{II} + {}^xA_{II} + {}^xG_{II})$, and

${}^xG_{II} \leq 0.40\ (x_{PII} + {}^xA_{II} + {}^xG_{II})$.

Also for supply of pears: ${}^xP_I + {}^xP_{II} + {}^xP_{III} \leq 80$,

for supply of apples: ${}^xA_I + {}^xA_{II} + {}^xA_{III} \leq 120$,

and for supply of grapes: ${}^xG_I + {}^xG_{II} + {}^xG_{III} \leq 40$.

Objective is to maximize Z

$$= ₹\ 10\ [7\ \{({}^xP_I + {}^xA_I + {}^xG_I) + 10\ ({}^xP_{II} + {}^xA_{II} + {}^xG_{II}) + 6\ ({}^xP_{III} + {}^xA_{III} + {}^xG_{III}) - 4\ ({}^xP_I + {}^xP_{II} + {}^xP_{III}) - 6\ ({}^xA_I + {}^xA_{II} + {}^xA_{III}) - 10\ ({}^xG_I + {}^xG_{II} + {}^xG_{III})\}].$$

65. A fertilizer company has only 1,000 tonnes of nitrate, 2,000 tonnes of phosphate and 500 tonnes of potash available per month. It uses these to make three basic fertilizers, namely 5—5—5, 5—10—5 and 10—10—5, where the numbers in each case represent the percentage by weight of nitrate, phosphate and potash in each of the mixtures. The costs of materials are

Ingredient	:	*Nitrate*	*Phosphate*	*Potash*	*Inert ingredients*
Cost (₹/tonne)	:	800	200	500	25

The three fertilizers sell at ₹ 300, ₹ 250 and ₹ 400 per tonne respectively. There is a constraint that at least 5,000 tonnes of 5—10—5 fertilizer must be produced per month. Construct L.P. model to determine the amount of each fertilizer that must be produced per month to maximize the monthly profit. [*P.T.U.M. Tech. Dec., 2011*]

[**Hint:** Let x_1, x_2 and x_3 be the amount in tonnes per month of fertilizer 5—5—5, 5—10—5 and 10—10—5 respectively. Then objective is to

$$\text{maximize } Z = \left(300 - \frac{5}{100}\times 800 - \frac{5}{100}\times 200 - \frac{5}{100}\times 500 - \frac{85}{100}\times 25\right)x_1$$

$$+ \left(250 - \frac{5}{100}\times 800 - \frac{10}{100}\times 200 - \frac{5}{100}\times 500 - \frac{80}{100}\times 25\right)x_2$$

$$+ \left(400 - \frac{10}{100}\times 800 - \frac{10}{100}\times 200 - \frac{5}{100}\times 500 - \frac{75}{100}\times 25\right)x_3$$

$$= 203.75x_1 + 145x_2 + 256.25x_3.$$

Constraints are

$$\frac{5}{100}x_1 + \frac{5}{100}x_2 + \frac{10}{100}x_3 \leq 1{,}000$$

or
$$x_1 + x_2 + 2x_3 \leq 20{,}000,$$

$$\frac{5}{100}x_1 + \frac{10}{100}x_2 + \frac{10}{100}x_3 \leq 2{,}000$$

or
$$x_1 + 2x_2 + 2x_3 \leq 40{,}000,$$

$$\frac{5}{100}x_1 + \frac{5}{100}x_2 + \frac{5}{100}x_3 \leq 500$$

or
$$x_1 + x_2 + x_3 \leq 10{,}000,$$

$$x_2 \geq 5{,}000,$$

$$x_1, x_2, x_3 \geq 0.]$$

66. A ship has three cargo holds, forward, aft and centre; the capacity limits are:

Forward	2,000 tonnes	1,00,000 m³
Centre	3,000 tonnes	1,35,000 m³
Aft	1,500 tonnes	30,000 m³

The following cargoes are offered; the ship owners may accept all or any part of each commodity:

Commodity	*Amount (tonnes)*	*Volume per tonne (m^3)*	*Profit per tonne (₹)*
A	6,000	60	60
B	4,000	50	80
C	2,000	25	50

In order to preserve the trim of the ship, the weight in each hold must be proportional to the capacity in tonnes. The objective is to maximize the profit. Formulate the linear programming model for this problem. [*Madras M.Sc. (Appl. Math.) 1983; I.I.T. (M. Tech.) 1980*]

[**Hint:** Let x_{1A}, x_{2A}, x_{3A} be the weights (in tonnes) of the commodity A to be accommodated in *farward, centre* and *aft* portions respectively. Similarly, let x_{1B}, x_{2B}, x_{3B} and x_{1C}, x_{2C}, x_{3C} be the corresponding weights (in tonnes) of *B* and *C*.

Objective function:

Maximize $z = 60\,(x_{1A} + x_{2A} + x_{3A}) + 80\,(x_{1B} + x_{2B} + x_{3B}) + 50\,(x_{1C} + x_{2C} + x_{3C})$.

Constraints:

$$\left.\begin{aligned} x_{1A} + x_{2A} + x_{3A} &\le 6{,}000 \\ x_{1B} + x_{2B} + x_{3B} &\le 4{,}000 \\ x_{1C} + x_{2C} + x_{3C} &\le 2{,}000 \end{aligned}\right\} \quad \textit{(commodity cargo)}$$

$$\left.\begin{aligned} x_{1A} + x_{1B} + x_{1C} &\le 2{,}000 \\ x_{2A} + x_{2B} + x_{2C} &\le 3{,}000 \\ x_{3A} + x_{3B} + x_{3C} &\le 1{,}500 \end{aligned}\right\} \quad \textit{(weight capacity)}$$

$$\left.\begin{aligned} 60\,x_{1A} + 50\,x_{1B} + 25\,x_{1C} &\le 1{,}00{,}000 \\ 60\,x_{2A} + 50\,x_{2B} + 25\,x_{2C} &\le 1{,}35{,}000 \\ 60\,x_{3A} + 50\,x_{3B} + 25\,x_{3C} &\le 30{,}000 \end{aligned}\right\} \quad \textit{(volume capacity)}$$

$$x_{ij} \ge 0 \; (i = 1, 2, 3;\; j = A, B, C).]$$

67. A contractor has been assigned the excavation work of a canal and of the headworks on a project. In order to ensure a balanced progress on the entire work the management has imposed certain conditions on his working. The excavation of the canal is more profitable than that of the headworks, but he has to abide by the conditions of contract. In addition, he has his own limitations on manpower and equipment. It is desired to find the optimum amount of excavation on the two works which he should undertake so that his profits are maximized and he satisfies the constraints of the contract and of the resources. These constraints are given below:

(*i*) The difference in the quantity of earthwork done on the two works does not exceed 2 units in a day.

(*ii*) The difference between the quantity of canal excavation and of twice the headworks excavation does not exceed 1 unit in a day.

(*iii*) Each unit of canal excavation done in a day requires one unit of manpower and one unit of machines; and each unit of headworks excavation requires 2 units of manpower and one unit of machines. Maximum available manpower is 10 units and machines 6 units.

The contractor stipulates a profit of 2 units for each unit of canal excavation and half of this for each unit of headworks excavation.

[**Hint:** Let the quantity of canal excavation that the contractor should do every day be x_1 units, and quantity of headworks excavation be x_2 units. It is obvious that the variables x_1 and x_2 are non-negative. The objective function is $z = 2x_1 + x_2$ (maximize) and the constraint relationships are:

$$x_1 + 2x_2 \le 10, \quad \textit{(manpower constraint)}$$
$$x_1 + x_2 \le 6, \quad \textit{(machine constraint)}$$
$$x_1 - x_2 \le 2, \quad \textit{(contract constraint)}$$
$$x_1 - 2x_2 \le 1, \quad \textit{(contract constraint)}$$
$$x_1, x_2 \ge 0.]$$

68. Rolls of paper having a fixed length and width of 180 cm are being manufactured by a paper mill. These rolls have to be cut to satisfy the following demand:

Width:	80 cm	45 cm	27 cm
No. of rolls:	200	120	130

Obtain the linear programming formulation of the problem to determine the cutting pattern, so that the demand is satisfied and wastage of paper is a minimum.

[**Hint:** Various alternatives for the number of rolls are given below:

Feasible patterns of cutting	*No. of rolls cut*	*Wastage per roll (cm)*	*Rolls obtained from each mother roll of width 180 cm*		
			80 cm	*45 cm*	*27 cm*
80 + 80	x_1	20	2	—	—
80 + 45 + 45	x_2	10	1	2	—
80 + 45 + 27 + 27	x_3	1	1	1	2
80 + 27 + 27 + 27	x_4	19	1	—	3
45 + 45 + 45 + 45	x_5	0	—	4	—
45 + 45 + 45 + 27	x_6	18	—	3	1
45 + 45 + 27 + 27 + 27	x_7	9	—	2	3
45 + 27 + 27 + 27 + 27 + 27	x_8	0	—	1	5
27 + 27 + 27 + 27 + 27 + 27	x_9	18	—	—	6

Thus the linear programming problem is:

Minimize $z = 20x_1 + 10x_2 + x_3 + 19x_4 + 18x_6 + 9x_7 + 18x_9$,

subject to the constraints:

$2x_1 + x_2 + x_3 + x_4 \geq 200,$ (*80 cm rolls*)

$2x_2 + x_3 + 4x_5 + 3x_6 + 2x_7 + x_8 \geq 120,$ (*45 cm rolls*)

$2x_3 + 3x_4 + x_6 + 3x_7 + 5x_8 + 6x_9 \geq 130,$ (*27 cm rolls*)

$x_j \geq 0;\ j = 1, 2, 3, ..., 9.$]

69. A manufacturing company produces three types of parts for automatic washing machines. It purchases castings of the parts from a local foundry and then finishes the parts with the help of drilling, shaping and polishing machines.

The selling prices of parts *A*, *B* and *C* respectively are ₹ 46, ₹ 55 and ₹ 75. All parts made can be sold. Castings for parts *A*, *B* and *C* cost ₹ 31, ₹ 35 and ₹ 55 respectively.

The company has only one machine of each type. Costs per hour to run each of the three machines are ₹ 100 for drilling, ₹ 150 for shaping and ₹ 150 for polishing. The capacities (parts per hour) for each part on each machine are given in the table below.

Machine	*Capacity per hour*		
	Part A	*Part B*	*Part C*
Drilling	25	40	25
Shaping	25	20	20
Polishing	40	30	40

The management of the company wants to know how many parts of each type it should produce per hour in order to maximize profit for an hour's run. Formulate the problem as the L.P. model.

[*H.P.U B.Tech, Nov., 2015; P.T.U.M. Tech. April, 2012; D.U.MBA, 2003, 2000*]

[**Hint:** Let x_1, x_2 and x_3 denote the number of parts *A*, *B* and *C* to be produced per hour. Then

$$\text{profit} = ₹ \left[\left\{(46-31)-\left(\frac{100}{25}+\frac{150}{25}+\frac{150}{40}\right)\right\}.x_1\right.$$

$$+ \left\{(55-35)-\left(\frac{100}{40}+\frac{150}{20}+\frac{150}{30}\right)\right\}.x_2$$

$$+ \left\{(75-55) - \left(\frac{100}{25} + \frac{150}{20} + \frac{150}{40}\right)\right\} . x_3$$

$$= ₹\,(1.25x_1 + 5x_2 + 4.75x_3),$$

subject to constraints $\frac{x_1}{25} + \frac{x_2}{40} + \frac{x_3}{25} \le 1,$

$$\frac{x_1}{25} + \frac{x_2}{20} + \frac{x_3}{20} \le 1,$$

$$\frac{x_1}{40} + \frac{x_2}{30} + \frac{x_3}{40} \le 1,$$

$x_1, x_2, x_3 \ge 0.$]

70. A mutual fund company has cash resources of ₹ 200 million for investment in a diversified portfolio. Table below shows the opportunities available, their estimated annual yields, risk factors and term period details.

Formulate the L.P. model to find the optimal portfolio that will maximize return, considering the following policy guidelines:

Investment type	*Annual yield (%)*	*Risk factor*	*Time period (years)*
Bank deposit	9.5	0.02	6
Treasury notes	8.5	0.01	4
Corporate deposit	12.0	0.08	3
Blue-chip stock	15.0	0.25	5
Speculative stocks	32.5	0.45	3
Real estate	35.0	0.40	10

(*i*) All the funds available may be invested.

(*ii*) Weighted average period of at least 5 years should be the planning horizon.

(*iii*) Weighted average risk factor must not exceed 0.20.

(*iv*) Investment in real estate and speculative stocks together must not be more than 25% of the money invested in total.

[*P.T.U. M.Tech. Nov., 2012*]

(*Ans.* Maximize $Z = \frac{9.5}{100}x_1 + \frac{8.5}{100}x_2 + \frac{12}{100}x_3 + \frac{15}{100}x_4 + \frac{32.5}{100}x_5 + \frac{35}{100}x_6,$

subject to constraints $x_1 + x_2 + x_3 + x_4 + x_5 + x_6 = 200,$

$$0.02x_1 + 0.01x_2 + 0.08x_3 + 0.25x_4 + 0.45x_5 + 0.40x_6 \le 0.2 \times 200,$$

$$6x_1 + 4x_2 + 3x_3 + 5x_4 + 3x_5 + 10x_6 \ge 5 \times 200,$$

$$x_5 + x_6 \le 0.25 \times 200,$$

$x_1, x_2, x_3, x_4, x_5, x_6$, each ≥ 0.)

71. A used-car dealer wishes to stock up his lot to maximize his profit. He can select cars A, B and C which are valued wholesale at ₹ 50,000, ₹ 70,000 and ₹ 80,000 respectively. These can be sold at ₹ 60,000, ₹ 85,000 and ₹ 1,05,000 respectively. For each type of car the probabilities of sale are

Type of car :	*A*	*B*	*C*
Prob. of sale in 90 days :	0.7	0.8	0.6

For every two cars of type B, he should buy one car of type A or C. If he has ₹ 10,00,000 to invest, what should he buy to maximize his expected gain? Write the mathematical model only.

[*Madurai U.B.E. (Mech.) 1977, 76*]

[**Hint:** Let x_1, x_2, x_3 be the cars of type *A*, *B* and *C* to be purchased. Gain per car of type *A*, *B* and *C* will be ₹ 10,000, ₹ 15,000 and ₹ 25,000 respectively. Therefore, the mathematical model is

maximize $Z = ₹ [0.7 \times 10{,}000\, x_1 + 0.8 \times 15{,}000\, x_2 + 0.6 \times 25{,}000\, x_3]$

$= ₹ (7{,}000x_1 + 12{,}000x_2 + 15{,}000x_3)$,

subject to constraints $50{,}000x_1 + 70{,}000\,(2x_2) \le 10{,}00{,}000$,

$70{,}000\,(2x_2) + 80{,}000x_3 \le 10{,}00{,}000$,

$x_1, x_2, x_3 \ge 0$.]

72. Evening shift resident doctors in a Govt. hospital work five consecutive days and then have two days off. Their five days of work can start on any day of the week and the schedule rotates indefinitely. The hospital requires the following minimum number of doctors working:

Sunday	*Monday*	*Tuesday*	*Wednesday*	*Thursday*	*Friday*	*Saturday*
35	55	60	50	60	50	45

No more than 40 doctors can start their five working days' schedule on the same day. Formulate the L.P. model to minimize the number of doctors to be employed by the hospital.

[*P.T.U. B.Tech. (Prod.) Nov., 2012; P.U.B.E. (E. and Ec.) April, 2008*]

[**Hint**. Minimize $Z = x_1 + x_2 + x_3 + x_4 + x_5 + x_6 + x_7$,

subject to constraints which may be constructed as follows: x_1 doctors join duty on Sunday. x_2 and x_3 doctors who joined duty last Monday and Tuesday will have off on Sunday.

$\therefore$ For Sunday, $x_1 + x_4 + x_5 + x_6 + x_7 \ge 35$.

Similarly for Monday, $x_2 + x_5 + x_6 + x_7 + x_1 \ge 55$,

for Tuesday, $x_3 + x_6 + x_7 + x_1 + x_2 \ge 60$,

for Wednesday, $x_4 + x_7 + x_1 + x_2 + x_3 \ge 50$,

for Thursday, $x_5 + x_1 + x_2 + x_3 + x_4 \ge 60$,

for Friday, $x_6 + x_2 + x_3 + x_4 + x_5 \ge 50$,

and for Saturday, $x_7 + x_3 + x_4 + x_5 + x_6 \ge 45$,

where $x_1, x_2, ..., x_7$, each ≤ 40 and ≥ 0.]

73. *PQR* Coffee Company mixes South Indian, Assamese and Imported Coffee to make two brands of coffee, Plains X and Plains X X. The characteristics used in blending the coffees include strength, acidity and caffeine. The test results of the available supplies of South Indian, Assamese and Imported coffees are shown in the following table:

	Price/kg (₹)	*Strength index*	*Acidity index*	*Per cent caffeine*	*Supply available (kg)*
South Indian	30	6	4.0	2.0	40,000
Assamese	40	8	3.0	2.5	20,000
Imported	35	5	3.5	1.5	15,000

The requirements for plains X and Plains XX coffees are given in the following table:

Plains coffee	*Price/kg (₹)*	*Min. strength*	*Max. acidity*	*Max. per cent caffeine*	*Quantity demanded (kg)*
X	45	6.5	3.8	2.2	35,000
XX	55	6.0	3.5	2.0	25,000

Assume that 35,000 kg of Plains X and 25,000 kg of Plains XX can be sold. Formulate the L.P. model to maximize profit. [*P.T.U. M.Tech. Nov., 2012*]

[**Hint:** Let x_{ij} ; $i = 1, 2, 3$ and $j = 1, 2$ be the quantities in kg of three types of coffees to make Plains X and XX respectively. Then L.P. model can be expressed as

maximize $Z = ₹ [\{45\,(x_{11} + x_{21} + x_{31}) + 55\,(x_{12} + x_{22} + x_{32})\} - \{30\,(x_{11} + x_{12})$

$+ 40\,(x_{21} + x_{22}) + 35\,(x_{31} + x_{32})\}]$,

subject to constraints $6x_{11} + 8x_{21} + 5x_{31} \ge 6.5\,(x_{11} + x_{21} + x_{31})$,

$$6x_{12} + 8x_{22} + 5x_{32} \geq 6\ (x_{12} + x_{22} + x_{32}),$$
$$4x_{11} + 3x_{21} + 3.5x_{31} \leq 3.8\ (x_{11} + x_{21} + x_{31}),$$
$$4x_{12} + 3x_{22} + 3.5x_{32} \leq 3.5\ (x_{12} + x_{22} + x_{32}),$$
$$2x_{11} + 2.5x_{21} + 1.5x_{31} \leq 2.2\ (x_{11} + x_{21} + x_{31}),$$
$$2x_{12} + 2.5x_{22} + 1.5x_{32} \leq 2.0\ (x_{12} + x_{22} + x_{32}),$$
$$x_{11} + x_{21} + x_{31} \geq 35{,}000,$$
$$x_{12} + x_{22} + x_{32} \geq 25{,}000,$$
$$x_{11} + x_{12} \leq 40{,}000,$$
$$x_{21} + x_{22} \leq 20{,}000,$$
$$x_{31} + x_{32} \leq 15{,}000,$$
$$x_{11}, x_{21}, x_{31}\ ;\ x_{12}, x_{22}, x_{32}, \text{ each} \geq 0.]$$

74. A factory has just purchased a machine which will be required for a period of 8 years. The annual maintenance cost goes on increasing as the machine gets older. At the end of any year the machine can be sold and a new one purchased in its place. The following information is available: Purchase price of the machine at any time is P, S_i = salvage value of selling a machine i years old, C_i = annual maintenance cost for a machine i years old.

Formulate a linear programming model to find an optimal replacement policy.

[*P.T.U. MBA May, 2001*]

75. An engineering company is planning to diversify its operations during the year 2007–08. The company has allocated capital expenditure budget equal to ₹ 5.15 lakhs in the year 2007 and ₹ 6.50 lakhs in the year 2008. The company has five investment projects under consideration. The estimated net returns at the present value and expected cash expenditures on each project in the two years are as follows :

Project	*Estimated net returns ('000 ₹)*	*Cash expenditure ('000 ₹)*	
		Year 2007	*Year 2008*
A	240	120	320
B	390	550	594
C	80	118	202
D	150	250	340
E	182	324	474

Formulate this capital budgeting problem as the L.P. model to maximize the net return.

[**Hint:** Let x_1, x_2, x_3, x_4 and x_5 be the *proportion* of investment in project *A, B, C, D* and *E* respectively. Therefore, the L.P. model is

maximize $Z = ₹\ 1{,}000\ (240x_1 + 390x_2 + 80x_3 + 150x_4 + 182x_5)$,

subject to $120x_1 + 550x_2 + 118x_3 + 250x_4 + 324x_5 \leq 515$,

$320x_1 + 594x_2 + 202x_3 + 340x_4 + 474x_5 \leq 650$,

$x_1 + x_2 + x_3 + x_4 + x_5 = 1$,

where x_1, x_2, x_3, x_4, x_5, each ≥ 0.]

76. *ABC* paints company manufactures three grades of paints—Venus, Diana and Aurora. The plant operates on a three-shift basis and the following data are available from the production records :

Requirement of resource	*Grade*			*Availability (capacity/month)*
	Venus	*Diana*	*Aurora*	
Special additive (kg/litre)	0.30	0.15	0.75	600 tonnes
Milling (kilolitres per machine shift)	2.0	3.0	5.0	100 machine shifts
Packing (kilolitres per shift)	12.0	12.0	12.0	80 shifts

There are no limitations on other resources. The particulars of sales forecasts and estimated contribution to overheads and profits are given below.

	Venus	*Diana*	*Aurora*
Maximum possible sales per month (kilolitres)	100	400	600
Contribution (₹/kilolitre)	4,000	3,500	2,000

Due to commitments already made, a minimum of 200 kilolitres per month of Aurora paint has to be necessarily supplied during the next year.

Just as the company was able to finalise the monthly production programme for the next 12 months, an offer was received from a nearby competitor for hiring 40 machine shifts per month of milling capacity for grinding Diana paint, that can be spared for at least a year. However, due to additional handling and the profit margin of the competitor involved by using this facility, the contribution from Diana paint will get reduced by ₹ 1 per litre. Formulate the L.P. model for determining the monthly production programme to maximize contribution.

[Delhi U.MBA, 1999, 98]

[Hint: Let x_1, x_2, x_3 and x_4 represent the quantities in kilolitres of Venus, Diana manufactured using company's facilities, Diana manufactured using hired facilities and Aurora respectively. Then the L.P. model is

maximize $Z =$ ₹ $(4{,}000x_1 + 3{,}500x_2 + 2{,}500x_3 + 2{,}000x_4)$,

subject to $0.30x_1 + 0.15x_2 + 0.15x_3 + 0.75x_4 \leq 600$, (special additive constraint)

$\frac{x_1}{2}+\frac{x_2}{3}+\frac{x_4}{5} \leq 100$, (own milling facility constraint)

$\frac{x_3}{3} \leq 40$, (hired milling facility constraint)

$\frac{x_1}{12}+\frac{x_2+x_3}{12}+\frac{x_4}{12} \leq 80$, (packing constraint)

$x_1 \leq 100$, (Venus marketing constraint)

$x_2 + x_3 \leq 400$, (Diana marketing constraint)

and $x_4 \geq 200$, (Aurora marketing constraint)

$x_4 \leq 600$, (Aurora marketing constraint)

x_1, x_2, x_3, x_4, each > 0.

77. A company is producing three chemicals CH–1, CH–2 and CH–3. These chemicals may be produced by any of the four processes P_1, P_2, P_3 and P_4. These processes are using different technology and methods to produce the chemicals CH–1, CH–2 and CH–3. Also these processes are independent of each other. The input requirements of these processes are given below.

Input requirements of processes (units/run)

Input chemical	*A*	*B*	*C*	*D*
Process P_1	8	8	6	2
Process P_2	6	4	3	5
Process P_3	5	5	7	4
Process P_4	3	6	4	8
Price of input/unit (₹)	4	8	6	5
Max. availability (units)	1,000	1,200	1,500	1,400

If a process is run once, the output obtained is as follow :

Output of chemicals by the processes (units/run)

Output chemical	*CH-1*	*CH-2*	*CH-3*	*Process cost/run*
Process P_1	2	3	4	₹ 20
Process P_2	5	2	5	₹ 25
Process P_3	4	6	3	₹ 30
Process P_4	4	4	7	₹ 40
Prices of chemicals (₹/ unit)	40	80	60	
Orders already received	200	300	100	

Formulate a suitable linear programming model to maximize the total profit [*P.U.M.B.A. Feb., 2009*]

[**Hint:** Let the processes P_1, P_2, P_3 and P_4 be run x_1, x_2, x_3 and x_4 times respectively. Then the L.P. model is

$$\text{maximize } Z = ₹ \ [\{40(2x_1+5x_2+4x_3+4x_4)+80(3x_1+2x_2+6x_3+4x_4)+60(4x_1+5x_2+3x_3+7x_4)\}$$
$$-(20x_1+25x_2+30x_3+40x_4)$$
$$-\{4(8x_1+6x_2+5x_3+3x_4)+8(8x_1+4x_2+5x_3+6x_4)+6(6x_1+3x_2+7x_3+4x_4)+5(2x_1+5x_2+4x_3+8x_4)\}]$$
$$= ₹ \ (398x_1+536x_2+668x_3+736x_4),$$

subject to constraints

$$8x_1+6x_2+5x_3+3x_4 \le 1{,}000,$$
$$8x_1+4x_2+5x_3+6x_4 \le 1{,}200,$$
$$6x_1+3x_2+7x_3+4x_4 \le 1{,}500,$$
$$2x_1+5x_2+4x_3+8x_4 \le 1{,}400,$$
$$2x_1+5x_2+4x_3+4x_4 \ge 200,$$
$$3x_1+2x_2+6x_3+4x_4 \ge 300,$$
$$4x_1+5x_2+3x_3+7x_4 \ge 100,$$

where x_1, x_2, x_3, x_4, each ≥ 0.]

2.7 ADVANTAGES OF LINEAR PROGRAMMING METHODS

Following are the main advantages of linear programming methods:

1. It helps in attaining the optimum use of productive factors. Linear programming indicates how a manager can utilize his productive factors most effectively by a better selection and distribution of these elements. For example, more efficient use of manpower and machines can be obtained by the use of linear programming.

2. It improves the quality of decisions. The individual who makes use of linear programming methods becomes more objective than subjective. The individual having a clear picture of the relationships within the basic equations, inequalities or constraints can have a better idea about the problem and its solution.

3. It also helps in providing better tools for adjustments to meet changing conditions. It can go a long way in improving the knowledge and skill of future executives.

4. Most business problems involve constraints like raw materials availability, market demand, etc. which must be taken into consideration. Just because we can produce so many units of products

does not mean that they can be sold. Linear programming can handle such situations also since it allows modification of its mathematical solutions.

5. It highlights the bottlenecks in the production processes. When bottlenecks occur, some machines cannot meet demand while others remain idle, at least part of the time. Highlighting of bottlenecks is one of the most significant advantages of linear programming.

2.8 LIMITATIONS OF LINEAR PROGRAMMING MODEL

This model, though having a wide field, has the following limitations:

1. For large problems having many limitations and constraints, the computational difficulties are enormous, even when assistance of large digital computers is available. The approximations required to reduce such problems to meaningful sizes may yield the final results far different from the exact ones.

2. Another limitation of linear programming is that it may yield fractional valued answers for the decision variables, whereas it may happen that only integer values of the variables are logical. For instance, in finding how many lathes and milling machines to be produced, only integer values of the decision variables, say x_1 and x_2 are meaningful. Except when the variables have large values, rounding the solution values to the nearest integers will not yield an optimal solution. Such situations justify the use of special techniques like integer programming.

3. It is applicable to only static situations since it does not take into account the effect of time. The O.R. team must difine the objective function and constraints which can change due to internal as well as external factors.

4. It assumes that the values of the coefficients of decision variables in the objective function as well as in all the constraints are known with certainty. Since in most of the business situations, the decision variable coefficients are known only probabilistically, it cannot be applied to such situations.

5. In some situations it is not possible to express both the objective function and constraints in linear form. For example, in production planning we often have non-linear constraints on production capacities like setup and takedown times which are often independent of the quantities produced. The misapplication of linear programming under non-linear conditions usually results in an incorrect solution.

6. Linear programming deals with problems that have a single objective. Real life problems may involve multiple and even conflicting objectives. One has to apply goal programming under such situations.

When comparison is made between the advantages and disadvantages/limitations of linear programming, its advantages clearly outweigh its limitations. It must be clearly understood that linear programming techniques, like other mathematical tools only help the manager to take better decisions ; they are in no way a substitute for the manager.

2.9 GRAPHICAL METHOD OF SOLUTION

Once a problem is formulated as mathematical model, the next step is to solve the problem to get the optimal solution. A linear programming problem with only two variables presents a simple case, for which the solution can be derived using a *graphical or geometrical method.* Though, in actual practice such small problems are rarely encountered, the graphical method provides a pictorial representation of the solution process and a great deal of insight into the basic concepts used in solving large L.P. problems. This method consists of the following steps:

1. *Represent the given problem in mathematical form i.e.*, formulate the mathematical model for the given problem.

2. *Draw the* x_1 *and* x_2*-axes.* The non-negativity restrictions $x_1 \geq 0$ and $x_2 \geq 0$ imply that the values of the variables x_1 and x_2 can lie only in the first quadrant. This eliminates a number of infeasible alternatives that lie in 2nd, 3rd and 4th quadrants.

3. *Plot each of the constraint on the graph**. The constraints, whether equations or inequalities are plotted as equations. For each constraint, assign any arbitrary value to one variable and get the value of the other variable. Similarly, assign another arbitrary value to the other variable and find the value of the first variable. Plot these two points and connect them by a straight line. Thus each constraint is plotted as line in the first quadrant.

4. *Identify the feasible region (or solution space) that satisfies all the constraints simultaneously.* For $\geq$ type constraint, the area on or above the constraint line *i.e.*, away from the origin and for $\leq$ type constraint, the area on or below the constraint line *i.e.*, towards origin will be considered. The area common to all the constraints is called feasible region and is shown shaded. Any point on or within the shaded region represents a feasible solution to the given problem. Though a number of infeasible points are eliminated, the feasible region still contains a large number of feasible points. Feasible region is also called *convex polygen*. Which is a convex set formed by the intersection of finite number of closed half-planes.

5. *Use iso-profit (cost) function line approach. For this, plot the objective function* by assuming Z = 0. This will be a line passing through the origin. As the value of Z is increased from zero, the line starts moving to the right, parallel to itself. Draw lines parallel to this line till the line is farthest way from the origin (for a maximization problem). For a minimization problem, the line will be nearest to the origin. The point of the feasible region through which this line passes will be the optimal point. It is possible that this line may coincide with one of the edges of the feasible region. In that case, every point on that edge will give the same maximum/minimum value of the objective function and will be the optimal point.

Alternatively use extrema point enumeration approach. For this, find the co-ordinates of each *extreme point* (or *corner point* or *vertex*) of the feasible region. Find the value of the objective function at each extreme point. The point at which objective function is maximum/minimum is the optimal point and its co-ordinates give the optimal solution.

EXAMPLE 2.9-1

A firm manufactures two products A & B on which the profits earned per unit are ₹ 3 and ₹ 4 respectively. Each product is processed on two machines M_1 and M_2. Product A requires one minute of processing time on M_1 and two minutes on M_2, while B requires one minute on M_1 and one minute on M_2. Machine M_1 is available for not more than 7 hr 30 min while machine M_2 is available for 10 hr during any working day. Find the number of units of products A and B to be manufactured to get maximum profit. [*Madhurai U. M. Com., 1997; P.U.B.E. (Mech.) Nov., 1996*]

Formulation of Linear Programming Model

Let x_1 and x_2 denote the number of units of products *A* and *B* to be produced per day.

Objective is to maximize the profit.

i.e., maximize $Z = 3x_1 + 4x_2$. ... (2.1)

Constraints are on the time available for machines M_1 and M_2.

$$\left.\begin{array}{l} i.e., \text{ for machine } M_1, 1.x_1 + 1x_2 \leq 450, \text{ and} \\ \text{for machine } M_2, 2x_1 + 1.x_2 \leq 600, \end{array}\right] \quad \text{... (2.2)}$$

where $x_1, x_2 \geq 0$. ... (2.3)

Thus the problem is to maximize equation (2.1) subject to relations (2.2) and (2.3). This will be done graphically.

Solution of L.P. Model

The non-negativity restrictions $x_1 \geq 0$ and $x_2 \geq 0$ imply that values of the variables x_1 and x_2 can lie only in the first quadrant (x_1, x_2 plane). This is shown by shaded area of figure 2.2. Other quadrants do not satisfy the non-negativity restrictions and hence the pt. (x_1, x_2) cannot lie in them. Therefore, a number of alternatives are eliminated.

* A constraint involving two variables is also called a *half-plane*. The corresponding equality or a line is known as the boundary of the half-plane.

The effect of the remaining constraints can now be added to figure 2.2. This is done by plotting all the constraints with their inequality sign changed into equality sign. The direction in which each constraint holds good is then determined from the direction of the inequality and is indicated by an arrow on its associated straight line. The constraint conditions define the boundary of the region containing feasible solution.

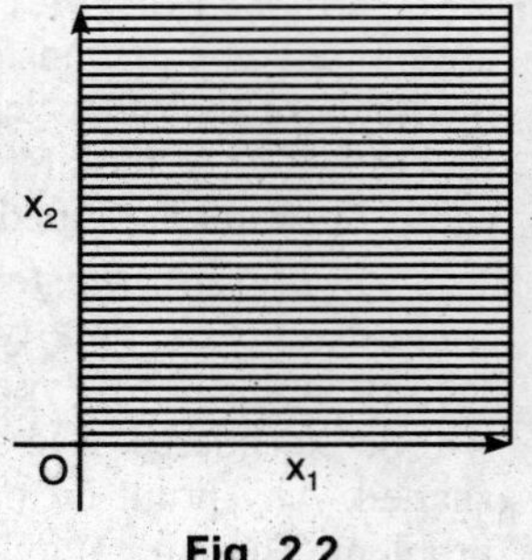

Fig. 2.2

For example, the constraints are $x_1 + x_2 \leq 450$ and $2x_1 + x_2 \leq 600$. We plot line $x_1 + x_2 = 450$ by joining two convenient points, say (0,450) and (450,0) and line $2x_1 + x_2 = 600$ by joining points, say (0,600) and (300,0). Then any point lying on or below the line $x_1 + x_2 = 450$ satisfies the constraint $x_1 + x_2 \leq 450$. Similarly, any point lying on or below the line $2x_1 + x_2 = 600$ satisfies the constraint $2x_1 + x_2 \leq 600$. This is clearly indicated by the direction of arrowheads attached to the lines. The shaded area in figure 2.3 satisfies both the constraints $x_1 + x_2 \leq 450$ and $2x_1 + x_2 = 600$ and also the non-negativity restrictions $x_1 \geq 0, x_2 \geq 0$. This area is called the *solution space* or the *region of feasible solutions*. Any point in this shaded region is a *feasible solution* to the given problem.

To Find Optimal Solution

Method 1: Our problem is to find the point (or points) in the feasible region, which maximizes (or maximize) the objective function (*i.e.*, profit). To do this, we notice that when Z is made zero, equation (2.1) becomes $3x_1 + 4x_2 = 0$ and this is represented by the dotted line AB passing through origin O. Its slope *i.e.*, tangent of the angle with X-axis is (– 3/4) = – 0.75*. As the value of Z is

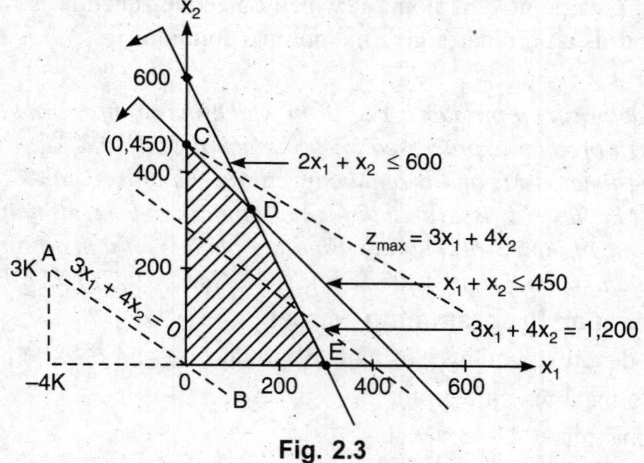

Fig. 2.3

increased from zero, the dotted line AB starts moving to the right, parallel to itself. Greater the value that Z can assume, more will be the company's profit. We go on drawing lines parallel to this line till the line is farthest away from the origin and passes through only one point of the feasible region. This is the point where maxima is attained. It is possible that such a line may be one of the edges of the feasible region. In that case every point on that edge gives the same maximum value of the objective function.

Another method to plot the dotted line for $Z = 3x_1 + 4x_2$ is to put $3x_1 + 4x_2 = 0$, giving $\frac{x_1}{x_2} = \frac{-4}{3}$. We plot 4 units of length on the negative side of the x_1-axis and then 3 units of length along the x_2-axis. The point so obtained when joined with the origin, represents the line $3x_1 + 4x_2 = 0$.

*An easy method to plot the dotted line for the objective function $Z = 3x_1 + 4x_2$ is to assign any value to Z, say $30 \times 40 = 1{,}200$ and to plot the line $3x_1 + 4x_2 = 1{,}200$. A dotted line is then drawn through the origin parallel to this line.

In the present example, maximum is obtained at the corner point C (0,450), which means that only product B should be manufactured and 450 units of this product B should be produced. The daily profit will be Z = ₹ (0 + 4 × 450) = ₹ 1,800. This solution corresponding to point C (0, 450), which maximizes the objective function, is called *optimal solution.*

Method 2: The four vertices of the convex region OCDE are O (0, 0), C (0, 450), D (150, 300) and E (300, 0). Values of the objective function $Z = 3x_1 + 4x_2$ at these vertices are

$$Z(O) = 0,\ Z(C) = 1{,}800,\ Z(D) = 450 + 1{,}200 = 1{,}650,\ Z(E) = 900.$$

Thus the maximum value of Z is ₹ 1,800 and it occurs at the vertex C (0, 450).

Hence the solution to the problem is

$$x_1 = 0,\ x_2 = 450 \text{ and } Z_{max} = ₹\ 1{,}800.$$

Note that coordinates of point D can be found easily by solving $x_1 + x_2 = 450$ and $2x_1 + x_2 = 600$ simultaneously. These equations represent the two constraint lines that intersect at point D.

EXAMPLE 2.9-2

Find the maximum value of

$$Z = 2x_1 + 3x_2,$$

$$\text{subject to } x_1 + x_2 \le 30,$$

$$x_2 \ge 3,$$

$$x_2 \le 12,$$

$$x_1 - x_2 \ge 0,$$

$$0 \le x_1 \le 20.$$

[P.U.B.E. (Mech.) 2012; J.N.T.U. Hyderabad B.Tech. May, 2011; P.T.U. (B.Tech.) 2010, 2001; Nellore M.B.A., 2002]

Solution

The solution space satisfying the given constraints and meeting the non-negativity restrictions $x_1 \ge 0$ and $x_2 \ge 0$ is shown shaded in Fig. 2.4. Any point in this shaded region is a feasible solution to the given problem.

The co-ordinates of the five vertices of the convex region ABCDE are A(3, 3), B(12, 12), C(18, 12), D(20, 10) and E(20, 3).

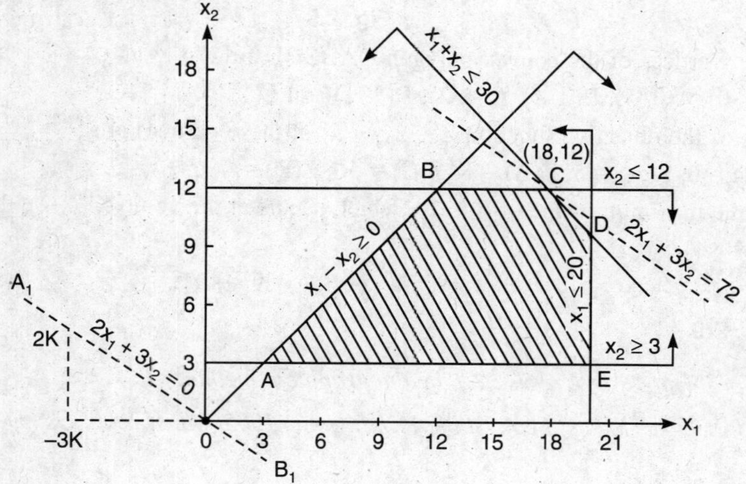

Fig. 2.4

Values of the objective function $Z = 2x_1 + 3x_2$ at these vertices are Z(A) = 15, Z(B) = 60, Z(C) = 72, Z(D) = 70 and Z(E) = 49.

Since the maximum value of Z is 72, which occurs at the point C(18,12), the solution to the given problem is $x_1 = 18$, $x_2 = 12$, $Z_{max} = 72$.

EXAMPLE 2.9-3

$$\text{Maximize } Z = 2x_1 + x_2,$$
$$\text{subject to } x_1 + 2x_2 \leq 10,$$
$$x_1 + x_2 \leq 6,$$
$$x_1 - x_2 \leq 2,$$
$$x_1 - 2x_2 \leq 1,$$
$$x_1, x_2 \geq 0.$$

[Mumbai U. B.Com. April, 2013; Dayalbagh Edu. Inst. Agra Dec., 2006; P.U. B.Com. Sept., 2004]

Solution

The solution space satisfying the given constraints and meeting the non-negativity restrictions $x_1 \geq 0$ and $x_2 \geq 0$ is shown shaded in Fig. 2.5. Any point in this shaded region is a feasible solution to the given problem.

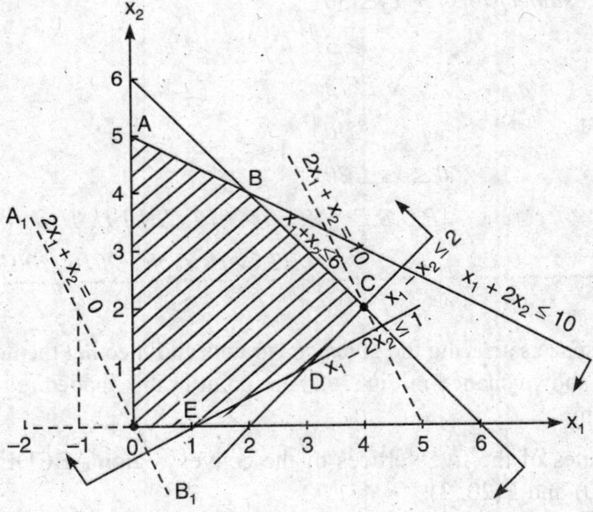

Fig. 2.5

The six vertices of the convex polygon OABCDE are

O(0, 0), A(0, 5), B(2, 4), C(4, 2), D(3, 1) and E(1, 0).

Values of the objective function $Z = 2x_1 + x_2$ at these vertices are

Z(O) = 0, Z(A) = 5, Z(B) = 8, Z(C) = 10, Z(D) = 7, Z(E) = 2.

Since the maximum value of Z is 10, which occurs at the vertex C(4, 2), the solution to the given problem is

$$x_1 = 4, x_2 = 2 \text{ and } Z_{max} = 10.$$

EXAMPLE 2.9-4

Solve problem 18 of exercise 2.1 by the graphical method.

[H.P.U. B.Tech. (Mech.) Sept., 2009; P.U. B.Com., 2005; MBA, 2000; G.N.D.U. B.Com., 2003]

Solution

The L.P. model for the given problem is

$$\text{maximize } Z = 3x_1 + 4x_2,$$

subject to

$$5x_1 + 4x_2 \le 200,$$
$$3x_1 + 5x_2 \le 150,$$
$$5x_1 + 4x_2 \ge 100,$$
$$8x_1 + 4x_2 \ge 80,$$
$$x_1, x_2 \ge 0.$$

The solution space satisfying the given constraints and meeting the non-negativity restrictions $x_1 \ge 0$ and $x_2 \ge 0$ is shown shaded in Fig. 2.6.

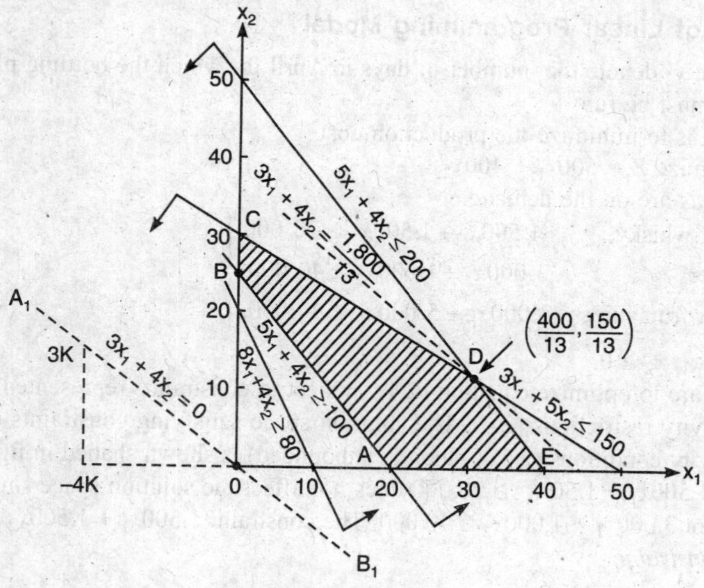

Fig. 2.6

Any point in the shaded region is a feasible solution to the given problem. The co-ordinates of the vertices of this convex region ABCDE are

$$A(20, 0),\ B(0, 25),\ C(0, 30),\ D\left(\frac{400}{13}, \frac{150}{13}\right) \text{ and } E(40, 0).$$

Values of the objective function $Z = 3x_1 + 4x_2$ at these vertices are

$$Z(A) = 60,\ Z(B) = 100,\ Z(C) = 120,\ Z(D) = \frac{1{,}800}{13},\ Z(E) = 120.$$

Since the maximum value of Z is $\frac{1{,}800}{13}$, which occurs at the vertex D $\left(\frac{400}{13}, \frac{150}{13}\right)$, the solution to the given problem is

$$x_1 = \frac{400}{13},\ x_2 = \frac{150}{13} \text{ and } Z_{max} = ₹\ \frac{1{,}800}{13} = ₹\ 138.46.$$

EXAMPLE 2.9-5

Mohan Meakins Breveries Ltd. has two bottling plants, one located at Solan and the other at Mohan Nagar. Each plant produces three drinks, whisky, beer and fruit juices named A, B and C respectively. The number of bottles produced per day are as follows:

	Plant at	
	Solan (S)	*Mohan Nagar (M)*
Whisky, A	*1,500*	*1,500*
Beer, B	*3,000*	*1,000*
Fruit juices, C	*2,000*	*5,000*

A market survey indicates that during the month of April, there will be a demand of 20,000 bottles of whisky, 40,000 bottles of beer and 44,000 bottles of fruit juices. The operating costs per day for plants at Solan and Mohan Nagar are 600 and 400 monetary units. For how many days each plant be run in April so as to minimize the production cost, while still meeting the market demand ? [*P.U.B.E. (Elect.) 2001; Pune U.MBA, 2000*]

Formulation of Linear Programming Model

Let x_1 and x_2 denote the number of days in April for which the bottling plants at Solan and Mohan Nagar must be run.

Objective is to minimize the production cost.

i.e., minimize $Z = 600x_1 + 400x_2$. ... (2.4)

Constraints are on the demand.

$$\left.\begin{array}{ll} \text{i.e., for whisky,} & 1,500x_1 + 1,500x_2 \geq 20,000, \\ \text{for beer,} & 3,000x_1 + 1,000x_2 \geq 40,000, \\ \text{and for fruit juices,} & 2,000x_1 + 5,000x_2 \geq 44,000, \end{array}\right\} \quad \text{... (2.5)}$$

where $x_1, x_2 \geq 0$. ... (2.6)

Thus we are to optimize equation (2.4), subject to constraints represented by relations (2.5) and non-negativity restrictions (2.6). The solution space satisfying constraints (2.5) and meeting the non-negativity conditions (2.6) (which is unbounded) is shown shaded in figure 2.7. Note that the constraint $1,500x_1 + 1,500x_2 \geq 20,000$ does not affect the solution space since it is dominated by the constraint $3,000x_1 + 1,000x_2 \geq 40,000$. The constraint $1,500x_1 + 1,500x_2 \geq 20,000$ is called a *redundant constraint*.

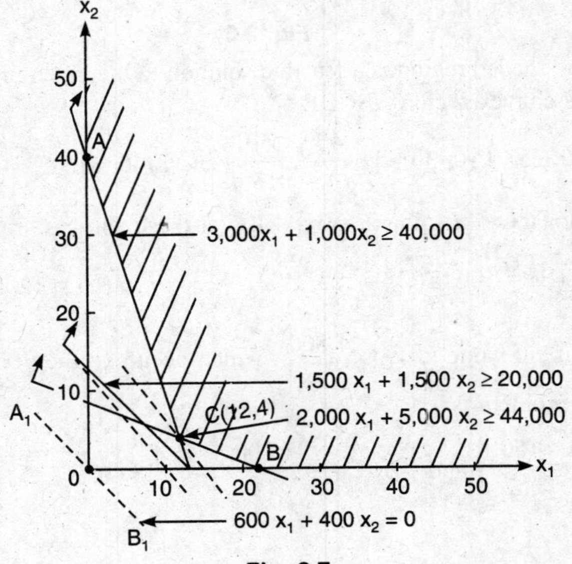

Fig. 2.7

To Find Optimal Solution

Method 1. The objective function, when Z = 0, gives the equation $600x_1 + 400x_2 = 0$ or $x_1/x_2 = -\frac{2}{3}$. The corresponding point (–2, 3) is plotted, which when joined with the origin O gives the dotted line A_1B_1. As Z is increased from zero, the dotted line A_1 B_1 moves to the right, parallel to itself. Since we are interested in minimizing Z, we increase the value of Z till the dotted line passes through the *nearest corner* of the shaded region from the origin. This gives the minimum value of Z, while keeping x_1 and x_2 within the region of feasible solutions. The coordinates of this point C are (12, 4). Thus production cost will be minimum if plants at Solan and Mohan Nagar are run for 12 days and 4 days respectively, giving the production cost as 600 × 12 + 400 × 4 = 7,200 + 1,600 = 8,800 monetary units. Substituting the values of x_1 and x_2 in constraints (2.5) we find that market demand is also met. The coordinates of the point C *i.e.*, the values of x_1 and x_2 can also be found by solving directly the equations $3{,}000x_1 + 1{,}000x_2 = 40{,}000$ and $2{,}000x_1 + 5{,}000x_2 = 44{,}000$ which intersect at that point.

Method 2. The three vertices of the convex set ACB are A(0, 40), B(22, 0) and C(12, 4).
Values of the objective function $Z = 600x_1 + 400x_2$ at these vertices are
Z(A) = 16,000, Z(B) = 13,200 and Z(C) = 7,200 + 1,600 = 8,800.
Thus the minimum value of Z is 8,800 monetary units and it occurs at the vertex C(12, 4).
Hence the solution to the problem is

$$x_1 = 12 \text{ days},$$
$$x_2 = 4 \text{ days},$$
and $$Z_{min} = 8{,}800 \text{ monetary units}.$$

EXAMPLE 2.9-6

Find the minimum value of

$$Z = 5x_1 - 2x_2,$$

subject to $$2x_1 + 3x_2 \geq 1,$$
$$x_1, x_2 \geq 0.$$

[*P.T.U. B.Tech. (Prod.) Nov., 2012*; *Madurai B.E. (Mech.) 1976*]

Solution

The solution space satisfying the given constraint and meeting the non-negativity restrictions $x_1 \geq 0$ and $x_2 \geq 0$ is shown shaded in Fig. 2.8. Any point in the shaded region is a feasible solution to the given problem.

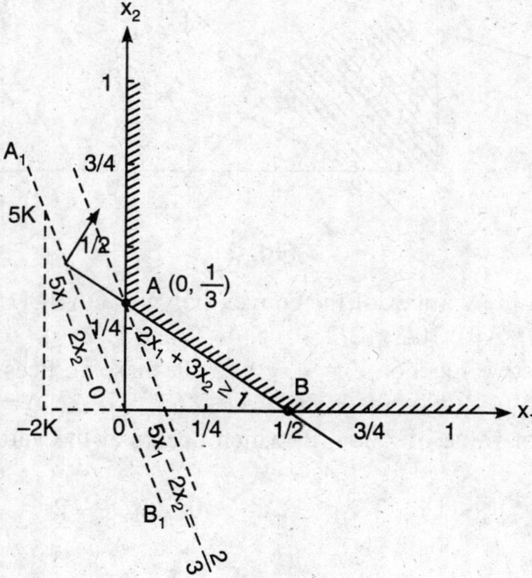

Fig. 2.8

The coordinates of the two vertices of the unbounded convex region are

$$A\left(0, \frac{1}{3}\right) \text{ and } B\left(\frac{1}{2}, 0\right).$$

Values of the objective function $Z = 5x_1 - 2x_2$ at these vertices are

$$Z(A) = -\frac{2}{3}, Z(B) = \frac{5}{2}.$$

Since the minimum value of Z is – 2/3 which occurs at the vertex A(0, 1/3), the solution to the given problem is

$$x_1 = 0, x_2 = \frac{1}{3}, Z_{min} = -\frac{2}{3}.$$

EXAMPLE 2.9-7

Find the minimum value of

$$Z = -x_1 + 2x_2,$$

subject to

$$-x_1 + 3x_2 \leq 10,$$
$$x_1 + x_2 \leq 6,$$
$$x_1 - x_2 \leq 2,$$
$$x_1, x_2 \geq 0.$$

[*Gujarat Tech. U.B.E. Dec., 2012; J.N.T.U. Hyderabad B.Tech. June, 2009; P.U. B.Com. April, 2006, 03*]

Solution

The solution space satisfying the given constraints and meeting the non-negativity restrictions $x_1 \geq 0$, $x_2 \geq 0$ is shown shaded in Fig. 2.9. Any point in this feasible region is a feasible solution to the given problem.

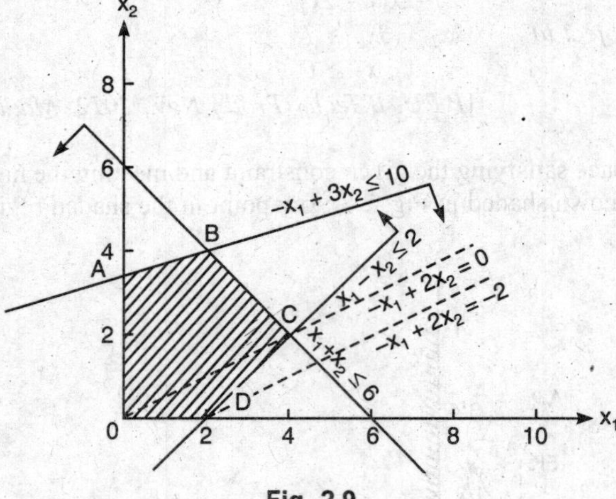

Fig. 2.9

The coordinates of the vertices of the convex polygon OABCD are

O(0, 0), A(0, 10/3), B(2, 4), C(4, 2) and D(2, 0).

Values of the objective function $Z = -x_1 + 2x_2$ at these vertices are

Z(O) = 0, Z(A) = 20/3, Z(B) = 6, Z(C) = 0, Z(D) = – 2.

Since the minimum value of Z is – 2, which occurs at the vertex D(2, 0), the solution to the given problem is

$$x_1 = 2, x_2 = 0, Z_{min} = -2.$$

EXAMPLE 2.9-8

Solve problem 10 of exercise 2.1 by the graphical method.

[P.U. B.Com. April, 2006, 03]

Formulation of L.P. Model

Let x_1 and x_2 denote the number of old hens and young hens that must be bought.

Objective is to maximize the profit per week. Since old hens lay 3 eggs/week and the young ones lay 5 eggs/week, the total number of eggs laid per week is $3x_1 + 5x_2$ which yields earnings/week of ₹ $[0.3(3x_1 + 5x_2)]$. As a hen costs ₹ 1 to be fed, the total cost of feeding the hens per week is ₹ $[1(x_1 + x_2)]$.

Thus the profit earned per week is ₹ $[0.3 (3x_1 + 5x_2) - 1(x_1 + x_2)]$ = ₹ $[- 0.1x_1 + 0.5 x_2]$.

Thus the objective function is

$$\text{maximize } Z = ₹ [- 0.1x_1 + 0.5x_2],$$

where $x_1, x_2 \geq 0$.

Constraints are

on the amount of money available, $2x_1 + 5x_2 \leq 80$,

on the number of hens that can be housed, $x_1 + x_2 \leq 20$,

on the minimum profit to be achieved, $- 0.1x_1 + 0.5x_2 \geq 6$.

Solution

The solution space satisfying the constraints $2x_1 + 5x_2 \leq 80$, $x_1 + x_2 \leq 20$, $- 0.1x_1 + 0.5x_2 \geq 6$ and meeting the non-negativity restrictions $x_1 \geq 0$, $x_2 \geq 0$ is shown shaded in Fig. 2.10.

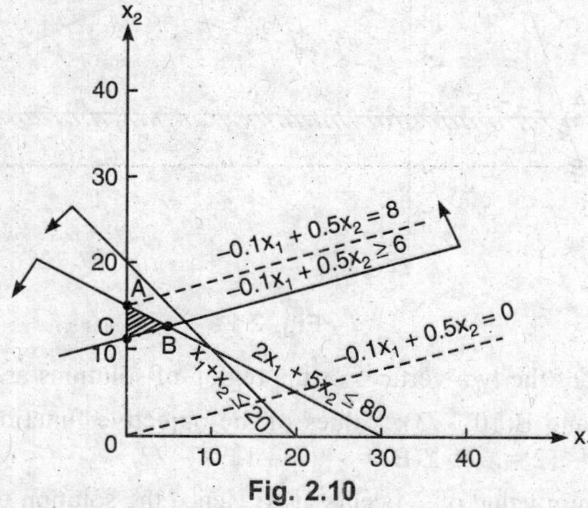

Fig. 2.10

The coordinates of the vertices of the convex polygon ABC are A(0, 16), B(20/3, 40/3) and C(0, 12).

Values of the objective function $Z = - 0.1x_1 + 0.5x_2$ at these vertices are Z(A) = ₹ 8, Z(B) = ₹ [– 2/3 + 20/3] = ₹ 6, Z(C) = ₹ 6.

Since the maximum value of Z is ₹ 8, which occurs at the vertex A(0, 16), the solution to the given problem is

$$x_1 = 0, x_2 = 16, Z_{max} = ₹\ 8.$$

EXAMPLE 2.9-9

Solve the following problem graphically:

$$\textit{Maximize } Z = - x_1 + 4x_2,$$

$$\textit{subject to} \quad - 3x_1 + x_2 \leq 6,$$

$$x_1 + 2x_2 \leq 4,$$
$$x_2 \leq -3,$$

no lower bound constraint for x_1.

[P.T.U. B.E. (Ec. & Comm.) Dec., 2011; B.Tech. (C.Sc.) 2010; H.P.U. B.Tech. (Mech.) June, 2007]

Solution

The third constraint can be rewritten as $-x_2 \geq 3$. The solution space satisfying the constraints is shown shaded in Fig. 2.11.

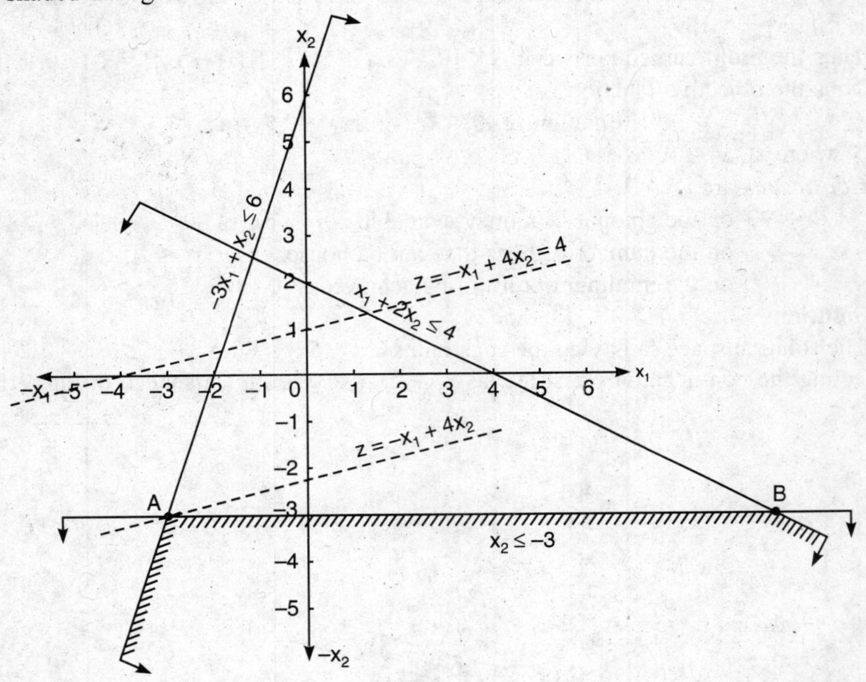

Fig. 2.11

The coordinates of the two vertices of the region of solutions are:

A(– 3, – 3) and B(10, – 3). Values of the objective function $Z = -x_1 + 4x_2$ at these vertices are Z(A) = 3 – 12 = – 9, Z(B) = – 10 – 12 = – 22.

Thus the maximum value of Z occurs at A. Hence the solution to the problem is

$$x_1 = -3, x_2 = -3;\ Z_{max} = -9.$$

EXAMPLE 2.9-10

A local travel agent is planning a charter trip to a major sea resort. The eight day/seven night package includes the fare for round-trip travel, surface transportation, board and lodging and selected tour options. The charter trip is restricted to 200 persons and past experience indicates that there will not be any problem for getting 200 persons. The problem for the travel agent is to determine the number of Deluxe, Standard and Economy tour packages to offer for this charter. These three plans differ according to seating and service for the flight, quality of accommodations, meal plans and tour options. The following table summarizes the estimated prices for the three packages and the corresponding expenses for the travel agent. The travel agent has hired an aircraft for the flat fee of ₹ 2,00,000 for the entire trip.

Tour Plan	*Prices and costs for tour packages per person*		
	Price (₹)	*Hotel costs (₹)*	*Meals & other expenses (₹)*
Deluxe	*10,000*	*3,000*	*4,750*
Standard	*7,000*	*2,200*	*2,500*
Economy	*6,500*	*1,900*	*2,200*

In planning the trip, the following considerations must be taken into account:

(*i*) *At least 10 per cent of the packages must be deluxe type.*

(*ii*) *At least 35 per cent but not more than 70 per cent must be of the standard type.*

(*iii*) *At least 30 per cent must be of the economy type.*

(*iv*) *The maximum number of deluxe packages available in any aircraft is restricted to 60.*

(*v*) *The hotel desires that at least 120 of the tourists should be on the deluxe and standard packages together.*

The travel agent wishes to determine the number of packages to offer in each type so as to maximize the total profit.

(*a*) *Formulate the above as a linear programming problem.*

(*b*) *Restate the above linear programming problem in terms of two decision variables, taking advantage of the fact that 200 packages will be sold.*

(*c*) *Find the optimum solution using graphical method for the restated linear programming problem and interpret your results.* [*Dayalbagh Edu. Inst. Agra MBA, 2005; Delhi U. MBA, 2004*]

Solution

(***a***) Let x_1, x_2 and x_3 represent the number of Deluxe, Standard and Economy tour packages. Then the problem can be expressed as

$$\text{maximize } Z = ₹\ [x_1(10{,}000 - 3{,}000 - 4{,}750) + x_2(7{,}000 - 2{,}200 - 2{,}500) + x_3(6{,}500 - 1{,}900 - 2{,}200) - 2{,}00{,}000]$$
$$= ₹\ (2{,}250x_1 + 2{,}300x_2 + 2{,}400x_3 - 2{,}00{,}000),$$

subject to the following constraints:

(*i*) $\dfrac{x_1}{x_1 + x_2 + x_3} \geq 0.10$ or $9x_1 - x_2 - x_3 \geq 0.$

(*ii*) $\dfrac{x_2}{x_1 + x_2 + x_3} \geq 0.35$ or $-7x_1 + 13x_2 - 7x_3 \geq 0$, and

$\dfrac{x_2}{x_1 + x_2 + x_3} \leq 0.70$ or $-7x_1 + 3x_2 - 7x_3 \leq 0.$

(*iii*) $\dfrac{x_3}{x_1 + x_2 + x_3} \geq 0.30$ or $-3x_1 - 3x_2 + 7x_3 \geq 0.$

(*iv*) $x_1 \leq 60.$

(*v*) $x_1 + x_2 \geq 120$m.

(*vi*) $x_1 + x_2 + x_3 = 200$, where $x_1, x_2, x_3 \geq 0.$

(***b***) $x_3 = 200 - x_1 - x_2$

∴ Objective function is to

$$\text{maximize } Z = ₹\ [2{,}250x_1 + 2{,}300x_2 + 2{,}400\ (200 - x_1 - x_2) - 2{,}00{,}000]$$
$$= ₹\ (-\ 150x_1 - 100x_2 + 2{,}80{,}000).$$

The constraints can be expressed as

(*i*) $9x_1 - x_2 - (200 - x_1 - x_2) \geq 0$ or $x_1 \geq 20.$

(*ii*) $-7x_1 + 13x_2 - 7(200 - x_1 - x_2) \geq 0$ or $x_2 \geq 70$, and
$-7x_1 + 3x_2 - 7(200 - x_1 - x_2) \leq 0$ or $x_2 \leq 140$.
(*iii*) $-3x_1 - 3x_2 + 7(200 - x_1 - x_2) \geq 0$ or $x_1 + x_2 \leq 140$.
(*iv*) $x_1 \leq 60$.
(*v*) $x_1 + x_2 \geq 120$.

(c) The region of feasible solutions satisfying all the above constraints and meeting the non-negativity restrictions is shown shaded in Fig. 2.12. The coordinates of the vertices of the closed polygon ABCDE are

A(20, 100), B(20, 120), C(60, 80), D(60, 70) and E(50, 70).

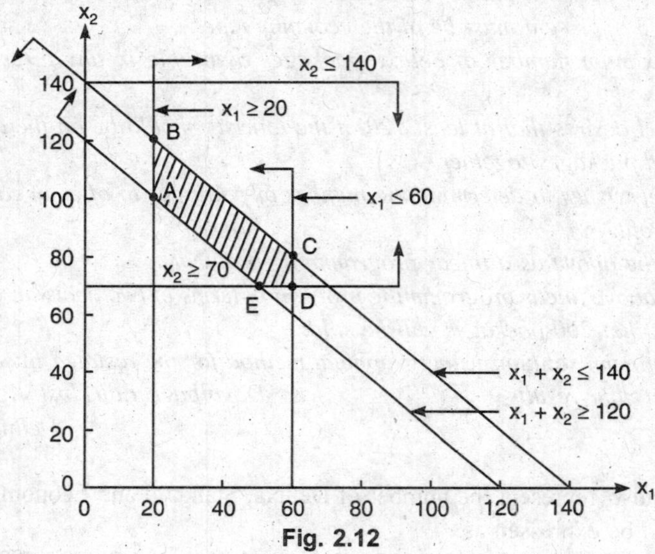

Fig. 2.12

Values of the objective function at these vertices are

Z_A = ₹ (– 150 × 20 – 100 × 100 + 2,80,000) = ₹ 2,67,000,
Z_B = ₹ (– 150 × 20 – 100 × 120 + 2,80,000) = ₹ 2,65,000,
Z_C = ₹ (– 150 × 60 – 100 × 80 + 2,80,000) = ₹ 2,63,000,
Z_D = ₹ (– 150 × 60 – 100 × 70 + 2,80,000) = ₹ 2,64,000,
and Z_E = ₹ (– 150 × 50 – 100 × 70 + 2,80,000) = ₹ 2,65,500.

∴ A(20, 100) is the optimal point which means that the number of Deluxe, Standard and Economy packages should be 20, 100 and 80 respectively to earn maximum profit of ₹ 2,67,000.

EXAMPLE 2.9-11

The standard weight of a special purpose brick is 5 kg and it contains two basic ingredients B_1 and B_2. B_1 costs ₹ 5/kg and B_2 costs ₹ 8/kg. Strength considerations dictate that the brick contains not more than 4 kg of B_1 and a minimum of 2 kg of B_2. Since the demand for the product is likely to be related to the price of the brick, find graphically the minimum cost of the brick satisfying the above conditions. [*P.T.U. MBA, Feb., 2011*]

Formulation of L.P. Model

Let the quantities in kg of ingredients B_1 and B_2 to be used to make the bricks be x_1 and x_2 respectively.

Objective is to minimize the cost of the brick.

i.e., minimize $Z = 5x_1 + 8x_2$.

Constraints are

on the quantity of ingredient B_1 : $x_1 \leq 4$,

on the quantity of ingredient B_2 : $x_2 \geq 2$,
on the weight of the brick : $x_1 + x_2 = 5$,
where $x_1, x_2 \geq 0$.

Solution

The given constraints are plotted in Fig. 2.13. *Since the third constraint is an equality constraint, the feasible region reduces to a line AB which has extreme points A(3, 2) and B(0, 5).*

Values of the objective function $Z = 5x_1 + 8x_2$ at these points are

$$Z(A) = 15 + 16 = 31,$$
$$Z(B) = 0 + 40 = 40.$$

Since the minimum value of Z is ₹ 31 which occurs at the point A(3, 2), the solution to the given problem is

$$x_1 = 3 \text{ kg},$$
$$x_2 = 2 \text{ kg},$$
$$Z_{min} = ₹\ 31.$$

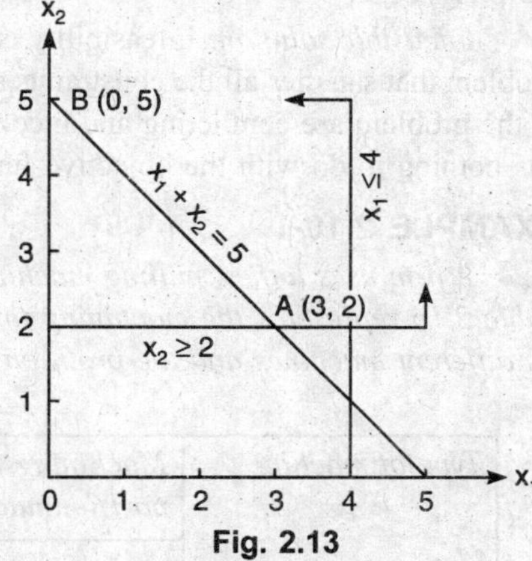

Fig. 2.13

The above examples indicate that the search for the optimum is reduced to finding *only the vertices* (corner points) of the solution space. Mathematically, a corner point is known as an *extreme point.* Once all the extreme points are known, the one that gives the best value of the objective function is the optimum. Sections 2.13 and 2.16 show that the *simplex method* consists of determining some of these vertices (extreme points) in a selective manner.

2.10 SOME EXCEPTIONAL CASES

In section 2.9 we discussed a number of linear programming problems and optimal solution for each of them was unique. This was because the objective function line passed only through the extreme point located at the intersection of the two constraint lines (half planes). However, it may not be so for every problem. In general, a linear programming problem may have

(*i*) a definite and unique optimal solution,
(*ii*) an infinite number of optimal solutions (multiple optimal solutions),
(*iii*) an unbounded solution,
(*iv*) no feasible solution (infeasible solution), and
(*v*) a single solution.

The first case was covered in the previous section. A few examples are presented here to cover the remaining cases.

Multiple optimal solutions: A L.P. problem may have the same optimal value of the objective function at more than one extreme point. For this, two conditions must be satisfied:

(*i*) The objective function, when plotted, should be parallel to a constraint that forms the boundary (edge) of the feasible region. In other words, the slope of the objective function is same as that of one of the *binding constraints*. A constraint is said to be *binding* or *active* if at optimality, left-hand side of the constraint equals right-hand side. *Such a constraint passes through one of the extreme points of the feasible region, which is the optimal point.* If the coordinates of the optimal point are substituted in the constraint and L.H.S. = R.H.S., then the constraint is a binding constraint.

(*ii*) The constraint should form a boundary of the feasible region in the direction of the optimal movement of the objective function line *i.e.*, the constraint should be an active constraint.

Unbounded solution: It exists when an L.P. problem has no limit on the constraints *i.e.*, the feasible region is not bounded in any respect. Variables x_1 and/or x_2 can have any value in the unbounded feasible region and theoretically, their value/values can increase to infinity. Value of the objective function may be finite or infinite. When it is infinite, the problem is said to have unbounded solution. *Unboundedness of the solution indicates that the problem has not been properly formulated. One or more of constraints have been inadvertently ignored while formulating the L.P. model.*

Infeasible solution: Infeasibility is a condition that exists when there is no solution to an L.P. problem that satisfies all the constraints and non-negativity restrictions. It means that the constraints in the problem are conflicting and inconsistent. Infeasibility depends solely on the constraints and has nothing to do with the objective function.

EXAMPLE 2.10-1

A firm uses lathes, milling machines and grinding machines to produce two machine parts. Table 2.16 represents the machining times required for each part, the machining times available on different machines and the profit on each machine part.

Table 2.16

Type of machine	*Machining time required for the machine part (minutes)*		*Maximum time available per week (minutes)*
	I	*II*	
Lathes	*12*	*6*	*3,000*
Milling machines	*4*	*10*	*2,000*
Grinding machines	*2*	*3*	*900*
Profit per unit	*₹ 40*	*₹ 100*	

Find the number of parts I and II to be manufatured per week to maximize the profit.

[*H.P.U. B.Tech. (Mech.) Nov., 2014*]

Formulation of Linear Programming Model

Let the number of parts I and II to be manufactured per week be x_1 and x_2 respectively.

Objective is to maximize the profit.

i.e., maximize $Z = 40x_1 + 100x_2$, ... (2.7)

where $x_1, x_2 \geq 0$. ... (2.8)

Constraints are on the time available on each machine.

$$\left.\begin{aligned} &\text{Thus for lathes,} && 12x_1 + 6x_2 \leq 3,000, \\ &\text{for milling machines,} && 4x_1 + 10x_2 \leq 2,000, \\ &\text{and for grinding machines,} && 2x_1 + 3x_2 \leq 900. \end{aligned}\right] \quad \text{... (2.9)}$$

Thus the problem is to determine the values of x_1 and x_2 which meet the non-negativity conditions (2.8), satisfy the constraints (2.9) and maximize equation (2.7).

Solution of L.P. Model

The solution space satisfying the constraints (2.9) and meeting the non-negativity conditions (2.8) is shown shaded in Fig. 2.14. Note that the constraint $2x_1 + 3x_2 \leq 900$ does not affect the solution space and is, thus, *a redundant constraint*.

The four vertices of the convex set OABC are O(0, 0), A(0, 200), B(187.5, 125), C(250, 0). Values of the objective function $Z = 40x_1 + 100x_2$ at these vertices are

Z(O) = 0, Z(A) = 20,000, Z(B) = 20,000, Z(C) = 10,000.

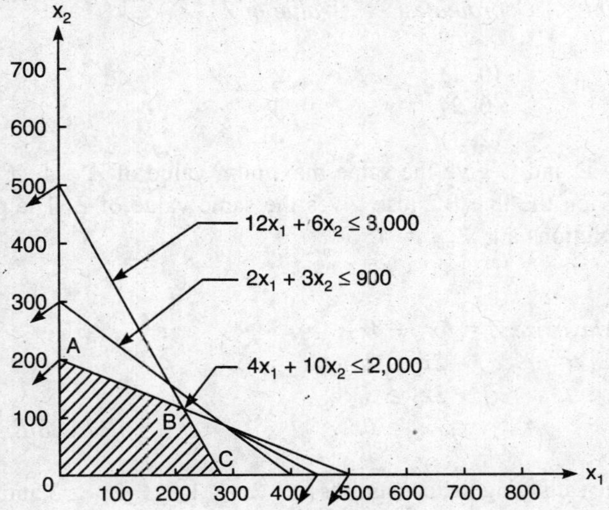

Fig. 2.14

Thus maximum value of Z occurs at two vertices A and B of the convex shaded region OABC.

∴ The two points A and B give the maximum value of Z. It follows that every linear convex combination of these points will also give the same maximum value of Z. Therefore, there is no unique optimal solution to the problem *i.e.*, the problem has multiple optimal solutions and any point between A and B on the line AB can be taken as an optimal solution with a profit value of ₹ 20,000.

EXAMPLE 2.10-2

Solve the following problem graphically:

$$\text{Max } Z = -x_1 + 2x_2,$$

$$\text{subject to} \quad x_1 - x_2 \le -1,$$

$$-0.5x_1 + x_2 \le 2,$$

$$x_1, x_2 \ge 0.$$

[*H.P.U. B.Tech. (Mech.) June, 2015; P.T.U. B.Com. Dec., 2011; P.U.B.Com. April, 2007; Sept., 2006; B.E. (C.S. and E.) Dec., 2004*]

Solution

R.H.S. of the first constraint is negative. Multiplying both sides of the constraint by – 1, it takes the form

$$-x_1 + x_2 \ge 1.$$

The solution space satisfying the constraints and meeting the non-negativity restrictions is shown shaded in Fig. 2.15.

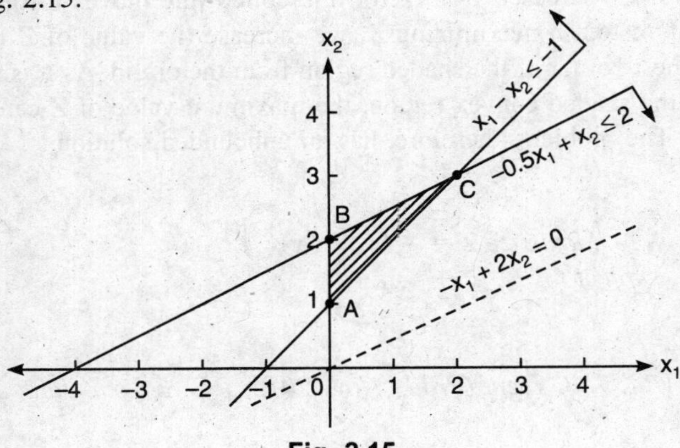

Fig. 2.15

Values of the objective function at the vertices of the closed region ABC are

Extreme Point (Vertex)	*Coordinates*	*Value of Z*
A	(0, 1)	2
B	(0, 2)	4
C	(2, 3)	4

Thus both points B and C give the same maximum value of Z = 4. It follows that every point between B and C on the line BC also gives the same value of Z. The problem, therefore, has multiple optimal solutions and $Z_{max} = 4$.

EXAMPLE 2.10-3

$$\text{Maximize } Z = 5x_1 + 4x_2,$$
$$\text{subject to} \quad x_1 - 2x_2 \leq 1,$$
$$x_1 + 2x_2 \geq 3,$$
$$x_1, x_2 \geq 0.$$

[P.T.U.B.E. April, 2013; 2001]

Solution

The solution space satisfying the constraints $x_1 - 2x_2 \leq 1$, $x_1 + 2x_2 \geq 3$ and the non-negativity conditions $x_1 \geq 0$, $x_2 \geq 0$ is shown shaded in Fig. 2.16. This shaded convex region is unbounded.

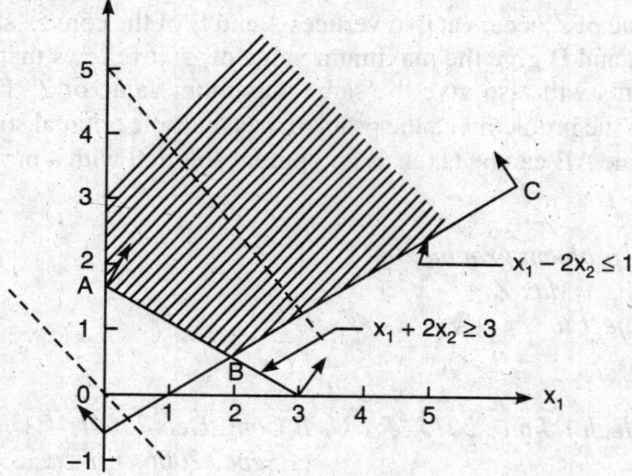

Fig. 2.16

The objective function, when Z = 0, gives the equation $5x_1 + 4x_2 = 0$, or $\frac{x_1}{x_2} = -\frac{4}{5}$. The corresponding point (–4, 5) is plotted, which when joined with origin, gives the plot of the dotted line $5x_1 + 4x_2 = 0$. As Z is increased from zero, this dotted line moves to the right, parallel to itself. Since we are interested in maximizing Z, we increase the value of Z till the dotted line passes through the farthest corner of the shaded region from the origin. As it is not possible to get the farthest corner for the shaded convex region, the maximum value of Z cannot be found as it occurs at infinity only. The problem, therefore, has an unbounded solution.

EXAMPLE 2.10-4

$$\text{Maximize } Z = -4x_1 + 3x_2,$$
$$\text{subject to} \quad x_1 - x_2 \leq 0,$$
$$x_1 \leq 4,$$
$$x_1, x_2 \geq 0.$$

[P.T.U. B. Tech. (Prod.) Nov., 2012; P.U. B.Com. Jan., 2005; Sept., 2005]

Solution

The solution space satisfying the constraints $x_1 - x_2 \leq 0, x_1 \leq 4$ and meeting the non-negativity restrictions $x_1 \geq 0, x_2 \geq 0$ is shown shaded in Fig. 2.17. *The line $x_1 - x_2 = 0$ is drawn by joining points (0, 0) and say (1, 1). This line has a slope of 45° and since $x_1 - x_2 \leq 0$ i.e., $x_1 \leq x_2$, the arrowhead associated with the line is in the upward direction.*

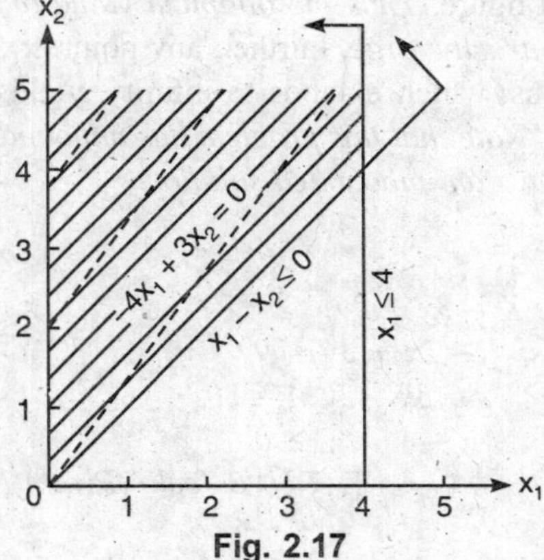

Fig. 2.17

To plot the line Z = $-4x_1 + 3x_2$, we assume Z = 0, giving $-4x_1 + 3x_2 = 0$ or $\frac{x_1}{x_2} = \frac{3}{4}$. The corresponding point (3, 4) is obtained, which when joined with origin, represents the dotted line $-4x_1 + 3x_2 = 0$. Lines are then drawn parallel to this line for increasing value of Z. Clearly, Z can be made large arbitrarily and the problem has no finite maximum value of Z.

The problem, therefore, has an unbounded solution. *Value of variable x_1 is limited to 4, while value of variable x_2 can be increased indefinitely.*

EXAMPLE 2.10-5

$$\text{Maximize } Z = -x_1 + 4x_2,$$
$$\text{subject to} \quad 3x_1 - x_2 \geq -3,$$
$$-0.3x_1 + 1.2x_2 \leq 3,$$
$$x_1, x_2 \geq 0.$$

Solution

The solution space satisfying the constraints $3x_1 - x_2 \geq -3$, $-0.3x_1 + 1.2x_2 \leq 3$ and meeting the non-negativity restrictions $x_1 \geq 0, x_2 \geq 0$ is shown shaded in Fig. 2.18.

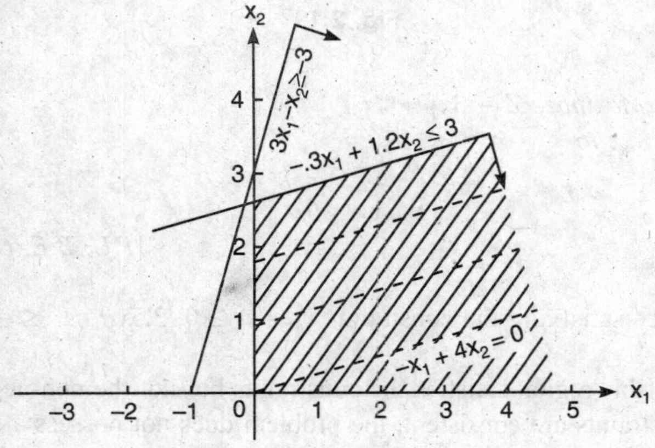

Fig. 2.18

Note that since the first constraint is $3x_1 - x_2 \geq -3$ (R.H.S. is negative), the direction of the arrowhead associated with this line is towards the origin.

For Z = 0, the objective function becomes $-x_1 + 4x_2 = 0$, which yields $x_1/x_2 = 4/1$. Thus the dotted line passing through origin O(0, 0) and the point (4, 1) represents $-x_1 + 4x_2 = 0$. The value of Z can be increased by drawing lines parallel to this line and the maximum value is limited by the upper edge of the shaded figure. *Thus the optimum value of Z is 10. However, values of variables x_1, x_2 can be made arbitrarily large.* Further, any point (x_1, x_2) lying on the upper edge of the region of feasible solutions, which extends to infinity, yields the same optimal value of Z = 10 for the objective function. *Note that this problem has unbounded feasible region. But since value of Z is finite, it does not have an unbounded solution.*

EXAMPLE 2.10-6

$$\text{Maximize } Z = 3x + 2y,$$
$$\text{subject to} \quad -2x + 3y \leq 9,$$
$$3x - 2y \leq -20,$$
$$x, y \geq 0.$$

[P.T.U. B.Tech. (Prod.) Nov. 2012; MBA May, 2002]

Solution

Fig. 2.19 indicates two shaded regions, one satisfying the constraint $-2x + 3y \leq 9$ and the other satisfying the constraint $3x - 2y \leq -20$. These two shaded regions in the first quadrant do not overlap with the result that there is no point (*x*, *y*) common to both the shaded regions. The problem cannot be solved graphically (or by any other method of solving L.P. problems) *i.e.*, the feasible solution to the problem does not exist or the problem has infeasible solution.

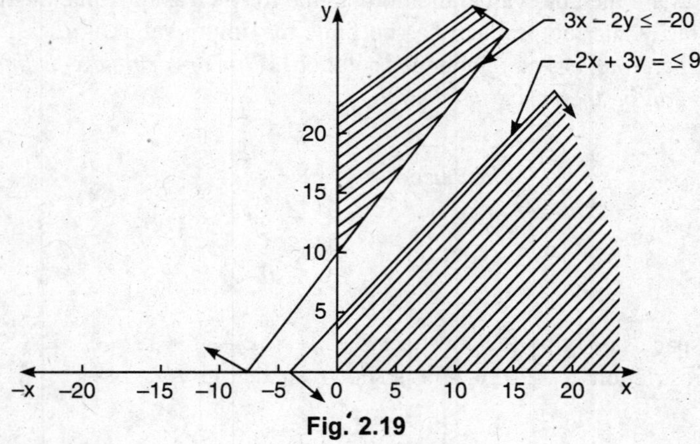

Fig. 2.19

EXAMPLE 2.10-7

$$\text{Maximize } Z = 3x_1 + 4x_2,$$
$$\text{subject to} \quad x_1 - x_2 \geq 0,$$
$$2.5x_1 - x_2 \leq -3,$$
$$x_1, x_2 \geq 0.$$

[P.U. B.E. (Mech.) Dec., 1982]

Solution

The solution space satisfying the constraints $x_1 - x_2 \geq 0$, $2.5x_1 - x_2 \leq -3$ is shown shaded in Fig. 2.20.

Any point within this region satisfies the constraints but not the non-negativity restrictions. Thus although the constraints are consistent, the problem does not possess a feasible solution.

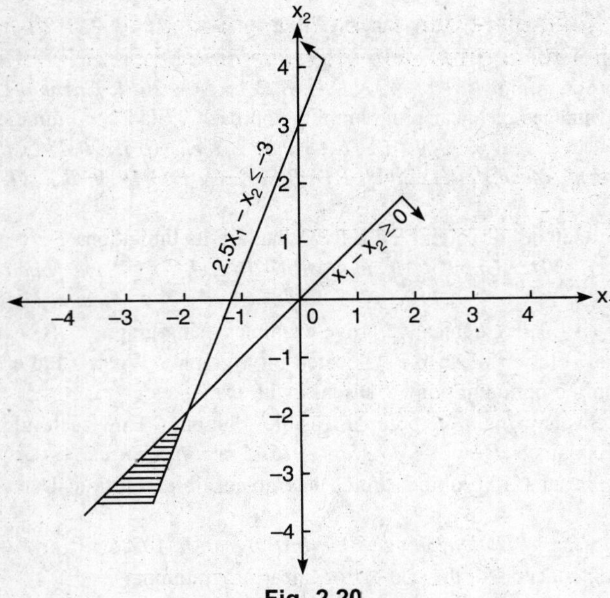

Fig. 2.20

EXAMPLE 2.10-8

$$\begin{aligned} \textit{Maximize } Z &= 5x_1 + 8x_2, \\ \textit{subject to } \quad 3x_1 + 5x_2 &= 18, \\ 5x_1 + 3x_2 &= 14, \\ x_1, x_2 &\geq 0. \end{aligned}$$

Solution

Fig. 2.21 shows the graphical solution. The feasible region reduces to the point A (1, 3). Thus *the problem has just a single solution*

$$x_1 = 1, x_2 = 3, Z = 5 + 24 = 29.$$

As there is nothing to be maximized, such a problem is not of much intrest from point of view of operations research.

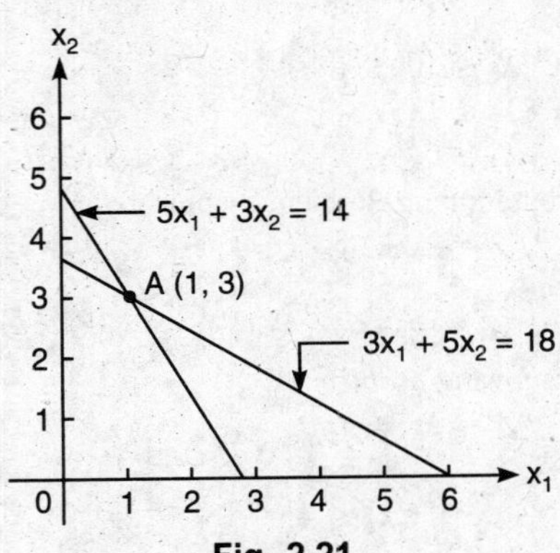

Fig. 2.21

Evidently, there were two variables x_1 and x_2 in the above examples and the problems were, therefore, two-dimensional and were simple to be represented (by the two axes lying in a plane) and solved graphically. Now, as the number of variables increases to 3, 4, ... we come across 3-dimensional, 4-dimensional, . . problems which become quite laborious to be solved by graphical methods. In such cases *simplex technique* helps us in

(*i*) starting with a feasible solution,

(*ii*) searching optimal solution in a systematic way.

EXERCISES 2.2

1. (*a*) What is linear programming ? (*G.N.D.U. B.Com. Nov. 2014; Chennai U. B.B.A. Nov., 2010*]
(*b*) What are the advantages of linear programming approach ? State the limitations of L.P.
[*J.N.T.U. Hyderabad B.Tech. April, 2011; Delhi U. M.Com., 2007; P.T.U. B.Tech. (Mech.) 2011; 2008; P.U. B.E. (E. & Ec.) 1999; B.E. (T. & I.T.) Nov., 2004 ; BBA, 2005*]
2. Explain the 'graphic method' of solving an L.P.P. What are its limitations ?
[*B.P.U.T., 2012; Univ. of Mumbai MBA, 2012; J.N.T.U. Hyderabad B. Tech. May, 2011; Chennai Univ. B.B.A. Nov., 2010*]
3. How will you solve an L.P.P. graphically ? Give examples using graph. [*G.N.D.U. B.Com., 1995*]
4. Where is the optimal solution of an L.P.P. located on a graph ? What is the effect of changing the objective function on the optimum point ? Discuss with examples.
5. Why do some problems have multiple optimal feasible solutions ? How such information is useful for decision-making ? Explain. [*P.U. UIAMS May, 2015; Dayal bagh Edu. Inst. Agra MBA Dec., 2014*]
6. Explain with example an L.P. problem which has no feasible solution. Use graphical method to explain.
[*G.N.D.U. B.Com., Sept. 2011; Dayalbagh Edu. Inst. Agra MBA Dec. 2014; P.U.B.E. (Mech.) 2000*]
7. Explain the following concepts in the context of linear programming:
(*i*) Objective function (*ii*) Convex polygon
(*iii*) Redundant constraint [*IGNOU M.C.A., 2003*]
8. What do you mean by infeasibility and unboundedness in linear programming ? Illustrate graphically.
[*P.U. UIAMS MBA May, 2015; Dayalbagh Edu. Inst. Agra MBA Dec., 2014; G.N.D.U. B.Com. Sept. 2012; April 2012; Gujarat Tech. U.B.E. Dec., 2012; P.T.U. MBA, 2014; 2008*]
9. Describe the complete procedure of finding graphical solution of an L.P.P. What do you understand by 'convex region'? Discuss one special case in the graphical solution of such a problem.
[*Gujarat Tech. U. MBA Dec., 2010*]
10. Explain the conditions of inconsistency and redundancy in L.P.P.
[*G.N.D.U. B.Com. Nov., 2014; V.T.U. Karnataka B.E. June, 2012*]
11. Solve the following L.P. problem :
Maximize $Z = 5X_1 + 2X_2$,
subject to
$2X_1 + 7X_2 \leq 100$,
$3X_1 + 8X_2 \leq 135$,
and $X_1, X_2 \geq 0$. [*J.N.T.U. Hyderabad B.Tech. May, 2009*]
12. Solve the following Linear Programming Problem graphically:
Maximize $Z = 2x + 3y$,
subject to the constraints
$x + 2y \leq 10,\ 2x + y \leq 14,\ x, y \geq 0$. [*Kuru. U. B.E. (Mech.) June, 2012*]

Use graphical method to solve the following problems :

13. Maximize $Z = 2x_1 + 3x_2$,
subject to constraints $x_1 + x_2 \leq 1$,
$3x_1 + x_2 \leq 4$,
$x_1, x_2 \geq 0$.
[*Meerut B.Sc. (Math.) 1970*]
(*Ans.* $x_1 = 0, x_2 = 1$; $Z_{max} = 3$.)
14. Maximize $Z = 5x_1 + 3x_2$,
subject to $3x_1 + 5x_2 \leq 15$,
$5x_1 + 2x_2 \leq 10$,
$x_1, x_2 \geq 0$. [*B.P.U.T., 2010; G.N.D.U. B.Com; Sept., 2006*]
$\left(Ans.\ x_1 = \frac{20}{19}, x_2 = \frac{45}{19}; Z_{max} = \frac{235}{19}. \right)$

15. Maximize $Z = 6x_1 + 8x_2,$
subject to
$$5x_1 + 10x_2 \le 60,$$
$$4x_1 + 4x_2 \le 40,$$
$$x_1, x_2 \ge 0.$$
[Chennai U.B.C.A. Nov., 2010]
(*Ans.* $x_1 = 8, x_2 = 2; Z_{max} = 64.$

16. Maximize $Z = 5x_1 + 3x_2,$
subject to
$$x_1 + x_2 \le 6,$$
$$0 \le x_1 \le 3,$$
$$0 \le x_2 \le 3,$$
$$2x_1 + 3x_2 \ge 3.$$
[P.T.U. BCA, 2010]
(*Ans.* $x_1 = 3, x_2 = 3; Z_{max} = 24.$)

17. Minimize $Z = 20x_1 + 10x_2,$
subject to
$$x_1 + 2x_2 \le 40,$$
$$3x_1 + x_2 \ge 30,$$
$$4x_1 + 3x_2 \ge 60,$$
$$x_1, x_2 \ge 0.$$
[J.N.T.U. MBA June, 2012; G.N.D.U. B.Com. Sept., 2012; V.T.U. Karnataka B.E. Dec., 2011; P.U. M.B.A., 2003]
(*Ans.* $x_1 = 6, x_2 = 12; Z_{min} = 240.$)

18. Maximize $Z = x_1 + \frac{x_2}{2},$
subject to
$$3x_1 + 2x_2 \le 12,$$
$$5x_1 \le 10,$$
$$x_1 + x_2 \le 8,$$
$$-x_1 + x_2 \ge 4,$$
$$x_1, x_2 \ge 0.$$
[P.U.B.E. (Mech.) Nov., 1979]
(*Ans.* $x_1 = 0.8, x_2 = 4.8; Z_{max} = 3.2.$)

19. Minimize $Z = 60x + 40y,$
subject to
$$30x + 10y \ge 240,$$
$$10x + 10y \ge 160,$$
$$20x + 60y \ge 480,$$
$$x, y \ge 0.$$
[P.U. B. Com., 2006]
(*Ans.* $x = 4, y = 12; Z_{min} = 720.$)

20. Minimize $Z = 4x_1 + x_2,$
subject to
$$3x_1 + 4x_2 \ge 20,$$
$$-x_1 - 5x_2 \le -15,$$
$$x_1, x_2 \ge 0.$$
[P.U. B. Com., 2006]
(*Ans.* $x_1 = 0, x_2 = 5; Z_{min} = 5.$)

21. Minimize $Z = 3x_1 + 2x_2,$
subject to
$$8x_1 + x_2 \ge 8,$$
$$2x_1 + x_2 \ge 6,$$
$$x_1 + 3x_2 \ge 6,$$
$$x_1 + 6x_2 \ge 8,$$
$$x_1, x_2 \ge 0.$$
[P.U. B.E. (Mech.) Dec., 1985]
(*Ans.* $x_1 = 2.4, x_2 = 1.2; Z_{min} = 9.6.$)

22. Maximize $Z = 3x + 9y,$
subject to
$$x + 4y \le 8,$$
$$x + 2y \le 4,$$
$$x, y \ge 0.$$
[Nagpur Univ. B.E., 2003]
(*Ans.* $x = 0, y = 2; Z_{max} = 18.$)

23. Maximize $Z = 6x_1 + 4x_2,$
subject to
$$2x_1 + 3x_2 \geq 30,$$
$$3x_1 + 2x_2 \leq 24,$$
$$x_1 + x_2 \geq 3,$$
$$x_1, x_2 \geq 0.$$

[*P.U.B.Com., 2002*]
(*Ans.* $x_1 = 12/5$, $x_2 = 42/5$; $Z_{max} = 48$.)

24. Maximize $Z = 2x_1 + x_2,$
subject to
$$x_1 + 2x_2 \leq 10,$$
$$x_1 + x_2 \leq 6,$$
$$x_1 - x_2 \leq 2,$$
$$x_1 - 2x_2 \leq 1,$$
$$x_1, x_2 \geq 0.$$

[*P.U.B.Com., 2002*]
(*Ans.* $x_1 = 4$, $x_2 = 2$; $Z_{max} = 10$.)

25. Minimize $Z = 5x_1 + 6x_2,$
subject to
$$2x_1 + 5x_2 \geq 1{,}500,$$
$$3x_1 + x_2 \geq 1{,}200,$$
where
$$x_1, x_2 \geq 0.$$

[*G.N.D.U. B.Com., Sept., 2009; P.U.B.B.A., 2001*]
$$\left(Ans.\ x_1 = \frac{4{,}500}{13},\ x_2 = \frac{2{,}100}{13};\ Z_{min} = \frac{35{,}100}{13}.\right)$$

26. Maximize $Z = -150x_1 - 100x_2 + 2{,}80{,}000,$
subject to
$$20 \leq x_1 \leq 60,$$
$$70 \leq x_2 \leq 140,$$
$$120 \leq x_1 + x_2 \leq 140,$$
$$x_1, x_2 \geq 0.$$

[*P.U.B. Com., 2000*]
(*Ans.* $x_1 = 20$, $x_2 = 100$, $Z_{max} = 2{,}67{,}000$.)

27. Maximize $Z = 3x_1 + 2x_2,$
subject to
$$2x_1 + x_2 \leq 10,$$
$$x_1 + 3x_2 \leq 6,$$
$$x_1, x_2 \geq 0.$$

[*P.U.B. Com., 1999*]
$$\left(Ans.\ x_1 = \frac{24}{5},\ x_2 = \frac{2}{5};\ Z_{max} = \frac{76}{5}.\right)$$

28. Maximize $Z = 3x_1 + 2x_2,$
subject to
$$-2x_1 + x_2 \leq 1,$$
$$x_1 \leq 2,$$
$$x_1 + x_2 \leq 3,$$
$$x_1, x_2 \geq 0.$$

[*Pbi.U. MCA, 2001*]
(*Ans.* $x_1 = 2$, $x_2 = 1$; $Z_{max} = 8$.)

29. (*a*) Minimize $Z = 2x_1 + x_2,$
(*b*) Maximize $Z = 2x_1 + 3x_2,$
constraints are
$$x_1 - 3x_2 \leq 6,$$

$$2x_1 + 4x_2 \geq 8,$$
$$x_1 - 3x_2 \geq -6,$$
$$x_1, x_2 \geq 0.$$

[*P.U.B.E. (Elect.) 2001*]

(*Ans.* (*a*) $x_1 = 0$, $x_2 = 2$; $Z_{min} = 2$, (*b*) Unbounded.)

30. Maximize $Z = 80x_1 + 120x_2$,
subject to
$$x_1 + x_2 \leq 9,$$
$$20x_1 + 50x_2 \leq 360,$$
$$x_1 \geq 2,$$
$$x_2 \geq 3,$$
$$x_1, x_2 \geq 0.$$

[*M.G.U. Kerala M.Com. June, 2010; P.U.B.Com. April, 2003*]

(*Ans.* $x_1 = 3$, $x_2 = 6$; $Z_{max} = 960$.)

31. Consider the following L.P.P. graphically:
Maximize $Z = 50x_1 + 60x_2$,
subject to
$$2x_1 + 3x_2 \leq 1{,}500,$$
$$3x_1 + 2x_2 \leq 1{,}500,$$
$$x_1 \leq 400,$$
$$x_2 \leq 400,$$
$$2x_1 \leq 3x_2,$$
$$x_1, x_2 \geq 0.$$

(*i*) Construct the constraint lines on the graph.
(*ii*) Mark the feasible region area.
(*iii*) Graph at least two isoprofit lines and mark direction of improvement of Z.
(*iv*) Obtain the optimal solution for the problem.

[*Karn. U.B.E. (Mech.) 1995*]

(*Ans.* (*iv*) $x_1 = 300$, $x_2 = 300$; $Z_{max} = 33{,}000$.)

32. Apply graphical method to solve the L.P.P. :
Maximize $Z = x_1 - 2x_2$,
subject to
$$-x_1 + x_2 \leq 1,$$
$$6x_1 + 4x_2 \geq 24,$$
$$0 \leq x_1 \leq 5,\ 2 \leq x_2 \leq 4.$$

[*P.T.U. MCA, 2010*]

(*Ans.* $x_1 = 5$, $x_2 = 2$; $Z_{max} = 1$.)

33. Solve the following L.P.P. graphically :
Maximize $Z = 4x_1 + 6x_2$,
subject to
$$x_1 + x_2 = 5,$$
$$x_1 > 2,$$
$$x_2 < 4,$$
$$x_1, x_2 \geq 0.$$

[*P.T.U. MBA, 2005*]

(*Ans.* $x_1 = 2$, $x_2 = 3$; $Z_{max} = 26$.)

34. Maximize $Z = 5x_2 - x_1$,
subject to
$$2x_1 - x_2 \geq -2,$$
$$-0.2x_1 + x_2 \leq 2,$$
$$x_1, x_2 \geq 0.$$

[*P.U.B.E. (Mech.) Nov., 1981*]

(*Ans.* x_1, x_2 can be arbitrarily large; $Z_{max} = 10$.)

35. Maximize $Z = x_1 + 0.5x_2,$

subject to

$$3x_1 + 2x_2 \le 6,$$
$$x_1 \le 2,$$
$$x_1 + x_2 \le 8,$$
$$-x_1 + x_2 \ge 4,$$
$$x_1, x_2 \ge 0.$$

[*P.U.B.E. (**Mech.**) May, 1982*]

(*Ans.* Infeasible solution.)

36. Maximize $Z = 2x_1 + x_2,$

subject to

$$\frac{3}{2}x_1 + x_2 \le 6,$$
$$x_1 \le 2,$$
$$x_1 + x_2 \ge 7,$$
$$-x_1 + x_2 \ge 4,$$

and

$$x_1, x_2 \ge 0.$$

(*Ans.* Infeasible solution.)

37. Maximize $Z = 3x_1 + 4x_2,$

subject to

$$x_1 - x_2 \le -1,$$
$$x_1 \ge x_2,$$
$$x_1, x_2 \ge 0.$$

[*Univ. of Madras B.Sc. (Math.) Nov. 2012*]

(*Ans. Solution does not exist.*)

38. Maximize $Z = 8x_1 + x_2,$

subject to

$$8x_1 + x_2 \le 8,$$
$$2x_1 + x_2 \le 6,$$
$$3x_1 + x_2 \le 6,$$
$$x_1 + 6x_2 \le 8,$$
$$x_1, x_2 \ge 0.$$

(*Ans.* Infinite number of optimal solutions exist.)

39. Maximize $Z = 4x_1 + 5x_2,$

subject to

$$x_1 + x_2 \ge 1,$$
$$-2x_1 + x_2 \le 1,$$
$$4x_1 - x_2 \ge 1,$$
$$x_1, x_2 \ge 0.$$

[*R.E.C. Hamirpur, 1995*]

(*Ans.* Unbounded solution.)

40. Find the maximum as well as minimum value of the objective function

$$Z = 4x + 5y,$$

subject to

$$2x + y \le 6,$$
$$x + 2y \le 5,$$
$$x - 2y \le 2,$$
$$-x + y \le 2,$$
$$x + y \ge 1,$$

and

$$x, y \ge 0.$$

[*P.U.B.E. (E. & Ec.) 1999; NIIFT Mohali, 1999*]

$$\left(Ans.\ x = \frac{7}{3},\ y = \frac{4}{3},\ Z_{\max} = 16;\ x = 1,\ y = 0,\ Z_{\min} = 4.\right)$$

41. Find the maximum as well as minimum value of the objective function

$$Z = -3x + 6y,$$

subject to
$$x + 2y + 1 \geq 0,$$
$$-4x + y + 23 \geq 0,$$
$$2x + y - 4 \geq 0,$$
$$x - 4y + 13 \geq 0,$$
$$x - y + 1 \geq 0,$$
and
$$x \geq 0, y \geq 0.$$

(*Ans.* $x = 3, y = 4, Z_{max} = 15; x = 5.75, y = 0; Z_{min} = 17.25$.)

42. Minimize $Z = x + y$,

subject to
$$5x + 10y \leq 50,$$
$$x + y \geq 1,$$
$$y \leq 4,$$
$$x, y \geq 0.$$

[*Gujarat Tech. U. MBA Dec., 2010*]

(*Ans.* Multiple optimal solutions;
$x = 0, y = 1, Z_{min} = 1; x = 1, y = 0, Z_{min} = 1$.)

43. A person requires 10, 12 and 12 units of chemicals A, B and C respectively for his gardens. A liquid product contains 5, 2 and 1 units of A, B and C respectively per jar. A dry product contains 1, 2 and 4 units of A, B and C per carton. If the liquid product sells for ₹ 3 per jar and the dry product sells for ₹ 2 per carton, how many of each should be purchased to minimize the cost and meet the requirements? Formulate the above problem as a LPP and solve it by graphical method.

[*J.N.T.U. Hyderabad B.Tech. June, 2009*]

44. ABC company owns a paint factory that produces both exterior and interior paints for wholesale distribution. The basic raw materials A and B are used to manufacture the paints. The maximum availability of A is 6 tonne/day and that of B is 8 tonne/day. The requirements of raw materials/tonne of interior and exterior paints are given below:

Raw material	*Exterior paint*	*Interior paint*
A	1	2
B	2	1

Market survey has established that the daily demand for interior paint cannot exceed that of exterior paint by more than 1 tonne. The survey also shows that maximum demand for interior paint is limited to 2 tonnes per day. The wholesale price/tonne is ₹ 3,000 for exterior and ₹ 2,000 for interior paints. How much interior and exterior paint the company should produce to maximize the gross income? Formulate the above data as LPP and solve graphically. [*V.T.U. Karnataka B.E. June, 2012*]

45. Solution space identified by a set of constraints is shown in Fig. 2.22. If one more constraint $x_1 + x_2 \geq 3$ is to be included, then is there any change in the solution space? If so, show the new feasible zone. With respect to the new feasible zone, state the redundant constraint or constraints if there are any.

[*V.T.U. Karnataka B.E. Jan., 2010*]

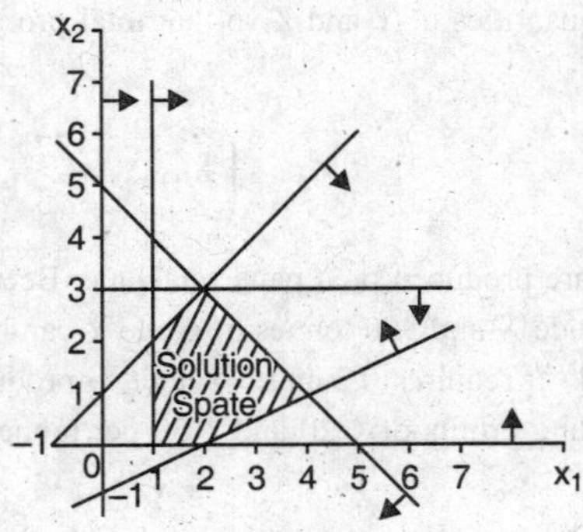

Fig. 2.22

46. Two products A and B are to be manufactured. One unit of product A requires 2.4 minutes of punch press time and 5 minutes of assembly time. The profit for product A is ₹ 0.60 per unit. One unit of product B requires 3 minutes of punch press time and 2.5 minutes of welding time. The profit for product B is ₹ 0.70 per unit. The capacity of the punch press deptt. available for these products is 1,200 minutes/week. The welding deptt. has an idle capacity of 600 minutes/week and assembly deptt. has 1,500 minutes/week.

(*i*) Formulate the problem as linear programming problem.

(*ii*) Determine the quantities of products A and B so that total profit is maximized.

[P.T.U. B.Tech. (Mech.) Dec., 2011]

(*Ans.* $x_A = 300$, $x_B = 160$ units; Z_{max} = ₹ 292.)

47. A feed mixing operation can be described in terms of two activities. The required mixture must contain four kinds of ingredients *w*, *x*, *y* and *z*. Two basic feeds A and B, which contain the required ingredients are available in the market. 1 kg of A contains 0.1 kg of *w*, 0.1 kg of *y* and 0.2 kg of *z*. Likewise, 1 kg of feed B contains 0.1 kg of *x*, 0.2 kg of *y* and 0.1 kg of *z*. The daily per head requirement is of at least, 0.4 kg of *w*, 0.6 kg of *x*, 2 kg of *y* and 1.6 kg of *z*. Feed A can be bought for £0.07 per kg and B for £0.05 per kg. Determine the quantity of feeds A and B in the mixture in order that the total cost is minimum. *[P.U.B.E. (Mech.) Nov., 1976]*

$$\left(Ans.\ x_A = \frac{16}{3}, x_B = \frac{22}{3}; Z_{min} = £\ 0.74.\right)$$

48. A firm manufactures two items. It purchases castings which are then machined, bored and polished. Castings for items A and B cost ₹ 3 and ₹ 4 respectively and are sold at ₹ 6 and ₹ 7 each respectively. Running costs of the three machines are ₹ 20, ₹ 14 and ₹ 17.50 per hour respectively. What product mix maximizes the profit ? Capacities of the machines are

	Part A	*Part B*
Machining capacity	25/hr	40/hr
Boring capacity	28/hr	35/hr
Polishing capacity	35/hr	25/hr

[C.A. May, 1998]

$$\left(Ans.\ x_1 = 16\frac{29}{31}, x_2 = 12\frac{28}{31}.\right)$$

49. A company is manufacturing products Y and Z. One unit of product Y requires 4.8 minutes of machining and 10 minutes of assembly time. The profit for product Y is ₹ 0.70 per unit. Product Z requires 6 minutes of machining time and 5 minutes of welding time for manufacturing one unit. Profit for Z is ₹ 0.90 per unit. The capacity of the machining deptt. available for these products is 1,400 minutes per week. The welding deptt. has an idle capacity of 800 minutes/week and assembly deptt. has 1,800 minutes/week. Determine the quantities of Y and Z so that total profit is maximized.

[P.U.B.E. (Mech.) 1979]

$$\left(Ans.\ Y = \frac{275}{3}, Z = 160 \text{ units}; P_{max} = ₹\ 208.17.\right)$$

50. Two grades of paper X and Y are produced on a paper machine. Because of raw material restrictions, not more than 400 tonnes of grade X and 300 tonnes of grade Y can be produced in a week. There are 160 production hours in a week. It requires 0.2 and 0.4 hour to produce one tonne of products X and Y respectively with corresponding profits of ₹ 20 and ₹ 50 per tonne. Find the optimum product mix using the graphic method. *[G.N.D.U. BBA April, 1997]*

(*Ans.* X = 200 tonnes, Y = 300 tonnes, Z_{max} = ₹ 19,000.)

51. A farm is engaged in breeding pigs. The pigs are fed on various products grown on the farm. Because of the need to ensure certain nutrient constituents, it is necessary to buy additionally one or two products, which we shall call A and B. The nutrient constituents (vitamins and proteins) in each unit of the products are given below.

Nutrient	*Nutrient contents in the products*		*Minimum amount of nutrients*
	A	*B*	
1	36	6	108
2	3	12	36
3	20	10	100

Product A costs ₹ 20 per unit and product B costs ₹ 40 per unit. How much of products A and B be purchased at the lowest possible cost so as to provide the pigs, nutrients not less than that given in the table. [*C.A. May, 2002; Nov., 2001*]

(*Ans.* $x_A = 4$ units, $x_B = 2$ units; Z_{max} = ₹ 160.)

52. The ABC Electric Appliance Company produces two products: refrigerators and ranges. Production takes place in two separate departments. Refrigerators are produced in deptt. I and ranges are produced in deptt. II. The company's two products are produced and sold on a weekly basis. The weekly production cannot exceed 25 refrigerators in deptt. I and 35 ranges in deptt. II, because of limited available facilities in the two deptts. The company regularly employs a total of 60 workers in the two deptts. A refrigerator requires 2 man-weeks of labour, while a range requires 1 man-week of labour. A refrigerator contributes a profit of ₹ 60 and a range contributes a profit of ₹ 40. Formulate the problem as L.P. problem. How many units of refrigerators and ranges should the company produce to realise a maximum profit ? [*Delhi M.B.A., 1985*]

(*Ans.* (*a*) Maximize $Z = 60x_1 + 40x_2$,

subject to

$$x_1 \le 25,$$
$$x_2 \le 35,$$
$$2x_1 + x_2 \le 60,$$
$$x_1, x_2 \ge 0.$$

(*b*) 12.5 refrigerators and 35 ranges, Z_{max} = ₹ 2,150).

53. A company produces two types of leather belts, say types A and B. Belt A is of a superior quality and belt B is of a lower quality. Profits on the two types of belts are 40 and 30 paise per belt respectively. Each belt of type A requires twice as much time as required by a belt of type B. If all belts were of type B, the company could produce 1,000 belts per day. The supply of leather, however, is sufficient only for 800 belts per day. Belt A requires a fancy buckle and only 400 fancy buckles are available for this per day. For belt of type B, only 700 buckles are available per day. How should the company manufacture the two types of belts in order to have a maximum overall profit ?

[*P.U.B.E. (Mech.) Dec., 2012; P.T.U. B. Tech. (Mech.) 2008*]

(*Ans.* $x_A = 200$, $x_B = 600$; Z_{max} = ₹ 260.)

[Hint: Maximize $Z = 0.4x_A + 0.3x_B$,

subject to

$$2x_A + x_B \le 1{,}000,$$
$$x_A + x_B \le 800,$$
$$x_A \le 400,$$
$$x_B \le 700,$$
$$x_A, x_B \ge 0.]$$

54. The ABC company wishes to plan its advertising strategy. There are two media under consideration, call them magazines I and II respectively. Magazine I has a reach of 2,000 potential customers and magazine II has a reach of 2,500 potential customers. The cost per page of advertising is ₹ 400 and

₹ 600 in magazines I and II respectively. The firm has a monthly budget of ₹ 6,000. There is an important requirement that the total reach for the income group under ₹ 20,000 per annum should not exceed 4,000 potential customers. The reach in magazines I and II for this income group is 400 and 200 potential customers. How many pages should be bought in the two magazines to maximize the total reach ? *[Delhi Dip. in Mkt. and Salesman, 1975]*

[**Hint:** Maximize Z = $2,000x_{I} + 2,500x_{II}$, subject to $400x_I + 600x_{II} \leq 6,000$, $400x_I + 200x_{II} \leq 4,000$, $x_I, x_{II} \geq 0$.]

(*Ans.* $x_1 = 7.5$, $x_2 = 5$; Z_{max} ₹ 27,500)

55. A plant manufactures two products A and B. The profit contribution of each product has been estimated as ₹ 20 for product A and ₹ 24 for product B. Each product passes through three departments of the plant. The time required for each product and total time available in each department are as follows:

	Hours required		
Department	*Product A*	*Product B*	*Available hours during the month*
1	2	3	1,500
2	3	2	1,500
3	1	1	600

The company has a contract to supply at least 250 units of product B per month. Formulate the problem as a linear programming model and solve by graphical method.

[P.U. B.Com., 2006]

(*Ans.* (*i*) Maximize $Z = 20x_A + 24x_B$,

subject to
$$2x_A + 3x_B \leq 1,500,$$
$$3x_A + 2x_B \leq 1,500,$$
$$x_A + x_B \leq 600,$$
$$x_B \geq 250,$$
$$x_A, x_B \geq 0.$$

(*ii*) $x_A = \dfrac{1,000}{3}$, $x_B = 250$; Z_{max} = ₹ $\dfrac{38,000}{3}$.)

56. On completing the construction of a house a person discovers that 100 square feet of plywood scrap and 80 square feet of white pine scrap are in usable form for the construction of tables and book cases. It takes 16 square feet of plywood and 8 square feet of white pine to make a table ; 12 square feet of plywood and 16 square feet of white pine are required to construct a book case. By selling the finished product to a local furniture store the person can realize a profit of ₹ 250 on each table and ₹ 290 on each book case. How may the person most profitably use the left-over wood ? Use graphical method to solve the problem. *[P.T.U. B.Tech. (Mech.) 2009]*

(*Ans.* $x_1 = 4$, $x_2 = 3$; Z_{max} = ₹ 1,870.)

57. The sales manager of a company has budgeted ₹ 1,20,000 for an advertising programme for one of the firm's products. The selected advertising programme consists of running advertisements in two different magazines. The advertisement for magazine 1 costs ₹ 2,000 per run while the advertisement for magazine 2 costs ₹ 5,000 per run. Past experience has indicated that at least 20 runs in magazine 1, and at least 10 runs in magazine 2 are necessary to penetrate the market with any appreciable effect. Also, experience has indicated that there is no reason to make more than 50 runs in either of the two magazines. How many runs in magazine 1 and how many in magazine 2 should be made ?

(*Ans.* Magazine 1: 20 to 35 runs; Magazine 2: 10 to 16 runs.)

58. A factory is to produce two products P_1 and P_2. The products require machining on two critical machines M_1 and M_2. Product P_1 requires 5 hr on machine M_1 and 3 hr on machine M_2. Product P_2 requires 4 hrs. on machine M_1 and 6 hr on machine M_2. Machine M_1 is available for 120 hr per week during regular working hours and 50 hr on overtime. Weekly machine hours on M_2 are limited to 150 hr on regular working hours and 40 hr on overtime. Product P_1 earns a unit profit of ₹ 8 if produced on regular time, ₹ 6 if produced on overtime on one machine and ₹ 4 if produced on overtime on both machines. Product P_2 earns a unit profit of ₹ 10 if produced on regular time, ₹ 8 if produced on overtime on both machines.

Formulate an L.P. model for designing an optimum production schedule for maximizing the profit.

[P.U.B.E. (Prod.) 1977]

59. A manufacturer of a line of patent medicines is preparing a production plan on medicines A and B. There are sufficient ingredients available to make 20,000 bottles of A and 40,000 bottles of B but there are only 45,000 bottles into which either of the medicines can be put. Furthermore, it takes 3 hours to prepare enough material to fill 1,000 bottles of A, it takes 1 hour to prepare enough material to prepare 1,000 bottles of B and there are 66 hours available for this operation. The profit is ₹ 8 per bottle for A and ₹ 7 per bottle for B.

(*a*) Formulate this problem as linear programming problem.

(*b*) How should the manufacturer schedule the production in order to maximize his profit ?

[H.P.U. B.Tech. (Mech.) 2009]

(*Ans:* (*a*) Maximize $Z = 8x_A + 7x_B$,

subject to $x_A \leq 20{,}000$,

$x_B \leq 40{,}000$,

$x_A + x_B \leq 45{,}000$,

$$\frac{3}{1{,}000}x_A + \frac{1}{1{,}000}x_B \leq 66$$

or $3x_A + x_B \leq 66{,}000$,

$x_A, x_B \geq 0$.

(*b*) $x_A = 10{,}500$, $x_B = 34{,}500$; Z_{max} = ₹ 3,25,500.)

60. A factory has decided to diversify its activities. The data collected for the sales and production departments are summarised below:

Potential demand exists for two products A and B. Market can absorb any quantity of A, whereas the share of B for this organisation is expected to be not more than 400 units per month. For every three units of B produced there is one unit of a by-product which sells at ₹ 3/unit and only 100 units of this by-product can be sold per month. Contribution per unit of products A and B is expected to be ₹ 6 and ₹ 8 respectively. These products require three different processes and the time required per unit of product is given in the table below:

Process	*Product A*	*Product B*	*Available hours*
I	2	3	900
II	1	2	600
III	2	2	1,200

Find the product mix to optimise the contribution.

[H.P.U. B.Tech. (Mech.) June, 2010]

(*Ans.* Multiple optimal solutions.

Solution I : $x_1 = 450$, $x_2 = 0$; Z_{max} = ₹ 2,700.

Solution II: $x_1 = 0$, $x_2 = 300$; Z_{max} = ₹ 2,700.)

61. A company is manufacturing two products X and Y, which are processed through three departments A, B and C. The data for the two products are given below :

Data	*Product X*	*Product Y*
Selling price per unit	₹ 200	₹ 240
Cost :		
(*i*) Material/unit	₹ 45	₹ 50
(*ii*) Departmental overheads/hour		
Department A	₹ 16	₹ 10
Department B	₹ 22.50	₹ 13.50
Department C	₹ 10	₹ 30
(*iii*) General variable overheads/unit	₹ 33	₹ 42

Fixed overheads are ₹ 2,750 per annum. Table below shows the available man-hours and rate per hour in departments A, B and C :

Department	*Available man-hours*	*Rate per hour*
A	800	₹ 2.00
B	600	₹ 2.25
C	720	₹ 2.50

Find the product mix to maximize the net profit. [*H.P. U. B.Tech. (Mech.) Nov., 2010*]

(*Ans.* (*i*) Max $Z = (200 - 45 - 6.50 - \frac{16}{2} - \frac{22.50}{2.25} - \frac{10}{2.50})x + (240 - 50 - 11.50 - \frac{10}{2} - \frac{13.50}{2.25} - \frac{30}{2.50})y$

$= 100x + 125y,$

subject to $8x + 5y \le 800,$

$10x + 6y \le 600,$

$4x + 12y \le 720,$

$x, y \ge 0,$

(*ii*) $x = 30, y = 50$; Z_{max} = ₹ 6,500.)

[**Hint:** Divide the departmental overheads by the rate per hour to find the processing time for the two products in three departments :

Deptt.	*X*	*Y*
A	8	5
B	10	6
C	4	12]

62. A company has 8 grade I and 10 grade II inspectors for quality control inspection. At least 1,800 pieces must be inspected in an 8-hour day. Grade I inspector can check 25 pieces an hour with an accuracy of 98%. Grade II inspector can check 15 pieces an hour with an accuracy of 95%.
The wage rate of a grade I inspector is ₹ 4 per hour, while that of grade II inspector is ₹ 3 per hour. Any error made by an inspector costs ₹ 2 to the company. Determine graphically the optimal assignment of inspectors that will minimize the daily inspection cost.

(*Ans.* (*i*) Min. $Z = 40x_1 + 36x_2,$

subject to $5x_1 + 3x_2 \ge 45,$

$x_1 \le 8,$

$x_2 \le 10,$

$x_1, x_2 \ge 0.$

(*ii*) $x_1 = 8, x_2 = \frac{5}{3}$; Z_{min} = ₹ 380.)

63. Solve graphically problem 10 of exercise 2.1. [*Raj. M.Phil. (ABST) 1993*]

(*Ans.* $x_1 = 10, x_2 = 20$; Z_{max} = ₹ 260.)

64. Solve graphically problem 57 of exercise 2.1.

(*Ans.* $x_1 = 400, x_2 = 0$; Z_{max} = ₹ 40,000.)

65. An advertising firm desires to reach two types of audiences—customers with annual income of more than ₹ 40,000 (target audience A) and customers with annual income of less than ₹ 40,000 (target audience B). The total advertising budget is ₹ 2,00,000. One programme of T.V. advertising costs ₹ 50,000 while one programme of radio advertising costs ₹ 20,000. Contract conditions ordinarily require that there should be at least 3 programmes on T.V. and no more than 5 on radio. Survey indicates that

one T.V. programme reaches 7,50,000 customers in target audience A and 1,50,000 in target audience B. One radio programme reaches 4,00,000 customers in target audience A and 2,60,000 in target audience B. Formulate the mathematical model and determine the media mix to maximize the number of customers reached. Use graphic method. *[D.U. MBA, 2005; C.A. Nov., 1999]*

(*Ans.* (*i*) Max. $Z = 9{,}00{,}000x_1 + 6{,}60{,}000x_2$,
subject to $5x_1 + 2x_2 \le 20$,
$x_1 \ge 3$,
$x_2 \le 5$,
$x_1, x_2 \ge 0$.
(*ii*) $x_1 = A$, $x_2 = O$, $Z_{max} = 36{,}00{,}000$.)

66. Suppose you have inherited ₹ 1,00,000 from your father-in-law that can be invested in a combination of only two stock portfolios, with the maximum investment allowed in either portfolio set at ₹ 75,000. The first portfolio has an average rate of return of 10%, whereas the second has 20%. In terms of risk factors associated with these portfolios, the first has a risk rating of 4 (on a scale 0 to 10), and the second has 9. Since you wish to maximize your return, you will not accept an average rate of return below 12% or a risk factor above 6. How much should you invest in each portfolio ? Formulate this as L.P.P. and solve by graphic method. *[P.U.M.Com., 2001]*

[**Hint:** Let x_1 and x_2 be the amount to be invested in the two stock portfolios. Then the mathematical model for the problem is

Maximize $Z = 0.1x_1 + 0.2x_2$,
subject to $x_1 + x_2 \le 1{,}00{,}000$,
$x_1 \le 75{,}000$,
$x_2 \le 75{,}000$,
$0.1x_1 + 0.2x_2 \ge 0.12\,(x_1 + x_2)$ or $-0.02x_1 + 0.08x_2 \ge 0$,
$4x_1 + 9x_2 \le 6\,(x_1 + x_2)$ or $-2x_1 + 3x_2 \le 0$,
$x_1, x_2 \ge 0$.

Solution by graphical method yields x_1 = ₹ 60,000, x_2 = ₹ 40,000; Z_{max} = ₹ 14,000.]

67. An animal feed company must produce exactly 200 kg of a mixture consisting of ingredients X_1 and X_2. The ingredient X_1 costs ₹ 3 per kg and X_2 costs ₹ 5 per kg. Not more than 80 kg of X_1 can be used and at least 60 kg of X_2 must be used. Find the minimum cost mixture.
[P.T.U. MBA Dec., 2013; P.U. B.B.A. Sept., 2008]

(*Ans.* (*i*) Min. $Z = 3x_1 + 5x_2$,
subject to $x_1 + x_2 = 200$,
$x_1 \le 80$,
$x_2 \ge 60$,
$x_1, x_2 \ge 0$.
(*ii*) $x_1 = 80$kg, $x_2 = 120$kg; Z_{min} = ₹ 840.)

68. A firm manufactures two types of shafts A and B. For any month it must produce 250 shafts A and 100 shafts B. The maximum total requirement of shafts A and B is 1,250 and minimum total requirement is 500.

Both shafts are to be processed on machines M_1 and M_2. Total number of machines M_1 and M_2 available are 15 each. Processing times in hours for each shaft on machines M_1 and M_2 are as follows:

	A	*B*
M_1	1.5	2
M_2	1	1.5
Profit/unit (₹)	400	600

If the firm has 25 working days a month, each of 8 hours, formulate the mathematical model for the problem and solve it by graphical method. *[P.U.B.E. (E. & Ec.) 2000]*

(*Ans.* Max $Z = 400x_1 + 600x_2$,
subject to $x_1 \ge 250$,
$x_2 \ge 100$,
$x_1 + x_2 \le 1{,}250$,
$x_1 + x_2 \ge 500$,
$1.5x_1 + 2x_2 \le 3{,}000$,
$x_1 + 1.5x_2 \le 3{,}000$,
$x_1, x_2 \ge 0$.
$x_1, = 250$, $x_2 = 1{,}000$; Z_{max} = ₹ 7,00,000.)

69. A firm makes products A and B and has a total production capacity of 9 tonnes per day, A and B requiring the same production capacity. The firm has a permanent contract to supply at least 2 tonnes of A and 3 tonnes of B per day to another company. Each tonne of A requires 20 machine-hour production time and each tonne of B requires 50 machine-hour production time, the daily maximum possible production time available is 360 hours. Profit per unit of product A is ₹ 80 and that of B is ₹ 120. Formulate the L.P.P. and solve it graphically. [*P.U.B.Com, April, 2004*]

(*Ans.* (*i*) Max. Z = ₹ $(80x_1 + 120x_2)$,

subject to $x_1 + x_2 \le 9,$

$x_1 \ge 2,$

$x_2 \ge 3,$

$20x_1 + 50x_2 \le 360,$

$x_1, x_2 \ge 0.$

(*ii*) $x_1 = 3, x_2 = 6$; Z_{max} = ₹ 960.)

70. A manufacturer of packing material manufactures two types of packing tins, round and flat. Major production facilities involved are cutting and joining. The cutting department can process 300 round tins or 500 flat tins per hour. The joining department can process 500 round tins or 300 flat tins per hour. If the contribution towards profit for a round tin is the same as that of a flat tin, what is the optimum production level ?

(*Ans.* $x_1 = 187.5, x_2 = 187.5$; $Z_{max} = 375$.)

[Hint. Let x_1 and x_2 be the number of round tins and flat tins manufactured per hour. Since the contribution towards profit is identical for both the products, the objective function can be expressed as $x_1 + x_2$. Hence the problem can be formulated as

maximize $Z = x_1 + x_2,$

subject to $\dfrac{x_1}{300} + \dfrac{x_2}{500} \le 1,$

$\dfrac{x_1}{500} + \dfrac{x_2}{300} \le 1,$

$x_1, x_2 \ge 0.$]

71. A farmer has 150 acres of land suitable for cultivating crops A and B. The cost of cultivating crop A is ₹ 400 per acre whereas that of crop B is ₹ 600 per acre. The farmer has a maximum of ₹ 74,000 available for land cultivation. Each acre of crop A requires 20 hours of labour and each acre of crop B requires 25 hours of labour. The farmer has a maximum of 2,300 hours of labour available. He also has decided that he will cultivate at least 70 acres of crop A. If he expects to make a profit of ₹ 150 per acre on crop A and ₹ 200 per acre on crop B, how many acres of each crop should he plant in order to maximize his profit? Formulate this as the L.P.P. model and solve it graphically. [*Mumbai U. MBA, 2010*]

(*Ans.* Maximize $Z = 150x_A + 200x_B,$

subject to $2x_A + 3x_B \le 370,$

$x_A + x_B \le 150,$

$4x_A + 5x_B \le 460,$

$x_A \ge 70,$

$x_A, x_B \ge 0; x_A = 70, x_B = 36$.)

2.11 THE GENERAL LINEAR PROGRAMMING PROBLEM

The general linear programming problem can be expressed as follows :

Find the values of variables $x_1, x_2, ..., x_n$ which maximize (or minimize) an objective function which is a linear function of variables, such as

$$Z = c_1x_1 + c_2x_2 + ... + c_n x_n, \quad ... (2.10)$$

subject to the constraints

$$\left.\begin{array}{l} a_{11}x_1 + a_{12}x_2 + \ldots + a_{1n}x_n \; (\le, =, \ge) \; b_1, \\ a_{21}x_1 + a_{22}x_2 + \ldots + a_{2n}x_n \; (\le, =, \ge) \; b_2, \\ \vdots \qquad\qquad\qquad\qquad \vdots \\ a_{m1}x_1 + a_{m2}x_2 + \ldots + a_{mn}x_n \; (\le, =, \ge) \; b_m, \end{array}\right\} \quad \ldots (2.11)$$

and meet the non-negativity restrictions

$$x_1, x_2, \ldots, x_n \ge 0. \quad \ldots (2.12)$$

For each constraint one and only one of signs ($\le$, $=$, $\ge$) holds but the sign may vary from one constraint to another. Because of the variety of notations in common use, one finds the general L.P.P. stated in many forms. Some of them are

(*i*) *Compact form by using the sigma sign* :

Maximize (or minimize) $\quad Z = \sum_{j=1}^{n} c_j \, x_j ,$

subject to $\quad \sum_{j=1}^{n} a_{ij} \, x_j \; (\le, =, \ge) \; b_i, \; i = 1, 2, \ldots, m,$

and $\quad x_j \ge 0, \; j = 1, 2, \ldots, n.$

Here, variables x_j ($j = 1, 2, \ldots, n$) are called *decision variables*, and c_j, a_{ij} and b_i ($i = 1, 2, \ldots, m$); $j = (1, 2, \ldots, n)$ are constants determined from the statement of the problem. The constants c_j represent the net unit contribution of decision variables x_j to the value of the objective function and are called *objective function coefficients*, constants b_i denote the total availability of the ith resource and are called *stipulations* and constants a_{ij} stand for the amount of resource, say i consumed in making one unit of product j and are called *structural coefficients*. Also in general L.P.P., $m < n$.

(*ii*) *Matrix-vector form* :

Maximize (or minimize) $Z = \mathbf{c}\boldsymbol{x}$,

subject to $\quad \boldsymbol{A}\boldsymbol{x} \; (\le, =, \ge) \; \boldsymbol{b},$

and $\quad \boldsymbol{x} \ge \mathbf{0},$

where **A** is a ($m \times n$) matrix, $\boldsymbol{x}$ is a ($n \times 1$) column vector, $\boldsymbol{b}$ is a ($m \times 1$) column vector and $\boldsymbol{c}$ is a ($1 \times n$) row vector. In other words

$$\mathbf{A}_{(m \times n)} = \begin{bmatrix} a_{11} & a_{12} & \ldots & a_{1n} \\ a_{21} & a_{22} & \ldots & a_{2n} \\ \vdots & & & \\ a_{m1} & a_{m2} & \ldots & a_{mn} \end{bmatrix},$$

$$\mathbf{A}_{(m \times n)} =$$

$$\boldsymbol{x}_{(n \times 1)} = \begin{bmatrix} x_1 \\ x_2 \\ \vdots \\ x_n \end{bmatrix},$$

$$\boldsymbol{b}_{(m \times 1)} = \begin{bmatrix} b_1 \\ b_2 \\ \vdots \\ b_m \end{bmatrix},$$

and $\quad \boldsymbol{c}_{1 \times n} = (c_1, c_2, \ldots, c_n),$

where **A** is called the *coefficient matrix*, $\boldsymbol{x}$ is the *decision vector*, $\boldsymbol{b}$ is the *requirement vector*, $\boldsymbol{c}$ is the *cost* (*price or profit*) *vector* of the L.P. problem and **0** is an n-dimensional null column vector.

A typical element a_{ij} of the matrix **A** indicates the amount of ith type of resource necessary to manufacture one unit of product j. Hence in a way, these elements represent the activity of the operational system. Therefore, matrix **A** is also called the *activity matrix* and its elements are called *activity coefficients*. For an identical reason, vector $\boldsymbol{b}$ is also referred to as the *resource vector* or *availability vector*.

(*iii*) In some situations, it is convenient to define a new unrestricted variable x_0 which is equal to the value of the objective function. Then the problem can be stated as

$$\text{Maximize (or minimize)} \quad Z = x_0,$$

$$\text{subject to} \quad x_0 - \sum_{j=1}^{n} c_j x_j = 0,$$

$$\sum_{j=1}^{n} a_{ij} x_j \ (\leq, =, \geq)\ b_i,\ i = 1, 2, \ldots m,$$

$$\text{and} \quad x_j \geq 0,\ j = 1, 2, \ldots, n.$$

2.12 CANONICAL AND STANDARD FORMS OF LINEAR PROGRAMMING PROBLEM

After formulating the linear programming problem, the next step is to obtain its solution. But before any analytic method is used to obtain the solution, the problem must be available in a particular form. Two forms are dealt with here, the *canonical form* and the *standard form*. While the canonical form is helpful in dealing with *duality theory*, to be discussed in section 6.1, the standard form is used to develop the general procedure for solving any linear programming problem.

2.12-1 The Canonical Form

The general linear programming problem discussed in section 2.11 can always be put in the following form, called the *canonical form*:

$$\text{Maximize } Z = \sum_{j=1}^{n} c_j x_j,$$

$$\text{subject to } \sum_{j=1}^{n} a_{ij} x_j \leq b_i, \qquad i = 1, 2, \ldots, m,$$

$$x_j \geq 0, \qquad j = 1, 2, \ldots, n.$$

The characteristics of this form are

(*a*) objective function is of maximization type,

(*b*) all constraints are of the ($\leq$) type (except non-negativity restrictions which are of ($\geq$) type),

(*c*) all decision variables are non-negative.

Any linear programming problem can be put in the canonical form by the use of some elementary transformations.

1. *The minimization* of a function, $f(x)$, is equivalent to the *maximization* of the negative expression of this function, $-f(x)$. For example, the linear objective function

$$\text{minimize } Z = c_1x_1 + c_2x_2 + \ldots + c_nx_n$$

is equivalent to

$$\text{maximize } G = -Z = -c_1x_1 - c_2x_2 - \ldots - c_nx_n,$$

with $Z = -G$. Therefore, for all linear programming problems the objective function can be expressed in the maximization form.

2. An inequality constraint of ($\geq$) type can be changed to an inequality of ($\leq$) type by multiplying both sides of the inequality by -1. For example, the linear constraint

$$a_1x_1 + a_2x_2 \geq b$$

is equivalent to

$$-a_1x_1 - a_2x_2 \le -b.$$

3. An equation may be replaced by two weak inequalities in opposite directions. For example, $a_1x_1 + a_2x_2 = b$ is equivalent to the two simultaneous constraints

$$a_1x_1 + a_2x_2 \le b \quad \text{and} \quad a_1x_1 + a_2x_2 \ge b$$

or

$$a_1x_1 + a_2x_2 \le b \quad \text{and} \quad -a_1x_1 - a_2x_2 \le -b.$$

4. A inequality constraint with absolute form on the left-hand side can be expressed as a combination of two regular inequalities. For example, for $b \ge 0$,

$$|a_1x_1 + a_2x_2| \le b$$

is equivalent to

$$a_1x_1 + a_2x_2 \le b \quad \text{and} \quad a_1x_1 + a_2x_2 \ge -b.$$

Similarly, for $q \ge 0$,

$$|p_1x_1 + p_2x_2| \ge q$$

is equivalent to

$$p_1x_1 + p_2x_2 \ge q \quad \text{and} \quad p_1x_1 + p_2x_2 \le -q.$$

5. So far, we have assumed the decision variables $x_1, x_2, ..., x_n$ to be all non-negative. It is possible, in actual practice, that a variable may be unconstrained (unrestricted)in sign, *i.e.*, it may be positive, zero or negative (theoretically its value may vary from $-\infty$ to $+\infty$). If a variable is unconstrained, it is expressed as the difference between two non-negative variables. For example, if x is an unconstrained variable, then it can be expressed as

$$x = x' - x'', \quad \text{where} \quad x' \ge 0 \text{ and } x'' \ge 0.$$

Value of x is positive, zero or negative depending upon whether x' is larger, equal to or smaller than x''.

Remark : A minimization problem can also be in canonical form if all its variables are non-negative and all its constraints are of ($\ge$) type.

2.12-2 The Standard Form

The general L.P. problem discussed in section 2.11 can always be put in the following form, called the standard form :

$$\text{Maximize (or minimize) } Z = \sum_{j=1}^{n} c_j x_j,$$

subject to

$$\sum_{j=1}^{n} a_{ij} x_j = b_i, \; i = 1, 2, ..., m,$$

$$x_j \ge 0, \; j = 1, 2, ..., n,$$

and

$$b_i \ge 0.$$

In the matrix-vector form, the standard form of the general L.P. problem can be expressed as

$$\text{Maximize (or minimize) } Z = \mathbf{cx},$$

subject to

$$\mathbf{Ax} = \mathbf{b},$$
$$\mathbf{x} \ge \mathbf{0},$$
$$\mathbf{b} \ge \mathbf{0}.$$

The main characteristics of the standard form are

1. All variables are non-negative.
2. The right-hand side of each constraint is non-negative.
3. All constraints are expressed as equations.
4. Objective function may be of maximization or minimization type.

Any L.P. problem can be put in standard form with the help of some elementary transformations.

1. As already explained, any unrestricted (also called unconstrained) variable x_j can be expressed as the difference of two non-negative variables

$$i.e., x_j = x_j' - x_j''; x_j' \geq 0, x_j'' \geq 0.$$

2. If right-hand side of a constraint is negative, it is multiplied on both sides by – 1 to make it +ve. This will, of course, reverse the sign of inequality.

3. The inequality constraints are changed to equality constraints by adding or subtracting a non-negative variable from the left-hand sides of such constraints. These new variables are called *slack variables* or simply *slacks*. They are added if the constraints are (≤) and subtracted if the constraints are (≥). Since in the case of (≥) constraints the subtracted variable represents the surplus of left-hand side over right-hand side, it is commonly known as *surplus variable* and is, in fact, a negative slack. Both decision variables as well as the slack and surplus variables are called the *admissible variables*. Slack and surplus variables are as much a part of the problem as decision variables and are treated in the same manner while finding a solution to the problem. These variables can remain positive throughout the process of solution and their values in the optimal solution give useful information about the problem.

For example, the constraint

$$a_1x_1 + a_2x_2 \leq b, \qquad b \geq 0$$

is changed in the standard form to $a_1x_1 + a_2x_2 + s_1 = b$, where $s_1 \geq 0$. Also constraint

$$p_1x_1 + p_2x_2 \geq q, \qquad q \geq 0$$

is changed to $p_1x_1 + p_2x_2 - s_2 = q$, where $s_2 \geq 0$.

The quantities s_1 and s_2 are variables and their values depend upon the values assumed by other $x's$ in a particular equation.

Physically, the slack variables can be looked upon as dummy (fictitious) products, yielding zero profit (or incurring zero cost), where each unit of these products requires one unit of a particular resource and zero unit of the remaining available resources. Similarly, the surplus variables can be interpreted as free products, yielding zero profit (or incurring zero cost), where each unit of these products requires one unit of particular resource and zero unit of the remaining available resources.

Before trying for the solution of the linear programming problem, it must be expressed in the standard form. The information given by the standard form is then expressed in the "*table form*" or "*matrix form*".

Let us consider the general linear programming problem

$$\text{maximize} \qquad Z = \sum_{j=1}^{n} c_j x_j ,$$

$$\text{subject to} \qquad \sum_{j=1}^{n} a_{ij} x_j \leq b_i, \ (b_i \geq 0), \qquad i = 1, 2, 3, ..., m,$$

$$x_j \geq 0, \qquad j = 1, 2, 3, ..., n.$$

This is expressed in the standard form as

$$\text{maximize } Z = \sum_{j=1}^{n} c_j x_j ,$$

$$\text{subject to} \qquad \sum_{j=1}^{n} a_{ij} x_j + s_i = b_i, \qquad i = 1, 2, 3, ..., m,$$

$$x_j \geq 0, \qquad j = 1, 2, 3, ..., n,$$

$$s_i \geq 0, \qquad i = 1, 2, 3, ..., m.$$

Such an L.P. problem formed after the introduction of slack or surplus variables is called *reformulated L.P. problem*.

Now, solving the L.P. problem means determining the set of nonnegative values of variables x_j and s_i which will maximize Z while satisfying the constraint equations. The concept is simple but we have a set of m equations with $(m + n)$ unknowns and an infinite number of solutions is possible. Clearly a hit and trial method for finding the optimal solution is not feasible. There is a definite need for an efficient and systematic procedure which will yield the desired solution in a finite number of trials. An iterative procedure called *simplex technique* helps us to reach the optimal solution (if it exists) in a finite number of iterations.

EXAMPLE 2.12-1

Express the following L.P. problem in standard form :

Maximize $Z = 7x_1 + 5x_2,$

subject to $2x_1 + 3x_2 \le 20,$

$3x_1 + x_2 \ge 10,$

$x_1, x_2 \ge 0.$

Solution. Introducing slack and surplus variables, the problem can be expressed in standard form as

maximize $Z = 7x_1 + 5x_2,$

subject to $2x_1 + 3x_2 + s_1 = 20,$

$3x_1 + x_2 - s_2 = 10,$

$x_1, x_2, s_1, s_2 \ge 0.$

EXAMPLE 2.12-2

Express the following linear programming problem in the standard form :

Maximize $Z = 3x_1 + 2x_2 + 5x_3,$

subject to $2x_1 - 3x_2 \le 3,$

$x_1 + 2x_2 + 3x_3 \ge 5,$

$3x_1 + 2x_3 \le 2,$

$x_1 \ge 0, x_2 \ge 0.$

Solution. Here x_1 and x_2 are restricted to be non-negative, while x_3 is unrestricted.

Let us express x_3 as $x_3' - x_3''$, where $x_3' \ge 0$ and $x_3'' \ge 0$. Thus the above problem can be written as

maximize $Z = 3x_1 + 2x_2 + 5x_3' - 5x_3'',$

subject to $2x_1 - 3x_2 \le 3,$

$x_1 + 2x_2 + 3x_3' - 3x_3'' \ge 5,$

$3x_1 + 2x_3' - 2x_3'' \le 2,$

where $x_1 \ge 0, x_2 \ge 0, x_3' \ge 0, x_3'' \ge 0.$

Introducing slack variables, the standard form is

maximize $Z = 3x_1 + 2x_2 + 5x_3' - 5x_3'',$

subject to $2x_1 - 3x_2 + s_1 = 3,$

$x_1 + 2x_2 + 3x_3' - 3x_3'' - s_2 = 5,$

$3x_1 + 2x_3' - 2x_3'' + s_3 = 2,$

where $x_1 \ge 0, x_2 \ge 0, x_3' \ge 0, x_3'' \ge 0, s_1 \ge 0, s_2 \ge 0$ and $s_3 \ge 0.$

EXAMPLE 2.12-3

Express the following linear programming problem in the standard form :

Determine x_1, x_2, x_3 *so as to*

maximize $Z = 3x_1 + 2x_2 + 5x_3,$

subject to $2x_1 + 3x_2 - 2x_3 \le 40,$

$4x_1 - 2x_2 + x_3 \le 24,$

$x_1 - 5x_2 - 6x_3 \ge 2,$

$x_1 \ge 0.$ *[P.T.U. B. Tech. (C.Sc.) 2010]*

Solution. Here only x_1 is restricted to be non-negative, while x_2 and x_3 are unrestricted. Let us express

$$x_1 \text{ as } = y_1, \text{ where } y_1 \geq 0,$$
$$x_2 = y_2 - y_3, \text{ where } y_2, y_3 \geq 0,$$
and
$$x_3 = y_4 - y_5, \text{where } y_4, y_5 \geq 0.$$

Thus the given problem can be written as

$$\begin{aligned} \text{maximize} \quad & Z = 3y_1 + 2y_2 - 2y_3 + 5y_4 - 5y_5, \\ \text{subject to} \quad & 2y_1 + 3y_2 - 3y_3 - 2y_4 + 2y_5 \leq 40, \\ & 4y_1 - 2y_2 + 2y_3 + y_4 - y_5 \leq 24, \\ & y_1 - 5y_2 + 5y_3 - 6y_4 + 6y_5 \geq 2, \\ \text{where} \quad & y_1, y_2, y_3, y_4, y_5, \text{ all } \geq 0. \end{aligned}$$

Introducing the slack variables, the standard form is

$$\begin{aligned} \text{maximize} \quad & Z = 3y_1 + 2y_2 - 2y_3 + 5y_4 - 5y_5, \\ \text{subject to} \quad & 2y_1 + 3y_2 - 3y_3 - 2y_4 + 2y_5 + s_1 = 40, \\ & 4y_1 - 2y_2 + 2y_3 + y_4 - y_5 + s_2 = 24, \\ & y_1 - 5y_2 + 5y_3 - 6y_4 + 6y_5 - s_3 = 2, \\ \text{where} \quad & y_1, y_2, y_3, y_4, y_5, s_1, s_2, s_3, \text{ all } \geq 0. \end{aligned}$$

EXAMPLE 2.12-4

Reformulate the problem into standard form :

$$\begin{aligned} \textit{Minimize} \quad & Z = 2x_1 + 3x_2, \\ \textit{subject to} \quad & 2x_1 - 3x_2 - x_3 = -4, \\ & 3x_1 + 4x_2 - x_4 = -6, \\ & 2x_1 + 5x_2 + x_5 = 10, \\ & 4x_1 - 3x_2 + x_6 = 18, \\ \textit{where} \quad & x_3, x_4, x_5, x_6 \textit{ all } \geq 0. \end{aligned}$$

Solution. Here x_3, x_4, x_5, x_6 (which are all non-negative) are the slack variables. The decision variables x_1, x_2 are unrestricted in sign.

Putting $x_1 = y_1 - y_2, x_2 = y_3 - y_4, x_3 = y_5, x_4 = y_6, x_5 = y_7$ and $x_6 = y_8$, the problem in standard form is

$$\begin{aligned} \text{minimize} \quad & Z = 2y_1 - 2y_2 + 3y_3 - 3y_4, \\ \text{subject to} \quad & -2y_1 + 2y_2 + 3y_3 - 3y_4 + y_5 = 4, \\ & -3y_1 + 3y_2 - 4y_3 + 4y_4 + y_6 = 6, \\ & 2y_1 - 2y_2 + 5y_3 - 5y_4 + y_7 = 10, \\ & 4y_1 - 4y_2 - 3y_3 + 3y_4 + y_8 = 18, \\ \text{where} \quad & y_1, y_2, y_3, y_4, y_5, y_6, y_7, y_8, \text{ all } \geq 0. \end{aligned}$$

Remark. When $x_1 = y_1 - y_2$, it can be seen that for any value of x_1, there will be an infinite number of combinations of (y_1, y_2) which satisfy this equation. However, if values of y_1 and y_2 are given, there will be only one value of x_1. Therefore, if an optimal solution to the new problem is obtained which contains specific values of $y_1, y_2, \ldots$ the corresponding unique values of $x_1, x_2, \ldots$ will also give an optimal solution for the given problem. Thus an optimal solution to the new problem is also an optimal solution to the original problem.

EXAMPLE 2.12-5

Express the following L.P. problem in standard form :

$$\begin{aligned} \textit{Maximize} \quad & Z = 3x_1 + 5x_2 + 2x_3, \\ \textit{subject to} \quad & x_1 + 2x_2 - x_3 \geq -4, \\ & -5x_1 + 6x_2 + 7x_3 \geq 5, \\ & 2x_1 + x_2 + 3x_3 = 10, \\ & x_1, x_2 \geq 0, \; x_3 \textit{ unrestricted in sign.} \end{aligned}$$

Solution. Here only x_3 is unrestricted variable. Let us express $x_3 = x_4 - x_5$, where $x_4 \geq 0$, $x_5 \geq 0$. Thus the problem can be expressed as

$$\begin{array}{lll} \text{maximize} & Z = 3x_1 + 5x_2 + 2x_4 - 2x_5, & \\ \text{subject to} & x_1 + 2x_2 - x_4 + x_5 & \geq -4, \\ & -5x_1 + 6x_2 + 7x_4 - 7x_5 & \geq 5, \\ & 2x_1 + x_2 + 3x_4 - 3x_5 & = 10, \\ & x_1, x_2, x_4, x_5 & \geq 0. \end{array}$$

Multiplying both sides of the first constraint by -1, it takes the form

$$-x_1 - 2x_2 + x_4 - x_5 \leq 4.$$

Adding slack variable s_1 to this constraint and subtracting slack variable s_2 from the second constraint, the problem can be expressed in standard form as

$$\begin{array}{lll} \text{maximize} & Z = 3x_1 + 5x_2 + 2x_4 - 2x_5, & \\ \text{subject to} & -x_1 - 2x_2 + x_4 - x_5 + s_1 & = 4, \\ & -5x_1 + 6x_2 + 7x_4 - 7x_5 - s_2 & = 5, \\ & 2x_1 + x_2 + 3x_4 - 3x_5 & = 10, \\ & x_1, x_2, x_4, x_5, s_1, s_2 \geq 0. & \end{array}$$

EXAMPLE 2.12-6

Express the following L.P. problem in the standard matrix form :

$$\begin{array}{lll} \textit{Maximize} & Z = 4x_1 + 2x_2 + 6x_3, & \\ \textit{subject to} & 2x_1 + 3x_2 + 2x_3 & \geq 6, \\ & 3x_1 + 4x_2 & = 8, \\ & 6x_1 - 4x_2 + x_3 & \leq 10, \\ & x_1, x_2, x_3 \geq 0. & \end{array}$$

Solution. The problem can be expressed in the standard form and then represented in the matrix form as follows :

$$\begin{array}{lll} \text{maximize} & Z = 4x_1 + 2x_2 + 6x_3 + 0x_4 + 0x_5, & \\ & = (4, 2, 6, 0, 0)\,[x_1, x_2, x_3, x_4, x_5], & \\ \text{subject to} & 2x_1 + 3x_2 + 2x_3 - x_4 & = 6, \\ & 3x_1 + 4x_2 & = 8, \\ & 6x_1 - 4x_2 + x_3 + x_5 & = 10, \\ & x_1, x_2, \ldots, x_5 \geq 0. & \end{array}$$

These constraints can be expressed as

$$\begin{pmatrix} 2 & 3 & 2 & -1 & 0 \\ 3 & 4 & 0 & 0 & 0 \\ 6 & -4 & 1 & 0 & 1 \end{pmatrix} \begin{pmatrix} x_1 \\ x_2 \\ x_3 \\ x_4 \\ x_5 \end{pmatrix} = \begin{pmatrix} 6 \\ 8 \\ 10 \end{pmatrix}.$$

Thus the given problem in the matrix form is

$$\begin{array}{ll} & \text{maximize } Z = \mathbf{cx}, \\ & \text{subject to } A\mathbf{x} = \mathbf{b}, \\ & \mathbf{x} \geq \mathbf{0}, \\ \text{where} & \mathbf{x} = [x_1, x_2, x_3, x_4, x_5], \\ & \mathbf{c} = (4, 2, 6, 0, 0), \\ & \mathbf{b} = \begin{bmatrix} 6 \\ 8 \\ 10 \end{bmatrix}, \end{array}$$

and $$\mathbf{A} = \begin{pmatrix} 2 & 3 & 2 & -1 & 0 \\ 3 & 4 & 0 & 0 & 0 \\ 6 & -4 & 1 & 0 & 1 \end{pmatrix}.$$

2.13 THEORY OF SIMPLEX METHOD

Simplex method, also called *simplex technique or simplex algorithm* was developed in 1947 by G.B. Dantzig, an American mathematician. It has the advantage of being universal, *i.e.*, any linear model for which the solution exists, can be solved by it. In principle, it consists of starting with a certain solution of which all that we know is that it is basic feasible, *i.e.*, it satisfies the constraints as well as non-negativity conditions ($x_j \geq 0, j = 1, 2, 3, ..., n$). We, then, improve upon this solution at consecutive stages, until, after a certain finite number of stages, we arrive at the optimal solution. The method also helps the decision-maker to identify the redundant constraints, an unbounded solution, multiple solutions and an infeasible solution.

The simplex method provides an algorithm which consists in moving from one vertex of the region of feasible solutions to another in such a manner that the value of the objective function at the succeeding vertex is less in a minimization problem (or more in a maximization problem) than at the preceding vertex. This procedure of jumping from one vertex to another is then repeated. Since the number of vertices is finite, this method leads to an optimal vertex in a finite number of steps. The basis of the simplex method consists of two fundamental conditions:

1. *The feasibility condition* : It ensures that if the starting solution is basic feasible, only basic feasible solutions will be obtained during computation.

2. *The optimality condition* : It guarantees that only better solutions (as compared to the current solution) will be encountered.

Simplex method makes use of the following three points in achieving a systematic reduction from an infinite number of solutions to a finite number of promising solutions:

1. If there are m equality constraints and $m + n$ is the number of variables ($m \leq n$), a start for the optimal solution is made by putting n unknowns (variables) [out of ($m + n$) unknowns] equal to zero and then solving for the m equations in remaining m unknowns, provided that the solution exists and is unique. The n zero variables are called *nonbasic variables* and the remaining m variables are called *basic* variables which form a *basic solution*. If the solution yields all non-negative basic variables, it is called *basic feasible solution;* otherwise it is *infeasible*. This step reduces the number of alternatives for the optimal solution from infinite to a finite number, whose maximum limit can be

$$^{m+n}C_m = \frac{(m+n)!}{m!\,n!}.$$

The resulting number of alternative solutions is still too large to be computationally feasible and is reduced by the 2nd condition.

2. We know that in a linear programming problem, all the variables must be non-negative. Since the basic solutions selected by condition 1 above are not necessarily non-negative, the number of alternatives can be further reduced by eliminating all *infeasible basic solutions* (solutions having variables of values less than zero). In the simplex method this is achieved by starting with a basic solution which is non-negative (≥ 0). A condition, called *feasibility condition* is then provided which ensures that the next basic solution to be selected from all the possible basic solutions is always feasible (≥ 0). This solution is called *basic feasible solution.* If all the basic variables are greater than zero (> 0), the solution is called *non-degenerate*; if some of them are zero, the solution is called *degenerate.* It will be shown in section 2.16 that a new basic feasible solution can be obtained from the previous one by setting *one of the m* basic variables equal to zero and

replacing it by a new non-basic variable. The basic variable set equal to zero is called a "*leaving variable*", while the new one is called an "*entering variable*".

3. The entering variable can be so selected that it improves the value of objective function so that the new solution is better than the previous one. This is achieved by the use of another condition called *optimality condition* which selects that entering variable which produces the largest *per unit* gain in the objective function. This procedure is repeated successively until no further improvement in the value of the objective function is possible. The final solution is, then, called an *optimal basic feasible solution* or simply *optimal solution*. This is the solution which optimizes the objective function equation, and satisfies all the constraints as well as the non-negativity conditions. This is, of course, true only if the objective function has a finite value.

The foregoing discussion shows that simplex method procedure is principally a *screening process* since it eliminates the solutions that are not promising solutions for the optimal solution.

2.14 SOME IMPORTANT DEFINITIONS

Consider the general linear programming problem involving n variables and m constraints $(m \leq n)$:

Determine the values of variables $x_1, x_2, ..., x_n$ which

$$\begin{aligned} \text{maximize} \quad & Z = c_1x_1 + c_2x_2 + ... + c_nx_n, \\ \text{subject to} \quad & a_{11}x_1 + a_{12}x_2 + ... + a_{1n}x_n \leq b_1, \\ & a_{21}x_1 + a_{22}x_2 + ... + a_{2n}x_n \leq b_2, \\ & \vdots \qquad\qquad\qquad\qquad\qquad \vdots \\ & a_{m1}x_1 + a_{m2}x_2 + ... + a_{mn}x_n \leq b_m, \\ \text{where} \quad & x_1, x_2, ..., x_n \geq 0. \end{aligned}$$

Introducing slack variables $x_{n+1}, x_{n+2}, ..., x_{n+m}$ in the constraints, it can be put in the following standard form :

$$\text{maximize} \quad Z = c_1x_1 + c_2x_2 + ... + c_nx_n, \qquad ... (2.13)$$

$$\text{subject to} \quad \left.\begin{aligned} a_{11}x_1 + a_{12}x_2 + ... + a_{1n}x_n + x_{n+1} &= b_1, \\ a_{21}x_1 + a_{22}x_2 + ... + a_{2n}x_n + x_{n+2} &= b_2, \\ \vdots \qquad\qquad\qquad &\vdots \\ a_{m1}x_1 + a_{m2}x_2 + ... + a_{mn}x_n + x_{n+m} &= b_m, \end{aligned}\right\} \qquad ... (2.14)$$

$$\text{where} \quad x_1, x_2, ..., x_n, x_{n+1}, x_{n+2}, ..., x_{n+m} \geq 0. \qquad ... (2.15)$$

1. *Solution*: A set of variables $[x_1, x_2, ..., x_{n+m}]$ is called a solution to L.P. problem if it satisfies the constraints (2.14).

2. *Feasible solution*: A set of variables $[x_1, x_2, ..., x_{n+m}]$ is called a feasible solution to L.P. problem if it satisfies the constraints (2.14) as well as non-negativity restrictions (2.15).

3. *Basic solution*: A solution obtained by setting any n variables (among $m + n$ variables) equal to zero and solving for remaining m variables (provided the determinant of the coefficients of these m variables is non-zero) is called a *basic solution*. These m variables (some of them may be zero) are called *basic variables* and the remaining n variables that have been put equal to zero each are called *non-basic variables*.

The number of basic solutions thus obtained will at most be ${}^{m+n}c_m = \dfrac{(m+n)!}{m!\,n!}$, which is the number of combinations of $m + n$ things taken m at a time.

4. *Basic feasible solution*: It is a basic solution that also satisfies the non-negativity restrictions (2.15). All variables in a basic feasible solution are ≥ 0. Every basic feasible solution of a problem

is an extreme point of the convex set of feasible solutions and every extreme point is a basic feasible solution of the set of constraints.

5. *Non-degenerate basic feasible solution*: It is a basic feasible solution in which all the m basic variables are positive (> 0) and the remaining n variables are zero each.

6. *Degenerate basic feasible solution*: It is a basic feasible solution in which one or more of the m basic variables are equal to zero.

7. *Optimal basic feasible solution*: It is the basic feasible solution that also optimizes the objective function (2.13).

8. *Unbounded solution*: If the value of the objective function can be increased or decreased indefinitely, the solution is called unbounded solution.

Unless otherwise stated, solution means a feasible solution.

9. *Set of points*: Just as a linear equation in x_1, x_2 such as $a_1x_1 + a_2x_2 = b$ represents a line in two-dimensions, so also a linear equation in x_1, x_2 and x_3, such as

$$a_1x_1 + a_2x_2 + a_3x_3 = b$$

or $\qquad \boldsymbol{ax} = b,$

where $\qquad \boldsymbol{a} = (a_1, a_2, a_3),$

and $\qquad \boldsymbol{x} = (x_1, x_2, x_3),$

represents a plane. Both of them are considered as *set of points*. Thus a line represents a set of points that satisfy the equation $a_1x_1 + a_2x_2 = b$, while a plane represents a set of points that satisfy $\boldsymbol{ax} = b$.

10. *Convex sets*: A set (of points) $\boldsymbol{S}$ is said to be a convex set if for any two points in the set, the line joining these two points lies entirely in the set. Fig. 2.23 (*a*) thus represents convex sets. On the other hand Fig. 2.23 (*b*) represents non-convex sets as they do not satisfy the above condition.

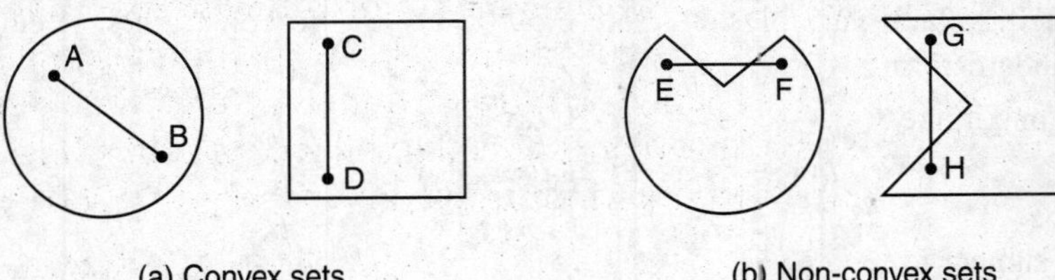

(a) Convex sets (b) Non-convex sets

Fig. 2.23

2.15 ANALYTICAL METHOD OR TRIAL AND ERROR METHOD

Graphical method cannot be applied to solve L.P. problems involving more than 2 variables. In such cases, analytical method (also called trial and error method) is quite helpful. This method also forms a good basis to grasp the more powerful simplex method. This method will be explained with the help of a few examples.

EXAMPLE 2.15-1

Solve example 2.9-1 by the trial and error method.

Solution

Linear programming model for the problem is

maximize $\qquad Z = 3x_1 + 4x_2,$

subject to $\qquad x_1 + x_2 \leq 450,$

$\qquad 2x_1 + x_2 \leq 600,$

where $\qquad x_1, x_2 \geq 0.$

The problem is first expressed in standard form by the introduction of slack variables s_1 and s_2 as shown below :

maximize $Z = 3x_1 + 4x_2 + 0s_1 + 0s_2$,
subject to $x_1 + x_2 + s_1 = 450$,
$2x_1 + x_2 + s_2 = 600$,
$x_1, x_2, s_1, s_2 \geq 0$.

The slack variables represent dummy (fictitious or imaginary) products with zero profit per unit. Here total number of variables, $m + n = 4$ and number of constraints, $m = 2$. A basic solution can be obtained by setting the n (2) variables equal to zero and then solving the constraint equations. The total number of basic solutions will be

$$^4C_2 = \frac{4!}{2!(4-2)!} = \frac{4 \times 3 \times 2 \times 1}{(2 \times 1) \times (2 \times 1)} = 6.$$

Table 2.17 gives a summary of the characteristics of the various basic solutions.

TABLE 2.17

S.No. of the basic solution	*Basic variables*	*Non-basic variables*	*Values of the basic variables given by the constraint equations*	*Value of the objective function*	*Is the solution feasible? (are all $x_j \geq 0$?)*	*Is the solution non-degenerate (are all basic variables > 0?)*	*Is the solution feasible and optimal?*
1	x_1, x_2	s_1, s_2	$x_1 + x_2 = 450$ $2x_1 + x_2 = 600$ $\therefore x_1 = 150, x_2 = 300$	1,650	Yes	Yes	No
2	x_1, s_1	x_2, s_2	$x_1 + s_1 = 450$ $2x_1 = 600$ $\therefore x_1 = 300, s_1 = 150$	900	Yes	Yes	No
3	x_1, s_2	x_2, s_1	$x_1 = 450$ $2x_1 + s_2 = 600$ $\therefore x_1 = 450, s_2 = -300$	—	No	No	No
4	x_2, s_1	x_1, s_2	$x_2 + s_1 = 450$ $x_2 = 600$ $\therefore x_1 = -150$	—	No	No	No
5	x_2, s_2	x_1, s_1	$x_2 = 450$ $x_2 + s_2 = 600$ $\therefore s_2 = 150$	1,800	Yes	Yes	Yes
6	s_1, s_2	x_1, x_2	$s_1 = 450, s_2 = 600$	0	Yes	Yes	No

Out of these solutions, solutions in which all basic variables x_j are ≥ 0 will be basic feasible; solutions in which all basic variables are > 0 will be non-degenerate basic feasible and the basic feasible solution that optimizes the objective function will be the optimal basic feasible solution. It may be seen that solutions 1, 2, 5 and 6 are basic feasible; they are also non-degenerate. Out of these, solution 5 gives the maximum value of the objective function Z and is, therefore, the optimal solution. Solutions 3 and 4 are infeasible and are to be discarded from consideration. Thus the optimal solution to the problem is

$x_1 = 0, x_2 = 450$; $Z_{max} = ₹\ 1,800$.

EXAMPLE 2.15-2

Find all the basic solutions to the following problem :

Maximize $Z = x_1 + 3x_2 + 3x_3$,
subject to $x_1 + 2x_2 + 3x_3 = 4$,
$2x_1 + 3x_2 + 5x_3 = 7$.

Also find which of the basic solutions are
 (i) basic feasible,
 (ii) non-degenerate basic feasible, and
 (iii) optimal basic feasible.

Solution. Since $m + n = 3$ and $m = 2$ in this problem, a basic solution can be obtained by setting the n variables equal to zero and then solving the constraint equations. The total number of basic solutions is

$$^3C_2 = \frac{3!}{2!1!} = 3.$$

Out of these solutions, solutions in which all basic variables (x_j) are ≥ 0 will be basic feasible; solutions in which all basic variables are > 0 will be non-degenerate basic feasible and the basic feasible solution that optimizes the objective function will be the optimal basic feasible solution. Table 2.18 gives a summary of the characteristics of the various basic solutions.

TABLE 2.18

S.No. of the basic solution	*Basic variables*	*Non-basic variables*	*Values of the basic variables given by the constraint equations*	*Value of the objective function*	*Is the solution feasible? (are all $x_j \geq 0$?)*	*Is the solution non-degenerate (are all basic variables > 0?)*	*Is the solution feasible and optimal?*
1	x_1, x_2	x_3	$x_1 + 2x_2 = 4$ $2x_1 + 3x_2 = 7$ $\therefore\ x_1 = 2, x_2 = 1$	5	Yes	Yes	Yes
2	x_1, x_3	x_2	$x_1 + 3x_3 = 4$ $2x_1 + 5x_3 = 7$ $\therefore\ x_1 = 1, x_3 = 1$	4	Yes	Yes	No
3	x_2, x_3	x_1	$2x_2 + 3x_3 = 4$ $3x_2 + 5x_3 = 7$ $\therefore\ x_2 = -1, x_3 = 2$	—	No	No	No

It may be seen that the first two solutions are basic feasible; they are also non-degenerate basic feasible solutions. The first solution, of course, is the optimal one.

Thus the optimal solution is $x_1 = 2, x_2 = 1, x_3 = 0$ with $Z_{max} = 5$.

EXAMPLE 2.15-3

A firm manufactures four different machine parts M_1, M_2, M_3 and M_4 made of copper and zinc. The amounts of copper and zinc required for each machine part, their exact availability and the profit earned from one unit of each machine part are as follows :

	M_1 (kg)	*M_2 (kg)*	*M_3 (kg)*	*M_4 (kg)*	*Exact availability (kg)*
Copper	*5*	*4*	*2*	*1*	*100*
Zinc	*2*	*3*	*8*	*1*	*75*
Profit (₹)	*12*	*8*	*14*	*10*	

How many of each part be manufactured to maximize profit ? For this problem find
 (i) basic solutions,
 (ii) basic feasible solutions,

(iii) non-degenerate basic feasible solutions, and

(iv) optimal basic feasible solution. [*P.U.B.E. (Elect.) 1996*]

Solution. Let x_1, x_2, x_3 and x_4 represent the quantities to be manufactured of machine parts M_1, M_2, M_3 and M_4 respectively. Then the linear programming problem is

$$\text{maximize} \quad Z = 12x_1 + 8x_2 + 14x_3 + 10x_4,$$

$$\text{subject to} \quad 5x_1 + 4x_2 + 2x_3 + x_4 = 100,$$

$$2x_1 + 3x_2 + 8x_3 + x_4 = 75,$$

$$\text{where} \quad x_1, x_2, x_3, x_4, \text{ all} \geq 0.$$

Here $m + n = 4$ and $m = 2$. A basic solution can be obtained by setting the $(n = 2)$ non-basic variables equal to zero and then solving the constraint (containing the basic variables) equations. The total number of basic solutions is

$$^4C_2 = \frac{4!}{2!2!} = 6.$$

Table 2.19 gives a summary of the characteristics of the various solutions.

TABLE 2.19

S.No. of the basic solution	*Basic variables*	*Non-basic variables*	*Values of the basic variables given by the constraint equations*	*Value of the objective function*	*Is the solution feasible? (are all $x_j \geq 0$?)*	*Is the solution non-degenerate? (are all basic variables > 0?)*	*Is the solution feasible and optimal?*
1	x_1, x_2	x_3, x_4	$5x_1 + 4x_2 = 100$ $2x_1 + 3x_2 = 75$ $\therefore\ x_1 = 0, x_2 = 25$	200	Yes	No	No
2	x_1, x_3	x_2, x_4	$5x_1 + 2x_3 = 100$ $2x_1 + 8x_3 = 75$ $\therefore\ x_1 = 325/18$ $x_3 = 175/36$	5,125/18	Yes	Yes	No
3	x_1, x_4	x_2, x_3	$5x_1 + x_4 = 100$ $2x_1 + x_4 = 75$ $\therefore\ x_1 = 25/3,$ $x_4 = 175/3$	2,050/3	Yes	Yes	Yes
4	x_2, x_3	x_1, x_4	$4x_2 + 2x_3 = 100$ $3x_2 + 8x_3 = 75$ $\therefore\ x_2 = 25, x_3 = 0$	200	Yes	No	No
5	x_2, x_4	x_1, x_3	$4x_2 + x_4 = 100$ $3x_2 + x_4 = 75$ $\therefore\ x_2 = 25, x_4 = 0$	200	Yes	No	No
6	x_3, x_4	x_1, x_2	$2x_3 + x_4 = 100$ $8x_3 + x_4 = 75$ $\therefore\ x_3 = -25/6,$ $x_4 = 325/3$	—	No	No	No

From the table the following inferences can be drawn:

1. Basic solutions are no. 1, 2, 3, 4, 5 and 6.

2. Basic feasible solutions are no. 1, 2, 3, 4 and 5.
3. Non-degenerate basic feasible solutions are no. 2 and 3.
4. Optimal basic feasible solution is no. 3, which gives
$x_1 = 25/3, x_2 = 0, x_3 = 0, x_4 = 175/3$ and $Z_{max} = 2{,}050/3$.

This trial and error method, however, suffers from the following inefficiencies :

1. In linear programming problems where m and n are large, solving numerous sets of simultaneous equations would be extremely cumbersome and time-consuming.

2. Scanning the profit column (value of objective function) in table 2.19, we find that its value changes from 200 to 5,125/18 to 2050/3 to 200 *i.e.*, there are ups and downs. There is need for a method that would ensure that successive solutions yield higher profit, culminating into the optimal one.

3. Some of the sets yield infeasible solutions. There should be means to detect such sets and not to solve them at all.

The simplex method, to be discussed soon, overcomes all these drawbacks.

EXAMPLE 2.15-4

Show, using matrix-vector notation, that the following system of linear equations has degenerate solutions :

$$2x_1 + x_2 - x_3 = 2,$$
$$3x_1 + 2x_2 + x_3 = 3.$$

[*Madurai B.Sc. (Math.) 1984*]

Solution. The given system of equations can be written as

$$\boldsymbol{Ax} = \boldsymbol{b},$$

where $\boldsymbol{A} = \begin{bmatrix} 2 & 1 & -1 \\ 3 & 2 & 1 \end{bmatrix}, \boldsymbol{x} = \begin{bmatrix} x_1 \\ x_2 \\ x_3 \end{bmatrix}$ and $\boldsymbol{b} = \begin{bmatrix} 2 \\ 3 \end{bmatrix}$.

Since A is of the order 2×3, there can be $^3C_2 = \dfrac{3!}{2!1!} = 3$ submatrices of the order 2×2.

They are

$$\begin{bmatrix} 2 & 1 \\ 3 & 2 \end{bmatrix}, \begin{bmatrix} 1 & -1 \\ 2 & 1 \end{bmatrix} \text{ and } \begin{bmatrix} 2 & -1 \\ 3 & 1 \end{bmatrix}.$$

Any one of them can be taken as our basis matrix **B**. The variables not associated with the columns of these submatrices are respectively x_3, x_1 and x_2.

Considering $\mathbf{B} = \begin{pmatrix} 2 & 1 \\ 3 & 2 \end{pmatrix}$,

a basic solution to the given system is obtained by setting $x_3 = 0$ and solving the system

$$\begin{pmatrix} 2 & 1 \\ 3 & 2 \end{pmatrix}\begin{pmatrix} x_1 \\ x_2 \end{pmatrix} = \begin{pmatrix} 2 \\ 3 \end{pmatrix}$$

or

$$2x_1 + x_2 = 2,$$
$$3x_1 + 2x_2 = 3,$$

which gives the basic solution to the problem :

$$x_1 = 1, x_2 = 0 \text{ (basic)}; x_3 = 0 \text{ (non-basic)}.$$

Similarly, considering the other two submatrices, we get solutions :

$$x_2 = 5/3, x_3 = -1/3 \text{ (basic)}; x_1 = 0 \text{ (non-basic) and}$$
$$x_1 = 1, x_3 = 0 \text{ (basic)}; x_2 = 0 \text{ (non-basic)}.$$

Since in two of these basic feasible solutions, one basic variable is zero, they are degenerate solutions. The second solution [0, 5/3, – 1/3] is not feasible. Thus the remaining two degenerate basic feasible solutions are

(1, 0, 0) and (1, 0, 0).

EXAMPLE 2.15-5

Find all the basic feasible solutions of the equations

$$2x_1 + 6x_2 + 2x_3 + x_4 = 3,$$
$$6x_1 + 4x_2 + 4x_3 + 6x_4 = 2.$$

[*Madurai B.Sc. (Appl. Math.) 1984; Delhi B.Sc. (Math.) 1983*]

Solution. The given system of equations can be presented in the following matrix form :

$$\mathbf{A}\boldsymbol{x} = \boldsymbol{b},$$

where $\mathbf{A} = \begin{pmatrix} 2 & 6 & 2 & 1 \\ 6 & 4 & 4 & 6 \end{pmatrix}$, $\boldsymbol{x} = \begin{pmatrix} x_1 \\ x_2 \\ x_3 \\ x_4 \end{pmatrix}$ and $\boldsymbol{b} = \begin{pmatrix} 3 \\ 2 \end{pmatrix}$.

Since $\mathbf{A}$ is of order 2 × 4, we can take any of the following ${}^4C_2 = \dfrac{4!}{2!2!} = 6$, 2 × 2 submatrices as our basis matrix $\mathbf{B}$:

$$\begin{pmatrix} 2 & 6 \\ 6 & 4 \end{pmatrix}, \begin{pmatrix} 2 & 2 \\ 6 & 4 \end{pmatrix}, \begin{pmatrix} 2 & 1 \\ 6 & 6 \end{pmatrix}, \begin{pmatrix} 6 & 2 \\ 4 & 4 \end{pmatrix}, \begin{pmatrix} 6 & 1 \\ 4 & 6 \end{pmatrix} \text{ and } \begin{pmatrix} 2 & 1 \\ 4 & 6 \end{pmatrix}.$$

The variables not associated with the first submatrix are x_3 and x_4. The basic solution to the given system is obtained by setting $x_3 = 0$, $x_4 = 0$ and solving the system.

$$\begin{pmatrix} 2 & 6 \\ 6 & 4 \end{pmatrix}\begin{pmatrix} x_1 \\ x_2 \end{pmatrix} = \begin{pmatrix} 3 \\ 2 \end{pmatrix}.$$

Solving this system of equations, a basic solution to the given system of equations is

$x_1 = 0, x_2 = 1/2$ (basic); $x_3 = x_4 = 0$ (non-basic).

Similarly, the other five solutions are

$x_1 = -2, x_3 = 7/2$ (basic); $x_2 = x_4 = 0$ (non-basic),

$x_1 = 8/3, x_4 = -7/3$ (basic); $x_2 = x_3 = 0$ (non-basic),

$x_2 = 1/2, x_3 = 0$ (basic); $x_1 = x_4 = 0$ (non-basic),

$x_2 = 1/2, x_4 = 0$ (basic); $x_1 = x_3 = 0$ (non-basic),

$x_3 = 2, x_4 = -1$ (basic); $x_1 = x_2 = 0$ (non-basic).

Out of the these six solutions, solutions (– 2, 0, 7/2, 0), (8/3, 0, 0, – 7/3) and (0, 0, 2, – 1) are not feasible. Also in each of the remaining three basic feasible solutions, at least one of the basic variables is zero. Hence the degenerate basic feasible solutions of the given system are

(0, 1/2, 0, 0), (0, 1/2, 0, 0) and (0, 1/2, 0, 0).

EXAMPLE 2.15-6

Is the following solution

$$x_1 = 1, \; x_2 = \frac{1}{2}, \; x_3 = x_4 = x_5 = 0$$

a basic solution of the equations

$$x_1 + 2x_2 + x_3 + x_4 = 2,$$
$$x_1 + 2x_2 + \frac{1}{2}x_3 + x_5 = 2\ ?$$

[*Madurai B.Sc. (Appl. Math.) 1983*]

Solution

The given system of equations can be presented in the following matrix form :

$$\mathbf{A}\boldsymbol{x} = \boldsymbol{b}, \text{ where } \quad \mathbf{A} = \begin{pmatrix} 1 & 2 & 1 & 1 & 0 \\ 1 & 2 & \frac{1}{2} & 0 & 1 \end{pmatrix}, \boldsymbol{x} = \begin{pmatrix} x_1 \\ x_2 \\ x_3 \\ x_4 \\ x_5 \end{pmatrix} \text{ and } \boldsymbol{b} = \begin{pmatrix} 2 \\ 2 \end{pmatrix}.$$

Since **A** is of order 2 × 5, we can take any of the following $^5C_2 = \dfrac{5!}{3!2!} = 10, 2 \times 2$ submatrices as our basis matrix **B** :

$$\begin{bmatrix} 1 & 2 \\ 1 & 2 \end{bmatrix}, \begin{bmatrix} 1 & 1 \\ 1 & \frac{1}{2} \end{bmatrix}, \begin{bmatrix} 1 & 1 \\ 1 & 0 \end{bmatrix}, \begin{bmatrix} 1 & 0 \\ 1 & 1 \end{bmatrix}, \begin{bmatrix} 2 & 1 \\ 2 & \frac{1}{2} \end{bmatrix}, \begin{bmatrix} 2 & 1 \\ 2 & 0 \end{bmatrix}, \begin{bmatrix} 2 & 0 \\ 2 & 1 \end{bmatrix}, \begin{bmatrix} 1 & 1 \\ \frac{1}{2} & 0 \end{bmatrix}, \begin{bmatrix} 1 & 0 \\ \frac{1}{2} & 1 \end{bmatrix} \text{ and } \begin{bmatrix} 1 & 0 \\ 0 & 1 \end{bmatrix}.$$

Out of these ten submatrices, the first submatrix may be dropped from consideration. Considering the remaining submatrices, the solutions are

$x_1 = 2, x_3 = 0$ (basic); $x_2 = x_4 = x_5 = 0$ (non-basic),
$x_1 = 2, x_4 = 0$ (basic); $x_2 = x_3 = x_5 = 0$ (non-basic),
$x_1 = 2, x_5 = 0$ (basic); $x_2 = x_3 = x_4 = 0$ (non-basic),
$x_2 = 1, x_3 = 0$ (basic); $x_1 = x_4 = x_5 = 0$ (non-basic),
$x_2 = 1, x_4 = 0$ (basic); $x_1 = x_3 = x_5 = 0$ (non-basic),
$x_2 = 1, x_5 = 0$ (basic); $x_1 = x_3 = x_4 = 0$ (non-basic),
$x_3 = 4, x_4 = -2$ (basic); $x_1 = x_2 = x_5 = 0$ (non-basic),
$x_3 = 2, x_5 = 1$ (basic); $x_1 = x_2 = x_4 = 0$ (non-basic),
$x_4 = 2, x_5 = 2$ (basic); $x_1 = x_2 = x_3 = 0$ (non-basic).

Clearly none of these corresponds to the given solution, *viz.*, $x_1 = 1, x_2 = 1/2, x_3 = x_4 = x_5 = 0$. Hence the given solution is not basic.

EXERCISES 2.3

1. Express the linear programming problem in generalised matrix form.
[*P.T.U. MBA May, 2014; Mumbai U. B.Com. April, 2013; IGNOU MBA Dec., 2006*]
2. Explain canonical and standard forms of L.P. problems.
[*P.T.U. BCA, 2010; MCA, 2010*]
3. Define the following :
(*i*) Basic solution (*ii*) Basic feasible solution (*iii*) Degenerate solution (*iv*) Non-degenerate solution (*v*) Optimal feasible solution.
[*Univ. of Madras B.Sc. (Math.) Nov., 2012; P.T.U.B. Tech. (Mech.) Dec., 2011; BCA, 2013; J.N.T.U. Hyderabad B.Tech. (Mech.) May, 2012; April, 2011; L.U. B.Com. 2010; G.N.D.U. B.Com., 2006, 03, 00; P.U.B.E. (T. & I.T.) Nov., 2004; B.E. (Mech.) 2000; B.Com. April, 2007; Sept., 2006; 2000; P.T.U. B.Tech. (C.Sc.) 2010, 2009; MBA June, 2003*]
4. Write short notes on
(*i*) Types of variables used in L.P.P.
(*ii*) Basic solution of L.P.P. [*P.U.B.E. (C.S. & E.) Dec., 2004; B.Com. April, 2002*]
5. Why is simplex method a better technique than graphical method for most real cases ?
[*GNDU B.Com., 1995*]
6. How can you handle unrestricted variables in the solution of L.P. problems ?
[*P.U. B.Com. April, 2004*]
7. Give general form of L.P.P. [*J.N.T.U. Hyderabad B.Tech., 2011*]

8. Reduce the following linear programming problem to the standard form :
Determine $x_1 \geq 0,\ x_2 \geq 0,\ x_3 \geq 0$
so as to maximize $A = 5x_1 + 3x_2 + 4x_3$,
subject to the constraints
$$2x_1 - 5x_2 \leq 6,$$
$$2x_1 + 3x_2 + x_3 \geq 5,$$
$$3x_1 + 4x_3 \leq 3.$$
(*Ans.* Maximize $A = 5x_1 + 3x_2 + 4x_3$,
subject to $2x_1 - 5x_2 + s_1 = 6$,
$2x_1 + 3x_2 + x_3 - s_2 = 5$,
$3x_1 + 4x_3 + s_3 = 3$,
$x_1, x_2, x_3, s_1, s_2, s_3 \geq 0$.)

9. Reduce the following linear programming problem to the standard form :
Determine $x_1 \geq 0,\ x_2 \geq 0,\ x_3$
so as to minimize $G = 2x_1 + x_2 + 3x_3$,
subject to the constraints
$$-5x_1 + 2x_2 \leq 5,$$
$$3x_1 + 2x_2 + 4x_3 \geq 7,$$
$$2x_1 + 5x_3 \leq 3.$$
(*Ans.* Minimize $G = 2y_1 + y_2 + 3y_3 - 3y_4$,
subject to $-5y_1 + 2y_2 + y_5 = 5$,
$3y_1 + 2y_2 + 4y_3 - 4y_4 - y_6 = 7$,
$2y_1 + 5y_3 - 5y_4 + y_7 = 3$,
$y_1, y_2, ..., y_7 \geq 0$.)

10. Put the following problem in the standard form :
Maximize $Z = 4x_1 + x_2 - 3x_3$,
subject to
$$x_1 + 5x_2 - 3x_3 \leq 20,$$
$$2x_1 + 7x_2 + 2x_3 \leq 10,$$
$$x_1 - 5x_2 - 3x_3 \geq 3,$$
$$x_1 \geq 0.$$
(*Ans.* Maximize $Z = 4y_1 + y_2 - y_3 - 3y_4 + 3y_5$,
subject to $y_1 + 5y_2 - 5y_3 - 3y_4 + 3y_5 + y_6 = 20$,
$2y_1 + 7y_2 - 7y_3 + 2y_4 - 2y_5 + y_7 = 10$,
$y_1 - 5y_2 + 5y_3 - 3y_4 + 3y_5 - y_8 = 3$,
$y_1, y_2, ..., y_8 \geq 0$.)

11. Express the following problem in the standard form :
Maximize $Z = 2x_1 + 5x_2$,
subject to
$$x_1 + 2x_2 - x_3 = -4,$$
$$3x_1 + 4x_2 - x_4 = -7,$$
$$x_1 + 2x_2 + x_5 = 9,$$
$$5x_1 - 2x_2 + x_6 = 17.$$
$$x_3, x_4, x_5, x_6 \geq 0.$$
(*Ans.* Minimize $Z = 2y_1 - 2y_2 + 5y_3 - 5y_4$,
subject to $-y_1 + y_2 - 2y_3 + 2y_4 + y_5 = 4$,
$-3y_1 + 3y_2 - 4y_3 + 4y_4 + y_6 = 7$,
$y_1 - y_2 + 2y_3 - 2y_4 + y_7 = 9$,
$5y_1 - 5y_2 - 2y_3 + 2y_4 + y_8 = 17$,
$y_1, y_2, ..., y_8 \geq 0$.)

12. Express the following L.P. problem in the matrix form :
Minimize $Z = 4x_1 + 5x_2 + 6x_3$,
subject to
$$2x_1 + 3x_3 \geq 6,$$
$$2x_1 + 3x_2 + 2x_3 = 8,$$
$$5x_1 - 2x_2 + 5x_3 \leq 10,$$
$$x_1, x_2, x_3 \geq 0.$$
(*Ans.* Minimize $Z = (4, 5, 6, 0, 0)\ (x_1, x_2, x_3, x_4, x_5)$,

$$\text{subject to} \begin{pmatrix} 2 & 0 & 3 & -1 & 0 \\ 2 & 3 & 2 & 0 & 0 \\ 5 & -2 & 5 & 0 & 1 \end{pmatrix} \begin{pmatrix} x_1 \\ x_2 \\ x_3 \\ x_4 \\ x_5 \end{pmatrix} = \begin{pmatrix} 6 \\ 8 \\ 10 \end{pmatrix}.$$

$x_1, x_2, ..., x_5 \geq 0$.)

13. Obtain all the basic solutions to the following system of linear equations :

$$x_1 + 2x_2 + x_3 = 4,$$
$$2x_1 + x_2 + 5x_3 = 5.$$

Which of them are basic feasible solutions and which are non-degenerate basic solutions ? Is the non-degenerate solution feasible ?

[*Kuru. U.B.E. (E. & Ec.) 1988; Meerut M.Sc. (Math.) 1974*]

(*Ans.* (*a*) (*i*) $x_1 = 2, x_2 = 1, x_3 = 0$,
(*ii*) $x_1 = 5, x_2 = 0, x_3 = -1$,
(*iii*) $x_1 = 0, x_2 = 5/3, x_3 = 2/3$;
(*b*) (*i*) and (*iii*);
(*c*) (*i*) and (*iii*);
(*d*) Yes.)

14. Compute all the basic feasible solutions to the L.P. problem :

Maximize $Z = 2x_1 + 3x_2 + 4x_3 + 7x_4$,
subject to the constraints $2x_1 + 3x_2 - x_3 + 4x_4 = 8$,
$x_1 - 2x_2 + 6x_3 - 7x_4 = -3$,
$x_1, x_2, x_3, x_4 \geq 0$,

and choose that one which maximizes Z.

[*Roorkee (B.E.) 1991; Meerut (B.Sc.) 1990; Meerut M.Sc. (Math.) 1988, 83*]

(*Ans.* (*i*) $x_1 = 1, x_2 = 2, x_3 = 0, x_4 = 0$

(*ii*) $x_1 = \frac{22}{9}, x_2 = 0, x_3 = 0, x_4 = \frac{7}{9}$

(*iii*) $x_1 = 0, x_2 = \frac{45}{16}, x_3 = \frac{7}{16}, x_4 = 0$

(*iv*) $x_1 = 0, x_2 = 0, x_3 = \frac{44}{17}, x_4 = \frac{45}{17}$; $Z_{max} = \frac{491}{17}$.)

15. What do you mean by an optimal basic feasible solution to an L.P. problem ? Is the solution $x_1 = 1$, $x_2 = \frac{1}{2}$, $x_3 = x_4 = x_5 = 0$ a basic solution to the equations

$$x_1 + 2x_2 + x_3 + x_4 = 2,$$

and

$$x_1 + 2x_2 + \frac{1}{2} x_3 + x_5 = 2 \ ?$$

[*Delhi B.Sc. (Math.) 1975*]

(*Ans.* No.)

16. Find all the basic feasible solutions of the equations

$$2x_1 + 6x_2 + 2x_3 + x_4 = 3,$$
$$6x_1 + 4x_2 + 4x_3 + 6x_4 = 2.$$

[*Delhi B.Sc. (Math.) 1978*]

(*Ans.* (*i*) $x_1 = 0, x_2 = \frac{1}{2}, x_3 = x_4 = 0$,

(*ii*) $x_2 = \frac{1}{2}$, $x_3 = 0$, $x_1 = x_4 = 0$,

(*iii*) $x_2 = \frac{1}{2}$, $x_4 = 0$, $x_1 = x_3 = 0$.)

17. Determine the optimum solution for the following L.P.P. by enumerating all the basic solutions :

$$\text{Maximize } Z = 2x_1 - 4x_2 + 5x_3 - 6x_4,$$
$$\text{subject to} \quad x_1 + 4x_2 - 2x_3 + 8x_4 \le 2,$$
$$-x_1 + 2x_2 + 3x_3 + 4x_4 \le 1,$$
$$x_1, x_2, x_3, x_4 \ge 0.$$

[*IGNOU MBA, 2001*]

(*Ans.* $x_1 = 8$, $x_2 = 0$, $x_3 = 3$, $x_4 = 0$; $Z_{max} = 31$.)

18. The following table gives the calorie values and the protein contents of five types of foods along with their costs. Find the amount of each type of food to be purchased in order to meet exactly the daily requirements of a person at minimum cost. Assume that a person, on the average, requires 3,000 calories and 100 grams of proteins.

	Bread	*Meat*	*Potatoes*	*Cabbage*	*Milk*
Calories	2,500	3,000	600	100	600
Proteins (gm)	80	150	20	10	40
Cost/kg (₹)	3	10	1	2	3

Also find

(*i*) basic feasible solutions,

(*ii*) non-degenerate basic feasible solutions,

(*iii*) optimal basic feasible solution.

(*Ans.* 1. $x_1 = \frac{10}{9}$, $x_2 = \frac{2}{27}$; $Z = 4\frac{2}{27}$; other non-basic variables zero.)

2. $x_1 = 0$, $x_3 = 5$; $Z = 5$; -do-

3. $x_1 = \frac{20}{17}$, $x_4 = \frac{10}{17}$; $Z = 4\frac{12}{17}$; -do-

4. $x_1 = \frac{15}{13}$, $x_5 = \frac{5}{26}$; $Z = 4\frac{1}{26}$; -do-

5. $x_2 = 0$, $x_3 = 5$; $Z = 5$; -do-

6. $x_2 = \frac{4}{3}$, $x_4 = -10$; $Z = -6\frac{2}{3}$; -do-

7. $x_2 = 2$, $x_5 = -5$; $Z = 5$; -do-

8. $x_3 = 5$, $x_4 = 0$; $Z = 5$; -do-

9. $x_3 = 5$, $x_5 = 0$; $Z = 5$; -do-

10. $x_4 = -30$, $x_5 = 10$; $Z = -30$; -do-

(*i*) No. 1, 2, 3, 4, 5, 8, 9.

(*ii*) No. 1, 3, 4.

(*iii*) No. 4; $x_1 = \frac{15}{13}$, $x_2 = 0$, $x_3 = 0$, $x_4 = 0$, $x_5 = \frac{5}{26}$; $Z_{min} = 4\frac{1}{26}$.)

2.16 THE SIMPLEX METHOD (TECHNIQUE OR ALGORITHM)

The graphical method discussed in sections 2.9 and 2.10 cannot be applied when the number of variables involved in the L.P. problem is more than three or rather two, since even with three variables the graphical solution becomes tedius as it involves intersection of planes in three dimensions. The simplex method, developed by Prof. George B. Dantzig, can be used to solve any L.P. problem (for which the solution exists) involving any number of variables and constraints (hundreds or even thousands!).

The computational procedure in the simplex method is based on the fundamental property that *the optimal solution to an L.P. problem, if it exists, occurs only at one of the corner points of the feasible region.* The simplex method always starts with initial basic feasible solution *i.e.*, origin, which is one of the corner points of the feasible region. This solution is then tested *i.e.*, it is ascertained whether improvement in the value of the objective function is possible by moving to the next corner point of the feasible region. If so, the solution at this point is obtained. This search for better corner point is repeated, till after a finite number of trials, the optimal solution, if it exists, is obtained. This technique will be explained by considering a few examples.

EXAMPLE 2.16-1

Solve example 2.9-1 by the simplex method.

Solution [*Gujarat Tech. U.B.E. Dec., 2012; Dayalbagh Edu. Inst. Agra Dec., 2006*]

Linear programming model for the problem is

maximize $Z = 3x_1 + 4x_2$, (Objective function) ... (2.16)

subject to $x_1 + x_2 \leq 450$, (Machine M_1 time constraint) ... (2.17)

$2x_1 + x_2 \leq 600$, (Machine M_2 time constraint)

where $x_1, x_2 \geq 0$. ... (2.18)

Step 1. Express the problem in standard form

The given problem is said to be expressed in standard form if the given (decision) variables are non-negative, right-hand side of the constraints are non-negative and the constraints are expressed as equations. Since the first two conditions are met with in the problem, non-negative slack variables s_1 and s_2 are added to the left-hand side of the first and second constraints respectively to convert them into equations. *Values of s_1 and s_2 vary with the values that x_1 and x_2 take in any solution. Slack variables represent unutilised capacity or resources. In the current problem s_1 denotes the time (in minutes) for which machine M_1 remains unutilised or idle; similarly s_2 denotes the idle time for machine M_2. Since slack variables represent idle resources, they contribute zero to the objective function. Accordingly, they are associated with zero coefficients in the objective function.* Accordingly, the problem in standard form, can be written as

maximize $Z = 3x_1 + 4x_2 + 0s_1 + 0s_2$, ... (2.19)

subject to $\left.\begin{aligned} x_1 + x_2 + s_1 &= 450, \\ 2x_1 + x_2 + s_2 &= 600, \end{aligned}\right\}$ ... (2.20)

where $x_1, x_2, s_1, s_2 \geq 0$. ... (2.21)

Step 2. Find initial basic feasible solution

In the simplex method a start is made with a feasible solution, which we shall get by assuming that the profit earned is zero. This will be so when decision variables x_1 and x_2 are each equal to zero. *These variables with zero values are called non-basic variables.* Substituting $x_1 = x_2 = 0$ in equations (2.20) yields $s_1 = 450$, $s_2 = 600$, which is called the initial basic feasible solution. Note that $Z = 0$ for this solution. *Variables s_1 and s_2 are called basic variables and they form the basis.*

In physical terms, it means neither of the two products are produced, the entire time available for machines M_1 and M_2 is unused and since nothing is being done, the profit earned is zero.

The problem in standard form and the solution obtained above are now expressed in the form of a table, called the simplex table (or tableau) 2.20.

TABLE 2.20

Contribution/unit c_j	*Basis (Basic variables)*	3	4	0	0	
		Body matrix		*Identity matrix*		
c_B		x_1	x_2	s_1	s_2	b
0	s_1	1	1	1	0	450
0	s_2	2	1	0	1	600

Interpretation of the data in the above table is given below. Other simplex tables will have similar interpretations.

(*i*) The first row indicates the coefficients c_j of the variables in the objective function equation (2.19). These coefficients remain unchanged in the subsequent tables. They represent the profit/cost per unit to the objective function of each of the variables. The second row indicates the variables in the problem for which c_j coefficients have already been written.

(*ii*) The first column (c_B-column) represents the coefficients of the current basic variables in the objective function. The second column is the *basis* column (or *product mix* column). It represents the basic variables of the current solution. The basic variables are the slack variables s_1 and s_2.

(*iii*) The *body matrix* (also called *coefficient matrix*) under non-basic variables x_1 and x_2 represents their coefficients a_{ij} in the constraints (2.20). These coefficients represent the amount of resource required to a make a unit of the product. For example, coefficients 1 under x_1-column and 1 under x_2-column in s_1-row represent that time required on machine M_1 to make a unit of product A and to make a unit of product B is one minute each. Likewise, to make a unit of product A requires two minutes on machine M_2 and to make a unit of product B requires one minute on machine M_2 respectively. These coefficients may be positive, zero or negative in a problem. They are called *exchange coefficients* or *substitution rates.*

(*iv*) The *identity matrix* represents the coefficients of slack variables in the constraints (2.20). Note that every simplex table will have identity matrix under the basic variables. The identity matrix is also called *unit matrix* or *basis matrix.* It is always a square matrix and its size is determined by the number of constraints.

(*v*) The *b*-column is the last column of table 2.20. This is also called *quantity column* or *solution values* (x_B) *column.* This column indicates the quantities of the available resources or R.H.S. values of the constraints or values of the basic variables, s_1 and s_2 in the initial basic feasible solution found earlier.

Variables not entered under the basis column are non-basic variables and their values are zero. For example, variables x_1 and x_2 are not listed under basis column of the table 2.20 as they are currently non-basic variables and their values are zero each.

Step 3. Perform optimality test

The next step is to ascertain whether the initial basic feasible solution found in step 2 can be improved or not. This solution involves zero profit; an improved solution should result in profit higher than zero. Two more rows are now added to the table 2.20. These are shown in table 2.21.

TABLE 2.21

	c_j	3	4	0	0		
c_B	Basis	x_1	x_2	s_1	s_2	b	θ
0	s_1	1	(1)	1	0	450	450 ← (*key row*)
0	s_2	2	1	0	1	600	600
	Z_j	0	0	0	0	0	(Profit lost/unit)
(N.E.R.)	c_j-Z_j	3	4	0	0		(Net profit/unit)
			↑ K				

Z_j-row coefficients under any column are obtained by adding the products of elements under that column with the corresponding c_B values *i.e.*, $Z_j = \sum c_B a_{ij}$, where a_{ij} is the matrix element in the *i*th row and *j*th column. For example, $Z_l = 0 \times 1 + 0 \times 2 = 0$. Likewise the Z_j values for each other variable column are calculated. Z_j value under *b*-column represents the current profit *i.e.*, zero. Since in the initial simplex table, values under c_B-column are zeros, all Z_j values will be zeros. Values in the Z_j-row are the amounts by which contribution (or profit) would be reduced if one unit of the corresponding variable x_1, x_2, etc. was added to the product mix. *In other way, Z_j values represent the contribution lost per unit of the variables.*

The last row (base row) in the table is c_j-Z_j row, also called the *index row* or *net evaluation row (N.E.R.)*. It is obtained by subtracting columnwise the Z_j values from the c_j values. This row determines whether or not the current solution is optimal. Coefficients in this row represent the *net profit* (*or net contribution or net marginal improvement*) in the value of the objective function Z for each unit of the respective column variable introduced into the solution. For instance, as per the current solution, $x_1 = 0$, $x_2 = 0$ and Z = 0. c_j-Z_j row indicates that if a unit of product A is produced, the profit will increase by ₹ 3 (for, say 10 units, the profit will increase by ₹ 30 and so on). Likewise, production of a unit of product B will increase the profit Z by ₹ 4. Note that c_j-Z_j values are meaningful only for the non-basic variables x_1 and x_2. For a basic variable, $Z_j = 1.c_j = c_j$ so that c_j-$Z_j = c_j - c_j = 0$. A positive coefficient in the c_j-Z_j row indicates the amount by which the profit will be increased if a unit of the corresponding variable is introduced into the solution; a negative coefficient indicates the amount by which the profit will be decreased if a unit of the corresponding variable is introduced into the solution. These coefficients or elements under slack variables s_1 and s_2-columns are also known as *shadow prices or accounting values or imputed values of the resources.*

The elements in the c_j-Z_j row are, therefore, examined; in case they are negative or zero, the current solution is optimal and in case any element is positive, it is not optimal and there is scope for improvement. Since two elements 3 and 4 under x_1 and x_2 variable columns are positive, the solution is not optimal and we proceed to the next step.

Step 4. Iterate towards an optimal solution

At each iteration, the simplex method moves the current basic feasible solution to an improved basic feasible solution. This is done by replacing one current basic variable by a new non-basic variable as explained below :

(*i*) *Selection of the entering variable*

For this we observe c_j-Z_j for different columns and mark the column for maximum positive value. The variable heading that column is the one which should enter the solution *i.e.*, the corresponding product should be produced. This variable is called *entering variable or incoming variable* and the column in which it occurs is called the *key column* (*or pivot column*) and is marked as 'K'. If more than one variable appears with the same maximum value, any one of these variables may be selected arbitrarily as the incoming variable. When no more positive values remain in the c_j-Z_j row (in some succeeding simplex table), the profit attained is maximum and optimal solution is achieved.

In table 2.21, highest positive value is 4, accordingly x_2 is the entering variable and this column is marked as key column.

(*ii*) *Selection of the leaving variable*

Variable x_2 is now going to enter the basis column in the next table. Obviously it will either replace the current basic variable s_1 or s_2. To determine which of the slack variables be replaced (removed or made zero or made non-basic), elements under *b*-column (quantity column) are divided by the corresponding elements of the key column and the row containing the minimum *non-negative ratio* is marked. The column containing these ratios, marked as θ-column in table 2.21 is also called *minimum ratio* or *replacement ratio column*. These ratios indicate the number of units of a variable (product) that can be produced by trading all of the current level of basic variables. This limits the number of units of the incoming variable that can be produced from the exchange. The current basic variable is, then, to be replaced and is called *leaving* (*outgoing or departing*) variable and is to be made zero. The row so marked is called the *key* (*or pivot*) *row*.

Zero is considered as non-negative and negative ratios are discarded. In case all ratios are negative or infinity, the solution is unbounded. The element lying at the intersection of key column and key row is called *key* (*or pivot*) *element* and is enclosed in ( ).

Note that the next solution (to be obtained soon) will be feasible only if row containing minimum (non-negative) ratio is selected as key row; in case a row containing higher (non-negative) ratio is marked as key row, the next solution will become infeasible and there will be some negative value in the *b*-column (quantity column) which is illogical.

In table 2.21, replacement ratios are $\frac{450}{1} = 450$ and $\frac{600}{1} = 600$; s_1 is the outgoing variable and (1) is the key element. The other elements in the key column are called *intersectional elements.*

(*iii*) *Evaluating* (*updating*) *the new solution or preparing the new simplex table*

Table 2.22 is now derived from table 2.21 by performing some row operations. First, basis column now contains variable x_2 in place of s_1. Corresponding c_B coefficient is changed from 0 to 4. Since in table 2.22 x_2 is the basic variable, x_2-column must be made an identity column ; key element if not unity is made unity and other intesectional elements are made zeros by suitable row operations.

In table 2.21, key element is already (1), accordingly elements 1, (1), 1, 0, 450 of s_1-row are retained as such as the elements 1, 1, 1, 0, 450 of x_2-row of table 2.22. The intersectional element 1 in x_2-column is now made zero by subtracting the key element 1 from it. However, this subtraction is to be done for all the elements of s_2-row of table 2.21 to get elements of s_2-row of table 2.22. Accordingly, the elements of s_2-row of table 2.22 will be 2 – 1 = 1, 1 – 1 = 0, 0 – 1 = – 1, 1 – 0 = 1 and 600 – 450 = 150. Table 2.22 can now be completed and is shown below:

TABLE 2.22

	c_j	3	4	0	0		
c_B	Basis	x_1	x_2	s_1	s_2	b	
4	x_2	1	1	1	0	450	
0	s_2	1	0	– 1	1	150	
	Z_j	4	4	4	0	1,800	*2nd feasible solution*
	c_j–Z_j	– 1	0	– 4	0		*(Optimal solution)*

This completes the *first iteration* (*stage*). The second feasible solution is represented by table 2.22.

Step 5. Perform Optimality test for second feasible solution

Compute $Z_j \left(= \sum c_B \, a_{ij} \right)$ elements for variable columns. They are 4, 4, 4, 0, 1800 Value of Z_j under *b*-column represents the value of objective function as per the second solution. Note that the profit has increased from 0 to ₹ 1,800 after the iteration. Next compute c_j-Z_j row. Elements in this row are 3 – 4 = – 1, 4 – 4 = 0, 0 – 4 = – 4 and 0 – 0 = 0 Since all elements are either zero or negative, the second feasible solution is optimal. The computational procedure comes to an end.

Values of the basic variables are seen in the *b*-column (quantity column). Values of other non-basic variables are zero each.

Hence the optimal solution is ,

$x_1 = 0,$

$x_2 = 450,$

$Z_{max} = ₹\ 1,800.$

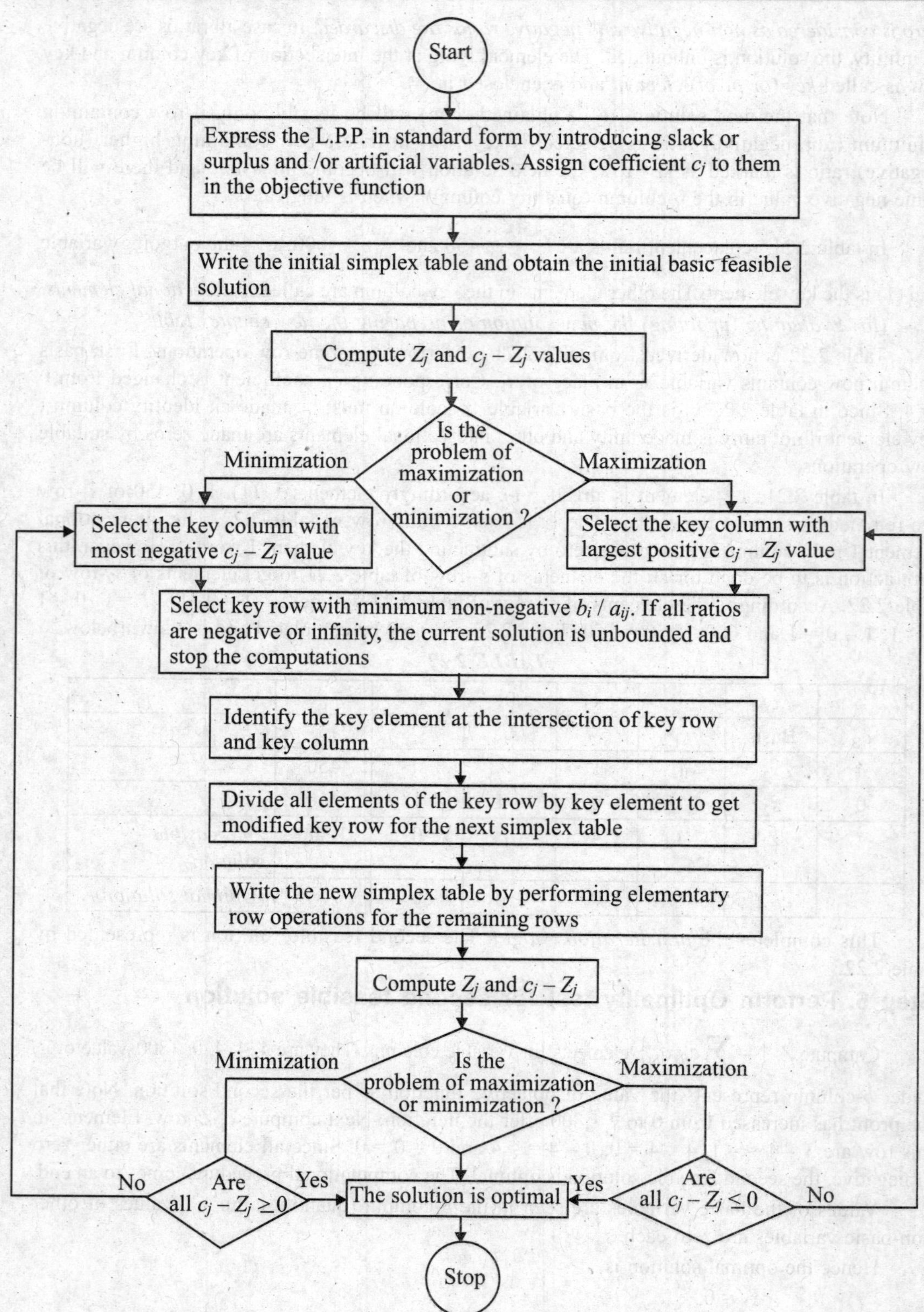

Fig. 2.24. Flow Chart for the Simplex Algorithm

The company should, therefore, not produce product A at all, it should produce 450 units of product B to get maximum daily profit of ₹ 1,800.

Remarks 1. The optimal solution obtained above satisfies the non-negativity restrictions (2.21), the constraints (2.20) and gives the maximum possible value of Z. No other set of values of x_1 and x_2 results in as high a profit (₹ 1,800) as this set.

2. In table 2.22, slack variable s_1 does not exist in the basis column. This means that capacity of machine M_1 resource is fully utilised, that is, available time of 450 minutes on this machine is completely used in making the products. However s_2 exists in the basis column and its value is 150. This means that 150 minutes of time on machine M_2 remain unutilised.

3. Elements in c_j-Z_j row under slack variables indicate the *shadow* prices (*also called accounting values or imputed values*) of the resources of machines M_1 and M_2 respectively. – 4 under variable s_1-column means that if the time available on machine M_1 is used a minute less, the decrease of profit will be ₹ 4. In other words, if M_1 is made available for a minute more, the profit will increase by ₹ 4. Therefore, if the company wants to increase its resource capacities, it should be for machine M_1. Capacity of machine M_2 has not been utilised fully; there will be no use increasing it further. ₹ 4 and ₹ 0 are called the shadow prices of machine M_1 resource and machine M_2 resource respectively.

The flow chart of the simplex method (algorithm) is shown in Fig. 2.24.

EXAMPLE 2.16-2

Use simplex method to solve the following problem :

$$\text{Maximize } Z = 2x_1 + 5x_2,$$

$$\text{subject to} \quad x_1 + 4x_2 \le 24, \quad 3x_1 + x_2 \le 21, \quad x_1 + x_2 \le 9, \quad x_1, x_2 \ge 0.$$

[P.U. B.Com. April, 2005]

Solution. It consists of the following steps (for details refer to example 2.16-1) :

Step 1. Express the problem in standard form

Introducing slack variables s_1, s_2 and s_3 the problem can be expressed in the following standard form :

$$\text{Maximize } Z = 2x_1 + 5x_2 + 0s_1 + 0s_2 + 0s_3,$$

$$\text{subject to} \quad x_1 + 4x_2 + s_1 = 24, \quad 3x_1 + x_2 + s_2 = 21, \quad x_1 + x_2 + s_3 = 9, \quad x_1, x_2, s_1, s_2, s_3 \ge 0.$$

The slack variables can be treated as imaginary products, contributing zero profits. Accordingly, they are assigned zero coefficients in the objective function.

Step 2. Find initial basic feasible solution

We shall start with a basic solution which we shall get by assuming that profit earned is zero. This will be so when non-basic variables x_1 and x_2 are each equal to zero. Setting $x_1 = 0$, $x_2 = 0$, the constraints yield the following initial basic feasible solution (*i. b. f. s.*):

$$s_1 = 24,\ s_2 = 21,\ s_3 = 9 \text{ and } Z = 0.$$

The above information can be expressed in the form of a table, called simplex table (table 2.23). The non-basic variables x_1 and x_2 are each zero. If any of them is made positive, Z will increase. This can be achieved by changing the basis of table 2.23 *i.e.*, by including x_1, x_2 in place of some basic variables (s_1, s_2 or s_3), which form the present basis.

TABLE 2.23

		c_j	2	5	0	0	0			
F.R.	c_B	Basis	x_1	x_2	s_1	s_2	s_3	b	θ	
	0	s_1	1	(4)	1	0	0	24	6	←
1/4	0	s_2	3	1	0	1	0	21	21	
1/4	0	s_3	1	1	0	0	1	9	9	
		Z_j	0	0	0	0	0	0		
		c_j-Z_j	2	5	0	0	0			
				↑K			*Initial basic feasible solution*			

Step 3. Perform optimality test

By performing the optimality test we can find whether the current feasible solution can be improved or not. This is done by computing c_j-Z_j, where $Z_j = \sum c_B\, a_{ij}$. Here a_{ij} is the matrix element in the ith row and jth column. If c_j-Z_j is positive under any column, the current feasible solution is not optimal and at least one better solution is possible. This is shown in table 2.23. Since c_j-Z_j is positive under x_1 and x_2-columns, *i.b.f.s.* is not optimal and can be improved.

Step 4. Iterate towards an optimal solution

Mark the key column, key row and key element as shown in table 2.23. x_2-column is the key column, s_1-row is the key row and (4) is the key element. x_2 is the incoming variable which replaces the outgoing variable s_1 in the next table (table 2.24). The incoming basic variable should appear *only* in the first (key) row with unit coefficient. Therefore, key element (4) is made 1 in that table. For this elements of s_1-row of table 2.23 are divided by 4 each and written as elements of x_2-row in table 2.24. The intersectional elements 1 and 1 of key column x_2 are now made zero each in table 2.24. For this, first the elements of key row in table 2.23 are multiplied by a *proper multiple* (also called *fixed ratio*) and then are *subtracted* from elements of s_2-row. Proper multiple or fixed ratio (F.R.) is always equal to intersectional element divided by key element. This is repeated for s_3-row as well. The fixed ratios $\frac{1}{4}, \frac{1}{4}$ are entered in the first column of table 2.23 against s_2-row and s_3-row. These row operations lead to the following elements of s_2-row and s_3-row of table 2.24.

$$s_2\text{-row}: \; 3-\frac{1}{4}=\frac{11}{4}, 1-\frac{4}{4}=0, 0-\frac{1}{4}=-\frac{1}{4}, 1-\frac{0}{4}=1, 0-\frac{0}{4}=0, 21-\frac{24}{4}=15;$$

$$s_3\text{-row}: \; 1-\frac{1}{4}=\frac{3}{4}, 1-\frac{4}{4}=0, 0-\frac{1}{4}=-\frac{1}{4}, 0-\frac{0}{4}=0, 1-\frac{0}{4}=1, 9-\frac{24}{4}=3.$$

TABLE 2.24

		c_j	2	5	0	0	0		
F.R.	c_B	Basis	x_1	x_2	s_1	s_2	s_3	b	θ
1/3	5	x_2	1/4	1	1/4	0	0	6	24

$11/3$	0	s_2	$11/4$	0	$-1/4$	1	0	15	$60/11$
	0	s_3	$(3/4)$	0	$-1/4$	0	1	3	4 ←
		Z_j	$5/4$	5	$5/4$	0	0	30	
		c_j-Z_j	$3/4$	0	$-5/4$	0	0		*Second feasible solution*
			↑K						

Step 5. Check second feasible solution for optimality

Z_j values and c_j-Z_j values for various variable-columns are calculated in table 2.24. Since c_j-Z_j value under x_1-column is positive, the second feasible solution is not optimal.

Step 6. Iterate towards an optimal solution

x_1-column is marked as the key column. x_1 is the incoming variable. Replacement ratios are $\frac{6}{1/4} = 24$, $\frac{15}{11/4} = \frac{60}{11}$, $\frac{3}{3/4} = 4$. Since 4 is the minimum non-negative ratio, s_3-row is marked as the key row. s_3 is the outgoing variable. It is replaced by x_1 in table 2.25. Elements of s_3-row in table 2.24 are multiplied by 4/3 to make the key element 1 in table 2.25 and the values are entered as the elements of x_1-row in this table. Next, the intersectional elements $\frac{1}{4}, \frac{11}{4}$ of x_1-column in table 2.24 are to be made zeros in table 2.25. To make $\frac{1}{4}$ as 0, elements of s_3-row of table 2.24 are multiplied by the fixed ratio $\frac{1/4}{3/4} = \frac{1}{3}$ and the values are then subtracted from the elements of x_2-row to get the new elements of x_2-row in table 2.25. These elements are

$\frac{1}{4}-\frac{1}{3}\left(\frac{3}{4}\right) = 0, 1-\frac{1}{3}(0) = 1, \frac{1}{4}-\frac{1}{3}\left(-\frac{1}{4}\right) = \frac{1}{4}+\frac{1}{12} = \frac{1}{3}, 0-\frac{1}{3}(0) = 0, 0-\frac{1}{3}(1) = -\frac{1}{3}, 6-\frac{1}{3}(3) = 5.$

Similarly, elements of s_2-row in table 2.25 will be

$\frac{11}{4}-\frac{11}{3}\left(\frac{3}{4}\right) = 0, 0-\frac{11}{3}(0) = 0, \; -\frac{1}{4}-\frac{11}{3}\left(-\frac{1}{4}\right) = -\frac{1}{4}+\frac{11}{12} = \frac{8}{12} = \frac{2}{3}, 1-\frac{11}{3}(0) = 1,$

$0-\frac{11}{3}(1) = -\frac{11}{3}, 15-\frac{11}{3}(3) = 4$. Table 2.25 is now completed.

TABLE 2.25

	c_j	2	5	0	0	0	
c_B	Basis	x_1	x_2	s_1	s_2	s_3	b
5	x_2	0	1	$1/3$	0	$-1/3$	5
0	s_2	0	0	$2/3$	1	$-11/3$	4
2	x_1	1	0	$-1/3$	0	$4/3$	4
	Z_j	2	5	1	0	1	33
c_j-Z_j	0	0	-1	0	-1	*Third feasible solution (optimal solution)*	

Step 7. Check third feasible solution for optimality

Z_j-row and c_j–Z_j-row values are calculated in table 2.25. Since all c_j-Z_j values are negative or zero, third feasible solution is optimal. The optimal solution is given by

$$\left.\begin{array}{l} x_1 = 4, \\ x_2 = 5, \\ s_2 = 4, \end{array}\right\} \text{(basic)} \qquad \left.\begin{array}{l} s_1 = 0, \\ s_3 = 0, \end{array}\right\} \text{(non-basic)}$$

$$Z = 33.$$

EXAMPLE 2.16-3

Solve example 2.6-1 by simplex method.

[*G.N.D.U. B.Com. April, 2008; P.U.B.Com April, 2008*]

Solution. (Refer examples 2.16.1 and 2.16.2 for details) The linear programming model for this problem is

$$\begin{aligned} \text{maximize } Z &= 4x_1 + 3x_2 + 6x_3, \\ \text{subject to } & 2x_1 + 3x_2 + 2x_3 \le 440, \\ & 4x_1 + 3x_3 \le 470, \\ & 2x_1 + 5x_2 \le 430, \\ & x_1, x_2, x_3 \ge 0. \end{aligned}$$

Step 1. Express the problem in standard form

Introducing slack variables s_1, s_2 and s_3 the problem can be expressed in the following standard form :

$$\begin{aligned} \text{maximize } Z &= 4x_1 + 3x_2 + 6x_3 + 0s_1 + 0s_2 + 0s_3, \\ \text{subject to } & 2x_1 + 3x_2 + 2x_3 + s_1 = 440, \\ & 4x_1 + 3x_3 + s_2 = 470, \\ & 2x_1 + 5x_2 + s_3 = 430, \\ & x_1, x_2, x_3, s_1, s_2, s_3 \ge 0. \end{aligned}$$

Step 2. Find initial basic feasible solution

Let decision variables $x_1 = x_2 = x_3 = 0$. Substituting these values in the constraints, we get the following *i.b.f.s.* :

$s_1 = 440$, $s_2 = 470$, $s_3 = 430$; Z = 0.

The problem in standard form and its solution are expressed in the form a table (table 2.26).

TABLE 2.26

		c_j	4	3	6	0	0	0		
F.R.	c_B	Basis	x_1	x_2	x_3	s_1	s_2	s_3	b	θ
2/3	0	s_1	2	3	2	1	0	0	440	220
	0	s_2	4	0	(3)	0	1	0	470	470/3←
	0	s_3	2	5	0	0	0	1	430	∞
		Z_j	0	0	0	0	0	0	0	
		c_j-Z_j	4	3	6	0	0	0		
					↑K				*i.b.f.s.*	

Step 3. Perform optimality test

Add Z_j and c_j-Z_j rows to table 2.26. Since c_j-Z_j is positive under x_1, x_2, x_3-columns *i.b.f.s.* is not optimal and can be improved.

Step 4. Iterate towards an optimal solution

Mark the key column, key row and key element. x_3 and s_2 are incoming and outgoing

TABLE 2.27

F.R.	c_B	c_j / Basis	4 / x_1	3 / x_2	6 / x_3	0 / s_1	0 / s_2	0 / s_3	b	θ
	0	s_1	−2/3	(3)	0	1	−2/3	0	380/3	380/9 ←
	6	x_3	4/3	0	1	0	1/3	0	470/3	∞
5/3	0	s_3	2	5	0	0	0	1	430	86
		Z_j	8	0	6	0	2	0	940	
		c_j-Z_j	− 4	3	0	0	− 2	0	*Second feasible*	
				↑K					*solution*	

variables respectively and (3) is the key element in table 2.26. Variable s_2 is to be replaced by x_3. Elements of s_2-row are divided by 3 to make key element unity. Intersectional element 2 in key column is to be made zero. Fixed ratio is $\frac{2}{3}$. Key row is, therefore, multiplied by $\frac{2}{3}$ and the values are subtracted from the elements of s_1-row. The other intersectional element is 0 and requires no row operations. Elements of s_3-row are, therefore, retained as such in table 2.27. All the above operations are represented in this table.

Step 5. Repeat steps 3 and 4

Steps 3 and 4 are now repeated alternately till optimal solution is obtained. $Z_j = \sum c_B\, a_{ij}$ row and c_j-Z_j row are now added to table 2.27. Since c_j-Z_j is positive under x_2-column, this solution is not optimal and is to be improved.

The key column, key row and key element have been marked. x_2 is incoming variable, s_1 is outgoing variable and (3) is the key element. s_1 is replaced by x_2 and necessary row operations have been made in table 2.28.

TABLE 2.28

c_B	c_j / Basis	4 / x_1	3 / x_2	6 / x_3	0 / s_1	0 / s_2	0 / s_3	b
3	x_2	$-\frac{2}{9}$	1	0	$\frac{1}{3}$	$-\frac{2}{9}$	0	$\frac{380}{9}$
6	x_3	$\frac{4}{3}$	0	1	0	$\frac{1}{3}$	0	$\frac{470}{3}$
0	s_3	$\frac{28}{9}$	0	0	$-\frac{5}{3}$	$\frac{10}{9}$	1	$\frac{1,970}{9}$
	Z_j	$\frac{22}{3}$	3	6	1	$\frac{4}{3}$	0	$\frac{3,200}{3}$
	c_j-Z_j	$-\frac{10}{3}$	0	0	− 1	$-\frac{4}{3}$	0	*Optimal solution*

$Z_j = \sum c_B\, a_{ij}$ and c_j-Z_j rows are now added to table 2.28. Since all c_j-Z_j elements are either zero or negative, the table represents an optimal solution. The optimal solution is

$$x_1 = 0,\ x_2 = \frac{380}{9},\ x_3 = \frac{470}{3};\ Z_{max} = \frac{3,200}{3}.$$

Also $$s_1 = 0,\ s_2 = 0,\ s_3 = \frac{1,970}{9}.$$

EXAMPLE 2.16-4

Three grades of coal A, B and C contain phosphorus and ash as impurities. In a particular industrial process, fuel up to 100 ton (maximum) is required which should contain ash not more than 3% and phosphorus not more than 0.03%. It is desired to maximize the profit while satisfying these conditions. There is an unlimited supply of each grade. The percentage of impurities and the profits of grades are given below.

Coal	*Phosphorus (%)*	*Ash (%)*	*Profits in rupees per ton*
A	*0.02*	*3.0*	*12.00*
B	*0.04*	*2.0*	*15.00*
C	*0.03*	*5.0*	*14.00*

Find the proportions in which the three grades be used.

[*H.P.U. B.Tech. (Mech.) Sept.; 2013; P.U.B.E: (Ec. and Comm.) Dec., 2011*]

Formulation of the Linear Programming Model

Let x_1, x_2 and x_3 respectively be the amounts in tons of grades A, B and C used.

Objective is to maximize the profit.

i.e., maximize $Z = 12x_1 + 15x_2 + 14x_3$. ... (2.22)

Constraints are

(*i*) phosphorus content must not exceed 0.03%.

Therefore $0.02x_1 + 0.04x_2 + 0.03x_3 \leq 0.03\ (x_1 + x_2 + x_3)$

or $2x_1 + 4x_2 + 3x_3 \leq 3(x_1 + x_2 + x_3)$

or $-x_1 + x_2 \leq 0.$ ... (2.23*a*)

(*ii*) ash content must not exceed 3%.

Therefore $3x_1 + 2x_2 + 5x_3 \leq 3(x_1 + x_2 + x_3)$

or $-x_2 + 2x_3 \leq 0.$ ... (2.23*b*)

(*iii*) total quantity of fuel required is not more than 100 ton.

Therefore $x_1 + x_2 + x_3 \leq 100,$ ... (2.23c)

where $x_1, x_2, x_3 \geq 0.$ ... (2.24)

Thus the problem is to maximize equation (2.22) subject to constraints (2.23*a*), (2.23*b*), (2.23*c*) and non-negativity restrictions (2.24).

Solution of the L.P. Model

Step 1. Introducing slack variables s_1, s_2 and s_3, the problem can be expressed in the following standard form :

$$\begin{aligned} \text{Maximize } Z &= 12x_1 + 15x_2 + 14x_3 + 0s_1 + 0s_2 + 0s_3, \\ \text{subject to } \quad & -x_1 + x_2 + s_1 = 0, \\ & -x_2 + 2x_3 + s_2 = 0, \\ & x_1 + x_2 + x_3 + s_3 = 100, \\ & x_1, x_2, x_3, s_1, s_2, s_3 \geq 0. \end{aligned}$$

Step 2. Substituting $x_1 = 0$, $x_2 = 0$, $x_3 = 0$ in the constraints yields the following initial basic feasible solution :

$s_1 = 0$, $s_2 = 0$, $s_3 = 100$; $Z = 0$.

Note that basic variables s_1 and s_2 are zero each; the solution is, therefore, *degenerate*. Table 2.29 represents the above information.

TABLE 2.29

	c_j	12	15	14	0	0	0		
c_B	Basis	x_1	x_2	x_3	s_1	s_2	s_3	b	θ
0	s_1	– 1	(1)	0	1	0	0	0	0←

0	s_2	0	– 1	2	0	1	0	0	– (negative ratio)
0	s_3	1	1	1	0	0	1	100	100
	Z_j	0	0	0	0	0	0	0	
	c_j-Z_j	12	15	14	0	0	0		*i.b.f.s*
			↑K						

Step 3. Z_j and c_j-Z_j rows are now added to table 2.29. Since elements in c_j-Z_j row are positive, *i.b.f.s* is not optimal and is to be improved.

Step 4. Mark x_2-column as the key column. Now find the replacement ratios. They are $\frac{0}{1} = 0$, $\frac{0}{-1}$, a negative ratio (denominator being negative) and $\frac{100}{1} = 100$. *Out of these the negative ratio is to be discarded* (Refer step 4 (*ii*) of example 2.16-1). Minimum non-negative ratio is 0 and s_1 is the key row. Variable s_1 is replaced by x_2 in table 2.30. Necessary row operations have been performed. Repeating steps 3 and 4 alternately yields the succeeding tables 2.31 and 2.32.

TABLE 2.30

F.R.	c_B	Basis	x_1	x_2	x_3	s_1	s_2	s_3	b	θ
		c_j	12	15	14	0	0	0		
1/2	15	x_2	–1	1	0	1	0	0	0	– (negative ratio)
1/2	0	s_2	– 1	0	2	1	1	0	0	– (negative ratio)
	0	s_3	(2)	0	1	– 1	0	1	100	50←
		Z_j	– 15	15	0	15	0	0	0	
		c_j-Z_j	27	0	14	– 15	0	0		
			↑K							*Second feasible (degenrate) solution*

Note that in table 2.30, fixed ratios are $\frac{1}{2}, \frac{1}{2}$. Key row is multiplied by these ratios and the values are *added to* elements of x_2-row and s_2-row in table 2.30 to get intersectional elements – 1, – 1 in it as zeros, in table 2.31. Variable s_3 is replaced by x_1 in this table.

TABLE 2.31

F.R.	c_B	Basis	x_1	x_2	x_3	s_1	s_2	s_3	b	θ
		c_j	12	15	14	0	0	0		
$1/5$	15	x_2	0	1	$1/2$	$1/2$	0	$1/2$	50	100
	0	s_2	0	0	$(5/2)$	$1/2$	1	$1/2$	50	20 ←
$1/5$	12	x_1	1	0	$1/2$	$-1/2$	0	$1/2$	50	100
		Z_j	12	15	$27/2$	$3/2$	0	$27/2$	1,350	
		c_j-Z_j	0	0	$1/2$	$-3/2$	0	$-27/2$		
					↑K					*Third feasible (non-degenerate) solution*

In table 2.31 key element is $\frac{5}{2}$. Replace s_2 by x_3. This is done in table 2.32.

TABLE 2.32

	c_j	12	15	14	0	0	0	
c_B	Basis	x_1	x_2	x_3	s_1	s_2	s_3	b
15	x_2	0	1	0	$2/5$	$-1/5$	$2/5$	40
14	x_3	0	0	1	$1/5$	$2/5$	$1/5$	20
12	x_1	1	0	0	$-3/5$	$-1/5$	$2/5$	40
	Z_j	12	15	14	$8/5$	$1/5$	$68/5$	1,360
	c_j-Z_j	0	0	0	$-8/5$	$-1/5$	$-68/5$	*(Optimal solution)*

Optimal solution is

$x_1 = 40$ tons, $x_2 = 40$ tons, $x_3 = 20$ tons ; $Z_{max} = ₹\ 1{,}360$.

EXAMPLE 2.16-5

Solve by simplex method the following L.P. problem :

$$\text{Minimize } Z = x_1 - 3x_2 + 3x_3,$$

$$\text{subject to} \quad \begin{aligned} 3x_1 - x_2 + 2x_3 &\le 7, \\ 2x_1 + 4x_2 &\ge -12, \\ -4x_1 + 3x_2 + 8x_3 &\le 10, \\ x_1, x_2, x_3 &\ge 0. \end{aligned}$$

[P.T.U. MBA May, 2014; H.P.U. B.Tech. (Mech.) 2015, 12; Kuru. U.B.E. (Mech. June, 2012; J.N.T.U. Hyderabad B.Tech. (Mech.) May, 2012; P.U. B.Com. Sept., 2005]

Solution

Step 1. Set-up the problem in standard form

As the right-hand side of the second constraint is negative , it is made positive by multiplying the constraint on both sides by – 1. This will reverse the inequality sign also. Thus this constraint takes the form

$$-2x_1 - 4x_2 \le 12.$$

Introducing slack variables s_1, s_2 and s_3, the problem can be expressed in the following standard form :

$$\text{Minimize } Z = x_1 - 3x_2 + 3x_3 + 0s_1 + 0s_2 + 0s_3,$$

$$\text{subject to} \quad \begin{aligned} 3x_1 - x_2 + 2x_3 + s_1 &= 7, \\ -2x_1 - 4x_2 + s_2 &= 12, \\ -4x_1 + 3x_2 + 8x_3 + s_3 &= 10, \\ x_1, x_2, x_3, s_1, s_2, s_3 &\ge 0. \end{aligned}$$

Step 2. Find initial basic feasible solution

Putting $x_1 = 0$, $x_2 = 0$, $x_3 = 0$ in the constraints we get *i.b.f.s.* as

$$s_1 = 7,\ s_2 = 12,\ s_3 = 10\ ;\ Z = 0.$$

TABLE 2.33

		c_j	1	– 3	3	0	0	0		
F.R.	c_B	Basis	x_1	x_2	x_3	s_1	s_2	s_3	b	θ
1/3	0	s_1	3	– 1	2	1	0	0	7	– 7
4/3	0	s_2	– 2	– 4	0	0	1	0	12	– 3
	0	s_3	– 4	(3)	8	0	0	1	10	$10/3$ ←
		Z_j	0	0	0	0	0	0	0	
		c_j-Z_j	1	– 3	3	0	0	0		
				↑K						

Step 3. Perform optimality test

$Z_j = \sum c_B\, a_{ij}$ and c_j-Z_j rows are added to table 2.33.

Note that the objective is to *minimize Z*. Therefore, *if any c_j-Z_j coefficient is negative, the solution is not optimal. The column having most negative c_j-Z_j value will be the key column.* Accordingly, x_2-column is marked the key column. Replacement ratios are – 7, – 3, and $\frac{10}{3}$. As $\frac{10}{3}$ is the only non-negative ratio, s_3-row is marked the key row and (3) is the key element.

Step 4. Iterate towards an optimal solution

Variable s_3 is replaced by x_2 by performing the row operations in the usual ways. Solution will become optimal when all c_j-Z_j coefficients become *zero or positive*. Iterations yield the following tables :

TABLE 2.34

		c_j	1	– 3	3	0	0	0			
F.R.	c_B	Basis	x_1	x_2	x_3	s_1	s_2	s_3	b	θ	
	0	s_1	$(5/3)$	0	$14/3$	1	0	$1/3$	$31/3$	$31/5$	←
$22/5$	0	s_2	$-22/3$	0	$32/3$	0	1	$4/3$	$76/3$	$-38/11$	
$4/5$	– 3	x_2	$-4/3$	1	$8/3$	0	0	$1/3$	$10/3$	$-5/2$	
		Z_j	4	– 3	– 8	0	0	– 1	– 10		
		c_j-Z_j	– 3	0	11	0	0	1			
			↑K								

TABLE 2.35

	c_j	1	– 3	3	0	0	0	
c_B	Basis	x_1	x_2	x_3	s_1	s_2	s_3	b
1	x_1	1	0	$14/5$	$3/5$	0	$1/5$	$31/5$
0	s_2	0	0	$156/5$	$22/5$	1	$14/5$	$354/5$
– 3	x_2	0	1	$32/5$	$4/5$	0	$3/5$	$58/5$

Z_j	1	− 3	$-82/5$	$-9/5$	0	$-8/5$	$-143/5$	
c_j-Z_j	0	0	$97/5$	$9/5$	0	$8/5$		*Optimal solution*

∴ Optimal solution to the problem is

$$x_1 = \frac{31}{5},\ x_2 = \frac{58}{5},\ x_3 = 0\ ;\ Z_{\min} = -\frac{143}{5}.$$

EXAMPLE 2.16-6

A food processing company produces three canned fruit products : mixed fruit, fruit cocktail and fruit delight. The main ingredients in each product are pears and peaches. Each product is produced in lots and must go through three processes, mixing, canning and packaging. The resource requirement for each product and each process are shown in the following L.P. formulation :

Maximize $Z = 10x_1 + 6x_2 + 8x_3$, *(profit, ₹)*

subject to $20x_1 + 10x_2 + 16x_3 \le 320$, *(pears, kg)*

$10x_1 + 20x_2 + 16x_3 \le 400$, *(peaches, kg)*

$x_1 + 2x_2 + 2x_3 \le 43$, *(mixing, hr)*

$x_1 + x_2 + x_3 \le 60$, *(canning, hr)*

$2x_1 + x_2 + x_3 \le 40$, *(packaging, hr)*

$x_1, x_2, x_3 \ge 0.$

Final simplex table 2.35(*a*)

		c_j	10	6	8	0	0	0	0	0
c_B	Basic Variables B	Solution values $b\ (=X_b)$	x_1	x_2	x_3	s_1	s_2	s_3	s_4	s_5
10	x_1	8	1	0	$8/15$	$1/15$	$1/30$	0	0	0
6	x_2	16	0	1	$8/15$	$-1/30$	$1/15$	0	0	0
0	s_3	3	0	0	$2/15$	0	$-1/10$	1	0	0
0	s_4	36	0	0	$-1/15$	$1/30$	$1/30$	0	1	0
0	s_5	8	0	0	$-8/15$	$1/10$	0	0		1
	Z_j		10	6	$128/15$	$7/15$	$1/15$	0	0	0
	c_j - Z_j		0	0	$-8/15$	$-7/15$	$-1/15$	0	0	0

On the basis of above information, answer the following questions :

(*i*) *Is the above solution feasible ?*

(*ii*) *Is the above solution optimal ? If yes, what is it ?*

(*iii*) *Is the above solution unbounded ?*

(*iv*) *Is the above solution degenerate ?*

(*v*) *Does't have multiple solutions ?*

(*vi*) *Determine the amount of used and unused resources.* [P.U. M.B.A. Feb., 2009]

Solution

(*i*) Yes, the above solution is feasible as values of all the variables are non-negative (≥ 0).

(*ii*) Yes, since $c_j - Z_j$ coefficients for the given maximization problem are either negative or zero, the solution is optimal.
The optimal solution is x_1 = 8 kg, x_2 = 16 kg, x_3 = 0, s_1 = 0, s_2 = 0; s_3 = 3 hr, s_4 = 36 hr, s_5 = 8 hr and Z_{max} = ₹ (10 × 8 + 6 × 16 + 8 × 0) = ₹ 176.

(*iii*) The above solution is not unbounded since values of all variables as well as Z_{max} are finite.

(*iv*) No, the above solution is non-degenerate since none of the basic variables has zero value.

(*v*) No, it does not have multiple solutions since $c_j - Z_j$ coefficients under none of the non-basic variables x_3, s_1 and s_2 have zero values.

(*vi*) Since s_1 = 0, all the 320 kg of pears are used in making the canned fruit products. Since s_2 = 0, all the 400 kg of peaches are also used. Since s_3 = 3 hr, mixing process remains unused for 3 hours. Since s_4 = 36 hr, time available for canning process remains unused for 36 hours. Since s_5 = 8 hr, time available for packaging process remains unused for 8 hours.

2.17 ARTIFICIAL VARIABLES TECHNIQUES

In the earlier problems, the constraints were of (≤) type (with non-negative right-hand sides). The introduction of slack variables readily provided the initial basic feasible solution. There are, however, many linear programming problems where slack variables cannot provide such a solution. In these problems at least one of the constraints is of (≥) or (=) type. In such cases, we introduce another type of variables called *artificial variables*. *These variables are fictitious and have no physical meaning. They assume the role of slack variables in the first iteration, only to be replaced at a later iteration. Thus they are merely a device to get the starting basic feasible solution so that simplex algorithm can be applied as usual to get optimal solution.* There are two (closely related) techniques available to solve such problems. They are

1. The *big M-method* or *M-technique* or *method of penalties* due to A. Charnes.
2. The *two-phase method* due to Dantzig, Orden and Wolfe.

2.17-1 The Big M-Method

This method consists of the following basic steps :

Step 1. Express the linear programming problem in standard form by introducing slack variables. These variables are added to the left-hand sides of the constraints of (≤) type and subtracted from the constraints of (≥) type.

Step 2. Add non-negative variables to the left-hand sides of all the constraints of *initially* (≥) or (=) type. These variables are called *artificial variables. The purpose of introducing the artificial variables is just to obtain an initial basic feasible solution.* They have, however, two drawbacks:

(*i*) They are fictitious, have no physical meaning or economic significance and have no relevance to the problem.

(*ii*) Their introduction (addition) violates the equality of constraints that has been already established in step 1.

They are, therefore, rightly termed as artificial variables as opposed to other real decision variables in the problem. Therefore, we must get rid of these variables and must not allow them to appear in the final solution. To achieve this, these variables are assigned a very large per unit penalty in the objective function. This penalty is designated by – M for maximization problems and + M for minimization problems, where M > 0. Value of M is much higher than the cost coefficients of other variables and for hand calculations it is not necessary to assign any specific value to it.

Step 3. Solve the modified linear programming problem by the simplex method.

The artificial variables are a computational device. They keep the starting equations in balance and provide a mathematical trick for getting a starting solution. By having a high penalty cost it is ensured that they will not appear in the final solution i.e., they will be driven to zero when the objective function is optimized by using the simplex method.

While making iterations, using the simplex method, one of the following three cases may arise:

1. If no artificial variable remains in the basis and the optimality condition is satisfied, then the solution is an optimal feasible solution to the given problem. Also, the original constraints are consistent and none of them is redundant.

2. If at least one artificial variable appears in the basis at zero level (with zero value in *b*-column) and the optimality condition is satisfied, then the solution is optimal feasible (though degenerate) solution to the given problem. The constraints are consistent though redundancy may exist in them. By redundancy is meant that the problem has more than the required number of constraints.

3. If at least one artificial variable appears in the basis at a non-zero level (with positive value in *b*-column) and the optimality condition is satisfied, then the original problem *has no feasible solution*; for if a feasible solution existed, the artificial variables could be driven to zero, yielding an improved value of the objective function. The problem has no feasible solution either because the constraints are inconsistent or because there are solutions, but none is feasible. In economic terms this means that the resources of the system are not sufficient to meet the expected demands. The final solution to the problem is not optimal since the objective function contains an unknown quantity M. Such a solution satisfies the constraints but does not optimize the objective function and is also called *pseudo-optimal solution*.

Remarks: 1. Slack variables are added to (the left-hand sides of) the constraints of (≤) type and subtracted from the constraints of (≥) type.

2. Artificial variables are added to the constraints of (≥) and (=) type. Equality constraints require neither slack nor surplus variables.

3. Variables, other than the artificial variables, (slack, surplus and variables given in the problem) once driven out in an iteration, may re-enter in a subsequent iteration. But, an artificial variable, once driven, can never re-enter, because of the large penalty coefficient M associated with it in the objective function. Advantage can be taken of this fact by not computing its column in iterations subsequent to the one from which it was driven out.

4. For computer solutions, some specific value has to be assigned to M. Usually, the largest value that can be represented in the computer is used.

EXAMPLE 2.17-1

Food X contains 6 units of vitamin A per gram and 7 units of vitamin B per gram and costs 12 paise per gram. Food Y contains 8 units of vitamin A per gram and 12 units of vitamin B per gram and costs 20 paise per gram. The daily minimum requirement of vitamin A and vitamin B is 100 units and 120 units respectively. Find the minimum cost of product mix by the simplex method. [*P.U. B. Com. April, 2007*]

Solution. Let x_1 and x_2 be the grams of food X and Y to be purchased. Then the problem can be formulated as follows :

$$\begin{aligned} \text{Minimize } Z &= 12x_1 + 20x_2, \\ \text{subject to } \quad & 6x_1 + 8x_2 \geq 100, \\ & 7x_1 + 12x_2 \geq 120, \\ & x_1, x_2 \geq 0. \end{aligned}$$

Step 1. Express the problem in standard form

Slack variables s_1 and s_2 are *subtracted* from the left-hand sides of the constraints to convert them to equations. These variables are also called *negative slack variables* or *surplus variables*. Variable s_1 represents units of vitamin A in product mix *in excess* of the minimum requirement of 100, s_2 represents units of vitamin B in product mix *in excess* of requirement of 120. Since they represent 'free' foods, the cost coefficients associated with them in the objective function are zeros. The problem, therefore, can be written as follows :

$$\text{Minimize } Z = 12x_1 + 20x_2 + 0s_1 + 0s_2,$$
$$\text{subject to} \quad 6x_1 + 8x_2 - s_1 = 100,$$
$$7x_1 + 12x_2 - s_2 = 120,$$
$$x_1, x_2, s_1, s_2 \geq 0.$$

Step 2. Find initial basic feasible solution

Putting $x_1 = x_2 = 0$, we get $s_1 = -100$, $s_2 = -120$ as the first basic solution but it is not feasible as s_1 and s_2 have negative values that do not satisfy the non-negativity restrictions. Therefore, we introduce artificial variables A_1 and A_2 in the constraints, which take the form

$$6x_1 + 8x_2 - s_1 + A_1 = 100,$$
$$7x_1 + 12x_2 - s_2 + A_2 = 120,$$
$$x_1, x_2, s_1, s_2, A_1, A_2 \geq 0.$$

Now artificial variables with values greater than zero violate the equality in constraints established in step 1. Therefore, A_1 and A_2 should not appear in the final solution. To achieve this, they are assigned a large unit penalty (a large positive value, + M) in the objective function, which can be written as

$$\text{minimize } Z = 12x_1 + 20x_2 + 0s_1 + 0s_2 + MA_1 + MA_2.$$

Problem, now, has six variables and two constraints. Four of the variables have to be zeroised to get initial basic feasible solution to the 'artificial system'. Putting $x_1 = x_2 = s_1 = s_2 = 0$, we get

$$A_1 = 100, A_2 = 120, Z = 220\text{ M}.$$

Note that we are starting with a very heavy cost (compare it with zero profit in maximization problem) which we shall minimize during the solution procedure. Table 2.36 represents the problem and its solution.

Step 3. Perform optimality test

TABLE 2.36

		c_j	12	20	0	0	M	M		
F.R.	c_B	Basis	x_1	x_2	s_1	s_2	A_1	A_2	b	θ
2/3	M	A_1	6	8	– 1	0	1	0	100	25/2
	M	A_2	7	(12)	0	– 1	0	1	120	10 ←
		Z_j	13M	20M	– M	– M	M	M	220 M	
		c_j-Z_j	12-13M	20-20M	M	M	0	0		
				↑K						*Initial solution*

Since c_j-Z_j is *negative* under x_1, x_2-columns, initial solution is not optimal and can be improved. c_j-Z_j is most negative under x_2-column. x_2-column is the key column, A_2-row is the key row and (12) is the key element. *Since A_2 is leaving variable, column A_2 is deleted from the next tables.*

Step 4. Iterate towards on optimal solution

Performing iterations results in the following tables:

TABLE 2.37

		c_j	12	20	0	0	M		
F.R.	c_B	Basis	x_1	x_2	s_1	s_2	A_1	b	θ
	M	A_1	(4/3)	0	– 1	2/3	1	20	15 ←

$7/16$	20	x_2	$7/12$	1	0	$-1/12$	0	10	$120/7$
		Z_j	$\frac{35}{3}+\frac{4}{3}M$	20	$-M$	$-\frac{5}{3}+\frac{2}{3}M$	M	200 + 20M	
		c_j-Z_j	$\frac{1}{3}-\frac{4}{3}M$ ↑K	0	M	$\frac{5}{3}-\frac{2}{3}M$	0		

c_B	Basis	x_1	x_2	s_1	s_2	b
12	x_1	1	0	$-3/4$	$1/2$	15
20	x_2	0	1	$7/16$	$-3/8$	$5/4$
	Z_j	12	20	$-1/4$	$-3/2$	205
	c_j-Z_j	0	0	$1/4$	$3/2$	

∴ Optimal solution is

$$x_1 = 15,\ x_2 = 5/4\ ;\ Z_{min} = 205 \text{ Paise} = ₹\ 2.05.$$

Hence 15 grams of food X and $\frac{5}{4}$ grams of food Y should be the required product mix with minimum cost of ₹ 2.05.

EXAMPLE 2.17-2

Maximize $Z = 3x_1 - x_2,$

subject to
$$2x_1 + x_2 \leq 2,$$
$$x_1 + 3x_2 \geq 3,$$
$$x_2 \leq 4,$$
$$x_1, x_2 \geq 0.$$

[*P.T.U. BCA, 2011; B.Tech., 2010; Gujarat Tech. U.B.E. Dec., 2012; Dayalbagh Edu. Inst. Agra MBA, Dec., 2013; H.P.U. B. Tech. (Mech.) Dec., 2009*]

Solution

Step 1. Set-up the problem in standard form

Introducing slack, surplus and artificial variables, the problem can be expressed in the following standard form :

Maximize $Z = 3x_1 - x_2 + 0s_1 + 0s_2 + 0s_3 - MA_1,$

subject to
$$2x_1 + x_2 + s_1 = 2,$$
$$x_1 + 3x_2 - s_2 + A_1 = 3,$$
$$x_2 + s_3 = 4,$$
$$x_1, x_2, s_1, s_2, s_3, A_1 \geq 0.$$

Step 2. Find initial basic feasible solution

Substituting $x_1 = x_2 = s_2 = 0$, the following initial basic feasible solution to the problem is obtained :

$$s_1 = 2,\ A_1 = 3,\ s_3 = 4\ ;\ Z = -3M.$$

Step 3. Perform optimality test

Since c_j-Z_j is positive under some variable columns, table 2.38 is not optimal and can be improved.

Step 4. Iterate towards an optimal solution

Successive iterations yielc the following tables :

TABLE 2.38

	c_j	3	– 1	0	0	0	– M		
c_B	Basis	x_1	x_2	s_1	s_2	s_3	A_1	b	θ
0	s_1	2	1	1	0	0	0	2	2
– M	A_1	1	(3)	0	– 1	0	1	3	1←
0	s_3	0	1	0	0	1	0	4	4
	$Z_j = \Sigma c_B a_{ij}$	– M	– 3M	0	M	0	– M	– 3M	
	c_j-Z_j	3 + M	– 1 + 3M	0	– M	0	0		
			↑K					*Initial solution*	

TABLE 2.39

	c_j	3	– 1	0	0	0			
c_B	Basis	x_1	x_2	s_1	s_2	s_3	b	θ	
0	s_1	$\left(5/3\right)$	0	1	$1/3$	0	1	$3/5$	←
– 1	x_2	$1/3$	1	0	$-1/3$	0	1	3	
0	s_3	$-1/3$	0	0	$1/3$	1	3	– 9	
	$Z_j = \Sigma c_B a_{ij}$	$-1/3$	– 1	0	$1/3$	0	– 1		
	c_j-Z_j	$10/3$	0	0	$-1/3$	0			
		↑K					*Second basic feasible solution*		

TABLE 2.40

	c_j	3	– 1	0	0	0	
c_B	Basis	x_1	x_2	s_1	s_2	s_3	b
3	x_1	1	0	$3/5$	$1/5$	0	$3/5$
– 1	x_2	0	1	$-1/5$	$-2/5$	0	$4/5$
0	s_3	0	0	$1/5$	$2/5$	1	$16/5$
	$Z_j = \Sigma c_B a_{ij}$	3	– 1	2	1	0	1
	c_j-Z_j	0	0	– 2	– 1	0	
					Optimal basic feasible solution		

Optimal solution is given by

$$x_1 = \frac{3}{5},\ x_2 = \frac{4}{5}\ ;\ Z_{\max} = 1.$$

EXAMPLE 2.17-3

Maximize $Z = x_1 + 2x_2 + 3x_3 - x_4,$

subject to $x_1 + 2x_2 + 3x_3 = 15,$
$2x_1 + x_2 + 5x_3 = 20,$
$x_1 + 2x_2 + x_3 + x_4 = 10,$
$x_1, x_2, x_3, x_4 \geq 0.$

[*P.T.U. B.Tech. (Mech.) Nov., 2012; BCA, 2010; R.T.M. Nagpur U.B.E. (Mech.) 2011; Dec., 2003; J.N.T.U. Hyderabad B.Tech. May, 2011; M.D.U.B.E. (Mech.) Dec., 2006; P.T.U.B.E. (Mech.) 2010; May, 2006, C.Sc., 2009; P.U.B.B.A., 2001*]

Solution

Step 1. Introducing artificial variables A_1, A_2, A_3, the given problem in standard form is

maximize $Z = x_1 + 2x_2 + 3x_3 - x_4 - MA_1 - MA_2 - MA_3,$

subject to $x_1 + 2x_2 + 3x_3 + 0x_4 + A_1 + 0A_2 + 0A_3 = 15,$
$2x_1 + x_2 + 5x_3 + 0x_4 + 0A_1 + A_2 + 0A_3 = 20,$
$x_1 + 2x_2 + x_3 + x_4 + 0A_1 + 0A_2 + A_3 = 10,$
$x_1, x_2, x_3, x_4, A_1, A_2, A_3 \geq 0.$

Step 2. Initial basic (non-degenerate) solution to the artificial system is

$x_1 = x_2 = x_3 = x_4 = 0,$
$A_1 = 15,$
$A_2 = 20,$
$A_3 = 10,$
$Z = -45\text{ M}.$

Table 2.41 represents this solution.

TABLE 2.41

	c_j	1	2	3	– 1	– M	– M	– M		
c_B	Basis	x_1	x_2	x_3	x_4	A_1	A_2	A_3	b	θ
– M	A_1	1	2	3	0	1	0	0	15	5
– M	A_2	2	1	(5)	0	0	1	0	20	4 ←
– M	A_3	1	2	1	1	0	0	1	10	10
	Z_j	– 4M	– 5M	– 9M	– M	– M	– M	– M	– 45M	
	$c_j–Z_j$	1 + 4M	2 + 5M	3 + 9M	– 1 + M	0	0	0		
				↑						

Initial solution

Since $c_j–Z_j$ is positive under some variable columns, table 2.41 is not optimal.

Step 3. Performing iterations to get an optimal solution results in the following tables :

TABLE 2.42

	c_j	1	2	3	– 1	– M	– M		
c_B	Basis	x_1	x_2	x_3	x_4	A_1	A_3	b	θ
– M	A_1	$-1/5$	$(7/5)$	0	0	1	0	3	$15/7$ ←
3	x_3	$2/5$	$1/5$	1	0	0	0	4	20
– M	A_3	$3/5$	$9/5$	0	1	0	1	6	$10/3$
	Z_j	$\frac{6-2M}{5}$	$\frac{3-16M}{5}$	3	– M	– M	– M	12–9M	
	$c_j–Z_j$	$\frac{-1+2M}{5}$	$\frac{7+16M}{5}$	0	– 1 + M	0	0		
			↑						

Second solution

TABLE 2.43

	c_j	1	2	3	– 1	– M	1	
c_B	Basis	x_1	x_2	x_3	x_4	A_3	b	θ
2	x_2	$-1/7$	1	0	0	0	$15/7$	∞
3	x_3	$3/7$	0	1	0	0	$25/7$	∞
– M	A_3	$6/7$	0	0	(1)	1	$15/7$	$15/7$ ←
	$Z_j = \Sigma c_B a_{ij}$	$\frac{7-6M}{7}$	2	3	– M	– M	$\frac{105-15M}{7}$	
	c_j–Z_j	$\frac{6M}{7}$	0	0	–1+M	0		
					↑		*Third solution*	

TABLE 2.44

	c_j	1	2	3	– 1		
c_B	Basis	x_1	x_2	x_3	x_4	b	θ
2	x_2	$-1/7$	1	0	0	$15/7$	– 15
3	x_3	$3/7$	0	1	0	$25/7$	$25/3$
– 1	x_4	$(6/7)$	0	0	1	$15/7$	$5/2$ ←
	$Z_j = \Sigma c_B a_{ij}$	$1/7$	2	3	– 1	$90/7$	
	c_j–Z_j	$6/7$	0	0	0		
		↑				*4th basic feasible solution*	

TABLE 2.45

	c_j	1	2	3	– 1	
c_B	Basis	x_1	x_2	x_3	x_4	b
2	x_2	0	1	0	$1/6$	$5/2$
3	x_3	0	0	1	$-1/2$	$5/2$
1	x_1	1	0	0	$7/6$	$5/2$
	$Z_j = \Sigma c_B a_{ij}$	1	2	3	0	15
	c_j–Z_j	0	0	0	– 1	
					Optimal basic feasible solution	

∵ c_j–Z_j is either zero or negative under all columns, the optimal basic feasible solution has been obtained. Optimal values are

$$x_1 = \frac{5}{2}, x_2 = \frac{5}{2}, x_3 = \frac{5}{2}, x_4 = 0.$$

Also $\quad A_1 = A_2 = A_3 = 0$ and $Z_{max} = 15$.

EXAMPLE 2.17-4

An Air Force is experimenting with three types of bombs P, Q and R in which three kinds of explosives, viz. A, B and C will be used. Taking the various factors into account, it has been decided to use at the maximum 600 kg of explosive A, at least 480 kg of explosive B and exactly 540 kg of explosive C. Bomb P requires 3, 2, 2 kg, bomb Q requires 1, 4, 3 kg and bomb R requires 4, 2, 3 kg of explosives A, B and C respectively. Bomb P is estimated to give the equivalent of a 2 ton explosion, bomb Q, a 3 ton explosion and bomb R, a 4 ton explosion respectively. Under what production schedule can the Air Force make the biggest bang?

[P.T.U.B. Tech. Dec., 2011; G.N.D.U. B.Com. Sept. 2010; SVSM PGDM, 2009; P.U.B. Tech. (T.I.T.) Dec., 2008]

Solution. Let x_1, x_2 and x_3 be the number of bombs of type P, Q and R respectively. Then linear programming model for the problem is given by

$$\begin{aligned} \text{maximize } Z &= 2x_1 + 3x_2 + 4x_3, \\ \text{subject to } \quad & 3x_1 + x_2 + 4x_3 \leq 600, \\ & 2x_1 + 4x_2 + 2x_3 \geq 480, \\ & 2x_1 + 3x_2 + 3x_3 = 540, \\ & x_1, x_2, x_3 \geq 0. \end{aligned}$$

Step 1. Introducing slack, surplus and artificial variables, the problem is expressed in the following standard form :

$$\begin{aligned} \text{Maximize } Z &= 2x_1 + 3x_2 + 4x_3 + 0s_1 + 0s_2 - MA_1 - MA_2, \\ \text{subject to } \quad & 3x_1 + x_2 + 4x_3 + s_1 = 600, \\ & 2x_1 + 4x_2 + 2x_3 - s_2 + A_1 = 480, \\ & 2x_1 + 3x_2 + 3x_3 + A_2 = 540, \\ & x_1, x_2, x_3, s_1, s_2, A_1, A_2 \geq 0. \end{aligned}$$

Step 2. Substituting $x_1 = x_2 = x_3 = s_2 = 0$ in the above artificial system, the following initial solution is obtained :

$$s_1 = 600,\ A_1 = 480,\ A_2 = 540\ ;\ Z = -\ 1{,}020\ M.$$

Step 3. Table 2.46 represents the above information. This table is not optimal and can be improved.

Step 4. Successive iterations are represented in the subsequent tables.

TABLE 2.46

	c_j	2	3	4	0	0	– M	– M		
c_B	Basis	x_1	x_2	x_3	s_1	s_2	A_1	A_2	b	θ
0	s_1	3	1	4	1	0	0	0	600	600
– M	A_1	2	(4)	2	0	– 1	1	0	480	120←
– M	A_2	2	3	3	0	0	0	1	540	180
	Z_j	–4M	–7M	–5M	0	M	–M	–M	–1,020M	
	c_j–Z_j	2+4M	3+7M	4+5M	0	–M	0	0		
			↑					*Initial solution*		

TABLE 2.47

	c_j	2	3	4	0	0	– M		
c_B	Basis	x_1	x_2	x_3	s_1	s_2	A_2	b	θ
0	s_1	$5/2$	0	$7/2$	1	$1/4$	0	480	960/7
3	x_2	$1/2$	1	$1/2$	0	$-1/4$	0	120	240
– M	A_2	$1/2$	0	$(3/2)$	0	$3/4$	1	180	120 ←

Z_j	$\frac{3}{2}-\frac{M}{2}$	3	$\frac{3}{2}-\frac{3M}{2}$	0	$-\frac{3}{4}-\frac{3M}{4}$	−M	360–180M
c_j-Z_j	$\frac{1}{2}+\frac{M}{2}$	0	$\frac{5}{2}+\frac{3M}{2}$ ↑	0	$\frac{3}{4}+\frac{3M}{4}$	0	*Second solution*

TABLE 2.48

	c_j	2	3	4	0	0	
c_B	Basis	x_1	x_2	x_3	s_1	s_2	b
0	s_1	$4/3$	0	0	1	$-3/2$	60
3	x_2	$1/3$	1	0	0	$-1/2$	60
4	x_3	$1/3$	0	1	0	$1/2$	120
	Z_j	$7/3$	3	4	0	$1/2$	660
	c_j-Z_j	$-1/3$	0	0	0	$-1/2$	*Optimal solution*

∴ Optimal solution is $x_1 = 0$, $x_2 = 60$, $x_3 = 120$; $Z_{max} = 660$.

EXAMPLE 2.17-5

Each unit of a chemical Xylol, processed in department 1; jointly yields two units of intermediate P and one unit of intermediate Q. Intermediate P has to be further processed in department 2 to make it a saleable product A, while unprocessed P would be a waste. Intermediate Q is sold as such to another company. The selling prices are ₹ 500 per unit of A and ₹ 400 per unit of Q. The processing of Xylol and P requires a common product facility at the rate of 60 minutes per unit of Xylol and 20 minutes per unit of P. The processing costs are ₹ 600 per unit of Xylol and ₹ 200 per unit of P. For the coming production period, the supply of Xylol is limited to 3,000 units and the production capacity to 4,500 hours. Required:

(i) Find the optimum production plan and the overall profitability.

(ii) Which resource restricts the achievement of profit target of 12 lakhs?

(iii) Suggest a way of achieving ths target. [*C.A. (Final) June, 2002*]

Solution

Let x_X, x_A, x_P and x_Q be the number of units of chemical Xylol used and products A, P and Q produced.

Profit/unit of product A = ₹ (500 − 200) = ₹ 300,
profit/unit of product Q = ₹ 400,
processing cost/unit of Xylol = ₹ 600.
Therefore, objective function becomes:

Max. $Z = 300\, x_A + 400\, x_Q - 600 x_X$.

Each unit of Xylol yields 2 units of P and one unit of Q.

$$\therefore \frac{x_X}{1} = \frac{x_P}{2} = \frac{x_Q}{1} \quad \therefore \quad x_P - 2x_X = 0 \text{ and } x_Q - x_X = 0$$

Also $x_P = x_A$ as unprocessed P would be a waste.

∴ $x_A - 2x_X = 0$ and $x_Q - x_X = 0$ are the two constraints.

Other constraints are $x_X \le 3{,}000$,

and $\frac{60}{60}x_X + \frac{20}{60}x_P \le 4{,}500$

or $\quad x_X + \frac{1}{3} x_P \leq 4{,}500$ or $x_X + \frac{x_A}{3} \leq 4{,}500.$

Thus the L.P. model can be expressed as

$$\text{Max. } Z = 300\,x_A + 400\,x_Q - 600\,x_X,$$
subject to
$$x_X \leq 3{,}000,$$
$$\frac{x_A}{3} + x_x \leq 4{,}500,$$
$$x_A - 2x_x = 0,$$
$$x_Q - x_x = 0,$$
where $\quad x_X, x_A, x_Q \geq 0.$

Introducing slack variable s_1 to the first constraint, s_2 to the second and artificial variable A_1 to the third constraint, the problem can be expressed as

$$\text{Maximize } Z = 300x_A + 400x_Q - 600x_X + 0s_1 + 0s_2 - MA_1,$$
subject to
$$x_X + s_1 = 3{,}000,$$
$$\frac{1}{3}x_A + x_X + s_2 = 4{,}500,$$
$$x_A - 2x_X + A_1 = 0,$$
$$x_Q - x_X = 0,$$
$$x_A, x_Q, x_X, s_1, s_2, A_1 \geq 0.$$

Note that artificial variable is not introduced in the last constraint since x_Q does not occur in any other constraint and, therefore, can be treated as a basic variable. Let $x_A = x_X = 0$. Then *i.b.f.s.* is

$s_1 = 3{,}000$; $s_2 = 4{,}500$; $A_1 = 0$; $x_Q = 0$; $Z = 0$.

Solution by simplex method yields the following tables :

TABLE 2.49

	c_j	300	400	– 600	0	0	– M		
c_B	Basis	x_A	x_Q	x_X	s_1	s_2	A_1	b	θ
0	s_1	0	0	1	1	0	0	3,000	∞
0	s_2	1/3	0	1	0	1	0	4,500	13,500
–M	A_1	(1)	0	– 2	0	0	1	0	0 ←
400	x_Q	0	1	– 1	0	0	0	0	–
	Z_j	– M	400	–400+2M	0	0	–M	0	
	$c_j - z_j$	300+M ↑	0	–200–2M	0	0	0		*i.b.f.s*

TABLE 2.50

	c_j	300	400	–600	0	0		
c_B	Basis	x_A	x_Q	x_X	s_1	s_2	b	θ
0	s_1	0	0	1	1	0	3,000	3,000
0	s_2	0	0	(5/3)	0	1	4,500	2,700 ←
300	x_A	1	0	– 2	0	0	0	– 0
400	x_Q	0	1	– 1	0	0	0	– 0
	Z_j	300	400	– 1,000	0	0	0	
	$c_j - Z_j$	0	0	400 ↑	0	0		*2nd b.f.s.*

TABLE 2.51

	c_j	300	400	–600	0	0	
c_B	Basis	x_A	x_Q	x_X	s_1	s_2	b
0	s_1	0	0	0	1	$-3/5$	300
– 600	x_X	0	0	1	0	$3/5$	2,700
300	x_A	1	0	0	0	$6/5$	5,400
400	x_Q	0	1	0	0	$3/5$	2,700
	Z_j	300	400	– 600	0	240	10,80,000
	$c_j–Z_j$	0	0	0	0	– 240	*Optimal solution*

(*i*) ∴ Optimal product mix is

x_A = 5,400 units, x_Q = 2,700 units, x_X = 2,700 units,

s_1 = 300 units, Z_{max} = ₹ 10.8 lakhs.

(*ii*) s_1 = 300 units of material remain unused. So it does not restrict the achievement of target.

s_2 = 0. This resource is fully used. It has opportunity cost of ₹ 240/hr and restricts the achievement of target.

(*iii*) *Let the production capacity resource increase by Δs_2 hours. Maximum value of Δs_2 is restricted by the fact that the new value of s_1 should remain ≥ 0.

$$i.e., \; 300 - \frac{3}{5}\,\Delta s_2 \geq 0 \quad \text{or} \quad -\frac{3}{5}\,\Delta s_2 \geq -300 \quad \text{or} \quad \Delta s_2 \leq 500.$$

Therefore, additional production capacity of 500 hours can be used.

Incremental profit = ₹ (500 × 240) = ₹ 1.2 lakhs.

Total profit = ₹ (10.8 + 1.2) = ₹ 12 lakhs.

With production capacity of 4,500 + 500 = 5,000 hours, the new values of variables x_X, x_A and x_Q become :

$$x_X' = x_X + \frac{3}{5} \times 500 = 2,700 + 300 = 3,000 \text{ units},$$

$$x_A' = x_A + \frac{6}{5} \times 500 = 5,400 + \frac{6}{5} \times 500 = 6,000 \text{ units},$$

$$x_Q' = x_Q + \frac{3}{5} \times 500 = 2,700 + \frac{3}{5} \times 500 = 3,000 \text{ units},$$

Z = ₹ [– 600 × 3,000 + 300 × 6,000 + 400 × 3,000.]

= ₹ 12 lakhs.

2.17-2 The Two-Phase Method

In the preceding section we observed that it was frequently necessary to add artificial variables to the constraints to obtain an initial basic feasible solution to an L.P. problem. If the problem is to be solved, the artificial variables must be driven to zero. The two-phase method is another method to handle these artificial variables. Here the L.P. problem is solved in two phases.

* *For details refer to topic 6.6 on sensitivity analysis.*

Phase I

In this phase we find an *i.b.f.s.* to the original problem. For this all artificial variables are to be driven to zero. To do this an *artificial objective function* (w) is created which is the sum of all the artificial variables. This *new* objective function is then *minimized,* subject to the constraints of the given (original) problem, using the simplex method. At the end of phase I, three cases arise:

1. If the minimum value of $w > 0$, and at least one artificial variable appears in the basis at a positive level, then the given problem has no feasible solution and the procedure terminates.

2. If the minimum value of $w = 0$, and no artificial variable appears in the basis, then a basic feasible solution to the given problem is obtained. The artificial variable column (s) is/are deleted for phase II computations.

3. If the minimum value of $w = 0$ and one or more artificial variables appear in the basis at zero level, then a feasible solution to the original problem is obtained. However, we must take care of this artificial variable and see that it never becomes positive during phase II computations. Zero cost coefficient is assigned to this artificial variable and it is retained in the initial table of phase II. If this variable remains in the basis at zero level in all phase II computations, there is no problem. However, the problem arises if it becomes positive in some iteration. In such a case, a slightly different approach is adopted in selecting the outgoing variable. The lowest non-negative replacement ratio criterion is not adopted to find the outgoing variable. Artificial variable (or one of the artificial variables if there are more than one) is selected as the outgoing variable. The simplex method can then be applied as usual to obtain the optimal basic feasible solution to the given L.P. problem.

Phase II

When phase I results in (2) or (3), we go on to phase II to find optimum solution to the given L.P. problem. The basic feasible solution found at the end of phase I is now used as a starting solution for the original problem. In other words, the final table of phase I becomes the starting table of phase II in which the *artificial* (*auxiliary*) *objective function* is replaced by the original objective function. The simplex method is then applied to arrive at the optimum solution. Artificial variables which do not appear in the basis may be deleted.

Remarks: 1. In phase I, the iterations are stopped as soon as the value of the new (artificial) objective function becomes zero because this is its minimum value. There is no need to continue till the optimality is reached if this value becomes zero earlier than that.

2. Note that the new objective function is always of minimization type regardless of whether the original problem is of maximization or minimization type.

EXAMPLE 2.17-6

Use the two-phase simplex method to

maximize $Z = 5x_1 + 3x_2,$

subject to the constraints $2x_1 + x_2 \leq 1,$

$x_1 + 4x_2 \geq 6,$

$x_1, x_2, \geq 0.$

[*P.T.U. B.Tech. (C.Sc.) 2010; Nellore M.B.A., 2002*]

Solution

Phase I

It consists of the following steps:

Step 1. Set-up the Problem in the Standard Form

The original objective function $Z = 5x_1 + 3x_2$ is temporarily set aside during the phase I solution. The given constraints, after the introduction of slack, surplus and artificial variables take the form :

$$2x_1 + x_2 + s_1 = 1,$$
$$x_1 + 4x_2 - s_2 + A_1 = 6,$$
$$x_1, x_2, s_1, s_2, A_1 \geq 0.$$

The new objective function is

$$\text{minimize } w = A_1.$$

Now the simplex method requires that a variable which appears in one equation must appear in all the equations. This is done by proper placement of zero coefficients. Thus the problem for phase I in standard form becomes

$$\text{minimize } w = 0x_1 + 0x_2 + 0s_1 + 0s_2 + A_1,$$
$$\text{subject to } \quad 2x_1 + x_2 + s_1 + 0s_2 + 0A_1 = 1,$$
$$x_1 + 4x_2 + 0s_1 - s_2 + A_1 = 6,$$
$$x_1, x_2, s_1, s_2, A_1 \geq 0.$$

Step 2. Find an Initial Basic Feasible Solution

Substituting $x_1 = x_2 = s_2 = 0$ in the constraint equations we get $s_1 = 1$, $A_1 = 6$ as the initial basic feasible solution. Table 2.52 represents this solution.

TABLE 2.52

	c_j	0	0	0	0	1			
c_B	Basis	x_1	x_2	s_2	s_1	A_1	b	θ	
0	s_1	2	(1)	0	1	0	1	1	←
1	A_1	1	4	– 1	0	1	6	3/2	
	$Z_j = \Sigma c_B a_{ij}$	1	4	– 1	0	1	6		
	$c_j – Z_j$	– 1	– 4	1	0	0			
			↑						

Initial b.f.s. for phase I problem

Step 3. Perform Optimality Test

Since $c_j – Z_j$ is negative under some columns (minimization problem), table 2.52 is not optimal.

Step 4. Iterate Towards an Optimal Solution

In table 2.52, x_2 is incoming variable, s_1 is outgoing variable and (1) is the key element. In table 2.53, s_1 is replaced by x_2.

TABLE 2.53

	c_j	0	0	0	0	1	
c_B	Basis	x_1	x_2	s_2	s_1	A_1	b
0	x_2	2	1	0	1	0	1
1	A_1	– 7	0	– 1	– 4	1	2
	$Z_j = \Sigma c_B a_{ij}$	– 7	0	– 1	– 4	1	2
	$c_j – Z_j$	7	0	1	4	0	

Optimal basic feasible solution for phase I problem

∵ $c_j – Z_j$ is either positive or zero under all columns, an optimal basic feasible solution to the auxiliary L.P.P. has been obtained.

However, since $w = A_1 = 2$ (> 0) and artificial variable A_1 appears in the basis at a positive level ($A_1 = 2$), the given problem *does not possess a feasible solution* and the procedure stops.

EXAMPLE 2.17-7

Use the two-phase simplex method to

$$\text{maximize } Z = 5x_1 - 4x_2 + 3x_3,$$
$$\text{subject to } \quad 2x_1 + x_2 - 6x_3 = 20,$$
$$6x_1 + 5x_2 + 10x_3 \leq 76,$$
$$8x_1 - 3x_2 + 6x_3 \leq 50,$$
$$x_1, x_2, x_3 \geq 0.$$

[*H.P.U. B.Tech. (Mech.) Nov., 2007*]

Solution

PHASE I: It consists of the following steps:

Step 1. Set-up the Problem in the Standard Form

The given constraints, after the introduction of slack and artificial variables take the form

$$2x_1 + x_2 - 6x_3 + A_1 = 20,$$
$$6x_1 + 5x_2 + 10x_3 + s_2 = 76,$$
$$8x_1 - 3x_2 + 6x_3 + s_3 = 50,$$
$$x_1, x_2, x_3, s_2, s_3, A_1 \geq 0.$$

The new (artificial) objective function is

$$\text{minimize } w = A_1.$$

The new objective function is also called the *infeasibility form or auxiliary (dummy) objective function.* Thus the problem for phase I in standard form can be written as

$$\text{minimize } w = 0x_1 + 0x_2 + 0x_3 + 0s_2 + 0s_3 + A_1,$$
$$\text{subject to } \quad 2x_1 + x_2 - 6x_3 + 0s_2 + 0s_3 + A_1 = 20,$$
$$6x_1 + 5x_2 + 10x_3 + s_2 + 0s_3 + 0A_1 = 76,$$
$$8x_1 - 3x_2 + 6x_3 + 0s_2 + s_3 + 0A_1 = 50,$$
$$x_1, x_2, x_3, s_2, s_3, A_1 \geq 0.$$

Step 2. Find an Initial Basic Feasible Solution

Setting variables $x_1 = x_2 = x_3 = 0$, the basic feasible solution to the auxiliary problem is

$$x_1 = x_2 = x_3 = 0,$$
$$A_1 = 20,$$
$$s_2 = 76,$$
$$s_3 = 50.$$

Table 2.54 represents this solution.

TABLE 2.54

	c_j	0	0	0	0	0	1		
c_B	Basis	x_1	x_2	x_3	s_2	s_3	A_1	b	θ
1	A_1	2	1	– 6	0	0	1	20	10
0	s_2	6	5	10	1	0	0	76	$38/3$
0	s_3	(8)	– 3	6	0	1	0	50	$25/4$ ←
Z_j		2	1	– 6	0	0	1	20	
$c_j – Z_j$		– 2	– 1	6	0	0	0		
		↑							

Initial b.f.s. for phase I problem

Step 3. Perform Optimality Test

Since $c_j – Z_j$ is negative under some variable columns, table 2.54 is not optimal.

Step 4. Iterate Towards an Optimal Solution

In table 2.54, x_1 is the incoming variable, s_3 is the outgoing variable and (8) is the key element. This element is made unity in table 2.55. Performing iterations to get an optimal solution results in the following tables :

TABLE 2.55

	c_j	0	0	0	0	0	1		
c_B	Basis	x_1	x_2	x_3	s_2	s_3	A_1	b	θ
1	A_1	0	($7/4$)	$-15/2$	0	$-1/4$	1	$15/2$	$30/7$ ←
0	s_2	0	$29/4$	$11/2$	1	$-3/4$	0	$77/2$	$154/29$
0	x_1	1	$-3/8$	$3/4$	0	$1/8$	0	$25/4$	$-50/3$
	Z_j	0	$7/4$	$-15/2$	0	$-1/4$	1	$15/2$	
	$c_j–Z_j$	0	$-7/4$ ↑	$15/2$	0	$1/4$	0		

Second b.f.s. for phase I problem

TABLE 2.56

	c_j	0	0	0	0	0	1	
c_B	Basis	x_1	x_2	x_3	s_2	s_3	A_1	b
0	x_2	0	1	$-30/7$	0	$-1/7$	$4/7$	$30/7$
0	s_2	0	0	$256/7$	1	$2/7$	$-29/7$	$52/7$
0	x_1	1	0	$-6/7$	0	$1/14$	$3/14$	$55/7$
Z_j		0	0	0	0	0	0	0
$c_j–Z_j$		0	0	0	0	0	1	

Opimal b.f.s. for phase I problem

Since $c_j–Z_j$ is non-negative under all columns, table 2.56 is optimal. Also, since $w_{min} = 0$ and no artificial variable appears in the basis, this table gives a b.f.s. to the original problem.

PHASE II: Phase II of the simplex method finds optimal solution to the original problem. Objective function for the initial table of phase II is the objective function of the original (given problem). The remaining part of initial table for phase II is the last table for phase I, with the only difference that Z_j and $c_j–Z_j$ rows in the last table for phase I are changed to account for the changes in the cost coefficients. Table 2.57 represents the initial table for phase II computations. *Note that since basis column in table 2.56 contains no artificial variable, it is not considered in table 2.57.*

TABLE 2.57

	c_j	5	– 4	3	0	0	
c_B	Basis	x_1	x_2	x_3	s_2	s_3	b
– 4	x_2	0	1	$-30/7$	0	$-1/7$	$30/7$
0	s_2	0	0	$256/7$	1	$2/7$	$52/7$

5	x_1	1	0	$-6/7$	0	$1/14$	$55/7$
	Z_j	5	-4	$90/7$	0	$13/14$	$155/7$
	$c_j - Z_j$	0	0	$-69/7$	0	$-13/14$	

Optimal b.f.s. for the original problem

Since $c_j - Z_j$ is either negative or zero under all variable columns, table 2.57 gives optimal basic feasible solution for the original problem. The optimal solution is

$$x_1 = \frac{55}{7},\ x_2 = \frac{30}{7},\ x_3 = 0\ ;\ Z_{max} = \frac{155}{7} = 22\frac{1}{7}.$$

EXAMPLE 2.17-8

Use two-phase simplex method to

$$\text{maximize } Z = 3x_1 + 2x_2 + 2x_3,$$
$$\text{subject to } \quad 5x_1 + 7x_2 + 4x_3 \leq 7,$$
$$-4x_1 + 7x_2 + 5x_3 \geq -2,$$
$$3x_1 + 4x_2 - 6x_3 \geq \frac{29}{7},$$
$$x_1, x_2, x_3 \geq 0.$$

[V.T.U. Karnataka B.E. June, 2010; P.U.B.E. (E. & Ec.) April, 2006; B.E. (T. & I.T.) Nov., 2004]

Solution

Phase I

It consists of the following steps:

Step 1. Set-up the Problem in the Standard Form

The second constraint is multiplied by – 1 on both sides and expressed as

$$4x_1 - 7x_2 - 5x_3 \leq 2.$$

The given constraints, after the introduction of slack, surplus and artificial variables take the form

$$5x_1 + 7x_2 + 4x_3 + s_1 = 7,$$
$$4x_1 - 7x_2 - 5x_3 + s_2 = 2,$$
$$3x_1 + 4x_2 - 6x_3 - s_3 + A_1 = \frac{29}{7},$$
$$x_1, x_2, x_3, s_1, s_2, s_3, A_1 \geq 0.$$

The new (artificial) objective function is

$$\text{minimize } w = A_1.$$

Thus the problem for phase I in standard form is

$$\text{minimize } w = 0x_1 + 0x_2 + 0x_3 + 0s_1 + 0s_2 + 0s_3 + A_1,$$
$$\text{subject to } \quad 5x_1 + 7x_2 + 4x_3 + s_1 + 0s_2 + 0s_3 + 0A_1 = 7$$
$$4x_1 - 7x_2 - 5x_3 + 0s_1 + s_2 + 0s_3 + 0A_1 = 2,$$
$$3x_1 + 4x_2 - 6x_3 + 0s_1 + 0s_2 - s_3 + A_1 = \frac{29}{7},$$
$$x_1, x_2, x_3, s_1, s_2, s_3, A_1 \geq 0.$$

Step 2. Find an Initial Basic Feasible Solution

Setting variables $x_1 = x_2 = x_3 = s_3 = 0$, the basic feasible solution to the auxiliary problem is

$$x_1 = x_2 = x_3 = s_3 = 0,$$
$$s_1 = 7,$$
$$s_2 = 2,$$
$$A_1 = \frac{29}{7}.$$

Table 2.58 represents this solution.

TABLE 2.58

	c_j	0	0	0	0	0	0	1			
c_B	Basis	x_1	x_2	x_3	s_1	s_2	s_3	A_1	b	θ	
0	s_1	5	(7)	4	1	0	0	0	7	1	←
0	s_2	4	–7	–5	0	1	0	0	2	$-2/7$	
1	A_1	3	4	– 6	0	0	– 1	1	$29/7$	$29/28$	
	Z_j	3	4	– 6	0	0	– 1	1	$29/7$		
	$c_j–Z_j$	– 3	– 4	6	0	0	1	0			
			↑								

Initial b.f.s. for phase I problem

Step 3. Perform Optimality Test

Since $c_j–Z_j$ is negative under some variable columns, table 2.58 is not optimal.

Step 4. Iterate Towards an Optimal Solution

In table 2.58, x_2 is incoming variable, s_1 is outgoing variable and (7) is the key element. This element is made unity in table 2.59. Performing iteration to get an optimal solution results in the following table :

TABLE 2.59

	c_j	0	0	0	0	0	0	1			
c_B	Basis	x_1	x_2	x_3	s_1	s_2	s_3	A_1	b	θ	
0	x_2	$5/7$	1	$4/7$	$1/7$	0	0	0	1	$7/5$	
0	s_2	9	0	– 1	1	1	0	0	9	1	
1	A_1	$(1/7)$	0	$-58/7$	$-4/7$	0	– 1	1	$1/7$	1	←
	Z_j	$1/7$	0	$-58/7$	$-4/7$	0	– 1	1			
	$c_j–Z_j$	$-1/7$	0	$58/7$	$4/7$	0	1	0			
		↑									

Second b.f.s for phase I problem

In table 2.59, there is tie between the s_2 and A_1-rows for the key row. Following the method described in section 2.18.2, A_1-row is selected as the key row. Thus $\left(\frac{1}{7}\right)$ is the key element. The simplex method is continued and the following table is obtained :

TABLE 2.60

c_B	c_j / Basis	0 / x_1	0 / x_2	0 / x_3	0 / s_1	0 / s_2	0 / s_3	b
0	x_2	0	1	42	3	0	5	2/7
0	s_2	0	0	521	37	1	63	0
0	x_1	1	0	− 58	− 4	0	− 7	1
	Z_j	0	0	0	0	0	0	0
	c_j–Z_j	0	0	0	0	0	0	

Optimal b.f.s. for the auxiliary problem

Since c_j–Z_j is zero under all variable columns, table 2.60 is optimal. Also since $w_{\min} = 0$ and no artificial variable appears in the basis, this table gives a b.f.s. to the original problem.

Phase II

The original objective function is

$$\text{maximize } Z = 3x_1 + 2x_2 + 2x_3 + 0s_1 + 0s_2 + 0s_3.$$

We are to maximize it subject to the original constraints. Using the solution of table 2.60 as the starting solution for phase II and carrying out computations to get optimal solution results in the following tables:

TABLE 2.61

c_B	c_j / Basis	3 / x_1	2 / x_2	2 / x_3	0 / s_1	0 / s_2	0 / s_3	b	θ	
2	x_2	0	1	42	3	0	5	2/7	1/147	
0	s_2	0	0	(521)	37	1	63	0	0	←
3	x_1	1	0	–58	– 4	0	– 7	1	– 1/58	
	Z_j	3	2	– 90	– 6	0	– 11	25/7		
	c_j–Z_j	0	0	92	6	0	11			
				↑						

Initial b.f.s. for the original problem

TABLE 2.62

c_B	c_j / Basis	3 / x_1	2 / x_2	2 / x_3	0 / s_1	0 / s_2	0 / s_3	b
2	x_2	0	1	0	9/521	–42/521	–41/521	2/7
2	x_3	0	0	1	37/521	1/521	63/521	0
3	x_1	1	0	0	62/521	58/521	7/521	1
	Z_j	3	2	2	278/521	92/521	65/521	25/7
	c_j–Z_j	0	0	0	–278/521	–92/521	–65/521	

Optimal b.f.s. to the given problem

Since $c_j - Z_j$ is either negative or zero under all variable columns, table 2.62 gives the optimal basic feasible solution to the given problem, which is

$$x_1 = 1, x_2 = \frac{2}{7}, x_3 = 0, Z_{max} = \frac{25}{7} = 3\frac{4}{7}.$$

EXAMPLE 2.17-9

Use the two-phase simplex method to

$$\text{maximize } Z = 2x_1 + x_2 + \frac{1}{4}x_3,$$
$$\text{subject to} \quad 4x_1 + 6x_2 + 3x_3 \leq 8,$$
$$3x_1 - 6x_2 - 4x_3 \leq 1,$$
$$2x_1 + 3x_2 - 5x_3 \geq 4,$$
$$x_1, x_2, x_3 \geq 0.$$

[*P.T.U. M.Tech. Dec., 2011*]

Solution

PHASE I. It consists of the following steps:

Step 1. Set-up the Problem in the Standard Form

The given constraints, after the introduction of slack, surplus and artificial variables, take the form

$$4x_1 + 6x_2 + 3x_3 + s_1 = 8,$$
$$3x_1 - 6x_2 - 4x_3 + s_2 = 1,$$
$$2x_1 + 3x_2 - 5x_3 - s_3 + A_1 = 4,$$
$$x_1, x_2, x_3, s_1, s_2, s_3, A_1 \geq 0.$$

The new (artificial) objective function is

$$\text{minimize } w = A_1.$$

Thus the problem for phase I in standard form is

$$\text{minimize } w = 0x_1 + 0x_2 + 0x_3 + 0s_1 + 0s_2 + 0s_3 + A_1,$$
$$\text{subject to} \quad 4x_1 + 6x_2 + 3x_3 + s_1 + 0s_2 + 0s_3 + 0A_1 = 8,$$
$$3x_1 - 6x_2 - 4x_3 + 0s_1 + s_2 + 0s_3 + 0A_1 = 1,$$
$$2x_1 + 3x_2 - 5x_3 + 0s_1 + 0s_2 - s_3 + A_1 = 4,$$
$$x_1, x_2, x_3, s_1, s_2, s_3, A_1 \geq 0.$$

Step 2. Find an Initial Basic Feasible Solution

Setting variables $x_1 = x_2 = x_3 = s_3 = 0$, the basic feasible solution to the auxiliary problem is

$$x_1 = x_2 = x_3 = s_3 = 0,$$
$$s_1 = 8,$$
$$s_2 = 1,$$
$$A_1 = 4,$$
$$w = 4.$$

Table 2.63 represents this solution.

TABLE 2.63

	c_j	0	0	0	0	0	0	1		
c_B	Basis	x_1	x_2	x_3	s_1	s_2	s_3	A_1	b	θ
0	s_1	4	(6)	3	1	0	0	0	8	$4/3$ ←
0	s_2	3	−6	−4	0	1	0	0	1	$-1/6$
1	A_1	2	3	−5	0	0	−1	1	4	$4/3$

Z_j	2	3	– 5	0	0	– 1	1	4
$c_j–Z_j$	– 2	– 3	5	0	0	1	0	
		↑						

Initial b.f.s. for phase I problem

Step 3. Perform Optimality Test

Since $c_j–Z_j$ is negative under some variable columns, table 2.63 is not optimal.

Step 4. Iterate Towards on Optimal Solution

In table 2.63, there is tie among s_1- and A_1-rows. Choosing s_1-row arbitrarily as the key row and performing iteration to get an optimal solution results in the following table :

TABLE 2.64

	c_j	0	0	0	0	0	0	1	
c_B	Basis	x_1	x_2	x_3	s_1	s_2	s_3	A_1	b
0	x_2	$2/3$	1	$1/2$	$1/6$	0	0	0	$4/3$
0	s_2	7	0	– 1	1	1	0	0	9
1	A_1	0	0	$-13/2$	$-1/2$	0	– 1	1	0
	Z_j	0	0	$-13/2$	$-1/2$	0	– 1	1	0
	$c_j–Z_j$	0	0	$13/2$	$1/2$	0	1	0	

Optimal b.f.s. for phase I problem

Since $c_j–Z_j$ is non-negative under all variable columns, an optimal basic feasible solution to the auxiliary problem has been obtained. However, since $w_{\min} = 0$ and the artificial variable A_1 appears in the basis at zero level, this solution may or *may not be the feasible solution to the given (original) problem.* To obtain an optimum basic feasible solution to it, we move to phase II.

PHASE II. We assign the actual costs associated with the original variables and *assign zero cost to artificial variable A_1 which appeared at zero level in phase I.* The objective function to the original problem can thus be written as

$$Z = 2x_1 + x_2 + \frac{1}{4}x_3 + 0s_1 + 0s_2 + 0s_3 + 0A_1.$$

We wish to maximize this objective function subject to the given constraints by applying the simplex method. The optimum basic feasible solution, if any, thus obtained will be an optimal basic feasible solution to the original problem.

TABLE 2.65

	c_j	2	1	1/4	0	0	0	0		
c_B	Basis	x_1	x_2	x_3	s_1	s_2	s_3	A_1	b	θ
1	x_2	$2/3$	1	$1/2$	$1/6$	0	0	0	$4/3$	2
0	s_2	(7)	0	– 1	1	1	0	0	9	$9/7$ ←
0	A_1	0	0	$-13/2$	$-1/2$	0	– 1	1	0	–
	Z_j	$\frac{2}{3}$	1	$1/2$	$1/6$	0	0	0	$4/3$	

$c_j - Z_j$	$4/3$ ↑	0	$-1/4$	$-1/6$	0	0	0

Initial b.f.s. to the original problem

TABLE 2.66

c_B	c_j Basis	2 x_1	1 x_2	1/4 x_3	0 s_1	0 s_2	0 s_3	0 A_1	b
1	x_2	0	1	$25/42$	$1/14$	$-2/21$	0	0	$10/21$
2	x_1	1	0	$-1/7$	$1/7$	$1/7$	0	0	$9/7$
0	A_1	0	0	$-13/2$	$-1/2$	0	-1	1	0
	Z_j	2	1	$13/42$	$5/14$	$4/21$	0	0	$64/21$
	$c_j - Z_j$	0	0	$-5/84$	$-5/14$	$-4/21$	0	0	

Optimal b.f.s. to the original problem

Since $c_j - Z_j$ is either zero or negative under all variable columns, table 2.66 gives optimal b.f.s. to the original problem, which is

$$x_1 = \frac{9}{7}, x_2 = \frac{10}{21}, x_3 = 0; Z_{max} = \frac{64}{21} = 3\frac{1}{21}.$$

EXAMPLE 2.17-10

Use the two-phase simplex method to

$$\textit{maximize } Z = x_1 + 1.5x_2 + 5x_3 + 2x_4,$$
$$\textit{subject to } \quad 3x_1 + 2x_2 + x_3 + 4x_4 \le 6,$$
$$2x_1 + x_2 + 5x_3 + x_4 \le 4,$$
$$2x_1 + 6x_2 - 4x_3 + 8x_4 = 0,$$
$$x_1 + 3x_2 - 2x_3 + 4x_4 = 0.$$
$$x_1, x_2, x_3, x_4 \ge 0.$$

Solution

PHASE I. It consists of the following steps:

Step 1. Set-up the Problem in Standard Form

Phase I problem, in standard form, can be expressed as

$$\text{minimize } w = 0x_1 + 0x_2 + 0x_3 + 0s_1 + 0s_2 + A_1 + A_2,$$
$$\text{subject to } \quad 3x_1 + 2x_2 + x_3 + 4x_4 + s_1 + 0s_2 + 0A_1 + 0A_2 = 6,$$
$$2x_1 + x_2 + 5x_3 + x_4 - 0s_1 + s_2 + 0A_1 + 0A_2 = 4,$$
$$2x_1 + 6x_2 - 4x_3 + 8x_4 + 0s_1 + 0s_2 + A_1 + 0A_2 = 0,$$
$$x_1 + 3x_2 - 2x_3 + 4x_4 + 0s_1 + 0s_2 + 0A_1 + A_2 = 0,$$
$$x_1, x_2, x_3, x_4, s_1, s_2, A_1, A_2 \ge 0.$$

Step 2. Find an Initial Basic Feasible Solution

The initial b.f.s. to the phase I problem is

$$x_1 = x_2 = x_3 = x_4 = 0,$$
$$s_1 = 6,$$
$$s_2 = 4,$$
$$A_1 = 0,$$

$$A_2 = 0,$$
$$w_{min} = 0.$$

In this solution, $w_{min} = 0$ and each of the basic artificial variable is at zero level. Therefore, computation of phase I is not required and we can directly start with phase II.

Note that the last equation is just one-half the third one. This clearly indicates redundancy in the constraints. The last constraint equation, which is redundant, can be dropped. However, instead of dropping this constraint, we shall retain it to show what happens in the two-phase method.

PHASE II. Table 2.67 is constructed to represent initial b.f.s. for phase II.

TABLE 2.67

	c_j	1	3/2	5	2	0	0	0	0		
c_B	Basis	x_1	x_2	x_3	x_4	s_1	s_2	A_1	A_2	b	θ
0	s_1	3	2	1	4	1	0	0	0	6	6
0	s_2	2	1	5	1	0	1	0	0	4	$4/5$
0	A_1	2	6	(−4)	8	0	0	1	0	0	− 0 ←
0	A_2	1	3	−2	4	0	0	0	1	0	− 0
	Z_j	0	0	0	0	0	0	0	0	0	
	$c_j–Z_j$	1	$3/2$	5	2	0	0	0	0		
				↑							

Initial b.f.s. for the original problem

Step 1. Perform Optimality Test

Since $c_j–Z_j$ is positive under some columns, table 2.67 is not optimal.

Step 2. Iterate Towards an Optimal Solution

In table 2.67, x_3 is incoming variable. By the minimum ratio rule, s_2 is the outgoing variable. *However, if s_2 is replaced by x_3, both artificial variables attain positive values in the new table. Therefore, a slightly different approach is used to choose the outgoing variable.*

Without caring for the simplex criterion for selection of the outgoing variable, we choose one of the artificial variables, say A_1, arbitrarily to leave the basis.

This is shown in table 2.67. The key element is (– 4). This is made unity in table 2.68. Also A_1 is replaced by x_3.

TABLE 2.68

	c_j	1	3/2	5	2	0	0	0	0		
c_B	Basis	x_1	x_2	x_3	x_4	s_1	s_2	A_1	A_2	b	θ
0	s_1	$7/2$	$7/2$	0	6	1	0	$1/4$	0	6	1
0	s_2	$9/2$	$17/2$	0	(11)	0	1	$5/4$	0	4	$4/11$ ←
5	x_3	$-1/2$	$-3/2$	1	− 2	0	0	$-1/4$	0	0	− 0
0	A_2	0	0	0	0	0	0	$-1/2$	1	0	–
	Z_j	$-5/2$	$-15/2$	5	−10	0	0	$-5/4$	0	0	
	$c_j–Z_j$	$7/2$	9	0	12	0	0	$5/4$	0		
					↑						

Second b.f.s. for the original problem

Step 3. Perform Optimality Test

A_2-row contains only zeros for all columns of the legitimate variables. Thus A_2 will always be in the basis. Hence this row is crossed so that the succeeding tables will have one row less than this table. Since $c_j–Z_j$ is either positive or zero under all columns, table 2.68 is not optimal. Further, since A_1 is eliminated from solution and A_2-row is crossed out, A_1 and A_2-columns are deleted in the succeeding tables. Performing row operations, the following table is obtained :

TABLE 2.69

	c_j	1	3/2	5	2	0	0	
c_B	Basis	x_1	x_2	x_3	x_4	s_1	s_2	b
0	s_1	$23/22$	$-25/22$	0	0	1	$-6/11$	$42/11$
2	x_4	$9/22$	$17/22$	0	1	0	$1/11$	$4/11$
5	x_3	$7/22$	$1/22$	1	0	0	$2/11$	$8/11$
	Z_j	$53/22$	$39/22$	5	2	0	$12/11$	$48/11$
	$c_j–Z_j$	$-31/22$	$-6/22$	0	0	0	$-12/11$	

Optimal b.f.s. to the original problem

Table 2.69 gives the following optimal b.f.s. to the original problem:

$$x_1 = 0,\ x_2 = 0,\ x_3 = \frac{8}{11},\ x_4 = \frac{4}{11};\ Z_{max} = \frac{48}{11} = 4\frac{4}{11}.$$

2.17-3 Comparison Between the Big M-Method and the Two-Phase Method

Following observations can be made by comparing the two simplex methods :

1. The basic approach to both the methods is same. Both add artificial variables to convert the problem in standard form and then eliminate them from the solution.

2. The number of iterations are equal.

3. The big M-method solves the L.P. problem in one pass, whereas the two-phase method solves it in two stages as two linear problems.

4. The big M-method is computationally inconvenient due to the existence of the large number, M. The two-phase method does not involve M during computations.

5. The big M-method presents a difficulty when the problem is solved on digital computer. While using the digital computer, M must be assigned a specific value much larger than the other objective function coefficients. Since a computer has only a fixed number of digits, the large difference in the value of M and other coefficients can create problem. Therefore, for computer calculations the two-phase method has been commonly used.

2.18 SPECIAL CASES IN THE SIMPLEX METHOD APPLICATION

This section deals with a number of special cases that arise in the application of the simplex method.

2.18-1 Tie in the Choice of Entering Variable

The non-basic variable that enters the basis is the one that gives the largest per unit improvement in the objective function. Variable having maximum positive value in a maximization problem and the maximum negative value in a minimization problem in $c_j–Z_j$ row is the entering variable. A tie in the choice of entering variable exists when more that one variable has the same largest positive (or negative) value. To break the tie any one of them is selected arbitrarily as the entering variable, though a wrong choice may increase the number of iterations to reach the optimal solution. Unfortunately there is no method to predict this beforehand. However, if there is a tie between a decision variable and a slack/ surplus variable, select the decision variable.

2.18-2 Tie in the Choice of Leaving Variable (Degeneracy)

Degeneracy in linear programming is said to occur when one or more basic variables have zero value. Degeneracy may arise

(*i*) at the initial stage when at least one basic variable is zero in the initial basic feasible solution. This will be so if the right-hand side of a constraint is zero.

(*ii*) at any subsequent iteration stage when there is tie among the minimum non-negative replacement ratios. Arbitrary selection of the outgoing variable is often suggested. This will result in the other tied variable becoming zero in the next table and the solution is said to be degenerate. There is no assurance that the value of the objective function will improve, since new solution may remain degenerate. This seriously reduces the efficiency of the simplex method. More serious, however, is the condition of '*cycling*' or '*circling*' in which the same sequence of simplex iterations are repeated endlessly without improving the solution. Fortunately the problems in which cycling occurs are very rare. In fact it is difficult to find a practical problem in which cycling occurs.

However, the number of iterations required to reach optimal solution can be reduced by applying the following simple procedure, called *perturbation method* by A. Charnes:

1. Divide each element in the tied rows by the *positive coefficients* of the key-column in that row.
2. Compare the resulting ratios, column by column, first in the identity and then in the body of the simplex table, from left to right.
3. The row which first contains the smallest algebraic ratio contains the outgoing variable. The simplex method is then continued to reach optimal solution.

The above procedure is applicable to any iteration. If any artificial variable is one of the tied variables, it should be immediately selected to leave the basis without following the above procedure.

So, there is nothing alarming about dealing with a degenerate solution with the exception of a small inconvenience. From the practical stand point, the degeneracy condition reveals that the problem has at least one *redundant constraint*. This means that the corresponding resources are superfluous. The knowledge that some resources are superfluous can be valuable during the implementation of the solution.

The phenomenon of *resolution of degeneracy* will be now explained by considering a few examples.

EXAMPLE 2.18-1

$$\begin{aligned} \text{Maximize } Z &= 2x_1 + 3x_2 + 10x_3, \\ \text{subject to } \quad & x_1 + 2x_3 = 0, \\ & x_2 + x_3 = 1, \\ & x_1, x_2, x_3 \geq 0. \end{aligned}$$

[*Meerut B.Sc. (Math.) 1970*]

Solution

Step 1. Set-up the Problem in the Standard Form

The given problem can be expressed as

$$\begin{aligned} \text{maximize } Z &= 2x_1 + 3x_2 + 10x_3, \\ \text{subject to } \quad & x_1 + 0x_2 + 2x_3 = 0, \\ & 0x_1 + x_2 + x_3 = 1. \\ & x_1, x_2, x_3 \geq 0. \end{aligned}$$

Note that there is no need to introduce artificial variables as x_1 and x_2 are themselves forming identity matrix $\begin{bmatrix} 1 & 0 \\ 0 & 1 \end{bmatrix}$ *and can be treated as basic variables.*

Step 2. Find an Initial Basic Feasible Solution

Setting $x_3 = 0$, the basic feasible (degenerate) solution to the problem is

$x_1 = 0$ (basic),
$x_2 = 1$ (basic),
$x_3 = 0$ (non-basic),
$Z = 3$.

Table 2.70 represents this solution.

TABLE 2.70

	c_j	2	3	10			
c_B	Basis	x_1	x_2	x_3	b	θ	
2	x_1	1	0	(2)	0	0	←
3	x_2	0	1	1	1	1	
	Z_j	2	3	7	3		
	$c_j–Z_j$	0	0	3			
				↑			*Initial b.f.s.*

Step 3. Perform Optimality Test

Since $c_j–Z_j$ is positive under x_3-column, table 2.70 is not optimal.

Step 4. Iterate Towards an Optimal Solution

Performing iteration to get an optimal solution results in the following table :

TABLE 2.71

	c_j	2	3	10	
c_B	Basis	x_1	x_2	x_3	b
10	x_3	$1/2$	0	1	0
3	x_2	$-1/2$	1	0	1
	Z_j	$7/2$	3	10	3
	$c_j–Z_j$	$-3/2$	0	0	
					Optimal b.f.s.

Table 2.71 is optimal and the optimal b.f.s. is

$x_1 = 0$ (non-basic),
$x_2 = 1$ (basic),
$x_3 = 0$ (basic),
$Z_{max} = 3$.

The above solution is, however, degenerate because basic variable x_3 has zero value. Note that the value of Z in table 2.70 as well as table 2.71 is same. Thus we have obtained the optimal degenerate solution from a degenerate solution without improving the value of Z. In other words, it is possible to move from one table to another without any improvement in the obejctive function.

EXAMPLE 2.18-2

$$\begin{aligned} \textit{Maximize } Z &= 2x_1 + x_2, \\ \textit{subject to } & 4x_1 + 3x_2 \le 12, \\ & 4x_1 + x_2 \le 8, \\ & 4x_1 - x_2 \le 8, \\ & x_1, x_2 \ge 0. \end{aligned}$$

[*P.T.U.M. Tech. April, 2012; P.U.B. Com., 2006*]

Solution

Step 1. Set-up the Problem in the Standard Form

The problem, in the standard form, can be expressed as

$$\begin{aligned} \text{maximize } Z &= 2x_1 + x_2 + 0s_1 + 0s_2 + 0s_3, \\ \text{subject to } & 4x_1 + 3x_2 + s_1 + 0s_2 + 0s_3 = 12, \\ & 4x_1 + x_2 + 0s_1 + s_2 + 0s_3 = 8, \\ & 4x_1 - x_2 + 0s_1 + 0s_2 + s_3 = 8, \\ & x_1, x_2, s_1, s_2, s_3 \ge 0. \end{aligned}$$

Step 2. Find an Initial Basic Feasible Solution

The initial b.f.s. is

$$\begin{aligned} x_1 &= x_2 = 0 \text{ (non-basic)}, \\ s_1 &= 12 \text{ (basic)}, \\ s_2 &= 8 \text{ (basic)}, \\ s_3 &= 8 \text{ (basic)}, \\ Z &= 0. \end{aligned}$$

Table 2.72 represents this solution.

TABLE 2.72

	c_j	2	1	0	0	0		
c_B	Basis	x_1	x_2	s_1	s_2	s_3	b	θ
0	s_1	4	3	1	0	0	12	3
0	s_2	4	1	0	1	0	8	2
0	s_3	(4)	– 1	0	0	1	8	2 ←
	Z_j	0	0	0	0	0	0	
	$c_j – Z_j$	2	1	0	0	0		
		↑						*Initial b.f.s.*

Step 3. Perform Optimality Test

Since $c_j – Z_j$ is positive under some variable columns, table 2.72 is not optimal.

Step 4. Iterate Towards an Optimal Solution

In table 2.72, x_1 is the incoming variable. As s_2 and s_3 are tied rows, perturbation method by A. Charnes is applied to determine the outgoing variable. The first column of the identity has elements 0 and 0 in the tied rows. Dividing them by the corresponding elements of key column, the resulting ratios are 0 and 0. Hence first column of the identify fails to identify the outgoing variable. The second column of the identity has elements 1 and 0 in the tied rows. Dividing them by the corresponding elements of the key column, the resulting ratios are 1/4, 0. As s_3-row yields the smaller ratio, it is marked as key row and (4) is the key element.

Performing iterations to get an optimal solution results in the following tables :

TABLE 2.73

c_B	c_j / Basis	2 / x_1	1 / x_2	0 / s_1	0 / s_2	0 / s_3	b	θ
0	s_1	0	4	1	0	− 1	4	1
0	s_2	0	(2)	0	1	− 1	0	0 ←
2	x_1	1	$-1/4$	0	0	$1/4$	2	− 8
	Z_j	2	$-1/2$	0	0	$1/2$	4	
	$c_j–Z_j$	0	$3/2$ ↑	0	0	$-1/2$		

Second b.f.s.

TABLE 2.74

c_B	c_j / Basis	2 / x_1	1 / x_2	0 / s_1	0 / s_2	0 / s_3	b	θ
0	s_1	0	0	1	− 2	(1)	4	4 ←
1	x_2	0	1	0	$1/2$	$-1/2$	0	− 0
2	x_1	1	0	0	$1/8$	$1/8$	2	16
	Z_j	2	1	0	$3/4$	$-1/4$	4	
	$c_j–Z_j$	0	0	0	$-3/4$	$1/4$ ↑		

Third b.f.s.

TABLE 2.75

c_B	c_j / Basis	2 / x_1	1 / x_2	0 / s_1	0 / s_2	0 / s_3	b
0	s_3	0	0	1	− 2	1	4
1	x_2	0	1	$1/2$	$-1/2$	0	2
2	x_1	1	0	$-1/8$	$3/8$	0	$3/2$
	Z_j	2	1	$1/4$	$1/4$	0	5
	$c_j–Z_j$	0	0	$-1/4$	$-1/4$	0	

Optimal b.f.s

Table 2.75 gives the following optimal b.f.s.:

$$x_1 = 3/2,$$
$$x_2 = 2,$$
$$Z_{max} = 5.$$

EXAMPLE 2.18-3

Maximize $Z = 5x_1 - 2x_2 + 3x_3,$

subject to $2x_1 + 2x_2 - x_3 \geq 2,$

$$3x_1 - 4x_2 \le 3,$$
$$x_2 + 3x_3 \le 5,$$
$$x_1, x_2, x_3 \ge 0.$$

[P.U.B.E. (Ec. and Comm.) Nov., 2011; (T.I.T.) Nov., 2006]

Solution

Step 1. Set-up the Problem in the Standard Form

The problem can be expressed in the standard form as

maximize $Z = 5x_1 - 2x_2 + 3x_3 + 0s_1 + 0s_2 + 0s_3 - MA_1$,

subject to $2x_1 + 2x_2 - x_3 - s_1 + 0s_2 + 0s_3 + A_1 = 2$,

$3x_1 - 4x_2 + 0x_3 + 0s_1 + s_2 + 0s_3 + 0A_1 = 3$,

$0x_1 + x_2 + 3x_3 + 0s_1 + 0s_2 + s_3 + 0A_1 = 5$,

$x_1, x_2, x_3, s_1, s_2, s_3, A_1 \ge 0$.

Step 2. Find an Initial Basic Feasible Solution

The i.b.f.s. is

$x_1 = x_2 = x_3 = s_1 = 0$ (non-basic),

$A_1 = 2$,

$s_2 = 3$,

$s_3 = 5$,

$Z = -2M$.

Table 2.76 represents this solution.

TABLE 2.76

	c_j	5	–2	3	0	0	0	– M		
c_B	Basis	x_1	x_2	x_3	s_1	s_2	s_3	A_1	b	θ
– M	A_1	(2)	2	–1	– 1	0	0	1	2	1 ←
0	s_2	3	– 4	0	0	1	0	0	3	1
0	s_3	0	1	3	0	0	1	0	5	∞
	Z_j	–2M	– 2M	M	M	0	0	– M	– 2M	
	$c_j–Z_j$	5+2M	–2+2M	3–M	– M	0	0	0		
		↑								

Initial solution

Step 3. Perform Optimality Test

Since $c_j–Z_j$ is positive under some variable columns, table 2.76 is not optimal.

Step 4. Iterate Towards an Optimal Solution

In table 2.76, x_1 is the incoming variable. A_1- and s_2-rows are tied. *But since A_1 is an artificial variable, it is chosen as the outgoing variable (the perturbation method need not be applied) and (2) is the key element.* Making this element unity and performing iterations to get an optimal solution results in the following tables :

TABLE 2.77

	c_j	5	–2	3	0	0	0		
c_B	Basis	x_1	x_2	x_3	s_1	s_2	s_3	b	θ
5	x_1	1	1	$-\frac{1}{2}$	$-\frac{1}{2}$	0	0	1	– 2
0	s_2	0	– 7	$\left(\frac{3}{2}\right)$	$\frac{3}{2}$	1	0	0	0 ←

0	s_3	0	1	3	0	0	1	5	$5/3$
	Z_j	5	5	$-5/2$	$-5/2$	0	0	5	
	c_j-Z_j	0	− 7	$11/2$	$5/2$	0	0		
				↑					

Second b.f.s.

TABLE 2.78

	c_j	5	−2	3	0	0	0		
c_B	Basis	x_1	x_2	x_3	s_1	s_2	s_3	b	θ
5	x_1	1	$-4/3$	0	0	$1/3$	0	1	$-3/4$
3	x_3	0	$-14/3$	1	1	$2/3$	0	0	− 0
0	s_3	0	(15)	0	− 3	− 2	1	5	$1/3$ ←
	Z_j	5	$-62/3$	3	3	$11/3$	0	5	
	c_j-Z_j	0	$56/3$	0	− 3	$-11/3$	0		
			↑						

Third b.f.s.

TABLE 2.79

	c_j	5	−2	3	0	0	0		
c_B	Basis	x_1	x_2	x_3	s_1	s_2	s_3	b	θ
5	x_1	1	0	0	$-4/15$	$7/45$	$4/45$	$13/9$	$-65/12$
3	x_3	0	0	1	$(1/15)$	$2/45$	$14/45$	$14/9$	$70/3$ ←
− 2	x_2	0	1	0	$-1/5$	$-2/15$	$1/15$	$1/3$	$-5/3$
	Z_j	5	− 2	3	$-11/15$	$53/45$	$56/45$	$101/9$	
	c_j-Z_j	0	0	0	$11/15$	$-53/45$	$-56/45$		
					↑				

Fourth b.f.s.

TABLE 2.80

	c_j	5	−2	3	0	0	0	
c_B	Basis	x_1	x_2	x_3	s_1	s_2	s_3	b
5	x_1	1	0	4	0	$1/3$	$4/3$	$23/3$
0	s_1	0	0	15	1	$2/3$	$14/3$	$70/3$
− 2	x_2	0	1	3	0	0	1	5
	Z_j	5	− 2	14	0	$5/3$	$14/3$	$85/3$
	c_j-Z_j	0	0	− 11	0	$-5/3$	$-14/3$	

Optimal b.f.s.

∴ Optimal solution is

$$x_1 = \frac{23}{3}, x_2 = 5, x_3 = 0 ; Z_{max} = \frac{85}{3} = 28\frac{1}{3}.$$

EXAMPLE 2.18-4

Solve the following problem :

Maximize $Z = 1,000x_1 + 4,000x_2 + 5,000x_3,$

subject to $3x_1 + 3x_3 \leq 22,$

$x_1 + 2x_2 + 3x_3 \leq 14,$

$3x_1 + 2x_2 \leq 14,$

$x_1, x_2 \geq 0.$

Solution

Step 1. Set-up the Problem in Standard Form

The problem can be expressed in standard form as

maximize $Z = 1,000x_1 + 4,000x_2 + 5,000x_3 + 0s_1 + 0s_2 + 0s_3,$

subject to $3x_1 + 3x_3 + s_1 = 22,$

$x_1 + 2x_2 + 3x_3 + s_2 = 14,$

$3x_1 + 2x_2 + s_3 = 14,$

$x_1, x_2, x_3, s_1, s_2, s_3 \geq 0.$

Step 2. Find an Initial Basic Feasible Solution

The i.b.f.s. is

$$x_1 = x_2 = x_3 = 0, s_1 = 22, s_2 = 14, s_3 = 14, Z = 0.$$

Table 2.81 represents this solution.

TABLE 2.81

	c_j	1,000	4,000	5,000	0	0	0		
c_B	Basis	x_1	x_2	x_3	s_1	s_2	s_3	b	θ
0	s_1	3	0	3	1	0	0	22	22/3
0	s_2	1	2	(3)	0	1	0	14	14/3 ←
0	s_3	3	2	0	0	0	1	14	∞
	z_j	0	0	0	0	0	0	0	
	$c_j–Z_j$	1,000	4,000	5,000	0	0	0		
				↑					*Initial b.f.s.*

Step 3. Perform Optimality Test

Since $c_j–Z_j$ is positive under some variable columns, i.b.f.s. is not optimal.

Step 4. Iterate Towards an Optimal Solution

Performing iteration to get optimal solution results in the following table:

TABLE 2.82

	c_j	1,000	4,000	5,000	0	0	0		
c_B	Basis	x_1	x_2	x_3	s_1	s_2	s_3	b	θ
0	s_1	2	– 2	0	1	– 1	0	8	– 4
5,000	x_3	1/3	2/3	1	0	1/3	0	14/3	7

0	s_3	3	(2)	0	0	0	1	14	7 ←
	Z_j	$5{,}000/3$	$10{,}000/3$	5,000	0	$5{,}000/3$	0	$70{,}000/3$	
	$c_j–Z_j$	$-2{,}000/3$	$2{,}000/3$	0	0	$-5{,}000/3$	0		
			↑						Second b.f.s.

In table 2.82, s_1-*column, the first column of identity matrix* has elements 0 and 0 in the tied rows. Dividing them by the corresponding elements of the key column, the resulting ratios are 0 and 0. *Hence first column of identity matrix fails to identify the outgoing variable.* s_2*-column has elements* $\frac{1}{3}$ *and 0 in the tied rows. Dividing them by the corresponding elements of key column, the resulting ratios are* $\frac{1}{2}$ *and 0. As* s_3*-row yields the smaller ratio, it is marked as key row and (2) is the key element.* Further iteration yields the following table :

TABLE 2.83

	c_j	1,000	4,000	5,000	0	0	0	
c_B	Basis	x_1	x_2	x_3	s_1	s_2	s_3	b
0	s_1	5	0	0	1	– 1	1	22
5,000	x_3	$-2/3$	0	1	0	$1/3$	$-1/3$	0
4,000	x_2	$3/2$	1	0	0	0	$1/2$	7
	$c_j–Z_j$	$-5{,}000/3$	0	0	0	$-5{,}000/3$	$-1{,}000/3$	28,000
								Optimal b.f.s.

Table 2.83 yields the following optimal solution :

$$x_1 = 0;\ x_2 = 7,\ x_3 = 0\ ;\ Z_{max} = 28{,}000.$$

2.18-3 Infinite Number of Optimal Solutions (Multiple Optimal Solutions)

It was seen in section 2.10 of graphical method that when the objective function is parallel to a binding constraint, it will have the *same optimal value* at more than one corner point. Any point on the *line segment* AB of example 2.10-1 represents an alternate optimal solution with the same objective value Z = 20,000.

In the optimal simplex table, if a non-basic variable has zero coefficient in the $c_j–Z_j$ row, there exists an alternate optimal solution. It is because that non-basic variable can enter the basis without changing the value of Z, but causing a change in the values of the basic variables. This variable may be a decision or slack or surplus variable.

From practical standpoint, multiple optimal solutions are useful because they allow us to choose among the many alternatives without sacrificing the objective value. In a product mix problem, for instance, the most preferred (or suitable) combination of products may be chosen among multiple alternatives.

EXAMPLE 2.18-5

Solve the following L.P. problem by simplex method:

$$\begin{aligned} \text{maximize } Z &= 4x_1 + 10x_2, \\ \text{subject to } \quad & 2x_1 + x_2 \le 10, \\ & 2x_1 + 5x_2 \le 20, \\ & 2x_1 + 3x_2 \le 18, \\ & x_1, x_2 \ge 0. \end{aligned}$$

(i) Indicate that this problem has an alternate optimal basic feasible solution.
(ii) Find that optimal solution.
(iii) Hence show that this problem has multiple optimal solutions.

[*P.T.U.M. Tech. April, 2012; Univ. of Madras M. Com. April, 2012; Kuru. U.B.E. (Mech.) June, 2012; H.P.U.B.Tech. (Mech.) Nov., 2006*]

Solution

Step 1. Set-up the Problem in the Standard Form

Introducing slack variables s_1, s_2, s_3 the problem can be expressed in the standard form as

$$\begin{aligned} \text{maximize } Z &= 4x_1 + 10x_2 + 0s_1 + 0s_2 + 0s_3, \\ \text{subject to } \quad & 2x_1 + x_2 + s_1 + 0s_2 + 0s_3 = 10, \\ & 2x_1 + 5x_2 + 0s_1 + s_2 + 0s_3 = 20, \\ & 2x_1 + 3x_2 + 0s_1 + 0s_2 + s_3 = 18, \\ & x_1, x_2, s_1, s_2, s_3 \geq 0. \end{aligned}$$

Step 2. Find an Initial Basic Feasible Solution

The i.b.f.s. is

$$x_1 = 0, x_2 = 0, s_1 = 10, s_2 = 20, s_3 = 18, Z = 0.$$

Table 2.84 represents this solution.

TABLE 2.84

	c_j	4	10	0	0	0		
c_B	Basis	x_1	x_2	s_1	s_2	s_3	b	θ
0	s_1	2	1	1	0	0	10	10
0	s_2	2	(5)	0	1	0	20	4 ←
0	s_3	2	3	0	0	1	18	6
	Z_j	0	0	0	0	0	0	
	$c_j–Z_j$	4	10	0	0	0		
			↑				*Initial basic feasible solution*	

Step 3. Perform Optimality Test

Since $c_j–Z_j$ is positive under some variable columns, table 2.84 is not optimal.

Step 4. Iterate Towards an Optimal Solution

In table 2.84, x_2 is incoming variable, s_2 is outgoing variable and (5) is the key element. In table 2.85, s_2 is replaced by x_2.

TABLE 2.85

	c_j	4	10	0	0	0		
c_B	Basis	x_1	x_2	s_1	s_2	s_3	b	θ
0	s_1	$(8/5)$	0	1	$-1/5$	0	6	$15/4$ ←
10	x_2	$2/5$	1	0	$1/5$	0	4	10
0	s_3	$4/5$	0	0	$-3/5$	1	6	$15/2$
	Z_j	4	10	0	2	0	40	
	$c_j–Z_j$	0	0	0	– 2	0		
		↑					*Optimal basic feasible solution*	

Step 5. Perform Optimality Test

Since $c_j – Z_j$ is either negative or zero under all variable columns, table 2.85 is optimal. The optimal solution is

$$x_1 = 0 \text{ (non-basic)},$$
$$x_2 = 4 \text{ (basic)},$$
$$s_1 = 6 \text{ (basic)},$$
$$s_2 = 0 \text{ (non-basic)},$$
$$s_3 = 6 \text{ (basic)},$$
$$Z_{max} = 40.$$

(*i*) In table 2.85, element of net evaluation row ($c_j – Z_j$ row) under x_1-column (corresponding to the non-basic variable x_1) is zero. It indicates that by introducing x_1 into solution, there will be no improvement in the value of the objective function Z. In other words, it indicates the existence of *an alternate* optimal basic feasible solution.

(*ii*) Choosing x_1 as the incoming variable and slack s_1 as the outgoing variable in table 2.85 and carrying out the iteration yields table 2.86.

TABLE 2.86

	c_j	4	10	0	0	0	
c_B	Basis	x_1	x_2	s_1	s_2	s_3	b
4	x_1	1	0	$5/8$	$-1/8$	0	$15/4$
10	x_2	0	1	$-1/4$	$1/4$	0	$5/2$
0	s_3	0	0	$-1/2$	$-1/2$	1	3
	Z_j	4	10	0	2	0	40
	$c_j – Z_j$	0	0	0	–2	0	

Alternate optimal basic feasible solution

Table 2.86 gives the following alternate optimal basic feasible solution:

$$x_1 = \frac{15}{4} \text{ (basic)},$$
$$x_2 = \frac{5}{2} \text{ (basic)},$$
$$s_1 = 0 \text{ (non-basic)},$$
$$s_2 = 0 \text{ (non-basic)},$$
$$s_3 = 3 \text{ (basic)},$$
$$Z_{max} = 40.$$

Note that the maximum value of the objective function remains the same. The above two are the basic feasible optimal solutions. Now if two basic feasible optimal solutions are known, an infinite number of non-basic feasible optimal solutions can be derived by taking any weighted average of these two solutions.

For example, if

$$X_1 = \begin{pmatrix} 0 \\ 4 \\ 6 \\ 0 \\ 6 \end{pmatrix} \text{ and } X_2 = \begin{pmatrix} 15/4 \\ 5/2 \\ 0 \\ 0 \\ 3 \end{pmatrix},$$

then $$X^* = \lambda X_1 + (1-\lambda) X_2, \text{ where } 0 \le \lambda \le 1$$

$$= \begin{pmatrix} \frac{15}{4}(1-\lambda) \\ 4\lambda + \frac{5}{2}(1-\lambda) \\ 6\lambda \\ 0 \\ 6\lambda + 3(1-\lambda) \end{pmatrix} = \begin{pmatrix} \frac{15}{4}(1-\lambda) \\ \frac{5}{2} + \frac{3}{2}\lambda \\ 6\lambda \\ 0 \\ 3 + 3\lambda \end{pmatrix}, \text{ where } 0 \le \lambda \le 1.$$

It can be seen that X^* gives the same maximum value 40 of Z for all values $0 \le \lambda \le 1$. The problem, therefore, has multiple optimal solutions.

2.18-4 Unbounded Solution

An unbounded solution in the simplex technique occurs when it is not possible to determine the basic variable that should leave the basis. This happens when all the *constraint coefficients* of the non-basic variable that is to enter the basis are *negative or zero* so that there is no minimum non-negative ratio. In such a case, the value of the entering variable can be increased indefinitely without violating any of the constraints, meaning that the solution space is *unbounded* in at least one direction. As a result, the obejctive value may increase (maximization case) or decrease (minimization case) indefinitely. In this case, both the solution space and the optimum objective value are unbounded. However, it is not necessary that if the solution space is unbounded, the optional objective value must also be unbounded (refer examples 2.10-3 to 2.10-5).

Unboundedness in a problem indicates only one thing : the model is poorly constructed. One or more non-redundant constraints are not included and the parameters (constants) of some constraints are not estimately correctly.

EXAMPLE 2.18-6

Show that there is an unbounded solution to the following L.P. problem:

Maximize $Z = 4x_1 + x_2 + 3x_3 + 5x_4,$

subject to the constraints

$$4x_1 - 6x_2 - 5x_3 - 4x_4 \ge -20,$$
$$-3x_1 - 2x_2 + 4x_3 + x_4 \le 10,$$
$$-8x_1 - 3x_2 + 3x_3 + 2x_4 \le 20,$$
$$x_1, x_2, x_3, x_4 \ge 0.$$

[*Pbi. U.B. Tech. 1999*]

Solution

Step 1. Set-up the Problem in the Standard Form

Multiplying the first constraint throughout by – 1, we get

$$-4x_1 + 6x_2 + 5x_3 + 4x_4 \le 20.$$

Introducing slack variables s_1, s_2, s_3, the problem can be expressed in standard form as

maximize $Z = 4x_1 + x_2 + 3x_3 + 5x_4 + 0s_1 + 0s_2 + 0s_3,$

subject to

$$-4x_1 + 6x_2 + 5x_3 + 4x_4 + s_1 + 0s_2 + 0s_3 = 20,$$
$$-3x_1 - 2x_2 + 4x_3 + x_4 + 0s_1 + s_2 + 0s_3 = 10,$$
$$-8x_1 - 3x_2 + 3x_3 + 2x_4 + 0s_1 + 0s_2 + s_3 = 20,$$
$$x_1, x_2, x_3, x_4, s_1, s_2, s_3 \ge 0.$$

Step 2. Find an Initial Basic Feasible Solution

Setting decision variables x_1, x_2, x_3, x_4 each equal to zero, the basic (non-degenerate) feasible solution is

$$x_1 = x_2 = x_3 = x_4 = 0 \text{ (non-basic)},$$
$$s_1 = 20 \text{ (basic)},$$

$s_2 = 10$ (basic),
$s_3 = 20$ (basic),
$Z = 0.$

Table 2.87 represents this solution.

TABLE 2.87

	c_j	4	1	3	5	0	0	0		
c_B	Basis	x_1	x_2	x_3	x_4	s_1	s_2	s_3	b	θ
0	s_1	– 4	6	5	(4)	1	0	0	20	5 ←
0	s_2	–3	– 2	4	1	0	1	0	10	10
0	s_3	– 8	– 3	3	2	0	0	1	20	10
	Z_j	0	0	0	0	0	0	0	0	
	c_j–Z_j	4	1	3	5	0	0	0		
					↑					

Initial basic feasible solution

Step 3. Perform Optimality Test

Since c_j–Z_j is positive under some variable columns, table 2.87 is not optimal.

Step 4. Iterate Towards an Optimal Solution

In table 2.87, x_4 is incoming variable, s_1 is outgoing variable and (4) is the key element. In table 2.88, s_1 is replaced by x_4.

TABLE 2.88

	c_j	4	1	3	5	0	0	0		
c_B	Basis	x_1	x_2	x_3	x_4	s_1	s_2	s_3	b	θ
5	x_4	– 1	$3/2$	$5/4$	1	$1/4$	0	0	5	– 5
0	s_2	– 2	$-7/2$	$11/4$	0	$-1/4$	1	0	5	$-5/2$
0	s_3	– 6	– 6	$1/2$	0	$-1/2$	0	1	10	$-5/3$
	Z_j	– 5	$15/2$	$25/4$	5	$5/4$	0	0	25	
	c_j–Z_j	9	$-13/2$	$-13/4$	0	$-5/4$	0	0		
		↑								

Second basic feasible solution

Step 5. Perform Optimality Test

Since c_j–Z_j is positive under x_1-column, table 2.88 is not optimal.

Step 6. Iterate Towards an Optimal Solution

In table 2.88, x_1 is the incoming variable. However, since all replacement ratios are negative (it is because all the constraint coefficients under x_1-column are negative), x_1 value can be increased indefinitely without violating any of the constraints. Because each unit increase in x_1 will increase Z by 9, an infinite increase in x_1 will also result in an infinite increase in Z. The problem, therefore, has no bounded solution and further computations stop.

EXAMPLE 2.18-7

Maximize $Z = 107x_1 + x_2 + 2x_3,$
subject to $14x_1 + x_2 - 6x_3 + 3x_4 = 7,$

$$16x_1 + \frac{1}{2}x_2 - 6x_3 \leq 5,$$
$$3x_1 - x_2 - x_3 \leq 0,$$
$$x_1, x_2, x_3, x_4 \geq 0.$$

[*V.T.U. Karnataka B.E. Dec., 2011; H.P.U.B. Tech. (Mech.) June, 2007; P.U.B. Com. Sept., 2005*]

Step 1. Set-up the Problem in the Standard Form

The first constraint is of equality form. It can be divided throughout by 3 to give unit coefficient to x_4.

i.e.,
$$\frac{14}{3}x_1 + \frac{1}{3}x_2 - 2x_3 + x_4 = \frac{7}{3}.$$

Variable x_4, now, occurs in constraint 1 with unit coefficient and it occurs in no other constraint and hence can be treated as a slack variable. Introducing slack variables, say x_5 and x_6 in second and third constraints, the problem can be expressed in standard form as

maximize $Z = 107x_1 + x_2 + 2x_3 + 0x_4 + 0x_5 + 0x_6,$

subject to
$$\frac{14}{3}x_1 + \frac{1}{3}x_2 - 2x_3 + x_4 + 0x_5 + 0x_6 = \frac{7}{3},$$
$$16x_1 + \frac{1}{2}x_2 - 6x_3 + 0x_4 + x_5 + 0x_6 = 5,$$
$$3x_1 - x_2 - x_3 + 0x_4 + 0x_5 + x_6 = 0,$$
$$x_1, x_2, x_3, x_4, x_5, x_6 \geq 0.$$

Step 2. Find an Initial Basic Feasible Solution

Setting decision variables x_1, x_2, x_3 each equal to zero, the basic (degenerate) feasible solution is

$$x_1 = x_2 = x_3 = 0 \text{ (non-basic)},$$
$$x_4 = 7/3 \text{ (basic)},$$
$$x_5 = 5 \text{ (basic)},$$
$$x_6 = 0 \text{ (basic)},$$
$$Z = 0.$$

This solution is represented in table 2.89.

TABLE 2.89

	c_j	107	1	2	0	0	0		
c_B	Basis	x_1	x_2	x_3	x_4	x_5	x_6	b	θ
0	x_4	$14/3$	$1/3$	-2	1	0	0	$7/3$	$1/2$
0	x_5	16	$1/2$	-6	0	1	0	5	$5/16$
0	x_6	(3)	-1	-1	0	0	1	0	0 ←
	Z_j	0	0	0	0	0	0	0	
	c_j–Z_j	107	1	2	0	0	0		
		↑							

Initial basic feasible solution

Step 3. Perform Optimality Test

Since c_j–Z_j is positive under some variable columns, table 2.89 is not optimal.

Step 4. Iterate Towards an Optimal Solution

In table 2.89, x_1 is incoming variable, x_6 is outgoing variable and (3) is the key element. In table 2.90, x_6 is replaced by x_1.

TABLE 2.90

	c_j	107	1	2	0	0	0		
c_B	Basis	x_1	x_2	x_3	x_4	x_5	x_6	b	θ
0	x_4	0	$17/9$	$-4/9$	1	0	$-14/9$	$7/3$	$-21/4$
0	x_5	0	$35/6$	$-2/3$	0	1	$-16/3$	5	$-15/2$
107	x_1	1	$-1/3$	$-1/3$	0	0	$1/3$	0	-0
	Z_j	107	$-107/3$	$-107/3$	0	0	$107/3$	0	
	c_j-Z_j	0	$110/3$	$113/3$	0	0	$-107/3$		
				↑					

Second basic feasible solution

Step 5. Perform Optimality Test

Since c_j-Z_j is positive under some variable columns, table 2.90 is not optimal.

Step 6. Iterate Towards an Optimal Solution

In table 2.90, x_3 is the incoming variable. However, since all replacement ratios (in θ-column) are negative, the problem has an unbounded solution.

2.18-5 Infeasible Solution

If all the constraints are not satisfied simultaneously, the model has no feasible solution. If all the constraints are of ≤ type (assuming that right-hand side constants are non-negative), such a situation of infeasible solution will not arise since inclusion of slack variables will provide a feasible solutioin. For ≥ and = type constraints, artificial variables are used. Although high penalty coefficient M is associated with artificial variables in the objective function to reduce them to zero at the optimum, this can occur only if the model has a feasible space. If not, at least one artificial variable will have positive value at the optimum iteration. Though optimality condition is satisfied, objective value will contain the penalty coefficient M. Such a solution is also called *pseudo-optimal solution.*

EXAMPLE 2.18-8

Use penalty method to

$$\text{minimize } Z = x_1 + 2x_2 + x_3,$$

$$\text{subject to} \quad x_1 + \frac{x_2}{2} + \frac{x_3}{2} \leq 1,$$

$$\frac{3}{2}x_1 + 2x_2 + x_3 \geq 8,$$

$$x_1, x_2, x_3 \geq 0.$$

[*P.T.U.B. Tech. April, 2012; H.P.U. B.Tech. (Mech.) June, 2010*]

Solution

Step 1. Set-up the Problem in Standard Form

Introducing slack variable s_1 in the first constraint and surplus variable s_2 in the second, the problem is expressed in the following standard form :

$$\text{minimize } Z = x_1 + 2x_2 + x_3 + 0s_1 + 0s_2,$$

subject to $x_1 + \frac{x_2}{2} + \frac{x_3}{2} + s_1 = 1,$

$$\frac{3}{2}x_1 + 2x_2 + x_3 - s_2 = 8,$$

$$x_1, x_2, x_3, s_1, s_2 \geq 0.$$

Step 2. Find an Initial Basic Feasible Solution

Setting $x_1 = x_2 = x_3 = 0$, yields the initial solution

$$s_1 = 1, s_2 = -8,$$

which is not feasible since s_2 is negative. Introducing artificial variable, the problem takes the form :

minimize $Z = x_1 + 2x_2 + x_3 + 0s_1 + 0s_2 + MA_1,$

subject to $x_1 + \frac{x_2}{2} + \frac{x_3}{2} + s_1 = 1,$

$$\frac{3}{2}x_1 + 2x_2 + x_3 - s_2 + A_1 = 8,$$

$$x_1, x_2, x_3, s_1, s_2, A_1 \geq 0.$$

The initial basic feasible solution to the artificial system is

$$x_1 = 0, x_2 = 0, x_3 = 0, s_2 = 0, s_1 = 1, A_1 = 8, Z = 8M.$$

Table 2.91 represents this solution.

TABLE 2.91

	c_j	1	2	1	0	0	M		
c_B	Basis	x_1	x_2	x_3	s_1	s_2	A_1	b	θ
0	s_1	1	$(1/2)$	$1/2$	1	0	0	1	2 ←
M	A_1	$3/2$	2	1	0	− 1	1	8	4
	Z_j	$\frac{3}{2}M$	2M	M	0	− M	M	8M	
	$c_j–Z_j$	$1-\frac{3}{2}M$	2−2M	1−M	0	M	0		
			↑						

Initial solution

Step 3. Perform Optimality Test

Since $c_j–Z_j$ is negative under some variable columns, table 2.91 is not optimal.

Step 4. Iterate Towards an Optimal Solution

Performing iteration to get an optimal solution results in the following table :

TABLE 2.92

	c_j	1	2	1	0	0	M	
c_B	Basis	x_1	x_2	x_3	s_1	s_2	A_1	b
2	x_2	2	1	1	2	0	0	2
M	A_1	$-\frac{5}{2}$	0	− 1	− 4	− 1	1	4
	Z_j	$4-\frac{5}{2}M$	2	2−M	4−4M	− M	M	4 + 4M
	$c_j–Z_j$	$-3+\frac{5}{2}M$	0	−1+M	−4+4M	M	0	

Second solution

Since $c_j–Z_j$ is non-negative under all columns, table 2.92 is optimal. *However, since A_2 appears in the basis at a positive value (4), the given problem has no feasible solution.* Thus table 2.92 does not give an optimal b.f.s. but a *pseudo-optimal solution.*

2.18-6 Unrestricted (or Unconstrained) Variables

So far we have solved problems in which decision variables $x_1, x_2, ...$ were non-negative. In practice, a variable may be unrestricted (or unconstrained) in sign *i.e.*, it may have a positive, zero or negative value. Since the use of simplex method requires that all the decision variables must have non-negative values at each iteration, to solve such a problem, the unrestricted variable is expressed as a difference of two non-negative variables. Thus unrestricted variable

$$x_1 = y_1 - y_2 \,;\, y_1 \geq 0,\, y_2 \geq 0.$$

Value of x_1 will be positive, zero or negative depending upon whether y_1 is larger, equal to or smaller than y_2.

EXAMPLE 2.18-9

$$\begin{aligned} \textit{Maximize } Z &= 2x_1 + 5x_2, \\ \textit{subject to} \quad & x_1 + 2x_2 \leq 8, \\ & x_1 \leq 4, \\ & 0 \leq x_2 \leq 3, \\ & x_1 \textit{ unrestricted.} \end{aligned}$$

[P.T.U. B. Tech. April, 2012]

Solution

Step 1. Set-up the Problem in Standard Form

Since x_1 is unrestricted, let

$$\begin{aligned} x_1 &= y_1 - y_2, \\ x_2 &= y_3, \\ y_1, y_2, y_3 &\geq 0. \end{aligned}$$

Therefore, the given problem can be written as

$$\begin{aligned} \text{maximize } Z &= 2y_1 - 2y_2 + 5y_3, \\ \text{subject to} \quad & y_1 - y_2 + 2y_3 \leq 8, \\ & y_1 - y_2 \leq 4, \\ & y_3 \leq 3, \\ & y_1, y_2, y_3 \geq 0. \end{aligned}$$

In standard form the problem can be written as

$$\begin{aligned} \text{maximize } Z &= 2y_1 - 2y_2 + 5y_3 + 0s_1 + 0s_2 + 0s_3, \\ \text{subject to} \quad & y_1 - y_2 + 2y_3 + s_1 = 8, \\ & y_1 - y_2 + s_2 = 4, \\ & y_3 + s_3 = 3, \\ & y_1, y_2, y_3, s_1, s_2, s_3 \geq 0. \end{aligned}$$

Step 2. Find Initial Basic Feasible Solution

Setting $y_1 = y_2 = y_3 = 0$, $s_1 = 8$, $s_2 = 4$, $s_3 = 3$, Z = 0.

Step 3. Perform Optimality Test

TABLE 2.93

	c_j	2	– 2	5	0	0	0		
c_B	Basis	y_1	y_2	y_3	s_1	s_2	s_3	b	θ
0	s_1	1	– 1	2	1	0	0	8	4
0	s_2	1	– 1	0	0	1	0	4	∞

0	s_3	0	0	(1)	0	0	1	3	3 ←
	Z_j	0	0	0	0	0	0	0	
	$c_j–Z_j$	2	– 2	5	0	0	0		
				↑					*Initial b.f.s.*

Step 4. Iterate Towards an Optimal Solution

TABLE 2.94

	c_j	2	– 2	5	0	0	0		
c_B	Basis	y_1	y_2	y_3	s_1	s_2	s_3	b	θ
0	s_1	(1)	– 1	0	1	0	– 2	2	2 ←
0	s_2	1	– 1	0	0	1	0	4	4
5	y_3	0	0	1	0	0	1	3	∞
	Z_j	0	0	5	0	0	5	15	
	$c_j–Z_j$	2	– 2	0	0	0	– 5		
		↑							*Second b.f.s.*

TABLE 2.95

	c_j	2	– 2	5	0	0	0	
c_B	Basis	y_1	y_2	y_3	s_1	s_2	s_3	b
2	y_1	1	– 1	0	1	0	– 2	2
0	s_2	0	0	0	– 1	1	2	2
5	y_3	0	0	1	0	0	1	3
	Z_j	2	– 2	5	2	0	1	19
	$c_j–Z_j$	0	0	0	– 2	0	– 1	
								Optimal b.f.s.

∴ $y_1 = 2, y_2 = 0, y_3 = 3, Z_{max} = 19.$

Therefore, the optimal solution to the given problem is

$$x_1 = y_1 - y_2 = 2 - 0 = 2,$$
$$x_2 = y_3 = 3,$$
$$Z_{max} = 19.$$

EXAMPLE 2.18-10

Minimize $Z = 2x_1 + 3x_2,$

subject to $x_1 - 2x_2 \leq 0,$

$-2x_1 + 3x_2 \geq -6,$

x_1, x_2 *unrestricted.*

Solution

Step 1. Set-up the Problem in the Standard Form

Since b_2 is negative (– 6), we multiply both sides of the second constraint by – 1 to obtain

$$2x_1 - 3x_2 \leq 6.$$

As variables x_1 and x_2 are unrestricted, we express them as

$$x_1 = y_1 - y_2,$$

and $$x_2 = y_3 - y_4,$$

where y_1, y_2, y_3, y_4, all ≥ 0.

Thus the given problem is transformed to

minimize $Z = 2y_1 - 2y_2 + 3y_3 - 3y_4$,

subject to $y_1 - y_2 - 2y_3 + 2y_4 \leq 0$,

$2y_1 - 2y_2 - 3y_3 + 3y_4 \leq 6$,

where y_1, y_2, y_3, y_4, all ≥ 0.

Introducing slack variables, the problem may be written as

minimize $Z = 2y_1 - 2y_2 + 3y_3 - 3y_4 + 0s_1 + 0s_2$,

subject to $y_1 - y_2 - 2y_3 + 2y_4 + s_1 = 0$,

$2y_1 - 2y_2 - 3y_3 + 3y_4 + s_2 = 6$,

where $y_1, y_2, y_3, y_4, s_1, s_2$, all ≥ 0.

Step 2. Find an Initial Basic Feasible Solution

The initial b.f.s. is

$$y_1 = y_2 = y_3 = y_4 = 0 \text{ (non-basic)},$$
$$s_1 = 0 \text{ (basic)},$$
$$s_2 = 6 \text{ (basic)},$$
$$Z = 0.$$

Table 2.96 represents this solution.

TABLE 2.96

	c_j	2	– 2	3	– 3	0	0		
c_B	Basis	y_1	y_2	y_3	y_4	s_1	s_2	b	θ
0	s_1	1	– 1	– 2	(2)	1	0	0	0 ←
0	s_2	2	– 2	– 3	3	0	1	6	2
	Z_j	0	0	0	0	0	0	0	
	$c_j–Z_j$	2	– 2	3	– 3	0	0		
					↑			*Initial b.f.s.*	

Step 3. Perform Optimality Test

Since $c_j–Z_j$ is negative under some columns, table 2.96 is not optimal.

Step 4. Iterate Towards an Optimal Solution

Performing iteration to get an optimal solution results in the following table:

TABLE 2.97

	c_j	2	– 2	3	– 3	0	0		
c_B	Basis	y_1	y_2	y_3	y_4	s_1	s_2	b	θ
– 3	y_4	$\frac{1}{2}$	$-\frac{1}{2}$	– 1	1	$\frac{1}{2}$	0	0	– 0
0	s_2	$\frac{1}{2}$	$-\frac{1}{2}$	0	0	$-\frac{3}{2}$	1	6	– 12
	Z_j	$-\frac{3}{2}$	$\frac{3}{2}$	3	– 3	$-\frac{3}{2}$	0	0	
	$c_j–Z_j$	$\frac{7}{2}$	$-\frac{7}{2}$	0	0	$\frac{3}{2}$	0		
			↑						*Second b.f.s.*

In table 2.97, y_2-column is the key column. To find the outgoing variable we find replacement ratios. Since both the replacement ratios are negative, y_2 can be increased indefinitely, and *objective function can be decreased indefinitely*. In order words, the given L.P. problem has an unbounded solution.

2.18-7 Variables with Lower Bounds

Sometimes, lower bounds may be specified in a linear programming problem. For example, it may be specified that $x_1 \geq c_1, x_2 \geq c_2$. Such constraints can be easily handled by substituting $x_1 = c_1 + y_1$ and $x_2 = c_2 + y_2$, where $y_1, y_2 \geq 0$ in the model and solving it in terms of y_1 and y_2.

EXAMPLE 2.18-11

For a company engaged in the manufacture of three products X, Y and Z, the available data are given below. Determine the product mix to maximize the profit.

TABLE 2.98

Operations	*Time in hours required per unit of* X	Y	Z	*Total available hours per month*
1	*1*	*2*	*2*	*200*
2	*2*	*1*	*1*	*220*
3	*3*	*1*	*2*	*180*
Profit/unit (₹)	*10*	*15*	*8*	
Minimum sales requirements/month in units	*10*	*20*	*30*	

[*P.U.B.E. (E.& Ec.) April, 2008*]

Solution

Let x, y, z denote the number of units produced per month of products X, Y and Z respectively. Objective is to maximize the monthly profit.

i.e., maximize $Z = 10x + 15y + 8z$.

Time constraints for the three operations are

$$x + 2y + 2z \leq 200,$$
$$2x + y + z \leq 220,$$
$$3x + y + 2z \leq 180.$$

Minimum sales requirements give the following constraints:

$$x \geq 10,$$
$$y \geq 20,$$
$$z \geq 30.$$

Solution of this problem will need introduction of 3 slack, 3 surplus and 3 artificial variables. The problem will involve, therefore, 12 variables and 6 constraints and will require sufficient time for solution by simplex method.

The time and effort for solution can be considerably reduced if variables x, y and z having lower bounds of 10, 20 and 30 respectively are substituted as follows:

$$x = 10 + x_1,$$
$$y = 20 + x_2,$$
$$z = 30 + x_3,$$

where $x_1, x_2, x_3 \geq 0.$

Substituting these values in the model, it takes the form :

$$\text{Maximize } Z = 10\,(10 + x_1) + 15\,(20 + x_2) + 8\,(30 + x_3)$$

$$= 10x_1 + 15x_2 + 8x_3 + 640,$$

subject to $(10 + x_1) + 2\,(20 + x_2) + 2\,(30 + x_3) \le 200,$

$2\,(10 + x_1) + (20 + x_2) + (30 + x_3) \le 220,$

$3\,(10 + x_1) + (20 + x_2) + 2\,(30 + x_3) \le 180,$

where $x_1, x_2, x_3 \ge 0.$

or Maximize $Z = 10x_1 + 15x_2 + 8x_3 + 640,$

subject to $x_1 + 2x_2 + 2x_3 \le 90,$

$2x_1 + x_2 + x_3 \le 150,$

$3x_1 + x_2 + 2x_3 \le 70,$

$x_1, x_2, x_3 \ge 0.$

Adding slack variables s_1, s_2 and s_3, we get

maximize $Z = 10x_1 + 15x_2 + 8x_3 + 640 + 0s_1 + 0s_2 + 0s_3$

or maximize $Z' = Z - 640 = 10x_1 + 15x_2 + 8x_3 + 0s_1 + 0s_2 + 0s_3,$

subject to $x_1 + 2x_2 + 2x_3 - s_1 = 90,$

$2x_1 + x_2 + x_3 + s_2 = 150,$

$3x_1 + x_2 + 2x_3 - s_3 = 70,$

$x_1, x_2, x_3, s_1, s_2, s_3 \ge 0.$

Initial basic feasibe solution is obtained by setting $x_1 = x_2 = x_3 = 0$. The solution is $s_1 = 90$, $s_2 = 150$, $s_3 = 70$, $Z' = 0$. This solution and further improved solutions are given in the following tables :

TABLE 2.99

	c_j	10	15	8	0	0	0		
c_B	Basis	x_1	x_2	x_3	s_1	s_2	s_3	b	θ
0	s_1	1	(2)	2	1	0	0	90	45 ←
0	s_2	2	1	1	0	1	0	150	150
0	s_3	3	1	2	0	0	1	70	70
	Z_j	0	0	0	0	0	0	0	
	$c_j–Z_j$	10	15	8	0	0	0		
			↑					*Initial b.f.s.*	

TABLE 2.100

	c_j	10	15	8	0	0	0		
c_B	Basis	x_1	x_2	x_3	s_1	s_2	s_3	b	θ
15	x_2	$1/2$	1	1	$1/2$	0	0	45	90
0	s_2	$3/2$	0	0	$-1/2$	1	0	105	70
0	s_3	$(5/2)$	0	1	$-1/2$	0	1	25	10 ←
	Z_j	$15/2$	15	15	$15/2$	0	0	675	
	$c_j–Z_j$	$5/2$	0	− 7	$-15/2$	0	0	*Second b.f.s*	
		↑							

TABLE 2.101

	c_j	10	15	8	0	0	0	
c_B	Basis	x_1	x_2	x_3	s_1	s_2	s_3	b
15	x_2	0	1	$4/5$	$3/5$	0	$-1/5$	40
0	s_2	0	0	$-3/5$	$-1/5$	1	$-3/5$	90
10	x_1	1	0	$2/5$	$-1/5$	0	$2/5$	10
	Z_j	10	15	16	7	0	1	700
	$c_j–Z_j$	0	0	– 8	– 7	0	– 1	
								Optimal b.f.s.

∴ Optimal solution is $x_1 = 10, x_2 = 40, x_3 = 0, Z' = 700$.

Substituting these values,

$$x = 10 + x_1 = 10 + 10 = 20 \text{ units,}$$
$$y = 20 + x_2 = 20 + 40 = 60 \text{ units,}$$
$$z = 30 + x_3 = 30 + 0 = 30 \text{ units,}$$
$$Z_{max} = Z' + 640 = ₹\ (700 + 640) = ₹\ 1{,}340.$$

∴ The optimal product mix is to produce 20 units of X, 60 units of Y and 30 units of Z to get the maximum profit of ₹ 1,340.

EXAMPLE 2.18-12

Consider the problem

$$\text{minimize } Z = x_2 - 3x_3 + 2x_5,$$
$$\text{subject to} \quad x_1 + 3x_2 - x_3 + 2x_5 = 7,$$
$$-2x_2 + 4x_3 + x_4 = 12,$$
$$-4x_2 + 3x_3 + 8x_5 + x_6 = 10,$$
$$x_1, x_2, ..., x_6 \geq 0.$$

Convert it into a maximization problem and solve by the simplex method.

[H.P.U. B.Tech. (Mech.) June, 2010; P.U. B.E. (Mech.) Nov., 2006]

Solution

The given minimization problem can be converted into equivalent maximization problem by multiplying the objective function by – 1.

Thus minimize $Z = x_2 - 3x_3 + 2x_5$ is equivalent to maximize $Z' (= -Z) = -x_2 + 3x_3 - 2x_5$.

There is no need to add artificial variables to the constraints. Variables x_1, x_4, x_6 occur only in the first, second and third constraint respectively. Since they form unit matrix $\begin{bmatrix} 1 & 0 & 0 \\ 0 & 1 & 0 \\ 0 & 0 & 1 \end{bmatrix}$ in the constraints and occur in the objective function with zero coefficients, they can be treated as slack variables. The constraints may be rearranged and the model can be written as

$$\text{maximize } Z' = -x_2 + 3x_3 - 2x_5 + 0x_1 + 0x_4 + 0x_6,$$
$$\text{subject to} \quad 3x_2 - x_3 + 2x_5 + x_1 = 7,$$
$$-2x_2 + 4x_3 + x_4 = 12,$$
$$-4x_2 + 3x_3 + 8x_5 + x_6 = 10,$$
$$x_1, x_2, ..., x_6 \geq 0.$$

Setting $x_2 = x_3 = x_5 = 0$, i.b.f.s. is $x_1 = 7, x_4 = 12, x_6 = 0, Z = 0$. This solution as well as further improved solutions are given by the following tables :

TABLE 2.102

	c_j	−1	3	−2	0	0	0		
c_B	Basis	x_2	x_3	x_5	x_1	x_4	x_6	b	θ
0	x_1	3	−1	2	1	0	0	7	−7
0	x_4	−2	(4)	0	0	1	0	12	3 ←
0	x_6	−4	3	8	0	0	1	10	$10/3$
	Z_j	0	0	0	0	0	0	0	
	$c_j–Z_j$	−1	3 ↑	−2	0	0	0	*Initial b.f.s.*	
0	x_1	$(5/2)$	0	2	1	$1/4$	0	10	4 ←
3	x_3	$-1/2$	1	0	0	$1/4$	0	3	−6
0	x_6	$-5/2$	0	8	0	$-3/4$	1	1	$-2/5$
	Z_j	$-3/2$	3	0	0	$3/4$	0	9	
	$c_j–Z_j$	$1/2$ ↑	0	−2	0	$-3/4$	0	*Second b.f.s.*	
−1	x_2	1	0	$4/5$	$2/5$	$1/10$	0	4	
3	x_3	0	1	$2/5$	$1/5$	$3/10$	0	5	
0	x_6	0	0	10	1	$-1/2$	1	11	
	Z_j	−1	3	$2/5$	$1/5$	$4/5$	0	11	
	$c_j–Z_j$	0	0	$-12/5$	$-1/5$	$-4/5$	0	*Optimal b.f.s.*	

Hence optimal solution is

$x_2 = 4, x_3 = 5, x_5 = 0, x_1 = 0, x_4 = 0, x_6 = 11; Z'_{max} = 11.$

$\therefore Z'_{min} = - Z'_{max} = - 11.$

2.19 SOLUTION OF SIMULTANEOUS EQUATIONS BY SIMPLEX METHOD

Artificial variables $A_1, A_2, \ldots$ are introduced in the constraint equations. A *dummy* objective function (of maximization type) is introduced in which all decision variables $x_1, x_2, \ldots$ are assigned zero objective coefficients and artificial variables $A_1, A_2, \ldots$ are each assigned −1 coefficient in the objective function. The linear model is, then, solved by the simplex method and the optimal values of the variables provide the solution to the given system of equations.

EXAMPLE 2.19-1

Use the simplex method to solve the following system of linear equations :

$$x_1 - x_3 + 4x_4 = 3,$$
$$2x_1 - x_2 = 3,$$
$$3x_1 - 2x_2 - x_4 = 1,$$
$$x_1, x_2, x_3, x_4 \geq 0.$$

[*Meerut M.Com. Jan., 1998*]

Solution. Since the objective function is not prescribed, a dummy objective function is introduced as

$$\begin{aligned} &\text{maximize } Z = 0x_1 + 0x_2 + 0x_3 + 0x_4 - A_1 - A_2 - A_3, \\ &\text{subject to} \quad x_1 - x_3 + 4x_4 + A_1 = 3, \\ &\qquad 2x_1 - x_2 + A_2 = 3, \\ &\qquad 3x_1 - 2x_2 - x_4 + A_3 = 1, \\ &\qquad x_1, x_2, x_3, x_4, A_1, A_2, A_3 \geq 0. \end{aligned}$$

Letting $x_1 = x_2 = x_3 = x_4 = 0$, i.b.f.s. is $A_1 = 3$, $A_2 = 3$, $A_3 = 1$; $Z = -7$.

The initial and subsequent simplex tables are given below.

TABLE 2.103

	c_j	0	0	0	0	− 1	− 1	− 1		
c_B	Basis	x_1	x_2	x_3	x_4	A_1	A_2	A_3	b	θ
− 1	A_1	1	0	− 1	4	1	0	0	3	3
− 1	A_2	2	− 1	0	0	0	1	0	3	$3/2$
− 1	A_3	(3)	− 2	0	− 1	0	0	1	1	$1/3$ ←
	Z_j	− 6	3	1	− 3	− 1	− 1	− 1	− 7	
	c_j–Z_j	6	− 3	− 1	3	0	0	0		
		↑								
− 1	A_1	0	$2/3$	− 1	$(13/3)$	1	0		$8/3$	$8/13$ ←
− 1	A_2	0	$1/3$	0	$2/3$	0	1		$7/3$	$7/2$
0	x_1	1	$-2/3$	0	$-1/3$	0	0		$1/3$	− 1
	Z_j	0	− 1	1	− 5	− 1	− 1		− 5	
	c_j–Z_j	0	1	− 1	5	0	0			
					↑					
	c_j	0	0	0	0	− 1	− 1	− 1		
c_B	Basis	x_1	x_2	x_3	x_4	A_1	A_2	A_3	b	θ
0	x_4	0	$(2/13)$	$-3/13$	1		0		$8/13$	4 ←
− 1	A_2	0	$3/13$	$2/13$	0		1		$25/13$	$25/3$
0	x_1	1	$-8/13$	$-1/13$	0		0		$7/13$	$-7/8$
	Z_j	0	$-3/13$	$-2/13$	0		− 1		$-25/13$	
	c_j–Z_j	0	$3/13$	$2/13$	0		0			
			↑							

0	x_2	0	1	$-3/2$	$13/2$	0	4	$-8/3$
-1	A_2	0	0	$(1/2)$	$-3/2$	1	1	2 ←
0	x_1	1	0	-1	4	0	3	-3
	Z_j	0	0	$-1/2$	$3/2$	-1	-1	
	c_j-Z_j	0	0	$1/2$ ↑	$-3/2$	0		
0	x_2	0	1	0	2		7	
0	x_3	0	0	1	-3		2	
0	x_1	1	0	0	1		5	
	Z_j	0	0	0	0			
	c_j-Z_j	0	0	0	0		*Optimal solution*	

Thus solution of the system of simultaneous equations is

$$x_1 = 5,\ x_2 = 7,\ x_3 = 2,\ x_4 = 0.$$

2.20 SOME ADDITIONAL POINTS

1. It may be desired to convert a maximization problem into a minimization one and vice versa. Mathematically, this can be accomplished by reversing the sign of *just* the objective function (Refer Ex. 2.18-12).

2. Whether to introduce slack or surplus or artificial variables depends on the type of inequality and has nothing to do with the type of the problem *i.e.*, whether maximization or minimization.

3. It may be noted that except the artificial variables, others (slack, surplus and decision variables), once driven out of solution, may re-enter in a subsequent iteration. Advantage can be taken of this fact by omitting its column in all subsequent iterations once an artificial variable is driven out (Refer Ex. 2.17-1 to 2.17-5 and 2.19-1).

4. Sometimes, lower bounds may be specified in a linear programming problem. For example, it may be stipulated that x_1 cannot be less than c_1 and x_2 cannot be less than c_2 *i.e.*, $x_1 \geq c_1$, $x_2 \geq c_2$. Such constraints can be easily handled by substituting $x_1 = c_1 + y_1$, $x_2 = c_2 + y_2$ in the model and then solving it in terms of y_1 and y_2 (Refer Ex. 2.18-11).

5. In all the simplex tables there must be an identity matrix of size $p \times p$, where p is the number of constraints. The columns that constitute such an identity matrix need not be adjacent.

6. When the objective function contains a constant term, the simplex method may be applied by excluding the constant and the optimal solution may be obtained. This constant is then added at the end to find the optimal value of the objective function (Refer Ex. 2.18-11)

7. The graphical method, the trial and error method, the simplex technique, the revised simplex method and the dual approach (to be discussed later in Chapter 6) are just the different ways of solving a linear programming problem. The reader may solve a problem in more than one way for the sake of practice and verification of the answer.

8. The *b*-column (quantity column) values can never be negative. Any negative value in *b*-column during computations indicates error in calculations. The solution should be checked and error must be corrected before proceeding further in computations.

9. Z-value in a subsequent table will be at least (maximization problem) or at most (minimization problem) equal to the value in the previous table.

10. If any solution violates any of the constraints, there is error in computations, which must be checked and corrected before proceeding further.

2.21 COMPUTATIONAL EFFICIENCY OF THE SIMPLEX TECHNIQUE

From theoretical point of view, the simplex technique is not an efficient method as it strives to reach an optimal solution by changing only one basic variable at a time. Clearly, a method can reach faster an optimal solution if it changes more than one basic variable at a time. Many variants to the simplex technique have been tried but none has resulted in appreciable decrease in the total computational time and the basic simplex method is still regarded as the best method to solve any linear programming problem.

The computational efficiency of the simplex method depends upon

(1) the number of iterations required to reach the optimal solution, and

(2) the total computational time required to solve the problem.

Solution of a large number of practical problems shows that for a standard linear programme with m constraints and n variables, the number of iterations required lies between m and $3m$, the average being $2m$; while the computational time required is approximately m^3. For instance, if a problem has twice the number of constraints than the other, the computer time taken to solve the former will be about 8 times that of the latter.

As the number of iterations and hence the computational efficiency of the simplex method depends upon the number of constraints rather than the number of variables, the number of constraints should be kept as small as possible by avoiding all unnecessary or redundant constraints during the formulation of the problem.

EXERCISES 2.4

1. Explain simplex method of solving linear programming problem.
[P.U.B.E. (Mech.) 2012; Univ. of Madras BBA April, 2012; Nov., 2010; P.T.U. B.Tech. (Mech.) 2008; Chennai Univ. B.B.A. Nov., 2010; P.U.M.Com., 2002]

2. What is the difference between simplex solution procedure for a maximization and a minimization problem ? Using the concept of net contribution, explain why the criterion for optimality for a maximization problem is different from a minimization problem. *[P.U.M.Com., 2001]*

3. Define the following and indicate their significance to decision-making with linear programming and simplex method :

(*i*) Key column (*ii*) Key row (*iii*) Degeneracy (*iv*) Cycling (*v*) Infeasibility.
[P.T.U.B.E. May, 2012; P.U.M.Com., 2001]

4. Discuss the simplex method where it indicates existence of multiple optimal, unbounded and infeasible solution of an L.P.P. *[G.N.D.U. B.Com. Sept., 2009; P.T.U. B.Tech. (C.Sc.) 2009]*

5. Explain the significance of the following variables with examples. When is each used and why ? What value does each carry in the objective function ?

(*i*) Slack variables (*ii*) Surplus variables (*iii*) Artificial variables.
[P.T.U. MBA May, 2015; V.T.U. Karnataka, 2012; G.N.D.U. B.Com. 2014, 13, 08, 07, 05; Univ. of Mumbai MBA, 2012; Univ. of Madras B.Sc. (Math.) Nov., 2012; Osmania U.MBA, 2012; L.U. B.Com. 2010; P.U. M.B.A. Feb., 2009; Chennai U.B.C.A. Nov., 2010; Dayalbagh Edu. Inst. Agra M. Tech. Dec., 2007; P.T.U. MBA, 2008; B. Tech., 2006]

6. Explain the concept of degeneracy in simplex method. How is it resolved?
[H.P.U. B.Tech. (Mech.) 2012; R.U. MBA June, 2011; Gujarat Tech. U.B.E. Dec., 2012; P.U.B.Com. April, 2008; G.N.D.U. B.Com. April 2015, 2016; P.T.U. B. Tech. (Mech.) May, 2007]

7. (*a*) What is cycling ? State the rules to avoid cycling.
[Pbi. U. MCA, 2001; K.U.M. Sc., 2001]

(*b*) What is pseudo-optimal solution? *[Univ. of Madras B.Sc. (Math.) Nov., 2012]*

8. (*a*) Explain the following with reference to L.P.P. :

(*i*) Entering variable (*ii*) Leaving variable *[I.I.M.S. Kolkata, 1996]*

(*b*) What are unrestricted variables? How do you handle them for solution of its problem by simplex method? *[H.P.U. B.Tech. (Mech.) 2012]*

9. (*a*) What do the coefficients within a simplex table represent ? Why is it necessary to compute a new set for each table in the analysis ?

(*b*) What is a dummy objective function ? Why is it used and what does it accomplish ?

10. What is the role of surplus variables in the simplex method ? [*Chennai U., 2002*]

11. Write the steps involved in two-phase simplex method.

[*G.N.D.U. B.Com. Sept., 2012; Sept., 2007; M.G.U. Kerala M.Com. June 2012; Nellore MBA, 2002*]

12. How do you identify the presence of multiple optima in the simplex method ?

[*P.T.U. B.Tech. (CH.) 2009*]

13. Name three basic parts of the simplex technique. [*P.T.U. B.Tech. (Mech.) 2009*]

Solve the following problems by the simplex method :

14. Maximize $Z = 2x_1 + x_2$,
subject to $x_1 + 2x_2 \leq 10$,
$x_1 + x_2 \leq 6$,
$x_1 - x_2 \leq 2$,
$x_1 - 2x_2 \leq 1$,
$x_1, x_2 \geq 0$.

[*Karn. U.B.E. (Mech.) 1997*]

(*Ans.* $x_1 = 4, x_2 = 2; Z_{max} = 10.$)

15. Solve the following L.P. problem using simplex method :
Maximize $Z = 10x_1 + 15x_2 + 20x_3$,
subject to $2x_1 + 4x_2 + 6x_3 \leq 24$,
$3x_1 + 9x_2 + 6x_3 \leq 30$,
$x_1, x_2, x_3 \geq 0$. [*Chennai U.B.C.A. Nov., 2010*]

16. Maximize $Z = 3x_1 + 2x_2 + 5x_3$,
subject to $x_1 + x_2 + x_3 \leq 9$,
$2x_1 + 3x_2 + 5x_3 \leq 30$,
$2x_1 - x_2 - x_3 \leq 8$,
$x_1, x_2, x_3 \geq 0$.

[*NIIFT Mohali, 1998; P.U.B.E. (Prod.) April, 1997*]

(*Ans.* $x_1 = 5, x_2 = 0, x_3 = 4; Z_{max} = 35.$)

17. Maximize $Z = 5x_1 + 3x_2 + 7x_3$,
subject to $x_1 + x_2 + 2x_3 \leq 28$,
$3x_1 + 2x_2 + x_3 \leq 26$,
$x_1 + x_2 + x_3 \leq 18$,
$x_1, x_2, x_3 \geq 0$.

What will be the solution if the first constraint changes to $x_1 + x_2 + 2x_3 \leq 26$.

[*P.U.B.E. (Prod.) 1997*]

(*Ans.* (*i*) $x_1 = 6, x_2 = 0, x_3 = 8; Z_{max} = 86.$

(*ii*) $x_1 = \frac{26}{5}, x_2 = 0, x_3 = \frac{52}{5}; \; Z_{max} = \frac{494}{5}$.)

18. Maximize $Z = 2x_1 + x_2 - 3x_3 + 5x_4$,
subject to $x_1 + 7x_2 + 3x_3 + 7x_4 \leq 46$,
$3x_1 - x_2 + x_3 + 2x_4 \leq 8$,
$2x_1 + 3x_2 - x_3 + x_4 \leq 10$,
$x_1, x_2, x_3, x_4 \geq 0$. [*P.U.B.E. (Mech.) Nov., 1994*]

(*Ans.* $x_1 = 0, x_2 = 12/7, x_3 = 0, x_4 = 34/7; Z_{max} = 26.$)

19. Maximize $Z = 2x_1 + 4x_2 + x_3 + x_4$,
subject to $x_1 + 3x_2 + x_4 \leq 4$,
$2x_1 + x_2 \leq 3$,
$x_2 + 4x_3 + x_4 \leq 3$,
$x_j \geq 0 \; (j = 1, 2, 3, 4)$.

[*Karn. U.B.Tech. (Mech.) May, 1989*]

(*Ans.* $x_1 = 1, x_2 = 1, x_3 = \frac{1}{2}, x_4 = 0; Z_{max} = \frac{13}{2}$.)

20. Minimize $x_0 = x_1 - 3x_2 + 2x_3$,
subject to $3x_1 - x_2 + 2x_3 \geq 7$,
$-2x_1 + 4x_2 \leq 12$,
$-4x_1 + 3x_2 + 8x_3 \leq 10$,
$x_1, x_2, x_3 \geq 0$.

[P.T.U. B.Tech. (Mech.) 2012; J.N.T.U. Anantapur MBA August, 2010; IGNOU MBA Dec., 2006; R.C.C. CHD., 2002; NIIFT Mohali, 2000]

(*Ans.* $x_1 = 4, x_2 = 5, x_3 = 0$; $Z_{min} = -11$.)

21. Maximize $Z = 3x_1 + 4x_2 + x_3 + 5x_4$,
subject to $8x_1 + 3x_2 + 2x_3 + 2x_4 \leq 10$,
$2x_1 + 5x_2 + x_3 + 4x_4 \leq 5$,
$x_1 + 2x_2 + 5x_3 + x_4 \leq 6$,
$x_1, x_2, x_3, x_4 \geq 0$.

[Meerut B.Sc. (Math.) 1970]

(*Ans.* $x_1 = \frac{15}{14}, x_2 = 0, x_3 = 0, x_4 = \frac{5}{7}$; $Z_{max} = \frac{95}{14}$.)

22. Maximize $Z = 2x_1 + 3x_2 + x_3 + 7x_4$,
subject to $8x_1 + 3x_2 + 4x_3 + x_4 \leq 6$,
$2x_1 + 6x_2 + x_3 + 5x_4 \leq 3$,
$x_1 + 4x_2 + 5x_3 + 2x_4 \leq 7$,
$x_1, x_2, x_3, x_4 \geq 0$.

(*Ans.* $x_1 = x_2 = x_3 = 0, x_4 = \frac{3}{5}$; $Z_{max} = 4.2$.)

23. Give an outline of the simplex method for solving an L.P.P. and solve :
Maximize $Z = 4x_1 + 5x_2 + 9x_3 + 11x_4$,
subject to constraints $x_1 + x_2 + x_3 + x_4 \leq 15$,
$7x_1 + 5x_2 + 3x_3 + 2x_4 \leq 120$,
$3x_1 + 5x_2 + 10x_3 + 15x_4 \leq 100$,
$x_j \geq 0$ $(j = 1, 2, 3, 4.)$

[J.N.T.U. Hyderabad B.Tech. Nov., 2012; R.T.M. Nagpur U. B.Tech. June, 2006]

(*Ans.* $x_1 = \frac{50}{7}, x_2 = 0, x_3 = \frac{55}{7}, x_4 = 0$; $Z_{max} = \frac{695}{7}$.)

24. Maximize $Z = 3x_1 + 2x_2$,
subject to $x_1 + x_2 \leq 4$,
$x_1 - x_2 \leq 2$,
$x_1, x_2 \geq 0$.

[I.A.S. (Math.) 1992]

(*Ans.* $x_1 = 3, x_2 = 1$; $Z_{max} = 11$.)

25. Maximize $Z = 3x_1 + 2x_2 + 5x_3$,
subject to $x_1 + 2x_2 + x_3 \leq 430$,
$3x_1 + 2x_3 \leq 460$,
$x_1 + 4x_2 \leq 420$,
$x_1, x_2, x_3 \geq 0$.

[B.P.U.T., 2011]

(*Ans.* $x_1 = 0, x_2 = 100, x_3 = 230$; $Z_{max} = 1{,}350$.)

26. Maximize $Z = 3x_1 + 5x_2 + 4x_3$,
subject to $2x_1 + 3x_2 \leq 8$,
$2x_2 + 5x_3 \leq 10$,
$3x_1 + 2x_2 + 4x_3 \leq 15$,
$x_1, x_2, x_3 \geq 0$.

[R.T.M. Nagpur B.E. (Mech.) Sept., 2010; P.T.U.B. Tech. (Mech.) Dec., 2006]

(*Ans.* $x_1 = \frac{89}{41}, x_2 = \frac{50}{41}, x_3 = \frac{62}{41}$; $Z_{max} = \frac{765}{41}$.)

27. Maximize $Z = 5x_1 + 3x_2$,
subject to $x_1 + x_2 \le 2$,
$5x_1 + 2x_2 \le 10$,
$-2x_1 - 8x_2 \ge -12$,
$x_1, x_2 \ge 0$.

[P.U.B. Com. April, 2009; Sept., 2006; April, 2006; M.Com. Sept., 2004]

(*Ans.* $x_1 = 2, x_2 = 0$; $Z_{max} = 10$.)

28. Maximize $Z = 4x + 10x_2$,
subject to $2x + x_2 \le 50$,
$2x_1 + 5x_2 \le 100$,
$2x_1 + 3x_2 \le 90$,
$x_1, x_2 \ge 0$.

[B.P.U.T., 2010; P.U.B.E. (T. & I.T.) Nov., 2004]

(*Ans.* $x_1 = 0, x_2 = 20$; $Z_{max} = 200$.)

29. Maximize $Z = 10x_1 + 6x_2 + 11x_3$,
subject to $4x_1 + 6x_2 + 7x_3 \le 210$,
$9x_1 + x_2 + 5x_3 \le 190$,
$13x_2 + 2x_3 \le 175$,
$x_1 \ge 0, x_2 \ge 0, x_3 \ge 1$.

[P.U.B.E. (Ec.) 2002]

[**Hint.** Let $x_3 = 1+x_4$, where $x_4 \ge 0$.]

(*Ans.* $x_1 = \dfrac{280}{43}$, $x_2 = 0$, $x_3 = \dfrac{1{,}130}{43}$; $Z_{max} = \dfrac{15{,}230}{43}$.)

30. Solve the following LPP by simplex method:
Maximize $Z = 2x_1 + x_2 + x_3$,
subject to $4x_1 + 6x_2 + 3x_3 \le 8$,
$3x_1 - 6x_2 - 4x_3 \le 1$,
$2x_1 + 3x_2 - 5x_3 \le 4$,
x_1, x_2 and $x_3 \ge 0$.

[J.N.T.U. Hyderabad B.Tech. June, 2009]

31. Solve using simplex method:
Maximize $Z = 30x_1 + 23x_2 + 29x_3$,
subject to $6x_1 + 5x_2 + 3x_3 \le 26$,
$4x_1 + 2x_2 + 5x_3 \le 7$,
$x_1, x_2, x_3 \ge 0$.

[J.N.T.U. Hyderabad B.Tech. June, 2009]

32. Solve the L.P. problem:
Maximize $Z = 3x_1 + 2x_2$,
subject to $x_1 + 2x_2 \le 430$,
$3x_1 + 2x_2 \le 460$,
$3x_1 + x_2 \le 420$ and $x_1, x_2 \ge 0$.

[R.T.M. Nagpur U.B. Tech. Dec., 2006]

33. Solve the following L.P.P. by simplex method:
Maximize $Z = 3x_1 + 4x_2$,
subject to constraints $x + 3x_2 \le 48$,
$2x_1 + x_2 \le 40$,
$2x_1 + 5x_2 \le 160$,
$x_1, x_2 \ge 0$.

[R.T.M. Nagpur U.B. Tech. Dec., 2005]

34. Maximize using simplex method:
$Z = 30x_1 + 40x_2 + 20x_3 + 10x_4$,
subject to $2x_4 + 10x_1 + 12x_2 + 7x_3 \le 10{,}000$,
$3x_4 + 7x_1 + 10x_2 + 8x_3 \le 8{,}000$,
$x_1 + x_2 + x_3 + x_4 \le 1{,}000$,
$x_1, x_2, x_3, x_4 \ge 0$.

[R.T.M. Nagpur U.B. Tech. Dec., 2004]

35. Maximize $Z = 6x_1 + 20x_2 + 248,$
subject to $2x_1 + x_2 \le 6,$
$3x_1 + 4x_2 \le 16,$
$x_1, x_2 \ge 0.$

[*P.U.M.Com., 2001*]

(*Ans.* $x_1 = 8/5, x_2 = 14/5; Z_{max} = 313.60.$)

36. Maximize $Z = 2x_1 + 2x_2 + 3,$
subject to $-x_1 + 2x_2 \le 4,$
$-x_1 + x_2 \le 5,$
$4x_1 - x_2 \le 10,$
$x_1, x_2 \ge 0.$

[*DOEACC, 1995*]

(*Ans.* $x_1 = 24/7, x_2 = 26/7; Z_{max} = 121/7.$)

37. Maximize $Z = 6x_1 + 7x_2 + 9x_3,$
subject to $3x_1 + 7x_2 + 6x_3 \le 255,$
$5x_1 + 8x_2 + 9x_3 \le 424,$
$11x_1 + 6x_2 + 8x_3 \le 235,$
$x_1, x_2, x_3 \ge 0.$

[*P.U.B.E. (Ec.) 2001, 2000*]

(*Ans.* $x_1 = 0, x_2 = \frac{785}{26}, x_3 = \frac{175}{26}; Z_{max} = \frac{3{,}535}{13}.$)

38. Maximize $Z = 2x_1 + x_2,$
subject to $4x_1 + 3x_2 \le 12,$
$4x_1 + x_2 \le 8,$
$4x_1 - x_2 \le 8,$
$x_1, x_2 \ge 0.$

[*P.U.B. Com. March, 2006*]

(*Ans.* $x_1 = \frac{3}{2}, x_2 = 2; Z_{max} = 5.$)

39. Maximize $Z = x_1 + 2x_2,$
subject to $-x_1 + 2x_2 \le 8,$
$x_1 + 2x_2 \le 12,$
$x_1 - 2x_2 \le 3,$
$x_1, x_2 \ge 0.$

Obtain an alternative optimal b.f.s. if it exists.

[*B.P.U.T. 6th Sem., 2011, Univ. of Madras B.Sc. (Mech.) Nov., 2012; H.P.U.B. Tech. (Mech.) Nov., 2010*]

(*Ans.* (*i*) $x_1 = \frac{15}{2}, x_2 = \frac{9}{4}, s_1 = 11, s_2 = 0, s_3 = 0; Z_{max} = 12.$

(*ii*) $x_1 = 2, x_2 = 5, s_1 = 0, s_2 = 0, s_3 = 11; Z_{max} = 12.$)

40. Maximize $Z = 20x_1 + 25x_2,$
subject to $12x_1 + 16x_2 \le 100,$
$16x_1 + 8x_2 \le 80,$
$x_1, x_2 \ge 0.$

[*P.U. MBA, 2000*]

(*Ans.* $x_1 = 3, x_2 = 4; Z_{max} = 160.$)

41. Use simplex method to solve the following L.P.P. :

Maximize $Z = 30x_1 + 40x_2,$
subject to $60x_1 + 120x_2 \le 12{,}000,$
$8x_1 + 5x_2 \le 600,$
$3x_1 + 4x_2 \le 500,$
$x_1, x_2 \ge 0.$

[*Osmania U. MBA, 2010*]

$\left(\text{Ans. } x_1 = \frac{200}{11}, x_2 = \frac{1{,}000}{11}; Z_{max} = \frac{46{,}000}{11}.\right)$

42. Solve by simplex method:

Maximize $Z = 10x_1 + 6x_2 + 4x_3$,
subject to $x_1 + x_2 + x_3 \le 100$,
$10x_1 + 4x_2 + 5x_3 \le 600$,
$2x_1 + 2x_2 + 6x_3 \le 300$,
$x_1, x_2, x_3 \ge 0$.

Does the problem have unique solution ? Give reasons

[G.N.D.U. B.Com. April, 2009; Mumbai U. MBA, 2010]

43. Show by the simplex method that the following L.P.P. has multiple optimal solutions :

Minimize $Z = -40x_1 - 100x_2$,
subject to $10x_1 + 5x_2 \le 250$,
$2x_1 + 5x_2 \le 100$,
$2x_1 + 3x_2 \le 90$,
$x_1, x_2 \ge 0$.

(*Ans.* (*i*) $x_1 = 0, x_2 = 20; Z_{min} = -2,000$.
(*ii*) $x_1 = 75/4, x_2 = 25/2; Z_{min} = -2,000$.)

44. Solve by the simplex method :

Maximize $Z = 3x_1 + 2x_2$,
subject to $-x_1 + 2x_2 + x_3 = 4$,
$3x_1 + 2x_2 + x_4 = 14$,
$x_1 - x_2 + x_5 = 3$,
$x_j \ge 0, j = 1, 2, ..., 5$.

[P.U.M.Sc. (I.T.) 2003; G.N.D.U. B. Com. April, 1994]

(*Ans.* Multiple optimal solutions. Two of them are :

(*i*) $x_1 = \frac{5}{2}, x_2 = \frac{13}{4}; x_3 = 0; x_4 = 0; x_5 = \frac{15}{4}; Z_{max} = 14$.

(*ii*) $x_1 = 4, x_2 = 1; x_3 = 0; x_4 = 0; x_5 = 0; Z_{max} = 14$.)

45. Show by simplex method that the following problem has an unbounded optimal solution :

Maximize $x_0 = 2x_1 + x_2$,
subject to $x_1 - x_2 \le 10$,
$2x_1 - x_2 \le 40$,
$x_1, x_2 \ge 0$.

46. Show that the L.P.P.

maximize $Z = 2x_1 + 3x_2 + 4x_3 + x_4$,
subject to $-x_1 - 5x_2 - 9x_3 + 6x_4 \le 2$,
$3x_1 - x_2 + x_3 + 3x_4 \le 10$,
$2x_1 + 3x_2 - 7x_3 + 8x_4 \le 0$,
$x_1, x_2, x_3, x_4 \ge 0$,

Has an unbounded solution.

47. Use the Charnes penalty method to

maximize $Z = 3x_1 - x_2$,
subject to constraints
$2x_1 + x_2 \ge 2$,
$x_1 + 3x_2 \le 3$,
$x_2 \le 4$.
$x_1, x_1 \ge 0$.

[P.T.U.B. Tech. April, 2012]

(*Ans.* $x_1 = 3, x_2 = 0; Z_{max} = 9$.)

48. Use the M-technique to

minimize $Z = 4x_1 + x_2$,
subject to $3x_1 + x_2 = 3$,
$4x_1 + 3x_2 \ge 6$,
$x_1 + 2x_2 \le 3$,
$x_1, x_2 \ge 0$.

[P.T.U. B.Tech. (CH) April, 2012, 2009; Nagpur U.B.E., 2003; P.U.B.E. (Mech.) 2002; B.Com. Sept., 2004; April, 2001]

(*Ans.* $x_1 = \frac{3}{5}, x_2 = \frac{6}{5}; Z_{max} = \frac{18}{5}$.)

49. Solve the following problem using the big M-method:

Maximize $Z = 6x_1 - 3x_2 + 2x_3$,
subject to $2x_1 + x_2 + x_3 \le 16$,
$3x_1 + 2x_2 + x_3 \le 18$,
$x_2 - 2x_3 \ge 8$,
$x_1, x_2, x_3 \ge 0$.

[P.T.U. B.Tech. (Prod.) Nov., 2012]

(*Ans.* $x_1 = \frac{2}{3}, x_2 = 8, x_3 = 0$; $Z_{max} = -20$.)

50. Use the Charnes penalty method to solve the problem :

Maximize $Z = 4x_1 + 5x_2 + 2x_3$,
subject to $2x_1 + x_2 + x_3 \le 10$,
$x_1 + 3x_2 + x_3 \le 12$,
$x_1 + x_2 + x_3 = 6$,
$x_1, x_2, x_3 \ge 0$.

[Karn. U.B.E. (Mech.) 1998; P.U.B.E. (Mech.) 1995]

(*Ans.* $x_1 = 3, x_2 = 3, x_3 = 0$; $Z_{max} = 27$.)

51. Solve the following problem by using x_4, x_5 and x_6 for the starting basic feasible solution :

Maximize $Z = 3x_1 + x_2 + 2x_3$,
subject to $12x_1 + 3x_2 + 6x_3 + 3x_4 = 9$,
$8x_1 + x_2 - 4x_3 + 2x_5 = 10$,
$3x_1 - x_6 = 0$,
$x_1, x_2, ..., x_6 \ge 0$.

[G.J.U. Hisar B.E., 1996]

(*Ans.* $x_1 = x_2 = x_4 = x_6 = 0, x_3 = \frac{3}{2}, x_5 = 8$; $Z_{max} = 3$.)

[**Hint.** Divide first constraint equation by 3, second by 2 and third by – 1].

52. Minimize $Z = 2x_1 + 9x_2 + x_3$,
subject to the constraints
$x_1 + 4x_2 + 2x_3 \ge 5$,
$3x_1 + x_2 + 2x_3 \ge 4$,
$x_1, x_2, x_3 \ge 0$.

[P.T.U. B.Tech. (Prod.) Nov., 2012]

(*Ans.* $x_1 = 0, x_2 = 0, x_3 = \frac{5}{2}$; $Z_{max} = \frac{5}{2}$.)

53. Solve using simplex algorithm :

Minimize $C = 2x_1 + 4x_2$,
subject to $2x_1 + x_2 \ge 14$,
$x_1 + 3x_2 \ge 18$,
$x_1 + x_2 \ge 12$,
$x_1 + x_2 \ge 0$,

[P.T.U. MBA, 2009]

(*Ans.* $x_1 = 9, x_2 = 3$; $C_{min} = 30$.)

54. Solve the following L.P. problem :

Minimize $Z = 3x_1 + 2x_2 + x_3$,
subject to $x_1 + 4x_2 + 3x_3 \ge 50$,
$2x_1 + x_2 + x_3 \ge 30$,
$-3x_1 - 2x_2 - x_3 \le -40$,
$x_1, x_2, x_3 \ge 0$.

[P.U.B. Com. Sept., 2000; ICWA (Final) Dec., 1992]

(*Ans.* $x_1 = \frac{25}{3}, x_2 = \frac{5}{3}, x_3 = \frac{35}{3}$; $Z_{min} = 40$.)

55. Maximize $Z = 4x_1 + 5x_2 - 3x_3 + 50$,
subject to $x_1 + x_2 + x_3 = 10$,
$x_1 - x_2 \ge 1$,
$2x_1 + 3x_2 + x_3 \le 40$,
$x_1, x_2, x_3 \ge 0$.

[G.N.D.U. B.Com. April, 2012; R.T.M. Nagpur B.Tech., 2004]

(*Ans.* $x_1 = \frac{11}{2}, x_2 = \frac{9}{2}, x_3 = 0$; $Z_{max} = \frac{189}{2}$.)

56. Solve by the Big M-method :

$$\text{Maximize } Z = x_1 + 2x_2 + 3x_3 - x_4,$$
$$\text{subject to} \quad x_1 + 2x_2 + 3x_3 = 15,$$
$$2x_1 + x_2 + 5x_3 = 20,$$
$$x_1 + 2x_2 + x_3 + x_4 = 10,$$
$$x_1, x_2, x_3, x_4 \geq 0.$$

[*P.T.U.B.Tech. (Mech.) May, 2006*]

(*Ans.* $x_1 = x_2 = x_3 = \dfrac{5}{2}$, $x_4 = 0$; $Z_{max} = 15$.)

57. Use the Big M-method to

$$\text{minimize } Z = 60x_1 + 80x_2,$$
$$\text{subject to} \quad x_1 \leq 400,$$
$$x_2 \geq 200,$$
$$x_1 + x_2 = 500,$$
$$x_1, x_2 \geq 0.$$

[*G.N.D.U. B.Com., Sept., 2007; P.U.B.Com. April, 2003*]

(*Ans.* $x_1 = 300$, $x_2 = 200$; $Z_{min} = 34{,}000$.)

58. Use the simplex method to solve the problem :

$$\text{Minimize } C = 8x + 5y,$$
$$\text{subject to} \quad 20x + 12y \geq 200,$$
$$8x \geq 40,$$
$$6y \geq 30,$$
$$x, y \geq 0.$$

[*P.U.B.E., 2001*]

(*Ans.* $x = 7$, $y = 5$; $C_{min} = 81$.)

59. Solve the following L.P.P. using the simplex method :

$$\text{Maximize } Z = 6x_1 + 4x_2,$$
$$\text{subject to} \quad 2x_1 + 3x_2 \leq 30,$$
$$3x_1 + 2x_2 \leq 24,$$
$$x_1 + x_2 \geq 3,$$
$$x_1, x_2 \geq 0.$$

Is the solution unique ? If not, give two different solutions.

[*G.N.D.U. B.Com April, 2006; P.U.B.Com., 2006, 2000*]

(*Ans.* (*i*) $x_1 = \dfrac{12}{5}$, $x_2 = \dfrac{42}{5}$; $Z_{max} = 48$.

(*ii*) $x_1 = 8$, $x_2 = 0$; $Z_{max} = 48$.)

60. Use the simplex method to

$$\text{minimize } Z = 3x_1 + 4x_2,$$
$$\text{subject to} \quad 4x_1 + x_2 \geq 30,$$
$$-x_1 - x_2 \leq -18,$$
$$x_1 + 3x_2 \geq 28,$$
$$x_1, x_2 \geq 0.$$

[*P.U.B. Com. April, 2008; G.N.D.U. B.Com., April, 2007*]

(*Ans.* $x_1 = 13$, $x_2 = 5$; $Z_{min} = 59$.)

61. Solve the L.P.P. :

$$\text{Minimize } Z = x_1 - 2x_2 - 3x_3,$$
$$\text{subject to} \quad 2x_1 + x_2 + 3x_3 = 2,$$
$$2x_1 + 3x_2 + 4x_3 = 1,$$
$$x_1, x_2, x_3 \geq 0.$$

[*G.N.D.U. B.Com., April, 2008*]

(*Ans. Infeasible solution.*)

62. Maximize by the simplex method :

$$Z = 3x_1 + 2x_2 + 2x_3,$$
subject to
$$5x_1 + 7x_2 + 4x_3 \le 7,$$
$$4x_1 - 7x_2 - 5x_3 \le 2,$$
$$3x_1 + 4x_2 - 6x_3 \ge 3,$$
$$x_1, x_2, x_3 \ge 0.$$

[*P.U.B. E. (Mech.) 1998*]

(*Ans.* $x_1 = 0$, $x_2 = \frac{27}{29}$, $x_3 = \frac{7}{58}$; $Z_{max} = \frac{61}{29}$.)

63. Solve the following problem :

Maximize $Z = x_1 + 2x_2 + 3x_3$,
subject to
$$x_1 - x_2 + x_3 \ge 4,$$
$$x_1 + x_2 + 2x_3 \le 8,$$
$$x_1 - x_3 \ge 2,$$
$$x_1, x_2, x_3 \ge 0.$$

[*G.N.D.U. B.Com., April, 2011; April, 2010; P.U.B.Com. April, 2010; B.E. (Mech.) 2000*]

(*Ans.* $x_1 = \frac{18}{5}$, $x_2 = \frac{6}{5}$, $x_3 = \frac{8}{5}$; $Z_{max} = \frac{54}{5}$.)

64. Maximize $Z = 4x_1 + 3x_2 + 5x_3$,
subject to
$$x_1 + 3x_2 + 2x_3 \le 10,$$
$$2x_1 + 2x_2 + x_3 \ge 6,$$
$$x_1 + 2x_2 + 3x_3 = 14,$$
$$x_1, x_2, x_3 \ge 0.$$

[*P.U.M.E. (Mech.) 1996*]

65. Solve by the big M-method :

Maximize $Z = 4x_1 + 5x_2 - 3x_3$,
subject to
$$x_1 + x_2 + x_3 = 10,$$
$$x_1 - x_2 \ge 1,$$
$$2x_1 + 3x_2 + x_3 \le 40,$$
$$x_1, x_2, x_3 \ge 0.$$

[*G.N.D.U. B.Com., Sept., 2007; R.T.M. Nagpur U.B. Tech. Dec., 2004; Dayalbagh Edu. Inst. Agra MBA May, 2005*]

(*Ans.* $x_1 = x_1 = 11/2$, $x_2 = 9/2$, $x_3 = 0$; $Z_{max} = 44.5$.)

66. Solve by the simplex method :

Minimize $Z = 4x_1 - 3x_2 + 7x_3 - x_4$,
subject to
$$7x_1 + 3x_2 \le 400,$$
$$5x_1 + 4x_3 \ge 250,$$
$$x_1 + x_4 = 43,$$

x_1, x_2, x_3 and x_4 are non-negative and none is below 20.

[**Hint.** Let $x_1 = 20 + x$, $x_2 = 20 + y$, $x_3 = 20 + z$, $x_4 = 20 + t$. Substitute the values in the model and then solve.]

67. Solve the following L.P.P. by the simplex method :

Maximize $Z = 40x_1 + 35x_2$,
subject to
$$2x_1 + 3x_2 \le 60,$$
$$4x_1 + 3x_2 \le 96,$$
$$x_1 \ge 10,$$
$$x_2 \ge 5.$$

[**Hint.** Substitute $x_1 = 10 + x$, $x_2 = 5 + y$ in the model and then solve.]

(*Ans.* $x_1 = 18$, $x_2 = 8$; $Z_{max} = 1{,}000$.)

68. Maximize $Z = 3x_1 + 5x_2 + 4x_3$,
subject to
$$x_1 + x_2 + x_3 = 10,$$
$$2x_1 + x_2 + 2x_3 \ge 16,$$
$$x_1 + 4x_2 + 3x_3 \le 24,$$
$$x_1, x_2, x_3 \ge 0.$$

[*P.U.M.E. (Mech.) May, 1995*]

69. Show two iterations of the simplex algorithm to solve the following problem :

Maximize $Z = 3x_1 + x_2 + 4x_3$,
subject to $3x_1 + x_2 + 2x_3 = 32$,
$2x_1 + 3x_2 + x_3 \le 44$,
$x_1 + x_2 + 3x_3 \le 36$,
$x_1 \ge 2,\ x_2 \ge 2,\ x_3 \ge 2$.

[Hint. Put $x_1 = 2 + x$, $x_2 = 2 + y$, $x_3 = 2 + z$ in the model and then solve.]

70. Solve the following L.P.P. by the simplex method :

Minimize $Z = 3x_1 + 4x_2 + 5x_3$,
subject to $x_1 + x_2 + 2x_3 \ge 30$,
$2x_1 + x_2 + x_3 \ge 35$,
$x_1, x_2, x_3 \ge 0$.

Identify the basic and non-basic variables in the final solution. What are the base row coefficients of non-basic variables ? How are they useful for sensitivity analysis ?

[P.T.U. MBA June, 2001]

71. Solve the following L.P. problem by Big M-method:

Maximize $Z = 2x_1 + 3x_2 + 4x_3$,
subject to $3x_1 + x_2 + 4x_3 \le 600$,
$2x_1 + 4x_2 + 2x_3 \ge 480$,
$2x_1 + 3x_2 + 3x_3 = 540$,
$x_1, x_2, x_3 \ge 0$.

[G.N.D.U. B.Com., Sept., 2013; V.T.U. Karnataka B.E. June, 2011]

72. Use the Big M-method to solve the following L.P. problem:

Maximize $Z = 2x_1 + x_2 + 3x_3$,
subject to the constraints
$x_1 + x_2 + 2x_3 \le 5$,
$2x_1 + 3x_2 + 4x_3 = 12$,
and $x_1, x_2, x_3 \ge 0$.

[R.T.M. Nagpur B.E. (Mech.) Dec., 2008]

73. Solve the following L.P. problem by simplex method:

Minimize $Z = 5x_1 + 3x_2$,
subject to the constraints
$2x_1 + 4x_2 \le 12$,
$2x_1 + 2x_2 = 10$,
$5x_1 + 2x_2 \ge 10$ and $x_1, x_2 \ge 0$.

[R.T.M. Nagpur U.B.Tech. (Mech.) June, 2007]

74. Use Big M-method to solve the following L.P. problem:

Maximize $Z = 2x_1 + x_2$,
subject to constraints
$x_1 + x_2 \ge 15$,
$2x_1 + 3x_2 \ge 24$,
and $x_1, x_2 \ge 0$.

[R.T.M. Nagpur U.B. Tech. Dec., 2005]

75. Minimize using simplex method:

$C = 12x_1 + 20x_2 + 18x_3$,
subject to $4x_2 + 6x_1 + 8x_3 \ge 100$,
$3x_3 + 7x_1 + 12x_2 \ge 120$,
$5x_3 + 4x_1 + 3x_2 \ge 80$,
$x_1, x_2, x_3 \ge 0$.

[R.T.M. Nagpur U.B. Tech. Dec., 2004]

76. (a) With reference to the solution of L.P.P by simplex method/table, when do you conclude as follows: (i) LPP has no limit for the improvement of the objective function (ii) L.P.P. has no feasible solution.

[V.T.U. Karnataka B.E. Jan., 2010]

(b) Use simplex method to solve the following L.P.P. :

Minimize $Z = 20x_1 + 10x_2$,

subject to $x_1 + x_2 \le 40,$
$3x_1 + x_2 \ge 30,$
$4x_1 + 3x_2 \ge 60,$
$x_1, x_2 \ge 0.$

[Osmania U. MBA, 2010]
(Ans. $x_1 = 6, x_2 = 12; Z_{min} = 240.$*)*

77. Use the two-phase method to

minimize $Z = x_1 + x_2,$
subject to $2x_1 + x_2 \ge 4,$
$x_1 + 7x_2 \ge 7,$
$x_1, x_2 \ge 0.$

[Univ. of Madras B.Sc. (Math.) Nov., 2012]
(Ans. $x_1 = \frac{21}{13}, x_2 = \frac{10}{13}; Z_{max} = \frac{31}{13}.$*)*

78. Solve the following linear programming problem, using the two phases of the simplex method :

Minimize $Z = 2x_1 + x_2,$
subject to $5x_1 + 10x_2 - x_3 = 8,$
$x_1 + x_2 + x_4 = 1,$
and x_1, x_2, x_3, x_4, all $\ge 0.$

(Ans. $x_1 = 0, x_2 = \frac{4}{5}, x_3 = 0, x_4 = \frac{1}{5}; Z_{min} = \frac{4}{5}.$*)*

79. Solve the following problem using the two-phase simplex method :

Minimize $Z = 8x_1 + 4x_2 + 2x_3,$
subject to $4x_1 + 2x_2 + x_3 \le 8,$
$3x_1 + 2x_2 \le 10,$
$x_1 + x_2 + x_3 \ge 4,$
$x_1, x_2, x_3 \ge 0.$

[H.P.U.B.Tech. (Mech.) Nov., 2010]

80. Using the two-phase method,

maximize $Z = 5x - 2y + 3z,$
subject to $2x + 2y - z \ge 2,$
$3x - 4y \le 3,$
$y + 3z \le 5,$
where $x, y, z \ge 0.$

[G.N.D.U. B.Com., 1999]
(Ans. $x = \frac{23}{3}, y = 5, z = 0; Z_{max} = \frac{85}{3}.$*)*

81. Solve the following problem by the two-phase method :

Minimize $Z = -x_1 - x_2,$
subject to $x_1 - x_2 - x_3 = 1,$
$-x_1 + x_2 + 2x_3 - x_4 = 1,$
$x_j \ge 0 \,;\, j = 1, 2, 3, 4.$

[P.U.B.E. (Mech.) Dec., 2012 (C.S. & E.) Dec., 2004]
(Ans. Unbounded solution.*)*

82. Minimize $Z = \frac{15}{2}x_1 - 3x_2,$

subject to the constraints
$3x_1 - x_2 - x_3 \ge 3,$
$x_1 - x_2 + x_3 \ge 2,$
$x_1, x_2, x_3 \ge 0.$

Use the two-phase method.

[Roorkee M.Sc. (Math.) 1974]
(Ans. $x_1 = \frac{5}{4}, x_2 = 0, x_3 = \frac{3}{4}; Z_{min} = \frac{75}{8}.$*)*

83. Solve the following L.P. problem using two-phase method :

Minimize $Z = 12x_1 + 18x_2 + 15x_3$,

subject to $4x_1 + 8x_2 + 6x_3 \geq 64$,

$3x_1 + 6x_2 + 12x_3 \geq 96$,

$x_1, x_2, x_3 \geq 0$. *[Chennai U.B.C.A. Nov., 2010]*

84. Minimize $Z = 2x_1 + 3x_2 + 2x_3 - x_4 + x_5$,

subject to the constraints

$3x_1 - 3x_2 + 4x_3 + 2x_4 - x_5 = 0$,

$x_1 + x_2 + x_3 + 3x_4 + x_5 = 2$,

and $x_j \geq 0, j = 1$ to 5.

(*Ans.* $x_1 = x_2 = x_3 = 0, x_4 = \frac{2}{5}, x_5 = \frac{4}{5}; Z_{min} = \frac{2}{5}$.)

85. Use the two-phase method to solve the problem :

Minimize $Z = x_1 - 2x_2 - 3x_3$,

subject to $-2x_1 + x_2 + 3x_3 = 2$,

$2x_1 + 3x_2 + 4x_3 = 1$,

$x_1, x_2, x_3 \geq 0$.

[J.N.T.U. Hyderabad B.Tech. May, 2011; G.N.D.U. B.Com., 2008]

(*Ans. Infeasible solution.*)

86. A company manufactures three types of leather belts, namely A, B and C. The unit profits from these three varieties are ₹ 10, ₹ 5 and ₹ 7 respectively. Leather is sufficient for only 800 belts per day (all types together). Belt A requires thrice the time of belt B and belt C requires twice the time of B. If all the belts of type B are produced, a maximum of 1,000 belts per day can be produced. Belt A requires a fancy buckle and 150 such buckles per day are available. There are sufficient number of buckles for the other varieties. Determine how many belts of each type be produced to maximize the total profit.

(*Ans.* Max $Z = 10x_1 + 5x_2 + 7x_3$,

subject to $x_1 + x_2 + x_3 \leq 800$,

$3x_1 + x_2 + 2x_3 \leq 1{,}000$,

$x_1 \leq 150$,

$x_1, x_2, x_3 \geq 0$.)

87. Suppose an L.P.P. is given by

Maximize $Z = CX$,

subject to $AX = B$,

where $C = (c_1, c_2, c_3, ...)$,

$X = (x_1, x_2, x_3, ...)'$,

A = the coefficient matrix,

$B = (b_1, b_2, b_3, ...)'$,

$X_j \geq 0$.

What is the basic feasible solution ? How does the simplex algorithm find the leaving variable and the entering variable to find a new basis ?

How does the simplex method find the value of Z for any set of basic variables ?

[P.U.M.E. (Mech.) 1996]

88. A factory works 8 hours a day, producing three products viz. A, B and C. Each of these products is processed in three different operations viz. 1, 2 and 3. The processing times in minutes for each of these products in each of the operations are given below along with utilisation of the processes and the cost and price in rupees for each of these three products which have unlimited demand.

Product	*Processing time (min) in operation*			*Cost/unit*	*Price/unit*
	1	2	3	(₹)	(₹)
A	4	3	1	10	16
B	2	1	4	8	12
C	3	4	5	5	10
Utilisation	80%	70%	90%		

(*i*) Determine the optimal product mix using the simplex method.

(*ii*) Give the interpretations for the values obtained in the final simplex table. [*ICWA, 1996*]

89. Food X contains 6 units of Vitamin A per gram and 7 units of Vitamin B per gram and costs 12 paise per gram. Food Y contains 8 units of Vitamin A per gram and 12 units of Vitamin B and costs 20 paise per gram. The daily minimum requirements of Vitamin A and Vitamin B are 100 units and 120 units respectively. Find the minimum cost of product mix. Use simplex method.

[*J.N.T.U. Hyderabad B. Tech. (C.Sc.) Dec., 2011*]

90. Sainath & Co. manufactures two brands of a product, namely Shivnath and Harinath. Both these models have to undergo the operations on three machines, lathe, milling and grinding. Each unit of Shivnath gives a profit of ₹ 45 and requires 2 hours on lathe, 3 hours on milling and 1 hour on grinding. Each unit of Harinath can give a profit of ₹ 70 and requires 5, 5, and 4 hours on lathe, milling and grinding respectively. Due to prior commitment, the use of lathe hours is restricted to a maximum of 70 in a week. The operators to operate milling machines are hired for 120 hours/week. Due to scarce availability of skilled manpower for grinding machine, the grinding hours are limited to 100 hours/week. Formulate the data into an LPP and solve. [*J.N.T.U. Hyderabad B. Tech. (C.Sc.) Dec., 2011*]

91. A person requires 10,12 and 12 units of chemicals A, B and C respectively for his garden. A liquid product contains 5, 2 and one units of A, B and C respectively per jar. A dry product contains 1, 2 and 4 units of A, B and C per carton. If the liquid product sells for ₹ 3 per jar and the dry product sells for ₹ 2 per carton, how many of each should be purchased to minimize the cost and meet the requirements?

[*R.T.M. Nagpur U.B. Tech. (Mech.) Dec., 2006*]

92. A firm makes two types of furniture : chairs and tables. The contribution to profit by each product as calculated by the accounting department is ₹ 20 per chair and ₹ 30 per table. Both products are to be processed on three machine M_1, M_2, and M_3. The time required in hours by each product and total time available in hours per week on each machine are as follows:

Machine	*Chair*	*Table*	*Available time (Hr)*
M_1	3	3	36
M_2	5	2	50
M_3	2	6	60

How should the manufacturer schedule his production in order to maximize profit ?

[*R.T.M. Nagpur U.B.Tech. June, 2005*]

93. A firm uses lathes, milling machines and grinding machines to produce two machine parts. The table below represents the machining times required for each part, the machining times available on different machines and the profit on each machine part:

Type of machine	*Machining time required for the machine part (minutes)*		*Maximum time available per week (minutes)*
	I	*II*	
Lathes	12	6	3,000
Milling machines	4	10	2,000
Grinding machines	2	3	900
Profit per unit	₹ 40	₹ 100	

Using graphical method, find the number of parts I and II to be manufactured per week to maximize the profit.

[*R.T.M. Nagpur U.B. Tech. June., 2006*]

94. A company possesses two manufacturing plants, each of which can produce three products X, Y & Z from a common raw material. However, the proportions in which the products are produced are different in each plant and so are the plant operating costs per hour. Data on production per hour and costs are given below, together with current orders in hand for each product. You are required to use graphical method to find out the number of production hours needed to fulfil the orders on hand at minimum cost.

Plant	Products			Operating cost per hour (₹)
	X	Y	Z	
A	2	4	3	9
B	4	3	2	10
Orders in hand	50	24	60	

[*R.T.M. Nagpur U.B. Tech. June, 2005*]

95. A manufacturing firm produces two machine parts P_1 and P_2 using milling and grinding machines. The different machining times required for each part, the machining times available on different machines and the profit on each machine part are as given below:

Machine	*Manufacturing time required (minutes)*		*Maximum time available per week (minutes)*
Lathe	10	5	2,500
Milling machine	4	10	2,000
Grinding machine	1	1.5	450
Profit per unit (₹)	50	100	

Determine the number of pieces of P_1 and P_2 to be manufactured per week to maximize profit.

[*R.T.M. Nagpur U.B. Tech. Dec., 2003*]

96. A firm has 240, 370 and 180 kg of wood, plastic and steel respectively. The firm produces two products A and B. Each unit of A requires 1, 3 and 2 kg of wood, plastic and steel respectively. The corresponding requirement for each unit of B is 3, 4 and 1 kg respectively. If A sells for ₹ 4 and B sells for ₹ 6 per unit, what product mix should the firm produce to have maximum gross income ? Formulate this as L.P.P. and solve. [*G.N.D.U. B.Com. April, 2004*]

(*Ans.* Maximize $Z = 4x_1 + 6x_2$,
subject to $x_1 + 3x_2 \le 240$,
$3x_1 + 4x_2 \le 370$,
$2x_1 + x_2 \le 180$,
$x_1, x_2 \ge 0$;
$x_1 = 30, x_2 = 70; Z_{max} =$ ₹ 540.)

97. Diet for a sick person must contain at least 4,000 units of vitamins, 50 units of minerals and 1,400 calories. Two foods A and B are available at a cost of ₹ 4 and ₹ 3 per unit respectively. If one unit of A contains 200 units of vitamins, 1 unit of mineral and 40 calories and one unit of B contains 100 units of vitamins, 2 units of minerals and 40 calories, what combination of foods be used to have the least cost? [*G.N.D.U. B.Com. April, 2010*]

(*Ans.* Minimize $Z =$ ₹ $(4x_1 + 3x_2)$,
subject to $200x_1 + 100x_2 \ge 4{,}000$,
$x_1 + 2x_2 \ge 50$,
$40x_1 + 40x_2 \ge 1{,}400$,
$x_1, x_2 \ge 0$;
$x_1 = 5, x_2 = 30; Z_{min} =$ ₹ 110.)

98. An advertising agency wishes to reach two types of audiences: customers with monthly income greater than ₹ 15,000 (target audience A) and customers with monthly income less than ₹ 15,000 (target audience B). The total advertising budget is ₹ 2,00,000. One programme of T.V. advertising costs ₹ 50,000; while one programme of radio advertising costs ₹ 20,000. For contract reasons, at least 3 programmes ought to be on T.V. and the number of radio programmes must be limited to 5. Surveys indicate that a single T.V. programme reaches 4,50,000 customers in target audience A and 50,000 in target audience B. One radio programme reaches 20,000 in target audience A and 80,000 in target audience B. Determine the media mix to maximize the total reach.

[*R.T.M. Nagpur U.B. Tech. Dec., 2005*]

(*Ans.* Maximize $Z = 5{,}00{,}000\ x_1 + 1{,}00{,}000\ x_2$,
subject to $50{,}000\ x_1 + 20{,}000\ x_2 \le 2{,}00{,}000$
$x_1 \ge 3$,
$x_2 \le 5$,
$x_1, x_2 \ge 0$;
$x_1 = 4,\ x_2 = 0;\ Z_{max} = 20{,}00{,}000$.)

99. XYZ company makes three different types of boats. All can be made profitably in this company, but the company's monthly production is constrained by the limited amount of labour, wood and screws available each month. The director will choose the combination of boats that maximizes the revenue in view of the information given in the following table:

Input	*Row boat*	*Canoe*	*Kayak*	*Monthly availability*
Labour	12	7	9	1,260 hours
Wood	22	18	16	19,008 board feet
Screws	2	4	3	396 kg
Selling price (₹)	4,000	2,000	5,000	

(i) Formulate the above problem as a linear programming problem.
(ii) Solve by simplex method and find the optimal solution.
(iii) How many kilograms of screws will be used to make all the boats given in the optimal solution?

[*Mumbai U. MBA, 2010*]

(*Ans.* (i) Maximize $Z = 4{,}000\ x_1 + 2{,}000\ x_2 + 5{,}000\ x_3$,
subject to $12x_1 + 7x_2 + 9x_3 \le 1{,}260$,
$22x_1 + 18x_2 + 16x_3 \le 19{,}008$,
$2x_1 + 4x_2 + 3x_3 \le 396$,
$x_1, x_2 \ge 0$;
(ii) $x_1 = 12,\ x_2 = 0,\ x_3 = 124;\ Z_{max}$ = ₹ 6,68,000.
(iii) 396 kg.)

100. Govt. has chosen three celebrities to appeal to public on T.V. for collecting money for a cancer hospital. Kapil, Sachin and Sushmita are to appeal on T.V. Kapil wants that he be given double the time than Sachin. Total time taken by Kapil and Sachin must be at least twice the time taken by Sushmita. Based on a pre-show survey it is believed that 40, 50 and 60 thousand viewers will watch the program for each minute of Kapil, Sachin and Susmita. If total time of the show is 30 minutes and 3 minutes are for direct requests to viewers, find the time alloted to each to get maximum number of viewers.

[*P.U.B.E. (Elect.) 1999*]

(*Ans.* Max Z = $10^4\ (4t_1 + 5t_2 + 6t_3)$,
subject to $t_1 = 2t_2$ or $t_1 - 2t_2 = 0$,
$t_1 + t_2 \ge 2t_3$ or $t_1 + t_2 - 2t_3 \ge 0$,
$t_1 + t_2 + t_3 \le 30 - 3$ or $t_1 + t_2 + t_3 \le 27$,
$t_1,\ t_2,\ t_3 \ge 0$;
$t_1 = 12$ min, $t_2 = 6$ min, $t_3 = 9$ min.)

101. Three types of cutting tools are produced in a factory using a lathe, a grinder and a polisher. The duration in hours required to produce one batch of tools on each of these machines are given in the following table along with costs, selling prices of each batch of tools and the minimum number of hours available on each machine per week.

Tool type	*Processing time (hr) per batch on a*			*Cost (₹) per batch*	*Selling prices (₹) per batch*
	Lathe	*Grinder*	*Polisher*		
A	7	2	5	100	145

B	3	3	8	65	100
C	4	4	2	80	120
Max. hr per week	50	40	80		

(*i*) Determine the optimum production schedule and maximum profit per week.

(*ii*) The factory wants to double the capacity of grinder at an additional cost of ₹ 50 per week. Should it go for it ? Substantiate your result.

[*I.C.W.A. (Final) June, 1993*]

102. A pharmaceutical company produces two popular drugs A and B which are sold at the rate of ₹ 9.60 and ₹ 7.80 respectively. The main ingredients are *x*, *y* and *z* and they are required in the following proportions :

Drugs	*x%*	*y%*	*z%*
A	50	30	20
B	30	30	40

The total available quantities (gm) of different ingredients are 1,600 in *x*, 1,400 in *y* and 1,200 in *z*. The costs of *x*, *y* and *z* per gm are ₹ 8, ₹ 6 and ₹ 4 respectively. Estimate the most profitable quantities of A and B to produce, using the simplex method.

[*I.C.W.A. (Final) 1994*]

(*Ans.* Max $Z = \{9.60 - (8 \times .5 + 6 \times .3 + 4 \times .2)\}.x_1$
$+ \{7.80 - (8 \times .3 + 6 \times .3 + 4 \times .4)\}.x_2$
$= 3x_1 + 2x_2,$

subject to $0.5x_1 + 0.3x_2 \le 1{,}600,$
$0.3x_1 + 0.3x_2 \le 1{,}400,$
$0.2x_1 + 0.4x_2 \le 1{,}200,$
$x_1, x_2 \ge 0;$
$x_1 = 2{,}000,\ x_2 = 2{,}000;\ Z_{max} =$ ₹ 10,000.)

103. A firm produces three products. These products are processed on three different machines. The time required to manufacture one unit of each of the three products and the daily capacity of the three machines are given in table 2.104 below.

TABLE 2.104

Machine	*Time per unit (minutes)*			*Machine capacity (minutes/day)*
	Product 1	*Product 2*	*Product 3*	
M_1	2	3	2	440
M_2	4	—	3	470
M_3	2	5	—	430

It is required to determine the daily number of units to be manufactured for each product. The profit per unit for products 1, 2 and 3 is ₹ 4, ₹ 3 and ₹ 6 respectively. It is assumed that all the amounts produced are consumed in the market.

[*P.U. B.Com. April, 2008; (Mech.) 1977, 79*]

(*Ans.* $x_1 = 0,\ x_2 = \frac{380}{9},\ x_3 = \frac{470}{3};\ Z_{max} =$ ₹ 1,066.67.)

104. A company has the option of using one or more of different types of production processes. The first and second processes result in product P_1, while third and fourth result in product P_2. For each process, input (resources) are

(*i*) labour measured in man-weeks,

(*ii*) kg of materials, K and

(*iii*) boxes of materials, B.

As each process varies in its input requirements, the profits obtained for each process are different even for processes producing the same item. The amounts of manpower and both kinds of materials are limited. The data are given in table 2.105.

TABLE 2.105

Item	One unit of product P_1		One unit of product P_2		Total available resources
	Process 1	Process 2	Process 3	Process 4	
Man-weeks	1	1	1	1	15 (max.)
Kg of materials, K	7	5	3	3	120 (max.)
Boxes of materials, B	3	5	10	15	100 (max.)
Unit profit (₹)	4	5	9	11	

What is the optimum production level of each process to get maximum profit ?

(*Ans.* $x_1 = \frac{50}{7}, x_2 = 0, x_3 = \frac{55}{7}, x_4 = 0; Z_{max} = ₹\ \frac{695}{7}$.)

105. A firm manufactures three products P_1, P_2 and P_3. The minimum number of units of P_1, P_2 and P_3 that must be produced are 100, 200 and 150 respectively. These products require two types of raw materials M_1 and M_2 which the firm can purchase upto a maximum of 500 and 400 units respectively. Design a production plan so as to maximize the profit if the respective individual profits of P_1, P_2 and P_3 are ₹ 2, ₹ 5 and ₹ 4 respectively. Consumption of raw materials is shown below.

TABLE 2.106

Raw material	Consumption of raw materials per unit product		
	P_1	P_2	P_3
M_1	$\frac{1}{2}$	1	1
M_2	2	$\frac{1}{2}$	$\frac{1}{5}$

(*Ans.* $x_1 = 100, x_2 = 300, x_3 = 150; Z_{max} = ₹\ 2{,}300$.)

[**Hint.** Maximize $Z = 2x_1 + 5x_2 + 4x_3$,

subject to $\frac{x_1}{2} + x_2 + x_3 \le 500$,

$2x_1 + \frac{x_2}{2} + \frac{x_3}{5} \le 400$,

$x_1 \ge 100$,

$x_2 \ge 200$,

$x_3 \ge 150$.]

106. A small scale industrialist produces four types of machine components M_1, M_2, M_3 and M_4 made of steel and brass. The amounts of steel and brass required for each component and the number of man-weeks of labour required to manufacture and assemble one unit of each component are as follows:

TABLE 2.107

	M_1	M_2	M_3	M_4	Availability
Steel	6	5	3	2	100 kg
Brass	3	4	9	2	75 kg
Man-weeks	1	2	1	2	20

The labour is restricted to 20 man-weeks, steel is restricted to 100 kg per week and brass to 75 kg per week. The industrialist's profit on each unit of M_1, M_2, M_3 and M_4 is ₹ 6, ₹ 4, ₹ 7 and ₹ 5 respectively. How many of each type of machine components should he produce to maximize his profit and how much is his profit ?

[*P.U.B.E. (Mech.) 1978*]

(*Ans.* $M_1 = 15, M_2 = 0, M_3 = \frac{10}{3}, M_4 = 0; Z_{max} =$ ₹ $\frac{340}{3}$ per week.)

107. A manufacturer of leather belts makes three types of belts A, B and C which are processed on three machines M_1, M_2 and M_3. Belt A requires 2 hours on machine M_1 and 3 hours on machine M_3. Belt B requires 3 hours on machine M_1, 2 hours on machine M_2, and 2 hours on machine M_3 and belt C requires 5 hours on machine M_2 and 4 hours on machine M_3. There are 8 hours of time per day available on machine M_1, 10 hours of time per day available on machine M_2 and 15 hours of time per day available on machine M_3. The profit gained from belt A is ₹ 3.00 per unit, from belt B is ₹ 5.00 per unit and from belt C is ₹ 4.00 per unit. What should be the daily production of each type of belt so that the profit is maximum ?

[*P.U.B.E. (Mech.) 1979*]

(*Ans.* $A = \frac{89}{41}, B = \frac{50}{41}$ and $C = \frac{62}{41}; Z_{max} = \frac{765}{41}$.)

108. A manufacturer produces three products A, B and C. Each product requires processing on two machines I and II. The time required to produce one unit of each product on a machine is

Product	*Time to produce one unit (hr)*	
	Machine I	*Machine II*
A	0.5	0.6
B	0.7	0.8
C	0.9	1.05

There are 850 hours available on each machine. The operating cost is ₹ 5/hr for machine I and ₹ 4/hr for machine II. The market requirements are at least 90 units of A, at least 80 units of B and at least 60 units of C. The manufacturer wishes to meet the requirements at minimum cost. Solve the problem by the simplex method.

[*Delhi M.B.A., 1975*]

[**Hint.** Minimize $Z = (0.5 \times 5 + 0.6 \times 4)x_A + (0.7 \times 5 + 0.8 \times 4)x_B + (0.9 \times 5 + 1.05 \times 4)x_C$

$= 4.9x_A + 6.7x_B + 8.7x_C,$

subject to $0.5x_A + 0.7x_B + 0.9x_C \le 850,$

$0.6x_A + 0.8x_B + 1.05x_C \le 850,$

$x_A \ge 90, x_B \ge 80, x_C \ge 60.$]

109. A factory has decided to diversify its activities. The data collected by sales and production departments is summarised below.

Potential demand exists for three products A, B and C. Market can take any amount of A and C whereas the share of B for this organisation is expected to be not more than 400 units a month. For every three units of C produced, there will be one unit of a by-product which sells at a contribution of ₹ 3 a unit and only 100 units of this by-product can be sold per month. Contribution per unit of products A, B and C is expected to be ₹ 6, ₹ 8 and ₹ 4 respectively.

These products require three different processes and the time required per unit product is given in the table below.

TABLE 2.108

Process	*Hours/unit*			*Available hours*
	Product A	*Product* B	*Product* C	
I	2	3	1	900
II	–	1	2	600
III	3	2	2	1,200

Determine the optimum product mix for maximizing the contribution.

[*Bombay Dip. Ind. Man., 1974*]

[**Hint.** Maximize $Z = 6x_A + 8x_B + 4x_C + \frac{x_C}{3} \times 3 = 6x_A + 8x_B + 5_{xC}$,

subject to
$$2x_A + 3x_B + x_C \leq 900,$$
$$x_B + 2x_C \leq 600,$$
$$3x_A + 2x_B + 2x_C \leq 1,200,$$
$$x_B \leq 400,$$
$$\frac{x_C}{3} \leq 100$$
or
$$x_C \leq 300,$$
$$x_A, x_B, x_C \geq 0.]$$

$$\left(Ans.\ x_A = \frac{1,800}{11}, x_B = \frac{1,200}{11}, x_C = \frac{2,700}{11}; Z_{\max} = ₹\frac{33,900}{11}.\right)$$

110. A company manufactures products A, B, C and D which are processed by planner, milling, drilling and assembly departments. The requirements per unit of product in hours and contribution are as follows:

TABLE 2.109

	Department				*Contribution/ unit*
	Planner	*Milling*	*Drilling*	*Assembly*	
Product A	0.5	2.0	0.5	3.0	₹ 8
Product B	1.0	1.0	0.5	1.0	₹ 9
Product C	1.0	1.0	1.0	2.0	₹ 7
Product D	0.5	1.0	1.0	3.0	₹ 6

Capacities of various departments and minimum sales requirements are

TABLE 2.110

Department	*Capacity (hours)*	*Minimum sales requirements*	
Planner	1,800	Product A	100 units
Milling	2,800	Product B	600 units
Drilling	3,000	Product C	500 units
Assembly	6,000	Product D	400 units

(*a*) Determine the number of products A, B, C and D to be manufactured to maximize production.
(*b*) Determine the total maximum contribution for products A, B, C and D.

(*c*) Determine the slack time in each department. [*P.U. M.Sc. (Math.) 1975*]

[**Hint.** Maximize $Z = 8x_1 + 9x_2 + 7x_3 + 6x_4$,

subject to
$$0.5x_1 - x_2 + x_3 + 0.5x_4 \le 1,800,$$
$$2x_1 + x_2 + x_3 + x_4 \le 2,800,$$
$$0.5x_1 + 0.5x_2 + x_3 + x_4 \le 3,000,$$
$$3x_1 + x_2 + 2x_3 + 3x_4 \le 6,000,$$
$$x_1 \ge 100,\ x_2 \ge 600,\ x_3 \ge 500,\ x_4 \ge 400.$$

Slack time in each deptt. is the value of slack variable for it.]

111. Maximize $Z = 8x_2$,

subject to
$$x_1 - x_2 \ge 0,$$
$$2x_1 + 3x_2 \le -6,$$
x_1, x_2 unrestricted. [*Meerut (Math.) 1993*]

(*Ans* $x_1 = -\frac{6}{5}, x_2 = -\frac{6}{5}; Z_{max} = -\frac{48}{5}$.)

112. Maximize $Z = 2x_1 + x_2 + 4x_3$,

subject to
$$-2x_1 + 4x_2 \le 4,$$
$$x_1 + 2x_2 + x_3 \ge 5,$$
$$2x_1 + 3x_3 \le 2,$$
$x_1, x_2 \ge 0$, x_3 unrestricted.

113. Maximize $Z = 2x_1 - 2x_2 + 3x_3$,

subject to
$$2x_1 + 3x_2 - x_3 \le 30,$$
$$3x_1 - 2x_2 + x_3 \le 24,$$
$$x_1 - 4x_2 - 6x_3 \ge 2,$$
$$x_1 \ge 0.$$

114. Minimize $Z = 4x_1 + 2x_2$,

subject to
$$3x_1 + x_2 \ge 27,$$
$$-x_1 - x_2 \le 21,$$
$$x_1 + 2x_2 \ge 30,$$
x_1 and x_2 unrestricted in sign.

[*G.N.D.U. B.Com. April, 2014, 2007*]

(*Ans.* $x_1 = \frac{24}{5}, x_2 = \frac{63}{5}; Z_{min} = \frac{222}{5}$.)

The Transportation Model

3.1 INTRODUCTION TO THE MODEL

In the previous chapter the general nature of the linear programming problem and its solution by the graphical, simplex and other methods was discussed. It was stated that the simplex algorithm could be used to solve any linear programming problem for which the solution exists. However, as the number of variables and constraints increase, the computation by this method becomes more and more laborious. Therefore, wherever possible, we try to simplify the calculations. One such model requiring simplified calculations is the *distribution model or the transportation model.* It deals with the transportation *of a product* available at several sources to a number of different destinations. The name "transportation model" is, however, misleading. This model can be used for a wide variety of situations such as scheduling, production, investment, plant location, inventory control, employment scheduling, personnel assignment, product mix problems and many others, so that the model is really not confined to transportation or distribution only.

The origin of transportation models dates back to 1941 when F.L. Hitchcock presented a study entitled 'The Distribution of a Product from Several Sources to Numerous Localities.' The presentation is regarded as the first important contribution to the solution of transportation problems. In 1947, T.C. Koopmans presented a study called 'Optimum Utilization of the Transportation System'. These two contributions are mainly responsible for the development of transportation models which involve a number of shipping sources and a number of destinations. Each shipping source has a certain capacity and each destination has a certain requirement associated with a certain cost of shipping from the sources to the destinations. The objective is to minimize the cost of transportation while meeting the requirements at the destinations. Transportation problems may also involve movement of a product from plants to warehouses, warehouses to wholesalers, wholsalers to retailers and retailers to customers.

3.2 ASSUMPTIONS IN THE TRANSPORTATION MODEL

1. Total quantity of the item available at different sources is equal to the total requirement at different destinations.
2. Item can be transported conveniently from all sources to destinations.
3. The unit transportation cost of the item from all sources to destinations is certainly and pecisely known.
4. The transportation cost on a given route is directly proportional to the number of units shipped on that route.
5. The objective is to minimize the total transportation cost for the organisation as a whole and not for individual supply and distribution centres.

3.3 DEFINITION OF THE TRANSPORTATION MODEL

Transportation models deal with problems concerning as to what happens to the effectiveness function when we associate each of a number of origins (sources) with each of a possibly different number of destinations (jobs). The total movement from each origin and the total movement to each destination is given and it is desired to find how the associations be made subject to the limitations on totals. In such problems, sources can be divided among the jobs or jobs may be done with a combination of sources. The distinct feature of transportation problems is that sources and jobs must be expressed in terms of *only one kind of unit.*

Suppose that there are m sources and n destinations. Let a_i be the number of supply units available at source $i(i = 1, 2, 3, \ldots, m)$ and let b_j be the number of demand units required at destination $j(j = 1, 2, 3, \ldots, n)$. Let c_{ij} represent the unit transportation cost for transportating the units from source i to destination j. The objective is to determine the number of units to be transported from source i to destination j so that the total transportation cost is minimum. In addition, the supply limits at the sources and the demand requirements at the destinations must be satisfied exactly.

If $x_{ij}(x_{ij} \geq 0)$ is the number of units shipped from source i to destination j, then the *equivalent linear programming model* will be

Find $x_{ij}(i = 1, 2, 3, \ldots, m; j = 1, 2, 3, \ldots, n)$ in order to

minimize $$Z = \sum_{i=1}^{m} \sum_{j=1}^{n} c_{ij} x_{ij},$$

subject to $$\sum_{j=1}^{n} x_{ij} = a_i, \quad i = 1, 2, 3, \ldots, m,$$

and $$\sum_{i=1}^{m} x_{ij} = b_j, \quad j = 1, 2, 3, \ldots, n,$$

where $$x_{ij} \geq 0.$$

The two sets of constraints will be consistent *i.e.*, the system will be in balance if

$$\sum_{i=1}^{m} a_i = \sum_{j=1}^{n} b_j.$$

Equality sign of the constraints causes one of the constraints to be redundant (and hence it can be deleted) so that the problem will have $(m + n - 1)$ constraints and $(m \times n)$ unknowns.

Note that a transportation problem will have a *feasible solution* only if the above restriction is satisfied. Thus, $\sum_{i=1}^{m} a_i = \sum_{j=1}^{n} b_j$ *is necessary as well as a sufficient condition* for a transportation problem to have a feasible solution. Problems that satisfy this condition are called *balanced* transportation problems. Techniques have been developed for solving *balanced or standard* transportation problems only. It follows that any non-standard problem in which the supplies and demands do not balance, must be converted to a balanced tansportation problem before it can be solved. This conversion can be achieved by the use of a dummy source/destination.

The above information can be put in the form of a general matrix shown below:

TABLE 3.1

		Destinations 1	2	3	...*j*...	*n*	*Supply*
	1	C_{11} x_{11}	C_{12} x_{12}	C_{13} x_{13}	C_{1j} x_{1j}	C_{1n} x_{1n}	a_1
	2	C_{21} x_{21}	C_{22} x_{22}	C_{23} x_{23}	C_{2j} x_{2j}	C_{2n} x_{2n}	a_2
Sorces or Origins	3	C_{31} x_{31}	C_{32} x_{32}	C_{33} x_{33}	C_{3j} x_{3j}	C_{3n} x_{3n}	a_3
	⋮ *i*	C_{i1} x_{i2}	C_{i2} x_{i2}	C_{i3} x_{i3}	C_{ij} x_{ij}	C_{in} x_{in}	⋮ a_i
	⋮ *m*	C_{m1} x_{m1}	C_{m2} x_{m2}	C_{m3} x_{m3}	C_{mj} x_{mj}	C_{mn} x_{mn}	⋮ a_m
Demand		b_1	b_2	b_3	.... b_j	b_n	

In table 3.1, c_{ij}, $i = 1, 2, \ldots, m$; $j = 1, 2, \ldots, n$, is the unit shipping cost from the *i*th origin to *j*th destination, x_{ij} is the quantity shipped from the *i*th origin to *j*th destination, a_i is the supply available at origin *i* and b_j is the demand at destination *j*.

Definitions

A few terms used in connection with transportation models are defined below.

1. **Feasible Solution.** A feasible solution to a transportation problem is a set of non-negative allocations, x_{ij} that satisfies the rim (row and column) restrictions.
2. **Basic Feasible Solution.** A feasible solution to a transportation problem is said to be a basic feasible solution if it contains no more than $m + n - 1$ non-negative allocations, where *m* is the number of rows and *n* is the number of columns of the transportation problem.
3. **Optimal Solution.** A feasible solution (not necessarily basic) that minimizes (maximizes) the transportation cost (profit) is called an optimal solution.
4. **Non-degenerate Basic Feasible Solution.** A basic feasible solution to a $(m \times n)$ transportation problem is said to be non-degenerate if,
   (*a*) the total number of non-negative allocations is exactly $m + n - 1$ (*i.e.*, number of independent constraint equations), and
   (*b*) these $m + n - 1$ allocations are in independent positions.
5. **Degenerate Basic Feasible Solution.** A basic feasible solution in which the total number of non-negative allocations is less than $m + n - 1$ is called degenerate basic feasible solution.

3.4 MATRIX TERMINOLOGY

The matrix used in the transportation models consists of squares called 'cells', which when stacked form 'columns' vertically and 'rows' horizontally.

The cell located at the intersection of a row and a column is designated by its row and column headings. Thus the cell located at the intersection of row A and column 3 is called cell (A, 3). Unit costs are placed in each cell.

TABLE 3.2

	Warehouses 1	2	3	4	*Output*
Plants A	2	3	11	4	15
B	5	6	8	7	20
Demand	10	5	12	8	35 (*Total*)

3.5 FORMULATION AND SOLUTION OF TRANSPORTATION MODELS

In this section we shall consider a few examples which will make clear the technique of formulation and solution of transportation models.

EXAMPLE 3.5-1 (Transportation Problem)

A dairy firm has three plants located in a state. Daily milk production at each plant is as follows:

Plant 1 ... 6 million litres,
plant 2 ... 1 million litres, and
plant 3 ... 10 million litres.

Each day the firm must fulfil the needs of its four distribution centres. Milk requirement at each centre is as follows:

Distribution centre 1 ... 7 million litres,
distribution centre 2 ... 5 million litres,
distribution centre 3 ... 3 million litres, and
distribution centre 4 ... 2 million litres.

Cost of shipping one million litres of milk from each plant to each distribution centre is given in the following table in hundreds of rupees:

TABLE 3.3

		Distribution centres			
		1	*2*	*3*	*4*
	1	*2*	*3*	*11*	*7*
Plants	*2*	*1*	*0*	*6*	*1*
	3	*5*	*8*	*15*	*9*

(*i*) *Show that the problem represents a network situation.*
(*ii*) *Formulate the mathematical model for the problem.*
(*iii*) *The dairy firm wishes to determine as to how much should be the shipment from which milk plant to which distribution centre so that the total cost of shipment is the minimum. Determine the optimal transportation policy.*

[*Chennai U., 2002; NIIFT Mohali, 2000*]

Solution. (*i*) Let us represent the example graphically:

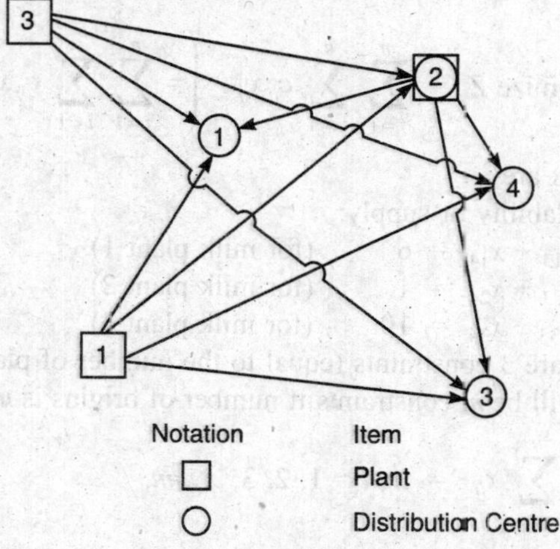

Fig. 3.1

We find that the above situation takes the shape of a network.

(*ii*) Formulation of Model

Step 1:

Key decision to be made is to find how much quantity of milk from which plant to which distribution centre be shipped so as to satisfy the constraints and minimize the cost. Thus the variables in the situation are: $x_{11}, x_{12}, x_{13}, x_{14}, x_{21}, x_{22}, x_{23}, x_{24}, x_{31}, x_{32}, x_{33}$ and x_{34}. These variables represent the quantities of milk to be shipped from different plants to different distribution centres and can be represented in the form of a matrix shown below:

TABLE 3.4

		Distribution centres			
		1	2	3	4
	1	x_{11}	x_{12}	x_{13}	x_{14}
Plants	2	x_{21}	x_{22}	x_{23}	x_{24}
	3	x_{31}	x_{32}	x_{33}	x_{34}

In general, we can say that the key decision to be made is to find the quantity of units to be transported from each origin to each destination. Thus, if there are m origins and n destinations, then x_{ij} are the decision variables (quantities to be found), where

$$i = 1, 2, \ldots, m,$$

and
$$j = 1, 2, \ldots, n.$$

Step 2:

Feasible alternatives are sets of values of x_{ij}, where $x_{ij} \geq 0$.

Step 3:

Objective is to minimize the cost of transportation.

i.e., minimize
$$\begin{aligned} Z = {} & 2x_{11} + 3x_{12} + 11x_{13} + 7x_{14} \\ & + x_{21} + 0x_{22} + 6x_{23} + x_{24} \\ & + 5x_{31} + 8x_{32} + 15x_{33} + 9x_{34}. \end{aligned}$$

In general, we can say that if c_{ij} is the unit cost of shipping from ith source to jth destination, the objective is

$$\text{minimize } Z = \sum_{i=1}^{m} \sum_{j=1}^{n} c_{ij} x_{ij} \quad \left(= \sum_{j=1}^{n} \sum_{i=1}^{m} c_{ij} x_{ij} \right).$$

Step 4: *Constraints* are

(*i*) because of availability or supply:

$$x_{11} + x_{12} + x_{13} + x_{14} = 6, \quad \text{(for milk plant 1)}$$
$$x_{21} + x_{22} + x_{23} + x_{24} = 1, \quad \text{(for milk plant 2)}$$
$$x_{31} + x_{32} + x_{33} + x_{34} = 10. \quad \text{(for milk plant 3)}$$

Thus, in all, there are 3 constraints (equal to the number of plants).

In general, there will be m constraints if number of origins is m, which can be expressed as

$$\sum_{j=1}^{n} x_{ij} = a_i, \; i = 1, 2, 3, \ldots, m.$$

(*ii*) because of requirement or demand:

$$x_{11} + x_{21} + x_{31} = 7, \quad \text{(for distribution centre 1)}$$
$$x_{12} + x_{22} + x_{32} = 5, \quad \text{(for distribution centre 2)}$$
$$x_{13} + x_{23} + x_{33} = 3, \quad \text{(for distribution centre 3)}$$
$$x_{14} + x_{24} + x_{34} = 2. \quad \text{(for distribution centre 4)}$$

In general, there are n constraints if the number of destinations is n, which can be expressed as

$$\sum_{i=1}^{m} x_{ij} = b_j, j = 1, 2, 3, \ldots, n.$$

Thus we find that the given situation involves (3 × 4 = 12) variables and (3 + 4 = 7) constraints. *In general*, such a situation will involve ($m \times n$) variables and ($m + n$) constraints. However, because the transportation model is always balanced, one of these constraints must be redundant. Thus, the model has $m + n - 1$ independent constraint equations, which means that the starting basic feasible solution consists of $m + n - 1$ basic variables.

It can be easily seen that in this model the objective function as well as the constraints are linear functions of the variables and, therefore, the model is a linear programming model and can be solved by simplex method. However, as a large number of variables are involved, computations required will be much more. The following points may be noted in a transportation model:

1. All supply as well as demand constraints are of equality type.
2. They are expressed in terms of only one kind of unit (million litres of milk in this problem).
3. Each variable occurs only once in the supply constraints and only once in the demand constraints.
4. Each variable in the constraints has unit coefficient only.

Therefore, the transportation model is a *special case of general L.P. model* wherein the above four conditions hold good and can be solved by a special technique called the transportation technique which is easier and shorter than the simplex technique.

(*iii*) Solution of the Transportation Model

The solution involves making a transportation table (in the form of a matrix), finding a feasible solution, performing optimality test and iterating towards optimal solution if required.

Step I: Make a Transportation Table

This consists in expressing supply from origins, requirements at destinations and cost of shipping from origins to destinations in the form of a matrix shown below.

A check is made to find if total supply and demand are equal. If yes, the problem is said to be a *balanced or self contained or standard problem*. If not, a dummy origin or destination (as the case may be) is added to balance the supply and demand. Table 3.5 represents the transportation table for the given problem.

TABLE 3.5

Distribution centres (Destinations)

		1	2	3	4	*Supply*	
	1	2	3	11	7	6	Total supply = 6 + 1 + 10 = 17
Plants (Origins)	2	1	0	6	1	1	
	3	5	8	15	9	10	Total requirement = 7 + 5 + 3 + 2 = 17
Requirement		7	5	3	2	17 (Total)	

Step II: Find a Basic Feasible Solution

This can be easily obtained by applying a technique which has been developed by Dantzig and which Charnes and Cooper refer to as "the north-west corner rule". Other methods for finding the initial feasible solutions are also described. In all these techniques it is assumed at the beginning that the transportation table is blank *i.e.*, initially all $x_{ij} = 0$.

The difference among these methods is the "quality" of the initial basic feasible solution they produce, in the sense that a better starting solution will involve a smaller objective value (minimization problem). In general, the Vogel's approximation method yields the best starting solution and the north-west corner method yields the worst. However, the latter is easier, quick and involves the least computations to get the initial solution.

(1) North-West Corner Rule or North-West Corner Method (NWCM)

This rule may be stated as follows:

(*i*) Start in the north-west (upper left) corner of the requirements table *i.e.*, the transportation matrix framed in step I and compare the supply of plant 1 (call it S_1) with the requirement of distribution centre 1 (call it D_1).

(*a*) If $D_1 < S_1$ *i.e.*, if the amount required at D_1 is less than the number of units available at S_1, set x_{11} equal to D_1, find the balance supply and demand and proceed to cell (1, 2) (*i.e.*, proceed horizontally).

TABLE 3.6

Distribution centres

		1	2	3	4	*Supply*
Plants	1	2 (6)	3	11	7	6/0
	2	1 (1)	0	6	1	1/0
	3	5	8 (5)	15 (3)	9 (2)	10/5/2/0
Requirement		7/1/0	5/0	3/0	2/0	

(*b*) If $D_1 = S_1$, set x_{11} equal to D_1, compute the balance supply and demand and proceed to cell (2, 2) (*i.e.*, proceed diagonally).

(*c*) If $D_1 > S_1$, set x_{11} equal to S_1, compute the balance supply and demand and proceed to cell (2, 1) (*i.e.*, proceed vertically).

(*ii*) Continue in this manner, step by step, away from the north-west corner until, finally, a value is reached in the south-east corner.

Thus in the present example (see table 3.6), one proceeds as follows:

(*i*) set x_{11} equal to 6, namely, the smaller of the amounts avaiblable at S_1 (6) and that needed at D_1 (7) and

(*ii*) proceed to cell (2, 1) (rule *c*). Compare the number of units available at S_2 (namely 1) with the amount required at D_1 (1) and accordingly set $x_{21} = 1$.

(*iii*) proceed to cell (3, 2) (rule *b*). Now supply from plant S_3 is 10 units while the demand for D_2 is 5 units; accordingly set x_{32} equal to 5.

(*iv*) proceed to cell (3, 3) (rule *a*) and allocate 3 there.

(*v*) proceed to cell (3, 4) (rule *a*) and allocate 2 there.

It can be easily seen that the proposed solution is a feasible solution since all supply and demand constraints are fully satisfied.

The following points may be noted in connection with this method:

(*i*) The quantities allocated are put in parenthesis and they represent the values of the corresponding decision variables. These cells are called *basic or allocated or occupied or loaded cells.* Cells without allocations are called *non-basic or vacant or empty or unoccupied or unloaded* cells. Values of the corresponding variables are all zero in these cells.

(*ii*) This method of allocation does not take into account the transportation cost and, therefore, may not yield a good (most economical) initial solution. The transportation cost associated with this solution is

$$Z = ₹\ [2 \times 6 + 1 \times 1 + 8 \times 5 + 15 \times 3 + 9 \times 2] \times 100 = ₹\ 11{,}600.$$

(2) Row Minima Method

This method consists in allocating as much as possible in the lowest cost cell of the first row so that either the capacity of the first plant is exhausted or the requirement at *j*th distribution centre is satisfied or both. In case of tie among the lowest cost cells in the row, select arbitrarily. Three cases arise:

(*i*) if the capacity of the first plant is completely exhausted, cross off the first row and proceed to the second row.

(*ii*) if the requirement at *j*th distribution centre is satisfied, cross off the *j*th column and reconsider the first row with the remaining capacity.

(*iii*) if the capacity of the first plant as well as the requirement at *j*th distribution centre are completely satisfied, cross off the row as well as the *j*th column and move down to the second row.

Continue the process for the resulting reduced transportation table until all the *rim conditions* (supply and requirement conditions) are satisfied.

TABLE 3.7

Distribution centres

Plants	1	2	3	4	*Supply*
1	2 (6)	3	11	7	6/0
2	1	0 (1)	6	1	1/0
3	5 (1)	8 (4)	15 (3)	9 (2)	10/9/5/2/0
Requirement	7/1/0	5/4/0	3/0	2/0	

In this problem, we first allocate to cell (1, 1) in the first row as it contains the minimum cost 2. We allocate min. (6, 7) = (6) in this cell. This exhausts the supply capacity of plant 1 and thus the first row is crossed off. The next allocation, in the resulting reduced matrix is made in cell (2, 2) of row 2 as it contains the minimum cost 0 in that row. We allocate min. (1, 5) = (1) in this cell. This exhausts the supply capacity of plant 2 and thus the second row is crossed off. The next allocation, in the resulting reduced matrix is made in cell (3, 1) of row 3 as it contains the minimum cost 5 in that row. We allocate min. (10, 1) = (1) in this cell. This exhausts the requirement condition of distribution centre 1 and hence the first column is crossed off. Proceeding in this way we allocate (4), (2) and (3) units to cells (3, 2), (3, 4) and (3, 3) till all the rim conditions are met with. The resulting matrix is shown in table 3.7.

The transportation cost associated with this solution is

$$Z = ₹\ [2 \times 6 + 0 \times 1 + 5 \times 1 + 8 \times 4 + 15 \times 3 + 9 \times 2] \times 100 = ₹\ 11{,}200,$$

which is less than the cost associated with solution obtained by N-W corner method.

(3) Column Minima Method

This method consists in allocating as much as possible in the lowest cost cell of the first column so that either the demand of the first distribution centre is satisfied or the capacity of the *i*th plant is exhausted or both. In case of tie among the lowest cost cells in the column, select arbitrarily. Three cases arise:

(*i*) if the requirement of the first distribution centre is satisfied, cross off the first column and move right to the second column.

(*ii*) if the capacity of *i*th plant is satisfied, cross off *i*th row and reconsider the first column with the remaining requirement.

(*iii*) if the requirement of the first distribution centre as well as the capacity of the *i*th plant are completely satisfied, cross off the column as well as the *i*th row and move right to the second column.

Continue the process for the resulting reduced transportation table until all the rim conditions are satisfied.

TABLE 3.8

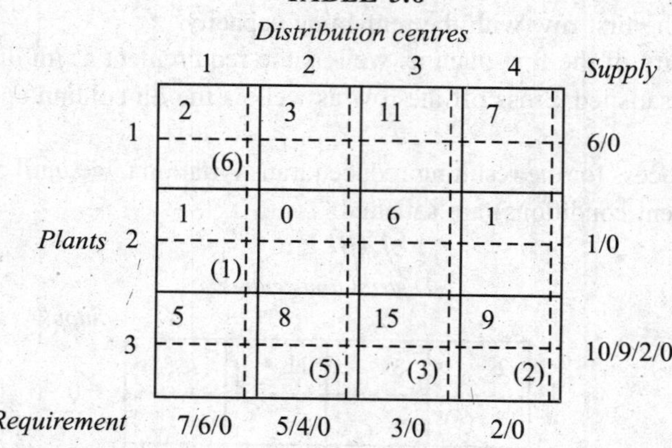

Plants \ Distribution centres	1	2	3	4	Supply
1	2 (6)	3	11	7	6/0
2	1 (1)	0	6	1	1/0
3	5	8 (5)	15 (3)	9 (2)	10/9/2/0
Requirement	7/6/0	5/4/0	3/0	2/0	

In the given problem we allocate first to cell (2, 1) in the first column as it contains the minimum cost 1. We allocate min. (1, 7) = (1) in this cell. This exhausts the supply capacity of plant 2 and thus the second row is crossed off. The next allocation in the resulting reduced matrix is made in cell (1, 1) of column 1 as it contains the second lowest cost 2 in that column. We allocate min. (6, 6) = (6) in this cell. This exhausts the supply capacity of plant 1 as well as the requirement of distribution centre 1. Therefore, we cross off first row and first column and move on to the second column. Proceeding in this way we allocate (5), (3) and (2) to cells (3, 2), (3, 3) and (3, 4) till all the rim conditions are met with. The resulting matrix is shown in table 3.8.

The transportation cost associated with this solution is

$$Z = ₹\ [2 \times 6 + 1 \times 1 + 8 \times 5 + 15 \times 3 + 9 \times 2] \times 100 = ₹\ 11{,}600,$$

which is same as the cost associated with solution obtained by N-W corner method.

(4) Least-Cost Method (or Matrix Minima Method or Lowest Cost Entry Method)

This method consists in allocating as much as possible in the lowest cost cell/cells and then further allocation is done in the cell/cells with second lowest cost and so on. *In case of tie among the cost, select the cell where allocation of more number of units can be made.* Consider the matrix for the problem under study.

TABLE 3.9

		Distribution centres 1	2	3	4	*Supply*
	1	2 (6)	3	11	7	6/0
Plants	2	1	0 (1)	6	1	1/0
	3	5 (1)	8 (4)	15 (3)	9 (2)	10/9/5/3/0
Requirement		7/1/0	5/4/0	3/0	2/0	

Here, the lowest cost cell is (2, 2) and maximum possible allocation (meeting supply and requirement positions) is made here. Evidently, maximum feasible allocation in cell (2, 2) is (1). This meets the supply position of plant 2. Therefore, row 2 is crossed out, indicating that no allocations are to be made in cells (2, 1), (2, 3) and (2, 4).

The next lowest cost cell (excluding the cells in row 2) is (1, 1); maximum possible allocation of (6) is made here and row 1 is crossed out. Next lowest cost cell in row 3 is (3, 1) and allocation of (1) is done here. Likewise, allocations of (4), (2) and (3) are done in cells (3, 2), (3, 4) and (3, 3) respectively. The transportation cost associated with this solution is

$$Z = ₹\ (2 \times 6 + 0 \times 1 + 5 \times 1 + 8 \times 4 + 15 \times 3 + 9 \times 2) \times 100$$
$$= ₹\ (12 + 0 + 5 + 32 + 45 + 18) \times 100 = ₹\ 11,200,$$

which is less than the cost associated with the solution obtained by N-W corner method.

(5) Vogel's Approximation Method (VAM) or Penalty Method or Regret Method

Vogel's approximation method is a heuristic method and is preferred to the methods described above. In the transportation matrix if an allocation is made in the second lowest cost cell instead of the lowest, then this allocation will have associated with it a penalty corresponding to the difference of these two costs due to 'loss of advantage'. That is to say, if we compute the difference between the two lowest costs for each row and column, we find the opportunity cost relevant to each row and column. It would be most economical to make allocation against the row or column with the highest opportunity cost. For a given row or column, the allocation should obviously be made in the least cost cell of that row or column. Vogel's approximation method, therefore, makes effective use of the cost information and yields a better initial solution than obtained by the other methods. This method consists of the following substeps:

Substep 1: Write down the cost matrix as shown below.

TABLE 3.10

		Distribution centres 1	2	3	4	*Supply*
	1	2	3	11	7	6 [1]
Plants	2	1	0	6	1 (1)	1/0 [1]
	3	5	8	15	9	10 [3]
Requirement		7 [1]	5 [3]	3 [5]	2/1 [6] ↑	

Enter the difference between the smallest and second smallest element in each column below the corresponding column and the difference between the smallest and second smallest element in each row to the right of the row. Put these numbers in brackets as shown. For example, in column 1, the two lowest elements are 1 and 2 and their difference is 1 which is entered as [1] below column 1. Similarly, the two smallest elements in row 2 are 0 and 1 and their difference 1 is entered as [1] to the right of row 2. A row or column "difference" can be thought of a penalty for making allocation in second smallest cost cell instead of smallest cost cell. In other words this difference indicates the unit penalty incurred by failing to make an allocation to the smallest cost cell in that row or column. In case the smallest and second smallest elements in a row/column are equal, the penalty should be taken as zero.

Substep 2: Select the row or column with the greatest difference and allocate as much as possible within the restrictions of the *rim conditions* to the lowest cost cell in the row or column selected.

In case of tie among the highest penalties, select the row or column having minimum cost. In case of tie in the minimum cost also, select the cell which can have maximum allocation. If there is tie among maximum allocation cells also, select the cell arbitrarily for allocation. Following these rules yields the best possible initial basic feasible solution and reduces the number of iterations required to reach the optimal solution.

Thus since [6] is the greatest number in brackets, we choose column 4 and allocate as much as possible to the cell (2, 4) as it has the lowest cost 1 in column 4. Since supply is 1 while the requirement is 2, maximum possible allocation is (1).

Substep 3: Cross off the row or column completely satisfied by the allocation just made. For the assignment just made at (2, 4), supply of plant 2 is completely satisfied. So, row 2 is crossed out and the shrunken matrix is written below.

TABLE 3.11

	1	2	3	4	
1	2	3 (5)	11	7	6/1 [1]
3	5	8	15	9	10 [3]
	7 [3]	5/0 [5] ↑	3 [4]	1 [2]	

This matrix consists of the rows and columns where allocations have not yet been made, including revised row and column totals which take the already made allocation into account.

Substep 4: Repeat steps 1 to 3 until all assignments have been made.

(*a*) Column 2 exhibits the greatest difference of [5]. Therefore, we allocate (5) units to cell (1, 2), since it has the smallest transportation cost in column 2. Since requirements of column 2 are completely satisfied, this column is crossed out and the reduced matrix is written again as table 3.12.

TABLE 3.12

	1	3	4	
1	2 (1)	11	7	1/0 [5] ←
3	5	15	9	10 [4]
	7/6 [3]	3 [4]	1 [2]	

(*b*) Differences are recalculated. The maximum difference is [5]. Therefore, we allocate (1) to the cell (1, 1) since it has the lowest cost in row 1. Since requirements of row 1 are fully satisfied, it is crossed out and the reduced matrix is written below.

In table 3.13, it is possible to find row differences but it is not possible to find column differences. Therefore, remaining allocations in this table are made by following the *least cost method.*

TABLE 3.13

	1	3	4	
3	5 (6)	15 (3)	9 (1)	10/4/3/0
	6/0	3/0	1/0	

(*c*) As cell (3, 1) has the lowest cost 5, maximum possible allocation of (6) is made here. Likewise, next allocation of (1) is made in cell (3, 4) and (3) in cell (3, 3) as shown.

All allocations made during the above procedure are shown below in the allocation matrix.

TABLE 3.14

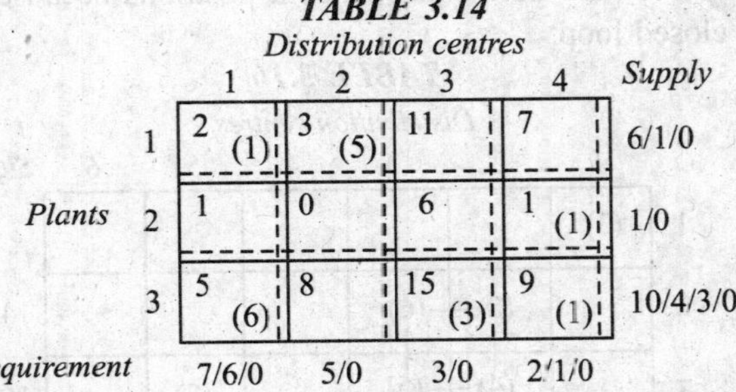

		Distribution centres				
		1	2	3	4	Supply
Plants	1	2 (1)	3 (5)	11	7	6/1/0
	2	1	0	6	1 (1)	1/0
	3	5 (6)	8	15 (3)	9 (1)	10/4/3/0
Requirement		7/6/0	5/0	3/0	2/1/0	

The above repetitions can be made in a single matrix as shown in table 3.15.

TABLE 3.15

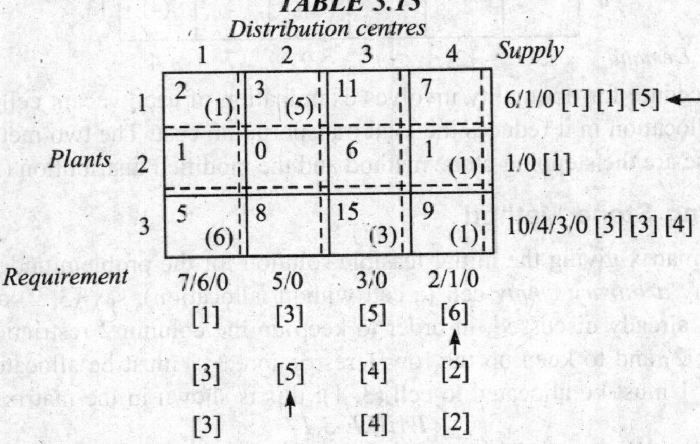

		Distribution centres				
		1	2	3	4	Supply
Plants	1	2 (1)	3 (5)	11	7	6/1/0 [1] [1] [5] ←
	2	1	0	6	1 (1)	1/0 [1]
	3	5 (6)	8	15 (3)	9 (1)	10/4/3/0 [3] [3] [4]
Requirement		7/6/0	5/0	3/0	2/1/0	
		[1]	[3]	[5]	[6] ↑	
		[3]	[5] ↑	[4]	[2]	
		[3]		[4]	[2]	

The cost of transportation associated with the above solution is

$$Z = ₹\,(2 \times 1 + 3 \times 5 + 1 \times 1 + 5 \times 6 + 15 \times 3 + 9 \times 1) \times 100$$

$$= ₹\,(2 + 15 + 1 + 30 + 45 + 9) \times 100 = ₹\,10,200,$$

which is evidently the least of all the values of transportation cost found by different methods. Since Vogel's approximation method results in the most economical initial feasible solution, we shall use this method for finding such a solution for all transportation problems henceforth.

Step III: Perform Optimality Test

Make an optimality test to find whether the obtained feasible solution is optimal or not. An optimality test can, of course, be performed only on that feasible solution in which

(*a*) number of allocations is $m + n - 1$, where m is the number of rows and n is the number of columns. In the given situation, m = 3 and $n = 4$ and number of allocations is 6 which is equal to $(m + n - 1)$ ($\because$ $3 + 4 - 1 = 6$). Hence optimality test can be performed.

(*b*) these $(m + n - 1)$ allocations should be in independent positions.

A look at the feasible solution of the problem under consideration indicates that all the allocations are in independent positions as it is impossible to increase or decrease any allocation without either changing the position of the allocations or violating the row and column restrictions. For example, if the allocation in cell (1, 1) is changed from (1) to (3), the allocation in cell (1, 2) must be changed from (5) to (3) in order to satisfy the row restriction. Similarly, the allocation in cell (3, 1) must be changed from (6) to (4) in order to meet the column restriction. This will, in turn, require changes in the allocations of cell (3, 3) and/or cell (3, 4).

A simple rule for allocations to be in independent positions is that it is impossible to travel from any allocation(thereby forming a closed loop), back to itself by a series of horizontal and vertical jumps from one occupied cell to another, without a direct reversal of route. For instance, the occupied cells in table 3.16 are not in independent positions because the cells (2, 2), (2, 3), (3, 3) and (3, 2) form a closed loop.

TABLE 3.16

Distribution centres

	1	2	3	4	5	6	*Supply*
Plants 1	(3)						3
2		(8)	(6)				14
3		(4)	(5)		(7)		16
4				(9)		(4)	13
Demand	3	12	11	9	7	4	

Now test procedure for optimality involves examination of each vacant cell to find whether or not making an allocation in it reduces the total transportation cost. The two methods commonly used for this purpose are the stepping-stone method and the modified distribution (MODI) method.

1. The Stepping Stone Method

Consider the matrix giving the initial feasible solution for the problem under consideration. Let us start with any *arbitrary empty* cell (a cell without allocation), say (3, 2) and allocate + 1 unit to this cell. As already discussed, in order to keep up the column 2 restriction, – 1 must be allocated to cell (1, 2) and to keep up the row 1 restriction, + 1 must be allocated to cell (1, 1) and consequently – 1 must be allocated to cell (3, 1); this is shown in the matrix below.

TABLE 3.17

	1	2	3	4	
1	2 (1)+1	3 –1(5)	11	7	6
2	1	0	6	1 (1)	1
3	5 (6) –1	8 +1	15 (3)	9 (1)	10
	7	5	3	2	

The net change in transportation cost as a result of this perturbation is called the evaluation of the empty cell in question.

$\therefore$ Evaluation of cell (3, 2) $= ₹\ 100 \times (8 \times 1 - 5 \times 1 + 2 \times 1 - 5 \times 1)$
$= ₹\ (0 \times 100) = ₹\ 0.$

Thus the total transportation cost increases by ₹ 0 for each unit allocated to cell (3, 2). Likewise, the net evaluation (also called *opportunity cost*) is calculated for every empty cell. For this the following simple procedure may be adopted.

Starting from the chosen empty cell, trace a path in the matrix consisting of a series of alternate horizontal and vertical lines. The path begins and terminates in the chosen cell. All other corners of the path lie in the cells for which allocations have been made. The path may skip over any number of occupied or vacant cells. Mark the corner of the path in the chosen vacant cell as positive and other corners of the path alternately –ve, +ve, –ve and so on. Allocate 1 unit to the chosen cell; subtract and add 1 unit from the cells at the corners of the path, maintaining the row and column requirements. The net change in the total cost resulting from this adjustment is called the evaluation of the chosen empty cell. Evaluations of the various empty cells (in hundreds of rupees) are:

Cell (1, 3) $= c_{13} - c_{33} + c_{31} - c_{11} = 11 - 15 + 5 - 2 = -1$,
Cell (1, 4) $= c_{14} - c_{34} + c_{31} - c_{11} = 7 - 9 + 5 - 2 = +1$,
Cell (2, 1) $= c_{21} - c_{24} + c_{34} - c_{31} = 1 - 1 + 9 - 5 = +4$,
Cell (2, 2) $= c_{22} - c_{24} + c_{34} - c_{31} + c_{11} - c_{12} = 0 - 1 + 9 - 5 + 2 - 3 = +2$,
Cell (2, 3) $= c_{23} - c_{24} + c_{34} - c_{33} = 6 - 1 + 9 - 15 = -1$,
Cell (3, 2) $= c_{32} - c_{31} + c_{11} - c_{12} = 8 - 5 + 2 - 3 = +2$.

If any cell evaluation is negative, the cost can be reduced so that the solution under consideration can be improved *i.e.*, it is not optimal. On the other hand, if all cell evaluations are positive or zero, the solution in question will be optimal. Since evaluations of cells (1, 3) and (2, 3) are –ve, initial basic feasible solution given in table 3.15 is not optimal.

Now in a transportation problem involving m rows and n columns, the total number of empty cells will be $m.n - (m + n - 1) = (m - 1)(n - 1)$. Therefore, there are $(m - 1)(n - 1)$ such cell evaluations which must be calculated and for large problems, the method can be quite inefficient. This method is named 'stepping stone' since only occupied cells or 'stepping stones' are used in the evaluation of vacant cells.

2. The Modified Distribution (MODI) Method or the u-v Method

In the stepping stone method, a closed path is traced for each unoccupied cell. Cell evaluations are found and the cell with the most negative evaluation becomes the basic cell. In the modified distribution method, cell evaluations of all the unoccupied cells are calculated simultaneously and only one closed path for the most negative cell is traced. Thus it provides considerable time saving over the stepping stone method. This method consists of the following substeps:

Substep 1: Set up a cost matrix containing the unit costs associated with the cells for which allocations have been made. This matrix for the present example is

TABLE 3.18

2	3		
			1
5		15	9

Cost matrix for allocated cells only

Substep 2: Introduce dual variables corresponding to the supply and demand constraints. If there are m origins and n destinations, there will be $m + n$ dual variables. Let u_i ($i = 1, 2, \ldots, m$) and v_j ($j = 1, 2, \ldots, n$) be the dual variables corresponding to supply and demand constraints. Variables u_i and v_j are such that $u_i + v_j = c_{ij}$ for all occupied cells.

Therefore, enter a set of numbers u_i ($i = 1, 2, 3$) along the left of the matrix and v_j ($j = 1, 2, 3, 4$) across the top of the matrix so that their sums equal the costs entered in substep 1.

Thus, $u_1 + v_1 = 2,$
$u_1 + v_2 = 3,$
$u_2 + v_4 = 1,$
$u_3 + v_1 = 5,$
$u_3 + v_3 = 15,$
and $u_3 + v_4 = 9.$

Since number of dual variables are $m + n$ ($3 + 4 = 7$ in the present problem) and number of allocations (in a non-degenerate solution) are $m + n - 1$ ($3 + 4 - 1 = 6$ in the present problem), one variable is assumed arbitrarily. Let $v_1 = 0$. Therefore, from the above equations

$u_1 = 2,\ v_2 = 1,\ u_3 = 5,\ v_3 = 10,\ v_4 = 4,\ u_2 = -3.$

The values of these dual variables satisfy the complementary slackness theorem which states that if primal constraints are equations, dual variables are unrestricted in sign (Refer section 6.1.3). Therefore, the matrix may be written as

TABLE 3.19

u_i \ v_j	0	1	10	4
2	2	3		
–3				1
5	5		15	9

Now for any vacant (empty) cell, $u_i + v_j$ is called the *implicit cost*, whereas c_{ij} is called the *actual cost* of the cell. The two costs are compared and $c_{ij} - (u_i + v_j)$ are calculated for each empty cell. If all $c_{ij} - (u_i + v_j) \geq 0$, then by the application of complementary slackness theorem it can be shown that the corresponding solution is optimum. If any $c_{ij} - (u_i + v_j) < 0$, the solution is not optimal. $c_{ij} - (u_i + v_j)$ is called the *evaluation of the cell (i, j) or opportunity cost of cell (i, j)*. Thus we have the following three substeps:

Substep 3: Fill the vacant cells with the sums of u_i and v_j. This is shown in table 3.20.

TABLE 3.20

u_i \ v_j	0	1	10	4
2	·	·	12	6
–3	–3	–2	7	·
5	·	6	·	·

Substep 4: Subtract the cell values of the matrix of substep 3 from the original cost matrix.

TABLE 3.21

·	·	11–12	7–6
1+3	0+2	6–7	·
·	8–6	·	·

→

TABLE 3.22

·	·	–1	1
4	2	–1	·
·	2	·	·

Cell evaluation matrix

The resulting matrix is called *cell evaluation matrix*.

Substep 5: Signs of the values in the cell evaluation matrix indicate whether optimal solution has been obtained or not. The signs have the following significance:

(*a*) A negative value in an unoccupied cell indicates that a better solution can be obtained by allocating units to this cell.

(*b*) A positive value in an unoccupied cell indicates that a poorer solution will result by allocating units to the cell.

(*c*) A zero value in an unoccupied cell indicates that another solution of the same total value can be obtained by allocating units to this cell. In the present example since two cell evaluations are negative, it is possible to obtain a better solution by making these cells as basic cells.

Step IV: Iterate Towards an Optimal Solution

This involves the following substeps:

Substep 1: From the cell evaluation matrix, identify the cell with the most negative cell evaluation. This is the *rate* by which total transportation cost can be reduced if one unit is allocated to this cell; in case more units are allocated, the cost will come down proportionately. Therefore, as many units as possible (keeping in mind the rim conditions) will be allocated to this cell to bring down the cost by maximum amount. *In case of tie in the cell evaluation, the cell wherein maximum allocation can be made is selected. In case of tie among cells that have the same maximum allocation, select arbitrarily.* This cell is now called the *identified cell.* With refrence to the simplex method, this identified cell is currently the non-basic cell that has been decided to be made basic (decided to enter the solution) by making allocation in it. In the present problem both the tied cells will have the same maximum allocation of 1 unit. Hence cell (1, 3) is selected arbitrarily.

Substep 2: Write down again the initial basic feasible solution that is to be improved. Check mark (√) the identified cell. This is shown in table 3.23.

TABLE 3.23

		Distribution centres				
		1	2	3	4	
	1	1 −	5	√ +		6
Milk plants	2				1	1
	3	6 +		3 −	1	10
		7	5	3	2	

Having decided the vacant cell that is to be made basic, the next thing is to decide which basic cell should be made non-basic by changing its present allocation to zero. For this we go to substep 3.

Substep 3: Trace a closed path in the matrix. This closed path has the following characteristics:

(*i*) It begins and terminates in the identified cell.

(*ii*) It consists of a series of alternate horizontal and vertical lines only (no diagonals).

(*iii*) It can be traced clockwise or anticlockwise.

(*iv*) All other corners of the path lie in the allocated cells only.

(*v*) The path may skip over any number of allocated or vacant cells.

(*vi*) There will always be one and only one closed path, which may be traced.

The closed path has even number of corners (4, 6, 8, ...) and any allocated cell can be considered only once. The closed path may or may not be square or rectangular in shape; it may have a peculiar configuration and the lines may even cross over.

Substep 4: Mark the identified cell as positive and each occupied cell at the corners of the path alternately –ve, +ve, –ve and so on.

Substep 5: Make a new allocation in the identified cell by entering the smallest allocation on the path that has been assigned a *–ve* sign. Add and subtract this new allocation from the cells at the corners of the path, maintaining the row and column requirements. This causes allocation in one basic cell to become zero and allocations in other cells remain non-negative. The basic cell whose allocation has been made zero, leaves the solution.

TABLE 3.24

1 – 1	5	+1		6
			1	1
6 + 1		3 – 1	1	10
7	5	3	2	

→

TABLE 3.25

	5	1		6
			1	1
7		2	1	10
7	5	3	2	

2nd feasible solution

Since cell evaluation (in hundreds of rupees) is – 1 and 1 unit has been reallocated, the total transportation cost should come down by ₹ (100 × 1) = ₹ 100. This can be vertified by actually calculating the total cost for table 3.25.

The total cost of transportation for this 2nd feasible solution is

$$= ₹\,(3 \times 5 + 11 \times 1 + 1 \times 1 + 7 \times 5 + 2 \times 15 + 1 \times 9) \times 100$$
$$= ₹\,(15 + 11 + 1 + 35 + 30 + 9) \times 100 = ₹\,10{,}100,$$

which is less than that for the first (starting) feasible solution by ₹ 100.

Step V: Check for Optimality

Let us check whether the solution obtained above is optimal or not. This shall be checked by repeating the steps under 'check for optimality' already made. In the above feasible solution,

(*a*) number of allocations is $(m + n - 1)$ *i.e.*, 6,

(*b*) these $(m + n - 1)$ allocations are in independent positions.

Above conditions being satisfied, an optimality test can be performed as follows:

Substep 1: Set up the cost matrix containing the costs associated with the cells for which allocations have been made.

Substep 2: Enter a set of numbers v_j along the top of the matrix and a set of number u_i at the left side so that their sum is equal to costs entered in matrix of substep 1, shown below.

TABLE 3.26

v_j / u_i	0	2	10	4
1		3	11	
–3				1
5	5		15	9

Thus,
$$u_1 + v_2 = 3, \qquad u_3 + v_1 = 5,$$
$$u_1 + v_3 = 11, \qquad u_3 + v_3 = 15,$$
$$u_2 + v_4 = 1, \quad \text{and} \quad u_3 + v_4 = 9.$$

Let $v_1 = 0$.

Then
$$u_3 = 5, \qquad u_2 = -3,$$
$$v_3 = 10, \qquad u_1 = 1,$$
$$v_4 = 4, \qquad v_2 = 2.$$

These values are shown enetered in matrix 3.26.

Substep 3: Fill the vacant cells with the sums of u_i and v_j.

TABLE 3.27

u_i \ v_j	0	2	10	4
1	1	·	·	5
–3	–3	–1	7	·
5	·	7	·	·

Substep 4: Subtract the cell values of this matrix from the original cost matrix.

TABLE 3.28

2 – 1	·	·	7 – 5
1 + 3	0 + 1	6 – 7	·
·	8 – 7	·	·

→

TABLE 3.29

1	·	·	2
4	1	–1	·
·	1	·	·

Cell evaluation matrix

This matrix 3.29 is called cell evaluation matrix.

Substep 5: Since one cell value is *–ve*, the 2nd feasible solution is not optimal.

Step VI: Iterate Towards an Optimal Solution

This involves the following substeps:

Substep 1: In the cell evaluation matrix, identify the cell with the most negative entry. It is the cell (2, 3).

Substep 2: Write down again the feasible solution in question (*i.e.*, second feasible solution).

TABLE 3.30

	5	1	
		+ √	– 1
7		– 2	+ 1

Mark the empty cell (√) for which the evaluation is negative. This is called identified cell.

Substep 3: Trace the path shown in the matrix.

Substep 4: Mark the identified cell as *+ve* and others alternately *–ve* and *+ve*.

Substep 5: Make the new allocation in the identified cell by entering the smallest allocation on the path which has been assigned negative sign. Subtract and add this amount from other cells. Tables 3.31 and 3.32 result.

TABLE 3.31

·	5	1	
		+ 1	1 – 1
7		2 – 1	1 + 1

→

TABLE 3.32

	5	1	
		1	
7		1	2

Third feasible solution

For this allocation matrix the transportation cost is

$$Z = ₹\ (5 \times 3 + 1 \times 11 + 1 \times 6 + 1 \times 15 + 2 \times 9 + 7 \times 5) \times 100 = ₹\ 10,000.$$

Thus it is a better solution. Let us see if it is an optimal solution.

Step VII: Test for Optimality

In the above feasible solution

(*a*) number of allocations is $m + n - 1$ *i.e.*, 6.

(*b*) These $m + n - 1$ allocations are in independent positions. Hence repeat the following substeps:

Substep 1: Set up the cost matrix containing costs associated with cells for which allocations have been made. This is table 3.33.

TABLE 3.33

u_i \ v_j	0	2	10	4
1		3	11	
–4			6	
5	5		15	9

Substep 2: Enter a set of number v_j and u_i such that

$u_1 + v_2 = 3$, $u_3 + v_1 = 5$,

$u_1 + v_3 = 11$, $u_3 + v_3 = 15$,

$u_2 + v_3 = 6$, and $u_3 + v_4 = 9$.

Let $v_1 = 0$.

Then, $u_3 = 5$, $u_2 = -4$,

$v_3 = 10$, $u_1 = 1$,

$v_4 = 4$, and $v_2 = 2$.

The resulting matrix is shown in table 3.34.

TABLE 3.34

u_i \ v_j	0	2	10	4
1	1	·	·	5
–4	–4	–2	·	0
5	·	7	·	·

Substep 3: Fill up the vacant cells also as shown above.

Substep 4: Subtract the cell values of the above matrix from the original cost matrix. Tables 3.35 and 3.36 result.

TABLE 3.35

2 – 1	·	·	7 – 5
1 + 4	0 + 2	·	1 – 0
·	8 – 7	·	·

→

TABLE 3.36

1	·	·	2
5	2	·	1
·	1	·	·

Cell evaluation matrix

Substep 5: Since all the cell values are positive, the third feasible solution given by table 3.37 is the optimal solution.

TABLE 3.37

		Distribution centres				
		1	2	3	4	Supply
	1	2	3 (5)	11 (1)	7	6
Plants	2	1	0	6 (1)	1	1
	3	5 (7)	8	15 (1)	9 (2)	10
Requirement		7	5	3	2	

Therefore the optimal solution is:

Milk plant	*Distribution centre*	*No. of units transported*	*Transportation cost/unit* (₹)	*Total transportation cost* (₹)
1	2	5	300	1,500
	3	1	1,100	1,100
2	3	1	600	600
3	1	7	500	3,500
	3	1	1,500	1,500
	4	2	900	1,800
				₹ 10,000

3.5-1 Degeneracy in Transportation Problem

We have seen that in case of simplex algorithm, the basic feasible solution may become degenerate at the initial stage or at some intermediate stage of computation. In a transportation problem with m origins and n destinations if a basic feasible solution has less than $m + n - 1$ allocations (occupied cells), the problem is said to be a *degenerate transportation problem.*

While in the simplex method degeneracy does not cause any serious difficulty, it can cause computational problem in transportation technique. In stepping stone method it will not be possible to make close paths (loops) for each and every vacant cell and hence evaluations of all the vacant cells cannot be calculated. If modified distribution method is applied, it will not be possible to find all the dual variables u_i and v_j since the number of allocated cells and their c_{ij} values is not enough. It is thus necessary to identify a degenerate transportation problem and take appropriate steps to avoid computational difficulty. Degeneracy can occur in the initial solution or during some subsequent iteration.

1. *Degeneracy in the initial solution:* Normally, while finding the initial solution (by any of the methods), any allocation made either satisfies supply or demand, but not both. If, however, both supply and demand are satisfied simultaneously, row as well as column are cancelled simultaneously and the number of allocations become one less than $m + n - 1$. If this phenomenon occurs twice, the number of allocations become two less than $m + n - 1$ and so on. This *degeneracy is resolved* or the above degenerate solution is made non-degenerate in the following manner:

First of all the requisite number of vacant cells *with least unit costs* are chosen so that (in case of tie choose arbitrarily):

(*i*) these cells plus the existing number of allocations are equal to $m + n - 1$.

(*ii*) these $m + n - 1$ cells are in independent positions *i.e.*, no closed path (loop) can be formed among them. If a loop is formed the cell/cells with next lower cost is/are chosen so that no loop is formed among them. This can always be done if the solution we start with contains allocated cells in independent positions.

Now allocate an infinitesimally small but positive value ε (Greek letter epsilon) to each of the chosen cells. Subscripts are used when more than one such letter is required (*e.g.*, ε_1, ε_2, etc.). These ε's are then treated like any other positive basic variable and are kept in the transportation array (matrix) until temporary degeneracy is removed or until the optimal solution is reached, whichever occurs first. At that point we set each $\varepsilon = 0$. Notice that ε is infinitesimally small and hence its effect can be neglected when it is added to or subtracted from a positive value (*e.g.* $10 + \in = 10$, $5 - \in = 5$, $\in + \in = 2\in$, $\in - \in = 0$). Consequently, they do not appreciably alter the physical nature of the original set of allocations but do help in carrying out further computations such as optimality test.

2. *Degeneracy during some subsequent iteration:* Sometimes even if the starting feasible solution is non-degenerate, degeneracy may develop later at some subsequent iteration. This happens when the selection of the entering variable (least value in the closed path that has been assigned a negative sign), causes two or more current basic variables (allocated cell values) to become zero. In this case we allocate ∈ to *recently vacated cell with least cost* so that there are exactly $m + n - 1$ allocated cells in independent positions and the procedure can then be continued in the usual manner.

3.5.2 Transportation Algorithm

Transportation algorithm for a minimization problem as discussed earlier can be summarized in the following steps:

1. Construct the transportation matrix. For this enter the supply a_i from the origins, demand b_j at the destinations and the unit costs c_{ij} in the various cells.
2. Find initial basic feasible solution by Vogel's approximation method or any of the other given methods.
3. Perform optimality test using modified distribution method. For this, find dual variables u_i and v_j such that $u_i + v_j = c_{ij}$ for occupied cells. Starting with, say, $v_1 = 0$, all other variables can be evaluated.
4. Compute the cell evaluations $= c_{ij} - (u_i + v_j)$ for vacant cells. If all cell evaluations are positive or zero, the current basic feasible solution is optimal. In case any cell evaluation is negative, the current solution is not optimal.
5. Select the vacant cell with the most negative evaluation. This is called identified cell.
6. Make as much allocation in the identified cell as possible so that it becomes basic *i.e.*, enters the basis. Construct a closed loop connecting this cell to the others basic cells. Reallocate the maximum possible number of units to these cells, keeping in mind the rim conditions. This will make allocation in one basic cell zero and in other basic cells the allocations will remain non-negative (≥ 0). The basic cell whose allocation becomes zero will leave the basis.
7. Return to step 3, repeat the process till optimal solution is obtained.

EXAMPLE 3.5-2 (Transportation Problem with Degeneracy)

A company has four warehouses and six stores. The warehouses altogether have a surplus of 22 units of a given commodity, divided among them as follows:

Warehouses	*1*	*2*	*3*	*4*
Surplus	*5*	*6*	*2*	*9*

The six stores altogether need 22 units of the commodity. Individual requirements at stores 1, 2, 3, 4, 5 and 6 are 4, 4, 6, 2, 4 and 2 units respectively.

Cost of shipping one unit of commodity from warehouse i to store j in rupees is given in the matrix below.

TABLE 3.38

		Stores					
		1	2	3	4	5	6
Warehouses	1	9	12	9	6	9	10
	2	7	3	7	7	5	5
	3	6	5	9	11	3	11
	4	6	8	11	2	2	10

(i) Formulate the mathematical model for the problem.

(ii) How should the products be shipped from the warehouses to the stores so that the transportation cost is minimum?

Explain degeneracy in transportation technique in the context of this problem. How is degeneracy resolved? *[PTU B. Tech., 2000]*

(*i*) Formulation of the Model

Step 1

Key decision to be made is to find how many units of the commodity be shipped from which warehouse to which store so that cost of transportation is minimum. Let x_{ij} represent the decision variables *i.e.*, number of units to be shipped.

Here, $i = 1, 2, 3, 4; j = 1, 2, 3, 4, 5, 6.$

Step 2

Feasible alternatives are sets of values of x_{ij}, where $x_{ij} \geq 0$.

Step 3

Objective is to minimize the transportation cost *i.e.*,

$$\text{minimize } Z = \sum_{i=1}^{4} \sum_{j=1}^{6} c_{ij} x_{ij},$$

where c_{ij} is the unit cost of shipping from ith warehouse to jth store.

Step 4

Constraints are

(*i*) because of surplus or supply:

$$x_{11} + x_{12} + x_{13} + x_{14} + x_{15} + x_{16} = 5 \text{ i.e., } \sum_{j=1}^{6} x_{1j} = 5.$$

$$\text{Similarly } \sum_{j=1}^{6} x_{2j} = 6, \sum_{j=1}^{6} x_{3j} = 2 \ \& \sum_{j=1}^{6} x_{4j} = 9.$$

(*ii*) because of requirement or demand:

$$x_{11} + x_{21} + x_{31} + x_{41} = 4 \text{ i.e., } \sum_{i=1}^{4} x_{i1} = 4.$$

$$\text{Similarly } \sum_{i=1}^{4} x_{i2} = 4, \sum_{i=1}^{4} x_{i3} = 6, \sum_{i=1}^{4} x_{i4} = 2, \sum_{i=1}^{4} x_{i5} = 4 \ \& \sum_{i=1}^{4} x_{i6} = 2.$$

Thus, the given situation involves 4 × 6 (= 24) variables and 4 + 6 (= 10) constraints.

(ii) Solution of the Model

The solution involves making a transportation table (in the form of a matrix), finding a feasible solution, performing optimality test and iterating towards optimal solution if required.

Step I: Make a Transportation Table

This involves expressing surplus (supply) from warehouses, demand at the stores, and unit cost of shipping from warehouses to stores in the form of a matrix (Table 3.39). A check is made to balance the surplus and demand.

TABLE 3.39

Stores (destinations)

		1	2	3	4	5	6	*Surplus (supply)*	
	1	9	12	9	6	9	10	5	
	2	7	3	7	7	5	5	6	Total surplus = 22
Ware-houses (origins)	3	6	5	9	11	3	11	2	
	4	6	8	11	2	2	10	9	Total requi-rement = 22
Requirement (demand)		4	4	6	2	4	2		

Thus supply and demand are balanced.

Step II: Find Initial Basic Feasible Solution

Table 3.40 represents initial basic feasible solution obtained by applying Vogel's approximation method as explained below:

TABLE 3.49

Stores

		1	2	3	4	5	6	*Supply*
	1	9	12	9 (5)	6	9	10	5/0 [3] [3] [0] [0] [0] [0]
	2	7	3 (4)	7	7	5	5 (2)	6/4/0 [2] [2] [2] [4] ←
Wareho-uses	3	6 (1)	5	9 (1)	11	3	11	2/1/0 [2] [2] [2] [1] [3] [3] ←
	4	6 (3)	8	11	2 (2)	2 (4)	10	9/7/3/0 [0] [0] [4] ← [2] [5] ←
Demand		4/1/0	4/0	6/1/0	2/0	4/0	2/0	*Initial basic feasible solution*
		[0]	[2]	[2]	[4]	[1]	[5]	
		[0]	[2]	[2]	[4]	[1]	↑	
		[0]	[2]	[2]	↑	[1]		
		[0]	[2]	[2]				
		[0]		[0]				
		[3]		[0]				

1. Row and column penalties are calculated. First allocation of (2) units is made in the least cost cell (2, 6) in column 6 corresponding to the highest penalty 5. Balance supply is 4 and balance demand is 0 and column 6 is cancelled.

2. Row penalties are calculated again. Second allocation of (2) units is made in the least cost cell (4, 4) of column 4 corresponding to the highest penalty of 4. Balance supply is 7, balance demand is 0 and column 4 is also cancelled.
3. Row penalties are calculated again. Third allocation of (4) units is made in the least cost cell (4, 5) of row 4. Balance supply is 3 and balance demand is 0 and column 5 is also cancelled.
4. Row penalties are calculated again. Fourth allocation of (4) units is made in the least cost cell (2, 2) in row 2 corresponding to the highest penalty of 4. The balance supply as well as demand are 0 each and row 2 as well as column 2 are cancelled. The solution to be obtained will be degenerate.
5. Row as well as column penalties are calculated again. Fifth allocation of (3) units is made in cell (4, 1) in row 4 corresponding to the highest penalty of 5. Balance demand is 1, balance supply is 0 and row 4 is cancelled.
6. Column penalties are calculated again. There is tie among the highest penalties 3 for row 3 as well as column 1. Considering either, the lowest cost cell is (3, 1) with unit cost of 6. Sixth allocation of (1) unit is made in cell (3, 1). Balance supply is 1, balance demand is 0 and column 1 is also cancelled.
7. Now column penalty is 0 but row penalty cannot be calculated.

Remaining allocations are made as per the least cost method. Since the unit cost of either of the cells is 9, cell (1, 3) is chosen arbitrarily and (5) units are allocated to this cell. Balance supply is 0 and balance demand is 1.

Lastly (1) unit is allocated to the cell (3, 3). Balance supply as well as demand is 0. Now no surplus unit is left and also the demand of all the six stores is met with.

The cost of transportation associated with the above solution is

$$Z = ₹\,(9 \times 5 + 3 \times 4 + 5 \times 2 + 6 \times 1 + 9 \times 1 + 6 \times 3 + 2 \times 2 + 2 \times 4)$$
$$= ₹\,(45 + 12 + 10 + 6 + 9 + 18 + 4 + 8) = ₹\,112.$$

Step III: Perform Optimality Test

Make an optimality test to find whether the obtained feasible solution is optimal or not. An optimality test can, however, be performed on that feasible solution in which

(*a*) number of allocations is $m + n - 1$.

In the given situation $m = 4$, $n = 6$. $\therefore m + n - 1 = 4 + 6 - 1 = 9$.

Now the number of allocations = 8 (< 9). Therefore optimality test cannot be performed as such. Such a solution is called a *degenerate solution.*

(*b*) these $m + n - 1$ allocations must be in independent positions.

In the present example the allocations are in independent positions as it is impossible to increase or decrease any allocation without either changing the positions of allocations or violating the row and column restrictions.

Since number of allocations is eight, there is need for making one infinitesimal allocation. Out of the unoccupied cells, cell (3, 5) has the least cost of ₹ 3. The infinitesimal allocation should be made in this cell. However, allocating ε to this cell forms a closed loop among the cells (3, 1), (3, 5), (4, 5) and (4, 1) so that allocation in these cells do not remain in independent postitions. Therefore, no allocation is made in cell (3, 5). There are two next higher cost cells, *viz.* cell (2, 5) and (3, 2) each with a cost of ₹ 5. Allocation in either of these cells does not result in closed loop. Hence the infinitesimal allocation can be made in either of these two cells. Let us make the allocation in cell (2, 5). Table 3.41 formed thereby is shown below. Cell (2, 5) with allocation ∈ is as good as any real allocated cell and no distinction will be made between this cell and other allocated cells in carrying out further computations.

TABLE 3.41

	1	2	3	4	5	6
1			5			
2		4			ε	2
3	1		1			
4	3			2	4	

Now optimality test can be applied. Proceeding as in example 3.5-1, we get the following tables:

TABLE 3.42

	1	2	3	4	5	6
1			9			
2		3			5	5
3	6		9			
4	6			2	2	

Initial cost matrix for the allocated cells

TABLE 3.43

u_i \ v_j	0	–6	3	–4	–4	–4
6			9			
9		3			5	5
6	6		9			
6	6			2	2	

TABLE 3.44

Table 3.44

u_i \ v_j	0	–6	3	–4	–4	–4
6	6	0	·	2	2	2
9	9	·	12	5	·	·
6	·	0	·	2	2	2
6	·	0	9	·	·	2

$u_i + v_j$ matrix for unallocated cells

TABLE 3.45

3	12	·	4	7	8
–2	·	–5	2	·	·
·	5	·	9	1	9
·	8	2	·	·	8

Cell evaluation matrix

Since cells (2, 1) and (2, 3) have negative values, the current feasible solution is not optimal.

Step IV: Iterate Towards an Optimal Solution

Proceeding as in example 3.5-1, we get the following tables:

TABLE 3.46

	1	2	3	4	5	6
1			5			
2		4	+ ✓		– ε	2
3	+ 1		– 1			
4	– 3			2	+ 4	

Initial basic feasible solution with closed path

TABLE 3.47

	1	2	3	4	5	6
1			5			
2		4	+ε		ε – ε	2
3	1 + ε		1–ε			
4	3 – ε			2	4 + ε	

→

TABLE 3.48

	1	2	3	4	5	6
1			5			
2		4	ε			2
3	1		1			
4	3			2	4	

2nd feasible solution

As can be seen, this new allocation gives the same cost of transportation (₹ 112) as the old one. But this places us in a position to carry further iterations.

Step V: Test for Optimality

In the above solution

(*a*) number of allocations are $m + n - 1$ (= 9),

(*b*) these $m + n - 1$ allocations are in independent positions.

Therefore, optimality test can be applied. It can be done by the Modified Distribution (MODI) method which consists of substeps 1 through 5, details of which are given in example 3.5-1.

TABLE 3.49

u_i \ v_j	0	−1	3	−4	−4	1
6			9			
4		3	7			5
6	6		9			
6	6			2	2	

$u_i + v_j$ matrix for occupied cells

TABLE 3.50

u_i \ v_j	0	−1	3	−4	−4	1
6	6	5	·	2	2	7
4	4	·	·	0	0	·
6	·	5	·	2	2	7
6	·	5	9	·	·	7

$u_i + v_j$ matrix for vacant cells

TABLE 3.51

3	7	·	4	7	3
3	·	·	7	5	·
·	0	·	9	1	4
·	3	2	·	·	3

Cell evaluation matrix

Since all the cell values are non-negative, the 2nd feasible solution is an optimal solution. Since the above matrix contains a zero entry, there exist alternative optimal solutions. Thus the optimal solution for our problem is

TABLE 3.52

		Stores						
		1	2	3	4	5	6	*Supply*
Warehouses	1	9	12	9 (5)	6	9	10	5
	2	7	3 (4)	7	7	5	5 (2)	6
	3	6 (1)	5	9 (1)	11	3	11	2
	4	6 (3)	8	11	2 (2)	2 (4)	10	9
Demand		4	4	6	2	4	2	

Total cost of transportation = ₹ 112.

In solving this problem, infinitesimal allocation was made in cell (2, 5). If this allocation is made in cell (3, 2), the same optimal solution (as above) is obtained without having to make any iteration.

EXAMPLE 3.5-3

Find the optimum solution to the following transportation problem in which the cells contain the unit transportation cost in rupees.

TABLE 3.53

	W_1	W_2	W_3	W_4	W_5	*Available*
F_1	7	6	4	5	9	40
F_2	8	5	6	7	8	30
F_3	6	8	9	6	5	20
F_4	5	7	7	8	6	10
Required	30	30	15	20	5	100 (Total)

[*Kuru. U.B.E. (Mech.) June, 2013; P.T.U. B.Tech. (Mech.) 2010; P.U.B.E.(E.&Ec.) Nov., 2011; B.Com. Sept., 2004, Jan., 2005, April, 2007; Jammu U.B.E.(Mech.) 2004*]

Solution

Step I: Make the Transportation Matrix

This step is not necessary in the current problem.

Step II: Find a Basic Feasible Solution

We shall use Vogel's approximation method to find initial basic feasible solution. The method consists of substeps 1, 2, 3 and 4 already explained in examples 3.5-1 and 3.5-2.

TABLE 3.54

	W_1	W_2	W_3	W_4	W_5	*Available*
F_1	7 (5)	6	4 (5)	5 (20)	9	40/25/5/0 [1] [1] [2]←[2]←
F_2	8	5 (30)	6	7	8	30/0 [1] [2] ←
F_3	6 (15)	8	9	6	5 (5)	20/15/0 [1] [1] [1] [1]←
F_4	5 (10)	7	7	8	6	10/0 [1] [1] [1] [1]
Required	30/25/15/0	30/0	15/0	20/0	5/0	
	[1]	[1]	[2] ↑	[1]	[1]	
	[1]	[1]		[1]	[1]	
	[1]			[1]	[1]	
	[1]				[1]	

The degenerate basic feasible solution is given by Table 3.54.

Step III: Perform Optimality Test

From the above matrix we find that

(*a*) required number of allocations = $m + n - 1 = 4 + 5 - 1 = 8$.

Actual number of allocations = 7.

∴ We shall allocate a very small positive value ε to one of cells (F_1, W_2), (F_2, W_3), (F_3, W_4) and (F_4, W_5), each of which has the same minimum transportation cost of ₹ 6 (out of the unoccupied cells). Allocations to either of cells (F_3, W_4) and (F_4, W_5) results in closed loops and hence no allocations will be made in these cells. Thus ε can be allocated to either cell (F_1, W_2) or (F_2, W_3). Let us allocate it to cell (F_2, W_3) so that the number of allocated cells becomes 8. This is shown in Table 3.55.

TABLE 3.55

	W_1	W_2	W_3	W_4	W_5	*Available*
F_1	7 (5)	6	4 (15)	5 (20)	9	40
F_2	8	5 (30)	6 (ε)	7	8	30
F_3	6 (15)	8	9	6	5 (5)	20
F_4	5 (10)	7	7	8	6	10
Required	30	30	15	20	5	

Initial basic feasible solution

(*b*) these 8 allocations are in independent positions. Therefore, optimality test can be performed. This consists of the following substeps:

Substeps 1, 2, 3, 4 and 5, details of which are given in example 3.5-1.

TABLE 3.56

u_i \ v_j	0	–4	–3	–2	–1
7	7		4	5	
9		5	6		
6	6				5
5	5				

Matrix of $u_i + v_j$ for allocated cells

→

TABLE 3.57

u_i \ v_j	0	–4	–3	–2	–1
7	·	3	·	·	6
9	9	·	·	7	8
6	·	2	3	4	·
5	·	1	2	3	4

Matrix with cell values of $u_i + v_j$ for empty cells

TABLE 3.58

	W_1	W_2	W_3	W_4	W_5
F_1	·	3	·	·	3
F_2	–1	·	·	0	0
F_3	·	6	6	2	·
F_4	·	6	5	5	2

Cell evaluation matrix

As cell value in cell (F_2, W_1) is negative, the initial basic feasible solution given by table 3.55 is not optimal.

Step IV: Iterate Towards an Optimal Solution

This involves substeps 1, 2, 3, 4 and 5, details of which are given in example 3.5-1.

TABLE 3.59

− 5		15 +	20	
+ ✓	30	ε −		
15				5
10				

Initial feasible solution with closed path

TABLE 3.60

5 − ε		15 + ε	20	
ε	30			
15				5
10				

→

TABLE 3.61

5		15	20	
ε	30			
15				5
10				

2nd feasible solution

Step V: Test for Optimality

Repeating step III we get the following tables:

TABLE 3.62

u_i \ v_j	0	−3	−3	−2	−1
7	7		4	5	
8	8	5			
6	6				5
5	5				

Matrix of (u_i, v_j) for allocated cells

→

TABLE 3.63

u_i \ v_j	0	−3	−3	−2	−1
7	·	4	·	·	6
8	·	·	5	6	7
6	·	3	3	4	·
5	·	2	2	3	4

Matrix with cell values ($u_i + v_j$) for empty cells

TABLE 3.64

·	2	·	·	3
·	·	1	1	1
·	5	6	2	·
·	5	5	5	2

Cell evaluation matrix

As all cell values are positive, the second feasible solution is optimal. Therefore optimal transportation policy is

TABLE 3.65

	W_1	W_2	W_3	W_4	W_5	*Available*
F_1	7 (5)	6	4 (15)	5 (20)	9	40
F_2	8	5 (30)	6	7	8	30
F_3	6 (15)	8	9	6	5 (5)	20
F_4	5 (10)	7	7	8	6	10
Required	30	30	15	20	5	

Total transportation cost

$= ₹ [7 \times 5 + 4 \times 15 + 5 \times 20 + 5 \times 30 + 6 \times 15 + 5 \times 5 + 5 \times 10]$

$= ₹ [35 + 60 + 100 + 150 + 90 + 25 + 50] = ₹ 510.$

EXAMPLE 3.5-4

Find the basic feasible solution of the following transportation problem by north-west corner rule. Also find the optimal transportation plan.

TABLE 3.66

	1	*2*	*3*	*4*	*5*	*Available*
A	*4*	*3*	*1*	*2*	*6*	*80*
B	*5*	*2*	*3*	*4*	*5*	*60*
C	*3*	*5*	*6*	*3*	*2*	*40*
D	*2*	*4*	*4*	*5*	*3*	*20*
Required	*60*	*60*	*30*	*40*	*10*	*200 Total*

[P.T.U. B.Tech. (Mech. Engg.) 2010; BCA, 2009; P.U. B.Com. Jan., 2005; G.N.D.U. B.Com. Sept., 2003]

Solution

Step I: Make a Transportation Table

This step is not necessary in the current problem.

Step II: Find Basic Feasible Solution

By following the north-west corner rule (explained in example 3.5-1), we get the non-degenerate initial basic feasible solution shown below.

TABLE 3.67

	1	2	3	4	5	Available
A	4 (60)	3 (20)	1	2	6	80/20/0
B	5	2 (40)	3 (20)	4	5	60/20/0
C	3	5	6 (10)	3 (30)	2	40/30/0
D	2	4	4	5 (10)	3 (10)	20/10/0
Required	60/0	60/40/0	30/10/0	40/10/0	10/0	

Initial basic feasible solution

Step III: Test for Optimality

Required number of allocations = $m + n - 1 = 4 + 5 - 1 = 8$.

Actual number of allocations = 8.

These 8 allocations are in independent positions. Therefore optimality test can be performed. This step consists of substeps 1, 2, 3, 4 and 5, details of which are given in example 3.5-1.

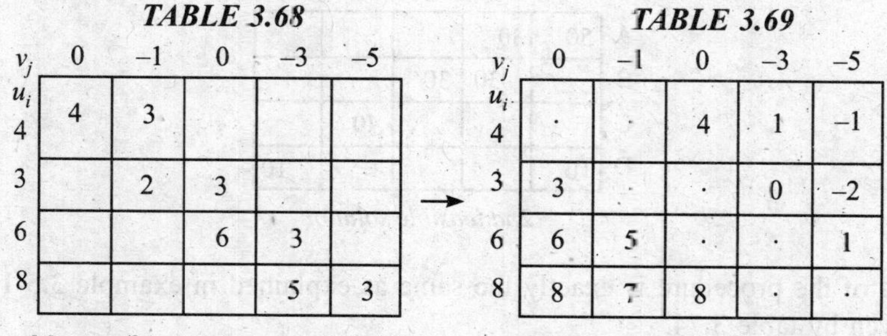

TABLE 3.68

u_i \ v_j	0	−1	0	−3	−5
4	4	3			
3		2	3		
6			6	3	
8				5	3

Matrix of (u_i, v_j) for occupied cells

→

TABLE 3.69

u_i \ v_j	0	−1	0	−3	−5
4	·	·	4	1	−1
3	3	·	·	0	−2
6	6	5	·	·	1
8	8	7	8	·	·

Matrix of $(u_i + v_j)$ for empty cells

TABLE 3.70

·	·	−3	1	7
2	·	·	4	7
−3	0	·	·	1
−6	−3	−4	·	·

Cell evaluation matrix

As many cell values are negative, initial basic feasible solution is not optimal.

Step IV: Iterate Towards an Optimal Solution

This involves substeps 1, 2, 3, 4 and 5, details of which are given in example 3.5-1.

TABLE 3.71

	1	2	3	4	5
A	− 60	20 +			
B		40 −	20 +		
C			10 −	30 +	
D	+ ✓			10 −	10

Initial feasible solution with closed path

TABLE 3.72

	1	2	3	4	5
A	50	30			
B		30	30		
C			*	40	
D	10			*	10

2nd feasible solution

In the second feasible solution the number of occupied cells (allocations) becomes less than $m + n - 1$ (= 8) on account of simultaneous vacation of two cells (C, 3) and (D, 4) as indicated by*.

This degeneracy can be overcome by allocating ε to cell (D, 4) which has the lower cost out of the two recently vacant cells. This is shown in table 3.73.

TABLE 3.73

	1	2	3	4	5
A	50	30			
B		30	30		
C				40	
D	10			ε	10

2nd feasible solution

The rest of the procedure is exactly the same as explained in example 3.5-1. The optimal solution is given by table 3.74.

TABLE 3.74

	1	2	3	4	5	Available
A	4 (10)	3	1 (30)	2 (40)	6	80
B	5	2 (60)	3	4	5	60
C	3 (30)	5	6	3	2 (10)	40
D	2 (20)	4	4	5	3	20
Required	60	60	30	40	10	200 (Total)

Optimal solution

EXAMPLE 3.5-5

Is

TABLE 3.75

		50	20
55			
30	35		25

an optimal solution of the transportation problem:

TABLE 3.76

					Available units
	6	1	9	3	70
	11	5	2	8	55
	10	12	4	7	90
Required units	85	35	50	45	215

If not, modify it to obtain the optimal solution.

[*P.U. UIAMS MBA May, 2015*]

Solution

Step I: Perform Optimality Test

Here actual number of allocations = the required number $m + n - 1 = 3 + 4 - 1 = 6$ and they are in independent positions. Therefore optimality test can be performed. It consists of substeps 1 through 5, details of which are given in example 3.5-1.

TABLE 3.77

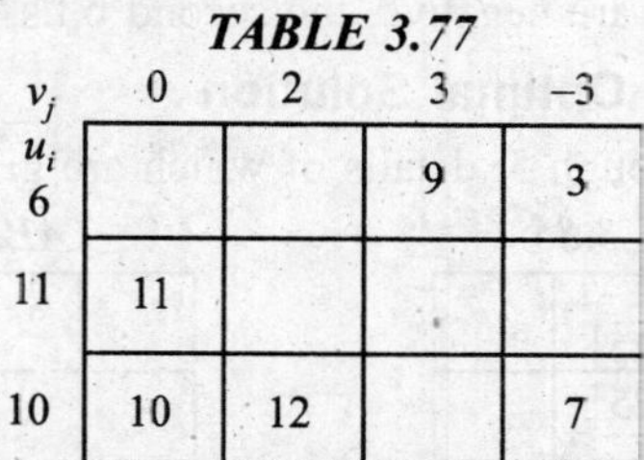

u_i \ v_j	0	2	3	−3
6			9	3
11	11			
10	10	12		7

$(u_i + v_j)$ matrix for occupied cells

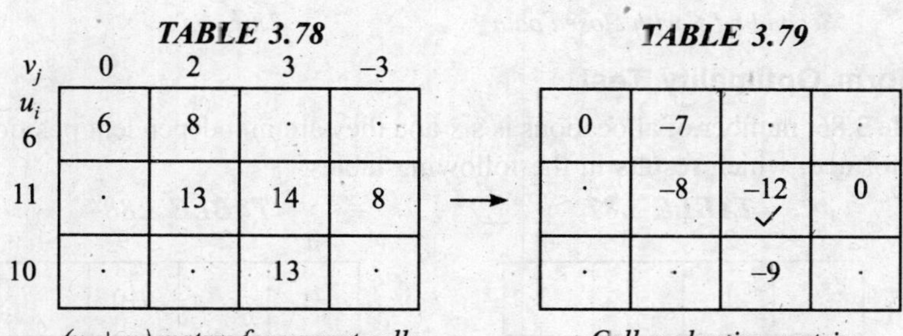

TABLE 3.78

u_i \ v_j	0	2	3	−3
6	6	8	·	·
11	·	13	14	8
10	·	·	13	·

$(u_i + v_j)$ matrix for vacant cells

→

TABLE 3.79

0	−7	·	·
·	−8	−12 ✓	0
·	·	−9	·

Cell evaluation matrix

Since some cell evaluations are negative, the given solution is not optimal.

Step II: Iterate Towards an Optimal Solution

It consists of substeps 1 through 5, details of which are given in example 3.5-1.

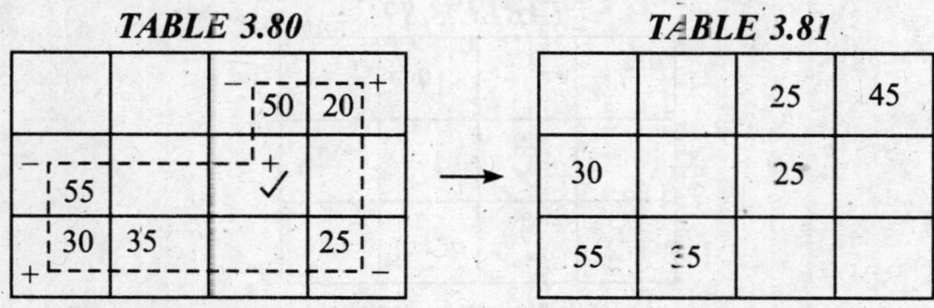

TABLE 3.80

		− 50	20 +
− 55		+ ✓	
+ 30	35		25 −

Initial b.f.s. with closed path

→

TABLE 3.81

		25	45
30		25	
55	35		

Second b.f.s.

Step III: Perform Optimality Test

Since in table 3.81, number of allocations is six and they are in independent positions, optimality test can be performed and the following tables are obtained:

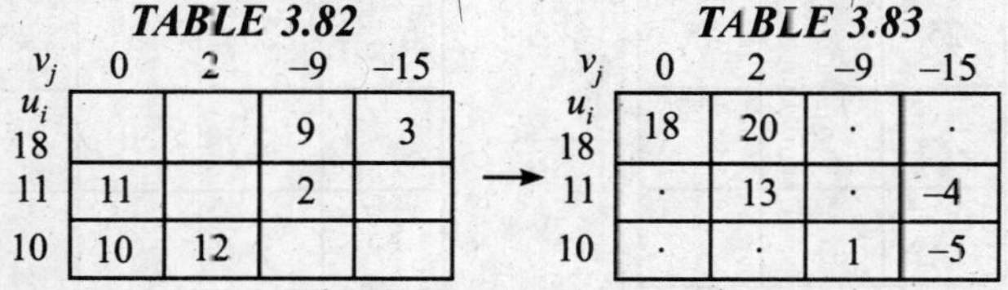

TABLE 3.82

u_i \ v_j	0	2	−9	−15
18			9	3
11	11		2	
10	10	12		

$(u_i + v_j)$ matrix for occupied cells

→

TABLE 3.83

u_i \ v_j	0	2	−9	−15
18	18	20	·	·
11	·	13	·	−4
10	·	·	1	−5

$(u_i + v_j)$ matrix for vacant cells

TABLE 3.84

−12	−19✓	·	·
·	−8	·	12
·	·	3	12

Cell evaluation matrix

Since some cell evaluations are negative, the second b.f.s. is not optimal.

Step IV: Iterate Towards an Optimal Solution

It consists of substeps 1 through 5, details of which are given in example 3.5-1.

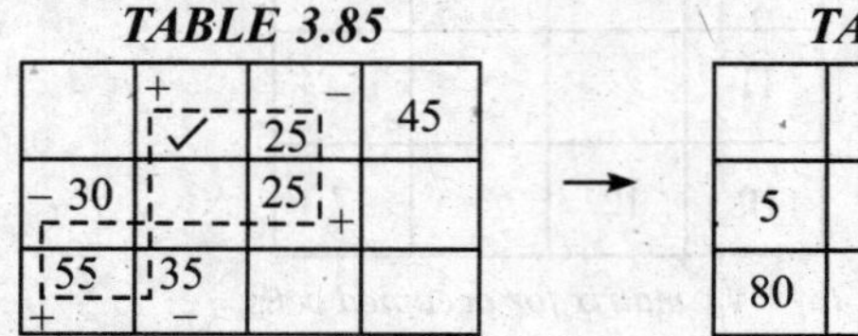

TABLE 3.85

	+ ✓	− 25	45
− 30		25 +	
55 +	35 −		

Second b.f.s. with closed path

→

TABLE 3.86

	25		45
5		50	
80	10		

Third b.f.s.

Step V: Perform Optimality Test

As in table 3.86, number of allocations is six and they are in independent positions, optimality test can be performed, which results in the following tables:

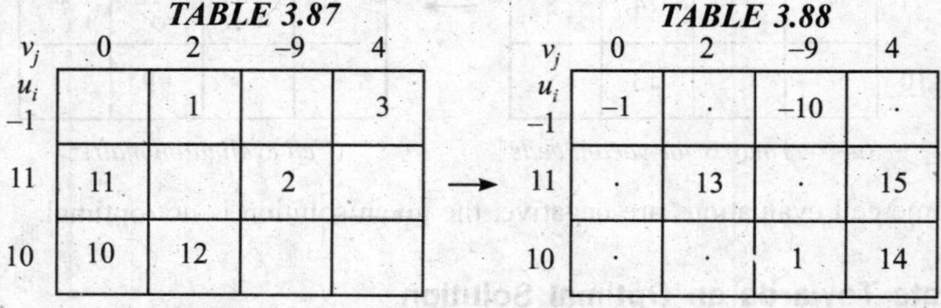

TABLE 3.87

u_i \ v_j	0	2	−9	4
−1		1		3
11	11		2	
10	10	12		

(u_i, v_j) matrix for occupied cells

→

TABLE 3.88

u_i \ v_j	0	2	−9	4
−1	−1	·	−10	·
11	·	13	·	15
10	·	·	1	14

(u_i + v_j) matrix for vacant cells

TABLE 3.89

7	·	19	·
·	−8 ✓	·	−7
·	·	3	−7

Cell evaluation matrix

Since some cell evaluations are negative, third b.f.s. is not optimal.

Step VI: Iterate Towards an Optimal Solution

It consists of substeps 1 through 5, details of which are given in example 3.5-1.

TABLE 3.90

	25		45
− 5	✓ +	50	
+ 80	10 −		

Third b.f.s. with closed path

→

TABLE 3.91

	25		45
	5	50	
85	5		

Fourth b.f.s

Step VII : Perform Optimality Test

Table 3.91 has six allocations in independent positions. The optimality test can, therefore, be performed and consists of the following tables:

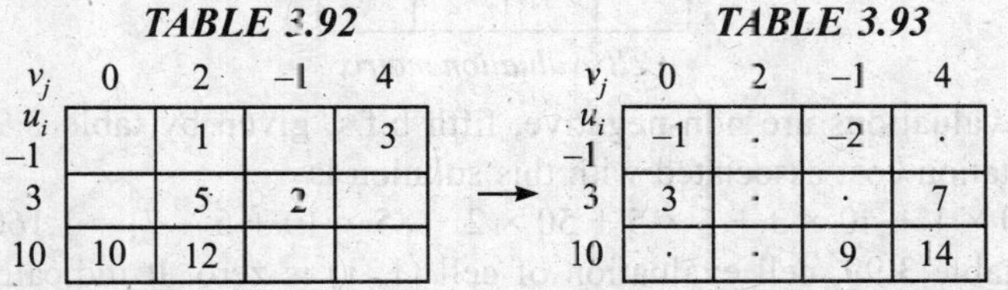

TABLE 3.92

u_i \ v_j	0	2	−1	4
−1		1		3
3		5	2	
10	10	12		

(u_i, v_j) matrix for occupied cells

TABLE 3.93

u_i \ v_j	0	2	−1	4
−1	−1	·	−2	·
3	3	·	·	7
10	·	·	9	14

$(u_i + v_j)$ matrix for vacant cells

TABLE 3.94

7	·	11	·
8	·	·	1
·	·	−5	−7 ✓

Cell evaluation matrix

Since some cell evaluations are negative, fourth b.f.s. is not optimal.

Step VIII: Iterate Towards an Optimal Solution

It consists of substeps 1 through 5, details of which are given in example 3.5-1.

TABLE 3.95

	+ 25		− 45
	5	50	
85	− 5		✓ +

Fourth b.f.s. with closed path

TABLE 3.96

	30		40
	5	50	
85			5

Fifth b.f.s.

Step IX: Perform Optimality Test

Table 3.96 has six allocations in independent positions. The optimality test can, therefore, be performed and consists of the following tables:

TABLE 3.97

u_i \ v_j	0	−5	−8	−3
6		1		3
10		5	2	
10	10			7

(u_i, v_j) matrix for occupied cells

TABLE 3.98

u_i \ v_j	0	−5	−8	−3
6	6	·	−2	
10	10	·	·	7
10	·	5	2	

$(u_i + v_j)$ matrix for vacant cells

TABLE 3.99

0	·	11	·
1	·	·	1
·	7	2	·

Cell evaluation matrix

As all cell evaluations are non-negative, fifth b.f.s. given by table 3.96 is optimal. The minimum transportation cost associated with this solution is

$$Z_{min} = [30 \times 1 + 40 \times 3 + 5 \times 5 + 50 \times 2 + 85 \times 10 + 5 \times 7] = 1{,}160.$$

Remark. In table 3.99, cell evaluation of cell (1, 1) is zero. It indicates the existence of alternate optimal solution at the same cost. Alternate optimal solutions or programmes are useful since they provide the programmer with a wider selection of 'best' choices and offer him the opportunity to consider secondary objectives as well. These alternate optimal solutions are obtained the same way as that used for normal optimal solutions by treating zero in the optimal cost evaluation matrix exactly the same way as negative entries.

So, we treat cell (1, 1) with zero evaluation as identified cell, make the shifts in allocations as indicated by closed path in table 3.100 and get alternate optimal solution (table 3.101).

TABLE 3.100

+ ✓	30		40 –
	5	50	
– 85			5 +

Optimal b.f.s. with closed path

TABLE 3.101

40	30		
	5	50	
45			45

Alternate optimal solution

Total transportation cost associated with this solution

$$= [40 \times 6 + 30 \times 1 + 5 \times 5 + 50 \times 2 + 45 \times 10 + 45 \times 7]$$
$$= [240 + 30 + 25 + 100 + 450 + 315] = 1{,}160.$$

In fact, we can find not only two but a large number (theoretically, infinite number) of optimal solutions. Instead of shifting 40 units, we can shift 39 or 38 or 37 … units and shall again arrive at optimal solutions at the same cost.

In general, derived programme $= \lambda x_1 + (1 - \lambda)x_2$,

where x_1 and x_2 are the first and second optimal programmes and parameter λ lies between 0 and 1. So, whenever an optimal solution contains vacant cell/cells with zero evaluations, there is a great flexibility in distribution at minimum cost.

EXAMPLE 3.5-6

Solve the following transportation problem where cell entries are unit costs.

TABLE 3.102

	D_1	D_2	D_3	D_4	D_5	*Available*
O_1	68	35	4	74	15	18
O_2	57	88	91	3	8	17
O_3	91	60	75	45	60	19
O_4	52	53	24	7	82	13
O_5	51	18	82	13	7	15
Required	16	18	20	14	14	82 / 82

[*H.P.U.B. Tech. (Mech.) 2012; P.U.B.E. (Mech.) Nov., 2006*]

Solution

Step I: Find Initial Basic Feasible Solution

The initial solution obtained by Vogel's approximation method is given below:

TABLE 3.103

	D_1	D_2	D_3	D_4	D_5	*Available*
O_1	68	35	4 (18)	74	15	18/0 [11]
O_2	57	88	91	3 (3)	8 (14)	17/3/0 [5] [5] [54] ←
O_3	91 (16)	60 (3)	75	45	60	19/16/0 [15] [15] [15]
O_4	52	53	24 (2)	7 (11)	82	13/11/0 [17] [45] ←
O_5	51	18 (15)	82	13	7 (ε)	15/0 [6] [6]
Required	16/0	18/3/0	20/2/0	14/3/0	14/0	*Initial basic feasible solution*
	[1]	[17]	[20] ↑	[4]	[1]	
	[1]	[35]	[51] ↑	[4]	[1]	
	[6]	[42] ↑		[10]	[1]	
	[34]	[28]		[42]	[52] ↑	

The solution is degenerate since number of allocations are 8 whereas $m + n - 1 = 5 + 5 - 1 = 9$.

Step II: Perform Optimality Test

The above solution is made feasible (non-degenerate) by allocating $\in$ units to the least cost, vacant independent cell (O_5, D_5) in table 3.103. Optimality test is performed below:

TABLE 3.104

	0	–31	–30	–47	–42
34			4		
50				3	8
91	91	60			
54			24	7	
49		18			7

(u_i, v_j) matrix for occupied cells of i.b.f.s.

→

TABLE 3.105

	0	–31	–30	–47	–42
34	34	3	·	–13	–8
50	50	19	20	·	·
91	·	·	61	44	49
54	54	23	·	·	12
49	49	·	19	2	·

(u_i + v_j) matrix for vacant cells

TABLE 3.106

34	32	·	87	23
7	69	71	·	·
·	·	14	1	11
✓–2	30	·	·	70
2	·	63	11	·

Cell evaluation matrix

Since one cell evaluation is negative, initial basic feasible solution is not optimal.

Step III: Iterate Towards an Optimal Solution

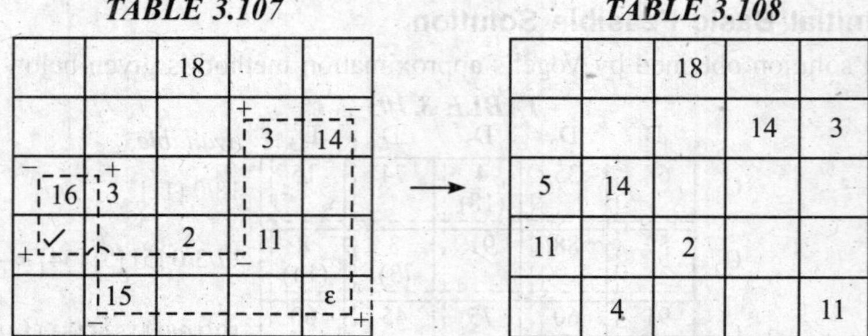

TABLE 3.107

		18		
			3	14
16	3			
✓		2	11	
	15			ε

Initial b.f.s. with closed path

TABLE 3.108

		18		
			14	3
5	14			
11		2		
	4			11

Second b.f.s.

Step IV: Perform Optimality Test

In table 3.108, number of allocations are 9 and they are in independent positions. The solution is basic feasible and is checked for optimality in the tables below:

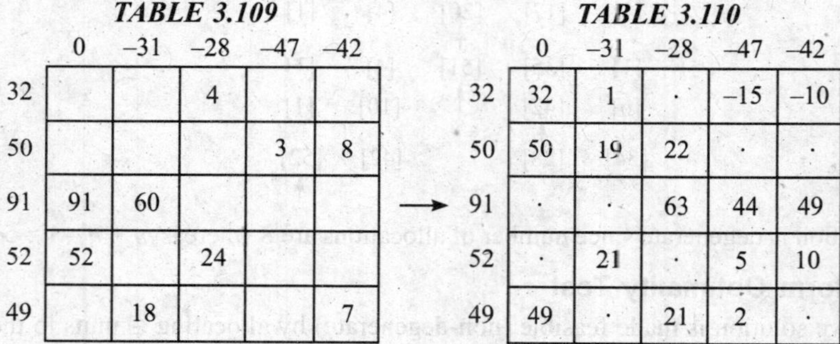

TABLE 3.109

	0	−31	−28	−47	−42
32			4		
50				3	8
91	91	60			
52	52		24		
49		18			7

$(u_i + v_j)$ matrix for occupied cells of 2nd b.f.s.

TABLE 3.110

	0	−31	−28	−47	−42
32	32	1	·	−15	−10
50	50	19	22	·	·
91	·	·	63	44	49
52	·	21	·	5	10
49	49	·	21	2	·

$(u_i + v_j)$ matrix for vacant cells

TABLE 3.111

36	34	·	89	25
7	69	69	·	·
·	·	12	1	11
·	32	·	2	72
2	·	61	11	·

Cell evaluation matrix

As all cell evaluations are non-negative, second b.f.s. given by table 3.108 is optimal. The minimum transportation cost associated with this solution is

$$Z_{min} = [18\times4 + 14\times3 + 3\times8 + 5\times91 + 14\times60 + 11\times52 + 2\times24 + 4\times18 + 11\times7]$$
$$= [72 + 42 + 24 + 455 + 840 + 572 + 48 + 72 + 77] = 2{,}202.$$

3.6 VARIANTS IN TRANSPORTATION PROBLEMS

The following variations in the transportation problem will now be considered:

1. Unbalanced transportation problem.
2. Maximization problem.

3. Different production costs.
4. No allocation in a particular cell/cells.
5. Overtime production.

3.6-1 The Unbalanced Transportation Problem

In the problems discussed so far, the total availability from all the origins was equal to the total demand at all the destinations *i.e.*, $\sum_{i=1}^{m} a_i = \sum_{j=1}^{n} b_j$. Such problems are called *balanced transportation problems.* In many real life situations, however, the total availability may not be equal to the total demand *i.e.*, $\sum_{i=1}^{m} a_i \neq \sum_{j=1}^{n} b_j$; such problems are called *unbalanced transportation problems.* In these problems either some available resources will remain unused or some requirements will remain unfilled.

Since a feasible solution exists only for a balanced problem, it is necessary that the total availability be made equal to the total demand. If *total capacity or availability is more than the demand* and if there are no costs associated with the failure to use the excess capacity, we add a *dummy (fictitious) destination* to take up the excess capacity and the costs of shipping to this destination are set equal to zero. The zero cost cells are *treated the same way as real cost cells and the* problem is solved as a balanced problem. If there is, however, a cost associated with unused capacity (*e.g.*, maintenance cost) and it is linear, it too can be easily treated.

In case the total demand is more than the availability, we add a *dummy origin* (*source*) to "fill" the balance requirement and the shipping costs are again set equal to zero. However, in real life, the cost of unfilled demand is seldom zero since it may involve lost sales, lesser profits, possibility of losing the customer or even business or the use of a more costly substitute. Solution of the problem under such situations may be more involved.

EXAMPLE 3.6-1 (Unbalanced Supply and Demand)

A product is produced by four factories A, B, C and D. The unit production costs in them are ₹ 2, ₹ 3, ₹ 1 and ₹ 5 respectively. Their production capacities are: factory A – 50 units, B – 70 units, C – 30 units and D – 50 units. These factories supply the product to four stores, demands of which are 25, 35, 105 and 20 units respectively. Unit transport cost in rupees from each factory to each store is given in the table below.

TABLE 3.112

		Stores 1	2	3	4
Factories	A	2	4	6	11
	B	10	8	7	5
	C	13	3	9	12
	D	4	6	8	3

Determine the extent of deliveries from each of the factories to each of the stores so that the total production and transportation cost is minimum.

[*H.P.U. B.Tech. (Mech.) Sept. 2013; Mumbai U.MBA, 2010; V.T.U. Karnataka B.E. June, 2010; SVSM PGDM, 2009; P.U.B. Com., 2006; Jan., 2005; NIIFT Mohali, 2000, PTU. M.B.A., 2002*]

Solution. First of all we shall compile a new table of unit costs which consists of both production and transportation costs. The new table or matrix is given below.

TABLE 3.113

		Stores 1	2	3	4	Production capacity
Factories	A	2 + 2	4 + 2	6 + 2	11 + 2	50
	B	10 + 3	8 + 3	7 + 3	5 + 3	70
	C	13 + 1	3 + 1	9 + 1	12 + 1	30
	D	4 + 5	6 + 5	8 + 5	3 + 5	50
Demand		25	35	105	20	

Step I: Make the Transportation Matrix

Let us again write down the above matrix (Table 3.113).

		Stores 1	2	3	4	Production capacity
Factories	A	4	6	8	13	50
	B	13	11	10	8	70
	C	14	4	10	13	30
	D	9	11	13	8	50
Demand		25	35	105	20	

Here total production capacity = 200 units,

total demand = 185 units,

surplus capacity = 15 units.

Thus, production capacity and demand are not balanced in this case and we have a surplus of 15 units of the product. Therefore, we create a fictitious (dummy) destination (store). The associated cost coefficients are taken as zero.

Therefore, our starting cost matrix becomes

TABLE 3.114

		Stores 1	2	3	4	d	Capacity
Factories	A	4	6	8	13	0	50
	B	13	11	10	8	0	70 Total capacity = 200
	C	14	4	10	13	0	30 Total demand = 200
	D	9	11	13	8	0	50
Demand		25	35	105	20	15	

Step II: Find a Basic Feasible Solution

We shall use Vogel's approximation method to find the initial feasible solution. The method consists of substeps 1,2,3 and 4 already explained in example 3.5-1.

TABLE 3.115

Stores

Factories	1	2	3	4	*d*	*Capacity*	
A	4 (25)	6 (5)	8 (20)	13	0	50/25/20/0	[4] [2] [2] [2] [5] ←
B	13	11	10 (70)	8	0	70/0	[8] [2] [2] [2] [2] [2]
C	14	4 (30)	10	13	0	30/0	[4] [6] ←
D	9	11	13 (15)	8 (20)	0 (15)	50/35/15/0	[8] [1] [1] [3] [5] [5] ←
Demand	25/0	35/5/0	105/85/15/0	20/0	15/0	*Initial basic feasible solution*	
	[5]	[2]	[2]	[0]	[0]		
	[5]	[2]	[2]	[0]			
	[5]	[5]	[2]	[0]			
	↑	[5]	[2]	[0]			
		↑	[2]	[0]			
			[3]	[0]			

Step III: Perform Optimality Test

From the above matrix we find that

(*a*) number of allocations = $m + n - 1 = 4 + 5 - 1 = 8$,

(*b*) these $m + n - 1$ allocations are in independent positions.

Therefore optimality test can be performed. This consists of substeps 1, 2, 3, 4 and 5, details of which are explained in example 3.5-1.

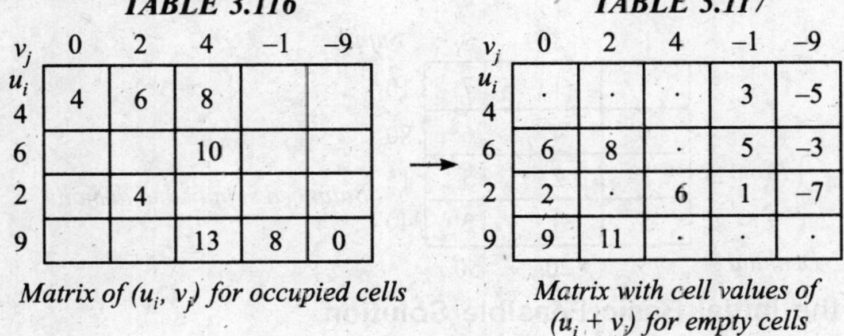

TABLE 3.116

u_i \ v_j	0	2	4	−1	−9
4	4	6	8		
6			10		
2		4			
9			13	8	0

Matrix of (u_i, v_j) for occupied cells

→

TABLE 3.117

u_i \ v_j	0	2	4	−1	−9
4	·	·	·	3	−5
6	6	8	·	5	−3
2	2	·	6	1	−7
9	9	11	·	·	·

Matrix with cell values of ($u_i + v_j$) for empty cells

TABLE 3.118

·	·	·	10	5
7	3	·	3	3
12	·	4	12	7
0	0	·	·	·

Cell evaluation matrix

Since cell values are non-negative, the first feasible solution is optimal. Since table 3.118 contains zero entries, there exist alternate optimal solutions. The practical significance of demand being 15 units less than production capacity is that the company may cut down the production of 15 units at the factory where it is uneconomical *i.e.*, at factory D.

The optimum (minimum) transportation plus production cost

$$Z = ₹\,(4 \times 25 + 6 \times 5 + 8 \times 20 + 10 \times 70 + 4 \times 30 + 13 \times 15 + 8 \times 20 + 0 \times 15)$$
$$= ₹\,(100 + 30 + 160 + 700 + 120 + 195 + 160 + 0)$$
$$= ₹\,1{,}465.$$

EXAMPLE 3.6-2

Consider the following unbalanced transportation problem:

TABLE 3.119

		To 1	2	3	Supply
From	1	5	1	7	10
	2	6	4	6	80
	3	3	2	5	15
Demand		75	20	50	

Since there is not enough supply, some of the demands at these destinations may not be satisfied. Suppose there are penalty costs for every unsatisfied demand unit which are given by 5, 3 and 2 for destination 1, 2, and 3 respectively. Find the optimal solution.

[R.T.M. Nagpur U.B.E. (Mech.) Sept., 2010]

Solution. Generally, an unbalnaced transportation problem is balanced by adding a row or a column, as the case may be, with cost values equal to zero. However, if we are given some other information, it must be taken into account. Here, penalty for not satisfying the demand at the destinations is given. So, the transportation plan to be decided would be such as to minimize the cost of transportation and penalty.

Step I: Prepare a Transportation Table

Since there is not enough supply, we introduce a dummy source whose 'transportation costs' are 5, 3 and 2 respectively and the supply is 145 – 105 = 40 units. The modified (balanced) transprotation problem is represented by table 3.120.

TABLE 3.120

		To 1	2	3	Supply
From	1	5	1	7	10
	2	6	4	6	80
	3	3	2	5	15
	d	5	3	2	40
Demand		75	20	50	

Balanced supply and demand

Step II: Find the Initial Basic Feasible Solution

Using Vogel's approximation method, an initial basic feasible solution is obtained which is given in table 3.121.

TABLE 3.121

		To 1	2	3	Supply	
From	1	5	1 (10)	7	10/0	[4] ←
	2	6 (60)	4 (10)	6 (10)	80/70/60/0	[2] [2] [2]
	3	3 (15)	2	5	15/0	[1] [1] [1]
	d	5	3	2 (40)	40/0	[1] [1]
Demand		75/60/0	20/10/0	50/10/0		
		[2]	[1]	[3]		
		[2]	[1]	[3]		
		[3]	[2]	↑		
		↑		[1]		

Step III: Perform Optimality Test

Since actual number of allocations = required number of allocations = $m + n - 1 = 4 + 3 - 1 = 6$, and they are in independent positions, the optimality test can be performed. It consists of substeps 1 through 5 explained in example 3.5-1 and represented in the tables below.

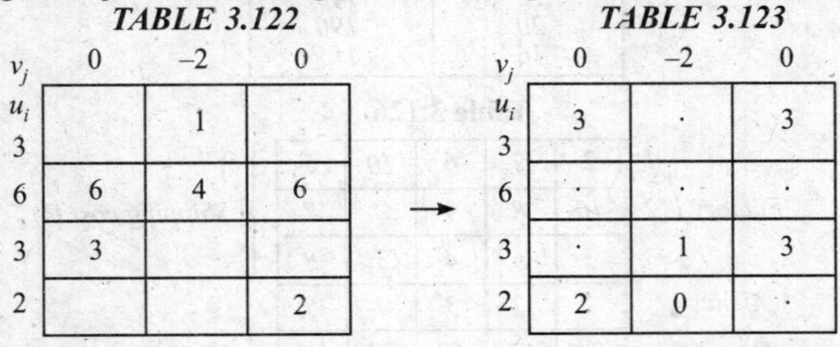

TABLE 3.122

u_i \ v_j	0	–2	0
3		1	
6	6	4	6
3	3		
2			2

(u_i, v_j) *matrix for occupied cells*

→

TABLE 3.123

u_i \ v_j	0	–2	0
3	3	·	3
6	·	·	·
3	·	1	3
2	2	0	·

$(u_i + v_j)$ *matrix for vacant cells*

TABLE 3.124

2	·	4
·	·	·
·	1	2
3	3	·

Cell evaluation matrix

Since all cell evaluations are positive, initial basic feasible solution given by table 3.121 is optimal. The transportation and penalty cost associated with this solution is

$= 1 \times 10 + 6 \times 60 + 4 \times 10 + 6 \times 10 + 2 \times 40 + 3 \times 15$

$= 10 + 360 + 40 + 60 + 80 + 45 = 595.$

3.6-2 The Maximization Problem

The transportation problem may involve maximization of profit rather than minimization of cost. Such a problem may be solved in one of the following ways:

(*a*) As maximization of a function is equivalent to minimization of negative of that function, the given problem may be converted into a minimization problem by multiplying the profit matrix by – 1. Minimization of this negative profit matrix by the usual method will be equivalent to the maximization of the given problem.

(*b*) It may be converted into a minimization problem, by subtracting all the profits from the highest profit in the matrix. The problem can then be solved by the usual methods.

(*c*) It may be solved as a maximization problem itself. However, while finding the initial basic feasible solution, allocations are to be made in highest profit cells, rather than in lowest cost cells. Also solution will be optimal when all cell evaluations are *non-positive* (≤ 0).

Examples will be now considered to explain each of the above procedures.

EXAMPLE 3.6-3 (Profit Maximization Problem)

A company has 3 factories manufacturing the same product and 5 sales agencies in different parts of the country. Production costs differ from factory to factory and the selling prices from agency to agency. The shipping cost per unit product from each factory to each agency is known. Given the following data, find the production and distribution schedules most profitable to the company.

TABLE 3.125

Factory i	*Production cost/unit (₹)*	*Max. capacity (No. of units)*
1	*18*	*140*
2	*20*	*190*
3	*16*	*115*

Table 3.126

1	*2*	*2*	*6*	*10*	*5*	
Factory i 2	*10*	*8*	*9*	*4*	*7*	*Shipping cost (₹)*
3	*5*	*6*	*4*	*3*	*8*	
Ajency j	*1*	*2*	*3*	*4*	*5*	
Demand	*74*	*94*	*69*	*39*	*119*	
Selling price (₹)	*35*	*37*	*36*	*39*	*34*	

Solution

Step I: Prepare the Transportation Table

First we are to construct a profit matrix in which

profit/unit = sales price/unit – production cost/unit – transportation cost/unit.

Thus, profit/unit from factory 1 to sales agency 1 = ₹ (35–18–2) = ₹ 15, profit/unit from factory 1 to sales agency 2 = ₹ (37–18–2) = ₹ 17, and so on.

The resulting profit matrix is shown in table 3.127.

TABLE 3.127

Sales agencies

Factories	1	2	3	4	5	*Production capacity*
1	35–18–2 = 15	37–18–2 = 17	36–18–6 = 12	39–18–10 = 11	34–18–5 = 11	140
2	35–20–10 = 5	37–20–8 = 9	36–20–9 = 7	39–20–4 = 15	34–20–7 = 7	190
3	35–16–5 = 14	37–16–6 = 15	36–16–4 = 16	39–16–3 = 20	34–16–8 = 10	115
Demand	74	94	69	39	119	445 / 395

In table 3.127, total production capacity = 445 units,

total demand = 395 units.

∴ Surplus capacity = 50 units.

Therefore, we create a dummy sales agency to take up the excess capacity of 50 units. The associated unit profit is zero in each cell. Therefore, we have the profit table 3.128 to maximize.

TABLE 3.128

Table 3.128

Sales agencies

Factories	1	2	3	4	5	Dm	*Capacity*
1	15	17	12	11	11	0	140
2	5	9	7	15	7	0	190
3	14	15	16	20	10	0	115
Demand	74	94	69	39	119	50	445/445

Balanced maximization problem

Step II: Convert the Maximization Problem to Minimization Problem

For this the above profit matrix is converted into a *loss matrix* by changing the signs of all the cell values as shown in table 3.129.

TABLE 3.129

Table 3.129

Sales agencies

		1	2	3	4	5	Dm	*Capacity*
Factories	1	–15	–17	–12	–11	–11	0	140
	2	–5	–9	–7	–15	–7	0	190
	3	–14	–15	–16	–20	–10	0	115
Demand		74	94	69	39	119	50	

We can now proceed with this matrix for minimization of loss. Since it is slightly cumbersome to work with negative values, they can be made positive by adding, say 20, the highest negative number to each cell value. This leads to the *relative loss* table 3.130.

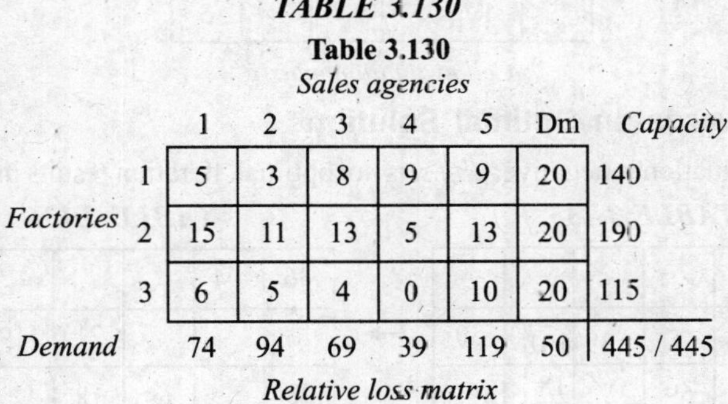

TABLE 3.130

Table 3.130

Sales agencies

		1	2	3	4	5	Dm	*Capacity*
Factories	1	5	3	8	9	9	20	140
	2	15	11	13	5	13	20	190
	3	6	5	4	0	10	20	115
Demand		74	94	69	39	119	50	445 / 445

Relative loss matrix

Table 3.130 represents a balanced minimization problem. The optimal production plus transportation schedule is now determined for this problem. Schedule that minimizes the losses will maximize the total profit. Dummy cells are treated at par with other real cells during computations.

Step III: Find Initial Basic Feasible Solution

Initial b.f.s. obtained by Vogel's approximation method is represented in table 3.131.

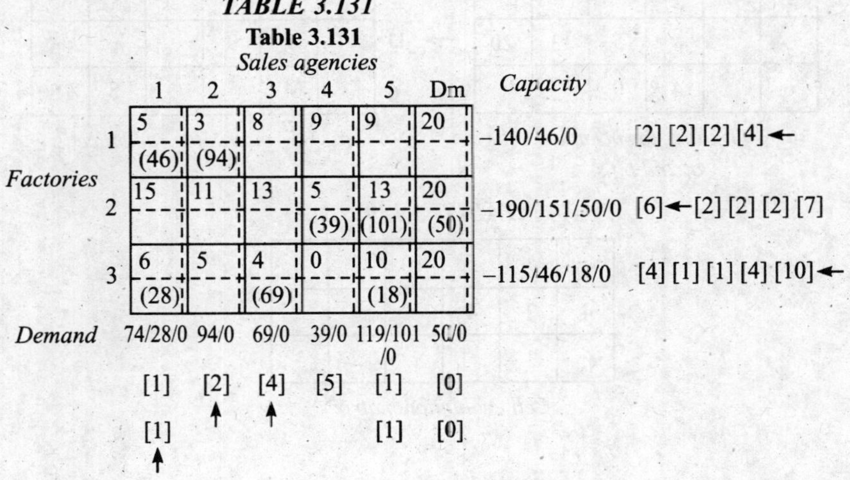

TABLE 3.131

Table 3.131

Sales agencies

		1	2	3	4	5	Dm	*Capacity*	
Factories	1	5 (46)	3 (94)	8	9	9	20	–140/46/0	[2] [2] [2] [4] ←
	2	15	11	13	5 (39)	13 (101)	20 (50)	–190/151/50/0	[6] ← [2] [2] [2] [7]
	3	6 (28)	5	4 (69)	0	10 (18)	20	–115/46/18/0	[4] [1] [1] [4] [10] ←
Demand		74/28/0	94/0	69/0	39/0	119/101/0	50/0		
		[1]	[2] ↑	[4] ↑	[5]	[1]	[0]		
		[1] ↑				[1]	[0]		

Step IV: Perform Optimality Test

Since number of allocations are 8(= $m + n - 1 = 3 + 6 - 1$) and they are in independent positions, optimality test can be performed which yields the following tables:

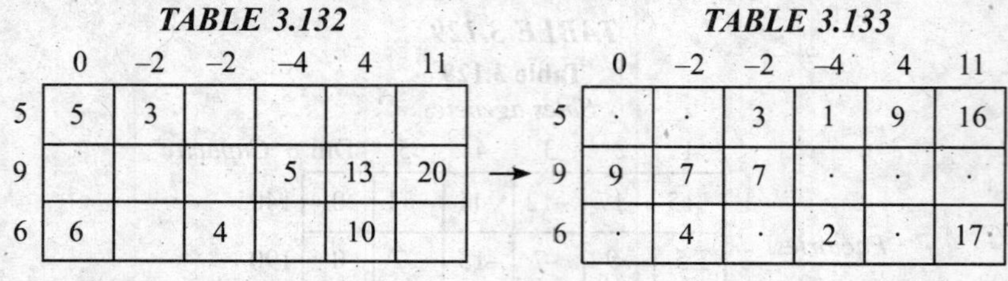

TABLE 3.132

	0	–2	–2	–4	4	11
5	5	3				
9				5	13	20
6	6		4		10	

Unit loss matrix for occupied cells of i.b.f.s.

→

TABLE 3.133

	0	–2	–2	–4	4	11
5	·	·	3	1	9	16
9	9	7	7	·	·	·
6	·	4	·	2	·	17

$(u_i + v_j)$ matrix for empty cells

TABLE 3.134

·	·	5	8	0	4
6	4	6	·	·	·
·	1	·	–2✓	·	3

Cell evaluation matrix

Step V: Iterate Towards an Optimal Solution

Since one cell evaluation is negative, *i.b.f.s.* is not optimal. Iteration results in the following tables:

TABLE 3.135

46	94				
			– 39	+ 101	50
28		69	+ ✓	– 18	

i.b.f.s. with closed path

→

TABLE 3.136

46	94				
			21	119	50
28		69	18		

Second b.f.s.

Step VI: Perform Optimality Test

Table 3.136 is now checked for optimality. The following tables are obtainted:

TABLE 3.137

	0	–2	–2	–6	2	9
5	5	3				
11				5	13	20
6	6		4	0		

$(u_i + v_j)$ matrix for occupied cells of 2nd b.f.s.

→

TABLE 3.138

	0	–2	–2	–6	2	9
5	·	·	3	–1	7	14
11	11	9	9	·	·	·
6	·	4	·	·	8	15

$(u_i + v_j)$ matrix for vacant cells

TABLE 3.139

·	·	5	10	2	6
4	2	4	·	·	·
·	1	·	·	2	5

Cell evaluation matrix

As all cell evaluations are positive, second *b.f.s.* given by table 3.136 is optimal. The *profit* associated with this optimal production-cum-distribution schedule as obtained from tables 3.128 and 3.136 is

$$= ₹ [15 \times 46 + 17 \times 94 + 15 \times 21 + 7 \times 119 + 0 \times 50 + 14 \times 28 + 16 \times 69 + 20 \times 18]$$

$$= ₹ [690 + 1{,}598 + 315 + 833 + 0 + 392 + 1{,}104 + 360] = ₹ 5{,}292.$$

Note that production capacity of factory 2 remains unused by 50 units and yields no profit.

EXAMPLE 3.6-4 (Maximization Problem)

A company wishes to determine an investment strategy for each of the next four years. Five investment types have been selected, investment capital has been allocated for each of the coming four years and maximum investment levels have been established for each investment type. An assumption is that amounts invested in any year will remain invested until the end of the planning horizon of four years. The following table summarizes the data for this problem. The values in the body of the table represent net return on investment of one rupee upto the end of the planning horizon. For example, a rupee invested in investment type B at the beginning of year 1 will grow to ₹ 1.90 by the end of the fourth year, yielding a net return of ₹ 0.90.

TABLE 3.140

Investment made at the beginning of the year	*Net return data on investment type*					*Rupees available (in 000's)*
	A	*B*	*C*	*D*	*E*	
1	*0.80*	*0.90*	*0.60*	*0.75*	*1.00*	*500*
2	*0.55*	*0.65*	*0.40*	*0.60*	*0.50*	*600*
3	*0.30*	*0.25*	*0.30*	*0.50*	*0.20*	*750*
4	*0.15*	*0.12*	*0.25*	*0.35*	*0.10*	*800*
Maximum rupee investment (in 000's)	*750*	*600*	*500*	*800*	*1,000*	*2,650/3,650*

The objective in this problem is to determine the amount to be invested at the beginning of each year in each investment to maximize the net rupee return for the four-year period.

Solution

Step I: Prepare the Transportation Table

We note that this transportation problem is unbalanced. Amount available is less than required by ₹ 1,000 thousands. Dummy row is added; return for every cell of this row is taken as zero.

TABLE 3.141

	Net return data on investment type					*Available rupees (000's)*
Year	A	B	C	D	E	
1	0.80	0.90	0.60	0.75	1.00	500
2	0.55	0.65	0.40	0.60	0.50	600
3	0.30	0.25	0.30	0.50	0.20	750
4	0.15	0.12	0.25	0.35	0.10	800
Dm	0	0	0	0	0	1,000
Max.rupees investment (000's)	750	600	500	800	1,000	3,650/3,650

Balanced maximization problem

Step II: Convert the Maximization Problem into Minimization Problem

This is done by subtracting all the elements from the highest value which is 1.00. The resulting *loss matrix* is given in table 3.142. The losses have been multiplied by 100 each to do away with decimals. The table, therefore, represents the unit losses in paise.

TABLE 3.142

Net loss in paise on investment type

	Year	A	B	C	D	E	*Rs. available (000's)*	
	1	20	10	40	25	0 (500)	500/0	[10]
	2	45	35 (100)	60	40	50 (500)	600/100/0	[5] [5]
	3	70	75	70	50 (750)	80	750/0	[20] [20] ←
	4	85 (250)	88	75 (500)	65 (50)	90	800/750/250/0	[10] [10] [10] [3]
Max. rupees investment (000's)	Dm	100 (500)	100 (500)	100	100	100	1,000/500/0	[0] [0] [0] 0]
		750 /500/0	600 /500/0	500/0	800 /50/0	1,000 /500/0		
		[25]	[25]	[20]	[15]	[50] ↑		
		[25]	[40] ↑	[10]	[10]	[30] ↑		
		[15]	[13]	[5]	[15]			
		[15]	[12]	[25]	[35]			

Step III: Find Initial Basic Feasible Solution

Initial *b.f.s.* obtained by Vogel's method is represented in table 3.142.

Step IV: Perform Optimality Test

Since number of allocations are 9(= $m + n - 1 = 5 + 5 - 1$) and they are in independent positions, optimality test can be performed and involves the tables below:

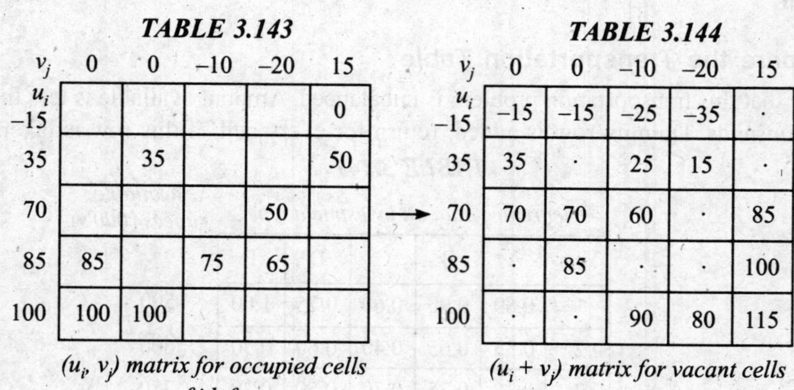

TABLE 3.143

u_i \ v_j	0	0	−10	−20	15
−15					0
35		35			50
70				50	
85	85		75	65	
100	100	100			

(u_i, v_j) matrix for occupied cells of i.b.f.s.

→

TABLE 3.144

u_i \ v_j	0	0	−10	−20	15
−15	−15	−15	−25	−35	·
35	35	·	25	15	·
70	70	70	60	·	85
85	·	85	·	·	100
100	·	·	90	80	115

(u_i + v_j) matrix for vacant cells

TABLE 3.145

35	25	65	60	·
10	·	35	25	·
0	5	10	·	–5
·	3	·	·	–10
·	·	10	20	✓ –15

Cell evaluation matrix

Since some cell evaluations are negative, *i.b.f.s.* is not optimal.

Step V: Iterate Towards an Optimal Solution

Iteration involves the following tables:

TABLE 3.146

				500
	+ 100	·		– 500
			750	
250		500	50	
500	– 500			✓ +

Initial b.f.s. with closed path

→

TABLE 3.147

				500
	600			* ε
			750	
250		500	50	
500	*			500

Second (degenerate) solution

On reallocating 500, two cells marked * become vacant while cell (5, 5) becomes basic and the solution becomes degenerate (Table 3.147). Out of the two recently vacant cells, cell (2, 5) has a unit loss of 50 Paise while cell (D_m, 2) has a loss of 100 Paise; ∈ is, therefore, allocated to cell (2, 5) in table 3.147 to make the solution non-degenerate.

This solution is checked for optimality. It is found to be non-optimal. After one more iteration, the optimal solution obtained is given below:

TABLE 3.148

				500
ε	600			
			750	
250		500	50	
500				500

Optimal solution

The net return on investment for the 4-year period, as obtained from tables 3.141 and 3.148 is found to be

$$= ₹\ [500 \times 1 + 600 \times 0.65 + 750 \times 0.50 + 250 \times 0.15 + 500 \times 0.25 + 50 \times 0.35] \times 1{,}000$$

$$= ₹\ [500 + 390 + 375 + 375 + 125 + 175] \times 1{,}000 = ₹\ 19{,}40{,}000.$$

EXAMPLE 3.6-5 (Profit Maximization Problem)

A company manufacturing air coolers has two plants located at Mumbai and Kolkata with a capacity of 200 units and 100 units per week respectively. The company supplies the air coolers to its four show rooms situated at Ranchi, Delhi, Lucknow and Kanpur which have a maximum demand of 75, 100, 100 and 30 units respectively. Due to the differences in raw material cost and transportation cost, the profit per unit in rupees differs which is shown in the table below.

TABLE 3.149

	Ranchi	*Delhi*	*Lucknow*	*Kanpur*
Mumbai	*90*	*90*	*100*	*110*
Kolkata	*50*	*70*	*130*	*85*

Plan the production programme so as to maximize the profit. The company may have its production capacity at both plants partly or wholly unused.

[H.P.U. B.Tech. June, 2015; P.T.U. MBA May, 2014; P.U.B. Com. April, 2007]

Solution. It consists of the following steps:

Step I: Make the Transportation Matrix

For the given data, the transportation matrix is as shown below:

TABLE 3.150

	Ranchi	*Delhi*	*Lucknow*	*Kanpur*	*Supply*	
Mumbai	90	90	100	110	200	Total supply = 300 units
Kolkata	50	70	130	85	100	Total demand = 305 units
Demand	75	100	100	30		

Thus, supply and demand are not balanced. As the demand is more than supply, a dummy source is introduced to meet the extra demand and zero profit coefficients are introduced since nothing is produced at the dummy source and, therefore, nothing can be sold. The resulting matrix is shown in table 3.151.

TABLE 3.151

	Ranchi	*Delhi*	*Lucknow*	*Kanpur*	*Supply*
Mumbai	90	90	100	110	200
Kolkata	50	70	130	85	100
Dummy source	0	0	0	0	5 *Balanced maximization problem*
Demand	75	100	100	30	

Step II: Find Initial Basic Feasible Solution

We shall use Vogel's approximation method to find the initial feasible solution. This method consists of substeps 1, 2, 3 and 4 already explained in example 3.5-1.

Note that we are dealing with maximization problem. Hence we shall enter the difference between the *highest* and the *second highest* elements in each row to the right of the row and the difference between the highest and the second highest elements in each column below the corresponding column. Each of these differences represents the *unit profit lost* for not allocating to the highest profit cell. Thus, while making allocations, at first we select cell (2, 3) with highest entry in row 2 which corresponds to the highest difference of [45]. Same is true for other allocations in table 3.152.

TABLE 3.152

	Ranchi	Delhi	Lucknow	Kanpur	Supply
Mumbai	90 (70)	90 (100)	100	110 (30)	200/170/70/0 [10] [20] [0]
Kolkata	50	70	130 (100)	85	100/0 [45] ←
Dummy source	0 (5)	0	0	0	5/0 [0] [0] [0]
Demand	75/5/0 [40] [90] [90] ↑	100/0 [20] [90] [90] ↑	100/0 [30]	30/0 [25] [110] ↑	

Step III: Perform Optimality Test

Required number of allocations = $m + n - 1 = 3 + 4 - 1 = 6$.

Actual number of allocations = 5.

Therefore we allocate very small positive number ε to cell (1, 3) [cell having *maximum profit* out of vacant cells] so that the number of allocations becomes 6. This is shown in table 3.153. These 6 allocations are in independent positions. Therefore optimality test can be performed. This consists of substeps 1, 2, 3, 4 and 5, details of which are given in example 3.5-1.

TABLE 3.153

	Ranchi	Delhi	Lucknow	Kanpur	Supply
Mumbai	90 (70)	90 (100)	100 (ε)	110 (30)	200
Kolkata	50	70	130 (100)	85	100
Dummy source	0 (5)	0	0	0	5
Demand	75	100	100	30	

Initial basic feasible solution

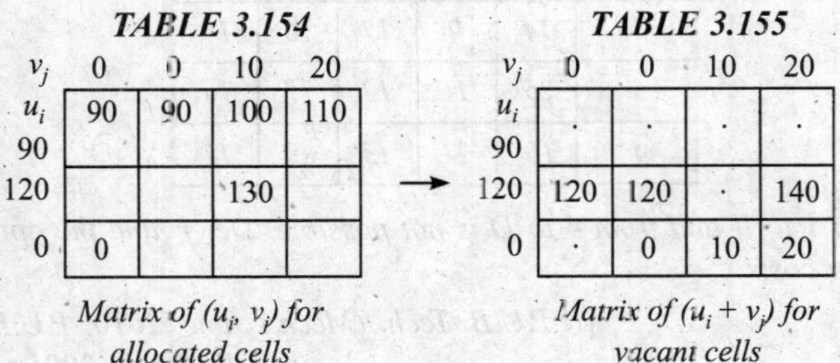

TABLE 3.154

u_i \ v_j	0	0	10	20
90	90	90	100	110
120			130	
0	0			

Matrix of (u_i, v_j) for allocated cells

→

TABLE 3.155

u_i \ v_j	0	0	10	20
90	·	·	·	·
120	120	120	·	140
0	·	0	10	20

Matrix of $(u_i + v_j)$ for vacant cells

TABLE 3.156

·	·	·	·
−70	−50	·	−55
·	0	−10	−20

Cell evaluation matrix

Since all cell values are *either negative or zero* (maximization problem), the initial basic feasible solution of table 3.153 is optimal. The demand at Ranchi is left unsatisfied by 5 units. The profit corresponding to the above scheme is

$$Z_{max} = ₹\,[90 \times 70 + 90 \times 100 + 110 \times 30 + 130 \times 100 + 0 \times 5] = ₹\,31,600.$$

3.6-3 Different Production costs

Sometimes a particular product may be manufactured at and then transported from different production plants. The production cost could be different in different units due to various reasons *e.g.*, new and more automation will bring down the product cost. In such problems the manufacturing cost is added to the transportation cost while finding the optimal solution (Refer examples 3.6-1 and 3.6-3). If in a transportation problem along with the variable production costs, fixed costs at various production plants are also given, the latter are neglected and no consideration is given to them while solving the problem (Refer exercise 30 (*b*)).

3.6-4 No Allocation in Particular Cell/Cells

In a transportation problem, some routes may be prohibited due to reasons such as road blockage, strike by route carriers, floods, etc. To avoid allocation in a particular cell/cells, a heavy penalty cost (M or ∞) is assigned to that cell/cells and then the problem is solved in the usual manner.

EXAMPLE 3.6-6

A company has factories at four different places, which supply warehouses A, B, C, D and E. Monthly factory capacities are 200, 175, 150 and 325 units respectively. Monthly warehouse requirements are 110, 90, 120, 230 and 160 units respectively. Unit shipping costs are given in table 3.157. The costs are in rupees.

TABLE 3.157

To / *From*	*A*	*B*	*C*	*D*	*E*
1	*13*	--	*31*	*8*	*20*
2	*14*	*9*	*17*	*6*	*10*
3	*25*	*11*	*12*	*17*	*15*
4	*10*	*21*	*13*	--	*17*

Shipment from 1 to B and from 4 to D is not possible. Determine the optimum distribution to minimize shipping costs.

[*H.P.U.B. Tech. (Mech.) June 2010; P.U.B.E.(Mech.) 2002; B.E.(Prod.) 2001; B.E.(Elect.) 2003*]

Solution

Step I: Set up the Transportation Table

Here, total capacity = 200 + 175 + 150 + 325 = 850 units,

total demand = 110 + 90 + 120 + 230 + 160 = 710 units.

Since demand is less than the capacity, a dummy warehouse *d* is created to absorb this additional capacity of 140 units. The associated cost elements will be all zero. Further to avoid allocation in cells (1, B) and (4, D), a very heavy penalty, + M is allocated to these cells. The modified transportation matrix is shown in table 3.158.

TABLE 3.158

To / *From*	A	B	C	D	E	*d*	*Capacity*
1	13	M	31	8 (200)	20	0	200/0(8) (5)
2	14	9	17	6 (30)	10 (145)	0	175/145/0 (6) (3) (3) (1)
3	25	11 (10)	12	17	15	0 (140)	150/10/0 (11)←(1) (1) (1) (1) (1)
4	10 (110)	21 (80)	13 (120)	M	17 (15)	0	325/215/200/80/0 (10) (3) (3) (3) (3) (4)
Demand	110/0	90 /80/0	120/0	230 /30/0	160 /15/0	140/0 (0)	*Initial basic feasible solution*
	(3)	(2)	(1)	(2)	(5)		
	(3)	(2)	(1)	(2)	(5)		
	(4)	(2)	(1)	(11)	(5)		
	(4)	(2)	(1)	↑	(5)		
	(15)	(10)	(1)		↑		
	↑	(10)	(1)		(2)		
		↑			(2)		

Step II: Find the Initial Basic Feasible Solution

Using Vogel's approximation method, the initial basic feasible solution is obtained. This is shown in table 3.158.

MODI method is now used to find optimal solution. This solution obtained after a few iterations is shown in table 3.159.

TABLE 3.159

To / *From*	A	B	C	D	E	*d*	*Capacity*
1	13	M	31	8 (200)	20	0	200
2	14	9	17	6 (30)	10 (145)	0	175
3	25	11 (90)	12 (45)	17	15 (15)	0	150
4	10 (110)	21	13 (75)	M	17	0 (140)	325
Demand	110	90	120	230	160	140	

EXAMPLE 3.6-7 (Overtime Production)

A company has factories at A, B and C which supply warehouses at D, E, F and G. The factory capacities are 230, 280 and 180 respectively for regular production. If overtime production is utilised, the capacities can be increased to 300, 360 and 190 respectively. Increment unit overtime costs are ₹ 5, ₹ 4 and ₹ 6 respectively. The current warehouse requirements are 165, 175, 205 and 165 respectively. Unit shipping costs in rupees between the factories and the warehouses are

TABLE 3.160

To / *From*	*D*	*E*	*F*	*G*
A	*6*	*7*	*8*	*10*
B	*4*	*10*	*7*	*6*
C	*3*	*22*	*2*	*11*

Determine the optimum distribution for the company to minimize costs.
[*R.T.M. Nagpur U.B. Tech. Dec., 2003; June, 2003*]

Solution

Step I: Set up the Transportation Table

Overtime production can be represented as additional factories, producing the item at their corresponding higher costs. For istance, shipping cost for the overtime shipment from factory A to warehouses D, E, F and G will be 6 + 5 = 11, 7 + 5 = 12, 8 − 5 = 13 and 10 + 5 = 15 rupees respectively. Similarly, from factory B to these warehouses it will be ₹ 8, 14, 11 and 10 respectively and from C to them it will be ₹ 9, 28, 8 and 17 respectively. Hypothetical factories for overtime production will have capacities of 70, 80 and 10 units respectively. As the total capacity is higher than the total demand, a dummy warehouse *d* is created to absorb this excess capacity of (300 + 360 + 190) – (165 + 175 + 205 + 165) = 140 units. The modified matrix is shown in table 3.161.

TABLE 3.161

To / *From*	D	E	F	G	*d*	*Capacity*
A	6	7 (175)	8 (25)	10	0 (30)	230
B	4 (115)	10	7	6 (165)	0	280
C	3	22	2 (180)	11	0	180
A_1	11	12	13	15	0 (70)	70
B_1	8 (50)	14	11	10	0 (30)	80
C_1	9	28	8	17	0 (10)	10
Demand	165	175	205	165	140	*Initial b.f.s.*

Step II: Find the Initial Basic Feasible Solution

This solution obtained by following the Vogel's approximation method is shown in table 3.161.

Step III: Perform Optimality Test

The above solution is not optimal. The optimal solution after one iteration is shown in table 3.162.

TABLE 3.162

From \ To	D	E	F	G	d	Capacity
A	6 (30)	7 (175)	8 (25)	10	0	230
B	4 (115)	10	7	6 (165)	0	280
C	3	22	2 (180)	11	0	180
A_1	11	12	13	15	0 (70)	70
B_1	8 (20)	14	11	10	0 (60)	80
C_1	9	28	8	17	0 (10)	10
Demand	165	175	205	165	140	*Optimal solution*

3.7 ADDITIONAL PROBLEMS

EXAMPLE 3.7-1

A company has seven manufacturing units situated in different parts of the country. Due to recession it is proposed to close four of these and to concentrate production in the remaining three units. Production in these units will actually be increased from present levels and would require an increase in the personnel employed in them. Personnel at the closed units expressed their desire for moving to any one of the remaining units and the company is willing to provide them removal (transfer) costs.

The retraining expenses would have to be incurred as the technology in these units are different. Not all existing personnel can be absorbed by transfer and a number of redundancies will arise, cost of redundancy is given as a general figure at each unit closed.

		A	*B*	*C*	*D*
No. employed :		*200*	*400*	*300*	*200*
		(These units A, B, C and D are to be closed)			
Retraining costs in ₹ '000/person		*A*	*B*	*C*	*D*
Transfer to	*E*	*0.5*	*0.4*	*0.6*	*0.3*
	F	*0.6*	*0.4*	*0.6*	*0.3*
	G	*0.5*	*0.3*	*0.7*	*0.3*
Removal costs in ₹ '000/person		*A*	*B*	*C*	*D*
Transfer to	*E*	*2.5*	*3.6*	*3.4*	*4.7*
	F	*2.4*	*4.6*	*3.4*	*1.7*
	G	*2.5*	*2.7*	*3.3*	*2.7*
Redundancy payments in		*A*	*B*	*C*	*D*
₹ '000/person	*:*	*6.0*	*5.0*	*6.0*	*7.0*
Additional personnel required at units	*:*	*E*	*F*	*G*	
Required	*:*	*350*	*450*	*200*	

(i) Obtain a solution to the problem of the cheapest means to transfer personnel from units closed to units which will be expanded.

(*ii*) *State with reason whether or not the solution obtained is optimal and unique.*
(*iii*) *State the costs of the initial and final solutions.* [*I.C.W.A., 1990; I.C.M.A., 1990*]

Solution. (*i*) First, the cost matrix is constructed in which cost = retraining cost + removal (transfer) cost. This is shown in the table below.

TABLE 3.163

From

		A	B	C	D	*Demand*
	E	3	4	4	5	350
To	F	3	5	4	2	450
	G	3	3	4	3	200
Supply		200	400	300	200	1,000 / 1,100

As the total number of persons at A, B, C and D is 1,100 while required at E, F and G is 1,000, the extra 100 persons will become redundant. To balance the supply and demand, a dummy manufacturing unit D_m is, therefore, introduced to take up these 100 persons at the costs of redundancy given in the problem. Thus the following matrix is constructed. Initial basic feasible solution is now obtained by V.A.M.

Table 3.164

From

		A	B	C	D	*Demand*	
	E	3 (200)	4 (100)	4 (50)	5	350/150/100/0	(1) (1) (1) ← (0)
	F	3	5	4 (250)	2 (200)	450/250/0	(1) (1) (1) (1) ←
To	G	3	3 (200)	4	3	200/0	(0) (0) (1)
	D_m	6	5 (100)	6	7	100/0	(1) (1) (0) (1)
Supply		200/0	400 /200/100/0	300 /50/0	200/0		
		(0)	(1) ↑	(0)	(1) ↑	*Initial b.f.s.*	
		(0)	(1)	(0)			
			(1)	(2)			

Test for optimality

No. of allocations = 7 = $m + n - 1$ (= 4 + 4 – 1) and they are in independent positions. Hence optimality test can be applied. It consists of the following tables:

TABLE 3.165

v_j / u_i	0	1	1	–1
3	3	4	4	
3			4	2
2		3		
4		5		

(u_i, v_j) *matrix for occupied cells*

→

TABLE 3.166

v_j / u_i	0	1	1	–1
3	·	·	·	2
3	3	4	·	·
2	2	·	3	1
4	4	·	5	3

($u_i + v_j$) *matrix for vacant cells*

TABLE 3.167

·	·	·	3
0	1	·	·
1	·	1	2
2	·	1	4

Cell evaluation matrix

Since all cell evaluations are non-negative, *i.b.f.s.* is optimal. Thus the optimal policy of transferring persons is

From	*To*	*Total cost (₹ 000's)*
A	E	3 × 200 = 600
B	E	4 × 100 = 400
	G	3 × 200 = 600
	D_m	5 × 100 = 500
C	E	4 × 50 = 200
	F	4 × 250 = 1,000
D	F	2 × 200 = 400
		Total : 3,700

Thus when manufacturing unit B is closed, 100 extra persons there will become redundant. The cost of redundancy there will be ₹ 5,00,000 as shown in the table above.

(*ii*) The solution obtained is optimal but not unique. Zero evaluation of cell (F, A) indicates the existence of an alternate optimal solution.

(*iii*) Costs are same *i.e.*, ₹ 37,00,000.

EXAMPLE 3.7-2

ABC manufacturing company wishes to develop a monthly production schedule for the next three months. Depending upon the sales commitments, the company can either keep the production constant, allowing fluctuations in inventory, or inventories can be maintained at a constant level, with fluctuating production. Fluctuating production necessitates in working overtime, the cost of which is estimated to be double the normal production cost of ₹ 12 per unit. Fluctuating inventories result in inventory carrying cost of ₹ 2 per unit per month. If the company fails to fulfil its sales commitment, it incurs a shortage cost of ₹ 4 per unit per month. The production capacities for the next three months are shown below:

	Production capacity		
Month	*Regular*	*Overtime*	*Sales*
1	*50*	*30*	*60*
2	*50*	*0*	*120*
3	*60*	*50*	*40*

Determine the optimal production schedule.

[*H.P.U.B. Tech. (Mech.) Nov., 2006; AMIE, 2005; D.U. MBA, 2001*]

Solution. Here regular and overtime production capacity is the source and the sales is the destination. The costs for different cells may be computed as follows:

(*i*) For items produced and sold in the same month, there will be no inventory carrying cost. Thus the costs for cells (1, 1), (2, 2) and (3, 3) are ₹ 12 each and for cells $(1_1, 1)$ and $(3_1, 3)$ for overtime production will be ₹ 24 each.

(*ii*) For items produced in a particular month and sold in subsequent months, additional inventory cost of ₹ 2 per unit per month will be incurred. Thus cells (1, 2), (1, 3), (2, 3), (1_1, 2) and (1_1, 3) will have costs of ₹ 14, ₹ 16, ₹ 14, ₹ 26 and ₹ 28 respectively.

(*iii*) For items produced in a particular month to meet the backlog of sales during previous months, in addition to the production costs (normal or overtime), shortage costs of ₹ 4 per unit per month will be incurred. Therefore, for cells (2, 1), (3, 2), (3, 1), (3_1, 2) and (3_1, 1) the costs will be ₹ 16, ₹ 16, ₹ 20, ₹ 28 and ₹ 32 respectively. Thus the equivalent transportation matrix for the given problem will be the one shown in table 3.168. As total production capacity is 240 units and sales are 220 units, a dummy column is added to take up the remaining 20 units and to make it a balanced problem.

TABLE 3.168

Sale in month

Production in month	1	2	3	Dummy	*Production capacity*
1	12	14	16	0	50
2	16	12	14	0	50
3	20	16	12	0	60
1_1	24	26	28	0	30
3_1	32	28	24	0	50
Sales	60	120	40	20	

Table 3.169 represents the *i.b.f.s.* obtained by applying the Vogel's approximation method.

TABLE 3.169

Sale in month

Production in month	1	2	3	Dummy	*Production capacity*	
1	12 (50)	14	16	0	50/0	[12] [2]
2	16	12 (50)	14	0	50/0	[12] [2]
3	20	16 (20)	12 (40)	0	60/20/0	[12] [4] [4]
1_0	24 (10)	26 (20)	28	0	30/20/0	[24] [2] [2]
3_0	32	28 (30)	24	0 (20)	50/30/0	[24] ← [4] [4]
Sales	60 /10/0	120/70 /50/30 /0	40/0	20/0		
	[4]	[2]	[2]	[0]		
	[4] ↑	[4]	[2]			
	[4]	[10] ↑	[16] ↑			
	[8] ↑	[2]				

The above solution is found to be optimal. There exists alternate optimal solution as well. This optimal production schedule involves a cost of ₹ 3,600.

EXAMPLE 3.7-3

A manufacturer must produce a product in sufficient quantitiy to meet his sales contracts in next four months. The production capacity and unit cost of production vary from month to month.

The product produced in one month may be held for sale in later months but at an estimated storage cost of ₹ 1 per unit per month. No storage cost is incurred for goods sold in the same month in which they are produced. The necessary data are given below.

TABLE 3.170

Month	*Contracted sales*	*Maximum production*	*Unit cost of production (₹)*
1	*20*	*40*	*14*
2	*30*	*50*	*16*
3	*50*	*30*	*15*
4	*40*	*50*	*17*

How much should the manufacturer produce each month to minimize total cost?

[*P.T.U.M. Tech. April, 2012; H.P.U.B.E. (Mech.) Nov., 2015, 2008; P.U.B.E. (T.I.T.) Dec., 2008; M.D.U Rohtak B.E. (Mech.) Dec., 2006*]

Solution: The product produced in month 1 will have a total cost of ₹ 14, ₹ 15, ₹ 16 and ₹ 17 if sold in the 1st, 2nd, 3rd and 4th month respectively. This forms the first row of matrix 3.171. Product produced in month 2 cannot be sold in the first month. Hence cell (2, 1) in the matrix is assigned infinite cost. The product will have a total cost of ₹ 16, ₹ 17 and ₹ 18 if sold in 2nd, 3rd and 4th month respectively. Hence the 2nd row of the matrix is prepared accordingly. The rest of the table is completed in the same manner. Finally, a dummy market is included in the table to absorb the excess supply of 30 units of the product. Table 3.171 can now be solved by Vogel's method.

TABLE 3.171

Month	1	2	3	4	Dm	*Maximum production*
1	14	15	16	17	0	40
2	∞	16	17	18	0	50
3	∞	∞	15	16	0	30
4	∞	∞	∞	17	0	50
Contracted sales	20	30	50	40	30	

Table 3.172 represents the initial *b.f.s.* obtained by applying Vogel's approximation method.

TABLE 3.172

Month	1	2	3	4	Dm	*Maximum production*	
1	14 (20)	15 (20)	16	17	0	40/20/0	[14] [15] [1] ←
2	∞	16 (10)	17 (20)	18 (20)	0	50/40/20/0	[16] [16] [1]
3	∞	∞	15 (30)	16	0	30/0	[15] [15] [1]
4	∞	∞	∞	17 (20)	0 (30)	50/20/0	[17] [17] ← [∞] ←
Contracted sales	20/0	30/10/0	50/20/0	40/20/0	30/0		
	[∞] ↑	[1]	[1]	[1]	[0]		
		[1]	[1]	[1]			
		[1]	[1]	[1]			

This solution when checked by MODI method is found to be non-optimal. Cell (... has gained negative evaluation. After one iteration, the following optimal production schedul...

1 – 1 : 20, 1 – 2 : 20, 2 – 2 : 10, 2 – 3 : 20, 2 – Dm : 20, 3 – 3 : 30, 4 – 4 : 40, 4 – Dm : 10; Total cost = ₹ 2,210.

EXAMPLE 3.7-4

Strong-hold Construction Company is interested in taking loans from banks for some of its projects P, Q, R, S and T. The rates of interest and the lending capacity differ from bank to bank. All these projects are to be completed. The relevant details are provided in the following table. Assuming the role of a consultant, advise this company as to how it should take the loans so that the total interest payable will be the least. Are there alternate optimal solutions? If so, indicate one such solution.

	Interest rate in percentage for project					*Max. credit (in thousands of rupees)*
Bank	*P*	*Q*	*R*	*S*	*T*	
Pvt. bank	*20*	*18*	*18*	*17*	*17*	*Any amount*
Nationalised bank	*16*	*16*	*16*	*15*	*16*	*400*
Cooperative bank	*15*	*15*	*15*	*13*	*14*	*250*
Amount required (in thousands of rupees)	*200*	*150*	*200*	*125*	*75*	

[*P.T.U. M. Tech. April, 2012; P.U.B.E. (T.I.T.) Nov., 2006; H.P. B.Tech. (Mech.) June, 2007*]

Solution. The total amount required for the five projects is ₹ 750 thousands. Since Pvt. bank can lend any amount, we allocate ₹ [750 – (400 + 250) = 100] thousands to this bank. The balanced problem is shown below. The initial *b.f.s.* is found by Vogel's approximation method.

TABLE 3.173

Table 3.173

Projects

Banks	P	Q	R	S	T	*Max. Credit (thousands)*	
Pvt. (*P*)	20	18 (100)	18	17	17	100/0	(0) (1) (0) (0)
Nationalised (*N*)	16 (200)	16 (50)	16 (150)	15	16	400/200/50/0	(1) (0) (0) (0)
Cooperative (*C*)	15	15	15 (50)	13 (125)	14 (75)	250/125/50/0	(1) (1) (0)
Amount required (thousands)	200/0	150 /100/0	200/150 /0	125/0	75/0		
	(1)	(1)	(1)	(2) ↑	(2) ↑	*Initial basic feasible solution*	
	(4) ↑	(2)	(2) ↑				

Test for optimality

No. of allocated cells = 7 = 3 + 5 – 1 (= *m* + *n* – 1) and they are in independent positions. Therefore optimality test can be applied. It yields the following tables:

TABLE 3.174

u_i \ v_j	0	0	0	–2	–1
18		18			
16	16	16	16		
15			15	13	14

(u_i, v_j) *matrix for allocated cells*

→

TABLE 3.175

u_i \ v_j	0	0	0	–2	–1
18	18	·	18	16	17
16	·	·	·	14	15
15	15	15	·	·	·

$(u_i + v_j)$ *matrix for vacant cells*

TABLE 3.176

2	·	0	1	0
·	·	·	1	1
0	0	·	·	·

Cell evaluation matrix

Since all cell values are non-negative, i.b.f.s. is optimal. Total interest as per the above allocation

$$= ₹\ [100 \times 0.18 + 200 \times 0.16 + 50 \times 0.16 + 150 \times 0.16 + 50 \times 0.15 + 125 \times 0.13 + 75 \times 0.14] \times 1{,}000$$

$$= ₹\ [18 + 32 + 8 + 24 + 7.5 + 16.25 + 10.5] \times 1{,}000 = ₹\ 1{,}16{,}250.$$

Further, since some of the cell evaluations are zero, alternate optimal solutions exist. To get one such solution, we include, say, cell (P, T) as the basic cell and reallocate as indicated below:

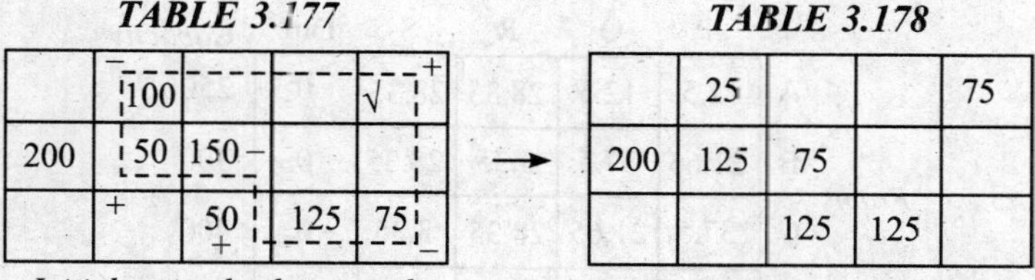

TABLE 3.177

	− 100			√ +
200	50	150 −		
	+	50 +	125	75 −

Initial optimal solution with reallocation

→

TABLE 3.178

	25			75
200	125	75		
		125	125	

Alternate optimal solution

Total interest as per the alternate solution

$$= ₹\ [25 \times 0.18 + 200 \times 0.16 + 125 \times 0.16 + 75 \times 0.16 + 125 \times 0.15 + 125 \times 0.13 + 75 \times 0.17] \times 1{,}000$$

$$= ₹\ [4.5 + 32 + 20 + 12 + 18.75 + 16.25 + 12.75] \times 1{,}000 = ₹\ 1{,}16{,}250.$$

Since the total interest remains same, the alternate solution is also optimal.

EXAMPLE 3.7-5

A complay has factories at A, B and C which supply warehouses at P, Q, R and S. Weekly factory capacities are 250, 300 and 400 units respectively for normal shift. Factories A and B are capable of overtime production of 50 and 75 units per week with an incremental cost of ₹ 4 and ₹ 5 respectively. The current warehouse requirements are 200, 275, 275 and 300 units. The positions of the points A, B, C; P, Q, R and S are as shown below:

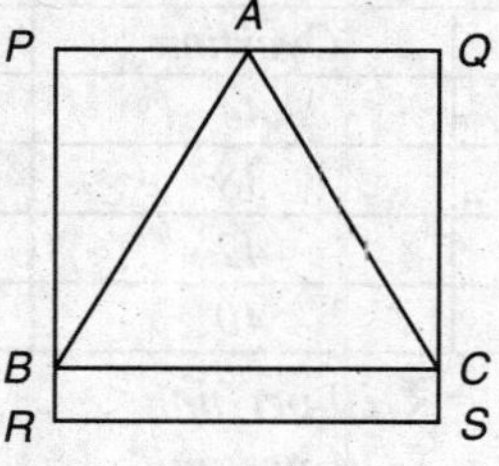

Fig. 3.2

Roads PQ, QS, SR and RP form a square of 10 km side, whereas roads AB, BC and CA form an equilateral triangle. A lies midway between P and Q. Transportation cost is estimated at ₹ 2.50 per kilometer. Determine the optimum distribution for minimum cost.

Solution: First find the length of each road and represent it in the form of a matrix. This is shown below:

TABLE 3.179

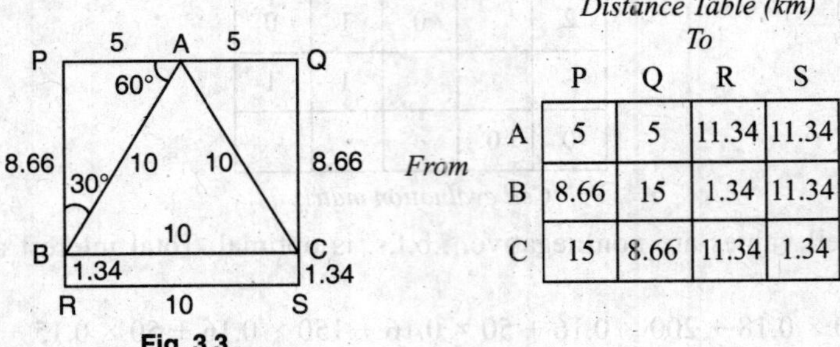

Fig. 3.3

Distance Table (km)

		To			
		P	Q	R	S
From	A	5	5	11.34	11.34
	B	8.66	15	1.34	11.34
	C	15	8.66	11.34	1.34

The final cost table is then prepared according to the given data, which can be minimized in the usual manner.

TABLE 3.180

Cost Table (₹)

		To					
		P	Q	R	S	Dm	*Capacity*
From	A	12.5	12.5	28.35	28.35	0	250
	B	21.65	37.5	3.35	28.35	0	300
	C	37.5	21.65	28.35	3.35	0	400
	A_0	16.5	16.5	32.35	32.35	0	50
	B_0	26.65	42.5	8.35	33.35	0	75
Requirement		200	275	275	300	25	1,075 / 1,075

EXAMPLE 3.7-6 (Production Scheduling Problem)

A company has a manufacturing plant which has the following regular production capacity during a quarter. Additional capacity can be obtained by the use of overtime but it increases the production cost. The forecast demand for the following quarter is also given below. The company starts with an initial inventory from the past quarter and requires a final inventory at the end of the quarter. Items which are produced but not immediately used can be stored with a storage charge. Data is given in the table below:

TABLE 3.181

Production capacity			*Forecast demand*	
Month	*Regular*	*Overtime*	*Month*	*Demand*
Jan.	*200*	*44*	*Jan.*	*200*
Feb.	*190*	*38*	*Feb.*	*150*
March	*210*	*42*	*March*	*250*
April	*200*	*40*	*April*	*250*

Regular production cost = *₹ 10 per unit*
Overtime production cost = *₹ 14 per unit*
Initial inventory = *100 units*
Final inventory = *125 units*
Storage cost on items produced on regular basis = *10% per unit per month*
Storage cost on items produced on overtime basis = *14.3% per unit per month*

Determine the production schedule in order to minimize the total cost of production and storage.

Solution. The following points may be noted to set-up the transportation table for the problem:

1. If full overtime capacity is used, the availability will be 100 + 800 + 164 = 1,064 units, whereas forecast demand plus final inventory is only 850 + 125 = 975 units. Hence a dummy destination (month) will be assumed to take up the balance 89 units. The cost in the associated dummy cells, will be assumed to be zero.
2. Forecast demand for January is 200 units. Since initial inventory is 100 units, the effective demand for this month is 100 units only.
3. Items that are produced in January and are also used in January have unit production cost of ₹ 10 and ₹ 14 for regular and overtime production respectively. Same is true for the months of Feb., March and April.
4. Items that are produced in January but are used in February, will have to be stored for a month, increasing the production-cum storage cost to (₹ 10 + ₹ $\frac{10\times10}{100}$) = ₹ 11 and (₹ 14 + ₹ $\frac{14\times14.3}{100}$) = ₹ 16 respectively for regular and overtime production. If used in March, the costs will increased to ₹ 12 and ₹ 18 and if used in April, they will become ₹ 13 and ₹ 20 respectively.
5. Final inventory at the end of the quarter (*i.e.*, April) is 125 units. The cost coefficients in the cells will be same as in April.
6. Items produced in February cannot be supplied in January. Shortages are not permitted as shortage cost or opportunity cost is not given. Hence infinite cost is assigned to such cells. Same is true for other months.

Table 3.182 represents the entire information.

TABLE 3.182

Forecast demand in month

		Jan.	*Feb.*	*Mar.*	*Apr.*	*Final Inv.*	Dm	*Production capacity*
Jan.	R	10 (100)	11	12	13 (50)	13 (50)	0	200/100/50/0 [10] [11] [1] [1] [0]
	OT	14	16	18	20	20	0 (44)	44/0 [14]←
Feb.	R	∞	10 (112)	11 (40)	12	12 (38)	0	190/78/38/0 [10] [10] [1] [1] [0]
	OT	∞	14 (38)	16	18	18	0	38/0 [14] [14] [2]←
Mar.	R	∞	∞	10 (210)	11	11	0	210/0 [10] [10] [1]←
	OT	∞	∞	14	16	16	0 (42)	42/0 [14] [14]←
Apr.	R	∞	∞	∞	10 (200)	10	0	200/0 [10] [10] [0]
	OT	∞	∞	∞	14	14 (37)	0 (3)	40/37/0 [14] [14]←[0] [0] [0]
		100/0	150/112/0	250/40/0	250/50/0	125/87/37/0	89/45/3/0	
		(4)	(1)	(1)	(1)	(1)	(0)	
		∞ ↑	(1)	(1)	(1)	(1)	(0)	
			(1)	(1)	(1)	(1)	(0)	
			(1)	(1)	(1)	(1)		
			(1)	(1)	(2)	(2)		
			(1)	(1)	(1)	(1)		

Vogel's approximation method has been applied to find initial b.f.s. (Table 3.182). Problem can now be solved in the usual manner.

3.8 LEAST-TIME TRANSPORTATION PROBLEMS

There are some transportation problems where the objective is to minimize *time* rather than transportation cost. Such problems are usually encountered in hospital management, military services, fire services, etc. where the speed of delivery or time of supply is more important than the transportation cost.

Now, while solving problems where the objective is to minimize time for each route, the cost per unit is replaced by the time required to ship the quantity x_{ij} from origin i to destination j, where $i = 1, 2, 3, \ldots, m$ and $j = 1, 2, 3, \ldots, n$. The corresponding transportation matrix is given below.

TABLE 3.183

Table 3.183

	1	2	3	...	n	a_i
1	t_{11}	t_{12}	t_{13}	...	t_{1n}	a_1
2	t_{21}	t_{22}	t_{23}	...	t_{2n}	a_2
3	t_{31}	t_{32}	t_{33}	...	t_{3n}	a_3
:	:	:	:	:	:	:
m	t_{m1}	t_{m2}	t_{m3}	...	t_{mn}	a_m

$$\text{and } \sum_{i=1}^{m} a_i = \sum_{j=1}^{n} b_j.$$

Note that the time of shipment is independent of the number of units shipped. Also since shipments from origins to destinations can be done at the same time on different routes, the shipment time of the total plan is not the sum total of the times of the individual routes. In fact, the shipment of a feasible plan will be complete when the shipment with the largest time on some route in the plan is complete. Such problems, therefore, require a different solution procedure.

Let T_k be the largest time associated with kth feasible plan. Our objective is, therefore, to find out a plan for which T_k is minimum of all values of k. The procedure for getting minimum T_k consists of the following steps:

Step I

Find an initial basic feasible solution. This is obtained by using the same method as for the normal transportation technique.

Step II

Find T_k corresponding to the current feasible solution and cross out all the non-basic cells for which $t_{ij} \geq T_k$.

Step III

Draw a closed path (as in the normal transportation technique) for the basic variable associated with T_k such that when the values at the corner elements are shifted around, this basic variable reduces to zero and no variable becomes negative. This procedure ends if no such closed path can be traced out, otherwise repeat step II.

EXAMPLE 3.8-1

A military equipment is to be transported from three origins to four destinations. The supply at the origins, the demand at the destinations and time of shipment is shown in the table below. The units to be shipped as obtained by rule are given in parentheses. Work out a transportation plan so that the total time required for shipment is minimum.

TABLE 3.184

Destinations

		1	2	3	4	a_i
	1	10 (12)	0 (3)	20	11	15
Origins	2	1	7 (5)	9 (15)	20 (5)	25
	3	12	14	16	18 (5)	5
	b_j	12	8	15	10	45 (Total)

[*Pbi.U. B. Tech., 1999*]

Solution. In this table

$x_{11} = 12, x_{12} = 3, x_{22} = 5, x_{23} = 15, x_{24} = 5$ and $x_{34} = 5$ and all other variables are zero.

The shipping times are $t_{11} = 10, t_{12} = 0, t_{22} = 7, t_{23} = 9, t_{24} = 20$ and $t_{34} = 18$. Therefore, all the shipments of this plan will be complete after

$$T_1 = \max (t_{11}, t_{12}, t_{22}, t_{23}, t_{24}, t_{34}) = t_{24} = 20 \text{ time units.}$$

Therefore, the cell (1, 3) is crossed out according to step II, since it has $t_{13} = 20$ (= T_1). The closed path for x_{24} is shown in the table below.

TABLE 3.185

	1	2	3	4
1	10 (12)	0 − (3)	~~20~~	11 +
2	1	7 + (5)	9 (15)	20 (5) −
3	12	14	16	18 (5)

It is clear from the closed path that x_{24} can be decreased by only three units, for, otherwise x_{12} will become negative. The new solution is shown in table 3.186.

TABLE 3.186

	1	2	3	4
1	10 (12)	0	~~20~~	11 (3)
2	1	7 (8)	9 (15)	20 (2)
3	12	14	16	18 (5)

For table 3.186, T_2 is still equal to 20. The next closed path is shown in table 3.187 where x_{24} is decreased further by 2 units, thereby reducing it to zero. This is shown in table 3.188.

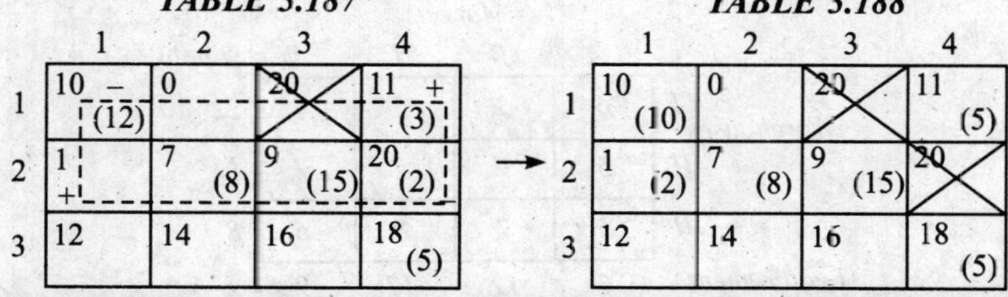

TABLE 3.187

	1	2	3	4
1	10 − (12)	0	~~20~~	11 + (3)
2	1 +	7 (8)	9 (15)	20 (2) −
3	12	14	16	18 (5)

→

TABLE 3.188

	1	2	3	4
1	10 (10)	0	~~20~~	11 (5)
2	1 (2)	7 (8)	9 (15)	~~20~~
3	12	14	16	18 (5)

In table 3.188, $T_3 = t_{34} = 18$, corresponding to x_{34}. The closed path for x_{34} is shown in table below.

TABLE 3.189

	1	2	3	4
1	10 − (10)	0	20 ╳	11 + (5)
2	1 (2)	7 (8)	9 (15)	20 ╳
3	12 +	14	16	18 − (5)

TABLE 3.190

	1	2	3	4
1	10 (5)	0	20 ╳	11 (10)
2	1 (2)	7 (8)	9 (15)	20 ╳
3	12 (5)	14	16	18 ╳

x_{34} can be reduced by 5 units, thus reducing it to zero. So it is crossed out and the resulting solution is shown in table 3.190.

Now $T_4 = t_{31} = 12$. Hence cells (3, 2) and (3, 3) are crossed out since t_{32} and t_{33} are both > t_{31}. This is shown in table 3.191.

TABLE 3.191

	1	2	3	4
1	10 (5)	0	20 ╳	11 (10)
2	1 (2)	7 (8)	9 (15)	20 ╳
3	12 (5)	14 ╳	16 ╳	18 ╳

Since no closed path can be traced for x_{31}, the iterative procedure ends here. Thus the above plan is optimal and the total shipment time is 12 units. Details of the plan are

$x_{11} = 5$ with $t_{11} = 10$, $x_{22} = 8$ with $t_{22} = 7$,

$x_{14} = 10$ with $t_{14} = 11$, $x_{23} = 15$ with $t_{23} = 9$,

$x_{21} = 2$ with $t_{21} = 1$, $x_{31} = 5$ with $t_{31} = 12$.

3.9 POST OPTIMALITY ANALYSIS IN TRANSPORTATION

The transportation models studied above will normally be valid for a limited period only. In actual practice, the reasource capacities and/or destination requirements may vary with time. Likewise, there may be some changes in the transportation cost. Such changes may affect the optimal allocation and the associated transportation cost. One way to study the effect of these changes is to solve the problem a new. Many a times, however, it may not be necessary to do so and the new optimal solution may be obtained by simply incorporating the changes in the current optimal solution, seeing the effects of these changes and carrying out iterations if required.

3.9-1 Changes in Resource Capacities and/or Destination Requirements

EXAMPLE 3.9-1

The following table shows all the necessary information on the available supply from each warehouse, the requirement of each market and the unit transportation cost in rupees from each warehouse to each market.

TABLE 3.192

		Markets				
		A	*B*	*C*	*D*	*Supply*
Warehouses	*I*	6	3	5	4	22
	II	5	9	2	7	15
	III	5	7	8	6	8
Requirement		7	12	17	9	

The shipping clerk has worked out the following schedule from experience: 12 units from I to B, 1 unit from I to C, 9 units from I to D, 15 units from II to C, 7 units from III to A and 1 unit from III to C.

(a) Check if the clerk has made the optimal schedule.

(b) Find the optimal schedule and minimum total shipping cost.

[M.G.U. Kerala M.Com. June, 2010]

(c) If the clerk is approached by a carrier of route III to B who offers to reduce his rate in the hope of getting some business, by how much must the rate be reduced by the driver before the clerk should consider giving him business?

(d) If the supply from warehouse II reduces to 12 units and simultaneously the requirement of market C reduces to 14 units, find the optimal transportation schedule.

[P.U.B.E. (E. & Ec.) April, 2006]

(e) Further, if supply from warehouse I also reduces to 18 units and simultaneously the requirement of market C reduces further to 10 units, will the optimal solution of part (d) change?

(f) If the supply of warehouse II is increased [w.r.t. optimal solution for part (b)] by 1 unit and simultaneously the demand of market C is also increased by 1 unit, will the optimal solution change?

(g) If the supply of warehouse II increases by 3 units [instead of 1 unit in part (f)] and demand of market D also increases by 3 units, will there be change in the optimal solution?

Solution. (*a*) The given basic feasible solution is shown in table 3.193.

TABLE 3.193

Markets

Warehouses	A	B	C	D	*Supply*
I	6	3 (12)	5 (1)	4 (9)	22
II	5	9	2 (15)	7	15
III	5 (7)	7	8 (1)	6	8
Requirement	7	12	17	9	

The total transportation cost= ₹ [3 × 12 + 5 × 1 + 4 × 9 + 2 × 15 + 5 × 7 + 8 × 1]

= ₹ [36 + 5 + 36 + 30 + 35 + 8] = ₹ 150.

The following tables are obtained while checking the optimality of the above feasible solution:

TABLE 3.194

u_i \ v_j	0	1	3	2
2		3	5	4
–1			2	
5	5		8	

(u_i, v_j) matrix for occupied cells

→

TABLE 3.195

u_i \ v_j	0	1	3	2
2	2	·	·	·
–1	–1	0	·	1
5	·	6	·	7

(u_i + v_j) matrix for empty cells

TABLE 3.196

	A	B	C	D
I	4	·	·	·
II	6	9	·	6
III	·	1	·	–1

Cell evaluation matrix

Since cell (III, D) has a negative value, table 3.193 is not optimal.

(*b*) Iteration towards the optimal solution involves the following tables:

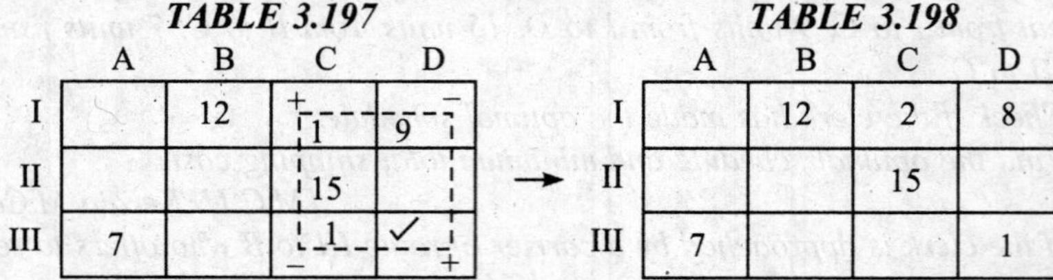

TABLE 3.197

	A	B	C	D
I		12	+ 1	– 9
II			15	
III	7		– 1	✓ +

Initial basic feasible solution with closed path

→

TABLE 3.198

	A	B	C	D
I		12	2	8
II			15	
III	7			1

Second basic feasible solution (optimal b.f.s)

Checking the optimality of second basic feasible solution involves the following tables:

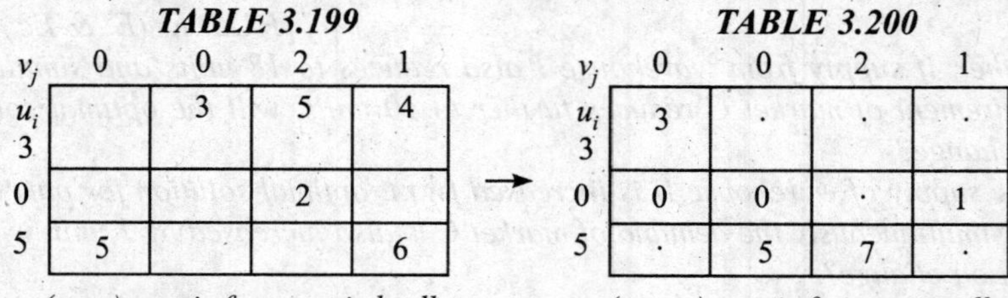

TABLE 3.199

u_i \ v_j	0	0	2	1
3		3	5	4
0			2	
5	5			6

(u_i, v_j) matrix for occupied cells

→

TABLE 3.200

u_i \ v_j	0	0	2	1
3	3	·		·
0	0	0	·	1
5	·	5	7	·

(u_i + v_j) matrix for vacant cells

TABLE 3.201

	A	B	C	D
I	3	·	·	·
II	5	9	·	6
III	·	2	1	·

Cell evaluation matrix

Since all cell values in table 3.201 are positive, second basic feasible solution given by table 3.198 is optimal.

Minimum transportation cost = ₹ [3 × 12 + 5 × 2 + 4 × 8 + 2 × 15 + 5 × 7 + 6 × 1]

= ₹ 149.

(*c*) If the clerk decides to ship all the eight units from III to B instead of 7 units to A and 1 unit to D, it will involve shifting of 7 units from (I, B) to (I, A) and 1 unit to (I, D) which results in the following table:

TABLE 3.202

		Markets			
Warehouses	A	B	C	D	*Supply*
I	6 (7)	3 (4)	5 (2)	4 (9)	22
II	5	9	2 (15)	7	15
III	5	7 (8)	8	6	8
Requirement	7	12	17	9	

Total transportation cost will become

= ₹ [6 × 7 + 3 × 4 + 5 × 2 + 4 × 9 + 2 × 15 + 7 × 8]

= ₹ [42 + 12 + 10 + 36 + 30 + 56] = ₹ 186.

∴ Additional transportation cost = ₹ (186 – 149) = ₹ 37.

∴ The carrier of III to B must reduce the rate by ₹ 37/8 or ₹ 4.63 so that the total cost of transportation remains the same and the clerk can give him business.

(*d*) The modified transportation table is shown below:

TABLE 3.203

	A	B	C	D	*Supply*
I	6	3 (12)	5 (2)	4 (8)	22
II	5	9	2 (12)	7	12
III	5 (7)	7	8	6 (1)	8
Requirement	7	12	14	9	

As the allocated cells remain unchanged, the above modification does not change the optimal schedule.

(*e*) In this case adjustment cannot be made by considering cell (I, C) alone, since allocation in this cell is 2 units only. Even if allocation in this cell is cancelled and allocation in cell (II, C) is also reduced to 10 units to match the requirement of market C, it results in imbalance in the allocated cells of warehouses I and III and it becomes necessary to make changes in allocations, check the solution for optimality and iterate if required.

(*f*) The modified transportation matrix is shown in table 3.204. Since the changes are confined to allocated cells only, the present changes do not affect the optimal allocation plan.

TABLE 3.204

	A	B	C	D	*Supply*
I	6	3 (12)	5 (2)	4 (8)	22
II	5	9	2 (16)	7	16
III	5 (7)	7	8	6 (1)	8
Requirement	7	12	18	9	

(*g*) Since it is not possible to confine the changes to allocated cells only, the optimal solution will change and it is necessary to make changes in the allocations, check the resulting solution for optimality and iterate if required.

3.9-2 Changes in Transportation Costs

An increase in the costs of empty cells will not change the current optimal solution as the current cost itself is too high, that is why there has been no allocations in these cells.

However, a reduction in costs of empty cells or an increase in costs of allocated cells is likely to change the transportation schedule. In this case the problem is reconsidered with the *current optimal solution.* New values of u_i and v_j numbers are computed and evaluations of the empty cells are determined. If they are all non-negative, the current solution still remains optimal. If not, a new solution is obtained which is then tested for optimality.

EXAMPLE 3.9-2

The following table gives the optimal cost of manufacturing and transporting from factories A, B, C and D to destinations E, F, G, H and J as ₹ 6,530.

(a) *Suppose some new equipments are installed that reduce the variable operating cost by ₹ 2 in factory B, will the optimal shipping schedule change?*

(b) *Is there an alternate optimal solution to part (a)? If so, find it.*

(c) *Suppose freight charges from A to E are reduced by ₹ 2 a unit, will it change the shipping schedule? If so, what is the new shipping schedule?*

(d) *If the demand at G increases from 50 units to 60 units, what will be the shipping schedule if there is no increase in supply from any factory?*

TABLE 3.205

		E	F	G	H	J	Supply
Factories	A	8	10 (100)	12	17	15	100
	B	15	13 (70)	18	11	9 (80)	150
	C	14 (70)	20	6 (50)	10	13 (40)	160
	D	13	19	7	6 (210)	12 (70)	280
Demand		70	170	50	210	190	

(*e*) *If demand at G increases to 60 units as well as the supply at factory D is increased by 10 units to meet this increased demand, find the optimal shipping schedule.*

Solution. (*a*) Incorporating the reduced operating cost in factory B and performing the optimality test we get the following tables:

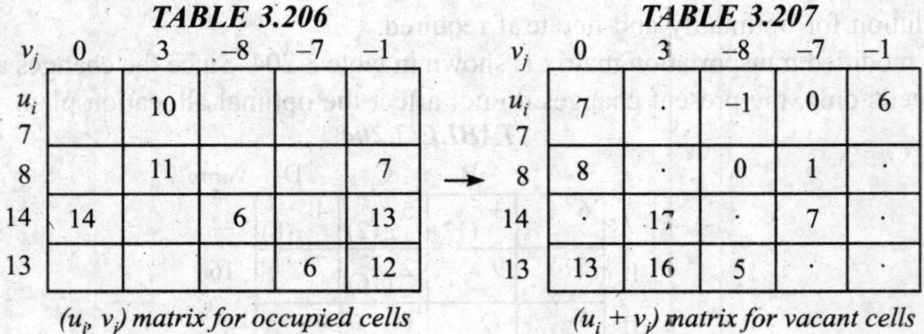

TABLE 3.206

u_i \ v_j	0	3	–8	–7	–1
7		10			
8		11			7
14	14		6		13
13				6	12

(u_i, v_j) matrix for occupied cells

→

TABLE 3.207

u_i \ v_j	0	3	–8	–7	–1
7	7	·	–1	0	6
8	8	·	0	1	·
14	·	17	·	7	·
13	13	16	5	·	·

$(u_i + v_j)$ matrix for vacant cells

TABLE 3.208

	E	F	G	H	J
A	1	·	13	17	9
B	5	·	16	8	·
C	·	3	·	3	·
D	0	3	2	·	·

Cell evaluation matrix

Since all the cell evaluations are positive, the solution is still optimal.

(*b*) In table 3.208, cell evaluation for non-basic cell (D, E) is zero. It means that making an allocation in this cell will not increase the total shipment cost. Trace a closed path treating cell (D, E) as identified cell. This is shown in table 3.209.

TABLE 3.209

	E	F	G	H	J
A		100			
B		70			80
B	– 70		50		+ 40
D	+ ✓			210	– 70

→

TABLE 3.210

	E	F	G	H	J
A		100			
B		70			80
C			50		110
D	70			210	

Alternate optimal solution

Table 3.210 represents the alternate optimal solution.

(*c*) Here cell (A, E) has a cost of ₹ 6 instead of ₹ 8. Therefore, subtracting table 3.207 from table 3.205, after this modification yields table 3.211.

TABLE 3.211

–1	·	13	17	9
7	·	18	10	·
·	3	·	3	·
0	3	2	·	·

Cell evaluation matrix

Thus the present shipping schedule is not optimal. The optimal shipping schedule can be now found by making an iteration. This solution is given by table 3.212.

TABLE 3.212

6 (70)	10 (30)	12	17	15
15	13 (140)	18	11	9 (10)
14	20	6 (50)	10	13 (110)
13	19	7	6 (210)	12 (70)

(*d*) Table 3.213 shows + 10 and – 10 adjustments. Finally, it is to be seen whether table 3.214 is optimal or not. This is left as an exercise for the reader.

TABLE 3.213

8	10 (100)	12	17	15	100
15	13 (70–10)	18	11	9 (80+10)	150
14 (70)	20	6 (50+10)	10	13 (40–10)	160
13	19	7	6 (210)	12 (70)	280
70	170 –10	50 +10	210	190	

→

TABLE 3.214

8	10 (100)	12	17	15	100
15	13 (60)	18	11	9 (90)	150
14 (70)	20	6 (60)	10	13 (30)	160
13	19	7	6 (210)	12 (70)	280
70	160	60	210	190	

(*e*) In this case making + 10 and – 10 adjustments yields tables 3.215 and 3.216.

TABLE 3.215

8	10 (100)	12	17	15	100
15	13 (70)	18	11	9 (80)	150
14 (70)	20	6 (50+10)	10	13 (40–10)	160
13	19	7	6 (210)	12 (70+10)	280 +10
70	170	50 +10	210	190	

→

TABLE 3.216

8	10 (100)	12	17	15	100
15	13 (70)	18	11	9 (80)	150
14 (70)	20	6 (60)	10	13 (30)	160
13	19	7	6 (210)	12 (80)	290
70	170	60	210	190	

Finally, it is to be checked whether table 3.216 is optimal or not. This is left as an exercise.

3.10 THE TRANS-SHIPMENT PROBLEM

The transportation problem assumes that direct routes exist from each source to each destination. However, there are situations in which units may be shipped from one source to another or to other destinations before reaching their final destination. This is called a trans-shipment problem. For example, movement of material involving two different modes of transport—road and railways or between stations connected by broad gauge and metre gauge lines will necessarily require trans-shipment. For the purpose of trans-shipment the distinction between a source and destination is dropped so that a transportation problem with m sources and n destinations gives rise to a trans-shipment problem with $m + n$ sources and $m + n$ destinations. The basic feasible solution to such a problem will involve $[(m + n) + (m + n) - 1]$ or $2m + 2n - 1$ basic variables and if we omit the variables appearing in the $(m + n)$ diagonal cells, we are left with $m + n - 1$ basic variables.

In the trans-shipment problem, as each source or destination is a potential point of supply as well as demand, the total supply, say of N units, is added to the actual supply of each source, as well as to the actual demand at each destination. Also the 'demand' at each source and 'supply' at each destination are set equal to N.

Therefore, we may assume the supply and demand of each location to be fictitious one. These quantities (N) may be regarded as *buffer stocks* and each of these buffer stocks should at least be equal to the total supply/demand in the given problem.

The given trans-shipment problem can, therefore, be regarded as the extended transportation problem and can hence be solved by the transportation technique. In the final solution, units transported from a point to itself *i.e.*, in diagonal cells are ignored as they do not have any physical meaning as there is no transportation involved.

EXAMPLE 3.10-1

A firm has two factories X and Y and three retail stores A, B and C. The number of units of a product available at factories X and Y are 200 and 300 respectively, while demanded at retail stores are 100, 150 and 250 respectively. Rather than shipping directly from sources to destinations, it is decided to investigate the possibility of trans-shipment. Find the optimal shipping schedule. The transportation costs in rupees per unit are given below.

TABLE 3.217

		Factory		Retail store		
		X	Y	A	B	C
Factory	X	0	6	7	8	9
	Y	6	0	5	4	3
Retail store	A	7	2	0	5	1
	B	1	5	1	0	4
	C	8	9	7	6	0

Solution. For this trans-shipment problem, buffer stock = total supply = total demand = 500 units. Adding 500 units to each supply/demand point, we get table 3.218. Initial b.f.s. obtained by the Vogel's approximation method is also shown.

TABLE 3.218

From \ To	X	Y	A	B	C	Supply
X	0 (500)	6	7 (200)	8	9	700
Y	6	0 (500)	5	4 (50)	3 (250)	800
A	7	2	0 (400)	5 (100)	1	500
B	1	5	1	0 (500)	4	500
C	8	9	7	6	0 (500)	500
Demand	500	500	600	650	750	

The optimal solution obtained after one iteration is given in table 3.219. The diagonal allocations in this table may be ignored since they have no physical meaning. The remaining allocations may be interpreted as follows:

TABLE 3.219

From \ To	X	Y	A	B	C
X	0 (500)	6	7 (100)	8 (100)	9
Y	6	0 (500)	5	4 (50)	3 (250)
A	7	2	0 (500)	5	1
B	1	5	1	0 (500)	4
C	8	9	7	6	0 (500)

Factory X supplies 100 units each to retail stores A and B. Factory Y supplies 50 units to retail store B and 250 units to C.

EXAMPLE 3.10-2

Table 3.220 represents the supply from the plants, the requirement at the distribution centres and the unit transportation costs.

TABLE 3.220

Plants \ Distribution centres	*A*	*B*	*C*	*Supply*
1	*11*	*13*	*25*	*150*
2	*13*	*15*	*35*	*300*
Requirement	*150*	*150*	*150*	

When each plant is also considered a destination and each distribution centre is also considered as origin, some additional cost data are necessary, which are given in the tables below:

TABLE 3.221

From plant \ To Plant	*A*	*B*
A	*0*	*75*
B	*11*	*0*

TABLE 3.222

From dist. centre \ To dist. centres	*A*	*B*	*C*
A	*0*	*33*	*11*
B	*11*	*0*	*13*
C	*75*	*13*	*0*

TABLE 3.223

From dist. centre \ To Plant	*1*	*2*
A	*13*	*25*
B	*35*	*13*
C	*55*	*65*

Find the optimal shipping schedule for the trans-shipment problem.

Solution. From the given four tables we get the following transportation formulation of the trans-shipment problem:

TABLE 3.224

From \ To	1	2	A	B	C	Supply
1	0 (150)	75	11 (300)	13 (150)	25	600
2	11 (300)	0 (450)	13	15	35	750
A	13	25	0 (300)	33	11 (150)	450
B	35	13	11	0 (450)	13	450
C	55	65	75	13	0 (450)	450
Requirement	450	450	600	600	600	

A buffer stock of 450 units, which is the total supply as well as total requirement in the original tranportation problem, is added to each row and column of the trans-shipment problem. The optimal solution is also given in table 3.224. The diagonal allocations in the table may be igonred since they have no physical meaning. The remaining allocations may be interpreted as follows:

(*i*) Plant 2 supplies 300 units to plant 1. This increases the supply capacity of plant 1 to 450 units including the 150 units originally available in it.

(*ii*) Plant 1 transports 300 units to distribution centre A and 150 units to B.

(*iii*) Distribution centre A sends 150 units to C out of 300 units available in it.

The total cost of trans-shipment $= 11 \times 300 + 13 \times 150 + 11 \times 300 + 11 \times 150 = 10{,}200$.

3.11 DUAL OF THE TRANSPORTATION PROBLEM

We know any linear programming problem has its dual. Since the transportation problem is a special type of L.P. problem, it also has its dual with usual interpretations and applications. To illustrate let us consider example 3.5-1 along with the transportation cost table 3.3. The mathematical model (Primal) for this problem is rewritten below:

Minimize $Z = 2x_{11} + 3x_{12} + 11x_{13} + 7x_{14} + x_{21} + 0x_{22} + 6x_{23} + x_{24} + 5x_{31} + 8x_{32} + 15x_{33} + 9x_{34}$,

subject to constraints

$$x_{11} + x_{12} + x_{13} + x_{14} = 6,$$
$$x_{21} + x_{22} + x_{23} + x_{24} = 1,$$
$$x_{31} + x_{32} + x_{33} + x_{34} = 10,$$
$$x_{11} + x_{21} + x_{31} = 7,$$
$$x_{12} + x_{22} + x_{32} = 5,$$
$$x_{13} + x_{23} + x_{33} = 3,$$
$$x_{14} + x_{24} + x_{34} = 2,$$

where $x_{ij} \geq 0$; $i = 1, 2, 3$; $j = 1, 2, 3, 4$.

Now the dual of this L.P. problem can be written as

maximize $Z' = 6u_1 + u_2 + 10u_3 + 7v_1 + 5v_2 + 3v_3 + 2v_4$,

subject to

$$u_1 + v_1 \leq 2,$$
$$u_1 + v_2 \leq 3,$$
$$u_1 + v_3 \leq 11,$$
$$u_1 + v_4 \leq 7,$$
$$u_2 + v_1 \leq 1,$$
$$u_2 + v_2 \leq 0,$$

$$u_2 + v_3 \leq 6,$$
$$u_2 - v_4 \leq 1,$$
$$u_3 + v_1 \leq 5,$$
$$u_3 + v_2 \leq 8,$$
$$u_3 + v_3 \leq 15,$$
$$u_3 + v_4 \leq 9,$$

where the dual variables u_i, v_j are unrestricted in sign,

$i = 1, 2, 3; j = 1, 2, 3, 4.$

Interpretation of the Dual

1. The dual variables u_i and v_j are the row numbers and column numbers respectively in table 3.19, used in solving the problem by the modified distribution method. In the dual u_i may be interpreted as the value of the product, free on board, at the ith origin and, therefore, may be called *location rent* and v_j can be interpreted as its value (delivered) at the jth destination and, therefore, may be termed *market price*. Hence Z' which represents the sum of these two factors is to be maximized. The constraints of the dual indicate that to allocate in a cell, the transportation cost in that cell should not be more than the sum of these two factors for that cell.

2. We know that in case of linear programming, the final (optimal) simplex table also represents the optimal solution of the dual without actually solving it. Likewise, the optimal (final) transportation table of the primal represents the optimal solution of the associated dual. For the problem under consideration, the optimal dual solution as given by table 3.34 is

$u_1 = 1, u_2 = -4, u_3 = 5, v_1 = 0, v_2 = 2, v_3 = 10, v_4 = 4.$

$$\text{Value of } Z'_{\max} = ₹\,100[6 \times 1 - 1 \times 4 + 10 \times 5 + 7 \times 0 + 5 \times 2 + 3 \times 10 + 2 \times 4]$$
$$= ₹\,100[6 - 4 + 50 + 0 + 10 - 30 + 8]$$
$$= ₹\,10{,}000, \text{ which is same as } Z_{\min}.$$

EXERCISES

1. Explain the following in the context of Transportation Problem:
   (*i*) Stepping Stone Method.
   (*ii*) Degenerate Transportation Problem.
   (*iii*) Modified Distribution Method.
   [*Pondicherry U.M.B.A. August, 2006; IGNOU MCA, 2003; P.U. BBA, 2001*]
2. Explain steps involved in V.A.M.
   [*P.U.B.E. (Ec. & Comm.) Nov., 2011; G.N.D.U. B.Com, April, 2013; April, 2008; Sept., 2007; J.N.T.U. Hyderabad B.Tech. Nov., 2010; G.N.D.U. B.com. April, 2006; P.U. M.B.A. Feb, 2009; BBA, 2001*]
3. Can degeneracy occur in a transportation problem? Justify your answer.
   [*Univ. of Madras B.Sc. (Math.) 2012'; K.U.M.Sc. 2001*]
4. What is degeneracy in transportation problems? How is it resolved?
   [*G.N.D.U. B.Com. Nov., 2014; April, 2014; Sept., 2012; April, 2012; Sept., 2011; Sept., 2010, Sept 2008; R.U. MBA., Dec., 2011; Univ. of Madras B.Sc. (Math.) Nov., 2012; R.T.M. Nagpur U.B.Tech. (Mech.) June, 2007; June, 2006; Dec., 2003; June, 2003; P.T.U. MBA, 2009; B. Tech. (C.Sc.) 2009; G.J.U. MBA Nov., 2003; NIIFT Mohali, 2000*]
5. Explain transportation problem giving examples.
   [*J.N.T.U. MBA, June 2012; Univ. of Madras B.Sc. (Math.) Nov., 2012; BBA Nov., 2010; BCA Nov., 2012; P.T.U.B. Tech. (Mech.) Dec., 2011; P.T.U. B.Tech. (C.Sc.) 2010; Chennai Univ. BBA Nov., 2010; BCA Nov., 2010; P.U.B.Com., 2000*]
6. (*a*) How will you define transportation model? Explain its application.
   (*b*) How will you define trans-shipment model? Explain its application. [*H.P.U.MCA, 1999*]
   (*c*) What is looping in transportation problem? [*P.T.U. MCA, 2010*]
7. Write mathematical model for general transportation problem.
   [*Mumbai U. B.Com. April, 2013; V.T.U. Karnataka B.Tech. (Mech.) 2012; IGNOU MBA June, 2007*]
8. What do you understand by a balanced and an unbalanced transportation problem? How an unbalanced problem is tackled?
   [*V.T.U. Karnataka B.E. June, 2012; G.N.D.U. B.Com., Sept., 2011; April, 2008; M.G.U. Kerala, M. Com. June 2010; P.T.U. BCA, 2010; R.T.M. Nagpur B.E. (Mech.) Dec., 2008; June, 2005; G.J.U. MBA Nov., 2003*]

9. What are the conditions for the application of the optimality test in case of transportation problem? Briefly explain as to why these conditions should be satisfied?
   [G.N.D.U. B.Com. April, 2010; Sept., 2009; Sept, 2007; P.T.U. MCA, 2010; B.Tech., 2010]
10. What is transportation problem? How is it a special case of L.P. problem?
   [V.T.U. Karnataka, B.Tech. (Mech.) 2012; P.T.U. MBA, 2006]
11. (*a*) Explain north-west corner rule for finding initial solution for a transportation problem.
   [G.N.D.U. B.Com., April, 2013; J.N.T.U. Hyderabad B.Tech. May, 2011; April 2011; P.U. MBA Feb., 2009; August, 2006; B. Com. Sept., 2004; P.T.U. B.E. (Mech.) 2011; MBA, 2008]
   (*b*) Describe least cost method for solving transportation problem.
   [Mumbai U. B.Com; April 2013]
12. (*a*) Explain stepping stone method for checking the solution for optimality in transportation problems. *[P.T.U. MCA, 2010; P.U. B. Com. Jan., 2005]*
   (*b*) Explain Vogel's approximation method. *[Mumbai U. MBA, 2010; J.N.T.U. Hyderbad B.Tech. (Mech.) May, 2012; May, 2011; P.U. MBA Feb., 2009]*
13. Explain briefly the following:
   (*i*) MODI method. *[G.N.D.U. B.Com. April, 2008]*
   (*ii*) Loops in transportation problem. *[G.N.D.U. B.Com. April, 2010; Sept., 2008]*
14. What do you understand from a transportation model of O.R.? List various methods of solving a transportation problem. Which is the best method of solving transportation problem and why?
   [Mumbai U. B.com., April, 2013; R.U. MBA June, 2014; P.U. MBA August, 2006]
15. (*a*) Give three variations in transportation problems. How are these resolved?
   [P.U.B.E.(Mech.) 1997]
   (*b*) Define trans-shipment problem.
   [P.T.U. MCA, 2010; MBA Sept., 2006; R.T.M. Nagpur U.B.E. (I.T.) 2009]
16. Describe a general transportation problem. Explain how to determine an initial basic feasible solution to the problem using Vogel's method. *[I.I.M.S. Kolkata, 1996]*
17. Give an algorithm to solve a transportation problem. *[P.T.U.B. Tech. (Mech.) 2008]*
18. Write a short note on dual of transportation model.
19. Explain sensitivity analysis in transportation problem when the changes take place in
   (*i*) source capacities.
   (*ii*) destination requirements.
   (*iii*) unit transportation costs.
20. Explain, with the help of an example, the procedure to solve a maximization type of transportation problem.
21. What is a trans-shipment problem? How is it different from a transportation problem ? Explain how it can be formulated and solved as a transportation problem.
   [P.T.U. MBA Feb., 2011; G.N.D.U. B.Com. Sept., 2010; R.T.M. Nagpur U.B.E. (Mech.) Sept., 2010; I.T., 2009; Dec., 2005; Gujarat T.U. MBA, 2011]
22. Explain any three methods of finding initial feasible solution of a transportation problem.
   [Univ. of Mumbai PGDM, 2012; Univ of Madras M.Com. April, 2012]
23. Determine an initial basic feasible solution to the following transportation problem using north-west corner rule:

TABLE 3.225

	To					Available
From	3	4	6	8	9	20
	2	10	1	5	8	30
	7	11	20	40	3	15
	2	1	9	14	16	13
Demand	40	6	8	18	6	

[P.T.U.B.E. (Mech.) May, 2006]

(*Ans.* $x_{11} = 20, x_{21} = 20, x_{22} = 6, x_{23} = 4, x_{33} = 4, x_{34} = 11, x_{44} = 7$ and $x_{45} = 6$.)

24. Find the feasible solution of the following transportation problem using north-west corner method:

TABLE 3.226

		To				
		W_1	W_2	W_3	W_4	*Supply*
	F_1	14	25	45	5	6
Factory	F_2	65	25	35	55	8
	F_3	35	3	65	15	16
Requirement		4	7	6	13	30 (Total)

[*NIIFT Mohali, 1999*]

(*Ans.* $x_{11} = 4, x_{12} = 2, x_{22} = 5, x_{23} = 3, x_{33} = 3, x_{34} = 13.$)

25. Determine an initial basic feasible solution to the following transportation problem using row minima method:

TABLE 3.227

		To			*Availability*
	5	2	4	3	22
From	4	8	1	6	15
	4	6	7	5	8
Demand	7	12	17	9	

[*M.G.U. Kerala M.Com., June, 2010; G.N.D.U. B.Com. April, 2008*]

(*Ans.* $x_{12} = 12, x_{13} = 1, x_{14} = 9, x_{23} = 15, x_{31} = 7, x_{33} = 1.$)

26. Determine an initial basic feasible solution to the following transportation problem using the row minima method:

TABLE 3.228

		To		*Available*
	3	8	5	5
From	5	5	3	8
	7	6	9	7
	4	9	5	14
Required	7	9	18	

[*Lucknow U. B.Com., 2010*]

(*Ans.* $x_{11} = 5, x_{23} = 8, x_{32} = 7, x_{41} = 2, x_{42} = 2, x_{43} = 10.$)

27. Determine an initial basic feasible solution to the following transportation problem using column minima method:

TABLE 3.229

		To		*Available*
	10	13	6	10
From	16	7	13	12
	8	22	2	8
Requirement	6	11	13	30 (Total)

(*Ans.* $x_{13} = 10, x_{22} = 11, x_{23} = 1, x_{31} = 6, x_{33} = 2.$)

28. Determine an initial basic feasible solution to the following transportation problem using column minima method:

TABLE 3.230

		Destination				
		D_1	D_2	D_3	D_4	*Availability*
Origin	O_1	1	2	1	4	20
	O_2	3	3	2	1	40
	O_3	4	2	5	9	20
	O_4	5	3	6	10	20
Requirement		20	40	30	10	

[*P.U.B. Com. April, 2008*]

(*Ans.* $x_{11} = 20, x_{23} = 30, x_{24} = 10, x_{32} = 20, x_{42} = 20$.)

29. Find the initial basic feasible solution to the following transportation problem by:

(*a*) minimum cost method,

(*b*) north-west corner rule.

State which of the methods is better.

TABLE 3.231

	To			*Supply*
From	2	7	4	5
	3	3	1	8
	5	4	7	7
	1	6	2	14
Demand	7	9	18	

[*L.U. B.Com., 2010; Pondicherry U.M.B.A. June, 2007*]

(*Ans.* (*a*) $x_{12} = 2, x_{13} = 3, x_{23} = 8, x_{32} = 7, x_{41} = 7, x_{43} = 7$.

(*b*) $x_{11} = 5, x_{21} = 2, x_{22} = 6, x_{32} = 3, x_{33} = 4, x_{43} = 14$; First.)

30. Find the initial basic feasible solution of the following transportation problem by Vogel's approximation method:

TABLE 3.232

		Warehouse				
		W_1	W_2	W_3	W_4	*Capacity*
	F	19	30	50	10	7
Factory	F_2	70	30	40	60	9
	F_3	40	8	70	20	18
Requirement		5	8	7	14	34 (Total)

[*P.U.B.E. (Mech.) 2012; R.U. MBA June, 2011; R.T.M. Nagpur U.B.E. (Mech.) 2011; U.P. Tech. U. Lucknow, 2010; G.N.D.U. B.Com. April, 2006*]

(*Ans.* $x_{11} = 5, x_{14} = 2, x_{23} = 7, x_{24} = 2, x_{32} = 8, x_{34} = 10$.)

31. Determine an initial basic feasible solution to the following T.P. using:

(*a*) north-west corner rule,

(*b*) Vogel's approximation method.

TABLE 3.233

Destination

		A_1	B_1	C_1	D_1	E_1	*Supply*
	A	2	11	10	3	7	4
Origin	B	1	4	7	2	1	8
	C	3	9	4	8	12	9
Demand		3	3	4	5	6	

[*Univ. of Madras B.Sc. (Math.) Nov., 2012; J.N.T.U. Hyderabad B.Tech. August, 2011; B.P.U.T., 2010*]

(*Ans.* (*a*) $x_{11} = 3, x_{12} = 1, x_{22} = 2, x_{23} = 4, x_{24} = 2, x_{34} = 3, x_{35} = 6$; 153

(*b*) $x_{14} = 4, x_{22} = 2, x_{25} = 6, x_{31} = 3, x_{32} = 1, x_{33} = 4, x_{34} = 1$.)

32. Find an initial basic feasible solution to the following T.P. using Vogel's approximation method:

TABLE 3.234

Destination

		1	2	3	4	*Availability*
	A	7	2	5	5	30
Origin	B	4	4	6	5	15
	C	5	3	3	2	10
	D	4	–1	4	2	20
Requirement		20	25	15	15	

[*P.U.B. Com. April, 2008, 2006*]

(*Ans.* $x_{11} = 5, x_{12} = 5, x_{13} = 15, x_{14} = 5, x_{21} = 15, x_{34} = 10, x_{42} = 20$.)

33. Find an optimal solution to the following transportation cost problem:

TABLE 3.235

Destination

		X	Y	Z	*Supply*
	A	2	7	4	50
Source	B	3	3	7	70
	C	5	4	1	80
	D	1	6	2	140
Demand		70	90	180	

[*P.T.U.B.Tech. (Mech.) April, 2012; Dec., 2011*]

(*Ans. A – X*: 50, *B – Y* : 70, *C – Y* : 20, *C – Z* : 60, *D – X*: 20, *D – Z*: 120; 770.)

34. Solve the following transportation problem:

TABLE 3.236

To

		1	2	3	4	*Supply*
	A	7	3	8	6	60
From	B	4	2	5	10	100
	C	2	6	5	1	40
Demand		20	50	50	80	

[*P.T.U. MBA May, 2005; G.N.D.U. B.Com. Sept., 2008*]

(*Ans. A* – 2 : 20, *A* – 4 : 40, *B* – 1 : 20, *B* – 2:30, *B* – 3:50, *C* – 4:40; 730.)

35. A distribution system has the following data:

Factory	*Capacity (units)*	*Warehouse*	*Demand (units)*
A	45	I	25
B	15	II	55
C	40	III	20

The transportation cost/unit (₹) associated with each route is as follows:

TABLE 3.237

	I	II	III
A	10	7	8
B	15	12	9
C	7	8	12

Find the optimum transportation schedule and the minimum total cost of transportation.

[*G.N.D.U. B.Com. May, 1999*]

(*Ans.* A-II : 40, A-III : 5, B-III : 15, C-I : 25, C-II : 15; Z_{min} = ₹ 750.)

36. A cement factory manager is considering the most econimical schedule to transport cement from his three manufacturing centres *P*, *Q* and *R* to depots *A*, *B*, *C*, *D* and *E*. The weekly production and demand along with the transportation cost per ton (₹) are given below:

TABLE 3.238

	A	B	C	D	E	*Supply (tons)*
P	4	1	3	4	4	60
Q	2	3	2	2	3	35
R	3	3	2	4	4	40
Demand (tons)	22	45	20	18	30	

What should be the distribution schedule?

[*P.T.U. B.Tech. April, 2012*]

(*Ans. P-B* : 45, *P-E* : 15, *Q-A* : 2, *Q-D* : 18, *Q-E* : 15, *R-A* : 20, *R-C* : 20; ₹ 290.)

37. Given below is a table taken from the solution process of a transportation problem:

TABLE 3.239

		Distribution Centres				
		1	2	3	4	*Availability*
	A	10	8 (5,000)	7	12	5,000
Factories	B	12	13	6 (4,500)	10 (1,500)	6,000
	C	8 (7,000)	10 (500)	12	14 (1,500)	9,000
Demand		7,000	5,500	4,500	3,000	

Answer the following questions:

(*a*) Is the solution feasible ?

(*b*) Is the solution degenerate ?

(*c*) Is the solution optimal? If not, find the optimal solution.

(*d*) Is there alternate optimal solution ? If yes, find that solution.

[*H.P.U. B.Tech. (Mech.) Nov., 2014; J..N.T.U. Hyderabad MBA April, 2012*]

(*Ans. A*-2 : 3,500, *A*-3 : 1,500, *B*-3 : 3,000, *B*-4 : 3,000, *C*-1: 7,000, *C*-2 : 2,000; Z_{min} = ₹ 1,62,500; No alternate optimal solution.)

38. National Oil Company has three refineries and four depots. The capacity of each refinery, transportation cost in ₹ /ton and requirement at each depot are given in the following table. Determine the optimum allocation of output.

TABLE 2.240

		Depot				
		D_1	D_2	D_3	D_4	*Capacity (tons)*
	R_1	5	7	13	10	700
Refinery	R_2	8	6	14	13	400
	R_3	12	10	9	11	800
Requirement (tons)		300	600	700	400	

[P.T.U. B.Tech. (Prod.) Nov., 2012; P.U. B.Com., Sept., 2010; G.N.D.U. B.Com. Sept., 2010]

(*Ans.* R_1-D_1 : 300, R_1-D_2 : 200, R_1-D_4 : 200, R_2-D_2 : 400, R_3-D_3: 700, R_3-D_4 : 100, D_m-D_4 = 100; Z_{min} = ₹ 14,700.)

39. Factories A, B and C supply to warehouses P, Q, R and S. The monthly production capacity (tons) of each factory and monthly requirements (tons) for each warehouse and the transportation costs in ₹ /ton are given in the following table:

TABLE 2.241

		Factories			
		A	B	C	*Production capacity (tons)*
	P	4	3	7	60
Warehouse	Q	5	8	4	50
	R	2	4	7	140
	S	5	8	4	50
Requirement (tons)		120	80	200	

Starting with Vogel's method, find the most economical transportation plan.

[P.U.M.Com. Sept, 2004]

(*Ans.* A-R : 120, B-P : 60, B-R : 20, C-Q : 50, C-S : 50, C-D_m : 100; Z_{min} = ₹ 900.)

40. Find the initial basic feasible solution to the following transportation problem. Is it optimal one ?

TABLE 3.242

		To				
		D_1	D_2	D_3	D_4	*Available (units)*
	O_1	5	4	2	1	130
From	O_2	2	3	7	5	100
	O_3	5	4	5	6	30
Demand (units)		40	50	70	100	

[Gujarat Technological U.MBA Dec., 2010]

41. Solve the following transportation problem using V.A.M. :

TABLE 3.243

	Cost of transportation (₹)				*Supply*
	P	Q	R	S	
A	10	18	11	7	20
B	9	12	14	6	40
C	8	9	12	10	35
Demand	16	18	31	30	

[H.P.U. B.Tech. (Mech.) June, 2015; Osmania U.MBA July, 2010]

42. A company has received a contract to supply gravel for three new construction projects located in cities A, B and C. The construction engineers have estimated the required amount of gravel at these construction projects as given below:

Project locations	:	A	B	C
Daily requirement (in truck loads)	:	144	204	82

The company has three gravel pits located in towns X, Y and Z. The gravel required for construction is supplied by these pits.

The amount of gravel that can be supplied is as follows :

Pit	:	X	Y	Z
Amount available (in truck loads)	:	152	164	154

The company has calculated the delivery cost given as follows:

TABLE 3.244

Pit	Project location		
	A	B	C
X	10	30	30
Y	70	110	70
Z	30	70	110

(i) Find the optimum solution and the minimum total cost.

(ii) Find alternate solution if it exists.

(iii) Find the unused capacities of the pits.

[*R.T.M. Nagpur B.Tech. Dec., 2004; Mumbai U. MBA, 2010*]

43. Goods are to be shipped from three warehouses W_1, W_2 and W_3 to six customers C_1, C_2, C_3, ..., C_6. The availabilities at the warehouses are 100, 120 and 150 units respectively, while the demands of customers are 50, 40, 50, 90, 60 and 80 units respectively. The unit costs of transporation are as given in the following table. Is it possible to have more than one optimal solution?

TABLE 3.245

Customers

		C_1	C_2	C_3	C_4	C_5	C_6
	W_1	15	25	18	35	40	23
Warehouses	W_2	22	36	40	60	50	38
	W_3	26	38	45	52	45	48

[*V.T.U. Karnataka B.E. June, 2012*]

44. Obtain the initial solution by VAM and optimal solution by MODI method for the transportation problem shown below:

TABLE 3.246

Unit transportation cost (₹) to markets

		A	B	C	*Supply*
	W_1	5	4	6	65
Warehouses	W_2	7	4	7	42
	W_3	8	6	7	43
Demand		70	30	50	

[*V.T.U. Karnataka B.E. June, 2011*]

45. The following information is available concerning the operation of a manufacturing company:

TABLE 3.247

Period	Units in order	Production capacity		Excess over cost per unit (₹)	Storage cost per unit (₹)
		Regular time	Over time		
Month 1	800	920	920	1.25	0.5
Month 2	1400	250	250	1.25	0.5

Formulate the problem as a transportation problem and determine the optimal solution.

[*V.T.U. Karnataka B.E. Dec., 2010*]

46. A problem of scheduling the weekly production of certain items for the next four weeks is to be solved. The production cost of the item is ₹ 10 for the first two weeks and ₹ 15 for the last two weeks. The weekly demands are 500, 800, 1000 and 900 units which must be met. The plant can produce a maximum of 700 units per week. In addition, the company can use overtime during second and third weeks. This increases the weekly production by an additional 200 units, but the production cost increases by ₹ 5 per unit. Excess production can be stored at a unit cost of ₹ 3 per week. How should the production be scheduled so as to minimize the total cost?

[*V.T.U. Karnataka B.E. Jan., 2010*]

47. A company has three factories A, B and C manufacturing the same product and five sales agencies in different parts of the country. Production cost differs from factories and selling price from agencies. Find out initial basic feasible solution in terms of profit by basic VAM.

Factory	Production cost (₹/unit)
A	5
B	6
C	2

TABLE 3.248

Agency	A	B	C	Selling price (₹ /unit)	Demand (units)
1	3	9	4	30	80
2	1	7	5	32	100
3	5	8	3	37	75
4	7	3	2	34	35
5	4	6	7	29	125
Production capacity (units)	*100*	*200*	*125*		

[*R.T.M. Nagpur U.B.E. (I.T.) 2009*]

48. Determine the optimum basic feasible solution to the following transportation problem:

TABLE 3.249

		To A	B	C	*Available*
From	1	50	30	220	1
	2	90	45	170	3
	3	250	200	50	4
Required		4	2	2	

[*J.N.T.U Hyderabad B.Tech. (C.Sc.) Dec., 2011*]

49. Optimize the following transportation problem:

TABLE 3.250

	D_1	D_2	D_3	Supply
S_1	8	5	6	120
S_2	15	10	12	80
S_3	3	9	10	80
Demand	150	80	50	

[J.N.T.U. Hyderabad B.Tech. (C.Sc.) Dec., 2011; April, 2011; Nov., 2010]

50. ABC agency transports material from one place to the other on commission basis. The following are the estimated commissions per unit of material to be transported from plants P_1, P_2 and P_3 to market centers M_1, M_2 and M_3. Optimize the commission to be earned by the agency (note that there is no route available to transport from P_2 to M_1).

TABLE 3.251

	M_1	M_2	M_3	Supply
P_1	6	9	8	120
P_2	–	4	2	80
P_3	11	5	4	80
Demand	150	70	60	280

[J.N.T.U. Hyderabad B.Tech. (C.Sc.) Dec., 2011; April, 2011]

51. Find the optimal cost of the following transportation matrix:

TABLE 3.252

	D_1	D_2	D_3	D_4	Supply
O_1	12	18	13	20	50
O_2	17	11	16	15	60
O_3	11	10	14	13	40
Demand	20	25	10	35	

[J.N.T.U. Hyderabad B.Tech. (C.Sc.) Dec., 2011]

52. A manufacturer has distribution centres located at Agra, Allahabad and Kolkata. These centers have available 40, 20 and 40 units of the product respectively. His retail outlets at A, B, C, D and E require 25, 10, 20, 30, and 15 units of the product, respectively. The shipping cost per unit (in rupees) between each centre and outlet is given in the following table:

TABLE 3.253

Distribution centres	Retail outlets				
	A	B	C	D	E
Agra	55	30	40	50	40
Allahabad	35	30	100	45	60
Kolkata	40	60	95	35	30

Determine the optimal shipping cost.

[J.N.T.U. Hyderabad B.Tech. May, 2011; P.U. B.Com. April, 2009; R.T.M. Nagpur B.E. (Mech.) Dec., 2008, 2005]

(*Ans.* ₹ 3,600.)

53. Shifttrans Transportation Company has four terminals *A*, *B*, *C* and *D*. At the start of first day of week, there are 8, 8, 6 and 3 vehicles available at terminals *A*, *B*, *C* and *D* respectively. During the previous night, 2, 12, 5 and 6 vehicles were loaded at plants *P*, *Q*, *R* and *S* respectively. The

distances (in km) between the terminals and plants are given in the table. Based upon the foregoing information, what vehicles should be sent to which plants to minimize total distance?

TABLE 3.254

	P	Q	R	S
A	22	46	16	40
B	41	15	50	40
C	82	32	48	60
D	40	40	36	30

[J.N.T.U. Hyderabad B.Tech. Nov., 2010]

54. A steel company has three hearth furnaces and five rolling mills. Transportation costs in ₹ per ton for shipping steel from furnaces to rolling mills are shown in the following table. Determine the minimum transportation cost.

TABLE 3.255

	Mills 1	2	3	4	5	*Availability*
Furnaces 1	40	20	30	20	60	8
Furnaces 2	52	42	50	22	12	12
Furnaces 3	60	50	45	72	35	14
Requirements	4	4	6	8	8	

[J.N.T.U. Hyderabad B.Tech. June, 2009]

(*Ans.* 1–1:4, 1–4:4, 2–4:4, 2–5:8, 3–2:4, 3–3:6, 3–D_M:4; = ₹ 894.)

55. (a) How transportation problem is solved when demand and supply are not equal ?

(b) The Transafe Transport Company has trucks available at four different localities A, B, C and D and the number of trucks at these localities are 5, 10, 7 and 3 respectively. The three customers P, Q and R require 5, 8 and 10 trucks respectively. Variable costs (in hundreds of rupees) of getting trucks to the customers are given below. Find the optimal transportation cost.

TABLE 3.256

From/To	P	Q	R
A	7	3	6
B	4	6	8
C	5	8	4
D	8	4	3

[J.N.T.U. Hyderabad B.Tech. June, 2009]

56 There are three parties who supply the following quantities of coal and three consumers who require the coal as follows:

Party 1	:	14 tons	Consumer A	:	6 tons
Party 2	:	12 tons	Consumer B	:	10 tons
Party 3	:	5 tons	Consumer C	:	15 tons

The cost matrix is as shown below:

TABLE 3.257

	A	B	C
1	6	8	4
2	4	9	3
3	1	2	6

Find the schedule of a transportation policy which minimizes the cost.

[J.N.T.U. Hyderabad B.Tech. June, 2009]

57. Solve the following transportation problem:

TABLE 3.258

	D_1	D_2	D_3	D_4	D_5	Availability
O_1	4	7	3	8	2	4
O_2	1	4	7	3	8	7
O_3	7	2	4	7	7	9
O_4	4	8	2	4	7	2
Demand	8	3	7	2	2	22

[*J.N.T.U. Hyderabad B.Tech. June, 2009*]

58. Solve the following transportation problem. The matrix shows the cost of transportation.

TABLE 3.259

From	To			Supply
	1	2	3	
A	10	18	9	100
B	4	3	11	200
C	6	9	15	400
Demand	250	150	300	700

[*J.N.T.U. Hyderabad B.Tech. May, 2009*]

59. A company has factories F_1, F_2 and F_3 which supply to warehouses W_1, W_2 and W_3. Weekly factory capacities are 200, 160 and 90 units respectively. Weekly warehouse requirements are 180, 120 and 150 units respectively. Unit shipping costs (in rupees) are as follows :

TABLE 3.260

Warehouse

		W_1	W_2	W_3	Supply
Factory	F_1	16	20	12	200
	F_2	14	8	18	160
	F_3	26	24	16	90
	Demand	180	120	150	

Determine the optimal distribution for this company to minimize total shipping cost.

[*R.T.M. Nagpur U.B.Tech. (Mech.) June, 2007*]

60. The figures in the body of the table below are proportional to the cost of transportation of the tonne of food grain form the port given by the row heading to the destination given by the column heading. Find the optimum transportation schedule.

TABLE 3.261

Ports/Destinations	Delhi	Ranchi	Mysore	Nagpur	Stock (in 000's tonnes)
Bombay	9	5	8	5	225
Calcutta	9	10	13	7	75
Madras	14	5	3	7	100
Requirements (000's tonnes)	125	80	95	100	400

[*R.T.M. Nagpur U.B. Tech. Dec., 2006*]

61. The XYZ Tobacco Company purchases tobacco and stores in warehouses located in the following four cities:

TABLE 3.262

Wharehouse location	*Capacity (tons)*
City A	90
City B	50
City C	80
City D	60

The warehouses supply tobacco to cigarette companies situated at three cities that have the following demand :

Cigarette company	*Demand (tons)*
Bharat	120
Janata	100
Red Lamp	110

The following railroad shipping costs per ton (in hundred rupees) have been determined :

TABLE 3.263

From \ *To*	*Bharat*	*Janata*	*Red Lamp*
A	7	10	5
B	12	9	4
C	7	3	11
D	9	5	7

Because of railroad construction, shipments are temporarily prohibited from warehouse at City A to Bharat Cigarette Company. Find the optimal distribution for XYZ Tobacco Company.

[*R.T.M. Nagpur U.B. Tech. June, 2006*]

62. Solve the following transportation problem using VAM for initial solution:

TABLE 3.264

From \ *To*	*A*	*B*	*C*	*D*	*Total available*
P	14	11	13	14	60
Q	12	13	12	12	35
R	13	15	12	14	80
Total required	32	45	30	28	

Find the optimal cost by any method.

[*R.T.M. Nagpur U.B.Tech. Dec., 2004*]

63. Solve the following transportation problem whose cost matrix, availability at each plant and requirements at each warehouse are given as follows :

TABLE 3.265

Plant	*Warehouse*				*Availability*
	W_1	W_2	W_3	W_4	
P_1	190	300	500	100	70
P_2	700	300	400	600	90
P_3	400	100	600	200	180
Requirement	50	80	70	140	–

[*Chennai U.B.B.A. Nov., 2010*]

64. Find the initial basic feasible solution to the following transportation problem using
(*a*) Vogel's approximation method,
(*b*) Row minima method.

TABLE 3.266

Destination

		I	II	III	IV	V	Supply
	A	2	11	10	3	7	4
Origin	B	1	4	7	2	1	8
	C	3	9	4	8	12	9
Demand		3	3	4	5	6	

[Chennai U.B.C.A. Nov., 2010]

65. Solve the following transportation problem in which the cell entries are unit transportation costs:

TABLE 3.267

Destination

		D_1	D_2	D_3	D_4	Supply
	O_1	6	4	1	5	14
Origin	O_2	8	9	2	7	16
	O_3	4	3	6	4	5
Required		6	10	15	4	

[P.T.U. MCA, 2010]

66. Consider the following transportation table. The costs are given in rupees, the supply and demand are in units. Determine the optimum solution.

TABLE 3.268

Source \ Destination	1	2	3	4	5	Supply
I	40	36	26	38	30	160
II	38	28	34	34	198	280
III	36	38	24	28	30	240
Demand	160	160	200	120	240	680 / 880

[P.T.U. B.Tech. Dec., 2011; Chennai U.B.B.A. Nov., 2010]

(Ans. $x_{I5} = 160$, $x_{II2} = 160$, $x_{II4} = 120$, $x_{III3} = 200$, $x_{III5} = 40$.)

67. Find the optimal solution to the following transportation problem :

TABLE 3.269

Factories	P	Q	R	S	Availability
A	10	8	7	12	500
B	12	13	6	10	500
C	8	10	12	14	900
Demand	700	550	450	300	1900 / 2000

[P.T.U. B.Tech. (C.Sc.) 2010]

68. (*a*) Describe the steps involved in solving a transportation problem.

[*P.T.U. B. Tech. (Mech.) 2009*]

(*b*) Solve the following cost-minimizing transportation problem :

TABLE 3.270

	D_1	D_2	D_3	D_4	D_5	D_6	*Available*
O_1	2	1	3	3	2	5	50
O_2	3	2	2	4	3	4	40
O_3	3	5	4	2	4	1	60
O_4	4	2	2	1	2	2	30
Required	30	50	20	40	30	10	180

[*J.N.T.U. Hyderabad B.Tech. May, 2011; April, 2011; P.T.U. B. Tech. (Mech.) 2009*]

69. A company is spending ₹ 1,000 on transportation of its units from three plants to four distribution centres. The supply and demand of units, with unit cost of transportation are given as follows:

TABLE 3.271

	D_1	D_2	D_3	D_4	*Supply (units)*
P_1	19	30	50	12	7
P_2	70	30	40	60	10
P_3	40	10	60	20	18
Demand (units)	5	8	7	15	

Find the maximum savings by optimal scheduling. [*P.U. B.Com., Sept., 2009*]

(*Ans.* ₹ 201.)

70. Goods have to be transported from factories F_1, F_2 and F_3 to warehouses W_1, W_2, W_3 and W_4. The transportation cost per unit, capacities and requirements are given in the following table :

TABLE 3.272

	W_1	W_2	W_3	W_4	*Capacity*
F_1	95	105	80	15	12
F_2	115	180	40	30	7
F_3	195	180	95	70	5
Requirement	5	4	4	11	

Find the distribution with minimum cost. [*P.T.U. B.Tech. (Mech.) 2005*]

71. Find the optimum solution to the following transportation problem :

TABLE 3.273

From \ *To*	*Sales Office* A	B	C	*Total Supply*
Factory A	1	2	15	100
Factory B	3	2	1	130
Factory C	12	5	5	75
Factory D	3	1	2	95
Total demand	120	80	200	

[*P.T.U. MBA, 2005*]

72. Solve the transportation problem for which the cost, origin availabilities and destination requirements are given below.

TABLE 3.274

	D_1	D_2	D_3	D_4	D_5	D_6	a_i
O_1	1	2	1	4	5	2	30
O_2	3	3	2	1	4	3	50
O_3	4	2	5	9	6	2	75
O_4	3	1	7	3	4	6	20
b_j	20	40	30	10	50	25	175 (Total)

[*P.U.B.E. (Mech.) Dec., 2012*]

(*Ans.* $x_{11} = 20, x_{13} = 10, x_{23} = 20, x_{24} = 10, x_{25} = 20,$
$x_{32} = 40, x_{35} = 10, x_{36} = 25, x_{45} = 20.$)

73. (*a*) Give a mathematical formulation of the transportation and simplex methods. What are the differences in the nature of problems that can be solved by these methods?

[*Pbi. B. Tech., 1999*]

(*b*) A company has three production shops supplying a product to five warehouses. The cost of production varies from shop to shop and so does the unit transportation cost from a shop to a warehouse. Each shop has a specific production capacity and each warehouse has certain amount of requirement. The unit transportation costs are given below :

TABLE 3.275

		Warehouse					
		I	*II*	*III*	*IV*	*V*	*Capacity*
	A	6	4	4	7	5	100
Shop	*B*	5	6	7	4	8	125
	C	3	4	6	3	4	175
Demand		60	80	85	105	70	

The cost of manufacturing the product at different production shops is

TABLE 3.276

		Variable cost (₹)	*Fixed cost* (₹)
	A	14	7,000
Shop	*B*	16	4,000
	C	15	5,000

Find the optimum quantity to be supplied from each shop to different warehouses at minimum total cost. [*J.N.T.U. Hyderabad MCA Feb., 2012*]

[Hint. Neglect the fixed costs while solving the problem.]

(*Ans. A* to II 15, *A* to III 85, *B* to II 20, *B* to IV 105,
C to I 60, *C* to II 45 and *C* to V 70; Z_{min} = ₹ 7,605.)

74. Given below is the unit costs array with supplies a_i, $i = 1, 2, 3$ and demands b_j, $j = 1, 2, 3$ and 4.

TABLE 3.277

		Sink 1	2	3	4	a_i
	1	8	10	7	6	50
Source	2	12	9	4	7	40
	3	9	11	10	8	30
	b_j	25	32	40	23	120 (Total)

Find the optimal solution to the above Hitchcock problem. [*P.U.B. Com., 2006*]

(*Ans.* $x_{11} = 25, x_{12} = 2, x_{14} = 23, x_{23} = 40, x_{32} = 30$; $Z_{min} = 848$.)

75. Find the optimum solution for the following transportation problem in which the cell values are unit transportation costs in rupees.

TABLE 3.278

		To A	B	C	*Total*
	I	1	2	3	50
From	II	3	2	1	80
	III	4	5	6	75
	IV	3	1	2	95
Total		120	80	100	

[*IGNOU MBA Dec.,2006*]

76. A departmental store wishes to purchase the following quantities of ladies' dresses:

Dress type:	A	B	C	D
Quantity:	150	100	75	250

Tenders are submitted by three different manufacturers who undertake to supply not more than the quantities below (all types of dresses combined):

Manufacturer:	W	X	Y
Total quantity:	350	250	150

The store estimates that its *profit* per dress will vary with the manufacturer as shown in the matrix below. How should orders be placed?

TABLE 3.279

		Dress A	B	C	D
	W	2.75	3.50	4.25	2.25
Manufacturer	X	3.00	3.25	4.50	1.75
	Y	2.50	3.50	4.75	2.00

[*NIIFT Mohali, 1998*]

(*Ans.* $x_{WB} = 25, x_{WD} = 250, x_{WDm} = 75, x_{XA} = 150, x_{XDm} = 100, x_{YB} = 75,$
$x_{YC} = 75$; ₹ 1,718.75.)

77. Solve the following transportation problem to minimize the total transportation cost :

TABLE 3.280

To warehouses

		A	B	C	D	E	*Plant capacity*
	1	1	2	6	2	3	800
From plants	2	3	4	5	8	1	600
	3	3	1	1	2	6	200
	4	4	7	3	5	4	400
Demand		400	100	700	300	500	

[*Dayalbagh Edu. Inst. Agra MBA May, 2005*]

(**Ans.** x_{1A}= 400, x_{1B} = 100, x_{1D} = 300, x_{2C} = 100, x_{2E} = 500, x_{3C} = 200, x_{4C} = 400; Z_{min} = 3,600.)

78. A manufacturer of jeans is interested in developing an advertising campaign that will reach four different age groups. Advertising can be conducted through T.V., radio and magazines. The following table gives the estimated cost in paise per exposure for each age group according to the medium employed. In addition, maximum exposure levels possible in each of the medium, namely T.V., radio and magazines are 40, 30 and 20 millions respectively. Also the minimum desired exposures within each age group, namely 13–18, 19–25, 26–35, 36 and older are 30, 25, 15 and 10 millions. The objective is to minimize the cost of attaining the minimum exposure level in each age group.

TABLE 3.281

Media	*Age groups*			
	13–18	19–25	26–35	36 and older
T.V.	12	7	10	10
Radio	10	9	12	10
Magazines	14	12	9	12

Formulate the above as a transportation problem and find the optimal solution.

[*M.G.U. Kerala, M.Com., June, 2011*]

(*Ans. T.V. to 19–25 : 25, T.V. to 36 and older : 10, radio to 13–18 : 30, magazines to 26–35 : 15;* Z_{min} = *₹ 7.10 million.*)

79. A fertilizer company has three plants A, B and C which supply to six major distribution centres 1, 2, 3, 4, 5 and 6. The table below gives the transportation costs per case, the plant annual capacities and predicted annual demands at different centres in terms of thousands of cases. The variable production costs per case are ₹ 8.50, ₹ 9.40 and ₹ 7.20 respectively at plants A, B and C. Determine the minimum cost production and transportation allocation.

TABLE 3.282

Transportation cost, ₹ per case

Major distribution centres

		1	2	3	4	5	6	*Annual production in thousands of cases*
	A	2.50	3.50	5.50	4.50	1.50	4.00	2,200
Plants	B	4.60	3.60	2.60	5.10	3.10	4.10	3,400
	C	5.30	4.30	4.80	2.30	3.30	2.80	1,800
Annual demand in thousands of cases		850	750	420	580	1,020	920	

Prove that if the variable production costs are the same at every plant, one can obtain an optimal allocation by using transportations costs only. [*Gujarat Univ.B.E.(Mech.) 1976*]

80. Describe the transportation problem. Give method of finding an initial feasible solution. Explain what is meant by an optimality test. Give the method of improving over the initial solution to reach the optimal feasible solution. *[Bombay M.Com., 1975]*

81. The unit costs of transportation from site i to site j are given below. At site $i = 1, 2, 3$, stocks of 150, 200 and 170 units respectively are available. 300 units are to be sent to site 4 and the rest to site 5. Find the cheapest way of doing this.

TABLE 3.283

From \ To	1	2	3	4	5
1	–	3	4	10	7
2	1	–	2	16	6
3	7	4	–	12	13
4	8	3	9	–	5
5	2	1	7	5	–

[P.U.M.B.A., 2001]

[Hint: In accordance with the restrictions of supply and demand, table 3.283 reduces to the following table:

From \ To	4	5	*Available*
1	10	7	150
2	16	6	200
3	12	13	170
Required	300	220	

The above table can now be easily solved.]

(Ans. $x_{14} = 130, x_{15} = 20, x_{25} = 200, x_{34} = 170$; 4,680.)

82. A production control superintendent finds the following information on his desk: In departments A, B and C, the number of surplus pallets is 18, 27 and 21 respectively. In departments G, H, I and J, the number of pallets required is 14, 12, 23 and 17 respectively. The *time* in minutes to move a pallet from one department to another is given below.

TABLE 3.284

From \ *To*	G	H	I	J
A	13	25	12	21
B	18	23	14	9
C	23	15	12	16

What is the optimal distribution plan to minimize the moving *time*?

[P.U.B. Com., 2006]

(Ans. $x_{AG} = 14, x_{AI} = 4, x_{BI} = 10, x_{BJ} = 17, x_{CH} = 12, x_{CI} = 9$.)

83. The following table gives the cost of transporting material from supply points A, B, C and D to demand points E, F, G, H and J.

TABLE 3.285

From \ To	E	F	G	H	J
A	8	10	12	17	15
B	15	13	18	11	9
C	14	20	6	10	13
D	13	19	7	6	12

The present allocation is as follows:

A to E 90, A to F 10, B to F 150, C to F 10, C to G 50, C to J 120, D to H 210, D to J 70.

(*a*) Check if this allocation is optimum. If not, find an optimum schedule.

(*b*) If in the above problem the transportation cost from A to G is reduced to 10, what will be the new optimum schedule? *[H.P.U.B. Tech. (Mech.) Sept., 2009]*

(*Ans.* (*a*) No; A to F 100, B to F 70, B to J 80, C to E 90, C to G 50, C to J 40, D to H 210 and D to J 70.

(*b*) same as in (*a*).)

84. Solve the following transportation problem:

TABLE 3.286

From \ To	A	B	C	D	E	*Supply*
1	20	19	14	21	16	40
2	15	15	–	19	16	60
3	18	20	18	20	–	90
Demand	30	40	70	40	60	

[P.T.U. B.Tech. (Prod.) Nov., 2012, P.U.B.E., 2001]

(*Ans.* $x_{1C} = 40$, $x_{2B} = 40$, $x_{2E} = 20$, $x_{3A} = 30$, $x_{3C} = 30$, $x_{3D} = 30$, $x_{DmD} = 10$, $x_{DmE} = 40$; $Z_{min} = 3{,}160$.

Alternate optimal solution: $x_{1C} = 10$, $x_{1E} = 30$, $x_{2B} = 40$, $x_{2E} = 20$, $x_{3A} = 30$, $x_{3C} = 60$, $x_{DmD} = 40$, $x_{DmE} = 10$; $Z_{min} = 3{,}160$.)

85. Solve the following transportation problem for minimum total transportation cost. The values in the body of the matrix represent the unit transportation costs in rupees.

TABLE 3.287

	D_1	D_2	D_3	D_4	*Supply*
O_1	12	7	10	10	40
O_2	10	9	12	10	30
O_3	14	12	9	12	20
Demand	30	25	15	10	

[G.N.D.U. B.Com. Sept., 2001; P.U.B.E.(Mech.) 2000]

(*Ans.* $O_1D_2 = 25$, $O_1D_4 = 10$, $O_1D_m = 5$, $O_2D_1 = 30$, $O_3D_3 = 15$, $O_3D_m = 5$; Z_{min} = ₹ 710.)

86. Solve the following transportation problem using Vogel's method in order to minimize the total transportation cost:

TABLE 3.288

Destination

		D_1	D_2	D_3	D_4	D_5	*Availability*
	O_1	3	5	8	9	11	20
Origin	O_2	5	4	10	7	10	40
	O_3	2	3	8	7	7	30
Demand		10	15	25	30	40	

[*P.U.B.E.(E. & Ec.) 1999*]

(*Ans.* $O_1D_1 = 10$, $O_1D_2 = 5$, $O_1D_3 = 5$, $O_2D_2 = 10$, $O_2D_4 = 30$, $O_3D_5 = 30$, $O_{Dm}D_3 = 20$, $O_{Dm}D_5 = 10$; $Z_{min} = 555$.)

87. A manufacturing company has three factories F_1, F_2 and F_3 with monthly manufacturing capacities of 7,000, 4,000 and 10,000 units of a product. The product is to be supplied to seven stores. The manufacturing cost of these factories are slightly different but the important factor is the shipping cost from each factory to a particular store. Table 3.289 represents the factory capacities, store requirements and unit cost in rupees of shipping from each factory to each store and slack. Here, slack is the difference between the total factory capacity and the total store requirement.

TABLE 3.289

		S_1	S_2	S_3	S_4	S_5	S_6	S_7	*Slack*	*Factory capacity*
	F_1	5	6	4	3	7	5	4	0	7,000
Factory	F_2	9	4	3	4	3	2	1	0	4,000
	F_3	8	4	2	5	4	8	3	0	10,000
Store demand		1,000	2,000	4,500	4,000	2,000	3,500	3,000	1,000	

Work out a transportation plan so as to minimize the transportation cost.

[*J.N.T.U. Hyderabad B.Tech. Nov., 2010*]

(*Ans.* $F_1S_1 = 1{,}000$, $F_1S_4 = 4{,}000$, $F_1S_7 = 1{,}000$, F_1 slack $= 1{,}000$, $F_2S_6 = 3{,}500$, $F_2S_7 = 500$, $F_3S_2 = 2{,}000$, $F_3S_3 = 4{,}500$, $F_3S_5 = 2{,}000$ and $F_3S_7 = 1{,}500$.)

88. Consider four bases of operations B_i and three targets T_j. The tons of bombs per aircraft from any base that can be delivered to any target are given in the following table:

TABLE 3.290

Target (T_j)

		1	2	3
	1	8	6	5
	2	6	6	6
Base (B_i)	3	10	8	4
	4	8	6	4

The daily sortie capability of each of the four bases is 150 sorties per day. The daily requirement in sorties over each individual target is 200. Find the allocation of sorties from each base to each target which *maximizes* the total tonnage over all the three targets explaining each step.

[*G.N.D.U.B. Com. Sept., 2006*]

(*Ans.* $x_{11} = 50$, $x_{12} = 100$, $x_{21} = 150$, $x_{33} = 150$, $x_{42} = 100$, $x_{43} = 50$; $Z_{opt} = 3{,}300$.)

89. General Electrodes is a big electrode manufacturing company. It has two factories and three main distribution centres in three cities. The supply and demand conditions for units of electrodes (truckloads) are given below along with unit cost of transportation. How should the trips be

scheduled so that the cost of transportation is minimized?

The present cost of transportation is around ₹ 3,100 per month. What can be the maximum savings by proper scheduling?

TABLE 3.291

Centres	:	A	B	C
Requirement	:	50	50	150
Cost per trip from X plant	:	25	35	10
Cost per trip from Y plant	:	20	5	80
Capacity of plant X	:	150 units of electrodes		
Capacity of plant Y	:	100 units of electrodes		

[*Mumbai Dip. Opr Manag.,* 1972]

(*Ans.* XC = 150, YA = 50, YB = 50; $Z_{\min}$ = ₹ 2,750; max. savings = ₹ 350.)

90. A company has decided to manufacture some or all of five new products at three of its plants. The production capacity of each of these three plants is as follows:

Plant no.	*Production capacity in total number of units*
1	40
2	60
3	90

Sales potential of the five products is as follows:

Product no.	1	2	3	4	5
Market potential in units	30	40	70	40	60

Plant no. 3 cannot produce product no. 5. The variable cost per unit for the respective plant and product combination is given below.

Product no.	1	2	3	4	5
Plant no. 1	20	19	14	21	16
Plant no. 2	15	20	13	9	16
Plant no. 3	18	15	18	20	—

Based on above data, determine the optimum product to plant combination by using linear programming.

[*Karn. U.B.E.(Mech.) 1998*]

(*Ans.* $x_{13} = 30, x_{15} = 10, x_{23} = 20, x_{24} = 40, x_{31} = 30,$ $x_{32} = 40, x_{33} = 20, x_{D5} = 50; Z_{min} = 2{,}700.$)

91. A company has three plants at locations A, B and C which supply to warehouses located at D, E, F, G and H. Monthly plant capacities are 1800, 2500 and 2900 units respectively. Monthly warehouse requirements are 1400, 1400, 1500, 1400 and 1800 units respectively. Unit transportation costs are given below.

TABLE 3.292

	D	E	F	G	H
A	5	8	6	6	3
B	4	7	7	6	5
C	8	4	6	6	4

Determine an optimum distribution to minimize the total transportation cost.

[*P.U. B.Com. Sept, 2012; J.N.T.U. Anantapur MBA, 2010; V.T.U. Karnataka B.E. Dec., 2011; P.T.U. MBA June, 2003; D.U. MBA, 2001*]

(*Ans.* A-H:1800; B–D:1400, B–G:1100, C-E:1400, C-F:1200, C-G:300, D_M–F = 300)

92. Consider the following problem:

Minimize $Z = 4x_{11} + 3x_{12} + 7x_{13} + 2x_{14} + x_{21} + 8x_{22} + 10x_{23} + 7x_{24} + 3x_{31} + 5x_{32} + 4x_{33} + 8x_{34},$

subject to
$$x_{11} + x_{12} + x_{13} + x_{14} \le 10,$$
$$x_{21} + x_{22} + x_{23} + x_{24} \le 15,$$
$$x_{31} + x_{32} + x_{33} + x_{34} \le 15,$$
and
$$x_{11} + x_{21} + x_{31} \ge 7,$$

$$x_{12} + x_{22} + x_{32} \geq 12,$$
$$x_{13} + x_{23} + x_{33} \geq 8,$$
$$x_{14} + x_{24} + x_{34} \geq 10,$$
$$x_{22} \geq 2,$$

$x_{ij} \geq 0$ for all $i, j(i = 1, 2, 3; j = 1, 2, 3$ and $4)$.

Describe if the above problem can be solved as a transportation model. If the answer is yes, find an initial starting solution by any method. [*M.D.U.B. Tech. (Mech.) Nov., 2010*]

93. Solve the following transportation problem using Vogel's method for initial solution:

TABLE 3.293

Destinations

		D_1	D_2	D_3	D_4	D_5	D_6	*Supply* a_i
Origins	O_1	5	10	15	8	9	7	30
	O_2	14	13	10	9	20	21	40
	O_3	15	11	13	25	8	12	10
	O_4	9	19	12	8	6	13	100
	Demand b_j	50	20	10	35	15	50	

[*H.P.U.B. Tech. (Mech.) Dec., 2009; P.U.B.E.(C.S.&E.) Dec., 2004*]

94. A particular product is manufactured in factories A, B and C and is sold at centres 1, 2, 3, 4 and 5. The cost in ₹ of product per unit and capacity in units is given. Also are given the sale price/unit at the centres, demand at them and the unit transportation cost in ₹.

TABLE 3.294

Production cost/unit (₹)	*Capacity (units)*	*Factory*
20	150	A
22	200	B
18	125	C

1	1	5	9	4	*Shipping costs* (₹/*unit*)
9	7	8	3	6	
4	5	3	2	7	
1	2	3	4	5	*Agency*
80	100	75	45	125	*Demand*
30	32	31	34	29	*Sale price* (₹/*unit*)

Find the production and distribution schedule most profitable to the company.

[*P.T.U. M.Tech. Nov., 2012, MBA, May, 2006*]

(*Ans.* $x_{11} = 50$, $x_{12} = 100$, $x_{24} = 25$, $x_{25} = 125$, $x_{2D} = 50$, $x_{31} = 30$, $x_{33} = 75$, $x_{34} = 20$; Z_{max} = ₹ 3,670.)

95. A transport company engaged in carrying parcels has three branches to serve five customers. The distance (km) from each branch to each of the customers is given below:

TABLE 3.295

Branches	*Customers*					*No. of trucks available*
	A	B	C	D	E	
I	10	8	12	9	3	15
II	4	4	6	6	7	12
III	15	7	11	13	8	16
No. of trucks required	8	8	4	7	6	

(*i*) Find out using VAM the allocation of trucks from branches to customers in order to minimize the total cost of transportation assuming that the cost is proportional to distance. What is the minimum required distance (km) to be run by the trucks?

(*ii*) If an arrival of a V.V.I.P. blocks the traffic from branch I to customers C and D and from branch II to customers D and E, what should be the optimal allocation in order to minimize the total transportation cost? *[ICWA (Final) June, 1993]*

(*Ans.* D_{min} = 195 km; Z_{min} = 221 km.)

96. Priyanka Iron and Steel Company has 3 open hearth furnaces and 5 rolling mills. Transportation cost (₹ per quintal) for transporting steel from furnaces to rolling mills is shown in the table below.

TABLE 3.296

Table 3.267

		Rolling mills					
		M_1	M_2	M_3	M_4	M_5	*Capacity*
	F_1	4	2	3	2	6	8
Furnaces	F_2	5	4	5	2	1	12
	F_3	6	5	4	7	3	14
Requirement		4	4	6	8	8	

What is the optimum schedule? *[P.U.M.Com. April, 2004]*

(*Ans.* F_1M_2 = 4, F_1M_4 = 4, F_2M_4 = 4, F_2M_5 = 8, F_3M_1 = 4, F_3M_3 = 6, F_3D_m = 4; Z_{min} = ₹ 80.)

97. A company has three factories A, B and C which supply to four warehouses P, Q, R and S. The monthly production capacity in tons at A, B and C is 120, 80 and 200 respectively. The monthly requirement in tons for the warehouses P, Q, R and S is 60, 50, 140 and 50 respectively. The transportation cost in ₹ per ton is given in the matrix below.

TABLE 3.297

		Factories		
		A	*B*	*C*
	P	4	3	7
Warehouses	Q	5	8	4
	R	2	4	7
	S	5	8	4

Using V.A.M. determine the transportation schedule that minimizes the total transportation cost. *[P.U.M. Com. Sept., 2004]*

(*Ans.* x_{PB} = 60, x_{QC} = 50, x_{RA} = 120, x_{RB} = 20, x_{SC} = 50, x_{DmC} = 100; Z_{min} = ₹ 900.)

98. Find the optimal solution to the following transportation problem:

TABLE 3.298

		Centres			
Factories	*P*	*Q*	*R*	*S*	*Availability*
A	10	8	7	12	500
B	12	13	6	10	600
C	8	10	12	14	900
Demand	700	550	450	300	

[*H.P.U.B. Tech. Nov., 2007; P.U.M.B.A., 2000*]

(*Ans. A-Q* : 350, *A-R* : 150, *B-R* : 300 *B-S* : 300, *C-P* : 700, *C-Q* : 200; 16,250.)

99. A company has three plants at locations A, B and C which supply warehouses located at D, E, F, G and H. Monthly plant capacities are 800, 500 and 900 units respectively. Monthly warehouse requirements are 400, 350, 300, 250 and 900. The unit transportation costs in rupees are given below:

TABLE 3.299

		To				
		D	E	F	G	H
	A	8	8	9	4	3
From	B	5	8	5	11	6
	C	8	9	7	3	3

Determine an optimum distribution for the company in order to minimize the total transportation cost. How much is the cost? [*P.U.B.E.(Mech.) 1998*]

(*Ans.* x_{AE} = 350, x_{AH} = 450, x_{BD} = 400, x_{BF} = 100, x_{CF} = 200, x_{CG} = 250, x_{CH} = 450; Z_{min} = ₹ 10,150.)

100. A furniture manufacturing company has three plants which manufacture two principal products, a standard card table and a deluxe card table. New deluxe card table will be introduced which must be considered in terms of selling prices and costs. The selling prices are:

Standard card table : ₹ 15.25,

deluxe card table : ₹ 19.15,

new deluxe card table : ₹ 21.95.

The requirements in units of three models are:

Standard card table : 450,

deluxe card table : 1050,

new deluxe card table : 600.

The variable costs of models and plant capacities are given below:

TABLE 3.300

		Variables costs			
		Standard	*Deluxe*	*New deluxe*	*Available Capacity*
	A	8.00	8.50	9.25	800
Plants	B	7.95	8.60	9.20	600
	C	8.10	8.45	9.30	700

Solve this by transportation method for the greatest contribution.

[*Karn.U.B.E.(Mech.) 1997*]

(*Ans.* x_{AS} = 450, x_{AD} = 350, x_{CD} = 700, x_{BND} = 600; Z_{max} = ₹ 22,130.)

101. Solve the following transportation problem:

TABLE 3.301

		Godowns 1	2	3	4	5	6	Stock available
Factories	1	7	5	7	5	5	3	60
	2	9	11	6	11	–	5	20
	3	11	10	6	2	2	8	90
	4	9	10	9	6	9	12	50
Demand		60	20	40	20	40	40	

[*C.A. Nov., 1989*]

State whether the solution obtained is unique. (*Ans.* (*i*) $x_{12} = 20$, $x_{16} = 40$, $x_{21} = 10$, $x_{23} = 10$, $x_{33} = 30$, $x_{34} = 20$, $x_{35} = 40$, $x_{41} = 50$, $Z_{min} = 1{,}120$ (*ii*) No.)

102. XYZ Co. has provided the following data seeking your advice on the optimum investment strategy:

TABLE 3.302

Investment made at the beginning of the year	*Net data on return (in paise) of selected investments*				*Amount available (₹ in lakhs)*
	P	*Q*	*R*	*S*	
1	95	80	70	60	70
2	75	65	60	50	40
3	70	45	50	40	90
4	60	40	40	30	30
Maximum investment (₹ in lakhs)	40	50	60	60	

The following additional information is also provided:

— P, Q, R and S represent the selected investments.

— The company has decided to have four years investment plan.

— The policy of the company is that the amount invested in any year will remain so until the end of the fourth year.

— The values (paise) in the table represent net returns on investment of one rupee till the end of the planning horizon. Determine the optimal investment strategy.

(*Ans.* $x_{1P} = 40$, $x_{1Q} = 30$, $x_{2Q} = 20$, $x_{2R} = 20$, $x_{3R} = 40$, $x_{3S} = 50$, $x_{4S} = 10$ lakhs; Z_{max} = ₹ 1,30,00,000.)

103. A company has four factories situated in four different locations in the country and four sales agencies located in four other locations in the country. The cost of production (₹/unit), the sale price (₹/unit), shipping cost (₹/unit) in the cells of the matrix, monthly capacities and monthly requirements are given below:

TABLE 3.303

Factory	*Sale agency* 1	2	3	4	*Monthly capacity (units)*	*Cost of production*
A	7	5	6	4	10	10
B	3	5	4	2	15	.15
C	4	6	4	5	20	16
D	8	7	6	5	15	15

Monthly
demand: 8 12 18 22 at sale agency 1, 2, 3 and 4 respectively.
Sale price: 20 22 25 18 at sale agency 1, 2, 3 and 4 respectively.

Find the monthly production and distribution schedule which will maximize profit.

[*P.U. B.Com. Sept., 2007*]

(*Ans.* $x_{A2} = 10, x_{B4} = 15, x_{C1} = 8, x_{C3} = 12, x_{D2} = 2, x_{D3} = 6, x_{D4} = 7; Z_{max}$ = ₹ 155.)

104. A particular product is manufactured in factories A, B, C and D and is sold at centres 1, 2 and 3. The cost in ₹/unit product and capacity in kg/unit time of each plant is given below:

Factory	*Cost (₹/unit)*	*Capacity (kg/unit time)*
A	12	100
B	15	20
C	11	60
D	13	80

The sale price in ₹/unit and the demand in kg/unit time are as follows:

Sale centre	*Sale price (₹/unit)*	*Demand (kg/unit time)*
1	15	120
2	14	140
3	16	60

Find the optimal sales distribution.

(*Ans.* $x_{A1} = 100, x_{B2} = 20, x_{C3} = 60, x_{D1} = 20, x_{D2} = 60, x_{Dm2} = 60; Z_{max}$ = ₹ 680.)

105. Priyanshu Enterprise has 3 auditors. Each auditor can work upto 160 hours during the next month, during which time 3 projects must be completed. Project 1 will take 130 hours, project 2 will take 140 hours and project 3 will take 160 hours. The amount in rupees per hour that can be billed for assigning each auditor to each project is given below:

TABLE 3.304

		Project	
Auditor	1	2	3
1	1,200	1,500	1,900
2	1,400	1,300	1,200
3	1,600	1,400	1,500

Find the optimal solution. Also find the *maximum* total billings during the next month.

[*G.N.D.U. B.Com. Nov., 2014*]

(*Ans.* $x_{13} = 160, x_{22} = 110, x_{31} = 130, x_{32} = 30$; ₹ 6,97,000)

106. Define the transportation problem. Give the optimum location of a warehouse with the following information:

TABLE 3.305

Fixed factories & markets	*Cartesian coordinates*		*Production (units)*	*Consumption (units)*	*Transportation cost (per ton/km)*
	X	*Y*			
F_1	2	3	5,000		₹ 5
F_2	1	1	5,000		₹ 4
M_1	7	2		2,000	₹ 3
M_2	3	7		2,000	₹ 3
M_3	5	5		1,000	₹ 3

Calculate the total transportation cost for optimal solution. [*P.U.MBA, 1997*]

107. Four suppliers have submitted sealed bids that quote the price per case of harinets delivered to four regional stores of the army. The bids are summarised in the following table. The regional stores' requirements as well as the supplying capacities of the suppliers are also shown. Supplier 4 has quoted for only region 1. Because of previous contractual obligations, region 3 will have to get a minimum of 200 cases from supplier 2.

TABLE 3.306

		Region				
		R_1	R_2	R_3	R_4	*Max. supply (cases)*
	S_1	30	25	40	35	800
Supplier	S_2	35	32	38	40	1,000
	S_3	28	30	35	38	1,500
	S_4	25	—	—	—	600
Required (cases)		1,000	800	1,200	750	

(*a*) Formulate this problem as a transportation model including all the constraints.

(*b*) Find the initial basic solution using V.A.M.

(*c*) Use MODI method to establish whether the above solution obtained is optimal or not.

[*Karn. U.B.E.(Mech.)1995*]

108. A food processing firm has compiled the following data for future monthly production requirements and production costs in regular and overtime.

TABLE 3.307

Month	*Quantity*	*Cost per unit (₹)*	
		Regular	*Overtime*
September	4,000	20	30
October	5,200	25	35
November	5,000	24	34
December	3,700	26	36
January	4,200	20	30
February	3,000	20	30

The production capacity of the firm is 6,000 units in regular time and 3,000 units in overtime. The cost of carrying storage is ₹ 7.50 per unit per month. If at the end of August, there are 3,500 units in stock at a cost of ₹ 25 each, what is the optimum production schedule and total associated cost? No inventory is required at the end of six months.

[*Kuru. U.M.Tech. May, 1998*]

109. A company maintains a stable workforce and uses inventory, overtime and subcontracting to meet demand requirements. Stock-outs are not permitted and demand must be satisfied through in-house production or subcontracting. The following data are available for next six months:

TABLE 3.308

Month	*Expected demand (units)*	*Regular capacity (units)*	*Overtime capacity (units)*	*Subcontracting capacity (units)*
January	940	620	200	250
February	475	500	150	250
March	730	550	150	250
April	790	575	150	250
May	895	600	200	250
June	915	600	200	250

Beginning inventory at the start of January is 350 units. Desired ending inventory is 300 units. The relevant cost data are as follows:

Regular cost/unit : ₹ 90

Overtime cost/unit : ₹ 135

Subcontracting cost/unit : ₹ 150

Inventory holding cost/unit/month : ₹ 5

Determine the production plan that will satisfy demand at minimum cost.

[IGNOU MBA June, 1999]

110. The following table shows all the necessary information on the available supply to each warehouse, the requirement of each market and the unit transportation cost in rupees from each warehouse to each market.

TABLE 3.309

Market

	I	II	III	IV	*Supply*
Warehouse A	5	2	4	3	22
B	4	8	1	6	15
C	4	6	7	5	8
Requirement	7	12	17	9	

The shipping clerk has worked out the following schedule from experience:

12 units from A to II, 1 unit from A to III, 9 units from A to IV, 15 units from B to III, 7 units from C to I and 1 unit from C to III.

(*a*) Check and see if the clerk has made the optimal schedule.

(*b*) Find the optimum schedule and minimum total shipping cost.

(*c*) If the clerk is approached by a carrier of route C to II who offers to reduce his rate in the hope of getting some business, by how much must the rate be reduced before the clerk should consider giving him an order?

[Dayalbagh Edu. Inst. Agra MBA Dec., 2013]

(*Ans.* (*a*) No. (*b*) A to II 12, A to III 2, A to IV 8, B to III 15, C to 17 and C to IV 1 unit; Z_{min} = ₹ 104. (*c*) ₹ 4.)

111. A company has factories at A, B and C which supply warehouses at D, E, F and G. Monthly factory capacities are 250, 300 and 400 units respectively for regular production. If overtime production is utilised, factories A and B can produce 50 and 75 additional units respectively at overtime incremental costs of ₹ 4 and ₹ 5 respectively. The current warehouse requirements are 200, 225, 275 and 300 units respectively. Unit transportation costs in rupees from factories to warehouses are as follows:

TABLE 3.310

From \ *To*	D	E	F	G
A	11	13	17	14
B	16	18	14	10
C	21	24	13	10

Determine the optimum distribution for this company to minimize costs.

[J.N.T.U. MBA June, 2012; P.T.U. B.Tech., 2010; D.U.B.E. (E. and Ec.) April, 2008; Pondicherry U. M.B.A. June, 2007, Nagpur U.B.E., 2003; J.U.B.E.(Mech.) 2004]

[**Hint:** First, table 3.311 is made which takes into account the overtime production and the corresponding production costs.

TABLE 3.311

	D	E	F	G	*Supply*
A	11	13	17	14	250
A_0	15	17	21	18	50
B	16	18	14	10	300
B_0	21	23	19	15	75
C	21	24	13	10	400
Demand	200	225	275	300	

In the above table, total supply = 1,075 units,

total demand = 1,000 units.

Therefore, we add a dummy warehouse with demand of 75 units and cost coefficients zero in each of its cells. Table 3.312 results.

TABLE 3.312

	D	E	F	G	*Dummy*	*Supply*
A	11	13	17	14	0	250
A_O	15	17	21	18	0	50
B	16	18	14	10	0	300
B_O	21	23	19	15	0	75
C	21	24	13	10	0	400
Demand	200	225	275	300	75	

The initial feasible solution can now be obtained and can be optimized using MODI method.]

(*Ans.* $x_{AD} = 150, x_{AE} = 100, x_{BE} = 125, x_{BG} = 175, x_{CF} = 275,$
$x_{CG} = 125, x_{A_0D} = 50, x_{B_0D_m} = 75;$ Z_{min} = ₹ 12,525.)

112. A company has plants at A, B and C which have capacities to produce 300 kg, 200 kg and 500 kg respectively of a particular chemical per day. The production costs per kg in these plants are ₹ 0.70, ₹ 0.60 and ₹ 0.66 respectively. Four bulk consumers have placed orders for the product on the following basis:

		Kg required per day	*Price offered ₹/kg*
	I	400	1.00
	II	250	1.00
Consumer	III	350	1.02
	IV	150	1.03

Shipping costs (in paise per kg) from plants to consumers are given in the table below:

		To			
		I	II	III	IV
	A	3	5	4	6
From	B	8	11	9	12
	C	4	6	2	8

Work out an optimal schedule for the above situation. Under what conditions would you change the schedule? [*H. P.U. B.Tech. (Mech.) June, 2010*]

113. A military equipment is to be transported from origins 1, 2, 3 to destinations 1, 2, 3 and 4. The supply at the origins, the demand at the destinations and *time* of shipment is shown in table 3.313. Work out a transportation plan so that the *time* required for shipment is the minimum.

TABLE 3.313

		Destination				
		1	2	3	4	Supply
Origin	1	10	22	0	22	8
	2	15	20	12	8	13
	3	20	12	10	15	11
Demand		5	11	8	8	

(*Ans.* $x_{11} = 5, x_{13} = 3, x_{23} = 5, x_{24} = 8, x_{32} = 11$.)

114. A company produces a small component for an industrial product and distributes it to five wholesalers at a fixed delivered price of ₹ 250 per unit. Sales forecasts indicate that monthly deliveries will be 300, 300, 100, 500 and 400 units to wholesalers 1, 2, 3, 4 and 5 respectively. The direct costs of production of each unit are ₹ 100, ₹ 90 and ₹ 80 at plants 1, 2 and 3 respectively. The transportation costs of shipping a unit from plants to wholesalers are given below:

TABLE 3.314

		Wholesalers				
		1	2	3	4	5
Plants	1	5	7	10	15	15
	2	8	6	9	12	14
	3	10	9	8	10	15

Find how many components each plant must supply to each wholesaler to maximize the profit? What is the maximum total profit? Take the monthly production capacities of plants 1, 2 and 3 as 500, 100 and 1,250 units respectively. [*P.U.B.E.(E.&Ec.) 1996*]

(*Ans.* $x_{11} = 250, x_{22} = 100, x_{31} = 50, x_{32} = 200, x_{33} = 100,$
$x_{34} = 500, x_{35} = 400; Z_{max} =$ ₹ 2,50,500.)

115. Suppose that England, France and Spain produce all the wheat, barley and oats in the world. The world demand for wheat requires 125 acres of land, for barley and oats the land required is 60 acres and 70 acres respectively. The total amount of land available for this purpose in England, France and spain is 70 acres, 110 acres and 80 acres respectively. The number of hours of labour needed in England, France and Spain to produce an acre of wheat is 18 hours, 13 hours and 16 hours respectively. Similarly, for barley the labour-hours needed are 15 hours, 12 hours and 12 hours respectively. For oats they are 12 hours, 10 hours and 16 hours respectively in the three countries. The labour cost/hour in producing wheat in England, France and spain is ₹ 30, ₹ 24 and ₹ 33 respectively. Likewise, labour cost/hour in producing barley is ₹ 27, ₹ 30 and ₹ 28 and in producing oats is ₹ 23, ₹ 25 and ₹ 21 respectively in the three countries. The problem is to allocate land use in each country so as to meet world's food requirements and minimize the total labour cost.

(a) Formulate the problem as transportation problem.

(b) Solve the problem for the optimum cost. [*Mumbai U. MBA, 2010*]

116. Solve the following trans-shipment problem:

TABLE 3.315

		Destinations				
		S_1	S_2	D_1	D_2	Available
Sources	S_1	0	2	3	4	5
	S_2	2	0	2	4	25
	D_1	3	2	0	1	
	D_2	4	4	1	0	
Required				20	10	

(*Ans.* $S_2 - D_1 : 25, S_1 - D_2 : 5; D_1 - D_2 = 5; Z_{min} = 75$.)

117. Given the following data, determine the optimum transportation routes:

TABLE 3.316

Destinations

		S_1	S_2	D_1	D_2	*Capacity*
	S_1	0	2	2	1	8
	S_2	1	0	2	3	3
Sources	D_1	2	2	0	2	
	D_2	1	3	2	0	
Demand				7	4	

(*Ans.* $S_1 - D_1 : 4$, $S_1 - D_2 : 4$, $S_2 - D_1 = 3$; $Z_{min} = 18$.)

118. Maruti Machines Company has plants at Delhi, Kolkata and Mumbai. Its major distribution centres are located at Bangalore and Jaipur. The capacities of the three plants during the next quarter are 1,000, 1,500 and 1,200 machines. The quarterly demand at the two distribution centres is 2,300 and 1,400 machines. The transportation cost per machine per km is ₹ 0.08. The distance in km between the plants and distribution centres is as given below:

TABLE 3.317

	Delhi	*Kolkata*	*Mumbai*	*Bangalore*	*Jaipur*
Delhi	—	3,000	2,000	3,000	500
Kolkata	3,000	—	2,500	2,000	2,500
Mumbai	2,000	2,500	—	1,000	1,500
Bangalore	3,000	2,000	1,000	—	2,500
Jaipur	500	2,500	1,500	2,500	—

Give the minimum transportation cost distribution schedule in case the entire supply from all the sources could pass through any source or destination, before it is redistributed.

(*Ans.* Delhi – Jaipur: 1,000, Kolkata – Jaipur : 1,300, Kolkata – Bangalore : 200, Mumbai – Bangalore : 1,200.)

119. (*a*) Consider the following trans-shipment problem with two sources and three destinations; the cost for shipments (in rupees) in given below:

TABLE 3.318

		Source		*Destination*			*Supply*
		S_1	S_2	D_1	D_2	D_3	
Source	S_1	0	80	10	20	30	100 + 300
	S_2	10	0	20	50	40	200 + 300
	D_1	20	30	0	4	10	300
Destination	D_2	40	20	10	0	20	300
	D_3	60	70	80	20	0	300
Demand		300	300	100 + 300	100 – 300	100 + 300	

Determine the optimal shipping schedule.

(b) Compare the stepping stone and the MODI methods of testing the optimality of a solution to a transportation problem. Give suitable illustration.

[*R.T.M. Nagpur U.B. Tech. Dec., 2005*]

The Assignment Model

In Chapters 2 and 3 we discussed the simplex and the transportation techniques for solving linear programming problems. However, there are some special cases of linear programming problems whose solutions can be obtained by special techniques They are easier to apply and greatly reduce the computational work required by the simplex and the transportation techniques. This chapter deals with one such special case—*the assignment problem* which finds many applications in allocation and scheduling, for example in assigning salesmen to different regions, vehicles and drivers to different routes, products to factories, jobs to machines, contracts to bidders and research problems to teams, etc. Assignment is generally made on one-to-one basis and if there are more jobs to do than can be done, one can decide which job to leave undone or what resource to add.

4.1 DEFINITION OF THE ASSIGNMENT MODEL

An assignment problem concerns as to what happens to the effectiveness function when we associate each of a number of 'origins' with each of the *same* number of 'destinations'. Each resource or facility (origin) is to be associated with one and only one job (destination) and associations are to be made in such a way so as to maximize (or minimize) the total effectiveness. Resources are not divisible among jobs, nor are jobs divisible among resources.

The assignment problem may be defined as follows:

Given n facilities and n jobs and given the effectiveness of each facility for each job, the problem is to assign each facility to one and only one job so as to optimize the given measure of effectiveness.

Table 4.1 represents the assignment of n facilities (machines) to n jobs. c_{ij} is cost of assigning ith facility to jth job and x_{ij} represents the assignment of ith facility to jth job. If ith facility can be assigned to jth job, $x_{ij} = 1$, otherwise zero. The objective is to make assignments that minimize the total assignment cost or maximize the total associated gain.

TABLE 4.1

		Jobs				
		1	2	···	n	a_i Supply
	1	c_{11}	c_{12}	···	c_{1n}	1
	2	c_{21}	c_{22}	···	c_{2n}	1
Facilities	⋮	⋮	⋮	⋮	⋮	⋮
	n	c_{n1}	c_{n2}	···	c_{nn}	1
Demand b_j		1	1	···	1	

Thus an assignment problem can be represented by $n \times n$ matrix which constitutes $n!$ possible ways of making assignments. One obvious way to find the optimal solution is to write all the $n!$ possible arrangements, evaluate the cost of each and select the one involving the minimum cost. However, this *enumeration method* is extremely slow and time consuming even for small values of n. For example, for $n = 10$, a common situation, the number of possible arrangements is

10! = 3,628,800. Evaluation of so large a number of arrangements will take a prohibitively large time. This confirms the need for an efficient computational technique for solving such problems.

4.2 MATHEMATICAL REPRESENTATION OF THE ASSIGNMENT MODEL

Mathematically, the assignment model can be expressed as follows:

Let x_{ij} denote the assignment of facility i to job j such that

$$x_{ij} = \begin{cases} 0, \text{ if the } i\text{th facilitiy is not assigned to } j\text{th job,} \\ 1, \text{ if the } i\text{th facility is assigned to } j\text{th job.} \end{cases}$$

Then, the model is given by

$$\text{minimize } Z = \sum_{j=1}^{n} \sum_{i=1}^{n} c_{ij} x_{ij} \left\{ = \sum_{i=1}^{n} \sum_{j=1}^{n} c_{ij} x_{ij} \right\},$$

subject to constraints $\sum_{j=1}^{n} x_{ij} = 1, i = 1, 2, 3, \ldots, n$, (one job is assigned to the ith facility)

$$\sum_{i=1}^{n} x_{ij} = 1, j = 1, 2, 3, \ldots, n, \text{ (one facility is assigned the } j\text{th job)}$$

and $x_{ij} = 0$ or 1 (or $x_{ij} = x_{ij}^2$).

We see that if the last condition is replaced by $x_{ij} \geq 0$, we have transportation model with all requirements and available resources equal to 1.

4.3 COMPARISON WITH THE TRANSPORTATION MODEL

An assignment model may be regarded as a special case of the transportation model. Here, (refer table 4.1) facilities represent the 'sources' and jobs represent the 'destinations'. Number of sources is equal to the number of destinations, supply at each source is unity ($a_i = 1$ for all i) and demand at each destination is also unity ($b_j = 1$, for all j). The cost of 'transporting' (assigning) facility i to job j is c_{ij} and the number of units allocated to a cell can be either one or zero, *i.e.* they are non-negative quantities.

However the *transportation algorithm* is not very useful to solve this model because of degeneracy. In this model, when an assignment is made, the row as well as column requirements are satisfied simultaneously (rim conditions being always unity), resulting in degeneracy. Thus the assignment problem is a completely degenerate form of the transportation problem. In $n \times n$ problem, there will be n assignments instead of $n + n - 1$ or $2n - 1$ and we will have to fill in $2n - 1 - n = n - 1$ epsilons which will make the computations quite combersome. However, the special structure of the assignment model allows a more convenient and simple method of solution.

The technique used for solving assignment model makes use of two theorems:

Theorem I

It states "In an assignment problem, if we add or subtract a constant to every element of a row (or column) in the cost matrix, then an assignment which minimizes the total cost on one matrix also minimizes the total cost on the other matrix".

Let c_{ij} represent the original cost elements of the matrix. If constants u_i and v_j are subtracted from the ith row and jth column respectively, the new cost elements will be

$$c'_{ij} = c_{ij} - u_i - v_j.$$

If Z is the original objective function, the new objective function will be

$$Z' = \sum_{i=1}^{n} \sum_{j=1}^{n} (c_{ij} - u_i - v_j) x_{ij}$$

$$= \sum_{i=1}^{n}\sum_{j=1}^{n} c_{ij}x_{ij} - \sum_{i=1}^{n} u_i \sum_{j=1}^{n} x_{ij} - \sum_{j=1}^{n} v_j \sum_{i=1}^{n} x_{ij}.$$

Now with reference to section 4.2,

$$Z = \sum_{i=1}^{n}\sum_{j=1}^{n} c_{ij}x_{ij},$$

and

$$\sum_{i=1}^{n} x_{ij} = \sum_{j=1}^{n} x_{ij} = 1.$$

$$\therefore \quad Z' = Z - \sum_{i=1}^{n} u_i - \sum_{j=1}^{n} v_j = Z - \text{constant}$$

or Z' is minimum when Z is minimum. This proves the theorem.

Likewise, if in an assignment problem some cost elements are negative, we may convert them into an equivalent assignment problem where all the cost elements are non-negative by *adding* a suitably large constant to the elements of the relevant row.

Theorem II

It states "If all $c_{ij} \geq 0$ and we can find a set $x_{ij} = x_{ij}^*$ such that $\sum_{i=1}^{n} \sum_{j=1}^{n} c_{ij}x_{ij}^* = 0$, then this solution is optimal."

The result follows automatically since as neither of c_{ij} is negative, the value of $Z = \sum_{i=1}^{n} \sum_{j=1}^{n} c_{ij}x_{ij}$ cannot be negative.

Hence its minimum value is zero which is attained when $x_{ij} = x_{ij}^*$. Thus the present solution is an optimal solution.

The above two theorems indicate that if one can create a new c'_{ij} matrix with zero entries, and if these zero elements, or a subset thereof, constitute feasible solution, then this feasible solution is the optimal solution.

Thus the method of solution consists of adding (in case matrix contains some negative elements) or subtracting constant from rows and columns until sufficient number of c'_{ij}s become zero to yield a solution with a value of zero.

4.4 SOLUTION OF THE ASSIGNMENT MODELS

The technique of solution of the assignment models will be made clear now. Since the solution applies the concept of opportunity costs, a brief description of this concept may be useful. The cost of any action consists of opportunities that are sacrificed in taking that action. Consider the following table which contains the cost in rupees of processing each of jobs *A*, *B* and *C* on machines *X*, *Y* and *Z*.

TABLE 4.2

		Machines		
		X	Y	Z
	A	25	15	22
Jobs	B	31	20	19
	C	35	24	17

Suppose it is decided to process job *A* on machine X. The table shows that the cost of this assignment is ₹ 25. Since machine Y could just as well process job A for ₹ 15, clearly assigning job *A* to machine X is not the best decision. Therefore, when job *A* is arbitrarily assigned to machine X, it is done by sacrificing the opportunity to save ₹ 10 (₹ 25 – ₹ 15). The sacrifice is referred to as an *opportunity cost.* The decision to process job *A* on machine X precludes the assignment of this job to machine Y, given the constraint that one and only one job can be assigned to a machine. Thus opportunity cost of assignment of job *A* to machine X is ₹ 10 with respect to the lowest cost assignment for job A. Likewise, a decision to assign job *A* to machine Z would involve an opportunity cost of ₹ 7 (₹ 22 – ₹ 15). Finally, since assignment of job A to machine Y is the best assignment, the opportunity cost of this assignment is zero (₹ 15 – ₹ 15). More precisely these costs can be called the *machine-opportunity costs* with regard to job A. Similarly, if the lowest cost of row B is subtracted from all the costs in this row, we would have the machine-opportunity costs with regard to job B. The same step in row C would give the machine-opportunity costs for job C. This is represented in the following table:

TABLE 4.3

Machines

		X	Y	Z
	A	10	0	7
Jobs	B	12	1	0
	C	18	7	0

Machine-opportunity cost table

In addition to these machine-opportunity costs, there are *job-opportunity costs* also. Job A, B or C, for instance, could be assigned to machine X. The assignment of job B to machine X involves a cost of ₹ 31, while the assignment of job A to machine X costs only ₹ 25. Therefore, the opportunity cost of assigning job B to machine X is ₹ 6 (₹ 31 – ₹ 25). Similarly, the opportunity cost of assigning job C to machine X is ₹ 10 (₹ 35 – ₹ 25). A zero opportunity cost is involved in the assignment of job A to machine X, since this is the best assignement for machine X (column X). Hence job-opportunity costs for each column (each machine) are obtained by subtracting the lowest cost entry in each column from all the cost entries in that column. If the lowest entry in each column of table 4.3 is subtracted from all the cost entries of that column, the resulting table is called *total opportunity cost table.*

TABLE 4.4

Machines

		X	Y	Z
	A	10–10=0	0–0=0	7–0=7
Jobs	B	12–10=2	1–0=1	0–0=0
	C	18–10=8	7–0=7	0–0=0

Total opportunity cost table

It may be recalled that the objective is to assign the jobs to the machines so as to minimize *total costs.* With the total opportunitiy cost table this objective will be achieved if the jobs are assigned to the machines in such a way as to obtain a total opportunity cost of zero. The total opportunity cost table contains four cells with zeros, each indicating a zero opportunity cost for that cell (assignment). Hence job A could be assigned to machine X or Y and job B to machine Z, all assignments having zero opportunity costs. This way job C, however, could not be assigned to any machine with a zero opportunity cost since assignment of job B to machine Z precludes the assignment of job C to this machine. Clearly, to make an optimal assignment of the three jobs to the three machines, there must be three zero cells in the table such that a complete assignment to these cells can be made with a total opportunity cost of zero.

There is, in fact, a convenient method for determining whether an optimal assignment can be made. This method consists of drawing minimum number of lines covering all zero cells in the total opportunity cost table. If the minimum number of lines equals the number of rows (or columns) in the table, an optimal assignment can be made and the problem is solved. If, however, the minimum number of lines is less than the number of rows (or columns), an optimal assignment cannot be made. In this case there is need to develop a new total opportunity cost table. In the present example, since it requires only two lines to cross (cover) all zeros, and there are three rows, an optimal assignment is not possible. Clearly, there is a need to modify the total opportunity cost table by including some assignment not in the rows and columns covered by the lines. Of course, the assignment chosen should have the least opportunity cost. In the present case it is the assignment of job B to machine Y with an opportunity cost of 1. In other words, we would like to change the opportunity cost for this assignment from 1 to zero.

TABLE 4.5

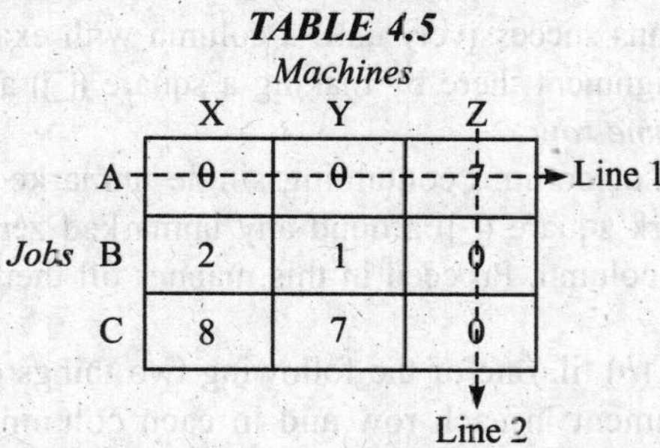

Machines

		X	Y	Z	
	A	0	0	7	→ Line 1
Jobs	B	2	1	0	
	C	8	7	0	
				Line 2	

To accomplish this we (*a*) choose the smallest element in the table not covered by a straight line and subtract this element from all other elements not having a line through them (*b*) add this smallest element to all elements lying at the intersection of any two lines. The revised total opportunity cost table is shown below.

TABLE 4.6

Machines

		X	Y	Z
	A	0	0	7+1=8
Jobs	B	2–1=1	1–1=0	0
	C	8–1=7	7–1=6	0

Revised opportunity cost table

The test for optimal assignment described above is applied again to the revised opportunity cost table. As the minimum number of lines covering all zeros is three and there are three rows (or columns), an optimal assignment can be made. The optimal assignments are A to X, B to Y and C to Z.

In larger problems, however, the assignments may not be readily apparent and there is need for more systematic procedure.

4.5 THE HUNGARIAN METHOD FOR SOLUTION OF THE ASSIGNMENT PROBLEMS

The Hungarian method suggested by Mr. Köning of Hungary or the *Reduced matrix method* or the *Flood's technique* is used for solving assignment problems since it is quite efficient and results in subtantial time saving over the other techniques. It involves a rapid reduction of the original matrix and finding of a set of n independent zeros, one in each row and column, which results in an optimal solution. The method consists of the following steps:

1. *Prepare a square matrix.* This step will not be required for $n \times n$ assignment problems. For $m \times n$ ($m \neq n$) problems, a dummy column or a dummy row, as the case may be, is added to make the matrix square.

2. *Reduce the matrix.* Subtract the smallest element of each row from all the elements of the row. So there will be at least one zero in each row. Examine if there is at least one zero in each column. If not, subtract the minimum element of the column(s) not containing zero from all the elements of that column(s). This step reduces the elements of the matrix until zeros, called *zero opportunity costs,* are obtained in each column.

3. *Check whether an optimal assignment can be made in the reduced matrix or not.* For this proceed as follows:

(*a*) Examine rows successively until a row with exactly one unmarked zero is obtained. Make an assignment to this single zero by making square (□) around it. Cross (×) all other zeros in the *same column* as they will not be considered for making any more assignments in that column. Proceed in this way until all rows have been examined.

(*b*) Now examine columns successively until a column with exactly one unmarked zero is found. Make an assignment there by making a square (□) around it and cross (×) any other zeros in the *same row.*

In case there is no row or column containing single unmarked zero (they contain more than one unmarked zero), mark square (□) around any unmarked zero arbitrarily and cross (×) all other zeros in its row *and* column. Proceed in this manner till there is no unmarked zero left in the cost matrix.

Repeat substeps (*a*) and (*b*) till one of the following two things occur:

(*i*) There is one assignment in each row and in each column. In this case the optimal assignment can be made in the current solution, *i.e.*, the current feasible solution is an optimal solution. The minimum number of lines crossing all zeros is n, the order of the matrix.

(*ii*) There is some row and/or column without assignment. In this case optimal assignment cannot be made in the current solution. The minimum number of lines crossing all zeros have to be obtained in this case by following step 4.

4. *Find the minimum number of lines crossing all zeros.* This consists of the following substeps:

(*a*) Mark (√) the rows that do not have assignments.

(*b*) Mark (√) the columns (not already marked) that have zeros in marked rows.

(*c*) Mark (√) the rows (not already marked) that have assignments in marked columns.

(*d*) Repeat substeps (*b*) and (*c*) till no more rows or columns can be marked.

(*e*) Draw straight lines through all unmarked rows and marked columns. This gives the minimum number of lines crossing all zeros. If this number is equal to the order of the matrix, then it is an optimal solution, otherwise go to step 5.

5. *Iterate towards the optimal solution.* Examine the uncovered elements. Select the smallest element and subtract it from all the uncovered elements. Add this smallest element to every element that lies at the intersection of two lines. Leave the remaining elements of the matrix as such. This yields second basic feasible solution.

6. Repeat steps 3 through 5 successively until the number of lines crossing all zeros becomes equal to the order of the matrix. In such a case every row and column will have one assignment. This indicates that an optimal solution has been obtained. The total cost associated with this solution is obtained by adding the original costs in the assigned cells.

Flow chart of these steps is shown in Fig. 4.1 below.

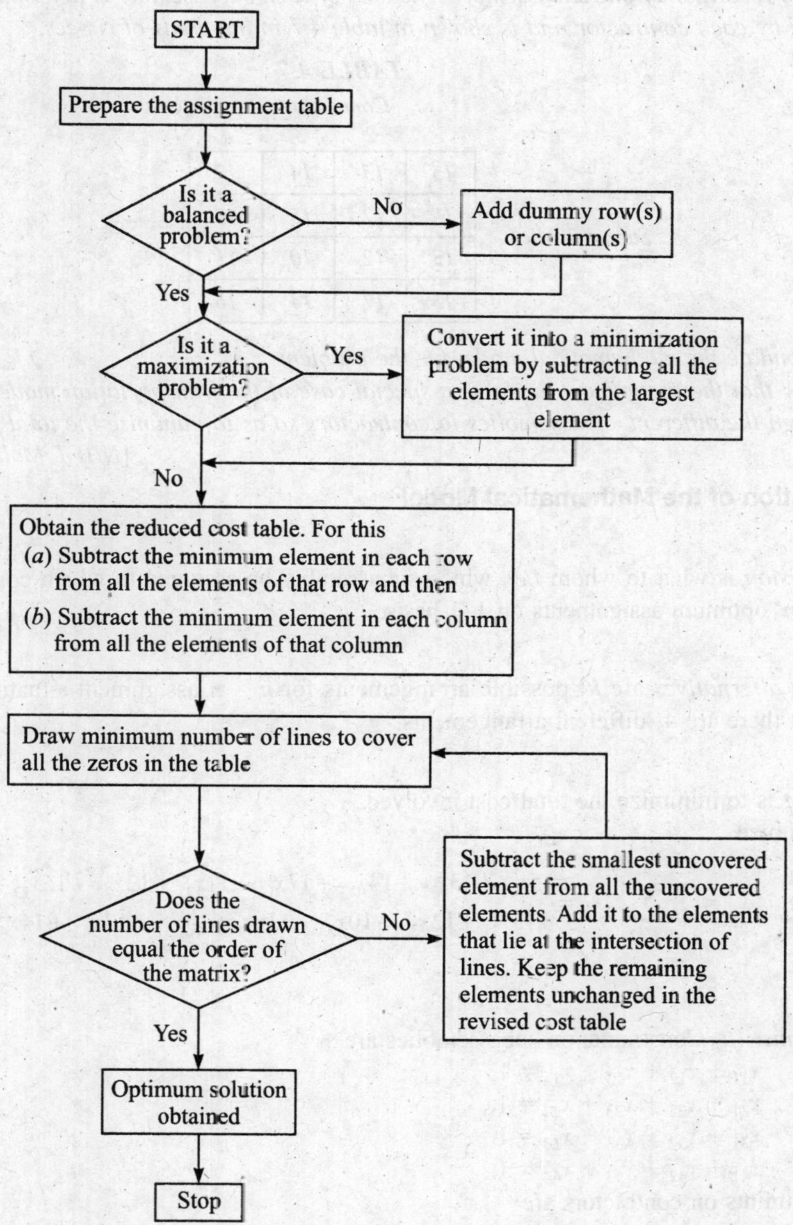

Fig. 4.1. Flow chart for the Hungarian method

4.6 FORMULATION AND SOLUTION OF THE ASSIGNMENT MODELS

In this section we shall consider a few examples which will make clear the techniques of formulation and solution of the assignment models.

EXAMPLE 4.6-1 (Assignment Problem)

A machine tool company decides to make four subassemblies through four contractors. Each contractor is to receive only one subassembly. The cost of each subassembly is determined by the bids submitted by each contractor and is shown in table 4.7 in hundreds of rupees.

TABLE 4.7

		Contractors			
		1	2	3	4
Subassemblies	1	15	13	14	17
	2	11	12	15	13
	3	13	12	10	11
	4	15	17	14	16

(i) Formulate the mathematical model for the problem.
(ii) Show that the assignment model is a special case of the transportation model.
(iii) Assign the different subassemblies to contractors so as to minimize the total cost.

[NIIFT Mohali, 2000]

(*i*) Formulation of the Mathematical Model

Step I

Key decision is what to whom *i.e.*, which subassembly be assigned to which contractor or what are the '*n*' optimum assignments on 1–1 basis.

Step II

Feasible alternatives are $n!$ possible arrangements for $n \times n$ assignment situation. In the given situation there are 4! different arrangements.

Step III

Objective is to minimize the total cost involved
i.e., minimize

$$Z=\sum_{i=1}^{n}\sum_{j=1}^{n} c_{ij}x_{ij} = \sum_{i=1}^{4}\sum_{j=1}^{4} c_{ij}x_{ij} = \begin{array}{l}15x_{11}+13x_{12}+14x_{13}+17x_{14}+11x_{21}+12x_{22}+15x_{23}+13x_{24}\\ +13x_{31}+12x_{32}+10x_{33}+11x_{34}+15x_{41}+17x_{42}+14x_{43}+16x_{44}.\end{array}$$

Step IV

Constraints: (*a*) Constraints on subassemblies are

$$x_{11}+x_{12}+x_{13}+x_{14}=1,$$
$$x_{21}+x_{22}+x_{23}+x_{24}=1,$$
$$x_{31}+x_{32}+x_{33}+x_{34}=1,$$
$$x_{41}+x_{42}+x_{43}+x_{44}=1.$$

(*b*) Constraints on contractors are

$$x_{11}+x_{21}+x_{31}+x_{41}=1,$$
$$x_{12}+x_{22}+x_{32}+x_{42}=1,$$
$$x_{13}+x_{23}+x_{33}+x_{43}=1,$$
$$x_{14}+x_{24}+x_{34}+x_{44}=1.$$

(*ii*) Comparing this model with the transportation model, we find that $a_i = 1$, $i = 1, 2, 3, 4$ and $b_j = 1$, $j = 1, 2, 3, 4$. Thus, the assignment model can be represented as in table 4.8.

Therefore, the assignment model is a special case of the transportation model in which (*a*) all right-handside constants in the constraints are unity *i.e.*, $a_i = 1$, $b_j = 1$.

TABLE 4.8

	Contractors (facilities, agents or means) 1	2	3	4	Supply a_i
Subassemblies 1	15	13	14	17	1
(jobs, tasks 2	11	12	15	13	1
or requirements) 3	13	12	10	11	1
4	15	17	14	16	1
Demand b_j	1	1	1	1	

(*b*) all coefficients of x_{ij} in the constraints are unity.

(*c*) $m = n$.

(*iii*) Solution of the Model

We shall apply the *Flood's Technique* for solving the assignment problems. This technique also known as the *Hungarian Method* or the *Reduced Matrix Method* consists of the following steps:

Step I

Prepare a Square Matrix: Since the situation involves a square matrix, this step is not necessary.

Step II

Reduce the Matrix: This involves the following substeps:

Substep 1: In the effectiveness matrix, subtract the minimum element of each row from all the elements of that row. The resulting reduced matrix will have at least one zero element in each row. Check if there is at least one zero element in each column also. If so, stop here. If not, proceed to substep 2.

Substep 2: Mark the columns that do not have zero element. Now subtract the minimum element of each such coulmn from all the elements of that column.

In the given situation, the minimum element in first row is 13. So, we subtract 13 from all the elements of the first row. Similarly we subtract 11, 10 and 14 from all the elements of row 2, 3 and 4 respectively. This gives at least one zero in each row as shown in table 4.9.

TABLE 4.9

	Contractors 1	2	3	4
Subassemblies 1	2	0	1	4
2	0	1	4	2
3	3	2	0	1
4	1	3	0	2

In table 4.9 column 4 has no zero element. We go to substep 2 and subtract the minimum element 1 from all its elements. Table 4.10 represents the resulting reduced matrix that contains at least one zero element in each row and in each column.

TABLE 4.10

	1	2	3	4
1	2	0	1	3
2	0	1	4	1
3	3	2	0	0
4	1	3	0	1

Initial basic feasible solution

Step III

Check if Optimal Assignment can be made in the Current Solution or not

Basis for making this check is that if the minimum number of lines crossing all zeros is less than n (in our example $n = 4$), then an optimal assignment cannot be made in the current solution. If it is equal to n (= 4), then optimal assignment can be made in the current solution.

Approach for obtaining minimum number of lines crossing all zeros consists of the following substeps:

Substep 1: Examine rows successively until a row with exactly one unmarked zero is found. Make a square (□) around this zero, indicating that an assignment will be made there. Mark (×) all other zeros in the *same column* showing that they cannot be used for making other assignments. Proceed in this manner until all rows have been examined.

In the given problem, row 1 has a single unmarked zero in column 2. Make an assignment there by enclosing this zero by a square (□). It means subassembly 1 is assigned to contractor 2. Since contractor 2 has been assigned subassembly 1 and as a contractor can be assigned only one subassembly, any other zero in column 2 is crossed. Since there is no other zero in this column, crossing is not required. Next, row 2 has a single unmarked zero in column 1, make an assignment. Row 4 has a single unmarked zero in column 3, make an assignment and cross the 2nd zero in column 3. Now, row 3 has a single unmarked zero in column 4, make an assignment here. This is shown in the matrix below.

TABLE 4.11

Contractors

Subassemblies	1	2	3	4
1	2	[0]	1	3
2	[0]	1	4	1
3	3	2	~~0~~ (×)	[0]
4	1	3	[0]	1

Substep 2: Next examine columns for single unmarked zeros, making them (□) and also marking (×) any other zeros in their rows.

In case there is no row or column containing single unmarked zero (there are more than one unmarked zeros), mark (□) one of the unmarked zeros arbitraily and (×) all other zeros in its row *and* column. Repeat the process till no unmarked zero is left in the cost matrix.

Substep 3: Repeat substeps 1 and 2 successively till one of the two things occurs:

(*a*) there may be no row and no column without assignment *i.e.*, there is one assignment in each row and in each column. In such a case the optimal assignment can be made in the current solution *i.e.*, the current feasible solution is an optimal solution. The minimum number of lines crossing all zeros will be equal to 'n'.

(*b*) there may be some row and/or column without assignment. Hence optimal assignment cannot be made in the current solution. The minimum number of lines crossing all zeros have to be obtained in this case.

In the present example, substeps 2 and 3 are not necessary since there is no column left unmarked. Since there is one assignment in each row and in each column, the optimal assignment can be made in the current solution. Thus minimum total cost is

= ₹ (13 × 1 + 11 × 1 + 11 × 1 + 14 × 1) × 100 = ₹ 4,900,

and the optimal assignment policy is

Subassembly	1 –	Contractor	2,
”	2 –	”	1,
”	3 –	”	4,
”	4 –	”	3.

The minimal cost of ₹ 4,900 can also be determined by summing up all the elements that were subtracted during the solution procedure *i.e.*, [(13 + 11 + 10 + 14) + 1] × 100 = ₹ 4,900.

EXAMPLE 4.6-2

Four different jobs can be done on four different machines. The set-up and take-down time costs are assumed to be prohibitively high for changeovers. The matrix below gives the cost in rupees of producing job i on machine j.

TABLE 4.12

		Machines			
		M_1	M_2	M_3	M_4
Jobs	J_1	5	7	11	6
	J_2	8	5	9	6
	J_3	4	7	10	7
	J_4	10	4	8	3

(i) How should the jobs be assigned to the various machines so that the total cost is minimized? Also formulate the mathematical model for the problem. [P.U. B.Com. April, 2007; B.E.(C.Sc.&E.) Dec., 2004; P.T.U. MBA May, 2002]

(ii) Explain the rationale of assignment algorithm.

Solution

(i) FORMULATION OF THE MODEL

Step I

Key decision is to find what job be assigned to which machine *i.e.*, what are the '*n*' optimum assignments on 1–1 basis.

Step II

Feasible alternatives are 4! possible arrangements for the given 4 × 4 assignment situation.

Step III

Objective is to minimize the total cost involved.

$$i.e., \text{minimize } Z = \sum_{i=1}^{4}\sum_{j=1}^{4} c_{ij}x_{ij} = \begin{array}{l} 5x_{11} + 7x_{12} + 11x_{13} + 6x_{14} + 8x_{21} + 5x_{22} + 9x_{23} + 6x_{24} \\ + 4x_{31} + 7x_{32} + 10x_{33} + 7x_{34} + 10x_{41} + 4x_{42} + 8x_{43} + 3x_{44}. \end{array}$$

Step IV

Constraints are

(*a*) due to jobs:

$$\begin{aligned} x_{11} + x_{12} + x_{13} + x_{14} &= 1, \\ x_{21} + x_{22} + x_{23} + x_{24} &= 1, \\ x_{31} + x_{32} + x_{33} + x_{34} &= 1, \\ x_{41} + x_{42} + x_{43} + x_{44} &= 1. \end{aligned}$$

(*b*) due to machines:

$$x_{11} + x_{21} + x_{31} + x_{41} = 1,$$
$$x_{12} + x_{22} + x_{32} + x_{42} = 1,$$
$$x_{13} + x_{23} + x_{33} + x_{43} = 1,$$
$$x_{14} + x_{24} + x_{34} + x_{44} = 1.$$

Also $x_{ij} = 0$ or 1.

Thus the problem is to optimize (minimize) the above objective function Z subject to the above constraints.

SOLUTION OF THE MODEL

The Hungarian method or the reduced matrix method will be used to solve the above model. This method consists of the following steps:

Step I

Prepare a Square Matrix: Since the situation involves a square matrix, this step is not necessary.

Step II

Reduce the Matrix: This involves the following substeps:

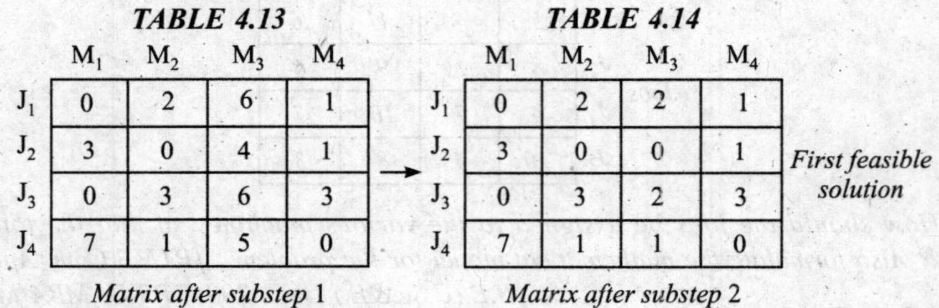

TABLE 4.13

	M_1	M_2	M_3	M_4
J_1	0	2	6	1
J_2	3	0	4	1
J_3	0	3	6	3
J_4	7	1	5	0

Matrix after substep 1
(*contains no zero in column* 3)

→

TABLE 4.14

	M_1	M_2	M_3	M_4
J_1	0	2	2	1
J_2	3	0	0	1
J_3	0	3	2	3
J_4	7	1	1	0

Matrix after substep 2

First feasible solution

Substep 1: In the effectiveness matrix, subtract the minimum element of each row from all the elements of the row. See if there is at least one zero in each row and in each column. If it is so, stop here. If not, proceed to substep 2.

Substep 2: Now subtract the minimum element of the column not containing a zero element from all the elements of the column.

Following these substeps we get table 4.13 which further leads to table 4.14.

Step III

Check if Optimal Assignment can be made in the Current Solution or not

Substep 1: Examine rows successively until a row with exactly one unmarked zero is found. Mark (□) this zero, indicating that an assignment will be made there. Mark (×) all other zeros in the *same column* showing that they cannot be used for making other assignments. Proceed in this manner until all rows have been examined.

TABLE 4.15

	M_1	M_2	M_3	M_4
J_1	[0]	2	2	1
J_2	3	[0]	0 (×)	1
J_3	0 (×)	3	2	3
J_4	7	1	1	[0]

Substep 2: Next examine columns for single unmarked zeros, marking them (□) and also marking (×) any other zeros in their rows.

Substep 3: In the present example, after following substeps 1 and 2 we find that their repetition is unnecessary and also row 3 and column 3 are without any assignments (table 4.15). Hence we proceed as follows to find the minimum number of lines crossing all zeros:

TABLE 4.16

	M_1	M_2	M_3	M_4	
J_1	[0]	2	2	1	✓
J_2	3	[0]	~~0~~	1	
J_3	~~0~~	3	2	3	✓
J_4	7	1	1	[6]	
	✓				

Substep 4: Mark (√) the rows for which assignment has not been made. In our problem it is the third row.

Substep 5: Mark (√) columns (not already marked) which have zeros in marked rows. Thus column 1 is marked (√).

Substep 6: Mark (√) rows (not already marked) which have assignments in marked columns. Thus row 1 is marked (√).

Substep 7: Repeat substeps 5 and 6 until no more marking is possible. In the present case this repetition is not necessary.

Substep 8: Draw lines through all unmarked rows and through all marked columns. This gives the minimum number of lines crossing all zeros. If the procedure is correct, there will be as many lines as the number of assignments. In this example, number of such lines is 3 which is less than $n(n = 4$ here). Hence optimal assignment is not possible in the current solution. Further reduction of table 4.16 is necessary.

Step IV

Iterate Towards Optimality

Examine the elements that do not have a line through them. Select the smallest of these elements and subtract it from all the elements that do not have a line through them. Add this smallest element to every element that lies at the intersection of two lines. Leave the remaining elements of the matrix unchanged. Proceeding in this manner we get the following matrix:

TABLE 4.17

	M_1	M_2	M_3	M_4
J_1	0	1	1	0
J_2	4	0	0	1
J_3	0	2	1	2
J_4	8	1	1	0

Second feasible solution

Step V

Check if Optimal Assignment can be made in the Current Feasible Solution or not

Repeating step III *i.e.*, substeps 1 through 8 therein, we get table 4.18.

TABLE 4.18

	M_1	M_2	M_3	M_4	
J_1	~~0~~	1	1	~~0~~	✓
J_2	4	[0]	~~0~~	1	
J_3	[0]	2	1	2	✓
J_4	8	1	1	[0]	✓
	✓			✓	

Since the minimum number of lines passing through all zeros is 3(< 4), optimal assignment cannot be made in the current solution.

Step VI

Iterate Towards Optimality

Repeating step IV, we get table 4.19.

TABLE 4.19

	M_1	M_2	M_3	M_4
J_1	[0]	~~0~~	~~0~~	~~0~~
J_2	5	[0]	~~0~~	2
J_3	~~0~~	1	[0]	2
J_4	8	~~0~~	~~0~~	[0]

Third feasible solution

Step VII

Check if Optimal Assignment can be made in the Current Feasible Solution or not

Repeat step III *i.e.*, substeps 1 through 8 therein. Since there is no row with exactly one unmarked zero, we start considering the columns. We find there is no column as well with single unmarked zero. Therefore, we make assignment *arbitrarily* in any zero and cross the remaining zeros in the same column *as well as* the same row. Let us make assignment at zero in cell (J_1, M_1) arbitrarily and cross the remaining zeros in column 1 and row 1. See now if there is exactly one zero (unmarked) in any row or in any column. We find row 3 has a single zero in column 3. We make assignment here in cell (J_3, M_3) and cross remaining zeros in column 3. Next assignment is made in cell (J_2, M_2) in row 2 and the remaining zeros in column 2 are crossed. Last assignment is made in cell (J_4, M_4).

As there is assignment in each row and in each column, optimal assignment can be made in the current solution. Hence optimal assignment policy is

Job J_1 should be assinged to machine M_1,

J_2 should be assigned to machine M_2,

J_3 should be assigned to machine M_3,

J_4 should be assigned to machine M_4,

and optimum cost = ₹ (5 + 5 + 10 + 3) = ₹ 23.

(ii) RATIONALE OF THE ASSIGNMENT ALGORITHM

Step I: The relative cost of assigning facility i to job j is not changed by the subtraction of a constant from a row or column of the original cost matrix. That is why we can subtract elements from rows and columns to get at least one zero in each row and in each column.

Step II: An optimal assignment exists if total reduced cost of assignment is zero. This is the case when the minimum number of lines necessary to cover all zeros is equal to the order of the matrix. If, however, it is less, further reduction of the cost matrix is necessary.

Step III: The underlying logic of this step can be explained considering, say, table 4.16 in which only 3 lines can be drawn. Therefore, optimal assignment is not possible and further reduction is required. This is done by subtracting the smallest non-zero element 1 from all the elements of the table. This yields the following table:

TABLE 4.20

	M_1	M_2	M_3	M_4
J_1	–1	1	1	0
J_2	2	–1	–1	0
J_3	–1	2	1	2
J_4	6	0	0	–1

This table contains negative elements. Since the objective is to obtain an assignment policy with total reduced cost of zero, the negative elements must be eliminated. This can be done by adding 1 to each of the rows and columns crossed by the three lines of table 4.16. This results in the following table:

TABLE 4.21

	M_1	M_2	M_3	M_4
J_1	0	1	1	0
J_2	4	0	0	1
J_3	0	2	1	2
J_4	8	1	1	0

All this, in fact, amounts to step IV (iterate towards optimality) *i.e.*, subtract the smallest non-zero uncovered element from all the uncovered elements, add it to the elements that lie at the intersection of lines and leave the remaining elements of the matrix unchanged. That is why table 4.21 is identical to table 4.17.

EXAMPLE 4.6-3

Solve the following assignment problem:

TABLE 4.22

	I	*II*	*III*	*IV*	*V*
1	*11*	*17*	*8*	*16*	*20*
2	*9*	*7*	*12*	*6*	*15*
3	*13*	*16*	*15*	*12*	*16*
4	*21*	*24*	*17*	*28*	*26*
5	*14*	*10*	*12*	*11*	*13*

[P.U. B.E. (Mech.) 2012; B.Com. April, 2008]

Solution

Step I: Reduce the Matrix

Subtract the minimum element of each row from all the elements of the row. Then subtract the minimum element of each column from all the elements of the column. Thus tables 4.23 and 4.24 are obtained.

TABLE 4.23

	I	II	III	IV	V
1	3	9	0	8	12
2	3	1	6	0	9
3	1	4	3	0	4
4	4	7	0	11	9
5	4	0	2	1	3

Matrix containing zero in every row

TABLE 4.24

	I	II	III	IV	V	
1	2	9	[0]	8	9	✓
2	2	1	6	[0]	6	
3	[0]	4	3	~~0~~	1	
4	3	7	~~0~~	11	6	✓
5	3	[0]	2	1	~~0~~	
			✓			

Matrix containing zero in every row as well as column

Step II: Check if Optimal Assignment can be made in the Current Feasible Solution or not

As the number of assignments in table 4.24 is 4 which is less than $n(= 5)$, the order of the matrix, optimal assignment is not possible in the current solution. We now draw the minimum number of lines crossing all zeros. Proceeding as in section 4.5 or example 4.6-2, it is found that the minimum number of lines crossing all zeros is 4.

Step III: Iterate Towards Optimality

In table 4.24, the minimum element that does not have a line through it is 2. Subtract it from all the elements which do not have a line through them. Add it to all the elements that lie at the intersection of two lines and leave the remaining elements of the matrix unchanged. We get table 4.25, which is the second basic feasible solution.

TABLE 4.25

	I	II	III	IV	V
1	0	7	0	6	7
2	2	1	8	0	6
3	0	4	5	0	1
4	1	5	0	9	4
5	3	0	4	1	0

Second b.f.s.

Step IV: Check if Optimal Assignment can be made in the Current Feasible Solution or not

TABLE 4.26

	I	II	III	IV	V	
1	~~0~~	7	~~0~~	6	7	✓
2	2	1	8	[0]	6	✓
3	[0]	4	5	~~0~~	1	✓
4	1	5	[0]	9	4	✓
5	3	[0]	4	1	~~0~~	
	✓		✓	✓		

As the number of assignments in table 4.26 is 4, which is less than $n(= 5)$, the order of the matrix, optimal assignment is not possible in table 4.26. Proceeding as in section 4.5 or example 4.6-2, it is found that the minimum number of lines crossing all zeros is 4.

Step V: Iterate Towards Optimality

In table 4.26, the minimum element that does not have a line through it is 1. Adding it to elements that lie at the intersection of two lines, subtracting it from elements that do not have a line through them and keeping the remaining elements of the matrix unchanged, we get table 4.27.

TABLE 4.27

	I	II	III	IV	V
1	[0]	6	~~0~~	6	6
2	2	[0]	8	~~0~~	5
3	~~0~~	3	5	[0]	~~0~~
4	1	4	[0]	9	3
5	4	~~0~~	5	2	[0]

Optimal b.f.s.

Step VI: Check if Optimal Assignment can be made in the Current Feasible Solution or not

As the number of assignments is 5 which is also the order of the matrix, table 4.27 gives optimal b.f.s. The associated minimum cost is

$$Z_{\min} = 11 + 7 + 12 + 17 + 13 = 60.$$

EXAMPLE 4.6-4

Five wagons are available at stations 1, 2, 3, 4 and 5. These are required at five stations I, II, III, IV and V. The mileages between various stations are given by the table below. How should the wagons be transported so as to minimize the total mileage covered?

TABLE 4.28

	I	*II*	*III*	*IV*	*V*
1	*10*	*5*	*9*	*18*	*11*
2	*13*	*9*	*6*	*12*	*14*
3	*3*	*2*	*4*	*4*	*5*
4	*18*	*9*	*12*	*17*	*15*
5	*11*	*6*	*14*	*19*	*10*

[*P.U.B. Com. April, 2008*]

Solution

Step I: Reduce the Matrix

Proceeding as in example 4.6-2 we get tables 4.29 and 4.30.

TABLE 4.29

	I	II	III	IV	V
1	5	0	4	13	6
2	7	3	0	6	8
3	1	0	2	2	3
4	9	0	3	8	6
5	5	0	8	13	4

Matrix containing zero in every row

→

TABLE 4.30

	I	II	III	IV	V	
1	4	[0]	4	11	3	✓
2	6	3	[0]	4	5	
3	[0]	~~0~~	2	~~0~~	~~0~~	
4	8	~~0~~	3	6	3	✓
5	4	~~0~~	8	11	1	✓
		✓				

Matrix containing zero in every row as well as column

Step II: Check if Optimal Assignment is Possible in the Current Feasible Solution or not

Proceeding as in examples 4.6-1 and 4.6-2, the minimum number of lines crossing all zeros as given by table 4.30 is 3. Hence optimal assignment is not possible in the current solution.

Step III: Iterate Towards Optimality

Proceeding as in example 4.6-2, we get table 4.31.

TABLE 4.31

	I	II	III	IV	V
1	3	0	3	10	2
2	6	4	0	4	5
3	0	1	2	0	0
4	7	0	2	5	2
5	3	0	7	10	0

Step IV: Check if Optimal Assignment can be made in the Current Feasible Solution or not

Proceeding as in example 4.6-2, the minimum number of lines crossing all zeros as given by table 4.32 is 4. Hence optimal assignment is not possible in the current solution.

TABLE 4.32

	I	II	III	IV	V	
1	3	[0]	3	10	2	✓
2	6	4	[0]	4	5	
3	[0]	1	2	~~0~~	~~0~~	
4	7	~~0~~	2	5	2	✓
5	3	~~0~~	7	10	[0]	
		✓				

Step V: Iterate Towards Optimality

Proceeding as in example 4.6-2, we get table 4.33.

TABLE 4.33

	I	II	III	IV	V
1	1	0	1	8	0
2	6	6	0	4	5
3	0	3	2	0	0
4	5	0	0	3	0
5	3	2	7	10	0

Step VI: Check if Optimal Assignment can be made in the Current Feasible Solution or not

Proceeding as in example 4.6-2, the minimum number of lines crossing all zeros as given by table 4.34 is 4. Hence optimal assignment is not possible in the current solution.

TABLE 4.34

	I	II	III	IV	V	
1	1	[0]	1	8	~~0~~	✓
2	6	6	[0]	4	5	✓
3	[0]	3	2	~~0~~	~~0~~	
4	5	~~0~~	~~0~~	3	~~0~~	✓
5	3	2	7	10	[0]	✓
		✓	✓			

Step VII: Iterate Towards Optimality

Proceeding as in example 4.6-2, we get table 4.35.

TABLE 4.35

	I	II	III	IV	V
1	0	0	1	7	0
2	5	6	0	3	5
3	0	4	3	0	1
4	4	0	0	2	0
5	2	2	7	9	0

Step VIII: Check if Optimal Assignment can be made in the Current Feasible Solution or not

Proceeding as in example 4.6-2, we find that there is an assignment in every row and column. Hence table 4.36 gives optimal assignment policy. The minimum mileage associated with this solution is

$$Z_{min} = 10 + 6 + 4 + 9 + 10 = 39.$$

TABLE 4.36

	I	II	III	IV	V
1	[0]	~~0~~	1	7	~~0~~
2	5	6	[0]	3	5
3	~~0~~	4	3	[0]	1
4	4	[0]	~~0~~	2	~~0~~
5	2	2	7	9	[0]

Optimal Solution

4.7 VARIATIONS OF THE ASSIGNMENT PROBLEM

1. *Non-square matrix (Unbalanced assignment problem).* Such a problem is found to exist when the number of facilities is not equal to the number of jobs. Since the Hungarian method of solution requires a square matrix, fictitious facilities or jobs, as the case may be, added and zero costs be assigned to the corresponding cells of the matrix. These cells are then treated the same way as the real cost cells during the solution procedure.

2. *Maximization problem.* Sometimes the assignment problem may deal with maximization of the objective function. The maximization problem has to be changed to minimization before

the Hungarian method may be applied. This transformation may be done in either of the following two ways:

(*a*) by subtracting all the elements from the largest element of the matrix,

(*b*) by multiplying the matrix elements by – 1.

The Hungarian method can then be applied to this equivalent minimization problem to obtain the optimal solution.

3. *Restrictions on assignments.* Sometimes technical, space, legal or other restrictions do not permit the assignment of a particular facility to a particular job. Such problems can be solved by assigning a very heavy cost (infinite cost) *i.e.*, ∞ or M to the corresponding cell. Such a job will then be automatically excluded from further consideration (making assignments).

4. *Alternate optimal solutions.* Sometimes, it is possible to have two or more ways to strike off all zero elements in the reduced matrix for a given problem. In such cases, there will be alternate optimal solutions with the same cost. Alternate optimal solutions offer a great flexibility to the management since it can select the one which is most suitable to its requirement.

All the above variations will now be explained by considering examples.

EXAMPLE 4.7-1

(Assignment Problem—Non-Square Matrix)

A company has one surplus truck in each of the cities A, B, C, D and E and one deficit truck in each of the cities 1, 2, 3, 4, 5 and 6. The distance between the cities in kilometres is shown in the matrix below (Table 4.37). Find the assignment of trucks from cities in surplus to cities in deficit so that the total distance covered by vehicles is minimum.

TABLE 4.37

	1	*2*	*3*	*4*	*5*	*6*
A	*12*	*10*	*15*	*22*	*18*	*8*
B	*10*	*18*	*25*	*15*	*16*	*12*
C	*11*	*10*	*3*	*8*	*5*	*9*
D	*6*	*14*	*10*	*13*	*13*	*12*
E	*8*	*12*	*11*	*7*	*13*	*10*

[P.T.U. B.Tech. (Mech.) Nov., 2012; P.U.B.Com.Sept., 2004]

Solution

Step I

Prepare a Square Matrix: As the situation involves a non-square matrix, it has to be modified to a square matrix by adding dummies. Add a dummy city with surplus vehicle. Since there is no distance associated with it, the corresponding cell values are made all zeros.

TABLE 4.38

		Cities in deficit					
		1	2	3	4	5	6
	A	12	10	15	22	18	8
	B	10	18	25	15	16	12
Cities with surplus	C	11	10	3	8	5	9
	D	6	14	10	13	13	12
	E	8	12	11	7	13	10
	Dummy	0	0	0	0	0	0

Step II

Reduce the Matrix: Proceeding as in example 4.6-2, we get table 4.39.

TABLE 4.39

	1	2	3	4	5	6
A	4	2	7	14	10	0
B	0	8	15	5	6	2
C	8	7	0	5	2	6
D	0	8	4	7	7	6
E	1	5	4	0	6	3
Dummy	0	0	0	0	0	0

Matrix after substep 1 (contains zero in each row and in each column)

(Initial feasible solution)

Step III

Check if Optimal Assignment can be made in the Current Solution or not

Proceeding as in example 4.6-2, the minimum number of lines crossing all zeros are given by table 4.40.

TABLE 4.40

	1	2	3	4	5	6	
A	4	2	7	14	10	[0]	
B	[0]	8	15	5	6	2	✓
C	8	7	[0]	5	2	6	
D	~~0~~	8	4	7	7	6	✓
E	1	5	4	[0]	6	3	
Dummy	~~0~~	[0]	~~0~~	~~0~~	~~0~~	~~0~~	
	✓						

As the minimum number of lines crossing all zeros is 5(< 6), optimal assignment cannot be made in the current feasible solution.

Step IV: Iterate Towards an Optimal Solution

Proceeding as in example 4.6-2, we get table 4.41.

TABLE 4.41

	1	2	3	4	5	6
A	6	2	7	14	10	0
B	0	6	13	3	4	0
C	10	7	0	5	2	6
D	0	6	2	5	5	4
E	3	5	4	0	6	3
Dummy	2	0	0	0	0	0

Second feasible solution

Step V: Check if Optimal Assignment can be made in the Current Feasible Solution or not

TABLE 4.42

	1	2	3	4	5	6	
A	6	2	7	14	10	[0]	✓
B	[0]	6	13	3	4	~~0~~	✓
C	10	7	[0]	5	2	6	
D	~~0~~	6	2	5	5	4	✓
E	3	5	4	[0]	6	3	
Dummy	2	[0]	~~0~~	~~0~~	~~0~~	~~0~~	
	✓					✓	

As the minimum number of lines crossing all zeros is 5(< 6), optimal assignment cannot be made in the current solution.

Step VI: Iterate Towards an Optimal Solution

TABLE 4.43

	1	2	3	4	5	6
A	6	0	5	12	8	0
B	0	4	11	1	2	0
C	12	7	0	5	2	8
D	0	4	0	3	3	4
E	5	5	4	0	6	5
Dummy	4	0	0	0	0	2

Third feasible solution

Step VII: Check if Optimal Assignment can be made in the Current Feasible Solution or not

TABLE 4.44

	1	2	3	4	5	6
A	6	[0]	5	12	8	~~0~~
B	~~0~~	4	11	1	2	[0]
C	12	7	[0]	5	2	8
D	[0]	4	~~0~~	3	3	4
E	5	5	4	[0]	6	5
Dummy	4	~~0~~	~~0~~	~~0~~	[0]	2

Since there is no row and no column without assignment, the third feasible solution is the optimal solution. The optimal assignment pattern is

city A should supply the vehicle to city 2,
city B should supply the vehicle to city 6,
city C should supply the vehicle to city 3,
city D should supply the vehicle to city 1,
city E should supply the vehicle to city 4, and
minimum distance travelled = (10 + 12 + 3 + 6 + 7) km = 38 km.
No truck is supplied to city 5.

EXAMPLE 4.7-2 (Non-Square Matrix)

A fast-food chain wants to build four stores. In the past the chain has used six different construction companies, and having been satisfied with each, has invited them to bid for each job. The final bids (in thousands of rupees) are shown in the following table:

TABLE 4.45

Construction companies

Stores	1	2	3	4	5	6
1	85.3	90	87.5	82.4	89.1	91.3
2	78.9	84.5	99.4	80.4	89.3	88.4
3	82.0	31.3	28.5	66.5	80.4	109.7
4	84.3	34.6	86.2	83.3	85.0	85.5

Since the fast-food chain wants to have each of the new stores ready as quickly as possible, it will allot at most one job to a construction company. What assignment will result in the minimum total cost?

Solution

Step I

Prepare a Square Matrix: As the problem involves a non-square 4 × 6 matrix, two dummy stores, say D_1 and D_2 are added with zero cost for each associated cell. Also all the elements are multiplied by 10 and the cost in hundreds of rupees is given by the matrix given below.

TABLE 4.46

Construction companies

Stores	1	2	3	4	5	6
1	853	900	875	824	891	913
2	789	845	994	804	893	884
3	820	313	285	665	804	1097
4	843	346	862	833	850	855
D_1	0	0	0	0	0	0
D_2	0	0	0	0	0	0

Step II

Reduce the Matrix: Performing row reductions yields table 4.47.

TABLE 4.47

Construction companies

Stores	1	2	3	4	5	6
1	29	76	51	[0]	67	89
2	[0]	56	205	15	104	95
3	535	28	[0]	380	519	812
4	497	[0]	516	487	504	509
D_1	~~0~~	~~0~~	~~0~~	~~0~~	[0]	~~0~~
D_2	~~0~~	~~0~~	~~0~~	~~0~~	~~0~~	[0]

Initial feasible solution (optimal solution)

Step III

Check if Optimal Assignment can be made in the Current Solution or not

Proceeding as in example 4.6-2, we find that there is an assignment in every row and column. Hence table 4.47 gives optimal assignment policy:

Store	*Construction company*	*Cost* (₹)
1	4	82,400
2	1	78,900
3	3	28,500
4	2	34,600
		₹ 2,24,400

EXAMPLE 4.7-3 (Non-Square Matrix)

A manufacturer of complex electronic equipment has just received a sizable contract and plans to subcontract part of the job. He has solicited bids for 6 subcontracts from 3 firms. Each job is sufficiently large and any firm can take only one job. The table below shows the bids as well as the cost estimates (in lakhs of rupees) for doing the job internally. Not more than three jobs can be performed internally.

TABLE 4.48

Firm \ Job	1	2	3	4	5	6
1	44	67	41	53	48	64
2	46	69	40	45	45	68
3	43	73	37	51	44	62
Internal	50	65	35	50	46	63

Find the optimal assignment that will result in minimum total cost.

Solution

Step I

Prepare a Square Matrix: The problem involves a non-square 4 × 6 matrix. As three jobs can be performed internally, table 4.48 may be completed to yield a square matrix 4.49.

TABLE 4.49

Firms	Jobs 1	2	3	4	5	6
1	44	67	41	53	48	64
2	46	69	40	45	45	68
3	43	73	37	51	44	62
I_1	50	65	35	50	46	63
I_2	50	65	35	50	46	63
I_3	50	65	35	50	46	63

Step II

Reduce the Matrix: Performing row and column reductions we get tables 4.50 and 4.51 respectively.

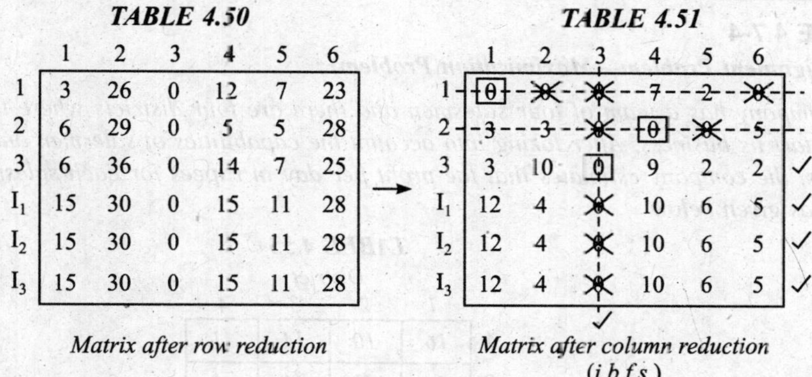

TABLE 4.50

	1	2	3	4	5	6
1	3	26	0	12	7	23
2	6	29	0	5	5	28
3	6	36	0	14	7	25
I_1	15	30	0	15	11	28
I_2	15	30	0	15	11	28
I_3	15	30	0	15	11	28

Matrix after row reduction

TABLE 4.51

	1	2	3	4	5	6	
1	[0]	×0	×0	7	2	×0	
2	3	3	×0	[0]	×0	5	
3	3	10	[0]	9	2	2	✓
I_1	12	4	×0	10	6	5	✓
I_2	12	4	×0	10	6	5	✓
I_3	12	4	×0	10	6	5	✓

Matrix after column reduction (i.b.f.s.)

Step III

Check if Optimal Assignment can be made in the Current Reduced Matrix or not: Proceeding as in example 4.6-2, the minimum number of lines covering all zeros is only 3(< 6). Hence optimal assignment cannot be made in the current feasible solution.

Step IV

Iterate towards an Optimal Solution: Proceeding as in example 4.6-2, we get table 4.52. Further iterations yield tables 4 53 and 4.54.

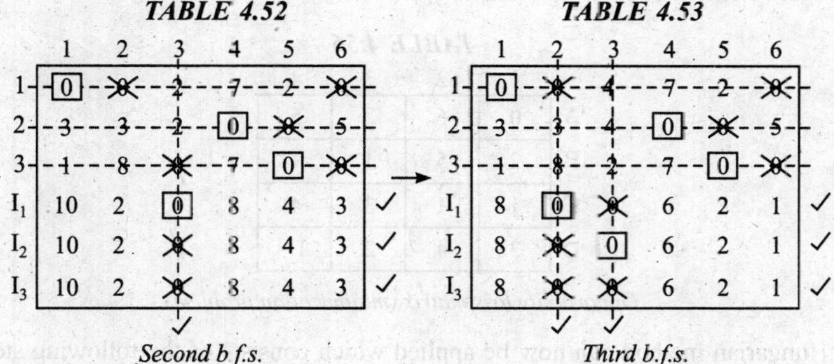

TABLE 4.52

	1	2	3	4	5	6	
1	[0]	×0	2	7	2	×0	
2	3	3	2	[0]	×0	5	
3	1	8	×0	7	[0]	×0	
I_1	10	2	[0]	8	4	3	✓
I_2	10	2	×0	8	4	3	✓
I_3	10	2	×0	8	4	3	✓

Second b.f.s.

TABLE 4.53

	1	2	3	4	5	6	
1	[0]	×0	4	7	2	×0	
2	3	3	4	[0]	×0	5	
3	1	8	2	7	[0]	×0	
I_1	8	[0]	×0	6	2	1	✓
I_2	8	×0	[0]	6	2	1	✓
I_3	8	×0	×0	6	2	1	✓

Third b.f.s.

TABLE 4.54

Firms \ Jobs	1	2	3	4	5	6
1	[0]	1	5	7	2	×0
2	3	4	5	[0]	×0	5
3	1	9	3	7	[0]	×0
I_1	7	[0]	×0	5	1	×0
I_2	7	×0	[0]	5	1	×0
I_3	7	×0	×0	5	1	[0]

Optimal solution

Table 4.54 gives optimal assignement policy. The associated minimum optimal cost is ₹ (44 + 45 + 44 + 65 + 35 + 63) = ₹ 296 lakh.

EXAMPLE 4.7-4

(Assignment Problem—Maximization Problem)

A company has a team of four salesmen and there are four districts where the company wants to start its business. After taking into account the capabilities of salesmen and the natrue of districts, the company estimates that the profit per day in rupees for each salesman in each district is as given below.

TABLE 4.55

Salesman	District 1	2	3	4
A	16	10	14	11
B	14	11	15	15
C	15	15	13	12
D	13	12	14	15

Find the assignment of salesmen to various districts which will yield maximum profit.

[P.T.U. B.Tech. (Mech.) Nov., 2012]

Solution. As the given problem is of maximization type, it has to be changed to minimization type before solving it by the Hungarian method. This is achieved by subtracting all the elements of the matrix from the largest element in it. Thus subtracting all the elements of profit table 4.55 from the largest element 16, the equivalent 'opportunity loss' matrix is given by table 4.56.

TABLE 4.56

	1	2	3	4
A	0	6	2	5
B	2	5	1	1
C	1	1	3	4
D	3	4	2	1

Opportunity loss matrix (minimization problem)

The Hungarian method can now be applied which consists of the following steps:

Step I

Prepare a Square Matrix: This step is not required here.

Step II

Reduce the Matrix: Proceeding as in example 4.6-2, we get table 4.57.

TABLE 4.57

	1	2	3	4
A	0	6	2	5
B	1	4	0	0
C	0	0	2	3
D	2	3	1	0

Matrix after substep I (initial feasible solution)

Step III

Check if Optimal Assignment can be made in the Current Feasible Solution or not

Proceeding as in example 4.6-2, we get table 4.58.

TABLE 4.58

	1	2	3	4
A	[0]	6	2	5
B	1	4	[0]	~~0~~
C	~~0~~	[0]	2	3
D	2	3	1	[0]

As there is one assignment in each row and in each column, optimal assignment can be made in the current feasible solution. Assignment policy shall be

salesman A should be assigned district 1,
salesman B should be assigned district 3,
salesman C should be assigned district 2,
salesman D should be assigned district 4.
Maximum profit per day = ₹ (16 + 15 + 15 + 15) = ₹ 61.

EXAMPLE 4.7-5 (Maximization Problem)

A company has four territories open and four salesmen available for assignment. The territories are not equally rich in their sales potential. It is estimated that a typical salesman operating in each territory would bring in the following annual sales:

Territory	:	*I*	*II*	*III*	*IV*
Annual sales (₹)	:	*60,000*	*50,000*	*40,000*	*30,000*

The four salesmen are also considered to differ in ability; it is estimated that working under the same conditions, their yearly sales would be proportionately as follows:

Salesman	:	*A*	*B*	*C*	*D*
Proportion	:	*7*	*5*	*5*	*4*

If the criterion is maximum expected total sales, the intutive answer is to assign the best salesman to the richest territory, the next best salesman to the second richest territory and so on. Verify this answer by the assignment method.

[*M.G.U. Kerala M.Com. June, 2010; D.U. MBA, 2000*]

Solution

Step I: Prepare a Square Matrix

The sum of sales of the four salesmen = 7 + 5 + 5 + 4 = 21. Taking the sale of ₹ 10,000 as one unit of sale, the annual sales of the four salesmen in the four territories are

$$\text{for } A: \frac{7}{21} \times 6, \frac{7}{21} \times 5, \frac{7}{21} \times 4, \frac{7}{21} \times 3,$$

$$\text{for } B: \frac{5}{21} \times 6, \frac{5}{21} \times 5, \frac{5}{21} \times 4, \frac{5}{21} \times 3,$$

$$\text{for } C: \frac{5}{21} \times 6, \frac{5}{21} \times 5, \frac{5}{21} \times 4, \frac{5}{21} \times 3,$$

and $$\text{for } D: \frac{4}{21} \times 6, \frac{4}{21} \times 5, \frac{4}{21} \times 4, \frac{4}{21} \times 3.$$

In order to avoid the fractional values of annual sales of each salesman in each territory, it will be rather convenient to consider the sales for 21 years. The problem is to determine the assignments which make the total sales maximum, and the effectiveness matrix is given by

TABLE 4.59

Territories

Salesmen	I	II	III	IV
A	42	35	28	21
B	30	25	20	15
C	30	25	20	15
D	24	20	16	12

Maximization problem

Step II: Convert the Maximization Problem into Minimization

The above maximization problem can be converted into the equivalent minimization problem by subtracting all the matrix elements from the highest element which is 42. Table 4.60 shows the resulting matrix.

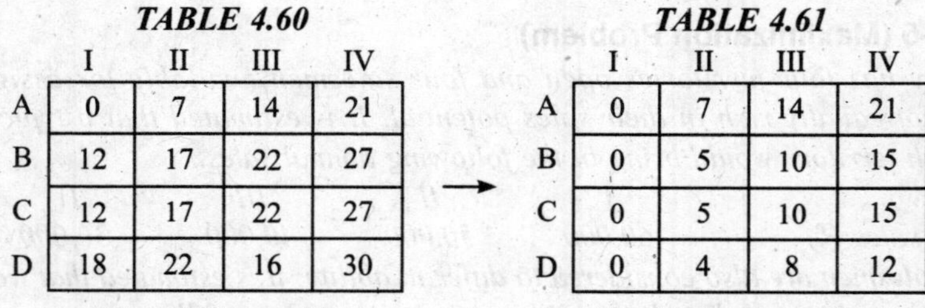

TABLE 4.60

	I	II	III	IV
A	0	7	14	21
B	12	17	22	27
C	12	17	22	27
D	18	22	16	30

Minimization problem

→

TABLE 4.61

	I	II	III	IV
A	0	7	14	21
B	0	5	10	15
C	0	5	10	15
D	0	4	8	12

Matrix after row reduction

Step III: Reduce the Matrix

Reduction of the matrix 4.60 by the usual method yields tables 4.61 and 4.62.

TABLE 4.62

	I	II	III	IV	
A	[0]	3	6	9	✓
B	~~0~~	1	2	3	✓
C	~~0~~	1	2	3	✓
D	~~0~~	[0]	~~0~~	~~0~~	
	✓				

Initial basic feasible solution

Step IV: Check if Optimal Assignment can be made in the Current Feasible Solution or not

Proceeding as in example 4.6-2, the minimum number of lines covering all zeros are only 2(< 4). Hence optimal assignment cannot be made in the current feasible solution.

Step V: Iterate towards an Optimal Solution

Proceeding as in example 4.6-2 we get table 4.63 and thereafter table 4.64, which is optimal.

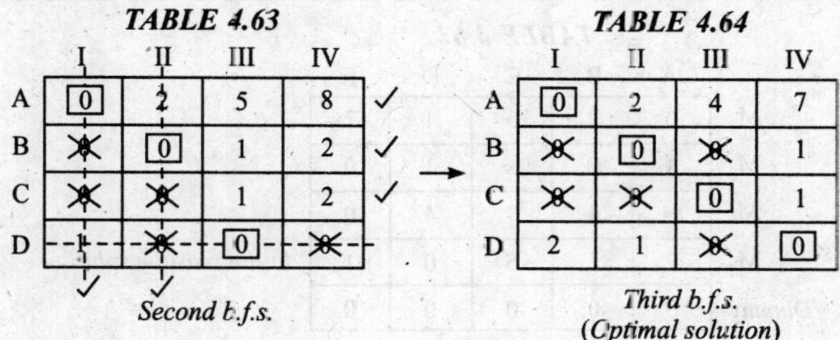

Maximum annual sales are = ₹ $\frac{1}{21}$(42 + 25 + 20 + 12) × 10,000

= ₹ 47,142.86.

EXAMPLE 4.7-6

(*Assignment Problem—Restrictions on Assignments*)

Four new machines M_1, M_2, M_3 and M_4 are to be installed in a machine shop. There are five vacant places A, B, C, D and E available. Because of limited space, machine M_2 cannot be placed at C and M_3 cannot be placed at A. C_{ij}, the assignment cost of machine i to place j in rupees is shown below.

TABLE 4.65

	A	*B*	*C*	*D*	*E*
M_1	4	6	10	5	6
M_2	7	4	–	5	4
M_3	–	6	9	6	2
M_4	9	3	7	2	3

Find the optimal assignment schedule.

[H.P.U. B.Tech. (Mech.) Nov., 2014; V.T.U. Karnataka B.Tech. (Mech.) 2012; P.T.U. B.Tech., 2010; L.U. B.Com., 2010]

Solution: Step I. Prepare a Square Matrix

As the given matrix is non-square, we add a dummy machine and associate zero cost with the corresponding cells. As machine M_2 cannot be placed at C and M_3 cannot be placed at A, we assign infinite cost (∞) in cells (M_2, C) and (M_3, A), resulting in the following matrix:

TABLE 4.66

	A	B	C	D	E
M_1	4	6	10	5	6
M_2	7	4	∞	5	4
M_3	∞	6	9	5	2
M_4	9	3	7	2	3
Dummy machine	0	0	0	0	0

Step II: Reduce the Matrix

Proceeding as in example 4.6-2, the following matrix results:

TABLE 4.67

	A	B	C	D	E
M_1	0	2	6	1	2
M_2	3	0	∞	1	0
M_3	∞	4	7	4	0
M_4	7	1	5	0	1
Dummy	0	0	0	0	0

Initial feasible solution

Matrix after substep I

Step III

Check if Optimal Assignment can be made in the Current Feasible Solution or not

Proceeding as in example 4.6-2, we get table 4.68.

TABLE 4.68

	A	B	C	D	E
M_1	[0]	2	6	1	2
M_2	3	[0]	∞	1	~~0~~
M_3	∞	4	7	4	[0]
M_4	7	1	5	[0]	1
Dummy	~~0~~	~~0~~	[0]	~~0~~	~~0~~

As there is no row and no column without assignment, optimal assignment can be made in the initial feasible solution. The optimal assignment of various machines is as follows:

Machine M_1 to place A,
machine M_2 to place B,
machine M_3 to place E,
machine M_4 to place D,
and place C will remain vacant.
Total assignment cost = ₹ (4 + 4 + 2 + 2) = ₹ 12.

EXAMPLE 4.7-7 (Alternate Optimal Solutions)

Solve the minimal assignment problem whose effectiveness matrix is

TABLE 4.69

	1	*2*	*3*	*4*
I	*2*	*3*	*4*	*5*
II	*4*	*5*	*6*	*7*
III	*7*	*8*	*9*	*8*
IV	*3*	*5*	*8*	*4*

[*H.P.U. B.Tech. (Mech.) June, 2015*]

Solution

Step I: Prepare a Square Matrix

This step is not required in this problem.

Step II: Reduce the Matrix

Proceeding as in example 4.6-2, the following tables are obtained:

TABLE 4.70

	1	2	3	4
I	0	1	2	3
II	0	1	2	3
III	0	1	2	1
IV	0	2	5	1

Matrix with zero in each row

→

TABLE 4.71

	1	2	3	4
I	[0]	✗	✗	2
II	✗	[0]	✗	2
III	✗	✗	[0]	✗
IV	✗	1	3	[0]

Matrix with zero in each row and each column (optimal solution)

Step III: Check if Optimal Assignment can be made in the Current Feasible Solution or not

There is no row or column with single unmarked zero. *This indicates existence of alternate optimal solutions*. Therefore, make assignment arbitrarily in cell (I, 1) say and cross off remaining zeros in row I *and* column 1. Next make assignment in a single unmarked zero in cell (IV, 4). Then make assignment *arbitrarily* in cell (II, 2) say. Last assignment is made in the left out cell (III, 3) of table 4.71. Z_{min} from table 4.71 = 2 + 5 + 9 + 4 = 20.

Likewise, if we first make assignment, say, in cell (IV, 1), we get an alternate optimal solution shown in table 4.72. Many more alternative optimal solutions can be determined.

TABLE 4.72

	1	2	3	4
I	✗	[0]	✗	2
II	✗	✗	[0]	2
III	✗	✗	✗	[0]
IV	[0]	1	3	✗

Alternative optimal solution

Table 4.72 also gives Z_{min} = 3 + 6 + 8 + 3 = 20.

EXAMPLE 4.7-8 (A Typical Assignment Problem)

A trip from Chandigarh to Delhi takes six hours by bus. A typical table of the bus service in both directions is given below.

TIME TABLE

Departure from Chandigarh	*Chandigarh-Delhi Service-line or route number*	*Arrival at Delhi*
06:00	a	12:00
07:30	b	13:30
11:30	c	17:30
19:00	d	01:00
00:30	e	06:30

Arrival at Chandigarh	*Delhi-Chandigarh Service-line or route number*	*Departure from Delhi*
11:30	1	05:30
15:00	2	09:00
21:00	3	15:00
00:30	4	18:30
06:00	5	00:00

The cost of providing this service by the transport company depends upon the time spent by the bus crew (driver and conductor) away from their places in addition to service times. There are five crew. There is a constraint that every crew should be provided with more than 4 hours of rest before the return trip again and should not wait for more than 24 hours for the return trip. The company has residential facilities for the crew at Chandigarh as well as at Delhi. Suggest an optimal assignment of the crew.

[R.T.M. Nagpur U.B.Tech. Dec., 2005; Nellore MBA, 2002]

Solution. As service time is constant, it does not affect the key decision. If all the crew are asked to reside at Chandigarh (so that they start from and come back to Chandigarh with minimum halt time at Delhi), then waiting time at Delhi for different service line connections will be as given by table 4.73.

TABLE 4.73

	1	2	3	4	5
a	17.5	21	3	6.5	12
b	16	19.5	1.5	5	10.5
c	12	15.5	21.5	1	6.5
d	4.5	8	14	17.5	23
e	23	2.5	8.5	12	17.5

Similarly, if crew are assumed to reside at Delhi (so that they start from and come back to Delhi with halt for minimum time at Chandigarh), then waiting time at Chandigarh for different service line connections is given by table 4.74.

TABLE 4.74

	1	2	3	4	5
a	18.5	15	9	5.5	0
b	20	16.5	10.5	5	1.5
c	0	20.5	14.5	11	5.5
d	7.5	4	22	18.5	13
e	13	9.5	3.5	0	18.5

As the crew can be asked to reside either at Chandigarh or Delhi, minimum waiting time from the above tables can be obtained for the different route connections by choosing minimum value out of the two waiting times, provided the value is more than 4 hours (minimum desired rest). These values of waiting times are shown in table 4.75.

TABLE 4.75

	1	2	3	4	5
a	17.5	15	9	5.5	12
b	16	16.5	10.5	5	10.5
c	12	15.5	14.5	11	5.5
d	4.5	8	14	17.5	13
e	13	9.5	8.5	12	17.5

The Hungarian method can now be applied for finding the optimal route connections which give minimum overall waiting time and hence the minimum cost of bus service operations. It consists of the following steps:

Step I: Prepare a Square Matrix

This step is not necessary here.

Step II: Reduce the Matrix

Proceeding as in example 4.6-2, we get table 4.76.

TABLE 4.76

	1	2	3	4	5
a	12	9.5	3.5	0	6.5
b	11	11.5	5.5	0	5.5
c	6.5	10	9	5.5	0
d	0	3.5	9.5	13	8.5
e	4.5	1	0	3.5	9

Matrix after substep 1

After substep 2 we get the following matrix:

TABLE 4.77

	1	2	3	4	5
a	12	8.5	3.5	0	6.5
b	11	10.5	5.5	0	5.5
c	6.5	9	9	5.5	0
d	0	2.5	9.5	13	8.5
e	4.5	0	0	3.5	9

Initial feasible solution

Step III: Check if Optimal Assignment can be made in the Current Feasible Solution or not

Proceeding as in example 4.6-2, we get table 4.78.

TABLE 4.78

	1	2	3	4	5	
a	12	8.5	3.5	[0]	6.5	✓
b	11	10.5	5.5	~~0~~	5.5	✓
c	6.5	9	9	5.5	[0]	
d	[0]	2.5	9.5	13	8.5	
e	4.5	[0]	~~0~~	3.5	9	
				✓		

As the minimum number of lines crossing all zeros is 4 *i.e.*, less than 5, optimal assignment cannot be made in the current feasible solution.

Step IV: Iterate Towards an Optimal Solution

Proceeding as in example 4.6-2, we get table 4.79.

TABLE 4.79

	1	2	3	4	5
a	8.5	5	0	0	3
b	7.5	7	2	0	2
c	6.5	9	9	9	0
d	0	2.5	9.5	16.5	8.5
e	4.5	0	0	7	9

Step V: Check if Optimal Assignment can be made in the Current Feasible Solution or not

TABLE 4.80

	1	2	3	4	5
a	8.5	5	[0]	~~0~~	3
b	7.5	7	2	[0]	2
c	6.5	9	9	9	[0]
d	[0]	2.5	9.5	16.5	8.5
e	4.5	[0]	~~0~~	7	9

As there is no row or column without assignment, optimal assignment is possible in the current solution.

∴ We get the following information:

TABLE 4.81

Crew	*Residence at*	*Service number*	*Waiting time (hours)*
1	Chandigarh	*d*1	4.5
2	Delhi	2*e*	9.5
3	Delhi	3*a*	9.0
4	Chandigarh	*b*4	5.0
5	Delhi	5*c*	5.5

Total minimum waiting time = (4.5 + 9.5 + 9 + 5 + 5.5) hours = 33.5 hours.

EXAMPLE 4.7-9

An airline that operates 7 days a week has the time table shown below. Crew must have a minimum layover of 5 hours between flights. Obtain the pairing of flights that minimizes layover time away from home assuming that the crew can be based at either of the two cities. The crew will be based at the city that results in smaller layover.

TABLE 4.82

Delhi – Jaipur			*Jaipur – Delhi*		
Flight no.	*Depart*	*Arrive*	*Flight no.*	*Depart*	*Arrive*
1	7:00AM	8:00AM	*101*	8:00AM	9:15AM
2	8:00AM	9:00AM	*102*	8:30AM	9:45AM
3	1:30PM	2:30PM	*103*	12 Noon	1:15PM
4	6:30PM	7:30PM	*104*	5:30PM	6:45PM

[*R.T.M. Nagpur U.B. Tech. Dec., 2003; P.U. B.Com. Jan., 2005; B.E.(Mech.) 2000*]

Solution. Let us assume that each plane makes one forward and one return trip only and that a plane flying from one city to the other must come back to the starting city at the earliest possible opportunity to keep the layover time minimum.

If all the crew start from Delhi, then layover time at Jaipur for various pairing of flights is given by table 4.83.

TABLE 4.83

Layover time at Jaipur

	101	102	103	104
1	24	24.5	28	9.5
2	23	23.5	27	8.5
3	17.5	18	21.5	27
4	12.5	13	16.5	22

TABLE 4.84

Layover time at Delhi

	101	102	103	104
1	21.75	21.25	17.75	12.25
2	22.75	22.25	18.75	13.25
3	28.25	27.75	24.25	18.75
4	9.25	8.75	5.25	23.75

Similarly, if all the crew is based at Jaipur, then layover time at Delhi for various pairing of flights is given by table 4.84.

As the crew can be either based at Delhi or Jaipur, they will obviously be based at the city that results in smaller layover time. We, therefore, pick up the smaller layover time for all pairing of flights from tables 4.83 and 4.84 and represent them in table 4.85.

TABLE 4.85

	101	102	103	104
1	21.75	21.25	17.75	9.5
2	22.75	22.25	18.75	8.5
3	17.5	18	21.5	18.75
4	9.25	8.75	5.25	22

The Hungarian method is now applied for finding the optimal pairings and successive tables obtained are given below:

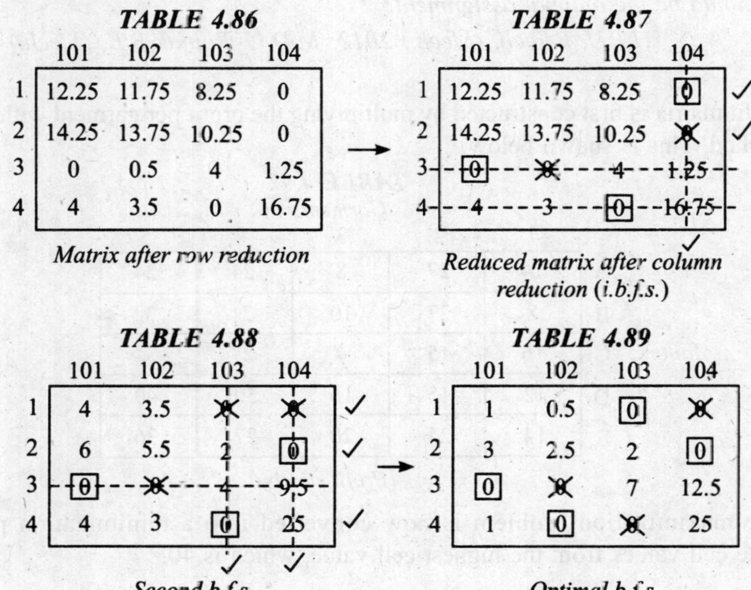

TABLE 4.86

	101	102	103	104
1	12.25	11.75	8.25	0
2	14.25	13.75	10.25	0
3	0	0.5	4	1.25
4	4	3.5	0	16.75

Matrix after row reduction

TABLE 4.87

	101	102	103	104	
1	12.25	11.75	8.25	[0]	✓
2	14.25	13.75	10.25	~~0~~	✓
3	[0]	~~0~~	4	1.25	
4	4	3	[0]	16.75	
				✓	

Reduced matrix after column reduction (i.b.f.s.)

TABLE 4.88

	101	102	103	104	
1	4	3.5	~~0~~	~~0~~	✓
2	6	5.5	2	[0]	✓
3	[0]	~~0~~	4	9.5	
4	4	3	[0]	25	✓
			✓	✓	

Second b.f.s.

TABLE 4.89

	101	102	103	104
1	1	0.5	[0]	~~0~~
2	3	2.5	2	[0]
3	[0]	~~0~~	7	12.5
4	1	[0]	~~0~~	25

Optimal b.f.s.

The best pairing of flights that results in minimum total layover time is given in table 4.90.

TABLE 4.90

Flight pair	*Crew based at city*	*Layover time (hours)*
103 – 1	Jaipur	17.75
2 – 104	Delhi	8.50
3 – 101	Delhi	17.50
102 – 4	Jaipur	8.75
	Total :	52.50

The problem has alternate optimal pairing of flights also.

4.8 ADDITIONAL PROBLEMS

EXAMPLE 4.8-1

A small garment making unit has five tailors stitching five different types of garments. All the five tailors are capable of stitching all the five types of garments. The output per day per tailor and the profit (₹) for each type of garment are given below:

TABLE 4.91

Tailors	*Garments* 1	2	3	4	5
A	*7*	*9*	*4*	*8*	*6*
B	*4*	*9*	*5*	*7*	*8*
C	*8*	*5*	*2*	*9*	*8*
D	*6*	*5*	*8*	*10*	*10*
E	*7*	*8*	*10*	*9*	*9*
Profit (₹) per garment	*2*	*3*	*2*	*3*	*4*

(i) Which type of garment should be assigned to which tailor in order to maximize profit, assuming that there are no other constraints?

(ii) If tailor D is absent for a specified period and no other substitute tailor is available, what should be the optimal assignment?

[H.P.U. B.Tech. (Mech.) 2012; M.D.U. Rohtak B.E. (Mech.) Dec., 2006]

Solution

(*i*) The profit matrix is first constructed by multiplying the profit per garment with the number of garments stitched. This is shown below:

TABLE 4.92

Tailors	Garments 1	2	3	4	5
A	14	27	8	24	24
B	8	27	10	21	32
C	16	15	4	27	32
D	12	15	16	30	40
E	14	24	20	27	36

Profit matrix

The above maximization problem is now converted into a minimization problem by subtracting all the cell values from the highest cell value, which is 40.

TABLE 4.93

	Garments 1	2	3	4	5
Tailors A	26	13	32	16	16
B	32	13	30	19	8
C	24	25	36	13	8
D	28	25	24	10	0
E	26	16	20	13	4

Opportunity loss matrix

This matrix is then reduced to get zero in each row and in each column and then allocations are made.

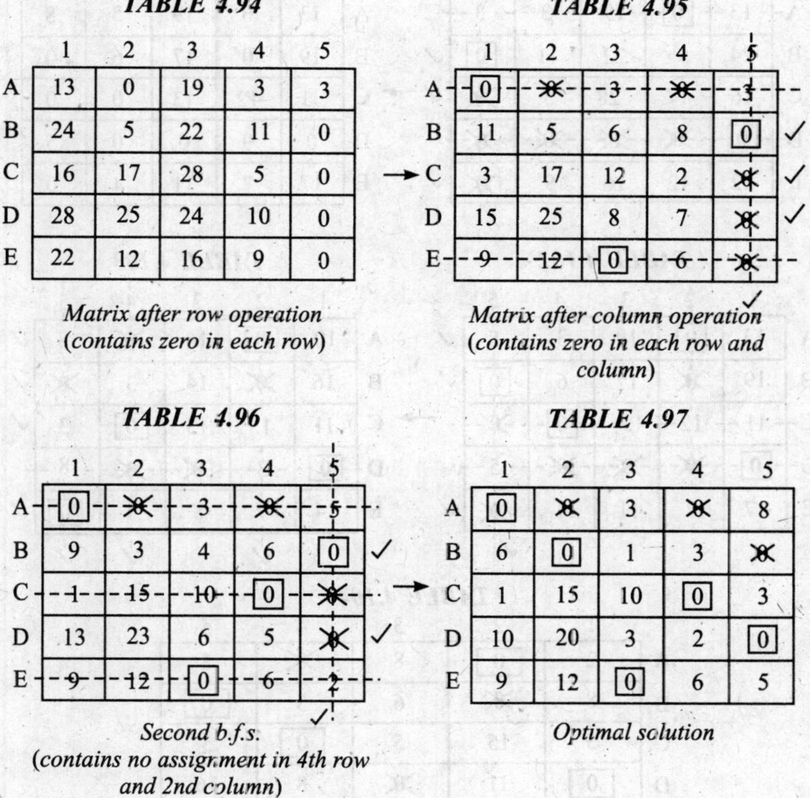

TABLE 4.94

	1	2	3	4	5
A	13	0	19	3	3
B	24	5	22	11	0
C	16	17	28	5	0
D	28	25	24	10	0
E	22	12	16	9	0

Matrix after row operation (contains zero in each row)

TABLE 4.95

	1	2	3	4	5	
A	[0]	~~0~~	3	~~0~~	3	
B	11	5	6	8	[0]	✓
→ C	3	17	12	2	~~0~~	✓
D	15	25	8	7	~~0~~	✓
E	9	12	[0]	6	~~0~~	
					✓	

Matrix after column operation (contains zero in each row and column)

TABLE 4.96

	1	2	3	4	5	
A	[0]	~~0~~	3	~~0~~	5	
B	9	3	4	6	[0]	✓
C	1	15	10	[0]	~~0~~	
D	13	23	6	5	~~0~~	✓
E	9	12	[0]	6	2	
					✓	

Second b.f.s. (contains no assignment in 4th row and 2nd column)

TABLE 4.97

	1	2	3	4	5
A	[0]	~~0~~	3	~~0~~	8
B	6	[0]	1	3	~~0~~
→ C	1	15	10	[0]	3
D	10	20	3	2	[0]
E	9	12	[0]	6	5

Optimal solution

Thus the optimal assignment policy is

Tailor	*Garment type*	*Profit* (₹)
A	1	14
B	2	27
C	4	27
D	5	40
E	3	20
	Total :	128

(*ii*) It tailor D is absent, the profit earned by him will be zero and the profit matrix becomes

TABLE 4.98

	1	2	3	4	5
A	14	27	8	24	24
B	8	27	10	21	32
C	16	15	4	27	32
D	0	0	0	0	0
E	14	24	20	27	36

Profit matrix

TABLE 4.99

	1	2	3	4	5
A	22	9	28	12	12
B	28	9	26	15	4
C	20	21	32	9	4
D	36	36	36	36	36
E	22	12	16	9	0

Equivalent loss matrix

TABLE 4.100

	1	2	3	4	5	
A	13	[0]	19	3	3	
B	24	5	22	11	[0]	✓
C	16	17	28	5	~~0~~	✓
D	[0]	~~0~~	~~0~~	~~0~~	~~0~~	
E	22	12	16	9	~~0~~	✓
					✓	

TABLE 4.101

	1	2	3	4	5
A	13	0	19	3	8
B	19	0	17	6	0
C	11	12	13	0	0
D	0	0	0	0	5
E	17	7	11	4	0

TABLE 4.102

	1	2	3	4	5	
A	13	[0]	19	3	8	✓
B	19	~~0~~	17	6	[0]	✓
C	11	12	13	[0]	~~0~~	
D	[0]	~~0~~	~~0~~	~~0~~	5	
E	17	7	11	4	~~0~~	✓
		✓			✓	

TABLE 4.103

	1	2	3	4	5	
A	10	[0]	16	~~0~~	8	✓
B	16	~~0~~	14	3	~~0~~	✓
C	11	15	13	[0]	3	✓
D	[0]	3	~~0~~	~~0~~	8	
E	14	7	8	1	[0]	✓
		✓		✓	✓	

TABLE 4.104

	1	2	3	4	5
A	2	[0]	8	~~0~~	8
B	8	~~0~~	6	3	[0]
C	3	15	5	[0]	3
D	[0]	11	~~0~~	8	16
E	6	7	[0]	1	~~0~~

Optimal solution

Thus the optimal assignment policy is

Tailor	*Garment type*	*Profit* (₹)
A	2	27
B	5	32
C	4	27
E	3	20
	Total :	106

Garment 1 remains unstitched since tailor D is absent.

EXAMPLE 4.8-2

Welldone Company has taken the third floor of a multi-storeyed building for rent with a view to locate one of their zonal offices. There are five main rooms on this floor to be assigned to five managers. Each room has its own advantages and disadvantages. Some have windows, some are closer to the washrooms or to the canteen or secretarial pool. The rooms are all of different sizes and shapes. Each of the five managers were asked to rank their room preferences amongst the rooms 301, 302, 303, 304 and 305.

Their preferences were recorded in a table as indicated below.

TABLE 4.105

MANAGER				
M_1	M_2	M_3	M_4	M_5
302	302	303	302	301
303	304	301	305	302
304	305	304	304	304
	301	305	303	
		302		

Most of the managers did not list all the five rooms since they were not satisfied with some of these rooms and they left off these from the list. Assuming that their preferences can be quantified by numbers, find out as to which manager should be assigned to which room so that their total preference ranking is minimum.

[*J.N.T.U. Hyderabad B.Tech. (C.Sc.) Dec., 2011*]

Solution. We first formulate the assignment problem in terms of preference ranking. This is shown below.

TABLE 4.106

	Managers				
Room nos	M_1	M_2	M_3	M_4	M_5
301	–	4	2	–	1
302	1	1	5	1	2
303	2	–	1	4	–
304	3	2	3	3	3
305	–	3	4	2	–

We have to find assignment so that the total preference ranking is minimum. In a cell (–) indicates that no assignment is to be made in that particular cell. This (–) is substituted by a very large no. M in the cells where no assignment is made and the following table is obtained:

TABLE 4.107

	M_1	M_2	M_3	M_4	M_5
301	M	4	2	M	1
302	1	1	5	1	2
303	2	M	1	4	M
304	3	2	3	3	3
305	M	3	4	2	M

Solution by reduced matrix method consists of the following tables:

TABLE 4.108

	M_1	M_2	M_3	M_4	M_5
301	M	3	1	M	0
302	0	0	4	0	1
303	1	M	0	3	M
304	1	0	1	1	1
305	M	1	2	0	M

Matrix after row operation
(Contains zero in each row & column)

→

TABLE 4.109

	M_1	M_2	M_3	M_4	M_5
301	M	3	1	M	[0]
302	[0]	~~0~~	4	~~0~~	1
303	1	M	[0]	3	M
304	1	[0]	1	1	1
305	M	1	2	[0]	M

Optimal solution

Thus the optimal assignment policy is 301–M_5, 302–M_1, 303–M_3, 304–M_2 and 305–M_4 and the total minimum ranking is 1 + 1 + 1 + 2 + 2 = 7.

EXAMPLE 4.8-3

The captain of a cricket team has to allot five middle batting positions to five batsmen. The average runs scored by each batsman at these positions are as follows:

TABLE 4.110

Batsman	*Batting position*				
	I	*II*	*III*	*IV*	*V*
P	*40*	*40*	*35*	*25*	*50*
Q	*42*	*30*	*16*	*25*	*27*
R	*50*	*48*	*40*	*60*	*50*
S	*20*	*19*	*20*	*18*	*25*
T	*58*	*60*	*59*	*55*	*53*

(i) Find the assignment of batsmen to positions which would give the maximum number of runs. [*Gujarat Tech. U.B.E. Dec., 2012; G.N.D.U. B.Com. April 2011; P.T.U. B.Tech. Dec., 2011*]

(ii) If another batsman 'U' with the following average runs in batting positions as given below:

Batting positions	:	*I*	*II*	*III*	*IV*	*V*
Average runs	:	*45*	*52*	*38*	*50*	*49*

is added to the team, should he be included to play in the team? If so, who will be replaced by him?

Solution. (*i*) Subtracting all cell elements from the largest element which is 60, the equivalent minimization problem is

TABLE 4.111

Batting position

Batsman		I	II	III	IV	V
	P	20	20	25	35	10
	Q	18	30	44	35	33
	R	10	12	20	0	10
	S	40	41	40	42	35
	T	2	0	1	5	7

Minimization problem

Solution by reduced matrix method consists of the following tables:

TABLE 4.112

	I	II	III	IV	V
P	10	10	15	25	0
Q	0	12	26	17	15
R	10	12	20	0	10
S	5	6	5	7	0
T	2	0	1	5	7

Matrix after row operation
(Contains zero in each row)

TABLE 4.113

	I	II	III	IV	V
P	10	10	14	25	0
Q	0	12	25	17	15
R	10	12	19	0	10
S	5	6	4	7	0
T	2	0	0	5	7

Matrix after column operation
(Contains zero in every row and column)

TABLE 4.114

	I	II	III	IV	V	
P	10	10	14	25	[0]	✓
Q	[0]	12	25	17	15	
R	10	12	19	[0]	10	
S	5	6	4	7	~~0~~	✓
T	2	[0]	~~0~~	5	7	
					✓	

Initial basic feasible solution
(Contains no assignment in 4th row and 3rd column)

TABLE 4.115

	I	II	III	IV	V
P	6	6	10	21	[0]
Q	[0]	12	25	17	19
R	10	12	19	[0]	14
S	1	2	[0]	3	~~0~~
T	2	[0]	~~0~~	5	11

Second basic feasibe solution
(Optimal solution)

∴ Optimal assignment policy is

Batsman	*Batting position*	*No. of runs*
P	V	50
Q	I	42
R	IV	60
S	III	20
T	II	60
		232

(*ii*) Assignment matrix if batsman 'U' is also included in the team takes the form

TABLE 4.116

Batting position

Batsman	I	II	III	IV	V
P	40	40	35	25	50
Q	42	30	16	25	27
R	50	48	40	60	50
S	20	19	20	18	25
T	58	60	59	55	53
U	45	52	38	50	49

Making this matrix a square matrix and then subtracting all the elements from the highest element which is 60, we get a balanced minimization problem that can be solved by the Hungarian method. The following tables are obtained:

TABLE 4.117

	I	II	III	IV	V	Dm
P	40	40	35	25	50	0
Q	42	30	16	25	27	0
R	50	48	40	60	50	0
S	20	19	20	18	25	0
T	58	60	59	55	53	0
U	45	52	38	50	49	0

Balanced maximization problem

TABLE 4.118

	I	II	III	IV	V	Dm
P	20	20	25	35	10	60
Q	18	30	44	35	33	60
R	10	12	20	0	10	60
S	40	41	40	42	35	60
T	2	0	1	5	7	60
U	15	8	22	10	11	60

Balanced minimization problem

TABLE 4.119

	I	II	III	IV	V	Dm
P	10	10	15	25	0	50
Q	0	12	26	17	15	42
R	10	12	20	0	10	60
S	5	6	5	7	0	25
T	2	0	1	5	7	60
U	7	0	14	2	3	52

Partially reduced matrix

TABLE 4.120

	I	II	III	IV	V	Dm
P	10	10	14	25	[0]	25
Q	[0]	12	25	17	15	17
R	10	12	19	[0]	10	35
S	5	6	4	7	~~0~~	[0]
T	2	~~0~~	[0]	5	7	35
U	7	[0]	13	2	3	27

Optimal solution

∴ Optimal assignment policy when batsman 'U' is included is

Batsman	*Batting position*	*No. of runs*
P	V	50
Q	I	42
R	IV	60
S	D_m	0
T	III	59
U	II	52
		263

Since number of runs increases by including batsman 'U', he should be included in the team. Batsman 'S' will be replaced by him.

EXAMPLE 4.8-4

A solicitors firm employs typists on hourly piece rate basis for their work. There are five typists and their charges and speeds are different. According to an earlier understanding only one job is given to one typist and the typist is paid for full hour even if he works for a fraction of an hour. Find the least cost allocation for the following data:

Typist	*Rate/hour (₹)*	*No. of pages typed/hour*
A	*5*	*12*
B	*6*	*14*
C	*3*	*8*
D	*4*	*10*
E	*4*	*11*

Job	*Number of page*
P	*199*
Q	*175*
R	*145*
S	*298*
T	*178*

[*V.T.U. Karnataka B.E. June, 2011; R.T.M. Nagpur U.B.E. (I.T.) 2009; P.T.U. B.Tech. (Mech. Engg.) 2010; Dayalbagh Edu. Inst. Agra MBA May, 2005; P.U. BBA, 2001*]

Solution

Step 1. Write the Assignment Matrix: The assignment matrix will represent the costs involved if each of the typists A, B, C, D and E is assigned each of the jobs P, Q, R, S and T. For example if typist A is assigned job P, time taken by him will be $\frac{199}{12} = 16\frac{7}{12}$ hours. Since the typist is to be paid for full hour even if he works for fraction of an hour, A is to be paid for 17 hours. As his rate per hour is ₹ 5, he will be paid ₹ 85 in all. Similarly other costs are evaluated and represented in the table below:

TABLE 4.121

		Jobs				
		P	Q	R	S	T
	A	85	75	65	125	75
	B	90	78	66	132	78
Typists	C	75	66	57	114	69
	D	80	72	60	120	72
	E	76	64	56	112	68

Step 2. Solve by the Hungarian Method: Solution of the problem by the Hungarian method results in the following optimal solution after two iterations:

TABLE 4.122

		Jobs				
		P	Q	R	S	T
	A	2	1	2	3	[0]
	B	4	1	[0]	7	~~0~~
Typists	C	8	[0]	2	~~0~~	2
	D	[0]	1	~~0~~	1	~~0~~
	E	3	~~0~~	3	[0]	3

Thus optimal assignment policy is

Typist	*Job*	*Cost* (₹)
A	T	75
B	R	66
C	Q	66
D	P	80
E	S	112
	Total :	₹ 399

Alternate optimal assignment policy is:

Typist	*Job*	*Cost* (₹)
A	T	75
B	R	66
C	S	114
D	P	80
E	Q	64
	Total :	₹ 399

EXAMPLE 4.8-5

A firm marketing a product has four salesmen S_1, S_2, S_3 and S_4. There are three customers C_1, C_2 and C_3. The probability of making a sale to a customer depends upon the salesman-customer support. The table below represents the probability with which each of the salesmen can sell to each of the customers:

TABLE 4.123

Salesmen

		S_1	S_2	S_3	S_4
	C_1	0.7	0.4	0.5	0.8
Customers	C_2	0.5	0.8	0.6	0.7
	C_3	0.3	0.9	0.6	0.2

If only one salesman is to be assigned to one customer, what combination of salesmen and customers shall be optimal? Profit obtained by selling one unit to C_1 is ₹ 500, to C_2 is ₹ 450 and to C_3 is ₹ 540. What is the total expected profit?

[G.N.D.U. B.Com. April 2012; P.U. B.Com, April 2009; H.P.U. B.E. (Mech.) 2008]

Solution. First step is to prepare the assignment matrix that represents the *expected profits* for each salesman-customer combination. Expected profits are obtained by multiplying the given profits with the associated probabilities. Table 4.124 represents their values.

TABLE 4.124

Salesmen

		S_1	S_2	S_3	S_4
	C_1	350	200	250	400
Customers	C_2	225	360	270	315
	C_3	162	486	324	108

Unbalanced maximization problem

Table 4.124 represents a non-square 3 × 4 matrix. A dummy customer is, therefore, added. The associated expected profits for this row will be zeros. The problem is then changed to minimization type by subtracting all the elements from the highest element 486. The resulting matrix is then solved by the Hungarian method. After two iterations the following optimal solution is obtained:

TABLE 4.125

Salesmen

		S_1	S_2	S_3	S_4
	C_1	50	245	150	[0]
	C_2	45	✗	[0]	✗
Customers	C_3	234	[0]	72	288
	Dm	[0]	45	✗	✗

Total expected profit = ₹ 1,156.

EXAMPLE 4.8-6

A firm produces four products. There are four operators who are capable of producing each of them. The processing time varies from operator to operator. The firm works 8 hours a day and allows 30 minutes for lunch. The processing times in minutes and profits of each of the product are given below:

TABLE 4.126

Operators	*Products*			
	A	*B*	*C*	*D*
1	*15*	*9*	*10*	*6*
2	*10*	*6*	*9*	*6*
3	*25*	*15*	*15*	*9*
4	*15*	*9*	*10*	*10*
Profit (₹/unit)	*8*	*6*	*5*	*4*

Find the optimal assignment of products to operators.

[P.U.B.E. (E. & Ec.) April, 2008; H.P.U. B.Tech. (Mech.) June, 2007]

Solution. The net working time is 450 minutes per day. The number of products that can be produced by each operator in 450 minutes are given in table 4.127. These values are then multiplied by the profit/unit to get profits for each operator-product combination (table 4.128). The maximization problem is converted to minimization and then solved by the Hungarian method.

TABLE 4.127

Operators	*Products*			
	A	B	C	D
1	30	50	45	75
2	45	75	50	75
3	18	30	30	50
4	30	50	45	45

TABLE 4.128

Operators	*Products*			
	A	B	C	D
1	240	300	225	300
2	360	450	250	300
3	144	180	150	200
4	240	300	225	180

After one iteration, optimal solution is obtained which is represented in table 4.129.

TABLE 4.129

Operators	*Products*			
	A	B	C	D
1	~~0~~	~~0~~	21	[0]
2	30	[0]	146	150
3	~~0~~	24	[0]	4
4	[0]	~~0~~	21	120

The optimal assignment is

Operator	*Product*	*Profit* (₹)
1	D	300
2	B	450
3	C	150
4	A	240
	Total =	1,140

4.9 SENSITIVITY ANALYSIS IN THE ASSIGNMENT PROBLEMS

The structure of the assignment problem is such that there is not much scope for sensitivity analysis. Small changes in the conditions (such as one operator doing two jobs) can be accommodated by adding one more row/column for the operator.

Addition/subtraction of a constant throughout a row or column does not affect the optimal assignment. However, same proportional change in a row or column can make a difference. Hence in assignment problems, there is no scope for changing the level of assignments.

EXERCISES 4.1

1. Give the mathematical formulation of an assignment problem. Explain how to view the problem in terms of an L.P.P. set-up.
[Mumbai U. B.Com. April, 2013; Chennai U.BCA Nov., 2010; J.N.T.U. Hyderabad B.Tech. April, 2011;R.T.M. Nagpur B.E. (Mech.) 2008, 05; K.U. M.Sc., 2001; P.T.U. M.B.A. Dec., 2002]
2. State the assignment model. Describe an algorithm for the solution of the assignment problem.
[G.N.D.U. B.Com. Sept., 2006; P.T.U. MBA Feb., 2011 B.Com. May 2004; Mumbai U. MBA, 2010; R.T.M. Nagpur U.B.Tech. Dec., 2003; P.U. M.Com. Sept., 2004; Pondicherry U.M.B.A. June, 2007]
3. Write short note on the assignment problem and its applications.
[G.N.D.U. B.Com. Sept., 2012; R.U. MBA June 2011; Univ. of Mumbai PGDM, 2012; J.N.T.U. Hyderabad MBA April 2012; B.Tech. Nov., 2010; Chennai U.B.C.A. Nov., 2010]
4. Explain the following in the context of assignment problem:
(*i*) Balanced assignment problem
(*ii*) The Hungarian method
[G.N.D.U. B.Com., April, 2013; Sept., 2010; J.N.T.U. Anantapur MBA August, 2010]
(*iii*) An infeasible assignment *[IGNOU MCA, 2003]*
5. Can you solve the assignment problem by the linear programming approach? If yes, give the method. *[P.U.B.E.(Mech.)1997]*
6. State the common and distinguishing features of the assignment and the transportation models.
[M.G.U. Kerala M.Com. June, 2012; V.T.U. Karnataka B.E. June, 2012; Dec., 2011; June, 2011; June, 2010; G.N.D.U.B.Com., 2009; P.T.U. MCA, 2010; MBA, 2009; Pondicherry U.M.B.A. August, 2006; Nagpur U. B.E.(Mech.) 2003; P.U.B.E.(Mech.) Nov., 2006; 2002; M.B.A. August, 2006]
7. What is the optimality criterion in the assignment problem?
[H.P.U. B.Tech. (Mech.) 2012; B.T.U. Karnataka B.Tech. (Mech.) 2012; G.N.D.U. B.Com. April, 2011; April 2009, Sept 2007; J.N.T.U. Hyderabad B. Tech. Sept. 2011]
8. What is the unbalanced assignment problem? How is it solved by the Hungarian method?
[B.P.U.T., 2010; G.N.D.U.B.Com. Sept., 2011; April, 2009; Sept. 2008; Osmania U. MBA, 2010; P.T.U. MBA, 2008; P.U.B.Com. April, 2004; April, 2003]
9. Show that the assignment model is a special case of the transportation model.
[P.T.U. B.Tech. (Mech.) May, 2007; G.N.D.U. B.Com. April, 2006; April, 2004]
10. How will you handle the following situations in an assignment problem ?
(*i*) maximization (*ii*) unbalanced problem (*iii*) impossible assignment.
[G.N.D.U. B.Com. April, 2012, Sept., 2010; Sept., 2009; P.U. MBA Feb., 2009]
11. (a) Explain unbalanced assignment problem. *[Univ. of Madras B.Sc. (Math.) Nov., 2012; G.N.D.U. B.Com. April 2010; April 2006; R.T.M. Nagpur U.B.Tech. June, 2006]*
(b) Briefly discuss the various steps in drawing minimum number of lines.
[G.N.D.U. B.Com. Sept., 2011, 2008]

Section 4.6

12. Consider the problem of assigning five operators to five machines. The assignment costs are given below.

TABLE 4.130

		Operators				
		I	II	III	IV	V
	A	10	5	13	15	16
	B	3	9	18	3	6
Machines	C	10	7	2	2	2
	D	5	11	9	7	12
	E	7	9	10	4	12

Assign the operators to different machines so that total cost is minimized.
[P.U.B.E. (Mech.) April, 1976]
(*Ans.* A–II, B–V, C–III, D–I, E–IV; 22.)

13. Suggest optimum assignment of 4 workers A, B, C and D to 4 jobs I, II, III, IV. The time taken by different workers in completing the different jobs is given below.

TABLE 4.131

Workers \ Jobs	I	II	III	IV
A	8	10	12	16
B	11	11	15	8
C	9	6	5	14
D	15	14	9	7

Also find the total time taken in completing the jobs [*Chennai U.B.B.A. Nov., 2010*]

(*Ans.* A-I, B-II, C-III, D-IV; 31.)

14. Solve the following assignment problem. The matrix entries are processing times in hours.

TABLE 4.132

Job \ Operator	1	2	3	4	5
1	20	22	35	22	18
2	4	26	24	24	7
3	23	14	17	19	19
4	17	15	16	18	15
5	16	19	21	19	25

[*P.T.U.B. Tech. April, 2012; Chennai U. B.C.A. Nov., 2010*]

(*Ans*. 1–5, 2–1, 3–2,4–3, 5–4; 7 hours.)

15. A project work consists of four jobs for which four contractors have submitted tenders. Find the assignment which minimizes the total cost of the project when each contractor is to be assigned one job.

TABLE 4.133

Contractors \ Jobs	1	2	3	4
1	10	24	30	15
2	16	22	28	12
3	12	20	32	10
4	9	26	34	16

[*R.T.M. Nagpur U.B.Tech. June, 2005; P.T.U. B.Tech. (C.Sc.) 2009*]

(*Ans.* Multiple optimal solutions. One optimal policy is $1 \to 2,\ 2 \to 3,\ 3 \to 4,\ 4 \to 1$; 66.)

16. (*a*) If in an assignment problem we add a constant to every element of a row (or column) in the effectiveness matrix, prove that an assignment that minimizes the total effectiveness in one matrix also minimizes the total effectiveness in the other matrix.

[*Sambalpur Univ. May, 1977*]

(*b*) A national car-rental service has a surplus of one car in each of the cities 1, 2, 3, 4, 5, 6 and a deficit of one car in each of the cities 7, 8, 9, 10, 11, 12. The distances in miles between cities with a surplus and cities with a deficit are displayed in matrix 4.135. How should the cars be despatched so as to minimize the total mileage travelled?

TABLE 4.134

		To 7	8	9	10	11	12
	1	41	72	39	52	25	51
	2	22	29	49	65	81	50
From	3	27	39	60	51	32	32
	4	45	50	48	52	37	43
	5	29	40	39	26	30	33
	6	82	40	40	60	51	30

[*P.T.U. MBA Feb., 2011*]

(*Ans.* 1–11, 2–8, 3–7, 4–9, 5–10, 6–12; Z_{min} = 185 miles.)

17. Using the following cost matrix determine optimal job assignment and the associated cost:

TABLE 4.135

		Jobs 1	2	3	4	5
Machinists	A	10	3	3	2	8
	B	9	7	8	2	7
	C	7	5	6	2	4
	D	3	5	8	2	4
	E	9	10	9	6	10

[*P.T.U.B. Tech. April, 2012; G.N.D.U.B. Com. April, 2008*]

(*Ans.* A-2, B-4, C-5, D-1, E-3; 21.)

18. Consider the problem of assigning five jobs to five persons. The assignment costs are given as follows:

TABLE 4.136

		Jobs 1	2	3	4	5
Persons	A	8	4	2	6	1
	B	0	9	5	5	4
	C	3	8	9	2	6
	D	4	3	1	0	3
	E	9	5	8	9	5

Determine the optimal assignment policy.

[*Univ. of Madras B.Sc. (Math.) Nov., 2012; P.T.U. B.Tech. April, 2012; May, 2011, G.N.D.U. B.Com., 2009 P.U. B.Com. April, 2009*]

(*Ans.* A-5, B-1, C-4, D-3, E-2; 9.)

19. Solve the following assignment problem. Asssign one machine to one worker so that time in hours in minimized.

TABLE 4.137

	M_1	M_2	M_3	M_4	M_5
A	3	2	7	4	8
B	5	4	3	8	5
C	3	7	9	1	2
D	4	2	6	5	7
E	2	8	4	6	6

[*P.T.U. B.Tech. April, 2012; Gujarat Technological U.MBA Dec., 2010*]

(*Ans.* A-M_4, B-M_3, C-M_5, D-M_2, E-M_1; 13 hours.)

20. (*a*) Distinguish between transportation model and assignment model. [*P.T.U. MBA May, 2015*]

(*b*) Four different jobs are to be done on four different machines. The setup and production times are prohibitively high for changeover. Table 4.138 indicates the cost of producing job *i* on machine *j* in rupees.

TABLE 4.138

Machines

Jobs	1	2	3	4
1	5	7	11	6
2	8	5	9	6
3	4	7	10	7
4	10	4	8	3

Assign jobs to different machines so that the total cost is minimized.

[*P.T.U. MBA Feb., 2011; P.U.B.E.(T.&I.T.) Nov., 2004; Nagpur U. B.E.(Mech.) 2003; NIIFT Mohali, 2001*]

(*Ans.* 1–1, 2–2, 3–3, 4–4; Z_{min} = ₹ 23.)

21. Six machines M_1, M_2, M_3, M_4, M_5 and M_6 are to be located in six places P_1, P_2, P_3, P_4, P_5 and P_6. C_{ij}, the cost of locating machine M_i at place P_j is given in the matrix below:

TABLE 4.139

	P_1	P_2	P_3	P_4	P_5	P_6
M_1	20	23	18	10	16	20
M_2	50	20	17	16	15	11
M_3	60	30	40	55	8	7
M_4	6	7	10	20	25	9
M_5	18	19	28	17	60	70
M_6	9	10	20	30	40	55

Formulate an L.P. model to determine an optimal assignment. Write the objective function and the constraints in detail. Define any symbol used. Find an optimal layout by assignment technique of linear programming.

[*P.U.B.E. (Mech.) Nov. 2002*]

(*Ans.* $M_1 - P_4$, $M_2 - P_6$, $M_3 - P_5$, $M_4 - P_3$, $M_5 - P_1$, $M_6 - P_2$; Z_{min} = 67.)

22. (*a*) Discuss assignment model. Indicate a method of solving an assignment problem.

[*P.U.B.E. (Mech.) April 1978*]

(*b*) A company is faced with the problem of assigning six different machines to five different jobs. The costs estimated in hundreds of rupees are given in the table below.

TABLE 4.140

Machines \ Jobs	1	2	3	4	5
1	2.5	5	1	6	2
2	2	5	1.5	7	3
3	3	6.5	2	8	3
4	3.5	7	2	9	4.5
5	4	7	3	9	6
6	6	9	5	10	6

Solve the problem assuming that the objective is to minimize the total cost.

[*P.T.U. B.Tech. April, 2012*]

(*Ans.* 1 – 4, 2 – 1, 3 – 5, 4 – 3, 5 – 2, 6 – Dummy; Z_{min} = ₹ 2,000.)

23. Five new machines are to be located in a machine shop. There are five possible locations in which the machines can be located. C_{ij}, the cost of placing machine i in place j is given in the table below.

TABLE 4.141

Machine \ Place	1	2	3	4	5
1	15	10	25	25	10
2	1	8	10	20	2
3	8	9	17	20	10
4	14	10	25	27	15
5	10	8	25	27	12

It is required to place the machines at suitable places so as to minimize the total cost.

(*i*) Formulate an L.P. model to find an optimal assignment.

(*ii*) Solve the problem by assignment technique of L.P. [*H.P.U. B.Tech. (Mech..) June, 2010; P.U.B.E.(Prod.) May, 2002*]

(*Ans.* 1 – 5, 2 – 3, 3 – 4, 4 – 2, 5 – 1; Z_{min} = 60.)

24. Find the optimal assignment for the assignment problem with the following cost matrix:

TABLE 4.142

	I	II	III	IV
A	5	3	1	8
B	7	9	2	6
C	6	4	5	7
D	5	7	7	6

[*J.N.T.U. Anantapur MBA August, 2010*]

(*Ans.* A – III, B – IV, C – II, D – 1; Z_{min} = 16.)

25. A project consists of four major jobs for which four contractors have submitted tenders. The tender amounts quoted in lakhs of rupees are given in the matrix below. Find the assignment that minimizes the total cost of the project. Each contractor has to be assigned only one job.

TABLE 4.143

		Job			
		a	*b*	*c*	*d*
	1	10	24	30	15
	2	16	22	28	12
Contractor	3	12	20	32	10
	4	9	26	34	16

[*H.P.U. B.Tech. June, 2015*]

(*Ans.* 1 – *b*, 2 – *c*, 3 – *d*, 4 – *a*; Z_{min} = 71.)

26. Solve the following assignment problem:

TABLE 4.144

	I	II	III	IV	V
1	11	17	8	16	20
2	9	7	12	6	15
3	13	16	15	12	16
4	21	24	17	28	26
5	14	10	12	11	15

[*H.P.U. B.Tech. Nov., 2015, P.U.B. Com. April, 2001; NIIFT Mohali, 2000*]

(*Ans.* 1 – I, 2 – IV, 3 – V, 4 – III, 5 – II; Z_{min} = 60.)

27. A team of 5 horses and 5 riders has entered a jumping show contest. The number of penalty points to be expected when each rider rides any horse is shown below.

TABLE 4.145

		Rider				
		R_1	R_2	R_3	R_4	R_5
	H_1	5	3	4	7	1
	H_2	2	3	7	6	5
Horse	H_3	4	1	5	2	4
	H_4	6	8	1	2	3
	H_5	4	2	5	7	1

How should the horses be allotted to the riders so as to minimize the expected loss of the team?

[*P.T.U. B.Tech. (Prod.) Nov., 2012; H.P.U.B. Tech. (Mech.) Nov., 2010*]

(*Ans.* $H_1 - R_5$, $H_2 - R_1$, $H_3 - R_4$, $H_4 - R_3$, $H_5 - R_2$; Z_{min} = 8.)

28. Find the minimum cost solution for the 5 × 5 assignment problem whose cost coefficients are as given below.

TABLE 4.146

	1	2	3	4	5
1	–2	–4	–8	–6	–1
2	0	–9	–5	–5	–4
3	–3	–8	–9	–2	–6
4	–4	–3	–1	0	–3
5	–9	–5	–8	–9	–5

[*J.N.T.U. Hyderabad B. Tech. May, 2009*]

(*Ans.* 1 – 3, 2 – 2, 3 – 5, 4 – 1, 5 – 4; Z_{min} = – 36.)

[**Hint.** Add 9 to all elements and then solve.]

29. Five employees of a company are to be assigned to five jobs, which can be done by any of them. The workers get different wages per hour. These are ₹ 5 per hour for A, B and C each and ₹ 3 per hour for D and E each. The amount of time in hours taken by each employee to do a given job is given in the table below. Determine the assignment pattern that (*a*) minimizes the total time taken (*b*) minimizes the total cost of getting the five jobs done.

TABLE 4.147

Job \ Employee	A	B	C	D	E
1	7	9	3	3	2
2	6	1	6	6	5
3	3	4	9	10	7
4	1	5	2	2	4
5	6	6	9	4	2

[*IGNOU MBA, 2002*]

(*Ans.* (*a*) 1– C, 2 – B, 3 – A, 4 – D, 5 – E; 11 hours.
(*b*) 1– D, 2 – B, 3 – A, 4 – C, 5 – E; ₹ 47.)

30. A sales manager has to assign 4 salesmen to 4 territories. The possible profit for each salesman in each territory is given below. Find the assignment that maximizes the profit.

TABLE 4.148

Salesmen \ Territories	A	B	C	D
1	35	27	28	37
2	28	37	29	40
3	35	24	32	33
4	24	32	25	28

[*J.N.T.U. Hyderabad B.Tech. Sept., 2011; Osmania U.MBA, 2010; P.U. B.Com. Sept., 2006; B.B.A. June, 2001*]

31. Solve the following assignment problem to minimize time:

TABLE 4.149

Men \ Jobs	1	2	3	4	5
1	2	9	3	7	1
2	6	8	7	6	1
3	4	6	5	3	1
4	4	2	7	3	1
5	5	3	9	5	1

(*Ans.* 1–1, 2–5, 3–3, 4–4, 5–2; 14. Also 1-3, 2-5, 3-1, 4-4, 5-2; 14.)

32. Six salesmen are to be allocated to six sales regions so that the cost of allocation of the job will be minimum. Cost matrix is given below.
   (*a*) Find the allocation to give minimum cost. What is the cost?
   (*b*) If the matrix represents earnings, find the optimum earnings.

TABLE 4.150

Salesman \ Region	I	II	III	IV	V	VI
A	15	35	0	25	10	45
B	40	5	45	20	15	20
C	25	60	10	65	25	10
D	25	20	35	10	25	60
E	30	70	40	5	40	50
F	10	25	30	40	50	15

[P.U.B.E.(Elect.) 2001]

33. Solve the following assignment problem for minimum optimal cost:

TABLE 4.151

From City \ To City	1	2	3	4	5	6
A	12	10	15	22	18	8
B	10	18	25	15	16	12
C	11	10	3	8	5	9
D	6	14	10	13	13	12
E	8	12	11	7	13	10

[P.U.B.Com. Sept., 2004]

(*Ans.* A – 2, B – 6, C – 3, D – 1, E – 4; 38.)

34. Find the optimal assignment and the assignment cost for 8 jobs J_1, J_2, ..., J_8 to be assigned to eight operators O_1, O_2, ..., O_8 when the assignment cost is as follows:

TABLE 4.152

	J_1	J_2	J_3	J_4	J_5	J_6	J_7	J_8
O_1	11	7	12	14	16	18	20	18
O_2	12	17	11	17	13	15	16	12
O_3	13	21	10	16	21	19	17	11
O_4	14	19	18	13	10	45	12	18
O_5	15	16	13	12	20	16	13	19
O_6	16	12	21	18	30	17	15	20
O_7	17	17	25	14	40	18	16	21
O_8	18	18	17	16	50	19	17	18

[P.U.B.E.(E.&Ec.) 2002]

(*Ans.* $O_1 - J_1$, $O_2 - J_3$, $O_3 - J_8$, $O_4 - J_5$, $O_5 - J_7$, $O_6 - J_2$, $O_7 - J_4$, $O_8 - J_6$; 101.)

Section 4.7-1

35. A company has four machines to do three jobs. Each job can be assigned to one and only one machine. The cost of each job on each machine is given in the following table:

TABLE 4.153

Machine

Job		W	X	Y	Z
	A	18	24	28	32
	B	8	13	17	19
	C	10	15	19	22

What are the job assignments which will minimize the cost?

[*J.N.T.U. Hyderabad MBA April, 2012*]

(*Ans.* A – W, B – X, C – Y; Z_{min} = 50.)

36. Assign four trucks 1, 2, 3 and 4 to vacant spaces, 7, 8, 9, 10, 11 and 12 so that the distance travelled is minimized. The matrix below shows the distance.

TABLE 4.154

	1	2	3	4
7	4	7	3	7
8	8	2	5	5
9	4	9	6	9
10	7	5	4	8
11	6	3	5	4
12	6	8	7	3

[*Karn.U.B.E.(Mech.)1995; Pb. Univ. B. Com. April, 2006*]

(*Ans.* 7 – 3, 8 – 2, 9 – 1, 12 – 4; Z_{min} = 12.)

37. A city corporation has decided to carry out road repairs on four main arteries of the city. The govt. has agreed to make a special grant of ₹ 50 lakh towards the cost with a condition that the repairs must be done at the lowest cost and quickest time. If conditions warrant, a supplementary token grant will also be considered favourably. The corporation has floated tenders and five contractors have sent in their bids. In order to expedite work, one road will be awarded to only one contractor.

TABLE 4.155

Cost of repairs on road (₹ lakhs)

		R_1	R_2	R_3	R_4
	C_1	9	14	19	15
	C_2	7	17	20	19
Contractor	C_3	9	18	21	18
	C_4	10	12	18	19
	C_5	10	15	21	16

(*i*) Find the best way of assigning the repairs to the contractors and the associated cost.

(*ii*) If it is necessary to seek supplementary grant, what should be the amount sought?

(*iii*) Which of the five contractors will be unsuccessful in his bid?

[*AMIE, 2005*]

(*Ans.* (*i*) C_1R_3 : 19, C_2R_1 : 7, C_4R_2 : 12, C_5R_4 : 16; ₹ 54 lakh.

(*ii*) ₹ 4 lakh. (*iii*) C_3.)

38. A company is faced with the problem of assigning six different machines to four different jobs. The costs, in hundreds of rupees, are estimated as follows:

TABLE 4.156

		Job 1	2	3	4
Machine	1	6	5	1	6
	2	2	5	3	7
	3	3	7	2	8
	4	7	7	5	9
	5	12	8	8	6
	6	6	9	5	10

Solve the problem and find the minimum total assignment cost. How will you proceed if machine no. 4 is out of order? Find the increase in minimum total assignment cost in this case.

[*P.U.B.E.(Mech.) 1998*]

(*Ans.* (*i*) 1 – 2, 2 – 1, 3 – 3, 4 – D_1, 5 – 4, 6 – D_2; Z_{min} = ₹ 1,500.
(*ii*) 1 – 2, 2 – 1, 3 – 3, 5 – 4, 6 – D; Z_{min} = ₹ 1,500.)

39. The personnel manager of ABC company wants to relocate Mr. X, Y and Z to regional offices. However, the firm also has an opening in its Chennai office and would send one of the three to that branch if it were more economical than a move to Delhi, Mumbai or Kolkata. It will cost ₹ 2,000 to relocate Mr. X to Chennai, ₹ 1,600 to relocate Mr. Y there and ₹ 3,000 to move Mr. Z.

TABLE 4.157

Hiree \ Office	Delhi	Mumbai	Kolkata
Mr. X	1,600	2,200	2,400
Mr. Y	1,000	3,200	2,600
Mr. Z	1,000	2,000	4,600

What is the optimum assignment of personnel to offices? [*Nagpur U. MBA, 1998*]

40. A company has four vehicles to be run on four routes. The distance in km for each route and the kms run per litre of diesel for each vehicle in each of the routes are given below.

TABLE 4.158

		Km per litre in the route of 1	2	3	4
Vehicles	A	4	5	5	3
	B	4.5	6	5	3.5
	C	5	5.5	6	4
	D	4.8	5.8	5.5	3
Distance covered per day (km)		300	250	150	150

Which vehicle should be assigned to which route in order to minimize the total consumption of diesel by all the four vehicles?

[*R.E.C. Hamirpur, 1995; ICWA (Final) June, 1991*]

(*Ans.* A – 3, B – 2, C – 4, D – 1; 171.42 litres.)

Section 4.7-2

41. A department has four subordinates and four tasks to be performed. The subordinates differ in efficiency and tasks differ in their intrinsic difficulty. The estimates of the profit in rupees each man would earn is given in the effectiveness matrix. How should the tasks be allocated, one to each man, so as to maximize the total earnings?

TABLE 4.159

Subordinate \ Task	5	6	7	8
1	5	40	20	5
2	25	35	30	25
3	15	25	20	10
4	15	5	30	15

[*NIIFT Mohali, 1998*]

(*Ans.* 1 – 6, 2 – 8, 3 – 5, 4 – 7; Z_{max} = ₹ 110.)

42. A company has five jobs to be done. The following matrix shows the return in rupees of assigning *i*th machine (*i* = 1, 2, ..., 5) to the *j*th job (*j* = 1, 2, ..., 5). Assign the five jobs to the five machines so as to maximize the total expected profit.

TABLE 4.160

Machine \ Job	1	2	3	4	5
1	5	11	10	12	4
2	2	4	6	3	5
3	3	12	5	14	6
4	6	14	4	11	7
5	7	9	8	12	5

[*P.U. B.Com., April, 2014; Sept., 2013; V.T.U. Karnataka B.E. Dec., 2011*]

(*Ans.* 1 – 3, 2 – 5, 3 – 4, 4 – 2, 5 – 1, Z_{max} = ₹ 50.)

43. The owner of a small machine shop has four machinists available to assign to jobs for the day. Five jobs are offered with the expected profit in rupees for each machinist on each job being as follows. Find the assignment of machinists to jobs that will result in the maximum profit. Which job should be declined?

TABLE 4.161

Machinist \ Job	A	B	C	D	E
1	6.20	7.80	5.00	10.10	8.20
2	7.10	8.40	6.10	7.30	5.90
3	8.70	9.20	11.10	7.10	8.10
4	4.80	6.40	8.70	7.70	8.00

[*P.T.U. MCA, 2010*]

(*Ans.* 1 – D, 2 – B, 3 – C, 4 – E; Job A; Z_{max} = ₹ 37.60.)

44. Alpha corporation has four plants, each of which can manufacture any one of the four products. Production costs differ from one plant to another and so do sales revenue. Given the revenue and cost data below, obtain which product each plant should produce to maximize profit.

TABLE 4.162

Plant	*Sales revenue (₹ '000s) per product*			
	1	2	3	4
A	50	68	49	62
B	60	70	51	74
C	55	67	53	70
D	58	65	54	69

Plant	Production cost (₹ '000s) per product			
	1	2	3	4
A	49	60	45	61
B	55	63	45	69
C	52	62	49	68
D	55	64	48	66

[*J.N.T.U. Hyderabad B.Tech. (C.Sc.) Dec., 2011*]

(*Ans.* A – 2, B – 4, C – 1, D – 3; Z_{max} = ₹ 22,000.)

45. Solve the following assignment problem to maximize sales:

TABLE 4.163

Territories

Salesmen	I	II	III	IV	V
A	10	15	17	14	14
B	6	18	10	12	16
C	8	5	13	13	6
D	12	11	16	10	12

If salesman B cannot be assigned to territory II for certain reason, will the optimal assignment change? If so, what will be the new assignment and total sales?

[*G.N.D.U. B.Com. Sept., 2011; April, 2010; P.U. B.Com. April, 2010; April, 2004*]

(*Ans.* (i) A-V, B-II, C-IV, D-III; 61.
(ii) A-II, B-V, C-IV, D-III; 60.)

46. The processing times (minutes) taken by 5 operators to make 5 different products are given below. The effective working hours in a day are 6.

TABLE 4.164

Operators	*Products*				
	1	2	3	4	5
A	10	12	18	15	9
B	12	10	20	18	10
C	8	9	15	10	8
D	9	8	24	12	12
E	10	15	18	12	10

Profits per product are ₹ 4, 2, 3, 3 and 4 for products 1, 2, 3, 4 and 5 respectively. Find the allocation of operators to products so as to maximize the total profit.

[*H.P.U. B.Tech. (Mech.) Sept., 2013*]

(*Ans.* A – 5, B – 3, C – 1, D – 2, E – 4; Z_{max} = ₹ 574.)

47. Four jobs are to be done on four differnt machines. Assign the jobs so as to maximize the total profit.

TABLE 4.165

Machine

Job	M_1	M_2	M_3	M_4
J_1	15	11	13	15
J_2	17	12	12	13
J_3	14	15	10	14
J_4	16	13	11	17

[*U.P.U. MBA, 2010*]

(*Ans.* J_1-M_3, J_2-M_1, J_3-M_2, J_4-M_4; Z_{max} = 62.)

48. Suggest optimum solution to the following assignment problem to get maximum sales:

TABLE 4.166

Markets (Sales in lakhs of rupees)

		I	II	III	IV
Salesmen	*A*	44	80	52	60
	B	60	56	40	72
	C	36	60	48	48
	D	52	76	36	40

(*Ans.* A-II, B-IV, C-III, D-I, ₹ 252 lakh.)

49. Five different machines can do any of the five required jobs, with different profit resulting from each assignment. Find the assignment that maximizes the total profit.

TABLE 4.167

Machines

		A	B	C	D	E
Jobs	1	30	37	40	28	40
	2	40	24	27	21	36
	3	40	32	33	30	35
	4	25	38	40	36	36
	5	29	62	40	34	39

[*P.T.U. B.Tech. (Prod.) Nov., 2012; Mumbai U. MBA, 2010; G.N.D.U.B. Com. April, 2007*]

(*Ans.* 1-C, 2-E, 3-A, 4-D, 5-B; 214.)

50. In a factory working for 8 hours a day, processing times (minutes) for each product by each of 5 operators are given below:

TABLE 4.168

Product

		A	B	C	D
Operator	1	4	2	4	1
	2	2	3	3	2
	3	4	3	2	2
	4	3	2	3	1
	5	2	3	4	1
Profit/unit (₹)		2	3	4	1

Find out which product be assigned to which operator so that the total profit is maximized and state the total profit per day. [*H.P.U. B.Tech. (Mech.) Nov., 2010*]

[**Hint.** First find the number of units of each product each operator can produce in a day and then make the profit table. (*Ans.* 1-B, 2-E, 3-C, 4-D, 5-A; Z_{min} = ₹ 2,640.)

51. An engineer has four mechanics X, Y, Z and K to be put on four jobs R_1, R_2, R_3 and R_4. All the jobs will be started at the same time. Probabilities of completion are given below. Decide which mechanic he should put on which job so that the profit is maximized.

TABLE 4.169

Jobs

		R_1	R_2	R_3	R_4
Mechanics	X	0.4	0.3	0.2	0.6
	Y	0.2	0.2	0.15	0.3
	Z	0.15	0.1	0	0.2
	K	0.1	0	0	0.2
Gain (₹)		1,000	1,500	5,000	8,000

State the logic of your procedure. What is the maximum gain? [*P.U.B.E.(Mech.) 1997*]

52. A machine shop has four machines (M_1 to M_4) available for fabrication of products as per customer specifications. On one occasion, orders have been received for five jobs (J_1 to J_5). Each job requires one machine and no machine can do more than one job. The expected profits in rupees by machine-job combinations are shown in the table below.

TABLE 4.170

	J_1	J_2	J_3	J_4	J_5
M_1	740	940	980	1,120	600
M_2	860	1,000	720	900	720
M_3	580	750	960	930	1,000
M_4	1,050	1,100	980	850	1,300

Find the optimal assignment of the jobs to the machines. Which job will not be accepted? If just before commencement of the jobs it becomes known that job 2 is cancelled, what will be its impact on the assignments and overall profits? [*C.A.(Final) June, 2003*]

53. An airline company has drawn up a new flight schedule involving five flights. To assist in allocating five pilots to the flights, it has asked them to state their preference scores by giving each flight a number out of 10. The higher the number, the greater is the preference. Some of these flights are unsuitable to some pilots owing to domestic reasons.

TABLE 4.171

		Flight number				
		1	2	3	4	5
	A	8	2	–	5	4
	B	10	9	2	8	4
Pilot	*C*	5	4	9	6	–
	D	3	6	2	8	7
	E	5	6	10	4	3

What would be the allocation of the pilots to flights in order to meet as many preferences as possible? [*H.P.U.B. Tech. (Mech.) June, 2010*]

(*Ans. A*–1, *B*–2, *C*–4, *D*–5, *E*–3; Z_{max} = 40.)

Section 4.7-3

54. Consider the problem of assigning five operators to five machines. The assignment costs are given in table 4.172.

TABLE 4.172

		Machine				
		M_1	M_2	M_3	M_4	M_5
	A	7	7	–	4	8
	B	9	6	4	5	6
Operator	C	11	5	7	–	5
	D	9	4	8	9	4
	E	8	7	9	11	3

Operator A cannot be assigned to machine M_3 and operator C cannot be assigned to machine M_4. Find the optimum assignment schedule.

[*J.N.T.U. Hyderabad B. Tech. Nov., 2010; P.U.B.Com., 2002; Jan., 2005; April, 2006; Sept., 2006*]

(*Ans.* A – M_4, B – M_3, C – M_2, D – M_1, E – M_5; Z_{min} = 25.)

55. Five mechanics are available to work on five machines and the respective cost in rupees for each mechanic-machine combination is given in the matrix below. A sixth machine is available to replace one of the existing machines and the associated costs are given in table 4.173. Determine
(*i*) whether the new machine can be accepted.
(*ii*) the optimal assignments and the associated costs.

TABLE 4.173

		Machine					
		1	2	3	4	5	6
Mechanic	A	19	15	–	16	13	22
	B	13	–	15	–	21	14
	C	15	17	19	20	12	18
	D	20	22	16	18	17	–
	E	–	16	14	19	18	15
	Dummy	0	0	0	0	0	0

[*P.U.B.E.(Elect.) 1999; Karn.U.B.E.(Mech.) 1998; Dayalbagh Edu. Inst. M. Tech., 1998*]

(*Ans.* Yes; A – 2, B – 1, C – 5, D – 3, E – 6; Z_{min} = ₹ 71.)

[**Hint.** First solve the 6 × 6 matrix given by table 4.173. Z_{min} is found to be ₹ 71. Next solve the 5 × 5 matrix obtained by deleting the last row and last column of the above table. Z_{min} for this matrix is ₹ 72. Hence sixth machine can be accepted since it reduces the assignment cost by ₹ 1.]

56. Solve the following assignment problem:

TABLE 4.174

	To	A_1	B_1	C_1	D_1	E_1
From	A	–	7	6	8	4
	B	7	–	8	5	6
	C	6	8	–	9	7
	D	8	5	9	–	8
	E	4	6	7	8	–

[*P.U.B.Com., 2002*]

(*Ans.* A – C_1, B – D_1, C – E_1, D – B_1, E – A_1; 27.)

57. ABC company has to work out the assignment of 5 different jobs to 5 different machines. The cost of the machine per unit of the job and setup costs of the jobs on machines are given in tables below. The jobs are to be made in batch sizes shown against them. Setup cost is independent of the previous setup. Determine the optimal assignment plan.

TABLE 4.175

		Jobs				
		J_1	J_2	J_3	J_4	J_5
Machines	M_1	0.8	1.1	0.7	1.6	6.2
	M_2	1.2	0.9	1.2	0.8	5.4
	M_3	2.1	2	1	2.2	5.1
	M_4	—	1.6	2	1.9	3.6
	M_5	3.2	2	2	2	2.6
Batch size		100	100	150	100	50

TABLE 4.176

Jobs

		J_1	J_2	J_3	J_4	J_5
	M_1	60	70	70	30	40
	M_2	40	50	50	20	80
Machines	M_3	30	40	40	40	100
	M_4	—	90	60	50	60
	M_5	80	100	80	60	60

[*P.U.B.E.(Mech.) 1997*]

58. An airline that operates between Delhi (A) and Kolkata (B) has the timetable as shown in table 4.177. Crew must have a minimum layover of 5 hours between flights. Obtain the pairing of flights that minimizes layover time away from home. Note that crew flying from A to B and back can be based either at A or at B. For any given pairing, they will be based at the city that results in the smaller layover.

TABLE 4.177

Delhi—Kolkata

Flight number	*Departure*	*Arrival*
1	6:00 A.M.	7:00 A.M.
2	7:30 A.M.	8:30 A.M.
3	10:30 A.M.	11:30 A.M.
4	2:00 P.M.	3:00 P.M.
5	6:00 P.M.	7:00 P.M.
6	11:30 P.M.	0:30 A.M.

Kolkata—Delhi

Flight number	*Departure*	*Arrival*
101	8:00 A.M.	9:15 A.M.
102	9:00 A.M.	10:15 A.M.
103	11:30 A.M.	0:45 P.M.
104	3:00 P.M.	4:15 P.M.
105	7:30 P.M.	8:45 P.M.
106	10:00 P.M.	11:15 P.M.

[*P.U.B.E.(Mech.) 1995*]

59. XYZ airline operating 7 days a week has given the following timetable. Crew must have a minimum layover of 5 hours between flights. Obtain the pairing of flights that minimizes layover time away from home. For any given pairing the crew will be based at the city that results in the smaller layover.

TABLE 4.178

Chennai – Mumbai			*Mumbai – Chennai*		
Flight no.	*Departure*	*Arrival*	*Flight no.*	*Departure*	*Arrival*
A_1	6 A.M.	8 A.M.	B_1	8 A.M.	10 A.M.
A_2	8 A.M.	10 A.M.	B_2	9 A.M.	11 A.M.
A_3	2 P.M.	4 P.M.	B_3	2 P.M.	4 P.M.
A_4	8 P.M.	10 P.M.	B_4	7 P.M.	9 P.M.

[*C.A. May, 2000*]

(*Ans.* $A_1 - B_3$, $A_2 - B_4$, $A_3 - B_1$, $B_2 - A_4$; 40 hours.)

Section 4.8

60. The personnel manager of a medium size company decides to recruit two employees D and E in a particular section of the organisation. The section has five fairly defined tasks 1, 2, 3, 4 and 5; and three employees A, B and C are already employed in the section. Looking to the rather specialised nature of task 3 and the special qualifications of the recruit D for task 3, the manager decides to assign

task 3 to employee D and then assign the remaining tasks to remaining employees so as to maximize the total effectiveness. The index of effectiveness of each employee for different tasks is as under.

TABLE 4.179

		Task				
		1	2	3	4	5
	A	25	55	60	45	30
	B	45	65	55	35	40
Employee	C	10	35	45	55	65
	D	40	30	70	40	60
	E	55	45	40	55	10

Assign the tasks for maximizing total effectiveness. Critically examine whether the decision of the manager to assign task 3 to employee *D* was correct.

[*D.U.MBA, 2000*]

(*Ans.* A – 4, B – 2, C – 5, D – 3, E – 1; Yes; Z_{max} = 300.)

61. A production centre wants to assign seven operators to seven different jobs A, B, C, D, E, F and G. The times taken by them for each job are as follows:

TABLE 4.180

		Operator						
		O_1	O_2	O_3	O_4	O_5	O_6	O_7
	A	23	12	45	39	54	21	18
	B	45	38	18	31	53	33	54
	C	38	41	31	38	54	19	45
Job	D	13	45	27	45	45	38	38
	E	38	34	36	30	38	41	21
	F	38	54	54	29	42	30	44
	G	45	45	23	17	45	39	49

Assign the jobs so that total operation time is minimum. Find the minimum total time for all the jobs. Find the increase in the minimum total time for all the jobs if job B has already been assigned to operator O_7.

[*P.U. B.E.(Ec.) 2001*]

(*Ans.* (*a*) A – O_2, B – O_3, C – O_6, D – O_1, E – O_7, F – O_5, G – O_4; 142.
(*b*) A – O_2, B – O_7, C – O_6, D – O_1; E – O_5, F – O_4, G – O_3; 46.)

62. Four persons P_1, P_2, P_3 and P_4 have to do five jobs J_1, J_2, J_3, J_4 and J_5. Each job is to be done by one person only. Each person does exactly one job except P_2 who can do 2 jobs. Cost involved in assigning a job to a person is given in the table below. Find an optimal assignment which minimizes the total cost.

TABLE 4.181

	J_1	J_2	J_3	J_4	J_5
P_1	6	4	5	7	8
P_2	7	5	8	6	9
P_3	8	6	7	9	10
P_4	5	7	8	4	6

[**Hint.** Add one more row for P_2 in table 4.181 and then solve.] [*DOEACC, 1995*]

63. The estimated sales (tons) per month in four different cities by five different managers are given below:

TABLE 4.182

Managers	*Cities*			
	A	B	C	D
P	13	15	12	14
Q	12	14	10	12
R	16	18	14	14
S	15	15	13	13
T	14	15	14	12

(*i*) Find out the assignment of managers to cities in order to maximize sales.

(*ii*) Due to certain reason it has been decided to post manager R to city B. Find out the allocation of the remaining managers to the remaining cities with minimum loss of sales. What would be the loss of sales?

(*iii*) If the policy of the management is to send one of the managers other than R for improving sales performance, who would be sent without losing the sales? [*ICWA June, 1993*]

(*Ans.* (i) P-D, Q-Dm, R-B, S-A, T-C; 61 tons.
(ii) No loss of sales.
(iii) Q.)

64. A company has four job orders. This company operates on project basis and has three project teams available. Each team must be assigned only one job order. The following table provides estimates of man-days of development and engineering time required.

TABLE 4.183
Development time
(Man-days)

	A	B	C	D
1	8	6	9	5
Teams 2	6	3	7	8
3	5	2	9	9

TABLE 4.184
Engineering time
(Man-days)

	A	B	C	D
1	3	3	5	4
2	5	9	8	7
3	6	9	10	6

Development expense : ₹ 120 per man-day
Engineering expense : ₹ 100 per man-day
Returns for company : Job A – ₹ 2,000; Job B – ₹ 1,800;
Job C – ₹ 2,100; Job D – ₹ 1,900.

(*a*) Which team should be assigned to which job to maximize profits?

(*b*) If team 3 cannot be assigned to job A, will there be a change in maximum profit?

[*Karn.U.B.E.(Mech.) 1995*]

65. To stimulate interest and provide an atmosphere for intellectual discussion, a finance faculty in a management school decides to hold special seminars on four contemporary topics: leasing, portfolio management, private mutual funds, swaps and options. Such seminars should be held once a week in the afternoons. However, scheduling these seminars (one for each topic and not more than one seminar per afternoon) has to be done carefully so that the number of students unable to attend is kept to a minimum. A careful study indicates that the number of students who cannot attend a particular seminar on a specific day is as follows:

TABLE 4.185

Day	*Leasing*	*Portfolio management*	*Private mutual funds*	*Swaps and options*
Monday	50	40	60	20
Tuesday	40	30	40	30
Wednesday	60	20	30	20
Thursday	30	30	20	30
Friday	10	20	10	30

Find an optimal schedule of the seminars. Also find out the total number of students who will be missing at least one seminar. [*C.A. Nov., 1992*]

(*Ans.* Monday : swaps and options, Tuesday : No seminar, Wednesday : portfolio management, Thursday : private mutual funds, Friday : leasing; 70.)

66. Four operators O_1, O_2, O_3 and O_4 are available to a manager who has to get four jobs J_1, J_2, J_3 and J_4 done by assigning one job to each operator. Given the times needed by different operators for different jobs in the matrix below:

TABLE 4.186

	J_1	J_2	J_3	J_4
O_1	12	10	10	8
O_2	14	12	15	11
O_3	6	10	16	4
O_4	8	10	9	7

(*i*) How should the manager assign the jobs so that the total time needed for all the four jobs is minimum?

(*ii*) If job J_2 is not to be assigned to operator O_2, what should be the assignment and how much additional total time will be required? [*M.G.U. Kerala M.Com. June, 2012*]

[**Hint.** For part (*ii*) change time in cell (O_2, J_2) to infinity and re-solve the problem.]

(*Ans.* (*i*) $O - J_3$, $O_2 - J_2$, $O_3 - J_4$, $O_4 - J_1$; 34.
(*ii*) $O_1 - J_2$, $O_2 - J_4$, $O_3 - J_1$, $O_4 - J_3$; 2.)

67. The marketing manager of a company is faced with the problem of assigning 5 regional managers to six zones. From past experience he knows that the efficiency percentage judged by sales, market share, operating costs, etc. depends upon the regional manager-zone combination given below:

TABLE 4.187

Zones

Regional manager	I	II	III	IV	V	VI
A	71	89	85	80	76	78
B	79	83	67	74	72	83
C	73	70	81	82	76	89
D	91	94	84	89	81	80
E	88	89	77	87	67	74

You are to advise the marketing manager which zone should be managed by a junior manager due to non-availability of a regional manager, so that overall efficiency is maximized. [*G.N.D.U. B.Com. Sept., 2008*]

(*Ans.* A – III, B – II, C – VI, D – I, E – IV, 435; Zone V.)

68. A manufacturing company has four zones A, B, C and D and four sales engineers P, Q, R and S respectively for assignment. Since the zones are not equally rich in sales potential, it is estimated that a particular engineer operating in a particular zone will bring the following sales:

Zone A	:	₹ 4,20,000
Zone B	:	₹ 3,36,000
Zone C	:	₹ 2,94,000
Zone D	:	₹ 4,62,000

The engineers have different sales ability. Working under the same conditions, their yearly sales are proportional to 14, 9, 11 and 8 respectively. The criterion of maximum expected total sales to be met by assigning the best engineer to the richest zone, the next best to the second richest zone and so on. Find the optimum assignment and the maximum sales. [*C.A. May, 1998*]

(*Ans.* P – D, Q – B, R – A, S – C; ₹ 3,92,000.)

69. A small school has five teachers teaching five different subjects. All the five teachers are capable of teaching all the five subjects. The output per day per teacher and course coverage (%) for each subject are given as follows:

TABLE 4.188

Teacher	*Subjects*				
	1	2	3	4	5
A	7	9	4	8	6
B	4	9	5	7	8
C	8	5	7	9	8
D	6	5	8	10	10
E	7	8	10	9	9
Course coverage (%)	2	3	2	3	4

(*i*) Which subject should be assigned to which teacher in order to maximize course coverage, assuming that there are no other constraints?

(*ii*) If teacher D is absent for a specified period and no other substitute teacher is available what should be the optimal assignment? [*P.U.B.E. (Mech.) Nov., 2006*]

[**Hint.** (*ii*) Take all cell values in row D as zeros and re-solve the problem.]

(*Ans.* (*i*) A – 1, B – 2, C – 4, D – 5, E – 3; 108%.

(*ii*) A – 2, B – 5, C – 4, E – 3; 106%; subject 1 remains uncovered.)

70. Five lathes are to be allotted to five operators (one for each). The following table gives weekly output figures (in pieces):

TABLE 4.189

Weekly output on lathe

		L_1	L_2	L_3	L_4	L_5
	P	20	22	27	32	36
Operator	Q	19	23	29	34	40
	R	23	28	35	39	34
	S	21	24	31	37	42
	T	24	28	31	36	41

Profit per piece is ₹ 25. Find the maximum profit.

[*R.T.M. Nagpur U.B. Tech. Dec., 2006*]

71. A firm produces four products. There are four operators who are capable of producing any of these four products. The processing time varies from operator to operator. The firm records 8 hours a day and allows 30 minutes for lunch. The processing time in minutes and the profit for each of the product are given below:

TABLE 4.190

Operators	*Products*			
	A	B	C	D
1	15	9	10	6
2	10	6	9	6
3	25	15	15	9
4	15	9	10	10
Profit (₹ per unit)	8	6	5	4

Find the optimal assignment of products to operators. [*R.T.M. Nagpur U.B.Tech. June, 2006*]

72. A head of department in a college has the problem of assigning courses to teachers with a view to maximising educational quality in his department. He has available to him one professor, two associate professors and one teaching assistant (T.A.). Four courses must be offered and after appropriate evaluation, he has arrived at the following relative ratings (100 = best rating) regarding the ability of each instructor to teach each of the four courses.

TABLE 4.191

	Course 1	*Course 2*	*Course 3*	*Course 4*
Prof 1	60	40	60	70
Assoc. Prof 2	20	60	50	70
Assoc. Prof 3	20	30	40	60
T.A.	30	10	20	40

How should he assign his staff to the courses to realise his objective ?

[*R.T.M. Nagpur B.E. (Mech.) Dec., 2008*]

73. In the modification of a plant layout of a factory, four new machines M_1, M_2, M_3 and M_4 are to be installed in a machine shop. There are five vacant places A, B, C, D and E available. Because of limited space, machine M_2 cannot be placed at C and M_3 cannot be placed at A. The cost of locating a machine at a place (in hundred rupees) is shown below.

TABLE 4.192

		Location				
		A	B	C	D	E
Machine	M_1	9	11	15	10	11
	M_2	12	9	–	10	9
	M_3	–	11	14	11	7
	M_4	14	8	12	7	8

Find the optimal assignment schedule.

[*R.T.M. Nagpur U.B. Tech. (Mech.) June, 2007; Dec., 2004*]

74. Solve the following assignment problem:

TABLE 4.193

Operator / *Machine*	*A*	*B*	*C*	*D*	*E*
M_1	16	13	17	19	20
M_2	13	12	13	16	17
M_3	14	11	15	17	18
M_4	5	5	8	8	11
M_5	6	4	7	8	10

[*R.T.M. Nagpur U.B. Tech. Dec., 2004*]

75. The owner of a small machine shop has machinists available to do jobs for the day. Five jobs are offered with expected profit for each machinist on each job as follows:

TABLE 4.194

	1	2	3	4
A	32	41	57	18
B	48	54	62	34
C	20	31	81	57
D	71	43	41	47
E	52	29	51	50

Find by using assignment method, the assignment of machinists to jobs that will result in the maximum profit. *[V.T.U. Karnataka B.E. June, 2010]*

76. A university examination panel has five examiners. The examiners are to be assigned to two practical examinatiozzs, two each for each practical exam. University desires to assign examiners such that the total distance travelled by all the examiners is minimum. The distance each examiner would have to travel to each practical examination centre is given below. Solve the problem.

TABLE 4.195

Examiners

		E_1	E_2	E_3	E_4	E_5
Practicals	A	20	40	60	20	70
	B	45	90	70	60	15

[V.T.U. Karnataka B.E. Jan., 2010]

77. Check if the following assignment is optimal. If not, find the optimal assignment.

TABLE 4.196

Jobs

		J_1	J_2	J_3	J_4	J_5
Men	M_1	$\boxed{20}$	15	14	–	30
	M_2	24	–	31	28	$\boxed{19}$
	M_3	32	$\boxed{21}$	–	20	27
	M_4	–	20	$\boxed{12}$	16	19
	M_5	31	26	25	$\boxed{21}$	–

[J.N.T.U. Hyderabad B.Tech. (C.Sc.) Dec., 2011]

78. Five lecturers have to deal a subject common to five different branches of engineering. Due to understanding level of the branches and the efficiency of lecture, the probable number of periods of 45 minutes required for each lecturer is given in the following matrix. A particular lecturer, namely, Mrs. Aparna refuses to go to CSE branch and IT students do not accept Mr. Prasad. Obtain an optimal arrangement.

TABLE 4.197

	ECE	EEE	CSE	IT	MECH
Mrs. Aparna	50	50	–	20	60
Dr. Raju	70	40	20	30	40
Mr. Prasad	90	30	50	–	30
Mr. Rajesh	70	20	60	70	20
Mr. Laxman	60	50	70	90	10

[*J.N.T.U. Hyderabad B.Tech. (C.Sc.) Dec., 2011*]

79. (a) Give the mathematical formulation of an assignment problem.

(b) Solve the assignment problem given in the table below. The figures in the table represent the time required for each combination.

TABLE 4.198

		Persons			
		1	2	3	4
Jobs	I	12	30	21	15
	II	18	33	9	31
	III	44	25	24	21
	IV	23	30	28	14

[*J.N.T.U. Hyderabad B.Tech. May, 2011; April, 2011*]

80. A company is faced with the problem of assigning 4 machines to 6 different jobs (one machine to one job only). The profits are estimated as follows. Solve the problem to maximize the total profits.

TABLE 4.199

3	7	3	6	5	5
6	1	8	4	2	7
2	4	5	3	4	6
6	4	8	7	3	4

[*P.T..U. MBA Dec., 2014; J.N.T.U. Hyderabad B.Tech. Nov., 2010*]

(*Ans.* A–2, B–3, C–6, D–4; D_{m1}–1, D_{m2}–5; ₹ 28.)

81. (a) Explain the assignment algorithm.

(b) Five workers are available to work with five machines and the respective costs (in rupees) associated with each worker & m/c assignment are given below. A sixth machine is available to replace one of the existing machines and the associated costs are also given below.

TABLE 4.200

		Machines					
		M_1	M_2	M_3	M_4	M_5	M_6
Workers	W_1	12	3	6	–	5	8
	W_2	4	11	–	5	–	3
	W_3	8	2	10	9	7	5
	W_4	–	7	8	6	12	10
	W_5	5	8	9	4	6	–

(i) Determine whether the new machine can be accepted.

(ii) Also find the optimal assignment. [*J.N.T.U. Hyderabad B.Tech. June, 2009*]

4.10 THE TRAVELLING SALESMAN PROBLEM (Shortest Cyclic Route Models)

There are a number of cities a salesman must visit. The distance (or time or cost) between every pair of cities is known. He starts from his home city, passes through each city once and only once and returns to his home city. The problem is to find the routes shortest in distance (or time or cost).

If the distance (or time or cost) between every pair of cities is independent of the direction of travel, the problem is said to be *symmetrical*. If for one or more pairs of cities the distance (or time or cost) varies with the direction, the problem is called *asymmetrical*. For example, it takes more time to go up a hill between two stations than come down the hill between them; similarly, a flight may take more time against the wind direction compared to that in the direction of wind.

If the salesman is to visit only two cities there is, of course, no choice. If the number of cities is three (A, B and C), of which the starting base is A, there are two possible routes A → B → C and A → C → B. For four cities, there are 6 possible routes:

A → B → C → D, A → B → D → C, A → C → B → D, A → C → D → B, A → D → B → C and A → D → C → B.

For eleven cities there are more than $3\frac{1}{2}$ million possible routes and for 21 cities, there are $20! = 2.4329 \times 10^{18}$ different routes. Even a fast electronic computer testing a route every micro second and working 8 hours a day for 365 days a year, would take around 2,31,440 years to find the best solution! In general, for n cities there are $(n - 1)!$ possible routes. It may be noted that since the salesman has to visit all the n cities, the shortest route will be independent of the selection of the starting city.

Obviously, the problem is to find the best route without trying each one. Unfortunately, there is no analytical method which can be used satisfactorily. However, a few computational techniques for solving the problem have been suggested.

Such types of problems arise in the following areas of management:

1. Postal deliveries
2. Inspection
3. School bus routing
4. Televison relays
5. Assembly lines, etc.

Mathematical Statement of the Travelling Salesman Problem

Mathematically, the problem may be stated as follows:

If c_{ij} is the cost of going from city i to city j and $x_{ij} = 1$, if the salesman goes directly from city i to j and zero otherwise, then the problem is to find x_{ij} which minimize

$$Z = \sum_{i=1}^{n} \sum_{j=1}^{n} c_{ij} x_{ij},$$

subject to
$$\sum_{j=1}^{n} x_{ij} = 1,$$

$$\sum_{i=1}^{n} x_{ij} = 1,$$

and
$$x_{ij} = 0 \text{ or } 1;\ i = 1, 2, \ldots, n;\ j = 1, 2, \ldots, n,$$

with the (two) additional constraints that no city is to be visited twice before the tour of all the cities is completed and that going from city i directly to i is not permitted, which means $c_{ii} = \infty$.

The equivalent production problem is: n items are to be produced on a machine in continuation. The set-up cost if item i is followed by j is c_{ij}. $x_{ij} = 1$ if item i is followed by j directly and zero otherwise. Each item is to be produced only once, *i.e.* item i is not to be produced again after item i, *i.e.* $c_{ii} = \infty$. Thus the travelling salesman problem or the multiple product production problem can be put in the form of an assignment problem as shown in table 4.201.

TABLE 4.201

		To city (or item)				
		1	2	3	...	n
From city (or item)	1	∞	C_{12}	C_{13}	...	C_{1n}
	2	C_{21}	∞	C_{23}	...	C_{2n}
	3	C_{31}	C_{32}	∞	...	C_{3n}
	⋮	⋮	⋮	⋮	⋮	⋮
	n	C_{n1}	C_{n2}	C_{n3}	...	∞

It may be noted that there must be only one x_{ij} for each value of i and each value of j. The problem is to find the n elements, one in each row and in each column so as to minimize the sum total of the associated costs shown in the matrix above. The problem is similar to the assignment problem discussed earlier with the difference that there is the additional constraint that no city is to be visited again before the tour of all the cities is completed (or no item is to be produced twice till all the items have been produced).

The above assignment problem can be solved and it can be hoped that the solution will satisfy the additional constraint. If it does not, it can be adjusted by inspection. The method, however, works well for small problems only. For large problems, a more systematic approach, developed by J.D.C. Little and his colleagues is used.

EXAMPLE 4.10-1

A salesman wants to visit cities 1, 2, 3 and 4. He does not want to visit any city twice before completing the tour of all the cities and wishes to return to his home city, the starting station. Cost of going from one city to another in rupees is given in table 4.202. Find the least cost route.

TABLE 4.202

		To city			
		1	2	3	4
From city	1	0	30	80	50
	2	40	0	140	30
	3	40	50	0	20
	4	70	80	130	0

Solution. This travelling salesman problem can be first solved as assignment problem. If the optimal assignment table also satisfies the additional constraint that no city is to be visited twice before completing the tour of all the cities, it is also the optimal solution to the given travelling salesman problem. If it does not, it can be adjusted.

As going from city $1 \to 1$, $2 \to 2$, etc. is not allowed, assign a large penalty $c_{ii} = \infty$ to these cells in table 4.184. The resulting table will have all diagonal elements ∞. Subtract the smallest element of each row from all the elements of the row and, if necessary, the smallest element of each column from all the elements of the column. This yields tables 4.203 and 4.204.

TABLE 4.203

	1	2	3	4
1	∞	0	50	20
2	10	∞	110	0
3	20	30	∞	0
4	0	10	60	∞

Reduced matrix with zero in every row

→

TABLE 4.204

	1	2	3	4
1	∞	0	0	20
2	10	∞	60	0
3	20	30	∞	0
4	0	10	10	∞

Reduced matrix with zero in every row and column

Check if optimal assignment can be made in the current reduced matrix. This is shown in table 4.205 through 4.207.

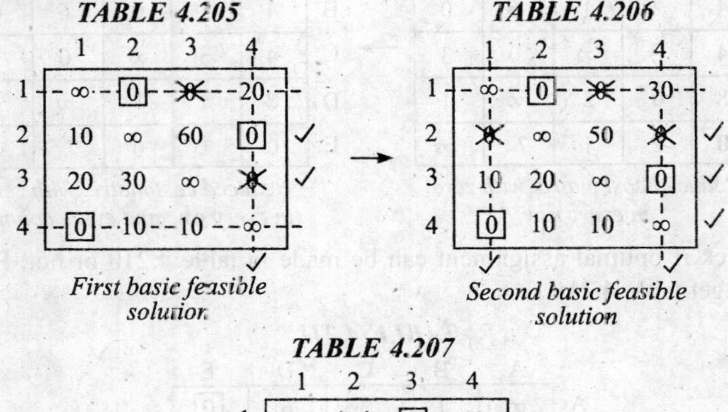

TABLE 4.205

	1	2	3	4	
1	∞	[0]	×	20	
2	10	∞	60	[0]	✓
3	20	30	∞	×	✓
4	[0]	10	10	∞	
				✓	

First basic feasible solution

→

TABLE 4.206

	1	2	3	4	
1	∞	[0]	×	30	
2	×	∞	50	×	✓
3	10	20	∞	[0]	✓
4	[0]	10	10	∞	✓
	✓			✓	

Second basic feasible solution

TABLE 4.207

	1	2	3	4
1	∞	×	[0]	40
2	[0]	∞	40	×
3	10	10	∞	[0]
4	×	[0]	×	∞

Optimal solution

Table 4.207 provides an optimal solution to the assignment problem. According to it the salesman should visit city 1 → 3 → 4 → 2 → 1 and this involves a cost of ₹ (80 + 20 + 80 + 40) = ₹ 220. This solution also satisfies the additional constraint of the travelling salesman problem. Thus the least cost route is 1 → 3 → 4 → 2 → 1 at a cost of ₹ 220.

EXAMPLE 4.10-2

A salesman wants to visit cities A, B, C, D and E. He does not want to visit any city twice before completing his tour of all the cities and wishes to return to the point of starting journey. Cost of going from one city to another (in rupees) is shown in table 4.208. Find the least cost route.

TABLE 4.208

	A	*B*	*C*	*D*	*E*
A	*0*	*2*	*5*	*7*	*1*
B	*6*	*0*	*3*	*8*	*2*
C	*8*	*7*	*0*	*4*	*7*
D	*12*	*4*	*6*	*0*	*5*
E	*1*	*3*	*2*	*8*	*0*

[*R.T.M. Nagpur U.B.E. (Mech.) 2011; D.U. MBA, 2000; P.U.B.E.(Mech.) Nov., 2002; B.E.(Prod.) 2001*]

Solution

Method 1. As going from A → A, B → B, etc. is not allowed, assign a large penalty (cost of journey), for these cells in the cost matrix. The problem is first solved as an assignment problem. If this optimal solution also satisfies the additional constraint, it is also the optimal solution to the given problem; if not, it can be adjusted by inspection. Reduce the cost matrix by subtracting the lowest element in each row from all the elements of the row. Then subtract the lowest element in each column (if required) from all the elements of the column till there is zero in every row and every column. Tables 4.209 and 4.210 result.

TABLE 4.209

	A	B	C	D	E
A	∞	1	4	6	0
B	4	∞	1	6	0
C	4	3	∞	0	3
D	8	0	2	∞	1
E	0	2	1	7	∞

Reduced cost matrix with zero in every row

→

TABLE 4.210

	A	B	C	D	E
A	∞	1	3	6	0
B	4	∞	0	6	0
C	4	3	∞	0	3
D	8	0	1	∞	1
E	0	2	0	7	∞

Reduced cost matrix with zero in every row and every column

We now check if optimal assignment can be made in table 4.210 or not. Proceeding as in example 4.6-2 we get table 4.211.

TABLE 4.211

	A	B	C	D	E
A	∞	1	3	6	[0]
B	4	∞	[0]	6	~~0~~
C	4	3	∞	[0]	3
D	8	[0]	1	∞	1
E	[0]	2	~~0~~	7	∞

This table provides an optimum solution to the assignment problem but not to the travelling salesman problem as it gives *A → E, E → A, B → C, C → D, D → B* as the solution which means that the salesman should go from A to E and then come back to *A* without visiting cities *B, C* and *D*. This violates the additional constraint that the salesman is not to visit any city twice before completing his tour of all the cities. Therefore, we now try to find *the next best solution* that also satisfies this additional constraint. The next minimum (non-zero) element in the matrix is 1. So, we shall try to bring element 1 into the solution. However, this element 1 occurs in three different cells. We shall consider all the three cases until an acceptable solution is obtained.

Case 1. We make 'unity assignment' in cell (*A, B*) instead of zero assignment in cell (*A, E*). Accordingly, zero assignment in cell (*D, B*) is changed to 'unity assignment' in cell (*D, E*). The resulting table is shown below.

TABLE 4.212

	A	B	C	D	E
A	∞	[1]	3	6	~~0~~
B	4	∞	[0]	6	~~0~~
C	4	3	∞	[0]	3
D	8	~~0~~	1	∞	[1]
E	[0]	2	~~0~~	7	∞

The resulting feasible solution is A → B, B → C, C → D, D → E, E → A and it involves a cost of ₹ (2 + 3 + 4 + 5 + 1) = ₹ 15.

Case 2. In table 4.211 we make 'unity assignment' in cell (D, C) instead of zero assignment in cell (D, B). As a result we have to make assignments in cell (B, E) instead of cell (B, C) and in cell (A, B) instead of cell (A, E). Table 4.213 is obtained.

TABLE 4.213

	A	B	C	D	E
A	∞	[1]	3	6	~~0~~
B	4	∞	~~0~~	6	[0]
C	4	3	∞	[0]	3
D	8	~~0~~	[1]	∞	1
E	[0]	2	~~0~~	7	∞

The resulting solution is A → B → E → A, C → D → C, which is not feasible as it does not satisfy the additional constraint.

Case 3. In table 4.211 we make 'unity assignment' in cell (D, E) instead of zero assignment in cell (D, B). Accordingly, zero assignment in cell (A. E) is changed to 'unity assignment' in cell (A, B). The resulting table is same as table 4.194 which gives the feasible solution A →B, B → C, C → D, D → E, E → A with a cost ₹ 15. Hence the least cost route is A → B → C → D → E → A with cost of ₹ 15.

Method 2. The problem is first solved by the Hungarian method. The optimal solution for the equivalent assignment problem is given in table 4.211. The assignments are A → E → A; B → C → D → B and they involve a cost of ₹ (1 + 3 + 4 + 4 + 1) = ₹ 13. In this assignment we have, two separate circuits which does not meet the condition of having one closed circuit (path). Somehow we should link the two circuits with the least increase in cost. The two circuits are

B ⟶ C ⟶ D   A ⟶ E

The two circuits may be combined as shown below. We should squeeze the link A – E in between B – C or C – D or D – B so as to have a single circuit.

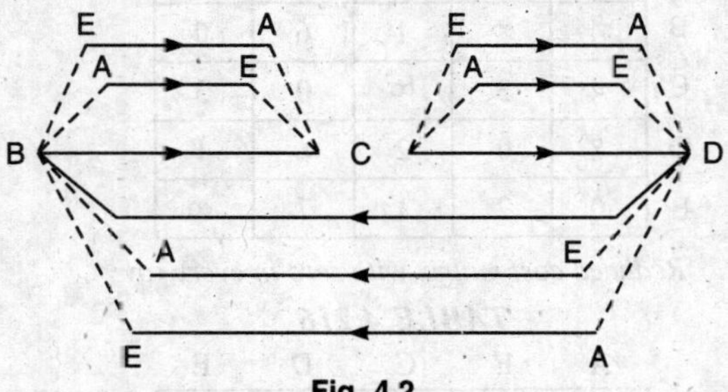

Fig. 4.2

Now the least extra cost on the dotted routes will have to be chosen to find the minimum further cost to be paid to meet the additional constraint. So we compute for each alternative the extra cost from the final optimal table 4.211:

BA and EC : 4 + 0 = 4,
BE and AC : 0 + 3 = 3,
CA and ED : 4 + 7 = 11,
CE and AD : 3 + 6 = 9,
DE and AB : 1 + 1 = 2,
DA and EB : 8 + 2 = 10.

Thus among the various ways of breaking a chain and linking, the combination of DE and AB gives the lowest increase of ₹ 2. Therefore, we will use this link in order to make one complete circuit and the cost will increase by ₹ 2. Thus the travelling salesman should follow the route B → C → D → E → A → B involving a total cost of ₹ (13 + 2) = ₹ 15. Since the salesman has to visit all the 5 cities, the shortest cost route will be independent of the starting city and, therefore, the lowest cost route can be said to be A → B → C → D → E → A.

Method 3. The iterative procedure developed by Little, Musty, Sweeney and Karel (1963) will be used to solve this problem. This is called the *Little's method* or *the Branch and Bound method.* This method consists of the following steps:

Step 1

(*i*) As going from A → A, B → B, etc. is not allowed, assign a large penalty (cost of journey), ∞ for these cells in the cost matrix, which we shall call set S. We get table 4.214 shown below representing the cost matrix (C_{ij}).

TABLE 4.214

	A	B	C	D	E
A	∞	2	5	7	1
B	6	∞	3	8	2
C	8	7	∞	4	7
D	12	4	6	∞	5
E	1	3	2	8	∞

Cost matrix (C_{ij})

(*ii*) *Reduce the matrix:* Subtract the lowest element in each row from all the elements of the row. Then subtract the lowest element in each column (if required) from all the elements of the column, till there is a zero in every row and every column. The total reduction *r* is the sum of the elements subtracted. We call the resulting matrix as (C'_{ij}).

TABLE 4.215

	A	B	C	D	E
A	∞	1	4	6	0
B	4	∞	1	6	0
C	4	3	∞	0	3
D	8	0	2	∞	1
E	0	2	1	7	∞

Reduced cost matrix with zero in every row

TABLE 4.216

	A	B	C	D	E
A	∞	1	3	6	0
B	4	∞	0	6	0
C	4	3	∞	0	3
D	8	0	1	∞	1
E	0	2	0	7	∞

Reduced cost matrix (C'_{ij}) *with zero in every row and every column*

∴ Total reduction $r = (1 + 2 + 4 + 4 + 1) + 1 = 12 + 1 = 13.$

Step 2

Find the penalty of *not using* each zero cell in (C'_{ij}). We argue that if we do not use the link (h, k), we must use other element in row h and some element in column k. Thus the cost of not using (h, k) is at least equal to the sum of the smallest element in row h and the smallest element in column k. These penalties have been recorded in the top left corners of the zero cells in table 4.217.

TABLE 4.217

	A	B	C	D	E
A	∞	1	3	6	(1) 0
B	4	∞	(0) 0	6	(0) 0
C	4	3	∞	(9) ✓ 0	3
D	8	(2) 0	1	∞	1
E	(4) 0	2	(0) 0	7	∞

For example, consider zero in cell (A, E). The sum of smallest elements in row A and column E [excluding zero in cell (A, E)] is 1 + 0 = 1. For cell (B, C), the sum is = 0 + 0 = 0 and for cell (C, D), the sum is = 3 + 6 = 9 and so on.

Step 3

Let (h, k) be the zero entry with the highest penalty. In case of tie, select arbitrarily. We now divide the given set S into two subsets: S (h, k) which contains the link (h, k) and S $\overline{(h, k)}$, which does not contain the link (h, k). We next calculate *lower bounds* on the costs of all routes in each subset.

We know that if (h, k) is not used, in addition to the reduction r, there will be cost of at least P_{hk}. Therefore, the lower bound $\theta\,\overline{(h, k)}$ is given by

$$\theta\,\overline{(h, k)} = r + P_{hk}.$$

In the present example r = 13 and P_{cd} = 9. ∴ $\theta\,\overline{(C, D)}$ = 13 + 9 = 22.

∴ Total cost of the *route not containing the highest penalty link* = $\theta\,\overline{(C, D)}$ = 22.

Step 4

Find the total cost of route containing the highest penalty link *i.e.*, lower bound for S (h, k). This is done as follows:

We observe that if we use the link (h, k), we cannot use the link (k, h); for, if we use (h, k) and (k, h) we would go from h to k and back to h without visiting other cities. We avoid the use of (k, h) by assigning a very heavy cost *i.e.*, $C'_{kh} = \infty$. Moreover, if we use (h, k) we will not use any other link in row h and column k. This is ensured by deleting row h and column k. In the remaining matrix we select our element from each row and column so that the cost will be at least the amount by which the remaining matrix can be reduced. Let this be r_{hk}. Then the lower bound θ (h, k) for S (h, k) is given by $\theta(h, k) = r + r_{hk}$.

In the example, $C'_{DC} = \infty$ and we delete row C and column D. The resulting matrix (Table 4.219) can be reduced by only zero, giving θ (C, D) = 13 + 0 = 13.

The results obtained in steps 3 and 4 are recorded in figure 4.3.

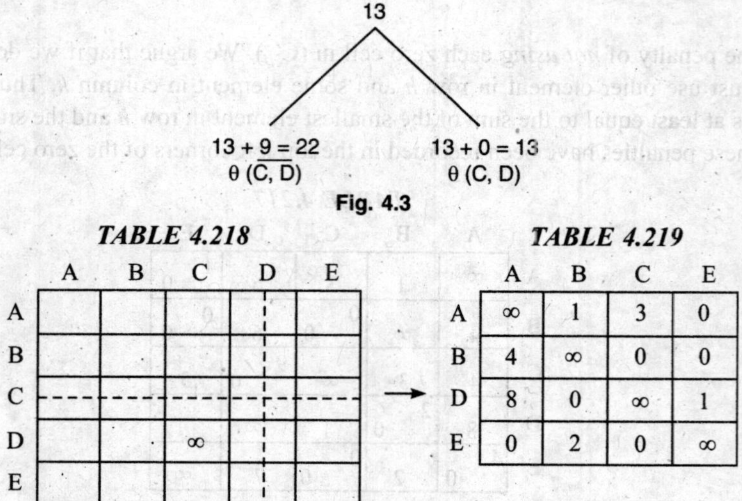

Fig. 4.3

TABLE 4.218

	A	B	C	D	E
A					
B					
C					
D			∞		
E					

TABLE 4.219

	A	B	C	E
A	∞	1	3	0
B	4	∞	0	0
D	8	0	∞	1
E	0	2	0	∞

Step 5

Find out of θ ($\overline{C, D}$) and θ (C, D), the one which is lower for further partitioning the subset S (*h*, *k*). If θ (C, D) is lower, return to step 2 and repeat it on the cost matrix obtained in step 4 (Table 4.219). If θ ($\overline{C, D}$) is chosen, return to the original reduced matrix (or step 1), put cost in cell (C, D) = ∞ and repeat the steps from 2 onwards.

In the example, θ (C, D) is chosen as it is lower. Applying step 2 we get table 4.220 in which penalties have been recorded in the top left corners of cells with zero entries.

TABLE 4.220

	A	B	C	E
A	∞	1	3	(1) 0
B	4	∞	(0) 0	(0) 0
D	8	(2) 0	∞	1
E	(4) ✓0	2	(0) 0	∞

Step 6

Cell (E, A) has the highest penalty of 4. We, now, divide the subset S (*h*, *k*) into two parts, one containing the cell (E, A) and the other not containing the cell (E, A) and calculate lower bounds on the costs of all routes in each part.

Total cost of route not containing the highest penalty link = θ ($\overline{E, A}$) = 13 + 4 = 17.

Step 7

Find the total cost of route containing the highest penalty link. This is done as follows: if we can use the link (E, A), we cannot use the link (A, E). Thus we put $C'_{AE} = \infty$ and delete row E and column A. In the remaining matrix we select one element from each row and column so that the cost will be at least the amount by which the remaining matrix can be reduced.

In the present example, lower bound for the matrix of table 4.219 *i.e.*, the total cost of route containing the highest penalty link (E, A) is = θ (E, A) = 13 + 1 = 14, as the resulting matrix (Table 4.221) can be reduced by 1 in row A.

The results obtained in steps 6 and 7 are recorded in figure 4.4 and tables 4.221 and 4.222.

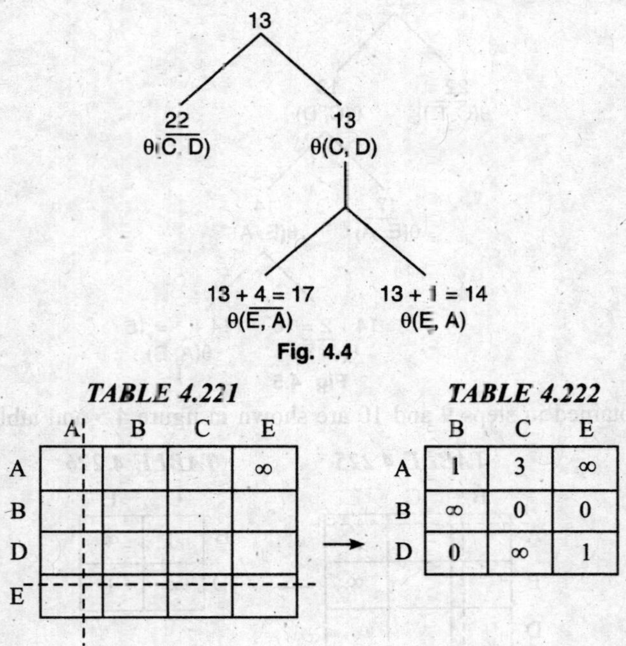

Fig. 4.4

TABLE 4.221

	A	B	C	E
A				∞
B				
D				
E				

TABLE 4.222

	B	C	E
A	1	3	∞
B	∞	0	0
D	0	∞	1

Step 8

Choose out of θ (E, A), and θ (E, A), the one which is lower.

Since θ (E, A) is lower, we return to step 2 and repeat it on the cost matrix obtained in step 7 (Table 4.222), after reducing it so that each row and column contains zero entry (Table 4.223) cell. Penalties have been recorded in the top left corners of the cells with zero entries in table 4.224.

TABLE 4.223

	B	C	E
A	0	2	∞
B	∞	0	0
D	0	∞	1

→

TABLE 4.224

	B	C	E
A	[2] ✓0	2	∞
B	∞	[2] 0	[1] 0
D	[1] 0	∞	1

Step 9

Cell (A, B) has the highest penalty of 2 [cell (B, C) also has the same penalty of 2; out of these two cells, we choose cell (A, B) arbitrarily].

∴ Cost of route not containing the cell (A, B); $\theta\,(\overline{A, B}) = 14 + 2 = 16.$

Step 10

If we use the link (A, B), we have the chain (E, A), (A, B). Hence we must exclude the link (B, E). Thus we put $C'_{BE} = \infty$. We delete row A and column B. The resulting matrix (Table 4.226) can be reduced by 1.

∴ Cost of route containing the cell (A, B); θ (A, B) = 14 + 1 = 15.

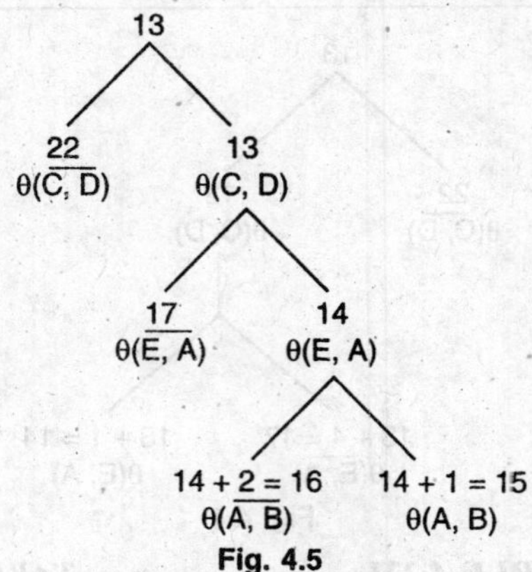

Fig. 4.5

The results obtained in steps 9 and 10 are shown in figure 4.5 and tables 4.225 and 4.226.

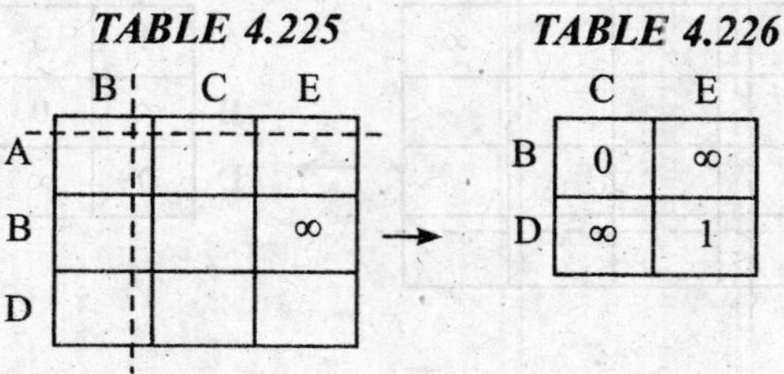

TABLE 4.225

	B	C	E
A			
B			∞
D			

→

TABLE 4.226

	C	E
B	0	∞
D	∞	1

Step 11

Reduce the matrix of step 10 so that each row and each column has at least one zero entry cell. This is shown in table 4.227.

TABLE 4.227

	C	E
B	∞ ✓ 0	∞
D	∞	∞ 0

Penalties are recorded on the top left corners of the cells containing zero entries in table 4.209.

Step 12

Let us choose cell (B, C) containing a penalty of ∞.

∴ Cost of route not containing the cell (B, C) *i.e.*, θ $(\overline{B, C})$ = 15 + ∞ = ∞.

Step 13

Delete row B and column C and we get table 4.228.

TABLE 4.228

	C	E
B		
D		0

Cost of route containing cell (B, C) *i.e.*, θ (B, C) = 15 + 0 = 15.

The results of steps 12 and 13 are shown in figure 4.6.

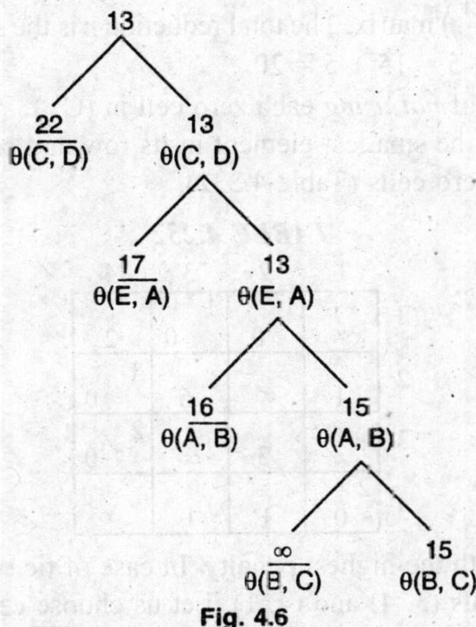

Fig. 4.6

∴ The least cost route is C → D → E → A → B → C.

Total cost of journey = cell (C, D) + cell (D, E) + cell (E, A) + cell (A, B) + cell (B, C)

= ₹ (4 + 5 + 1 + 2 + 3) = ₹ 15.

EXAMPLE 4.10-3

A salesman wants to visit cities 1, 2, 3 and 4. He does not want to visit any city twice before completing the tour of all the cities and wishes to return to his home city, the starting station. Cost of going from one city to another in rupees is given in table 4.229. Find the least cost route by the branch and bound method.

TABLE 4.229

From city \ To city	*1*	*2*	*3*	*4*
1	–	*3*	*8*	*5*
2	*4*	–	*14*	*3*
3	*4*	*5*	–	*2*
4	*7*	*8*	*13*	–

[*H.P.U.B.Tech. (Mech.) June, 2007; P.U.B.E. (T.I.T) Nov., 2006; B.E. (Mech.) Nov., 2006*]

Solution. 1. *Reduce the matrix:* As going from 1 → 1, 2 → 2, etc. is not allowed, assign a large penalty cost $C_{ii} = \infty$ to these cells in table 4.229. Performing row reduction and then column reduction, tables 4.230 and 4.231 are obtained.

TABLE 4.230

	1	2	3	4
1	∞	0	5	2
2	1	∞	11	0
3	2	3	∞	0
4	0	1	6	∞

Reduced matrix with zero in every row

→

TABLE 4.231

	1	2	3	4
1	∞	0	0	2
2	1	∞	6	0
3	2	3	∞	0
4	0	1	1	∞

Reduced matrix with zero in every row and every column

Table 4.231 represents (C'_{ij}) matrix. The total reduction r is the sum of the elements subtracted.

$\therefore r = (3 + 3 + 2 + 7) + 5 = 15 + 5 = 20.$

2. Calculate the penalty of *not using* each zero cell in (C'_{ij}). Penalty of not using a zero cell is at least equal to the sum of the smallest element in its row and column. Record these penalties in the top left corners of the zero cells (Table 4.232).

TABLE 4.232

	1	2	3	4
1	∞	^{1} 0	^{1} 0	2
2	1	∞	6	^{1} 0
3	2	3	∞	^{2} ✓ 0
4	^{2} 0	1	1	∞

3. Select the zero cell with the highest penalty. In case of tie select arbitrarily. In the present example there is tie among cells (3, 4) and (4, 1). Let us choose cell (3, 4). Divide the given set S into two subsets: S (3, 4) containing the cell (3, 4) and $S(\overline{3, 4})$ not containing the cell (3, 4). Next calculate *lower bounds* on the costs of all routes in each subset.

The lower bound $\theta(\overline{3, 4})$ if cell (3, 4) is not used = r + maximum penalty = 20 + 2 = 22.

∴ Cost of the route *not containing* the highest penalty link, $\theta(\overline{3, 4}) = 22$.

4. Find the cost of the route *containing* the highest penalty link, θ (3, 4). The method to obtain it is described below:

If we use link (h, k), we cannot use the link (k, h); because if we use (h, k) and (k, h) both, it amounts to going from h to k and then back to h without visiting other cities. The use of (k, h) is avoided by assigning it a very heavy cost, *i.e.*, $C'_{kh} = \infty$. Further, if we use link (3, 4), we will not use any other link in row 3 and column 4. This is ensured by deleting row 3 and column 4. Also we find the cost at which the matrix can be reduced. Then,

$$\theta\,(3, 4) = r + \text{cost of reducing the matrix.}$$

Substituting $C'_{43} = \infty$ and deleting row 3 and column 4, we find that the matrix (Table 4.234) can be reduced by 1 in row 2.

∴ Lower bound θ (3, 4) = 20 + 1 = 21.

The results obtained is steps 3 and 4 are shown in Fig. 4.7 and tables 4.233 and 4.234.

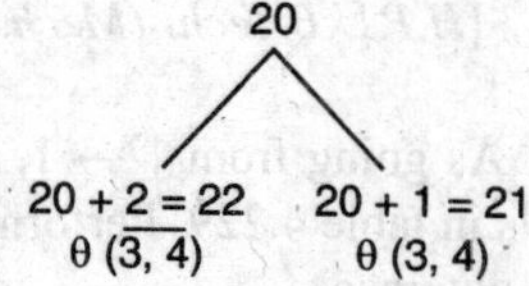

Fig. 4.7

TABLE 4.233

	1	2	3	4
1				
2				
3				
4			∞	

→

TABLE 4.234

	1	2	3
1	∞	0	0
2	1	∞	6
4	0	1	∞

Table 4.234 does not contain zero in every row. Table 4.235 is obtained by subtracting minimum element 1 from elements of row 2.

TABLE 4.235

	1	2	3
1	∞	$^{1}0$	$^{5}0$ ✓
2	$^{5}0$	∞	5
4	$^{1}0$	1	∞

5. Select out of $\theta(\overline{3, 4})$ and θ (3, 4), the one which is smaller for further partitioning the subset (h, k). If θ (3, 4) is smaller, return to step 2 and apply it to the cost matrix obtained in step 4 (Table 4.234). If $\theta(\overline{3, 4})$ is smaller, return to the original reduced matrix of step 1, assign cost to cell (3, 4) = ∞ and repeat steps 2 onwards.

Here θ (3, 4) is chosen since it is lower. Apply step 2 to table 4.235 to record penalties of zero cells. There is tie among cells (1, 3) and (2, 1). We arbitrarily choose cell (1, 3). Since $\theta(3,4)$ is lower, further branching will emerge from leg or link θ (3, 4).

6. Cell (1, 3) has the highest penalty of 5. Subset (h, k) is now divided into two parts, one containing the cell (1, 3) and the other not containing the cell (1, 3). Lower bounds are then calculated on the costs of all the routes in each part.

Total cost of route not containing the link (1, 3) = $\theta(\overline{1, 3})$ = 21 + 5 = 26.

7. Find the total cost of route containing the highest penalty link (1, 3). This is obtained as follows:

If we choose link (1, 3), we cannot choose link (3, 1). Thus we should put $C'_{31} = \infty$ and delete row 1 and column 3. However, there is actually no need of putting $C'_{31} = \infty$ as cell (3, 1) does not exist in table 4.235.

Referring to table 4.235, the total cost of route containing the link (1, 3) = 21 + 1 = 22, since the matrix 4.237 can be reduced only by 1 in column 2.

The results obtained in steps 6 and 7 are recorded in Fig. 4.8 and tables 4.236 and 4.237.

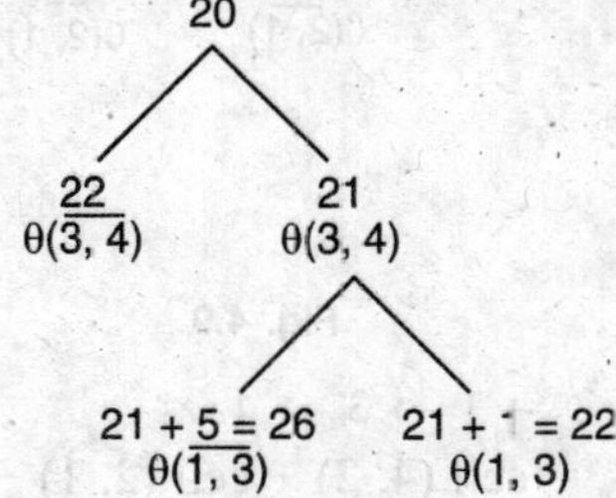

Fig. 4.8

TABLE 4.236

	1	2	3
1			
2			
4			

→

TABLE 4.237

	1	2
2	0	∞
4	0	1

8. Choose out of $\theta(\overline{1, 3})$ and θ (1, 3), the one which is lower for further branching. Reduce table 4.237 by subtracting element 1 from the elements of column 2. This is shown in table 4.238. Penalties have been recorded in the top left corners of the zero cells.

TABLE 4.238

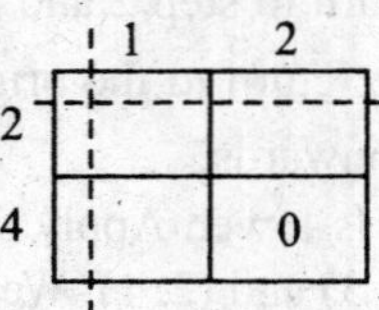

	1	2
2	∞ ✓ 0	∞
4	0 0	∞ 0

9. There is tie among cells (2, 1) and (4, 2); we choose cell (2, 1) arbitrarily.

Cost of route not containing the cell (2, 1); $\theta(\overline{2,1}) = 22 + \infty = \infty$.

10. Delete row 2 and column 1 and we get table 4.239.

TABLE 4.239

	1	2
2		
4		0

Cost of route containing the cell (2, 1); θ (2, 1) = 22 + 0 = 22.

The results of steps 9 and 10 are shown in Fig. 4.9. After deleting row 2 and column 1, we are left with only one choice, *i.e.*, cell (4, 2).

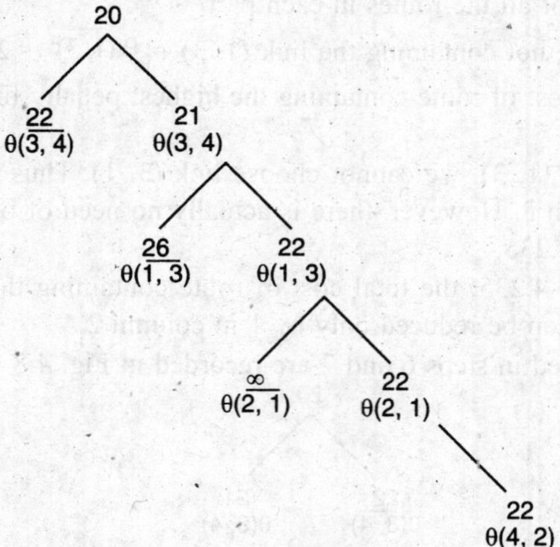

Fig. 4.9

∴ Least cost route is 4 → 2 → 1 → 3 → 4.

Total cost of the journey = cell (4, 2) + cell (2, 1) + cell (1, 3) + cell (3, 4)

= 8 + 4 + 8 + 2 = 22.

EXAMPLE 4.10-4

Products 1, 2, 3, 4 and 5 are to be processed on a machine. The setup costs in rupees per change depend upon the product presently on the machine and the set-up to be made and are given by the following data:

$C_{12} = 16$, $C_{13} = 4$, $C_{14} = 12$, $C_{23} = 6$, $C_{34} = 5$, $C_{25} = 8$, $C_{35} = 6$, $C_{45} = 20$; $C_{ij} = C_{ji}$, $C_{ij} = \infty$ *for all values of i and j not given in the data. Find the optimum sequence of products in order to minimize the total set-up cost.* [*G.N.D.U. B.Com. April, 2013*]

Solution. Determination of optimum order of processing the products so that the set-up costs are minimum is a travelling salesman problem. The set-up (changeover) costs between the products are analogous to distances between the cities. Each product must be produced only once and the production must return to the first product.

We first begin to solve this problem as an assignment problem. The given data are expressed in the form of a table (Table 4.240).

TABLE 4.240

	1	2	3	4	5
1	∞	16	4	12	∞
2	16	∞	6	∞	8
3	4	6	∞	5	6
4	12	∞	5	∞	20
5	∞	8	6	20	∞

Hungarian method or reduced matrix method will be used to obtain optimal assignment. This method consists of the following steps:

Step I

Prepare a Square Matrix: This step is not necessary in this example.

Step II

Reduce the Matrix: Proceeding as in example 4.6-2, we get table 4.241.

TABLE 4.241

	1	2	3	4	5
1	∞	12	0	8	∞
2	10	∞	0	∞	2
3	0	2	∞	1	2
4	7	∞	0	∞	15
5	∞	2	0	14	∞

Matrix after substep I (Contains zero in each row)

After substep 2 we get the following matrix:

TABLE 4.242

	1	2	3	4	5
1	∞	10	0	7	∞
2	10	∞	0	∞	0
3	0	0	∞	0	0
4	7	∞	0	∞	13
5	∞	0	0	13	∞

Matrix after substep 2 (Contains zero in each row and in each column) Initial feasible solution

Step III

Check if Optimal Assignment can be made in the Current Feasible Solution or not

Proceeding as in example 4.6-2 we get

TABLE 4.243

	1	2	3	4	5	
1	∞	10	[0]	7	∞	✓
2	10	∞	~~0~~	∞	[0]	
3	[0]	~~0~~	∞	~~0~~	~~0~~	
4	7	∞	~~0~~	∞	13	✓
5	∞	[0]	~~0~~	13	∞	
			✓			

As the minimum number of lines crossing all zeros is 4 *i.e.*, less than 5, optimal assignment cannot be made in the current feasible solution.

Step IV

Iterate towards an Optimal Solution

Proceeding as in example 4.6-2 we get

TABLE 4.244

	1	2	3	4	5
1	∞	3	0	0	∞
2	10	∞	7	∞	0
3	0	0	∞	0	0
4	0	∞	0	∞	6
5	∞	0	7	13	∞

Second feasible solution

Step V

Check if Optimal Assignment can be made in the Current Feasible Solution or not

TABLE 4.245

	1	2	3	4	5
1	∞	3	[0]	~~0~~	∞
2	10	∞	7	∞	[0]
3	~~0~~	~~0~~	∞	[0]	~~0~~
4	[0]	∞	~~0~~	∞	6
5	∞	[0]	7	13	∞

As there is no row or column without assignment, optimal assignment is possible in the current solution. Table 4.245, however, provides an optimal solution to the assignment problem but not to the given travelling salesman problem (sequencing problem) as it gives $1 \rightarrow 3$, $3 \rightarrow 4$, $4 \rightarrow 1$, $2 \rightarrow 5$ and $5 \rightarrow 2$ as the solution which means that the products should be processed in the order $1 \rightarrow 3 \rightarrow 4 \rightarrow 1$, without processing the products 2 and 5. This violates the additional constraint that each product must be processed only once and only after having processed all the products, the production should return to product 1. So we try to find the *'next best' solution* that also satisfies this additional constraint.

The next minimum (non-zero) element is 3 in cell (1, 2). We make assignment to entry 3 in this cell instead of zero assignment in cell (1, 3). Accordingly, zero assignment in cell (5, 2) is changed to assignment in cell (5, 3) with entry 7. This gives table 4.246.

TABLE 4.246

	1	2	3	4	5
1	∞	[3]	~~0~~	~~0~~	∞
2	10	∞	7	∞	[0]
3	~~0~~	~~0~~	∞	[0]	~~0~~
4	[0]	∞	~~0~~	∞	6
5	∞	~~0~~	[7]	13	∞

The resulting feasible solution 1 – 2, 2 – 5, 5 – 3, 3 – 4, 4 – 1 is also the optimal solution. Thus the optimal sequence for the processing of products is 1 – 2 – 5 – 3 – 4 – 1 and it involves a cost of ₹ (16 + 8 + 5 + 12 + 6) = ₹ 47.

EXERCISES 4.2

1. What is the travelling salesman problem? Which situations can be treated as the travelling salesman problem? How does its solution differ from the solution of the assignment problem?

   [*H.P.U. B.Tech. (Mech.) 2012; Chennai U. B.C.A. Nov., 2010; P.T.U. B. Tech. (Mech.) May, 2012; May, 2011; MBA, 2005; P.U.B.E.(Mech.) Nov., 2006, G.J.U. MBA Nov., 2003*]

2. What is the travelling salesman model? What are its practical applications? Describe the role of branch and bounding to solve the travelling salesman's model.

   [*P.T.U. MBA May, 2001; P.U.B.E.(Prod.) 2001*]

3. What is the travelling salesman problem? What is the current status of the solvability of the travelling salesman problem? What are the problems beling faced in the research?

   [*P.T.U. MBA Sept., 2006; P.U. M.Sc.(I.T.) 2003*]

4. A machine operator processes five types of items on his machine each week and must choose a sequence for them. The setup cost per change depends on the items presently on the machine and the set-up to be made, according to the following table:

TABLE 4.247

From item \ To item	*A*	*B*	*C*	*D*
A	∞	4	7	3
B	4	∞	6	3
C	7	6	∞	7
D	3	3	7	∞

   If he processes each type of item once and only once each week, how should he sequence the items on his machine?

   [*J.N.T.U. Hyderabad B.Tech. Nov., 2010*]

   (*Ans.* A → D → B → C → A and A → C → B → D → A; min. cost = 19.)

5. Given the matrix of set-up costs below, show how to sequence production so as to minimize set-up cost per cycle.

TABLE 4.248

To

From	A	B	C	D	E
A	∞	3	6	2	3
B	3	∞	5	2	3
C	6	5	∞	6	4
D	2	2	6	∞	6
E	3	3	4	6	∞

[*H.P.U. B.Tech. June, 2015; P.U.B. Com. April, 2007; G.N.D.U. B.Com. April, 2006*]

(*Ans.* A → D → B → C → E → A or A → E → C → B → D → A; min. cost = 16.)

6. Solve the travelling salesman problem given by the following data: $C_{12} = 20$, $C_{13} = 4$, $C_{14} = 10$, $c_{23} = 5$, $c_{34} = 6$, $c_{25} = 10$, $c_{35} = 6$, $c_{45} = 20$, where $c_{ij} = c_{ji}$ and there is no route between cities i and j if a value of c_{ij} is not shown.

[*P.U.B.E. (Mech.) 2012*]

(*Ans.* 1 → 3 → 2 → 5 → 4 → 1; 49. Also 1 → 4 → 5 → 2 → 3 → 1; 49.)

7. Find the least cost for the travelling salesman problem shown below.

TABLE 4.249

	P	Q	R	S	T
P	0	12	15	17	11
Q	16	0	13	18	12
R	18	17	0	14	17
S	22	14	16	0	15
T	11	13	12	18	0

[*P.U. B.E.(Mech.) Dec., 1987*]

(*Ans.* 65.)

8. Solve the following travelling salesman problem so as to minimize the cost per cycle:

TABLE 4.250

To city

From city	1	2	3	4	5
1	∞	10	25	25	10
2	1	∞	10	15	2
3	8	9	∞	20	10
4	14	10	24	∞	15
5	10	8	25	27	∞

[*Pbi. U. MCA, 1997*]

(*Ans.* 1 → 5 → 2 → 3 → 4 → 1; 62.)

9. Solve the following travelling salesman problem to minimize the distance (in km) travelled:

TABLE 4.251

To city

From city	A	B	C	D	E
A	–	12	24	25	15
B	6	–	16	18	7
C	10	11	–	18	12
D	14	17	22	–	16
E	12	13	23	25	–

[*ICWA June, 1997*]

(*Ans* A → B → C → D → E → A or A → B → E → C → D → A; 74 km.)

10. A travelling salesman has planned to visit 5 cities. He would like to start from a particular city, visit each city only once and return to the starting city. The travelling cost in rupees is given in the table below. Find the least cost route.

TABLE 4.252

To

From	A	B	C	D	E
A	–	7	5	3	5
B	7	–	8	4	3
C	5	8	–	6	2
D	3	4	6	–	2
E	5	3	2	2	–

[*IGNOU MCA, 2001*]

(*Ans.* A → D → B → E → C → A or A → C → E → B → D → A; ₹ 17.)

11. For the matrix shown below find the least cost route for the travelling salesman problem:

TABLE 4.253

To city

From city	1	2	3	4	5	6
1	∞	12	7	6	5	5
2	9	∞	13	5	13	10
3	6	13	∞	7	10	8
4	4	9	10	∞	6	9
5	5	13	7	6	∞	4
6	5	11	9	6	5	∞

[*P.U.B.E.(Mech.) 2001*]

(*Ans.* 5 – 3 – 2 – 4 – 1 – 6 – 5; ₹ 39.)

12. A sales girl is scheduled to visit six different cities A, B, C, D, E and F. The distance matrix in kilometres for all the cities is given below:

TABLE 4.254

To

From	A	B	C	D	E	F
A	–	139	112	110	132	112
B	139	–	122	105	109	110
C	112	122	–	117	126	108
D	110	105	117	–	134	111
E	132	109	126	134	–	118
F	112	110	108	111	118	–

She plans to start her journey from city A and to return to this city after visiting all the cities without visiting any city more than once. Find the sequence of the cities for her visit programme for minimum total distance travelled. What is the total distance travelled?

[*P.U.B.E.(Mech.) 1998*]

13. Six different jobs J_1, J_2, J_3, J_4, J_5 and J_6 are to be worked on a machine tool capable of having different fixtures for different jobs. The setting time for each job depends on the job preceding it. This being so, a sequence of jobs is to be decided which gives the total minimum elapsed time. It is necessary that a job once undertaken will not be handled again till all other jobs are finished. The setting times are given below:

TABLE 4.255

Next jobs

Jobs before	J_1	J_2	J_3	J_4	J_5	J_6
J_1	–	17	20	22	6	18
J_2	21	–	18	23	17	16
J_3	23	22	–	19	22	19
J_4	27	19	21	–	20	21
J_5	16	18	17	23	–	17
J_6	18	16	20	24	19	–

[*P.U. B.E.(Mech.) Dec., 1986*]

14. Find the least cost route for the travelling salesman problem shown below:

TABLE 4.256

To city

From city	1	2	3	4	5	6	7
1	∞	8	14	8	6	10	3
2	8	∞	12	7	6	5	5
3	10	9	∞	13	5	13	10
4	7	6	13	∞	7	10	8
5	7	4	9	10	∞	6	9
6	8	5	13	7	6	∞	4
7	4	5	11	9	6	5	∞

[*P.U. B.E. (Mech.) May, 1983*]

(*Ans.* 1 → 7 → 2 → 6 → 4 → 3 → 5 → 1; Least Cost = 45.)

15. A machine operator processes 5 types of items on his machine each week, and must choose a sequence for them. The set-up cost per change depends on the item presently on the machine and the set-up to be made according to the table below. If he processes each type once and only once each week, how should he sequence the items on his machine in order to minimize the total set-up cost?

TABLE 4.257

	A	B	C	D	E
A	∞	4	7	3	4
B	4	∞	6	3	4
C	7	6	∞	7	5
D	3	3	7	∞	7
E	4	4	5	7	∞

[*V.T.U. Karnataka B.E. Dec., 2011*]

16. Solve the following travelling salesman problem by branch-and-bound method:

TALE 4.258

	A	B	C	D	E	F
A	–	2	7	1	8	12
B	12	–	6	8	9	10
C	3	11	–	15	7	1
D	12	6	1	–	7	10
E	5	12	13	10	–	4
F	4	7	8	12	15	–

[*R.T.M. Nagpur U.B.E. (Mech.) Sept., 2010*]

17. The expected times required to be taken by a salesman in travelling from one city to another are given in the table below. How should the salesman plan his trip so that he covers each of these cities not more than once and completes his trip in minimum possible time required for travelling?

TABLE 4.259

To city

		A	B	C	D	E
	A	–	10	13	11	12
	B	10	–	12	10	12
From city	C	13	12	–	13	11
	D	11	10	13	–	10
	E	12	12	11	10	–

[*J.N.T.U. Hyderabad B.Tech. April, 2011*]

18. (a) What is a travelling salesman problem?
    (b) Solve the following travelling salesman problem:

TABLE 4.260

From \ To	A	B	C	D
A	–	46	16	40
B	41	–	50	40
C	82	32	–	60
D	40	40	36	–

[*H.P.U. B.Tech. Nov., 2015; J.N.T.U. Hyderabad B.Tech. June, 2009*]

19. What is a travelling salesman problem ? Solve the following problem:
    You are required to design a complete route for a salesman who begins from city 1. The distances in km between the cities are given in the table.

TABLE 4.261

Form city \ To city	1	2	3	4	5	6
1	–	25	18	35	50	39
2	21	–	28	16	30	13
3	22	28	–	14	16	20
4	35	12	14	–	12	12
5	50	30	16	12	–	8
6	39	15	20	12	7	–

[*Gujrat Technological U.MBA Dec., 2010*]

Sequencing Models and Related Problems

The sequencing problem involves the determination of an optimal order or sequence of performing a series of jobs by a number of facilities (that are arranged in a specific order) so as to optimize the total time or cost. Sequencing problems may be classified into two groups :

1. In the first group, there are n different jobs to be performed, where each job requires processing on some or all of m different types of machines. The order in which these machines are to be used for processing each job (for example, each job is to be processed first on machine A, then on B and thereafter on C *i.e.* in the order ABC) is given. Also, the expected or actual processing time of each job on each machine is known. We can also determine the effectiveness for any given sequence of jobs at each of the machines and we wish to select from the $(n!)^m$ *theoretically feasible* alternatives, the one which is both *technologically feasible* and optimizes the effectiveness measure (*e.g.* minimizes the total elapsed time from the start of the first job on the first machine to the completion of the last job on the last machine as well as idle time of machines). A technologically feasible sequence is one which satisfies the constraints (if any) on the order in which each job must be performed through the m machines. The technology of manufacturing processes renders many sequences technologically infeasible. For example, a part must be degreased before it is painted; similarly, a hole must be drilled before it is threaded.

Although, theoretically, it is always possible to select the best sequence by testing each one; in practice, it is impossible because of the large number of computations involved. For example, if there are 4 jobs to be processed on each of the 5 machines (*i.e.* $n = 4$ and $m = 5$), the total number of theorically possible different sequences will be $(4!)^5 = 7,962,624$. Of course, as already said, some of them may not be feasible because the required operations must be performed in a specified order. Obviously, any technique which helps us arrive at an optimal (or at least approximately so) sequence without trying all or most of the possibilities will be quite valuable.

2. The second group of problems deals with job shops having a number of machines and a list of tasks to be performed. Each time a task is completed by a machine, the next task to be started on it has got to be decided. Thus the list of tasks will change as fresh orders are received.

Unfortunately, both types of problems are intrinsically difficult. While solutions are possible for some simple cases of the first type, only some empirical rules have been developed for the second type till now.

5.1 SEQUENCING PROBLEMS

In sequencing problems, there are two or more customers to be served (or jobs to be done) and one or more facilities (machines) are available for this purpose. We want to know when each job is to begin and what its due date is. We also want to know which facilities are required to do each job, in which order these facilities are required and how long each operation is to take.

Sequencing problems have been most commonly encountered in 'production shops' where different products are to be processed over various combinations of machines.

It may be noted the sequencing problems can arise even where *one service facility* is involved. Since the total elapsed time (also called makespan) is fixed and equal to the sum of processing times for all the jobs for all possible sequences, some other optimality criteria *e.g.*, minimizing the mean flow time or some function of lateness of the jobs may be applied in such problems.

The various optimality criteria normally resorted to are :

1. Minimizing total elapsed time (or makespan).
2. Minimizing mean flow time (or mean time in the job shop).
3. Minimizing idle time of machines.
4. Minimizing total tardiness : Lateness of a job is defined as the difference between the actual completion time of the job and its due date. If lateness is positive, it is termed as tardiness. Total tardiness is the sum of tardiness over all the jobs in the set.
5. Minimizing number of tardy jobs.
6. Minimizing in-process inventory cost.
7. Minimizing the cost of being late.

A general sequencing problem may be defined as follows :

Let there be n jobs (1, 2, 3, ..., n), each of which has to be processed, one at a time, on each of the m machines (A, B, C, ...). The order of processing each job through the machines is given (for example, job 1 is processed on machines A, C, B, in this order). Also, the time required for processing each job on each machine is given. The problem is to find among $(n!)^m$ *possible sequences, that technologically feasible sequence for processing the jobs which gives the minimum total elapsed time for all the jobs.*

Symbolically,

Let A_i = time required for job i on machine A,

B_i = time required for job i on machine B, etc., and

T = total elapsed time for jobs 1, 2, ..., n *i.e.*, time from start of the first job to completion of the last job.

The problem is to determine a sequence $(i_1, i_2, ..., i_n)$ where $(i_1, i_2, ..., i_n)$ is a permutation of integers (1, 2, ..., n) which will minimize T.

Elements of sequencing problem: The following elements characterise a sequencing problem :

1. *Number of machines*: It refers to the number of service facilities through which a job must pass before it is completed.
2. *Processing order*: It refers to the order in which machines are required for completing the job. If each job is to be proceed first on machine A, then on B and thereafter on C, the processing order is ABC.
3. *Processing time*: It is the time required by a job on each machine.
4. *Idle time*: It is the time for which a machine remains idle during the total elapsed time.
5. *Total elapsed time*: It is the time period from the start of processing of first job on the first machine to the completion of the last job on the last machine. It is equal to processing time plus idle time on each machine.
6. *No passing rule*: No passing means maintaining the order in which jobs are to be processed on two machines. For instance, if n jobs are to be processed on two machines A and B in the order AB, then each job must go first to machine A and then to machine B.

Analytic methods have been developed for solving only five simple cases :

(1) n jobs and one machine A.

(2) n jobs and two machines A and B; all jobs processed in the order, say AB, other limitations described in section 5.4.

(3) n jobs and three machines A, B and C; all jobs processed in the order, say ABC, other limitations described in section 5.5.

(4) two jobs and m machines; each job to be processed through the machines in a prescribed order, not necessarily the same for both jobs.

(5) n jobs and m machines A, B, C, ..., K; all jobs processed in the order, say ABC ... K, other limitations described in section 5.7.

5.2 ASSUMPTIONS IN SEQUENCING PROBLEMS

The following simplifying assumptions are usually made while dealing with sequencing problems :

(*i*) only one operation is carried out on a machine at a particular time.

(*ii*) each operation, once started, must be completed.

(*iii*) an operation must be completed before its succeeding opeation can start.

(*iv*) only one machine of each type is available.

(*v*) a job is processed as soon as possible, but only in the order specified.

(*vi*) processing times are independent of order of performing the operations.

(*vii*) the transportation time *i.e.* the time required to transport jobs from one machine to another is negligible.

(*viii*) jobs are completely known and are ready for processing when the period under consideration starts.

(*ix*) the cost of in-process inventory for each job is same and negligibly small.

5.3 PROCESSING OF *n* JOBS THROUGH ONE MACHINE

The case when a number of jobs is to be processed on a single facility is quite common in actual practice. Some of the examples are : a number of patients waiting for a doctor, a number of programs waiting to get on a computer, a number of cars to be serviced at a service station, a number of different jobs to be machined on a lathe, a number of broken down machines to be repaired by a mechanic and the like.

Since *the total elapsed time* (also called *makespan*) is fixed and equal to the sum of processing times for all the jobs for all possible sequences, some other optimally criteria *e.g.*, minimizing the mean flow time or some function of lateness of the jobs may be applied in such problems.

The various optimally criteria normally resorted to are :

1. Minimizing total elapsed time (or makespan).
2. Minimizing mean flow time (or mean time in the job shop).
3. Minimizing idle time of machines.
4. Minimizing total *tardiness* : Lateness of a job is defined as the difference between the actual completion time of the job and its due date. If lateness is positive, it is termed as tardiness. Total tardiness is the sum of tardiness over all the jobs in the set.
5. Minimizing number of tardy jobs.
6. Minimizing in-process inventory cost.
7. Minimizing the cost of being late.

Consider a *static* job shop wherein n different jobs with known processing times require processing on a single machine. The job shop is static in the sense that any new job that arrives does not disturb the processing of these n jobs. So it is assumed that new job arrivals wait for being considered in the next batch of jobs after the processing of the current n jobs is completed. Let

n = number of different jobs,

t_i = processing time of job i,

W_i = waiting time (before processing) for job i,

F_i = flow time of job $i = W_i + t_i$,

c_i = completion time of job i,
d_i = due date of job i,
L_i = lateness of job $i = c_i - d_i$,
E_i = earliness of job $i = d_i - c_i$,
T_i = tardiness of job i,
and N_T = number of tardy jobs.

A. *Shortest Processing Time (SPT) Rule*

(*a*) Sequencing the jobs in a way that the job with least processing time is picked up first, followed by the one with the next smallest processing time and so on is known as SPT sequencing and achieves the following objectives :

(*i*) minimizing mean waiting time,
(*ii*) minimizing mean flow time,
(*iii*) minimizing mean latesness,
(*iv*) minimizing the mean number of jobs waiting as in-process inventory.

(*b*) In case importance of the jobs varies, a weight w_i is assigned to each job, a larger value indicating greater importance. Processing times are divided by the weights and jobs sequenced in order of increasing $\dfrac{t_i}{w_i}$.

The weighted mean flow time,

$$\text{WMFT} = \frac{\sum_{i=1}^{n} w_i F_i}{\sum_{i=1}^{n} w_i}.$$

This rule is called *weighted shortest processing time* (*WSPT*) *rule.*

EXAMPLE 5.3-1

Six jobs A, B, C, D, E and F have arrived at one time to be processed on a single machine. Assuming that no new jobs arrive thereafter, determine

Job	:	*A*	*B*	*C*	*D*	*E*	*F*
Processing time (minutes)	:	*7*	*6*	*8*	*4*	*3*	*5*

(i) optimal sequence as per SPT rule,
(ii) completion times of the jobs,
(iii) mean flow time,
(iv) average in-process inventory.

Solution

(*i*) As per SPT rule optimal sequence is : E – D – F – B – A – C.

(*ii*) Completion times of the jobs are : 3, 7, 12, 18, 25 and 33 minutes respectively.

(*iii*) Mean flow time is : $\dfrac{3+7+12+18+25+33}{6} = \dfrac{98}{6} = \dfrac{49}{3} = 16.33$ minutes.

(*iv*) Number of jobs waiting as in-process inventory are 6 during time 0–3, 5 during 3–7, 4 during 7–12, 3 during 12–18, 2 during 18–25 and 1 during 25–33 minutes.

$$\therefore \quad \text{Average in-process inventory} = \frac{6\times 3+5\times 4+4\times 5+3\times 6+2\times 7+1\times 8}{3+4+5+6+7+8}$$

$$= \frac{18+20+20+18+14+8}{33} = \frac{98}{33} = 3 \text{ jobs (approx.).}$$

EXAMPLE 5.3-2

Eight jobs 1, 2, ..., 8 are to be processed on a single machine. The processing times, due dates and importance weights of the jobs are represented in table 5.1.

TABLE 5.1

Job	*Processing time* t_i *(minutes)*	*Due date* d_i *(minutes)*	*Importance weight* w_i	$\frac{t_i}{w_i}$
1	*5*	*15*	*1*	*5.0*
2	*8*	*10*	*2*	*4.0*
3	*6*	*15*	*3*	*2.0*
4	*3*	*25*	*1*	*3.0*
5	*10*	*20*	*2*	*5.0*
6	*14*	*40*	*3*	*4.7*
7	*7*	*45*	*2*	*3.5*
8	*3*	*50*	*1*	*3.0*

Assuming that no new jobs arrive thereafter, determine using SPT rule and WSPT rule

(i) optimal sequence,

(ii) completion time of the jobs,

(iii) mean flow time as well as weighted mean flow time,

(iv) average in-process inventory,

(v) lateness, mean lateness and maximum lateness,

(vi) number of jobs actually late.

Solution

1. *SPT Rule*

(*i*) Optimal sequence is 4–8–1–3–7–2–5–6.

(*ii*) Completion times of these jobs are : 3, 6, 11, 17, 24, 32, 42 and 56 minutes respectively.

(*iii*) Mean flow time $= \frac{3+6+11+17+24+32+42+56}{8} = \frac{191}{8} = 23.875$ minutes.

(*iv*) Number of jobs waiting as in-process inventory are 8 during time 0–3, 7 during 3–6, 6 during 6–11, 5 during 11–17, 4 during 17–24, 3 during 24–32, 2 during 32–42 and 1 during 42–56 minutes.

∴ Average in-process inventory

$$= \frac{8\times3+7\times3+6\times5+5\times6+4\times7+3\times8+2\times10+1\times14}{3+3+5+6+7+8+10+14} = \frac{191}{56} = 3.41 \text{ jobs.}$$

(*v*) Lateness of the various jobs is given by :

Job no.	:	4	8	1	3	7	2	5	6
Lateness (minutes)	:	– 22	– 44	– 4	2	– 21	22	22	16

Mean lateness $= \frac{-22-44-4+2-21+22+22+16}{8} = -\frac{29}{8} = -3.625$ minutes.

Maximum lateness = 22 minutes.

(*vi*) Number of jobs actually late = 4.

2. *WSPT Rule*

(*i*) $\frac{t_i}{w_i}$ is calculated for each job and is shown in the last column of table 5.1. The optimal sequence as per non-decreasing $\frac{t_i}{w_i}$ values is 3–4–8–7–2–6–1–5.

(*ii*) Completion times of these jobs are 6, 9, 12, 19, 27, 41, 46 and 56 minutes respectively.

(*iii*) Mean flow time $= \frac{6+9+12+19+27+41+46+56}{8} = 27$ minutes.

Weighted mean flow time $= \frac{3\times6+1\times9+1\times12+2\times19+2\times27+3\times41+1\times46+2\times56}{3+1+1+2+2+3+1+2}$

$= \frac{412}{15} = 27.47$ minutes.

(*iv*) Number of jobs waiting as in-process inventory are 8 during time 0–6, 7 during 6–9, 6 during 9–12, 5 during 12–19, 4 during 19–27, 3 during 27–41, 2 during 41–46 and 1 during 46–56 minutes.

∴ Average in-process inventory

$= \frac{8\times6+7\times3+6\times3+5\times7+4\times8+3\times14+2\times5+1\times10}{6+3+3+7+8+14+5+10} = \frac{216}{56} = 3.86$ jobs.

(*v*) Lateness of the various jobs is given by

Job no.	:	3	4	8	7	2	6	1	5
Lateness (minutes)	:	– 9	– 16	– 38	– 26	17	1	31	36

Mean lateness $= \frac{-9-16-38-26+17+1+31+36}{8} = -\frac{4}{8} = -0.5$ minutes.

Maximum lateness = 36 minutes.

(*vi*) Number of jobs actually late = 4.

B. Earliest Due Date (EDD) Rule

According to this rule jobs are sequenced in the order of non-decreasing due dates. This rule minimizes the maximum job lateness as well as maximum job tardiness. However, this rule tends to make more jobs tardy and increases the mean tardiness.

EXAMPLE 5.3-3

Solve example 5.3-2 by applying EDD rule. Compare the results with those obtained from SPT rule.

Solution

(*i*) Optimal sequence as per EDD rule is 2–1–3–5–4–6–7–8.

(*ii*) Completion times of these jobs are 8, 13, 19, 29, 32, 46, 53 and 56 minutes respectively.

(*iii*) Mean flow time $= \frac{8+13+19+29+32+46+53+56}{8} = \frac{256}{8} = 32$ minutes.

(*iv*) Number of jobs waiting as in-process inventory are 8 during time 0–8, 7 during 8–13, 6 during 13–19, 5 during 19–29, 4 during 29–32, 3 during 32–46, 2 during 46–53 and 1 during 53–56 minutes.

∴ Average in-process inventory

$$= \frac{8\times8+7\times5+6\times6+5\times10+4\times3+3\times14+2\times7+1\times3}{8+5+6+10+3+14+7+3} = \frac{256}{56} = 4.57 \text{ jobs.}$$

(*v*) Lateness of the various jobs is given by :

Job no.	:	1	2	3	4	5	6	7	8
Lateness	:	– 2	– 2	4	7	9	6	8	6

$$\text{Mean lateness} = \frac{-2-2+4+7+9+6+8+6}{8} = \frac{36}{8} = 4.5 \text{ minutes.}$$

Maximum lateness = 9 minutes.

(*vi*) Number of jobs actually late = 6.

Thus EDD rule has reduced the maximum lateness from 22 minutes to 9 minutes. However, it has increased the mean lateness from – 3.625 minutes to 4.5 minutes. Also the number of late jobs has increased from 4 to 6.

C. Slack Time Remaining (STR) Rule

Slack time for a job is defined as the due date of the job minus its processing time. Sequencing the jobs in such a way that the jobs with the least slack time are picked up first for processing, followed by the one with the next smallest slack time and so on is called the slack time remaining (STR) rule.

EXAMPLE 5.3-4

The information regarding jobs to be scheduled through one machine is given below.

Job	:	*A*	*B*	*C*	*D*	*E*	*F*	*G*
Processing time (days)	:	*4*	*12*	*2*	*11*	*10*	*3*	*6*
Due date (days)	:	*20*	*30*	*15*	*16*	*18*	*5*	*9*

(*i*) *What is the first come, first served (FCFS) schedule ?*

(*ii*) *What is the shortest processing time (SPT) schedule ?*

(*iii*) *What is the slack time remaining (STR) schedule ?*

(*iv*) *What is the earliest due date (EDD) schedule ?*

(*v*) *What are the mean flow times for each of the schedules above ?*

Solution

(*i*) *First come, first served schedule*

The FCFS schedule is A → B → C → D → E → F → G and the processing times will be as follows :

Job	*Machine*	
	In	*Out*
A	0	4
B	4	16
C	16	18
D	18	29
E	29	39
F	39	42
G	42	48

(ii) Shortest processing time schedule

The SPT schedule is C → F → A → G → E → D → B and the processing times will be as follows :

Job	*Machine In*	*Machine Out*
C	0	2
F	2	5
A	5	9
G	9	15
E	15	25
D	25	36
B	36	48

(iii) Slack time remaining schedule

Slack time for each job is first calculated as shown below.

Job	*Processig time*, t_i (*days*)	*Due date* d_i (*days*)	*Slack time* (*days*) (d_i–t_i)
A	4	20	16
B	12	30	18
C	2	15	13
D	11	16	5
E	10	18	8
F	3	5	2
G	6	9	3

Accordingly the STR schedule is F → G → D → E → C → A → B and the processing times will be

Job	*Machine In*	*Machine Out*
F	0	3
G	3	9
D	9	20
E	20	30
C	30	32
A	32	36
B	36	48

(iv) Earliest due date (EDD) schedule

The EDD schedule is F → G → C → D → E → A → B and the processing times will be

Job	*Machine In*	*Machine Out*
F	0	3
G	3	9
C	9	11
D	11	22
E	22	32
A	32	36
B	36	48

(*v*) *Mean flow times for the various schedules are*

(*a*) ***FCFS schedule*** : According to this schedule completion times of the jobs are 4, 16, 18, 29, 39, 42 and 48 respectively. Accordingly, mean flow time is

$$= \frac{4+16+18+29+39+42+48}{7} = \frac{196}{7} = 28 \text{ days.}$$

(*b*) ***SPT schedule*** : According to this schedule completion times of the jobs are 2, 5, 9, 15, 25, 36 and 48 respectively. Accordingly mean flow time is

$$= \frac{2+5+9+15+25+36+48}{7} = \frac{140}{7} = 20 \text{ days.}$$

(*c*) ***STR schedule*** : According to this schedule completion of jobs will occur at times 3, 9, 20, 30, 32, 36 and 48 respectively. The mean flow time will be

$$= \frac{3+9+20+30+32+36+48}{7} = \frac{178}{7} = 25.43 \text{ days.}$$

(*d*) ***EDD schedule*** : According to this schedule completion of jobs will occur at times 3, 9, 11, 22, 32, 36 and 48 respectively. The mean flow time will be

$$= \frac{3+9+11+22+32+36+48}{7} = \frac{161}{7} = 23 \text{ days.}$$

5.4 PROCESSING *n* JOBS THROUGH TWO MACHINES

There are n different jobs to be processed on two machines and it is desired to determine the optimal sequence of jobs that minimizes T, the total elapsed time from the start of the first job on first machine to the completion of the last job on second machine. The total elapsed time includes the idle time, if any.

The following conditions are assumed :

(*i*) Only two machines are involved, A and B.

(*ii*) Each job is processed in the order AB *i.e.*, whichever job is processed first on machine A must also be processed first on machine B and so on; no passing being allowed.

(*iii*) Set-up times of machines A and B are independent of the sequence in which the jobs are taken up.

(*iv*) In-process storage space is available and the cost of in-process inventory is either same for each job or is too small to be considered. This, however, is correct only for processes involving short duration. For longer processes, inventory cost must also be considered.

(*v*) Order of completion of jobs has no significance *i.e.*, no job is required more urgently than the other.

(*vi*) The actual or expected processing times $A_1, A_2, ..., A_n; B_1, B_2, ..., B_n$ are known and represented by a table of the type shown below.

TABLE 5.2

Machine times for n jobs and two machines

Job i	*A*	*B*
1	A_1	B_1
2	A_2	B_2
3	A_3	B_3
⋮	⋮	⋮
i	A_i	B_i
⋮	⋮	⋮
n	A_n	B_n

It can be shown that the shortest elapsed time occurs when all jobs are processed on the two machines in the same order. The solution procedure given below (without proof) is due to S.M. Johnson and R. Bellman. It consists of the following steps:

Step 1: Examine the columns of processing times on machines A and B and find the smallest value [Min (A_i, B_i)].

Step 2 : If this value falls in column A, schedule this job first on machine A. If this value falls in column B, schedule this job last on machine A (because of the given order AB). If there are equal minimal values (there is tie) one in each column, schedule the one in the first column first on machine A; and the one in the second column, last on machine A. If both equal values are in the first column (A), select the one with lowest entry in column B first. If the equal values are in the second column (B), select the one with the lowest entry in column A first.

Step 3 : Cross out the job assigned and continue the process (repeat steps 1 and 2), placing the jobs next to first or next to last till all the jobs are scheduled. The resulting sequence will minimize T.

EXAMPLE 5.4-1

A machine operator has to perform two operations, turning and threading, on a number of different jobs. The time required to perform these operations (in minutes) for each job is known. Determine the order in which the jobs should be processed in order to minimize the total time required to turn out all the jobs.

TABLE 5.3

Job	*Time for turning (minutes)*	*Time for threading (minutes)*
1	*3*	*8*
2	*12*	*10*
3	*5*	*9*
4	*2*	*6*
5	*9*	*3*
6	*11*	*1*

Also find the total processing time and idle times for turning and threading operations.

[*V.T.U. Karnataka B.E. June, 2011; J.N.T.U. Hyderabad B.Tech. (C.Sc.) Dec., 2011 ; P.U.B.Com. Sept., 2006*]

Solution

The solution procedure is described below :

By examining the columns, we find the smallest value. It is threading time of 1 minute for job 6 in second column. Thus we schedule job 6 last for turning (and thereafter for threading) as shown below.

					6

The reduced set of processing times becomes

Job	*Turning time (minutes)*	*Threading Time (minutes)*
1	3	8
2	12	10
3	5	9
4	2	6
5	9	3

The smallest value is turning time of 2 minutes for job 4 in first column. Thus we schedule job 4 first as shown below.

4					6

The reduced set of processing times becomes

Job	*Turning time (minutes)*	*Threading Time (minutes)*
1	3	8
2	12	10
3	5	9
5	9	3

There are two equal minimal values : turning time of 3 minutes for job 1 in first column and threading time of 3 minutes for job 5 in second column. According to the rules, job 1 is scheduled next to job 4 and 5 next to job 6 as shown below.

4	1			5	6

The reduced set of processing times becomes

Job	*Turning time (minutes)*	*Threading Time (minutes)*
2	12	10
3	5	9

The smallest value is turning time of 5 minutes for job 3 in first column. Therefore, we schedule job 3, next to job 1 and we get the optimal sequence as

4	1	3	2	5	6

Now we can calculate the elapsed time corresponding to the optimal sequence, using the individual processing times given in the problem. The details are shown in table 5.4.

TABLE 5.4

Job	*Turning operation*		*Threading operation*	
	Time in	*Time out*	*Time in*	*Time out*
4	0	2	2	8
1	2	5	8	16
3	5	10	16	25
2	10	22	25	35
5	22	31	35	38
6	31	42	42	43

Thus the minimum elapsed time is 43 minutes. Idle time for turning operation is 1 minute (from 42nd minute to 43rd minute) and for threading operation is 2 + 4 = 6 minutes (from 0 – 2 and 38 – 42 minutes).

Remarks : 1. Turning operation remains idle for 1 minute if the cycle is repeated because processing in new cycle can start only when the processing of last job of previous cycle is completed *i.e.*, after 43 minutes.

2. A job may be held in inventory before going to a machine. For example, job 1 is free from turning operation after 5th minute and threading operation will start on it after 8th minute. Therefore it will be kept in inventory for 3 minutes. It is assumed that storage space is available and cost of holding inventory for each job is either same or negligible. Similarly, jobs 3, 2 and 5 are held in inventory for 6, 3 and 4 minutes respectively.

3. It may be observed that the total elapsed time is equal to the sum of processing time and idle time of turning operation or threading operation.

4. The total elapsed time can also be calculated using Gantt chart as shown in Fig. 5.1.

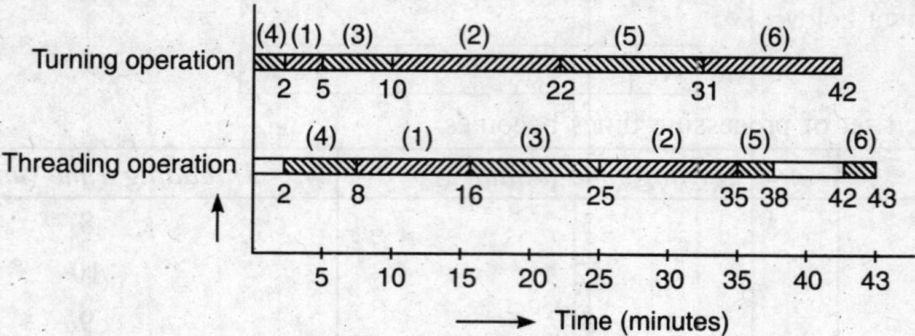

Fig. 5.1. Gantt chart

EXAMPLE 5.4-2

There are seven jobs, each of which has to go through the machines A and B in the order AB. Processing times in hours are given as

Job :	*1*	*2*	*3*	*4*	*5*	*6*	*7*
Machine A :	*3*	*12*	*15*	*6*	*10*	*11*	*9*
Machine B :	*8*	*10*	*10*	*6*	*12*	*1*	*3*

(a) *Determine a sequence of these jobs that will minimize the total elapsed time T. Also find T and idle time for machines A and B.*

[*J.N.T.U. Hyderabad B.Tech. (C.Sc.) Dec., 2011; P.U.B.Com. Jan., 2005*]

(b) *If the order is revised to BA, what difference will it make to the calculated results?*

[*Dayalbagh Edu. Inst. Agra B.Sc. Engg. & M.Tech. Dec., 2012*]

Solution

(a) By examining the processing times we find the smallest value. It is 1 hour for job 6 on machine *B*. Thus we schedule job 6 last on machine *A* as shown below.

					6

The reduced set of processing times becomes

Job :	1	2	3	4	5	7
Machine A :	3	12	15	6	10	9
Machine B :	8	10	10	6	12	3

There are two equal minimal values : processing time of 3 hours for job 1 on machine *A* and processing time of 3 hours for job 7 on machine *B*. According to rules, job 1 is scheduled first and job 7 next to job 6 as shown below.

1					7	6

The reduced set of processing times becomes

Job :	2	3	4	5
Machine A :	12	15	6	10
Machine B :	10	10	6	12

Again there are two equal minimal values : processing time of 6 hours for job 4 on machine *A as well as* on machine *B*. We may choose *arbitrarily* to process (schedule) job 4 *next to job 1 or next to job 7* as shown below.

1	4				7	6

or

1				4	7	6

The reduced set of processing times becomes

Job :	2	3	5
Machine A :	12	15	10
Machine B :	10	10	12

There are three equal minimal values : processing time of 10 hours for job 5 on machine A and for jobs 2 and 3 on machine B. According to rules, job 5 is scheduled next to job 4 in the first schedule or next to job 1 in the second schedule. Job 2 then is scheduled next to job 7 in the first schedule or next to job 4 in the second schedule. The optimal sequences are shown below.

1	4	5	3	2	7	6

or

1	5	3	2	4	7	6

Now we can calculate the elapsed time corresponding to either of the optimal sequences, using the individual processing times given in the problem. The elapsed time and idle times for machines A and B will be same for either sequence. The details corresponding to the first schedule are shown in table 5.5.

TABLE 5.5

Job	*Machine A*		*Machine B*		*Idle for machine B*
	Time in	*Time out*	*Time in*	*Time out*	
1	0	3	3	11	3
4	3	9	11	17	0
5	9	19	19	31	2
3	19	34	34	44	3
2	34	46	46	56	2
7	46	55	56	59	0
6	55	66	66	67	7

Thus the minimum elapsed time is 67 hours. Idle time for machine A is 1 hour (66th-67th hour) and for machine B is 17 hours.

(b) Problem can be resolved for the order BA of the machines. It can be seen that optimal job sequence is 6–7–2–3–5–4–1 or 6–7–4–2–3–5–1, but the idle times for the machines remain unchanged.

EXAMPLE 5.4-3

A refrigeration company has six plants located in different parts of a city. Every year it is necessary for each plant to be completely overhauled. The overhauling is carried out in two stages A and B, and each stage requires a crew of workmen with completely different skills. The work on stage B can start only when stage A has been completed. The plant has to be closed for the entire period of the overhauling. The company, at present, is following the schedule of the overhaul of the six plants as given below :

Time required by the crew (days)

Plant :	P_1	P_2	P_3	P_4	P_5	P_6
Crew A :	*12*	*9*	*10*	*8*	*10*	*10*
Crew B :	*10*	*7*	*9*	*14*	*6*	*8*

(i) Determine the optimal sequence.

(ii) If downtime of any of the six plants costs ₹ 5,000 per day, idle time for crew A costs ₹ 1,500 per day and idle time for crew B costs ₹ 2,500 per day, which of the two schedules, the present one or the one determined in part (i), will be more economical? What are their respective costs ?

Solution

Present Schedule

Downtime of the plants and idle time in days for crew A and B are calculated in table 5.6.

TABLE 5.6

Plant	Crew A		Crew B		Down	Idle time	
	Start	Finish	Start	Finish	time	Crew A	Crew B
P_1	0	12	12	22	22	–	12
P_2	12	21	22	29	17	–	–
P_3	21	31	31	40	19	–	2
P_4	31	39	40	54	23	–	–
P_5	39	49	54	60	21	–	–
P_6	49	59	60	68	19	9	–
Total					121	9	14

∴ Total cost = ₹ [121 × 5,000 + 9 × 1,500 + 14 × 2,500] = ₹ 6,53,500.

Optimal Schedule

Applying the rule by Johnson and Bellman explained in section 5.4, the optimal sequence is $P_4 \to P_1 \to P_3 \to P_6 \to P_2 \to P_5$. Down time of the plants and idle time in days for crew A and B for this schedule are calculated in table 5.7.

TABLE 5.7

Plant	Crew A		Crew B		Down	Idle time	
	Start	Finish	Start	Finish	time	Crew A	Crew B
P_4	0	8	8	22	22	–	8
P_1	8	20	22	32	24	–	–
P_3	20	30	32	41	21	–	–
P_6	30	40	41	49	19	–	–
P_2	40	49	49	56	16	–	–
P_5	49	59	59	65	16	6	3
Total					118	6	11

∴ Total cost = ₹ [118 × 5,000 + 6 × 1,500 + 11 × 2,500] = ₹ 6,26,500.

∴ Optimal sequence is more economical as it reduces the total cost by ₹ 27,000.

EXAMPLE 5.4-4

A manufacturing company processes 6 different jobs on two machines A and B. Number of units of each job and its processing times on A and B are given in table 5.8. Find the optimal sequence, the total minimum elapsed time and idle time for either machine.

TABLE 5.8

Job no.	No. of units of each job	Processing time	
		Machine A (minutes)	Machine B (minutes)
1	3	5	8
2	4	16	7
3	2	6	11
4	5	3	5
5	2	9	7.5
6	3	6	14

[P.U.B.Com. April, 2004]

Solution. By examining the processing times we find that the smallest value is 3 minutes for job 4 on machine A. Thus we schedule job 4 first on machine A as shown.

4					

Repeating the procedure detailed in section 5.4, we get the following assignments :

4	1				

4	1	3	6		

4	1	3	6	5	2
5	3	2	3	2	4

The optimal sequence as well as the number of units of each job are shown above. The optimal sequence is

First : 5 units of job 4,
Second : 3 units of job 1,
Third : 2 units of job 3,
Fourth : 3 units of job 6,
Fifth : 2 units of job 5,
and Sixth : 4 units of job 2.

Table 5.9 is now constructed to determine the total elapsed time.

TABLE 5.9

Job no.	Unit no. of	Machine A Time in (minutes)	Machine A Time out (minutes)	Machine B Time in (minutes)	Machine B Time out (minutes)	Idle time of machine B (minutes)
4	1st	0	3	3	8	3
	2nd	3	6	8	13	–
	3rd	6	9	13	18	–
	4th	9	12	18	23	–
	5th	12	15	23	28	–
1	1st	15	20	28	36	–
	2nd	20	25	36	44	–
	3rd	25	30	44	52	–
3	1st	30	36	52	63	–
	2nd	36	42	63	74	–
6	1st	42	48	74	88	–
	2nd	48	54	88	102	–
	3rd	54	60	102	116	–
5	1st	60	69	116	123.5	–
	2nd	69	78	123.5	131	–
2	1st	78	94	131	138	–
	2nd	94	110	138	145	–
	3rd	110	126	145	152	–
	4th	126	142	152	159	–

From this table the total minimum elapsed time is 159 minutes, idle time for machine A is 17 minutes and for machine B is 3 minutes.

5.5 PROCESSING *n* JOBS THROUGH THREE MACHINES

This sequenecing problem is competely described as follows :

(*i*) only three machines A, B and C are involved,

(*ii*) each job is processed in the prescribed order ABC (first on machine A, then on B and thereafter on C),

(*iii*) no passing of jobs is permitted (*i.e.*, the same order over each machine is maintained), and

(*iv*) the actual or expected processing times $A_1, A_2, ..., A_n$; $B_1, B_2, ..., B_n$ and $C_1, C_2, ..., C_n$ are known and represented by a table of the type shown below.

TABLE 5.10

Machine times for n jobs and three machines			
Job	*A*	*B*	*C*
1	A_1	B_1	C_1
2	A_2	B_2	C_2
3	A_3	B_3	C_3
⋮	⋮	⋮	⋮
i	A_i	B_i	C_i
⋮	⋮	⋮	⋮
n	A_n	B_n	C_n

The problem, again, is to find the optimum sequence of jobs which minimizes T.

No general solution is available at present for such a case. However, the method of section 5.4 can be extended to cover the special cases where either one or both of the following conditions hold good (if neither of the conditions holds good, the method fails and the optimal sequence has to be found by enumerating all the sequences).

(1) the minimum time on machine *A* is ≥ maximum time on machine *B*, and

(2) the minimum time on machine *C* is ≥ maximum time on machine *B*.

The method, described here without proof, is to replace the problem by an equivalent prolem involving *n* jobs and two machines. These two (fictitious) machines are denoted by *G* and *H* and their corresponding processing times are given by

$$G_i = A_i + B_i, \ H_i = B_i + C_i.$$

If this new problem with the prescribed order *GH* is solved by the method of section 5.4, the resulting optimal sequence will also be optimal for the original problem.

EXAMPLE 5.5-1

A machine operator has to perform three operations: turning, threading and knurling on a number of different jobs. The time required to perform these operations (in minutes) for each job is known. Determine the order in which the jobs should be processed in order to minimize the total time required to turn out all the jobs. Also find the idle times for the three operations.

TABLE 5.11

Job	*Time for turning (minutes)*	*Time for threading (minutes)*	*Time for knurling (minutes)*
1	*3*	*8*	*13*
2	*12*	*6*	*14*
3	*5*	*4*	*9*
4	*2*	*6*	*12*
5	*9*	*3*	*8*
6	*11*	*1*	*13*

[*G.N.D.U. BBA April, 2008*]

Solution

Here, min $A_i = 2$, max $B_i = 8$, and min $C_i = 8$. Since min C_i = max B_i, we can solve this example by the procedure described in section 5.5.

The equivalent problem involving 6 jobs and two fictitious operations G and H becomes

Processing times for 6 jobs and two fictitious operations

Job	G_i = *Turning + Threading (minutes)*	H_i = *Threading + knurling (minutes)*
1	11	21
2	18	20
3	9	13
4	8	18
5	12	11
6	12	14

Examining the columns G_i and H_i, we find that the smallest value is 8 under operation G_i in row 4. Thus we schedule job 4 first (on operation G_i and thereafter on H_i) as shown below.

4					

The reduced set of processing times becomes

Job	G_i	H_i
1	11	21
2	18	20
3	9	13
5	12	11
6	12	14

The next smallest value is 9 under column G_i for job 3. Hence we schedule job 3 as shown below.

4	3				

The reduced set of processing times becomes

Job	G_i	H_i
1	11	21
2	18	20
5	12	11
6	12	14

There are two equal minimal values : processing time of 11 minutes under column G_i for job 1 and processing time of 11 minutes under column H_i for job 5. According to the rules, job 1 is scheduled next to job 3 and 5 is scheduled last as shown below.

4	3	1			5

The reduced set of processing times becomes

Job	G_i	H_i
2	18	20
6	12	14

The smallest value is 12 under column G_i for job 6. Hence we schedule job 6 next to job 1 and the optimal sequence becomes

4	3	1	6	2	5

Now we may calculate the elapsed time corresponding to the optimal sequence, using the individual processing times given in the problem. The details are shown in table 5.12.

TABLE 5.12

Job	Turning operation		Threading operation		Knurling operation	
	Time in	Time out	Time in	Time out	Time in	Time out
4	0	2	2	8	8	20
3	2	7	8	12	20	29
1	7	10	12	20	29	42
6	10	21	21	22	42	55
2	21	33	33	39	55	69
5	33	42	42	45	69	77

Thus the minimum elapsed is 77 minutes. Idle time for turning operation is 77 – 42 = 35 minutes, for threading operation is 2 + 1 + 11 + 3 + (77 – 45) = 17 + 32 = 49 minutes and for knurling operation is 8 minutes.

EXAMPLE 5.5-2

There are five jobs, each of which is to be processed through three machines A, B, and C in the order ABC. Processing times in hours are

TABLE 5.13

Job	A	B	C
1	3	4	7
2	8	5	9
3	7	1	5
4	5	2	6
5	4	3	10

Determine the optimum sequence for the five jobs and the minimum elapsed time. Also find the idle time for the three machines and waiting time for the jobs.

Solution

Here, min A_i = 3, max B_i = 5, and min C_i = 5. Since min C_i = max B_i, we can solve this example by the procedure described in section 5.5.

The equivalent problem involving 5 jobs and two fictitious machines G and H becomes

Machine times for five jobs and two fictitious machines

Job	G ($G_i = A_i + B_i$)	H ($H_i = B_i + C_i$)
1	7	11
2	13	14
3	8	6
4	7	8
5	7	13

Examining columns G_i and H_i, we find that the smallest value of machining time is 6 hours under column H_i for job 3. Thus we schedule job 3 last (on machine G and thereafter on H) as shown below.

				3

Further examining the columns G_i and H_i, we find that the next smallest value of machining time is 7 hrs. under column G_i for jobs 1, 4 and 5. Since all the values are in the same column G_i, we schedule job 4 first since it has lowest entry 8 in column H_i, job 1 next as it has next higher entry 11 in column H_i and job 5 next to job 1 since it has still higher entry 13 in column H_i. This is shown below.

4	1	5		3

Job 2 is now scheduled next to job 3 and the optimal sequence becomes

4	1	5	2	3

Obviously, the other optimal solutions, because of ties will be

4	5	1	2	3

,

1	4	5	2	3

,

1	5	4	2	3

,

5	1	4	2	3

,

and

5	4	1	2	3

.

The minimum elapsed time can now be calculated corresponding to any optimal sequence, say first using the individual machining times given in the problem. The details are shown in table 5.14.

TABLE 5.14

Job	*Machine A*		*Machine B*		*Machine C*	
	Time in	*Time out*	*Time in*	*Time out*	*Time in*	*Time out*
4	0	5	5	7	7	13
1	5	8	8	12	13	20
5	8	12	12	15	20	30
2	12	20	20	25	30	39
3	20	27	27	28	39	44

The minimum elapsed time is 44 hours, idle time for machine *A* is 44 – 27 = 17 hours, for machine *B* is 5 + 1 + 5 + 2 + (44 – 28) = 29 hours and for machine *C* is 7 hours. Minimum elapsed time and idle times for machines *A*, *B* and *C* will be same for other optimal sequences.

There is no waiting of jobs between machines *A* and *B*, the jobs have to wait for loading on machine *C* for (1 + 5 + 5 + 11) = 22 hours resulting in some in-process inventory cost.

EXAMPLE 5.5-3

Find the sequence that minimizes the total elapsed time required to complete the following tasks. Each task is processed in any two of the machines A, B and C in any order.

		Task						
		1	*2*	*3*	*4*	*5*	*6*	*7*
	A	*12*	*6*	*5*	*3*	*5*	*7*	*6*
Machine	*B*	*7*	*8*	*9*	*8*	*7*	*8*	*3*
	C	*3*	*4*	*11*	*5*	*2*	*8*	*4*

[*G.N.D.U.B Com. April, 2010; P.U.B.Com., 2002*]

Solution. There are 6 possible ways of processing the tasks :

(*i*) *Each task is processed by machines A and B in the order AB.*

By examining the processing times we find that the smallest value is 3 for task 4 on machine *A* as well as for task 7 on machine *B*. Thus we schedule tasks 4 and 7 as shown below.

4						7

Repeating the process as detailed in section 5.4, we get the following sequence :

4	5	3	2	6	1	7

Total elapsed time is calculated in the table below.

TABLE 5.15

Task	Machine A		Machine B	
	Time in	Time out	Time in	Time out
4	0	3	3	11
5	3	8	11	18
3	8	13	18	27
2	13	19	27	35
6	19	26	35	43
1	26	38	43	50
7	38	44	50	53

∴ Total elapsed time = 53.

(*ii*) *Each task is processed by machines A and B in the order BA*

		Task						
		1	2	3	4	5	6	7
Machine	*B*	7	8	9	8	7	8	3
	A	12	6	5	3	5	7	6

Proceeding as in section 5.4, we get the following sequence :

7	1	6	2	3	5	4

Note that this sequence is just the opposite of the one obtained in part (*i*).
Total elapsed time is now calculated as usual in the order *BA*.
Total elapsed time is found to be = 53.

(*iii*) *Each tasked is processed by the machines B and C in the order BC*

		Task						
		1	2	3	4	5	6	7
Machine	*B*	7	8	9	8	7	8	3
	C	3	4	11	5	2	8	4

Proceeding as in case (*i*) above, the optimal sequence is :

7	6	3	4	2	1	5

Total elapsed time = 52.

(*iv*) *Each task is processed by the machines B and C in the order CB*
Concluding from cases (*i*) and (*ii*) we can say that optimal sequence is :

5	1	2	4	3	6	7

Total elapsed time = 52

(*v*) *Each task is processed by the machines A and C in the order AC*
The optimal sequence and total elapsed time can be found to be :

4	3	6	7	2	1	5

T.E.T. = 46.

(*vi*) *Each task is processed by the machines A and C in the order CA*
The optimal sequence and the total elapsed time are :

5	1	2	7	6	3	4

T.E.T. = 46.

From the above six cases it is concluded that tasks should be processed on machines A and C in the order AC or CA. The optimal sequences are 4–3–6–7–2–1–5 or 5–1–2–7–6–3–4 with minimum total elapsed time 46.

5.6 PROCESSING TWO JOBS THROUGH *m* MACHINES

This sequencing problem is described as follows:

(*a*) there are m machines, denoted by $A, B, C, ..., K$,

(*b*) only two jobs are to be performed: job 1 and job 2,

(*c*) the technological ordering of each of the two jobs through m machines is known. This ordering may or may not be the same for both jobs. Alternative ordering is not permissible for either job.

(*d*) the actual or expected processing times $A_1, B_1, C_1, ..., K_1; A_2, B_2, C_2, ..., K_2$ are known, and

(*e*) each machine can work only one job at a time and storage space for in-process inventory is available.

The problem is to minimize the total elapsed time T *i.e.*, to minimize the time from the start of first job to the completion of the second job.

Such a problem can be solved by graphical method which is simple and provides good (though not necessarily optimal) results.

EXAMPLE 5.6-1

Using graphical method, determine the optimal sequence needed to process jobs 1 and 2 on five machines, A, B, C, D and E. For each machine find the job which should be done first. Also calculate the total time needed to complete both the jobs.

TABLE 5.16

Job 1	*Sequence* :	*A*	*B*	*C*	*D*	*E*
	Time (hr) :	*1*	*2*	*3*	*5*	*1*
Job 2	*Sequence* :	*C*	*A*	*D*	*E*	*B*
	Time (hr) :	*3*	*4*	*2*	*1*	*5*

[*P.T.U. MBA Dec., 2014*]

Solution

The graphical procedure is described with the help of the following steps :

Step 1

Draw two axes at right angles to each other. Represent processing time on job 1 along horizontal axis and processing time on job 2 along vertical axis. Scale used must be same for both the jobs.

Step 2

Layout the machine times for the two jobs on corresponding axes in the given technological order. This is shown in figure 5.2.

Step 3

Machine A requires 1 hour for job 1 and 4 hours for job 2. A rectangle LMNP is, thus, constructed for machine A. Similar rectangles are constructed for machines B, C, D and E as shown.

Step 4

Make a program by starting from origin (O) and moving through the various stages of completion (points) till the point marked 'finish' is reached. Choose path consisting only of horizontal, vertical and 45° lines. A horizontal line represents work on job 1 while job 2 remains idle; a vertical line represents work on job 2 while job 1 remains idle and a 45° line to the base represents simultaneous work on both jobs.

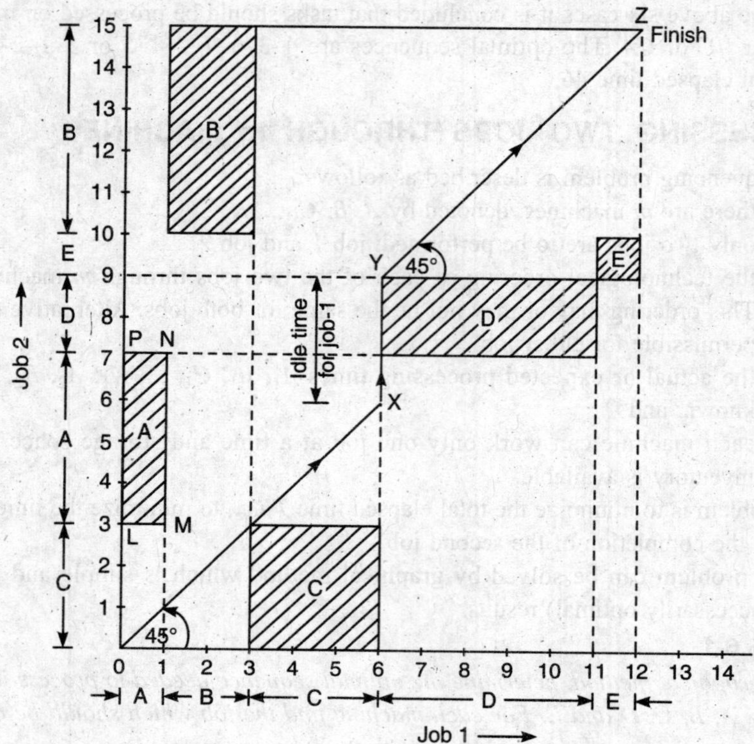

Fig. 5.2. Graphic solution of 2 job and 5 machine problem.

Step 5

Find the optimal path (program). An optimal path is one that minimizes idle time for job 1 (vertical movement). Likewise, an optimal path is one that minimizes idle time for job 2 (horizontal movement). Obviously, the optimal path is one which coincides with 45° line to the maximum extent.

Further, both jobs cannot be processed simultaneously on one machine. Graphically, this means that diagonal movement through the blocked out areas is not allowed.

A good path, accordingly, is chosen by eye and drawn on the graph (path OXYZ).

Step 6

Find the elapsed time. It is obtained by adding the idle time for either job to the processing time for that job. The idle time for the chosen path is found to be 3 hours for job 1.

$\therefore$ Total elapsed time = 12 + 3 = 15 hours (considering job 1)

= 15 + 0 = 15 hours (considering job 2).

Step 7

The optimal schedule corresponding to the chosen path is shown in Fig. 5.3.

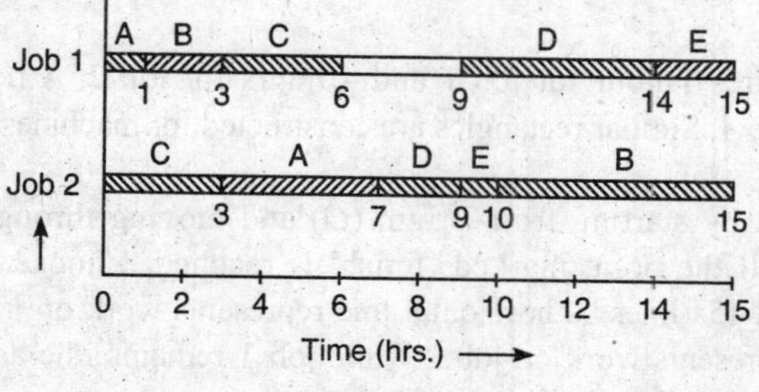

Fig. 5.3

The optimal sequence or schedule on various machines for the two jobs as evident from Fig. 5.3 is :

	Machine A	:	job 1 precedes job 2,
	machine B	:	job 1 precedes job 2,
	machine C	:	job 2 precedes job 1,
	machine D	:	job 2 precedes job 1,
and	machine E	:	job 2 precedes job 1.

EXAMPLE 5.6-2

Use graphical method to minimize the time required to process the following jobs on the machines. For each machine specify the job which should be done first. Also calculate the total elapsed time to complete both jobs.

TABLE 5.17

		Machines				
Job 1	*Sequence:*	*A*	*B*	*C*	*D*	*E*
	Time (hr):	*6*	*8*	*4*	*12*	*4*
Job 2	*Sequence:*	*B*	*C*	*A*	*D*	*E*
	Time (hr):	*10*	*8*	*6*	*4*	*12*

[*V.T.U. Karnataka B.E. June, 2011; P.U.B. (E. & Ec.) April, 2006*]

Solution

Step 1

Draw two axes at right angles to each other. Represent processing time on job 1 along horizontal axis and processing time on job 2 along vertical axis. Scale used must be same for both jobs.

Step 2

Lay out the machine times for the two jobs on corresponding axes in the given technological order. This is shown in Fig. 5.4.

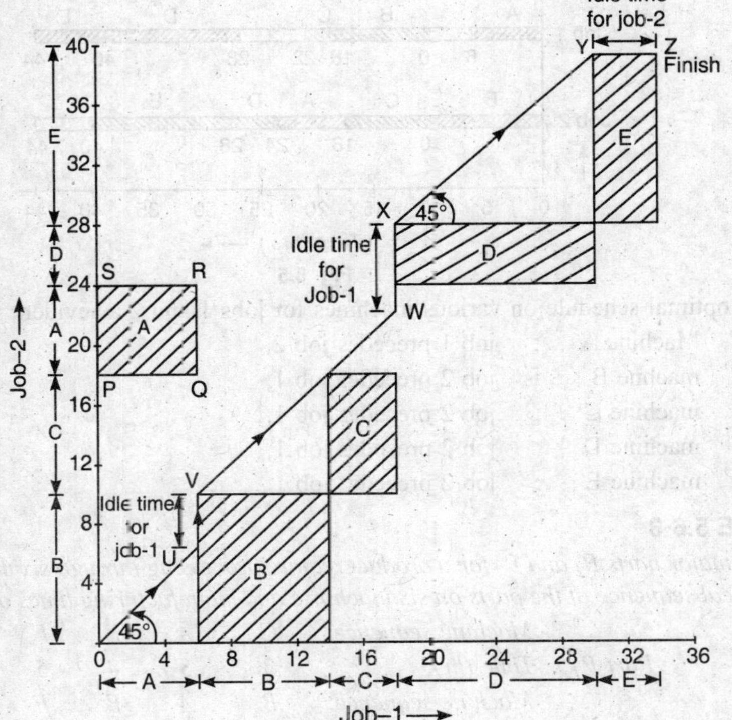

Fig. 5.4. Graphical solution of 2 job and 5 machine problem.

Step 3

Machine A requires 6 hours for job 1 and 6 hours for job 2. A square $PQRS$ is, thus, constructed for machine A. Similarly, rectangles are constructed for machines B, C, D and E as shown.

Step 4

Make a program by starting with zero time (origin O) and moving through the various stages of completion (points) till the point marked 'finish' is reached. Choose path consisting only of horizontal, vertical and 45° lines. A horizontal line represents work on job 1 while job 2 remains idle; a vertical line represents work on job 2 while job 1 remains idle and a 45° line to the base represents simultaneous work on both the jobs.

Step 5

Find the optimal path (program). An optimal path is one that minimizes idle time on job 1 as well as job 2. Obviously, the optimal path is one which coincides with 45° line to the maximum extent. Further, both jobs cannot be processed simultaneously on one machine. Graphically, this means that diagonal movement through the blocked out areas is not allowed. A good path, accordingly, is chosen by eye and drawn on the graph (path OUVWXYZ).

Step 6

Find the elapsed time. It is obtained by adding the idle time for either job to the processing time for that job.

The idle time for the chosen path is found to be 4 + 6 = 10 hours for job 1 and 4 hours for job 2.

∴ Total elapsed time = 34 + 10 = 44 hrs. (considering job 1)

= 40 + 4 = 44 hrs. (considering job 2).

Step 7

The optimal schedule corresponding to the chosen path is shown in Fig. 5.5.

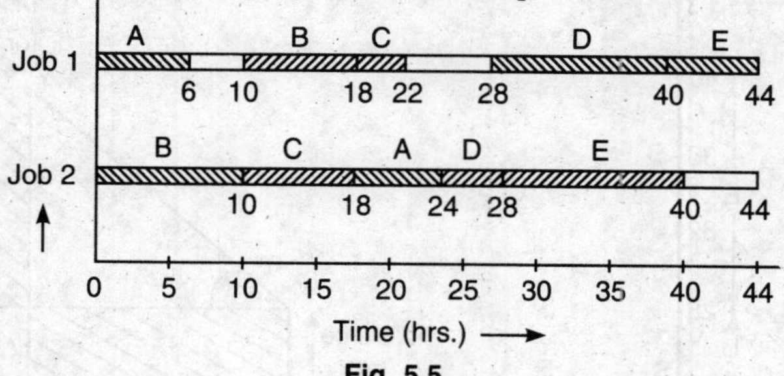

Fig. 5.5

The optimal schedule on various machines for jobs 1 and 2 as evident from Fig. 5.5 is

	Machine A	:	job 1 precedes job 2,
	machne B	:	job 2 precedes job 1,
	machine C	:	job 2 precedes job 1,
	machine D	:	job 2 precedes job 1,
and	machine E	:	job 2 precedes job 1.

EXAMPLE 5.6-3

Two major parts P_1 and P_2 for a product require processing through six machine centres. The technological sequence of the parts on six machines and manufacturing times on each machine are

	Machine sequence:	*C*	*A*	*E*	*F*	*D*	*B*
Part P_1	*Time (hr):*	2	3	4	5	6	1
	Machine sequence:	*B*	*A*	*E*	*F*	*C*	*D*
Part P_2	*Time (hr):*	3	2	5	3	2	3

What would be the optimal scheduling to minimize the total processing time for these two parts ? Find also the total elapsed time. For each machine specify the part that should be processed first.

[P.U.M.Com. April, 2004]

Solution

Mark the processing times for parts P_1 and P_2 on the horizontal and vertical axes according to the given technological ordering of the machines.

Construct the rectangular blocks by pairing the same machines as shown in Fig. 5.6. Now mark a path from the origin O to the point of Finish moving as much as possible along the 45° line.

Idle time for part P_1 is 2 hours and for part P_2 is $2 + 2 + 1 = 5$ hours.

$\therefore$ Total elapsed time $= 21 + 2 = 23$ hours (considering part P_1)

$= 18 + 5 = 23$ hours (considering part P_2).

The optimal schedule corresponding to the chosen path can be drawn and it can be shown that on

Machine A : part P_1 precedes part P_2,

Machne B : part P_2 precedes part P_1,

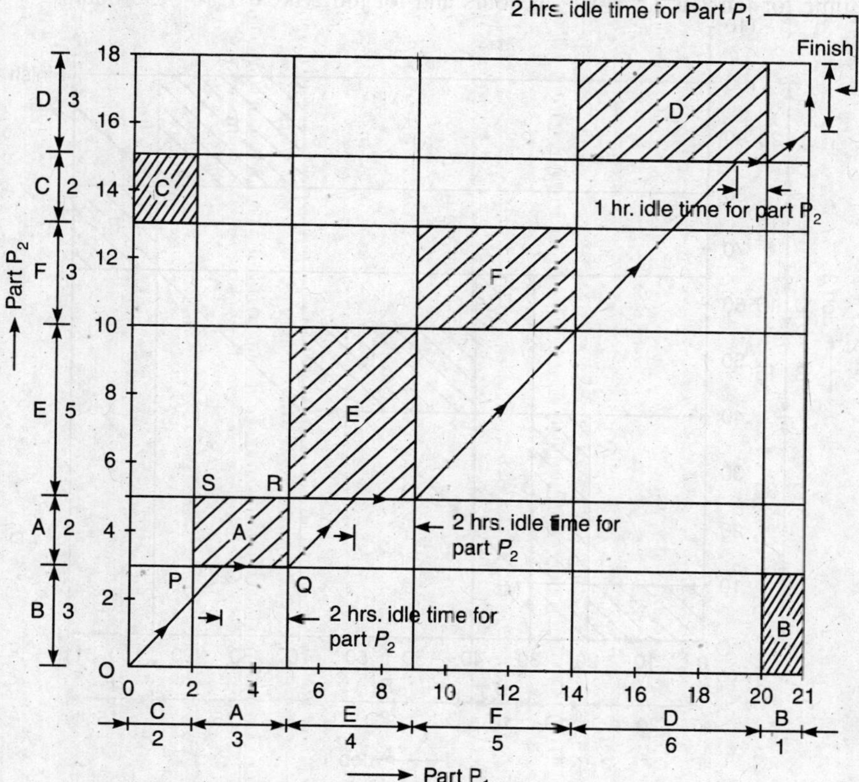

Fig. 5.6. Graphical solution of 2 part and 6 machine problem.

Machine C : part P_1 precedes part P_2,

Machine D : part P_1 precedes part P_2,

Machine E : part P_1 precedes part P_2,

and Machine F : part P_1 precedes part P_2.

EXAMPLE 5.6-4

A workshop has six machines A, B, C, D, E and F. Two jobs have to be processed through each of these machines. The processing time on each machine and technological sequence of jobs is given below.

Job 1 : $A \to C \to D \to B \to E \to F,$

Job 2 : $A \to C \to B \to D \to F \to E.$

	Time in hours on machine					
	A	*B*	*C*	*D*	*E*	*F*
Job 1	*20*	*30*	*10*	*10*	*25*	*15*
Job 2	*10*	*15*	*30*	*10*	*20*	*15*

In which order should the jobs be done on each of the machines to minimize the total time required to process the jobs ? Also find the minimum elapsed time.

Solution

Mark the processing times for jobs 1 and 2 on the horizontal and vertical axes according to the given technological ordering of the machines.

Construct the rectangular blocks by pairing the same machines as shown in Fig. 5.7. Now mark a path from the origin O to the point of finish moving as much as possible along the 45° line. Idle time for job 1 is 15 + 5 = 20 hours and for job 2 is 20 + 10 = 30 hours.

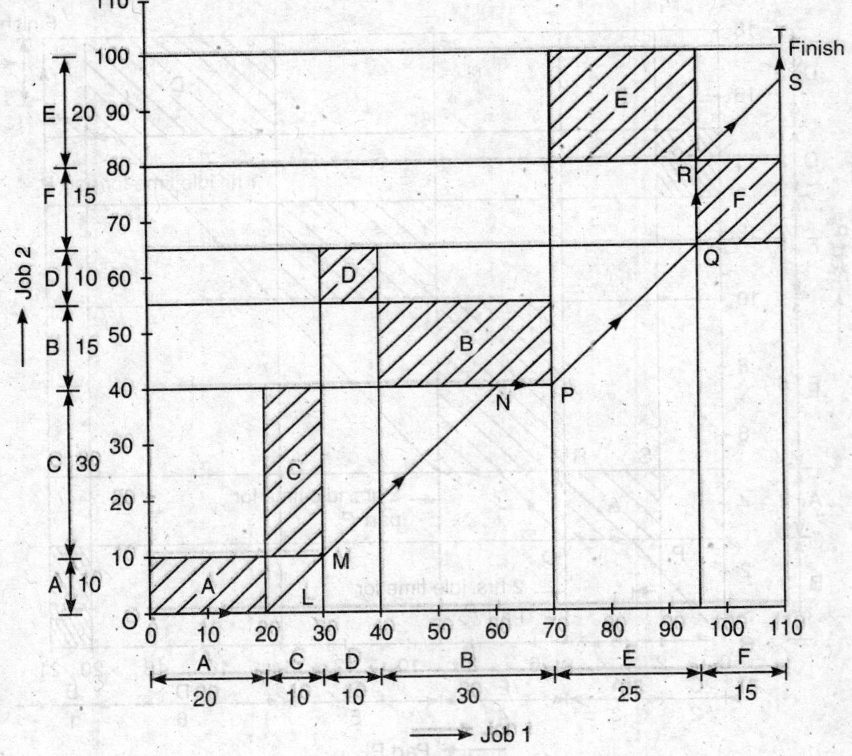

Fig. 5.7.

$\therefore$ Total elapsed time = 110 + 20 = 130 hours (considering job 1)

= 100 + 30 = 130 hours (considering job 2).

5.7 PROCESSING *n* JOBS THROUGH *m* MACHINES

This sequencing problem is described as follows :

(*i*) there are *n* jobs to be performed, denoted by 1, 2, 3, ..., *i*, ..., *n*.

(*ii*) there are m machines, denoted by A, B, C, ..., K.

(*iii*) each job is to be processed in the prescribed order, say ABC ...K.

(*iv*) no passing of jobs is permitted (*i.e.*, same order over each machine is maintained).

(*v*) the actual or expected processing times $A_1, A_2, ..., A_n; B_1, B_2, ..., B_n; C_1, C_2, ..., C_n; ..., K_1, K_2, ..., K_n$ are known and represented by a table of the type shown below.

TABLE 5.18

Machine times for n jobs and m machines

Job	*A*	*B*	*C*	...	*K*
1	A_1	B_1	C_1	...	K_1
2	A_2	B_2	C_2	...	K_2
3	A_3	B_3	C_3	...	K_3
⋮	⋮	⋮	⋮	⋮	⋮
i	A_i	B_i	C_i	⋮	K_i
⋮	⋮	⋮	⋮	⋮	⋮
n	A_n	B_n	C_n	...	K_n

The problem, as before, is to find the optimum sequence of jobs which minimizes T.

CASE I

Method of section 5.5 can be applied (extended) to cover the special cases where either *one* or *both* of the following conditions hold gold (if neither of the conditions holds good, the method fails) :

(*i*) the minimum time on machine A is ≥ maximum time on machines B, C, ..., K – 1,

(*ii*) the minimum time on machine K is ≥ maximum time on machines B, C, ..., K – 1.

The method is to replace the m machine problem by an equivalent two machine problem. These two (fictitious) machines are denoted by a and b and their corresponding processing times are given by

$$a_i = A_i + B_i + ... + (K-1)_i,$$
$$b_i = B_i + C_i + ... + (K-1)_i + K_i.$$

If this new problem with the prescribed order ab is solved by the method of section 5.5, the resulting optimal sequence will also be optimal for the original problem.

Further, if

$$B_i + C_i + ... + (K-1)_i = k,$$

where k is a fixed positive constant for all jobs (i = 1, 2, 3, ..., n), then the given problem can be solved simply as n job two machine problem (where the two machines are A and K in the order AK) as per the method of section 5.4.

EXAMPLE 5.7-1

Four jobs 1, 2, 3 and 4 are to be processed on each of the five machines A, B, C, D and E in the order ABCDE. Find the total minimum elapsed time if no passing of jobs is permitted. Also determine idle time for each machine.

TABLE 5.19

M/c / *Job*	*A*	*B*	*C*	*D*	*E*
1	*7*	*5*	*2*	*3*	*9*
2	*6*	*6*	*4*	*5*	*10*
3	*5*	*4*	*5*	*6*	*8*
4	*8*	*3*	*3*	*2*	*6*

Solution

Here, min $A_i = 5$, min $E_i = 6$ and max $(B_i, C_i, D_i) = 6, 5, 6$ respectively. Since min E_i = max (B_i, D_i), we can solve this problem by the procedure described in section 5.7.

The equivalent problem involving 4 jobs and 2 fictitious machines *a* and *b* becomes

Job	*Machine a*	*Machine b*
1	17	19
2	21	25
3	20	23
4	16	14

Examining the columns we find that the optimal sequence is

1	3	2	4

Now we may calculate the total elapsed time corresponding to the optimal sequence, using the individual processing times given in the original problem. The details are shown in table 5.20.

TABLE 5.20

M / c *Job*	*A*	*B*	*C*	*D*	*E*
1	0 – 7	7 – 12	12 – 14	14 – 17	17 – 26
3	7 – 12	12 – 16	16 – 21	21 – 27	27 – 35
2	12 – 18	18 – 24	24 – 28	28 – 33	35 – 45
4	18 – 26	26 – 29	29 – 32	33 – 35	45 – 51

Thus the minimize elapsed time is 51 time units. Idle time on machine

A = 51 – 26 = 25 time units,

B = 7 + 2 + 2 + (51 – 29) = 33 time units,

C = 12 + 2 + 3 + 1 + (51 – 32) = 37 time units,

D = 14 + 4 + 1 + (51 – 35) = 35 time units,

and E = 17 + 1 = 18 time units.

EXAMPLE 5.7-2

Four jobs 1, 2, 3 and 4 are to be processed on each of the four machines A, B, C and D in the order ABCD. The processing times in minutes are given in table 5.21. Find, for no passing, the minimum elapsed time and idle time for each machine.

TABLE 5.21

M / c *Job*	*A*	*B*	*C*	*D*
1	*58*	*14*	*14*	*48*
2	*30*	*10*	*18*	*32*
3	*28*	*12*	*16*	*44*
4	*64*	*16*	*12*	*42*

Solution

Here, min $A_i = 28$, min $D_i = 32$ and max $(B_i, C_i) = 16, 18$ respectively. Since min (A_i, D_i) > max (B_i, C_i), we can solve this problem by the procedure described in section 5.7. The problem can be converted into a four job and two machine problem.

Further, since $B_1 + C_1 = B_2 + C_2 = B_3 + C_3 = B_4 + C_4 = 28$, a fixed positive constant, the given problem reduces to that of finding the optimal sequence for 4 jobs and 2 machines A and

D in the order AD. Machines B and C do not have any effect on the optimality of the sequence.

Examining columns A and D only, the optimal sequence is given by

3	2	1	4

Now we may calculate the total elapsed time corresponding to the optimal sequence, using the individual processing times given in the original problem. The details are shown in table 5.22.

TABLE 5.22

M / c *Job*	*A*	*B*	*C*	*D*
3	0 – 28	28 – 40	40 – 56	56 – 100
2	28 – 58	58 – 68	68 – 86	100 – 132
1	58 – 116	116 – 130	130 – 144	144 – 192
4	116 – 180	180 – 196	196 – 208	208 – 250

Thus the minimum elapsed time is 4 hr and 10 min. Machines A, B, C and D remain idle for 70, 198, 190 and 84 minutes respectively.

EXAMPLE 5.7-3

Determine an optimal sequence for the following sequencing problem.

TABLE 5.23

Machine (Time in hours)

Job	M_1	M_2	M_3	M_4
A	*20*	*10*	*9*	*20*
B	*17*	*7*	*15*	*17*
C	*21*	*8*	*10*	*21*
D	*25*	*5*	*9*	*25*

Solution *[P.U. B.E. (C.&E.) April, 2008]*

Here, min M_{i1} = 17, min M_{i4} = 17 and max M_{i2} = 10, M_{i3} = 15. Since min (M_{i1}, M_{i4}) > max (M_{i2}, M_{i3}), this problem can be solved by the procedure described in section 5.7. Thus if G_i and H_i are the two fictitious machines, such that

$M_{ig} = M_{i1} + M_{i2} + M_{i3}$ and $M_{iH} = M_{i2} + M_{i3} + M_{i4}$, then the given problem can be represented as the following equivalent problem involving 4 jobs and 2 fictitious machines:

Job	*Machine*	
	G_i	H_i
A	39	39
B	39	39
C	39	39
D	39	39

Here, Since $G_i = H_i$, i = 1, 2, 3, 4 and $M_{i1} = M_{i4}$, there will be 4! (= 24) schedules each giving us an optimal sequence, They are

ABCD, ABDC, ACBD, ACDB, ADBC, ADCB,
BACD, BADC, BCAD, BCDA, BDAC, BDCA,
CABD, CADB CBAD, CBDA, CDAB, CDBA,
DABC, DACB, DBAC, DBCA, DCAB, DCBA.

Each of the above optimal sequences yields the same total elapsed time given, say, by table 5.24.

TABLE 5.24
Machines (time in hours)

Job	M_1	M_2	M_3	M_4
A	0 – 20	20 – 30	30 – 39	39 – 59
B	20 – 37	37 – 44	44 – 59	59 – 76
C	37 – 58	58 – 66	66 – 76	76 – 97
D	58 – 83	83 – 88	88 – 97	97 – 122

Thus the total minimum elapsed time for each of the above 24 sequences is 122 hours.

CASE II

Sequencing problems involving *n* jobs and *m* machines wherein neither of the conditions described in case I earlier are satisfied can be solved by the procedure described below.

Step 1. The given $n \times m$ problem is split into a number of $n \times 2$ subproblems. The number of such problems will be $m - 1$. Thus a 3-machine problem will involve $3 - 1 = 2$ subproblems, a 4-machine problem will involve $4 - 1 = 3$ subproblems and so on.

For example, a 4-machine problem involving machines A, B, C and D will yield the following 2-machine subproblems :

1. Involving machines A and D
2. Involving machines A + B and C + D
3. Involving machines A + B + C and B + C + D.

Step 2. Each 2-machine subproblem is solved as per the method of section 5.4.

Step 3. All the solutions are examined. The sequence that involves the least processing time or cost is the optimal.

EXAMPLE 5.7-4

Five jobs 1, 2, ..., 5 are to be processed on four machines A, B, C, and D. Their processing times are given in table 5.25. Determine the optimal sequence, minimum elapsed time and idle time for each machine.

TABLE 5.25

Job	*Processing times in hours* A	B	C	D
1	*7*	*15*	*14*	*21*
2	*11*	*18*	*18*	*6*
3	*2*	*13*	*11*	*16*
4	*14*	*4*	*27*	*14*
5	*18*	*11*	*32*	*16*

Solution

Step 1. Here min $A_i = 2$, max $B_i = 18$, max $C_i = 32$, min $D_i = 6$. Since neither of the conditions are satisfied, the problem is split up into the following three 2-machine subproblems:

Subproblem 1

Job	*Processing times on machines* A	D
1	7	21
2	11	6
3	2	16
4	14	14
5	18	16

Subproblem 2

Job	*Processing times on machines* A + B	C + D
1	22	35
2	29	24
3	15	27
4	18	41
5	29	48

Subproblem 3

Job	*Processing times on machines* A + B + C	B + C + D
1	36	50
2	47	42
3	26	40
4	45	45
5	61	59

Step 2. Optimal sequence is now determined for each subproblem. They are

1. For subproblem 1 : 3 → 1 → 4 → 5 → 2
2. For subproblem 2 : 3 → 4 → 1 → 5 → 2
3. For subproblem 3 : 3 → 1 → 4 → 5 → 2

Step 3. Total processing time is now calculated for each different sequence.

Sequence 3 → 1 → 4 → 5 → 2

Sequence	A	B	C	D
3	0–2	2–15	15–26	26–42
1	2–9	15–30	30–44	44–63
4	9–23	30–34	44–71	71–85
5	23–41	41–52	71–103	103–119
2	41–52	52–70	103–121	121–127

∴ Total elapsed time is 127 hours.

Sequence 3 → 4 → 1 → 5 → 2

Sequence	A	B	C	D
3	0–2	2–15	15–26	26–42
4	2–16	16–20	26–53	53–67
1	16–23	23–38	53–67	67–88
5	23–41	41–52	67–99	99–115
2	41–52	52–70	99–117	117–123

∴ Total elapsed time is 123 hours.

Hence Optimal sequence : 3 → 4 → 1 → 5 → 2,
minimum elapsed time : 123 hours,
idle time for machine A : 123 – 52 = 71 hours,
idle time for machine B : 2 + 1 + 3 + 3 + (123 – 70) = 62 hours,
idle time for machine C : 15 + (123 – 117) = 21 hours,
and idle time for machine D : 26 + 11 + 11 + 2 = 50 hours.

5.8 SOLUTION OF COMPLICATED SEQUENCING PROBLEMS

Previous sections dealt with only simple sequencing problems. However, the problem may become complex due to a number of factors. Some of them are described here.

(*i*) *Overlap.* Sometimes a job may involve the processing of a number of similar items. Situations may arise wherein a few first items coming out of one operation may go in for second before remaining items in the lot could go in for the first operartion.

(*ii*) *Movement time.* Movement of jobs from one facility to another may take a considerable amount of time and it has to be incorporated into the model

(*iii*) *Rework.* If one of the sequencing operations is inspection, the defective items may have to be sent back to an operation performed earlier for reprocess, resulting in either a delay or splilting the jobs into two lots.

(*iv*) *Expediting.* If a particular job is urgently required, it may have to be given priority and be processed earlier.

(*v*) *Machine breakdown.* A machine may breakdown or the operator may be injured or absent from work.

(*vi*) *Material shortage.* The material required for carrying out a particular operation may not be readily available.

(*vii*) *Variable processing times.* In multi-shift plants, the time required to perform an operation may vary from shift to shift. These times and the costs associated with them may even be of probabilistic nature.

There are two approaches for solution of these complex problems. One approach is to split the problem into simpler subproblems, which are then handled individually. This approach is, however, open to all the defects of suboptimization, which lowers the overall system effectiveness.

The other approach involves the use of *Monte Carlo technique.* This simulation technique involves the probability distribution of the various characteristics of the problem, such as availability of each machine, processing time on each machine, more than one machine of the same type, various alternative routes for the jobs, variations in working pace of operators from shift to shift and the like.

Simulation offers a very promising technique for solving complex sequencing problems. However, simulation may involve computation of a large amount of data. Therefore, efforts have been made to reduce the number of sequencings to be tested and also the number of trials required to test each sequence. High speed electronic computers have been used for simulation trials of complex sequencing problems and further developments are expected in the days to come.

5.9 PROBLEMS RELATED TO SEQUENCING (ROUTING PROBLEMS IN NETWORKS)

Routing problems in networks are the problems related to sequencing and, of late, they have been receiving increased attention. Such problems usually occur in the areas of transportation and communication. A network problem involves the determination of a route from city i (origin) to city j (destination) for which there exist a number of alternative paths at various stages of the journey. The cost of journey, which may be function of distance, time or money, is different for different routes and the problem is to find the minimum cost route. Theoretically, the procedure involves determination of the cost of all the possible routes and selecting the one with minimum cost. However, in actual practice the number of such feasible alternatives is too large to be tried one by one. For instance, with 6 alternative paths, the number of possibilities is $5! = 120$, with 9 paths the number becomes $8! = 40,320$, while for 21 paths it increases to 2.4329×10^{18}. This proves the necessity of a more efficient method to find the optimal path.

There are many problems associated with networks, out of which the following two are important :

1. The travelling salesman problem (discussed earlier in section 4.10).
2. The minimal path problem.

5.10 MINIMAL PATH PROBLEM (SHORTEST ACYCLIC ROUTE MODELS)

The travelling salesman problem is a routing problem involving rather severe constraints. *Another routing problem arises when we wish to go from one place to another or to several other places and we are to select the shortest route (involving least distance or time or cost) out of many alternatives, to reach the desired station. Such acyclic route network problems can be easily solved by graphical method.*

A *network* is defined as a set of points or *nodes* which are connected by lines or *links*. A way of going from one node (*the origin*) to another (*the destination*) is called a *route or path.* The links in a network may be one way (in either direction) or two way (in both directions). The numbers on the links in the network represent the time, cost or distance involved in traversing them. It is assumed that the way in which we enter a node has no effect on the way of leaving it—an assumption which does not hold good in travelling salesman problem.

EXAMPLE 5.10-1

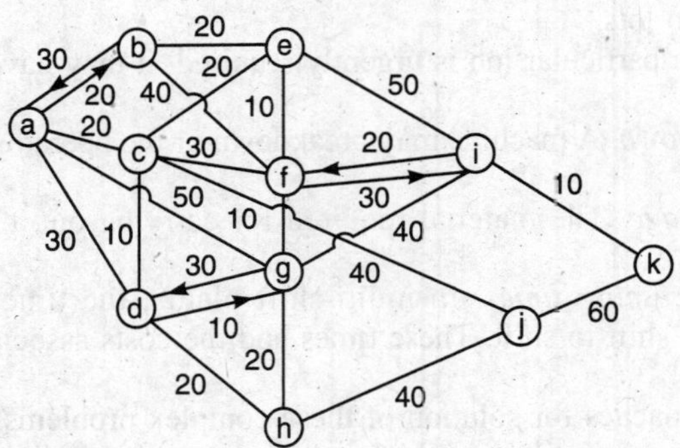

Fig. 5.8

A person wishes to reach the destination 'k' while starting from the station 'a' in the network shown in figure 5.8. Links work in both directions unless marked otherwise.

The numbers on the links represent cost (in rupees) of going from one node to another. Find the route that involves the least cost.

Solution. It is the shortest route problem but does not have the restrictions imposed in a travelling salesman problem. For instance, it is not necessary to include all the nodes in the optimal shortest route; moreover, it is not a cyclic route problem as it is not required to come back to the starting point '*a*'.

Obviously, in order to find the shortest route between '*a*' and '*k*' we must find the shortest route from '*a*' to every other point in the network. The graphical method used for this purpose consists of the following steps :

Step 1. Starting with the origin '*a*', draw all links by which one can go from '*a*' to other nodes and represent the cost from '*a*' on each of these nodes. This is shown in figure 5.9.

Step 2. In case there are links between any of the nodes obtained in step 1, determine for each of these links if the indirect route from '*a*' is shorter than the direct route. Draw the shorter route as a solid line and the longer route as a dotted line. Insert the shortest cost found on each such node.

For example, the cost of going from '*a*' to '*g*' through '*d*' is lower than the cost of going from '*a*' to '*g*' directly. Hence link *ag* is drawn dotted. In case of a tie both links are drawn solid. Thus one can go from '*a*' to '*d*' directly or through '*c*' at the same cost. Hence the links connecting them are drawn solid, as shown in figure 5.10.

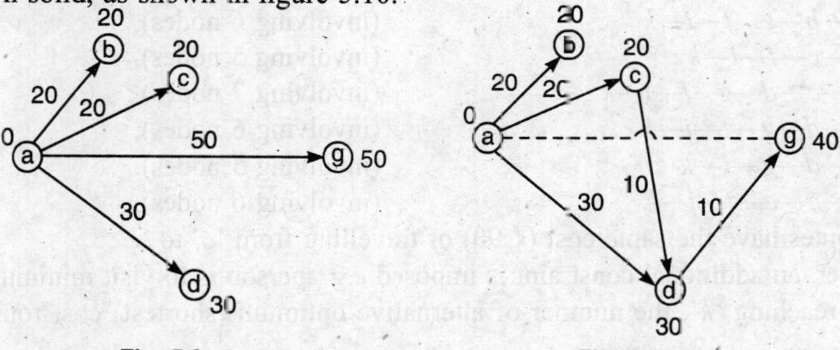

Fig. 5.9 Fig. 5.10

Step 3. Add nodes to which one can go from the nodes represented in step 2 and repeat step 2. This is shown in figure 5.11.

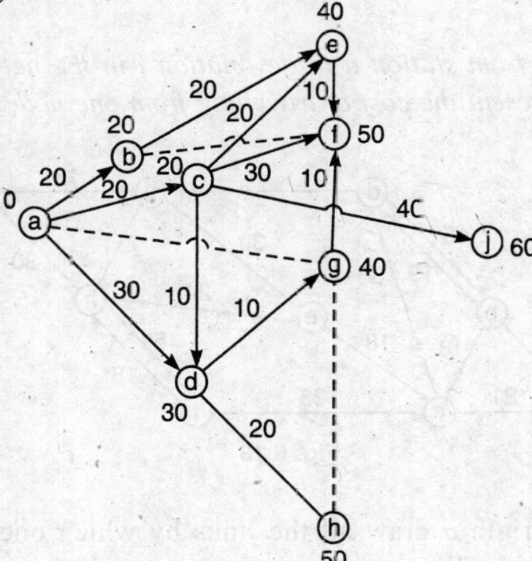

Fig. 5.11

Step 4. Continue till completed. This is shown in figure 5.12. Solid lines show the routes that can be taken from '*a*' to every other node. Evidently there are a number of alternative paths giving least cost. They are

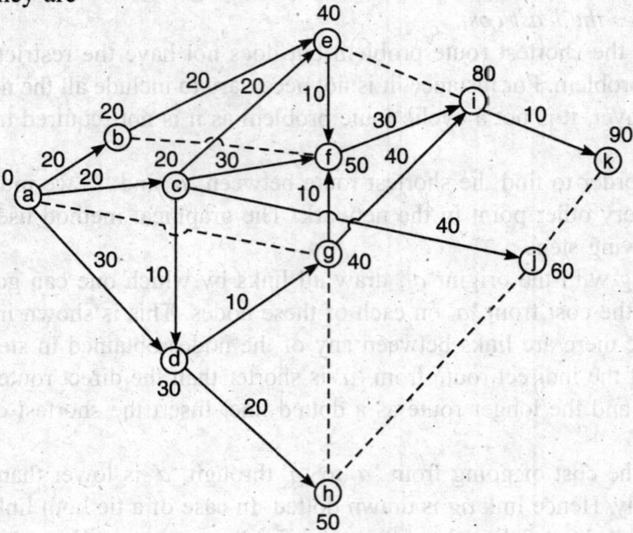

Fig. 5.12

(*i*) *a—b—e—f—i—k*	(involving 6 nodes),
(*ii*) *a—c—f—i—k*	(involving 5 nodes),
(*iii*) *a—c—d—g—f—i—k*	(involving 7 nodes),
(*iv*) *a—d—g—f—i—k*	(involving 6 nodes),
(*v*) *a—d—g—i—k*	(involving 5 nodes),
(*vi*) *a—c—e—f—i—k*	(involving 6 nodes),

All the routes have the same cost (₹ 90) of travelling from '*a*' to '*k*'.

If, however, an additional constraint is imposed *e.g.*, person is to visit minimum number of stations before reaching '*k*', the number of alternative optimum (shortest) cost routes decreases to only two :

(*i*) *a—c—f—i—k,*
(*ii*) *a—d—g—i—k.*

EXAMPLE 5.10-2

A person wishes to go from station a to destination i in the network shown in Fig. 5.13. The number on the links represent the cost of travelling from one node to another. Find the least cost route.

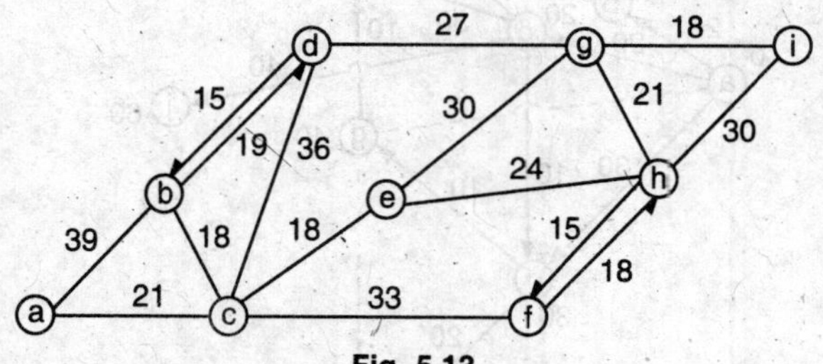

Fig. 5.13

Solution

1. Starting from the origin *a* draw all the links by which one can go from *a* to other nodes and show the cost of travelling each path from *a* on all these nodes. This is shown in Fig. 5.14.

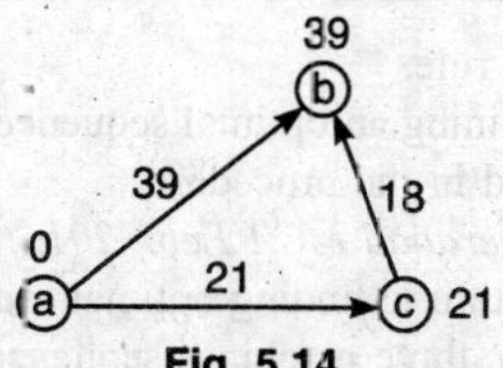

Fig. 5.14

2. See if there are links between any of the nodes of step 1. If so, determine for all such links whether the indirect route from *a* is shorter than the direct route. Represent the shorter route by a solid line and the longer route by a dotted line. Insert the shorter cost thus found on each such node.

3. Add nodes to which one can go from the nodes drawn in step 2 and repeat step 2. This is shown in Fig. 5.15. Here, nodes *d, e, f* have been added. Cost of reaching node *d* from *b* is ₹ (39 + 19) = ₹ 58, while from *c* is ₹ (21 + 36) = ₹ 57. Hence link *bd* is drawn dotted and link *cd* is drawn solid. The lower cost of ₹ 57 is entered above the node *d*. Likewise, cost of ₹ 39 and ₹ 54 is entered on nodes *e* and *f*.

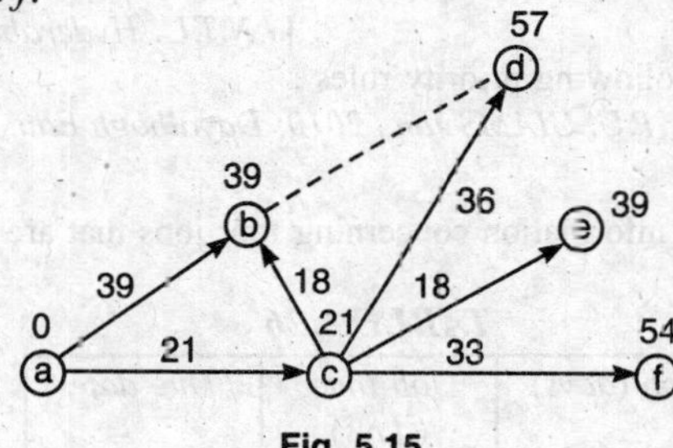

Fig. 5.15

4. Continue the process till node *i* is reached. This is shown in Fig. 5.16. Solid lines show the routes that can be taken from *a* to every other node. The least cost route is *a-c-e-g-i* with a total cost of ₹ 87.

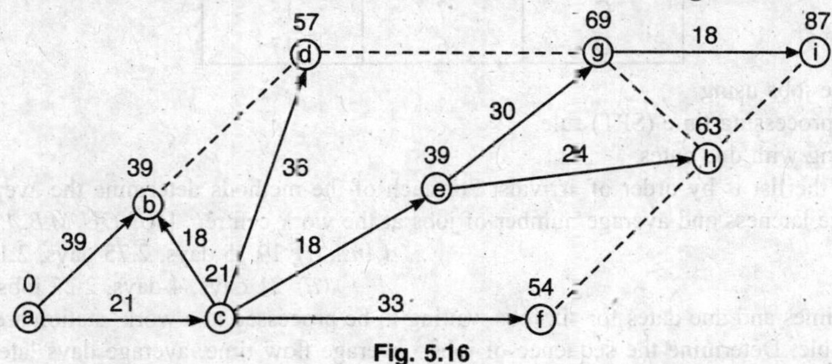

Fig. 5.16

EXERCISES

1. Explain sequencing problem in proper details.
[*P.T.U. MBA May, 2015; Chennai U.B.C.A., 2010; B.Sc. (Math.) Nov., 2012; R.U. B.Com. Dec., 2011; P.U. B.Com. Sept., 2004, 2002; K.U.M.Sc., 2001*]
2. Explain the importance of sequencing problem. What are various methods of solving sequencing problems ? Briefly explain them. [*P.U.B.E. (Mech.) 1997*]
3. Give three different examples of sequencing problem from your daily life. Explain the process of solving sequencing problem. [*P.U.B.Com., 2000*]
4. Explain the following terms in the context of sequencing problems :
(*a*) Total elapsed time and idle time.
(*b*) Processing order. [*GNDU B.Com., 1995*]
5. State the assumptions made in sequencing. [*J.N.T.U. Hyderabad MBA Nov., 2012; R.U. MBA June, 2011; Dec., 2011; V.T.U. Karnataka B.E. June, 2011; Dec., 2010; P.U.B.Com. Sept., 2004*]

6. Write the assumptions for Johnson's rule. [P.T.U. MBA Dec., 2014]
7. Give Johnson's procedure for determining an optimal sequence for processing n jobs on two machines. Give the justification of the rule used in the procedure. [J.N.T.U. Hyderabad MCA Feb., 2012; B.Tech. (C.Sc.) Dec., 2011; May, 2011]
8. When can we apply Johnson's algorithm in finding optimal ordering of n jobs through three machines? Explain the procedure to solve n-job, three machines sequencing problem. [Univ. of Madras B.Sc. (Math.) Nov., 2012; J.N.T.U. Hyderabad B.Tech. (C.Sc.) Dec., 2011; Chennai U., 2002; R.C.C.CHD., 2002]
9. How will you process n jobs through m machines ? Discuss. [Kuru.U.B.E. (Mech.) 1992]
10. Explain how you sequence 2 jobs on m machines. [P.T.U. MBA Dec., 2014; Univ. of Madras B.Sc. (Math.) Nov., 2012]
11. What is the difference between a travelling salesman problem and the shortest-route problem ? Briefly discuss the solution procedure of a shortest-route problem. [P.U.B.E. (Elect.) 1996; B.E. (Mech.) 1996, 95; K.U.B.E. (Mech.) 1992]
12. Discuss the situations leading to multiple optimal solutions in sequencing problems. [J.N.T.U. Hyderabad B.Tech. (C.Sc.) Dec., 2011]
13. Briefly describe each of the following priority rules : (i) SPT (ii) FCFS (iii) EDD. [P.U. UIAMS Jan., 2010; Dayalbagh Edu. Inst. Agra M.Tech. Dec., 2012]

Section 5.3

14. The following table contains information concerning four jobs that are awaiting processing at a work centre.

TABLE 5.26

Job (days)	Job time (days)	Due date
A	14	20
B	10	16
C	7	15
D	6	17

Sequence the jobs using

(*i*) Shortest processing time (SPT) rule.

(*ii*) Processing with due dates.

Assume the list is by order of arrivals. For each of the methods determine the average job flow time, average lateness and average number of jobs at the work centre. [IGNOU M.B.A. Dec., 2004]

(*Ans.* (*i*) 19.75 days, 2.75 days, 2.135 jobs;
(*ii*) 21 days, 4 days, 2.27 jobs.)

15. Processing times and due dates for six jobs waiting to be processed at a work station are given in the following table. Determine the sequence of jobs, average flow time, average days late and average number of jobs at the work station for each of the following rules :

(*i*) FCFS (*ii*) SPT (*iii*) EDD.

TABLE. 5.27

Job	Processing time (days)	Due date (days)
A	4	14
B	16	32
C	8	8
D	20	34
E	10	30
F	18	30

[Dayalbagh Edu. Inst. Agra, M.B.A. Dec., 2007]

(*Ans.* (*i*) A – B – C – D– E– F, 39 days, 18 days, 3.08.
(*ii*) A – C – E – B– F– D, 34.67 days, 13 days, 2.74.
(*iii*) C – A – E – F– B– D, 35.67 days, 12.67 days, 2.82.)

16. For the following data concerning 10 jobs to be processed on one processor determine the minimum flow time schedule. What is the minimum mean flow time ?

TABLE 5.28

Job i	1	2	3	4	5	6	7	8	9	10
Processing time t_i (hours)	5	6	11	8	12	14	7	10	6	12
Importance weight w_i	3	2	1	3	2	1	3	2	1	3
Due date d_i (hours)	30	30	40	80	100	70	90	80	40	90

17. A job shop incurs a cost of ₹ C per day for each day a job is in the shop. At the beginning of a month there are five jobs in the shop. The data for these jobs are given below :

TABLE 5.29

Job	:	1	2	3	4	5
Processing time (days)	:	5	3	10	2	4
Due date (days)	:	10	15	20	9	7

If cost per day is ₹ 50 for each job, what schedule will minimize the total cost ? Suppose job *i* costs ₹ C_i per day for each day it is in the shop. If C_i = ₹ 30, 10, 20, 5 and 50 for i = 1, 2, 3, 4 and 5 respectively, which schedule will minimize the total cost ? [*R.C.C. CHD, 2002*]

18. A bomb squad faces the following situation: A terrorist has planted 5 bombs in an airport building endangering lives and property. The squad has located all five bombs and must now proceed to dismantle them. Because of limited staffing, the bombs can be dismantled only sequentially. Unfortunately, there is not much time left, and squad must choose judiciously the order in which bombs will be dismantled. The following data represents a reliable estimate by the squad :

TABLE 5.30

Bomb	:	1	2	3	4	5
Time to dismantle (hr)	:	3	1	2	4	1
Time remaining before the bomb will explode (hr)	:	9	11.25	11	6	5

What sequence for dismantling the bombs would you recommend to the squad ? What should be the criterion that the squad must optimize ? [*R.C.C. CHD. MCA, 2001*]

19. A custom furniture shop has the five jobs below to be done and it is desired to find the sequence through which they should be processed.

Job	:	A	B	C	D	E
Days to finish	:	2	8	6	4	1
Date promised (in days from today)	:	5	8	12	10	4

Determine the sequence of the jobs, the average flow time, average days late and average number of jobs at the work centre for the following rules :
(a) FCFS (b) EDD (c) SPT.

[*Dayalbagh Edu. Inst. Agra B.Sc. Engg.Tech. Dec., 2011*]
(*Ans.* (a) A-B-C-D-E, 13.8 days, 6.6 days, 3.2.
(b) E-A-B-D-C, 10.2 days, 3.4 days, 2.4.
(c) E-A-D-C-B, 9 days, 2.8 days, 2.143.)

Section 5.4

20. Five jobs must pass through a lathe and a surface grinder, in that order. The processing times in hours are shown below. Determine a minimum makespan sequence of the jobs. Draw the Gantt chart and determine the makespan and machine idle time.

TABLE 5.31

Job	:	1	2	3	4	5
Lathe	:	4	1	5	2	5
Surface grinder	:	3	2	4	3	6

[R.C.C.CHD. MCA, 2001]

21. Find the sequence that minimizes the total elapsed time to complete the following jobs. Each job is processed in the order (*i*) AB (*ii*) BA.

TABLE 5.32

Jobs (Processing times in minutes)

		1	2	3	4	5	6	7
Machines	*A*	12	6	5	11	5	7	6
	B	7	8	9	4	7	8	3

Determine the sequence for the jobs so as to minimize the process time. Also find total elapsed time.

[P.U.B.Com., 2001]

(*Ans.* (*i*) 3–5–2–6–1–4–7 ; 51 min ; 3 min. (*ii*) 7–4–1–6–2–5–3 ; 55 min ; 9 min.)

22. We have five jobs, each of which must go through the two machines *A* and *B* in the order *AB*. Processing times are given in the table below.

TABLE 5.33

Processing time in hours

Job	1	2	3	4	5
Machine A	5	1	9	3	10
Machine B	2	6	7	8	4

Determine a sequence for the five jobs that will minimize the elapsed time *T*.

[U.P.U. MBA, 2010; P.U.B.Com. Sept., 2009; April, 2007; G.N.D.U. B.Com., 2006, 2005; P.T.U. B.Tech. (Mech.) Dec., 2006]

(*Ans.* 2–4–3–5–1; $T_{\min}$ = 30 hours.)

23. A bookbinder has one printing press, one binding machine and manuscripts of a number of different books. The times required in minutes to perform the printing and binding operations for each book are known. We wish to determine the order in which books should be processed in order to minimize the total time required to turn out all the books.

TABLE 5.34

Book	:	1	2	3	4	5	6
Printing time	:	30	120	50	20	90	110
Binding time	:	80	100	90	60	30	10

[J.N.T.U. Hyderabad B.Tech. June, 2009; P.U.B. Com., 2006]

(*Ans.* 4–1–3–2–5–6; $T_{\min}$ = 430 minutes.)

24. A ready-made garment manufacturer has to process 7 items through two stages of production, *viz.* cutting and sewing. The time taken for each of these items at the different stages is given below in appropriate units.

TABLE 5.35

Item	:	1	2	3	4	5	6	7
Cutting time	:	5	7	3	4	6	7	12
Sewing time	:	2	6	7	5	9	5	8

Find the order in which these items are to be processed through these stages so as to minimize the total processing time.

[P.U.B.Com.Jan., 2005]

(*Ans.* 3–4–5–7–2–6–1.)

25. A company has eight large machines which receive preventive maintenance. The maintenance team is divided into two crew *A* and *B*. Crew *A* takes the machine 'power' and replaces parts according to a given

maintenance schedule. The second crew resets the machine and puts it back into operation. At all times the no passing rule is considered to be in effect. The servicing times for each machine are given below.

TABLE 5.36

Machine	*a*	*b*	*c*	*d*	*e*	*f*	*g*	*h*
Crew A	5	4	22	16	15	11	9	4
Crew B	6	10	12	8	20	7	2	21

Determine the optimal sequence of scheduling the factory maintenance crew to minimize their idle time and represent it on a chart. [*P.U.B. Com. April, 2008*]

(*Ans. b–a–e–c–d–f–h–g.*)

26. Seven jobs, each of which has to go through the machines M_1 and M_2 in the order $M_2 M_1$, have the following processing times in hours :

TABLE 5.37

Job	:	A	B	C	D	E	F	G
Machine M_1	:	3	12	15	6	10	11	9
Machine M_2	:	8	10	10	6	12	1	3

(*i*) Determine the optimal sequence that will minimize the total elapsed time. Also find idle time of each machine.

(*ii*) If the order is reversed to $M_1 M_2$, what difference will it make to the calculated results ?

[*J.N.T.U. Hyderabad MBA April, 2012, 2008; Daylabagh Edu. Inst. Agra MBA Nov., 2012; April, 2008; P.U.B.Com. 2008, April, 2003*]

27. A bookbinder has one printing press, one book binding machine and manuscripts of 7 different books. The time required for performing printing and binding operations for different books are shown below.

TABLE 5.38

Book	*Printing time (days)*	*Binding time (days)*
1	20	25
2	90	60
3	80	75
4	20	30
5	120	90
6	15	35
7	65	50

Determine the optimal sequence, total elapsed time and idle time for either operation.

[*P.U.M.Com. Sept., 2004*]

(*Ans.* 6–1–4–5–3–2–7; 460 days; 50 days; 90 days.)

28. Determine an optimal sequence to process the various types of fan blades each day from the following information so as to minimize the total elapsed time :

TABLE 5.39

Types of fan blades	*No. to be processed each day*	*Processing time on*	
		Machine A (minutes)	*Machine B (minutes)*
1	4	4	8
2	6	12	6
3	5	14	16
4	2	20	22
5	4	8	10
6	3	18	2

Also work out the total elapsed time for the optimal sequence. What is the total idle time on the machines ? [*P.U.B. Com. March, 2006*]

(*Ans.* 1→5→3→4→2→6; 286 minutes; 2 minutes; 48 minutes.)

29. In a factory there are six jobs to perform which should go through two machines M_1 and M_2 in that order. The processing times in hours for these jobs are given below:

TABLE 5.40

		Jobs					
		J_1	J_2	J_3	J_4	J_5	J_6
Machines	M_1	1	3	8	5	6	3
	M_2	5	6	3	2	2	10

Determine the optimal sequence, the total elapsed time and idle time on each machine.

(*Ans.* J_1-J_2-J_6-J_3-J_5-J_4; 29 hr ; 3 hr ; 1 hr.)

30. Find the optimal sequence, the total time required to complete the tasks and idle time on each machine for the following data:

TABLE 5.41

		Tasks								
		A	B	C	D	E	F	G	H	I
Machines	I	2	5	4	9	6	8	7	5	4
	II	6	8	7	4	3	9	3	8	11

[*J.N.T.U. Hyderabad MBA June, 2012; B.Tech. (C.Sc.) Dec., 2011; P.U.B.Com. Sept., 2004*]

(*Ans.* A-C-I-B-H-F-D-G-E; 61; 11; 2.)

31. What are the assumptions made in sequencing problems? Sai Automobile Works has six cars for repair. The repair consists of two-step procedure viz. dent removing and painting. The time estimates are as follows :

TABLE 5.42

Car Number	1	2	3	4	5	6
Time Estimate (Dent removing)	16	10	11	13	8	18
Time Estimate (Painting)	15	9	15	11	12	14

Find the correct sequence of operations and prepare Gantt chart and schedule chart so as to minimise the idle time. [*J.N.T.U. Hyderabad B.Tech. (C.Sc.) Dec., 2011*]

32. Find the sequence that minimizes the total elapsed time, given the processing times in hours required to complete the following jobs as shown in the table below. Also compute the total elapsed time and idle time for each machine.

TABLE 5.43

Job:	1	2	3	4	5	6
Machine I:	4	8	3	6	7	5
Machine II:	6	33	7	2	8	4

[*J.N.T.U. Hyderabad B.Tech. May, 2011*]

33. Find the sequence that minimizes the total elapsed time required to complete the following tasks in the sequence M_1M_2:

TABLE 5.44

Job	1	2	3	4	5	6
Machine M_1	2	6	9	3	2	4
Machine M_2	10	8	10	7	9	12

Also find the total elapsed time and idle time of each machine.

[*J.N.T.U. Hyderabad B.Tech. June, 2009*]

Section 5.5

34. A foreman wants to process four different jobs on three machines: a shaping machine, a drilling machine and a tapping machine, the sequence of operations being shaping-drilling-tapping. Decide the optimal sequence for the four jobs to minimize the time elapsed from the start of first job to the end of last job if the process times are

TABLE 5.45

Job	*Shaping (minutes)*	*Drilling (minutes)*	*Tapping (minutes)*
1	13	3	18
2	18	8	4
3	8	6	13
4	23	6	8

(*Ans.* 3–1–4–2; T_{min} = 74 minutes; Idle times: 12, 51, 31 minutes respectively.)

35. If a third stage of production is added, *viz.* pressing and packing with the processing times of exercise no. 24, find the order in which these seven items are to be processed so as to minimize the time taken to process all the items through all the three stages.

Item :	1	2	3	4	5	6	7
Pressing and packing time :	10	12	11	13	12	10	11

[*P.U.B.B.A., 1999*]

(*Ans.* 1–4–3–5–2–5–7; T_{min} = 86 time units; Idle times: 42, 44, 7 time units respectively.)

36. Find the sequence, for the following eight jobs, that will minimize the total elapsed time for the completion of all the jobs. Each job is processed in the same order *CAB*. Entries give the time in hours on the machines.

TABLE 5.46

Jobs		1	2	3	4	5	6	7	8
Times	*A*	4	6	7	4	5	3	6	2
on	*B*	8	10	7	8	11	8	9	13
machines	*C*	5	6	2	3	4	9	15	11

[*V.T.U. Karnataka B.E. Dec., 2010; G.N.D.U.B.Com. April, 2005*]

(*Ans.* 4–1–3–5–2–8–7–6; T_{min} = 81 hours.)

37. Find the sequence that minimizes the total time in hours required to complete the following tasks :

TABLE 5.47

Tasks :	A	B	C	D	E	F	G
Machine I :	3	8	7	4	9	8	7
Machine II :	4	3	2	5	1	4	3
Machine III :	6	7	5	11	5	6	12

What is the minimum elapsed time ?

[*R.U. MBA Dec., 2011; B.P.U.T., 2010; G.N.D.U.B. Com. April, 2008; P.U.B. Com. April, 2006, 2000*]

(*Ans.* (*i*) A–D–G–F–B–C–E
(*ii*) A–D–G–B–F–C–E; 59 hours.)

38. Find the sequence that minimizes the total elapsed time required to complete the following jobs on three machines. Give the necessary condition for the method.

TABLE 5.48

	Jobs:	J_1	J_2	J_3	J_4	J_5	J_6	J_7	J_8
Time on	A_1:	2	7	6	7	10	3	10	12
machines	A_2:	4	5	8	9	7	6	9	11
	A_3:	5	6	4	8	3	9	11	7

[*P.U.B. Com., 2006*]

39. Following table shows processing time in hours for 7 jobs on 3 machines. The order of processing is *ACB*. Determine optimum sequence and minimum elapsed time.

TABLE 5.49

		Job 1	2	3	4	5	6	7
Machine	A	7	8	1	1	2	7	10
	B	7	11	9	7	10	9	8
	C	5	2	1	3	7	6	3

[*Karn. U.B.E. (Mech.) 1996*]

40. Six jobs have to be processed on three machines *A*, *B* and *C* in the order *ACB*. The time taken by each job on each machine is indicated below. Each machine can process only one job at a time. Find the optimal sequence, total elapsed time and idle time on each machine.

TABLE 5.50

Job		:	J_1	J_2	J_3	J_4	J_5	J_6
Processing time	A	:	12	8	7	11	10	5
in hr on	B	:	7	10	9	6	10	4
machine	C	:	3	4	2	5	15	4

[*G.N.D.U. B.Com. April, 2010; 2007*]

41. A book binder has one printing press, one binding machine and one finishing machine and manuscripts of a number of different books. The time required for printing, binding and finishing of each book is known. Determine the order in which the books be processed to minimize the total elapsed time. Also find this time.

TABLE 5.51

Book	Processing time (minutes)				
	1	2	3	4	5
Printing time	40	90	80	60	50
Binding time	50	60	20	30	40
Finishing time	80	100	60	70	100

[*V.T.U. Karnataka B.E. June, 2012; R.U. MBA June, 2011; U.P.U. MBA, 2009*]

(*Ans.* 1-4-5-2-3; 510 min; 140 min; 90 min.)

42. Six jobs have to be processed on three machines A, B and C in the order ACB. Time taken by each job on each machine is indicated below.

TABLE 5.52

		Jobs J_1	J_2	J_3	J_4	J_5	J_6
Machines	A	12	8	7	11	10	5
	B	7	10	9	6	10	5
	C	3	4	2	5	1.5	4

Determine the sequence to minimize the total processing time.

[*G.N.D.U.B. Com. April, 2010*]

(*Ans.* J_3-J_2-J_5-J_4-J_1-J_6 or J_6-J_3-J_5-J_2-J_4-J_1.)

43. Find the optimum sequence when the jobs are to be processed on machines *A*, *B* and *C* in the order *ABC*. Time given is in hours.

TABLE 5.53

Jobs	Machines A	B	C
1	3	8	13
2	12	6	14
3	5	4	9
4	2	6	12
5	9	3	8
6	11	1	13
7	8	8	20

[*G.N.D.U. BBA April, 2008*]

(*Ans.* 4-3-1-6-7-2-5.)

44. Determine the optimal sequence of jobs that minimizes the total elapsed time. Jobs are to be processed on three machines M_1, M_2 and M_3 in the order M_1 M_2 M_3.

TABLE 5.54

Machines	Jobs A	B	C	D	E	F	G
M_1	3	8	7	4	9	8	7
M_2	4	3	2	5	1	4	3
M_3	6	7	5	11	5	6	12

[*G.N.D.U.B. Com. April, 2008*]

(*Ans.* A-G-D-F-B-C-E.)

45. Determine the optimal sequence for the eight jobs. Time required in minutes by each job is given. Also find the total elapsed time.

TABLE 5.55

Machines	Jobs 1	2	3	4	5	6	7	8
M_1	14	10	10	13	12	11	9	9
M_2	11	14	10	9	14	14	7	10
M_3	9	8	10	11	12	7	8	9

[*Osmania U.Hyderabad MBA July, 2010*]

46. There are five jobs, each of which must go through machines A, B and C in the order ABC. Processing times are given in the table below:

TABLE 5.56

Job	Processing times (hr)		
	A	B	C
1	8	5	4
2	10	6	9
3	6	2	8
4	7	3	6
5	11	4	5

Determine a sequence for five jobs that will minimize the elapsed time T.

[*J.N.T.U. Hyderbad B.Tech. (Mech.) May, 2012; V.T.U. Karnataka B.Tech. June, 2010*]

47. There are five jobs, each of which is to be processed through three machines A, B and C in the order ABC. Processing times in hours are

TABLE 5.57

Job	A	B	C
1	3	4	7
2	8	5	9
3	7	1	5
4	5	2	6
5	4	3	10

Determine the optimum sequence for the five jobs and the minimum elapsed time. Also find the idle time for the three machines and waiting time for the jobs.

[*J.N.T.U. Hyderabad B.Tech. Sept., 2011*]

Section 5.6

48. Use graphical method to minimize the time needed to process the following jobs on machines *A*, *B*, *C*, *D* and *E*. Find the total time elapsed to complete both jobs. Also find for each job, the machine on which it should be processed first.

TABLE 5.58

Job 1 Sequence :	*A*	*B*	*C*	*D*	*E*
Time (hr). :	2	3	5	2	1
Job 2 Sequence :	*D*	*C*	*A*	*B*	*E*
Time (hr) :	6	2	3	1	3

(*Ans.* T_{min} = 16 hr; *A*(1), *B*(1), *C*(1), *D*(2), *E*(1 or 2).]

49. There are two jobs to be processed through four machines *A*, *B*, *C*, and *D*. The prescribed technological orders are

Job 1 : ABCD

Job 2 : DBAC

Processing times in hours are given in the following table :

TABLE 5.59

Job	*Machine A*	*B*	*C*	*D*
1	2	4	5	1
2	6	4	2	3

Calculate the total minimum elapsed time to complete the two jobs.

[*Chennai B.Sc. (Math.) 1984*]

(*Ans.* T_{min} = 21 hrs.)

50. There are two jobs to be processed through five machines *A*, *B*, *C*, *D* and *E*. The prescribed technological order is

Job 1 :	*A*	*B*	*C*	*D*	*E*
Job 2 :	*B*	*C*	*A*	*D*	*E*

The process times in hours are given in table 5.60.

TABLE 5.60

Job 1		*Job 2*	
Sequence of machines	*Time*	*Sequence of machines*	*Time*
A	3	*B*	5
B	4	*C*	4
C	2	*A*	3
D	6	*D*	2
E	2	*E*	6

Find out the optimal sequencing of jobs on machines and the minimum time required to process these jobs. [U.P.U. MBA, 2010]

(*Ans.* T_{min} = 22 hr; $A(1)$, $B(2)$, $C(2)$, $D(1)$, $E(2)$.)

51. The time spent in processing of two jobs on six machines A, B, C, D, E, F and the necessary technological ordering of machines are as follows :

TABLE 5.61

Job 1	*Sequence*	*A*	*B*	*C*	*D*	*E*	*F*
	Time (min)	20	10	10	30	25	15
Job 2	*Sequence*	*A*	*C*	*B*	*D*	*F*	*E*
	Time (min)	10	30	15	10	15	20

Use graphical method to determine an optimal sequence of jobs which minimizes elapsed time. [Karn. U.B.E. (Mech.) 1997]

52. Determine the least time in which the two jobs can be performed on the eight machines. The processing times and the machine sequence for the jobs are given below :

TABLE 5.62

	M/c sequence	:	*A*	*B*	*C*	*D*	*E*	*F*	*G*	*H*
Job 1	*Time (hr)*	:	6	4	5	5	7	2	1	5
	M/c sequence	:	*C*	*B*	*A*	*D*	*E*	*G*	*F*	*H*
Job 2	*Time (hr)*	:	5	6	3	4	4	6	1	4

[P.U. MBA, 1997]

53. Determine the minimum elapsed time for completing the following two jobs. Details of processing time and the sequence of operations are given below:

Job 1 : A – 4 to C – 2 to D – 6 to E – 3 to B – 2
Job 2 : C – 8 to A – 3 to D – 4 to B – 2 to E – 3

Also determine the sequences of jobs on each machine. [V.T.U. Karnataka B.E. June, 2012]

54. It is required to process the following two jobs on various machines shown below:

TABLE 5.63

	Sequence	A	B	C	D	E
Job I	*Time (in hr)*	7	9	5	13	5
	Sequence	B	C	A	D	E
Job II	*Time (in hr)*	11	9	7	5	13

Find for each machine which job should be done first and calculate the total elapsed time. [V.T.U. Karnataka B.E. Jan., 2010]

Section 5.7

55. There are four jobs each of which has to be processed on machines A, B, C, D, E and F in the order A B C D E F. Processing time in hours is given in table 5.64. Find out the optimal sequencing of jobs, minimum time required to process these jobs and the idle time for each of the machines.

TABLE 5.64

Job	*A*	*B*	*C*	*D*	*E*	*F*
1	15	8	6	14	6	26
2	17	7	9	10	15	22
3	21	7	12	9	11	19
4	18	6	11	12	14	17

[Karn. U.B.E. (Mech.) 1998; P.U.B.E. (Mech.) Nov., 1994]

(*Ans.* 1–2–4–3; T_{min} = 133 hr ; Idle times: 62, 105, 95, 88, 87 and 49 hr respectively.)

56. Solve the following sequencing problem giving an optimal solution when no passing is allowed:

TABLE 5.65

		Job				
		1	2	3	4	5
Machine	A	14	7	12	8	10
	B	5	6	4	7	3
	C	3	2	4	1	5
	D	10	12	8	15	16

(*Ans.* 2–4–5–1–3; T_{min} = 76 time units;
Idle times: 25, 51,
61, 15 time units respectively.)

57. Find an optimal sequence for the following sequencing problem of four jobs and five machines when passing is not allowed :

TABLE 5.66

Job:	1	2	3	4
Machine M_1:	6	5	4	7
Machine M_2:	4	5	3	2
Machine M_3:	1	3	4	2
Machine M_4:	2	4	5	1
Machine M_5:	8	9	7	5

Also find the total elapsed time.

[*Osmania M.Sc.* (*Math.*) *1982*]
(*Ans.* 1–3–2–4; 43 hours.)

58. There are 4 jobs each of which has to go through the machines $M_1, M_2, ..., M_6$ in the order $M_1 M_2 ... M_6$. Processing times in minutes are given. Determine the sequence of these four jobs which minimizes the total elapsed time *T*.

TABLE 5.67

		Machines					
		M_1	M_2	M_3	M_4	M_5	M_6
	A	20	10	9	4	12	27
Jobs	*B*	19	8	11	8	10	21
	C	13	7	10	7	9	17
	D	22	6	5	6	10	14

(*Ans. C–A–B–D; T_{min}* = 130 minutes.)

59. Six jobs 1, 2, 3, 4, 5 and 6 are to be processed on five machines *A*, *B*, *C*, *D* and *E* in the order *BCDEA*. Find the optimal sequence of jobs, minimum time to process these jobs and the idle time for each of the machines. The processing times in hours are given below.

TABLE 5.68

		Time in hours on machines				
		A	B	C	D	E
	1	8	6	1	2	5
	2	13	7	2	4	1
Jobs	3	8	18	5	5	4
	4	11	15	2	6	3
	5	13	8	6	5	6
	6	9	11	4	6	7

[*P.U.B.E. (Mech.) May, 1994*]

60. Suggest optimum assignment of 4 workers A, B, C and D to 4 jobs I, II, III and IV. The time taken by different workers in completing the different jobs is given below:

TABLE 5.69

		Jobs			
		I	II	III	IV
Workers	A	8	10	12	16
	B	11	11	15	8
	C	9	6	5	14
	D	15	14	9	7

Also find the total time taken in completing the jobs. *[Chennai U. BBA Nov., 2010]*

Section 5.10

61. Find the shortest route from '*a*' to '*i*' by using graphical method. The numbers on the links represent the distance in kilometres.

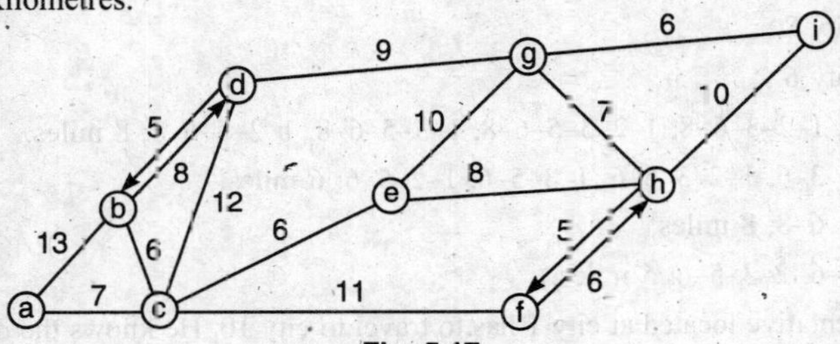

Fig. 5.17

(*Ans. a-c-e-g-i;* 29 km.)

62. Find the shortest route from '0' to '8' by using graphical method. The numbers on the links represent the distance in kilometres.

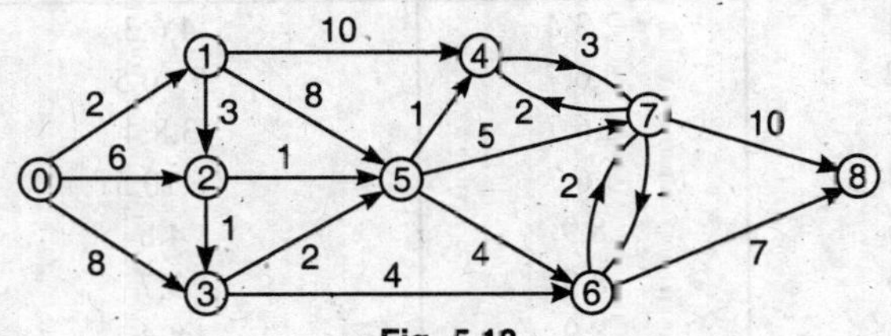

Fig. 5.18

(*Ans.* 0-1-2-3-6-8; 17 km; 0-1-2-5-6-8.)

63. Find the shortest route from *a* to *k* by using graphical method. The numbers on the links represent the distance in kilometres.

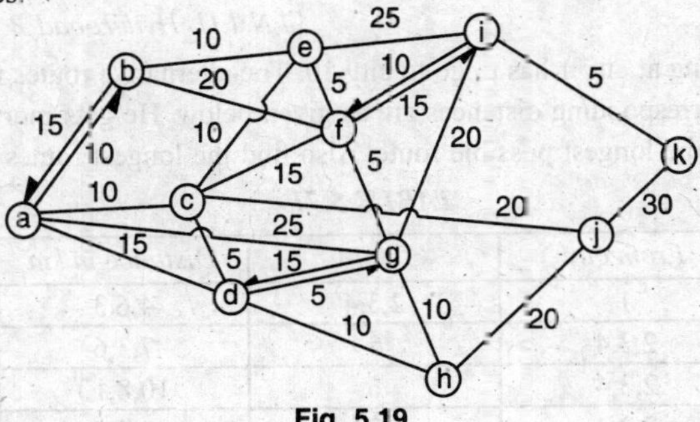

Fig. 5.19

(*Ans.* (*i*) *a-b-e-f-i-k,*
(*ii*) *a-c-f-i-k,*
(*iii*) *a-c-d-g-f-i-k,*
(*iv*) *a-d-g-f-i-k,*
(*v*) *a-d-g-i-k;*
(*vi*) *a-c-e-f-i-k*; 45 km.)

64. The network in Fig. 5.20 represents the distances in miles between various cities i, $i = 1, 2, 3, ..., 8$. Find the shortest route between the following pairs of cities :

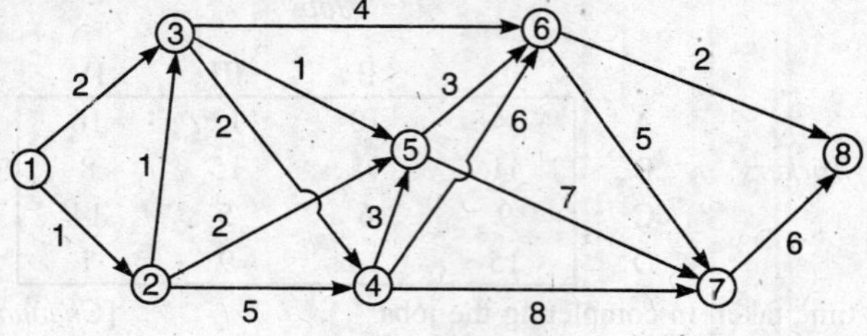

Fig. 5.20

(*i*) City 1 to city 8.
(*ii*) City 1 to city 6.
(*iii*) City 4 to city 8.
(*iv*) City 2 to city 6. [*H.P.U. MCA, 1999*]

(*Ans.* (*i*)1–3–6–8, 1–2–3–6–8, 1–2–3–5–6–8, 1–3–5–6–8, 1–2–5–6–8; 8 miles.
(*ii*) 1–3–6, 1–2–3–6, 1–2–3–5–6, 1–3–5–6, 1–2–5–6; 6 miles.
(*iii*) 4–6–8, 4–5–6–8; 8 miles.
(*iv*) 2–3–6, 2–5–6, 2–3–5–6; 5 miles.)

65. A medical representative located at city 1 has to travel to city 10. He knows the distance of alternative routes from city 1 to city 10. Find the shortest possible route. Also find the shortest routes from any city to city 10. The possible routes and corresponding distances are as given below:

TABLE 5.70

From city	*To city*	*Corresponding distance in km*
1	2,3,4	4,6,3
2	5,6,7	7,10,5
3	5,6,7	3,8,4
4	5,6,7	6,10,5
5	8,9	4,8
6	8,9	3,7
7	8,9	8,4
8	10	7
9	10	9

[*J.N.T.U. Hyderabad B.Tech. (C.Sc.) Dec., 2011*]

66. A representative residing at city 1 has to go to city 10. The alternative routes from city 1 to city 10, the possible routes and corresponding distances are as given below. He gets more travelling allowances if he travels more. Find the longest possible route. Also find the longest routes from any city to city 10.

TABLE 5.71

From city	*To city*	*Distance in km*
1	2,3,4	4,6,3
2,3,4	5	7,3,6
2,3,4	6	10,8,10
2,3,4	7	5,4,5
5,6,7	8	4,3,8
5,6,7	9	8,7,4
8,9	10	7,9

[*J.N.T.U. Hyderabad B.Tech. (C.Sc.) Dec., 2011*]

67. In 18th century, when transportation systems were not developed, a family wanted to travel from their home to reach a friend's home in other part of the country. They had a choice of alternate routes and haltages between their home and the destination. The costs of travel from each point to the other point on route, based on such factors as distance, difficulty, mode of transportation, etc. are given below:

TABLE 5.72

	1	2	3	4	5	6	7	8	9	10
1	–	7	5	4	–	–	–	–	–	–
2	–	–	–	–	8	3	9	–	–	–
3	–	–	–	–	10	7	6	–	–	–
4	–	–	–	–	4	5	6	–	–	–
5	–	–	–	–	–	–	–	6	8	–
6	–	–	–	–	–	–	–	7	4	–
7	–	–	–	–	–	–	–	3	6	–
8	–	–	–	–	–	–	–	–	–	5
9	–	–	–	–	–	–	–	–	–	4

Find the safest route so that the total travelling cost is minimum.

[J.N.T.U. Hyderabad B.Tech. May, 2011; April, 2011]

68. A distance network consists of 11 nodes which are distributed as shown in the table below. Find the shortest path from node 1 to node 11 and also the corresponding distances.

TABLE 5.73

Arc	*Distance*	*Arc*	*Distance*
1-2	8	5-7	8
1-3	7	5-8	1
1-4	4	6-9	3
1-5	2	6-10	5
2-6	4	7-9	5
3-6	8	7-10	1
3-7	4	8-10	5
4-7	6	9-11	5
		10-11	5

[J.N.T.U. Hyderabad B.Tech. June, 2009]

Advanced Topics in Linear Programming

6.1 DUALITY IN LINEAR PROGRAMMING

For every L.P. problem (linear programme) there is a related unique L.P. problem (another linear programme) involving the same data which also describes the original problem (programme).

The given original programme is called the *primal programme* (P). This programme can be rewritten by transposing (reversing) the rows and columns of the algebraic statement of the problem. Inverting the programme in this way results in *dual programme* (D). The variables of the dual programme (problem) are known as *dual variables* or *shadow prices* of the various resources. A solution to the dual programme may be found in a manner similar to that used for the primal. The two programmes have very closely related properties so that *optimal* solution of the dual problem gives complete information about the *optimal* solution of the primal problem and vice versa.

Duality is an extremely important and interesting feature of linear programming. The various useful aspects of this property are

(*i*) If the primal problem contains a large number of rows (constraints) and a smaller number of columns (variables), the computational procedure can be considerably reduced by converting it into dual and then solving it. Hence it offers an advantage in many applications.

(*ii*) It gives additional information as to how the optimal solution changes as a result of the changes in the coefficients and the formulation of the problem. This forms the basis of *post optimality or sensitivity analysis*.

(*iii*) Duality in linear programming has certain far reaching consequences of economic nature. This can help managers to compare the alternative courses of action and their relative values.

(*iv*) Calculation of the dual checks the accuracy of the primal solution.

(*v*) Duality in linear programming shows that each linear programme is equivalent to a two-person zero-sum game. This indicates that fairly close relationships exist between linear programming and the theory of games.

(*vi*) Duality is not restricted to linear programming problems only but finds application in economics, physics and other fields. In economics it is used in the formulation of input and output systems. In physics it is used in the series circuit and parallel circuit theory.

(*vii*) Economic interpretation of the dual helps the management in making future decisions.

(*viii*) Duality is used to solve L.P. problems (by the *dual simplex method*) in which the initial solution is infeasible.

(*ix*) The solution of the dual problem can be used by the decision-maker for planning or augmenting (increasing) the resources.

6.1-1 Dual Problem when Primal is in Canonical Form

The general linear programming problem in canonical form as discussed in section 2.12-1 is

$$\begin{aligned}
&\text{maximize} && Z = c_1x_1 + c_2x_2 + c_3x_3 + \dots + c_nx_n,\\
&\text{subject to} && a_{11}x_1 + a_{12}x_2 + a_{13}x_3 + \dots + a_{1n}x_n \le b_1,\\
& && a_{21}x_1 + a_{22}x_2 + a_{23}x_3 + \dots + a_{2n}x_n \le b_2,\\
& && \dots\dots\dots\dots\dots\dots\dots\dots\\
& && \dots\dots\dots\dots\dots\dots\dots\dots\\
& && a_{m1}x_1 + a_{m2}x_2 + a_{m3}x_3 + \dots + a_{mn}x_n \le b_m,\\
&\text{where} && x_1, x_2, x_3, \dots, x_n, \text{ all} \ge 0.
\end{aligned} \qquad \dots(6.1)$$

If the above problem is referred to as primal, then its associated dual will be

$$\begin{aligned}
&\text{minimize} && W = b_1y_1 + b_2y_2 + b_3y_3 + \dots + b_my_m,\\
&\text{subject to} && a_{11}y_1 + a_{21}y_2 + a_{31}y_3 + \dots + a_{m1}y_m \ge c_1,\\
& && a_{12}y_1 + a_{22}y_2 + a_{32}y_3 + \dots + a_{m2}y_m \ge c_2,\\
& && \dots\dots\dots\dots\dots\dots\dots\dots\\
& && \dots\dots\dots\dots\dots\dots\dots\dots\\
& && a_{1n}y_1 + a_{2n}y_2 + a_{3n}y_3 + \dots + a_{mn}y_m \ge c_n,\\
&\text{where the dual variables} && y_1, y_2, y_3, \dots, y_m, \text{ all} \ge 0.
\end{aligned} \qquad \dots(6.2)$$

Equations (6.1) and (6.2) are called *symmetric primal-dual pairs.*

The above pair of programmes can be written as

Primal	*Dual*
maximize $Z = \sum_{j=1}^{n} c_j x_j$,	minimize $W = \sum_{i=1}^{m} b_i y_i$,
subject to $\sum_{j=1}^{n} a_{ij} x_j \le b_i$, $i = 1,2,3, \dots, m,$	subject to $\sum_{i=1}^{m} a_{ij} y_i \ge c_j$, $j = 1,2,3, \dots, n,$
where $x_j \ge 0$, $j = 1,2,3, \dots, n.$	where $y_i \ge 0$, $i = 1,2,3, \dots, m.$

From the above two programmes, the following *rules* to construct the dual are clear:

(1) If the primal contains n variables and m constraints, the dual will contain m variables and n constraints.

(2) The maximization problem in the primal becomes the minimization problem in the dual and vice versa.

(3) The maximization problem has (≤) constraints while the minimization problem has (≥) cosntraints.

(4) Constraints of ≤ type in the primal become ≥ type in the dual and vice versa.

(5) The coefficient matrix of the constraints of the dual is the transpose of the primal.

(6) A new set of variables appear in the dual.

(7) The constants $c_1, c_2, c_3, \dots, c_n$ in the objective function of the primal appear in the right-hand side of the constraints of the dual.

(8) The constants $b_1, b_2, b_3, \dots, b_m$ in the right-hand side of the constraints of the primal appear in the objective function of the dual.

(9) The variables in both problems are non-negative.

The constraint relationships of the primal and dual can be represented in a single table such as table 6.1.

TABLE 6.1

	x_1	x_2	x_3	…	x_n	
y_1	a_{11}	a_{12}	a_{13}	⋯	a_{1n}	$\le b_1$
y_2	a_{21}	a_{22}	a_{23}	⋯	a_{2n}	$\le b_2$
y_3	a_{31}	a_{32}	a_{33}	⋯	a_{3n}	$\le b_3$
⋮	⋮	⋮	⋮	⋮	⋮	⋮
y_m	a_{m1}	a_{m2}	a_{m3}	⋯	a_{mn}	$\le b_m$
	$\ge c_1$	$\ge c_2$	$\ge c_3$	⋯	$\ge c_n$	

The primal-dual relationships can also be summarized as below:

Primal	*Dual*
(*i*) Maximization problem	Minimization problem
(*ii*) n variables and m constraints	m variables and n constraints
(*iii*) $\le$ type constraints	$\ge$ type constraints
(*iv*) Objective function coefficients	R.H.S. constants of the constraints
(*v*) R.H.S. constants of the constraints	Objective function coefficients
(*vi*) = type ith constraint	unrestricted ith variable
(*vii*) Variable x_j unrestricted	jth constraint = type

EXAMPLE 6.1-1.1

Construct the dual to the primal problem

maximize $Z = 3x_1 + 5x_2,$

subject to
$$2x_1 + 6x_2 \le 50,$$
$$3x_1 + 2x_2 \le 35,$$
$$5x_1 - 3x_2 \le 10,$$
$$x_2 \le 20,$$
where $x_1 \ge 0,\ x_2 \ge 0.$ *[NIIFT Mohali, 2000]*

Solution

Let y_1, y_2, y_3 and y_4 be the corresponding dual variables, then the dual problem is given by

minimize $W = 50y_1 + 35y_2 + 10y_3 + 20y_4,$

subject to
$$2y_1 + 3y_2 + 5y_3 \ge 3,$$
$$6y_1 + 2y_2 - 3y_3 + y_4 \ge 5,$$
where y_1, y_2, y_3, y_4, all ≥ 0.

As the dual problem has lesser number of constraints than the primal (2 instead of 4), it requires lesser work and effort to solve it. This follows from the fact that the computational difficulty in the linear programming problem is mainly associated with the number of constraints rather than number of variables.

EXAMPLE 6.1-1.2

Construct the dual of the problem

minimize $Z = 3x_1 - 2x_2 + 4x_3,$

subject to the constraints
$$3x_1 + 5x_2 + 4x_3 \ge 7,$$
$$6x_1 + x_2 + 3x_3 \ge 4,$$
$$7x_1 - 2x_2 - x_3 \le 10,$$
$$x_1 - 2x_2 + 5x_3 \ge 3,$$
$$4x_1 + 7x_2 - 2x_3 \ge 2,$$
$$x_1, x_2, x_3 \ge 0.$$
[Meerut B.Sc. (Math.) 1970]

Solution

As the given problem is of minimization, all constraints should be of ≥ type. Multiplying the third constraint by – 1 on both sides, we get

$$-7x_1 + 2x_2 + x_3 \geq -10.$$

The dual of the given problem will be

$$\begin{aligned} \text{maximize} \quad & W = 7y_1 + 4y_2 - 10y_3 + 3y_4 + 2y_5, \\ \text{subject to} \quad & 3y_1 + 6y_2 - 7y_3 - y_4 + 4y_5 \leq 3, \\ & 5y_1 + y_2 + 2y_3 - 2y_4 + 7y_5 \leq -2, \\ & 4y_1 + 3y_2 + y_3 + 5y_4 - 2y_5 \leq 4, \\ & y_1, y_2, y_3, y_4, y_5, \text{ all} \geq 0, \end{aligned}$$

where y_1, y_2, y_3, y_4, and y_5 are the dual variables associated with the first, second, third, fourth and fifth constraint respectively.

EXAMPLE 6.1-1.3

Construct the dual of the problem

$$\begin{aligned} \textit{maximize} \quad & Z = 3x_1 + 17x_2 + 9x_3, \\ \textit{subject to} \quad & x_1 - x_2 + x_3 \geq 3, \\ & -3x_1 + 2x_3 \leq 1, \\ & x_1 \geq 0,\ x_2 \geq 0,\ x_3 \geq 0. \end{aligned}$$

Solution

Firstly the ≥ constraint is converted into ≤ constraint by multiplying both sides by –1.

i.e., $-x_1 + x_2 - x_3 \leq -3$.

Now the dual of the given problem is

$$\begin{aligned} \text{minimize} \quad & W = -3y_1 + y_2, \\ \text{subject to} \quad & -y_1 - 3y_2 \geq 3, \\ & y_1 \geq 17, \\ & -y_1 + 2y_2 \geq 9, \\ & y_1 \geq 0,\ y_2 \geq 0. \end{aligned}$$

6.1.2 Dual Problem when Primal is in the Standard Form

As discussed in section 2.12-2, all constraints are equations (=) in standard form. In this section we shall find that an equality constraint in the primal corresponds to an unconstrained variable in the dual and vice versa. Consider the problem

$$\begin{aligned} \text{maximize} \quad & Z = c_1x_1 + c_2x_2, \\ \text{subject to} \quad & a_{11}x_1 + a_{12}x_2 = b_1, \\ & a_{21}x_1 + a_{22}x_2 \leq b_2, \\ & x_1 \geq 0,\ x_2 \geq 0. \end{aligned}$$

The first constraint of equality form, when expressed in canonical form is equivalent to

$$a_{11}x_1 + a_{12}x_2 \leq b_1 \text{ and } a_{11}x_1 + a_{12}x_2 \geq b_1.$$

Or it can be expressed as

$$\begin{aligned} & a_{11}x_1 + a_{12}x_2 \leq b_1, \\ & -a_{11}x_1 - a_{12}x_2 \leq -b_1. \end{aligned}$$

Let y'_1, y''_1 and y_2 be the dual variables associated with the first, second and third constraints. Then the dual problem is

$$\begin{aligned} \text{minimize} \quad & W = b_1(y'_1 - y''_1) + b_2y_2, \\ \text{subject to} \quad & a_{11}(y'_1 - y''_1) + a_{21}y_2 \geq c_1, \\ & a_{12}(y'_1 - y''_1) + a_{22}y_2 \geq c_2, \\ & y'_1 \geq 0,\ y''_1 \geq 0,\ y_2 \geq 0. \end{aligned}$$

Note that the term $(y'_1 - y''_1)$ occurs in the objective function as well as all the constraints of the dual. This will always be true whenever there is an equality constraint in the primal. If we put $y'_1 - y''_1 = y_1$, then the new variable y_1, which is the difference between two non-negative variables, becomes unrestricted in sign and the dual problem becomes

$$\begin{aligned} &\text{minimize} && W = b_1y_1 + b_2y_2, \\ &\text{subject to} && a_{11}y_1 + a_{21}y_2 \geq c_1, \\ & && a_{12}y_1 + a_{22}y_2 \geq c_2, \end{aligned}$$

y_1 unrestricted in sign, $y_2 \geq 0$.

This shows that the dual variable which corresponds to an equality constraint must be unrestricted in sign. Conversely, when a primal variable is unrestricted in sign, its dual constraint must be in equality form.

In general, if the primal problem in standard form is

$$\text{maximize} \quad Z = \sum_{j=1}^{n} c_j x_j,$$

$$\text{subject to} \quad \sum_{j=1}^{n} a_{ij} x_j = b_i, \quad i = 1, 2, 3, \ldots, m,$$

$$x_j \geq 0, \qquad j = 1, 2, 3, \ldots, n;$$

then the dual problem is

$$\text{minimize} \quad W = \sum_{i=1}^{m} b_i y_i,$$

$$\text{subject to} \quad \sum_{i=1}^{m} a_{ij} y_i \geq c_j, \qquad j = 1, 2, 3, \ldots n,$$

y_i are unrestricted in sign for all i.

On the other hand , if the primal problem is

$$\text{maximize} \quad Z = \sum_{j=1}^{n} c_j x_j,$$

$$\text{subject to} \quad \sum_{j=1}^{n} a_{ij} x_j \leq b_i, \qquad i = 1, 2, 3, \ldots m,$$

x_j are unrestricted in sign for all j,

then the dual problem is given by

$$\text{minimize} \quad W = \sum_{i=1}^{m} b_i y_i,$$

$$\text{subject to} \quad \sum_{i=1}^{m} a_{ij} y_i = c_j, \qquad j = 1, 2, 3, \ldots, n,$$

$$y_i \geq 0, \; i = 1, 2, 3, \ldots, m.$$

Note that in this case the dual is in the standard form.

From the above discussion it is concluded that we can work with any of the forms of primal while dealing with duality theory.

EXAMPLE 6.1-2.1

Construct the dual of the problem

$$\begin{aligned} &\textit{maximize} && Z = 3x_1 + 10x_2 + 2x_3, \\ &\textit{subject to} && 2x_1 + 3x_2 + 2x_3 \leq 7, \\ & && 3x_1 - 2x_2 + 4x_3 = 3, \\ & && x_1 \geq 0, x_2 \geq 0, x_3 \geq 0. \end{aligned}$$

[*NIIFT Mohali, 2000*]

Solution

As the given problem is of maximization, all constraints should be of ≤ type. The constraint $3x_1 - 2x_2 + 4x_3 = 3$ can be expressed as a pair of inequalities

$$3x_1 - 2x_2 + 4x_3 \le 3 \text{ and } 3x_1 - 2x_2 + 4x_3 \ge 3$$

or $$3x_1 - 2x_2 + 4x_3 \le 3 \text{ and } -3x_1 + 2x_2 - 4x_3 \le -3$$

Let y_1, y'_2 and y''_2 be the associated non-negative dual variables. Then the dual of the problem is

$$\begin{aligned} \text{minimize} \quad & W = 7y_1 - 3(y'_2 - y''_2), \\ \text{subject to} \quad & 2y_1 - 3(y'_2 - y''_2) \ge 3, \\ & 3y_1 - 2(y'_2 - y''_2) \ge 10, \\ & 2y_1 - 4(y'_2 - y''_2) \ge 2, \\ \text{where} \quad & y_1, y'_2, y''_2 \ge 0. \end{aligned}$$

Substituting $y_2' - y_2'' = y_2$, where y_2 is unrestricted in sign, the dual problem becomes

$$\begin{aligned} \text{minimize} \quad & W = 7y_1 - 3y_2, \\ \text{subject to} \quad & 2y_1 - 3y_2 \ge 3, \\ & 3y_1 - 2y_2 \ge 10, \\ & 2y_1 + 4y_2 \ge 2, \end{aligned}$$

where $y_1 \ge 0$, y_2 unrestricted in sign.

EXAMPLE 6.1-2.2

Construct the dual of the problem

$$\begin{aligned} \textit{minimize} \quad & Z = x_2 + 3x_3, \\ \textit{subject to} \quad & 2x_1 + x_2 \le 3, \\ & x_1 + 2x_2 + 6x_3 \ge 5, \\ & -x_1 + x_2 + 2x_3 = 2, \\ & x_1, x_2, x_3 \ge 0. \end{aligned}$$

[Univ. of Madras B.Sc. (Math.) Nov., 2012; P.U.B. Com. Sept., 2004]

Solution

As the given problem is of minimization, all constraints should be of ≥ type. Multiplying the first constraint by –1 on both sides we get

$$-2x_1 - x_2 \ge -3.$$

The constraint $-x_1 + x_2 + 2x_3 = 2$ can be expressed as a pair of inequalities

$$-x_1 + x_2 + 2x_3 \ge 2 \text{ and } -x_1 + x_2 + 2x_3 \le 2$$

or $$-x_1 + x_2 + 2x_3 \ge 2 \text{ and } x_1 - x_2 - 2x_3 \ge -2.$$

Thus the given problem becomes

$$\begin{aligned} \text{minimize} \quad & Z = 0x_1 + x_2 + 3x_3, \\ \text{subject to} \quad & -2x_1 - x_2 \ge -3, \\ & x_1 + 2x_2 + 6x_3 \ge 5, \\ & -x + x_2 + 2x_3 \ge 2, \\ & x_1 - x_2 - 2x_3 \ge -2, \\ & x_1, x_2, x_3 \ge 0. \end{aligned}$$

Let y_1, y_2, y'_3 and y''_3 be the associated non-negative dual variables. Then the dual of the problem is

$$\begin{aligned} \text{maximize} \quad & W = -3y_1 + 5y_2 + 2y'_3 - 2y''_3, \\ \text{subject to} \quad & -2y_1 + y_2 - y'_3 + y''_3 \le 0, \\ & -y_1 + 2y_2 + y'_3 - y''_3 \le 1, \\ & 6y_2 + 2y'_3 - 2y''_3 \le 3, \\ & y_1, y_2, y'_3, y''_3, \text{ all} \ge 0 \end{aligned}$$

Substituting $y'_3 - y_3'' = y_3$ where y_3 is unrestricted in sign, the dual problem becomes

$$\begin{aligned} \text{maximize} \quad & W = -3y_1 + 5y_2 + 2y_3, \\ \text{subject to} \quad & -2y_1 + y_2 - y_3 \le 0, \\ & -y_1 + 2y_2 + y_3 \le 1, \\ & 6y_2 + 2y_3 \le 3, \\ & y_1, y_2, \ge 0,\ y_3 \text{ unrestricted in sign.} \end{aligned}$$

EXAMPLE 6.1-2.3

Construct the dual of the primal problem

$$\begin{aligned} \textit{maximize} \quad & Z = 2x_1 + x_2 + x_3, \\ \textit{subject to} \quad & x_1 + x_2 + x_3 \ge 6, \\ & 3x_1 - 2x_2 + 3x_3 = 3, \\ & -4x_1 + 3x_2 - 6x_3 = 1, \\ & x_1, x_2, x_3 \ge 0. \end{aligned}$$

[P.U.B. Com. April, 2006]

Solution

As the given problem is of maximization, all cosntraints should be ≤ type. Multiplying the first constraint by – 1 on both sides we get

$$-x_1 - x_2 - x_3 \le -6.$$

The equation $3x_1 - 2x_2 + 3x_3 = 3$ can be expressed as a pair of inequalities

$$3x_1 - 2x_2 + 3x_3 \le 3 \text{ and } 3x_1 - 2x_2 + 3x_3 \ge 3$$

or $3x_1 - 2x_2 + 3x_3 \le 3$ and $-3x_1 + 2x_2 - 3x_3 \le -3$.

Similarly, the equation $-4x_1 + 3x_2 - 6x_3 = 1$ can be expressed as

$$-4x_1 + 3x_2 - 6x_3 \le 1 \text{ and } 4x_1 - 3x_2 + 6x_3 \le -1.$$

Thus the given problem becomes

$$\begin{aligned} \text{maximize} \quad & Z = 2x_1 + x_2 + x_3, \\ \text{subject to} \quad & -x_1 - x_2 - x_3 \le -6, \\ & 3x_1 - 2x_2 + 3x_3 \le 3, \\ & -3x_1 + 2x_2 - 3x_3 \le -3, \\ & -4x_1 + 3x_2 - 6x_3 \le 1, \\ & 4x_1 - 3x_2 + 6x_3 \le -1. \\ & x_1, x_2, x_3 \ge 0. \end{aligned}$$

Let $y_1, y'_2, y''_2, y'_3, y''_3$ be the associated non-negative dual variables. Then the dual of this problem is

$$\begin{aligned} \text{minimize} \quad & W = -6y_1 + 3(y'_2 - y''_2) + (y'_3 - y_3''), \\ \text{subject to} \quad & -y_1 + 3(y'_2 - y_2'') - 4(y'_3 - y_3'') \ge 2, \\ & -y_1 - 2(y'_2 - y_2'') + 3(y'_3 - y_3'') \ge 1, \\ & -y_1 + 3(y'_2 - y_2'') - 6(y'_3 - y_3'') \ge 1, \\ & y_1, y'_2, y_2'', y'_3, y''_3, \text{ all} \ge 0. \end{aligned}$$

Substituting $y'_2 - y_2'' = y_2$ and $y'_3 - y_3'' = y_3$, where y_2 and y_3 are both unrestricted in sign, the dual problem becomes

$$\begin{aligned} \text{minimize} \quad & W = -6y_1 + 3y_2 + y_3, \\ \text{subject to} \quad & -y_1 + 3y_2 - 4y_3 \ge 2, \\ & -y_1 - 2y_2 + 3y_3 \ge 1, \\ & -y_1 + 3y_2 - 6y_3 \ge 1, \end{aligned}$$

$y_1 \ge 0$, y_2 and y_3 unrestricted in sign.

EXAMPLE 6.1-2.4

Obtain the dual of the following primal problem:

$$\textit{Minimize} \quad Z = 3x_1 - 2x_2 + x_3,$$

subject to $2x_1 - 3x_2 + x_3 \leq 5,$
$4x_1 - 2x_2 \geq 9,$
$-8x_1 + 4x_2 + 3x_3 = 8,$
$x_1, x_2 \geq 0$, x_3 *is unrestricted.*

[*V.T.U. Karnataka B.E. June, 2011; P.U. B.Com. April, 2008*]

Solution

Since x_3 is unrestricted, let it be replaced by $x'_3 - x_3''$, where $x'_3 \geq 0, x_3'' \geq 0$. Then the given problem becomes

minimize $Z = 3x_1 - 2x_2 + x'_3 - x_3'',$
subject to $2x_1 - 3x_2 + x'_3 - x_3'' \leq 5,$
$4x_1 - 2x_2 \geq 9,$
$-8x_1 + 4x_2 + 3x'_3 - 3x_3'' = 8,$
$x_1, x_2, x'_3, x_3'' \geq 0.$

Since it is a minimization problem, the first constraint is multiplied by -1 on both sides to give

$$-2x_1 + 3x_2 - x'_3 + x_3'' \geq -5.$$

The equation $-8x_1 + 4x_2 + 3x'_3 - 3x_3'' = 8$ can be expressed as a pair of inequalities

$-8x_1 + 4x_2 + 3x'_3 - 3x_3'' \geq 8$ and $-8x_1 + 4x_2 + 3x'_3 - 3x_3'' \leq 8$

or $-8x_1 + 4x_2 + 3x'_3 - 3x_3'' \geq 8$ and $8x_1 - 4x_2 - 3x'_3 + 3x_3'' \geq -8.$

Thus the given problem becomes

minimize $Z = 3x_1 - 2x_2 + x'_3 - x_3'',$
subject to $-2x_1 + 3x_2 - x'_3 + x_3'' \geq -5,$
$4x_1 - 2x_2 \geq 9,$
$-8x_1 + 4x_2 + 3x'_3 - 3x_3'' \geq 8,$
$8x_1 - 4x_2 - 3x'_3 + 3x_3'' \geq -8,$
$x_1, x_2, x'_3, x_3'' \geq 0.$

Let y_1, y_2, y'_3, y_3'' be the associated non-negative dual variables. Then the dual of this problem is

maximize $W = -5y_1 + 9y_2 + 8(y_3' - y_3''),$
subject to $-2y_1 + 4y_2 - 8(y_3' - y_3'') \leq 3,$
$3y_1 - 2y_2 + 4(y_3' - y_3'') \leq -2,$
$-y_1 + 3(y_3' - y_3'') \leq 1,$
$y_1 - 3(y_3' - y_3'') \leq -1,$
$y_1, y_2, y_3', y_3'' \geq 0.$

Replacing $y'_3 - y_3''$ by y_3, where y_3 is unrestricted in sign and combining the last two inequalities so as to form an equation, this dual may be written as

maximize $W = -5y_1 + 9y_2 + 8y_3,$
subject to $-2y_1 + 4y_2 - 8y_3 \leq 3,$
$3y_1 - 2y_2 + 4y_3 \leq -2,$
$-y_1 + 3y_3 = 1,$
$y_1, y_2 \geq 0$, y_3 unrestricted in sign.

EXAMPLE 6.1-2.5

Obtain the dual of the primal problem

maximize $Z = x_1 + 3x_2 - 2x_3 + 5x_4,$
subject to $3x_1 - x_2 + x_3 - 4x_4 = 2,$
$5x_1 + 3x_2 - x_3 - 2x_4 = 3,$
$x_1, x_2 \geq 0$, x_3, x_4 *unrestricted in sign.*

Solution

The first equality constraint can be expressed as a pair of inequalities :

$$3x_1 - x_2 + x_3 - 4x_4 \le 2,$$

and $$-3x_1 + x_2 - x_3 + 4x_4 \le -2.$$

The second equality constraint may also be expressed as a pair of inequalities :

$$5x_1 + 3x_2 - x_3 - 2x_4 \le 3,$$

and $$-5x_1 - 3x_2 + x_3 + 2x_4 \le -3.$$

Unrestricted variables x_3 as well as x_4 are replaced by the difference of non-negative variables.

i.e., $$x_3 = x'_3 - x_3'',$$
$$x_4 = x'_4 - x_4'',$$

where $$x'_3, x_3'', x'_4, x_4'' \ge 0.$$

Thus the primal problem is

maximize $$Z = x_1 + 3x_2 - 2x'_3 + 2x_3'' + 5x'_4 - 5x_4'',$$

subject to
$$3x_1 - x_2 + x'_3 - x''_3 - 4x'_4 + 4x_4'' \le 2,$$
$$-3x_1 + x_2 - x'_3 + x_3'' + 4x'_4 - 4x_4'' \le -2,$$
$$5x_1 + 3x_2 - x'_3 + x_3'' - 2x'_4 + 2x_4'' \le 3,$$
$$-5x_1 - 3x_2 + x'_3 - x_3'' + 2x'_4 - 2x_4'' \le -3,$$
$$x_1, x_2, x'_3, x_3'', x'_4, x_4'' \ge 0.$$

Let y'_1, y_1'', y'_2 and y_2'' be the associated non-negative dual variables. Then the dual is

minimize $$W = 2(y'_1 - y_1'') + 3(y'_2 - y''_2),$$

subject to
$$3(y'_1 - y_1'') + 5(y'_2 - y_2'') \ge 1,$$
$$-(y'_1 - y_1'') + 3(y'_2 - y_2'') \ge 3,$$
$$(y'_1 - y_1'') - (y'_2 - y_2'') \ge -2,$$
$$-(y'_1 - y_1'') + (y'_2 - y_2'') \ge 2,$$
$$-4(y'_1 - y_1'') - 2(y'_2 - y_2'') \ge 5,$$
$$4(y'_1 - y_1'') + 2(y'_2 - y_2'') \ge -5,$$
$$y'_1, y_1'', y'_2, y_2'' \ge 0.$$

Replacing $y'_1 - y_1''$ by y_1 and $y'_2 - y_2''$ by y_2, where y_1 and y_2 are unrestricted in sign and combining the third and fourth constraints as well as fifth and sixth cosntraints so as to form equality constraints, the dual takes the form

minimze $$W = 2y_1 + 3y_2,$$

subject to
$$3y_1 + 5y_2 \ge 1,$$
$$-y_1 + 3y_2 \ge 3,$$
$$y_1 - y_2 = -2,$$
$$-4y_1 - 2y_2 = 5,$$
y_1, y_2 unrestricted in sign.

6.1-3 Duality Theorems

This section presents some of the fundamental theorems which describe the relationship between the primal problem and its dual.

Theorem 1. *The dual of the dual is the primal.*

Proof. Let the primal problem in canonical form be

maximize $$Z = c_1x_1 + c_2x_2 + \ldots + c_nx_n,$$

subject to
$$a_{11}x_1 + a_{12}x_2 + \ldots + a_{1n}x_n \le b_1,$$
$$a_{21}x_1 + a_{22}x_2 + \ldots + a_{2n}x_n \le b_2,$$
$$\vdots \qquad\qquad \vdots \qquad\qquad \vdots \qquad \vdots \qquad \ldots(6.3)$$
$$a_{m1}x_1 + a_{m2}x_2 + \ldots + a_{mn}x_n \le b_m,$$

where $$x_1, x_2, \ldots, x_n \text{ all} \ge 0;$$

then the dual of this problem is

$$\begin{aligned}
\text{minimize} \quad & W = b_1y_1 + b_2y_2 + \ldots + b_my_m, \\
\text{subject to} \quad & a_{11}y_1 + a_{21}y_2 + \ldots + a_{m1}y_m \geq c_1, \\
& a_{12}y_1 + a_{22}y_2 + \ldots + a_{m2}y_m \geq c_2, \\
& \quad \vdots \qquad\quad \vdots \qquad\qquad\quad \vdots \qquad\quad \vdots \\
& a_{1n}y_1 + a_{2n}y_2 + \ldots + a_{mn}y_m \geq c_n,
\end{aligned} \qquad \ldots (6.4)$$

where $y_1, y_2, \ldots, y_m$, all ≥ 0 are the associated dual variables.

Multiplying each of the relations (6.4) throughout by –1 we obtain

$$\begin{aligned}
\text{minimize} \quad & (-W) = -b_1y_1 - b_2y_2 - \ldots - b_my_m, \\
\text{subject to} \quad & -a_{11}y_1 - a_{21}y_2 - \ldots - a_{m1}y_m \leq -c_1, \\
& -a_{12}y_1 - a_{22}y_2 - \ldots - a_{m2}y_m \leq -c_2, \\
& \quad \vdots \qquad\quad \vdots \qquad\qquad\quad \vdots \qquad\quad \vdots \\
& -a_{1n}y_1 - a_{2n}y_2 - \ldots - a_{mn}y_m \leq -c_n, \\
\text{where} \quad & y_1, y_2, \ldots, y_m, \text{ all } \geq 0.
\end{aligned} \qquad \ldots (6.5)$$

By constructing the dual of relations (6.5) and multiplying throughout by –1 we obtain a system identical to relations (6.3). This proves the theorem.

From the above theorem, we conclude that it is immaterial which programme is called the primal and which one is called the dual. We may call programme (6.4) as the primal and (6.3) as the dual. In fact (6.3) and (6.4) are called pair of dual problems.

Theorem 2. *The value of the objective function Z for any feasible solution of the primal is ≤ the value of the objective function W for any feasible solution of the dual.*

Proof. The general linear programming problem (primal) involving *n* decision variables and *m* constraints in canonical form is given by relations (6.3) and its associated dual involving *m* decision variables and *n* constraints is given by relations (6.4).

Multiply the first inequality of (6.3) by y_1, the second inequality of (6.3) by y_2, etc., and add them all. We get

$$\begin{aligned}
&(a_{11}x_1y_1 + a_{12}x_2y_1 + \ldots + a_{1n}x_ny_1) + (a_{21}x_1y_2 + a_{22}x_2y_2 \\
&\quad + \ldots + a_{2n}x_ny_2) + \ldots + (a_{m1}x_1y_m + a_{m2}x_2y_m + \ldots \\
&\quad + a_{mn}x_ny_m) \leq b_1y_1 + b_2y_2 + \ldots + b_my_m.
\end{aligned} \qquad \ldots (6.6)$$

Similarly, multiply the first inequaltiy of (6.4) by x_1, the second inequality by x_2, etc., and add them all. We get

$$\begin{aligned}
&(a_{11}x_1y_1 + a_{21}x_1y_2 + \ldots + a_{m1}x_1y_m) + (a_{12}x_2y_1 + a_{22}x_2y_2 \\
&\quad + \ldots + a_{m2}x_2y_m) + \ldots + (a_{1n}x_ny_1 + a_{2n}x_ny_2 + \ldots \\
&\quad + a_{mn}x_ny_m) \geq c_1x_1 + c_2x_2 + \ldots + c_nx_n.
\end{aligned} \qquad \ldots (6.7)$$

Now the sums on the left-hand side of inequalities (6.6) and (6.7) are equal.

Hence

$$c_1x_1 + c_2x_2 + \ldots + c_nx_n \leq b_1y_1 + b_2y_2 + \ldots + b_my_m.$$

i.e., $Z \leq W$. $\qquad \ldots (6.8)$

In other words, any feasible solution to the primal is less than or equal to any feasible solution to the dual. Thus if the feasible solution to the dual approximates ∞, the primal can have no feasible solution. Similarly, if the feasible solution to the primal approximates + ∞, the dual can have no feasible solution. In either case, there is no finite optimum for the primal or the dual. If, however, both problems have finite optimal solutions, it can be reasonably expected that these two solutions are the same. This important conclusion leads to the following theorems :

Theorem 3. *If either the primal or the dual problem has an unbounded solution, then the solution to the other problem is infeasible.*

It results directly from the above paragraph.

Theorem 4. *(Main Duality Theorem or Fundamental Theorem of Duality) If both the primal and the dual problems have feasible solutions, then both have optimal solutions and max. Z = min. W.*

Proof. When both the primal and the dual problems have feasible solutions, then from theorem 2, there is a lower bound on the minimum value of W as well as an upper bound on the maximum value of Z. In other words, neither the primal nor the dual have an unbounded solution. Therefore, both must have optimal solutions.

The symmetric primal dual programmes in matrix-vector notation are

Primal

maximize $Z = \mathbf{cx}$,
subject to $\mathbf{Ax} \leq \mathbf{b}$,
$\mathbf{x} \geq \mathbf{0}$.

Dual

minimize $\mathbf{W} = \mathbf{yb}$,
subject to $\mathbf{yA} \geq \mathbf{c}$,
$\mathbf{y} \geq \mathbf{0}$.

Let the finite optimal solution to the primal be

$$\mathbf{x_B} = \mathbf{B^{-1}\,b},$$

and the corresponding optimal value of the primal objective function be

$$Z = \mathbf{c_B\,x_B}$$
$$= \mathbf{c_B\,(B^{-1}\,b)}$$

The corresponding conditions for optimality are

$[Z_j - c_j] \geq 0$

or $[\mathbf{c_B\,B^{-1}\,A - c,\ c_B\,B^{-1}}] \geq \mathbf{0}$.

or $\mathbf{c_B\,B^{-1}\,A - c \geq 0,\ c_B\,B^{-1} \geq 0}$.

Now to verify that the associated optimal dual solution is $\mathbf{y_B = c_B\,B^{-1}}$, only observe that the above relation then demonstrates that the feasibility conditions for the dual problem are satisfied.

The corresponding value of the dual objective function is given by

$$\overline{\mathbf{W}} = \mathbf{y_B\,b = (c_B\,B^{-1})\,b}$$
$$= \mathbf{c_B\,(B^{-1}\,b) = c_B x_B}$$
$$= \text{max. } \mathbf{Z}.$$

Now it only remains to be shown that $\overline{\mathbf{W}}$ is also the optimal value of the dual objective function. From theorem 2, for all feasible x_j and y_i,

$$\mathbf{Z \leq W},$$

which will also be true for extreme optimal and dual values.

i.e., max. $\mathbf{Z} \leq$ min. $\mathbf{W}$

or $\overline{\mathbf{W}} \leq$ min. $\mathbf{W}$

But $\overline{\mathbf{W}}$ cannot be less than min. $\mathbf{W}$

$\therefore$ max. $\mathbf{Z}$ = min. $\mathbf{W}$.

Theorem 5 (Complementary Slackness Theorem)

It states that

1. *If a primal variable is positive, then the corresponding dual constraint is an equation at the optimum.*
2. *If the primal constraint is a strict inequality, then the corresponding dual variable is zero at the optimum.*
3. *If a dual variable is positive, then the corresponding primal constraint is an equation at the optimum.*
4. *If a dual constraint is a strict inequality, then the corresponding primal variable is zero at the optimum.*

Proof. The general primal problem and its associated dual in canonical form are given by relations (6.3) and (6.4) respectively. To express them in standard form, slack variables

$x'_1, x'_2, ..., x'_m$ are added to the primal whereas slack variables $y'_1, y'_2, ..., y'_n$ are subtracted from the dual. Thus the primal looks like

$$\begin{aligned} \text{maximize} \quad & Z = c_1x_1 + c_2x_2 + ... + c_nx_n, \\ \text{subject to} \quad & a_{11}x_1 + a_{12}x_2 + ... + a_{1n}x_n + x'_1 = b_1, \\ & a_{21}x_1 + a_{22}x_2 + ... + a_{2n}x_n + x'_2 = b_2, \\ & \vdots \\ & a_{m1}x_1 + a_{m2}x_2 + ... + a_{mn}x_n + x'_m = b_m, \\ & x_1, x_2, ..., x_n, x'_1, x'_2, ..., x'_m \geq 0; \end{aligned} \quad ... (6.9)$$

and the associated dual takes the form

$$\begin{aligned} \text{minimize} \quad & W = b_1y_1 + b_2y_2 + ... + b_my_m, \\ \text{subject to} \quad & a_{11}y_1 + a_{21}y_2 + ... + a_{m1}y_m - y'_1 = c_1, \\ & a_{12}y_1 + a_{22}y_2 + ... + a_{m2}y_m - y'_2 = c_2, \\ & \vdots \\ & a_{1n}y_1 + a_{2n}y_2 + ... + a_{mn}y_m - y'_n = c_n, \\ & y_1, y_2, ..., y_m, y'_1, y'_2, ..., y'_n \geq 0. \end{aligned} \quad ... (6.10)$$

Multiplying the first constraint in (6.9) by y_1, the second constraint by y_2, and so on, and adding them all, we get

$$\begin{aligned} & (a_{11}x_1y_1 + a_{12}x_2y_1 + ... + a_{1n}x_ny_1) + (a_{21}x_1y_2 + a_{22}x_2y_2 + ... + a_{2n}x_ny_2) \\ & \quad + ... + (a_{m1}x_1y_m + a_{m2}x_2y_m + ... + a_{mn}x_ny_m) \\ & = (x'_1y_1 + x'_2y_2 + ... + x'_my_m) + (b_1y_1 + b_2y_2 + ... + b_my_m). \end{aligned}$$

Similarly, multiplying the first constraint in (6.10) by x_1, the second constraint by x_2 and so on, and adding them all, we get

$$\begin{aligned} & (a_{11}x_1y_1 + a_{21}x_1y_2 + ... + a_{m1}x_1y_m) + (a_{12}x_2y_1 + a_{22}x_2y_2 + ... + a_{m2}x_2y_m) \\ & \quad + ... + (a_{1n}x_ny_1 + a_{2n}x_ny_2 + ... + a_{mn}x_ny_m) \\ & = (x_1y'_1 + x_2y'_2 + ... + x_ny'_n) + (c_1x_1 + c_2x_2 + ... + c_nx_n). \end{aligned}$$

Since sums on the L.H.S of these two equations are equal,

$$\begin{aligned} & (b_1y_1 + b_2y_2 + ... + b_my_m) - (x'_1y_1 + x'_2y_2 + ... + x'_my_m) \\ = \; & (x_1y'_1 + x_2y'_2 + ... + x_ny'_n) + (c_1x_1 + c_2x_2 + ... + c_nx_n), \end{aligned}$$

or $W - Z = (x'_1y_1 + x'_2y_2 + ... + x'_my_m) + (x_1y'_1 + x_2y'_2 + ... + x_ny'_n)$.

When an optimal solution is obtained, let

$$Z_{max} = \overline{Z},$$

$$W_{min} = \overline{W},$$

and let the corresponding values of the variables be

$$\overline{x}_1, \overline{x}_2, ..., \overline{x}_n, \overline{x}'_1 \overline{x}'_2 ..., \overline{x}'_m;$$

$$\overline{y}_1, \overline{y}_2 ..., \overline{y}_m, \overline{y}'_1 \overline{y}'_2 ..., \overline{y}'_n.$$

Now from theorem 4,

$$Z_{max} = W_{min}$$

or

$$\overline{Z} = \overline{W}$$

$$\therefore (\overline{x}'_1\,\overline{y}_1 + \overline{x}'_2\,\overline{y}_2 + ... + \overline{x}'_m\,\overline{y}_m) + (\overline{x}_1\,\overline{y}'_1 + \overline{x}_2\overline{y}'_2 + ... + \overline{x}_n\,\overline{y}'_n) = 0. \quad ... (6.11)$$

Since all variables are non-negative, each product in (6.11) must be zero.

$$\therefore \quad \overline{x}'_i\,\overline{y}_i = 0, \text{ for all } i = 1, 2, ..., m,$$

$$\overline{x}_j\,\overline{y}'_j = 0, \text{ for all } j = 1, 2, ..., n.$$

Now, when $\overline{x}'_i\,\overline{y}_i = 0$, for all $i = 1, 2, ..., m$,

$$\overline{x}'_i = 0, \text{ if } \overline{y}_i > 0.$$

and $\quad \overline{y}_i = 0, \text{ if } \overline{x}'_i > 0;$

and when $\quad \overline{x}_j\overline{y}'_j = 0, \text{ for all } j = 1, 2 ..., n,$

$$\bar{x}_j = 0, \text{ if } \bar{y}'_j > 0,$$

and $$\bar{y}'_j = 0, \text{ if } \bar{x}_j > 0.$$

6.1-4 Correspondence Between Primal and Dual Optimal Solutions

1. Values for the non-basic variables of the primal are given by the base row of the dual solution, under the slack variables (if there are any), neglecting the –ve sign if any and under the artificial variables (if there is no slack variable in a constraint) neglecting the –ve sign if any, after deleting the constant M.
2. Values for the slack variables of the primal are given by the base row under the non-basic variables of the dual solution neglecting the –ve sign if any.
3. The value of the objective function is same for primal and dual solutions.

The above properties will be clear from the following examples.

EXAMPLE 6.1-4.1

A feed mixing operation can be described in terms of the two activities. The required mixture must contain four kinds of ingredients w, x, y and z. Two basic feeds A and B, which contain the required ingredients are available in the market. One kg of A contains 0.1 kg of w, 0. 1 kg of y and 0.2 kg of z. Likewise, one kg of feed B contains 0.1 kg of x, 0.2 kg of y and 0.1 kg of z. The daily per head requirement is of at least 0.4 kg of w, 0.6 kg of x, 2 kg of y and 1.8 kg of z. Feed A can be bought for £ 0.07 per kg and B can be bought for £ 0.05 per kg The availabilities, requirements and costs are summarized in the table below.

TABLE 6.2

Ingredient	*Feed A (kg)*	*Feed B (kg)*	*Requirement (kg)*
w	*0.1*	*0.0*	*0.4*
x	*0.0*	*0.1*	*0.6*
y	*0.1*	*0.2*	*2.0*
z	*0.2*	*0.1*	*1.8*
Cost	*£0.07*	*£0.05*	

Determine the quantities of feeds A and B in the mixture so that the total cost is minimum.

Solution. Formulation of L.P. model

Step 1 : *key decision* is to find the quantities of feeds A and B in the mixture.

Step 2 : Let these quantities in kg be x_1 and x_2.

Step 3 : *Feasible alternatives* are sets of values of x_1 and x_2,

$$\text{where } x_1 \geq 0, x_2 \geq 0. \qquad ...(6.12)$$

Step 4 : *Objective* is to minimize the cost.

i.e., minimize $$Z = 0.07x_1 + 0.05x_2. \qquad ... (6.13)$$

Step 5 : *Constraints* are imposed by the requirements. They are

$$0.1x_1 + 0x_2 \geq 0.4, \qquad ... (6.14\ a)$$
$$0x_1 + 0.1x_2 \geq 0.6, \qquad ... (6.14\ b)$$
$$0.1x_1 + 0.2x_2 \geq 2.0, \qquad ... (6.14\ c)$$
$$0.2x_1 + 0.1x_2 \geq 1.8. \qquad ... (6.14\ d)$$

Thus we get a linear optimization model in which we are to minimize equation (6.13) subject to constraints (6.14 *a*), (6.14 *b*), (6.14 *c*), (6.14 *d*) and the non-negativity restrictions (6.12).

SOLUTION OF THE MODEL

Method (I) : Using the Primal Problem

Step 1. Express the problem in standard form

Introducing surplus variables the problem may be written as

$$\text{minimize} \quad Z = 0.07x_1 + 0.05x_2 + 0s_1 + 0s_2 + 0s_3 + 0s_4,$$
$$\text{subject to} \quad 0.1x_1 + 0x_2 - s_1 = 0.4,$$
$$0x_1 + 0.1x_2 - s_2 = 0.6,$$
$$0.1x_1 + 0.2x_2 - s_3 = 2.0,$$
$$0.2x_1 + 0.1x_2 - s_4 = 1.8,$$

where, $x_1, x_2, s_1, s_2, s_3, s_4 \geq 0$.

Step 2. Find initial basic feasible solution

Putting $x_1 = x_2 = 0$, we get $s_1 = -0.4$, $s_2 = -0.6$, $s_3 = -2.0$, $s_4 = -1.8$ as the initial solution which is infeasible. Introducing artificial variables we get an 'artificial system' given by

$$\text{minimize} \quad Z = 0.07x_1 + 0.05x_2 + 0s_1 + 0s_2 + 0s_3 + 0s_4 + MA_1 + MA_2 + MA_3 + MA_4,$$
$$\text{subject to} \quad 0.1x_1 + 0x_2 - s_1 + A_1 = 0.4,$$
$$0x_1 + 0.1x_2 - s_2 + A_2 = 0.6,$$
$$0.1x_1 + 0.2x_2 - s_3 + A_3 = 2.0,$$
$$0.2x_1 + 0.1x_2 - s_4 + A_4 = 1.8,$$

where, $x_1, x_2, s_1, s_2, s_3, s_4, A_1, A_2, A_3, A_4 \geq 0$.

Setting $x_1 = x_2 = s_1 = s_2 = s_3 = s_4 = 0$, we get $A_1 = 0.4$, $A_2 = 0.6$, $A_3 = 2.0$ and $A_4 = 1.8$ as the b.f.s. to the artificial system.

The above information can be represented in the form of table 6.3.

TABLE 6.3

	c_j	0.07	0.05	0	0	0	0	M	M	M	M		
c_B	Basis	x_1	x_2	s_1	s_2	s_3	s_4	A_1	A_2	A_3	A_4	b	θ
M	A_1	0.1	0	–1	0	0	0	1	0	0	0	0.4	∞
M	A_2	0	(0.1)	0	–1	0	0	0	1	0	0	0.6	6 ←
M	A_3	0.1	0.2	0	0	–1	0	0	0	1	0	2	10
M	A_4	0.2	0.1	0	0	0	–1	0	0	0	1	1.8	18
	Z_j	0.4M	0.4M	– M	– M	– M	– M	M	M	M	M		
	$c_j - Z_j$	0.07–0.4M	0.05–0.4M	M	M	M	M	0	0	0	0		
			↑										

Initial solution

Step 3. Perform optimality test

Since $c_j - Z_j$ is negative under some columns, table 6.3 is not optimal.

Step 4. Iterate towards an optimal solution

Performing iterations to get an optimal solution results in the tables below.

TABLE 6.4

	c_j	0.07	0.05	0	0	0	0	M	M	M	M		
c_B	Basis	x_1	x_2	s_1	s_2	s_3	s_4	A_1	A_2	A_3	A_4	b	θ
M	A_1	0.1	0	–1	0	0	0	1	0	0	0	0.4	∞
0.05	x_2	0	1	0	–10	0	0	0	10	0	0	6	$-\frac{3}{5}$
M	A_3	0.1	0	0	(2)	–1	0	0	–2	1	0	0.8	$\frac{2}{5}$ ←
M	A_4	0.2	0	0	1	0	–1	0	–1	0	1	1.2	$\frac{6}{5}$
	Z_j	0.4M	0.05	–M	–0.5+3M	–M	–M	M	0.5–3M	M	M	0.3+2.4M	
	$c_j - Z_j$	0.07–0.4M	0	M	0.5–3M	M	M	0	–0.5+4M	0	0		
					↑								

Second solution

TABLE 6.5

	c_j	0.07	0.05	0	0	0	0	M	M	M	M	
c_B	Basis	x_1	x_2	s_1	s_2	s_3	s_4	A_1	A_2	A_3	A_4	b
0.07	x_1	1	0	0	0	$10/3$	$-20/3$	0	0	$-10/3$	$20/3$	$16/3$
0.05	x_2	0	1	0	0	$-20/3$	$10/3$	0	0	$20/3$	$-10/3$	$22/3$
0	s_2	0	0	0	1	$-2/3$	$1/3$	0	–1	$2/3$	$-1/3$	$1/3$
0	s_1	0	0	1	0	$1/3$	$-2/3$	–1	0	$-1/3$	$2/3$	$1/3$
	Z_j	0.07	0.05	0	0	–0.1	– 0.3	0	0	0.1	0.3	
	$c_j - Z_j$	0	0	0	0	0.1	0.3	M	M	M–0.1	M–0.3	

Optimal basic feasible solution

Note that table 6.5 is obtained after *making three iterations* on table 6.4.

∴ Optimal quantities of feeds A and B in the mixture are 16/3 kg and 22/3 kg respectively.

Total minimum cost of the mixture $= £\left[0.07 \times \frac{16}{3} + 0.05 \times \frac{22}{3}\right]$

$= £\ 0.74.$

Method II : Using the Dual Problem

The primal problem is

$$\begin{aligned}\text{minimize} \quad & Z = 0.07x_1 + 0.05x_2,\\ \text{subject to} \quad & 0.1x_1 + 0x_2 \geq 0.4,\\ & 0x_1 + 0.1x_2 \geq 0.6,\\ & 0.1x_1 + 0.2x_2 \geq 2.0,\\ & 0.2x_1 + 0.1x_2 \geq 1.8,\\ & x_1 \geq 0, x_2 \geq 0.\end{aligned}$$

The dual of this problem will be

$$\begin{aligned}\text{maximize} \quad & W = 0.4y_1 + 0.6y_2 + 2y_3 + 1.8y_4,\\ \text{subject to} \quad & 0.1y_1 + 0y_2 + 0.1y_3 + 0.2y_4 \leq 0.07,\\ & 0y_1 + 0.1y_2 + 0.2y_3 + 0.1y_4 \leq 0.05,\\ & y_1, y_2, y_3, y_4, \text{ all} \geq 0.\end{aligned}$$

Step 1. Express the problem in standard form

Adding the slack variables s_1 and s_2, the constraints become

$$0.1y_1 + 0y_2 + 0.1y_3 + 0.2y_4 + s_1 = 0.07,$$
$$0y_1 + 0.1y_2 + 0.2y_3 + 0.1y_4 + s_2 = 0.05,$$

and the objective function becomes

$$\begin{aligned}\text{maximize} \quad & W = 0.4y_1 + 0.6y_2 + 2y_3 + 1.8y_4 + 0s_1 + 0s_2,\\ \text{where} \quad & y_1, y_2, y_3, y_4, s_1, s_2, \text{ all} \geq 0.\end{aligned}$$

Step 2. Find initial basic feasible solution

Setting $y_1 = y_2 = y_3 = y_4 = 0$, we get $s_1 = 0.07$, $s_2 = 0.05$ as the b.f.s. to the dual problem. The above information is represented in the form of table 6.6.

Step 3. Perform optimality test

Since $c_j - Z_j$ is positive under some columns, table 6.6 is not optimal.

Step 4. Iterate towards an optimal solution

Performing iterations to get an optimal solution results in the tables below.

TABLE 6.6

	c_j	0.4	0.6	2	1.8	0	0		
c_B	Basis	y_1	y_2	y_3	y_4	s_1	s_2	b	θ
0	s_1	0.1	0	0.1	0.2	1	0	0.07	0.7
0	s_2	0	0.1	(0.2)	0.1	0	1	0.05	0.25 ←
	Z_j	0	0	0	0	0	0		
	$c_j - z_j$	0.4	0.6	2	1.8	0	0		
				↑ K					

Initial basic feasible solution

TABLE 6.7

c_B	Basis	y_1	y_2	y_3	y_4	s_1	s_2	b	θ
0	s_1	0.1	–0.05	0	(0.15)	1	–0.5	0.045	0.3 ← (Key row)
2	y_3	0	0.5	1	0.5	0	5	0.25	0.5
	$c_j - Z_j$	0.4	–0.4	0	0.8	0	–10		
					↑ K				

Iterating again, the final optimal table 6.8 is obtained.

TABLE 6.8

	c_j	0.4	0.6	2	1.8	0	0	
c_B	Basis	y_1	y_2	y_3	y_4	s_1	s_2	b
1.8	y_4	$2/3$	$-1/3$	0	1	$20/3$	$-10/3$	0.3
2	y_3	$-1/3$	$2/3$	1	0	$-10/3$	$20/3$	0.1
	Z_j	$1.6/3$	$2.2/3$	2	1.8	$16/3$	$22/3$	
	$c_j - Z_j$	$-0.4/3$	$-0.4/3$	0	0	$-16/3$	$-22/3$	

Optimal basic feasible solution

The optimal b.f.s. is thus given by

$$y_1 = 0, y_2 = 0, y_3 = 0.1, y_4 = 0.3,$$
$$W_{max} = £\ [2 \times 0.1 + 1.8 \times 0.3] = £\ 0.74.$$

Optimal values of x_1 and x_2 are given under the slacks of the dual with changed sign of coefficients in $c_j - Z_j$ row.

∴ Optimal values of x_1 and x_2 are 16/3 and 22/3 respectively *i.e.*, optimal quantities of feeds A and B in the mixture are 16/3 kg and 22/3 kg respectively.

Similarly, optimal values of dual variables y_1, y_2, y_3 and y_4 ($y_1 = 0$, $y_2 = 0$, $y_3 = 0.1$ and $y_4 = 0.3$ from table 6.8) could be obtained from the optimal primal solution given by table 6.5 either under the slack variables s_1, s_2, s_3 and s_4 or under the corresponding artificial variables A_1, A_2, A_3 and A_4 with changed sign after deleting the constant M.

Note. In example 6.1-4.1, the primal problem contains 2 variables and 4 constraints which are of ≥ type. The simplex table was lengthy; involved 10 variable columns, 4 basic variable rows and required 4 iterations to reach optimality. In contrast, the dual problem contained 4 variables and 2 constraints of ≤ type. The simplex table was much smaller as it involved only 6 variable columns, 2 basic variable rows and required just 2 iterations to reach the optimal solution. *Therefore, when primal problem involves larger number of constraints of ≥ type and smaller number of variables, it is most advantageous to form the dual problem and solve the dual rather than solving the primal problem. This is one of the main advantages of duality theory.*

EXAMPLE 6.1-4.2

Solve the following l.p.p. by using its dual:

Maximize $Z = 5x_1 - 2x_2 + 3x_3,$

subject to $2x_1 + 2x_2 - x_3 \geq 2,$

$3x_1 - 4x_2 \leq 3,$

$x_2 + 3x_3 \leq 5,$

$x_1, x_2, x_3 \geq 0.$ [*H.P.U. B.Tech. Nov., 2015*]

Solution

The given problem can be written as

maximize $Z = 5x_1 - 2x_2 + 3x_3,$

subject to $-2x_1 - 2x_2 + x_3 \leq -2,$

$3x_1 - 4x_2 \leq 3,$

$x_2 + 3x_3 \leq 5,$

$x_1, x_2, x_3 \geq 0.$

The associated dual is given by

minimize $W = -2y_1 + 3y_2 + 5y_3,$

subject to $-2y_1 + 3y_2 \geq 5,$

$-2y_1 - 4y_2 + y_3 \geq -2,$

$y_1 + 3y_3 \geq 3,$

$y_1, y_2, y_3 \geq 0.$

The solution of the dual by simplex method consists of the following steps :

Step 1. Express the problem in standard form

Multiplying the second constraint by –1, it can be written as

$$2y_1 + 4y_2 - y_3 \leq 2.$$

Introducing slack, surplus and artificial variables, we get an artificial system given by

minimize $W = -2y_1 + 3y_2 + 5y_3 + 0s_1 + 0s_2 + 0s_3 + MA_1 + MA_2,$

subject to $-2y_1 + 3y_2 - s_1 + A_1 = 5,$

$2y_1 + 4y_2 - y_3 + s_2 = 2,$

$y_1 + 3y_3 - s_3 + A_2 = 3,$

$y_1, y_2, y_3, s_1, s_2, s_3, A_1, A_2 \geq 0.$

Step 2. Find initial basic feasible solution

Putting $y_1 = y_2 = y_3 = s_1 = s_3 = 0$, we get $A_1 = 5, s_2 = 2, A_2 = 3$ as the b.f.s. to the artificial system.

The above information can be represented in the form of a matrix or table.

TABLE 6.9

	c_j	–2	3	5	0	0	0	M	M		
c_B	Basis	y_1	y_2	y_3	s_1	s_2	s_3	A_1	A_2	b	θ
M	A_1	–2	3	0	–1	0	0	1	0	5	5/3
0	s_2	2	(4)	–1	0	1	0	0	0	2	1/2 ←
M	A_2	1	0	3	0	0	–1	0	1	3	∞
	Z_j	–M	3M	3M	–M	0	–M	M	M		
	$c_j - Z_j$	–2+M	3–3M	5–3M	M	0	M	0	0		
			↑								

Initial solution

Step 3. Perform optimality test

Since $c_j - Z_j$ is negative under some columns, table 6.9 is not optimal.

Step 4. Iterate towards an optimal solution

Iterating thrice, the final cptimal table 6.10 is obtained.

TABLE 6.10

	c_j	−2	3	5	0	0	0	M	M	
c_B	Basis	y_1	y_2	y_3	s_1	s_2	s_3	A_1	A_2	b
0	s_3	− 15	0	0	−4	−3	1	4	−1	11
3	y_2	$-2/3$	1	0	$-1/3$	0	0	$1/3$	0	$5/3$
5	y	$-14/3$	0	1	$-4/3$	−1	0	$4/3$	0	$14/3$
Z_j		$-76/3$	3	5	$-23/3$	−5	0	$23/3$	0	
$c_j - Z_j$		$70/3$	0	0	$23/3$	5	0	$-23/3$ +M	M	

Optimal basic feasible solution

The optimal solution is

$$y_1 = 0,\ y_2 = 5/3,\ y_3 = 14/3;\ W_{min} = 3 \times \frac{5}{3} + 5 \times \frac{14}{3} = \frac{85}{3}.$$

The optimal basic feasible solution for the given primal problem as obtained from table 6.10 is

$$x_1 = 23/3,\ x_2 = 5,\ x_3 = 0,\ Z_{max} = 85/3.$$

EXAMPLE 6.1-4.3

Write the dual corresponding to

$$x_1 + x_2 + 2x_3 \le 120,$$
$$3x_1 - 2x_2 - x_3 \ge 90,$$
$$2x_1 + 4x_2 + 2x_3 = 100,$$
$$5x_1 + 8x_2 + 10x_3 = \text{maximum } Z,$$
$$x_1, x_2, x_3 \ge 0.$$

Use simplex method and cbtain the zeroth and first iterates of the dual.

[H.P.U. B.Tech. June, 2015; P.T.U. B.Tech. (Prod.) May, 2011]

Solution

The primal problem may be written as

maximize $Z = 5x_1 + 8x_2 + 10x_3,$

subject to $x_1 + x_2 + 2x_3 \le 120,$

$- 3x_1 + 2x_2 + x_3 \le - 90,$

$2x_1 + 4x_2 + 2x_3 \le 100,$

$- 2x_1 - 4x_2 - 2x_3 \le -100,$

$x_1, x_2, x_3 \ge 0.$

Let y_1, y_2, y'_3 and y_3'' be the associated dual variables. Then the dual problem is

minimize $W = 120y_1 - 90y_2 + 100\,(y'_3 - y_3''),$

subject to $y_1 - 3y_2 + 2(y'_3 - y_3'') \ge 5,$

$y_1 + 2y_2 + 4\,(y'_3 - y_3'') \ge 8,$

$2y_1 + y_2 + 2\,(y'_3 - y_3'') \ge 10,$

$y_1, y_2, y'_3, y_3'' \ge 0.$

The solution of this dual problem by simplex method consists of the following steps :

Step 1. Set up the Problem in the Standard Form

Introducing surplus and artificial variables, we get an 'artificial system' given by

minimize $W = 120y_1 - 90y_2 + 100y'_3 - 100y_3'' + 0s_1 + 0s_2 + 0s_3 + MA_1 + MA_2 + MA_3,$

subject to $y_1 - 3y_2 + 2y'_3 - 2y_3'' - s_1 + 0s_2 + 0s_3 + A_1 + 0A_2 + 0A_3 = 5,$
$y_1 + 2y_2 + 4y'_3 - 4y_3'' + 0s_1 - s_2 + 0s_3 + 0A_1 + A_2 + 0A_3 = 8,$
$2y_1 + y_2 + 2y'_3 - 2y_3'' + 0s_1 + 0s_2 - s_3 + 0A_1 + 0A_2 + A_3 = 10,$
$y_1, y_2, y'_3, y_3'', s_1, s_2, s_3, A_1, A_2, A_3 \geq 0.$

Step 2. Find an Initial Basic Feasible Solution

Setting variables $y_1, y_2, y'_3, y_3'', s_1, s_2, s_3$ each equal to zero, the initial b.f.s. to the 'artificial system' is

$$y_1 = y_2 = y'_3 = y_3'' = s_1 = s_2 = s_3 = 0,$$
$$A_1 = 5,$$
$$A_2 = 8,$$
$$A_3 = 10,$$
$$W = 23M.$$

Table 6.11 is the zeroth iterate and represents this solution.

TABLE 6.11

	c_j	120	–90	100	–100	0	0	0	M	M	M		
c_B	Basis	y_1	y_2	y_3'	y_3''	s_1	s_2	s_3	A_1	A_2	A_3	b	θ
M	A_1	1	–3	2	–2	–1	0	0	1	0	0	5	5/2
M	A_2	1	2	(4)	–4	0	–1	0	0	1	0	8	2←
M	A_3	2	1	2	–2	0	0	–1	0	0	1	10	5
	Z_j	4M	0	8M	–8M	–M	–M	–M	M	M	M	23M	
	$c_j–Z_j$	120–4M	–90	100–8M	–100+8M	M	M	M	0	0	0		
				↑									

Zeroth iterate (Initial solution)

Step 3. Perform Optimality Test

Since $c_j - Z_j$ is negative under some columns, table 6.11 is not optimal.

Step 4. Iterate Towards an Optimal Solution

Performing iteration to get the *first iterate* results in the following table:

TABLE 6.12

	c_j	120	–90	100	–100	0	0	0	M	M	M		
c_B	Basis	y_1	y_2	y'_3	y_3''	s_1	s_2	s_3	A_1	A_2	A_3	b	θ
M	A_1	$(\frac{1}{2})$	–4	0	0	–1	$\frac{1}{2}$	0	1	$-\frac{1}{2}$	0	1	2 ←
100	y'_3	$\frac{1}{4}$	$\frac{1}{2}$	1	–1	0	$-\frac{1}{4}$	0	0	$\frac{1}{4}$	0	2	8
M	A_3	$\frac{3}{2}$	0	0	0	0	$\frac{1}{2}$	–1	0	$-\frac{1}{2}$	1	6	4
	Z_j	25+2M	50–4M	100	–100	–M	–25+M	–M	M	25–M	M	200+7M	
	$c_j - Z_j$	95–2M	–140+4M	0	0	M	25–M	M	0	–25+2M	0		
		↑											

First iterate (Second solution)

Table 6.12 is the first iterate and yields the following solution to the dual problem :

$$A_1 = 1,$$
$$y'_3 = 2,$$
$$A_3 = 6,$$
$$W = 200 + 7M.$$

EXAMPLE 6.1-4.4

Use duality to solve the problem

minimize $Z = x_1 - x_2,$

subject to $2x_1 - x_2 \geq 2,$

$-x_1 + x_2 \geq 1,$
$x_1, x_2 \geq 0.$

[*P.T.U. MBA Feb., 2011, H.P.U. B.E. (Mech.) 2008, 2009*]

Solution

The dual of the given primal problem is

maximize $\quad W = 2y_1 + y_2,$
subject to $\quad 2y_1 - y_2 \leq 1,$
$-y_1 + y_2 \leq -1,$
$y_1, y_2 \geq 0.$

Step 1. Set up the problem in the standard form

Multiplying the second dual constraint throughout by −1, it becomes

$$y_1 - y_2 \geq 1.$$

Introducing slack, surplus and artificial variables, the dual 'artificial system' in standard form can be expressed as

maximize $\quad W = 2y_1 + y_2 + 0s_1 + 0s_2 - MA_1,$
subject to $\quad 2y_1 - y_2 + s_1 = 1,$
$y_1 - y_2 - s_2 + A_1 = 1,$
$y_1, y_2, s_1, s_2, A_1 \geq 0.$

Step 2. Find an initial basic feasible solution

This is obtained by setting non-basic variables y_1, y_2, s_2 each equal to zero. This gives the basic solution for the 'artificial system' as

$y_1 = y_2 = 0,$
$s_1 = 1,$
$s_2 = 0, A = 1,$
$W = -M.$

Since the basic variables s_1, A_1 are > 0, the above basic solution for the artificial system is also feasible and non-degenerate. The initial simplex table can now be constructed using s_1, A_1 as basic variables.

TABLE 6.13

	c_j	2	1	0	0	−M		
c_B	Basis	y_1	y_2	s_1	s_2	A_1	b	θ
0	s_1	(2)	−1	1	0	0	1	1/2 ←
−M	A_1	1	−1	0	−1	1	1	1
	$Z_j = \sum c_B.a_{ij}$	−M	M	0	M	−M	−M	
	$c_j - Z_j$	2+M	1−M	0	−M	0		
		↑						

Initial solution

Step 3. Perform optimality test

This is done by computing $c_j - Z_j$. Since $c_j - Z_j$ is positive under y_1-column, initial solution given by table 6.13 is not optimal.

Step 4. Iterate towards on optimal solution

Table 6.14 is obtained by replacing s_1 by y_1.

TABLE 6.14

	c_j	2	1	0	0	−M	
c_B	Basis	y_1	y_2	s_1	s_2	A_1	b

2	y_1	1	$-\frac{1}{2}$	$\frac{1}{2}$	0	0	$\frac{1}{2}$
–M	A_1	0	$-\frac{1}{2}$	$-\frac{1}{2}$	–1	1	$\frac{1}{2}$
	Z_j	2	$-1+\frac{M}{2}$	$1+\frac{M}{2}$	M	–M	$1-\frac{M}{2}$
	$c_j - Z_j$	0	$2-\frac{M}{2}$	$-1-\frac{M}{2}$	–M	0	

Second solution

Since $c_j - Z_j$ is either zero or negative under all columns, but artificial variable A_1 appears in the basis at non-zero level $\frac{1}{2}$, the dual problem has no feasible solution. It follows that the given primal problem also has *infeasible solution.*

6.1-5 Economic interpretation of the dual variables

Dual variables have an interesting interpretation from the cost or economic point of view. To illustrate this point let us consider example 2.9-5 again.

The L.P. model for this (primal) problem is

$$\begin{aligned} \text{minimize} \quad & Z = 600x_1 + 400x_2, \\ \text{subject to} \quad & 1{,}500x_1 + 1{,}500x_2 \geq 20{,}000, \\ & 3{,}000x_1 + 1{,}000x_2 \geq 40{,}000, \\ & 2{,}000x_1 + 5{,}000x_2 \geq 44{,}000, \\ & x_1, x_2 \geq 0. \end{aligned}$$

The dual of this primal is

$$\text{maximize} \quad W = 20{,}000y_1 + 40{,}000y_2 + 44{,}000y_3, \quad \text{...(6.11)}$$
$$\text{subject to} \quad 1{,}500y_1 + 3{,}000y_2 + 2{,}000y_3 \leq 600, \quad \text{...(6.12)}$$
$$1{,}500y_1 + 1{,}000y_2 + 5{,}000y_3 \leq 400, \quad \text{...(6.13)}$$
$$y_1, y_2, y_3 \geq 0. \quad \text{...(6.14)}$$

Optimal solution to the primal has been obtained in example 2.9-5 and is

$$x_1 = 12 \text{ days},$$
$$x_2 = 4 \text{ days},$$
$$Z_{min} = 8{,}800 \text{ monetary units.}$$

Optimal solution to the dual is found to be (left as an exercise for the reader)

$$y_1 = 0,$$
$$y_2 = \frac{11}{65},$$
$$y_3 = \frac{3}{65},$$
$$W_{max} = 8{,}800.$$

Now, as the R.H.S. of constraints (6.12) and (6.13) denotes monetary units, the L.H.S. must also be expressed in monetary units. In the first term 1,500 y_1 of the first constraint, 1,500 is the number of bottles of whisky produced per day. Hence, y_1 must denote the cost of producing one bottle of whisky. Similarly y_2 denotes the cost of producing a bottle of beer and y_3 denotes the cost of producing a bottle of fruit juices. y_1, y_2 and y_3 are called the *shadow prices* of whisky, beer and fruit juices respectively. They represent not the *actual market prices* but the *true accounting values* or the *imputed values* of the three drinks.

The objective function of the dual is to maximize the total accounting values of the drinks produced per month. The two constraints of the dual ensure that the total accounting value of the daily output of each plant must remain less than the daily cost of operating the plant. The shadow prices represent the values that the company should set on its resources in order to reflect their value to society, while the constraints ensure that the internal price cannot be set to get more value from a drink than what the company puts into it. It means that in a situation of equilibrium, the laws of economics for society do not require any profit.

The values of $y_1 = 0$, $y_2 = 11/65$ and $y_3 = 3/65$ represent the shadow prices of whiskey, beer and fruit-juices respectively. $y_1 = 0$ means that the accounting value of whisky is zero and that it is produced in surplus as a by-product.

EXAMPLE 6.1-5.1

A company makes three products X, Y and Z out of three raw materials A, B and C. The number of units of raw materials required to produce one unit of the product is as given in the table below.

	X	*Y*	*Z*
A	*1*	*2*	*1*
B	*2*	*1*	*4*
C	*2*	*5*	*1*

The unit profit contribution of the products X, Y and Z is ₹ 40, 25 and 50 respectively. The number of units of raw materials available are 36, 60 and 45 respectively.

(i) Determine the product mix that will maximize the total profit.

(ii) From the final simplex table, write the solution to the dual and give the economic interpretation.

Solution

(*i*) Let the company produce x, y and z units of the products X, Y and Z respectively. Then the problem can be expressed mathematically as

$$\begin{aligned} &\text{maximize} \quad P = 40x + 25y + 50z, \\ &\text{subject to} \quad x + 2y + z \le 36, \\ &\qquad 2x + y + 4z \le 60, \\ &\qquad 2x + 5y + z \le 45, \\ &\qquad x, y, z \ge 0. \end{aligned}$$

Adding slack variables s_1, s_2 and s_3, we get

$$\begin{aligned} &\text{maximize} \quad P = 40x + 25y + 50z + 0s_1 + 0s_2 + 0s_3, \\ &\text{subject to} \quad x + 2y + z + s_1 = 36, \\ &\qquad 2x + y + 4z + s_2 = 60, \\ &\qquad 2x + 5y + z + s_3 = 45, \\ &\qquad x, y, z, s_1, s_2, s_3 \ge 0. \end{aligned}$$

Initial basic feasible solution is $x = y = z = 0$, $s_1 = 36$, $s_2 = 60$, $s_3 = 45$ and P = 0. This solution and further improved solutions are given in the following tables :

TABLE 6.15

	c_j	40	25	50	0	0	0		
c_B	Basis	x	y	z	s_1	s_2	s_3	b	θ
0	s_1	1	2	1	1	0	0	36	36
0	s_2	2	1	(4)	0	1	0	60	15 ←
0	s_3	2	5	1	0	0	1	45	45
	Z_j	0	0	0	0	0	0	0	
	$c_j - Z_j$	40	25	50	0	0	0		
				↑					

TABLE 6.16

	c_j	40	25	50	0	0	0		
c_B	Basis	x	y	z	s_1	s_2	s_3	b	θ
0	s_1	$\frac{1}{2}$	$\frac{7}{4}$	0	1	$-\frac{1}{4}$	0	21	42
50	z	$\frac{1}{2}$	$\frac{1}{4}$	1	0	$\frac{1}{4}$	0	15	30
0	s_3	$(\frac{3}{2})$	$\frac{19}{4}$	0	0	$-\frac{1}{4}$	1	30	20 ←
	Z_j	25	$\frac{25}{2}$	50	0	$\frac{25}{2}$	0	750	
	$c_j–Z_j$	15	$\frac{25}{2}$	0	0	$-\frac{25}{2}$	0		
		↑							

TABLE 6.17

	c_j	40	25	50	0	0	0	
c_B	Basis	x	y	z	s_1	s_2	s_3	b
0	s_1	0	$\frac{1}{6}$	0	1	$-\frac{1}{6}$	$-\frac{1}{3}$	11
50	z	0	$-\frac{4}{3}$	1	0	$\frac{1}{3}$	$-\frac{1}{3}$	5
40	x	1	$\frac{19}{6}$	0	0	$-\frac{1}{6}$	$\frac{2}{3}$	20
	Z_j	40	60	50	0	10	10	1,050
	$c_j - Z_j$	0	–35	0	0	–10	–10	

∴ **Optimal solution to the given (primal) problem is**

$$x = 20 \text{ units}, y = 0, z = 5 \text{ units}; P_{max} = ₹\ 1{,}050.$$

(*ii*) The dual problem is

minimize $\quad W = 36y_1 + 60y_2 + 45y_3,$

subject to

$$y_1 + 2y_2 + 2y_3 \geq 40,$$
$$2y_1 + y_2 + 5y_3 \geq 25,$$
$$y_1 + 4y_2 + y_3 \geq 50,$$
$$y_1, y_2, y_3 \geq 0.$$

From table 6.17, $y_1 = 0$, $y_2 = 10$, $y_3 = 10$, $W_{min} = ₹\ 1{,}050$.

Economic Interpretation

Suppose the manager of the company wants to sell the three raw materials *A, B* and *C* instead of using them for making products *X, Y* and *Z* and, then, by selling the products earn a profit of ₹ 1,050. Suppose the selling prices were ₹ y_1, ₹ y_2 and ₹ y_3 per unit of raw materials A, B and C respectively. Then the cost to the purchaser of all the three raw materials will be ₹ $(36y_1 + 60y_2 + 45y_3)$. Of course, the purchaser will like to set the selling prices of A, B and C so that the total cost is minimum. So the objective function will be to minimize $36y_1 + 60y_2 + 45y_3$.

Table 6.17 indicates that the marginal values of raw materials, *A, B* and *C* are ₹ 0, ₹ 10 and ₹ 10 per unit respectively. Thus if the manager sells the raw materials *A, B* and *C* at price ₹ 0, ₹ 10 and ₹ 10 per unit respectively, he will get the same contribution of ₹ 1,050 which he is going to get if he uses these resources for producing products *X, Y* and *Z* and then sells them.

EXAMPLE 6.1-5.2

A company manufactures three products : tables, chairs and racks. The resource utilisation, resource availability and profit/unit of each product are given below :

TABLE 6.18

Product	Resource Requirement			Profit / unit
	Timber (cubic feet)	Time in manufacturing department (hours)	Time in finishing department (hours)	(₹)
Table	10	7	2	12
Chair	2	3	4	3
Rack	1	2	1	1
Available	100	77	80	

(i) Formulate it as a linear programming problem.
(ii) Write its dual.
(iii) Find the optimal solution to the given problem.
(iv) From the final optimal table, find the solution to the dual problem.
(v) What are the shadow prices of the resources?
(vi) Give economic interpretation of the dual problem.

Solution

(*i*) Let x_1, x_2, and x_3 denote the number of units of tables, chairs and racks to be produced by the company. Then the L.P. problem is

maximize $Z = 12x_1 + 3x_2 + x_3$,
subject to
$10x_1 + 2x_2 + x_3 \le 100$,
$7x_1 + 3x_2 + 2x_3 \le 77$,
$2x_1 + 4x_2 + x_3 \le 80$,
$x_1, x_2, x_3 \ge 0$.

(*ii*) Dual problem can be expressed as

minimize $Z' = 100y_1 + 77y_2 + 80y_3$,
subject to
$10y_1 + 7y_2 + 2y_3 \ge 12$,
$2y_1 + 3y_2 + 4y_3 \ge 3$,
$y_1 + 2y_2 + y_3 \ge 1$,
$y_1, y_2, y_3 \ge 0$.

(*iii*) The primal problem can be solved by using the simplex method. The final optimal table is

TABLE 6.19

	c_j	12	3	1	0	0	0	
c_B	Basis	x_1	x_2	x_3	s_1	s_2	s_3	b
12	x_1	1	0	$-1/16$	$3/16$	$-1/8$	0	$73/8$
3	x_2	0	1	$13/16$	$-7/16$	$5/8$	0	$35/8$
0	s_3	0	0	$-17/8$	$11/8$	$-9/4$	1	$177/4$
	Z_j	12	3	$27/16$	$15/16$	$3/8$	0	
	$c_j - Z_j$	0	0	$-11/16$	$-15/16$	$-3/8$	0	

Optimal solution to the given problem is

$$x_1 = \frac{73}{8},\ x_2 = \frac{35}{8},\ x_3 = 0\ ;\ Z_{max} = ₹\left(\frac{876}{8} + \frac{105}{8}\right) = ₹\ 122.63.$$

(*iv*) Optimal solution to the dual problem is

$$y_1 = \frac{15}{16}, y_2 = \frac{3}{8}, y_3 = 0 \ ; \ Z'_{min} = ₹ \left[100 \times \frac{15}{16} + 77 \times \frac{3}{8} + 80 \times 0\right] = ₹\ 122.63.$$

(*v*) Shadow prices of the resources are

timber $= ₹\ \frac{15}{16}$ per cubit foot,

time in manufacturing deptt. $= ₹\ \frac{3}{8}$ per hour,

time in finishing deptt. = Nil (because there is already unused capacity of $\frac{177}{4}$ hours in this department).

Note that racks are not to be produced as $c_j - Z_j$ value in the optimal table $\left(\frac{-11}{16}\right)$ indicates that every rack produced would cause a loss of ₹ $\frac{11}{16}$ in the profit.

(*vi*) Economic interpretation of the dual problem can be explained as follows :

Suppose this manufacturing company is thinking of renting its production facilities and selling out timber to some other firm, say *ABC* company, instead of using them by itself and then selling the products — tables, chairs and racks to get a profit of ₹ 122.63. Then *ABC* company is interested in minimizing the sum to be paid (cost to it), while the parent manufacturing company will be interested in knowing the rates it should charge for timber/cubic feet and production time/hour in manufacturing as well as finishing departments.

Let y_1 be the price of timber/cubic feet, y_2 be the charges/hour of manufacturing department and y_3 be the charges/hour of finishing department. Then the total amount *ABC* company would have to pay is $100\,y_1 + 77y_2 + 80\,y_3$ and its objective is to

minimize $Z' = 100y_1 + 77y_2 + 80\,y_3$.

Having known this total cost, *ABC* company would be interested in knowing the values of y_1, y_2 and y_3 respectively. The total this company has to pay to make a table is ₹ $(10y_1 + 7y_2 + 2y_3)$. As the parent company can earn a profit of ₹ 12 / table if it produces by itself, *ABC* company has no option but to settle for paying a minimum of ₹ 12 / table.

$\therefore \quad 10y_1 + 7y_2 + 2y_3 \geq 12.$

Similarly, $\quad 2y_1 + 3y_2 + 4y_3 \geq 3,$

$\qquad y_1 + 2y_2 + y_3 \geq 1,$

where $\quad y_1, y_2, y_3 \geq 0.$

EXERCISES 6.1

1. What is duality theory ? What are the rules to form a dual problem from the primal problem ? What are the advantages of duality ?
   [*M.G.U. Kerala M.Com. June, 2012; P.T.U. M.Tech. Dec., 2011; Osmania MBA, 2010; J.N.T.U. Hyderabad B.Tech. Nov., 2010; H.P.U. B.Tech. (Mech.) Sept., 2013; June, 2010; Chennai U. B.Sc. (Math.) Nov., 2012; B.C.A. Nov., 2010; P.T.U. MBA, 2009; P.U.B.E. (Mech.) Nov., 2002; B.E.(E. and Ec.) 2001; P.T.U. B.Tech., 2001; P.U. B.Com. April., 2007; Sept., 2006; Jan., 2005*]
2. Explain the meaning of duality in L.P. What are the advantages of solving a minimization problem by converting it into a maximization problem ? [*P.U.B.E.(Mech.) 1997*]
3. What is duality? What is the significance of dual variables in simplex solution ?
   [*P.T.U. MBA May, 2014; Univ. of Madras B.Sc. (Math.) Nov., 2012; J.N.T.U. Hyderabad B.Tech. April, 2011; M.D.U. Rohtak B.E. (Mech.) Dec., 2006; G.N.D.U. B.Com., 2004*]

4. Discuss the various relations regarding primal and dual problems.
[P.T.U. MCA. 2010; P.U.B.Com. April, 2004; 2000]
5. Explain the primal-dual relationships. How can dual problem be useful in management decision-making ?
[U.P.U. MBA, 2010; P.U. B.Com. April, 2008; M.D.U. Rohtak B.E. (Mech.) Dec., 2006]
6. Explain the relationship between each number in a primal and corresponding number in the dual. [P.U. MBA Feb., 2009]
7. What is duality in L.P. problems? If the dual of an L.P.P. is solved, where will we get the values of decision variables of the primal L.P.P. ? [P.T.U. B.Tech. (C.Sc.) 2009]
8. Prove that dual of a dual is primal. [G.N.D.U. B.Com., 2005; P.U. B.B.A., 2001]
9. What are the fundamental theorems of duality? [P.U. B.Com. April, 2001]
10. Explain the economic interpretation of duality.
[P.T.U. M.Tech. Nov., 2012; G.N.D.U.B. Com. Sept., 2004]
11. Discuss, in brief, duality in linear programming. Explain how the concept of duality can be useful in managerial decision-making. [U.P.U. MBA, 2009]
12. What do you understand by duality ? Write some important features of primal and dual problems.
[Univ. of Madras B.Sc. (Math.) Nov., 2012; Gujarat U.MBA Dec., 2010; R.T.M. Nagpur B.E. (Mech.) Dec., 2008]
13. Prove that
   (i) If an L.P.P. has an optimal feasible solution, its dual also has an optimal feasible solution. [DOEACC, 1999; GNDU B.Com., 1995]
   (ii) If either problem has an unbounded optimal solution, then the other problem has no feasible solution at all.
   (iii) Both problems may be infeasible *i.e.*, they may not have any solution.
   [Kuru. U. M.Sc. (Stat.) 1978, 75; Delhi O.R., 1978]
   (iv) Necessary and sufficient condition for any L.P.P and its dual to have optimal solutions is that both have feasible solutions. [Meerut M.Sc.(Math.) 1971]
14. State complementary slackness theorem. Show that if in an optimal basic feasible solution of primal problem, a legitimate non-slack variable is basic, then for corresponding optimal feasible solution of the dual, the corresponding constraint is satisfied as an equation.
[P.U.B.E. (T.&I.T.) Nov., 2004]
15. State and prove the weak duality theorem. Using it, show that if the primal problem is unbounded, then the dual problem is infeasible.
[Univ. of Madras B.Sc. (Math.) Nov., 2012; P.U.B.E.(C.S.&E.) Dec., 2004]

Section 6.1-1

16. Form the dual of the following primal problem :

$$\begin{aligned} \text{Minimize} \quad & Z = 20x_1 + 40x_2, \\ \text{subject to} \quad & 2x_1 + 20x_2 \geq 40, \\ & 20x_1 + 3x_2 \geq 20, \\ & 4x_1 + 15x_2 \geq 30, \\ & x_1, x_2 \geq 0. \end{aligned}$$

[Chennai U.B.C.A. Nov., 2010]

[*Ans.* Maximize $Z' = 40y_1 + 20y_2 + 30y_3$, subject to $2y_1 + 20y_2 + 4y_3 \leq 20$, $20y_1 + 3y_2 + 15y_3 \leq 40$, $y_1, y_2, y_3 \geq 0$.)

17. Write the dual of the following L.P. problem:

$$\begin{aligned} \text{Minimize} \quad & Z = 7x_1 + 3x_2 + 8x_3, \\ \text{subject to} \quad & 8x_1 + 2x_2 + x_3 \geq 3, \\ & 3x_1 + 6x_2 + 4x_3 \geq 4, \\ & 4x_1 + x_2 + 5x_3 \geq 1, \\ & x_1 + 5x_2 + 2x_3 \geq 7, \\ & x_1, x_2, x_3 \geq 0. \end{aligned}$$

[Delhi B.Sc. (Math.) 1974]

(*Ans.* Maximize $W = 3y_1 + 4y_2 + y_3 + 7y_4$,
subject to $8y_1 + 3y_2 + 4y_3 + y_4 \le 7$,
$2y_1 + 6y_2 + y_3 + 5y_4 \le 3$,
$y_1 + 4y_2 + 5y_3 + 2y_4 \le 8$,
y_1, y_2, y_3, y_4, all ≥ 0.)

18. Write the dual of the problem :

Maximize $Z = 2x_1 + 5x_2 + 3x_3$,
subject to
$2x_1 + 4x_2 - x_3 \le 8$,
$-2x_1 - 2x_2 + 3x_3 \ge -7$,
$x_1 + 3x_2 - 5x_3 \ge -2$,
$4x_1 + x_2 + 3x_3 \le 4$,
$x_1, x_2, x_3 \ge 0$.

(*Ans.* Minimize $W = 8y_1 + 7y_2 + 2y_3 + 4y_4$,
subject to $2y_1 + 2y_2 - y_3 + 4y_4 \ge 2$,
$4y_1 + 2y_2 - 3y_3 + y_4 \ge 5$,
$-y_1 - 3y_2 + 5y_3 + 3y_4 \ge 3$,
$y_1, y_2, y_3, y_4 \ge 0$.)

19. Obtain the dual problem of the following L.P.P. :

Maximize $f(x) = 2x_1 + 5x_2 + 6x_3$,
subject to
$5x_1 + 6x_2 - x_3 \le 3$,
$-2x_1 + x_2 + 4x_3 \le 4$,
$x_1 - 5x_2 + 3x_3 \le 1$,
$-3x_1 - 3x_2 + 7x_3 \le 6$,
$x_1, x_2, x_3 \ge 0$.

Also verify that the dual of the dual problem is the primal problem.

[*Madurai B.Sc. (Appl. Math.) 1984*]

(*Ans.* Minimize $f(y) = 3y_1 + 4y_2 + y_3 + 6y_4$,
subject to $5y_1 - 2y_2 + y_3 - 3y_4 \ge 2$,
$6y_1 + y_2 - 5y_3 - 3y_4 \ge 5$,
$-y_1 + 4y_2 + 3y_3 + 7y_4 \ge 6$,
$y_1, y_2, y_3, y_4 \ge 0$.)

20. Formulate the following linear problem into its dual form :

Minimize $Z = 3x_1 - 2x_2 + 4x_3$,
subject to
$3x_1 + 5x_2 + 4x_3 \ge 7$,
$6x_1 + x_2 + 3x_3 \ge 4$,
$7x_1 - 2x_2 - x_3 \le 10$,
$x_1 - 2x_2 + 5x_3 \ge 3$,
$4x_1 + 7x_2 - 2x_3 \ge 2$,
$x_1, x_2, x_3 \ge 0$.

[*R.U. MBA June, 2011; Dec., 2011*]

(*Ans.* Maximize $W = 7y_1 + 4y_2 - 10y_3 + 3y_4 + 2y_5$,
subject to $3y_1 + 6y_2 - 7y_3 + y_4 + 4y_5 \le 3$,
$5y_1 + y_2 + 2y_3 - 2y_4 + 7y_5 \le -2$,
$4y_1 + 3y_2 + y_3 + 5y_4 - 2y_5 \le 4$,
$y_1, y_2, y_3, y_4, y_5 \ge 0$.)

21. Write the dual of the following L.P.P. :

Maximize $Z = x_1 - x_2 + 3x_3$,
subject to
$x_1 + x_2 + x_3 \le 10$,
$2x_1 - x_3 \le 2$,
$2x_1 - 2x_2 + 3x_3 \le 6$,
$x_1, x_2, x_3 \ge 0$.

[*J.N.T.U. Hyderabad MBA June, 2012*]

(*Ans.* Minimize $W = 10y_1 + 2y_2 + 6y_3$,
subject to $y_1 + 2y_2 + 2y_3 \ge 1$,
$y_1 - 2y_3 \ge -1$,
$y_1 - y_2 + 3y_3 \ge 3$,
$y_1, y_2, y_3 \ge 0$.)

22. Write the dual of the following L.P.P. :

Minimize $Z = 80x_1 + 90x_2 + 100x_3,$
subject to $2x_1 + 5x_2 - 3x_3 \leq 100,$
$8x_1 + 9x_2 \geq 50,$
$5x_1 + 6x_2 + 10x_3 \leq 150,$
$x_1, x_2, x_3 \geq 0.$

[Mumbai U. MBA, 2010]

(*Ans.* Maximize $Z' = -100y_1 + 50y_2 - 150y_3,$
subject to $-2y_1 + 8y_2 - 5y_3 \leq 80,$
$-5y_1 + 9y_2 - 6y_3 \leq 90,$
$3y_1 - 10y_3 \leq 100,$
$y_1, y_2, y_3 \geq 0.$)

23. Write the dual of the following L.P.P. :

Maximize $Z = 40x_1 + 25x_2 + 50x_3,$
subject to $x_1 + 2x_2 + x_3 \leq 36,$
$2x_1 + x_2 + 4x_3 \leq 60,$
$2x_1 + 5x_2 + x_3 \leq 45,$
$x_1, x_2, x_3 \geq 0.$

[Mumbai U. MBA, 2010]

(*Ans.* Minimize $Z' = 36y_1 + 60y_2 + 45y_3,$
subject to $y_1 + 2y_2 + 2y_3 \geq 40,$
$2y_1 + y_2 + 5y_3 \geq 25,$
$y_1 + 4y_2 + y_3 \geq 50,$
$y_1, y_2, y_3 \geq 0.$)

24. Write the dual of the following L.P.P. :

Maximize $Z = -3x_1 + 4x_2,$
subject to $2x_1 + 3x_2 \leq 16,$
$5x_1 + 2x_2 \geq 20,$
$x_1, x_2 \geq 0.$

[U.P.U. MBA, 2009]

(*Ans.* Minimize $Z' = 16y_1 - 20y_2,$
subject to $2y_1 - 5y_2 \geq -3,$
$3y_1 - 2y_2 \geq 4,$
$y_1, y_2 \geq 0.$)

25. Write the dual of the following problem :

Maximize $Z = 10y_1 + 8y_2 - 6y_3,$
subject to $3y_1 + y_2 - 2y_3 \leq 10,$
$-2y_1 + 3y_2 - y_3 \geq 12,$
$y_1, y_2, y_3 \geq 0.$

[Gujarat U. MBA Dec., 2010]

(*Ans.* Minimize $Z' = 10x_1 - 12x_2,$
subject to $3x_1 + 2x_2 \geq 10,$
$x_1 - 3x_2 \geq 8,$
$-2x_1 + x_2 \geq -6,$
$x_1, x_2 \geq 0.$)

Section 6.1-2

26. Construct the dual of the problem :

Maximize $Z = 4x_1 + 5x_2 + 12x_3,$
subject to $2x_1 + x_2 + x_3 \leq 4,$
$3x_1 - 2x_2 + x_3 = 3,$
$x_1, x_2, x_3 \geq 0.$

[P.U. B.Com. April, 2006]

(*Ans.* Minimize $W = 4y_1 + 3y_2,$
subject to $2y_1 + 3y_2 \geq 4,$
$y_1 - 2y_2 \geq 5,$
$y_1 + y_2 \geq 12,$
$y_1 \geq 0$, y_2 unrestricted in sign.)

27. Construct the dual of the linear programming problem :

Minimize $Z = 10x_1 - 6x_2 - 8x_3,$
subject to $x_1 - 3x_2 + x_3 = 5;$
$-2x_1 + x_2 + 3x_3 = 8,$
$x_1, x_2, x_3 \geq 0.$

(*Ans.* Maximize $W = 5y_1 + 8y_2,$
subject to $y_1 - 2y_2 \leq 10,$
$-3y_1 + y_2 \leq -6,$
$y_1 + 3y_2 \leq -8,$
y_1, y_2 unrestricted in sign.)

28. Obtain the dual of the problem:

Minimize $Z = x_3 + x_4 + x_5$,
subject to $x_1 - x_3 + x_4 - x_5 = -2$,
$x_2 - x_3 - x_4 + x_5 = 1$,
$x_1, x_2, x_3, x_4, x_5 \geq 0$.

[*Gauhati M.Sc. (Stat.) 1975*]

(*Ans.* Maximize $W = -2y_1 + y_2$,
subject to $-y_1 - y_2 \leq 1$,
$y_1 - y_2 \leq 1$,
$-y_1 + y_2 \leq 1$,
y_1, y_2 unrestricted in sign.)

29. Write the dual of :

Maximize $Z = 3x_1 + x_2 + x_3 - x_4$,
subject to $x_1 + 5x_2 + 3x_3 + 4x_4 \leq 5$,
$x_1 + x_2 = -1$,
$x_3 - x_4 \leq -5$,
$x_j \geq 0; j = 1, 2, 3, 4$.

[*Mumbai B.Sc. (Stat.) 1976*]

(*Ans.* Minimize $W = 5y_1 - y_2 - 5y_3$,
subject to $y_1 + y_2 \geq 3$,
$5y_1 + y_2 \geq 1$,
$3y_1 + y_3 \geq 1$,
$4y_1 - y_3 \geq -1$,
$y_1, y_3 \geq 0$, y_2 unrestricted.)

30. Construct the dual of the problem:

Maximize $Z = 6x_1 + 4x_2 + 6x_3 + x_4$,
subject to the constraints
$4x_1 + 4x_2 + 4x_3 + 8x_4 = 21$,
$3x_1 + 17x_2 + 80x_3 + 2x_4 \leq 48$,
$x_1, x_2 \geq 0$,
x_3, x_4 are unrestricted.

[*Delhi M.Sc. (Math.) 1972*]

(*Ans.* Minimize $W = 21y_1 + 48y_2$,
subject to $4y_1 + 3y_2 \geq 6$,
$4y_1 + 17y_2 \geq 4$,
$4y_1 + 80y_2 = 6$,
$8y_1 + 2y_2 = 1$,
y_1 unrestricted in sign, $y_2 \geq 0$.)

31. Construct the dual of the following L.P.P. :

Maximize $Z = 3x_1 + 17x_2 + 9x_3$,
subject to $x_1 - x_2 + x_3 \geq 3$,
$-3x_1 + 2x_3 \leq 1$,
$2x_1 + x_2 - 5x_3 = 1$,
$x_1, x_2, x_3 \geq 0$.

[*P.U. B.Com. April, 2006*]

(*Ans.* Minimize $Z' = -3y_1 + y_2 + y_3$,
subject to $-y_1 - 3y_2 + 2y_3 \geq 3$,
$y_1 + y_3 \geq 17$,
$-y_1 + 2y_2 - 5y_3 \geq 9$,
$y_1, y_2 \geq 0, y_3$ unrestricted in sign.)

32. Construct the dual of the following problem:

Maximize $Z = 3x_1 + 10x_2 + 2x_3$,
subject to $2x_1 + 3x_2 + 2x_3 \leq 7$,
$3x_1 - 2x_2 + 4x_3 = 3$,
$x_1, x_2, x_3 \geq 0$.

[*P.U. B.Com. April, 2008*]

(*Ans.* Minimize $Z' = 7y_1 + 3y_2$,
subject to $2y_1 + 3y_2 \geq 3$,
$3y_1 - 2y_2 \geq 10$,
$2y_1 + 4y_2 \geq 2$,
$y_1 \geq 0, y_2$
unrestricted in sign.)

33. Obtain the dual of the following L.P.P:

Maximize $Z = 2x_1 + 3x_2 - x_3$,
subject to $4x_1 + 3x_2 + x_3 = 6$,
$x_1 + 2x_2 + 5x_3 = 9$,
$x_1, x_2, x_3 \geq 0$.

[*G.N.D.U. B.Com. Sept., 2005*]

(*Ans.* Minimize $Z = 6y_1 + 9y_2$,
subject to $4y_1 + y_2 \geq 2$,
$3y_1 + 2y_2 \geq 3$,
$y_1 + 5y_2 \geq -1$,
y_1, y_2 both unrestricted in sign.)

34. Write the dual of the following L.P.P. :

Minimize $Z = 4x_1 + 5x_2 - 3x_3$,
subject to $x_1 + x_2 + x_3 = 22$,
$3x_1 + 5x_2 - 2x_3 \leq 65$,
$x_1 + 7x_2 + 4x_3 \geq 120$,
$x_1, x_2 \geq 0$, x_3 unrestricted.

[*G.N.D.U. B.Com. April, 2006*]

(*Ans.* Maximize $Z' = 22y_1 - 65y_2 + 120y_3$,
subject to $y_1 - 3y_2 + y_3 \leq 4$,
$y_1 - 5y_2 + 7y_3 \leq 5$,
$y_1 + 2y_2 + 4y_3 \leq -3$,
y_1 unrestricted in sign ; $y_2, y_3 \geq 0$.)

35. Obtain the dual of the following LP problem:

Minimize $Z = 2x_1 + 3x_2 + 4x_3$,
subject to $2x_1 + 3x_2 + 5x_3 \geq 2$,
$3x_1 + x_2 + 7x_3 = 3$,
$x_1 + 4x_2 + 6x_3 \leq 5$,
$x_1, x_2 \geq 0$ and x_3 is unrestricted.

[*V.T.U. Karnataka B.E. June, 2010*]

(*Ans.* Maximize $Z' = 2y_1 + 3y_2 - 5y_3$,
subject to $2y_1 + 3y_2 - y_3 \leq 2$,
$3y_1 + y_2 - 4y_3 \leq 3$,
$5y_1 + 7y_2 - 6y_3 \leq 4$,
$y_1, y_3 \geq 0$; y_2
unrestricted in sign.)

36. Construct the dual of the problem:

Maximize $Z = 4x_1 + 2x_2$,
subject to $x_1 - 2x_2 \geq 2$,
$x_1 + 2x_2 = 8$,
$x_1 - x_2 \leq 10$,
$x_1 \geq 0$, x_2 unrestricted in sign.

[*P.U.B.E. (Prod.) 1997*]

(*Ans.* Minimize $W = -2y_1 + 8y_2 + 10y_3$,
subject to $-y_1 + y_2 + y_3 \geq 4$,
$2y_1 + 2y_2 - y_3 = 2$,
$y_1, y_3 \geq 0$, y_2 unrestricted in sign.)

37. Construct the dual of :

Maximize $Z = 4x_1 + x_2 + 7x_3,$

subject to $x_1 + x_2 + x_3 = 10$

$5x_1 - x_2 + x_3 \geq 12,$

$x_1 + 7x_2 - 3x_3 \leq 4,$

$x_1, x_2, x_3 \geq 0.$

[*Chennai U. B.B.A. Nov., 2010*]

(*Ans.* Minimize $Z' = 10y_1 - 12y_2 + 4y_3,$
subject to $y_1 - 5y_2 + y_3 \geq 4,$
$y_1 + 2y_2 + 7y_3 \geq 1,$
$y_1 - y_2 - 3y_3 \geq 7,$
y_1 unrestricted, $y_2, y_3 \geq 0.$)

38. Obtain the dual of the problem:

Maximize $Z = 4x_1 + 3x_2 - x_3 + x_4 + 4x_5,$

subject to $2x_1 - x_2 + 3x_3 + x_4 - x_5 = 2,$

$x_1 + x_2 + 2x_3 + x_4 - 9x_5 = 6,$

$x_1, x_2, x_3, x_4 \geq 0$, x_5 unrestricted.

[*Delhi B.Sc. (Math.) 1979*]

(*Ans.* Minimize $W = 2y_1 + 6y_2,$
subject to $2y_1 + y_2 \geq 4,$
$-y_1 + y_2 \geq 3,$
$3y_1 + 2y_2 \geq -1,$
$y_1 + y_2 \geq 1,$
$-y_1 - 9y_2 = 4,$
y_1, y_2 unrestricted in sign.)

39. Construct the dual of the following primal problem :

Maximize $Z = x_1 + x_2 + 2x_3,$

subject to $2x_1 - 3x_2 + 2x_3 = 4,$

$x_1 + x_2 + x_3 \geq 6,$

$4x_1 - 3x_2 - 5x_3 = 1,$

$x_1, x_2, x_3 \geq 0.$

[*P.U. B.E.(Mech.) Dec., 1984*]

(*Ans.* Minimize $W = 4y_1 - 6y_2 + y_3,$
subject to $2y_1 - y_2 + 4y_3 \geq 1,$
$-3y_1 - y_2 - 3y_3 \geq 1,$
$2y_1 - y_2 - 5y_3 \geq 2,$
$y_2 \geq 0$, y_1 and y_3 unrestricted.)

40. Costruct the dual problem for the following :

Maximize $Z = 16x_1 + 14x_2 + 36x_3 + 6x_4,$

subject to $14x_1 + 4x_2 + 14x_3 + 8x_4 = 21,$

$13x_1 + 17x_2 + 80x_3 + 2x_4 \leq 48,$

$x_1, x_2 \geq 0$; x_3, x_4 unrestricted .

[*P.U. B.E.(Mech.) Dec., 1982*]

(*Ans.* Minimize $W = 21y_1 + 48y_2,$
subject to $14y_1 + 13y_2 \geq 16,$
$4y_1 + 17y_2 \geq 14,$
$14y_1 + 80y_2 = 36,$
$8y_1 + 2y_2 = 6,$
y_1 unrestricted, $y_2 \geq 0.$)

41. Write the dual of:

Minimize $Z = x_1 + x_2 + x_3,$

subject to $x_1 - 3x_2 + 4x_3 = 5,$

$x_1 - 2x_2 \leq 3,$

$2x_2 - x_3 \geq 4,$

$x_1, x_2, \geq 0$, x_3 unrestricted.

[*Pbi. U. MCA, 1997*]

(*Ans.* Maximize $W = 5y_1 - 3y_2 + 4y_3,$
subject to $y_1 - y_2 \leq 1,$
$-3y_1 + 2y_2 + 2y_3 \leq 1,$
$4y_1 - y_3 = 1,$
$y_2, y_3 \geq 0$, y_1 unrestricted.)

42. Write the dual of :

Minimize $Z = 3x_1 + 5x_2 + 6x_3,$
subject to
$x_1 + 4x_2 + 6x_3 \leq 5,$
$2x_1 + 3x_2 + 5x_3 \geq 4,$
$3x_1 + x_2 + 7x_3 = 3,$
$x_1, x_2 \geq 0,$ x_3 unrestricted.

[*Karn. U. B.E.(Mech.) 1995*]

(*Ans.* Maximize $Z' = -5y_1 + 4y_2 + 3y_3,$
subject to $-y_1 + 2y_2 + 3y_3 \leq 3,$
$-4y_1 + 3y_2 + y_3 \leq 5,$
$-6y_1 + 5y_2 + 7y_3 = 6,$
$y_1, y_2 \geq 0,$ y_3 unrestricted.)

Section 6.1-4

43. Construct the dual of the following L.P.P. and solve both the primal and the dual :

Minimize $Z = 4x_1 + 2x_2 + 3x_3,$
subject to the constraints
$2x_1 + 4x_3 \geq 5,$
$2x_1 + 3x_2 + x_3 \geq 4,$
$x_1, x_2, x_3 \geq 0.$

[*J.N.T.U. Hyderabad B.Tech. Nov., 2010*]

(*Ans.* Primal : $x_1 = 0, x_2 = \frac{11}{12}, x_3 = \frac{5}{4}; Z_{min} = \frac{67}{12};$

Dual : $y_1 = \frac{7}{12}, y_2 = \frac{2}{3}; W_{max} = \frac{67}{12}$.)

44. Construct the dual of the following L.P.P. and solve both the primal and the dual :

Maximize $Z = 5x_1 + 12x_2 + 4x_3,$
subject to
$x_1 + 2x_2 + x_3 \leq 5,$
$2x_1 - x_2 + 3x_3 = 2,$
$x_1, x_2, x_3 \geq 0.$

[*P.U. B.Com. April, 2006*]

(*Ans.* Primal : $x_1 = \frac{9}{5}, x_2 = \frac{8}{5}, x_3 = 0 ; Z_{max} = \frac{141}{5};$

Dual : $y_1 = \frac{29}{5}, y_2 = y'_2 - y''_2 = 0 - \frac{2}{5} = -\frac{2}{5};$

$W_{min} = \frac{141}{5}$.)

45. Find the dual of the following set of inequalities and solve it :

$2x_1 + 3x_2 \leq 12,$
$-3x_1 + 2x_2 \leq -4,$
$3x_1 - 5x_2 \leq 2,$
x_1 unrestricted, $x_2 \geq 0.$

(*Ans.* $x_1 = \frac{36}{13}, x_2 = \frac{28}{13}$.)

[*Hint* : Add the objective function maximize $Z = 0x_1 + 0x_2$.]

46. Using duality, find the optimal solution to the problem:

Maximize $Z = 3x_1 - 2x_2,$
subject to
$x_1 + x_2 \leq 5,$
$-x_2 \leq -1,$
$0 \leq x_1 \leq 4,$
$0 \leq x_2 \leq 6.$

[*P.U. B.Com., 2002; MBA, 2001*]

(*Ans.* $x_1 = 4, x_2 = 1; z_{max} = 10.$)

47. Solve the following primal. Also find its dual and solve it.

Maximize $Z = 10y_1 - y_2 - 9y_3 - 8y_4$,
subject to
$2y_1 - y_2 - 3y_3 - y_4 + 2 = 0$,
$5y_1 - 2y_2 - 3y_4 + 5 = 0$,
$-7y_1 + 4y_2 - y_3 - 4y_4 + 1 \geq 0$,
$-3y_1 - 2y_2 - 5y_3 - 6y_4 + 10 \geq 0$,
y_1, y_2, y_3, y_4, all ≥ 0.

(*Ans.* Primal : $y_1 = \frac{1}{7}$, $y_2 = \frac{8}{7}$, $y_3 = 0$, $y_4 = \frac{8}{7}$; $Z_{max} = -\frac{62}{7}$;

Dual : $x_1 = \frac{111}{7}$, $x_2 = -\frac{57}{7}$, $x_3 = \frac{1}{7}$, $x_4 = 0$; $W_{min} = -\frac{62}{7}$.)

48. Solve the following by its dual only :

Minimize $Z = 10x_1 + 15x_2 + 30x_3$,
subject to
$x_1 + 3x_2 + x_3 \geq 90$,
$2x_1 + 5x_2 + 3x_3 \geq 120$,
$x_1 + x_2 + x_3 \geq 60$,
$x_1, x_2, x_3 \geq 0$.

[*Jammu U.B.E. (Mech.) 2004*]

(*Ans.* $y_1 = \frac{5}{2}$, $y_2 = 0$, $y_3 = \frac{15}{2}$; $Z'_{max} = 675$;

$x_1 = 45$, $x_2 = 15$, $x_3 = 0$; $Z_{min} = 675$.)

49. Consider the problem :

Maximize $Z = 5x_1 + 8x_2$,
subject to
$x_1 + x_2 \leq 2$,
$x_1 - 2x_2 \geq 0$,
$-x_1 + 4x_2 \leq 1$,
$x_1, x_2 \geq 0$.

What is the dual of the above problem? Find the solution of the primal problem by solving its dual.

[*P.U.B.E. (Mech.) Nov., 2002, 2000*]

(*Ans.* $x_1 = 7/5$, $x_2 = 3/5$; $Z_{max} = 59/5$.)

50. Write the dual of the following L.P. Problem :

Maximize $Z = 3x_1 + 5x_2 + 4x_3$,
subject to
$2x_1 + 3x_2 \leq 8$,
$2x_2 + 5x_3 \leq 10$,
$3x_1 + 2x_2 + 4x_3 \leq 15$,
$x_1, x_2, x_3 \geq 0$.

The optimal simplex table of the above problem with x_4, x_5, x_6 as slack variables is given below.

TABLE 6.20

	x_1	x_2	x_3	x_4	x_5	x_6	b
x_1	1	0	0	–2/41	–12/41	15/41	65/41
x_2	0	1	0	15/41	8/41	10/41	50/41
x_3	0	0	1	–2/41	–12/41	15/41	80/41
$c_j - Z_j$	–	–	–	–45/41	–24/41	–11/41	Z = 765/41

From this table find the optimal values of the dual variables and verify the duality theorem.

[*I.S.I., 1962*]

(*Ans.* $y_1 = 45/41$, $y_2 = 24/41$, $y_3 = 11/41$; $W_{min} = \frac{765}{41} = x_1 = \frac{65}{41}$, $x_2 = \frac{50}{41}$, $x_3 = \frac{80}{41}$; $Z_{max} = \frac{765}{41}$.)

51. Apply to concept of duality, solve the L.P.P. :

Maximise $Z = 3x_1 + x_2$,
subject to
$x_1 - x_2 \leq 1$,
$x_1 + x_2 \leq 4$,
$x_1 - 3x_2 \leq 3$;
$x_1, x_2 \geq 0$.

[*Univ. of Madras B.Sc. (Math.) Nov., 2012; J.N.T.U. Hyderabad B.Tech. April, 2011*]

52. Apply the simplex method to solve the following :

Maximize $Z = 30x_1 + 23x_2 + 29x_3$,
subject to $6x_1 + 5x_2 + 3x_3 \le 26$,
$4x_1 + 2x_2 + 5x_3 \le 7$,
every $x_j \ge 0$.

Also read the solution to the dual of the above problem from the final table.

[*Agra M. Stat.*, 1973]

(*Ans.* Primal : $x_1, = 0, x_2 = \frac{7}{2}, x_3 = 0;\ Z_{max} = \frac{161}{2}$;
Dual : $y_1 = 0, y_2 = \frac{23}{2};\ W_{min} = \frac{161}{2}$.)

53. Write the dual of the following L.P.P. :

Minimize $Z = 20x + 16y$,
subject to $x + y \le 12$,
$2x + y \ge 17$,
$2x \ge 5$,
$y \ge 6$,
$x, y \ge 0$,

and solve it by the simplex method. [*P.U.B.E.(Mech.)* 1997]

(*Ans.* $x = 5, y = 7;\ Z_{max} = 212$.)

54. Write the dual of the following L.P.P. :

Minimize $Z = y_1 + 0.4y_2$,
subject to $0.1y_1 + 0.2y_2 \ge 2$,
$0.2y_1 + 0.1y_2 \ge 1.7$,
$0.1y_2 \ge 0.6$,
$0.1y_1 \ge 0.4$,
$y_1, y_2 \ge 0$.

Solve it by the simplex method. [*P.U.B.E.(Mech.)* 1997]

(*Ans.* $y_1 = 4, y_2 = 9;\ Z_{min} = 7.6$.)

55. State the dual of the following and solve the same by the simplex method :

Maximize $Z = 2x_1 + 3x_2 + 4x_3$,
subject to $2x_1 + 3x_2 + 5x_3 \ge 2$,
$3x_1 + x_2 + 7x_3 \le 3$,
$x_1 + 4x_2 + 6x_3 \le 5$,
$x_1, x_2 \ge 0$, x_3 unrestricted. [*I.I.M.S. Kolkata*, 1996]

56. Write the dual of the following L.P.P. :

Maximize $Z = 4x_1 + 2x_2$,
subject to $-x_1 - x_2 \le -3$,
$-x_1 + x_2 \le -2$,
$x_1, x_2 \ge 0$.

Hence or otherwise find the solution of the primal. [*P.U.MBA*, 2003]

(*Ans.* Unbounded solution.)

57. Solve the following L.P.P. by simplex method, after converting it into dual problem:

Maximize $Z = 25x_1 + 10x_2$,
subject to $x_1 + x_2 = 50$,
$x_1 \ge 20$,
$x_2 \le 40$,
$x_1, x_2 \ge 0$. [*P.U.B. Com. April*, 2004]

(*Ans.* $x_1 = 20, x_2 = 30;\ z_{min} = 800$.)

58. Obtain the dual of the following L.P.P. and then solve the dual:

Maximize $Z = 2x_1 + 5x_2 + 6x_3$,
subject to $5x_1 + 6x_2 - x_3 \le 3$,
$2x_1 + x_2 + 4x_3 \le 4$,

$x_1 - 5x_2 + 3x_3 \leq 1,$
$-3x_1 - 3x_2 + 7x_3 \leq 6,$
$x_1, x_2, x_3 \geq 0.$ [*P.U. B.E.(T.& I.T.) Nov., 2004*]

59. A pension fund manager is considering investing in two shares A and B. It is estimated that

(*a*) Share A will earn a dividend of 12% per annum and share B 4% per annum.

(*b*) Growth in the market value in one year of share A will be 10 paise per ₹ 1 invested and in B 40 paise per ₹ 1 invested.

He wants to invest the minimum total sum which will give dividend income of at least ₹ 600 per annum and growth in one year of at least ₹ 1,000 on the initial investment. You are required to

(*i*) state the mathematical formulation of the problem.

(*ii*) compute the minimum sum to be invested to meet the manager's objective by using the simplex method on the dual problem. [*P.T.U. MBA May, 2002*]

(*Ans.* (*i*) Minimize $Z = x_1 + x_2$,
subject to $0.12x_1 + 0.04x_2 \geq 600$,
$0.1x_1 + 0.4x_2 \geq 1,000$,
$x_1, x_2 \geq 0$.

(*ii*) $x_1 = ₹ \frac{50,000}{11}, x_2 = ₹ \frac{15,000}{11}; Z_{min} = ₹ \frac{65,000}{11}$.)

60. In order to produce 1,000 tonnes of non-oxidizing steel for engine valves, at least the following quantities of manganese (Mn), chromium (Cr) and molybdenum (Mb) are needed :

Mn 50 kg, Cr 60 kg and Mb 70 kg.

These metals are available in packages A, B and C having different proportions of Mn, Cr and Mb and also differing in prices as under :

Contents in kg per packet

Package	*Mn*	*Cr*	*Mb*	*Price per packet (₹)*
A	10	10	5	45
B	10	15	5	60
C	5	5	25	75

How many packets of packages A, B and C should be purchased to minimize cost? What is the possible cost? Solve through dual only. [*Gujrat Univ. B.E. April, 1976*]

61. (*a*) Write the dual of the following primal problem. Also give the interpretation of both primal and dual problem in general.

Minimize $Z = 3x_1 + 2.25\,x_2$,
subject to $2x_1 + 4x_2 \geq 40$,
$3x_1 + 2x_2 \geq 50$,
$x_1, x_2 \geq 0$.

(*b*) Solve the dual problem given in (*a*) through the simplex method. [*IGNOU MBA June, 2007*]

(*Ans.* (*a*) $x = 15, x_2 = 2.5; Z_{min} = 50.625$.
(*b*) $y = 3/32, y_2 = 15/16; Z'_{max} = 50.625$.)

62. Use dual to solve the following L.P.P. :

Minimize $Z = x_1 + x_2$,
subject to $2x_1 + x_2 \geq 4$,
$x_1 + 7x_2 \geq 7$,
$x_1, x_2 \geq 0$.

[*G.N.D.U. B.Com. April, 2010*]

(*Ans.* $x_1 = 21/13, x_2 = 10/13; Z_{min} = 31/13$.)

63. ABC company combines factors *X* and *Y* to form a product which must weigh 50 kg. At least 20 kg of *X* and not more than 40 kg of *Y* can be used. *X* costs ₹ 25 per kg and *Y* costs ₹ 10 per kg. Use duality to find the amount of factors *X* and *Y* which should be used to manufacture the product [*P.U.B. Com. April, 2010*]

(*Ans.* Minimize $Z = 25x + 10y$,
subject to $x + y \geq 50$,
$x \geq 20$,

$y \le 40,$
$x, y \ge 0;$
$x = 20, y = 30; Z_{min}$ = ₹ 800.)

64. The following is the final simplex table of exercise 23. Write the optimum solution of primal as well as dual.

	c_j	40	25	50	0	0	0	
c_B	Basis	x_1	x_2	x_3	s_1	s_2	s_3	b
0	s_1	0	1/6	0	1	–1/6	–1/3	11
50	x_3	0	–4/3	1	0	1/3	–1/3	5
40	x_1	1	19/6	0	0	–1/6	2/3	20
	$c_j–Z_j$	0	–35	0	0	–10	–10	

[*Mumbai U. MBA, 2010*]
(*Ans.* $x_1 = 20, x_2 = 0, x_3 = 5; Z_{max} = 1{,}050.$
$y_1 = 0, y_2 = 10, y_3 = 10; Z'_{min} = 1{,}050.$)

65. (a) Find the graphical solution to the following L.P.P. :
Minimize $Z = x + y,$
subject to $5x + 10y \le 50,$
$x + y \ge 1,$
$y \le 4,$
$x, y \ge 0.$

(b) Also write the dual of this problem. [*Gujarat Technological U. MBA Dec., 2010*]
(*Ans.* (*a*) $x = 1, y = 0; Z_{min} = 1$ and $x = 0, y = 1; Z_{min} = 1;$
so multiple optimal solutions.
(*b*) Maximize $Z' = -50y_1 + y_2 - 4y_3,$
subject to $-5y_1 + y_2 \le 1,$
$-10y_1 + y_2 - y_3 \le 1,$
$y_1, y_2, y_3 \ge 0.$)

66. Show that both the primal and the dual of the following L.P.P. have the same optimal 'Z' and the solution can be read from the primal solution:
Maximize $Z = 2x_1 + x_2,$
subject to constraints $x_1 + 5x_2 \le 10, x_1 + 3x_2 \le 6,$
$2x_1 + 2x_2 \le 8, x_1, x_2 \ge 0.$ [*V.T.U. Karnataka B.E. June, 2012*]

67. Find the optimum value of Z for the following L.P.P. by inspecting its dual only:
Minimize $Z = 4x_1 + 5x_2 + 3x_3 + 4x_4,$
such that $2x_1 + 6x_2 + 3x_3 + 4x_4 \ge 50,$
and $x_1, x_2, x_3, x_4 \ge 0.$ [*V.T.U. Karnataka B.E. Jan., 2010*]

68. Write the dual for the following L.P.P. Solve the primal and read the solution of both primal and dual problems.
Maximize $Z = 2x_1 + x_2,$
subject to constraints $x_1 + 2x_2 \le 10,$
$x_1 + x_2 \le 6,$
$x_1 - x_2 \le 2, x_1 - 2x_2 \le 1$ and $x_1, x_2 \ge 0.$
[*V.T.U. Karnataka B.E Dec., 2010*]

69. Applying the concept of duality, solve the L.P.P. :
Maximize $Z = 3x_1 + x_2,$
subject to $x_1 - x_2 \le 1,$
$x_1 + x_2 \le 4,$
$x_1 - 3x_2 \le 3,$
$x_1, x_2 \ge 0.$ [*J.N.T.U. Hyderabad B.Tech. April, 2011*]

70. (*a*) What is the principle of duality in L.P.P. ? Explain its advantages.
(*b*) Use duality to solve the L.P.P:
Minimize $Z = 8x_1 - 2x_2 - 4x_3,$
subject to $x_1 - 4x_2 - 2x_3 \ge 2,$
$x_1 + x_2 - 3x_3 \ge -1,$
$-3x_1 - x_2 + x_3 \ge -1,$
$x_1, x_2, x_3 \ge 0.$ [*J.N.T.U. Hyderabad B.Tech. Nov., 2010*]

6.2 THE DUAL SIMPLEX METHOD

In this section we introduce a different simplex algorithm that is motivated by the relationship between the primal and dual problems. The algorithm is designed to solve a class of L.P. models efficiently. It is used to solve problems which start *dual feasible, i.e.*, whose primal is optimal but infeasible . In this method the solution starts better than optimum but infeasible and remains infeasible until the true optimum is reached at which the solution becomes feasible. Thus, whereas the regular simplex method starts with a basic feasible but non-optimal solution and works towards optimality, the dual simplex method starts with a basic infeasible but optimal solution and works towards feasibility.

The dual simplex method was first discovered by C.E. Lemke, a student of Charnes. It is applicable to maximization as well as minimization problems. The constraints are converted into $\leq$ type and slack variables are added to set up the problem in the standard form. The initial simplex table is constructed and if any b_i is negative and the optimality condition is satisfied, then the given problem can be solved by the dual simplex method. Note that a negative right-handside element signifies that the corresponding slack variable is negative.

The dual simplex method is quite similar to the regular simplex method and once they are started, the only difference lies in the criterion used for selecting a variable to enter the basis and to leave the basis. In the dual simplex method this criterion is for the dual while in regular simplex method the criterion is for the primal. Further, in the dual simplex method we first determine the variable to leave the basis and then the variable to enter the basis, while reverse is done in the case of the regular simplex method.

6.2-1 Applications of the Dual Simplex Method

In general it is not always easy to find a dual feasible basis. For many practical problems the initial table is neither primal feasible nor dual feasible. Hence as a rule the regular (primal) simplex method is preferred over the dual simplex method for solving the general L.P. problem. However, there are instances when the dual simplex method has a distinct advantage over the primal simplex method. These are the problems in which a dual feasible table is readily available to start the dual simplex method. Various applications of the dual simplex method include :

1. Sensitivity analysis when the right-hand side vector b_i changes or when new constraints are added. If the newly added constraint is not satisfied by the optimal solution, the problem remains optimal but it becomes infeasible. The dual simplex method can then be applied to clear the infeasibility.
2. Parametric programming.
3. Integer programming algorithms.
4. Some non-linear programming algorithms.
5. It eliminates the introduction of artificial variables in the L.P. problems. This is the advantage over the regular simplex method.

6.2-2 Dual Simplex Algorithm

The dual simplex algorithm (technique) to solve an L.P. problem consists of the following steps :

Step 1. Convert the problem into maximization problem if it is initially in the minimization form.

Step 2. Convert $\geq$ type constraints, if any, into $\leq$ type by multiplying both sides of such constraints by – 1.

Step 3. Convert the inequality constraints into equalities by addition of slack variables and obtain the initial solution. Express the above information in the form of a table known as the dual simplex table.

Step 4. Compute $c_j - Z_j$ for every column. Three cases arise :

(*a*) If all $c_j - Z_j$ are either negative or zero and all b_i are non-negative, the solution obtained above is the optimal basic feasible solution.

(*b*) If all $c_j - Z_j$ are either negative or zero and at least one b_i is negative, then proceed to step 5.

(*c*) If any $c_j - Z_j$ *is positive, the method fails.*

Step 5. Select the row that contains the most negative b_i. This row is called the key row or the pivot row. The corresponding basic variable leaves the basis. This is called *dual feasibility condition.*

Step 6. Look at the elements of the key row.

(*a*) If all elements are non-negative, the problem *does not have a feasible solution.*

(*b*) If at least one element is negative, find the ratios of the corresponding elements of $c_j - Z_j$ row to these elements. Ignore the ratios associated with positive or zero elements of the key row. Choose the smallest of these ratios. The corresponding column is the key column and the associated variable is the entering variable. This is called *dual optimality condition.* Mark the key element or the pivot element.

Step 7. Make the key element unity. Perform the row operations as in the regular simplex method and repeat iteraions until either an optimal feasible solution is obtained in a finite number of steps or there is an indicat on of the non-existence of a feasible solution. Flow chart of these steps is shown in Fig. 6.1.

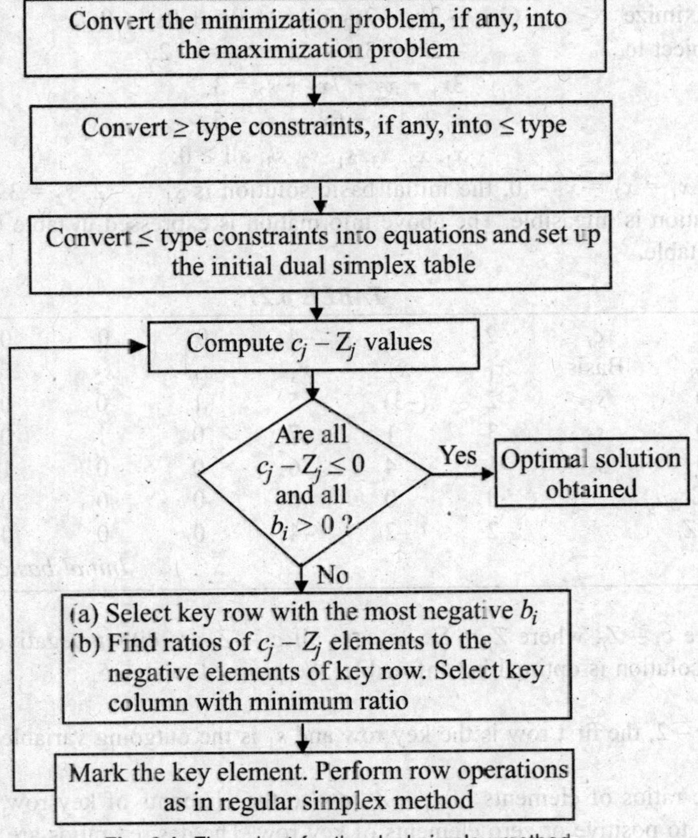

Fig. 6.1. Flow chart for the dual simplex method.

This technique will now be explained by considering a few examples.

EXAMPLE 6.2-1

Solve by dual simplex method the following problem :

Minimize $Z = 2x_1 + 2x_2 + 4x_3,$

subject to

$2x_1 + 3x_2 + 5x_3 \geq 2,$

$3x_1 + x_2 + 7x_3 \leq 3$

$x_1 + 4x_2 + 6x_3 \leq 5,$

$x_1, x_2, x_3 \geq 0.$

[P.T.U. M.Tech. Dec., 2011; P.U.B.E. (T. & I.T.) Nov., 2004]

Solution

It consists of the following steps :

Step 1

The given minimization problem is converted into maximization problem by writing

maximize $G = -Z = -2x_1 - 2x_2 - 4x_3.$

Step 2

The first constraint is of ≥ type. It is converted into ≤ type by multiplying throughout by –1. Thus the constraint becomes

$$-2x_1 - 3x_2 - 5x_3 \leq -2.$$

Step 3

The problem in canonical form is now converted into standard form by adding slack variables s_1, s_2 and s_3 in the constraints. Thus the problem is expressed as

maximize $G = -2x_1 - 2x_2 - 4x_3 + 0s_1 + 0s_2 + 0s_3,$

subject to

$-2x_1 - 3x_2 - 5x_3 + s_1 = -2,$

$3x_1 + x_2 + 7x_3 + s_2 = 3,$

$x_1 + 4x_2 + 6x_3 + s_3 = 5,$

$x_1, x_2, x_3, s_1, s_2, s_3,$ all $\geq 0.$

Putting $x_1 = x_2 = x_3 = 0$, the initial basic solution is $s_1 = -2$, $s_2 = 3$, $s_3 = 5$. Since s_1 is negative, solution is infeasible. The above information is expressed in table 6.21, called starting dual simplex table.

TABLE 6.21

	c_j	–2	–2	–4	0	0	0		
c_B	Basis	x_1	x_2	x_3	s_1	s_2	s_3	b	
0	s_1	–2	(–3)	–5	1	0	0	–2	←
0	s_2	3	1	7	0	1	0	3	
0	s_3	1	4	6	0	0	1	5	
$Z_j = \Sigma c_B a_{ij}$		0	0	0	0	0	0	0	
$c_j - Z_j$		–2	–2	–4	0	0	0		
			↑						

Initial basic infeasible solution

Step 4

Compute $c_j - Z_j$, where $Z_j = \Sigma c_B\, a_{ij}$. As all $c_j - Z_j$ are either negative or zero and b_1 is negative, the solution is optimal but infeasible. We proceed to step 5.

Step 5

As $b_1 = -2$, the first row is the key row and s_1 is the outgoing variable.

Step 6

Find the ratios of elements of $c_j - Z_j$ row to the elements of key row. Neglect the ratios corresponding to positive or zero elements of key row. The desired ratios are

$$\frac{-2}{-2} = 1, \quad \frac{-2}{-3} = \frac{2}{3} \text{ and } \frac{-4}{-5} = \frac{4}{5}.$$

Since $\frac{2}{3}$ is the smallest ratio, 'x_2' column is the key column; x_2 is the incoming variable and (–3) is the key element.

Step 7

Replace s_1 by x_2. This is shown in table 6.22.

TABLE 6.22

	c_j	–2	–2	–4	0	0	0	
c_B	Basis	x_1	x_2	x_3	s_1	s_2	s_3	b
–2	x_2	$2/3$	1	$5/3$	$-1/3$	0	0	$2/3$
0	s_2	$7/3$	0	$16/3$	$1/3$	1	0	$7/3$
0	s_3	$-5/3$	0	$-2/3$	$4/3$	0	1	$7/3$
	$Z_j = \Sigma c_B a_{ij}$	$-4/3$	–2	$-10/3$	$2/3$	0	0	$-4/3$
	$c_j – Z_j$	$-2/3$	0	$-2/3$	$-2/3$	0	0	

Optimal basic feasible solution

As all $c_j - Z_j$ are negative or zero and all b_i are positive, the solution given by table 6.22 is optimal. The optimal solution is

$$x_1 = 0,$$
$$x_2 = \frac{2}{3},$$
$$x_3 = 0,$$
$$\max. G = -2 \times 0 - 2 \times \frac{2}{3} - 4 \times 0 = -\frac{4}{3}$$

or
$$\min. Z = \frac{4}{3}.$$

EXAMPLE 6.2-2

Use dual simplex method to

maximize $Z = -3x_1 - 2x_2,$

subject to

$$x_1 + x_2 \geq 1,$$
$$x_1 + x_2 \leq 7,$$
$$x_1 + 2x_2 \geq 10,$$
$$x_2 \leq 3,$$
$$x_1, x_2, \geq 0.$$

[*P.T.U.-M.Tech. Nov., 2012; M.D.U. Rohtak B.E. (Mech.) Dec., 2006*]

Solution

Proceeding as in example 6.2-1 we express the given problem as

maximize $Z = -3x_1 - 2x_2,$

subject to

$$-x_1 - x_2 \leq -1,$$
$$x_1 + x_2 \leq 7,$$
$$-x_1 - 2x_2 \leq -10,$$
$$x_2 \leq 3,$$
$$x_1, x_2 \geq 0.$$

Adding slack variables the problem can be expressed as

maximize $Z = -3x_1 - 2x_2 + 0s_1 + 0s_2 + 0s_3 + 0s_4,$

subject to $-x_1 - x_2 + s_1 = -1,$

$$x_1 + x_2 + s_2 = 7,$$
$$-x_1 - 2x_2 + s_3 = -10,$$
$$x_2 + s_4 = 3,$$
$$x_1, x_2, s_1, s_2, s_3, s_4 \geq 0.$$

The initial basic infeasible solution is $x_1 = 0, x_2 = 0, s_1 = -1, s_2 = 7, s_3 = -10, s_4 = 3$. This is expressed in table 6.23.

TABLE 6.23

	c_j	−3	−2	0	0	0	0		
c_B	Basis	x_1	x_2	s_1	s_2	s_3	s_4	b	
0	s_1	−1	−1	1	0	0	0	−1	
0	s_2	1	1	0	1	0	0	7	
0	s_3	−1	(−2)	0	0	1	0	−10	←
0	s_4	0	1	0	0	0	1	3	
	$Z_j = \Sigma c_B a_{ij}$	0	0	0	0	0	0	0	
	$c_j - Z_j$	−3	−2	0	0	0	0		*First basic infeasible solution*
			↑						

$$\frac{c_j - Z_j}{a_{ij}} = \frac{-3}{-1} = 3, \text{ for } x_1 - \text{column and}$$
$$= \frac{-2}{-2} = 1, \text{ for } x_2 - \text{column.}$$

∴ x_2-column is the key column and (−2) is the key element. s_3 is replaced by x_2 in table 6.24.

TABLE 6.24

	c_j	−3	−2	0	0	0	0		
c_B	Basis	x_1	x_2	s_1	s_2	s_3	s_4	b	
0	s_1	$-\frac{1}{2}$	0	1	0	$-\frac{1}{2}$	0	4	
0	s_2	$\frac{1}{2}$	0	0	1	$\frac{1}{2}$	0	2	
−2	x_2	$\frac{1}{2}$	1	0	0	$-\frac{1}{2}$	0	5	
0	s_4	$\left(-\frac{1}{2}\right)$	0	0	0	$\frac{1}{2}$	1	−2	←
$Z_j = \Sigma c_B a_{ij}$		−1	−2	0	0	1	0	−10	
$c_j - Z_j$		−2	0	0	0	−1	0		
$\frac{c_j - Z_j}{a_{ij}}$		4	-	-	-	-	-		
		↑							*Second basic infeasible solution*

Replace s_4 and x_1. This is shown in table 6.25.

TABLE 6.25

	c_j	−3	−2	0	0	0	0		
c_B	Basis	x_1	x_2	s_1	s_2	s_3	s_4	b	
0	s_1	0	0	1	0	−1	−1	6	
0	s_2	0	0	0	1	1	1	0	
−2	x_2	0	1	0	0	0	1	3	
−3	x_1	1	0	0	0	−1	−2	4	
$Z_j = \Sigma c_B a_{ij}$		−3	−2	0	0	3	4	−18	
	$c_j - Z_j$	0	0	0	0	−3	−4		*Optimal feasible solution*

Table 6.25 gives the optimal feasible solution, which is

$$x_1 = 4,\ x_2 = 3 \text{ and } Z_{max} = -3 \times 4 - 2 \times 3 = -18$$

To reinforce the understanding of the dual simplex method, Fig. 6.2 shows graphically the path followed by the algorithm in the solution of this problem. The algorithm starts at extreme point

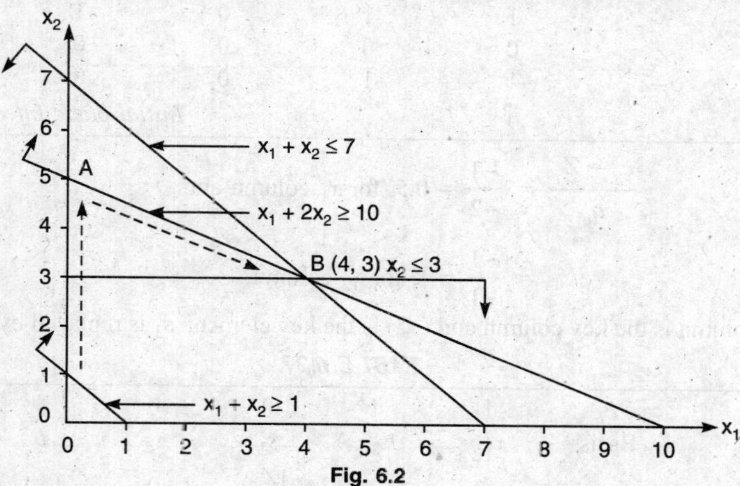

Fig. 6.2

O (which is infeasible and better than optimum since $Z = 0$), then moves to A (which is still infeasible and better than optimum since $Z = -10$), and finally becomes feasible at B. At this point, the process ends with B as the feasible optimal solution. Note that the region of feasible solution in this problem is just the point B.

EXAMPLE 6.2-3

Use dual simplex method to solve the L.P.P. :

Minimize $\quad Z = x_1 + x_2,$

subject to $\quad 2x_1 + x_2 \geq 2,$

$\quad -x_1 - x_2 \geq 1,$

$\quad x_1,\ x_2 \geq 0.$

[P.U.B.E. (T.I.T.) Nov., 2006]

Solution

Proceeding as in example 6.2-1 we express the given problem as

maximize $\quad Z' = -Z = -x_1 - x_2,$

subject to $\quad -2x_1 - x_2 \leq -2,$

$\quad x_1 + x_2 \leq -1,$

$\quad x_1,\ x_2 \geq 0.$

Adding slack variables s_1, s_2 the problem can be expressed as

maximize $\quad Z' = -x_1 - x_2 + 0s_1 + 0s_2,$

subject to $\quad -2x_1 - x_2 + s_1 = -2,$

$\quad x_1 + x_2 + s_2 = -1,$

$\quad x_1,\ x_2,\ s_1,\ s_2 \geq 0.$

The initial basic solution is $x_1 = 0,\ x_2 = 0,\ s_1 = -2,\ s_2 = -1,\ Z' = 0$, which is infeasible. This is expressed in table 6.26. As b_1 is the most negative, s_1-row is the key row and s_1 is the outgoing variable.

TABLE 6.26

	c_j	−1	−1	0	0		
c_B	Basis	x_1	x_2	s_1	s_2	b	
0	s_1	(−2)	−1	1	0	−2	←
0	s_2	1	1	0	1	−1	
	Z_j	0	0	0	0	0	
	$c_j – Z_j$	−1	−1	0	0		
		↑					

Initial basic infeasible solution

$$\frac{c_j - Z_j}{a_{ij}} = \frac{-1}{-2} = 0.5, \text{ for } x_1\text{-column and}$$

$$= \frac{-1}{-1} = 1, \text{ for } x_2\text{-column.}$$

∴ x_1-column is the key column and (−2) is the key element. s_1 is replaced by x_1 in table 6.27.

TABLE 6.27

	c_j	−1	−1	0	0		
c_B	Basis	x_1	x_2	s_1	s_2	b	
−1	x_1	1	$1/2$	$-1/2$	0	1	
0	s_2	0	$1/2$	$1/2$	1	−2	←
	Z_j	−1	$-1/2$	$1/2$	0	−1	
	$c_j – Z_j$	0	$-1/2$	$-1/2$	0		

Second basic infeasible solution

Compute $c_j – Z_j$ row. Since $c_j – Z_j$ coefficients are either negative or zero under all columns and b_2 is negative, the second basic solution is optimal but infeasible.

Since b_2 is negative, mark the second row as the key row which yields s_2 as the outgoing variable. But since s_2 –row contains no negative coefficient, no other variable enters the basis. Thus the given L.P.P. has no feasible solution.

EXAMPLE 6.2-4

Use dual simplex method to solve the following L.P. problem :

Minimize $Z = 3x_1 + 2x_2 + x_3 + 4x_4,$

subject to $2x_1 + 4x_2 + 5x_3 + x_4 \geq 10,$

$3x_1 - x_2 + 7x_3 - 2x_4 \geq 2,$

$5x_1 + 2x_2 + x_3 + 6x_4 \geq 15,$

$x_1, x_2, x_3, x_4 \geq 0.$

[*P.T.U. M.Tech. Nov. 2012; P.U. B.E. (T.I.T.) DEC., 2008*]

Solution

Proceeding as in example 6.2-1, we express the given problem as

maximize $Z' = -Z = -3x_1 - 2x_2 - x_3 - 4x_4,$

subject to $-2x_1 - 4x_2 - 5x_3 - x_4 \leq -10,$

$-3x_1 + x_2 - 7x_3 + 2x_4 \leq -2,$

$-5x_1 - 2x_2 - x_3 - 6x_4 \leq -15,$

$x_1, x_2, x_3, x_4 \geq 0.$

Adding slack variables s_1, s_2, s_3, the problem can be expressed as

maximize $\quad Z' = -3x_1 - 2x_2 - x_3 - 4x_4 + 0s_1 + 0s_2 + 0s_3,$

subject to $\quad -2x_1 - 4x_2 - 5x_3 - x_4 + s_1 = -10,$

$-3x + x_2 - 7x_3 + 2x_4 + s_2 = -2,$

$-5x_1 - 2x_2 - x_3 - 6x_4 + s_3 = -15,$

$x_1, x_2, x_3, x_4, s_1, s_2, s_3 \geq 0.$

The initial basic infeasible solution is $x_1 = x_2 = x_3 = x_4 = 0$, $s_1 = -10$, $s_2 = -2$, $s_3 = -15$, $Z' = 0$. This is expressed in table 6.28. As b_3 is the most negative, s_3-row is the key row and s_3 is the outgoing variable.

TABLE 6.28

	c_j	−3	−2	−1	−4	0	0	0		
c_B	Basis	x_1	x_2	x_3	x_4	s_1	s_2	s_3	b	
0	s_1	−2	−4	−5	−1	1	0	0	−10	
0	s_2	−3	1	−7	2	0	1	0	−2	
0	s_3	(−5)	−2	−1	−6	0	0	1	−15	←
	Z_j	0	0	0	0	0	0	0	0	
	c_j–Z_j	−3	−2	−1	−4	0	0	0		
	$\dfrac{c_j - Z_j}{a_{ij}}$	0.6	1	1	0.67	–	–	–		
		↑								

Initial basic infeasible solution

Since $\dfrac{c_j - Z_j}{a_{ij}}$ is minimum under x_1-column, x_1 is the incoming variable. Variable s_3 is replaced by x_1 in table 6.29.

TABLE 6.29

	c_j	−3	−2	−1	−4	0	0	0	
c_B	Basis	x_1	x_2	x_3	x_4	s_1	s_2	s_3	b
0	s_1	0	$-16/5$	$(-23/5)$	$7/5$	1	0	$-2/5$	−4 ←
0	s_2	0	$11/5$	$-32/5$	$28/5$	0	1	$-3/5$	7
−3	x_1	1	$2/5$	$1/5$	$6/5$	0	0	$-1/5$	3
	Z_j	−3	$-6/5$	$-3/5$	$-18/5$	0	0	$3/5$	−9
	c_j–Z_j	0	$-4/5$	$-2/5$	$-2/5$	0	0	$-3/5$	
				↑					

Second basic infeasible solution

In table 6.29, b_1 is the only negative element. Therefore, s_1-row is the key row and s_1 is the outgoing variable. $\dfrac{c_j - Z_j}{a_{ij}}$ values are :

$$\frac{-\frac{4}{5}}{-\frac{16}{5}} = \frac{1}{4}, \quad \frac{-\frac{2}{5}}{-\frac{23}{5}} = \frac{2}{23}.$$

Since $\frac{2}{23}$ is the smaller ratio, x_3-column is the key column and x_3 is the incoming variable. s_1 is replaced by x_3 in table 6.30.

TABLE 6.30

	c_j	−3	−2	−1	−4	0	0	0	
c_B	Basis	x_1	x_2	x_3	x_4	s_1	s_2	s_3	b
−1	x_3	0	$16/23$	1	$-7/23$	$-5/23$	0	$2/23$	$20/23$
0	s_2	0	$153/23$	0	$84/23$	$-32/23$	1	$-1/23$	$289/23$
−3	x_1	1	$6/23$	0	$29/23$	$1/23$	0	$-5/23$	$65/23$
	Z_j	−3	$-34/23$	−1	$-80/23$	$2/23$	0	$13/23$	$-215/23$
	c_j-Z_j	0	$-12/23$	0	$-12/23$	$-2/23$	0	$-13/23$	

Optimal b.f.s.

Table 6.30 gives the optimal feasible solution

$$x_1 = \frac{65}{23}, x_2 = 0, x_3 = \frac{20}{23}, x_4 = 0, Z_{max}' = -\frac{215}{23} \text{ or } Z_{min} = \frac{215}{23}.$$

EXERCISES 6.2

1. What is duality ? Explain dual simplex algorithm briefly. *[Pbi. U. MCA, 2001]*
2. Write the various steps involved in the dual simplex method. *[P.U.B.E. (T.I.T.) Dec., 2008; Nellore MBA, 2002]*
3. Explain how to examine the existence or otherwise of primal feasible solution with the help of dual simplex algorithm. *[Kuru. U. M.Sc. (Math.) 2001]*
4. What is the essential difference between regular simplex and dual simplex method? *[P.T.U. M.Tech. Nov., 2012; P.U.B.E. (T.I.T.) Nov., 2006]*
5. Describe the flow chart for the dual simplex method. *[Kuru. U. B.E. (Mech.) June, 2012]*
6. Use dual simplex method to

   minimize $Z = 2x_1 + x_2$,
   subject to $3x_1 + x_2 \geq 3$,
   $4x_1 + 3x_2 \geq 6$,
   $x_1 + 2x_2 \leq 3$,
   $x_1, x_2 \geq 0$.

   [P.U.B.E. (C.S. & E.) 2004]

   $\left(\textit{Ans. } x_1 = \frac{3}{5}, x_2 = \frac{6}{5}; Z_{min} = \frac{12}{5}.\right)$
7. Solve the following problem by dual simplex method :

   minimize $Z = 20x_1 + 2x_2$,
   subject to $x_1 + x_2 \geq 12$,
   $2x_1 + x_2 \geq 17$,
   $x_1 \geq 2.5$,
   $x_2 \geq 6$,
   $x_1, x_2 \geq 0$.

   (*Ans.* $x_1 = 5, x_2 = 7$; $Z_{min} = 114$.)
8. Solve by dual simplex method the problem

   minimize $Z = 10x_1 + 6x_2 + 2x_3$,
   subject to $-x_1 + x_2 + x_3 \geq 1$,
   $3x_1 + x_2 - x_3 \geq 2$,

$x_1, x_2, x_3 \geq 0.$ [P.T.U.B.Tech. (C.Sc.) 2009]

$\left(\textit{Ans. } x_1 = \frac{1}{4}, x_2 = \frac{5}{4}, x_3 = 0; Z_{\min} = 10.\right)$

9. Use dual simplex method to solve :

Minimize $Z = 5x_1 + 6x_2 + 3x_3,$
subject to $5x_1 + 5x_2 + 3x_3 \geq 50,$
$x_1 + x_2 - x_3 \geq 20,$
$7x_1 + 6x_2 - 9x_3 \geq 30,$
$5x_1 + 5x_2 + 5x_3 \geq 35,$
$2x_1 + 4x_2 - 15x_3 \geq 10,$
$12x_1 + 10x_2 \geq 90,$
$x_2 - 10x_3 \geq 20,$
$x_1, x_2, x_3 \geq 0.$

10. Solve the following problem using dual simplex method :

Maximize $Z = -6x_1 - 7x_2 - 3x_3 - 5x_4,$
subject to $2x_1 + 5x_2 + x_3 + x_4 \geq 8,$
$x_2 + 5x_3 - 6x_4 \geq 10,$
$5x_1 + 6x_2 - 3x_3 + 4x_4 \geq 12,$
$x_1, x_2, x_3, x_4 \geq 0.$

[Kuru. U.B.E. (Mech.) June, 2012]

$\left(\textit{Ans. } x_1 = 0, x_2 = \frac{30}{11}, x_3 = \frac{16}{11}, x_4 = 0; Z_{\max} = -\frac{258}{11}.\right)$

11. Use dual simplex method to solve

minimize $Z = x_1 + 2x_2 + 3x_3,$
subject to $2x_1 - x_2 + x_3 \geq 4,$
$x_1 + x_2 + 2x_3 \leq 8,$
$x_2 - x_3 \geq 2,$
$x_1, x_2, x_3 \geq 0.$

[Univ. of Madras B.Sc. (Math.) Nov., 2012; P.T.U. M.Tech. Dec., 2011; B.E. (Mech.) May, 2011]

12. Use dual simplex method to solve

minimize $Z = x_1 + 4x_2 + 3x_4,$
subject to $x_1 + 2x_2 - x_3 + x_4 \geq 3,$
$-2x_1 - x_2 + 4x_3 + x_4 \geq 2,$
$x_1, ..., x_4 \geq 0.$ [B.P.U.T., 2012]

(Ans. $x_1 = 7, x_2 = 0, x_3 = 4, x_4 = 0 ; Z_{\min} = 7.$)

13. Use dual simplex method to solve

maximize $Z = -2x_1 - x_3,$
subject to $x_1 + x_2 - x_3 \geq 5,$
$x_1 - 2x_2 + 4x_3 \geq 8,$
$x_1, x_2, x_3 \geq 0.$ [Kuru. U., 2002]

(Ans. $x_1 = 0, x_2 = 14, x_3 = 9; Z_{\min} = -9.$)

14. Use dual simplex method to solve

minimize $Z = 3x_1 + x_2,$
subject to $x_1 + x_2 \geq 1,$
$2x_1 + 3x_2 \geq 2,$
$x_1, x_2 \geq 0.$ [P.U. B.E. (Mech.) 2012]

(Ans. $x_1 = 0, x_2 = 1; Z_{\min} = 1.$)

15. Use dual simplex method to solve

minimize $Z = 6x_1 + 7x_2 + 3x_3 + 5x_4,$
subject to $5x_1 + 6x_2 - 3x_3 + 4x_4 \geq 12,$
$x_2 + 5x_3 - 6x_4 \geq 10,$
$2x_1 + 5x_2 + x_3 + x_4 \geq 8,$
$x_1, x_2, x_3, x_4 \geq 0.$ [Meerut U. B.Sc. (Hons.) 1991, 90]

16. Solve the following L.P.P. by dual simplex method:

Minimize $Z = 3x_1 + 2x_2$,
subject to
$3x_1 + x_2 \geq 3$,
$4x_1 + 3x_2 \geq 6$,
$x_1 + x_2 \leq 3$,
$x_1, x_2 \geq 0$. [*V.T.U. Karnataka B.E. Jan., 2010*]

*6.3 THE REVISED SIMPLEX METHOD

The simplex method discussed in chapter 2 performs calculations on the entire table during each iteration. If a linear programming problem involving a large number of variables and constraints is to be solved by this method, it will require a large storage space and time on a computer. Some computational techniques have been developed which require much less computer storage and time than that required by the simplex method. The three important and efficient computational techniques are: *the revised simplex method or simplex method with multipliers, the bounded variables method and the decomposition method.* These techniques will now be discussed in details.

While solving a problem with simplex method, successive iterations are obtained by using row operations. This requires storing the entire table in the memory of the computer, which may not be feasible for very large problems. Luckily, it is really not necessary to calculate the entire table during each interation. The only information needed in moving from one table to the next is

(1) The $c_j–Z_j$ row to determine the non-basic variable that enters the basis.

(2) The pivot column.

(3) The current basic variables and their values (right-hand side constants) to determine the minimum positive ratio and thereby to determine the basic variable that leaves the basis.

In the revised simplex method, the above information is directly obtained from the *original equations* of the problem by making use of the current basis matrix $\boldsymbol{B}$ and its inverse $\boldsymbol{B}^{-1}$. This method will now be illustrated with the help of some examples.

EXAMPLE 6.3-1

Use the revised simplex method to solve the following problem :

Maximize $Z = 6x_1 + 3x_2 + 4x_3 - 2x_4 + x_5$,
subject to $2x_1 + 3x_2 + 3x_3 + x_4 = 10$,
$x_1 + 2x_2 + x_3 + x_5 = 8$,
$x_1, ..., x_5 \geq 0$.

Solution

Since variable x_4 appears only in the first constraint equation with a unit coefficient, it is a basic variable in that equation. Similarly, x_5 is a basic variable. The basic feasible solution is $x_1 = x_2 = x_3 = 0$, $x_4 = 10$ and $x_5 = 8$. For easy reference the tables of the regular simplex method are shown below.

TABLE 6.31

	c_j	6	3	4	–2	1		
c_B	Basis	x_1	x_2	x_3	x_4	x_5	b	θ
–2	x_4	2	3	(3)	1	0	10	10/3 ←
1	x_5	1	2	1	0	1	8	8
	$Z_j=\Sigma c_B a_{ij}$	–3	–4	–5	-2	1	–12	
	$c_j–Z_j$	9	7	9	0	0		
				↑				

Initial basic feasible solution

*The reader should refer to appendix A-2 while going through sections 6.3 and 6.4.

TABLE 6.32

c_B	c_j / Basis	6 / x_1	3 / x_2	4 / x_3	−2 / x_4	1 / x_5	b	θ
4	x_3	$(2/3)$	1	1	$1/3$	0	$10/3$	5 ←
1	x_5	$1/3$	1	0	$-1/3$	1	$14/3$	14
	$Z_j = \Sigma c_B a_{ij}$	3	5	4	1	1	18	
	$c_j - Z_j$	3 ↑	−2	0	−3	0		

Second feasible solution

TABLE 6.33

c_B	c_j / Basis	6 / x_1	3 / x_2	4 / x_3	−2 / x_4	1 / x_5	b
6	x_1	1	$3/2$	$3/2$	$1/2$	0	5
1	x_5	0	$1/2$	$-1/2$	$-1/2$	1	3
	$Z_j = \Sigma c_B a_{ij}$	6	$19/2$	$17/2$	$5/2$	1	33
	$c_j - Z_j$	0	$-13/2$	$-9/2$	$-9/2$	0	

Optimal solution

∴ Optimal solution is $x_1 = 5, x_2 = x_3 = x_4 = 0, x_5 = 3,$
and $Z_{max} = 6 \times 5 + 1 \times 3 = 33.$

The revised simplex method works on the principle that any table corresponding to a basic feasible solution can be obtained directly from the *original equations* by matrix-vector operations. Let the column vectors $\mathbf{P}_1$, $\mathbf{P}_2$, $\mathbf{P}_3$ $\mathbf{P}_4$ and $\mathbf{P}_5$ denote the original columns of x_1, x_2, x_3, x_4 and x_5 and let the column vector $\mathbf{b}$ represent the right-hand side constants. Thus

$$\mathbf{P}_1 = \begin{bmatrix} 2 \\ 1 \end{bmatrix}, \mathbf{P}_2 = \begin{bmatrix} 3 \\ 2 \end{bmatrix}, \mathbf{P}_3 = \begin{bmatrix} 3 \\ 1 \end{bmatrix}, \mathbf{P}_4 = \begin{bmatrix} 1 \\ 0 \end{bmatrix}, \mathbf{P}_5 = \begin{bmatrix} 0 \\ 1 \end{bmatrix} \text{ and } \mathbf{b} = \begin{bmatrix} 10 \\ 8 \end{bmatrix}.$$

Table 6.32 in which x_3 and x_5 are the basic variables may be generated directly by matrix theory as follows:

Define a *basis matrix* **B** whose elements are the original columns of the basic variables x_3 and x_5. Thus

$$\mathbf{B} = [\mathbf{P}_3, \mathbf{P}_5] = \begin{bmatrix} 3 & 0 \\ 1 & 1 \end{bmatrix}.$$

The inverse of the basis matrix, denoted by $\mathbf{B}^{-1}$ is obtained as follows :
Since $|\mathbf{B}| = 3 \times 1 - 1 \times 0 = 3 - 0 = 3$ $(\neq 0)$, **B** is nonsingular and hence B^{-1} exists.

$$(\mathbf{BI}) = \begin{bmatrix} 3 & 0 & : & 1 & 0 \\ & & : & & \\ 1 & 1 & : & 0 & 1 \end{bmatrix}.$$

Divide the first row by 3 : $\begin{bmatrix} 1 & 0 & : & \frac{1}{3} & 0 \\ & & : & & \\ 1 & 1 & : & 0 & 1 \end{bmatrix}.$

Subtract first row from the second : $\begin{bmatrix} 1 & 0 & : & \frac{1}{3} & 0 \\ & & : & & \\ 0 & 1 & : & -\frac{1}{3} & 1 \end{bmatrix}$.

Then $\mathbf{B}^{-1} = \begin{bmatrix} \frac{1}{3} & 0 \\ -\frac{1}{3} & 1 \end{bmatrix}$.

Then according to matrix theory any column in table 6.32 can be obtained by premultiplying the corresponding original column in table 6.31 by the inverse of the basis matrix, $\mathbf{B}^{-1}$. For example.

$$\overline{\mathbf{P}}_1 = \mathbf{B}^{-1}\mathbf{P}_1 = \begin{bmatrix} \frac{1}{3} & 0 \\ -\frac{1}{3} & 1 \end{bmatrix} \begin{bmatrix} 2 \\ 1 \end{bmatrix} = \begin{bmatrix} 2 \times \frac{1}{3} + 1 \times 0 \\ 2\left(-\frac{1}{3}\right) + 1 \times 1 \end{bmatrix} = \begin{bmatrix} \frac{2}{3} \\ \frac{1}{3} \end{bmatrix},$$

$$\overline{\mathbf{P}}_2 = \mathbf{B}^{-1}\mathbf{P}_2 = \begin{bmatrix} \frac{1}{3} & 0 \\ -\frac{1}{3} & 1 \end{bmatrix} \begin{bmatrix} 3 \\ 2 \end{bmatrix} = \begin{bmatrix} 1 \\ 1 \end{bmatrix}, \text{ etc.}$$

and $$\overline{\mathbf{b}} = \mathbf{B}^{-1}\mathbf{b} = \begin{pmatrix} \frac{1}{3} & 0 \\ -\frac{1}{3} & 1 \end{pmatrix} \begin{pmatrix} 10 \\ 8 \end{pmatrix} = \begin{pmatrix} \frac{10}{3} \\ \frac{14}{3} \end{pmatrix},$$

where $\overline{\mathbf{P}}_1, \overline{\mathbf{P}}_2$, etc. represent the column vectors and $\overline{\mathbf{b}}$ represents the right-hand side constants of table 6.32.

We know that there are two key steps in the simplex method, namely, the determination of the nonbasic variable that enters the basis and the basic variable that leaves the basis. These two steps are carried out in the revised simplex method as shown below.

In the regular simplex method, the $\overline{c}_j - \overline{Z}_j$) row for table 6.32 is calculated as follows:

$$(\overline{c}_j - \overline{Z}_j) = c_j - \Sigma c_B a_{ij} = c_j - c_B \overline{\mathbf{P}}_j.$$

Also $$\overline{\mathbf{P}}_j = \mathbf{B}^{-1}\mathbf{P}_j.$$

$\therefore$ $$(\overline{c}_j - \overline{Z}_j) = c_j - c_B\mathbf{B}^{-1}\mathbf{P}_j.$$

Let the vector $\boldsymbol{\pi}$ denote $c_B\mathbf{B}^{-1}$. The elements of vector $\boldsymbol{\pi}$ are called *the simplex multipliers.*

$\therefore$ $$(\overline{c}_j - \overline{Z}_j) = c_j - \boldsymbol{\pi}\mathbf{P}_j, \text{ for all } j.$$

For example in table 6.32,

$$\boldsymbol{\pi} = (\pi_1, \pi_2) = c_B\mathbf{B}^{-1} = (4, 1)\begin{pmatrix} 1/3 & 0 \\ -1/3 & 1 \end{pmatrix} = (1, 1).$$

$\therefore$ $$(\overline{c}_j - \overline{Z}_1) = c_1 - \boldsymbol{\pi}\mathrm{P}_1 = 6 - (1, 1)\begin{pmatrix} 2 \\ 1 \end{pmatrix} = 6 - (2 + 1) = 3,$$

$$(\bar{c}_2 - \bar{Z}_2) = c_2 - \boldsymbol{\pi}P_2 = 3 - (1, 1)\begin{pmatrix}3\\2\end{pmatrix} = 3 - (3 + 2) = -2,$$

$$(\bar{c}_4 - \bar{Z}_4) = c_4 - \boldsymbol{\pi}P_4 = -2 - (1, 1)\begin{pmatrix}1\\0\end{pmatrix} = -2 - 1 = -3.$$

The incoming non-basic variable is the one corresponding to the maximum positive value of $(\bar{c}_j - \bar{Z}_j)$. As $\bar{c}_1 - \bar{Z}_1$ has the maximum positive value (3), x_1 is the non-basic variable that enters the basis of table 6.32.

Next we are to find the basic variable that is to leave the basis by the minimum positive ratio rule. For this we have to determine the elements in x_1-column and the right-hand side constants for table 6.32. As already shown,

$$\bar{\mathbf{P}}_1 = \mathbf{B}^{-1}\mathbf{P}_1 = \begin{pmatrix}1/3 & 0\\-1/3 & 1\end{pmatrix}\begin{pmatrix}2\\1\end{pmatrix} = \begin{pmatrix}2/3\\1/3\end{pmatrix},$$

and $$\bar{\mathbf{b}} = \mathbf{B}^{-1}\mathbf{b} = \begin{pmatrix}1/3 & 0\\-1/3 & 1\end{pmatrix}\begin{pmatrix}10\\8\end{pmatrix} = \begin{pmatrix}10/3\\14/3\end{pmatrix}.$$

The first row gives minimum positive ratio 5 and hence the basic variable x_3 will be replaced by x_1. Hence the new set of basic variables are x_1 and x_5.

The next new basis matrix $\mathbf{B} = (\mathbf{P}_1, \mathbf{P}_5) = \begin{pmatrix}2 & 0\\1 & 1\end{pmatrix}.$

$\mathbf{B}^{-1}$ can be computed as follows :

$\because$ $|\mathbf{B}| = 2 - 0 = 2\ (\neq 0)$, $\mathbf{B}$ is non-singular and hence $\mathbf{B}^{-1}$ exists.

$$(\mathbf{BI}) = \begin{pmatrix}2 & 0 & : & 1 & 0\\ & & : & & \\1 & 1 & : & 0 & 1\end{pmatrix}$$

Divide the first row by 2 : $\begin{pmatrix}1 & 0 & : & 1/2 & 0\\ & & : & & \\1 & 1 & : & 0 & 1\end{pmatrix}.$

Subtract first row from the second : $\begin{pmatrix}1 & 0 & : & 1/2 & 0\\ & & : & & \\0 & 1 & : & -1/2 & 1\end{pmatrix}.$

$$\therefore \qquad \mathbf{B}^{-1} = \begin{pmatrix}1/2 & 0\\-1/2 & 1\end{pmatrix}.$$

The new right-hand side constants are

$$\bar{\mathbf{b}} = \mathbf{B}^{-1}\mathbf{b} = \begin{pmatrix}1/2 & 0\\-1/2 & 1\end{pmatrix}\begin{pmatrix}10\\8\end{pmatrix} = \begin{pmatrix}5\\3\end{pmatrix}.$$

Thus the new basic feasible solution is

$$x_1 = 5,\ x_2 = x_3 = x_4 = 0,\ x_5 = 3 \text{ and } Z_{\max} = 33.$$

To check the optimality of this solution we need $(\bar{c}_j - \bar{Z}_j)$ coefficients for x_2, x_3 and x_4 columns.

$$(\bar{c}_j - \bar{Z}_j) = c_j - \boldsymbol{\pi}P_j,$$

where, $\boldsymbol{\pi} = (\pi_1, \pi_2) = c_B\mathbf{B}^{-1} = (6, 1)\begin{pmatrix}\frac{1}{2} & 0\\-\frac{1}{2} & 1\end{pmatrix} = \left(\frac{5}{2}, 1\right).$

$$\therefore \quad (\overline{c}_2 - \overline{Z}_2) = c_2 - \boldsymbol{\pi}\mathbf{P}_2 = 3 - \left(\frac{5}{2}, 1\right)\begin{bmatrix}3\\2\end{bmatrix}$$

$$= 3 - \frac{19}{2} = -\frac{13}{2},$$

$$(\overline{c}_3 - \overline{Z}_3) = c_3 - \boldsymbol{\pi}\mathbf{P}_3 = 4 - \left(\frac{5}{2}, 1\right)\begin{bmatrix}3\\1\end{bmatrix} = 4 - \frac{17}{2} = -\frac{9}{2},$$

$$(\overline{c}_4 - \overline{Z}_4) = c_4 - \boldsymbol{\pi}\mathbf{P}_4 = -2 - \left(\frac{5}{2}, 1\right)\begin{bmatrix}1\\0\end{bmatrix} = -2 - \frac{5}{2} = -\frac{9}{2}.$$

As all $(\overline{c}_j - \overline{Z}_j)$ coefficients are negative, the current solution is optimal.

From the above discussion it may be concluded that any information contained in a simplex table can be obtained directly from the original equations if the inverse of the basis matrix of that table is known. This, in turn, can be obtained from the original equations if the current basic variables in that table are known. Thus the revised simplex method can generate any information that is available in the regular simplex method. However, it generates only the relevant information that is required to perform the simplex steps.

Actually, while solving a problem by revised simplex method, the inverse of the basis matrix is not obtained by inverting the matrix of basic columns because inverting a matrix is costly and needs more time on a digital computer. *The inverse of the basis matrix, at each step, is obtained by a simple pivot operation on the previous inverse.* To illustrate this we refer back to the tables 6.31 to 6.33 already computed.

In the initial basic feasible solution of table 6.31, x_4 and x_5 are the basic variables. The initial basis matrix is

$$[\mathbf{P}_4, \mathbf{P}_5] = \begin{bmatrix}1 & 0\\0 & 1\end{bmatrix} = \mathbf{I} \text{ (identity matrix).}$$

The new column coefficients corresponding to x_4 and x_5 in any subsequent table are obtained by premultiplying $\mathbf{P}_4$ and $\mathbf{P}_5$ by the inverse of current basis matrix. Thus

$$\overline{\mathbf{P}}_4 = \mathbf{B}^{-1}\,\mathbf{P}_4 \text{ and } \overline{\mathbf{P}}_5 = \mathbf{B}^{-1}\,\mathbf{P}_5.$$

$$\therefore \quad [\,\overline{\mathbf{P}}_4, \overline{\mathbf{P}}_5\,] = \mathbf{B}^{-1}\,[\mathbf{P}_4, \mathbf{P}_5] = \mathbf{B}^{-1}\,\mathbf{I} = \mathbf{B}^{-1}.$$

Thus the 'x_4' and 'x_5'-columns in any table give the inverse of the basis for that table. For instance, in table 6.32, the 'x_4' and 'x_5'-columns are given by

$$\begin{bmatrix}\frac{1}{3} & 0\\ -\frac{1}{3} & 1\end{bmatrix},$$

which was the computed inverse of the basis for the table. The same is true for table 6.33 as well. Thus the new basis inverse can be easily obtained by considering the columns of initial basic variables and updating them by pivot operation. Similarly, the right-hand side constants of any table can be obtained by updating their values by the pivot operation at each iteration. Thus the revised simplex method makes use of a reduced simplex table which contains the columns of the initial basic variables, the right-hand side constants along with current basic variables. This reduced simplex table corresponding to table 6.32 is shown below.

TABLE 6.34

Basis	$\mathbf{B}^{-1}$		Constants $\mathbf{b}$
x_3	$1/3$	0	$10/3$
x_5	$-1/3$	1	$14/3$

From $\mathbf{B}^{-1}$, the simplex multipliers and the $(\bar{c}_j - \bar{Z}_j)$ coefficients are calculated. This results in selecting x_1 as the entering variable. The 'x_1'-column (pivot column) for table 6.32 is then computed as follows :

$$\bar{\mathbf{P}}_1 = \mathbf{B}^{-1}\mathbf{P}_1 = \begin{bmatrix} \frac{1}{3} & 0 \\ -\frac{1}{3} & 1 \end{bmatrix}\begin{bmatrix} 2 \\ 1 \end{bmatrix} = \begin{bmatrix} \frac{2}{3} \\ \frac{1}{3} \end{bmatrix}.$$

Knowing $\bar{\mathbf{P}}_1$ and $\bar{\mathbf{b}}_1$, the minimum positive ratio test can be performed, which identifies x_3 as the outgoing variable. This means that the pivot column $\begin{pmatrix} \frac{2}{3} \\ \frac{1}{3} \end{pmatrix}$ should be reduced to $\begin{pmatrix} 1 \\ 0 \end{pmatrix}$. This can be done by

(1) Multiplying the first row by $\frac{3}{2}$.

(2) Multiplying this modified row by $\frac{1}{3}$ and subtracting it from the second row.

The pivot operation, when carried on the reduced table 6.34 yields the following table :

TABLE 6.35

Basis	$\mathbf{B}^{-1}$		$\mathbf{b}$
x_1	$1/2$	0	5
x_5	$-1/2$	1	3

The new basic feasible solution is $x_1 = 5$, $x_5 = 3$, $x_2 = x_3 = x_4 = 0$. The new inverse of the basis is $\begin{bmatrix} 1/2 & 0 \\ -1/2 & 1 \end{bmatrix}$. Using the new basis inverse, the simplex multipliers and $(\bar{c}_j - \bar{Z}_j)$ coefficients can be calculated to check the optimality of the solution provided by table 6.35.

EXAMPLE 6.3-2

Use revised simplex method to solve the L.P.P. :

Maximize $Z = 2x_1 + x_2$,

subject to $3x_1 + 4x_2 \le 6$,

$6x_1 + x_2 \le 3$,

$x_1, x_2 \ge 0$.

[*Kerala M.Sc. (Math.) 1984, Lucknow M.B.A., 1980*]

Solution

The problem can be expressed in standard form as

$$\begin{aligned} \text{maximize} \quad & Z = 2x_1 + x_2 + 0x_3 + 0x_4, \\ \text{subject to} \quad & 3x_1 + 4x_2 + x_3 + 0x_4 = 6, \\ & 6x_1 + x_2 + 0x_3 + x_4 = 3, \\ & x_1, x_2, x_3, x_4 \geq 0. \end{aligned}$$

Let $\mathbf{P}_1$, $\mathbf{P}_2$, $\mathbf{P}_3$, $\mathbf{P}_4$ and $\mathbf{b}$ denote the column vectors corresponding to x_1, x_2, x_3, x_4 and the right-hand side constants respectively. Then

$$\mathbf{P}_1 = \begin{bmatrix} 3 \\ 6 \end{bmatrix}, \mathbf{P}_2 = \begin{bmatrix} 4 \\ 1 \end{bmatrix}, \mathbf{P}_3 = \begin{bmatrix} 1 \\ 0 \end{bmatrix}, \mathbf{P}_4 = \begin{bmatrix} 0 \\ 1 \end{bmatrix} \text{ and } \mathbf{b} = \begin{bmatrix} 6 \\ 3 \end{bmatrix}.$$

Since (x_3, x_4) form the initial basis,

$$\mathbf{B}_{(2\times 2)} = [\mathbf{P}_3, \mathbf{P}_4] = \begin{bmatrix} 1 & 0 \\ 0 & 1 \end{bmatrix} = \mathbf{I}.$$

$\therefore \quad \mathbf{B}^{-1} = \mathbf{I}$ and $\overline{\mathbf{b}} = \mathbf{B}^{-1}\mathbf{b} = \mathbf{b}$.

The initial table of the revised simplex method is given below. The last two columns of this table are added later.

TABLE 6.36

Basis	$\mathbf{B}^{-1}$		*Constants*	*Variable to enter*	*Pivot column*
x_3	1	0	6	x_1	3
x_4	0	1	3		(6)

Iteration 1

The simplex multipliers are

$$\begin{aligned} \boldsymbol{\pi} &= (\pi_1, \pi_2) = c_B\,\mathbf{B}^{-1} \\ &= (0, 0)\begin{bmatrix} 1 & 0 \\ 0 & 1 \end{bmatrix} = (0, 0). \end{aligned}$$

$$\therefore \quad \overline{c}_1 - \overline{Z}_1 = c_1 - \boldsymbol{\pi}\mathbf{P}_1 = 2 - (0, 0)\begin{bmatrix} 3 \\ 6 \end{bmatrix} = 2,$$

$$\overline{c}_2 - \overline{Z}_2 = c_2 - \boldsymbol{\pi}\mathbf{P}_2 = 1 - (0, 0)\begin{bmatrix} 4 \\ 1 \end{bmatrix} = 1.$$

Since $\overline{c}_1 - \overline{Z}_1$ has more positive value, x_1 is variable that enters the basis. The pivot (key) column is

$$\overline{\mathbf{P}}_1 = \mathbf{B}^{-1}\mathbf{P}_1 = \begin{bmatrix} 1 & 0 \\ 0 & 1 \end{bmatrix}\begin{bmatrix} 3 \\ 6 \end{bmatrix} = \begin{bmatrix} 3 \\ 6 \end{bmatrix}.$$

The entering variable x_1 and the elements in the pivot column are now entered in table 6.36. Applying the minimum positive ratio rule, the ratios are (2, 1/2). Hence x_4 is the outgoing variable and (6) is the key element.

Now the pivot column $\begin{bmatrix} 3 \\ (6) \end{bmatrix}$ must be reduced to $\begin{bmatrix} 0 \\ 1 \end{bmatrix}$. This is obtained by

(*i*) multiplying row 2 by $\frac{1}{2}$ and subtracting from row 1, and

(*ii*) dividing row 2 by 6.

The new $\mathbf{B}^{-1}$ and right-hand constants are given in table 6.37.

TABLE 6.37

Basis	B^{-1}		*Constants*	*Variable to enter*	*Pivot column*
x_3	1	$-1/2$	$9/2$	x_2	$(7/2)$
x_1	0	$1/6$	$1/2$		$1/6$

Iteration 2

The simplex multipliers corresponding to table 6.37 are

$$\boldsymbol{\pi} = (\pi_1, \pi_2) = c_B\,\mathbf{B}^{-1} = (0, 2)\begin{bmatrix} 1 & -\frac{1}{2} \\ 0 & \frac{1}{6} \end{bmatrix} = \left(0, \frac{1}{3}\right).$$

$$\therefore \qquad \overline{c}_2 - \overline{Z}_2 = c_2 - \boldsymbol{\pi}\mathbf{P}_2 = 1 - \left(0, \frac{1}{3}\right)\begin{bmatrix} 4 \\ 1 \end{bmatrix} = 1 - \left(0 - \frac{1}{3}\right) = \frac{2}{3},$$

$$\overline{c}_4 - \overline{Z}_4 = c_4 - \boldsymbol{\pi}\mathbf{P}_4 = 0 - \left(0, \frac{1}{3}\right)\begin{bmatrix} 0 \\ 1 \end{bmatrix} = 0 - \left(0 + \frac{1}{3}\right) = -\frac{1}{3}.$$

Since $\overline{c}_2 - \overline{Z}_2$ is positive, x_2 is the variable that enters the basis. The pivot column is

$$\overline{\mathbf{P}}_2 = \mathbf{B}^{-1}\mathbf{P}_2 = \begin{bmatrix} 1 & -\frac{1}{2} \\ 0 & \frac{1}{6} \end{bmatrix}\begin{bmatrix} 4 \\ 1 \end{bmatrix} = \begin{bmatrix} 4 - \frac{1}{2} \\ 0 + \frac{1}{6} \end{bmatrix} = \begin{bmatrix} \frac{7}{2} \\ \frac{1}{6} \end{bmatrix}.$$

The entering variable x_2 and the elements in the pivot column are now entered in table 6.37. Applying the minimum positive ratio rule, the ratios are (9/7 3). Hence x_3 is outgoing variable and $\left(\frac{7}{2}\right)$ is the key element.

Now the pivot column $\begin{bmatrix} \left(\frac{7}{2}\right) \\ \frac{1}{6} \end{bmatrix}$ must be reduced to $\begin{bmatrix} 1 \\ 0 \end{bmatrix}$. This is done by

(*i*) multiplying row 1 by $\frac{1}{21}$ and subtracting from row 2, and

(*ii*) multiplying row 1 by $\frac{2}{7}$.

The new $\mathbf{B}^{-1}$ and right-hand side constants are represented in table 6.38.

TABLE 6.38

Basis	B^{-1}		*Constants*
x_2	$2/7$	$-1/7$	$9/7$
x_1	$-1/21$	$4/21$	$2/7$

The simplex multipliers corresponding to table 6.38 are

$$\boldsymbol{\pi} = (\pi_1, \pi_2) = c_B\,\mathbf{B}^{-1} = (1, 2)\begin{bmatrix} \frac{2}{7} & -\frac{1}{7} \\ -\frac{1}{21} & \frac{4}{21} \end{bmatrix}$$

$$= \left(\frac{2}{7} - \frac{2}{21}, -\frac{1}{7} + \frac{8}{21}\right) = \left(\frac{4}{21}, \frac{5}{21}\right).$$

$$\therefore \qquad \overline{c}_3 - \overline{Z}_3 = c_3 - \boldsymbol{\pi}\mathbf{P}_3 = 0 - \left(\frac{4}{21}, \frac{5}{21}\right)\begin{bmatrix}1\\0\end{bmatrix} = -\frac{4}{21},$$

$$\overline{c}_4 - \overline{Z}_4 = c_4 - \boldsymbol{\pi}\mathbf{P}_4 = 0 - \left(\frac{4}{21}, \frac{5}{21}\right)\begin{bmatrix}0\\1\end{bmatrix} = \frac{5}{21}.$$

Since $\overline{c}_3 - \overline{Z}_3$ and $\overline{c}_4 - \overline{Z}_4$ are negative, table 6.38 gives optimal solution, which is

$$x_1 = \frac{2}{7},\ x_2 = \frac{9}{7};\ Z_{\max} = 2 \times \frac{2}{7} + 1 \times \frac{9}{7} = \frac{13}{7}.$$

EXAMPLE 6.3-3

Solve by revised simplex method the problem:

$$\begin{aligned} \textit{Maximize} \qquad & Z = x_1 + 2x_2 + 3x_3 - x_4, \\ \textit{subject to} \qquad & x_1 + 2x_2 + 3x_3 = 15, \\ & 2x_1 + x_2 + 5x_3 = 20, \\ & x_1 + 2x_2 + x_3 + x_4 = 10, \\ & x_1, x_2, x_3, x_4 \geq 0. \end{aligned}$$

[*Meerut, 1971, 72*]

Solution

Variable x_4 occurs only in the third constraint with unit coefficient. Therefore, x_4 is a basic variable. Introducing artificial variable x_5 and x_6 in the first and second constraints leads to the following standard form of the problem:

$$\begin{aligned} \text{Maximize} \qquad & Z = x_1 + 2x_2 + 3x_3 - x_4 - \mathrm{M}x_5 - \mathrm{M}x_6, \\ \text{subject to} \qquad & x_1 + 2x_2 + 3x_3 + 0x_4 + x_5 + 0x_6 = 15, \\ & 2x_1 + x_2 + 5x_3 + 0x_4 + 0x_5 + x_6 = 20, \\ & x_1 + 2x_2 + x_3 + x_4 + 0x_5 + 0x_6 = 10, \\ & x_1, x_2, \ldots, x_6 \geq 0. \end{aligned}$$

Let $\mathbf{P}_1, \ldots, \mathbf{P}_6$ and $\mathbf{b}$ denote the column vectors corresponding to $x_1, \ldots, x_6$ and the right-hand side constants respectively. Then

$$\mathbf{P}_1 = \begin{bmatrix}1\\2\\1\end{bmatrix}, \mathbf{P}_2 = \begin{bmatrix}2\\1\\2\end{bmatrix}, \mathbf{P}_3 = \begin{bmatrix}3\\5\\1\end{bmatrix}, \mathbf{P}_4 = \begin{bmatrix}0\\0\\1\end{bmatrix}, \mathbf{P}_5 = \begin{bmatrix}1\\0\\0\end{bmatrix}, \mathbf{P}_6 = \begin{bmatrix}0\\1\\0\end{bmatrix} \text{ and } \mathbf{b} = \begin{bmatrix}15\\20\\10\end{bmatrix}.$$

Now (x_4, x_5, x_6) form the initial basis.

$$\therefore \qquad \mathbf{B}_{(3 \times 3)} = [\mathbf{P}_4, \mathbf{P}_5, \mathbf{P}_6] = \begin{bmatrix}0&1&0\\0&0&1\\1&0&0\end{bmatrix} = \mathbf{I}.$$

$$\therefore \quad \mathbf{B}^{-1} = \mathbf{I} \text{ and } \overline{\mathbf{b}} = \mathbf{B}^{-1}\mathbf{b} = \mathbf{b}.$$

The initial table of the revised simplex method is given below. The last two columns of this table are added later.

TABLE 6.39

Basis	$\mathbf{B}^{-1}$			*Constants*	*Variable to enter*	*Pivot column*
x_4	0	1	0	15		(5)
x_5	0	0	1	20	x_3	1
x_6	1	0	0	10		3

Iteration 1

The simplex multipliers are

$$\boldsymbol{\pi} = (\pi_1, \pi_2, \pi_3) = c_B\,\mathbf{B}^{-1}$$

$$= (-1, -\mathrm{M}, -\mathrm{M})\begin{bmatrix}0 & 1 & 0\\0 & 0 & 1\\1 & 0 & 0\end{bmatrix} = (-\mathrm{M}, -1, -\mathrm{M}).$$

$$\therefore \quad \overline{c}_1 - \overline{Z}_1 = c_1 - \boldsymbol{\pi}\mathbf{P}_1 = 1 - (-\mathrm{M}, -1, -\mathrm{M})\begin{bmatrix}1\\2\\1\end{bmatrix}$$

$$= 1 - (-\mathrm{M} - 2 - \mathrm{M}) = 3 + 2\mathrm{M},$$

$$\overline{c}_2 - \overline{Z}_2 = c_2 - \boldsymbol{\pi}\mathbf{P}_2 = 2 - (-\mathrm{M}, -1, -\mathrm{M})\begin{bmatrix}2\\1\\2\end{bmatrix}$$

$$= 2 - (-2\mathrm{M} - 1 - 2\mathrm{M}) = 3 + 4\mathrm{M},$$

$$\overline{c}_3 - \overline{Z}_3 = c_3 - \boldsymbol{\pi}\mathbf{P}_3 = 3 - (-\mathrm{M}, -1, -\mathrm{M})\begin{bmatrix}3\\5\\1\end{bmatrix}$$

$$= 3 - (-3\mathrm{M} - 5 - \mathrm{M}) = 8 + 4\mathrm{M}.$$

Since $\overline{c}_3 - \overline{Z}_3$ is most positive, x_3 is the variable that enters the basis. The pivot column is

$$\overline{\mathbf{P}}_3 = \mathbf{B}^{-1}\mathbf{P}_3 = \begin{bmatrix}0 & 1 & 0\\0 & 0 & 1\\1 & 0 & 0\end{bmatrix}\begin{bmatrix}3\\5\\1\end{bmatrix} = \begin{bmatrix}5\\1\\3\end{bmatrix}.$$

The entering variable x_3 and the elements in the pivot column are now entered in table 6.39. Applying the minimum positive ratio rule, the ratios are $(3, 20, \frac{10}{3})$. Hence x_4 is the outgoing variable. This is shown by putting the corresponding pivot element in brackets *i.e.*, (5). Now the pivot column $\begin{bmatrix}(5)\\1\\3\end{bmatrix}$ must be reduced to $\begin{bmatrix}1\\0\\0\end{bmatrix}$. This is obtained by

(*i*) dividing row 1 by 5,
(*ii*) subtracting the reduced row 1 from row 2, and
(*iii*) multiplying the reduced row 1 by 3 and subtracting from row 3. The new $\mathbf{B}^{-1}$ and constants are given in table 6.40.

TABLE 6.40

Basis	$\mathbf{B}^{-1}$			*Constants*	*Variable to enter*	*Pivot column*
x_3	0	$1/5$	0	3		$1/5$
x_5	0	$-1/5$	1	17	x_2	$9/5$
x_6	1	$-3/5$	0	1		$\left(\frac{7}{5}\right)$

Iteration 2

The simplex multipliers corresponding to table 6.40 are

$$\boldsymbol{\pi} = (\pi_1, \pi_2, \pi_3) = c_B\,\mathbf{B}^{-1} = (3, -M, -M)\begin{bmatrix} 0 & 1/5 & 0 \\ 0 & -1/5 & 1 \\ 1 & -3/5 & 0 \end{bmatrix} = \left[-M, \frac{3}{5} + \frac{4}{5}M, -M\right].$$

$$\therefore \quad \overline{c}_1 - \overline{Z}_1 = c_1 - \boldsymbol{\pi}\mathbf{P}_1 = 1 - \left(-M, \frac{3}{5} + \frac{4}{5}M, -M\right)\begin{bmatrix} 1 \\ 2 \\ 1 \end{bmatrix}$$

$$= 1 - \left[-M + \frac{6}{5} + \frac{8}{5}M - M\right] = -\frac{1}{5} + \frac{2}{5}M,$$

$$\overline{c}_2 - \overline{Z}_2 = c_2 - \boldsymbol{\pi}\mathbf{P}_2 = 2 - \left(-M, \frac{3}{5} + \frac{4}{5}M, -M\right)\begin{bmatrix} 2 \\ 1 \\ 2 \end{bmatrix}$$

$$= 2 - \left[-2M + \frac{3}{5} + \frac{4}{5}M - 2M\right] = \frac{7}{5} + \frac{16}{5}M,$$

$$\overline{c}_4 - \overline{Z}_4 = c_4 - \boldsymbol{\pi}\mathbf{P}_4 = -1 - \left(-M, \frac{3}{5} + \frac{4}{5}M, -M\right)\begin{bmatrix} 0 \\ 0 \\ 1 \end{bmatrix}$$

$$= -1 - [0 + 0 - M] = -1 + M.$$

Since $\overline{c}_2 - \overline{Z}_2$ is most positive, x_2 is the variable that enters the basis. The pivot column is

$$\overline{\mathbf{P}}_2 = \mathbf{B}^{-1}\mathbf{P}_2 = \begin{bmatrix} 0 & 1/5 & 0 \\ 0 & -1/5 & 1 \\ 1 & -3/5 & 0 \end{bmatrix}\begin{bmatrix} 2 \\ 1 \\ 2 \end{bmatrix} = \begin{bmatrix} 1/5 \\ 9/5 \\ 7/5 \end{bmatrix}.$$

The replacement ratios are $(15, \frac{85}{9}, \frac{5}{7})$. Thus variable x_6 leaves the basis. *Since x_6 is artificial variable, it will be excluded from further consideration.* The pivot column $\begin{bmatrix} 1/5 \\ 9/5 \\ (7/5) \end{bmatrix}$ must be reduced to $\begin{bmatrix} 0 \\ 0 \\ 1 \end{bmatrix}$. This is done by

(*i*) dividing row 3 by 7/5,

(*ii*) dividing row 3 by 7 and subtracting from row 1, and
(*iii*) multiplying row 3 by 9/7 and subtracting from row 2.

The new $\mathbf{B}^{-1}$ and constants are given in table 6.41.

TABLE 6.41

Basis	$\mathbf{B}^{-1}$			*Constants*	*Variable to enter*	*Pivot column*
x_3	–1/7	2/7	0	20/7		0
x_5	–9/7	4/7	1	110/7	x_4	(1)
x_2	5/7	–3/7	0	5/7		0

Iteration 3

The simplex multipliers of table 6.41 are

$$\boldsymbol{\pi} = (\pi_1, \pi_2, \pi_3) = (3, -\text{M}, 2)\begin{bmatrix} -\frac{1}{7} & \frac{2}{7} & 0 \\ -\frac{9}{7} & \frac{4}{7} & 1 \\ \frac{5}{7} & -\frac{3}{7} & 0 \end{bmatrix}$$

$$= \left(-\frac{3}{7} + \frac{9}{7}\text{M} + \frac{10}{7}, \frac{6}{7} - \frac{4}{7}\text{M} - \frac{6}{7}, -\text{M}\right) = \left(1 + \frac{9}{7}\text{M}, -\frac{4}{7}\text{M}, -\text{M}\right).$$

$$\therefore \quad \overline{c}_1 - \overline{Z}_1 = c_1 - \boldsymbol{\pi}\mathbf{P}_1 = 1 - \left(1 + \frac{9}{7}\text{M}, -\frac{4}{7}\text{M}, -\text{M}\right)\begin{bmatrix}1\\2\\1\end{bmatrix}$$

$$= 1 - \left[1 + \frac{9}{7}\text{M} - \frac{8}{7}\text{M} - \text{M}\right] = \frac{6}{7}\text{M},$$

$$\overline{c}_4 - \overline{Z}_4 = c_4 - \boldsymbol{\pi}\mathbf{P}_4 = -1 - \left(1 + \frac{9}{7}\text{M}, -\frac{4}{7}\text{M}, -\text{M}\right)\begin{bmatrix}0\\0\\1\end{bmatrix} = -1 + \text{M}.$$

$\overline{c}_6 - \overline{Z}_6$ is not calculated since x_6 is an artificial variable. Since $\overline{c}_4 - \overline{Z}_4$ is most positive, x_4 enters the basis and the pivot column becomes

$$\overline{\mathbf{P}}_4 = \mathbf{B}^{-1}\mathbf{P}_4 = \begin{bmatrix} -\frac{1}{7} & \frac{2}{7} & 0 \\ -\frac{9}{7} & \frac{4}{7} & 1 \\ \frac{5}{7} & -\frac{3}{7} & 0 \end{bmatrix}\begin{bmatrix}0\\0\\1\end{bmatrix} = \begin{bmatrix}0\\1\\0\end{bmatrix}.$$

The replacement ratios are $\left(\infty, \frac{110}{7}, \infty\right)$. Hence x_5 is the variable that leaves the basis. Since x_5 is artificial variable, it is excluded from further consideration. The pivot column is $\begin{bmatrix}0\\(1)\\0\end{bmatrix}$. The B^{-1} and constants are given in table 6.42.

TABLE 6.42

Basis		$\mathbf{B}^{-1}$		*Constants*	*Variable to enter*	*Pivot column*
x_3	–1/7	2/7	0	20/7		(3/7)
x_4	–9/7	4/7	1	110/7	x_1	6/7
x_2	5/7	–3/7	0	5/7		–1/7

Iteration 4

The simplex multipliers for table 6.42 are

$$\boldsymbol{\pi} = (\pi_1, \pi_2, \pi_3) = c_B\,\mathbf{B}^{-1} = (3, -1, 2)\begin{bmatrix} -\frac{1}{7} & \frac{2}{7} & 0 \\ -\frac{9}{7} & \frac{4}{7} & 1 \\ \frac{5}{7} & -\frac{3}{7} & 0 \end{bmatrix}$$

$$= \left(-\frac{3}{7}+\frac{9}{7}+\frac{10}{7}, \frac{6}{7}-\frac{4}{7}-\frac{6}{7}, -1\right) = \left[\frac{16}{7}, -\frac{4}{7}, -1\right].$$

$$\therefore \quad \overline{c}_1 - \overline{Z}_1 = c_1 - \boldsymbol{\pi}\mathbf{P}_1 = 1 - \left(\frac{16}{7}, -\frac{4}{7}, -1\right)\begin{bmatrix}1\\2\\1\end{bmatrix} = 1 - \left[\frac{16}{7} - \frac{8}{7} - 1\right] = \frac{6}{7}.$$

$\overline{c}_5 - \overline{Z}_5$ and $\overline{c}_6 - \overline{Z}_6$ are not calculated since x_5 and x_6 are artificial variables. Since $\overline{c}_1 - \overline{Z}_1$ is positive, x_1 enters the basis and the pivot column becomes

$$\overline{\mathbf{P}}_1 = \mathbf{B}^{-1}\mathbf{P}_1 = \begin{bmatrix} -\frac{1}{7} & \frac{2}{7} & 0 \\ -\frac{9}{7} & \frac{4}{7} & 1 \\ \frac{5}{7} & -\frac{3}{7} & 0 \end{bmatrix}\begin{bmatrix}1\\2\\1\end{bmatrix} = \begin{bmatrix}\frac{3}{7}\\ \frac{6}{7}\\ -\frac{1}{7}\end{bmatrix}.$$

The replacement ratios are $\left(\frac{20}{3}, \frac{55}{3}, -5\right)$. Thus x_3 is the outgoing variable. The pivot column $\begin{bmatrix}(3/7)\\6/7\\-1/7\end{bmatrix}$ must be reduced to $\begin{bmatrix}1\\0\\0\end{bmatrix}$.

This is done by

(*i*) multiplying row 1 by 7/3,

(*ii*) multiplying row 1 by 2 and subtracting it from row 2, and

(*iii*) dividing row 1 by 3 and adding it to row 3.

The new $\mathbf{B}^{-1}$ and constants are given in table 6.43.

TABLE 6.43

Basis	$\mathbf{B}^{-1}$			*Constants*
x_1	$-1/3$	$2/3$	0	$20/3$
x_4	-1	0	1	10
x_2	$2/3$	$-1/3$	0	$5/3$

The simplex multipliers corresponding to table 6.43 are

$$\boldsymbol{\pi} = (\pi_1, \pi_2, \pi_3) = c_B\,\mathbf{B}^{-1} = (1, -1, 2)\begin{bmatrix} -\frac{1}{3} & \frac{2}{3} & 0 \\ -1 & 0 & 1 \\ \frac{2}{3} & -\frac{1}{3} & 0 \end{bmatrix} = (2, 0, -1).$$

$$\therefore \quad \bar{c}_3 - \bar{Z}_3 = c_3 - \boldsymbol{\pi}\mathbf{P}_3 = 3 - (2, 0, -1)\begin{bmatrix} 3 \\ 5 \\ 1 \end{bmatrix} = 3 - (6 + 0 - 1) = -2.$$

Since $\bar{c}_3 - \bar{Z}_3$ is negative. table 6.43 gives optimal solution, which is

$$x_1 = \frac{20}{3},\ x_2 = \frac{5}{3},\ x_3 = 0,\ x_4 = 10,\ x_5 = 0,\ x_6 = 0, \text{ and}$$

$$Z_{\max} = 1 \times \frac{20}{3} - 1 \times 10 + 2 \times \frac{5}{3} = \frac{20}{3} - 10 + \frac{10}{3} = 0.$$

EXAMPLE 6.3-4

Solve the following L.P.P. by the revised simplex method :

Minimize $\quad Z = -4x_1 + x_2 + 2x_3,$

subject to

$$2x_1 - 3x_2 + 2x_3 \le 12,$$
$$-5x_1 + 2x_2 + 3x_3 \ge 4,$$
$$3x_1 - 2x_3 = -1,$$
$$x_1, x_2, x_3 \ge 0.$$

[*P.U.B.E. (T. and I.T.) Nov., 2004*]

Solution

In standard form the problem can be expressed as

minimize $\quad Z = -4x_1 + x_2 + 2x_3,$

subject to

$$2x_1 - 3x_2 + 2x_3 + x_4 = 12,$$
$$-5x_1 + 2x_2 + 3x_3 - x_5 = 4,$$
$$-3x_1 + 2x_3 = 1,$$
$$x_1, \ldots, x_5 \ge 0.$$

Since the second and third equations do not contain basic variables, artificial variables x_6 and x_7 are added and the problem takes the form

minimize $\quad Z = -4x_1 + x_2 + 2x_3 + 0x_4 + 0x_5 + Mx_6 + Mx_7,$

subject to

$$2x_1 - 3x_2 + 2x_3 + x_4 = 12,$$
$$-5x_1 + 2x_2 + 3x_3 - x_5 + x_6 = 4,$$
$$-3x_1 + 2x_3 + x_7 = 1,$$
$$x_1, \ldots, x_7 \ge 0.$$

Let $\mathbf{P}_1, \ldots, \mathbf{P}_7$ and $\mathbf{b}$ denote the column vectors corresponding to $x_1, \ldots, x_7$ and the right-hand side constants respectively. Then

$$\mathbf{P}_1 = \begin{bmatrix} 2 \\ -5 \\ -3 \end{bmatrix}, \mathbf{P}_2 = \begin{bmatrix} -3 \\ 2 \\ 0 \end{bmatrix}, \mathbf{P}_3 = \begin{bmatrix} 2 \\ 3 \\ 2 \end{bmatrix},$$

$$\mathbf{P}_4 = \begin{bmatrix} 1 \\ 0 \\ 0 \end{bmatrix}, \mathbf{P}_5 = \begin{bmatrix} 0 \\ -1 \\ 0 \end{bmatrix}, \mathbf{P}_6 = \begin{bmatrix} 0 \\ 1 \\ 0 \end{bmatrix}, \mathbf{P}_7 = \begin{bmatrix} 0 \\ 0 \\ 1 \end{bmatrix} \text{ and } \mathbf{b} = \begin{bmatrix} 12 \\ 4 \\ 1 \end{bmatrix}.$$

Now (x_4, x_6, x_7) form the initial basis.

$$\therefore \quad \mathbf{B}_{(3\times 3)} = [\mathbf{P}_4, \mathbf{P}_6, \mathbf{P}_7] = \begin{bmatrix} 1 & 0 & 0 \\ 0 & 1 & 0 \\ 0 & 0 & 1 \end{bmatrix} = \mathbf{I},$$

$$\therefore \quad \mathbf{B}^{-1} = \mathbf{I} \text{ and } \overline{\mathbf{b}} = \mathbf{B}^{-1}\mathbf{b} = \mathbf{b}.$$

The initial table of the revised simplex method is given below. The last two columns of this table are added later.

TABLE 6.44

Basis	$\mathbf{B}^{-1}$			*Constants*	*Variable to enter*	*Pivot column*
x_4	1	0	0	12		2
x_6	0	1	0	4	x_3	3
x_7	0	0	1	1		(2)

Iteration 1

The simplex multipliers are

$$\boldsymbol{\pi} = (\pi_1, \pi_2, \pi_3) = c_B\,\mathbf{B}^{-1} = (0, \text{M}, \text{M}) \begin{bmatrix} 1 & 0 & 0 \\ 0 & 1 & 0 \\ 0 & 0 & 1 \end{bmatrix} = (0, \text{M}, \text{M}).$$

$$\therefore \quad (\overline{c}_1 - \overline{Z}_1) = c_1 - \boldsymbol{\pi}\mathbf{P}_1 = -4 - (0, \text{M}, \text{M}) \begin{bmatrix} 2 \\ -5 \\ -3 \end{bmatrix} = 8\text{M} - 4,$$

$$(\overline{c}_2 - \overline{Z}_2) = c_2 - \boldsymbol{\pi}\mathbf{P}_2 = 1 - (0, \text{M}, \text{M}) \begin{bmatrix} -3 \\ 2 \\ 0 \end{bmatrix} = 1 - 2\text{M},$$

$$(\overline{c}_3 - \overline{Z}_3) = c_3 - \boldsymbol{\pi}\mathbf{P}_3 = 2 - (0, \text{M}, \text{M}) \begin{bmatrix} 2 \\ 3 \\ 2 \end{bmatrix} = 2 - 5\text{M},$$

$$(\overline{c}_5 - \overline{Z}_5) = c_5 - \boldsymbol{\pi}\mathbf{P}_5 = 0 - (0, \text{M}, \text{M}) \begin{bmatrix} 0 \\ -1 \\ 0 \end{bmatrix} = \text{M}.$$

Since $(\overline{c}_3 - \overline{Z}_3)$ is most negative, x_3 is the variable that enters the basis. The pivot column is

$$\overline{\mathbf{P}}_3 = \mathbf{B}^{-1}\mathbf{P}_3 = \begin{bmatrix} 1 & 0 & 0 \\ 0 & 1 & 0 \\ 0 & 0 & 1 \end{bmatrix}\begin{bmatrix} 2 \\ 3 \\ 2 \end{bmatrix} = \begin{bmatrix} 2 \\ 3 \\ 2 \end{bmatrix}.$$

The entering variable x_3 and the elements in the pivot column are now entered in table 6.44. Applying the minimum positive ratio rule, the ratios are (6, 4/3, 1/2). Hence x_7 is the outgoing variable. This is shown by putting the corresponding pivot element in brackets *i.e.*, (2). *Since x_7 is an artificial variable, it will be discarded from further consideration*. Now the pivot column $\begin{bmatrix} 2 \\ 3 \\ (2) \end{bmatrix}$ must be reduced to $\begin{bmatrix} 0 \\ 0 \\ 1 \end{bmatrix}$.

This is obtained by

(*i*) subtracting row 3 from row 1,

(*ii*) multiplying row 3 by 3/2 and subtracting from row 2,

(*iii*) dividing row 3 by 2

The new $\mathbf{B}^{-1}$ and constants are given in table 6.45.

TABLE 6.45

Basis	$\mathbf{B}^{-1}$			*Constants*	*Variable to enter*	*Pivot column*
x_4	1	0	–1	11		– 3
x_6	0	1	$-3/2$	$5/2$	x_2	(2)
x_3	0	0	$1/2$	$1/2$		0

Iteration 2

The simplex multipliers corresponding to table 6.45 are

$$\boldsymbol{\pi} = (\pi_1, \pi_2, \pi_3) = c_B B^{-1} = (0, \text{M}, 2)\begin{bmatrix} 1 & 0 & -1 \\ 0 & 1 & -\frac{3}{2} \\ 0 & 0 & \frac{1}{2} \end{bmatrix} = \left(0, \text{M}, 1 - \frac{3\text{M}}{2}\right).$$

$$\therefore \quad (\overline{c}_1 - \overline{Z}_1) = c_1 - \boldsymbol{\pi}\text{P}_1 = -4 - \left(0, \text{M}, 1 - \frac{3\text{M}}{2}\right)\begin{bmatrix} 2 \\ -5 \\ -3 \end{bmatrix}$$

$$= -4 - \left\{-5\text{M} - 3 + \frac{9\text{M}}{2}\right\} = -1 + \frac{1}{2}\text{M},$$

$$(\overline{c}_2 - \overline{Z}_2) = c_2 - \boldsymbol{\pi}\text{P}_2 = 1 - (0, \text{M}, 1 - \frac{3}{2}\text{M})\begin{bmatrix} -3 \\ 2 \\ 0 \end{bmatrix} = 1 - \{2\text{M}\} = 1 - 2\text{M},$$

$$(\overline{c}_5 - \overline{Z}_5) = c_5 - \boldsymbol{\pi}\text{P}_5 = 0 - (0, \text{M}, 1 - \frac{3}{2}\text{M})\begin{bmatrix} 0 \\ -1 \\ 0 \end{bmatrix} = 0 - \{-\text{M}\} = \text{M}.$$

$(\overline{c}_7 - \overline{Z}_7)$ is not calculated since x_7 is an artificial variable. Since $(\overline{c}_2 - \overline{Z}_2)$ is the most negative, x_2 enters the basis and the pivot column becomes

$$\overline{\mathbf{P}}_2 = \mathbf{B}^{-1}\mathbf{P}_2 = \begin{bmatrix} 1 & 0 & -1 \\ 0 & 1 & -\frac{3}{2} \\ 0 & 0 & \frac{1}{2} \end{bmatrix} \begin{bmatrix} -3 \\ 2 \\ 0 \end{bmatrix} = \begin{bmatrix} -3 \\ 2 \\ 0 \end{bmatrix}.$$

The replacement ratios are $\left(-\frac{11}{3}, \frac{5}{4}, \infty\right)$. Hence x_6 is the variable that leaves the basis (x_6 will be discarded from further consideration). This is shown by putting the corresponding pivot element in brackets *i.e.*, (2). The pivot column $\begin{bmatrix} -3 \\ (2) \\ 0 \end{bmatrix}$ is now reduced to $\begin{bmatrix} 0 \\ 1 \\ 0 \end{bmatrix}$. This is done by

(*i*) multiplying row 2 by 3/2 and adding it to row 1,
(*ii*) dividing row 2 by 2.

The new $\mathbf{B}^{-1}$ and constants are given in table 6.46.

TABLE 6.46

Basis	$\mathbf{B}^{-1}$			*Constants*	*Variable to enter*	*Pivot column*
x_4	1	$3/2$	$-13/4$	$59/4$		$(17/4)$
x_2	0	$1/2$	$-3/4$	$5/4$	x_1	$-1/4$
x_3	0	0	$1/2$	$1/2$		$-3/2$

Iteration 3

The simplex multipliers of table 6.46 are

$$\boldsymbol{\pi} = (\pi_1, \pi_2, \pi_3) = c_B\,\mathbf{B}^{-1} = (0, 1, 2) \begin{bmatrix} 1 & \frac{3}{2} & -\frac{13}{4} \\ 0 & \frac{1}{2} & -\frac{3}{4} \\ 0 & 0 & \frac{1}{2} \end{bmatrix} = \left(0, \frac{1}{2}, \frac{1}{4}\right).$$

$$\therefore \quad (\overline{c}_1 - \overline{Z}_1) = c_1 - \boldsymbol{\pi}\mathbf{P}_1 = -4 - \left(0, \frac{1}{2}, \frac{1}{4}\right) \begin{bmatrix} 2 \\ -5 \\ -3 \end{bmatrix} = -4 - \left\{-\frac{5}{2} - \frac{3}{4}\right\} = -\frac{3}{4},$$

$$(\overline{c}_5 - \overline{Z}_5) = c_5 - \boldsymbol{\pi}\mathbf{P}_5 = 0 - \left(0, \frac{1}{2}, \frac{1}{4}\right) \begin{bmatrix} 0 \\ -1 \\ 0 \end{bmatrix} = \frac{1}{2}.$$

Since $(\overline{c}_1 - \overline{Z}_1)$ is the most negative, x_1 enters the basis and the pivot column becomes

$$\overline{\mathbf{P}}_1 = \mathbf{B}^{-1}\mathbf{P}_1 = \begin{bmatrix} 1 & \frac{3}{2} & -\frac{13}{4} \\ 0 & \frac{1}{2} & -\frac{3}{4} \\ 0 & 0 & \frac{1}{2} \end{bmatrix} \begin{bmatrix} 2 \\ -5 \\ -3 \end{bmatrix} = \begin{bmatrix} \frac{17}{4} \\ -\frac{1}{4} \\ -\frac{3}{2} \end{bmatrix}.$$

The replacement ratios are $(\frac{59}{17}, -5, -\frac{1}{3})$. Hence x_4 is the variable that leaves the basis.

The pivot column $\begin{bmatrix} \left(\frac{17}{4}\right) \\ -\frac{1}{4} \\ -\frac{3}{2} \end{bmatrix}$ must be reduced to $\begin{bmatrix} 1 \\ 0 \\ 0 \end{bmatrix}$.

This is done by

(*i*) multiplying row 1 by $\frac{1}{17}$ and adding it to row 2,

(*ii*) multiplying row 1 by $\frac{6}{17}$ and adding it to row 3,

(*iii*) dividing row 1 by $\frac{17}{4}$.

The new $\mathbf{B}^{-1}$ and constants are given in table 6.47.

TABLE 6.47

Basis		$\mathbf{B}^{-1}$		*Constants*
x_1	$4/17$	$6/17$	$-13/17$	$59/17$
x_2	$1/17$	$10/17$	$-16/17$	$36/17$
x_3	$6/17$	$9/17$	$-11/17$	$97/17$

The simplex multipliers of table 6.47 are

$$\boldsymbol{\pi} = (\pi_1, \pi_2, \pi_3) = c_B\,\mathbf{B}^{-1} = (-4, 1, 2) \begin{bmatrix} \frac{4}{17} & \frac{6}{17} & -\frac{13}{17} \\ \frac{1}{17} & \frac{10}{17} & -\frac{16}{17} \\ \frac{6}{17} & \frac{9}{17} & -\frac{11}{17} \end{bmatrix} = \left[-\frac{3}{17}, \frac{4}{17}, \frac{14}{17}\right].$$

$$\therefore \qquad (\overline{c}_4 - \overline{Z}_4) = c_4 - \boldsymbol{\pi}\mathbf{P}_4 = 0 - \left(\frac{-3}{17}, \frac{4}{17}, \frac{14}{17}\right)\begin{bmatrix} 1 \\ 0 \\ 0 \end{bmatrix} = \frac{3}{17},$$

$$(\overline{c}_5 - \overline{Z}_5) = c_5 - \boldsymbol{\pi}\mathbf{P}_5 = 0 - \left(\frac{-3}{17}, \frac{4}{17}, \frac{14}{17}\right)\begin{bmatrix} 0 \\ -1 \\ 0 \end{bmatrix} = \frac{4}{17}.$$

Since $(\bar{c}_4 - \bar{Z}_4)$ as well as $(\bar{c}_5 - \bar{Z}_5)$ are non-negative, table 6.47 gives optimal solution, which is $x_1 = \frac{59}{17}, x_2 = \frac{36}{17}, x_3 = \frac{97}{17}, x_4 = 0, x_5 = 0, x_6 = 0, x_7 = 0$ and optimal value of objective function is

$$Z_{min} = -4 \times \frac{59}{17} + 1 \times \frac{36}{17} + 2 \times \frac{97}{17} = -\frac{6}{17}.$$

6.3-1 Advantages and Disadvantages of the Revised Simplex Method over the Regular Simplex Method

Advantages

1. The number of arithmetic operations in the revised simplex method may be lesser than in the regular simplex method, depending on the size $(m \times n)$ of the problem and the sparsity (fraction of coefficients) of its c_j, a_{ij} and b_i elements.
2. The revised simplex method works with a reduced table as it stores only the basic variables, the basis inverse and the R.H.S. constants. Hence less new information needs to be stored in the memory of the computer from one iteration to the other.
3. Since computations in the revised simplex method are based on the basis inverse and the original data only, machine roundoff error is controlled by controlling the accuracy of basis inverse. This is a distinct advantage over the regular simplex method, where there is a propagation of roundoff error.
4. The theory of the revised simplex method, especially the importance of the basis inverse and the simplex multipliers is quite helpful in understanding sensitivity analysis and parametric programming.

Disadvantages

The above advantages of the revised simplex method are realised only for computations by a digital computer. For hand calculations, a lot of side computations are required. Computational mistakes are also likely to be more in this method.

EXERCISES 6.3

1. Explain the revised simplex method and compare it with the regular simplex method. *[B.P.U.T., 2012]*
2. What are the advantages of the revised simplex method over the standard simplex method ? *[P.T.U. MCA, 2010; P.U.B.E. (T. & I.T.) Nov., 2004; B.E. (C. Sc. and E.) Dec., 2004]*
3. Use revised simplex method to solve the following problem :

   Minimize $Z = 2x_1 + x_2,$

   subject to $3x_1 + x_2 = 3,$

   $4x_1 + 3x_2 \geq 6,$

   $x_1 + 2x_2 \leq 3,$

   $x_1, x_2 \geq 0.$

   [Kuru. U. B. Tech. (Mech.) 1989]

   $\left(Ans.\ x_1 = \frac{3}{5}, x_2 = \frac{6}{5}; Z_{min} = \frac{12}{5}.\right)$
4. Solve the following problem by the revised simplex method :

   Maximize $x_0 = 6x_1 - 2x_2 + 3x_3,$

   subject to $2x_1 - x_2 + 2x_3 \leq 2,$

   $x_1 + 4x_3 \leq 4,$

   $x_1, x_2, x_3 \geq 0.$

   [Madurai M. Sc. (Appl. Sc.) 1983 ; Roorkee M.E. (Elect.) 1977]

   (Ans. $x_1 = 4, x_2 = 6, x_3 = 0; x_{omax} = 12.$*)*

5. Solve by the revised simplex method, the problem

maximize $Z = x_1 + x_2 + 3x_3$,

subject to constraints

$3x_1 + 2x_2 + x_3 \leq 3$,
$2x_1 + x_2 + 2x_3 \leq 2$,
$x_1, x_2, x_3 \geq 0$.

[*Kuru. U. M. Tech. Dec., 1988 ; Dec., 1983*]

(*Ans.* $x_1 = 0, x_2 = 0, x_3 = 1$; $Z_{max} = 3$.)

6. Use the revised simplex method to solve the problem

maximize $Z = 30x_1 + 23x_2 + 29x_3$,

subject to $6x_1 + 5x_2 + 3x_3 \leq 26$,
$4x_1 + 2x_2 + 5x_3 \leq 7$,
$x_1, x_2, x_3 \geq 0$.

[*Kuru. U. M. Tech. May, 1988 ; Agra M. Stat., 1973*]

(*Ans.* $x_1 = 0, x_2 = 7/2, x_3 = 0$; $Z_{max} = 161/2$.)

7. Use the revised simplex method to

minimize $Z = 2x_1 + 3x_2 + 2x_3 - x_4 + x_5$,

subject to $3x_1 - 3x_2 + 4x_3 + 2x_4 - x_5 = 0$,
$x_1 + x_2 + x_3 + 3x_4 + x_5 = 2$,
$x_1, ..., x_5 \geq 0$.

(*Ans.* $x_1 = x_2 = x_3 = 0$ (non-basic variables),
$x_4 = 2/5, x_5 = 4/5$ (basic variables),
$Z_{min} = 2/5$.)

8. Use the revised simplex method to

maximize $Z = x_1 + 2x_2$,

subject to $x_1 + x_2 \leq 3$,
$x_1 + 2x_2 \leq 5$,
$3x_1 + x_2 \leq 6$,
$x_1, x_2 \geq 0$.

[*Meerut M. Sc. (Math.) 1969, 1970 (S)*]

(*Ans.* $x_1 = 1, x_2 = 2, x_3 = 0$; $Z_{max} = 5$.)

9. Solve, by using the revised simplex method, the problem :

Minimize $Z = x_1 + x_2$,

subject to $x_1 + 2x_2 \geq 7$,
$4x_1 + x_2 \geq 6$,
$x_1, x_2 \geq 0$.

[*P.T.U. MCA, 2010*]

(*Ans.* $x_1 = 5/7, x_2 = 22/7$; $Z_{min} = 27/7$.)

10. Solve the following problem by the revised simplex method :

Maximize $Z = 2x_1 + x_2 + 2x_3$,

subject to $4x_1 + 3x_2 + 8x_3 \geq 12$,
$4x_1 + x_2 + 12x_3 \leq 8$,
$4x_1 - x_2 + 3x_3 \leq 8$,
$x_1, x_2, x_3 \geq 0$.

(*Ans.* $x_1 = \frac{3}{2}, x_2 = 2, x_3 = 0$; $Z_{max} = 5$.)

11. Solve the problem by the revised simplex method :

Minimize $Z = -3x_1 + x_2 + x_3$,

subject to $x_1 - 2x_2 + x_3 \leq 11$,
$-4x_1 + x_2 + 2x_3 \geq 3$,
$2x_1 - x_3 = -1$,
$x_1, x_2, x_3 \geq 0$.

(*Ans.* $x_1 = 4, x_2 = 1, x_3 = 9$; $Z_{min} = -2$.)

12. Using artificial variables, solve by the revised simplex method :

Maximize $Z = -2x_1 - 4x_2 - x_3,$

subject to
$$x_1 + 2x_2 - x_3 \le 5,$$
$$2x_1 - x_2 + 2x_3 = 2,$$
$$-x_1 + 2x_2 + 2x_3 \ge 1,$$
$$x_1, x_2, x_3 \ge 0.$$

(*Ans.* $x_1 = 0, x_2 = 0, x_3 = 1$; $Z_{max} = -1$).

13. The following L.P.P. is fed to a computer for solution :

Maximize $Z = 3x_1 + 2x_2,$

subject to
$$-x_1 + 2x_2 + x_3 = 4,$$
$$3x_1 + 2x_2 + x_4 = 14,$$
$$x_1 - x_2 + x_5 = 3,$$
$$x_1, x_2, x_3, x_4, x_5 \ge 0.$$

Using the revised simplex method, the computer has the following information corresponding to the basis **B** at some stage :

$$X_{\mathbf{B}} = (x_3, x_4, x_1),$$

and
$$\mathbf{B}^{-1} = \begin{bmatrix} 1 & 0 & 1 \\ 0 & 1 & -3 \\ 0 & 0 & 1 \end{bmatrix}.$$

(*i*) Compute the current b.f.s. and simplex multipliers corresponding to basis **B**.

(*ii*) Show that the present solution is not optimal. Which variable should be introduced into the basis ?

(*iii*) Find the new inverse of the basis and the new simplex multipliers.

(*iv*) Write the new b.f.s. Is it optimal ? Why or why not ?

14. Solve the following L.P.P. by the revised simplex method:

Minimize $Z = -4x_1 + x_2 + 2x_3,$

subject to
$$2x_1 - 3x_2 + 2x_3 \le 12,$$
$$-5x_1 + 2x_2 + 3x_3 \ge 4,$$
$$3x_1 - 2x_3 = -1,$$
$$x_1, x_2, x_3 \ge 0.$$

[*P.U.B.E. (T. and I.T.) Nov., 2004*]

$\left(Ans.\ x_1 = {}^{59}\!/_{17}, x_2 = {}^{36}\!/_{17}, x_3 = {}^{97}\!/_{17}; Z_{min} = -{}^{6}\!/_{17}\right)$

6.4 THE BOUNDED VARIABLES PROBLEM

A linear programming problem may have, in addition to the regular constraints, lower or upper bounds on some or all the variables *i.e.*, constraints of the type

$$l_j \le x_j \le u_j,$$

where x_j is the jth variable of the problem and l_j and u_j are its lower and upper bounds respectively.

The lower bound constraint can be handled directly by substituting

$$l_j = x_j - x_j' \text{ or } x_j = l_j + x_j', \text{ where } x_j' \ge 0.$$

For an upper bound constraint of the type $x_j \le u_j$, the substitution $x_j = u_j - x_j''$, $x_j'' \ge 0$ does not guarantee that x_j will remain non-negative. This difficulty is overcome by using a special technique *called bounded variable simplex method*, which consists of the following steps :

Step 1

If R.H.S. of any constraint is negative, make it positive by multiplying the constraint by – 1.

Step 2

Convert the inequalities of the constraints into equations by the addition of suitable slacks and/or surplus variables and obtain an initial basic feasible solution.

Step 3

If any variable is at a positive lower bound, it should be substituted at its lower bound.

Step 4

Calculate the net evaluation $c_j - Z_j$. For a maximization problem, if $c_j - Z_j \leq 0$ for the non-basic variables at their upper bound, optimum basic feasible solution is attained. If not, go to step 5. Reverse is true for a minimization problem.

Step 5

Select the most positive of $c_j - Z_j$.

Step 6

Let x_j be a nonbasic variable at zero level which is selected to enter the solution. Let $(\boldsymbol{X_B})_i = (\boldsymbol{X_B^*})_i$ be the ith variable of the current basic solution $\boldsymbol{X_B}$.

Compute the quantities

$$\theta_1 = \min_i \left\{ \frac{(\boldsymbol{X_B^*})_i}{a_{ij}}, a_{ij} > 0 \right\},$$

$$\theta_2 = \min_i \left\{ \frac{u_i - (\boldsymbol{X_B^*})_i}{-a_{ij}}, a_{ij} < 0 \right\},$$

$$\text{and } \theta = \min.\ (\theta_1, \theta_2, u_j),$$

where u_j is the upper bound for the variable x_j. Let $(\boldsymbol{X_B})_r$ be the variable corresponding to $\theta = \min.\ (\theta_1, \theta_2, u_j)$. Then

(*i*) if $\theta = \theta_1$, then $(\boldsymbol{X_B})_r$ leaves the solution and x_j enters by using the regular row operations of the simplex method.

(*ii*) if $\theta = \theta_2$, $(\boldsymbol{X_B})_r$ leaves the solution and x_j enters; then $(\boldsymbol{X_B})_r$ being non-basic at its upper bound must be substituted out by using

$$(\boldsymbol{X_B})_r = u_r - (\boldsymbol{X_B})'_r, \text{ where } 0 \leq (\boldsymbol{X_B})'_r < u_r.$$

(*iii*) if $\theta = u_j$, then x_j is substituted at its upper bound difference $u_j - x_j'$, while remaining non-basic.

EXAMPLE 6.4-1

Using bounded variable simplex method, solve the L.P.P.:

Maximize $\quad Z = 3x_1 + x_2 + x_3 + 7x_4,$

subject to the constraints

$$2x_1 + 3x_2 - x_3 + 4x_4 \leq 40,$$
$$-2x_1 + 2x_2 + 5x_3 - x_4 \leq 35,$$
$$x_1 + x_2 - 2x_3 + 3x_4 \leq 100,$$
$$x_1 \geq 2,\ x_2 \geq 1,\ x_3 \geq 3,\ x_4 \geq 4.$$

[Meerut B.Sc. (Math.) 1972]

Solution

Since x_1, x_2, x_3, and x_4 have positive lower bounds, they must be substituted at their lower bounds.

$$\text{Let } x_1 = 2 + y_1,$$
$$x_2 = 1 + y_2,$$
$$x_3 = 3 + y_3,$$
$$x_4 = 4 + y_4.$$

The given problem becomes

maximize $\quad Z = 3\,(2 + y_1) + (1 + y_2) + (3 + y_3) + 7\,(4 + y_4)$

$= 38 + 3y_1 + y_2 + y_3 + 7y_4.$

i.e., maximize $\quad Y = (Z - 38) = 3y_1 + y_2 + y_3 + 7y_4,$

subject to $\quad 2\,(2 + y_1) + 3\,(1 + y_2) - (3 + y_3) + 4\,(4 + y_4) \leq 40$

i.e., $\quad 2y_1 + 3y_2 - y_3 + 4y_4 \leq 20,$

$-2\,(2 + y_1) + 2\,(1 + y_2) + 5\,(3 + y_3) - (4 + y_4) \leq 35$

i.e., $-2y_1 + 2y_2 + 5y_3 - y_4 \le 26,$

$(2 + y_1) + (1 + y_2) - 2(3 + y_3) + 3(4 + y_4) \le 100$

i.e., $y_1 + y_2 - 2y_3 + 3y_4 \le 91,$

$y_1, y_2, y_3, y_4 \ge 0.$

This problem can now be solved by regular simplex method. The solution is left as an exercise for the reader. The optimal solution is

$$y_1 = 63/4,\ y_2 = 0,\ y_3 = 23/2 \text{ and } y_4 = 0.$$

$$\therefore \quad x_1 = 63/4 + 2 = 71/4,$$

$$x_2 = 0 + 1 = 1,$$

$$x_3 = 23/2 + 3 = 29/2,$$

$$x_4 = 0 + 4 = 4,$$

$$Z_{max} = 3 \times \frac{71}{4} + 1 \times 1 + \frac{1 \times 29}{2} + 4 \times 7 = \frac{387}{4}.$$

EXAMPLE 6.4-2

Solve the following L.P.P. by the bounded variable simplex method :

Maximize $Z = 3x_1 + 5x_2 + 3x_3,$

subject to $x_1 + 2x_2 + 2x_3 \le 14,$

$2x_1 + 4x_2 + 3x_3 \le 23,$

$0 \le x_1 \le 4,\ 0 \le x_2 \le 5 \text{ and } 0 \le x_3 \le 3.$

[*Bharthiar M.Sc. (Math.) 1988*]

Solution

The given constraint inequalities can be converted into equalities by introducing slack variables s_1 and s_2 and the problem becomes

maximize $Z = 3x_1 + 5x_2 + 3x_3 + 0s_1 + 0s_2,$

subject to $x_1 + 2x_2 + 2x_3 + s_1 = 14,$

$2x_1 + 4x_2 + 3x_3 + s_2 = 23,$

$0 \le x_1 \le 4,\ 0 \le x_2 \le 5,\ 0 \le x_3 \le 3,\ s_1 \ge 0,\ s_2 \ge 0.$

The basic variables are $s_1 = 14$ and $s_2 = 23$. Since no upper bounds are specified for these basic variables, we arbitrarily assume their upper bounds to be ∞ each. The above information can be put in the form of a table shown below.

TABLE 6.48

	c_j	3	5	3	0	0			
c_B	Basis	x_1	x_2	x_3	s_1	s_2	X_B^*	θ′	$u_i - (X_B^*)_i$
0	s_1	1	2	2	1	0	14	7	∞–14 = ∞
0	s_2	2	4	3	0	1	23	23/4	∞–23 = ∞
$Z_j = \Sigma c_B a_{ij}$		0	0	0	0	0			
$c_j - Z_j$		3	5 ↑	3	0	0			
	u_j	4	5	3	∞	∞			

Iteration 1

x_2 is the incoming variable, since $c_2 - Z_2$ is most positive.

Now θ_1 = min. (7, 23/4) = 23/4, (corresponding to s_2)

$\theta_2 = \infty$, since all elements in 'x_2'-column are non-negative, and $u_2 = 5$.

$$\therefore \quad \theta = \text{min. } (\theta_1, \theta_2, u_2)$$

$$= \text{min. } (23/4, \infty, 5)$$

$$= 5.$$

Since $\theta = u_2$, x_2 is substituted at its upper bound difference *i.e.*, $x_2 = 5 - x_2'$ but it remains non-basic. The problem thus becomes

$$\begin{array}{lll} & \text{maximize} & Z = 3x_1 + 5(5 - x_2') - 3x_3 + 0s_1 + 0s_2 \\ \text{or} & \text{maximize} & Z' = Z - 25 = 3x_1 - 5x_2' + 3x_3 + 0s_1 + 0s_2, \\ & \text{subject to} & x_1 + 2(5 - x_2') + 2x_3 + s_1 + 0s_2 = 14 \\ \text{or} & & x_1 - 2x_2' + 2x_3 + s_1 + 0s_2 = 4, \\ \text{and} & & 2x_1 + 4(5 - x_2') + 3x_3 + 0s_1 + s_2 = 23 \\ \text{or} & & 2x_1 - 4x_2' + 3x_3 - 0s_1 + s_2 = 3, \\ & & x_1, x_2', x_3, s_1, s_2 \geq 0. \end{array}$$

The new simplex table becomes

TABLE 6.49

	c_j	3	−5	3	0	0				
c_B	Basis	x_1	x_2'	x_3	s_1	s_2	X_B^*	θ'		$u_i - (X_B^*)_i$
0	s_1	1	− 2	2	1	0	4	4		$\infty - 4 = \infty$
0	s_2	(2)	− 4	3	0	1	3	3/2	←	$\infty - 3 = \infty$
$Z_j = \Sigma c_B a_{ij}$		0	0	0	0	0				
$c_j - Z_j$		3	− 5	3	0	0				
		↑								
	u_j	4	5	3	∞	∞				

Iteration 2

Now let x_1 be the incoming variable.

Then $\theta_1 = \min. (4, 3/2) = 3/2$, (corresponding to s_2)

$\theta_2 = \infty$, since all elements in 'x_1'-column are non-negative, and $u_1 = 4$.

$\therefore \quad \theta = \min. (3/2, \infty, 4) = 3/2$.

Since $\theta = \theta_1$, introduce x_1 and drop s_2. This yields

TABLE 6.50

	c_j	3	−5	3	0	0			
c_B	Basis	x_1	x_2'	x_3	s_1	s_2	X_B^*	$u_i - (X_B^*)_i$	
0	s_1	0	0	1/2	1	−1/2	5/2	$\infty - 5/2 = \infty$	
3	x_1	1	(−2)	3/2	0	1/2	3/2	4–3/2 = 5/2	←
$Z_j = \Sigma c_B a_{ij}$		3	−6	9/2	0	3/2			
$c_j - Z_j$		0	1	−3/2	0	−3/2			
			↑						
	u_j	4	5	3	∞	∞			

Iteration 3

x_2' is the entering variable.

$$\theta_1 = \infty,$$

$$\theta_2 = \frac{4 - 3/2}{-(-2)} = 5/4, \text{ (corresponding to } x_1)$$

$$u_2 = 5.$$

$\therefore \theta = \min. (\infty, 5/4, 5) = 5/4$. Since $\theta = \theta_2$, introduce x_2' into the basis and drop x_1 and then substitute it out at its upper bound $4 - x_1'$. Thus by removing x_1 and introducing x_2', the table becomes

TABLE 6.51

c_B	Basis	x_1	x'_2	x_3	s_1	s_2	X_B^*
0	s_1	0	0	1/2	1	–1/2	5/2
–5	x'_2	–1/2	1	–3/4	0	–1/4	–3/4

Now substituting $x_1 = 4 - x'_1$, the final table becomes

TABLE 6.52

	c_j	–3	–5	3	0	0	
c_B	Basis	x'_1	x'_2	x_3	s_1	s_2	X_B^*
0	s_1	0	0	1/2	1	–1/2	5/2
–5	x'_2	1/2	1	–3/4	0	–1/4	5/4
$Z_j = \Sigma c_B a_{ij}$		–5/2	–5	15/4	0	5/4	
$c_j – Z_j$		–1/2	0	–3/4	0	–5/4	

Optimal feasible solution

∴ Optimal solution is $x'_1 = 0$, $x'_2 = 5/4$, $x_3 = 0$.

In terms of original variables, the solution is

$$x_1 = 4 - 0 = 4,$$
$$x_2 = 5 - 5/4 = 15/4,$$
$$x_3 = 0, \text{ and } Z_{max} = 3 \times 4 + 5 \times 15/4 + 3 \times 0 = 123/4.$$

EXERCISES 6.4

1. State the computational procedure for resolving a linear programming problem with upper bound conditions.
2. Solve the following problem by lower and upper bounding technique:

Maximize $Z = 4y_1 + 4y_2 + 3y_3$,
subject to $-y_1 + 2y_2 + 3y_3 \le 15$,
$-y_2 + y_3 \le 4$,
$2y_1 + y_2 - y_3 \le 6$,
$y_1 - y_2 + 2y_3 \le 10$,
$0 \le y_1 \le 8, 0 \le y_2 \le 4, 0 \le y_3 \le 4$.

(*Ans.* $y_1 = 17/5$, $y_2 = 16/5$, $y_3 = 4$; $Z_{max} = 192/5$.)

3. Solve the following linear programming problem by using bounded variable simplex method :

Maximize $Z = 4y_1 + 2y_2 + 6y_3$,
subject to $4y_1 - y_2 \le 9$,
$-y_1 + y_2 + 2y_3 \le 8$,
$-3y_1 + y_2 + 4y_3 \le 12$,
$1 \le y_1 \le 3, 0 < y_2 \le 5, 0 \le y_3 \le 2$.

(*Ans.* $y_1 = 3$, $y_2 = 5$, $y_3 = 2$; $Z_{max} = 34$.)

4. Solve the following L.P.P. by using the bounded variable technique :

Maximize $Z = 3x_1 + 2x_2$,
subject to $x_1 - 3x_2 \le 3$,
$x_1 - 2x_2 \le 4$,
$2x_1 + x_2 \le 20$,
$x_1 + 3x_2 \le 30$,
$-x_1 + x_2 \le 6$,
$0 \le x_1 \le 8$,
$0 \le x_2 \le 6$.

(*Ans.* $x_1 = 7$, $x_2 = 6$; $Z_{max} = 33$.)

5. Solve the following L.P.P. by using the bounded variable technique :

Maximize $Z = 2x_1 + x_2$,

subject to
$x_1 + 2x_2 \leq 10$,
$x_1 + x_2 \leq 6$,
$x_1 - x_2 \leq 2$,
$x_1 - 2x_2 \leq 1$,
$0 \leq x_1 \leq 3,\ 0 \leq x_2 \leq 2$.

6. Use the bounded variable technique to solve

maximize $Z = x_2 + 3x_3$,

subject to
$x_1 + x_2 + x_3 \leq 10$,
$x_1 - 2x_3 \geq 0$,
$2x_2 - x_3 \leq 10$,
$0 \leq x_1 \leq 8,\ 0 \leq x_2 \leq 4,\ x_3 \geq 0$.

[*Bharthidasan B.Sc. (Math.) 1990*]

7. Solve the following problem by the bounded algorithm :

minimize $Z = 6x_1 - 2x_2 - 3x_3$,

subject to
$2x_1 + 4x_2 + 2x_3 \leq 8$,
$x_1 - 2x_2 + 3x_3 \leq 7$,
$0 \leq x_1 \leq 2,\ 0 \leq x_2 \leq 2,\ 0 \leq x_3 \leq 1$.

(*Ans.* $x_1 = 0,\ x_2 = \frac{3}{2},\ x_3 = 1;\ Z_{\min} = -6.$)

8. Use the bounded algorithm to solve

minimize $Z = 3x_1 + 5x_2 + 2x_3$,

subject to
$x_1 + 2x_2 + 2x_3 \leq 10$,
$2x_1 + 4x_2 + 3x_3 \leq 15$,
$0 \leq x_1 \leq 4,\ 0 \leq x_2 \leq 3,\ 0 \leq x_3 \leq 3$.

(*Ans.* $x_1 = 4,\ x_2 = \frac{7}{4},\ x_3 = 0;\ Z_{\min} = \frac{83}{4}.$)

9. Solve the following L.P.P. by the upper bounding algorithm :

Maximize $Z = 3x_1 + 5x_2 + 2x_3$,

subject to
$x_1 + x_2 + 2x_3 \leq 14$,
$2x_1 + 4x_2 + 3x_3 \leq 43$,
$0 < x_1 \leq 4,\ 7 \leq x_2 \leq 10,\ 0 \leq x_3 \leq 3$.

(*Ans.* $x_1 = 4,\ x_2 = \frac{35}{4},\ x_3 = 0;\ Z_{\max} = \frac{223}{4}.$)

6.5 THE DECOMPOSITION METHOD

Some linear programming problems, in practice, may involve a large number of variables and/ or constraints and require considerable computation time. The coefficient matrix, normally, contains many zero-elements. Such problems, with special structure, can be solved by the decomposition method developed by Dantzig and Wolf. This method splits the original problem into partial problems, finds the solution for each and then finds the solution to the given problem according to certain rules.

Consider, for example, a central office of a business organisation that controls the activities of its two branches. A certain part of the resources is directly controlled by the central office but the other parts are the responsiblities of the branches. Let componnets of $\mathbf{b}_0$ denote the capacities of the resouces of the central office, and components of $\mathbf{b}_1$ and $\mathbf{b}_2$ represent the capacities of the resources of the branches. Further, let matrices $\mathbf{A}_1$ and $\mathbf{A}_2$ contain the technological coefficients of the central resources and matrices $\mathbf{B}_1$ and $\mathbf{B}_2$ refer to the technological coefficients of the resources of the branches. Then the system of inequalities

$$\mathbf{A}_1\mathbf{x}_1 + \mathbf{A}_2\mathbf{x}_2 \leq \mathbf{b}_0,$$

$$\mathbf{x}_1, \mathbf{x}_2 \geq \mathbf{0},$$

is called the *central system of constraints* and the systems

$$\mathbf{B}_1\mathbf{x}_1 \leq \mathbf{b}_1,$$
$$\mathbf{x}_1 \geq \mathbf{0},$$

and

$$\mathbf{B}_2\mathbf{x}_2 \leq \mathbf{b}_2,$$
$$\mathbf{x}_2 \geq \mathbf{0},$$

are the *systems of constraints of the branches*. If the inner products $\mathbf{c}_1\mathbf{x}_1$ and $\mathbf{c}_2\mathbf{x}_2$ describe the economic results of the two branches, then $\mathbf{c}_1\mathbf{x}_1 + \mathbf{c}_2\mathbf{x}_2$ represents the total result of the organisation. The complete linear programming model for this example can be expressed as

maximize $Z = \mathbf{c}_1\mathbf{x}_1 + \mathbf{c}_2\mathbf{x}_2,$

subject to $\mathbf{A}_1\mathbf{x}_1 + \mathbf{A}_2\mathbf{x}_2 \leq \mathbf{b}_0,$

$\mathbf{B}_1\mathbf{x}_1 \leq \mathbf{b}_1,\ \mathbf{B}_2\mathbf{x}_2 \leq \mathbf{b}_2,$

$\mathbf{x}_1, \mathbf{x}_2 \geq 0.$

The decomposition method reflects the aim of co-ordinating the activities of the branches for the overall benefit of the organisation. It may be noted that this model involves constraints consisting of two independent sets of inequalities. The first set, consisting of a compiling constraint, involves all the design variables $\mathbf{x}_1$ and $\mathbf{x}_2$, while the second set consists of two different groups of constraints, each group involving the design variables ($\mathbf{x}_1$ or $\mathbf{x}_2$) of that group only.

The general form of the above model is

maximize $Z = \sum_{j=1}^{n} \mathbf{c}_j\mathbf{x}_j,$

subject to $\mathbf{A}_1\mathbf{x}_1 + \mathbf{A}_2\mathbf{x}_2 + ... + \mathbf{A}_n\mathbf{x}_n \leq \mathbf{b}_0,$

$\mathbf{B}_1\mathbf{x}_1 \leq \mathbf{b}_1,$

$\mathbf{B}_2\mathbf{x}_2 \leq \mathbf{b}_2,$

$\vdots$

$\mathbf{B}_n\mathbf{x}_n \leq \mathbf{b}_n,$

$\mathbf{x}_1, \mathbf{x}_2, ..., \mathbf{x}_n \geq 0.$

In the matrix-vector form the problem may be expressed as

maximize $Z = \sum_{j=1}^{n} \mathbf{c}_j\mathbf{x}_j\,,$

subject to

$$\begin{bmatrix} \mathbf{A}_1 & \mathbf{A}_2 & \mathbf{A}_3 & \cdots & \mathbf{A}_n \\ \mathbf{B}_1 & \mathbf{0} & \mathbf{0} & \cdots & \mathbf{0} \\ \mathbf{0} & \mathbf{B}_2 & \mathbf{0} & \cdots & \mathbf{0} \\ \mathbf{0} & \mathbf{0} & \mathbf{B}_3 & \cdots & \mathbf{0} \\ \vdots & \vdots & \vdots & & \vdots \\ \mathbf{0} & \mathbf{0} & \mathbf{0} & \cdots & \mathbf{B}_n \end{bmatrix} \begin{bmatrix} \mathbf{x}_1 \\ \mathbf{x}_2 \\ \mathbf{x}_3 \\ \vdots \\ \mathbf{x}_n \end{bmatrix} \leq \begin{bmatrix} \mathbf{b}_0 \\ \mathbf{b}_1 \\ \mathbf{b}_2 \\ \vdots \\ \mathbf{b}_n \end{bmatrix}.$$

$$x_j \geq 0, j = 1, 2, ..., n.$$

For the general decomposition principle as applied to the above problem the interested readers may refer to 'Linear Programming' by G. Hadley (35) as well as to G.B. Dantzig and P. Wolf : 'A decomposition Principle for Linear Programe', *J. Operations Research*, **8**, 1, p 101-111, 1960.

6.6 SENSITIVITY ANALYSIS

Once the optimal solution to a linear programming problem has been attained, two situations may arise which require additional computations :

1. During the formulation it is assumed that the parameters such as market demand, equipment capacity, resource consumption, resource availability, the relevant costs or profits are all known with certainty and do not change over time. In actual practice the markets fluctuate, material and labour costs go up or down, production times change and equipment availability varies from time to time. It is, therefore, desirable to study how the *current* optimal solution changes when the parameters of the problem get changed. In these problems this information may be more important than the single result provided by the optimal solution. Such an analysis converts the static linear programming solution into a dynamic tool to study the effect of changing conditions such as in business and industry.

2. The second situation is rather unpleasant, yet one may be encountered with it quite often. After attaining the optimal solution, one may discover that a wrong value of a cost coefficient was used or a particular variable or constraint was omitted or one or more of right-hand constants used were wrong.

The changes in parameters of the problem may be discrete or continuous. The study of the effect of discrete changes in parameters on the optimal solution is called the *sensitivity analysis* or the *post optimality analysis*, while that of continuous changes in parameters is called *parametric programming*. One way to determine the effects of parameter changes is to solve the problem anew, which may be computationally inefficient. Alternatively, the *current* optimal solution may be investigated, making use of the properties of the simplex criterion. The second method reduces additional computations considerably and hence forms the subject of the present discussion.

The changes in the parameters of a linear programming problem include:

1. Changes in the right-hand side of the constraints or availability of resources (b_i).
2. Changes in the cost / profit coefficients or cost/profit contribution per unit of decision variables (c_j).
3. Addition of new variables.
4. Changes in the coefficients of constraints or consumption of resources per unit of decision variables (a_{ij}).
5. Addition of new constraints.
6. Deletion of variables.
7. Deletion of constraints.

Generally, these parameter changes result in one of the following three cases :

1. The optimal solution remains unchanged *i.e.*, the basic variables and their values remain unchanged.
2. The basic variables remain unchanged but their values change.
3. The basic variables as well as their values are changed.

While dealing with these changes, one important objective is to find the maximum extent to which a parameter or a set of parameters can be changed so that the current optimal solution remains optimal. In other words, the objective is to determine how *sensitive* is the optimal solution to the changes in those parameters. Such an analysis is called *sensitivity analysis*.

In this topic we shall see how to minimize the additional computations necessary to study the changes in various parameters. In many cases it may not be necessary to solve the problem all over again. A small amount of computational work applied to the optimal solution will suffice. However, when large modifications in parameters are made, the post-optimal computations may become so tedious that there is no alternative but to go back to the beginning and resolve the problem.

6.6-1 Changes in the Right-Hand Side of the Constraints b_i (Availability of Resources)

Suppose that an optimal solution to a linear programming problem has already been found and it is desired to find the effect of increasing or decreasing some resource. Clearly, this will affect not only the objective function but also the solution. Large changes in the limiting resources may even change the variables in the solution since one or more current basic variables become negative. Dual simplex method is used to remove infeasibility and to get a feasible optimal solution.

EXAMPLE 6.6-1.1

(a) Solve the problem

$$\text{maximize} \quad Z = 5x_1 + 12x_2 + 4x_3,$$
$$\text{subject to} \quad x_1 + 2x_2 + x_3 \le 5,$$
$$2x_1 - x_2 + 3x_3 = 2,$$
$$x_1, x_2, x_3 \ge 0.$$

(b) Discuss the effect of changing the requirement vector from $\begin{bmatrix} 5 \\ 2 \end{bmatrix}$ *to* $\begin{bmatrix} 7 \\ 2 \end{bmatrix}$ *on the optimum solution.*

(c) Discuss the effect of changing the requirement vector from $\begin{bmatrix} 5 \\ 2 \end{bmatrix}$ *to* $\begin{bmatrix} 3 \\ 9 \end{bmatrix}$ *on the optimum solution.*

(d) Which resource should be increased and how much to achieve the best marginal increase in the value of the objective function ?

[*Dayalbagh Edu. Inst. M. Tech., 1998*]

Solution

(*a*) The standard form of this problem is

$$\text{maximize} \quad Z = 5x_1 + 12x_2 + 4x_3 + 0x_4 - Mx_5,$$
$$\text{subject to} \quad x_1 + 2x_2 + x_3 + x_4 = 5,$$
$$2x_1 - x_2 + 3x_3 + x_5 = 2,$$
$$x_1, x_2, x_3, x_4, x_5 \ge 0.$$

Putting $x_1 = x_2 = x_3 = 0$ in the constraint equations, we get $x_4 = 5$ and $x_5 = 2$ as the initial basic solution which can be expressed in the form of a simple matrix or table. Performing iterations yields the tables given below.

TABLE 6.53

	c_j	5	12	4	0	–M		
c_B	Basis	x_1	x_2	x_3	x_4	x_5	b	θ
0	x_4	1	2	1	1	0	5	5
–M	x_5	2	–1	(3)	0	1	2	2/3 ← *key row*
$Z_j = \Sigma c_B\, a_{ij}$		–2M	M	–3M	0	–M		
$\bar{c}_j = c_j - Z_j$		5+2M	12–M	4+3M	0	0		
				↑K				*Initial feasible solution*

TABLE 6.54

	c_j	5	12	4	0	–M			
c_B	Basis	x_1	x_2	x_3	x_4	x_5	b	θ	
0	x_4	$1/3$	$(7/3)$	0	1	$-1/3$	$13/3$	$13/7$	← Key row
4	x_3	$2/3$	$-1/3$	1	0	$1/3$	$2/3$	-2	
$Z_j = \Sigma c_B a_{ij}$		$8/3$	$-4/3$	4	0	$4/3$			
$\overline{c}_j = c_j - Z_j$		$7/3$	$40/3$	0	0	$-M - 4/3$			
			↑K						

Second feasible solution

TABLE 6.55

	c_j	5	12	4	0	– M			
c_B	Basis	x_1	x_2	x_3	x_4	x_5	b	θ	
12	x_2	$1/7$	1	0	$3/7$	$-1/7$	$13/7$	13	
4	x_3	$(5/7)$	0	1	$1/7$	$2/7$	$9/7$	$9/5$	←*Key row*
$Z_j = \Sigma c_B a_{ij}$		$32/7$	12	4	$40/7$	$-4/7$			
$\overline{c}_j = c_j - Z_j$		$3/7$	0	0	$-40/7$	$-M + 4/7$			
		↑K							

Third feasible solution

TABLE 6.56

	c_j	5	12	4	0	– M	
c_B	Basis	x_1	x_2	x_3	x_4	x_5	b
12	x_2	0	1	$-1/5$	$2/5$	$-1/5$	$8/5$
5	x_1	1	0	$7/5$	$1/5$	$2/5$	$9/5$
$Z_j = \Sigma c_B a_{ij}$		5	12	$23/5$	$29/5$	$-2/5$	
$\overline{c}_j = c_j - Z_j$		0	0	$-3/5$	$-29/5$	$-M + 2/5$	

Optimal feasible solution

Thus the optimal solution is $x_1 = 9/5$, $x_2 = 8/5$, $x_3 = 0$,
$Z_{max} = 5 \times 9/5 + 12 \times 8/5 + 0 = 141/5$.

(*b*) New values of the current basic variables are given by

$$\begin{bmatrix} x_2 \\ x_1 \end{bmatrix} = \mathbf{B}^{-1}\mathbf{b} = \begin{bmatrix} \frac{2}{5} & -\frac{1}{5} \\ \frac{1}{5} & \frac{2}{5} \end{bmatrix} \begin{bmatrix} 7 \\ 2 \end{bmatrix} = \begin{bmatrix} \frac{14}{5} - \frac{2}{5} \\ \frac{7}{5} + \frac{4}{5} \end{bmatrix} = \begin{bmatrix} \frac{12}{5} \\ \frac{11}{5} \end{bmatrix}.$$

Since both x_1 and x_2 are non-negative, the current basic solution consisting of x_1 and x_2 remains feasible and optimal at the new values $x_1 = 11/5$, $x_2 = 12/5$ and $x_3 = 0$. The new optimum value of Z is $5 \times 11/5 + 12 \times 12/5 + 4 \times 0 = 199/5$.

(*c*) New values of the current basic variables are

$$\begin{bmatrix} x_2 \\ x_1 \end{bmatrix} = \mathbf{B}^{-1}\mathbf{b} = \begin{bmatrix} \frac{2}{5} & -\frac{1}{5} \\ \frac{1}{5} & \frac{2}{5} \end{bmatrix}\begin{bmatrix} 3 \\ 9 \end{bmatrix} = \begin{bmatrix} \frac{6}{5}-\frac{9}{5} \\ \frac{3}{5}+\frac{18}{5} \end{bmatrix} = \begin{bmatrix} -\frac{3}{5} \\ \frac{21}{5} \end{bmatrix}.$$

Since x_2 becomes –ve, the *current optimal solution becomes infeasible.* As discussed in section 6.2, dual simplex method may be used to clear infeasibility of the problem. Table 6.56 is modified and written as below.

TABLE 6.57

	c_j	5	12	4	0	–M		
c_B	Basis	x_1	x_2	x_3	x_4	x_5	b	
12	x_2	0	1	$\left(-\frac{1}{5}\right)$	$\frac{2}{5}$	$-\frac{1}{5}$	$-\frac{3}{5}$	← *Key row*
5	x_1	1	0	$\frac{7}{5}$	$\frac{1}{5}$	$\frac{2}{5}$	$\frac{21}{5}$	
$Z_j = \Sigma c_B a_{ij}$		5	12	$\frac{23}{5}$	$\frac{29}{5}$	$-\frac{2}{5}$		
$\bar{c}_j = c_j - Z_j$		0	0	$-\frac{3}{5}$	$-\frac{29}{5}$	$-M+\frac{2}{5}$		
				↑K				

As $b_1 = -\frac{3}{5}$, the first row is the key row and x_2 is the outgoing variable. Find the ratios of nonbasic elements of $\bar{c}_j$ row to the elements of key row. Neglect the ratios corresponding to positive or zero elements of key row and choose the lowest ratio. The desired ratio is $\frac{-3/5}{-1/5} = 3.$ Hence 'x_3'-column is the key column, x_3 is the incoming variable and $\left(-\frac{1}{5}\right)$ is the key element.

Replace x_2 by x_3. This is shown in table 6.58.

TABLE 6.58

	c_j	5	12	4	0	–M	
c_B	Basis	x_1	x_2	x_3	x_4	x_5	b
4	x_3	0	-5	1	–2	1	3
5	x_1	1	7	0	3	–1	0
$Z_j = \Sigma c_B a_{ij}$		5	15	4	7	–1	
$\bar{c}_j = c_j - Z_j$		0	-3	0	–7	–M+1	

As all elements in $\bar{c}_j$ -row are negative or zero and all b_i are positive, the solution given by table 6.58 is optimal. The optimal solution is

$$x_1 = 0,\ x_2 = 0,\ x_3 = 3,$$
$$Z_{\max} = 5\ (0) + 12\ (0) + 4 \times 3 = 12.$$

(*d*) In order to find the resource that should be increased (or decreased), we shall write the dual objective function, which is

$$G = 5y_1 + 2y_2,$$

where $y_1 = 29/5$ and $y_2 = 2/5$ are the optimal dual variables (see table 6.56). Thus the first resource should be increased as each additional unit of the first resource increases the objective function by 29/5. Next we are to find how much the first resource should be increased so that each additional unit continues to increase the objective function by 29/5. This requirement will be met so long as the primal problem remains feasible. If Δ be increase in the first resource, it can be determined from the condition

$$\begin{bmatrix} x_2 \\ x_1 \end{bmatrix} = \mathbf{B}^{-1}\mathbf{b} = \begin{bmatrix} 2/5 & -1/5 \\ 1/5 & 2/5 \end{bmatrix}\begin{bmatrix} 5+\Delta \\ 2 \end{bmatrix}$$

$$= \begin{bmatrix} 10/5 + 2\Delta/5 - 2/5 \\ 5/5 + \Delta/5 + 4/5 \end{bmatrix} = \begin{bmatrix} \dfrac{8+2\Delta}{5} \\ \dfrac{9+\Delta}{5} \end{bmatrix} \geq \begin{bmatrix} 0 \\ 0 \end{bmatrix}.$$

As x_1 and x_2 remain feasible (≥ 0) for all values of $\Delta \geq 0$, the first resource can be increased indefinitely while maintaining the condition that each additional unit will increase the objective function by 29/5.

(*e*) The second resource should be decreased as each additional unit of the second resource decreases the objective function by 2/5. Let Δ be the decrease in the second resource. To find its extent, we make use of the condition that the current solution remains feasible so long as

$$\begin{bmatrix} x_2 \\ x_1 \end{bmatrix} = \mathbf{B}^{-1}\mathbf{b} = \begin{bmatrix} 2/5 & -1/5 \\ 1/5 & 2/5 \end{bmatrix}\begin{bmatrix} 5 \\ 2-\Delta \end{bmatrix}$$

$$= \begin{bmatrix} 10/5 - 2/5 + \Delta/5 \\ 5/5 + 4/5 - 2\Delta/5 \end{bmatrix} = \begin{bmatrix} \dfrac{8+\Delta}{5} \\ \dfrac{9-2\Delta}{5} \end{bmatrix} \geq \begin{bmatrix} 0 \\ 0 \end{bmatrix}.$$

Evidently x_1 remains positive only so long as $\dfrac{9-2\Delta}{5} \geq 0$ or $\Delta \leq 9/2$.

If $\Delta > 9/2$, x_1 becomes negative and must leave the solution.

EXAMPLE 6.6-1.2

Given the following L.P. problem :

Maximize $Z = -x_1 + 2x_2 - x_3,$

subject to $3x_1 + x_2 - x_3 \leq 10,$

$-x_1 + 4x_2 + x_3 \geq 6,$

$x_2 + x_3 \leq 4,$

$x_1, x_2, x_3 \geq 0,$

and the optimal solution given by table 6.59, find the separate ranges of b_1, b_2 and b_3 consistent with the optimal solution.

TABLE 6.59

	c_j	−1	2	−1	0	0	0	−M	
c_B	Basis	x_1	x_2	x_3	x_4	x_5	x_6	A_2	b
0	x_4	3	0	−2	1	0	−1	0	6
2	x_2	0	1	1	0	0	1	0	4
0	x_5	1	0	3	0	1	4	−1	10
	Z_j	0	2	2	0	0	2	0	
	$\overline{c}_j$	−1	0	−3	0	0	−2	−M	

[*Meerut M. Sc. (L.P.) 1993*]

Solution

To find variation in b_1 : Let b_1 become $10 + \Delta b_1$. To find the range of variation of b_1, we make use of the condition that the current solution remains feasible so long as

$$\begin{bmatrix} x_4 \\ x_2 \\ x_5 \end{bmatrix} = \mathbf{B}^{-1}\mathbf{b} = \begin{bmatrix} 1 & 0 & -1 \\ 0 & 0 & 1 \\ 0 & -1 & 4 \end{bmatrix} \begin{bmatrix} 10 + \Delta b_1 \\ 6 \\ 4 \end{bmatrix} \geq \begin{bmatrix} 0 \\ 0 \\ 0 \end{bmatrix}.$$

This gives $10 + \Delta b_1 - 4 \geq 0$

or $\Delta b_1 \geq -6$ or $-6 \leq \Delta b_1$.

Since there is no upper bound to Δb_1,

$$-6 \leq \Delta b_1 \leq \infty$$

or $$4 \leq b_1 \leq \infty,$$

To find variation in b_2 :

Let b_2 become $6 + \Delta b_2$. Then

$$\begin{bmatrix} x_4 \\ x_2 \\ x_5 \end{bmatrix} = \mathbf{B}^{-1}\mathbf{b} = \begin{bmatrix} 1 & 0 & -1 \\ 0 & 0 & 1 \\ 0 & -1 & 4 \end{bmatrix} \begin{bmatrix} 10 \\ 6 + \Delta b_2 \\ 4 \end{bmatrix} \geq \begin{bmatrix} 0 \\ 0 \\ 0 \end{bmatrix}.$$

This gives $-6 - \Delta b_2 + 16 \geq 0$

or $10 \geq \Delta b_2$

or $\Delta b_2 \leq 10$.

Since there is no lower bound to Δb_2,

$$-\infty \leq \Delta b_2 \leq 10$$

or $$-\infty \leq b_2 \leq 16.$$

To find variation in b_3 :

Let b_3 become $4 + \Delta b_3$. Then

$$\begin{bmatrix} x_4 \\ x_2 \\ x_5 \end{bmatrix} = \mathbf{B}^{-1}\mathbf{b} = \begin{bmatrix} 1 & 0 & -1 \\ 0 & 0 & 1 \\ 0 & -1 & 4 \end{bmatrix} \begin{bmatrix} 10 \\ 6 \\ 4 + \Delta b_3 \end{bmatrix} \geq \begin{bmatrix} 0 \\ 0 \\ 0 \end{bmatrix}.$$

This yields

$10 - 4 - \Delta b_3 \geq 0$ or $\Delta b_3 \leq 6$,

$4 + \Delta b_3 \geq 0$ or $\Delta b_3 \geq -4$, and

$-6 + 16 + 4\,\Delta b_3 \geq 0$ or $\Delta b_3 \geq -\dfrac{5}{2}$.

$\therefore \quad -\dfrac{5}{2} \leq \Delta b_3 \leq 6$ or $\dfrac{3}{2} \leq b_3 \leq 10$.

Remark : The above two examples used the matrix-vector form of L.P.P. to determine the effects of changes in b_i. The same results could be obtained without using this form. Next example is intended to serve this purpose.

EXAMPLE 6.6-1.3

A factory manufactures three products A, B and C for which the data is given in the table below. Find the optimal product mix if the profit/unit is ₹ 32, ₹ 30 and ₹ 40 for product A, B and C respectively.

TABLE 6.60

	Product A	B	C	Available resources
Material required (kg/unit)	*5*	*4*	*3*	*2,500 kg*
Machine hours required/unit	*2*	*3*	*1*	*1,275 hours*
Labour hours required/unit	*3*	*2*	*4*	*2,100 hours*

(i) Find the optimal solution if machine hours available increase by 75 i.e., they become 1,350.

(ii) Find the optimal solution if labour hours available decrease by 100 i.e., they become 2,000.

(iii) Find the optimal solution if 10 units of product A are to be produced.

Solution

Mathematical model for the problem can be written as

$$\begin{aligned} \text{maximize} \quad & Z = 32x_1 + 30x_2 + 40x_3, \\ \text{subject to} \quad & 5x_1 + 4x_2 + 3x_3 \le 2{,}500, \\ & 2x_1 + 3x_2 + x_3 \le 1{,}275, \\ & 3x_1 + 2x_2 + 4x_3 \le 2{,}100, \\ & x_1, x_2, x_3 \ge 0. \end{aligned}$$

Initial basic feasible solution will be $x_1 = 0, x_2 = 0, x_3 = 0, s_1 = 2{,}500, s_2 = 1{,}275, s_3 = 2{,}100$ and $Z = 0$ and is represented in table 6.61.

TABLE 6.61

	c_j	32	30	40	0	0	0		
c_B	Basis	x_1	x_2	x_3	s_1	s_2	s_3	b	θ
0	s_1	5	4	3	1	0	0	2,500	2,500/3
0	s_2	2	3	1	0	1	0	1,275	1,275
0	s_3	3	2	(4)	0	0	1	2,100	525 ←
	Z_j	0	0	0	0	0	0	0	
	$\overline{c}_j = c_j - Z_j$	32	30	40 ↑	0	0	0		

After two iterations, the following optimal table is obtained :

TABLE 6.62

	c_j	32	30	40	0	0	0	
c_B	Basis	x_1	x_2	x_3	s_1	s_2	s_3	b
0	s_1	$3/2$	0	0	1	-1	$-1/2$	125
30	x_2	$1/2$	1	0	0	$2/5$	$-1/10$	300
40	x_3	$1/2$	0	1	0	$-1/5$	$3/10$	375
	Z_j	35	30	40	0	4	9	24,000
	$c_j - Z_j$	-3	0	0	0	-4	-9	

∴ Optimal solution is $x_1 = 0$, $x_2 = 300$ units, $x_3 = 375$ units, $Z_{max} =$ ₹ 24,000. In producing these products all the machine hours and labour hours available are consumed. However, 125 kg of material remains unutilized; only 2,375 kg of it is used.

(*i*) In table 6.62, s_2-column shows that if one machine hour is increased, 1 kg of material will remain unconsumed, product B will increase by $\frac{2}{5}$ unit and C will reduce by $-\frac{1}{5}$ unit. Therefore, if machine hours available are increased by 75, x_2 will increase by $\frac{2}{5} \times 75 = 30$ units and x_3 will decrease by $\frac{1}{5} \times 75 = 15$ units. Thus the optimal solution will be $x_1 = 0, x_2 = 330, x_3 = 360$. Further, if one machine hour remains unused, there is a loss of ₹ 4. In other words, for every additional machine hour used, there is gain of ₹ 4; the profit, therefore, will increase by ₹ 75 × 4 = ₹ 300 to attain a value of ₹ 24,300. This can also be calculated for the new solution as ₹ (0 × 125 + 30 × 330 + 40 × 360) = ₹ 24,300.

(*ii*) In table 6.62, s_3-column shows that if one labour hour available is less, it would change the value of x_2 by $-1 \times \left(-\frac{1}{10}\right) = \frac{1}{10}$ units and of x_3 by $-1 \times \frac{3}{10} = -\frac{3}{10}$ units. Therefore, a reduction of 100 labour hours in availability will increase x_2 by $\frac{1}{10} \times 100 = 10$ units and decrease x_3 by $\frac{3}{10} \times 100 = 30$ units. Also the profit will reduce by ₹ 100 × 9 = ₹ 900 and the new optimal solution would be

$$x_1 = 0,\ x_2 = 310 \text{ units},\ x_3 = 345 \text{ units};\ Z_{max} = ₹\ 23{,}100.$$

(*iii*) In table 6.62, x_1-column shows that when one unit of product A is produced, it would reduce the production of B and C each by $\frac{1}{2}$ unit. Therefore, if $x_1 = 10$, $x_2 = 300 - \frac{1}{2} \times 10 = 295$, $x_3 = 375 - \frac{1}{2} \times 10 = 370$. The profit reduces by ₹ 3 per unit of x_1 produced and hence will come down by ₹ 30 and become ₹ 23,970. This can also be calculated for the new solution as ₹ (10 × 32 + 30 × 295 + 40 × 370) = ₹ 23,970.

6.6-2 Changes in the Cost/Profit Coefficients c_j

Changes in the coefficients of the objective function may take place due to a change in cost or profit of either basic variables or non-basic variables. Each of these two cases will first be considered separately. The discussion, will then, be followed by a combined case. All the three cases will be studied by considering a few examples.

EXAMPLE 6.6-2.1

A company wants to produce three products A, B and C. The unit profits on these products are ₹ 4, ₹ 6 and ₹ 2 respectively. These products require two types of resources — man-power and material. The following L.P. model is formulated for determining the optimal product mix:

$$\text{maximize} \quad Z = 4x_1 + 6x_2 + 2x_3,$$
$$\text{subject to} \quad x_1 + x_2 + x_3 \le 3, \text{ (manpower)}$$
$$x_1 + 4x_2 + 7x_3 \le 9, \text{ (material)}$$
$$x_1, x_2, x_3 \ge 0,$$

where x_1, x_2, x_3 are the number of products A, B and C produced.

(a) Find the optimal product mix and the corresponding profit to the company.

(b) (i) Find the range on the values of non-basic variable coefficient c_3 such that the current optimal product mix remains optimal.

(ii) *What happens if c_3 is increased to ₹ 12 ? What is the new optimal product mix in this case ?* *[M.D.U. Rohtak B.E. (Mech.) Dec., 2006]*

(c) (i) *Find the range on basic variable coefficient c_1 such that the current optimal product mix remains optimal.*

(ii) *Find the effect when c_1 = ₹ 8 on the optimal product mix.*

(d) *Find the effect of changing the objective function to $Z = 2x_1 + 8x_2 + 4x_3$ on the current optimal product mix.* *[P.T.U. MBA June, 2003]*

Solution

The standard form of the problem is

$$\text{maximize} \quad Z = 4x_1 + 6x_2 + 2x_3 + 0x_4 + 0x_5,$$
$$\text{subject to} \quad x_1 + x_2 + x_3 + x_4 = 3,$$
$$x_1 + 4x_2 + 7x_3 + x_5 = 9,$$
$$x_1, x_2, x_3, x_4, x_5 \geq 0.$$

Putting $x_1 = x_2 = x_3 = 0$ in the constraint equations, we get $x_4 = 3$ and $x_5 = 9$ as the initial basic feasible solution which can be expressed in the form of a simple matrix or table as shown below. Performing iterations we get the remaining tables.

TABLE 6.63

	c_j	4	6	2	0	0			
c_B	Basis	x_1	x_2	x_3	x_4	x_5	b	θ	
0	x_4	1	1	1	1	0	3	3	
0	x_5	1	(4)	7	0	1	9	9/4	←
$Z_j = \Sigma c_B a_{ij}$		0	0	0	0	0			
$\bar{c}_j = c_j - Z_j$		4	6	2	0	0			
			↑						

Initial feasible solution

TABLE 6.64

	c_j	4	6	2	0	0			
c_B	Basis	x_1	x_2	x_3	x_4	x_5	b	θ	
0	x_4	$(3/4)$	0	$-3/4$	1	$-1/4$	$3/4$	1	←
6	x_2	$1/4$	1	$7/4$	0	$1/4$	$9/4$	9	
$Z_j = \Sigma c_B a_{ij}$		$3/2$	6	$21/2$	0	$3/2$			
$\bar{c}_j = c_j - Z_j$		$5/2$	0	$-17/2$	0	$-3/2$			
		↑							

Second feasible solution

TABLE 6.65

	c_j	4	6	2	0	0	
c_B	Basis	x_1	x_2	x_3	x_4	x_5	b
4	x_1	1	0	-1	$4/3$	$-1/3$	1
6	x_2	0	1	2	$-1/3$	$1/3$	2
$Z_j = \Sigma c_B a_{ij}$		4	6	8	$10/3$	$2/3$	
$\bar{c}_j = c_j - Z_j$		0	0	-6	$-10/3$	$-2/3$	

Optimal feasible solution

∴ Optimal solution is $x_1 = 1$, $x_2 = 2$, $x_3 = 0$ and Z_{max} = ₹ $(4 \times 1 + 6 \times 2 + 2 \times 0)$ = ₹ 16.

Effect of changing the objective function coefficient of a non-basic variable

(*b*) (*i*) The coefficient c_3 corresponds to the non-basic variable x_3 for product C. In the optimal product mix shown in table 6.65, product C is not produced because of the low associated profit of ₹ 2 per unit (c_3). Clearly, if c_3 further decreases, it will have no effect on the current optimal product mix. However, if c_3 is increased beyond a certain value, it may become profitable to produce the product C.

As a rule, the sensitivity of the current optimal solution is determined by studying how the current optimal solution given in table 6.65 changes as a result of changes in the input data. When value of c_3 changes, the value of net evaluation (relative profit coefficient) of the nonbasic variable x_3 *i.e.*, $\overline{c}_3$ in table 6.65 also changes. The table will remain optimal, as long as $\overline{c}_3$ remains non-positive.

∴ For table 6.65 to remain optimal, $\overline{c}_3 \le 0$

$$\text{or} \quad c_3 - (4, 6)\begin{bmatrix} -1 \\ 2 \end{bmatrix} \le 0$$

$$\text{or} \quad c_3 - (-4 + 12) \le 0$$

$$\text{or} \quad c_3 \le 8.$$

This means that as long as the unit profit of product C is less than ₹ 8, it is not profitable to produce it. The current optimal solution remains optimal.

(*ii*) If
$$c_3 = 12, \ \overline{c}_3 = c_3 - (4, 6)\begin{bmatrix} -1 \\ 2 \end{bmatrix}$$
$$= 12 - (-4 + 12) = 12 - 8 = 4.$$

As $\overline{c}_3$ becomes positive, the current product mix given by table 6.65 does not remain optimal. The optimal profit can be increased further by producing product C. Non-basic variable x_3 can enter the solution to increase Z. This is shown in table 6.66.

TABLE 6.66

	c_j	4	6	12	0	0			
c_B	Basis	x_1	x_2	x_3	x_4	x_5	b	θ	
4	x_1	1	0	–1	$4/3$	$-1/3$	1	–1	
6	x_2	0	1	(2)	$-1/3$	$1/3$	2	1	←
$Z_j = \Sigma c_B a_{ij}$		4	6	8	$10/3$	$2/3$			
$\overline{c}_j = c_j - Z_j$		0	0	4 ↑	$-10/3$	$-2/3$			

Replace x_2 by x_3.

TABLE 6.67

	c_j	4	6	12	0	0	
c_B	Basis	x_1	x_2	x_3	x_4	x_5	b
4	x_1	1	$1/2$	0	$7/6$	$-1/6$	2
12	x_3	0	$1/2$	1	$-1/6$	$1/6$	1
$Z_j = \Sigma c_B a_{ij}$		4	8	12	$8/3$	$4/3$	
$\overline{c}_j = c_j - Z_j$		0	–2	0	$-8/3$	$-4/3$	

Optimal feasible solution

∴ New optimal product mix is $x_1 = 2, x_2 = 0, x_3 = 1$ and Z_{max} = ₹ (4 × 2 + 6 × 0 + 12 × 1) = ₹ 20.

Effect of changing the objective function coefficient of a basic variable

(*c*) (*i*) Clearly, when c_1 decreases below a certain level, it may no longer remain profitable to produce product A. On the other hand, if c_1 increases beyond a certain value, it may becomes so profitable that it is most paying to produce only product A. In either case the optimal product mix will change and hence there is lower as well as upper limit on c_1 within which the optimal product mix will not be affected.

Referring again to table 6.65, it can be seen that any variation in c_1 (and/or in c_2 also) will not change $\bar{c}_1$ and $\bar{c}_2$ (*i.e.*, they remain zero), while $\bar{c}_3, \bar{c}_4, \bar{c}_5$ will change. However, as long as $\bar{c}_j$ ($j = 3, 4, 5$) remain non-positive, table 6.65 will remain optimal. $\bar{c}_3, \bar{c}_4$ and $\bar{c}_5$ can be expressed as functions of c_1 as follows :

$$\bar{c}_3 = 2 - (c_1, 6)\begin{bmatrix}-1\\2\end{bmatrix} = 2 - (-c_1 + 12) = c_1 - 10,$$

$$\bar{c}_4 = 0 - (c_1, 6)\begin{bmatrix}\frac{4}{3}\\-\frac{1}{3}\end{bmatrix} = 0 - \left(\frac{4}{3}c_1 - 2\right) = -\frac{4}{3}c_1 + 2,$$

$$\bar{c}_5 = 0 - (c_1, 6)\begin{bmatrix}-\frac{1}{3}\\\frac{1}{3}\end{bmatrix} = 0 - \left(-\frac{1}{3}c_1 + 2\right) = \frac{1}{3}c_1 - 2.$$

For $\bar{c}_3$ to be ≤ 0, $c_1 - 10 \leq 0$ or $c_1 \leq 10$,

for $\bar{c}_4$ to be ≤ 0, $-\frac{4}{3}c_1 + 2 \leq 0$ or $c_1 \geq \frac{3}{2}$,

for $\bar{c}_5$ to be ≤ 0, $\frac{1}{3}c_1 - 2 \leq 0$ or $c_1 \leq 6$.

∴ Range on c_1 for the optimal product mix to remain optimal is $\frac{3}{2} \leq c_1 \leq 6$. Thus so long as c_1 lies within these limits, the optimal solution in table 6.65 viz., $x_1 = 1, x_2 = 2, x_3 = 0$ remains optimal. However, within this range, as the value of c_1 is changed, Z_{max} undergoes a change. For example, when $c_1 = 3$, Z_{max} = ₹ (3 × 1 + 6 × 2) = ₹ 15.

(*ii*) When $c_1 = 8,\ \bar{c}_3 = c_1 - 10 = 8 - 10 = -2,$

$$\bar{c}_4 = -\frac{4}{3}c_1 + 2 = -\frac{4}{3} \times 8 + 2 = -\frac{26}{3},$$

$$\bar{c}_5 = \frac{1}{3}c_1 - 2 = \frac{8}{3} - 2 = +\frac{2}{3},$$

$$\bar{c}_1 = \bar{c}_2 = 0.$$

As $\bar{c}_5$ becomes positive, the solution given in table 6.65 no longer remains optimal. Slack variable x_5 enters the solution. This is shown in table 6.68.

TABLE 6.68

	c_j	8	6	2	0	0		
c_B	Basis	x_1	x_2	x_3	x_4	x_5	b	θ
8	x_1	1	0	–1	$4/3$	$-1/3$	1	–3
6	x_2	0	1	2	$-1/3$	$(1/3)$	2	6 ←

$Z_j = \Sigma c_B a_{ij}$		8	6	4	$26/3$	$-2/3$	
$\bar{c}_j = c_j - Z_j$		0	0	-2	$-26/3$	$2/3$ ↑	

Replace x_2 by x_5.

TABLE 6.69

	c_j	8	6	2	0	0	
c_B	Basis	x_1	x_2	x_3	x_4	x_5	b
8	x_1	1	1	1	1	0	3
0	x_5	0	3	6	-1	1	6
$Z_j = \Sigma c_B a_{ij}$		8	8	8	8	0	
$\bar{c}_j = c_j - Z_j$		0	-2	-6	-8	0	

Optimal feasible solution

Thus the optimal product mix changes to $x_1 = 3$, $x_2 = 0$ and $x_3 = 0$ units with $Z_{\max} =$ ₹ 24.

Effect of changing the objective function coefficients of basic as well as non-basic variables

(*d*) The effect on the optimal product mix can be determined by checking whether the $\bar{c}_j$-row in table 6.65 remains non-positive.

$$\bar{c}_1 = 0,\ \bar{c}_2 = 0,$$

$$\bar{c}_3 = 4 - (2, 8)\begin{bmatrix}-1\\2\end{bmatrix} = 4 - (-2 + 16) = -10 < 0,$$

$$\bar{c}_4 = 0 - (2, 8)\begin{bmatrix}\frac{4}{3}\\-\frac{1}{3}\end{bmatrix} = 0 - \left(\frac{8}{3} - \frac{8}{3}\right) = 0,$$

$$\bar{c}_5 = 0 - (2, 8)\begin{bmatrix}-\frac{1}{3}\\\frac{1}{3}\end{bmatrix} = 0 - (-2/3 + 8/3) = -2 < 0.$$

Hence the optimal solution does not change. The optimal product mix remains $x_1 = 1$, $x_2 = 2$, $x_3 = 0$ and $Z_{\max} =$ ₹ $(1 \times 2 + 2 \times 8 + 0 \times 4) =$ ₹ 18. There is indication of an alternate optimal solution since $\bar{c}_4 = 0$.

EXAMPLE 6.6-2.2

Given the L.P. problem

maximize $Z = -x_1 + 2x_2 - x_3,$

subject to $3x_1 + x_2 - x_3 \le 10,$

$-x_1 + 4x_2 + x_3 \ge 6,$

$x_2 + x_3 \le 4,$

$x_1, x_2, x_3 \ge 0,$

determine the effect of discrete changes in c_j ($j = 1, 2, ..., 6$) on the optimal basic feasible solution given by table 6.70.

TABLE 6.70

	c_j	−1	2	−1	0	0	0	−M	
c_B	Basis	x_1	x_2	x_3	x_4	x_5	x_6	A_1	b
0	x_4	3	0	−2	1	0	−1	0	6
2	x_2	0	1	1	0	0	1	0	4
0	x_5	1	0	3	0	1	4	−1	10
	Z_j	0	2	2	0	0	2	0	8
	$\bar{c}_j$	−1	0	−3	0	0	−2	−M	

Solution

x_1 is a non-basic variable with $c_1 = -1$. If c_1 further decreases, x_1 will not enter the basis and hence will not affect the optimality of the solution. There is, thus, no lower limit on the value of c_1. However, if c_1 increases and exceeds a certain value, it may become profitable to have x_1 in the basis. There is, thus, an upper limit on the value of c_1.

Table 6.70 remains optimal if $\bar{c}_1$ remains non-positive.

i.e., $$\bar{c}_1 \le 0$$

or $$c_1 - (0, 2, 0)\begin{bmatrix}3\\0\\1\end{bmatrix} \le 0$$

or $$c_1 \le 0.$$

x_2 is a basic variable. The table remains optimal so long as $\bar{c}_j$ coefficient for the non-basic variables remain non-positive *i.e.,* so long as

$$\bar{c}_1 = -1 - (0, c_2, 0)\begin{bmatrix}3\\0\\1\end{bmatrix} \le 0 \text{ or } -1 < 0, \text{ which is so,}$$

$$\bar{c}_3 = -1 - (0, c_2, 0)\begin{bmatrix}-2\\1\\3\end{bmatrix} \le 0 \text{ or } -1 - c_2 \le 0 \text{ or } c_2 \ge -1,$$

$$\bar{c}_6 = 0 - (0, c_2, 0)\begin{bmatrix}-1\\1\\4\end{bmatrix} \le 0 \text{ or } 0 - c_2 \le 0 \text{ or } c_2 \ge 0,$$

$$\bar{c}_7 = -M - (0, c_2, 0)\begin{bmatrix}0\\0\\-1\end{bmatrix} \le 0 \text{ or } -M - 0 \le 0 \text{ or } -M \le 0, \text{ which is so.}$$

∴ $$c_2 \ge 0.$$

x_3 is a non-basic variable. To find its limiting value,

$$\bar{c}_3 \le 0$$

or $$c_3 - (0, 2, 0)\begin{bmatrix}-2\\1\\3\end{bmatrix} \le 0 \text{ or } c_3 - 2 \le 0 \text{ or } c_3 \le 2.$$

x_4 is a basic variable. Its limiting value is obtained from $\bar{c}_1, \bar{c}_3, \bar{c}_6$ and $\bar{c}_7$ as follows :

$$\overline{c}_1 = -1 - (c_4, 2, 0)\begin{bmatrix}3\\0\\1\end{bmatrix} \le 0 \text{ or } -1 - 3c_4 \le 0 \text{ or } c_4 \ge -\frac{1}{3},$$

$$\overline{c}_3 = -1 - (c_4, 2, 0)\begin{bmatrix}-2\\1\\3\end{bmatrix} \le 0 \text{ or } -1 + 2c_4 - 2 \le 0 \text{ or } c_4 \le \frac{3}{2},$$

$$\overline{c}_6 = 0 - (c_4, 2, 0)\begin{bmatrix}-1\\1\\4\end{bmatrix} \le 0 \text{ or } 0 + c_4 - 2 \le 0 \text{ or } c_4 \le 2, \text{ and}$$

$$\overline{c}_7 = -M - (c_4, 2, 0)\begin{bmatrix}0\\0\\-1\end{bmatrix} \le 0 \text{ or } -M \le 0, \text{ which is true.}$$

∴ Limits for c_4 are

$$-\frac{1}{3} \le c_4 \le \frac{3}{2}.$$

x_5 is a basic variable. Its limiting value is obtained from $\overline{c}_1, \overline{c}_3, \overline{c}_6$ and $\overline{c}_7$ as follows:

$$\overline{c}_1 = -1 - (0, 2, c_5)\begin{bmatrix}3\\0\\1\end{bmatrix} \le 0 \text{ or } -1 - c_5 \le 0 \text{ or } c_5 \ge -1,$$

$$\overline{c}_3 = -1 - (0, 2, c_5)\begin{bmatrix}-2\\1\\3\end{bmatrix} \le 0 \text{ or } -1 - (2 + 3c_5) \le 0 \text{ or } c_5 \ge -1,$$

$$\overline{c}_6 = 0 - (0, 2, c_5)\begin{bmatrix}-1\\1\\4\end{bmatrix} \le 0 \text{ or } 0 - (2 + 4c_5) \le 0 \text{ or } c_5 \ge -\frac{1}{2},$$

$$\overline{c}_7 = -M - (0, 2, c_5)\begin{bmatrix}0\\0\\-1\end{bmatrix} \le 0 \text{ or } -M + c_5 \le 0 \text{ or } c_5 \le M.$$

$$\therefore \qquad -\frac{1}{2} \le c_5 \text{ or } c_5 \ge -\frac{1}{2}.$$

x_6 is a non-basic variable. To find its limiting value, $\overline{c}_6 \le 0$

$$\text{or} \quad c_6 - (0, 2, 0)\begin{bmatrix}-1\\1\\4\end{bmatrix} \le 0 \text{ or } c_6 - 2 \le 0 \text{ or } c_6 \le 2.$$

EXAMPLE 6.6-2.3

Consider the L.P. problem

$$\text{maximize} \quad Z = 3x_1 + 5x_2 + 4x_3,$$
$$\text{subject to} \quad 2x_1 + 3x_2 \le 8,$$

$$2x_2 + 5x_3 \le 10,$$
$$3x_1 + 2x_2 + 4x_3 \le 15,$$
$$x_1, x_2, x_3 \ge 0.$$

The optimal table is given below.

TABLE 6.71

	c_j	3	5	4	0	0	0	
c_B	Basis	x_1	x_2	x_3	x_4	x_5	x_6	b
5	x_2	0	1	0	$15/41$	$8/41$	$-10/41$	$50/41$
4	x_3	0	0	1	$-6/41$	$5/41$	$4/41$	$62/41$
3	x_1	1	0	0	$-2/41$	$-12/41$	$15/41$	$89/41$
	Z_j	3	5	4	$45/41$	$24/41$	$11/41$	$765/41$
	$\bar{c}_j$	0	0	0	$-45/41$	$-24/41$	$-11/41$	

(a) How much c_3 and c_4 can be increased till the optimal solution given by table 6.71 ceases to be optimal? Also find the new value of the objective function if possible.

(b) Find the range over which b_2 can be changed maintaining the feasibility of the solution. [Chennai B.Sc. (Math.) 1976 ; Delhi B.Sc. (Math.) 1995]

Solution

(a) (i) Variation in c_3 : x_3 is a basic variable. To find its limiting value(s), $\bar{c}_j$ coefficients should be calculated. c_3 can be changed only as long as $\bar{c}_j$ coefficients for the non-basic variables (for $j = 4, 5, 6$) remain non-positive.

i.e.,
$$\bar{c}_4 = 0 - (5, c_3, 3)\begin{bmatrix}15/41\\-6/41\\-2/41\end{bmatrix} \le 0 \text{ or } -\left[\frac{75}{41} - \frac{6}{41}c_3 - \frac{6}{41}\right] \le 0 \text{ or } c_3 \le \frac{23}{2},$$

$$\bar{c}_5 = 0 - (5, c_3, 3)\begin{bmatrix}8/41\\5/41\\-12/41\end{bmatrix} \le 0 \text{ or } -\left[\frac{40}{41} + \frac{5}{41}c_3 - \frac{36}{41}\right] \le 0 \text{ or } c_3 \ge -\frac{4}{5},$$

$$\bar{c}_6 = 0 - (5, c_3, 3)\begin{bmatrix}-10/41\\4/41\\15/41\end{bmatrix} \le 0 \text{ or } -\left[-\frac{50}{41} + \frac{4}{41}c_3 + \frac{45}{41}\right] \le 0 \text{ or } c_3 \ge \frac{5}{4}.$$

$$\therefore \qquad \frac{5}{4} \le c_3 \le \frac{23}{2}.$$

Value of the objective function varies from $\dfrac{594.5}{41}$ to $\dfrac{1,230}{41}$.

(ii) Variation in c_4 : x_4 is a non-basic variable. Value of x_4 can be increased only so long as $\bar{c}_4$ remains ≤ 0.

or
$$c_4 - (5, 4, 3)\begin{bmatrix}15/41\\-6/41\\-2/41\end{bmatrix} \le 0$$

or $$c_4 - \left[\frac{75}{41} - \frac{24}{41} - \frac{6}{41}\right] \leq 0$$

or $$c_4 \leq \frac{45}{41}.$$

There is no limit on the lower value of c_4.

$\therefore$ $$-\infty \leq c_4 \leq \frac{45}{41}.$$

The value of the objective function remains $\frac{765}{41}$.

(*b*) $$\mathbf{B}^{-1} = \begin{bmatrix} \frac{15}{41} & \frac{8}{41} & -\frac{10}{41} \\ -\frac{6}{41} & \frac{5}{41} & \frac{4}{41} \\ -\frac{2}{41} & -\frac{12}{41} & \frac{15}{41} \end{bmatrix}$$

Therefore, the new values of the current basic variables when b_2 changes from 10 to 10 + Δb_2, say, are given by

$$\begin{bmatrix} x_2 \\ x_3 \\ x_1 \end{bmatrix} = \mathbf{B}^{-1}\mathbf{b} = \begin{bmatrix} \frac{15}{41} & \frac{8}{41} & -\frac{10}{41} \\ -\frac{6}{41} & \frac{5}{41} & \frac{4}{41} \\ -\frac{2}{41} & -\frac{12}{41} & \frac{15}{41} \end{bmatrix} \begin{bmatrix} 8 \\ 10 + \Delta b_2 \\ 15 \end{bmatrix} \geq \begin{bmatrix} 0 \\ 0 \\ 0 \end{bmatrix}$$

or $$\frac{120}{41} + \frac{80}{41} + \frac{8}{41}\Delta b_2 - \frac{150}{41} \geq 0 \text{ or } \Delta b_2 \geq -\frac{25}{4},$$

$$-\frac{48}{41} + \frac{50}{41} + \frac{5}{41}\Delta b_2 + \frac{60}{41} \geq 0 \text{ or } \Delta b_2 \geq -\frac{62}{5},$$

$$-\frac{16}{41} - \frac{120}{41} - \frac{12}{41}\Delta b_2 + \frac{225}{41} \geq 0 \text{ or } \Delta b_2 \leq \frac{89}{12}.$$

$\therefore$ Limiting range for Δb_2 is $-\frac{25}{4} \leq \Delta b_2 \leq \frac{89}{12}$

or $$\frac{15}{4} \leq b_2 \leq \frac{209}{12}.$$

6.6-3 Addition of a New Variable

Addition of a new variable in physical sense means introduction of a new product to the current product mix. Intuitively, it is desirable only if it is profitable *i.e.*, if it improves the optimal value of the objective function.

EXAMPLE 6.6-3.1

Referring to example 6.6-2.1, let us suppose that Research and Development department of the company has proposed a fourth product D which requires 1 unit of manpower and 1 unit of material and earns a unit profit of ₹ 3 when sold in the market. It is desired to find whether it is profitable to produce product D.

Solution

Addition of this product in the already existing product mix is equivalent to addition of a new variable (say x_6) and a column $\begin{bmatrix}1\\1\end{bmatrix}$ in the initial table (table 6.63). Now the present optimal product mix given by the table 6.65 remains optimal so long as the relative profit coefficient (net evaluation) of this new product, say $\bar{c}_6$ remains non-positive.

Now from the revised simplex method we know that

$$\bar{c}_6 = c_6 - c_B\,\bar{\mathbf{P}}_6 = c_6 - c_B\,.\,\mathbf{B}^{-1}\mathbf{P}_6 = c_6 - \boldsymbol{\pi}\mathbf{P}_6,$$

where $c_6 = ₹\ 3$, $\mathbf{P}_6 = \begin{bmatrix}1\\1\end{bmatrix}$ and π is the simplex multiplier corresponding to the current optimal solution contained in table 6.65 and is given by

$$\boldsymbol{\pi} = c_B\,\mathbf{B}^{-1}$$

$$= (4, 6)\begin{bmatrix}\frac{4}{3} & -\frac{1}{3}\\ -\frac{1}{3} & \frac{1}{3}\end{bmatrix} = \left(\frac{10}{3}, \frac{2}{3}\right).$$

$$\therefore \qquad \bar{c}_6 = 3 - \left(\frac{10}{3}, \frac{2}{3}\right)\begin{bmatrix}1\\1\end{bmatrix} = 3 - \left(\frac{10}{3} + \frac{2}{3}\right) = -1.$$

As $\bar{c}_6$ is non-positive, the present optimal solution does not change even after the product D is introduced. As product D cannot improve the present value of the maximum profit, it should not be produced.

If, however, $\bar{c}_6$ turns out to be positive, it follows that product D can increase the value of maximum profit; simplex method can then be applied to find the new optimal solution.

EXAMPLE 6.6-3.2

Consider the problem

$$\begin{aligned} &\textit{maximize} && Z = 45x_1 + 100x_2 + 30x_3 + 50x_4,\\ &\textit{subject to} && 7x_1 + 10x_2 + 4x_3 + 9x_4 \le 1{,}200,\\ &&& 3x_1 + 40x_2 + x_3 + x_4 \le 800,\\ &&& x_1, x_2, x_3, x_4 \ge 0. \end{aligned}$$

The optimal table for this problem is given below.

TABLE 6.72

	c_j	45	100	30	50	0	0	
c_B	Basis	x_1	x_2	x_3	x_4	x_5	x_6	b
30	x_3	$5/3$	0	1	$7/3$	$4/15$	$-1/15$	$400/3$
100	x_2	$1/30$	1	0	$-1/30$	$-1/150$	$2/75$	$40/3$
$\bar{c}_j = c_j - Z_j$		$-25/3$	0	0	$-50/3$	$-22/3$	$-2/3$	

If a new variable x_7 is added to this problem with a column $\begin{bmatrix}10\\10\end{bmatrix}$ and $c_7 = 120$, find the change in the optimal solution.

Solution

$$\bar{c}_7 = c_7 - c_B\,\bar{\mathbf{P}}_7 = c_7 - c_B\,.\,\mathbf{B}^{-1}\,.\,\mathbf{P}_7 = c_7 - \boldsymbol{\pi}\mathbf{P}_7,$$

where $c_7 = 120$, $\mathbf{P}_7 = \begin{bmatrix}10\\10\end{bmatrix}$ and $\boldsymbol{\pi}$, the simplex multiplier corresponding to the original optimal solution in table 6.72 is given by

$$\boldsymbol{\pi} = (\pi_1, \pi_2) = c_B\,\mathbf{B}^{-1} = (30,100)\begin{bmatrix}\frac{4}{15} & -\frac{1}{15}\\ -\frac{1}{150} & \frac{2}{75}\end{bmatrix} = \left(\frac{22}{3}, \frac{2}{3}\right).$$

$$\therefore \qquad \bar{c}_7 = c_7 - \boldsymbol{\pi}\mathbf{P}_7 = 120 - \left(\frac{22}{3}, \frac{2}{3}\right)\begin{bmatrix}10\\10\end{bmatrix} = 120 - \left(\frac{220}{3} + \frac{20}{3}\right) = +40.$$

Since $\bar{c}_7$ is positive, the existing optimal solution can be improved.

$$\text{Now} \qquad \bar{\mathbf{P}}_7 = \mathbf{B}^{-1}\mathbf{P}_7 = \begin{bmatrix}\frac{4}{15} & -\frac{1}{15}\\ -\frac{1}{150} & \frac{2}{75}\end{bmatrix}\begin{bmatrix}10\\10\end{bmatrix} = \begin{bmatrix}2\\ \frac{1}{5}\end{bmatrix}.$$

Now we start with the original optimal table (table 6.72) and add entries corresponding to variable x_7 as follows :

TABLE 6.73

c_B	c_j Basis	45 x_1	100 x_2	30 x_3	50 x_4	0 x_5	0 x_6	120 x_7	b	θ	
30	x_3	$5/3$	0	1	$7/3$	$4/15$	$-1/15$	2	$800/3$	$400/3$	
100	x_2	$1/30$	1	0	$-1/30$	$-1/150$	$2/75$	$(1/5)$	$40/3$	$200/3$	←Key row
$\bar{c}_j = c_j - Z_j$		$-25/3$	0	0	$-50/3$	$-22/3$	$-2/3$	+40			
								↑K			

Replace x_2 by x_7.

TABLE 6.74

c_B	c_j Basis	45 x_1	100 x_2	30 x_3	50 x_4	0 x_5	0 x_6	120 x_7	b
30	x_3	$4/3$	−10	1	$8/3$	$1/3$	$-1/3$	0	$400/3$
120	x_7	$1/6$	5	0	$-1/6$	$-1/30$	$2/15$	1	$200/3$
$Z_j = \Sigma c_B a_{ij}$		60	300	30	60	6	6	120	
$\bar{c}_j = c_j - Z_j$		−15	−200	0	−10	−6	−6	0	

Optimal feasible solution

Since $\bar{c}_j$ is negative, table 6.74 gives the optimal solution with $x_3 = 400/3$, $x_7 = 200/3$ (basic variables), $x_1 = x_2 = x_4 = x_5 = x_6 = 0$ (non-basic variables) and $Z_{max} = 30 \times 400/3 + 120 \times 200/3 = 4{,}000 + 8{,}000 = 12{,}000$.

6.6-4 Changes in the Coefficients of the Constraints (Technological Coefficients) a_{ij}

When changes take place in the constraint coefficients of a *non-basic variable* in a current optimal solution, feasibility of the solution is not affected. The only effect, if any, may be on the optimality of the solution. This effect can be studied by following the steps given in section 6.6-3.

However, if the constraint coefficients of a *basic variable* get changed, things become more complicated since the feasibility of the current optimal solution may also be affected (lost). The basic matrix is affected, which, in turn, may affect all the quantities given in the current optimal table. Under such circumstances, it may be better to solve the problem all over again.

EXAMPLE 6.6-4.1

Find the effect of the following changes in the original optimal table 6.72 of problem 6.6-3.2 :

(a) 'x_1'-column in the problem changes from $\begin{bmatrix} 7 \\ 3 \end{bmatrix}$ *to* $\begin{bmatrix} 7 \\ 5 \end{bmatrix}$.

(b) 'x_1'-column changes from $\begin{bmatrix} 7 \\ 3 \end{bmatrix}$ *to* $\begin{bmatrix} 5 \\ 8 \end{bmatrix}$.

Solution

(*a*) x_1 is a non-basic variable in the optimal solution.

$$\overline{c}_1 = c_1 - c_B\,\overline{\mathbf{P}}_1 = c_1 - c_B\,\mathbf{B}^{-1}\mathbf{P}_1$$

$$= c_1 - \boldsymbol{\pi}\mathbf{P}_1, \text{ where } c_1 = 45,\ \mathbf{P}_1 = \begin{bmatrix} 7 \\ 5 \end{bmatrix},$$

$$\text{and } \boldsymbol{\pi} = c_B\boldsymbol{B}^{-1} = (30, 100)\begin{bmatrix} \frac{4}{15} & -\frac{1}{15} \\ -\frac{1}{150} & \frac{2}{75} \end{bmatrix} = \left(\frac{22}{3}, \frac{2}{3}\right).$$

$$\therefore\ \overline{c}_1 = 45 - \left(\frac{22}{3}, \frac{2}{3}\right)\begin{bmatrix} 7 \\ 5 \end{bmatrix} = 45 - \left(\frac{154}{3} + \frac{10}{3}\right) = 45 - \frac{164}{3} = -\frac{29}{3}$$

Since $\overline{c}_1$ remains non-positive, the origianl optimum solution remains optimum for the new problem also.

(*b*) $\overline{c}_1 = c_1 - c_B\,\overline{\mathbf{P}}_1 = c_1 - c_B\boldsymbol{B}^{-1}\mathbf{P}_1$

$$= c_1 - \boldsymbol{\pi}\mathbf{P}_1 = 45 - \left(\frac{22}{3}, \frac{2}{3}\right)\begin{bmatrix} 5 \\ 8 \end{bmatrix} = 45 - \left(\frac{110}{3} + \frac{16}{3}\right) = +\,3.$$

As $\overline{c}_1$ is positive, the existing optimum solution can be improved.

$$\text{Now } \overline{\mathbf{P}}_1 = \mathbf{B}^{-1}\mathbf{P}_1 = \begin{bmatrix} \frac{4}{15} & -\frac{1}{5} \\ -\frac{1}{150} & \frac{2}{75} \end{bmatrix}\begin{bmatrix} 5 \\ 8 \end{bmatrix} = \begin{bmatrix} \frac{4}{5} \\ \frac{27}{150} \end{bmatrix}.$$

Now we start with the original optimal table (table 6.72) and incorporate the changes due to variable x_1.

TABLE 6.75

	c_j	45	100	30	50	0	0		
c_B	Basis	x_1	x_2	x_3	x_4	x_5	x_6	b	θ
30	x_3	$4/5$	0	1	$7/3$	$4/15$	$-1/15$	$800/3$	$1,000/3$
100	x_2	$(27/150)$	1	0	$-1/30$	$-1/150$	$2/75$	$40/3$	$2,000/27$ ← key row
	$\bar{c}_j = c_j - Z_j$	+3 ↑K	0	0	$-50/3$	$-22/3$	$-2/3$		

Replace x_2 by x_1.

TABLE 6.76

	c_j	45	100	30	50	0	0	
c_B	Basis	x_1	x_2	x_3	x_4	x_5	x_6	b
30	x_3	0	$-40/9$	1	$67/27$	$8/27$	$-5/27$	$5,600/27$
45	x_1	1	$50/9$	0	$-5/27$	$-1/27$	$4/27$	$2,000/27$
$Z_j = \Sigma c_B a_{ij}$		45	$350/3$	30	$595/9$	$65/9$	$10/9$	
$\bar{c}_j = c_j - Z_j$		0	$-50/3$	0	$-145/9$	$-65/9$	$-10/9$	

Optimal feasible solution

Since $\bar{c}_j$ is non-positive, table 6.76 gives the optimal solution with

$$x_1 = \frac{2,000}{27},\ x_3 = \frac{5,600}{27} \quad \text{(basic variables)},$$

$$x_2 = x_4 = x_5 = x_6 = 0 \quad \text{(non-basic variables)},$$

$$Z_{\max} = \frac{2,000}{27} \times 45 + \frac{5,600}{27} \times 30 = \frac{10,000}{3} + \frac{56,000}{9} = \frac{86,000}{9}.$$

6.6-5 Addition of a New Constraint

Addition of a new constraint may or may not affect the feasibility of the current optimal solution. For this, it is sufficient to check whether new constraint is satisfied by the current optimal solution or not. If it is satisfied, the inclusion of the constraint has no effect on the current optimal solution *i.e.*, it remains feasible as well as optimal. If, however, the constraint is not satisfied, the current optimal solution becomes infeasible. Dual simplex method is then used to find the new optimal solution.

EXAMPLE 6.6-5.1

(a) In problem 6.6-2.1 an administrative constraint is added. Products A, B and C require 2, 3 and 2 hours of administrative services, while the total available administrative hours are 10. How does the optimal solution given by table 6.65 change ?

(b) If the total available administrative time is 4 hours, find the new optimal solution.

Solution

(*a*) The optimal feasible solution given by table 6.65 is $x_1 = 1, x_2 = 2, x_3 = 0$; while the additional constraint is $2x_1 + 3x_2 + 2x_3 \le 10$. As this constraint is satisfied by the optimal solution, the solution remains feasible and optimal for the modified problem.

(*b*) As the additional constraint $2x_1 + 3x_2 + 2x_3 \le 4$ is not satisfied by the current optimal solution, table 6.65 is no longer optimal for the modified problem. In order to find the new optimal solution, we add the new constraint as the third row in table 6.77. Using s_3 as the slack variable for this constraint, the (modified) optimal table may be written as

TABLE 6.77

c_B	c_j Basis	4 x_1	6 x_2	2 x_3	0 x_4	0 x_5	0 x_6	b
4	x_1	1	0	–1	$4/3$	$-1/3$	0	1
6	x_2	0	1	2	$-1/3$	$1/3$	0	2
0	x_6	2	3	2	0	0	1	4
$Z_j = \Sigma c_B a_{ij}$		4	6	8	$10/3$	$2/3$	0	
$\overline{c}_j = c_j - Z_j$		0	0	–6	$-10/3$	$-2/3$	0	

Since x_1 and x_2 are in the basic solution, their corresponding coefficients in the basic constraint must be zero. To eliminate the coefficients of x_1 and x_2, we multiply the first row by –2, the second row by –3 and add them to the third row. Table 6.78 represents the new table after the row operations. Note that $\overline{c}_j$ -row is not affected since the new basic variable x_6 is the slack variable.

TABLE 6.78

c_B	c_j Basis	4 x_1	6 x_2	2 x_3	0 x_4	0 x_5	0 x_6	b	
4	x_1	1	0	–1	$4/3$	$-1/3$	0	1	
6	x_2	0	1	2	$-1/3$	$1/3$	0	2	
0	x_6	0	0	(–6)	$-5/3$	$-1/3$	1	–4	← *Key row*
$Z_j = \Sigma c_B a_{ij}$		4	6	8	$10/3$	$2/3$	0		
$\overline{c}_j = c_j - Z_j$		0	0	–6	$-10/3$	$-2/3$	0		
				↑K					

In table 6.78, $\overline{c}_j$ -row is optimal, but since b_3 is negative, the current basic solution is infeasible. In other words, table 6.78 is dual feasible and, therefore, dual simplex method is applied to find the new optimal solution.

Evidently x_6 is the variable that leaves the basis. The ratios for the non-basic variables are 1, 2, 2 respectively. The variable x_3 which corresponds to the minimum ratio is the entering variable. The key element, –6 has been shown bracketed. Regular simplex method is used to find the optimal solution.

Replace x_6 by x_3.

TABLE 6.79

c_B	c_j Basis	4 x_1	6 x_2	2 x_3	0 x_4	0 x_5	0 x_6	b
4	x_1	1	0	0	$29/18$	$-5/18$	$-1/6$	$5/3$
6	x_2	0	1	0	$-8/9$	$2/9$	$1/3$	$2/3$
2	x_3	0	0	1	$5/18$	$1/18$	$-1/6$	$2/3$
$Z_j = \Sigma c_B a_{ij}$		4	6	2	$5/3$	$1/3$	1	
$\overline{c}_j = c_j - Z_j$		0	0	0	$-5/3$	$-1/3$	–1	

Optimal feasible solution

Table 6.79 is optimal and the optimal product mix is to produce 5/3 units of product A, 2/3 units of product B and 2/3 units of product C with the new maximum profit = ₹ (4 × 5/3 + 6 × 2/3 + 2 × 2/3) = ₹ 12. Thus the addition of a new constraint decreases the optimum profit from ₹ 16 (table 6.65) to ₹ 12. This is true of every linear programming problem. In general, whenever a new constraint is added to a linear programming problem, the old optimal value will always be better or at least equal to the new optimal value. In other words, addition of a new constraint cannot improve the optimal value of any linear programming problem.

The idea of adding new constraints can sometimes be used to reduce the computational time and hence cost of solving a linear programming problem. As the computational effort in solving a linear programming problem increases with the number of constraints, it will be advantageous to identify and delete the constraints that are not binding. Such constraints are called *inactive or secondary constraints*. These may pertain to resources which can be obtained easily or can be directly controlled. The new problem with fewer number of constraints is then solved. After the optimal solution is obtained, the secondary constraints are added to verify whether the optimal solution satisfies them or not. If not, the dual simplex method is applied to get the new optimal solution. No doubt, the overall saving in computational time and cost will depend on how accurately the initial judgements were made while identifying the secondary constraints.

6.6-6 Deletion of a Variable

Deletion of a *non-basiç variable* is a totally superfluous operation and does not affect the feasibility and/or optimality of the current optimal solution. However, deletion of a *basic variable* may affect the optimality and a new optimum solution may have to be found out. For this, a heavy penality –M (+ M in case of minimization problems) is assigned to the variable under consideration and the new optimum solution is obtained by applying regular simplex method to the (modified) current optimum table.

EXAMPLE 6.6-6.1

Consider the optimal table 6.79 of example 6.6-5.1. If product B is not to be produced, so that variable x_2 is to be deleted from this table, find the optimum solution to the resulting L.P. problem.

Solution

Since x_2 is a basic variable, we assign a penalty –M to x_2 in table 6.79 since the given L.P. problem is of maximization type. The resulting modified table is shown below.

TABLE 6.80

	c_j	4	–M	2	0	0	0			
c_B	Basis	x_1	x_2	x_3	x_4	x_5	x_6	b	θ	
4	x_1	1	0	0	$29/18$	$-5/18$	$-1/6$	$\frac{5}{3}$	–10	
–M	x_2	0	1	0	$-8/9$	$2/9$	$(1/3)$	$2/3$	2	← *Key row*
2	x_3	0	0	1	$5/18$	$1/18$	$-1/6$	$2/3$	–4	
$Z_j = \Sigma c_B a_{ij}$		4	–M	2	$7+8/9\,M$	$-1-2/9\,M$	$-1-M/3$			
$\bar{c}_j = c_j - Z_j$		0	0	0	$-7-8/9\,M$	$1+2/9\,M$	$1+M/3$			
							↑K	*Initial feasible solution*		

Replace x_2 by x_6.

TABLE 6.81

	c_j	4	–M	2	0	0	0			
c_B	Basis	x_1	x_2	x_3	x_4	x_5	x_6	b	θ	
4	x_1	1	$1/2$	0	$7/6$	$-1/6$	0	2	–12	
0	x_6	0	3	0	$-8/3$	$(2/3)$	1	2	3	← *Key row*
2	x_3	0	$1/2$	1	$-1/6$	$1/6$	0	1	6	
$Z_j = \Sigma c_B a_{ij}$		4	3	2	$13/3$	$-1/3$	0			
$\overline{c}_j = c_j - Z_j$		0	–M–3	0	$-13/3$	$1/3$	0			
						↑K				

2nd feasible solution

Replace x_6 by x_5.

TABLE 6.82

	c_j	4	–M	2	0	0	0	
c_B	Basis	x_1	x_2	x_3	x_4	x_5	x_6	b
4	x_1	1	$5/4$	0	$1/2$	0	$1/4$	$5/2$
0	x_5	0	$9/2$	0	–4	1	$3/2$	3
2	x_3	0	$-1/4$	1	$1/2$	0	$-1/4$	$1/2$
$Z_j = \Sigma c_B a_{ij}$		4	$9/2$	2	3	0	$1/2$	
$\overline{c}_j = c_j - Z_j$		0	$-M-9/2$	0	–3	0	$-1/2$	

New optimal feasible solution

∴ New optimal solution is $x_1 = \frac{5}{2}, x_2 = 0, x_3 = \frac{1}{2}$; Z_{max} = ₹ $(4 \times \frac{5}{2} + 2 \times \frac{1}{2})$ = ₹ 11.

6.6-7 Deletion of a Constraint

The constraint to be deleted may be either binding or unbinding on the optimal solution. The deletion of an unbinding constraint can only enlarge the feasible region but will not affect the optimal solution. This can be easily verified graphically. Moreover, if the constraint under consideration has a slack or surplus variable of zero value in the basis matrix, it cannot be binding and hence will not affect the optimal solution.

The deletion of a binding constraint will, however, cause postoptimality problem. The simplest way to proceed in this case is via the addition of one or two new variables. For example, the constraint

$$a_{i1}x_1 + a_{i2}x_2 + ... + a_{in}x_n = b_i$$

can be written as

$$a_{i1}x_1 + a_{i2}x_2 + ... + a_{in}x_n + x_{n+1} - x_{n+2} = b_i \; ; \; x_{n+1}, x_{n+2} \geq 0,$$

where x_{n+1} and x_{n+2} are slack and surplus variables respectively. The problem can then be solved by the procedure laid down in section 6.6-3 for addition of new variables.

EXERCISES 6.6

1. What do you understand by sensitivity analysis ? Explain how it is carried out. [B.P.U.T. 6th Sem., 2011; IGNOU MBA June, 2007; P.T.U. MBA Sept., 2006; P.U. M.Com. Sept., 2004]
2. What is sensitivity analysis ? Discuss the effect of (i) variation of b_i (ii) variation of c_j. [P.T.U. B.Tech. (C.Sc.) 2010, (Mech.) May, 2007, 2006]
3. Write short note on shadow prices in simplex algorithm. What is their role in sensitivity analysis ? [P.T.U. B.Tech. (Mech.) May, 2006]
4. What do you mean by sensitivity analysis ? Discuss it with respect to (i) Change in constraint matrix (ii) Addition of a new constraint. [Meerut M.Sc. (Math.) 1979]
5. Describe the role of duality theory in sensitivity analysis. [P.U. B.E. (Prod.) 1977]
6. Explain with suitable examples the basic philosophy behind sensitivity analysis. [P.T.U. MBA May, 2014]
7. Explain the basic concepts of sensitivity analysis. What are the different factors affecting the given solutions and how do we resolve them ? Give a brief comment on each of them. [Gujarat Tech. U. MBA Dec., 2010]

Section 6.6-1

8. The optimal solution to the following L.P.P. :

Maximize $Z = 35x_1 + 50x_2$,

subject to $4x_1 + 6x_2 \le 120$,
$x_1 + x_2 \le 20$,
$2x_1 + 3x_2 \le 40$,
$x_1, x_2 \ge 0$,

is given below with slack variables x_3, x_4 and x_5 :

TABLE 6.83

	c_j	35	50	0	0	0	
c_B	Basis	x_1	x_2	x_3	x_4	x_5	b
0	x_3	0	0	1	0	–2	40
35	x_1	1	0	0	3	–1	20
50	x_2	0	1	0	–2	1	0
	$\bar{c}_j$	0	0	0	–5	–15	

If the R.H.S. of the constraints is changed from $(120, 20, 40)^T$ to $(75, 15, 50)^T$, find the new optimum solution. (*Ans.* $x_1 = \frac{15}{2}, x_2 = \frac{15}{2}$; $Z_{max} = \frac{1,275}{2}$.)

9. Solve the problem : Maximize $Z = 2x_1 + 3x_2$, subject to $x_1 + 2x_2 \le 8$, $3x_1 + 2x_2 \le 15$; $x_1, x_2 \ge 0$. If the new requirement vector is $(4, 20)^T$, find the new optimal solution.

(*Ans.* (i) $x_1 = \frac{7}{2}, x_2 = \frac{9}{4}$; $Z_{max} = \frac{55}{4}$.

(ii) $x_1 = 4, x_2 = 0$; $Z_{max} = 8$.)

10. Solve the problem : Minimize $Z = -x_1 + 2x_2 + 3x_3$, subject to $-x_1 + x_2 + x_3 \ge 3$, $x_1 + 2x_2 + x_3 \le 10$; $x_1, x_2, x_3 \ge 0$. If the R.H.S. of the first constraint is changed from 3 to 7, find the new optimum solution.

(*Ans.* (i) $x_1 = 0, x_2 = 3, x_3 = 0$; $Z_{min} = 6$.

(ii) $x_1 = 0, x_2 = 3, x_3 = 4$; $Z_{min} = 18$.)

11. Discuss the effect of discrete changes in the requirement vectors for the following L.P.P. :

Maximize $Z = 3x_1 + 4x_2 + x_3 + 7x_4$,

subject to $8x_1 + 3x_2 + 4x_3 + x_4 \le 7$,
$2x_1 + 6x_2 + x_3 + 5x_4 \le 3$,

$x_1 + 4x_2 + 5x_3 + 2x_4 \le 8,$
$x_1, x_2, x_3, x_4 \ge 0.$

[*Meerut M.Sc. (Math.) 1992 ; Madurai B.Sc. (Math.) 1983*]

(*Ans.* $-\frac{32}{5} \le \Delta b_1 \le 5, -\frac{5}{4} \le \Delta b_2 \le \frac{84}{5}, -\frac{126}{19} \le \Delta b_3$.)

12. Solve the following L.P.P. and find the range over which b_2 can be changed maintaining the feasibility of the solution:

Maximize $Z = 3x_1 + 5x_2 + 4x_3,$
subject to
$2x_1 + 3x_2 \le 8,$
$2x_2 + 5x_3 \le 10,$
$3x_1 + 2x_2 + 4x_3 \le 15,$
$x_1, x_2, x_3 \ge 0.$

(*Ans.* $x_1 = \frac{89}{41}, x_2 = \frac{50}{41}, x_3 = \frac{62}{41}, Z_{max} = \frac{765}{41}; -\frac{25}{4} \le \Delta b_2 \le \frac{89}{12}$.)

13. For the L.P.P.

maximize $Z = 3x_1 + 4x_2 + 6x_3 + 10x_4,$
subject to
$x_1 + x_2 + x_3 + x_4 \le 12,$
$6x_1 + 4x_2 + 2x_3 + x_4 \le 90,$
$2x_1 + 4x_2 + 9x_3 + 10x_4 \le 70,$
$x_1, x_2, x_3, x_4 \ge 0,$

find the ranges within which availability of resources can change, maintaining the feasibility of the solution.

(*Ans.* $-5 \le \delta_1 < \frac{187}{29}$; $\delta_2 \ge -\frac{187}{4}$; $-46 \le \delta_3 \le 50$.)

Section 6.6-2

14. (*a*) Solve the problem :

Maximize $Z = x_1 + 1.5x_2,$
subject to
$2x_1 + 2x_2 \le 160,$
$x_1 + 2x_2 \le 120,$
$4x_1 + 2x_2 \le 280,$
$x_1, x_2 \ge 0.$

(*b*) Over what values of profit for x_2 will the present solution be still optimal ?

(*c*) Determine the optimal range for c_1.

(*Ans.* (*a*) $x_1 = 40, x_2 = 40; Z_{max} = 100.$
(*b*) $1 \le c_2 \le 2.$
(*c*) $3/4 \le c_1 \le 3/2$.)

15. Solve the problem :

(*a*) Maximize $Z = 45x_1 + 100x_2 + 30x_3 + 50x_4,$
subject to
$7x_1 + 10x_2 + 4x_3 + 9x_4 \le 1{,}200,$
$3x_1 + 40x_2 + x_3 + x_4 \le 800,$
$x_1, x_2, x_3, x_4 \ge 0.$

(*b*) Find the effect of
(*i*) changing the cost coefficients c_1 and c_4 from 45 and 50 to 40 and 60 respectively.
(*ii*) changing c_1 to 40 and c_2 to 90.
(*iii*) changing c_3 from 30 to 24.

[*Kuru. U. M.Tech. (Mech.) 1989, 88*]

(*Ans.* (*a*) $x_1 = 0, x_2 = \frac{40}{3}, x_3 = \frac{800}{3}, x_4 = 0; Z_{max} = \frac{28{,}000}{3}$.

(*b*) (*i*) Same as in part (*a*).

(*ii*) $x_1 = 0, x_2 = \frac{40}{3}, x_3 = \frac{800}{3}, x_4 = 0; Z_{max} = 9{,}200.$

(*iii*) $x_1 = 160, x_2 = 8, x_3 = 0, x_4 = 0; Z_{max} = 8{,}000$.)

16. Consider the problem

maximize $Z = 2x_2 - 5x_3,$
subject to $x_1 + x_3 \le 2,$
$2x_1 + x_2 + 6x_3 \le 6,$
$x_1 - x_2 + 3x_3 = 0,$
$x_1, x_2, x_3 \ge 0.$

(*a*) Write the dual from the standard form.
(*b*) Solve the primal and hence find the solution to the dual.
(*c*) Suppose that the coefficients of x_2 and x_3 in the objective function are changed from (2, – 5) to (1, 1), find the new solution.

[*Ans.* (*a*) Minimize $W = 2y_1 + 6y_2,$
subject to $y_1 + 2y_2 + y_3 \ge 0,$
$y_2 - y_3 \ge 2,$
$y_1 + 6y_2 + 3y_3 \ge -5,$
$y_1, y_2 \ge 0$, y_3 unrestricted.
(*b*) $y_1 = 0, y_2 = 2/3, y_3 = -4/3, W_{min} = 4.$
(*c*) Unbounded.)

17. (*a*) Solve the problem

maximize $Z = x_1 + 5x_2 + 3x_3,$
subject to $x_1 + 2x_2 + x_3 = 3,$
$2x_1 - x_2 = 4,$
$x_1, x_2, x_3 \ge 0.$

(*b*) If the objective function is changed to
maximize $Z = 2x_1 + 5x_2 + 2x_3$, find the new optimal solution.

(*Ans.* (*a*) $x_1 = 2, x_2 = 0, x_3 = 1; Z_{max} = 5.$
(*b*) $x_1 = 11/5, x_2 = 2/5, x_3 = 0; Z_{max} = 32/5.$)

18. For the problem

minimize $Z = x_2 - 3x_3 + 2x_5,$
subject to $3x_2 - x_3 + 2x_5 \le 7,$
$-2x_2 + 4x_3 \le 12,$
$-4x_2 + 3x_3 + 8x_5 \le 10,$
$x_2, x_3, x_5 \ge 0,$

the optimal table is

TABLE 6.84

	c_j	0	1	–3	0	2	0	
c_B	Basis	x_1	x_2	x_3	x_4	x_5	x_6	b
1	x_2	$2/5$	1	0	$1/10$	$4/5$	0	4
–3	x_3	$1/5$	0	1	$3/10$	$2/5$	0	5
0	x_6	1	0	0	$-1/2$	10	1	11
	$\bar{c}_j$	$1/5$	0	0	$4/5$	$12/5$	0	

(*a*) Formulate the dual problem for this primal problem.
(*b*) What are the optimal values of dual variables ?
(*c*) How much must c_5 be decreased before x_5 goes into solution ?
(*d*) How much can 7 in first constraint be increased before the basis would change ?

[*Kerala B.E., 1984 ; Dibrugarh M.Sc. (Stat.) 1976 ; Roorkee M.E. (Mech.) 1977*]

(*Ans.* (*a*) Maximize $W = -7y_1 - 12y_2 - 10y_3,$
subject to $-3y_1 + 2y_2 + 4y_3 \le 1,$
$-y_1 + 4y_2 + 3y_3 \ge 3,$
$-2y_1 - 8y_3 \le 2,$
$y_1, y_2, y_3 \ge 0.$

(b) $y_1 = 1/5, y_2 = 4/5, y_3 = 0.$
(c) $\Delta c_5 > 12/5.$
(d) $\Delta b_1 < -1.$)

19. A plant is engaged on the production of two products which are processed through three departments; the number of hours available in each department is indicated in the table below.

TABLE 6.85

Department	Product A	Product B	Max. hours available (per week)
I	7	8	1,600
II	8	12	1,600
III	15	16	1,600

(a) If the profit for the product is ₹ 6 for a unit of product A, but only ₹4 for a unit of product B, what quantities per week should be planned to maximize profit ? Illustrate the problem graphically.
(b) Capacity can be increased in one department only. In which department should it be done and why ? To what extent should the capacity be increased ?
(c) If the cost per hour in department I is ₹ 25, in department II, ₹ 40 and in department III, ₹ 50, what quantities should be planned to minimize the cost of production ?

[Bombay Dip. Op. Man., 1973]

20. A furniture manufacturer makes x_1 chairs, x_2 tables and x_3 sideboards. He has formulated the following model for his production programme :

Maximize $Z = 20x_1 + 15x_2 + 15x_3,$
subject to $8x_1 + 2x_2 + 8x_3 \le 100$ (wood),
$4x_1 + 4x_2 + 4x_3 \le 60$ (labour),
$x_1, x_2, x_3 \ge 0.$

The dual linear programme is to

minimize $W = 100y_1 + 60y_2,$
subject to $8y_1 + 4y_2 \ge 20$, (chair),
$2y_1 + 4y_2 \ge 15$ (table),
$8y_1 + 4y_2 \ge 15$ (sideboard),
$y_1, y_2 \ge 0;$

and the solution to the dual is

TABLE 6.86

	c_j	100	60	0	0	0	M	M	M	
c_B	Basis	y_1	y_2	s_1	s_2	s_3	A_1	A_2	A_3	b
0	s_2	0	–3	$-1/4$	1	0	$1/4$	–1	0	$75/64$
0	s_3	0	0	–1	0	1	1	0	–1	5
100	y_1	1	$\frac{1}{2}$	$-1/8$	0	0	$1/8$	0	0	$115/48$
	$\bar{c}_j$	0	10	$25/2$	0	0	$-25/2$ +M	M	M	$11,500/48$

(a) Determine the ranges for the capacity of the inputs.
(b) Determine the ranges for the contributions of x_1, x_2 and x_3 over which the present product mix remains optimal.

21. Maximize $Z = 3x_1 + 5x_2 + 4x_3$, subject to $2x_1 + x_2 + x \le 5,$
$x_1 + 4x_2 + 2x_3 \le 16,\ x_1 + 2x_2 + 3x_3 \le 9;\ x_1, x_2, x_3 \ge 0.$
Find the range of variation of the objective function coefficients and the right-hand side of the constraints for which the current optimal solution remains unchanged.

[P.U.M.E. (Mech.) May, 1995]

22. Given the L.P.P. : Maximize $Z = 3x_1 + 5x_2$, subject to constraints :
$$3x_1 + 2x_2 \leq 18,\ x_1 \leq 4,\ x_2 \leq 6 \text{ and } x_1, x_2 \geq 0,$$
(*i*) determine an optimal solution to the L.P.P.
(*ii*) discuss the effect on the optimality of the solution when the objective function is reduced to $Z = 3x_1 + x_2$. [*Meerut (Math.) 1974*]
(*Ans.* (*i*) $x_1 = 2, x_2 = 6$; $Z_{max} = 36$.
(*ii*) $x_1 = 2, x_2 = 6$; $Z_{max} = 12$.)

23. For Ex. 22 find the range for the coefficient of x_2 in the objective function without affecting the optimal solution.
[*IAS, 1996 ; Madurai B.Sc. (Appl. Math.) 1984 ; Delhi B.Sc. (Math.) 1987*]

24. JOBCO produces two products on two machines. A unit of product 1 requires 2 hours on machine 1 and 1 hour on machine 2. For product 2, a unit requires 1 hour on machine 1 and 3 hours on machine 2. The revenues per unit of products 1 and 2 are \$30 and \$20 respectively. The total daily processing time available for each machine is 8 hours.
(a) Use the graphical method of L.P.P. to determine the number of units of products 1 and 2 that maximizes the revenue.
(b) Determine the dual prices for machine 1 and the feasibility range of it.
(c) Suppose that the unit revenue of product 2 is changed to \$ 40. Will the current optimum solution remain the same ? If not, determine the new optimum solution.
[*Gujarat Technological U. MBA Jan., 2011*]

Section 6.6-3

25. Solve the L.P.P. : Maximize Z = $3y_1 + 5y_2$, subject to $y_1 + y_3 = 4$, $3y_1 + 2y_2 + y_4 = 18$; $y_1, y_2, y_3, y_4 \geq 0$.
If a new variable y_5 is introduced in the above L.P.P. with profit 7, so that the new problem becomes : Maximize $Z' = 3y_1 + 5y_2 + 7y_5$, subject to $y_1 + y_3 + y_5 = 4$, $3y_1 + 2y_2 + y_4 + 2y_5 = 18$; $y_1, ..., y_5 \geq 0$, find the solution to the new problem. (*Ans.* $y_1 = y_3 = y_4 = 0, y_2 = 5, y_5 = 4$; $Z'_{max} = 53$.)

26. A manufacturing company produces two products, each of which requires stamping, assembly and painting operations. Total productive capacity by operation if it were devoted solely to one product or the other is

TABLE 6.87

Operation	*Productive capacity (units/week)*	
	Product A	*Product B*
Stamping	500	700
Assembly	650	330
Painting	450	700

Demand for the two products is unlimited and the profits on A and B are ₹ 20 and ₹ 15 respectively. The company wants to expand its product line. Its marketing manager has determined that there is an unlimited market for a third product C. The productive capacity for this product is

TABLE 6.88

Operation	*Product C (units/week)*
Stamping	200
Assembly	180
Painting	120

The unit profit for product C is estimated to be ₹ 16. Should the company extend its product line by including product C ?

27. A company manufactures three products A, B and C using three types of inputs X, Y and Z in different proportions. The following matrix gives requirements of various inputs (in kg) per unit production (one kg) of the three products.

TABLE 6.89

Inputs

Product	*X*	*Y*	*Z*
A	4	8	8
B	4	6	4
C	8	4	0

The per unit profits for the three products are ₹ 20, ₹ 40 and ₹ 10 respectively. The company has 800 kg of input X, 1,800 kg of input Y and 500 kg of input Z. The following final simplex table gives the optimal solution :

TABLE 6.90

	c_j	20	40	10	0	0	0	
c_B	Basis	x_1	x_2	x_3	s_1	s_2	s_3	b
10	x_3	–1/2	0	1	1/8	0	–1/8	75/2
0	s_2	–2	0	0	–1/2	1	–1	900
40	x_2	2	1	0	0	0	1/4	125
	$\bar{c}_j$	–55	0	0	–5/4	0	–35/4	

(*a*) Determine

(*i*) the ranges for the capacities of inputs,

(*ii*) the ranges for the contribution of A, B and C over which the present product mix remains optimal.

(*b*) A new product D is proposed to be added. The input requirements for it are 3 of X, 4 of Y and 6 of Z and the unit profit is ₹ 25. Is it worthwhile adding this product ?

28. Referring to Ex. 13, a new product x_5 with input requirement vector $\begin{bmatrix} 1 \\ 3 \\ 3 \end{bmatrix}$ is being considered for inclusion into the existing product mix. What should be its contribution/unit so that it may be included ? (*Ans.* $c_5 \geq 31/8$.)

29. A manufacturer can produce four products using three resources namely labour, raw material and machine time. The unit contributions and the technological constraints are given below in the form of an L.P.P. :

Maximize $Z = 3x_1 + 3x_2 + 4x_3 + 7x_4$, subject to $x_1 + x_2 + x_3 + x_4 \leq 9$, $5x_1 + 3x_2 + 2x_3 + x_4 \leq 60$, $x_1 + 3x_2 + 5x_3 + 8x_4 \leq 50$; $x_1, x_2, x_3, x_4 \geq 0$.

(*i*) Find the optimal product mix.

(*ii*) Suppose a fifth product represented by variable x_8 is to be included in the optimal product mix, what should be its unit contribution if the resource requirements for this product are $\frac{7}{4}$ units, 3 units and 7 units of labour, material and machine time respectively ?

(*Ans.* (*i*) $x_1 = \frac{22}{7}$, $x_2 = x_3 = 0$, $x_4 = \frac{41}{7}$; $Z_{max} = \frac{353}{7}$. (*ii*) $c_8 > 8.25$.)

Section 6.6-4

30. Consider the problem

$$\begin{aligned} \text{maximize} \quad & Z = 3x_1 + 2x_2 + 5x_3, \\ \text{subject to} \quad & x_1 + 2x_2 + x_3 \leq 430, \\ & 3x_1 + 2x_3 \leq 460, \\ & x_1 + 4x_2 \leq 420, \\ & x_1, x_2, x_3 \geq 0. \end{aligned}$$

The optimal solution to this problem is given by the following table :

TABLE 6.91

c_B	c_j Basis	3 x_1	2 x_2	5 x_3	0 s_1	0 s_2	0 s_3	b
2	x_2	$-1/4$	1	0	$1/2$	$-1/4$	0	100
5	x_3	$3/2$	0	1	0	$1/2$	0	230
0	s_3	2	0	0	-2	1	1	20
$Z_j = \Sigma c_B a_{ij}$		7	2	5	1	2	0	
$\overline{c}_j = c_j - Z_j$		-4	0	0	-1	-2	0	

Suppose that the constraint coefficients of 'x_1'-column are changed from $(1, 3, 1)^T$ to $(1, 1, 6)^T$ in the starting matrix and profit coefficients of x_2 and x_3 are changed from (2, 5) to (1, 3), find the new optimal solution.

(*Ans.* $x_1 = 4$, $x_2 = 99$, $x_3 = 228$; $Z_{\max} = 795$.)

31. **Referring to example 6.6-2.3, find the limits for the changes in a_{14} and a_{24} so that the new solution remains an optimal feasible solution.**
32. **In Ex: 29, $a_{33} = 5$ and x_3 is a non-basic variable. What should be the value of a_{33} so that x_3 becomes a basic variable ?**

(*Ans.* $a_{33} \le \frac{11}{4}$.)

33. **In Ex. 29, find the change in coefficient a_{32} of non-basic variable x_2 so that it may become a basic variable.**

(*Ans.* $a_{32} \le \frac{22}{7}$.)

34. **Consider the following L.P.P. : Maximize $Z = 20x_1 + 10x_2$, subject to $x_1 + 2x_2 \le 40$, $3x_1 + 2x_2 \le 60$; $x_1, x_2 \ge 0$. Find the optimal solution. Also determine the optimal solution if x_2-column changes from $\begin{bmatrix} 2 \\ 2 \end{bmatrix}$ to $\begin{bmatrix} 2 \\ 1 \end{bmatrix}$.**

(*Ans.* (*i*) $x_1 = 20$, $x_2 = 0$; $Z_{\max} = 400$.
(*ii*) $x_1 = 10$, $x_2 = 15$; $Z_{\max} = 350$.)

35. **The optimal table for the following L.P.P : Maximize $Z = 3x_1 + x_2$, subject to $x_1 + x_2 \le 6$, $2x_1 + 3x_2 \le 8$; $x_1, x_2 \ge 0$ is given below, where x_3 and x_4 are slack variables.**

TABLE 6.92

c_B	c_j Basis	3 x_1	1 x_2	0 x_3	0 x_4	b
0	x_3	0	$-1/2$	1	$-1/2$	2
3	x_1	1	$3/2$	0	$1/2$	4
	$\overline{c}_j = c_j - Z_j$	0	$-7/2$	0	$-3/2$	

Suppose the constraint coefficients of x_2 are changed from $\begin{bmatrix} 1 \\ 3 \end{bmatrix}$ to $\begin{bmatrix} 2 \\ 0 \end{bmatrix}$, find the new optimal solution.

(*Ans.* $x_1 = 4$, $x_2 = 1$; $Z_{\max} = 13$.)

36. **Consider the following L.P.P. : Maximize $Z = 3x_1 + 2x_2$, subject to $4x_1 + 3x_2 \le 120$, $x_1 + 3x_2 \le 60$; $x_1, x_2 \ge 0$. If the technological coefficients of x_2 are changed from $\begin{bmatrix} 3 \\ 3 \end{bmatrix}$ to $\begin{bmatrix} 2 \\ 1 \end{bmatrix}$, find the new optimal solution.**

(*Ans.* $x_1 = 0$, $x_2 = 60$; $Z_{\max} = 120$.)

37. Consider the following L.P.P. : Minimize $Z = -x_1 + 2x_2 + 3x_3$, subject to $-x_1 + x_2 + x_3 \geq 3$, $x_1 + 2x_2 + x_3 \leq 10$; $x_1, x_2, x_3 \geq 0$. If the technological coefficients of x_1 are changed from $\begin{bmatrix}-1\\1\end{bmatrix}$ to $\begin{bmatrix}2\\1\end{bmatrix}$, find the new optimal solution.

(*Ans.* $x_1 = 10, x_2 = 0, x_3 = 0$; $Z_{min} = -10$.)

38. The following mathematical formulation describes a problem of allocating three resources to the annual production of four commodities by a manufacturing firm. The amounts of four products to be produced are represented by x_1, x_2, x_3 and x_4 respectively. The objective function reflects the profit contribution in rupees of these products.

Maximize $Z = 2x_1 - x_2 + 3x_3 - 2x_4$,

subject to
$$x_1 + 3x_2 - x_3 + 2x_4 \leq 7 \text{ (resource A)},$$
$$-x_1 + 2x_2 + 4x_3 \leq 12 \text{ (resource B)},$$
$$-x_1 - 4x_2 + 3x_3 + 8x_4 \leq 10 \text{ (resource C)}.$$

If you add x_5, x_6 and x_7 as slack variables, you have at the final iteration of the simplex method,

$$Z_0 + \frac{7}{5}x_1 + \frac{12}{5}x_4 + \frac{1}{5}x_5 + \frac{4}{5}x_6 = 11,$$
$$\frac{3}{10}x_1 + x_2 + \frac{4}{5}x_4 + \frac{2}{5}x_5 + \frac{1}{10}x_6 = 4,$$
$$-\frac{1}{10}x_1 - x_3 + \frac{2}{5}x_4 + \frac{1}{5}x_5 + \frac{3}{10}x_6 = 5,$$
$$\frac{1}{2}x_1 + 10x_4 + x_5 - \frac{1}{2}x_6 + x_7 = 11,$$

where Z_0 represents the profit of the program.

(*i*) State optimal values for each x_j and the objective function. Is the optimal solution unique ?

(*ii*) For each of the variables x_1 and x_3 give an interval for its objective function coefficients such that the basic solution in part (*i*) remains optimal.

(*iii*) If the availability of resource A is increased from 7 units to 8 units, what would happen to the value of Z_0 ?

(*iv*) Write the dual problem. Indicate optimal values for the dual variables and calculate the associated value of the dual objective function.

(*v*) Write an economic interpretation of each dual variable.

(*vi*) Suppose the Research and Development deptt. proposes a new product x_8 whose production coefficients in the constraints for resources A, B and C are 5, –3 and 1 respectively and the objective function coefficient is 2, can the solution in part (*i*) be improved ? If so, show how ? If not, indicate what happens if x_8 is introduced into the basis.

(*vii*) If instead of a new product, the R and D department discovers a new process of manufacturing the first product x_1 which is represented by

$$\mathbf{P}_1 = \begin{bmatrix}1+\delta\\-1\\-1\end{bmatrix},$$

how small can δ be such that the solution in part (*i*) remains optimal ?

[*B.U.M.M.S., 1973*]

39. Consider the linear programming problem

maximize $Z = 2x_2 - 5x_3$,

subject to
$$x_1 + x_3 \geq 2,$$
$$2x_1 + x_2 + 6x_3 \leq 6,$$
$$x_1 - x_2 + 3x_3 = 0,$$
$$x_1, x_2, x_3 \geq 0.$$

The final table yielding the optimal solution is

TABLE 6.93

	c_j	0	2	–5	0	0	–M	–M	
c_B	Basis	x_1	x_2	x_3	s_1	s_2	A_1	A_3	b
2	x_2	0	1	0	0	1/3	0	–2/3	2
0	s_1	0	0	2	1	1/3	–1	1/3	0
0	x_1	1	0	3	0	1/3	0	1/3	2
	Z_j	0	2	0	0	2/3	0	–4/3	4
	$\bar{c}_j$	0	0	–5	0	–2/3	–M	–M+4/3	

(*a*) What are the shadow prices (optimal values of the dual variables) of each of the constraints in the primal ?

(*b*) Over what range of coefficients for each variable in the objective function will the optimal solution remain optimal ?

(*c*) Over what range of constraint constants will the optimal solution remain feasible ?

(*d*) Over what range of technical coefficients of x_3 in the second constraint will x_3 remain non-basic? In the first constraint ? In the second constraint ?

Section 6.6-5

40. If in Ex. 37, instead of changing x_1-column coefficients, a new constraint $x_1 + x_3 \geq 2$ is added, find the new optimal solution.

(*Ans.* $x_1 = 0, x_2 = 1, x_3 = 2; Z_{min} = 8$.)

41. If in Ex. 36, instead of changing x_2-column coefficients, a new constraint $x_1 \leq 25$ is added, find the new optimal solution.

(*Ans.* $x_1 = 25, x_2 = \frac{20}{3}; Z_{max} = \frac{265}{3}$.)

42. Find the optimal solution for the problem : Minimize $Z = x_1 - 2x_2 - x_3$, subject to $x_1 + x_2 + x_3 \leq 6, x_1 - 2x_2 \leq 4 ; x_1, x_2 \geq 0$. If a new constraint $- x_2 + 2x_3 \geq 4$ is added to the problem, find the new optimal solution.

(*Ans.* $x_1 = 0, x_2 = \frac{8}{3}, x_3 = \frac{10}{3}; Z_{min} = -\frac{26}{3}$.)

43. Consider the following table which represents an optimal solution to some L.P.P. :

TABLE 6.94

	c_j	2	4	1	3	2	0	0	0	
c_B	Basis	x_1	x_2	x_3	x_4	x_5	x_6	x_7	x_8	b
2	x_1	1	0	0	–1	0	1/2	1/5	–1	3
4	x_2	0	1	0	2	1	–1	0	1/2	1
1	x_3	0	0	1	–1	–2	5	–3/10	2	7
	$\bar{c}_j$	0	0	0	–2	0	–2	–1/10	–2	17

If the additional constraint $2x_1 + 3x_2 - x_3 + 2x_4 + 4x_5 \leq 5$ is annexed to the system, will there be any change in the optimal solution ? Justify your answer. [*Meerut M.Sc. (Math.) 1972*]

(*Ans.* No change.)

44. Consider the optimum table of Ex. 43. If an additional constraint $2x_1 + 3x_2 - x_3 + 2x_4 + 4x_5 \leq 1$ is added to the system, would there be any change in the optimum solution? Determine the new optimum solution.

(*Ans.* $x_1 = 3, x_2 = 0, x_3 = 9, x_5 = 1 ; Z_{max} = 17$.)

45. A firm produces three items A, B and C and requires two types of resources — man-hours and raw material. The following L.P. problem has been formulated to determine the optimum production schedule that maximizes the total profit :

Maximize $Z = 3y_1 + y_2 + 5y_3$,

subject to $6y_1 + 3y_2 + 5y_3 \le 45$ (man-hours),

$3y_1 + 4y_2 + 5y_3 \le 30$ (raw material),

$y_1, y_2, y_3 \ge 0$,

where y_1, y_2, y_3 are the number of items A, B and C. The optimal solution with y_4 and y_5 as slack variables is

TABLE 6.95

c_B	c_j / Basis	3 y_1	1 y_2	5 y_3	0 y_4	0 y_5	b
3	y_1	1	$-1/3$	0	$1/3$	$-1/3$	5
5	y_3	0	1	1	$-1/5$	$2/5$	3
$\overline{c}_j = c_j - Z_j$		0	-3	0	0	-1	

(*a*) Find the range on the unit profit of product A. If $c_1 = 4$, what is the optimal solution?

(*b*) If additional 10 units of raw material can be obtained at a cost of ₹ 12, is it profitable to do so ?

(*c*) If the available raw material is increased to 50 units, what is the optimal solution ?

(*d*) Due to 'technological breakthrough' the raw material required by item B is reduced to 2 units. Will it affect the optimal solution ?

(*e*) If a supervision constraint, $2y_1 + y_2 + 3y_3 \le 20$ is added to the original problem, how is the optimal solution affected ?

46. A manufacturer produces four products A, B, C and D by using two types of machines (lathes and milling machines). The times required on the two machines to manufacture one unit of each of the four products, the profit per unit of the product and the total time available on the two types of machines per day are given below.

TABLE 6.96

Machines	*Product time required per unit (minutes)*				*Total time available per day (minutes)*
	A	B	C	D	
Lathe	4	9	7	10	5,500
Milling machine	2	1	3	20	3,500
Profit/unit (₹)	15	25	25	65	

(*a*) Find the number of units of the various products to be produced for maximizing profit.

(*b*) Find the effect of increasing the profit per unit of product C to ₹ 30.

(*c*) Find the effect of changing the profit per unit of product A and B to ₹ 10 and ₹ 30 respectively.

(*d*) Find the effect of changing the total time available per day on the two machines to 3,500 and 5,500 minutes respectively.

(*e*) If a new product E, which requires 7 minutes/unit on lathe and 4 minutes/unit on milling machine can also be produced, will it be worthwhile to produce it if it brings a profit of ₹ 30 per unit ?

(*f*) If products A, B, C and D require 3, 4, 5 and 2 minutes/unit respectively on grinding machine in addition to the present operations, find the optimal solution. The total time available per day on grinding machine is 3,000 minutes.

(*g*) If product A requirs 3 minutes on lathe and 3 minutes on milling machine (instead of 4 and 2 minutes respectively) per unit, find the new optimum solution.

47. Consider the L.P.P. : Maximize $Z = 3x_1 + 4x_2 + x_3 + 7x_4$, subject to $8x_1 + 3x_2 + 4x_3 + x_4 \leq 7$, $2x_1 + 6x_2 + x_3 + 5x_4 \leq 3$, $x_1 + 4x_2 + 5x_3 + 2x_4 \leq 8$; $x_1, x_2, x_3, x_4 \geq 0$.
   (*a*) Determine the optimal solution.
   (*b*) Discuss the effect of discrete changes in b_i (i = 1, 2, 3).
   (*c*) Discuss the effect of discrete changes in c_j on the optimal solution of part (*a*), where j = 1, 4, 7.
   (*d*) Discuss the effect of discrete changes in activity coefficient a_{24}.
   (*e*) If an additional constraint $2x_1 + 3x_2 + x_3 + 5x_4 \leq 4$ is added to the system, will there be any change in the current optimal solution of part (*a*).
   (*f*) If an additional constraint $2x_1 + 3x_2 + x_3 + 5x_4 \leq 2$ is added, what will be the effect?

(*Ans.* (*a*) $x_1 = \frac{16}{19}, x_2 = 0, x_3 = 0, x_4 = \frac{5}{19}$; $Z_{\max} = \frac{83}{19}$.

(*b*) $-\frac{32}{5} \leq \Delta b_1 \leq 5, -\frac{5}{4} \leq \Delta b_2 \leq \frac{84}{5}, -\frac{126}{19} \leq \Delta b_3$.

(*c*) $-\frac{1}{5} \leq \Delta c_1 \leq 53, -\frac{169}{42} \leq \Delta c_4 \leq \frac{1}{2}, -\frac{1}{9} \leq \Delta c_7 \leq 1$.

(*d*) $-\frac{1}{3} \leq a_{24} \leq \frac{169}{23}$.

(*e*) No; value of $Z_{\max} = \frac{83}{19}$.

(*f*) $x_1 = \frac{33}{38}, x_4 = \frac{1}{19}, x_7 = \frac{267}{38}, x_6 = 1$; $Z_{\max} = \frac{113}{38}$.)

48. Solve the L.P.P. : Maximize $Z = 8x_1 + 9x_2$, subject to $5x_1 + 4x_2 \leq 40$, $x_1 + 2x_2 \leq 12$, $5x_1 + 19x_2 \leq 95$; $x_1, x_2 \geq 0$. Use sensitivity analysis to modify the optimal solution as follows:
   (*i*) Add the constraint $4x_1 + 5x_2 \leq 40$.
   (*ii*) Now delete the constraint $5x_1 + 4x_2 \leq 40$. [*Roorkee M.Sc. (Appl. Math.) 1996*]

Section 6.6-6

49. Solve the problem : Maximize $Z = 3x_1 + 4x_2 + x_3 + 7x_4$, subject to $8x_1 + 3x_2 + 4x_3 + x_4 \leq 7$, $2x_1 + 6x_2 + x_3 + 5x_4 \leq 3$, $x_1 + 4x_2 + 5x_3 + 2x_4 \leq 8$; $x_1, x_2, x_3, x_4 \geq 0$.
   Discuss the effect of deleting variable x_4 on the optimal solution.

(*Ans.* (*i*) $x_1 = \frac{16}{19}, x_4 = \frac{5}{19}, x_7 = \frac{126}{19}$; $Z_{\max} = \frac{83}{19}$.

(*ii*) $x_1 = \frac{11}{14}, x_2 = \frac{5}{21}, x_7 = \frac{5,123}{58}$; $Z_{\max} = \frac{139}{42}$.)

50. If in the optimal table 6.94 of Ex. 43, variable x_2 is deleted, find its effect on the optimal solution.
(*Ans.* $x_1 = 3, x_3 = 9, x_4 = 0, x_5 = 1$; $Z_{\max} = 17$.)

6.7 PARAMETRIC LINEAR PROGRAMMING

Section 6.6 on sensitivity analysis discussed the effect of discrete changes in the input coefficients of the linear programming problem on its optimal solution. Further, these input coefficients (c_j or b_i or a_{ij}) were changed one at a time. However, if there is continuous change in the values of the these coefficients or if simultaneous variations (changes in all components of c_j or b_i or a_{ij}) occur in their values, none of the results of section 6.6 are valid.

Parametric linear programming investigates the effect of *predetermined continuous* variations of these coefficients on the optimal solution. It is simply an extension of sensitivity analysis and aims at finding the various basic solutions that become optimal, one after the other, as the coefficients of the problem change continuously. The coefficients change as a linear function of a single parameter, hence the name parametric linear programming for this computational technique. As in sensitivity analysis, the purpose of this technique is to reduce the additional computations required to obtain the changes in the optimal solution. The various types of parametric problems that one may come across are :

1. *Parametric cost problem* : in which the cost coefficients c_j vary linearly as a function of parameter λ.
2. *Parametric right-hand side problem* : in which the resources availability coefficients b_i vary linearly as a function of parameter λ.
3. *Parametric problem involving linear variations in the non-basic vector $\mathbf{P}_j$ of A.*
4. *Parametric problem involving simultaneous linear variations in c_j, b_i and $\mathbf{P}_j$.*

This text covers type 1 and type 2 parametric problems in details. For the remaining types, the interested readers may refer to (74).

6.7-1 Parametric Cost Problem

Let the linear programming problem before parametrization be

$$\begin{aligned} &\text{minimize} && Z = \mathbf{CX}, \\ &\text{subject to} && \mathbf{AX} = \mathbf{b}, \\ &&& \mathbf{X} \geq \mathbf{0}, \end{aligned}$$

where $\mathbf{C}$ is the given cost vector.

Let this cost vector change to $\mathbf{C} + \lambda\mathbf{C}'$ so that the parametric cost problem becomes

$$\begin{aligned} &\text{minimize} && \mathbf{Z} = (\mathbf{C} + \lambda\mathbf{C}')\,\mathbf{X}, \\ &\text{subject to} && \mathbf{AX} = \mathbf{b}, \\ &&& \mathbf{X} \geq \mathbf{0}, \end{aligned}$$

where $\mathbf{C}'$ is the given predetermined cost variation vector and λ is an unknown (positive or negative) parameter. As λ changes, the cost coefficients of all variables also change. We wish to determine the family of optimal solutions as λ changes from $-\infty$ to $+\infty$.

This problem is solved by using the simplex method and sensitivity analysis. When $\lambda = 0$, the parametric cost problem reduces to the original L.P. problem; simplex method is used to find its optimal solution. Let $\mathbf{B}$ and $\mathbf{X_B}$ represent the optimal basis matrix and the optimal basic feasible solution respectively for $\lambda = 0$. The net evaluations or relative cost coefficients are all non-negative (minimization problem) and are given by

$$\overline{c}_j = c_j - Z_j = c_j - \sum c_B\, a_{ij} = c_j - c_{\mathbf{B}}\,\overline{\mathbf{P}}_j,$$

where c_{B} is the cost vector of the basic variables and $\overline{\mathbf{P}}_j$ is the jth column (corresponding to the variable x_j) in the optimal table.

As λ changes from zero to a positive or negative value, the feasible region and values of the basic variables $\mathbf{X_B}$ remain unaltered, but the relative cost coefficients change. For any variable x_j, the relative cost coefficient is given by

$$\begin{aligned} \overline{c}_j\;(\lambda) &= (c_j + \lambda c_j') - (c_{\mathbf{B}} + \lambda c_{\mathbf{B}}')\,\overline{\mathbf{P}}_j \\ &= (c_j - c_{\mathbf{B}}\overline{\mathbf{P}}_j) + \lambda\,(c_j' - c_{\mathbf{B}}'\overline{\mathbf{P}}_j) = \overline{c}_j + \lambda\,\overline{c}'_j. \end{aligned}$$

Since vectors $\mathbf{C}$ and $\mathbf{C}'$ are known, $\overline{c}_j$ and $\overline{c}'_j$ can be determined. For the current minimization problem, $\overline{c}_j\;(\lambda)$ must be non-negative for the solution to be optimal [$\overline{c}_j\,(\lambda)$ must be non-positive for a maximization problem]. Thus

$$\overline{c}_j\,(\lambda) \geq 0,\; \overline{c}_j + \lambda\,\overline{c}'_j \geq 0.$$

In other words, for a given solution we can determine the range for λ within which the solution remains optimal.

EXAMPLE 6.7-1.1

Consider the linear programming problem

maximize $Z = 4x_1 + 6x_2 + 2x_3$,

subject to $x_1 + x_2 + x_3 \leq 3$,

$x_1 + 4x_2 + 7x_3 \leq 9$,

$x_1, x_2, x_3 \geq 0$.

The optimal solution to this problem is given by the following table:

TABLE 6.97

c_B	c_j / Basis	4 x_1	6 x_2	2 x_3	0 x_4	0 x_5	b
4	x_1	1	0	–1	$4/3$	$-1/3$	1
6	x_2	0	1	2	$-1/3$	$1/3$	2
$Z_j = \sum c_B a_{ij}$		4	6	8	$10/3$	$2/3$	
$\bar{c}_j = c_j - Z_j$		0	0	–6	$-10/3$	$-2/3$	

Solve this problem if the variation cost vector $C' = (2, -2, 2, 0, 0)$. Identify all critical values of the parameter λ.

Solution

The given parametric cost problem is

maximize $Z = (4 + 2\lambda)x_1 + (6 - 2\lambda)x_2 + (2 + 2\lambda)x_3 + 0x_4 + 0x_5$,

subject to $x_1 + x_2 + x_3 + x_4 = 3$,

$x_1 + 4x_2 + 7x_3 + x_5 = 9$,

$x_1, x_2, x_3, x_4, x_5 \geq 0$.

When $\lambda = 0$, the problem reduces to the L.P. problem, whose optimal solution is given by table 6.97. The relative profit coefficients in this optimal table are all non-positive. For values of λ other than zero, the relative profit coefficients become linear functions of λ. To compute them, we, first, add a new relative profit row called $\bar{c}'_j$ -row to table 6.97. This is shown in table 6.98.

TABLE 6.98

c'_B	c_B	c'_j / c_j / Basis	2 4 x_1	– 2 6 x_2	2 2 x_3	0 0 x_4	0 0 x_5	b
2	4	x_1	1	0	–1	$4/3$	$-1/3$	1
– 2	6	x_2	0	1	2	$-1/3$	$1/3$	2
	$\bar{c}_j$		0	0	–6	$-10/3$	$-2/3$	$Z = 16$
	$\bar{c}'_j$		0	0	8	$-10/3$	$4/3$	$Z' = -2$

In table 6.98, $\bar{c}'_j$ is calculated just as $\bar{c}_j$ row except that vector **C** is replaced by **C′**. For example,

$$\bar{c}_2 = c_2 - Z_2 = c_2 - \sum c_B a_{i2} = c_2 - c_B \bar{\mathbf{P}}_2 = 6 - (4, 6)\begin{bmatrix}0\\1\end{bmatrix} = 6 - 6 = 0.$$

$$\therefore \quad \bar{c}'_1 = c'_1 - c'_B \bar{P}_1 = 2 - (2, -2)\begin{bmatrix}1\\0\end{bmatrix} = 0,$$

$$\bar{c}'_2 = -2 - (2, -2)\begin{bmatrix}0\\1\end{bmatrix} = 0,$$

$$\bar{c}'_3 = 2 - (2, -2)\begin{bmatrix}-1\\2\end{bmatrix} = 2 - (-2 - 4) = 8,$$

$$\bar{c}'_4 = 0 - (2, -2)\begin{bmatrix}\frac{4}{3}\\-\frac{1}{3}\end{bmatrix} = -\left(\frac{8}{3} + \frac{2}{3}\right) = -\frac{10}{3},$$

$$\bar{c}'_5 = 0 - (2, -2)\begin{bmatrix}-\frac{1}{3}\\\frac{1}{3}\end{bmatrix} = -\left(-\frac{2}{3} - \frac{2}{3}\right) = \frac{4}{3},$$

$$Z' = 1 \times 2 - 2 \times 2 = -2.$$

Table 6.98 represents a basic feasible solution for the given parametric cost problem. It is given by

$$x_1 = 1, x_2 = 2, x_3 = x_4 = x_5 = 0.$$

Value of the objective function, $Z(\lambda) = Z + \lambda Z' = 16 - 2\lambda$.

The relative profit coefficients, which are linear functions of λ, are given by

$$\bar{c}_j(\lambda) = \bar{c}_j + \lambda \bar{c}'_j, \; j = 1, 2, 3, 4, 5.$$

Table 6.98 will be optimal if $\bar{c}_j(\lambda) \leq 0$ for $j = 3, 4, 5$. Thus we can determine the range of λ for which table 6.98 remains optimal as follows:

$$\bar{c}_3(\lambda) = \bar{c}_3 + \lambda \bar{c}'_3 = -6 + 8\lambda \leq 0 \text{ or } \lambda \leq 3/4,$$

$$\bar{c}_4(\lambda) = \bar{c}_4 + \lambda \bar{c}'_4 = -\frac{10}{3} - \frac{10}{3}\lambda \leq 0 \text{ or } \lambda \geq -1,$$

$$\bar{c}_5(\lambda) = \bar{c}_5 + \lambda \bar{c}'_5 = -\frac{2}{3} + \frac{4}{3}\lambda \leq 0 \text{ or } \lambda \leq \frac{1}{2}.$$

Thus $x_1 = 1, x_2 = 2, x_3 = x_4 = x_5 = 0$ is an optimal solution for the given parametric problem for all values of λ between -1 and $1/2$ and $Z_{max} = 16 - 2\lambda$.

For $\lambda > 1/2$, the relative profit coefficient of the non-basic variable x_5, namely $\bar{c}_5(\lambda)$ becomes positive and table 6.98 no longer remains optimal. Regular simplex method is used to iterate towards optimality. x_5 is the entering variable and computation of 'θ' -column indicates x_2 to be the variable that leaves the basis matrix so that the key element is $\frac{1}{3}$. The key element is made unity and x_2 is replaced by x_5 in table 6.99.

TABLE 6.99

		c'_j	2	−2	2	0	0	
		c_j	4	6	2	0	0	
c'_B	c_B	Basis	x_1	x_2	x_3	x_4	x_5	b
2	4	x_1	1	1	1	1	0	3
0	0	x_5	0	3	6	−1	1	6
		$\bar{c}_j$	0	2	−2	−4	0	Z = 12
		$\bar{c}'_j$	0	−4	0	−2	0	Z′ = 6

Table 6.99 will be optimal if $\overline{c}_j(\lambda) \le 0$, for $j = 2, 3, 4$.

Now
$$\overline{c}_2(\lambda) = \overline{c}_2 + \lambda \overline{c}'_2 = 2 - 4\lambda \le 0 \quad \therefore \lambda \ge \frac{1}{2},$$
$$\overline{c}_3(\lambda) = \overline{c}_3 + \lambda \overline{c}'_3 = -2 \le 0, \text{ which is true,}$$
$$\overline{c}_4(\lambda) = \overline{c}_4 + \lambda \overline{c}'_4 = -4 - 2\lambda \le 0 \quad \therefore \lambda \ge -2.$$

$\therefore$ For all $\lambda < \frac{1}{2}$, the optimal solution is given by

$$x_1 = 3, x_2 = x_3 = x_4 = 0, x_5 = 6 \text{ and } Z_{max} = 12 + 6\lambda.$$

For $\lambda < -1$, the relative profit coefficient of the non-basic variable x_4, namely $\overline{c}_4(\lambda)$ becomes positive and again table 6.98 no longer remains optimal. x_4 becomes the entering variable and x_1 the leaving variable. Key element is 4/3. This element is made unity and x_1 is replaced by x_4 in table 6.100.

TABLE 6.100

		c'_j	2	–2	2	0	0	
		c_j	4	6	2	0	0	
c'_B	c_B	Basis	x_1	x_2	x_3	x_4	x_5	b
0	0	x_4	$3/4$	0	$-3/4$	1	$-1/4$	$3/4$
–2	6	x_2	$1/4$	1	$7/4$	0	$1/4$	$9/4$
		$\overline{c}_j$	$5/2$	0	$-17/2$	0	$-3/2$	$Z = 27/2$
		$\overline{c}'_j$	$5/2$	0	$11/2$	0	$1/2$	$Z' = -9/2$

Table 6.100 will be optimal if $\overline{c}'_1(\lambda) \le 0$ for $j = 1, 3, 5$.

Now
$$\overline{c}_1(\lambda) = \overline{c}_1 + \lambda \overline{c}'_1 = \frac{5}{2} + \frac{5}{2}\lambda \le 0 \qquad \therefore \quad \lambda \le -1,$$
$$\overline{c}_3(\lambda) = \overline{c}_3 + \lambda \overline{c}'_3 = -\frac{17}{2} + \frac{11}{2}\lambda \le 0 \qquad \therefore \lambda \le \frac{17}{11},$$
$$\overline{c}_5(\lambda) = \overline{c}_5 + \lambda \overline{c}'_5 = -\frac{3}{2} + \frac{1}{2}\lambda \le 0 \qquad \therefore \lambda \le 3.$$

$\therefore$ For all $\lambda \le -1$, the optimal solution is given by

$$x_1 = 0, x_2 = \frac{9}{4}, x_3 = 0, x_4 = \frac{3}{4}, x_5 = 0 \text{ and } Z_{max} = \frac{27}{2} - \frac{9}{2}\lambda.$$

Thus tables 6.98, 6.99 and 6.100 give families of optimal solutions for $-1 \le \lambda \le \frac{1}{2}$, $\lambda \ge \frac{1}{2}$ and $\lambda \le -1$ respectively.

EXAMPLE 6.7-1.2

Consider the parametric problem

maximize $\quad Z = (3 - 6\lambda)x_1 + (2 - 2\lambda)x_2 + (5 + 5\lambda)x_3,$

subject to $\quad x_1 + 2x_2 + x_3 \le 430,$

$3x_1 + 2x_3 \le 460,$

$x_1 + 4x_2 \le 420,$

$x_1, x_2, x_3 \ge 0.$

Perform a complete parametric analysis and identify all the critical values of the parameter λ.
[*Shivaji M.Sc. (Math.) 1977*]

Solution

The given parametric problem is

$$\begin{aligned}\text{maximize} \quad & Z = (3 - 6\lambda)x_1 + (2 - 2\lambda)x_2 + (5 + 5\lambda)x_3 + 0x_4 + 0x_5 + 0x_6,\\ \text{subject to} \quad & x_1 + 2x_2 + x_3 + x_4 = 430,\\ & 3x_1 + 2x_3 + x_5 = 460,\\ & x_1 + 4x_2 + x_6 = 420,\\ & x_1, x_2, x_3, x_4, x_5, x_6 \geq 0.\end{aligned}$$

When $\lambda = 0$, the parametric problem reduces to a simple L.P. problem, whose optimal solution is given by table 6.101 (left as an exercise for the reader). The relative profit coefficients in this table are all non-positive.

TABLE 6.101

	c_j	3	2	5	0	0	0	
c_B	Basis	x_1	x_2	x_3	x_4	x_5	x_6	b
2	x_2	$-1/4$	1	0	$1/2$	$-1/4$	0	100
5	x_3	$3/2$	0	1	0	$1/2$	0	230
0	x_6	2	0	0	−2	1	1	20
$Z_j = \sum c_B a_{ij}$		7	2	5	1	2	0	1,350
$\bar{c}_j = c_j - Z_j$		−4	0	0	−1	−2	0	

For values of λ other than zero, the relative profit coefficients become linear functions of λ. To compute them we first add a new relative profit row called $\bar{c}'_j$ -row to table 6.101. This is shown in table 6.102.

TABLE 6.102

		c'_j	− 6	−2	5	0	0	0	
		c_j	3	2	5	0	0	0	
c'_B	c_B	Basis	x_1	x_2	x_3	x_4	x_5	x_6	b
−2	2	x_2	$-1/4$	1	0	$1/2$	$-1/4$	0	100
5	5	x_3	$3/2$	0	1	0	$1/2$	0	230
0	0	x_6	2	0	0	−2	1	1	20
		$\bar{c}_j$	−4	0	0	−1	−2	0	Z = 1,350
		$\bar{c}'_j$	−14	0	0	1	−3	0	Z′ = 950

In table 6.102, $\bar{c}'_j$ is calculated just as $\bar{c}_j$ -row except that vector **C** is replaced by **C′**. For example,

$$\bar{c}'_1 = \bar{c}_1 - c'_B \,\bar{\mathbf{P}}_1 = -6 - (-2, 5, 0)\begin{bmatrix} -1/4 \\ 3/2 \\ 2 \end{bmatrix} = -6 - \left(\frac{1}{2} + \frac{15}{2} + 0\right) = -14, \text{ etc.}$$

and $\quad Z' = -2 \times 100 + 5 \times 230 = 950.$

Table 6.102 represents the basic feasible solution for the given parametric problem. It is given by

$$x_1 = 0,\ x_2 = 100,\ x_3 = 230,\ x_4 = x_5 = 0,\ x_6 = 20\ ;\ Z(\lambda) = Z + \lambda Z' = 1{,}350 + 950\,\lambda.$$

The relative profit coefficients, which are linear functions of λ, are given by

$$\bar{c}_j(\lambda) = \bar{c}_j + \lambda \bar{c}'_j,\ j = 1, 2, \ldots, 6.$$

Table 6.102 will be optimal if $\bar{c}_j(\lambda) \le 0$ for $j = 1, 4, 5$. Thus we can determine the range of λ for which table 6.102 remains optimal. This is done as follows:

$$\bar{c}_1(\lambda) = \bar{c}_1 + \lambda \bar{c}'_j = -4 - 14\lambda \le 0 \text{ or } \lambda \ge -\frac{2}{7},$$

$$\bar{c}_4(\lambda) = \bar{c}_4 + \lambda \bar{c}'_4 = -1 + \lambda \le 0 \text{ or } \lambda \le 1,$$

$$\bar{c}_5(\lambda) = \bar{c}_5 + \lambda \bar{c}'_5 = -2 - 3\lambda \le 0 \text{ or } \lambda \ge -\frac{2}{3},$$

Thus $x_1 = 0,\ x_2 = 100,\ x_3 = 230,\ x_4 = x_5 = 0,\ x_6 = 20$ is an optimal solution for the given parametric problem for all values of λ between – 2/3 and 1 and $Z_{max} = 1{,}350 + 950\lambda$.

For $\lambda > 1$, the relative profit coefficient of the non-basic variable x_4, namely $\bar{c}_4(\lambda)$ becomes positive and table 6.102 no longer remains optimal. Regular simplex method is used to find the optimal solution. x_4 is the entering variable and computation of replacement ratio (θ) column indicates x_2 to be the variable that leaves the basis. The key element is $\frac{1}{2}$. This key element is made unity and x_2 is replaced by x_4 in table 6.103.

TABLE 6.103

		c'_j	– 6	– 2	5	0	0	0	
		c_j	3	2	5	0	0	0	
c'_B	c_B	Basis	x_1	x_2	x_3	x_4	x_5	x_6	b
0	0	x_4	$-1/2$	2	0	1	$-1/2$	0	200
5	5	x_3	$3/2$	0	1	0	$1/2$	0	230
0	0	x_6	1	4	0	0	0	1	420
		$\bar{c}_j$	$-9/2$	2	0	0	$-5/2$	0	Z = 1,150
		$\bar{c}'_j$	$-27/2$	–2	0	0	$-5/2$	0	Z′ = 1,150

Table 6.103 will be optimal if $\bar{c}_j(\lambda) \le 0$ for $j = 1, 2, 5$.

Now
$$\bar{c}_1(\lambda) = \bar{c}_1 + \lambda \bar{c}'_1 = -\frac{9}{2} - \frac{27}{2}\lambda \le 0 \text{ or } \lambda \ge -\frac{1}{3},$$

$$\bar{c}_2(\lambda) = \bar{c}_2 + \lambda \bar{c}'_2 = 2 - 2\lambda \le 0 \text{ or } \lambda \ge 1, \text{ which is true,}$$

$$\bar{c}_5(\lambda) = \bar{c}_5 + \lambda \bar{c}'_5 = -\frac{5}{2} - \frac{5}{2}\lambda \le 0 \text{ or } \lambda \ge -1.$$

∴ For all values of $\lambda \ge 1$, the optimal solution is given by

$$x_1 = x_2 = 0,\ x_3 = 230,\ x_4 = 200,\ x_5 = 0,\ x_6 = 420;\ Z_{max} = 1{,}150\,(1 + \lambda).$$

For $\lambda < -\frac{2}{3}$, the relative profit coefficient of the non-basic variable x_5, namely $\bar{c}_5(\lambda)$ becomes positive and again table 6.102 no longer remains optimal. x_5 becomes the entering variable and x_6 the leaving variable. Key element is 1. Replacing x_6 by x_5 we get table 6.104.

TABLE 6.104

		c'_j	−6	−2	5	0	0	0	
		c_j	3	2	5	0	0	0	
c'_B	c_B	Basis	x_1	x_2	x_3	x_4	x_5	x_6	b
−2	2	x_2	$1/4$	1	0	0	0	$1/4$	105
5	5	x_3	$1/2$	0	1	0	0	$-1/2$	220
0	0	x_5	2	0	0	−2	1	1	20
		$\bar{c}_j$	0	0	0	−5	0	2	Z = 1,310
		$\bar{c}'_j$	−8	0	0	−5	0	3	Z′ = 890

Table 6.104 will be optimal if $\bar{c}_j(\lambda) \leq 0$ for $j = 1, 4, 6$.

Now
$$\bar{c}_1(\lambda) = \bar{c}_1 + \lambda \bar{c}'_1 = 0 - 8\lambda \leq 0 \text{ or } \lambda \geq 0,$$
$$\bar{c}_4(\lambda) = -5 - 5\lambda \leq 0 \text{ or } \lambda \geq -1,$$
$$\bar{c}_6(\lambda) = 2 + 3\lambda \leq 0 \text{ or } \lambda \leq -\frac{2}{3}.$$

Thus for $-1 \leq \lambda \leq -\frac{2}{3}$, the optimal solution s given by

$$x_1 = 0, x_2 = 105, x_3 = 220, x_4 = 0, x_5 = 20, x_6 = 0; Z_{max} = 1{,}310 + 890\,\lambda.$$

Thus tables 6.102, 6.103 and 6.104 give families of optimal solutions for $-\frac{2}{3} \leq \lambda \leq 1$, $\lambda \geq 1$, $-1 \leq \lambda \leq -\frac{2}{3}$. The critical values of λ are $-\frac{2}{3}$, 1.

6.7-2 Parametric Right-Hand Side Problem

The right-hand side constants in a linear programming problem represent the limits in the resources and the outputs. In some practical problems all the resources are not independent of one another. A shortage of one resource may cause shortage of other resources at varying levels. Same is true for outputs also. For example, consider a firm manufacturing electrical appliances. A shortage in electric power will decrease the demand of all the electric items produced, in varying degrees depending upon the electric energy consumed by them. In all such problems, we are to consider simultaneous changes in the right-hand side constants, which are functions of one parameter and study how the optimal solution is affected by these changes.

Let the linear programming problem before parameterization be

$$\begin{aligned} \text{maximize} \quad & \mathbf{Z} = \mathbf{cX}, \\ \text{subject to} \quad & \mathbf{AX} = \mathbf{b}, \\ & \mathbf{X} = \mathbf{0}, \end{aligned}$$

where **b** is the known requirement (right-hand side) vector. Let this requirement vector **b** change to $\mathbf{b} + \lambda\mathbf{b}'$ so that parametric right-hand side problem becomes

$$\begin{aligned} \text{maximize} \quad & Z = \mathbf{cX}, \\ \text{subject to} \quad & \mathbf{AX} = \mathbf{b} + \lambda\mathbf{b}', \\ & \mathbf{X} \geq \mathbf{0}, \end{aligned}$$

where $\mathbf{b}'$ is the given and predetermined variation vector and λ is an unknown parameter. As λ changes, the right-hand constants also change. We wish to determine the family of optimal solutions as λ changes from $-\infty$ to $+\infty$.

When $\lambda = 0$, the parametric problem reduces to the original L.P. problem; simplex method is used to find its optimal solution.

Let $\mathbf{B}$ and $\mathbf{X_B}$ represent the optimal basis matrix and the optimal basic feasible solution respectively for $\lambda = 0$. Then $\mathbf{X_B} = \mathbf{B}^{-1}\,\mathbf{b}$. As λ changes from zero to a positive or negative value, the values of the basic variables change and the new values are given by

$$\mathbf{X_B} = \mathbf{B}^{-1}\,(\mathbf{b} + \lambda\mathbf{b}') = \mathbf{B}^{-1}\,\mathbf{b} + \lambda\mathbf{B}^{-1}\mathbf{b}' = \bar{\mathbf{b}} + \lambda\,\bar{\mathbf{b}}'.$$

A change in λ has no effect on the values of relative profit coefficients $\bar{c}_j$ *i.e.*, $\bar{c}_j$ values remain non-positive (maximization problem). For a given basis matrix $\mathbf{B}$, values of $\bar{\mathbf{b}}$ and $\bar{\mathbf{b}}'$ can be calculated. The solution $\mathbf{X_B} = \bar{\mathbf{b}} + \lambda\bar{\mathbf{b}}'$ is feasible and optimal as long as $\bar{\mathbf{b}} + \lambda\,\bar{\mathbf{b}}' \geq 0$. In other words, for a given solution we can determine the range for λ within which the solution remains optimal.

EXAMPLE 6.7-2.1

Consider the linear programming problem

maximize $Z = 4x_1 + 6x_2 + 2x_3,$

subject to $x_1 + x_2 + x_3 \leq 3,$

$x_1 + 4x_2 + 7x_3 \leq 9,$

$x_1, x_2, x_3 \geq 0.$

The optimal solution to this problem is given by

TABLE 6.105

	c_j	4	6	2	0	0	
c_B	*Basis*	x_1	x_2	x_3	x_4	x_5	b
4	x_1	1	0	-1	$4/3$	$-1/3$	1
6	x_2	0	1	2	$-1/3$	$1/3$	2
$Z_j = \sum c_B\, a_{ij}$		4	6	8	$10/3$	$2/3$	
$\bar{c}_j = c_j - Z_j$		0	0	-6	$-10/3$	$-2/3$	

Solve the problem if the variation right-hand side vector $b' = \begin{bmatrix} 3 \\ -3 \end{bmatrix}$. *Perform complete parametric analysis and identify all critical values of parameter* λ.

Solution

The given parametric right-hand side problem is

maximize $Z = 4x_1 + 6x_2 + 2x_3 + 0x_4 + 0x_5,$

subject to $x_1 + x_2 + x_3 + x_4 = 3 + 3\lambda,$

$x_1 + 4x_2 + 7x_3 + x_5 = 9 - 3\lambda,$

$x_1, x_2, x_3, x_4, x_5 \geq 0.$

When $\lambda = 0$, the problem reduces to the L.P. problem whose optimal solution is given by table 6.105. For values of λ other than zero, the values of right-hand constants change because of the variation vector $\mathbf{b}'$. This is shown in the expanded table 6.106.

TABLE 6.106

	c_j	4	6	2	0	0		
c_B	Basis	x_1	x_2	x_3	x_4	x_5	$\bar{\mathbf{b}}$	$\bar{\mathbf{b}}'$

4	x_1	1	0	−1	$4/3$	$-1/3$	1	5
6	x_2	0	1	2	$(-1/3)$	$1/3$	2	−2 ←*Key row*
	$\bar{c}_j$	0	0	−6	$-10/3$	$-2/3$	Z = 16	Z′ = 8
					↑K			

The vectors $\bar{\mathbf{b}}$ and $\bar{\mathbf{b}}'$ are computed as follows :

$$\bar{\mathbf{b}} = \mathbf{B}^{-1}\mathbf{b} = \begin{bmatrix} \frac{4}{3} & -\frac{1}{3} \\ -\frac{1}{3} & \frac{1}{3} \end{bmatrix} \begin{bmatrix} 3 \\ 9 \end{bmatrix} = \begin{bmatrix} 1 \\ 2 \end{bmatrix},$$

$$\bar{\mathbf{b}}' = \mathbf{B}^{-1}\mathbf{b}' = \begin{bmatrix} \frac{4}{3} & -\frac{1}{3} \\ -\frac{1}{3} & \frac{1}{3} \end{bmatrix} \begin{bmatrix} 3 \\ -3 \end{bmatrix} = \begin{bmatrix} 5 \\ -2 \end{bmatrix}$$

For a fixed λ, the value of basic variables in table 6.106 are given by

$$x_1 = \bar{b}_1 + \lambda \bar{b}_1' = 1 + 5\lambda,\; x_2 = \bar{b}_2 + \lambda \bar{b}_2' = 2 - 2\lambda.$$

$\bar{c}_j$ values are not affected as long as the basis consists of variables x_1 and x_2. As λ changes, values of basic variables x_1 and x_2 change and table 6.106 remains optimal as long as the basis (x_1, x_2) remains feasible. In other words, table 6.106 remains optimal as long as

$$x_1 = 1 + 5\lambda \geq 0 \text{ or } \lambda \geq -\frac{1}{5},$$

$$x_2 = 2 - 2\lambda \geq 0 \text{ or } \lambda \leq 1.$$

Therefore, table 6.106 remains optimal as λ varies from −1/5 to 1. Thus for all $-1/5 \leq \lambda \leq 1$, the optimal solution is given by

$$x_1 = 1 + 5\lambda,\; x_2 = 2 - 2\lambda,\; x_3 = x_4 = x_5 = 0,\; Z_{max} = 16 + 8\lambda.$$

For λ > 1, the basic variable x_2 becomes negative. Although this makes table 6.106 infeasible for the primal, it remains feasible for the dual since all $\bar{c}_j$ coefficients are non-positive. Dual simplex method can, therefore, be applied to find the new optimal solution for λ > 1. Evidently x_2 is the variable that leaves the basis. The ratios of the non-basic variables are −3, 10, − 2. Thus variable x_4 is the entering variable. The key element −1/3 has been shown bracketed. Regular simplex method is now used to find the new optimal solution. In table 6.107, the key element has been made unity and x_2 is replaced by x_4.

TABLE 6.107

	c_j	4	6	2	0	0		
c_B	Basis	x_1	x_2	x_3	x_4	x_5	$\bar{\mathbf{b}}$	$\bar{\mathbf{b}}'$
4	x_1	1	4	7	0	1	9	−3
0	x_4	0	−3	−6	1	−1	−6	6
$Z_j = \sum c_B a_{ij}$		4	16	28	0	4		
$\bar{c}_j = c_j - Z_j$		0	−10	−26	0	−4		

The basic solution given by table 6.107 is

$$x_1 = 9 - 3\lambda,\; x_2 = 0,\; x_3 = 0,\; x_4 = -6 + 6\lambda,\; x_5 = 0,\; Z_{max} = 36 - 12\lambda.$$

This solution is optimal as long as the basic variables x_1 and x_4 remain non-negative *i.e.*, as long as

$$x_1 = 9 - 3\lambda \geq 0 \text{ or } \lambda \leq 3,$$
$$x_4 = -6 + 6\lambda \geq 0 \text{ or } \lambda \geq 1.$$

Thus the above solution is optimal for all $1 \leq \lambda \leq 3$.

For $\lambda > 3$, the basic variable x_1 becomes negative. As there is no negative coefficient in the first row, the primal solution is infeasible. Hence there exists no optimal solution to the problem for all $\lambda > 3$.

For $\lambda \leq -1/5$, the basic variable x_1 in table 6.106 becomes negative. Although this makes table 6.106 infeasible for the primal, it remains feasible for the dual, since all $\overline{c}_j$ coefficients are non-positive. Dual simplex method can, therefore, be applied to find the new optimal solution for $\lambda \leq -1/5$. Evidently x_1 is the variable that leaves the basis. The ratios of non-basic variables are 6, –5/2, 2. Thus variable x_5 is the entering variable and –1/3 is the key element. This element is made unity in table 6.108. Also x_1 is replaced by x_5.

TABLE 6.108

	c_j	4	6	2	0	0		
c_B	Basis	x_1	x_2	x_3	x_4	x_5	$\mathbf{\overline{b}}$	$\mathbf{\overline{b}'}$
0	x_5	–3	0	3	–4	1	–3	–15
6	x_2	1	1	1	1	0	3	3
$Z_j = \sum c_B a_{ij}$		6	6	6	6	0		
$\overline{c}_j = c_j - Z_j$		–2	0	–4	–6	0		

The basic solution given by table 6.108 is

$$x_1 = 0, x_2 = 3 + 3\lambda, x_3 = 0, x_4 = 0, x_5 = -3 - 15\lambda,$$

and $\quad Z_{\max} = 18 + 18\lambda.$

This solution is optimal so long as

$$x_2 = 3 + 3\lambda \geq 0 \text{ or } \lambda \geq -1,$$
$$x_5 = -3 - 15\lambda \geq 0 \text{ or } \lambda \leq -1/5.$$

Thus the above solution is optimal for all $-1 \leq \lambda \leq -1/5$.

For $\lambda < -1$, the basic variable x_2 in table 6.108 becomes negative. As there is no negative coefficient in the second row, the primal solution is infeasible. Hence there exists no optimal solution to the problem for all $\lambda < -1$. Thus tables 6.106, 6.107 and 6.108 give families of optimal solutions for $-\frac{1}{5} \leq \lambda \leq 1, 1 \leq \lambda \leq 3$ and $-1 \leq \lambda \leq -\frac{1}{5}$ respectively.

EXAMPLE 6.7-2.2

Consider the parametric problem

$$\text{maximize} \quad Z = 3x_1 + 2x_2 + 5x_3,$$
$$\text{subject to} \quad x_1 + 2x_2 + x_3 \leq 430 + \theta,$$
$$3x_1 + 2x_3 \leq 460 - 4\theta,$$
$$x_1 + 4x_2 \leq 420 - 4\theta,$$
$$x_1, x_2, x_3 \geq 0.$$

Determine the critical values (range) of θ *for which the solution remains optimal basic feasible.*

Solution

The given parametric right-hand side problem can be expressed in standard form as maximize $Z = 3x_1 + 2x_2 + 5x_3 - 0x_4 + 0x_5 + 0x_6,$

subject to $x_1 + 2x_2 + x_3 + x_4 = 430 + \theta,$

$3x_1 + 2x_3 + x_5 = 460 - 4\theta,$

$x_1 + 4x_2 + x_6 = 420 - 4\theta,$

$x_1, x_2, x_3, x_4, x_5, x_6 \geq 0.$

When θ = 0, the problem reduces to the L.P. problem whose optimal solution is given by table 6.109.

TABLE 6.109

	c_j	3	2	5	0	0	0	
c_B	Basis	x_1	x_2	x_3	x_4	x_5	x_6	b
2	x_2	$-1/4$	1	0	$1/2$	$-1/4$	0	100
5	x_3	$3/2$	0	1	0	$1/2$	0	230
0	x_6	2	0	0	−2	1	1	20
$Z_j = \sum c_B a_{ij}$		7	2	5	1	2	0	1,350
$\bar{c}_j = c_j - Z_j$		−4	0	0	−1	−2	0	

For values of θ other than zero, the values of right-hand side constants change because of the variation vector **b′**. This is shown in the expanded table 6.110.

TABLE 6.110

	c_j	3	2	5	0	0	0		
c_B	Basis	x_1	x_2	x_3	x_4	x_5	x_6	$\bar{\mathbf{b}}$	$\bar{\mathbf{b}}'$
2	x_2	$-1/4$	1	0	$1/2$	$-1/4$	0	100	$\frac{3}{2}$
5	x_3	$3/2$	0	1	0	$1/2$	0	230	−2
0	x_6	2	0	0	(−2)	1	1	20	−10←
	$\bar{c}_j$	−4	0	0	−1	−2	0	Z = 1,350	Z′ = −7
					↑				

The vectors $\bar{\mathbf{b}}$ and $\bar{\mathbf{b}}'$ in table 6.110 are computed as follows :

$$\bar{\mathbf{b}} = \mathbf{B}^{-1}\mathbf{b} = \begin{bmatrix} \frac{1}{2} & -\frac{1}{4} & 0 \\ 0 & \frac{1}{2} & 0 \\ -2 & 1 & 1 \end{bmatrix} \cdot \begin{bmatrix} 430 \\ 460 \\ 420 \end{bmatrix} = \begin{bmatrix} 100 \\ 230 \\ 20 \end{bmatrix},$$

$$\bar{\mathbf{b}}' = \mathbf{B}^{-1}\mathbf{b}' = \begin{bmatrix} \frac{1}{2} & -\frac{1}{4} & 0 \\ 0 & \frac{1}{2} & 0 \\ -2 & 1 & 1 \end{bmatrix} \cdot \begin{bmatrix} 1 \\ -4 \\ -4 \end{bmatrix} = \begin{bmatrix} \frac{3}{2} \\ -2 \\ -10 \end{bmatrix}.$$

For a fixed θ, values of the basic variables in table 6 110 are given by

$$x_2 = 100 + \frac{3}{2}\theta,$$

$$x_3 = 230 - 2\,\theta,$$
$$x_6 = 20 - 10\,\theta.$$

$\overline{c}_j$ values are not affected so long as the basis consists of x_2, x_3 and x_6 . As θ changes, values of the basic variables x_2, x_3 and x_6 change and table 6.110 remains optimal as long as the basis (x_2, x_3, x_6) remains feasible. In other words, table 6.110 remains optimal as long as

$$x_2 = 100 + \frac{3}{2}\theta \geq 0 \text{ or } \theta \geq -\frac{200}{3},$$
$$x_3 = 230 - 2\,\theta \geq 0 \text{ or } \theta \leq 115,$$
$$x_6 = 20 - 10\,\theta \geq 0 \text{ or } \theta \leq 2.$$

Therefore, table 6.110 remains optimal as θ varies from $-\frac{200}{3}$ to 2. Thus for all $-\frac{200}{3} \leq \theta \leq 2$, the optimal solution is given by

$$x_2 = 100 + \frac{3}{2}\theta,$$
$$x_3 = 230 - 2\theta,$$
$$x_6 = 20 - 10\theta,$$
$$Z_{max} = 1{,}350 - 7\theta.$$

For $\theta > 2$, the basic variable x_6 becomes negative. Although this makes table 6.110 infeasible for the primal, it remains feasible for the dual, since all $\overline{c}_j$ coefficients are negative. Dual simplex method, can, therefore, be applied to find the new optimal solution for $\theta > 2$. Evidently x_6 is the variable that leaves the basis. The ratios of the non-basic variables are –2 , 1/2, –2. Thus x_4 is the incoming variable. The key element –2 has been shown bracketed. Regular simplex method is now applied to find the new optimal solution. In table 6.111 the key element is made unity and x_6 is replaced by x_4.

TABLE 6.111

	c_j	3	2	5	0	0	0		
c_B	Basis	x_1	x_2	x_3	x_4	x_5	x_6	$\overline{\mathbf{b}}$	$\overline{\mathbf{b}}'$
2	x_2	1/4	1	0	0	0	1/4	105	–1
5	x_3	3/2	0	1	0	1/2	0	230	–2
0	x_4	–1	0	0	1	–1/2	–1/2	–10	5
	Z_j	8	2	5	0	5/2	1/2	1,360	–12
	$\overline{c}_j$	–5	0	0	0	–5/2	–1/2		

The basic solution given by table 6.111 is

$$x_1 = 0,$$
$$x_2 = 105 - \theta,$$
$$x_3 = 230 - 2\,\theta,$$
$$x_4 = -10 + 5\,\theta,$$
$$x_5 = x_6 = 0\,,$$
$$Z_{max} = 1{,}360 - 12\,\theta.$$

This solution is optimal as long as the basic variables x_2, x_3 and x_4 remain non-negative *i.e.*, as long as

$$x_2 = 105 - \theta \geq 0 \text{ or } \theta \leq 105,$$
$$x_3 = 230 - 2\theta \geq 0 \text{ or } \theta \leq 115,$$
$$\mathbf{x_4 = -10 + 5\theta \geq 0 \text{ or } \theta \geq 2.}$$

Thus the above solution is optimal for all $2 \leq \theta \leq 105$.

For $\theta > 105$, the basic variable x_2 becomes negative. As there is no negative coefficient in the first row, the primal solution is infeasible. Hence there exists no optimal solution to the problem for all $\theta > 105$.

For $\theta < -\frac{200}{3}$, the basic variable x_2 in table 6.110 becomes negative. Dual simplex method can be applied to find the new optimal solution for $\theta < -\frac{200}{3}$.

Evidently x_2 is the variable that leaves the basis. The ratios of the non-basic variables are 16, – 2, 8. Thus x_5 is the incoming variable and –1/4 is the key element. This element is made unity in table 6.112. Also x_2 is replaced by x_5.

TABLE 6.112

	c_j	3	2	5	0	0	0		
c_B	Basis	x_1	x_2	x_3	x_4	x_5	x_6	$\bar{\mathbf{b}}$	$\bar{\mathbf{b}}'$
0	x_5	1	–4	0	–2	1	0	–400	–6
5	x_3	1	2	1	1	0	0	430	1
0	x_6	1	4	0	0	0	1	420	–4
	Z_j	5	10	5	5	0	0	2,150	5
	$\bar{c}_j$	–2	–8	0	–5	0	0		

The basic solution given by table 6.112 is

$$x_1 = x_2 = 0,$$
$$x_3 = 430 + \theta,$$
$$x_4 = 0,$$
$$x_5 = -400 - 6\,\theta,$$
$$x_6 = 420 - 4\,\theta,$$
$$Z_{max} = 2,150 + 5\,\theta.$$

This solution is optimal so long as

$$x_3 = 430 + \theta \geq 0 \text{ or } \theta \geq -430,$$
$$x_5 = -400 - 6\,\theta \geq 0 \text{ or } \theta \leq -\frac{200}{3},$$
$$x_6 = 420 - 4\,\theta \geq 0 \text{ or } \theta \leq 105.$$

Thus the above solution is optimal for all $-430 \leq \theta \leq -\frac{200}{3}$.

For $\theta < -430$, the basic variable x_3 in table 6.112 becomes negative. As there is no negative coefficient in the second row, the primal solution is infeasible. Hence there exists no optimal solution to the problem for all $\theta < -430$.

Thus tables 6.110, 6.111 and 6.112 give families of optimal feasible solution for $-\frac{200}{3} \leq \theta \leq 2$, $2 \leq \theta \leq 105$ and $-430 \leq \theta \leq -\frac{200}{3}$ respectively.

EXERCISES 6.7

1. Explain parametric linear programming. How does it differ from sensitivity analysis?
2. What are different types of parametric linear programming problems? Explain their solution procedures.

Section 6.7-1

3. Consider the parametric linear programming problem

minimize $Z = (\theta - 1)x_1 + x_2,$
subject to $x_1 + 2x_2 \le 10,$
$2x_1 + x_2 \le 11,$
$x_1 - 2x_2 \le 3,$
$x_1, x_2, \ge 0.$

Perform a complete parametric programming analysis. Identify all critical values of the parameter θ and the optimal basic solutions.

[*Sambalpur M.Sc. (Math.) 1977*]

(*Ans.* $x_1 = 0, x_2 = 5$ for $0 \le \theta \le 3/2$;
$x_1 = 4, x_2 = 3$ for $3/2 \le \theta \le 3$;
$x_1 = 5, x_2 = 1$ for $3 \le \theta$.)

4. Consider the parametric problem

maximize $Z = (3 + 3\theta)\, x_1 + 2x_2 + (5 - 6\theta)x_3,$
subject to $x_1 + 2x_2 + x_3 \le 430,$
$3x_1 + 2x_3 \le 460,$
$x_1 + 4x_2 \le 420,$
$x_1, x_2, x_3 \ge 0,$

where θ is a non-negative parameter. Perform a complete parametric programming analysis.

(*Ans.* For $0 \le \theta \le \frac{1}{3}$: $(x_1, x_2, x_3) = (0, 100, 230)$; $Z_{max} = 1{,}350 - 1{,}380\,\theta$;

for $\frac{1}{3} \le \theta \le \frac{5}{12}$; $(x_1, x_2, x_3) = (10, 102.5, 215)$; $Z_{max} = 1{,}310 - 1{,}260\,\theta$;

for $\theta \ge \frac{5}{12}$: $(x_1, x_2, x_3) = \left(\frac{460}{3}, \frac{200}{3}, 0\right)$; $Z_{max} = \frac{1{,}780}{3} + 460\theta$.)

5. Solve the parametric cost problem

minimize $Z = (2 + \lambda)x_1 + (1 + 4\lambda)x_2,$
subject to $3x_1 + x_2 \ge 3,$
$4x_1 + 3x_2 \ge 6,$
$x_1 + 2x_2 \le 3,$
$x_1, x_2 \ge 0,$

and λ is a non-negative parameter.

6. Perform a complete parametric programming analysis of the following L.P. problem:

minimize $Z = \lambda x - y,$
subject to $3x - y \ge 5,$
$2x + y \le 3,$
$-\infty \le \lambda \le \infty.$

[*Meerut M.Sc. (Math.) 1973*]

(*Ans.* For $-2 \le \lambda \le 3$: $x = \frac{8}{5}, y = -\frac{1}{5}$; $Z_{min} = \frac{1}{5} + \frac{8}{5}\lambda$;

for $\lambda = 3$ a multiple solution exists.)

7. The following table gives an optimal solution to a linear programming problem :

TABLE 6.113

	c_j	4	6	2	0	0	
c_B	Basis	x_1	x_2	x_3	x_4	x_5	b
4	x_1	1	0	1	3	–1	1
6	x_2	0	1	1	–1	2	2
	$\bar{c}_j$	0	0	– 8	– 6	– 8	Z = 16

where x_4 and x_5 are slack variables.

(*a*) How much can c_3 be increased before the current solution becomes non-optimal? Find an optimal solution when $c_3 = 12$.

(*b*) Find the range on c_1 for the given basis to the optimal.

(*c*) Find the range on b_2 for the given basis to be optimal.

(*d*) Find the optimal solution by dual simplex method when b_2 is increased by 2 units.

(*e*) Find the range on λ for which the given solution is still optimum if C is replaced by $C + \lambda C'$, where $C' = (0, 0, 1, -1, 2)$ and $-\infty \le \lambda \le \infty$.

8. Perform a complete parametric programming analysis and identify all the critical values of the parameter λ for the problem

$$\begin{aligned} \text{maximize} \quad & Z = (3 - 6\lambda)x_1 + (2 - 2\lambda)x_2 + (5 + 5\lambda)x_3, \\ \text{subject to} \quad & x_1 + 2x_2 + x_3 \le 430, \\ & 3x_1 + 2x_3 \le 460, \\ & x_1 + 4x_2 \le 420, \\ & x_1, x_2, x_3 \ge 0. \end{aligned}$$

[*Shivaji M.Sc. (Math.) 1977*]

(*Ans.* For $-2/3 \le \lambda \le 1$: $(x_1, x_2, x_3) = (0, 100, 230)$, $Z_{max} = 1{,}350 + 950\lambda$;
For $\lambda \ge 1$: $(x_1, x_2, x_3) = (0, 0, 230)$, $Z_{max} = 1{,}150(1 + \lambda)$;
For $-1 \le \lambda \le -2/3$: $(x_1, x_2, x_3) = (0, 105, 220)$, $Z_{max} = 1{,}310 + 890\lambda$.)

9. For the following linear programming problem

$$\begin{aligned} \text{minimize} \quad & Z = \lambda x_1 - \lambda x_2 - x_3 + x_4, \\ \text{subject to} \quad & 3x_1 - 3x_2 - x_3 + x_4 \ge 5, \\ & 2x_1 - 2x_2 + x_3 - x_4 \le 3, \\ & x_1, x_2, \ldots, x_4 \ge 0, \end{aligned}$$

find the range of λ over which the solution remains basic feasible and optimal.

(*Ans.* For $-2 \le \lambda \le 3$: $(x_1, x_2, x_3, x_4) = (8/5, 0, 0, 1/5)$, $Z_{min} = 1/5 + 8/5\,\lambda$;
for $\lambda > 3$ no solution exists.)

10. Solve the parametric cost problem

$$\begin{aligned} \text{minimize} \quad & Z = (2 + \lambda)x_1 + (1 + 4\lambda)x_2, \\ \text{subject to} \quad & 3x_1 + x_2 \ge 3, \\ & 4x_1 + 3x_2 \ge 6, \\ & x_1 + 2x_2 \le 3, \\ & x_1, x_2 \ge 0, \end{aligned}$$

where λ is a non-negative parameter.

11. Study the variation in the optimal solution of the following parameterized L.P., given $t \ge 0$:

$$\begin{aligned} \text{Minimize} \quad & Z = (4 - t)x_1 + (1 - 3t)x_2 + (2 - 2t)x_3, \\ \text{subject to} \quad & 3x_1 + x_2 + 2x_3 = 3, \\ & 4x_1 + 3x_2 + 2x_3 \ge 6, \\ & x_1 + 2x_2 + 5x_3 \le 4, \\ & x_1, x_2, x_3 \ge 0. \end{aligned}$$

(*Ans.* $x_1 = \dfrac{2}{5}$, $x_2 = \dfrac{9}{5}$, $x_3 = 0$; $Z_{min} = \dfrac{17 - 29t}{5}$.)

Section 6.7-2

12. Solve the problem

$$\begin{aligned} \text{maximize} \quad & Z = 3x_1 + 2x_2 + 5x_3, \\ \text{subject to} \quad & x_1 + 2x_2 + x_3 \le 430 + 500\lambda, \\ & 3x_1 + 2x_3 \le 460 + 100\lambda, \\ & x_1 + 4x_2 \le 420 - 200\lambda, \\ & x_1, x_2, x_3 \ge 0, \end{aligned}$$

where λ is a non-negative parameter.

(*Ans.* For $0 \le \lambda \le 1/55$: $(x_1, x_2, x_3) = (0, 100 + 225\lambda, 230 + 50\lambda)$
and $Z_{max} = 1{,}350 + 700\lambda$;
for $1/55 \le \lambda \le 2.1$: $(x_1, x_2, x_3) = (0, 105 - 50\lambda, 230 + 50\lambda)$
and $Z_{max} = 1{,}360 + 150\lambda$;
for $\lambda > 2.1$: no feasible solution exists.)

13. Minimize $Z = 4y_1 + y_2,$
subject to
$$3y_1 + y_2 = 3 + 3\lambda,$$
$$4y_1 + 3y_2 \geq 6 + 2\lambda,$$
$$y_1 + 2y_2 \leq 3 + 4\lambda,$$
$$y_1, y_2, \lambda \geq 0.$$

14. Given the L.P. problem
maximize $Z = 7y_1 + 4y_2 + 6y_3 + 5y_4,$
subject to
$$2y_1 + y_2 + 2y_3 + y_4 \leq 6 + \theta,$$
$$y_1 - 2y_2 + 2y_3 + 4y_4 \leq 20 - \theta,$$
$$3y_1 + y_2 - 3y_3 + 2y_4 \leq 40 - \theta,$$
$$y_1, y_2, y_3, y_4 \geq 0,$$
perform a complete parametric programming analysis and identify all the critical values of the parameter θ.

15. Solve the following L.P.P.:
Minimize $Z = (2 + \lambda)x_1 + (4 - \lambda)x_2 + (4 - 2\lambda)x_3 - (3 - 3\lambda)x_4,$
subject to
$$x_1 + x_2 + x_3 = 4 - \lambda,$$
$$2x_1 + 4x_2 + x_4 = 8 - \lambda,$$
$$x_1, x_2, ..., x_4 \geq 0,$$
where λ is a non-negative parameter. Study the variations of the optimal solution with λ.

16. Maximize $Z = 3x_1 + 2x_2 + 5x_3,$
subject to
$$x_1 + 2x_2 + x_3 \leq 40 - t,$$
$$3x_1 + 2x_3 \leq 60 + 2t,$$
$$x_1 + 4x_2 \leq 30 - 7t,$$
$$x_1, x_2, x_3, t \geq 0.$$

(*Ans.* For $0 \leq t \leq \frac{10}{3}$: $x_1 = 0, x_2 = 5 - t, x_3 = 30 + t$; $Z_{\max} = 160 + 3t$;

for $\frac{10}{3} \leq t \leq \frac{30}{7}$: $x_1 = 0, x_2 = \frac{30 - 7t}{4}, x_3 = 30 + t$; $Z_{\max} = 165 + \frac{3}{2}t$;

for $t > \frac{30}{7}$: no feasible solution exists.)

17. Study the variation in optimal solution of the following parameterized L.P., given $t \geq 0$:
Minimize $Z = 4x_1 + x_2 + 2x_3,$
subject to
$$3x_1 + x_2 + 2x_3 = 3 + 3t,$$
$$4x_1 + 3x_2 + 2x_3 \geq 6 + 2t,$$
$$x_1 + 2x_2 + 5x_3 \leq 4 - t,$$
$$x_1, x_2, x_3 \geq 0.$$

18. Minimize $Z = 3x_1 + 2x_2,$
subject to
$$3x_1 + x_2 \geq 3 + 2t,$$
$$4x_1 + 3x_2 \geq 6 + 2t,$$
$$x_1 + x_2 \leq 3 - 4t,$$
$$x_1, x_2 \geq 0 \; ; -\infty \leq t \leq \infty.$$

(*Ans.* For $0 \leq t \leq \frac{3}{8}$: $x_1 = \frac{3 + 7t}{5}, x_2 = \frac{6 - 11t}{5}, Z_{\min} = \frac{21 - t}{5}$;

for $\frac{3}{8} \leq t \leq \frac{2}{5}$: $x_1 = -3 + 11t, x_2 = 6 - 15t, Z_{\min} = 3 + 3t$.)

19. Maximize $Z = (4 - 100\lambda)y_1 + (8 - 4\lambda)y_2,$
subject to
$$y_1 + y_2 \leq 6,$$
$$2y_1 + y_2 \leq 4 - \lambda,$$
$$y_1, y_2 \geq 0.$$

Study the variations in the optimal solution with parameter λ, where $-\infty \le \lambda \le \infty$.

20. For Ex. 7, find the range on λ for which the given basis (x_1, x_2) is still optimal if the original **b** vector is replaced by $\mathbf{b} + \lambda\,\mathbf{b}'$, where $\mathbf{b}' = \begin{bmatrix} 1 \\ -1 \end{bmatrix}$ and $-\infty < \lambda < \infty$. Also find the optimal solution when $\lambda = 1/2$. (Assume that (x_4, x_5) forms the initial basis.)

6.8 GOAL PROGRAMMING

In chapter 2 we studied in detail, the linear programming technique as a tool for management decisions. However, a difficulty with linear programming is that objective function is measured in only *one dimension* such as profit or loss or production capacity, etc. It is impossible in linear programming to have *multiple objectives* unless they can be measured in the same units. Organisations often, due to the pressure of society and statutory regulations, have *several objectives* generally not measurable in the same units (e.g., these objectives may have units of measurement as rupees, hours, tons, etc.) These objectives may even be conflicting. For example, different objectives set by a company could be employment stability, high product quality, maximization of profit, better industrial and labour relations, minimization of noise level, etc. In such situations, it may be impossible to find a single solution that optimizes the conflicting objectives. Instead we may seek a *compromise solution* based on the relative importance of each objective.

Goal programming, developed by Charnes and Cooper, presents a technique for solving such multiobjective models. The principal idea is to convert the original multiple objectives into a single goal. The resulting model yields what is usually termed as an *efficient solution* because it may not be optimum with respect to *all* the conflicting objectives of the problem.

This technique uses the simplex method for finding the *near optimum solution* of a single dimensional or multidimensional objective function subject to a set of linear constraints. All management goals with their assigned priorities are incorporated into the objective function and only the environmental conditions *i.e.*, those outside the management control are treated as constraints. The objective function contains the *deviational variables* that represent each goal or subgoal. The deviational variables are represented in two dimensions— a positive and a negative deviation from each subgoal and / or constraint and the objective function involves the minimization of these deviations.

Goal programming asks management of the organisation to set some estimated targets for each goal and assign priorities to them *i.e.*, to rank them in order of importance. The management only has to say which goal is more important than the other; it need not say how much more.

With this information in hand, goal programming tries to *minimize* the deviations from the targets that were set. It begins with the most important goal and continues in such a way that a less important goal is considered only after the more important ones are satisfied or have reached the point beyond which no further improvements are desired. In the final solution all the goals may not be fulfilled to the fullest extent (of estimated targets); however, the deviations will be the minimum possible.

Steps in Goal Programming Model Formulation

1. Define the variables and the constants

The first step is to define the relevant variables and the right-hand side constants. The right-hand side constants may be either available resources or specified goal levels. It requires careful analysis of the problem to identify the relevant variables that affect the specified goals.

2. Formulate constraints

Formulate the constraints in the same manner as in ordinary L.P. problem. For each constraint, develop an equation by introducing deviational variables D_u and D_o, whee D_u represents the amount by which goal is underachieved and D_o represents the amount by which goal is overachieved (right-hand side of each constraint).

3. Develop the objective function

The objective function must be developed by analysing the specified goals. Priority factors should be assigned to the variables that are relevant to the goal attainment. Differential weights must be assigned to deviational variables having the same priority.

EXAMPLE 6.8-1

A company manufactures two products, radios and transistors, which must be processed through assembly and finishing departments. Assembly has 90 hours available, finishing can handle up to 72 hours of work. Manufacturing one radio requires 6 hours in assembly and 3 hours in finishing. Each transistor requires 3 hours in assembly and 6 hours in finishing. If profit is ₹ 120 per radio and ₹ 90 per transistor, determine the best combination of radios and transistors to realize profit of ₹ 2,100.

Solution

This is a *single goal* (profit) problem. Let

D_u = amount by which profit goal is underachieved,

D_o = amount by which profit goal is overachieved.

The given problem can be expressed as the following goal problem :

Minimize $Z = D_u$, (underachievement of the profit target)

subject to $120x_1 + 90x_2 + D_u - D_o = 2{,}100$,

($\because$ profit earned + underachievement − overachievement = target)

$6x_1 + 3x_2 \le 90$, (assembly department constraint)

$3x_1 + 6x_2 \le 72$, (finishing department constraint)

$x_1, x_2, D_u, D_o \ge 0.$

Adding slack variables, assembly and finishing department constraints can be expressed as

$$6x_1 + 3x_2 + s_1 = 90,$$
$$3x_1 + 6x_2 + s_2 = 72,$$
$$x_1, x_2, s_1, s_2 \ge 0.$$

$\therefore$ The goal programming problem can be expressed as

minimize $Z = 0x_1 + 0x_2 + 0s_1 + 0s_2 + D_u + 0D_o$,

subject to $120x_1 + 90x_2 + D_u - D_o = 2{,}100.$

$6x_1 + 3x_2 + s_1 = 90,$

$3x_1 + 6x_2 + s_2 = 72,$

$x_1, x_2, s_1, s_2, D_u, D_o \ge 0.$

Simplex method can now be employed to solve the problem. This is shown in tables 6.114 through 6.116.

TABLE 6.114

	c_j	0	0	0	0	1	0		
c_B	Basis	x_1	x_2	s_1	s_2	D_u	D_o	b	θ
1	D_u	120	90	0	0	1	−1	2,100	$35/2$
0	s_1	(6)	3	1	0	0	0	90	15 ←
0	s_2	3	6	0	1	0	0	72	24
Z_j		120	90	0	0	1	−1		
$\bar{c}_j$		−120	−90	0	0	0	1		
		↑							

Initial basic feasible solution

TABLE 6.115

	c_j	0	0	0	0	1	0		
c_B	Basis	x_1	x_2	s_1	s_2	D_u	D_o	b	θ
1	D_u	0	30	−20	0	1	−1	300	10
0	x_1	1	$\frac{1}{2}$	$\frac{1}{6}$	0	0	0	15	30
0	s_2	0	$\left(\frac{9}{2}\right)$	$\frac{1}{2}$	1	0	0	27	6 ←
	Z_j	0	30	−20	0	1	−1		
	$\bar{c}_j$	0	−30	20	0	0	1		
			↑						

Second basic feasible solution

TABLE 6.116

	c_j	0	0	0	0	1	0	
c_B	Basis	x_1	x_2	s_1	s_2	D_u	D_o	b
1	D_u	0	0	$-\frac{50}{3}$	$-\frac{20}{3}$	1	−1	120
0	x_1	1	0	$\frac{2}{9}$	$-\frac{1}{9}$	0	0	12
0	x_2	0	1	$-\frac{1}{9}$	$\frac{2}{9}$	0	0	6
	Z_j	0	0	$-\frac{50}{3}$	$\frac{20}{3}$	1	−1	
$\bar{c}_j$		0	0	$\frac{50}{3}$	$\frac{20}{3}$	0	1	

Optimal basic feasible solution

Thus the optimal solution is

$$x_1 = 12, x_2 = 6, D_{u_{min}} = ₹\ 120.$$

$D_{u_{min}}$ = ₹ 120 means that the target profit of ₹ 2,100 is underachieved by ₹ 120 *i.e.*, profit actually earned (by manufacturing 12 radios and 6 transistors) is ₹ 2,100 – ₹ 120 = ₹ 1,980.

EXAMPLE 6.8-2

If in example 6.8-1, the company sets two equally ranked goals, one to reach a profit goal of ₹ 1,500 and the other to meet a radio goal of 10, find the optimal solution.

Solution

Since the two goals are equally ranked, a Re. 1 deviation from the profit target is just as important (in the goal programming model) as a deviation of 1 radio. Let

D_{up} = amount by which the profit goal is underachieved,
D_{op} = amount by which the profit goal is overachieved,
D_{ur} = amount by which the radio goal is underachieved,
D_{or} = amount by which the radio goal is overachieved.

Then the objective function and constraints for the goal programming model are

minimize $Z = D_{up} + D_{ur}$,

subject to

$$120x_1 + 90x_2 + D_{up} - D_{op} = 1{,}500,$$
$$x_1 + D_{ur} - D_{or} = 10,$$
$$6x_1 + 3x_2 \le 90,$$
$$3x_1 + 6x_2 \le 72,$$
$$x_1, x_2, D_{up}, D_{op}, D_{ur}, D_{or} \ge 0.$$

Adding slack variables, assembly and finishing department constraints can be written as

$$6x_1 + 3x_2 + s_1 = 90,$$

$$3x_1 + 6x_2 + s_2 = 72,$$
$$x_1, x_2, s_1, s_2 \geq 0.$$

Simplex method can now be employed to solve the problem. This is shown in tables 6.117 through 6.119.

TABLE 6.117

c_B	c_j / Basis	0 / x_1	0 / x_2	0 / s_1	0 / s_2	1 / D_{up}	0 / D_{op}	1 / D_{ur}	0 / D_{or}	b	θ	
1	D_{up}	120	90	0	0	1	–1	0	0	1,500	25/2	
1	D_{ur}	(1)	0	0	0	0	0	1	–1	10	10	←
0	s_1	6	3	1	0	0	0	0	0	90	15	
0	s_2	3	6	0	1	0	0	0	0	72	24	
	Z_j	121	90	0	0	1	–1	1	–1			
	$\bar{c}_j$	–121 ↑	–90	0	0	0	1	0	1			

Initial basic feasible solution

TABLE 6.118

c_B	c_j / Basis	0 / x_1	0 / x_2	0 / s_1	0 / s_2	1 / D_{up}	0 / D_{op}	1 / D_{ur}	0 / D_{or}	b	θ	
1	D_{up}	0	90	0	0	1	–1	–120	(120)	300	5/2	←
0	x_1	1	0	0	0	0	0	1	–1	10	–10	
0	s_1	0	3	1	0	0	0	– 6	6	30	5	
0	s_2	0	6	0	1	0	0	–3	3	42	14	
	Z_j	0	90	0	0	1	–1	–120	120			
	$\bar{c}_j$	0	–90	0	0	0	1	121	–120 ↑			

2nd b.f.s.

TABLE 6.119

c_B	c_j / Basis	0 / x_1	0 / x_2	0 / s_1	0 / s_2	1 / D_{up}	0 / D_{op}	1 / D_{ur}	0 / D_{or}	b
0	D_{or}	0	$\frac{3}{4}$	0	0	$\frac{1}{120}$	$-\frac{1}{120}$	–1	1	$\frac{5}{2}$
0	x_1	1	$\frac{3}{4}$	0	0	$\frac{1}{120}$	$-\frac{1}{120}$	0	0	$\frac{25}{2}$
0	s_1	0	$-\frac{3}{2}$	1	0	$-\frac{1}{20}$	$\frac{1}{20}$	0	0	15
0	s_2	0	$\frac{15}{4}$	0	1	$-\frac{1}{40}$	$\frac{1}{40}$	0	0	$\frac{1}{40}$
	Z_j	0	0	0	0	0	0	0	0	
	$\bar{c}_j$	0	0	0	0	1	0	1	0	

Optimal b.f.s.

It may be noticed from table 6.119 that the goal of 10 radios is achieved and in fact bettered (25/2 – 10 = 5/2); 5/2 appears in this table as D_{or} (overachievement of radios). Profit goal of ₹ 1,500 is also reached since both D_{up} and D_{op} are zero (because they are not in the final solution) and, therefore, profit is exactly ₹ 1,500.

EXAMPLE 6.8-3

Suppose for example 6.8-1, the company has established the following goals and has assigned them priorities P_1, P_2, P_3 (where P_1 is most important) as follows :

Priority	*Goal*
P_1	*Produce to meet a radio goal of 13*
P_2	*Reach a profit goal of ₹ 1,950*
P_3	*Produce to meet a transistor goal of 5.*

Find the optimum solution.

Solution

Let

D_{up} = amount by which the profit goal is underachieved,
D_{op} = amount by which the profit goal is overachieved,
D_{ur} = amount by which the radio goal is underachieved;
D_{or} = amount by which the radio goal is overachieved,
D_{ut} = amount by which the transistor goal is underachieved,
D_{ot} = amount by which the transistor goal is overachieved.

Then the objective function and constraints for the goal programming model are

minimize $Z = P_1 D_{ur} + P_2 D_{up} + P_3 D_{ut}$,

subject to

$120x_1 + 90x_2 + D_{up} - D_{op} = 1{,}950$, (profit goal)
$x_1 + D_{ur} - D_{ot} = 13$, (radio goal)
$x_2 + D_{ut} - D_{or} = 5$, (transistor goal)
$6x_1 + 3x_2 + s_1 = 90$, (assembly constraint)
$3x_1 + 6x_2 + s_2 = 72$, (finishing constraint)
$x_1, x_2, s_1, s_2, D_{up}, D_{op}, D_{ur}, D_{or}, D_{ut}, D_{ot} \geq 0$.

The P's used here are called *pre-emptive priority factors;* in the goal programming algorithm that follows it is assumed that the priority ranking is absolute *i.e.*, P_1 goals are more important than P_2 goals and P_2 goals will not be achieved until P_1 goals have been achieved; same is true for P_3 goals. These P's are not assigned any actual values, they just indicate that one goal is more important than the other.

Table 6.120 represents the initial simplex table for this problem. This table has a number of characteristics:

TABLE 6.120

	c_j	0	0	0	0	P_2	0	P_1	0	P_3	0		
c_B	Basis	x_1	x_2	s_1	s_2	D_{up}	D_{op}	D_{ur}	D_{or}	D_{ut}	D_{ot}	b	θ
P_2	D_{up}	120	90	0	0	1	–1	0	0	0	0	1,950	65/4
P_1	D_{ur}	(1)	0	0	0	0	0	1	–1	0	0	13	13 ←
P_3	D_{ut}	0	1	0	0	0	0	0	0	1	–1	5	∞
0	s_1	6	3	1	0	0	0	0	0	0	0	90	15
0	s_2	3	6	0	1	0	0	0	0	0	0	72	24
P_3	Z_j	0	1	0	0	0	0	0	0	1	–1		
	$\overline{c}_j$	0	–1	0	0	0	0	0	0	0	1		
P_2	Z_j	120	90	0	0	1	–1	0	0	0	0		
	$\overline{c}_j$	–120	–90	0	0	0	1	0	0	0	0		
P_1	Z_j	1	0	0	0	0	0	1	–1	0	0		
	$\overline{c}_j$	–1	0	0	0	0	0	0	1	0	0	*Initial b.f.s.*	
		↑											

1. Each of the priorities P_1, P_2 and P_3 has separate Z_j and $\overline{c}_j$ rows. It is because the goals do not have the same dimension (units) and, therefore, cannot be just added. For example, we cannot add deviations from the profit goal (₹) to the deviations from the radio goal (number). These separate priority rows are required to keep track of the things. The priority rows are generally written from bottom to top in order of priority.
2. The $\overline{c}_j$ value for any column is shown in the priority rows at the bottom of the table. For instance, $\overline{c}_j$ value for x_1-column is contained in the P_2 and P_1 rows at the bottom and is read as $-120\ P_2 - P_1$; likewise the $\overline{c}_j$ value for x_2-column is read as $-\ P_3 - 90\ P_2$.
3. To select the incoming variable, we start with the most important priority (P_1 here) and mark the most negative $\overline{c}_j$ value in that row. If there is no negative value in that row, we move to the next most important priority (P_2 here) and mark the most negative $\overline{c}_j$ value in that row.
4. To mark the outgoing variable the usual minimum ratio rule is used. Thus D_{ur} is the outgoing variable in table 6.120.
5. A negative $\overline{c}_j$ value that has a positive $\overline{c}_j$ value in one of the P-rows *underneath* it is disregarded because such a positive value would mean that the deviations from the lower (and more important) goal would be *increased* if that variable is brought into the solution. Once the initial simplex table is set up, we proceed just as we have done in simplex method, keeping in mind the above five characteristics. Tables 6.121 through 6.123 represent the various iterations.

TABLE 6.121

	c_j	0	0	0	0	P_2	0	P_1	0	P_3	0		
c_B	Basis	x_1	x_2	s_1	s_2	D_{up}	D_{op}	D_{ur}	D_{or}	D_{ut}	D_{ot}	b	θ
P_2	D_{up}	0	90	0	0	1	−1	−120	120	0	0	390	3
0	x_1	1	0	0	0	0	0	1	−1	0	0	13	−13
P_3	D_{ut}	0	1	0	0	0	0	0	0	1	−1	5	∞
0	s_1	0	3	1	0	0	0	−6	(6)	0	0	12	2 ←
0	s_2	0	6	0	1	0	0	−3	3	0	0	33	11
P_3	Z_j	0	1	0	0	0	0	0	0	1	−1		
	$\overline{c}_j$	0	−1	0	0	0	0	0	0	0	1		
P_2	Z_j	0	90	0	0	1	−1	−120	120	0	0		
	$\overline{c}_j$	0	−90	0	0	0	1	120	−120	0	0		
									↑				
P_1	Z_j	0	0	0	0	0	0	0	0	0	0		
	$\overline{c}_j$	0	0	0	0	0	0	1	0	0	0		*2nd b.f.s.*

TABLE 6.122

	c_j	0	0	0	0	P_2	0	P_1	0	P_3	0		
c_B	Basis	x_1	x_2	s_1	s_2	D_{up}	D_{op}	D_{ur}	D_{or}	D_{ut}	D_{ot}	b	θ
P_2	D_{up}	0	30	−20	0	1	−1	0	0	0	0	150	5
0	x_1	1	$\frac{1}{2}$	$\frac{1}{6}$	0	0	0	0	0	0	0	15	30
P_3	D_{ut}	0	1	0	0	0	0	0	0	1	−1	5	5

0	D_{or}	0	$\left(\frac{1}{2}\right)$	$\frac{1}{6}$	0	0	0	–1	1	0	0	2	4 ←
0	s_2	0	$\frac{9}{2}$	$-\frac{1}{2}$	1	0	0	0	0	0	0	27	6
P_3	Z_j	0	1	0	0	0	0	0	0	1	–1		
	$\bar{c}_j$	0	–1	0	0	0	0	0	0	0	1		
P_2	Z_j	.0	30	–20	0	1	–1	0	0	0	0		
	$\bar{c}_j$	0	–30 ↑	20	0	0	1	0	0	0	0		
P_1	Z_j	0	0	0	0	0	0	0	0	0	0		
	$\bar{c}_j$	0	0	0	0	0	0	1	0	0	0		*3rd b.f.s*

TABLE 6.123

	c_j	0	0	0	0	P_2	0	P_1	0	P_3	0	
c_B	Basis	x_1	x_2	s_1	s_2	D_{up}	D_{op}	D_{ur}	D_{or}	D_{ut}	D_{ot}	b
P_2	D_{up}	0	0	–30	0	1	–1	60	–60	0	0	30
0	x_1	1	0	0	0	0	0	1	–1	0	0	13
P_3	D_{ut}	0	0	$-\frac{1}{3}$	0	0	0	2	–2	1	–1	1
0	x_2	0	1	$\frac{1}{3}$	0	0	0	–2	2	0	0	4
0	s_2	0	0	–2	1	0	0	9	–9	.0	0	9
P_3	Z_j	0	0	$-\frac{1}{3}$	0	0	0	2	–2	1	–1	
	$\bar{c}_j$	0	0.	$\frac{1}{3}$	0	0	0	–2	2	0	1	
P_2	Z_j	0	0	–30	0	1	–1	60	–60	0	0	
	$\bar{c}_j$	0	0	30	0	0	1	–60	60	0	0	
P_1	Z_j	0	0	0	0	0	0	0	0	0	0	
	$\bar{c}_j$	0	0	0	0	0	0	1	0	0	0	*Optimal b.f.s.*

Table 6.123 gives $x_1 = 13$, $x_2 = 4$ as the solution.

Notice that there are still negative $\bar{c}_j$ values in P_2 and P_3 rows (–60 and –2 respectively). However, since in both of them there is a positive value in P_1 row below them (1), we disregard both of them.

It may be noted from table 6.123 that the goals have been met to different extents. The most important goal (produce 13 radios) has been achieved. The second important goal (reach ₹ 1,950 profit) has been missed by ₹ 30 [we generated a profit of ₹ (120 × 13 + 90 × 4) = ₹ 1,920 only]. The deviation, however is less, being about 1.5%. Notice that this deviation shows up as D_{up} in the final table. The lowest-ranked goal (produce 5 transistors) is missed by 1 transistor. Here, too, the deviation shows up as D_{ut} in table 6.123. Finally, notice that there are 9 hours unutilized in finishing. While it might appear that these should have been utilised, it must not be forgotten that to manufacture another transistor, for example, would also require time in assembly, where all the time has already been used.

6.8-1 Graphical Method for Goal Programming

Linear goal programming problems involving two decision variables can be solved by the graphical method also. The graphical method helps the reader to have a deeper insight into the problem. This method is based on well defined logical steps and results in reducing the computational effort. It is used to minimize the total deviation from a set of multiple goals. The deviation from the goal with the highest priority is minimized to the fullest possible extent before deviation from the next goal is minimized.

EXAMPLE 6.8-4

A small furnishing company manufactures tables and chairs. Each chair requires 4 man-hours of labour while each table requires 5 man-hours of labour. If only 40 man-hours are available each week and the owner of the company would neither hire additional labour nor utilise overtime, formulate the linear goal programming problem and solve it. Both the table and the chair fetch a profit of ₹ 100 each. The owner has a target to earn a profit of ₹ 2,000 per week. Also he would like to supply 10 chairs, if possible, per week to a sister concern.

Solution

The goals of the company and their assigned priorities are

Priority	*Goal*
1st	To avoid hiring extra labour or utilise overtime
2nd	To reach a profit goal of ₹ 2,000 a week
3rd	To supply 10 chairs a week to the sister concern.

Let x_1 and x_2 denote the number of chairs and tables to be produced per week. If u_i and O_i represent the amount by which the ith goal is underachieved and overachieved respectively, then the goals (expressed as constraints in order of priority) are

$$g_1 : 4x_1 + 5x_2 + u_1 - O_1 = 40, \qquad \text{(man-hour goal)}$$
$$g_2 : 100x_1 + 100x_2 + u_2 - O_2 = 2{,}000, \qquad \text{(profit goal)}$$
$$g_3 : x_2 + u_3 - O_3 = 10. \qquad \text{(chair goal)}$$

To achieve the first goal completely, the overtime O_1 must be minimized. Similarly, the second goal will be fulfilled when the underachievement in profit, u_2 is minimized and the chair goal will be attained when underachievement u_3 is minimized. Therefore, the objective function of the problem may be written as

$$\text{minimize} \qquad Z = \{O_1, u_2, u_3\},$$
$$\text{subject to} \qquad 4x_1 + 5x_2 + u_1 - O_1 = 40,$$
$$100x_1 + 100x_2 + u_2 - O_2 = 2{,}000,$$
$$x_2 + u_3 - O_3 = 10,$$
$$x_1, x_2, u_1, u_2, u_3, O_1, O_2, O_3, \text{ each} \geq 0.$$

To solve this problem graphically, the variables x_1 and x_2 are plotted along the horizontal and vertical axes respectively. The three goal constraints are plotted as straight lines by assuming each $u_i = O_i = 0$. Arrows ($\leftarrow$ or $\rightarrow$) are then associated with each line to represent underachievement or overachievement of the goal (Fig. 6.3 (*a*)).

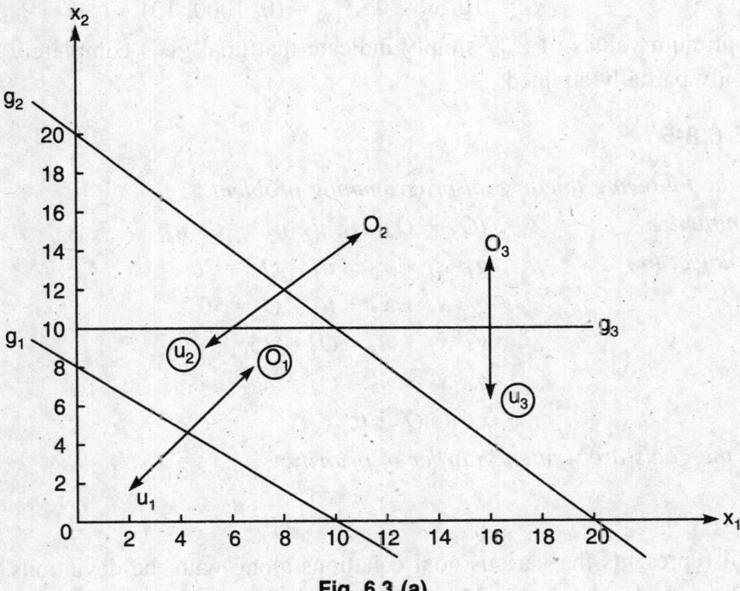

Fig. 6.3 (a)

Man-hour goal (g_1) is the most important and is the first to be considered. Since this goal is achieved when O_1 is minimized, we may set $O_1 = 0$ as its minimum value. The region satisfying $x_1, x_2 \geq 0$ and $O_1 = 0$ is shown shaded in Fig. 6.3(*b*). Any point within this region satisfies the man-hour goal and minimizes O_1 at the priority level one.

The next important goal is the profit goal (g_2) and to attain it we must minimize u_2. Clearly, u_2 cannot be decreased down to zero since this would degrade our previous solution — a higher priority goal. The minimum value of u_2 without affecting the previously attained higher goal is the point ($x_1 = 10$, $x_2 = 0$) and is marked in Fig. 6.3 b.

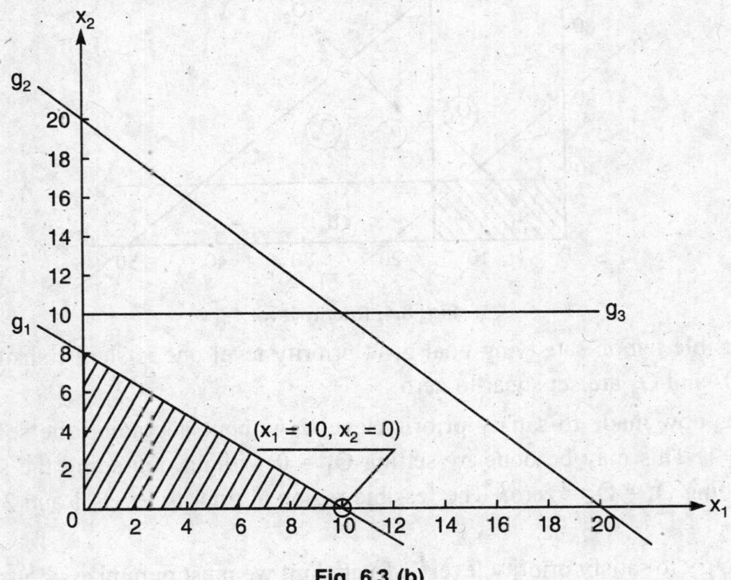

Fig. 6.3 (b)

The last important goal (in the order of priority) is g_3 to satisfy which we must minimize u_3. However, any minimization of u_3 would require a movement from the solution previously determined and would degrade at least one higher priority goal already attained. Therefore, the optimal solution to the problem is

$$x_1 = 10, x_2 = 0, Z_{min} = (0, 1000, 10).$$

The optimum values of Z_{min} simply indicate that goal g_1 is completely attained, while g_2 and g_3 are only partially attained.

EXAMPLE 6.8-5

Solve the following linear goal programming problem :

minimize $\quad Z = (O_3 + O_4, O_1, u_2, u_3 + 8/5\, u_4),$

subject to

$$g_1: x_1 + x_2 + u_1 - O_1 = 20,$$
$$g_2: x_1 + x_2 + u_2 - O_2 = 50,$$
$$g_3: x_1 + u_3 - O_3 = 15,$$
$$g_4: x_2 + u_4 - O_4 = 8,$$
$$x_i, u_i, O_i \geq 0,$$

where the goals are written in order of priority.

Solution

Fig. 6.4 represents the various goal equations along with the deviations to be minimized. The highest priority goal g_1, is considered first. This can be achieved by minimizing $O_3 + O_4$ *i.e.*, by setting $O_3 = O_4$ = zero.

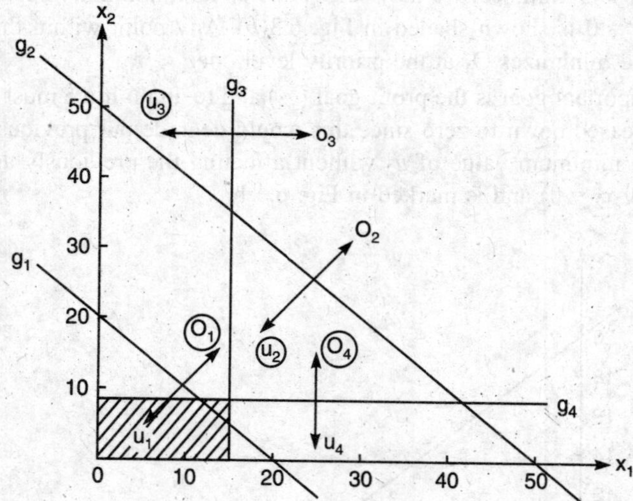

Fig. 6.4. Priority level 1.

The feasible region satisfying goal g_1 at priority level one is shown shaded in fig. 6.4 for which both O_3 and O_4 are set squal to zero.

Effort is now made to satisfy priority level 2 without degrading the solution reached at priority level 1. This may be done by setting $O_1 = 0$ without degrading the solution obtained earlier (by setting $O_3 = O_4$ = zero.) The feasible region at priority levels 1 and 2 is shown shaded in Fig. 6.5.

Next we try to satisfy priority level 3. To attain it we must minimize u_2. u_2, however, cannot be set to zero since it would degrade our solutions previously attained at both priority levels 1 and 2. Since g_1 and g_2 goal lines are parallel, the feasible region minimizing u_2 without degrading the previously attained higher priority goals is given by the line segment AB in Fig. 6.5.

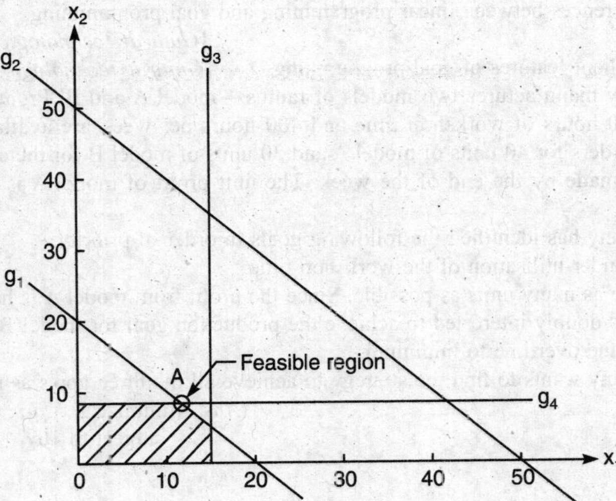

Fig. 6.5 Priority Levels 1 and 2.

Finally to achieve g_4 at priority level 4, we must minimize u_3 and u_4. Evidently u_4 is to be considered 8/5 times more important than u_3. The final solution (without degrading earlier ones) is attained at A where we set $u_4 = 0$. u_3 is not set equal to zero because of priority of u_4 over u_3.

As a result, the final solution is given by point A in Fig. 6.6.

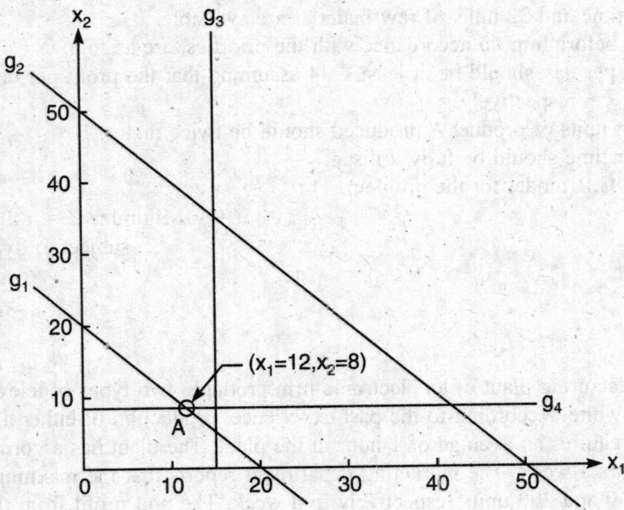

Fig. 6.6 All Priority Levels.

It is $$x_1 = 12, x_2 = 8, Z_{min} = (0, 0, 30, 3).$$

Thus first and second priority goals are attained fully, while the third and fourth priority goals are attained as best as possible.

EXERCISES 6.8

1. Explain graphical method for solving linear goal programming problem.
   [*P.T.U. B. Tech. (C.Sc.) 2009*]
2. What is goal programming ? When is it applicable ?
   [*Osmania U. MBA, 2010; Pondicherry U.M.B.A. June, 2007, 2006; P.U. MBA August, 2006, IGNOU MBA Dec., 2006*]

3. Write differences between linear programming and goal programming.
[*Gujarat Technological U. MBA, Jan., 2011*]
4. Explain salient features of goal programming. [*Gujarat Technological U. MBA Dec., 2010*]
5. A company manufactures two models of radios – model A and B. Production of model A or B requires 10 hours of workshop time and 400 hours per week are available. The company has received orders for 40 units of model A and 30 units of model B for the current week and supply has to be made by the end of the week. The unit profit of model A is ₹ 500 and that of B is ₹ 1,000.

The company has identified the following goals in order of priority:

(*i*) To avoid under-utilisation of the workshop time.

(*ii*) To produce as many units as possible. Since the profit from model A is half that of model B, the company is doubly interested to achieve the production goal for model B relative to model A.

(*iii*) To reduce the overtime to minimum.

The company wants to find the strategy to achieve all the three goals as nearly as possible.

(*Ans.* Minimize $Z = p_1u_1 + p_2u_2 + 2p_2u_3 + p_3O_1$,
subject to $10x_1 + 10x_2 + u_1 - O_1 = 400$,
$x_1 + u_2 - O_2 = 40$,
$x_2 + u_3 - O_3 = 30$,
$x_1, x_2, u_1, u_2, u_3, O_1, O_2, O_3 \geq 0$.)

6. (*a*) "Goal programming appears to be the most appropriate, flexible and powerful technique for complex decision problems involving multiple conflicting objectives". Discuss.
[*Pondicherry MBA August, 2006*]

(*b*) A manufacturer produces two products A and B using two limited resources–labour and raw material. A unit of product A requires 2 hours of labour time and 3 units of raw material while a unit of product B requires 4 hours of labour time and 4 units of raw material. Everyday 28 hours of labour time and 32 units of raw material are available.

The goals before him, in accordance with the priorties, are as follows :

(*i*) The profit per day should be at least ₹ 44 assuming that the profit per unit of products A and B is ₹ 8 and ₹ 6 respectively.

(*ii*) Number of units of product A produced should be twice that of B.

(*iii*) The labour time should be fully utilised.

Formulate G.P. model for the problem.

(*Ans.* Minimize $Z = p_1u_1 + p_2(u_2 + O_2) + p_3u_3$,
subject to $8x_1 + 6x_2 + u_1 - O_1 = 44$,
$x_1 - 2x_2 + u_2 - O_2 = 0$,
$2x_1 + 4x_2 + u_3 - O_3 = 28$,
$3x_1 + 4x_2 \leq 32$,
$x_1, x_2, u_1, u_2, u_3, O_1, O_2, O_3 \geq 0$.)

7. The manufacturing plant of an electronic firm produces two types of television sets – colour and black-and-white. According to the past experience, production of either a colour or a black-and-white set requires an average of 1 hour in the plant. The plant has a normal production capacity of 400 hours a week. The marketing department reports that the maximum demand for the two types is 240 and 300 units respectively in a week. The unit profit from the sale of colour set is ₹ 800, while from black-and-white set is ₹ 400.

The chairman of the company has set the following goals arranged in the order of preference to the organisation :

(*i*) To avoid any under-utilisation of the normal production capacity.

(*ii*) To sell as many units as possible. Since profit from colour set is twice that from black-and-white, the desire is to produce the former as double of the latter type of television.

(*iii*) To minimize overtime as much as possible.

Formulate the G.P. model for the problem.

(*Ans.* Minimize $Z = p_1u_1 + 2p_2u_2 + p_2u_3 + p_3O_1$,
subject to $x_1 + x_2 + u_1 - O_1 = 400$,
$x_1 + u_2 - O_2 = 240$,
$x_2 + u_3 - O_3 = 300$,
$x_1, x_2, u_1, u_2, u_3, O_1, O_2, O_3 \geq 0$.)

8. An advertising company with 18 employees has received a contract to promote a new product. The company can advertise by radio and television. The following table provides data about the number of persons reached by each type of advertisement, the cost and labour requirement:

TABLE 6.124

	Data/min of advertisement	
	Radio	*Television*
Exposure (in lakhs of persons)	60	100
Cost (in thousands of rupees)	80	200
Assigned employees	2	4

The contract prohibits the company from using more than 8 minutes on radio advertisement. The company has a goal to reach at least 500 lakhs of persons. It has set a budget goal of ₹ 10 lakhs for the project. The first goal is more important to the company than the second. Formulate G.P. model to find the time in minutes to be devoted to advertisement by radio and television.

(*Ans.* Minimize $Z = p_1u_1 + p_2O_2$,
subject to $60x_1 + 100x_2 + u_1 - O_1 = 500$,
$80x_1 + 200x_2 + u_2 - O_2 = 1{,}000$,
$x_1 \le 8$,
$2x_1 + 4x_2 \le 18$,
$x_1, x_2, u_1, u_2, O_1, O_2 \ge 0$.)

9. Two products are manufactured on two sequential machines. The following table gives the machining times in minutes per unit for the two products.

TABLE 6.125

Machine	*Product 1*	*Product 2*
1	6	4
2	8	3

The daily production quota for the two products are 100 and 80 units respectively. Each machine runs 8 hours a day. Overtime, though not desirable, may be used if necessary, to meet the production quota. Formulate the problem as a G.P. model.

(*Ans.* Minimize $Z = u_1 + u_2 + O_3 + O_4$,
subject to $x_1 + u_1 - O_1 = 100$,
$x_2 + u_2 - O_2 = 80$,
$6x_1 + 4x_2 + u_3 - O_3 = 480$,
$8x_1 + 3x_2 + u_4 - O_4 = 480$,
$x_1, x_2, u_1, u_2, u_3, u_4, O_1, O_2, O_3, O_4 \ge 0$.)

10. A camera company manufactures two types of cameras – the standard model and the deluxe model. The production of one unit of the standard model requires 3 hours in department I and 4 hours in department II. Production of a unit of deluxe model requires 4 hours and 3 hours in department I and II respectively. Currently 100 hours are available in each department. Profit on standard camera is ₹ 300/ unit, while on deluxe camera is ₹ 400/unit. Management of the company has set the following goals :

P_1 (Priority 1) : Avoid overtime operations in each department.

P_2 (Priority 2) : According to the sales department, a minimum of 10 cameras of each type can be sold weekly. Management would like to meet these sales goals. Since production time may limit producing this number of each model and since the deluxe model has a higher profit margin, the sales goals should be weighted by the profit contribution for the respective model *i.e.*, ₹ 300 for standard and ₹ 400 for deluxe model.

P_3 (Priority 3) : Maximize profits.

Construct the G.P. model for the problem. The target amount is ₹ 90,000.

(*Ans.* Minimize $Z = p_1O_1 + p_1O_2 + 300\,p_2u_3 + 400\,p_2u_4 + p_3u_5$,
subject to $3x_1 + 4x_2 + u_1 - O_1 = 100$,
$4x_1 + 3x_2 + u_2 - O_2 = 100$,
$x_1 + u_3 - O_3 = 10$,
$x_2 + u_4 - O_4 = 10$,
$300x_1 + 400x_2 + u_5 - O_5 = 90{,}000$,
$x_1, x_2, u_1, u_2, u_3, u_4, u_5, O_1, O_2, O_3, O_4, O_5 \ge 0$.)

Note : ₹ 90,000 has been taken as an arbitratry high profit goal to include u_5 in the objective function.

11. A company manufactures three types of lamps: a desk lamp, a bedside lamp and a floor lamp. The lamps are all solid brass and produced in two distinct steps: turning and finishing. The schedule for labour and material inputs and availability of each type is as follows :

TABLE 6.126

	Desk lamp	*Bedside lamp*	*Floor lamp*	*Availability*
Turning labour	1 hr	3 hr	2 hr	1,500/month
Finishing labour	2 hr	2 hr	4 hr	1,000/month
Brass	2 kg	1.5 kg	3 kg	3,000/month

Profit contribution of each type is ₹ 400, ₹ 500 and ₹ 650 respectively. The company has two equally desirable goals: minimizing the idle time in finishing and making a monthly profit of ₹ 1,00,000. Set-up the problem as a goal program and find the optimal solution.

(*Ans.* Minimize $Z = u_1 + u_2$,
subject to $x_1 + 3x_2 + 2x_3 \le 1{,}500$,
$2x_1 + 2x_2 + 4x_3 + u_1 - O_1 = 1{,}000$,
$2x_1 + 1.5x_2 + 3x_3 \le 3{,}000$,
$400x_1 + 500x_2 + 650x_3 + u_2 - O_2 = 1{,}00{,}000$,
$x_1, x_2, x_3, u_1, u_2, O_1, O_2 \ge 0$.)

12. A textile company produces two types of materials, a strong upholstery material and a regular dress material. The upholstery material is produced according to direct orders from furniture manufacturers. The dress material, on the other hand, is distributed to retail fabric stores. The average production rates for the upholstery material and for the dress material are identical: 1,000 meters per hour. By running two shifts, the operational capacity of the plant is 80 hr per week. The marketing department reports that the maximum estimated sale for the following week is 70,000 metres of the upholstery material and 45,000 metres of the dress material. According to the accounts department, the approximate profit from a metre of upholstery material is ₹ 2.50 and from a metre of dress material is ₹ 1.50.

The president of the company believes that a good employer-employee relationship is an important factor for business success. Hence, he decides that a stable employment level is a primary goal for the firm. Therefore, wherever there is demand exceeding normal production capacity, he simply expands production capacity by providing overtime. However, he also feels that overtime operation of the plant for more than 10 hr per week should be avoided because of the accelerating costs. The president has the following goals:

(*i*) The first goal is to avoid any underutilisation of production capacity (*i.e.*, to maintain stable employment at normal capacity.)
(*ii*) The second goal is to limit the overtime operation of the plant to 10 hr.
(*iii*) The third goal is to achieve the sales goals of 70,000 meters of upholstery material and 45,000 metres of dress material.
(*iv*) The last goal is to minimize the overtime operation of the plant as much as possible.

Formulate and solve this problem as a linear goal programming problem. [*Delhi M.B.A., 1975*]

13. Construct a goal programming model using the following data. Show the deviational variables in the constraints.

Resource type	*Product 1*	*Product 2*	*Available resource*
Labour hours	2	4	600
Material 1 (kg)	4	5	1,000
Material 2 (kg)	5	4	1,200
Profit/unit (₹)	20	32	

It is known that production of one unit of product 1 would require 0.3 person and production of one unit of prodcut 2 would require 0.75 person. The manager has set-up two goals:
(i) profit of ₹ 5,400 and
(ii) a total staff of 108 persons. [*Gujarat Technological U. MBA Dec., 2010*]

(*Ans.* Minimize $Z = u_1 + O_2$,
subject to $20x_1 + 32x_2 + u_1 - O_1 = 5{,}400$,
$0.3x_1 + 0.75x_2 + u_2 - O_2 = 108$,
$2x_1 + 4x_2 \le 600$,
$4x_1 + 5x_2 \le 1{,}000$,
$5x_1 + 4x_2 \le 1{,}200$,
$x_1, x_2, u_1, u_2, O_1, O_2 \ge 0$.)

14. Find x_1, x_2 to
minimize $Z = \{u_1, u_2\}$,
and satisfy the goals

$$x_1 + x_2 + u_1 - O_1 = 20,$$
$$4x_1 + 5x_2 + u_2 - O_2 = 150,$$
$$x_1, x_2, u_1, u_2, O_1, O_2 \geq 0.$$

[*P.T.U. B.Tech. (C.Sc.) 2009*]

15. Find x_1, x_2 to
minimize $Z = \{3O_1 + 3O_2, u_3, u_4\}$,
and satisfy the goals

$$x_1 + x_2 + u_1 - O_1 = 8,$$
$$x_1 + u_2 - O_2 = 3,$$
$$3x_1 + 5x_2 + u_3 - O_3 = 65,$$
$$x_1 + x_2 + u_4 - O_4 = 10,$$
$$x_1, x_2, u_1, u_2, u_3, u_4, O_1, O_2, O_3, O_4 \geq 0.$$

16. Solve the goal programming problem :
Minimize $Z = p_1u_1 + p_2(u_2 + O_2) + p_3u_3$,
subject to

$$8x_1 + 6x_2 + u_1 - O_1 = 36,$$
$$x_1 - 2x_2 + u_2 - O_2 = 0,$$
$$2x_1 + 4x_2 + u_3 = 20,$$
$$3x_1 + 4x_2 + u_4 = 24,$$
$$x_1, x_2, u_1, u_2, u_3, u_4, O_1, O_2 \geq 0.$$

(*Ans.* $x_1 = \frac{24}{5}, x_2 = \frac{12}{5}, O_1 = \frac{84}{5}, u_3 = \frac{4}{5}$; Profit $= \frac{264}{5}$.)

17. Solve the following goal programming problem :
Minimize $Z = u_1 + O_1 + u_2 + O_2$,
subject to

$$10x_1 + 12x_2 + u_1 - O_1 = 6{,}650,$$
$$x_1 + x_2 + u_2 - O_2 = 625,$$
$$2x_1 + 3x_2 \leq 1{,}500,$$
$$3x_1 + 2x_2 \leq 1{,}500,$$
$$x_1, x_2, u_1, u_2, O_1, O_2 \geq 0.$$

(*Ans.* $x_1 = 300, x_2 = 300, u_1 = 50, u_2 = 25, Z_{min} = 75$.)

18. Solve the G.P. problem :
Minimize $Z = p_1O_1 + p_2O_2 + 30p_2u_3 + 40p_2u_4 + p_3u_5$,
subject to

$$2x_1 + 4x_2 + u_1 - O_1 = 80,$$
$$3x_1 + 3x_2 + u_2 - O_2 = 80,$$
$$x_1 + u_3 - O_3 = 10,$$
$$x_2 + u_4 - O_4 = 10,$$
$$30x_1 + 40x_2 + u_5 - O_5 = 1{,}200,$$
$$x_1, x_2, u_1, ..., u_5, O_1, ..., O_5 \geq 0.$$

(*Ans.* $x_1 = \frac{40}{3}, x_2 = \frac{40}{3}, O_3 = \frac{10}{3}, O_4 = \frac{10}{3}, u_5 = \frac{800}{3}$,
all other deviational variables = 0; Profit $= \frac{2{,}800}{3}$.)

19. The Harrison Electric Co., located in Chicago's Old Town area, produces two products popular with home renovators: old fashioned chandeliers and ceiling fans. Both chandeliers and fans require a two-step production process involving wiring and assembly. It takes 2 hours to wire each chandelier and 3 hours to wire a ceiling fan. Final assembly of chandeliers and fans requires 6 and 5 hours respectively. The production capability is such that only 12 hours of wiring time and 30 hours of assembly time are available. Each chandelier produced brings the company a profit of \$7 and each fan a profit of \$6. Harrison's management wants to achieve several goals, arranged in order of their importance to the company.
Goal 1: To produce profit of \$30, if possible, during the production period.
Goal 2: To fully utilize the available wiring department hours.
Goal 3: To avoid overtime in the assembly department.

Goal 4: To meet a contract requirement to produce at least 7 ceiling fans.
Formulate and solve the problem as a goal programming model.

[*Gujarat Technological U. MBA Jan., 2011*]

6.9 LINEAR FRACTIONAL PROGRAMMING

Problems concerning optimization of two linear fractions subject to a set of linear constraints are called linear fractional programming problems. These problems may be stated as

$$\text{Optimize} \qquad Z = \frac{\mathbf{c}'\mathbf{x} + \alpha}{\mathbf{d}'\mathbf{x} + \beta},$$

$$\text{subject to} \qquad \mathbf{A}\mathbf{x} \le \mathbf{b},\ \mathbf{x} \ge 0,$$

where (*i*) **x, c, d** are $n \times 1$ vectors,

(*ii*) **A** is an $m \times n$ matrix,

(*iii*) **b** is an $m \times 1$ vector,

(*iv*) **c′**, **d′** are transpose of vectors **c** and **d**,

and (*v*) α, β are scalars.

A linear fractional programming problem can be expressed as an equivalent linear problem with an additional constraint and an additional variable. The usual simplex method may then be applied to find the optimal solution.

EXAMPLE 6.9-1

$$\textit{Minimize} \qquad Z(x) = \frac{-2x_1 + x_2 + 2}{x_1 + 3x_2 + 4},$$

subject to constraints

$$-x_1 + x_2 \le 4,$$
$$2x_1 + x_2 \le 14,$$
$$x_2 \le 6,$$
$$x_1, x_2 \ge 0.$$

Solution

Initial solution given by $x_1 = 0$, $x_2 = 0$ is feasible for the given problem and at this point (0, 0) the denominator $x_1 + 3x_2 + 4 \ge 0$. Thus the denominator is positive over the entire feasible region (*i.e.*, for all non-negative values of x_1 and x_2).

$$\text{Let} \qquad t = \frac{1}{x_1 + 3x_2 + 4},$$

$$\text{and} \qquad y_1 = tx_1,$$
$$y_2 = tx_2.$$

Then the equivalent linear programming problem is

$$\text{minimize} \qquad Z(y) = -2y_1 + y_2 + 2t,$$

$$\text{subject to} \qquad -\frac{y_1}{t} + \frac{y_2}{t} \le 4$$

$$\text{or} \qquad -y_1 + y_2 - 4t \le 0,$$
$$2y_1 + y_2 - 14t \le 0,$$
$$y_2 - 6t \le 0,$$
$$y_1 + 3y_2 + 4t = 1, \qquad [\because t(x_1 + 3x_2 + 4) = 1]$$
$$y_1, y_2, t \ge 0.$$

This problem can be solved by the simplex technique. The optimal solution is found to be

$$y_1 = 7/11,\ y_2 = 0,\ t = 1/11.$$

Hence the optimal solution to the given fractional problem is

$$x = \frac{y_1}{t} = 7, x_2 = \frac{y_2}{t} = 0; \; Z_{\min}(x) = \frac{-2\times7+0+2}{7+0+4} = -\frac{12}{11}.$$

EXERCISES 6.9

1. Maximize $Z(x) = \dfrac{5x_1 + 3x_2}{5x_1 + 2x_2 + 1}$,

   subject to $3x_1 + 5x_2 \leq 15,$
   $5x_1 + 2x_2 \leq 10,$
   $x_1, x_2 \geq 0.$

   [Aligarh M.Sc. (Math.) 1973]

   (*Ans.* $x_1 = 0, x_2 = 3, Z_{\max} = \frac{9}{7}$.)

2. Maximize $Z = \dfrac{-3x_1 - x_2}{x_1 + 2x_2 + 5}$,

   subject to $x_1 + x_2 \geq 1,$
   $2x_1 + 3x_2 \geq 2,$
   $x_1, x_2 \geq 0.$

   [Delhi M.Sc. (O.R.) 1968]

3. Maximize $Z = \dfrac{2x_1 + 3x_2}{x_1 + x_2 + 7}$, subject to constraints :

   $3x_1 + x_2 \leq 4, x_1 + x_2 \leq 1; x_1, x_2 \geq 0.$

   [Aligarh M.Sc. (Math.) 1972]

4. Minimize $Z = \dfrac{-x_1 + 2x_2}{5x_1 + 3x_2 + 2}$, subject to constraints :

   $3x_1 + 6x_2 \leq 8, 5x_1 + 2x_2 \leq 10; x_1, x_2 \geq 0.$

   [Delhi M.Sc. (O.R.) 1976]

6.10 INTEGER PROGRAMMING

Prior sections have treated problems wherein all basic variables (including slack or surplus variables) were permitted to take any non-negative real (continuous or fractional) values. It was done since in many situations it is quite possible and appropriate to have fractional solutions. For instance, it is quite possible to use 9.85 kg of raw material, 3.62 man-hours and 3.46 metre length of a sheet in a project. However, there are many problems, especially in business and industry, in which only integral values for the variables in optimal solutions make sense. For example, it is not possible to run 8.6 buses on a route or to open 5.4 branches of a bank or to employ 2.5 lathes in a workshop for manufacturing a product.

A linear programming problem in which some or all of the varialbes must take non-negative integer (discrete) values is commonly referred to as *integer linear programming problem.* When all the variables are constrained to be integers, it is called an *all (pure)-integer programming problem,* and in case only some of the variables are restricted to have integer values, the problem is said to be a *mixed integer programming problem.* In some situations each variable can take on the values of either zero or one, as in 'do' and 'not to do' type decisions; such problems are referred to as *zero-one programming problems*.

Strictly speaking, if in an L.P. problem we restrict the variables to be non-negative integers, the problem becomes non-linear. However, it is convenient to still call it an integer linear programming problem because after dropping integer restrictions on the variables, the objective function as well as the constraints remain linear in form.

One obvious and common approach to solve an integer linear programming problem is to ignore the integer restrictions on the variables and to solve the resulting L.P. problem by any of the techniques described earlier, and then to round off or truncate the fractional values of the variables in the optimal solution to the nearest integers. This method, however, gives satisfactory results only if the values of the variables are very large so that rounding off or truncating results in negligible change. For example, if the optimum value of the decision variable comes out to be $4549\frac{5}{8}$, it can be easily rounded off to 4549 or 4550 without much error. However, for smaller values, rounding or truncating may produce a solution totally different from the *true* optimal integer solution. Some of the constraints may be violated (solution may become infeasible) since rounding off certain variables may require substantial changes in the values of the other variables to satisfy all the constraints. For example, consider the constraints

$$-x_1 + x_2 \leq 5\frac{1}{2},$$

$$x_1 + x_2 \leq 10\frac{1}{2}$$

having non-integer optimal solution as $x_1 = 5/2$ and $x_2 = 8$. Here rounding off x_1 to 2 or 3 or any other integer value violates one or the other constraint. Even if the rounded off solution satisfies the constraints, there is no guarantee that it is the *true optimal integer solution*. For instance, consider the problem

$$\begin{aligned} &\text{maximize} && Z = 3x_1 + 10x_2, \\ &\text{subject to} && x_1 + 5x_2 \leq 12, \\ &&& x_1 \leq 3, \\ &&& x_1, x_2 \text{ non-negative integers.} \end{aligned}$$

The optimal non-integer solution of the above problem obtained in figure 6.7 is

$$x_1 = 3, x_2 = 1.8, Z_{\max} = 27.$$

If the non-integer variable is rounded off to 2, it violates the feasibility. Rounding off x_2 to 1 satisfies both the constraints but gives $Z_{\max} = 19$, which is far less than the true optimal integer solution $x_1 = 2$, $x_2 = 2$ and $Z_{max} = 26$.

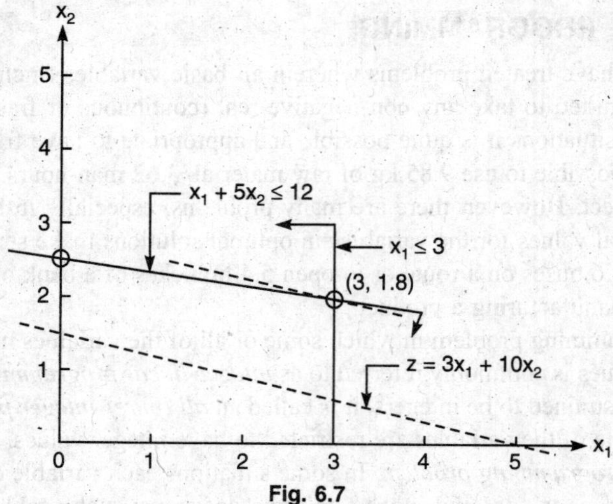

Fig. 6.7

In addition, for large problems this method may be computationally expensive. For instance, if the optimal L.P. solution is $x_1 = 3.4$, $x_2 = 2.6$ and $Z_{max} = 8.6$, one has to try four alternatives, namely (3, 2), (3, 3), (4, 2) and (4, 3). The one which is feasible (satisfies all the constraints) and is closeset to the optimal value of 8.6 of the objective function will be the *approximate* integer solution. As the variables increase in number, the number of alternatives increases tremendously.

For 3 variables, the number of alternatives is $2^3 = 8$, and for 11 variables it becomes $2^{11} = 2048$! And even after examining all such alternatives, the optimal integer solution to the problem is not guaranteed. All these difficulties justify the need for developing a systematic and efficient procedure for obtaining the *exact* optimal integer solution to such problems. A considerable number of algorithms have been developed for this purpose. Unfortunately none possesses computational efficiency that is even remotely comparable to the simplex method (except on special types of problems), so they ordinarily are limited to relatively small problems having a few dozen variables. Despite decades of extensive research, computational experience with integer programming algorithms has been less than satisfactory. To date, there does not exist an I.P. computer code that can solve integer programming problems consistently. Therefore, this remains an active area of research and progress continues to be made in developing more efficient algorithms.

6.10-1 Applications of Integer Programming

Integer programming is a valuable tool in operations research, having tremendous potential for applications. Such problems occur quite frequently in business and industry. All assignment and transportation problems are integer programming problems. It was demonstrated in assignment problems that their decision variables are either zero or one *i.e.*,

$$x_{ij} = 0 \text{ or } 1.$$

Other examples are capital budgeting and production scheduling problems. In fact, any situation involving decisions of the type "either to do a job or not to do" ("either – or") can be viewed as an I.P. problem. In all such situations,

$$x_j = \begin{bmatrix} 1 \text{ (if } j\text{th activity is performed),} \\ 0 \text{ (if } j\text{th activity is not performed)}\cdot \end{bmatrix}$$

In addition, all allocation problems involving the allocation of men and machines give rise to integer programming problems, since such commodities can be assigned only in integers and not in fractions.

6.10-2 Formulation Possibilities Through Mixed Integer Programming

Integer programming formulations of situations in which variables are inherently discrete in nature do not pose any problem. However, there are numerous situations wherein the variables are not discrete. Nevertheless, these problems fit into the linear programming format except for some minor disparity. Fortunately, certain formulation possibilities are available for circumventing some of these disparities. These involve the introduction of one or more artificial variables that are restricted to be integers. This reduces the problem to be a mixed integer programming problem in the desired format. As progress continues in the development of efficient algorithms, this approach is attaining increasing practical importance. Some of the problems handled by this approach are now described.

Either – or Constraints

Consider the case wherein it is possible to make a choice between two constraints so that either one or the other constraint may hold. For instance, choice may be possible between the two available resources so that it is necessary for only one of the resource availability constraints to hold mathematically. Let the two constraints be

either $\quad 3x_1 + 2x_2 \le 12,$

or $\quad 4x_1 + x_2 \le 15.$

It is desired to reformulate these constraints to fit into the linear programming format. If M is an extremely large number, these constraints can be expressed as

$$\text{either} \quad 3x_1 + 2x_2 \le 12, \quad \text{and} \quad 4x_1 + x_2 \le 15 + M$$

$$\text{or} \quad 3x_1 + 2x_2 \le 12 + M, \quad \text{and} \quad 4x_1 + x_2 \le 15,$$

since the addition of M to the right-hand side of such constraints has the effect of eliminating them. This formulation is equivalent to the set of constraints

$$3x_1 + 2x_2 \le 12 + y\,M,$$
$$4x_1 + x_2 \le 15 + (1 - y)\,M,$$
$$y = 0, 1,$$

which can be expressed in a mixed integer linear programming format as

$$3x_1 + 2x_2 - My \le 12,$$
$$4x_1 + x_2 + My \le 15 + M,$$
$$y \le 1,$$
$$y \ge 0 \text{ and integer.}$$

Since the artificial variable y is either 0 or 1, this formulation guarantees that only one of the original constraints holds.

K out of N constraints Must Hold

Consider a case wherein it is desired that only K out of the N constraints must hold (K < N). Let these N constraints be denoted by

$$f_1(x_1, x_2, ..., x_n) \le b_1,$$
$$f_2(x_1, x_2, ..., x_n) \le b_2,$$
$$\vdots \qquad \vdots$$
$$f_N(x_1, x_2, ..., x_n) \le b_N.$$

Using the logic of the preceding section, the equivalent formulation is

$$f_1(x_1, x_2, ..., x_n) \le b_1 + My_1,$$
$$f_2(x_1, x_2, ..., x_n) \le b_2 + My_2,$$
$$\vdots \qquad \vdots$$
$$f_N(x_1, x_2, ..., x_n) \le b_N + My_N,$$
$$\sum_{i=1}^{N} y_i = \text{N} - \text{K},$$
$$y_i \le 1,$$
$$y_i \ge 0, y_i \text{ integer for } i = 1, 2, ..., \text{N}.$$

Since the constraints on y_i guarantee that K of these artificial variables will be zero and remaining equal to 1, K of the original constraints will remain unchanged and the rest will, in effect, be eliminated.

EXAMPLE 6.10-1 (Assignment Problem)

There are n jobs to be manufactured and n machines are available. Each job can be processed on each of the machines. The cost of processing is represented by the table below. If

TABLE 6.127

Machines \ Jobs	1	2	⋯	n
1	c_{11}	c_{12}	⋯	c_{1n}
2	c_{21}	c_{22}	⋯	c_{2n}
⋮	⋮	⋮	⋮	⋮
n	c_{n1}	c_{n2}	⋯	c_{nn}

one job is to be processed on one machine only, the problem is to determine the optimal assignment policy that will turn out all the jobs at minimum total cost. Formulate this problem as I.P. model.

Formulation as I.P. Problem

Let
$$x_{ij} = \begin{cases} 1, \text{ if } i\text{th machine is assigned the } j\text{th job,} \\ 0, \text{ if } i\text{th machine is not assigned the } j\text{th job.} \end{cases}$$

Then the I.P. model is given by

$$\text{minimize} \quad Z = \sum_{i=1}^{n} \sum_{j=1}^{n} c_{ij}\, x_{ij} = \sum_{j=1}^{n} \sum_{i=1}^{n} c_{ij}\, x_{ij},$$

subject to the constrainte

$$\sum_{j=1}^{n} x_{ij} = 1, \; i = 1, 2, ..., n;$$

$$\sum_{i=1}^{n} x_{ij} = 1, \; j = 1, 2, ..., n.$$

EXAMPLE 6.10-2 (Travelling Salesman Problem)

A book salesman who lives at city 1 must call once a month on four customers located in cities 2, 3, 4 and 5. The following table gives the distance in kilometers among the different cities.

TABLE 6.128

		To City 1	2	3	4	5
From City	1	–	210	150	250	110
	2	210	–	100	80	130
	3	150	100	–	60	105
	4	250	80	60	–	90
	5	110	130	105	90	–

The objective is to minimize the total distance travelled by the salesman. Formulate the problem as I.P. model.

Formulation as I.P. Problem

As travelling from city i to i is not possible, a prohibitively high cost c_{ii} = M, i = 1, 2, ..., 5 is assigned to the diagonal cells.

Let $$x_{ij} = \begin{cases} 1, & \text{if the salesman travels from city } i \text{ to city } j, \\ 0, & \text{otherwise.} \end{cases}$$

The necessary condition for a complete route is that city i connects to one city only and that city j is reached from exactly one city. Then I.P. model for the problem is

$$\begin{aligned} \text{minimize} \quad Z = \; & [210x_{12} + 150x_{13} + 250x_{14} + 110x_{15} + 210x_{21} + 100x_{23} + 80x_{24} \\ & + 130x_{25} + 150x_{31} + 100x_{32} + 60x_{34} + 105x_{35} + 250x_{41} + 80x_{42} \\ & + 60x_{43} + 90x_{45} + 110x_{51} + 130x_{52} + 105x_{53} + 90x_{54} \\ & + M\,(x_{11} + x_{22} + x_{33} + x_{44} + x_{55})] \text{ km}, \end{aligned}$$

$$\begin{aligned} \text{subject to} \quad & x_{11} + x_{12} + x_{13} + x_{14} + x_{15} = 1, \\ & x_{21} + x_{22} + x_{23} + x_{24} + x_{25} = 1, \\ & x_{31} + x_{32} + x_{33} + x_{34} + x_{35} = 1, \\ & x_{41} + x_{42} + x_{43} + x_{44} + x_{45} = 1, \\ & x_{51} + x_{52} + x_{53} + x_{54} + x_{55} = 1, \\ & x_{11} + x_{21} + x_{31} + x_{41} + x_{51} = 1, \\ & x_{12} + x_{22} + x_{32} + x_{42} + x_{52} = 1, \\ & x_{13} + x_{23} + x_{33} + x_{43} + x_{53} = 1, \end{aligned}$$

$$x_{14} + x_{24} + x_{34} + x_{44} + x_{54} = 1,$$

and $$x_{15} + x_{25} + x_{35} + x_{45} + x_{55} = 1.$$

EXAMPLE 6.10-3 (Capital Budgeting Problem)

A company manufacturing chemicals has 4 independent investment projects and must allocate a fixed capital budget to one or more of them so that the company's total assets are maximized. The estimated investments and the anticipated cash outflows associated with these projects are given in the table below.

TABLE 6.129

Project	*Investment (₹ lakhs)*		*Cash inflows (₹ lakhs)*
	1st year	*2nd year*	
A	*60*	*160*	*105*
B	*108*	*140*	*140*
C	*200*	*150*	*80*
D	*90*	*70*	*100*

The company has earmarked ₹ 600 lakhs for investment in the first year and ₹ 700 lakhs in the second year. If projects A and C are mutually exclusive, how should the investment be made so that the company's total assets are maximized ?

Formulation as I.P. Problem

Let $$x_j = \begin{cases} 1, \text{ if there is investment on the } j\text{th project} \\ 0, \text{ otherwise } (j = 1, 2, 3, 4) \end{cases}$$
for projects A, B, C, and D.

Then the objective is

maximize $Z = 105x_1 + 140x_2 + 80x_3 + 100x_4$.

The constraints are on availability of the funds for the two years and can be expressed as

$60x_1 + 108x_2 + 200x_3 + 90x_4 \leq 600,$

and $160x_1 + 140x_2 + 150x_3 + 70x_4 \leq 700.$

Since projects A and C are mutually exclusive,

$$x_1 + x_3 = 1.$$

Remark : In the above three situations variables were discrete and hence there was no difficulty in I.P. model formulations. Difficulty arises in situations where direct I.P. formulations are not possible. Codification of variables is helpful in such situations. A few situations that require codification and transformation are now presented.

EXAMPLE 6.10-4 (Fixed Charge Problem)

(a) Consider a production planning problem wherein it is required to produce n items. Let the production of the jth item involve two types of set-up costs, the fixed cost K_j ($K_j \geq 0$) independent of the quantity produced and a variable cost c_j per unit. If x_j is the number of units of the jth item produced, the production cost function for the jth item may be written as

$$C_j(x_j) = \begin{cases} K_j + c_j x_j, & x_j > 0, \\ 0, & x_j = 0. \end{cases}$$

The objective function then becomes

minimize $$Z = \sum_{j=1}^{n} C_j(x_j)$$

$$= \sum_{j=1}^{n} (K_j + c_j x_j).$$

The corresponding constraint is

$$\sum_{j=1}^{n} x_j \geq n, \quad x_j \geq 0 \quad \text{and integer.}$$

It may be noted that the objective function is non-linear because of the fixed cost K_j involved. This difficulty can, however, be overcome by reformulation of the problem as a mixed integer programming problem with the introduction of auxiliary binary variables y_j, given by

$$y_j = \begin{cases} 1, \text{ if } x_j > 0, \\ 0, \text{ if } x_j = 0. \end{cases}$$

These conditions can be expressed as a single linear constraint

$$x_j \leq My_j,$$

in which M denotes a very large number (exceeding the largest feasible value of x_j for all j). The model can, therefore, be expressed as

minimize $\quad Z = \sum_{j=1}^{n} (K_j y_j + c_j x_j),$

subject to $\quad \sum_{j=1}^{n} x_j \geq n,$

$$x_j \leq M\,y_j,$$
$$x_j \geq 0 \text{ and integer,}$$
$$y_j = 1 \text{ or } 0 \text{ for all } j.$$

Note that although the original fixed charge problem has nothing to do with integer problem, the "transformed" problem is a zero-one mixed integer problem.

(*b*) *Consider the following production data :*

Product	*Profit / unit (₹)*	*Direct labour requirement (hours)*
1	*11*	*16*
2	*14*	*20*
3	*9*	*10*

Fixed cost (₹)	*Direct labour requirement (hours)*
10,000	*Up to 15,000*
18,000	*15,000 to 30,000*
25,000	*30,000 to 60,000*

Formulate an integer programming problem to determine the production schedule so as to maximize the total net profit.

Formulation as I.P. Problem

Let x_1, x_2, x_3 be the number of units of the product 1, 2 and 3 respectively to be produced. Further, let $y_j, j = 1, 2, 3$ be the binary integer variable corresponding to the fixed cost of ₹ 10,000, ₹ 18,000 and ₹ 25,000 respectively, where $y_j = 0$ or 1.

Then the integer L.P. problem can be expressed as

maximize $Z = 11x_1 + 14x_2 + 9x_3 - 10{,}000y_1 - 18{,}000y_2 - 25{,}000y_3,$

subject to the constraints

$$16x_1 + 20x_2 + 10x_3 \leq 15{,}000y_1 + 30{,}000y_2 + 60{,}000y_3,$$
$$y_1 + y_2 + y_3 = 1,$$
where $x_1,\ x_2, x_3 \geq 0,$
$$y_j = 0 \text{ or } 1,\ j = 1, 2, 3.$$

EXAMPLE 6.10-5 (Fixed Cost/Variable Cost Problem)

A company is having 3 machines to produce 8,000 units with fixed setup cost, variable production cost/unit and maximum production as given below:

Machine	*Setup cost (₹)*	*Production cost per unit (₹)*	*Maximum production (units)*
1	*10,000*	*5*	*6,000*
2	*7,000*	*4*	*5,000*
3	*6,000*	*8*	*4,000*

Formulate an integer programming problem to minimize the total cost.

Formulation as I.P. Problem

Let x_1, x_2 and x_3 be the number of units to be produced on machines 1, 2 and 3 respectively and y_1, y_2 and y_3 be the binary integer variables corresponding to machines 1, 2 and 3 respectively. If a machine is used, the binary variable has value 1, otherwise zero.

∴ Fixed cost $= 10{,}000\ y_1 + 7{,}000\ y_2 + 6{,}000\ y_3$.

Variable cost $= 5x_1 + 4x_2 + 8x_3$.

∴ The integer programming problem can be expressed as:

Minimize $Z = 5x_1 + 4x_2 + 8x_3 + 10{,}000\ y_1 + 7{,}000\ y_2 + 6{,}000\ y_3,$

subject to $x_1 + x_2 + x_3 \geq 8{,}000,$ (production constraint)

$$\left.\begin{array}{l} x_1 \leq 6{,}000, \\ x_2 \leq 5{,}000, \\ x_3 \leq 4{,}000, \end{array}\right\} \quad \text{(capacity constraints)}$$

where $x_1, x_2, x_3 \geq 0\ ;\ y_1, y_2, y_3 = 0$ or 1.

EXAMPLE 6.10-6 (Job Sequencing Problem)

Three products A, B and C are to be produced using four machines. The technological sequence and the processing times on the machines for the three products are shown in Fig. 6.8.

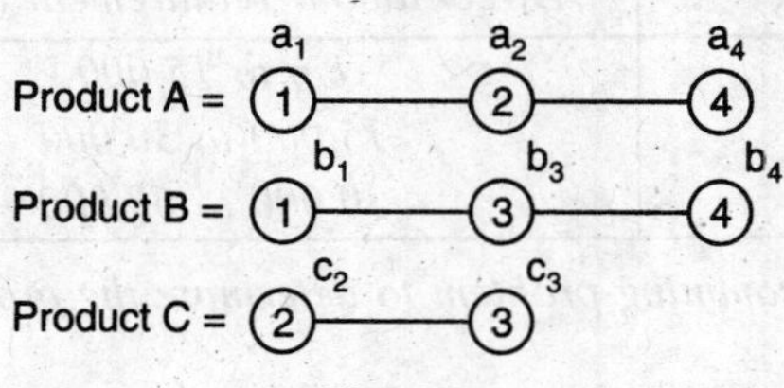

Fig. 6.8

For instance, product A is processed on machine 1 for a_1 hours, then on machine 2 for a_2 hours and finally on machine 4 for a_4 hours. Each machine processes only one product at a time and must complete its processing before taking up the next one. Further product B must be completed in not more than d hours from the start. Determine the optimal sequence in which the products be processed in order to complete all the products in the least possible time.

Formulation as I.P. Problem

Let x_{A_j} denote the time (measured from zero datum) at which the processing of product A starts on machine j ($j = 1, 2, 4$). Likewise x_{B_j} and x_{C_j} are defined.

The technological sequence in which the three products are to be machined results in the first set of constraints. Product A is processed first on machine 1, then on machine 2, and finally on machine 4. In other words

$$x_{A_1} + a_1 \le x_{A_2}$$

and $$x_{A_2} + a_2 \le x_{A_4}.$$

Similarly for products B and C, we get

$$x_{B_1} + b_1 \le x_{B_3},$$

$$x_{B_3} + b_3 \le x_{B_4},$$

$$x_{C_2} + c_2 \le x_{C_3}.$$

The next set of constraints is due to the fact that no machine can work on more than one product at a time. For example, machine 1 can process either product A or B at a given time. In other words either product A precedes B on machine 1 or vice versa. Thus we have an "either-or" type constraint for machine 1 given by

$$x_{A_1} + a_1 \le x_{B_1},$$

or $$x_{B_1} + b_1 \le x_{A_1}.$$

The above "either-or" constraint can be modified to the following two constraints with the help of a binary integer variable :

$$x_{A_1} + a_1 - x_{B_1} \le M\, y_1,$$

and $$x_{B_1} + b_1 - x_{A_1} \le (1 - y_1)\, M,$$

$$0 \le y_1 \le 1,\ y_1 \text{ integer}.$$

The first constraint becomes effective when $y_1 = 0$, implying that product A precedes B, while the second constraint becomes effective when $y_1 = 1$, implying that product B precedes A on machine 1.

Likewise, for machines 2, 3 and 4 we obtain

$$x_{A_2} + a_2 - x_{C_2} \le M\, y_2,$$

$$x_{C_2} + c_2 - x_{A_2} \le (1 - y_2)\, M,$$

$$x_{B_3} + b_3 - x_{C_3} \le M\, y_3,$$

$$x_{C_3} + c_3 - x_{B_3} \le (1 - y_3)\, M,$$

$$x_{A_4} + a_4 - x_{B_4} \le M\, y_4,$$

$$x_{B_4} + b_4 - x_{A_4} \le (1 - y_4)\, M,$$

$$0 \le y_2, y_3, y_4 \le 1,\ y_2, y_3, y_4 \text{ integers}.$$

Further, the time constraint for product B yields

$$x_{B_4} + b_4 \le d.$$

To write the objective function, note that product A will be completed at time $x_{A_4} + a_4$, product B a $x_{B_4} + b_4$ and product C at $x_{C_3} + c_3$. If Z denotes the time by which all the three products are completed, then the objective is to minimize Z, where

$$Z = \max\left(x_{A_4} + a_4,\ x_{B_4} + b_4,\ x_{C_3} + c_3\right).$$

This non-linear objective function forms a further set of three constraints

$$Z \geq x_{A_4} + a_4,$$

$$Z \geq x_{B_4} + b_4,$$

and $$Z \geq x_{C_3} + c_3.$$

Therefore, the complete formulation of the mixed integer problem is to minimize Z subject to the above constraints, $0 \leq y_i \leq 1$, y_i integer for $i = 1, 2, 3, 4$ and all other variables just non-negative.

EXAMPLE 6.10-7 (Warehouse Location Problem)

A company has plans to open two new warehouses in an area. Three sites S_1, S_2 and S_3 are under consideration. Four customers with demands D_1, D_2, D_3 and D_4 are to be supplied. Any two sites can supply all the demands but while site S_1 can supply all customers, site S_2 can supply only D_1, D_2 and D_4 and site S_3 can supply only D_2, D_3 and D_4. C_{ij} denotes the unit transportation cost from site S_i to customer D_j. The following data are given for each site :

TABLE 6.130

Site	*Capacity* (₹)	*Initial capital investment* (₹)	*Unit operating cost* (₹)
S_1	C_1	K_1	O_1
S_2	C_2	K_2	O_2
S_3	C_3	K_3	O_3

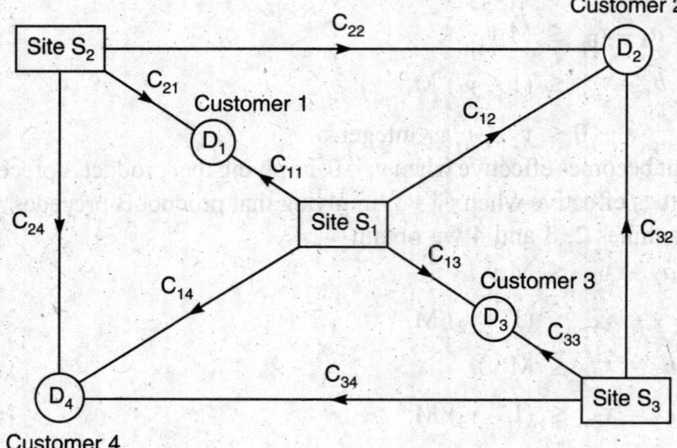

Fig. 6.9

Select the proper sites for the two warehouses that minimize the total investment, operation and transportation costs.

Formulation as I.P. Problem

Each warehouse site has a fixed initial capital cost which is independent of the quantity stored along with variable operating and transportation costs which are proportional to the quantity shipped. The total cost function is therefore non-linear and binary integer variables can be used to formulate this problem as an I.P. problem.

If the binary integer variable y_i denotes the decision to select or not to select the site s_i, then

$$y_i = \begin{cases} 1, \text{ if site } s_i \text{ is selected,} \\ 0, \text{ if otherwise.} \end{cases}$$

If x_{ij} represents the quantity shipped from site S_i to customer D_j, then the supply constraint for site S_1 is

$$x_{11} + x_{12} + x_{13} + x_{14} \le C_1 y_1.$$

When $y_1 = 1$, site S_1 is selected and the quantity shipped cannot exceed the capacity C_1. However, when $y_1 = 0$, the non-negative variables $x_{11}, x_{12}, x_{13}, x_{14}$ will automatically be zero implying that no shipment is possible from site S_1.

Likewise, constraints for sites S_2 and S_3 are

$$x_{21} + x_{22} + x_{24} \le C_2 y_2,$$
$$x_{32} + x_{33} + x_{34} \le C_3 y_3.$$

Since only two sites are to be selected, we have the additional constraint

$$y_1 + y_2 + y_3 = 2.$$

The constraints on demand can be expressed as

$$x_{11} + x_{21} = D_1 \quad \text{(for customer 1)},$$
$$x_{12} + x_{22} + x_{32} = D_2 \quad \text{(for customer 2)},$$
$$x_{13} + x_{33} = D_3 \quad \text{(for customer 3)},$$
$$x_{14} + x_{24} + x_{34} = D_4 \quad \text{(for customer 4)}.$$

To formulate the objective function, we note that the total cost of investment, operation and transportation for site S_1 is

$K_1 y_1 + O_1 (x_{11} + x_{12} + x_{13} + x_{14}) + C_{11}x_{11} + C_{12}x_{12} + C_{13}x_{13} + C_{14}x_{14}$. The total cost function for sites S_2 and S_3 can similarly be written. Thus the objective function equation can be expressed as

$$\text{minimize} \quad Z = K_1 y_1 + O_1 (x_{11} + x_{12} + x_{13} + x_{14}) + C_{11}x_{11} + C_{12}x_{12} + C_{13}x_{13} + C_{14}x_{14}$$
$$+ K_2 y_2 + O_2 (x_{21} + x_{22} + x_{24}) + C_{21}x_{21} + C_{22}x_{22} + C_{24}x_{24}$$
$$+ K_3 y_3 + O_3 (x_{32} + x_{33} + x_{34}) + C_{32}x_{32} + C_{33}x_{33} + C_{34}x_{34}.$$

The above objective function is, therefore, to be minimized subject to the following constraints :

$$x_{11} + x_{12} + x_{13} + x_{14} \le C_1 y_1,$$
$$x_{21} + x_{22} + x_{24} \le C_2 y_2,$$
$$x_{32} + x_{33} + x_{34} \le C_3 y_3,$$
$$y_1 + y_2 + y_3 = 2,$$
$$x_{11} + x_{21} = D_1,$$
$$x_{12} + x_{22} + x_{32} = D_2,$$
$$x_{13} + x_{33} = D_3,$$
$$x_{14} + x_{24} + x_{34} = D_4,$$
$$y_i = 1 \text{ or } 0,\ x_{ij} \ge 0, y_i \text{ integer for } i = 1, 2, 3.$$

Example 6.10-8 (Caterer Problem)

A caterer is to organise garden parties for a week. He needs a total of 160, 120, 60, 80, 90, 100 and 105 fresh napkins during the seven days of the week. Each new napkin costs ₹ 2. He can also use soiled napkins after getting them washed from a laundry. Ordinarily, washing charges are ₹ 0.35 per napkin and they are returned after 4 days. However, the laundry also provides express service at a cost of ₹ 0.60 per napkin, in which case they are returned after 2 days. Determine the planning schedule the caterer should adopt to buy or send napkins to the laundry so as to minimize the cost if he has no napkins at the beginning of the week.

Formulation as I.P. Problem

Let z denote the number of purchased napkins and x_j, y_j denote the number of washed napkins obtained after ordinary washing and express washing respectively on any day. Then the total supply S_j on any day will be

$$S_j = z + \sum_{j=1}^{7} (x_j + y_j).$$

If the initial inventory level for the napkins is u_0, the fact that requirement for each day must be met can be expressed as

$$u_0 + S_j \geq D_j, j = 1, 2, ..., 7,$$

where D_j denotes the cumulative demand of the napkins.

The objective is to minimize the cost *i.e.*,

$$\text{minimize} \qquad Z = 2z + 0.35 \sum_{j=1}^{7} x_j + 0.60 \sum_{j=1}^{7} y_j ,$$

Thus the problem is to find the non-negative integer values of z, x_j and y_j so as to minimize the cost Z while satisfying the above constraints. As the inventory level u_0 is given to be zero, the various constraints can be written as

$$S_1 = z + x_1 + y_1 \geq D_1$$
$$\geq 160,$$
$$S_2 = z + x_1 + x_2 + y_1 + y_2 \geq D_2$$
$$\geq 280,$$
$$S_3 = z + x_1 + x_2 + x_3 + y_1 + y_2 + y_3 \geq D_3$$
$$\geq 340,$$
$$S_4 = z + x_1 + x_2 + x_3 + x_4 + y_1 + y_2 + y_3 + y_4 \geq D_4$$
$$\geq 420,$$
$$S_5 = z + x_1 + x_2 + x_3 + x_4 + x_5 + y_1 + y_2 + y_3 + y_4 + y_5 \geq D_5$$
$$\geq 510,$$
$$S_6 = z + x_1 + x_2 + x_3 + x_4 + x_5 + x_6 + y_1 + y_2 + y_3 + y_4 + y_5 + y_6 \geq D_6$$
$$\geq 610,$$
$$S_7 = z + x_1 + x_2 + x_3 + x_4 + x_5 + x_6 + x_7 + y_1 + y_2 + y_3 + y_4 + y_5 + y_6 + y_7 \geq D_7$$
$$\geq 715.$$

Since there is no supply of napkins given for ordinary washing for the first four days,

$$x_1 = x_2 = x_3 = x_4 = 0.$$

Likewise since there is no supply of napkins given for express washing for the first two days,

$$y_1 = y_2 = 0.$$

Accordingly the constraints reduce to

$$z \geq 160 \qquad \text{(redundant)},$$
$$z \geq 280,$$
$$z + y_3 \geq 340,$$
$$z + y_3 + y_4 \geq 420,$$
$$z + x_5 + y_3 + y_4 + y_5 \geq 510,$$
$$z + x_5 + x_6 + y_3 + y_4 + y_5 + y_6 \geq 610,$$
$$z + x_5 + x_6 + x_7 + y_3 + y_4 + y_5 + y_6 + y_7 \geq 715.$$

Further, out of these constraints the first becomes redundant and can be deleted. The new objective function is given by

$$\text{minimize} \qquad Z = 2z + 0.35\,(x_5 + x_6 + x_7) + 0.60\,(y_3 + y_4 + y_5 + y_6 + y_7).$$

Thus the problem is to find non-negative integer values of z, x_j, y_j that minimize this objective function, while satisfying the above constraints. The problem involves 9 variables and 6 constraints and can be solved as an I.P. problem.

6.10-3 Methods of Integer Programming

A systematic procedure for solving pure integer programming problems was first suggested by R.E. Gomory in 1958. He, later on extended the procedure to cover mixed integer programming problems. Named as *cutting plane algorithm,* the method consists in first solving the integer programming problem as ordinary continuous L.P. problem and then introducing additional constraints one after the other to *cut* (eliminate) certain parts of the solution space until an integral solution is obtained.

Another method called the *branch and bound algorithm* originally developed by A.H. Land and A.G. Doig and later modified by R.J. Dakin is more efficient and is more widely used for solving all integer and mixed integer programming problems. In this method, too, the problem is solved as ordinary continuous L.P. problem and then the solution space is systematically 'partitioned' into subproblems by deleting parts that contain no feasible integer solutions.

The third algorithm, called *additive algorithm* due to E. Balas is an efficient and interesting algorithm for solving pure zero-one linear programming problems. The *generalised penalty function method* has also been developed to solve all integer and mixed integer programming problems.

6.10-4 The Concept of Cutting Plane Algorithms

To illustrate the concept of cutting plane, let us consider the problem

maximize $\quad Z = 5x_1 + 7x_2,$

subject to $\quad -2x_1 + 3x_2 \leq 6,$

$6x_1 + x_2 \leq 30,\ x_1, x_2 \geq 0$ and integer.

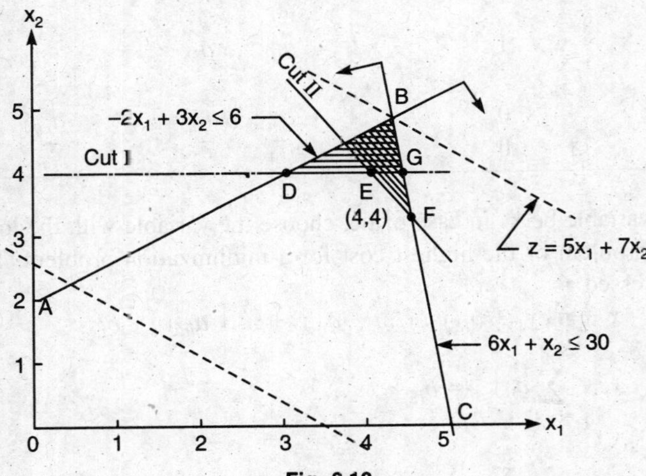

Fig. 6.10

The solution space of the problem is the region OABC in Fig. 6.10. The non-integer optimal solution represented by point B is

$$x = \frac{21}{5},\ x_2 = \frac{24}{5},\ Z_{\max} = \frac{273}{5} = 54.6.$$

The cutting plane algorithm modifies the solution space by adding *cuts* that produce an optimal integer extreme point. Fig. 6.10 gives an example of two such cuts. Cut I, when added, produces the (continuous) L.P. optimum at G with $x_1 = \frac{13}{3}$, $x_2 = 4$, $Z = \frac{149}{3} = 49.67$. Then we add cut II, which together with cut I and the original constraints, produces the L.P. optimum at E with $x_1 = 4$, $x_2 = 4$ and $Z = 48$, which is all integer, as desired. The new feasible convex region reduces to OADEFC.

Two things deserve consideration while selecting the cuts (or the additional constraints) :

1. The new feasible region, obtained by changing the boundaries of the solution space, must remain a convex set.
2. The "sliced off" portion should not contain any feasible integer solutions to the original problem.

The method developed by Gomory is used to develop (secondary) constraints for all integer and mixed integer programming problems.

6.10-5 Gomory Fractional (All Integer) Algorithm

Gomory cutting plane algorithm starts by solving the continuous L.P. problem. From the optimum L.P. table is selected a row, called the *source row,* for which the basic variable is noninteger. The desired cut is then constructed from the fractional components of the coefficients of the source row. For this reason, it is referred to as the *fractional cut.*

To see how Gomory constraints are generated, consider table 6.131 which contains non-integer solution of an ordinary L.P. problem. This table contains $(m + n)$ variables, of which x_i $(i = 1, 2, ..., m)$ are basic and y_j $(j = 1, 2, ..., n)$ are non-basic. Some or all of these basic variables have non-integer values. The basic variable with the largest fractional value is selected.

TABLE 6.131

Basis	x_1	x_2	...	x_i	...	x_m	y_1	y_2	...	y_j	...	y_n	b
x_1	1	0		0		0	a_{11}	a_{12}		a_{1j}		a_{1n}	b_1
x_2	0	1		0		0	a_{21}	a_{22}		a_{2j}		a_{2n}	b_2
⋮													⋮
x_i	0	0		1		0	a_{i1}	a_{i2}		a_{ij}		a_{in}	b_i
⋮													⋮
x_m	0	0		0		1	a_{m1}	a_{m2}		a_{mj}	.	a_{mn}	b_m
$\bar{c}_j$	0	0	...	0	...	0	$\bar{c}_1$	$\bar{c}_2$	...	$\bar{c}_j$	...	$\bar{c}_n$	

Let this basic variable be x_i. In case of tie, choose the variable with the lowest contribution for a maximization problem or the highest cost for a minimization problem. The *i*th constraint equation can be expressed as

$$x_i + a_{i1}y_1 + a_{i2}y_2 + ... + a_{ij}y_j + ... + a_{in}y_n = b_i$$

or
$$x_i + \sum_{j=1}^{n} a_{ij}y_j = b_i$$

or
$$x_i = b_i - \sum_{j=1}^{n} a_{ij}y_j, \; b_i \text{ non-integer. (source row)}$$

Let
$$b_i = (b_i)_i + f_i,$$
and
$$a_{ij} = (a_{ij})_i + f_{ij},$$

where $(b_i)_i$ and $(a_{ij})_i$ are the integers obtained by truncating the fractional parts f_i and f_{ij} from b_i and a_{ij} respectively. Here $0 < f_i < 1$ *i.e.,* f_i is a *strictly positive fraction* and $0 \leqslant f_{ij} < 1$ *i.e.,* f_{ij} is a non-negative fraction. For instance,

b_i	$(b_i)_i$	f_i
$7/2$	3	$1/2$
$-4\,1/4$	-5	$3/4$
$-3/4$	-1	$1/4$
-1	-1	0

The source row can now be writtean as

$$x_i = (b_i)_i + f_i - \sum_{j=1}^{n} \{(a_{ij})_i + f_{ij}\}\, y_j$$

$$= (b_i)_i + f_i - \sum_{j=1}^{n} (a_{ij})_i y_j - \sum_{j=1}^{n} f_{ij} y_j .$$

$$\therefore \quad f_i - \sum_{j=1}^{n} f_{ij} y_j = x_i - (b_i)_i + \sum_{j=1}^{n} (a_{ij})_i y_j .$$

Since for the optimal integer solution all variables x_i and y_j are integers, it follows that R.H.S. of the above equation must be an integer. Therefore, L.H.S. of the equation is also an integer.

$$\therefore \quad f_i - \sum_{j=1}^{n} f_{ij} y_j \text{ is an integer.}$$

Further, since f_{ij} are non-negative fractions and y_j are non-negative integers, $\sum_{j=1}^{n} f_{ij} y_j$ is ≥ 0.

Since f_i is strictly positive fraction, the quantity $f_i - \sum_{j=1}^{n} f_{ij} y_j$ can be written as

$$f_i - \sum_{j=1}^{n} f_{ij} y_j \leq f_i$$

or $$f_i - \sum_{j=1}^{n} f_{ij} y_j < 1. \qquad \text{[Since } f_i < 1\text{, being a positive fraction]}$$

As the quantity $f_i - \sum_{j=1}^{n} f_{ij} y_j$ has to be an integer,

$$f_i - \sum_{j=1}^{n} f_{ij} y_j \leq 0.$$

Adding a non-negative slack s_i, Gomory's constraint equation becomes

$$f_i - \sum_{j=1}^{n} f_{ij} y_j + s_i = 0 \text{ or } s_i = \sum_{j=1}^{n} f_{ij} y_j - f_i, \text{ (fractional cut)}$$

where s_i must also be an integer by definition. This equation is called *fractional cut*. Since y_j are non-basic variables, they are all zero.

$$\therefore \quad s_i = -f_i, \text{ which is infeasible.}$$

This means that optimal L.P. solution does not satisfy the new additional Gomory constraint. Dual simplex method can now be used to clear this infeasibility. In effect, it is equivalent to cutting off the solution space towards the optimal integer solution.

Table 6.132 is obtained after adding the fractional cut to table 6.131.

TABLE 6.132

Basis	x_1	x_2	...	x_i	...	x_m	y_1	y_2	...	y_j	...	y_n	s_i	b
x_1	1	0		0		0	a_{11}	a_{12}		a_{1j}		a_{1n}	0	b_1
x_2	0	1		0		0	a_{21}	a_{22}		a_{2j}		a_{2n}	0	b_2
$\vdots$													$\vdots$	$\vdots$
x_i	0	0		1		0	a_{i1}	a_{i2}		a_{ij}		a_{in}	0	b_i
$\vdots$													$\vdots$	$\vdots$
x_m	0	0		0		1	a_{m1}	a_{m2}		a_{mj}		a_{mn}	0	b_m
$\bar{c}_j$	0	0	...	0	...	0	$\bar{c}_1$	$\bar{c}_2$	...	$\bar{c}_j$	...	$\bar{c}_n$		
s_i	0	0	...	0	...	0	$-f_{i1}$	$-f_{i2}$	...	$-f_{ij}$	...	$-f_{in}$	1	$-f_i$

Dual simplex method is now applied to table 6.132 and a new optimal solution is obtained. If this solution happens to be all integer, nothing more is required to be done. But if the solution is non-integer, a new Gomory constraint is derived from table 6.132 and the dual simplex method is applied again to clear infeasibility. This procedure is repeated until either an optimal integer solution is obtained or the dual simplex method indicates the non-existence of a feasible solution.

A few important points in connection with Gomory's all-integer algorithm need mentioning here.

1. This algorithm is called "fractional" because all the non-zero coefficients of the generated cut are less than one (fractions).

2. It appears, as a first thought, that while solving the integer programming problem by this method, the size of the problem can grow very large since one slack and one constraint is added to the problem with the addition of each fractional cut. This, however, is not true. In fact, the total number of constraints in any modified table cannot exceed $(m + n)$, the total number of variables in the original problem. It is so because if the modified table, at any time, has more than $(m + n)$ constraints, one or more of slacks s_i associated with fractional cuts must become basic and get replaced. The equations associated with these slacks become redundant and can be dropped, thereby leaving only $(m + n)$ constraints in the table.

3. This algorithm, however, suffers from a few disadvantages. The first is associated with the round-off errors evolved during numerical computations. These errors may give an entirely different and incorrect optimal integer solution. This difficulty can be avoided by storing the coefficients as fractions instead of as decimal quantities. However, after a number of computations, the size of numerators and denominators of these fractions may become too large for the capacity of the computer. This problem can, however, be overcome by using "all-integer integer" algorithm developed by Gomory.

4. While solving the integer programming problem by this algorithm, the problem remains infeasible (since no feasible integer solution is obtained) until the optimal integer solution is attained. Therefore, there is no good integer solution which can be regarded as approximate optimal integer solution in case the computations have to be terminated at any in-between stage.

The various steps involved in solving an all-integer programming problem by the Gomory's cutting plane method are summarized below.

(*i*) *Integerise the constraints* : Transform the constraints so that all the coefficients are whole numbers. For example the constraint equation

$$\frac{7}{4}x_1 + \frac{1}{5}x_2 + \frac{3}{4}x_3 = \frac{17}{5}$$

can be expressed as

$$35x_1 + 4x_2 + 15x_3 = 68.$$

(*ii*) *Solve using the simplex method* : Ignoring integrality restriction, find the optimal solution to the problem using the simplex method. If the solution is all-integer, it is an optimal basic feasible integer solution. If not, proceed to step (*iii*). Ignore non-integer values for slack variables since they represent unused resources only.

(*iii*) *Develop a cutting plane* : From the final simplex table select the constraint with the largest fractional value. In case of a tie, choose the constraint having the lowest contribution (maximization problem) or the highest cost (minimization problem). Alternatively, select the constraint with

$$\max \frac{f_i}{\sum_{j=1}^{n} f_{ij}}.$$

If the coefficient is negative, express it as the sum of a negative integer and a non-negative fraction. Construct the Gomory's constraint

$$s_i = \sum_{j=1}^{n} f_{ij} y_j - f_i$$

and add it to the final simplex table. Add an additional column for s_i also.

(*iv*) *Solve using the dual simplex method* : Solve the augmented I.P.P. obtained above by the dual simplex method so that the outgoing variable is s_i. If the optimal solution thus obtained has all-integral values, it is an optimal feasible solution for the given I.P.P. If not, repeat step (*iii*) until an optimal feasible integer solution is obtained.

EXAMPLE 6.10-9

Maximize $Z = 5x_1 + 7x_2$,

subject to $-2x_1 + 3x_2 \le 6$,

$6x_1 + x_2 \le 30$,

$x_1, x_2 \ge 0$ *and integer.*

[*Dayalbagh Edu. Inst. M. Tech., 1998*]

Solution

Ignoring integrality restriction, the problem can be expressed in standard form as

maximize $Z = 5x_1 + 7x_2 + 0s_1 + 0s_2$,

subject to $-2x_1 + 3x_2 + s_1 = 6$,

$6x_1 + x_2 + s_2 = 30$,

$x_1, x_2, s_1, s_2 \geqslant 0$.

Putting $x_1 = x_2 = 0$ in the constraint equations yields $s_1 = 6$, $s_2 = 30$ as the initial b.f.s. Solution of the problem by the simplex method is given in tables 6.133 through 6.135.

TABLE 6.133

	c_j	5	7	0	0			
c_B	Basis	x_1	x_2	s_1	s_2	b	θ	
0	s_1	-2	(3)	1	0	6	2	←
0	s_2	6	1	0	1	30	30	
	Z_j	0	0	0	0			
	$\bar{c}_j$	5	7	0	0			
			↑					

Initial basic feasible solution

Replace s_1 by x_2.

TABLE 6.134

	c_j	5	7	0	0			
c_B	Basis	x_1	x_2	s_1	s_2	b	θ	
7	x_2	$-2/3$	1	$1/3$	0	2	-3	
0	s_2	$(20/3)$	0	$-1/3$	1	28	$21/5$	←
	Z_j	$-14/3$	7	$7/3$	0	14		
	$\bar{c}_j$	$29/3$	0	$-7/3$	0			
		↑						

Second basic feasible solution

Replace s_2 by x_1.

TABLE 6.135

	c_j	5	7	0	0	
c_B	Basis	x_1	x_2	s_1	s_2	b
7	x_2	0	1	$3/10$	$1/10$	$24/5$
5	x_1	1	0	$-1/20$	$3/20$	$21/5$
Z_j		5	7	$37/20$	$29/20$	$273/5$
$\overline{c}_j$		0	0	$-37/20$	$-29/20$	

Optimal feasible non-integer solution

Table 6.135 gives the optimum continuous solution

$$x_1 = 21/5,\ x_2 = 24/5,\ Z_{\max} = 273/5.$$

The pure integer cut is developed under the assumption that all the variables are integer. Note also that since the original objective coefficients are integer, the value of Z associated with the integer solution must also be integer.

To construct Gomory's constraint, select x_2-row which has the larger fractional part, $\frac{4}{5}$. Each of *non-integer* coefficients are factored into *integer and fractional* components, ensuring that *fractional components are strictly positive.* Accordingly, x_2-row is written as

$$(1+0)x_2 + \left(0+\frac{3}{10}\right)s_1 + \left(0+\frac{1}{10}\right)s_2 = 4 + \frac{4}{5}.$$

The Gomory's constraint to be added is

$$s_i = \sum_{j=1}^{n} f_{ij}\, y_j - f_i$$

or
$$s' = \frac{3}{10}s_1 + \frac{1}{10}s_2 - \frac{4}{5}$$

or
$$-\frac{3}{10}s_1 - \frac{1}{10}s_2 + s' = -\frac{4}{5}.$$

Alternatively the Gomory's constraint may be constructed as follows :
x_2-row, having the larger fractional part 4/5, is rewritten as

$$x_2 + \frac{3}{10}s_1 + \frac{1}{10}s_2 = \frac{24}{5} \qquad \text{... } (i)$$

or
$$(1+0)x_2 + \left\{0+\frac{3}{10}\right\}s_1 + \left(0+\frac{1}{10}\right)s_2 = 4 + \frac{4}{5}.$$

Accordingly, the following equation is generated :

$$x_2 + 0s_1 + 0s_2 + s' = 4. \qquad \text{... } (ii)$$

Subtracting (*i*) from (*ii*), we get the required cut,

$$-\frac{3}{10}s_1 - \frac{1}{10}s_2 + s' = -\frac{4}{5}.$$

The modified simplex table after inserting this equation in table 6.135 becomes

TABLE 6.136

	c_j	5	7	0	0	0	
c_B	Basis	x_1	x_2	s_1	s_2	s'	b
7	x_2	0	1	$3/10$	$1/10$	0	$24/5$
5	x_1	1	0	$-1/20$	$3/20$	0	$21/5$
0	s'	0	0	$(-3/10)$	$-1/10$	1	$-4/5$ ←
	Z_j	5	7	$37/20$	$29/20$	0	$273/5$
	$\bar{c}_j = c_j - Z_j$	0	0	$-37/20$	$-29/20$	0	
				↑			

Since basic variable s′ is negative, table 6.136 gives infeasible solution for the given (primal) problem. However, since all $\bar{c}_j$ coefficients are either zero or negative, it is feasible for the dual and dual simplex method can be applied to find the new optimal solution. Key column, key row and key element are marked in table 6.136. Regular simplex method is now applied to find the new optimal solution.

Replace s' by s_1.

TABLE 6.137

	c_j	5	7	0	0	0	
c_B	Basis	x_1	x_2	s_1	s_2	s'	b
7	x_2	0	1	0	0	1	4
5	x_1	1	0	0	$1/6$	$-1/6$	$13/3$
0	s_1	0	0	1	$1/3$	$-10/3$	$8/3$
Z_j		5	7	0	$5/6$	$37/6$	$149/3$
$\bar{c}_j$		0	0	0	$-5/6$	$-37/6$	

Optimal feasible non-integer solution

In table 6.137, x_1 has non-integer value 13/3. Non-integer value of s_1 is not to be considered since it is a slack variable. Second Gomory's constraint is now constructed. x_1 - equation is

$$x_1 + \frac{1}{6}s_2 - \frac{1}{6}s' = \frac{13}{3},$$

which can be written as

$$(1+0)x_1 + \left(0 + \frac{1}{6}\right)s_2 + \left(-1 + \frac{5}{6}\right)s' = 4 + \frac{1}{3}.$$

The Gomory's constraint to be added is

$$s'' = \frac{1}{6}s_2 + \frac{5}{6}s' - \frac{1}{3}$$

or

$$-\frac{1}{6}s_2 - \frac{5}{6}s' + s'' = -\frac{1}{3}.$$

Inserting this constraint equation in table 6.137, the modified simplex table becomes

TABLE 6.138

	c_j	5	7	0	0	0	0		
c_B	Basis	x_1	x_2	s_1	s_2	s'	s''	b	
7	x_2	0	1	0	0	1	0	4	
5	x_1	1	0	0	$1/6$	$-1/6$	0	$13/3$	
0	s_1	0	0	1	$1/3$	$-10/3$	0	$8/3$	
0	s''	0	0	0	$(-1/6)$	$-5/6$	1	$-1/3$	←
	Z_j	5	7	0	$5/6$	$37/6$	0	$149/3$	
	$\overline{c}_j$	0	0	0	$-5/6$	$-37/6$	0		
					↑				

Replace s'' by s_2.

TABLE 6.139

	c_j	5	7	0	0	0	0	
c_B	Basis	x_1	x_2	s_1	s_2	s'	s''	b
7	x_2	0	1	0	0	1	0	4
5	x_1	1	0	0	0	–1	1	4
0	s_1	0	0	1	0	–5	2	2
0	s_2	0	0	0	1	5	– 6	2
Z_j		5	7	0	0	2	5	48
$\overline{c}_j$		0	0	0	0	–2	–5	

Optimal integer solution

Table 6.139 yields optimal integer solution

$$x_1 = 4,\ x_2 = 4,\ Z_{max} = 48.$$

Note. It can be easily verified that the addition of above two constraints "cuts" the solution space as desired (see Fig. 6.10). The first constraint

$$-\frac{3}{10}s_1 - \frac{1}{10}s_2 + s' = -\frac{4}{5}$$

can be expressed in terms of x_1 and x_2 only by substituting the values of s_1 and s_2.

Now $\quad s_1 = 6 + 2x_1 - 3x_2,$

and $\quad s_2 = 30 - 6x_1 - x_2.$

$$\therefore \quad -\frac{3}{10}(6 + 2x_1 - 3x_2) - \frac{1}{10}(30 - 6x_1 - x_2) + s' = -\frac{4}{5}$$

or $\quad s' + x_2 = 4$, which is equivalent to $x_2 \le 4$.

Similarly, the second constraint

$$-\frac{1}{6}s_2 - \frac{5}{6}s' + s'' = -\frac{1}{3} \text{ is equivalent to}$$

$$-\frac{1}{6}(30 - 6x_1 - x_2) - \frac{5}{6}(4 - x_2) + s'' = -\frac{1}{3}$$

or $\quad x_1 + x_2 + s'' = 8$ or $x_1 + x_2 \le 8$.

Fig. 6.10 shows that the addition of these two constraints results in new optimal extreme point (4, 4).

EXAMPLE 6.10-10

Maximize $Z = 3x_1 + x_2 + 3x_3,$

subject to $-x_1 + 2x_2 + x_3 \le 4,$

$$2x_2 - \frac{3}{2}x_3 \le 1,$$

$$x_1 - 3x_2 + 2x_3 \le 3,$$

$x_1, x_2, x_3 \ge 0$ *and integer.*

[*R.U. M.Sc. (Math.) 2011; Jammu U. B.E. (Mech.) 2004*]

Solution

Since, for the application of cutting plane method, all the coefficients and constants in each constraint must be whole numbers, the second constraint must be transformed to

$$4x_2 - 3x_3 \le 2.$$

Ignoring the integrality restriction, the problem can be expressed in the standard form as

maximize $Z = 3x_1 + x_2 + 3x_3 + 0s_1 + 0s_2 + 0s_3,$

subject to $-x_1 + 2x_2 + x_3 + s_1 = 4,$

$$4x_2 - 3x_3 + s_2 = 2,$$

$$x_1 - 3x_2 + 2x_3 + s_3 = 3,$$

$$x_1, x_2, x_3, s_1, s_2, s_3 \ge 0.$$

Solution of the problem by the simplex method is given in tables 6.140 through 6.143.

TABLE 6.140

	c_j	3	1	3	0	0	0			
c_B	Basis	x_1	x_2	x_3	s_1	s_2	s_3	b	θ	
0	s_1	– 1	2	1	1	0	0	4	– 4	
0	s_2	0	4	– 3	0	1	0	2	∞	
0	s_3	(1)	– 3	2	0	0	1	3	3	←
	Z_j	0	0	0	0	0	0			
	$\overline{c}_j$	3	1	3	0	0	0			
		↑								

Initial basic feasible solution

(*ii*) Replace s_3 by x_1.

TABLE 6.141

	c_j	3	1	3	0	0	0			
c_B	Basis	x_1	x_2	x_3	s_1	s_2	s_3	b	θ	
0	s_1	0	– 1	3	1	0	1	7	–7	
0	s_2	0	(4)	– 3	0	1	0	2	1/2	←
3	x_1	1	– 3	2	0	0	1	3	– 1	
	Z_j	3	– 9	6	0	0	3			
	$\overline{c}_j$	0	10	–3	0	0	–3			
			↑							

Second basic feasible solution

(*ii*) Replace s_2 by x_2.

TABLE 6.142

	c_j	3	1	3	0	0	0			
c_B	Basis	x_1	x_2	x_3	s_1	s_2	s_3	b	θ	
0	s_1	0	0	$\left(9/4\right)$	1	$1/4$	1	$15/2$	$10/3$	←
1	x_2	0	1	$-3/4$	0	$1/4$	0	$1/2$	$-2/3$	
3	x_1	1	0	$-1/4$	0	$3/4$	1	$9/2$	– 18	

Z_j		3	1	$-3/2$	0	$5/2$	3
$\bar{c}_j$		0	0	$9/2$	0	$-5/2$	-3
				↑			

Third basic feasible solution

(*ii*) Replace s_1 by x_3.

TABLE 6.143

	c_j	3	1	3	0	0	0	
c_B	Basis	x_1	x_2	x_3	s_1	s_2	s_3	b
3	x_3	0	0	1	$4/9$	$1/9$	$4/9$	$10/3$
1	x_2	0	1	0	$1/3$	$1/3$	$1/3$	3
3	x_1	1	0	0	$1/9$	$7/9$	$10/9$	$16/3$
	Z_j	3	1	3	2	3	5	
	$\bar{c}_j$	0	0	0	-2	-3	-5	

Optimal feasible non-integer solution

∴ The optimal non-interger solution is

$$x_1 = \frac{16}{3},\ x_2 = 3,\ x_3 = \frac{10}{3},\ Z_{\max} = 29.$$

To construct Gomory's constraint, the constraint equation with the largest fractional part is selected. Since, here x_1-row as well as x_3-row have the same fractional part 1/3, tie can be broken by choosing the row with maximum $\dfrac{f_i}{\sum_{j=1}^{n} f_{ij}}$.

Now taking x_1-row as the source row, we get from table 6.143,

$$x_1 + \frac{1}{9}s_1 + \frac{7}{9}s_2 + \frac{10}{9}s_3 = 5 + \frac{1}{3}$$

$$\text{or} \quad \frac{1}{9}s_1 + \frac{7}{9}s_2 + \frac{10}{9}s_3 = \frac{1}{3}.$$

$$\therefore \quad \frac{f_i}{\sum_{j=1}^{n} f_{ij}} \text{ for } x_1\text{-row} = \frac{1/3}{\frac{1}{9}+\frac{7}{9}+\frac{10}{9}} = \frac{1}{6}.$$

Similarly, taking x_3-row as the source row, we have from table 6.143,

$$x_3 + \frac{4}{9}s_1 + \frac{1}{9}s_2 + \frac{4}{9}s_3 = \frac{10}{3} = 3 + \frac{1}{3}$$

$$\text{or} \quad \frac{4}{9}s_1 + \frac{1}{9}s_2 + \frac{4}{9}s_3 = \frac{1}{3}.$$

$$\therefore \quad \frac{f_i}{\sum_{j=1}^{n} f_{ij}} \text{ for } x_3\text{ - row} = \frac{1/3}{\frac{4}{9}+\frac{1}{9}+\frac{4}{9}} = \frac{1}{3}.$$

Since x_3-row gives a stronger cut, it is selected as the source row and can be written as

$$(1+0)x_3 + \left(0+\frac{4}{9}\right)s_1 + \left(0+\frac{1}{9}\right)s_2 + \left(0+\frac{4}{9}\right)s_3 = 3 + \frac{1}{3}.$$

The Gomory's constraint to be added is

$$s_i = \sum_{j=1}^{n} f_{ij} y_j - f_i$$

or
$$s' = s_1 + \frac{1}{9}s_2 + \frac{4}{9}s_3 - \frac{1}{3}$$

or
$$-\frac{4}{9}s_1 - \frac{1}{9}s_2 - \frac{4}{9}s_3 + s' = -\frac{1}{3}.$$

The modified simplex table after inserting this equation in table 6.143 becomes

TABLE 6.144

c_B	c_j / Basis	3 x_1	1 x_2	3 x_3	0 s_1	0 s_2	0 s_3	0 s'	b	
3	x_3	0	0	1	4/9	1/9	4/9	0	10/3	
1	x_2	0	1	0	1/3	1/3	1/3	0	3	
3	x_1	1	0	0	1/9	7/9	10/9	0	16/3	
0	s'	0	0	0	(−4/9)	−1/9	−4/9	1	−1/3	←
	Z_j	3	1	3	2	3	5	0	29	
	$\bar{c}_j$	0	0	0	−2	−3	−5	0		
					↑					

Since s' is negative and all $\bar{c}_j$ coefficients in table 6.144 are non-positive, dual simplex method can be applied to find the new optimal solution. Ratios for the non-basic variables are 9/2, 27, 45/4. Thus s_1 is the entering variable and $\left(-\frac{4}{9}\right)$ is the key element. s' is replaced by s_1 in table 6.145.

TABLE 6.145

c_B	c_j / Basis	3 x_1	1 x_2	3 x_3	0 s_1	0 s_2	0 s_3	0 s'	b
3	x_3	0	0	1	0	0	0	1	3
1	x_2	0	1	0	0	1/4	0	3/4	11/4
3	x_1	1	0	0	0	3/4	1	1/4	21/4
0	s_1	0	0	0	1	1/4	1	−9/4	3/4
	Z_j	3	1	3	0	5/2	3	9/2	55/2
	$\bar{c}_j$	0	0	0	0	−5/2	−3	−9/2	

Non-integer optimal feasible solution

Since the solution is still non-integer, second Gomory's constraint must be added. Now x_2-row has the largest fractional part, 3/4 and is chosen as the source row. Non-integer value of s_1 is not considered since it is a slack variable. To construct second Gomory's constraint x_2-row is written as

$$x_2 + \frac{1}{4}s_2 + \frac{3}{4}s' = \frac{11}{4}$$

or $$(1+0)\,x_2 + \frac{1}{4}s_2 + \frac{3}{4}s' = 2 + \frac{3}{4}.$$

∴ Gomory's constraint is given by

$$s'' = \frac{1}{4}s_2 + \frac{3}{4}s' - \frac{3}{4}$$

or $$-\frac{1}{4}s_2 - \frac{3}{4}s' + s'' = -\frac{3}{4}.$$

Adding this constraint to table 6.145, the modified simplex table becomes

TABLE 6.146

	c_j	3	1	3	0	0	0	0	0		
c_B	Basis	x_1	x_2	x_3	s_1	s_2	s_3	s'	s''	b	
3	x_3	0	0	1	0	0	0	1	0	3	
1	x_2	0	1	0	0	$1/4$	0	$3/4$	0	$11/4$	
3	x_1	1	0	0	0	$3/4$	1	$1/4$	0	$21/4$	
0	s_1	0	0	0	1	$1/4$	1	$-9/4$	0	$3/4$	
0	s''	0	0	0	0	$-1/4$	0	$(-3/4)$	1	$-3/4$	←
	Z_j	3	1	3	0	$5/2$	3	$9/2$	0	$55/2$	
	$\bar{c}_j$	0	0	0	0	$-5/2$	−3	$-9/2$	0		
								↑			

In table 6.146, s'' is the outgoing variable. Applying dual simplex method, ratios for the non-basic variables are 10, 6. Hence s' is the incoming variable and $\left(-\frac{3}{4}\right)$ is the key element. s'' is replaced by s' in table 6.147.

TABLE 6.147

	c_j	3	1	3	0	0	0	0	0	
c_B	Basis	x_1	x_2	x_3	s_1	s_2	s_3	s'	s''	b
3	x_3	0	0	1	0	$-1/3$	0	0	$4/3$	2
1	x_2	0	1	0	0	0	0	0	1	2
3	x_1	1	0	0	0	$2/3$	1	0	$1/3$	5
0	s_1	0	0	0	1	1	1	0	−3	3
0	s'	0	0	0	0	$1/3$	0	1	$-4/3$	1
	Z_j	3	1	3	0	1	3	0	6	23
	$\bar{c}_j$	0	0	0	0	−1	−3	0	−6	

Optimal feasible integer solution

Table 6.147 gives all-integer optimal solution

$$x_1 = 5,\ x_2 = 2,\ x_3 = 2;\ Z_{max} = 23.$$

EXAMPLE 6.10-11

Consider the problem :

Maximize $Z = 2x_1 + 20x_2 - 10x_3,$

subject to $2x_1 + 20x_2 + 4x_3 \le 15,$

$6x_1 + 20x_2 + 4x_3 = 20,$

$x_1, x_2, x_3 \ge 0$ *and integer.*

Solve the problem as a continuous linear program; then show that it is impossible to obtain feasible integer solution by using simple rounding. Solve the problem using any integer problem algorithm. [*Sri Venkt. M.Sc. (Stat.) 1977*]

Solution

Ignoring the integrality restriction, the problem can be expressed in the standard form as

maximize $Z = 2x_1 + 20x_2 - 10x_3 + 0s_1 - MA_1,$

subject to $2x_1 + 20x_2 + 4x_3 + s_1 = 15,$

$6x_1 + 20x_2 + 4x_3 + A_1 = 2\ 0,$

$x_1, x_2, x_3, s_1, A_1 \ge 0.$

Putting $x_1 = x_2 = x_3 = 0$ in the constraint equations we get $s_1 = 15$, $A_1 = 20$ as the initial solution which is expressed in table 6.148.

TABLE 6.148

	c_j	2	20	–10	0	–M		
c_B	Basis	x_1	x_2	x_3	s_1	A_1	b	θ
0	s_1	2	(20)	4	1	0	15	3/4 ←
–M	A_1	6	20	4	0	1	20	1
	Z_j	–6M	–20M	–4M	0	–M	–20M	
	$\overline{c}_j$	2 + 6M	20 + 20M	–10 + 4M	0	0		
			↑					

Initial solution

After two iterations the following optimal table is obtained :

TABLE 6.149

	c_j	2	20	–10	0	
c_B	Basis	x_1	x_2	x_3	s_1	b
20	x_2	0	1	1/5	3/40	5/8
2	x_1	1	0	0	–1/4	5/4
	Z_j	2	20	4	1	15
	$\overline{c}_j$	0	0	–14	–1	

Non-integer optimal feasible solution

Note that A_1-column has been dropped in table 6.149 from further consideration. This table gives non-integer optimal solution as

$$x_1 = \frac{5}{4} = 1\frac{1}{4},\ x_2 = \frac{5}{8},\ x_3 = 0;\ Z = 15.$$

The rounded solution $x_1 = 1$, $x_2 = 1$, $x_3 = 0$ satisfies neither of the constraints while $x_1 = 1$, $x_2 = 0$, $x_3 = 0$, $Z = 2$ satisfies the first but not the second constraint. Hence, it is not possible to obtain feasible integer solution by using simple rounding. To obtain integer solution, we must construct Gomory's constraint. First row is selected since it has the larger fractional part, 5/8. The x_2-equation corresponding to this row is

$$x_2 + \frac{1}{5}x_3 + \frac{3}{40}s_1 = \frac{5}{8},$$

which can be written as

$$(1+0)x_2 + \left(0+\frac{1}{5}\right)x_3 + \left(0+\frac{3}{40}\right)s_1 = \frac{5}{8}.$$

Therefore, the Gomory's constraint to be added is

$$s' = \frac{1}{5}x_3 + \frac{3}{40}s_1 - \frac{5}{8}$$

or

$$-\frac{1}{5}x_3 - \frac{3}{40}s_1 + s' = -\frac{5}{8}.$$

Inserting this constraint equation in table 6.149, the modified simplex table becomes

TABLE 6.150

	c_j	2	20	−10	0	0		
c_B	Basis	x_1	x_2	x_3	s_1	s'	b	
20	x_2	0	1	1/5	3/40	0	5/8	
2	x_1	1	0	0	−1/4	0	5/4	
0	s'	0	0	−1/5	(−3/40)	1	−5/8	←
	Z_j	2	20	4	1	0	15	
	$\overline{c}_j$	0	0	−14	−1	0		
					↑			

Since s' is negative and all $\overline{c}_j$ coefficients in table 6.150 are non-positive, dual simplex method can be applied to find the new optimal solution. Ratios for the non-baisc variables are 70, 40/3. Thus s_1 is the incoming variable, s' the outgoing variable and (−3/40) is the key element. In table 6.151, s' is replaced by s_1.

TABLE 6.151

	c_j	2	20	−10	0	0	
c_B	Basis	x_1	x_2	x_3	s_1	s'	b
20	x_2	0	1	0	0	1	0
2	x_1	1	0	2/3	0	−10/3	10/3
0	s_1	0	0	8/3	1	−40/3	25/3
Z_j		2	20	4/3	0	40/3	20/3
$\overline{c}_j$		0	0	−34/3	0	−40/3	

Non-integer optimal feasible solution

As the solution is still non-integer, one more Gomory's constraint must be added. Now x_1-row as well as s_1-row have the same fractional part 1/3. However, x_1 has a contribution of 2, while s_1 has a zero contribution. Since s_1 has a lower contribution, s_1-row is selected. s_1-equation corresponding to this row is

$$\frac{8}{3}x_3 + s_1 - \frac{40}{3}s' = \frac{25}{3},$$ which can be written as

$$\left(2+\frac{2}{3}\right)x_3 + (1+0)s_1 + \left(-14+\frac{2}{3}\right)s' = \left(8+\frac{1}{3}\right).$$

The corresponding fractional cut is

$$s'' = \frac{2}{3}x_3 + \frac{2}{3}s' - \frac{1}{3} \quad \text{or} \quad -\frac{2}{3}x_3 - \frac{2}{3}s' + s'' = -\frac{1}{3}.$$

Inserting this additional constraint in table 6.151, the modified simplex table becomes

TABLE 6.152

c_B	c_j Basis	2 x_1	20 x_2	–10 x_3	0 s_1	0 s'	0 s''	b
20	x_2	0	1	0	0	1	0	0
2	x_1	1	0	2/3	0	–10/3	0	10/3
0	s_1	0	0	8/3	1	–40/3	0	25/3
0	s''	0	0	(–2/3)	0	–2/3	1	–1/3 ←
	Z_j	2	20	4/3	0	40/3	0	20/3
	$\overline{c}_j$	0	0	–34/3 ↑	0	–40/3	0	

Since s'' is negative and all non-basic $\overline{c}_j$ coefficients are non-positive, application of dual simplex method to table 6.152 yields the following table:

TABLE 6.153

c_B	c_j Basis	2 x_1	20 x_2	–10 x_3	0 s_1	0 s'	0 s''	b
20	x_2	0	1	0	0	1	0	0
2	x_1	1	0	0	0	–4	1	3
0	s_1	0	0	0	1	–16	4	7
–10	x_3	0	0	1	0	1	–3/2	1/2
	Z_j	2	20	–10	0	2	17	1
	$\overline{c}_j$	0	0	0	0	–2	–17	

Non-integer optimal feasible solution

Since the solution is still non-integer, a third fractional cut needs to be constructed. x_3-equation corresponding to the fourth row is

$$x_3 + s' - \frac{3}{2}s'' = \frac{1}{2}\text{, which can be written as}$$

$$(1 + 0)\,x_3 + (1 + 0)s' + \left(-2+\frac{1}{2}\right)s'' = \frac{1}{2}.$$

The corresponding fractional cut is

$$s''' = \frac{1}{2}s'' - \frac{1}{2} \text{ or } -\frac{1}{2}s'' + s''' = -\frac{1}{2}.$$

Inserting this additional constraint in table 6.153, the modified simplex table becomes

TABLE 6.154

c_B	c_j Basis	2 x_1	20 x_2	–10 x_3	0 s_1	0 s'	0 s''	0 s'''	b
20	x_2	0	1	0	0	1	0	0	0
2	x_1	1	0	0	0	–4	1	0	3
0	s_1	0	0	0	1	–16	4	0	7
–10	x_3	0	0	1	0	1	$-3/2$	0	$1/2$
0	s'''	0	0	0	0	0	$(-1/2)$	1	$-1/2$ ←
	Z_j	2	20	–10	0	2	17	0	1
	$\overline{c}_j$	0	0	0	0	–2	–17 ↑	0	

Applying the dual simplex method to table 6.154 we get

TABLE 6.155

c_B	c_j Basis	2 x_1	20 x_2	–10 x_3	0 s_1	0 s'	0 s''	0 s'''	b
20	x_2	0	1	0	0	1	0	0	0
2	x_1	1	0	0	0	–4	0	2	2
0	s_1	0	0	0	1	–16	0	8	3
–10	x_3	0	0	1	0	1	0	–3	2
0	s''	0	0	0	0	0	1	–2	1
Z_j		2	20	–10	0	2	0	34	–16
$\bar{c}_j$		0	0	0	0	–2	0	–34	

Optimal feasible integer solution

The optimal feasible integer solution given by table 6.155 is

$$x_1 = 2, x_2 = 0, x_3 = 2, Z_{max} = -16.$$

It may be noted that in all the three problems dicussed *the optimum solution is all integer i.e., values of decision variables, slacks and objective function are integer.*

6.10-6 The Mixed Algorithm

In mixed integer problems only some of the variables are constrained to be integers. As in the case of pure integers, the problem is first solved as a continuous linear programming problem and then secondary cuts corresponding to the integer variables are added one by one. The value of the objective function in the optimum solution of the mixed integer programming problem is always superior to or at least equal to that of all integer problem, and is always inferior to or equal to that of the continuous L.P. problem.

EXAMPLE 6.10-12

Maximize $Z = 4x_1 + 6x_2 + 2x_3,$

subject to $4x_1 - 4x_2 \le 5,$

$-x_1 + 6x_2 \le 5,$

$-x_1 + x_2 + x_3 \le 5,$

$x_1, x_2, x_3 \ge 0;$ x_1, x_3 *integer.*

[*P.U. B.E. (T.I.T.) Nov., 2006*]

Solution

The optimal solution to this problem obtained by ignoring the integrality condition is given in the following simplex table :

TABLE 6.156

c_B	c_j Basis	4 x_1	6 x_2	2 x_3	0 s_1	0 s_2	0 s_3	b
4	x_1	1	0	0	3/10	1/5	0	5/2
6	x_2	0	1	0	1/20	1/5	0	5/4
2	x_3	0	0	1	1/4	0	1	25/4

Optimal feasible non-integer solution

Variables x_1 and x_3 are constrained to be integers. To construct Gomory's constraint, select x_1-row which has the larger fractional part, 1/2. This row can be written as

$$(1+0)x_1 + \left(0+\frac{3}{10}\right)s_1 + \left(0+\frac{1}{5}\right)s_2 = 2 + \frac{1}{2},$$

The Gomory's constraint to be added is

$$s' = \frac{3}{10}s_1 + \frac{1}{5}s_2 - \frac{1}{2}$$

or
$$-\frac{3}{10}s_1 - \frac{1}{5}s_2 + s' = -\frac{1}{2}.$$

Adding this constraint to table 6.156, we get

TABLE 6.157

c_B	c_j Basis	4 x_1	6 x_2	2 x_3	0 s_1	0 s_2	0 s_3	0 s'	b	
4	x_1	1	0	0	3/10	1/5	0	0	5/2	
6	x_2	0	1	0	1/20	1/5	0	0	5/4	
2	x_3	0	0	1	1/4	0	1	0	25/4	
0	s'	0	0	0	(−3/10)	−1/5	0	1	−1/2	←
	Z_j	4	6	2	2	2	2	0		
	$\bar{c}_j$	0	0	0	−2	−2	−2	0		
	ratio	–	–	–	20/3 ↑	10	–	–		

Replace s' by s_1.

TABLE 6.158

c_B	c_j *Basis*	4 x_1	6 x_2	2 x_3	0 s_1	0 s_2	0 s_3	0 s'	b
4	x_1	1	0	0	0	0	0	1	2
6	x_2	0	1	0	0	1/6	0	1/6	7/6
2	x_3	0	0	1	0	−1/6	1	5/6	35/6
0	s_1	0	0	0	1	2/3	0	−10/3	5/3

Taking x_3-row as the source row, we have

$$(1+0)x_3 + \left(-1+\frac{5}{6}\right)s_2 + (1+0)s_3 + \left(0+\frac{5}{6}\right)s' = 5 + \frac{5}{6}.$$

∴ The Gomory's constraint is

$$s'' = \frac{5}{6}s_2 + \frac{5}{6}s' - \frac{5}{6} \text{ or } -\frac{5}{6}s_2 - \frac{5}{6}s' + s'' = -\frac{5}{6}.$$

This constraint is now added to table 6.158 and we get

TABLE 6.159

	c_j	4	6	2	0	0	0	0	0		
c_B	Basis	x_1	x_2	x_3	s_1	s_2	s_3	s'	s''	b	
4	x_1	1	0	0	0	0	0	1	0	2	
6	x_2	0	1	0	0	$1/6$	0	$1/6$	0	$7/6$	
2	x_3	0	0	1	0	$-1/6$	1	$5/6$	0	$35/6$	
0	s_1	0	0	0	1	$2/3$	0	$-10/3$	0	$5/3$	
0	s''	0	0	0	0	$(-5/6)$	0	$-5/6$	1	$-5/6$	←
	Z_j	4	6	2	0	$2/3$	2	$20/3$	0		
	$\bar{c}_j$	0	0	0	0	$-2/3$	–2	$-20/3$	0		
	Ratio	–	–	–	–	$4/5$	–	8	–		
						↑					

Replace s'' by s_2.

TABLE 6.160

	c_j	4	6	2	0	0	0	0	0	
c_B	Basis	x_1	x_2	x_3	s_1	s_2	s_3	s'	s''	b
4	x_1	1	0	0	0	0	0	1	0	2
6	x_2	0	1	0	0	0	0	0	$1/5$	1
2	x_3	0	0	1	0	0	1	1	$-1/5$	6
0	s_1	0	0	0	1	0	0	–4	$4/5$	1
0	s_2	0	0	0	0	1	0	1	$-6/5$	1

Optimal integer solution

Table 6.160 gives optimal integer solution

$$x_1 = 2, x_2 = 1, x_3 = 6 \; ; Z_{max} = 26.$$

6.10-7 Branch-and-Bound (B & B) Algorithm

Branch-and-bound algorithm is the most widely used method for solving pure as well as mixed integer problems in practice. Most commercial computer codes use this method for solving I.P. Problems.

In this method also, the problem is first solved as a continuous L.P. problem ignoring the integrality condition. If the solution is infeasible or unbounded, then the given L.P.P. also has an infeasible or unbounded solution. If the solution satisfies the integer restrictions, the optimal integer solution has been obtained. If in the optimal solution some variable, say x_j is not an integer, then

$$x_j^{\bullet} < x_j < +1,$$

where $x_j^{\bullet}$ and $x_j^{\bullet} + 1$ are consecutive non-negative integers.

It follows that any feasible integer value of x_j must satisfy one of the two conditions, namely $$x_j \le x_j^{\bullet} \text{ or } x_j \ge x_j^{\bullet} + 1.$$

since variable has no integer value between $x_j^{\bullet}$ and $x_{j+1}^{\bullet}$.

These two conditions are mutually exclusive and when applied separately to the continuous L.P. problem, form two different subproblems (also called *nodes*). Thus the original problem is '*branched*' or '*partitioned*' into two subproblems. Geometrically it means that the branching process eliminates that portion of the feasible region that contains no feasible integer solution.

For instance, let the continuous optimal solution to a problem be

$$x_1 = 5\frac{1}{2},\ x_2 = 0,\ Z_{\max} = 55.$$

Now $$x_1 = 5\frac{1}{2} \text{ gives } 5 < x_1 < 6.$$

For an integer valued solution,

$$\text{either } x_1 \leq 5 \text{ or } x_1 \geq 6,$$

and we search for optimum value of Z either in the first region ($x_1 \leq 5$) or in the second region ($x_1 \geq 6$).

This branching process yields two subproblems, one by adding the constraint $x_j \leq x_j^{\bullet}$ and the other by adding the constraint $x_j \geq x_j^{\bullet} + 1$ to the original set of constraints. Each of these subproblems is then solved separately as a linear program, using the same objective function of the original problem. If any subproblem yields an optimal integer solution, it is not further branched. However, if it yields a non-integer solution, it is further branched into two subproblems. This branching process is continued, until each problem terminates with either integer valued optimal solution or there is evidence that it cannot yield a better solution. Whenever a *better* integer solution is found for any subproblem, it replaces the one previously found. The integer valued solution, among all the subproblems that gives the most optimum value of the objective function is selected as the optimum solution.

Main drawback of this algorithm is that it requires the optimum solution of each subproblem and in large problems it could be very time-consuming. However, the computational efficiency of this algorithm is increased by applying the concept of "bounding". According to this concept, whenever the continuous optimum solution of a subproblem yields a value of the objective function lower than that of the best available integer solution (maximization case), it is useless to explore the problem any further. This subproblem is said to be *fathomed* and is dropped from further consideration. Thus once a feasible integer solution is obtained , its associated objective function can be used as a lower bound (maximization case) to delete inferior subproblems. Hence efficiency of a branch and bound algorithm depends upon how soon the successive subproblems are fathomed.

If the objective function is to be minimized, the procedure remains the same except that upper bounds are used. Thus the value of the first integral solution becomes an upper bound for the problem and the programs are eliminated when their objective function values are greater than the current upper bound.

This algorithm can be extended directly to the mixed integer problems (in which only some of the variables are integer). If a variable is continuous, we simply never select it as a branching variable. A subproblem provides a new bound on the objective value if the values of all the discrete variables are integer and the objective value is better than the existing bound.

EXAMPLE 6.10-13

Maximize $Z = 2x_1 + 3x_2,$

subject ot $6x_1 + 5x_2 \leq 25,$

$x_1 + 3x_2 \leq 10,$

x_1, x_2 *non-negative integers.* [*J.U. B.E. (Mech.) 2006, 2004*]

Solution

The given problem is first solved as a continuous linear programming problem ignoring the integrality condition. Any of the methods, graphical or simplex could be used, however the graphical method will be used here. The non-integer optimal solution given in Fig. 6.11 is

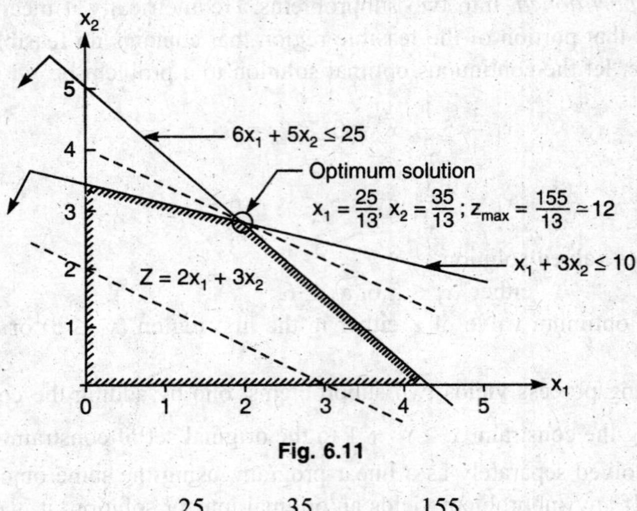

Fig. 6.11

$$x_1 = \frac{25}{13}, x_2 = \frac{35}{13}; Z_{max} = \frac{155}{13} \sim 12.$$

This is the starting solution and is represented on the tree diagram given in Fig. 6.16. It can be observed that addition of integer restrictions can only make L.P. solution worse. Hence *upper bound* on the value of Z for the integer problem is 12. Since the solution is non-integer with both x_1 and x_2 having fractional values, any variable may be arbitrarily selected for branching. If x_2 is selected, then

$$x_2 = \frac{35}{13} \text{ gives } 2 < x_2 < 3.$$

For an integer solution, a value of greater than 2 and less than 3 being ruled out, we can specify that either $x_2 \le 2$ or it is ≥ 3. These can be used to partition the solution space of the given problem into two distinct subproblems.

Thus we add a new constraint either $x_2 \le 2$ or $x_2 \ge 3$ to the original L.P. problem, yielding two subproblems:

Subproblem 1		*Subproblem 2*	
Maximize	$Z = 2x_1 + 3x_2,$	Maximize	$Z = 2x_1 + 3x_2,$
subject to	$6x_1 + 5x_2 \le 25,$	subject to	$6x_1 + 5x_2 \le 25,$
	$x_1 + 3x_2 \le 10,$		$x_1 + 3x_2 \le 10,$
	$x_2 \le 2,$		$x_2 \ge 3,$
	x_1, x_2 non-negative integers.		x_1, x_2 non-negative integers.

These subproblems are again solved by ignoring the integrality condition. The solution of subproblem 1 given in Fig. 6.12 is

$$x_1 = 2.5, x_2 = 2 ; Z_{max} = 11.$$

Similarly, the optimal solution obtained graphically in Fig. 6.13 for subproblem 2 is

$$x_1 = 1, x_2 = 3 ; Z_{max} = 11.$$

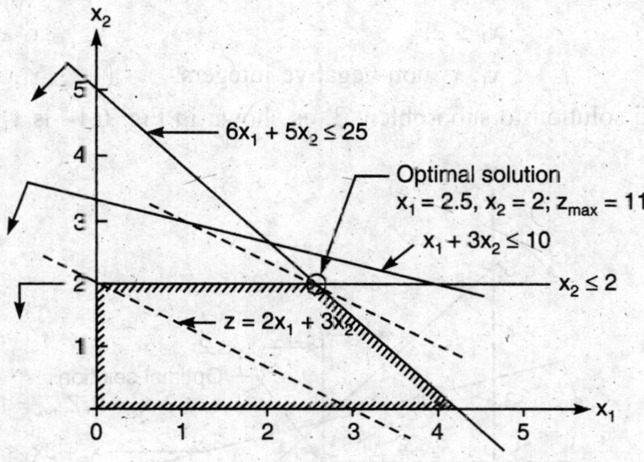

Fig. 6.12

This is a feasible integer solution to the given problem. Since variables x_1 and x_2 are integers, there is no need to branch subproblem 2 further. Note that $Z_{max} = 11$ is a *lower bound* on the maximum value of Z for the future solutions. Also by the above partitioning we have not ruled out any integer solution to the original (given) problem.

Thus $\qquad Z_L = 11.$

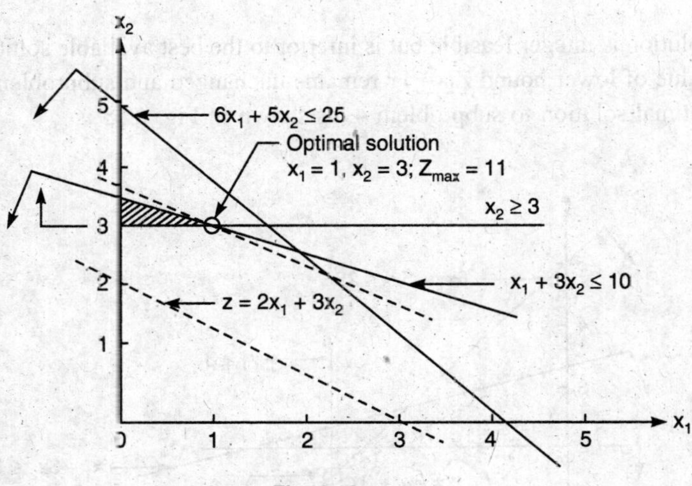

Fig. 6.13

Subproblem 1 is now the only candidate for branching. The optimum continuous solution to this problem give $Z_{max} = 11$, which is not inferior to the lower bound. Therefore, it can be branched into further subproblems. Since x_1 is the only fractional valued variable, this will act as the branching variable and the new subproblems will have one of the following additional constraints :

Since $\quad x_1 = 2.5, \quad$ either $\quad x_1 \le 2,$

or $\quad x_1 \ge 3.$

Thus the subproblems emanating from it are

Subproblem 3		*Subproblem 4*	
Maximize	$Z = 2x_1 + 3x_2,$	Maximize	$Z = 2x_1 + 3x_2,$
subject to	$6x_1 + 5x_2 \le 25,$	subject to	$6x_1 + 5z_2 \le 25,$
	$x_1 + 3x_2 \le 10,$		$x_1 + 3x_2 \le 10,$
	$x_2 \le 2,$		$x_2 \le 2,$

$x_1 \leq 2,$ $x_1 \geq 3,$

x_1, x_2 non-negative integers. x_1, x_2 non-negative integers.

The optimal solution to subproblem 3, as shown in Fig. 6.14 is $x_1 = 2, x_2 = 2; Z_{max} = 10$.

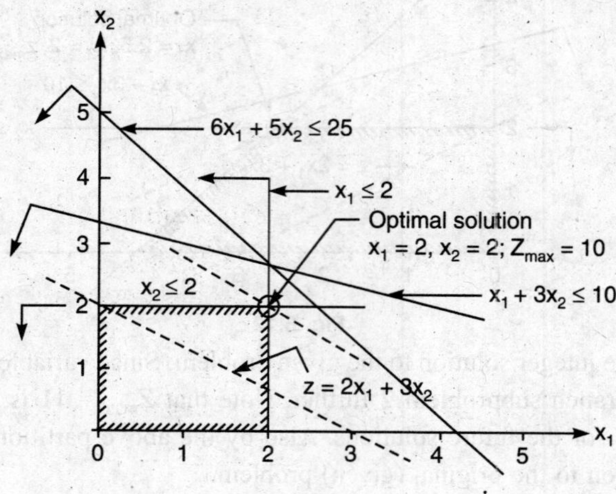

Fig. 6.14

This solution is integer feasible but is inferior to the best available solution already obtained. Hence the value of lower bound $Z_L = 11$ remains unchanged and subproblem 3 is also fathomed.

The optimal solution to subproblem 4, as shown in Fig. 6.15 is

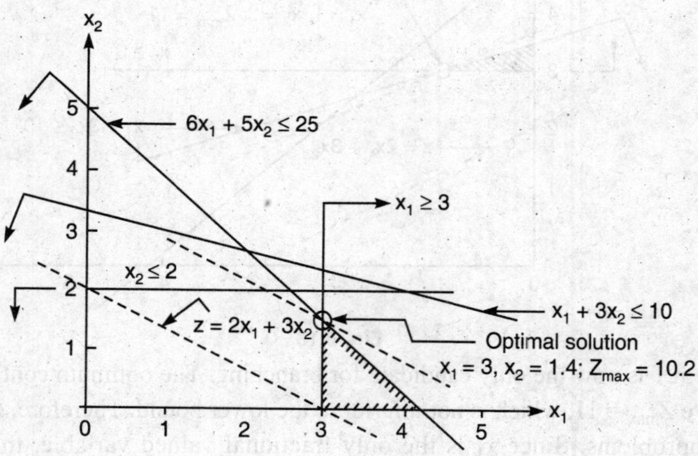

Fig. 6.15

$$x_1 = 3, x_2 = 1.4; Z_{max} = 10.2.$$

Since the solution is non-integer, subproblem 4 can be further branched with x_2 as the branching variable. But the value of its objective function ($Z_{max} = 10.2$) is inferior to the lower bound and hence this does not promise a solution better than the one already obtained. Therefore, this subproblem is also fathomed. Now there is no subproblem which can be further branched and the best available solution corresponding to subproblem 2 is the integer optimal solution of the problem.

i.e., $$x_1 = 1, x_2 = 3; Z_{max} = 11.$$

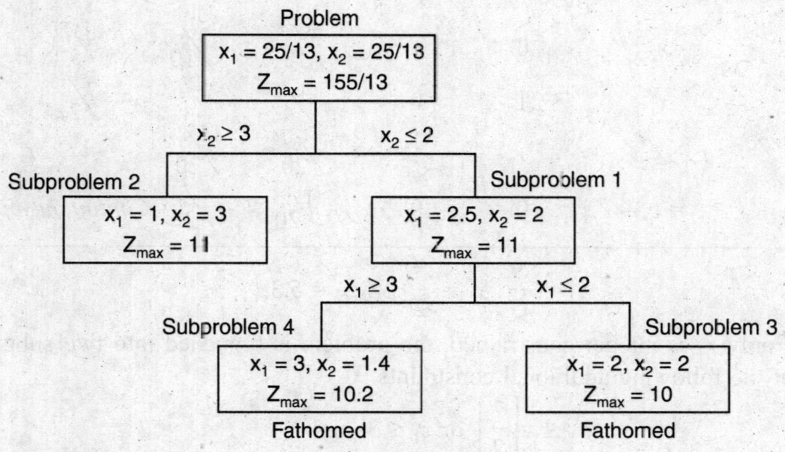

Fig. 6.16

Fig. 6.16 summarizes the generated subproblems in the form of a *tree*.

Example 6.10.13 was solved using graphical method. We present below a mixed-integer problem and solve it by the simplex method.

EXAMPLE 6.10-14

Solve the following mixed integer problem by the branch-and-bound technique :

Maximize $Z = x_1 + x_2,$

subject to $2x_1 + 5x_2 \leq 16,$

$6x_1 + 5x_2 \leq 30,$

$x_2 \geq 0,$

$x_1 \geq 0$ *and integer.*

[*R.U. M.Sc. (Math.) 2011; P.U. B.E. (T.I.T.) Dec., 2006*]

Solution

The continuous optimal solution of the problem has been obtained in table 6.161 as

$$x_1 = \frac{7}{2} \text{ and } x_2 = \frac{9}{5}, \text{ giving } Z_{\max} = \frac{53}{10} = 5.3.$$

TABLE 6.161

	c_j	1	1	0	0			
c_B	Basis	x_1	x_2	s_1	s_2	b_i	θ	
0	s_1	2	5	1	0	16	8	
0	s_2	(6)	5	0	1	30	5	←
	Z_j	0	0	0	0			
	$\overline{c}_j = c_j - Z_j$	1	1	0	0			
		↑						
0	s_1	0	$(10/3)$	1	$-1/3$	6	$9/5$	←
1	x_1	1	$5/6$	0	$1/6$	5	6	
	Z_j	1	$5/6$	0	$1/6$			
	$\overline{c}_j = c_j - Z_j$	0	$1/6$	0	$-1/6$			
			↑					

1	x_2	0	1	$3/10$	$-3/10$	$9/5$	
1	x_1	1	0	$-1/4$	$1/4$	$7/2$	
	Z_j	1	1	$1/20$	$3/20$		
	$\bar{c}_j = c_j - Z_j$	0	0	$-1/20$	$-3/20$		*Continuous optimal solution*

$$\therefore \qquad x_2 = \frac{9}{5},\ x_1 = \frac{7}{2};\ Z_{max} = 5.3.$$

Since only x_1 is integer constrained, the problem is branched into two subproblems, each using one of the following additional constraints :

$$x_1 \le \left[\frac{7}{2}\right] \text{ or } x_1 \le 3, \text{ and}$$

$$x_1 \ge \left[\frac{7}{2}\right] + 1 \text{ or } x_1 \ge 4.$$

Optimal solution to the problem

$$\begin{aligned} \text{maximize} \quad & Z = x_1 + x_2, \\ \text{subject to} \quad & 2x_1 + 5x_2 \le 16, \\ & 6x_1 + 5x_2 \le 30, \\ & x_1 \le 3, \\ & x_2 \ge 0, \end{aligned}$$

is obtained in table 6.162 as $x_1 = 3$ and $x_2 = 2$, giving $Z_{max} = 5$. Since it satisfies the condition of x_1 being integer, it is the best solution available so far, and lower bound $Z_L = 5$.

TABLE 6.162

	c_j	1	1	0	0	0			
c_B	Basis	x_1	x_2	s_1	s_2	s_3	b_i	θ	
0	s_1	2	5	1	0	0	16	8	
0	s_2	6	5	0	1	0	30	5	
0	s_3	(1)	0	0	0	1	3	3	←
	Z_j	0	0	0	0	0			
	$\bar{c}_j = c_j - Z_j$	1	1	0	0	0			
		↑							
0	s_1	0	(5)	1	0	–2	10	2	←
0	s_2	0	5	0	1	–6	12	$12/5$	
1	x_1	1	0	0	0	1	3	–	
	Z_j	1	0	0	0	1			
	$\bar{c}_j = c_j - Z_j$	0	1	0	0	–1			
			↑						
1	x_2	0	1	$1/5$	0	$-2/5$	2		
0	s_2	0	0	–1	1	–4	2		
1	x_1	1	0	0	0	1	3		
	Z_j	1	1	$1/5$	0	$3/5$			
	$\bar{c}_j = c_j - Z_j$	0	0	$-1/5$	0	$-3/5$			

$\therefore \quad x_1 = 3, x_2 = 2; Z_{max} = 5.$

Optimal solution to the problem

$$\begin{aligned} \text{maximize} \quad & Z = x_1 + x_2, \\ \text{subject to} \quad & 2x_1 + 5x_2 \le 16, \\ & 6x_1 + 5x_2 \le 30, \\ & x_1 \ge 4, \\ & x_2 \ge 0, \end{aligned}$$

is obtained in table 6.163 as $x_1 = 4$ and $x_2 = \frac{6}{5}$, which gives $Z_{max} = \frac{26}{5} = 5.2$. This solution also satisfies the condition of x_1 being non-negative integer and the value of $Z = 5.2$ is better than the lower bound. Therefore, this branch is also fathomed. Therefore, the optimal solution to the given problem is $x_1 = 4$, $x_2 = 6/5$ and $Z_{max} = 5.2$.

TABLE 6.163

	c_j	1	1	0	0	0	–M			
c_B	Basis	x_1	x_2	s_1	s_2	s_3	A_1	b_i	θ	
0	s_1	2	5	1	0	0	0	16	8	
0	s_2	6	5	0	1	0	0	30	5	
–M	A_1	(1)	0	0	0	–1	1	4	4	←
	Z_j	–M	0	0	0	M	–M			
	$\bar{c}_j = c_j - Z_j$	1+M	1	0	0	–M	0			
		↑								
0	s_1	0	5	1	0	2		8	$8/5$	
0	s_2	0	(5)	0	1	6		6	$6/5$	←
1	x_1	1	0	0	0	–1		4	–	
	Z_j	1	0	0	0	–1				
	$\bar{c}_j = c_j - Z_j$	0	1	0	0	1				
			↑							
0	s_1	0	0	1	–1	–4		2		
1	x_2	0	1	0	$1/5$	$6/5$		$6/5$		
1	x_1	1	0	0	0	–1		4		
	Z_j	1	1	0	$1/5$	$1/5$				
	$\bar{c}_j = c_j - Z_j$	0	0	0	$-1/5$	$-1/5$				

The optimal mixed-integer solution is

$$\therefore \; x_1 = 4, x_2 = \frac{6}{5}; \; Z_{max} = \frac{26}{5} = 5.2.$$

6.10-8 Additive Algorithm for Zero-One Programming

The linear programming problem in which all the variables are constrained to take values of 0 or 1 only, is called a *zero-one* (*or binary*) *L.P. problem*. A number of real-life managerial problems fall into this category. The assignment problem discussed in chapter 4 is the best example of this type. Problems of capital budgeting, project selection, facility location, machine/job sequencing, etc. involve zero-one integer solutions.

A study of the various techniques available for solving binary problems is essential because

(*i*) a certain class of non-linear integer programming problems can be converted into equivalent binary problems.

(*ii*) a number of industrial and managerial problems can be formulated as binary problems.

Such problems can be solved by Gomory's cutting plane method or branch and bound method with the additional constraint that all the variables have values of 0 or 1. However, since these algorithms were developed primarily to solve general integer L.P. problems, they do not take advantage of the special features of zero-one L.P. problems. A number of efficient algorithms have been proposed to solve such problems, of which the additive algorithm by E. Balas is the one most commonly used and will be discussed here.

If a problem involves n binary variables, an explicit enumeration process will involve testing all the 2^n possible solutions against the stated objective function and constraints. However, the additive algorithm cleverly discards some of the solutions so that in the final analysis only a few of 2^n solutions require to be investigated explicitly.

The method begins by setting all the n variables equal to zero and systematically assigns the value 1 to one or more variables in such a way that after trying only a few of 2^n alternatives, there results either an optimal solution or an evidence of the existence of no feasible solution. As the operations involved are only additions and subtractions, this algorithm is called *additive algorithm.*

In order to employ this algorithm, the continuous version of the zero-one problem must start dual feasible *i.e.*, it should be optimal but infeasible. The integer problem must be of minimization type, all objective function coefficients should be non-negative and constratins should be ≤ type *i.e.*,

$$\text{Minimize} \quad Z = \sum_{j=1}^{n} c_j x_j,$$

$$\text{subject to} \quad \sum_{j=1}^{n} a_{ij} x_j \le b_i,$$

$$x_j = 0 \text{ or } 1 \text{ for } j = 1, 2, ..., n,$$

$$c_j \ge 0 \text{ for all } j.$$

Any L.P. problem can be converted into the above form by the following operations:

(*i*) Change the sign of the objective function if it is of maximization type.

(*ii*) Replace all equality constraints by two weak inequalities, one of ≤ type and the other of ≥ type.

(*iii*) Multiply all ≥ type constratints by – 1 to convert them to ≤ type.

(*iv*) Define a new variable y_j such that

$$y_j = \begin{cases} x_j \text{ if } c_j \ge 0 \text{ in the minimization problem,} \\ 1 - x_j \text{ if } c_j \le 0 \text{ in the minimization problem,} \end{cases}$$

where y_j is the binary variable in objective function as well as constraints. Slack variables s_i can be now added to constratins to put them into the form

$$\sum_{j=1}^{n} a_{ij} x_j + s_i = b_i.$$

If the problem is primal feasible (in addition to being dual feasible), nothing more needs to be done since the minimum in terms of new variables is achieved by assigning zero value to all the variables. However, if it is optimal infeasible, additive algorithm can be used to find the optimum. As in B and B, the *branching* in this algorithm is also based on the use of branching variable x_j. However, since x_j is a binary variable two branches are associated, one for $x_j = 0$ and the other for $x_j = 1$. *Bounding* is treated in the same manner as in the B and B; an improved integer solution forms an upper bound on the minimum value of the objective function. The fathoming of the subproblem can take place in one of the three ways :

1. The subproblem yields a feasible integer solution.
2. The subproblem does not lead to a feasible solution.
3. The subproblem does not yield a better upper bound.

These rules are the same as in B and B. The main difference is that L.P. problems are not solved ; instead, we use heuristics.

EXAMPLE 6.10-15

Convert the following 0-1 problem to satisfy the starting requirements of the additive algorithm :

Maximize $Z = -3x_1 + 4x_2,$

subject to

$$2x_1 + x_2 = 5,$$
$$3x_1 + 5x_2 \geq 6,$$
$$x_1, x_2 = (0, 1).$$

Solution

1. Multiply objective function by –1 to convert it to minimization.
$\therefore$ We get minimize $Z' = (-Z) = 3x_1 - 4x_2.$
2. Make all the constraints of $\leq$ type. Replace the first equality constraint by two weak inequalities in opposite directions. We get
$$2x_1 + x_2 \leq 5 \text{ and } 2x_1 + x_2 \geq 5, \text{ which is equivalent to}$$
$$2x_1 + x_2 \leq 5 \text{ and } -2x_1 - x_2 \leq -5.$$
The second constraint is multiplied on both sides by –1 to yield
$$-3x_1 - 5x_2 \leq -6.$$
3. Using slack variables s_1, s_2 and s_3 in the constraints the problem is expressed as
minimize $Z' = 3x_1 - 4x_2,$
subject to
$$2x_1 + x_2 + s_1 = 5,$$
$$-2x_1 - x_2 + s_2 = -5$$
$$-3x_1 - 5x_2 + s_3 = -6,$$
$$x_1, x_2 = (0, 1) \; ; \; s_1, s_2, s_3 \geq 0.$$
4. Since coefficient of x_2 in the objective function is negative, substitute $x_2 = 1 - y_2$ and $x_1 = y_1$ in the above problem and we get
minimize $Z'' = Z' + 4 = 3y_1 + 4y_2,$
subject to
$$2y_1 - y_2 + s_1 = 4,$$
$$-2y_1 + y_2 + s_2 = -4$$
$$-3y_1 + 5y_2 + s_3 = -1,$$
$$y_1, y_2 = (0, 1) \; ; \; s_1, s_2, s_3 \geq 0.$$

EXAMPLE 6.10-16

Maximize $Z = x_1 + 2x_2 - 3x_3,$

subject to

$$20x_1 + 15x_2 - x_3 \leq 10,$$
$$12x_1 - 3x_2 - 4x_3 \leq 20,$$
$$3x_1 + 5x_2 + x_3 \leq 6,$$
$$x_j = 0 \text{ or } 1 \text{ for all } j.$$

Solution

As explained earlier the problem must be in minimization form with all positive coefficients in the objective function and constraints of $\leq$ type.

Thus the objective function can be written as

minimize $Z' = -x_1 - 2x_2 + 3x_3.$

To convert the negative coefficients in the objective function to positive, make the following substitution:

$$x_j = \begin{cases} y_j \text{ if } c_j \text{ is} \geq 0, \\ 1 - y_j \text{ if } c_j \leq 0, \end{cases}$$

where y_j is binary variable. Since x_1, x_2 have negative coefficients while x_3 has a positive coefficient, substitute

$$x_1 = 1 - y_1,\ x_2 = 1 - y_2 \text{ and } x_3 = y_3.$$

This transforms the objective function to

minimize $\quad Z' = -(1 - y_1) - 2(1 - y_2) + 3y_3 = y_1 + 2y_2 + 3y_3 - 3.$

The constant – 3 can be dropped since it will not make any difference, being independent of the values of y_j. Thus we have

minimize $\quad Z'' = (Z' + 3) = y_1 + 2y_2 + 3y_3.$

The constraints can be written as

$$20(1 - y_1) + 15(1 - y_2) - y_3 \leq 10 \text{ or } -20y_1 - 15y_2 - y_3 \leq -25,$$
$$12(1 - y_1) - 3(1 - y_2) - 4y_3 \leq 14 \text{ or } -12y_1 + 3y_2 - 4y_3 \leq 5,$$
$$3(1 - y_1) + 5(1 - y_2) + y_3 \leq 6 \text{ or } -3y_1 - 5y_2 + y_3 \leq -2.$$

Using the slack variable s_1, the first constraint may be written as

$$-20y_1 - 15y_2 - y_3 + s_1 = -25$$

or $\quad s_1 = -25 + 20y_1 + 15y_2 + y_3 \geq 0. \quad (\because s_1 \geq 0) \quad ...(i)$

Similarly $\quad s_2 = 5 + 12y_1 - 3y_2 + 4y_3 \geq 0, \quad ...(ii)$

$\quad s_3 = -2 + 3y_1 + 5y_2 - y_3 \geq 0. \quad ...(iii)$

Now the problem is in the proper format to use implicit enumeration. The initial solution is obtained by setting $y_1 = y_2 = y_3 = 0$, which gives $Z'' = 0$. The values of slack variables are then given by

$$s_1 = -25,\ s_2 = 5,\ s_3 = -2.$$

The above solution is represented by node 1 in Fig. 6.17. Since s_1, s_3 values are negative, this is not a feasible solution. The variables y_1, y_2 and y_3 are all *free* at this stage to take 0 or 1 values and hence are called *free variables*.

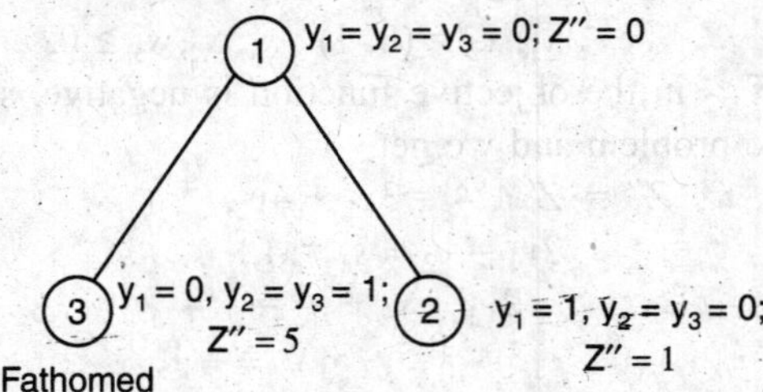

Fig. 6.17

Now check if the violated constraints (*i*) and (*iii*) can be satisfied by assigning a value of 1 to each of the variables having positive coefficients in these constraints. There is no use in assigning value of 1 to the variables with negative coefficients since that will only worsen the feasibility.

Now substituting $\quad y_1 = y_2 = y_3 = 1$ in constraint (*i*) gives $s_1 = 11 > 0$,

and substituting $\quad y_1 = y_2 = 1$ in constrating (*iii*) gives $s_3 = 6 > 0$.

This indicates that there is possibility of a feasible solution emanating from node 1.

Measure of infeasibility : To move the solution towards feasibility, some of the variables have to be raised to level 1. A number of heuristic procedures have been proposed to select the variable from the set of free variables. One method is to select the variable which will minimize the total infeasibility over all the constratins. The infeasibility for a non-negative constraint is zero and for a negative constraint it is the amount that must be added to make it zero. If v_j measures the total infeasibility when variable y_j is raised to level 1, then v_j is defined as

$$v_j = \sum_{\text{All } j} \min \{0, (s_i - a_{ij})\}.$$

For the example being considered,

$$v_1 = (-25 + 20) + 0 + 0 = -5,$$
$$v_2 = (-25 + 15) + 0 + 0 = -10,$$
$$v_3 = (-25 + 1) + 0 + (-2 - 1) = -27.$$

Now variable giving smallest infeasibility is selected to take the value 1. In case of tie, the variable with the smallest cost coefficient is chosen. Since v_1 is the smallest infeasibility, variable y_1 is selected to take the value 1, while variables y_2 and y_3 remain free variables. This solution corresponding to node 2 in Fig. 6.17 is

$$y_1 = 1, y_2 = y_3 = 0, Z'' = 1.$$

This solution when substituted in constraints (*i*), (*ii*) and (*iii*) gives

$$s_1 = -25 + 20 - 5,$$
$$s_2 = 5 + 12 = 17,$$
$$s_3 = -2 + 3 = 1.$$

Thus the above solution (node 2) is infeasible but the constraint (*i*) can be satisfied by setting the free variables having positive coefficients equal to 1. Hence there is possibility of a feasible solution emanating from node 2.

Now $y_1 = 1$ and one of the variables y_2 and y_3 is to be assigned the value 1.

For the example being considered,

$$v_2 = 0 + 0 + 0 = 0,$$
$$v_3 = -4 + 0 + 0 = -4.$$

Since v_2 is the smallest infeasibility, y_2 is selected to take the value 1 (in addition to y_1), while variable y_3 remains free. This corresponds to node 4 in Fig. 6.18 which gives the solution $y_1 = y_2 = 1, y_3 = 0, Z'' = 3$.

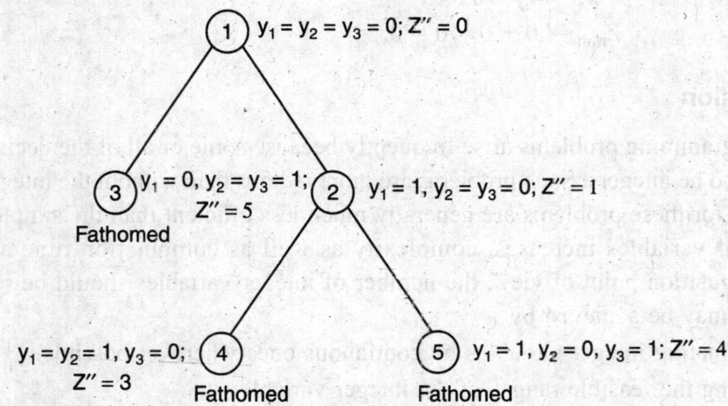

Fig. 6.18

This solution when substituted in constratints (*i*), (*ii*) and (*iii*) gives

$$s_1 = -25 + 20 + 15 = 10,$$
$$s_2 = 5 + 12 - 3 = 14,$$
$$s_3 = -2 + 3 + 5 = 6.$$

This solution is feasible. This is recorded as the best available solution so far. The value of the objective function corresponding to this solution will act as an upper bound for the future solutions. Thus $Z_u = 3$.

Since any solution with $y_1 = y_2 = 1$ and some other variable raised to 1 will destroy the optimality, there is no need to examine any solution emanating from node 4. In other words, all solutions emanating from node 4 have been implicitly enumerated. Node 4 is, then, said to be fathomed.

Now we go back to node 2. This is called *backtracking.* The other solution emanating from this node 2 is

$$y_1 = 1, y_2 = 0, y_3 \text{ free to take 0 or 1.}$$

This corresponds to node 5. When $y_3 = 0$ we get infeasible solution [constraints (*i*), (*ii*) and (*iii*) yield $s_1 = -5$, $s_2 = 17$, $s_3 = 1$] and when $y_3 = 1$, the optimality is destroyed (since $y_1 = 1$, $y_2 = 0$, $y_3 = 1$ yields $Z'' = 1 + 0 + 3 = 4$, which is higher than the min $Z_u = 3$). There is no need of checking the feasibility condition of this solution ($y_1 = 1, y_2 = 0, y_3 = 1$). Thus, since node 5 does not promise a better solution, it is fathomed.

Backtracking to node 1, we have node 3 emanating from node 1. The solution corresponding to node 3 is

$$y_1 = 0, y_2 \text{ and } y_3 \text{ free to take 0 or 1.}$$

Now we check the possibilities of getting a feasible solution emanating from node 3.

When $y_1 = 0$, $y_2 = 1$ and y_3 is set at 1, from constraints (*i*), (*ii*) and (*iii*) we get

$$s_1 = -25 + 0 + 15 + 1 = -9,$$
$$s_2 = 5 + 0 - 3 + 4 = 6,$$
$$s_3 = -2 + 0 + 5 - 1 = 2.$$

Since this does not give a feasible solution, node 3 is fathomed.

Thus the optimal solution is

$$y_1 = y_2 = 1, y_3 = 0 \; ; \; Z''_{max} = 3.$$

This solution can now be translated in terms of original variables as follows :

$$x_1 = 1 - y_1 = 1 - 1 = 0,$$
$$x_2 = 1 - y_2 = 1 - 1 = 0,$$
$$x_3 = y_3 = 0,$$
$$Z_{min} = 0 + 0 - 0 = 0.$$

6.10-9 Conclusion

Integer programming problems arise frequently because some or all of the decision variables may be restricted to be integers. Such problems are more tedious than without the integer restriction, so the algorithms for these problems are generally much less efficient than the simplex algorithm. As the number of variables increases, complexity as well as computation time also increase. Hence from computation point of view, the number of integer variables should be reduced as far as possible. This may be achieved by

(*i*) approximating integer variables by continuous ones wherever possible.

(*ii*) restricting the feasible ranges of the integer variables.

(*iii*) avoiding the use of non-linearity in the model.

Computer codes for integer programming algorithms are now commonly available in mathematical programming software packages. These algorithms, usually, are based on the branch and bound technique and variations thereof. Though some of the early algorithms used the cutting plane approach, they met with only limited success which strongly depended upon the special structure of the problem.

Though I.P. problems form an important category, efficient solution algorithms are still lacking. Not much theoretical breakthrough in this area is expected, instead more efficient computers may increase the efficiency of I.P. algorithms.

Some algorithms have been developed for integer non-linear programming but as yet considerabiy less progress has been made compared to the integer linear programming.

EXERCISES 6.10

1. Write a short note on integer programming model.
[*P.T.U. MCA, 2010; B.Tech. (Mech.) May, 2007; P.U.B.E. (Pod.) 2001*]
2. Define and briefly explain I.P.P., all I.P.P. and mixed I.P.P.
[*Univ. of Madras B.Sc. (Math.) Nov., 2012; Pbi. U. MCA, 2001*]
3. What is the concept involved in the Gomory's cutting plane method ?
[*Chennai U., 2002*]
4. Explain two examples to explain the need for integr programming problem.
[*Bharathiar U. Coimbatore B.Sc. April, 2011*]
5. Describe a method of solving mixed I.P.P. [*Chennai U. B.Sc. (Math.) 1984*]
6. Explain the branch-and-bound method in integer programming.
[*IGNOU MBA June, 2007*]
7. Explain some of the practical applications of integer programming.
[*Chennai B.E. (Ind. Engg.) 1979*]
8. Write short note on zero-one programming. [*Meerut M.Sc. (Math.) 1984*]
9. (*a*) Discuss the need of integer programming in mathematical programming.
(*b*) Illustrate with numerical examples the possible consequences which may involve if one solves an integer L.P. problem ignoring 'the integer constraints' and then rounding off the non-integer values of the optimum solution to integers.
[*IGNOU MBA Dec., 2006*]
(*c*) Describe the principle of "valid cut" used in solving integer programming problem.
[*Indore M.Sc. (Stat.) 1975*]
10. Explain the methods used in solving integer programming problems.
[*V.T.U. Karnataka B.E. June, 2012; Jan., 2010*]

Section 6.10-1

11. Consider the problem of assigning three jobs to three men. Each man is capable of doing all the jobs; however, the time taken by the different men on each job is different and can be assumed to be known. The assignment has to be done so that each job is assigned only once, each man gets only one job and the total time taken by all the jobs is minimized. Formulate it as an I.P. problem with decision variables defined as

$$x_{ij} = \begin{cases} 1, \text{ if the } i\text{th man is assigned to job } j, \\ 0, \text{ otherwise.} \end{cases}$$

[*IGNOU MCA, 2001*]
12. A sales representative of a pharmaceutical company has been assigned a region and he must visit *n* cities in this region once in a quarter, starting from and returning to the regional headquarters. Formulate this as an I.P. problem to minimize the distance travelled.
13. A company is facing a budgeting problem. The data relating to the problem is given in table 6.164. The present values of the budget constraints are ₹ 60,000 in the first year and ₹ 30,000 in the second year. Assuming that the projects under consideration are independent of each other, formulate the problem as I.P. problem.

TABLE 6.164

Projects	*Present value of outlay required in period 1 (000's of rupees)*	*Present value of outlay required in period 2 (000's of rupees)*	*Net present value of the cash inflow (000's of rupees)*
1	18	3	12
2	38	7	9
3	46	4	13
4	16	6	12
5	46	24	40
6	8	2	18

7	6	7	17
8	50	18	25
9	13	3	26

(*Ans.* Max $Z = 12x_1 + 9x_2 + 13x_3 + 12x_4 + 40x_5 + 18x_6 + 17x_7 + 25x_8 + 26x_9$,
subject to $18x_1 + 38x_2 + 46x_3 + 16x_4 + 46x_5 + 8x_6 + 6x_7 + 50x_8 + 13x_9 \leq 60$,
$3x_1 + 7x_2 + 4x_3 + 6x_4 + 24x_5 + 2x_6 + 7x_7 + 18x_8 + 3x_9 \leq 30$,
$x_1, ..., x_9 = (0, 1.)$

14. A refrigeration and air-conditioning company has been awarded a contract for the air-conditioning of a new computer installation. The company has to make a choice between two alternatives :
(*a*) hire one or more refrigeration technicians for six hours a day or
(*b*) hire one or more part-time refrigeration apprentice technicians for four hours a day.
The rate of wages of a refrigeration technician is ₹ 20 per hour, while the corresponding rate of appentice technician is ₹ 8 per hour. The company wants to engage the technicians on work for not more than 25 man-hours per day and also limit the charges to technicians to ₹ 440. The company estimates that the productivity of a refrigeration technician is eight units and that of a part-time apprentice technician is three units. Formulate the integer programming problem to enable the company to select the optimum number of technicians and apprentices.
[*IGNOU MBA, 2002*]

(*Ans.* Maximize Z (total productivity) $= 8x_1 + 3x_2$,
subject to $120x_1 + 32x_2 \leq 440$,
$6x_1 + 4x_2 \leq 25$,
$x_1, x_2 \geq 0$ and integer.)

15. Gapco manufactures three products whose daily labour and raw material requirements are given in the following table :

TABLE 6.165

Product	*Required daily labour (hours/unit)*	*Required daily raw material (kg/unit)*
1	3	4
2	4	3
3	5	6

The profits per unit of the three products are ₹ 25, ₹ 30 and ₹ 22 respectively. Gapco has two options for locating the plant.

TABLE 6.166

Location	*Available daily labour (hours)*	*Available daily raw material (kg)*
1	100	100
2	90	120

Formulate the problem as a mixed I.P. and determine the optimum location of the plant.
(*Ans.* Location 2 ; $x_1 = 26, x_2 = 3, x_3 = 0$; Z_{max} = ₹ 740.)

Section 6.10-5

16. Solve the problem by Gomory's algorithm :
Maximize $Z = 3x_1 + 4x_2$,
subject to $x_1 + x_2 \leq 4$,
$3/5x_1 + x_2 \leq 3$,
$x_1, x_2 \geq 0$ and integer.
(*Ans.* $x_1 = 3, x_2 = 1; Z_{max} = 13$.)

17. Solve by cutting plane algorithm :
Maximize $Z = 7x_1 + 10x_2$,
subject to $-x_1 + 3x_2 \leq 6$,

$7x_1 + x_2 \leq 35,$

$x_1, x_2 \geq 0$ and integer. [*V.T.U. Karnataka B.E. Dec., 2010*]

(*Ans.* $x_1 = 4, x_2 = 3; Z_{max} = 58.$)

18. Solve the following problem by the fractional cut and compare the true optimum integer solution with the solution obtained by rounding the continuous optimum:

Maximize $Z = 3x_1 + x_2 + 3x_3,$

subject to $-x_1 + 2x_2 + x_3 \leq 4,$

$4x_2 - 3x_3 \leq 2,$

$x_1 - 3x_2 + 2x_3 \leq 3,$

$x_1, x_2, x_3 \geq 0$ and integer.

(*Ans.* (*i*) $x_1 = 5, x_2 = 2, x_3 = 2; Z_{max} = 23.$

(*ii*) $x_1 = 5, x_2 = 3, x_3 = 3, Z = 27$; infeasible.)

19. Use Gomory's cutting plane algorithm to solve :

Maximize $Z = 2x_1 + x_2,$

subject to $2x_1 + 5x_2 \leq 17,$

$3x_1 + 2x_2 \leq 10,$

$x_1, x_2 \geq 0$ and integer.

(*Ans.* $x_1 = 3, x_2 = 0; Z_{max} = 6.$)

20. Use the cut algorithm to solve :

Maximize $Z = 3x_1 + 4x_2,$

subject to $2x_1 + x_2 \leq 6,$

$2x_1 + 3x_2 \leq 9,$

$x_1, x_2 \geq 0$ and integer.

(*Ans.* $x_1 = 0, x_2 = 3; Z_{max} = 12.$)

21. Use cutting plane method to solve :

Maximize $Z = x_1 + 2x_2,$

subject to $x_1 + x_2 \leq 7,$

$2x_1 \leq 11,$

$2x_2 \leq 7,$

$x_1, x_2 \geq 0$ and integer. [*Chennai U. B.E. (Mech. and Prod.) 1991*]

(*Ans.* $x_1 = 4, x_2 = 3; Z_{max} = 10.$)

22. Find the optimum integer solution to the I.P.P. :

Maximize $Z = x_1 + x_2,$

subject to $3x_1 + 2x_2 \leq 5,$

$x_2 \leq 2,$

$x_1, x_2 \geq 0$ and integer.

[*V.T.U. Karnataka B.E. June, 2010;*
P.T.U. B.Tech. (C.Sc.) 2009]

(*Ans.* $x_1 = 0, x_2 = 2; Z_{max} = 2.$)

23. Solve the I.P.P. :

Maximize $Z = 2x_1 + 2x_2,$

subject to $5x_1 + 3x_2 \leq 8,$

$x_1 + 2x_2 \leq 4,$

$x_1, x_2 \geq 0$ and integer. [*Madurai U. M.Sc. (Appl. Sc.) 1983*]

(*Ans.* $x_1 = 1, x_2 = 1; Z_{max} = 4.$)

24. Maximize $Z = x_1 + x_2,$

subject to $3x_1 + 2x_2 \leq 20,$

$6x_1 + 5x_2 \leq 25,$

$x_1 + 3x_2 \leq 10,$

x_1, x_2 non-negative integers.

(*Ans.* Continuous solution : $x_1 = 25/13, x_2 = 35/13;$

integer optimal solution : (1, 3), (2, 2), (3, 1), (4, 0); $Z_{max} = 4.$)

25. Solve the following problem by the Gomory algorithm :

Maximize $Z = 2x_1 + 10x_2 + x_3$,
subject to
$5x_1 + 2x_2 + x_3 \leq 15$,
$2x_1 + x_2 + 7x_3 \leq 20$,
$x_1 + 3x_2 + 2x_3 \leq 25$,
all variables non-negative and integral.

(*Ans.* $x_1 = 0, x_2 = 7, x_3 = 1$; $Z_{max} = 71$.)

26. Solve by the Gomory algorithm :

Minimize $Z = 20x_1 + 22x_2 + 18x_3$,
subject to
$4x_1 + 6x_2 + x_3 \geq 54$,
$4x_1 + 4x_2 + 6x_3 \geq 65$,
x_1, x_2, x_3, each ≤ 7,
all variables non-negative and integral.

(*Ans.* $x_1 = 2, x_2 = 7, x_3 = 5$; $Z_{min} = 284$.)

27. Solve the following integer programming problem :

Maximize $Z = x_1 + 2x_2$,
subject to
$x_1 + 2x_2 \leq 12$,
$4x_1 + 3x_2 \leq 14$,
$x_1, x_2 \geq 0$ and integer. [*Chennai U., 2002*]

28. A manufacturer of baby dolls makes two types of dolls : doll *x* and doll *y*. Processing of these two dolls is done on two machines, A and B. Doll *x* requires 2 hours on machine A and 6 hours on machine B. Doll *y* requires 5 hours on machine A and also 5 hours on machine B. There are 16 hours of time available on machine A and 30 hours on machine B. The profit gained on both the dolls is same *i.e.*, Re. 1 per doll. What should be the daily production of each of the two dolls ?

(*a*) Set up and solve the L.P. problem.

(*b*) If the optimal solution is not integer-valued, use the Gomory technique to find the optimal solution. [*Delhi M.B.A., 1973*]

(*Ans.* $x_1 = 3, x_2 = 2$; $Z_{max} = 5$.)

29. Explain Gomory's method for solving all I.P.P. and hence solve the following :

Maximize $Z = 2x_1 + 6x_2$,
subject to
$3x_1 + x_2 \leq 5$,
$4x_1 + 4x_2 \leq 9$,
$x_1, x_2 \geq 0$ and integer. [*Kuru. U. M.E. (Mech.) 1988*]

30. Solve the following linear programming problem by Gomory technique:

Maximize $Z = 3x_2$,
subject to
$3x_1 + 2x_2 \leq 7$,
$-x + x_2 \leq 2$,
$x_1, x_2 \geq 0$ and are integers.

[*V.T.U. Karnataka B.E. June, 2011*]

Section 6.10-6

31. Solve the following mixed integer problem by the method of cutting planes :

Maximize $Z = x_1 + x_2$,
subject to
$2x_1 + 5x_2 \leq 16$,
$6x_1 + 5x_2 \leq 30$,
x_1 non-negative integer, $x_2 \geq 0$.

[*Bharathiar U. Coimbatore B.Sc. April, 2011; P.U.B.E. (T.I.T.) Nov., 2005*]

(*Ans.* $x_1 = 4, x_2 = 6/5$; $Z_{max} = 26/5$.)

32. The non-integer optimal solution of a maximization L.P.P. is given in table 6.167. Find the optimal solution in which x_1 is integer.

TABLE 6.167

	c_j	6	4	1	0	0	0	
c_B	Basis	x_1	x_2	x_3	s_1	s_2	s_3	b
0	s_1	0	$-1/2$	$1/2$	1	$-1/2$	0	$15/2$
6	x_1	1	$5/6$	$1/6$	0	$1/6$	0	$25/6$
0	s_3	0	$13/6$	$17/6$	0	$-1/6$	1	$15/6$

[*P.U.M.E. (Mech.) 1987*]

(*Ans.* $x_1 = 4, x_2 = \frac{1}{5}, x_3 = 0; Z_{max} = 24.8.$)

33. Solve the following mixed integer problem :

Maximize $Z = -3x_1 + x_2 + 3x_3,$
subject to
$$-x_1 + 2x_2 + x_3 \le 4,$$
$$2x_2 - \frac{3}{2}x_3 \le 1,$$
$$x_1 - 3x_2 + 2x_3 \le 3,$$
$x_1, x_2 \ge 0$, x_3 non-negative integer.

[*P.U.M.E. (Mech.) Jan., 1986*]

(*Ans.* $x_1 = 0, x_2 = 1, x_3 = 2$; $Z_{max} = 7.$)

Section 6.10-7

34. Show graphically that the following problem has no feasible integer solution :

Maximize $Z = 2x_1 + x_2,$
subject to
$$10x_1 + 10x_2 \le 9,$$
$$10x_1 + 5x_2 \ge 1,$$
x_1, x_2 non-negative integers.

Verify the solution algebrically by using
(*a*) the fractional algorithm,
(*b*) the branch and bound algorithm.

[*Bharathiar U. Coimbatore B.Sc. April, 2011*]

35. Solve the following problem by branch-and-bound method :

Maximize $Z = 3x_1 + x_2 + 3x_3,$
subject to
$$-x_1 + 2x_2 + x_3 \le 4,$$
$$4x_2 - 3x_3 \le 2,$$
$$x_1 - 3x_2 + 2x_3 \le 3,$$
x_1, x_3 non-negative integers, $x_2 \ge 0$.

(*Ans.* $x_1 = 5, x_2 = 11/4, x_3 = 3; Z_{max} = 26\frac{3}{4}.$)

36. Maximize $Z = x_1 + x_2,$
subject to
$$4x_1 - x_2 \le 10,$$
$$2x_1 + 5x_2 \le 10,$$
$$4x_1 - 3x_2 \le 6,$$
$$x_1, x_2 = 0, 1, 2, 3, \ldots .$$

Use the branch-and-bound technique.

[*I.I.Sc. D.O.M., 1977*]

37. Maximize by the branch-and-bound technique,

$$Z = 7x_1 + 9x_2,$$

subject to $-x_1 + 3x_2 \le 6,$
$7x_1 + x_2 \le 35,$
$0 \le x_1, x_2 \le 7,$
x_1, x_2 are integers.

[Kuru U. B.E. (Mech.) June, 2012; B.P.U.T., 2010]
(Ans. $x_1 = 4, x_2 = 7; Z_{max} = 91$.)

38. (*a*) Explain the branch-and-bound method of solving integer programming problem.
[IGNOU MBA Dec., 2006]

(*b*) Use the branch-and-bound technique to
maximize $Z = 2y_1 + 6y_2,$
subject to $3y_1 + y_2 \le 5,$
$4y_1 + 4y_2 \le 9,$
$y_1, y_2 = 0, 1, 2, 3, \ldots$.

39. Solve the following problem by branch-and-bound technique :
Maximize $Z = x_1 + x_2,$
subject to $3x_1 + 2x_2 \le 12,$
$x_2 \le 2,$
$x_1, x_2 \ge 0$ and are integers. *(Ans.* $x_1 = 2, x_2 = 2; Z_{max} = 4$.)
[V.T.U. Karnataka B.E. June, 2012]

40. Solve by the branch-and-bound method,
maximize $Z = 3x_1 + x_2 + 3x_3,$
subject to $-x_1 + 2x_2 + x_3 \le 4,$
$4x_2 - 3x_3 \le 2,$
$x_1 - 3x_2 + 2x_3 \le 3,$
$x_1, x_2, x_3 \ge 0$ and integer.

Compare the rounded optimal solution and the integer optimal solution.
(Ans. Rounded solution : $x_1 = 5, x_2 = x_3 = 3, Z = 2$; infeasible.
Integer optimal solution : $x_1 = 5, x_2 = 2, x_3 = 2; Z_{max} = 23$.)

41. Solve the following mixed integer problem by the branch-and-bound algorithm :
Minimize $Z = 10x_1 + 9x_2,$
subject to $x_1 \le 8,$
$x_2 \le 10,$
$5x_1 + 3x_2 \ge 45,$
$x_1, x_2 \ge 0, x_2$ integer.

42. Maximize $Z = 3x_1 + 3x_2 + 13x_3,$
subject to $-3x_1 + 6x_2 + 7x_3 \le 8,$
$5x_1 - 3x_2 + 7x_3 \le 8,$
$0 \le x_j \le 5,$
all x_j are integers for $j = 1, 2, 3.$

43. Use branch-and-bound technique to solve
maximize $Z = 3x_1 + 4x_2 + 5x_3,$
subject to $x_1 + x_2 + x_3 \le 10.5,$
$2x_1 + x_2 + 5x_3 \le 15,$
x_1, x_2 non-negative integer ; $x_3 \ge 0.$ *[Pbi. U. MCA, 2001]*

44. Use I.P. branch-and-bound algorithm to solve the problem :
Maximize $Z = 5x_1 + 4x_2,$
subject to $x_1 + x_2 \le 5,$
$10x_1 + 6x_2 \le 45,$
x_1, x_2 non-negative integers.

Use x_1 as branching variable.

[P.U. B.E. (Mech.) 2012; V.T.U. Karnataka B.E. Jan., 2010;
P.U.B.E. (C.S. and E.) Dec., 2004]
(Ans. $x_1 = 3, x_2 = 2; Z_{max} = 23$.)

45. Use branch-and-bound algorithm to solve

maximize $Z = 5x_1 + 4x_2 + 4x_3 + 2x_4,$

subject to $x_1 + 3x_2 + 2x_3 + x_4 \leq 10,$

$5x_1 + x_2 + 3x_3 + 2x_4 \leq 15,$

$x_1 + x_2 + x_3 + x_4 \leq 6,$

$x_1, x_2, x_3, x_4 \geq 0$ and integer.

[P.U.B.E. (T. and I.T.) Nov., 2004]

46. Solve the following problem by B and B method :

Maximize $Z = x_1 + 2x_2 + 5x_3,$

subject to $| -x_1 + 10x_2 - 3x_3 \geq 15,$

$2x_1 + x_2 + x_3 \leq 10,$

$x_1, x_2, x_3 \geq 0$ and integer.

(*Ans.* $x_1 = x_2 = 0, x_3 = 10; Z_{max} = 50.$)

47. Use B and B method to solve

maximize $Z = 6x_1 + 8x_2,$

subject to $4x_1 + 16x_2 \leq 32,$

$14x_1 + 4x_2 \leq 28,$

$x_1, x_2 \geq 0$ and integer.

[B.P.U.T. 6th Sem., 2011]

(*Ans.* $x_1 = 0, x_2 = 2; Z_{max} = 16.$)

48. Solve by B and B technique

maximize $Z = 2x_1 + 3x_2,$

subject to $5x_1 + 7x_2 \leq 35,$

$4x_1 + 9x_2 \leq 36,$

$x_1, x_2 \geq 0$ and integer.

(*Ans.* $x_1 = 4, x_2 = 2$; $Z_{max} = 14.$)

49. Solve by B and B technique

maximize $Z = 5x_1 + 3x_2,$

subject to $4x_1 + 2x_2 \leq 25,$

$x_1 \leq 5, x_2 \leq 8,$

$x_1, x_2 \geq 0$ and integer.

[P.U. B.E. (Mech.) 2012; Kuru. U. B.E. (Mech.) June, 2012]

(*Ans.* $x_1 = 2, x_2 = 8$; $Z_{max} = 34.$)

50. Use branch-and-bound method to solve the following linear programming problem :

Minimize $Z = 4x_1 + 3x_2,$

subject to $5x_1 + 3x_2 \geq 30,$

$x_1 \leq 4,$

$x_2 \leq 6,$

$x_1, x_2 \geq 0$ and are integers.

[V.T.U. Karnataka B.E. June, 2011]

Section 6.10-8

51. Solve by the additive algorithm the problem

maximize $Z = 3x_1 + x_2 + 3x_3,$

subject to $-x_1 + 2x_2 + x_3 \leq 4,$

$4x_2 - 3x_3 \leq 2,$

$x_1 - 3x_2 + 2x_3 \leq 3,$

$x_1, x_2, x_3 = (0, 1).$

(*Ans.* $x_1 = x_2 = x_3 = 1; Z_{max} = 7.$)

52. Solve by the additive algorithm the problem

minimize $Z = -5x_1 + 7x_2 + 10x_3,$

subject to $-x_1 - 3x_2 + 5x_3 \geq 0,$

$2x_1 + 6x_2 - 3x_3 \geq 4,$

$$-x_2 + 2x_3 \geq 2,$$
$$x_1, x_2, x_3 = (0, 1).$$

(*Ans.* No feasible solution.)

53. Show by the additive algorithm that the following problem has no feasible solution :

Maximize $Z = 2x_1 + x_2$,
subject to $10x_1 + 10x_2 \leq 9$,
$10x_1 + 5x_2 \geq 1$,
$x_1, x_2 = (0, 1)$.

54. Minimize $Z = -5x_1 + 7x_2 + 10x_3 - 3x_4 + x_5$,
subject to $x_1 + 3x_2 - 5x_3 + x_4 + 4x_5 \geq 0$,
$2x_1 + 6x_2 - 3x_3 + 2x_4 + 2x_5 \geq 4$,
$x_2 - 2x_3 - x_4 + x_5 \leq -2$,
$x_j = 0$ or $1, j = 1, 2, ..., 5$.

(*Ans.* $x_1 = x_2 = x_3 = x_4 = 1, x_5 = 0; Z_{min} = 9$.)

55. Maximize $Z = 3x_1 + 2x_2 - 5x_3 - 2x_4 + 3x_5$,
subject to $x_1 + x_2 + x_3 + 2x_4 + x_5 \leq 4$,
$7x_1 + 3x_3 - 4x_4 + 3x_5 \leq 8$,
$11x_1 - 6x_2 + 3x_4 - 3x_5 \geq 3$,
$x_j = 0$ or 1 for all j.

(*Ans.* $x_1 = x_2 = 1, x_3 = x_4 = x_5 = 0; Z_{max} = 5$.)

56. Maximze $Z = 3x_1 + 6x_2 + 3x_3 + 6x_4 + 13x_5$,
subject to $-3x_1 - 6x_2 + 6x_3 + 12x_4 + 7x_5 \leq 8$,
$6x_1 + 12x_2 - 3x_3 - 6x_4 + 7x_5 \leq 8$,
$x_j = 0$ or 1 for $j = 1, 2, ..., 5$.

(*Ans.* $x_1 = x_2 = x_3 = x_4 = 0, x_5 = 1; Z_{max} = 13$.)

Dynamic Programming

While considering the situations of allocation, transportation, assignment, scheduling and planning, it was assumed that the values of decision variables do not change over the planning horizon. Thus these problems were of static nature and were solved as specific situations occurring at a certain moment. However, we come across a number of situations where the decision variables vary with time, and these situations are considered to be dynamic in nature. The technique dealing with these types of problems is called *dynamic programming.* It will be shown in the body of the chapter that time element is not an essential variable, rather *any multistage situation in which a series of decisions are to be made is considered a dynamic programming problem.*

7.1 INTRODUCTION

In optimization problems involving a large number of decision variables or the inequality constraints, it may not be possible to use the methods of calculus for obtaining a solution. Classical mathematics handles the problems in a way to find the optimal values for all the decision variables simultaneously which for large problems rapidly increases the computations that become uneconomical or difficult to handle even by the available computers. The obvious solution is to split up the original large problem into small subproblems involving a few variables and that is precisely what the dynamic programming does. It uses recursive equations to solve a large, complex problem, broken into a series of interrelated decision stages (subproblems) wherein the outcome of the decision at one stage affects the decisions at the remaining stages.

Dynamic programming is a mathematical technique dealing with the optimization of multistage decision problems. The technique was originated in 1952 by Richard Bellman and G.B. Dantzig, and was initially referred to as the *stochastic linear programming*. Today dynamic programming has been developed as a mathematical technique to solve a wide range of decision problems and it forms an important part of every operation researcher's tool kit.

Though the originator of the technique, Richard Bellman, himself, has said, "we have coined the term 'dynamic programming' to emphasize that there are problems in which time plays an essential role", yet, in many dynamic programming problems time is not a relevant variable. For example, a decision regarding allocation of a fixed quantity of resources to a number of alternative uses constitutes one decision to be taken at one time, but the situation can be handled as a dynamic programming problem. As another instance, suppose a company has marked capital C to be spent on advertising its products through three different media *i.e.*, of newspaper, radio and television. In each media the advertisement can appear a number of times per week. Each appearance has associated with it certain costs and returns. How many times the product should be advertised in each media so that the returns are maximum and the total cost is within the prescribed limit ? In this situation time is not a variable, but the problem can be divided into stages and solved by dynamic programming.

7.2 DISTINGUISHING CHARACTERISTICS OF DYNAMIC PROGRAMMING

The important features of dynamic programming which distinguish it from other quantitative techniques of decision-making can be summarized as follows :

1. *Dynamic programming splits the original large problem into smaller subproblems (also called stages)* involving only a few variables, wherein the outcome of decision at one stage affects the decisions at the remaining stages.
2. *It involves a multistage process of decision-making*. The points at which decisions are called for are called stages. The stages may be certain time intervals or certain sub-divisions of the problems, for which independent feasible decisions are possible. Each stage can be thought of having a beginning and an end. The stages come in a sequence, the end of a stage forming the beginning of the next stage.
3. *In dynamic programming, the variable that links up two stages is called a state variable.* At any stage, the status of the problem can be described by the values the state variable can take. These values are referred to as states. Each stage may have, associated with it, a certain number of states. It is not essential to know about the previous decisions and how the states arise. This enables us to consider decisions one at a time.
4. *In dynamic programming the outcome of decisions depends upon a small number of variables*; that is, at any stage only a few variables should define the problem. For example, in the production smoothening problem, all that one needs to know at any stage is the production capacity, cost of production in regular and overtime, storage costs and the time remaining to the last decision.
5. *A stage decision does not alter the number of variables on which the outcome depends, but only changes the numerical value of these variables*. For the production smoothening problem, the number of variables which describe the problem *i.e.*, production capacity, production costs, storage costs and time to the last decision, remain the same at all stages. No variable is added or dropped. The effect to decision at any stage will be to alter the used production capacity, storage cost, production cost and time remaining to the last decision.
6. *Principle of Optimality. Dynamic programming is based on Bellman's Principle of Optimality, which states, "An optimal policy (a sequence of decisions) has the property that whatever the initial state and decision are, the remaining decisions must constitute an optimal policy with regard to the state resulting from the first decision"*. This principle implies that a wrong decision taken at one stage does not prevent from taking of optimum decisions for the remaining stages. For example, in a production scheduling problem, wrong decisions made during first and second months do not prevent taking correct decisions during third, fourth month, etc. Using this principle of optimality, we find the best policy by solving one stage at a time, and then adding a series of one-stage-problems until the overall optimum of the original problem is attained.
7. *Bellman's principle of optimality forms the basis of dynamic programming technique.* With this principle in mind, *recursive equations* are developed to take optimal decision at each stage. A recursive equation expresses subsequent state conditions and it is based on the fact that a policy is 'optimal' if the decision made at each stage results in overall optimality over all the stages and not only for the current stage.
8. *Dynamic programming provides a systematic procedure wherein starting with the last stage of the problem and working backwards one makes an optimal decision for each stage of the problem*. The information for the last stage is the information derived from the previous stages. It may be noted that D.P. problems can also be solved by working forward *i.e.*, starting with the first stage and then working forward upto the last stage.

7.3 DYNAMIC PROGRAMMING APPROACH

Before discussing the solutions to numerical problems, it will be worthwhile to know a little more about some fundamental concepts of dynamic programming. The first concept is *stage.* As already discussed, the problem is broken down into subproblems and each subproblem is referred to as a stage. A stage signifies a portion of decision problem for which a separate decision can be made. At each stage there are a number of alternatives and the decision-making process involves the selection of one feasible alternative which may be called as *stage decision.* The stage decision may not be optimal for the considered stage, but contributes to make an overall optimal decision for the entire problem.

The other important concept is *state.* A state represents the status of the problem at a particular stage. The variables which specify the condition of decision process and summarize the current '*status*' of the system are called *state variables.* For example, in the capital budgeting problem, the capital is the state variable. The amount of capital allocated to the present stage and the preceding stages (or the capital remaining) defines the status of the problem. The number of state variables should be as small as possible. With the increase in number of state variables, increases the difficulty of problem solving.

The procedure adopted in the analysis of dynamic programming problems can be summarized as follows :

1. Define the problem variables, determine the objective function and specify the constraints.
2. Define the stages of the problem. Determine the state variables whose values constitute the state at each stage and the decision required at each stage. Specify the relationship by which the state at one stage can be expressed as a function of the state and decisions at the next stage.
3. Develop the recursive relationship for the optimal return function which permits computation of the optimal policy at any stage. Decide whether to follow the forward or the backward method to solve the problem. Specify the optimal return function at stage 1, since it is generally a bit different from the general optimal return function for the other stages.
4. Make a tabular representation to show the required values and calculations for each stage.
5. Find the optimal decision at each stage and then the overall optimal policy. There may be more than one such optimal policy.

7.4 FORMULATION OF DYNAMIC PROGRAMMING PROBLEMS

Consider a situation wherein a certain quantity 'R' of a resource (such as men, machines, money, materials, etc.) is to be distributed among 'n' number of different activities. The return 'P' depends upon the activities and the quantities of resource allotted to them and the objective is to maximize the total return.

If $p_i(R_i)$ denotes the return form the ith activity with the resource R_i, then the total return may be expressed as

$$P(R_1, R_2, ..., R_n) = p_1(R_1) + p_2(R_2) + ... + p_n(R_n). \quad ...(7.1)$$

The quantity of resource R is limited, which gives rise to the constraint

$$R = R_1 + R_2 + ... + R_n, \quad R_i \geq 0,\ i = 1, 2, ..., n. \quad ...(7.2)$$

The problem is to maximize the total return given by equation (7.1) subject to constraint (7.2).

$$\text{If } f_n(R) = \max_{0 \leq R_i \leq R} [P(R_1, R_2, ..., R_n)] = \max_{0 \leq R_i \leq R} [p_1(R_1) + p_2(R_2) + ... + p_n(R_n)], \quad ...(7.3)$$

then $f_n(R)$ is the maximum return from the distribution of the resource R to the n activities. Let us now allocate the resource to the activities, one by one, starting from the last *i.e.*, nth activity. An expression connecting $f_n(R)$ and $f_{n-1}(R)$ for arbitrary values of R and n may now be obtained with the help of principle of optimality. If R_n is the quantity of resource allocated to the nth activity such that $0 \leq R_n \leq R$, then regardless of the values of R_n, a quantity $(R - R_n)$ of the resource will be distributed amongst the remaining $(n - 1)$ activities. Let $f_{n-1}(R - R_n)$ denote the return from the $(n-1)$ activities, then the total return from all the n activities will be

$$p_n(R_n) + f_{n-1}(R - R_n).$$

An optimal choice of R_n will maximize the above function and thus the fundamental dynamic programming model may be expressed as

$$f_n(R) = \underset{0 \le R_n \le R}{\text{Max.}} \ [p_n(R_n) + f_{n-1}(R - R_n)], \ n = 2, 3, ..., \qquad ... (7.4)$$

where $f_1(R)$, when $n = 1$ is obtained from equation (7.3) as

$$f_1(R) = p_1(R). \qquad ... (7.5)$$

Equation (7.5) gives the return from the first activity when whole of the resource R is allotted to it. Once $f_1(R)$ is known, equation (7.4) provides a relation to evaluate $f_2(R)$, $f_3(R)$, ... This recursive process ultimately leads to the value of $f_{n-1}(R)$ and finally $f_n(R)$ at which the process stops.

EXAMPLE 7.4-1 (Employment Smoothening Problem)

A firm has divided its marketing area into three zones. The amount of sales depends upon the number of salesmen in each zone. The firm has been collecting the data regarding sales and salesmen in each area over a number of past years.

The information is summarized in table 7.1. For the next year firm has only 9 salesmen and the problem is to allocate these salesmen to three different zones so that the total sales are maximum.

TABLE 7.1

Profits in thousands of rupees

No. of salesmen	*Zone 1*	*Zone 2*	*Zone 3*
0	30	35	42
1	45	45	54
2	60	52	60
3	70	64	70
4	79	72	82
5	90	82	95
6	98	93	102
7	105	98	110
8	100	100	110
9	90	100	110

[*P.T.U. MBA May, 2002*]

Solution. In this problem the three zones represent the three stages and the number of salesmen represent the state variables.

Stage 1: We start with zone 1. The amount of sales corresponding to different number of salesmen allocated to zone 1 are given in table 7.1 and are reproduced in table 7.2.

TABLE 7.2

Zone 1

No. of salesmen :	0	1	2	3	4	5	6	7	8	9
Profit (000' *of* ₹) :	30	45	60	70	79	90	98	105	100	90

Stage 2: Now consider the first two zones, zone 1 and 2. Nine salesmen can be divided among two zones in 10 different ways : as 9 in zone 1 and 0 in zone 2, 8 in zone 1 and 1 in zone 2, 7 in zone 1 and 2 in zone 2, etc. Each combination will have associated with it certain returns. The returns for all number of salesmen (total) 9, 8, 7, ..., 0 are shown in table 7.3.

For a particular number of salesmen, the profits for all possible combinations can be read along the diagonal. Max. profits are marked by*.

TABLE 7.3

Zone 1	x_1:	0	1	2	3	4	5	6	7	8	9
	$f_1(x_1)$:	30	45	60	70	79	90	98	105	100	90
Zone 2 x_2	$f_2(x_2)$										
0	35	65*	80*	95*	105*	114	125*	133	140	135	125
1	45	75	90	105*	115*	124	135*	143*	150	145	
2	52	82	97	112	122	131	142	150	157		
3	64	94	109	124	134	143*	154*	162			
4	72	102	117	132	142	151	162				
5	82	112	127	142	152	161					
6	93	123	138	153	163*						
7	98	128	143	158							
8	100	130	145								
9	100	130									

Stage 3: Now consider the distribution of 9 salesmen in three zones 1, 2 and 3. The decision at this stage will result in allocating certain number of salesmen to zone 3 and the remaining to zone 2 and 1 combined; and then by following the backward process, they will be distributed to zones 2 and 1.

For total of 9 salesmen to be allocated to the three zones, the returns are shown in table 7.4 below.

TABLE 7.4

No. of salesmen :	0	1	2	3	4	5	6	7	8	9
Total profit $f_2(x_2) + f_1(x_1)$:	65	80	95	105	115	125	135	143	154	163
Salesmen in zone 2 + *zone* 1:	0+0	0+1	0+2	0+3	1+3	0+5	1+5	3+4	3+5	6+3
$(x_2 + x_1)$				1+2				1+6		
No. of salesmen in Zone 3:	9	8	7	6	5	4	3	2	1	0
Profit $f_3(x_3)$:	110	110	110	102	95	82	70	60	54	42
Total profit $f_3(x_3) + f_2(x_2)$ $+ f_1(x_1)$	175	190	205	207	210*	207	205	203	208	205

From table 7.4, the maximum profit for 9 salesmen is ₹ 2,10,000 if 5 salesmen are allotted to zone 3 and from the remaining four, 1 is allotted to zone 2 and 3 to zone 1.

EXAMPLE 7.4-2 (Capital Budgeting Problem)

A manufacturing company has three sections producing automobile parts, bicycle parts and sewing machine parts respectively. The management has allocated ₹ 20,000 for expanding the production facilities. In the auto parts and bicycle parts sections, the production can be increased either by adding new machines or by replacing some old inefficient machines by automatic machines. The sewing machine parts section was started only a few years back and thus the additional amount can be invested only by adding new machines to the section. The cost of adding and replacing the machines, along with the associated expected returns in the different sections is given in table 7.5. Select a set of expansion plans which may yield the maximum return.

TABLE 7.5

Alternatives		Auto parts section		Bicycle parts section		Sewing machine parts section	
		Cost (₹)	Return (₹)	Cost (₹)	Return (₹)	Cost (₹)	Return (₹)
1.	No expansion	0	0	0	0	0	0
2.	Add new machines	4,000	8,000	8,000	12,000	2,000	8,000
3.	Replace old m/cs	6,000	10,000	12,000	18,000	—	—

Solution

Here each section of the company is a stage. At each stage there are a number of alternatives for expansion. Capital represents the state variable. Let us consider the first stage – the auto parts section. There are three alternatives : no expansion, add new machines and replace old machines. The amount that may be allocated to stage 1 may vary from 0 to ₹ 20,000; of course, it will be overspending if it is more than ₹ 6000. The returns of the various alternatives are given in table 7.6.

TABLE 7.6

Stage 1 : Auto parts section

State x_1 (000' of ₹)	Evaluation of alternatives (Values in thousands of rupees) 1	2	3	Optimal solution	
	Cost $C_{11} = 0$ Return	Cost $C_{12} = 4$ Return	Cost $C_{13} = 6$ Return	Optimal Return	Decision
0	0	—	—	0	1
2	0	—	—	0	1
4	0	8	—	8	2
6	0	8	10	10	3
8	0	8	10	10	3
10	0	8	10	10	3
12	0	8	10	10	3
14	0	8	10	10	3
16	0	8	10	10	3
18	0	8	10	10	3
20	0	8	10	10	3

When the capital allocated is zero or ₹ 2,000, only first alternative (no expansion) is possible. Return is, of course, zero. When the amount allocated is ₹ 4,000, alternatives 1 and 2 are possible with returns of ₹ 0 and ₹ 8,000. So we select alternative 2 and when the amount allocated is ₹ 6,000, all the three alternatives are possible, giving returns of zero, ₹ 8,000 and ₹ 10,000 respectively. So we select alternative 3 with return of ₹ 10,000 and so on.

Stage 2: Let us now move to stage 2. Here, again, three alternatives are available. The computations are carried out in table 7.7.

TABLE 7.7

Stage 2 : Bicycle parts section (+ Auto parts section)

State x_2 (000' of ₹)	Evaluation of alternatives (Values in thousands of rupees)			Optimal solution	
	1	2	3		
	Cost $C_{21} = 0$ Return	Cost $C_{22} = 8$ Return	Cost $C_{23} = 12$ Return	Optimal Return	Decision
0	0 + 0 = 0	—	—	0	1
2	0 + 0 = 0	—	—	0	1
4	0 + 8 = 8	—	—	8	1
6	0 + 10 = 10	—	—	10	1
8	0 + 10 = 10	12 + 0 = 12	—	12	2
10	0 + 10 = 10	12 + 0 = 12	—	12	2
12	0 + 10 = 10	12 + 8 = 20	18 + 0 = 18	20	2
14	0 + 10 = 10	12 + 10 = 22	18 + 0 = 18	22	2
16	0 + 10 = 10	12 + 10 = 22	18 + 8 = 26	26	3
18	0 + 10 = 10	12 + 10 = 22	18 + 10 = 28	28	3
20	0 + 10 = 10	12 + 10 = 22	18 + 10 = 28	28	3

Here state x_2 represents the total amount allocated to the current stage (stage 2) and the preceding stage (stage 1). Similarly, the return also is the sum of the current stage and the preceding stage (Principle of optimality). Thus when $x_2 <$ ₹ 8,000, only the first alternative (no expansion) is possible. But with $x_2 =$ ₹ 8,000, a return of ₹ 12,000 is possible by selecting the second alternative (add new machines). With $x_2 =$ ₹ 12,000, three alternatives are possible with the maximum return of ₹ 20,000 from alternative 2. The optimal policy consists of a set of two decisions, namely adopt alternative 2 at second stage (table 7.7) and again alternative 2 at the first stage (table 7.6).

Stage 3: The computations for stage 3 are given in table 7.8.

TABLE 7.8

Stage 3 : Sewing m/c parts section (+ Bicycle parts section + Auto parts section)

State x_3 (000' of ₹)	Evaluation of alternatives (Values in thousands of rupees)		Optimal solution	
	Cost $C_{31} = 0$ Return	Cost $C_{32} = 2$ Return	Optimal Return	Decision
0	0 + 0 = 0	—	0	1
2	0 + 0 = 0	8 + 0 = 8	8	2
4	0 + 8 = 8	8 + 0 = 8	8	1, 2
6	0 + 10 = 10	8 + 8 = 16	16	2
8	0 + 12 = 12	8 + 10 = 18	18	2
10	0 + 12 = 12	8 + 12 = 20	20	2
12	0 + 20 = 20	8 + 12 = 20	20	1, 2
14	0 + 22 = 22	8 + 20 = 28	28	2
16	0 + 26 = 26	8 + 22 = 30	30	2
18	0 + 28 = 28	8 + 26 = 34	34	2
20	0 + 28 = 28	8 + 28 = 36	36	2

For x_3 = 20,000, the optimal decision for stage 3 is alternative 2, which gives a total return of ₹ 36,000. This involves a cost of ₹ 2,000 and leaves ₹ 18,000 to be allotted for stages 2 and 1 combined. From table 7.7, for allocation of ₹ 18,000, alternative 3 is to be chosen which costs ₹ 12,000. For remaining sum of ₹ 6,000, from table 7.6, decision alternative 3 is to be selected. Thus the optimal policy of expanding production facilities is 3–3–2, which can be elaborated as : replace old machines with automatics in auto parts section, replace old machines with automatics in bicycle parts section, and add new machines to the sewing machines parts section. This policy gives the optimal return of ₹ 36,000.

EXAMPLE 7.4-3

The owner of a chain of four grocery stores has purchased six crates of fresh strawberries. The following table gives the estimated profits at each store when it is allocated various number of boxes :

TABLE 7.9

		Stores			
		1	*2*	*3*	*4*
	0	*0*	*0*	*0*	*0*
	1	*4*	*2*	*6*	*2*
	2	*6*	*4*	*8*	*3*
Number of	*3*	*7*	*6*	*8*	*4*
boxes	*4*	*7*	*8*	*8*	*4*
	5	*7*	*9*	*8*	*4*
	6	*7*	*10*	*8*	*4*

The owner does not wish to split crates between stores, but is willing to make zero allocations. Find the allocation of six crates so as to maximize the profits.

[P.T.U. M.Tech. April, 2012]

Solution

This problem is similar to the allocation of salesmen to different zones. Here stores represent the stages and number of boxes represent the state variables. Thus the problem involves 4 stages and 6 state variables. Let x_1, x_2, x_3 and x_4 be the number of crates allocated to the 4 stores and $f_1(x_1)$, $f_2(x_2)$, $f_3(x_3)$ and $f_4(x_4)$ be the respective profits. Then the problem is

$$\text{maximize } Z = f_1(x_1) + f_2(x_2) + f_3(x_3) + f_4(x_4),$$
$$\text{subject to} \quad x_1 + x_2 + x_3 + x_4 \le 6,$$
$$\text{where} \quad x_1, x_2, x_3, x_4 \text{ are non-negative integers.}$$

Stage 1: The estimated profits corresponding to different number of boxes allocated to store 1 are given in table 7.9 and are reproduced in table 7.10.

TABLE 7.10

Store 1

No. of boxes, x_1	:	0	1	2	3	4	5	6
Profit $f_1(x_1)$	:	0	4	6	7	7	7	7

Stage 2: Now consider the first two stores, store 1 and 2. Six boxes can be divided among the two sotres in 7 different ways : as 6 in store 1 and 0 in store 2, 5 in store 1 and 1 in store 2, etc. Each combination will have associated with it certain profits. The profits for all the total number of boxes, such as 6, 5, 4, ..., 0 are shown in table 7.11.

TABLE 7.11

Store 1 x_1:		0	1	2	3	4	5	6
$f_1(x_1)$:		0	4	6	7	7	7	7
Store 2 x_2	$f_2(x_2)$							
0	0	0*	4*	6*	7	7	7	7
1	2	2	6*	8*	9	9	9	
2	4	4	8*	10*	11	11		
3	6	6	10*	12*	13			
4	8	8	12*	14*				
5	9	9	13					
6	10	10						

For a particular number of boxes, the profits for all possible combinations can be read along the diagonal. Maximum profits are marked by *. Thus the optimal profits and corresponding allocations of boxes to the two stores are given by :

TABLE 7.12

Boxes	:	0	1	2	3	4	5	6
$f_2(x_2) + f_1(x_1)$	:	0	4	6	8	10	12	14
$x_2 + x_1$	:	0 + 0	0 + 1	1 + 1 0 + 2	2 + 1 1 + 2	3 + 1 2 + 2	4 + 1 3 + 2	4 + 2

Stage 3: Now consider the distribution of 6 boxes to three stores 1, 2 and 3. The decision at this stage will result in allocating certain number of boxes to store 3 and the remaining to stores 2 and 1 combined and then by following the backward process, they will be distributed to stores 2 and 1. The profits for all the total number of boxes, such as 6, 5, 4, ..., 0 are shown in table 7.13.

TABLE 7.13

Store	*Boxes* $(x_2 + x_1)$	0	1	2	3	4	5	6
1+2	$f_2(x_2)+f_1(x_1)$	0	4	6	8	10	12	14
Store 3 x_3	$f_3(x_3)$							
0	0	0*	4	6	8	10	12	14
1	6	6*	10*	12*	14*	16*	18*	
2	8	8	12*	14*	16*	18*		
3	8	8	12	14	16			
4	8	8	12	14				
5	8	8	12					
6	8	8						

For any particular number of boxes, the profits for all possible combinations can be read along the diagonal. Maximum profits are marked by *. Thus the optimal profits and corresponding allocations of boxes to the three stores are given by table 7.14.

TABLE 7.14

Boxes	:	0	1	2	3	4	5	6
$f_3(x_3) + f_2(x_2) + f_1(x_1)$	:	0	6	10	12	14	16	18
$x_3 + (x_2 + x_1)$	:	0 + 0	1 + 0	1 + 1	2 + 1 1 + 2	2 + 2 1 + 3	2 + 3 1 + 4	2 + 4 1 + 5

Stage 4: Now consider the distribution of 6 boxes to four stores. The corresponding profits for all possible combinations are given in table 7.15.

TABLE 7.15

Boxes $\sum_{j=1}^{3} x_j$	:	0	1	2	3	4	5	6
$\sum_{j=1}^{3} f_j(x_j)$	:	0	6	10	12	14	16	18
x_4	:	6	5	4	3	2	1	0
$f_4(x_4)$	:	4	4	4	4	3	2	0
$\sum_{j=1}^{4} f_j(x_j)$	:	4	10	14	16	17	18*	18*

Thus the maximum possible profit is 18 for $x_4 = 1$ or 0. Going back, eight optimal allocations can be traced, each yielding profit of 18.

TABLE 7.16

		x_1^*	x_2^*	x_3^*	x_4^*
	1	1	2	2	1
	2	1	3	1	1
	3	1	3	2	0
Possible	4	1	4	1	0
optimal	5	2	1	2	1
allocations	6	2	2	1	1
	7	2	2	2	0
	8	2	3	1	0

EXAMPLE 7.4.4

An oil company has 8 units of money available for exploration of three sites. If oil is present at a site, the probability of finding it depends upon the amount allocated for exploiting the site, as given below.

TABLE 7.17

	Units of money allocated								
	0	*1*	*2*	*3*	*4*	*5*	*6*	*7*	*8*
Site 1	*0.0*	*0.0*	*0.1*	*0.2*	*0.3*	*0.5*	*0.7*	*0.9*	*1.0*
Site 2	*0.0*	*0.1*	*0.2*	*0.3*	*0.4*	*0.6*	*0.7*	*0.8*	*1.0*
Site 3	*0.0*	*0.1*	*0.1*	*0.2*	*0.3*	*0.5*	*0.8*	*0.9*	*1.0*

The probability that the oil exists at sites 1, 2 and 3 is 0.4, 0.3 and 0.2 respectively. Find the optimal allocation of money.

[*Kuru. U.M.Tech. (Mech.) May, 1994; P.U.M.E. (Mech.) Dec., 1988*]

Solution. In this oil exploration problem, the objective is to maximize the probability of finding oil by allocating the available amount of money to the three potential oil sites.

Let x_1, x_2 and x_3 be the units of money allocated to the sites 1, 2 and 3 respectively, and $p_1(x_1)$, $p_2(x_2)$ and $p_3(x_3)$ be the corresponding probabilities of finding oil, if it exists. Then actual probabilities of finding oil at the three sites are $p_1(x_1) \times 0.4$, $p_2(x_2) \times 0.3$ and $p_3(x_3) \times 0.2$.

Thus the objective function can be written as

$$\text{maximize } Z = 0.4\, p_1(x_1) + 0.3\, p_2(x_2) + 0.2\, p_3(x_3),$$

subject to constraint $\quad x_1 + x_2 + x_3 \le 8,$

where x_1, x_2, x_3 are non-negative integers.

The probabilities of finding the oil, taking into consideration the availabilities of oil at different sites, in the percentage form can be expressed as below.

TABLE 7.18

Units of money allocated

	0	1	2	3	4	5	6	7	8
Site 1, $f_1(x_1)$:	0	0	4	8	12	20	28	36	40
Site 2, $f_2(x_2)$:	0	3	6	9	12	18	21	24	30
Site 3, $f_3(x_3)$:	0	2	2	4	6	10	16	18	20

Here the three sites are regarded as the three stages and the money allocated is the state variable.

Stage 1: We start with site 1. The actual probabilities of finding the oil when expressed as percentages are shown in table 7.19.

TABLE 7.19

Site 1

Units of money allocated:	0	1	2	3	4	5	6	7	8
$f_1(x_1)$:	0	0	4	8	12	20	28	36	40

Stage 2: Now consider the first two sites 1 and 2. Eight units of money can be divided among the two sites in 9 different ways as shown in table 7.20.

TABLE 7.20

x_2	x_1 / $f_1(x_1)$ / $f_2(x_2)$	0	1	2	3	4	5	6	7	8
	$f_1(x_1)$	0	0	4	8	12	20	28	36	40
0	0	0*	0	4	8	12*	20*	28*	36*	40*
1	3	3*	3	7	11	15	23	31	39	
2	6	6*	6	10	14	18	26	34		
3	9	9*	9	13	17	21	29			
4	12	12*	12	16	20	24				
5	18	18	18	22	26					
6	21	21	21	25						
7	24	24	24							
8	30	30								

The opitmal values of $f_2(x_2) + f_1(x_1)$ are given in table 7.21.

TABLE 7.21

Units of money :	0	1	2	3	4	5	6	7	8
$f_2(x_2) + f_1(x_1)$:	0	3	6	9	12	20	28	36	40
$x_2 + x_1$:	0+0	1+0	2+0	3+0	4+0 0+4	0+5	0+6	0+7	0+8

Stage 3: Now consider the allocation of 8 units of money to the three sites. The corresponding probabilities expressed as percentages are shown in table 7.22.

TABLE 7.22

Units of money :	0	1	2	3	4	5	6	7	8
$f_2(x_2) + f_1(x_1)$:	0	3	6	9	12	20	28	36	40
$x_2 + x_1$:	0+0	1+0	2+0	3+0	4 + 0 0 + 4	0+5	0+6	0+7	0+8
x_3 :	8	7	6	5	4	3	2	1	0
$f_3(x_3)$:	20	18	16	10	6	4	2	2	0
$f_3(x_3) + f_2(x_2) + f_1(x_1)$:	20	21	22	19	18	24	30	38	40

Thus the maximum probability is 40%, which is obtained if $x_3 = 0$, $x_2 = 0$ and $x_1 = 8$ *i.e.*, if entire 8 units of money are allocated to site 1 only.

EXAMPLE 7.4-5

A company manufacturing a certain product has a contract of supplying 40 units at the end of month 1 and 60 units at the end of month 2. The cost of manufacturing x units in any month is $c(x) = 100x + 0.4x^2$. The company has enough production facilities to manufacture 100 units a month. If the company produces more than 40 units in month 1, any excess units can be carried over to month 2. However, there is an inventory carrying cost of ₹ 1.60 for each unit carried over from month 1 to 2. How many units should the company produce each month to minimize the total cost assuming that there is no initial inventory ?

Solution. Here month 1 and month 2 are the two stages and the number of units to be produced each month are the state variables. Let x_1 and x_2 be the number of units of the product to be produced in month 1 and 2 respectively and W be the amount of inventory at the end of month 1, which is to be carried to month 2.

Then $x_1 = 40 + W$ and $x_2 = 60 - W$.

Cost incurred in month 1, $c_1(x_1) = 100x_1 + 0.4x_1^2 = 100(40 + W) + 0.4(40 + W)^2$

$$= 4{,}640 + 132W + 0.4W^2,$$

and cost incurred in month 2, $c_2(x_2) = 100x_2 + 0.4x_2^2 = 100(60 - W) + 0.4(60 - W)^2$

$$= 7{,}440 - 148W + 0.4W^2$$

∴ Total cost incurred in the two months, including the inventory carrying cost,

$$c_1(x_1) + c_2(x_2) = 12{,}080 - 16W + 0.8W^2 + 1.60W.$$

This cost is minimum if $\frac{d}{dW}(12{,}080 - 16W + 0.8W^2 + 1.60W) = 0$

or if $-16 + 1.6W + 1.60 = 0$

or if $W = 9$ units. ∴ $x_1 = 49$ units, $x_2 = 51$ units.

Minimum total cost $= 12{,}080 - 16 \times 9 + 0.8 \times 9^2 + 1.60 \times 9 =$ ₹ 12,015.20.

EXAMPLE 7.4-6

A manufacturer has entered into a contract for the supply of the following number of units of a product at the end of each month:

Month :	*Jan.*	*March*	*August*	*October*	*November*	*December*
No. of units :	*10*	*5*	*20*	*3*	*6*	*30*

The units manufactured during a month are available for supply at the end of the month or they may be kept in storage at a cost of ₹ 2 per unit per month. Each time the manufacture of a batch of units is undertaken, there is a set-up cost of ₹ 400. Determine the production schedule which will minimize the total cost. [*P.T.U. M.Tech. Dec., 2011; P.U. B.E. T.I.T. Dec., 2008*]

Solution. Here the six months represent the 6 stages and number of units to be manufactured are the state variables. We shall start from the last month of December and move backwards.

Month of December

The best decision is to produce 30 units with a cost of ₹ 400 towards the set-up cost and there is no storage cost.

Month of November

There are two alternatives :

1. Produce (6 + 30) = 36 units to satisfy the demand of November and December.
   Total cost = ₹ (400 + 30 × 2 × 1) = ₹ 460.
2. Produce 6 units in Nov. + 30 units in Dec. involving 2 set-ups and no storage cost.
   Total cost = ₹ (400 + 400) = ₹ 800.

∴ The optimum decision is to produce 36 units in Nov. and no units in Dec.

Month of October

Various alternatives are :

1. Produce (3 + 6 + 30) = 39 units in Oct.
   Total cost = ₹ (400 + 6 × 2 × 1 + 30 × 2 × 2) = ₹ 532.
2. Produce (3 + 6) = 9 units in Oct. and 30 units in Dec.
   Total cost = ₹ (400 × 2 + 6 × 2 × 1) = ₹ 812.
3. Produce 3 units in Oct. and 36 units in Nov.
   Total cost = ₹ (400 × 2 + 30 × 2 × 1) = ₹ 860.

Note that as per the decision made in Nov., producing 3 units in Oct., 6 in Nov. and 30 in Dec. is already ruled out as it involves higher cost.

Thus optimum decision is to produce 39 units in Oct. and nothing in Nov. and Dec.

Month of August

The various possible alternatives are :

1. Produce (20 + 3 + 6 + 30) = 59 units in August.
   Total cost = ₹ (400 + 3 × 2 × 2 + 6 × 2 × 3 + 30 × 2 × 4) = ₹ 688.
2. Produce (20 + 3 + 6) = 29 units in August and 30 in Dec.
   Total cost = ₹ [(400 × 2) + 3 × 2 × 2 + 6 × 2 × 3] = ₹ 848.
3. Produce (20 + 3) = 23 units in August and 36 in Nov.
   Total cost = ₹ [400 × 2 + 3 × 2 × 2 + 30 × 2 × 1] = ₹ 872.
4. Produce 20 units in August and 39 units in Oct.
   Total cost = ₹ [400 × 2 + 6 × 2 × 1 + 30 × 2 × 2] = ₹ 932.

Thus optimum decision is to produce 59 units in August and none in the following months.

Month of March

The various possible alternatives are :

1. Produce all (5 + 20 + 3 + 6 + 30) = 64 units in March.
   Total cost = ₹ [400 + 20 × 2 × 5 + 3 × 2 × 7 + 6 × 2 × 8 + 30 × 2 × 9]
   = ₹ 1,278.
2. Produce (5 + 20 + 3 + 6) = 34 units in March and 30 in Dec.
   Total cost = ₹ [400 × 2 + 20 × 2 × 5 + 3 × 2 × 7 + 6 × 2 × 8] = ₹ 1,138.
3. Produce (5 + 20 + 3) = 28 units in March and 36 units in Nov.
   Total cost = ₹ [400 × 2 + 20 × 2 × 5 + 3 × 2 × 7 + 30 × 2 × 1] = ₹ 1,102.

4. Produce (5 + 20) = 25 units in March and 39 units in Oct.

   Total cost = ₹ [400 × 2 + 20 × 2 × 5 + 6 × 2 × 1 + 30 × 2 × 2] = ₹ 1,132.

5. Produce 5 units in March and 59 units in August.

   Total cost = ₹ [400 × 2 + 3 × 2 × 2 + 6 × 2 × 3 + 30 × 2 × 4] = ₹ 1,088.

∴ The optimum decision is to produce 5 units in March and 59 units in August. The total cost involved is ₹ 1,088.

Month of January

The various possible alternatives are :

1. Produce all 74 units in January.

   Total cost = ₹ [400 + 5 × 2 × 2 + 20 × 2 × 7 + 3 × 2 × 9 + 6 × 2 × 10 + 30 × 2 × 11]
   = ₹ 1,534.

2. Produce (10 + 5 + 20 + 3 + 6) = 44 units in January and 30 units in December.

   Total cost = ₹ [400 × 2 + 5 × 2 × 2 + 20 × 2 × 7 + 3 × 2 × 9 + 6 × 2 × 10]
   = ₹ 1,274.

3. Produce (10 + 5 + 20 + 3) = 38 units in Janaury and 36 units in Nov.

   Total cost = ₹ [400 × 2 + 5 × 2 × 2 + 20 × 2 × 7 + 3 × 2 × 9 + 30 × 2 × 1]
   = ₹ 1,214.

4. Produce (10 + 5 + 20) = 35 units in January and 39 units in Oct.

   Total cost = ₹ [400 × 2 + 5 × 2 × 2 + 20 × 2 × 7 + 6 × 2 × 1 + 30 × 2 × 2]
   = ₹ 1,232.

5. Produce (10 + 5) = 15 units in January and 59 units in August.

   Total cost = ₹ [400 × 2 + 5 × 2 × 2 + 3 × 2 × 2 + 6 × 2 × 3 + 30 × 2 × 4]
   = ₹ 1,108.

6. Produce 10 units in January, 5 units in March and 59 units in August.

   Total cost = ₹ [400 × 3 + 3 × 2 × 2 + 6 × 2 × 3 + 30 × 2 × 4] = ₹ 1,488.

Thus optimum decision is to produce 15 units in Jan. and 59 units in August.

Therefore, the best production schedule that will minimize total cost and satisfy the demand from January till December is to produce 15 units in January and 59 units in August.

EXAMPLE 7.4-7

A salesman is planning a business tour from Mumbai to Kolkata in the course of which he proposes to cover one city from each of the company's different marketing zones en route. As he

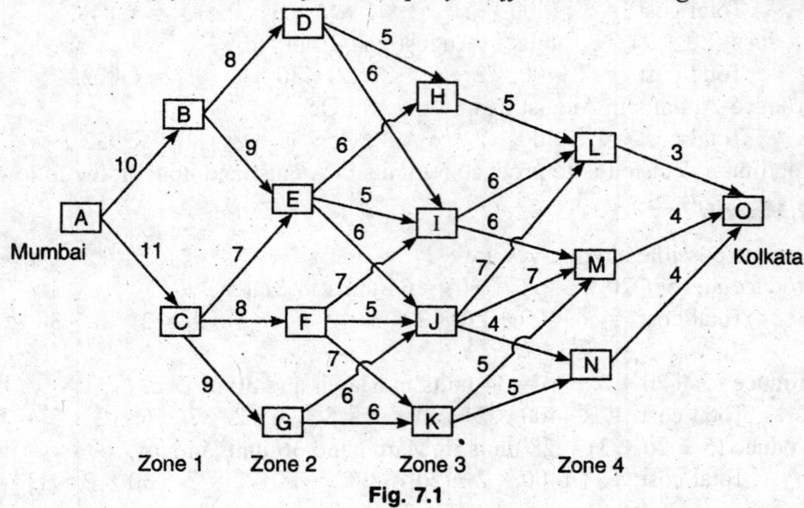

Fig. 7.1

has limited time at his disposal, he has to complete his tour in the shortest possible time. The network in Fig. 7.1 shows the number of days' time involved for covering any of the various intermediate cities (time includes travel as well as working time). Determine the optimum tour plan.

Solution. Starting from A, the cities of various marketing zones may be considered as distinct stages.

Stage 1 : B or C ?
Stage 2 : D, E, F or G ?
Stage 3 : H, I, J or K ?
Stage 4 : L, M or N ?
Stage 5 : Best route to O.

Stage 1: At this stage it is not known whether B lies on the overall shortest route; but if it does, the shortest route from A to B is AB.

$$\left.\begin{array}{l}\text{A to B} = 6\\ \text{A to C} = 11\end{array}\right\} \text{ the only routes.}$$

Stage 2: It is not known whether D lies on the overall shortest route; but if it does, the only route from A is ABD, involving a total travel time of = 10 + 8 = 18 days.

Similarly, ABE = 10 + 9 = 19
ACE = 11 + 7 = 18
ACF = 11 + 8 = 19
ACG = 11 + 9 = 20.

From the above, shortest routes are :

$$\left.\begin{array}{l}\text{A to D} = 18\\ \text{A to E} = 18\\ \text{A to F} = 19\\ \text{A to G} = 20.\end{array}\right\}$$

Stage 3: It is not known whether H lies on the overall shortest route; but if it does, is it through D or E ?

Both D and E are reached in 18 days by the quickest route from A (from the optimal result from stage 2).

Therefore ADH = 18 + 5 = 23
AEH = 18 + 6 = 24
Similarly, ADI = 18 + 6 = 24
AEI = 18 + 5 = 23
AFI = 19 + 7 = 26
AEJ = 18 + 6 = 24
AFJ = 19 + 5 = 24
AGJ = 20 + 6 = 26
AFK = 19 + 7 = 26
AGK = 20 + 6 = 26.

From the above, shortest routes from A are

$$\left.\begin{array}{l}\text{A to H} = 23\\ \text{A to I} = 23\\ \text{A to J} = 24\\ \text{A to K} = 26.\end{array}\right\}$$

Stage 4: Proceeding in the same way as for stage 3, we have

AHL = 23 + 5 = 28
AIL = 23 + 6 = 29

$$AJL = 24 + 7 = 31$$
$$AIM = 23 + 6 = 29$$
$$AJM = 24 + 7 = 31$$
$$AKM = 26 + 5 = 31$$
$$AJN = 24 + 4 = 28$$
$$AKN = 26 + 5 = 31.$$

∴ The shortest routes from A are

$$\left.\begin{array}{r} \text{A to L} = 28 \\ \text{A to M} = 29 \\ \text{and A to N} = 28. \end{array}\right\}$$

Final stage: There are three alternatives to reach O from the 4th stage *viz*. LO, MO and NO. Using the optimal times at 4th stage,

$$\left.\begin{array}{r} ALO = 28 + 3 = 31 \\ AMO = 29 + 4 = 33 \\ ANO = 28 + 4 = 32. \end{array}\right\}$$

Thus the shortest time from A to O = 31. Now we retrace the steps backwards along the network to identify the intermediate cities along the shortest route.

A – O — Final
A – L – O — Stage 4
A – H – L – O — Stage 3
A – D – H – L – O — Stage 2
A – B – D – H – L – O — Optimal route.

The problem of finding the shortest route is known as the *stage coach problem.*

EXAMPLE 7.4-8

A dealer has to dispose of certain goods within 5 weeks' time. The market prices are fluctuating from week to week. It is estimated that the chances of getting ₹ 2,000 for the whole stock are 45%, chances of getting ₹ 2,500 are 35% and chances for getting ₹ 3,000 are 20%. If the goods are not sold in the first 4 weeks, then they will have to be disposed of in the fifth week at the prevailing market price in that week. When should the stocks be sold ?

[P.T.U. M.Tech. April, 2012]

Solution. The five weekly periods can be treated as five stages and the sale prices are the state variables. At each stage the dealer has to make a choice among the alternatives 'sell' and 'wait'. If the prevailing market price is more than that he expects in the following weeks, he should 'sell' and if it is less, he should 'wait'.

These types of problems can be conveniently handled by starting from the last stage and solving by the *backward induction* or *backward process.*

Fifth Week (*stage*): As it is essential to sell the stocks by the fifth week, he will get ₹ 2,000 or ₹ 2,500 or ₹ 3,000 depending upon the price prevailing in the market in that week.

Fourth Week (*stage*): The prevailing price may be ₹ 2,000, ₹ 2,500 or ₹ 3,000. If it is ₹ 3,000, he will naturally sell the stock. If it is less than ₹ 3,000, he may decide to sell or wait. He will sell if the market price in 4th week is more than the expected return in the 5th week, otherwise he will wait.

Now expected return in the 5th week = ₹ [2,000 × .45 + 2,500 × .35 + 3,000 × .20]
= ₹ 2,375.

Thus if the market price in the 4th week is ₹ 3,000 or ₹ 2,500 he should sell; otherwise he should wait.

Third week (*stage*): If the prevailing price is ₹ 3,000 he should sell. If the price is less, he will still sell if he can get more than the expected return in the 4th week; otherwise he will wait.

Expected return in the 4th week = ₹ [3,000 × .20 + 2,500 × .35 + 2,375 × .45]
= ₹ 2,544.

Thus if the market price in the 3rd week is ₹ 3,000, he should sell; otherwise he should wait.

Second week (*stage*): If the prevailing price is ₹ 3,000 he should sell. If not, he should see the expected return in the third week.

Expected return in the 3rd week = ₹ [3,000 × 0.20 + 2,544 × 0.35 + 2,544 × 0.45]
= ₹ 2,635.

So, he should wait.

First week (*stage*): If the prevailing price is ₹ 3,000 he should sell; if not, expected return in the 2nd week will determine his decisioin.

Expected return in the 2nd week = ₹ [3000 × .20 + 2,635 × .35 + 2,635 × .45]
= ₹ 2,708.

So, he should wait.

Thus we reach at the following optimal decision policy: The dealer should sell goods if the market price in the first, second and third weeks is ₹ 3,000; otherwise wait. In the fourth week, if he can get ₹ 2,500 or ₹ 3,000 he should sell; if it is less than ₹ 2,500 he should wait. If the goods remain unsold upto the 5th week he should dispose of the stock at whatever value he gets in that week.

EXAMPLE 7.4-9 (Cargo-Loading Problem)

In a cargo loading problem, there are 4 items of different weights/unit and different value/unit as given below.

Item (i)	*Weight / unit (w_i kg/unit)*	*Value / unit (p_i ₹/unit)*
1	*1*	*1*
2	*3*	*5*
3	*4*	*7*
4	*6*	*11*

The maximum cargo load is restricted to 17. How many units of each item be loaded to maximize the value ? *[P.U. B.E. (T.I.T.) Nov., 2005]*

Solution. It is a four-stage problem, each item represents a stage. The state of the system is represented by the weight capacity available for allocation to stages 1, 2, 3, 4 and is denoted by x_i which varies from 0 to 17. If a_i is the number of units of item i, then the problem is

$$\text{maximize } Z = \sum_{i=1}^{4} a_i \, p_i ,$$

$$\text{subject to } \sum_{i=1}^{4} a_i \, w_i \leq W .$$

Stage 1: Here, $w_1 = 1$ kg/unit, $p_1 =$ ₹ 1/unit; $\dfrac{W}{w_1} = \dfrac{17}{1} = 17.$

$\therefore$ $a_1 = 0, 1, 2, ..., 17.$

Stage 2: Here, $w_2 = 3$kg/unit, $p_2 =$ ₹ 5/unit ; $\dfrac{W}{w_2} = \dfrac{17}{3}$

$= 5.67$ (= 5, integral value).

$\therefore$ $a_2 = 0, 1, 2, ..., 5.$

TABLE 7.23

x_i	Stage 1		Stage 2		Stage 3		Stage 4		$f_i^*(x_i)$
	$w_1 = 1, p_1 = 1$ $a_1 = 0,1,2, ...,17$		$w_2 = 3, p_2 = 5$ $a_2 = 0,1,2, ..., 5$		$w_3 = 4, p_3 = 7$ $a_3 = 0,1,2,3,4$		$w_4 = 6, p_4 = 11$ $a_4 = 0,1,2$		
	a_1	$f_1(x_1)$	a_2	$f_2(x_2)$	a_3	$f_3(x_3)$	a_4	$f_4(x_4)$	
0	0	0*	0	—	0	—	0	—	0
1	1	1*	0	—	0	—	0	—	1
2	2	2*	0	—	0	—	0	—	2
3	3	3	1	5+0=5*	0	—	0	—	5
4	4	4	1	5+1=6	1	7+0=7*	0	—	7
5	5	5	1	5+2=7	1	7+1=8*	0	—	8
6	6	6	2	10+0=10	1	7+2=9	1	11+0=11*	11
7	7	7	2	10+1=11	1	7+5=12*	1	11+1=12*	12
8	8	8	2	10+2=12	2	14+0=14*	1	11+2=13	14
9	9	9	3	15+0=15	2	14+1=15	1	11+5=16*	16
10	10	10	3	15+1=16	2	14+2=16	1	11+7=18*	18
11	11	11	3	15+2=17	2	14+5=19*	1	11+8=19*	19
12	12	12	4	20+0=20	3	21+0=21	2	22+0=22*	22
13	13	13	4	20+1=21	3	21+1=22	2	22+1=23*	23
14	14	14	4	20+2=22	3	21+2=23	2	22+2=24*	24
15	15	15	5	25+0=25	3	21+5=26	2	22+5=27*	27
16	16	16	5	25+1=26	4	28+0=28	2	22+7=29*	29
17	17	17	5	25+2=27	4	28+1=29	2	22+8=30*	30

Stage 3: Here, $w_3 = 4$ kg/unit, $p_3 =$ ₹ 7/unit; $\dfrac{W}{w_3} = \dfrac{17}{4} = 4.25.$

$\therefore$ $a_3 = 0, 1, 2, 3, 4.$

Stage 4: Here, $w_4 = 6$ kg/unit, $p_4 =$ ₹ 11/unit; $\dfrac{W}{w_4} = \dfrac{17}{6} = 2.83.$

$\therefore$ $a_4 = 0, 1, 2.$

Let $f_1(x_1)$, $f_2(x_2)$, $f_3(x_3)$ and $f_4(x_4)$ be the values of the loaded items at stage 1, 2, 3 and 4 respectively. The computation for different stages are given in table 7.23.

As seen from the table, for total load of 17 kg, the maximum value of cargo items is ₹ 30 (= 22 + 8 = 22 + 7 + 1), which is achieved if we load 1 unit of item 1, 1 unit of item 3 and 2 units of item 4.

EXAMPLE 7.4-10 (Selection of Advertising Media)

A cosmetics manufacturing company is interested in selecting the advertising media for its product and the frequency of advertising in each media. The data collected over the past two years regarding the frequency of advertising in three media of newspaper, radio and television and the related sales of the product give the following results:

TABLE 7.24

Expected sales in thousands of rupees

Frequency/week	*Television*	*Radio*	*Newspaper*
1	*220*	*150*	*100*
2	*275*	*250*	*175*
3	*325*	*300*	*225*
4	*350*	*320*	*250*

The cost of advertising in newspaper is ₹ 500 per appearance, while in radio and in television, it is ₹ 1,000 and ₹ 2,000 respectively. The budget provides ₹ 4,500 per week for advertisement. The problem is of determining the optimal combination of advertising media and advertising frequency. *[P.T.U. M.Tech. Nov., 2012]*

Solution

The problem can be decomposed into three stages corresponding to the three media of advertising. In each media four alternatives (frequencies) are possible. Each alternative, has associated with it certain cost and return (expected sales). Here again, the capital marked for allocation to different media is the state variable. A combination of media and frequency is to be selected in such a way as to maximize the total sales with expenditure not exceeding the specified limit of ₹ 4,500.

Let us consider the advertising media of television as the first stage. If x_1 is the capital allocated to stage 1, and R_{1j} (C_{1j}) is the return (expected sales) corresponding to cost C_{1j}, then, the optimal return is

$$f_1(x_1) = \max [R_{1j}(C_{1j})],$$
$$j = 0, 1, 2, 3, 4, \text{ with } 0 \le x_1 \le C.$$

By applying this equation at various levels of expenditure, the various alternatives are evaluated and the one giving the largest expected sales is selected. The selected frequencies and the optimal return for different values of x_1 are given in table 7.25.

TABLE 7.25

Stage 1

State x_1	*Cost per appearance = ₹ 2,000* *Return (in thousands of rupees)*	*Frequency*
500	—	0
1,000	—	0
1,500	—	0
2,000	220	1
2,500	220	1
3,000	220	1
3,500	220	1
4,000	275	2
4,500	275	2

For x_1 = 0, ₹ 500, ₹ 1,000 and ₹ 1,500; it is not possible to advertise in this media, since the cost of one appearance per week is ₹ 2,000. For x_1 = ₹ 2,000, ₹ 2,500, ₹ 3,000 and ₹ 3,500, the product can be advertised only once, giving a return of ₹ 2,20,000.

With x_1 = ₹ 4,000, ₹ 4,500, two appearances can occur giving a return of ₹ 2,75,000.

TABLE 7.26

Stage 2

Cost per appearance = ₹ 1,000
Return in thousands of rupees

State x_2	*0*	*1*	*2*	*3*	*4*	*Return*	*Freq.*
500	0	0	—	—	—	0	0
1,000	0	**150**	—	—	—	150	1
1,500	0	**150+0**	—	—	—	150	1
2,000	220	150+0	**250**	—	—	250	2
2,500	220	150+0	**250+0**	—	—	250	2
3,000	220	**150+220**	250+0	300	—	370	1
3,500	220	**150+220**	250+0	300+0	—	370	1
4,000	275	150+220	**250+220**	300+0	320	470	2
4,500	275	**150+220**	250+220	300+0	320+0	470	2

Now let us move to the second stage. Again for advertising in radio, four alternatives (frequencies) are possible. Here, the state x_2 will signify the expenditure incurred at the first stage and at the current stage.

At any value of state x_2 $(0 \le x_2 \le C)$,

$$\text{optimal return } f_2(x_2) = \max [R_{2j}(C_{2j}) + f_1(x_1)], \text{ for } j = 0 \text{ to } 4$$
$$= \max [R_{2j}(C_{2j}) + f_1(x_2 - C_{2j})], \text{ for } j = 0 \text{ to } 4.$$

The evaluation of altrenatives is carried in the tabular form shown in table 7.26. To illustrate, at $x_2 = 3{,}000$, four alternatives are possible, *i.e.*, do not advertise, advertise once, twice or thrice. It is not possible to advertise four times because that needs a sum of ₹ 4,000. If we do not purchase any advertisement (frequency = 0), the amount of ₹ 3,000 can purchase one advertisement in media T, giving expected sales of ₹ 2,20,000. If one advertisement is purchased in media R, this will cost ₹ 1,000, and with amount of ₹ 2,000 left one advertisement can be purchased in media T, giving total return of ₹ (150 + 220) × 1,000 = ₹ 3,70,000. If two advertisements are purchased in R, costing ₹ 2,000, the balance amount of ₹ 1,000 will be of no use in media T, and thus will give total sales as ₹ (250 + 0) × 1,000 = ₹ 2,50,000. The maximum return comes when we purchase one advertisement in media R. This is the optimal decision for x_2 = ₹ 3,000.

Now we move to the third stage.

$$f_3(x_3) = \max [R_{3j}(C_{3j}) + f_2(x_2)], \text{ for } j = 0 \text{ to } 4$$
$$= \max [R_{3j}(C_{3j}) + f_2(x_3 - C_{3j})], \text{ for } j = 0 \text{ to } 4.$$

TABLE 7.27

Cost per appearance = ₹ 500

Stage 3 *Return in thousands of rupees*

State x_3	*0*	*1*	*2*	*3*	*4*	*Optimal Decision* *Total sales*	*Frequency*
500	0	**100**	—	—	—	100	1
1,000	150	100+0	**175**	—	—	175	2
1,500	150	**100+150**	175+0	225	—	250	1
2,000	250	100+150	**175+150**	225+0	250	325	2
2,500	250	100+250	175+150	**225+150**	250+0	375	3
3,000	370	100+250	**175+250**	225+150	250+150	425	2
3,500	370	100+370	175+250	**225+250**	250+150	475	3
4,000	470	100+370	**175+370**	225+250	250+250	545	2
4,500	470	100+470	175+370	**225+370**	250+250	595	3

The computations are given in table 7.27. For the allocated capital of ₹ 4,500, the maximum sales that can be expected are of ₹ 5,95,000. From table 7.27, the optimal decision is : purchase three advertisements in newspaper. This will cost ₹ 1,500. The amount left is ₹ 3,000, and corresponding to that at stage 2, the optimal decision is : purchase one advertisement in radio. This costs ₹ 1,000 which leaves behind an amount of ₹ 2,000 which can purchase one advertisement in television (stage 1).

Similarly, if the firm wants to spend only ₹ 4,000 per week, the optimal policy will be : purchase two advertisements in newspaper costing ₹ 1,000, one in radio costing ₹ 1,000, and one in television costing ₹ 2,000. This will give an optimal expected sales worth ₹ 5,45,000.

EXAMPLE 7.4-11

A man is engaged in buying and selling identical items. He operates from a warehouse that can hold 500 items. Each month he can sell any quantity that he chooses to stock at the beginning of the month. Each month, he can buy as much as he wishes for delivery at the end of the month, so long as his stock does not exceed 500 items. For the next four months he has the following error-free forecasts of cost and selling prices :

Month :	*1*	*2*	*3*	*4*
Cost :	*27*	*26*	*24*	*28*
Selling price :	*28*	*25*	*25*	*27*

If he currently has a stock of 200 units, what quantities should he sell and buy in the next four months ? Find the solution using dynamic programming.

[Agra (M.Stat.) 1974; I.S.I. Dip. (Oprn. Mgmt.) 1978; Kuru.U., 1979]

Solution

The problem can be analysed by treating the four months as the four stages.

Let x_i be the number of items to be sold during the month i,
y_i be the number of items to be ordered during the month i,
b_i be the stock level in the beginning of month i,
p_i be the selling price in month i,
c_i be the purchase price in month i,
w be the warehouse capacity, which is 500.

The problem will be solved starting with the 4th month and then proceeding backward.

If $f_n(b_n)$ is the return when there are n more months to follow and the initial stock at the beginning of month n is b_n, then n varies from 1 to 4 as the months vary from 4th to 1st.

n :	4	3	2	1
Month :	I	II	III	IV

The recursive equations can be written as

At stage 1:

$$f_1(b_n) = \max_{x_n, y_n} [p_1 x_n - c_1 y_n],$$

where $x_n \le b_n$ and $b_n - x_n + y_n \le W$.

For any other stage,

$$f_n(b_n) = \max_{x_n, y_n} [p_n x_n - c_n y_n + f_{n-1}(b_n - x_n + y_n)].$$

When n = 1,

$$f_1(b_1) = \max_{x_1, y_1} [p_1 x_1 - c_1 y_1].$$

Since c_1 is positive, to maximize $f_1(b_1)$, $y_1 = 0$; and since no stock should be left at the end of the 4th month, the amount to be sold during the month should be equal to be the amount at the beginning of the month, *i.e.* $x_1 = b_1$.

$$\therefore \quad f_1(b_1) = p_1 b_1 = 27 b_1.$$

When n = 2,

$$\begin{aligned} f_2(b_2) &= \max_{x_2, y_2} [p_2 x_2 - c_2 y_2 + f_1(b_1)] \\ &= \max_{x_2, y_2} [p_2 x_2 - c_2 y_2 + f_1(b_2 - x_2 + y_2)] \\ &= \max_{x_2, y_2} [25 x_2 - 26 y_2 + 27(b_2 - x_2 + y_2)] \\ &= \max_{x_2, y_2} [y_2 - 2x_2 + 27 b_2]. \end{aligned}$$

Since

$$\begin{aligned} y_2 &\le W - b_2 + x_2 \\ &\le 500 - b_2 + x_2, \end{aligned}$$

$$\begin{aligned} f_2(b_2) &= \max_{x_2} [500 - b_2 + x_2 - 2x_2 + 27 b_2] \\ &= \max_{x_2} [26 b_2 - x_2 + 500]. \end{aligned}$$

To maximize $f_2(b_2)$, x_2 can be taken as zero.

$$\therefore \quad f_2(b_2) = 26b_2 + 500.$$

When n = 3,

$$f_3(b_3) = \max_{x_3, y_3} [p_3x_3 - c_3y_3 + f_2(b_2)]$$

$$= \max_{x_3, y_3} [25x_3 - 24y_3 + 26b_2 + 500].$$

Now $\quad b_2 = b_3 - x_3 + y_3.$

$$\therefore \quad f_3(b_3) = \max_{x_3, y_3} [25x_3 - 24y_3 + 26(b_3 - x_3 + y_3) + 500]$$

$$= \max_{x_3, y_3} [26b_3 - x_3 + 2y_3 + 500],$$

and $\quad y_3 \leq 500 - b_3 + x_3.$

$$\therefore \quad f_3(b_3) = \max_{x_3} [26b_3 - x_3 + 2(500 - b_3 + x_3) + 500]$$

$$= \max_{x_3} [24b_3 + x_3 + 1{,}500].$$

Now to maximize $f_3(b_3)$, x_3 should be maximum permissible, which is b_3 since $x_3 \leq b_3$.

$$\therefore \quad f_3(b_3) = 25b_3 + 1{,}500.$$

When n = 4,

$$f_4(b_4) = \max_{x_4, y_4} [p_4x_4 - c_4y_4 + f_3(b_3)]$$

$$= \max_{x_4, y_4} [28x_4 - 27y_4 + 25b_3 + 1{,}500].$$

But $\quad b_3 = b_4 - x_4 + y_4.$

$$\therefore \quad f_4(b_4) = \max_{x_4, y_4} [28x_4 - 27y_4 + 25(b_4 - x_4 + y_4) + 1{,}500]$$

$$= \max_{x_4, y_4} [25b_4 + 3x_4 - 2y_4 + 1{,}500].$$

To maximize $f_4(b_4)$, y_4 should be zero as $y_4 \geq 0$, and x_4 which is $\leq b_4$, should at maximum be equal to b_4.

i.e., $\quad y_4 = 0$ and $x_4 = b_4$, which gives

$$f_4(b_4) = 28b_4 + 1{,}500.$$

Now, it is given that stock level at the beginning of the first month is 200.

Thus $\quad b_4 = 200.$

$$\therefore \quad f_4(b_4) = 28 \times 200 + 1{,}500 = 7{,}100,$$

$$x_4 = 200,\ y_4 = 0,$$

$$b_3 = b_4 - x_4 + y_4 = 0,$$

$$x_3 = b_3 = 0,$$

$$y_3 = 500 - b_3 + x_3 = 500,$$

$$b_2 = b_3 - x_3 + y_3 = 500,$$

$$x_2 = 0,\ y_2 = 500 - b_2 + x_2 = 0,$$

$$b_1 = b_2 - x_2 + y_2 = 500,$$

$$x_1 = b_1 = 500, \text{ and}$$

$$y_1 = 0.$$

The optimal policy can be expressed as

Month :	I	II	III	IV
n :	4	3	2	1
Purchase :	0	500	0	0
Sale :	200	0	0	500

7.5 OPTIMAL SUBDIVISION PROBLEM

This problem deals with the division of a given quantity into a given number of parts. Let Q be the quantity to be divided in n number of parts $(u_1, u_2, ..., u_n)$. Then problem can be expressed as

$$\text{maximize } \prod_{i=1}^{n} u_i \quad \text{or maximize } u_1.u_2.u_3.... u_n,$$

$$\text{subject to } \sum_{i=1}^{n} u_i = Q,$$

$$u_i \geq 0, \quad i = 1, 2, ..., n.$$

The problem can be handled by dynamic programming, by considering each part as a stage. The alternatives at each stage are infinite, since u_i is continuous and may assume any non-negative value, satisfying the constraints

$$\sum_{i=1}^{n} u_i = Q.$$

The state of the system x_i, at any stage i, represents the part of resource Q, allocated to stage 1 through i inclusive. The recursion formula is then given as

$$f_1(x_1) = \max_{u_i = x_1} \{u_1\}, \qquad ... (7.6)$$

$$f_i(x_i) = \max_{0 \leq u_i \leq x_i} \{u_i f_{i-1}(x_i - u_i)\},$$

$$= \max_{u_i} \{u_i (x_i - u_i)\}. \qquad ... (7.7)$$

EXAMPLE 7.5-1

Determine the value of u_1, u_2, u_3 so as to maximize $(u_1 . u_2 . u_3)$, subject to $u_1 + u_2 + u_3 = 10$ and $u_1, u_2, u_3 \geq 0$.

[*R.T.M. Nagpur U.B.E. (Mech.) 2011; J.N.T.U. Hyderabad B.Tech. April, 2011; Nagpur U. (B.E.) 2003; R.C.C. CHD, 2002; PTU B. Tech., 2000*]

Solution. In this example Q = 10, is to be divided into three parts u_1, u_2 and u_3 such that their product is maximum.

This D.P. problem can be regarded as a three-stage problem with sate variables x_1, x_2, x_3 and returns $f_1(x_1)$, $f_2(x_2)$ and $f_3(x_3)$ respectively.

At stage 3, $x_3 = u_1 + u_2 + u_3$,

at stage 2, $x_2 = x_3 - u_3 = u_1 + u_2$,

at stage 1, $x_1 = x_2 - u_2 = u_1$.

$$\therefore \quad f_1(x_1) = u_1 = x_2 - u_2,$$

$$f_2(x_2) = \max \{u_2(x_2 - u_2)\}, \; 0 \leq u_2 \leq x_2,$$

$$= \max \{u_2 x_2 - u_2^2\}, \; 0 \leq u_2 \leq x_2.$$

Differentiating w.r.t. u_2, and equating the differential to zero,

$$\frac{\partial f_2(x_2)}{\partial u_2} = x_2 - 2u_2 = 0 \quad \text{or} \quad u_2 = \frac{x_2}{2}.$$

$$\therefore \quad f_2(x_2) = \frac{x_2}{2}\left(x_2 - \frac{x_2}{2}\right) = \frac{x_2^2}{4}.$$

Now $$f_3(x_3) = \max_{u_3}\left\{u_3.\frac{x_2^2}{4}\right\} = \max_{u_3}\left\{u_3.\frac{(x_3-u_3)^2}{4}\right\}.$$

Differentiating w.r.t. u_3 and equating to zero,

$$\frac{\partial}{\partial u_3}\left[\frac{(u_3x_3^2 + u_3^3 - 2u_3^2x_3)}{4}\right] = 0$$

$$\begin{aligned}
\text{or} \quad & x_3^2 + 3u_3^2 - 4u_3x_3 = 0 \\
\text{or} \quad & x_3^2 - 3u_3x_3 + 3u_3^2 - u_3x_3 = 0 \\
\text{or} \quad & x_3(x_3 - 3u_3) - u_3(x_3 - 3u_3) = 0 \\
\text{or} \quad & (x_3 - u_3)(x_3 - 3u_3) = 0.
\end{aligned}$$

$\therefore$ Either $u_3 = x_3$ which is trivial since

$$x_3 = u_1 + u_2 + u_3;$$

$$\text{or} \quad u_3 = \frac{x_3}{3} = \frac{10}{3}.$$

$$\therefore \quad x_2 = 10 - \frac{10}{3} = \frac{20}{3},$$

and $u_2 = \frac{x_2}{2} = \frac{10}{3}$ and hence $u_1 = \frac{10}{3}$.

$$\therefore \quad u_1 = u_2 = u_3 = \frac{10}{3},$$

and maximum product $= u_1 \cdot u_2 \cdot u_3 = \frac{1{,}000}{27}$.

EXAMPLE 7.5-2

Let us consider the general case of dividing Q into n parts $u_1, u_2, ..., u_n$ so as to maximize $\prod_{i=1}^{n} u_i$, $u_i \geq 0$.

[*J.N.T.U. Hyderabad B.Tech. Nov., 2010*]

Solution

Using the recursive equations (7.6) and (7.7),

$$f_1(x_1) = \max_{u_1}\{u_1\},$$

$$f_i(x_i) = \max_{0 \le u_i \le x_i}\{u_i f_{i-1}(x_i - u_i)\}$$

For i = 1, $f_1(x_1) = x_1$ which means $u_1^* = x_1$.

For i = 2, $f_2(x_2) = \max_{0 \le u_2 \le x_2}\{u_2 . f_1(x_2 - u_2)\}$

$$= \max \{u_2 \cdot f_1(x_2 - u_2)\},$$

$$= \{u_2 \cdot (x_2 - u_2)\}, \quad \text{since } f_1\,(x_2 - u_2) = x_2 - u_2.$$

Differentiating w.r.t. u_2 and equating to zero,

$$\frac{\partial}{\partial u_2}(u_2 x_2 - u_2^2) = 0$$

or $$x_2 - 2u_2 = 0 \quad \text{or} \quad u_2{}^* = \frac{x_2}{2}$$

$$\therefore \quad f_2\,(x_2) = \frac{x_2}{2}\left(x_2 - \frac{x_2}{2}\right) = \left(\frac{x_2}{2}\right)^2.$$

It can be shown that the second derivative is negative, which is a sufficient condition for maxima.

Since $$x_2 = u_1 + u_2,$$

$$u_1 = x_2 - u_2 = x_2 - \frac{x_2}{2} = \frac{x_2}{2}.$$

Thus for a two-stage problem,

$$u_1 = u_2 = \frac{x_2}{2}.$$

For i = 3, $$f_3\,(x_3) = \max_{u_3} \{u_3 \,.\, f_2\,(x_3 - u_3)\}$$

$$= \max\left\{u_3 \cdot \left(\frac{x_3 - u_3}{2}\right)^2\right\}, \text{since } f_2\,(x_2) = \left(\frac{x_2}{2}\right)^2.$$

Differentiating w.r.t. u_3, and equating to zero,

$$\frac{\partial}{\partial u_3}\left[\frac{(u_3 x_3^2 + u_3^3 - 2u_3^2 x_3)}{4}\right] = 0$$

or $$x_3{}^2 + 3u_3{}^2 - 4u_3 x_3 = 0,$$

which gives either $u_3 = x_3$ or $u_3 = \dfrac{x_3}{3}$.

Since only $u_3 = \dfrac{x_3}{3}$ satisfies the sufficiency condition for a maxima,

(also $u_3 \neq x_3$ since $u_1 + u_2 + u_3 = x_3$)

$$f_3\,(x_3) = \frac{x_3}{3}\frac{\left(x_3 - \frac{x_3}{3}\right)^2}{4} = \left(\frac{x_3}{3}\right)^3.$$

$$\therefore \quad u_3{}^* = \frac{x_3}{3}.$$

Since $$x_3 = u_1 + u_2 + u_3,$$

$$x_2 = u_1 + u_2 = x_3 - u_3 = x_3 - \frac{x_3}{3} = \frac{2}{3}x_3.$$

But $$u_1 = u_2 = \frac{x_2}{2} = \frac{x_3}{3}.$$

$\therefore$ For a three-stage problem, $u_1 = u_2 = u_3 = \dfrac{x_3}{3}$ with $f_3\,(x_3) = \left(\dfrac{x_3}{3}\right)^3.$

For an n-stage problem,

$u_1 = u_2 = u_3 \ldots = u_n = \dfrac{x_n}{n}$ with $f_n(x_n) = \left(\dfrac{x_n}{n}\right)^n$.

But $\quad x_n = Q.$

$$\therefore \quad u_1 = u_2 = u_3 = \ldots = u_n = \frac{Q}{n}, \text{ and } f_n(Q) = \left(\frac{Q}{n}\right)^n.$$

Remark : Since $f_n(Q) = \left(\dfrac{Q}{n}\right)^n = \left(\dfrac{\sum_{i=1}^{n} u_i}{n}\right)^n$,

and
$$f_n(Q) = \max \{u_1 . u_2 . u_3 \ldots u_n\}$$
$$= \max_{u_i} \left[\prod_{i=1}^{n} u_i\right] \geq \prod_{i=1}^{n} u_i,$$
$$\frac{\sum_{i=1}^{n} u_i}{n} \geq \left(\prod_{i=1}^{n} u_i\right)^{1/n}.$$

$\therefore$ Arithmetic mean $\geq$ Geometric mean.

This inequality is known as Cauchy's geometric-arithmetic mean inequality, which states that arithmetic mean of 'n' numbers is always greater than their geometric mean except when all the numbers are equal.

EXAMPLE 7.5-3

$$\textit{Minimize } Z = y_1^2 + y_2^2 + y_3^2,$$
$$\textit{subject to} \quad y_1 + y_2 + y_3 \geq 15,$$
$$y_1, y_2, y_3 \geq 0.$$

[*J.N.T.U. Hyderabad B.Tech. April, 2011; P.T.U. MBA May, 2002*]

Solution

Let the state variables be x_1, x_2 and x_3 such that,

$$x_3 = y_1 + y_2 + y_3,$$
$$x_2 = x_3 - y_3 = y_1 + y_2, \text{ and}$$
$$x_1 = x_2 - y_2 = y_1.$$

The recursive equations are

$$f_3(x_3) = \min_{y_3} \{y_3^2 + f_2(x_2)\},$$
$$f_2(x_2) = \min_{y_2} \{y_2^2 + f_1(x_1)\}, \text{ and}$$
$$f_1^*(x_1) = \min_{y_1} \{y_1^2\} = y_1^2.$$

Since $x_1 = x_2 - y_2$ and $f_1(x_1) = y_1^2$,

$$f_2(x_2) = \min_{y_2} \{y_2^2 + (x_2 - y_2)^2\}.$$

Differentiating $\{y_2^2 + (x_2 - y_2)^2\}$ w.r.t. y_2 and equating to zero,

$$2y_2 + 2(x_2 - y_2)(-1) = 0$$

$$\text{or} \quad -2x_2 + 4y_2 = 0$$

$$\text{or} \quad y_2 = \frac{x_2}{2}.$$

$$\therefore \quad f_2^*(x_2) = \left(\frac{x_2}{2}\right)^2 + \left(x_2 - \frac{x_2}{2}\right)^2 = \frac{x_2^2}{2}.$$

$$\text{Now} \quad f_3(x_3) = \min_{y_3}\left\{y_3^2 + f_2(x_2)\right\}.$$

$$\text{Since} \quad x_2 = x_3 - y_3 \quad \text{and} \quad f_2(x_2) = \frac{x_2^2}{2},$$

$$f_3(x_3) = \min_{y_3}\left\{y_3^2 + \frac{(x_3 - y_3)^2}{2}\right\}.$$

Differentiating $\left\{y_3^2 + \dfrac{(x_3 - y_3)^2}{2}\right\}$ w.r.t. y_3 and equating to zero,

$$2y_3 - (x_3 - y_3) = 0$$

$$\text{or} \quad y_3 = \frac{x_3}{3}.$$

$$\therefore \quad f_3^*(x_3) = \left(\frac{x_3}{3}\right)^2 + \frac{\left(x_3 - \dfrac{x_3}{3}\right)^2}{2} = \frac{x_3^2}{3}.$$

Since $x_3 = y_1 + y_2 + y_3 \geq 15$, for minimization of $f_3(x_3)$, $y_1 + y_2 + y_3 = 15$ or $x_3 = 15$.

$$\therefore \quad f_3^*(x_3) = \frac{(15)^2}{3} = 75,$$

$$\text{and} \quad y_3 = \frac{x_3}{3} = 5,$$

$$y_2 = \frac{x_2}{2} = \frac{x_3 - y_3}{2} = \frac{15 - 5}{2} = 5,$$

$$y_1 = x_2 - y_2 = 10 - 5 = 5.$$

Thus minimum value of $y_1^2 + y_2^2 + y_3^2 = 75$ with $y_1 = y_2 = y_3 = 5$.

EXAMPLE 7.5-4

Minimize $y_1^2 + y_2^2 + y_3^2$,
subject to $y_1 + y_2 + y_3 = 10$,

when (a) y_1, y_2, y_3 are non-negative,
(b) y_1, y_2, y_3 are non-negative integers.

Solution

(*a*) When y_1, y_2, y_3 are continuous non-negative variables, the solution can be obtained in the same way as in example 7.5-3.

$$\text{Minimum value of } y_1^2 + y_2^2 + y_3^2 = \frac{(10)^2}{3} = \frac{100}{3},$$

$$\text{with} \quad y_1 = y_2 = y_3 = \frac{10}{3}.$$

(*b*) When the variables y_1, y_2 and y_3 are non-negative integers, the problem can conveniently be solved by the tabular or enumeration method, treating it as a three-stage problem.

At stage 1, the state variable x_1 can take any integer value from 0 to 10, with return,

$$f_1(x_1) = \underset{0 \le y_1 \le 10}{\text{minimum}} \{y_1^2\} = y_1^2.$$

At stage 2,

$$f_2(x_2) = \underset{0 \le y_2 \le 10}{\text{minimum}} \{y_2^2 + f_1^*(x_2 - y_2)^2\}.$$

The computations for 2nd stage are shown below, where the minimum $f_2(x_2)$ values are identified by asterisks.

y_2	y_2^2 \ y_1	0	1	2	3	4	5	6	7	8	9	10
	y_1^2	0	1	4	9	16	25	36	49	64	81	100
0	0	0*	1*	4	9	16	25	36	49	64	81	100
1	1	1*	2*	5*	10	17	26	37	50	65	82	
2	4	4	5*	8*	13*	20	29	40	53	68		
3	9	9	10	13*	18*	25*	34	45	58			
4	16	16	17	20	25*	32*	41*	52				
5	25	25	26	29	34	41*	50*					
6	36	36	37	40	45	52						
7	49	49	50	53	58							
8	64	64	65	68								
9	81	81	82									
10	100	100										

The optimal values of $f_2(x_2)$ are

y_2	0	1	2	3	4	5	6	7	8	9	10
$f_2^*(x_2)$	0	1	2	5	8	13	18	25	32	41	50

At stage 3,

$$f_3(x_3) = \min \{y_3^2 + f_2^*(x_2)\}$$
$$= \min \{y_3^2 + f_2^*(x_3 - y_3)^2\}$$

y_3	0	1	2	3	4	5	6	7	8	9	10
$x_3 - y_3$	10	9	8	7	6	5	4	3	2	1	0
y_3^2	0	1	4	9	16	25	36	49	64	81	100
$f_2^*(x_3 - y_3)^2$	50	41	32	25	18	13	8	5	2	1	0
$f_3(x_3)$	50	42	36	34*	34*	38	44	54	66	82	100

$$f_3^*(x_3) = 34 \quad \text{for} \quad y_3^* = 3 \text{ or } 4.$$

For $y_3^* = 3, f_2^*(x_2) = 25$, for which $y_1 = 3$ and $y_2 = 4$

or $y_1 = 4$ and $y_2 = 3$.

For $y_3^* = 4, f_2^*(x_2) = 18$, for which $y_1 = 3, y_2 = 3$.

Thus minimum value of 34 corresponds to

$(y_1, y_2, y_3) = (3, 3, 4), (3, 4, 3), (4, 3, 3)$.

EXAMPLE 7.5-5

Using Bellman's principle of optimality,

minimize $Z = y_1 + y_2 + y_3 + ... + y_n$,

subject to $y_1 . y_2 . y_3 ... y_n = b$,

$y_i \ge 0 \; ; \; i = 1, 2, ..., n.$

[*Bharathiar U. Coimbatore B.Sc. April, 2011*]

Solution

This problem comprises of factorising a constant b into n factors, such that the sum of the factors is minimum. It can be treated as an n-stage dynamic programming problem.

Let $f_n(b)$ be the minimum attainable value of $\sum_{i=1}^{n} y_i$, when $y_1, y_2, ..., y_n$ are factors of b.

Considering the problem as single-stage, *i.e.*, $n = 1$,

$$f_1(b) = b$$

or
$$f_1(b) = \min_{y_1 = b}\{y_1\}.$$

Considering the problem as two-stage, *i.e.*, $n = 2$ and factorising b into two factors y_1 and y_2,

$$y_1 \cdot y_2 = b.$$

If
$$y_2 = x, \quad y_1 = \frac{b}{x}$$

and
$$f_2(b) = \min\{y_1 + y_2\} = \min\{y_2 + y_1\}$$
$$= \min_{0 \le x \le b}\left\{x + \frac{b}{x}\right\}$$

or
$$f_2(b) = \min_{0 \le x \le b}\left\{x + f_1^*\left(\frac{b}{x}\right)\right\}, \text{ since } f_1\left(\frac{b}{x}\right) = \frac{b}{x}.$$

Next consider $n = 3$ with $y_1 \cdot y_2 \cdot y_3 = b$.

If
$$y_3 = x, \quad y_1 \cdot y_2 = \frac{b}{x} \text{ and}$$
$$f_3(b) = \min\{y_1 + y_2 + y_3\} = \min\{y_3 + y_1 + y_2\}$$
$$= \min\left\{x + f_2^*\left(\frac{b}{x}\right)\right\}.$$

In the general form, for an i-stage problem,

$$f_i(b) = \min\left\{x + f_{i-1}^*\left(\frac{b}{x}\right)\right\},$$

where
$$y_i = x \text{ and } y_1 \cdot y_2 \cdot y_3 \ldots y_{i-1} = \frac{b}{x}.$$

Now the optimal policy can be determined.

$$f_1^*(b) = b, \quad f_2(b) = \min\left\{x + f_1^*\left(\frac{b}{x}\right)\right\}$$
$$= \min_{0 \le x \le b}\left\{x + \frac{b}{x}\right\}, \quad \text{since } f_1^*(b) = b.$$

Differentiating $\left\{x + \frac{b}{x}\right\}$ w.r.t. x and equating to zero,

$$1 - \frac{b}{x^2} = 0 \quad \text{or} \quad x = b^{1/2}.$$

$$\therefore \quad f_2^*(b) = b^{1/2} + \frac{b}{b^{1/2}} = 2\,b^{1/2}.$$

Now
$$f_3(b) = \min_{0\le x\le b}\left\{x + f_2^*\left(\frac{b}{x}\right)\right\}$$
$$= \min_{0\le x\le b}\left\{x + 2\left(\frac{b}{x}\right)^{\frac{1}{2}}\right\}, \quad \text{since } f_2^*(b) = 2b^{1/2}.$$

Differentiating $x + 2\left(\frac{b}{x}\right)^{\frac{1}{2}}$ w.r.t. x and equating to zero,
$$1 - b^{\frac{1}{2}}x^{\frac{-3}{2}} = 0 \quad \text{or} \quad x = b^{\frac{1}{3}}.$$

$$\therefore \quad f_3^*(b) = b^{\frac{1}{3}} + 2\left(\frac{b}{b^{\frac{1}{3}}}\right)^{\frac{1}{2}} = 3b^{\frac{1}{3}} \text{ and so on.}$$

For n-stage problem,
$$f_n^*(b) = nb^{\frac{1}{n}} \quad \text{and} \quad x = b^{\frac{1}{n}}.$$

Hence the optimal solution is
$$y_1 = y_2 = y_3 = \ldots = y_n = b^{\frac{1}{n}},$$
and
$$f_n^*(b) = nb^{\frac{1}{n}}.$$

EXAMPLE 7.5-6

Solve the following problem :
$$\text{Minimize } Z = \sum_{i=1}^{n} y_i^2,$$
$$\text{subject to} \quad \prod_{i=1}^{n} y_i = b,$$
$$y_i \ge 0;\ i = 1, 2, \ldots, n.$$

[P.U.B.E. (T.I.T.) Nov., 2006]

Solution. This problem can be treated as n-stage dynamic programming problem. Let $f_n(b)$ be the minimum attainable value of Z, when b is factorised into n parts.

For n = 1, $y_1 = b$,

and hence
$$f_1^*(b) = \min_{y_1 = b}\left[y_1^2\right] = b^2.$$

For n = 2, $y_1 y_2 = b$.

Let $y_2 = x$, $y_1 = b/x$.

Then
$$f_2(b) = \min\,[y_1^2 + y_2^2] = \min\,[y_2^2 + y_1^2]$$
$$= \min_{0\le x\le b}\left[x^2 + \left(\frac{b}{x}\right)^2\right]$$

or
$$f_2^*(b) = \min_{0\le x\le b}\left[x^2 + f_1^*\left(\frac{b}{x}\right)\right], \quad \text{since } f_1(b) = b^2.$$

For n = 3, $y_1 \cdot y_2 \cdot y_3 = b$.

Let $\quad y_3 = x, \quad y_1 y_2 = \frac{b}{x}.$

Then

$$f_3(b) = \min\,[y_1^2 + y_2^2 + y_3^3] = \min[y_3^2 + y_1^2 + y_2^2]$$

$$= \min_{0 \le x \le b}\left[x^2 + f_2^*\left(\frac{b}{x}\right)\right].$$

Thus for i-stage problem,

$$f_i(b) = \min_{0 \le x \le b}\left[x^2 + f_{i-1}^*\left(\frac{b}{x}\right)\right].$$

The optimal policy can now be determined.

$$f_1^*(b) = b^2,$$

$$f_2(b) = \min_{0 \le x \le b}\left[x^2 + f_1(b)\right]$$

$$= \min_{0 \le x \le b}\left[x^2 + \left(\frac{b}{x}\right)^2\right], \quad \text{since } f_1(b) = b^2.$$

Differentiating $\left\{x^2 + \frac{b^2}{x^2}\right\}$ w.r.t. x and equating to zero,

$$2x - \frac{2b^2}{x^3} = 0 \quad \text{or} \quad x^4 = b^2$$

or

$$x = b^{\frac{1}{2}} \quad \therefore \quad y_1 = y_2 = b^{\frac{1}{2}},$$

and

$$f_2^*(b) = \left(b^{\frac{1}{2}}\right)^2 + \left(\frac{b}{b^{\frac{1}{2}}}\right)^2 = 2\left(b^{\frac{1}{2}}\right)^2.$$

Now,

$$f_3(b) = \min_{0 \le x \le b}\left[x^2 + f_2\left(\frac{b}{x}\right)\right]$$

$$= \min_{0 \le x \le b}\left[x^2 + 2\frac{b}{x}\right], \quad \text{since } f_2(b) = 2b.$$

Differentiating $\left\{x^2 + \frac{2b}{x}\right\}$ w.r.t. x and equating to zero,

$$2x - \frac{2b}{x^2} = 0 \quad \text{or} \quad x = b^{\frac{1}{3}}.$$

$$\therefore \quad y_3 = x = b^{\frac{1}{3}} \quad \text{and} \quad y_1 \cdot y_2 = \frac{b}{x} = b^{\frac{2}{3}}.$$

$$\therefore \quad y_1 = y_2 = b^{\frac{1}{3}} \quad \text{since } y_1 = y_2$$

and

$$f_3^*(b) = \left(b^{\frac{1}{3}}\right)^2 + 2\frac{b}{b^{\frac{1}{3}}} = 3b^{\frac{2}{3}}.$$

Continuing in the same way,

$$f_n^*(b) = nb^{\frac{2}{n}},$$

and $\quad y_1 = y_2 = y_3 = \ldots = y_n = b^{\frac{1}{n}}.$

EXAMPLE 7.5-7

Solve the following problem :

$$\text{Maximize } Z = u_1^2 + u_2^2 + u_3^2,$$
$$\text{subject to} \quad u_1 \cdot u_2 \cdot u_3 = 6,$$
$$u_1, u_2, u_3 \text{ all positive integers.}$$

Solution

It can be treated as a three-stage problem.

Let

$$x_3 = u_1 \cdot u_2 \cdot u_3 = 6,$$

$$x_2 = u_1 \cdot u_2 = \frac{6}{u_3}, \text{ and}$$

$$x_1 = u_1 = \frac{x_2}{u_2}.$$

Stage 1: $x_1 = u_1$, where u_1 can vary from 1 to 6.

$$\therefore \quad f_1(x_1) = \max_{0 \le x \le 6} \{x_1^2\} = \max_{0 \le u_1 \le 6} \{u_1^2\} \quad \text{with } u_1 \text{ integer.}$$

u_1	:	1	2	3	4	5	6
$f_1^*(x_1)$	:	1	4	9	16	25	36

Stage 2:

$$x_2 = u_1 u_2 = 6 \text{ with } u_1, u_2 \text{ integers.}$$
$$u_1 = 1 \quad 2 \quad 3 \quad 4 \quad 5 \quad 6$$
$$u_2 = \frac{6}{u_1} = 6 \quad 3 \quad 2 \quad - \quad - \quad 1$$

$$\therefore \quad f_2(x_2) = \max\,[u_2^2 + f_1^*(x_1)] = \max\left[u_2^2 + \left(\frac{x_2}{u_2}\right)^2\right].$$

u_2	u_2^2 \ u_1 / $f_1(x_1)$	1 / 1	2 / 4	3 / 9	6 / 36
1	1	2*	5*	10*	37*
2	4	5*	8	13	
3	9	10*	13		
6	36	37*			

$\therefore$ The optimal values of $f_2(x_2)$ are

x_2	:	1	2	3	6
$f_2^*(x_2)$	:	2	5	10	37

Stage 3:

$$x_3 = u_1 u_2 u_3 = 6,$$

$$u_3 = \frac{6}{u_1 u_2} = \frac{6}{x_2}.$$

$$\therefore \quad f_3(x_3) = \max\left[u_3^2 + \left(\frac{6}{x_2}\right)^2\right] = \max\,[u_3^2 + f_2^*(x_2)].$$

u_3	x_2 / $f_2^*(x_2)$ / u_3^2	1 / 2	2 / 5	3 / 10	6 / 37
1	1	3*	6*	11*	38*
2	4	6	9	14	
3	9	11	14		
6	36	38*			

∴ The optimal values of $f_3(x_3)$ are

x_3 :	1	2	3	6
$f_3^*(x_3)$:	3	6	11	38

For $x_3 = 6$, optimal Z = 38 with $u_3 = 1$ or 6.

Proceeding backwards, following sets of values for u_1, u_2, u_3 can be traced:
$(u_1, u_2, u_3) = (1, 6, 1); (1, 1, 6); (6, 1, 1)$.

EXAMPLE 7.5-8

Use dynamic programming to show that $\sum_{i=1}^{n} p_i \log p_i$ *subject to the constraint* $\sum_{i=1}^{n} p_i = 1$, $p_i \geq 0$ *for all i is minimum when* $p_1 = p_2 = ... = p_n = \frac{1}{n}$.

[*IAS, 1983; Delhi M.Sc. (Math.) 1968, 76; Meerut M.Sc. (Math.) 1985*]

Solution

This problem can be treated as an *n*-stage dynamic programming problem.

Let $f_n(1)$ be the minimum attainable value of $\Sigma\, p_i \log p_i$.

When n = 1, $p_1 = 1$.

$$\therefore \quad f_1^*(1) = \min [p_1 \log p_1] = 1 \log 1.$$

When n = 2, $p_1 + p_2 = 1$.

$$\therefore \quad f_2(1) = \min [p_1 \log p_1 + p_2 \log p_2] = \min [p_2 \log p_2 + p_1 \log p_1].$$

If $\quad p_2 = z, p_1 = 1 - z$.

$$\therefore \quad f_2(1) = \min_{0 \leq z \leq 1} [z \log z + (1-z) \log (1-z)]$$

$$= \min_{0 \leq z \leq 1} [z \log z + f_1(1-z)],$$

since $\quad f_1(1-z) = (1-z) \log (1-z)$.

By simple calculus, it can be shown that the function $f(z) = z \log z + (1-z) \log (1-z)$ is minimum for $z = 1/2$. Thus for a two-stage problem,

$$p_1 = p_2 = \frac{1}{2},$$

and $$f_2^*(1) = \frac{1}{2} \log \frac{1}{2} + \frac{1}{2} \log \frac{1}{2} = 2\left(\frac{1}{2} \log \frac{1}{2}\right).$$

Next, when n = 3, $p_1 + p_2 + p_3 = 1$.

If $\quad p_3 = z, p_1 + p_2 = 1 - z$.

$$f_3(1) = \min [p_3 \log p_3 + p_2 \log p_2 + p_1 \log p_1]$$

$$= \min_{0 \leq z \leq 1} [z \log z + f_2(1-z)].$$

Since $$f_2(1) = 2\left(\frac{1}{2}\log\frac{1}{2}\right),$$

$$f_2(1-z) = 2\frac{1-z}{2}\log\frac{1-z}{2}.$$

$$\therefore \quad f_3(1) = \min_{0\le z\le 1}\left[z\log z + 2\left(\frac{1-z}{2}\right)\log\left(\frac{1-z}{2}\right)\right].$$

Again by differential calculus, it can be shown that

$f(z) = z\log z + 2\left(\frac{1-z}{2}\right)\log\left(\frac{1-z}{2}\right)$ is minimum for $z = \frac{1}{3}$, which gives

$$p_1 = p_2 = p_3 = \frac{1}{3},$$

and $$f_3^*(1) = \frac{1}{3}\log\frac{1}{3} + 2\left(\frac{1}{3}\right)\log\left(\frac{1}{3}\right) = 3\left(\frac{1}{3}\log\frac{1}{3}\right).$$

For n-stage problem, the result can be generalised as

$$p_1 = p_2 = \ldots = p_n = \frac{1}{n},$$

and $$f_n^*(1) = n\left(\frac{1}{n}\log\frac{1}{n}\right).$$

EXAMPLE 7.5-9

$$\textit{Maximize } Z = \sum_{i=1}^{n} b_i x_i,$$

$$\textit{subject to } \sum_{i=1}^{n} x_i = c\,;\; x_i \ge 0,\; i = 1, 2, \ldots, n.$$

[Delhi M.Sc. (Math.) 1966; Meerut M.Sc. (Math.) 1974]

Solution

Let $f_n(c)$ be the return function.

For n = 1, i.e., a single stage,

$$x_1 = c.$$

$$\therefore \quad f_1^*(c) = \max_{x_1=c}[b_1 x_1] = b_1 c.$$

For n = 2, $x_1 + x_2 = c.$

$$\therefore \quad f_2(c) = \max[b_1x_1 + b_2x_2].$$

Let $x_2 = z$ and $x_1 = c - z$.

$$\therefore \quad f_2(c) = \max_{0\le z\le c}[b_2 z + b_1(c-z)]$$

$$= \max_{0\le z\le c}[b_2 z + f_1(c-z)], \text{ because } f_1(c) = b_1 c.$$

For n = i, the general recursive equation is

$$f_i(c) = \max_{0\le z\le c}[b_i z + f_i(c-z)].$$

Again, when n = 2,

$$f_2(c) = \max_{0\le z\le c}[b_2 z + b_1(c-z)]$$

$$= \max_{0 \le z \le c} \left[(b_2 - b_1)z + b_1 c)\right].$$

The function $\{(b_2 - b_1) z + b_1 c\}$ will be maximum when z takes its maximum value c and $(b_2 - b_1) > 0$.

$\therefore \quad f_2^* (c) = [(b_2 - b_1) c + b_1 c] = b_2 c,$

and $\quad x_2 = z = c, x_1 = 0.$

When n = 3, $x_1 + x_2 + x_3 = c.$

Taking $\quad x_3 = z, \quad x_1 + x_2 = c - z,$

$$f_3 (c) = \max_{0 \le z \le c} \left[(b_3 z + f_2^*(c - z)\right].$$

$$= \max_{0 \le z \le c} \left[(b_3 z + b_2 (c - z)\right], \quad \text{because} \quad f_2^* (c) = b_2 c$$

$$= \max_{0 \le z \le c} \left[(b_3 - b_2)z + b_2 c)\right].$$

The function $f_3 (c)$ will be maximum when z takes its maximum value of c and $(b_3 - b_2) > 0$, which gives

$f_3^* (c) = b_3 c,$

$x_3 = z = c$ and $x_1 = x_2 = 0.$

Generalising the result for n-stage problem,

$f_n (c) = b_n c,$

$x_n = c, x_1 = x_2 = x_3 = ... = x_{n-1} = 0.$

Thus the optimal policy is

$(x_1, x_2, x_3, ..., x_{n-1}, x_n) = (0, 0, 0, ..., 0, c)$, with $f_n (c) = b_n c$.

7.6 SYSTEM RELIABILITY

EXAMPLE 7.6-1

An electronic device consists of four components, each of which must function for the system to function. The system reliability can be improved by installing parallel units in one or more of the components. The reliability (R) of a component with one, two or three parallel units and the corresponding cost (C) are given in table 7.28. The maximum amount available for this device is 100. The problem is to determine the number of parallel units in each component.

TABLE 7.28

Number of units	*Components*							
	1		*2*		*3*		*4*	
	R	*C*	*R*	*C*	*R*	*C*	*R*	*C*
1	*0.70*	*10*	*0.50*	*20*	*0.70*	*10*	*0.60*	*20*
2	*0.80*	*20*	*0.70*	*40*	*0.90*	*30*	*0.70*	*30*
3	*0.90*	*30*	*0.80*	*50*	*0.95*	*40*	*0.90*	*40*

[P.U.M.E. (Mech.) 1987]

Solution

The reliability of a system is the product of the reliability of its components. If $R_i \, u_i$ is the reliability of component having u_i units in parallel, then the reliability of the system comprising of n components in series is $\prod_{i=1}^{n} R_i . u_i$. The problem, then, becomes

$$\text{maximize } R = \prod_{i=1}^{n} R_i . u_i ,$$

$$\text{subject to} \quad \sum_{i=1}^{n} C_i . u_i \le C ,$$

where $C_i \cdot u_i$ is the cost of components, when it has u_i units in parallel, and C is the total capital available. The problem can be solved by considering the components as stages and the capital allocated as state of the system, x_i. The state x_i ($0 \le x_i \le C$) is the capital allocated to stages 1 through i, inclusive. The reliability of the components of the return function at stage i may be expressed as $f_i(x_i)$.

The recursive equations can be written as

$$f_1(x_1) = \max_{u_i} \{R_i \cdot u_i\}, 0 \le C_1 \cdot u_1 \le x_1 ;$$

$$f_i(x_i) = \max_{u_i} \{R_i \cdot u_i \times f_{i-1}(x_i - C_i \cdot u_i)\}, 0 \le C_i \cdot u_i \le x_i .$$

Since the return functions of different components are multiplied by each other, the procedure is called *multiplicative decomposition.*

In the given example, device will consist of at least one unit in each component.

$\therefore \quad C_{11} \le x_1 \le C - C_{21} - C_{31} - C_{41}$ or $10 \le x_1 \le 50$,

$C_{11} + C_{12} \le x_2 \le C - C_{31} - C_{41}$ or $30 \le x_2 \le 70$,

$C_{11} + C_{12} + C_{13} \le x_3 \le C - C_{41}$ or $40 \le x_3 \le 80$,

$C_{11} + C_{12} + C_{13} + C_{14} \le x_4 \le C$ or $60 \le x_4 \le 100$.

The computations for different stages are given below in the tabular form.

TABLE 7.29

Stage 1

	$f_1(u_1/x_1) = R_1 \cdot u_1$			Optimal solution	
x_i	$u_1 = 1$ R = 0.7, C = 10	$u_1 = 2$ R = 0.8, C = 20	$u_1 = 3$ R = 0.9, C = 30	$f_1(x_1)$	u_1^*
10	.7	—	—	.7	1
20	.7	.8	—	.8	2
30	.7	.8	.9	.9	3
40	.7	.8	.9	.9	3
50	.7	.8	.9	.9	3

Stage 2

	$f_2(u_2/x_2) = R_2 . u_2 \cdot f_1^*(x_2 - C_2 \cdot u_2)$			Optimal solution	
x_i	$u_2 = 1$ R = 0.5,C = 20	$u_2 = 2$ R = 0.7,C = 40	$u_2 = 3$ R = 0.8, C = 50	$f_2(x_2)$	u_2^*
30	.5 × .7	—	—	.35	1
40	.5 × .8	—	—	.40	1
50	.5 × .9	.7 × .7	—	.49	2
60	.5 × .9	.7 × .8	.8 × .7	.56	2,3
70	.5 × .9	.7 × .9	.8 × .8	.64	3

Stage 3

x_i	$f_3(u_3/x_3) = R_3 \cdot u_3 \times f_2^*(x_3 - C_3 \cdot u_3)$			Optimal solution	
	$u_3 = 1$ R = 0.7, C = 10	$u_3 = 2$ R = 0.9, C = 30	$u_3 = 3$ R = 0.95, C = 40	$f_3(x_3)$	u_3^*
40	.7 × .35 = .245	—	—	.245	1
50	.7 × .40 = .280	—	—	.280	1
60	.7 × .49 = .343	.9 × .35 = .315	—	.343	1
70	.7 × .56 = .392	.9 × .40 = .360	.95 × .35 = .3325	.392	1
80	.7 × .64 = .448	.9 × .49 = .441	.95 × .40 = .380	.448	1

Stage 4

x_i	$f_4(u_4/x_4) = R_4 \cdot u_4 \times f_3^*\ (x_4 - C_4 \cdot u_4)$			Optimal solution	
	$u_4 = 1$ R = 0.6, C = 20	$u_4 = 2$ R = 0.7, C = 30	$u_4 = 3$ R = 0.9, C = 40	$f_4(x_4)$	u_4^*
60	.6 × .245 = .147	—	—	.147	1
70	.6 × .280 = .168	.7 × .245 = .1715	—	.1715	2
80	.6 × .343 = .2058	.7 × .280 = .196	.9 × .245 = .2205	.2205	3
90	.6 × .392 = .2352	.7 × .343 = .2401	.9 × .280 = .252	.252	1
100	.6 × .448 = .2688	.7 × .392 = .2744	.9 × .343 = .3087	.3087	3

Optimal value of $f_4\ (x_4) = 0.3087$ with $u_4^* = 3$ and $x_4 = 100$, is obtained from $f_3\ (x_3) = 0.343$ which has $u_3^* = 1$ and $f_2\ (x_2) = .49$, which is for $u_2^* = 2$ and then $u_1^* = 1$. Thus the optimal allocation is : 3 units in parallel should be installed on component four, 1 unit on component three, 2 units on component two and 1 unit on component one.

7.7 SOLUTION OF L.P.P. BY DYNAMIC PROGRAMMING

The linear programming problem in the general form is

$$\begin{aligned} \text{maximize} \quad & Z = c_1x_1 + c_2x_2 + \dots + c_nx_n, \\ \text{subject to} \quad & a_{11}x_1 + a_{12}x_2 + \dots + a_{1n}x_n \le b_1, \\ & a_{21}x_1 + a_{22}x_2 + \dots + a_{2n}x_n \le b_2, \\ & \vdots \qquad\qquad\qquad\qquad\qquad \vdots \\ & a_{m1}x_1 + a_{m2}x_2 + \dots + a_{mn}x_n \le b_m, \\ & x_1, x_2, \dots, x_n \ge 0. \end{aligned}$$

This problem involving m resources and n decision variables can be formulated as a dynamic programming problem as follows :

Each activity j ($j = 1, 2, \dots, n$) is considered a stage. Then the problem can be regarded as n-stage problem and decision variables (alternatives) are the levels of activities x_j (≥ 0) at stage j. Since x_j is continuous, each activity has infinite number of alternatives (values of x_j) within the feasible space.

Allocation problems are a particular type of L.P. problems that require allocation of available resources to the activities. The constants $b_1, b_2, \dots, b_m$ are the amounts of the available resources. The state of the system at any stage is given by the amount allocated at that stage and left for the remaining stages. The state would be thus an m-dimensional vector $(b_1, b_2, \dots, b_m)$.

Let $f_n\ (b_1, b_2, \dots, b_m)$ be the optimal value of the objective function defined above for stages $x_1, x_2, \dots, x_n$ for states $b_1, b_2, \dots, b_m$. Using forward computational procedure, the recursive equation can be written as

$$f_j\ (b_1, b_2, \dots, b_m) = \max_{0 \le x_j \le b} \left[c_jx_j + f_{j-1}\ (b_1 - a_{1j}x_j, b_2 - a_{2j}x_j, \dots, b_m - a_{mj}x_j) \right].$$

The maximum value of b that x_j can assume is

$$b = \min\left[\frac{b_1}{a_{1j}}, \frac{b_2}{a_{2j}}, \ldots, \frac{b_m}{a_{mj}}\right].$$

EXAMPLE 7.7-1

Use dynamic programming to solve the following L.P.P. :

$$\begin{aligned} \text{Maximize } Z &= 3x_1 + 5x_2, \\ \text{subject to } \quad & x_1 \leq 4, \\ & x_2 \leq 6, \\ & 3x_1 + 2x_2 \leq 18, \\ & x_1, x_2 \geq 0. \end{aligned}$$

[*J.N.T.U. Hyderbad B.Tech. Nov., 2010*]

Solution

There are two variables and hence the problem can be treated as a two-stage dynamic programming problem. Both x_1 and x_2 being continuous, represent the infinite number of alternatives within the feasible space. The three constraints can be regarded as three resources, say b_1, b_2 and b_3 which are to be allocated to x_1 and x_2 at different stages. The state of the system at a stage would be given by the amount of resources allocated at that stage and left for the remaining stages. Therefore, the states of the equivalent D.P. problem are $b_1 = 4$, $b_2 = 6$ and $b_3 = 18$.

Stage 1

The optimal value of f_1 (b_1, b_2, b_3) at stage 1 is given by

$$f_1(b_1, b_2, b_3) = \max_{0 \leq x_1 \leq b} [3x_1],$$

where $b_1 = 4$, $b_2 = 6$, $b_3 = 18$.

The feasible value of x_1 is non-negative and satisfies all the three constraints.

But the maximum value of b that x_1 can assume is $= \min\left(\frac{4}{1}, \frac{6}{0}, \frac{18}{3}\right) = 4.$

$$\therefore \quad f_1(4, 6, 18) = \max_{0 \leq x_1 \leq 4} [3x_1] = 3\min\left[4, \frac{18 - 2x_2}{3}\right],$$

$$\text{where} \quad x_1^0 = \min\left[4, \frac{18 - 2x_2}{3}\right] = 4.$$

Stage 2

The recursive equation for optimization of this two-stage problem is

$$\begin{aligned} f_2(4, 6, 18) &= \max_{0 \leq x_2 \leq b} [5x_2 + 3x_1] \\ &= \max_{0 \leq x_2 \leq b} \left[5x_2 + 3\min\left(4, \frac{18 - 2x_2}{3}\right)\right]. \end{aligned}$$

But the maximum value of b that x_2 can assume is $\min\left(\frac{4}{0}, \frac{6}{1}, \frac{18}{2}\right) = 6.$

$$\therefore \quad f_2(4, 6, 18) = \max_{0 \leq x_2 \leq 6} \left[5x_2 + 3\min\left(4, \frac{18 - 2x_2}{3}\right)\right].$$

$$\text{Now}\quad \min\left(4, \frac{18-2x_2}{3}\right) = \begin{cases} 4 & \text{, if } 0 \le x_2 \le 3, \\ \dfrac{18-2x_2}{3} & \text{, if } 3 < x_2 \le 6. \end{cases}$$

$$\therefore\quad 5x_2 + 3\min\left(4, \frac{18-2x_2}{3}\right) = \begin{cases} 5x_2 + 12 & \text{, if } 0 \le x_2 \le 3, \\ 3x_2 + 18 & \text{, if } 3 < x_2 \le 6. \end{cases}$$

$$\therefore\quad f_2(4, 6, 18) = \max \begin{bmatrix} 27 & \text{, at } x_2 = 3, \\ 36 & \text{, at } x_2 = 6, \end{bmatrix}$$

$$= 36.$$

$$\therefore x_2^* = 6,\quad Z_{max} = 36 \text{ and } x_1^* = \min\left[4, \frac{18-2x_2}{3}\right] = \min\left[4, \frac{18-12}{3}\right] = 2.$$

EXAMPLE 7.7-2

Solve the following L.P.P. by the method of dynamic programming:

$$\textit{Maximize } Z = 2x_1 + 5x_2,$$
$$\textit{subject to}\quad 2x_1 + x_2 \le 430,$$
$$2x_2 \le 460,$$
$$x_1, x_2 \ge 0.$$

[J.N.T.U. Hyderabad B.Tech. Nov., 2010; P.U.B.E (T. and I.T.) Nov., 2004]

Solution

The problem involves two decision variables and two resources b_1 and b_2. Therefore, the states of the equivalent D.P. problem are $b_1 = 430$, $b_2 = 460$.

Stage 1

$$f_1(b_1, b_2) = \max_{0 \le x_1 \le b} [2x_1].$$

The maximum value of b that x_1 can assume is $= \min\left(\dfrac{430}{2}, \dfrac{460}{0}\right)$

$$= \min(215, \infty) = 215.$$

$$\therefore\quad f_1(430, 460) = \max_{0 \le x_1 \le 215} [2x_1] = 2\min\left[\frac{430-x_2}{2}, \infty\right]$$

and $\quad x_1^0 = 215.$

Stage 2

The recursive equation is

$$f_2(b_1, b_2) = \max_{0 \le x_2 \le b} [5x_2 + 2z_1]$$

$$\text{or}\quad f_2(430, 460) = \max_{0 \le x_2 \le b}\left[5x_2 + 2\min\left(\frac{430-x_2}{2}, \infty\right)\right].$$

But the maximum value of b that x_2 can assume is $\min\left(\dfrac{430}{1}, \dfrac{460}{2}\right) = 230.$

$$\therefore\quad f_2(430, 460) = \max_{0 \le x_2 \le 230}\left[5x_2 + 2\min\left(\frac{430-x_2}{2}, \infty\right)\right].$$

$$\text{Now}\quad \min\left(\frac{430-x_2}{2}, \infty\right) = \frac{430-x_2}{2} = 100,\quad 0 \le x_2 \le 230.$$

$$\therefore\ 5x_2 + 2\min\left(\frac{430-x_2}{2}, \infty\right) = 5x_2 + 200,\quad 0 \le x_2 \le 230.$$

$$\therefore \quad f_2(430, 460) = 5x_2 + 200 = 5 \times 230 + 200 = 1{,}150 + 200 = 1{,}350.$$

$$\therefore \quad x_2^* = 230, Z_{\max} = 1{,}350 \text{ and } x_1^* = \frac{430 - 230}{2} = 100.$$

EXAMPLE 7.7-3

Solve the following L.P.P. by dynamic programming :

$$\text{Maximize } Z = 50x_1 + 100x_2,$$
$$\text{subject to } \quad 10x_1 + 5x_2 \le 2{,}500,$$
$$4x_1 + 10x_2 \le 2{,}000,$$
$$x_1 + \frac{3}{2}x_2 \le 450,$$
$$x_1, x_2 \ge 0.$$

Solution

The problem involves two decision variables and three resources b_1, b_2 and b_3. Therefore, the states of the equivalent D.P. problem are $b_1 = 2{,}500$, $b_2 = 2{,}000$ and $b_3 = 450$.

Stage 1

$$f_1(b_1, b_2, b_3) = \max_{0 \le x_1 \le b} [50x_1],$$

where the maximum is to be taken over $0 \le 10x_1 \le 2{,}500$; $0 \le 4x_1 \le 2{,}000$ and $0 \le x_1 \le 450$.

The maximum value of b that x_1 can assume is $= \min\left(\frac{2{,}500}{10}, \frac{2{,}000}{4}, \frac{450}{1}\right) = 250.$

$$\therefore \quad f_1(2{,}500, 2{,}000, 450) = \max_{0 \le x_1 \le 250} [50x_1]$$

$$= 50 \min\left[\frac{2{,}500 - 5x_2}{10}, \frac{2{,}000 - 10x_2}{4}, \frac{450 - 3/2x_2}{1}\right]$$

and $\quad x_1^0 = 250.$

Stage 2

The recursive equation is

$$f_2(b_1, b_2, b_3) = \max_{0 \le x_2 \le b} [100x_2 + 50x_1]$$

or $\quad f_2(2{,}500, 2{,}000, 450)$

$$= \max_{0 \le x_2 \le b}\left[100x_2 + 50 \cdot \min\left(\frac{2{,}500 - 5x_2}{10}, \frac{2{,}000 - 10x_2}{4}, \frac{450 - 3/2x_2}{1}\right)\right].$$

Now the maximum value of b that x_2 can assume is

$$= \min\left(\frac{2{,}500}{5}, \frac{2{,}000}{10}, \frac{450}{3/2}\right) = \min(500, 200, 300) = 200.$$

$\therefore \; f_2(2{,}500, 2000, 450)$

$$= \max_{0 \le x_2 \le 200}\left[100x_2 + 50 \min\left(\frac{2{,}500 - 5x_2}{10}, \frac{2{,}000 - 10x_2}{4}, \frac{450 - 3/2x_2}{1}\right)\right].$$

$$\text{Now } \min\left[\frac{2{,}500 - 5x_2}{10}, \frac{2{,}000 - 10x_2}{4}, \frac{450 - 3/2x_2}{1}\right] = \begin{cases} \dfrac{2{,}500 - 5x_2}{10}, & \text{if } 0 \le x_2 \le 125, \\ \dfrac{2{,}000 - 10x_2}{4}, & \text{if } 125 < x_2 \le 200. \end{cases}$$

$$\therefore \quad f_2\,(2{,}500, 2{,}000, 450) = \max \begin{cases} 100x_2 + 50 \cdot \dfrac{2{,}500 - 5x_2}{10}, \text{ if } 0 \le x_2 \le 125, \\ 100x_2 + 50 \cdot \dfrac{2{,}000 - 10x_2}{4}, \text{ if } 125 < x_2 \le 200. \end{cases}$$

$$= \max \begin{cases} 75x_2 + 12{,}500 \;; \text{ if } 0 \le x_2 \le 125, \\ 25{,}000 - 25x_2 \;, \text{ if } 125 < x_2 \le 200. \end{cases}$$

$$= \max \begin{cases} 21{,}875 \text{ at } x_2 = 125, \\ 21{,}875 \text{ at } x_2 = 125. \end{cases}$$

$$= 21{,}875.$$

$$\therefore \quad Z_{max} = 21{,}875;\ x_2^* = 125,\ x_1^* = \min\left[\frac{2{,}500 - 5x_2^*}{10}, \frac{2{,}000 - 10x_2^*}{4}, \frac{450 - 3/2x_2^*}{1}\right]$$

$$\text{or} \quad x_1^* = \min\left[\frac{2{,}500 - 5 \times 125}{10}, \frac{2{,}000 - 10 \times 125}{4}, 450 - \frac{3}{2} \times 125\right]$$

$$= \min\ [187.5, 187.5, 262.5]$$

$$= 187.5.$$

7.8 APPLICATIONS OF DYNAMIC PROGRAMMING

We have discussed some over-simplified examples from the various fields of applications of dynamic programming. Many more applications are found for this decision-making technique. Whereas the linear programming has found its applications in large-scale complex situations, dynamic programming has more applications in smaller-scale systems. Following are a few of the large number of fields in which dynamic programming has ben successfully applied:

1. **Production.** In the production area, this technique has been employed for *production, scheduling* and *employment smoothening,* in the face of widely fluctuating demand requirements.

2. **Inventory Control.** This technique has been used to determine the optimum inventory level and for formulating the inventory reordering rules, indicating when to replenish an item and by what amount.

3. **Allocation of Resources.** It has been employed for allocating the scarce resources to different alternative uses, such as allocating salesmen to different sales zones and *capital budgeting procedures.*

4. **Selection of advertising media.** (See example 7.4.10)

5. **Spare part level determination** to guarantee high efficiency utilisation of expensive equipment.

6. **Equipment replacement policies.** To determine at which stage equipment is to be replaced for optimal return from the facilities.

7. Scheduling methods for routine and major overhauls on complex machinery.

8. Systematic plan or search to discover the whereabouts of a valuable resource.

These are only a few of the wide range of situations to which dynamic programming has been successfully applied. Many real operating systems call for thousands of such decisions. The dynamic programming models make it possible to make all these decisions, of course with the help of computers. These decisions individually may not appear to be of much economic benefit, but in aggregate they exert a major influence on the economy of a firm.

7.9 DETERMINISTIC DYNAMIC PROGRAMMING

In deterministic dynamic programming the decisions are under the control of the decision-maker and outcomes of the decisions have values which are fixed and certain. The number of decisions to be made may be finite or infinite. Example 7.4–1 on allocation of nine salesmen to three zones involves revenues which are fixed and known with certainty and hence forms a deterministic D.P. problem. The problem involves three stages and hence 3 decisions. However, in many situations the number of decisions to be taken could be infinite. For instance, the intention of the management of an organisation quite often is to remain in business indefinitely. Likewise, objective of a production manager is to minimize the production costs over indefinite future period.

In such situations, since each decision stage will involve some cost, the cost of all the decision policies will always be unlimited and it is futile to talk of choosng a policy that minimizes the total cost of all the decisions. Two approaches are followed in such cases :

The first approach discounts the costs to be incurred in future. This approach is justified when the decisions to be made are not very frequent, say not more than once or twice a year. Here, the costs incurred in the current year will have more influence on the decisions than the costs incurred next year and so on.

The second approach is used when the decisions are to be made frequently, say once a week or fortnight, so that discounting the costs each week over long indefinite periods will be too long and cumbersome. In such cases a policy that minimizes the average cost per decision rather than the total cost is selected.

7.10 PROBABILISTIC DYNAMIC PROGRAMMING

In probabilistic dynamic programming the outcomes of the decisions are not certain and are associated with probabilities. These situations also may involve finite or infinite number of decisions.

(*i*) *Finite number of decisions* : In such cases *decision tree approach* is used. Decision tree diagram is a graphical representation of various decisions, alternatives and their outcomes in a decision-making problem. In constructing a decision tree there are certain conventions to be followed. The tree is constructed by starting from left and moving towards right. The sqare box ❑ denotes a decision point at which the available strategies are considered. The circle O represents the chance node or event. The various outcomes or states of nature emanate from this chance node. These states of nature are represented by straight lines. Probabilities are associated with these outcomes.

Suppose a company manufacturing toys is to decide whether to introduce the deluxe model or popular model. From market survey, the probabilities of market demand alongwith the associated profit or loss from sales for both the models is known. To analyse the problem and to decide the optimum strategy, the problem can be represented as a decision tree shown in Fig. 7.2. There are two branches at the decision node 1, each branch representing a strategy. Similarly, at each of the two chance nodes A and B, there are three branches representing outcomes.

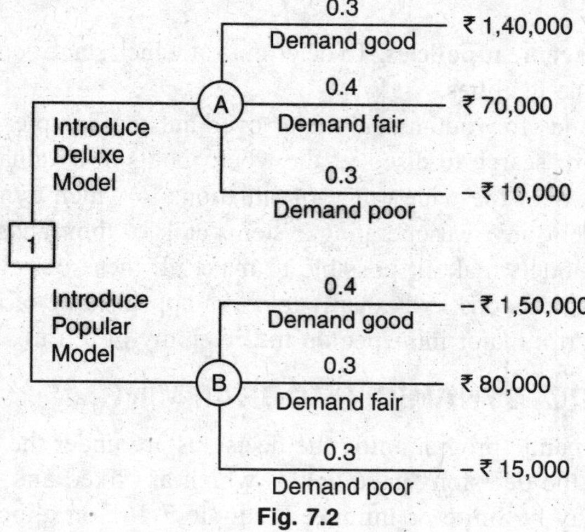

Fig. 7.2

Thus the decision tree shows the structure of the decision problem. To carry out the decision analysis, conditional payoffs are estimated for every combinatioin of actions and events. The payoffs can be either positive or negative. Also probabilities for each event must be assessed by the decision-maker. Analysis of the decision tree is done by following roll back method or backward pass method as shown below.

Expected payoff at chance node A = ₹ [0.3 × 1,40,000 + 0.4 × 70,000 – 0.3 × 10,000]
= ₹ (42,000 + 28,000 – 3,000) = ₹ 67,000.

Expected payoff at chance node B = ₹ [0.4 × 1,50,000 + 0.3 × 80,000 – 0.3 × 15,000]
= ₹ [60,000 + 24,000 – 4,500] = ₹ 79,500.

∴ Expected payoff at decision node 1 = Max ₹ [67,000; 79,500]
= ₹ 79,500.

Therefore, the company should produce the popular model.

(*ii*) *Infinite number of decisions*

There are situations in which the outcomes are probabilistic and the same decision is to be made at regular intervals and this process continues indefinitely *e.g.*, problems involving maintenance, replacement of equipment, etc. The approach in such situations is to maximize the outcome per decision rather than the total outcome over an idefinite period.

EXERCISES

1. What is dynamic programming ? Write step-by-step procedure to solve a general problem by D.P. approach. [*P.T.U. B.Tech. (Mech.) May, 2012; J.N.T.U. Hyderabad B.Tech. (Mech.) May, 2012; P.U. M.B.A., Feb., 2009; M.Sc. (I.T.) 2003*]

2. What is dynamic programming and what sort of problems can be solved by it ? State Bellman's principle of optimality and explain why it holds. [*P.T.U. B.Tech. (Mech.) Dec., 2011; 2008; K.U.M.Sc., 2001*]

3. Discuss dynamic programming application to business and develop the recursive relation used in dynamic programming formulation. [*P.T.U. MBA Dec., 2002*]

4. What is the need of dynamic programming and how is it different from linear programming ? Write some applications of dynamic programming. [*J.N.T.U. Hyderabad B.Tech. (Mech.) May, 2012; P.T.U. B.Com. May, 2011; M.B.A., 2009; P.U.B.E. (T. and I.T.) Nov., 2004*]

5. Write short note on dynamic programming and its applications. [*P.T.U. MBA May, 2006*]

6. Explain the following in the context of dynamic programming :
(*i*) Principle of optimality (*ii*) State (*iii*) Stage. [*Gujarat Tech. U.B.E. Dec., 2012; IGNOU MCA, 2003*]

7. Explain Bellman's principle of optimality. [*J.N.T.U. Hyderabad B.Tech. (Mech.) May, 2012; Bharathiar U. Coimbatore B.Sc. April, 2011; R.T.M. Nagpur U.B.E. (Mech.) 2011; P.T.U.B.E. (Mech.) 2009; May 2006; Nagpur U.B.E. (Mech.) 2003; R.C.C. CHD., 2002; P.T.U.B.E., 2001*]

8. Write short note on characteristics of dynamic programming. [*SVSM, PGDM, 2009; P.T.U. M.Tech. Nov., 2012; B.Tech. (Mech.) Dec., 2006*]

9. What do you understand by forward and backward algorithms ? [*J.N.T.U. Hyderabad B.Tech. Nov., 2011; P.U.B.E. (Prod.) 2001, K.U.M.Sc., 2001*]

10. (*a*) What is dynamic recursive relation ? Describe the general process of backward recursion. [*P.T.U. MBA June, 2003*]

(*b*) Explain briefly deterministic and probabilistic dynamic programming. [*P.T.U. B.Tech. (Mech.) April, 2013; P.U. B.E. (T.I.T.) Nov., 2006*]

11. With the help of an example, describe in detail dynamic programming method for solving the L.P.P. [*P.T.U. MCA, 2010*]

12. Explain the general algorithm for solving a dynamic programming problem. [*Bharathiar U.Coimbatore B.Sc. April, 2011*]

Section 7.4

13. A food processing firm has compiled the following data for future monthly production requirements and production costs in regular and overtime periods.

TABLE 7.30

Month	*Quantity (units)*	*Cost per unit*	
		Regular (₹)	*Overtime* (₹)
September	4,000	20	30
October	5,200	25	35
November	5,000	24	34
December	3,700	26	36
January	4,200	20	30
February	3,000	20	30

The production capacity of the firm is 6,000 units in regular time and 3,000 units in overtime. The cost of carrying storage is ₹ 7.50 unit per month. If at the end of August, there are 3,500 units in stock at a cost of ₹ 25 each, what is optimal production schedule and the total associated cost ? Note that no inventory is required at the end of six months.

14. A drug manufacturing concern has ten medical representatives working in three sales areas. The profitability for each representative in three sales areas is as follows :

TABLE 7.31

No. of representatives		0	1	2	3	4	5	6	7	8	9	10
Profitability (thousands of rupees)	*Area 1*	15	22	30	38	45	48	54	60	65	70	70
	Area 2	26	35	40	46	55	62	70	76	83	90	95
	Area 3	30	38	44	50	60	65	72	80	85	90	85

Determine the optimum allocation of medical representatives in order to maximize the profits.
What will be the optimum allocation if the number of representatives available at present is only six?

(*Ans.* (3, 6, 1), ₹ 2,46,000; (4, 1, 1); ₹ 1, 18,000.)

15. A student of OR has five days at his disposal to revise the subject before examination. The course is divided into four sections. He decides to devote a whole day to the study of some section so that he may study a section for one day, two days, three days, etc., or not at all. The expected grade points he will get for different alternative arrangements are as follows :

TABLE 7.32

Study days	*Course sections*			
	I	*II*	*III*	*IV*
0	1	1	0	0
1	2	1	0	1
2	2	2	1	2
3	3	3	2	2
4	4	3	3	3
5	4	4	3	4

How should he distribute the available days to the different sections of the course so that he maximizes his grade point average ? (*Ans.* 12 ways, max. grade point average = 6.)

16. A company has three media A, B and C available for advertising its product. The data collected over the past years about the relationship between the sales and frequency of advertisement in the different media are as follows :

TABLE 7.33

Frequency/ month	*Estimated sale (units) per month*		
	A	B	C
1	125	180	300
2	225	290	350
3	260	340	450
4	300	370	500

The cost of advertisement is ₹ 5,000 in medium A, ₹ 10,000 in medium B and ₹ 20,000 in medium C. The total budget allocated for advertising the product is ₹ 40,000. Determine the optimal combination of advertising media and frequency. (*Ans.* Once in C, once in B, twice in A.)

17. In an investment project, only 8 units of money are available for allocation in unit amounts to three investment programmes. The return function for each programme is given in table 7.34. The function $g_i(x)$ represents the return from investing x units of money in ith investment programme (i = 1, 2, 3.). What is the optimal investment policy ?

TABLE 7.34

x	0	1	2	3	4	5	6	7	8
$g_1(x)$	0	5	15	40	80	90	95	98	100
$g_2(x)$	0	5	15	40	60	70	73	74	75
$g_3(x)$	0	4	26	40	45	50	51	52	53

(*Ans.* 4 units to programme 1, 4 to programme 2 and none to 3.)

18. A research project has been assigned to three teams, working on three different approaches. An assessment of their work shows that their chances of completing the work within the stipulated period are only 60%, 70% and 80% respectively. Three more scientists are available in the organisation, who can be allocated to the teams to accelerate the work. The estimated probabilities of completing the work when 0, 1, 2, and 3 scientists are added to each team are given in table 7.35. The problem is to determine the allocation of three additional scientists so as to maximize the probabilities of success of all the three teams.

TABLE 7.35

		Teams		
		1	2	3
Number of additional scientists	0	.60	.70	.80
	1	.70	.85	.90
	2	.80	.90	.95
	3	.90	.95	.98

(*Ans.* 2 scientists to team 1, 1 scientist to team 2 and none to team 3; 54.4%.)

19. Find the shortest path from 1 to 12 through the network given in Fig. 7.3.

(*Ans.* 1–3–6–10–12, cost = 12.)

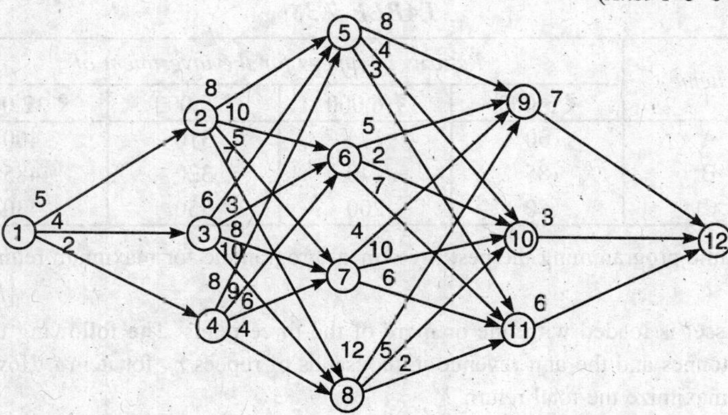

Fig. 7.3

20. In exercise 19 find the longest path connecting 1 and 12.

(*Ans.* 1–3–8–9–12, cost = 33.)

21. Production is to be planned for a four-period horizon. There is no initial inventory and the final inventory is to be zero. No shortages are allowed. Production and inventory costs have the following forms :

TABLE 7.36

Period (t)	*Demand* (D_t)	*Set-up cost* (A_t)	*Unit production cost* (c_t)	*Unit holding cost per period* (h_t)
1	20	₹ 30	₹ 3	₹ 2
2	30	40	3	1
3	40	30	4	1
4	30	50	4	1

(*a*) Formulate the above as a dynamic programming problem *i.e.*, establish the recurrence relation to be used for solving the problem.

(*b*) Obtain the optimal production quantity in each period of the planning horizon. Also compute the total cost of the optimal plan. [*R.C.C. CHD. MCA, 2001*]

22. A contractor has to supply the following number of items at the end of each month :

TABLE 7.37

Month	*Month number*	*Number of items*
Jan.	1	85
Feb.	2	180
March	3	300
April	4	375
May	5	375
June	6	285
		1,600

Production during a month is available for supply at the end of the month. The stock holding cost per item per month is ₹ 1. The set-up cost is ₹ 900 per set-up and the production cost is ₹ 2 per item. What should be the optimal policy of production in various months so that the total cost involved is minimized?

[*DOEACC, 1995*]

23. Mr. Gupta wants to invest ₹ 12,000 in the three schemes, namely A, B and C to have the best return. Investment in schemes A and B can only be done in multiples of ₹ 3,000. The returns from the three schemes are given in the following table :

TABLE 7.38

Scheme	*Returns in rupees for the investment of*			
	₹ 3,000	₹ 6,000	₹ 9,000	₹ 12,000
A	60	175	310	400
B	85	140	320	485
C	50	200	350	430

Find by dynamic programming the best investment programme for maximum returns.

[*P.T.U. MCA, 2002*]

24. A 4-tonne vessel is loaded with one or more of the three items. The following table gives the unit weight w_i in tonnes and the unit revenue in thousands of rupees r_i, for item i. How should the vessel be loaded to maximize the total return ?

TABLE 7.39

Item i	w_i	r_i
1	2	31
2	3	47
3	1	44

[P.U.B.E. (C.Sc. and E.) Dec., 2004]
(*Ans.* 2 units of item 1 only ; ₹ 62,000.)

25. A manufacturing firm has a contract to supply lathe chucks as per the following schedule. The product made during a month will be supplied at the end of the month. The set-up cost is ₹ 1,000, while the inventory carrying cost is ₹ 1.00 per piece per month. In which month should the batches be produced and of what size, so that the total of set-up and inventory carrying costs are minimized?

TABLE 7.40

Month	No. of items
January	100
February	200
March	300
April	400
May	400
June	300

[J.N.T.U. Hyderabad B.Tech. May, 2011]

26. (*a*) What do you mean by forward and backward recursion in dynamic programming?
(*b*) Suppose that a person wants to select the shortest highway route between two cities. The network shown below provides the possible routes between the starting city at node 1 and the destination city at node 7. The routes pass through intermediate cities designated by nodes 2 to 6. Solve the problem of finding the shortest route using dynamic programming.

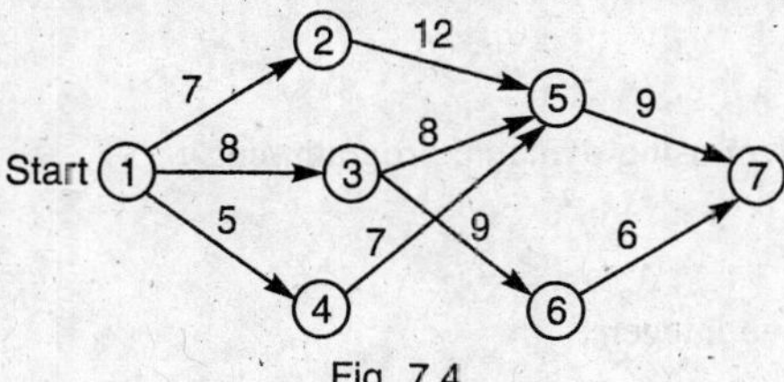

Fig. 7.4

[J.N.T.U. Hyderabad B.Tech. Nov., 2010]

27. Find number of each of three items to be included in a package so that value of the package will be maximum. Total weight of package must not exceed 5 kg.

TABLE 7.41

Items	Weight in kg	Value in ₹
1	1	30
2	3	80
3	2	65

[J.N.T.U. Hyderabad B.Tech. Nov., 2010]

28. (*a*) State Bellman's principle of optimatity and explain by an illustrative example how it can be used to solve multistage problem with finite number of stages.

[J.N.T.U. Hyderabad B.Tech. June, 2009]

(*b*) A government space project is conducting research on a certain engineering problem that must be solved before man can fly to moon safely. These research teams are currently trying three different approaches for solving this problem. The estimate has been made that under present circumstances, the possibility that the respective teams, call them A, B and C, will not succeed are 0.4, 0.6 and

0.8 respectively. Thus the current probability that all three teams will fail = (0.40) × (0.60) × (0.80) = 0.192. Since the objective is to minimize this probability, the decision has been made to assign two or more top scientists among the three teams in order to lower it as much as possible. The following table gives the estimated probability that the respective team will fail when 0,1 or 2 additional scientists are added to that team.

TABLE 7.42

		A	B	C
No. of new scientists:	0	0.40	0.60	0.80
	1	0.20	0.40	0.50
	2	0.15	0.20	0.30

How should the additional scientists be allocated to the team ?

[J.N.T.U. Hyderabad B.Tech. June, 2009]

Section 7.5

29. Use dynamic programming to

$$\text{maximize } Z = x_1 \cdot x_2 \cdot x_3,$$
$$\text{subject to } x_1 + x_2 + x_3 = 5,$$
$$x_1, x_2, x_3 \geq 0.$$

[K.U.M.Sc., 2001]

(*Ans.* $x_1 = x_2 = x_3 = 5/3$; $Z_{max} = 125/27$.)

30. Use dynamic programming to find the value of :

$$\text{Maximize } Z = Y_1 \cdot Y_2 \cdot Y_3,$$
$$\text{subject to } Y_1 + Y_2 + Y_3 = 2,$$
$$\text{where } Y_1, Y_2, Y_3 \geq 0.$$

[P.T.U. M.B.A. June, 2003]

31. Maximize $Z = x_1 \cdot x_2 \cdot x_3,$

subject to $x_1 + x_2 + x_3 = 10,$

$x_1, x_2, x_3 \geq 0.$

32. Solve the following problem using dynamic programming :

$$\text{Maximize } Z = y_1^2 + y_2^2 + y_3^2,$$
$$\text{subject to } y_1 \cdot y_2 \cdot y_3 \leq 4,$$

where y_1, y_2, y_3 are positive integers.

[Pbi.U. MCA, 1997]

(*Ans.* y_1, y_2, y_3 = (1, 4, 1); (1, 1, 4); (4, 1, 1); $Z_{max} = 18$.)

33. Minimize $\sum y_n^2$ such that

$y_1 \cdot y_2 \cdot y_3 \cdot \ldots y_n = 6,$

$y_1, y_2, \ldots, y_n \geq 0.$

[Kuru.U.B.E. (Mech.) 1988]

34. Solve the following problem by D.P. approach :

$$\text{Minimize } \sum_{i=1}^{10} y_i^2 ,$$

subject to $y_1 + y_2 + y_3 + \ldots + y_{10} = 8,$

$y_i \geq 0, i = 1, 2, \ldots, 10.$

(*Ans.* $y_i = 0.8$, $i = 1, 2, \ldots, 10$; $Z_{max} = 6.4$.)

35. Solve the following problem by dynamic programming :

$$\text{Minimize } Z = 2x_1 + 3x_2 + 20x_3,$$
$$\text{subject to } x_1 + x_2 + x_3 = 12,$$
$$x_1, x_2, x_3 \geq 0.$$

36. Solve the following problem using dynamic programming :

$$\text{Minimize } Z = \sum_{j=1}^{n} y_j^2,$$

$$\text{subject to} \quad \prod_{j=1}^{n} y_j = b, \quad y_j \geq 0 \text{ for all } j.$$ [*Pbi.U.MCA, 1997; DOEACC, 1995*]

(*Ans.* $y_j = b^{\frac{1}{n}}$; $Z_{\min} = n \cdot b^{\frac{2}{n}}$.)

37. Minimize $Z = 2x_1^2 + 3x_2^2 + x_3^2$,
subject to $x_1 + x_2 + x_3 = 10$,
where x_1, x_2, x_3 are +ve integers. [*P.U.M.E. (Mech.) May, 1995*]

38. Formulate the following problem as a dynamic programming problem and find the optimal solution:

Maximize $Z = (x_1+2)^2 + x_2x_3 + (x_4 - 5)^2$.
subject to $x_1 + x_2 + x_3 + x_4 \leq 5$,
x_i $(i = 1, 2, 3, 4)$ non-negative integers.

(*Ans.* $x_1 = 5$, $x_2 = x_3 = x_4 = 0$.)

39. Minimize $12x_1^3 + 27x_2^3 + 147x_3^3$ in non-negative x_i such that $\Sigma x_i = 1$.

(*Ans.* $x_1 = 0$, $x_2 = 0$, $x_3 = 1$.)

Section 7.6

40. Resolve the reliability problem of section 7.6 for the following data :

TABLE 7.43

Components

u_i	1		2		3		4	
	R	C	R	C	R	C	R	C
1	.70	4	.60	2	.90	3	.80	3
2	.75	5	.80	4	—	—	.80	5
3	.85	7	—	—	—	—	—	—

Total capital available C = 15.

[*Ans.* $(u_1, u_2, u_3, u_4) = (2, 2, 1, 1)$.]

41. Consider the problem of designing an electronic device consisting of three main components. The three components are arranged in series so that the failure of one of the components will result in the failure of the whole device. Therefore, it is decided that the reliability (probability of no failure) of the device can be improved by installing parallel (stand-up) units on each component. Each component may have at most three units installed in parallel. The total capital (in thousands of rupees) available for the device is 10. Following data are available :

TABLE 7.44

m_i	$i = 1$		$i = 2$		$i = 3$	
	r_1	c_1	r_2	c_2	r_3	c_3
1	0.5	2	0.7	3	0.6	1
2	0.7	4	0.8	5	0.8	2
3	0.9	5	0.9	6	0.9	3

Here m_i is the number of parallel units placed with the ith component, r_i is the reliability of the ith component and c_i is its cost. Determine m_i which will maximize the total reliability of the system.

(*Ans.* $m_1 = 3$, $m_2 = 1$, $m_3 = 2$; max. reliability = 0.504.)

42. Consider the problem of designing electronic devices to carry five power cells, each of which must be located within three electronic systems. If one system's power fails, it is powered on an auxiliary basis by the cells of the remaining systems. The probability that any particular system will experience a power failure depends on the number of cells originally assigned to it. Estimated power failure probabilities for a particular system are given below.

TABLE 7.45

Power cells	*Probability of system power failure*		
	System 1	*System 2*	*System 3*
1	0.50	0.60	0.40
2	0.15	0.20	0.25
3	0.04	0.10	0.10
4	0.02	0.05	0.05
5	0.01	0.02	0.01

Determine the number of power cells to be assigned to each system to maximize the overall system reliability.

(*Ans.* $x_1 = 3, x_2 = 1, x_3 = 1, f_1(5) = 0.0096$.)

43. There are n machines which can perform two jobs. If x of them do the first job, they produce goods worth $g(x) = 3x$, and if y of them perform the second job, they produce goods worth $h(y) = 2.5y$. Machines are subject to depriciation so that after performing the first job only $a\,(x) = \frac{x}{3}$ machines remain available and after performing the second job $b\,(y) = \frac{2y}{3}$ machines remain available in the beginning of the second year. The process is repeated with the remaining machines. Obtain the maximum total return after three years and also find the optimal policy in each year.

[*Meerut M.Sc. (Math.) 1986*]

(*Ans.* First year : $x_1 = 0, y_1 = m$; *Second year :* $x_2 = 0,\ y_2 = 2/3\ m$;
Third year: $x_3 = 4m/9,\ y_3 = 0$; $F_3^*\,(s_1) = 5.5\ m$.)

Section 7.7

Solve the following L.P.P. by dynamic programming method :

44. Maximize $Z = 8x_1 + 7x_2$,
subject to $2x_1 + x_2 \le 8,\ 5x_1 + 2x_2 \le 15\ ;\ x_1, x_2 \ge 0$.

[*I.I.Sc. (Indl. Mangt.) 1977; Cochin Dip. Oper. and Comp. Appl., 1981*]

(*Ans.* $x_1 = 0, x_2 = 7.5$; $Z_{max} = 52.5$.)

45. Maximize $Z = 4x_1 + 14x_2$,
subject to $2x_1 + 7x_2 \le 21,\ 7x_1 + 2x_2 \le 21\ ;\ x_1, x_2 \ge 0$.

(*Ans.* $x_1 = 0, x_2 = 3$; $Z_{max} = 42$.)

46. Maximize $Z = 3x_1 + 4x_2$,
subject to $2x_1 + x_2 \le 40,\ 2x_1 + 5x_2 \le 180;\ x_1, x_2 \ge 0$. [*Bharathiar U. Coimbatore B.Sc. April, 2011; P.U.B.E. (Prod.) 2001*]

(*Ans.* $x_1 = \frac{5}{2}$, $x_2 = 35$; $Z_{max} = 147.5$.)

47. Maximize $Z = x_1 + 9x_2$,
subject to $2x_1 + x_2 \le 25,\ x_2 \le 11;\ x_1, x_2 \ge 0$. [*Delhi M.Sc. (Math.) 1974*]

(*Ans.* $x_1 = 7, x_2 = 11$; $Z_{max} = 106$.)

48. Maximize $Z = 2x_1 + 4x_2$,
subject to $2x_1 + 3x_2 \le 48,\ x_1 + 3x_2 \le 42,\ x_1 + x_2 \le 21;\ x_1, x_2 \ge 0$.

[*B.I.T. Ranchi B.E. (Prod.) 1984*]

(*Ans.* $x_1 = 6, x_2 = 12$; $Z_{max} = 60$.)

49. Maximize $Z = 10x_1 + 30x_2$,
subject to $3x_1 + 6x_2 \leq 168$, $12x_2 \leq 240$; $x_1, x_2 \geq 0$.

[*R.T.M. Nagpur U.B.E. (Mech.) Sept., 2010; J.N.T.U. Hyderabad B.Tech. June, 2009; May, 2009*]

50. Solve the following LPP by dynamic programming :
Maximize $Z = 50x_1 + 100x_2$,
subject to $2x_1 + 3x_2 \leq 48$,
$x_1 + 3x_2 \leq 42$,
$x_1 + x_2 \leq 21$,
$x_1, x_2 \geq 0$. [*J.N.T.U. Hyderabad B.Tech. May, 2011*]

51. Use D.P. method to
minimize $Z = x_1 + 3x_2 + 4x_3$,
subject to $2x_1 + 4x_2 + 3x_3 \geq 60$,
$3x_1 + 2x_2 + x_3 \geq 60$,
$2x_1 + x_2 + 3x_3 \geq 90$,
$x_1, x_2, x_3 \geq 0$. [*J.N.T.U. Hyderabad B.Tech. April, 2011*]

Probability Theory

8.1 TERMINOLOGY IN PROBABILITY THEORY

Before a formal definition of probability can be given, it is necessary to introduce a few basic terms.

Experiment. An *experiment* is an operation whose output cannot be predicted with certainty.

Outcome. Output of an experiment is called *outcome.* The number of outcomes depends upon the nature of the experiment and may be finite or infinite. For example, consider the experiment of hitting a particular target by a marksman. There are only two outcomes, either hit or miss. However, if the experiment involves the measurement of time between successive failures of an electronic equipment, the outcomes are given by time-to-failure, which can have any positive real values.

Sample Space. The set of all possible outcomes of a given experiment is called the *sample space* or the *event space* or the *probability space.* We now consider a few examples which will explain the above definitions.

EXAMPLE 8.1–1

A single, regular die consisting of 6 faces is rolled once. Thus the experiment is the roll of the die. A sample space for this experiment could be

$$S = \{1, 2, 3, 4, 5, 6\},$$

where integers 1 to 6 represent the face which may come up when the die stops.

EXAMPLE 8.1-2

Consider an experiment of tossing a coin once. The possible outcomes of this experiment are

(*a*) the coin lies with its head H up,

(*b*) the coin lies with its tail T up.

The chances of the coin resting on its edge are extremely small and hence this outcome is neglected. The associated sample space is

$$S = \{H, T\}.$$

EXAMPLE 8.1-3

Consider the experiment of tossing of two coins. The possible outcomes are HH, HT, TH and TT. The associated sample space for the experiment is

$$S = \{HH, HT, TH, TT\}.$$

EXAMPLE 8.1-4

Consider the experiment of selection of one card from a standard deck of 52 and let it be assumed that the cards are numbered from 1 to 52. The associated sample space is

$$S = \{1, 2, 3, ..., 52],$$

since the selected card must correspond to one of these integers.

Finite and Infinite Sample Spaces

A sample space is called *finite* if the number of possible outcomes in the sample space is finite, otherwise it is called *infinite*. The four examples cited above have finite sample space.

Discrete and Continuous Sample Spaces

A sample space is called *discrete* if it contains only finite or infinite but countable number of possible outcomes, otherwise it is called *continuous*.

EXAMPLE 8.1-5

In the random experiment of counting the number of persons coming per hour for tickets at the booking window of cinema hall, the sample space S = {1, 2, 3, ...} is discrete.

EXAMPLE 8.1-6

In the experiment of measuring the time t between successive failures of an electronic equipment, the sample space is

$$S = \{0 \leq t \leq \infty\},$$

which is continuous.

Event

An *event* or *sample point* is a subset of sample space. Every subset is an event. An event *occurs* if any one of its elements is the outcome of the experiment.

Elementary Event

An *Elementary event* or *simple event* is a subset containing a single sample point. The sample space S itself is called the *certain event* or *sure event*. An event that contains no sample point is called *impossible event* and is denoted by ϕ.

EXAMPLE 8.1-7

When a single, regular die is rolled once, the associated sample space is

$$S = \{1, 2, 3, 4, 5, 6\}.$$

Then each of the subsets

A = {1}, B = {2, 4, 6}, C = {1, 3, 5}, D = {1, 2, 4, 5}, E = {2, 3, 4, 5}, is an event. In fact these are not the only events (there are many more), since these are not the only subsets of S. Evidently A is an elementary event. Events A, B, C, D and E are different because their subsets are different. If we actually roll the die once and we get face 1 up, then events A, C and D are said to have occurred, since all these events have 1 as an element. Similarly, if we get the face 3 up, events C & E are said to have occurred as they have 3 as an element. Event F = ϕ = {7} is, obviously, an impossible event.

EXAMPLE 8.1-8

Let the experiment involve selection of one student from the total number of 1,500 students on the rolls of a college. The sample space will be represented by

$$S = \{1, 2, 3, ..., 1{,}500\}.$$

Then the subsets

A = {1, 100}, B = {10}, C = {2, 5, 16, 80, 400}, D = {201, 202, 203, ..., 1,000} etc., are all events. If the student numbered 80 happens to be selected, then event C is said to have occurred; if student numbered 1,350 happens to be selected, none of the events A, B, C and D has occurred since this number is not contained by any of them.

EXAMPLE 8.1-9

If a trial consists of rolling of two dice simultaneously, then since each die can show one of the faces 1 to 6, there are 36 possible outcomes and the sample space is

$$S = \{x_1, x_2\}, \text{ where } x_1 = 1, 2, ..., 6; x_2 = 1, 2, ..., 6.$$

And let, events A, B and C be such that

A occurs if the sum of two dice is 4,
B occurs if the sum of two dice is 9,
C occurs if the two dice have the same number.

Then these events are subsets

$$A = \{(1, 3), (2, 2), (3, 1)\}$$
$$B = \{(3, 6), (4, 5), (5, 4), (6, 3)\},$$
$$C = \{(1, 1)\}, (2, 2), (3, 3), (4, 4), (5, 5), (6, 6)\}.$$

EXAMPLE 8.1-10

Consider again the experiment of measuring time between successive failures of an electronic equipment with sample space

$$S = \{0 \le t \le \infty\}.$$

Then event with inter-failure time of 10 is $A = \{0 \le t \le 10\}$.

Mutually Exclusive Events

Two events A and B are said to be *mutually exclusive* or *disjoint* if they do not have simple events in common. In other words A and B are mutually exclusive events if they cannot occur simultaneously.

Independent Events

An event A is said to be *independent* of event B if the probability that A occurs is not affected by whether B has or has not occurred.

8.2 DEFINITION OF PROBABILITY

Probability of an event has been defined in the following three ways :

1. The a-priori Probability

If there are *n mutually exclusive, exhaustive* and *equally likely* outcomes of an experiment and if *m* of them are favourable to an event A, then the probability of occurrence of A, denoted by P (A) is defined as the ratio $\frac{m}{n}$.

i.e.,
$$P(A) = \frac{m}{n}, \quad \text{where } 0 \le m \le n, \quad n > 0. \qquad ... (8.1)$$

EXAMPLE 8.2-1

A card is drawn from a deck of cards. What is the probability that the card drawn is a heart? What is the probability that the card drawn is an ace ?

Solution

In drawing a card there are 52 mutually exclusive and equally likely cases and there are 13 cases favourable to the drawing of a heart; hence the probability of drawing a heart is 13/52 = 1/4. For the second event, there are 4 cases favourable to the drawing of an ace, hence the probability is 4/52 = 1/13.

EXAMPLE 8.2-2

An urn contains 10 black, 15 white and 5 red balls. What is the probability of drawing a black, a white or a red ball ?

Solution

There are 30 equally likely cases. Out of these 30 cases, there are 10, 15 and 5 cases favourable respectively to a black, a white or a red ball. Hence the probability of drawing a black, white or a red ball is 1/3, 1/2 and 1/6 respectively.

The probability defined as above is called *a-priori probability* or *mathematical probability.* This definition works well with games of chance—tossing of an ideal coin, rolling of a die or playig a game of cards. In fact this definition is true only for those cases where the outcomes are equally likely and this may not always be true.

EXAMPLE 8.2-3

In a class of 50 students what is the probability that a particular student X will pass an examination ?.

Solution

There are obviously two cases; either the student will pass or fail. In finding the probability of passing, the two cases cannot be taken as equally likely to give a value of 1/2 since X may be a hardworking and intelligent student and probability of his passing may be 1.

2. The a-posteriori Probability

This is also called *statistical* or *empirical probability.* It overcomes the shortcomings of the previous definition of probability. If n represents *sufficiently large* number of trials made to see whether an event A occurs or not and m represents the number of trials in which it is observed to occur, then the probability of occurrence of A is given by

$$P(A) = \lim_{n \to \infty} \frac{m}{n} \quad \text{... (8.2)}$$

provided the circumstances from trial to trial remain the same.

Clearly, $0 \leq P(A) \leq 1$,

where $P(A) = 0$ signifies that the event is impossible, while $P(A) = 1$ signifies that it is certain. For example, the probability of the event that rolled die will show a "seven" is zero (impossible), while the probability that a tossed coin will turn up a head or a tail is one (certain).

3. Axiomatic Definition of Probability

With every event A in a finite sample space S, we associate a real number P (A), which is called the probability of event A if it satisfies the following axioms:

(*i*) $0 \leq P(A) \leq 1$, for each subset A of S, which implies that probability of an event always varies from 0 to 1.

(*ii*) $P(S) = 1$, where S is the sample space, also called *certain event.*

(*iii*) $P(\phi) = 0$, where ϕ is the *impossible event.*

(*iv*) P (A or B) = P (A) + P (B), where A and B are two *mutually exclusive* events.

8.3. LAWS OF PROBABILITY

Now we shall study the various laws of probability. The proofs given refer to the first definition of probability (mathematical probability). However, these laws can be proved by using the second definition of probability (statistical probability) with requisite modifications.

8.3-1 Complementary Events

When an event A fails to occur, one may say that event 'non-A' has occurred. The event 'non-A' is called *the complementary event* of A and is represented by $\bar{A}$ or A′. For example, in flipping up of an ideal coin, the event that head appears is complementary to the event that tail appears.

1st Law

If p is the probability of event A and q is the probability of its complementary event $\bar{A}$, *then*

$$p = 1 - q \quad \text{or} \quad P(A) = 1 - P(\bar{A}). \qquad \text{... (8.3)}$$

Proof. Let n be the total number of possible outcomes, of which m are favourable to the occurrence of event A. Then, obviously, the remaining $n - m$ outcomes are favourable to 'non-A' or $\bar{A}$

$$\therefore \qquad q = P(\bar{A}) = \frac{n-m}{n} = 1 - \frac{m}{n} = 1 - p = 1 - P(A).$$

EXAMPLE 8.3-1

An illiterate servant is given 5 cards addressed to 5 different persons residing in the same city. What is the probability that the servant hands over the card to a wrong person ?

Solution

All possible different ways to distribute 5 cards to 5 different persons are (5!) or 120. There is only one way of handing over the cards to all the five right addresses. Let this event be A.

Then $$p = P(A) = \frac{1}{120}.$$

The probability of handing over cards to wrong addresses,

$$q = 1 - p = 1 - \frac{1}{120} = \frac{119}{120}.$$

8.3-2 Mutually Exclusive Events

Two events A and B are said to be *mutually exclusive* if the occurrence of A precludes the occurrence of B and vice versa *i.e.*, if they cannot occur *simultaneously.* For example, in the random experiment of tossing an unbiased coin, the two events defined by

A = Head appears, B = Tail appears are mutually exclusive.

2nd Law (Law of Addition)

If A and B are two mutually exclusive events with probabilities p_1 *and* p_2 *respectively, then the probability of either of them (A or B) is equal to the sum of their individual probabilities.*

i.e., $$p = p_1 + p_2 \quad \text{or} \quad P(A \text{ or } B) = P(A) + P(B). \qquad \text{... (8.4)}$$

Proof. Let n be the total number of possible outcomes, of which m_1 are favourable to A and m_2 are favourable to B. Then

$$p_1 = \frac{m_1}{n} \quad \text{and} \quad p_2 = \frac{m_2}{n}.$$

Since A and B are mutually exclusive, m_1 outcomes favourable to A are not favourable to B and vice versa. Hence there are exactly $m_1 + m_2$ outcomes favourable to the event 'A or B'.

$$\therefore \qquad p = \frac{m_1 + m_2}{n} = \frac{m_1}{n} + \frac{m_2}{n} = p_1 + p_2$$

or $\qquad$ P (A or B) = P (A) + P (B).

Generalising, if $A_1, A_2, A_3, ..., A_n$ are the mutually exclusive events with probability $p_1, p_2, p_3, ..., p_n$, then

$$P (A_1 \text{ or } A_2, ..., \text{or } A_n) = P (A_1) + P (A_2) + ... + P (A_n)$$

or $$p = p_1 + p_2 + ... + p_n. \qquad ... (8.5)$$

EXAMPLE 8.3-2

An urn contains 4 white and 6 black balls. What is the probability that the ball drawn is white or black ?

Solution

Since the ball drawn can be either white or black, the probability is 4/10 + 6/10 = 1.

8.3-3 Mutually Exclusive and Exhaustive Events

Events $A_1, A_2, A_3, ..., A_n$ are called mutually exclusive and exhaustive events if

(*i*) when one of them occurs, none out of the remaining will occur,

(*ii*) one or the other event must occur in any trial.

For example, in the trial of tossing of a fair coin, the events that head appears and tail appears are two mutually exclusive and exhaustive events, as the chances of the coin resting on its edge are almost zero.

3rd Law

If $A_1, A_2, A_3, ..., A_n$ are n mutually exclusive and exhaustive events with probabilities $p_1, p_2, ..., p_n$ respectively, then

$$p_1 + p_2 + p_3 + ... + p_n = 1. \qquad ... (8.6)$$

Proof. Let n be the total number of possible outcomes, of which m_1 are favourable to event A_1, m_2 to A_2, ..., m_n to A_n, so that

$$p_1 = \frac{m_1}{n}, p_2 = \frac{m_2}{n}, ..., p_n = \frac{m_n}{n}.$$

As the events are mutually exclusive, m_1 outcomes are favourable only to A_1 and not to A_2, ..., A_n and so on. Moreover, they are also exhaustive.

Now $$m_1 + m_2 + ... + m_n = n \quad \text{or} \quad \frac{m_1}{n} + \frac{m_2}{n} + ... + \frac{m_n}{n} = 1$$

or $$p_1 + p_2 + ... + p_n = 1 \quad \text{or} \quad P (A_1) + P (A_2) + ... + P (A_n) = 1.$$

EXAMPLE 8.3-3

The experience data for welders in a fabrication shop are given below. What is the probability that a welder selected at random will have 6 or more years of experience?

Years of experience	*Number*	*Probability*
0–2	5	*5/50 = 1/10 = 0.1*
3–5	10	*10/50 = 1/5 = 0.2*
6–8	15	*15/50 = 3/10 = 0.3*
More than 8	20	*20/50 = 2/5 = 0.4*
	50	

Solution

$$P\,(6 \text{ or more}) = P\,(6 \text{ to } 8) + P\,(\text{more than } 8) = 0.3 + 0.4 = 0.7.$$

8.3-4 Mutually Independent Events

Two events A and B are said to be independent events if the occurrence or non-occurrence of A does not depend upon the occurrence of B and vice versa.

4th Law

If two events A and B are mutually independent with individual probabilities p_1 and p_2 respectively, then the probability p of their simultaneous occurrence is equal to the product of their individual probabilties.

i.e., $$P\,(A \text{ and } B) = P\,(A)\cdot P\,(B) \quad \text{or} \quad P\,(AB) = P\,(A)\cdot P\,(B)$$

or $$p = p_1 \cdot p_2. \qquad \text{... (8.7)}$$

Proof. Let n_1 and m_1 be the total number of possible and favourable outcomes for event A and n_2 and m_2 for event B so that

$$p_1 = \frac{m_1}{n_1} \quad \text{and} \quad p_2 = \frac{m_2}{n_2}.$$

As the two events are independent, n_1 possible outcomes for event A can be associated with each of the n_2 possible cases for event B, so that the total number of possible cases for 'A and B' is $n_1 n_2$. Similarly, the total number of favourable cases for 'A and B' is $m_1 m_2$.

∴ Probability of 'A and B'

$$p = \frac{m_1 m_2}{n_1 n_2} = \frac{m_1}{n_1} \cdot \frac{m_2}{n_2} = p_1 p_2.$$

or $$P\,(A \text{ and } B) = P\,(A)\cdot P\,(B) \quad \text{or} \quad P\,(AB) = P\,(A)\cdot P\,(B).$$

Similarly, if there are three mutually independent events A, B and C (this means that the probability of any one of these taking place does not depend upon whether the remaining two have taken place), then

$$P\,(A \text{ and } B \text{ and } C) = P\,(A \text{ and } B)\cdot P\,(C) \quad \text{or} \quad P\,(ABC) = P\,(A)\cdot P(B)\cdot P\,(C). \qquad \text{... (8.8)}$$

Generalising, for n mutually independent events $A_1, A_2, ..., A_n$ with individual probabilities of p_1 $p_2, ..., p_n$ respectively, the probability of event '$A_1, A_2, ...$ and A_n', is the product $p_1 p_2 ... p_n$.

i.e., $$P\,(A_1, A_2, ..., \text{and } A_n) = P\,(A_1)\cdot P\,(A_2) ... P\,(A_n). \qquad \text{... (8.9)}$$

Thus the probability for joint occurrence of any number of mutually independent events is equal to the product of the probabilities of these events.

EXAMPLE 8.3-4.1

A worker is to look after three machines. In any given hour, the probability of first machine not requiring worker's attention is 0.8, for the second machine it is 0.85 and for the third it is 0.75. What is the probability that none of the machines will require the worker's attention during a given hour ?

Solution

Assuming that the machines work independently of each other, the required probability is

$$= (0.8)\,(0.85)\,(0.75) = 0.51.$$

EXAMPLE 8.3-4.2

In the previous problem, what is the probability that at least one of the three machines will not require the worker's attention during a given hour ?

Solution

In this problem we are to deal with probability of the form P (A or B or C) and hence we first think of the addition rule. However, this rule cannot be applied directly, since any two of the three events are mutually compatible (nothing prevents any two of the machines from working normally during a given hour). Moreover, the sum of the three given probabilities also exceeds unity.

However, the probability of the first machine requiring the worker's attention is 0.2, for the second machine it is 0.15 and for the third it is 0.25. Since the three events are mutually independent, the probability that all the three events will take place is

$$(0.2)\ (0.15)\ (0.25) \ = \ 0.0075.$$

But the events "all the three machines will require attention" and "at least one of the three will work quietly" are mutually incompatible. Hence their sum must be unity and, therefore, the probability that at least one machine will not require attention is

$$1 - 0.0075 = 0.9925.$$

As this value is very near to unity, the probability that at least one machine will not require the worker's attention is almost a certainty. Thus at least one machine will operate normally during a given hour.

EXAMPLE 8.3-4.3

An urn contains 5 white and 8 black balls. Another urn contains 6 white and 10 black balls. One ball is taken out from each of the urns. What is the probability that the balls taken out are both white ?

Solution

Probability of white ball from first urn = 5/13 and probability of white ball from second urn = 6/16. Now the colour of the ball drawn from the second urn does not depend upon the colour of the ball drawn from the first urn. Hence the two events are independent and the required probability is

$$\left(\frac{5}{13}\right)\left(\frac{6}{16}\right) = \frac{15}{104}.$$

EXAMPLE 8.3-4.4

The probability of shooting down an enemy aircraft by one rifle shot is 0.004. Find the probability of shooting down the plane with simultaneous shots from 250 rifles.

Solution

Probability of not shooting down the aircraft with a single shot is 1 – 0.004 = 0.996. Since the events are independent, the probability that it will not be downed by 250 shots = $(0.996)^{250}$.

∴ The probability that at least one of 250 shots will down the plane

$$= \ 1 - (0.996)^{250} = 1 - 0.367 = 0.633.$$

8.4 MODIFIED ADDITION LAW

The previous sections dealt with the laws governing the probability of compound events consisting of mutually exclusive or mutually independent events. However, there may be many events which are neither mutually exclusive nor independent. The modified addition law for such events states:

The probability that at least one of the events A and B occurs is obtained by adding the probability that A occurs and the probability that B occurs and then subtracting the probability that both A and B occur.

i.e., P (A or B) = P (A) + P (B) – P (AB). ... (8.10)

Proof. The various possible combinations of two events A and B are

(*i*) A occurs and B occurs (n_{11}),

(*ii*) A occurs and B does not occur (n_{12}),

(*iii*) A does not occur and B occurs (n_{21}),

(*iv*) A does not occur and B does not occur (n_{22}).

Let n be the total number of possible outcomes of the combination of A and B and let n_{11}, n_{12}, n_{21} and n_{22} represent the possible outcomes that favour occurrence of (*i*), (*ii*), (*iii*) and (*iv*) respectively. Here subscript 1 stands for the occurrence of event A or B and subscript 2 stands for the non-occurrence of event A or B. For example, n_{12} represents the number of possible outcomes in which even A occurs and event B does not occur.

Since event 'A or B' means one of the above combinations (*i*) (*ii*) and (*iii*), the number of possible outcomes favourable to 'A or B' is $n_{11} + n_{12} + n_{21}$.

$$\therefore \quad P(A \text{ or } B) = \frac{n_{11} + n_{12} + n_{21}}{n} = \frac{(n_{11} + n_{12}) + (n_{11} + n_{21}) - n_{11}}{n}$$

$$= \frac{n_{11} + n_{12}}{n} + \frac{n_{11} + n_{21}}{n} - \frac{n_{11}}{n} = P(A) + P(B) - P(AB).$$

Generalising, the modified addition law for three events becomes P (A or B or C) = P (A) + P (B) + P (C) – [P (AB) + P (BC) + P (AC)] + P (ABC). ... (8.11)

Proof. Let us consider events 'B or C' as event D. Then applying the modified addition law for two events A and D, we get

P (A or D) = P (A) + P (D) – P (AD),

P (D) = P (B or C) = P (B) + P (C) – P (BC)

and P (AD) = P (A & 'B or C') = P (AB or AC)

= P (AB) + P (AC) – P (ABC).

∴ P (A or D) = P (A) + P (B) + P (C) – P (BC) – P (AD)

or P (A or B or C) = P (A) + P (B) + P (C)

– [P (AB) + P (BC) + P (CA)] + P (ABC).

EXAMPLE 8.4-1

Calculate the probability of drawing either an ace or a spade in a pack of cards.

Solution

$$P(\text{Ace or Spade}) = P(\text{Ace}) + P(\text{Spade}) - P(\text{Ace and Spade}) = \frac{4}{52} + \frac{13}{52} - \frac{1}{52} = \frac{16}{52} = \frac{4}{13}.$$

8.5 LAW OF CONDITIONAL PROBABILITY

Sometimes it may be given that event A has occurred and it may be required to find the probability that B also occurs. For example, it may be given that the card drawn from a deck of 52 cards is red and it may be required to find the probability that the card drawn is a king of hearts. Or, it may be found on medical research that a randomly selected person has a family history of leprosy and further it may be required to find the probability of this particular person also to suffer from leprosy. In such situations we are, obviously, given that an event A has occurred and we are to find the probability that B also occurs.

The event B is dependent on A and occurs only if A has occurred. The probability attached to such an event is called *conditional probability.* It is denoted by P (B/A) *i.e.*, probability of B given that A has occurred and is expressed as

$$P(B/A) = \frac{P(AB)}{P(A)}. \qquad \text{... (8.12)}$$

Proof. Let n denote the total number of possible outcomes of which m are favourable to event A. The cases favourable to A and B are to be found from the m cases favourable to A. Let m_1 be the number of such cases. Then from the definition of probability,

$$P(AB) = \frac{m_1}{n}.$$

This can also be written as

$$P(AB) = \frac{m}{n} \cdot \frac{m_1}{m},$$

where m/n is the probability of A. To understand the second factor, we observe that assuming the occurrence of A, there are only m equally likely cases left, out of which m_1 are favourable to B. Hence ratio m_1/m represents the conditional probability P (B/A) of B assuming that A has actually occurred.

Thus $\frac{m}{n} = P(A)$ and $\frac{m_1}{m} = P(B/A)$. $\therefore$ $P(AB) = P(A) \cdot P(B/A)$.

Similarly, $$P(AB) = P(B) \cdot P(A/B). \qquad \text{... (8.13)}$$

Thus probability of the product AB of the two events is equal to the product of probability of event A and conditional probability of B under the condition A or is equal to the product of probability of event B and conditional probability of A under the condition B. This is called law of conditional probability or compound probability.

This result can be easily extended to three or more events. For example, let us consider three events A, B and C. The occurrence of A and B and C is evidently equivalent to the occurrence of the compound event AB and C. Therefore, we have

$$P(ABC) = P(AB) \cdot P(C/AB).$$

Also $$P(AB) = P(A) \cdot P(B/A).$$

$\therefore$ $$P(ABC) = P(A) \cdot P(B/A) \cdot P(C/AB). \qquad \text{... (8.14)}$$

This formula means: *Probability of the product of three events is equal to the product of probability of first event, conditional probability of second event when the first event has occurred, and conditional probability of the third event when the product of the first and the second events has occurred.*

Generalising, if $A_1, A_2, ..., A_n$ are the random events, then

$$P(A_1 \cdot A_2 \ldots A_n) = P(A_1) \cdot P(A_2/A_1) \cdot P(A_3/A_1A_2) \ldots P(A_n/A_1 \ldots A_{n-1}). \qquad \text{... (8.15)}$$

If events A and B are *independent,* the conditional probability P (B/A) is the same as the probability of B, P (B) found without any reference to A. Hence the compound probability of two independent events can be written as

$$P(AB) = P(A) \cdot P(B),$$

a result already proved under section 8.3-4. This result, obviously, can be extended to three or more events.

8.6 BAYES' THEOREM

If $A_1, A_2, ..., A_n$ are mutually exclusive events whose union is the sample space S, where P $(A_i) \neq 0$ for $i = 1, 2, ..., n$ and if B is any random event for which $P(B) = 0$, then for all i

$$P(A_i/B) = \frac{P(A_i) \cdot P(B/A_i)}{P(A_1) \cdot P(B/A_1) - P(A_2) \cdot P(B/A_2) + \ldots + P(A_n) \cdot P(B/A_n)}. \qquad \text{... (8.16)}$$

Proof. Evidently, Bayes' theorem concerns with finding the conditional probability (A_i/B). The probability of compound event A_iB can be written in two forms:

$$P(A_iB) = P(A_i) \cdot P(B/A_i)$$

or

$$P(A_iB) = P(B) \cdot P(A_i/B).$$

Equating the right-hand sides, we derive the following expression for the unknown probability $P(A_i/B)$:

$$P(A_i/B) = \frac{P(A_i) \cdot P(B/A_i)}{P(B)}. \quad \text{... (8.17)}$$

Since event B can occur in mutually exclusive forms

$$A_1B, A_2B, ..., A_nB,$$

by applying the theorem of total probability, we get

$$P(B) = P(A_1) \cdot P(B/A_1) + P(A_2) \cdot P(B/A_2) + ... + P(A_n) \cdot P(B/A_n).$$

Substituting the value of P(B) in equation (8.17), we get

$$P(A_i/B) = \frac{P(A_i) \cdot P(B/A_i)}{P(A_1) \cdot P(B/A_1) + P(A_2) \cdot P(B/A_2) + ... + P(A_n) \cdot P(B/A_n)}.$$

8.7 RANDOM VARIABLES

A random variable is also called *variate, chance variable* or *stochastic variable.* It is real valued function defined over the sample space of an experiment. Thus random variable is a variable whose value is a number determined by the outcome of an experiment with which is associated a sample space.

EXAMPLE 8.7-1

In the experiment of rolling of a die, the random variable is represented by the set of outcomes {1, 2, 3, 4, 5, 6}. In the experiment of tossing of a coin, the outcomes, head (H) and tail (T) can be represented as a random variable by assigning 0 to H and 1 to T.

8.8 DISCRETE RANDOM VARIABLES

A random variable x is called *discrete* if the number of possible values of x (*i.e.*, the range space) is finite or countably infinite *i.e.*, possible values of x may be $x_1, x_2, ..., x_n, ...$ The list terminates in the finite case, while it continues indefinitely in the countably infinite case.

A discrete variable takes specific values at discrete points on the real line. For instance, number of members of a family, number of students in a class, number of passengers in a bus, tossing of a coin and rolling of a die, all are examples of discrete variables.

8.9 CONTINUOUS RANDOM VARIABLES

A random variable is called *continuous* if its range space is an interval or a collection of intervals. A continuous variable can assume any value over a continuous range of the real line. For instance, heights of school children, temperatures and barometric pressures of different cities are examples of continuous variables.

8.10 PROBABILITY DISTRIBUTION OF A DISCRETE RANDOM VARIABLE

Let x be a discrete random variable on a sample space S of at most a countably infinite number of values $x_1, x_2, ..., x_n, ...$ With each possible outcome x_i, we associate a number $P(x_i)$ and call it the probability of x_i. The number $P(x_i)$ must satisfy the following two conditions:

(*i*) $P(x_i) \geq 0$, for all values of i,

(ii) $\sum_{i=1}^{n} P(x_i) = 1$. ... (8.18)

The function P is called *probability function* of the random variable *x*.

EXAMPLE 8.10-1

A pair of fair dice is rolled once. Let x be the random variable whose value for any outcome is the sum of the two numbers on the dice.

(i) Find the probability function of x. Construct the probability table and a probability chart.

(ii) Find the probability that x is an odd number.

(iii) Find $P(3 \le x_i \le 9)$ and $P(0 \le x_i \le 4)$.

Solution

(*i*) As *x* is the random variable whose value for any outcome is the sum of the two numbers on the dice, the range for *x* is

(2, 3, 4, ..., 11, 12).

Event for which x = 2 is (1, 1) *i.e.*, one,

events for which x = 3 are (1, 2,), (2, 1) *i.e.*, two,

x = 4 are (1, 3), (2, 2), (3, 1) *i.e.*, three,

x = 5 are (1, 4), (2, 3), (3, 2), (4, 1) *i.e.*, four,

x = 6 are (1, 5), (2, 4), (3, 3), (4, 2), (5, 1) *i.e.*, five,

x = 7 are (1, 6), (2, 5), (3, 4), (4, 3), (5, 2), (6, 1) *i.e.*, six,

x = 8 are (2, 6), (3, 5), (4, 4), (5, 3), (6, 2) *i.e.*, five,

x = 9 are (3, 6), (4, 5), (5, 4), (6, 3) *i.e.*, four,

x = 10 are (4, 6), (5, 5), (6, 4) *i.e.*, three,

x = 11 are (5, 6), (6, 5) *i.e.*, two,

event for which x = 12 is (6, 6) *i.e.*, one.

Thus the probability distribution is as shown in table 8.1 below.

TABLE 8.1

x	2	3	4	5	6	7	8	9	10	11	12
P(x)	$\frac{1}{36}$	$\frac{2}{36}$	$\frac{3}{36}$	$\frac{4}{36}$	$\frac{5}{36}$	$\frac{6}{36}$	$\frac{5}{36}$	$\frac{4}{36}$	$\frac{3}{36}$	$\frac{2}{36}$	$\frac{1}{36}$

The probability distribution is represented on the chart as shown in figure 8.1.

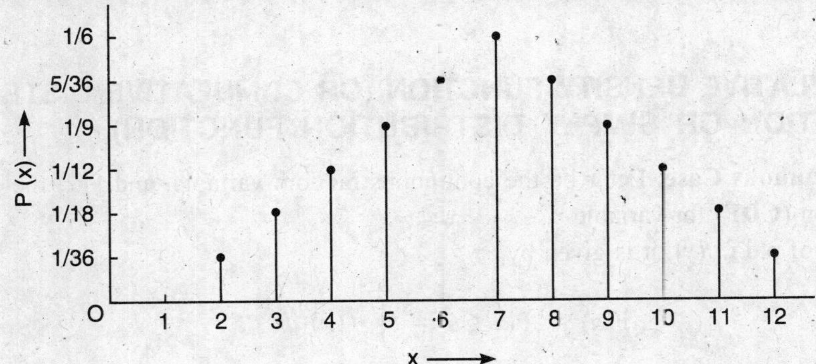

Fig. 8.1

(*ii*) Probability that x is an odd number is

$$P(x = 3) + P(x = 5) + P(x = 7) + P(x = 9) + P(x = 11)$$

$$= \frac{2}{36} + \frac{4}{36} + \frac{6}{36} + \frac{4}{36} + \frac{2}{36} = \frac{1}{2}.$$

(*iii*)

$$P(3 \le x_i \le 9) = \sum_{i=3}^{9} P(x_i) = [P(x = 3) + P(x = 4) + P(x = 5)$$

$$+ P(x = 6) + P(x = 7) + P(x = 8) + P(x = 9)]$$

$$= \frac{2}{36} + \frac{3}{36} + \frac{4}{36} + \frac{5}{36} + \frac{6}{36} + \frac{5}{36} + \frac{4}{36} = \frac{29}{36}.$$

$$P(0 \le x_i \le 4) = \sum_{i=2}^{4} P(x_i) = [P(x = 2) + P(x = 3) + P(x = 4)]$$

$$= \frac{1}{36} + \frac{2}{36} + \frac{3}{36} = \frac{1}{6}.$$

8.11 PROBABILITY DISTRIBUTION OF A CONTINUOUS RANDOM VARIABLE

If x is a continuous random variable, it will have infinite number of values in any interval howsoever small. The probability that this variable lies in the infinitesimal interval $(x, x + dx)$ is expressed $f(x) \cdot dx$, where the function $f(x)$ is called *probability density function* (p.d.f.). If x is a continuous random variable in the range $(-\infty, \infty)$ its p.d.f. $f(x)$ must satisfy the following two conditions:

(*i*) $f(x) \ge 0, \quad -\infty < x < \infty,$

(*ii*) $$\int_{-\infty}^{+\infty} f(x) \cdot dx = 1. \qquad \text{... (8.19)}$$

The first condition in both discrete and continuous distributions means that p.d.f. is always positive (otherwise the probability of some events will be negative), while the second condition means that the sum of all probabilities is unity.

A knowledge of p.d.f. helps one to calculate all the other types of probabilities. For example, it can be shown that

$$P(a < x < b) = \int_a^b f(x) \cdot dx = F(b) - F(a).$$

8.12 CUMULATIVE DENSITY FUNCTION (OR CUMULATIVE DISTRIBUTION FUNCTION OR SIMPLY DISTRIBUTION FUNCTION)

(*a*) **Continuous Case.** Let x be the continuous random variable, and $F(x)$ the cumulative density function (**CDF**) for variable x, $-\infty < x < \infty$.

In terms of p.d.f. $f(x)$, it is given by

$$F(a) = P(x \le a) = \int_{-\infty}^{a} f(x) \cdot dx. \qquad \text{... (8.20)}$$

Evidently F(a) represents the area enclosed under $f(x)$ within the range $-\infty < x < a$.

Also, when $x = a$, $P(x = a) = 0$, since the enclosed area is zero.

Further, if a and b are two real numbers such that $-\infty < a < b < \infty$, the probability of the event $a < x < b$ is given by

$$P(a < x < b) = \int_a^b f(x)\cdot dx = \int_{-\infty}^b f(x)\cdot dx - \int_{-\infty}^a f(x)\cdot dx = F(b) - F(a). \quad \text{... (8.21)}$$

The cumulative distribution function F(a) has the following properties:

$$\left.\begin{aligned} &(i) \quad \lim_{a\to\infty} F(a) = \lim_{a\to\infty} \int_{-\infty}^{a} f(x)\cdot dx = 1, \\ &(ii) \quad \lim_{a\to-\infty} F(a) = \lim_{a\to-\infty} \int_{-\infty}^{a} f(x)\cdot dx = 0. \end{aligned}\right] \quad \text{... (8.22)}$$

These properties indicate that F(a) is a *monotone, non-decreasing* function of a.

Lastly, from the relationship between $f(x)$ and F(x), it can be concluded that

$$f(x) = \frac{d}{dx}[F(x)]. \quad \text{... (8.23)}$$

It follows that the probability law of a random variable x is defined completely by either $f(x)$ or F(x).

(*b*) **Discrete Case.** Let x be a random variable, a be a real number and F(a) the probability that x takes values less than or equal to a *i.e.*,

$$F(a) = P(x \le a). \quad \text{... (8.24)}$$

Then the function F(a) as defined above is called *cumulative distribution function* of x.

Thus various results for CDF in the discrete case can be obtained by simply substituting P(x) for $f(x)$ in all the above properties. Obviously, integration will be replaced by summation and differentiation by differences. The CDF will be step function since the p.d.f. is defined at discrete points only.

EXAMPLE 8.12-1

A fair die is rolled once. The faces are numbered 1, 2, ..., 6 and the probability of any face coming up is same i.e., 1/6. Find the CDF and represent it graphically.

Solution

The various events with their associated probabilities are

x	1	2	3	4	5	6
P(x)	1/6	1/6	1/6	1/6	1/6	1/6

Then
$$F(x) = \sum_{i=1}^{i=x} 1/6 = \frac{x}{6},\ x = 1, 2, 3, ..., 6.$$

The complete CDF is shown in Fig. 8.2.

The CDF curve is a step curve consisting of horizontal line segments only.

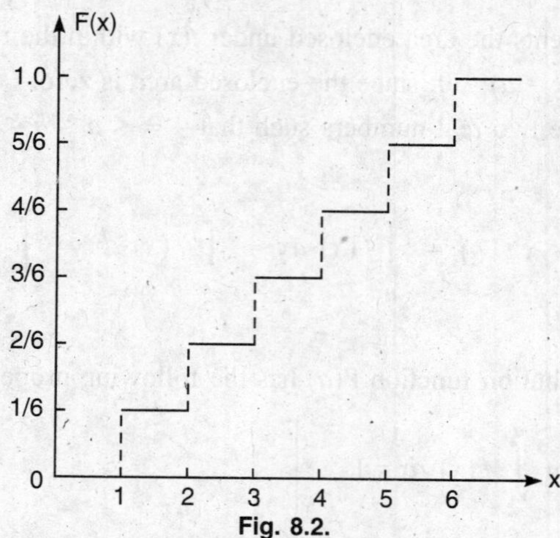

Fig. 8.2.

8.13 MATHEMATICAL EXPECTATION OF A RANDOM VARIABLE

It has been shown in the previous sections that if x is a discrete random variable, either distribution function P(x) or probability function p can be used to evaluate probability statements about x. If, however, x is a continuous random variable, either distribution function F(x) or density function $f(x)$ can be used to evaluate probability statements about x. However, very often the *average* or *expected value* of x and not merely the probability statement of x, in a certain interval is asked for.

If x is a *discrete random variable* which takes mutually exclusive values $x_1, x_2, ..., x_n$ with associated probability functions $P(x_1), P(x_2), ..., P(x_n)$, then the mathematical expectation of x, denoted by E(x) is given by

$$E(x) = x_1 P(x_1) + x_2 P(x_2) + ... + x_n P(x_n) = \sum_{i=1}^{n} xP(x), \quad ... (8.25)$$

so long as the sum is absolutely convergent.

This number is also called the *expected value or mean value of* x.

Similarly, if x is the *continuous random variable* with probability density function $f(x)$, the expected value of x is defined as

$$E(x) = \int_{-\infty}^{\infty} x \cdot f(x) \cdot dx, \quad ... (8.26)$$

so long as the integral is absolutely convergent. If integral or the sum is not absolutely convergent, the expected value does not exist.

The above results for expectation of a random variable can be easily extended to the expectation of a function of the random variable. Let x be the discrete random variable with possible values $x_1, x_2, ..., x_n$ occurring with probability functions $P(x_1), P(x_2), ..., P(x_n)$ respectively. Let H(x) be a function of x, then H(x) is also a discrete random variable and its expected value is given by

$$E[H(x)] = H(x_1) \cdot P(x_1) + H(x_2) \cdot P(x_2) + ... + H(x_n) \cdot P(x_n)$$

$$= \sum_{i=1}^{n} H(x_i) \cdot P(x_i), \quad ... (8.27)$$

provided the series is absolutely convergent.

If x is a continuous random variable with probability density function $f(x)$, then integration rather than summation will be used to get the expected value of H(x).

Then $$E[H(x)] = \int_{-\infty}^{\infty} H(x) \cdot f(x) \cdot dx, \qquad \text{... (8.28)}$$

provided the integral is absolutely convergent.

Laws of Mathematical Expectation

1. E(k) = k *i.e.*, expectation of a constant = constant itself.
2. E(kx) = k E(x) *i.e.*, expectation of a product of a constant and chance variable = product of constant and expectation of chance variable.
3. E($x \pm y \pm z \pm$ ...) = E(x) ± E(y) ± E(z) ± ...
   i.e., expectation of sum (or difference) = sum (or difference) of expectations.
4. E(xyz...) = E(x)·E(y) E(z) ....
   i.e., expectation of a product of independent chance variables = product of their expectations.
5. E($k \pm lx$) = $k \pm l$ E(x), where k and l are constants.

EXAMPLE 8.13-1

A doctor recommends a patient to go on a particular diet for two weeks and there is equal likelihood for the patient to lose his weight between 2 kg and 4 kg. What is the average amount the patient is expected to lose on this diet ?

Solution

$$f(x) = \frac{1}{2}, 2 < x < 4;$$
$$= 0, \text{ otherwise.}$$

The weight expected to be lost

$$= E(x) = \int_2^4 x \cdot \frac{1}{2} dx = \left[\frac{x^2}{4}\right]_2^4 = \frac{1}{4}[4^2 - 2^2] = 3 \text{ kg.}$$

EXAMPLE 8.13-2

In the game of rolling a fair die with faces numbered 1 to 6, a person gets as many rupees as the number of the face that turns up. What is the mathematical expectation of his earnings ?

Solution

The possible earnings together with their associated probabilities are given below.

x_i	1	2	3	4	5	6
P(x_i)	1/6	1/6	1/6	1/6	1/6	1/6

$$\therefore E(x) = \sum_{i=1}^{6} x_i P(x_i) = 1.\frac{1}{6} + 2.\frac{1}{6} + 3.\frac{1}{6} + 4.\frac{1}{6} + 5.\frac{1}{6} + 6.\frac{1}{6} = \frac{7}{2} = ₹\ 3.50.$$

EXAMPLE 8.13-3

In the game of rolling two dice simultaneously, a person is to get as many rupees as the sum of the numbers on the faces of the two dice. What is the mathematical expectation of his earnings ?

Solution

As discussed in example 8.10-1, the various possible earnings together with their associated probabilities are

x_i	2	3	4	5	6	7	8	9	10	11	12
$P(x_i)$	$\frac{1}{36}$	$\frac{2}{36}$	$\frac{3}{36}$	$\frac{4}{36}$	$\frac{5}{36}$	$\frac{6}{36}$	$\frac{5}{36}$	$\frac{4}{36}$	$\frac{3}{36}$	$\frac{2}{36}$	$\frac{1}{36}$

$$\therefore \qquad E(x) = \sum_{i=2}^{12} x_i\, P(x_i) = 2.\frac{1}{36} + 3.\frac{2}{36} + 4.\frac{3}{36} + 5.\frac{4}{36} + 6.\frac{5}{36} + 7.\frac{6}{36}$$

$$+ 8.\frac{5}{36} + 9.\frac{4}{36} + 10.\frac{3}{36} + 11.\frac{2}{36} + 12.\frac{1}{36} = ₹\ 7.$$

8.14 CENTRAL TENDENCY

Having collected the data for a random variable x, and analysed it in the form of frequency distribution, the next step is to find the *nature of distribution. Central tendency*—a property for values of x to tend towards the centre is quite important in this context. The three most important measures of central tendency are *mean, mode* and *median.*

Mean. If x is the random variable, then its expected value $E(x)$ itself is called the *mean* or *average* value of x and denoted by $\bar{x}$. Mean value of the random variable locates the middle of its probability function.

Mode. The mode of a random variable x is that value of the variable which occurs with the greatest frequency and is denoted by $\bar{x}$. It is possible that a particular distribution may not have a mode, or if it has a mode, it may not be unique. A distribution is called unimodal, bimodal, trimodal, ... depending upon whether it has one, two, three, ... modes.

For a discrete distribution, mode $\bar{x}$ is determined by the following inequalities:

$$P(x = x_i) \le P(x = \bar{x}), \quad x_i \le \bar{x},$$

and
$$P(x = x_j) \le P(x = \bar{x}), \quad x_j \ge \bar{x}. \qquad \text{... (8.29)}$$

For a continuous distribution it is determined by the following equations/inequations:

$$\frac{d}{dx}[f(x)] = 0, \quad \text{and} \quad \frac{d^2}{dx^2}[f(x)] = 0. \qquad \text{... (8.30)}$$

Median. For a discrete or continuous distribution of a random variable x, the median is defined as the variate—value X which satisfies the following inequalities:

$$P(x \le X) = \frac{1}{2}, \quad \text{and } P(x \ge X) = \frac{1}{2}. \qquad \text{... (8.31)}$$

It is denoted by $\bar{x}$. Thus if a continuous distribution function has a p.d.f. $f(x)$ in the range (a, b) then $\bar{x}$ is given by

$$\int_a^{\tilde{x}} f(x)dx = \frac{1}{2} = \int_b^{\tilde{x}} f(x) \cdot dx. \qquad \text{... (8.32)}$$

Note. If mean and median are known, the mode can be calculated from the empirical formula

Mean – Mode = 3(Mean – Median).

8.15 DISPERSION OR VARIABILITY

The probability function of a random variable x indicates the possible values that x can have together with their associated probabilities. The mean or E(x) indicates where the centre of the mass of the probability function is located. It gives a quick picture of the long-run average result when an experiment is repeated a large number of times. However, it gives no idea as to how results of one performance vary from the other.

The property which indicates the degree of variability of data about the central value is called *dispersion.* Two important measures of dispersion are *mean deviation* and *standard deviation* (*or variance*).

(*i*) **Mean Deviation.** Mean deviation (M.D.), '$\delta(a)$' of a sample or population from a value 'a' is defined as

(*a*) $$\delta(a) = E(|x-a|) = \frac{1}{N}\sum f_i\,|x_i - a|. \qquad \text{... (8.33)}$$

The above equation (8.33) is a general expression applicable to all statistics.

For example, mean deviation from mean is given by

$$\delta(\bar{x}) = E(|x - \bar{x}|),$$

and mean deviation from median is given by

$$\delta(\bar{x}) = E(|x - \bar{x}|).$$

Unless otherwise mentioned, $\delta(a)$ stands for mean deviation from the mean *i.e.*, $\delta(\bar{x})$.

Though mean deviation is a good measure of dispersion, it is difficult to be treated mathematically.

(*ii*) **Variance.** If x is a random variable whose possible values $x_1, x_2, ..., x_n$ occur with probabilities $f(x_1), f(x_2), ..., f(x_n)$, then the variance of x is denoted by Var (x) or σ_x^2 or S^2 and is defined by

$$\text{Var}(x) = \sigma_x^2 = E(x-\mu)^2 = \frac{1}{N}\sum_{i=1}^{n} f(x_i)(x_i - \mu)^2, \qquad \text{... (8.34)}$$

(For a population with mean E(x) = μ).

$$\text{and Var}(x) = S^2 = E(x-\bar{x})^2 = \frac{1}{N}\sum_{i=1}^{n} f(x_i)\cdot(x_i - \bar{x})^2. \qquad \text{... (8.35)}$$

(For a large sample with mean E(x) = $\bar{x}$).

Calculations of Variance

For a population, Var(x)

$$\begin{aligned} &= \sigma_x^2 = E(x-\mu)^2 = E(x^2 - 2\mu x + \mu^2) \\ &= E(x^2) - 2\mu\, E(x) + \mu^2 = E(x^2) - 2\mu^2 + \mu^2 \\ &= E(x^2) - \mu^2 = E(x^2) - [E(x)]^2. \qquad \text{... (8.36)} \end{aligned}$$

$\therefore$ Variance can be calculated as average of squares of x minus square of the average of x.

For a large sample,

$$\text{Var}(x) = S^2 = \frac{1}{N}\sum_{i=1}^{n} f(x_i)(x_i - \bar{x})^2 = \frac{1}{N}\sum_{i=1}^{n}(x_i^2 - 2x_i\cdot\bar{x} + \bar{x}^2)\cdot f(x_i)$$

$$= \frac{1}{N}\left[\sum_{i=1}^{n} x_i^2 f(x_i) - 2\bar{x}\sum_{i=1}^{n} x_i f(x_i) + \bar{x}^2\sum_{i=1}^{n} f(x_i)\right]$$

$$= \frac{1}{N}\left[\sum_{i=1}^{n} x_i^2\cdot f(x_i) - 2\bar{x}\cdot\bar{x} + \bar{x}^2\cdot 1\right]$$

$$= \frac{1}{N}\left[\sum_{i=1}^{n} x_i^2 f(x_i) - \bar{x}^2\right]. \quad \text{... (8.37)}$$

Variance is also called *second moment of dispersion.*

(*iii*) **Standard Deviation.** The positive square root of variance is called standard deviation (S.D.) and is denoted by σ_x or S.

Thus $\sigma_x = +\sqrt{\text{Var}(x)} = [E(x-\mu)^2]^{1/2} = \sqrt{\frac{\sum(x_i-\mu)^2}{n}}$. (for a population)

... (8.38)

To calculate standard deviation we trace the following five steps:

1. Subtract the mean from each value of the data.
2. Square each of the difference obtained in step 1.
3. Add together all the squared differences.
4. Divide the sum of all the squared differences by the number of values.
5. Take the square root of the quotient obtained in step 4.

Standard deviation is also $= [E(x-\bar{x})^2]^{1/2}$. (for a large sample) ... (8.39)

If random variable x is expressed in some units, units of variance will be squares of the units of x. However, units of standard deviation are the same as the units of x and hence S.D. is of more interest to calculate dispersion.

EXAMPLE 8.15-1

Calculate variance and standard deviation of the random variable x defined in example 8.13-1.

Solution

$$\text{Variance } \sigma_x^2 = \int_2^4 (x-3)^2 \cdot \frac{1}{2}\, dx$$

$$= \frac{1}{2}\left[\frac{(x-3)^3}{3}\right]_2^4 = \frac{1}{6}[(1)^3 - (-1)^3] = \frac{1}{3},$$

and $\sigma = \frac{1}{\sqrt{3}}$.

EXAMPLE 8.15-2

Calculate variance and standard deviation of the random variable x defined in example 8.13-3.

Solution

x_i	2	3	4	5	6	7	8	9	10	11	12
$f(x_i)$	$\frac{1}{36}$	$\frac{2}{36}$	$\frac{3}{36}$	$\frac{4}{36}$	$\frac{5}{36}$	$\frac{6}{36}$	$\frac{5}{36}$	$\frac{4}{36}$	$\frac{3}{36}$	$\frac{2}{36}$	$\frac{1}{36}$

As already calculated in example 8.13-3, mean $E(x) = 7$.

$$E(x^2) = 2^2.\frac{1}{36} + 3^2.\frac{2}{36} + 4^2.\frac{3}{36} + 5^2.\frac{4}{36} + 6^2.\frac{5}{36} + 7^2.\frac{6}{36} + 8^2.\frac{5}{36} + 9^2.\frac{4}{36} + 10^2.\frac{3}{36} + 11^2.\frac{2}{36} + 12^2.\frac{1}{36} = 54.8.$$

$\therefore$ $\qquad \text{Var}(x) = E(x^2) - [E(x)]^2 = 54.8 - 49 = 5.8,$

and $\qquad \text{S.D.} = \sqrt{5.8} = 2.4.$

EXAMPLE 8.15-3

A box contains electric bulbs, proportion p of which are defective. A bulb is drawn at random; if x has value 1 when the bulb is defective and zero otherwise, obtain the variance of x.

Solution

x: 1 $\qquad$ 0

$P(x)$: p $\qquad$ $1 - p (= q)$

$\therefore \quad E(x) = 1.p + 0.q = p,$

$E(x^2) + 1^2.p + 0^2.q = p.$

$\therefore \quad \text{Var}(x) = E(x^2) - [E(x)]^2 = p - p^2 = p(1 - p) = pq.$

EXAMPLE 8.15-4

Mean and variance of x are 25 and 2 respectively. Find

(i) $E(x^2)$,

(ii) $Var(3x - 2)$,

(iii) σ_{3x-2},

(iv) $Var(-x)$,

(v) σ_{-x}.

Solution

(i) $\text{Var}(x) = E(x^2) - [E(x)]^2$

$\therefore 2 = E(x^2) - (25)^2$

$\therefore E(x)^2 = 627.$

(ii) $\text{Var}(3x - 2) = \text{Var}(3x) = 9\ \text{Var}(x) = 9 \times 2 = 18.$

(iii) $\sigma_{3x-2} = +\sqrt{18} = 4.24.$

(iv) $\text{Var}(-x) = \text{Var}(x) = 2.$

(v) $\sigma_{-x} = +\sqrt{2} = 1.414.$

8.16 DISCRETE PROBABILITY DISTRIBUTIONS

In this section a brief account is given of a few discrete probability distributions which have a wider use in practice.

8.16-1 Bernoulli Trials and Binomial Distribution

Bernoulli Trial. It is an experiment which has only two possible outcomes, success (S) and failure (F). Various examples of Bernoulli trials are : tossing of a coin (head or tail), firing a target (hit or miss), fighting an election (win or not win), playing a game (win or lose), etc. In fact, any chance mechanism whose outcomes can be grouped into two classes may be regarded as a Bernoulli trial.

Binomial Distribution. We make n trials. The result of each trial is random and can either be success or failure. Let p be the probability of success and $q = (1 - p)$ be the probability of failure. The results of n trials are independent *i.e.* the outcome of any particular trial depends neither on the outcomes of the previous trials nor the trials that follow. The probability of getting k successes in n trials can be found as follows :

Without loss of generality, it can be assumed that the first k trials result in success and the remaining $n-k$ trials result in failure. By compound probability theorem, the probability of this event $= (p.p... \ k \text{ times}).(q.q. \ ... \ n-k \text{ times}) = p^k \times q^{n-k}$.

Now out of n trials, the k successes can happen in any one of ${}^nC_k$ different ways. For each way of getting k successes the probability is $p^k \cdot q^{n-k}$. Hence the probability of getting k successes in n trials is

$$f = P(x = k) \ = \ {}^nC_k \cdot p^k \cdot q^{n-k}, \ k = 0, 1, 2, ..., n. \qquad ... (8.40)$$

The quantities n and p are called parameters of binomial distribution. The random variable k is discrete as it takes integer values only. If p and q are equal, the binomial distribution is symmetrical, otherwise it is skewed. The limiting form of a binomial distribution when $n \to \infty$ is a continuous p.d.f. known as normal distribution.

Properties of binomial distribution are

$$\text{mean } \mu \ = \ np,$$
$$\text{variance } \sigma_x^2 \ = \ npq,$$
$$\text{standard deviation } \sigma_x \ = \ \sqrt{npq}\,.$$

Applications: The binomial distribution finds use in many scientific and engineering applications. It is used extensively in statistical quality control and acceptance sampling to classify a lot as defective or non-defective. Medical applications as success or failure of surgery, cure or no cure of a patient and military applications as hit or miss of a target, are characterised by binomial distribution.

EXAMPLE 8.16-1.1

Consider the tossing of a fair coin. Find the probability of getting exactly two heads (in any order) on the 3 tosses of the fair coin.

Solution

Here p = characteristic probability or probability of success = 0.5,
q = $1 - p$ = the probability of failure = 0.5,
k = the number of successes desired = 2,
n = the number of trials to be undertaken = 3.

$$\text{Probability of } k \text{ successes in } n \text{ trials} = {}^nC_k \, p^k q^{n-k} = \frac{n!}{k!(n-k)!} \cdot p^k q^{n-k}.$$

$$\therefore \text{ Probability of 2 successes in 3 trials} = \frac{3!}{2!(3-2)!} \cdot (0.5^2)(0.5^1) = \frac{6}{2 \times 1} \times .25 \times .5 = 0.375.$$

∴ The chances of getting 2 heads on 3 tosses of a fair coin are 0.375.

EXAMPLE 8.16-1.2

Some field representatives of the Environmental Protection Agency are doing spot checks of water pollution in streams. Historically, 8 out of 10 such tests produce favourable results i.e., no pollution. If the field group is going to perform 6 tests, find the chances of getting exactly three favourable results from this group of tests.

Solution

Here $p = 0.8$, $q = 0.2$, $k = 3$, $n = 6$.

$$\text{Probability of } k \text{ successes in } n \text{ trials} = {}^nC_k \, p^k q^{n-k} = \frac{n!}{k!(n-k)!} \cdot p^k q^{n-k}.$$

$\therefore$ Probability of 3 favourable tests out of 6 = $\frac{6!}{3!\cdot 3!}\cdot(0.8)^3(0.2)^3 = \frac{720}{6\times 6}(0.512)(0.008)$

$= 0.08192.$

EXAMPLE 8.16-1.3

Five employees are required to operate a chemical process; the process cannot be started until all 5 work stations are manned. Employee records indicate that there is 0.3 chance of any one employee being late, and we know that they all come to work independently of each other. Management is interested in knowing the probabilities of 0, 1, 2, 3, 4 or 5 employees being late, so that a decision concerning the number of back-up personnel can be made. Draw the probability distribution illustrating this situation.

Solution

Here $p = 0.3$, $q = 0.7$, $n = 5$.

We would make a separate calculation for each k from 0 through 5. Probability of k successes in n trials = ${}^nC_k p^k q^{n-k} = \frac{n!}{k!(n-k)!}p^k q^{n-k}$.

$$\therefore \text{P}(0) = \frac{5!}{0!5!}(0.3)^0(0.7)^5 = \frac{120}{1\times 120}\ (1)\ (0.1681) = 0.1681,$$

$$\text{P}(1) = \frac{5!}{1!4!}(0.3)^1(0.7)^4 = \frac{120}{1\times 24}\ (0.3)\ (0.7)^4 = 0.360,$$

$$\text{P}(2) = \frac{5!}{2!3!}\ (0.3)^2\ (0.7)^3 = \frac{120}{2\times 6}\ (0.09)\ (0.343) = 0.3087,$$

$$\text{P}(3) = \frac{5!}{3!2!}\ (0.3)^3\ (0.7)^2 = \frac{120}{6\times 2}\ (0.027)\ (0.49) = 0.1323,$$

$$\text{P}(4) = \frac{5!}{4!1!}\ (0.3)^4\ (0.7)^1 = \frac{120}{24\times 1}\ (0.0081)\ (0.7) = 0.0284,$$

$$\text{P}(5) = \frac{5!}{5!0!}\ (0.3)^5\ (0.7)^0 = \frac{120}{120\times 1}\ (0.00243)\ (1) = 0.0024.$$

If the results of the above six independent calculations are graphed, this binomial distribution would appear as shown in Fig. 8.3.

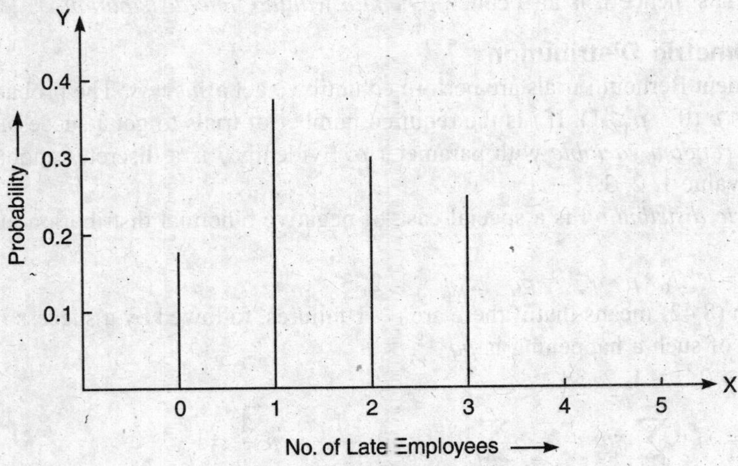

Fig. 8.3

EXAMPLE 8.16-1.4

If on an average 8 ships out of 10 arrive safely at a port, find the mean and standard deviation of the number of ships arriving safely out of a total of 1,600 ships. [*Delhi M.Com. 1983*]

Solution

Here $p = 8/10 = 0.8$, $q = 0.2$, $n = 1{,}600$.

$\therefore$ Mean $= np = 1{,}600 \times 0.8 = 1280$,

standard deviation $= \sqrt{npq} = \sqrt{1{,}600 \times 0.8 \times 0.2} = 16$.

EXAMPLE 8.16-1.5

The incidence of occupational disease in an industry is such that the workers have a 20% chance of suffering from it. What is the probability that out of six workers 4 or more will contract the disease ?

Solution

Probability that 4 or more workers will contract the disease

$= 1 -$ (probability that 4 or less workers will contract the disease)

$= 1 - {}^nC_k\, p^k \cdot q^{n-k}$.

Here $p = 0.2$, $q = 0.8$, $n = 6$, $k = 4, 3, 2, 1, 0$.

$$\begin{aligned}\therefore \text{The required probability} &= 1 - [{}^6C_4 \cdot (0.2)^4 \cdot (0.8)^2 + {}^6C_3(0.2)^3\,(0.8)^3 + {}^6C_2(0.2)^2(0.8)^4 \\ &\quad + {}^6C_1(0.2)^1\,(0.8)^5 + {}^6C_0(0.2)^0\,(0.8)^6] \\ &= 1 - [0.0157 + 0.0819 + 0.2457 + 0.3932 + 0.2622] \\ &= 1 - 0.9987 = 0.0013.\end{aligned}$$

8.16-2 Negative Binomial Distribution (Pascal Distribution)

In binomial distribution n, the number of trials is fixed and the random variable is the number of successes (or failures) to occur. In *negative binomial distribution*, the random variable is given by the number of independent trials to be carried out until a given number of successes (or failures) occur. If j denotes the number of trials necessary for c, a fixed number of successes, then probability of j trials until c successes occur = probability of $(c - 1)$ successes in $(j - 1)$ trials $\times$ probability of a success in the jth trial.

$$\begin{aligned}\therefore \quad P(x = j) &= [{}^{j-1}C_{c-1} \cdot p^{c-1} \cdot q^{j-c}] \cdot p. \\ &= {}^{j-1}C_{c-1}\, p^c \cdot q^{j-c}, \quad j = c,\ c + 1\ c + 2, \ldots \qquad \ldots (8.41)\end{aligned}$$

Obviously, $P(x = j)$ is the probability that one must wait to get c successes (or failures) in j independent trials; hence it is also called *binomial waiting time distribution.*

8.16-3 Geometric Distribution

Independent Bernoulli trials are performed until we get a *success*. The probability of success on each trial is p $(0 < p \leq 1)$. If j is the required number of trials to get a success, then j is called the *geometric random variable* with parameter p. Evidently j is a discrete random variable as it can have any value 1, 2, 3,... .

Geometric distribution is a special case of negative binomial distribution and occurs when $c = 1$, *i.e.*,

$$P(x = j) = {}^{j-1}C_0 \times p \times q^{j-1} = pq^{j-1}, \quad j = 1, 2, 3, \ldots . \qquad \ldots (8.42)$$

Equation (8.42) means that if there are $j - 1$ failures, followed by a success on jth trial, then the possibility of such a happening is pq^{j-1}.

$P(x = j) \geq 0, j = 1, 2, 3, \ldots$.

$$\sum_{j=1}^{\infty} P(x = j) = \sum_{j=1}^{\infty} pq^{j-1} = p\sum_{j=1}^{\infty} q^{j-1} = p \cdot \frac{1}{1-q} = p \cdot \frac{1}{p} = 1..$$

Properties of geometric distribution are

$$\text{mean} = \frac{1}{p},$$

$$\text{variance} = \frac{q}{p^2},$$

$$\text{standard deviation} = \frac{\sqrt{q}}{p}.$$

8.16-4 Hypergeometric Distribution

Binomial distribution is applicable to an experiment in which the probability of success is same for all trials. However, if it varies from trial to trial, *hypergeometric distribution* is more suitable.

From a lot of N items, of which N_1 are good and N_2 $(= N - N_1)$ defective, we choose n $(\leq N)$ items at random *without* replacement. Then the probability that the sample contains k items of the first category and $n - k$ of the second is given by

$$P(x = k) = \frac{{}^{N_1}C_k \cdot {}^{N_2}C_{n-k}}{{}^{N}C_n}, \quad k = 0, 1, 2, ..., n. \qquad ... (8.43)$$

Properties of hypergeometric distribution are

$$\text{mean} = \frac{n N_1}{N},$$

$$\text{variance} = \frac{N_1 N_2 \cdot n(N - n)}{N^2 \cdot (N - 1)},$$

$$\text{standard deviation} = \frac{1}{N} \cdot \sqrt{\frac{N_1 N_2 \cdot n(N - n)}{N - 1}}.$$

If there are m categories instead of two (good and defective), the hypergeometric distribution may be generalised to the following form:

$$\frac{{}^{N_1}C_{k_1} \cdot {}^{N_2}C_{k_2} \cdots {}^{N_m}C_{km}}{{}^{N}C_n}. \qquad ... (8.44)$$

8.16-5 Multinomial Distribution

It is obtained from generalisation of binomial distribution. Let the sample space of an experiment be divided into s mutually exclusive events $A_1, A_2, ..., A_k$ with probabilities $p_1, p_2, ..., p_k$, where $p_1 + p_2 + ... + p_k = 1$.

Then in n repeated trials, the probability of A_1 occurring n_1 times, A_2 occurring n_2 times, ..., A_k occurring n_k times is

$$\frac{n!}{n_1!\, n_2! ... n_k!} \cdot p_1^{n} \cdot p_2^{n_2} \cdots p_k^{n_k}, \qquad ... (8.45)$$

where $n_1 + n_2 + ... + n_k = n$.

The above expression is called *multinomial distribution* since its terms are precisely the terms in the expression of $(p_1 + p_2 + ... + p_k)^n$. If $k = 2$, this distribution reduces to binomial distribution.

8.16-6 Poisson Distribution

In binomial distribution it was possible to count the number of successes (number of times the event occurred) as well as failures (event did not occur) in a finite number of trials. However, there are many random phenomena wherin it is possible to prescribe the number of times an event occurs but not the number of times it does not occur. For example, number of patients arriving at a doctor's clinic in, say, 30 minutes interval can be counted but it is not possible to count how many have not arrived. Likewise, number of vehicles arriving at a road crossing can be recorded but not the number of vehicles which do not arrive there. These are examples of occurrence of an *isolated event* in a *continuum of time*. A typical application of the Poisson distribution occurs in analysing queuing problems.

Suppose we use the number of patients arriving at a doctor's clinic as an illustration of Poisson distribution characteristics:

1. The average arrival of patients per 30-minute interval can be estimated from the past data.
2. If we divide the 30-minute interval into smaller intervals of, say, one second each, we find that the following statements are true:
   (*a*) The probability that exactly one patient will arrive at the clinic per second is a very small number and is constant for every 1-second interval.
   (*b*) The probability that two or more patients will arrive within a 1-second interval is so small that it can be safely neglected.
   (*c*) The number of patients who arrive in a 1-second interval is independent of where that 1-second interval is within the larger 30-minute interval.
   (*d*) The number of patients who arrive in any 1-second interval is not dependent on the number of arrivals in any other 1-second interval.

In this illustration the number of trials (or subdivisions) n is large (1800); if λ is the number of patients arriving in 1-second interval, $p = \frac{\lambda}{n}$ (or $\lambda = np$). Under the condition that $n \to \infty$, $p \to 0$ but $np = \lambda$, a finite positive value, the binomial distribution approximates to Poisson distribution. For binomial distribution,

$$P(x = k) = {}^nC_k \, p^k \cdot q^{n-k}, \quad k = 0, 1, 2, ..., n$$

$$= {}^nC_k \left(\frac{\lambda}{n}\right)^k \cdot \left(1 - \frac{\lambda}{n}\right)^{n-k}, \quad k = 0, 1, 2, ..., n.$$

It can be shown that as $n \to \infty$,

$$P(x = k) = \frac{\lambda^k \cdot e^{-\lambda}}{k!}, \quad k = 0, 1, 2, ..., \qquad ... (8.46)$$

which is the Poisson distribution. Here

λ = the average (mean) of the distribution,
k = the specific value of the discrete random variable in which we are interested,
e = 2.718, the base of natural logarithms.

Properties of the Poisson distribution are

$$\text{mean} = \lambda,$$
$$\text{variance} = \lambda,$$
$$\text{standard deviation} = \sqrt{\lambda}.$$

This distribution finds application in a wide variety of situations in which some kind of *event occurs repeatedly but haphazardly.* Some of the situations are

1. Number of telephone calls arriving a telephone exchange per unit time.
2. Number of α-particles emitted by a radioactive substance.
3. Number of deaths occurring due to, say, heart disease in a city having large population.
4. Number of typing errors per page in a big text.

5. Number of defects occurring in the long length of cloth being manufactured in a factory.
6. Number of vehicles arriving at a road intersection, customers arriving at a service counter, broken-down machines waiting repairs, letters waiting to be typed by the typist, etc.

EXAMPLE 8.16-6.1

Consider an emergency room of a small rural hospital where the past records indicate an average of 5 arrivals daily. The demand for emergency room service at this hospital is distributed according to a Poisson distribution. Calculate the probability of exactly 0, 1, 2, 3, 4 and 5 arrivals. What is the probability of more than 3 arrivals ?

Solution

$$P(x = k) = \frac{\lambda^k e^{-\lambda}}{k!}. \text{ Here, } \lambda = 5, k = 0, 1, 2, 3, 4 \text{ and } 5.$$

$$\therefore \quad P(0) = \frac{5^0 \cdot e^{-5}}{0!} = \frac{1.(0.00674)}{1} = 0.00674,$$

$$P(1) = \frac{5^1 \cdot e^{-5}}{1!} = \frac{5 \times 0.00674}{1} = 0.03370,$$

$$P(2) = \frac{5^2 \cdot e^{-5}}{2!} = \frac{25 \times 0.00674}{2} = 0.08425,$$

$$P(3) = \frac{5^3 \cdot e^{-5}}{3!} = \frac{125 \times 0.00674}{6} = 0.14042,$$

$$P(4) = \frac{5^4 \cdot e^{-5}}{4!} = \frac{625 \times 0.00674}{24} = 0.17552,$$

$$P(5) = \frac{5^5 \cdot e^{-5}}{5!} = \frac{3125 \times 0.00674}{120} = 0.17552.$$

Probability of more than three arrivals = 1 – sum of probabilities of 0, 1, 2 and 3 arrivals
= 1 – (0.00674 + 0.03370 + 0.08425 + 0.14042)
= 1 – 0.26511 = 0.73489

In other words, there will be more than 3 arrivals per day slightly less than three-quarters of the time.

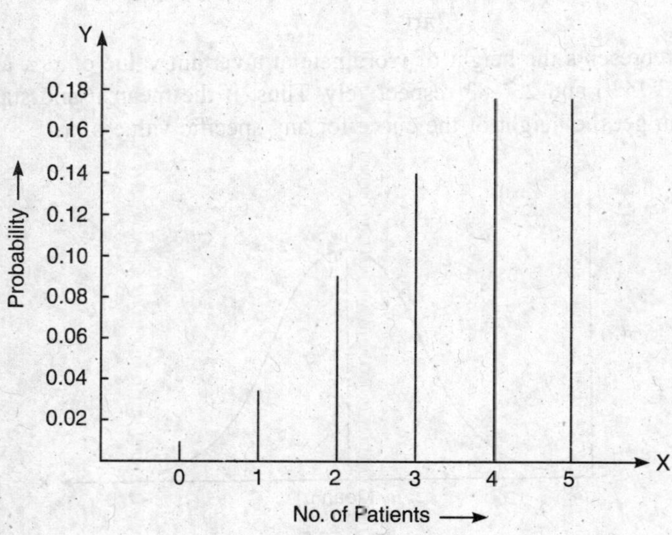

Fig. 8.4

Fig. 8.4 represents graphically the Poisson probability distribution of demand for emergency room services. This distribution is only for 0 through 5 calls for emergency room service; it would, of course, be possible to determine the required probability values and thus the graphic distribution for any number of arrivals with additional calculation.

8.17 CONTINUOUS PROBABILITY DISTRIBUTIONS

In discrete probability distributions, the probability is clustered at certain points. For these distributions,

$$P(x = x_i) = P_i,$$

and $$\Sigma P_i = 1, \text{ where } i = 1, 2, ..., n. \quad ... (8.47)$$

In continuous probability distributions, the probability is distributed continuously and uniformly over the whole area of the curve $y = f(x)$. Therefore, to find the probability that x lies between any two values a and b, one has to find the area enclosed between the x-axis, curve $y = f(x)$ and the ordinates $x = a$ and $x = b$. This area is mathematically given by the integral

$$\int_a^b f(x).dx.$$

Similarly, probability that x lies between x and $x + \delta x$ is given by the area of the elementary strip of base δx, constructed near the point x. This area decreases with decrease in the value of δx, and will become zero when $\delta x \to 0$ so that the probability that x takes a particular value, say $x = k$ is zero. Thus in case of a continuous distribution, probability at a point is zero, while it is finite for a finite interval. Now we shall discuss a few important continuous probability distributions.

8.17-1 Normal Distribution

The normal (or Gaussian) distribution or curve (also called normal probability curve, probability curve, error curve, etc.) is the best known continuous distribution and occupies a very important position. It is important for a manager because many phenomena follow this distribution. Almost all probability distributions tend to normal distribution under certain limiting conditions.

A variable is said to be normally distributed if its curve appears as shown in Fig. 8.5. This curve has the following expression :

$$f(x) = \frac{1}{\sqrt{2\pi\sigma^2}} \cdot e^{-\frac{(x-\mu)^2}{2\sigma^2}}, -\infty < x < \infty, \quad ...(8.48)$$

where $f(x)$ represents the height of y-ordinate at a certain value of x. π and e are constants having values of 3.1416 and 2.7183 respectively. Thus, if the mean μ and standard deviation σ are known, we can get the height of the curve for any specific value of x.

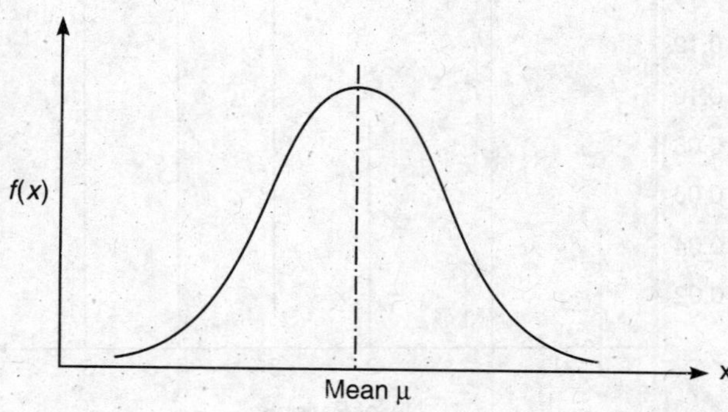

Fig. 8.5

The shape of this curve depends upon these two parameters and for different values of μ and σ, we get different normal curves. Fig. 8.6 shows the dependence on σ. The three normal curves have the same value of μ (μ = 0) but different values of σ, namely ½, 1 and 2 respectively. The parameter σ controls the relative flatness of the curve. As σ decreases, the curve becomes more sharply peaked and as σ increases the curve becomes more flatter.

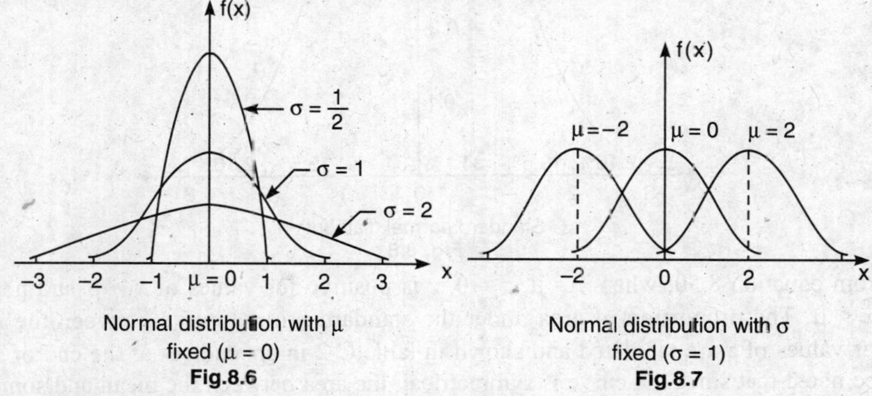

Normal distribution with μ fixed (μ = 0)
Fig.8.6

Normal distribution with σ fixed (σ = 1)
Fig.8.7

If σ is kept constant and μ is varied (Fig. 8.7), the shape of the curve remains the same but its midpoint moves to the location of μ. Note that while μ can have any value (+ or –), σ is always positive.

The notation N(μ, σ^2) is usually used to represent a normal distribution with mean μ and stranded deviation σ. This distribution has the following characteristics (Fig. 8.5) :

1. Its mean = μ, variance = σ^2 and standard deviation = σ.
2. It is unimodal, bell shaped and symmetrical about the mean. That is, if the curve is folded along the line $x = \mu$, the two halves will coincide.
3. The mean, mode and median all coincide at $x = \mu$.
4. The total area under the curve is divided evenly because of the symmetry. 50% of area is to the right of the vertical line at $x = \mu$ and 50% is to its left.
5. Variable x, being continuous, can take any value between –∞ and ∞. As such, the curve approaches closely but never touches the x-axis.
6. As σ and μ control the shape of the curve, for different combinations of σ and μ, we will have different normal curves. Thus, the normal distribution is a family of distributions in which a member is distinguished from the others depending upon the values of μ and σ it has. One such distinguished member is obtained by assuming μ = 0 and σ = 1 and is known as *standard normal distribution*. It has the following expression :

$$f(z) = \frac{1}{\sqrt{2\pi}} \cdot e^{-z^2/2}, -\infty < z < \infty, \quad \text{...(8.49)}$$

in which variable z is known as *standard normal variate* and is defined as

$$z = \frac{x - \mu}{\sigma}. \quad \text{...(8.50)}$$

7. If we construct two vertical lines at a distance of one standard deviation on either side of the mean (Fig. 8.8), then the area enclosed by these lines under the curve is found to be equal to 68.2% of the total area. If we draw these vertical lines at a distance of two standard deviations an either side of the mean, the area inclosed is 95.4% and for distance of three standard deviations the area covered is 99.73% of the total area under the curve *i.e.*, μ ± 3σ covers 99.73% of the area under the curve. Thus although, theoretically, the range of z is from –∞ to ∞, for all practical purposes it lies within ± 3.

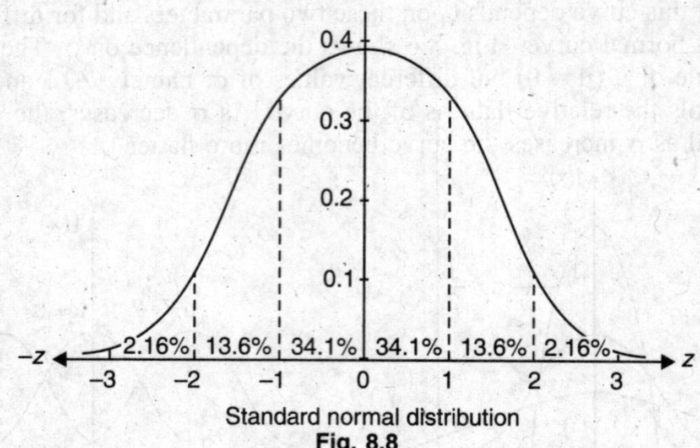

Standard normal distribution

Fig. 8.8

From equation 8.50, when $x = \mu$, $z = 0$, z is positive for values of $x > \mu$ and negative for values $x < \mu$. The proportion of area under the standard normal curve between the mean and particular values of z are tabulated and shown in table C-2 in appendices at the end of this book. It may be noted that since the curve is symmetrical, the area between the mean and some positive value of z is same as that for the negative value of z.

Importance of Normal Distribution

1. In limiting form, almost all distributions tend to normal distribution.
2. When a variable is not normally distributed, it can be made normally distributed with the help of some suitable transformations.
3. The distribution of sample mean, sample variance, etc. converge to normal when sample size is large and as such this distribution forms the basis for tests of significance.

EXAMPLE 8.17-1.1

A project yields an average cash flow of ₹ 500 lakhs with a standard deviation of ₹ 60 lakhs. Calculate the following probabilities.:

(a) cash flow will be more than ₹ 560 lakhs.

(b) cash flow will be less than ₹ 420 lakhs.

(c) cash flow will lie between ₹ 460 lakhs and ₹ 540 lakhs.

(d) cash flow will be more than ₹ 680 lakhs.

[Dayalbagh Edu. Inst. Agra M.Com. Dec., 2008]

Solution

We first reduce the distribution to the standard normal distribution and then with the help of statistical table C–2, find out the area under the curve or the required probabilties.

Now
$$z = \frac{x - \mu}{\sigma} = \frac{x - 500}{60}.$$

(*a*) For $x = 560$, the standard normal variate reduces to

$$z = \frac{560 - 500}{60} = 1.$$

For z = 1 from table C–2, the area on the right-hand side of $z = 1$ is 0.1587, which is also the probability that the cash flow will be more than ₹ 560 lakhs. This is shown in Fig. 8.9 (*a*).

(*b*) Here,
$$z = \frac{420 - 500}{60} = \frac{-80}{60} = -1.33.$$

The negative sign indicates that the area under consideration is to the left of the mean. Now from the tables we can find the area to the left of the point B corresponding to $z = 1.33$. This is 0.9082 of the total area under the curve. Therefore, area under the curve to the right of point B $= 1 - 0.9082 = .0918$. By symmetry, this is equal to the area under the curve to the left of point A corresponding to $z = -1.33$.

∴ Probability that the cash flow will be less than ₹ 420 lakhs = 0.0918. This is shown in Fig. 8.9 (*b*).

(*c*) Here,

$$z_1 = \frac{460-500}{60} = -\frac{40}{60} = -0.66,$$

$$z_2 = \frac{540-500}{60} = \frac{40}{60} = 0.66.$$

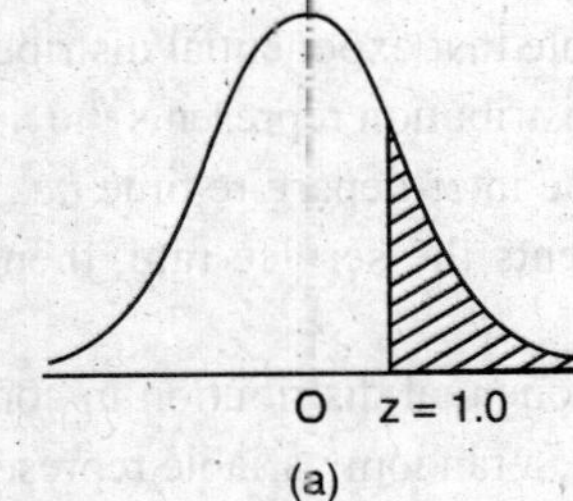

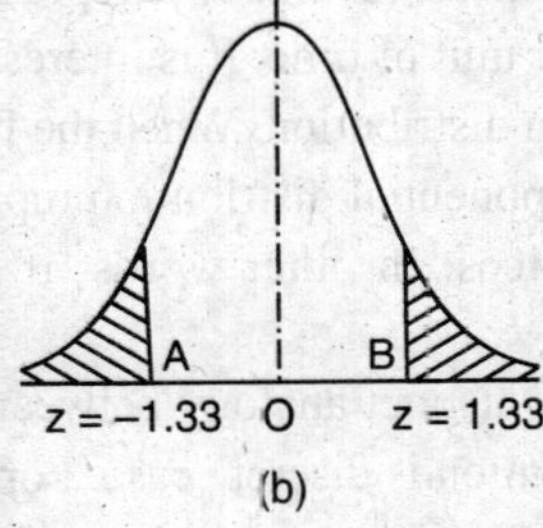

Fig. 8.9

∴ Area of the curve to the left of the point at $z_2 = 0.66$ is $= 0.7454$, and area of the curve to the left of the point corresponding to $z_1 = -0.66$ is $= 0.5 - (0.7454 - 0.5) = 1 - 0.7454 = 0.2546$.

∴ Area under the curve between z_1 and $z_2 = 0.7454 - 0.2546 = 0.4908$.

∴ The probability of cash flow being between ₹ 460 lakhs and ₹ 540 lakhs is 0.49. This is shown in Fig. 8.10 (*a*).

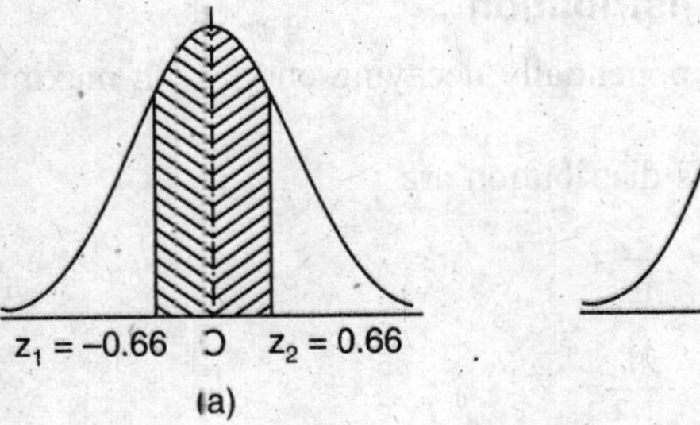

Fig. 8.10

(*d*) Here,

$$z = \frac{680-500}{60} = \frac{180}{60} = 3.0$$

Referring to the table, the area beyond 3.0 is $1 - 0.99865 = 0.00135$ (see Fig. 8.10 (*b*)), hence the probability of cash flow being more than ₹ 680 lakhs is 0.00135.

8.17-2 Exponential Distribution (Negative Exponential Distribution)

A continuous random variable x, with its *p.d.f.* defined by

$$f(x) = \begin{cases} \mu e^{-\mu x}, & \text{if } x > 0; \\ 0, & \text{otherwise,} \end{cases} \qquad \text{... (8.51)}$$

where parameter $\mu > 0$, is said to have an *exponential distribution. P.d.f.* for this distribution is shown in Fig. 8.11.

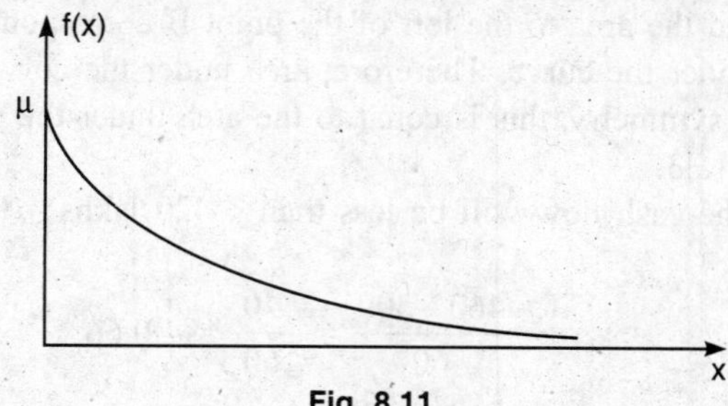

Fig. 8.11

Exponential distribution is often encountered in queuing problems as a probability model for service time. Its mean (average) μ represents 'the rate of service' *i.e.*, the average number of customers served per unit of time. It is interesting to note that exponential distribution is intimately related to the Poisson distribution. When the Poisson distribution represents the *number* of arrivals per unit time, the exponential distribution represents the inter-departure time *i.e.*, the *time between two* successive services. In other words, if μ represents the service rate, then x represents the inter-departure time.

There is also a distinct analogy between the exponential distribution in continuous case and the geometric distribution is discrete case. For example, a random variable representing the *number* of trials before the first failure in the geometric distribution is analogous to the variable representing *time-to-failure* in the exponential distribution. In the limiting case as $p \to 0$ and inter-trial time $\to$ 0, geometric distribution takes the form of exponential distribution.

Exponential distribution applies to events that are subject to a constant chance of failure, such as life testing electronic components.

Properties of the Exponential Distribution

1. The density function is an exponentially decaying curve with maximum μ at $x = 0$ (see Fig. 8.11).

2. The mean and variance of this distribution are

$$E(x) = \frac{1}{\mu},$$

$$V(x) = \frac{1}{\mu^2}.$$

3. The cumulative distribution function F(x) is given by

$$F(x) = P(X \le x) = \int_0^x f(x) \cdot dx = \int_0^x \mu \cdot e^{-\mu x} \cdot dx = 1 - e^{-\mu x}.$$

No special table is needed for the calculation of probabilities of the exponential distribution. The logarithmic table is sufficient for this purpose.

8.17-3 Rectangular Distribution (Uniform or Homogeneous Distribution)

A continuous random variable x is said to have *rectangular* or *uniform distribution* if its density function is given by

$$f(x) = \begin{cases} \frac{1}{b-a}, a < x < b \\ 0, \text{otherwise}, \end{cases} \qquad \text{... (8.52)}$$

where a, $b > 0$ are some constants.

This distribution is called uniform distribution because its density function is uniform (constant) in the interval (a, b).

The distribution function F(x) is given by

$$F(x) = \int_{-\infty}^{x} f(x) \cdot dx$$

$$= \begin{cases} 0 & , \quad x < a, \\ \dfrac{x-a}{b-a} & , \quad a < x < b, \\ 1 & , \quad x \geq b. \end{cases}$$

The function F(x) varies linearly in the interval (a, b).

Figures 8.12 and 8.13 show the density function $f(x)$ and distribution function F(x) in the interval (a, b).

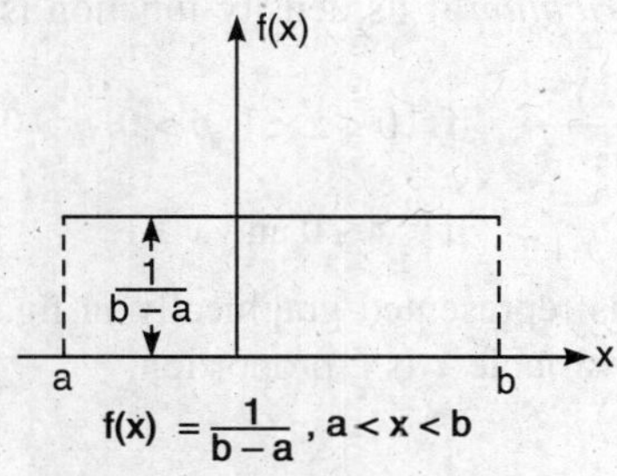

Fig. 8.12

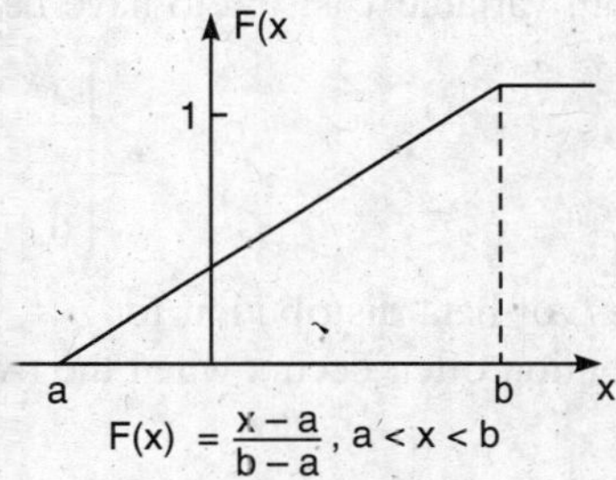

Fig. 8.13

Properties of rectangular distribution are

$$\text{mean} = \frac{a+b}{2},$$

$$\text{variance} = \frac{(b-a)^2}{12},$$

$$\text{standard deviation} = \frac{b-a}{2\sqrt{3}}.$$

Rectangular distribution finds its application in statistical problems.

8.17-4 Gamma Distribution

A continuous random variable x is said to have *gamma* or *Erlang distribution* if it assumes only non-negative values and its *p.d.f.* is given by

$$f(x) = \begin{cases} \dfrac{\mu(\mu x)^{n-1} e^{-\mu x}}{(n-1)!}, & \text{if } 0 < x < \infty; \\ 0, \text{ otherwise.} \end{cases} \qquad \text{... (8.53)}$$

The parameters μ and n are non-negative parameters. When $n = 1$, the above *p.d.f.* is reduced to the exponential *p.d.f.* The gamma distribution is applied to waiting-time models in life testing, waiting time until death, etc. If there are n independent and identically distributed exponential random variables, the distribution representing the *summation* of these variables is the gamma distribution. This distribution (sum of exponential random variables) is analogous to the negative binomial (sum of geometric random variables) distribution. For $n = 1$ and $\mu = 0.5$, the graph for *p.d.f.* of gamma distribution is shown in figure 8.14

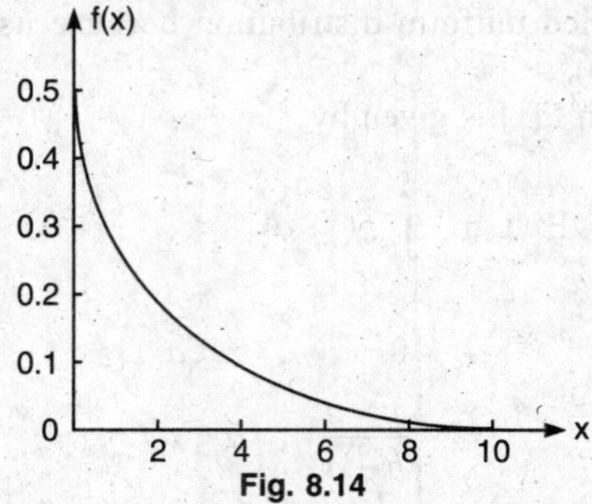

Fig. 8.14

As in Poisson distribution, so also in gamma distribution, the mean and variance are equal. This distribution possesses the additive property.

8.17-5 Beta Distribution

A random variable x is said to have *beta distribution* if its density function is given by

$$f(x) = \begin{cases} \dfrac{x^{p-1} \cdot (1-x)^{q-1}}{\beta(p,q)}, & \text{if } \ 0 < x < 1;\, p > 0,\, q > 0, \\ 0, & \text{if } \ x \le 0 \text{ and } x \ge 1. \end{cases} \quad \ldots (8.54)$$

The *p.d.f.* of beta distribution for $p = q = 2$ is represented graphically in figure 8.15. This type of distribution often occurs when the random variable x is a proportion.

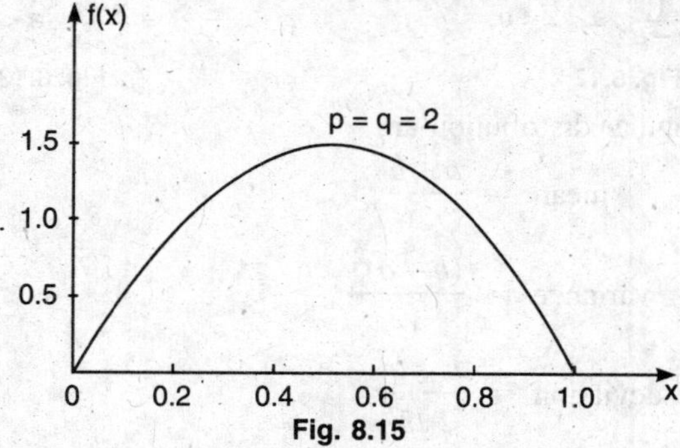

Fig. 8.15

Properties of beta distribution are

$$\text{mean} = \frac{p}{p+q},$$

$$\text{variance} = \frac{p(p+1)}{(p+q)(p+q+1)},$$

$$\text{standard deviation} = \sqrt{\frac{p(p+1)}{(p+q)\,(p+q+1)}}.$$

EXERCISES

1. What are the axioms of probability ? [*Kanpur U., 1996*]
2. Define conditional probability and outline its properties. [*P.T.U. MCA, 2010*]
3. What do you understand by the following terms ?:
   Random experiment, event, mutually exclusive events, exhaustive events, complementary events, equally likely events and independent events. [*P.U. MFC, 2002*]

4. (*a*) Explain with examples the rules of addition and multiplication theory of probability. [*Rohtak U. MBA, 1981*]

(*b*) Write short notes on sample space and probability. [*P.T.U. MCA, 2010*]

5. Differentiate between

(*i*) Mutually exclusive events and non-exclusive events.

(*ii*) Conditional and joint probabilities. [*P.T.U. MCA, 2010*]

6. What do you understand by the term 'probability' ? Discuss its importance in business decision-making. What are the different approaches to probability ? [*Dayalbagh Edu. Inst. Agra M.Com. Dec., 2007*]

7. State and explain Baye's theorem. [*Delhi MBA, 1982*]

8. Explain what is meant by probability distribution of a random variable ? How is it useful in decision - making ? [*Delhi U. M.Com., 1983*]

9. Define binomial distribution and indicate its chief characteristics. Under what conditions does it tend to Poisson distribution ? [*P.U.MFC, 2002*]

10. Difine Poisson probability model. State some business and economic situations where it can be usefully employed. [*Delhi U.M.Com., 1980; Chennai M.Com., 1983*]

11. Give examples of situations where exponential distribution may be used, explaining clearly the various variables and parameters.

12. What is a uniform distribution ? Where is it found useful ? [*C.A. May, 1982*]

13. What are the chief properties of normal distribution ? Describe briefly the importance of normal distribution in statistical analysis. [*Delhi U. MBA, 1982*]

14. State the distinctive features of the binomial, Poisson and normal probability distributions. When does a binomial or Poisson distribution tend to a normal distribution ? [*BHU MBM, 1977; Delhi U. M.Com., 1978*]

15. Why does the normal distribution hold the most honourable position in probability theory ? [*Delhi U. M.Com., 1975*]

Section 8.1

16. What is the sample space for the experiment which consists of drawing one ball from an urn containing 8 balls of which 3 are green and 5 are red ? The balls have been numbered 1 through 8.

(*Ans.* S = {1, 2, ..., 8}.)

17. For problem 16 define the events as subsets:

A: a green ball is drawn,

B: a red ball is drawn.

(*Ans.* A = {1, 2, 3}; B = {4, 5, 6, 7, 8}.)

18. What is the sample space for the experiment which consists of drawing 2 balls with replacement from an urn containing 8 balls ? The balls are numbered 1 through 8.

(*Ans.* $S = \{(x_1, x_2): x_i = 1, 2, ..., 8; i = 1, 2\}$.)

19. For exercise 18 define the events as subsets :

A : the first ball is green,

B : the second ball is green,

C : both balls are green.

(*Ans.* $A = \{x_1, x_2) : x_1 = 1, 2, 3; x_2 = 1, 2, ..., 8\}$,
$B = \{(x_1, x_2) : x_1 = 1, 2, ..., 8; x_2 = 1, 2, 3\}$,
$C = \{(x_i, x_2) : x_i = 1, 2, 3; i = 1, 2\}$.)

Section 8.2

20. What is the probability of obtaining 9, 10 and 11 points with 3 dice ?

$$\left(\textit{Ans.} \frac{25}{216}, \frac{27}{216}, \frac{27}{216}.\right)$$

21. What is the probability of getting 2 tails and 2 heads when 4 coins are tossed ?

$$\left(\textit{Ans.} \frac{3}{8}.\right)$$

Section 8.3-8.7

22. There are 26 persons in a birthday party. What is the probability that at least two of them have the same birthday ? (*Ans.* 0.6.)

23. A coin is so weighted that head is thrice as likely to appear as tail. What is P(H) and P(T)?

$$\left(Ans.\ \frac{3}{4}, \frac{1}{4}\right)$$

24. An urn contains 3 green and 5 red balls. One ball is drawn, its colour unnoted and laid aside. Then another ball is drawn, find the probability that it is green or red. How does the probability change if the colour of the ball is noted ?

$$\left(Ans.\ \frac{3}{8}, \frac{5}{8}; \frac{2}{7}\right)$$

25. If the probability that A will solve a problem is 1/4 and the probability that B will solve is 3/4, what is the probability that the problem is at all solved ?

$$\left(Ans.\ \frac{13}{16}\right)$$

26. A die is so weighted that all even numbers have the same chance of appearing, all odd numbers have the same chance of appearing, while an even number is twice as likely to appear as an odd number. Find the probability that

(*i*) a prime number appears,
(*ii*) an even number appears,
(*iii*) an odd number appears,
(*iv*) an odd prime number appears.

(*Ans.* 4/9, 2/3, 1/3, 2/9.)

27. A pair of fair dice is rolled once. What is the probability that the sum is equal to each of the integers from 2 to 127 ?

(*Ans.*

s	2	3	4	5	6	7	8
p	$\frac{1}{36}$	$\frac{2}{36}$	$\frac{3}{36}$	$\frac{4}{36}$	$\frac{5}{36}$	$\frac{6}{36}$	$\frac{5}{36}$

9	10	11	12
$\frac{4}{36}$	$\frac{3}{36}$	$\frac{2}{36}$	$\frac{1}{36}$

)

28. A die is so located that the probability of a particular number appearing is proportional to the number. What is the probability of all single element events? What is the probability of occurrence of an even number and of a number greater than 4?

$$\left(Ans.\ \frac{1}{21}, \frac{2}{21}, \frac{3}{21}, \frac{4}{21}, \frac{5}{21}, \frac{6}{21}; \frac{12}{21}; \frac{11}{21}\right)$$

29. Three players A, B and C play a sequence of games. It is so decided that winner of each game scores one point and he who first scores three points is the final winner. A wins the first and third games while B wins the second. What is the probability that C is the final winner?

$$\left(Ans.\ \frac{2}{27}\right)$$

30. An urn contains 1 white and 2 black balls, while another contains 2 white and 1 black ball. One ball is transferred from the first urn into the second, after which a ball is drawn from the second urn. What is the probability that it is black?

$$\left(Ans.\ \frac{5}{12}\right)$$

31. An urn contains a white and b black balls. Balls are drawn one by one until only those of the same colour are left. What is the probability that they are white?

$$\left(Ans.\ \frac{a}{a+b}\right)$$

32. Eight white and 2 black balls are randomly laid out in a row. What is the probability that the two black balls are side by side? What is the probability that they occupy the end positions?

$$\left(Ans. \frac{1}{5}, \frac{1}{45}.\right)$$

33. An urn contains 2 white and 5 black balls. A ball is selected at random. If the ball drawn is black, it is replaced and two additional black balls are added to the urn; if the ball drawn is white, it is neither replaced nor additional balls are added. A ball is then drawn from the urn for the second time. What is the probability that it is black?

$$\left(Ans. \frac{50}{63}.\right)$$

34. An urn contains a fair coin and a two-headed coin. A coin is selected at random and tossed. If head appears, the other coin is tossed; if tail appears, the same coin is tossed.

(*i*) Find the probability that head appears on the second toss.

(*ii*) If head appears on the second toss, find the probability that it also appeared on the first toss.

$$\left(Ans. \frac{5}{8}, \frac{4}{5}.\right)$$

35. Certain mass-produced articles, of which 0.5% are defective, are packed in cartons each containing 130 articles. What proportion of cartons is free from defective articles? Also find out the proportion of cartons containing 2 or more defectives. *[IGNOU MBA, 2002]*

[**Hint.** $\lambda = \frac{0.5}{100} \times 130 = 0.65,$

$$p_0 = \frac{e^{-\lambda}.\lambda^x}{x!} = \frac{e^{-0.65} \times 0.65^0}{0!} = 0.522,$$

$$p_1 = \frac{e^{-0.65} \times 0.65^1}{1!} = 0.339,$$

$\therefore \quad p = 1 - (p_0 + p_1) = 1 - (0.522 + 0.339) = 0.139.$]

36. The latest nationwide political poll indicates that for Americans, who are randomly selected, the probability that they are conservatives is 0.55, the probability that they are liberal is 0.30 and the probability that they are middle of the road is 0.15. Answer the following questions pertaining to a randomly selected group of 10 Americans:

(a) What is probability that four are liberals?

(b) what is the probability that none are conservative?

(c) What is the probability that two are middle of the road?

(d) What is the probability that at least eight are liberal?

[Dayalbagh Edu. Inst. Agra M.B.A. Dec., 2012]

(*Ans.* (a) 20% (b) 0.034% (c) 27.59% (d) 0.159%.)

Section 8.11

37. Find the value of c so that the following $f(x)$ is a p.d.f. :

$$f(x) = \begin{cases} \frac{c}{x^2}, 10 \le x \le 20; \\ 0, \quad \text{otherwise.} \end{cases}$$

(*Ans.* $c = 20$.)

38. The following p.d.f. of the discrete random variable x represents the weekly demand of a certain item:

x	0	1	2	3
P(x)	*0.15*	*0.25*	*0.35*	*0.45*

If the weekly demands are independent and identical, find the p.d.f. for a two-week demand.

Decision Theory, Games, Investment Analysis and Annuity

The previous chapters dealt with formulation and solution of models under conditions of *perfect* information. This is usually referred to as decision making under *certainty.* Many managerial decisions, however, are made with some uncertainty. Managers, for example, authorise substantial financial investments with less than complete information about product demand. As the decisions taken by a manager govern the fortunes of business—right decisions will have a salutary effect while the wrong ones may prove to be disastrous, it is extremely important to choose the appropriate decision. Decision theory provides a rational approach to the managers in dealing with problems confronted with partial, imperfect or uncertain future conditions.

9.1 STEPS IN DECISION THEORY APPROACH

The decision theory approach generally involves four steps. We shall introduce these by considering a manufacturing company that is thinking of several alternative methods to increase its production to meet the increasing market demand.

Step 1. List all the viable alternatives

The first action a decision-maker must take is to list all the *viable alternatives* that can be considered in the decision. For instance, for the company considered above, there may be only the following three options:

1. Expand the present plant
2. Construct a new plant
3. Subcontract production for extra demand.

These alternatives are also termed as *courses of actions* or simply *actions* or *acts* or *strategies* and are known to and under the control of the decision-maker.

Step 2. Identify the expected future events

The second step for the decision-maker is to list all the *future events* that may occur. Often it is possible to identify most of the events that *can* occur; the difficulty is to identify *which particular event will* occur. These future events (not under the control of decision-maker) are termed as *states of nature* or *outcomes* in decision theory. Of course, out of this list, only one of the *events will* occur. For the manufacturing company considered above, the greatest uncertainty will be about product demand. The future events related to the demand may be

1. High demand
2. Moderate demand
3. Low demand
4. No demand.

Step 3. Construct a payoff table

The decision-maker now constructs a *payoff* table (table representing profit, benefit, etc.) or *conditional gain* or *conditional profit table* for each possible combination of alternative course of action and state of nature. Table 9.1 represents 12 possible payoffs for the manufacturing company's expansion decision.

TABLE 9.1

Alternatives	*States of nature (product demand)*			
	High	*Moderate*	*Low*	*Nil*
Expand	₹ 50,000	₹ 25,000	– ₹ 25,000	– ₹ 45,000
Construct	₹ 70,000	₹ 30,000	– ₹ 40,000	– ₹ 80,000
Subcontract	₹ 30,000	₹ 15,000	– ₹ 1,000	– ₹ 10,000

Step 4. Select optimum decision criterion

Finally, the decision-maker will choose *criterion* which results in largest pay off. The criterion may be economic, quantitative or qualitative (*e.g.*, market share, profit, fragrance of a perfume, etc).

9.2 DECISION-MAKING ENVIRONMENTS

Decisions are made under four types of environments that differ according to the *degree of certainty*. The degree of certainty may vary from complete certainty to complete uncertainty. The region that lies in between correspond to decision making under risk.

1. *Decision-making under conditions of certainty*

In this environment, only one state of nature exists for each alternative *i.e.*, there is complete certainty about the future. It is easy to analyse the situation and make good decisions. Since the decision-maker has perfect knowledge about the future outcomes, he simply chooses the alternative having optimum payoff. Examples include cost-volume-profit analysis when information about them is certainly and precisely known, linear programming when resources required, resources available, cost or profit per unit of the product are known with certainty.

2. *Decision-making under conditions of uncertainty*

Here, more than one states of nature exist but the decision-maker lacks sufficient knowledge to allow him assign probabilities to the various states of nature.

3. *Decision-making under conditions of risk*

Here also, more than one states of nature exist but the decision-maker has sufficient information to allow him assign probabilities to each of these states.

4. *Decision-making under conditions of conflict*

Situations exist in which two (or more) opponents with *conflicting objectives* try to make decisions with each trying to gain at the cost of the other(s). Examples include situations such as two players struggling to win at chess, candidates fighting an election, two enemies planning war tactics, firms struggling to maintain their market shares, etc. These situations are different since the decision-maker is working against an intelligent apponent. They are called decision-making under conflict or under partial uncertainty. The theory governing these types of decision problems is called *theory of games* and will be taken up later in this chapter.

9.3 DECISION-MAKING UNDER CONDITIONS OF CERTAINTY

Since under this environment, only *one* state of nature exists, the decision-maker simply picks up the best payoff in *that* one column and chooses the associated alternative. For example, if the company knew that the demand would be *high*, it would choose the alternative 'construct' to get the highest payoff ₹ 70,000; if it knew that the demand would be low, it would choose alternative 'subcontract' to keep the losses lowest to ₹ 1,000.

Under conditions of certainty, the particular state of nature is associated with probability 1. Though the state of nature is only one, possible alternatives could be numerous. Linear programming, transportation and assignment techniques, input-output analysis, activity analysis and economic order quantity models are used for such situations. Few complex managerial decision-making problems, however, ever enjoy the luxury of having complete information about the future and thus decision-making under certainty is of little consequential interest.

9.4 DECISION-MAKING UNDER CONDITIONS OF UNCERTAINTY

Under conditions of uncertainty, the decision-maker has a knowledge about the states of nature that happen but lacks the knowledge about the probabilities of their occurrence. Situations like launching a new product fall under this category. The insufficient data lead to a more complex decision model and, perhaps, a less satisfactory solution. However, one uses scientific methods to exploit the available data to the fullest extent.

Under conditions of uncertainty, a few decision criteria are available which could be of help to the decision-maker and a choice among them is determined by the company's policy and attitude of the decision-maker.

9.4-1 Maximax Criterion or Criterion of Optimism

This criterion provides the decision-maker with *optimistic* criterion. He finds the maximum possible payoff for each possible alternative and then chooses the alternative with maximum payoff within this group. Table 9.1 is repeated here as table 9.2 to illustrate this method. The maximax payoff is ₹ 70,000 corresponding to the alternative 'construct'.

TABLE 9.2

Alternatives	*States of nature (product demand)*				*Maximum of row*	
	High ₹	*Moderate* ₹	*Low* ₹	*Nil* ₹	₹	
Expand	50,000	25,000	– 25,000	– 45,000	50,000	
Construct	70,000	30,000	– 40,000	– 80,000	**70,000**	← *Maximax*
Subcontract	30,000	15,000	– 1,000	– 10,000	30,000	

When dealing with *costs*, the minimum of each alternative is considered and then the alternative which minimizes the above minimum costs is selected. This is called *minimin* criterion.

9.4-2 Maximin Criterion or Criterion of Pessimism (Wald Criterion)

This criterion provides the decision-maker with *pessimistic* criterion. To use this criterion, the decision-maker maximizes his minimum possible payoffs. He finds first the minimum possible payoff for each alternative and then chooses the alternative with maximum payoff within this group. The maximin payoff to the company as obtained from table 9.3 is –₹ 10,000 corresponding to the alternative 'subcontract'.

TABLE 9.3

Alternatives	*States of nature (product demand)*				*Minimum of row*	
	High ₹	*Moderate* ₹	*Low* ₹	*Nil* ₹	₹	
Expand	50,000	25,000	– 25,000	– 45,000	– 45,000	
Construct	70,000	30,000	– 40,000	– 80,000	– 80,000	
Subcontract	30,000	15,000	– 1,000	– 10,000	– **10,000**	← *Maximin*

Thus this criterion identifies the worst outcome of each alternative and then selects the best of those worst outcomes.

When dealing with *costs,* the maximum cost associated with each alternative is considered and the alternative that minimizes the above maximum costs is selected. This is called *minimax* criterion.

9.4-3 Minimax Regret Criterion (Savage Criterion)

This decision criterion was developed by L.J. Savage. He pointed out that the decision-maker might experience regret after the decision has been made and the states of nature *i.e.*, events have occurred. Thus the decision-maker should attempt to minimize regret before actually selecting a particular alternative (strategy). The basic steps involved in this criterion are :

1. Determine the amount of regret corresponding to each event for every alternative. The regret for *j*th event corresponding to *i*th alternative is given by
   *i*th regret = (maximum payoff – *i*th payoff) for the *j*th event.
2. Determine the maximum regret amount for each alternative.
3. Choose the alternative which corresponds to the minimum of the above maximum regrets.

TABLE 9.4

Alternatives	*States of nature (product demand)*				*Maximum of row*	
	High ₹	*Moderate* ₹	*Low* ₹	*Nil* ₹	₹	
Expand	20,000	5,000	24,000	35,000	**35,000**	← *Minimax*
Construct	0	0	39,000	70,000	70,000	
Subcontract	40,000	15,000	0	0	40,000	

Amounts of regrets for table 9.1 are represented in table 9.4. This table shows that the company will minimize its regret to ₹ 35,000 by selecting alternative 'Expand'. It may be observed that while the other decision rules do not take into account the cost of *opportunity lost* by making the wrong decision, the minimax regret criterion does so.

9.4-4 Hurwicz Criterion (Criterion of Realism)

Also called the *weighted average criterion*, it is a compromise between the maximax (optimistic) and maximin (pessimistic) decision criteria. This criterion is based on Hurwicz's concept of *coefficient of optimism* (*or pessimism*). This concept allows the decision-maker to take into account both the maximum and minimum for each alternative and assign them weights according to *his* degree of optimism (or pessimism). The alternative which maximizes the sum of these weighted payoffs is then selected. The criterion of realism consists of the following steps:

1. Choose an appropriate degree of optimism α, so that $(1 - \alpha)$ represents the degree of pessimism. α is called *coefficient* or *index of optimism.*
2. Determine the maximum as well as minimum of each alternative and obtain
   $$P = \alpha . \text{ maximum} + (1 - \alpha) \text{ minimum}.$$
3. Choose the alternative that yields the maximum value of P.

Table 9.1 is reproduced here as table 9.5 to explain the above concepts, wherein α is assumed to be 0.8.

TABLE 9.5

Alternatives	*States of nature (product demand)*				*Maximum of row*	*Minimum of row*	*P = α . max + (1 – α) min*
	High ₹	*Moderate* ₹	*Low* ₹	*Nil* ₹	₹	₹	₹
Expand	50,000	25,000	– 25,000	– 45,000	50,000	– 45,000	31,000
Construct	70,000	30,000	– 40,000	– 80,000	70,000	– 80,000	**40,000**
Subcontract	30,000	15,000	– 1,000	– 10,000	30,000	– 10,000	22,000

When $\alpha = 0$, the criterion is too pessimistic; when $\alpha = 1$, it is too optimistic. A value of α between zero and one may be selected depending upon whether the decision-maker leans towards pessimism or optimism. In the absence of strong feeling one way or the other, a value of $\alpha = 1/2$ seems to be a reasonable choice.

9.4-5 Laplace Criterion or Criterion of Rationality (Bayes' Criterion)

This criterion is based upon what is known as the *principle of insufficient reason.* Since the probabilities associated with the occurrence of various events are unknown, there is not enough information to conclude that these probabilities will be different. This criterion assigns equal probabilities to all the events of each alternative decision and selects the alternative associated with the maximum *expected payoff*. Symbolically, if n denotes the number of events and P's denote the payoffs, then expected value for strategy, say s_1 is

$$\frac{1}{n}\,[P_1 + P_2 + \ldots + P_n].$$

Table 9.1 is reproduced as table 9.6 to explain the above criterion.

TABLE 9.6

Alternatives	*States of nature (product demand)*				*Expected payoff*
	High ₹	*Moderate* ₹	*Low* ₹	*Nil* ₹	₹
Expand	50,000	25,000	– 25,000	– 45,000	$\frac{1,000}{4}$ [50 + 25 – 25 – 45] = – 1,250
Construct	70,000	30,000	– 40,000	– 80,000	$\frac{1,000}{4}$ [70 + 30 – 40 – 80] = – 5,000
Subcontract	30,000	15,000	– 1,000	– 10,000	$\frac{1,000}{4}$ [30 + 15 – 1 – 10] = **8,500**

Thus the alternative 'subcontract' results in maximum average payoff of ₹ 8,500.

EXAMPLE 9.4-1

The following matrix gives the payoff of different strategies (alternatives) S_1, S_2, S_3 against conditions (events) N_1, N_2, N_3 and N_4 :

TABLE 9.7

	N_1	N_2	N_3	N_4
S_1	₹ 4,000	₹ – 100	₹ 6,000	₹ 18,000
S_2	20,000	5,000	400	0
S_3	20,000	15,000	– 2,000	1,000

Indicate the decision taken under the following approach :

(i) Pessimistic (ii) Optimistic (iii) Regret and (iv) Equal probability.

[*Bangalore M.B.A., 1977*]

Solution

For the given payoff matrix, the values corresponding to pessimistic, optimistic and equal probability criteria are given below.

TABLE 9.8

	Pessimistic (maximin) value	*Optimistic (maximax) value*	*Equal probability value* $= 1/n\ (P_1 + P_2 + ... + P_n)$
S_1	– ₹ 100	₹ 18,000	₹ 1/4 (4,000 – 100 + 6,000 + 18,000) = ₹ 6,975
S_2	**₹ 0**	**₹ 20,000**	₹ 1/4 (20,000 + 5,000 + 400 + 0) = ₹ 6,350
S_3	– ₹ 2,000	**₹ 20,000**	₹ 1/4 (20,000 + 15,000 – 2,000 + 1,000) = **₹ 8,500**

Thus under pessimistic approach, S_2 is the optimal decision; under optimistic approach, S_2 or S_3 are the decision alternatives and under equal probability approach, S_3 is the alternative to be selected.

Table 9.9 represents the regret for every event and for each alternative calculated by the expression:

$$i\text{th regret} = (\text{maximum payoff} - i\text{th payoff}) \text{ for the } j\text{th event.}$$

TABLE 9.9

	N_1 *Regret (₹)*	N_2 *Regret (₹)*	N_3 *Regret (₹)*	N_4 *Regret (₹)*	*Maximum regret (₹)*
S_1	16,000	15,100	0	0	**16,000**
S_2	0	10,000	5,600	18,000	18,000
S_3	0	0	8,000	17,000	17,000

The decision alternative S_1 would be chosen since it corresponds to the minimal of the maximum possible regrets.

EXAMPLE 9.4-2

Given the following payoff function for each act a_1 and a_2,

$$Q_{a_1} = -25 + 40x,$$
$$Q_{a_2} = -80 + 29x,$$

(i) find the break even value of x.

(ii) If x = 5, which is the better act?

(iii) If x = 5, what is the regret of the poor strategy?

(iv) If x = – 10, which is the better act?

(v) If x = – 10, what is the regret of the poor strategy?

Solution

(*i*) For break even point,

$$Q_{a_1} = Q_{a_2} \text{ or } -25 + 40x = -80 + 29x \text{ or } x = -5.$$

$\therefore x = -5$ is the break even point.

(*ii*) When $x = 5$, $Q_{a_1} = -25 + 200 = 175$,

$$Q_{a_2} = -80 + 145 = 65.$$

$\therefore a_1$ is the better act

(*iii*) For $x = 5$, the regret of the poor strategy $a_2 = 175 - 65 = 110$.

(*iv*) When $x = -10$, $Q_{a_1} = -25 - 400 = -425$,

$$Q_{a_2} = -80 - 290 = -370.$$

$\therefore a_2$ is the better act.

(*v*) For $x = -10$, the regret of the poor strategy $a_1 = -370 - (-425) = 55$.

EXAMPLE 9.4-3

A steel manufacturing company is concerned with the possibility of a strike. It will cost an extra ₹ 20,000 to acquire an adequate stockpile. If there is a strike and the company has not stockpiled, management estimates an additional expense of ₹ 60,000 on account of lost sales. Should the company stockpile or not if it is to use

(i) Optimistic criterion (ii) Wald criterion (iii) Savage criterion (iv) Hurwicz criterion for $\alpha = 0.4$ *(v) Laplace criterion?* *[P.T.U. B.Tech. (Mech.) Nov., 2012]*

Solution

Conditional cost table is constructed using the given data.

TABLE 9.10

Conditional cost table (₹)

States of nature	*Alternatives*	
	Stockpile, A_1	*Do not stockpile,* A_2
Strike, S_1	20,000	60,000
No strike, S_2	20,000	0

(*i*) *Optimistic Criterion* : Since the table represents costs, *minimin criterion* will be used. Here minimum of alternative A_1 is ₹ 20,000 and of A_2 is ₹ 0. Therefore, company should select alternative A_2 *i.e.*, it should not stockpile and associated cost is ₹ 0.

(*ii*) *Wald Criterion* : Again since the table represents costs, *minimax criterion* will be used. Maximum of alternative A_1 is ₹ 20,000 and of A_2 is ₹ 60,000. Therefore, company should select alternative A_1 *i.e.*, it should stockpile and associated cost is ₹ 20,000.

(*iii*) *Savage Criterion* (*Minimax Regret Criterion*) : Conditional regret table is first constructed. For S_1-row, regret will be cost minus the minimum cost of ₹ 20,000; for S_2-row it will be cost minus the minimum cost of ₹ 0.

TABLE 9.11

Conditional regret table (₹)

States of nature	*Alternatives*	
	Stockpile, A_1	*Do not stockpile,* A_2
Strike, S_1	0	40,000
No strike, S_2	20,000	0

Maximum regret for alternative A_1 is ₹ 20,000 and for A_2 is ₹ 40,000. Therefore, company should choose alternative A_1 with minimax regret of ₹ 20,000.

(*iv*) *Hurwicz Criterion* (*Weighted Average Criterion*) : For $\alpha = 0.4$, the cost associated with alternative A_1 = ₹ (20,000 × 0.4 + 20,000 × 0.6) = ₹ 20,000; cost associated with alternative A_2 = ₹ (60,000 × 0.4 + 0 × 0.6) = ₹ 24,000. Therefore, the company should stockpile and associated cost is ₹ 20,000.

(*v*) *Laplace Criterion* (*Equal Probability Criterion*) : Equal probability cost for alternative A_1 = ₹ $\frac{1}{2}$ (20,000 + 20,000) = ₹ 20,000; equal probability cost for alternative

$A_2 = ₹\ \frac{1}{2}\ (60,000 + 0) = ₹\ 30,000.$

Therefore, the company should stockpile and associated cost is ₹ 20,000.

EXAMPLE 9.4-4

A manufacturer makes a product, of which the principal ingradient is a chemical X. At present, the manufacturer spends ₹ 1,000 per year on supply of X, but there is a possibility that the price may soon increase to four times its present value because of a worldwide shortage of the chemical. There is another chemical Y, which the manufacturer could use in conjunction with a third chemical Z in order to give the same effect as chemical X. Chemicals Y and Z would together cost the manufacturer ₹ 3,000 per year and their prices are not likely to increase. What action should the manufacturer take ? Apply the maximin and minimax criteria for decision-making and give two sets of solutions. If the coefficient of optimism is 0.4, find the course of action that minimizes the cost. [*ICWA Dec., 1988*]

Solution

Maximin Criterion

Since maximin criterion can be applied only to profit payoff table, the following table is setup in which negative cost values represent profits.

TABLE 9.12

States of nature	*Courses of action*	
	Use X (A_1)	*Use Y and Z (A_2)*
Price of X increases	– 4,000	–3,000
Price of X does not increase	– 1,000	– 3,000

Column minimum : – 4,000 **– 3,000** (Maximin)

Maximum of column minima is – 3,000. Hence the manufacturer should use Y and Z.

Minimax Criterion

The corresponding opportunity loss is shown below.

TABLE 9.13

States of nature	*Courses of action*	
	Use X	*Use Y and Z*
Price increases	1,000	0
Price does not increase	0	2,000
Column maxima	**1,000** (Minimax)	2,000

As minimax regret is ₹ 1,000, he should use X.

Hurwicz Criterion

For $\alpha = 0.4$, payoff associated with alternative A_1
$= 0.4\ (-\ 1,000) + 0.6\ (-\ 4,000) = -\ ₹\ 2,800.$

For $\alpha = 0.4$, payoff associated with alternative $A_2 = 0.4\ (-\ 3,000) + 0.6\ (-3,000)$
$= -\ ₹\ 3,000.$

Since A_1 gives a higher payoff, according to Hurwicz criterion, the manufacturer should use chemical X.

EXAMPLE 9.4-5

A factory manufactures three types of boxes. The fixed and variable costs are given.

TABLE 9.14

	Fixed cost (₹)	Variable cost (₹) per unit
Type 1	20,000	10
Type 2	30,000	8
Type 3	50,000	5

The likely demands under three situations are given below.

		Units
Poor demand	:	2,000
Moderate demand	:	5,000
High demand	:	10,000

If the sale price of each type is ₹ 20, prepare the payoff table.

Solution

Let B_1, B_2, B_3 be the three types of boxes and D_1, D_2 and D_3 denote the three levels of demand. Then

$$\text{payoff} = \text{sales revenue} - \text{fixed cost} - \text{variable cost.}$$

Calculating the payoff in thousands of rupees, we have

$$B_1D_1 = 2 \times 20 - 20 - 2 \times 10 = 0,$$
$$B_2D_1 = 2 \times 20 - 30 - 2 \times 8 = 40 - 46 = -6,$$
$$B_3D_1 = 2 \times 20 - 50 - 2 \times 5 = 40 - 60 = -20,$$
$$B_1D_2 = 5 \times 20 - 20 - 5 \times 10 = 100 - 70 = 30,$$
$$B_2D_2 = 5 \times 20 - 30 - 5 \times 8 = 100 - 70 = 30,$$
$$B_3D_2 = 5 \times 20 - 50 - 5 \times 5 = 100 - 75 = 25,$$
$$B_1D_3 = 10 \times 20 - 20 - 10 \times 10 = 200 - 120 = 80,$$
$$B_2D_3 = 10 \times 20 - 30 - 10 \times 8 = 200 - 110 = 90,$$
and
$$B_3D_3 = 10 \times 20 - 50 - 10 \times 5 = 200 - 100 = 100.$$

The payoff table is shown below.

TABLE 9.15
Payoff ('000 ₹)

Demand	Acts		
	B_1 (₹)	B_2 (₹)	B_3 (₹)
D_1	0	– 6	– 20
D_2	30	30	25
D_3	80	90	100

9.5 DECISION-MAKING UNDER CONDITIONS OF RISK

Most business decisions may have to be made under conditions of risk. Here more than one states of nature exist and the decision-maker has sufficient information to assign probabilities to each of these states. These probabilities could be obtained from the past records or from simply the subjective judgement of the decision-maker. Under conditions of risk, a number of decision criteria are available which could be of help to the decision-maker.

9.5-1 Expected Value Criterion

This criterion requires the calculation of the expected value of each decision alternative which is the sum of the weighted payoffs for that alternative, where the weights are the probabilities assigned to the states of nature that can happen. Also known as *expected monetary value (EMV) criterion*, it consists of the following steps :

1. Construct a conditional pay-off table listing the alternative decisions and the various states of nature. Enter the conditional profit for each decision-event combination along with the associated probabilities.
2. Calculate the EMV for each decision alternative by multiplying the conditional profits by assigned probabilities and adding the resulting conditional values.
3. Select the alternative that yields the highest EMV.

EXAMPLE 9.5-1

A newspaper boy has the following probabilities of selling a magazine:

No. of copies sold	*Probability*
10	*0.10*
11	*0.15*
12	*0.20*
13	*0.25*
14	*0.30*
	1.00

Cost of a copy is 30 paise and sale price is 50 paise. He cannot return unsold copies. How many copies should he order ? [*C.A. (Nov.) 1979*]

Solution

The no. of copies for purchase and for sales which have meaning to the newsboy are 10, 11, 12, 13 or 14. These are his sales magnitudes. There is no reason for him to buy less than 10 or more than 14 copies. Table 9.16, *the conditional profit table,* shows the profit resulting from any possible combination of supply and demand. Stocking of 10 copies each day will always result in a profit of 200 paise irrespective of the demand. For instance, even if the demand on some day is 13 copies, he can sell only 10 and hence his conditional profit is 200 paise.

When he stocks 11 copies, his profit will be 220 paise on days when buyers request 11, 12, 13 or 14 copies. But on days when he has 11 copies on stock and buyers buy only 10 copies, his profit decreases to 170 paise. The profit of 200 paise on the 10 copies sold must be reduced by 30 paise, the cost of one copy left unsold. The same will be true when he stocks 12, 13 or 14 copies. Thus the conditional profit in paise is given by

$$\text{Payoff} = 20 \times \text{copies sold} - 30 \times \text{copies unsold.}$$

TABLE 9.16

Conditional profit table (Paise)

Possible demand (no. of copies)	*Probability*	*Possible stock action*				
		10 copies	*11 copies*	*12 copies*	*13 copies*	*14 copies*
10	0.10	200	170	140	110	80
11	0.15	200	220	190	160	130
12	0.20	200	220	240	210	180
13	0.25	200	220	240	260	230
14	0.30	200	220	240	260	280

Next, the expected value of each decision alternative is obtained by multiplying its conditional profit by the associated probability and adding the resulting values. This is shown in table 9.17.

TABLE 9.17

Expected profit table (Paise)

Possible demand	*Probability*	*Expected profit from stocking*				
		10 copies	*11 copies*	*12 copies*	*13 copies*	*14 copies*
10	0.10	20	17	14	11	8
11	0.15	30	33	28.5	24	19.5
12	0.20	40	44	48	42	36
13	0.25	50	55	60	65	57.5
14	0.30	60	66	72	78	84
Total expected profit (Paise)		200	215	**222.5**	220	205

The newsboy must, therefore, order 12 copies to earn the highest possible average daily profit of 222.5 paise. This stocking will maximize the total profits *over a period of time*. Of course, there is no guarantee that he will make a profit of 222.5 paise, say, tomorrow. However, if he stocks 12 copies each day in future under the conditions given, he will have average profit of 222.5 paise per day. This is the best he can do because the choice of any one of the other four possible stock actions will result in a lower daily profit.

9.5-2 Expected Opportunity Loss (EOL) Criterion

An alternative approach (to maximizing EMV approach) is to minimize expected opportunity loss (EOL). Expected opportunity loss (or *expected value of regret)* represents the amount by which maximum possible profit will be reduced under various possible stock actions. The course of action that minimizes these losses or reductions is the optimal decision alternative. The procedure to calculate expected opportunity losses is as follows:

1. Prepare the conditional profit table for each decision-event combination and write the associated probabilities.
2. For each event, determine the *conditional opportunity loss (COL)* by subtracting the payoff from the maximum payoff for that event.
3. Calculate the expected opportunity loss (EOL) for each decision alternative by multiplying the COL's by the associated probabilities and then adding the values.
4. Select the alternative that yields the lowest EOL.

EXAMPLE 9.5-2

Solve example 9.5-1 by EOL criterion.

Solution

TABLE 9.18

Conditional profit table (Paise)

Possible demand (no. of copies) (Event)	*Probability*	*Possible stock action (alternative)*				
		10 copies	*11 copies*	*12 copies*	*13 copies*	*14 copies*
10	0.10	200	170	140	110	80
11	0.15	200	220	190	160	130
12	0.20	200	220	240	210	180
13	0.25	200	220	240	260	230
14	0.30	200	220	240	260	280

The best alternative for demand of 10 copies is to order 10 copies resulting in optimal profit of 200 paise. The conditional opportunity loss for each stock action (alternative) for this event is obtained just by subtracting the respective conditional profits from 200 paise. Likewise, for demand of 11, 12, 13 and 14 copies subtract the conditional pay-off values for each of these rows from the maxima of that row. The resulting conditional opportunity loss (COL) table is shown below.

TABLE 9.19

Conditional loss table (Paise)

Possible demand (no. of copies) (Event)	*Probability*	*Possible stock action (alternative)*				
		10 copies	*11 copies*	*12 copies*	*13 copies*	*14 copies*
10	0.10	0	30	60	90	120
11	0.15	20	0	30	60	90
12	0.20	40	20	0	30	60
13	0.25	60	40	20	0	30
14	0.30	80	60	40	20	0

Expected opportunity loss (EOL) can now be computed by multiplying the probability of each of state of nature with the appropriate loss value and adding the resulting products. For instance for holding a stock of 10 copies,

$$\text{EOL} = 0.10 \times 0 + 0.15 \times 20 + 0.20 \times 40 + 0.25 \times 60 + 0.30 \times 80$$
$$= 0 + 3 + 8 + 15 + 24 = 50 \text{ paise.}$$

EOL values for various stock actions are computed in table 9.20.

TABLE 9.20

Expected loss table (Paise)

Possible demand (no. of copies) (Event)	*Probability*	*Possible stock action (alternative)*				
		10 copies	*11 copies*	*12 copies*	*13 copies*	*14 copies*
10	0.10	0	3	6	9	12
11	0.15	3	0	4.5	9	13.5
12	0.20	8	4	0	6	12
13	0.25	15	10	5	0	7.5
14	0.30	24	18	12	6	0
EOL (paise)		50	35	**27.5**	30	45

The optimum stock action is the one which will minimize expected opportunity losses; this action calls for the stocking of 12 copies each day, at which point there is minimum expected loss of 27.5 paise.

Note. It may be pointed out that EMV and EOL decision criteria are completely consistent and yield the same optimal decision alternative. However, while EOL decision alternative will be always based on finding the minimum EOL value under EOL criterion irrespective of whether the problem is of maximizing expected profit or minimizing expected loss; under EMV criterion, the decision alternative will be based on either largest EMV value or smallest EMV value depending upon the type of problem (whether it is of maximization or minimization type).

9.5-3 Expected Value of Perfect Information (EVPI)

In the newsboy problem discussed above, the occurrence of states of nature was associated with probability. *Complete and accurate information about the future demand*, referred to as *perfect information*, would remove all uncertainty from the problem. With this perfect information he would *know in advance* how many copies were going to be demanded each day. Under such circumstances he would stock each day the *exact* number of copies required that day. For a sale of 10 copies, he would stock 10 copies and realize a profit of 200 paise; for a sale of 11 copies, he would stock 11 copies and realize a profit of 220 paise and so on. Table 9.21 shows the conditional profit values under condition of perfect information.

TABLE 9.21

Conditional profit table under certainty (Paise)

Possible demand (no. of copies) (Event)	*Possible stock action (alternative)*				
	10 copies	*11 copies*	*12 copies*	*13 copies*	*14 copies*
10	200	–	–	–	–
11	–	220	–	–	–
12	–	–	240	–	–
13	–	–	–	260	–
14	–	–	–	–	280

The expected profit under perfect information (EPPI) can now be computed. As shown in table 9.22, with perfect information the newsboy could count on making an average profit of 250 paise a day. This is the *maximum profit possible.*

TABLE 9.22

Expected profit table with perfect information (Paise)

Market size (no. of copies)	*Conditional profit under certainty*	*Probability of market size*	*Expected profit with perfect information*
10	200	0.10	20
11	220	0.15	33
12	240	0.20	48
13	260	0.25	65
14	280	0.30	84
			EPPI = 250

The best expected daily profit without perfect information was found to be 222.5 paise (table 9.17). The difference of 27.5 paise is the maximum amount the newsboy will be willing to pay, per day, to a *perfect predictor* because this is the maximum amount by which he can increase his expected daily profit. This difference is *the expected value of perfect information* and is referred to as EVPI. There is no sense in paying more than 27.5 paise to the predictor since that will lower the expected daily profit. It may be noted that in example 9.5-2, 27.5 paise was the minimum expected loss (EOL). Thus it may be concluded that EVPI is equal to the minimum EOL.

EVPI is an important concept in decision analysis. For a given problem, EVPI represents the maximum amount a person should pay to get additional information on which may be based the decision alternative.

EXAMPLE 9.5-3

A dairy firm wants to determine the quantity of butter it should produce to meet the demand. Past records have shown the following demand patterns:

Quantity required (kg)	*No. of days demand occurred*
15	*6*
20	*14*
25	*20*
30	*80*
35	*40*
40	*30*
50	*10*

The stock levels are restricted to the range 15 to 50 kg due to inadequate storing facilities. Butter costs ₹ 40 per kg and is sold at ₹ 50 per kg.

(i) Construct a conditional profit table.

(ii) Determine the action alternative associated with the maximization of expected profit.

(iii) Determine EVPI. *[P.T.U. B.Tech. (Mech.) Nov., 2012; SVSM PGDM, 2009]*

Solution

(*i*) Clearly, the dairy firm would not produce butter less than 15 kg and more than 50 kg. From the data given in the problem, we can calculate the conditional profit values for each stock action and event (demand) combination. If CP denotes the conditional profit, S the quantity in stock and D the demand, then

$$CP = \begin{cases} 10S, \text{ when } D \geq S, \\ 50D - 40S, \text{ when } D < S. \end{cases}$$

The resulting payoff table is given below. Also the quantity of butter required for 6 days out of a total of 200 days is 15 kg means that the demand of 15 kg has an associated probability of 6/200 = 0.03. Similarly, probabilities associated with other demand levels can be calculated and are shown in column (*i*) of table 9.23.

TABLE 9.23

Conditional profit table

Possible demand (event) (kg)	*Probability*	*Possible stock action (alternative) (kg)*						
		15	20	25	30	35	40	50
	(i)	*(ii)*	*(iii)*	*(iv)*	*(v)*	*(vi)*	*(vii)*	*(viii)*
		₹	₹	₹	₹	₹	₹	₹
15	0.03	150	– 50	– 250	– 450	– 650	– 850	– 1,250
20	0.07	150	200	0	– 200	– 400	– 600	– 1,000
25	0.10	150	200	250	50	– 150	– 350	– 750
30	0.40	150	200	250	300	100	– 100	– 500
35	0.20	150	200	250	300	350	150	– 250
40	0.15	150	200	250	300	350	400	0
50	0.05	150	200	250	300	350	400	500

TABLE 9.24

Expected profit table

Possible demand (event) (kg)	*Probability (i)*	*Possible stock action (alternative) (kg)* 15 *(i)×(ii)* ₹	20 *(i)×(iii)* ₹	25 *(i)×(iv)* ₹	30 *(i)×(v)* ₹	35 *(i)×(vi)* ₹	40 *(i)×(vii)* ₹	50 *(i)×(viii)* ₹
15	0.03	4.50	– 1.50	– 7.50	– 13.50	– 19.50	– 25.50	– 37.50
20	0.07	10.50	14.00	0.00	– 14.00	– 28.00	– 42.00	– 70.00
25	0.10	15.00	20.00	25.00	5.00	– 15.00	– 35.00	– 75.00
30	0.40	60.00	80.00	100.00	120.00	40.00	– 40.00	– 200.00
35	0.20	30.00	40.00	50.00	60.00	70.00	30.00	– 50.00
40	0.15	22.50	30.00	37.50	45.00	52.50	60.00	0.00
50	0.05	7.50	10.00	12.50	15.00	17.50	20.00	25.00
EMV (₹)		150.00	192.50	**217.50**	**217 .50**	117.50	– 32.50	– 407.50

(*ii*) The calculations for expected payoffs and EMV for each action are shown in table 9.24. Since the maximum EMV is ₹ 217.50 for stock of 25 as well as 30 kg of butter, the dairy firm may produce 25 kg or 30 kg of butter and can expect an average daily profit of ₹ 217.50.

(*iii*) The EVPI is calculated from table 9.25.

TABLE 9.25

Expected profit table with perfect information

Market size (event)	*Conditional profit under certainty (₹)*	*Probability of market size*	*Expected profit with perfect information (₹)*
15	150	0.03	4.50
20	200	0.07	14.00
25	250	0.10	25.00
30	300	0.40	120.00
35	350	0.20	70.00
40	400	0.15	60.00
50	500	0.05	25.00
			EPPI = 318.50

The expected value of perfect information is given by

$$\text{EVPI} = \text{EPPI} - \text{max. EMV} = ₹\ (318.50 - 217.50) = ₹\ 101.$$

9.5-4 EMV for Items that have a Salvage Value

In the discussion so far, it has been assumed that the product being stocked was completely worthless if not sold on the 'selling' day. This assumption, that the product has no salvage value, is not always realistic. If the product does have a salvage value, then it must be considered in calculating the conditional profits for each stock action.

EXAMPLE 9.5-4

An ice-cream retailer buys ice cream at a cost of ₹ 5 per cup and sells it for ₹ 8 per cup; any remaining unsold at the end of the day can be disposed of at a salvage price of ₹ 2 per cup. Past sales have ranged between 15 and 18 cups per day; there is no reason to believe that sales volume will take on any other magnitude in future. Find the EMV if the sale history has the following probabilities:

Market Size	:	*15*	*16*	*17*	*18*
Probability	:	*0.10*	*0.20*	*0.40*	*0.30*

[*P.T.U. BCA, 2010*]

Solution

From the data given in the problem, we can calculate the conditional profit values for each stock action and event (market size) combination If CP denotes the conditional profit, S the quantity in stock and D the market demand, then

$$CP = \begin{cases} (8-5)\,S = 3S, \text{ when } D \geq S, \\ 8D - 5S + 2\,(S-D), \text{ when } D < S. \end{cases}$$

The resulting pay-off matrix is given below. A stock of 15 cups each day will result in daily profit of ₹ 45 irrespective of the demand. A stock of 16 cups each day will result in a profit of ₹ 48 when the demand is 16 cups or more. But when the demand is 15 cups, the conditional profit will be ₹ [8 × 15 – 5 × 16 + 2 × (16 – 15)] = ₹ 42. The conditional profits for each stock action-event combination can, therefore, be calculated.

TABLE 9.26

Conditional profit table

Possible demand (event)	*Probability*	*Possible stock action (alternative)*			
	(i)	15 *(ii)* ₹	16 *(iii)* ₹	17 *(iv)* ₹	18 *(v)* ₹
15	0.10	45	42	39	36
16	0.20	45	48	45	42
17	0.40	45	48	51	48
18	0.30	45	48	51	54

The expected pay-offs and the EMV for each stock action can now be calculated.

TABLE 9.27

Expected profit table

Possible demand (event)	*Probability (i)*	*Possible stock action (alternative)*			
		15 *(i)×(ii)* ₹	16 *(i)×(iii)* ₹	17 *(i)×(iv)* ₹	18 *(i)×(v)* ₹
15	0.10	4.50	4.20	3.90	3.60
16	0.20	9.00	9.60	9.00	8.40
17	0.40	18.00	19.20	20.40	19.20
18	0.30	13.50	14.40	15.30	16.20
	EMV (₹)	45.00	47.40	**48.60**	47.40

From table 9.27, max. EMV = ₹ 48.60 for stock action of 17 ice-cream cups each day.

9.5-5 Use of Incremental (Marginal) Analysis

In many decision making problems, the use of conditional profit and expected profit tables would be quite cumbersome because of the large number of computations required. Example 9.5-4, for instance, with 4 demand levels and 5 possible stock actions involved the calculation of 20 conditional profits. For 100 values of demand levels and stock actions the calculations involved would be tremendous! This excessive computational work can be avoided by *incremental or marginal approach.* According to this approach, any additional unit purchased will either be sold or remain unsold. If p represents the probability of selling one additional unit, then $(1 - p)$ must be the probability of not selling it. If the additional unit is sold, the conditional profit will increase as a result of the profit earned from this unit. This is termed as *incremental (marginal) profit,* IP. If the additional unit is not sold, the conditional profit reduces and the amount of reduction is called the *incremental (marginal) loss,* IL resulting from stocking of an item that is not sold.

Additional units should be stocked so long as the expected incremental profit from stocking each of them is more than the expected incremental loss from stocking each. The expected incremental profit from stocking and selling an additional unit is the incremental profit of the unit multiplied by the probability that the unit would be sold *i.e.*, p(IP). The expected incremental loss from stocking and not selling an additional unit is the incremental loss incurred if the unit remains unsold multiplied by the probability that the unit would not be sold *i.e.*, $(1 - p)$(IL). Thus the units should be stocked upto the point where

$$p(\text{IP}) = (1 - p)\ (\text{IL})$$

or

$$p(\text{IP} + \text{IL}) = \text{IL} \quad \text{or} \quad p = \frac{\text{IL}}{\text{IP} + \text{IL}}.$$

The letter p represents the minimum required probability of selling at least an additional unit to justify the stocking of that additional unit. Additional units should be stocked so long as the probability of selling at least an additional unit is greater than p.

EXAMPLE 9.5-5

A milkman buys milk at ₹12 per litre and sells for ₹ 15 per litre. Unsold milk has to be thrown away. The daily demand has the following probability distribution:

Demand (litres)	:	*46*	*48*	*50*	*52*	*54*	*56*	*58*	*60*	*62*	*64*
Probability	:	*0.01*	*0.03*	*0.06*	*0.10*	*0.20*	*0.25*	*0.15*	*0.10*	*0.05*	*0.05*

If each day's demand is independent of previous day's demand, how many litres should be ordered every day ?

[*Rajasthan M.B.A., 1982*]

Solution

Here IP = ₹ (15 – 12) = ₹ 3,

and IL = ₹ 12.

The milkman should stock additional litres of milk so long as the probability of selling at least an additional litre of milk is greater than p, where

$$p = \frac{\text{IL}}{\text{IP} + \text{IL}} = \frac{12}{12 + 3} = 0.8.$$

The value of 0.8 for p implies that in order to justify the stocking of an additional unit, there must be at least 0.8 cumulative probability of selling that unit. The cumulative probabilities of sales are computed in table 9.28. Additional units should be stocked so long as the probability of selling at least an additional unit is greater than p. The optimum number of litres of milk to be stocked is 54. If the number is increased to 56, the cumulative probability will become 0.60, which is less than the required value of 0.8.

TABLE 9.28

Cumulative probabilities of sales

Sales (litres of milk)	*Probability of this sales level*	*Cumulative probability that sales will be at this level or higher*
46	0.01	1.00
48	0.03	0.99
50	0.06	0.96
52	0.10	0.90
54	0.20	0.80
56	0.25	0.60
58	0.15	0.35
60	0.10	0.20
62	0.05	0.10
64	0.05	0.05

For $p = 0.8$,

expected incremental profit $= p\,(\text{IP}) =$ ₹ $0.8 \times 3 =$ ₹ 2.40,

expected incremental loss $= (1-p)\,(\text{IL}) =$ ₹ $0.2 \times 12.00 =$ ₹ 2.40.

For 56 litres of stock level, expected incremental loss will be more than expected incremental gain.

The use of incremental analysis yields the same solution as provided by the EMV and EOL approaches. However, the computational effort required in this approach is much less.

9.6 MAXIMUM LIKELIHOOD CRITERION

According to this criterion, the decision-maker just selects the state of nature that has the highest probability of occurrence and then picks the decision alternative which will yield the highest payoff in that state of nature. For instance, referring to table 9.25 of example 9.5-4, the ice-cream retailer would choose the demand level of 17 cups that corresponds to the highest probability of 0.40 and having selected that, would decide in favour of stock action of 17 cups since it results in the largest conditional profit of ₹ 51 in that state of nature.

This decision criterion produces valid results when the probability of one state of nature is much more than any other and when the conditional values are not too much different This criterion, however, may result in serious errors when a large number of states of nature exist and each of them is associated with a small and nearly equal probability of occurrence.

9.7 EXPECTED VALUE CRITERION FOR CONTINUOUSLY DISTRIBUTED RANDOM VARIABLES

The situations considered so far in this chapter involved *discrete* random variables. Many real situations, however, are concerned with continuously distributed random variables. The expected value criterion discussed earlier can be applied for such situations also.

EXAMPLE 9.7-1

A vegetable seller buys tomatoes for ₹ 45 a box and sells them for ₹ 80 per box. If the box is not sold on the first selling day, it is worth ₹ 15 as salvage. The past records indicate that demand is normally distributed, with a mean of 30 boxes daily and a standard deviation of 9 boxes. How many boxes should he stock ?

Solution

Minimum required probability of selling at least an additional unit (box) to justify the stocking of that unit is

$$p = \frac{\text{IL}}{\text{IP} + \text{IL}} = \frac{(45-15)}{(80-45)+(45-15)} = \frac{30}{35+30} = \frac{30}{65} = 0.462.$$

This value of probability means that the vegetable seller must be 0.462 sure of selling at least an additional unit before it would pay him to stock that unit. In Fig. 9.1 is shown the 0.462 probability on the normal distribution curve of the past demand. The required 0.462 probability is the shaded area. The vegetable seller should stock additional boxes until he reaches point A; if he stocks more units, the probability will fall below 0.462.

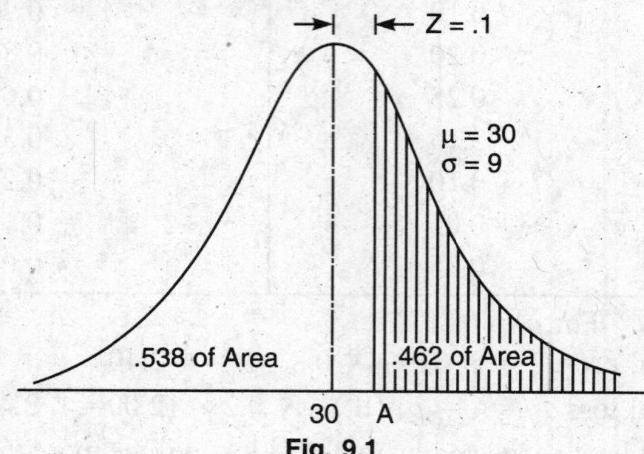

Fig. 9.1

Since the shaded area under the normal curve in Fig. 9.1 is 0.462 of the total area, the open area must be 1.000 – 0.462 = 0.538 of the area under the curve. From table C-2 in the appendix, the normal deviate $z = 0.1$ for value of 0.538. This means that point A is 0.1 standard deviation to the right of the mean.

Since the standard deviation of the distribution of past demand is 9 boxes, point A can be located as follows:

$$\begin{aligned}\text{Point A} &= \text{mean} + \text{standard deviation}\\ &= 30 + 0.1 \times 9 = 30.9 \simeq 31 \text{ boxes.}\end{aligned}$$

Thus the fruit seller should stock 31 boxes.

9.8 ADDITIONAL EXAMPLES

EXAMPLE 9.8-1

Under an employment promotion programme, it is proposed to allow sale of newspapers on the buses during off-peak hours. The vendor can purchase the newspapers at a special concessional rate of 25 paise per copy against the selling price of 40 paise. Any unsold copies are, however, a dead loss. The vendor has estimated the following probability distribution for the number of copies demanded:

Number of copies	:	*15*	*16*	*17*	*18*	*19*	*20*
Probability	:	*0.04*	*0.19*	*0.33*	*0.26*	*0.11*	*0.07*

(a) How many copies should he order so that his expected profit will be maximum ?

(b) Compute EPPI.

(c) The vendor is thinking of spending on a small market survey to obtain additional information regarding the demand levels. How much should he be willing to spend on such a survey ? [*P.T.U. M.Tech. April, 2012; M.D.U. Rohtak B.E. (Mech.) Dec., 2006*]

Solution

From the data given in the problem, we can calculate the conditional profit values for each action-event combination. If CP denotes the conditional profit, S the quantity in stock and D the demand, then

$$\text{CP} = \begin{cases} (40-25)\,\text{S} = 15\text{S}, \text{ when D} \geq \text{S}, \\ 40\text{D} - 25\text{S}, \text{ when D} < \text{S}. \end{cases}$$

The resulting conditional profit matrix is shown in table 9.29.

TABLE 9.29

Conditional profit table

Demand (event)	*Probability*	*Possible stock action (alternative)*					
		15	16	17	18	19	20
	(*i*)	(*ii*) ₹	(*iii*) ₹	(*iv*) ₹	(*v*) ₹	(*vi*) ₹	(*vii*) ₹
15	0.04	2.25	2.00	1.75	1.50	1.25	1.00
16	0.19	2.25	2.40	2.15	1.90	1.65	1.40
17	0.33	2.25	2.40	2.55	2.30	2.05	1.80
18	0.26	2.25	2.40	2.55	2.70	2.45	2.20
19	0.11	2.25	2.40	2.55	2.70	2.85	2.60
20	0.07	2.25	2.40	2.55	2.70	2.85	3.00

The expected payoffs and the EMV for each stock action can now be calculated.

TABLE 9.30

Expected profit table

Demand (event)	*Probability*	*Possible stock action (alternative)*					
		15	16	17	18	19	20
	(*i*)	(*i*)×(*ii*) ₹	(*i*)×(*iii*) ₹	(*i*)×(*iv*) ₹	(*i*)×(*v*) ₹	(*i*)×(*vi*) ₹	(*i*)×(*vii*) ₹
15	0.04	0.09	0.08	0.07	0.06	0.05	0.04
16	0.19	0.43	0.46	0.41	0.36	0.31	0.27
17	0.33	0.74	0.79	0.84	0.76	0.68	0.59
18	0.26	0.58	0.62	0.66	0.70	0.64	0.57
19	0.11	0.25	0.26	0.28	0.30	0.31	0.29
20	0.07	0.16	0.17	0.18	0.19	0.20	0.21
EMV (₹)	2.25	2.38	2.44	2.37	2.19	1.97	

(*a*) The vendor should order 17 copies to get maximum expected daily profit of ₹ 2.44.

(*b*) EPPI is computed as below.

TABLE 9.31

Event	*Probability*	*Payoff under perfect information* (₹)	*Expected payoff under perfect information* (₹)
15	0.04	2.25	0.09
16	0.19	2.40	0.46
17	0.33	2.55	0.84
18	0.26	2.70	0.70
19	0.11	2.85	0.31
20	0.07	3.00	0.21
		EPPI (₹)	2.61

Thus EPPI = ₹ 2.61.

(*c*) EVPI = EPPI – max expected EMV = ₹ (2.61 – 2.44) = ₹ 0.17.

Thus the vendor should not spend more than ₹ 0.17 for market survey.

EXAMPLE 9.8-2

A bicycle repairman has an opportunity to purchase a stock of discontinued bicycles. They were originally supposed to be sold for ₹ 400 each. The repairman is offered all five bicycles for ₹ 500, which makes his cost for each bicycle ₹ 100. If he sells them, he believes, he can get ₹ 250 for each bicycle, thereby making a profit of ₹ 150. He has two options: either to buy all the discontinued bicycles or not to buy at all. There are six states of nature; these being the demand for 0, 1, 2, 3, 4 and 5 bicycles.

(i) Prepare the payoff as well as regret tables for the problem.

(ii) If the repairman has the option of buying any number of bicycles (0 to 5), find the average expected payoff and average expected regret for each stock action.

[PTU. B.Tech., 2000]

Solution

(*i*) The conditional profits are given by

$$CP = \begin{cases} 150S, \text{ when } D \geq S, \\ 250D - 100S, \text{ when } D < S, \end{cases}$$

where S is the no. of bicycles in stock and D is the demand. The following conditional profit table is obtained:

TABLE 9.32

Conditional profit table

Demand (event)	*Stock action*	
	Buy none ₹	*Buy all* ₹
0	0	– 500
1	0	– 250
2	0	0
3	0	250
4	0	500
5	0	750

The regret table can now be prepared.

TABLE 9.33

Regret table

Demand (event)	*Stock action*	
	Buy none ₹	*Buy all* ₹
0	0	500
1	0	250
2	0	0
3	250	0
4	500	0
5	750	0

(*ii*) When the repairman has the option of buying any number (from 0 to 5) of bicycles, there are six stock actions (alternatives) and six events. The payoff as well as regret tables are shown below. Also average expected payoff and average expected regret for each stock action is calculated assuming the same probability 1/6 for each event.

TABLE 9.34

Payoff table

Demand (event)	Stock action					
	0 ₹	*1* ₹	*2* ₹	*3* ₹	*4* ₹	*5* ₹
0	0	– 100	– 200	– 300	– 400	– 500
1	0	150	50	– 50	– 150	– 250
2	0	150	300	200	100	0
3	0	150	300	450	350	250
4	0	150	300	450	600	500
5	0	150	300	450	600	750
Average (₹)	0	108.33	175	200	183.33	125

TABLE 9.35

Regret table

Demand (event)	Stock action					
	0 ₹	*1* ₹	*2* ₹	*3* ₹	*4* ₹	*5* ₹
0	0	100	200	300	400	500
1	150	0	100	200	300	400
2	300	150	0	100	200	300
3	450	300	150	0	100	200
4	600	450	300	150	0	100
5	750	600	450	300	150	0
Average (₹)	375	266.67	200	175	191.67	250

Tables 9.34 and 9.35 suggest an optimum stock level of 3 discontinued bicycles. This stock action results in the highest average pay-off of ₹ 200 or the lowest average regret of ₹ 175.

EXAMPLE 9.8-3

A TV dealer finds that the cost of a TV in stock for a week is ₹ 30 and the cost of a unit shortage is ₹ 70. For one particular model of TV the probability distribution of weekly sales is as follows:

Weekly sales	:	*0*	*1*	*2*	*3*	*4*	*5*	*6*
Probability	:	*0.10*	*0.10*	*0.20*	*0.25*	*0.15*	*0.15*	*0.05*

How many units per week should the dealer order? Also find EVPI.

[P.T.U.M. Tech. Dec., 2011; U.P.U. MBA, 2009; M.D.U. Rohtak B.E. (Mech.) Dec., 2006]

Solution

Here, the stocking cost = ₹ 30/week and shortage cost = ₹ 70. The *cost* table is constructed below. Also the expected costs for various strategies are calculated.

$$\text{Conditional cost} = \begin{cases} 30.S + 70\,(D - S), & \text{when } D \geq S, \\ 30.S, & \text{when } D < S. \end{cases}$$

TABLE 9.36
Cost table

Weekly sales	*Probability*	*Weekly stock action*						
		0 ₹	*1* ₹	2 ₹	3 ₹	4 ₹	5 ₹	6 ₹
0	0.10	0	30	60	90	120	150	180
1	0.10	70	30	60	90	120	150	180
2	0.20	140	100	60	90	120	150	180
3	0.25	210	170	130	90	120	150	180
4	0.15	280	240	200	160	120	150	180
5	0.15	350	310	270	230	190	150	180
6	0.05	420	380	340	300	260	220	180
Expected cost (₹)		203	170	144	132	137.50	153.50	180

Thus the TV dealer should order 3 units/week. ECPI table can now be prepared from cost table.

TABLE 9.37
Expected cost for perfect information

Demand	*Probability*	*Minimum Cost* ₹	*ECPI*
0	0.10	0	0
1	0.10	30	3
2	0.20	60	12
3	0.25	90	22.50
4	0.15	120	18
5	0.15	150	22.50
6	0.05	180	9
			87.00

Thus EVPI =Min. expect cost – ECPI = ₹ (132 – 87) = ₹ 45.

EXAMPLE 9.8-4

The sales manager of Beta Co. is highly experienced in the fad market. He is sure that the sales of JUMBO (during the period it has especial appeal) will not be less than 25,000 units. Plant capacity limits total production to a maximurn of 80,000 units during JUMBO's brief life. According to the sales manager, there are 2 chances in 5 for a sales volume of 50,000 units. The probability that it will be more than 50,000 units is 4 times the probability that it will be less than 50,000. If sales exceed 50,000 units, volumes of 60,000 and 80,000 are equally likely. A 70,000 unit volume is 4 times as likely as either. It costs ₹ 30 to produce a unit of JUMBO whereas its selling price is estimated at ₹ 50 per unit. Initial investment is estimated at ₹ 8,00,000. Should the venture of production be undertaken ?

Solution

Prob. (50,000) = 2/5 = 0.40.

∴ Prob. (less than or more than 50,000) = 0.60.

Prob. (less than 50,000) : Prob. (more than 50,000) :: 1 : 4.

∴ Prob. (less than 50,000) = 0.60 × 1/5 = 0.12,

Prob. (more than 50,000) = 0.60 × 4/5 = 0.48.

Prob. (60,000) : Prob. (70,000) : Prob. (80,000) :: 1 : 4: 1.

∴ Prob. (60,000) = 0.48 × 1/1 + 4 + 1 = 0.08,

Prob. (70,000) = 0.48 × 4/1 + 4 + 1 = 0.32,

Prob. (80,000) = 0.08.

Thus we have complete probability distribution of sales except that for sales less than 50,000, we have a summarized probability of 0.12. For sales less than 50,000 units, let us assume a sales volume of 25,000 units.

TABLE 9.38

Payoff table in thousands of rupees

Demand (Event)	*Probability*	*Stock action*				
		< 50,000 (take it 25,000) ₹	*50,000* ₹	*60,000* ₹	*70,000* ₹	*80,000* ₹
<50,000 (worst 25,000)	0.12	500	– 250	– 550	– 850	– 1,150
50,000	0.40	500	1,000	700	400	100
60,000	0.08	500	1,000	1,200	900	600
70,000	0.32	500	1,000	1,200	1,400	1,100
80,000	0.08	500	1,000	1,200	1,400	1,600
Expected payoff		500	850	790	690	430

Thus the optimum expected payoff is ₹ 8,50,000. Since it is more than the initial investment of ₹ 8,00,000, the venture should be undertaken.

EXAMPLE 9.8-5

Your company manufactures goods for a market in which the technology of the products is changing rapidly. The research and development department has produced a new product which appears to have potential for commercial exploitation. A further ₹ 60,000 is required for development testing.

The company has 100 customers and each customer might purchase, at the most, one unit of the product. Market research suggests a selling price of ₹ 6,000 for each unit with total variable costs of manufacturing and selling estimated at ₹ 2,000 for each unit.

As a result of previous experience of this type of market, it has been possible to derive a probability distribution relating to the proportion of customers who will buy the product, which is as follows:

TABLE 9.39

Proportion of customers	*Probability*
0.04	0.1
0.08	0.1
0.12	0.2
0.16	0.4
0.20	0.2

Determine the expected opportunity losses, given no further information than that stated above and state, whether or not, the company should develop the product.

[*I.C.M.A. (London) Nov., 1978*]

Solution

If p denotes the proportion of customers who purchase the new product, then the conditional profit will be given by

$$CP = ₹\ (6,000 - 2,000)\ (p \times 100) - 60,000 = ₹\ 1,000\ (400p - 60).$$

The conditional profit table can now be constructed. The company has two alternative courses of action: to develop the product or not to develop the product. From the conditional profit table, the opportunity loss table can be derived and expected opportunity losses can be found.

TABLE 9.40

Conditional profit table

State of nature (Proportion of customers)	*Probability*	*Alternative actions*	
		Do not develop (A_1) ₹	*Develop (A_2)* ₹
0.04	0.1	0	– 44,000
0.08	0.1	0	– 28,000
0.12	0.2	0	– 12,000
0.16	0.4	0	4,000
0.20	0.2	0	20,000

TABLE 9.41

Opportunity loss table

Proportion of customers	*Probability*	*Alternative actions*	
		Do not develop (A_1) ₹	*Develop (A_2)* ₹
0.04	0.1	0	44,000
0.08	0.1	0	28,000
0.12	0.2	0	12,000
0.16	0.4	4,000	0
0.20	0.2	20,000	0

$\therefore$ EOL (A_1) = 0.4 (4,000) + 0.2 (20,000) = ₹ 5,600,

EOL (A_2) = 0.1 (44,000) + 0.1 (28,000) + 0.2 (12,000) = ₹ 9,600.

Since A_1 gives the lower EOL of ₹ 5,600, the best decision is not to develop the product.

EXAMPLE 9.8-6

A company has recently installed new machinery but has not yet decided on the appropriate number of a certain spare part required for repairs.

Spare parts cost £ 2,000 each but are only available if ordered now. If the plant failed and there was no spare part available, the cost to the business of mending the plant rises to £ 15,000. The plant has an estimated life of 10 years and the probability distribution of failures during this time, based on the experience with similar plants, is as follows:

TABLE 9.42

No. of failures over ten years period	:	*0*	*1*	*2*	*3*	*4*	*5 and over*
Probability	:	*0.1*	*0.4*	*0.3*	*0.1*	*0.1*	*nil*

Calculate

(a) The expected number of failures in the ten-year period.

(b) The optimal number of spares that should be purchased now.

(c) The expected cost of the ordering policy chosen.

(d) The value of perfect information of the number of failures in ten-year life.

[*P.T.U. M.Tech. April, 2012*]

Solution

(*a*) Expected number of failures

$$= 0 \times 0.1 + 1 \times 0.4 + 2 \times 0.3 + 3 \times 0.1 + 4 \times 0.1 = 1.7.$$

(*b*) The *cost* table for each combination of number of spare parts purchased and number of failures is shown below. As an example, the conditional cost for 3 spare parts purchased and 4 failures is.

$$= 3 \times £\ 2{,}000 + (4 - 3) \times £\ 15{,}000 = £\ 21{,}000.$$

TABLE 9.43

Conditional cost table (thousands of pounds)

No. of failures	*Probability*	*Alternative actions (spares purchased)*				
		0	*1*	*2*	*3*	*4*
0	0.1	£ 0	£ 2	£ 4	£ 6	£ 8
1	0.4	15	2	4	6	8
2	0.3	30	17	4	6	8
3	0.1	45	32	19	6	8
4	0.1	60	47	34	21	8
Expected cost (£)	25.5	14	8.5	7.5	8	

∴ Optimal no. of spare parts to be purchased is 3.

(*c*) The expected cost of ordering policy chosen = £ 7,500.

(*d*) Expected cost under perfect information (ECPI)

$$= £\ 1{,}000\ (0.1 \times 0 + 0.4 \times 2 + 0.3 \times 4 + 0.1 \times 6 + 0.1 \times\ 8) = £\ 3{,}400.$$

∴ EVPI = Optimum expected cost under uncertainty – ECPI = £ (7,500 – 3,400) = £ 4,100.

EXAMPLE 9.8-7

XYZ company manufactures parts for passanger cars and sells them in lots of 10,000 parts each. The company has the policy of inspecting each lot before it is shipped to the customer. Five inspection ratings established for quality control represent the percentage of defective items contained in each lot. The management is considering two possible courses of action :

(i) Shut down the entire plant operations and thoroughly inspect each machine. This action costs ₹ 600.

(ii) Continue production but offer the customer a refund of ₹ 1 for each defective item that is detected and returned.

Rating	*Proportion of defective items*	*Frequency*
Excellent (A)	*0.02*	*25*
Good (B)	*0.05*	*30*
Acceptable (C)	*0.10*	*20*
Fair (D)	*0.15*	*20*
Poor (E)	*0.20*	*5*

What is the optimum decision for the company ? Also find the EVPI.

[*M.S Baroda MBA, 1995*]

Solution

For the first course of action, the cost is ₹ 600 irrespective of the rating of the lot. For the second, the cost will depend upon the rating : for rating A of the lot it will be ₹ (10,000 × 0.02 × 1) = ₹ 200. Likewise, it is calculated for each rating and is represented in table 9.44.

TABLE 9.44

Rating	*Proportion of defective items*	*Probability*	*Cost (₹)*		*Opportunity loss (₹)*	
			Inspect	*Refund*	*Inspect*	*Refund*
A	0.02	0.25	600	200	400	0
B	0.05	0.30	600	500	100	0
C	0.10	0.20	600	1,000	0	400
D	0.15	0.20	600	1,500	0	900
E	0.20	0.05	600	2,000	0	1,400
Expected value			600	800	130	330

Since expected inspection cost is less, the plant should be shut down for inspection.

EVPI = minimum expected opportunity loss = ₹ 130.

EXAMPLE 9.8-8

Total cost of a product is given by 1,000 + bx, while the total revenue is given by 20x, where x is the number of units of the product. The variable 'b' is the variable cost per unit and has the following probability distribution:

'b' (₹)	*Probability*
5	*0.1*
6	*0.5*
7	*0.4*

Compute:

(a) Expected profit assuming that 500 units will be sold.

(b) Expected profit assuming that there is 0.5 probability of selling 500 units and 0.5 probability of selling no units. [*J.N.V. Jodhpur M.Com., 1994*]

Solution

(*a*) Expected cost = ₹ [0.1 (1,000 + 5 × 500) + 0.5 (1,000 + 6 × 500) + 0.4 (1,000 + 7 × 500)]

= ₹ [0.1 × 3,500 + 0.5 × 4,000 + 0.4 × 4,500]

= ₹ (350 + 2,000 + 1,800) = ₹ 4,150.

Expected revenue = ₹ (20 × 500) = 10,000.

∴ Expected profit = ₹ (10,000 – 4,150) = ₹ 5,850.

(*b*) Expected revenue = ₹ [20 × 500 × 0.5 + 20 × 0 × 0.5] = ₹ 5,000.

∴ Expected profit = ₹ (5,000 – 4,150) = ₹ 850.

EXAMPLE 9.8-9

A stall at a certain railway station sells for 80 paise a copy of daily newspaper for which it pays 50 paise. Unsold papers are returned for a refund of 25 paise a copy. Daily sales and corresponding probabilities are as follows :

Daily sales :	*500*	*600*	*700*
Probability :	*0.5*	*0.3*	*0.2*

(i) How many copies should it ordr each day to get maximum expected profit?

(ii) If unsold copies cannot be returned and are useless, what should be the optimal order each day ? Use increment analysis.

[*P.T.U. M.Tech. Dec., 2011*]

Solution

(*a*) Here IP = ₹ (0.80 – 0.50) = ₹ 0.30,

IL = ₹ (0.50 – 0.25) = ₹ 0.25.

The stall should order additional copy so long as the probability of selling at least an additional copy is greater than p, where

$$p = \frac{\text{IL}}{\text{IP} + \text{IL}} = \frac{0.25}{0.30 + 0.25} = \frac{0.25}{0.55} = 0.45.$$

Thus to justify the ordering of an additional copy, there must be at least 0.45 cumulative probability of selling that copy. Cumulative probabilities are computed below :

Daily sales	*Probability*	*Cumulative probability*
500	0.5	1.0
600	0.3	0.5
700	0.2	0.2

∴ Optimal number of copies to be ordered is 600.

(*b*) When unsold copies are non-refundable,

IL = ₹ 0.50.

$$\therefore \quad p = \frac{\text{IL}}{\text{IP} + \text{IL}} = \frac{0.50}{0.30 + 0.50} = \frac{0.50}{0.80} = 0.625.$$

∴ Optimal order size = 500 copies.

EXAMPLE 9.8-10

An investment company is considering which of the two methods should it adopt to market its investment services to the public : direct mailing or newspaper advertisement. The company has a budget of ₹ 1,50,000 for this purpose. Cost of direct mailing is 30 paise for each 'shot'. Past experience indicates a response rate of between 6% and 12% with an average of 8%. The chances of the lower, higher and average response rate actually occurring are estimated to be 15%, 20% and 65% respectively.

Newspaper advertisements have also been used in the past and they also produce varying response rates. The company would give a weekly insertion in Sunday newspapers, thereby totalling 52 insertions in a year. Response rates vary between 700 and 2,000 per insertion with average of 1,350. The chances of these response rates actually occurring are 30%, 20% and 50% respectively. In either case, only 40% of the responses are expected to produce a sale. Each sale yields a net income of ₹ 10. Which method should the company adopt?

Solution

Direct mailing

$$\text{Number of shots} = \frac{1,50,000}{0.30} = 5,00,000.$$

Number of responses will be

Low : 0.06 × 5,00,000 = 30,000,
High : 0.12 × 5,00,000 = 60,000,
Average : 0.08 × 5,00,000 = 40,000.

Since only 40% of the responses produce a sale and each sale yields a net income of ₹ 10, net annual incomes will be

Low : ₹ 30,000 × 0.4 × 10 = ₹ 1,20,000,
High : ₹ 60,000 × 0.4 × 10 = ₹ 2,40,000,
Average : ₹ 40,000 × 0.4 × 10 = ₹ 1,60,000.

Newspaper advertisements

Net annual income for each type of response is

Low : 700 × (0.4 × 10) × 52 = ₹ 1,45,600,

High : 2,000 × (0.4 × 10) × 52 = ₹ 4,16,000,

Average : 1,350 × (0.4 × 10) × 52 = ₹ 2,80,800.

EMV for both the methods is computed in table 9.45.

TABLE 9.45

EMV in 000's of Rupees

Response	*Direct mailing*			*Newspaper advertisements*		
	Income	*Probability*	*Expected payoff*	*Income*	*Probability*	*Expected payoff*
Low	120	0.15	18	145.6	0.30	43.68
High	240	0.20	48	416.0	0.20	83.20
Average	160	0.65	104	280.8	0.50	140.40
EMV			170			267.28

∴ The company should choose the second method *i.e.*, newspaper advertisements.

EXAMPLE 9.8-11

A toy manufacturer is considering a project of manufacturing Tippi-Toes, a dancing doll with three different movement designs. The dolls are sold at an average price of ₹ 10. The first movement design using gears and levels will require the lowest tooling and setup cost of ₹ 1,00,000 and ₹ 5 per unit of variable cost. Second design with spring action will have fixed cost of ₹ 1,60,000 and variable cost of ₹ 4 per unit. Third design with weights and pulleys will have a fixed cost of ₹ 3,00,000 and variable cost of ₹ 3 per unit. One of the following demand events can occur for Tippi-Toes with the associated probabilities :

Type of demand	*Units required*	*Probability*
Light	*25,000*	*0.10*
Moderate	*1,00,000*	*0.70*
Heavy	*1,50,000*	*0.20*

(i) Construct payoff table for the above project.

(ii) Which is the optimum design ?

(iii) How much the decision-maker could afford to pay to obtain perfectly correct information about demand ?

Solution

Payoffs for the above three demand events for the three movement designs of the dolls can be calculated as follows :

Payoff = Revenue – Total variable cost – Fixed cost.

∴ Payoff for light demand, design 1

= ₹ (25,000 × 10 – 25,000 × 5 – 1,00,000) = ₹ 25,000.

Payoff for moderate demand, design 1

= ₹ (1,00,000 × 10 – 1,00,000 × 5 – 1,00,000) = ₹ 4,00,000.

Payoff for heavy demand, design 1

= ₹ (1,50,000 × 10 – 1,50,000 × 5 – 1,00,000) = ₹ 6,50,000.

Payoff for light demand, design 2

= ₹ (25,000 × 10 – 25,000 × 4 – 1,60,000) = – ₹ 10,000.

Payoff for moderate demand, design 2

= ₹ (1,00,000 × 10 – 1,00,000 × 4 – 1,60,000) = ₹ 4,40,000.

Payoff for heavy demand, design 2

= ₹ (1,50,000 × 10 – 1,50,000 × 4 – 1,60,000) = ₹ 7,40,000.

Payoff for light demand, design 3

= ₹ (25,000 × 10 – 25,000 × 3 – 3,00,000) = – ₹ 1,25,000.

Payoff for moderate demand, design 3

= ₹ (1,00,000 × 10 – 1,00,000 × 3 – 3,00,000) = ₹ 4,00,000.

Payoff for heavy demand, design 3

= ₹ (1,50,000 × 10 – 1,50,000 × 3 – 3,00,000) = ₹ 7,50,000.

(*i*) The conditional payoff table for Tippi-Toes decision is given below :

TABLE 9.46

Conditional payoff table (₹)

Demand	*Probability*	*Design with*		
		Gears and levels	*Spring action*	*Weights and pulleys*
Light	0.10	25,000	– 10,000	– 1,25,000
Moderate	0.70	4,00,000	4,40,000	4,00,000
Heavy	0.20	6,50,000	7,40,000	7,50,000
Expected payoff		4,12,500	4,55,000	4,17,500

(*ii*) ∴ The toy manufacturer should go in for spring action design for the doll.

(*iii*) Expected payoff with perfect information

= ₹ (25,000 × 0.10 + 4,40,000 × 0.70 + 7,50,000 × 0.20)

= ₹ 4,60,500.

∴ EVPI = ₹ (4,60,500 – 4,55,000) = ₹ 5,500.

Thus ₹ 5,500 is the maximum amount the decision-maker would be willing to pay to obtain perfect information about the demand of the doll.

EXAMPLE 9.8-12

A company is faced with the problem of determining the optimum number of a certain magazine to order. The magazine costs ₹ 5 and sells at ₹ 10 per copy. If the company orders more copies than it can sell, the unsold copies can be returned under the prior wholesale contract for a refund under the following formula : upto first 500 copies, refund is ₹ 3 for each unsold copy; between 501 to 1,000 copies, refund is ₹ 2 for each copy and for over 1,000 copies, it is ₹ 1 per copy. The sale record of past 100 weeks is given:

No. of copies sold/week	:	*4,000*	*5,000*	*6,000*	*7,000*	*8,000*
No. of weeks	:	*10*	*25*	*35*	*20*	*10*

(i) What is the optimum decision ?

(ii) Compute the expected maximum profit. [P.T.U. M.Tech. Nov., 2012]

Solution

If 4,000 copies are ordered, net profit for each of the five levels of demand will be ₹ 4,000 × 5 = ₹ 20,000.

If 5,000 copies are ordered, net profit if demand turns out to be for 4,000 copies will be ₹ (4,000 × 5 – 500 × 2 – 500 × 3) = ₹ 17,500. If the demand is for 5,000 copies or more, all the 5,000 copies will be sold, resulting in net profit of ₹ (5,000 × 5) = ₹ 25,000. Similarly, the net profit can be computed for all demand levels for order sizes of 6,000 ; 7,000 and 8,000 copies. The conditional net profit table below represents the values for each combination of demand level and order size.

TABLE 9.47

Conditional net profit table (thousands of rupees)

Demand	*Probability*	*No. of copies ordered*				
		4,000	5,000	6,000	7,000	8,000
4,000	0.10	20	17.50	13.50	9.50	5.50
5,000	0.25	20	25	22.50	18.50	14.50
6,000	0.35	20	25	30	27.50	23.50
7,000	0.20	20	25	30	35	32.50
8,000	0.10	20	25	30	35	40
Expected net profit		20	24.25	26.475	25.70	22.90

(*i*) Thus optimum decision is to order 6,000 copies.
(*ii*) Maximum expected profit is ₹ 26,475.

EXAMPLE 9.8-13

The XYZ company has total excess cash funds of ₹ 60,000 to invest in various projects during this month and the next, according to the cash-flow statement prepared by the accounts department. The firm has been offered the following investment opportunities : It can participate immediately (at the start of this month) in a project by investing ₹ 60,000, which is equally likely to result in a net profit of ₹ 20,000 or a loss of ₹ 10,000 within the month. In effect, the company will be able to reclaim its principal, with either a profit or a loss, by the month's end. At the same time, the firm is informed that in one month from now, it will be given the opportunity of investing ₹ 55,000 in another investment which is equally likely to result in a net profit of ₹ 15,000 or a net loss of ₹ 5,000.

Assuming that this company examines its cash position every two months to determine the feasibility of investing excess cash, advise this company as to whether it should invest in project 1 of this month or invest in project 2 of next month or invest in projects 1 and 2 together if the objective is to maximize the expected profits over the next two months.

[*C.A. Nov., 1991*]

Solution

Expected profits if invested in project 1 this month

= ₹ [0.5 × 20,000 + 0.5 (–10,000)] = ₹ 5,000.

Expected profits if invested in project 2 next month

= ₹ [0.5 × 15,000 + 0.5 (–5,000)] = ₹ 5,000.

Expected profits if invested in projects 1 and 2 together are calculated in the table below :

TABLE 9.48

State of nature	*Joint probability*	*Pay-off* ₹	*Expected profits* ₹
Profits in project 1 and in project 2	0.5 × 0.5 = 0.25	20,000 + 15,000 = 35,000	0.25 × 35,000 = 8,750
Profit in project 1 and loss in project 2	0.5 × 0.5 = 0.25	20,000 – 5,000 = 15,000	0.25 × 15,000 = 3,750
Loss in project 1	0.5	– 10,000	0.5 × (– 10,000) = – 5,000
			7,500

Note that if there is loss of ₹ 10,000 in project 1, there is not enough cash to invest in project 2.

Hence the company is advised to invest in project 1 and project 2 together in order to maximize its profits over the next two months.

EXERCISES 9.1

1. What is decision-making ? Explain and differentiate this under the conditions of certainty and uncertainty. *[P.T.U. M.Tech. Dec., 2011; May, 2011; U.P.U. MBA, 2010; M.D.U. Rohtak B.E. (Mech.) Dec., 2006]*
2. What are the different environments in which decisions are made ? *[H.P.U. B.Tech. (Mech.) 2012; Bharathiar U. Dip. in QR. April, 2011; P.T.U. B.Tech. (Mech.) Dec., 2011; May, 2011 ; May, 2010]*
3. Explain the different methods useful for decision-making under uncertainty. *[P.T.U. M.G.U. Kerala M.Com., June 2012; P.T.U. B.Tech. (Mech.) 2012; M.Tech. Dec., 2011; MBA, Dec., 2013; 2009; B.Tech. (Mech.) 2008]*
4. Write notes on : (*a*) Laplace criterion (*b*) Minimax regret criterion (*c*) Criterion of Bayes and (*d*) Criterion of realism. *[Calicut M Com., 1992; Kerala M.Com., 1991]*
5. Explain with suitable examples the maximin, the minimax and the regret criteria in decision-making. *[Univ. of Mumbai MBA, 2012]*
6. With the help of an example, describe in detail decision-making under risk. *[P.T.U. MCA, 2010]*
7. What is EMV ? How is it computed to be used as a criterion of decision-making and when ? *[M.D.U. MBA, 2010; P.T.U. MBA, 2009; Chennai U. B.B.A. Nov., 2010]*
8. Write short note on the value of perfect information. *[U.P.U. MBA, 2010; B.P.U.T. 2010; P.T.U. MBA, 2009; P.U.B.E. (Prod.) 2001]*
9. What is meant by statistical decision analysis? How is it different from other methods used in decision-making? Describe some methods which are useful in decision-making under uncertainty. *[G.J.U.B.E., 1998]*
10. Explain how statistical analysis can be helpful to business managers in decision-making under uncertainty. *[C.A. (Nov.) 1984]*
11. Explain clearly the following terms:
    (*i*) Action space (*ii*) State of nature (*iii*) Payoff table and (*iv*) Opportunity loss. *[Maharishi Dayanand University M.BA.,1982]*
12. Indicate the difference between decision-making under risk and uncertainty in statistical decision theory. *[P.U. UIAMS MBA May, 2015; Bharathiar U. Coimbatore B.Sc. April, 2011; P.T.U. B.Tech. (Mech.) 2009; MBA Dec., 2002]*
13. Explain the various steps involved in the Decision Theory Approach. Which are the decision criteria available for the condition of uncertainty? *[P.T.U. MBA Dec., 2013; Kuru. U.B.E. (Mech.) June, 2012]*
14. What is meant by decision-making under uncertainty ? Explain minimax regret criterion and Laplace criterion of decision-making. *[Mumbai U. MBA, 2012, 2010]*
15. Write short note on various methods useful for decision-making under uncertainty. *[P.T.U. MBA, 2009; B.Tech., 2008]*

Section 9.4

16. A training programme is to be met with a batch size of a_1, a_2, a_3 and a_4 which meets the expenses. s_1, s_2, s_3 and s_4 indicate the level of attendance. The table below indicates the additional cost incurred due to the level of attendance in different batches.

TABLE 9.49

	s_1	s_2	s_3	s_4
a_1	6	11	19	26
a_2	7	6	11	22
a_3	20	17	11	20
a_4	29	21	18	14

Find the optimum batch size using Laplace, minimax and maximin criteria.

[*G.N.D.U. MBA April, 2001*]

(*Ans.* a_2 ; a_4 ; a_4.)

17. The following matrix gives the payoff of different strategies S_1, S_2, S_3 against different conditions N_1, N_2, N_3 and N_4.

TABLE 9.50

	N_1	N_2	N_3	N_4
S_1	4,000	– 100	6,000	18,000
S_2	20,000	5,000	400	0
S_3	20,000	15,000	– 2,000	1,000

(*a*) Indicate the decision taken under the following approach:
(*i*) Pessimistic (*ii*) Optimistic (*iii*) Regret and (*iv*) Equal probability.
(*b*) Explain briefly the principle involved in each approach. [*St. Joseph (Bangalore) M.B.A., 1977*]

(*Ans.* (*i*) S_2 (*ii*) S_2 or S_3 (*iii*) S_1 (*iv*) S_3.)

18. Dr. Thomas has been thinking about starting his own independent nursing home. The problem is to decide how large the nursing home should be. The annual returns will depend on both the size of nursing home and a number of marketing factors. After a careful analysis, Dr. Thomas developed the following table:

TABLE 9.51

Size of nursing home	*Good market* (₹)	*Fair market* (₹)	*Poor market* (₹)
Small (S)	50,000	20,000	– 10,000
Medium(M)	70,000	35,000	– 25,000
Large (L)	90,000	35,000	– 45,000
Very large (VL)	2,00,000	25,000	– 1,20,000

(*a*) What is the maximax decision ?
(*b*) What is the maximin decision ?
(*c*) What is equally likely decision ?
(*d*) What is the criterion of realism decision? Use $\alpha = 0.8$.
(*e*) Develop an opportunity loss table and determine the minimax decision.

(*Ans.* (*a*) VL (*b*) S (*c*) VL (*d*) VL (*e*) L or VL.)

19. The research department of M/s Hindustan Lever has recommended to the marketing department to launch a shampoo of three different types. The marketing manager has to decide one of the types of shampoo to be launched under the following estimated payoffs for various levels of sales:

TABLE 9.52

Type of shampoo	*Estimated levels of sales*		
	15,000	10,000	5,000
1. *Egg shampoo*	30	10	10
2. *Clinic shampoo*	40	15	5
3. *Deluxe shampoo*	55	20	3

What will be the marketing manager's decision if (*i*) maximin (*ii*) minimax (*iii*) maximax (*iv*) Laplace (*v*) Regret criterion is applied ? [*Sardar Patel B.E. (Mech.) 1984*]

(*Ans.* (*i*) 1, (*ii*) 1, (*iii*) 3, (*iv*) 3, (*v*) 3.)

20. A food product company is contemplating the introduction of a revolutionary new product with new packaging to replace the existing product at a large increase in price (S_1) or a moderate change in composition of the existing product with a new packaging at a small increase in price (S_2) or a small change in the composition of the existing product with a negligible increase in price (S_3). The three states of nature are : (*i*) high increase in sales (N_1), (*ii*) no change in sales (N_2) and (*iii*) decrease in sales (N_3). The marketing department of the company worked out the payoffs in terms of yearly net profits for each course of action for these events. This is represented in the following table:

TABLE 9.53

States of nature	*Courses of action*		
	S_1	S_2	S_3
N_1	₹ 7,00,000	₹ 5,00,000	₹ 3,00,000
N_2	3,00,000	4,50,000	3,00,000
N_3	1,50,000	0	3,00,000

Which strategy should the company choose on the basis of (*a*) maximin criterion (*b*) maximax criterion (*c*) minimax regret criterion and (*d*) Laplace criterion ? [*M.D. MBA, 1983*]

(*Ans.* (*a*) S_3 (*b*) S_1 (*c*) S_1 (*d*) S_1.)

21. XYZ Informatics Corporation summarizes international financial information reports on a weekly basis, prints sophisticated data and forecasts, which are purchased weekly by mutual funds, banks and insurance companies. This information is very expensive and the demand for the report is limited to a maximum of 30 units per week. The possible demands are 0, 10, 20 or 30 per week. The profit per report sold is ₹ 30 and the loss per report unsold at the end of the week is ₹ 20. No production of extra reports during a week is possible. Further, there is a penalty cost of ₹ 250 for not meeting the demand. Unsold reports cannot be carried over to the next week. Using the payoff table, find the number of reports to be produced if (*i*) maximin strategy is adopted (*ii*) maximax strategy is adopted. (*Ans.* (*i*) 10, – ₹ 200 (*ii*) 30, ₹ 900.)

22. A gambler at a horse race is considering placing a bet on a specific horse. There are four possible alternatives and four states of nature with the following payoffs :

TABLE 9.54

Strategies	*States of nature*			
	A wins	*B wins*	*C wins*	*All lose*
Bet A	7	– 2	– 2	– 2
Bet B	3	3	– 2	– 2
Bet C	2	2	2	– 2
Do not bet	0	0	0	0

(*a*) What is the maximin strategy ? (*b*) What strategy should be selected as per Hurwicz criterion with $\alpha = 0.5$? (*c*) What is the best strategy by Savage criterion ? (*a*) What is the best strategy by Laplace criterion ? (*Ans.* (*a*) Do not bet (*b*) Bet A (*c*) Bet B (*d*) Bet C.)

23. A decision problem has been expressed in the following payoff table :

TABLE 9.55

	Outcome		
Action	*I*	*II*	*III*
A	10	20	26
B	30	30	60
C	40	30	20

(*a*) What is the minimax payoff action ? (*b*) What is the minimum opportunity loss action?

[*Poona MBA, 1983*]

(*Ans.* (*a*) A (*b*) B)

Section 9.5-9.8

24. A person has the choice of running a hot-snack stall or an ice-cream and cold-drink stall at a certain holiday resort during the coming summer season. If the weather during the season is cool and rainy, he can expect to make a profit of ₹ 15,000 and if it is warm, he can expect to make a profit of only ₹ 3,000 by running a hot-snack stall. On the other hand, if his choice is to run an ice-cream and cold-drink shop, he can expect to make a profit of ₹ 18,000 if the weather is warm and only ₹ 3,000 if the weather is cool and rainy. The meteorological authorities predict that there is 40% chance of the weather being warm during the coming season. Should he opt for running the hot-snack stall or the ice-cream stall ? *[P.U. MBA Feb., 2009]*
[**Hint.** The payoff table will be as shown below].

TABLE 9.56

State of nature	*Probability*	*Action*			
		Hot-snack stall (Profit)		*Ice-cream stall (Profit)*	
		Conditional	*Expected*	*Conditional*	*Expected*
Warm	0.4	₹ 3,000	₹ 1,200	₹18,000	₹7,200
Cool and rainy	0.6	₹ 15,000	₹ 9,000	₹ 3,000	₹ 1,800
			₹ 10,200		₹ 9,000

Thus he should open hot-snack stall.]

25. An investor was considering stock purchases in two companies. He determined the following payoff table contingent upon whether company A or B wins a competition for share of the market.

TABLE 9.57

State	**Strategies**	
	a_1 *(Invest in A)*	a_2 *(Invest in B)*
Q_1 : A wins	30	0
Q_2 : B wins	40	80

(*a*) What is the maximin strategy ? The maximax strategy ?
(*b*) At what probability of A's winning is the expected value of the two strategies the same?

(Ans. (*a*) a_1, a_2 (*b*) 4/7.)

[**Hint.** $30p + 40(1-p) = 0p + 80(1-p)$.]

26. Following are the records of demand of an item for the past 300 days:

TABLE 9.58

Demand in units	*No.of days*	*Probability*
10,000	18	0.06
11,000	90	0.30
12,000	120	0.40
13,000	60	0.20
14,000	12	0.04
	300	1.00

(*i*) What is the expected demand ?
(*ii*) It costs ₹ 15 to make an item which sells for ₹ 20 normally, but at the end of the day any surplus has to be disposed of at ₹ 10 per item. What is the optimum output ?

[P.T.U.B. Tech. (Mech.) Dec., 2011]

(Ans. (*i*) 11,860 (*ii*) 12,000 with EMV = ₹ 55,800.)

27. A newspaper boy buys his newspaper for ₹ 0.20 each and sells it for ₹ 0.40 each. Any paper not sold by the end of the day becomes useless for him. His problem is to determine the optimum number of papers that he should buy. If he stocks more, his profits are reduced to the extent of

cost of unsold newspapers, and if he stocks less, he loses the opportunity to earn more profits. An analysis of past records shows the probability distribution of demand of newspapers as given in the table below.

TABLE 9.59

Demand	*Probability*
0	0.20
10	0.25
20	0.40
30	0.10
40	0.05

Find the optimum number of newspapers he should stock. (*Ans.* 20.)

28. Indicate which of the following acts are inadmissible and assign reasons for the same :

TABLE 9.60

Events	*Acts*			
	A_1	A_2	A_3	A_4
E_1	100	101	50	25
E_2	80	30	20	10
E_3	20	19	40	– 5

(*Ans.* A_3 is inadmissible since A_1 has higher maximum as well the minimum payoff.)

29. Decide in the following situations:

TABLE 9.61

	Acts	
Events	A_1	A_2
E_1	1	– 2
E_2	– 1	100

(*i*) Which act gives the maximin payoff ?
(*ii*) What is the expected payoff if the probability of event E_1 is 0.99 ?
(*iii*) Which act has the maximum payoff if the event probabilities are equal ?

(*Ans.* (*i*) A_1 (*ii*) A_1 = 0.98, A_2 = – 0.98 (*iii*) A_2 with 49.)

30. Indicate minimax opportunity loss act and calculate the lowest expected opportunity loss from the following opportunity loss table:

TABLE 9.62

		Acts		
Events	*Probability*	A_1	A_2	A_3
E_1	0.4	10	0	20
E_2	0.5	0	30	40
E_3	0.1	50	5	0

(*Ans.* A_2, A_1 with 9.)

31. Wings Corner wants to decide how many men's shirts to order for the Diwali season. For a particular type of shirt, Wings must order in lots of 50 shirts. If it orders 50 shirts, cost is ₹ 60 per shirt; if it orders 100 shirts, cost is ₹ 55 per shirt, and if it orders 150 or more shirts, the cost is ₹ 50 per shirt. Wings' selling price is ₹ 95, but any leftover at the end of the season will be sold at 50 per cent discount. It is assumed that demand will be either 50, 100, 150, 200 or 250 shirts and that the Corner will not suffer any loss of goodwill if it runs out-of-stock. It must place the entire order for the season at the beginning, with no opportunity for reordering. Wings has estimated the probability of demand as follows:

Demand	:	50	100	150	200	250
Probability	:	0.15	0.25	0.25	0.20	0.15

(*i*) Use a payoff table to determine the order quantity that will maximize the expected contribution.
(*ii*) Calculate the expected value of perfect information.

[**Hint.** CP = (95 – Purchase price)S, when D ≥ S,

95 D – (Purchase price)S + 47.50 (S – D), when D < S.

The payoff table obtained is shown below.

TABLE 9.63

Demand	*Cost/shirt* ₹	*Probability*	*Stock action*				
			50 ₹	*100* ₹	*150* ₹	*200* ₹	*250* ₹
50	60	0.15	1,750	1,625	2,000	1,875	1,750
100	55	0.25	1,750	4,000	4,375	4,250	4,125
150	50	0.25	1,750	4,000	6,750	6,625	6,500
200	50	0.20	1,750	4,000	6,750	9,000	8,875
250	50	0.15	1,750	4,000	6,750	9,000	11,250

The problem can now be solved easily.]

32. A mineral processing company wants to decide about the number of spare-gear trains it has to order at the time of placing order for a high horsepower gearbox connected to a grinding unit. Although the life of a gear can be as high as 30 years and more, sudden failures cannot be ruled out. In case of failure, it would be expensive and time consuming to get a spare gear train. The cost would be ₹ 2,00,000 including the loss of production due to downtime of the equipment. If ordered out with the gearbox, a gear train would cost only ₹ 10,000. The following data are based on an analysis of past failures of 100 gearboxes:

No. of spare-gear trains required	*No. of gearboxes requiring the spares*
0	93
1	4
2	1
3	1
4	1

Advise the optimal order size. [*Poona M.B.A.,1982*]

[**Hint.** The cost table constructed for the problem is shown below.

TABLE 9.64

Cost table (thousands of rupees)

Demand	*Probability*	*No. of spare-gear trains in stock*				
		0	*1*	*2*	*3*	*4*
0	0.93	₹ 0	₹ 10	₹ 20	₹ 30	₹ 40
1	0.04	200	10	20	30	40
2	0.01	400	210	20	30	40
3	0.01	600	410	220	30	40
4	0.01	800	610	420	230	40

The problem can now be solved by the usual method.]

33. A payoff matrix has to be prepared with three alternative products A_1, A_2 and A_3. The respective costs of these products are ₹ 2, ₹ 2.50 and ₹ 4 per unit and their selling prices are ₹ 3, ₹ 4 and ₹ 5 per unit respectively.

The normal production capacity of the plant for production of each of the products A_1, A_2 and A_3 is 3,000, 2,000 and 1,000 units respectively. Calculate payoffs if the states of demand are high (S_1), moderate (S_2) and low (S_3) with respective demand levels of 3,000, 2,000 and 1,000 units. The stocks unsold will be worth half the cost price for the next period.

[**Hint.** The payoff table can be prepared in the usual manner.]

TABLE 9.65

Payoff table

Demand	Production alternatives		
	A_1 3,000	A_2 2,000	A_3 1,000
S_1 (3,000)	₹ 3,000	₹ 3,000	₹ 1,000
S_2 (2,000)	1,000	3,000	1,000
S_3 (1,000)	– 1,000	250	1,000

34. A well-known department store advertises female fashion garments from time to time in the Sunday press. Only one garment is advertised on each occasion. The statistical probability of demand at various levels after each advertisement is as follows:

TABLE 9.66

Demand (No. of garments)	*After advertising in one newspaper*	*After advertising in two newspapers*
30	0.10	0.00
40	0.25	0.15
50	0.40	0.35
60	0.25	0.40
70	0.00	0.10

The garment advertised to sell at ₹ 35 costs ₹ 15 to make and can be disposed of, if unsold, for ₹ 10.

(*a*) Calculate how many garments should be purchased by the stores in order to maximize expected gross profit after advertising in

(*i*) one newspaper

(*ii*) two newspapers.

(*b*) Calculate the amount, if any, of the expected net profit under conditions (*i*) and (*ii*) of part (*a*).

[**Hint.** Prepare the payoff table as usual. Then calculate EMV for probabilities of demand on advertising in one newspaper and two newspapers independently.]

(*Ans.* (*a*) (*i*) 60, (*ii*) 60.
(*b*) (*i*) ₹ 900 (*ii*) ₹ 1,037.50.)

35. The daily demand of cars for hiring in a city is as follows:

Demand : 12 13 14 15 16
Probability : 0.2 0.1 0.3 0.3 0.1

The parking charges per car are ₹ 100 per day if a car is not hired. For hiring a car, a company gets ₹ 250 rent per car per day. If a car is hired, the company does not have to pay parking charges. The company wants to enter into business in the city. Construct a payoff table and determine how many cars the company should have, based on EMV criterion. [*Mumbai U. MBA, 2010*]

36. Given the payoff table :

TABLE 9.67

State of nature	*Probability*	*Act*		
		x	*y*	*z*
P	0.3	–120	–80	100
Q	0.5	200	400	–300
R	0.2	260	–260	600

Using the expected monetary values, decide which act can be chosen as the best. [*C.A. June, 1993*]

(*Ans.* y; EMV = 124.)

37. A newspaper agent's experience shows that the daily demand of the newspapers in his area has the following probability distribution :

Daily demand	:	300	400	500	600	700
Probability	:	0.1	0.3	0.4	0.1	0.1

He sells the newspapers for ₹ 2 each, while he buys each at ₹ 1. Unsold copies are traded as scrap and each such copy fetches 10 paise. Assuming that he stocks the newspapers in multiples of 100 only, how many should he stock so that his expected profit is maximum ?

[*I.C.W.A. Dec., 1997*]

(*Ans.* 500; EMV = ₹ 405.)

38. A company is trying to manufacture a new type of toy. The company is to decide whether to bring out a full, partial or minimal production line. There are three levels of product acceptance and the company has estimated their probability of occurrence. Management of the company will make the decision on the basis of maximizing the expected profit from the first year of production. The relevant data are shown in the following table where in first year profits in thousands of rupees are given.

TABLE 9.68

State of nature :	*Good*	*Fair*	*Poor*
Full	90	60	–15
Partial	80	65	–10
Minimal	60	50	0

(i) What is the optimum production line and its expected profit ?
(ii) What is the optimum EOL and the optimum course of action ?

[*I.C.W.A. June, 1998*]

(*Ans.* (i) Partial; ₹ 38,000 (ii) Partial; ₹ 6,000.)

39. A major consumer goods manufacturer wishes to decide which of two new products to bring out in the market and what level of advertising to use. The profit table for these products is as follows (profits are in units of ₹ 10,000):

TABLE 9.69

Demand	*Product 1*			*Product 2*		
	A_1	A_2	A_3	A_1	A_2	A_3
S_1, *High*	140	160	200	200	210	230
S_2, *Average*	100	130	160	160	170	190
S_3, *Low*	80	120	140	120	130	140

where A_1 = low expenditure advertising programme,
A_2 = medium expenditure advertising programme, and
A_3 = high expenditure advertising programme.

The prior probability distributions of demand are

TABLE 9.70

S_i	*Product 1* $p(S_i)$	*Product 2* $p(S_i)$
S_1	0.4	0.2
S_2	0.5	0.2
S_3	0.1	0.6

(*a*) Which product and advertising level would you recommend ?
(*b*) What is the expected value of perfect information for each product ?

(*Ans.* (*a*) Product 1 with high expenditure advertising programme.
(*b*) EVPI for product 1 = 174 – 174 = 0,
EVPI for product 2 = 168 – 168 = 0.)

40. A retailer has to decide on the optimal number of units to be stocked in respect of a certain item

under the following circumstances:

(*a*) Cost price in season: ₹ 12.

(*b*) Selling price in season: ₹ 18.

(*c*) Bargain price after season: ₹ 9.

(*d*) Cost of holding an item in inventory beyond the season is ₹ 1.

The distribution of demand based on past data is shown below.

Demand	:	7	8	9	10	11
Probability	:	0.20	0.20	0.25	0.15	0.20

Determine the optimal act based on the expected monetary value criterion.

[**Hint.** Conditional profit = ₹ [(18 – 12). units sold – (12 – 9 + 1). units unsold.]

(*Ans.* 9 units, EMV = ₹ 48.)

41. A company operates a photographic developing and printing business at a holiday resort. It employs assistants on a full-time basis at ₹ 3/hr each but when the volume of work is large, it can let out the surplus work to another firm at ₹ 5/hr per employee. The demand figures for the past season are as follows and there is no reason to consider that conditions will be different for the current season.

No. of full-time assistants required	:	5	6	7	8	9	10
No. of days	:	10	34	46	58	37	15

Setup a conditional cost table which illustrates the cost of selecting the various alternative number of full-time assistants within the given range of activity and state which number of assistants employed on a full-time basis would minimize costs over the season. Calculate the expected value of perfect information.

[**Hint.** Conditional cost table is represented by table 9.71.

TABLE 9.71

Assistants required	*Probability*	*Full-time assistants employed*					
		5	*6*	*7*	*8*	*9*	*10*
5	0.05	₹ 15	₹ 18	₹ 21	₹ 24	₹ 27	₹ 30
6	0.17	20	18	21	24	27	30
7	0.23	25	23	21	24	27	30
8	0.29	30	28	26	24	27	30
9	0.185	35	33	31	29	27	30
10	0.075	40	38	36	34	32	30

The expected cost table can now be prepared and EVPI can be computed.]

(*Ans.* ₹ 2.58.)

42. The demand pattern of the cakes made in a bakery is as follows :

No. of cakes demanded	:	0	1	2	3	4	5
Probability	:	0.05	0.10	0.25	0.30	0.20	0.10

If the preparation cost is ₹ 3 per unit and selling price is ₹ 4 per unit, how many cakes should the baker make to maximize his profit ? Use incremental analysis.

[*Poona M.B.A., 1983*]

(*Ans.* 2.)

43. A factory has to choose one out of two products for manufacture. Products and states of nature are given below :

		States of nature		
		Good	*Fair*	*Poor*
Products	A	0.60	0.25	0.15
	B	0.70	0.20	0.10

Profit expectations are as follows :

		States of nature		
		Good	*Fair*	*Poor*
Products	A	₹ 25,000	₹ 10,000	₹ 2,000
	B	₹ 40,000	₹ 15,000	– ₹ 1,000

What is optimal strategy by expected value method ?

[*G.J.U.B.E. (Mech.) 1996*]

(*Ans.* Product B ; V_A = ₹ 17,800 ; V_B = ₹ 30,900.)

44. A milkman buys milk at ₹ 10 per litre and sells it at ₹ 12 if sold on the same day ; if not, it can be sold at ₹ 9 per litre the next day. Demand of milk lies between 45 litres and 60 litres per day and its probabilities are uniformly distributed over this demand. If each day's demand is independent of the previous day's demand, how many litres should be ordered every day?

[*P.U.B.E. (Mech.) Nov., 1996*]

45. A large restaurant purchases cakes daily from a local bakery. The cakes cost ₹ 10 each and sell at ₹ 15 each. If the cakes are not sold on the same day, they are sold in another outlet for ₹ 8 each. The relative frequency distribution for the restaurant sales is given below :

Daily sales (dozens)	:	30	31	32	33	34	35	36
Relative frequency	:	0.01	0.09	0.16	0.25	0.30	0.11	0.08

You are required to state :

(*i*) Optimum quantity which the buyer wants to purchase to maximize the expected profit.

(*ii*) How much the buyer could afford to pay for perfectly correct information for sales ?

[*ICWA (Final) June, 1993*]

46. Pragati Construction is considering the purchase of one of the four available tracts of land. The future profit that will be realised on the tracts depends upon the geographical area that will hav the greatest population growth during the next two years. Potential profits in thousands of rupees are given in the table below. Management believes that each of the four areas is equally likely to be the area that experiences greatest growth.

TABLE 9.72

Tract	*Profit if greatest growth occurs in the (000's)*			
	North	*East*	*South*	*West*
A_1	₹ 70	₹ 70	₹ 50	₹ 30
A_2	50	90	50	30
A_3	30	60	60	60
A_4	50	20	80	80

(*i*) What probability assessments should be assigned to states of nature ?

(*ii*) Determine the expected value of perfect information.

(*iii*) Develop a loss matrix and determine the EVPI by computing expected losses.

(*Ans.* (*i*) 0.25, 0.25, 0.25, 0.25. (*ii*) ₹ 22, 500. (*iii*) ₹ 22, 500.)

47. Seller of a perishable item purchases them @ ₹ 10 per item and sells them @ ₹ 13 per item, if sold the same day. Items not demanded the same day are sold early morning next day @ ₹ 8 per item. The demand is known to vary over 10, 11, 12 and 13 items per day with probabilities of 0.2, 0.4, 0.3 and 0.1 respectively. The seller has only ₹ 120 to invest for the item. Based on expected value criterion, using tree diagram or otherwise, decide what he should do. Should he be sorry for not being able to purchase 13 items due to shortage of money ? Justify your answer.

[*C.A. May, 1994*]

(*Ans.* 11 or 12 items ; ₹ 32 ; No.)

[**Hint.** Expected payoff is maximum in case he purchases 11 or 12 items *i.e.*, ₹ 32. He should not feel sorry for not being able to purchase 13 items as its expected profit is ₹ 30.50, which is less than that for 11 or 12 items.]

48. A small industry finds from the past data that the cost of making an item is ₹ 25. The selling price of the item is ₹ 30; if it is not sold within a week, it could be disposed of at ₹ 20 at the end of the week. Data for sales is given below.

Weekly sales	:	≤ 3	4	5	6	7	≥ 8
No. of weeks	:	0	10	20	40	30	0

Find the optimum number of items per week the industry should produce.

[*P.T.U. B.Tech., 2010; Chennai U. B.B.A. Nov., 2010*]

(*Ans.* 6.)

49. A wholesaler of sports goods has an opportunity to buy 5,000 pairs of skis that have been declared surplus by the government. The wholesaler will pay ₹ 50 per pair and can obtain ₹ 100 a pair by selling skis to retailers. The wholesaler is in doubt as to how many pairs he will be able to sell. Any skis left over can be sold to discount outlets at ₹ 20 a pair. The wholesaler assigns probabilites to demand as follows

Retailer's demand (pairs)	*Probability*
1,000	0.6
3,000	0.3
5,000	0.1

(*a*) Compute the conditional monetary and expected monetary values.
(*b*) Compute the expected profit with a perfect predicting device.
(*c*) Compute the EVPI. [*Bangalore MBA, 1983*]

(*Ans.* (*a*) EMV : ₹ 50, 54, 10 thousands.
(*b*) ₹ 1,00,000. (*c*) ₹ 46,000.)

50. A distributor of a certain product incurs holding cost of ₹ 100 per unit per week and shortage cost of ₹ 300 per unit. The data on the sales of the product are given below.

Weekly sales (units)	:	0	1	2	3	4	5	6	7	8
No. of weeks	:	0	0	5	10	15	15	5	0	0

How many units should the distributor buy every week ? Also find EVPI.

[*C.A. Nov., 1986*]

(*Ans.* 5, ₹ 120.)

51. Narula Pastry shop makes pastries and sells them at ₹ 30 per dozen in special boxes containing one dozen each. The cost of pastries to the bakery is ₹ 15 per dozen. At the end of the week, the slightly stale pastries are sold off at ₹ 10 per dozen. The salaries, rent and other overhead expenses attributable to the pastry production are ₹ 2 per dozen. Fresh pastries are sold in the Narula special boxes which cost 50 paise each. Stale pastries are sold wrapped in ordinary paper. The probability distribution of demand for pastries in the past is as follows :

Demand in dozens	:	0	1	2	3	4	5
Probability	:	0.02	0.15	0.18	0.50	0.10	0.05

(*a*) Construct the payoff table (*b*) Construct the loss table (c) Compute the expected profits (*d*) What is the optimum stock level ? (*e*) What is the EVPI ?

(*Ans.* (*d*) 3 dozens (*e*) ₹ 6.28.)

[**Hint.** Conditional payoffs are given by

$$\text{CP} = \begin{cases} (30-15-2-0.50)\,\text{S} = \text{Rs.}\,12.50\,\text{S} & \text{when D} \ge \text{S}, \\ 12.50\,\text{D} - (15-10+2)\,(\text{S}-\text{D}) = 12.50D - 7\,(S-D) & \text{when D} < \text{S}.\end{cases}$$]

52. A company finds that certain parts supplied by a contractor in batches of 800 each turn out to be defective and as a result there is loss of ₹ 12 per defective part. It is realised that if an engineer is posted to the contractor, this will reduce the defective parts to 2% which is acceptable to the company. However, it will require an additional expenditure of ₹ 200 per batch. On the basis of the past experience, following are the probabilities of the defective parts :

Defective parts (%)	:	2	4	6	8	10
Probability	:	0.1	0.2	0.3	0.3	0.1

Should the company post the engineer ?

(*Ans.* Yes, saving = ₹ 208.)

[**Hint.** Expected no. of defective parts = 0.1 × 2 + 0.2 × 4 + 0.3 × 6 + 0.3 × 8 + 0.1 × 10 = 6.2%

$\therefore$ Loss due to defective parts = ₹ 800 × $\frac{6.2}{100}$ × 12 = ₹ 600.

Loss if engineer is posted = ₹ (800 × $\frac{2}{100}$ × 12 + 200) = ₹ 392.]

53. A manager is faced with the problem of choosing one of the three products for manufacturing. The demand for each product may turn out to be good, moderate or poor. The probability for each state of nature is estimated as follows :

TABLE 9.73

Product	*Demand*		
	Good	*Moderate*	*Poor*
X	0.70	0.20	0.10
Y	0.50	0.30	0.20
Z	0.40	0.50	0.10

The estimated profit or loss under these states is

TABLE 9.74

	Payoff for demand (₹)		
	Good	*Moderate*	*Poor*
X	30,000	20,000	10,000
Y	60,000	30,000	20,000
Z	40,000	10,000	– 15,000

Advise the manager about the choice of the product.

[*ICWA (Final) Dec., 1991*]
(*Ans.* Y, EMV = ₹ 43,000.)

54. XYZ company manufactures parts for cars and sells them in lots of 10,000 parts each. The company has a policy of inspecting each lot before it is actually shipped to the retailer. Five inspection categories established for quality control represent the percentage of defective parts in each lot.

Rating	:	*Excellent (A)*	*Good (B)*	*Acceptable (C)*	*Fair (D)*	*Poor (E)*
Proportion of defective items	:	0.02	0.05	0.10	0.15	0.20
Frequency	:	25	30	20	20	5

The management is considering two courses of action : (*i*) to shut down the entire plant operations and thoroughly inspect each machine and (*ii*) to continue production as it now exists but offer the customer a refund for defective items that are detected and subsequently returned. The first alternative will cost ₹ 680 while the second will cost the company ₹ 1.20 for each defective item returned. Find optimum policy and EVPI.

[**Hint.** Refer to example 9.8-7.]

55. The probability of demand for lorries for hiring on any day in a given district is as follows :

No. of loarries demanded	:	0	1	2	3	4
Probability	:	0.1	0.2	0.3	0.2	0.2

Lorries have a fixed cost of ₹ 90 each day to keep the daily hire charges (net of variable costs of running) as ₹ 200. If the lorry-hire company owns 4 lorries, what is its daily expectation ? If the company is about to go into business and currently has no lorries, how many lorries should it buy ?

[*CA May, 1985*]

[**Hint.** For a lorry, the fixed cost is ₹ 90 and revenue is ₹ 200. With 4 lorries the payoff values will be

No. of lorries demanded :	0	1	2	3	4
Payoff :	0 – 90 × 4	200 – 90 × 4	400 – 90 × 4	600 – 90 × 4	800 – 90 × 4
	= – 360	= – 160	= 40	= 240	= 440

∴ Daily expectation =0.1 (–360) + 0.2 (–160) + 0.3 (40) + 0.2 (240) + 0.2 (440) = ₹ 80.

To determine the number of lorries to be bought, the following conditional pay-off table is prepared:

TABLE 9.75

Demand	*Probability*	*Conditional pay-offs due to decision to purchase lorries (action) (₹)*				
		0	1	2	3	4
0	0.1	0	– 90	–180	–270	–360
1	0.2	0	110	20	–70	–160
2	0.3	0	110	220	130	40
3	0.2	0	110	220	330	240
4	0.2	0	110	220	330	440
	EMV :	0	90	**140**	130	80

∴ The company should buy 2 lorries.]

56. Mr. X quite often flies from city A to city B. He can use the airport bus which costs ₹ 25; but if he takes it, there is chance of 0.08 that he will miss the flight. The stay in a hotel costs ₹ 270 with a 0.96 chance of being on time for the flight. For ₹ 350 he can use a taxi which will make 99 per cent chance of being on time for the flight. If Mr. X catches the plane on time, he will conclude a business transaction which will produce a profit of ₹ 10,000, otherwise he will lose it. What should be his course of action ? Answer on the basis of EMV criterion.

[*CA May, 1990*]

[Hint. Payoff table and EMV for the problem are given in the table below :

TABLE 9.76

States of nature	*Courses of action*					
	Bus		*Stay in hotel*		*Taxi*	
	Prob.	*Cost (₹)*	*Prob.*	*Cost (₹)*	*Prob.*	*Cost (₹)*
Catches the flight	0.92	10,000–25 = 9,975	0.96	10,000–270 = 9,730	0.99	10,000–350 = 9,650
Misses the flight	0.08	–25	0.04	–270	0.01	–350
EMV		9,175		9,330		9,550

∴ He should use the taxi; EMV will be ₹ 9,550.]

57. A retail store is trying to determine the optimal daily order size for a perishable item. The store buys the item at the rate of ₹ 60 per kg and sells at the rate of ₹ 90 per kg.

If the order size is more than demand, the excess quantity can be sold at ₹ 75 per kg in a secondary market; otherwise, the opportunity cost for the store is ₹ 10 per kg for the unsatisifed portion of the demand. Based on the past experience, it is found that the demand varies from 50 kg to 200 kg in steps of 50 kg. The possible values of the order size are from 100 kg to 300 kg in steps of 100 kg. Determine the optimal order size which will maximize the daily profit of the store using:

(i) Laplace criterion.

(ii) Maximum criterion. [*Bharathiar U.Dip. in OR April, 2001*]

9.9 VARIATIONS OF THE EXPECTED VALUE CRITERION

This section is devoted to three issues relating to the expected value criterion. The first issue deals with determination of *posterior* probabilities based on experimentation, the second is devoted to *decision trees* and the third issue deals with *utility versus the actual value of money.*

9.9-1 Posterior Probabilities and Bayesian Analysis

In the preceding analysis of decision-making under risk, the probabilities used in the expected value criterion are usually obtained from the past historical data. These probabilities are called *prior probabilities* and the analysis that uses them to find expected payoffs is known as *prior analysis.*

If the prior analysis results in high expected opportunity loss (EOL) or EVPI, it may be desirable to obtain additional information through sampling or experimentation or test research. Prior probabilities may then be revised in the light of this additional information by using *Bayes theorem* to yield *posterior probabilities* or *Bayes probabilities.*

Revised analysis of the problem using these probabilities is called *posterior analysis* or *Bayesian analysis*. This analysis gives a revised value of EMV which is expected to be better than the EMV based on prior analysis. The difference between the two should at least be equal to the cost of obtaining the additional information (known as cost of sampling), otherwise it may not be worth to carry out posterior analysis.

EXAMPLE 9.9-1.1

A company receives shipments of certain items. It should decide whether to accept or reject the shipment, on the basis of inspection of a sample selected from the shipment. From the past experience, it is known that the percentage of defective items in a batch of shipment is either 0, 2 or 5, the probabilities for which are 0.5, 0.3 and 0.2 respectively. The company can accept only those batches which have no defectives. The cost of rejecting a good batch i.e., batch with no defectives is ₹ 200. The cost of accepting a defective batch is ₹ 600.

A sample of 10 items has been selected from the shipment and two items are found to be defective. The conditional probabilities of getting 2 defectives in a sample of 10 items from a batch of 0, 2% and 5% defectives are calculated as 0.083, 0.185 and 0.265 respectively. Determine whether the shipment should be accepted. [*C.A. Nov., 1989*]

Solution

The following table summarizes the given information:

State (Per cent defectives)	*Prior probability*	*Conditional probability*	*Action (cost in ₹)*	
			Accept	*Reject*
0	0.5	0.083	0	200
2	0.3	0.185	400	0
5	0.2	0.265	600	0

First the posterior probabilities are calculated. The necessary computations are given in the table below:

State	*Prior probability* (1)	*Conditional probability* (2)	*Joint probability* (1) × (2) = (3)	*Posterior probability* (4) = (3) ÷ 0.15
0	0.5	0.083	0.0415	0.277
2	0.3	0.185	0.0555	0.370
5	0.2	0.265	0.0530	0.353
			0.1500	

$\therefore$ E_1 (accept) = 0.277 × 0 + 0.370 × 400 + 0.353 × 600 = ₹ 360.

E_2 (reject) = 0.277 × 200 + 0.370 × 0 + 0.353 × 0 = ₹ 55.40.

Since E_2 results in lower cost, the company should reject the shipment.

EXAMPLE 9.9-1.2

A manufacturing company is considering the introduction of a new product to its existing product range. The company is to make decision on the market survey of the demand for the product which is as follows:

Event (sales)	*Probability*	*Action*	
		Manufacture	*Do not manufacture*
		(Profit in thousands of rupees)	
High	*0.25*	*180*	*0*
Low	*0.75*	*– 50*	*0*

The company wants to have further information on which to base the decision and contacts a consultant cell. The consultant cell provides the following additional information:

Event (sales)	*Sales forecast (Probability)*		
	High	*Indecisive*	*Low*
High	*0.5*	*0.3*	*0.2*
Low	*0.1*	*0.5*	*0.4*

If the consultant cell charges ₹ 10,000 for providing the information,

(a) determine the decision company should take with prior information as well as with additional information.

(b) Perform a complete posterior analysis and state whether it will be economical to engage the consultants.

Solution

(*a*) The EMV calculations with prior information are given below.

Event (sales)	*Probability*	*Action*	
		Manufacture	*Do not manufacture*
		(Profit in thousands of rupees)	
High	0.25	180	0
Low	0.75	– 50	0
	EMV (prior)	7.5	0

Thus the decision of the manufacturing company, based on EMV criterion would be to manufacture the product to earn an expected profit of ₹ 7,500. EVPI will be ₹ [(180 × 0.25 + 0 × 0.75) – 7.5] × 1,000 = ₹ 37,500.

(*b*) The probability information supplied by the consultant cell is in the form of *conditional probabilities* often called *'likelihoods'*. With this additional information, the company will revise prior event probabilities to get joint probabilities, marginal probabilities and finally posterior probabilities as follows:

Event (sales)	*Prior probabilities*	*Conditional probabilities*			*Joint probabilities*		
		(H)	*(I)*	*(L)*	*(H)*	*(I)*	*(L)*
High	0.25	0.5	0.3	0.2	0.125	0.075	0.050
Low	0.75	0.1	0.5	0.4	0.075	0.375	0.300
		Marginal probabilities			0.200	0.450	0.350

Event (sales)	*Posterior probabilities* (H)	(I)	(L)
High	0.125/0.2 = 0.625	0.167	0.143
Low	0.075/0.2 = 0.375	0.833	0.857

These posterior probabilities are now used to compute revised EMV, revised EVPI and the optimal action. The sales forecasts (likelihoods) High, Indecisive and Low will be considered individually.

Sales forecasts (likelihood) high

Event (sales)	*Posterior probability*	*Action* A_1	A_2
High	0.625	180	0
Low	0.375	– 50	0
	EMV:	**93.75**	0

Sales forecasts (likelihood) indecisive

Event (sales)	*Posterior probability*	*Action* A_1	A_2
High	0.167	180	0
Low	0.833	– 50	0
	EMV:	–11.59	**0**

Sales forecasts (likelihood) low

Event (sales)	*Posterior probability*	*Action* A_1	A_2
High	0.143	180	0
Low	0.857	–50	0
	EMV:	– 17.11	**0**

From the above EMV values of the optimal acts, the posterior EMV is calculated as follows:

Likelihood	*Marginal probability*	*Action*	*Optimal EMV*	*Expected EMV*
H	0.200	A_1	93.75	18.75
I	0.450	A_2	0	0
L	0.350	A_2	0	0
			Posterior EMV :	18.75

∴ Posterior EMV = ₹ 18.75 × 1,000 = ₹ 18,750.

Thus from the information provided by the consultants, the company has EMV increased from ₹ 7,500 to ₹ 18,750.

∴ The maximum that this company shall be willing to pay the consultant cell is ₹ (18,750 – 7,500) = ₹ 11,250.

Thus EVPI for the additional information = ₹ 11,250.

Since the consultants' charges are ₹ 10,000, the company should go in for their advice and get the additional information. By doing so, the company gains ₹ 1,250.

EXAMPLE 9.9-1.3

A firm is currently considering the purchase of new equipment to manufacture parts required by the north sea oil development programme. There are three types of equipment which could be purchased :

(1) Conventional manual operation (CMO)

(2) Numerically controlled (NC)

(3) Computer numerically controlled (CNC).

The capital cost of the equipment rises from (1) through (3). The profit resulting from whichever course of action is finally taken depends on the size of the market to be supplied; at present this is uncertain. The market has been classified into three broad categories: poor, fair and good. The profits (losses are given a negative sign) are shown for each market size/machine tool type in the table below:

Equipment	*Profit (£ million)*		
	Market		
	Poor	*Fair*	*Good*
CMO	*0.5*	*1.0*	*1.5*
NC	*0*	*1.5*	*2.5*
CNC	*– 1.5*	*0.5*	*3.5*

The chances of the market being poor, fair or good are assessed at 30%, 50% and 20% respectively by the firm's management.

A market research group could be employed to provide information on which market will be realised. Past experience with work from this group shows that its information cannot be relied on to be absolutely accurate. The management assesses the following chances of it indicating a poor (I), fair (II) and good (III) market when these are the actual states of the market, to be as follows:

Actual state	*Indicated state*		
	I	*II*	*III*
Poor	*0.7*	*0.2*	*0.1*
Fair	*0.2*	*0.7*	*0.1*
Good	*0*	*0.2*	*0.8*

You are required to

(a) Prepare the conditional/expected opportunity loss table based on the market assessment made by the firm.

(b) Calculate the expected value of perfect information.

(c) Prepare the conditional expected opportunity loss table on the information which might be available from the market research; and

(d) State the maximum amount it would be worthwhile for the firm to pay for the market research.

[ICMA London Nov., 1977]

Solution

(*a*) The conditional profit table is given below:

Market	*Probability*	*Buying decision*		
		CMO	*NC*	*CNC*
Poor	0.3	0.5	0	– 1.5
Fair	0.5	1.0	1.5	0.5
Good	0.2	1.5	2.5	3.5

Opportunity loss table is now constructed by subtracting the profits for each event (market position) from the highest profit for that event.

Market	Probability	Buying decision		
		CMO	NC	CNC
Poor	0.3	0	0.5	2.0
Fair	0.5	0.5	0	1.0
Good	0.2	2.0	1.0	0
Expected opportunity loss:		0.65	**0.35**	1.1

(*b*) EVPI is the EOL for the optimal act *i.e.,* £ 0.35 million corresponding to buying of numerically controlled (NC) equipment.

(*c*) The joint probabilities and their marginal probabilities are then computed.

Market	Prior probabilities	Conditional probabilities			Joint probabilities		
		(I)	(II)	(III)	(I)	(II)	(III)
Poor	0.3	0.7	0.2	0.1	0.21	0.06	0.03
Fair	0.5	0.2	0.7	0.1	0.10	0.35	0.05
Good	0.2	0	0.2	0.8	0	0.04	0.16
Marginal probabilities:					0.31	0.45	0.24

The required posterior probabilities are now obtained by dividing each joint probability by the corresponding marginal probability.

Market	Posterior probabilities		
	(I)	(II)	(III)
Poor	0.21/0.31= 0.68	0.13	0.12
Fair	0.10/0.31 = 0.32	0.78	0.21
Good	0/0.31 = 0	0.09	0.67

Posterior analysis is now performed:

For State (I)

Market	Posterior probability	Buying decision		
		CMO	NC	CNC
Poor	0.68	0	0.5	2.0
Fair	0.32	0.5	0	1.0
Good	0	2.0	1.0	0
	EOL:	**0.16**	0.34	1.68

For State(II)

Market	Posterior probability	Buying decision		
		CMO	NC	CNC
Poor	0.13	0	0.5	2.0
Fair	0.78	0.5	0	1.0
Good	0.09	2.0	1.0	0
	EOL:	0.57	**0.155**	1.04

For State (III)

Market	Posterior probability	Buying decision		
		CMO	NC	CNC
Poor	0.12	0	0.5	2.0
Fair	0.21	0.5	0	1.0
Good	0.67	2.0	1.0	0
	EOL:	1.445	0.73	**0.45**

It is observed from the above posterior analysis that when the given information is state (I), the firm will buy CMO, when the given information is state (II), the firm will buy NC; and when it is state (III), the firm will buy CNC.

(*d*) We now calculate the revised (posterior) EOL and then the expected value of market research.

State	*Marginal probability*	*Buying decision*	*Optimal EOL*	*Expected EOL*
I	0.31	CMO	0.16	0.05
II	0.45	NC	0.155	0.07
III	0.24	CNC	0.45	0.11
			Posterior EOL :	0.23

Thus EOL can be reduced from £0.35 million to £0.23 million by conducting the market research. The net gain from market research is £0.12 million, which is the expected value for market research *i.e.*, the maximum amount the firm shall be willing to pay to the market research group as the price for providing additional information.

EXERCISES 9.2

Section 9.9-1

1. Costman Ltd. is considering the introduction of a new product to its existing product range. It has defined two levels of sales as 'High' and 'Low' on which to base its decision and has estimated the chances that each market level will occur together with their costs and consequent profits and losses. This information is summarised below:

Event (sales)	*Probability*	*Action*	
		Market product £ 000's	*Do not market product £ 000's*
High	0.3	150	0
Low	0.7	– 40	0

The company's marketing manager suggests a market research survey be undertaken to provide further information on which to base the decision. On past experience with a certain market research organisation, the marketing manager assesses its ability to give good information in the light of subsequent actual sales achievements as follows:

Market research survey outcome	*Actual sales*	
	Market 'high'	*Market 'low'*
'High' sales forecast	0.5	0.1
Indecisive survey report	0.3	0.4
'Low' sales forecast	0.2	0.5

Given that to undertake the market research survey will cost £20,000, state whether or not there is a case for employing the market research organisation.

[*Delhi U. MBA, 2000*]

(*Ans.* Prior EVPI = £28,000,
posterior EVPI = £18,350; no case.)

2. A company is thinking about introducing a new tennis racket. The company wants to decide whether to bring out a full, partial or minimal product line to start with. The market response may be 'good', 'fair' or 'poor' and their probabilities of occurrence have been estimated. The company shall make its decision on the basis of expected profit from the first year. The relevant data are shown below:

Market	*Probability*	*Anticipated first year profit (₹ 000's) Product line*		
		Full	*Partial*	*Minimal*
Good	0.2	180	140	100
Fair	0.4	150	120	90
Poor	0.4	– 65	– 20	0

(*a*) Determine the optimal action and its EMV.

(*b*) The marketing deptt. of the company suggests a test marketing analysis at a cost of ₹ 15,000, whereby it will determine whether the consumer reaction is favourable or unfavourable. An analysis of the results of similar tests yields the following additional information:

Market response	*Probability of favourable test marketing reaction*
Good	0.85
Fair	0.62
Poor	0.21

Perform a complete posterior analysis and state whether test marketing analysis be undertaken or not.

3. Expected return (in million rupees) from the sale of three machines A, B and C under expected market conditions as poor (S_1), fair (S_2) and good (S_3) are given below.

States	*Return (in million rupees)*		
	Poor (S_1)	*Fair* (S_2)	*Good* (S_3)
A	0.5	1.0	1.5
B	0.0	1.5	2.5
C	– 1.5	0.5	3.5

Chances of market at states S_1, S_2 and S_3 are 30%, 50% and 20% respectively. But the market research conducted subsequently finds the actual chances of states of the market as follows :

State of nature (Market sale)	X_1 *(Poor)*	X_2 *(Fair)*	X_3 *(Good)*
S_1	0.7	0.2	0.1
S_2	0.2	0.7	0.1
S_3	0.0	0.2	0.8

Find (*i*) conditional and expected loss table (*ii*) EVPI (*iii*) Expected loss table on the basis of the results of market research (*iv*) Economic cost of market research.

(*Ans.* (*ii*) EVPI = ₹ 35,000 (*iv*) ₹ 12,000.)

4. The following table gives partial information regarding the opportunity loss of accepting colour television sets offered to a company for retail sales:

Proportion of defective parts	*Prior probability*	*Opportunity loss* (₹)
0.15	0.4	0
0.20	0.3	1,00,000
0.25	0.2	1,50,000
0.30	0.1	2,00,000

A preliminary sample of 20 television sets indicates that five sets are defective. The probabilities of obtaining five defectives out of 20 with population probabilities being 0.15, 0.20, 0.25 and 0.30 are 0.103, 0.175, 0.202 and 0.179 respectively. Compute the EOL before and after sampling.

(*Ans.* ₹ 80,000 ; ₹ 97,930.)

5. A farmer is attempting to decide which of the three crops he should plant on his 100-acre farm. The profit from each crop is strongly dependent on the rainfall during the growing season. He has categorised the rainfall as substantial, moderate or light. He estimates his profit for each crop as shown in the table :

Rainfall	*Estimated profit (₹)*		
	Crop A	*Crop B*	*Crop C*
Substantial	7,000	2,500	4,000
Moderate	3,500	3,500	4,000
Light	1,000	4,000	3,000

Depending on the weather in the previous seasons and the current projection for the coming season, he estimates the probability of substantial rainfall as 0.2, that of moderate rainfall as 0.3 and that of light rainfall as 0.5.

Furthermore, services of forecasters could be employed to provide a detailed survey of the current rainfall prospects as given in the table below

Actual rainfall	*Rainfall prediction*		
	Substantial	*Moderate*	*Light*
Substantial	0.70	0.25	0.05
Moderate	0.30	0.60	0.10
Light	0.10	0.20	0.70

(*a*) From the available data, determine the optimal decision as to which crop to plant.
(*b*) Determine whether it would be economical for the farmer to hire the services of a forecaster.

(*Ans.* (*a*) Crop B, ₹ 3,550; EVPI = ₹ 1,050.
(*b*) Yes; Saving = ₹ 5.70.)

9.9-2 Decision Trees

The decision problems discussed so far dealt with only single-stage decision-making. The payoffs, alternatives, states of nature and the associated probabilities were not subjected to changes. We now consider situations that involve *multiple stages.* They are characterised by a sequence of decisions with each decision influencing the next. Such problems, called *sequential decision problems,* are analysed best with the help of decision trees.

A decision tree is a graphical representation of the decision process indicating decision alternatives, states of nature, probabilities attached to the states of nature and conditional benefits and losses. *It consists of a network of nodes and branches*. Two types of nodes are used: decision node represented by a square and state of nature (chance or event) node represented by a circle. Alternative courses of action (strategies) originate from the decision node as main branches (decision branches). At the end of each decision branch, there is a state of nature node from which emanate chance events in the form of sub-branches (chance branches). The probabilities associated with the chance events are shown alongside these branches. At the terminal of the chance branches are shown the values of the outcome (payoffs). A branch that forms the end of the decision tree *i.e.*, not followed by a decision or chance node is called a *terminal branch.*

The general approach used in decision tree analysis is to work *backward* through the tree from right to left, computing the expected value (also called *position value*) of each chance node. We, then, choose the particular branch leaving a *decision node* which leads to the *chance node* with the highest expected value. This is known as *roll back or fold back process.*

Illustration: Suppose we have the decision-making problem represented by the following table:

TABLE 9.77
Conditional profits

States of nature	*Probability*	*Alternative*	
		(A_1) Produce 25 units	*(A_2) Produce 75 units*
S_1 *(High demand)*	0.6	4,000	10,000
S_2 *(Low demand)*	0.4	2,000	– 5,000

The decision tree for the above problem is shown in Fig. 9.2. For a decision alternative (strategy) the EMV is calculated by summing the products of payoff of each state and its probability.

For example, EMV of decision alternative A_1 (or node A) is

$= ₹ (4,000 \times 0.6 + 2,000 \times 0.4) = ₹ 3,200.$

Similarly, EMV of decision alternative A_2 (or node B) is

$= ₹ (10,000 \times 0.6 - 5,000 \times 0.4) = ₹ 4,000.$

Since alternative A_2 yields higher EMV, 75 units should be produced.

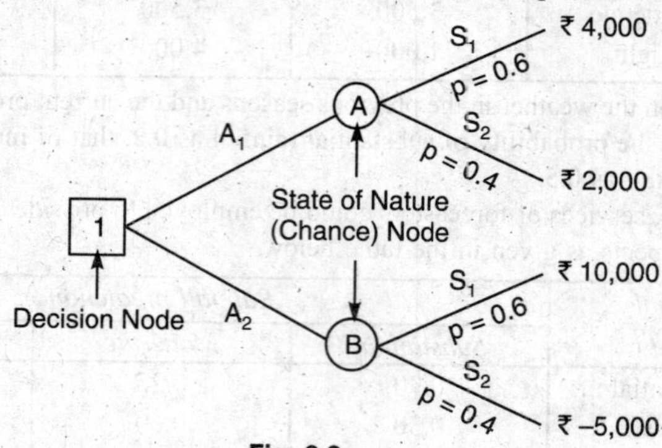

Fig. 9.2

Decision trees are useful for representing the interrelated, sequential and multidimensional aspects of a decision-making problem. By drawing a decision tree, one is in a position to visualise the entire complexity of the decision problem in all its dimensions as also the actual processes and stages for arriving at the final decision.

Steps in Decision Tree Analysis

1. Identify the decision points and the alternative courses of action at each decision point systematically.
2. At each decision point, determine the probability and the payoff associated with each course of action.
3. Commencing from the extreme right end, compute the expected payoffs (EMV) for each course of action.
4. Choose the course of action that yields the best payoff for each of the decisions.
5. Proceed backwards to the next stage of decision points.
6. Repeat above steps till the first decision point is reached.
7. Finally, identify the courses of action to be adopted from the beginning to the end under different possible outcomes for the situation as a whole.

9.9-2.1 Advantages and Limitations of the Decision Tree Approach

Advantages of the Decision Tree Approach

1. It structures the decision process and helps decision-making in an orderly, systematic and sequential manner.
2. It requires the decision-maker to examine all possible outcomes, whether desirable or undesirable.
3. It communicates the decision-making process to others in an easy and clear manner, illustrating each assumption about the future.
4. It displays the logical relationship between the parts of a complex decision and identifies the time sequence in which various actions and subsequent events would occur.
5. It is especially useful in situations wherein the initial decision and its outcome affects the subsequent decisions. It can be applied in various fields such as introduction of a new product, marketing, make or buy decisions, investment decisions, etc.

Limitations of the Decision Tree Approach

1. Decision tree diagrams become more complicated as the number of decision alternatives increases and more variables are introduced.

2. It becomes highly complicated when interdependent alternatives and dependent variables are present in the problem.
3. It assumes that utility of money is linear with money.
4. It analyses the problem in terms of expected values and thus yields an 'average' valued solution.
5. There is often inconsistency in assigning probabilities for different events.

EXAMPLE 9.9-2.1

A client asks an estate agent to sell three properties A, B and C for him and agrees to pay him 5% commission on each sale. He specifies certain conditions. The estate agent must sell property A first, and this he must do within 60 days. If and when A is sold, the agent receives his 5% commission on that sale. He can then either back out at this stage or nominate and try to sell one of the remaining two properties within 60 days. If he does not succeed in selling the nominated property in that period, he is not given the opportunity to sell the other. If he does sell it in the period, he is given the opportunity to sell the third property on the same conditions. The following table summarises the prices, selling costs (incurred by the estate agent whenever a sale is made) and the estate agent's estimated probability of making a sale.

TABLE 9.78

Property	*Prices of property*	*Selling costs*	*Probability of sale*
A	*₹ 12,000*	*₹ 400*	*0.7*
B	*25,000*	*225*	*0.6*
C	*50,000*	*450*	*0.5*

(i) Draw up an appropriate decision tree for the estate agent.
(ii) What is the estate agent's best strategy under EMV approach?

Solution

The estate agent gets 5% commission if he sells the properties and satisfies the specified conditions. The amount he receives as commission on sale of properties A, B and C will be ₹ 600, ₹ 1,250 and ₹ 2,500 respectively. Since the selling costs incurred by him are ₹ 400, ₹ 225 and ₹ 450, his conditional profits from sale of properties A, B and C are ₹ 200, ₹ 1,025 and ₹ 2,050 respectively. The decision tree for the problem is shown in Fig. 9.3.

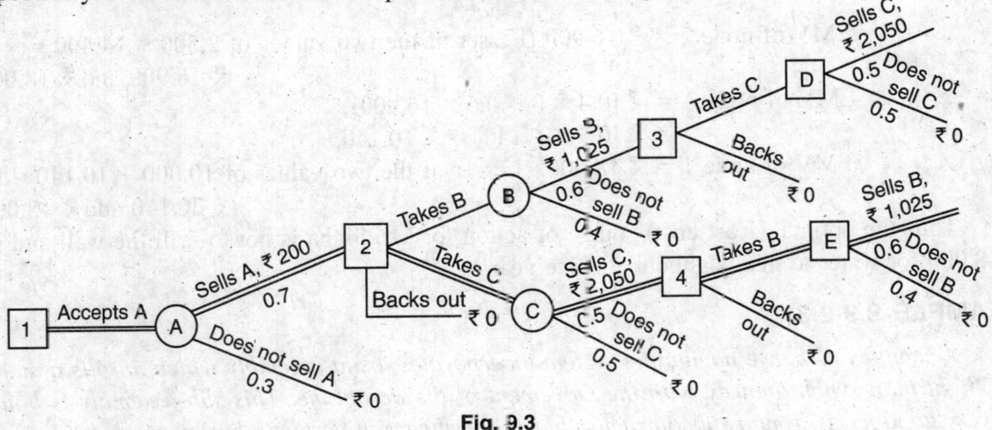

Fig. 9.3

EMV of node D = ₹ (0.5 × 2,050 + 0.5 × 0) = ₹ 1,025.
EMV of node E = ₹ (0.6 × 1,025 + 0.4 × 0) = ₹ 615.
EMV of node 3 = Max ₹ (1,025 0) = ₹ 1,250.
EMV of node 4 = Max. ₹ (615, 0) = ₹ 615.
EMV of node B = ₹ [0.6 (1,025 + 1,025) + 0.4 × 0] = ₹ 1,230.
EMV of node C = ₹ [0.5 (2,050 + 615) + 0.5 × 0] = ₹ 1,332.50.

∴ EMV of node 2 = ₹ 1,332.50. (Higher of the EMV at B and C).

∴ EMV of node A = ₹ [0.7(200 + 1,332.50) + 0.3 × 0] = ₹ 1,072.75.

∴ EMV of node 1 = ₹ 1,072.75.

The optimal strategy path is drawn in bold lines. Thus the optimum strategy for the estate agent is to sell A; if he sells A then try to sell C and if he sells C, then try to sell B to get an optimum expected amount of ₹ 1,072.75.

EXAMPLE 9.9-2.2

Mr. Sinha had to decide whether or not to drill a well on his farm. In his village, only 40% of the wells drilled were successful at 200 feet of depth. Some of the farmers who did not get water at 200 feet, drilled further up to 250 feet but only 20 % struck water at 250 feet. Cost of drilling is ₹ 50 per foot. Mr. Sinha estimated that he would pay ₹ 18,000 during a 5-year period in the present value terms, if he continues to buy water from the neighbour rather than go for the well which would have a life of 5 years. Mr. Sinha has three decisions to make: (a) should he drill up to 200 feet and (b) if no water is found at 200 feet, should he drill up to 250 feet? (c) should he continue to buy water from his neighbour ? [P.T.U. B.Tech., 2001]

Solution

Decision tree diagram for the above problem is shown in Fig. 9.4.

The cost associated with each outcome is written on the decision tree.

EMV of node B = ₹ [0.2 × 0 + 0.8 × 18,000]
= ₹ 14,400.

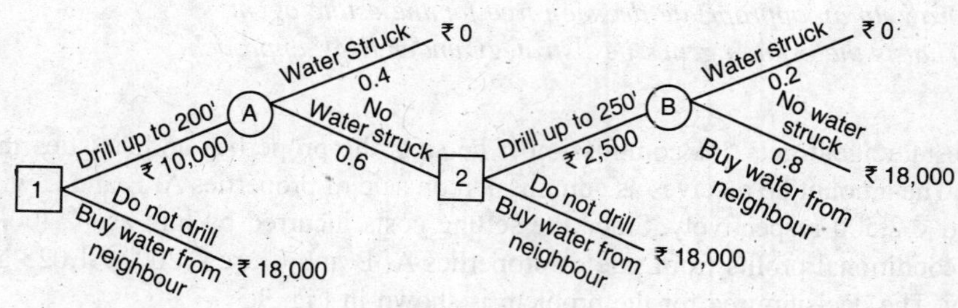

Fig. 9.4

∴ EMV of node 2 = ₹ 16,900 (Lesser of the two values of 2,500 + 14,400 = ₹ 16,900 and ₹ 18,000).

∴ EMV of node A = ₹ [0.4 × 0 + 0.6 × 16,900]
= ₹ [0 + 10, 1404 = ₹ 10,140.

∴ EMV of node 1 = ₹ 18,000. [Lesser of the two values of 10,000 + 10,140 = ₹ 20,140 and ₹ 18,000.]

Thus the optimal (least cost) course of action for Mr. Sinha is not to drill the well and pay ₹ 18,000 for water to his neighbour for five years.

EXAMPLE 9.9-2.3

A complex airborne navigating system incorporates a sub-assembly which unrolls a map of the flight plan synchronously with the movement of the aeroplane. This sub-assembly is bought on very good terms from a subcontractor, but is not always in perfect adjustment on delivery. The sub-assemblies can be readjusted on delivery to guarantee accuracy at a cost of ₹ 50 per sub-assembly. It is not, however, possible to distinguish visually those sub-assemblies that need adjustment.

Alternatively, the sub-assemblies can each be tested electronically at a cost of ₹ 10 per sub-assembly tested. Past experience shows that about 30% of those supplied are defective; the probability of the test indicating a bad adjustment when the sub-assembly is faulty is 0.8, while the probability that the test indicates a good adjustment when the sub-assembly is properly adjusted is 0.7. If the adjustment is not made and the sub-assembly is found to be faulty when the system has its final check, the cost of subsequent rectification will be ₹ 140.

Draw up an appropriate decision tree to show the alternatives open to the purchaser and use it to determine his appropriate course of action. [*C.A. May, 1982*]

Solution

The decision tree diagram for the problem is shown in Fig. 9.5.

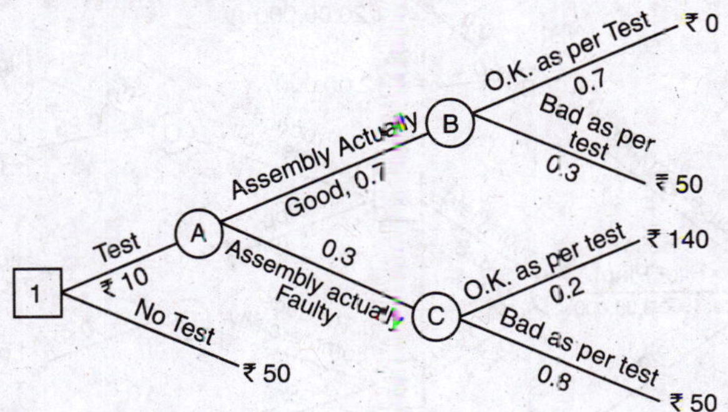

Fig. 9.5

EMV of node B = ₹ [0.7 × 0 + 0.3 × 50] = ₹ 15.
EMV of node C = ₹ [0.2 × 140 + 0.8 × 50] = ₹ 68.
EMV of node A = ₹ [0.7 × 15 + 0.3 × 68] = ₹ 30.90.
EMV of node 1 via the branch 'Test' = ₹ [10 + 30.90] = ₹ 40.90.
EMV of node 1 via the branch 'No Test' = ₹ 50.

∴ Optimal EMV of node 1 is ₹ 40.90 corresponding to the optimal decision 'Test the sub-assemblies'.

EXAMPLE 9.9-2.4

A large steel manufacturing company has three options with regard to production: (i) produce commercially (ii) build pilot plant (iii) stop producing steel. The management has estimated that their pilot plant, if built, has 0.8 chance of high yield and 0.2 chance of low yield. If the pilot plant does show a high yield, management assigns a probability of 0.75 that the commercial plant will also have a high yield. If the pilot plant shows a low yield, there is only a 0.1 chance that the commercial plant will show a high yield. Finally, management's best assessment of the yield on a commercial-size plant without building a pilot plant first has a 0.6 chance of high yield. A pilot plant will cost ₹ 3,00,000. The profits earned under high and low yield conditions are ₹ 1,20,00,000 and – ₹ 12,00,000 respectively. Find the optimum decision for the company. [*P.T.U.B.E., 2001*]

Solution

Fig. 9.6 represents the decision tree diagram for the problem.

EMV of chance node C = ₹ [0.75 × 1,20,00,000 – 0.25 × 12,00,000]
= ₹ [90,00,000 – 3,00,000] = ₹ 87,00,000.

EMV of chance node D = ₹ [0.1 × 1,20,00,000 – 0.9 × 12,00,000]
= ₹ [12,00,000 – 10,80,000] = ₹ 1,20,000.

EMV of decision node 2 = ₹ 87,00,000.

EMV of decision node 3 = ₹ 1,20,000.

EMV of chance node A = ₹ (0.8 × 87,00,000 + 0.2 × 1,20,000]
= ₹ [69,60,000 + 24,000] = ₹ 69,84,000.

EMV of chance node B = ₹ [0.6 × 1,20,00,000 – 0.4 × 12,00,000]
= ₹ [72,00,000 – 4,80,000] = ₹ 67,20,000.

EMV of decision node 1 if pilot plant is built

= ₹ 69,84,000 – ₹ 3,00,000

= ₹ 66,84,000.

∴ EMV of decision node 1 for alternative 'produce commercially'

= ₹ 67,20,000.

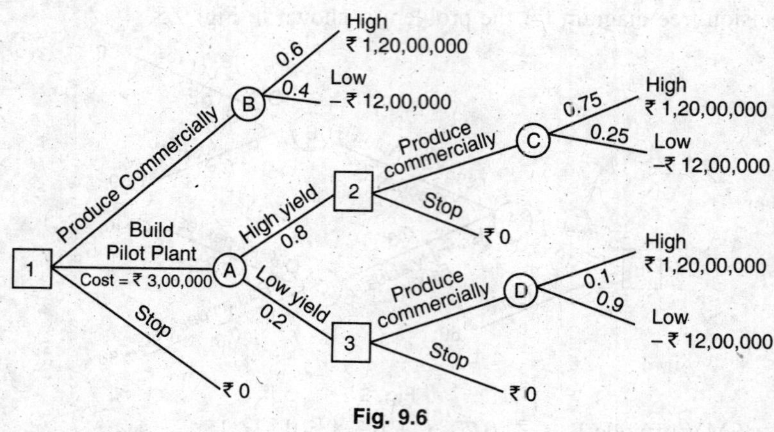

Fig. 9.6

∴ The company should not build the pilot plant but should produce commercially.

EXAMPLE 9.9-2.5

A company is currently working with a process, which, after paying for materials, labour, etc. brings a profit of ₹ 12,000. The company has the following alternatives:

(i) The company can conduct research R_1 which is expected to cost ₹ 10,000 and has 90% probability of success. If successful, the gross income will be ₹ 26,000.

(ii) The company can conduct research R_2, expected to cost ₹ 6,000 and has a probability of 60% success. If successful, the gross income will be ₹ 24,000.

(iii) The company can pay ₹ 5,000 as royalty of a new process which will bring a gross income of ₹ 20,000.

(iv) The company may continue the current process.

Because of limited resources, only one of the two types of research can be carried out at a time. Draw the decision tree and find the optimal strategy for the company.

[P.U. UIAMS MBA May, 2015; P.T.U. B.Tech., 2010; P.U. MBA Feb., 2009]

Solution

The decision tree diagram is shown in Fig. 9.7. Point 1 is the decision box. The four alternatives available to the company are shown emanating from it. Upon failure of a particular research, say R_1, there are again three alternatives: conduct research R_2, pay royalty or continue the existing process. If R_2 fails after failure of R_1, the company is left with only two choices, *i.e.*, either to pay royalty or continue the existing process.

EMV of decision node 4 = Max. ₹ [12,000, (20,000 – 5,000)] = ₹ 15,000.

EMV of decision node 5 = Max. ₹ [12,000, (20,000 – 5,000)] = ₹ 15,000.

EMV of chance node C = ₹ [0.4 × 15,000 + 0.6 × 24,000] = ₹ 20,400.

EMV of chance node D = ₹ [0.9 × 26,000 + 0.1 × 15,000] = ₹ 24,900.

EMV of decision node 2 = Max. ₹ [12,000, (20,000 – 5000), (20,400 – 6,000)]

= ₹ 15,000.

EMV of decision node 3 = Max. ₹ [12,000, (20,000 – 5,000), (24,900 – 10,000)]

= ₹ 15,000.

EMV of chance node A = ₹ [0.9 × 26,000 + 0.1 × 15,000] = ₹ 24,900.

EMV of chance node B = ₹ [0.6 × 24,000 + 0.4 × 15,000] = ₹ 20,400.

$$\begin{aligned}\text{EMV of decision node 1} &= \text{Max. ₹ } [(24{,}900 - 10{,}000), 12{,}000, \\ &\quad (20{,}000 - 5{,}000), (20{,}400 - 6{,}000)] \\ &= \text{₹ } 15{,}000.\end{aligned}$$

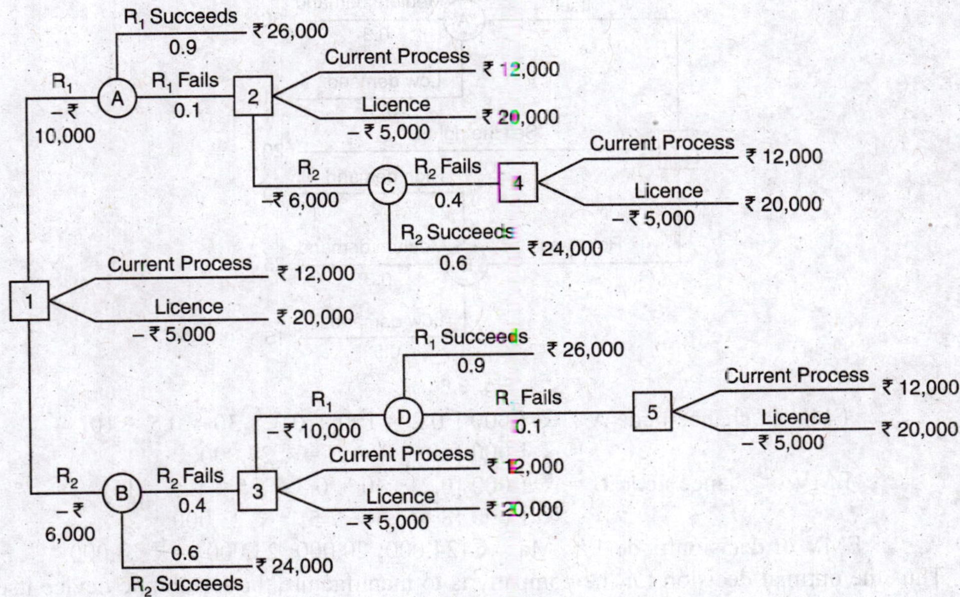

Fig. 9.7

Thus the company should pay ₹ 5,000 as royalty of the new process to earn maximum expected profit of ₹ 15,000.

EXAMPLE 9.9-2.6

A company dealing with newly invented telephonic device is faced with the problem of selecting the following strategies:

(i) manufacture the device itself,

(ii) to be paid on a royalty basis by another manufacturer,

(iii) sell the rights for its invention for a lump sum.

The profit in thousands of rupees that can be expected in each case and the probabilities associated with the sales volume are shown in the following table:

TABLE 9.79

Event	*Probability*	*Manufacture itself*	*Royalties*	*Sell the rights*
High demand	*0.2*	*100*	*40*	*20*
Medium demand	*0.3*	*30*	*25*	*20*
Low demand	*0.5*	*– 10*	*15*	*20*

(a) Represent the company's problem in the form of a decision tree.

(b) Extend the diagram further for the following additional information:

(i) If the company manufactures itself and sales are medium or high, it has the opportunity of developing a new version of its telephone.

(ii) From past experience, it estimates that there is 50% chance of successful development.

(iii) If the cost of development is ₹ 20 and the returns (after deducting the development cost) are ₹ 35 and ₹ 10 for high and medium demand respectively.

Solution

(*a*) The decision tree diagram for the problem is shown in Fig. 9.8.

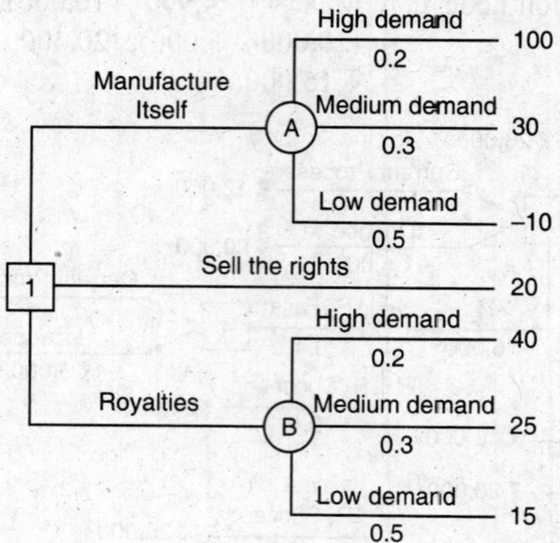

Fig. 9.8

EMV of chance node A = ₹ 1,000 [0.2 × 100 + 0.3 × 30 – 0.5 × 10]
= ₹ 1,000 [20 + 9 – 5] = ₹ 24,000.

EMV of chance node B = ₹ 1,000 [0.2 × 40 + 0.3 × 25 + 0.5 × 15]
= ₹ 1,000 [8 + 7.5 + 7.5] = ₹ 23,000.

∴ EMV of decision node 1 = Max. ₹ [24,000; 20,000; 23,000] = ₹ 24,000.

Thus the optimal decision for the company is to manufacture the telephonic device itself to get the maximum expected profit of ₹ 24,000.

(*b*) The decision tree diagram with the additional information is shown in Fig. 9.9.

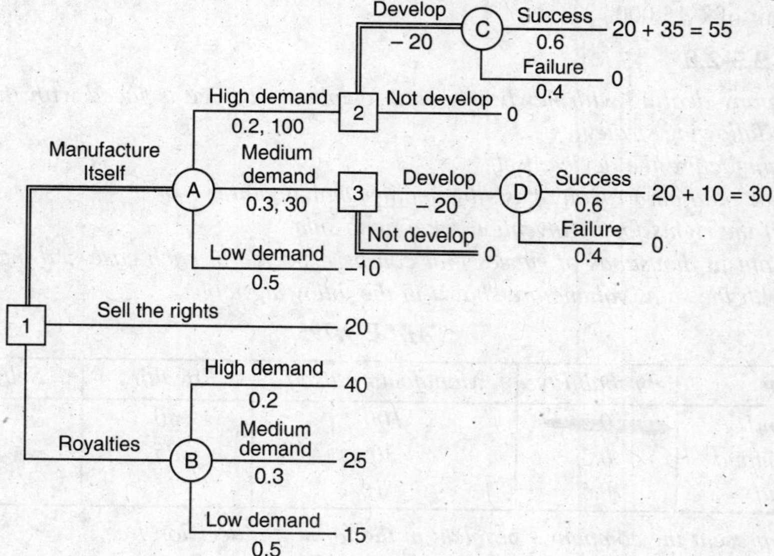

Fig. 9.9

EMV of chance node C = ₹ 1,000 [0.6 × 55 + 0.4 × 0] = ₹ 33,000.

EMV of chance node D = ₹ 1,000 [0.6 × 30 + 0.4 × 0] = ₹ 18,000.

EMV of decision node 2 = Max. ₹ 1,000 [(33 – 20), 0] = ₹ 13,000.

EMV of decision node 3 = Max. ₹ [(18,000 – 20,000), 0] = ₹ 0.

EMV of chance node A = ₹ [0.2 × 1,13,000 + 0.3 × 30,000 – 0.5 × 10,000]
= ₹ 26,600.

EMV of chance node B = ₹ [0.2 × 40,000 + 0.3 × 25,000 + 0.5 × 15,000]
= ₹ 23,000.

∴ EMV of decision node 1 = Max. ₹ [26,600; 20,000; 23,000] = ₹ 26,600.

Thus the optimum expected profit to the company is ₹ 26,600. To earn this amount, the company should manufacture the telephonic device itself. Further, it should develop the new version of telephone if the demand is high and should not develop it when the demand is medium. This is shown by bold lines on the tree diagram.

EXAMPLE 9.9-2.7

The Oil India Corporation is considering whether to go for an offshore oil drilling contract to be awarded in Bombay High. If the bid value would be ₹ 600 million with a 65% chance of gaining the contract, they may set up a new drilling operation or move already existing operation which has proved successful, to the new site. The probability of success and expected returns are as follows:

TABLE 9.80

Outcome	New drilling operation		Existing operation	
	Probability	Expected revenue (₹ million)	Probability	Expected revenue (₹ million)
Success	0.75	800	0.85	700
Failure	0.25	200	0.15	250

If the corporation do not bid or lose the contract, they can use the ₹ 600 million to modernize their operation. This would result in a return of either 5% or 8% on the sum invested with probabilities of 0.45 and 0.55. Assume that all costs and revenues have been discounted to the present value.

(i) Construct a decision tree for the problem showing clearly the course of action.

(ii) By applying an appropriate decision criteria recommend whether or not the Oil India Corporation should bid the contract.

(iii) What would be the financial return if they bid? [I.C.W.A. (Final) June, 1990]

Solution

The decision tree for the problem is shown in Fig. 9.10.

E.M.V. at node C = ₹ (0.75 × 800 + 0.25 × 200) million = ₹ 650 million.

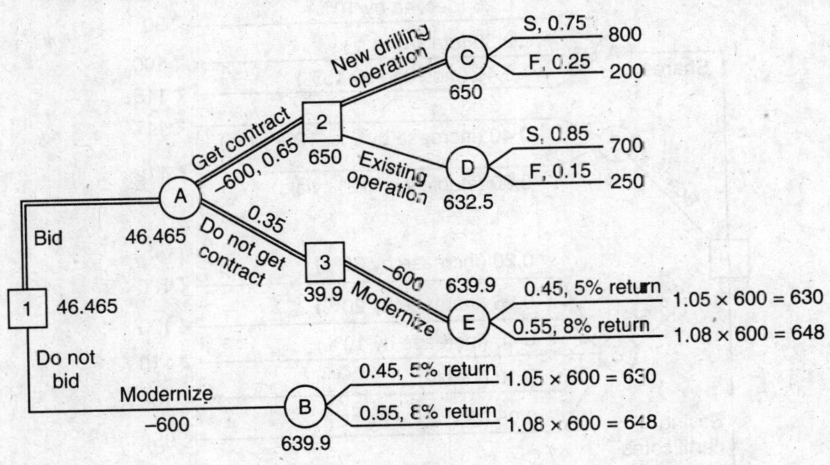

Fig. 9.10

E.M.V. at node D = ₹ (0.85 × 700 + 0.15 × 250) million = ₹ 632.5 million.

E.M.V. at node E = ₹ (0.45 × 630 + 0.55 × 648) million = ₹ 639.9 million.

E.M.V. at node 2 = Maximum of ₹ (650,632.5) million = ₹ 650 million.
E.M.V. at node 3 = ₹ (639.9 – 600) = ₹ 39.9 million.
E.M.V. at node A = ₹ (0.65 × 50 + 0.35 × 39.9) million = ₹ 46.465 million.
E.M.V. at node B = ₹ (0.45 × 630 + 0.55 × 648) million = ₹ 639.9 million.
E.M.V. at node 1 = Maximum of ₹ (46.465,639.9 – 600) million
= ₹ 46.465 million.

(*ii*) Thus the company should bid and if it gets the contract, it should setup a new drilling operation; if it does not get the contract, it should modernize its operation.

(*iii*) The financial return is $\frac{46.465}{600} \times 100 = 7.74\%$.

EXAMPLE 9.9-2.8

The investment staff of TNC Bank is considering four investment proposals for a client: shares, bonds, real estate and savings certificates. These investments will be held for one year. The past data regarding the four proposals are given below:

Shares: There is 25 per cent chance that shares will decline by 10 per cent, a 30 per cent chance that they will remain stable and a 45 per cent chance that they will increase in value by 15 per cent. Also the shares under consideration do not pay any dividends.

Bonds: These bonds stand a 40 per cent chance of increase in value by 5 per cent and 60 per cent chance of remaining stable and they yield 12 per cent.

Real Estate: This proposal has a 20 per cent chance of increasing 30 per cent in value, a 25 per cent chance of increasing 20 per cent in value, a 40 per cent chance of increasing 10 per cent in value, a 10 per cent chance of remaining stable and a 5 per cent chance of losing 5 per cent of its value.

Saving Certificates: These certificates yield 8.5 per cent with certainty.

Use a decision tree to structure the alternatives available to the investment staff, and using the expected value criterion, choose the alternative with the highest expected value.

[*P.T.U. MBA Dec., 2013*]

Solution

Assuming that we have ₹ 100 to invest, the required decision tree is shown in Fig. 9.11.

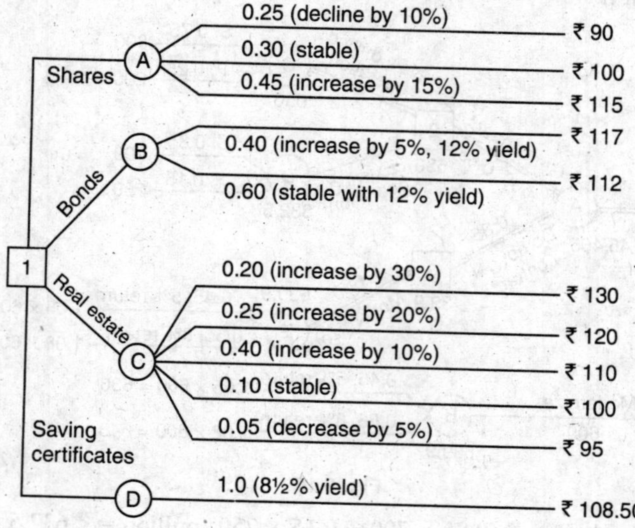

Fig. 9.11

E.M.V. at node A = 0.25 × 90 + 0.30 × 100 + 0.45 × 115
= ₹ (22.5 + 30 + 51.75) = ₹ 104.25.

E.M.V. at node B = 0.40 × 117 + 0.60 × 112 = ₹ (46.8 + 67.2) = ₹ 114.

E.M.V. at node C = 0.2 × 130 + 0.25 × 120 + 0.40 × 110 + 0.1 × 100 + 0.05 × 95
= ₹ [26 + 30 + 44 + 10 + 4.75] = ₹ 114.75.

E.M.V. at node D = ₹ 108.50.

∴ The alternative of real estate yields the highest expected value of ₹ 114.75.

EXAMPLE 9.9-2.9

The daily demand for the breads in the city can assume one of the following values : 3,400; 3,600; 3,700 or 3,800 breads with the probabilities 0.18, 0.12, 0.20 and 0.50. If the stockist stocks more than the need, he can return them at a discount price of ₹ 8 per bread. Assuming that he pays ₹ 8.50 per bread and sells it for ₹ 9.50 per bread, find the optimum stock level by using a decision tree representation. [P.T.U. MCA, 2002]

Solution

The decision tree diagram for the problem is shown in Fig. 9.12.

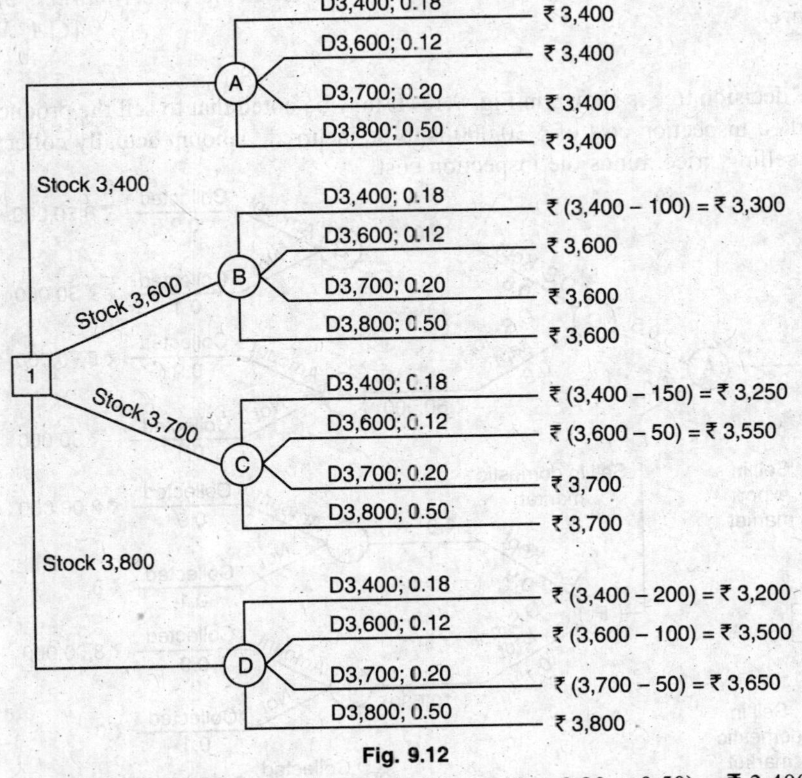

Fig. 9.12

EMV at chance node A = ₹ 3,400 (0.18 + 0.12 + 0.20 + 0.50) = ₹ 3,400.

EMV at chance node B = ₹ [3,300 × 0.18 + 3,600 (0.12 + 0.20 + 0.50)]
= ₹ 3,546.

EMV at chance node C = ₹ [3,250 × 0.18 + 3,550 × 0.12 + 3,700 (0.20 + 0.50)]
= ₹ 3,601.

EMV at chance node D = ₹ [3,200 × 0.18 + 3,500 × 0.12 + 3,650 × 0.20 +
3,800 × 0.50] = ₹ 3,626.

∴ The optimum stock level is 3,800 breads.

EXAMPLE 9.9-2.10

A businessman has an option of selling a product in domestic market or in export market. The available relevant data are given below.

TABLE 9.81

Items	*For export market*	*For domestic market*
Probability of selling	*0.6*	*1.0*
Probability of keeping delivery schedule	*0.8*	*0.9*
Penalty of not meeting delivery schedule	*₹ 50,000*	*₹ 10,000*
Selling price	*₹ 9,00,000*	*₹ 8,00,000*
Cost of third party inspection	*₹ 30,000*	*Nil*
Probability of collection of sale amount	*0.9*	*0.9*

If the product is not sold in export market, it can always be sold in domestic market. There are no other implications like interest and time.

(i) Draw the decision tree using the data given above.

(ii) Should the businessman go for selling the product in the export market? Justify your answer.

[*C.A., May, 1997*]

Solution

(*i*) The decision tree is shown in Fig. 9.13. It may be noted that to sell the product in export market, inspection cost of ₹ 30,000 is to be incurred. Amount actually collected will be the selling price minus the inspection cost.

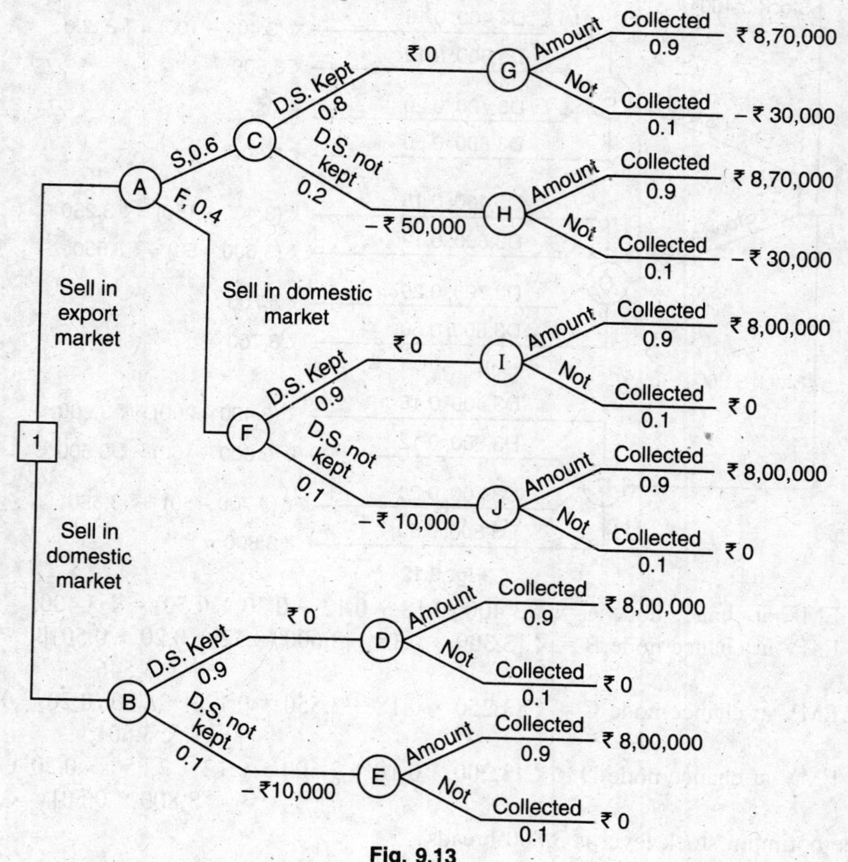

Fig. 9.13

(*ii*) EMV at chance node I = ₹ (0.9 × 8,00,000) = ₹ 7,20,000.
EMV at chance node J = ₹ 7,20,000.
EMV at chance node G = ₹ (0.9 × 8,70,000 – 0.1 × 30,000) = ₹ 7,80,000.
EMV at chance node H = ₹ 7,80,000.
EMV at chance node F = ₹ (0.9 × 7,20,000 + 0.1 × 7,10,000) = ₹ 7,19,000.
EMV at chance node C = ₹ (0.8 × 7,80,000 + 0.2 × 7,30,000) = ₹ 7,70,000.
EMV at chance node D = ₹ (0.9 × 8,00,000) = ₹ 7,20,000.
EMV at chance node E = ₹ 7,20,000.
EMV at chance node A = ₹ (0.6 × 7,70,000 + 0.4 × 7,19,000) = ₹ 7,49,600.
EMV at chance node B = ₹ (0.9 × 7,20,000 + 0.1 × 7,10,000) = ₹ 7,19,000.
∴ EMV at decision node 1 = Max. ₹ [7,49,600; 7,19,000] = ₹ 7,49,600.

Therefore, the businessman should go for selling the product in the export market.

EXAMPLE 9.9-2.11

Growth rate of ABC company in past years has been slower than the average for the industry. The company is considering two alternatives to rectify the situation: (i) expand the number of product lines and (ii) increase inventories for better service.

There is 70% chance that the economy will go into growth stage, in which case there is 80% chance for increased demand. If the demand increases, a profit of ₹ 10,00,000 is expected. However, if the demand does not increase, profit of only ₹ 8,00,000 is expected. If inventories are increased, a profit of ₹ 9,00,000 is anticipated in case of increase in demand; otherwise ₹ 6,00,000 will be realised.

In the event, the economy does not grow, a mild recession is anticipated. In this case, there is 50-50 chance for either high or low demand. The profits are then estimated to be:

Expansion with high demand = ₹ 7,50,000,
Expansion with low demand = ₹ 6,00,000,
Inventories with high demand = ₹ 5,50,000,
Inventories with low demand = ₹ 4,00,000.

Profit figures are the forcasts after one year of operation. The product expansion policy requires ₹ 1,00,000 in cash now. Keeping inventories will cost ₹ 10,000 for the year, payable at the year end. The company is using an interest rate of 10% for its analysis. Should the company expand its products or work with inventories?

Solution

The decision tree diagram for the problem is shown in Fig. 9.14.

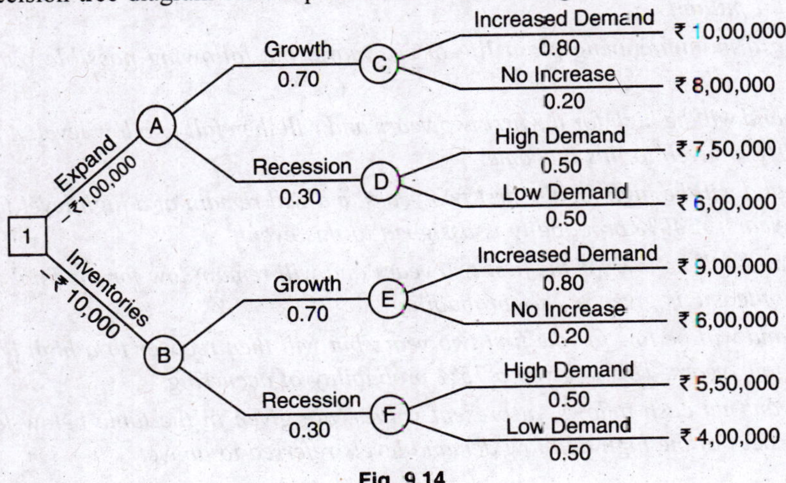

Fig. 9.14

E.M.V. at chance node C one year hence = ₹ (0.80 × 10,00,000 + 0.20 × 8,00,000)
= ₹ 9,60,000.

E.M.V. at chance node D one year hence = ₹ (0.50 × 7,50,000 + 0.50 × 6,00,000)
= ₹ 6,75,000.

E.M.V. at chance node E one year hence = ₹ (0.80 × 9,00,000 + 0.20 × 6,00,000)
= ₹ 8,40,000.

E.M.V. at chance node F one year hence = ₹ (0.50 × 5,50,000 + 0.50 × 4,00,000)
= ₹ 4,75,000.

E.M.V. at chance node A one year hence = ₹ (0.70 × 9,60,000 + 0.30 × 6,75,000)
= ₹ 8,74,500.

E.M.V. at chance node B one year hence = ₹ (0.70 × 8,40,000 + 0.30 × 4,75,000)
= ₹ 7,30,500.

E.M.V. at present at decision node 1 if the company expands the number of product lines

$$= ₹ \left[\frac{100}{110}(8{,}74{,}500) - 1{,}00{,}000\right]$$

$$= ₹ (7{,}95{,}000 - 1{,}00{,}000) = ₹ 6{,}95{,}000.$$

Note that expansion cost of ₹ 1,00,000 has to be incurred immediately at time zero.

E.M.V., at present, at decision node 1 if the company increases inventories for better service

$$= ₹ \left[\frac{100}{110}(7{,}30{,}500 - 10{,}000)\right] = ₹ 6{,}55{,}000.$$

Note that cost of inventories is payable at year end and hence has to be discounted @10% to get its present value.

∴ The company should expand the number of product lines. The expected net present value of profits to the company is ₹ 6,95,000.

EXAMPLE 9.9-2.12

A manufacturer of electrical components for the motor vehicle industry is faced with the problem of building a new plant for the manufacture of electronic components for vehicles. Estimates of the size of the new plant to be built have been made and two sizes selected based on forecasts of future new vehicle demands. A large plant is estimated to cost ₹ 3 million and a small plant ₹ 1.4 million.

Based on a manufacturing plant life of six years, the following possible outcomes are assessed:

(i) Demand will be high for the first two years and will then fall to a low level. A probability of 20% is given to this outcome.

(ii) Demand will be high for the first two years and will remain at a high level for the final four years. A 40% probability is assigned to this event.

(iii) Demand will be low for the first two years and will remain low for the final four years. This outcome is given a 25% probability.

(iv) Demand will be low for the first two years but will then recover to a high level for the final four years. This is given a 15% probability of occurring.

The relevant net cash inflows, at present values, are given in the table below for the two alternate plant sizes at the high and low demand levels referred to above:

TABLE 9.82

Size of Plant	Demand	Net cash inflow at present values	
		Years 1 and 2 (₹ thousands)	Year 3 to 6 (₹ thousands)
Large	High	2,088	3,132
	Low	522	783
Small	High	870	1,305
	Low	696	1,044

The net present values above have been calculated for the two periods covered by the predictions, at the rate of 10% per annum which is the expected cost of capital.

(a) Draw the decision tree diagram for the above information.

(b) Evaluate the deicision tree and advise management which plant if either, should be built.

Solution

The possible outcomes for the next 6 years are listed as

Outcome	*Years 1 and 2*	*Years 3 to 6*	*Probability*
1	High	Low	0.20
2	High	High	0.40
3	Low	Low	0.25
4	Low	High	0.15

Fig. 9.15 represents the decision tree for the problem.

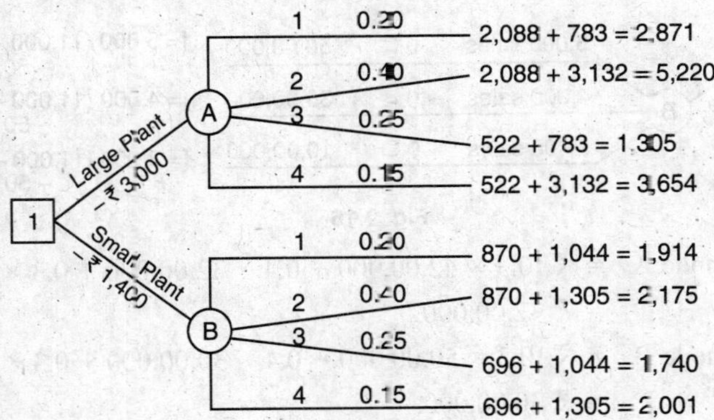

Fig. 9.15

The outcomes for each plant for the years 1 to 6 result in returns shown in Fig. 9.15 in thousands of rupees. For instance, if large plant is built, high demand for first two years followed by low demand for years 3 to 6 will result in return of ₹ (2,088 + 783) = ₹ 2,871 thousand. The returns for the remaining outcomes can, likewise, be calculated.

Expected net present value of chance node A

= ₹ (2,871 × 0.20 + 5,220 × 0.40 + 1,305 × 0.25 + 3,654 × 0.15) thousand

= ₹ 3,536.55 thousand = ₹ 35,36,550.

ENPV of chance node B = ₹ (1,914 × 0.20 + 2,175 × 0.40 + 1,740 × 0.25 + 2,001 × 0.15) thousand

= ₹ 1987.95 thousand = ₹ 19,87,950.

ENPV of decision node 1

$$= \text{Max. ₹ } [(35,36,550 - 30,00,000); (19,87,950 - 14,00,000)]$$
$$= \text{Max. ₹ } [5,36,550; 5,87,950] = \text{₹ } 5,87,950.$$

Therefore, in order to maximize expected net present value, the smaller plant should be built.

EXAMPLE 9.9-2.13

The Indian Yacht Company has developed a new cabin cruiser which they have earmarked for the medium to large boat market. A market analysis has a 30% probability of annual sales being 5,000 boats, a 40% probability of 4,000 annual sales and a 30% probability of 3,000 annual sales. This company can go into limited production, where variable costs are ₹ 10,000 per boat, and fixed costs are ₹ 8,00,000 annually. Alternatively, they can go into full scale production, where variable costs are ₹ 9,000 per boat, and fixed costs are ₹ 50,00,000 annually. If the new boat is to be sold for ₹ 11,000, should the company go into limited or full scale production when their objective is to maximize the expected profits?

Solution

The various alternatives available to the company and the associated payoffs are shown in the decision tree given below:

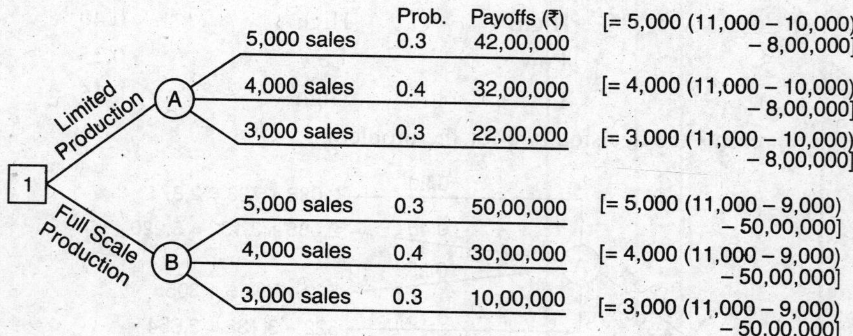

Fig. 9.16

E.M.V. of chance node A $= \text{₹ } [0.3 \times 42,00,000 + 0.4 \times 32,00,000 + 0.3 \times 22,00,000]$
$= \text{₹ } 32,00,000.$

E.M.V. of chance node B $= \text{₹ } [0.3 \times 50,00,000 + 0.4 \times 30,00,000 + 0.3 \times 10,00,000]$
$= \text{₹ } 30,00,000.$

∴ E.M.V. of decision node 1 $= \text{₹ } 32,00,000.$

Hence the company should go into limited production and realise an expected annual profit of ₹ 32,00,000.

EXAMPLE 9.9-2.14

A company is contemplating whether to produce a new product. If it decides to produce the product it must either instal a new division which needs a cash outlay of four lakh rupees or work overtime with overtime expenses of ₹ 1.5 lakhs. If the company decides to instal a new division, it needs the approval of Govt. and the company feels that there is 70% chance of getting the approval. A market survey has revealed the following facts regarding the magnitude of sales for the new product:

Magnitude of sales	*Probability*	*Resulting profit (in ₹ lakhs)*
High	*0.45*	*15*
Medium	*0.30*	*7*
Low	*0.20*	*3*
Nil	*0.05*	*– 5 (loss)*

However, by resorting to overtime, the company will not be in a position to meet the high magnitude of sales. It will be able to satisfy upto the level of medium magnitude only, even if high magnitude of sales result. Solve the problem to suggest the option to be selected.

[*C.A. (Final) Nov., 1989*]

Solution

The decision tree is shown in Fig. 9.17.

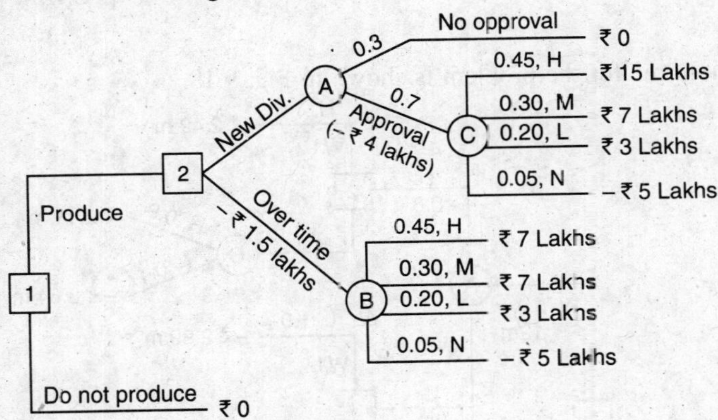

Fig. 9.17

E.M.V. at node C = ₹ (0.45 × 15 + 0.30 × 7 + 0.20 × 3 – 0.05 × 5) lakhs
= ₹ 9.2 lakhs.

E.M.V. at node A = ₹ [0.3 × 0 + 0.7 × (9.2 – 4)] lakhs = ₹ 3.64 lakhs.

E.M.V. at node B = ₹ (0.45 × 7 + 0.30 × 7 + 0.20 × 3 – 0.05 × 5) lakhs
= ₹ 5.6 lakhs.

∴ E.M.V. at node 2 = Maximum of [₹ 3.64, ₹ (5.6 – 1.5)] lakhs = ₹ 4.1 lakhs.

∴ E.M.V. at node 1 = Maximum of [₹ (4.1,0)] lakhs = ₹4.1 lakhs.

Thus the company should produce the new product and work overtime to earn maximum expected profit of ₹ 4.1 lakhs.

EXAMPLE 9.9-2.15

Matrix company is planning to launch a new product, which can be introduced initially in Western India or in the entire country. If the product is introduced only in Western India, the investment outlay will be ₹ 12 million. After two years, the company can evaluate the project to determine whether it should cover the entire country. For such expansion it will have to incur an additional investment of ₹ 10 million. To introduce the product in the entire country right in the beginning would involve an outlay of ₹ 20 million. The product, in any case, will have a life of 5 years, after which the plant will have zero value.

If the product is introduced only in Western India, demand would be high or low with the probabilities of 0.8 and 0.2 respectively and annual cash inflows of ₹ 4 million and ₹ 2.5 million respectively.

If the product is introduced in the entire country right in the beginning, the demand would be high or low with probabilities of 0.6 and 0.4 respectively and annual cash inflows of ₹ 8 million and ₹ 5 million respectively.

Based on the observed demand in Western India, if the product is introduced in the entire country, the following probabilities would exist for high and low demand on an all India basis:

Western India	*All India* High demand	*All India* Low demand
High demand	0.90	0.10
Low demand	0.40	0.60

The hurdle rate applicable to this project is 12%.

(a) Set up the decision tree for the investment situation.

(b) Advise Matrix company on the investment policy it should follow. Support your advice with appropriate reasoning.

[*I.C.W.A. (Final) June, 1990*]

Solution

The decision tree for the problem is shown in Fig. 9.18.

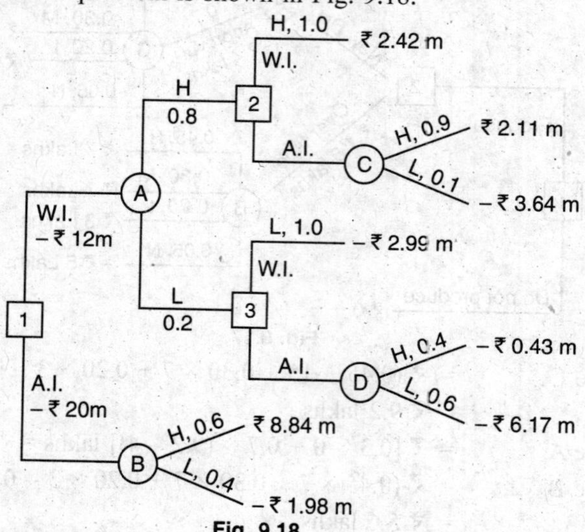

Fig. 9.18

Cash flow table is shown below.

TABLE 9.83

Branch	*Cash flow in millions of rupees in year* 0	1	2	3	4	5	*Net present value at K = 12%*
1	– 12	4	4	4	4	4	2.42*
2	– 12	4	– 6	8	8	8	2.11
3	– 12	4	– 6	5	5	5	– 3.64
4	– 12	2.5	2.5	2.5	2.5	2.5	– 2.99
5	– 12	2.5	– 7.5	8	8	8	– 0.43
6	– 12	2.5	– 7.5	5	5	5	– 6.17
7	– 20	8	8	8	8	8	8.84
8	– 20	5	5	5	5	5	– 1.98

$$\text{*Net present value for branch 1} = -12 + \frac{4}{1.12} + \frac{4}{1.12^2} + \frac{4}{1.12^3} + \frac{4}{1.12^4} + \frac{4}{1.12^5}$$

$$= -12 + \frac{4}{1.12}\ (1 + 1.12^{-1} + 1.12^{-2} + \ldots \text{ upto 5 terms})$$

$$= -12 + 4 \times 1.12^{-1} \left[\frac{1-1.12^{-5}}{1-1.12^{-1}}\right]$$

$$= -12 + 4\ .\ \frac{1-1.12^{-5}}{0.12} = 2.42.$$

Net present values for other branches have been similarly calculated and represented on the decision tree diagram.

E.M.V. at node C = ₹ (0.9 × 2.11 – 0.1 × 3.64) = ₹ 1.54 m.
E.M.V. at node D = ₹ (– 0.4 × 0.43 – 0.6 × 6.17) = – ₹ 3.87 m.
∴ E.M.V. at node 2 = Max. of ₹ [2.42; 1.54] m = ₹ 2.42 m.
E.M.V. at node 3 = Max. of ₹ [– 2.99; – 3.87] m = – ₹ 2.99 m.
E.M.V. at node A = ₹ (0.8 × 2.42 – 0.2 × 2.99) m = ₹ 1.34 m.
E.M.V. at node B = ₹ (0.6 × 8.84 – 0.4 × 1.98) = ₹ 4.51 m.
∴ E.M.V. at node 1 = maximum of ₹ (1.34; 4.51) m = ₹ 4.51 m.

Thus the company should initially launch the new product in the entire country to earn the maximum expected amount of ₹ 4.51 million.

EXAMPLE 9.9-2.16

An oil drilling company is considering the purchase of mineral rights on a property for ₹ 100 lakhs. The price includes tests to indicate whether the property has type A geological formation or type B geological formation. The company will be unable to tell the geological formation until the purchase is made. It is known, however, that 40% of the land in this area has type A formation and 60% type B formation. If the company decides to drill on the land it will cost ₹ 200 lakhs. If the company does drill, it may hit an oil well, a gas well or a dry hole. Drilling experience indicates that the probability of striking an oil well is 0.4 on type A and 0.1 on type B formation. Probability of hitting gas is 0.2 on type A and 0.3 on the type B formation. The estimated discounted cash value from an oil well is ₹ 1,000 lakhs and from a gas well is ₹ 500 lakhs. This includes everything except cost of mineral rights and cost of drilling. Use decision tree approach and recommend whether the company should purchase the mineral rights. [I.C.W.A. June, 1987]

Solution

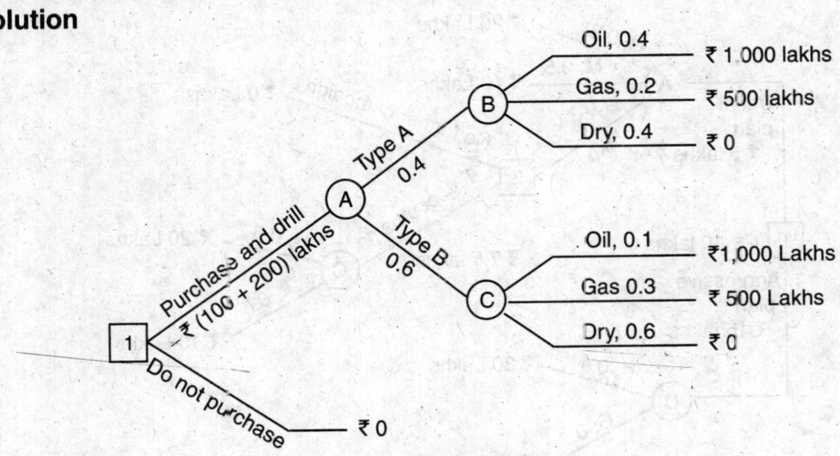

Fig. 9.19

The decision tree for the problem is shown in Fig. 9.19.

E.M.V. at node B = ₹ (0.4 × 1,000 + 0.2 × 500 + 0.4 × 0) lakhs
= ₹ 500 lakhs.

E.M.V. at node C = ₹ (0.1 × 1,000 + 0.3 × 500 + 0.6 × 0) lakhs
= ₹ 250 lakhs.

∴ E.M.V. at node A = ₹ (0.4 × 500 + 0.6 × 250) lakhs
= ₹ 350 lakhs.

∴ E.M.V. at node 1 = Maximum of ₹ (350 – 100 – 200, 0) lakhs
= ₹ 50 lakhs.

Thus the company should purchase the mineral rights and drill the land till the well is struck and the expectd returns will be ₹ 50 lakhs.

EXAMPLE 9.9-2.17

The Sensual Cosmetic Co. has developed a new perfume which management feels has a tremendous potential. It not only interacts with the weaver's body chemistry to create a unique fragrance but is especially long lasting. A total of ₹ 10 lakhs has already been spent on its development. Two marketing plans have been devised :

(*i*) *The first plan follows the company's usual policy of giving small samples of the new product when other items in the company's product lines are purchased and placing advertisements in women's magazines. This plan would cost ₹ 5 lakhs and it is believed that it might result in a high, moderate or low market response with probability of 0.2, 0.5 and 0.3 respectively. The net profit excluding development and promotion costs in these cases would be ₹ 20 lakhs, ₹ 10 lakhs and ₹ 1 lakh respectively. If it later appeared that the market response is going to be low, it will still be possible to launch a T.V. add. campaign. This would cost another ₹ 7.5 lakhs. It would change the market response to high or moderate as previosly described but with probability of 0.5 each.*

(*ii*) *The second marketing plan is much more aggressive than the first. The expenditure would be ₹ 15 lakhs but the market response would be either excellent or good, with probabilities of 0.4 and 0.6 respectively. The profit excluding development and promotion costs would be ₹ 30 lakhs and ₹ 25 lakhs for the two outcomes. Advise on the sequence of strategy to be followed by the company.*

Solution

The decision tree for the problem is shown in Fig. 9.20.

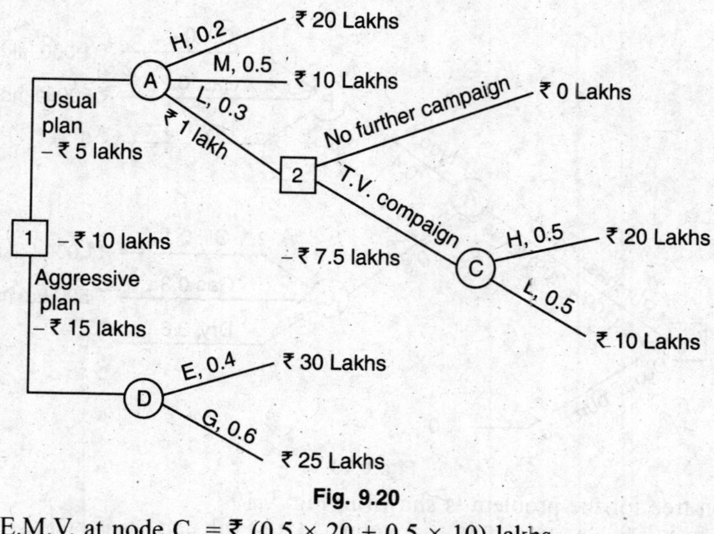

Fig. 9.20

E.M.V. at node C = ₹ (0.5 × 20 + 0.5 × 10) lakhs
= ₹ 15 lakhs.

E.M.V. at node 2 = ₹ (15 – 7.5) lakhs
= ₹ 7.5 lakhs.

E.M.V. at node A = ₹ [0.2 × 20 + 0.5 × 10 + 0.3 (1 + 7.5)] lakhs
= ₹ 11.55 lakhs.

E.M.V. at node B = ₹ (0.4 × 30 + 0.6 × 25) lakhs
= ₹ 27 lakhs.

E.M.V. at node 1 = Maximum of ₹ (11.55 – 5; 27 – 15) lakhs – ₹ 10 lakhs
= ₹ (12 – 10) lakhs = ₹ 2 lakhs.

Thus the company should go in for aggressive plan to earn maximum expected profit of ₹ 2 lakhs.

EXAMPLE 9.9-2.18

A company has two options : either invest in a large plant (investment ₹ 50 lakhs) or in a small plant (outlay ₹ 25 lakhs). In the latter option, after year 1, depending on market response, it can expand by investing ₹ 30 lakhs further. Market survey puts the market response into two categories : good and bad. The chances of good response initially are 0.6 and of bad response are 0.4. However, if the initial response is good, subsequent response will be good with probability of 0.9. Similarly, if initial response is bad, subsequent response is likely to be bad with probability of 0.9. The estimated payoffs are given below :

		Small plant		*Large plant*	
		Good	*Bad*	*Good*	*Bad*
Initial year	-	*15*	*5*	*20*	*5*
Subsequent years (Cumulative)	-	*60*	*20*	*80*	*20*

Advise the company the option it should adopt.

[I.C.W.A. Dec., 1988]

Solution

The decision tree for the problem is shown in Fig. 9.21.

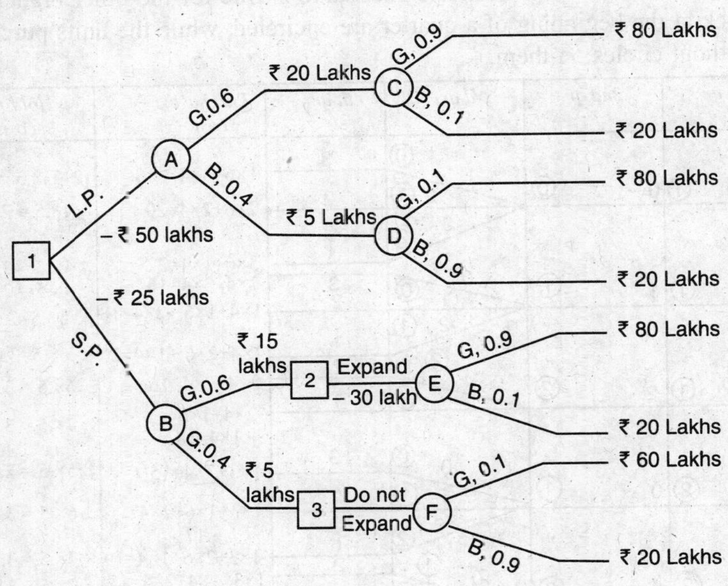

Fig. 9.21

E.M.V. at node C = ₹ (0.9 × 80 + 0.1 × 20) lakhs = ₹ 74 lakhs.

E.M.V. at node D = ₹ (0.1 × 80 + 0.9 × 20) lakhs = ₹ 26 lakhs.

E.M.V. at node E = ₹ (0.9 × 80 + 0.1 × 20) lakhs = ₹ 74 lakhs.

E.M.V. at node F = ₹ (0.1 × 60 + 0.9 × 20) lakhs = ₹ 24 lakhs.
E.M.V. at node 2 = ₹ (74 – 30) lakhs = 44 lakhs.
E.M.V. at node 3 = ₹ 24 lakhs.
E.M.V. at node A = ₹ [0.6 (74 + 20) + 0.4 (26 + 5)] lakhs
= ₹ 68.8 lakhs.
E.M.V. at node B = ₹ [0.6 (44 + 15) + 0.4 (24 + 5)] lakhs
= ₹ 47 lakhs.
E.M.V. at node 1 = Maximum of ₹ [68.8 – 50) ; (47 – 25)] lakhs
= ₹ 22 lakhs.

Thus the optimal strategy is to go in for a small plant initially and expand later if initial response is good and do not expand if initial response is bad. This strategy results in expected profit of ₹ 22 lakhs.

EXAMPLE 9.9-2.19

A paper mill uses 1 unit of pulp per quarter. The storage capacity for the pulp in the mill is 2 units of pulp. Pulp may be bought (in complete units only) at the following prices, the money unit being arbitrary. The price depends upon the quarter of the year in which the purchase is made.

Quarter	:	*1*	*2*	*3*	*4*
Purchase price (Per unit of pulp)	:	*3*	*4*	*6*	*4*

There is also a holding (or stock) charge of 0.5 per unit per quarter, the charge being based on the stock in hand at the beginning of each quarter. During a quarter, addition to stock can be made at any time. It is thus possible to leave the stock at capacity (if desired) at the end of the quarter. The mill has capacity stock stored (2 units) at the beginning of the year and must leave the same situation at the end of the year. Under these constraints, what is the most rotional series of decisions for the mill manager to make? [I.C.W.A. Dec., 1984]

Solution

The situation is represented by the decision tree shown in Fig. 9.22. The explanation is given below for the first branch of the decision tree; same is true for the other branches. The number of units in stock at the beginning of a quarter are encircled, while the units purchased during the quarter are without circles on them.

1st qr	*2nd qr*	*3rd qr*	*4th qr*	*Purchase cost*	*Holding cost*	*Total cost*
② 0	① 0	⓪ 1	⓪ 3	1×6+3×4 = 18	(2+1)×.5 = 1.5	19.5
		2	① 2	2×6+2×4=20	4×.5 = 2.0	22.0
		3	② 1	3×6+1×4=22	5×.5 = 2.5	24.5
② 0	① 1	① 0	⓪ 3	1×4+3×4=16	4×.5 = 2.0	18.0
		1	① 2	1×4+1×6 +2×4=18	5×.5=2.5	20.5
		2	② 1	1×4+2×6 +1×4=20	6×.5=3.0	23.0
② 0	① 2	② 0	① 2	2×4+2×4=16	6×.5 = 3.0	19.0
		1	② 1	2×4+1×6 + 1×4=18	7×.5 = 3.5	21.5
② 1	② 0	① 0	⓪ 3	1×3+3×4=15	5×.5 = 2.5	17.5
		1	① 2	1×3+1×6+2×4 =17	6×.5 = 3.0	20.0
		2	② 1	1×3+2×6+1×4=19	7×.5 = 3.5	22.5
② 1	② 1	② 0	① 2	1×3+1×4+2×4=15	7×.5 = 3.5	18.5
		1	② 1	1×3+1×4+1×6 +1×4 = 17	8×.5 = 4.0	21.0

Fig. 9.22

Starting with a stock of 2 units of pulp at the beginning of the first quarter, if nothing is purchased during this quarter, the number left at the beginning of second quarter will be 1 since one unit of pulp is consumed during each quarter. Likewise, if nothing is purchased during the second quarter, the number left at the beginning of the third quarter will be zero. Now there are three options : purchase 1, 2 or 3 units represented by the three branches in the third quarter. The number of units left accordingly at the beginning of the fourth quarter will be 0, 1 and 2 respectively. Since there is consumption of one unit during the quarter and there must remain 2 units in stock at the end of the fourth quarter, the number of units to be purchased will be 3, 2 and 1 respectively.

Since one unit is purchased during the third quarter and 3 units are purchased during the fourth quarter, the purchase cost for the top decision branch is

$$= 1 \times 6 + 3 \times 4 = 18 \text{ monetary units.}$$

Further, as the total number of units in stock during the four quarters is $2 + 1 + 0 + 0 = 3$, the stock holding cost

$$= 3 \times 0.5 = 1.5 \text{ monetary units.}$$

$\therefore$ Total cost $= 18 + 1.5 = 19.5$ monetary units

The procedure is repeated for the remaining branches of the decision tree.

From the total cost column, the minimum cost is 17.5 monetary units when 1 unit is purchased during the first quarter and 3 units are purchased during the fourth quarter.

EXERCISES 9.3

1. What do you understand by decision tree analysis? What is node in a decision tree? What is backward pass? [*Univ. of Mumbai MBA, 2012; J.N.T.U. Hyderabad B.Tech. (Mech.) May, 2012; P.T.U. MBA, 2006; M.G.U. Kerala M.Com. June, 2010; C.A. (Final) May, 2000*]
2. What is the concept of decision tree analysis? What are the basic steps involved in the construction of such a tree? Explain how expected payoff is optimized. Suitable examples may be assumed. [*P.T.U. MBA May, 2015; M.G.U. Kerla M.Com., 2012; U.P.U. MBA, 2009; P.U.B.E. (Prod.) 2001*]
3. Explain the construction of a decision tree. What do you mean by it? What are the advantages and limitations of the decision tree approach? [*Univ. of Mumbai MBA, 2012*]
4. A businessman has two independent investments A and B available to him, but he lacks the capital to undertake both of them simultaneously. He can choose to take A first and then stop, or if A is successful, then take B or vice versa. The probability of success of A is 0.7, while for B it is 0.4. Both investments require an initial capital outlay of ₹ 2,000 and both return nothing if the venture is unsuccessful. Successful completion of A will return ₹ 3,000 (over cost) and successful completion of B will return ₹ 5,000 (over cost). Draw the decision tree and determine the best strategy. [*P.T.U. MBA Dec., 2014; U.P. Tech. U.MBA, 2010*]
(*Ans.* Accept A first and if successful, accept B;EMV = ₹ 2,000.)
5. A company owns a lease on a certain property. It may sell the lease for ₹ 12,000 or it may drill the said property for oil. Various possible drilling results along with the probabilities of happening and rupee consequences are as under :

TABLE 9.84

Possible results	*Probability*	*Rupee consequences*
Dry well	0.10	– 1,00,000
Gas well only	0.40	45,000
Oil and gas combination	0.30	98,000
Oil well	0.20	1,99,000

Draw a decision tree diagram for the above problem and calculate EMV for the act 'drill'. Should the company drill or sell? [*Poona M.B.A., 1982*]
6. A manager has a choice between (*i*) A risky contract promising ₹ 7 lakhs with probability 0.6 and ₹ 4 lakhs with probability 0.4. (*ii*) A diversified portfolio consisting of two contracts with

independent outcomes and each promising ₹ 3.5 lakhs with probability 0.6 and ₹ 2 lakhs with probability 0.4. Construct a decision tree using EMV criterion. Can you arrive at the decision using EMV criterion? [*Poona M.B.A.,1982*]

7. Mr. Basu is interested in developing and marketing a new drug. The cost of extensive research to develop the drug would be ₹ 1,00,000. The manager of research programme said that there is 60% chance that the drug will be developed successfully. The market potential is assessed as follows with present value of profits:

TABLE 9.85

Market conditions	*Probability*	*Present value of profits*
Large market potential	0.1	₹ 5,00,000
Moderate market potential	0.6	2,20,000
Low market potential	0.3	80,000

The present value figures do not include the cost of research. While Mr. Basu was considering this proposal, another similar proposal came up which also required the investment of ₹ 1,00,000. The present value of profit for the second proposal was ₹ 1,20,000. The return on the investment in the second proposal is almost certain.

(*i*) Draw a decision tree for Mr. Basu indicating all choices and events.
(*ii*) What decision Mr. Basu should take regarding the investment of ₹ 1,00,000?
(*iii*) If Mr. Basu is a risk averter, should he change the decision given by you?

[*Bombay Univ. M.M.S., 1982*]

8. An oil company has recently acquired rights in a certain area to conduct surveys and test drillings to lead to lifting oil where it is found in commercially exploitable quantities. The area is already considered to have good potential for finding oil in commercial quantities. At the outset, the company has the choice to conduct further geological tests or to carry out a drilling programme immediately. On the known conditions, the company estimates that there is a 70 : 30 chance of further tests showing a 'success'.
Whether the tests show the possibility of ultimate success or not or even if no tests are undertaken at all, the company could still pursue its drilling programmes or alternatively consider selling its rights to drill in the area. Thereafter, however, if it carries out the drilling programme, likelihood of final success or failure is considered dependent on the foregoing stages. Thus

(*i*) if 'successful' tests have been carried out, the expectation of success in drilling is given as 80 : 20,
(*ii*) if the tests indicate 'failure', then the expectation of success in drilling is given as 20 : 80,
(*iii*) if no tests have been carried out at all, the expectation of success in drilling is given as 55 : 45.

Costs and revenues have been estimated for all possible outcomes and the net present value of each is given below.

TABLE 9.86

Outcome	*Net present value (£m)*
Success :	
With prior tests	100
Without prior tests	120
Failure :	
With prior tests	– 50
Without prior tests	– 40
Sale of exploitation rights:	
Prior tests show 'success'	65
Prior tests show 'failure'	15
Without prior tests	45

(*a*) Draw up a decision (probability) tree diagram to represent the above information.
(*b*) Evaluate the tree in order to advise the management of the company on its best course of action.
(*c*) Discuss the value of decision trees in providing management with guidance for decision-making. Give examples of any situations where you consider their use would be of benefit.

[*CMA London May,1981*]

9. A company manufacturing three brands B_1, B_2 and B_3 of a highly competitive consumer product has to decide about its pricing strategy. Unfortunately they have discovered after a lapse of 6 to

8 months that their costs are out of line. They now have the following options :

(*a*) Raise the prices of all brands in stages over a period of one year.

(*b*) Raise the prices of all brands sharply to ensure good margins, though this would mean an initial loss of sales.

(*c*) Raise the price of one brand at a time making the change at two monthly intervals (note: stop increasing the prices if at any stage payoff is negative).

The probability and associated payoffs are given below.

TABLE 9.87

	Probability	*Pay-off* (₹)
Strategy (a)	0.70	50,000
	030	70,000
Strategy (b)	0.15	2,00,000
	0.30	50,000
	0.20	30,000
	0.20	10,000
	0.15	– 1,00,000
Strategy (c)	0.60	50,000
(*i*) Raise B_1	0.40	– 20,000
(*ii*) If successful with B_1, raise B_2	0.50	75,000
	0.50	– 30,000
(*iii*) If successful with B_1 and B_2, raise B_3	0.30	75,000
	0.70	– 50,000

Draw a decision tree and recommend an optimal decision. [*B.U.D.M.A., 1971*]

10. Mr. X is trying to decide whether to travel to Sri Lanka from Delhi to negotiate the sale of a shipment of China novelties. He holds the novelties in stock and is fairly confident, but by no means sure, that if he makes the trip he will sell the novelties at a price that will given him a profit of ₹ 30,000. He puts the probability of obtaining the order at 0.6. If he does not make the trip, he will certainly not get the order.

If the novelties are not sold in Sri Lanka there is an Indian customer who will certainly buy them at a price that leaves him a profit of ₹ 15,000 and his offer will be open at least till Mr. X returns from Sri Lanka. Mr X estimates the expenses of trip to Sri Lanka at ₹ 2,500. He is, however, concerned that his absence, even for only three days, may lead to production inefficiencies in the factory. These could cause him to miss the deadline on another contract, with the consequence that a late penalty of ₹ 10,000 will be invoked. Mr. X assesses the probability of missing the deadline under these circumstances at 0.4. Further, he believes that in his absence there will be a lower standard of housekeeping in the factory, and the raw material and labour costs on the other contract will rise by about ₹ 2,000 above the budgeted figure.

Draw an appropriate decision tree for Mr. X's problem and, using EMV as the appropriate criterion for decision, find the appropriate initial decision. (*Ans.* Proceed to Sri Lanka; EMV = ₹ 15,500.)

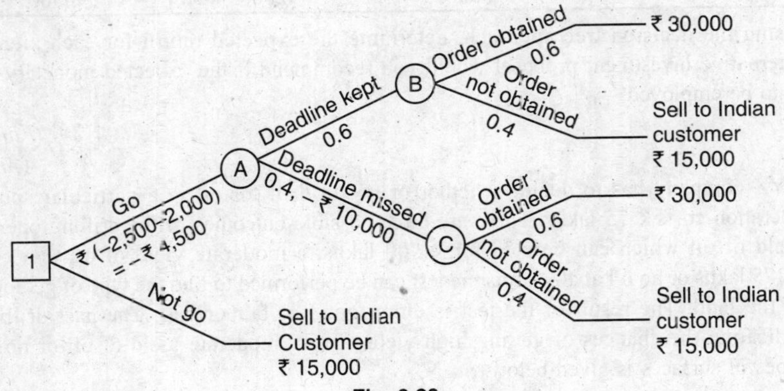

Fig. 9.23

11. A firm making widgets has been considering the likely demand for widgets over the next 6 years and thinks that the demand pattern will be as follows :

	High demand for 6 years	:	Prob. 0.5,
	low demand for 6 years	:	Prob. 0.3,
and	high demand for 3 years followed by low demand for 3 years	:	Prob. 0.2.

No possibility is envisaged for other types of demand. Enlargement of capacity is required and the following options are available :

Option A : Install fully automatic facilities at the cost of ₹ 5.4 million.

Option B : Install semi-automatic facilities at the cost of ₹ 4 million.

Option C : Install the semi-automatic facilities immediately as in option B and upgrade to fully automatic at an additional cost of ₹ 2 million in 3 years time provided demand has been high for 3 years.

The returns expected for the various demand and capacity options are estimated to be

		If high	*If low*
Option A	:	₹ 1.6 million p.a.	₹ 0.6 million p.a.
Option B	:	₹ 0.9 million p.a. for 3 years, then 0.5 m.p.a. for 3 years.	₹ 0.8 million p.a.
Option C	:	₹ 0.9 m. p.a. for 3 years, then ₹ 1.1 m. p.a. for 3 years.	₹ 0.8 m. p.a. for 3 years, then ₹ 0.3 m. p.a. for 3 years.

What decision should the firm take?

[*C.A. (Final) June, 1992*]

(*Ans.* Install fully-automatic machine immediately; E.M.V. = ₹ 1.8 million.)

12. Growfast company is evaluating four single-period investment opportunities whose returns are based on the state of the economy. The possible states of the economy and the associated probability distribution is as follows :

State	:	*Fair*	*Good*	*Great*
Probability	:	0.2	0.5	0.3

The returns for each investment opportunity and each state of the economy are as follows :

TABLE 9.88

Alternative	*State of economy*		
	Fair	*Good*	*Great*
W	₹ 1,000	₹ 3,000	₹ 6,000
X	500	4,500	6,800
Y	0	5,000	8,000
Z	– 4,000	6,000	8,500

Using the decision tree approach, determine the expected return for each alternative. Which alternative investment proposal would you recommend if the expected monetary value criterion is to be employed?

[*C.A. (Final) Nov., 1992*]

(*Ans.* Y; ₹ 4,900.)

13. XYZ company has to decide whether or not to drill for oil in a particular spot. The drilling operation costs ₹ 75 lakhs. There are three possible outcomes of the drilling operations : a high yield of oil which can be sold for ₹ 200 lakhs, a moderate yield of oil that can be sold for ₹ 175 lakhs or no oil at all. A seismic test can be performed to find the type of geological formation of the land. The result of the test is either good or fair or bad. The past drilling experience indicating the chances of getting high yield of oil, moderate yield of oil or no oil on various types of surfaces is given below.

Seismic test	*High yield*	*Moderate yield*	*No oil*	*Total*
Good	50%	25%	25%	100%
Fair	30%	30%	40%	100%
Bad	10%	20%	70%	100%

It is also known that chances of this land giving good, fair or bad reading in the seismic test are 40%, 30% and 30% respectively. XYZ company wants to know whether or not to drill on this land.

(*Ans.* Perform seismic test, E.M.V. = 38.75 lakhs.)

14. A land owner has an option to sell rights for oil exploration. If he sells the rights, he can get ₹ 8 lakhs and further ₹ 63 lakhs if oil is found. However, as an alternative he can himself conduct a test whether oil exists, the cost of which is ₹ 15 lakhs. If the test succeeds, he can expect a revenue of ₹ 135 lakhs by selling oil.
 (i) Represent this situation by a decision tree.
 (ii) Suggest the best decision for the land owner.
 Assume that the probability that the oil exists is 0.4. [*Mumbai U. MBA, 2010*]

9.9-3 Utility Theory

In the preceding sections, expected monetary value (EMV) criterion has been applied to find the optimum decision alternative under conditions of risk. However, the decision-maker may not be always interested in optimizing the *face value* of money. There may be objectives or preferences other than money. In such cases, the *utility* rather than the *actual value* of money may be used in the analysis. Utility of money is the *measure of preference* of individuals having various alternatives available to them. Consider the following illustration :

If a person is asked to choose between the two alternatives: a tax-free gift of ₹ 10,000 or a 5% chance of getting ₹ 2,50,000 and 95% chance of getting nothing, he would, most likely, choose the first alternative even though its expected payoff is ₹ 10,000 as against ₹ (2,50,000 × 0.05 + 0 × 0.95) = ₹ 12,500 for the second alternative. This points out the inadequacy of E.M.V. approach. This apparent paradox is explained by *utility theory.* Basically it states that each rupee is not equally valuable to an individual. For example, hundred rupees is worth much less to an individual who has lots of a money than it is to a poor. The worth of money may be different to different persons and even to the same person in different situations. A company with strong financial position may opt for a risky venture since it can absorb the loss if worst happens, while a company with poor financial position will avoid all risky ventures.

The determination of utility is subjective. It depends upon our attitude of accepting risk. The utility theory approach attempts to determine a utility function or a utility curve for a decision-maker. This function (or curve) converts money into an *arbitrary utility measure*.

The choice between alternatives is then made based on maximizing expected utility instead of maximizing expected return (EMV).

Some typical utility curves are shown in Fig. 9.24.

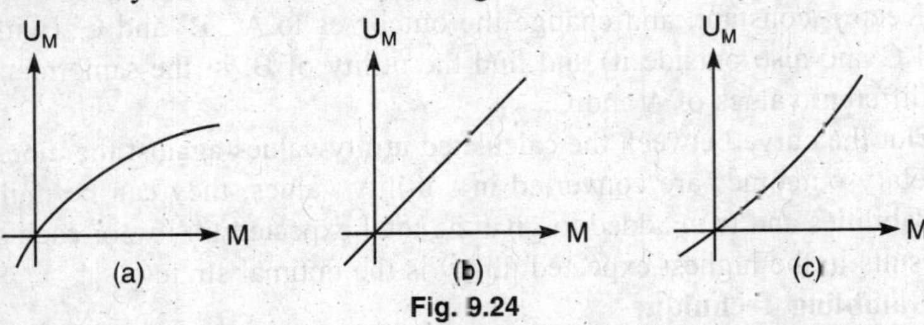

Fig. 9.24

Fig. 9.24 (*a*) shows a typical utility curve where the slope decreases as money values increase. Such a curve will be followed by an individual who is 'risk avoider' or conservative. Firms with unsound financial positions would prefer to follow this curve. Fig. 9.24 (*b*) shows the utility curve for a decision-maker who says that every rupee amount is equally valuable. In this case, expected utility would give the same results as expected return (EMV) analysis. This may be a realistic form of curve for large companies and the government who are generally 'risk neutral'. That is why large companies practice self-insurance and individuals do not. In Fig. 9.24(*c*), the slope of the curve increases faster than the money value. This utility curve is for a 'risk taker' or for a person with 'high aspiration level'.

In actual practice, a utility curve may be a combination of the above types as an individual may be a 'risk taker for smaller amounts and a 'risk avoider' when large amounts are involved. In this case, the utility curve will follow an elongated S-shape.

9.9-3. Methods of Measuring Utility

1. Von Neumann and Morgenstern Method

Consider a situation in which an individual is offered two alternatives involving three outcomes ₹ 5,000, ₹ 2,500 and ₹ 0:

(*i*) a sure gift (guaranteed cash) of ₹ 2,500.

(*ii*) winning ₹ 5,000 with probability 0.5 and ₹ 0 with probability 0.5.

Assume that he opts for the sure gift of ₹ 2,500. Decrease this sure gift to ₹ 2,000 and again ask him his choice. He still dreads the 50/50 gamble and opts for the first alternative. Go on this way, decreasing the sure gift, until the individual is indifferent to the two alternatives. This point is called the *certainty monetary equivalent* (C.M.E.) of the gamble. Let us assume that this individual's certainty monetary equivalent to the gamble is ₹ 1,200. Now arbitrary utility values are assigned to the outcomes of the gamble. Let a utility of 5 be assigned to ₹ 5,000 and 0 be assigned to ₹ 0. As the individual is indifferent to

(*i*) a sure gift (guaranteed cash) of ₹ 1,200 and

(*ii*) winning of ₹ 5,000 with probability 0.5 and ₹ 0 with probability 0.5, the utility of ₹ 1,200 with probability 1 equals the utility of ₹ 5,000 with probability 0.5 and nothing with probability 0.5. Symbolically,

$$1.\ U_{1,200} = \frac{1}{2}\ U_{5,000} + \frac{1}{2}\ U_0 \text{ or } U_{1,200} = \frac{1}{2} \times 5 + \frac{1}{2} \times 0 = 2.5.$$

In the above situation, we assumed outcomes of ₹ 5,000, ₹ 2,500 and ₹ 0 respectively. To explain the general procedure, let us consider a situation in which the individual is to choose among the two alternatives involving outcomes A, B and C :

(*i*) a sure gift of B,

(*ii*) winning A with probability p and C with probability $(1 - p)$.

The procedure consists of the following steps :

Step 1. Assign arbitrary utility values to A and C (the highest and the lowest outcomes).

Step 2. Select a value of p preferably near 0.5.

Step 3. Determine the amount B such that its utility equals the utility of alternative (*ii*).

i.e., $$U_B = pU_A + (1 - p)\ U_C.$$

Step 4. Keep p constant, and change the outcomes to A′, B′ and C′ (within the interval between A and C and also outside it) and find the utility of B′ in the same manner. Repeat the procedure for different values of A and C.

Step 5. Plot the curve between the calculated utility values against the monetary outcomes. Once the monetary outcomes are converted into utility values, they can be multiplied by their associated probabilities and then added to give the total expected utility for each strategy and the strategy that results in the highest expected utility is the optimal strategy.

2. Standard Gambling Technique

The standard gambling technique is precisely a modification over CME approach. Here the amounts A and C are fixed while p is varied until the person is indifferent to a certain return B and a gamble of winning A with probability p and C with probability $(1 - p)$ *i.e.*,

$$U_B = pU_A + (1 - p)U_C.$$

Thus p is calculated and the procedure is repeated for different values of B to get additional utility points between the interval A and C and then the utility curve is plotted.

3. Logarithmic Utility Function

An individual is, in general, a risk avoider. His utility curve is the one shown in Fig. 9.20(*a*) whose slope decreases as the money values increase *i.e.*, each extra rupee has diminishing returns in terms of utility. Such a curve can be well represented by a logarithmic curve. Thus for 'risk avoiders' the utility function can be given by

$$U_x = \log (x + 1),$$

where x is the monetary amount.

EXAMPLE 9.9-3.1

A businessman is thinking whether to invest in bonds with an assured return or in a new venture that is likely to fetch him ₹ 20,000 or nothing with equal probabilities. The businessman says he would prefer an assured return if it is ₹ 10,000 or more, would be indifferent to the two alternatives if the assured return is ₹ 8,000 and would opt for the risky alternative if this amount is less than ₹ 6,000.

The businessman had purchased a minicomputer last year which is lying with him unused at present. The minicomputer can fetch him a profit of ₹ 8,000 by way of consultancy. He says that he would not like to sell the computer but would be indifferent to an offer of ₹ 3,000.

Recently a Govt agency invited bid offers for a contract worth a profit of ₹ 8,000. Bidding expenses are reimbursable if the contract materialises and not otherwise. There is an equal chance of winning or losing the bid. After thinking over the possibilities, the businessman says that he would be indifferent to submitting the bid at a bidding expense of ₹ 2,000. Construct the businessman's utility curve by using the CME technique.

Solution

Let arbitrary utility values of 100 and 0 be assigned to the most favourable and least favourable outcomes.

$$\therefore \quad U_{20,000} = 100 \text{ utiles}, \; U_0 = 0 \text{ utile}.$$

According to the problem,

$$U_{8,000} = 0.5\, U_{20,000} + 0.5\, U_0 = 0.5 \times 100 + 0.5 \times 0 = 50 \text{ utiles}.$$

Further, as the businessman is indifferent between his utilities for ₹ 3,000 and of a chance of ₹ 8,000 or nothing,

$$U_{3,000} = 0.5\, U_{8,000} + 0.5\, U_0 = 0.5 \times 50 + 0.5 \times 0 = 25 \text{ utiles}.$$

By choosing to enter the bid at an expense of ₹ 2,000, he may either gain ₹ 8,000 or lose (bidding expenses of) ₹ 2,000 with equal probability. Since he is indifferent to submitting the bid,

$$U_0 = 0.5\, U_{8,000} + 0.5\, U_{-2,000}.$$

$$\therefore \quad 0 = 0.5 \times 50 + 0.5\, U_{-2,000} \text{ or } U_{-2,000} = -\,50 \text{ utiles}.$$

Thus we have the following points for the businessman's utility curve :

Amount (₹)	*Utility* (*utiles*)
20,000	100
8,000	50
3,000	25
0	0
– 2,000	– 50

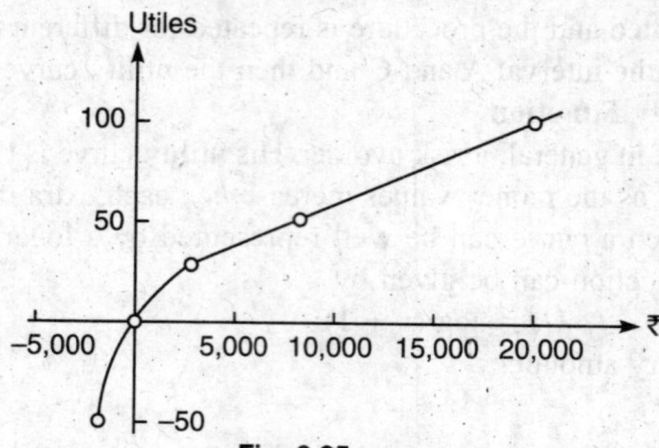

Fig. 9.25

The utility curve is plotted in Fig. 9.25. From this curve we can make a reasonble estimate of the businessman's behaviour when faced with risky ventures.

EXAMPLE 9.9-3.2

An opportunity is offered at a cost of ₹ 22 to participate in a venture with probability 0.1 of gaining ₹ 100 and probability 0.9 of gaining ₹ 10. Bose has a utility function for money given by $U_M = M + 0.01M^2$, where M is the amount of money.

(a) Would you expect Bose to participate in the venture?

(b) Aiyer has a utility function $U_M = \log M$. How much would he be willing to pay to buy this venture?

Solution

(*a*)

$$U_{22} = 22 + 0.01 \times 22^2 = 26.84,$$
$$U_{100} = 100 + 0.01 \times 100^2 = 200,$$
$$U_{10} = 10 + 0.01 \times 10^2 = 11.$$

∴ Utility of participating in the venture = 0.1 × 200 + 0.9 × 11 = 29.9.

Since it is more than U_{22}, Bose should participate in the venture.

(*b*) Let C be the cost that Aiyer should be willing to pay.

Then $U_{100} = \log 100 = 2$, $U_{10} = \log 10 = 1$.

∴ $U_C = \log C = 0.1 \times 2 + 0.9 \times 1 = 1.1$

∴ C = antilog 1.1 = ₹ 12.88.

EXAMPLE 9.9-3.3

Corporation XYZ is considering an investment which would utilise all its funds available for investment. The researches expect either of the two instantaneous events to occur, with the results shown in the table below.

Event	*Conditional net monetary value (₹)*	*Probability of event*
A	*10,00,000*	*0.70*
B	*– 50,000*	*0.30*

Assume that the firm has a utility function which may be approximated as follows:

$$U = -0.001\,Y^2, \quad \text{if } Y < -1{,}500,$$
$$= Y, \quad \text{if } Y > 1{,}500.$$

(a) Is it desirable to undertake the venture on the basis of the assumed utility function?

(b) What would be the decision if the expected payoff criterion is used?

Solution

(*a*) $U_A = Y = 10,00,000$ utiles,

$U_B = -0.001\ (-50,000)^2 = -25,00,000$ utiles.

∴ Utility of the venture $= 0.7\ U_A + 0.3\ U_B$

$= 0.7 \times 10,00,000 + 0.3\ (-25,00,000) = -50,000$ utiles.

Since the utility of the venture is negative, it is not desirable to undertake the venture.

(*b*) E.M.V. = ₹ (10,00,000 × 0.7 – 50,000 × 0.3) = ₹ 6,85,000

(a highly positive value).

Thus according to expected payoff criterion, the venture should be undertaken. This contradictory result represents the inadequacy of the expected payoff criterion.

EXAMPLE 9.9-3.4

The net return of an opportunity can be ₹ 95 with a probability of 0.2 or ₹ 15 with a probability of 0.3 or ₹ 5 with a probability of 0.5. How much would an individual having a utility function of log (M + 5), where M is the monetary amount, be willing to pay to buy this opportunity? [*C.A. (Final) May, 1990*]

Solution

Let C be the amount which the individual would be willing to pay for the opportunity.

Now $U_M = \text{Log}\ (M + 5)$.

∴ $U_{95} = \log (100) = 2$,

$U_{15} = \log (20) = 1.301$,

$U_5 = \log (10) = 1$.

∴ $U_C = \log (C + 5) = 0.2 \times 2 + 0.3 \times 1.301 + 0.5 \times 1 = 1.2903$

or $C + 5 = \text{antilog}\ 1.2903 =$ ₹ 19.51 or C = ₹ 14.51.

Thus the person would be willing to pay ₹ 14.51 to buy the opportunity.

EXAMPLE 9.9-3.5

Mr. XX has an after-tax annual income of ₹ 90,000 and is considering to buy accident insurance for his car. The probability of accident during the year is 0.1 (assume that at most one accident will occur), in which case the damage to the car will be ₹ 11,600. With a utility function of $U(x) = \sqrt{x}$, *what is the insurance premium he will be willing to pay?*

[*C.A. (Final) Nov., 1990*]

Solution

Let A represent the venture when Mr. XX does not buy the accident insurance for his car. Then, in case of accident ($p = 0.1$), he would spend ₹ 11,600 on damages and will be left with ₹ 78,400. In case of no accident, ($p = 0.9$), he retains ₹ 90,000. Then

$U_A = U_{78,400} \times 0.1 + U_{90,000} \times 0.9.$

Now $U(x) = U_x = \sqrt{x}$.

∴ $U_{78,400} = \sqrt{78,400} = 280$ utiles,

$U_{90,000} = \sqrt{90,000} = 300$ utiles.

∴ $U_A = 280 \times 0.1 + 300 \times 0.9 = 298$ utiles.

∴ Amount x which will give the same utility as that of venture

A = $(298)^2$ = ₹ 88,804. [$\because U(x) = \sqrt{x}$ or $x = [U(x)]^2$]

Thus Mr. XX will be indifferent to an amount of ₹ 88,804 with certainty and the venture A.

∴ The amount he will be willing to pay as car premium

= ₹ (90,000 – 88,804) = ₹ 1,196.

EXAMPLE 9.9-3.6

An investor has ₹ 10,000 to invest in common stock. His selection is between companies C and D. He feels that for each of the investments he has a 0.7 probability of doubling his money and 0.3 probability of losing half his money depending upon the company's stock rising or falling respectively. His choices are

(i) invest the entire money in either C or D.

(ii) invest ₹ 5,000 in one company and not invest in the other.

(iii) invest ₹ 5,000 in C and ₹ 5,000 in D.

If his utility values for changes in assets are ₹ 10,000 = 1;

₹ 5,000 = 0.9; ₹ 2,500 = 0.7; ₹ 0 = 0.4; – ₹ 2,500 = 0.2; – ₹ 5,000 = 0, what investment plan should he choose to maximize his expected utility ? Assume that rise or fall of either stock is independent of the other.

[C.A. (Final) Dec., 1990]

Solution

The expected utility for each investment plan is shown in the table below.

TABLE 9.89

Investment plan	*Outcome*	*Probability*	*Changes in assets (₹)*	*Utility value*	*Expected utility*
1. Invest ₹ 10,000 in C	Doubling the money	0.7	10,000	1	0.7×1 = 0.7
	Losing half the money	0.3	– 5,000	0	0.3×0 = 0
					Total: 0.7
2. Invest ₹ 10,000 in D	Doubling the money	0.7	10,000	1	0.7×1 = 0.7
	Losing half the money	0.3	– 5,000	0	0.3×0 = 0
					Total: 0.7
3. Invest ₹ 5,000 in C and not in D	Doubling the money	0.7	5,000	0.9	0.7×0.9 = 0.63
	Losing half the money	0.3	– 2,500	0.2	0.3×0.2 = 0.06
					Total: 0.69
4. Invest ₹ 5,000 in D and not in C	Doubling the money	0.7	5,000	0.9	0.7×0.9 = 0.63
	Losing half the money	0.3	– 2,500	0.2	0.3×0.2 = 0.06
					Total: 0.69
5. Invest ₹ 5,000 in C and ₹ 5,000 in D	Doubling the money	0.7×0.7 = 0.49	10,000	1	0.49×1 = 0.49
	Doubling in C & losing in D	0.7×0.3 = 0.21	2,500	0.7	0.21×0.7 = 0.147
	Doubling in D & losing in C	0.7×0.3 = 0.21	2,500	0.7	0.21×0.7 = 0.147
	Losing half the money	0.3×0.3 = 0.09	–5,000	0	0.09×0 = 0.00
					Total: 0.784

Hence optimal decision is : invest ₹ 5,000 in C and ₹ 5,000 in D.

EXERCISES 9.4

1. What is the significance of utility as a basis of decision-making? State the assumptions underlying the theory of utility.

2. Explain the Von Neuman Morgenstern method for measuring utility.

[*M.D.U. Rohtak B.E. Dec., 2006*]

3. A decision-maker has the following utilities over the relevant portion of his overall assets scale:

Assets (₹)	:	50,000	60,000	70,000	80,000	90,000
Utility	:	0.32	0.46	0.59	0.67	0.72

The decision-maker currently possesses total assets of ₹ 70,000. He is offered a place in the lottery where he has a chance of 0.6 of winning ₹ 10,000 and 0.4 of losing ₹ 10,000. Should the decision-maker accept the offer?

[**Hint.** $U_{70,000} = 0.59$.

$U_{lottery} = 0.6\ U_{80,000} + 0.4\ U_{60,000} = 0.6 \times 0.67 + 0.4 \times 0.46 = 0.586$.]

(*Ans.* No, he should not accept.)

4. A person has assets of ₹ 50,000 and is offered a deal, which in his opinion, has probability 0.3 of resulting in a loss of ₹ 50,000 and 0.7 of resulting in a profit of ₹ 50,000. His utility function is as follows:

Assets (₹)	:	0	10,000	25,000	50,000	75,000	1,00,000
Utility	:	0	0.4	0.6	0.8	0.9	1.0

What should be his decision?

[**Hint.** $U_{50,000} = 0.8$

$U_{lottery} = 0.3\ U_0 + 0.7\ U_{1,00,000}$ (*Ans.* No, he should not accept.)

$= 0.3 \times 0 + 0.7 \times 1 = 0.7$.]

5. Mr. Naresh is offered an opportunity to participate in a project that may give him a profit of ₹ 500 with probability of 0.1 and ₹ 50 with a probability of 0.9. His utility function is given by

$$U(x) = x + 0.01\ x^2.$$

If the cost of entering the project is ₹ 125, should he participate in the project?

[**Hint.** $U(125) = 125 + 0.01\ (125)^2 = 281.25$.

$U_{project} = 0.1\ [U(500)] + 0.9\ [U(50)]$

$= 0.1\ [500 + 0.01\ (500)^2] + 0.9\ [50 + 0.01\ (50)^2]$

$= 300 + 67.5 = 367.5$.]

(*Ans.* Yes, he should participate in the project.)

6. M/s Gulshan Toys is considering to bring a new type of animated doll. The company is to decide whether to bring out a full, partial or minimum product line. It has categorised three possible levels of product acceptance and has estimated their probability of occurrence. Gulshan's management will make its decision on the basis of maximizing the expected utility of the anticipated profit from the first year of production. The relevant product data are shown below.

TABLE 9.90

Product acceptance	*Probability*	*Production line*		
		Full	*Partial*	*Minimal*
Excellent	0.20	75	60	50
Good	0.35	65	45	30
Poor	0.45	– 30	– 15	0

M/s Gulshan Toys has evaluated the following utility function in terms of the first year profit :

Profit (000's of ₹)	:	80	70	60	50	40	30	20	10	0	–10	–20	–30
Utility	:	40	37	34	30	25	20	14	7	0	–10	–25	–45

Determine the optimal product line. What is the expected utility ? What is the cash amount associated with this utility value ? How can this cash amount be interpreted? On the basis of maximizing EMV, the optimal decision was to bring out a partial product line.

(*Ans.* Minimal line, EUV = 13.)

7. An individual whose current assets amount to ₹ 80,000 has the following utility function over the relevant portion of his overall assets scale :

Assets (0000's of ₹)	:	6	7	8	9	10	11
Utility	:	0.24	0.38	0.50	0.60	0.67	0.72

(*a*) He is offered a bet in which he has 60% chance of gaining ₹ 20,000 and 40% chance of losing ₹ 20,000. Should he accept the offer?

(*b*) Alternatively, he is offered participation in two bets each involving a gain of ₹ 10,000 with a probability of 0.6 and a loss of ₹ 10,000 with a probability of 0.4. Should he decide differently than in case (*a*)?

(*Ans.* (*a*) No (*b*) Accept the offer.)

9.10 THE THEORY OF GAMES

The theory of games (or *game theory or competitive strategies*) is a mathematical theory that deals with the general features of competitive situations. *This theory is helpful when two or more individuals or organisations with conflicting objectives try to make decisions*. In such situations, a decision made by one decision-maker affects the decision made by one or more of the remaining decision-makers and the final outcome depends upon the decision of all the parties. Such situations often arise in the fields of business, industry, economics, sociology and military training. This theory is applicable to a wide variety of situations such as two players struggling to win at chess, candidates fighting an election, two enemies planning war tactics, firms struggling to maintain their market shares, launching advertisement campaigns by companies marketing competing product, negotiations between organisations and unions, etc. These situations differ from the ones we have discussed so far wherein *nature* was viewed as a *harmless opponent*.

The theory of games is based on the *minimax principle* put forward by J. Von Neumann which implies that each competitor will act so as to minimize his maximum loss (or maximize his minimum gain) or achieve *best of the worst*. So far only simple competitive problems have been analysed by this mathematical theory. The theory does not describe how a game should be played; it describes only the procedure and principles by which plays should be selected.

Though the theory of games was developed by Von Neumann (called father of game theory) in 1928, it was only after 1944 when he and Morgenstern published their work named '*Theory of Games and Economic Behaviour*', that the theory received its proper attention. Since, so far the theory has been capable of analysing very simple situations only, there has remained a wide gap between what the theory can handle and the most actual situations in business and industry. So, the primary contribution of game theory has been its concepts rather than its formal application to the solution of real problems.

9.11 CHARACTERISTICS OF GAMES

A competitive game has the following characteristics :

(*i*) There are *finite* number of participants or competitors. If the number of participants is 2, the game is called two-person game; for number greater than two, it is called *n*-person game.

(*ii*) Each participant has available to him a list of *finite* number of possible courses of action. The list may not be same for each participant.

(*iii*) Each participant knows all the *possible choices* available to others but does not know which of them is going to be chosen by them.

(iv) *A play* is said to *occur* when each of the participants chooses one of the courses of action available to him. The choices are assumed to be made simultaneously so that no participant knows the choices made by others until he has decided his own.

(v) Every combination of courses of action determines an outcome which results in gains to the participants. The gain may be positive, negative or zero. Negative gain is called a loss.

(vi) The gain of a participant depends not only on his own actions but also those of others.

(vii) The gains (payoffs) for each and every play are fixed and specified in advance and are known to each player. Thus each player knows fully the information contained in the payoff matrix.

(viii) The players make individual decisions without direct communication.

9.12 GAME MODELS

There are various types of game models. They are based on the factors like the number of players participating, the sum of gains or losses and the number of strategies available, etc.

1. *Number of persons* : If a game involves only two players, it is called two-person game; if there are more than two players, it is named *n*-person game. An *n*-person game does not imply that exactly *n* players are involved in it. Rather it means that the participants can be classified into *n* mutually exclusive groups, with all members in a group having identical interests.
2. *Sum of payoffs* : If the sum of payoffs (gains and losses) to the players is zero, the game is called zero-sum or constant-sum game, otherwise non zero-sum game.
3. *Number of strategies* If the number of strategies (moves or choices) is finite, the game is called a finite game; if not, it is called infinite game.

9.13 DEFINITIONS

1. *Game* : It is an activity, between two or more persons, involving actions by each one of them according to a set of rules, which results in some gain (+ve, –ve or zero) for each. If in a game the actions are determined by skills, it is called a *game of strategy*, if they are determined by chance, it is termed as a *game of chance.* Further a game may be *finite* or *infinite*. A finite game has a finite number of *moves* and *choices*, while an infinite game contains an infinite number of them.
2. *Player* : Each participant or competitor playing a game is called a *player.* Each player is equally intelligent and rational in approach.
3. *Play* : A play of the game is said to *occur* when each player chooses one of his courses of action.
4. *Strategy* : It is the predetermined rule by which a player decides his course of action from his list of courses of actions during the game. To decide a particular strategy, the player need not know the other's strategy.
5. *Pure strategy* : It is the decision rule to always select a particular course of action. It is usually represented by a number with which the course of action is associated.
6. *Mixed strategy* : It is decision, in advance of all plays, to choose a course of action for each play in accordance with some probability distribution. Thus, a mixed strategy

is a selection among pure strategies with some fixed probabilities (proportions). The advantage of a mixed strategy, after the pattern of the game has become evident, is that the opponents are kept guessing as to which course of action will be adopted by a player.

Mathematically, a mixed strategy of a player with *m* possible courses of actions is a set X of *m* non-negative numbers whose sum is unity, where each number represents the probability with which each course of action (pure strategy) is chosen. Thus if x_i is the probability of choosing course *i*, then

$$X = (x_1, x_2, ..., x_m),$$

where $$\sum_{i=1}^{m} x_i = 1$$

and $$x_i \geq 0, i = 1, 2, ..., m.$$

Evidently a pure strategy is a special case of mixed strategy in which all but one x_i are zero. A player may be able to choose only *m* pure strategies but he has an infinite number of mixed strategies to choose from.

7. *Optimal strategy* : The strategy that puts the player in the most preferred position irrespective of the strategy of his opponents is called an optimal strategy. Any deviation from this strategy would reduce his payoff.
8. *Zero-sum game* : It is a game in which the sum of payments to all the players, after the play of the game, is zero. In such a game, the gain of players that win is exactly equal to the loss of players that lose *e.g.*, two candidates fighting elections, wherein the gain of votes by one is the loss of votes to the other.
9. *Two-person zero-sum game* : It is a game involving only two players, in which the gain of one player *equals* the loss to the other. It is also called a *rectangular game* or *matrix game* because the payoff matrix is rectangular in form. If there are *n* players and the sum of the game is zero, it is called *n*-person zero-sum game. The characteristics of a two-person zero-sum game are
   (*a*) only two players are involved,
   (*b*) each player has a finite number of strategies to use,
   (*c*) each specific strategy results in a payoff,
   (*d*) total payoff to the two players at the end of each play is zero.
10. *Nonzero-sum game* : Here a third party (*e.g.* the 'house' or a 'kitty') receives or makes some payment. A payoff matrix for such a game is shown below. The left-hand entry in each cell is the payoff to A,

TABLE 9.91

		Player B 1	2
Player A	1	2, 2	– 6, 6
	2	6, – 6	– 2, – 2

and the right-hand entry is the payoff to B. Note that for play combination (1, 1) and (2, 2) the sums of the payoffs are not equal to zero.

11. *Payoff* : It is the outcome of the game. *Payoff (gain or game) matrix* is the table showing the amounts received by the player named at the left-hand side after all possible plays of the game. The payment is made by player named at the top of the table.

Let player A have m courses of action and player B have n courses of action. Then the game can be described by a pair of matrices which can be constructed as described below.

(*a*) Row designations for each matrix are the courses of action available to player A.

(*b*) Column designations for each matrix are the courses of action available to player B.

(*c*) The cell entries are the payments to A for one matrix and to B for the other matrix. The cell entry a_{ij} is the payment to A in A's payoff matrix when A chooses the course of action i and B chooses the course of action j.

(*d*) In a two-person zero-sum game, the cell entries in B's payoff matrix will be the negative of the corresponding cell entries in A's payoff matrix. A is called maximizing player as he would try to maximize the gains, while B is called minimizing player as he would try to minimize his losses.

TABLE 9.92

		Player B				
		1	2	3 ...	j ...	n
	1	a_{11}	a_{12}	a_{13} ...	a_{1j} ...	a_{1n}
	2	a_{21}	a_{22}	a_{23} ...	a_{2j}...	a_{2n}
Player A	3	a_{31}	a_{32}	a_{33} ...	a_{3j}...	a_{3n}
	⋮	⋮	⋮	⋮	⋮	⋮
	i	a_{i1}	a_{i2}	a_{i3} ...	a_{ij}...	a_{in}
	⋮	⋮	⋮	⋮	⋮	⋮
	m	a_{m1}	a_{m2}	a_{m3} ...	a_{mj}...	a_{mn}

A's payoff matrix

TABLE 9.93

		Player B				
		1	2	3	...j	... n
	1	$-a_{11}$	$-a_{12}$	$-a_{13}$	... $-a_{1j}$	... $-a_{1n}$
	2	$-a_{21}$	$-a_{22}$	$-a_{23}$	... $-a_{2j}$	... $-a_{2n}$
	3	$-a_{31}$	$-a_{32}$	$-a_{33}$	... $-a_{3j}$	... $-a_{3n}$
Player A	⋮	⋮	⋮	⋮	⋮	⋮
	i	$-a_{i1}$	$-a_{i2}$	$-a_{i3}$	... $-a_{ij}$	... $-a_{in}$
	⋮	⋮	⋮	⋮	⋮	⋮
	m	$-a_{m1}$	$-a_{m2}$	$-a_{m3}$	... $-a_{mj}$	... $-a_{mn}$

B's payoff matrix

Thus the sum of payoff matrices for A and B is a null matrix. Here, the objective is to determine the optimum strategies of both the players that result in optimum payoff to each, irrespective of the strategy used by the other.

Henceforth, we shall usually omit B's payoff matrix, keeping in mind that it is just the negative of A's payoff matrix.

To explain the above concepts let us consider the following example :

EXAMPLE 9.13-1

Table 9.94 illustrates a game, where competitors A and B are assumed to be equal in ability and intelligence. A has a choice of strategy 1 or strategy 2, while B can select strategy 3 or 4.

TABLE 9.94

Competitor B

		Strategy 3	*Strategy* 4	*Minimum of row*
Competitor A	*Strategy* 1	+4	+6	4
	Strategy 2	+3	+5	3
Maximum of column		4	6	

Both competitors know the payoffs for every possible strategy. It should be noted that the game favours competitor A since all values are positive. Values that favour B would be negative. Based upon these conditions, game is biased against B. However, since B must play the game, he will play to minimize his losses. There are, in all, 2 × 2 = 4 possible combinations of their strategies.

The various possible strategies for the two competitors are :

(1) A wins the highest game value if he plays strategy 1 all the time since it has higher values than strategy 2.

(2) B realizes this situation and plays strategy 3 in order to minimize his losses since the value of 4 in strategy 3 is lower than the value of 6 in strategy 4.

The game value must be 4 since A wins 4 points while B loses 4 points each time the game is played. The *'game value' is the average winnings per play over a long number of plays*. The game illustrated in table 9.94 is a two-person zero-sum game since A wins 4 points in each play while B loses the same amount. A game is solved when the following has been determined:

(*a*) the average amount per play that A will win in the long run if A and B use their best strategies. As explained earlier, it is called the value of the game.

(*b*) the strategy that A should use to ensure that his average gain per play is at least equal to the value of the game.

(*c*) the strategy that B should use to ensure that his average loss per play is no more than the value of the game.

9.14 RULES FOR GAME THEORY

The preceding two-person zero-sum game could be easily solved because of the distribution of values within the game matrix. However, some specific rules must be employed to solve other two-person zero-sum games containing the same number or larger number of rows and columns. The basic rules employed in solving such games are described below.

9.15 RULE 1. LOOK FOR A PURE STRATEGY (SADDLE POINT)

EXAMPLE 9.15-1 (Two-Person Zero-Sum Game with Saddle Point)

In a certain game, player A has three possible choices L, M and N, while player B has two possible choices P and Q. Payments are to be made according to the choices made.

TABLE 9.95

Choices	*Payment*
L, P	*A pays B ₹ 3*
L, Q	*B pays A ₹ 3*
M, P	*A pays B ₹ 2*
M, Q	*B pays A ₹ 4*
N, P	*B pays A ₹ 2*
N, Q	*B pays A ₹ 3*

What are the best strategies for players A and B in this game? What is the value of the game for A and B?

Solution

The above payments can be easily arranged in the form of a matrix. Let positive number represent a payment from B to A and negative number a payment from A to B. We, then, have the payoff matrix shown in table 9.96.

Minimax and maximin values are also shown on the matrix. When player A plays his first strategy (namely L), he may gain – 3 or 3 depending upon player B's selected strategy. He can guarantee, however, a gain of at least min. {– 3, 3} = – 3 regardless of B's selected strategy. Similarly, if A plays his second strategy (namely M), he guarantees an income of at least min. {– 2, 4} = – 2; if he plays his third strategy (namely N) he guarantees an income of at least min. {2, 3} = 2. Thus the minimum value in each row represents the minimum gain guaranteed to A if he plays his *pure (grand) strategies.*

These values are indicated in the matrix under 'Minimum of row'. Now, player A, by selecting his third strategy (N), is maximizing his minimum gain. This gain is given by max. {– 3, – 2, 2} = 2. This selection of player A is called the *maximin strategy* and his corresponding gain is called the *maximin or lower value* of the game.

TABLE 9.96

		Player B *Plans (choices)*		
		P	Q	*Minimum of row*
Player A (plans choices)	L	– 3	3	– 3
	M	– 2	4	– 2
	N	2	3	(2) *maximin*
Miximum of column		(2) *minimax*	4	

Player B, on the other hand, wants to minimize his losses. He realizes that if he plays his first pure strategy (namely P), he can lose no more than max. {–3, –2, 2} = 2, regardless of A's selections. Similarly, if he plays his second pure strategy (Q), the maximum he loses is max. {3, 4, 3} = 4. These values are indicated in the above matrix by 'Maximum of column'. Player B will select the strategy that minimizes his maximum loss. This is given by strategy P and his corresponding loss is given by min. {2, 4} = 2. Player B's selection is called the *minimax strategy* and his corresponding loss is called the *minimax (or upper) value* of the game.

It is seen from the conditions governing the minimax criterion that the minimax (upper) value is *greater than or equal to* the maximin (lower) value. When the two are equal (minimax value = maximin value), the corresponding pure strategies are called *optimal strategies* and the game is said to have a *saddle point or equilibrium point* and is called a *stable game*. The value of the game is given by the saddle point and is equal to the maximin and minimax values. Thus the saddle point is the point of intersection of the two courses of action and the gain at this point is the value of the game. The game is said to be *fair* if maximin value = minimax value = 0, and is said to be *strictly determinable* if maximin value = minimax value ≠ 0. Note that neither player can improve his position by selecting any other strategy. Saddle point is the number which is *lowest in its row and highest in its column.*

In the above example, minimax value = maximin value = 2. The value of the game is thus equal to 2. The game has a saddle point given by the entry (N, P) of the matrix. As the game value is 2, (and not zero), the game is not fair, though it is strictly determinable.

The saddle point solution guarantees that neither player is tempted to select a better strategy. If B moves to the other strategy Q, player A may move to strategy M, which means that B will lose ₹ 4, rather than ₹ 2 at present. Likewise, A does not want to use a different strategy because if A moves to strategy, say L, player B will adopt strategy P so that A will lose ₹ 3, rather than winning ₹ 2 presently.

We summarise below the steps required to detect a saddle point:

(1) At the right of each row, write the row minimum and ring the largest of them.

(2) At the bottom of each column, write the column maximum and ring the smallest of them.

(3) If these two elements are same, the cell where the corresponding row and column meet is a saddle point and the element in that cell is the value of the game.

(4) If the two ringed elements are unequal, there is no saddle point, and the value of the game lies between these two values.

(5) If there are more than one saddle points then there will be more than one solutions, each solution corresponding to each saddle point.

We give below a few more examples of games. Saddle points, if they exist, have been ringed. Optimum strategies and game values are also indicated.

$$\begin{array}{cc} & B \\ A & \begin{bmatrix} -4 & 3 \\ -3 & -7 \end{bmatrix} \end{array}$$

No saddle point exists since there is no element which is both the lowest in its row and highest in its column.

$$\begin{array}{ccl} & B & \\ A & \begin{bmatrix} 3 & 2 \\ -2 & -3 \\ -4 & -5 \end{bmatrix} & \begin{array}{l} (2) \\ -3 \\ -5 \end{array} \\ & \begin{array}{cc} 3 & (2) \end{array} & \end{array}$$

Strategies: A, row 1 and B, column 2.
Saddle point : (1, 2)
Game value: + 2.

$$\begin{array}{ccl} & B & \\ A & \begin{bmatrix} 1 & 13 & 11 \\ -9 & 5 & -11 \\ 0 & -3 & 13 \end{bmatrix} & \begin{array}{l} (1) \\ -11 \\ -3 \end{array} \\ & \begin{array}{ccc} (1) & 13 & 13 \end{array} & \end{array}$$

Saddle point: (1, 1)
Strategies: A, row 1; B, column 1.
Game value: + 1.

$$\begin{array}{ccl} & B & \\ A & \begin{bmatrix} 16 & 4 & 0 & 14 & -2 \\ 10 & 8 & 6 & 10 & 12 \\ 2 & 6 & 4 & 8 & 14 \\ 8 & 10 & 2 & 2 & 0 \end{bmatrix} & \begin{array}{l} -2 \\ (6) \\ 2 \\ 0 \end{array} \\ & \begin{array}{ccccc} 16 & 10 & (6) & 14 & 14 \end{array} & \end{array}$$

Saddle point: (2, 3)
Strategies: A, row 2; B, column 3.
Game value: + 6.

If there is no saddle point, neither player can optimize his chances by using a pure strategy; they must mix some or all of their courses of action, resulting in *mixed strategies*. Methods of finding mixed strategies will be discussed later in this chapter.

Note. *Always look for a saddle point while attempting to solve a game. If the given problem has a saddle point but is solved by other methods, the resulting solution will be incorrect.*

EXAMPLE 9.15-2

Consider the game G with the following payoff

TABLE 9.97

Player B

Player A		B_1	B_2
	A_1	2	6
	A_2	–2	λ

(a) Show that G is strictly determinable, whatever λ may be.

(b) Determine the value of G.

[*Univ. of Madras BBA April, 2012*]

Solution

(*a*) Ignoring whatever the value of λ may be, the given payoff matrix represents

TABLE 9.98

	B_1	B_2	*Row minima*
A_1	2	6	2
A_2	–2	λ	–2
Column maxima	2	6	

∴ Maximin value = 2 and minimax value = 2.

∴ The game G is strictly determinable, whatever λ may be.

(*b*) Value of the game = 2,

strategies: A, row 1; B, column 1.

EXAMPLE 9.15-3

For what value of λ, the game with following payoff matrix is strictly determinable?

TABLE 9.99

Player B

Player A		B_1	B_2	B_3
	A_1	λ	6	2
	A_2	–1	λ	–7
	A_3	–2	4	λ

Solution

Ignoring whatever the value of λ may be, the given payoff matrix represents

TABLE 9.100

	B_1	B_2	B_3	*Row minima*
A_1	λ	6	2	2
A_2	–1	λ	–7	–7
A_3	–2	4	λ	–2
Column maxima	–1	6	2	

∴ Maximin value = 2 and minimax value = – 1.

∴ Value of the game lies between – 1 and 2 *i.e.*, $-1 \le V \le 2$.

∴ For strictly determinable game since maximin value = minimax value, we must have $-1 \le \lambda \le 2$.

EXAMPLE 9.15-4

Find the ranges of values of p and q which will render the entry (2, 2) a saddle point for the game.

TABLE 9.101

Player B

		B_1	B_2	B_3
Player A	A_1	2	4	5
	A_2	10	7	*q*
	A_3	4	*p*	6

[*Sri Venkateshwar M. Sc. (Stat.) 1977*]

Solution

First ignoring the values of *p* and *q* we determine the maximin and minimax values of payoff matrix as follows:

TABLE 9.102

	B_1	B_2	B_3	*Row minima*
A_1	2	4	5	2
A_2	10	7	*q*	7
A_3	4	*p*	6	4
Column maxima	10	7	6	

Since the entry (2, 2) is saddle point for the game,

∴ maximin value = 7,

minimax value = 7.

This imposes the condition on *p* as $p \le 7$ and on *q* as $q \ge 7$.

Hence the range of *p* and *q* will be $p \le 7$, $q \ge 7$.

EXAMPLE 9.15-5

The payoff matrix of a game is given below. Find the solution of the game to A and B.

TABLE 9.103

				B			
		I	*II*	*III*	*IV*	*V*	*Row minima*
	I	–4	–2	–2	3	1	–4
A	*II*	1	0	–1	0	0	(–1)
	III	–6	–5	–2	–4	4	–6
	IV	3	1	–6	0	–8	–8
Column maxima		3	1	(–1)	3	4	

[*G.N.D.U. B.Com. Sept., 2014; Sept., 2013; P.U. B.Com April, 2014; Sept., 2013*]

Solution

The matrix has a saddle point in cell (II, III). Value of the game is –1 to A and +1 to B. The optimum strategies for players A and B are II and III respectively.

9.16 RULE 2. REDUCE GAME BY DOMINANCE

If no pure strategies exist, the next step is to eliminate certain strategies (rows and/or columns) by dominance. Rows and/or columns of the payoff matrix that are inferior to at least one of the remaining rows and/or columns are deleted from further consideration. The resulting game can be solved for some mixed strategy.

EXAMPLE 9.16-1 (3 x 3 Game, Matrix Reduction by Dominance)

Two players P and Q play a game. Each of them has to choose one of the three colours, white (W), black (B) and red (R) independently of the other. Thereafter the colours are compared. If both P and Q have chosen white (W, W), neither wins anything. If player P selects white and player Q black (W, B), player P loses ₹ 2 or player Q wins the same amount and so on. The complete payoff table is shown below (Table 9.104). Find the optimum strategies for P and Q and the value of the game.

TABLE 9.104

		Colour chosen by Q		
		W	*B*	*R*
Colour chosen by P	*W*	*0*	*–2*	*7*
	B	*2*	*5*	*6*
	R	*3*	*–3*	*8*

Solution

This matrix has no saddle point. Evidently, player Q will not play strategy R since this will result in heaviest losses to him and highest gains to player P. He can do better by playing columns W or B. Thus column R is to be deleted and strategy R is called dominated strategy.

The dominance rule for columns is : Every value in the dominating column(s) must be less than or equal to the corresponding value of the dominated column. The resulting matrix is

TABLE 9.105

		Q	
		W	B
P	W	0	–2
	B	2	5
	R	3	–3

From table 9.105, it is clear that player P will not play row W since it will give him returns lower than given by row B. Hence row W is dominated by row B and can be deleted.

The dominance rule for rows is: Every value in the dominating row(s) must be greater than or equal to the corresponding value of the dominated row. The resulting matrix is

TABLE 9.106

		Player Q	
		W	B
Player P	B	2	5
	R	3	–3

This 2 × 2 matrix can be easily solved as discussed later.

Dominance need not be based on the superiority of *pure strategies* only.

A given strategy is also said to be dominated if it is inferior to some *convex linear combination* (*e.g.*, average) of two or more pure strategies. To illustrate this let us consider the following game:

TABLE 9.107

		B		
		1	2	3
A	1	6	1	3
	2	0	9	7
	3	2	3	4

This game has no saddle point. Further, none of the pure strategies of A is inferior to any of his other pure strategies. However, average of A's first and second pure strategies gives us

$$\left(\frac{6+0}{2}, \frac{1+9}{2}, \frac{3+7}{2}\right) = (3, 5, 5).$$

This is obviously superior to A's third pure strategy. Therefore, the third strategy may be deleted from the matrix. The resulting matrix becomes

TABLE 9.108

		B		
		1	2	3
A	1	6	1	3
	2	0	9	7

Remark : 1. *It should be noted that a game reduced by dominance may disclose a saddle point which was not found in the original matrix under rule 1 (look for a pure strategy or saddle point). This is not necessarily a true saddle point since it may not be the least value in its row and the highest value in its column as per the original matrix. Therefore, this pseudo-saddle point is ignored and the reduced game should be solved for mixed strategies.*

2. *The rules of dominance discussed above are used when the payoff matrix is a profit matrix for player A (and a loss matrix for player B); if otherwise, the rules get reversed.*

Note: *Always look for dominance when solving a game.*

9.17 RULE 3. SOLVE FOR A MIXED STRATEGY

In cases where there is no saddle point and dominance has been used to reduce the game matrix, players will resort to mixed strategies. A few different methods will be described to optimize the winning of each player and to solve the game. One of the players must determine what proportion of time to play each row while the other must know what portion of the time to play each column. The payoffs obtained will be the *expected payoffs* and the value of the game will be the *expected value* of the game. Such games are called *unstable games*.

9.18 MIXED STRATEGIES (2 × 2 GAMES)

Arithmetic and algebraic methods are used for finding optimum strategies as well as game value for a 2 × 2 game. Each of these methods will be described in some details now.

9.18-1 Arithmetic Method (Odds Method or Short Cut Method) for Finding Optimum Strategies and Game Value

It provides an easy method for finding the optimum strategies for each player in a 2 × 2 game without a saddle point. It consists of the following steps:

(*i*) subtract the two digits in column 1 and write the difference under column 2, ignoring sign.

(*ii*) subtract the two digits in column 2 and write the difference under column 1, ignoring sign.

(*iii*) similarly proceed for the two rows.

These values are called *oddments*. They are the frequencies with which the players must use their courses of action in their optimum strategies.

EXAMPLE 9.18-1.1 (Two-person zero-sum game without saddle point)

In a game of matching coins, player A wins ₹ 2 if there are two heads, wins nothing if there are two tails and loses Re. 1 when there are one head and one tail. Determine the payoff matrix, best strategies for each player and the value of game to A.

[*V.T.U. Karnataka B.E. June, 2010*]

Solution

The payoff matrix for A will be

TABLE 9.109

		Player B	
		H	T
Player A	H	2	–1
	T	–1	0

Since there is no saddle point, the optimal strategies will be mixed strategies. Using the steps described above we get

TABLE 9.110

		Player B			
		H	T		
Player A	H	2	–1	1	1/3 + 1 = 0.25
	T	–1	0	3	3/3 + 1 = 0.75
		1	3		
		0.25	0.75		

Thus for optimum gains, player A should use strategy H for 25% of the time and strategy T for 75% of the time, while player B should use strategy H 25% of the time and strategy T 75% of the time.

To obtain the value of the game any of the following expressions may be used:

Using A's oddments

B plays H; value of the game, $V = ₹\left(\dfrac{1 \times 2 - 3 \times 1}{3+1}\right) = ₹\left(-\dfrac{1}{4}\right)$.

B plays T; value of the game, $V = ₹\left(\dfrac{1 \times -1 + 3 \times 0}{3+1}\right) = ₹\left(-\dfrac{1}{4}\right)$

Using B's oddments

A plays H; value of the game, $V = ₹\left(\dfrac{1 \times 2 - 1 \times 3}{3+1}\right) = ₹\left(-\dfrac{1}{4}\right)$

A plays T; value of the game, $V = ₹\left(\dfrac{-1 \times 1 + 0 \times 3}{1+3}\right) = ₹\left(-\dfrac{1}{4}\right)$.

The above values of V are equal only if sum of the oddments vertically and horizontally are equal. Cases in which it is not so are treated later.

Thus the full solution of the game is

A (1, 3); B (1, 3); V = ₹ (– 1/4).

This is the value of the game to A *i.e.,* A gains ₹ (–1/4) *i.e.,* he loses ₹ 1/4 which B, in turn, gets. Arithmetic method is easier than algebraic method but it cannot be applied to larger games.

EXAMPLE 9.18-1.2

Reduce the following game by dominance and find the game value:

TABLE 9.111

		Player B			
		I	*II*	*III*	*IV*
	I	3	2	4	0
Player A	*II*	3	4	2	4
	III	4	2	4	0
	IV	0	4	0	8

[P.U. B.Com. April 2014; G.N.D.U. B.Com. April, 2014; Dayalbagh Edu. Inst. Agra MBA Dec., 2013; J.N.T.U. Hyderabad MCA Feb. 2012; V.T.U. Karnataka B.E. June, 2012; P.T.U. B.Tech. (Mech.) 2010; B.Tech. (C.Sc.) 2009; G.N.D.U. B.Com. 2004, 02; P.U. M.Com., 2004, 2003; B.Com. April, 2007; April, 2006; Sept., 2004]

Solution

This matrix has no saddle point. We now try to reduce the size of given payoff matrix by using the concept of dominance.

From player A's point of view, row I is dominated by row III. Row I is, therefore, deleted resulting in the following reduced matrix:

TABLE 9.112

		Player B			
		I	II	III	IV
	II	3	4	2	4
Player A	III	4	2	4	0
	IV	0	4	0	8

From player B's point of view, column I is dominated by III. Column I is, therefore, deleted and the following payoff matrix results:

TABLE 9.113

		Player B		
		II	III	IV
	II	4	2	4
Player A	III	2	4	0
	IV	4	0	8

In the above matrix no single row (or column) dominates another row (column). However, column II is dominated by the average of columns III and IV, which is

$$\begin{bmatrix} \dfrac{2+4}{2} \\ \dfrac{4+0}{2} \\ \dfrac{0+8}{2} \end{bmatrix} = \begin{bmatrix} 3 \\ 2 \\ 4 \end{bmatrix}.$$

Hence column II is deleted, resulting in the following matrix :

TABLE 9.114

		Player B	
		III	IV
	II	2	4
Player A	III	4	0
	IV	0	8

Again, row II is dominated by the average of III and IV rows, which gives $\left(\dfrac{4+0}{2}, \dfrac{0+8}{2}\right)$ = (2, 4). Therefore, row II is deleted and 2 × 2 game matrix results.

TABLE 9.115

		Player B	
		III	IV
	III	4	0
Player A	IV	0	8

The above 2 × 2 matrix can be solved by arithmetic method which consists of the following steps:

(*i*) subtract the two digits in column III and write them under column IV, ignoring sign.
(*ii*) subtract the two digits in column IV and write them under column III, ignoring sign.
(*iii*) similarly proceed for the two rows. Thus we get

TABLE 9.116

		Player B		
		III	IV	
	III	4	0	8 2/3
Player A	IV	0	8	4 1/3
		8	4	
		2/3	1/3	

Thus the complete solution to the given problem is:
Optimal strategy for player A: (0, 0, 2/3, 1/3),
optimal strategy for player B: (0, 0, 2/3, 1/3),
value of the game (for A): $\dfrac{8 \times 4 + 0 \times 4}{8+4} = 8/3.$

EXAMPLE 9.18-1.3

Reduce the following game by dominance property and solve it:

TABLE 9.117

Player B

		1	2	3	4	5
	I	1	3	2	7	4
Player A	II	3	4	1	5	6
	III	6	5	7	6	5
	IV	2	0	6	3	1

[*G.N.D.U. B.Com. April, 2011; P.U. B.Com. April, 2011; April, 2006*]

Solution

Here, row IV is dominated by row III. Deleting row IV we get

TABLE 9.118

Player B

		1	2	3	4	5
	I	1	3	2	7	4
Player A	II	3	4	1	5	6
	III	6	5	7	6	5

Now, column 4 is dominated by columns 1 and 2, also column 5 is dominated by column 2. Therefore, deleting columns 4 and 5 we have

TABLE 9.119

Player B

		1	2	3
	I	1	3	2
Player A	II	3	4	1
	III	6	5	7

In the above matrix, row I as well as II are dominated by row III. Therefore, we delete rows I and II and get

TABLE 9.120

Player B

		1	2	3
Player A	III	6	5	7

Out of the three strategies available to player B, he will use no. 2 in order to minimize his losses. Therefore, the solution to the problem is

Optimal strategy for A: III, optimal strategy for B: 2; game value (for A): 5.

Remark: *Reduction of this problem by the rules of dominance has resulted in saddle point (III, 2). This is because the original problem has the saddle point. It was reduced as per the statement of the problem; otherwise it should have been directly solved using the saddle point method.*

EXAMPLE 9.18-1.4

Solve the following game by using the principle of dominance:

TABLE 9.121

		Player B					
		I	*II*	*III*	*IV*	*V*	*VI*
	1	4	2	0	2	1	1
	2	4	3	1	3	2	2
Player A	*3*	4	3	7	–5	1	2
	4	4	3	4	–1	2	2
	5	4	3	3	–2	2	2

[*G.N.D.U. B.Com. April, 2011; P.U. B.Com. April, 2012; V.T.U. Karnataka B.E. June, 2011*]

Solution

The above payoff matrix has no saddle point. From player A's point of view, row 1 is dominated by row 2 and row 5 is dominated by row 4. Accordingly, rows 1 and 5 are deleted. The following reduced matrix results.

TABLE 9.122

		Player B					
		I	II	III	IV	V	VI
	2	4	3	1	3	2	2
Player A	3	4	3	7	–5	1	2
	4	4	3	4	–1	2	2

From player B's point of view, columns I and II are dominated by columns IV, V and VI; also column VI is dominated by column V. Therefore, columns I, II and VI are deleted, resulting in

TABLE 9.123

		Player B		
		III	IV	V
	2	1	3	2
Player A	3	7	–5	1
	4	4	–1	2

Now none of single row (or column) dominates another row (or column). However, column V is dominated by the average of columns III and IV, which is

$$\begin{bmatrix} \dfrac{1+3}{2} \\ \dfrac{7-5}{2} \\ \dfrac{4-1}{2} \end{bmatrix} = \begin{bmatrix} 2 \\ 1 \\ 3/2 \end{bmatrix}.$$

Accordingly, column V is deleted and the following matrix is obtained:

TABLE 9.124

		Player B	
		III	IV
	2	1	3
Player A	3	7	–5
	4	4	–1

Further, row 4 is dominated by the average of row 2 and 3. Hence row 4 is deleted. The resulting 2 × 2 game is shown below.

TABLE 9.125

		Player B	
		III	IV
	2	1	3
Player A	3	7	–5

Solving this game by arithmetic method we have

TABLE 9.126

		Player B				
		III	IV			
	2	1	3	12	6	6/7
Player A	3	7	–5	2	1	1/7
		8	6			
		4	3			
		4/7	3/7			

Therefore, optimal strategy for A: (0, 6/7, 1/7, 0, 0),
optimal strategy for B: (0, 0, 4/7, 3/7, 0, 0),

game value: $\dfrac{1\times8+3\times6}{8+6}=\dfrac{26}{14}=\dfrac{13}{7}$.

EXAMPLE 9.18-1.5

A and B play a game in which each has three coins a 5p, a l0p and a 20p. Each player selects a coin without the knowledge of the other's choice. If the sum of the coins is an odd amount, A wins B's coin; if the sum is even, B wins A's coin. Find the best strategy for each player and the value of the game. [*Univ. of Mumbai PGDM, 2012; J.N.T.U. Hyderabad B.Tech. (C.Sc.) Dec., 2011; May, 2009; R.U. M.Sc. (Math.) 2011; G.N.D.U. B.Com., Sept., 2010; Sept., 2008; 2006; P.T.U. B.Tech. (Mech.) 2010; P.U. B.Com. April, 2011; Sept., 2009 Sept., 2006; April, 2007; April, 2006*]

Solution

A's payoff matrix for the given problem is shown in table 9.127.

TABLE 9.127

			Player B		
			(5)	(10)	(20)
			I	II	III
	(5)	I	–5	10	20
Player A	(10)	II	5	–10	–10
	(20)	III	5	–20	–20

This game has no saddle point. Column III is dominated by column II and is, therefore, deleted. This yields table 9.128.

TABLE 9.128

			Player B (5) I	(10) II
	(5)	I	–5	10
Player A	(10)	II	5	–10
	(20)	III	5	–20

Row III is dominated by row II and the following 2 × 2 matrix is obtained:

TABLE 9.129

			Player B (5) I	(10) II		
Player A	(5)	I	–5	10	15	1/2
	(10)	II	5	–10	15	1/2
			20	10		
			2/3	1/3		

On solving by arithmetic method, the following solution is obtained :
Optimal strategy for player A: (1/2, 1/2, 0),
optimal strategy for player B: (2/3, 1/3, 0), and

value of the game for player A: $\dfrac{-5 \times 15 + 5 \times 15}{15 + 15} = 0.$

Thus the optimal strategies are that none of the players should choose 20 p coin. Player A should select 5p and 10p coins equally *i.e.*, each for half of the time while player B should select 5p coin for 2/3rd of the time and 10p coin for 1/3rd of the time.

EXAMPLE 9.18-1.6

Solve the following game :

TABLE 9.130

		Player B B_1	B_2
	A_1	30	2
Player A	A_2	4	14
	A_3	6	9

[*P.T.U. M.Tech. Dec., 2011*]

Solution

This game has no saddle point. None of the single row dominates another row. However, sum of $\frac{1}{4}$ of row A_1 and $\frac{3}{4}$ of row A_2 yields

$$30 \times \tfrac{1}{4} + 4 \times \tfrac{3}{4} = \tfrac{42}{4} = \tfrac{21}{2},$$

and $2 \times \tfrac{1}{4} + 14 \times \tfrac{3}{4} = \tfrac{44}{4} = 11.$

These values are conistently higher than the elements of row A_3. Thus row A_3 is dominated and is therefore deleted, yielding:

TABLE 9.131

		Player B			
		B_1	B_2		
Player A	A_1	30	2	10	$5/19$
	A_2	4	14	28	$14/19$
		12	26		
		$6/19$	$13/19$		

On solving by arithmetic method, the following solution is obtained:

Optimal strategy for player A: $\left(5/19, 14/19, 0\right)$,

optimal strategy for player B: $\left(6/19, 13/19\right)$,

game value : $30 \times 6/19 + 2 \times 13/19 = 206/19$.

EXAMPLE 9.18-1.7

A company is currently involved in negotiations with its union on the upcoming wage contract. Positive signs in table 9.132 represent wage increase while negative sign represents wage reduction. What are the optimal strategies for the company as well as the union? What is the game value ?

TABLE 9.132

Conditional costs to the company (₹ in lakhs)

		Union strategies			
		U_1	U_2	U_3	U_4
Company strategies	C_1	+ 0.25	+ 0.27	+ 0.35	– 0.02
	C_2	+ 0.20	+ 0.16	+ 0.08	+ 0.08
	C_3	+ 0.14	+ 0.12	+ 0.15	+ 0.13
	C_4	+ 0.30	+ 0.14	+ 0.19	+ 0.00

[*Delhi U. M.B.A., 1994*]

Solution

Since in a game matrix, player to its left is a maximizing player and the one at the top is a minimizing player, table 9.132 is transposed and rewritten as table 9.133 since the company's interest is to minimize the wage increase while union's interest is to get the maximum wage increase.

TABLE 9.133

		Company strategies			
		C_1	C_2	C_3	C_4
Union strategies	U_1	0.25	0.20	0.14	0.30
	U_2	0.27	0.16	0.12	0.14
	U_3	0.35	0.08	0.15	0.19
	U_4	– 0.02	0.08	0.13	0.00

In table 9.133, row U_4 is dominated by row U_1 as well as U_3. It is, therefore, deleted to give table 9.134.

TABLE 9.134

Company strategies

		C_1	C_2	C_3	C_4
Union	U_1	0.25	0.20	0.14	0.30
strategies	U_2	0.27	0.16	0.12	0.14
	U_3	0.35	0.08	0.15	0.19

In table 9.134, column C_1 is dominated by C_2 as well as C_3, while C_4 is dominated by C_3. Deleting columns C_1 and C_4 we get

TABLE 9.135

Company strategies

		C_2	C_3
	U_1	0.20	0.14
Union	U_2	0.16	0.12
strategies	U_3	0.08	0.15

In table 9.135, row U_2 is dominated by U_1 and is, therefore, deleted to give

TABLE 9.136

Company strategies

		C_2	C_3		
Union	U_1	0.20	0.14	0.07	$7/13$
strategies	U_3	0.08	0.15	0.06	$6/13$
		0.01	0.12		
		$1/13$	$12/13$		

Arithmetic method yields the following solution:

Optimal strategy for the company : $\left(0, \frac{1}{13}, \frac{12}{13}, 0\right)$,

optimal strategy for the union : $\left(\frac{7}{13}, 0, \frac{6}{13}, 0\right)$,

value of the game : ₹ $\left(0.20 \times \frac{1}{13} + 0.14 \times \frac{12}{13}\right)$ lakh $=$ ₹ $\frac{1.88}{13}$ lakh.

9.18-2 Algebraic Method for Finding Optimum Strategies and Game Value

While applying this method it is assumed that x represents the fraction of time (frequency) for which player A uses strategy 1 and $(1 - x)$ represents the fraction of time (frequency) for which he uses strategy 2. Similarly, y and $(1 - y)$ represent the fraction of time for which player B uses strategies 1 and 2 respectively.

EXAMPLE 9.18-2.1 (Two-person zero-sum game without saddle point)

The two armies are at war. Army A has two airbases, one of which is thrice as valuable as the other. Army B can destroy an undefended airbase, but it can destroy only one of them. Army A can also defend only one of them. Find the best strategy for A to minimize its losses.

[P.U. B.Com. April, 2008]

Solution

Since both armies have only two possible courses of action, the gain matrix for army A is

TABLE 9.137

			Army B	
			1 *Attack the smaller airbase*	2 *Attack the larger airbase*
Army A	*Defend smaller airbase*	1	*0* *Both survive*	*–3* *The larger one destroyed*
	Defend larger airbase	2	*–1* *The smaller one destroyed*	*0* *Both survive*

There is no saddle point. Under this method, army A wants to divide its plays between the two rows so that the expected winnings by playing the first row are exactly equal to the expected winnings by playing the second row irrespective of what army B does. In order to arrive at the optimum strategies for Army A, it is necessary to equate its expected winnings when army B plays column 1 to its expected winnings when army B plays column 2.

i.e., when $0x + (-1)(1-x) = -3x + 0(1-x)$

or when $-1 + x = -3x$ *i.e.,* $4x = 1 \therefore x = 1/4$.

Thus army A should play first row 1/4th of the time and second row 3/4th ($= 1 - x$) of the time.

Similarly, army B wants to divide its time between columns 1 and 2 so that the expected winnings are same by playing each column, no matter what army A does. Optimum strategies for army B will be found by equating its expected winnings when army A plays row 1 to its expected winnings when army A plays row 2.

i.e., when $0.y - 3(1-y) = -1.y + 0(1-y)$

or when $-3 + 3y = -y$

or when $4y = 3$, or when $y = 3/4$.

Thus army B should play first column 3/4th of the time and second column 1/4th ($= 1 - y$) of the time. These optimum strategies can be shown on the gain matrix, which becomes

TABLE 9.138

		Army B		
		1	2	
Army A	1	0	–3	1/4
	2	–1	0	3/4
		3/4	1/4	

The game value can be found either for army A or for army B.

Game value for army A: While army B plays column 1, 3/4 of time, army A wins zero for 1/4 time and – 1 for 3/4 time; also while army B plays column 2 for 1/4 of time, army A wins –3 for 1/4 time and zero for 3/4 time.

∴ Total expected winnings for army A are

$$\text{game value} = \frac{3}{4}\left(0 \times \frac{1}{4} - 1 \times \frac{3}{4}\right) + \frac{1}{4}\left(-3 \times \frac{1}{4} + 0 \times \frac{3}{4}\right) = -\frac{9}{16} - \frac{3}{16} = -\frac{3}{4}.$$

Game value for army B: While army A plays row 1, 1/4 of time, army B wins zero for 3/4 of time and –3 for 1/4 of time; also while army A plays row 2, 3/4 of time, army B wins –1 for 3/4 of time and zero for 1/4 of time.

$$\therefore \text{ Game value for army B} = \frac{1}{4}\left(\frac{3}{4}\times 0 - 3\times\frac{1}{4}\right) + \frac{3}{4}\left[\frac{3}{4}\times(-1) + 0\times\frac{1}{4}\right]$$

$$= \frac{1}{4}\left(-\frac{3}{4}\right) + \frac{3}{4}\left(-\frac{3}{4}\right) = -\frac{3}{16} - \frac{9}{16} = -\frac{12}{16} = -\frac{3}{4}.$$

Thus the full solution of the game is

army A: $\left(\frac{1}{4}, \frac{3}{4}\right)$, army B: $\left(\frac{3}{4}, \frac{1}{4}\right)$, game value $= -\frac{3}{4}$.

EXAMPLE 9.18-2.2

For any 2 × 2 two-person zero-sum game without any saddle point, having payoff matrix for player A as

TABLE 9.139

		Player B	
		B_1	B_2
	A_1	a_{11}	a_{12}
Player A	A_2	a_{21}	a_{22}

find the optimal mixed strategies and value of the game. [*IAS, 1987*]

Solution

Let x and $(1 - x)$ be the probabilities of selecting strategies A_1 and A_2 by player A, and y and $(1 - y)$ be the probabilities of selecting strategies B_1 and B_2 by player B.

Then the expected value of the game to player A is given by

$$E(x, y) = x\, y\, a_{11} + (1 - x)\, y\, a_{21} + x\,(1 - y)\, a_{12} + (1 - x)(1 - y)\, a_{22}.$$

In order to determine the optimum values of x and y, we now differentiate $E(x, y)$ partially w.r.t x and y.

$$\therefore \quad \frac{\partial}{\partial x}[E(x, y)] = ya_{11} - ya_{21} + (1 - y)a_{12} - (1 - y)a_{22},$$

and $$\frac{\partial}{\partial y}[E(x, y)] = xa_{11} + (1 - x)a_{21} - xa_{12} - (1 - x)a_{22}.$$

By setting $\frac{\partial}{\partial x}[E(x, y)] = 0$ and $\frac{\partial}{\partial y}[E(x, y)] = 0$, we get

$$y\,(a_{11} - a_{21} - a_{12} + a_{22}) = a_{22} - a_{12}$$

or $$y = \frac{a_{22} - a_{12}}{a_{11} + a_{22} - (a_{12} + a_{21})},$$

and $$x\,(a_{11} - a_{21} - a_{12} + a_{22}) = a_{22} - a_{21}$$

or $$x = \frac{a_{22} - a_{21}}{a_{11} + a_{22} - (a_{12} + a_{21})}.$$

Substituting these values of x, y in $E(x, y)$, the required value of the game is

$$V = E(x, y) = \frac{a_{11}a_{22} - a_{12}a_{21}}{(a_{11} + a_{22}) - (a_{12} + a_{21})}.$$

EXAMPLE 9.18-2.3

A game has the payoff matrix $A = \begin{pmatrix} 0 & 1 \\ 2 & 1 \end{pmatrix}$. *Show that E (x, y) = 1– 2y (x – 1/2) and deduce that in the solution of the game, the second player follows a pure strategy while the first has infinite number of mixed strategies.*

[B.H.U. (Stat.) 1968]

Solution

Suppose A uses his first and second pure strategies with probabilities x and $(1 - x)$ and B uses mixed strategy $(y, 1 - y)$. Then the expected payoff is given by

$$E(x, y) = 0.x.y + 1.x.(1 - y) + 2.(1 - x).y + 1.(1 - x)(1 - y)$$
$$= 1 - 2y\,(x - \tfrac{1}{2}).$$

Then using the results of example 9.18-2.2,

$$y_1 = y = \frac{a_{22} - a_{12}}{(a_{11} + a_{22}) - (a_{12} + a_{21})} = \frac{1 - 1}{(0 + 1) - (1 + 2)} = 0,$$

$$y_2 = 1 - y_1 = 1,$$

and $$x_1 = x = \frac{a_{22} - a_{21}}{(a_{11} + a_{22}) - (a_{12} + a_{21})} = \frac{1 - 2}{-2} = \tfrac{1}{2},$$

$$x_2 = 1 - x_1 = 1 - \tfrac{1}{2} = \tfrac{1}{2},$$

value of game, $$V = \frac{a_{11}a_{22} - a_{12}a_{21}}{(a_{11} + a_{22}) - (a_{12} + a_{21})} = \frac{0 \times 1 - 1 \times 2}{-2} = 1.$$

Thus B's optimum strategy is (0, 1) which means that B should always use his second pure strategy. Also A's optimum mixed strategy is $\left(\tfrac{1}{2}, \tfrac{1}{2}\right)$.

Now we also know that if B follows his optimum strategy, A can use his supporting strategies, either singly or in any proportion. Thus B has one optimum pure strategy, while A has infinite number of optimum mixed strategies.

9.19 MIXED STRATEGIES (2 × n GAMES OR m × 2 GAMES)

These are the games in which one player has only two courses of action open to him while his opponent may have any number. To solve such games, the first step is to look for a saddle point; if there is one, the game is readily solved. If not, the next step is to reduce the given matrix to 2 × 2 size by the rules of dominance. If the matrix can be reduced to 2 × 2 size, it can be easily solved by the arithmetic or other methods described in section 9.18. If, however, the given matrix cannot be reduced to 2 × 2 size, it can be still solved by algebraic method, method of subgames and graphical method. Each of these methods will now be explained to some length.

9.19-1 Algebraic Method for 2 × n or m × 2 games

The payoffs for a rectangular game can always be given by $m \times n$ matrix, where player A has m possible courses of action and player B has n possible courses of action and the payoff matrix is (a_{ij}). This is shown in table 9.140 below.

TABLE 9.140

				B			
		1	2	··	j	···	n
	1	a_{11}	a_{12}	··	a_{1j}	···	a_{1n}
	2	a_{21}	a_{22}	··	a_{2j}	···	a_{2n}
	⋮		⋮	⋮		⋮	
A	i	a_{i1}	a_{i2}	··	a_{ij}	···	a_{in}
			⋮	⋮		⋮	
	m	a_{m1}	a_{m2}	··	a_{mj}	···	a_{mn}

It can be shown mathematically that

1. Each rectangular game has a specific value V. This value is unique.
2. There exists for player A a best strategy X *i.e.,* there exist frequencies $x_1, x_2, ..., x_m$ such that $x_1 + x_2 + ... + x_m = 1$ and such that if he plays strategy 1 with frequency x_1, strategy 2 with frequency x_2, ..., strategy m with frequency x_m, then he can assure himself at least an expected gain of V, where V is the value of the game.
3. Similarly for player B, there exists a best strategy,

$$Y = (y_1, y_2, ..., y_n), \sum_{j=1}^{n} y_j = 1,$$

such that if he plays strategies 1, 2, ..., *n,* with frequencies $y_1, y_2, ..., y_n$ respectively, he can assure himself *at most* a loss of V.

It can be shown that the unknown (frequencies) $x_1, x_2, ..., x_m; y_1, y_2, ..., y_n$ and V can be found from the following relations:

$$x_1 + x_2 + ... + x_m = 1, x_i \geq 0, \qquad ... (9.1)$$

$$y_1 + y_2 + ... + y_n = 1, y_j \geq 0, \qquad ... (9.2)$$

$$x_1 a_{1j} + x_2 a_{2j} + ... + x_m a_{mj} \geq V, \text{ for } j = 1, 2, ..., n, \qquad ... (9.3)$$

$$y_1 a_{i1} + y_2 a_{i2} + ... + y_n a_{in} \leq V, \text{ for } i = 1, 2, ..., m. \qquad ... (9.4)$$

Relation (9.3) actually represents n inequalities, one inequality for each j. Similarly, relation (9.4) represents m inequalities. We, thus, have $m + n - 1$ unknowns with $m + n + 2$ relations (with added restrictions $x_i \geq 0$, $y_j \geq 0$ since negative frequencies have no meaning).

The *algebraic method* is a direct method to solve for the unknowns from relations (9.1), (9.2), (9.3) and (9.4). It must be borne in mind that each rectangular game has a value, namely V, which exists and is unique. Therefore, the idea is to find such value V which satisfies all the four relations. The first obvious step is to assume that relations (9.3) and (9.4) are equalities. We shall consider an example to describe how algebraic method can help to solve $2 \times n$ or $m \times 2$ games.

EXAMPLE 9.19-1.1

Solve by algebraic method the game for which the payoff matrix is given in table 9.141.

TABLE 9.141

		B	
		1	*2*
	1	–2	–4
A	*2*	–1	3
	3	1	2

Solution

From the above discussion, we get the following relations for the unknowns x_1, x_2, x_3; y_1, y_2 and V:

$$x_1 + x_2 + x_3 = 1, \qquad \text{... (9.5)}$$
$$y_1 + y_2 = 1, \qquad \text{... (9.6)}$$
$$x_1(-2) + x_2(-1) + x_3(1) \geq V, \qquad \text{... (9.7)}$$
$$x_1(-4) + x_2(3) + x_3(2) \geq V, \qquad \text{... (9.8)}$$
$$y_1(-2) + y_2(-4) \leq V, \qquad \text{... (9.9)}$$
$$y_1(-1) + y_2(3) \leq V, \qquad \text{... (9.10)}$$
$$y_1(1) + y_2(2) \leq V. \qquad \text{... (9.11)}$$

Thus we have six unknowns x_1, x_2, x_3; y_1, y_2 and V and seven relations.

Now the first step towards solution is to assume all the inequalities as equalities and we get

$$x_1 + x_2 + x_3 = 1, \qquad \text{... (9.12)}$$
$$y_1 + y_2 = 1, \qquad \text{... (9.13)}$$
$$-2x_1 - x_2 + x_3 = V, \qquad \text{... (9.14)}$$
$$-4x_1 + 3x_2 + 2x_3 = V, \qquad \text{... (9.15)}$$
$$-2y_1 - 4y_2 = V, \qquad \text{... (9.16)}$$
$$-y_1 + 3y_2 = V, \qquad \text{... (9.17)}$$
$$y_1 + 2y_2 = V. \qquad \text{... (9.18)}$$

Now considering equations (9.13), (9.16) and (9.17),

$$y_2 = 1 - y_1,$$
$$-2y_1 - 4(1 - y_1) = V \text{ or } -2y_1 - 4 + 4y_1 = V \text{ or } 2y_1 - 4 = V,$$

and $\quad -y_1 + 3(1 - y_1) = V$ or $-y_1 + 3 - 3y_1 = V$ or $-4y_1 + 3 = V$.

$\therefore \quad 2y_1 - 4 = -4y_1 + 3$ *i.e.*, $6y_1 = 7$ or $y_1 = 7/6$.

This is unacceptable, since frequency y_1 cannot be greater than 1 ($0 \leq y_1 \leq 1$). Therefore, if we assume relations (9.9) and (9.10) as equalities, we do not get a solution.

A general procedure is, then, to assume one inequality and the other relations as equalities. If we again meet with a contradiction, we assume other inequalities until a solution is finally reached.

However, these computations can be made simpler with the help of the following theorems:

Theorem 1 states that : if $x_1a_{1j} + x_2a_{2j} + ... + x_ma_{mj} > V$, then $y_j = 0$.

Theorem 2 states that : if $y_1a_{i1} + y_2a_{i2} + ... + y_na_{in} < V$, then, $x_i = 0$.

Let us apply these theorems to our problem. We, therefore, proceed as follows:

(1) Thus if $-2x_1 - x_2 + x_3 > V$, then $y_1 = 0$. Therefore, equations (9.16), (9.17) and (9.18) can be true only if $y_2 = 0$.
$\therefore y_1 + y_2 = 0$, which is contradicted by equation (9.13).

(2) Similarly, a contradiction is obtained if $-4x_1 + 3x_2 + 2x_3 > V$.

(3) If $-2y_1 - 4y_2 < V$, then $x_1 = 0$ and equations (9.12), (9.14) and (9.15) will lead to contradiction. Proceeding in this manner, we finally find that only the following relations lead to a solution:

$$x_1 + x_2 + x_3 = 1, \qquad \text{...(9.12)}$$
$$y_1 + y_2 = 1, \qquad \text{...(9.13)}$$
$$-2x_1 - x_2 + x_3 = V, \qquad \text{...(9.14)}$$
$$-4x_1 + 3x_2 + 2x_3 > V, \qquad \text{...(9.15}a\text{)}$$
$$-2y_1 - 4y_2 < V, \qquad \text{...(9.16}a\text{)}$$
$$-y_1 + 3y_2 < V, \qquad \text{...(9.17}a\text{)}$$
$$y_1 + 2y_2 = V. \qquad \text{...(9.18)}$$

From relation (9.15*a*), $y_2 = 0$, so that $y_1 = 1$. Further, from relation (9.16*a*), $x_1 = 0$ and from relation (9.17*a*), $x_2 = 0$, so that $x_3 = 1$. Substituting the values of y_1 and y_2 in (9.18), V = 1. Therefore, the final solution is given by

$x_1 = 0, x_2 = 0, x_3 = 1\ \ y_1 = 1, y_2 = 0$ and V = 1.

i.e., optimum strategy for A is, A (0, 0, 1),

optimum strategy for B is, B (1, 0),

game value = + 1.

Evidently, the algebraic solution of the game is very lengthy and the computations become much more complex as the number of possible choices for A & B increase.

Remark. *The above problem can be easily solved by locating the saddle point. However, it has been solved by algebraic method just to illustrate the method.*

9.19-2 Method of Subgames for 2 × n or m × 2 Games

This method subdivides the given 2 × *n* or *m* × 2 game into a number of 2 × 2 subgames, each of which is then solved and then the optimal strategies are determined. While trying to solve, *first find out for each subgame if a saddle point exists and the subgame has a pure strategy. In case there is no saddle point, then solve the subgame by arithmetic or algebraic method.* Examples 9.19-2.1 and 9.19-2.2 explain this method.

EXAMPLE 9.19-2.1 (2 × 3 Game, No Dominance)

Two airlines operate the same air route, both trying to get as large a market as possible. Based on a certain market, daily gains and losses in rupees are shown in table 9.142 in which positive values favour airline A and negative values favour airline B. Find the solution for the game.

TABLE 9.142

		Airline B		
		Does nothing	*Advertises special rates*	*Advertises special features (i.e., movies, fine food)*
Airline A	*Advertises special rates*	*275*	*–50*	*–75*
	Advertises special features (i.e., movies, fine food)	*125*	*130*	*150*

[P.U.B.Com. April, 2006]

Solution

We see that the game has no saddle point, nor it can be reduced by dominance. This game can be solved by algebraic method described in section 9.19-1, but we shall solve this game here by the method of subgames.

This 2 × 3 game can be thought of as three 2 × 2 subgames:

Subgame 1:

		B	
		1	2
A	1	275	–50
	2	125	130

(Ignoring column 3)

Subgame 2:

		B 1	3	
A	1	275	–75	(Ignoring column 2)
	2	125	150	

Subgame 3:

		B 2	3	
A	1	–50	–75	(Ignoring column 1)
	2	130	150	

Airline B which has more number of columns (than the number of rows for A), has more flexibility, generally resulting in a better strategy. In order to find optimum strategy for airline B, all the above three 2 × 2 subgames must be solved for their strategies and game values. We shall solve them by arithmetic method.

Subgame 1:

		B 1	2			
A	1	275	–50	5	1	1/66
	2	125	130	325	65	65/66
		180	150			
		6	5			
		36	30			
		36/66	30/66			

There is no saddle point.

∴ The strategy for A is, A (1/66, 65/66),
the strategy for B is, B (36/66, 30/66, 0),

$$\text{game value} = ₹\left(\frac{275 \times 1 + 125 \times 65}{66}\right) = ₹\ 127.27.$$

Subgame 2:

		B 1	3			
A	1	275	–75	25	1	1/15
	2	125	150	350	14	14/15
		225	150			
		3	2			
		3/5	2/5			
		9/15	6/15			

There is no saddle point.

Thus strategies are: A (1/15, 14/15),
B (9/15, 0, 6/15),

$$\text{value of the game, V} = ₹\left(\frac{275 \times 3 - 75 \times 2}{5}\right) = ₹\left(\frac{825 - 150}{5}\right) = ₹\ 135.$$

Subgame 3 :

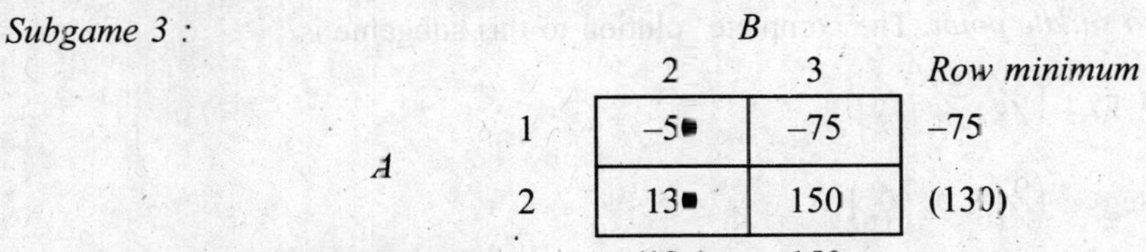

		B: 2	3	Row minimum
A	1	–50	–75	–75
	2	130	150	(130)
Column maximum		(130)	150	

Thus this subgame has a saddle point (2, 2). Thus solution is

A (0, 1), B (0, 1, 0), V = ₹ 130.

Now, since airline B has the flexibility to play any two out of the courses of action available to it, it will play those strategies for which the loss occurring to the airline is minimum. As the values for all the subgames are positive, airline A is the winner. Hence airline B will play subgame 1 for which the loss is minimum *i.e.,* ₹ 127.27.

Hence the complete solution to the problem is

strategies: A (1/66, 65/66), B (36/66, 30/66, 0).

game value V = ₹ 127.27.

Remark: *Subgame 3 has a saddle point, hence arithmetic or algebraic method should not be applied to solve it. If it is applied, the resulting solution will be incorrect.*

EXAMPLE 6.19-2.2

Solve the following 2 × n game by the method of subgames:

TABLE 9.143

		Player B: B_1	B_2	B_3
Player A	A_1	*1*	*3*	*11*
	A_2	*8*	*5*	*2*

[J.N.T.U. Hyderabad B.Tech. May, 2011; P.U. B.Com. April, 2008]

Solution

Table 9.143 has no saddle point. Also it cannot be reduced by the property of dominance. The given 2 × 3 game matrix can be split up into three 2 × 2 subgames. Using arithmetic method, the following subgames and their solutions are obtained:

Subgame 1

		B: B_1	B_2	Row minimum	
A	A_1	1	3	1	*(Ignoring*
	A_2	8	5	(5)	*column B_3)*
Column maximum		8	(5)		

This subgame has a saddle point (A_2, B_2). Thus solution is

A : strategy A_2,

B : strategy B_2,

game value: 5.

Subgame II

		B: B_1	B_3				
A	A_1	1	11	6	3	3/8	*(Ignoring*
	A_2	8	2	10	5	5/8	*column B_2)*
		9	7				
		9/16	7/15				

It has no saddle point. The complete solution to this subgame is

A's strategy : $\left(\frac{3}{8}, \frac{5}{8}\right)$,

B's strategy : $\left(\frac{9}{16}, 0, \frac{7}{16}\right)$,

game value : $\frac{1\times 6 + 10\times 8}{6+10} = \frac{86}{16} = 5.375.$

Subgame III

		B				
A	A_1	B_2	B_3	3	3/11	*(Ignoring*
	A_2	3	11	8	8/11	*column B_1)*
		5	2			
		9	2			
		9/11	2/11			

It has no saddle point. The complete solution to this subgame is

A's strategy : $\left(\frac{3}{11}, \frac{8}{11}\right)$,

B's strategy : $\left(0, \frac{9}{11}, \frac{2}{11}\right)$,

game value: $\frac{3\times 3 + 5\times 8}{3+8} = \frac{9+40}{11} = 4.46.$

Now player B has the flexibility to play any two out of the courses of action available to him. However, he will play those strategies for which the loss occurring to him is the minimum. Since the values for all the subgames are positive, player A is the winner. Therefore, player B will play subgame III for which his loss is minimum. Hence the complete solution to the problem is

$$A\left(\frac{3}{11}, \frac{8}{11}\right),\ B\left(0, \frac{9}{11}, \frac{2}{11}\right);\ V = 4.46.$$

9.19-3 Graphical Method for 2 × n or m × 2 Games

Graphical method is applicable to only those games in which one of the players has two strategies only. The advantage of this method is that it is relatively fast. It reduces the $2 \times n$ or $m \times 2$ game to 2×2 size by *identifying and eliminating the dominated strategies* and then solves it by the analytical (algebraic or arithmetic) methods discussed earlier. The resulting solution is also the solution to the original problem. The method is interesting as it explains the idea of the saddle point graphically. Consider the following $2 \times n$ game :

TABLE 9.144

	B			
	y_1	y_2	…	y_n
A x_1	a_{11}	a_{12}	…	a_{1n}
$x_2 = 1 - x_1$	a_{21}	a_{22}	…	a_{2n}

It is assumed that the game has no saddle point. Player A has two strategies A_1 and A_2 which he mixes with probabilities x_1 and $x_2 = 1 - x_1$, where $0 \le x_1 \le 1$. Player B has n strategies B_1, B_2, ..., B_n which he mixes with probabilities $y_1, y_2, ..., y_n$, where $y_1, y_2, ..., y_n$, each ≥ 0 and $y_1 + y_2 + ... + y_n = 1$. The objective is to determine the optimal values of x_1 and x_2.

Expected payoffs for A corresponding to the pure strategies of B are given below.

TABLE 9.145

B's pure strategies	*A's expected payoffs*
1	$a_{11}x_1 + a_{21}(1 - x_1) = (a_{11} - a_{21})x_1 + a_{21}$
2	$a_{12}x_1 + a_{22}(1 - x_1) = (a_{12} - a_{22})x_1 + a_{22}$
⋮	⋮
n	$a_{1n}x_1 + a_{2n}(1 - x_1) = (a_{1n} - a_{2n})x_1 + a_{2n}$

Thus A's expected payoffs vary linearly with x_1. Now, according to the maximin criterion for mixed strategies, A should select that value of x_1 which maximizes his minimum expected payoff. This may be done by plotting the above lines as a function of x_1. This is shown in figure 9.26. When A chooses strategy A_1, $x_1 = 1$ and the probability with which he chooses strategy A_2 *i.e.*, $x_2 = 0$. Probability x_1 is represented by the horizontal line and strategies A_2 and A_1 are represented by two vertical lines unit distance apart. A's expected payoffs are represented by the sloping lines. A number is allotted to each line corresponding to B's pure strategy. The lower boundary (envelope) of these lines (shown by heavy lines) gives the minimum expected payoff to A as a function of x_1. Since A is maximizing player, the highest point on this lower boundary (shown by a dot), then gives the maximin expected payoff to A and hence the optimum value $x_1 = (x_1^*)$.

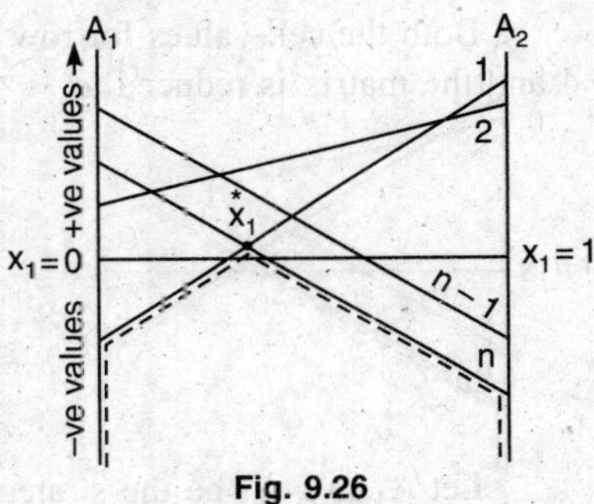

Fig. 9.26

The two optimum strategies for B are given by the two lines which pass through this *maximin point.* Thus the 2 × n game is reduced to 2 × 2 game which can be easily solved by the methods already described.

The importance of the maximin point is that it is the highest level, on the average, at which B can hold A's winnings. Similarly, it is the level at which A can hold B to minimize his losses. In other words, it just indicates how far one player can go before he is restrained by his opponent's defensive strategy. It is the average payoff around which the game revolves.

In the same way, we can treat (m × 2) games. For these (m × 2) games, we shall get *minimax point* which will be the lowest point on the upper boundary (instead of highest point on the lower boundary). Thus we conclude that any (2 × n) or (m × 2) game can be reduced to (2 × 2) game. To explain the graphical method, we shall consider a few examples.

EXAMPLE 9.19-3.1

Solve the game given in table 9.146 by the graphical method.

TABLE 9.146

		B			
		y_1	y_2	y_3	y_4
A	x_1	19	6	7	5
	x_2	7	3	14	6
	x_3	12	8	18	4
	x_4	8	7	13	–1

[P.U. B.Com. April, 2007]

Solution

The first step is to look for a saddle point. It does not exist in this problem. The second step is to see if the game can be reduced by dominance. All the cell values in column 2 as well as 4 are less than the corresponding values in columns 1 and 3. Hence columns 1 and 3 are dominated by columns 2 and 4 and the reduced matrix becomes

TABLE 9.147

		B	
		y_2	y_4
	x_1	6	5
A	x_2	3	6
	x_3	8	4
	x_4	7	–1

Both the cell values for row 3 are higher than those for row 4. Hence row 3 dominates row 4 and the matrix is reduced to

TABLE 9.148

		B	
		y_2	$y_4 = 1 - y_2$
	x_1	6	5
A	x_2	3	6
	x_3	8	4

Let A_1, A_2, A_3 be the strategies which A mixes with probabilities x_1, x_2 and x_3 and B_2, B_4 be the strategies which B mixes with probabilities y_2 and $y_4 = 1 - y_2$. When B adopts strategy B_2 , $y_2 = 1$ and the probability with which he will adopt strategy B_4 *i.e.*, $y_4 = 0$.

This matrix can be solved now by graphical method. B's expected payoffs corresponding to A's pure strategies are given below.

A's pure strategies	*B's expected payoffs*
1	$6y_2 + 5\,(1 - y_2) = y_2 + 5$
2	$3y_2 + 6\,(1 - y_2) = -\,3y_2 + 6$
3	$8y_2 + 4\,(1 - y_2) = 4y_2 + 4$

These three straight lines can be plotted as functions of y_2 as follows:

Draw two lines B_4 and B_2 parallel to each other one unit apart and mark a scale on each of them (Figure 9.26). To represent A's first strategy, join mark 6 on B_2 with mark 5 on B_4; to represent A's second strategy, join mark 3 on B_2 with mark 6 on B_4; and so on and bound the figure from above as shown since B is a minimizing player.

Since player B wishes to minimize his maximum expected losses, the two lines which intersect at the lowest point of the upper bound (envelope) show the two courses of action A should choose in his best strategy *i.e.*, A_1 and A_2. We can, thus, immediately reduce the 3 × 2 game to 2 × 2 game which can be easily solved by arithmetic method. The resulting 2 × 2 game is shown in table 9.149.

TABLE 9.149

		B			
		2	4		
	1	6	5	3	3/4
A	2	3	6	1	1/4
		1	3		
		1/4	3/4		

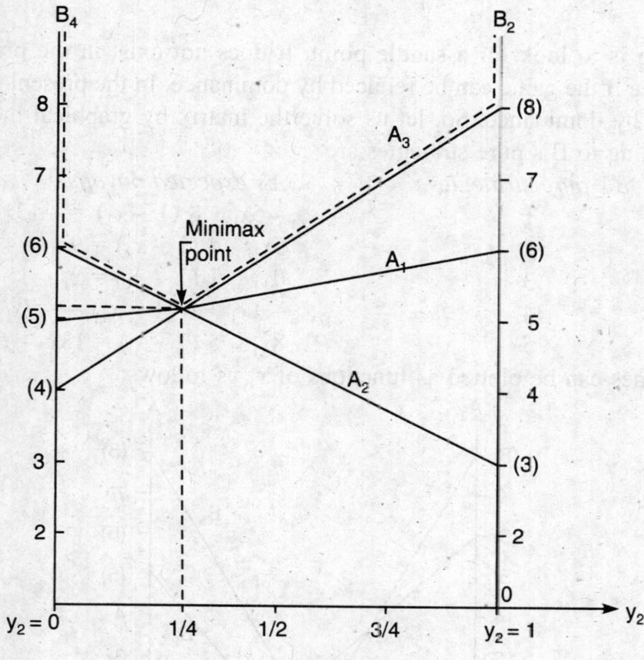

Fig. 9.27

∴ Optimum strategies are

A (3/4, 1/4, 0, 0),
B (0, 1/4, 0, 3/4),

value of the game is, $V = \frac{6 \times 1 + 3 \times 5}{1+3} = \frac{21}{4} = 5\frac{1}{4}$.

Remarks. 1. There is an alternative approach to plot B's expected payoffs as lines for each of A's pure strategy. For strategy 1 of A, equation $y_2 + 5$ represents B's expected payoff. When $y_2 = 0$, payoff = 5 and when $y_2 = 1$, payoff = 6. Thus we join mark 6 on B_2 with mark 5 on B_4. Similarly, other lines are plotted.

2. The optimal strategies of player B and value of the game can also be determined by either of the following two ways :

(*a*) The two coordinates of the minimax point give the optimal value of y_2 (and hence of $y_4 = 1 - y_2$ too) and value of the game. In Fig. 9.27, minimax point has coordinates ($^1/_4$, $^{21}/_4$). ∴ $y_2 = {}^1/_4$ (and hence $y_4 = 1 - {}^1/_4 = {}^3/_4$) and $V = {}^{21}/_4$.

(*b*) Optimal value of y_2 can also be obtained by solving algebraically the equations of the two strategies A_1 and A_2 that intersect at the minimax point. Thus when $y_2 + 5 = -3y_2 + 6$, $y_2 = {}^1/_4$ (and hence $y_4 = 1 - {}^1/_4 = {}^3/_4$). Value of the game (payoff) is obtained by substituting value of $y_2 = {}^1/_4$ in any of these equations.

EXAMPLE 9.19-3.2

Solve the following 2 × 5 game by graphical method:

TABLE 9.150

		Player B				
		1	*2*	*3*	*4*	*5*
Player A x_1	*1*	*–5*	*5*	*0*	*–1*	*8*
$x_2 = 1 - x_1$	*2*	*8*	*–4*	*–1*	*6*	*–5*

[*G.N.D.U. B.Com. April, 2010; P.U. B.Com., Sept., 2012; April, 2012; 2006; B.B.A., 2001*]

Solution

The first step is to look for a saddle point. It does not exist in the present problem. The second step is to see if the game can be reduced by dominance. In the present problem, the matrix cannot be reduced by dominance. So, let us solve the matrix by graphical method. A's expected payoffs corresponding to B's pure strategies are

B's pure strategies	*A's expected payoffs*
1	$-5x_1 + 8(1-x_1) = -13x_1 + 8$
2	$5x_1 - 4(1-x_1) = 9x_1 - 4$
3	$0x_1 - 1(1-x_1) = x_1 - 1$
4	$-1x_1 + 6(1-x_1) = -7x_1 + 6$
5	$8x_1 - 5(1-x_1) = 13x_1 - 5$

These five lines can be plotted as functions of x_1 as follows:

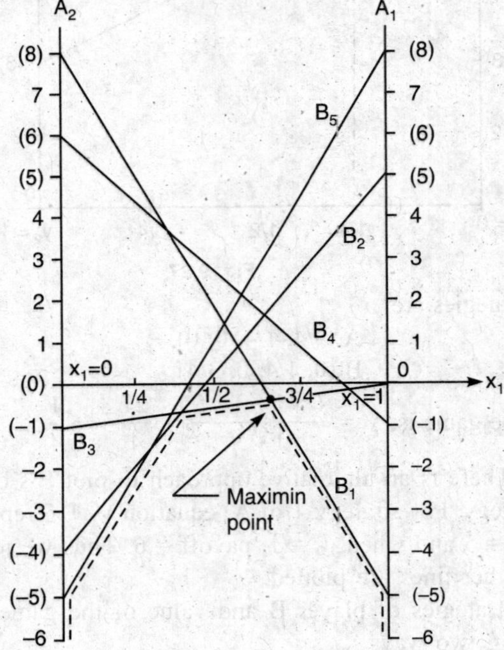

Fig. 9.28

Draw two parallel lines A_2 and A_1 one unit apart and mark a scale on each of them (Fig. 9.28). To represent B's first strategy, join mark – 5 on A_1 with mark 8 on A_2; to represent B's second strategy, join mark 5 on A_1 with mark – 4 on A_2 and so on (for the remaining three strategies) and bound the figure from below.

Since player A wishes to maximize his minimum expected payoff, the two lines which intersect at the highest point of the lower bound show the two courses of action B should choose in his best strategy, which are B_1 and B_3. We can thus immediately reduce the 2 × 5 game to 2 × 2 game which can be easily solved, say, by arithmetic method. The resulting 2 × 2 game is shown in table 9.151.

TABLE 9.151

		B			
		1	3		
A	1	–5	0	9	9/14
	2	8	–1	5	5/14
		1	13		
		1/14	13/14		

∴ Optimum strategies are

A (9/14, 5/14), B (1/14, 0, 13/14, 0, 0).

value of the game is, $V = \dfrac{-5 \times 1 + 0 \times 13}{1 + 13} = \dfrac{-5}{14}$.

EXAMPLE 9.19-3.3

Solve the following game:

TABLE 9.152

		B		
		y_1	y_2	y_3
A	x_1	6	4	3
	$x_2 = 1 - x_1$	2	4	8

Solution

This game does not have a saddle point, nor it can be reduced by dominance. A's expected payoffs corresponding to B's pure strategies are

B's pure strategies	*A's expected payoffs*
1	$6x_1 + 2(1 - x_1) = 4x_1 + 2$
2	$4x_1 + 4(1 - x_1) = 4$
3	$3x_1 + 8(1 - x_1) = -5x_1 - 8$

These three lines are shown plotted in Fig. 9.29. The figure is bound from below. There are two maximum points C and D giving the same value of the game.

(*i*) *Point C* : Strategies B_1 and B_2 are chosen by B and the following 2 × 2 game is to be solved :

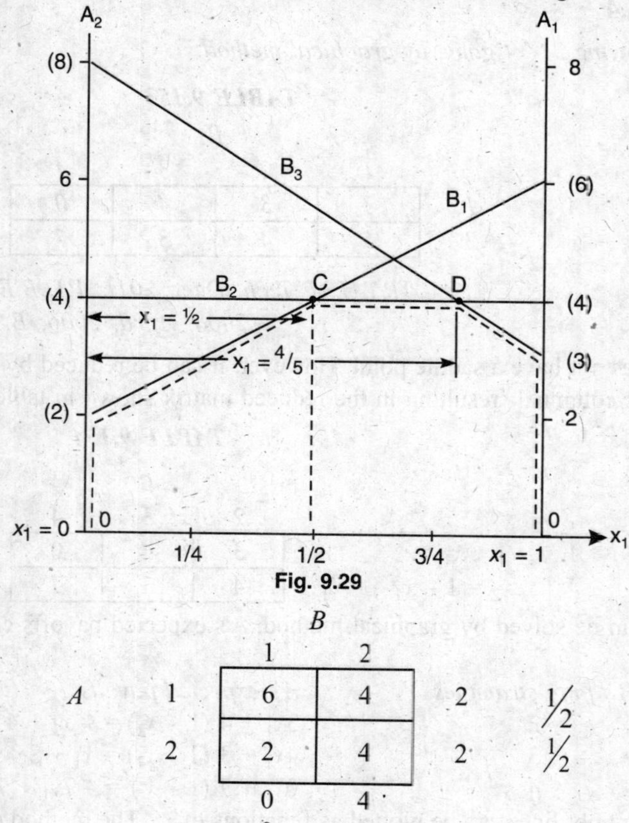

Fig. 9.29

		B 1	2		
A	1	6	4	2	½
	2	2	4	2	½
		0	4		
		0	1		

$\therefore$ Optimal solution is : A $\left(\frac{1}{2}, \frac{1}{2}\right)$, B (0, 1, 0) ; V = 4.

(*ii*) *Point D* : Strategies B_2 and B_3 are mixed by B and the following 2 × 2 game is to be solved:

		B 2	3		
A	1	4	3	4	$\frac{4}{5}$
	2	4	8	1	$\frac{1}{5}$
		5	0		
		1	0		

$\therefore$ Optimal solution is A $\left(\frac{4}{5}, \frac{1}{5}\right)$, B (0, 1, 0) ; V = 4.

As evident from Fig. 9.25, any value of x_1 between the points C and D shall be optimal for A. Value of x_1 at points C and D is $\frac{1}{2}$ and $\frac{4}{5}$ respectively. Thus, optimal strategy for A is any pair of (x_1, $x_2 = 1 - x_1$), where $\frac{1}{2} \le x_1 \le \frac{4}{5}$ or $0.5 \le x_1 \le 0.8$. Optimal strategy for B is (0, 1, 0) and value of game is 4.

Note: *If there happen to be more than two lines passing through the maximin (or minimax) point, then any two lines having opposite signs for their slopes will yield an alternative optimal solution.*

EXAMPLE 9.19-3.4

Solve the following 2 × 4 game by graphical method:

TABLE 9.153

		B 1	2	3	4
A	*1*	*3*	*3*	*4*	*0*
	2	*5*	*4*	*3*	*7*

Solution

[*P.T.U.M. Tech. Dec., 2011; P.U.B.E. (E. & Ec.) April, 2008; April, 2006; B. Com. Sept., 2005*]

This game does not have a saddle point. However, it can be reduced by dominance because column 2 dominates column 1, resulting in the reduced matrix shown in table 9.154.

TABLE 9.154

			B 2	3	4
A	x_1	1	3	4	0
	$x_2 = 1 - x_1$	2	4	3	7

This matrix can be solved by graphical method. A's expected payoffs corresponding to B's pure strategies are

B's pure strategies	*A's expected payoffs*
2	$3x_1 + 4(1 - x_1) = -x_1 + 4$
3	$4x_1 + 3(1 - x_1) = x_1 + 3$
4	$0x_1 + 7(1 - x_1) = -7x_1 + 7$

These three straight lines can be plotted as functions of x_1. The method of plotting them has already been described; and they appear as shown in figure 9.30.

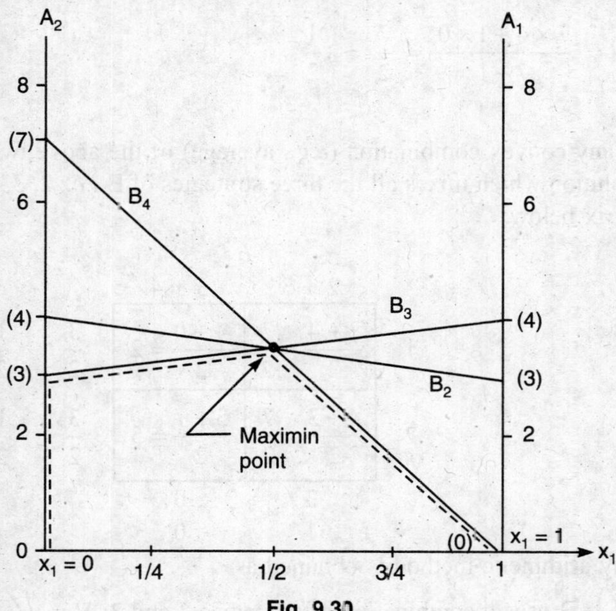

Fig. 9.30

Figure is to be bound from below as shown. All the three lines pass through the maximin point. As mentioned earlier, any two lines having opposite signs for their slopes will yield an alternative optimal solution. This means that the combination of B_2 and B_4 must be excluded as both have the same sign for their slopes. So the game reduces to two 2×2 games which can be easily solved, say, by arithmetic method.

(*i*)

		B 2	3		
A	1	3	4	1	1/2
	2	4	3	1	1/2
		1	1		
		1/2	1/2		

A's optimum strategy : A (1/2, 1/2),

B's optimum strategy : B (0, 1/2, 1/2, 0),

$$\text{game value, V} = \frac{3 \times 1 + 4 \times 1}{1+1} = \frac{7}{2} = 3\frac{1}{2}.$$

(*ii*)

		B 3	4			
A	1	4	0	4	1/2	4/8
	2	3	7	4	1/2	4/8
		7	1			
		7/8	1/8			

A's optimum strategy : A (4/8, 4/8),

B's optimum strategy : B (0, 0, 7/8, 1/8),

$$\text{game value, V} = \frac{7\times4+1\times0}{7+1} = \frac{7}{2} = 3\frac{1}{2}.$$

Remark:

1. Note that any convex combination (*e.g.*, average) of the above two matrices is also an optimal solution which mixes all the three strategies of B *i.e.*, 2, 3, and 4. This is shown in the matrix below.

		B			
		2 + 3	3 + 4		
A	1	$\frac{3+4}{2}=\frac{7}{2}$	$\frac{4+0}{2}=2$	$\frac{3}{2}$	$\frac{1}{2}$
	2	$\frac{4+3}{2}=\frac{7}{2}$	$\frac{3+7}{2}=5$	$\frac{3}{2}$	$\frac{1}{2}$
		3	0		
		1	0		

Solution by arithmetic method is obtained as

A $\left(\frac{1}{2}, \frac{1}{2}\right)$, B uses a combination of strategies 2 and 3; V = $\frac{7}{2}$.

2. The above matrix has a saddle point. Since graphical method *eliminates the dominated strategies*, this saddle point for the reduced matrix is not the true saddle point for the original (given) problem and is to be ignored. Thus once a game is reduced by graphical method to 2 × 2 size, it should be solved only by an *analytical method*.

9.20 MIXED STRATEGIES (3 × 3 OR HIGHER GAMES)

To solve 3 × 3 or higher games also, the first step is to look for a saddle point; if there is one, the game is readily solved. If not, the next step is to reduce the given matrix to 2 × 2 size matrix or 2 × n (or m × 2) matrix by applying the rules of dominance. If the matrix can be reduced to 2 × 2 size, it can be easily solved by the methods described under section 9.18. If the matrix can only be reduced to 2 × n (or m × 2) size matrix, it can still be solved by applying the methods described under section 9.19. However, if the final matrix is of 3 × 3 or higher size, it can be solved by algebraic method, method of matrices, method of linear programming and by iterative method of approximate solution.

Algebraic method has already been described for 2 × n (or m × 2) games under section 9.19. The method can be extended to 3 × 3 or higher games and will not be discussed here. The remaining three methods will now be described in some details.

9.20-1 Method of Matrices

This method will be illustrated with the help of a few examples.

EXAMPLE 9.20-1.1

Solve the game given by table 9.155.

TABLE 9.155

		B			
		1	*2*	*3*	
A	*1*	7	*1*	7	*1*
	2	*9*	*–1*	*1*	*–1*
	3.	5	7	6	(5)
		9	(7)	(7)	

Solution

The first step is to look for a saddle point. It does not exist in this problem. The game value lies between 5 and 7. The next step is to see if the given matrix can be reduced by dominance. We see that it cannot be reduced. So let us solve this matrix by the method of matrices. Subtract each row from the row above (*i.e.*, subtract 2nd row from the first and third row from the second) and write down the values below the matrix. Similarly, subtract each column from the column to its left (*i.e.*, subtract second column from the first and third column from the second) and write down the results to the right of the matrix. Thus we get table 9.156.

TABLE 9.156

		B 1	2	3		
	1	7	1	7	6	–6
A	2	9	–1	1	10	–2
	3	5	7	6	–2	1
		–2	2	6		
		4	–8	–5		

Next, calculate the oddments for A_1, A_2, A_3 and B_1, B_2, B_3.

Oddment for A_1 = determinant $\begin{vmatrix} 10 & -2 \\ -2 & 1 \end{vmatrix} = 10 - 4 = 6,$

oddment for A_2 = determinant $\begin{vmatrix} 6 & -6 \\ -2 & 1 \end{vmatrix} = 12 - 6 = 6,$

oddment for A_3 = determinant $\begin{vmatrix} 6 & -6 \\ 10 & -2 \end{vmatrix} = -12 + 60 = 48,$

oddment for B_1 = determinant $\begin{vmatrix} 2 & 6 \\ -8 & -5 \end{vmatrix} = -10 + 48 = 38,$

oddment for B_2 = determinant $\begin{vmatrix} -2 & 6 \\ 4 & -5 \end{vmatrix} = 24 - 10 = 14,$

oddment for B_3 = determinant $\begin{vmatrix} -2 & 2 \\ 4 & -8 \end{vmatrix} = 16 - 8 = 8,$

Next, write down these oddments (as shown in table 9.157) neglecting their signs. Since both the sums of oddments are same (60 each), this is a solution to the game. If the sums are different, both players do not use all of their courses of actions in their best strategies and this method fails.

TABLE 9.157

		B 1	2	3				
	1	7	1	7	6	1	1/10	3/30
A	2	9	–1	1	6	1	1/10	3/30
	3	5	7	6	48	8	8/10	24/30
		38	14	8	60			
		19	7	4				
		19/30	7/30	4/30				

Thus optimum strategies are

A (3/30, 3/30, 24/30), B (19/30, 7/30, 4/30),

$$\text{game value, V} = \frac{7\times1+9\times1+5\times8}{1+1+8} = \frac{7+9+40}{10} = \frac{56}{10} = \frac{28}{5} = 5\frac{3}{5}.$$

EXAMPLE 9.20-1.2

Solve the following 3 × 3 game by the method of matrices :

TABLE 9.158

		B 1	2	3	
A	1	1	–1	–1	(–1)
	2	–1	–1	3	(–1)
	3	–1	2	–1	(–1)
		(1)	2	3	

[*Kuru. Univ., 1975*]

Solution

The given problem has no saddle point and as seen from table 9.158, the game value lies between –1 and 1. It cannot be reduced by dominance rules.

Subtract each row from the row above and each column from the column to its left and write the results as shown in table 9.159.

TABLE 9.159

		B 1	2	3		
A	1	1	–1	–1	2	0
	2	–1	–1	3	0	–4
	3	–1	2	–1	–3	3
		2	0	–4		
		0	–3	4		

$$\text{Oddment for } A_1 = \text{determinant} \begin{vmatrix} 0 & -4 \\ -3 & 3 \end{vmatrix} = 0 - 12 = -12,$$

$$\text{Oddment for } A_2 = \text{determinant} \begin{vmatrix} 2 & 0 \\ -3 & 3 \end{vmatrix} = 0 - 6 = -6,$$

$$\text{Oddment for } A_3 = \text{determinant} \begin{vmatrix} 2 & 0 \\ 0 & -4 \end{vmatrix} = -8 - 0 = -8,$$

$$\text{Oddment for } B_1 = \text{determinant} \begin{vmatrix} 0 & -4 \\ -3 & 4 \end{vmatrix} = 0 - 12 = -12,$$

$$\text{Oddment for } B_2 = \text{determinant} \begin{vmatrix} 2 & -4 \\ 0 & 4 \end{vmatrix} = 0 - 8 = -8,$$

$$\text{Oddment for } B_3 = \text{determinant} \begin{vmatrix} 2 & 0 \\ 0 & -3 \end{vmatrix} = -6 - 0 = -6.$$

Now we write these oddments, neglecting their signs as shown in table 9.160.

TABLE 9.160

		B					
		1	2	3			
A	1	1	–1	–1	12	12/26	6/13
	2	–1	–1	3	6	6/26	3/13
	3	–1	2	–1	8	8/26	4/13
		12	8	6	26		
		12/26	8/26	6/26			
		6/13	4/13	3/13			

Since the sum of vertical oddments is equal to the sum of horizontal oddments, this is the solution to the problem. The complete solution is

A's optimal strategies : $\left(\frac{6}{13}, \frac{3}{13}, \frac{4}{13}\right)$,

B's optimal strategies : $\left(\frac{6}{13}, \frac{4}{13}, \frac{3}{13}\right)$,

game value, V : $\dfrac{12\times1-6\times1-8\times1}{12+6+8} = -\dfrac{2}{26} = -\dfrac{1}{13}$.

Note. *The above method can be applied only when sum of vertical oddments is equal to the sum of horizontal oddments i.e.. if both players use all their plays in their best strategies. The method breaks down when the players do not use all their courses of action in their best strategies i.e., the sum of vertical oddments is not equal to the sum of horizontal oddments. In such a case, the method of linear programming may be applied.*

9.20-2 Method of Linear Programming

Game theory bears a strong relationship to linear programming, since every finite two-person zero-sum game can be expressed as a linear programme and conversely every linear programme can be represented as a game. Linear programming is the most general method of solving any two-person zero-sum game. If there is no saddle point, dominance is unsuccessful in reducing the game and the method of matrices also fails, then linear programming offers the best method of solution. We shall describe this method with the help of a few examples.

EXAMPLE 9.20-2.1

Two oil companies, Indian Oil Co. and Caltex, operating in a state are trying to increase their market share at the expense of the other. The Indian Oil Co. is considering possibilities of decreasing price, giving free soft drinks on ₹ 400 purchases of oil or giving away a drinking glass with each 40 litre purchase. Obviously, Caltex cannot ignore this and comes out with its own programme to increase its share in the market. The payoff matrix from the viewpoints of percentage increase or decrease in market shares is given in table 9.161.

TABLE 9.161

		CALTEX		
		Decrease price	*Free soft drinks on ₹ 400 purchase*	*Free drinking glass on 40 litres or more*
	Decrease price	4	1	–3
INDIAN OIL CO.	*Free soft drinks on ₹ 400 purchase*	3	1	6
	Free drinking glass on 40 litres or more	–3	4	–2

Determine the optimum strategies for the two oil companies.

Solution

Let us denote the Indian Oil Co. by A and Caltex by B. Let x_1, x_2, x_3 and y_1, y_2, y_3 be the probabilities by which A and B respectively select their strategies. The game has no saddle point and the game value lies between 1 and 4. The matrix cannot be reduced by the rules of dominance. The method of linear programming will be used to solve it.

Let the value of the game (to A) be V. Consider the game from B's point of view. B is trying to minimize V. then,

against A_1, $4y_1 + y_2 - 3y_3 \le V$,
against A_2, $3y_1 + y_2 + 6y_3 \le V$,
against A_3, $-3y_1 + 4y_2 - 2y_3 \le V$,
$y_1 + y_2 + y_3 = 1$, (Sum of probabilities must be equal to 1)
where $y_1, y_2, y_3 \ge 0$.

Divide each of above relations by V. Note that this division is valid only if V > 0. If, however, V < 0, the direction of inequality constraints must be reversed and if V = 0, division would be meaningless. However, both these cases can be easily solved by adding a positive constant K (where K > the negative game value) to all the entries of the matrix, thus ensuring that the game value *for the revised matrix is greater than zero.* After obtaining the optimal solution, the true value of the game can be obtained by subtracting K from the game value so obtained.

In general, if the maximin value of this game is non-negative, then the value of the game is greater than zero, provided the game does not have a saddle point.

Since maximin value is 1 in the present example, we get the following relations by dividing by V:

$$4.\frac{y_1}{V} + \frac{y_2}{V} - 3.\frac{y_3}{V} \le 1,$$

$$3.\frac{y_1}{V} + \frac{y_2}{V} + 6.\frac{y_3}{V} \le 1,$$

$$-3.\frac{y_1}{V} + 4.\frac{y_2}{V} - 2.\frac{y_3}{V} \le 1,$$

$$\frac{y_1}{V} + \frac{y_2}{V} + \frac{y_3}{V} = \frac{1}{V},$$

where $$\frac{y_1}{V}, \frac{y_2}{V}, \frac{y_3}{V} \ge 0.$$

Putting $\dfrac{y_j}{V} = Y_j, j = 1, 2, 3,$ we get

$$\left.\begin{aligned} 4Y_1 + Y_2 - 3Y_3 &\le 1, \\ 3Y_1 + Y_2 + 6Y_3 &\le 1, \\ -3Y_1 + 4Y_2 + 2Y_3 &\le 1, \end{aligned}\right\} \quad \text{... (9.19)}$$

$$Y_1 + Y_2 + Y_3 = \frac{1}{V}, \quad \text{... (9.20)}$$

where $Y_1, Y_2, Y_3 \ge 0.$

Since B is trying to minimize V, he must maximize 1/V. Thus the problem is to maximize objective function (equation 9.20) subject to constraints (9.19) which can be done by simplex method under the following steps:

Step I. Set up the Problem in the Standard Form

Introducing slack variables S_1, S_2 and S_3 the problem can be expressed in the standard form as

$$\begin{aligned} 4Y_1 + Y_2 - 3Y_3 + S_1 &= 1, \\ 3Y_1 + Y_2 + 6Y_3 + S_2 &= 1, \\ -3Y_1 + 4Y_2 - 2Y_3 + S_3 &= 1, \end{aligned}$$

and it is desired to maximize

$$\frac{1}{V} = Y_1 + Y_2 + Y_3 + 0S_1 + 0S_2 + 0S_3,$$

where $Y_1, Y_2, Y_3, S_1, S_2, S_3 \ge 0.$

Step 2. Find the Initial Basic Feasible Solution

Setting non-basic variables Y_1, Y_2, Y_3 each equal to zero, i.b.f.s. is

$$Y_1 = Y_2 = Y_3 = 0, S_1 = S_2 = S_3 = 1, \frac{1}{V} = 0.$$

Initial table can now be constructed using S_1, S_2, S_3 as basic variables.

TABLE 9.162

	c_j	1	1	1	0	0	0		
c_B	Basis	Y_1	Y_2	Y_3	S_1	S_2	S_3	b	θ
0	S_1	(4)	1	–3	1	0	0	1	1/4 ←
0	S_2	3	1	6	0	1	0	1	1/3
0	S_3	–3	4	–2	0	0	1	1	–1/3
$Z_j = \Sigma c_B a_{ij}$		0	0	0	0	0	0	0	
$c_j - Z_j$		1 ↑	1	1	0	0	0		
									i.b.f.s.

Step 3. Perform Optimality Test

Calculating $c_j - Z_j$ we find that it is positive under some columns. Hence table 9.162 is not optimal. Since there is tie for the incoming variable, Y_1 is arbitrarily selected as the incoming variable.

Step 4. Iterate Towards an Optimal Solution

Performing iterations we get the following tables:

TABLE 9.163

	c_j	1	1	1	0	0	0		
c_B	Basis	Y_1	Y_2	Y_3	S_1	S_2	S_3	b	θ
1	Y_1	1	$1/4$	$-3/4$	$1/4$	0	0	$1/4$	$-3/4$
0	S_2	0	$1/4$	$(33/4)$	$-3/4$	1	0	$1/4$	$1/33$ ←
0	S_3	0	$19/4$	$-17/4$	$3/4$	0	1	$7/4$	$-7/17$
	Z_j	1	$1/4$	$-3/4$	$1/4$	0	0	$1/4$	
	$c_j - Z_j$	0	$3/4$	$7/4$	$-1/4$	0	0		
				↑					

2nd b.f.s.

TABLE 9.164

	c_j	1	1	1	0	0	0		
c_B	Basis	Y_1	Y_2	Y_3	S_1	S_2	S_3	b	θ
1	Y_1	1	$3/11$	0	$2/11$	$1/11$	0	$3/11$	1
1	Y_3	0	$1/33$	1	$-1/11$	$4/33$	0	$1/33$	1
0	S_3	0	$(161/33)$	0	$4/11$	$17/33$	1	$62/33$	$62/161$ ←
	Z_j	1	$10/33$	1	$1/11$	$7/33$	0	$10/33$	
	$c_j - Z_j$	0	$23/33$	0	$-1/11$	$-7/33$	0		
			↑						

3rd b.f.s.

TABLE 9.165

	c_j	1	1	1	0	0	0	
c_B	Basis	Y_1	Y_2	Y_3	S_1	S_2	S_3	b
1	Y_1	1	0	0	$26/161$	$10/161$	$-9/161$	$27/161$
1	Y_3	0	0	1	$-15/161$	$19/161$	$-1/161$	$3/161$
1	Y_2	0	1	0	$12/161$	$17/161$	$33/161$	$62/161$
	Z_j	1	1	1	$23/161$	$46/161$	$23/161$	$92/161$
	$c_j - Z_j$	0	0	0	$-23/161$	$-46/161$	$-23/161$	

Optimal b.f.s.

Table 9.147 gives the following optimal solution:

$$Y_1 = 23/161,\ Y_2 = 62/161,\ Y_3 = 3/161;\ 1/V = 92/161 = 4/7.$$

∴ Value of the game, $V = 7/4$.

$$\because \quad \frac{y_j}{V} = Y_j,$$

$$y_1 = Y_1 \,.\, V = \frac{27}{161} \times \frac{7}{4} = \frac{27}{92},$$

$$y_2 = Y_2 \,.\, V = \frac{62}{161} \times \frac{7}{4} = \frac{31}{46} = \frac{62}{92},$$

$$y_3 = Y_3 \,.\, V = \frac{3}{161} \times \frac{7}{4} = \frac{3}{92}.$$

A's best strategies appear in $c_j - Z_j$ row of the optimal table 9.165 with changed signs under S_1, S_2 and S_3-columns.

$$\therefore \quad X_1 = 23/161,\; X_2 = 46/161,\; X_3 = 23/161.$$

$$\therefore \quad x_1 = X_1 \,.\, V = 23/161 \times 7/4 = 23/92 = 1/4,$$

$$x_2 = X_2 \,.\, V = 46/161 \times 7/4 = 1/2,$$

$$x_3 = X_3 \,.\, V = 23/161 \times 7/4 = 1/4.$$

$\therefore$ Best strategies for A (Indian Oil Co.) = (1/4, 1/2, 1/4),

best strategies for B (Caltex) = $\left(27/92, 62/92, 3/92\right)$, V (for A) = $7/4$.

EXAMPLE 9.20-2.2

Solve the game shown in table 9.166 by the L. P. method.

TABLE 9.166

		B 1	B 2	B 3
A	1	3	–4	2
A	2	1	–3	–7
A	3	–2	4	7

Solution

Let x_1, x_2, x_3 and y_1, y_2, y_3 be the probabilities with which A and B select their pure strategies. The game has no saddle point and the game value lies between – 2 and + 3. The matrix cannot be reduced by the rules of dominance. Further, it cannot be solved by the method of matrices, since the sums of oddments of A and B are not equal. L.P. method will be used to solve it. Since the value of the game lies between – 2 and + 3, it is possible that the value of the game (V) may be negative or zero. Therefore, a positive constant K is added to all the elements of the matrix, which is more than the maximin value *i.e.,* K must be > 2. Let K = 3. The given matrix is then modified to the one shown in table 9.167.

TABLE 9.167

		B 1	B 2	B 3
A	1	6	–1	5
A	2	4	0	–4
A	3	1	7	10

Let the value of the game to A be V. Consider the game from B's point of view. B is trying to minimize V. Then,

against A_1, $6y_1 - y_2 + 5y_3 \le V$,
against A_2, $4y_1 + 0y_2 - 4y_3 \le V$,
against A_3, $y_1 + 7y_2 + 10y_3 \le V$,
and $y_1 + y_2 + y_3 = 1$,
$y_1, y_2, y_3 \ge 0$.

Dividing each of the above relations by V,

$$\frac{6y_1}{V} - \frac{y_2}{V} + \frac{5y_3}{V} \le 1,$$

$$\frac{4y_1}{V} + \frac{0y_2}{V} - \frac{4y_3}{V} \le 1,$$

$$\frac{y_1}{V} + \frac{7y_2}{V} + \frac{10y_3}{V} \le 1,$$

$$\frac{y_1}{V} + \frac{y_2}{V} + \frac{y_3}{V} = \frac{1}{V},$$

where $\frac{y_1}{V}, \frac{y_2}{V}, \frac{y_3}{V} \ge 0.$

Substituting $\frac{y_j}{V} = Y_j, j = 1, 2, 3$, we get

$$\left.\begin{aligned} 6Y_1 - Y_2 + 5Y_3 &\le 1, \\ 4Y_1 + 0Y_2 - 4Y_3 &\le 1, \\ Y_1 + 7Y_2 + 10Y_3 &\le 1, \end{aligned}\right\} \qquad \text{... (9.21)}$$

$$Y_1 + Y_2 + Y_3 = \frac{1}{V}, \qquad \text{... (9.22)}$$

$$Y_1, Y_2, Y_3 \ge 0.$$

Since B is trying to minimize V, he must maximize $\frac{1}{V}$. Thus the problem is to maximize Eq. (9.22) subject to constraints (9.21). This is done by simplex method which consists of the following steps:

Step 1. Set up the Problem in the Standard Form

Introducing slack variables S_1, S_2 and S_3 the problem in standard form can be expressed as

$$6Y_1 - Y_2 + 5Y_3 + S_1 = 1,$$
$$4Y_1 + 0Y_2 - 4Y_3 + S_2 = 1,$$
$$Y_1 + 7Y_2 + 10Y_3 + S_3 = 1,$$

maximize $\frac{1}{V} = Y_1 + Y_2 + Y_3 + 0S_1 + 0S_2 + 0S_3$,

$Y_1, Y_2, Y_3, S_1, S_2, S_3 \ge 0.$

Step 2. Find an Initial Basic Feasible Solution

Setting non-basic variables Y_1, Y_2, Y_3 each equal to zero, the i.b.f.s. is

$$Y_1 = Y_2 = Y_3 = 0, S_1 = S_2 = S_3 = 1, \frac{1}{V} = 0.$$

Initial table can now be constructed using S_1, S_2, S_3 as basic variables.

TABLE 9.168

c_B	c_j / Basis	1 / Y_1	1 / Y_2	1 / Y_3	0 / S_1	0 / S_2	0 / S_3	b	θ
0	S_1	(6)	–1	5	1	0	0	1	1/6 ←
0	S_2	4	0	–4	0	1	0	1	1/4
0	S_3	1	7	10	0	0	1	1	1
	Z_j	0	0	0	0	0	0	0	
	$c_j - Z_j$	1	1	1	0	0	0		
		↑							*i.b.f.s.*

Step 3. Perform Optimality Test

Calculating $c_j - Z_j$ in table 9.168, we find that it is positive under some columns. Hence i.b.f.s. is not optimal. Since there is tie for the incoming variable, Y_1 is arbitrarily selected as the incoming variable.

Step 4. Iterate Towards an Optimal Solution

Performing iterations we get the following tables:

TABLE 9.169

c_B	c_j / Basis	1 / Y_1	1 / Y_2	1 / Y_3	0 / S_1	0 / S_2	0 / S_3	b	θ
1	Y_1	1	$-1/6$	$5/6$	$1/6$	0	0	$1/6$	–1
0	S_2	0	$2/3$	$-22/3$	$-2/3$	1	0	$1/3$	$1/2$
0	S_3	0	$(43/6)$	$55/6$	$-1/6$	0	1	$5/6$	$5/43$ ←
	Z_j	1	$-1/6$	$5/6$	$1/6$	0	0	$1/6$	
	$c_j - Z_j$	0	$7/6$	$1/6$	$-1/6$	0	0		
			↑						*2nd b.f.s.*

TABLE 9.170

c_B	c_j / Basis	1 / Y_1	1 / Y_2	1 / Y_3	0 / S_1	0 / S_2	0 / S_3	b
1	Y_1	1	0	$45/43$	$7/43$	0	$1/43$	$8/43$
0	S_2	0	0	$-352/43$	$-28/43$	1	$-4/43$	$11/43$
1	Y_2	0	1	$55/43$	$-1/43$	0	$6/43$	$5/43$
	Z_j	1	1	$100/43$	$6/43$	0	$7/43$	$13/43$
	$c_j - Z_j$	0	0	$-57/43$	$-6/43$	0	$-7/43$	*Optimal b.f.s.*

Table 9.170 yields the following optimal solution:

$$Y_1 = \frac{8}{43},\ Y_2 = \frac{5}{43},\ Y_3 = 0;\ \frac{1}{V} = Y_1 + Y_2 + Y_3 = \frac{8}{43} + \frac{5}{43} + 0 = 13/43$$

∴ Value of the game for the modified matrix, $V = 43/13$.

$$\because \quad \frac{y_j}{V} = Y_j \quad \therefore y_j = Y_j \,.\, V, \; j = 1, 2, 3.$$

$$\therefore \quad y_1 = Y_1 \,.\, V = \frac{8}{43} \times \frac{43}{13} = \frac{8}{13},$$

$$y_2 = Y_2 \,.\, V = \frac{5}{43} \times \frac{43}{13} = \frac{5}{13},$$

$$y_3 = Y_3 \,.\, V = 0.$$

A's best strategies appear in $c_j - Z_j$ row under S_1, S_2 and S_3-columns in table 9.170 with changed signs.

$$\therefore \quad X_1 = \frac{6}{43}, X_2 = 0, X_3 = \frac{7}{43}.$$

$$\therefore \quad x_1 = X_1 \,.\, V = \frac{6}{43} \times \frac{43}{13} = \frac{6}{13},$$

$$x_2 = X_2 \,.\, V = 0,$$

$$x_3 = X_3 \,.\, V = \frac{7}{43} \times \frac{43}{13} = \frac{7}{13}.$$

$\therefore$ Best strategies for A : $\left(6/13, 0, 7/13\right)$,

best strategies for B : $\left(8/13, 5/13, 0\right)$,

value of game for the given problem $= 43/13 - 3 = 4/13$.

EXAMPLE 9.20-2.3

Write both primal and dual L.P. problems corresponding to the following rectangular game:

TABLE 9.171

	Y			
	5	*7*	*4*	*10*
X	*4*	*3*	*7*	*9*
	1	*2*	*5*	*6*

Solution

Let x_1, x_2, x_3 and y_1, y_2, y_3, y_4 be the probabilities with which, A and B respectively, select their pure strategies. Then we can write

TABLE 9.172

		Y			
		y_1	y_2	y_3	y_4
	x_1	5	7	4	10
X	x_2	4	3	7	9
	x_3	1	2	5	6

Let the value of the game be V. Consider the game from Y's point of view. He is interested in determining strategies y_1, y_2, y_3 and y_4 that will minimize his maximum expected loss. Thus

against X_1, $\quad 5y_1 + 7y_2 + 4y_3 + 10y_4 \leq V$,

against X_2, $\quad 4y_1 + 3y_2 + 7y_3 + 9y_4 \leq V$,

against X_3, $y_1 + 2y_2 + 5y_3 + 6y_4 \le V$

$y_1 + y_2 + y_3 + y_4 = 1,$ (since sum of probabilities must be unity)

where y_1, y_2, y_3, y_4, all ≥ 0.

Since maximin value of the game is greater than zero, dividing by V we get the following relations:

$$5\frac{y_1}{V} + 7\frac{y_2}{V} + 4\frac{y_3}{V} + 10\frac{y_4}{V} \le 1,$$

$$4\frac{y_1}{V} + 3\frac{y_2}{V} + 7\frac{y_3}{V} + 9\frac{y_4}{V} \le 1,$$

$$\frac{y_1}{V} + 2\frac{y_2}{V} + 5\frac{y_3}{V} + 6\frac{y_4}{V} \le 1,$$

$$\frac{y_1}{V} + \frac{y_2}{V} + \frac{y_3}{V} + \frac{y_4}{V} = \frac{1}{V}.$$

where $\frac{y_1}{V}, \frac{y_2}{V}, \frac{y_3}{V}, \frac{y_4}{V}$ all ≥ 0.

Putting $\frac{y_j}{V} = Y_j$, $j = 1, 2, 3, 4$, we get

$$\left.\begin{array}{l} 5Y_1 + 7Y_2 + 4Y_3 + 10Y_4 \le 1, \\ 4Y_1 + 3Y_2 + 7Y_3 + 9Y_4 \le 1, \\ Y_1 + 2Y_2 + 5Y_3 + 6Y_4 \le 1, \end{array}\right] \quad \text{... (9.23)}$$

$$Y_1 + Y_2 + Y_3 + Y_4 = 1/V, \quad \text{... (9.24)}$$

where Y_1, Y_2, Y_3, Y_4, all ≥ 0. ... (9.25)

Since Y is trying to minimize V, he must maximize 1/V. Thus the problem is to maximize objective function (equation 9.24) subject to constraints (9.23) and the non-negativity restrictions (9.25).

Similarly, an L.P. problem can be developed for X's strategies. X is interested in determining strategies x_1, x_2, x_3 that will maximize his minimum expected gain V. Thus

against Y_1, $5x_1 + 4x_2 + x_3 \ge V$,

against Y_2, $7x_1 + 3x_2 + 2x_3 \ge V$,

against Y_3, $4x_1 + 7x_2 + 5x_3 \ge V$,

against Y_4, $10x_1 + 9x_2 + 6x_3 \ge V$,

$x_1 + x_2 + x_3 = 1,$

where x_1, x_2, x_3, all ≥ 0.

Dividing by V and substituting $x_i/V = X_i$, $i = 1, 2, 3$, we get

$$\left.\begin{array}{l} 5X_1 + 4X_2 + X_3 \ge 1, \\ 7X_1 + 3X_2 + 2X_3 \ge 1, \\ 4X_1 + 7X_2 + 5X_3 \ge 1, \end{array}\right] \quad \text{...(9.26)}$$

$$10X_1 + 9X_2 + 6X_3 \ge 1,$$

$$X_1 + X_2 + X_3 = 1/V, \quad \text{...(9.27)}$$

where X_1, X_2, X_3, all ≥ 0. ...(9.28)

Since X is trying to maximize V, he must minimize 1/V. Thus the problem is to minimize objective function equation (9.27) subject to constraints (9.26) and the non-negativity restrictions (9.28). If programme for X is regarded as primal, that for Y it is dual and vice versa. The solution of the dual programme can be obtained from the primal optimal simplex table.

EXAMPLE 9.20-2.4

In a game, the organizer can hide the prize in one of the five fox holes 1, 2, 3, 4 or 5 as shown in Fig. 9.31. A gunner has a single shot and may fire at any of the four spot A, B, C or D. The gunner will win a prize of 4 points if the prize is in a fox hole adjacent to the spot where the shot was fired, otherwise he will lose 6 points. For example, if a shot if fixed at spot B, the gunner wins the prize if the prize is in fox hole 2 or 3.

① A ② B ③ C ④ D ⑤

Fig. 9.31

(a) Assuming this to be a zero-sum game, construct the reward point matrix.
(b) Find and eliminate all dominated strategies.
(c) Write down each player's L.P.

[U.P. Tech. U. MBA, 2010]

Solution

(*a*) The reward point matrix is written below:

TABLE 9.173

		Organizer				
		1	2	3	4	5
	A	4	4	–6	–6	–6
Gunner	B	–6	4	4	–6	–6
	C	–6	–6	4	4	–6
	D	–6	–6	–6	4	4

(*b*) Every value in column 2 is equal to or higher than the corresponding value in column 1. Therefore, column 2 is dominated by column 1 and hence it is deleted. Also every value in column 4 is equal to or higher than the corresponding value in column 5 and hence column 4 is deleted, resulting in reduced matrix given by table 9.174.

TABLE 9.174

		Organizer		
		1	3	5
	A	4	–6	–6
Gunner	B	–6	4	–6
	C	–6	4	–6
	D	–6	–6	4

In table 9.174, row B has the same values as row C. Hence any of them may be deleted. Row C is deleted and we get the final reduced table 9.175.

TABLE 9.175

		Organizer (Y)		
		1	3	5
	A	4	–6	–6
Gunner	B	–6	4	–6
(X)	D	–6	–6	4

(*c*) Let x_1, x_2, x_3, and y_1, y_2, y_3 be the probabilities with which X and Y respectively select their pure strategies. The game has no saddle point and the game value lies between –6 and 4. Let the value of the game to X be V. Consider the game from Y's point of view. He is trying to minimize V.

Then,

against A, $4y_1, - 6y_2 - 6y_3 \leq V$,
against B, $-6y_1 + 4y_2 - 6y_3 \leq V$,
against D, $-6y_1 - 6y_2 + 4y_3 \leq V$,
and $y_1 + y_2 + y_3 = 1$,
$y_1, y_2, y_3 \geq 0$.

Similarly, from X's (Gunner's) point of view,

against 1, $4x_1 - 6x_2 - 6x_3 \geq V$,
against 3, $-6x_1 + 4x_2 - 6x_3 \geq V$,
against 5, $-6x_1 - 6x_2 + 4x_3 \geq V$,
and $x_1 + x_2 + x_3 = 1$,
$x_1, x_2, x_3 \geq 0$.

9.20-3 Iterative Method of Approximate Solution

Iterative method can be applied to solve 3 × 3 or higher games which cannot be solved by the method of matrices and are extremely tedious to be solved by method of linear programming. This method gives an approximate solution for the value of the game and the true value can be determined to any degree of accuracy. Optimum strategies can also be determined but not so satisfactorily. The method assumes that each player acts under the assumption that past is the best guide for the future and will play in such a manner so as to maximize the expected gain or to minimize the expected loss.

EXAMPLE 9.20-3.1

Find the value and optimum strategies of the rectangular game whose payoff matrix is given in table 9.176. Use iterative method of approximate solution.

TABLE 9.176

		B 1	B 2	B 3
A	1	2	0	0
	2	0	0	4
	3	0	3	0

Solution

In this method, player A selects any row arbitrarily and places it below the matrix. Let he select row 1. Player B examines this row and chooses a column corresponding to the *smallest* number in the row. Let it be column 3. Column 3 is then placed to the *right* of the matrix.

Player A examines this column and chooses a row corresponding to the *largest* number in this column. This is row 2. Row 2 is then added to the row last chosen and the sum of the two rows is placed beneath the row last chosen.

Player B chooses a column corresponding to the *smallest* number in the new row and adds this column to the column last chosen. In case of a tie, the player should choose the row or column different from his last choice. The procedure is repeated for a number of iterations. Ten iterations have been shown for the present example. The smallest number in each succeeding row and the largest number in each succeeding column have been ringed. The approximate strategies are determined by dividing the number of ringed elements in each row and in each column by the total number of iterations. Thus A's approximate strategies are (4/10, 3/10, 3/10) and B's approximate strategies are (5/10, 2/10, 3/10).

TABLE 9.177

		B 1	B 2	B 3											
A	1	2	0	0	0	0	0	2	4	(6)	(8)	(10)	(10)	10	4/10
	2	0	0	4	(4)	(4)	4	4	4	4	4	4	8	(12)	3/10
	3	0	3	0	0	3	(6)	(6)	(6)	6	6	6	6	6	3/10
		2	0	(0)											
		2	(0)	4											
		2	(0)	8											
		(2)	3	8											
		(2)	6	8											
		(2)	9	8											
		(4)	9	8											
		(6)	9	8											
		8	9	(8)											
		10	9	(8)											
		5/10	2/10	3/10											

The upper bound for the game value is determined by dividing the highest number in the last column (12), by the total number of iterations *i.e.,* 10 in this case. Similarly, the lower bound is determined by dividing the lowest number in the last row (8), by the total number of iterations, 10. Thus,

$$8/10 \le V \le 12/10 .$$

The approximate solution gets better with further iterations.

EXAMPLE 9.20-3.2

Solve the following game approximately :

TABLE 9.178

	Player B			
Player A	2	3	–1	0
	5	4	2	–2
	1	3	8	2

[*P.T.U. B.Tech. (C.Sc.) 2010*]

Solution

In this method, let player A select row 3, being the superior strategy over his other strategies and place it under the matrix. Player B examines this row and chooses column corresponding to the *smallest* number of this row. This is column 1. Column 1 is then placed to the right of the matrix. Player A examines this column and chooses a row corresponding to the *largest* number in this column. This is row 2. This row is then added to the row last chosen and the sum of the two rows is placed below the row last chosen. Player B then chooses the column corresponding to the smallest number in the new row and adds this column to the column last chosen. This procedure is repeated for a finite number of times. Ten iterations have been shown for the present example. The smallest number in each succeeding row and the largest number in each succeeding column have been ringed.

TABLE 9.179

	Player B														
	2	3	–1	0	2	2	2	2	2	2	2	4	6	8	0
Player A	5	4	2	–2	(5)	3	1	–1	–3	–5	–7	–2	3	8	$\frac{1}{10}$
	1	3	8	2	1	(3)	(5)	(7)	(9)	(11)	(13)	(14)	(15)	(16)	$\frac{9}{10}$
	(1)	3	8	2											
	6	7	10	(0)											
	7	10	18	(2)											
	8	13	26	(4)											
	9	16	34	(6)											
	10	19	42	(8)											
	11	22	50	(10)											
	(12)	25	58	12											
	(13)	28	66	14											
	(14)	31	74	16											
	$\frac{4}{10}$	0	0	$\frac{6}{10}$											

The approximate strategies are determined by dividing the *number* of ringed numbers in each row or column by the total number of ringed numbers. Thus A's approximate strategies are (0, 1/10,9/10) and B's approximate strategies are (4/10, 0, 0, 6/10).

The upper bound for the game value is determined by dividing the highest number in the last column (16) by the total number of iterations. Similarly, the lower bound is determined by dividing the lowest number in the last row (14) by the total number of iterations. Thus

$$\frac{14}{10} \leq V \leq \frac{16}{10}.$$

9.20.4 Summary of Systematic Methods for Solving Two-Person Zero-Sum Games

1. Look for a saddle point or points. If one is found, the game is readily solved.
2. Look for dominance. If dominance is found, delete the dominated row(s) and/or column(s). Each matrix so formed must be further checked for dominance.
3. If the size of the reduced matrix becomes (2 × 2), it can be solved by arithmetic and algebraic methods described in section 9.18.
4. If the size of the reduced matrix becomes (2 × *n*) or (*m* × 2), use graphical method to reduce it to (2 × 2) size matrix and then solve it by arithmetic or algebraic method. If graphical method is not to be applied, the game can still be solved by algebraic method and method of subgames. All these methods are described in section 9.19.
5. If the reduced size of the matrix becomes (3 × 3) or higher, algebraic method, method of matrices, simplex method of linear programming and iterative method of approximate solution can be used for solving it. These methods are described in section 9.20.

9.21 n-PERSON ZERO-SUM GAMES

These games are usually treated as if two coalitions are formed by the *n*-persons involved. The characteristics of such a game are values of the various games between every possible pair of coalitions. For example, for players A, B, C and D the following coalitions can be formed:

A against B, C, D;

B against A, C, D;
C against A, B, D;
D against A, B, C;
A, B against C, D;
A, C against B, D;
A, D against B, C.

If the value of the game for B, C, D coalition is V, then the value of the game for A is –V, since it is zero-sum game. Thus in a four-person zero-sum game there will be seven values or characteristics for the game, which are obtained from the seven different coalitions.

EXAMPLE 9.21-1

Find the values of the three-person zero-sum game in which player A has two choices X_1, X_2; player B has two choices Y_1, Y_2 and player C also has two choices Z_1 and Z_2. The payoff matrix is shown in table 9.180.

TABLE 9.180

Choice			*Payoff*		
A	*B*	*C*	*A*	*B*	*C*
X_1	Y_1	Z_1	3	2	–2
X_1	Y_1	Z_2	0	2	1
X_1	Y_2	Z_1	0	–1	4
X_1	Y_2	Z_2	1	3	–1
X_2	Y_1	Z_1	4	–1	0
X_2	Y_1	Z_2	–1	1	3
X_2	Y_2	Z_1	1	0	2
X_2	Y_2	Z_2	0	2	1

Solution

There are three possible coalitions:

1. A against B, C;
2. B against A, C;
3. C against A, B.

We shall solve each of the resulting game.

1. A against B, C. The payoff matrix in A's terms is shown in table 9.181.

TABLE 9.181

		B, C				
		Y_1,Z_1	Y_1,Z_2	Y_2,Z_1	Y_2,Z_2	
A	X_1	3	0	0	1	(0)
	X_2	4	–1	1	0	–1
		4	(0)	1	1	

The first step is to look for a saddle point. The game has a saddle point. Thus, we have the following solution for A against B, C :

A's best strategy is X_1,
B's and C's best combination of strategies is Y_1, Z_2,
value of the game for A is zero,
value of the game for B, C is zero.

2. B against A, C: The payoff matrix in B's terms is shown in table 9.182.

TABLE 9.182

		A, C			
		X_1,Z_1	X_1,Z_2	X_2,Z_1	X_2,Z_2
B	Y_1	2	2	–1	1
	Y_2	–1	3	0	2

The first step is to look for saddle point. In this game there is none. The next step is to reduce the game by the rules of dominance. Columns X_1, Z_2 and X_2, Z_2 are dominated and should, therefore, be deleted. The resulting reduced matrix is shown in table 9.183.

TABLE 9.183

		A, C			
		X_1, Z_1	X_2, Z_1		
B	Y_1	2	–1	1	1/4
	Y_2	–1	0	3	3/4
		1	3		
		1/4	3/4		

Solving this 2 × 2 game by arithmetic method we get the following result:

B's best strategy is to play choice Y_1 with a frequency of 1/4 and choice Y_2 with a frequency of 3/4. A's and C's best strategy is for C to play Z_1 and for A to play X_1 with a frequency of 1/4 and X_2 with a frequency of 3/4.

Value of the game for B $= \dfrac{2/4 - 3/4}{1/4 + 3/4} = -\dfrac{1}{4}$,

value of the game for A, C = 1/4.

3. C against A, B : The payoff matrix in C's terms is shown in table 9.184.

TABLE 9.184

		A, B			
		X_1,Y_1	X_1,Y_2	X_2,Y_1	X_2,Y_2
C	Z_1	–2	4	0	2
	Z_2	1	–1	3	1

The first step is to look for saddle point. In this case there is none. The next step is to reduce the game by the rules of dominance. Columns X_2, Y_1 and X_2, Y_2 are dominated by column X_1, Y_1 and the resulting reduced matrix is shown in table 9.185.

TABLE 9.185

		A, B			
		X_1, Y_1	X_1, Y_2		
C	Z_1	–2	4	2	2/8
	Z_2	1	–1	6	6/8
		5	3		
		5/8	3/8		

Solving it by the arithmetic method we get the following results:

C's best strategy is to play choice Z_1 with a frequency of 2/8 and choice Z_2 with a frequency of 6/8; A's and B's best strategy is for A to play X_1 and for B to play Y_1 with a frequency of 5/8 and Y_2 with a frequency of 3/8.

$$\text{Value of the game for C is} = \frac{-10/8+12/8}{5/8+3/8} = \frac{2/8}{1} = \frac{1}{4},$$

value of the game for A, B = – 1/4.

Therefore, the characteristics of the game are

$$V(A) = 0, \quad V(B, C) = 0,$$
$$V(B) = -1/4, \quad V(A, C) = 1/4,$$
$$V(C) = 1/4, \quad V(A, B) = -1/4.$$

9.22 LIMITATIONS OF GAME THEORY AND CONCLUDING REMARKS

Our discussion of game theory has been limited to two-person zero-sum games and *n*-person zero-sum games only. There are practically few applications of game theory to the real world situations. This is because of the following facts:

1. The environment in which management decisions are made is rarely a two-person; the government or society is often an external party involved in decision-making.
2. Sum of the gains and losses of the opponents may not be zero, resulting in nonzero-sum games.
3. In real life situations, it is very rare that both parties will have equal information and intelligence.
4. It is not easy to find the values of the payoff matrix accurately. Inaccurate values in the matrix will yield misleading results. To establish that one outcome is better than the other may not be difficult, but it is quite another thing to establish exactly how much better.
5. The solution to the games is based on the maximin or minimax principles according to which players will choose strategies that either maximize the minimum gains or minimize the maximum losses. In real life situations, managers may not adopt such conservative approach and may prefer to take risks. Moreover, the information regarding available strategies and payoffs may be incomplete and uncertain.
6. In real world, the selected strategy is usually continued for a sufficiently long period of time which amounts to long-term planning and for short durations this strategy may be wrong.

Game theory has not still reached its full potential. It may receive increasing application for solving O.R. marketing problems as more firms employ computers to simulate their operations. The wedlock of game theory with simulation for the solution of managerial marketing problems is likely to provide game theory the thrust necessary to become an important tool for quantitative decision-making.

9.23 BIDDING PROBLEMS

Business problems sometimes involve bidding for contracts. Companies often bid to get contracts, concessions and licences to use a patent, etc. The two types of bidding problems are

(*i*) Open or auction bids,

(*ii*) Closed bids.

In open bids, two or more bidders bid on an item of certain value until no body is willing to increase the bid. The last bid is, then, the winner bid.

In closed bids each bidder submits his bid in a closed envelope and the envelopes are opened all at one time and the highest (or lowest) bid is accepted. In this case none knows his opponent's bid.

Only some simple bidding problems can be solved by the game theory.

EXAMPLE 9.23-1

Two items of worth ₹ 100 and ₹ 150 each are to be auctioned at a public sale. There are only two bidders A and B. Bidder A has ₹ 125 and the bidder B has ₹ 155 with him. If each bidder wants to maximize his own return, what should be his strategy?

Solution

Let the successive increase of bids be λ. At any bid, each player has the option to increase the bid or to leave the opponent's bid stand. If B bids ₹ x on the first item (of value ₹ 100), then A has the following options:

If A lets B win the first item for ₹ x, then B will be left with ₹ $(155 - x)$ only for bidding on the second item *i.e.,* he cannot make a bid of more than ₹ $(155 - x)$ for the second item. Thus A will be positively able to win the second item for ₹ $(155 - x + \lambda)$. Therefore, A's gain by allowing B to win the first item for ₹ x will be

$$₹ [150 - (155 - x + \lambda)] = ₹ (x - \lambda - 5).$$

On the other hand, if A bids ₹ $(x + \lambda)$ for the first item and B lets him win the bid, then A's gain will be

$$₹ [100 - (x + \lambda)] = ₹ (100 - x - \lambda).$$

Now since A wants to maximize his return, he should bid ₹ $(x + \lambda)$ for the first item provided

$$100 - x - \lambda \geq x - \lambda - 5 \text{ or } x \leq ₹\ 52.50.$$

Thus A should bid for the first item till $x \leq$ ₹ 52.50. In case $x \geq$ ₹ 52.50, he should let B win it.

Similarly, B's gains in the two alternatives are

$$₹ [150 - (125 - y) - \lambda] \text{ and } ₹ (100 - y - \lambda),$$

where ₹ y denote A's bid for the first item. Thus B should bid ₹ $(y + \lambda)$ for the first item provided

$$100 - y - \lambda \geq 150 - (125 - y) - \lambda \text{ or } y \leq ₹\ 37.50.$$

Obviously, A will win the first item for ₹ 37.50 because he can increase his bid without any loss upto ₹ 52.50, and B will get the second item in ₹ (125 – 37.50) = ₹ 87.50 because A, after winning the first item in ₹ 37.50, cannot increase his bid for the second item beyond ₹ 87.50. Thus B will get the second item for ₹ 87.50. Therefore, gain to A is ₹ (100 – 37.50) = ₹ 62.50 and to B is ₹ (150 – 87.50) = ₹ 62.50.

EXAMPLE 9.23-2

Two items of values ₹ 100 and ₹ 120 respectively are to be bid simultaneously by two bidders A and B. Both players intend to devote a total sum of ₹ 130 to the two bids. If each uses a minimax criterion, find the resulting bids.

Solution

Here, the bids are closed since they are to be made simultaneously. Let A_1 and A_2 be the A's optimum bids for the first and second items respectively. Obviously, A's optimum bids are the ones that fetch the same profit to A on both the items. If p denotes the profit earned by a successful bid, then

$$2p = (100 - A_1) + (120 - A_2)$$

or $$2p = 220 - A_1 - A_2.$$

Since both A and B intend to devote only ₹ 130 for both the bids,

$$A_1 + A_2 = ₹130.$$

∴ $$2p = 220 - 130 = 90$$

or $$p = ₹\ 45.$$

Now $$p = 100 - A_1 \text{ or } A_1 = 100 - p = 100 - 45 = ₹\ 55.$$

Also $$p = 120 - A_2 \text{ or } A_2 = 120 - p = 120 - 45 = ₹\ 75.$$

Thus optimum bids for A are ₹ 55 and ₹ 75 for the first and second item respectively. Likewise, optimum bids for B can be determined which will also be ₹ 55 and ₹ 75 respectively for the two items.

EXERCISES 9.5

1. Write short note on applications of game theory. [*P.U. B.Com. April, 2004; Sept, 2004*]
2. For what type of business problems might game theory be helpful ? [*J.N.T.U. Hyderabad B.Tech. May, 2012; P.U. B.Com. Jan., 2005*]
3. Write any four limitations of game theory. [*P.U. B.Com. Sept., 2012; J.N.T.U. Hyderabad MBA June, 2012; B.Tech. (C.Sc.) Dec., 2011; P.T.U. B.Tech. (C.Sc.) 2010; MBA, 2008*]
4. Describe the role of theory of games for scientific decision-making. [*Kuru. U. B.Tech. (Mech.) May, 1989; M.Tech. Dec., 1988; May, 1988*]
5. Explain the assumptions underlying game theory. [*M.G.U., Kerala M.Com. June, 2012; J.N.T.U. Anantapur MBA August 2010; P.U. B.Com. Sept., 2012; April, 2007*]
6. What do you understand by zero-sum and nonzero-sum games ? What do you mean by strategy, dominance and saddle point ? [*R.U. M.Sc. (Math.) 2011; Mumbai U.MBA, 2010; Osmania U. MBA, 2010; J.N.T.U. Hyderabad B.Tech. May, 2009; P.T.U. MBA, 2008; P.U. B.Com. April, 2007; B.E.(Elect.) 2001; IGNOU MBA June, 2007*]
7. (*a*) State and prove minimax theorem for two-person zero-sum games.
   (*b*) Define the terms: payoff matrix, saddle point and dominance.
   [*Dayalbagh Edu. Inst. Agra M.B.A. Dec., 2012; J.N.T.U. Hyderabad MCA Feb., 2012; M.G.U. Kerala M.Com. June, 2012; P.T.U. M.Tech. Dec., 2011; Mumbai U. MBA, 2010 ; U.P. Tech. U. MBA, 2010; Karnataka B. E. June, 2010; U.P. Tech. U. MBA, 2010; V.T.U. Chennai U. B.B.A. Nov., 2010; SVSM PGDM, 2009; IGNOU MBA June, 2007; P.T.U. M.Tech. Nov., 2012; MBA, 2005; K.U. M.Sc., 2001; P.U. B.Com. Sept., 2006; March, 2006; Jan., 2005*]
8. Discuss the basic concepts of game theory giving examples. [*P.T.U. B.Tech., 2010; P.U. B. Com., 2000*]
9. Explain the following: (*i*) Minimax and maximin principles (*ii*) Pure and mixed strategies (*iii*) Two-person zero sum game.
   [*P.U. B.Com. Sept., 2014; April, 2013; JNTU Hydrabad B.Tech. (Mech.) May, 2012; Mumbai U. MBA, 2010; U.P. Tech. U. MBA, 2010; Dayalbagh Edu. Inst. Agra MBA Dec., 2012; Dec., 2011; 2007; IGNOU MBA Dec., 2006; P.T.U. M.Tech. Nov., 2012; (Mech.) 2010; MCA, 2010; MBA, 2009; B.Tech. (Mech.) 2007; J.N.T.U. Hyderabad B.Tech. (Mech.) May, 2012; May, 2011; Nov., 2010; June, 2009; P.U. MBA August, 2006; B.Com. April, 2003; Sept., 2004; M.Com. Sept., 2004*]
10. Discuss various methods of finding solutions to a given game. [*GNDU B.Com., 1991*]
11. Discuss the algebraic method for solving 2 × 2 games by taking a suitable example. [*J.N.T.U. Hyderabad B.Tech. Sept., 2011; P.U. B.Com. April, 2004; Sept., 2004*]
12. Explain the arithmetic method for finding optimal strategies for a 2 × 2 game. [*P.T.U. B. Tech. (C.Sc.) 2009*]
13. Explain graphical method to solve games. [*Karn. U.B.E. (Mech.) 1998; Madurai B.E. (Mech.) 1980*]
14. State the four properties which a competitive situation should have if it is to be called a competitive game. [*P.T.U. MBA Dec., 2014; J.N.T.U. Hyderabad B.Tech. April, 2011; Nov., 2010*]
15. What is a strictly determinable game ? A fair game ? What are the rules to find a saddle point ? [*J.N.T.U. Hyderabad B.Tech. April, 2011; P.T.U. MBA, 2008; P.U. B.Com. March, 2006*]
16. How is the concept of dominance used in simplifying the solution of a rectangular game?
   [*Dayalbagh Edu. Inst. Agra MBA Dec., 2014; P.U. B.Com. Nov., 2014; April, 2014; Sept., 2013; J.N.T.U. Hyderabad B.Tech. (C.Sc.) Dec., 2011; P.U.B.B.A., 2001; B.Com. April, 2006; April, 2004*]
17. Show how a game can be formulated as an L.P.P. [*IAS (Math.) 1999, Raj. U. M.Phil., 1990*]
18. Discuss equivalence of a matrix game and L.P. Explain the method of solving a game as L.P.P. [*J.N.T.U. Hyderabad B.Tech. Nov., 2010*]
19. Explain the interative method of getting an approximate solution to a game problem. [*Chennai M.Sc. (Stat.) 1979*]

20. For a two-person zero-sum game, the payoff matrix for player A is $\begin{bmatrix} a_{11} & a_{12} \\ a_{21} & a_{22} \end{bmatrix}$ with no saddle point. Obtain the optimal strategies (x_1, x_2) and (y_1, y_2).

[*Chennai U. M.Sc. (Math.) 1981*]

21. Define the following:
(i) Saddle point (ii) Pure strategy (iii) Mixed strategy (iv) Two-person zero-sum game.

[*P.T.U. MBA Dec., 2014; May, 2014, V.T.U. Karnataka B.E. June, 2012; J.N.T.U. Hyderabad B.Tech. Nov., 2011*]

22. Explain 'Theory of Games' and discuss in detail the importance of terminology used in game theory. [*Kuru. U.B.E. (Mech.) June, 2012*]

Section 9.15

23. The following games have saddle point solutions. Determine the saddle point and optimum strategies for each player.

(*a*)

	Y		
X	4	6	4
	2	10	0

(*b*)

	Y		
X	2	–1	3
	4	5	6

[*PTU B.Tech. (C.Sc.) 2010*]

(*c*)

	B	
A	1	4
	–1	–4
	–3	–2

(*d*)

	B	
A	4	4
	4	4

(*Ans.* (*a*) S.P. = 4, X_1, Y_1 or Y_3. (*b*) S.P. = 4, X_2, Y_1. (*c*) S.P. = 1, A_1, B_1. (*d*) S.P.= 4, A_1 or A_2; B_1 or B_2.)

24. Determine the optimum strategies and values of the following games:

(*a*)

	B			
A	–3	4	2	9
	7	8	6	10
	6	2	4	–1

[*J.N.T.U. Hyderabad B.Tech. June, 2009*]

(*b*)

	Y			
X	1	7	3	4
	5	6	4	5
	7	2	0	3

[*U.P. Tech. U.MBA, 2010*]

(*c*)

	B			
A	–1	9	6	8
	–2	10	4	6
	5	3	0	7
	7	–2	8	4

(*d*)

	B				
A	10	4	2	9	1
	7	6	5	7	8
	3	5	4	4	9
	6	7	3	3	2

(*Ans.* (*a*) A_2, B_3; V = 6. (*b*) X_2, Y_3; V = 4. (*c*) $0 \le V \le 7$. (*d*) A_2, B_3; V = 5.)

(*e*)

Firm B

	3	–1	4	6	7
Firm A	–1	8	2	4	12
	16	8	6	14	12
	1	11	–4	2	1

[*J.N.T.U. Hyderabad B.Tech. April, 2011; M.G.U. Kerala M.Com., June 2010; P.U. M.B.A. Feb., 2009; G.N.D.U.B. Com., 2007*]

(*Ans.* A_3, B_3; 6.)

25. Find the value of the games shown below. Also indicate whether they are fair or strictly determinable.

(*a*)

B

	1	9	6	0
A	2	3	8	–1
	–5	–2	10	–3
	7	4	–2	–5

(*b*)

B

	6	–2	–3	8
A	–1	–2	–7	0
	8	9	–6	–7
	9	5	–7	7

(*Ans.* (*a*) V = 0; A_1, B_4; fair. (*b*) V = –3; A_1, B_3; Strictly determinable.)

26. Solve the following game and find its value :

B

	–5	2	0	7
A	5	6	4	8
	4	0	2	–3

[*G.N.D.U. B.Com. April, 2006*]

(*Ans.* A_2, B_3 ; 4.)

27. Solve the following game :

		B 1	2	3	4	5
	I	4	4	2	–4	–6
A	II	8	6	8	–4	0
	III	10	2	4	–10	12

[*Dayalbagh Edu. Inst. Agra MBA, Dec., 2012; Dec., 2011*]

(*Ans.* A_{II}, B_4 ; –4.)

28. Find the range of values of p and q so that the entry (2, 2) is a saddle point in the following games:

(*a*)

B

	2	q	4
A	p	6	11
	7	3	4

(*b*)

Y

	0	2	3
X	8	5	q
	2	p	4

(*Ans.* (*a*) $p \ge 6$, $q \le 6$; (*b*) $p \le 5$, $q \ge 5$.)

Section 9.18-9.19

29. Two players A and B match coins. If the coins match, then A wins one unit of value; if the coins do not match, then B wins one unit of value. Determine optimum strategies for the players and the value of the game.

[*Delhi M.BA., 1972*]

(*Ans.* A (1/2, 1/2), B (1/2, 1/2); V = 0.)

30. Solve the game whose payoff matrix is

B

A		
	5	2
	3	4

by arithmetic method and verify the results by algebraic method. Calculate the game value.

[P.U. B.Com., Sept., 2008, 2006]

(*Ans.* A(1/4. 3/4), B (1/2, 1/2); V = 3.5.)

31. In a game of matching coins with two players suppose A wins one unit of value when there are two heads, wins nothing when there are two tails, and loses 1/2 unit of value when there are one head and one tail. Determine the payoff matrix, the best strategies for each player and the value of the game to A.

[*P.T.U. MBA May,* 2014; *IGNOU MBA Dec., 2006*]

(*Ans.* A(1/4, 3/4), B (1/4,3/4); V = –1/8.)

32. Use dominance property to solve the following game between two players A and B:

B

A			
	6	8	6
	4	12	2

[*Meerut M.Sc. (Math.) 1977*]

(*Ans.* A_1, B_3; V = 6.)

33. Solve the following game and find the game strategies and game value :

B

		1	2	3	4
	1	20	50	25	17
A	2	55	54	81	84
	3	45	44	80	73

[*P.T.U. MBA, 2008*]

(*Ans.* A_2, B_2; V = 54.)

34. Solve, by using dominance property, the following game:

B

		I	II	III
	I	1	7	2
A	II	6	2	7
	III	6	1	6

[*P.U. B.Com. Sept., 2007; P.T.U. MBA, 2005*]

(*Ans.* A(2/5, 3/5, 0), B(1/2, 1/2, 0); V = 4.)

35. Solve the following game by dominance method :

B

		I	II	III	IV
	I	[illegible]	8	3	13
	II	[illegible]	1	5	3
A	III	[illegible]	10	4	12
	IV	[illegible]	6	7	12

[*V.T.U. Karnataka B.E. (Mech.) Dec., 2012*]

36. (*a*) Define : (i) Saddle point (ii) Fair game.

(*b*) If the following payoff matrix has saddle point, determine the value of game and ranges of 'P' and 'Q'.

		B	
A	1	Q	6
	P	5	10
	6	2	3

[*V.T.U. Karnataka B.E. (Mech.) April, 2012*]

37. A game has the payoff matrix

$$A = \begin{bmatrix} 0 & 2 \\ 1 & 1 \end{bmatrix}.$$

Show that E(*x*, *y*) = 1 – 2*x* (*y* – 1/2) and deduce that in solution of the game, the first player follows a pure strategy while the second has infinite number of mixed startegies.

[*J.N.T.U. Hyderabad B.Tech. May, 2011; April, 2011; Nov., 2010*]

38. Distinguish between deterministic and probabilistic games. Children Srija and Himaja play a game and have some 25 paise coins and 50 paise coins. Each draws a coin from her bag without knowing other's choice. If the sum of coins drawn by both is even, Srija wins them; otherwise Himaja wins. Find the best strategy for each player and also find the value of the game.

[*J.N.T.U. Hyderabad B.Tech. (C.Sc.) Dec., 2011*]

39. Solve the following game by algebraic method :

		B 1	2
A	1	–2	–4
	2	–1	3
	3	1	2

[*J.N.T.U. Hyderabad MBA April, 2012; B.Tech. June, 2009*]

40. In a game of matching coins, player 'A' wins ₹ 8, if both coins show head and ₹ 1 if both are tails. Player B wins ₹ 3 when coins do not match. Given the choice of being player A or player B, which would you choose and what would be your strategy? [*V.T.U. Karnataka B.E. Jan., 2010*]

41. Solve the following game :

		B I	II	III	IV
A	1	20	15	12	35
	2	25	14	8	10
	3	40	2	19	5
	4	5	4	11	0

[*V.T.U. Karnataka B.E. Jan., 2010*]

42. Reduce the following game matrix by dominance and solve for optimal strategies :

		B b_1	b_2	b_3
A	a_1	9	8	–7
	a_2	3	–6	4
	a_3	6	7	7

[*R.U. MBA June, 2011; G.N.D.U. B.Com. April, 2008*]

(*Ans.* A(1/17, 0, 16/17), B(14/7, 0, 3/17); 105/17.)

43. Reduce the following games to 2 × 2 games and solve them :

(*a*)

	Y			
X	–2	–4	3	4
	–6	–5	2	1

(*Ans.* X(1, 0), Y(0, 1, 0, 0); V = –4).

(*b*)

	B		
A	6	–3	7
	–3	0	4

[*Chennai U.B.B.A. Nov., 2010*]
(*Ans.* A (1/4, 3/4), B (1/4, 3/4, 0); V = –3/4).

44. Find the solution of the following game:

	B		
A	1	3	11
	8	5	2

[*V.T.U. Karnataka B.E. Dec., 2010; Sambalpur Univ. May, 1977*]

$\left(Ans.\ A\left(\frac{6}{16}, \frac{10}{16}\right), B\left(\frac{9}{16}, 0, \frac{7}{16}\right); V = \frac{43}{8}.\right)$

45. (*a*) Explain clearly the following terms:
(1) Strategy
(2) Payoff matrix
(3) Saddle point. [*I.I.M.S. Calcutta, 1996*]

(*b*) Find the best strategy and the value of the following game:

		B		
		I	II	III
	I	–1	–2	8
A	II	7	5	–1
	III	6	0	12

[*Baroda Univ. April, 1973*]

$\left(Ans.\ A\left(0, \frac{12}{18}, \frac{6}{18}\right), B\left(0, \frac{13}{18}, \frac{5}{18}\right); V = \frac{10}{3}.\right)$

46. (*a*) What is game theory ? Include in your answer various approaches in solving for strategies and game values. [*Baroda Univ. B.E. May, 1975*]

(*b*) Describe the role of 'Theory of Games' for scientific decision-making.

(*c*) Describe how a 'Two-person zero-sum game' can be solved by linear programming. [*P.U.B.E. (Prod., 1977*]

47. Consider the game

		B		
		1	2	3
	1	5	50	50
A	2	1	1	0.1
	3	10	1	10

Verify that the strategies (1/6, 0, 5/6) for player A and (49/54, 5/54, 0) for B are optimal and find the value of the game. $\left(Ans.\ V = \frac{55}{6}.\right)$

48. Find the optimum strategies for X and Y and the value of the game:

	Y		
X	–6	10	11
	–1	–2	–3
	–1	–2	–4

[B.P.U.T., 2010]

$\left(Ans.\ X\left(\frac{2}{19}, \frac{17}{19}, 0\right), Y\left(\frac{14}{19}, 0, \frac{5}{19}\right); V = -\frac{29}{19}.\right)$

49. Find the optimum strategies for Y and the value of the game.

	Y				
X	4	–1	4	–1	2
	2	2	3	–4	2
	1	–3	1	0	–4

(*Ans.* Y (0, 0, 0, 6/7, 1/7); V = – 4/7.)

50. Two firms are competing for business under the conditions such that one firm's gain is another firm's loss. Firm A's payoff matrix is given below :

		Firm B		
		No advertising	*Medium advertising*	*Heavy advertising*
Firm A	*No advertising*	10	5	–2
	Medium advertising	13	12	15
	Heavy advertising	16	14	10

Suggest optimal strategies for the two firms and the net outcome thereof.

[*Chennai U.B.B.A. Nov., 2010*]

$\left(Ans.\ A\left(0, \frac{4}{7}, \frac{3}{7}\right), B\left(0, \frac{5}{7}, \frac{2}{7}\right);\ V = \frac{90}{7}.\right)$

51. Solve the following 3 × 5 game using dominance property :

		Player B				
		1	2	3	4	5
Player A	1	6	15	30	21	6
	2	3	3	6	6	4
	3	12	12	24	35	3

[*Chennai U. B.C.A. Nov., 2010*]

(*Ans.* A(1, 0, 0), B(0, 0, 0, 0, 1) ; V = 6.)

52. Solve the following game :

		B			
		I	II	III	IV
A	I	6	4	8	0
	II	6	8	4	8
	III	8	4	8	0
	IV	0	8	0	16

[*P.U. B.Com., 2007; B.B.A., 2001*]

$\left(Ans.\ A\left(0, 0, \frac{2}{3}, \frac{1}{3}\right), B\left(0, 0, \frac{2}{3}, \frac{1}{3}\right); V = \frac{16}{3}.\right)$

53. Solve the following game:

Player B

Player A					
	10	81	32	43	93
	59	63	39	69	73
	71	20	05	27	84
	34	14	44	44	69

[P.U.B.E. (E. & Ec.) 2002]

(*Ans.* A(0, 33/43, 10/43, 0), B(17/23, 0, 6/23, 0, 0); 53.8.)

54. Find the values of X and Y so that the following game has a saddle point :

Player B

Player A			
	18	Y	36
	X	54	99
	63	27	36

[P.U.B.E. (E. & Ec.; 2001]

(*Ans.* $54 < X < 63$, $18 < Y < 54$.)

55. Solve the following game :

B

A				
	1	7	2	4
	0	3	7	8
	5	2	6	10

[P.U.B.Com., 1999]

$\left(Ans.\ A\left(\tfrac{1}{3}, 0, \tfrac{2}{3}\right), B\left(\tfrac{5}{9}, \tfrac{4}{9}, 0, 0\right); V = 3.67.\right)$

56. Reduce the following game to 2 × 2 game by using dominance and modified dominance property and then solve the game.

B

A	B_1	B_2	B_3	B_4
A_1	1	2	–1	2
A_2	3	1	2	3
A_3	–1	3	2	1
A_4	–2	2	0	–3

[G.N.D.U. B.Com. April, 2009]

$$\left(Ans.\ \begin{matrix} & B_1 & B_2 \\ A_2 & 3 & 1 \\ A_3 & -1 & 3 \end{matrix}, A\left(0, \frac{2}{3}, \frac{1}{3}, 0\right), B\left(\frac{1}{3}, \frac{2}{3}, 0, 0\right); \frac{5}{3}.\right)$$

57. Solve the following game after reducing it by dominance method :

B

A	I	II	III	IV	V	VI
1	4	2	0	2	1	1
2	4	3	1	3	2	2
3	4	3	7	–5	1	2
4	4	3	4	–1	2	2
5	4	3	2	–2	2	2

[G.N.D.U. B.Com. April, 2012; P.U. B.Com. April, 2004]

$\left(Ans.\ A\left(0, \tfrac{6}{7}, \tfrac{1}{7}, 0, 0\right), B\left(0, 0, \tfrac{4}{7}, \tfrac{3}{7}, 0, 0\right); \tfrac{13}{7}.\right)$

58. Two breakfast food manufacturers, ABC and XYZ are competing for an increased market share. The payoff matrix, represented in the following table, shows the increase in market share for ABC and decrease in market share for XYZ:

		XYZ			
		Give coupons	*Decrease price*	*Maintain present strategy*	*Increase advertising*
ABC	*Give coupons*	2	–2	4	1
	Decrease price	6	1	12	3
	Maintain present strategy	–3	2	0	6
	Increase advertising	2	–3	7	1

Simplify the problem by the rules of dominance and obtain optimal strategies for both the manufacturers and the value of the game.

[*R.U. MBA June, 2011; Mumbai U. MBA, 2010; P.T.U. MBA June, 2003*]

$\left(Ans.\ A\left(0, \frac{1}{2}, \frac{1}{2}, 0\right), B\left(0, \frac{1}{10}, \frac{9}{10}, 0\right); 1.5.\right)$

59. Consider the following payoff matrix for two firms. What is the best mixed strategy for both the firms and also find out the value of the game.

	Firm II		
	No advertising	*Medium advertising*	*Large advertising*
Firm I *No advertising*	60	50	40
Firm I Medium advertising	70	70	50
Firm I Large advertising	80	60	75

[*P.U.B.E. (Elect.) 2001*]

$\left(Ans.\ I\left(0, \frac{3}{7}, \frac{4}{7}\right), II\left(0, \frac{5}{7}, \frac{2}{7}\right); V = \frac{450}{7}.\right)$

60. Two separate firms, A and B, for years have been selling a competing product which forms part of both firms' total sales. The marketing executive of firm A raised the question, "What should be the firm's strategies in terms of advertising for the product in question?" The market research team of the firm A developed the following data for varying degrees of advertising:

(*a*) No advertising, medium advertising and large advertising for both firms will result in equal market shares.

(*b*) Firm A with no advertising: 40% of the market with medium advertising by firm B and 28% of the market with large advertising by firm B.

(*c*) Firm A using medium advertising: 70% of the market with no advertising by firm B and 45% of the market with large advertising by firm B.

(*d*) Firm A using large advertising: 75% of the market with no advertising by firm B and 47.5% of the market with medium advertising by firm B.

Based upon the foregoing information, answer the marketing executive's question.

(*e*) What advertising policy should firm A pursue when consideration is given to the following factors :

Selling price : ₹ 4.00 per unit, variable cost of product : ₹ 2.50 per unit, annual volume for firm A: 30,000 units, cost of annual medium advertising : ₹ 5,000 and cost of annual large advertising : ₹ 15,000 ? What contribution, before other fixed cost, is available to the firm?

[*Delhi U. MBA, 2000, 1998; AIMA (Dip. in Mgt.) 1989, 1988*]

[**Hint.** The payoff matrix for the game is

		Firm B		
		No advt. A_1	Medium advt. A_2	Large advt. A_3
	No advt. A_1	50	40	28
Firm A	*Medium advt.* A_2	70	50	45
	Large advt. A_3	75	47.5	50

This matrix can be solved and the answer is A (0, $^1/_3$, $^2/_3$), B(0, 2/3, 1/3) ; V = 48.3 per cent of market value.

For part (*e*) the following table is first prepared :

Market share of firm A

		Firm B		
		No advt.	*Medium advt.*	*Large advt.*
	No advt.	0.50 × 30,000 = 15,000	0.40 × 30,000 = 12,000	0.28 × 30,000 = 8,400
Firm A	*Medium advt.*	0.70 × 30,000 = 21,000	0.50 × 30,000 = 15,000	0.45 × 30,000 = 13,500
	Large advt.	0.75 × 30,000 = 22,500	0.475 × 30,000 = 14,250	0.50×30,000 = 15,000

Given that the expenditure on medium and large advertisements is ₹ 5,000 and ₹ 15,000 respectively, the net profit to firm A can be calculated as follows :

Net profit = (Sale price – Cost price) × Sales volume – Advertising expenditure.

The net profit to the firm is shown in the following table :

Profit to firm A

		Firm B		
		No. advt.	*Medium advt.*	*Large advt.*
	No. advt.	1.5 × 15,000 = 22,500	1.5 × 12,000 = 18,000	1.5×8,400 = 12,600
Firm A	*Medium advt.*	1.5 × 21,000 – 5,000 = 26,500	1.5 × 15,000 – 5,000 = 17,500	1.5×13,500 – 5,000 = 15,250
	Large advt.	1.5 × 22,500 – 15,000 = 18,750	1.5×14,250 – 15,000 = 6,375	1.5×15,000 – 15,000 = 7,500

The following observations can be made from the table above :

(*i*) If firm A chooses strategy of 'No advt.', then minimum profit is ₹ 12,600 because firm B can use the strategy of 'Large advt.'

(*ii*) If firm A chooses strategy of 'Medium advt.' then minimum profit is ₹ 15,250 because firm B can use the strategy of 'Large advt.'

(*iii*) If firm A chooses strategy of 'Large advt', then minimum profit is ₹ 6,375 because firm B can use the strategy of 'Medium advt.'

Based on these observations, firm A should adopt the policy of medium advertising.]

61. In an election of M.L.A., two political parties A and B are thinking of nominating a candidate in a closed session, whose results are to be announced simultaneously. The following odds are offered for the various possible combinations of candidates:

Party A	*Odds*	*Party B*
Sharma	3:1	Singh
Sharma	4:1	Gill

Sharma	1:3	Bajwa
Goel	3:7	Singh
Goel	3:2	Gill
Goel	1:4	Bajwa
Kapoor	4:1	Singh
Kapoor	1:4	Gill
Kapoor	1:3	Bajwa

The parties want to select candidate in accordance with standard minimax criterion. What are the optimal strategies for party A and B ? (*Ans.* A (Sharma), B (Bajwa); V = –0.50.)

[Hint: If the payoff for a party are taken as its probability of winning, the two payoff matrices in the 'game' would be

		Party B		
		Singh	Gill	Bajwa
Party A	Sharma	0.75	0.80	0.25
	Goel	0.30	0.60	0.20
	Kapoor	0.80	0.20	0.25

Payoff matrix for party A

and

		Party B		
		Singh	Gill	Bajwa
Party A	Sharma	0.25	0.20	0.75
	Goel	0.70	0.40	0.80
	Kapoor	0.20	0.80	0.75

Payoff matrix for party B

With these payoff matrices, the game is not zero-sum. The game can be converted to zero-sum by taking the payoffs to be *differences* between the corresponding win probabilities.

The payoff matrix for party A becomes

		Party B		
		Singh	Gill	Bajwa
Party A	Sharma	0.50	0.60	–0.50
	Goel	–0.40	0.20	–0.60
	Kapoor	0.60	–0.60	–0.50

This matrix can be solved for optimal strategies.]

62. In a well known children's game, each player says 'stone' or 'scissors' or 'paper'. If one says 'stone' and the other 'scissors' , then the former wins a rupee. Similarly 'scissors' beats 'paper' and 'paper' beats 'stones', *i.e.,* the player calling the former word wins a rupee. If the two players name the same item, then there is a tie *i.e.,* there is no payoff. Write down the payoff matrix, find the value of the game and hence write down the optimal strategies for both the players.

[*Bombay B.Sc. (Stat.) 1977*]

Section 9.19-3

63. Solve the following 2 × 3 game by reducing it by graphical method :

		Player B		
		B_1	B_2	B_3
Player A	A_1	1	3	11
	A_2	8	5	2

[*P.U. B.Com. April, 2008*]

64. Solve the following game :

Player B

Player A		I	II
	I	2	5
	II	2	3
	III	3	2
	IV	–2	8

[*P.U. B.Com. Sept., 2013; April, 2011; G.N.D.U. B.Com. April, 2010*]

65. Solve the following game for A using graphical Method:

Player A

Player B		A_1	A_2	A_3	A_4
	B_1	–7	7	–4	8
	B_2	6	–4	–2	6

[*P.U. B.Com. April, 2013; Sept., 2011; G.N.D.U. B.Com. April, 2008*]

[**Hint.** Transpose the matrix and then solve.]

66. Solve the following game :

Player B

Player A		
	[illegible]	–3
	[illegible]	5
	–[illegible]	6
	[illegible]	1
	[illegible]	2
	–5	0

[*J.N.T.U. Hyderabad B.Tech. (C.Sc.) Dec., 2011; G.N.D.U. B.Com. April, 2006*]

67. Solve the following game graphically:

Player B

Player A						
	8	–4	–3	1	–6	–8
	–7	–5	–1	–6	–3	4

[*G.N.D.U. B.Com., 2002*]

68. Solve the following game graphically :

Player B

Player A		1	2	3	4	5	6	7	8
	1	5	–3	2	1	3	0	4	–1
	2	–1	6	0	3	2	–2	3	3

[*G.N.D.U. B.Com. April, 2002*]

69. (a) What are the assumptions made in the theory of games?

(b) Obtain the optimal strategies for both players and the value of the game for two-person zero-sum game whose payoff matrix is given in the table below:

Player A	*Player B*	
	B_1	B_2
A_1	–6	7
A_2	4	–5
A_3	–1	–2
A_4	–2	5
A_5	7	–6

[*J.N.T.U. Hyderabad B.Tech. May, 2011; P.U. B.Com. Sept., 2006*]

70. (a) Define :
   (i) Competitive game
   (ii) Pure strategies
   (iii) Mixed strategies
   (iv) Two-person zero-sum (or rectangular) game
   (v) Payoff matrix.

(b) Players A and B, each take out one or two matches and guess how many matches the opponent has taken. If one of the players guesses correctly, then the loser has to pay him as many rupees as the sum of the number held by both players. Otherwise, the payoff is zero. Write down the payoff matrix and obtain the optimal strategies of both players.

[*J.N.T.U. Hyderabad B.Tech. April, 2011; Nov., 2010*]

71. Solve the following 2 × 3 game by method of subgames :

A \ B	1	2	3
1	–1	7	6
2	5	–3	3

[*J.N.T.U. Hyderabad B.Tech. June, 2009*]

72. Solve the following (2 × 4) game by graphical method :

Player A \ *Player B*	I	II	III	IV
I	2	1	0	–2
II	1	0	3	2

[*V.T.U. Karnataka B.E. June, 2012*]

73. Reduce the following game to '3 × 2' by dominance principle and then solve it by graphical method:

Player A \ *Player B*	y_1	y_2	y_3	y_4
x_1	19	6	7	5
x_2	7	3	14	6
x_3	12	8	18	4
x_4	8	7	13	–1

[*V.T.U. Karnataka B.E. June, 2011*]

74. Two companies are competing for the same product. Their different strategies are given in the following payoff matrix :

Company B \ *Company A*	a_1	a_2	a_3
b_1	4	–1	0
b_2	–1	4	2

What are the best strategies for both companies ? Find the value of the game.

[*J.N.T.U. Hyderabad B.Tech. (Mech.) May, 2012*]

75. (a) Distinguish between the games with saddle points and games without saddle points.

(b) Solve the following game graphically:

–6	0	6	–3/2
7	–3	–8	2

[*J.N.T.U. Hyderabad B.Tech. (C.Sc.) Dec., 2011*]

76. Solve the following games by reducing them to 2 × 2 games by graphical method:

(*a*)

B

A					
	3	0	6	–1	7
	–1	5	–2	2	1

[*J.N.T.U. Hyderabad B.Tech May, 2011; April, 2011; Nov., 2010*]

$\left(\textit{Ans.}\ A\left(\frac{3}{7}, \frac{4}{7}\right), B\left(\frac{3}{7}, 0, 0, \frac{4}{7}, 0\right), V = \frac{5}{7}.\right)$

(*b*)

B

A					
	0	4	–8	–5	1
	1	5	8	–4	0

[*P.T.U. B.Tech. April, 2012*]

(*Ans.* A_2, B_4 ; V = –4.)

(*c*)

B

A		
	2	3
	6	7
	–6	10
	–3	–2
	3	2

(*d*)

B

A		
	–4	3
	–7	1
	–2	–4
	–5	–2
	–1	–6

[*P.T.U.M.Tech. April, 2012; Dayalbagh Edu. Inst. Agra MBA May, 2005*]

(*Ans.* (c) A_2, B_1 ; V = 6. (*d*) $A\left(\frac{5}{12}, 0, 0, 0, \frac{7}{12}\right), B\left(\frac{9}{12}, \frac{3}{12}\right); V = -\frac{9}{4}.$)

(*e*)

B

A		I	II	III
	I	1	3	11
	II	8	5	2

[*V.T.U. Karnataka B.E. Dec., 2010*]

$\left(\textit{Ans.}\ A\left(\frac{3}{11}, \frac{8}{11}\right), B\left(0, \frac{2}{11}, \frac{9}{11}\right); V = \frac{49}{11}.\right)$

(*f*)

B

A		I	II	III	IV
	I	2	2	3	–1
	II	4	3	2	6

[*V.T.U. Karnataka B.E. Dec., 2011; P.T.U. M.Tech. Nov., 2012 MBA, 2009; GNDU B.Com., 2003*]

(*g*)

B

A		B_1	B_2	B_3
	A_1	20,000	30,000	60,000
	A_2	45,000	45,000	30,000

[*Bombay M.M.S., 1997*]

$\left(\textit{Ans.}\ (f)\ A\left(\frac{1}{2}, \frac{1}{2}\right), B\left(0, 0, \frac{7}{8}, \frac{1}{8}\right); V = 2\frac{1}{2}.\ \ (g)\ A\left(\frac{3}{11}, \frac{8}{11}\right), B\left(\frac{6}{11}, 0, \frac{5}{11}\right); V = 38,182.\right)$

77. Solve the following 2×5 game using graphical method :

		Player B				
		1	2	3	4	5
Player A	1	4	2	5	–6	6
	2	7	–9	7	4	8

[*P.T.U. M.Tech. Nov., 2012; B. Tech. April, 2012; Chennai U.B.C.A. Nov., 2010*]

$$\left(Ans.\ A\left(\frac{13}{21}, \frac{8}{21}\right), B\left(0, {}^{10}\!/_{21}, 0, {}^{11}\!/_{21}, 0\right); V = \frac{-46}{21}.\right)$$

Section 9.20-1

78. Solve the following game problem by the method of matrices :

	B		
A	1	0	2
	3	0	0
	0	2	1

[*J.N.T.U. Hyderabad B.Tech. Sept., 2011*]

$$\left(Ans.\ A\left({}^{1}\!/_{4}, {}^{1}\!/_{4}, {}^{1}\!/_{2}\right), B\left({}^{1}\!/_{3}, {}^{1}\!/_{3}, {}^{1}\!/_{3}\right); V = 1.\right)$$

79. Solve the following 3×3 game by the method of matrices :

	B		
A	1	–1	–1
	–1	–1	3
	–1	2	–1

$$\left(Ans.\ A\left({}^{6}\!/_{13}, {}^{3}\!/_{13}, {}^{4}\!/_{13}\right), B\left({}^{6}\!/_{13}, {}^{4}\!/_{13}, {}^{3}\!/_{13}\right); V = -{}^{1}\!/_{13}.\right)$$

80. Solve the following rectangular game by the method of matrices:

	B			
A	3	–1	1	2
	–2	3	2	3
	2	–2	–1	1

[*Kuru. U. B.Tech. (Mech.) May, 1989; M.Tech. Dec., 1988; Delhi B.Sc. (Math.) 1974*]

$$\left(Ans.\ A\left({}^{5}\!/_{9}, {}^{4}\!/_{9}, 0\right), B\left({}^{4}\!/_{9}, {}^{5}\!/_{9}, 0, 0\right); V = {}^{7}\!/_{9}.\right)$$

81. Solve the following game by the method of matrices:

		B		
		I	II	III
A	I	7	1	7
	II	9	–1	1
	III	5	7	6

$$\left(Ans.\ A\left({}^{3}\!/_{10}, {}^{3}\!/_{10}, {}^{4}\!/_{10}\right), B\left({}^{19}\!/_{30}, {}^{7}\!/_{30}, {}^{4}\!/_{30}\right); V = {}^{28}\!/_{5}.\right)$$

82. Solve the following 3 × 3 game by the method of matrices:

B

A			
	0	0	0
A	0	–1	–1
	0	1	–1

$\left(Ans.\ A\left(0, \tfrac{1}{2}, \tfrac{1}{2}\right), B\left(0, \tfrac{1}{2}, \tfrac{1}{2}\right); V = 0.\right)$

83. (a) Write a note on:

(i) Saddle point

(ii) Value of the game.

(b) For the following matrix of payoffs find saddle point. If there is no saddle point, find the optimal strategies, their frequencies and value of the game.

B

	0	1	2
A	1	–2	3
	2	4	–1

[*J.N.T.U. Hyderabad B.Tech. Nov., 2010*]

84. (a) Consider the following payoff matrix and determine the optimal strategy:

		B I	II	III
	I	6	9	4
A	II	5	10	7
	III	9	8	9

(b) Write a note on zero-sum games. [*J.N.T.U. Hyderabad B.Tech. June, 2010*]

Section 9.20-2

85. Solve the following game by linear programming:

B

	0	2	2
A	3	–1	3
	4	4	–2

[*Kuru. U. M.Tech. May, 1998*]

$\left(Ans.\ A\left(\tfrac{6}{11}, \tfrac{3}{11}, \tfrac{2}{11}\right), B\left(\tfrac{5}{22}, \tfrac{8}{22}, \tfrac{9}{22}\right); V = \tfrac{17}{11}.\right)$

86. Write both the primal and the dual L.P. programmes for the following payoff matrix:

2	1	0	–2
1	0	3	2

[*P.T.U. B.Tech. (Mech.) Dec., 2006*]

(*Ans.* Primal: Minimize $1/V = X_1 + X_2$,
s.t. $2X_1 + X_2 \geq 1$, $X_1 \geq 1$, $3X_2 \geq 1$,
$-2X_1 + 2X_2 \geq 1$; $X_1, X_2 \geq 0$.
Dual: Maximize $1/V = Y_1 + Y_2 + Y_3 + Y_4$,
s.t. $2Y_1 + Y_2 - 2Y_4 \leq 1$, $Y_1 + 3Y_3 + 2Y_4 \leq 1$;
$Y_1, Y_2, Y_3, Y_4 \geq 0$.)

87. Solve the following 3 × 3 game by linear programming:

		Player B	
Player A	1	–1	–1
	–1	–1	3
	–1	2	–1

[*Kuru. M.Sc. (Math.) 1975*]

$\left(Ans.\ A\left(\frac{6}{13}, \frac{3}{13}, \frac{4}{13}\right), B\left(\frac{6}{13}, \frac{4}{13}, \frac{3}{13}\right); V = -\frac{1}{13}.\right)$

88. Solve exercise no. 80 by the method of linear programming.

89. Write both the primal and dual L.P. programmes for the payoff matrix shown below.

		Y		
X	3	5	2	8
	2	6	5	1
	4	7	3	9

(*Ans.* Primal: Minimize $1/V = X_1 + X_2 + X_3$,
subject to $3X_1 + 2X_2 + 4X_3 \geq 1$,
$5X_1 + 6X_2 + 7X_3 \geq 1$,
$2X_1 + 5X_2 + 3X_3 \geq 1$.
$8X_1 + X_2 + 9X_3 \geq 1$,
$X_1, X_2, X_3 \geq 0$.
Dual: Maximize $1/V = Y_1 + Y_2 + Y_3 + Y_4$,
subject to $3Y_1 + 5Y_2 + 2Y_3 + 8Y_4 \leq 1$,
$2Y_1 + 6Y_2 + 5Y_3 + Y_4 \leq 1$,
$4Y_1 + 7Y_2 + 3Y_3 + 9Y_4 \leq 1$,
$Y_1, Y_2, Y_3, Y_4 \geq 0$.)

90. Solve the following game by L.P. technique:

		B	
A	1	–1	3
	3	5	–3
	6	2	–2

[*R.U. M.Sc. (Math.) 2011; Delhi U. B.Sc. (Stat.) 2000*]

$\left(Ans.\ A\left(\frac{2}{3}, \frac{1}{3}, 0\right), B\left(0, \frac{1}{2}, \frac{1}{2}\right); V = 1.\right)$

91. Formulate the following game as an L.P.P. and obtain its solution:

		B		
		B_1	B_2	B_3
A	A_1	8	9	3
	A_2	2	5	6
	A_3	4	1	7

[*Osmania U.MBA July, 2010*]

$\left(Ans.\ A\left(\frac{21}{52}, \frac{12}{52}, \frac{19}{52}\right), B\left(\frac{2}{13}, \frac{3}{13}, \frac{8}{13}\right); V = \frac{67}{13}.\right)$

92. Write both the primal and dual L.P. programmes for the following rectangular game. Solve the game by simplex method.

1	–1	3
3	5	–3
6	2	–2

93. There are two competing departmental stores R and C in a city. Both stores have equal reputation and the total number of customers is equally divided between the two. Both the stores plan to run annual discount sales in the last week of December. For this, they want to attract more number of customers by using advertisement through newspaper, radio and television. By seeing the market trend, the store R constructed the following payoff matrix where the numbers in the matrix indicate a gain or a loss of customers. Find optimal strategies for stores R and C by L.P. method.

	Store C		
Store R	40	50	–70
	10	25	–10
	100	30	60

[*P.U.B.E. (Mech.) 1978*]

$\left(\textit{Ans.}\ \mathrm{R}\left(\frac{1}{5}, 0, \frac{4}{5}\right), \mathrm{C}\left(0, \frac{13}{15}, \frac{2}{15}\right); \mathrm{V} = 34.\right)$

Section 9.20-3

94. The matrix of a certain 3 × 3 game is given below.

	Y		
X	2	0	1
	0	2	1
	3	0	0

Obtain an approximate solution by iteration.

$\left(\textit{Ans.}\ \mathrm{X}\left(\frac{3}{10}, \frac{6}{10}, \frac{1}{10}\right), \mathrm{Y}\left(\frac{3}{10}, \frac{5}{10}, \frac{2}{10}\right); 1 \le \mathrm{V} \le 1.2.\right)$

95. Solve exercise no. 78 by iterative method of approximate solution.

$\left(\textit{Ans.}\left(\frac{1}{4}, \frac{1}{4}, \frac{1}{2}\right), \mathrm{B}\left(\frac{1}{3}, \frac{1}{3}, \frac{1}{3}\right); \mathrm{V} = 1.\right)$

96. Use iterative method to find approximate solution for the following game:

	Y				
X	3	4	5	–2	3
	2	–2	1	0	–2
	1	–1	2	1	6

97. Solve the following game approximately:

	B		
A	1	–1	–1
	–1	–1	3
	–1	2	–1

[*Delhi B.Sc. (Stat.) 1999; Jodhpur U. M.Sc. (Math.) 1992*]

$\left(\textit{Ans.}\ \mathrm{A}\left(\frac{4}{10}, \frac{3}{10}, \frac{3}{10}\right), \mathrm{B}\left(\frac{4}{10}, \frac{2}{10}, \frac{4}{10}\right); -\frac{2}{10} \le \mathrm{V} \le \frac{2}{10}\right)$

Section 9.23

98. Two items of worth ₹ 75 and ₹ 125 are to be auctioned at a public sale. There are only two bidders A and B. Bidder A has ₹ 100 and B has ₹ 130. What should be their strategies if each bidder is interested in maximizing his return?

[*Meerut U. (Math.) 1998*]

(*Ans.* A : Purchase price = ₹ 25; gain = ₹ 50;
B : Purchase price = ₹ 75; gain = ₹ 50.)

99. Two objects of worth ₹ 80 and ₹ 100 are to be bid simultaneously by two bidders A and B. Both have intention of devoting a total sum of ₹ 110 to the two bids. If each uses a minimax criterion, find the resulting bids.

(*Ans.* A : Optimum bids : ₹ 45, ₹ 65;
B : Optimum bids : ₹ 45, ₹ 65.)

9.24 INTRODUCTION TO INVESTMENT ANALYSIS

Efficient allocation of funds is one of the most important functions of the financial management in modern times. This function involves the firm's decision to invest its funds in long-term assets and other profitable activities. Such investment decisions are of great significance for the firm as they affect its wealth, influence its size, set the pace and direction of its growth and determine its business risk. *Thus investment decisions involve the most efficient investment of the funds in long-term activities in anticipation of the expected flow of future benefits over a number of years.* The future benefits are measured in terms of cash flows. In the investment decisions, it is the flow of cash—outflow and inflow—and not the accrued earnings which is important.

Investment decisions influence the firm's wealth. If the investment proposals are profitable, the firm's wealth will increase, otherwise it will decrease. The investment decisions, thus, affect the value of the firm. Every firm would, therefore, like to undertake *investment analysis* which involves the consideration of investment proposals, estimation of cash flows for the proposals, evaluation of cash flows, selection of projects based on some criterion and finally the continuous revaluation of these projects.

9.25 METHODS OF INVESTMENT ANALYSIS

The most widely used methods of evaluating an investment proposal are

A. *Deterministic Models*
   1. Break-Even Analysis
   2. Payback Period method
   3. Average Rate of Return Method
   4. Discounted Cash Flow Methods
      (*a*) Net Present Value Method
      (*b*) Internal Rate of Return Method
   5. Discounted Payback Period Method

B. *Probabilistic Models*
   1. Risk Adjusted Discount Rate Method
   2. Certainty-Equivalent Approach
   3. Expected Monetary Value Method
   4. Hillier's and Hertz's Models

9.26 BREAK-EVEN ANALYSIS

The break-even analysis is the most widely known form of cost-volume-profit (CVP) analysis. That is why the two terms are used interchangeably by many. The break-even analysis provides a relationship between revenues and costs with respect to volume (quantity) of sales. It represents the level of sales at which costs and revenues are in equilibrium; the equilibrium point being known as the break-even point (BEP). At the break-even point, total revenue is equal to the total costs; it is a no-profit, no-loss point. This analysis assumes that the total costs can be separated as fixed costs and variable costs.

Two approaches can be used to determine the break-even point: 1. The formula approach 2. The chart approach.

1. *The Formula Approach:* The break-even point can be computed in terms of units or in terms of money value of sales volume or as percentage of estimated capacity.

(*i*) *In Units :* For a single-product firm, the break-even point in terms of units will be reached when the total earned revenue becomes equal to the total costs. If s denotes the unit selling price, v the unit variable cost, F the fixed costs and Q_B the break-even point (units), then

$$\text{total revenue} = Q_B \cdot s, \text{ and}$$

$$\text{total costs} = F + Q_B \cdot v.$$

Therefore, at break-even point,

$$Q_B \cdot s = F + Q_B \cdot v$$

or $$Q_B = \frac{F}{s - v} \qquad \text{... (9.29)}$$

or $$\text{break-even point (units)} = \frac{\text{Fixed costs}}{\text{selling price/unit} - \text{variable cost/unit}}.$$

(*ii*) *In Money Value:* The break-even point for a single-product firm can also be expressed in terms of rupee value of sales volume. If both sides of equation (9.29) are multiplied by the unit selling price, we get the break-even point in terms of rupees. Thus

$$R_B = Q_B \cdot s = \frac{F}{s - v} \cdot s$$

or $$\text{break-even point (rupees)} = R_B = \frac{F}{1 - \frac{v}{s}}. \qquad \text{...(9.30)}$$

As both the variable costs and sales revenue vary in direct proportion to sales volume, the above formula can also be used for a multi-product firm. For such a firm,

$$\text{break-even point (rupees)} = \frac{\text{Fixed costs}}{1 - \text{Total variable costs / Total sales revenue}}. \qquad \text{...(9.31)}$$

(*iii*) *As a Percentage of Capacity:* The break-even point as a percentage of capacity is obtained by dividing the break-even sales by the total estimated sales or capacity sales. Thus

$$\text{break-even point (as a percentage of capacity)} = \frac{\text{Break-even sales}}{\text{Capacity sales}} \times 100.$$

2. *The Chart Approach:* The break-even chart (BEC) represents a pictorial view of the relationships between costs, volume and profit. The break-even point in this chart is the one at which the total cost line and the total revenue line intersect. The break-even chart is constructed as follows:

(*i*) Represent the sales volume along the horizontal axis. The sales volume may be expressed in terms of units, rupees or as a percentage of capacity.

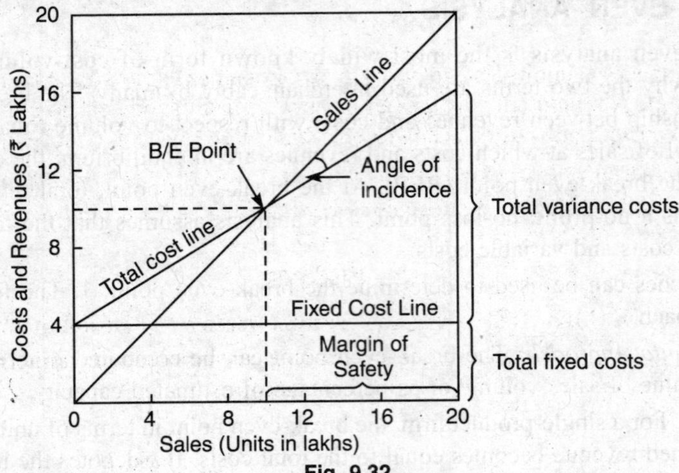

Fig. 9.32

(*ii*) Represent the revenues, fixed and variable costs along the vertical axis. A similar vertical line may be drawn on the right of the chart to complete the square.

(*iii*) Draw the fixed cost line parallel to the horizontal axis through the fixed cost point.

(*iv*) Draw the total revenue line and the total cost line. The point at which they intersect is the break-even point. The angle between these lines is called the angle of incidence. Larger this angle, larger are the profits and vice-versa. Managements aim to increase the angle of incidence to increase their rates of profits. The area between the lines to the left of this point is the *loss area* and represents the unrecovered fixed costs, while the area to its right is the *profit area (Fig.* 9.32) Profits are represented by the difference between total revenues and total costs.

The excess of actual or budgeted sales over the break-even sales is called *margin of safety.* The margin of safety ratio is expressed as

$$\text{M/s ratio} = \frac{\text{Budgeted sales} - \text{B/E sales}}{\text{Budgeted sales}}.$$

The margin of safety indicates the extent to which sales may fall before a firm suffers a loss. Larger the margin of safety, safer the firm.

To increase the margin of safety, the firm should try to increase output as well as sale price/ unit and reduce the fixed costs as well as variable costs.

Low break-even point and large angle of incidence in the break-even chart indicate that fixed costs are low and margin of safety is high. It is a sign of financial stability of the firm. Also, they indicate that high profits are earned over a large range of sales volume.

Assumptions in Break-Even Analysis

The above discussion of the break-even analysis is based on the following assumptions:

1. The total cost can be separated into fixed and variable costs.
2. The total fixed cost remains unchanged with changes in sales volume.
3. The variable cost per unit is constant and the total variable cost is proportional to the sales volume.
4. The selling price per unit is constant *i.e.*, it does not change with volume.
5. The firm manufactures only one product or if there are multiple products, the sales mix does not change.
6. All units produced are sold so that there is no opening or closing stock.

Utility of Break-Even Analysis

Break-even analysis is the most useful technique of profit planning and control. It is a device to explain the relationship between costs, volume and profits. The utility of the break-even analysis lies in the following advantages it has:

1. It is a simple device to understand complicated accounting data.
2. It is useful for studying the relationships between costs, volume and profits as it shows the effect on profits of the changes in the fixed costs, variable costs, selling price and volume of sales.
3. It is useful for forecasting costs and profits of various volumes of sales.
4. It is a tool for cost control as it shows the relative importance of the fixed costs and the variable costs.
5. Profitability of the various products can be studied and the most profitable product mix can be adopted.
6. It is a simple diagnostic tool. It indicates to management the causes of increasing break-even point and falling profits. An analysis of these causes can reveal to management what actions should be taken.
7. It provides basic information for further profit improvement studies and is a useful starting point for detailed investigations.
8. It is a useful method for considering the risk implications of alternative actions. From one alternative a firm may expect a higher profit and also a higher break-even point, while another alternative may produce comparatively lower profit but may also entail a lower break-even point. In taking a decision, the firm should not only consider the profits expected from the alternative but also the *probability* of reaching the break-even point. An alternative for which the *probability* of reaching the break-even point is higher should be preferred.

Limitations of Break-Even Analysis

1. It is difficult to separate costs into fixed and variable components.
2. The total fixed cost may not remain unchanged over the entire volume range.
3. The unit selling price and unit variable cost may not remain constant.
4. It is difficult to use for a multi-product firm.
5. It is a short-term concept and has limited use in long-term planning.
6. It is a static tool and shows the relationship between costs, volume and profits of a firm at a given point of time only.

EXAMPLE 9.26-1

A manufacturing firm produces a single product whose selling price is ₹ 16 per unit and the variable costs per unit are ₹ 12. If the annual fixed costs of the firm are estimated as ₹ 1,20,000, find the break-even point in units, in rupees and as a percentage of capacity if the firm has an estimated capacity of 50,000 units of the product. What is the margin of safety ?

Solution

Here, s = ₹ 16, v = ₹ 12 and F = ₹ 1,20,000.

$$\therefore \text{ Break-even point (units)}, \; Q_B = \frac{F}{s-v} = \frac{1,20,000}{16-12} = 30,000 \text{ units.}$$

$$\text{Break-even point (rupees)}, \; R_B = \frac{F}{1-\frac{v}{s}} = \frac{1,20,000}{1-12/16} = ₹\ 4,80,000.$$

$$\text{Break-even point (as a percentage of capacity)} = \frac{\text{Break-even sales}}{\text{Capacity sales}} = \frac{30,000}{50,000} = 60\%.$$

Margin of safety = 50,000 – 30,000 = 20,000 units.

EXAMPLE 9.26-2

Three firms X, Y and Z manufacture the same product. The selling price is ₹ 10 per unit of the product — equal for all firms. The fixed costs for firms X, Y and Z respectively are ₹ 1,00,000, ₹ 2,00,000 and ₹ 3,24,000; while the variable costs per unit are ₹ 8, ₹ 5 and ₹ 4 respectively. Determine the break-even points for all the firms. How much profits are earned by the firms if each of them sells 70,000 units? What will be the impact on their profits if sales (a) increase by 20 per cent (b) decrease by 20 per cent ?

Solution

1. The break-even points for the firms are

Firm X

$$\text{B/E point} = \frac{F}{s-v} = \frac{1,00,000}{10-8} = 50,000 \text{ units.}$$

Firm Y

$$\text{B/E point} = \frac{2,00,000}{10-5} = 40,000 \text{ units.}$$

Firm Z

$$\text{B/E point} = \frac{3,24,000}{10-4} = 54,000 \text{ units.}$$

2. The profits made by three firms at a sale of 70,000 units are

Firm X

Profit = (unit selling price – unit variable cost) × no. of units sold – total fixed costs

$= (s - v)\, n - F =$ ₹ [(10 – 8) × 70,000 – 1,00,000] = ₹ 40,000.

Firm Y

Profit = $(s - v)\, n - F =$ ₹ [(10 – 5) × 70,000 – 2,00,000]

= ₹ 1,50,000.

Firm Z

Profit = $(s - v)\, n - F =$ ₹ [(10 – 4) × 70,000 – 3,24,000] = ₹ 96,000.

3. When the sales increase by 20%, the effect on profits is shown below.

Firm X

Profit = [(10 – 8) × 70,000 × 1.2 – 1,00,000] = ₹ 68,000.

$$\therefore \text{Per cent increase in profit} = \frac{68,000 - 40,000}{40,000} \times 100 = 70\%.$$

Firm Y

Profit = ₹ [(10 – 5) × 70,000 × 1.2 – 2,00,000] = ₹ 2,20,000.

$$\therefore \text{Per cent increase in profit} = \frac{2,20,000 - 1,50,000}{1,50,000} \times 100 = 46.67\%.$$

Firm Z

Profit = ₹ [(10 – 4) × 70,000 × 1.2 – 3,24,000] = ₹ 1,80,000.

$$\therefore \text{Per cent increase in profit} = \frac{1,80,000 - 96,000}{96,000} \times 100 = 87.5\%.$$

4. When the sales decrease by 20 per cent the effect on profits will be as shown below.

Firm X

$$\text{Profit} = ₹\ [(10-8)\times 70\,000 \times 0.8 - 1{,}00{,}000] = ₹\ 12{,}000.$$

$$\therefore \text{ Per cent decrease in profit} = \frac{40{,}000-12{,}000}{40{,}000}\times 100 = 70\%.$$

Firm Y

$$\text{Profit} = ₹\ [(10-5)\times 70\,000 \times 0.8 - 2{,}00{,}000] = ₹\ 80{,}000.$$

$$\therefore \text{ Per cent decrease in profit} = \frac{1{,}50{,}000-80{,}000}{1{,}50{,}000}\times 100 = 46.67\%.$$

Firm Z

$$\text{Profit} = ₹\ [(10-4)\times 70{,}000 \times 0.8 - 3{,}24{,}000] = ₹\ 12{,}000.$$

$$\therefore \text{ Per cent decrease in profit} = \frac{96{,}000-12{,}000}{96{,}000}\times 100 = 87.5\%.$$

EXAMPLE 9.26-3

Suppose a firm has the following budget for a particular year:

Sales (1,00,000 units @ ₹ 20) = ₹ 20,00,000,
variable costs (1,00,000 units @ ₹ 10) = ₹ 10,00,000,
fixed costs = ₹ 4,00,000,
net profits = ₹ 6,00,000.

What shall be the impact on the firm's profits, if the following changes take place:

Increase in price: 20%,
decrease in sales volume: 25%,
increase in variable costs: 10%,
increase in fixed costs: 5%.

Solution

Selling price per unit, s = ₹ (20 × 1.2) = ₹ 24.

Sales volume, n = 1,00,000 × 0.75 = 75,000 units.

Variable cost/unit, v = ₹ (10 × 1.1) = ₹ 11.

Fixed costs, F = ₹ (4,00,000 × 1.05) = ₹ 4,20,000.

∴ Profit = $(s - v)\ n$ – F = ₹ [(24 – 11) × 75,000 – 4,20,000] = ₹ 5,55,000.

$$\therefore \text{ Per cent change in profit} = \frac{5{,}55{,}000-6{,}00{,}000}{6{,}00{,}000}\times 100 = -7.5\%.$$

EXAMPLE 9.26-4

A plant is manufacturing 3,000 heavy duty lathes per year and is operating at 75% of its capacity. The annual sales return is ₹ 1,05,00,000. The fixed cost of the plant is ₹ 40,00,000 and variable cost is ₹ 4,150 per unit. There is a proposal to utilise spare capacity by manufacturing precision lathes which would increase the fixed cost by ₹ 8,00,000 but reduce the variable cost by ₹ 750 per unit.

1. *Is the proposal economical ? Give reasons for your answer.*
2. *If a reduction in selling price by ₹ 500 per unit requires the plant to be run at 90% of its capacity to break-even, would this be a better proposal than the earlier one?*

Solution

Present plant capacity, n = 3,000 units.

$$\text{Profit} = (s - v)\, n - \text{F} \;=\; ₹ \left[\left(\frac{1,05,00,000}{3,000} - 4,150\right) \times 3,000 - 40,00,000\right]$$

$$= ₹\, [-650 \times 3,000 - 40,00,000] = -\, ₹\, 59,50,000.$$

$$\text{Break-even point} = \frac{\text{F}}{s - v} = \frac{40,00,000}{3,500 - 4,150} = \frac{80,000}{13} \text{ units.}$$

1. Full capacity of the plant, $n' = \dfrac{3,000}{0.75} = 4,000$ units.

Fixed cost, $\quad \text{F}' = ₹\, 48,00,000.$

Variable cost, $\quad v' = ₹\, (4,150 - 750) = ₹\, 3,400/\text{unit}.$

$$\therefore\ \text{Profit} = (s - v')\, n' - \text{F}' = ₹ \left[\left(\frac{1,05,00,000}{3,000} - 3,400\right) \times 4,000 - 48,00,000\right]$$

$$= ₹\, (100 \times 4,000 - 48,00,000) = -₹\, 44,00,000.$$

Thus the proposal is economical since it reduces the loss by ₹ 15,50,000.

2. Selling *price*, $s'' = ₹ \left[\dfrac{1,05,00,000}{3,000} - 500\right] = ₹\, 3,000.$

90% of break-even capacity, $n'' = 0.9 \times \dfrac{80,000}{13} = \dfrac{72,000}{13}$ units.

$$\therefore \qquad \text{Profit} = ₹ \left[(3,000 - 4,150) \times \frac{72,000}{13} - 40,00,000\right]$$

$$= ₹ \left[\frac{-1,150 \times 72,000}{13} - 40,00,000\right] = -\, ₹\, 1,03,69,230.$$

∴ This proposal results in very heavy losses and is not acceptable.

EXAMPLE 9.26-5

The Anita Shoe Store currently stocks three lines of lady shoes. Anita is considering dropping one line of shoes and adding two more. From the given data decide whether or not Anita should make this change. Give your reasons.

Shoes now stocked

Type	*Selling price(s)*	*Variable cost per pair (v)*	*Sales this year*
Flat	₹ *100*	₹ *60*	₹ *3,00,000*
Golf	*160*	*120*	*1,00,000*
Dress	*200*	*120*	*6,00,000*
Fixed costs: ₹ *3,00,000*			

Shoes stocked if proposal is accepted

Type	*Selling price(s)*	*Variable cost per pair(v)*	*Expected sales*
Flat	₹*100*	₹*60*	₹ *2,50,000*
Dress	*200*	*120*	*6,00,000*
Evening	*160*	*80*	*1,00,000*
Bed	*60*	*30*	*50,000*
Fixed costs: ₹ *3,00,000*			

Solution

Computation of net profit on shoes stocked

Type	*Sales this year*	*Sales units(n)*	*Contribution/unit* $(s-v)$	*Contribution*
Flat	₹ 3,00,000	3,000	₹ 40	₹ 1,20,000
Golf	1,00,000	625	40	25,000
Dress	6,00,000	3,000	80	2,40,000
				Total: ₹ 3,85,000

∴ Profit = Contribution – Fixed cost

= ₹ (3,85,000 – 3,00,000) = ₹ 85,000.

Computation of net profit on proposed shoes

Type	*Sales this year*	*Sales units(n)*	*Contribution/unit* $(s-v)$	*Contribution*
Flat	₹ 2,50,000	2,500	₹ 40	₹ 1,00,000
Dress	6,00,000	3,000	80	2,40,000
Evening	1,00,000	625	80	50,000
Bed	50,000	2,500/3	30	25,000
				Total: ₹ 4,15,000

∴ Profit = ₹ (4,15,000 – 3 00,000) = ₹ 1,15,000.

Thus Anita Shoe Store should make the change since it would yield an additional profit of ₹ (1,15,000 – 85,000) = ₹ 30,000.

EXAMPLE 9.26-6

Atlas Co. produces three types of cycle pedals A, B and C. They were produced at 100% capacity last year, which represented a ₹ 20,00,000 sales volume. All the units produced were sold. Fixed costs for the firm were ₹ 2,50,000. It was observed that type A pedals cost ₹ 12 per unit and sold at ₹ 20 per unit contributed ₹ 10,00,000 to the total sales; type B pedals cost ₹ 9 per unit and sold at ₹ 12 per unit contributed ₹ 6,00,000 to the total sales while type C pedals cost ₹ 4 per unit and sold for ₹ 8 per unit contributed ₹ 4,00,000 to the total sales. Determine (i) the break-even point (ii) the loss that would be expected if capacity were reduced by 10%.

Solution

This is a multi-product problem. To apply the concept of break-even analysis we need to find the contribution of each product not as a difference between the unit selling price and unit variable cost but as a percentage.

Product	*Unit selling price (₹)*	*Unit variable cost (₹)*	*Contribution per unit (₹)*	*Contribution as % age of selling price*	*Sales (₹)*	*Fraction of sales*	*Weighted %*
A	20	12	8	40%	10,00,000	0.50	20%
B	12	9	3	25%	6,00,000	0.30	7.5%
C	8	4	4	50%	4,00,000	0.20	10%
							Total: 37.5%

$$\text{Break-even point} = \frac{\text{Fixed cost}}{\text{Weighted per cent contribution}} = \frac{2,50,000}{37.5} = 6,666.7 \text{ units.}$$

Now sales volume at 100% capacity = ₹ 20,00,000.

∴ Profit at 100% capacity = Sales – Fixed costs – Variable costs

= ₹ [20,00,000 – 2,50,000 – (1 – 0.375) × 20,00,000]

= ₹ 5,00,000.

Sales volume at 90% capacity = ₹ (0.9 × 20,00,000) = ₹ 18,00,000.

∴ Profit at 90% capacity = ₹ [18,00,000 – 2,50,000 – (1 – 0.375) × 18,00,000]

= ₹ 4,25,000.

∴ Expected loss = ₹ (5,00,000 – 4,25,000) = ₹ 75,000.

$$\text{Per cent expected loss} = \frac{75,000}{5,00,000} \times 100 = 15\%.$$

9.27 PAYBACK PERIOD METHOD

Payback period is one of the most popular traditional methods of evaluating investment proposals. *It can be defined as the number of years required to recover the cash invested in a project.* If the annual cash inflows are same, the payback period can be computed by dividing cash invested by the annual cash inflow; if unequal, it can be calculated by adding up the cash inflows until the total is equal to the initial cash invested.

Payback period can be used as an accept or reject rule and also as a method of ranking projects. If the payback period calculated for a project is less than the maximum payback period set up by the management, the project is accepted; if not, it is rejected. As a ranking method it gives highest ranking to the project that has the shortest payback period and lowest ranking to the project with highest payback period.

Merits:

1. It is simple to understand and easy to calculate.
2. It is less costly than the other evaluation techniques.
3. It also makes clear that no project yields profit unless the payback period is over. It thus emphasises that projects in which cash inflow accrue quickly are profitable. It is quite useful for projects where the risk of obsolescence is high, *e.g.*, computers and aircraft manufacturing.

Demerits:

1. It takes no account of the cash inflows that accrue after the payback period and is not an appropriate method of measuring the profitability of an investment project.
2. It fails to consider the *magnitude* and *timing* of cash inflows *i.e.*, it gives equal weights to returns of equal amounts even though they take place in different periods.

EXAMPLE 9.27-1

A project requires a cash outlay of ₹ 60,000 and yields an annual cash inflow of ₹ 12,000 for 7 years. What is its payback period ?

Solution

$$\text{Payback period} = \frac{₹\ 60,000}{₹\ 12,000} = 5 \text{ years.}$$

EXAMPLE 9.27-2

An equipment costs ₹ 1,20,000 when installed. Old equipment can be sold for ₹ 20,000. The equipment will yield about ₹ 50,000 per year. If the corporate income tax rate is 50%, determine the payback period.

Solution

$$\text{Payback period} = \frac{\text{Net investment}}{\text{Annual aftertax earnings}}$$

$$= \frac{₹\ (1,20,000 - 20,000)}{₹\ (50,000 \times 0.5)} = 4 \text{ years.}$$

EXAMPLE 9.27-3

Calculate the payback period for a project which requires a cash outlay of ₹ 30,000 and generates cash inflows of ₹ 11,000, ₹ 10,000, ₹ 7,000 and ₹ 6,000.

Solution

When we add up the cash inflows, we find that ₹ 28,000 of the original outlay is recovered in the first three years. In the fourth year, the balance ₹ 2,000 of the original outlay needs to be recovered and the cash inflow during the year is ₹ 6,000. Assuming that the cash inflows occur uniformly during the year, the time required to recover ₹ 2,000 will be $\frac{₹\ 2,000}{₹\ 6,000} \times 12 = 4$ months.

Thus the payback period is 3 years and 4 months.

EXAMPLE 9.27-4

Calculate the payback periods of the following projects each requiring a cash outlay of ₹ 12,000. Suggest which one is acceptable if the standard payback period is 6 years.

	Cash inflows		
Year	*Project X*	*Project Y*	*Project Z*
1	*₹ 2,400*	*₹ 5,000*	*₹500*
2	*2,400*	*3,000*	*1,500*
3	*2,400*	*2,000*	*2,000*
4	*2,400*	*1,500*	*3,000*
5	*2,400*	*500*	*5,000*
6	*2,400*	*0*	*0*

Solution

Payback period

For project X $= \frac{12,000}{2,400} = 5$ years,

for project Y = ₹ (5,000 + 3,000 + 2,000 + 1,500 + 500)

= ₹ 12,000 is recovered in 5 years and

for project Z = ₹ (500 + 1,500 + 2,000 + 3,000 + 5,000)

= ₹ 12,000 is recovered also in 5 years.

Thus the payback period in each case is 5 years. As the actual payback period of every project is less than the standard payback period of 6 years, all projects are acceptable. However, intuitively project X is more desirable than project Y or Z as it yields cash inflows even after the payback period. Out of Y and Z, project Y should be preferred as larger cash inflows come earlier in its life as compared to project Z.

9.28 AVERAGE (ACCOUNTING) RATE OF RETURN METHOD

The accounting rate of return (ARR) is found by dividing the average annual net income (after taxes and depreciation) by the average cash outlay *i.e.,* average book value after depreciation. The accounting rate of return is thus an average rate and can be determined by the following equation:

$$\text{ARR} = \frac{\text{Average income}}{\text{Average investment}}$$

A variation of the ARR method is to divide the average earnings after taxes by the original cost of the project instead of average cost.

This method accepts all those projects whose ARR value is higher than the minimum rate established by the management and rejects those whose ARR value is lower. It also ranks the project as number one if it has highest ARR and lowest rank would be assigned to the project with lowest ARR.

Merits:

1. It is very simple to understand and use.
2. It can be easily calculated using the accounting data.
3. It uses the entire stream of incomes in calculating the accounting rate.

Demerits:

1. It uses accounting profits and not cash flows in comparing the projects.
2. It ignores the time value of money. Profits accruing in different periods are valued equally.
3. It does not allow for the fact that the profits can be reinvested.

EXAMPLE 9.28-1

Net investment for a new equipment is ₹ 1,00,000. Based on ten-year expectation, average earnings per year, after taxes and depreciation are estimated at ₹ 20,000. Find average rate of return.

Solution

$$\text{Average rate of return} = \frac{₹\ 20{,}000}{₹\ 1{,}00{,}000} \times 100 = 20\%.$$

EXAMPLE 9.28-2

A project costs ₹ 50,000 and has a scrap value of ₹ 10,000. Its stream of income before depreciation and taxes during first five years is ₹ 10,000; ₹ 12,000, ₹ 14,000, ₹ 16,000 and ₹ 20,000 respectively. Assume depreciation on straight line basis and 50% tax rate. Calculate the accounting rate of return for the project.

Solution

Depreciation for 5 years = ₹ (50,000 – 10,000) = ₹ 40,000.

∴ Depreciation per year = ₹ 40,000/5 = ₹ 8,000.

Calculation of Accounting Rate of Return

Period	*1* ₹	*2* ₹	*3* ₹	*4* ₹	*5* ₹	*Average* ₹
Earnings before dep. and taxes	10,000	12,000	14,000	16,000	20,000	14,400
Depreciation	8,000	8,000	8,000	8,000	8,000	8,000

Net earnings before taxes	2,000	4,000	6,000	8,000	12,000	6,400
Taxes @ 50%	1,000	2,000	3,000	4,000	6,000	3,200
Net earnings after taxes	1,000	2,000	3,000	4,000	6,000	3,200
Book value of investment:						
Beginning	50,000	42,000	34,000	26,000	18,000	
Ending	42,000	34,000	26,000	18,000	10,000	
Average	46,000	38,000	30,000	22,000	14,000	30,000

$$\text{Accounting rate of return} = \frac{₹\ 3,200}{₹\ 30,000} \times 100 = 10.67\%.$$

9.29 TIME-ADJUSTED OR DISCOUNTED CASH FLOW (DCF) METHODS

The methods discussed so far suffer from a serious drawback—they fail to recognise the time value of money in evaluating the investment worth of the projects.

Methods that fully recognise the time value of money are called *time-adjusted* or *discounted cash flow methods* or *present value methods.* They are

1. Net present value method
2. Internal rate of return method.

9.29-1 Net Present Value (NPV) Method

It is one of the discounted cash flow methods and fully recognises the time value of money. It correctly postulates that cash flows arising at different time periods differ in values and are comparable only when their equivalents–present values–are found out. It involves the following steps:

1. Select an appropriate rate of interest to discount cash flows. Generally this rate is the firm's *cost of capital* which equals the minimum rate of return expected by the investor.
2. Compute present value of cash inflows and outflows using the cost of capital as the discount rate. If all cash outflows are made in the initial year, then their present value will be equal to the cash actually spent.
3. Find out the net present value by subtracting the present value of cash outflows from the present value of cash inflows.
4. Accept the investment project if its net present value is positive or zero and reject it if its net present value is negative.

The equation for NPV, assuming that all cash outflows are made in the initial year t_o can be written as

$$\text{NPV} = \left[\frac{A_1}{1+k} + \frac{A_2}{(1+k)^2} + \ldots + \frac{A_n}{(1+k)^n}\right] - C$$

$$= \sum_{t=1}^{n} \frac{A_t}{(1+k)^t} - C, \qquad \ldots(9.32)$$

where $A_1, A_2, \ldots, A_n$ represent the cash inflows, k is the firm's cost of capital, C is the cash outlay and n is the expected life of the proposal.

Merits:

1. It recognises the time value of money.
2. It considers all cash flows over the entire life of the project.
3. It aims at maximizing the welfare of the owners of the organisation.

Demerits:

1. It is difficult to use.
2. It assumes that the discount rate—which is usually the firm's cost of capital—is known; but the cost of capital is difficult to understand and measure.
3. It may not give satisfactory answer when projects involving different amount of investment are compared. The project with higher NPV may not be desirable if it also requires a large investment.

EXAMPLE 9.29-1

Calculate the NPV for a project which initially costs ₹ 5,000 and generates year-end cash inflows of ₹ 1,800, ₹ 1,600, ₹ 1,400, ₹ 1,200 and ₹ 1,000 respectively in the five years of its life. Assume rate of return as 10%.

Solution

Calculation of the Net Present Value

Year	*Cash inflows*	*Discounting factor at 10%*	*Present value of cash inflows*
1	₹ 1,800	0.909	₹ 1,636
2	1,600	0.826	1,322
3	1,400	0.751	1,052
4	1,200	0.683	820
5	1,000	0.620	620
			₹ 5,450
			Less cash outlay 5,000
			NPV ₹ 450

EXAMPLE 9.29-2

The XYZ Co. Ltd. is considering three proposed investments A, B and C. Each requires an investment of ₹ 4,900 and each has an economic life of three years and total cash inflow over that period of ₹ 6,000. The pattern for each proposal differs as below.

Year	*Annual cash inflows*		
	A	*B*	*C*
1	*₹ 1,000*	*₹ 2,000*	*₹ 3,000*
2	*2,000*	*2,000*	*2,000*
3	*3,000*	*2,000*	*1,000*

Calculate the NPV of each proposal if the required rate of return is 10%.

[C.A (Final) Nov., 1976]

Solution

Calculation of the NPV of the Proposals

End of year	*Discounting factor at 10%*	*Proposal A Cash inflows*	*PV*	*Proposal B Cash inflows*	*PV*	*Proposal C Cash inflows*	*PV*
		₹	₹	₹	₹	₹	₹
1	0.909	1,000	909	2,000	1,818	3,000	2,727
2	0.826	2,000	1,652	2,000	1,652	2,000	1,652
3	0.751	3,000	2,253	2,000	1,502	1,000	751
			4,814		4,972		5,130
	Less cash outlay		4,900		4,900		4,900
	NPV		– 86		72		230

Thus proposal C is the best as it yields the maximum NPV of ₹ 230 among the three proposals.

9.30 INTERNAL RATE OF RETURN (IRR) METHOD

The internal rate of return is the rate that equals the present value of the cash inflows with the present value of cash outflows of an investment. Thus it is the rate at which the net present value of the investment is zero. It can be determined from the following equation:

$$C = \frac{A_1}{1+r} + \frac{A_2}{(1+r)^2} + \ldots + \frac{A_n}{(1+r)^n} = \sum_{t=1}^{n} \frac{A_t}{(1-r)^t}$$

or

$$\sum_{t=1}^{n} \frac{A_t}{(1+r)^t} - C = 0. \qquad \ldots(9.33)$$

It may be seen that the IRR formula is the same as used for the NPV method with the difference that in the NPV method the required rate of interest (cost of capital), k is known and the NPV is to be found out, while in the IRR method the value of r is to be determined at which the NPV is zero. The value of r in the IRR équation is determined by trial and error method. Some value of the rate of return is chosen and NPV of cash inflows is calculated. If this value is lower than the present value of cash outflows, a lower rate is tried; if this value is higher than the present value of cash outflows, a higher rate is tried. The process is repeated until the net present value becomes zero.

According to IRR method, a project is accepted if its internal rate of return is higher than or equal to the minimum required rate of return (*i.e.*, $r \geq k$); and the project is to be rejected if $r < k$.

Merits:

1. Like the NPV method, it considers the time value of money.
2. It considers cash flows over the entire life of the project.
3. It has psychological appeal to the users.

Demerits:

1. It is difficult to understand and use in practice.
2. It may yield results inconsistent with the NPV method if the projects differ in their expected lives or cash outlays or timing of cash flows.
3. It may not give unique answers in all situations.

EXAMPLE 9.30-1

A project costs ₹ 32,400 and is expected to generate cash flows of ₹ 16,000, ₹ 14,000 and ₹ 12,000 over its life of three years. Calculate the internal rate of return of the project.

Solution

Initially let us select a rate of 20% and calculate the NPV of the project.

Rate 20%

Year	*Cash inflows*	*Discount factor at 20%*	*Present value*
1	₹ 16,000	0.833	₹ 13,328
2	14,000	0.694	9,716
3	12,000	0.579	6,948
			29,992
		Less cash outlay	32,400
		NPV (–) ₹	2,408

Since NPV is negative, the rate assumed is higher. Therefore, lower rates should be tried. We now try 18%, 16% and 14% and get the following results:

Year	*Cash inflows* ₹	*D.F.at 18%*	*PV* ₹	*D.F.at 16%*	*PV* ₹	*D.F.at 14%*	*PV* ₹
1	16,000	0.847	13,552	0.862	13,792	0.877	14,032
2	14,000	0.718	10,052	0.743	10,402	0.769	10,766
3	12,000	0.609	7,308	0.641	7,692	0.675	8,100
			30,912		31,886		32,898
	Less cash outlay		32,400		32,400		32,400
	NPV		(–) ₹ 1,488		(–) ₹ 514		(+) ₹ 498

From the above observations it can be seen that the true rate of return lies between 16% and 14%. Let us try rate of 15%.

Rate 15%

Year	*Cash inflows*	*Discount factor at 15%*	*Present value*
1	₹ 16,000	0.870	₹ 13,920
2	14,000	0.756	10,584
3	12,000	0.658	7,896
			₹ 32,400
		Less cash outlay	32,400
		NPV	0

As NPV is zero at 15% rate, it is the true rate of return.

9.31 DISCOUNTED PAYBACK PERIOD METHOD

The payback period is defined as the number of years required to recover the original cash investment in a project. In case of the discounted payback period, we consider the discounted present values of future cash inflows and determine the number of years required to recover the initial investment. If discounted payback period is less than the desired payback period, the project is accepted, otherwise it is rejected.

EXAMPLE 9.31-1

The initial investment for a project is ₹ 12,000. If the cash inflows during its 5-year period are ₹ 4,000, ₹ 5,600, ₹ 5,000, ₹ 6,000 and ₹ 5,000 respectively, would you accept the project if the maximum desired payback period is 4 years? Assume that money has a value 10%.

Solution

Year	*Cash inflow*	*DF at 10%*	*Discounted present value (DPV)*	*Cumulative DPV*
1	₹ 4,000	0.909	₹ 3,636	₹ 3,636
2	5,600	0.826	4,626	8,262
3	5,000	0.751	3,755	**12,017**
4	6,000	0.683	4,098	16,115
5	5,000	0.621	3,105	19,220

It may be observed that the number of years required to recover the initial investment is 3 years. Thus the discounted payback period is 3 years. As the maximum payback period is 4 years, the project should be accepted.

9.32 PROBABILISTIC MODELS

In real world situations, the investment projects are exposed to risks. Risk exists because of inability of the decision-maker to make perfect forecasts. Forecasts cannot be made with perfection or certainty because the course of future events on which they depend is uncertain. We discuss below the various methods used for analysis of investment projects associated with risk.

9.33 RISK ADJUSTED DISCOUNT RATE

The economists think that to allow for risk, a businessman should have some premium over and above the usual discount had the project been riskfree; the greater the risk, the greater the associated risk premium. Therefore, to allow for the riskiness of future cash flows, *a risk premium rate* may be added to the otherwise risk-free discount rate.

According to the risk-adjusted discount rate method,

$$\text{NPV} = \sum_{t=1}^{n} \frac{A_t}{(1+k^*)^t} - C, \qquad \text{...(9.34)}$$

where risk-adjusted discount rate k^* = risk-free rate + risk-premium rate

$= i + \phi,$

$A_1, A_2, \ldots$ are the cash inflows and C is the initial capital outlay.

Merits:

1. It is simple and can be easily used.
2. It has an appeal for risk-averse businessman.

Demerits:

1. There is no easy way to determine the risk-premium rate and hence the risk-adjusted discount rate.
2. It assumes that the investors are risk-averse. Though it is generally true, there do exist risk-seekers in the world. Instead of demanding premium for taking risk, such persons may be willing to pay a premium to take risks.

EXAMPLE 9.33-1

An investment project costs ₹ 1,00,000 initially and is expected to generate cash flows in the next four years as per details given below. It was felt that the project is riskier and that the management would be willing to go in for that risk if an additional discount of 5% is paid as the risk-premium to them, in addition to a 10% risk-free discount. Using NPV method would you accept the proposal if

(i) it is considered to be risk free,

(ii) it is considered to be risky.

Year	:	*1*	*2*	*3*	*4*
Cash inflow	:	*₹ 50,000*	*₹ 40,000*	*₹20,000*	*₹ 20,000*

Solution

NPV of the project is computed below under risk as well as risk-free conditions. Here $i = 10\%$, $\phi = 5\%$ and hence $k^* = 15\%$.

Year	*Cash inflow*	*DF at 10%*	*PV*	*DF at 15%*	*PV*
1	₹ 50,000	0.909	₹ 45,450	0.870	₹43,500
2	40,000	0.826	33,040	0.756	30,240
3	20,000	0.751	15,020	0.658	13,160
4	20,000	0.683	13,660	0.572	11,440
			1,07,170		98,340
	Less cash outlay		1,00,000		1,00,000
		NPV	₹ 7,170		(–) ₹ 1,660

Thus the project is acceptable under condition of no risk but unacceptable under risk condition.

9.34 CERTAINTY-EQUIVALENT APPROACH

This approach accounts for the risk by applying a correction factor to all the future cash inflows, thereby reducing them to some conservative levels or to their certainty equivalents. According to it,

$$\text{NPV} = \sum_{t=1}^{n} \frac{\alpha_t A_t}{(1+i)^t} - C, \qquad \text{...(9.35)}$$

where A_t = the forecast of cash inflow without risk-adjustment,

α_t = the risk-adjustment factor or the certainty-equivalent coefficient, and

i = risk-free rate, assumed to be constant for all periods.

The certainty-equivalent coefficient α_t, varies inversely with risk and its value ranges between 0 and 1. A higher value of α_t is to be used for lower risk. The value is decided by the decision-maker subjectively or objectively.

The certainty-equivalent coefficient can be expressed as the ratio between certain cash flows and risky cash flows. That is

$$\alpha_t = \frac{A_t}{A_t^*} = \frac{\text{Certain cash flows}}{\text{Risky cash flows}}. \qquad \text{...(9.36)}$$

Merits: It recognises the risk explicitly in each cash flow.

Demerits:

1. The procedure of reducing the cash inflows may be inconsistent from investment to investment.

2. The person forecasting the cash inflows, well knowing that his estimates are going to be reduced, may inflate them in anticipation.

EXAMPLE 9.34-1

A company uses the certainty-equivalent approach in its evaluation of risky investments. Currently, the company has two alternative approaches. The expected net cash flows for the two projects are as follows:

Year	*Project A*	*Project B*
0	*(–) ₹ 15,000*	*(–) ₹ 20,000*
1	*7,500*	*12,500*
2	*7,500*	*10,000*
3	*7,500*	*7,500*
4	*5,000*	*5,000*

Risk analysis of the cash flow distribution has provided the following certainty-equivalents:

Year	*Project A*	*Project B*
0	*1.00*	*1.00*
1	*0.95*	*0.90*
2	*0.85*	*0.80*
3	*0.70*	*0.70*
4	*0.65*	*0.60*

If the after-tax risk free rate is 5% per annum, which of the two projects should be selected?

Solution

We compute the NPV for both the projects :

Project A

$$\text{NPV} = \frac{\alpha_1 A_1}{1+k} + \frac{\alpha_2 A_2}{(1+k)^2} + \frac{\alpha_3 A_3}{(1+k)^3} + \frac{\alpha_4 A_4}{(1+k)^4} - C$$

$$= \frac{0.95\times 7,500}{1.05} + \frac{0.85\times 7,500}{(1.05)^2} + \frac{0.70\times 7,500}{(1.05)^3} + \frac{0.65\times 5,000}{(1.05)^4} - 1.0\times 15000$$

= ₹ 4,775.

Project B

$$\text{NPV} = \frac{0.9\times 12,500}{1.05} + \frac{0.80\times 10,000}{(1.05)^2} + \frac{0.70\times 7,500}{(1.05)^3} + \frac{0.60\times 5,000}{(1.05)^4} - 1.0\times 20,000$$

= ₹ 4,973.

Therefore, project B should be selected.

9.35 EXPECTED MONETARY VALUE (EMV)

Future cash inflow may be treated as a random variable that assumes various values with time along with some probability attached to the event that it will assume a particular value. Once the probabilities are assigned to the future events, the next step is to compute the expected monetary value. This is found out by multiplying the monetary values of the possible events by the probabilities.

Thus, $$(\text{EMV})_t = \bar{A}_t = \sum_{i=1}^{n} A_{it}\, p_i, \qquad \text{...(9.37)}$$

where A_{it} is the cash inflow for the ith event in the tth time period.

For comparison of investment proposals, the expected NPV of each of them can then be computed as follows:

$$\text{Expected NPV} = \sum_t (PV \text{ of } \bar{A}_t) - C. \quad ...(9.38)$$

Though calculation of EMV is quite helpful in risk analysis, computation of *dispersion* of cash flows *i.e.,* the difference between the possible cash flows and their expected values gives better insight. A commonly used measure of risk is *standard deviation.* It measures the deviation or variance about the expected cash flow of each of the possible cash flows. It is calculated by the following formula:

$$\sigma = \sqrt{\sum_{i=1}^{n} (A_{it} - \bar{A}_t)^2 \, p_{it}} = \sqrt{\sum_{i=1}^{n} d_i^2 \, p_{it}} \,. \quad ...(9.39)$$

9.36 HILLIER AND HERTZ'S MODELS

The discounted cash flow method explained earlier has been further developed by Hillier and Hertz for probabilistic cash flows. Hillier postulates normal distribution for the expected NPV of the cash flows of the previous years and also puts forward formulae for computing the standard deviation, which can be used to compare the risk for various projects.

$$\text{Mean of NPV,} \quad M = \sum_{i=0}^{n} (1+r)^{-i} \, M_i \quad \text{and} \quad ...(9.40)$$

$$\text{variance of NPV,} \quad \sigma^2 = \sum_{i=0}^{n} (1+r)^{-2i} \,.\, \sigma_i^2 \,, \quad ...(9.41)$$

where M_i is the mean and σ_i the standard deviation of the cash flow distribution (assumed normal) of the ith period and r is the discounting factor.

Hertz endeavoured to find out the probability distribution of the NPV of an investment project concerning market introduction of a new product. He used simulation to get the results. He described input factors such as the market size, selling price, market growth rate, market share, total investment required, useful life of facilities, residual value of investment, operating costs and fixed costs by their frequency distributions. Random numbers were chosen and NPV was computed. This was repeated thousand times to derive the NPV histogram which was then approximated to a probability distribution. The shape of the distribution gave useful information to arrive at investment decisions.

EXAMPLE 9.36-1

A company has determined the following probabilities for net cash flows generated by a project:

Year 1		*Year 2*		*Year 3*	
Cash flow	*Probability*	*Cash flow*	*Probability*	*Cash flow*	*Probability*
₹2,000	*0.10*	*₹ 2,000*	*0.20*	*₹ 2,000*	*0.30*
4,000	*0.20*	*4,000*	*0.30*	*4,000*	*0.40*
6,000	*0.30*	*6,000*	*0.40*	*6,000*	*0.20*
8,000	*0.40*	*8,000*	*0.10*	*8,000*	*0.10*

Calculate the expected monetary values. Also calculate the present value of the expected cash flow using 10% discount rate.

Solution

The following table shows the calculation of the expected monetary value:

Year 1			Year 2			Year 3		
Cash flow ₹	*Probability*	*Expected Value* ₹	*Cash flow* ₹	*Probability*	*Expected value* ₹	*Cash flow* ₹	*Probability*	*Expected value* ₹
2,000	0.10	200	2,000	0.20	400	2,000	0.30	600
4,000	0.20	800	4,000	0.30	1,200	4,000	0.40	1,600
6,000	0.30	1,800	6,000	0.40	2,400	6,000	0.20	1,200
8,000	0.40	3,200	8,000	0.10	800	8,000	0.10	800
		6,000			4,800			4,200

From the expected value, the net present value (NPV) is calculated as follows:

Year	*Expected value*	*DF at 10%*	*Present value*
1	₹ 6,000	0.909	₹ 5,454.00
2	4,800	0.826	3,964.80
3	4,200	0.751	3,154.20
		PV of cash flow:	₹12,573.00

EXAMPLE 9.36-2

In example 9.36-1, determine the standard deviation about the expected value.

Solution

Let d_1, d_2 and d_3 denote the deviations of the returns from the mean for year 1, 2 and 3 respectively.

Calculation of Variances for Each Year

Year 1	Year 2	Year 3
$d_1^2 \times p$	$d_2^2 \times p$	$d_3^2 \times p$
$(2,000 - 6,000)^2 \times 0.10$	$(2,000 - 4,800)^2 \times 0.20$	$(2,000 - 4,200)^2 \times 0.30$
$(4,000 - 6,000)^2 \times 0.20$	$(4,000 - 4,800)^2 \times 0.30$	$(4,000 - 4,200)^2 \times 0.40$
$(6,000 - 6,000)^2 \times 0.30$	$(6,000 - 4,800)^2 \times 0.40$	$(6,000 - 4,200)^2 \times 0.20$
$(8,000 - 6,000)^2 \times 0.40$	$(8,000 - 4,800)^2 \times 0.10$	$(8,000 - 4,200)^2 \times 0.10$
$\sigma_1^2 = 4.0 \times 10^6$	$\sigma_2^2 = 3.36 \times 10^6$	$\sigma_3^2 = 3.56 \times 10^6$

Calculation of Standard Deviation

Year (*i*)	σ_i^2	$\frac{1}{(1+r)^{2i}}$	$\sigma_i^2 (1+r)^{-2i}$
1	4×10^6	0.826	3.304×10^6
2	3.36×10^6	0.683	2.295×10^6
3	3.56×10^6	0.564	2.008×10^6
		Total:	7.607×10^6

Standard deviation = ₹ $\sqrt{7.607 \times 10^6}$ = ₹ 2.758×10^3 = ₹ 2,758.

EXAMPLE 9.36-3

An investment proposal had the following discrete probability distributions of expected cash flows:

State (j)	*Year 1*		*Year 2*		*Year 3*	
	Return	*Prob.*	*Return*	*Prob.*	*Return*	*Prob.*
1	*₹ 50*	*0.10*	*₹ 20*	*0.10*	*–₹ 40*	*0.10*
2	*60*	*0.20*	*40*	*0.25*	*30*	*0.30*
3	*70*	*0.40*	*60*	*0.30*	*50*	*0.30*
4	*80*	*0.20*	*80*	*0.25*	*80*	*0.20*
5	*90*	*0.10*	*100*	*0.10*	*140*	*0.10*

Give (i) the expected return for each year and also net present worth of the total expected return (ii) standard deviation of the expected returns in each year and also standard deviation of the present value of expected returns. Assume discount rate 10%. [*CA. (Final) May, 1978*]

Solution

(*i*) *Computation of Expected Returns*

State j	*Year 1*			*Year 2*			*Year 3*		
	Return	*Prob.*	*Return × Prob.*	*Return*	*Prob.*	*Return ×Prob.*	*Return*	*Prob.*	*Return × Prob.*
1	₹ 50	0.10	₹ 5	₹ 20	0.10	₹ 2	–₹ 40	0.10	– ₹ 4
2	60	0.20	12	40	0.25	10	30	0.30	9
3	70	0.40	28	60	0.30	18	50	0.30	15
4	80	0.20	16	80	0.25	20	80	0.20	16
5	90	0.10	9	100	0.10	10	140	0.10	14
	Total		70			60			50

Year	*Expected returns*	*DF at 10%*	*Present value*
1	₹ 70	0.909	₹ 63.63
2	60	0.826	49.56
3	50	0.751	37.55

∴ Present worth of the total expected return = ₹ 150.74.

(*ii*) Denoting deviations of returns from the mean by d_1, d_2 and d_3 for years 1, 2, and 3 respectively, we get variances as follows:

State j	d_1	d_1^2	$d_1^2 p$	d_2	d_2^2	$d_2^2 p$	d_3	d_3^2	$d_3^2 p$
1	–20	400	40	–40	1,600	160	–90	8,100	810
2	–10	100	20	–20	400	100	–20	400	120
3	0	0	0	0	0	0	0	0	0
4	10	100	20	20	400	100	30	900	180
5	20	400	40	40	1,600	160	90	8,100	810
Total			$\sigma_1^2 = 120$			$\sigma_2^2 = 520$			$\sigma_3^2 = 1,920$

Year i	σ_i^2	$(1+r)^{-2i}$	$\sigma_i^2 \cdot (1+r)^{-2i}$
1	120	0.826	99.12
2	520	0.683	355.16
3	1,920	0.564	1,082.88

∴ Standard deviation of the present value of expected returns

$$= ₹\sqrt{99.12+355.16+1,082.88} = ₹\ 39.21.$$

EXAMPLE 9.36-4

Two mutually exclusive investment proposals are being considered. The following information is available:

	Project A	*Project B*
Cost	*₹ 20,000*	*₹ 20,000*
Life	*2 years*	*2 years*
Cash flow each year	*₹12,000*	*₹ 12,000*
Salvage value	*0*	*0*

Upon further analysis it was found that probability of cash inflow each year for the projects is as follows:

Project A		*Project B*	
Possible inflow	*Probability*	*Possible inflow*	*Probability*
₹10,000	*0.2*	*₹ 11,000*	*0.2*
12,000	*0.6*	*12,000*	*0.6*
14,000	*0.2*	*13,000*	*0.2*

Advise for selecting the proposal, assuming cost of capital 10% [*C.A. (Final) May, 1981*]

Solution

Project A

Inflow	*Prob.*	*Inflow × Prob.*	$d_1^2.p$
₹ 10,000	0.2	₹ 2,000	$(10,000 - 12,000)^2 \times 0.2 = 0.8 \times 10^6$
12,000	0.6	7,200	0
14,000	0.2		
		$M_1 = \frac{2,800}{12,000}$	$\sigma_1^2 = \frac{0.8\times10^6}{1.6\times10^6}$

Project B

Inflow	*Prob.*	*Inflow × Prob.*	d_2^2p
₹ 11,000	0.2	₹ 2,200	$(11,000 - 12,000)^2 \times 0.2 = 0.2 \times 10^6$
12,000	0.6	7,200	0
13,000	0.2	2,600	0.2×10^6
		$M_2 = 12,000$	$\sigma_2^2 = 0.4 \times 10^6$

Mean value of NPV and its variance for each project is calculated in table below.

Computation of Mean NPV and its S.D.

						Project A		*Project* B
Year i	M_i ₹	$(1+r)^{-i}$	$M_i(1+r)^{-i}$ ₹	$(1+r)^{-2i}$	σ_i^2	$(1+r)^{-2i}.\sigma_i^2$	σ_i^2	$(1+r)^{-2i}\sigma_i^2$
0	–20,000	1.000	–20,000	1.000	0	0	0	0
1	12,000	0.909	10,908	0.826	1.6×10^6	1.3216×10^6	0.4×10^6	0.3304×10^6
2	12,000	0.826	9,912	0.683	1.6×10^6	1.0928×10^6	0.4×10^6	0.2732×10^6
			Total: 820			2.4144×10^6		0.6036×10^6

Since variance of project B is less than that of project A, project B is to be preferred.

EXAMPLE 9.36-5

Three mutually exclusive investment proposals are being considered. The following information is available:

	Project A	*Project B*	*Project C*
Cost	*₹ 18,000*	*₹ 18,000*	*₹ 18,000*
Life	*2 years*	*2 years*	*2 years*
Cash flow each year	*₹ 12,000*	*₹ 12,000*	*₹ 12,000*

Upon further analysis it was found that the probability of cash inflow each year for projects A, B and C is as follows:

Project A		*Project B*		*Project C*	
Possible inflow	*Prob.*	*Possible inflow*	*Prob.*	*Possible inflow*	*Prob.*
₹ 6,000	*0.3*	*₹ 8,000*	*0.3*	*₹ 10,000*	*0.3*
12,000	*0.4*	*12,000*	*0.4*	*12,000*	*0.4*
18,000	*0.3*	*17,000*	*0.3*	*14,000*	*0.3*

Assuming cost of capital at 10%, advise the selection of project by giving the reasons for such action.

[*C.A.(Final) May, 1977*]

Solution

Project A

Possible inflow	*Prob.*	*Possible inflow × Prob.*	$d_1^2\, p$
₹ 6,000	0.3	₹ 1,800	$(6{,}000 - 12{,}000)^2 \times 0.3 = 10.8 \times 10^6$
12,000	0.4	4,800	0
18,000	0.3	5,400	10.8×10^6
		$M_1 = 12{,}000$	$\sigma_1^2 = 21.6 \times 10^6$

Project B

Possible inflow	*Prob.*	*Possible inflow × Prob.*	$d_2^2\ p$
₹ 8,000	0.3	₹ 2,400	$(8,000 - 12,300)^2 \times 0.3$ $= 5.547 \times 10^6$
12,000	0.4	4,800	0.036×10^6
17,000	0.3	5,100	6.627×10^6
		M_2= 12,300	$\sigma_2^2 = 12.210 \times 10^6$

Project C

Possible inflow	*Prob.*	*Possible inflow × Prob.*	$d_3^2 p$
₹ 10,000	0.3	₹ 3 000	$(10,000 - 12,000)^2 \times 0.3$ $= 1.2 \times 10^6$
12,000	0.4	4,800	0
14,000	0.3	4,200	1.2×10^6
		M_3=12,000	$\sigma_3^2 = 2.4 \times 10^6$

Calculation of Mean NPV and Its Variance

Year i	M_i	$(1 + r)^{-i}$	$M_i\ (1+r)^{-i}$	$(1 + r)^{-2i}$
0	– ₹ 18,000	1.000	– ₹ 18,000	1.000
1	12,000	0.909	10,908	0.826
2	12,000	0.826	9,912	0.683
	Total :		2,820	

Project A		*Project B*		*Project C*	
σ_1^2	$\sigma_1^2 .(1 + r)^{-2i}$	σ_2^2	$\sigma_2^2\ (1 + r)^{-2i}$	σ_3^2	$\sigma_3^2\ (1 + r)^{-2i}$
0	0	0	0	0	0
21.6×10^6	17.84×10^6	12.21×10^6	10.08×10^6	2.4×10^6	1.98×10^6
21.6×10^6	14.75×10^6	12.21×10^6	8.34×10^6	2.4×10^6	1.64×10^6
Total:	32.59×10^6		18.42×10^6		3.62×10^6

Since variance of project C is less than that of projects A and B, project C is preferred.

EXERCISES 9.6

1. What is investment analysis? Why is it of great significance to a firm?

   [*C.A. May, 1978*]

2. Discuss the importance of break-even analysis.

   [*Kuru. U.B. Tech. (Indl. Engg.) 1997 ; Karn . U.B. E. (Mech.) 1996*]

3. What is break-even analysis? How is it useful? Also explain as to how the break-even point of a multi-product can be calculated.

4. (*a*) List the different bases for comparison of different investment alternatives. Explain with examples.

   (*b*) Distinguish between rate of return and rate of interest.

   [*Karn. U.B.E. (Mech.) 1998*]

5. Clearly examine the net present value and internal rate of return methods used in appraising capital projects. Also discuss a few simple approaches for incorporating risk factor in such decision-making. *[Delhi U. M.Com., 1984]*
6. Discuss briefly the discounted cash flow method and its role in investment analysis.
7. Explain the concept of margin of safety. How can be the margin of safety be measured?
8. What do you mean by risk in investment proposals? How can it be measured ?
9. Discuss the discounted cash flow method and its role in investment decision.
10. ABC Ltd. is considering three projects. The expected cash flows are as follows :

	A	B	C
Initial investment	₹ 1,00,000	₹ 1,00,000	₹ 1,00,000
Annual cash inflows :			
Year 1	₹ 50,000	₹ 10,000	₹ 10,000
2	50,000	10,000	50,000
3	10,000	50,000	40,000
4	10,000	30,000	70,000
5	10,000	1,00,000	10,000

(*a*) Determine for each project (*i*) the payback period (*ii*) the internal rate of return (approximate) and (*iii*) the NPV, assuming the company's cost of capital as 10%.

(*b*) Rank the projects by the payback, NPV and IRR methods of capital budgeting.

11. The fixed costs for the year 2012-13 are ₹ 40,000. The sales for this period are of ₹ 1,00,000. The variable cost per unit is ₹ 2. Selling price of each product is ₹ 10 and the number of units involved coincides with the expected volume of output. Construct the break-even graph and determine:
    (*a*) Break-even point.
    (*b*) How many minimum number of products should be sold to earn profit?
    (*c*) Profit earned at a turnover of ₹ 80,000.
    (*d*) Margin of safety.
    (*e*) Angle of incidence.

(*Ans.* (*a*) 5,000 units, (*b*) 5,000 (*c*) ₹ 24,000 (*d*) 5,000 units (*e*) 34°.)

12. Three locations are being considered for a new plant. Fixed costs per year for the three locations are ₹ 30,000, ₹ 60,000 and ₹ 1,10,000 respectively. Variable costs in ₹/unit are 75, 45 and 25 respectively. The selling price of the product is ₹ 120. Find the most economical location for an expected volume of 2,000 units per year using the locational break-even analysis. *[IGNOU MBA June, 2000]*

(*Ans.* ₹ 60,000; ₹ 90,000; ₹ 80,000; location 2.)

13. A ball bearing manufacturing company is planning to install an additional plant which will require leasing new equipment for a monthly payment of ₹ 60,000. Variable cost would be ₹ 20 per item and each item would retail for ₹ 70.
    (*i*) How many ball bearings must be sold in order to break-even?
    (*ii*) What would be the profit (or loss) if 1,000 items are made and sold in a month ?
    (*iii*) How many items must be sold to realise a profit of ₹ 40,000 ?

[IGNOU MBA June, 2004]

(*Ans.* (*i*) 1,200 (*ii*) –₹ 10,000 (*iii*) 2,000.)

14. A manager has the option of purchasing one, two or three machines. Fixed costs and potential volumes are as follows :

Number of machines	*Total annual fixed costs (₹)*	*Corresponding range of output (no. of units)*
1	96,000	0 to 300
2	1,50,000	301 to 600
3	2, 00, 000	601 to 900

Variable cost is ₹ 100 per unit and revenue is ₹ 400 per unit.

(*i*) Determine the break-even point for each range.

(*ii*) If projected annual demand is between 580 and 660 units, how many machines should the manager purchase? [*IGNOU M.B.A. Dec., 2004*]

(*Ans.* 320, 500, 666.67 units; 2 machines.)

15. A firm is considering three capacity alternatives: A, B and C. Alternative A would have an annual fixed costs of ₹ 1,00,000 and variable cost of ₹ 20 per unit. Alternative B would have annual fixed costs of ₹ 1,20,000 and variable cost of ₹ 18 per unit. Alternative C would have fixed cost of Rs. 80,000 variable cost of ₹ 30 per unit. Revenue is expected to be ₹ 50 per unit. Which alternative has the lowest break-even quantity? Which alternative will produce the highest profits for an annual output of 10,000 units? Which alternative would require the lowest volume of output to generate an annual profit of ₹ 50,000? [*Dayalbagh Educational Inst. Agra M.Tech. Dec., 2012*]

(*Ans.* A with BEQ = 3,333.33 units, A as well as B with profit of ₹ 2,00,000 each; A with volume of 5,000 units.)

16. Alfa Infotech Ltd. has two investment proposals with the following cash flows:

Year	*Proposal A Cash flow (₹)*	*Proposal B Cash flow (₹)*
0	–4,00,000	–7,20,000
1	1,12,000	2,60,000
2	1,40,000	2,60,000
3	1,64,000	2,60,000
4	1,80,000	2,60,000

The cost of capital is 10% p.a. Assuming that both the proposals are equally risky, which proposal should be accepted? Justify your answer. [*Gujarat Technologicl U. MBA, 2011*]

17. Calculate the net present value of the following investment proposals and decide on the acceptance/rejection of these proposals. The discount rate is 10 per cent.

Proposal	*Investment (₹)*	*Net cash inflows (₹)*			
	0	1	2	3	4
I	20,000	8,000	8,000	8,000	8,000
II	20.000	6,000	8,000	10,000	10,000
III	20,000	4,000	8,000	10,000	10,000
IV	20,000	10,000	10,000	10,000	5,000

Also calculate the internal rate of return for these proposals.

18. Fill in the missing amounts in each of the four situations below. Each case is independent of others and only one product is being sold in each case.

Case	*Units sold*	*Sales*	*Variable expenses*	*Fixed expenses*	*Net income/ loss*
1	--	₹ 50 000	--	₹ 10,000	₹ 10,000
2	8,000	--	40,000	--	9,000
3	3,000	45,000	--	18,000	3,000
4	9,000	81,000	45,000	20,000	--

[*CA. (Final)Nov., 1978*]

(*Ans.* 1. Units sold cannot be determined, variable expenses : ₹ 30,000.

2. None of the missing amounts can be calculated.

3. ₹ 30,000.

4. ₹ 15,000.)

18. The Delta Corporation is considering an investment in one of the two mutually exclusive proposals: project A which involves an initial outlay of ₹ 1,70,000 and project B which has an outlay of ₹ 1,50,000 . The cetainty-equivalent approach is employed in evaluating risky investments. The current yield on treasury bills is 5% and the company uses this as the riskless rate. Expected values

of net cash flows with their respective certainty equivalents are given below.

	Project A		Project B	
Year	*Cash flow (₹)*	*Certainty equivalent*	*Cash flow (₹)*	*Certainty equivalent*
1	90,000	0.8	90,000	0.9
2	1,00,000	0.7	90,000	0.8
3	1,10,000	0.5	1,00,000	0.6

(*i*) Which project should be acceptable to the company ?

(*ii*) Which project is riskier? How do you know ?

(*iii*) If the company was to use the risk-adjusted discount rate method, which project would be analysed with higher rate ?

[**Hint.** (*i*) We compute the NPV for both the projects.

Project A

$$\text{NPV} = \frac{\alpha_1 A_1}{1+k} + \frac{\alpha_2 A_2}{(1+k)^2} + \frac{\alpha_3 A_3}{(1+k)^3} - C$$

$$= \frac{0.8 \times 90,000}{1.05} + \frac{0.7 \times 1,00,000}{(1.05)^2} + \frac{0.5 \times 1,10,000}{(1.05)^3} - 1,70,000 = ₹\ 9,574.$$

Project B

$$\text{NPV} = \frac{0.9 \times 90,000}{1.05} + \frac{0.8 \times 90,000}{(1.05)^2} + \frac{0.6 \times 1,00,000}{(1.05)^3} - 1,50,000 = ₹\ 44,279.$$

∴ Project B with higher NPV should be acceptable to the company.

(*ii*) Project A is riskier. It is because certainty equivalents associated with expected cash flow of project A are lower than those of project B.

(*iii*) project A being more risky would be analysed using higher discount rate.]

20. Assume that the cash flows of exercise 10 are independently and normally distributed with the following parametric values:

Period	0	1	2
Mean, M (₹)	– 1,600	1,500	1,000
Standard deviation, σ_i (₹)	400	500	600

(*a*) Compute the mean of the present value distribution.

(*b*) Compute the standard deviation of the present value distribution.

(*c*) Compute the probability of the investment having a net present value of zero or less.

(*d*) Compute the expected value of perfect information.

(*Ans.* (*a*) ₹ 590, (*b*) ₹ 780, (*c*) 0.224, (*d*) ₹ 100.)

21. Obtain expected DCF and associated risk as measured by the standard deviation for project A, if the cost of capital equals 10% and the probability distribution of cash flows is as given below.

Year 1		*Year 2*		*Year 3*	
Cash flows	*Probability*	*Cash flows*	*Probability*	*Cash flows*	*Probability*
₹ 1,000	0.10	₹ 1,900	0.20	₹1,500	0.10
1,500	0.20	2,500	0.30	2,250	0.70
2,000	0.40	2,750	0.20	2,500	0.10
2,500	0.20	3,150	0.30	3,000	0.10
3,000	0.10				

[*C.A. (Final) Nov., 1977*]

(*Ans.* ₹ 5,695, ₹ 675.)

22. An electronics company is considering investing in a new plant where it will produce either television components or computer components for a new as of yet untested computer. Their economist predicts that the returns from an investment in the television components will be independent of each other and have the following mean and variances:

Year	*Expected value*	*Variance*
1	₹ 1,00,000	₹20,000
2	80,000	15 000
3	2,00,000	30 000
4	2,00,000	40 000
5	2,00,000	50 000

The computer components' returns, on the other hand, are thought to be perfectly correlated with each other, as all of them will depend on the market's acceptance of the new computer. The returns on this investment have an expected value of ₹ 1,30,000 and a variance of ₹ 40,000 each year. Assume that both investments can be made for ₹ 5,00,000 each, and that the firm's cost of capital is 10%. Find the expected value and the variance of the net present value of (*a*) television project (*b*) computer project.

(*Ans.* (*a*) ₹ 67,980, ₹ 286
(*b*) –₹ 7,300, ₹ 758.)

23. Two mutually exclusive investment proposals are being considered. The following information is available:

	Project A	*Project B*
Cost	₹12,000	₹ 12,000
Life	2 years	2 years
Cash flow each year	₹ 8,000	₹ 8,000
Salvage value	0	0

Upon further analysis it was found that the cost of the project is a certain amount and so is the life of the project. However, the probabilities of cash inflow each year for projects A and B are as follows:

Project A		*Project B*	
Possible inflow	*Probability*	*Possible inflow*	*Probability*
₹4,000	0.2	₹7,000	0.2
8,000	0.6	8,000	0.6
12,000	0.2	9,000	0.2

Assuming cost of capital at 10%, advise the selection of the project.

[C.A. (Final) Nov., 1976]

24. A company is considering investing in two projects: Project A and B. However, project B can only be undertaken if there is a positive cash flow from A. The possible cash flows and their probabilities are as follows:

Project A

Cash inflow	*Probability*	*Date*
– ₹ 1,200	0.15	30th June, 2012
+ ₹ 2,500	0.45	30th June, 2012
– ₹ 100	0.40	30th June, 2012

Project B

Cash inflow	*Probability of B's cash inflow if A returns ₹ 2,500*	*Date*
+ ₹ 4,000	0.50	30th June, 2013
+ ₹ 500	0.25	30th June, 2013
–₹ 2,000	0.25	30th June, 2013

(*i*) Calculate the expected cash flow from project A on 30th June, 2012.

(*ii*) Calculate the NPV of the expected cash flow from project B on 30th June, 2013 using 10% interest rate.

(*iii*) What course of action would you recommend and why?

(*Ans.* (*i*) ₹ 905, (*ii*) ₹ 1,477,
(*iii*) invest in A as NPV is +ve, invest in B if A shows a +ve return.)

9.37 ANNUITY

An annuity is a series of payments or deposits of the same size made at equal intervals of time. Annuities are generally assumed to be made at the end of each period. They are of two types:

Certain annuity: When payments are supposed to be made over a certain period of time *e.g.*, payments of same size made in purchasing an equipment.

Contingent annuity: When payments are supposed to be made over an uncertain period *e.g.*, premium instalments of the L.I.C. policy of an individual as they are discontinued at the death of the person—an uncertain period.

Some terms commonly used in the context of annuities are

1. *Payment interval* : It is the time between successive payments.
2. *Term:* It is the time interval from the moment the first payment falls due to the moment the last payment interval ends.
3. *Annual rent:* It is the total sum of payments in one year.

9.37-1 Amount of an Annuity

It is the sum total of the accumulated values of all the payments made during the term of the annuity.

Let A = the constant periodic amount of each payment,
r = interest rate,
n = number of payment intervals (time periods),
S = the total accumulated amount, and
R = amount of Re. 1 in one year *i.e.,* $1 + r$.

Payment A made at the end of the 1st interval (year) remains invested for $(n - 1)$ years and shall accumulate to $A(1 + r)^{n-1} = AR^{n-1}$. Similarly, payment A made at the end of the 2nd year remains invested for $(n - 2)$ years and shall accumulate to AR^{n-2} and so on.

$$\therefore \quad S = AR^{n-1} + AR^{n-2} + AR^{n-3} + \ldots + AR^2 + AR + A$$

or
$$RS = AR^n + AR^{n-1} + AR^{n-2} + \ldots + AR^2 + AR.$$

Subtracting,
$$(R - 1)\,S = AR^n - A$$

or
$$S = \frac{A(R^n - 1)}{R - 1}.$$

The accumulated amount S may be used to payoff a debt or purchase a new equipment and is also called a *sinking fund.*

9.37-2 Present Value of an Annuity

It is the sum total of the present (discounted) values of all the payments made during the term of the annuity.

Let A = constant periodic amount of each payment,
r = interest rate,
n = number of payment intervals (time periods),

V = present value of the annuity, and

R = amount of Re. 1 in one year.

Present value of the first payment A made in the end of the first interval (year) is A/R = AR^{-1}. Similarly, present value of the second payment A made at the end of the second year is AR^{-2} and so on.

$$\therefore \quad V = AR^{-1} + AR^{-2} + ... + AR^{-(n-1)} + AR^{-n}$$

$$\text{or} \quad R.V. = A + AR^{-1} + AR^{-2} + ... - AR^{-(n-1)}.$$

Substracting, $(R-1)V = A - AR^{-n}$

$$\text{or} \quad V = \frac{A(1-R^{-n})}{R-1}.$$

9.37-3 Perpetual Annuity

An annuity that goes on for ever is called *perpetual annuity or perpetuity*. Since in this case $n \to \infty, \bar{R}^{-n} \to 0$ and, therefore, present value of perpetuity is

$$V = \frac{A}{R-1} = \frac{A}{(1+r)-1} = \frac{A}{r}$$

If mA is the present value of an annuity A, then the annuity is said to be worth m years' purchase.

∴ For perpetual annuity,

$$mA = \frac{A}{r} \quad \text{or} \quad m = \frac{1}{r}.$$

9.37-4 Present Value of Uneven Cash Inflows

Let $A_1, A_2, ..., A_n$ be the unequal cash inflows received at the end of year 1, 2, ..., n respectively. Then the present value of these sums at interest rate r is given by

$$V = \frac{A_1}{1+r} + \frac{A_2}{(1+r)^2} + ... + \frac{A_n}{(1+r)^n}$$

$$= A_1R^{-1} + A_2R^{-2} + ... + A_nR^{-n} = \sum_{t=1}^{n} A_tR^{-t}.$$

9.37-5 Deferred Annuity

It is an annuity which does not commence until after the lapse of a certain number of years. When an annuity is deferred for p years, it is said to commence after p years, and the first payment is made at the end of $(p + 1)$ years.

Let A = constant periodic amount of each payment,

r = interest rate,

p = no. of years for which the annuity is deferred,

n = no. of years for which the annuty is made,

V = present value of the annuity, and

R = amount of Re. 1 in one year.

The first payment is made at the end of $(p - 1)$ years.

Hence the present values of the first, second, third, . . . payments are given by $AR^{-(p+1)}$, $AR^{-(p+2)}$, $AR^{-(p+3)}$....

$$\therefore \quad V = AR^{-(p+1)} + AR^{-(p+2)} + AR^{-(p+3)} + ... + AR^{-(p+n)}$$

or $$RV = AR^{-p} + AR^{-(p+1)} + AR^{-(p+2)} + ... + AR^{-(p+n-1)}.$$

Subtracting, $$(R-1)\,V = AR^{-p} - AR^{-(p+n)} \text{ or } V = \frac{AR^{-p}(1-R^{-n})}{R-1}.$$

The present value of a *deferred perpetuity* to commence after p years will be

$$V = \frac{AR^{-p}}{R-1}.$$

EXAMPLE 9.37-1

(a) *A person deposits ₹ 1,200 in a bank for 4 years. How much will he get assuming an interest rate of 11 %?*

(b) *If the person plans investing ₹ 100 per year in a savings plan that earns 5% interest p.a. compounded annually, what is the sum of annuity payments at the end of 12 years?*

Solution

(a) The required sum is given by

$$S = P(1+r)^n = ₹\,1{,}200\,(1+0.11)^4$$
$$= ₹\,1{,}200\,(1.11)^4 = ₹\,1{,}821.68.$$

(b) Here, $A = ₹\,100$, $r = 5\% = 0.05$, $n = 12$ years, $R = 1.05$.

$$\therefore \quad S = \frac{A(R^n-1)}{R-1} = \frac{100\,(1.05^{12}-1)}{1.05-1} = ₹\,2{,}000\,(1.05^{12}-1) = ₹\,1{,}591.71.$$

EXAMPLE 9.37-2

(a) *Calculate the present value of ₹ 100 to be received at the end of (i) 5 years from now (ii) 10 years from now, assuming a time preference rate of 6% p.a.*

(b) *A project offers an annual return of ₹ 15,000 for 5 years. If the cost of money is 12%, what is the present value of the project ?*

(c) *Assuming a 10% discount rate, what is the present value of the perpetual annuity of ₹ 100 payable at the end of the first year, ₹ 200 payable at the end of the second year, and so on, increasing by ₹ 100 each year ?*

Solution

(a) (i) $$V = AR^{-n} = \frac{A}{R^n} = \frac{A}{(1+r)^n} = \frac{100}{(1.06)^5} = ₹\,74.73.$$

(ii) $$V = \frac{100}{(1.06)^{10}} = ₹\,55.84.$$

(b) $$V = \frac{A\left(1-R^{-n}\right)}{R-1} = \frac{15{,}000\left(1-1.12^{-5}\right)}{1.12-1} = 1{,}25{,}000\left(1-\frac{1}{1.12^5}\right)$$
$$= ₹\,54{,}071.64.$$

(c) $$V = 100\,R^{-1} + 200\,R^{-2} + 300\,R^{-3} + ... \text{ upto } \infty$$

or $$RV = 100 + 200\,R^{-1} + 300\,R^{-2} + ... \text{ upto } \infty.$$

Subtracting, $$V(R-1) = 100 + 100\,R^{-1} + 100\,R^{-2} + ... \text{ upto } \infty$$
$$= 100\,(1 + R^{-1} + R^{-2} + ... \text{ upto } \infty)$$
$$= 100\,\frac{1}{1-R^{-1}} = \frac{100R}{R-1}.$$

$$\therefore \quad V = \frac{100R}{(R-1)^2} = \frac{100\times 1.1}{(1.1-1)^2} = ₹11{,}000.$$

EXAMPLE 9.37-3

(*a*) *If money is worth 9%, compounded bimonthly, find the present value as well as the amount of an annuity whose annual rent is ₹ 1,800 which is payable bimonthly for 5 years.*

(*b*) *A person purchases a T.V. by making a cash payment of ₹ 5,000. In addition, he has to pay ₹ 1,000 at the end of each six months for 4 years. If money is worth 10%, compounded half-yearly, find the equivalent cash price for the T.V.*

(*c*) *Ramu has a capital of ₹ 20,000 for which he receives interest at 5%. If he spends ₹ 1,800 every year, show that he will be ruined before the end of the 17th year.*

Solution

(*a*) Here, $r = \frac{9}{6} = 1.5\% = 0.015,$

$$A = ₹\ \frac{1,800}{6} = ₹\ 300,$$

$$n = 5 \times 6 = 30 \text{ bimonths.}$$

$$\therefore \quad V = \frac{A(1-R^{-n})}{R-1} = \frac{300(1-1.015^{-30})}{1.015-1} = 20,000\left(1-\frac{1}{1.015^{30}}\right) = ₹\ 7,204.75.$$

$$S = \left(\frac{R^n-1}{R-1}\right) = \frac{300\,(1.015^{30}-1)}{1.015-1} = 20,000\,(1.563-1) = ₹\ 11,261.60.$$

(*b*) Required cash price = ₹ (5,000 + V),

where $V = \frac{A(1-R^{-n})}{R-1}.$

Here, A = ₹ 1,000, $n = 4 \times 2 = 8$, $r = \frac{10}{2} = 5\% = 0.05$, R = 1.05.

$$\therefore \quad V = \frac{1,000\,(1-1.05^{-8})}{1.05-1} = 20,000\left(1-\frac{1}{1.05^{8}}\right) = ₹\ 6,463.21.$$

∴ Cash price = ₹ (5,000 + 6,463.21) = ₹ 11,463.21.

(*c*) Spending ₹ 1,800 per year can be regarded as an annuity. The present value of this annuity for *n* years at 5% rate is given by

$$V = \frac{1,800\,(1-1.05^{-n})}{1.05-1} = 36,000\,(1-1.05^{-n}).$$

This must be equal to the capital of ₹ 20,000.

$$\therefore \quad 20,000 = 36,000\,(1-1.05^{-n})$$

or $\frac{5}{9} = 1-1.05^{-n}$ or $1.05^{-n} = \frac{4}{9}.$

Taking logs, $-n \log (1.05) = \log 4 - \log 9$

$\therefore \quad -n \times 0.0211892 = 0.6020599 - 0.9542425$ or $n = 16.62.$

∴ He will be ruined by the end of the 17th year.

EXAMPLE 9.37-4

(*a*) *Determine the present value discounted by 6% of an annuity of ₹ 400 for period of 3 years, commencing (i) 1 year's time, (ii) 4 year's time, (iii) 8 year's time.*

(*b*) *a, b, c year's purchase must be paid for an annuity to continue for n, 2n and 3n years respectively. Prove that* $a^2 - ab + b^2 = ac$.

Solution

(*a*) $$V = AR^{-p}\left(\frac{1-R^{-n}}{R-1}\right).$$

(*i*) $$V = 400\ .\ (1.06)^{-1}\ .\ \left(\frac{1-1.06^{-3}}{1.06-1}\right) = \frac{400}{1.06\times 0.06}\left(1-\frac{1}{1.06^3}\right) = ₹\ 1{,}008.68.$$

(*ii*) $$V = 400.\ (1.06)^{-4}\ .\ \left(\frac{1-1.06^{-3}}{1.06-1}\right) = \frac{400}{1.06^4\times 0.06}\left(1-\frac{1}{1.06^3}\right) = ₹\ 846.91.$$

(*iii*) $$V = \frac{400}{1.06^8\times 0.06}\left(1-\frac{1}{1.06^3}\right) = \frac{1{,}008.68}{1.06^7} = ₹\ 670.83.$$

(*b*) We are to prove that $a^2 - ab + b^2 = ac$ or equivalently, $a^2 + b^2 = a\ (b + c)$.

Now $$V = aA = \frac{A\left(1-R^{-n}\right)}{R-1}\ \therefore\ a = \frac{1-R^{-n}}{R-1},$$

$$V = bA = \frac{A\left(1-R^{-2n}\right)}{R-1}\ \therefore\ b = \frac{1-R^{-2n}}{R-1},$$

$$V = cA\ \frac{A\left(1-R^{-3n}\right)}{R-1}\ \therefore\ c = \frac{1-R^{-3n}}{R-1}.$$

$$\therefore\ \text{L.H.S.} = a^2 + b^2 = \left(\frac{1-R^{-n}}{R-1}\right)^2 + \left(\frac{1-R^{-2n}}{R-1}\right)^2$$

$$= \frac{1}{(R-1)^2}\ [(1-R^{-n})^2 + (1-R^{-2n})^2]$$

$$= \frac{1}{(R-1)^2}\ [1 - 2R^{-n} + R^{-2n} + 1 - 2R^{-2n} + R^{-4n}]$$

$$= \frac{1}{(R-1)^2}\ [2 - 2R^{-n} - R^{-2n} + R^{-4n}].$$

$$\text{R.H.S.} = a(b + c) = \left(\frac{1-R^{-n}}{R-1}\right)\left[\frac{1-R^{-2n}}{R-1} + \frac{1-R^{-3n}}{R-1}\right]$$

$$= \frac{(1-R^{-n})}{(R-1)^2}\ [2 - R^{-2n} - R^{-3n}]$$

$$= \frac{1}{(R-1)^2}\ [2 - R^{-2n} - R^{-3n} - 2R^{-n} + R^{-3n} + R^{-4n}]$$

$$= \frac{1}{(R-1)^2}\left[2 - 2R^{-n} - R^{-2n} + R^{-4n}\right].$$

$\therefore$ L.H.S. = R.H.S.

EXAMPLE 9.37-5

A man buys a car for ₹ 3,00,000. He estimates that its value will depreciate each year by 20% of its value in the beginning of the year. Find the depreciated value at the end of the 5 years.

If the man sets aside at the end of each of the 5 years a certain fixed sum (₹ A) to accumulate at 5.5% compound interest in order to be able to buy at the end of the 5 years another car costing ₹ 5,00,000 after allowing for the above depreciated value of the old car, find the value ₹ A of each payment.

Solution

Depreciated value of the old car after 5 years

$$= 3,00,000 \times (1 - \frac{r}{100})^n = ₹\ 3,00,000 \times (1 - \frac{20}{100})^5$$

$$= ₹\ 3,00,000 \times (0.8)^5 = ₹\ 98,304.$$

According to the problem,

$$₹\ (5,00,000 - 98,304) = A \cdot \left(\frac{R^n - 1}{R - 1}\right) \text{ or } ₹\ 4,01,696 = A\ \frac{1.055^5 - 1}{1.055 - 1}$$

or

$$A = ₹\ \left[\frac{4,01,696 \times 0.055}{1.055^5 - 1}\right] = ₹\ 71,974.50.$$

EXAMPLE 9.37-6

Accumulations in a provident fund are invested at the end of every year to earn 10% p.a. A person contributes $12\frac{1}{2}$ per cent of his salary to which the employer adds 10% every month. Find how much the accumulations will amount to at the end of 30 years of his service for every 100 rupees of his monthly salary.

Solution

Contribution towards provident fund per month = ₹ 22.50.

∴ Contribution towards provident fund per year = ₹ (22.50 × 12) = ₹ 270.

We have now to find the amount accumulated for an annuity of ₹ 270 every year at 10% for 30 years.

∴
$$S = \frac{A(R^n - 1)}{R - 1} = ₹\ \frac{270(1.1^{30} - 1)}{1.1 - 1} = ₹\ 2,700\ (1.1^{30} - 1) = ₹\ 44,413.38.$$

EXERCISES 9.7

1. What is annuity ? Distinguish between various types of annuities on the basis of (*i*) their terms and (*ii*) the payment times.
2. Derive expressions for obtaining (*i*) the amount of annuity (*ii*) The persent value of annuity (*iii*) the persent value of deferred annuity. [*L.U. B.Com., 2010*]
3. What is perpetuity ? Derive expression for present value of perpetuity at a given interest rate.
4. What is an annuity ? Write short notes on present value of an annuity and amount of an annuity. [*C.A. (Final) Dec., 1990*]
5. A person borrows ₹ 4,000 at 5% compound interest. If the principal and interest are to be repaid in 8 equal yearly instalments, find the amount of each instalment.

[**Hint.** $4,000 = \frac{A(1 - 1.05^{-8})}{1.05 - 1}$.] (*Ans.* ₹ 618.88.)

6. Calculate the sum of money received by a person retiring at the age of 58 years if he wants to commute his annual pension of ₹ 6,000 for a present payment when compound interest is reckoned at 8% and the expectation of his life is assessed at 10 years only.

[**Hint.** V = $\frac{6,000\left(1-1.08^{-10}\right)}{1.08-1}$.] (*Ans.* ₹ 40,260.50.)

7. A scooter is bought on instalment basis. ₹ 4,000 is paid initially at the time of signing the contract according to which four yearly instalments of ₹ 3,000 each are to be paid in addition at the end of each year. If interest is @ 8% per annum, what is the cash down price of the scooter?

[**Hint.** V = 4,000 + $\frac{3000\left(1-1.08\right)^{-4}}{1.08-1}$.] (*Ans.* ₹ 13,936.38.)

8. A firm sets aside for a reserve fund, a sum of ₹ 10,000 annually to enable it to payoff a debenture issue of ₹ 1,30,000 at the end of 10 years. Assuming that the reserve accumulates at 6% p.a. compound, find the surplus after paying off the debenture stock.

[**Hint.** Surplus = 10,000 $\frac{(1.06^{10}-1)}{1.06-1}$ – 1,30,000.] (*Ans.* ₹ 1,807.95.)

9. A man, on his 50th birthday decides to make a gift of ₹ 10,000 on his 60th birthday. He decides to save this amount by making equal annual payments upto and including his 60th birthday to a fund which gives 5% compound interest, the first payment being made at once. Calculate the amount of each annual payment.

[**Hint.** n = 11; 10,000 = A$\left(\frac{1.05^{11}-1}{1.05-1}\right)$.] (*Ans.* 703.89.)

10. A person purchases a car for ₹ 50,000. He estimates that its value will depreciate each year by 20 per cent of its value at the beginning of the year. Find the depreciated value of the car at the end of 5 years. It the person sets aside at the end of each of 5 years, a certain fixed sum to accumulate at 5% p.a. compound interest in order to be able to buy at the end of five years another car costing ₹ 80,000 (after allowing the above depreciated value of the old car), find the amount of his each payment.

[**Hint.** S = P$\left(1-\frac{20}{100}\right)^5$ = 50,00 $\left(1-\frac{20}{100}\right)^5$ = 16,384.

∴ (80,000 – 16,384) = A. $\left[\frac{1.05^5-1}{1.05-1}\right]$.] (*Ans.* ₹ 11,512.90.)

11. The accumulations in a provident fund are invested at the end of every year to earn interest @ 10% p.a. A person contributes $12\frac{1}{2}$ % of his salary to which the employer adds 10% every month. Find how much the accumulations will amount to at the end of 20 years of his service for every ₹ 1,000 of his monthly salary.

[**Hint.** M = $\left(1,000\times\frac{22.5}{100}\times12\right)\cdot\frac{1.1^{20}-1}{1.1-1}$.] (*Ans.* ₹ 1,54,642.49.)

12. A person has borrowed ₹ 50,00,000 from a bank to buy a house at 9% p.a. What should be the uniform yearly instalment so as to repay the loan at the end of four years? [*Mumbai U. MBA, 2010*]

13. Mr. X deposited ₹ 10,000 in a bank for 3 years offering interest at the rate of 6% p.a. compounded half yearly during first year, at the rate of 12% p.a., compounded quarterly during second year and at 10% p.a. compounded continually during third year. Find the balance after 3 years. [*L.U. B.Com., 2010*]

14. A company establishes a sinking fund to buy a machine of ₹ 2,50,000 after 4 years. Contributions to the fund are made at the end of every year. Find the amount of each annual deposit if the interest is 18%, compounded annually. [*L.U. B.Com., 2010*]

Queuing Models

The queuing theory or waiting line theory owes its development to A.K. Erlang. He, in 1903, took up the problem on congestion of telephone traffic. The difficulty was that during busy periods, telephone operators were unable to handle the calls the moment they were made, resulting in delayed calls. A.K. Erlang directed his first efforts at finding the delay for one operator and later on the results were extended to find the delay for several operators. The field of telephone traffic was further developed by Molins (1927) and Thornton D-Fry (1928). However, it was only after World War II that this early work was extended to other general problems involving queues or waiting lines.

Waiting lines or queues are omnipresent. Businesses of all types, industries, schools, hospitals, cafeterias, book stores, libraries, banks, post offices, petrol pumps, theatres – all have queuing problems. Queues are also found in industry — in shops where machines wait to be repaired, in tool cribs where mechanics wait to receive tools and in telephone exchanges where incoming calls wait to be handled by the operators. Further examples of queues, though less apparent are: waiting for a telephone operator to answer, a traffic light to change, the morning mail to be delivered and the like.

Waiting line problems arise either because

(*i*) there is too much demand on the facilities so that we say that there is an excess of waiting time or inadequate number of service facilities.

(*ii*) there is too less demand, in which case there is too much idle facility time or too many facilities.

In either case, the problem is to either *schedule arrivals* or *provide proper number of facilities or both* so as to obtain an optimum balance between the costs associated with waiting time and idle time.

Operations research can quite effectively analyse such queuing or congestion phenomena. However, a sound understanding of queuing theory combined with imagination is required to apply the theory to practical situations.

10.1 APPLICATIONS OF QUEUING MODELS

Waiting line or queuing theory has been applied to a wide variety of business situations. All situations where customers are involved such as restaurants, cafeterias, departmental stores, cinema halls, banks, post offices, petrol pumps, airline counters, patients in clinics, etc., are likely to have waiting lines. Generally, the customer expects a certain level of service, whereas the firm providing service facility tries to keep the costs minimum while providing the required service.

Waiting line theory is also widely used by manufacturing units. It has been popularly used in the area of tool cribs. There is a general complaint from the foremen that their workmen wait too long in line for tools and parts. Though the management wants to reduce the overhead charges, engaging more attendants can actually reduce overall manufacturing costs, since the workers will be working instead of standing in line.

Another problem that has been successfully solved by waiting line theory is the determination of the proper number of docks to be constructed for trucks or ships. Since both dock costs and demurrage costs can be very large, the number of docks should be such that the sum of the two costs is minimized.

Queuing methods have also been used for the problem of machine breakdowns and repairs. There are a number of machines that breakdown individually and at random times. The machines that breakdown form a waiting line for repairs by maintenance personnel and it is required to find the optimum number of repair personnel which makes the sum of the cost of repairmen and the cost of production loss from downtime, a minimum.

Queuing theory has been extended to decide wage incentive plans. For example, some workers are asked to operate, say, two machines while the others, four machines. Since the machines are identical, the base rate of payment is same for all workers. However, the incentive bonus for production in excess of quota is half as much per unit for operators with four machines as for those with two machines. Apparently, the arrangement appears to be fair. However, a study of downtime for repairs shows that while the two machines run by one man would have 12 per cent downtime, four machines run by one man would have 16% downtime. The reason is that two (or more) machines can breakdown at once in the four-machine group which is generally not true for two-machine group. Thus the worker operating four machines would have to operate at a higher efficiency than his counterpart in order to earn the same incentive. The problem was solved by paying the operators of the four-machine group a higher base rate determined by using the probabilities computed from queuing theory.

Queuing theory has also been applied for the solution of problems such as

1. Scheduling of mechanical transport fleets.
2. Scheduling distribution of scarce war material.
3. Scheduling of jobs in production control.
4. Minimization of congestion due to traffic delay at tool booths.
5. Solution of inventory control problems.

10.2 INTRODUCTION

Waiting lines or queues are familiar phenomena, which we observe quite frequently in our daily life. *The basic characteristics of a queuing phenomenon are*

1. Units arrive, at regular or irregular intervals of time, at a given point called the service centre. For example, trucks arriving a loading station, customers entering a department store, persons arriving a cinema hall, ships arriving a port, letters arriving a typist's desk, etc. All these units are called *entries* or *arrivals of customers.*
2. One or more *service channels* or *service stations* or *service facilities* (ticket windows, salesgirls, typists, docks, etc.) are assembled at the service centre. If the service station is empty (free), the arriving customer(s) will be served immediately; if not, the arriving customer(s) will wait in line until the service is provided. Once service has been completed, the customer leaves the system. Whenever we have customers coming to a service facility in such a way that either the customers or the facilities have to wait, we have a queuing problem. Figure. 10.1 shows the major *constituents* of a queuing system (or delay phenomenon). They are

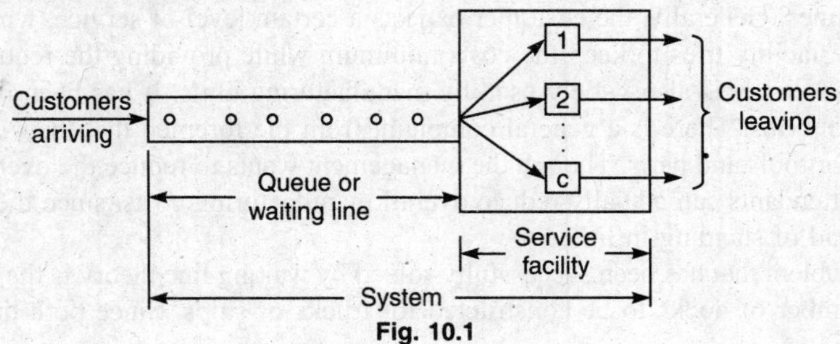

Fig. 10.1

1. **Customer:** The arriving unit that requires some service to be performed. As already described, the customers may be persons, machines, vehicles, parts, etc.
2. **Queue (Waiting line):** The number of customers waiting to be serviced. The queue does not include the customer(s) currently being serviced.
3. **Service Channel:** The process or facility which is performing the services to the customer. This may be single or multi-channel. The number of service channels is denoted by the symbol *c*.

10.3 ELEMENTS OF A QUEUING SYSTEM (STRUCTURE OF A QUEUING SYSTEM)

A queuing system is specified completely by seven main elements:

1. Input or arrival (inter-arrival) time distribution
2. Output or departure (service) time distribution
3. Service channels
4. Service discipline
5. Maximum number of customers allowed in the system
6. Calling source or population
7. Customer's behaviour.

1. Arrival Time Distribution. It represents the *pattern* in which the number of customers arrive at the service facility. Arrivals may also be represented by the *inter-arrival* time, which is the period between two successive arrivals.

Arrivals may be separated by equal intervals of time or by unequal but definitely known intervals of time or by unequal intervals of time whose probabilities are known; these are called random arrivals.

The rate at which customers arrive to be serviced, *i.e.,* number of customers arriving per unit of time is called *arrival rate.* When the arrival rate is random, the customers arrive in no logical pattern or order over time. This represents most cases in the business world.

When arrivals are random, we have to know the probability distribution describing arrivals, specifically *the time between arrivals.* Management scientists have demonstrated that random arrivals are often best described by the Poisson distribution, which was discussed in some details in chapter 8. Of course, arrivals are not always Poisson, and we need to be certain that the assumption of Poisson distribution is appropriate before we use it. Mean value of arrival rate is represented by λ. It may be noted that the Poisson distribution with mean arrival rate λ is equivalent to the (negative) exponential distribution of inter-arrival times with mean inter-arrival time $^1/_\lambda$.

2. Service (Departure) Time Distribution. It represents the *pattern* in which the number of customers leave the service facility. Departures may also be represented by the *service* (inter-departure) time, which is the time period between two successive services.

Service time may be constant or variable but known or random (variable with only known probability).

If service times are randomly distributed, we have to find out what probability distribution best describes their behaviour. In many cases where service times are random, management scientists have found that they are best described by the *exponential probability distribution.* If service times are exponentially distributed and arrival rates Poisson distributed, the mathematics necessary to study waiting line behaviour is somewhat easier to develop and use. Fig. 10.2 illustrates an exponential probability distribution of service times; from this we find that the probability of long service times is rather small.

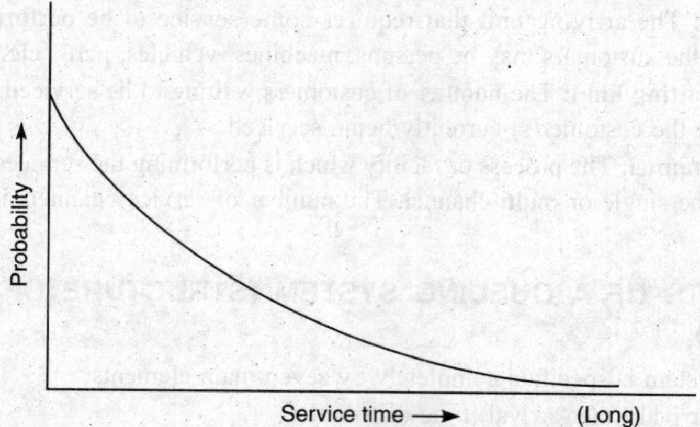

Fig. 10.2 Exponential distribution of service times.

The rate at which one service channel can perform the service, *i.e.,* number of customers served per unit of time is called *service rate.* This rate assumes the service channel to be always busy, *i.e.,* no idle time is allowed. Mean value of service rate is represented by μ. In business problems more cases of uniform service rate will be found than of uniform arrival rates.

3. Service Channels. The queuing system may have a single service channel. Arriving customers may form one line and get serviced, as in a doctor's clinic. The system may have a number of service channels, which may be arranged in parallel or in series or a complex combination of both. In case of parallel channels, several customers may be serviced simultaneously, as in a barber shop. For series channels, a customer must pass successively through all the channels before service is completed, *e.g.,* a product undergoing different processes over different machines or students, during admissions going through one counter after another before all admission formalities are complete. A queuing model is called *one server model,* when the system has one server only and a *multi-server model* when the system has a number of parallel channels each with one server.

Sometimes several service channels may feed into one subsequent service channel; for example, several ticket booths in a theatre may send all the ticket holders to a single ticket collector at the entrance of the theatre. On the other hand, sometimes, a single service channel may disperse customers among several channels that come after it; for example, an enquiry clerk in an office.

4. Service Discipline. Service discipline or order of service is the rule by which customers are selected from the queue for service. The most common discipline is 'first come, first served', according to which the customers are served in the order of their arrival, *e.g.,* cinema ticket windows, railway stations, banks, etc. The other discipline is 'last come, first served', as in a big godown, where the items arriving last are taken out first. Still other disciplines include 'service in random order (SIRO)' and 'priority'. 'Priority' is said to occur when an arriving customer is chosen for service ahead of some other customers already in the queue. A unit (customer) is said to have 'pre-emptive' priority if it not merely goes to the head of the queue but displaces any unit already being served when it arrives. Provided that the order of service is not related to service time, it does not affect the queue length or average waiting time but it does affect the time an individual customer has to wait. The service discipline, therefore, affects the derivation of equations used for analysis. In this text only the most common service discipline 'first come, first served' will be assumed for further discussion.

5. Maximum Number of Customers allowed in the System (Capacity of the System). Maximum number of customers in the system can be either finite or infinite. In some facilities, only a limited number of customers are allowed in the system and new arriving customers are not allowed to join the system unless the number becomes less than the limiting value.

6. Calling Source or Population. The arrival pattern of the customers depends upon the source which generates them. If there are only a few potential customers, the calling source (population) is called finite. If there are a large number of potential customers (say, over 40 or 50), it is usually said to be infinite. There is still another rule for categorising the source as finite or infinite. A finite source exists when an arrival affects the probability of arrival of potential future customers. For example, a battery of M running machines is a finite source, as far as machine repair situation is concerned. Before any machine breaks down, the calling source consists of M potential customers. As soon as a machine breaks down, it becomes a customer and hence cannot generate another 'call' until it gets serviced (repaired). An infinite source is said to exist when the arrival of a customer does not affect the rate of arrival of potential future customers.

7. Customer's behaviour: The customer's behaviour is also very important in the study of queues. If a customer decides not to enter the queue since it is too long, he is said to have *balked.* If a customer enters the queue, but after sometime loses patience and leaves it, he is said to have *reneged.* When there are two or more parallel queues and the customers move from one queue to the other, in the hope of reducing their waiting times they are said to be *jockeying.*

10.4 OPERATING CHARACTERISTICS OF A QUEUING SYSTEM

Analysis of a queuing system involves a study of its different operating characteristics. Some of them are

1. *Queue length* (L_q) – the average number of customers in the queue waiting to get service. This excludes the customer(*s*) being served.
2. *System length* (L_s) – the average number of customers in the system including those waiting as well as those being served.
3. *Waiting time in the queue* (W_q) – the average time for which a customer has to wait in the queue to get service.
4. *Total time in the system* (W_s) – the average total time spent by a customer in the system from the moment he arrives till he leaves the system. It is taken to be the waiting time plus the service time.
5. *Utilization factor* (ρ) – it is the proportion of time a server actually spends with the customers. It is also called *traffic intensity.*

10.5 WAITING TIME AND IDLE TIME COSTS

In order to solve a queuing problem, service facility must be manipulated so that an optimum balance is obtained between the cost of waiting time and the cost of idle time.

The cost of waiting customers generally includes either the indirect cost of lost business (because people go somewhere else, buy less than they had intended to, or do not come again in future) or direct cost of idle equipment and persons; for example, cost of truck drivers and equipment waiting to be unloaded or cost of operating an airplane or ship waiting to land or dock. The cost of lost business is not easy to assess. For example, vehicle drivers wanting petrol will avoid pumps having long queues. To determine how much business is lost, some type of experimentation and data collection is required.

The cost of idle service facilities is the payment to be made to the servers (engaged at the facilities) for the period for which they remain idle.

By increasing the investment in labour and equipment (service facilities), waiting time and the losses associated with it can be decreased. It is desirable, then, to obtain the minimum sum of these two costs; costs of investment and operation, and costs due to waiting. This optimum balance of costs can be obtained by *scheduling* the *flow* of *units* requiring service and/or *providing proper number of facilities.* If the facilities are not under control, flow of units may be scheduled to minimize the sum of waiting time and idle time costs. If the flow is not subject to control, that amount of equipment and personnel be employed which minimizes the overall costs of operation. If both can be controlled, one should schedule the input as well as provide facilities which minimize the overall cost.

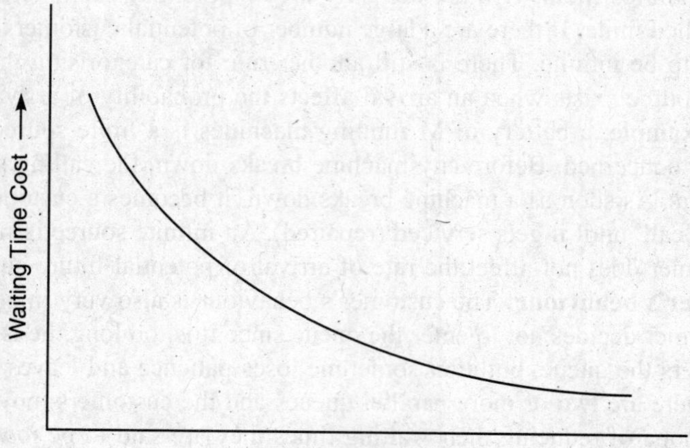

Fig. 10.3 Relationship between level of service and waiting time cost.

Fig. 10.3 illustrates the relationship between the level of service provided and the cost of *waiting time.* It is observed that as the level of service is increased (as more servers are provided), the cost of waiting time decreases.

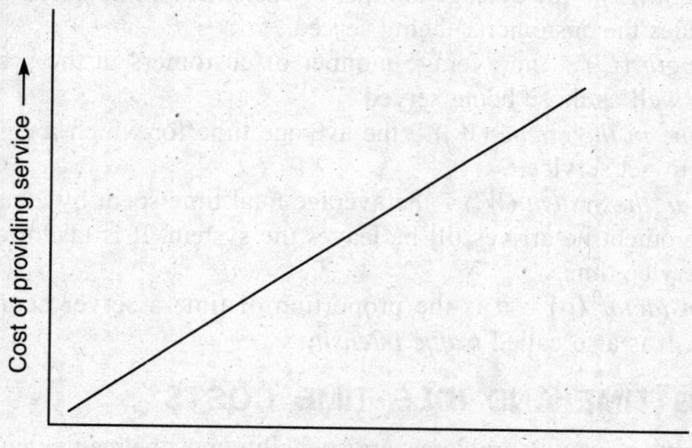

Fig. 10.4 Relationship between level of service and cost of providing service.

In Fig. 10.4 is illustrated the relationship between the level of service and the cost of *providing that* service. It is observed that as the level of service increases, so does the cost of providing that increased service.

In Fig. 10.5 the waiting time cost is added to the cost of providing service to establish a *total expected cost.* We see that the total expected cost is minimum at a service level denoted by point S. Thus the objective of the techniques explained in the remainder of this chapter is really to determine that particular level of service which minimizes the total cost of providing service and waiting for that service.

Let C_w = expected waiting cost/unit/unit time,

L_s = expected (average) number of units in the system,

and C_f = cost of servicing one unit.

Then expected waiting cost per unit time (period) $= C_w \cdot L_s = C_w \cdot \dfrac{\lambda}{\mu - \lambda}$, and expected service cost per unit time (period) $= C_f \cdot \mu$.

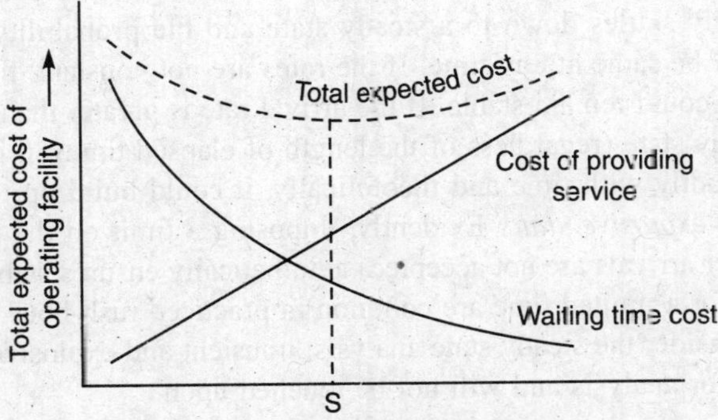

Fig. 10.5 Total cost of operating service facility.

$\therefore$ Total cost, $C = C_w \dfrac{\lambda}{\mu - \lambda} + \mu\, C_f.$

This will be minimum if $\dfrac{d}{d\mu}(C) = 0$

or if $- C_w \cdot \dfrac{\lambda}{(\mu - \lambda)^2} + C_f = 0$, which gives $\mu = \lambda \pm \sqrt{\dfrac{C_w}{C_f}}\,\lambda.$

Note that a plus and minus sign appear before the square root sign. A negative value of μ is not a possible answer in real life problems. μ given by the above equation is called *minimum cost service rate.*

EXAMPLE 10.5-1

Consider a situation in which the mean arrival rate is one customer every 4 minutes and the mean service time is $2\frac{1}{2}$ minutes. If the waiting cost is ₹ 5 per unit per minute and the minimum cost of servicing one unit is ₹ 4, find the minimum cost service rate.

Solution

Here, $\lambda = \dfrac{1}{4} = 0.25.$

$$\mu = \lambda \pm \sqrt{\frac{C_w}{C_f}.\lambda} = 0.25 \pm \sqrt{\frac{5 \times 0.25}{4}} = 0.25 \pm \sqrt{0.3125} = 0.25 \pm 0.56.$$

$\therefore$ $\mu = 0.81$ units/minute. $(\because \mu = -\,0.32$ is not a feasible solution.)

10.6 TRANSIENT AND STEADY STATES OF THE SYSTEM

Queuing theory analysis involves the study of system's behaviour over time. If the operating characteristics (behaviour of the system) vary with time, it is said to be in *transient state.* Usually a system is transient during the early stages of its operation, when its behaviour still depends upon the initial conditions (number of customers in the system) and the elapsed time. However, it is the 'long-run' behaviour or the *steady state condition* of the system which is more important. A system is said to be in steady state condition if its behaviour becomes independent of its initial conditions and of the elapsed time.

An essential condition for reaching a steady state is that the total elapsed time since the start of the operation must be sufficiently large (theoretically, it should tend to infinity). However, this is not the sufficient condition as the parameters of the system also affect its state *e.g.*, number of customers at the counter of a post office within 15 minutes of its opening.

For example, if the average arrival rate is less than average service rate and both are constant, the system eventually settles down to a steady state and the probability of finding a particular length of queue will be same at any time. If the rates are not constant, the system will not reach a steady state, but it could remain stable. If the arrival rate is greater than service rate, the system cannot attain a steady state (regardless of the length of elapsed time); it is rather unstable, queue length increases steadily with time and theoretically, it could build up to infinity. Such state of the system is called *explosive state.* Evidently, imposing a limit on the maximum length of the queue (so that further arrivals are not accepted) automatically ensures stability. Queuing situations which are unstable for a limited time are common in practice– rush-hour traffic is an example. In this text we shall consider the steady state analysis; transient and explosive states require complex mathematical tools for analysis and will not be touched upon.

10.7 KENDALL'S NOTATION FOR REPRESENTING QUEUING MODELS

D.G. Kendall (1953) and later A. Lee (1966) introduced useful notation for queuing models. The complete notation can be expressed as

$$(a/b/c) : (d/e/f),$$

where
- a = arrival (or inter-arrival) time distribution,
- b = departure (or service) time distribution,
- c = number of parallel service channels in the system,
- d = service discipline,
- e = maximum number of customers allowed in the system,
- f = calling source or population.

The following conventional codes are generally used to replace the symbols a, b and d:

Symbols for a and b

- M = Markovian (Poisson) arrival or departure distribution (or exponential interarrival or service time distribution),
- E_k = Erlangian or gamma interarrival or service time distribution with parameter k,
- GI = general independent arrival distribution,
- G = general departure distribution,
- D = deterministic interarrival or service times.

Symbols for d

- FCFS = first come, first served,
- LCFS = last come, first served,
- SIRO = service in random order,
- GD = general service discipline.

The symbols e and f represent a finite (N) or infinite (∞) number of customers in the system and calling source respectively. For instance, $(M/E_k/1) : (FCFS/N/\infty)$ represents Poisson arrival (exponential interarrival), Erlangian departure, single server, 'first come, first served' discipline, maximum allowable customers N in the system and infinite population model.

10.8 CLASSIFICATION OF QUEUING MODELS

The various types of queuing models can be classified as follows :

(*a*) Probabilistic Queuing Models

1. **Model I (Erlang Model) :** This model is symbolically represented by $(M/M/1) : (FCFS/\infty/\infty)$. This represents Poisson arrival (exponential interarrival), Poisson departure (exponential service time), single server, first come, first served service discipline, infinite

number of customers allowed in the system and infinite population. Since the Poisson and exponential distributions are related to each other, both of them are denoted by the symbol 'M' due to Markovian property of exponential distribution.

2. **Model II (General Erlang Model) :** Though this model is also represented by (M/M/1) : (FCFS/∞/∞), it is a general queuing model in which the arrival and service rates depend upon the length of the queue. Some persons desiring service may not join the queue since it is too long, thus affecting the arrival rate. Similarly, service rate is also affected by the length of the queue.
3. **Model III :** This model is represented by (M/M/1) : (SIRO/∞/∞). It is essentially the same as model I except that the service discipline is SIRO insetad of FCFS.
4. **Model IV :** This model is represented by (M/M/1) : (FCFS/N/∞). In this model the capacity of the system is limited or finite, say N. So the number of arrivals cannot exceed N.
5. **Model V :** This model is represented by (M/M/1) : (FCFS/n/M). It is finite-population or limited-source model. In this model the probability of an arrival depends upon the number of potential customers available to enter the system.
6. **Model VI :** This model is represented by (M/M/c) : (FCFS/∞/∞). This is same as model I except that there are c service channels working in parallel.
7. **Model VII :** This model is represented by (M/E_k/1) : (FCFS/∞/∞). In this model instead of exponential service time, there is Erlang service time with k phases.
8. **Model VIII :** This model is represented by (M/M/1) : (GD/m/n), where $m \le n$. It represents machine-repair problem with a single repairman. n is the total number of machines out of which m are brokendown and are forming a queue. GD represents a general service discipline.
9. **Model IX :** This model is represented by (M/M/c) : (GD/m/n), $m \le n$. It is same as model VIII except that there are c repairmen, $c < n$.
10. **Model X :** This is called power supply model.

(b) Deterministic Model

11. **Model XI :** This model is represented by (D/D/1) : (FCFS/∞/∞). In this model interarrival time as well as service time are fixed and known with certainty. The model is, therefore, called deterministic model.

(C) Mixed Queuing Model

12. **Model XII :** This model is represented by (M/D/1) : (FCFS/∞/∞). Here, arrival rate is Poisson distributed while the service rate is deterministic or constant.

10.9 SINGLE-CHANNEL QUEUING THEORY

A single-channel queuing problem results from random interarrival time and random service time at a single service station. The random arrival time can be described mathematically by a probability distribution. The most common distribution found in queuing problems is Poisson distribution. This is used in single-channel queuing problems for random arrivals where the service time is exponentially distributed. The sections ahead give the reader an insight into the true nature of operations research—the difficulties of developing OR models, the need for logical assumptions and the utilization of higher mathematics.

10.9-1 Models for Arrival and Service Times

Generally, arrivals do not occur at fixed regular intervals of times but tend to be clustered or scattered in some fashion. A *Poisson distribution* is a discrete probability distribution which predicts the number of arrivals in a given time. The Poisson distribution involves the probability of occurrence of an arrival. Poisson assumption is quite restrictive in some cases. It assumes that arrivals are random and independent of all other operating conditions. The mean arrival rate (*i.e.,* the average number of arrivals per unit of time) λ is assumed to be constant over time and is independent of the number of units already serviced, queue length or any other random property of the queue.

Since the mean arrival rate is constant over time, it follows that the probability of an arrival between time t and $t + dt$ is $\lambda \, . \, dt$.

Thus probability of an arrival in time $dt = \lambda \, dt$. ...(10.1)

The following characteristics of Poisson distribution are written here without proof :

Probability of n arrivals in time $t = \dfrac{(\lambda t)^n \, . \, e^{-\lambda t *}}{n\,!}$, $n = 0, 1, 2, ...,$ ...(10.2)

Probability density function of inter-arrival time (time interval between two consecutive arrivals)

$$= \lambda \, . \, e^{-\lambda t}. \qquad ...(10.3)$$

Finally, Poisson distribution assumes that the time period dt is very small so that $(dt)^2$, $(dt)^3$, etc. $\rightarrow 0$ and can be ignored.

Service time is the time required for completion of a service *i.e.,* it is the time interval between beginning of a service and its completion. The mean service rate is the average number of customers served per unit of time (assuming the service to be continuous throughout the entire time unit), while the average service time $1/\mu$ is the time required to serve one customer. The most common type of distribution used for service times is exponential distribution. It involves the probability of completion of a service. It should be noted that Poisson distribution cannot be applied to servicing because of the possibility of the service facility remaining idle for some time. Poisson distribution assumes fixed time interval of continuous servicing, which can never be assured in all services.

Mean service rate μ is also assumed to be constant over time and independent of the number of units already serviced, queue length or any other random property of the system. Thus probability that a service is completed between t and $t + dt$, provided that the service is continuous

$$= \mu dt.$$

Under the condition of continuous service, the following characteristics of exponential distribution are written, without proof :

Probability of n complete services in time $t = \dfrac{(\mu t)^n \, . \, e^{-\mu t}}{n\,!}$. ...(10.4)

Probability density function (*p.d.f*) of interservice time, *i.e.,* time between two consecutive services $= \mu \, . \, e^{-\mu t}$. ...(10.5)

Probability that a customer shall be serviced in more than time $t = e^{-\mu t}$. ...(10.6)

EXAMPLE 10.9-1.1

On an average, 6 customers reach a telephone booth every hour to make calls. Determine the probability that exactly 4 customers will reach in 30-minute period, assuming that arrivals follow Poisson distribution.

Solution

Here $\lambda = 6$ customers/hour,

$t = 30$ minutes $= 0.5$ hour,

$n = 4$,

$\lambda t = 6 \times 0.5 = 3$ customers.

$\therefore$ Probability of 4 customers arriving in 0.5 hour

*See appendix B.1 for derivation of the expression.

$$= \frac{(\lambda t)^n \cdot e^{-\lambda t}}{n!} = \frac{(3)^4 \cdot e^{-3}}{4!} = \frac{(3)^4 \cdot (2.718)^{-3}}{4!} = \frac{81 \times 0.0498}{24} = 0.168.$$

EXAMPLE 10.9-1.2

In a bank, 20 customers, on the average, are served by a cashier in an hour. If the service time has exponential distribution, what is the probability that

(*a*) *it will take more than 10 minutes to serve a customer ?*

(*b*) *a customer shall be free within 4 minutes ?*

Solution. (*a*) Here $\mu = 20$ customers/hour,

$$t = 10 \text{ minutes} = \frac{1}{6} \text{ hour.}$$

$\therefore$ Probability that it will take more than 10 minutes to serve a customer $= e^{-\mu t} = e^{-20 \times 1/6}$ $= e^{-10/3} = 0.0357.$

(*b*) Here $t = 4$ minutes $= \frac{1}{15}$ hour.

$\therefore$ Probability that a customer will be free within 4 minutes
$= 1 - e^{-\mu t} = 1 - e^{-20 \times 1/15} = 1 - e^{-4/3} = 1 - 0.264 = 0.736.$

EXERCISES 10.1

1. Discuss the costs associated with queuing system. Also explain the concepts of optimum servicing rate and optimum cost. [*IGNOU MBA June, 2007; Dec, 2006*]
2. In a bank operation, the arrival rate is 2 customers/minute. Determine the following :
   (*a*) The average number of arrivals during 5 minutes.
   (*b*) The probability that no arrivals will occur during the next 30 seconds.
   (*c*) The probability that at least one arrival will occur during the next 30 seconds.
   (*d*) The probability that the time between two successive arrivals is at least 3 minutes.
   [**Hint.** (*a*) $n = 2 \times 5 = 10.$
   (*b*) $p_0 = \frac{(\lambda t)^n \cdot e^{-\lambda t}}{n!} = \frac{\left(2 \times \frac{1}{2}\right)^0 \cdot e^{-2 \times \frac{1}{2}}}{0!} = e^{-1} = 0.367.$
   (*c*) $p = 1 - p_0 = 1 - 0.367 = 0.633.$
   (*d*) $p = e^{-\lambda t} = e^{-2 \times 3} = e^{-6} = 0.00248.$]
3. Inventory is withdrawn from a stock of 80 items according to Poisson distribution at the rate of 5 items per day. Detemine the following :
   (a) The probability that 10 items are withdrawn during the first 2 days.
   (b) The probability that no items are left at the end of 4 days.
   (c) The average number of items withdrawn over a 4-day period. [*P.U.B.E. (C.Sc.) Dec., 2004*]

10.9-2 Model-I. Single-Channel Poisson Arrivals with Exponential Service, Infinite Population Model [(M/M/I) : (FCFS/∞/∞)]

Let us consider a single-channel system with Poisson arrivals and exponential service time distribution. Both the arrivals and service rates are independent of the number of customers in the waiting line. Arrivals are handled on 'first come, first served' basis. Also the mean arrival rate λ is less than the mean service rate μ.

The following mathematical notation (symbols) will be used in connection with queuing models:

n = number of customers in the system (waiting line + service facility) at time t.
λ = mean arrival rate (number of arrivals per unit of time).

μ = mean service rate per busy server (number of customers served per unit of time).

λdt = probability that an arrival enters the system between t and $t + dt$ time interval *i.e.,* within time interval dt.

$1 - \lambda dt$ = probability that no arrival enters the system within interval dt plus higher order terms in dt.

μ = mean service rate per channel.

μdt = probability of one service completion between t and $t + dt$ time interval *i.e.,* within time interval dt.

$1 - \mu . dt$ = probability of no service rendered during the interval dt plus higher order terms in dt.

p_n = steady state probability of exactly n customers in the system.

$p_n(t)$ = transient state probability of exactly n customers in the system at time t, assuming the system started its operation at time zero.

$p_{n+1}(t)$ = transient state probability of having $n + 1$ customers in the system at time t.

$p_{n-1}(t)$ = transient state probability of having $n - 1$ customers in the system at time t.

$p_n(t + dt)$ = probability of having n customers in the system at time $t + dt$.

L_q = expected (average) number of customers in the queue.

L_s = expected number of customers in the system (waiting + being served).

W_q = expected waiting time per customer in the queue (expected time a customer keeps waiting in line).

W_s = expected time a customer spends in the system. (in waiting + being served)

L_n = expected number of customers waiting in line excluding those *times when the line is empty i.e.,* expected number in *non-empty queue* (expected number of customers in a *queue that is formed from time to time).*

W_n = expected time a customer waits in line if *he has to wait at all i.e.,* expected time in the queue for *non-empty queue.*

To determine the properties of the single-channel system, it is necessary to find an expression for the probability of n customers in the system at time t *i.e.,* $p_n(t)$, for, if $p_n(t)$ is known, the expected number of customers in the system and hence the other characteristics can be calculated. In place of finding an expression for $p_n(t)$, we shall first find the expression for $p_n(t + dt)$.

The probability of n units (customers) in the system at time $t + dt$ can be determined by summing up probabilities of all the ways this event could occur. The event can occur in four mutually exclusive and exhaustive ways:

TABLE 10.1

Event	*No. of units at time t*	*No. of arrivals in time dt*	*No. of services in time dt*	*No. of units at time t + dt*
1	n	0	0	n
2	$n + 1$	0	1	n
3	$n - 1$	1	0	n
4	n	1	1	n

Now we compute the probability of occurrence of each of the events, remembering that the probability of a service or arrival is μdt or λdt and $(dt)^2 \to 0$.

$\therefore$ Probability of event 1 = Probability of having n units at time t

× Probability of no arrivals

× Probability of no services

$$= p_n(t).(1 - \lambda dt)\ (1 - \mu dt)$$
$$= p_n(t)\ [1 - \lambda dt - \mu dt + \lambda\ \mu\ (dt)^2]$$
$$= p_n(t)\ [1 - \lambda dt - \mu dt].$$

Similarly, probability of event 2 $= p_{n+1}(t).\ (1 - \lambda dt)\ .\ (\mu dt)$
$= p_{n+1}(t)\ [\mu dt]$,

probability of event 3 $= p_{n-1}(t)\ [\lambda dt].(1 - \mu dt) = p_{n-1}(t)\ [\lambda dt]$,

probability of event 4 $= p_n(t)\ .\ (\lambda\ dt)\ (\mu\ .\ dt)$
$= p_n(t)\ .\ [\lambda\ .\ \mu\ (dt)^2] = 0.$

Note that other events are not possible because of the small value of dt that causes $(dt)^2$ to approach zero (as in event 4).

Since one and only one of the above events can happen, we can obtain $p_n(t + dt)$ [where $n > 0$} by adding the probabilities of above four events.

$\therefore\ p_n(t + dt) = p_n(t)\ [1 - \lambda dt - \mu dt] + p_{n+1}(t)\ [\mu dt] + p_{n-1}(t)\ [\lambda dt] + 0$

or $p_n(t + dt) = p_n(t) - p_n(t)\ [\lambda dt + \mu dt] + p_{n+1}(t)\ [\mu dt] + p_{n-1}(t)\ [\lambda dt]$

or $\dfrac{p_n\ (t + dt) - p_n(t)}{dt} = -\ (\lambda + \mu)\ .\ p_n(t) + \mu\ .\ p_{n+1}(t)\ .\ + \lambda p_{n-1}(t).$

Taking the limit when $dt \to 0$, we get the following differential equation which gives the relationship between p_n, p_{n-1}, p_{n+1} at any time t, mean arrival rate λ and mean service rate μ :

$$\frac{d}{dt}\ [p_n(t)] = \lambda p_{n-1}(t) + \mu p_{n+1}(t) - (\lambda + \mu) p_n(t), \quad \text{where } n > 0. \quad ...(10.7)$$

After solving for $p_n(t + dt)$ where $n > 0$, it is necessary to solve for $p_n(t + dt)$ where $n = 0$ *i.e.* to solve for $p_0\ (t + dt)$. If $n = 0$, only two mutually exclusive and exhaustive events can occur as shown in table 10.2.

TABLE 10.2

Event	*No. of units at time t*	*No. of arrivals in time dt*	*No. of services in time dt*	*No. of units at time t + dt*
1	0	0	–	0
2	1	0	1	0

$\therefore$ Probability of event 1 = Probability of having no unit at time t × Probability of no arrivals × Probability of no services

$= p_0(t) \times (1 - \lambda\ dt) \times 1$

and Probability of event 2 = Probability of having one unit at time t × Probability of no arrivals × Probability of one service

$= p_1(t) \times (1 - \lambda\ dt) \times (\mu\ dt).$

Note that if no units were in the system, the probability of no service would be 1. Probability of having no unit in the system at time $t + dt$ is given by summing up the probabilities of above two events.

$$\therefore \quad p_0(t + dt) = p_0(t)\ .\ (1 - \lambda dt) + p_1(t).(\mu dt)\ (1 - \lambda dt)$$
$$= p_0(t) - p_0(t).(\lambda dt) + p_1(t).(\mu dt)$$

or $\quad p_0(t + dt) - p_0(t) = -\ p_0(t).(\lambda dt) + p_1(t)\ (\mu dt)$

or $\quad \dfrac{p_0(t + dt) - p_0(t)}{dt} = \mu.p_1(t) - \lambda p_0(t).$

When $dt \to 0$, the differential equation which indicates the relationship between probabilities p_0 and p_1 at any time t, mean arrival rate λ and mean service rate μ, is

$$\frac{d}{dt}[p_0(t)] = \mu p_1(t) - \lambda p_0(t), \text{ where } n = 0. \qquad ...(10.8)$$

Equations (10.7) and (10.8) provide relationships *involving* the *probability density function* $p_n(t)$ for all values of n but still we do not know the value of $p_n(t)$.

Assuming the steady state condition for the system, when the probability of *having* n units (customers) in the system becomes independent of time, we get

$$p_n(t) = p_n, \quad \frac{d}{dt}[p_n(t)] = 0.$$

Therefore, for a steady state system the differential equations (10.7) and (10.8) reduce to difference equations (10.9) and (10.10) :

$$0 = \lambda p_{n-1} + \mu . p_{n+1} - (\lambda + \mu) p_n, \text{ where } n > 0, \qquad ...(10.9)$$

$$0 = \mu p_1 - \lambda p_0; \quad \text{where } n = 0. \qquad ...(10.10)$$

From equation (10.10), we have $p_1 = \dfrac{\lambda}{\mu} \cdot p_0$.

Putting $n = 1$ in equation (10.9), we have

$$0 = \lambda p_0 + \mu p_2 - (\lambda + \mu) p_1.$$

$$\therefore \quad p_2 = \frac{\lambda + \mu}{\mu} \cdot p_1 - \frac{\lambda}{\mu} \cdot p_0 = \frac{\lambda + \mu}{\mu} \cdot \left(\frac{\lambda}{\mu} \cdot p_0\right) - \frac{\lambda}{\mu} \cdot p_0$$

$$= \frac{\lambda}{\mu} \cdot p_0 \left(\frac{\lambda + \mu}{\mu} - 1\right) = \left(\frac{\lambda}{\mu}\right)^2 \cdot p_0 .$$

Similarly, for $n = 2$, equation (10.9) gives

$$p_3 = \left(\frac{\lambda}{\mu}\right)^3 \cdot p_0.$$

$$\vdots$$

$$p_n = \left(\frac{\lambda}{\mu}\right)^n p_0, \quad \text{where } n > 0. \qquad ...(10.11)$$

Equation (10.11) gives p_n in terms of p_0, λ and μ. Finally, an expression for p_0 in terms of λ and μ must be obtained. The easiest way to do this is to recognize that the probability that the channel is busy is the ratio of the arrival rate and service rate, $\left(\dfrac{\lambda}{\mu}\right)$. Thus p_0 is 1 minus this ratio.

i.e.
$$p_0 = 1 - \frac{\lambda}{\mu}. \qquad ...(10.12)$$

Hence
$$p_n = \left(\frac{\lambda}{\mu}\right)^n \cdot \left(1 - \frac{\lambda}{\mu}\right). \qquad ..(10.13)$$

Having known the value of p_n, we can find the various operating characteristics of the system.

1. *Expected number of units in the system (waiting + being served)*, L_s is obtained by using the definition of an expected value:

$$E(x) = \sum_{i=0}^{i=\infty} x_i \, p_i$$

$$\therefore \quad L_s = \sum_{n=0}^{n=\infty} n p_n$$

or $$L_s = \sum_{n=0}^{\infty} n\left(\frac{\lambda}{\mu}\right)^n\left(1-\frac{\lambda}{\mu}\right) = \left(1-\frac{\lambda}{\mu}\right).\sum_{n=0}^{\infty} n\left(\frac{\lambda}{\mu}\right)^n$$

$$= \left(1-\frac{\lambda}{\mu}\right)\left[0\left(\frac{\lambda}{\mu}\right)^0 + 1\left(\frac{\lambda}{\mu}\right) + 2\left(\frac{\lambda}{\mu}\right)^2 + 3\left(\frac{\lambda}{\mu}\right)^3 + \ldots\right]$$

$$= \left(1-\frac{\lambda}{\mu}\right)\left[0 + \frac{\lambda}{\mu} + 2\left(\frac{\lambda}{\mu}\right)^2 + 3\left(\frac{\lambda}{\mu}\right)^3 + \ldots\right].$$

The series within brackets is an infinite series of the form 0, a, $2a^2$, $3a^3$, ..., xa^x, ... For such an infinite series, if a is a constant and less than one, the sum is given by the formula

$$S_\infty = \frac{a}{(1-a)^2}.$$

$$\therefore \quad L_s = \left(1-\frac{\lambda}{\mu}\right)\left[\frac{\lambda/\mu}{(1-\lambda/\mu)^2}\right] = \frac{\lambda/\mu}{1-\lambda/\mu} = \frac{\lambda}{\mu-\lambda}. \quad \text{...(10.14)}$$

2. *Expected number of units in the queue,* L_q = Expected number of units in the system – Expected number in service (single server).

$$\therefore \quad L_q = L_s - \frac{\lambda}{\mu} = \frac{\lambda}{\mu-\lambda} - \frac{\lambda}{\mu} = \lambda\left[\frac{\mu-\mu+\lambda}{\mu(\mu-\lambda)}\right] = \frac{\lambda}{\mu}.\frac{\lambda}{\mu-\lambda}. \quad \text{...(10.15)}$$

Note that the expected number in service is 1 times the probability that the service channel is busy *i.e.,* $1 . \frac{\lambda}{\mu}$.

3. *Expected time per unit in the system (expected time a unit spends in the system),*

$$W_s = \frac{\text{Expected number of units in the system}}{\text{Arrival rate}} = \frac{L_s}{\lambda} = \frac{\lambda}{(\mu-\lambda).\lambda} = \frac{1}{\mu-\lambda}. \quad \text{...(10.16)}$$

4. *Expected waiting time per unit in the queue,* W_q = Expected time in system – time in service.

$$\therefore \quad W_q = W_s - \frac{1}{\mu} = \frac{1}{\mu-\lambda} - \frac{1}{\mu} = \frac{\lambda}{\mu}.\frac{1}{\mu-\lambda}. \quad \text{...(10.17)}$$

5. *Variance of queue length* :
By definition we have

$$\text{Var}(n) = E(n)^2 - [E(n)]^2 = \sum_{n=0}^{\infty} n^2 p_n - \left[\sum_{n=0}^{\infty} n\, p_n\right]^2$$

$$= \sum_{n=1}^{\infty} n^2 p_n - \left[\sum_{n=1}^{\infty} np_n\right]^2 \quad (\because \text{ for } n = 0, \text{ both terms are zero only})$$

$$= \sum_{n=1}^{\infty} n^2 . (1-\frac{\lambda}{\mu})(\frac{\lambda}{\mu})^n - [L_s]^2$$

$$= \left(1-\frac{\lambda}{\mu}\right)\sum_{n=1}^{\infty} n^2 . \left(\frac{\lambda}{\mu}\right)^n - \left(\frac{\lambda}{\mu-\lambda}\right)^2$$

$$= \left(1-\frac{\lambda}{\mu}\right)\left[1.\frac{\lambda}{\mu} + 2^2 . \left(\frac{\lambda}{\mu}\right)^2 + 3^2.\left(\frac{\lambda}{\mu}\right)^3 + \ldots\right] - (\frac{\lambda}{\mu-\lambda})^2$$

$$= \frac{\lambda}{\mu}\cdot\left(1-\frac{\lambda}{\mu}\right)\left[1+2^2\cdot\frac{\lambda}{\mu}+3^2\left(\frac{\lambda}{\mu}\right)^2+\ldots\right]-\left(\frac{\lambda}{\mu-\lambda}\right)^2$$

Let $\quad S = 1 + 2^2\,\frac{\lambda}{\mu} + 3^2\cdot\left(\frac{\lambda}{\mu}\right)^2 + \ldots = 1 + 2^2\rho + 3^2\rho^2 + \ldots \quad \left(\because \rho = \frac{\lambda}{\mu}\right)$

Integrating both sides w.r.t. ρ from 0 to ρ, we have

$$\int_0^{\rho} S\,.\,d\rho = \int_0^{\rho}(1+2^2\rho+3^2\rho^2+\ldots)\,d\rho = [\rho+2\rho^2+3\rho^3+\ldots]_0^{\rho}$$

$$= \rho + 2\rho^2 + 3\rho^3 + \ldots = \rho\,(1 + 2\rho + 3\rho^2 + \ldots)$$

$$= \rho\,.\,\frac{1}{(1-\rho)^2} = \frac{\rho}{(1-\rho)^2}.$$

Now differentiating both sides w.r.t. ρ, we have

$$S = \frac{1}{(1-\rho)^2} + \rho\,.\,(-2)\,.\,(1-\rho)^{-3}\,(-1) = \frac{1}{(1-\rho)^2}+\frac{2\rho}{(1-\rho)^3}=\frac{1+\rho}{(1-\rho)^3}=\frac{1+\lambda/\mu}{(1-\lambda/\mu)^3}.$$

$$\therefore \qquad \text{Var}(n) = \frac{\lambda}{\mu}\left(1-\frac{\lambda}{\mu}\right).\frac{\left(1+\frac{\lambda}{\mu}\right)}{\left(1-\frac{\lambda}{\mu}\right)^3}-\left(\frac{\lambda}{\mu-\lambda}\right)^2.$$

∴ Variance of queue length

$$= \frac{\lambda/\mu\,(1+\lambda/\mu)}{(1-\lambda/\mu)^2}-\frac{\frac{\lambda^2}{\mu^2}}{\left(1-\frac{\lambda}{\mu}\right)^2}=\frac{\frac{\lambda}{\mu}}{\left(1-\frac{\lambda}{\mu}\right)^2}. \qquad \ldots(10.18)$$

6. *Average length of non-empty queue (length of queue that is formed from time to time),* L_n : For a non-empty queue, the number of units in the system should be at least 2 (one in service and the other in the queue). Probability of a non-empty queue

$$= \sum_{n=0}^{\infty} p_n - (p_0 + p_1) = 1 - \left(p_0 + \frac{\lambda}{\mu}\,p_0\right) = 1 - p_0\left(1+\frac{\lambda}{\mu}\right)$$

$$= 1 - \left(1-\frac{\lambda}{\mu}\right)\left(1+\frac{\lambda}{\mu}\right) = \left(\frac{\lambda}{\mu}\right)^2.$$

Now average length of non-empty queue,

$$L_n = \frac{\text{Average length of queue}}{\text{Probability of non-empty queue}} = \frac{\frac{\lambda}{\mu}\cdot\frac{\lambda}{\mu-\lambda}}{\left(\frac{\lambda}{\mu}\right)^2} = \frac{\mu}{\mu-\lambda}. \qquad \ldots(10.19)$$

7. *Average waiting time in non-empty queue (average waiting time of an arrival who waits), or expected waiting time per busy period,*

$$W_n = \frac{1}{\mu-\lambda}. \qquad \ldots(10.20)$$

8. *Probability of queue being greater than or equal to k,*

$$p(\geq k) = \sum_{n=0}^{\infty} p_n - \sum_{n=0}^{n=k-1} p_n = 1 - [p_0 + p_1 + p_2 + \ldots + p_{k-1}]$$

$$= 1 - \left[p_0 + \frac{\lambda}{\mu} p_0 + \left(\frac{\lambda}{\mu}\right)^2 p_0 + \ldots + \left(\frac{\lambda}{\mu}\right)^{k-1} p_0 \right]$$

$$= 1 - p_0 \left[1 + \frac{\lambda}{\mu} + \left(\frac{\lambda}{\mu}\right)^2 + \ldots + \left(\frac{\lambda}{\mu}\right)^{k-1} \right]$$

$$= 1 - p_0 \cdot \frac{1 - \left(\frac{\lambda}{\mu}\right)^k}{1 - \frac{\lambda}{\mu}} = 1 - \left(1 - \frac{\lambda}{\mu}\right) \cdot \frac{1 - \left(\frac{\lambda}{\mu}\right)^k}{1 - \frac{\lambda}{\mu}} = \left(\frac{\lambda}{\mu}\right)^k . \qquad \text{...(10.21a)}$$

9. *Probability of queue being greater than k,*

$$p(> k) = \left(\frac{\lambda}{\mu}\right)^{k+1} \qquad \text{... (10.21b)}$$

10. *Probability that the queue is non-empty*

$$p(n > 1) = 1 - p_0 - p_1 = 1 - \left(1 - \frac{\lambda}{\mu}\right) - \frac{\lambda}{\mu}\left(1 - \frac{\lambda}{\mu}\right) = \left(\frac{\lambda}{\mu}\right)^2 . \qquad \text{. (10.21c)}$$

11. *Probability density function of waiting time (excluding service) distribution*

$$= \begin{cases} \frac{\lambda}{\mu}(\mu - \lambda) . e^{-(\mu - \lambda)t} , & t > 0 \\ \frac{\lambda}{\mu}(\mu - \lambda) , & t = 0. \end{cases} \qquad \text{...(10.22)}$$

12. *Probability density function of* (*waiting* + *service*) *time distribution*

$$= (\mu - \lambda) . e^{-(\mu - \lambda)t} . \qquad \text{...(10.23)}$$

10.9-3 An Explanatory Note on the Queuing Formulae

1. *Traffic intensity*. The ratio $\frac{\lambda}{\mu}$ is called the traffic intensity or the *utilisation factor* and it determines the degree to which the capacity of the service station is utilised (expected fraction of time the service facility is busy). For instance, if customers arrive at the rate of 9 per hour and the service rate is 10 per hour, the utilisation of the service facility is 9/10 = 90%.

2. *Average length of the queue* $= \frac{\lambda}{\mu} . \frac{\lambda}{\mu - \lambda}$.

Consider that a statistician observes the queue at a service facility after every one hour and that the length of the queue for, say, six observations is as follows:

Observation No.	*Queue*	*Service facility*	*Length of queue*
1	None	None	0
2	* *	*	2
3	None	*	0
4	* * * * *	*	5
5	* *	*	2
6	* * *	*	3
			Average = 12/6 = 2.

Thus the average queue length = 2.

3. *Average number of units in the system* = $\dfrac{\lambda}{\mu - \lambda}$.

For the above situation, this average

$$= \frac{(0+0)+(2+1)+(0+1)+(5+1)+(2+1)+(3+1)}{6} = \frac{17}{6}.$$

4. *Average length of non-empty queue* = $\dfrac{\lambda}{\mu - \lambda}$.

This will be calculated from observation no. 2, 4, 5 and 6, since during observations 1 and 3 the queue was empty, though during observation 3 there was a unit being served. For the above situation, then this average = $\dfrac{2+5+2+3}{4}$ = 3.

5. *Average waiting time of an arrival* = $\dfrac{\lambda}{\mu\,(\mu - \lambda)}$.

At times when there are no units in the system, the arriving unit will not have to wait. However, when there are units already in the system, the arriving unit will have to wait. As another example, let the waiting times of, say, 8 units observed be

= 10, 8, 3, 0, 5, 9, 0, 6 minutes.

Then the average waiting time = $\dfrac{10+8+3+0+5+9+0+6}{8} = \dfrac{41}{8} = 5.125$ minutes.

6. *Average waiting time of an arrival who waits* = $\dfrac{1}{\mu - \lambda}$.

In the above situation, ignoring the observations when the waiting time is zero, this average = 41/6 = 6.83 minutes.

7. *Average time an arrival spends in the system* = $\dfrac{1}{\mu - \lambda}$.

Here, along with the waiting times, the service times must also be given. Then this average

$$= \frac{\text{Total (waiting time + service time)}}{8} \text{ minutes.}$$

10.9-4 Assumptions and Limitations of Queuing Model

The various results of section 10.9.2 have been derived under the *following simplifying assumptions* :

1. The customers arrive for service at a single service facility at random according to Poisson distribution with mean arrival rate λ or equivalently, the inter-arrival times follow exponential distribution with mean 1/λ.
2. The service time has exponential distribution with mean service rate μ.

3. The service discipline followed is first come, first served.
4. Customer behaviour is normal *i.e.*, customers desiring service join the queue, wait for their turn and leave only after getting serviced; they do not resort to balking, reneging or jockeying.
5. Service facility behaviour is normal. It serves the customers continuously, without break, as long as there is queue. Also it serves only one customer at a time.
6. The waiting space available for customers in the queue is infinite.
7. The calling source (population) has infinite size.
8. The elapsed time since the start of the queue is sufficiently long so that the system has attained a steady state or stable state.
9. The mean arrival rate λ is less than the mean service rate μ.

However, in most of the actual business situations the above assumptions are hardly satisfied. The *various limitations* in a queuing model are :

1. The waiting space for the customers is usually limited.
2. The arrival rate may be state dependent. An arriving customer, on seeing a long queue, may not joint it and go away without getting service.
3. The arrival process may not be stationary. There may be peak period and slack period during which the arrival rate may be more or less than the average arrival rate.
4. The population of customers may not be infinite and the queuing discipline may not be first come, first served
5. Services may not be rendered continuously. The service facility may breakdown; also the service may be provided in batches rather than individually.
6. The queuing system may not have reached the steady state. It may be, instead, in transient state. It is commonly so when the queue just starts and the elapsed time is not sufficient.

EXAMPLE 10.9-4.1

A self-service store employs one cashier at its counter. Nine customers arrive on an average every 5 minutes while the cashier can serve 10 customers in 5 minutes. Assuming Poisson distribution for arrival rate and exponential distribution for service time, find

1. *Average number of customers in the system*
2. *Average number of customers in the queue or average queue length.*
3. *Average time a customer spends in the system.*
4. *Average time a customer waits before being served.*

[*J.N.T.U. Hyderabad B.Tech. (Mech.) May, 2012; May, 2011; P.T.U. B.E., 2001*]

Solution

Arrival rate $\lambda = 9/5 = 1.8$ customers/minute,
service rate $\mu = 10/5 = 2$ customers/minute.

1. Average number of customers in the system,

$$L_s = \frac{\lambda}{\mu - \lambda} = \frac{1.8}{2 - 1\,8} = 9.$$

2. Average number of customers in the queue,

$$L_q = \frac{\lambda^2}{\mu(\mu - \lambda)} = \frac{\lambda}{\mu} \cdot \frac{\lambda}{(\mu - \lambda)} = \frac{1.8}{2} \times \frac{1.8}{2 - 1.8} = 8.1.$$

3. Average time a customer spends in the system,

$$W_s = \frac{1}{\mu - \lambda} = \frac{1}{2 - 1\,8} = 5 \text{ minutes.}$$

4. Average time a costumer waits in the queue,

$$W_q = \frac{\lambda}{\mu}\left(\frac{1}{\mu - \lambda}\right) = \frac{1.8}{2}\left(\frac{1}{2 - 1.8}\right) = 4.5 \text{ minutes.}$$

EXAMPLE 10.9-4.2

A person repairing radios finds that the time spent on the radio sets has exponential distribution with mean 20 minutes. If the radios are repaired in the order in which they come in and their arrival is approximately Poisson with an average rate of 15 for 8-hour day, what is the repairman's expected idle time each day ? How many jobs are ahead of the average set just brought in ?

[P.U.B.E. (T.&I.T.) Nov., 2004; B.E. (Mech.) 2002 ; P.T.U. (B.Tech.) 2010; 2000; MBA May, 2002 ; IGNOU MBA, 2000]

Solution

$$\text{Arrival rate } \lambda = \frac{15}{8 \times 60} = \frac{1}{32} \text{ units/minute,}$$

$$\text{service rate } \mu = \frac{1}{20} \text{ units/minute.}$$

Number of jobs ahead of the set brought in = Average number of jobs in the system,

$$L_s = \frac{\lambda}{\mu - \lambda} = \frac{1/32}{1/20 - 1/32} = \frac{5}{3}.$$

Number of hours for which the repairman remains busy in an 8-hour day

$$= 8\ \frac{\lambda}{\mu} = 8 \times \frac{1/32}{1/20} = 8 \times \frac{20}{32} = 5 \text{ hours.}$$

∴ Time for which repairman remains idle in an 8-hour day

$$= 8 - 5 = 3 \text{ hours.}$$

EXAMPLE 10.9-4.3

A branch of Punjab National Bank has only one typist. Since the typing work varies in length (number of pages to be typed), the typing rate is randomly distributed approximating a Poisson distribution with mean service rate of 8 letters per hour. The letters arrive at a rate of 5 per hour during the entire 8-hour work day. If the typewriter is valued at ₹ 1.50 per hour, determine.

1. *Equipment utilization.*
2. *The per cent time that an arriving letter has to wait.*
3. *Average system time.*
4. *Average cost due to waiting on the part of typewriter i.e., it remaining idle.*

[H.P.U. B. Tech. (Mech.) Nov., 2007; Nagpur U.B.E. (Mech.) 2003]

Solution

Arrival rate, $\lambda = 5$ per hour,

service rate, $\mu = 8$ per hour.

1. Equipment utilization, $\rho = \dfrac{\lambda}{\mu} = \dfrac{5}{8} = 0.625.$

2. The per cent time an arriving letter has to wait

= per cent time the typewriter remains busy

= 62.5%.

3. Average system time,

$$W_s = \frac{1}{\mu - \lambda} = \frac{1}{8-5} = \frac{1}{3} \text{ hr.} = 20 \text{ minutes.}$$

4. Average cost due to waiting on the part of the typewriter per day

$$= 8 \times (1 - 5/8) \times ₹\,1.50 = ₹\,4.50.$$

EXAMPLE 10.9-4.4

The milk plant at a city distributes its products by trucks, loaded at the loading dock. It has its own fleet of trucks plus trucks of a private transport company. This transport company has complained that sometime its trucks have to wait in line and thus the company loses money paid for a truck and driver that is only waiting. The company has asked the milk plant management either to go in for a second loading dock or discount prices equivalent to the waiting time. The following data are available:

Average arrival rate (all trucks) = 3 per hour,
average service rate = 4 per hour.

The transport company has provided 40% of the total number of trucks. Assuming that these rates are random according to Poisson distribution, determine

1. *The probability that a truck has to wait.*
2. *The waiting time of a truck that waits.*
3. *The expected waiting time of company trucks per day.*

[*P.U.B.E. (Mech.) Nov., 2002*]

Solution

1. The probability that a truck has to wait for service = utilization factor = $\rho = \frac{\lambda}{\mu}$ = 3/4 = 0.75.
2. The waiting time of a truck that waits

$$= W_n = \frac{1}{\mu - \lambda} = \frac{1}{4-3} = \frac{1}{1} = 1 \text{ hour.}$$

3. Total expected waiting time of company trucks per day = Trucks/day × % of company trucks × expected waiting time per truck

$$= (3 \times 8) \times (0.40) \times \frac{\lambda}{\mu(\mu - \lambda)}$$

$$= 24 \times 0.40 \times \frac{3}{4(4-3)} = 7.2 \text{ hours/day.}$$

EXAMPLE 10.9-4.5

Arrival rate of telephone calls at a telephone booth are according to Poisson distribution, with an average time of 9 minutes between two consecutive arrivals. The length of telephone call is assumed to be exponentially distributed, with mean 3 minutes.

(a) *Determine the probability that a person arriving at the booth will have to wait.*

(b) *Find the average queue length that is formed from time to time.*

(c) *The telephone company will install a second booth when convinced that an arrival would expect to have to wait at least four minutes for the phone. Find the increase in flow rate of arrivals which will justify a second booth.*

(d) *What is the probability that an arrival will have to wait for more than 10 minutes before the phone is free ?*

(e) *What is the probability that he will have to wait for more than 10 minutes before the phone is available and the call is also complete ?*

(*f*) *Find the fraction of a day that the phone will be in use.*

[*V.T.U. Karnataka B.E. June, 2010; R.T.M. Nagpur U. B.Tech. (Mech.) June, 2007; Dec., 2005; P.T.U. B.Tech. (Mech.) 2008; MBA June, 2003*]

Solution

Here, arrival rate, $\lambda = 1/9$ per minute,
service rate, $\mu = 1/3$ per minute.

(*a*) Probability that a person will have to wait

$$= \frac{\lambda}{\mu} = \frac{1/9}{1/3} = \frac{1}{3} = 0.33.$$

(*b*) Average queue length that is formed from time to time

$$= \frac{\mu}{\mu - \lambda} = \frac{1/3}{1/3 - 1/9} = \frac{1/3}{2/9} = \frac{1}{3} \times \frac{9}{2} = 1.5 \text{ persons.}$$

(*c*) Let λ_1 be the new (increased) arrival rate to justify the installation of the second telephone booth.

Average waiting time in the queue $= \dfrac{\lambda_1}{\mu(\mu - \lambda_1)}$.

$$\therefore \quad 4 = \frac{\lambda_1}{1/3 \,.\, (1/3 - \lambda_1)}$$

or $\quad 1/9 - \dfrac{\lambda_1}{3} = \dfrac{\lambda_1}{4}$ or $\lambda_1 \times 7/12 = 1/9$.

$$\therefore \quad \lambda_1 = \frac{12}{7 \times 9} = \frac{4}{21} \text{ arrivals/minute.}$$

$\therefore$ Increase in flow rate of arrivals $= \dfrac{4}{21} - \dfrac{1}{9} = \dfrac{5}{63}$ per minute.

(*d*) Probability [waiting time ≥ 10] $= \displaystyle\int_{10}^{\infty} \frac{\lambda}{\mu} . (\mu - \lambda) . e^{-(\mu - \lambda)t} . dt$

$$= \frac{\lambda}{\mu} . (\mu - \lambda) . \left[\frac{e^{-(\mu - \lambda)t}}{-(\mu - \lambda)}\right]_{10}^{\infty}$$

$$= \frac{-\lambda}{\mu} \left[0 - e^{-(\mu - \lambda).10}\right]$$

$$= \frac{\lambda}{\mu} . e^{-(\mu - \lambda).10}$$

$$= \frac{1/9}{1/3} . e^{-\left(\frac{1}{3} - \frac{1}{9}\right).10} = \frac{1}{3} . e^{\frac{-20}{9}} = \frac{1}{30}.$$

(*e*) Probability [time in system ≥ 10] $= \displaystyle\int_{10}^{\infty} (\mu - \lambda) . e^{-(\mu - \lambda)t} . dt$

$$= (\mu - \lambda) . \left[\frac{e^{-(\mu - \lambda)t}}{-(\mu - \lambda)}\right]_{10}^{\infty}$$

$$= -\left[e^{-(\mu - \lambda)t}\right]_{10}^{\infty}$$

$$= -\left[0 - e^{-(\mu - \lambda).10}\right] = e^{-\left(\frac{1}{3} - \frac{1}{9}\right).10}$$

$$= e^{-20/9} = 0.1.$$

(*f*) The expected fraction of a day that the phone will be in use

$$= \frac{\lambda}{\mu} = 0.33.$$

EXAMPLE 10.9-4.6

In a large maintenance department, fitters draw parts from the parts-store which is at present staffed by one storeman. The maintenance foreman is concerned about the time spent by fitters getting parts and wants to know if the employment of a store labourer to assist the storeman would be worthwhile. On investigation it is found that

(*a*) *a simple queue situation exists,*
(*b*) *fitters cost ₹ 2.50 per hour,*
(*c*) *the storeman costs ₹ 2 per hour and can deal, on the average, with 10 fitters per hour,*
(*d*) *a labourer could be employed at ₹ 1.75 per hour and would increase the service capacity of the store to 12 per hour,*
(*e*) *on the average 8 fitters visit the stores each hour.*

[*Pondicherry MBA August, 2006*]

Solution

The problem can be solved by two methods:

Method 1: Here, we calculate the average *number of customers* in the system before and after the labourer is employed and compare the reduction in the resulting queuing cost with the increase in service cost.

Without labourer :

∴ Number of customers in the system, $L_s = \frac{\lambda}{\mu - \lambda} = \frac{8}{10 - 8} = 4.$

∴ Cost/hr = 4 × ₹ 2.50 = ₹ 10.

With labourer

$$\lambda = 8/\text{hr}, \mu = 12/\text{hr}.$$

∴ Number of customers in the system, $L_s = \frac{\lambda}{\mu - \lambda} = \frac{8}{12 - 8} = 2.$

Cost/hr = cost of fitters per hour + cost of labourer per hour
= 2 × ₹ 2.50 + ₹ 1.75 = ₹ 6.75.

Since there is net saving of ₹ 3.25, it is recommended to employ the labourer.

Method 2 : Here, we calculate the average *time* spent by the customers (fitters) in the system before and after the employment of the labourer, and again compare the reduction in the resulting queuing cost with the increase in the service cost.

Without labourer

$$\lambda = 8/\text{hr}, \mu = 10/\text{hr}.$$

∴ Average time spent by a fitter in the system $W_s = \frac{1}{\mu - \lambda} = \frac{1}{10 - 8} = 0.5$ hr.

∴ Cost/hr = 8 × 0.5 × ₹ 2.50 = ₹ 10.

With labourer

$$\lambda = 8/\text{hr}, \mu = 12/\text{hr}.$$

$\therefore$ Average time spent by a fitter in the system, $W_s = \dfrac{1}{\mu - \lambda} = \dfrac{1}{12-8} = \dfrac{1}{4}$ hr.

$\therefore$ Cost/hr = 8 × 1/4 × ₹ 2.50 + ₹ 1.75 = ₹ 6.75.

$\therefore$ It is recommended to employ the labourer.

EXAMPLE 10.9-4.7

On the average 96 patients per 24-hour day require the service of an emergency clinic. Also on the average, a patient requires 10 minutes of active attention. Assume that the facility can handle only one emergency at a time. Suppose that it costs the clinic ₹ 100 per patient treated to obtain an average servicing time of 10 minutes, and that each minute of decrease in this average time would cost the clinic ₹10 per patient treated. How much would have to be budgeted by the clinic to decrease the average size of the queue from $1\frac{1}{3}$ patients to $\frac{1}{2}$ patient?

[*Dayalagh Edu. Inst. Agra MBA Dec., 2011; H.P.U. B.Tech. (Mech.) Nov., 2006; P.T.U. B.Tech. (Mech.) Dec., 2006*]

Solution

Here, $\lambda = \dfrac{96}{24} = 4$ patients/hr, $\mu = \dfrac{1}{10} \times 60 = 6$ patients/hr.

Average number of patients in the queue

$$= \frac{\lambda}{\mu} \cdot \frac{\lambda}{\mu - \lambda} = \frac{4}{6} \cdot \frac{4}{6-4}$$

or $\quad L_q = \dfrac{4}{6} \times \dfrac{4}{2} = \dfrac{4}{3} = 1\dfrac{1}{3}$.

This number is to be reduced from $1\frac{1}{3}$ to $\frac{1}{2}$ (L_q'). This can be achieved by increasing the service rate to, say, μ'.

Now $\quad L_q' = \dfrac{\lambda}{\mu'} \cdot \dfrac{\lambda}{\mu' - \lambda}$.

$\therefore \quad \dfrac{1}{2} = \dfrac{4}{\mu'} \cdot \dfrac{4}{\mu' - 4}$

or $\quad \mu'^2 - 4\mu' - 32 = 0$ or $(\mu' - 8)(\mu' + 4) = 0$

or $\quad \mu' = 8$ patients/hr. $\quad$ ($\mu' = -4$ is illogical and hence neglected).

$\therefore$ Average time required by each patient = 1/8 hr = 15/2 minutes.

$\therefore$ Decrease in the time required to attend a patient $= 10 - \dfrac{15}{2} = \dfrac{5}{2}$ minutes.

Therefore, the budget required for each patient = ₹ (100 + 5/2 × 10) = ₹ 125.

Thus to decrease the size of the queue, the budget per patient should be increased from ₹ 100 to ₹ 125.

EXAMPLE 10.9-4.8

Workers come to tool store room to receive special tools (required by them) for accomplishing a particular project assigned to them. The average time between two arrivals is 60 seconds and the arrivals are assumed to be in Poisson distribution. The average service time (of the tool room attendant) is 40 seconds. Determine

(a) average queue length,

(b) *average length of non-empty queues,*

(c) *average number of workers in system including the worker being attended,*

(d) *mean waiting time of an arrival,*

(e) *average waiting time of an arrival (worker) who waits, and*

(f) *the type of policy to be established. In other words, determine whether to go in for an additional tool store room attendant which will minimize the combined cost of attendant's idle time and the cost of workers' waiting time. Assume the charges of a skilled worker ₹ 4 per hour and that of tool store room attendant ₹ 0.75 per hour.*

[*J.N.T.U. Hyderabad B.Tech. May, 2011; R.T.M. Nagpur U. B.Tech. June, 2006*]

Solution

Here, $\lambda = 1/60$ per second $= 1$ per minute,

$\mu = 1/40$ per second $= 1.5$ per minute.

(a) Average queue length, $L_q = \dfrac{\lambda}{\mu} \cdot \dfrac{\lambda}{\mu - \lambda} = \dfrac{1}{1.5} \cdot \dfrac{1}{1.5 - 1} = \dfrac{1}{0.75} = \dfrac{4}{3}$ workers.

(b) Average length of non-empty queues, $L_n = \dfrac{\mu}{\mu - \lambda} = \dfrac{1.5}{1.5 - 1} = 3$ workers.

(c) Average number of workers in the system, $L_s = \dfrac{\lambda}{\mu - \lambda} = \dfrac{1}{1.5 - 1} = 2$ workers.

(d) Mean waiting time of an arrival,

$$W_q = \frac{1}{\mu} \cdot \frac{\lambda}{\mu - \lambda} = \frac{1}{1.5} \times \frac{1}{1.5 - 1} = \frac{4}{3} \text{ minutes.}$$

(e) Average waiting time of an arrival who waits,

$$W_n = \frac{1}{\mu - \lambda} = \frac{1}{1.5 - 1} = 2 \text{ minutes.}$$

(f) Probability that the tool room attendant remains idle,

$$p_0 = 1 - \frac{\lambda}{\mu} = 1 - \frac{1}{1.5} = \frac{1}{3}.$$

∴ Idle time cost of the one attendent = 1/3 × 8 × ₹ 0.75 = ₹ 2/day.

Waiting time cost of workers = W_q × no. of workers arriving/day × cost of worker

$$= \left(\frac{4}{3} \times \frac{1}{60}\right) \times (8 \times 60) \times ₹\ 4 = ₹\ \frac{128}{3} = ₹\ 42.67\text{/day.}$$

∴ Total cost = ₹ (42.67 + 2) = ₹ 44.67/day.

Now the service rate, after the additional store room attendant is employed, is not given in the problem so that the total cost could be calculated and compared with the earlier total cost of ₹ 44.67/day. As the waiting time cost is much higher than the idle time cost, it is justified to employ an additional tool room attendant.

EXAMPLE 10.9-4.9

Customers arrive at a one window drive-in bank according to a Poisson distribution with mean 10 per hour. Service time per customer is exponential with mean 5 minutes. The space in front of the window, including that for the serviced car can accommodate a maximum of three cars. Other cars can wait outside this space.

(a) *What is the probability that an arriving customer can drive directly to the space in front of the window ?*

(b) *What is the probability that an arriving customer will have to wait outside the indicated space ?*

(c) *How long is an arriving customer expected to wait before starting service ?*

[*H.P.U. B.Tech. (Mech.) June, 2010; P.U.B.E. (T.I.T.) Nov., 2005; IGNOU MBA, 2002; P.U.B.E. (Prod.) 2001; J.U. B.E. (Mech.) 2004*]

Solution

Here, $\lambda = 10/\text{hour}$, $\mu = 60/5 = 12/\text{hour}$.

(*a*) The probability that an arriving customer can drive directly to the space in front of the window can be obtained by summing up the probabilities of the events in which this can happen. A customer can drive directly to the space if

(*i*) there is no customer car already

(*ii*) there is already 1 customer car

(*iii*) there are already 2 cars in the space.

Thus the required probability $= p_0 + p_1 + p_2$

$$= \left(1-\frac{\lambda}{\mu}\right) + \frac{\lambda}{\mu}\left(1-\frac{\lambda}{\mu}\right) + \left(\frac{\lambda}{\mu}\right)^2\left(1-\frac{\lambda}{\mu}\right)$$

$$= \left(1-\frac{\lambda}{\mu}\right)\left[1+\frac{\lambda}{\mu}+\frac{\lambda^2}{\mu^2}\right]$$

$$= \left(1-\frac{10}{12}\right)\left[1+\frac{10}{12}+\frac{100}{144}\right] = 0.42.$$

(*b*) The probability that an arriving customer has to wait outside the indicated space = 1 – 0.42 = 0.58.

(c) Average waiting time of a customer in the queue

$$= \frac{1}{\mu}.\frac{\lambda}{\mu-\lambda} = \frac{10}{12\,(12-10)} = 0.417 \text{ hours} = 25 \text{ minutes.}$$

EXAMPLE 10.9-4.10

A repairman is to be hired to repair machines which break down at an average rate of 3 per hour. The breakdowns follow Poisson distribution. Non-productive time of machines is considered to cost ₹ 16 per hour. Two repairmen have been interviewed : one is slow but cheap, while the other is fast but expensive. The slow repairman charges ₹ 8 per hour and he services brokendown machines at the rate of 4 per hour. The fast repairman demands ₹ 10 per hour and he services at an average rate of 6 per hour. Which repairman should be hired ? Assume an 8-hour working day.

[*H.P.U.B Tech. (Mech.) Dec., 2009*]

Solution

Here, $\lambda = 3/\text{hour}$,

idle time (down time) cost of the machine = ₹ 16/hour.

Slow repairman

$$\mu = 4/\text{hour}.$$

A machine remains unproductive from the moment it breakdown till it is repaired and starts working again *i.e.*, it remains unproductive for the time it waits for repairs plus the repair time or *for the time spent by it in the system.*

Average number of brokendown machines *in the system* $= \dfrac{\lambda}{\mu-\lambda} = \dfrac{3}{4-3} = 3.$

Machine hours lost in 8-hour day = 3 × 8 = 24 hours.

∴ Total cost/day = cost of idle machines + repairman charges

= ₹ (16 × 24 + 8 × 8) = ₹ (384 + 64) = ₹ 448.

Fast repairman

$\mu = 6/\text{hour}.$

Average number of brokendown machines in the system $= \dfrac{\lambda}{\mu - \lambda} = \dfrac{3}{6-3} = 1.$

Machine hours lost in 8-hour day = 1 × 8 = 8 hours.

∴ Total cost per day = cost of idle machines + repairman charges

= ₹ (16 × 8 + 10 × 8) = ₹ (128 + 80) = ₹ 208.

∴ Fast repairman should be engaged.

EXAMPLE 10.9-4.11

Customers arrive at a bank counter manned by a single cashier according to Poisson distribution with mean arrival rate 6 customers/hour. The cashier attends the customers on first come, first served basis at an average rate of 10 customers/hour with the service time exponential distribution. Find

(a) *the probability of the number of arrivals (0 through 5) during (i) 15-minute interval (ii) 30-minute interval.*

(b) *the probability that the queuing system is idle.*

(c) *the prbability associated with the number of customers (0 through 5) in the queuing system.*

(d) *the time a customer should expect to spend in the queue.*

(e) *the time a customer spends before leaving the bank counter.*

[P.T.U. B. Tech. April, 2012]

Solution

(*a*) Here $\lambda = 6$ customers/hour, $\mu = 10$ customers/hour, $\dfrac{\lambda}{\mu} = 0.6.$

(*i*) $t = 15$ minutes $= \dfrac{1}{4}$ hour, $\lambda t = \dfrac{6}{4} = 1.5$ customers.

Probability of n customers arriving in time $t = \dfrac{(\lambda t)^n \cdot e^{-\lambda t}}{n!}.$

∴ Probability of n customers arriving in 15 minutes $= \dfrac{(1.5)^n \cdot e^{-1.5}}{n!}$

Probabilities of 0, 1, 2, 3, 4 and 5 customers arriving during this time interval are shown in the second column of the table 10.3.

(*ii*) $t = 30$ minutes $= \dfrac{1}{2}$ hour, $\lambda t = \dfrac{6}{2} = 3$ customers.

Probability of n customers arriving in 30 minutes $= \dfrac{3^n \cdot e^{-3}}{n!}.$

Probabilities of 0, 1, 2, 3, 4 and 5 customers arriving during this time interval are shown in the third column of the table.

TABLE 10.3

Probabilities of arrival

n	*In 15 minutes*	*In 30 minutes*
0	0.223	0.050
1	0.335	0.149
2	0.251	0.224
3	0.126	0.224
4	0.047	0.168
5	0.014	0.101

(*b*) Probability that the queuing system is idle, $p_0 = 1 - \dfrac{\lambda}{\mu} = 1 - \dfrac{6}{10} = 0.4.$

(*c*) Probability of n customers in the queuing system,

$$p_n = \left(\frac{\lambda}{\mu}\right)^n . \left(1 - \frac{\lambda}{\mu}\right)$$

$$= (0.6)^n \,.\, (0.4) = 0.4 \cdot (0.6)^n.$$

Probabilities of 0, 1, 2, 3, 4 and 5 customers in the system are given below :

No. of customers	:	0	1	2	3	4	5
Probability	:	0.4	0.24	0.144	0.0864	0.05184	0.031104

(*d*) The time a customer spends in the queue,

$$W_q = \frac{\lambda}{\mu} . \frac{1}{\mu - \lambda} = 0.6 \,.\, \frac{1}{10 - 6} = 0.15 \text{ hour}$$

$$= 9 \text{ minutes.}$$

(*e*) The time a customer spends in the system,

$$W_s = \frac{1}{\mu - \lambda} = \frac{1}{10 - 6} = 0.25 \text{ hour} = 15 \text{ minutes.}$$

EXAMPLE 10.9-4.12

Customers arrive at the First Class Ticket Counter of a Theatre at the rate of 12 per hour. There is one clerk serving the customers at the rate of 30 per hour.

(*i*) *What is the probability that there is no customer at the counter (i.e., that the system is idle) ?*

(*ii*) *What is the probability that there are more than 2 customers at the counter ?*

(*iii*) *What is the probability that there is no customer waiting to be served ?*

(*iv*) *What is the probability that a customer is being served and no body is waiting ?*

[*P.T.U. M.Tech. Dec., 2011; SVSM PGDM, 2009; P.U. B.E. (T.I.T.) Dec., 2008*]

Solution

Here, $\lambda = 12$/hour, $\mu = 30$/hour.

(*i*) Probability that there is no customer in the system,

$$p_0 = 1 - \frac{\lambda}{\mu} = 1 - \frac{12}{30} = 0.6.$$

(*ii*) Probability that there are more than two customers at the counter

$$= p_3 + p_4 + p_5 + \ldots$$

$$= 1 - (p_0 + p_1 + p_2)$$

$$= 1 - \left[p_0 \left(1 + \frac{\lambda}{\mu} + \frac{\lambda^2}{\mu^2}\right) \right]$$

$$= 1 - \left[0.6 \left(1 + \frac{12}{30} + \frac{144}{900}\right) \right] = 0.064.$$

(*iii*) Probability that there is no customer waiting to be served

= probability that there is at most one customer at the counter

$$= p_0 + p_1 = 0.6 + 0.6 \left(\frac{12}{30}\right) = 0.84.$$

(*iv*) Probability that a customer is being served and no body is waiting $= p_1 = p_0 \cdot \dfrac{\lambda}{\mu}$

$$= 0.6 \left[\frac{12}{30}\right] = 0.24.$$

EXAMPLE 10.9-4.13

In the central railway station 15 computerised reservation counters are available. A customer can book his/her ticket in any train on any day in any one of these computerised reservation counters. The average time spent per customer by each clerk is 5 minutes. Average arrivals per hour during three types of activity periods have been calculated and customers have been surveyed to determine how long they are willing to wait during each type of period.

Type of period	*Arrivals/hr*	*Customer's acceptable waiting time*
Peak	*110*	*15 minutes*
Normal	*60*	*10 minutes*
Low	*30*	*5 minutes*

Making suitable assumptions on this queuing process, determine how many counters should be kept open during each type of period.

[*Univ. of Mumbai PGDM, 2012; M.D.U. Rohtak B.E. (Mech.) Dec., 2006*]

Solution

The following assumptions are made for performing various calculations :

1. The arrival of customers follows Poisson probability distribution with mean arrival rate λ.
2. The service time has exponential distribution, mean service rate being μ.
3. The service discipline is first come, first served.
4. The calling source (population) has infinite size.
5. There is no unusual customer behaviour.
6. There is no unusual server behaviour.
7. The mean arrival rate at any reservation counter is less than the mean service rate ($\lambda < \mu$).
8. A customer can book his/her ticket in any train on any day in any of the reservation counters *i.e.,* there are as many queues as the number of counters open. The queues are selected at random by the arrivals and there is no line-switching. The system is, therefore, not multi-channel and can be thought of and analysed as the one composed of a number of different single queuing systems operating together.

(*i*) *Peak period*

$$\lambda' = 110/\text{hr}, \ W_q = 15 \text{ minutes},$$

$$\mu = \frac{1}{5} \times 60 = 12/\text{hr}.$$

Now $\quad W_q = \frac{\lambda}{\mu}.\frac{1}{\mu - \lambda}$, where λ and μ are the arrival rate and service rate respectively at one counter.

$\therefore \quad \frac{15}{60} = \frac{\lambda}{12\,(12-\lambda)}.$

$\therefore \quad 3\,(12 - \lambda) = \lambda$

or $\quad \lambda = 9/\text{hr.}$

$\therefore$ No. of counters to be kept open $= \frac{110}{9} = 12.22 \sim 13.$

(*ii*) *Normal period*

Here, $\quad \lambda' = 60/\text{hr},\ W_q = 10$ minutes.

$$W_q = \frac{\lambda}{\mu}.\frac{1}{\mu - \lambda}.$$

$\therefore \quad \frac{10}{60} = \frac{\lambda}{12\,(12-\lambda)}.$

$\therefore \quad 2\,(12 - \lambda) = \lambda$

or $\quad \lambda = 8/\text{hr.}$

$\therefore$ No. of counters to be kept open $= \frac{60}{8} = 7.5 \sim 8.$

(*iii*) *Low period*

Here, $\quad \lambda' = 30/\text{hr},\ W_q = 5$ minutes.

$$W_q = \frac{\lambda}{\mu}.\frac{1}{\mu - \lambda}.$$

$\therefore \quad \frac{5}{60} = \frac{\lambda}{12\,(12-\lambda)}.$

$\therefore \quad (12 - \lambda) = \lambda$

or $\quad \lambda = 6/\text{hr.}$

$\therefore$ No. of counters to be kept open $= \frac{30}{6} = 5.$

EXAMPLE 10.9-4.14

Referring to example 10.9-4.9, how many spaces should be provided in front of the window so that all the arriving customers can wait in front of the window at least 20% of the time ?

Solution

Here, $\lambda = 10$ customers/hour, $\mu = \frac{1}{5} \times 60 = 12$ customers/hour.

$$p_0 = 1 - \frac{\lambda}{\mu} = 1 - \frac{10}{12} = 0.16\ ;\ p_1 = \frac{\lambda}{\mu}\ p_0 = \frac{10}{12} \times 0.16 = 0.13.$$

$\therefore$ Probability that there will be no car or one car in the space = 0.16 + 0.13 = 0.29.

Since it is more than 20%, there should be at least one car space in front of the window.

EXAMPLE 10.9-4.15

(*a*) *A typist at an office of a company receives on the average 20 letters per day for typing. The typist works 8 hours a day and it takes on the average 20 minutes to type a letter. The cost of a letter waiting to be mailed (opportunity cost) is 80 paise per hour and the cost of the equipment plus salary of the typist is ₹ 45 per day.*

(i) What is the typist's utilization rate ?

(ii) What is the average number of letters waiting to be typed ?

(iii) What is average waiting time needed to have a letter typed ?

(iv) What is the total daily cost of waiting letters to be mailed ? *[C.A. Nov., 1993]*

(b) In order to improve the typing service, the company has the choice to take lease of one of the two models of an automated typewriter. The daily costs and the resulting increase in efficiency of the typist are given below :

Model	*Additional cost/day*	*Increase in typist's efficiency*
I	*₹ 20*	*50%*
II	*₹ 25*	*75%*

What action should the company take to minimize the total daily cost of waiting letters to be mailed ?

Solution

Here, $\lambda = 20$ letters/day, $\mu = \frac{1}{20} \times 8 \times 60 = 24$ letters/day.

(*a*) (*i*) The typist's utilization rate $= \frac{\lambda}{\mu} = \frac{20}{24} = \frac{5}{6} = 0.833.$

(*ii*) The average number of letters waiting to be typed,

$$L_q = \frac{\lambda}{\mu} \cdot \frac{\lambda}{\mu - \lambda} = \frac{20}{24} \cdot \frac{20}{24 - 20} = \frac{5}{6} \times 5 = 4.17.$$

(*iii*) The average waiting time needed to have a letter typed

= waiting time in the queue + time to type the letter

$= \text{time spent in the system} = \frac{1}{\mu - \lambda} = \frac{1}{24 - 20} = \frac{1}{4}$ day = 2 hours.

(*iv*) The average number of waiting letters to be mailed

= the average number of letters in the system.

$$L_s = \frac{\lambda}{\mu - \lambda} = \frac{20}{24 - 20} = 5.$$

Now the total daily cost of waiting letters to be mailed = the average number of letters in the system × opportunity cost + cost of equipment and salary

$$= ₹\left[5 \times \left(\frac{80}{100} \times 8\right) + 45\right] = ₹\,(32 + 45) = ₹\,77.$$

(*b*) *Lease Model I*

Here, $\lambda = 20$ letters/day, $\mu = 24 \times 1.5 = 36$ letters/day.

$$L_s = \frac{\lambda}{\mu - \lambda} = \frac{20}{36 - 20} = \frac{20}{16} = \frac{5}{4} = 1.25.$$

∴ The total daily cost of waiting letters to be mailed

$$= ₹\left[1.25 \times \frac{80}{100} \times 8 + 45 + 20\right] = ₹\,(8 + 45 + 20) = ₹\,73.$$

Lease Model II

Here, $\lambda = 20$ letters/day, $\mu = 24 \times 1.75 = 42$ letters/day.

$$L_s = \frac{\lambda}{\mu - \lambda} = \frac{20}{42 - 20} = \frac{20}{22} = \frac{10}{11}.$$

∴ The total daily cost of waiting letters to be mailed

$$= ₹\left[\frac{10}{11}\times\frac{80}{100}\times 8+45+25\right] = ₹\ 75.82.$$

Comparing the two choices with the existing system, it is advisable to lease model I of the automated typewriter.

EXAMPLE 10.9-4.16

At what average rate must a clerk in a supermarket work in order to ensure a probability of 0.90 that a customer will not have to wait longer than 12 minutes ? Customers arrive at the counter in Poisson fashion with mean rate of 15 per hour. Service time has exponential distribution.

[*Meerut U. (Math.) 1999, 96*]

Solution

Here, λ = 15/hour = $\frac{15}{60} = \frac{1}{4}$/minute, probability (waiting time ≥ 12) = 1 – 0.90 = 0.10.

$$\therefore \qquad \int_{12}^{\infty}\frac{\lambda}{\mu}\,.\,(\mu-\lambda)\,.\,e^{-(\mu-\lambda)t}\,.\,dt = 0.10$$

$$\text{or} \qquad \frac{\lambda}{\mu}\,(\mu-\lambda)\,.\left[\frac{e^{-(\mu-\lambda)t}}{-(\mu-\lambda)}\right]_{12}^{\infty} = 0.10$$

$$\text{or} \qquad -\frac{1}{4\mu}\,[0-e^{-(\mu-.25)12}] = 0.10 \text{ or } e^{3-12\mu} = 0.4\,\mu \text{ or } \mu = \frac{1}{2.48}\text{/minute.}$$

$$\text{or} \qquad \mu = \frac{60}{2.48} = 24.2 \text{ customers/hour.}$$

EXAMPLE 10.9-4.17

The mean rate of arrival of planes at an airport during the peak period is 20/hour as per Poisson distribution. During congestion, the planes are forced to fly over the field in the stack awaiting the landing of other planes that had arrived earlier.

(*a*) *How many planes would be flying in the stack during good and in bad weather ?*

(*b*) *How long a plane would be in the stack and in the process of landing in good and in bad weather ?*

(*c*) *How much stack and landing time to allow so that priority to land out of order would have to be requested only once in 20 times ?*

Assume μ = *60 planes/hour in good weather and 30 planes/hour in bad weather.*

[*P.T.U. B.Tech. April, 2012*]

Solution

In good weather : λ = 20 planes/hour, μ = 60 planes/hour.

$$(a) \qquad L_q = \frac{\lambda}{\mu}\cdot\frac{\lambda}{\mu-\lambda} = \frac{20}{60}\cdot\frac{20}{60-20} = \frac{1}{6} \text{ planes.}$$

$$(b) \qquad W_s = \frac{1}{\mu-\lambda} = \frac{1}{60-20} = \frac{1}{40} \text{ hour} = \frac{60}{40} = 1.5 \text{ minutes.}$$

(*c*) The time taken by a plane during stack and landing can be found from :

$$\int_0^t (\mu-\lambda)\,.\,e^{-(\mu-\lambda)t}\,.\,dt = 1-\frac{1}{20} = \frac{19}{20} = 0.95,$$

$$\text{or } (\mu - \lambda) \cdot \left[\frac{e^{-(\mu-\lambda)t}}{-(\mu-\lambda)}\right]_0^t = 0.95,$$

which gives $e^{-(\mu-\lambda)t} = 0.05$ or $e^{-(60-20)t} = 0.05$ or $t = 0.075$ hour = 4.5 minutes.

In bad weather : $\lambda = 20$ planes/hour, $\mu = 30$ planes/hour.

(*a*) $$L_q = \frac{\lambda}{\mu} \cdot \frac{\lambda}{\mu - \lambda} = \frac{20}{30} \cdot \frac{20}{30-20} = \frac{4}{3} \text{ planes.}$$

(*b*) $$W_s = \frac{1}{\mu - \lambda} = \frac{1}{30-20} = 0.1 \text{ hour} = 6 \text{ minutes.}$$

(*c*) $$e^{-(\mu-\lambda)t} = 0.05 \text{ or } e^{-(30-20)t} = 0.05 \text{ or } e^{-10t} = 0.05$$

or $$t = 0.3 \text{ hour} = 18 \text{ minutes.}$$

EXAMPLE 10.9-4.18

A company is considering the construction of two repair facilities, each with different characteristics. On the average, 24 trucks require repairs each month and the arrivals are Poisson distributed. The loss of revenue (opportunity cost) to the firm of having a truck in repairs is estimated to be ₹ 300 per month. The two facilities which are under consideration have the following characteristics:

Characteristics		*Facility A*	*Facility B*
Installation cost	:	*₹ 2,00,000*	*₹ 6,00,000*
Labour cost per month	:	*₹ 80,000*	*₹ 80,000*
Repair rates (estimated)	:	*30 trucks/month*	*60 trucks/month*
Arrival rates (estimated)	:	*24 trucks/month*	*24 trucks/month*
Economic life	:	*4 years*	*4 years*

Determine which facility should be built by the company. *[P.T.U. M.Tech. April, 2012]*

Solution

$$\text{Total annual cost} = \frac{1}{4} \text{ (total installation cost)} + \text{annual labour cost}$$
$$+ \text{ annual cost of lost revenue due to down trucks.}$$

Facility A

$$\text{Annual installation cost} = ₹ \left(\frac{1}{4} \times 2,00,000\right) = ₹\ 50,000.$$

Annual labour cost = ₹ (12 × 80,000) = ₹ 9,60,000.

Computation of cost of down time of trucks

Expected number of trucks in the service facility,

$$L_s = \frac{\lambda}{\mu_1 - \lambda} = \frac{24}{30-24} = 4.$$

∴ Cost/year of lost revenue = 4 × (12 × 300) = ₹ 14,400.

∴ Total annual cost = ₹ (50,000 + 9,60,000 + 14,400) = ₹ 10,24,400.

Facility B

$$\text{Annual installation cost} = ₹ \left(\frac{1}{4} \times 6,00,000\right) = ₹\ 1,50,000.$$

Annual labour cost = ₹ (12 × 80,000) = ₹ 9,60,000.

Computation of cost of down time of trucks

Expected number of trucks in the service facility,

$$L_s = \frac{\lambda}{\mu_2 - \lambda} = \frac{24}{60 - 24} = \frac{2}{3}.$$

$\therefore$ Cost/year of lost revenue = $\frac{2}{3} \times (12 \times 300)$ = ₹ 2,400.

$\therefore$ Total annual cost = ₹ (1,50,000 + 9,60,000 + 2,400)
= ₹ 11,12,400.

As cost/year for facility A is lesser, the company should construct facility A.

EXAMPLE 10.9-4.19

Semi-finished components arrive at a workstation of an assembly line at an average rate of 2 per minute, Poisson distributed. A machine is to be installed at this workstation for the specific operation. Three alternative machines P, Q and R are available. The characteristics of the machines are given below. Whenever a component is idle awaiting the machine to get free, the cost is estimated at ₹ 18 per minute. Using the concept of single-channel queue system and considering all relevant costs, recommend the machine that would be the best for this work station:

Machine	:	*P*	*Q*	*R*
Fixed costs (₹/minute)	:	*36*	*60*	*90*
Variable costs (₹/minute)	:	*18*	*15*	*8*
Processing rate (Units/minute)	:	*3*	*6*	*12*

[*P.U.B.E. (T.I.T.) Nov., 2006; C.A. June, 2003*]

Solution

Here, $\lambda = 2$/minute.

Machine P

$\mu = 3$/minute.

Average number of components awaiting the machine to get free,

$$L_q = \frac{\lambda}{\mu}.\frac{\lambda}{\mu - \lambda} = \frac{2}{3}.\frac{2}{3-2} = \frac{4}{3}.$$

$$\therefore \quad \text{Cost/minute} = ₹ \left(\frac{4}{3} \times 18 + 36 + 18\right) = ₹ 78.$$

Machine Q

$\mu = 6$/minute.

$$L_q = \frac{\lambda}{\mu}.\frac{\lambda}{\mu - \lambda} = \frac{2}{6}.\frac{2}{6-2} = \frac{1}{3}.\frac{1}{2} = \frac{1}{6}.$$

$$\therefore \quad \text{Cost/minute} = ₹ \left(\frac{1}{6} \times 18 + 60 + 15\right) = ₹ 78.$$

Machine R

$\mu = 12$/minute.

$$L_q = \frac{\lambda}{\mu}.\frac{\lambda}{\mu - \lambda} = \frac{2}{12}.\frac{2}{12-2} = \frac{1}{6}.\frac{1}{5} = \frac{1}{30}.$$

$$\therefore \quad \text{Cost/minute} = ₹ \left(\frac{1}{30} \times 18 + 90 + 8\right) = ₹ 98.60.$$

$\therefore$ Either machine P or Q may be installed.

EXAMPLE 10.9-4.20

Goods trucks arrive randomly at a stockyard with a mean of 8 trucks/hour. A crew of four operatives can unload a truck in 6 minutes. Trucks waiting in queue to be unloaded are paid a waiting charge at the rate of ₹ 60 per hour. Operatives are paid a wage rate of ₹ 20 per hour. It is possible to augment the crew strength to 2 or 3 (of four operatives per crew) when the unloading time will be 4 minutes or 3 minutes respectively per truck. Find the optimal crew size.

[*P.T.U. M.Tech. April, 2012; V.T.U. Karnataka B.E. June, 2011; C.A. (Final) June, 2003*]

Solution

1- Crew strength :

$$\lambda = 8 \text{ trucks/hour},$$

$$\mu = \frac{1}{6} \times 60 = 10 \text{ trucks/hour.}$$

$$\text{Waiting time of a truck, } W_q = \frac{\lambda}{\mu}.\frac{1}{\mu - \lambda} = \frac{8}{10} \times \frac{1}{10 - 8} = \frac{2}{5} \text{ hour.}$$

$\therefore$ Waiting time of trucks/hour = Number of trucks arriving in one hour × W_q

$$= 8 \times \frac{2}{5} = \frac{16}{5} \text{ hours.}$$

$$\therefore \text{ Waiting time cost/hour} = ₹ \left(\frac{16}{5} \times 60\right) = ₹\ 192.$$

Operatives' wages/hour = ₹ (20 × 4) = ₹ 80.

$\therefore$ Total cost/hour = ₹ (192 + 80) = ₹ 272.

2 - Crew strength :

$$\lambda = 8 \text{ trucks/hour},$$

$$\mu = \frac{1}{4} \times 60 = 15 \text{ trucks/hour.}$$

$$W_q = \frac{\lambda}{\mu}.\frac{1}{\mu - \lambda} = \frac{8}{15} \times \frac{1}{15 - 8} = \frac{8}{105} \text{ hour.}$$

$$\therefore \text{ Waiting time of trucks/hour} = \frac{8}{105} \times 8 = \frac{64}{105} \text{ hour.}$$

$$\therefore \text{ Waiting time cost/hour} = ₹ \left(\frac{64}{105} \times 60\right) = ₹\ \frac{256}{7} = ₹\ 36.60.$$

Operatives' wages/hour = ₹ (20 × 8) = ₹ 160.

$\therefore$ Total cost/hour = ₹ 196.60.

3- Crew strength

$$\lambda = 8 \text{ trucks/hour},$$

$$\mu = \frac{1}{3} \times 60 = 20 \text{ trucks/hour.}$$

$$W_q = \frac{\lambda}{\mu}.\frac{1}{\mu - \lambda} = \frac{8}{20} \times \frac{1}{20 - 8} = \frac{1}{30} \text{ hour.}$$

$$\therefore \text{ Waiting time of trucks/hour} = ₹\ \frac{1}{30} \times 8 = \frac{4}{15} \text{ hour.}$$

$$\therefore \text{ Waiting time cost/hour} = ₹ \left(\frac{4}{15} \times 60\right) = ₹\ 16.$$

Operatives' wages/hour = ₹ (20 × 12) = ₹ 240.

∴ Total cost/hour = ₹ 256.

Therefore, optimal crew size is 2 (of 8 operatives).

EXERCISES 10.2

1. Define a queue and explain the various queue disciplines.
   [*Dayalbagh Edu.. Inst. Agra M.B.A. Dec., 2012; J.N.T.U. Hyderabad B.Tech. Sept., 2011; May, 2011; R.T.M. Nagpur U.B. Tech. (Mech.) June, 2007; P.T.U. MBA, 2002*]
2. Explain characteristics and classification of queuing models.
   [*P.T.U. MBA Dec., 2013; V.T.U. Karnataka B.E. June, 2012; Dec., 2011; June, 2010; Osmania U.MBA, 2010; R.T.M. Nagpur B.E. (Mech.) 2011; K.U.B.E. (Mech.) June, 2012; Chennai Univ. BBA Nov., 2010; Pondicherry U.M.B.A. August, 2006; Nagpur U. B.E., 2003 ; P.U. MBA August, 2006; B.E. (Mech.) 2002*]
3. Write a note on various assumptions made in single-channel queuing theory.
   [*P.T.U. MBA May, 2015; Dec., 2014; R.U. MBA Dec., 2011; R.T.M. Nagpur U. B.Tech. June, 2005; P.U. M.B.A., 2009; M.D.U. Rohtak B.E. (Mech.) Dec., 2006; P.U. B.E. (Mech.) 2002, 2000; P.T.U. M.Tech. Nov., 2012; B.Tech., 2000; ICWA, 1996*]
4. Discuss basic elements (or structure) of waiting line situations.
   [*Dayalbagh Edu. Inst. Agra MBA Dec., 2014; P.T.U. MBA Dec. 2013; R.U. MBA June, 2011; Dec., 2011; Gujarat Tech. U.B.E. Dec., 2012; U.P.U. MBA, 2010; P.T.U. MCA, 2010; M.D.U. Rohtak B.E. (Mech.) Dec., 2006; P.U.B.E. (T.I.T.) Nov., 2006*]
5. Explain the terms balking and queue discipline.
   [*P.T.U. B.Tech. (Mech.) May, 2011; MCA, 2010, MBA, 2009; P.U. B.E. (T.I.T.) Nov., 2006; BBA, 2001*]
6. Discuss the terms : traffic intensity, balking, reneging and jockeying.
   [*J.N.T.U. Hyderabad MBA Nov., 2012; V.T.U. Karnataka B.E. Dec., 2011; P.T.U. B.Tech. (Mech.) 2010; P.U. B.E. (T.I.T.) Nov., 2006; Dec., 2008*]
7. Explain the queue parameters. [*H.P.U. B.Tech. (Mech.) Sept., 2013; P.T.U. MBA, 2005; G.J. U. B.E. (Mech.) 1998*]
8. What is the use of single-server models? [*R.U. MBA June, 2011; Chennai Univ. B.B.A. Nov., 2010*]
9. Explain the following :
   (*i*) Arrival pattern (*ii*) Service discipline (*iii*) Service channel (*iv*) Service distribution.
   [*P.U. B.E. (Mech.) 2012*]
10. Give some applications of queuing theory.
    [*Dayalbagh Edu. Inst. J.N.T.U. Hyderabad MBA April, 2012; Agra MBA Dec., 2012; Univ. of Madras MBA Nov., 2012; P.T.U. MBA May, 2015; Nov., 2012; B.Tech. (Mech.) May, 2011; (C.Sc.) 2009; B.Tech. (Mech.) 2010, 2008; R.T.M. Nagpur U. B.Tech. Dec., 2006; M.D.U. Rohtak B.E. (Mech.) 2006*]
11. Explain the following with reference to queuing models :
    (*i*) M/M/2 (*ii*) Service discipline (*iii*) Kendal's notation.
    [*J.N.T.U. Hyderabad B.Tech. May, 2011; V.T.U. Karnataka B.E. Dec., 2010; P.T.U. M.Tech. Nov., 2012; B.Tech. (Mech.) May, 2006; P.U. B.E. (T.I.T.) Dec., 2008*]
12. Explain the queuing process.
    [*P.T.U. B.E. (Mech.) May, 2011; MBA Dec., 2014; Univ. of Madras MBA April, 2012*]
13. What is a queuing problem ? Explain queuing system, transient and steady state.
    [*P.T.U. B.Tech. (Mech.) 2011, 2009*]
14. "The assumptions in queuing theory are so restrictive as to render behaviour prediction of queuing system practically worthless." Discuss. [*P.T.U. MBA Dec., 2013*]
15. Give a general structure of the queuing system and explain it. Prove that if the number of arrivals follows Poisson process, then the inter-arrival times follow the exponential distribution.
    [*Pbi. U. MCA, 1997*]
16. Prove that if arrivals occur at random in time, then the number of arrivals occurring in a fixed time interval follows Poisson distribution. [*P.U. B.E. (Mech.) 1997*]
17. Discuss the arrival and service processes of waiting line models. Write the standard method of expressing the queuing problem. [*P.U. B.E. (Mech.) 2012; G.J.U. B.E. (Mech.) 1996*]

18. State some of the important distributions of arrival interval and service times used in queuing models.
[*P.T.U. B.Tech. (Mech.) Dec., 2006*]

19. If the probability of an arrival in time interval t and $t - \Delta t$ is $\lambda \, . \, \Delta t + 0 \, . \, (\Delta t)^2$, show that

$$p_n(t) = \frac{e^{-\lambda t} \, . (\lambda t)^n}{n\,!}, \; n = 0, 1, 2, ..., \infty.$$

[*Kuru. U. B.E. (Mech.) 1988*]

20. Give a relationship for expected number of customers in the queue for infinite population, single channel, Poisson arrivals and exponential service system. Also derive expressions for L_q, W_s and W_q for this system.
[*Karn. U. B.E. (Mech.) 1999, 95*]

21. Obtain the steady state equation for the model M/M/1 : FIFO and derive the formula for
    (*i*) average number of units in the queue.
    (*ii*) average waiting time of an arrival in the queue.
[*Nagpur U. B.E. 2003 ; P.U. B.E. (Prod.) 2001; P.T.U. MBA May, 2001*]

22. Prove that the probability of n customers in the system at any time in case of Poisson arrivals and exponential service times is given by

$$p_n = \left(\frac{\lambda}{\mu}\right)^n \cdot \left(1 - \frac{\lambda}{\mu}\right).$$

[*P.U.B.E. (Mech.) 1999, 95; B.E. (Elect.) 1996*]

23. What are the different classes of a queuing system ? Give examples for each one of them.
[*Univ. of Mumbai PGDM, 2012*]

Section 10.9-4

24. A repair shop attended by a single mechanic has an average of 4 customers per hour who bring small appliances for repair. The mechanic inspects them for defects and quite often can fix them right away or otherwise render a diagnosis. This takes him 6 minutes on the average. Arrivals are Poisson and service time has the exponential distribution. You are required to
    (*a*) find the proportion of time during which the shop is empty,
    (*b*) find the probability of finding at least one customer in the shop,
    (*c*) the average number of customers in the system,
    (*d*) the average time, including service, spent by a customer.
[*R.T.M. Nagpur B.E. (Mech.) Dec., 2008*]
(*Ans.* (*a*) 0.6 (*b*) $1 - p_0 = 0.4$ (*c*) 2/3 (*d*) 10 minutes.)

25. A duplicating machine maintained for office use is used and operated by people in the office who need to make copies, mostly secretaries. Since the work to be copied varies in length (number of pages of the original) and copies required, the service rate is randomly distributed but it does approximate a Poisson having a mean service rate of 10 jobs per hour. Generally, the requirements for use are random over the entire 8-hour working day but arrive at a rate of 5 per hour. Several people have noted that a waiting line develops occasionally and have questioned the policy of maintaining only one unit. If the time of a secretary is valued at ₹ 350 per hour, make an analysis to find
    (*a*) equipment utilisation,
    (*b*) the per cent time an arrival has to wait,
    (*c*) the average system time, and
    (*d*) the average cost of waiting and operating the machine.
(*Ans.* (*a*) 0.5 (*b*) 50% (*c*) 12 minutes
(*d*) cost/day $= (8 \times 5) \times \frac{1}{5} \times$ ₹ 350 = ₹ 2,800.)

26. In a bank, cheques are cashed at a single-teller counter. Customers arrive at the counter in a Poisson manner at an average rate of 30 customers per hour. The teller takes on an average $1\frac{1}{2}$ minute to cash a cheque. The service time is exponentially distributed.
(*a*) calculate the percentage of time the teller is busy.
(*b*) calculate the average time a customer is expected to wait. [*Chennai U.B.B.A. Nov., 2010*]
(*Ans.* (*a*) 75% (*b*) 6 minutes.)

27. Customers arrive at one-window drive according to a Poisson distribution with mean of 10 minutes. Service time per customer is exponential with mean of 6 minutes. The space in front of the window can accommodate only three vehicles including the serviced one. Other vehicles have to wait outside this space. Calculate the
(*a*) probability that an arriving customer can drive directly to the space in front of the window.
(*b*) probability that an arriving customer will have to wait outside the directed space.
[*P.T.U. B.Tech. Dec., 2011; U.P.U. MBA, 2009; P.U.B.Tech. (Mech.) 2009*]
(*Ans.* (*a*) 0.784 (*b*) 0.216.]

28. Data have been accumulated at a banking facility regarding the waiting time for delivery trucks to be loaded. The data show that the average arrival rate for the trucks at the loading dock is 2/hour. The average time to load a truck, using 2 loaders is 10 minutes so that the service rate is 3 trucks per hour. The management is considering hiring another loader at ₹ 5 per hour to reduce the loading time. Drivers are paid ₹ 4 per hour and truck utilisation is valued at ₹ 3 per hour. Should the additional loader be hired if an increase in the service rate to 4 trucks per hour would result ?
[*P.T.U.B. Tech. (Mech.) Dec., 2011*]
(*Ans.* ₹ 2/hour saving with new loader.)

[**Hint.** *Without additional loader*

$$L_s = \frac{\lambda}{\mu - \lambda} = \frac{2}{3-2} = 2.$$

$\therefore$ Cost/hr = ₹ 2 (3 + 4) = ₹ 14.

With additional loader

$$L_s = \frac{2}{4-2} = 1.$$

$\therefore$ Cost/hr = ₹ [1 (3 + 4) + 5] = ₹ 12.]

29. The tool room company's quality control department is manned by a single clerk who takes an average of 5 minutes in checking parts of each of the machine coming for inspection. The machines arrive once in every 8 minutes on the average. One hour of the machine is valued at ₹ 15 and the clerk's time is valued at ₹ 4 per hour. What are the average hourly queuing system costs associated with the quality control department ?
[*H.P.U. B.Tech. (Mech.) Nov., 2014; P.T.U. B.Tech. (Prod.) Nov., 2012; (Mech.) May, 2011*]

[**Hint.** $\lambda = \frac{60}{8} = 7.5\text{/hr}, \mu = \frac{60}{5} = 12\text{/hr}.$

$$W_s = \frac{1}{\mu - \lambda} = \frac{1}{12 - 7.5} = \frac{2}{9} \text{ hr.}$$

Average queuing cost/machine = ₹ $(15 \times \frac{2}{9})$ = ₹ $\frac{10}{3}$.

$\therefore$ Average queuing cost/hr = ₹ $(\frac{10}{3} \times 7.5)$ = ₹ 25.

Average cost of the clerk/hr = ₹ 4.

$\therefore$ Total cost for the deptt./hr = ₹ 29.]

30. Cars arrive at a toll gate according to Poisson distribution with mean 90/hr. Average time for passing through the gate is 38 seconds. Drivers complain of long waiting time. Authorities are willing to decrease the passing time through the gate to 30 seconds by introducing new automatic devices. This

can be justified only if under the old system, the number of waiting cars exceeds 5. In addition, the percentage of the gate's idle time under the new system should not exceed 10%. Can the new device be justified ?

[*P.T.U. B.Tech. (Prod.) Nov., 2012; May, 2011*]

[Hint. $\lambda = 90/\text{hr} = 1.5/\text{min.}, \mu = \frac{60}{38} = \frac{30}{19}/\text{min.}$

$$\therefore \quad L_q = \frac{\lambda}{\mu}.\frac{\lambda}{\mu-\lambda} = \frac{1.5 \times 19}{30} \cdot \frac{1.5}{\frac{30}{19} - 1.5} = 18.5 \ (> 5).$$

$$p_0 = 1 - \frac{\lambda}{\mu'} = 1 - \frac{1.5}{\frac{60}{30}} = 0.25 \ (> 0.10).$$

Since condition for Lq is satisfied but not for p_0, the new device is not justified.]

31. XYZ wholesale fruit and vegetable distributors employ one worker whose job is to load fruit and vegetables on outgoing company trucks. An average of 24 trucks per day or 3 per hour arrive at the loading gate according to a Poisson distribution. The worker loads them at a rate of 4 per hour following approximately exponential distribution in his service times.
   (*i*) Determine the operating characteristics of this loading gate problem. What is the probability that there will be more than 3 trucks either being loaded or waiting ?
   (*ii*) The distributors believe that adding a second fruit and vegetable loader will substantially improve the firm's efficiency. They estimate that a 2-person crew at the loading gate will double the loading rate. Analyse the effect on the queue of such a change and compare the results to those obtained in part (*i*).
   (*iii*) Truck drivers working for XYZ distributors earn ₹ 20 per hour on the average. Fruit loaders receive about ₹ 3 per hour. Truck drivers waiting in the queue or at the loading gate are drawing a salary but are productively idle and unable to generate revenue during that time. What would be the hourly cost savings to the firm associated with employing two loaders instead of one ?

(*Ans.* (*i*) $L_s = 3, L_q = 2.25, W_s = 1$ hr, $W_q = 3/4$ hr, $\rho = 0.75$, $p\,(> 3) = \rho^4 = (0.75)^4 = 0.316$.
(*ii*) $L_s = 0.6, L_q = 0.225, W_s = 0.2$ hr, $W_q = 0.075$ hr, $\rho = 0.375$, $p\,(> 3) = (0.375)^4 = 0.0198$.
(*iii*) (*a*) ₹ (3 × 20 + 3) = ₹ 63. (*b*) ₹ (0.6 × 20 + 6) = ₹ 18.
∴ Savings = ₹ 45.)

32. Arrivals at a telephone booth are considered to be Poisson with an average time of 10 minutes between one arrival and the next. The length of a phone call is assumed to be distributed exponentially with mean 3 minutes.
   (*a*) What is the probability that an arrival will have to wait more than 10 minutes before the phone is free ?
   (*b*) What is the probability that it will take him more than 10 minutes altogether to wait for phone and complete his call ?
   (*c*) Estimate the fraction of a day that the phone will be in use.
   (*d*) Find the average number of units in the system.
   (*e*) Find the probability that there will be 6 or more units waiting for the call.

[*V.T.U. Karnataka B.E. June, 2012; Dec., 2011; R.U. MBA June, 2011; R.T.M Nagpur U. B.E. (Mech.) Sept., 2010; Dec., 2006 2003, J.N.T.U. Hyderabad B.Tech. April, 2011; P.T.U. B.Tech. (Mech.) May, 2006*]

(*Ans.* (*a*) 0 03 (*b*) 0.1 (*c*) 0.3 (*d*) 0.43 (*e*) $(0.3)^6 = 0.00073$.)

[Hint. (*a*) p (waiting time ≥ 10) $= \int_{10}^{\infty} \frac{\lambda}{\mu} \cdot (\mu - \lambda) \cdot e^{-(\mu - \lambda)t} \cdot dt$

$$= -\frac{\lambda}{\mu}.[e^{-(\mu-\lambda)t}]_{10}^{\infty} = 0.3\ e^{-2.3} = 0.3 \times 0.1 = 0.03.$$

(*b*) p (waiting time in the system ≥ 10) $= \int_{10}^{\infty} (\mu - \lambda) \cdot e^{-(\mu - \lambda)t} \cdot dt = e^{-10(\mu - \lambda)} = e^{-2.3} = 0.1.$]

33. In a railway marshalling yard, goods trains arrive at a rate of 30 trains per day. Assuming that the inter-arrival time follows an exponential distribution and the service time distribution is also exponential with an average 36 minutes, calculate the following :

(*i*) Average number of trains in the system.

(*ii*) The probability that the queue size exceeds 10. (*iii*) If the input of trains increases to an average 33 per day, what will be the change in (i) and (*ii*) ?

[P.T.U. MBA May, 2014; B.Tech. (Mech.) Nov., 2012; 2010; P.U. B.E. (Mech.) 2012; V.T.U. Karnataka B.E. Dec., 2011; J.N.T.U. Hyderabad B.Tech. May, 2011; Nov., 2010; P.T.U. B.Tech. (C.Sc.) 2010; IGNOU MBA Dec., 2006; Dayalbagh Edu. Inst. Agra MBA May, 2005; R.C.C. CHD., 2002 ; P.T.U. B.Tech., 2001]

(*Ans.* (*i*) 3 (*ii*) $(0.75)^{10} = 0.056$ (*iii*) 4.8, $(0.83)^{10} = 0.155$.)

34. A repairman is to be hired to repair machines which break down at an average rate of 3/hour. The breakdowns follow Poisson distribution. Non-productive time of a machine is considered to cost ₹ 10 per hour. Two repairmen have been interviewed—one is slow but cheap, while the other is fast but expensive. The slow repairman charges ₹ 5 per hour and he services brokendown machines at the rate of 4 per hour. The fast repairman demands ₹ 7 per hour and he services at an average rate of 6 per hour. Which repairman should be hired ?

[P.T.U.B. Tech. April, 2012; Osmania U. MBA July, 2010]

(*Ans.* Fast repairman since it results in savings of ₹ (280 – 136) = ₹ 144 per day.)

35. Auto vehicles arrive at a petrol pump, having one petrol unit, in Poisson fashion with an average of 10 units per hour. The service time is distributed exponentially with a mean of 3 minutes. Find the following :

(*a*) Average number of units in the system.

(*b*) Average waiting time for customers.

(*c*) Average length of queue.

(*d*) Probability that a customer arriving at the pump will have to wait.

(*e*) The utilisation factor for the petrol pump.

(*f*) Probability that the number of customers in the system is 2.

[P.T.U. M.Tech. Dec., 2011; P.U. B.E., 2001]

(*Ans.* (*a*) 1 (*b*) 3 min (*c*) 0.5 (*d*) 0.5 (*e*) 0.5 (*f*) 0.125.)

36. A xerox machine in an office is operated by a person who does other jobs also. The average service time for a job is 6 minutes per customer. On an average, every 12 minutes, one customer arrives for xeroxing. Find

(*i*) the xerox machine utilisation,

(*ii*) percentage of time that an arrival has not to wait,

(*iii*) average time spent by a customer,

(*iv*) average queue length,

(*v*) the arrival rate if the management is willing to deploy the person exclusively for xeroxing when the average time spent by a customer exceeds 15 minutes.

[P.T.U. B.Tech. April, 2012; May, 2011; P.U. B.E. (Mech.) 2000]

(*Ans.* (*i*) 0.5 (*ii*) 50% (*iii*) 12 min (*iv*) 0.5 (*v*) 6/hr.)

37. Arrivals of machinists at a tool crib are considered to be Poisson distributed at an average rate of 6 per hour. The length of time a machinist must remain at the tool crib is exponentially distributed with the average time being 0.05 hour.

(*i*) What is the probability that a machinist arriving at the tool crib will have to wait ?

(*ii*) What is the average number of machinists at the tool crib ?

(*iii*) The company will install a second tool crib when convinced that a machinist would expect to have to spend at least 6 minutes waiting and being serviced at the tool crib. By how much should the flow of machinists to the tool crib increase to justify the addition of a second tool crib ?

[Dayalbagh Edu. Inst. M.Tech., 1998]

(*Ans.* (*i*) 0.3 (*ii*) $\frac{3}{7}$ (*iii*) 4/hour.)

38. Arrival rate of cars to a certain service station is according to Poisson distribution with an average time of 50 minutes between the two consecutive arrivals. The length of service needed by a car is assumed to be exponentially distributed with mean of 25 minutes.
(*a*) Determine the probability that a car arriving at the station will have to wait.
(*b*) Determine the probability that a car arriving at the station will have to wait for more than 10 minutes for the service.
(*c*) Determine the probability that a car arriving at the station will have to wait for more than 20 minutes for the service.
(*d*) Find the flow rate of the cars if the average waiting time of the cars is 35 minutes.
(*e*) What is the utilisation fraction of the service station ?
[*P.T.U. B.Tech. (Mech.) Nov., 2012*]
(*Ans.* (*a*) 0.5 (*b*) $\frac{0.5}{e^{0.2}} = 0.41$ (*c*) $\frac{0.5}{e^{0.42}} = 0.33$ (*d*) 1.4/hour (*e*) 0.5.)

39. Given average arrival rate = 8/hour, average service time = 5 minutes, calculate
(*i*) average queue length
(*ii*) average waiting time
(*iii*) idle time in 8-hour shift
(*iv*) utilisation rate of server.
[*G.J.U. B.E. (Mech.) 1998*]
(*Ans.* (*i*) $\frac{4}{3}$ (*ii*) 10 min (*iii*) $\frac{8}{3}$ hour (*iv*) $\frac{2}{3}$.)

40. A postal clerk can service a customer in 3 minutes, the service time being exponentially distributed. The inter-arrival time of customers is also exponentially distributed with an average of 12 minutes during the early morning slack period and an average of 5 minutes during the afternoon peak period. Assess the average queue length and the expected waiting time in the queue during the two periods.
[*Karn. U. B.E. (Mech.) 1997*]
(*Ans.* (*i*) $\frac{1}{12}$, 1 min (*ii*) 0.9, 4.5 min.)

41. A hospital is studying the proposal to reorganize its emergency service facility. The present arrival rate is one call every 15 minutes and the service rate is one call every 10 minutes. Current cost of service is ₹ 100/hour. Each delay in service costs ₹ 125. If the proposal is accepted, the service rate will become one call every six minutes. Can the reorganization be justified on a strictly cost basis only if the proposal increases the cost of service by 50% ? [*J.N.T.U. Hyderabad MBA April, 2012*]

42. A tractor operator has only one tractor and he operates it on the job order from farmers. The requisitions for the jobs arrive with Poisson distribution having interval time of 0.7 day. The average time to do a job is distributed exponentially with mean 0.5 day. Assuming that the tractor can take up the next job immediately on completion of the previsous job, determine the following :
(*i*) Will a queue be formed ?
(*ii*) If queue is formed will it statistically stabilize ?
(*iii*) What is the utilization factor of the tractor ?
(*iv*) What is the idle time in daily duty of 7 hours ?
(*v*) What is the mean number of job orders waiting ?
(*vi*) What is the mean waiting time for job orders in the system ?
(*vii*) What is the mean waiting time in the queue ?
[*P.U. B.E. (Mech.) 1997*]
(*Ans.* (*i*) yes (*ii*) yes (*iii*) $\frac{5}{7}$ (*iv*) 2 hours (*v*) 2.5 (*vi*) $\frac{7}{4}$ days (*vii*) $\frac{5}{4}$ days.)

43. A company's quality control department is manned by a single inspector who takes an average of 5 minutes in checking parts of each machine coming for inspection. The machines arrive once in every 8 minutes on the average. One hour of machine is value at ₹ 15 and the inspector's time is valued at ₹ 4 per hour. What are the hourly average queuing system costs associated with the quality control department ? [*J.N.T.U. Hyderabad B.Tech. Sept., 2011*]
(*Ans.* ₹ 29.)

44. Products are expected to arrive at a machining station at the average rate of 3 per hour. One of the following alternatives is to be selected for machining of the products :
    1. A single machine of type A.
    2. Two machines of type B.

    Machine A, on the average, can machine a product in 15 minutes. The average machining time on machine B is 30 minutes per product. Which of the above alternatives will reduce the average time a product waits before it is taken up for machining ? Assume Poisson pattern of arrivals and exponentially distributed service times.

    [*P.U. M.E. (Mech.) 1996*]

45. A bank plans to open a single-server drive in a banking facility at a particular centre. It is estimated that 28 customers will arrive each hour on an average. If on an average, it requires 2 minutes to process a customer transaction, determine
    (*i*) the proportion of time the system will be idle.
    (*ii*) on the average how long the customer will have to wait before reaching the server ?
    (*iii*) the length of the drive-way required to accommodate all the arrivals on the average if 20 feet driveway is required for each car that is waiting for service.

    [*P.U. M. Com. April, 2004*]

    (*Ans.* (*i*) $\frac{1}{15}$ (*ii*) 28 minutes (*iii*) 261.3 feet.)

46. At a one-man barber shop customers arrive according to Poisson distribution with a mean arrival rate of 5/hour. The hair-cutting time is exponentially distributed, with an average haircuit taking 10 minutes. Calculate the following:
    (*i*) Average number of customers in the shop and the average number of customers waiting for the haircut.
    (*ii*) The per cent of time an arrival can walk right in without having to wait.
    (*iii*) The percentage of customers who have to wait prior to getting into the barber's chair.

    [*Dayalbagh Edu. Inst. Agra MBA Dec., 2014; 2013; U.P.U. MBA, 2009*]

    (*Ans.* (*i*) 5, 25/6 (*ii*) 16.7% (*iii*) 83.3%.)

47. Assume that the goods trains are coming in a yard at the rate of 30 trains per day, inter-arrival time following an exponential distribution. The service time for each train is assumed to be exponential with an average of 36 minutes. If the yard can admit 9 trains at a time (there being 10 lines, one of which is reserved for shunting purposes), calculate the probability that the yard is empty. Also find the average queue length. [*Dayalbagh Edu. Inst. Agra MBA Dec., 2012*]

    (*Ans.* 0.25, 3 trains.)

48. (*a*) What is service discipline? State various disciplines with examples.
    (*b*) Patrons arrive at a reception counter at an average inter-arrival time of 2 minutes. The receptionist on duty takes an average of one minute per person. (Arrivals are as per poisson and services are as per exponential distribution).
    (*i*) What is the chance that a patron will straight away meet the receptionist?
    (*ii*) For what portion of time the receptionist is busy?
    (*iii*) What is the average queue length?
    (*iv*) What is the average number of patrons in the system?
    (*v*) What is the average waiting time of a patron?
    (*vi*) What average time a patron spends in the system?
    (*vii*) Suppose management wants to keep a second receptionist when the average waiting time of an arrival exceeds 1.5 minutes. Find what should be the inter-arrival time to justify a second receptionist ?

    [*V.T.U. Karnataka B.E. Jan., 2010*]

49. People arrive to purchase the cinema tickets at the First Class Ticket Counter of a theatre at the rate of 150 per hour. There is one clerk issuing the tickets at the rate of 400 per hour. Find:
    (*a*) The probability that there is no single person at the counter to purchase the ticket.
    (*b*) The probability that a person is being served and nobody is waiting.

(*c*) The probability that there is no person waiting to be served.

(*d*) The probability that there are more that 25 people at the counter.

[*J.N.T.U. Hyderabad B.Tech. June, 2009*]

50. In Hitech Software System Company, the function of computer systems fails on an average rate of 5 per hour. The idle time cost of a computer system is estimated to be ₹ 200 per hour. The company works 10 hours a day (including one-hour lunch break). The systems manager is considering two service engineers for rectifying the breakdown systems. The first service engineer takes about 50 minutes on an average to repair a system and charges ₹ 100 per hour for the service. The second service engineer takes about 40 minutes in repairing the system and charges ₹ 150 per hour for the service. Assuming the rate of computer system failures is as per Poisson distribution and the repair rate is exponentially distributed, which of the two service engineers should be engaged?

[*J.N.T.U. Hyderabad B.Tech. June, 2009*]

51. In a telephone exchange the arrival of calls follows Poisson distribution, with an average time of 8 minutes between two consecutive calls. The length of a call is exponentially distributed with mean 4 minutes. Determine

(*a*) the probability that a call arriving at the booth will have to wait.

(*b*) the average queue length that forms from time to time.

(*c*) the probability that an arrival will have to wait for more than 10 minutes before the phone is free.

(*d*) the hours of a day that the exchange will be in use.

[*J.N.T.U. Hyderabad B.Tech. June, 2009*]

52. (*a*) For a departmental store,

Mean arrival rate = 20 customers/hr.

Mean service rate = 24 customers/hr.

Calculate values for : ρ, L_s, W_s, L_q, W_q.

(*b*) State all models of queuing system with sketches.

[*R.T.M. Nagpur U. B.Tech. Dec., 2004*]

53. (*a*) Explain the need for studying queues.

(*b*) At the balcony ticket counter of a cinema hall, customers arrive at the rate of 12 per hour according to Poisson distribution. The single clerk at the counter serves the customers at the rate of 30 per hour.

(*i*) What is the probability that there is no customer at the counter ?

(*ii*) What is the probability that there are more than 2 customers at the counter?

Find :

(*i*) Average number of customers in the system (counter) and in the queue.

(*ii*) Average time a customer spends in the system and in the queue.

[*V.T.U. Karnataka B.E. June, 2011*]

54. In a machine shop, the inter-arrival times at the tool crib are exponential, with an average time of 10 minutes. The length of the service time is assumed to be exponential with a mean of 6 minutes. Find:

(i) The probability that a person arriving at the booth will have to wait.

(ii) Average length of the queue.

(iii) The probability that an arrival will have to wait for more than 12 minutes for service and to obtain his tools. [*V.T.U. Karnataka B.E. Dec., 2010*]

55. (*a*) Explain waiting line models with example based on structure.

(*b*) People arrive at a hotel in Poisson distributed arrival rate of 8 per hour. Service time distribution is closely approximated by negative exponential. The average service time is 5 min. Calculate :

(*i*) Utilization factor.

(ii) Probability that service provider is idle.

(*iii*) Average no. of customers in waiting line.

(*iv*) Average no. of customers in system.

(*v*) Average waiting time in queue.

(*vi*) Average waiting time in system.

[*R.T.M. Nagpur U.B.E. (I.T.) 2009*]

56. A T.V. repairman finds that the time spent on his jobs has an exponential distribution with mean 30 minutes. If he repairs sets in the order in which they come in, and if the arrival of sets is approximately as per Poisson distribution with an average rate of 10 per 8 hour day, what is repairman's expected idle time each day? How many jobs are ahead of the average set just brought in ?

[*B.P.U.T., 2012; J.N.T.U. Hyderabad B.Tech. April, 2011; Nov., 2010*]

57. In the above exercise no. 56, also determine :
(*i*) Probability that the length of queue is more than 5.
(*ii*) Probability that it will take more than two hours altogether to get the set repaired.
(*iii*) Time spent before the average set is taken for repairs.
(*iv*) Probability that there are 3 sets in his shop.

[*R.T.M. Nagpur U. B.Tech. June, 2005*]

58. In a factory the machines break down on an average rate of 10 machines/hour. The downtime cost of the machines is estimated to be ₹ 20/hour. The factory works 8 hours a day. The factory manager is considering two mechanics for repairing of machines. Mechanic A takes, on an average, 5 minutes in repairing a machine and demands wages @ ₹ 10/hour. Mechanic B takes 4 minutes only but demands wages @ ₹ 15/hour. Assuming that the machine breakdown rate is Poisson distributed and repair times follow exponential distribution, which of the two mechanics should be engaged ?

(*Ans.* Mechanic B; Cost ₹ 440/day.)

59. XYZ firm has, on the average, 45 pieces of an equipment requiring repairs per week. The probability of an equipment failure is approximately constant so that the arrivals are distributed according to the Poisson law. The repair time is exponentially distributed. The downtime cost of the equipment is estimated at ₹ 600 per day. There are 5 working days/week and the firm works 50 weeks per annum. The firm has two repiar facilities to choose from. The details are

		Facility F_1	F_2
Installation charges	:	₹ 7,20,000	₹ 12,00,000
Operating expenses p.a.	:	₹ 2,40,000	₹ 3,00,000
Economic life	:	6 years	6 years
Scrap value	:	Nil	Nil
Service rate	:	60/week	120/week

Assuming that there is no time value of money, which facility would you suggest the firm to choose?

(*Ans.* F_2.)

[**Hint.** Total annual cost for facility F_1

$$= \frac{7,20,000}{6} + 2,40,000 + (W_s \times \lambda) \times 50 \times (5 \times 600)$$

$$= 1,20,000 + 2,40,000 + \left(\frac{1}{60-45} \times 45\right) \times 50 \times 3,000 = ₹\ 8,10,000.$$

Total annual cost for facility F_2

$$= \frac{12,00,000}{6} + 3,00,000 + \left(\frac{1}{120-45} \times 45\right) \times 50 \times (5 \times 600)$$

$$= 2,00,000 + 3,00,000 + 90,000 = ₹\ 5,90,000.]$$

60. Telephone users arrive at a booth following a Poisson distribution with an average time of 5 minutes between one arrival and the next. The time taken for a telephone call is, on an average, 3 minutes and it follows an exponential distribution. What is the probability that the telephone booth is busy ? How many more booths should be established to reduce the system waiting time to less than or equal to half the present waiting time ?

[*H.P.U. B.Tech. (Mech.) June, 2015; P.T.U. M.Tech. Nov., 2012; K.U.B.E. (Mech.) June, 2012*]

[**Hint.** $p_{busy} = \frac{\lambda}{\mu} = \frac{12}{20} = 0.6$; $W_s = \frac{1}{\mu-\lambda} = \frac{1}{20-12} = \frac{1}{8}$ hour.

$$\therefore \quad \frac{1}{16} = \frac{1}{\mu'-\lambda} = \frac{1}{\mu'-12}.$$

$\therefore \qquad \mu' = 28\text{/hour. No. of booths} = \dfrac{28}{20} = 1.4 \simeq 2.]$

61. A road transport company has one reservation clerk on duty at a time. She handles information of bus schedules and makes reservations. Customers arrive at the rate of 8 per hour and the clerk can handle 12 customers on an average per hour. Answer the following:
   (*i*) What is the average number of customers waiting for the service of the clerk ?
   (*ii*) What is the average time a customer has to wait before getting service ?
   (*iii*) The management is contemplating to install a computer system to handle the information and reservations. This is expected to reduce the service time from 5 to 3 minutes. The additional cost of having the new system is ₹ 50. The waiting time cost works out to be 12 paise per minute spent waiting before being serviced. Should the company install the computer system ? Assume 8-hour working day.

[*Chennai U. MBA, 1997*]

(*Ans.* Yes; saving = ₹ 11.44.)

[**Hint.** (*iii*) $W_q = \dfrac{\lambda}{\mu(\mu - \lambda)} = \dfrac{8}{12.(12-8)} = \dfrac{1}{6}$ hour.

$\therefore$ Cost/day for the present system $= \left(\dfrac{1}{6} \times \lambda\right) \times 8 \times \dfrac{12}{100} = \left(\dfrac{1}{6} \times 8\right) \times 8 \times \dfrac{12 \times 60}{100} = ₹\ 76.80.$

With computer system, $\mu = \dfrac{60}{3} = 20\text{/hour.} \quad \therefore W_q = \dfrac{8}{20(20-8)} = \dfrac{1}{30}$ hour.

$\therefore$ Cost/day $= \left(\dfrac{1}{30} \times \lambda\right) \times 8 \times \dfrac{12}{100} + 50 = \left(\dfrac{1}{30} \times 8\right) \times 8 \times \dfrac{12 \times 60}{100} + 50 = ₹\ 65.36.$

$\therefore$ Net saving with computer system = ₹ 11.44.]

62. A firm has several machines and wants to instal its own service facility for the repair of its machines. The average breakdown rate of the machines is 3/day. The repair time has exponential distribution. The loss incurred due to the lost time of an inoperative machine is ₹ 40/day. There are two repair facilities available. Facility X has an installation cost of ₹ 20,000 and facility Y costs ₹ 40,000. The total labour cost per year for the two facilities is ₹ 5,000 and ₹ 8,000 respectively. Facility X can repair 4 machines daily while facility Y can repair 5 machines daily. The life span of both the machines is 4 years. Which facility should be installed ?

[*P.T.U. M.Tech. Nov., 2012*]

(*Ans.* Y.)

[**Hint.** Total annual cost for facility X

$$= \frac{20,000}{4} + 5,000 + L_s \times 40 \times 365$$

$$= 5,000 + 5,000 + \frac{\lambda}{\mu - \lambda} \times 40 \times 365 = 10,000 + \frac{3}{4-3} \times 40 \times 365$$

$$= ₹\ 53,800.$$

Total annual cost for facility Y

$$= \frac{40,000}{4} + 8,000 + \frac{3}{5-3} \times 40 \times 365 = ₹\ 39,900.]$$

63. In a tool crib manned by a single assistant, the operators arrive at the rate of 10 per hour. Each operator needs 3 minutes on an average to be served. Find out the loss of production due to waiting of an operator in a shift of 8 hours if the rate of production is 100 units per shift.

[*Pondicherry MBA August, 2006*]

64. A warehouse has only one loading dock manned by a 3-man crew. Trucks arrive at the loading dock at an average rate of 4 trucks per hour and the arrival rate is Poisson distributed. The loading of a truck takes 10 minutes on an average and can be assumed to be exponentially distributed. The operating cost

of a truck is ₹ 20 per hour and the members of the loading crew are paid at the rate of ₹ 6 each per hour. Would you advise the truck owner to add another crew of three persons ?

[*Univ. of Madras MBA April, 2012; R.U. MBA Dec., 2011*]

(*Ans.* Yes. Saving = ₹ 12/hour.)

[**Hint.** Here, $\lambda = 4$/ hour, $\mu = 6$/ hour.

For existing crew

Total cost / hour = Cost of loading crew + waiting time cost

= number of loaders × wage rate per hour + expected waiting time in the system × expected arrival.rate × waiting cost / hour.

$$= ₹ \left(6 \times 3 + \frac{1}{6-4} \times 4 \times 20\right) = ₹\ 58\text{/hour.}$$

For proposed crew

$$\text{Total cost/hour} = 6 \times 6 + \frac{1}{12-4} \times 4 \times 20 = ₹\ 46\text{/hour.}$$

∴ The truck owner should add another crew of three persons.]

10.9-5 Model II. Generalisation of Model (M/M/1): (FCFS/∞/∞) (Birth-Death Process)

In the queuing model discussed in Section 10.9-2, λ and μ were assumed to remain fixed during the queuing phenomenon. However, in actual practice, their values may not remain fixed. When λ is not fixed and depends upon the queue length, it will mean that some arrival interested in joining the queue may not join due to long queue. Likewise, if μ also depends on queue length, the service rate may be affected.

Hence in the general case, the differential equations (10.7) and (10.8) will take the form

$$\frac{d}{dt}\,[p_n(t)] = \lambda_{n-1}\, p_{n-1}(t) + \mu_{n+1}\, p_{n+1}(t) - (\lambda_n + \mu_n)\, p_n(t) \text{ for } n > 0,$$

and $$\frac{d}{dt}\,[p_0(t)] = \mu_1 p_1(t) - \lambda_0 p_0(t) \text{ for } n = 0.$$

∴ For steady state system,

$$0 = \lambda_{n-1} p_{n-1} + \mu_{n+1} p_{n+1} - (\lambda_n + \mu_n) p_n \text{ for } n > 0, \quad ...(10.24)$$

and $$0 = \mu_1 p_1 - \lambda_0 p_0 \text{ for } n = 0.$$

∴ $$p_1 = \frac{\lambda_0}{\mu_1} \cdot p_0. \quad ...(10.25)$$

For $n = 1$, equation (10.24) yields

$$0 = \lambda_0 p_0 + \mu_2 p_2 - (\lambda_1 + \mu_1) p_1$$

$$= \mu_1 p_1 + \mu_2 p_2 - (\lambda_1 + \mu_1) p_1 = \mu_2 p_2 - \lambda_1 p_1. \text{ [from = } n \text{ (10.25)]}$$

∴ $$p_2 = \frac{\lambda_1}{\mu_2} \cdot p_1 = \frac{\lambda_0}{\mu_1} \cdot \frac{\lambda_1}{\mu_2} \cdot p_0.$$

For $n = 2$, equation (10.24) yields

$$0 = \lambda_1 p_1 + \mu_3 p_3 - (\lambda_2 + \mu_2) p_2$$

$$= \mu_2 p_2 + \mu_3 p_3 - (\lambda_2 + \mu_2) p_2 = \mu_3 p_3 - \lambda_2 p_2.$$

∴ $$p_3 = \frac{\lambda_2}{\mu_3} \cdot p_2 = \frac{\lambda_0}{\mu_1} \cdot \frac{\lambda_1}{\mu_2} \cdot \frac{\lambda_2}{\mu_3} \cdot p_0.$$

In general, $$p_n = \frac{\lambda_0}{\mu_1} \cdot \frac{\lambda_1}{\mu_2} \cdots \frac{\lambda_{n-2}}{\mu_{n-1}} \cdot \frac{\lambda_{n-1}}{\mu_n} \cdot p_0. \quad ...(10.26)$$

Thus if p_0 is known, all p_i's can be evaluated. We know that

$$\sum_{n=0}^{\infty} p_n = 1$$

or $$p_0 + p_1 + p_2 + \ldots = 1$$

or $$p_0 \left[1 + \frac{\lambda_0}{\mu_1} + \frac{\lambda_0}{\mu_1} \cdot \frac{\lambda_1}{\mu_2} + \ldots\right] = 1$$

or $$p_0 S = 1, \quad \text{where } S = 1 + \frac{\lambda_0}{\mu_1} + \frac{\lambda_0}{\mu_1} \cdot \frac{\lambda}{\mu_2} + \ldots$$

$$\therefore \quad p_0 = \frac{1}{S}.$$

If S is a divergent series, then $p_0 = 0$ which is meaningless. However if S is convergent, p_0 will not vanish and shall have some value. A few different cases arise:

Case 1: If $\lambda_n = \lambda$ and $\mu_n = \mu$ *i.e.,* λ and μ are fixed and are independent of n, then series S is convergent if $\lambda/\mu < 1$.

Case 2 : $$\lambda_n = \frac{\lambda}{n+1} \text{ and } \mu_n = \mu \text{ (fixed)}.$$

In this case λ_n decreases as n increases *i.e.*, the arrival rate decreases with increase in queue length. In this case S becomes

$$S = 1 + \frac{\lambda}{\mu} + \frac{\lambda}{\mu} \cdot \frac{\lambda}{2\mu} + \frac{\lambda}{\mu} \cdot \frac{\lambda}{2\mu} \cdot \frac{\lambda}{3\mu} + \ldots$$

$$= 1 + \frac{\lambda}{\mu} + \frac{1}{1 \times 2} \cdot \left(\frac{\lambda}{\mu}\right)^2 + \frac{1}{1 \times 2 \times 3} \cdot \left(\frac{\lambda}{\mu}\right)^3 + \ldots$$

$$= 1 + \rho + \frac{\rho^2}{2!} + \frac{\rho^3}{3!} - \ldots = e^{\rho}.$$

$$\therefore \quad p_0 = \frac{1}{e^{\rho}} = e^{-\rho}. \qquad \ldots(10.27)$$

$$\therefore \quad p_1 = \frac{\lambda}{\mu} p_0 = \rho e^{-\rho},$$

$$p_2 = \frac{\rho^2}{2!} e^{-\rho},$$

$$\vdots$$

$$p_n = \frac{\rho^n}{n!} e^{-\rho}. \qquad \ldots(10.28)$$

p_i's in equation (10.28) are the values of a Poisson distribution with parameter ρ.

Case 3 : $\lambda_n = \lambda$ (fixed) and $\mu_n = n\mu$ *i.e.,* the service rate increases with increase in queue length. *This, in fact, is the problem of queue with infinite number of service channels.* The word 'infinite' means that service channels are available to each arrival. It does not, however, mean that all the infinite number of service channels will remain busy every time. It only means that if n customers arrive, then n service channels will be available for all $n = 0, 1, 2, \ldots, \infty$. Obviously, no queue will form since each arrival will immediately have the service facility. *Such a situation exists when the customers are using self-service.* Another such situation is that telephone (service stations) are always available to all the arriving persons. For this S becomes

$$S = 1 + \frac{\lambda}{\mu} + \frac{\lambda}{\mu}.\frac{\lambda}{2\mu} + \frac{\lambda}{\mu}.\frac{\lambda}{2\mu}.\frac{\lambda}{3\mu} + ...$$

$$= 1 + \frac{\lambda}{\mu} + \frac{1}{2!}\left(\frac{\lambda}{\mu}\right)^2 + \frac{1}{3!}\left(\frac{\lambda}{\mu}\right)^3 + ...$$

$$= 1 + \rho + \frac{\rho^2}{2!} + \frac{\rho^3}{3!} + ... = e^{\rho}.$$

$$\therefore \quad p_0 = \frac{1}{e^{\rho}} = e^{-\rho}.$$

$\therefore$ p_n (as in case 2) $= \dfrac{\rho^n}{n!} \,.\, e^{-\rho}$, which is a Poisson distribution.

EXAMPLE 10.9-5.1

A shipping company has a single unloading dock with ships arriving in a Poisson fashion at an average rate of 3/day. The unloading time distribution for a ship with n unloading crews is found to be exponential with average unloading time $^1/_{2n}$ days. The company has a large labour supply without regular working hours, and to avoid long waiting times, the company has a policy of using as many unloading crews as there are ships waiting in line or being unloaded. Find :

(a) the average number of unloading crews working at any time, and

(b) the probability that more than 4 crews will be needed.

[*DOEACC, 1996*]

Solution

Here, $\lambda = 3$ ships/day,

$\mu_n = n\mu$,

average unloading time with n crews $= \dfrac{1}{2n}$ days.

$\therefore$ Average unloading time with one crew $= \dfrac{1}{2}$ day.

$\therefore$ Mean unloading rate with one crew, $\mu = 2$ ships/day.

(*a*) Expected (average) number of unloading crews

$$= L_s = \sum_{n=0}^{\infty} np_n = \sum_{n=0}^{\infty} n\,.\frac{\rho^n}{n!}e^{-\rho} = e^{-\rho}\sum_{n=0}^{\infty}\frac{n}{n!}.\rho^n$$

$$= e^{-\rho}\left[0 + \rho + \frac{2}{2!}\rho^2 + \frac{3}{3!}\rho^3 + ...\infty\right]$$

$$= e^{-\rho}\left[\rho + \rho^2 + \frac{1}{2!}\rho^3 + ...\infty\right]$$

$$= e^{-\rho}.\,\rho[1 + \rho + \frac{\rho^2}{2!} + ...\infty] = e^{-\rho}.\,\rho\,.\,e^{\rho} = \rho$$

$$= \frac{\lambda}{\mu} = \frac{3}{2} = 1.5.$$

(*b*) Probability that more than 4 crews will be needed

= probability that there are at least 5 ships in the system

$$= \sum_{n=5}^{\infty} p_n = \sum_{n=0}^{\infty} p_n - \sum_{n=0}^{4} p_n$$

$$= 1 - (p_0 + p_1 + p_2 + p_3 + p_4)$$

$$= 1 - e^{-\rho}\left[1 + \rho + \frac{\rho^2}{2} + \frac{\rho^3}{3!} + \frac{\rho^4}{4!}\right] \quad (\because p_n = \frac{\rho^n \cdot e^{-\rho}}{n!}.)$$

$$= 1 - e^{-1.5}\left[1 + 1.5 - \frac{1.5^2}{2!} + \frac{1.5^3}{3!} + \frac{1.5^4}{4!}\right] = 0.019.$$

EXAMPLE 10.9-5.2

Problems arrive at a computer centre in a Poisson fashion at an average rate of 5/day. The rules of the computer centre are that any man waiting to get his problem solved must aid the man whose problem is currently being solved. If the time to solve a problem with one man has an exponential distribution with mean time of 1/3 day, and if the average solving time is inversely proportional to the number of people working on the problem, find the expected system time for a person entering the line.

[*J.N.T.U.Hyderabad B.Tech. May, 2011*]

Solution

Here, $\lambda = 5$ problems/day and $\mu = 3$ problems/day.

Then the expected number of persons working at any instant,

$$L_s = \sum_{n=0}^{\infty} n\, p_n = \sum_{n=0}^{\infty} n \,.\, \frac{\rho^n}{n!}\, e^{-\rho} = e^{-\rho} \sum_{n=0}^{\infty} \frac{n}{n!} . \rho^n$$

$$= \rho = \frac{\lambda}{\mu} \quad \text{(see example 10.9-5.1)}$$

$$= \frac{5}{3}.$$

Now $\quad W_s = \dfrac{L_s}{\lambda} = \dfrac{5/3}{5} = \dfrac{1}{3}$ day $= \dfrac{24}{3} = 8$ hours.

EXAMPLE 10.9-5.3

A cafeteria with self-service has an arrival rate of 12/hour. The average time taken by a person to collect and eat his meal is 20 minutes. Assuming that the interarrival times are exponentially distributed, how many seats must the cafeteria have to accomodate each customer with probability 0.95 ?

Solution

Here, $\lambda = 12$ customers/hour and $\mu = \dfrac{60}{20} = 3$ customers/hour.

Now it is required to find n so that $p_n = 0.95$.

$$p_n = \frac{\rho^n}{n!}\, e^{-\rho}, \quad \text{where } \rho = \frac{\lambda}{\mu} = 4.$$

$$\therefore \qquad 0.95 = \frac{4^n}{n!}\, e^{-4} = \frac{4^n}{n!} \times 0.0183 \qquad \therefore \quad \frac{4^n}{n!} = 51.9.$$

From hit and trial, $n = 7$.

So seven seats must be provided.

10.9-6 Model III. Single-Channel Poisson Arrivals, Exponential Service, Infinite Population, Service in Random Order Model (M/M/1) : (SIRO/∞/∞)

This model is essentially the same as model I of section 10.9-2 based on FCFS principle. As the derivation of p_n does not depend upon any specific queue discipline, p_n for SIRO rule is also given by

$$p_n = \left(\frac{\lambda}{\mu}\right)^n \cdot \left(1 - \frac{\lambda}{\mu}\right) = \rho^n (1 - \rho), \text{ for } n \geq 0.$$

It follows that all the results of model I are equally applicable to this case also. In fact, these results can be extended to any queue discipline namely, FCFS, LCFS, SIRO and GD.

10.9-7 Model IV. (M/M/1 : FCFS/N/∞) Finite Queue Length Model

This model differs from model I in that the maximum number of customers in the system is limited to N and hence the difference equations of model I are valid only so long as $n < N$.

Thus in this model, $\lambda_n = \lambda,\ \mu_n = \mu$ for $n < N$,

$\lambda_n = 0,\ \mu_n = \mu$ for $n \geq N$,

because when the number of customers in the system becomes N, no new arrivals can be accommodated.

The following system of differential equations holds good here :

$$\begin{aligned} p_0(t + dt) &= p_0(t)\,(1 - \lambda dt) + p_1(t)\,\mu dt\,.\,(1 - \lambda dt) \\ &= p_0(t) - \lambda dt\,.\,p_0(t) + \mu dt\,.\,p_1(t), \text{ for } n = 0; \\ p_n(t + dt) &= p_n(t)\,[1 - \lambda dt - \mu dt] + p_{n+1}(t)\,.\,\mu dt + p_{n-1}(t)\,\lambda dt \\ &= p_n(t) - (\lambda + \mu)\,dt\,p_n(t) + \mu dt p_{n+1}(t) + \lambda dt\,p_{n-1}(t), \text{ for } 1 \leq n \leq N - 1 \\ \text{and } p_N(t + dt) &= p_N(t)\,[1 - \lambda_N dt - \mu dt] + p_{N-1}(t)\,.\,\lambda dt \\ &= p_N(t) - \mu dt\,.\,p_N(t) + \lambda dt\,.\,p_{N-1}(t)\ [\because \text{For } n = N, \lambda_N = 0], \text{ for } n = N. \end{aligned}$$

Simplifying the above equations and taking the limit when $dt \to 0$, we get

$$\left.\begin{aligned} &\frac{d}{dt}[p_o(t)] = \mu p_1(t) - \lambda p_0(t), \quad \text{for } n = 0 \\ &\frac{d}{dt}[p_n(t)] = \mu p_{n+1}(t) - (\lambda + \mu)\,p_n(t) + \lambda p_{n-1}(t), \ \textit{for}\ 1 \leq n \leq N - 1 \\ \text{and } &\frac{d}{dt}[p_N(t)] = -\mu p_N(t) + \lambda p_{N-1}(t), \quad \textit{for } n = N. \end{aligned}\right\} \qquad ...(10.29)$$

Under steady state conditions, we have

$$\left.\begin{aligned} &0 = \mu p_1 - \lambda p_0 \ \textit{or}\ \mu p_1 = \lambda p_0, && \text{for} \quad n = 0 \\ &0 = \mu p_{n+1} - (\lambda + \mu) p_n + \lambda p_{n-1}, && \text{for} \quad 1 \leq n \leq N - 1 \\ \text{and} \quad &0 = -\mu p_N + \lambda p_{N-1} \text{ or } \mu p_N = \lambda p_{N-1}, && \text{for} \quad n = N. \end{aligned}\right] \qquad ...(10.30)$$

i.e.,

$$\left.\begin{aligned} p_1 &= \frac{\lambda}{\mu} p_0 = \rho p_0, \\ p_2 &= \left(\frac{\lambda}{\mu}\right)^2 p_0 = \rho^2 p_0, \\ &\vdots \\ p_n &= \left(\frac{\lambda}{\mu}\right)^n p_0 = \rho^n p_0, \\ &\vdots \\ p_N &= \left(\frac{\lambda}{\mu}\right)^N p_0 = \rho^N p_0 \end{aligned}\right\} \qquad ...(10.31)$$

Now for finding p_0, we use the relation

$$\sum_{n=0}^{N} p_n = 1 \text{ (Since the capacity of the system is N)}$$

or $\quad p_0 + p_1 + p_2 + ... + p_N = 1$

or $\quad p_0 (1 + \rho + \rho^2 + ... + \rho^N) = 1$

or $\quad p_0 \left(\frac{1-\rho^{N+1}}{1-\rho}\right) = 1$

or $$p_0 = \frac{1-\rho}{1-\rho^{N+1}}. \qquad ...(10.32)$$

$\therefore$ $$p_n = \frac{1-\rho}{1-\rho^{N+1}} . \rho^n, \; 0 \le n \le N. \qquad ...(10.33)$$

Characteristics of Model IV

1. Average number of customers in the system,

$$L_s = \sum_{n=0}^{N} np_n = \sum_{n=0}^{N} n . \left(\frac{1-\rho}{1-\rho^{N+1}}\right) \rho^n$$

$$= \frac{1-\rho}{1-\rho^{N+1}} . \sum_{n=0}^{N} n\rho^n$$

$$= \frac{1-\rho}{1-\rho^{N+1}} . [0 + \rho + 2\rho^2 + 3\rho^3 + ... + N \rho^N].$$

Now let $\quad S = \rho + 2\rho^2 + 3\rho^3 + ... - N \rho^N.$

$\therefore \quad \rho S = \rho^2 + 2\rho^3 + 3\rho^4 + ... + (N-1) \rho^N + N \rho^{N+1}.$

Subtracting we have,

$$(1-\rho) S = \rho + \rho^2 + \rho^3 + ... + \rho^N - N \rho^{N+1} = \rho . \left(\frac{1-\rho^N}{1-\rho}\right) - N \rho^{N+1}$$

or $$S = \rho . \left[\frac{1-\rho^N}{(1-\rho)^2}\right] - N . \frac{\rho^{N+1}}{1-\rho}.$$

$\therefore$ $$L_s = \frac{1-\rho}{1-\rho^{N+1}} \left[\rho . \frac{1-\rho^N}{(1-\rho)^2} - N . \frac{\rho^{N+1}}{1-\rho}\right]$$

$$= \frac{1}{1-\rho^{N+1}}\left[\rho \cdot \frac{1-\rho^{N}}{1-\rho} - N \cdot \rho^{N+1}\right]$$

$$= \frac{\rho - \rho^{N+1} - N\rho^{N+1} + N\rho^{N+2}}{(1-\rho^{N+1})(1-\rho)}$$

or $$L_s = \frac{\rho\,[1-(1+N)\,\rho^{N} + N\,\rho^{N+1}]}{(1-\rho)\,(1-\rho^{N+1})}. \qquad ...(10.34)$$

2. Average number of customers in the queue,

$$L_q = \sum_{n=1}^{N} (n-1)\,p_n = \sum_{n=1}^{N} np_n - \sum_{n=1}^{N} p_n$$

$$= \sum_{n=1}^{N} (0 + np_n) - \left[\sum_{n=0}^{N} p_n - p_0\right]$$

$$= \sum_{n=0}^{N} np_n - \sum_{n=0}^{N} p_n + p_0 = L_s - 1 + p_0$$

$$= \frac{\rho\,[1-(1+N)\rho^{N} + N\,\rho^{N+1}]}{(1-\rho)\,(1-\rho^{N+1})} - 1 + \frac{1-\rho}{1-\rho^{N+1}}$$

$$= \frac{\{\rho-(1+N)\rho^{N+1} + N\rho^{N+2}\} - \{1-\rho-\rho^{N+1}+\rho^{N+2}\} + \{1-2\rho+\rho^{2}\}}{(1-\rho)\,(1-\rho^{N+1})}$$

$$= \frac{\rho^{2} - N\,\rho^{N+1} + (N-1)\rho^{N+2}}{(1-\rho)\,(1-\rho^{N+1})}$$

$$= \frac{1 - N\,\rho^{N-1} + (N-1)\rho^{N}}{(1-\rho)\,(1-\rho^{N+1})} \cdot \rho^{2}. \qquad ...(10.35)$$

3. Average time a customer spends in the system,

$$W_s = \frac{L_s}{\lambda'}, \quad \text{where } \lambda' = \lambda\,(1 - p_N). \qquad ...(10.36)$$

4. Average waiting time in the queue,

$$W_q = \frac{L_q}{\lambda'}. \qquad ...(10.37)$$

EXAMPLE 10.9-7.1

Trains arrive at the yard every 15 minutes and the service time is 33 minutes. If the line capacity of the yard is limited to 4 trains, find

(i) the probability that the yard is empty,

(ii) the average number of trains in the system.

[*J.N.T.U. Hyderabad B.Tech. Nov., 2010; H.P.U. B.Tech. (Mech.) June, 2010; P.U.B.E. (Mech.) Nov., 1996*]

Solution

$$\lambda = 1/15 \text{ per minute},$$

$$\mu = 1/33 \text{ per minute}.$$

$$\therefore \quad \rho = \lambda/\mu = 33/15 = 2.2,$$

$$N = 4.$$

(*i*) $$p_0 = \frac{1-\rho}{1-\rho^{N+1}} = \frac{\rho-1}{\rho^{N+1}-1} = \frac{2.2-1}{2.2^5-1} = \frac{1.2}{51.5-1} = 0.0237.$$

(*ii*) Average number of trains in the system,

$$L_s = \sum_{n=0}^{N} np_n = 0 + p_1 + 2p_2 + 3p_3 + 4p_4$$

$$= p_0(\rho + 2\rho^2 + 3\rho^3 + 4\rho^4) \qquad (\because p_n = \rho^n \cdot p_0.)$$

$$= 0.0237[2.2 + 2 \times 2.2^2 + 3 \times 2.2^3 + 4 \times 2.2^4]$$

$$= 0.0237[2.2 + 9.68 + 31.94 + 93.70] = 3.26.$$

EXAMPLE 10.9-7.2

If for a period of 2 hours in a day (8 A.M. to 10 A.M.) trains arrive at the yard every 20 minutes but the service time is 36 minutes, calculate for this period

(a) the probability that the yard is empty,

(b) the average number of trains at the yard.

Line capacity of the yard is limited to 4 trains only.

[*H.P.U. B. Tech. (Mech.) Nov., 2010; Meerut M.Sc. (Math.) 2001*]

Solution

Here, $\lambda = \frac{60}{20} = 3$ trains/hour, $\mu = \frac{60}{36} = \frac{5}{3}$ trains/hour.

$$\therefore \quad \rho = \frac{\lambda}{\mu} = \frac{3 \times 3}{5} = 1.8.$$

(*a*) $$p_0 = \frac{1-\rho}{1-\rho^{N+1}} = \frac{\rho-1}{\rho^{N+1}-1} = \frac{1.8-1}{1.8^5-1} = \frac{0.8}{18.9-1} = 0.045.$$

$$\therefore \quad L_s = p_0 \sum_{n=0}^{4} n \cdot p_n = p_0 [0 + \rho + 2\rho^2 + 3\rho^3 + 4\rho^4] \ (\because p_n = \rho^n . p_0.)$$

$$= 0.045 \times 1.8 [1 + 2 \times 1.8 + 3 \times 1.8^2 + 4 \times 1.8^3]$$

$$= 0.081 [1 + 3.6 + 9.72 + 23.328] = 3.05 \text{ trains.}$$

EXAMPLE 10.9-7.3

At a railway station only one train is handled at a time. The railway yard is sufficient only for two trains to wait while the other is given signal to leave the station. Trains arrive at the station at an average rate of 6 per hour and the railway station can handle them on an average of 12 per hour. Assuming Poisson arrivals and exponential service distribution, find the steady state probabilities for the various number of trains in the system. Also find the average number of trains at the railway station and the average waiting time of a new train coming into the yard.

[*Univ. of Madras B.Sc. (Math.) Nov., 2012*]

Solution

Here, $\lambda = 6$ trains/hour, $\mu = 12$ trains/hour, $\rho = \frac{\lambda}{\mu} = \frac{6}{12} = 0.5.$

Since the maximum queue length is 2, the maximum number of trains in the system is 3 (= N).

Now, probability that there is no train in the system, $p_0 = \frac{1-\rho}{1-\rho^{N+1}}$.

$$\therefore \quad p_0 = \frac{1-0.5}{1-(0.5)^{3+1}} = \frac{0.5}{1-(0.5)^4} = 0.53.$$

Since $p_n = p_0 \cdot \rho^n$, $p_1 = 0.53 \times (.5)^1 = 0.265$, $p_2 = 0.53\ (.5)^2 = 0.13$, $p_3 = 0.53\ (.5)^3 = 0.066$

∴ Average number of trains in the system,

$$L_s = 1p_1 + 2p_2 + 3p_3$$

or $$L_s = 1 \times 0.265 + 2 \times 0.13 + 3 \times 0.066 = 0.723.$$

To find W_q

$$L_q = \frac{1 - N\rho^{N-1} + (N-1)\rho^N}{(1-\rho)(1-\rho^{N+1})} \cdot \rho^2 = \frac{1 - 3 \times 0.5^2 + 2 \times 0.5^3}{(1-0.5)[1-(0.5)^4]} \times (0.5)^2$$

$$= \frac{1 - 0.75 + 0.25}{0.5 \times 0.9375} \times 0.25 = 0.267.$$

$$\lambda' = \lambda\ (1 - p_N) = 6\ (1 - p_3) = 6\ (1 - 0.066) = 5.604.$$

$$\therefore \quad W_q = \frac{L_q}{\lambda'} = \frac{0.267}{5.604} = 0.0476 \text{ hours} = 2.85 \text{ minutes.}$$

EXERCISES 10.3

1. Obtain the steady state difference equations for the queuing model (M/M/1) : (FCFS/N/∞) in usual notations and solve them for p_0 and p_n. Also find the average number of units in the system and average queue length.

   [*P.U. B.E. (Mech.) Nov., 200*

2. A barber shop has space to accommodate only 10 customers. He can serve only one person at a time. If a customer comes to his shop and finds it full, he goes to the next shop. Customers randomly arrive at an average rate of 10 per hour and the barber's service time is exponential with an average of minutes per customer.
   (*i*) Write recurrence relations for the steady state, FCFS queuing system.
   (*ii*) Determine p_0 and p_n. [*J.N.T.U. Hyderabad B.Tech. April, 201*

3. For the (M/M/1) : (FCFS/k) queuing model, show that the steady state probability p_n is given by

$$p_n = \frac{1-\rho}{1-\rho^{k+1}} \cdot \rho^n,\ 0 \le n \le k.$$

   [*P.T.U. B.Tech., 200*

4. Patients arrive at a clinic according to Poisson distribution at the rate of 30 per hour. The waiting room does not accommodate more than 14 patients. Examination time per patient is exponential with mean rate 20 per hour.
   (*a*) Find the effective arrival rate at the clinic.
   (b) What is the probability that an arriving patient will not wait ?
   (c) What is the expected waiting time until a patient is discharged from the clinic ?
   [*J.N.T.U. Hyderabad B.Tech. Nov., 201*

5. In a car-wash service facility, cars arrive for service according to Poisson distribution with mean 5 per hour. The time for washing and cleaning each car has exponential distribution with mean 10 minutes per car. The facility cannot handle more than one car at a time and has a total of 5 parking spaces.
   (*a*) Find the effective arrival rate.
   (*b*) What is the probability that an arriving car will get service immediately upon arrival ?
   (*c*) Find the expected number of parking spaces occupied. [*Delhi U. B.Sc. (Stat.) 199*

6. Let there be an automobile inspection situation with 3 inspection stalls. The station can accomodate 4 cars waiting (7 in station) at one time. The arrival pattern is Poisson with a mean of 1 car every minute. The service time is exponential with mean of 6 minutes per car. Find the
   (*a*) expected number of customers in the queue; (*b*) expected number of customers in the system; (*c*) expected waiting time in the system; and (*d*) expected number of cars per hour that cannot enter the system. (*Ans.* (*a*) L_q = 3.09 cars (*b*) L_s = 6.06 cars (*c*) W_s = 12.3 minutes (*d*) 30.4 cars / hou

7. In a bank, customers arrive in a Poisson stream with mean 36 per hour. The service time per customer is negative exponential with mean 0.35 hour. Assuming that the system can accommodate at most 30 customers at a time, how many tellers should be provided under each of the following two conditions?
   (*a*) The probability of having more than $(x + 3)$ waiting customers is less than 0.2, where x is the number of tellers.
   (*b*) The expected number in the system does not exceed 3.

   [J.N.T.U. Hyderabad B.Tech. May, 2009]

8. (*a*) A child care shop dealing with children's requirements has one cashier who handles all customers' payments. The cashier takes on an average 4 minutes per customer. Customers come to cashier's area in random manner but on an average of 10 people per hour. The management received a large number of customers' complaints and decided to investigate the following questions:
   (*i*) What is the average length of the waiting line to be expected under the existing conditions?
   (*ii*) What portion of his time is the cashier expected to be idle?
   (*iii*) What is the average length of time that a customer would be expected to wait to pay for his purchase ?
   (*iv*) If it was decided that a customer would not tolerate a wait of more than 12 minutes, what is the probability that a customer would have to wait at least that length of time?

   (*b*) What is a queuing problem? Explain some of basic characteristics of a queuing system. What are some of the important assumptions in queuing models?

   [R.T.M. Nagpur U. B.Tech. Dec., 2004]

10.9-8 Model V. Single-Channel, Finite Population Model with Poisson Arrivals & Exponential Service Times (Limited Source Model) (M/M/1): (FCFS/n/M)

In some cases, units arrive from a limited pool of potential customers. Once a unit joins the queue, there is one less unit which could arrive and, therefore, the probability of an arrival is lowered. When a unit is served, it rejoins the pool of potential customers, and the probability of an arrival is, thereby, increased. As a rule of thumb, if the population is less than 40, the equations for a finite population should be used.

Although the concepts are same as those for infinite population, some of the terms are different and the equations required for analysis are different. One distinct difference is that the probability of an arrival depends upon the number of potential customers available to enter the system. Thus if the total customers' population is M and n represents the number of customers already in the queuing system, any arrival must come from M-n number that is not yet in the system.

To determine the properties of this system, it is necessary to find an expression for the probability of n customers in the system at time t *i.e.*, $p_n(t)$, for, if $p_n(t)$ is known, the expected number of customers in the system and other such like properties can be found. In place of finding an expression for $p_n(t)$, we shall initially find an expression for $p_n(t + dt)$.

The probability of n units in the system at time $t + dt$ can be determined by summing up probabilities of all the ways this event could occur. The event can occur in three mutually exclusive and exhaustive ways:

TABLE 10.4

Event	*No. of units at time t*	*No. of arrivals in time dt*	*No. of services in time dt*	*No. of units at time t + dt*
1	n	0	0	n
2	$n + 1$	0	1	n
3	$n - 1$	1	0	n

∴ Probability of event 1 $= p_n(t) \,.\, [1 - (\text{M} - n)\, \lambda\, dt]\, (1 - \mu dt)$

$= p_n(t) - p_n(t) \,.\, (\text{M} - n)\, \lambda dt - p_n(t) \,.\, \mu dt.$

Probability of event 2 $= p_{n+1}(t) \,.\, [1 - (M - n - 1)\lambda\, dt]\,(\mu dt)$
$= p_{n+1}(t) \,.\, \mu\, dt.$

Probability of event 3 $= p_{n-1}(t) \,.\, [(M - n + 1)\lambda\, dt]\,(1 - \mu\, dt)]$
$= p_{n-1}(t) \,.\, (M - n + 1)\lambda\, dt.$

$$\therefore \quad p_n(t + dt) = p_n(t) - p_n(t) \,.\, (M - n)\lambda\, dt - p_n(t) \,.\, \mu\, dt + p_{n+1}(t) \,.\, \mu\, dt + p_{n-1}(t)\,(M - n + 1) \,.\, \lambda\, dt$$

or
$$\frac{p_n(t + dt) - p_n(t)}{dt} = -p_n(t) \,.\, [\lambda(M - n) + \mu)] + p_{n+1}(t) \,.\, \mu + p_{n-1}(t)\,[(M - n + 1)\lambda].$$

Taking the limit when $dt \to 0$, we get

$$\frac{d}{dt}[p_n(t)] = -p_n(t)[(M - n)\lambda + \mu] + p_{n+1}(t) \,.\, \mu + p_{n-1}(t)[(M - n + 1)\lambda].$$

Assuming a steady state condition for the system when

$p_n(t) = p_n$ and $\frac{d}{dt}[p_n(t)] = 0$, we get

$$0 = -p_n[(M - n)\lambda + \mu] + p_{n+1}(\mu) + p_{n-1}[(M - n + 1)\lambda].$$

$$\therefore \quad p_{n+1} = p_n\left[(M - n)\frac{\lambda}{\mu} + 1\right] - p_{n-1}(M - n + 1)\frac{\lambda}{\mu}. \qquad ...(10.38)$$

This is a general expression for p_{n+1} as a function of p_n and p_{n-1}. Now we find an expression for p_n in terms of p_0, λ, μ and M.

Now, $p_0 = p_0,$

$$p_1 = p_0 M\left(\frac{\lambda}{\mu}\right), \qquad \text{[From equation (10.38) for } n = 0.]$$

$$p_2 = p_1\left[\frac{(M - 1)\lambda}{\mu} + 1\right] - p_0(M - 1 + 1)\frac{\lambda}{\mu}$$

(From equation 10.38 for $n = 1$.)

$$= p_0 M\left(\frac{\lambda}{\mu}\right)\left[\frac{(M - 1)\lambda}{\mu} + 1\right] - p_0 M\left(\frac{\lambda}{\mu}\right)$$

$$= p_0 M\left(\frac{\lambda}{\mu}\right)\left[\frac{(M - 1)\lambda}{\mu} + 1 - 1\right]$$

$$= p_0\frac{\lambda}{\mu} \,.\, M \,.\, (M - 1) \,.\, \frac{\lambda}{\mu}$$

$$= p_0\left(\frac{\lambda}{\mu}\right)^2 . \, M\,(M - 1),$$

$$\vdots$$

$$p_n = p_0\left(\frac{\lambda}{\mu}\right)^n . \, M \,.\, (M - 1)\,(M - 2)...(M - n + 1)$$

$$= p_0\left(\frac{\lambda}{\mu}\right)^n . \, \frac{M!}{(M - n)!} = p_0\,\frac{M!}{(M - n)!} \,.\, \left(\frac{\lambda}{\mu}\right)^n. \qquad ...(10.39)$$

Now we find p_0 in terms of λ, μ and M.

$$\sum_{n=0}^{n=M} p_n = \sum_{n=0}^{n=M} p_0\,\frac{M!}{(M - n)!}\left(\frac{\lambda}{\mu}\right)^n = 1.$$

1. ∴ Probability of an empty system,

$$p_0 = \frac{1}{\sum_{n=0}^{n=M} \frac{M!}{(M-n)!}\left(\frac{\lambda}{\mu}\right)^n}. \quad \text{...(10.40)}$$

2. Therefore, from equation (10.39) and equation (10.40), we have probability of n customers in the system,

$$p_n = \frac{\frac{M!}{(M-n)!}\left(\frac{\lambda}{\mu}\right)^n}{\sum_{n=0}^{n=M} \frac{M!}{(M-n)!}\cdot\left(\frac{\lambda}{\mu}\right)^n} = p_0 \cdot \frac{M!}{(M-n)!}\left(\frac{\lambda}{\mu}\right)^n. \quad \text{...(10.41)}$$

The following formulae are written here without proof :

3. Expected number of customers in the system,

$$L_s = \sum_{n=0}^{n=M} np_n = M - \frac{\mu}{\lambda}(1 - p_0). \quad \text{...(10.42)}$$

4. Expected number of customers in the queue,

$$L_q = M - \frac{\lambda + \mu}{\lambda}\ (1 - p_0). \quad \text{...(10.43)}$$

EXAMPLE 10.9-8.1

A mechanic repairs four machines. The mean time between service requirements is 5 hours for each machine and forms an exponential distribution. The mean repair time is 1 hour and also follows the same distribution pattern. Machine downtime costs ₹ 25 per hour and the mechanic costs ₹ 55 per day.

(a) Find the expected number of operating machines.

(b) Determine the expected downtime cost per day.

(c) Would it be economical to engage two mechanics, each repairing only two machines ?

[*P.T.U. MBA May, 2002*]

Solution

This situation involves finite population.

Arrival rate $\lambda = 1/5 = 0.2$,

service rate $\mu = 1/1 = 1$.

Let us first find the probability of an empty system,

$$p_0 = \frac{1}{\sum_{n=0}^{n=4} \frac{4!}{(4-n)!}\left(\frac{0.2}{1}\right)^n}$$

$$= \frac{1}{1 + 4(.2) + (4\times3)(.2)^2 + (4\times3\times2)\times(.2)^3 + (4\times3\times2\times1)(.2)^4} = 0.4.$$

(*a*) Expected number of broken-down machines in the system,

$$L_s = M - \frac{\mu}{\lambda}\ (1 - p_0)$$

$$= 4 - \frac{1}{0.2}\ (1 - 0.4) = 4 - 5 \times 0.6 = 4 - 3 = 1.$$

∴ Expected number of operating machines in the system = 4 – 1 = 3.

(*b*) Expected downtime cost per day (assuming an 8-hour day)

= 8 × expected number of broken-down machines × ₹ 25 per hour.

= 8 × 1 × 25 = ₹ 200 per day.

(*c*) When there are two mechanics each serving two machines, M = 2.

$$\therefore \quad p_0 = \frac{1}{\sum_{n=0}^{n=2} \frac{2!}{(2-n)!}\left(\frac{0.2}{1}\right)^n} = \frac{1}{1 + 2(.2) + 2 \times 1(.2)^2} = \frac{1}{1.48} = 0.68.$$

It is assumed that each mechanic with his two machines constitutes a separate system with no interplay. Expected number of machines in the system

$$= \text{M} - \frac{\mu}{\lambda} . (1 - p_0) = 2 - \frac{1}{0.2} (1 - .68) = 0.4.$$

∴ Expected downtime/day = 8 × 0.4 × number of mechanics

= 8 × 0.4 × 2 = 6.4 hr/day.

∴ Total cost with two mechanics

= ₹ (2 × 55 + 6.4 × 25)

= ₹ (110 + 160) = ₹ 270 per day.

Total cost with one mechanic = ₹ (55 + 200) = ₹ 255 per day.

Hence use of two mechanics is not economical.

EXERCISES 10.4

1. In a machine shop there are two identical machines. Products arrive for machining at the average rate of 4 products per hour. The average machining time is 24 minutes per product. The production manager complains of loss of production time and suggests the installation of a third machine. What is the average waiting time per product under the present circumstances ? What is it likely to be if a third machine is installed ? Assume Poisson pattern of arrival and exponentially distributed service times. [*P.T.U. MBA May, 2001*]

2. In a machine shop there are 10 identical machines. These machines are subjected to periodical breakdowns and require the service of a maintenance department. Each machine breaks down in a Poisson pattern. The time required to put a machine back into production line is exponentially distributed. Formulate a queuing model to determine the following :

   (*i*) Average downtime of the machines (W_s).

   (*ii*) Probability that all the machines are in working order (p_0).

   [*P.U. M.E. (Mech.) May, 1995*]

10.10 MODEL VI. MULTI-CHANNEL QUEUING THEORY (M/M/C) : (FCFS/∞/∞)

Multi-channel queuing theory treats the condition in which there are several service stations in parallel and each customer in the waiting line can be served by more than one station. Each service facility is prepared to deliver the same type of service. The new arrival selects one station without any external pressure. When a waiting line is formed, a single line usually breaks down into shorter lines in front of each service station. The arrival rate λ and service rate μ are mean values from Poisson distribution and exponential distribution respectively. Service discipline is first come, first served and customers are taken from a single queue *i.e.,* any empty channel is filled by the next customer in line. (See Fig. 10.1).

Let n = number of customers in the system,

p_n = probability of n customers in the system,

c = number of parallel service channels ($c > 1$),

λ = arrival rate of customers,

μ = service rate of individual channel.

When $n < c$, there is no queue because all arrivals are being serviced, and the rate of servicing will be $n\mu$ as only n channels are busy, each at the rate of μ. When $n = c$, all channels will be working and when $n > c$, there will be $(n - c)$ customers in the queue and rate of service will be $c\mu$ as all the c channels are busy. There will be three cases in this system. To determine the properties of multi-channel system, it is necessary to find an expression for the probability of n customers in the system at time t *i.e.*, $p_n(t)$.

Case 1 (When n = 0) :

Let us first find $p_0\,(t + dt)$. This event can occur only in two exclusive and exhaustive ways:

TABLE 10.5

Event	No. of units at time t	No. of arrivals in time dt	No. of services in time dt	No. of units at time t + dt
1	0	0	–	0
2	1	0	1	0

$$p_0(t + dt) = p_0(t) \,.\, (1 - \lambda dt) + p_1(t) \,.\, (1 - \lambda dt) \,.\, (\mu dt)$$
$$= p_0(t) - p_0(t) \,.\, \lambda dt + p_1(t) \,.\, (\mu dt).$$

$$\therefore \quad \frac{p_0(t + dt) - p_0(t)}{dt} = \mu p_1(t) - \lambda p_0(t).$$

Taking the limit $dt \to 0$, $\dfrac{d}{dt}\,[p_0(t)] = \mu\, p_1(t) - \lambda p_0(t)$.

Considering the steady state system, $0 = \mu p_1 - \lambda p_0$.

$$\therefore \quad p_1 = \frac{\lambda}{\mu} p_0. \qquad \text{...(10.44)}$$

Case 2. (When $1 \leq n \leq c - 1$) :

When n lies between 1 and $c - 1$, all customers arriving will be immediately served and n channels out of c will be busy. Let us first find $p_n\,(t + dt)$. This event can occur in three exclusive and exhaustive ways:

TABLE 10.6

Event	No. of units at time t	No. of arrivals in time dt	No. of services in time dt	No. of units at time t + dt
1	n	0	0	n
2	$n - 1$	1	0	n
3	$n + 1$	0	1	n

$$\therefore \quad p_n(t + dt) = p_n(t) \,.\, (1 - \lambda dt)\,(1 - n\mu dt)$$
$$+ p_{n-1}(t) \,.\, \lambda dt \,.\, [1 - (n - 1)\,\mu dt]$$
$$+ p_{n+1}(t)\,(1 - \lambda dt) \,.\, [(n + 1)\mu dt]$$
$$= p_n(t)\,[1 - (\lambda + n\mu)dt] + p_{n-1}(t) \,.\, \lambda dt + p_{n+1}(t) \,.\, (n + 1)\mu dt.$$

$$\therefore \quad \frac{p_n(t+dt) - p_n(t)}{dt} = -\,(\lambda + n\mu)\,p_n(t) + \lambda p_{n-1}(t) + (n+1)\mu \cdot p_{n+1}(t).$$

Considering the steady state system,

$$\lambda p_{n-1} - (\lambda + n\mu)p_n + (n + 1)\,\mu p_{n+1} = 0 \text{ for } 1 \leq n \leq c - 1. \qquad \text{...(10.45)}$$

Now equation (10.44) gives $p_1 = \dfrac{\lambda}{\mu} p_0$.

Putting $n = 1$ in equation (10.45), we get

$$\lambda p_0 - (\lambda + \mu)p_1 + 2\mu p_2 = 0$$

or $$\lambda p_0 - (\lambda + \mu)\, p_0 + 2\mu p_2 = 0$$

or $$-\frac{\lambda^2}{\mu} p_0 + 2\mu p_2 = 0$$

or $$p_2 = \frac{1}{2}\left(\frac{\lambda}{\mu}\right)^2 p_0 = \frac{1}{2!}\left(\frac{\lambda}{\mu}\right)^2 p_0.$$

Similarly, putting $n = 2$ in equation (10.45), we get

$$p_3 = \frac{1}{3!}\left(\frac{\lambda}{\mu}\right)^3 p_0.$$

In general, $$p_n = \frac{1}{n!}\left(\frac{\lambda}{\mu}\right)^n p_0 \text{ for } 1 \le n \le c-1. \qquad ...(10.46)$$

Case 3 (when $n \ge c$)

When $n = c - 1$, substituting it in equation (10.45), we get

$$\lambda p_{c-2} - [\lambda + (c-1)\mu]\, p_{c-1} + c\mu p_c = 0.$$

$$\therefore \quad p_c = \frac{1}{c\mu}[\lambda + (c-1)\mu]p_{c-1} - \frac{\lambda}{c\mu} p_{c-2}. \qquad ...(10.47)$$

Now from equation (10.46),

$$p_{c-1} = \frac{1}{(c-1)!}\cdot\left(\frac{\lambda}{\mu}\right)^{c-1} \cdot p_0$$

and $$p_{c-2} = \frac{1}{(c-2)!}\cdot\left(\frac{\lambda}{\mu}\right)^{c-2} \cdot p_0 .$$

$\therefore$ From equation (10.47),

$$p_c = \frac{1}{c\mu}[\lambda + (c-1)\mu]\cdot\frac{1}{(c-1)!}\cdot\left(\frac{\lambda}{\mu}\right)^{c-1} \cdot p_0 - \frac{\lambda}{c\mu}\cdot\frac{1}{(c-2)!}\cdot\left(\frac{\lambda}{\mu}\right)^{c-2} \cdot p_0$$

$$= \frac{\lambda}{c\mu}\cdot\frac{1}{(c-1)!}\cdot\left(\frac{\lambda}{\mu}\right)^{c-1} \cdot p_0 + \frac{(c-1)\,\mu}{c\mu\,(c-1)!}\cdot\left(\frac{\lambda}{\mu}\right)^{c-1} \cdot p_0 - \frac{\lambda}{c\mu}\cdot\frac{1}{(c-2)!}\cdot\left(\frac{\lambda}{\mu}\right)^{c-2} \cdot p_0$$

$$= \frac{1}{c!}\left(\frac{\lambda}{\mu}\right)^c p_0 + \frac{\lambda}{c\mu}\cdot\frac{1}{(c-2)!}\cdot\left(\frac{\lambda}{\mu}\right)^{c-2} \cdot p_0 - \frac{\lambda}{c\mu}\cdot\frac{1}{(c-2)!}\cdot\left(\frac{\lambda}{\mu}\right)^{c-2} \cdot p_0$$

$$= \frac{1}{c!}\left(\frac{\lambda}{\mu}\right)^c p_0 .$$

Similarly, when $n = c + 1$, substituting in equation (10.45) and simplifying, we get

$$p_{c+1} = \frac{\lambda}{c\mu} \cdot p_c = \frac{\lambda}{c\mu}\cdot\frac{(\lambda/\mu)^c}{c!} p_0 = \frac{1}{c\,.\,c!}\left(\frac{\lambda}{\mu}\right)^{c+1} \cdot p_0,$$

$$p_{c+2} = \frac{1}{c^2\,.\,c!}\left(\frac{\lambda}{\mu}\right)^{c+2} \cdot p_0,$$

In general, $$p_n = \frac{1}{c^{n-c}\,.\,c!}\cdot\left(\frac{\lambda}{\mu}\right)^n \cdot p_0 \text{, for } n \ge c. \qquad ...(10.48)$$

Thus equations (10.44), (10.47) and (10.48) give the value of p_n for $n = 0$, $1 \le n \le c - 1$

and $n \geq c$. It still remains to find the value of p_0 in terms of c, μ and λ. Then the values of p_n and p_0 can be used to develop the other equations. For finding the value of p_0, we use the relation

$$\sum_{n=0}^{\infty} p_n = 1$$

or $$\sum_{n=0}^{c-1} p_n + \sum_{n=c}^{\infty} p_n = 1$$

or $$\sum_{n=0}^{c-1} \frac{1}{n!}\left(\frac{\lambda}{\mu}\right)^n \cdot p_0 + \sum_{n=c}^{\infty} \frac{1}{c^{n-c}\ldots c!}\cdot\left(\frac{\lambda}{\mu}\right)^n \cdot p_0 = 1$$

or $$p_0\left[\sum_{n=0}^{c-1} \frac{1}{n!}\cdot\left(\frac{\lambda}{\mu}\right)^n + \sum_{n=c}^{\infty} \frac{c^c}{c^n\,.\,c!}\left(\frac{\lambda}{\mu}\right)^n\right] = 1$$

or $$p_0\left[\sum_{n=0}^{c-1} \frac{(\lambda/\mu)^n}{n!} + \frac{c^c}{c!}\sum_{n=c}^{\infty}\left(\frac{\lambda}{c\mu}\right)^n\right] = 1$$

or $$p_0\left[\sum_{n=0}^{c-1} \frac{(\lambda/\mu)^n}{n!} + \frac{c^c}{c!}\left\{\left(\frac{\lambda}{c\mu}\right)^c + \left(\frac{\lambda}{c\mu}\right)^{c+1} + \left(\frac{\lambda}{c\mu}\right)^{c+2} + \ldots\infty\right\}\right] = 1$$

or $$p_0\left[\sum_{n=0}^{c-1} \frac{(\lambda/\mu)^n}{n!} + \frac{c^c}{c!}\cdot\left(\frac{\lambda}{c\mu}\right)^c\left\{1 + \frac{\lambda}{c\mu} + \left(\frac{\lambda}{c\mu}\right)^2 + \ldots\infty\right\}\right] = 1$$

or $$p_0\left[\sum_{n=0}^{c-1} \frac{(\lambda/\mu)^n}{n!} + \frac{(\lambda/\mu)^c}{c!}\cdot\left(\frac{1}{1-\lambda/c\mu}\right)\right] = 1$$

or $$p_0\left[\sum_{n=0}^{c-1} \frac{(\lambda/\mu)^n}{n!} + \frac{(\lambda/\mu)^c}{c!}\cdot\left(\frac{c\mu}{c\mu-\lambda}\right)\right] = 1$$

or $$p_0 = \frac{1}{\displaystyle\sum_{n=0}^{c-1} \frac{(\lambda/\mu)^n}{n!} + \frac{(\lambda/\mu)^c}{c!}\cdot\frac{c\mu}{c\mu-\lambda}}. \qquad \ldots(10.49)$$

Now the various properties of the multi-channel system can be found out.

1. Expected (average) number of customers in the system,

$$^*L_s = \frac{\lambda\,.\,\mu\left(\dfrac{\lambda}{\mu}\right)^c}{(c-1)!\,(c\mu-\lambda)^2}\,p_0 + \frac{\lambda}{\mu}. \qquad \ldots(10.50)$$

2. Expected (average) number of customers waiting in the queue,

$$L_q = L_s - \text{average number being served}$$

$$= L_s - c\,.\,\frac{\lambda}{c\mu} = L_s - \frac{\lambda}{\mu}$$

$$= \frac{\lambda\mu\,.\left(\dfrac{\lambda}{\mu}\right)^c}{(c-1)!\,(c\mu-\lambda)^2}\cdot p_0. \qquad \ldots(10.51)$$

* For proof, see Philip M. Morse, *'Queues, Inventories and Maintenance'*, Wiley, New York, 1958.

3. Average time a customer spends in the system,

$$W_s = \frac{L_s}{\lambda} = \frac{\mu\left(\dfrac{\lambda}{\mu}\right)^c}{(c-1)!\,(c\mu-\lambda)^2} \cdot p_0 + \frac{1}{\mu}. \qquad \text{...(10.52)}$$

4. Average waiting time of a customer in the queue,

$$W_q = \frac{L_q}{\lambda} = \frac{\mu\left(\dfrac{\lambda}{\mu}\right)^c}{(c-1)!\,(c\mu-\lambda)^2} \cdot p_0. \qquad \text{...(10.53)}$$

5. Probability that a customer has to wait,

$$p\,(n \geq c) = \frac{\mu\,.\left(\dfrac{\lambda}{\mu}\right)^c}{(c-1)!\,(c\mu-\lambda)} \cdot p_0. \qquad \text{...(10.54)}$$

6. Probability that a customer enters the service without waiting,

$$1 - p\,(n \geq c) = 1 - \frac{\mu\,.\left(\dfrac{\lambda}{\mu}\right)^c}{(c-1)!\,(c\mu-\lambda)} \cdot p_0. \qquad \text{...(10.55)}$$

7. Average number of idle servers

$= c -$ (average number of customers served). ...(10.56)

8. Utilisation rate, $\rho = \dfrac{\lambda}{c\mu}$. ...(10.57)

9. Efficiency of M/M/c model $= \dfrac{\text{Average number of customers served}}{\text{Total number of customers}}$. ...(10.58)

EXAMPLE 10.10-1

A tax consulting firm has 3 counters in its office to receive people who have problems concerning their income, wealth and sales taxes. On the average 48 persons arrive in an 8-hour day. Each tax adviser spends 15 minutes on an average on an arrival. If the arrivals are Poissonly distributed and service times are according to exponential distribution, find

(a) the average number of customers in the system,
(b) average number of customers waiting to be served,
(c) average time a customer spends in the system,
(d) average waiting time for a customer,
(e) the number of hours each week a tax adviser spends performing his job,
(f) the probability that a customer has to wait before he gets service,
(g) the expected number of idle tax advisers at any specified time.

[*Jammu U.B.E. Mech., 2004*]

Solution

Here, $c = 3$, $\lambda = \dfrac{48}{8} = 6\text{/hour}$, $\mu = \dfrac{1}{15} \times 60 = 4\text{/hour}$, $\dfrac{\lambda}{\mu} = \dfrac{3}{2}$.

First of all, it is necessary to find the value of p_0 which is the probability of having no customer in the system.

$$p_0 = \frac{1}{\displaystyle\sum_{n=0}^{c-1} \frac{(\lambda/\mu)^n}{n!} + \frac{(\lambda/\mu)^c}{c!} \cdot \frac{c\mu}{c\mu-\lambda}} = \frac{1}{\displaystyle\sum_{n=0}^{2} \frac{(\lambda/\mu)^n}{n!} + \frac{(\lambda/\mu)^3}{3!} \cdot \frac{3\mu}{3\mu-\lambda}}$$

$$= \frac{1}{\left[1+\frac{\lambda}{\mu}+\frac{1}{2}\left(\frac{\lambda}{\mu}\right)^2\right]+\frac{(\lambda/\mu)^3}{6}\cdot\frac{3\mu}{3\mu-\lambda}}$$

$$= \frac{1}{\left(1+\frac{3}{2}+\frac{9}{8}\right)+\frac{27}{48}\cdot\frac{12}{12-6}} = \frac{1}{\frac{29}{8}+\frac{9}{8}} = \frac{8}{38} = \frac{4}{19} = 0.21.$$

(*a*) Average number of customers in the system,

$$L_s = \frac{\lambda\mu\left(\frac{\lambda}{\mu}\right)^c}{(c-1)!(c\mu-\lambda)^2}\cdot p_0 + \frac{\lambda}{\mu}$$

$$= \frac{6\times4\times(3/2)^3}{2!(12-6)^2}\times 0.21 + \frac{3}{2} = 1.74.$$

(*b*) Average number of customers waiting to be served,

$$L_q = L_s - \frac{\lambda}{\mu} = 1.74 - \frac{3}{2} = 0.24.$$

(*c*) Average time a customer spends in the system,

$$W_s = \frac{L_s}{\lambda} = \frac{1.74}{6} = 0.29 \text{ hour} = 17.4 \text{ minutes}.$$

(*d*) Average waiting time for a customer,

$$W_q = \frac{L_q}{\lambda} = \frac{0.24}{6} = 0.04 \text{ hour} = 2.4 \text{ minutes}.$$

(*e*) Utilisation factor, $\rho = \frac{\lambda}{c\mu} = \frac{6}{3\times4} = \frac{1}{2}$.

∴ Number of hours each day a tax adviser spends doing his job $= \frac{1}{2}\times 8 = 4$.

∴ On an average, a tax adviser is busy 4 × 5 = 20 hours based on 5-working day week.

(*f*) Probability that a customer has to wait,

$$p\,(n \geq c) = \frac{\mu\cdot\left(\frac{\lambda}{\mu}\right)^c}{(c-1)!(c\mu-\lambda)}\cdot p_0$$

$$= \frac{4\times\left(\frac{3}{2}\right)^3}{2!(12-6)}\times 0.21 = 0.236.$$

(*g*) We know that the probability of no customers in the system is p_0, which means that ll the three tax advisers are idle. We have to determine p_1 and p_2 *i.e.*, the probability that 2 tax dvisers and 1 tax adviser respectively are idle.

Now, $$p_n = \frac{1}{n!}\left(\frac{\lambda}{\mu}\right)^n p_0. \quad (n < c)$$

∴ $$p_1 = \frac{1}{1!}\left(\frac{3}{2}\right)\times 0.21 = 0.315,$$

$$p_2 = \frac{1}{2!}\left(\frac{3}{2}\right)^2 \times 0.21 \times = 0.236.$$

∴ Expected number of idle advisers at any specified time

$$= 3p_0 + 2p_1 + 1.p_2$$
$$= 3 \times 0.21 + 2 \times 0.315 + 1 \times 0.236 = 1.496 \sim 1.5.$$

Alternatively, utilisation factor $= \dfrac{\lambda}{c\mu} = \dfrac{6}{3 \times 4} = \dfrac{1}{2}$.

Thus each tax advisor is busy for half the time and hence also free for half the time.

∴ Expected number of idle tax advisors $= \dfrac{1}{2} \times 3 = 1.5$.

EXAMPLE 10.10-2

Ships arrive at a port at the rate of one in every 4 hours with exponential distribution of interarrival times. The time a ship occupies a berth for unloading has exponential distribution with an average of 10 hours. If the average delay of ships waiting for berths is to be kept below 14 hours, how many berths should be provided at the port ?

[*Kuru.U. B.E. (Mech.) June, 2012*]

Solution

Here, $\lambda = \dfrac{1}{4}$ per hour, $\mu = \dfrac{1}{10}$ per hour, $\dfrac{\lambda}{\mu} = \dfrac{5}{2}$.

For multi-channel queuing system, $\lambda/c\mu < 1$, to ensure that the queue does not explode.

$$\therefore \qquad \frac{1/4}{\frac{1}{10}.c} < 1 \text{ or } c > \frac{5}{2}.$$

Let us calculate the waiting time when $c = 3$.

$$\text{Now} \qquad p_0 = \frac{1}{\sum_{n=0}^{c-1} \frac{(\lambda/\mu)^n}{n!} + \frac{(\lambda/\mu)^c}{c!} . \frac{c\mu}{c\mu - \lambda}} = \frac{1}{\sum_{n=0}^{2} \frac{(5/2)^n}{n!} + \frac{\left(\frac{5}{2}\right)^3}{3!}\left(\frac{3/10}{3/10 - 1/4}\right)}$$

$$= \frac{1}{\left[1 + \frac{5}{2} + \frac{1}{2}.\left(\frac{5}{2}\right)^2\right] + \frac{125}{6 \times 8} \times \frac{3}{10} \times \frac{20}{1}} = \frac{1}{6.625 + 15.625} = 0.045.$$

Average waiting time of a ship,

$$W_q = \frac{\mu.(\lambda/\mu)^c}{(c-1)!(c\mu - \lambda)^2} p_0 = \frac{1/10 \times (5/2)^3}{2!(3/10 - 1/4)^2} \times 0.045 = 14.06 \text{ hours,}$$

which is greater than 14 hours. Hence 3 berths are inadequate.

Let $c = 4$. Then

$$p_0 = \frac{1}{\sum_{n=0}^{3} \frac{(5/2)^n}{n!} + \frac{(5/2)^4}{4!} \frac{3/10}{(3/10 - 1/4)}}$$

$$= \frac{1}{[1 + 5/2 + 1/2\,(5/2)^2 + 1/6(5/2)^3] + \frac{625}{24 \times 16} \times \frac{3}{10} \times \frac{20}{1}}$$

$$= \frac{1}{9.23 + 9.765} = 0.0526.$$

Average waiting time of a ship,

$$W_q = \frac{1/10 \times (5/2)^4}{3!(3/10 - 1/4)^2} \times 0.0526 = 13.7 \text{ hours},$$

which is less than the allowable time of 14 hours.

Hence, 4 berths must be provided at the port.

EXAMPLE 10.10-3

A library wants to improve its service facilities in terms of the waiting time of its borrowers. The library has two counters at present and borrowers arrive according to Poisson distribution with arrival rate 1 every 6 minutes and service time follows exponential distribution with a mean of 10 minutes. The library has relaxed its membership rules and a substantial increase in the number of borrowers is expected. Find the number of additional counters to be provided if the arrival rate is expected to be twice the present value and the average waiting time of the borrowers must be limited to half the present value.

Solution

Here, $\lambda = \frac{1}{6}$/minute = 10/hr, $\mu = \frac{1}{10}$/minute = 6/hr, $\frac{\lambda}{\mu} = \frac{10}{6} = \frac{5}{3}$, $c = 2$.

$$\therefore \qquad p_0 = \frac{1}{\sum_{n=0}^{c-1} \frac{(\lambda/\mu)^n}{n!} + \frac{(\lambda/\mu)^c}{c!} \cdot \frac{c\mu}{c\mu - \lambda}} = \frac{1}{\sum_{n=0}^{1} \frac{(5/3)^n}{n!} + \frac{(5/3)^2}{2!}\left(\frac{2 \times 6}{2 \times 6 - 10}\right)}$$

$$= \frac{1}{\left(1 + \frac{5}{3}\right) + \frac{25}{2 \times 9} \times 6} = 0.091.$$

Average waiting time of a borrower,

$$W_q = \frac{\mu \cdot (\lambda/\mu)^c}{(c-1)!(c\mu - \lambda)^2} \cdot p_0 = \frac{6\,(5/3)^2}{1!(12-10)^2} \times 0.091 = 0.379 \text{ hours}$$

$= 22.75$ minutes.

New arrival rate, $\qquad \lambda = 2 \times \frac{1}{6} = \frac{1}{3}$/minute = 20/hr, μ = 6/hr,

$$\therefore \qquad \frac{\lambda}{\mu} = \frac{20}{6} = \frac{10}{3}.$$

We shall calculate the average waiting time of a customer for different number of counters.

When $c = 3$, $\frac{\lambda}{c\mu} = \frac{20}{3 \times 6} = \frac{10}{9}$ (> 1), hence $c = 3$ will result in explosion of the queue.

When $c = 4$,

$$p_0 = \frac{1}{\sum_{n=0}^{3} \frac{(10/3)^n}{n!} + \frac{(10/3)^4}{4!}\left(\frac{24}{24-20}\right)} = \frac{1}{[1 + 10/3 + 1/2(10/3)^2 + 1/6(10/3)^3] + \frac{10{,}000}{24 \times 81} \times 6}$$

$= 0.0213.$

$\therefore$ Average waiting time of a borrower,

$$W_q = \frac{\mu . (\lambda/\mu)^c}{(c-1)!(c\mu - \lambda)^2} . p_0 = \frac{6 . (10/3)^4}{3!(24-20)^2} \times 0.0213$$

$$= 0.164 \text{ hour} = 9.86 \text{ minutes},$$

which is less than half the present value of 22.75 minutes. Hence it is necessary to provide 2 additional counters.

EXAMPLE 10.10-4.

A bank has two tellers working on savings accounts. The first teller handles withdrawals only while the second teller handles deposits only. It has been found that the service time distribution for the deposits and withdrawals both is exponential with mean service time 3 minutes per customer. Depositors are found to arrive in a Poisson fashion throughout the day with mean arrival rate 16 per hour. Withdrawers also arrive in a Poisson fashion with mean arrival rate 14 per hour.

(a) What would be the effect on the average waiting time for depositors and withdrawers if each teller could handle both withdrawals and deposits ?

(b) What would be the effect if this could only be accomplished by increasing the service time to 3.5 minutes ?

[Gujarat U. MBA, 1988; Delhi Univ. M.B.A., 1987; April, 1983]

Solution

Here, $\mu = \frac{1}{3}$/minute = 20/hour, $\lambda_1 = 16$/hour, $\lambda_2 = 14$/hour.

Average waiting time for depositors,

$$W_{q_1} = \frac{1}{\mu} . \frac{\lambda_1}{\mu - \lambda_1} = \frac{1}{20} \times \frac{16}{20-16} = \frac{1}{5} \text{ hours} = 12 \text{ minutes}.$$

Average waiting time for withdrawers,

$$W_{q_2} = \frac{1}{\mu} . \frac{\lambda_2}{\mu - \lambda_2} = \frac{1}{20} \times \frac{14}{20-14} = \frac{7}{60} \text{ hours} = 7 \text{ minutes}.$$

(*a*) Here, $\lambda = \lambda_1 + \lambda_2 = 16 + 14 = 30$/hour,

$$\mu = 20/\text{hour}, \lambda/\mu = 3/2, c = 2.$$

$$\therefore \quad p_0 = \frac{1}{\sum_{n=0}^{c-1} \frac{(\lambda/\mu)^n}{n!} + \frac{(\lambda/\mu)^c}{c!} . \frac{c\mu}{c\mu - \lambda}} = \frac{1}{\sum_{n=0}^{1} \frac{(3/2)^n}{n!} + \frac{(3/2)^2}{2!} . \frac{40}{40-30}}$$

$$= \frac{1}{(1 + 3/2) + \frac{9}{4 \times 2} \times \frac{40}{10}} = \frac{1}{7}.$$

$\therefore$ Average waiting time,

$$W_q = \frac{\mu . (\lambda/\mu)^c}{(c-1)!(c\mu - \lambda)^2} . p_0 = \frac{20 . (3/2)^2}{1!(40-30)^2} \times \frac{1}{7} = \frac{9}{140} \text{ hours} = \frac{27}{7} \text{ minutes} = 3.86 \text{ minutes}.$$

(*b*) When the service time is 3.5 minutes,

service rate $\mu = \frac{1}{3.5}$/minute $= \frac{60}{3.5} = \frac{120}{7}$/hour,

$$\lambda = 30/\text{hour}, \frac{\lambda}{\mu} = \frac{7}{4}, c = 2.$$

$$\therefore \quad p_0 = \frac{1}{\sum_{n=0}^{c-1} \frac{(\lambda/\mu)^n}{n!} + \frac{(\lambda/\mu)^c}{c!} \cdot \frac{c\mu}{c\mu - \lambda}} = \frac{1}{\sum_{n=0}^{1} \frac{(7/4)^n}{n!} + \frac{(7/4)^2}{2!} \cdot \left(\frac{240/7}{240/7 - 30}\right)}$$

$$= \frac{1}{\left(1 + \frac{7}{4}\right) + \frac{49}{2 \times 16} \times 8} = \frac{1}{15}.$$

∴ Average waiting time,

$$W_q = \frac{\mu(\lambda/\mu)^c}{(c-1)!(c\mu - \lambda)^2} \cdot p_0 = \frac{120/7(7/4)^2}{1!(240/7 - 30)^2} \times \frac{1}{15} = \frac{343}{1,800} \text{ hours} = 11.43 \text{ minutes.}$$

EXAMPLE 10.10-5

At present a servicing department provides answers through one channel, which on average can deal with 24 enquiries/hour at a cost of £3 per enquiry. Increasingly the customers are complaining that they have to wait for a long time and the department is considering alternative arrangements. There is either a two-channel system costing £100/hour and service rate of 15/hour in each, or a three-channel system costing £125 per hour and service rate of 10/hour in each. Customers arrive at the rate of 20/hour. Average time a customer is in this system

$$= \frac{(\rho k)^k}{k!(1-\rho)^2 \cdot k\mu} p_0 + \frac{1}{\mu},$$

where
$$p_0 = \frac{k!(1-\rho)}{(\rho k)^k + k!(1-\rho)\left\{\sum_{n=0}^{k-1} \frac{(\rho k)^n}{n!}\right\}}.$$

You are required to calculate

(a) the average time a customer is in the system under the present arrangement,

(b) the extra charges per enquiry that would need to be made to recover the extra cost of each of the two arrangements proposed,

(c) the implied value of customer's time per hour if they agree to pay the extra cost of the two-channel system.

[ICMA (London) Nov., 1977]

Solution

Here, λ = 20/hour, μ = 24/hour.

(*a*) Average time a customer spends in the system,

$$W_s = \frac{1}{\mu - \lambda} = \frac{1}{24 - 20} = \frac{1}{4} \text{ hour} = 15 \text{ minutes.}$$

(*b*) Present cost = £3 × 24 = £72/hour.

(*i*) Cost of 2-service channel system = £ 100/hour.

∴ Extra charges/enquiry = £ (100 – 72)/20 = £ 1.40.

(*ii*) Cost of 3-service channel system = £ 125/hour.

∴ Extra charges/enquiry = £ (125 – 72)/20 = £ 2.65.

(*c*) Here μ = 15/hour, k = 2.

$$\therefore \quad \rho = \frac{\lambda}{k\mu} = \frac{20}{2 \times 15} = \frac{2}{3}.$$

$$\therefore \quad p_0 = \frac{2!\left(1-\frac{2}{3}\right)}{\left(\frac{2}{3}\times 2\right)^2 + 2!\left(1-\frac{2}{3}\right)\left\{\sum_{n=0}^{1}\frac{(2/3\times 2)^n}{n!}\right\}}$$

$$= \frac{2\times 1/3}{\frac{16}{9} + 2\times\frac{1}{3}.\left\{1+\frac{1}{1!}\left(\frac{2}{3}\times 2\right)^1\right\}}$$

$$= \frac{2/3}{\frac{16}{9}+\frac{2}{3}.\left\{1+\frac{4}{3}\right\}} = \frac{2}{3}\times\frac{9}{30} = \frac{1}{5} = 0.2.$$

Average time spent in the system,

$$W_s = \frac{\left(\frac{2}{3}\times 2\right)^2}{2!\left(1-\frac{2}{3}\right)^2 (2\times 15)}\times 0.2 + \frac{1}{15}$$

$$= \frac{16}{9}\times\frac{1}{2}\times\frac{9}{30}\times 0.2 + \frac{1}{15} = \frac{1.8}{15} = 0.12 \text{ hours} = 7.2 \text{ minutes.}$$

∴ Customer's time saved = 15 – 7.2 = 7.8 minutes.

∴ The implied value of customer's time per hour = £ 1.40 × $\frac{60}{7.8}$ = £ 10.77.

EXAMPLE 10.10-6

A branch of Punjab National Bank has only one typist. Since the typing work varies in length (number of pages to be typed), the typing rate is randomly distributed approximating a Poisson distribution with mean service rate of 8 letters/hour. The letters arrive at a rate of 5/hour during the entire 8-hour work day. If the waiting time cost of the letters is ₹ 1.50 per hour, find the average system time and the total lost time cost.

There is a possibility of either installing an additional typewriter of the same type or replacing the present one by a better and faster typewriter. The data are given below.

TABLE 10.7

	Service rate μ per hour	*Daily rental cost (₹)*
Present typewriter	8	2.50
Proposed typewriter	12	4.50

Suggest the better alternative.

Solution

Here, λ = 5/hour; μ = 8/hour.

Average system time with present typewriter,

$$W_s = \frac{1}{\mu-\lambda} = \frac{1}{8-5} = \frac{1}{3} \text{ hour.}$$

∴ Lost time cost/day = 8 × 5 × 1/3 × ₹ 1.50 = ₹ 20.

∴ Total cost per day of the present typewriter

= rental cost + lost time cost

= ₹ 2.50 + ₹ 20.00 = ₹ 22.50.

If proposed better and faster typewriter is installed

Average system time, $W_s = \frac{1}{\mu - \lambda} = \frac{1}{12-5} = \frac{1}{7}$ hour.

Lost time cost per day = $(8 \times 5) \times \frac{1}{7} \times 1.50 = ₹\ \frac{60}{7} = ₹\ 8.57.$

Total cost per day = rental cost + lost time cost

= ₹ 4.50 + ₹ 8.57 = ₹ 13.07.

If additional typewriter of the same type is installed

To calculate the waiting time in the system for two machines, first let us find p_0.

$$p_0 = \frac{1}{\sum_{n=0}^{n=c-1} \frac{1}{n!}\left(\frac{\lambda}{\mu}\right)^n + \frac{1}{c!}\left(\frac{\lambda}{\mu}\right)^c \frac{c\mu}{c\mu - \lambda}}$$

$$= \frac{1}{\sum_{n=0}^{n=1} \frac{1}{n!}\left(\frac{5}{8}\right)^n + \frac{1}{2!}\left(\frac{5}{8}\right)^2 . \frac{2 \times 8}{2 \times 8 - 5}}$$

$$= \frac{1}{\frac{1}{0!}\left(\frac{5}{8}\right)^0 + \frac{1}{1!}\left(\frac{5}{8}\right)^1 + \frac{1}{2!}\left(\frac{5}{8}\right)^2 . \frac{16}{11}}$$

$$= \frac{1}{1 + \frac{5}{8} + \frac{25}{88}} = \frac{1}{\frac{88 + 55 + 25}{88}} = \frac{88}{168} = \frac{11}{21}.$$

Expected time spent in the system,

$$W_s = \frac{\mu (\lambda / \mu)^c\, p_0}{(c-1)!\,(c\mu - \lambda)^2} + \frac{1}{\mu}$$

$$= \frac{8 \times (5/8)^2 \times 11/21}{(2-1)!\,(2 \times 8 - 5)^2} + \frac{1}{8}$$

$$= \frac{25/8 \times 11/21}{11 \times 11} + \frac{1}{8} = \frac{25}{88 \times 21} + \frac{1}{8} = \frac{32}{231} \text{ hours} = 8.3 \text{ minutes.}$$

∴ Total cost per day = rental cost of two typewriters + cost of lost time

$$= ₹\left(2 \times 2.50 + 8 \times 5 \times \frac{32}{231} \times 1.50\right)$$

$$= ₹\left(5 + \frac{640}{77}\right) = ₹\ (5 + 8.31) = ₹\ 13.31.$$

∴ It is slightly less expensive to install a single proposed better and faster typewriter.

EXAMPLE 10.10-7

Solve example 10.9-4.4 assuming two equal sized docks.

Solution

Here, $\lambda = 3/\text{hour}$, $\mu = 4/\text{hour}$, $\lambda/\mu = 3/4$, $c = 2$.

1. The probability that a truck has to wait for service,

$$p\,(n \geq c) = \frac{\mu\,.\,(\lambda/\mu)^c}{(c-1)\,!\,(c\mu - \lambda)}\,.\,p_0,$$

where
$$p_0 = \frac{1}{\sum_{n=0}^{c-1} \frac{(\lambda/\mu)^n}{n!} + \frac{1}{c!}\left(\frac{\lambda}{\mu}\right)^c . \frac{c\mu}{c\mu - \lambda}}$$

$$= \frac{1}{\sum_{n=0}^{n=1} \frac{1}{n!}(3/4)^n + \frac{1}{2!}(3/4)^2 . \frac{2 \times 4}{2 \times 4 - 3}}$$

$$= \frac{1}{\frac{1}{0!}(3/4)^0 + \frac{1}{1!}(3/4)^1 + \frac{1}{2} \times \frac{9}{16} \times \frac{8}{5}}$$

$$= \frac{1}{1 + \frac{3}{4} + \frac{9}{20}} = \frac{1}{\frac{20 + 15 + 9}{20}} = \frac{20}{44} = \frac{5}{11}.$$

$\therefore$
$$p\,(n \geq c) = \frac{4\,.(3/4)^2}{1!\,(4 \times 2 - 3)} \times \frac{5}{11} = \frac{4 \times 9}{16 \times 5} \times \frac{5}{11} = \frac{9}{44} = 0.205.$$

2. The waiting time of a truck that waits is,

$$W_n = \frac{\text{Expected waiting time of truck, } W_q}{\text{Probability that a truck actually has to wait, } p_c}.$$

$\therefore$
$$W_n = \frac{\mu\,.\,(\lambda/\mu)^c \cdot p_0}{(c-1)\,!\,(c\mu - \lambda)^2} \times \frac{1}{p_c}$$

$$= \frac{4\,(3/4)^2}{1!\,(2 \times 4 - 3)^2} \times \frac{5}{11} \times \frac{44}{9} = 0.2 \text{ hours} = 12 \text{ minutes.}$$

3. Total expected waiting time of company trucks per day

= Trucks/day × % of company trucks × Expected waiting time/truck

= (3 × 8) × (0.40) × W_q = 24 × 0.40 × (p_c × W_n)

= 24 × 0.40 × 9/44 × 0.2 = 0.393 hours = 23.58 minutes.

EXERCISES 10.5

1. Obtain the system of steady state equations and hence find the values of p_0 and p_n for (M/M/C) : (FCFS/∞/∞) queuing system. *[Delhi M.Sc. (OR) 1992, 90]*

2. For the case of s channels, Poisson arrivals and exponential service times, show that the probability that an arrival has to wait is given by

$$p(n \geq s) = \frac{\mu . \left(\frac{\lambda}{\mu}\right)^s . p_0}{(s-1)!(s\mu - \lambda)}.$$ *[Delhi U., 1976]*

3. Derive a relationship for expected number of customers in queue for infinite population, multi-channel Poisson arrival and exponential service system. *[P.U. B.E. (Prod.) Oct., 1993; B.E. (Mech.) 1992]*

4. Write short note on multi-channel queue with infinite customer population. [P.U. B.E. (Prod.) 2001]

5. Assuming $\lambda = 12$/hr, $\mu = 5$/hr, $c = 3$, $p_0 = 0.056$, calculate
   (*i*) the average time a customer is in the system,
   (*ii*) the average number of customers in the system,
   (*iii*) whether any time would be saved for customers if the 3-channel system with service rate of 5/hr is replaced by a single channel system with an average service rate of 15/hr.

   (*Ans.* (*i*) 25 min (*ii*) 4.98 (*iii*) 5 min)

6. A bank has two counters for withdrawals. One counter handles withdrawals of value less than ₹ 1,000 and the other counter ₹ 1,000 and above. Analysis of service time shows an exponential distribution with mean service time of 6 minutes per customer for each counter. Arrival of customers follows Poisson distribution with mean 8 per hour for the first counter and 5 per hour for the second counter.
   (*a*) What are the average waiting times per customer of each counter?
   (*b*) If each counter could handle all withdrawals irrespective of their value, how would the average waiting time change ? [Kuru. U. B.E. (Mech.) 1995]

   (*Ans.* (*a*) 24 min, 6 min (*b*) 4.2 min)

7. A supermarket has two girls ringing up sales at the counters. If the service time for each customer is exponential with mean 4 minutes, and if people arrive in a Poisson fashion at the rate of 10/hour,
   (*a*) What is the probability of having to wait for the service ?
   (*b*) What is the expected percentage of idle time for each girl ?
   (*c*) Find the average queue length and the average number of units in the system.

   [Chennai U., 2002]

   (*Ans.* (*a*) 0.167 (*b*) 67%.)

[**Hint.** (*b*) Fraction of time the service channels remain busy,

$$\rho = \frac{\lambda}{c\mu} = \frac{10}{2 \times 15} = \frac{1}{3}.$$

$\therefore$ Fraction of time the service channels remain idle $= 1 - \rho = \dfrac{2}{3}$.

$\therefore$ Expected percentage of idle time for each girl $= \dfrac{2}{3} \times 100 = 67\%$.]

8. A telephone exchange has two long-distance operators. The telephone company finds that during the peak load, long distance calls arrive in a Poisson fashion at an average rate of 15 per hour. The length of service on these calls is approximately exponentially distributed with mean length 5 minutes.
   (*a*) What is the probability that a subscriber will have to wait for his long distance call during the peak hours of the day ?
   (*b*) If the subscribers will wait and serviced in turn, what is the expected waiting time ?

   [Delhi U. (Math.) 1979]

   (*Ans.* (*a*) 0.48 (*b*) 3.2 minutes.)

9. An insurance company has three claim adjusters in its branch office. People with claims against the company are found to arrive in a Poisson fashion at an average rate of 20 per 8-hour day. The amount of time that an adjuster spends with a claimant is found to have an exponential distribution with mean service time 40 minutes. Claimants are processed in the order of their appearance.
   (*a*) How many hours per week can an adjuster expect to spend with the claimants ?
   (*b*) How much time, on the average, does a claimant spend in the branch office ?

   [P.U. B.E. (Mech.) Nov., 1993]

10. Four counters are being run on the frontier of a country to check the passports and necessary papers of the tourists. The tourists choose a counter at random. If arrivals are Poisson at the rate λ and the service time is exponential with parameter $\dfrac{\lambda}{2}$, what is the steady state average queue at each counter?

    [Meerut U. 1984; Agra M.Sc. (Stat.) 1973]

    (*Ans.* 4/23.)

11. A petroleum company is considering expansion of its one unloading facility at its refinery. Due to random variations in weather, loading delays and other factors, ships arriving at the refinery to unload crude oil arrive at a rate of 5 ships per week. The service rate is 10 ships per week. Assume that arrivals follow a Poisson process and the service time is exponential.
    (*a*) Find the average time a ship must wait before beginning to deliver its cargo to the refinery.
    (*b*) If a second berth is rented what will be the average number of ships waiting before being unloaded?
    (*c*) What would be the average time a ship would wait before being unloaded with two berths ?
    (*d*) What is the average number of berths at any specified time ?

(*Ans.* (*a*) $\frac{1}{10}$ week (*b*) $\frac{1}{30}$ (*c*) $\frac{1}{150}$ week (*d*) 1.5.)

12. Determine the minimum number of parallel servers needed in each of the following (Poisson arrival/departure) situations to guarantee that the operation of the queuing situation will be stable :
    (*a*) Customers arrive every five minutes and are served at the rate of 10 customers per hour.
    (*b*) The average interarrival time is 2 minutes and the average service time is 6 minutes.
    (*c*) The arrival rate is 30 customers per hour and the service rate per server is 40 customers per hour.

(*Ans.* (*a*) $c \geq 2$ (*b*) $c \geq 4$ (*c*) $c \geq 1$.)

13. An insurance company has 3 claim adjusters in its main office. Customers are found to arrive in Poisson manner at the rate of 5 per hour for settling claims against the company. The service time is found to have exponential distribution with mean 25 minutes. Claimants are processed on first come, first served basis. Calculate
    (*a*) The average number of customers in the system.
    (*b*) The average time a customer spends in the system.
    (*c*) The average queue length.
    (*d*) The average waiting time for customers.
    (*e*) The number of hours per week spent on performing the job.
    (*f*) The probability that at least a claim adjuster is waiting for the customer.
    (*g*) Expected number of idle claim adjusters at any specific moment.

(*Ans.* (*a*) 3.18 (*b*) 13.21 minutes (*c*) 1.1 (*d*) 38.2 minutes
(*e*) 27.76 hours/week (*f*) 0.52 (*g*) 0.92.)

14. You have been asked to consider three systems for providing service when customers arrive with mean arrival rate of 24 per hour.
    (*i*) A single-channel system with mean service rate of 30 per hour at ₹ 5 per customer with a fixed cost of ₹ 50 per hour.
    (*ii*) A two-channel system in which the channels are in parallel, each with mean service rate of 15 per hour at ₹ 4 per customer and a fixed cost of ₹ 30 per hour per channel.
    (*iii*) A three-parallel channel system, each with mean service rate of 10 per hour at ₹ 3 per customer and fixed cost of ₹ 25 per hour per channel. The systems are identical in all other aspects with a single queue. Average time a customer is in the system is given by

$$\frac{\mu \cdot \left(\frac{\lambda}{\mu}\right)^c}{(c-1)!\,(c\mu-\lambda)^2} \cdot p_0 + \frac{1}{\mu}$$

and $p_0 = 0.2$ for $c = 1$, 0.111 for $c = 2$ and 0.056 for $c = 3$. You are required to calculate
    (*a*) the average time a customer is in the system when 1, 2 and 3 channels are in use.
    (*b*) the most economical system to adopt if the value of the customer's time is ignored. Also find the total cost per hour of the three systems. [*ICWA (Final) June, 1992*]

(*Ans.* (*a*) 10, 11.1 and 12.5 minutes (*b*) ₹ 170, ₹ 156 and
₹ 147; 3-channel system.)

10.11 ERLANG FAMILY DISTRIBUTION

The preceding sections in this chapter assumed the service time to follow exponential distribution. Even though this distribution serves as a good approximation for many practical situations, the exponential assumption of service time gives only one parameter (μ) of possible service time distributions. This assumption is found to be unduly restrictive, partly because the exponential distribution has the property that the larger service times are less probable than smaller service times. Moreover, for exponential distribution, the standard deviation is equal to the mean. As there would be situations where the mean and standard deviation differ substantially, the models have to be made more general by using a distribution which conforms closely to the practical problems and yet retains the simplicity of the properties of exponential distribution. Erlang service time distribution fulfills all these conditions and is very useful in queuing problems. It considers the service of an item to be executed in a number of phases immediately following each other, all phases have to be completed before the second unit can enter the service channel.

When a unit has to pass through k stages for its service, then these k stages of servicing are called k phases. The distribution of servicing time in each of these phases will be an independent variable and the distribution of the total servicing time of a unit in the system will be some combined distribution of time in all these phases. The average time taken by the unit in each phase is $1/\mu k$ and the service time distribution is given by

$$f_t = (\mu k)^k \cdot t^{k-1} \cdot \frac{e^{-\mu kt}}{(k-1)!}, \quad 0 \le t \le \infty. \qquad \text{...(10.59)}$$

For different values of k, we get different distributions. In other words, we get a family of distributions. However, all these distributions of Erlang family have the same average service time $1/\mu$. The standard deviation (σ) of the kth member of the family is given by $\frac{1}{\mu\sqrt{k}}$ and the mode is located at $t = \frac{k-1}{\mu k}$.

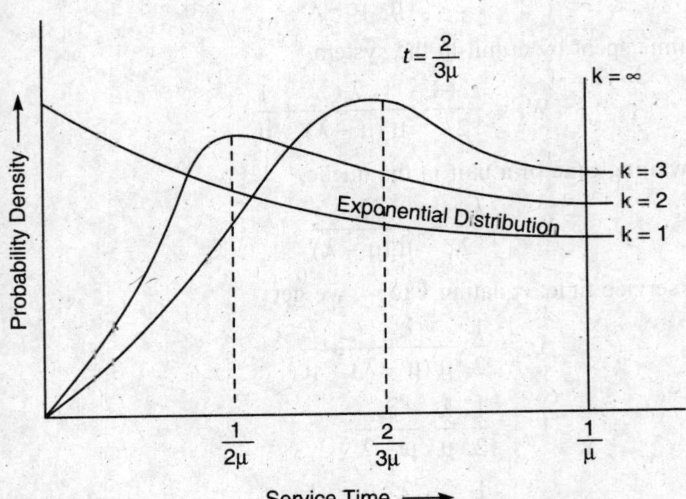

Fig. 10.6 The Erlang family of service time distribution.

Figure 10.6 shows the variation of density functions with increase in the value of k.

As seen in Fig. 10.6 when $k = 1$, mode is at $t = 0$, when $k = 2$ it is at $t = \frac{1}{2\mu}$ and when

$k = 3$, it is at $t = \dfrac{2}{3\mu}$.

For $k = \infty$, the variance is zero, service time is constant and is equal to $\dfrac{1}{\mu}$.

10.11-1 Model VII. $(M/E_k/1) : (FCFS/\infty/\infty)$ [Multi-Phase Service Model]

This is a queuing model with Poisson arrivals, Erlang service time with k phases, single channel, first come, first served discipline and infinite population.

In this model one unit is served in k phases. The arrival or departure of one unit, therefore, means an increase or decrease of k phases arranged in series one after the other in the system and the completion of service of one phase of a unit will mean the decrease of one phase in the system. If at any time there are m units waiting in the queue with one unit in service which has to still pass through s phases, then the total number of phases n in the system at that time will be given by

$$n = mk + s.$$

If μ denotes the number of units served per unit time, then $k\,\mu$ will be the number of phases served per unit time and we have

$$\lambda_n = \lambda,$$

$$\mu_n = \mu k.$$

The following formulae representing the characteristics of this model are written here without proof :

1. Average number of units in the system,

$$L_s = \frac{k+1}{2k}.\frac{\lambda}{\mu}.\frac{\lambda}{\mu-\lambda}+\frac{\lambda}{\mu}. \qquad ...(10.60)$$

2. Average number of units in the queue,

$$L_q = \frac{k+1}{2k}.\frac{\lambda}{\mu}.\frac{\lambda}{\mu-\lambda}. \qquad ...(10.61)$$

3. Average time spent by a unit in the system,

$$W_s = \frac{k+1}{2k}.\frac{\lambda}{\mu(\mu-\lambda)}+\frac{1}{\mu}. \qquad ...(10.62)$$

4. Average waiting time of a unit in the queue,

$$W_q = \frac{k+1}{2k}.\frac{\lambda}{\mu(\mu-\lambda)}. \qquad ...(10.63)$$

For constant service time, equating k to ∞, we get

$$L_s = \frac{1}{2}.\frac{\lambda^2}{\mu(\mu-\lambda)}+\frac{\lambda}{\mu}, \qquad ...(10.64)$$

$$L_q = \frac{1}{2}.\frac{\lambda}{\mu}.\frac{\lambda}{\mu-\lambda}, \qquad ...(10.65)$$

$$W_s = \frac{1}{2}.\frac{\lambda}{\mu(\mu-\lambda)}+\frac{1}{\mu}, \qquad ...(10.66)$$

$$W_q = \frac{1}{2}.\frac{1}{\mu}.\frac{\lambda}{\mu-\lambda}. \qquad ...(10.67)$$

When $k = 1$, the Erlang service time distribution reduces to exponential distribution and values of L_s, L_q, W_s and W_q are same as that of Model I discussed in section 10.9-2.

EXAMPLE 10.11-1.1

In a factory cafeteria the customers have to pass through three counters. The customers buy coupons at the first counter, select and collect the snacks at the second counter and collect tea at the third. The server at each counter takes on an average 1.5 minutes although the distribution of service time is approximately exponential. If the arrival of customers to the cafeteria is approximately Poisson at an average rate of 6 per hour, calculate

(a) the average time a customer spends waiting in the cafeteria,

(b) the average time of getting the service,

(c) the most probable time in getting the service.

Solution

Here no. of phases $k = 3$,

service time per phase = 1.5 minutes.

$\therefore$ Service time per customer = $1.5 \times 3 = 4.5$ minutes.

$$\therefore \qquad \mu = \frac{1}{4.5} \text{ customers/minute} = \frac{40}{3} \text{ customers/hour,}$$

$$\lambda = 6 \text{ customers/hour.}$$

(a) Average waiting time,

$$W_q = \frac{k+1}{2k} \cdot \frac{\lambda}{\mu} \cdot \frac{1}{\mu - \lambda} = \frac{3+1}{2 \times 3} \cdot \frac{6 \times 3}{40} \cdot \frac{1}{\frac{40}{3} - 6} = \frac{9}{220} \text{ hours} = \frac{27}{11} = 2.45 \text{ minutes.}$$

(b) Average time of getting the service *i.e.*, in collecting coupons, snacks, etc. is the mean of t when it is following the 3rd member of Erlang family ($\because k = 3$). Now average service time for an Erlang distribution is $1/\mu$.

$$\therefore \text{ Average time spent} = \frac{1}{\mu} = \frac{3}{40} \text{ hours} = 4.5 \text{ minutes.}$$

(c) The most probable time spent in getting the service is the modal value of t for the 3rd member of Erlang family.

$$\therefore \text{ Most probable time spent} = \frac{k-1}{\mu k} = \frac{3-1}{\frac{40}{3} \times 3} = \frac{1}{20} \text{ hour} = 3 \text{ minutes.}$$

EXAMPLE 10.11-1.2

Repairing a certain type of machine which breaks down in a given factory consists of 5 basic steps that must be performed sequentially. The time taken to perform each of the 5 steps is found to have an exponential distribution with mean 5 minutes and is independent of other steps. If these machines break down in a Poisson fashion at an average rate of two per hour and if there is only one repairman, what is the average idle time for each machine that has broken down ?

[*J.N.T.U. Hyderabad B.Tech. April, 2011*]

Solution

Here, no. of phases $k = 5$,

service time per phase = 5 minutes.

$\therefore$ Service time per unit = $5 \times 5 = 25$ minutes.

$$\therefore \qquad \mu = \frac{1}{25} \text{ units/minute} = \frac{12}{5} \text{ units/hour.}$$

$\lambda = 2$ units/hour.

Average idle time of the machine = Average time spent by the machine in the system,

$$W_s = \frac{k+1}{2k} \cdot \frac{\lambda}{\mu} \cdot \frac{1}{\mu - \lambda} + \frac{1}{\mu}$$

$$= \frac{5+1}{2 \times 5} \times \frac{2 \times 5}{12} \times \frac{1}{\frac{12}{5} - 2} + \frac{5}{12}$$

$$= \frac{1}{2} \times \frac{5}{2} + \frac{5}{12} = \frac{20}{12} = \frac{5}{3} \text{ hours} = 100 \text{ minutes.}$$

EXAMPLE 10.11-1.3

A colliery working one shift per day uses a large number of locomotives which break down at random intervals, on average one failing per 8-hour shift. The fitter carries out a standard maintenance schedule on each faulty locomotive. Each of the 5 main parts of this schedule takes an average of 1/2 hour but the time varies widely. How much time will the fitter have for other tasks and what is the average time a locomotive is out of service ?

Solution

Here, $k = 5$, $\lambda = \frac{1}{8}$/hour, service time per part $= \frac{1}{2}$ hour.

$\therefore$ Service time per locomotive $= \frac{5}{2}$ hours. $\quad \therefore \mu = \frac{2}{5}$/hour.

Fraction of time the fitter will have for other tasks = Fraction of time for which the fitter is idle

$$= 1 - \frac{\lambda}{\mu} = 1 - \frac{1/8}{2/5} = 1 - \frac{5}{16} = \frac{11}{16}.$$

$\therefore$ Time the fitter will have for other tasks in a day = 11/16 × 8 = 5.5 hours.

Average time a locomotive is out of service

= Average time spent by the locomotive in the system

$$= \frac{k+1}{2k} \cdot \frac{\lambda}{\mu} \cdot \frac{1}{\mu - \lambda} + \frac{1}{\mu} = \frac{5+1}{2 \times 5} \cdot \frac{1/8}{2/5} \cdot \frac{1}{\frac{2}{5} - \frac{1}{8}} + \frac{5}{2}$$

$$= \frac{6}{10} \times \frac{5}{16} \times \frac{40}{11} + \frac{5}{2} = 3.18 \text{ hours.}$$

EXAMPLE 10.11-1.4

An airline maintenance base has facilities only for overhauling one airline engine at a time. Hence, to return the airplanes into use at the earliest, the policy is to stagger the overhauling of the 4 engines of each airplane. In other words, only one engine is overhauled each time an airplane comes into the shop. Under this policy, airplanes have arrivals according to a Poisson process at a mean rate of l/day. The time required for an engine overhaul has an exponential distribution with a mean of 1/2 day.

A proposal has been made to change the policy so as to overhaul all four engines consecutively each time an aeroplane comes into the shop. It is pointed out that although this will quadruple the expected service time, each plane would need to come into the shop only one-fourth time as often. Compare the two alternatives on a meaningful basis.

Solution

The two alternatives will be compared on the basis of the waiting time cost of the airplanes requiring overhauling.

First alternative: This is M/M/1 : FCFS/∞/∞ queuing system.

∴ Expected number of airplanes in the system,

$$L_s = \frac{\lambda}{\mu - \lambda} = \frac{1}{2-1} = 1.$$

Second alternative: This is $M/E_k/1$: FCFS/∞/∞ queuing system.

Here, $\lambda = \frac{1}{4}$ airplanes/day,

no. of phases, $k = 4$,

mean service time per airplane $= \frac{1}{2} \times 4 = 2$ days.

∴ Mean service rate, $\mu = \frac{1}{2}$ airplane per day.

∴ Expected number of airplanes in the system,

$$L_s = \frac{k+1}{2k}\frac{\lambda}{\mu}.\frac{\lambda}{\mu-\lambda} + \frac{\lambda}{\mu} = \frac{5}{8} \times \frac{1/4}{1/2} \times \frac{1/4}{1/2 - 1/4} + \frac{1/4}{1/2}$$

$$= \frac{5}{8} \times \frac{1}{2} \times 1 + \frac{1}{2} = \frac{13}{16}.$$

Comparing the two, the second alternative results in smaller no. of planes requiring overhauling and hence lowers the waiting time cost and should, therefore, be adopted.

EXAMPLE 10.11-1.5

In a car manufacturing plant, a loading crane takes exactly 10 minutes to load a car into a wagon and again come back to the position of loading another car. If the arrivals of cars is a Poisson stream at an average of one every 20 minutes, calculate the average waiting time of a car.

Solution

Here, $\lambda = \frac{1}{20}$ cars/minute $= \frac{1}{20} \times 60 = 3$ cars/hour, service rate is constant, being equal to 6/hour. Therefore, $k = \infty$ and the average waiting time of a car is given by

$$W_q = \frac{1}{2}.\frac{\lambda}{\mu}.\frac{1}{\mu - \lambda}$$

$$= \frac{1}{2}.\frac{3}{6}.\frac{1}{6-3} = \frac{1}{12} \text{ hour} = 5 \text{ minutes.}$$

EXERCISES 10.6

1. Describe the use of Erlang distribution in queuing process.

[*Kerala U. M.Sc. (Stat.) 1983*]

2. Explain Erlang's queuing model and derive expressions for
   (*a*) the expected number of units in the system,
   (*b*) the expected number of units in the queue.

[*Bhopal U. M.Sc. (Stat.) 1985; Delhi U. M.Sc. (OR) 1992*]

3. Prove that for the Erlang distribution with parameters $\mu + k$, the mode is at $t = \dfrac{k-1}{\mu k}$.

[*Kuru. U. B.E. (Mech.) June, 2012*]

4. A hospital clinic has a doctor examining patients brought in for a general check-up. The doctor averages 4 minutes on each phase of the check-up although the distribution of time spent on each phase is approximately exponential. If each patient goes through four phases in the check-up and if the arrivals of the patients at the doctor's office are approximately Poisson at an average rate of 3 per hour, what is the average time spent by a patient waiting in the doctor's office? What is the average time spent in the examination ? What is the most probable time spent in the examination ? [*Delhi M.Sc. (Math.) 1973*]

(*Ans.* 16 minutes, 12 minutes.)

5. A warehouse in a small state receives orders for a certain item and sends them by a truck as soon as possible to the customers. The orders arrive in a Poisson fashion at a mean rate of 0.9 per day. Only one item at a time can be shipped by a truck from the warehouse, which is located in the central part of the state. Because the customers are located in various places in the state, the distribution of service time in days has a distribution with probability density $4t\, e^{-2t}$. What is the expected delay between the arrival of an order and the arrival of the item to the customer ? Service time here implies the time the truck takes to load, gets to the customer, unloads and returns to the warehouse. Loading and unloading times are small as compared to the travel time.

[**Hint.** $\mu = 1, \lambda = 0.9, k = 2.$

$$W_q = \frac{k+1}{2k} \cdot \frac{\lambda}{\mu(\mu-\lambda)} = \frac{3}{4} \times \frac{0.9}{0.1} = 6.75 \text{ days},$$

$$W_s = \frac{k+1}{2k} \cdot \frac{\lambda}{\mu(\mu-\lambda)} + \frac{1}{\mu} = \frac{27}{4} + \frac{1}{1} = 7.75 \text{ days.}]$$

6. A barber with one man takes *exactly* 25 minutes to complete one hair cut. If customers arrive in a Poisson fashion at an average rate of one every 40 minutes, how long on the average must a customer wait for service? [*J.N.T.U. Hyderabad B.Tech. Nov., 2010*]

(*Ans.* 20.8 minutes.)

7. At a certain airport it takes *exactly* 5 minutes to land an airplane, once it is given the signal to land. Although incoming planes have scheduled arrival times, the wide variability in arrival times produces an effect which makes the incoming planes appear to arrive in a Poisson fashion at an average rate of 6/hour. This produces occasional stack-ups at the airport which can be dangerous and costly. Under these circumstances, how much time will a pilot expect to spend circling the field waiting to land ?

[*Delhi M.Sc. (Math.) 1972*]

(*Ans.* 2.5 minutes.)

8. In a certain bank, the customers arrive according to Poisson distribution with a mean of 4 per hour. From observations on the teller's performance, the mean service time is estimated to be 10 minutes, with a variance of 25 minutes. It is felt that the Erlang would be a reasonable assumption for the distribution of the teller's service time. Also it is assumed that there is no limit on the number of customers. Bank officials wish to know, on the average, how long a customer must wait until he gets the service, and how many customers are waiting for service ? (*Ans.* 12.5 minutes, 5/6.)

[**Hint.** Use $\mu = \dfrac{1}{10}$ and $\sigma^2 = \dfrac{1}{k\mu^2} = 25$ to get $k = 4$.]

9. A barber runs his own saloon. It takes *exactly* 25 minutes to complete one hair cut. Customers arrive in a Poisson fashion with average rate of one every 35 minutes.
   (*a*) For what per cent of time would the barber be idle ?
   (*b*) What is the average time a customer spends in the shop ?

(*Ans.* (*a*) 29% (*b*) 56.25 minutes.)

[**Hint.** (*a*) Find $p_0 = 1 - \dfrac{\lambda}{\mu} = 1 - 0.71 = 0.29$. (*b*) Find $W_s = \dfrac{k+1}{2k} \cdot \dfrac{\lambda}{\mu(\mu-\lambda)} + \dfrac{1}{\mu}$, where $k = \infty$

$$= \frac{\lambda}{2\mu(\mu-\lambda)} + \frac{1}{\mu}.]$$

10. The repair of a lathe requires four steps to be completed one after another in a certain order. The time taken to perform each step follows exponential distribution with mean 10 minutes and is independent of the other steps. Machine breakdown follows Poisson process with mean 3 breakdowns per hour. Answer the following :
    (*a*) What is the expected idle time of the machine, assuming there is only one repairman available in the workshop ?
    (*b*) What is the expected number of brokendown machines in the queue ?
    (*Ans.* (*a*) 16.25 minutes (*b*) 0.3.)
11. A tailoring shop with one man takes *exactly* one day to stitch a suit. Customers' arrival follows a Poisson pattern with mean 1 in every 2 days. How long, on an average, a customer is expected to wait in such a situation ? (*Ans.* Half a day.)
12. At an automobile workshop, maintenance of vehicles is done in two stages. Service time of each stage is 1 hour with exponential form. If one vehicle is brought for maintenance every 4 hours at the workshop, determine expected number of vehicles in the queue and in the system ; expected waiting time in the queue and in the system.
    $\left(Ans.\ \frac{1}{16}, \frac{5}{16}; \frac{1}{4} \text{ hr}, \frac{5}{4} \text{ hr.}\right)$
13. Repair of a certain type of machine requires 3 steps to be completed sequentially. The time taken to perform each step follows an exponential distribution with mean $6\frac{2}{3}$ minutes and is independent of other steps. The machine breakdown follows a Poisson process at a rate of 1 per 2 hours. Assuming that there is only one repairman, find
    (*a*) the expected idle time of a machine.
    (*b*) the average waiting time of a brokendown machine in the queue
    (*c*) the expected number of brokendown machines in the queue.
    (*d*) the average number of machines that are not in operation.
    $\left(Ans.\ W_s = 22\frac{2}{3} \text{ minutes}, W_q = 2\frac{2}{3} \text{ minutes}, L_q = \frac{1}{45}, L_s = \frac{17}{90}.\right)$
14. The arrival of vehicles at a certain service facility is according to Poisson distribution with an average time of 120 minutes between two consecutive arrivals.
    The service is needed at two points, namely, A and B. The length of service needed to the vehicles at A is assumed to be exponentially distributed with mean of 35 minutes. The length of service needed to the vehicles at B is also assumed to be exponentially distributed with mean of 25 minutes. Determine
    (*a*) the probability that a vehicle arriving at the station will have to wait at both the points A and B.
    (*b*) the probability that a vehicle arriving at the station will have to spend at least 75 minutes in the system for the service.
    (*c*) the average waiting time for the vehicles at points A and B for the service.
    [*P.T.U. MBA Dec., 2003*]

10.12 MACHINE REPAIR PROBLEM

This problem, in the simplest form, consists of a system having n machines and a single mechanic to repair them. Since n is finite, it forms a finite population model. When a machine breaks down, it is repaired by the mechanic and if during this time another machine breaks down, it can be attended by the mechanic only afler the first one is repaired and, therefore, it forms a queue. If at any instant out of total n machines, m are in the queuing system for repair, then $(n - m)$ machines will be working and the breakdown rate will be proportional to $(n - m)$.

For any system, the rate of breakdown of machines depends upon the input distribution and the servicing time of the machine depends upon the output distribution. With one mechanic, the problem will be of single-channel and with more than one mechanic, it will be a multi-channel one. Further, if the machine is repaired in k phases, the output distribution will be Erlangian distribution.

10.12-1 Model VIII (M/M/1) : (GD/*m*/*n*)

Let there be n machines in the system. The arrival rate and service rate follow Poisson distribution with parameters λ and μ respectively. Now, if any machine is in working order at time t, then the probability that it will join the queue for repair in time dt will be $\lambda\, dt$. Likewise, if a machine is chosen for service at time t, then the probability that its service will be completed in time dt will be $\mu\, dt$.

Suppose that at any time t, m machines are broken down and are forming a queue for servicing, where $m \le n$. Let us first find $p_m\,(t + dt)$. This can happen in the following three exclusive ways:

TABLE 10.8

Event	*No. of units at time t*	*No. of arrivals in time dt*	*No. of services in time dt*	*No. of units at time t + dt*
1	m	0	0	m
2	$m - 1$	1	0	m
3	$m + 1$	0	1	m

$\therefore$ Probability of event 1 $= p_m(t)\,.\,(1 - \lambda_m dt)\,(1 - \mu dt)$

$= p_m(t)\,[1 - (\lambda_m + \mu)dt]$.

Similarly, probability of event 2

$= p_{m-1}(t)\,.\,\lambda_{m-1}dt\,.\,(1 - \mu dt)$

$= p_{m-1}(t)\,.\,\lambda_{m-1}dt$, and

probability of event 3 $= p_{m+1}(t)\,.\,[1 - \lambda_{m+1}(t)]\,.\,\mu dt = p_{m+1}(t)\,.\,\mu dt$.

$$\therefore \quad p_m(t + dt) = p_m(t)\,[1 - (\lambda_m + \mu)dt] + p_{m-1}(t)\,.\,\lambda_{m-1}dt + p_{m+1}(t)\,.\,\mu dt$$

$$\text{or} \quad \frac{p_m(t + dt) - p_m(t)}{dt} = -(\lambda_m + \mu)\,p_m(t) + \lambda_{m-1}\,p_{m-1}(t) + \mu\,.\,p_{m+1}(t).$$

When $dt \to 0$, we have

$$\frac{d}{dt}[p_m(t)] = -(\lambda_m + \mu)p_m(t) + \lambda_{m-1}\,.\,p_{m-1}(t) + \mu p_{m+1}(t).$$

For the steady state system,

$$0 = -(\lambda_m + \mu)p_m + \lambda_{m-1}\cdot p_{m-1} + \mu p_{m+1}.$$

Now, as the arrival rate is proportional to the number of machines working in order,

$$\lambda_m = (n - m)\,\lambda,$$

$$\lambda_{m-1} = (n - \overline{m - 1})\,\lambda = (n - m + 1)\,\lambda,$$

$$\lambda_n = 0.$$

Hence we have,

$$0 = -[(n - m)\lambda + \mu]p_m + (n - m + 1)\lambda\,.\,p_{m-1} + \mu p_{m+1}$$

$$\text{or} \quad [(n - m)\lambda + \mu]p_m = (n - m + 1)\lambda\,.\,p_{m-1} + \mu p_{m+1} \text{ for } 1 \le m < n. \qquad ...(10.68)$$

Likewise, when $m = 0$, we can write the expression for $p_0\,(t + dt)$ and following the above steps, it can be shown that

$$n\lambda p_0 = \mu p_1, \text{ for } m = 0. \qquad ...(10.69)$$

Further, when $m = n$,

$$p_n(t + dt) = p_n(t)\,[1 - (\lambda_n + \mu)dt] + p_{n-1}(t)\,.\,\lambda_{n-1}(t),$$

which can ultimately be expressed as

$$\mu p_n = \lambda p_{n-1}, \text{ for } m = n. \qquad ...(10.70)$$

When $m = 1$, equation (10.68) yields

$$[n-1)\lambda + \mu]p_1 = n\lambda p_0 + \mu p_2 = \mu p_1 + \mu p_2$$

or $$(n-1)\lambda p_1 = \mu p_2. \quad ...(10.71)$$

When $m = 2$, equation (10.68) yields

$$[(n-2)\lambda + \mu]p_2 = (n-1)\lambda \,.\, p_1 + \mu p_3 = \mu p_2 + \mu p_3$$

or $$(n-2)\lambda \,.\, p_2 = \mu p_3. \quad ...(10.72)$$

Similarly, for $m = 3, 4, ..., n-2, n-1$.

Thus we get the recurrence equation

$$(n-m)\,\lambda\, p_m = \mu p_{m+1}, \text{ for } m = 0, 1, 2, ..., n-1. \quad ...(10.73)$$

Substituting $m = n-1, n-2, ..., 1$, in equation (10.73), we get

$$\lambda \,.\, p_{n-1} = \mu p_n \text{ or } p_{n-1} = \frac{\mu}{\lambda} \cdot p_n,$$

$$2\lambda p_{n-2} = \mu p_{n-1} \text{ or } p_{n-2} = \frac{1}{2} \cdot \frac{\mu}{\lambda} \cdot p_{n-1} = \frac{1}{2!}\left(\frac{\mu}{\lambda}\right)^2 \cdot p_n,$$

$$3\lambda p_{n-3} = \mu p_{n-2} \text{ or } p_{n-3} = \frac{1}{3.2}\left(\frac{\mu}{\lambda}\right)^3 p_n = \frac{1}{3!}\left(\frac{\mu}{\lambda}\right)^3 \cdot p_n,$$

$$\vdots$$

$$p_{n-k} = \frac{1}{k!}\left(\frac{\mu}{\lambda}\right)^k \cdot p_n,$$

$$\vdots$$

$$p_0 = \frac{1}{n!}\left(\frac{\mu}{\lambda}\right)^n \cdot p_n. \quad ...(10.74)$$

Now $$\sum_{m=0}^{n} p_m = 1$$

i.e., $p_0 + p_1 + p_2 + ... + p_n = 1$

or $$\frac{1}{n!}\left(\frac{\mu}{\lambda}\right)^n p_n + \frac{1}{(n-1)!} \cdot \left(\frac{\mu}{\lambda}\right)^{n-1} \cdot p_n + ... + p_n = 1$$

or $$p_n = \frac{1}{1 + \frac{\mu}{\lambda} + ... + \frac{1}{(n-1)!} \cdot \left(\frac{\mu}{\lambda}\right)^{n-1} + \frac{1}{n!}\left(\frac{\mu}{\lambda}\right)^n}. \quad ...(10.75)$$

Here p_0 is the probability that all the machines in the system are in the working order and the repairman is idle.

Expected queue length

If at any time t there are m machines for repair in the queue including the one in service, then the queue length will be $(m-1)$ and the average queue length will be,

$$L_q = \sum_{m=1}^{n} (m-1)\, p_m$$

$$= \sum_{m=1}^{n} m p_m - \sum_{m=1}^{n} p_m$$

$$= \sum_{m=0}^{n} m p_m - \sum_{m=1}^{n} p_m \quad (\because m p_m = 0 \text{ or } m = 0)$$

$$= \sum_{m=0}^{n} mp_m - \left[\sum_{m=0}^{n} p_m - p_0\right]$$

$$= \sum_{m=0}^{n} mp_m - 1 + p_0. \quad \left(\because \sum_{m=0}^{n} p_m = 1\right) \qquad \text{...(10.76)}$$

Now from equation (10.73), we have by taking sum on both sides,

$$\sum_{m=0}^{n} (n-m)\lambda p_m = \sum_{m=0}^{n} \mu p_{m+1}$$

or

$$\lambda \sum_{m=0}^{n} mp_m = n\lambda \sum_{m=0}^{n} p_m - \mu \sum_{m=0}^{n} p_{m+1}$$

$$= n\lambda - \mu \sum_{m=0}^{n-1} p_{m+1} + \mu p_{m+1}$$

$$= n\lambda - \mu \sum_{m=0}^{n-1} p_{m+1}$$

($\because$ There are only m machines in the system)

$$= n\lambda - \mu\,(p_1 + p_2 + ... + p_n)$$

$$= n\lambda - \mu\,[(p_0 + p_1 + p_2 ... + p_n) - p_0]$$

$$= n\lambda - \mu\,(1 - p_0). \qquad \left(\because \sum_{m=0}^{n} p_m = 1\right)$$

$$\therefore \quad \sum_{m=0}^{n} mp_m = n - \frac{\mu}{\lambda}(1 - p_0).$$

Therefore, substituting the value of $\sum_{m=0}^{n} mp_m$ in equation (10.76), we have

$$L_q = n - \frac{\mu}{\lambda}(1 - p_0) - (1 - p_0)$$

$$= n - \left(\frac{\mu}{\lambda} + 1\right)(1 - p_0).$$

10.12-2 Model IX (M/M/c) : (GD/*m*/*n*)

Here, n : the total number of machines in the system,
c : number of repairmen $(c < n)$,
m : number of machines out of order at any time.

There can be two possibilities in this system.

Case I. $m \le c$: In this case no machine has to wait for repair but there is possibility that some repairmen may sit idle, this number being equal to $(c - m)$.

Case II. $m > c$: In this case, at any time t, c machines will be in service and $(m - c)$ will be waiting in line. If λ and μ are the parameters of input and output distribution, then

$$\lambda_m = n\lambda,\ \mu_m = 0 \qquad \text{for } m = 0, \qquad \text{...(10.77)}$$

$$\lambda_m = (n-m)\lambda,\ \mu_m = m\mu \qquad \text{for } 1 \le m \le c, \qquad \text{...(10.78)}$$

and

$$\lambda_m = (n-m)\lambda,\ \mu_m = c\mu \qquad \text{for } c \le m \le n. \qquad \text{...(10.79)}$$

Let us first find $p_m(t + dt)$ for $1 \le m \le c$. This can happen in the following three exclusive ways:

TABLE 10.9

Event	No. of units at time t	No. of arrivals in time dt	No. of services in time dt	No. of units at time $t + dt$
1	m	0	0	m
2	$m-1$	1	0	m
3	$m+1$	0	1	m

Probability of event 1 $= p_m(t)\,(1 - \lambda_m dt)\,(1 - \mu_m dt)$

$$= p_m(t)\,[1 - (n-m)\lambda\,.\,dt]\,[1 - m\mu\,.\,dt]$$

$$= p_m(t)\left[1 - \{(n-m)\lambda + m\mu\}dt\right].$$

Similarly, probability of event 2

$$= p_{m-1}(t)\,(\lambda_{m-1}dt)\,(1 - \mu_{m-1}dt)$$

$$= p_{m-1}(t)\,[(n - \overline{m-1})\,\lambda dt]\,[1 - (m-1)\mu\,.\,dt]$$

$$= p_{m-1}(t)\,.\,(n - m + 1)\lambda dt, \text{ and}$$

probability of event 3 $= p_{m+1}(t)\,[1 - (n - \overline{m+1})\,\lambda dt]\,.\,[(m+1)\mu dt]$

$$= p_{m+1}(t)\,.\,[(m+1)\mu dt].$$

$\therefore$
$$p_m(t+dt) = p_m(t)\,[1 - \{(n-m)\lambda + m\mu\}dt] + p_{m-1}(t)\,.\,(n-m+1)\lambda dt + p_{m+1}(t)\,.\,[(m+1)\mu dt].$$

Taking the limits $dt \to 0$, we get

$$\frac{d}{dt}[p_m(t)] = [-(n-m)\lambda + m\mu]p_m(t) + (n-m+1)\lambda\,.\,p_{m-1}(t) + (m+1)\mu\,.\,p_{m+1}(t), \text{ for } 1 \le m \le c. \quad \text{... (10.80)}$$

Similarly, $p_m(t+dt)$ for $c < m \le n$ can be written as

$$p_m(t+dt) = p_m(t)\,[1 - \{(n-m)\lambda + c\mu\}dt] + p_{m-1}(t)\,.\,(n-m+1)\lambda dt + p_{m+1}(t)\,.\,c\mu dt,$$

which when $dt \to 0$, gives

$$\frac{d}{dt}[p_m(t)] = [-(n-m)\lambda + c\mu]p_m(t) + (n-m+1)\lambda\,.\,p_{m-1}(t) + c\mu p_{m+1}(t), \text{ for } c < m \le n. \quad \text{...(10.81)}$$

Finally, $p_0\,(t+dt)$ can be expressed as

$$p_0(t+dt) = p_0(t)\,.\,(1 - \lambda_0 dt)\,.\,1 + p_1(t)\,.\,(1 - \lambda_1 dt)\,.\,\mu_1 dt$$

$$= p_0(t)\,.\,[1 - n\lambda\,.\,dt] + p_1(t)\,.\,\mu dt.$$

Taking the limits $dt \to 0$, we get

$$\frac{d}{dt}[p_0(t)] = -\,n\lambda\,.\,p_0(t) + \mu p_1(t), \text{ for } m = 0. \quad \text{...(10.82)}$$

For steady state system, equations (10.80), (10.81) and (10.82) reduce to

$$\left.\begin{aligned} n\lambda\,p_0 &= \mu p_1, \quad \text{for } m = 0;\\ [(n-m)\lambda - m\mu]p_m &= (n-m+1)\lambda\,.\,p_{m-1} + (m+1)\mu\,p_{m+1}, \quad \text{for } 1 \le m \le c;\\ \text{and } [(n-m)\lambda - c\mu]p_m &= (n-m+1)\lambda\,.\,p_{m-1} + c\mu p_{m+1}, \quad \text{for } c < m \le n. \end{aligned}\right] \quad \text{...(10.83)}$$

Equations (10.83) on simplification yield

$$\left.\begin{aligned} n\lambda p_0 &= \mu p_1 \quad \textit{for } m = 0;\\ (n-m)\lambda p_m &= (m+1)\mu p_{m+1}, \quad \textit{for } m \le c;\\ (n-m)\lambda p_m &= c\mu p_{m+1}, \quad \textit{for } m > c. \end{aligned}\right] \quad \text{...(10.84)}$$

To find the solution of steady state equations:
From the first equation of (10.84),

$$p_1 = n \cdot \frac{\lambda}{\mu} \cdot p_0.$$

Putting $m = 1$ in the second equation of (10.84),

$$2\mu p_2 = (n-1) \cdot \lambda p_1$$

or

$$2p_2 = (n-1) \cdot \frac{\lambda}{\mu} \cdot p_1.$$

Putting $m = 2$ in the second equation of (10.84),

$$3p_3 = (n-2)\frac{\lambda}{\mu} p_2$$

$$\vdots$$

$$(m+1)p_{m+1} = (n-m)\frac{\lambda}{\mu} p_m, \quad \text{for } 0 \le m \le c.$$

Similarly, from third equation of (10.84), we get

$$cp_{m+1} = (n-m)\frac{\lambda}{\mu} \cdot p_m, \qquad \text{for } c < m \le n.$$

Proceeding as in model VII, we get the following solution:

$$p_0 = \frac{1}{\sum_{m=0}^{c} {}^nC_m \left(\frac{\lambda}{\mu}\right)^m + \sum_{m=c+1}^{n} {}^nC_m \frac{(\lambda/\mu)^m \cdot m!}{c^{m-c} \cdot c!}}. \quad \text{...(10.85)}$$

$$p_m = \begin{cases} {}^nC_m \cdot \left(\frac{\lambda}{\mu}\right)^m \cdot p_0, & \text{for } 0 \le m \le c, \quad \text{...(10.86)} \\ {}^nC_m \frac{\left(\frac{\lambda}{\mu}\right)^m \cdot m!}{c^{m-c} \cdot c!} \cdot p_0, & \text{for } c < m \le n. \quad \text{...(10.87)} \end{cases}$$

10.13 MODEL X. POWER SUPPLY MODEL

This problem can also be analysed as a queuing problem. Let there be an electric circuit supplying power to 'a' consumers. Further, let the requirement and supply schedules follow Poisson distribution with parameters λ and μ respectively.

If at any time t, there are n consumers in the queue for the supply of current, then

$$\left.\begin{aligned} \lambda_n &= (a-n)\lambda, \\ \mu &= n\mu. \end{aligned}\right] \qquad \text{for } 0 \le n \le a.$$

The difference equations defining the system can be constructed as in section 10.9-2 to yield

$$\begin{aligned} p_0(t+dt) &= p_0(t)\,[1-\lambda_0 dt] + p_1(t) \cdot \mu_1 dt \\ &= p_0(t)\,[1-a\lambda dt] + p_1(t) \cdot \mu dt, \qquad \text{for } n = 0. \\ p_n(t+dt) &= p_n(t)\,[1-\lambda_n dt]\,[1-\mu_n dt] + p_{n-1}(t) \cdot \lambda_{n-1} \cdot dt + p_{n+1}(t) . \mu_{n+1} . dt \\ &= p_n(t)\,[1-(\lambda_n+\mu_n)dt] + p_{n-1}(t) \cdot \lambda_{n-1} \cdot dt + p_{n+1}(t) \cdot \mu_{n+1} \cdot dt \\ &= p_n(t)[1-\{(a-n)\lambda + n\mu\}dt] + p_{n-1}(t) \cdot (a-n+1)\lambda dt \\ &\qquad + p_{n+1}(t) \cdot (n+1)\mu \cdot dt, \text{ for } 1 \le n \le a-1, \end{aligned}$$

and

$$p_n(t+dt) = p_n(t)[1-a\mu dt] + p_{n-1}(t)\,(a-a+1)\lambda dt$$

$$= p_n(t)[1 - a\mu dt] + p_{n-1}(t) \,.\, \lambda dt, \text{ for } n = a.$$

Taking the limit as $dt \to 0$ and assuming a steady state system, the above equations yield

$$a\lambda p_0 = \mu p_1, \quad \text{for } n = 0;$$

$$[(a-n)\lambda + n\mu]p_n = (a-n+1)\lambda . p_{n-1} + (n+1) . \mu p_{n+1}, \text{ for } 1 \le n < a-1;$$

and
$$a\mu p_a = \lambda p_{a-1}, \text{ for } n = a.$$

The above three equations give the recurrence formula

$$(a-n)\lambda \,.\, p_n = (n+1)\mu \,.\, p_{n+1}, \qquad \text{for } n = 0, 1, 2, ..., a.$$

∴ For
$$n = 0, p_1 = a \,.\, \frac{\lambda}{\mu} \cdot p_0,$$

for
$$n = 1, p_2 = \frac{a-1}{2} \cdot \frac{\lambda}{\mu} \cdot p_1 = \frac{a(a-1)}{2!}\left(\frac{\lambda}{\mu}\right)^2 \cdot p_0,$$

for
$$n = 2, p_3 = \frac{a-2}{3} \cdot \frac{\lambda}{\mu} \cdot p_2 = \frac{a(a-1)(a-2)}{3!}\left(\frac{\lambda}{\mu}\right)^3 \cdot p_0,$$

$$\vdots$$

$$p_n = \frac{a-(n-1)}{n} \cdot \frac{\lambda}{\mu} \cdot p_{n-1}$$

$$= \frac{a(a-1)(a-2)\ldots(a-n+1)}{n!}\left(\frac{\lambda}{\mu}\right)^n p_0,$$

and
$$p_a = \frac{a(a-1)(a-2)\ldots 2.1}{a!} \cdot \left(\frac{\lambda}{\mu}\right)^a \cdot p_0 = \left(\frac{\lambda}{\mu}\right)^a \cdot p_0 .$$

Now
$$\sum_{n=0}^{a} p_n = 1.$$

$$\therefore \quad p_0 + p_1 + p_2 + \ldots + p_a = 1$$

or
$$p_0\left[1 + a\left(\frac{\lambda}{\mu}\right) + \frac{a(a-1)}{2!}\left(\frac{\lambda}{\mu}\right)^2 + \ldots + \left(\frac{\lambda}{\mu}\right)^a\right] = 1$$

or
$$p_0\left(1 + \frac{\lambda}{\mu}\right)^a = 1.$$

$$\therefore \quad p_0 = \frac{1}{\left(1 + \frac{\lambda}{\mu}\right)^a} = \left(\frac{\mu}{\mu + \lambda}\right)^a . \qquad \text{...(10.88)}$$

$$\therefore \quad p_n = \frac{a(a-1)(a-2)\ldots(a-n+1)}{n!} \cdot \left(\frac{\lambda}{\mu}\right)^a \cdot \left(\frac{\mu}{\mu+\lambda}\right)^c$$

$$= \frac{a!}{n!(a-n)!} \cdot \left(\frac{\lambda}{\mu}\right)^n \cdot \left(\frac{\mu}{\lambda+\mu}\right)^a = \frac{a!}{n!(a-n)!} \cdot \left(\frac{\lambda}{\mu}\right)^n \cdot \left(\frac{\mu}{\lambda+\mu}\right)^n \cdot \left(\frac{\mu}{\lambda+\mu}\right)^{a-n}$$

$$= {}^a c_n \cdot \left(\frac{\lambda}{\lambda+\mu}\right)^n \cdot \left(\frac{\mu}{\lambda+\mu}\right)^{a-n}, \qquad \text{...(10.89)}$$

which is a binomial distribution.

10.14 DETERMINISTIC MODELS

The simplest type of queuing problems, obviously, are the ones wherein probability distributions are not required to describe the arrival and service patterns. Here, the units arrive at fixed (constant) intervals of time and service times are also constant. Such models are, therefore, called deterministic models.

10.14-1 Model XI. D/D/1

In this model,

D : Deterministic interarrival time distribution,

D : Deterministic service time distribution,

1 : Single channel.

Consider the elementary case of a constant rate of arrivals to a single-channel having a constant service rate. These regularly spaced arrivals are to be served on FCFS basis. If the arrival rate is $\frac{1}{a}$, then the interarrival time will be a. Likewise, if $\frac{1}{b}$ is the service rate, the interservice time will be b. Three cases arise:

1. *When* $b < a$

Since service time is less than inter-arrival time, no unit will have to wait *i.e.,* queue length will be zero or it will go on diminishing if initially there is a queue.

2. *When* $b = a$

In this case if initially the queue length is zero, then no new arrival will have to wait, otherwise the queue length will remain constant.

3. When $b > a$

In this case the queue length will go on increasing indefinitely.

To show that queue length will go on diminishing when $b < a$

Let there be n units in the queue at time $t = 0$. Since $b < a$, one more unit from the queue will enter the service channel before new arrival takes place. There is a time lag of $(a - b)$ between the unit served and the new arrival. If there are $\frac{b}{a-b}$ arrivals, then in the time interval of new arrival, one extra unit can be served. Therefore, during the period $(n - 1)$ units are served, there will be only $(n-1)\frac{b}{a-b}$ new arrivals.

Total length of the queue = no. of units present in the queue + no. of new arrivals + one unit in service

$$= (n-1) + (n-1)\frac{b}{a-b} + 1$$

$$= \frac{na-b}{a-b}. \qquad \text{...(10.90)}$$

Therefore, after serving $\frac{na-b}{a-b}$ units, the queue will disappear.

Total time spent in service before a queue disappears,

$$T = \left(\frac{na-b}{a-b}\right)b. \qquad \text{...(10.91)}$$

EXAMPLE 10.14-1.1

A company manufacturing cold drinks uses c capping machine which caps bottles at the rate of 1 every 2 seconds. The bottles arrive at the rate of 1 bottle every 4 seconds. If in the beginning there are 20 bottles to be capped, how much time is required to service the bottles that are waiting?

[P.T.U. B.Tech. (C.Sc.) 2009]

Solution

Here, $b = 2$ seconds,

$a = 4$ seconds,

$n = 20$ bottles.

Since $b < a$, the initial queue will diminish as service proceeds and will eventually disappear. Time required to service the waiting bottles,

$$T = \left(\frac{na - b}{a - b}\right) . b = \left(\frac{20 \times 4 - 2}{4 - 2}\right) \times 2 = 78 \text{ seconds.}$$

10.14-2 Model XII. M/D/1

This model consists of Poisson arrivals, deterministic or constant service time and a single service channel. Here service time is not a random variable but is some constant. Without loss of generality, let us assume the service time to be unity so that $\mu = 1$. Let

(*a*) p_0 = probability that there is no unit in the system at the end of unit time. This can happen in two mutually exclusive and exhaustive ways:

(*i*) There is no unit in the system in the beginning of this period, also there is no arrival during the unit time. Probability of this event is (p_0 × probability of no arrival).

(*ii*) There is one unit in the beginning which is served in unit time and no unit arrived during this time. Probability of this event is (p_1 × probability of no arrival in unit time × probability of one service in unit time).

Now let the arrival rate be λ for Poisson arrivals. Then

probability of n arrivals in time $t = \dfrac{e^{-\lambda t} . (\lambda t)^n}{n}$.

$\therefore$ Probability of no arrival in unit time $= \dfrac{e^{-\lambda.1} . (\lambda . 1)^0}{0!} = e^{-\lambda}$.

$$\therefore p_0 = p_0 . e^{-\lambda} + p_1 . e^{-\lambda} . 1 = (p_0 + p_1)\, e^{-\lambda} = \sum_{i=0}^{1} p_i\, e^{-\lambda}. \quad ...(10.92)$$

(*b*) Let p_1 = probability of one unit in the system. This can happen in the following three mutually exclusive and exhaustive ways:

TABLE 10.10

Event	*No. of units at time t*	*No. of arrivals in time dt*	*No. of services in time dt*	*No. of units at time t + dt*
1	0	1	0	1
2	1	1	1	1
3	2	0	1	1

$\therefore$ Probability of event 1 $= p_0 . \lambda e^{-\lambda}$,

probability of event 2 $= p_1 . \lambda e^{-\lambda} . 1$,

probability of event 3 $= p_2 . e^{-\lambda}$.

$$\therefore p_1 = p_0 . \lambda e^{-\lambda} + p_1 \lambda e^{-\lambda} + p_2 e^{-\lambda}. \quad ...(10.93)$$

(*c*) Finally, let p_n = probability that there are n units in the system at the end of unit time interval.

This can happen in the following three mutually exclusive and exhaustive ways:

TABLE 10.11

Event	*No. of units at time t*	*No. of arrivals in time dt*	*No. of services in time dt*	*No. of units at time t + dt*
1	n	1	1	n
2	$n+1$	0	1	n
3	$n-1$	1	0	n

∴ Probability of event 1 = $p_n \,.\, \lambda e^{-\lambda} \,.\, 1$,
probability of event 2 = $p_{n+1} \,.\, e^{-\lambda}$,
probability of event 3 = $p_{n-1} \,.\, \lambda e^{-\lambda} \,.\, 0 = 0$.

∴ $$p_n = p_n \lambda e^{-\lambda} + p_{n+1} e^{-\lambda}. \qquad ...(10.94)$$

Average queue length and waiting time

$$L_q = \sum_{n=1}^{\infty} n p_n = p_1 + e^{-\lambda} \sum_{n=1}^{\infty} (\lambda p_n + p_{n+1}) n.$$

It can be shown that the above expression reduces to

$$L_q = \frac{(\lambda/\mu)^2}{2\left(1-\dfrac{\lambda}{\mu}\right)} = \frac{1}{2}\cdot\frac{\lambda}{\mu}\cdot\frac{\lambda}{\mu-\lambda}. \qquad ...(10.95)$$

Average waiting time,

$$W_q = \frac{(\lambda/\mu)^2}{2\lambda\left(1-\dfrac{\lambda}{\mu}\right)} = \frac{1}{2}\cdot\frac{\lambda}{\mu}\cdot\frac{1}{\mu-\lambda}. \qquad ...(10.96)$$

Above formulae are same as obtained for Erlang service time distribution when $k = \infty$ [(10.65) and (10.67)].

EXAMPLE 10.14-2.1

A firm is engaged in both shipping and receiving activities. The management is always interested in improving the efficiency of new innovations in loading and unloading procedures. The arrival distribution of trucks is found to be Poisson with arrival rate of 3 trucks per hour. The service time distribution is exponential with unloading rate of 4 trucks per hour. Determine

(i) expected number of trucks in the queue,
(ii) expected waiting time of the truck in the queue,
(iii) probability that the loading and unloading dock and workers will be idle,
(iv) what reductions in waiting time are possible if loading and unloading is standardised ?

Solution

This is an example of M/M/1 : FCFS/∞/∞ system

Here, λ = 3/hr, μ = 4/hr.

(*i*) $L_q = \dfrac{\lambda}{\mu}\cdot\dfrac{\lambda}{\mu-\lambda} = \dfrac{3}{4}\cdot\dfrac{3}{4-3} = 2.25.$

(*ii*) $W_q = \dfrac{1}{\mu}\cdot\dfrac{\lambda}{\mu-\lambda} = \dfrac{1}{4}\cdot\dfrac{3}{4-3} = \dfrac{3}{4}$ hour.

(*iii*) $p_0 = 1 - \frac{\lambda}{\mu} = 1 - \frac{3}{4} = 0.25.$

(*iv*) When service rate becomes constant with $\mu = 4$/hr, the system becomes M/D/1. Then from equation (10.96),

$$W_q = \frac{(\lambda/\mu)^2}{2\lambda.\left(1-\frac{\lambda}{\mu}\right)} = \frac{(3/4)^2}{2\times 3\times\left(1-\frac{3}{4}\right)} = \frac{9}{16}\times\frac{2}{3}=\frac{3}{8} \text{ hour.}$$

$\therefore$ Saving in waiting time $= \frac{3}{4} - \frac{3}{8} = \frac{3}{8} = 0.375$ hour = 22.5 minutes.

10.15 MONTE CARLO TECHNIQUE APPLIED TO QUEUING PROBLEMS*

The Monte Carlo technique is quite useful for analysing waiting line problems which are difficult or impossible to be analysed mathematically. *Simulated sampling methods*, for example, are quite helpful when the first come, first served assumption is not valid for a particular queuing problem. In many cases, the observed distributions for arrival times and service times cannot be fitted to certain mathematical distribution (Poisson and exponential distribution) and Monte Carlo approach is the only hope under such situations. Similarly, multi-channel queuing, in which departures from one queue form the arrivals for another, is another difficult area which can be easily handled by Monte Carlo technique.

Simulated sampling methods consist of replacing the actual universe of items by its theoretical counterpart, which is a universe described by some assumed probability distribution. A random number table is then used for sampling from this theoretical population. Such simulated sampling methods are called the *Monte Carlo methods*.

The Monte Carlo approach has many advantages over the ordinary sampling method of just looking at the actual situation and forming a history of arrivals, services, queue lengths and waiting times, etc. Firstly, with a digital computer, this approach can develop many months or years of data in only a few minutes. Secondly, it allows manipulation of those factors which can be controlled. For example, we can readily assess the effect of adding one or more service stations without actually having to install them. Similarly, changes in queue discipline can be tried out experimentally on paper, without any disruption of the actual process.

EXERCISES 10.7

1. Write short notes on
   (*i*) deterministic queues (*ii*) waiting line models.

   [ICWA June, 1991]

2. Discuss in detail a deterministic queuing model.

   [R.U. MBA June, 2011]

*For further details the reader is referred to Chapter 13 of this book.

Replacement Models

11.1 INTRODUCTION

Replacement models find applications in the following situations:

1. All industrial and military equipment gets worn with time and usage and it functions with decreasing efficiency. For example, a machine requires higher operating cost, a transport vehicle such as a car or airplane requires more and more maintenance cost, a railway timetable becomes more and more out of date with the passage of time. The ever increasing repair, maintenance and operating cost necessitates the replacement of the equipment. However, there is no sharp, clearly defined time which indicates the need for this replacement. The replacement policy, in this case, consists of calculating the increased operating cost, maintenance cost, forced idle time cost together with cost of the new equipment and scrap value of the old.

2. A separate but similar problem involves the replacement of items such as electric bulbs, radio tubes, television parts, etc. which do not deteriorate with time but suddenly fail. The problem, in this case, is of finding which items to replace and whether or not to replace them in a group and, if so, when. The objective is to minimize the sum of the cost of the item, cost of replacing the item and the cost associated with failure of item.

3. Another situation in which replacement becomes necessary is *obsolescence* due to new discoveries and better design of the equipment. The equipment needs replacement not because it no longer performs to the designed standards, but because more modern equipment performs higher standards. For example, an equipment may have an economic life of 20 years, yet it may become obsolete after 10 years because of better technical developments.

4. Still another situation involving replacement is the staff in an organisation that gradually decreases due to death, retrenchment and other reasons.

Thus in these situations there is need to formulate a replacement policy to determine the time or age at which the replacement of the given equipment is most economical, taking into consideration all the alternatives.

11.1-1 Types of Failures

There are two types of failures:

1. Gradual failure
2. Sudden failure

1. *Gradual Failure* : Gradual failure is progressive in nature. As the life of the equipment increases, its operational efficiency decreases. This results in
   (*a*) increased running (repair, maintenance and operating) costs.
   (*b*) decreased productivity.
   (*c*) decreased resale or scrap value.
   Machines, vehicles, tyres, tubes, pistons, piston rings, bearings, etc. fall in this category.

2. *Sudden Failure* : Some items do not deteriorate with time. They give the desired level of service for some period, after which they fail. The period of desired service is not constant but follows some frequency distribution which may be progressive, retrogressive or random in nature.

(*i*) *Progressive failure* : If the probability of failure of an item increases with increase in its life, then such a failure is called a progressive failure [Fig. 1.1 (*a*)]. Electric bulbs and tubes fall under this category of failure.

(*ii*) *Retrogressive failure* : If the probability of failure of an item is more in the beginning but decreases with the life of an item, then such a failure is called a retrogressive failure [Fig. 11.1 (*b*)]. Automobile engines fall under this category.

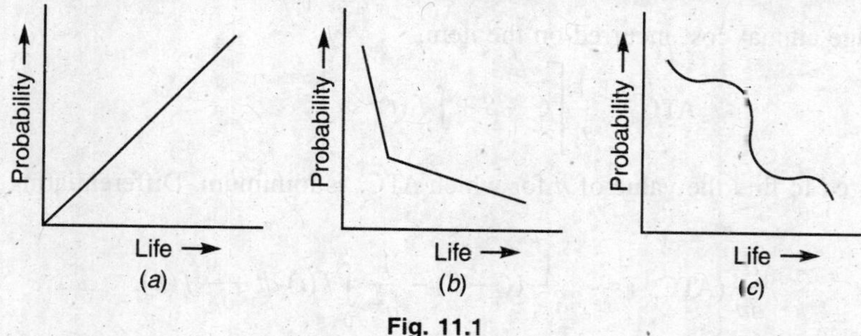

Fig. 11.1

(*iii*) *Random failure* : If the probability of failure of the item is due to random causes such as physical shock, irrespective of its age, then such a failure is called a random failure [Fig. 11.1 (*c*)]. Failure of vacuum tubes and electronic items is generally random in nature.

11.2 REPLACEMENT OF ITEMS THAT DETERIORATE *i.e.*, WHOSE MAINTENANCE COSTS INCREASE WITH TIME

Quite often the repair, maintenance and operating costs of items increase with time and a stage may come when these costs become so high that it is more economical to replace the item by a new one. Since these costs tend to increase with time, they are grouped while analysing a problem.

If these costs decrease or remain constant with time, the best policy is never to replace the item. However, this condition is hardly met with in practice. If these costs fluctuate with time, the item should be replaced only when they are increasing, of course, the analysis becomes more involved.

Generally, *all* costs that depend upon the *choice or age* of the equipment must be taken into account while analysing the decision of its replacement. However, in special situations, certain costs may not be considered. For example, costs (such as labour cost, electric cost, etc.) that do not change with the *age* of the equipment may not be included in calculations.

Now we shall consider a few cases of items that deteriorate with time and it will be assumed that suitable expressions for maintenance costs are available.

11.2-1 Replacement of Items whose Maintenance and Repair Costs Increase with Time, Ignoring Changes in the Value of Money During the Period

Let us first consider a simple situation which consists of minimizing the average annual cost of an equipment whose maintenance cost is a function increasing with time and whose scrap value is constant. As the time value of money is not to be considered, the interest rate is zero and the calculations can be based on *average annual cost.*

Case 1. When time '*t*' is a continuous variable

Let $\quad C$ = Capital cost of the item,

S = Scrap value of the item,

T_{ave} = Average annual total cost of the item,

n = Number of years the item is to be in use,

$f(t)$ = Operating and maintenance cost of the item at time t.

Annual cost of the item at any time t = capital cost – scrap value + maintenance cost at time t.

Now total maintenance cost incurred during n years $= \int_0^n f(t).\, dt.$

$\therefore$ Total cost incurred during n years, $TC = C - S + \int_0^n f(t).\, dt.$

$\therefore$ Average annual cost incurred on the item,

$$\text{ATC}_n = \frac{1}{n}\left[C - S + \int_0^n f(t).\, dt\right]. \qquad ...(11.1)$$

It is desired to find the value of n for which ATC_n is minimum. Differentiating ATC_n w.r.t. n we get

$$\frac{d}{dn}(\text{ATC}_n) = -\frac{1}{n^2}(C - S) - \frac{1}{n^2}\int_0^n f(t)\, dt + \frac{1}{n} f(n),$$

where $f(n)$ is operating and maintenance cost at time n *i.e.* the current maintenance cost.

For $\frac{d}{dn}(\text{ATC}_n) = 0$, we have

$$f(n) = \frac{1}{n}\left[C - S + \int_0^n f(t)\, dt\right] = \text{ATC}_n. \qquad ...(11.2)$$

Thus the item should be replaced when the average annual cost to date becomes equal to the current maintenance cost. Using this result we can decide when to replace an item provided an explicit expression is given for the maintenance and repair costs.

Case 2 : When time '*t*' is a discrete variable

In this case, the total cost incurred during n years,

$$\text{TC} = \text{C} - \text{S} + \sum_{t=0}^{n} f(t)\cdot \qquad ...(11.3)$$

$\therefore$ Average annual cost incurred on the item,

$$T_{\text{ave}} = \text{ATC}_n = \frac{1}{n}\left[C - S + \sum_{t=0}^{n} f(t)\right]\cdot \qquad ...(11.4)$$

We want to find the value of n for which ATC_n is minimum.

Thus we have the inequalities

$ATC_{n-1} > ATC_n < ATC_{n+1}$, which gives

$ATC_{n-1} - ATC_n > 0$

and $ATC_{n+1} - ATC_n > 0$.

Rewriting equation (11.4) for period $n + 1$, we get

$$ATC_{n+1} = \frac{1}{n+1}\left[C - S + \sum_{t=1}^{n+1} f(t)\right] = \frac{1}{n+1}\left[C - S + \sum_{t=1}^{n} f(t) + f(n+1)\right]$$

$$= \frac{n}{n+1}\left[\frac{1}{n}\left\{c - s + \sum_{t=1}^{n} f(t)\right\}\right] + \frac{f(n+1)}{n+1} = \frac{n}{n+1}.\, ATC_n + \frac{f(n+1)}{n+1}.$$

$$\therefore \quad ATC_{n+1} - ATC_n = \frac{n}{n+1}. ATC_n + \frac{f(n+1)}{n+1} - ATC_n$$

$$= \frac{f(n+1)}{n+1} + ATC_n \left(\frac{n}{n+1} - 1 \right) = \frac{f(n+1)}{n+1} - \frac{ATC_n}{n+1}.$$

Since $ATC_{n+1} - ATC_n > 0$, we get

$$\frac{f(n+1)}{n+1} - \frac{ATC_n}{n+1} > 0 \text{ or } f(n+1) - ATC_n > 0 \text{ or } f(n+1) > ATC_n.$$

Similarly, $ATC_{n-1} - ATC_n > 0$ yields $f(n) < ATC_{n-1}$. These results provide the following replacement policy :

(i) *If the running cost (operating and maintenance cost) for the next year, $f(n+1)$ is more than the average annual cost of nth year, ATC_n, then replace at the end of n years. That is*

$$f(n+1) > \frac{1}{n}\left[C - S + \sum_{t=0}^{n} f(t) \right].$$

(ii) *If the running cost of the present year is less than the previous year's average annual cost, ATC_{n-1}, then do not replace. That is*

$$f(n) < \frac{1}{n-1}\left[C - S + \sum_{t=0}^{n-1} f(t) \right].$$

The above policy implies that *n is optimal at the minimum average annual cost.*

Tabular method is used in this case. It has the advantage of being a simpler method. The examples that follow explain this method.

EXAMPLE 11.2-1

The cost of a machine is ₹ 6,100 and its scrap value is ₹ 100. The maintenance costs found from experience are as follows:

Year	*1*	*2*	*3*	*4*	*5*	*6*	*7*	*8*
Maintenance cost (₹)	*100*	*250*	*400*	*600*	*900*	*1,200*	*1,600*	*2,000*

When should the machine be replaced?

[M.G.U Kerala M.Com. June, 2010; J.N.T.U. Hyderabad B.Tech. (C.Sc.) Dec., 2011; June, 2009; P.T. U. B.E. (Mech.) 2008; May, 2006; MBA June, 2003]

Solution

Let it be profitable to replace the machine after n years. Then n is determined by the minimum value of T_{ave}. Values of T_{ave} for various years are computed in table 11.1.

TABLE 11.1

(1) *Years of service* (n)	(2) *Purchase price – scrap value* (C – S) ₹	(3) *Annual maintenance cost* $f(t)$ ₹	(4) *Summation of maintenance cost* $\sum_{t=0}^{n} f(t)$ ₹	(5) *Total cost* $C - S + \sum_{t=0}^{n} f(t)$ ₹	(6) *Average annual cost* $\frac{1}{n}\left[C - S + \sum_{t=0}^{n} f(t)\right]$ ₹
1	6,000	100	100	6,100	6,100
2	6,000	250	350	6,350	3,175

3	6,000	400	750	6,750	2,250
4	6,000	600	1,350	7,350	1,837.50
5	6,000	900	2,250	8,250	1,650
6	6,000	1,200	3,450	9,450	**1,575**
7	6,000	1,600	5,050	11,050	1,578
8	6,000	2,000	7,050	13,050	1,631

Table 11.1 shows that the average annual cost is minimum (₹ 1,575) during the sixth year and then rises. Hence the machine should be replaced after 6 years of its use.

EXAMPLE 11.2-2

The maintenance cost and resale value per year of a machine whose purchase price is ₹ 7,000 is given below.

TABLE 11.2

Year	*1*	*2*	*3*	*4*	*5*	*6*	*7*	*8*
Maintenance cost in ₹	*900*	*1,200*	*1,600*	*2,100*	*2,800*	*3,700*	*4,700*	*5,900*
Resale value in ₹	*4,000*	*2,000*	*1,200*	*600*	*500*	*400*	*400*	*400*

When should the machine be replaced ?

[J.N.T.U. Hyderabad B.Tech. Nov., 2010; R.T.M. Nagpur U.B. Tech. June, 2006]

Solution

Capital cost C = ₹ 7,000. Let it be profitable to replace the machine after n years. Then n should be determined by the minimum value of T_{ave}. Values of T_{ave} for various years are computed in table 11.3.

TABLE 11.3

(1) *Years of service*	(2) *Resale value* (₹)	(3) *Purchase price–resale value (C – S)* (₹)	(4) *Annual maintenance cost* $f(t)$ (₹)	(5) *Summation of maintenance cost* $\sum_{t=0}^{n} f(t)$ (₹)	(6) *Total cost* $\left[C-S+\sum_{t=0}^{n} f(t)\right]$ (₹)	(7) *Average annual cost* $\frac{1}{n}\left[C-S+\sum_{t=0}^{n} f(t)\right]$ (₹)
1	4,000	3,000	900	900	3,900	3,900
2	2,000	5,000	1,200	2,100	7,100	3,550
3	1,200	5,800	1,600	3,700	9,500	3,166.67
4	600	6,400	2,100	5,800	12,200	3,050
5	500	6,500	2,800	8,600	15,100	**3,020**
6	400	6,600	3,700	12,300	18,900	3,150
7	400	6,600	4,700	17,000	23,600	3,371.43
8	400	6,600	5,900	22,900	29,500	3,687.50

We observe from the table that average annual cost is minimum (₹ 3,020) in the 5th year. Hence the machine should be replaced at the end of 5 years of service.

EXAMPLE 11.2-3

The purchase price of a machine is ₹ 52,000. The installation charges amount to ₹ 14,400 and its scrap value is only ₹ 6,400. The maintenance cost in various years is given below:

Year	:	*1*	*2*	*3*	*4*	*5*	*6*	*7*	*8*
Maintenance cost	:	*1,000*	*3,000*	*4,000*	*6,000*	*8,400*	*11,600*	*16,000*	*19,200*

After how many years should the machine be replaced ? Assume that the machine replacement can be done only at the year ends. *[P.T.U. B.Tech. (Mech.) May, 2011]*

Solution

Here, cost of the machine. C = ₹ (52,000 + 14,400) = ₹ 66,400.

Scrap value, S = ₹ 6,400.

The optimum replacement period is determined as in table 11.4.

TABLE 11.4

(1) Years of service (n)	(2) Purchase price – resale value (C–S) ₹	(3) Annual maintenance cost $f(t)$ ₹	(4) Summation of maintenance cost $\sum_{t=0}^{n} f(t)$ ₹	(5) Total cost $C - S + \sum_{t=0}^{n} f(t)$ ₹	(6) Average annual cost $\frac{1}{n}\left[C - S + \sum_{t=0}^{n} f(t)\right]$ ₹
1	60,000	1,000	1,000	61,000	61,000
2	60,000	3,000	4,000	64,000	32,000
3	60,000	4,000	8,000	68,000	22,667
4	60,000	6,000	14,000	74,000	18,500
5	60,000	8,400	22,400	82,400	16,480
6	60,000	11,600	34,000	94,000	**15,667**
7	60,000	16,000	50,000	1,10,000	15,714
8	60,000	19,200	69,200	1,29,200	16,150

We observe from the table that average annual cost is minimum (₹ 15,667) in the sixth year. Hence the machine should be replaced at the end of 6 years of service.

EXAMPLE 11.2-4

A taxi owner estimates from his past records that the costs per year for operating a taxi whose purchase price when new is ₹ 60,000 are as given below.

Age	*1*	*2*	*3*	*4*	*5*
Operating cost (₹)	*10,000*	*12,000*	*15,000*	*18,000*	*20,000*

After 5 years, the operating cost is ₹ 6,000 k, where k = 6, 7, 8, 9, 10 (k denoting age in years). If the resale value decreases by 10% of purchase price each year, what is the best replacement policy? Cost of money is zero. *[P.T.U. MBA Dec., 2014]*

Solution

$$10\% \text{ of purchase price} = ₹\ 60{,}000 \times \frac{10}{100} = ₹\ 6{,}000.$$

Thus the resale value decreases by ₹ 6,000 every year, which means that (C – S) increases by ₹ 6,000 every year.

Average annual cost of the taxi is computed in the following table :

TABLE 11.5

(1) Years of service (n)	(2) Resale value (₹) (S)	(3) Purchase price–resale value (₹) (C – S)	(4) Annual operating cost (₹) f(t)	(5) Summation of operating cost (₹) $\sum_{t=0}^{n} f(t)$	(6) Total cost (₹) (3) + (5)	(7) Average annual cost (₹) (6)/(1)
1	54,000	6,000	10,000	10,000	16,000	**16,000**
2	48,000	12,000	12,000	22,000	34,000	17,000
3	42,000	18,000	15,000	37,000	55,000	18,333
4	36,000	24,000	18,000	55,000	79,000	19,750
5	30,000	30,000	20,000	75,000	1,05,000	21,000
6	24,000	36,000	36,000	1,11,000	1,47,000	24,500
7	18,000	42,000	42,000	1,53,000	1,95,000	27,857
8	12,000	48,000	48,000	2,01,000	2,49,000	31,125
9	6,000	54,000	54,000	2,55,000	3,09,000	34,333
10	0	60,000	60,000	3,15,000	3,75,000	37,500

Hence one year is the optimal replacement period.

EXAMPLE 11.2-5

Fleet cars have their costs increasing as they continue in service due to increased direct operating cost (gas and oil) and increased maintenance (repairs, tyres, batteries, etc.). The initial cost is ₹ 3,800 and the trade-in value drops as time passes until it reaches a constant value of ₹ 600. Given the cost of operating, maintaining and the trade-in value, determine the proper length of service before cars should be replaced.

Years of service	:	*1*	*2*	*3*	*4*	*5*
Year end trade-in value (₹)	:	*2,000*	*1,200*	*800*	*700*	*600*
Annual operating cost (₹)	:	*1,600*	*1,900*	*2,200*	*2,500*	*2,800*
Annual maintenance cost (₹)	:	*400*	*500*	*700*	*900*	*1,100*

Solution

Here, capital (initial) cost is ₹ 3,800, year end trade-in value is 'S' and running cost $f(t)$ (sum of annual operating cost + annual maintenance cost) can be calculated. Values of T_{ave} for various years are computed in table 11.6.

TABLE 11.6

(1) Years of service (n)	(2) Resale value (S) ₹	(3) Purchase price – resale value (C – S) ₹	(4) Annual running cost f(t) ₹	(5) Summation of running cost $\sum_{t=0}^{n} f(t)$ ₹	(6) Total cost $C - S + \sum_{t=0}^{n} f(t)$ ₹	(7) Average annual cost $\frac{1}{n}\left[C - S + \sum_{t=0}^{n} f(t)\right]$ ₹
1	2,000	1,800	2,000	2,000	3,800	3,800
2	1,200	2,600	2,400	4,400	7,000	3,500
3	800	3,000	2,900	7,300	10,300	**3,433**
4	700	3,100	3,400	10,700	13,800	3,450
5	600	3,200	3,900	14,600	17,800	3,560

The table shows that average annual cost is minimum (₹ 3,433) during third year. Hence the cars should be replaced at the end of three years.

EXAMPLE 11.2-6

(a) Machine A costs ₹ 9,000. Annual operating costs are ₹ 200 for the first year, and then increase by ₹ 2,000 every year. Determine the best age at which to replace the machine. If the optimum replacement policy is followed, what will be the average yearly cost of owning and operating the machine? Assume that the machine has no resale value when replaced and that future costs are not discounted.

(b) Machine B costs ₹ 10,000. Annual operating costs are ₹ 400 for the first year and then increase by ₹ 800 every year. You have now a machine of type A which is one year old. Should you replace it with B, and if so, when?

(c) Suppose you are just ready to replace machine A with another machine of the same type, when you hear that machine B will become available in a year. What would you do?

[J.N.T.U. Hyderabad B.Tech. June, 2009]

Solution

(*a*) It is given that machine A has no resale value when replaced. The average annual cost is computed in table 11.7.

TABLE 11.7

(1) Years of service (n)	(2) Resale value (S) (₹)	(3) Purchase price – resale value (C – S) (₹)	(4) Annual maintenance cost f (t) (₹)	(5) Summation of maintenance cost $\sum_{t=0}^{n} f(t)$ (₹)	(6) Total cost (3) + (5) (₹)	(7) Average annual cost (6)/(1) (₹)
1	Zero	9,000	200	200	9,200	9,200
2	Zero	9,000	2,200	2,400	11,400	5,700
3	Zero	9,000	4,200	6,600	15,600	**5,200**
4	Zero	9,000	6,200	12,800	21,800	5,450
5	Zero	9,000	8,200	21,000	30,000	6,000

From table 11.7 we find that machine A should be replaced at the end of 3 years and the average yearly cost of owning and operating the machine at this time of replacement is ₹ 5,200.

(*b*) The average annual cost for machine B is computed in table 11.8.

TABLE 11.8

(1) Years of service (n)	(2) Resale value (S) (₹)	(3) Purchase price–resale value (C – S) (₹)	(4) Annual maintenance cost f (t) (₹)	(5) Summation of maintenance cost $\sum_{t=0}^{n} f(t)$ (₹)	(6) Total cost (3)+(5) (₹)	(7) Average annual cost (6)/(1) (₹)
1	Zero	10,000	400	400	10,400	10,400
2	Zero	10,000	1,200	1,600	11,600	5,800
3	Zero	10,000	2,000	3,600	13,600	4,533.33
4	Zero	10,000	2,800	6,400	16,400	4,100
5	Zero	10,000	3,600	10,000	20,000	**4,000**
6	Zero	10,000	4,400	14,400	24,400	4,066.67

Table 11.8 indicates that machine B should be replaced at the end of 5 years. Moreover, since the lowest average cost of ₹ 4,000 for machine B is less than the lowest average cost of ₹ 5,200 for machine A, machine A should be replaced by machine B.

Now we have to determine as to when machine A should be replaced. *Machine A should be replaced when the cost for next year of running this machine becomes more than the average yearly cost for machine B.*

Now total cost of machine A in the first year = ₹ 9,200,
total cost of machine A in the second year = ₹ 11,400 – ₹ 9,200 = ₹ 2,200,
total cost of machine A in the third year = ₹ 4,200,
total cost of machine A in the fourth year = ₹ 6,200.

As the cost of running machine A in third year (₹ 4,200) is more than the average yearly cost for machine B (₹ 4,000); machine A should be replaced at the end of two years *i.e.*, one year after it is one year old (one year hence).

(*c*) As seen from part (*b*), machine A should be replaced one year hence and machine B will also be available at that time. Therefore, machine A should be replaced by machine B after one year from now.

EXAMPLE 11.2-7

(a) An autorickshaw driver finds from his previous records that the cost per year of running an autorickshaw whose purchase price is ₹ 7,000 is as given below.

Year	:	*1*	*2*	*3*	*4*	*5*	*6*	*7*	*8*
Running cost (₹)	:	*1,100*	*1,300*	*1,500*	*1,900*	*2,400*	*2,900*	*3,500*	*4,100*
Resale price (₹)	:	*3,100*	*1,600*	*850*	*475*	*300*	*300*	*300*	*300*

At what age is the replacement due ?

(b) Another person has three autorickshaws of the same purchase price and cost of running each as in part (a). Two of these vehicles are 2 years old and the third one is 1 year old. He is considering a new type of autorickshaw with 50% more capacity than one of the old ones at a unit price of ₹ 9,000. He estimates that the running costs and resale price for the new vehicle will be as follows:

Year	:	*1*	*2*	*3*	*4*	*5*	*6*	*7*	*8*
Running cost (₹)	:	*1,300*	*1,600*	*1,900*	*2,500*	*3,200*	*4,100*	*5,100*	*6,200*
Resale price (₹)	:	*4,100*	*2,100*	*1,100*	*600*	*400*	*400*	*400*	*400*

Assuming that the loss of flexibility due to fewer vehicles is of no importance, and that he will continue to have sufficient work for three of the old vehicles, what should be his policy?

[*J.N.T.U. Hyderabad B.Tech. June, 2009; P.U. Dec., 2003*]

Solution

(*a*) The average annual cost for old autorickshaw is computed in table 11.9.

TABLE 11.9

(1) *Years of service (n)*	*(2)* *Resale value (S)* (₹)	*(3)* *Purchase price–resale value* *(C–S)* (₹)	*(4)* *Annual maintenance cost* *f(t)* (₹)	*(5)* *Summation of maintenance cost* $\sum_{t=0}^{n} f(t)$ (₹)	*(6)* *Total cost* (3)+(5) (₹)	*(7)* *Average annual cost* (6)/(1) (₹)
1	3,100	3,900	1,100	1,100	5,000	5,000
2	1,600	5,400	1,300	2,400	7,800	3,900
3	850	6,150	1,500	3,900	10,050	3,350
4	475	6,525	1,900	5,800	12,325	3,081
5	300	6,700	2,400	8,200	14,900	2,980
6	300	6,700	2,900	11,100	17,800	**2,967**
7	300	6,700	3,500	14,600	21,300	3,043
8	300	6,700	4,100	18,700	25,400	3,175

Thus the old autorickshaw should be replaced at the end of 6th year.

(*b*) Now let us compute the average annual cost of the new autorickshaw of larger capacity. This is done in table 11.10.

TABLE 11.10

(1) Years of service (n)	(2) Resale value (S) (₹)	(3) Purchase price–resale value (C – S) (₹)	(4) Annual maintenance cost f (t) (₹)	(5) Summation of maintenance cost $\sum_{t=0}^{n} f(t)$ (₹)	(6) Total cost (3)+(5) (₹)	(7) Average annual cost (6)/(1) (₹)
1	4,100	4,900	1,300	1,300	6,200	6,200
2	2,100	6,900	1,600	2,900	9,800	4,900
3	1,100	7,900	1,900	4,800	12,700	4,233
4	600	8,400	2,500	7,300	15,700	3,925
5	400	8,600	3,200	10,500	19,100	**3,820**
6	400	8,600	4,100	14,600	23,200	3,867
7	400	8,600	5,100	19,700	28,300	4,043
8	400	8,600	6,200	25,900	34,500	4,312

As the new autorickshaw has 50% more capacity than the old one, the minimum average annual cost of ₹ 3,820 for the former is equivalent to ₹ 3,820 × 2/3 = ₹ 2,547 for the latter. Since this amount is less than ₹ 2,967 for it, the latter will be replaced by the new autorickshaw.

Having decided to replace the old vehicle by the new one, we now will determine as to when this replacement should be made. For uniformity we assume that all the three old autorickshaws will be replaced by two new larger ones since they have 50% more capacity.

The new vehicles will be purchased when the cost for the next year of running the three old vehicles becomes more than the average annual cost of the two new ones.

Total annual cost of one smaller auto rickshaw during first year = ₹ 5,000,
annual cost of one smaller autorickshaw during second year = ₹ 7,800 – ₹ 5,000 = ₹ 2,800,
annual cost of one smaller autorickshaw during third year = ₹ 2,250,
annual cost of one smaller autorickshaw during fourth year = ₹ 2,275,
annual cost of one smaller autorickshaw during fifth year = ₹ 2,575,
annual cost of one smaller autorickshaw during sixth year = ₹ 2,900 and so on.

Total cost one year hence for two smaller auto rickshaws aged two years and one autorickshaw aged one year = ₹ (2 × 2,250 + 2,800) = ₹ 7,300.

Similarly, total cost 2 years hence = ₹ (2 × 2,275 + 2,250) = ₹ 6,800,
total cost 3 years hence = ₹ (2 × 2,575 + 2,275) = ₹ 7,425,
total cost 4 years hence = ₹ (2 × 2,900 + 2,575) = ₹ 8,375 and so on.

And minimum average annual cost for two new autorickshaws = ₹ (2 × 3,820) = ₹ 7,640.

As the total cost of old autorickshaws is less than the minimum average cost of the new auto rickshaws till 3 years hence and becomes more only 4 years hence, the old auto rickshaws should be replaced by the new larger ones three years hence.

EXAMPLE 11.2-8

A company has a machine whose cost is ₹ 30,000. Its maintenance cost and resale value at the end of different years are as given below :

Year	:	*1*	*2*	*3*	*4*	*5*	*6*
Maintenance cost (₹)	:	*4,500*	*4,700*	*5,000*	*5,500*	*6,500*	*7,500*
Resale value (₹)	:	*27,000*	*25,300*	*24,000*	*21,000*	*18,000*	*13,000*

(a) What is the economic life of the machine and what is the minimum average cost ?

(b) The company has obtained a contract to supply the goods produced by the machine for 5 years from now. After 5 years, the company does not intend to use the machine. If the machine, at present, is one year old, what replacement policy should the company adopt if it intends to replace the machine not more than once ?

Solution

(*a*) The average annual cost of the machine is computed in table 11.11.

TABLE 11.11

(1) Year (n)	*(2) Depreciation (C–S)*	*(3) Annual maintenance cost*	*(4) Summation of maintenance cost*	*(5) Total cost*	*(6) Average annual cost*
		$f(t)$	$\sum_{t=0}^{n} f(t)$	(2) + (4)	(5) / (1)
	(₹)	(₹)	(₹)	(₹)	(₹)
1	3,000	4,500	4,500	7,500	7,500
2	4,700	4,700	9,200	13,900	6,950
3	6,000	5,000	14,200	20,200	**6,733**
4	9,000	5,500	19,700	28,700	7,175
5	12,000	6,500	26,200	38,200	7,640
6	17,000	7,500	33,700	50,700	8,450

Since the minimum average cost of ₹ 6,733 corresponds to year 3, the economic life of the machine is 3 years.

(*b*) First let us calculate the yearly cost (and also cumulative cost) of keeping this one year old machine in year 1, 2, ..., 5 hence of its life. This is done in table 11.12.

TABLE 11.12

Year	*Maintenance cost* (₹)	*Depreciation* (₹)	*Total cost* (₹)	*Cumulative total cost* (₹)
1	4,700	1,700	6,400	6,400
2	5,000	1,300	6,300	12,700
3	5,500	3,000	8,500	21,200
4	6,500	3,000	9,500	30,700
5	7,500	5,000	12,500	43,200

Alternate policies and costs associated with each one are as follows :

1. Keep old machine for zero year and the new one for full 5 years.

   Total cost = ₹ (0 + 38,200) = ₹ 38,200.

2. Keep old machine for 1 year and the new one for 4 years.

   Total cost = ₹ (6,400 + 28,700) = ₹ 35,100.

3. Keep old machine for 2 years and the new one for 3 years.

   Total cost = ₹ (12,700 + 20,200) = ₹ **32,900.**

4. Keep old machine for 3 years and the new one 2 years.

   Total cost = ₹ (21,200 + 13,900) = ₹ 35,100.

5. Keep old machine for 4 years and the new one for 1 year.

   Total cost = ₹ (30,700 + 7,500) = ₹ 38,200.

6. Keep old machine for 5 years and do not buy a new one.

   Total cost = ₹ (43,200 + 0) = ₹ 43,200.

∴ The company should keep the current machine running for two more years and then buy a new machine and use it for the remaining 3 years.

EXERCISES 11.1

1. List two uses of replacement model. [*P.T.U. MBA, 2005*]
2. Explain how the theory of replacement is used in replacement of items whose maintenance cost varies with time. [*Univ. of Madras MBA Nov., 2012; P.T.U. MBA Nov., 2012; B.Tech. (Mech.) May, 2012; J.N.T.U. Hyderabad B.Tech May, 2011; Nov., 2010; P.T.U. B.E. (Mech.) Dec., 2006; May, 2006; Nagpur U. B.E. (Mech.) 2003*]
3. For an equipment the maintenance cost is a function increasing with time and scrap value is constant. Ignoring time value of money and considering interest rate as zero, find at what time it is advisable to replace the equipment ? [*P.U. B.E. (Elect.) 1996; I.I.M.S. Kolkata, 1994*]
4. Describe with suitable illustrations, any two situations in which replacement of items is necessary. [*V.T.U. Karnataka B.E. Dec., 2011; J.N.T.U. Hyderabad B.Tech. May 2011; Mumbai U. MBA, 2010*]
5. Briefly explain costs which are relevant to decisions for replacement of depreciable costs. [*U.P.U. MBA, 2010*]
6. Explain the replacement problem. Discuss some important replacement situations and policies. [*P.T.U. MBA, 2015, Dec., 2014; Dec., 2013; B.Tech., 2010; J.N.T.U. Hyderabad B.Tech. May, 2011; R.T.M. Nagpur B.Tech. Dec., 2005; June, 2005; Dec., 2004; Dec., 2003*]
7. What are the reasons for replacement ? List and explain. [*V.T.U. Karnataka B.E. Dec., 2011*]
8. (*a*) Explain briefly the importance of replacement analysis.
   (*b*) What do you mean by 'Money value is not counted and counted' in replacement analysis ? [*J.N.T.U. Hyderabad B.Tech. June, 2009*]
9. Madras Cola Inc. uses a bottling machine that costs ₹ 50,000 when new. Table below gives the expected operating costs per year, the annual expected production per year and the salvage value of the machine. The wholesale price for a bottle of drink is ₹ 1.00.

Data Associated with age of bottling machine

Age	1	2	3	4	5
Operating costs (₹) :	7,000	8,000	10,000	14,000	20,000
Production (bottles) :	2,08,000	2,08,000	2,00,000	1,90,000	1,75,000
Salvage value (₹) :	30,000	19,000	15,000	12,000	10,000

When should the machine be replaced ? [*J.N.T.U. Hyderabad B.Tech. May, 2011*]

10. The cost of a new machine is ₹ 5,000. The maintenance cost of nth year is given by $R_n = 500\,(n-1)$; $n = 1, 2, \ldots$. Assuming that the money value will not change with time, after how many years will it be economical to replace the machine by a new one? [*J.N.T.U. Hyderabad B.Tech. May, 2009*]
11. The maintenance cost and resale value per year of a machine whose purchase price is ₹ 7,000 are given below:

Year :	1	2	3	4	5	6	7	8
Maintenance cost (₹) :	900	1,200	1,600	2,100	2,800	3,700	4,700	5,900
Resale value (₹) :	4,000	2,000	1,200	600	500	400	400	400

When should the machine be replaced? (*Ans.* End of 4th year.)

12. A manufacturing firm has come to know from the past records that a machine costing ₹ 56,000 is not working satisfactorily inspite of its regular maintenance. With a view to replacing this machine the following facts were obtained :

Year	*Annual running cost (₹)*	*Resale value (₹)*
1	7,000	28,000
2	9,100	14,000
3	11,900	8,400
4	15,400	4,200
5	20,300	3,500
6	26,600	3,000
7	33,600	3,000
8	42,000	3,000

When should the machine be replaced ? (*Ans.* End of 5th year.)

13. Suppose a machine costs ₹ 1,60,000. Its value, if sold, is ₹ 96,000 after one year, ₹ 72,000 after two years, ₹ 54,000 after three years and so on *i.e.*, after heavier depreciation in the first year, it loses 25% of the remaining value in each subsequent year. Its operating cost includes maintenance cost plus loss of output due to breakdown, etc. and is estimated to be ₹ 8,000 in the first year, ₹ 12,000 in the second year and so on, increasing by ₹ 4,000 each year. When should the machine be optimally replaced ? What is the corresponding minimum average cost ? [*Mumbai U. MBA, 2010*]

14. Obtain the economic life of the machine and minimum average cost from the following data. Purchase price is ₹ 20,000.

Year	: 1	2	3	4	5	6
Maintenance cost (₹)	: 1,500	1,700	2,000	2,500	3,500	5,500
Resale value (₹)	: 17,000	15,300	14,000	12,000	8,000	3,000

[*G.N.D.U.B. Com. Sept., 2002*]
(*Ans.* 3 years; ₹ 3,733.)

15. (*a*) Machine A costs ₹ 45,000 and the operating costs are estimated at ₹ 1,000 for the first year, increasing by ₹ 10,000 per year in the second and subsequent years. Machine B costs ₹ 50,000 and operating costs are ₹ 2,000 for the first year, increasing by ₹ 4,000 in second and subsequent years. If we now have a machine of type A, should we replace it with B ? If so, when ? Assume both the machines have no resale value and future costs are not discounted.
[*R.T.M. Nagpur U.B.E. (Mech.) 2011, 2008; J.N.T.U. Hyderabad B.Tech. May, 2011*]
(*b*) Explain with examples the failure mechanism of items. [*R.T.M. Nagpur B.E. (Mech.) 2008*]

16. A firm is thinking of replacing a particular machine whose cost price is ₹ 12,200. The scrap price of this machine is only ₹ 200. The maintenance costs are found to be as follows:

Year	: 1	2	3	4	5	6	7	8
Maintenance cost (₹)	: 200	500	800	1,200	1,800	2,500	3,200	4,000

Determine when the firm should get the machine replaced.
[*M.G.U. Kerala B.Com. June, 2012; Univ. of Madras MBA April, 2012; J.N.T.U. Hyderabad B. Tech. (C.Sc.) Dec., 2011*]
(*Ans.* C_{ave} = ₹ 3,167; 6th year.)

17. A fleet owner finds from his past records that the costs per year of running a truck whose purchase price is ₹ 6,000 are as given below:

Year	: 1	2	3	4	5	6	7
Running cost (in ₹)	: 1,000	1,200	1,400	1,800	2,300	2,800	3,400
Resale value (in ₹)	: 3,000	1,500	750	375	200	200	200

Determine at what age is the replacement due.
[*J.N.T.U. Hyderabad B.Tech. June, 2009; P.T.U. B.Tech. (Mech.) 2009; Dec., 2006; P.U.M. Com. Jan., 2006; Chennai U., 2002*]
(*Ans.* End of 5th year.)

18. The following table gives the running costs per year and resale prices of a certain equipment whose purchase price is ₹ 5,000 :

Year	: 1	2	3	4	5	6	7	8
Running costs (in ₹)	: 1,500	1,600	1,800	2,100	2,500	2,900	3,400	4,000
Resale value (in ₹)	: 3,500	2,500	1,700	1,200	800	500	500	500

At what year is the replacement due ? [*P.T.U. MBA May, 2006*]
(*Ans.* End of 4th year.)

19. A fleet owner finds from his past records that the costs per year of running a vehicle whose purchase price is ₹ 50,000 are as under :

Year	: 1	2	3	4	5	6	7
Running cost (₹)	: 5,000	6,000	7,000	9,000	11,500	16,000	18,000
Resale value (₹)	: 30,000	15,000	7,500	5,750	2,000	2,000	2,000

Thereafter, running cost increases by ₹ 2,000 per year but the resale value remains constant at ₹ 2,000. At what age is the replacement due ? [*J.N.T.U. Hyderabad B.Tech. (C.Sc.) Dec., 2011; April, 2011; P.T.U. B. Tech. (Mech.) Nov., 2012; Dec., 2011*]
(*Ans.* 6th year; ₹ 17,083.30.)

20. The data on the operating costs per year and resale price of equipment A whose purchase price is ₹ 10,000 are given below :

Year	:	1	2	3	4	5	6	7
Operating cost (₹)	:	1,500	1,900	2,300	2,900	3,600	4,500	5,500
Resale value (₹)	:	5,000	2,500	1,250	600	400	400	400

(*a*) What is the optimum period of replacement ?

(*b*) When equipment A is 2 years old, equipment B which is a new model for the same usage is available. The optimum period for replacement is 4 years with an average cost of ₹ 3,600. Should we change equipment A with B ? If so when ?

[*P.T.U. B.Tech. (Mech.) Nov., 2012; G.J.U. MBA Nov., 2003*]

(*Ans. (a) 5 years, ₹ 4,360 (b) 4 years (2 years hence.)*)

21. Machine A costs ₹ 3,600. Annual operating costs are ₹ 40 for the first year and then increase by ₹ 360 every year. Assuming that the machine has no resale value, determine the best replacement age. Another machine B which is similar to machine A costs ₹ 4,000. Annual running costs are ₹ 200 for the first year and then increase by ₹ 200 every year. It has resale value of ₹ 1,500, ₹ 1,000 and ₹ 500 if replaced at the end of first, second and third year respectively. After third year it has no resale value. Which machine would you prefer to purchase ? [*Guwahati M.C.A., 1992*]

22. An equipment which costs ₹ 15,000 has to be replaced with a new equipment. The following data have been estimated:

Year	:	1	2	3	4	5	6	7	8
Resale value (₹)	:	12,000	9,500	7,500	5,700	4,200	3,900	2,900	2,000
Annual maintenance cost (₹)	:	600	800	1,050	1,400	2,100	3,500	5,000	6,800

Ignore the time value of money and inflation. When should the equipment be replaced ?

[*ICWA (Final) June, 1989*]

(*Ans.* After 4 years; ₹ 3,287.50.)

23. The data collected in running a machine, the cost of which is ₹ 60,000 are given below:

Year	:	1	2	3	4	5
Resale value (₹)	:	42,000	30,000	20,400	14,400	9,650
Cost of spares (₹)	:	4,000	4,270	4,880	5,700	6,800
Cost of labour (₹)	:	14,000	16,000	18,000	21,000	25,000

Determine the optimum period for replacement of the machine. [*ICWA (Final) June, 1990*]

(*Ans.* After 4 years; ₹ 33,362.50.)

24. The following table gives the cost of spares per year, overhead cost of maintenance per year and the resale value of a certain equipment whose purchase price is ₹ 50,000:

Year	:	1	2	3	4	5
Cost of spares (₹)	:	10,000	12,000	14,000	15,000	17,000
Overhead maintenance cost (₹)	:	5,000	5,000	6,000	6,000	8,000
Resale value (₹)	:	40,000	32,000	28,000	25,000	22,000

Determine the optimum period for replacement. [*ICWA (Final) Dec., 1990*]

(*Ans.* After 4 years; ₹ 24,500.)

25. An auto owner finds from his past records that the cost per year of an auto whose purchase price is ₹ 60,000 is

Year	*Running cost (₹)*	*Resale price (₹)*
1	10,000	30,000
2	12,000	15,000
3	14,000	7,500
4	18,000	3,750
5	23,000	2,000
6	28,000	2,000
7	34,000	2,000
8	40,000	2,000

Determine at what age is its replacement due. [*P.T.U. MBA, 2008*]

(*Ans.* 5 years.)

11.2-2 Replacement of Items Whose Maintenance Costs Increase with Time and Value of Money also Changes with Time

As the money value changes with time, we must calculate the *present value or present worth* of the money to be spent a few years hence. If it is the interest rate (i may also be considered as the *rate of inflation* or the sum of the rates of *interest and inflation*) per year, a rupee invested at present will be equivalent to $(1 + i)$ a year hence, $(1 + i)^2$ two years hence, and $(1 + i)^n$ in n years time. In other words, making a payment of one rupee after n years is equivalent to paying $(1 + i)^{-n}$ now. The quantity $(1 + i)^{-n}$ is called the present worth or present value of one rupee spent n years from now.

Present value of a rupee spent n years hence $= (1 + i)^{-n} = v^n$,

where, $v = (1 + i)^{-1} = \dfrac{1}{1+i}$ is called *discount rate or discount factor or present worth factor (pwf)* and is always less than unity.

In order to find the optimal policy of replacement *i.e.*, when a manufacturer should replace a machine on which he is working, let us assume that the machine is replaced after n years. Let C be the purchase price of the machine and $R_1, R_2, \ldots, R_n$ be the running costs is 1st, 2nd,..., nth year respectively. Assuming that scrap value of the machine is zero and that all payments (cash outflows) are made at the beginning of each year, the present worth of expenditure in n years is

$$P_n = C + R_1 + vR_2 + v^2R_3 + \ldots + v^{n-1}.R_n. \qquad \ldots(11.5)$$

Thus P_n is the amount of money required *now* to pay all future costs of acquiring and operating the machine assuming that it is to be replaced after n years.

Now P_n increases as n increases which means that the present worth, if the machine is replaced after $n + 1$ years is greater than if it is replaced after n years. Thus for any additional amount spent we get an extra year's service. We are, therefore, interested in finding some function of *the replacement interval* which allows for this.

In order to do so, let us assume that the manufacturer invests the amount P_n by borrowing money at the interest rate i and repays it off in fixed annual payments, each of value x, throughout the life of the machine. Thus after n years he will have paid off the total cost P_n of the machine.

The present worth of fixed annual payments, each of value x, for n years is

$$x + vx + v^2x + \ldots + v^{n-1}x = \frac{1 - v^n}{1 - v}x.$$

Since this is equal to the sum P_n borrowed,

$$P_n = \frac{1 - v^n}{1 - v}x,$$

or

$$x = \frac{1 - v}{1 - v^n}P_n. \qquad \ldots(11.6)$$

Thus the best period to replace the machine is the period n which minimizes $x = \dfrac{1 - v}{1 - v^n}P_n$. However, since $(1 - v)$ is a positive constant, the period at which to replace the machine is the period n which minimizes the function $F_n = \dfrac{P_n}{1 - v^n}$.

Since n can have only discrete values, method of finite differences (appendix B) can be used to calculate its optimal value. By this method, n will be optimal *i.e.*, F_n will be minimum if

$$\Delta F_{n-1} < 0 < \Delta F_n. \qquad \ldots(11.7)$$

Now

$$\Delta F_n = F_{n+1} - F_n \qquad \ldots(11.8)$$

$$= \frac{P_{n+1}}{1 - v^{n+1}} - \frac{P_n}{1 - v^n} = \frac{(1 - v^n)P_{n+1} - (1 - v^{n+1})P_n}{(1 - v^{n+1})(1 - v^n)}$$

$$= \frac{1}{(1-v^{n+1})(1-v^n)} [(P_{n+1} - P_n) + (v^{n+1} P_n - v^n P_{n+1})] \quad ...(11.9)$$

Further, $\quad P_{n+1} = (C + R_1 + vR_2 + ... + v^{n-1} R_n) + v^n R_{n+1} = P_n + v^n R_{n+1}$.

From equation (11.9) we get

$$\Delta F_n = \frac{1}{(1-v^{n+1})(1-v^n)} [(v^n R_{n+1}) + v^{n+1} P_n - v^n \{P_n + v^n R_{n+1}\}]$$

$$= \frac{1}{(1-v^{n+1})(1-v^n)} [v^n R_{n+1} (1 - v^n) - v^n P_n (1 - v)]$$

$$= \frac{v^n (1-v)}{(1-v^{n+1})(1-v^n)} \left[\frac{1-v^n}{1-v} R_{n+1} - P_n\right] \quad ...(11.10)$$

$$= \text{a positive constant} \left[\frac{1-v^n}{1-v} R_{n+1} - P_n\right].$$

∴ ΔF_n has always the same sign as the quantity in brackets.

∴ From inequation (11.7), n will be optimal if

$$\frac{1-v^{n-1}}{1-v} R_n - P_{n-1} < 0 < \frac{1-v^n}{1-v} R_{n+1} - P_n. \quad ...(11.11)$$

From inequality (11.11) we have,

$$\frac{1-v^n}{1-v} R_{n+1} - P_n > 0$$

or $\quad R_{n+1} > P_n \cdot \dfrac{1-v}{1-v^n}$

or $\quad R_{n+1} > P_n \Big/ \dfrac{1-v^n}{1-v}$

or $\quad R_{n+1} > \dfrac{C + R_1 + vR_2 + v^2 R_3 + ... + v^{n-1} R_n}{1 + v + v^2 + ... + v^{n-1}} \quad ...(11.12a)$

or $\quad R_{n+1} > \dfrac{C + \sum_{r=1}^{n} R_r v^{r-1}}{\sum_{r=1}^{n} v^{r-1}} \quad ...(11.12b)$

or next periods cost > *weighted average* of previous costs, since the expression on the R.H.S. of inequation (11.12 *a*) is the weighted average of all costs upto and including period $n - 1$. The weights $1, v, v^2, ..., v^{n-1}$ are the *discount factors* applied to the costs in each period.

The other part of inequation (11.11) can, similarly, be expressed as

$$R_n < \frac{C + R_1 + vR_2 + v^2 R_3 + ... + v^{n-2} R_{n-1}}{1 + v + v^2 + ... + v^{n-2}} \quad ...(11.13a)$$

or $\quad R_n < \dfrac{C + \sum_{r=1}^{n} R_r v^{r-2}}{\sum_{r=1}^{n} v^{r-2}}. \quad ...(11.13b)$

From expressions (11.12*b*) and (11.13*b*) we conclude that

(a) *The machine should be replaced if the next period's cost is greater than the weighted average of previous costs.*

(b) *The machine should not be replaced if the next period's cost is less than the weighted average of previous costs.*

The corresponding value of the minimum annual payment x is obtained from equation (11.6) as

$$x = \frac{1-v}{1-v^n} \text{P}_n.$$

Further, if x_1 and x_2 are the minimum annual payments for two machines A and B, A will be preferred if $x_1 < x_2$ and vice versa.

It may be noted that the replacement policy of section 11.2-1 in which money value is ignored is a special case of this section. As interest rate $i \to 0$, the discount rate $v \to 1$ and expression (11.12 *a*) reduces to

$$R_{n+1} > \frac{\text{C} + \text{R}_1 + \text{R}_2 + ... + \text{R}_n}{1+1+1+...+n \text{ times}}$$

or
$$\text{R}_{n+1} > \frac{\text{P}_n}{n}, \text{ which is identical to equation (11.2).}$$

In actual practice, this type of replacement problem may be further complicated by the prevailing tax laws. A discussion of tax laws is beyond the scope of this book, but in any real problem the effect of taxes has got to be taken into account.

EXAMPLE 11.2-9

The yearly cost of two machines A and B, when money value is neglected is shown in table 11.13. Find their cost patterns if money value is 10% per year and hence find which machine is more economical.

TABLE 11.13

Year	*1*	*2*	*3*
Machine A (₹)	*1,800*	*1,200*	*1,400*
Machine B (₹)	*2,800*	*200*	*1,400*

[R.T.M. Nagpur U. B.Tech. June, 2006; P.T.U. B.E., 2001; Karn. U. B.E. (Mech.) 1998]

Solution

The total expenditure for each machine in three years when money value is not considered is ₹ 4,400. Thus the two machines are equally good if the money has no value over time. When the value of money is 10% per year, the discount rate

$$v = \frac{1}{1+0.10} = \frac{1}{1.1} = 0.9091.$$

The discounted cost patterns for machines A and B are shown in table 11.14.

TABLE 11.14

Year	1	2	3	*Total cost (₹)*
Machine A (Discounted cost in ₹)	1,800	1,200 × 0.9091 = 1,090.90	$1{,}400 \times 0.9091^2$ = 1,157.04	4,047,94
Machine B (Discounted cost in ₹)	2,800	200 × 0.9091 = 181.82	$1{,}400 \times 0.9091^2$ = 1,157.04	4,138.86

As total cost for machine A is less than that for machine B, machine A is more economical.

EXAMPLE 11.2-10

A machine costs ₹ 500. Operation and maintenance costs are zero for the first year and increase by ₹ 100 every year. If money is worth 5% every year, determine the best age at which the machine should be replaced. The resale value of the machine is negligibly small. What is the weighted average cost of owning and operating the machine? [*Gujarat Tech. U.B.E. Dec., 2012*]

Solution

Discount rate,

$$v = \frac{1}{1+r} = \frac{1}{1+0.05} = 0.9524.$$

To find the best replacement age, we enter the calculations in a table. Table 11.15 represents these calculations. From this table we find that

$$₹\ 200 < ₹\ 217.61 < ₹\ 300,$$

where ₹ 200 is the running cost of 3rd year and ₹ 300 is that of 4th year. Therefore, the machine should be replaced after *third year*. The weighted average cost of owning and operating the machine is ₹ 217.61.

TABLE 11.15

(1) Years of service (r)	(2) Maintenance cost (R_r) (₹)	(3) Discount factor (v^{r-1})	(4) Discounted cost $(R_r v^{r-1})$ (₹)	(5) Discounted total cost $C+\sum_{r=1}^{n} R_r v^{r-1}$ (₹)	(6) Cumulative discount factor $\sum_{r=1}^{n} v^{r-1}$	(7) Weighted average annual cost $\frac{C+\sum_{r=1}^{n} R_r v^{r-1}}{\sum_{r=1}^{n} v^{r-1}}$ (₹)
1	0	1.0000	0.00	500.00	1.0000	500.00
2	100	0.9524	95.24	595.24	1.9524	304.88
3	200	0.9070	181.40	776.64	2.3594	**217.61 Replace**
4	300	0.8638	259.14	1,035.78	3.7232	278.20
5	400	0.8227	329.08	1,364.86	4.5459	300.25

EXAMPLE 11.2-11

A manufacturer is offered two machines A and B. A has cost price of ₹ 2,500, its running cost is ₹ 400 for each of the first 5 years and increases by ₹ 100 every subsequent year. Machine B, having the same capacity as A, costs ₹ 1,250, has running cost of ₹ 600 for 6 years, increasing by ₹ 100 per year thereafter. If money is worth 10% per year, which machine should be purchased? Scrap value of both machines is negligibly small. [*DOEACC, 1997*]

Solution

As money is worth 10% per year, the discount rate for both machines is

$$v = \frac{1}{1+r} = \frac{1}{1+0.10} = 0.9091.$$

The calculations for machines A and B are entered in tables 11.16 and 11.17 respectively.

TABLE 11.16

Machine A

(1) *Years of service (r)*	(2) *Running cost (R_r)* (₹)	(3) *Discount factor (v^{r-1})*	(4) *Discounted running cost ($R_r v^{r-1}$)* (₹)	(5) $C + \sum_{r=1}^{n} R_r v^{r-1}$ (₹)	(6) $\sum_{r=1}^{n} v^{r-1}$	(7) $\frac{(5)}{(6)}$ (₹)
1	400	1.0000	400.00	2,900.00	1.0000	2,900.00
2	400	0.9091	363.64	3,263.64	1.9091	1,709.45
3	400	0.8264	330.56	3,594.20	2.7355	1,313.84
4	400	0.7513	300.52	3,894.72	3.4868	1,116.93
5	400	0.6830	273.20	4,167.92	4.1698	999.50
6	500	0.6209	310.45	4,478.37	4.7907	934.80
7	600	0.5645	338.70	4,817.07	5.3552	899.40
8	700	0.5132	359.24	5,176.31	5.8684	881.92
9	800	0.4665	373.20	5,549.51	6.3349	**875.86 Replace**
10	900	0.4241	381.69	5,931.20	6.7590	877.35

From Table 11.16, we conclude that for machine A, ₹ 800 < 875.86 < 900, where ₹ 800 is the running cost during 9th year and ₹ 900 is that in 10th year. Hence machine A should be replaced *after 9th year.*

TABLE 11.17

Machine B

(1) *Years of service (r)*	(2) *Running cost (R_r)* (₹)	(3) *Discount factor (v^{r-1})*	(4) *Discounted running cost ($R_r v^{r-1}$)* (₹)	(5) $C + \sum_{r=1}^{n} R_r v^{r-1}$ (₹)	(6) $\sum_{r=1}^{n} v^{r-1}$	(7) $\frac{(5)}{(6)}$ (₹)
1	600	1.0000	600.00	1,850.00	1.0000	1,850.00
2	600	0.9091	545.46	2,395.46	1.9091	1,254.75
3	600	0.8264	495.84	2,891.30	2.7355	1,056.95
4	600	0.7513	450.78	3,342.08	3.4868	958.49
5	600	0.6830	409.80	3,751.88	4.1698	899.77
6	600	0.6209	372.54	4,124.42	4.7907	860.92
7	700	0.5645	395.15	4,519.57	5.3552	843.96
8	800	0.5132	410.56	4,930.13	5.8684	**840.11 Replace**
9	900	0.4665	419.85	5,349.98	6.3349	844.52
10	1,000	0.4241	424.10	5,774.08	6.7590	854.28

Similarly, from table 11.17 for machine B we find that

₹ 800 < 840.11 < 900,

where ₹ 800 is the running cost in 8th year and ₹ 900 is that in 9th year. Hence machine B should be replaced *after 8th year.*

Further, since the weighted average cost in 9 years of machine A is ₹ 875.86 and weighted average cost in 8 years of machine B is ₹ 840.11, it is advisable to purchase *machine B.*

EXAMPLE 11.2-12

A manual stamper currently valued at ₹ 1,000 is expected to last 2 years and cost ₹ 4,000 per year to operate. An automatic stamper which can be purchased for ₹ 3,000 will last 4 years and can be operated at an annual cost of ₹ 3,000. If money carries the rate of interest 10% per annum, determine which stamper should be purchased.

Solution

The total present worth (discounted cost) of the manual stamper for two years is computed below.

TABLE 11.18

Year	*Cost (₹)*	*Discount factor*	*Discounted total cost (₹)*
1	1,000 + 4,000 = 5,000	1.0000	5,000
2	4,000	0.9091	3,636
			8,636

Total discounted cost of the automatic stamper for four years is computed below.

TABLE 11.19

Year	*Cost (₹)*	*Discount factor*	*Discounted total cost (₹)*
1	6,000	1.0000	6,000
2	3,000	0.9091	2,727
3	3,000	0.8264	2,479
4	3,000	0.7513	2,254
			13,460

∴ Average cost for 2 years = ₹ 6,730.

This shows that the apparent advantage is with the automatic stamper. But this comparison is unfair since the periods for which the costs are considered are different. If we consider the manual stamper also for 4 years, then its total discounted cost will be

TABLE 11.20

Year	*Cost (₹)*	*Discount factor*	*Discounted total cost (₹)*
1	5,000	1.0000	5,000
2	4,000	0.9091	3,636
3	5,000	0.8264	4,132
4	4,000	0.7513	3,005
			15,773

This proves conclusively that the automatic stamper should be installed.

EXAMPLE 11.2-13

The cost of a new machine is ₹ 5,000. The maintenance cost during the nth year is given by M_n = ₹ 500 (n – 1), where n = 1,2,3, ... If the discount rate per year is 0.05, after how many years will it be economical to replace the machine by a new one ?

[*J.N.T.U. Hyderabad B. Tech. Nov., 2010; R.T.M. Nagpur U. B.Tech. Dec., 2004*]

Solution

Since the discount rate of money is 0.05 per year, the present worth of the money to be spent after a year is

$$v = \frac{1}{1+.05} = 0.9523.$$

TABLE 11.21

Year (*r*) (1)	*Maintenance cost* (R_r) (2) (₹)	*Discount factor* (v^{r-1}) (3)	*Discounted maintenance cost* ($R_r v^{r-1}$) (4) (₹)	*Cumulative total discounted cost* $C+\sum_{r=1}^{n} R_r v^{r-1}$ (5) (₹)	*Cumulative discount factor* $\sum_{r=1}^{n} v^{r-1}$ (6)	*Weighted average annual cost* (7) $= \frac{(5)}{(6)}$ (7) (₹)
1	0	1.0000	0	5,000	1.0000	5,000
2	500	0.9523	476	5,476	1.9523	2,805
3	1,000	0.9070	907	6,383	2.8593	2,232
4	1,500	0.8638	1,296	7,679	3.7231	2,063
5	2,000	0.8227	1,645	9,324	4.5458	**2,051**
6	2,500	0.7835	1,959	11,283	5.3293	2,117

From table 11.21 it is clear that it will be economical to replace the machine at the end of 5th year.

EXAMPLE 11.2-14

A person is considering to purchase a machine for his factory. The related data about the alternative machines are as follows:

TABLE 11.22

	Machine A	*Machine B*	*Machine C*
Present investment (₹)	*10,000*	*12,000*	*15,000*
Total annual cost (₹)	*2,000*	*1,500*	*1,200*
Life (years)	*10*	*10*	*10*
Salvage value (₹)	*500*	*1,000*	*1,200*

As an adviser of the company, you have been asked to select the best machine considering 12% normal rate of return per year.

Given present worth factor @ 12% for 10 years = 5.650,
present worth factor @ 12% for 10th year = 0.322.

Solution

In this problem we shall calculate the present value of the total cost of each machine and the machine for which the present value is least is to be recommended. The calculations are given below:

TABLE 11.23

	Machine A	*Machine B*	*Machine C*
1. *Present investment* (₹)	10,000	12,000	15,000
2. *Present value of total annual cost* (₹)	2,000 ×5.650 = 11,300	1,500 × 5.650 = 8,475	1,200 × 5.650 = 6,780
3. *Present value of salvage value* (₹)	500 × 0.322 = 161	1,000 × 0.322 = 322	1,200 × 0.322 = 386.40
4. *Total cost* (1) + (2) – (3)	21,139	20,153	21,393.60

From the table it follows that machine B having the least present value of total cost should be purchased.

EXAMPLE 11.2-15

A scooter costs ₹ 6,000 when new. The running cost and salvage value (selling price) at the end of the year is given in table 11.24. If the interest rate is 10% per year and running costs are assumed to have occurred at mid year, find when the scooter should be replaced.

TABLE 11.24

Year	*1*	*2*	*3*	*4*	*5*	*6*	*7*
Running cost (₹)	*1,200*	*1,400*	*1,600*	*1,800*	*2,000*	*2,400*	*3,000*
Salvage value (₹)	*4,000*	*2,666*	*2,000*	*1,500*	*1,000*	*600*	*600*

[*J.N.T.U. Hyderabad B. Tech. May, 2011*]

Solution

As the interest rate is 10% per year, discount rate

$$v = \frac{1}{1+0.10} = 0.9091.$$

The running costs given in table 11.24 occur at mid-year and we can discount them to the start of the year by multiplying by $v^{1/2} = \sqrt{0.9091} = 0.95346$. The remaining calculations are shown in table 11.25. Costs have been calculated upto first decimal place only. It follows from the table that the scooter should be replaced after 5 years.

EXAMPLE 11.2-16

The cost of a new vehicle is ₹ 10,000. Compare the optimum period of replacement assuming the following cost information:

TABLE 11.26

Age of vehicle	*Repair cost/year (₹)*	*Salvage value at the end of the year (₹)*
1	*5,000*	*8,000*
2	*10,000*	*6,400*
3	*10,000*	*5,120*

Assume that repairs are made at the end of each year only if the vehicle is to be retained and are not necessary if the vehicle is to be sold for its salvage value. Assume discount rate of 10%. [*CA. (Final) Nov. 1982*]

Solution

Here, there are three replacement policies to be compared *viz.* replacement on a yearly, two-yearly and three-yearly basis. For this purpose, we shall consider a six-year period (LCM of 1, 2 and 3) so that each one of the policies would have completed a certain number of cycles. The calculations are shown in table 11.27.

TABLE 11.25

1	2	3	4	5	6	7	8	9	10	11	12
Year of service (r)	*Salvage value* (S_r) (₹)	*Running cost (mid-year)* (R'_r) (₹)	*Running cost (start of the year)* $(R_r = v^{1/2}R'_r)$ (₹)	(v^{r-1})	(v^r)	*Discounted running cost* $(R_r v^{r-1})$ (₹)	*Discounted salvage value* $(S_r v^r)$ (₹)	$C+\sum_{r=1}^{n} R_r v^{r-1}$ (₹)	$C+\sum_{r=1}^{n} R_r v^{r-1} - s_r v^r$ (₹)	$\sum_{r=1}^{n} v^r$	$\frac{(10)}{(11)}$ (₹)
1	4,000	1,200	1,144.2	1.0000	0.9091	1,144.2	3,636.4	7,144.2	3,507.8	0.9091	3,859.0
2	2,666	1,400	1,334.8	0.9091	0.8264	1,211.6	2,203.2	8,355.8	6,152.6	1.7355	3,544.2
3	2,000	1,600	1,525.6	0.8264	0.7513	1,260.8	1,502.6	9,616.6	8,114.0	2.4868	3,262.6
4	1,500	1,800	1,716.2	0.7513	0.6830	1,289.2	1,024.5	10,905.8	9,881.3	3.1698	3,117.2
5	1,000	2,000	1,907.0	0.6830	0.6209	1,302.4	620.9	12,208.2	11,587.3	3.7907	3,056.6
6	600	2,400	2,288.4	0.6209	0.5645	1,420.8	338.7	13,629.0	13,290.3	4.3552	**3,051.6**
7	600	3,000	2,860.4	0.5645	0.5132	1,614.7	307.9	15,243.7	14,935.8	4.8684	3,067.9

TABLE 11.27 Determination of Optimal Replacement Policy

Year	Purchase cost (₹)	Maintenance cost (₹)	Salvage value (₹)	Net cost (₹)	PV Factor	PV of cost (₹)
Yearly Replacement Policy						
0	10,000	–	–	10,000	1.0000	10,000.00
1	10,000	–	(8,000)	2,000	0.9091	1,818.20
2	10,000	–	(8,000)	2,000	0.8264	1,652.80
3	10,000	–	(8,000)	2,000	0.7513	1,502.60
4	10,000	–	(8,000)	2,000	0.6830	1,366.00
5	10,000	–	(8,000)	2,000	0.6209	1,241.80
6	–	–	(8,000)	(8,000)	0.5645	(4,516.00)
					Total cost	13,065.40
Two-Yearly Replacement Policy						
0	10,000			10,000	1.0000	10,000.00
1		5,000		5,000	0.9091	4,545.50
2	10,000		(6,400)	3,600	0.8264	2,975.00
3		5,000		5,000	0.7513	3,756.50
4	10,000		(6,400)	3,600	0.6830	2,458.80
5		5,000		5,000	0.6209	3,104.50
6	–		(6,400)	(6,400)	0.5645	(3,61,2.80)
					Total cost	23,227.50
Three-Yearly Replacement Policy						
0	10,000			10,000	1.0000	10,000.00
1		5,000		5,000	0.9091	4,545.50
2		10,000		10,000	0.8264	8,264.00
3	10,000		(5120)	4,880	0.7513	3,666.30
4		5,000		5,000	0.6830	3,415.00
5		10,000		10,000	0.6209	6,209.00
6			(5120)	(5,120)	0.5645	(2,890.20)
					Total cost	33,209.60

Since the total cost in respect of yearly replacement policy is the minimum, this is the optimal policy.

EXERCISES 11.2

1. Derive the expression for the condition to replace the equipment whose maintenance costs increase with time and the value of money also changes with time. [*Karn. U.B.E. (Mech.) 1996*]
2. Derive the following rules for minimizing costs in case of replacement of item whose maintenance costs increase with time :
   (*i*) Replace if the next period's cost is greater than the weighted average of the previous costs.
   (*ii*) Do not replace if the next period's cost is less than the weighted average of the previous costs. [*Raj.U. M.Phil., 1992*]
3. Find the optimum replacement policy which minimizes the total of all future discounted costs for an equipment which costs ₹ *a* and which needs maintenance costs of ₹ C_1, C_2, ..., C_n, etc. ($C_{n-1} > C_n$) during the first year, second year, etc., respectively; and further *d* is the depreciation value for unit of money during a year.

4. Purchase price of a machine is ₹ 3,000 and its running cost is given in the table below. If the discount rate is 0.90, find at what age the machine should be replaced.

Year	1	2	3	4	5	6	7
Running cost (₹)	500	600	800	1,000	1,300	1,600	2,000

[*Ranchi M.Sc. (Math.)* 1983]

(*Ans.* After 3 years.)

5. The cost of a new machine is ₹ 4,000. The maintenance cost of *n*th year is given by $R_n = 500\ (n - 1)$; $n = 1, 2, \ldots$. Suppose that the discount rate per year is 0.05. After how many years will it be economical to replace the machine by a new one ? [*R.T.M. Nagpur U. B.Tech. (Mech.) Dec., 2008*]

(*Ans.* After 4 years.)

6. A truck is priced at ₹ 60,000 and running costs are estimated at ₹ 6,000 for each of the first four years, increasing by ₹ 2,000 per year in the fifth and subsequent years. If money is worth 10% per year, when should the truck be replaced ? Assume that the truck will eventually be sold for scrap at a negligible price. [*M.G.U. Kerala M.Com., June, 2012*]

(*Ans.* After 9 years.)

7. A company has the option to buy one of the minicomputers: MINICOMP and CHIPCOMP. MINICOMP costs ₹ 5 lakhs, and running and maintenance costs are ₹ 60,000 for each of the first five years, increasing by ₹ 20,000 in the sixth and subsequent years. CHIPCOMP has the same capacity as MINICOMP but costs only ₹ 2,50,000. However, its running and maintenance costs are ₹ 1,20,000 per year in the first five years and increase by ₹ 20,000 per year thereafter. If the money is worth 10% per year, which computer should be purchased ? What are the optimal replacement periods for each computer? Assume that there is no salvage value for either computer. Explain your analysis. [*R.T.M. Nagpur U.B.Com. (Mech.) June, 2007*]

(*Ans.* MINICOMP : 9 years; ₹ 1,55,204
CHIPCOMP : 7 years; ₹ 1,73,219.)

8. The yearly cost of two machines A and B in rupees when money value is neglected is as follows:

Year	:	1	2	3	4	5
Machine A	:	1,800	1,200	1,400	1,600	1,000
Machine B	:	2,800	200	1,400	1,100	600

Find the cost patterns if money value is 10% per year and hence find which machine is more economical. [*Chennai B.E. (Mech.) 1999*]

9. A person is planning to purchase a car. A new car costs ₹ 1,20,000. The resale value of the car at the end of the year is 85% of the previous year. Maintenance and operation costs during the first year are ₹ 20,000 and they increase by 15% every year. The minimum resale value of the car can be ₹ 40,000.
(*a*) When should the car be replaced to minimize average annual cost ?
(*b*) If interest of 12% is assumed, when should the car be replaced ? [*Kerala U. M.Com., 1990*]

10. A firm pays ₹ 10,000 for its equipments; their operating and maintenance costs are about ₹ 2,500 per year for the first two years and then go up by approximately ₹ 1,500 per year. When such equipment be replaced, if the discount rate is 10% per year ? [*J.N.T.U. Hyderabad B.Tech. (Mech.) May, 2012*]

11. A pipeline is due for repairs. It will cost ₹ 10,000 and lasts for 3 years. Alternatively, a new pipeline can be laid at a cost of ₹ 30,000 and lasts for 10 years. Assuming cost of capital to be 10% and ignoring salvage value, which alternative should be chosen? [*J.N.T.U. Hyderabad B.Tech. Nov., 2011; May, 2009*]

12. The data collected in running a machine are given below :

Year	*Cost of spares and maintenance (₹)*	*Resale value (₹)*
1	16,000	42,000
2	18,000	30,000
3	21,000	20,500
4	25,000	14,500
5	30,000	10,000
6	36,000	8,000

Assuming the interest rate as 10% and cost of m/c as ₹ 60,000, determine the optimal replacement age of machine. [*R.T.M. Nagpur U. B.Tech. Dec., 2005; Dec., 2003*]

13. (*a*) What are the various costs that one should take into consideration while suggesting a replacement policy ?

(*b*) A fleet owner finds from his past records that the cost per year of an auto whose purchase price is ₹ 60,000 is as given below :

Year	*Running cost (₹)*	*Resale value (₹)*
1	10,000	30,000
2	12,000	15,000
3	14,000	7,500
4	18,000	3,750
5	23,000	2,000
6	28,000	2,000
7	34,000	2,000
8	40,000	2,000

Assuming rate of return as 8%, determine at what age is its replacement due.

[*R.T.M. Nagpur U. B.Tech. June, 2005*]

14. (*a*) What are the different costs that one should take into consideration while suggesting a replacement policy ?

(*b*) The data collected in running a machine are given below. Assuming the interest rate as 12% and cost of machine as ₹ 1,50,000, determine the optimal replacement age of the machine.

Year	*Running cost (₹)*	*Salvage value (₹)*
1	10,000	1,30,000
2	15,000	1,20,000
3	20,000	1,15,000
4	25,000	1,05,000
5	30,000	90,000
6	40,000	75,000
7	45,000	60,000
8	50,000	50,000

[*R.T.M. Nagpur U. B.Tech. June, 2003*]

15. An engineering company is offered a material handling equipment. It is purchased for ₹ 60,000 originally and maintenance costs are estimated to be ₹ 10,000 for each of the first 5 years, increasing by ₹ 3,000 every year thereafter. The company expects a return of 10% on all its investments. What is the optimum replacement period ? Assume that the maintenance costs are incurred at the end of the year.

[*Pbi.U. MBA, 1988*]

(*Ans.* End of 8th year; ₹ 19,311.)

16. XYZ Machine Tools seek your expert opinion for the optimum replacement period of a machine used by them. The data relevant for decision-making are given below :

(*i*) Capital cost of the machine is ₹ 10,000.

(*ii*) Operating cost is ₹ 500 in the first four years and then it increases by ₹ 300 each year.

(*iii*) Interest rate for the firm is 10% p.a.

[*D.U. MBA, 2008*]

(*Ans.* 10th year; ₹ 2,447.)

17. It is required to find the optimal replacement time of a certain type of equipment. The initial cost of equipment is C. Salvage value and repair cost are given by S(*t*) and R(*t*) respectively. The cost of capital is *r* per cent and T is the time period of replacement cycle.

(*i*) Show that the present value of all future costs associated with a policy of equipment replacement after time T is

$$\left(\frac{1}{1-e^{-rt}}\right)\left[C - S(t)\,e^{-rt} + \int_0^T R(t)e^{-rt}\,dt\right].$$

(*ii*) The optimal value of T is given by

$$R(t) - S'(t) + S(t)\, r = r^k / (1 - e^{-rt}),$$

where k is the present value of the cycle. [*I.S.I. Dip., 1976*]

18. If you wish to have a return of 10% per annum on your investment, which of the following plans would you prefer?

		Plan A	*Plan B*
		(*in rupees*)	
1st cost	:	2,00,000	2,50,000
Scrap value after 15 years	:	1,50,000	1,80,000
Excess of annual revenue over annual disbursement	:	25,000	30,000

[*Karn. U. B. E. (Mech.) 1995*]
(*Ans*. Plan A.)

11.3 REPLACEMENT OF ITEMS THAT FAIL SUDDENLY

In the previous section we considered replacement of items that deteriorate with time resulting in increasing maintenance and operation costs. The optimal lives of the items were found by balancing the increased running costs against decreased depreciation. However, there are many real life situations in which items do not deteriorate with time but fail suddenly. A system usually consists of a large number of low-cost items that are increasingly liable to failure with age (*e.g.*, failure of some resistor in a radio, television, computer, etc.). Sometimes, the failure of an item may cause a complete breakdown of the system. The costs of failure, in such a case will be quite higher than the cost of the item itself. For example, a tube or a condenser in an aircraft costs little, but its failure may result in total collapse of the aircraft. Similarly, failure of an industrial equipment such as a pump in a refinery may close down the entire system and may cause heavy losses due to loss in production, idle labour, wastage and other damages.

It is, therefore, quite important to know, *in advance*, as to when the failure is likely to take place so that item can be replaced before it actually fails. Rigorous inspection may be required to detect imminent failures and once they are detected, *preventive replacement* may be quite economical. Quite often, however, it may not be possible to predict the time of failure by direct inspection. In such cases, the time of failure can be predicted from the probability distribution of failure time obtained from past experience. The problem, then, is to find the optimal value of time t which minimizes the total cost involved in the system.

Two types of replacement policies are considered when dealing with such situations:

1. *Individual replacement policy* (*remedial replacement policy*) in which an item is replaced immediately after it fails.
2. *Group replacement policy* (*preventive replacement policy*) in which all items are replaced, at the end of an optimal time period, irrespective of whether they have failed or not, with a provision that if any item fails before the *optimal* time, it may be individually replaced.

11.3-1 Group Replacement Policy

Quite often a system consists of a *large number of identical, low-cost items* which are more and more likely to fail with time. It may be economical to replace all such items at fixed intervals. Such a policy of replacement is called *group replacement policy* and is particularly suitable when the cost of individual item is comparatively small. An important example is of replacing the street light bulbs.

Thus under this policy we replace all items at fixed interval '*t*' whether they have failed or not and at the same time go on replacing failed items as and when they fail during that interval. The problem is to determine the optimum group replacement time interval.

Let N : The total number of items in the system,
N_t : Number of items that fail during time t,

C(t) : The total cost of group replacement after a time t, so that average cost per unit time is $\dfrac{C(t)}{t}$,

C_1 : Cost of replacing an item when all the items in that group are replaced simultaneously,

C_2 : Cost of replacing an individual item on failure.

Then, clearly

$$C(t) = C_1N + C_2\,[N_1 + N_2 + ... + N_{t-1}].$$

$$\therefore \text{ Average cost per unit time} = \frac{C(t)}{t} = F(t) = \frac{C_1N + C_2(N_1 + N_2 + ... + N_{t-1})}{t}. \quad ...(11.14)$$

Now optimum group replacement time 't' will be that period which minimizes the average cost per unit time.

The condition for minimum F(t) is

$$\Delta\, F(t-1) < 0 < \Delta\, F(t). \quad ...(11.15)$$

Now

$$\Delta\, F(t) = F(t+1) - F(t)$$

$$= \frac{C(t+1)}{t+1} - \frac{C(t)}{t} = \frac{C(t) + C_2N_t}{t+1} - \frac{C(t)}{t}$$

$$= \frac{t\,\{C(t) + C_2N_t\} - C(t)\,\{t+1\}}{t\,(t+1)} = \frac{t\,C_2N_t - C(t)}{t(t+1)}$$

or

$$\Delta F(t) = \frac{C_2N_t - \dfrac{C(t)}{t}}{(t+1)}, \quad ...(11.16)$$

which must be greater than zero for minimum F(t).

i.e.,

$$\frac{C_2N_t - \dfrac{C(t)}{t}}{(t+1)} > 0$$

or

$$C_2N_t > \frac{C(t)}{t}. \quad ...(11.17)$$

Similarly from $\Delta F(t-1) < 0$, we can prove that

$$C_2N_{t-1} < \frac{C(t-1)}{t-1}. \quad ...(11.18)$$

From equations (11.17) and (11.18) we get the following group replacement policy:

1. *Group replacement should be made at the end of tth period if the cost of individual replacement for the tth period is more than the average cost per unit time through the end of t periods.*
2. *Group replacement should not be made at the end of tth period if the cost of individual replacement for the tth period is less than the average cost per unit time through the end of t periods.*

EXAMPLE 11.3-1

The following mortality rates have been observed for a certain type of light bulbs in an installation with 1,000 bulbs :

End of week	:	*1*	*2*	*3*	*4*	*5*	*6*
Probability of failure to date	:	*0.09*	*0.25*	*0.49*	*0.85*	*0.97*	*1.00*

There are a large number of such bulbs which are to be kept in working order. If a bulb fails in service, it costs ₹ 3 to replace but if all the bulbs are replaced in the same operation, it can be done for only ₹ 0.70 a bulb. It is proposed to replace all bulbs at fixed intervals, whether or not they have burnt out, and to continue replacing burnt out bulbs as they fail. (a) What is the best interval between group replacements ? (b) Also establish if the policy, as determined by you, is superior to the policy of replacing bulbs as and when they fail, there being nothing like 'group replacement'. (c) At what group replacement price per bulb, would a policy of strictly individual replacement become preferable to the adopted policy ?

Assume that all the bulbs failing during a week might fail at any time of the week and that the group replacements are made only at the end of a week.

Solution

Let p_i be the probability that a new light bulb fails during the ith week of its life. Then we get the following probability distribution of the lives of the bulbs :

$$p_1 = 0.09,$$
$$p_2 = 0.25 - 0.09 = 0.16,$$
$$p_3 = 0.49 - 0.25 = 0.24,$$
$$p_4 = 0.85 - 0.49 = 0.36,$$
$$p_5 = 0.97 - 0.85 = 0.12,$$
$$p_6 = 1.00 - 0.97 = 0.03.$$

Since the sum of all probabilities is unity, all probabilities higher than p_6 must be zero *i.e.*. $p_7 = p_8 = p_9$, etc.= 0. Thus all light bulbs are sure to burn out by the 6th week.

From this distribution we observe that 9 per cent of the bulbs are expected to burn out during the first week of their life. In the lot of 1,000 bulbs, therefore, 90 bulbs are expected to fail in the first week. Similarly, of this lot, 16% *i.e.*, 160 bulbs are expected to fail during the second week, 240 bulbs in the third week, 360 in the fourth week, 120 in the fifth week and the remaining 30 in the sixth week.

Of the 90 bulbs that would be replaced in the first week, 9 per cent *i.e.*, 8 bulbs would fail in the first week of their life, that is to say, in week 2, 16 per cent (= 14 bulbs) would fail in week 3, and so on. Similarly, of the total replacements numbering 168 (160 of the original lot plus 8 out of the 90 replacements in the first week) during the second week, 9 per cent will fail during the third week, 16 per cent during the fourth week and so on.

These number of failures (and hence number of replacements) in different weeks are calculated in table 11.28 below.

TABLE 11.28

Week (i)	*Expected number of failures (N_i)*
0	$N_0 = N_0 \qquad = 1{,}000,$
1	$N_1 = N_0p_1 = 1{,}000 \times 0.09 \qquad = 90,$
2	$N_2 = N_0p_2 + N_1p_1 = 1{,}000 \times 0.16 + 90 \times 0.09 \qquad = 168,$
3	$N_3 = N_0p_3 + N_1 p_2 + N_2p_1 = 1{,}000 \times 0.24 + 90 \times 0.16 + 168 \times 0.09 \qquad = 269,$
4	$N_4 = N_0p_4 + N_1p_3 + N_2p_2 + N_3p_1 = 1{,}000 \times 0.36 + 90 \times 0.24 + 168 \times 0.16 + 269 \times 0.09 \qquad = 432,$
5	$N_5 = N_0p_5 + N_1p_4 + N_2p_3 + N_3p_2 + N_4p_1 = 1{,}000 \times 0.12 + 90 \times 0.36 + 168 \times 0.24 + 269 \times 0.16 + 432 \times 0.09 \qquad = 274,$
6	$N_6 = N_0p_6 + N_1p_5 + N_2p_4 + N_3p_3 + N_4p_2 + N_5p_1 = 1{,}000 \times 0.03 + 90 \times 0.12 + 168 \times 0.36 + 269 \times 0.24 + 432 \times 0.16 + 274 \times 0.09 \qquad = 260,$
7	$N_7 = 0 + N_1p_6 + N_2p_5 + N_3p_4 + N_4p_3 + N_5p_2 + N_6p_1 = 90 \times 0.03 + 168 \times 0.12 + 269 \times 0.36 + 432 \times 0.24 + 274 \times 0.16 + 260 \times 0.09 \qquad = 291,$
and so on.	

Thus we find that the number of bulbs failing each week increases till the 4th week, then decreases and again increases from 7th week. Thus N_i will continue to oscillate till the system attains a steady state. Thereafter, the proportion of the bulbs failing each week will be the reciprocal of their average life.

Now we can determine the total and, thereby, the average weekly cost associated with the policy of replacing bulbs every week, every two weeks, ... and so on as per the group replacement policy; keeping in mind that replacement of all the 1,000 bulbs in one operation costs ₹ 0.70 per bulb and replacement of an individual bulb costs ₹ 3.

(*a*) *Determination of optimal group replacement interval*

Upto week	*Total cost of group replacement* (₹)	*Average cost per week* (₹)
1	1,000 × 0.70 + 90 × 3 = 970	970.00
2	1,000 × 0.70 + 3 (90 + 168) = 1,474	**737.00**
3	1,000 × 0.70 + 3 (90 + 168 + 269) = 2,281	760.33

As the average minimum cost is in the 2nd week, it is optimal to have a group replacement after every *two weeks*.

(*b*) When the policy of 'replacing the bulbs as and when they fail' is adopted, there are no group replacements and it becomes an individual replacement policy. Since it is assumed that a bulb can fail at any time during the week, it is necessary to first determine the average (mean or expected) life a light bulb.

$$\text{Average (expected) life of light bulbs} = \sum_{i=1}^{6} ip_i$$

$$= 1 \times 0.09 + 2 \times 0.16 + 3 \times 0.24 + 4 \times 0.36 + 5 \times 0.12 + 6 \times 0.03 = 3.35.$$

$$\therefore \text{Average number of failures per week} = \frac{1{,}000}{3.35} = 299.$$

∴ Cost of individual replacement of bulbs per week = ₹ 3 × 299 = ₹ 897.

Since the cost of group replacements per week is ₹ 737 and that of individual replacements is ₹ 897 per week, it is advisable to adopt the policy of group replacements.

(*c*) Let ₹ x be the group replacement price per bulb. Then,

$$₹\ 897 < \frac{1{,}000x + 3\,(90 + 168)}{2}.$$

$$\therefore \qquad x > ₹\ 1.02.$$

Therefore, when the group replacement price per bulb exceeds ₹ 1.02, the policy of strictly individual replacements becomes more economical.

EXAMPLE 11.3-2

Find the cost per period of individual replcement policy of an installation of 300 light bulbs, given the following:

(*i*) *Cost of replacing an individual bulb is* ₹ *2.*

(*ii*) *Conditional probability of failure is given below:*

Week no.	:	0	1	2	3	4
Conditional probability of failure	:	0	0.1	0.3	0.7	1.0

Also calculate the number of light bulbs that would fail during each of the four weeks.

[*P.T.U. B.Tech. April, 2012*]

Solution

Let p_i be the probability that a light bulb fails during the ith week of its life. Then

$$p_0 = 0,$$
$$p_1 = 0.1,$$
$$p_2 = 0.3 - 0.1 = 0.2,$$
$$p_3 = 0.7 - 0.3 = 0.4,$$

and $$p_4 = 1 - 0.7 = 0.3.$$

Since the sum of all the above probabilities is unity, all probabilities higher than p_4 must be zero. Thus all light bulbs are sure to burn out by the 4th week.

Let N_i represent the number of replacements made at the end of ith week when all the 300 bulbs are new initially. Then we have

Week	*Expected number of failures*	
0	N_0	$= 300$
1	$N_1 = N_0 p_1 = 300 \times 0.1$	$= 30$
2	$N_2 = N_0 p_2 + N_1 p_1 = 300 \times 0.2 + 30 \times 0.1 = 60 + 3$	$= 63$
3	$N_3 = N_0 p_3 + N_1 p_2 + N_2 p_1 = 300 \times 0.4 + 30 \times 0.2 + 63 \times 0.1$	$= 132$
4	$N_4 = N_0 p_4 + N_1 p_3 + N_2 p_2 + N_3 p_1 = 300 \times .3 + 30 \times 0.4 + 63 \times 0.2 + 132 \times 0.1$	$= 128$

∴ Number of light bulbs failing during week 1, 2, 3 and 4 are 30, 63, 132 and 128 respectively.

Thus we find that the number of bulbs failing each week increases till the 3rd week and then decreases during the 4th week.

$$\text{Average life of light bulbs} = \sum_{i=1}^{4} ip_i = 1 \times 0.1 + 2 \times 0.2 + 3 \times 0.4 + 4 \times 0.3 = 2.9 \text{ weeks.}$$

$$\therefore \text{ Average number of failures per week} = \frac{300}{2.9} = 103 \text{ (approx.)}.$$

∴ Cost of individual replacement of bulbs = ₹ 2 × 103 = ₹ 206/ week.

EXAMPLE 11.3-3

The typing pool of a large organisation employs 100 copy typists. The distribution of length of service is given in the following table:

Duration of employment in years	:	*1*	*2*	*3*	*4*	*5 or more*
Proportion of staff leaving in that year of employment	:	*30%*	*40%*	*20%*	*10%*	*0%*

Assuming that an employee leaving is replaced by another at the end of the year, determine

(i) the number of staff who leave in each of the first 8 years of the department's existence, assuming it started with 100 employees and this total number does not change.

(ii) the number leaving each year when the steady state situation is reached, and

(iii) the total annual cost of recruiting staff in the steady state if replacement of each new copy typist costs ₹ 200.

Solution

(*i*) It is given that initially there are 100 copy typists in the organisation and that no person stays in service for more than 5 years. The probabilities of leaving the service after 1, 2, ..., 5 years can be used to calculate the number of staff who leave the organisation in the first eight years of its existence.

Year	*No. of employees leaving by the end of the year*	*No. of new persons employed*
0	N_0 = Nil	$N_0 = 100$
1	$N_1 = N_0p_1 = 100 \times 0.30$	$N_1 = 30$
2	$N_2 = N_1p_1 + N_0p_2 = 30 \times .3 + 100 \times .4$	$N_2 = 49$
3	$N_3 = N_2p_1 + N_1p_2 + N_0p_3 = 49 \times .3 + 30 \times .4 + 100 \times .2$	$N_3 = 46.7$
4	$N_4 = N_3p_1 + N_2p_2 + N_1p_3 + N_0p_4 = 46.7 \times .3 + 49 \times .4 + 30 \times .2 + 100 \times .1$	$N_4 = 49.6$
5	$N_5 = N_4p_1 + N_3p_2 + N_2p_3 + N_1p_4 + N_0p_5 = 49.6 \times .3 + 46.7 \times .4 + 49 \times .2 + 30 \times .1 + 100 \times 0$	$N_5 = 46.4$
6	$N_6 = N_5p_1 + N_4p_2 + N_3p_3 + N_2p_4 + N_1p_5 + N_0p_6 = 46.4 \times .3 + 49.6 \times .4 + 46.7 \times .2 + 49 \times .1 + 30 \times 0 + 100 \times 0$	$N_6 = 48$
7	$N_7 = N_6p_1 + N_5p_2 + N_4p_3 + N_3p_4 + N_2p_5 = 48 \times .3 + 46.4 \times .4 + 49.6 \times .2 + 46.7 \times .1 + 49 \times 0$	$N_7 = 47.6$
8	$N_8 = N_7p_1 + N_6p_2 + N_5p_3 + N_4p_4 + N_3p_5 = 47.6 \times .3 + 48 \times .4 + 46.4 \times .2 + 49.6 \times .1 + 46.7 \times 0$	$N_8 = 47.7$

(*ii*) The expected length of service of any copy typist in the organisation

$$= 1 \times .3 + 2 \times .4 + 3 \times .2 + 4 \times .1 = 2.1 \text{ years.}$$

∴ Average number of employees leaving by the end of each year in steady state

$$= \frac{100}{2.1} = 47.62.$$

(*iii*) The annual cost of replacing a copy typist in steady state

= cost of replacement × average number of replacements in a year

= ₹ (200 × 47.62) = ₹ 9,524.

EXAMPLE 11.3-4

A unit of electrical equipment is subject to failure. The probability distribution of its age at failure is

Age at failure (weeks)	*2*	*3*	*4*	*5*
Probability	*0.2*	*0.4*	*0.3*	*0.1*

Initially 10,000 new units are installed and any unit which fails is replaced by a new unit at the end of the week in which it fails.

(a) *Calculate the expected number of units to be replaced in each of weeks 1 to 7. What rate of failures can be expected in the long run ?*

(b) *Among the 10,000 installed units at the start of week 8, how many can be expected to be aged zero week, 1 week, 2 weeks, 3 weeks or 4 weeks? Compare this with the expected frequency distribution in the long run.*

(c) *Replacement of individual units on failure costs 5 paise each. An alternative policy is to replace all units after a fixed number of weeks (at a cost of ₹300) and to replace any units failing before the replacement interval at the individual cost of 5 paise each at the end of week in which they fail. Should this preventive policy be adopted ? If so, after how many weeks should all units be replaced ?* [DOEACC, 1995]

Solution

(*a*) *Age of failure*

Weeks	:	1	2	3	4	5
Probability	:	0.0	0.2	0.4	0.3	0.1

Let N_i be the number of replacements made at the end of week *i*.

End of week	*Number of units replaced*	
0	N_0	$= 10{,}000$
1	$N_1 = N_0p_1 = 10{,}000 \times 0.0$	$= 0$
2	$N_2 = N_0p_2 + N_1p_1 = 10{,}000 \times .2 + 0$	$= 2{,}000$
3	$N_3 = N_0p_3 + N_1p_2 + N_2p_1 = 10{,}000 \times .4 + 0 \times .2 + 2{,}000 \times 0.0$	$= 4{,}000$
4	$N_4 = N_0p_4 + N_1p_3 + N_2p_2 + N_3p_1 = 10{,}000 \times .3 + 0$ $+ 2{,}000 \times .2 + 4{,}000 \times 0.0$	$= 3{,}400$
5	$N_5 = N_0p_5 + N_1p_4 + N_2p_3 + N_3p_2 + N_4p_1$ $= 10{,}000 \times .1 + 0 \times .3 + 2{,}000 \times .4 + 4{,}000 \times .2 + 3{,}400 \times 0.0$	$= 2{,}600$
6	$N_6 = N_0p_6 + N_1p_5 + N_2p_4 + N_3p_3 + N_4p_2 + N_5p_1$ $= 10{,}000 \times 0.0 + 0 + 2{,}000 \times .3 + 4{,}000 \times .4 + 3{,}400 \times .2$ $+ 2{,}600 \times 0.0$	$= 2{,}880$
7	$N_7 = N_0p_7 + N_1p_6 + N_2p_5 + N_3p_4 + N_4p_3 + N_5p_2 + N_6p_1$ $= 10{,}000 \times 0 + 2{,}000 \times .1 + 4{,}000 \times .3 + 3{,}400 \times .4 + 2{,}600 \times .2$ $+ 2{,}880 \times 0.0$	$= 3{,}280$

Mean life at failure $= 2 \times 0.2 + 3 \times 0.4 + 4 \times 0.3 + 5 \times 0.1 = 3.3$ weeks.

$\therefore$ Average rate of failures in the long run $= \dfrac{10{,}000}{3.3} = 3{,}030$ per week.

(*b*) Expected frequency distribution of ages at the beginning of 8th week:

Age (weeks)		*Number*
0	=	3,280
1	=	2,880
2	$\{1 - 0.2\} \times 2{,}600$ =	2,080
3	$\{1 - (0.2 + 0.4)\} \times 3{,}400$ =	1,360
4	$\{1 - (0.2 + 0.4 + 0.3)\} \times 4{,}000$ =	400
		10,000

Since 3,030 units are replaced on the average each week, the expected number of units at any time having age 0 and 1 week is 3,030 each. The long-run expected age distribution is, therefore, given by

Age (weeks)		*Number*
0		3,030
1		3,030
2	$\{1 - 0.2\} \times 3{,}030$ =	2,424
3	$\{1 - (0.2 + 0.4)\} \times 3{,}030$ =	1,213
4	$\{1 - (0.2 + 0.4 + 0.3)\} \times 3{,}030$ =	303
		10,000

(*c*) *Individual Replacement Policy*

With individual replacement, the average replacement cost is = ₹ (3,030 × 0.05) = ₹ 151.50 per week.

Group Replacement Policy

Units failing during a week are to be replaced at the end of that week. However, if at the end of a week there is group replacement, individual replacement need not be resorted to and individual replacement cost during that week will not be incurred *i.e.,* it will be zero.

End of week	*Total cost of group replacement*	*Average cost per week*
1	300	300
2	300 + 0 × 0.05 = 300	150
3	300 + (0 + 2,000) × 0.05 = 400	**133.33**
4	300 + (0 + 2,000 + 4,000) × 0.05 = 600	150

∴ The minimum cost replacement policy is group replacement every three weeks at a cost of ₹ 133.33 per week.

EXAMPLE 11.3-5

(a) At time zero, all items in a system are new. Each item has a probability p of failing immediately before the end of first month of life and a probability q (= 1 – p) of failing immediately before the end of the second month (i.e., all items fail by the end of the second month). If all items are replaced as they fail, show that the expected number of failures f(x) at the end of month x is given by

$$f(x) = \frac{N}{1+q}\,[1-(-q)^{x+1}],$$

where N is the number of items in the system.

(b) If the cost per item of individual replacement is C_1 and the cost per item of group replacement is C_2, find the condition under which

(i) a group replacement policy at the end of each month is the most profitable.

(ii) a group replacement policy at the end of every other month is the most profitable.

(iii) no group replacement policy is better than a policy of pure individual replacement.

[*Delhi M.Sc.* (*Math.*) 1971, 76; *Meerut M.Sc. (Stat.) 1970*]

Solution

(*a*) Let N_i be the number of items expected to fail at the end of *ith* month.

$$\therefore \quad N_1 = \text{Number of items expected to fail at the end of 1st month}$$
$$= N.p$$
$$= N(1-q),$$
$$N_2 = \text{Number of items expected to fail at the end of 2nd month}$$
$$= Nq + N_1 p$$
$$= Nq + N_1(1-q)$$
$$= Nq + N(1-q)^2$$
$$= N(1-q+q^2),$$
$$N_3 = \text{Number of items expected to fail at the end of 3rd month}$$
$$= N_1 q + N_2 p$$
$$= N(1-q)\,q + N(1-q+q^2)(1-q)$$
$$= N(1-q+q^2-q^3),$$
$$\vdots$$
$$N_n = N[1-q+q^2-q^3+\ldots+(-q)^n].$$
$$\therefore \quad f(x) = \text{Number of items expected to fail at the end of month } x$$
$$= N[1-q+q^2-q^3+\ldots+(-q)^x]$$
$$= N\left[\frac{1-(-q)^{x+1}}{1-(-q)}\right] = \frac{N}{1+q}\,[1-(-q)^{x+1}].$$

(*b*) Average life of an item = $1.p + 2q = 1(1-q) + 2q = 1 + q$.

$\therefore$ Average number of failures $= \dfrac{N}{1+q}$.

$\therefore$ Cost of individual replacement $= \dfrac{N}{1+q} C_1$.

(*i*) For a group replacement policy at the end of each month, the cost of replacement is NC_2. This replacement policy is most profitable if

$$\frac{N}{1+q} C_1 > NC_2.$$

(*ii*) For a group replacement policy at the end of every other month, the cost of replacement is $NC_2 + N_1C_1 = NC_2 + N.p.C_1$. Therefore, the average cost per month is $\dfrac{NC_2 + N.p.C_1}{2}$.

This replacement policy is most profitable if

$$\frac{N}{1+q} C_1 > \frac{NC_2 + N.p.C_1}{2}.$$

(*iii*) No group replacement policy is better than a policy of pure individual replacement if

$$NC_2 > \frac{N}{1+q} C_1$$

and $$\frac{NC_2 + N.p.C_1}{2} > \frac{N}{1+q} C_1.$$

EXERCISES 11.3

1. Explain how the theory of replacement is used in the replacement of items that fail suddenly.
[*P.T.U. B.Tech. (Mech.) April, 2013; MBA Nov., 2012; Univ. of Madras MBA Nov., 2012; J.N.T.U. Hyderabad B.Tech. May, 2011; Nov., 2010; R.T.M. Nagpur U. B.Tech. 2004, 03; Nagpur U. B.E. (Mech.) 2003*]
2. Why is replacement of items required ? Distinguish between individual replacement and group replacement policies. [*R.U. MBA June, 2011; J.N.T.U. Hyderabad B.Tech. (C.Sc.) Dec., 2011; P.T.U. B.Tech. (Mech.) 2011, 2010, 2001*]
3. Write a note on group replacement policy. [*J.N.T.U. Hyderabad B.Tech. (Mech.) May, 2012; R.T.M. Nagpur U.B.E.(I.T.) 2009; P.T.U. MBA, 2009*]
4. What is the objective of replacement analysis and what are the costs associated with sudden failure of items ? [*ICWA (Final) Dec., 1991*]
5. An electronic equipment has 5,000 IC's. If any one IC fails, it has to be replaced. Cost of replacing a single IC is ₹ 10. The data of failures are given below :

Month	:	1	2	3	4	5	6
% surviving at the end of each month	:	0.03	0.10	0.30	0.40	0.15	0.02

Obtain the best replacement policy to replace the individual IC's which fail during fixed interval. [*P.T.U. MBA, 2009*]

6. The following mortality rates have been observed for a certain type of light bulbs:

Week	:	1	2	3	4	5
Per cent failing by week end	:	10	25	50	80	100

There are 1,000 bulbs in use and it costs ₹ 2 to replace an individual bulb which has burnt out. If all bulbs were replaced simultaneously, it would cost 50 paise per bulb. It is proposed to replace all the bulbs at fixed intervals, whether or not they have burnt out, and to continue replacing burnt out bulbs as they fail. At what intervals should all the bulbs be replaced?

[*R.T.M. Nagpur U. B.E. (I.T.) 2009; G.N.D.U. B.Com., 2006*]

(*Ans.* Every two weeks.)

7. The probability of failure just before age n is shown below. If individual replacement costs ₹ 1.25 and group replacement costs ₹ 0.50 per item, find the optimal group replacement policy.

n	:	1	2	3	4	5	6	7	8	9	10	11
p_n	:	0.01	0.03	0.05	0.07	0.10	0.15	0.20	0.15	0.11	0.08	0.05

[*G.N.D.U. B.Com. April, 2004*]

(*Ans.* After every 6 weeks.)

8. The following failure rates have been observed for a certain type of light bulbs:

End of week	:	1	2	3	4	5	6	7	8
Probability of failure to date	:	0.05	0.13	0.25	0.43	0.68	0.88	0.96	1.00

The cost of replacing an individual failed bulb is ₹ 1.25. The decision is made to replace all bulbs simultaneously at fixed intervals, and also to replace individual bulbs as they fail in service. If the cost of group replacement is 30 paise per bulb, what is the best interval between group replacements? At what group replacement price per bulb would a policy of strictly individual replacement become preferable to the adopted policy ?

[*P.T.U. B.Tech. April, 2012; J.N.T.U. Hyderabad B.Tech. Nov., 2010; R.T.M. Nagpur B.E. (Mech.) Dec., 2008*]

(*Ans.* After every third week, 49 paise.)

9. A computer contains 10,000 resistors. When any resistor fails, it is replaced. The cost of replacing a resistor individually is ₹ 1 only. If all the resistors are replaced at the same time, the cost per resistor would be reduced to 35 paise. The per cent surviving at the end of month t is given below.

Month	:	0	1	2	3	4	5	6
Per cent surviving at the end of month	:	100	97	90	70	30	15	0

What is the optimum replacement plan?

[*M.G.U. Kerala M. Com June, 2012; V.T.U. Karnataka B.E. Dec., 2011; R.T.M. Nagpur U. B.Tech. (Mech.) Dec., 2008; Dec., 2001*]

(*Ans.* Replace every 3 months, ₹ 2183.61.)

10. A computer contains 20,000 resistors. When any resistor fails, it is replaced. The cost of replacing a resistor individually is ₹ 1. If all the resistors are replaced at the same time, the cost per resistor is reduced to ₹ 0.40. The per cent surviving at the end of month t and the probability of failure during month t are given below:

End of the month	:	0	1	2	3	4	5	6
Per cent surviving at the end of month	:	100	96	90	65	35	20	0
Probability of failure during the month t	:	0	0.04	0.06	0.25	0.30	0.15	0.20

What is the optimum replacement plan ? [*R.T.M. Nagpur U. B.Tech. June, 2003*]

11. The following failure rates have been observed for a certain type of transistors in a digital computer:

End of week	:	1	2	3	4	5	6	7	8
Prob. of failure	:	0.07	0.11	0.25	0.41	0.70	0.88	0.96	1.00

The cost of replacement of transistor individually on failure is ₹ 15/unit. A decision is made to replace all transistors simultaneously and to replace the individual transistors as they fail in service. If the cost of group replacement is ₹ 8/unit,

(*i*) What is the best interval between group replacement ?

(*ii*) Which policy of replacement is economical ?

(*iii*) If group replacement is economical at current costs, at what cost of individual replacement, group replacement would be uneconomical ?

(*iv*) How high can the cost/unit in group replacement be to make a preference for individual replacement policy ?

12. There are large number of light bulbs, all of which must be kept in working order. If a bulb fails in service it costs ₹ 2 to replace it. If all the bulbs are replaced in the same operation, it costs ₹ 1.40 per bulb. The following table shows proportion of bulbs failing in successive time intervals. Determine the best replacement policy and give reasons.

Week	:	1	2	3	4	5	6
Proportion of bulbs failing	:	0.09	0.16	0.24	0.36	0.12	0.03

[*Karn. U.B.E. (Mech.) 1997*]

13. A factory has a large number of bulbs, all of which must be in working condition. Mortality rate is given below:

Week	:	1	2	3	4	5	6
Proportion which failed	:	0.10	0.15	0.25	0.35	0.12	0.03

If a bulb fails in service, it costs ₹ 3.50 to replace; if all bulbs are replaced at a time, it costs ₹ 1.20 each. Find optimum replacement policy. *[P.U. MBA, 1996]*

14. A group process plant in an oil refinery is fitted with valves. Over a period of time, it has been observed that the failure pattern of 400 of these valves is

Month	:	1	2	3	4	5	6	7	8
No. of failures	:	8	20	48	104	120	56	32	12

If there are 500 valves and they cost ₹ 50 each to replace individually and ₹ 25 each to replace on a planned group maintenance system, what is the least expensive programme ? *[Karn. U. B.E. (Mech.) 1995]*

15. A computer has a large number of electronic tubes. They are subject to mortality as given below:

Period	*Age of failure (hours)*	*Prob. of failure*
1	0–200	0.10
2	200–400	0.26
3	400–600	0.35
4	600–800	0.22
5	800–1,000	0.07

If the tubes are replaced in groups, the cost of replacement is ₹ 15 per tube. Group replacement can be done at fixed intervals in the night shifts when the computer is not normally used. The replacement of individual tubes which fail in service costs ₹ 60 per tube. How frequently should the tubes be replaced ? *[R.T.M. Nagpur U. B.Tech. (Mech.) June, 2007]*

[**Hint.** Consider each block of 200 hours as one period and assume that there are 1,000 electronic tubes initially.]

(*Ans.* After every 2 periods, *i.e.*, after every 400 hours; cost = ₹ 10,500 per week.)

16. Following mortality rates have been observed for certain type of fuses:

Week	:	1	2	3	4	5
Per cent failing by the end of the week	:	5	15	35	75	100

There are 100 fuses in use and it costs ₹ 5 to replace an individual fuse. If all fuses were replaced simultaneously, it would cost ₹ 1.25 per fuse. It is proposed to replace all fuses at fixed intervals of time whether or not they have been burnt out, and to continue replacing burnt-out fuses as they fail. At what intervals the group replacement should be made? Also prove that this optimal policy is superior to the straightforward policy of replacing each fuse only when it fails.

[P.T.U. MBA May, 2015; J.N.T.U. B.Tech. Hyderabad May, 2011; Nov., 2010; G.N.D.U. B.Com., 2005]

(*Ans.* 2 weeks; ₹ 1,007.50/week.)

17. The maintenance engineer for a large construction company is examining alternatives open to him for the replacement of hydraulic hoses on the firm's 100 front-end loaders; each loader uses six hoses, which from historical maintenance records fail at this rate:

Month of use	:	*1*	*2*	*3*	*4*	*5*
Per cent requiring replacement by that month	:	*10*	*15*	*20*	*70*	*100*

The maintenance engineer learns that the 'in-the-field' replacement costs ₹ 80 per hose while it costs only ₹ 40 per hose if all the hoses are replaced at regular intervals during routine maintenance and service. Evaluate the alternatives open to this engineer and recommend a course of action.

[C.A. (Final) Nov., 1990]

(*Ans.* 3 months; ₹ 11,536/month.)

18. An organisation is considering periodic replacement of 2,000 units of an item which follows sudden failure mechanism. It is now following a policy of replacing its units as they fail at a cost of ₹ 800 per item. The organisation feels that it can cut its per item replacement cost by ₹ 150 by using the periodic replacement method. By making use of the information given in the table below, evaluate these alternatives and make a recommendation to this organisation:

End of month	:	1	2	3	4	5
Per cent of original items that fail during the month	:	10	20	40	70	100

[*C.A. (Final) Nov., 1991*]

(*Ans.* Individual replacement policy; ₹ 4,44,444.45.)

19. An automatic machine uses 250 moving parts as part of a complete assembly. The average cost of a failed moving part is ₹ 200. Removing the part and replacing it is time-consuming and disrupts manufacturing. Therefore, the management is considering a group replacement at a specific interval. Find out optimum replacement interval and additional cost, if any. Other details are :

Use in months	*Probability of failure*
1	0.05
2	0.05
3	0.10
4	0.15
5	0.25
6	0.40

Replacement cost per part (₹)

Replacement	*Purchase*	*Installation*	*Total*
Individual replacement	200	500	700
Group replacement	150	200	350

[*R.T.M. Nagpur B.E. (Mech.) Sept., 2010*]

20. (*a*) In the theory of replacement models, construct an equation for the cost of maintaining a system as a function of the control variable t (the number of periods between group replacement).

(*b*) It has been suggested by a data processing firm that they adopt a policy of periodically replacing all the 1,000 tubes in a certain piece of equipment. A tube is known to have the mortality distribution (probability of failure) shown in the table below :

Tube failures/week :	1	2	3	4	5
Probability of failure :	0.3	0.1	0.1	0.2	0.3

The cost of replacing the tubes on an individual basis is estimated to be ₹ 1.00 per tube and the cost of a group replacement is ₹ 0.30 per tube. Compare the cost of preventive replacement with that of remedial replacement. [*J.N.T.U. Hyderabad B.Tech. May, 2011; April, 2011; Nov., 2010*]

21. The management of a large hotel is considering the periodic replacement of light bulbs fitted in its rooms. There are 500 rooms in the hotel and each room has 6 bulbs. The management is now following the policy of replacing the bulbs as they fail at a total cost of ₹ 3 per bulb. The management feels that this cost can be reduced to ₹ 1 by adopting the periodic replacement method. On the basis of information given below, evaluate the alternatives and make a recommendation to the management.

Months of use :	1	2	3	4	5
Per cent of bulbs failing by that month :	10	20	50	80	100

[*J.N.T.U. Hyderabad B.Tech. April, 2011*]

22. An electric company, which generates and distributes electricity conducted a study on the life of poles. The appropriate data are given in the following table :

Years after installation :	1	2	3	4	5	6	7	8	9	10
Percentage poles failing :	1	2	3	5	7	12	20	30	16	4

(*a*) If the company now installs 5,000 poles and follows a policy of replacing poles only when they fail, how many poles are expected to be replaced each year during the next 10 years ? To simplify the computation, assume that failures occur and replacements are made only at the end of year.

(b) The cost of replacing an individual pole is ₹ 160. If we have a common group replacement policy, it costs ₹ 80 per pole. Find the optimal period for group replacement.

[*J.N.T.U. Hyderabad B.Tech. April, 2011; R.T.M. Nagpur U. B.Tech. Dec., 2004*]

23. A decision has to be made for group replacement versus individual replacement policy for 500 fluorescent tubes of a particular make in the university campus. Failure rates for the tubes were recorded as under:

End of month	1	2	3	4	5	6
Prob. of failure	0.11	0.30	0.25	0.20	0.10	0.04

Cost of replacing an individual tube is ₹ 55 and when replaced as a group it is ₹ 35. Find out whether group replacement policy is economical or not. If economical, at the end of which month should the tubes be replaced as a group ?

[*J.N.T.U. Hyderabad B.Tech. June, 2009*]

11.4 MORTALITY AND STAFFING PROBLEMS

Problems concerning mortality as well as recruitment and promotion of staff can, sometimes, be analysed in a manner similar to that used in replacement problems in industry. The next few examples will make the idea clear.

EXAMPLE 11.4-1

An airline requires 250 assistant hostesses, 350 hostesses and 50 supervisors. Girls are recruited at age 21 and, if in service, they retire at age 60. Given the 'life' table (table 11.29), determine

(i) How many girls should be recruited each year ?

(ii) At what age promotions should take place?

TABLE 11.29

Age (years)	*No. in service*	*Age (years)*	*No. in service*
21	1,000	41	120
22	700	42	112
23	500	43	105
24	400	44	100
25	300	45	92
26	260	46	88
27	230	47	80
28	210	48	72
29	195	49	65
30	180	50	60
31	170	51	53
32	165	52	45
33	160	53	40
34	155	54	32
35	150	55	26
36	145	56	20
37	140	57	18
38	135	58	15
39	130	59	10
40	125	60	–

Solution

If 1,000 girls had been recruited each year for the past 39 years, the total number of them serving upto the age of 59 years = 6,603. Total number of girls required in the airline

$$= 250 + 350 + 50 = 650.$$

(*i*) ∴ No. of girls to be recruited every year in order to maintain a strength of 650 = $\frac{1,000}{6,603}$ $\times$ 650 = 98 (approx.)

(*ii*) Let the assistant hostesses be promoted at the age x. Then upto age $x - 1$ year, number of assistant hostesses required = 250. Now out of 650 girls, 250 are assistant hostesses; therefore out of 1,000, their number is $\frac{250}{650} \times 1,000 = 385$ (approx.).

From table 11.29, this number is available upto the age of 24 years.

∴ Promotion of assistant hostesses is due in the *25th year.*

Now out of 650 girls, 350 are hostesses. Therefore, if we recruit 1,000 girls, the no. of hostesses will be $\frac{350}{650} \times 1,000 = 538$ (approx.)

∴ Total number of assistant hostesses and hostesses in a recruitment of 1,000 = 385 + 538 = 923.

∴ No. of supervisors required = 1,000 – 923 = 77.

From table 11.29, this number is available upto the age of 47 years.

∴ Promotion of hostesses is due in the *48th year.*

EXAMPLE 11.4-2

A faculty in a college is planned to rise to a strength of 50 staff members and then to remain at that level. The wastage of recruits depends upon their length of service and is as follows:

Year	:	*1*	*2*	*3*	*4*	*5*	*6*	*7*	*8*	*9*	*10*
Total % who left up to the end of year	:	*5*	*35*	*56*	*65*	*70*	*76*	*80*	*86*	*95*	*100*

(i) Find the number of staff members to be recruited every year.

(ii) If there are seven posts of Head of Deptt. for which length of service is the only criterion of promotion, what will be average length of service after which a new entrant should expect promotion?

Solution

Let us assume that the recruitment per year is 100. From above it is clear that the 100 who join in the first year will become zero in 10th year, the 100 who join in the 2nd year will (serve for 9 years and) become 5 at the end of the 10th year and the 100 who join in the 3rd year will (serve for 8 years and) become 14 at the end of the 10th year and so on. Thus, when the equilibrium is attained, the distribution of length of service of staff members will be as follows:

TABLE 11.30

Year	*No. of staff members*
0	100
1	95
2	65
3	44
4	35
5	30
6	24
7	20
8	14
9	5
10	0
Total	432

(*i*) Thus if 100 staff members are recruited every year, the total number of staff members 10 years hence = 432.

To maintain a strength of 50, the number to be recruited every year = $\frac{100}{432} \times 50 = 11.6$.

In the calculations above we have assumed that those staff members who completed x years' service but left before $x + 1$ years' service, actually left immediately before completing $x + 1$ years. If it is assumed that they left immediately after completing x years' service, the total number will become $432 - 100 = 332$ and the required intake will be $50 \times \frac{100}{332} = 15$. In actual practice, they may leave at any time in the year so that reasonable number of recruitments per year $= \frac{11.6 + 15}{2} = 13$ (nearly).

(*ii*) If we recruit 13 persons every year then we want 7 seniors. Hence if we recruit 100 every year then we shall require $\frac{7}{13} \times 100 = 54$ (approx.) seniors.

It can be seen from table 11.30 that 54 seniors will be available if we promote them during 6th year of their service ($\because$ $0 + 5 + 14 + 20 + 24 = 63 > 54$).

Therefore, the promotion of a newly recruited staff member will be due after completing 5 years and before putting in 6 years of service.

11.5 MISCELLANEOUS REPLACEMENT PROBLEMS

There are many replacement situations which do not clearly fall under the categories discussed in the previous sections. We shall consider two such problems here.

EXAMPLE 11.5-1

A piece of equipment either can fail completely, so that it has to be scrapped (no salvage value), or may suffer a minor defect which can be repaired. The probability that it will not have to be scrapped before age t is f(t) and the conditional probability that it will need a repair in the instant t to t + dt, knowing that it was in running order at age t, is r(t).dt. The probability of a repair or complete failure is dependent only on the age of the equipment and not on the previous repair history.

Each repair costs ₹ C, and complete replacement costs ₹ K. For some considerable time, the policy has been to replace only on failure.

(a) Derive a formula for the expected cost per unit time of the present policy of replacing only on failure.

(b) It has been suggested that it might be cheaper to scrap equipment at some fixed age T, thus avoiding the higher risk of repairs with advancing age. Show that the expected cost per unit time of such policy is

$$\frac{C \int_0^T f(u) \,.\, r(u) \,.\, du + K}{\int_0^T f(u) \,.\, du}.$$

[*Kuru. M.Sc. (Math.) 1975*]

Solution

Since $f(t)$ is the probability that the equipment will not have to be scrapped before age t, $\int_0^\infty f(t) \,.\, dt = 1$.

Further, it is given that the probability that equipment will need a repair in the interval t and $t + dt$ knowing that it was running at age t is $r(t) \cdot dt$.

(*a*) The probability that equipment will need a repair between age u and $u + du$ is $f(u) \cdot r(u) \cdot du$.

$\therefore$ Expected cost of repair $= C\int_0^\infty f(u) \cdot r(u) \cdot du$

and total expected cost $= \dfrac{C\int_0^\infty f(u) \cdot r(u) \cdot du + K}{\int_0^\infty f(u) \cdot du}$

$$= C\int_0^\infty f(u) \cdot r(u) \cdot du + K\,;\ \text{since } \int_0^\infty f(u) \cdot du = 1.$$

(*b*) If the equipment is scrapped at a fixed age T, the expected cost of repair is

$$C\int_0^T f(u) \cdot r(u) \cdot du$$

and the total expected cost up to age T is $C\int_0^T f(u) \cdot r(u) \cdot du + K$.

Expected cost per unit time is given by

$$F(t) = \frac{C\int_0^T f(u) \cdot r(u) \cdot du + K}{\int_0^T f(u) \cdot du}.$$

EXAMPLE 11.5-2

Automobile batteries are manufactured by a firm at a factory cost of ₹ 20 each. The mortality table for the battery life is given in table 11.31. The batteries are covered under a guarantee policy such that if a battery fails during the first month after purchase, full price of the new battery is refunded; a failure in second month carries a refund of 19/20 of the full price, in third month 18/20 and so on till the 20th month, during which a failure carries a refund of 1/20 of the full price. What should be the break-even selling price of the batteries ?

TABLE 11.31

Month	*Probability of failure in next month*	*Month*	*Probability of failure in next month*
0	0.05	11	0.01
1	0.00	12	0.01
2	0.00	13	0.01
3	0.00	14	0.01
4	0.00	15	0.015
5	0.00	16	0.020
6	0.00	17	0.025
7	0.00	18	0.030
8	0.00	19	0.035
9	0.00	20	0.785
10	0.00	and above	
		Total	1.000

Solution

Let p_i be the probability that a new battery will fail during $(i + 1)$th month after purchase and let X be the break-even price.

∴ Average refund for a battery that fails is

$$Y = \sum_{i=0}^{19} \frac{20-i}{20} X \cdot p_i.$$

$$\therefore \quad Y = X \left[0.05 \times 1 + 0.00 \left\{ \frac{19}{20} + \frac{18}{20} + \frac{17}{20} + \frac{16}{20} + \frac{15}{20} + \frac{14}{20} + \frac{13}{20} + \frac{12}{20} + \frac{11}{20} \right\} \right.$$

$$+ 0.01 \left\{ \frac{10}{20} + \frac{9}{20} + \frac{8}{20} + \frac{7}{20} \right\} + 0.015 \times \frac{6}{20} + 0.020 \times \frac{5}{20}$$

$$\left. + 0.025 \times \frac{4}{20} + 0.030 \times \frac{3}{20} + 0.035 \times \frac{2}{20} + 0.785 \times \frac{1}{20} \right]$$

$$= X \left[0.05 + \frac{0.34}{20} + \frac{0.09}{20} + \frac{0.10}{20} + \frac{0.10}{20} + \frac{0.09}{20} + \frac{0.07}{20} + \frac{0.785}{20} \right]$$

$$= X \left[\frac{2.575}{20} \right] = 0.12875 \text{ X}.$$

Now the break-even price X is the sum of the factory cost and the expected refund.

$$\therefore \quad X = 20 + 0.12875 \text{ X}$$

or $\quad X = ₹\,23$ (approx.).

11.6 RENEWAL THEORY

If the probability distribution of failure time of items is known, one can solve replacement problems analytically. The mathematical technique used to solve these replacement problems is called *renewal theory.* This theory treats the life of the item as a random variable. In statistical terminology, a *renewal* takes place when an old item is replaced by a new one or it is repaired so that the probability density function (p.d.f.) of its future life time is same as that of the new item. We give below the basic principle bypassing the details of a renewal process.

Renewal Density Theorem

Let the life of each item be denoted by random variable x_i, $i = 1, 2, 3, \ldots$ and let each item be replaced immediately on failure. Then, if we start using the first item at time $t = 0$, the nth will start being used at time $t = x_1 + x_2 + \ldots + x_{n-1}$. Let x_i be identically and independently distributed with probability distribution F_x and let the probability of event x be p_x.

The probability that a renewal occurs during a small interval $(t, t + dt)$ is called *replacement rate* at time t, where t is measured from the start of use of the first item. It is denoted by $h(t).dt$ and is called *renewal density function.*

Thus $h(t).dt$ = probability that a renewal occurs in time interval $(t, t + dt)$, and this probability = prob. that first machine fails in time interval $(t, t + dt)$

+ prob. that second machine fails in time interval $(t, t + dt)$ + ...

$$\therefore \quad h(t) = f_1(t) + f_2(t) + \ldots = \sum_{r=1}^{\infty} f_r(t), \quad \ldots(11.19)$$

where $f_1(t)$ = density function of a random variable with probability distribution F_x,

$f_2(t)$ = density function of the sum of 2 random variables with probability distribution F_x,

⋮

$f_r(t)$ = density function of $x_1 + x_2 + \ldots + x_r$ with probability distribution F_x.

The problem is to show that $h(t)$ becomes constant as $t \to \infty$. In other words, we are to prove that the probability of replacement in any small time interval tends to a constant. In order to prove this we use the Laplace transforms of h and f:

$$h^*(s) = \int_0^\infty e^{-st}\, h(t)\,.\, dt\,,$$

$$f^*(s) = \int_0^\infty e^{-st}\, f(t)\,.\, dt\,.$$

Using the property of Laplace transforms, equation (11.19) gives

$$h^*(s) = f^*(s) + [f^*(s)]^2 - \ldots$$

$$= \frac{f^*(s)}{1 - f^*(s)}.$$

Now ${}^*f(s) \to 1 - \mu + 0\,(s)$ as $s \to 0$,

where $\mu = \text{E}x_i$ is called the mean of an item.

$$\therefore \qquad \text{As } s \to 0,\ h^*(s) \to \frac{1 - \mu s + \ldots}{\mu s + \ldots} = \frac{1}{\mu s}.$$

$$\text{Now} \qquad \int_0^\infty \frac{1}{\mu}\, e^{-st}\,.\, dt = \frac{1}{\mu s}.$$

$$\therefore \qquad h\dagger(t) \to \frac{1}{\mu} \text{ as } t \to \infty.$$

(† The rigorous proof of this step is too involved to be included here) *i.e., the rate of renewal of an item tends to the reciprocal of the mean life of the item.*

EXAMPLE 11.6-1

A new item is placed in a system at time zero. The probability that the system again has a new item for the first time at time t is f(t). Certain costs are incurred during the interval 0 to t (called a cycle), the probabilities of which are known. Show that in the long run, the average cost per unit time is

$$\frac{C}{\bar{u}},$$

where C is expected cost over one cycle and $\bar{u}$ is expected duration of one cycle.

Solution

Let a be the long-run average cost per unit time. Then, for a long interval 0 to T, the costs incurred will be aT. Let the first item be replaced at time u and let the probability of this replacement be $f(u)$. Clearly, the costs incurred from time u onwards will be a (T – u). It follows that

$$a\text{T} = \sum_{u=0}^{\text{T}} a\,.\,(\text{T} - u)\,.\,f(u) + \text{C}, \qquad \ldots(11.20)$$

where C is the given expected cost over one cycle *i.e.,* over the time between placing a new item in the system and its first replacement or repair.

Now if T is large and the replacement occurs before T,

$$\sum_0^{\text{T}} f(u) = 1.$$

$$\therefore \qquad \sum_0^{\text{T}} aT\, f(u) = a\text{T},$$

and $\sum_{0}^{T} u.f(u).du = \bar{u}$ = average length of a cycle.

∴ From equation (11.20), we get

$$aT = \sum_{u=0}^{T} a(T-u)\, f(u) + C$$

$$= \sum_{0}^{T} aT\, f(u) - \sum_{u=0}^{T} auf(u) + C = aT - a\bar{u} + C.$$

∴ $$a\bar{u} = C \text{ or } a = \frac{C}{\bar{u}}.$$

i.e., the long-run average cost per unit time is the ratio of expected cost over a cycle to the expected duration of the cycle.

EXAMPLE 11.6-2

A new tyre costs ₹ 200 and retreading costs ₹ 65. A tyre must be replaced or retreaded when it wears smooth. However, retreading is possible only if the tyre walls have not deteriorated. For the data given in table 11.32 find the average cost per thousand km if

(a) the old tyre is always replaced by a new tyre,

(b) the old tyre is retreaded whenever possible. Of course, a tyre can be retreaded only once.

TABLE 11.32

Age (thousands of km)	:	*10*	*11*	*12*	*13*	*14*	*15*	*16*
Probability that tyre becomes smooth	:				*0.15*	*0.15*	*0.25*	*0.25*
Probability that smooth tyre can be retreaded	:				*0.8*	*0.8*	*0.7*	*0.7*
Probability of failure of a retreaded tyre	:	*0.1*	*0.15*	*0.2*				

Solution

Let us assume that smoothness occurs at the middle of km intervals. Then the average age in thousands of km at which a new tyre becomes smooth is

$$13.5 \times 0.15 + 14.5 \times 0.15 + 15.5 \times 0.25 + 16.5 \times 0.25 = 12.2.$$

Thus the cycle time is 12.2 thousand km and the cost per cycle is ₹ 200.

∴ Average cost per thousand km $= \dfrac{200}{12.2} =$ ₹ 16.40.

Similarly, the average age in thousands of km at which the tyre must be retreaded is $10.5 \times 0.1 + 11.5 \times 0.15 + 12.5 \times 0.2 = 5.275$.

∴ Average cost of retreading per thousand km

$$= \frac{65}{5.275} = ₹\ 12.32.$$

In order to find the cost per thousand km of new tyre and a retreaded one, whenever possible, we must find the total average life of both.

Now total average life of both = Average life of a new tyre + probability of using a retreaded tyre × average life of retreaded tyre.

Now probability of using a retreaded tyre

= Probability of smoothness at each age × probability that the tyre can be retreaded
= 0.15 × 0.8 + 0.15 × 0.8 + 0.25 × 0.7 + 0.25 × 0.7 = 0.24 + 0.35 = 0.59.

Total average life in thousand km till we again have new tyre

$$= 12.2 + 0.59 \times 5.275 = 12.2 + 3.11 = 15.31.$$

Expected cost over the cycle = ₹ (200 + 0.59 × 65) = ₹ 238.35.

∴ Average cost per thousand km if we retread whenever possible

$$= ₹\ \frac{238.35}{15.31} = ₹15.57.$$

EXERCISES 11.4

1. Define renewal function. What is renewal theory ? Derive the fundamental integral equation of the renewal theory for an ordinary renewal process. *[Raj. U.M. Phil., 1993, 92]*
2. Calculate the probability of staff resignation in each year from the following survival table :

Year	:	0	1	2	3	4	5	6	7	8	9	10
No. of original staff in service at the end of year	:	1,000	940	820	580	400	280	190	130	70	30	0

[Raj. U. M.Phil., 1993]

3. Truck tyres which fail in service can cause expensive accidents. A failure in service is estimated to cost ₹ 2,000 excluding the cost of replacing the blown tyre. A new tyre costs ₹ 800 and has the mortality shown in the table below. If the tyres are to be replaced after covering a certain fixed number of km or on failure, whichever occurs first, determine the replacement policy that minimizes the average cost per km.

Truck tyre mortality

Age at failure (km)	*Probability of failure*
≤ 10,000	0.000
10,001–13,000	0.035
13,001–16,000	0.083
16,001–19,000	0.190
19,001–22,000	0.475
22,001–25,000	0.217
	1.000

[**Hint.** Assume that failure takes place at the exact ages 11,500, 14,500, 17,500, etc.]

4. A certain piece of equipment is very difficult to adjust. During a period when no adjustment is made, the running cost increases linearly with time at the rate of ₹ b per hour. The running cost immediately after an adjustment is not known precisely until the adjustment has been made. Before the adjustment, the resulting running cost x is deemed to be a random variable x with density function $f(x)$. If each replacement costs ₹ k, when should replacement be made ? *[Meerut M.Sc. (Math.) 1970]*
5. If the life of electric light bulbs follows the distribution

$$f(x)\, dx = \lambda e^{-\lambda x}\, .\, dx \quad (\lambda > 0;\ 0 \le x < \infty),$$

find the renewal density $h(t)$ after the end of the period $(0, t)$.

If there are M points in a building, how many bulbs would you expect to replace within a period (t_1, t_2), where $t_2 > t_1$?

Inventory Models

This chapter presents the kind of analysis which develops mathematical models of inventory processes. Efforts will be made to develop not a single general model but a wide variety of models each for a specific situation.

An *Inventory* consists of *usable but idle resources* such as men, machines, materials or money. When the resource involved is a material, the inventory is also called *'stock'*. An inventory problem is said to the exist if either the resources are subjected to control or if there is at least one such cost that decreases as inventory increases. The objective is to minimize total (actual or expected) cost. However, in situations where inventory affects demand, the objective may also be to maximize profit.

12.1 NECESSITY FOR MAINTAINING INVENTORY

Though inventory of materials is an idle resource (since the materials lie idle and are not to be used immediately), almost every organisation must maintain it for efficient and smooth running of its operations. Without it no business activity can be performed, whether it is a service organisation like a hospital or a bank or it is a manufacturing or trading organisation. If an enterprise has no inventory of materials at all, on receiving a sales order it will have to place order for purchase of raw materials, wait of their receipt and then start production. The customer will thus have to wait for a long time for the delivery of the goods and may turn to other suppliers resulting in loss of business for the enterprise. Most organisations have 20 to 25 per cent of the total funds devoted to inventory. It may even increase to 70 per cent in case of pharmaceutical, chemical and paints industries. Maintaining an inventory is necessary because of the following reasons :

1. It helps in smooth and efficient running of an enterprise. It decouples the production from customers and vendors and simplifies the otherwise complex organisation for manufacture and reduces the coordination effort.
2. It provides service to the customer at a short notice. Timely deliveries can fetch more goodwill and orders.
3. In the absence of inventory, the enterprise may have to pay high prices because of piecemeal purchasing. Maintaining of inventory may earn price discount because of bulk purchasing. It also takes advantage of favourable market.
4. It reduces product costs since there is an added advantage of batching and long, uninterrupted production runs.
5. It acts as a buffer stock when raw materials are received late and shop rejections are too many.
6. Process and movement inventories (also called pipeline stocks) are quite necessary in big enterprises where significant amounts of times are required to tranship items from one location to another.
7. Bulk purchases will entail less orders and, therefore, less clerical costs. This applies to goods produced within the organisation as well. Less orders, as a result of larger lots, will entail lesser machine setups and other associated costs.
8. An organisation may have to deal with several customers and vendors who are not necessarily near it. Inventories, therefore, have to be built to meet the demand at least during the transit time.

9. It helps in maintaining economy by absorbing some of the fluctuations when the demand for an item fluctuates or is seasonal.

However, too often inventories are wrongly used as a substitute for management. For example, if there are large finished goods inventories, inaccurate sales forecasting by marketing deptt. may never be apparent. Similarly, a production foreman who has large in-process inventories may be able to hide his poor planning since there is always something to manufacture. Furthermore, inventory means unproductive 'tied up' capital of the enterprise. The capital could be usefully utilised in other ventures as well. With large inventory, there is always likelihood of obsolescence too. Also maintenance of inventory costs additional money to be spent on personnel, equipment, insurance, etc. Thus excess inventories are not at all desirable. This necessitates controlling the inventories in the most useful way.

Causes of Poor Inventory Control

1. Overbuying without regard to the forecast or proper estimate of demand to take advantage of favourable market.
2. Overproduction or production of goods much before the customer requires them.
3. Overstocking may also result from the desire to provide better service to the customers. Bulk production to cut down production costs will also result in large inventories.
4. Cancellation of orders and minimum quantity stipulations by the suppliers may also give rise to large inventories.

12.1-1 Classifications of Inventories

Inventories are generally classified into the following types :

1 Direct Inventories

They include items that are directly used for production and are classified as :

(*a*) *Production Inventory* : Items such as raw materials, components and subassemblies used to produce the final product.

(*b*) *Work-in-Process Inventory* : Items in semi-finished form or products at different stages of production.

(*c*) *Finished Goods Inventory* : This includes the final products ready for dispatch to consumers or distributors.

(*d*) *MRO Inventory* : Maintenance, repair and operating items such as spare parts and consumable stores that do not go into the final product but are consumed during the production process.

(*e*) *Miscellaneous Inventory* : All other items such as scrap, obsolete and unsaleable products, stationery and other items used in office, factory and sales department, etc.

2 Indirect Inventories

Indirect inventories may be classified as :

(*a*) *Transit or Pipeline Inventories* : Also called *movement inventories*, they consist of items that are currently under transportation *e.g.*, coal being transported from coalfields to a thermal plant.

(*b*) *Buffer Inventories* : They are required as protection against the uncertainties of supply and demand. A company may well know the average demand of an item that it needs; however, the actual demand may turn out to be quite different–it may well exceed the average value. Similarly, the average delivery period (lead time) may be known but due to some unforeseen reasons, the actual delivery period could be much more. Such situations require extra stock of the item to reduce the number of stock-outs or back-orders. This extra stock in excess of the average demand during the lead time is called *buffer stock* (or *safety stock* or *cushion stock*).

(*c*) *Decoupling Inventories* : They are required to decouple or disengage the different parts of the production system. For an item that requires processing on a series of different machines with different processing times, it is a must to have decoupling inventories of the item in between the various machines for smooth and continuous production. The decoupling inventories act as shock absorbers in case of varying work-rates, machine breakdowns or failures, etc.

(*d*) *Seasonal Inventories* : Some items have seasonal demands *e.g.*, demand of woollen textiles in winter, coolers and air conditioners in summer, raincoats in rainy season, etc. Inventories for such items have to be maintained to meet their high seasonal demand.

(*e*) *Lot Size Inventories* : Items are usually purchased in lots to
  (*i*) avail price discounts
  (*ii*) reduce transportation and purchase costs
  (*iii*) minimize handling and receiving costs.

Lot size or *cycle inventories* are, therefore, held by purchasing items in lots rather than their exact quantities required. For example, a textile industry may buy cotton in bulk during cotton season rather than buying it everyday.

(*f*) *Anticipation Inventories* : They are held to meet the anticipated demand. Purchasing of crackers well before Diwali, fans before the approaching summer, piling up of raw material in the face of imminent transporters' strike are examples of anticipation inventories.

12.2 INVENTORY COSTS

The four costs considered in inventory control models are :

1. Purchase costs
2. Inventory carrying or stock holding costs
3. Procurement costs (for bought-out items) or set-up costs (for made-in items) and
4. Shortage costs (due to disservice to the customers).

12.2-1 Purchase Costs

It is the price that is paid for purchasing/producing an item. It may be constant per unit or may vary with the quantity purchased / produced. If the cost / unit is constant, it does not affect the inventory control decision. However, the purchase cost is definitely considered when it varies as in quantity discount situations.

12.2-2 Inventory Carrying Costs (or Stock Holding Costs or Holding Costs or Storage Costs)

They arise on account of maintaining the stocks and the interest paid on the capital tied up with the stocks. They vary directly with the size of the inventory as well as the time for which the item is held in stock. Various components of the stockholding cost are :

1. *Cost of money or capital tied up in inventories.* This is, by far, the most important component. Money borrowed from the banks may cost interest of about 12%. But usually the problem is viewed in a slightly different way *i.e.,* how much the organisation would have earned, had the capital been invested in an alternative project such as developing a new product, etc. It is generally taken somewhere around 15% to 20% of the value of the inventories.
2. *Cost of storage space.* This consists of rent for space. Besides space expenses, this will also include heating, lighting and other atmospheric control expenses. Typical values may vary from 1 to 3% .
3. *Depreciation and deterioration costs.* They are especially important for fashion items or items undergoing chemical changes during storage. Fragile items such as crockery are liable to damage, breakage, etc. 0.2% to 1% of the stock value may be lost due to damage and deterioration.
4. *Pilferage cost.* It depends upon the nature of the item. Valuables such as gun metal bushes and expensive tools may be more tempting, while there is hardly any possibility of heavy casting or forging being stolen. While the former must be kept under lock and key, the latter may be simply dumped in the stockyard. Pilferage cost may be taken as 1% of the stock value.

5. *Obsolescence cost.* It depends upon the nature of the item in stock. Electronic and computer components are likely to be fast outdated. Changes in design also lead to obsolescence. It may be possible to quantify the percentage loss due to obsolescence and it may be taken as 5% of the stock value.
6. *Handling costs.* These include all costs associated with movement of stock, such as cost of labour, overhead cranes, gantries and other machinery used for this purpose.
7. *Record-keeping and administrative cost.* There is no use of keeping stocks unless one can easily know whether or not the required item is in stock. This signifies the need of keeping funds for record-keeping and necessary administration.
8. *Taxes and Insurance.* Most organisations have insurance cover against possible loss from theft, fire, etc. and this may cost 1% to 2% of the invested capital.

Inventory carrying cost C_1 is expressed either as per cent/unit time (*e.g.*, 20% per year) or in terms of monetary value/unit /unit time (*e.g.*, ₹ 5/unit/ year).

Example : If the average stock during a year is of value ₹ 20,000, the inventory carrying costs, being, say, equal to 20%, amount to ₹ $20,000 \times \frac{20}{100} =$ ₹ 4,000.

12.2-3 Procurement Costs or Set-up Costs

These include the fixed cost associated with placing of an order or setting up a machinery before starting production. They include costs of purchase, requisition, follow up, receiving the goods, quality control, cost of mailing, telephone calls and other follow-up actions, salaries of persons for accounting and auditing, etc. *Also called order costs or replenishment costs*, they are assumed to be independent of the quantity ordered or produced but directly proportional to the number of orders placed. At times, however, these costs may not bear any simple relationship to the number of orders. More than one stock item may be ordered on one set of the documents; the clerical staff is not divisible and without the existing staff increasing or decreasing, there may be considerable scope for changing the number of orders. In such a case, the acquisition cost relationship may be quadratic or stepped instead of a straight line. They are expressed in terms of ₹/order or ₹/set-up.

12.2-4 Shortage Costs or Stock-out Costs

These costs are associated with either a delay in meeting demands or the inability to meet it at all. Therefore, shortage costs are usually interpreted in two ways. In case the unfilled demand can be filled at a later stage (backlog case), these costs are proportional to quantity that is short as well as the delay time and are expressed as ₹/unit back ordered/unit time (*e.g.* ₹ 7/unit/year). They represent loss of goodwill and cost of idle equipment. In case the unfilled demand is lost (no backlog case), these costs become proportional to only the quantity that is short. These result in cancelled orders, lost sales, profit and even the business itself.

It follows from the above discussion that if the purchase cost is constant and independent of the quantity purchased, it is not considered in formulating the inventory control policy. The total variable inventory cost in this case is given by

Total variable inventory cost = Carrying cost + Ordering cost + Shortage cost.

However, if the unit cost depends upon the quantity purchased *i.e.*, price discounts are available, the purchase cost is definitely considered in formulating the inventory control policy. The total inventory cost in this case is then given by

Total inventory cost (including the cost of the item) = Purchase cost + Carrying cost + Ordering cost + Shortage cost.

12.3 INVENTORY CONTROL PROBLEM

The inventory control problem consists of determination of three basic factors :

1. When to order (produce or purchase) ?
2. How much to order ?
3. How much safety stock should be kept ?

When to order. This is related to the *lead time* (also called *delivery lag*) of an item. Lead time may be defined as the time interval between the placement of an order for an item and its receipt in stock. It may be replenishment order on an outside firm or within the works. There should be enough stock for each item so that customers' orders can be reasonably met from this stock until replenishment. This stock level, known as *reorder level*, has, therefore, to be determined for each item. It is determined by balancing the cost of maintaining these stocks and the disservice to the customer if his orders are not filled in time.

How much to order. As already discussed, each order has associated with it the ordering cost or acquisition cost. To keep it low, the number of orders should be as few as possible *i.e.,* the order size should be large. But large order size would imply high inventory carrying cost. Thus the problem of how much to order is solved by compromising between the acquisition costs and inventory carrying costs.

How much should be the safety stock. This is important to avoid overstocking while ensuring that no stock-outs take place.

The inventory control policy of an organisation depends upon the demand characteristics. The demand for an item may be independent or dependent. For instance, the demand for the different models of television sets manufactured by a company does not depend upon the demand of any other item, while the demand of its various components will depend upon the demand (and hence sale) of the television sets and may be arithmetically computed from the latter. The independent demand is usually ascertained by extrapolating the past demand history *i.e.,* by *forecasting.* The order level can be fixed from the demand forecasts and the lead time. Thus while in the case of dependent demand, simple arithmetic computations are enough to ascertain requirement of the components; in the case of independent demand items, statistical forecasting techniques have to be employed. The discussion of these forecasting techniques will be taken up later in this chapter. The family tree drawn in the next section gives an idea of the various inventory control policies.

12.4 CLASSIFICATION OF FIXED ORDER QUANTITY INVENTORY MODELS

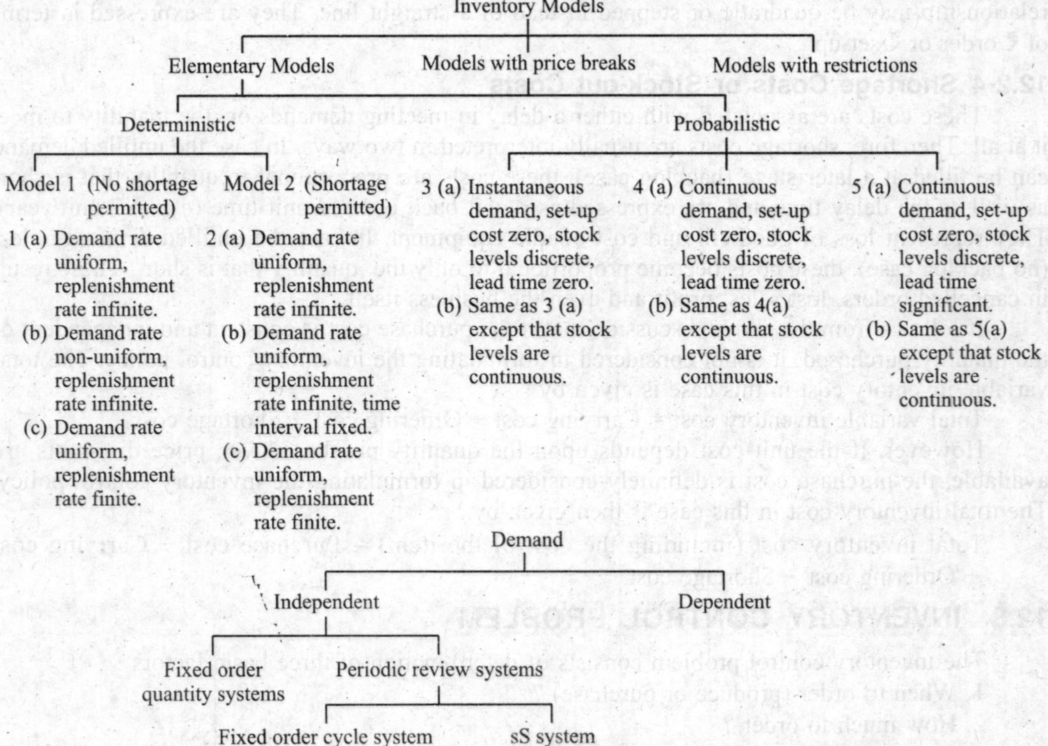

Fixed order quantity systems will now be discussed in detail. The periodic review systems will be taken up briefly towards the end of this chapter.

12.5 INVENTORY MODELS WITH DETERMINISTIC DEMAND

It is extremely difficult to formulate a single general inventory model which takes into account all variations in real systems. In fact, even if such a model were developed, it may not be analytically solvable. Thus inventory models are usually developed for some specific situations.

In this section we shall deal with situations in which demand is assumed to be fixed and completely known. Models for such situations are called *economic lot size models or economic order quantity models.*

12.5-1 Model 1 (a) Classical EOQ Model (Demand Rate Uniform, Replenishment Rate Infinite)

This is one of the simplest inventory models. A stockist has order to supply goods to customers at a uniform rate R per unit time. Hence demand is fixed and known. No shortages are allowed, consequently, the cost of shortage, C_2 is infinity. He places an order with the manufacturer every t time units, where t is fixed; and the ordering cost per order is C_3. Replenishment time is negligible *i.e.*, replenishment rate is infinite so that replenishment is instantaneous (lead time is zero). The holding cost is assumed to be proportional to the amount of inventory as well as the time inventory is held. Thus the cost of holding inventory I for time T is C_1IT, where C_1 is the cost of holding one unit in inventory for a unit of time. The cost coefficients C_1, C_2 and C_3 are assumed to be constants. The stockist's problem is to determine

(*i*) How frequently he should place the order.

(*ii*) How many units should be ordered in each order.

This model is illustrated schematically in figure 12.1.

If orders are placed at intervals t, a quantity $q = Rt$ must be ordered in each order. Since the stock in small time dt is $Rt\,dt$, the stock in time period t will be

$$\int_0^t R\,t.dt = \frac{1}{2}\,Rt^2 = \frac{1}{2}\,qt = \text{Area of inventory triangle OAP.}$$

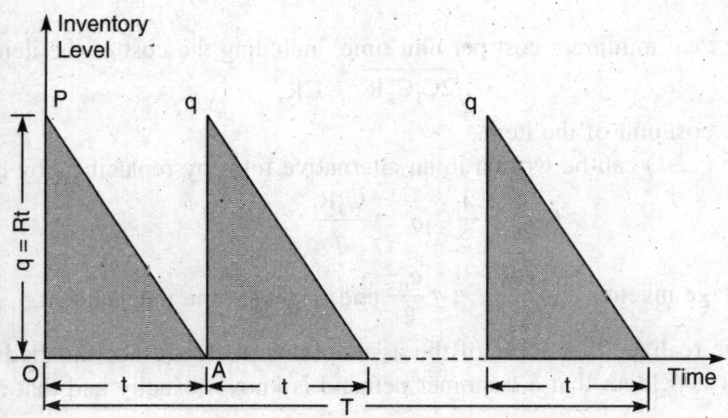

Fig. 12.1. Inventory situation for model 1 (a).

$\therefore$ Cost of holding inventory during time $t = \dfrac{1}{2}\,C_1Rt^2$.

Ordering cost to place an order $= C_3$.

$\therefore$ Total cost during time $t = \dfrac{1}{2}\,C_1Rt^2 + C_3$.

$\therefore$ Average total cost per unit time, $C(t) = \dfrac{1}{2}\,C_1Rt + \dfrac{C_3}{t}$. ...(12.1)

C will be minimum if $\frac{dC(t)}{dt} = 0$ and $\frac{d^2C(t)}{dt^2}$ is positive.

Differentiating equation (12.1) w.r.t.'t',

$$\frac{dC(t)}{dt} = \frac{1}{2}\, C_1R - \frac{C_3}{t^2} = 0, \text{ which gives } t = \sqrt{\frac{2C_3}{C_1R}}.$$

Differentiating equation (12.1) twice w.r.t. 't'

$\frac{d^2C(t)}{dt^2} = \frac{2C_3}{t^3}$, which is positive for value of t given by the above equation.

Thus C(t) is minimum for optimal time interval,

$$t_0 = \sqrt{\frac{2C_3}{C_1R}}. \qquad \text{...(12.2)}$$

Optimum quantity q_0 to be ordered during each order,

$$q_0 = R\, t_0 = \sqrt{\frac{2C_3R}{C_1}}, \qquad \text{...(12.3)}$$

which is known as the *optimal lot size (or economic order quantity) formula* due to R.H. Wilson. It is also called *Wilson's formula or square root formula or Harris lot size formula.*

Any other order quantity will result in a higher cost.

The resulting minimum average cost per unit time,

$$C_0(q) = \frac{1}{2}\, C_1R.\, \sqrt{\frac{2C_3}{C_1R}} + C_3.\, \sqrt{\frac{C_1R}{2C_3}}$$

$$= \frac{1}{\sqrt{2}}\sqrt{C_1C_3R} + \frac{1}{\sqrt{2}}\sqrt{C_1C_3R} = \sqrt{2C_1C_3R}. \qquad \text{...(12.4)}$$

This cost curve has the lowest value (Fig. 1.1) just above the intersection of the two cost curves viz, ordering cost curve and carrying cost curve. At the intersection point the two costs are equal.

Also the total minimum cost per unit time, including the cost of the item

$$= \sqrt{2C_1C_3R} + CR, \qquad \text{...(12.4a)}$$

where C is the cost/unit of the item.

Equation (12.1) can be written in an alternative form by replacing t by q/R as

$$C(q) = \frac{1}{2}\, C_1q + \frac{C_3R}{q}. \qquad \text{...(12.5)}$$

The average inventory is $\frac{q_0 + 0}{2} = \frac{q_0}{2}$ and is, thus, time independent.

It may be realized that some of the assumptions made are not satisfied in actual practice. For instance, it is seldom that a customer demand is known exactly and that replenishment time is negligible.

Corollary 1. In the above model if the order cost is $C_3 + bq$ instead of being fixed, where b is the order cost per unit item, we can prove that there is no change in the optimum order quantity due to the changed order cost.

Proof. The average cost per unit time, $C(q) = \frac{1}{2} C_1q + \frac{R}{q}(C_3 + bq)$. [From equation (12.5)]

For the minimum cost $\frac{dC(q)}{dq} = 0$ and $\frac{d^2C(q)}{dq^2}$ is positive.

i.e., $\frac{1}{2}C_1 - \frac{RC_3}{q^2} = 0$ or $q = \sqrt{\frac{2RC_3}{C_1}}$,

and $\frac{d^2C(q)}{dq^2} = \frac{2RC_3}{q^3}$, which is necessarily positive for above value of q.

$\therefore \qquad q_0 = \sqrt{\frac{2C_3R}{C_1}}$, which is same as equation (12.3).

Hence there is no change in optimum order quantity as a result of change in the order cost.

Corollary 2. In model 1 (*a*) discussed above, the lead time has been assumed to be zero. Most practical problems, however, have a positive lead time L from the time the order for the item is placed until it is actually delivered. The ordering policy of the above model, therefore, must satisfy the reorder point.

If L is the lead time in days and R is the inventory consumption rate in units per day, the total inventory requirements during the lead time = LR. Thus we should place an order q as soon as the stock level becomes LR. This is called reorder point p = LR.

In practice, this is equivalent to continuously observing the level of inventory until the reorder point is obtained. That is why the economic lot size model is also called *continous review model.* Figure 12.2 shows the reorder points.

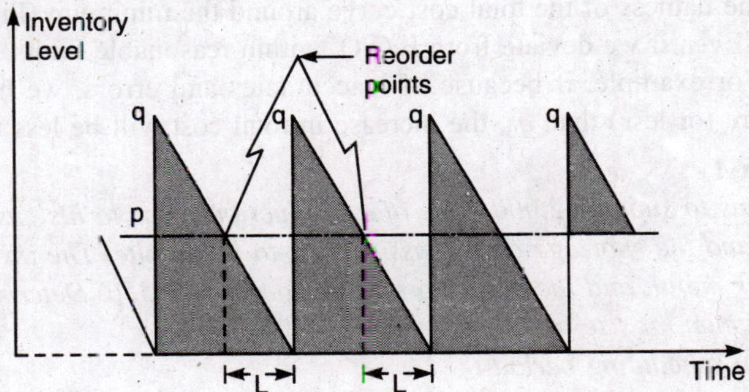

Fig. 12.2. Inventory situation with lead time.

If a buffer stock B is to be maintained, reorder point will be

$$p = B + LR. \qquad ...(12.6)$$

Furthermore, if d days are required for reviewing the system,

$$p = B + LR + \frac{Rd}{2} = B + R\left(L + \frac{d}{2}\right) \qquad ...(12.7)$$

Assumptions in E.O.Q. Formula

Following simplifying assumptions have been made while deriving the economic order quantity formula :

1. Demand is known and uniform (constant).
2. Shortages are not permitted ; as soon as the stock level becomes zero, it is instantaneously replenished.
3. Replenishment of stock is instantaneous or replenishment rate is infinite.
4. Lead time is zero. The moment the order is placed, the quantity ordered is received.
5. Inventory carrying cost per unit and ordering cost per order remain constant over time. The former is linearly related to the quantity ordered and the latter to the number of orders.
6. Cost of the item remains constant over time. There are no price-breaks or quantity discounts.
7. The item is purchased and replenished in lots or batches.
8. The inventory system pertains to a single item.

Limitations of (Objections to) E.O.Q. Formula

The E.O.Q. formula has a number of limitations. It has been highly controversial since a number of objections have been raised regarding its validity. Some of them are

1. In practice the demand is neither known with certainty nor it is uniform. If the fluctuations are mild, the formula can be applicable but for large fluctuations it loses its validity. Dynamic E.O.Q. models, instead, may have to be applied.
2. The ordering cost is difficult to measure. Also it may not be linearly related to the number of orders as assumed in the derivation of the model. The inventory carrying rate is still more difficult to measure and even to define precisely.
3. It is difficult to predict the demand. Present demand may be quite different from the past history. Hardly any prediction is possible for a new product to be introduced in the market.
4. The E.O.Q. model assumes instantaneous replenishment of the entire quantity ordered. In practice, the total quantity may be supplied in parts. E.O.Q. model is not applicable in such a situation.
5. Lead time may not be zero unless the supplier is next-door and has sufficient stock of the item, which is rarely so.
6. Price variations, quantity discounts and shortages may further ivalidate the use of the E.O.Q. formula.

However, the flatness of the total cost curve around the minimum (Fig. 1.1) is an answer to many objections. Even if we deviate from E.O.Q. within reasonable limits, there is no substantial change in cost. For example, if because of inaccuracies and errors, we have selected an order quantity 20% more (or less) than q_0, the increase in total cost will be less than 2%.

EXAMPLE 12.5-1

A stockist has to supply 12,000 units of a product per year to his customer. The demand is fixed and known and the shortage cost is assumed is to be infinite. The inventory holding cost is ₹ 0.20 per unit per month and the ordering cost per order is ₹ 350. Determine

(i) the optimum lot size q_0,

(ii) optimum scheduling period t_0,

(iii) minimum total variable yearly cost.

Solution

Supply rate, $\quad R = \dfrac{12,000}{12} = 1,000$ units/month,

C_1 = ₹ 0.20 per unit per month, C_3 = ₹ 350 per order.

$$(i)\quad q_0 = \sqrt{\frac{2C_3R}{C_1}} = \sqrt{\frac{2\times350\times1,000}{0.20}} = 1,870 \text{ units/order.}$$

$$(ii)\quad t_0 = \sqrt{\frac{2C_3}{C_1R}} = \sqrt{\frac{2\times350}{0.20\times1,000}} = 1.87 \text{ months} = 8.1 \text{ weeks between orders.}$$

$$(iii)\quad C_0 = \sqrt{2C_1C_3R} = \sqrt{2\times0.20\times12\times350\times(1,000\times12)} = ₹\ 4,490 \text{ per year.}$$

EXAMPLE 12.5-2

A particular item has a demand of 9,000 units/year. The cost of one procurement is ₹100 and the holding cost per unit is ₹ 2.40 per year. The replacement is instantaneous and no shortages are allowed. Determine

(i) the economic lot size,

(ii) the number of orders per year,

(iii) the time between orders,

(iv) the total cost per year if the cost of one unit is ₹ 1.

[*P.T.U. B.Tech. (Mech.) April, 2013; NIIFT Mohali, 2000*]

Solution

R = 9,000 units/year,

C_3 = ₹ 100/procurement, C_1 = ₹ 2.40/unit/year.

$$(i) \quad q_0 = \sqrt{\frac{2C_3R}{C_1}} = \sqrt{\frac{2\times100\times9,000}{2.40}} = 866 \text{ units/procurement}$$

$$(ii) \quad n_0 = \frac{1}{t_0} = \sqrt{\frac{C_1R}{2C_3}} = \sqrt{\frac{2.40\times9,000}{2\times100}} = \sqrt{108} = 10.4 \text{ orders/year.}$$

$$(iii) \quad t_0 = \frac{1}{n_0} = \frac{1}{10.4} = 0.0962 \text{ years} = 1.15 \text{ months between procurement.}$$

$$(iv) \quad C_0 = 9,000 \times 1 + \sqrt{2C_1C_3R}$$

$$= 9,000 + \sqrt{2\times2.40\times100\times9,000}$$

$$= 9,000 + 2,080 = ₹\ 11,080/\text{year.}$$

EXAMPLE 12.5-3

A stockist has to supply 400 units of a product every Monday to his customers. He gets the product at ₹ 50 per unit from the manufacturer. The cost of ordering and transportation from the manufacturer is ₹ 75 per order. The cost of carrying inventory is 7.5% per year of the cost of the product. Find

(i) the economic lot size,

(ii) the total optimal cost (including the capital cost),

(iii) the total weekly profit if the item is sold for ₹ 55 per unit.

[*NIFT Mohali, 2001; P.U. B.Com. Sept., 2005*]

Solution

R = 400 units/week,

C_3 = ₹ 75/ per order,

C_1 = 7.5% per year of the cost of the product

$$= ₹ \left(\frac{7.5}{100}\times50\right) \text{ per unit per year}$$

$$= ₹ \left(\frac{7.5}{100}\times\frac{50}{52}\right) \text{ per unit per week}$$

$$= ₹ \frac{3.75}{52} \text{ per unit per week.}$$

$$(i) \quad q_0 = \sqrt{\frac{2C_3R}{C_1}} = \sqrt{\frac{2\times75\times400\times52}{3.75}} = 912 \text{ units/order.}$$

$$(ii) \quad C_0 = 400 \times 50 + \sqrt{2C_1C_3R}$$

$$= 20,000 + \sqrt{\frac{2\times3.75}{52}\times75\times400}$$

$$= 20,000 + 65.80 = ₹\ 20,065.80 \text{ per week.}$$

(*iii*) Profit P = 55 × 400 – C_0 = 22,000 – 20,065.80 = ₹ 1,934.20 per week.

EXAMPLE 12.5-4

A stockist purchases an item at the rate of ₹ 40 per piece from a manufacturer. 2,000 units of the item are required per year. What should be the order quantity per order if the cost per order is ₹ 15 and the inventory charges per year are 20 paise ? [*J.N.T.U. Hyderabad B.Tech. Nov., 2010*]

Solution

$$R = 2,000 \text{ units/year},$$
$$C_3 = ₹\ 15 \text{ / order},$$
$$I = \text{Re. } 0.20 \text{ / year} \therefore C_1 = CI = ₹\ 0.20 \times 40 = ₹\ 8\text{/unit/year}.$$

$$\therefore \quad q_0 = \sqrt{\frac{2C_3R}{C_1}} = \sqrt{\frac{2 \times 15 \times 2,000}{8}} = 87 \text{ units/order}.$$

EXAMPLE 12.5-5

The demand for a commodity is 100 units per day. Every time an order is placed, a fixed cost of ₹ 400 is incurred. Holding cost is ₹ 0.08 per unit per day. If the lead time is 13 days, determine the economic lot size and the reorder point.

Solution

$$q_0 = \sqrt{\frac{2C_3R}{C_1}} = \sqrt{\frac{2 \times 400 \times 100}{0.08}} = 1,000 \text{ units}.$$

Length of cycle, $t_0 = \dfrac{1,000}{100} = 10$ days.

As the lead time is 13 days and cycle length is 10 days, reodering should occur when the level of inventory is sufficient to satisfy the demand for 13–10 = 3 days.

$\therefore$ Reorder point = 100 × 3 = 300 units.

It may be noted that the 'effective' lead time is taken equal to 3 days rather than 13 days. It is because the lead time is longer than t_0.

EXAMPLE 12.5-6

(a) Calculate the E.O.Q. in units and total variable cost for the following items, assuming an ordering cost of ₹ 5 and a holding cost of 10%.

Item	*Annual demand*	*Unit price (₹)*
A	*800 units*	*0.02*
B	*400 units*	*1.00*
C	*392 units*	*8.00*
D	*13,800 units*	*0.20*

(b) For the above problem, compute E.O.Q. in ₹ as well as in years of supply. Also calculate the E.O.Q. frequency for each of the four items.

Solution

(*a*) $$q_0 = \sqrt{\frac{2C_3R}{C_1}}, \quad C_0 = \sqrt{2C_1C_3R}.$$

Item A $$q_0 = \sqrt{\frac{2 \times 5 \times 800}{0.02 \times \frac{10}{100}}} = \sqrt{\frac{800}{0.002}} = 2,000 \text{ units},$$

$$C_0 = \sqrt{2 \times 5 \times 800 \times 0.02 \times \frac{10}{100}} = ₹\ 4.$$

Item B $$q_0 = \sqrt{\frac{2 \times 5 \times 400}{1.00 \times \frac{10}{100}}} = 200 \text{ units},$$

$$C_0 = \sqrt{2 \times 5 \times 400 \times 1.00 \times \frac{10}{100}} = ₹\ 20.$$

Item C $$q_0 = \sqrt{\frac{2 \times 5 \times 392}{8.00 \times \frac{10}{100}}} = 70 \text{ units},$$

$$C_0 = \sqrt{2 \times 5 \times 392 \times 8.00 \times \frac{10}{100}} = ₹\ 56.$$

Item D $$q_0 = \sqrt{\frac{2 \times 5 \times 13,800}{0.20 \times \frac{10}{100}}} = 2,627 \text{ units},$$

$$C_0 = \sqrt{2 \times 5 \times 13,800 \times 0.20 \times \frac{10}{100}} = ₹\ 52.54.$$

(b) E.O.Q. in ₹

for item A : 2,000 × 0.02 = 40,
for item B : 200 × 1= 200,
for item C : 70 × 8 = 560,
and for item D : 2,627 × 0.20 = 525.40.

E.O.Q. in years of supply

for item A : $\frac{2000}{800} = 2.5$ years,

for item B : $\frac{200}{400} = 0.5$ year,

for item C : $\frac{70}{392} = 0.18$ year,

and for item D : $\frac{2,627}{13,800} = 0.19$ year.

E.O.Q. frequency (number of orders per year)

for item A : $\frac{1}{1.25} = 0.4$,

for item B : $\frac{1}{0.5} = 2$,

for item C : $\frac{1}{0.18} = 5.6$,

and for item D : $\frac{1}{0.19} = 5.25$.

EXAMPLE 12.5-7

(a) Compute the E.O.Q. and the total variable cost for the following :

Annual demand	:	*25 units,*
unit price	:	*₹ 2.50,*
order cost	:	*₹ 4.00,*
storage rate	:	*1% per year,*
interest rate	:	*12% per year,*
obsolescence rate	:	*7% per year.*

(b) Compute the order quantity and the total variable cost that would result if an incorrect price of ₹ 1.60 were used for the item.

[*R.U. M.Sc. (Math.) 2011; NIIFT Mohali, 2001; P.T.U. MBA May, 2002*]

Solution

(*a*) $$C_1 = ₹\ \frac{(1+12+7)}{100} \times 2.50 = ₹\ 0.50 \text{ per unit per year.}$$

$$\therefore \quad q_0 = \sqrt{\frac{2C_3R}{C_1}} = \sqrt{\frac{2 \times 4 \times 25}{0.50}} = 20 \text{ units,}$$

$$C_0 = \sqrt{2C_1C_3R} = \sqrt{2 \times 4 \times 25 \times 0.50} = ₹\ 10.$$

(*b*) $$q = \sqrt{\frac{2 \times 4 \times 25}{\frac{20}{100} \times 1.60}} = 25 \text{ units. This is non-optimal size.}$$

$$\text{Ordering cost} = \frac{C_3R}{q} = \frac{4 \times 25}{25} = ₹\ 4.$$

$$\text{Stock holding cost} = \frac{1}{2}C_1 . q = \frac{1}{2} . \left(\frac{20}{100} \times 2.50\right) \times 25 = ₹\ 6.25.$$

Note that for calculating the stock holding cost, correct price is to be used. A clectrical error does not mean that the stock value changes. Price paid for the stocks shall still be ₹ 2.50 even though a less price of ₹ 1.60 is taken for E.O.Q. computations.

∴ Total variable cost/year = ₹ 10.25.

EXAMPLE 12.5-8

ABC manufacturing company purchases 9,000 parts of a machine for its annual requirement, ordering one month's usage at a time. Each part costs ₹ 20. The ordering cost per order is ₹ 15, and the carrying charges are 15% of the average inventory per year.

You have been asked to suggest a more economical purchasing policy for the company. What advice would you offer and how much would it save the company per year?

[*Dayalbagh Edu. Inst. Agra MBA May, 2013; SVSM PGDM, 2009; P.T.U.B.E. (Mech.) May, 2006; P.U.B.Com. April, 2006; Sept., 2004*]

Solution

Here, $$R = 9{,}000 \text{ parts/year,}$$

$$\therefore \quad q = \frac{9{,}000}{12} = 750 \text{ parts.}$$

$$C = ₹\ 20 \text{ part, } C_3 = ₹\ 15 \text{ /order,}$$

$$C_1 = ₹\ 20 \times \frac{15}{100} = ₹\ 3 \text{ / part/ year.}$$

$$\text{Total annual variable cost} = \frac{q}{2} . C_1 + \frac{R}{q} . C_3$$

$$= ₹ \left[\frac{750}{2} \times 3 + \frac{9{,}000}{750} \times 15\right] = ₹\ 1{,}305.$$

$$q_0 = \sqrt{\frac{2RC_3}{C_1}} = \sqrt{\frac{2 \times 9{,}000 \times 15}{3}} = 300 \text{ units.}$$

$$\text{Total annual variable cost} = \sqrt{2RC_1C_3} = \sqrt{2 \times 9{,}000 \times 3 \times 15} = ₹\ 900.$$

Hence if the company purchases 300 units each time and places 30 orders in the year, the net saving to the company will be ₹ (1,305 – 900) = ₹ 405 a year.

EXAMPLE 12.5-9

A company uses ₹ 10,000 worth of an item during the year. The ordering costs are ₹ 25 per order and carrying charges are 12.5% of the average inventory value. Find the economic order quantity, number of orders per year, time period per order and the total cost.

Solution

Here CR = ₹ 10,000, C_3 = ₹ 25/ order, I = 12.5% = 0.125.

Now E.O.Q. in units $= q_0 = \sqrt{\dfrac{2C_3R}{C_1}} = \sqrt{\dfrac{2C_3R}{CI}}$.

$\therefore$ E.O.Q. in rupees $= Cq_0 = C\sqrt{\dfrac{2C_3R}{CI}} = \sqrt{\dfrac{2C_3CR}{I}} = \sqrt{\dfrac{2\times25\times10{,}000}{0.125}} = ₹\ 2{,}000.$

Number of orders / year, $n_0 = \dfrac{R}{q_0} = \dfrac{CR}{Cq_0} = \dfrac{10{,}000}{2{,}000} = 5.$

Time period per order, $t_0 = \dfrac{1}{n_0} = \dfrac{1}{5}$ year = 73 days.

Annual variable cost $= \sqrt{2C_3C_1R} = \sqrt{2C_3CIR} = \sqrt{2C_3ICR}$

$= \sqrt{2\times25\times0.125\times10{,}000} = ₹\ 250.$

$\therefore$ Total annual cost $= CR + \sqrt{2C_3C_1R} = ₹\ (10{,}000 + 250) = ₹\ 10{,}250.$

EXAMPLE 12.5-10

A manufacturing company of microwave ovens uses ₹ 75,000 worth of LED readout circuits annually in its production process. Cost per order is ₹ 45 and the carrying charges assessed against this classification of inventory are 25% of the average balance per year. This company follows an E.O.Q. purchasing system and to date has not been offered any discounts on these circuits. Now the supplier has indicated that if the company would buy its circuits four times a year in equal quantities, a discount of 1.5% off the list price would be given in return. Would you advise this company to accept this offer ? In order to maintain the present total cost, what should be the minimum discount acceptable to the company if four orders of equal sizes are placed in a year?

[*Dayalbagh Edu. Inst. Agra MBA May, 2013*]

Solution

Here, CR = ₹ 75,000, C_3 = ₹ 45/order, I = 25% = 0.25.

$\therefore \quad C_0 = \sqrt{2RC_3CI} = \sqrt{2\times75{,}000\times45\times0.25} = ₹\ 1{,}299.04.$

$\therefore$ Total cost = ₹ (75,000 + 1,299.04) = ₹ 76,299.04.

To earn discount, quantity ordered, $q = \dfrac{R}{4}$. This is non-optimal size. Total cost when discount of 1.5% is availed of

$$= \frac{q}{2}CI + \frac{R}{q}\,.\,C_3 + CR = \frac{R}{4\times2}CI + \frac{R}{q}C_3 + CR$$

$$= CR\left(1+\frac{I}{8}\right) + \frac{R}{q}\,.\,C_3 = CR\left(1+\frac{I}{8}\right) + 4C_3$$

$$= ₹\left[0.985\times75{,}000\left(1+\frac{0.25}{8}\right)+4\times45\right]$$

$$= ₹\ (76{,}183.60 + 180) = ₹\ 76{,}363.60.$$

Therefore, the company should not accept the offer of 1.5% discount. Let x be the minimum per cent discount acceptable to the company.

Then $$76{,}299.04 = \frac{100-x}{100} \times 75{,}000\left(1+\frac{0.25}{8}\right) + 4 \times 45$$

$$= \frac{100-x}{100} \times 75{,}000 \times \frac{33}{32} + 180$$

or $$100 - x = \frac{76{,}119.04 \times 100 \times 32}{75{,}000 \times 33} = 98.416$$

or $$x = 1.584\%.$$

EXAMPLE 12.5-11

A company is considering the feasibility of changing suppliers for coupling hardware. Presently the company has an optimal purchasing policy with Ace Hardware at a discount of 1%. Current yearly purchases are ₹ 81,000 and the Administrative Charges are ₹ 125 per purchase and the carrying charges are 25% of the average inventory level.

Bids received from other suppliers are: Nutz Co. offers 5% discount if ordered twice a year and Grabbers Co. offers 3% discount if ordered four times a year. Should the company retain the present supplier or accept the proposed offers and , if so, which offer?

[*Dayalbagh Edu. Inst. Agra Dec., 2006*]

Solution

$$q_0 = \sqrt{\frac{2C_3R}{C_1}} = \sqrt{\frac{2C_3R}{CI}}$$

$$\text{E.O.Q. in rupees} = Cq_0 = C \cdot \sqrt{\frac{2C_3R}{CI}} = \sqrt{\frac{2CC_3R}{I}} = \sqrt{\frac{2CRC_3}{I}}$$

$$= \sqrt{\frac{2 \times 81{,}000 \times 125}{0.25}} = 9{,}000. \quad (\because \text{order value} = CR = ₹\ 81{,}000.)$$

$$\text{Total cost at 1\% discount} = \frac{1}{2}C_1q + C_3 \cdot \frac{R}{q} + CR$$

$$= \frac{1}{2}\, CIq + C_3 \cdot \frac{R}{q} + CR$$

$$= \frac{1}{2} \times 9{,}000 \times 0.25 \times 0.99 + 125 \times \frac{81{,}000}{9{,}000} + 81{,}000 \times 0.99$$

$$= ₹\ 82{,}428.75.$$

$$\text{Total cost at 5\% discount from Nutz Co. offer} = \frac{q}{2}\,CI + C_3 . \frac{R}{q} + CR$$

$$= \frac{81{,}000}{2 \times 2} \times 0.25 \times 0.95 + 2 \times 125 + 81{,}000 \times 0.95$$

$$= ₹\ 82{,}009.38.$$

$$\text{Total cost at 3\% discount from Grabbers Co. offer} = \frac{q}{2}\,CI + C_3 . \frac{R}{q} + CR$$

$$= \frac{81{,}000}{4 \times 2} \times 0.25 \times 0.97 + 4 \times 125 + 81{,}000 \times 0.97$$

$$= ₹\ 81{,}525.31.$$

The company should, therefore, accept the offer from Grabbers Co.

EXAMPLE 12.5-12

The purchase manager of an organisation has collected the following data for one of the A-class items :

Interest on the locked-up capital	*= 20%*
Order processing cost for each order	*= ₹ 100*
Inspection cost per lot	*= ₹ 50*
Follow up cost for each order	*= ₹ 80*
Pilferage while holding inventory	*= 5%*
Other holding cost	*= 15%*
Other procurement cost for each order	*= ₹ 170*
Annual demand	*= 1,000 units*
Cost per item	*= ₹ 10*
Discount for a minimum order quantity of 500 items	*= 10%*

What should be the ordering policy of the purchase manager?

[*ICWA (Final) Dec., 1991*]

Solution

Here, annual demand, R = 1,000 units,
cost per item, C = ₹ 10,
total acquisition cost, C_3 = ₹ (100 + 50 + 80 + 170) = ₹ 400 per order,
inventory carrying rate, I = (20 + 5 + 15) = 40%,
discount for minimum quantity of 500 items = 10%.

$$q_0 \text{ for unit cost of ₹ } 10 = \sqrt{\frac{2C_3R}{CI}} = \sqrt{\frac{2\times 400\times 1{,}000}{10\times 0.40}} = 447 \text{ units.}$$

Total cost if the purchase quantity is 447 units

$$= CR + \sqrt{2C_1C_3R} = ₹\ (CR + \sqrt{2CC_3RI}\,)$$
$$= ₹\ (9 \times 1{,}000 + \sqrt{2\times 10\times 400\times 1{,}000\times 0.4}\,)$$
$$= ₹\ (9{,}000 + 1{,}788.55) = ₹\ 10{,}788.85.$$

Unit cost when quantity ordered is 500 units = ₹ (10 × .90) = ₹ 9.

$$\text{Total cost} = CR + \frac{q}{2}CI + \frac{R}{q}\cdot C_3$$
$$= 9 \times 1{,}000 + \frac{500}{2} \times 9 \times 0.4 + \frac{1{,}000}{500} \times 400$$
$$= 9{,}000 + 900 - 800 = ₹\ 10{,}700.$$

Therefore, the purchase manager should place order for 500 items each time.

EXAMPLE 12.5-13

The purchasing manager of a distillery company is considering three sources of supply for oak barrels. The first supplier offers any quantity of barrels at ₹ 150 each. The second supplier offers barrels in lots of 150 or more at ₹ 125 per barrel. The third supplier offers barrels in lots of 250 or more at ₹ 100 each. The distillery uses 1,500 barrels a year at a constant rate. Carrying costs are 40 per cent, and it costs the purchasing company ₹ 400 to place an order. Calculate the total annual cost for the orders placed to the probable suppliers and find out the supplier to whom the orders should be placed. [*Dayalbagh Edu. Inst. Agra MBA May, 2014; P.U. B.Com April, 2008; April, 2006, B.E. (E. & Ec.) April, 2008*]

Solution

Here, annual demand, R = 1,500 barrels,
inventory rate, I = 40% = 0.4,
ordering cost, C_3 = ₹ 400 / order.

The cost/unit is shown in the table below.

Supplier	*Quantity of barrels*	*Cost/unit*
First	Any quantity	₹150
Second	150 and above	₹ 125
Third	250 and more	₹ 100

Total annual costs are calculated below for the three suppliers :

First supplier $q_0 = \sqrt{\dfrac{2RC_3}{CI}} = \sqrt{\dfrac{2\times 1,500\times 400}{150\times 0.4}}$ = 141.4 barrels (feasible).

$$\text{Total annual cost} = CR + \sqrt{2RC_3CI}$$
$$= 150 \times 1,500 + \sqrt{2\times 1,500\times 400\times 150\times 0.4}$$
$$= 2,25,000 + 8,484 = ₹\ 2,33,484.$$

Second supplier $q_0 = \sqrt{\dfrac{2\times 1,500\times 400}{125\times 0.4}}$ = 154.92 barrels (feasible)

$$\text{Total annual cost} = CR + \sqrt{2RC_3CI}$$
$$= 125 \times 1,500 + \sqrt{2\times 1,500\times 400\times 125\times 0.4}$$
$$= 1,87,500 + 7,746 = ₹\ 1,95,246.$$

Third supplier $q_0 = \sqrt{\dfrac{2\times 1,500\times 400}{100\times 0.4}}$ = 173.2 barrels.

(not feasible since min. quantity is 250 barrels)

∴ Minimum batch size for which order can be placed = 250 barrels.

$$\therefore \quad \text{Total annual cost} = CR + \frac{q}{2}CI + C_3 \cdot \frac{R}{q}$$
$$= 100 \times 1,500 + \frac{250}{2} \times 100 \times 0.4 + 400 \times \frac{1,500}{250}$$
$$= 1,50,000 + 5,000 + 2,400 = ₹\ 1,57,400.$$

Thus the order for 250 oak barrels each time should be placed with the third supplier as it involves the lowest annual cost.

EXAMPLE 12.5-14

A company plans to consume 700 pieces annually of a particular component. Past records indicate that its purchasing department spent ₹ 12,500 for placing 15,000 purchase orders. The average inventory was valued at ₹ 50,000 and the total storage cost was ₹ 7,500, which included wages, rent, taxes, insurance, etc. related to store department. The company borrows capital at 10 per cent a year. If the cost of the component is ₹ 12 and lot size is 10, determine the

(a) purchase price/year,
(b) purchase expenses/year,
(c) storage expenses/year,
(d) capital cost/ year,
(e) total cost/year.

Solution

(*a*) Purchase price/year $= ₹\ 12 \times 700 = ₹\ 8,400.$

(*b*) Ordering cost/order $= ₹\ \dfrac{12,500}{15,000} = ₹\ 0.83.$

$\therefore$ Purchase expenses/year = ₹ $\left(0.83\times\frac{700}{10}\right)$ = ₹ 58.33.

(c) Inventory carrying rate, $I = \frac{7,500}{50,000} \times 100 = 15\%$ / year.

$\therefore$ Storage expenses/year $= \frac{q}{2}$ CI = ₹ $\left(\frac{10}{2}\times 12\times\frac{15}{100}\right)$ = ₹ 9.

(d) Capital cost/year $= \frac{q}{2}$. C.I′ = ₹ $\left(\frac{10}{2}\times 12\times\frac{10}{100}\right)$ = ₹ 6.

(e) Total cost/year = ₹ [8,400 + 58.33 + 9 + 6] = ₹ 8,473.33.

EXAMPLE 12.5-15

A chemical company is considering the optimal batch size for reorder of concentrated sulphuric acid. The management accountant has supplied the following information :

(i) The purchase price of sulphuric acid is ₹ 150 per gallon.

(ii) The clerical and data processing costs are ₹ 500 per order.

All the transport is done by rail. A charge of ₹ 2,000 is made each time the special line to the factory is opened. A charge of ₹ 20 per gallon is also made. The company uses 40,000 gallons per year. Maintenance costs of stocks are ₹ 200 per gallon per year.

Each gallon requires 0.5 sq. ft. of storage space. If warehouse space is not used, it can be rented out to another company at ₹ 200 per sq. ft. per annum. Available warehouse space is 1,000 sq. ft., the overhead costs being ₹ 5,000 per annum. Calculate

(a) the economic reorder size.

(b) the minimum total annual cost of holding and reordering stock. [P.U. MBA, 2004]

Solution

Here, annual demand, R = 40,000 gallons,

Ordering cost, C_3 = ₹ (500 + 2,000) = ₹ 2,500/ order.

If the warehouse space is rented out, the company can get ₹ 200 per sq. ft. If it uses the space for storing sulphuric acid, it is not able to realise that amount.

$\therefore$ Carrying cost, C_1 = ₹ (200 + 0.5 × 200) = ₹ 300 / gallon / year.

Note that the rail transport cost of ₹ (20 × 40,000) = ₹ 8,00,000 as well as the overhead cost of ₹ 5,000 are fixed costs and are irrelevant for finding the economic order size.

$$(a)\quad \therefore\quad q_0 = \sqrt{\frac{2RC_3}{C_1}} = \sqrt{\frac{2\times 40,000\times 2,500}{300}} = 817 \text{ gallons.}$$

(b) Total annual cost = $CR + \sqrt{2RC_3C_1}$ + Rail transport cost + Storage overhead cost

$$= ₹\left[150\times 40,000 + \sqrt{2\times 40,000\times 2,500\times 300} + 20\times 40,000 + 5,000\right]$$

$$= ₹\,[60,00,000 + 2,44,950 + 8,00,000 + 5,000] = ₹\ 70,49,950.$$

EXAMPLE 12.5-16

A company uses an item at a uniform rate of 2,000 units per year. Delivery is instantaneous and no shortages are permitted. The ordering, receiving and hauling cost is ₹ 13 per order, while inspection cost is ₹ 12 per order. Interest costs ₹ 0.056 and deterioration and obsolescence costs ₹ 0.004 respectively per year for each item actually held in inventory plus ₹ 0.02 per year based on the maximum number of units in inventory. Calculate the E.O.Q. If lead time is 25 days, find reorder level. [P.T.U. B.Tech. April, 2012]

Solution

Here, R = 2,000 units/year, C_3 = ₹ (13 + 12) = ₹ 25/order. Inventory carrying cost based on actual *i.e.*, average inventory = ₹ (0.056 + 0.004) = ₹ 0.06/unit/year.

Inventory carrying cost based on maximum inventory = ₹ 0.02/unit/year.

$$\text{Annual variable cost} = C_3 \cdot \frac{R}{q} + 0.06 \cdot \frac{q}{2} + 0.02 \cdot q = \frac{25 \times 2{,}000}{q} + 0.05q.$$

For E.O.Q., $\dfrac{25 \times 2{,}000}{q} = 0.05q$ (Carrying cost = Ordering cost)

or $$q^2 = \frac{25 \times 2{,}000}{0.05} \text{ or } q = \sqrt{\frac{25 \times 2{,}000}{0.05}} = 1{,}000 \text{ units.}$$

∴ E.O.Q. = 1,000 units.

$$\text{Reorder level} = R \times L = 2{,}000 \times \frac{25}{365} = 137 \text{ units.}$$

EXAMPLE 12.5-17

A wholesaler supplies 30 stuffed dolls each weekday to various shops. Dolls are purchased from the manufacturer in lots of 120 each of ₹ 1,200 per lot. Every order incurs a handling charge of ₹ 60 plus a freight charge of ₹ 250 per lot. Multiple and fractional lots also can be ordered, and all orders are filled the next day. The incremental cost is ₹ 0.60 per year to store a doll in inventory. The wholesaler finances inventory investments by paying its holding company 2% monthly for borrowed funds. Find E.O.Q. and frequency of orders assuming 250 weekdays in a year. [*P.T.U. B.Tech. April, 2012*]

Solution

Annual demand, R = 30 × 250 = 7,500 units.

$$\text{Unit cost of purchase, } C = ₹\ \frac{1{,}200}{120} = ₹\ 10.$$

Ordering cost, C_3 = ₹ (60 + 250) = ₹ 310 / order.

$$\text{Inventory carrying cost, } C_1 = ₹ \left(0.60 + 10 \times \frac{2 \times 12}{100}\right) = ₹\ 3 / \text{unit / year.}$$

$$\therefore \quad q_0 = \sqrt{\frac{2RC_3}{C_1}} = \sqrt{\frac{2 \times 7{,}500 \times 310}{3}} = 1{,}245 \text{ units.}$$

$$n_0 = \frac{R}{q_0} = \frac{7{,}500}{1{,}245} \simeq 6 \text{ orders / year.}$$

$$t_0 = \frac{1}{n_0} = \frac{1}{6} \text{ years} = 2 \text{ months.}$$

∴ Order of 1,245 units should be placed every two months.

EXAMPLE 12.5-18

A company assembles a component which uses a part bought from an outside supplier at a cost of ₹ 5 per unit. Each month 18,000 components are produced at a steady rate throughout. There is a lead time of one month and the current practice for the company is to order 72,000 units at a time. This order is placed when the stock level falls to 48,000.

The supplier offers a 10% discount if orders are placed in lot sizes of 2,00,000 units and he is allowed a two-months delivery period. If the company wanted to change to these terms, it would require additional storage which would cost ₹ 24,000 per year and would incur additional handling charges of ₹ 0.05 per unit. The company would maintain the level of protection afforded by the use of safety stock.

The cost of placing an order is ₹ 200 and the cost of receiving delivery of an order is ₹ 800. The cost of capital normally used for inventory decisions is 12% per annum. You are required

(a) to calculate and state the annual cost following the current practice.

(b) to calculate and state the minimum annual cost if the extra storage space were available so that the discount for larger quantities could be considered.

Solution

(*a*) Here, q = 72,000 units, C_3 = ₹ (200 + 800) = ₹ 1,000/order,
C = ₹ 5/unit, I = 0.12, R = 18,000 × 12 = 2,16,000 units / year.

Now ROL = lead time demand + safety stock = LTD + SS

∴ 48,000 = 1 × 18,000 + SS

or SS = 30,000 units.

$$\therefore \text{ Total annual cost } = \left(\frac{q}{2}+\text{SS}\right)\text{CI}+\text{C}_3\,.\frac{R}{q}+CR$$

$$= ₹\left[\left(\frac{72,000}{2}+30,000\right)\times 5\times 0.12+1,000\times\frac{2,16,000}{72,000}+5\times 2,16,000\right]$$

= ₹ (39,600 + 3,000 + 10,80,000) = ₹ 11,22,600.

(*b*) *If orders of E.O.Q. are placed*

$$q_0=\sqrt{\frac{2RC_3}{CI}}=\sqrt{\frac{2\times 2,16,000\times 1,000}{5\times 0.12}}=26,833 \text{ units.}$$

$$\therefore \text{ Total annual cost } = \left(\frac{q}{2}+\text{SS}\right)\text{CI}+\text{C}_3\frac{R}{q}+CR$$

$$= ₹\left[\left(\frac{26,833}{2}+30,000\right)\times 5\times 0.12+1,000\times\frac{2,16,000}{26,833}+5\times 2,16,000\right]$$

= ₹ (26,050 + 8,050 + 10,80,000) = ₹ 11,14,100.

If orders of 2,00,000 units are placed

Here, C = ₹ (5×0.9) = ₹ 4.50 / unit,
q = 2,00,000 units,
LT = 2 months,
storage charges = ₹ 24,000/year,
handling charges = ₹ 0.05/unit.

∴ C_3 = ₹ (1,000 + 0.05 × 2,00,000) = ₹ 11,000/order.

Now ROL = LTD + SS.

∴ 48,000 = 2 × 18,000 + SS

or SS = 12,000 units.

$$\therefore \text{ Total annual cost } = \left(\frac{q}{2}+SS\right)\text{CI}+C_3\frac{R}{q}+\text{CR + annual charges}$$

$$= ₹\left[\left(\frac{2,00,000}{2}+12,000\right)\times 4.50\times 0.12+11,000\times\frac{2,16,000}{2,00,000}+4.50\times 2,16,000+24,000\right]$$

= ₹ (1,12,000 × 0.54 + 11,000 × 1.08 + 4.50 × 2,16,000 + 24,000)

= ₹ (60,480 + 11,880 + 9,72,000 + 24,000) = ₹ 10,68,360.

∴ Minimum annual cost of ₹ 10,68,360 is incurred if order quantity is 2,00,000 units.

EXERCISES 12.1

1. Define inventory. What are the advantages and disadvantages of having inventories? [*R.U. M.Sc. (Math.) 2011; P.T.U. MCA, 2010; M.B.A. Feb., 2009; B.Tech. (Mech.) 2009; P.U.B.Com. April, 2007; Pbi. U. MCA, 2001*]
2. How will you control the inventories of a manufacturing organisation? Discuss the various inventory costs associated with this organisation. [*P.T.U. B.Com., 2010; B.E. (Mech.) May, 2011, 2006; P.U. M.Com., 2002*]
3. Explain the following terms in inventory management :
   (*i*) Carrying cost (*ii*) Shortage cost (*iii*) Ordering cost.
   [*P.U.B.Com. April, 2007, 2004, 2000, 1996; G.J.U. MBA Nov., 2003; P.T.U. BCA, 2011; B.Tech. (Mech.) May, 2011; 2010; May, 2006; Dayalbagh Edu. Inst. Agra M.Tech. Dec., 2012; 2007*]
4. Write short notes on the following :
   (*i*) Necessity for inventory control [*P.U. MBA Feb., 2009*]
   (*ii*) Functions performed by inventory [*J.N.T.U. Hyderabad B.Tech. Nov., 2010; P.T.U. B.Tech. (Mech.) May, 2012; 2008*]
   (*iii*) Inventory costs and their components. [*Univ. of Madras MBA April, 2012; P.T.U. BBA 2011; MCA, 2010; B.Tech. (Mech.) Dec., 2006*]
5. (a) Most of the businessmen view inventory as a necessary evil. Do you agree with this? Explain. [*GNDU B.Com., 1996*]
   (b) What are the factor that contribute to the inventory carrying cost? [*Dayabagh Edu. Institutes, Agra, B.E. & M.Tech. Dec., 2012*]
6. What are advantages of proper inventory management ? [*Mumbai U. MBA, 2010*]
7. Classify inventory. [*J.N.T.U. Hyderabad B.Tech. Nov., 2010*]
8. Derive the EOQ formula $q_0 = \sqrt{\dfrac{2C_3R}{C_1}}$, where the symbols have usual meanings. State the assumptions and limitations in this formula.
   [*P.T.U. MBA, 2012; B.Tech., 2010; J.N.T.U. Hyderabad B.Tech. (C.Sc.) Dec., 2011; P.T.U.B.Tech. (Mech.) Dec., 2011; Dec., 2006; P.U. M.Com. March, 2006; 2004; B.Com., 2010; Sept., 2006; April, 2007; 2004; C.A.(Final) 2003*]
9. Represent in the form of a table the various types of inventory control models. [*IGNOU MBA June, 2007; Dec., 2006; P.U. B.Com. March, 2006; Sept., 2005*]
10. Explain economic lot size. [*P.T.U. B.Tech., 2010; MBA, 2009*]
11. Explain the basic characteristics of an inventory system. [*P.T.U. MBA, 2009*]
12. State the assumptions underlying the basic EOQ formula. [*P.T.U. BBA, 2011; MBA, 2008*]
13. In each of the following cases, stock is replenished instantaneously and no shortage is allowed. Find the economic lot size, the associated total cost and length of time between two orders.
    (*a*) C_3 = ₹ 100, C_1 = Re. 0.05 and R = 30 units/year.
    (*b*) C_3 = ₹ 50, C_1 = Re. 0.05 and R = 30 units/year.
    (*c*) C_3 = ₹ 100, C_1 = Re. 0.01 and R = 40 units/year.
    (*d*) C_3 = ₹ 100, C_1 = Re. 0.04 and R = 20 units/year. (*Ans.* (*a*) q_0 = 346, t_0 = 11.55, $C_0(q)$ = ₹ 17.30.)
14. In each case of exercise no. 11, determine the reorder level if lead time is 14 units.
15. A company purchases 10,000 items per year for use in its production shop. The unit cost is ₹ 10 per year, holding cost is ₹ 0.80 per month and cost of making a purchase is ₹ 200. Determine the following if no shortages are allowed :
    (*i*) The optimum order quantity,
    (*ii*) the optimum total yearly cost,
    (*iii*) the number of orders per year,
    (*iv*) the time between orders. [*NIIFT Mohali, 1998*]
16. A certain item costs ₹ 235 per ton. The monthly requirement is 5 tons and each time the stock is replenished, there is a setup cost of ₹ 1,000. The cost of carrying of inventory has been estimated at 10% of the value of the stock per year. What is the optimal order quantity? [*J.N.T.U Hyderabad B.Tech. (C.Sc.) Dec., 2011*]

17. The XYZ manufacturing company has determined, from an analysis of its accounting and production data for part number 625, that its cost to purchase is ₹ 36 per order and ₹ 2 per part. Its inventory carrying charges are 18% of the average inventory. The demand for this part is 10,000 units per annum. Find
    (*a*) what should the economic order quantity be ?
    (*b*) what is the optimal no. of days' supply per optimum order? [*Delhi M.B.A., 1975*]
    (*Ans.* 1.144 units, 0.1414 year.)
18. An aircraft company uses rivets at an approximate consumption rate of 2,500 kg per year. The rivets cost ₹ 30 per kg and the company personnel estimates that it costs ₹ 130 to place an order and the inventory carrying cost is 10% per year. How frequently should orders for rivets be placed and what quantities should be ordered? [*Meerut M.Sc. (Stat.) 1976*]
    (*Ans.* 466 kg, 5.3/year.)
19. Consider the inventory system with the following data in usual notations : R = 1,000 units/year, I = 0.30, P = ₹ 0.50 per unit, C_3 = ₹ 10, L = 2 years (lead time) and C_1 = IP. Determine
    (*i*) optimal order quantity,
    (*ii*) reorder point,
    (*iii*) minimum average cost. [*Delhi, 1968*]
    (*Ans.* 365 units, 2,000 units, ₹ 54.80.)
20. A stockist has to supply 400 units of a product every Monday to his customers. He gets the product at ₹ 50 per unit from the manufacturer. The cost of ordering and transportation from the manufacturer in ₹ 50 per order. The cost of carrying inventory is 75% per year of the cost of the product. Find
    (*i*) the economic lot size,
    (*ii*) the total optimal cost (including the capital cost). [*P.T.U. B.Tech. (Mech.) 2010*]
    (*Ans.* (*i*) 235.5 units (*ii*) ₹ 2,169.84/week.)
21. A computer company sells a particular type of personal computer. It costs the store ₹ 25,000 each time it places an order with the manufacturer. The annual carrying cost is ₹ 9,000. The manager estimates the annual demand of P.C.'s to be 1,200 units. Determine the optimal order quantity and the total minimum inventory cost. [*Osmania U. MBA, 2010*]
    (*Ans. 81.6 units;* ₹ *7,34, 757.50.*)
22. A shopkeeper has a uniform demand of an item at the rate of 50 items per month. He buys it from a supplier at the cost of ₹ 6 per item and the cost of ordering is ₹ 10 each time. If the stock holding costs are 20% per year of the stock value, how frequently should he replenish his stock ? Suppose the supplier offers a 5% discount on orders between 200 and 900 items and a 10% discount on orders exceeding or equal to 1,000 items, can the shopkeeper reduce his costs by taking advantage of either of these discounts ? [*P.T.U. MBA Feb., 2011; P.U.B.Com., 2010, 2004*]
    (*Ans.* 5% discount should be accepted.)
23. A company uses 8,000 units of a product as raw material, costing ₹ 10 per unit. The administrative cost per purchase in ₹ 40. The holding costs are 28% of the average inventory. The company is following an optimal purchasing policy and places orders according to the EOQ. It has been offered a quantity discount of 10% if it purchases its entire requirement only four times a year. Should the company accept this offer ? If not, what minimum discount should the company demand ?
    [*G.N.D.U. B.Com. April, 2008*]
24. The annual demand for an item is 3,200 units. The unit cost is ₹ 6 and inventory carrying charges are 25% per annum. If the cost of one procurement is ₹ 150, determine
    (*i*) Economic order quantity.
    (*ii*) Number of orders per year.
    (*iii*) Time between orders.
    (*iv*) The optimal cost. [*G.N.D.U.B.Com. April, 2007*]
25. A company requires 10,000 units of a material per annum. The cost per order is ₹ 50 and the storage cost is ₹ 5 per unit of average inventory. What quantity should be ordered to minimize the total cost ? Also find out the total variable inventory cost. [*G.N.D.U.B.Com. April, 2010*]
26. A factory requires 16,000 units of a part, costing ₹ 2 per unit. If carrying cost is 8% of the inventory value and ordering cost is ₹ 40 per order, calculate EOQ, optimum number of orders per annum, the total holding cost, the reorder level and the length of inventory cycle. What would be the saving if ordering is done as per EOQ instead of thrice per year ? [*G.N.D.U.B.Com. April, 2002*]
    (*Ans.* 2,829 units, 5.66 orders, ₹ 226.27, 64.5 days; ₹ 94.)

27. The production department for a company requires 3,600 kg of raw material for manufacturing a particular item per year. It has estimated that the cost of placing an order is ₹ 36 and the cost of carrying inventory is 25% of the investment in the inventories. The price is ₹ 10 per kg. The purchase manager wishes to determine an ordering policy for raw material.
[*R.T.M. Nagpur U.B.E. (Mech.) 2011; J.N.T.U. Hyderabad B.Tech. (C.Sc) Dec., 2011*]

28. Derive the expression for EOQ of Wilson - Harris Inventory Model. A company uses 10,000 units per year of an item. The purchase price is ₹ 1 per item. Ordering cost is ₹ 25 per order. Carrying cost per year is 12% of the inventory value. Find EOQ and the number of orders per year. The lead time is 4 weeks and assuming 50 working weeks per year, find the reorder point.
[*J.N.T.U. Hyderabad B.Tech. (C.Sc.) Dec., 2011*]

29. A company uses 24,000 units of a raw material which costs ₹ 12.50 per unit. Placing each order costs ₹ 22.50 and the carrying cost is 5.4% per year of the average inventory. Find the economic order quantity and the total inventory cost (including the cost of the material). Should the company accept the offer made by the supplier of a discount of 5% on the cost price on a single order of 24,000 units ?
[*J.N.T.U. Hyderabad B.Tech. (C.Sc.) Dec., 2011; April, 2011; Nov., 2010*]

30. A product 'X' is purchased by a company from outside suppliers. The consumption is 10,000 units per year. The cost of the item is ₹ 5 per unit and the ordering cost is estimated to be ₹ 100 per order. The cost of carrying inventory is 25%. If the consumption rate is uniform, determine the economic purchasing quantity. [*J.N.T.U. Hyderabad B.Tech. May, 2011*]

31. (*a*) Classify inventory.

    (*b*) Find the economic lot size that associates with total cost and the length of time between two orders, given that the set-up cost is ₹ 100, daily holding cost per unit of inventory is 5 paise and daily demand is approximately 30 units.[*J.N.T.U. Hyderabad B.Tech. Nov., 2010*]

32. Find the economic order quantity for the data given below :

    Annual demand : 2,400 units
    Unit cost of the item : ₹ 2 per unit
    Ordering cost : ₹ 30 per order
    Inventory holding cost : 20% of the unit cost. [*J.N.T.U. Hyderabad B.Tech. May, 2009*]

33. A company, which raises speciality cattle for low-fat beef, feeds its cattle on a strictly monitored schedule. The ranch uses 12,000 pounds of grain a year. The cost of ordering is $ 10 per order, and the cost of carrying inventory is $ 0.06 per pound per annum. What is the economic order quantity ? What is the minimum total inventory cost ? How many times should the ranch order grain during the year ? The ranch operates 360 days a year. What is the order cycle time in days between orders ? Is carrying cost greater than, equal to, or less than the ordering cost ?
[*Dayalbagh Edu. Inst. Agra B.Sc. Engg. & M.Tech. Dec., 2011*]
(*Ans.* 2,000 pounds, $ 120, 6/year, 60 days, equal.)

34. Determine the EOQ for the following data :

    Annual demand = ₹ 1,00,000 worth of an item
    Ordering cost = 1% of order value
    Carrying cost = 20% of average inventory value. [*P.U. B.Com., 2002*]
(*Ans.* ₹ 10,000.)

$$\text{[Hint. } q_0 = \sqrt{\frac{2C_3R}{C_1}} = \sqrt{\frac{2R \cdot \frac{Cq_0}{100}}{CI}} = \sqrt{\frac{2 \times 1{,}00{,}000 \times \frac{q_0}{100}}{20/100}} = \sqrt{10{,}000\, q_0}$$

$\therefore \quad q_0^2 = 10{,}000\, q_0$ or q_0 = ₹ 10,000 (order value).]

35. An item is used at a uniform rate of 50,000 units per year. No shortage is allowed and delivery is at an infinite rate. The ordering, receiving and handling cost is ₹ 13 per order, while inspection cost is ₹ 12 per order. Interest costs ₹ 0.056 and obsolescence costs ₹ 0.004 respectively per year for each item actually held in inventory plus ₹ 0.02 per year per unit based on the maximum number of units in inventory. Calculate EOQ. If lead time is 20 days, find reorder level. [*IGNOU MCA, 2003*]
(*Ans.* 5,590 units; 2,778 units.)

36. A motor company purchases 9,000 motor spare parts for its annual requirement, ordering one month usage at a time. Each spare part costs ₹ 20. The ordering cost/order is ₹ 15 and the carrying charges are 15% of the average inventory per year.
You have been asked to suggest more economical purchasing policy for the company. What advice would you offer and how much would it save the company per year?
[*Dayalbagh Edu. Inst. Agra MBA May, 2013; G.N.D.U. B.Com. April, 2006; P.T.U.B.Tech. (Mech.) May, 2006; P.U. B.Com., 2002*]
(*Ans.* Purchase 300 parts/ order; Annual savings ₹ 405.)

37. Thompson Tooling has a department of Defence Contract for 1,50,000 bushings a year. Thompson orders the metal for bushings in lots of 40,000 units from a supplier. It costs $ 40 to place an order and the estimated carrying charge is 20% of the unit cost, which is $ 0.15. Thompson wants to know what per cent their order quantity varies from optimal and what this variation is costing them, if any. Hence calculate the extra cost incurred by Thompson for not ordering in optimal lots. [*R.C.C. CHD., 2002*]
(*Ans.* 50% ; $ 150.)

38. A manufacturer uses ₹ 25,000 worth of an item during the year. He has estimated the ordering cost as ₹ 50 per order and carrying costs as 12.5% of average inventory value. Find the optimal order size, number of orders per year, time period per order and total cost. [*IGNOU MBA, 2002*]
[**Hint.** Here R = ₹ 25,000/year, C_3 = ₹ 50 / order, I = 12.5% / year.

$$\therefore \quad q_0 = \sqrt{\frac{2RC_3}{C_1}} = \sqrt{\frac{2.CR.C_3}{CC_1}} = \sqrt{\frac{2.CR.C_3}{C.CI}} = \frac{1}{C}\sqrt{\frac{2.CR.C_3}{I}}.$$

$$\therefore \quad Cq_0 = \sqrt{\frac{2.CR.C_3}{I}} = \sqrt{\frac{2 \times 25{,}000 \times 50}{12.5/100}} = ₹\ 3{,}162.\ \text{(order value)}$$

$$n_0 = \frac{R}{q_0} = \frac{25{,}000}{3{,}162} = 7.9/\text{year}.$$

$$t_0 = \frac{1}{n_0} = \frac{12}{7.9} = 1.52\ \text{months}.$$

$$C_0 = \sqrt{2\,R\,C_3\,C_1} = \sqrt{2 \times 25{,}000 \times 50 \times \frac{12.5}{100}} = ₹\ 559\ ]$$

39. Frequently the manager of an inventory system must make the decision whether to purchase or manufacture an item. Suppose that an item may be purchased for ₹ 25 per unit and manufactured at the rate of 10,000 units per year for ₹ 22 each. However, if purchased, the ordering cost is only ₹ 5 compared to a setup cost of ₹ 50 if it is manufactured. The yearly demand for this item is 2,500 units and the inventory holding cost rate is 10 per cent. What suggestion (make or buy) would you make to the manager in this case? [*R.C.C.CHD. MCA, 2001*]
(*Ans.* C_P = ₹ 62,750; C_M = ₹ 55,642; make.)

40. A company uses 1,200 units per month of an electronic component each costing ₹ 2. Placing each order costs ₹ 50 and the carrying cost is 6% per year of the average inventory.
(*i*) Find EOQ.
(*ii*) If the company gets 5% discount on single order, should it accept the discount offer?
(*iii*) Find discount percentage which matches EOQ ordering for a single order.
[*P.U. B.Com. April, 2003*]

41. A factory requires 1,500 units of an item per month, each costing ₹ 27. The cost per order is ₹ 150 and the inventory carrying charges work out to be 20% of the average inventory. Find out the EOQ and the number of orders per year. Would you accept a 2% price discount on a minimum supply quantity of 1,200 units? Compare the total cost in both the cases. [*DOEACC, 1997*]

42. In a warehouse the independent demand for a commonly used bolt is 500 units per month. The ordering cost is ₹ 30 per order placed. The carrying cost is 25% per year and each bolt costs 50 paise.
(*i*) Calculate the lot size for this product. State assumptions made in using formula.
(*ii*) How often is this product to be purchased?
(*iii*) If ordering cost is reduced to ₹ 5 per order, how will it change lot size and frequency of purchasing? [*IGNOU MBA June, 1998*]
(*Ans.* (*a*) (*i*) 1,697 units (*ii*) 3.5/year; 3.4 months. (*b*) (*i*) 693 units (*ii*) 8.66/ year; 1.38 months.)

43. A company works 50 weeks in a year. For a certain part, included in the assembly of several parts, there is an annual demand of 10,000 units. This part may be available from either an outside supplier or a subsidiary company. The following data relating to the part are given:

		From outside supplier (₹)	*From subsidiary company (₹)*
Purchase price/unit	:	12	13
Cost of placing an order	:	10	10
Cost of receiving an order	:	20	15
Storage and all carrying costs, including capital cost/unit/year	:	2	2

(*i*) What purchase quantity from which source would you recommend ?

(*ii*) What would be the minimum total cost ? [*ICWA June, 1989*]

(*Ans.* (*i*) 548 units/order from outside supplier (*ii*) ₹ 1,21,096.)

44. A purchase manager places order each time for a lot of 500 numbers of a particular item. From the available data the following results are obtained:

Inventory carrying cost = 40%,
ordering cost per order = ₹ 600,
cost per unit = ₹ 50,
annual demand = 1,000 units.

Find out the loss to the organisation due to his ordering policy. [*ICWA (Final) Dec., 1989*]

(*Ans.* ₹ 1,301.)

45. (*a*) What are the different costs associated with inventory control systems ? How are they obtained? Give both the analytical and graphical methods of determining economic order quantity.

(*b*) For one of the bought-out items, the following are the relevant data:

Ordering cost = ₹ 500, holding cost = 40%,
cost per item = ₹ 100, annual demand = 1,000.

The purchase manager placed 5 orders of equal quantity in one year in order to avail the discount of 5% on the cost of the item. Work out the gain or loss to the organisation due to his ordering policy for this item. [*ICWA (Final) Dec., 1990*]

(*Ans.* Gain of ₹ 5,024.55.)

46. The Inventory Company, after an analysis of its accounting and production records has determined that it uses ₹ 36,000 per year of a component part purchased at ₹ 18 per part. The purchasing cost is ₹ 40 per order and its annual inventory carrying charges are $16\frac{2}{3}$ % of the average inventory.

(*i*) Determine the most economic quantity to order at one time.

(*ii*) Determine the most economic number of times to order per year.

(*iii*) Determine the average days' supply for ordering the most economic quantity (year = 365 days).

(*iv*) Determine the optimum amount of rupees' worth of the units per order. [*C.A. (Final) Dec., 1990*]

(*Ans.* (*i*) 231 units (*ii*) 8.66 (*iii*) 42.15 days (*iv*) ₹ 4,158.)

47. Given the following data for a particular inventory item :

Usage	:	500 units/week
Ordering cost	:	₹ 40/order
Carrying cost	:	₹ 1/unit/week
Lead time	:	3 weeks
Price	:	₹ 50/unit.

Determine the following :

(*i*) E.O.Q. (*ii*) Cycle time (*iii*) Reorder point

(*iv*) Average inventory level

(*v*) Average weekly ordering cost

(*vi*) Average weekly carrying cost

(*vii*) Average weekly total cost including the cost of the item.

[*Dayalbagh Edu. Inst. Agra M.B.A. Dec., 2012, 2007*]

(*Ans.* 200 units, 0.4 days, 1,500 units, 100 units, ₹ 100, ₹ 100, ₹ 25,200.)

12.5-2 Model 1 (b) (Demand Rate Non-uniform, Replenishment Rate Infinite)

In this model all assumptions are same as in model 1 (*a*) with the exception that instead of uniform demand rate R, we are given some total demand D, to be satisfied during some long time period T. Thus demand rates are different in different order cycles.

Let q be the fixed quantity ordered each time the order is placed.

Number of orders, $\quad N = \dfrac{D}{q}.$

If t_1 is the time interval between orders 1 and 2, t_2 the time interval between orders 2 and 3 and so on, the total time T will be

$$= t_1 + t_2 + \ldots + t_n. \qquad \ldots(12.8)$$

This model is illustrated schematically in figure 12.3.

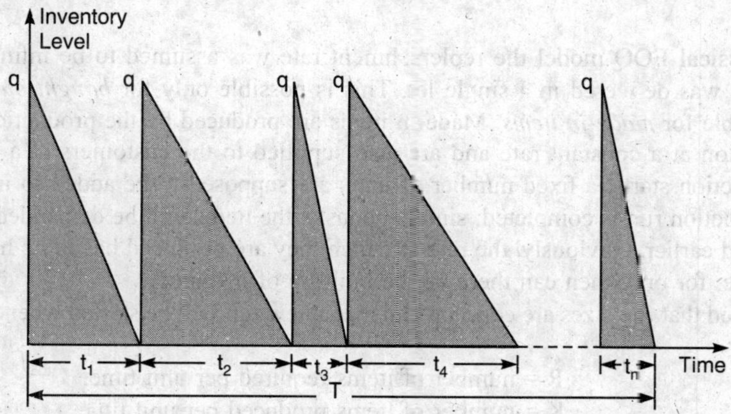

Fig. 12.3. Inventory situation for different rates of demand in different cycles.

Holding costs for time period T will be

$$= \left(\frac{1}{2}qt_1\right)C_1 + \left(\frac{1}{2}qt_2\right)C_1 \ldots + \left(\frac{1}{2}qt_n\right)C_1$$

$$= \frac{1}{2}q\,C_1\,(t_1 + t_2 + \ldots + t_n) = \frac{1}{2}q\,C_1T,$$

and the ordering cost will be

$$= C_3 \,.\, N$$

$$= C_3 \,.\, \frac{D}{q}, \text{ where } C_3 \text{ is the ordering cost per order.}$$

∴ Total cost equation for fixed order size q will be

$$C(q) = \frac{1}{2}q\,C_1T + C_3\frac{D}{q}. \qquad \ldots(12.9)$$

For minimum cost, $\dfrac{d}{dq}\,[C(q)] = 0$ and $\dfrac{d^2}{dq^2}\,[C(q)]$ should be positive.

∴ Differentiating equation (12.9) w.r.t. q,

$$\frac{d}{dq}\,[C(q)] = \frac{1}{2}C_1T - C_3\frac{D}{q^2} = 0 \qquad \therefore q = \sqrt{\frac{2C_3D}{C_1T}} = \sqrt{\frac{2C_3\,.\,D/T}{C_1}}$$

and $\qquad \dfrac{d^2}{dq^2}\,[C(q)] = \dfrac{2C_3D}{q^2}$, which is positive for the value of q given above.

$\therefore$ Optimal lot size, $q_0 = \sqrt{\dfrac{2C_3(D/T)}{C_1}}$, ...(12.10)

and minimum total cost,

$$C_0(q) = \frac{1}{2}C_1.T.\sqrt{\frac{2C_3(D/T)}{C_1}} + C_3D\sqrt{\frac{C_1}{2C_3(D/T)}}$$

$$= \sqrt{2C_1C_3(D/T)}. \quad \text{...(12.11)}$$

From equations (12.10) and (12.11) we find that results for this model can be obtained if the uniform demand rate R in model 1 *(a)* is replaced by *average* demand rate D/T.

12.5-3 Model 1 (c) (Demand Rate Uniform, Replenishment or Production Rate Finite)

In the classical EOQ model the replenishment rate was assumed to be infinite; the entire quantity ordered was delivered in a single lot. This is possible only for *bought-out items* and is simply unthinkable for *made-in items*. Made-in items are produced by the production department of the organisation at a constant rate and are also supplied to the customers at a constant rate. When the production starts, a fixed number of units are supposed to be added to inventory each day till the production run is completed; simultaneously, the items will be demanded at a constant rate, as stipulated earlier. Obviously, the rate at which they are produced has to be higher than the consumption rate, for only then can there be the built-up of inventory.

It is assumed that run sizes are constant and that a new run will be started whenever inventory is zero. Let

R = number of items required per unit time,
K = number of items produced per unit time,
C_1 = cost of holding per item per unit time,
C_3 = cost of setting up a production run,
q = number of items produced per run, $q = Rt$,
t = interval between runs.

Figure 12.4 shows the variation of inventory with time.

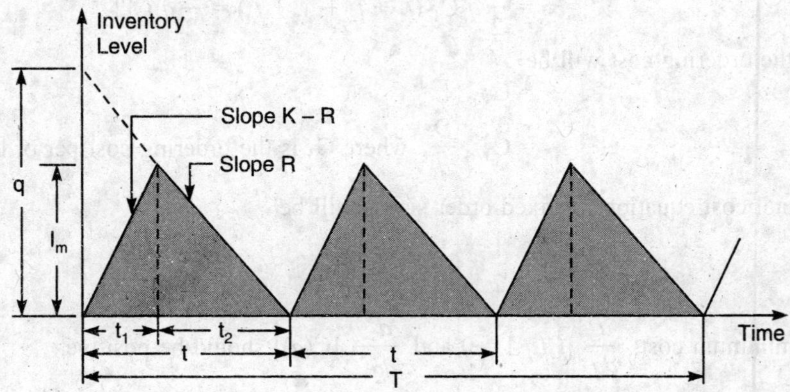

Fig. 12.4. Inventory situation with finite rate of production.

Here, each production run of length t consists of two parts t_1 and t_2, where

(i) t_1 is the time during which the stock is building up at a constant rate of K - R units per unit time,

(ii) t_2 is the time during which there is no production (or supply or replenishment) and inventory is decreasing at a constant demand rate R per unit time.

Let I_m be the maximum inventory available at the end of time t_1 which is expected to be consumed during the remaining period t_2 at the demand rate R.

Then $$I_m = (K - R)\, t_1 \quad \text{or} \quad t_1 = \frac{I_m}{K - R}. \qquad \text{...(12.12)}$$

Now the total quantity produced during time $t_1 = q$ and the quantity consumed during the same period is Rt_1, therefore the remaining quantity available at the end of time t_1 is

$$I_m = q - Rt_1 \qquad \text{...(12.13)}$$

$$= q - \frac{R \,.\, I_m}{K - R}$$

$$\therefore \quad I_m\left(1 + \frac{R}{K - R}\right) = q \quad \text{or} \quad I_m = \frac{K - R}{K} q. \qquad \text{...(12.14)}$$

Now holding cost per *production run i.e., for time period t*

$$= \frac{1}{2} \,.\, I_m \,.\, t \,.\, C_1$$

and set-up cost *per production run* = C_3.

∴ Total variable cost per production run $= \frac{1}{2}\; I_m \,.\, t \,.\, C_1 + C_3.$

∴ Total average cost *per unit time,*

$$C\,(I_m, t) = \frac{1}{2}\; I_m\, C_1 + C_3 / t \qquad \text{...(12.15)}$$

or $$C(q, t) = \frac{1}{2}\left(\frac{K - R}{K} \,.\, q\right) C_1 + \frac{C_3}{t}$$

or $$C(q) = \frac{1}{2}\left(\frac{K - R}{K} \,.\, q\right) C_1 + \frac{C_3}{q/R} \qquad (\because \; q = Rt)$$

$$= \frac{1}{2}\,\frac{(K - R)}{K}\, C_1 \,.\, q + \frac{C_3 R}{q}. \qquad \text{...(12.16)}$$

For minimum value of $C(q)$,

$$\frac{d}{dq}[C(q)] = \frac{1}{2}\,\frac{K - R}{K} \,.\, C_1 - \frac{C_3 R}{q^2} = 0, \text{ which gives}$$

$$q = \sqrt{\frac{2C_3 RK}{(K - R)C_1}} = \sqrt{\frac{2C_3}{C_1} \,.\, \frac{RK}{K - R}} = \sqrt{\frac{K}{K - R}} \,.\, \sqrt{\frac{2C_3 R}{C_1}}$$

and $$\frac{d^2}{dq^2}[C(q)] = \frac{2C_3 R}{q^3}, \text{ which is positive.}$$

Now, when the replenishment rate is finite, the economic order quantity q_0 is called optimum lot size.

∴ Optimum lot size, $$q_0 = \sqrt{\frac{2C_3}{C_1} \,.\, \frac{RK}{K - R}} = \sqrt{\frac{K}{K - R}} \,.\, \sqrt{\frac{2C_3 R}{C_1}} \qquad \text{...(12.17)}$$

Optimum time interval, $$t_0 = \frac{q_0}{R} = \sqrt{\frac{K}{K - R}} \,.\, \sqrt{\frac{2C_3}{C_1 R}}. \qquad \text{...(12.18)}$$

Optimum average cost/unit time, C_0

$$= \frac{1}{2}\,\frac{(K - R)}{K}\, C_1 \,.\, \sqrt{\frac{2C_3}{C_1} \,.\, \frac{RK}{K - R}} + C_3 R \sqrt{\frac{C_1 (K - R)}{2C_3 \,.\, RK}}$$

$$= \sqrt{2C_1 C_3 R \,.\, \frac{K - R}{K}} = \sqrt{\frac{K - R}{K}} \,.\, \sqrt{2C_1 C_3 R}. \qquad \text{...(12.19)}$$

Particular Cases: (*i*) If K = R, then $C_0 = 0$, which means that there will be no holding cost and no setup cost

(*ii*) If K = ∞, *i.e.*, production rate is infinite, this model reduces to model 1 (*a*).

EXAMPLE 12.5-17

A company has a demand of 12,000 units/year for an item and it can produce 2,000 such items per month. The cost of one setup is ₹ 400 and the holding cost/unit/month is ₹ 0.15. Find the optimum lot size and the total cost per year, assuming the cost of 1 unit as ₹ 4. Also find the maximum inventory, manufacturing time and total time.

[*P.T.U. B.Tech. (Mech.) Nov., 2012; J.N.T.U. Hyderabad B.Tech. April, 2011; Mumbai U. MBA, 2010*]

Solution

$$R = 12{,}000 \text{ units/year},$$
$$K = 2{,}000 \times 12 = 24{,}000 \text{ units/year},$$
$$C_3 = ₹\ 400\text{/setup},$$
$$C_1 = ₹\ 0.15 \times 12 = ₹\ 1.80\text{/unit/year}.$$

(*i*)
$$q_0 = \sqrt{\frac{K}{K-R}} \cdot \sqrt{\frac{2C_3R}{C_1}} = \sqrt{\frac{24{,}000}{24{,}000-12{,}000}} \cdot \sqrt{\frac{2 \times 400 \times 12{,}000}{1.80}}$$
$$= 3{,}264 \text{ units/setup}.$$

(*ii*)
$$C_0 = 12{,}000 \times 4 + \sqrt{2C_1C_3R} \cdot \sqrt{\frac{K-R}{K}}$$
$$= 48{,}000 + \sqrt{2 \times 1.80 \times 400 \times 12{,}000 \times \frac{12{,}000}{24{,}000}}$$
$$= 48{,}000 + 2{,}940 = ₹\ 50{,}940\text{/ year}.$$

(*iii*) Max. inventory $\quad I_{m_0} = \dfrac{K-R}{K} \cdot q_0 = \dfrac{24{,}000-12{,}000}{24{,}000} \times 3{,}264 = 1{,}632$ units.

(*iv*) Manufacturing time $t_1 = \dfrac{I_{m0}}{K-R} = \dfrac{1{,}632}{12{,}000} = 0.136$ years.

(*v*) Total time $\quad t_0 = \dfrac{q_0}{R} = \dfrac{3{,}264}{12{,}000} = 0.272$ years.

EXAMPLE 12.5-18

An item is produced at the rate of 50 items per day. The demand occurs at the rate of 25 items per day. If the setup cost is ₹ 100 per setup and holding cost is ₹ 0.01 per unit of item per day, find the economic lot size for one run, assuming that shortages are not permitted. Also find the time of cycle and minimum total cost for one run. [*Bombay B.Sc. (Stat.) 1975; Pune M.B.A., 1983*]

Solution

Here, $\quad K = 50$ items per day, $R = 25$ items per day,

$C_3 = ₹\ 100$ per setup, $C_1 = ₹\ 0.01$ per unit per day.

$$\therefore \quad q_0 = \sqrt{\frac{2C_3R}{C_1}} \cdot \sqrt{\frac{K}{K-R}} = \sqrt{\frac{2 \times 100 \times 25}{0.01} \times \frac{50}{25}} = 1{,}000 \text{ items}.$$

$$t_0 = \frac{q_0}{R} = \sqrt{\frac{2C_3}{C_1R}} \cdot \sqrt{\frac{K}{K-R}} = \sqrt{\frac{2 \times 100}{0.01 \times 25} \times \frac{50}{25}} = 40 \text{ days}.$$

$$\text{Minimum daily cost} = \sqrt{2C_1C_3R} \cdot \sqrt{\frac{K-R}{K}} = ₹\ \sqrt{2 \times 0.01 \times 100 \times 25 \times \frac{25}{50}} = ₹\ 5.$$

∴ Minimum total cost per run = ₹ 5 × 40 = ₹ 200.

12.5-4 Model 2 (a) (Demand Rate Uniform, Replenishment Rate Infinite, Shortages Allowed)

In the earlier models the shortages and hence back ordering was not permitted. Hence the models involved a trade-off between carrying cost and ordering cost. However, in actual practice shortages may take place and hence shortage cost also needs to be considered. Shortages may also be allowed to derive certain advantages. One advantage of allowing shortages is to increase the cycle time, and hence spreading the ordering (or setup) cost over a long period, thereby reducing the total ordering cost over the planning period. Another advantage is decreased net stock in inventory, resulting in reduced inventory carrying cost.

This model is just the extension of model 1 (*a*) allowing shortages. Let

R = number of items required per unit time *i.e.,* demand rate,
C_1 = cost of holding per item per unit time,
C_2 = shortage cost per item per unit time,
C_3 = ordering cost/order,
q = number of items ordered in one order,
q = Rt,
t = interval between orders,
I_m = number of items that form inventory at the beginning of time interval t.

Lead time is assumed to be zero. Figure 12.5 shows the variation of inventory with time.

It is assumed that when shortages occur and customers are not served immediately, they leave their orders with the supplier and these back orders are filled as soon as the stock is received, such as point *D* in the Fig. Out of the total quantity q received, all shortages equal to an amount '*s*' are first taken care and the remaining quantity $I_m = q - s$ forms the inventory for the next cycle.

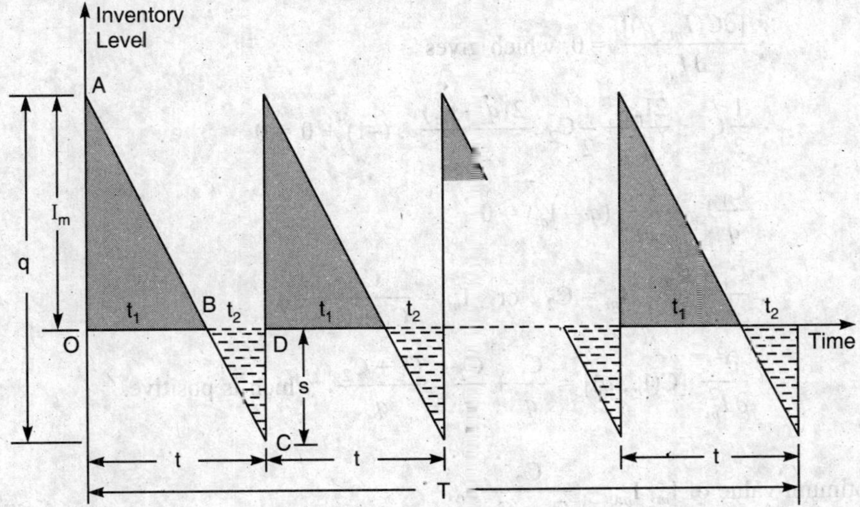

Fig. 12.5. Inventory situation for model 2 (a).

Here, the total time period T is divided into n equal time intervals, each of value t. The time interval t is further divided into two parts t_1 and t_2.

$$i.e., \quad t = t_1 + t_2,$$

where t_1 is the time interval during which items are drawn from inventory and t_2 is the interval during which the items are not filled. Using the relationship of similar triangles,

$$\frac{t_1}{t} = \frac{I_m}{q}. \qquad \therefore \; t_1 = \frac{I_m \cdot t}{q},$$

and $\dfrac{t_2}{t} = \dfrac{s}{q} = \dfrac{q - I_m}{q}$. $\therefore\ t_2 = \dfrac{q - I_m}{q} \cdot t$.

Now total inventory during time t = area of ΔOAB = $\dfrac{1}{2}\, I_m \cdot t_1$.

$\therefore$ Inventory holding cost during time $t = \dfrac{1}{2}\, C_1\, I_m \cdot t_1$.

Similarly, total shortage during time t = area of ΔBCD = $\dfrac{1}{2}(q - I_m)\, t_2$.

$\therefore$ Shortage cost during time $t = \dfrac{1}{2}\, C_2\,(q - I_m)\, t_2$,

and ordering cost during time $t = C_3$.

$\therefore$ Total cost during time $t = \dfrac{1}{2}\, C_1\, I_m\, t_1 + \dfrac{1}{2}\, C_2\,(q - I_m)\, t_2 + C_3$

or total average cost per unit time,

$$C(I_m, t) = \frac{1}{t}\left[\frac{1}{2} C_1 I_m t_1 + \frac{1}{2} C_2 (q - I_m) t_2\right] + \frac{C_3}{t} \qquad \text{...(12.20)}$$

$$= \frac{1}{t}\left[\frac{1}{2} C_1 I_m \cdot \frac{I_m \cdot t}{q} + \frac{1}{2} C_2 (q - I_m) \cdot \frac{q - I_m}{q} \cdot t\right] + \frac{C_3}{t}.$$

$$\therefore \quad C(I_m, q) = \frac{1}{2} C_1 \frac{I_m^2}{q} + \frac{1}{2} C_2 \cdot \frac{(q - I_m)^2}{q} + \frac{C_3 \cdot R}{q}. \qquad \text{...(12.21)}$$

Total average cost per unit time C (I_m, q) being a function of two variables I_m and q, has to be partially differentiated w.r.t. I_m and q separately and then put equal to zero.

i.e., $\dfrac{[\partial C(I_m, q)]}{\partial I_m} = 0$, which gives

$$\frac{1}{2} C_1 \cdot \frac{2 I_m}{q} + \frac{1}{2} C_2 \cdot \frac{2(q - I_m)}{q} \cdot (-1) + 0 = 0$$

or $$\frac{C_1}{q} I_m - \frac{C_2}{q}\,(q - I_m) = 0$$

or $$\frac{C_1 + C_2}{q} \cdot I_m = C_2 \quad \text{or} \quad I_m = \frac{C_2}{C_1 + C_2} \cdot q$$

and $$\frac{\partial^2}{\partial I_m^2}\,[C(I_m, q)] = \frac{C_1}{q} + \frac{C_2}{q} = \frac{C_1 + C_2}{q}, \text{ which is positive.}$$

$\therefore$ Optimum value of I_m, $I_{m0} = \dfrac{C_2}{C_1 + C_2}\, q_0$. ...(12.22)

Similarly, $\dfrac{\partial}{\partial q}\,[C(I_m, q)] = 0$, which gives

$$\frac{1}{2} C_1\, I_m^2 \left(-\frac{1}{q^2}\right) + \frac{1}{2} C_2 \cdot \frac{q \cdot 2 \cdot (q - I_m) - (q - I_m)^2 \cdot 1}{q^2} - \frac{C_3 R}{q^2} = 0$$

or $$C_1 I_m^2 - C_2 \{(q - I_m) \cdot (2q - q + I_m)\} + 2\, C_3\, R = 0$$

or $$C_1 I_m^2 - C_2 \cdot (q^2 - I_m^2) + 2 C_3 R = 0$$

or $$C_2 q^2 = (C_1 + C_2)\, I_m^2 + 2 C_3 R$$

or $$C_2 q^2 = (C_1 + C_2) \cdot \frac{C_2^2}{(C_1 + C_2)^2} \cdot q^2 + 2C_3R = \frac{C_2^2}{C_1 + C_2} \cdot q^2 + 2C_3R$$

or $$\left(C_2 - \frac{C_2^2}{C_1 + C_2} \right) q^2 = 2C_3R$$

or $$q^2 = \frac{C_1 + C_2}{C_1 C_2} \cdot 2C_3R \quad \text{or} \quad q = \sqrt{\frac{C_1 + C_2}{C_1 C_2}} \cdot \sqrt{2C_3R},$$

and it can be proved that $\frac{\partial^2}{\partial q^2} [C(I_m, q)]$ is positive.

∴ Optimal value of q,

$$q_0 = \sqrt{\frac{C_1 + C_2}{C_1 C_2}} \cdot \sqrt{2C_3R} = \sqrt{\frac{C_1 + C_2}{C_2}} \cdot \sqrt{\frac{2C_3R}{C_1}}. \qquad ...(12.23)$$

∴ From equation (12.22),

$$I_{m0} = \sqrt{\frac{C_2}{C_1 (C_1 + C_2)}} \cdot \sqrt{2C_3R} = \sqrt{\frac{C_2}{C_1 + C_2}} \cdot \sqrt{\frac{2C_3R}{C_1}}. \qquad ...(12.24)$$

Substituting values of I_{m0} and q_0 in equation (12.21), we get the minimum average cost per unit time as

$$C_0(I_m, q) = \frac{C_1}{2} \left\{ \frac{C_2}{C_1 + C_2} \right\}^2 \cdot q + \frac{C_2}{2} \cdot \frac{\left\{ q - \frac{c_2}{c_1 + c_2} q \right\}^2}{q} + C_3 \frac{R}{q}$$

$$= \frac{C_1}{2} \cdot \frac{C_2^2}{(C_1 + C_2)^2} \cdot q + \frac{C_2}{2} \cdot \frac{C_1^2}{(C_1 + C_2)^2} \cdot q + C_3 \cdot \frac{R}{q}$$

$$= \frac{C_1 C_2}{2 \cdot (C_1 + C_2)^2} \cdot q \ (C_1 + C_2) + C_3 \cdot \frac{R}{q}$$

$$= \frac{C_1 C_2}{2 \cdot (C_1 + C_2)} \cdot \sqrt{\frac{C_1 + C_2}{C_1 C_2}} \cdot \sqrt{2C_3R} + C_3R \cdot \frac{\sqrt{C_1 C_2}}{\sqrt{C_1 + C_2}} \cdot \frac{1}{\sqrt{2C_3R}}$$

$$= \frac{1}{\sqrt{2}} \sqrt{\frac{C_1 C_2}{C_1 + C_2}} \cdot \sqrt{C_3R} + \frac{1}{\sqrt{2}} \sqrt{\frac{C_1 C_2}{C_1 + C_2}} \cdot \sqrt{C_3R}.$$

∴ $$C_0(I_m, q) = \sqrt{\frac{C_1 C_2}{C_1 + C_2}} \cdot \sqrt{2C_3R}$$

$$= \sqrt{\frac{C_2}{C_1 + C_2}} \sqrt{2C_1C_3R} \qquad ...(12.25)$$

Optimal time interval t between runs is given by

$$t_0 = \frac{q_0}{R} = \sqrt{\frac{C_1 + C_2}{C_1 C_2}} \cdot \sqrt{\frac{2C_3}{R}}$$

$$= \sqrt{\frac{C_1 + C_2}{C_2}} \cdot \sqrt{\frac{2C}{C_1 R}} \qquad ...(12.26)$$

Particular cases (*i*) If shortages arc prohibited *i.e.,* $C_2 = \infty$, equations (12.23), (12.25) and (12.26) reduce to equations (12.3), (12.4) and (12.2) for model 1 (*a*), which must be true since model 1 (*a*) is a special case of model 2(*a*).

(*ii*) If $C_2 \neq \infty$ $\sqrt{\dfrac{C_2}{C_1 + C_2}} \cdot \sqrt{2C_1C_3R}$ from equation (12.25) < $\sqrt{2C_1C_3R}$ from equation (12.4).

$\therefore$ Total expected costs associated with policy of model 2 (*a*) are $\sqrt{\dfrac{C_2}{C_1 + C_2}}$ of the costs associated with policy of model 1 (*a*).

12.5-5 Model 2 (b) (Demand Rate Uniform, Replenishment Rate Infinite, Shortages Allowed, Time Interval Fixed)

Time interval t is fixed which means that inventory is to be replenished after every fixed time t. All other assumptions of model 2 (*a*) hold good.

Here, $t_1 = \dfrac{I_m \cdot t}{q}$, and $t_2 = \dfrac{q - I_m}{q} \cdot t$.

Total inventory during time $t = \dfrac{1}{2} I_m t_1$.

$\therefore$ Total inventory holding cost during time $t = \dfrac{1}{2} C_1 I_m t_1$.

Similarly, total shortage during time $t = \dfrac{1}{2} \cdot (q - I_m) t_2$.

$\therefore$ Total shortage cost during time $t = \dfrac{1}{2} C_2 \cdot (q - I_m) t_2$.

Now ordering cost C_3 and time interval t are both constant, hence the average cost per unit time $\dfrac{C_3}{t}$ is also constant and hence is not to be considered.

$\therefore$ Total average cost per unit time,

$$C(I_m) = \frac{1}{t}\left[\frac{1}{2} C_1 I_m t_1 + \frac{1}{2} C_2 (q - I_m) t_2\right]$$

$$= \frac{1}{t}\left[\frac{1}{2} C_1 I_m \cdot \frac{I_m t}{q} + \frac{1}{2} C_2 (q - I_m) \cdot \frac{q - I_m}{q} \cdot t\right].$$

$$\therefore \quad C(I_m) = \left[\frac{C_1}{2q} \cdot I_m^2 + \frac{C_2}{2q} (q - I_m)^2\right]. \qquad \text{...(12.27)}$$

Now $C(I_m)$ will be optimal if $\dfrac{d}{d\, I_m} [C(I_m)] = 0$ and $\dfrac{d^2}{d\, I_m^2} [C(I_m)]$ is positive.

$\dfrac{d}{d\, I_m} [C(I_m)] = 0$ gives

$$\frac{C_1}{2q} \cdot 2I_m + \frac{C_2}{2q} \cdot 2 (q - I_m)(-1) = 0$$

or $\quad C_1 I_m - C_2(q - I_m) = 0$

or $\quad I_m = \dfrac{C_2}{C_1 + C_2} \cdot q,$

and $\quad \dfrac{d^2}{d\, I_m^2} [C(I_m)] = \dfrac{C_1 + C_2}{q}$, which is positive.

∴ Optimum order quantity is given by

$$\left.\begin{aligned} I_{m0} &= \frac{C_2}{C_1 + C_2} . q \\ &= \frac{C_2}{C_1 + C_2} Rt. \end{aligned}\right] \quad ...(12.28)$$

The minimum average cost per unit time from equation (12.27) is given by

$$C_0(I_m) = \frac{C_1}{2q} . \left(\frac{C_2}{C_1 + C_2}\right)^2 q^2 + \frac{C_2}{2q} . \left(q - \frac{C_2}{C_1 + C_2} . q\right)^2$$

$$= \frac{1}{2} C_1 q . \left(\frac{C_2}{C_1 + C_2}\right)^2 + \frac{1}{2} C_2 q . \left(\frac{C_1}{C_1 + C_2}\right)^2$$

$$= \frac{1}{2} . \frac{C_1 C_2}{(C_1 + C_2)^2} . q (C_1 + C_2)$$

$$\left.\begin{aligned} &= \frac{1}{2} . \frac{C_1 C_2}{C_1 + C_2} . q \\ &= \frac{1}{2} . \frac{C_1 C_2}{C_1 + C_2} . Rt. \end{aligned}\right] \quad ...(12.29)$$

From equation (12.28) we observe that unless C_1 is zero, optimum order level I_m is less than the demand q during the time interval t. Therefore, it is advantageous to plan for shortages.

12.5-6 Model 2 (c) (Demand Rate Uniform, Production Rate Finite, Shortages Allowed)

This model has the same assumptions as in model 2(*a*) except that production rate is finite. Figure 12.6 shows the variation of inventory with time.

Referring to Figure 12.6, we find that inventory is zero in the beginning. It increases at constant rate (K – R) for time t_1 until it reaches a level I_m. There is no replenishment during time t_2, inventory decreases at constant rate R till it becomes zero. Shortage starts piling up at constant rate R during time t_3 until this backlog reaches a level s. Lastly, production starts and backlog is filled at a constant rate K – R during time t_4 till the backlog becomes zero. This completes one cycle; the total time taken during this cycle is

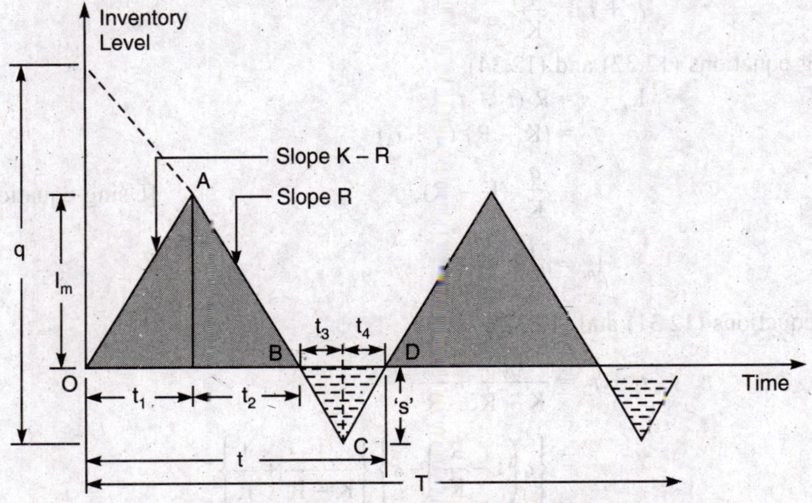

Fig. 12.6. Inventory situation for model 2 (c).

$$t = t_1 + t_2 + t_3 + t_4.$$

This cycle repeats itself over and over again.

Now holding cost during time interval t

$$= C_1 \,.\, \text{area of } \Delta \text{ OAB}$$

$$= C_1 \,.\, \frac{1}{2} \,.\, I_m (t_1 + t_2),$$

and shortage cost during time interval t

$$= C_2 \,.\, \text{area of } \Delta \text{ BCD}$$

$$= C_2 \,.\, \frac{1}{2} \,.\, s \,.\, (t_3 + t_4).$$

Also set-up cost during time interval $t = C_3$.

Total average cost per unit time,

$$C = \frac{\frac{1}{2} \cdot C_1 I_m (t_1 + t_2) + \frac{1}{2} C_2 \cdot s \cdot (t_3 + t_4) + C_3}{t_1 + t_2 + t_3 + t_4}. \qquad ...(12.30)$$

Now C is a function of six variables I_m, s, t_1, t_2, t_3, and t_4 but we can derive relationships which determine the values of I_m, t_1, t_2, t_3 and t_4 in terms of only two variables q and s. An inventory policy is given when we know how much to produce *i.e.*, q and when to start production, which can be found if s is known.

Now $\qquad I_m = (K - R)\, t_1, \qquad ...(12.31)$

also $\qquad I_m = R\, t_2. \qquad ...(12.32)$

$\therefore \qquad (K - R)\, t_1 = R\, t_2. \qquad ...(12.33)$

Further, $\qquad s = R\, t_3, \qquad ...(12.34)$

also $\qquad s = (K - R)\, t_4. \qquad ...(12.35)$

$\therefore \qquad (K - R)\, t_4 = R\, t_3. \qquad ...(12.36)$

Adding equations (12.33) and (12.36) we get

$$(K - R)\,(t_1 + t_4) = R(t_2 + t_3). \qquad ...(12.37)$$

The manufacturing rate multiplied by the manufacturing time gives the manufactured quantity.

$$\therefore \qquad q = K\, t_1 + K\, t_4 = (t_1 + t_4)\, K.$$

$$\therefore \qquad t_1 + t_4 = \frac{q}{K}. \qquad ...(12.38)$$

Adding equations (12.32) and (12.34),

$$I_m + s = R\,(t_2 + t_3)$$

$$= (K - R)\,(t_1 + t_4)$$

$$= \frac{q}{K}\,(K - R). \qquad \text{[Using equation (12.38)]}$$

$$\therefore \qquad I_m = q\left(1 - \frac{R}{K}\right) - s. \qquad ...(12.39)$$

From equations (12.31) and (12.32),

$$t_1 + t_2 = \frac{I_m}{K - R} + \frac{I_m}{R}$$

$$= \left\{q\left(1 - \frac{R}{K}\right) - s\right\}\left\{\frac{1}{K - R} + \frac{1}{R}\right\}. \qquad ...(12.40)$$

[Using equation (12.39)]

Similarly, $$t_3 + t_4 = \frac{s}{K-R} + \frac{s}{R} = s\left(\frac{1}{K-R} + \frac{1}{R}\right). \quad \text{...(12.41)}$$

and $$t_1 + t_2 + t_3 + t_4 = \left(\frac{1}{K-R} + \frac{1}{R}\right)\left\{q \cdot \frac{K-R}{K}\right\} = \frac{q}{R}. \quad \text{...(12.42)}$$

Substituting values of I_m, $t_1 + t_2$, $t_3 + t_4$ and $t_1 + t_2 + t_3 + t_4$ in equation (12.30), we get

$$C(q, s) = \frac{R}{q}\left[\frac{1}{2} \cdot C_1 \cdot \left\{q\left(1 - \frac{R}{K}\right) - s\right\} \cdot \left\{q\left(1 - \frac{R}{K}\right) - s\right\}\right.$$
$$\left.\left\{\frac{1}{K-R} + \frac{1}{R}\right\} + \frac{1}{2} C_2 \cdot s\left(\frac{1}{K-R} + \frac{1}{R}\right) \cdot s\right] + \frac{R}{q} C_3$$
$$= \frac{R}{q}\left[\frac{1}{2} \cdot \left(\frac{1}{K-R} + \frac{1}{R}\right)\right]\left[C \cdot \left\{q\left(1 - \frac{R}{K}\right) - s\right\}^2 + C_2 \cdot s^2\right] + \frac{R}{q} \cdot C_3.$$

$$\therefore \quad C(q, s) = \frac{R}{2q} \cdot \frac{K}{R(K-R)} \cdot \left[C_1 \left\{\left(q \cdot \frac{K-R}{K}\right) - s\right\}^2 + C_2 s^2\right] + \frac{R}{q} C_3$$

or $$C(q, s) = \frac{1}{2q} \cdot \frac{K}{K-R} \cdot \left[C_1 \left\{q \cdot \frac{K-R}{K} - s\right\}^2 + C_2 s^2\right] + \frac{R}{q} C_3. \quad \text{...(12.43)}$$

Now cost C (q,s) will be minimum if

$$\frac{\partial}{\partial q}[C(q, s)] = 0, \quad \frac{\partial^2}{\partial q^2}[C(q,s)] > 0$$

and $$\frac{\partial}{\partial s}[C(q, s)] = 0, \quad \frac{\partial^2}{\partial s^2}[C(q,s)] > 0.$$

Differentiating equation (12.43) partially w.r.t. s,

$$\frac{\partial}{\partial s}[C(q, s)] = \frac{1}{2q} \cdot \frac{K}{K-R} \cdot \left[2C_1\left(q \cdot \frac{K-R}{K} - s\right)(-1) + 2C_2 s\right] = 0$$

or $$2C_1 \cdot \left(q \cdot \frac{K-R}{K}\right) = 2(C_1 + C_2) \cdot s$$

or $$s = q \cdot \frac{K-R}{K} \cdot \frac{C_1}{C_1 + C_2}.$$

$$\frac{\partial^2}{\partial s^2}[C(q, s)] = \frac{1}{2q} \cdot \frac{K}{K-R}(2C_1 + 2C_2), \text{ which is positive.}$$

$$\therefore \quad s_0 = q \cdot \frac{K-R}{K} \cdot \frac{C_1}{C_1 + C_2} \quad \text{(12.44)}$$

Differentiating equation (12.43) partially w.r.t. q,

$$\frac{\partial}{\partial q}[C(q,s)] = -\frac{1}{2q^2} \cdot \frac{K}{K-R} \cdot \left[C_1\left(q \cdot \frac{K-R}{K} - s\right)^2 + C_2 s^2\right]$$
$$+ \frac{1}{2q} \cdot \frac{K}{K-R}\left[2C_1 \cdot \left(q \cdot \frac{K-R}{K} - s\right) \cdot \frac{K-R}{K}\right] - \frac{RC_3}{q^2} = 0,$$

which on simplification gives,

$$q = \sqrt{2C_3 \cdot \frac{C_1 + C_2}{C_1 C_2}} \cdot \sqrt{\frac{KR}{K - R}}.$$

It can be proved that $\frac{\partial^2}{\partial q^2}$ [C(q,s)] is positive, so that

$$q_0 = \sqrt{2C_3 \cdot \frac{(C_1 + C_2)}{C_1 C_2}} \cdot \sqrt{\frac{KR}{K - R}}$$

$$= \sqrt{\frac{C_1 + C_2}{C_2}} \cdot \sqrt{\frac{K}{K - R}} \cdot \sqrt{\frac{2C_3 R}{C_1}}. \qquad \text{...(12.45)}$$

From equation (12.44), $s_0 = \sqrt{2C_3 \cdot \frac{C_1}{(C_1 + C_2)\, C_2}} \cdot \sqrt{\frac{R\,(K - R)}{K}}.$ ...(12.46)

Substituting values of q_0 and s_0 in equation (12.30), and simplifying we get

$$C_0(q,s) = \sqrt{\frac{2C_1 C_2}{C_1 + C_2} \cdot C_3} \sqrt{\frac{R(K - R)}{K}}$$

$$= \sqrt{\frac{C_2}{C_1 + C_2}} \cdot \sqrt{\frac{K - R}{K}} \cdot \sqrt{2C_1 C_3 R}. \qquad \text{...(12.47)}$$

Optimum time interval t_0 is given by

$$t_0 = \frac{q_0}{R} = \sqrt{2C_3 \cdot \frac{(C_1 + C_2)}{C_1 C_2} \cdot \frac{K}{R(K - R)}}$$

$$= \sqrt{\frac{C_1 + C_2}{C_2}} \cdot \sqrt{\frac{K}{K - R}} \cdot \sqrt{\frac{2C_3}{C_1 R}} \qquad \text{...(12.48)}$$

and $I_{m0} = q_0\left(1 - \frac{R}{K}\right) - s_0$ [Equation (12.39)]

$$= \sqrt{\frac{2C_2 \cdot C_3}{C_1\,(C_1 + C_2)}} \cdot \sqrt{\frac{R\,(K - R)}{K}}$$

$$= \sqrt{\frac{C_2}{C_1 + C_2}} \cdot \sqrt{\frac{K - R}{K}} \cdot \sqrt{\frac{2C_3\, R}{C_1}}. \qquad \text{...(12.49)}$$

Particular cases

(*i*) If K = ∞, *i.e.*, production rate is infinity, equations (12.45), (12.49) and (12.47) giving q_0, I_{m0} and C_0 reduce to equations (12.23), (12.24) and (12.25) for model 2(*a*).

(*ii*) If $C_2 = \infty$, *i.e.*, no shortages are allowed, equations (12.45), (12.48) and (12.47) reduce to (12.17), (12.18) and (12.19) for model 1(*c*).

(*iii*) If K = ∞, $C_2 = \infty$, this model becomes model 1(*a*) and equations (12.45), (12.47) and (12.48) reduce to equations (12.3), (12.4) and (12.2) respectively.

EXAMPLE 12.5-19

Find the results of example 12.5-2 if in addition to the data given in that problem the cost of shortage is also given as ₹ 5 per unit per year.

Solution

$$R = 9{,}000 \text{ units/year}, \; C_3 = ₹\,100/\text{procurement},$$
$$C_1 = ₹\,2.40/\text{unit/year}, \; C_2 = ₹\,5/\text{unit/year}.$$

(*i*) From equation (12.23),

$$q_0 = \sqrt{\frac{C_1 + C_2}{C_2}}.\sqrt{\frac{2C_3 R}{C_1}} = \sqrt{\frac{2.40 - 5}{5}}.\sqrt{\frac{2 \times 100 \times 9{,}000}{2.40}}$$

$$= \sqrt{11{,}10{,}000} = 1{,}053 \text{ units/procurement.}$$

(*ii*) From equation (12.25).

$$C_0(I_m, q) = 9{,}000 \times 1 + \sqrt{\frac{C_2}{C_1 + C_2}}\sqrt{2C_1C_3R} = 9{,}000$$

$$+ \sqrt{\frac{5}{2.4 + 5}}.\sqrt{2 \times 2.4 \times 100 \times 9{,}000}$$

$$= ₹\,(9{,}000 + 1{,}710) = ₹\,10{,}710/\text{year.}$$

(*iii*) Number of orders/year, $n_0 = \dfrac{9{,}000}{1{,}053} = 8.55.$

(*iv*) Time between orders,

$$t_0 = \frac{1}{n_0} = \frac{1}{8.55} = 0.117 \text{ year} = 1.4 \text{ months.}$$

EXAMPLE 12.5-20

The data for this example are same as that of example 12.5-14 except that the shortage cost of one unit is ₹ 20 per year. Find the various results.

Solution

$$R = 12{,}000 \text{ units/year},$$
$$K = 2{,}000 \times 12 = 24{,}000 \text{ units/year},$$
$$C_3 = ₹\,400/\text{setup},$$
$$C_1 = ₹\,0.15 \times 12 = ₹\,1.80 \text{ per unit/year},$$
$$C_2 = ₹\,20 \text{ per year.}$$

(*i*) Using equation (12.45),

$$q_0 = \sqrt{\frac{2C_3R}{C_1}}.\sqrt{\frac{C_1 + C_2}{C_2}}.\sqrt{\frac{K}{K - R}}$$

$$= \sqrt{\frac{2 \times 400 \times 12{,}000}{1.80}}.\sqrt{\frac{1.80 + 20}{20}}.\sqrt{\frac{24{,}000}{24{,}000 - 12{,}000}}$$

$$= \sqrt{\frac{2 \times 400 \times 12{,}000}{1.80}}.\sqrt{\frac{10.9}{10}}.\sqrt{2} = 3{,}410 \text{ units.}$$

(*ii*) From equation (12.47),

$$C_0(q, s) = 12{,}000 \times 4 + \sqrt{2C_1\,C_3\,R}.\sqrt{\frac{C_2}{C_1 + C_2}}.\sqrt{\frac{K - R}{K}}$$

$$= 48{,}000 + \sqrt{2 \times 1.80 \times 400 \times 12{,}000}.\sqrt{\frac{20}{20 + 1.80}} \times \sqrt{\frac{24{,}000 - 12{,}000}{24{,}000}}$$

$$= 48{,}000 + \sqrt{2 \times 1.80 \times 400 \times 12{,}000}.\sqrt{\frac{10}{10.9}}.\frac{1}{\sqrt{2}} = ₹\,50,185/\text{ year.}$$

(*iii*) Using equation (12.49),

$$I_{m_0} = \sqrt{\frac{2C_3R}{C_1}}.\sqrt{\frac{C_2}{C_1+C_2}}.\sqrt{\frac{K-R}{K}}$$

$$= \sqrt{\frac{2\times 400\times 12,000}{1.80}}\times\sqrt{\frac{20}{1.80+20}}.\sqrt{\frac{24,000-12,000}{24,000}}$$

$$= \sqrt{\frac{2\times 400\times 12,000}{1.80}\times\frac{10}{10.9}\times\frac{1}{2}} = 1.564 \text{ units/production run.}$$

(*iv*) Manufacturing time interval, $t_1 + t_4$

$$= \frac{q_0}{K} \quad \text{[equation (12.38)]}$$

$$= \frac{3,410}{24,000} = 0.1421 \text{ year} = 1.7 \text{ months.}$$

(*v*) Total time interval, t_0 $= \dfrac{q_0}{R}$ [equation (12.48)]

$$= \frac{3,410}{12,000} = 0.2842 \text{ year} = 3.4 \text{ months.}$$

EXAMPLE 12.5-21

A contractor supplies diesel engines to a truck manufacturer at the rate of 20 per day. He has to pay a penalty of ₹ 10 per engine per day for missing the scheduled delivery date. Holding cost of a complete engine is ₹ 12 per month. The manufacturing of engines starts with the beginning of the month and is completed at the end of the month. What should be the inventory level at the beginning of each month ?

Solution

R = 20 engines/day, C_2 = ₹ 10 per engine per day,
C_1 = ₹ 12 per month = 12/30 = ₹ 0.40/day, t = 1 month = 30 days.

Using equation (12.28), $I_{m_0} = \dfrac{C_2}{C_1+C_2}.q = \dfrac{C_2}{C_1+C_2}.Rt$

$$= \frac{10}{0.40+10}\times 20\times 30 = 577 \text{ engines/month.}$$

Example 12.5-22

A dealer supplies you the following information with regard to a product dealt-in by him:

Annual demand	:	*10,000 units*
Ordering cost	:	*₹ 10 per order*
Inventory carrying cost	:	*20% of value of inventory per year*
Price	:	*₹ 20 per unit.*

The dealer is considering the possibility of allowing some back-order (stock-out) to occur. He has estimated that the annual cost of back-ordering will be 25% of the value of inventory.

(*i*) *What should be the optimum number of units of the product he should buy in one lot?*

(*ii*) *What quantity of the product should be allowed to be back-ordered, if any ?*

(*iii*) *What would be the maximum quantity of inventory at any time of the year ?*

(*iv*) *Would you recommend to allow back-ordering ? If so, what would be the annual cost saving by adopting the policy of back-ordering ?* [P.U.M.F.C., 2002]

Solution

Here R = 10,000 units/year,
C_3 = ₹ 10/order,

$$C_1 = CI = ₹\ 20 \times \frac{20}{100} = ₹\ 4/\text{unit/year},$$

$$C_2 = ₹\ 20 \times \frac{25}{100} = ₹\ 5/\text{unit/year}.$$

(*i*) q_0, allowing back-order $= \sqrt{\frac{C_1 + C_2}{C_2}} \cdot \sqrt{\frac{2RC_3}{C_1}}$

$$= \sqrt{\frac{4+5}{5}} \cdot \sqrt{\frac{2 \times 10,000 \times 10}{4}} = 300 \text{ units/order}.$$

(*ii*) Maximum quantity to be back-ordered, $s_0 = q_0 - I_{m_0}$,

where $I_{m_0} = \sqrt{\frac{C_2}{C_1 + C_2}} \cdot \sqrt{\frac{2RC_3}{C_1}}$

$$= \sqrt{\frac{5}{4+5}} \cdot \sqrt{\frac{2 \times 10,000 \times 10}{4}} = 167 \text{ units}.$$

$\therefore \quad s_0 = 300 - 167 = 133$ units.

(*iii*) Maximum inventory, $I_{m_0} = 167$ units.

(*iv*) Annual cost without back-order $= \sqrt{2RC_3C_1} = \sqrt{2 \times 10,000 \times 10 \times 4} = ₹\ 894.$

Annual cost allowing back-order $= \sqrt{\frac{C_2}{C_1 + C_2}} \cdot \sqrt{2RC_3C_1}$

$$= \sqrt{\frac{5}{4+5}} \cdot \sqrt{2 \times 10,000 \times 10 \times 4} = ₹\ 667.$$

$\therefore$ Saving in annual cost if back-order is allowed = ₹ 227.

EXERCISES 12.2

1. Formulate an inventory model in which demand is not uniform and production rate is infinite. *[P.U.MFC-1 April, 1999]*
2. Derive economic lot size formula for made-in items when lead time is zero and shortages are not allowed. *[J.N.T.U. Hyderabad MCA Feb., 2012; R.U. MSc. (Math.) 2011; P.U.M.Com. Sept., 2004; B.Com. Sept., 2004; P.T.U. B.Tech., 2001, 2000]*
3. (*a*) What do you understand by a fixed time period and fixed quantity models ? When would you use each of them ?
   (*b*) Derive the equation for EOQ under certainty.
   (*c*) How will this equation change under condition of uncertainty ? *[P.U. MBA, 1997]*
4. Derive EOQ model for deterministic demand when replenishment rate is infinite and shortages are permitted. *[J.N.T.U. Hyderabad B.Tech. May, 2011; P.T.U. B.Tech., 2001]*
5. Derive economic lot size formula for an inventory model with finite production rate and shortages permitted. *[K.U.M.Sc. (Math.) 2001]*
6. Discuss the concept of economic lot size. How is it determined ? What happens when total carrying cost per year is not equal to total ordering cost per year ? *[P.U.B.Com. Sept., 2001]*

Section 12.5-3

7. A contractor has to supply 10,000 bearings per day to an automobile manufacturer. He finds that, when he starts a production run, he can produce 25,000 bearings per day. The cost of holding a bearing in stock for one year is 2 paise, and the setup cost of a production run is ₹ 18. What is the optimum lot size and how frequently should production run be made?
   [ICWA Dec., 1993; Meerut M.Sc. (Math.) 1969; Delhi M.Com., 1975]
   (*Ans.* 1,05,000; 10.5 days.)

8. A product is produced at the rate of 50 items per day. The demand occurs at the rate of 30 items per day. Given that setup cost per order = ₹ 100 and holding cost per unit per unit time = ₹ 0.05, find the economic lot size and the associated total cost per cycle assuming that no shortage is allowed.

(*Ans.* 225, ₹ 11.)

9. A company manufactures refrigeration units in batches. The estimated demand is 10,000 units/year. It costs ₹ 100 to setup the manufacturing process and the carrying cost is ₹ 0.50 per unit per year. Once the production process has been setup, 80 units can be manufactured daily. The demand during the production day has been 60 units per day. How many units should the company produce in each batch ? How long will the production cycle last ? *[IGNOU MBA Dec., 1997]*

(*Ans.* 4,000 units; 50 days.)

10. The manager of a company manufacturing car parts has entered into a contract of supplying 1,000 numbers. per day of a particular part to a car manufacturer. He finds that his plant has a capacity of producing 2,000 numbers. per day of the part. The cost of the part is ₹ 50, cost of holding stock is 12% per annum and setup cost per production run is ₹ 100. What should be run size for each production run and total optimum cost/month ? How frequently should production runs be made ? Shortage is not permissible. *[Mumbai U.MBA, 2010]*

11. A product is sold at the rate of 50 pieces per day and is manufactured at the rate of 250 pieces per day. The setup cost of the machines is ₹ 1,000 and the storage cost is found to be ₹ 0.0015 per piece per day. With labour charges of ₹ 3.20 per piece, material cost at ₹ 2.10 per piece and overhead cost of ₹ 4.10 per piece, find the minimum cost batch size if the interest charges are 8 per cent (assume 300 working days in a year). Also compute the optimal number of orders in a year. *[J.U. MBA, 2004]*

[Hint. $R = 50 \times 300 = 15{,}000$ pieces / year, $K = 250 \times 300 = 75{,}000$ pieces / year,

$C_3 =$ ₹ 1,000/setup, $C_1 =$ ₹ $[0.0015 \times 300 + 0.08\ (3.20 + 2.10 + 4.10)]$

$=$ ₹ 12.02/year.

$$\therefore\ q_0 = \sqrt{\frac{K}{K-R}}\sqrt{\frac{2C_3R}{C_1}} = \sqrt{\frac{75{,}000}{75{,}000-15{,}000}}\sqrt{\frac{2\times 1{,}000\times 15{,}000}{12.02}}$$

$= 5{,}586$ pieces.

$$n_0 = \frac{R}{q_0} = \frac{15{,}000}{5{,}586} \simeq 3 \text{ cycles/year.]}$$

12. A company can produce a part it uses in an assembly operation at the rate of 50 an hour. The company operates 8 hours a day, 300 days a year. Daily usage of the part is 300 parts. The run size is 6,000 parts. The annual holding cost is ₹ 20 per unit and the setup cost is ₹ 1,000 per setup.
(*a*) How many runs per year will be there ?
(*b*) How many parts/day are being added to inventory, while production is occurring ?
(*c*) Assuming that production begins when there are no parts on hand, what is the maximum number of parts in inventory ?
(*d*) Every so often, preventive maintenance, which requires 6 working days, must be performed on it. Does this interrupt production cycles, or is there enough time between cycles to perform the maintenance ? Explain. *[Dayalbagh Edu. Inst. Agra B.B.M. May, 2008]*

[Hint. (*a*) $n = \dfrac{300 \times 300}{6{,}000} = 15.$

(*b*) Parts added/day to inventory $= 50 \times 8 - 300 = 100$ /day.

(*c*) $I_{mo} = \dfrac{K-R}{K} . q_0 = \dfrac{100}{400} \times 6{,}000 = 1{,}500$ parts.

(*d*) For demand of 300 parts / day, inventory of 1,500 parts will be able to meet the demand for 5 days. As preventive maintenance requires 6 days, production cycles will be interrupted.]

13. Find the most economic batch quantity of a product on a machine if the production rate of the item on the machine is 200 pieces/day and the demand is uniform at the rate of 100 pieces/day. The set-up cost is ₹ 200 per batch and the cost of holding one item in inventory is ₹ 0.81 per day. How will the batch quantity vary if the machine production rate was infinite ? *[J.N.T.U. Hyderabad B.Tech. April, 2011; Nov., 2010]*

Section 12.5-4

14. A contractor undertakes to supply diesel engines to a truck manufacturer at the rate of 25 per day. He finds that the cost of holding a completed engine in stock is ₹ 16 per month, and there is a clause in the contract penalising him ₹ 10 per engine per day late for missing the scheduled delivery date. Production of engines is in batches, and each time a new batch is started there are setup costs of ₹ 10,000. How frequently should batches be started, and what should be the initial inventory level at the time each batch is completed ? [*Baroda B.Sc. (Math.) 1978*]

(*Ans.* 40 days, 943 engines.)

15. A manufacturer receives an order for 6,890 items to be delivered over a period of a year as follows:
at the end of the 1st week: 5 items,
at the end of 2nd week: 10 items,
at the end of 3rd week: 15 items, etc.
The cost of carrying inventory is ₹ 2.60 per item per year and the cost of a setup is ₹ 450 per production run.
Compute costs for the following policies:
(1) Make all 6,890 at start of the year.
(2) Make 3,445 now and 3,445 in 6 months.
(3) Make 1/12th of the order each month.
(4) Make 1/52 of the order each week. (*Ans.* ₹ 12,000, ₹ 8,000, ₹ 9 000, ₹ 27,000 (approx.))

16. A manufacturer received an annual contract for supplying 4,000 gears to be delivered over a period of one year. Deliveries are to be affected as under:
First quarter –3,500, second quarter –4,500, third quarter –2,000, fourth quarter –4,000. The manufacturer wants to plan out his production on his vital machine which costs ₹ 590 for setting up. The cost of gear is ₹ 60 and inventory carrying cost comes to 10% per year. Calculate the annual cost for producing this quantity in a number of equal lots. What will be the minimum cost over the year ? Explain and derive the formula used. [*Baroda Univ., 1975*]

17. (*a*) Discuss in detail the inventory costs which are to be considered for determination of economic order quantity.
(*b*) The demand for a product is 25 units per month, and the items are withdrawn uniformly. The setup cost each time a production run is made is ₹ 15. The inventory holding cost is ₹ 0.30 per item per month. Assuming that shortages are not allowed, determine how often to make a production run and what size should it be. Prove the formula used. If shortages cost ₹ 1.50 per item/month, determine how often to make production run and what size should it be.

[*P.U.B.Com. Sept., 2000*]

(*Ans.* 50 units, 2 months; 54 units, 2.16 months.)

18. The annual demand for an automobile component unit is 36,000 units. The carrying cost is ₹ 0.5 per unit per year. The ordering cost is ₹ 25 per order and the shortage cost is ₹ 15 per unit per year. Find the optimal values of :
(*i*) Economic order quantity (*ii*) Maximum inventory (*iii*) Cycle time (*iv*) No. of orders.
[*J.N.T.U. Hyderabad B.Tech. (Mech.) May, 2012*]

Section 12.5-5–12.5-6

19. A product is produced at the rate of 50 items per day. The demand occurs at the rate of 30 items per day. Given that
set-up cost per order = ₹ 100,
holding cost per item per unit time = ₹ 0.05,
and shortages being allowed, what is the shortage cost per unit under optimal conditions if the lot size is 600 items. (*Ans.* ₹ 1/220.)

20. Consider the following data

Unit cost	:	₹ 100,
order cost	:	₹ 160,
inventory carrying cost	:	₹ 20,
back-order cost	:	₹ 10,
annual demand	:	1,000 units.

Compute the following:

(*i*) Minimum cost order quantity

(*ii*) Time between orders

(*iii*) Maximum number of back-orders

(*iv*) Maximum inventory level

(*v*) Overall annual cost. [*C.A. (Final) May, 1990*]

(*Ans.* (*i*) 219 units (*ii*) 2.63 months (*iii*) 146 units (*iv*) 73 units (*v*) ₹ 1,01,460.59.)

21. The demand for an item is 16,000 units per year. Its production rate is 900 units per month. The carrying cost is ₹ 400 per unit per year and the set-up cost is ₹ 3,000 per set-up. The penalty cost is ₹ 1,000 per unit per year. Find out :

    (*i*) Economic order quantity

    (*ii*) Number of orders per year

    (*iii*) Time between two consecutive orders. [*J.N.T.U. Hyderabad B.Tech. (Mech.) May, 2012*]

22. The demand for an item in a company is 18,000 units per year and the company can produce the item at a rate of 3,000 per month. The cost of one set-up is ₹ 500 and the holding cost of one unit per month is 15 paise. The shortage cost of one unit is ₹ 20 per year. Determine the optimum manufacturing quantity and the number of shortages. Also determine the manufacturing time and the time between set-ups. [*J.N.T.U. Hyderabad B.Tech. May, 2011*]

12.6 INVENTORY MODELS WITH PROBABILISTIC DEMAND

The models discussed in the previous sections are only artificial since in practical situations, demand is hardly known precisely. In most situations demand is probabilistic since only *probability distribution* of future demand, rather than the exact value of demand itself, is known. The probability distribution of future demand is usually determined from the data collected from past experience. In such situations we choose policies that minimize the *expected* costs rather than the actual costs. Expected costs are obtained by multiplying the actual costs for a particular situation with the probability of occurrence of that situation and then either summing or integrating according as the probability distribution is discrete or continuous.

12.6-1 Model 3(a) (Instantaneous Demand, Set-up Cost Zero, Stock Levels Discrete and Lead Time Zero)

This model deals with the inventory situation of items that require one time purchase only. Perishable items such as cut flowers, cosmetics, seasonal items such as calendars and diaries and spare parts fall under this category.

In this model the item is ordered at the beginning of the period to meet the demand during that period, the demand being instantaneous as well as discrete in nature. At the end of the period, there are two types of costs involved : over-stocking cost and under-stocking cost. They represent opportunity losses incurred when the number of units stocked is not exactly equal to the number of units actually demanded.

Let R = discrete demand rate with probability p_R,

I_m = discrete stock level for time interval t,

t = constant interval between orders,

C_1 = over-stocking cost (over-ordering cost). This is opportunity loss associated with each unit left unsold

$= C + C_h - V$,

C_2 = under-stocking cost (under-ordering cost). This is opportunity loss due to not meeting the demand.

$= S - C - C_h/2 + C_s$,

where C is the unit cost price, C_h the unit carrying cost, C_s the unit shortage cost, S the unit selling price and V is the salvage value. If value of any parameter is not given, it is taken as zero.

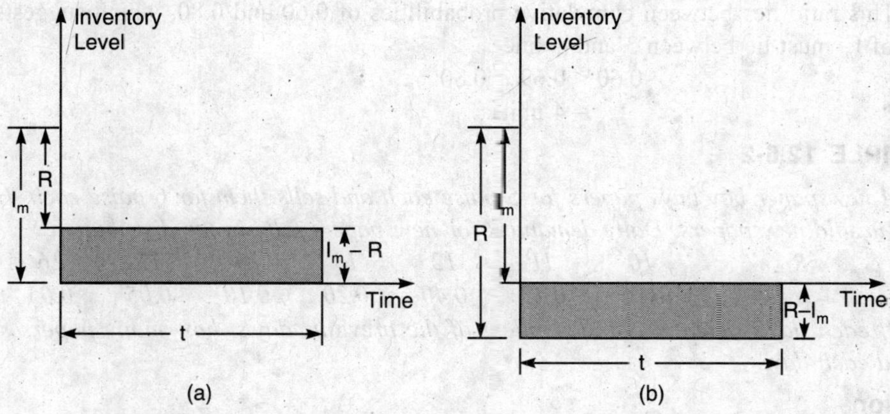

Fig. 12.7. Inventory situation for model 3(a), (a) $R \leq I_m$ (b) $R > I_m$.

Production is assumed to be instantaneous and lead time negligibly small. The problem is to determine the optimal inventory level I_m, where $R \leq I_m$ or $R > I_m$ at the beginning of each time interval. The variation of inventory with time for these two cases is shown in Fig. 12.7(*a*) and (*b*).

When $R \leq I_m$, as shown in figure 12.7(*a*), there are no shortages; when $R > I_m$, as shown in figure 12.7(*b*), shortages occur.

Then the optimal order quantity I_{m_0} is determined when value of cumulative probability distribution exceeds the ratio $\dfrac{C_2}{C_1 + C_2}$ by computing

$$p_{R \leq I_m - 1} < \frac{C_2}{C_1 + C_2} < p_{R \leq I_m}.$$

Example 12.6-1

A trader stocks a particular seasonal product at the beginning of the season and cannot reorder. The item costs him ₹ 25 and he sells it at ₹ 50 each. For any item that cannot be met on demand, the trader has estimated a goodwill cost of ₹ 15. Any item unsold will have a salvage value of ₹ 10. Holding cost during the period is estimated to be 10% of the price. The probability of demand is as follows :

Units stocked	:	2	3	4	5	6
Probability of demand	:	0.35	0.25	0.20	0.15	0.05

Determine the optimal number of items to be stocked.

Solution

Here, C = ₹ 25, S = ₹ 50, C_h = ₹ (0.10 × 25) = ₹ 2.50, C_s = ₹ 15 and V = ₹ 10.

$\therefore$ $C_1 = C + C_h - V$ = ₹ (25 + 2.50 – 10) = ₹ 17.50,

$C_2 = S - C - C_h/2 + C_s$ = ₹ $\left(50 - 25 - \dfrac{2.50}{2} + 15\right)$ = ₹ 38.75.

Cumulative probability of demand is now calculated.

Units stocked	:	2	3	4	5	6
Probability of demand, p_R	:	0.35	0.25	0.20	0.15	0.05
Cumulative probability of demand $\sum_{R=0}^{I_m} p_R$	:	0.35	0.60	0.80	0.95	1.00

Now $\dfrac{C_2}{C_1 + C_2} = \dfrac{38.75}{17.50 + 38.75} = 0.69.$

This ratio lies between cumulative probabilities of 0.60 and 0.80, which suggests that the value of I_m must lie between 3 and 4 since

$$0.60 < 0.69 < 0.80.$$

$$\therefore \quad I_{m_0} = 4 \text{ units.}$$

EXAMPLE 12.6-2

A newspaper boy buys papers for 5 paise each and sells them for 6 paise each. He cannot return unsold newspapers. Daily demand R for newspapers follows the distribution :

R	:	*10*	*11*	*12*	*13*	*14*	*15*	*16*
p_R	:	*0.05*	*0.15*	*0.40*	*0.20*	*0.10*	*0.05*	*0.05*

If each day's demand is independent of the previous day's, how many papers should be ordered each day?

Solution

Let I_m be the number of newspapers ordered per day and R be the demand for it *i.e.,* the number that are actually sold per day.

Now $\quad C_1 = ₹\, 0.05,$

$\quad C_2 = S - C = ₹\, (0.06 - 0.05) = ₹\, 0.01.$

The probabilities for demand are

R	:	10	11	12	13	14	15	16
p_R	:	0.05	0.15	0.40	0.20	0.10	0.05	0.05
$\sum_{R=0}^{I_m} p_R$	:	0.05	0.20	0.60	0.80	0.90	0.95	1.00

The desired optimum value for I_m is determined by the double inequality,

$$p_{R \le I_m - 1} < \frac{C_2}{C_1 + C_2} < p_{R \le I_m}.$$

$$\text{Now} \quad \frac{C_2}{C_1 + C_2} = \frac{0.01}{0.01 + 0.05} = \frac{1}{6} = 0.167.$$

This suggests that I_m must lie between 10 and 11 because

$$0.05 < 0.167 < 0.20.$$

$$\therefore \quad I_{m_0} = 11.$$

EXAMPLE 12.6-3

Some of the spare parts of a ship cost ₹ 50,000 each. These spare parts can only be ordered together with the ship. If not ordered at the time the ship is constructed, these parts cannot bt available on need. Suppose that a loss of ₹ 4,500,000 is suffered for each spare that is needed when none is available in the stock. Further suppose that the probabilities that the spares will be needed as replacement during the life term of the class of ship discussed are

Spares required	*Probability*
0	*0.900*
1	*0.040*
2	*0.025*
3	*0.020*
4	*0.010*
5	*0.005*
6 or more	*0.000*
Total	*1.000*

How many spare parts should be procured ? [*P.T.U. B.Tech. (Mech.) Nov., 2012*]

Solution

$$C_1 = ₹\ 50{,}000,$$
$$C_2 = C_s = ₹\ 4{,}500{,}000.$$
$$\frac{C_2}{C_1 + C_2} = \frac{4{,}500{,}000}{4{,}550{,}000} = 0.989.$$

Cumulative probability distribution is

Spares required :	0	1	2	3	4	5	6 or more
$\sum_{R=0}^{I_m} p_R$:	0.900	0.940	0.965	0.985	0.995	1.000	1.000

The desired optimum value for I_m is determined by the double inequality

$$p_{R \le I_m - 1} < \frac{C_2}{C_1 + C_2} < p_{R \le I_m}$$

This suggests that I_m must lie between 3 and 4 because 0.985 < 0.989 < 0.995.

$\therefore \quad I_{m_0} = 4.$

EXAMPLE 12.6-4

(a) A firm is to order a new lathe. Its power unit is an expensive part and can be ordered only with the lathe. Each of these units is uniquely built for a particular lathe and cannot be used on any other. The firm wants to know how many spare units should be incorporated in the order for each lathe. Cost of the unit when ordered with the lathe is ₹ 700. If a spare unit is needed (because of its failure during service) and is not available, the whole lathe becomes useless. The cost of the unit made to order and the down-time cost of the lathe is ₹ 9,300. The analysis of 100 similar units on similar lathes yields the following information given in table 12.1.

(b) If in the above problem the shortage cost of the part is unknown and the firm wants to maintain stock level of 4 parts, find the shortage cost

TABLE 12.1

No. of spare units required	*No. of lathes requiring indicated number of spare units*	*Estimated probability of occurrence of indicated number of failures*
0	*87*	*0.87*
1	*5*	*0.05*
2	*3*	*0.03*
3	*2*	*0.02*
4	*1*	*0.01*
5	*1*	*0.01*
6	*1*	*0.01*
7 or more	*0*	*0.00*

Solution

(*a*) The range of optimum value of stock level. I_m is given by

$$p_{R \le I_m - 1} < \frac{C_2}{C_1 + C_2} < p_{R \le I_m}.$$

Table 12.2 gives the data of table 12.1 after reformulation.

TABLE 12.2

I_m	R	p_R	$\sum_{R=0}^{I_{m0}} p_R$
0	0	0.87	0.87
1	1	0.05	0.92
2	2	0.03	0.95
3	3	0.02	0.97
4	4	0.01	0.98
5	5	0.01	0.99
6	6	0.01	1.00
7 or more		0.00	1.00
		1.00	

Here $C_1 = ₹\ 700$, $C_2 = C_s = ₹\ 9{,}300$.

$\therefore \quad \dfrac{C_2}{C_1 + C_2} = \dfrac{9{,}300}{700 + 9{,}300} = 0.93.$ ∴ Optimum value of $I_m = 2$, since $0.92 < 0.93 < 0.95$.

(*b*) Here $I_m = 4$.

$$\therefore \quad p_{R \le 3} < \frac{C_2}{700 + C_2} < p_{R \le 4}$$

$$\text{or} \quad 0.97 < \frac{C_2}{700 + C_2} < 0.98.$$

∴ The least value of C_2 is given by

$$\frac{C_2}{700 + C_2} = 0.97 \quad \text{or} \quad C_2 = \frac{700 \times 0.97}{0.03} = ₹\ 22{,}633.33,$$

and the greatest value of C_2 is given by

$$\frac{C_2}{700 + C_2} = 0.98 \quad \text{or} \quad C_2 = \frac{700 \times 0.98}{0.02} = ₹\ 34{,}300.$$

∴ The value of shortage cost ranges from ₹ 22,633.33 to ₹ 34,300.

EXAMPLE 12.6-5

The cost of holding an item in stock is ₹ 2 per unit and the shortage cost is ₹ 8. If ₹ 2 is the purchasing cost per unit, determine the optimal order level of inventory, given the following probability distribution:

R	:	*0*	*1*	*2*	*3*	*4*	*5*
p(R)	:	*0.05*	*0.25*	*0.20*	*0.15*	*0.20*	*0.15*

Solution

Here, $\quad C_h = ₹\ 2,\ C_s = ₹\ 8,\ C = ₹\ 2.$

$$\therefore \quad C_1 = C + C_h - V = ₹\ (2 + 2 - 0) = ₹\ 4,$$

$$C_2 = S - C - \frac{C_h}{2} + C_s = 0 - 2 - \frac{2}{2} + 8 = ₹\ 5.$$

$$\therefore \quad \frac{C_2}{C_1 + C_2} = \frac{5}{4+5} = \frac{5}{9} = 0.56.$$

Cumulative probability distribution is

R	:	0	1	2	3	4	5
$\sum_{R=0}^{I_m} p(R)$	:	0.05	0.30	0.50	0.65	0.85	1.00

The desired optimum value for I_m is determined by the double inequality

$$p_{R \le I_m - 1} < \frac{C_2}{C_1 + C_2} < p_{R \le I_m}.$$

This suggests that I_m must lie between 2 and 3 because $0.50 < 0.56 < 0.65$.

$\therefore \qquad I_{m_0} = 3.$

12.6-2 Model 3 (b) (Instantaneous Demand, No Set-up Cost, Stock Levels Continuous, Lead Time zero)

In this model, all conditions are same as in model 3(*a*) except that the stock levels are continuous (rather than discrete). Therefore, probability $f(R)\, dR$ will be used instead of p_R, where $f(R)$ is the probability density function of the demand rate R.

Then the optimal order quantity I_{m_0} is determined when the value of cumulative probability distribution is equal to $\frac{C_2}{C_1 + C_2}$ by computing

$$\int_{R=0}^{I_m} f(R)\,.\,dR = \frac{C_2}{C_1 + C_2}.$$

Example 12.6-6

A baking company sells one of its types of cakes by weight. It makes a profit of 95 paise a pound on every pound of cake sold on the day it is baked. It disposes of all cakes not sold on the day they are baked at a loss of 15 paise a pound. If demand is known to be rectangular between 3,000 and 4,000 pounds, determine the optimum amount to be baked.

[*Delhi M. Sc. (Math.) 1973*]

Solution

Penalty cost/unit of oversupply, $C_1 = ₹\ 0.15$,

Penalty cost/unit of undersupply, $C_2 = ₹\ 0.95$,

$R_1 = 3{,}000$ pounds,

$R_2 = 4{,}000$ pounds.

$$f(R) = \frac{1}{R_2 - R_1} = \frac{1}{1{,}000}.$$

Optimum value of I_m is given by

$$\int_0^{I_m} f(R)\,.\,dR = \frac{C_2}{C_1 + C_2}.$$

$$\therefore \quad \int_{3{,}000}^{I_m} \frac{1}{1{,}000}\,.\,dR = \frac{0.95}{0.15 + 0.95} = \frac{0.95}{1.1}.$$

$$\therefore \quad \frac{1}{1{,}000}\,[I_m - 3{,}000] = \frac{0.95}{1.1}$$

or $$I_m = \frac{950}{1.1} + 3{,}000 = 3{,}864 \text{ units}.$$

EXAMPLE 12.6-7

A baking company sells one of its types of cake by weight. It makes a profit of 95 paise a pound on every pound of cake sold on the day it is baked. It disposes of all cakes not sold on the day they are baked at a loss of 15 paise a pound. If demand is known to have probability density function

$$f(R) = 0.03 - 0.0003\ R,$$

find the optimum amount of cake the company should bake daily.

Solution

Using the relation

$$\int_0^{I_m} f(R)\,.\,dR = \frac{C_2}{C_1 + C_2},\ \text{we get}$$

$$\int_0^{I_m} (0.03 - 0.0003R)\,dR = \frac{0.95}{0.15 + 0.95} = \frac{0.95}{1.1}.$$

$$\therefore\quad 0.03\ I_m - \frac{0.0003\ I_m^2}{2} = \frac{0.95}{1.1}$$

or $\quad 0.03\ I_m - 0.00015\ I_m^{\ 2} = 0.8636$

or $\quad 3{,}000\ I_m - 15\ I_m^{\ 2} = 86{,}360$

or $\quad 200\ I_m - I_m^{\ 2} = 5{,}757$

or $\quad I_m^2 - 200\ I_m + 5{,}757 = 0$

or $\quad I_m = \dfrac{200 \pm \sqrt{(200)^2 - 4 \times 5{,}757}}{2} = 165.15$ or 34.85 pounds.

$I_m = 165.15$ pounds is not feasible since the given probability distribution of R is not applicable above 100 pounds.

$\therefore$ Optimum value of $I_m = 34.85$ pounds/day.

EXAMPLE 12.6-8

A fish stall sells a variety of fish at the rate of ₹ 5 per kg on the day of the catch. If the stall fails to sell the catch on the same day, it pays for storage at the rate of ₹ 0.30 per kg and the price fetched is ₹ 4.50 per kg on the next day. Past records show that there is an unlimited demand for fish one day old. The problem is to ascertain how much fish should be procured every day so that the total expected cost is minimum. It has been found from the past records that the daily demand follows an exponential distribution with

$$f(x) = 0.02\ e^{-0.02x},\ 0 \le x \le \infty.$$

[*Bombay B.Sc.(Stat.) 1984; B.Sc. (Appl. Comp.) 1984*]

Solution

The cost of over-stocking 1 kg of fish, C_1 = ₹ [0.30 + (5 – 4.50)] = ₹ 0.80.

$$\therefore\quad \int_0^{I_m} f(x)\,.\,dx = \frac{C_2}{C_1 + C_2}\ \text{yields}$$

$$\int_0^{I_m} 0.02\,e^{-0.02x}\,.\,dx = \frac{5}{5 + 0.80} = 0.862$$

or $\quad 0.02\left[\dfrac{e^{-0.02x}}{-0.02}\right]_0^{I_m} = 0.862$

or $\quad -\left[e^{-0.02 I_m} - 1\right] = 0.862$

$\therefore\quad e^{-0.02\ I_m} = 0.138 \quad \therefore\ I_{m_0} = 100.$

12.6-3 Model 4 (*a*) (Continuous Demand, Set-up Cost Zero, Stock Levels Discrete, Lead Time Zero)

This model is similar to model 3(*a*) with the difference that demand is continuous rather than instantaneous *i.e.,* withdrawals from stock are continuous rather than instantaneous. Also the rate of withdrawals is assumed to be constant.

The reorder time is assumed to be fixed and known; hence set-up cost is not included in calculations. Production is assumed to be instantaneous and lead time negligibly small.

The problem is to determine the optimal order level I_m where $R \le I_m$ or $R > I_m$, at the beginning of each time period. The variation of inventory with time for these two cases is shown in Fig. 12.8(*a*) and (*b*).

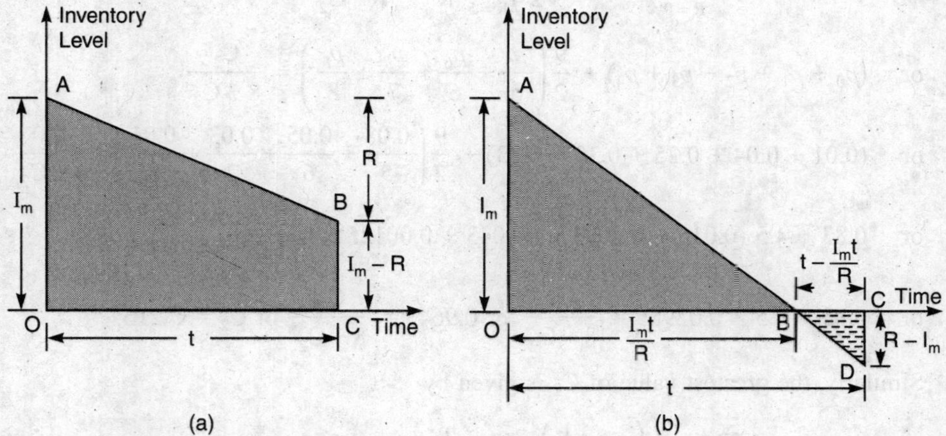

Fig. 12.8. Inventory situation for model 4(a); (a) $R \le I_m$ (b) $R > I_m$.

When $R \le I_m$ as shown in Fig. 12.8(*a*), there are no shortages; when $R > I_m$, as shown in figure 12.8(*b*), shortages occur.

It can be shown that for optimum stock level,

$$\sum_{R=0}^{I_m - 1} p_R + \left(I_m - \frac{1}{2}\right) \sum_{R=I_m}^{\infty} \frac{p_R}{R} < \frac{C_2}{C_1 + C_2} < \sum_{R=0}^{I_m} p_R + \left(I_m + \frac{1}{2}\right) \sum_{R=I_m+1}^{\infty} \frac{p_R}{R}$$

EXAMPLE 12.6-9

The probability distribution of monthly sales of a certain item is as follows:

Monthly sales :	0	1	2	3	4	5	6	7	8
Probability :	0.01	0.04	0.25	0.30	0.23	0.08	0.05	0.03	0.01

The cost of holding inventory is ₹ 8 per unit per month. A stock of 5 items is maintained at the start of each month. If the shortage cost is proportional to both time and quantity short, find the imputed cost of shortage of unit item for unit time.

Solution

As the problem is stated in discrete units, the answer will consist of a range of values for the imputed cost. Here,

optimum inventory, $I_m = 5$ units,
holding cost, $C_1 =$ ₹ 8 per unit per month.
Range of monthly sales = 0 to 8.
Probability p_R for sale R in each month is

p_0	p_1	p_2	p_3	p_4	p_5	p_6	p_7	p_8
0.01	0.04	0.25	0.30	0.23	0.08	0.05	0.03	0.01

Range of optimum value of I_m is given by

$$\sum_{R=0}^{I_m-1} p_R + \left(I_m - \frac{1}{2}\right) \sum_{R=I_m}^{\infty} \frac{p_R}{R} < \frac{C_2}{C_1 + C_2} < \sum_{R=0}^{I_m} p_R + \left(I_m + \frac{1}{2}\right) \sum_{R=I_m+1}^{\infty} \frac{p_R}{R}$$

$\therefore$ The least value of C_2 is given by

$$\sum_{R=0}^{I_m-1} p_R + \left(I_m - \frac{1}{2}\right) \sum_{R=I_m}^{\infty} \frac{p_R}{R} = \frac{C_2}{C_1 + C_2}$$

or
$$\sum_{R=0}^{4} p_R + \left(5 - \frac{1}{2}\right) \sum_{R=5}^{8} \frac{p_R}{R} = \frac{C_2}{8 + C_2}$$

or
$$(p_0 + p_1 + p_2 + p_3 + p_4) + \frac{9}{2}\left(\frac{p_5}{5} + \frac{p_6}{6} + \frac{p_7}{7} + \frac{p_8}{8}\right) = \frac{C_2}{8 + C_2}$$

or
$$(0.01 + 0.04 + 0.25 + 0.30 + 0.23) + \frac{9}{2}\left(\frac{0.08}{5} + \frac{0.05}{6} + \frac{0.03}{7} + \frac{0.01}{8}\right) = \frac{C_2}{8 + C_2}$$

or
$$0.83 + 4.5\ (0.016 + 0.0083 + 0.0043 + 0.00125) = \frac{C_2}{8 + C_2}$$

or
$$0.83 + 4.5 \times 0.02985 = \frac{C_2}{8 + C_2} \text{ or } 0.9643 = \frac{C_2}{8 + C_2} \text{ or } C_2 = ₹\ 216.$$

Similarly, the greatest value of C_2 is given by

$$\sum_{R=0}^{I_m} p_R + \left(I_m + \frac{1}{2}\right) \sum_{R=I_m+1}^{\infty} \frac{p_R}{R} = \frac{C_2}{C_1 + C_2}$$

or
$$\sum_{0}^{5} p_R + \left(5 + \frac{1}{2}\right) \sum_{R=6}^{8} \frac{p_R}{R} = \frac{C_2}{8 + C_2}$$

or
$$(p_0 + p_1 + p_2 + p_3 + p_4 + p_5) + \frac{11}{2}\left(\frac{p_6}{6} + \frac{p_7}{7} + \frac{p_8}{8}\right) = \frac{C_2}{8 + C_2}$$

or
$$(0.01 + 0.04 + 0.25 + 0.30 + 0.23 + 0.08) + \frac{11}{2}\left(\frac{0.05}{6} + \frac{0.03}{7} + \frac{0.01}{8}\right) = \frac{C_2}{8 + C_2}$$

or
$$0.91 + \frac{11}{2}\ (0.01385) = \frac{C_2}{8 + C_2} \text{ or } 0.91 + 0.076165 = \frac{C_2}{8 + C_2} \text{ or } C_2 = ₹\ 570.25.$$

$\therefore$ Range of values for the imputed cost C_2 is ₹ 216 < C_2 < ₹ 570.25.

12.6-4 Model 4 (b) (Continuous Demand, Set-up Cost Zero, Continuous Stock Levels, Lead Time Zero)

In this model, all conditions are same as in model 4 (*a*) except that the stock levels are continuous (rather than discrete). Therefore, probability $f(R)\, dR$ will be used instead of p_R, where $f(R)$ is the probability density function of the demand rate R.

Then the optimal order quantity I_{m_0} is given by

$$\int_0^{I_{m0}} f(R)\,.\,dR + \int_{I_{m0}}^{\infty} I_m\,.\,\frac{f(R)}{R}\,.\,dR = \frac{C_2}{C_1 + C_2}.$$

EXAMPLE 12.6-10

Let the probability density of demand of a certain item during a week be

$$f(x) = \begin{cases} 0.1, 0 \le x \le 10; \\ 0, \text{otherwise.} \end{cases}$$

This demand is assumed to occur with a uniform pattern over the week. Let the unit carrying cost of the item in inventory be ₹ 2 per week and unit shortage cost be ₹ 8 per week. How will you determine the optimal order level of the inventory ? [*Agra M. Stat., 1973*]

Solution

Here

$$f(x) = 0.1,\ 0 \le x \le 10,$$
$$C_1 = ₹\ 2\text{/week},$$
$$C_2 = ₹\ 8\text{/week}.$$

As the demand is uniform over the week, the optimum order level of the inventory, I_m, is given by

$$\int_0^{I_m} f(x)\ .\ dx + I_m \int_{I_m}^{\infty} \frac{f(x)}{x}\ .\ dx = \frac{C_2}{C_1 + C_2}$$

or
$$\int_0^{I_m} 0.1\, dx + I_m \int_{I_m}^{10} \frac{0.1}{x}\ .\ dx = \frac{8}{2+8}$$

or
$$0.1\ I_m + 0.1\ I_m (\log 10 - \log I_m) = 0.8$$

or
$$I_m + 2.3\ I_m - I_m \log I_m = 8$$

or
$$3.3\ I_m - I_m \log I_m = 8.$$

On solving the equation by trial and error method, we get $I_m = 4.5$.

EXERCISES 12.3

1. Discuss any stochastic model of inventory management. Derive the formula of optimum level of inventory. [*Dibrugarh M.Sc. (Stat.) 1994*]
2. Discuss the problem of inventory control when the stochastic demand is uniform, production is instantaneous and lead time is negligible (discrete case). [*Meerut M.Sc. (Math.) 1995*]
3. Discuss the continuous case of a probabilistic inventory model with instantaneous demand and no set-up cost. [*Dibrugarh M.Sc. (Stat.) 1994*]

Section 12.6-1 to 12.6-4

4. A newspaper boy buys papers for 30 paise and sells them for 70 paise each. He cannot return unsold newspapers. Daily demand has the following distribution:

No. of customers :	23	24	25	26	27	28	29	30	31	32
Probability :	0.01	0.03	0.06	0.10	0.20	0.25	0.15	0.10	0.05	0.05

If each day's demand is independent of the previous day's, how many papers should he order each day ? [*Meerut M.Sc. (Stat.) 1971, 74; Mumbai B.Sc. (Stat.) 1975*]

(*Ans* 28.)

5. The probability distribution of monthly sales of a certain item is as follows:

Monthly sales :	0	1	2	3	4	5	6
Probability :	0.01	0.06	0.25	0.35	0.20	0.03	0.10

The cost of carrying inventory is ₹ 30 per unit per month and the cost of unit shortage is ₹ 70 per month. Determine the optimum stock level which minimizes the total expected cost.

Delhi M.Sc. (Math.) 1976]

(*Ans.* 3.)

6. An electric company is about to order a new generator for its plant. One of the essential parts of the generator is expensive and complicated. Its failure cannot be foreseen and its failure leads to the breakdown of the generator. Each of these parts is uniquely built for a particular generator and

may not be used on any other. The cost of part when ordered with generator is ₹ 4,000. If a spare part is required and is not available, the cost of having the part to order plus the cost of downtime is ₹ 80,000. The planned life of the generator is 20 years and records of similar parts in similar generators give the following information:

No. of spare parts required in 20 years	*No. of generators requiring indicated no. of spares*	*Estimated probability of indicated no. of failures*
0	90	0.90
1	5	0.05
2	2	0.02
3	1	0.01
4	1	0.01
5	1	0.01
6 or more	0	0.00

How many spare parts should be incorporated in the order for each generator ? (*Ans.* 2.)

7. An ice-cream company sells one of its types of ice cream by weight. If the product is not sold on the day it is prepared, it can be sold at a loss of 50 paise per pound. There is, however, an unlimited market for one day old ice cream. On the other hand the company makes a profit of ₹ 3.20 on every pound of ice cream sold on the day it is prepared. Past daily orders form a distribution with

$$f(x) = 0.02 - 0.0002\,x,\ 0 \le x \le 100.$$

How many pounds of ice cream should the company prepare every day ?

[*Baroda B.Sc. (Math.) 1978; Agra M.Sc. (Stat.) 1974*]

(*Ans.* 63.3 pounds.)

8. A baking company sells cake by the pound. It makes a profit of 50 paise a pound on every pound sold on the day it is baked. It disposes of all cakes not sold on the day it is baked at a loss of 12 paise a pound. If the demand is known to be rectangular between 2,000 and 3,000 pounds, determine the optimum daily amount baked. [*J.N.T.U. Hyderabad B.Tech. Nov., 2010*]

(*Ans.* 2,807 pounds.)

9. An item is sold for ₹ 25 per unit and it costs ₹ 10. Unsold items can be sold for ₹ 4 each. It is assumed that there is no shortage penalty cost besides the lost revenue. The demand is known to be any value between 600 and 1,000 items.
Determine the optimum number of units of the item to be stocked. [*IGNOU MCA, 2003*]

(*Ans.* 886 units.)

10. Show that when considering the optimum level of inventory S_0, which minimizes the total expected cost in case of continuous (non-discrete) quantities, the condition to be satisfied is

$$F(S_0) = \frac{C_2}{C_1 + C_2},$$

where $$F(S_0) = \int_0^{s_0} f(r)\,.\,dr.$$

Here, $f(r)$ = the probability density function of requirement of quantity r,
C_2 = the shortage cost,
C_1 = the holding cost per unit of quantity per unit of time. [*Gujarat Univ. B.E., 1976*]

11. A shopkeeper has to decide how much quantity of bread he should stock every week. The quantity of bread demanded in any week is assumed to be a continuous random variable with a given probability function $f(x)$. Let '*a*' be the unit cost of purchasing bread and '*d*' be the unit penalty cost. Find the optimum quantity of bread to be stocked. [*I.S.I., 1962*]

12. The probability distribution of monthly sales of a certain item is as follows:

Monthly sales	0	1	2	3	4	5	6
Probability	0.02	0.05	0.03	0.27	0.20	0.10	0.06

The cost of carrying inventory is ₹ 10 per unit per month. The current policy is to maintain a stock of 4 items at the beginning of each month. Assuming that the cost of shortage is proportional to both time and quantity short, obtain the imputed cost of shortage of one item for one time unit.

[*Meerut M.Sc. (Stat.) 1970*]

(*Ans.* Between ₹ 17.78 and ₹ 52.50.)

13. An airline runs a school for air hostesses each month; it takes two months to assemble a group of girls and to train them. Past records of turnover in hostesses show that the probability of requiring x new trained hostesses in any one month is $g(x)$ [$x = 0, 1, 2, ...$], and the probability of requiring y new hostesses in any two-months period is $h(y)$. In the event that a trained hostess is not required for flying duties, the airline still has to pay her salary at the rate of C_1 per month. If insufficient hostesses are available, there is a cost of C_2 per girl short per month. Show how to determine decision rules for the size of classes. [*Meerut, 1971,75*]

14. Two products are stocked by a company. The company has limited space and cannot store more than 40 units. The demand distributions for the products are as follows:

First Product		*Second Product*	
Demand	*Probability of demand*	*Demand*	*Probability of demand*
0	0.10	0	0.05
10	0.20	10	0.20
20	0.35	20	0.40
30	0.25	30	0.20
40	0.10	40	0.15

The inventory carrying costs are ₹ 5 and ₹ 10 per unit of the ending inventories for the first and second products respectively. The shortage costs are ₹ 20 and ₹ 50 per unit of the ending shortages for the first and second products respectively. Find out the economic order quantities for both the products. (*Delhi M.BA., 1976*)

15. The uniform annual demands for two bulky items are 90 units and 160 units respectively. The carrying costs are ₹ 250 and ₹ 200 per ton per year and set-up costs are ₹ 50 and ₹ 40 per production respectively. No shortages are allowed. Space considerations restrict the average amount of inventory of both items to 4,000 c. ft. A ton of the first item occupies 1,000 c. ft., and a ton of the second item 500 c. ft. Find the optimal lot size. [*I.S.I., 1971*]
(*Ans.* 2 tons, 4 tons.)

12.7 INVENTORY MODELS WITH PRICE BREAKS

In the inventory models discussed so far the production or purchase cost per unit was assumed to be constant. It was not considered during their formulation since it did not affect the level of inventory. In this section we shall consider a class of inventory problems in which this cost is variable and depends upon the quantity manufactured or purchased. This usually happens when *discounts* are offered for the purchase of large quantities. These discounts take the form of *price breaks*. For example, the price breaks may be given as

₹ 1 per item for purchase of items upto 499,
₹ 0.95 per item for purchase of items from 500 upto 999.
₹ 0.90 per item for purchase of items 1,000 or more.

Clearly, the purchase cost $C(q)$ is a variable and is given by the expression

$$C(q) = \begin{cases} 1.q & 0 \le q \le 499, \\ 1 \times 500 + 0.95\,(q - 500) & 500 \le q \le 999, \\ 1 \times 500 + 0.95\,(1{,}000 - 500) - 0.90\,(q - 1{,}000) & q \ge 1{,}000. \end{cases}$$

Such a variable cost must be considered in the inventory model. Further, as this variable production or purchase cost per unit is more appropriate for purchased parts (because of quantity discounts), we shall, hereafter, refer only to purchased parts and the problem, then, is to determine

(*i*) how often the parts be purchased,

(*ii*) how many units should be purchased at anyone time.

12.7-1 Inventory Models with One Price Break

To understand how the optimal order quantity can be determined in such a case, let us consider example 12.7-1.

EXAMPLE 12.7-1

An automobile manufacturer purchases 2,400 castings over a period of 360 days. This requirement is fixed and known. These castings are subject to quantity discounts. Ordering cost is ₹ 70,000/order and storage cost per day is 0.12% of the unit cost. Determine the optimal purchase quantity if the supplier has offered the following unit prices for the castings :

$$\text{Unit price} = ₹\ 1{,}000 \text{ for } q < 1{,}000,$$
$$= ₹\ 950 \text{ for } q \geq 1{,}000.$$

Solution

First we calculate the EOQ if the unit price of castings is ₹ 950.

$$\text{EOQ for unit price of ₹ 950} = \sqrt{\frac{2RC_3}{C_1}} = \sqrt{\frac{2 \times 70{,}000 \times \frac{2{,}400}{360}}{\frac{0.12}{100} \times 950}} = 905 \text{ units.}$$

Therefore, the manufacturer should place order for 905 units. This, however, will not be acceptable to the supplier since he will charge ₹ 950/unit only if the order is placed for 1,000 or more units in an order. Therefore, this is an infeasible solution. To avail unit price of ₹ 950, the manufacturer must place an order of *at least* 1,000 units.

Total cost per day for order quantity of 1,000 units

$$= \frac{q}{2} CI + C_3 \cdot \frac{R}{q} + CR$$

$$= ₹ \left(\frac{1{,}000}{2} \times 950 \times \frac{0.12}{100} + 70{,}000 \times \frac{2{,}400}{360} \times \frac{1}{1{,}000} + 950 \times \frac{2{,}400}{360} \right)$$

$$= ₹\ (570 + 466.67 + 6{,}333.33) = ₹\ 7{,}370.$$

Next let us calculate the EOQ if the unit price of castings is ₹ 1,000.

$$\text{EOQ for unit price of ₹ 1,000} = \sqrt{\frac{2RC_3}{C_1}} = \sqrt{\frac{2 \times 70{,}000 \times \frac{2{,}400}{360}}{\frac{0.12}{100} \times 1{,}000}} = 882 \text{ units.}$$

Total cost per day for order quantity of 882 units

$$= \frac{q}{2} CI + C_3 \cdot \frac{R}{q} + CR$$

$$= ₹ \left(\frac{882}{2} \times 1{,}000 \times \frac{0.12}{100} + 70{,}000 \times \frac{2{,}400}{360} \times \frac{1}{882} + 1{,}000 \times \frac{2{,}400}{360} \right)$$

$$= ₹\ (529.20 + 529.20 + 6{,}666.67) = ₹\ 7{,}725.$$

Since the earlier cost is lower, the optimal order quantity is 1,000 units. The total cost curve (which is a stepped curve) is shown in Fig. 12.9.

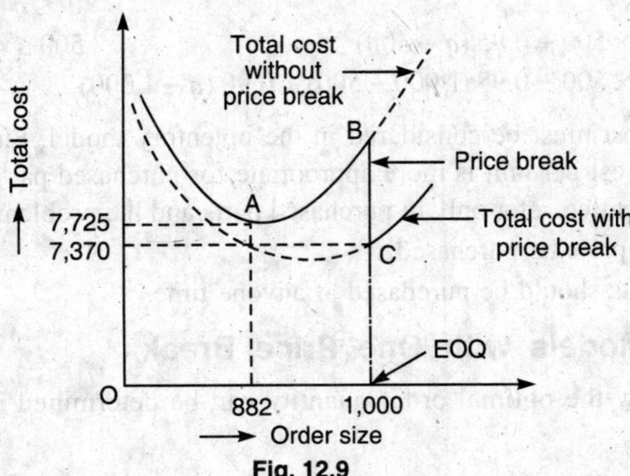

Fig. 12.9

Clearly, the curve shows a marked drop in the total cost due to price discount at a quantity of 1,000 units. At this level, the total cost is lower than the total cost corresponding to 882 units.

12.7-2 Inventory Models with Multiple Price Breaks

Sometimes the supplier may offer more than one price breaks. The solution procedure for such problems is the extension of that used for single price break.

We first determine the EOQ with the lowest cost price. If it is feasible *i.e.*, if the value falls in the slab of the lot size for this cost price, then this is the optimal order quantity. If it is infeasible, we determine EOQ with the next lowest cost price. If this too is infeasible, the next lowest cost is tried. The procedure is continued till the feasible EOQ is obtained. The total cost corresponding to this quantity level is then calculated. Also, the total cost of order quantities corresponding to cut-off points of the subsequent cost prices is calculated. The quantity corresponding to the minimum of these total costs is the optimal order quantity.

EXAMPLE 12.7-2

Find the optimal order quantity for a product for which the price breaks are as follows:

Quantity	*Unit cost*
$0 < q < 500$	*₹ 10,*
$500 \le q < 750$	*₹ 9.25,*
$750 \le q$	*₹ 8.75.*

The monthly demand for the product is 200 units, storage cost is 2% of the unit cost and cost of ordering is ₹ 100. [*Univ. of Madras B.Sc. (Math.) Nov., 2012; Chennai U., 2002; P.T.U. MBA May, 2002; P.U. B.Com., 2000*]

Solution

EOQ for unit price of ₹ 8.75 = $\sqrt{\dfrac{2C_3R}{C_1}} = \sqrt{\dfrac{2\times100\times200}{8.75\times0.02}}$ = 478 units (infeasible).

EOQ for unit price of ₹ 9.25 = $\sqrt{\dfrac{2\times100\times200}{9.25\times0.02}}$ = 465 units (infeasible).

EOQ for unit price of ₹ 10 = $\sqrt{\dfrac{2\times100\times200}{10\times0.02}}$ = 447 units (feasible).

Total cost/month for order quantity of 447 units (optimal size)

$$= \sqrt{2\,C_1C_3R} + CR = \sqrt{2\times(10\times0.02)\times100\times200} + 10\times200$$

= ₹ (89.45 + 2,000) = ₹ 2089.45.

Total cost/month for order quantity of 500 units (non-optimal size)

$$= \frac{q}{2}\,C_1 + C_3\,.\,\frac{R}{q} + CR$$

$$= ₹\left(\frac{500}{2}\times9.25\times0.02 + 100\times\frac{200}{500} + 9.25\times200\right)$$

= ₹ (46.25 + 40 + 1,850) = ₹ 1,936.25.

Total cost/month for order quantity of 750 units (non-optimal size)

$$= \frac{q}{2}\,C_1 + C_3\,.\,\frac{R}{q} + CR$$

$$= ₹\left(\frac{750}{2}\times8.75\times0.02 + 100\times\frac{200}{750} + 8.75\times200\right)$$

= ₹ (65.63 + 26.67 + 1,750) = ₹ 1,842.30.

∴ The optimal order quantity is 750 units. The total cost curve, which is a stepped curve is shown in Fig. 12.10.

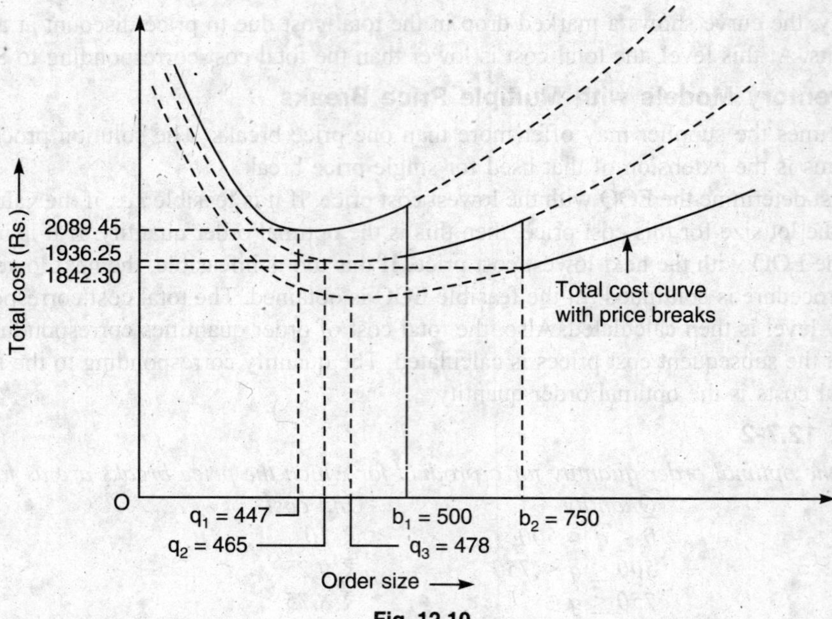

Fig. 12.10

EXAMPLE 12.7-3

Find the optimal order quantity for a product when the annual demand for the product is 500 units, the cost of storage per unit per year is 10% of the unit cost and ordering cost per order is ₹ 180. The unit costs are given below:

Quantity	*Unit cost*
$0 \le q_1 < 500$	₹ *25.00*
$500 \le q_2 < 1,500$	₹ *24.80*
$1,500 \le q_3 < 3,000$	₹ *24.60*
$3,000 \le q_4$	₹ *24.40*

[*J.N.T.U. Hyderabad B.Tech. April, 2011; P.U.B.Tech. (Mech.) Dec., 2006; B. Com. Jan., 2005*]

Solution

Here, R = 500 units, I = 0.10, C_3 = ₹ 180.

$$\text{EOQ for unit price of ₹ 24.40} = \sqrt{\frac{2C_3R}{C_1}} = \sqrt{\frac{2C_3R}{CI}} = \sqrt{\frac{2 \times 180 \times 500}{24.40 \times 0.10}} = 271.6 \text{ units.}$$

But this is not feasible because the unit price of ₹ 24.40 is not available for an order size of 271.6 units.

$$\text{EOQ for unit price of ₹ 24.60} = \sqrt{\frac{2 \times 180 \times 500}{24.60 \times 0.10}} = 270.5 \text{ units (infeasible).}$$

$$\text{EOQ for unit price of ₹ 24.80} = \sqrt{\frac{2 \times 180 \times 500}{24.80 \times 0.10}} = 269.4 \text{ units (infeasible).}$$

$$\text{EOQ for unit price of ₹ 25.00} = \sqrt{\frac{2 \times 180 \times 500}{25 \times 0.10}} = 268.3 \text{ units (feasible).}$$

Total annual cost for order quantity of 268.3 units (optimal size)

$$= \sqrt{2C_1C_3R} + CR = \sqrt{2 \times 25 \times 0.10 \times 180 \times 500} + 25 \times 500$$

$$= ₹\ (670.82 + 12,500) = ₹\ 13,170.82.$$

Total annual cost for quantity corresponding to cut-off point of 500 units

$$= \frac{q}{2} C_1 + C_3 . \frac{R}{q} + CR = \frac{500}{2} \times 24.80 \times 0.10 + 180 \times \frac{500}{500} + 24.80 \times 500$$

$= ₹ (620 + 180 + 12{,}400) = ₹ 13{,}200.$

Total annual cost for order quantity corresponding to cut-off point of 1,500 units

$$= ₹ \left(\frac{1{,}500}{2} \times 24.60 \times 0.10 + 180 \times \frac{500}{1{,}500} - 24.60 \times 500 \right)$$

$= ₹ (1{,}845 + 600 + 12{,}300) = ₹ 14{,}745.$

Total annual cost for order quantity corresponding to cut-off point of 3,000 units

$$= ₹ \left(\frac{3{,}000}{2} \times 24.40 \times 0.10 + 180 \times \frac{500}{3{,}000} + 24.40 \times 500 \right)$$

$= ₹ (3{,}660 + 30 + 12{,}200) = ₹ 15{,}890.$

Since the total cost is minimum at $q_0 = 268.3$ units, it represents the optimal order quantity.

EXERCISES 12.4

1. Discuss the solution procedure for an inventory problem with two price breaks. *[Kuru. U. M.Sc., 2001]*
2. Describe decision rules for a purchase inventory model with three price breaks. *[Delhi U. M.Sc. (Math.) 1975]*
3. Discuss briefly the impact of quantity discounts on EOQ and hence on inventory control procedure. *[P.U.B.Com. April, 1999]*

Section 12.7-1–12.7-2

4. A manufacturer of engines is required to purchase 2,400 castings per year. This requirement is assumed to be fixed and known. The manufacturer is given a lower price for quantity purchased within certain ranges. The problem is to determine the optimal purchase quantity.
   The following data are given :
   Time period T = 12 months,
   total demand R = 2,400 units,
   I = 2%,
   Setup cost per procurement, C_3 = ₹ 350,
   K_{11} = ₹ 10 $0 \le q < 500$,
   K_{12} = ₹ 9.25 $q \ge 500$. (*Ans.* 870.)
5. In exercise 4, if the setup cost per procurement is ₹ 100 only, find the optimal order quantity. (*Ans.* 500.)
6. If in exercise 5, the price break does not occur until q = 3,000 find the optimal lot size. (*Ans.* 447.)
7. The annual demand of a product is 10,000 units. Each unit costs ₹ 100 if orders are placed in quantities below 200 units but for orders of 200 or above the price is ₹ 95. The annual inventory holding cost is 10% of the value of the item and the ordering cost is ₹ 5 per order. Find the economic lot size. *[J.N.T.U. Hyderabad B.Tech. May, 2011]*
8. The demand for a product is 2,400 units over 360 days. The storage cost is 0.06% of the unit cost of the product and the ordering cost is ₹ 35,000. Find the optimal order quantity if the price breaks are as follows :

Quantity range	*Purchasing cost (₹)*
$0 \le q < 1{,}000$	1,000,
$1{,}000 \le q < 4{,}000$	925,
$4{,}000 \le q$	850.

9. A manufacturer's requirement for an item is 2,000 units per year. Ordering costs are ₹ 100 per order and inventory costs are 16% per year per unit of average inventory. Calculate the economic order quantity. If the price quoted is ₹ 10 each for quantities below 1,000 units, ₹ 9.50 for quantities between 1,000 and below 2,000 and ₹ 9.30 for lots of 2,000 or more, compute total ordering cost when ordering in lots of (*i*) 500 (*ii*) 1,000 and (*iii*) 2,000 units. *[Gwalior Univ., 1975]*

10. Find the optimal order quantity for a product for which the following data are given :

$R = 100$ units/week,
$C_3 = ₹\ 300$,
$I = 10\%$/unit/week,
$K_1 = ₹\ 1$ if $q < 500$,
₹ 0.95 if $500 \le q < 1{,}000$,
₹ 0.90 if $1{,}000 \le q$. [*P.U. B.E. (E.&Ec.) April, 2006; B. Com. April, 2006*]

(*Ans.* 1,000 units.)

11. Determine an optimal ordering rule for the following case:

$R = 5{,}000$ units/month,
$C_3 = ₹\ 50$ per order,
$P = ₹\ 0.50$ per unit per month.

Unit costs are

$K_{11} = ₹\ 1.50$ $\quad 0 \le q < 100$,
$K_{12} = ₹\ 1.40$ $\quad 100 \le q < 250$,
$K_{13} = ₹\ 1.30$ $\quad 250 \le q < 500$,
$K_{14} = ₹\ 1.00$ $\quad 500 \le q < 1{,}000$,
$K_{15} = ₹\ 0.90$ $\quad 1{,}000 \le q < 5{,}000$,
$K_{16} = ₹\ 0.85$. $\quad 5{,}000 \le q$.

12. Assume that the following quantity discount schedule for a particular bearing is available to a retail store:

Order size (units)	*Discount*
0–49	0%
50–99	5%
100–199	10%
200 and above	12%

The cost of a single bearing with no discount is ₹ 30. The annual demand is 250 units, ordering cost is ₹ 20 per order and annual inventory carrying cost is ₹ 4 per unit. Determine the optimal order quantity and the associated minimal total cost of inventory and purchasing cost, if shortages are not allowed. [*P.T.U. B.Tech. (Mech.) Nov., 2012*]

(*Ans.* 100 units; ₹ 7,000.)

13. A company requires 2,500 units of a special type of bolts per year. An offer has been received for supply of these at the rate of ₹ 5 per piece. The supplier has also offered a discount of 3% for purchase lot of size between 1,500-2,499 units. Any order of 2,500 units and above shall be supplied at a discount of 5% on the base price. If the company expects 20% return on its investments in working capital and the cost of transport of each lot from the supplier premises works out to ₹ 20 per lot, is it advantageous to change the order quantity and get discount ? If yes, how much ? [*IGNOU MBA, 2000*]

(*Ans.* No discount acceptable, 316; ₹ 12,816.)

14. A hardware store procures and sells hardware items. Following information is available :

Expected annual sales	:	8,000 units,
ordering cost	:	₹ 180 per order,
holding cost	:	10% of the average inventory value.

The item can be purchased according to the following schedule :

Lot size	*Unit price (₹)*
1 – 999	22.00
1,000 – 1,499	20.00
1,500 – 1,999	19.00
2,000 and above	18.50

Determine the best order size. [*G.N.D.U. B.Com. April, 2000*]

(*Ans.* 2,000 units, total cost = ₹ 1,50,570.)

15. A company decides to buy pistons from the market. The demand is 60 pistons per day. Ordering cost is ₹ 50 per order and the carrying cost is 15% of the price of the piston. Assume 300 working days in a year. Price schedule is given below :

Quantity ordered	*Unit price* (₹)
0 – 1,999	65
2,000 – 4,999	60
5,000 – 9,999	55
over 9,999	50

(*i*) What is the optimal order quantity?

(*ii*) What would be the minimum inventory cost for such an optimal order policy?

[*IGNOU MBA Dec., 1999*]

(*Ans*. Over 10,000; ₹ 9,37,590.)

16. In a warehouse the annual demand for an item is 12,500 units. The ordering cost is ₹ 5 per order. The inventory carrying cost is 25% per annum. There are three price breaks. Orders in the range of 1,000 – 4,999 units cost ₹ 0.48 per unit. Orders in the range of 5,000 – 9,999 units have a price of ₹ 0.42 per unit and orders of 10,000 or more units are priced at ₹ 0.36 per unit. What quantity should be ordered to minimize total annual cost ? [*IGNOU MBA June, 1998*]

(*Ans.* 10,000 units; ₹ 4,956.25.)

17. A company is requiring 1,000 units of a raw material per month. The ordering cost is ₹ 15 per order. The carrying cost in addition to ₹ 2 per unit is estimated to be 15% of average inventory per unit per year. The purchase price of raw material is ₹ 100 per unit. Find the economic lot size and the total cost. The company gets concession of 5% on purchase price if it orders 2,000 units or more but less than 5,000 units. Orders of 5,000 units or above get 2% commission in addition to 5%. Which of the three ways of the orders the company should adopt ? [*GNDU. B.Com., 1993*]

(*Ans.* 5,000 units; ₹ 11,55,911.)

18. A shopkeeper has a uniform demand of an item at the rate of 100 items per month. He buys it from a supplier at a cost of ₹ 12/item and the cost of ordering is ₹ 10/order. If the stock holding cost is 20% of average stock value, how frequently should he replenish his stocks ?
Further, suppose the supplier offers a 5% discount on orders between 200 and 999 items and a 10% discount on orders exceeding or equal to 1,000, can the shopkeeper reduce his cost by taking advantage of either of these discounts ? [*P.U. M.Com. April, 2006, 2004*]

(*Ans.* Accept 5% discount; ₹ 13,968.)

19. A soft-drink company buys a large number of pallets every year which it uses in the warehousing of its bottled products. A vendor has offered the company the following discount schedule for pallets :

Order quantity	*Price per unit*
Less than 500	₹ 10.00
500 – 999	₹ 9.50
1,000 – 1,499	₹ 9.15
1,500 and above	₹ 9.00

The average yearly replacement for the past two years has been 1,650 pallets, which looks realistic for this year. The cost per order is ₹ 12.50 and annual carrying costs are 18% of average inventory. What quantity should be ordered ? (*Ans.* 1,000 units.)

20. Estimated demand for gold-filled lockets at a jewellery shop is 2,500 lockets a year. The ordering cost is ₹ 2,250 and the following price schedule applies :

No. of lockets	*Price / locket*
1–599	₹ 4,500
600–1,199	₹ 4,000
1,200 or more	₹ 3,750

What order size will minimize total cost in each of the following cases :

(*i*) carrying cost is ₹ 900 per locket on an annual basis.

(*ii*) carrying cost is 20% of price on annual basis. [*Dayalbagh Edu. Inst. Agra B.B.M. May, 2007*]

(*Ans.* (*i*) 1,200 (*ii*) 1,200.)

21. Consider an item on which incremental quantity discounts are available. The first 10 units cost ₹ 100 each and additional units cost ₹ 95 each. Determine the optimal order quantity when λ = 500 units per year, i = 0.20, A = ₹ 50 per year per set-up. [*J.N.T.U. Hyderabad B.Tech. Nov., 2010*]

22. (*a*) Describe decision rules for a purchase inventory model with two price breaks without shortages.
(*b*) Find the optimum order quantity for the following price break inventory problem :

Annual demand :	200 units
Inventory carrying cost :	25%
Ordering cost :	₹ 20 per order
Quantity	*Price/unit*
$0 \le Q < 50$	₹ 10
$50 \le Q < 100$	₹ 9
$100 \le Q$.	₹ 8

[*J.N.T.U. Hyderabad B.Tech. June, 2009*]

23. A company consumes 200 items/month, working 30 days in a month. The cost of the item is ₹ 1,000. For a lot of more than 50, the price is ₹ 950. Find out the optimum purchase quantity if ordering cost is ₹ 10,000 and handling charges are 1% of unit cost per month. If the discounted price is available for a lot of more than 75 items, find the optimum purchase quantity. [*J.N.T.U. Hyderabad B.Tech. June, 2009*]

24. (*a*) Describe the basic characteristics of an inventory system.
(*b*) A firm producing transistor radios has estimated that it will require 12,000 transistor components for the next year's production. The cost of carrying inventory is estimated at 25% of the value of the inventory per year. There are two sources of supply: German firm and Japanese firm. The cost, insurance, and freight (CIF) price per component from German firm works out at ₹ 12 and from Japanese firm ₹ 10. The ordering cost works out at ₹ 120 per order. Which is the best source to buy from Germany or Japan ? In addition, if order quantity were at least 6,000 units, the CIF price would be ₹ 9 per item. [*J.N.T.U. Hyderabad B.Tech. June, 2009*]

12.8 MULTI-ITEM DETERMINISTIC MODEL

This model considers the inventory system consisting of several items. There are limitations on production facilities or storage capacity or time or money. This limitation results in an interaction between the different items so that it is not possible to consider each item separately. However, simple cases can be handled by using the *technique of Lagrange multipliers*.

Consider an inventory consisting of n items. For simplicity let us assume that production is instantaneous, there is no quantity discount and that no shortages are permitted. Further let us assume that the demand is known and uniform at a rate of R_i per unit time for the ith item. Let C_{1i} be the inventory holding cost per unit per unit time and C_{3i} be the setup cost per production run for the ith item.

Total cost of ith item per production run

$$= C_{1i}\left(\frac{1}{2}q_i t\right) + C_{3i}.$$

∴ Total cost of ith item per unit time

$$= \frac{1}{2} C_{1i}\, q_i + \frac{C_{3i}}{t}$$

or
$$C(q_i) = \frac{1}{2} C_{1i}\, q_i + C_3 \frac{R_i}{q_i}, \qquad \left(\because t = \frac{q_i}{R_i}\right)$$

where q_i is the order quantity for ith item.

∴ Total cost per unit time,

$$C(q_1, q_2, \ldots, q_n) = \sum_{i=1}^{n}\left(\frac{1}{2} C_{1i} q_i + \frac{C_{3i} R_i}{q_i}\right), \quad i = 1, 2, \ldots, n. \qquad \ldots(12.50)$$

To minimize this cost, we must differentiate it w.r.t. q_i and put it equal to zero.

i.e.,
$$\frac{\partial [C(q_1, q_2, \ldots, q_n)]}{\partial q_i} = \frac{1}{2} C_{1i} - \frac{C_{3i} R_i}{q_i^2} = 0,$$

which gives optimal value of q_i as

$$q_i^0 = \sqrt{\frac{2C_{3i} R_i}{C_{1i}}}, \quad i = 1, 2, \ldots, n. \qquad \ldots(12.51)$$

Limitation on Inventories

If, now, there is a limitation on inventories that restricts the average number of all types of stocked items to I_m, the cost $C(q_1, q_2, ..., q_n)$ must be minimized subject to the restriction that

$$\frac{1}{2}\sum_{i=1}^{n} q_i \leq I_m. \qquad ...(12.52)$$

If $\frac{1}{2}\sum_{i=1}^{n} q_i \leq I_m$, there is no problem; the optimum values given by equation (12.51) are the required values.

If $\frac{1}{2}\sum_{i=1}^{n} q_i > I_m$, *equality* condition must be obtained by reducing one or more of q_i^0s. We define a quantity λ such that

$$\lambda < 0 \text{ when } \sum_{i=1}^{n} q_i - 2I_m = 0,$$

$$\lambda = 0 \text{ when } \sum_{i=1}^{n} q_i - 2I_m < 0,$$

where λ is *Lagrangian multiplier.*

Then quantity $\lambda\left(\sum_{i=1}^{n} q_i - 2I_m\right)$ is identically equal to zero and it may be added to the cost equation (12.50) without changing the value of $C(q_1, q_2, ..., q_n)$.

$$\therefore \quad C(\lambda; q_1, q_2, ..., q_n) = \sum_{i=1}^{n}\left(\frac{1}{2}C_{1i}q_i + \frac{C_{3i}R_i}{q_i}\right) + \lambda\left(\sum_{i=1}^{n} q_i - 2I_m\right), i = 1, 2, ..., n. \qquad ...(12.53)$$

For optimum values of q_i we put $\frac{\partial[C(\lambda; q_1, q_2, ..., q_n)]}{\partial q_i}$

$$= \frac{1}{2}C_{1i} - \frac{C_{3i}R_i}{q_i^2} + \lambda = 0,$$

and $$\frac{\partial[C(\lambda; q_1, q_2, ..., q_n)]}{\partial \lambda} = \sum_{i=1}^{n} q_i - 2I_m = 0.$$

The second equation implies that q_i^0 must satisfy the inventory constraint in equality sense.

From the first equation, $$q_i^0 = \sqrt{\frac{2C_{3i}R}{C_{1i} + 2\lambda^0}} \qquad ...(12.54)$$

and from the second, $$\sum_{i=1}^{n} q_i^0 = 2I_m. \qquad ...(12.55)$$

Notice that q_i^0 is dependent on $\lambda°$, the optimal value of λ. Also for $\lambda° = 0$, q_i^0 gives the solution of the unconstrained case. The value of $\lambda°$ can be found by systematic trial and error. By definition, $\lambda < 0$ for the above minimization case. Thus if we try successive negative values of λ, its optimum value $\lambda°$ should result in simultaneous values of q_i^0, which satisfy the given constraint in equality sense. Thus determination of $\lambda°$ automatically yields q_i^0.

Limitation on Storage Area

Let A be the maximum storage area available for n items and a_i be the storage area required by one unit of ith item. If q_i is the order quantity for ith item, the storage requirement constraint becomes

$$\sum_{i=1}^{n} a_i q_i < A.$$

The Lagrangian function for this problem is

$$C(\lambda;\, q_1, q_2, \ldots, q_n) = \sum_{i=1}^{n}\left(\frac{1}{2}C_{1i}\, q_i + \frac{C_{3i}\, R_i}{q_i}\right) + \lambda\left(\sum_{i=1}^{n} a_i q_i - A\right),\quad i = 1, 2, \ldots, n. \qquad \ldots(12.56)$$

For optimum values of q_i, we put

$$\frac{\partial}{\partial q_i}[C(\lambda;\, q_1, q_2, \ldots, q_n)] = \frac{1}{2}C_{1i} - \frac{C_{3i}\, R_i}{q_i^2} + \lambda a_i = 0,$$

and $$\frac{\partial[C(\lambda;\, q_1, q_2, \ldots, q_n)]}{\partial\lambda} = \sum_{i=1}^{n} a_i\, q_i - A = 0,$$

which give $$q_i^0 = \sqrt{\frac{2C_{3i}\, R_i}{C_{1i} + 2\lambda^\circ a_i}},\quad i = 1, 2, \ldots, n, \qquad \ldots(12.57)$$

and $$\sum_{i=1}^{n} a_i\, q_i = A. \qquad \ldots(12.58)$$

The value of λ° can be found by systematic trial and error.

EXAMPLE 12.8-1

A company producing three items has limited storage space of averagely 750 items of all types. Determine the optimal production quantities for each item separately, when the following information is given:

Product	*1*	*2*	*3*
Holding cost, C_1 (₹)	*0.05*	*0.02*	*0.04*
Setup cost, C_3 (₹)	*50*	*40*	*60*
Demand rate	*100*	*120*	*75*

Solution

Using economic lot size formula (12.51), we get for

item 1 : $$q_1^0 = \sqrt{\frac{2C_{31}\, R_1}{C_{11}}} = \sqrt{\frac{2\times 50\times 100}{0.05}} = 447,$$

item 2 : $$q_2^0 = \sqrt{\frac{2\times 40\times 120}{0.02}} = 693,$$

item 3 : $$q_3^0 = \sqrt{\frac{2\times 60\times 75}{0.04}} = 474.$$

$\therefore$ Average inventory at any time $= \frac{1}{2}$ [447 + 693 + 474] = 807, which is greater than the limiting number of 750 items. Therefore, we use equation (12.54), which includes the parameter λ. Let $\lambda = 0.005$. Then using equation (12.54) we get for

item 1 : $$q_1^0 = \sqrt{\frac{2C_{31}\, R_1}{C_{11} + 2\lambda^\circ}} = \sqrt{\frac{2\times 50\times 100}{0.05 + 2\times 0.005}} = 409,$$

item 2 : $$q_2^0 = \sqrt{\frac{2\times 40\times 120}{0.02 + 2\times 0.005}} = 566,$$

item 3 : $$q_3^0 = \sqrt{\frac{2\times 60\times 75}{0.04 + 2\times 0.005}} = 424.$$

$\therefore$ Average inventory at any time $= \dfrac{1}{2}$ (409 + 566 + 424) = 700, which is less than the limiting value of 750 items.

$\therefore$ Smaller value of λ should be used in computations. The best way of finding it is by linear interpolation.

Figure 12.11 shows the variation of average inventory as a function of λ. Points A and B have coordinates (0, 807) and (0.005, 700) respectively and between these points the unknown curve can be approximated to a straight line. Point C, which corresponds to average inventory of 750 can be computed as follows:

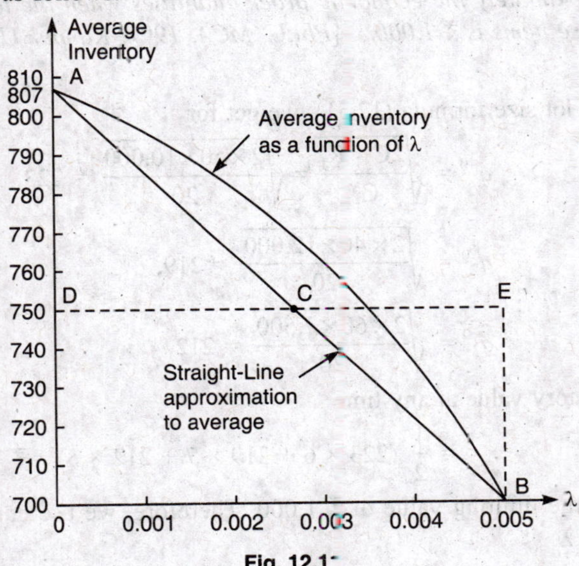

Fig. 12.11

From similar triangles ACD and BCE,

$$\frac{DC}{AD} = \frac{CE}{BE} = \frac{DE - DC}{BE}$$

or $$\frac{DC}{807 - 750} = \frac{0.005}{807 - 800}$$

or $$107\ DC = 57 \times 0.005$$

or $$DC = \frac{57 \times 0.005}{107} \sim 0.0027 \text{ or } \lambda^\circ \sim 0.0027.$$

Now $$q_i^0 = \sqrt{\frac{2C_{3i}\ R_i}{C_{1i} + 2\lambda^\circ}}.$$

$\therefore$ $$q_1^0 = \sqrt{\frac{2 \times 50 \times 100}{0.05 + 2 \times 0.0027}} = 425,$$

$$q_2^0 = \sqrt{\frac{2 \times 40 \times 120}{0.02 + 2 \times 0.0027}} = 615,$$

and $$q_3^0 = \sqrt{\frac{2 \times 60 \times 75}{0.04 + 2 \times 0.0027}} = 445.$$

$\therefore$ Average inventory $= \dfrac{1}{2}(425 + 615 + 445) = 742.5$, which is less than but quite close to 750.

EXAMPLE 12.8-2

Consider a shop which produces three items. The items are produced in lots. The demand rate for each item is constant and can be assumed to be deterministic. No back orders are to be allowed. The pertinent data for the items are given below.

Item	*1*	*2*	*3*
Holding cost (₹)	20	20	20
Setup cost (₹)	50	40	60
Unit cost (₹)	6	7	5
Demand rate per year	10,000	12,000	7,500

Determine approximately the economic order quantities when the total value of average inventory levels of these items is ₹ 1,000. [*Pbi.U. MCA, 1997; Kanpur U. M.Sc. (Math.) 1993*]

Solution

Using economic lot size formula (12.51), we get for

item 1 : $$q_1^0 = \sqrt{\frac{2C_{31}\ R_1}{C_{11}}} = \sqrt{\frac{2 \times 50 \times 10{,}000}{20}} = 223,$$

item 2 : $$q_2^0 = \sqrt{\frac{2 \times 40 \times 12{,}000}{20}} = 219,$$

item 3 : $$q_3^0 = \sqrt{\frac{2 \times 60 \times 7{,}500}{20}} = 212.$$

∴ Average inventory value at any time

$$= \frac{1}{2}\ (223 \times 6 + 219 \times 7 + 212 \times 5) = ₹\ 1{,}965.50,$$

which is greater than the limiting value of ₹ 1,000. Therefore, we use equation (12.54) which includes the parameter λ.

Let $\lambda = 30.$

Then using this equation we get for

item 1 : $$q_1^0 = \sqrt{\frac{2C_{31}\ R_1}{C_{11} + 2\lambda^\circ}} = \sqrt{\frac{2 \times 50 \times 10{,}000}{20 + 2 \times 30}} = 112,$$

item 2 : $$q_2^0 = \sqrt{\frac{2 \times 40 \times 12{,}000}{20 + 2 \times 30}} = 109.5,$$

item 3 : $$q_3^0 = \sqrt{\frac{2 \times 60 \times 7{,}500}{20 + 2 \times 30}} = 106.$$

∴ Average inventory value at any time

$$= \frac{1}{2}\ [112 \times 6 + 109.5 \times 7 + 106 \times 5] = ₹\ 984.25,$$

which is less than the limiting value of ₹ 1,000. Hence, smaller value of λ should be used.

Let $\lambda = 28.5.$

Then using equation (12.54) we get for

item 1 : $$q_1^0 = \sqrt{\frac{2C_{31}\ R_1}{C_{11} + 2\lambda^\circ}} = \sqrt{\frac{2 \times 50 \times 10{,}000}{20 + 2 \times 28.5}} = 114,$$

item 2 : $$q_2^0 = \sqrt{\frac{2 \times 40 \times 12{,}000}{20 + 2 \times 28.5}} = 111.6,$$

item 3 : $$q_3^0 = \sqrt{\frac{2\times 60\times 7{,}500}{20+2\times 28.5}} = 108.$$

∴ Average inventory value at any time

$$= \frac{1}{2}\ [114\times 6 + 111.6\times 7 + 108\times 5] = ₹\ 1{,}002.60.$$

This value is sufficiently close to the given amount of ₹ 1,000.

∴ Economic order quantities for the three items are 114, 111.6 and 108 units respectively.

EXAMPLE 12.8-3

A machine shop produces three products 1, 2 and 3 in lots. The shop has a warehouse whose total floor area is 4,000 sq. metres. The relevant data for the three items are given below :

Item	:	*1*	*2*	*3*
Annual demand (units/year)	:	*500*	*400*	*600*
Cost/unit (₹)	:	*30*	*20*	*70*
Setup cost/lot (₹)	:	*800*	*600*	*1,000*
Floor area required (sq. metres)	:	*5*	*4*	*10*

Inventory carrying rate is 20% per annum. Determine approximately the economic lot size for each item.

Solution

Using economic lot size formula (12.51) we get for

item 1 : $$q_1^0 = \sqrt{\frac{2C_{31}\ R_1}{C_{11}}} = \sqrt{\frac{2\times 800\times 500}{30\times 0.20}} = 365 \text{ units,}$$

item 2 : $$q_2^0 = \sqrt{\frac{2\times 600\times 400}{20\times 0.20}} = 346 \text{ units,}$$

item 3 : $$q_3^0 = \sqrt{\frac{2\times 1{,}000\times 600}{70\times 0.20}} = 293 \text{ units.}$$

∴ Floor area required = 5 × 365 + 4 × 346 + 10 × 293 = 6,139 sq. metres, which is more than the limiting value of 4,000 sq. metres. Therefore, we use equation (12.57) which includes Lagrange multiplier λ. Let $\lambda = 1$; then using equation (12.57) we get for

item 1 : $$q_1^0 = \sqrt{\frac{2C_{31}\ R_1}{C_{11} + 2\lambda a_1}} = \sqrt{\frac{2\times 800\times 500}{30\times 0.20 + 2\times 1\times 5}} = 223.6 \text{ units,}$$

item 2 : $$q_2^0 = \sqrt{\frac{2\times 600\times 400}{20\times 0.20 + 2\times 1\times 4}} = 200 \text{ units,}$$

item 3 : $$q_3^0 = \sqrt{\frac{2\times 1{,}000\times 600}{70\times 0.20 + 2\times 1\times 10}} = 188 \text{ units.}$$

∴ Floor area required = 5 × 223.6 + 4 × 200 + 10 × 188 = 3,798 sq. meters, which is less than the available space. Trying $\lambda = 0.8$ we, similarly, get $q_1^0 = 239$ units, $q_2^0 = 214$ units and $q_3^0 = 200$ units, for which the floor area required = (239 × 5 + 214 × 4 + 200 × 10) = 4,051 sq. metres, which is more than the available space. Trying for other values of λ in the range between 0.8 and 1, we find that the most suitable value is 0.835 for which $q_1^0 = 236$ units, $q_2^0 = 211$ units and $q_3^0 = 197$ units which occupy floor area of 3,994 sq. metres, which is quite close to and less than 4,000 sq. metres.

∴ $q_1^0 = 236$ units, $q_2^0 = 211$ units and $q_3^0 = 197$ units.

EXERCISES 12.5

1. Discuss a deterministic inventory system with multiple items and limited floor area.

[*Delhi U. M.Sc. (Stat.) 1995*]

Section 12.8

2. For an inventory problem with three items, the parameters of the problem are given below :

Item (*i*)	C_{3i} (₹)	R_i	C_{1i} (₹)	a_i (m^2)
1	10	2	0.30	1
2	5	4	0.10	1
3	15	4	0.20	1

If the total available storage area is 25 m^2, find the economic order quantities.

(*Ans.* 6.7, 7.6 and 10.6.)

3. Four different items are kept in a store. The demand rates are constant for the four items. Production rate is instantaneous and no shortages are permitted. The data for the problem are given below.

Item *i*	*Setup cost* C_{3i}	*Demand rate* R_i	*Holding cost* C_{1i}	*Annual demand*
1	₹ 50	20	₹ 0.20	5,000
2	100	10	0.10	10,000
3	20	10	0.10	5,000
4	90	5	0.20	7,500

Find the economic lot sizes if the total number of orders per year for the four items is limited to 200 only.

4. A small shop produces three machine parts 1, 2 and 3 in lots. The shop has only 650 sq ft of storage space. The appropriate data for three items are presented in the following table:

Item	1	2	3
Demand rate (units/year)	5,000	2,000	10,000
Procurement cost (₹)	100	200	75
Cost per unit (₹)	10	15	5
Floor space required (sq. ft/unit)	0.70	0.80	0.40

The carrying charges on each item are 20% of average inventory evaluation per annum. If no stock-outs are allowed, determine the optimal lot size for each item. [*DOEACC, 1995*]

12.9 FORECASTING OF DEMAND

Forecasting is the projection of the past data into future and, therefore, it has a wide field of applications. Implicit in forecasting is that there exists a pattern in the past demand data which can be extrapolated or generalised for the future with the desired measure of certainty. The word 'pattern' here requires a little elaboration. The demand of a period may be such that it can be related to that of the previous periods. In other words, the demand may have a regular time-dependent behaviour, *viz.,* stationary, rising, falling or seasonal. However, there may be cases where demand may be widely fluctuating. It may be 10 in January, 165 in February and drop down to 33 in March. There is no time-dependent pattern here *i.e.,* the demand is not regular. However even this widely fluctuating demand may be *stable* in the sense that its frequency distribution may conform to a standard distribution such as Poisson or Gamma. Such a demand pattern, though not regular, is stable in statistical sense. Forecasting can, therefore, be classified into:

1. Time Series Forecasting.
2. Probability Distribution Forecasting.

Since an inventory control problem is concerned with the two factors–when to order and how much to order, forecasting finds applicability in determination of both these parameters. It may be noted that in inventory control our concern is with short-term forecasting, over a month, week or even a day so as to ultimately fix the reorder level for each item.

12.10 FORECASTING METHODS

Forecasting methods consist of deriving suitable mathematical equations to describe the significant demand pattern. A forecasting method should fulfil the following general requirements:

1. It should describe the underlying pattern as quickly as possible.
2. Computations should be as easy as possible, especially in view of a large number of items which have to be handled even in a small organisation. It should, therefore, be possible to compute forecasts cheaply as well as quickly.
3. It should be possible to clearly spell out the forecasting technique so that computations can be carried out routinely by a computer or manually.
4. The number of involved variables should be small so that the storage space required in computer is minimum.
5. The forecasting model should be responsive to the demand behaviour and should quickly attune itself to the changed demand level. If the demand behaviour, hitherto more or less stable, starts fluctuating, the forecasting model should give lesser consideration to the older demand observations and more to the recent ones.

The various forecasting methods used in the context of inventory control will now be discussed.

12.10-1 Moving Average Method for Forecasting

This method can be used if the underlying demand pattern is stationary *i.e.*, having a constant mean level. It is logical to assume that as we go back in time, the older observations will have progressively less relevance to future forecasts. This is implicit in all the forecasting models. The moving average method accomplishes this rather crudely by averaging the data of a few recent periods and ignoring the older observations. Equal weightage is assigned to all the periods chosen for averaging.

Let m_t = moving average at time t,
y_t = demand in time t, and
n = moving average period.

Then
$$m_t = \frac{y_t + y_{t-1} + y_{t-2} + \ldots + y_{t-(n-1)}}{n} = \frac{1}{n} \sum_{x=t-n+1}^{t} y_x$$

$$\therefore \quad m_{t+1} = \frac{1}{n}\,[y_{t+1} + y_t + y_{t-1} + \ldots + y_{t-(n-2)}]$$

$$= \frac{1}{n}\,[y_{t+1} + (y_t + y_{t-1} + \ldots + y_{t-n+2} + y_{t-n+1}) - y_{t-n+1}]$$

$$= \frac{1}{n}\,[y_{t+1} + n\,.\,m_t - y_{t-n-1}]$$

$$= m_t + \frac{y_{t+1} - y_{t-n+1}}{n}$$

Thus the moving average at any time period is obtained by adding to the previous moving average, the contribution made by the demand in this period and subtracting the contribution made by the oldest demand.

The choice of n, the moving average period, is confronted with two conflicting considerations. A higher value of n results in better smoothing but it involves increased amount of historical data to be manipulated for forecasting purposes. There has to be a suitable compromise between these two considerations.

This method suffers from the following two drawbacks :

1. The moving average period, n has to be quite long for better results.
2. If the demand, instead of being stationary, depicts trends, the forecasts provided by this method will lag the original demand.

Hence this method is not favoured for inventory control and a far more versatile method—exponential smoothed average model is normally used. If a series has demand values of 40, 48, 54, 62, then

$$\text{moving average} = \frac{1}{4}\ (40 + 48 + 54 + 62) = \frac{1}{4}\ (204) = 51.$$

12.10-2 Exponential Smoothed Average Method

In the foregoing example, moving average

$$= \frac{1}{4}\ (40 + 48 + 54 + 62)$$
$$= \frac{1}{4} \times 40 + \frac{1}{4} \times 48 + \frac{1}{4} \times 54 + \frac{1}{4} \times 62$$
$$= W_1 \times 40 + W_2 \times 48 + W_3 \times 54 + W_4 \times 62,$$

where the weightages W_1, W_2, W_3 and W_4 assigned to each observation are equal and $\frac{1}{4}$ each, which is the reciprocal of the moving averages period. Since the sum of W_1, W_2, W_3 and W_4 is unity, the moving average is a *true* average.

Exponential smoothing is also an average in this sense. The most recent observation is attached the highest weightage and it decreases in geometric progression as we move towards the older observations. Ratio of the two consecutive weights here is $(1 - \alpha)$, where α is called *smoothing coefficient* whose value lies between 0 and 1. The exponential smoothed average u_t, which is the forecast for the next period $(t + 1)$ is computed as below.

Observation at period t (1)	*Assigned weightages* (2)	*Column* (3) = (1) × (2)
y_t	α	αy_t
y_{t-1}	$\alpha\ (1 - \alpha)$	$\alpha\ (1 - \alpha) y_{t-1}$
$\vdots$	$\vdots$	$\vdots$
y_{t-n}	$\alpha\ (1 - \alpha)^n$	$\alpha\ (1 - \alpha)^n\ y_{t-n}$
$\vdots$	$\vdots$	$\vdots$
$-\infty$	$-\infty$	0
		Sum = u_t

As the weightages in column (2) are decaying exponentially, the method is termed as the exponential smoothed average. To be of any practical use, the above expression for u_t has to be considerably simplified as follows:

$$\begin{aligned} u_t &= \alpha y_t + \alpha\ (1 - \alpha)\ y_{t-1} + \ldots\ \alpha\ (1 - \alpha)^n\ y_{t-n} + \ldots\infty \\ &= \alpha y_t + (1 - \alpha)\ [\alpha y_{t-1} + \alpha\ (1 - \alpha) y_{t-2} + \ldots + \alpha\ (1 - \alpha)^n\ y_{t-(n-1)} + \ldots] \\ &= \alpha y_t + (1 - \alpha)\ u_{t-1} \\ &= u_{t-1} + \alpha\ (y_t - u_{t-1}) \\ &= u_{t-1} + \alpha e_t, \end{aligned} \quad \ldots(12.59)$$

where $e_t = (y_t - u_{t-1})$ is called *error* and is the difference between the latest observation, y_t and its forecast a period earlier, u_{t-1}.

The computational procedure for finding u_t, thus, consists of the following steps :

1. Compute error e_t by subtracting the previous forecast from the latest observation.
2. Multiply error e_t by α. This is the correction to be applied to the past average.
3. Add this correction to the past average, u_{t-1}. This gives new average u_t as the forecast for the next period.

It was stated earlier that values of α lie between 0 and 1. When $\alpha = 0$, $\alpha e_t = 0$ which means that no account is taken of any difference between latest incoming observation and its forecast a period earlier. When $\alpha = 1$, correction $u_t = y_t$ which means that the latest incoming observation itself is taken as the forecast for the next period and the earlier observations are completely ignored.

Thus a low value of α gives more weightage to the past series and less weightage to the latest observation. Lower values α are, therefore, to be used when the series is rather stable and higher values when the series is rather fluctuating.

EXAMPLE 12.10-2.1

An initial forecast of 28 is given. If $\alpha = 0.1$, smooth exponentially the following series:
30, 30, 23, 28, 25, 24, 29, 25.

Solution

The computations are given in table 12.3 which is self-explanatory.

TABLE 12.3

S.No.	*Observation* y_t *(1)*	*Error* $e_t = y_t - u_{t-1}$ *(2) = (1) – (4)*	*Correction* αe_t *(3) = (2) × 0.1*	*Forecast* $u_t = u_{t-1} + \alpha e_t$ *(4) Initial = 28*
1	30	30 – 28 = 2	0.20	28.20
2	30	30 – 28.2 = 1.8	0.18	28.38
3	23	23 – 28.38 = – 5.38	– 0.54	27.84
4	28	28 – 27.84 = 0.16	0.02	27.86
5	25	25 – 27.86 = – 2.86	– 0.29	27.57
6	24	24 – 27.57 = – 3.57	– 0.36	27.21
7	29	29 – 27.21 = 1.79	0.18	27.39
8	25	25 – 27.39 = – 2.39	– 0.24	27.15

It can be observed from column (4) that the forecasts are fairly close to the given observations which are fluctuating around a stationary level of about 27. If the given series were depicting some trend, the forecasts would not have been so close to the observations and there would have been a systematic bias. The exponential smoothing method would not be much helpful in such a case.

12.10-3 Exponential Smoothed Average Method with Trend Correction

When the demand is depicting some trend *e.g.*, ramp or stepped or impulse increase, a *trend factor* λ_t, must also be considered in computations. The following equations (written without proof) may be used in such a case :

$$u_t = u_{t-1} + \alpha\,(y_t - u_{t-1}), \quad \text{...(12.60)}$$

$$\lambda_t = \alpha\,(u_t - u_{t-1}) + (1 - \alpha)\,\lambda_{t-1}, \quad \text{...(12.61)}$$

$$u'_t = u_t + \left(\frac{1-\alpha}{\alpha} + 1\right) . \lambda_t, \quad \text{...(12.62)}$$

where λ_{t-1} and λ_t are the initial trend and smoothed trend respectively. The computations for finding the exponential smoothed forecasts will be explained with the help of an example.

EXAMPLE 12.10-3.1

Find the exponential smoothed forecasts with trend correction for the sales data in column (2) of table 12.4. Assume

initial trend, $\lambda_0 = -2.00$,
initial average, $u_0 = 500$, $\alpha = 0.1$.

TABLE 12.4

Period (1)	*Sales* y_t (2)	*Smoothed average* u_t (3)	*Smoothed trend* λ_t (4)	*Forecast* u'_t (5)	*Forecast error* (5) – (2)
0	—	500	– 2.00	—	—
1	515	501.5	– 1.65	—	—
2	505	501.85	– 1.45	485.0	– 20
3	480	499.67	– 3.48	487.35	7.35
4	510	500.70	– 3.03	464.87	– 45.13
5	525	498.27	– 2.97	470.40	– 54.60
6	550	493.10	– 3:19	468.57	– 81.43

Solution

Equations (12.91), (12.92) and (12.93) are used to fill up the remaining columns of table 12.4.

For period 1 :

$u_1 = u_0 + \alpha\,(y_1 - u_0).$

Now $u_0 = 500,\ y_1 = 515$ and $\alpha = 0.1$.

$\therefore\quad u_1 = 500 + 0.1\,(515 - 500) = 500 + 1.5 = 501.5.$

$\lambda_1 = \alpha\,(u_1 - u_0) + (1 - \alpha)\,\lambda_0 = 0.1\,(501.5 - 500) + 0.9 \times (-2.00) = -1.65,$

$u'_1 = u_1 + \left(\dfrac{1-\alpha}{\alpha} + 1\right)\lambda_1 = 501.5 + 10\,(-1.65) = 485.0,$

$e_1 = 485 - 505 = -20.$

For period 2 :

$u_2 = u_1 + \alpha\,(y_2 - u_1) = 501.5 + 0.1\,(505 - 501.5) = 501.85,$

$\lambda_2 = \alpha\,(u_2 - u_1) + (1 - \alpha)\,\lambda_1 = 0.1\,(501.85 - 501.5) + 0.9\,(-1.65) = -1.45,$

$u'_2 = u_2 + 10\lambda_2 = 501.85 - 10 \times 1.45 = 487.35,$

$e_2 = 487.35 - 480 = 7.35.$

For period 3 :

$u_3 = u_2 + \alpha\,(y_3 - u_2) = 501.85 + 0.1\,(480 - 501.85) = 499.67,$

$\lambda_3 = \alpha\,(u_3 - u_2) + (1 - \alpha)\,\lambda_2 = 0.1\,(499.67 - 501.85) + 0.9\,(-1.45) = -3.48,$

$u'_3 = u_3 + 10\,\lambda_3 = 499.67 - 10 \times 3.48 = 464.87,$

$e_3 = 464.87 - 510 = -45.13.$

For period 4 :

$u_4 = u_3 + \alpha\,(y_4 - u_3) = 499.67 + 0.1\,(510 - 499.67) = 500.70,$

$\lambda_4 = \alpha\,(u_4 - u_3) + (1 - \alpha)\,\lambda_3 = 0.1\,(500.70 - 499.67) + 0.9\,(-3.48) = -3.03,$

$u'_4 = u_4 + 10\lambda_4 = 500.70 - 10 \times 3.03 = 470.40,$

$e_4 = 470.40 - 525 = -54.60.$

For period 5 :

$u_5 = u_4 - \alpha\,(y_5 - u_4) = 500.70 - 0.1\,(525 - 500.70) = 498.27,$

$\lambda_5 = \alpha\,(u_5 - u_4) + (1 - \alpha)\,\lambda_4 = 0.1\,(498.27 - 500.70) + 0.9\,(-3.03) = -2.97,$

$u'_5 = u_5 + 10\lambda_5 = 498.27 - 10 \times 2.97 = 468.57,$

$e_5 = 468.57 - 550 = -81.43.$

For period 6 :

$u_6 = u_5 - \alpha\,(y_6 - u_5) = 498.27 - 0.1\,(550 - 498.27) = 493.10,$

$\lambda_6 = \alpha\,(u_6 - u_5) + (1 - \alpha)\,\lambda_5 = 0.1\,(493.10 - 498.27) + 0.9\,(-2.97) = -3.19,$

$u'_6 = u_6 + 10\lambda_6 = 493.10 - 10 \times 3.19 = 461.20.$

12.11 WHEN TO ORDER

When the stock, being continuously depleted by the customers' demand, reaches the reorder level, an order of fixed size q is placed.

Lead time or Delivery Lag : *The time interval between placement of an order and receipt of goods against it is called lead time.* It is normally short in case of local supplier or off-the-shelf items and greater for made-to-order or out-station supplier. Lead time may not be a constant and is usually not so. For the same item and the same supplier it can vary from stage to stage. Lead time may, therefore, be a stochastic variable. This complicates the problem of accumulating the forecasts of demand over the period encompassed by the lead time. Lead time may also be exponentially forecast as is done for demand.

However, because of the mathematical complexities involved, it may be assumed to be a constant.

Reorder Level : *It is the stock level at which fresh orders should be placed with the suppliers for procuring additional inventory equal to the economic order quantity.* R.O.L. is so fixed that the customers can be 'reasonably' served from this stock until the replenishment of size q arrives against the order placed (Fig. 12.12). So the problem of when to order reduces to fixing R.O.L. with the operating policy that as the stocks cross this level an order is placed (on the vendor or within the works, of which the size is predetermined and fixed.)

We have already discussed the exponential smoothing method for demand. This method is particularly suitable for short-term forecasting, especially when several hundred or thousand items are involved. These short-term forecasts have, then, to be extended over the period encompassed by the lead time. For example, if the lead time is 2 months, we will have to accumulate the next 2 months' forecasts in order to find the forecast lead time demand.

R.O.L. = Lead time demand (LTD).

When the demand pattern is almost stationary and depicts no trend or seasonal variations,

$$\text{Lead time demand} = \text{Lead time} \times \text{average demand (LT} \times \text{R)} \quad ...(12.63)$$

$$\therefore \quad \text{R.O.L.} = \text{Lead time} \times \text{average demand.} \quad ...(12.64)$$

If the safety stock is provided, R.O.L. is given by,

$$\text{R.O.L.} = \text{Lead time demand} + \text{Safety stock (LTD + SS).} \quad ...(12.65)$$

Further, if time T is required for reviewing the system,

$$\text{R.O.L.} = \text{LTD} + \text{SS} + \frac{\text{R.T}}{2}. \quad ...(12.66)$$

If there is provision of safety stock,

$$\text{maximum inventory} = q + \text{SS}, \quad ...(12.67)$$

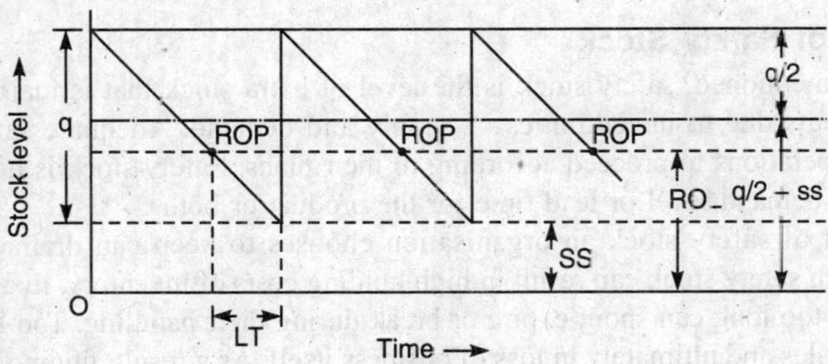

Fig. 12.12

$$\text{minimum inventory} = \text{SS}, \quad ...(12.68)$$

$$\text{average inventory} = \frac{\text{SS} + (q + \text{SS})}{2} = \frac{q}{2} + \text{SS}. \quad ...(12.69)$$

Fig. 12.12 represents an ideal inventory model wherein the actual demand is same as expected demand and there are no variations from the forecasts. Here, the moment the stock level (being depleted) reaches the R.O.L., order of the fixed size q (= EOQ) is placed; these points have been marked as reorder points (ROP). As soon as the stock level reaches the safety stock, the supplies are received, the stock level, thereby, reaching the maximum level q + SS.

However, a realistic inventory situation would look like the one depicted in Fig. 12.13. In this demand is not uniform. Three inventory cycles are shown. In the first cycle lead time demand (LTD) is just equal to the expected demand and as soon as the stock level reaches safety stock, fresh supplies are received. In the second cycle, lead time demand is more than the expected demand and, therefore, safety stock is used. The third cycle represents a condition where LTD is less than the expected demand.

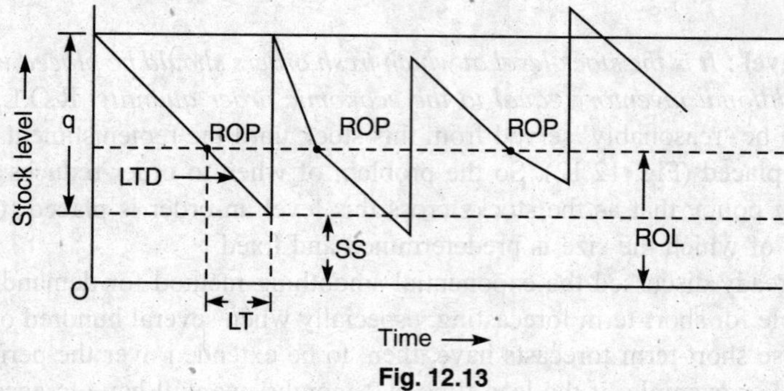

Fig. 12.13

Safety Stock : *Lead time demand is the stock level, which on the average, is sufficient to fill customers' orders as the stocks are being replenished.* 'On the average' implies that during this period of replenishment, 50% of the customers' orders can be filled while 50% may be either refused or back-ordered to be filled later. It is because the actual demand may be different from the predicted value. When R.O.L. = lead time demand, only 50% of the orders are expected to be filled during the replenishment period. This may not be acceptable to the management who may like to limit the 'disservice' to the customers down to 5 % or 10% at the cost of extra stocking. *This extra stock in excess of the lead time demand is called the safety stock* (or *buffer stock* or *cushion stock*).

Since safety stock is used only sparingly in extraordinary situations when the lead time demand exceeds the forecast demand, its amount must be judiciously decided. Its optimum value is determined by balancing its holding cost with the stock-out cost which may result if it is not provided.

Determination of Safety Stock

As already mentioned, safety stock is the level of extra stock that is maintained to reduce the risk of stockouts due to uncertainties of supply and demand. Adequate safety stock levels permit business operations to proceed according to their plans. Safety stock is held when there is uncertainty in the demand level or lead time for the product or both.

The amount of safety stock an organisation chooses to keep can dramatically affect its business. Too much safety stock can result in high holding costs of inventory. In addition, products that are stored for too long can spoil, expire or break during their handling. Too little safety stock can result in lost sales and ultimately in loss of business itself. As a result, finding the right balance between too much and too little safety stock is essential.

Safety stock is determined in one of the following manners:

1. In case demand rate varies but lead time remains constant,

$$\text{safety stock, S.S.} = (\text{maximum demand rate} - \text{average demand rate}) \times \text{lead time.} \quad \ldots(12.70)$$

2. In case lead time varies but demand rate remains constant,

$$\text{S.S.} = (\text{maximum lead time} - \text{average lead time}) \times \text{demand rate.} \qquad ...(12.71)$$

3. In case both demand rate and lead time vary,

$$\text{S.S.} = (\text{maximum demand rate} \times \text{maximum lead time}) - (\text{average demand rate} \times \text{average lead time}). \qquad ...(12.72)$$

4. If demand of a product is normally distributed with mean M and standard deviation σ_d and lead time is LT and service level is given, then for the given service level, service factor Z can be determined from table C-2 (towards the end of the book) and safety stock is given by

$$\text{S.S.} = Z \,.\, \sigma_d \,.\, \sqrt{\text{LT}}. \qquad ...(12.73)$$

5. Sometimes instead of standard deviation of demand, mean absolute deviation (MAD) of demand may be given. Then

$$\text{standard deviation, } \sigma_d = \sqrt{\frac{\pi}{2}} \,.\, \text{MAD}. \qquad ...(12.74)$$

$$\therefore \quad \text{Safety stock, S.S.} = Z \,.\, \sigma_d \,.\, \sqrt{\text{LT}},$$

$$\text{and reorder level, R.O.L.} = \text{M.LT} + \text{S.S.} = \text{M.LT} + Z \,.\, \sigma_d \,.\, \sqrt{\text{LT}}. \qquad ...(12.75)$$

The problem of 'when to order' is, therefore, to be solved statistically; the policy being to place an order when the depleting stocks cross the R.O.L. It is, therefore, necessary to fix R.O.L. and it is desirable to have a compromise between the inventory carrying costs and shortage costs due to disservice to the customers.

EXAMPLE 12.11-1

The average monthly consumption for an item is 300 units and the normal lead time is one month. If the maximum consumption has been upto 370 units per month and maximum lead time is $\frac{1}{2}$ months, what should be the buffer stock for the item ?

Solution

$$\text{Optimum buffer stock} = \text{Maximum lead lime demand} - \text{Normal lead time demand}$$

$$= \frac{3}{2} \times 370 - 1 \times 300 = 555 - 300 = 255 \text{ units.}$$

EXAMPLE 12.11-2

A firm uses every year 12,000 units of a raw material costing ₹ 1.25 per unit. Ordering cost is ₹ 15 per order and the holding cost is 5% per year of average inventory.

(i) Find the economic order quantity.

(ii) The firm follows E.O.Q. purchasing policy. It operates for 300 days per year. Procurement time is 14 days and safety stock is 400 units. Find the reorder point, the maximum inventory and the average inventory. [*Meerut M. Com., 1975*]

Solution

(i)

$$\text{E.O.Q.} = q_0 = \sqrt{\frac{2C_3R}{C_1}} = \sqrt{\frac{2 \times 15 \times 12{,}000}{5/100 \times 1.25}} = \sqrt{\frac{2 \times 15 \times 12{,}000 \times 100}{5 \times 1.25}}$$

$$= 2{,}400 \text{ units.}$$

(ii)

$$\text{Reorder level} = \text{safety stock} + \text{consumption during normal lead time}$$

$$= 400 + 14 \times \frac{12{,}000}{300} = 960 \text{ units.}$$

(*iii*) Maximum inventory = q_0 + S.S. = 2,400 + 400 = 2,800 units.

(*iv*) Minimum inventory = S.S. = 400 units.

$$\therefore \quad \text{Average Inventory} = \frac{2,800 + 400}{2} = 1,600 \text{ units.}$$

EXAMPLE 12.11-3

Calculate the various parameters for putting an item with following data on E.O.Q. system:

Annual consumption = 12,000 units at the cost of ₹ 7.50 per unit.

Setup cost = ₹ 6.00 and inventory holding cost = ₹ 0.12 per unit.

Normal lead time = 15 days and maximum lead time = 20 days.

[*NIIFT Mohali, 2000*]

Solution

The various parameters to be calculated for putting an item on E.O.Q. system are :

(*i*)
$$\text{E.O.Q.} = q_0 = \sqrt{\frac{2C_3R}{C_1}} = \sqrt{\frac{2 \times 6 \times 12,000}{0.12}} = 1,096 \text{ units.}$$

(*ii*)
$$\text{Optimum safety stock, S.S.} = \frac{(20-15)}{30} \times \frac{12,000}{12} = 167 \text{ units.}$$

(*iii*)
$$\text{R.O.L.} = \text{S.S.} + \text{consumption during normal lead time}$$
$$= 167 + \frac{15}{30 \times 12} \times 12,000 = 167 + 500 = 667 \text{ units.}$$

EXAMPLE 12.11-4

The following information is provided for an item:

Annual usage = 12,000 units, ordering costs = ₹ 60 per order, carrying costs 10%, unit cost of item = ₹ 10 and lead time = 10 days.

There are 300 working days/year. Determine E.O.Q. and number of orders per year. In the past two years the use rate has gone as high as 70 units per day. For a reordering system based on the inventory level, what should be the safety stock ? What should be the reorder level at this safety stock ? What would be the carrying costs for a year ?

[*Gujarat Tech. U.B.E. Dec., 2012*]

Solution

Here, C_3 = ₹ 60/order, R = 12,000 units/year,

$$C_1 = CI = ₹\ 10 \times \frac{10}{100} = ₹\ 1/\text{item/year.}$$

$$\therefore \quad \text{E.O.Q.} = q_0 = \sqrt{\frac{2C_3R}{C_1}} = \sqrt{\frac{2 \times 60 \times 12,000}{1}} = 1,200.$$

$$\text{No. of orders/year} = \frac{12,000}{1,200} = 10.$$

$$\text{Average usage} = \frac{12,000}{300} = 40 \text{ units/day.}$$

Maximum usage = 70 units/day.

∴ Safety stock = (70 – 40) × 10 = 300 units.

R.O.L. = Average lead time demand + S.S. = 40 × 10 + 300 = 700 units.

$$\text{Average inventory} = \frac{q_0}{2} + \text{S.S.} = \frac{1,200}{2} + 300 = 900 \text{ units.}$$

$$\therefore \text{Inventory carrying costs/year} = ₹\ 900 \times 10 \times \frac{10}{100} = ₹\ 900.$$

EXAMPLE 12.11-5

An automobile company has determined that 16 spare engines will result in a stock-out risk of 25% while 20 will reduce the risk to 15% and 24 to 10%. If the lead time is 3 months and the average usage is 6 engines/month. what should be the R.O.L. to maintain 85% service level?

Solution

Lead time demand = 3 × 6 = 18 engines.

Safety stock for 85% service or 15% disservice = 20 engines.

∴ R.O.L. = 18 + 20 = 38 engines.

EXAMPLE 12.11-6

A firm has normally distributed forecast of usage with MAD = 60 units. It desires a service level which limits stock-outs to one order cycle per year.

(a) How much safety stock should be kept if the order quantity is normally a week's supply?

(b) What will be the safety stock if the order quantity is 4 weeks' supply ?

Solution

(*a*) No. of orders/year = 52.

Since there is 1 stock-out per year, service level = $\frac{52-1}{52} \times 100 = 98\%$.

∴ Service factor Z = 2.05. (From table C-2 in the appendix)

Now $\sigma_d = \text{S.D.} = \sqrt{\frac{\pi}{2}}\,.\,\text{MAD} = \sqrt{\frac{\pi}{2}} \times 60 = 75 \text{ units}$

And $\text{S.S.} = Z\,.\,\sigma_d.$

∴ S.S. = 2.05 × 75 = 154 units.

(*b*) No. of orders/year = $\frac{52}{4} = 13$.

∴ Service level = $\frac{13-1}{13} \times 100 = 92.3\%$.

Service factor Z from table C-2 = 1.43.

Now $Z = \frac{\text{S.S.}}{\text{S.D.}}$

∴ S.S. = 1.43 × 75 = 107 units.

EXAMPLE 12.11-7

The average demand for an item is 120 units/year. The lead time is 1 month and the demand during lead time follows normal distribution with average of 10 units and standard deviation of 2 units. If the item is ordered once in 4 months and the policy of the company is that there should not be more than 1 stock-out every two years, determine the reorder level.

Solution

No. of orders in 2 years = $\frac{1}{4} \times (2 \times 12) = 6$.

∴ % service = $\frac{6-1}{6} \times 100 = 83.33$.

∴ Z from table C-2 = 0.97.

Now $\text{S.S.} = Z\,.\,\sigma_d.$

∴ S.S. = 0.97 × 2 = 1.94.

∴ R.O.L. = Lead time demand + S.S.

= 1 × 10 + 1.94 = 11.94 units.

EXAMPLE 12.11-8

A look at the past records gives the following distribution for lead time and daily demand during lead time:

Lead time distribution

Lead time (days)	:	0	1	2	3	4	5	6	7	8	9	10
Frequency	:	0	0	1	2	3	4	4	3	2	2	1

Demand rate distribution

Demand/day (units)	:	0	1	2	3	4	5	6	7
Frequency	:	3	5	4	5	2	3	2	1

What should be the buffer stock ?

Solution

First let us compute the average lead time.

Lead time (1)	*Frequency* (2)	*Col. (1) × Col. (2)* (3)
1	0	0
2	1	2
3	2	6
4	3	12
5	4	20
6	4	24
7	3	21
8	2	16
9	2	18
10	1	10
	22	129

$$\therefore \quad \text{Average lead time} = \frac{129}{22} = 5.86 \text{ days.}$$

Let us now compute the average demand rate.

Demand (1)	*Frequency* (2)	*Col.(1) × Col. (2)* (3)
0	3	0
1	5	5
2	4	8
3	5	15
4	2	8
5	3	15
6	2	12
7	1	7
	25	70

$$\therefore \quad \text{Average demand rate} = \frac{70}{25} = 2.8.$$

$\therefore$ Average lead time demand = 5.86 × 2.8 = 16.4 units.

Maximum lead time demand = Maximum lead time × Maximum demand rate

= 10 × 7 = 70 units.

$\therefore$ Buffer stock = 70 – 16.4 = 53.6 units.

EXAMPLE 12.11-9

A hotel is using around 400 napkins every day. The actual number varies with the guests on any day. Usage can be approximated by normal distribution with mean 400 and standard deviation of 9 napkins per day. The lead time is 3 days. If the hotel policy is to maintain the stockout risk to 5%, what is the number of napkins that must be on hand at reorder time and what would be the safety stock ?

[*Dayalbagh Edu. Inst. Agra BBM May, 2011*]

Solution

Here, M = R = 400 napkins/day, standard deviation, σ_d = 9 napkins/day, LT = 3 days.

Stockout risk = 5%. ∴ Service level = 95%.

From table C-2, service factor, Z = 1.645.

∴ Safety stock, S.S. = $Z \,.\, \sigma_d \,.\, \sqrt{LT} = 1.645 \times 9 \times \sqrt{3} = 26$ napkins.

∴ Reorder level, R.O.L. = Lead time demand + S.S.

= Average demand rate × lead time + S.S. = 400 × 3 + 26 = 1,226 napkins.

EXAMPLE 12.11-10

The demand per month for a product is distributed normally with a mean of 100 and standard deviation 25. The lead time distribution is given below. What service level will be afforded by a reorder level of 500 units ?

Lead time (months)	*Probability*
1	*0.10*
2	*0.20*
3	*0.40*
4	*0.20*
5	*0.10*

[*P.T.U. B.Tech. (Mech.) 2009; C.A. May, 1989*]

Solution

Here, mean M = 100 units, σ_d = 25 units, reorder level R.O.L. = 500 units.

Now
$$\text{R.O.L.} = \text{M.LT} + Z \,.\, \sigma_d \,.\, \sqrt{\text{LT}}.$$

∴ Safety factor,
$$Z = \frac{\text{R.O.L.} - \text{M.LT}}{\sigma_d \sqrt{\text{LT}}}.$$

This is calculated below for various values of lead time by using the iterative procedure:

TABLE 12.5

Lead time (months)	*Value of Z*	*Probability of service rendered (From table C-2)*	*Probability of lead time*	*Conditional prob. of expected service level*
1	$\frac{500 - 100 \times 1}{25\sqrt{1}} = 16$	100	0.10	10.0
2	$\frac{500 - 100 \times 2}{25\sqrt{2}} = 8.48$	100	0.20	20.0
3	$\frac{500 - 100 \times 3}{25\sqrt{3}} = 4.62$	100	0.40	40.0
4	$\frac{500 - 100 \times 4}{25\sqrt{4}} = 2.0$	97.7	0.20	19.54
5	$\frac{500 - 100 \times 5}{25\sqrt{5}} = 0$	50.0	0.10	50.0
		Total :		94.54

∴ Reorder level of 500 units will give a service level of 94.54%.

EXAMPLE 12.11-11

A drugstore stocks a popular brand of sunscreen. The average demand for the sunscreen is 6 bottles per day, with a standard deviation of 1.2 bottles. A vendor for the sunscreen producer checks the drugstore stock every 60 days. During one visit the drugstore had 8 bottles in stock. The lead time to receive an order is 5 days. Determine the order size for this period order that will enable the drugstore to maintain a 95% service level.

[*Dayalbagh Edu. Inst. Agra MBA May, 2010*]

Solution

Average demand , d = 6 bottles / day,
standard deviation, σ_d = 1.2 bottles,
time between checks, T = 60 days,
stock at hand, S = 8 bottles,
lead time, LT = 5 days,
service level = 0.95. ∴ Z = 1.65. (From table C-2)

$$\text{Order size} = d(LT+T)+Z\sqrt{LT+T}\,.\,\sigma_d - S$$
$$= 6\,(5+60)+1.65\sqrt{5+60}\times 1.2-8$$
$$= 390+1.65\times\sqrt{65}\times 1.2-8$$
$$= 390+15.96-8 = 397.96 \simeq 398 \text{ bottles.}$$

EXAMPLE 12.11-12

A company has compiled the following information regarding a component it wants to purchase:

The average usage is 120 units per day with standard deviation of 50 units per day based on the plant operating for 250 days per year. The acquisition cost per order is ₹ 20. Inventory holding cost is ₹ 1 per unit per year and the acquisition lead time is constant at 10 days. The company has determined the allowable stock-outs per year to be one. Using the information, determine

(i) the economic order quantity,
(ii) the required safety stock and the reorder level.

[*P.T.U.B.Tech. May, 2011*]

Solution

Here, R = 120 × 250 = 30,000 units/year,
C_3 = ₹ 20/order,
C_1 = ₹ 1/unit/year.

(*i*) ∴ $$\text{E.O.Q.} = \sqrt{\frac{2C_3R}{C_1}} = \sqrt{\frac{2\times 20\times 30{,}000}{1}} = 1095.45 \text{ units/order.}$$

(*ii*) Lead time = 10 days,
Standard deviation of daily demand = 50 units.
With E.O.Q. of 1095.45 units, the number of orders during the year

$$n_0 = \frac{30{,}000}{1095.45} = 27.386.$$

Since the company allows one stockout during the year, the service factor

$$= \frac{27.386-1}{27.386} = 0.9635.$$

For service level (probability of meeting the customer's demand) of 0.9635, the service factor or the normal deviate Z, as found from table C-2 is 1.79.

Now safety stock = $Z\,.\,\sigma_d\,.\,\sqrt{\text{LT}} = 1.79\times 50\times\sqrt{10} = 1.79\times 158.114 = 283$ units.
Reorder level = Expected demand during lead time + safety stock
= 120 × 10 + 283 = 1,483 units.

12.12 SELECTIVE INVENTORY MANAGEMENT TECHNIQUES

The inventory of an industrial organisation consists of hundreds and even thousands of items having widely varying costs, usage and lead time together with procurement and/or technical problems. It is neither desirable nor possible to exercise the same degree of control over all these items. The management should pay more attention to items whose usage value is high and less attention to items having low usage value. The organisation should, therefore, be selective in its approach towards inventory control and the techniques used are called selective inventory control techniques.

12.12-1 ABC Analysis

The ABC analysis is based on *Pareto's law* that a few high usage value items constitute a major part of the capital invested in inventories, whereas bulk of items having low usage value constitute insignificant part of the capital.

It contemplates to classify all the inventory items into three categories based on their usage values. Items of high usage value but small in number are classified as 'A' items and would be under strict control of top level management. 'C' items are large in number but require little capital and would be under simple control. Items of moderate value and size are classified as 'B' items and would attract reasonable attention of the middle level management. ABC analysis (Always Better Control analysis) is also known as *'control by importance and exception'* and *'proportional value analysis'*.

It has been found that normal inventory items in most organisations show the following distribution patterns:

A : 5 to 10% of the total number of items accounting for 70 to 80% of the annual usage value,

B : 10 to 20% accounting for about 15 to 20% of the annual usage value, and

C : 70 to 80% of the number of items accounting for 5 to 15% of the annual usage value.

In view of the several hundred and even thousand items stocked in most inventory situations, the ABC analysis may be carried out on a sample. Once a random sample has been obtained, the following steps may be performed for the ABC analysis:

1. Find the annual usage value of every item in the sample by multiplying the annual requirement by its unit cost.
2. Arrange these items in descending order of usage value computed above.
3. Accumulate the total number of items and the usage value.
4. Convert the accumulated totals of number of items and usage values into percentage of the grand totals.
5. Plot the two percentages on the graph paper (Fig. 12.14). The curve obtained is called *ABC distribution curve* or *Pareto curve* or *Lorentz curve* or the *curve of maldistribution*.
6. Mark the cut-off points X_1 and Y_1 where the curve changes its slope, dividing it into three segments A, B and C. These segments A, B and C for the sample are then generalised over the entire population of stock items.

Under ABC analysis, an organisation would devote much time and effort in the control of 'A' items. Extra care will be taken for determining the minimum and maximum inventory levels and reorder level etc. of the 'A' items whereas so much control may not be exercised on 'C' items. 'A' items have high inventory carrying costs and should, therefore, be procured in smaller lots. *Fixed- interval inventory control system* may be used for these items. 'C' items such as paper clips, rubber bands, nails, nuts, etc. require very little capital and hence have low inventory carrying costs and should be bought in bigger lots so that there are fewer orders and hence lower acquisition cost and also to take advantage of quantity discounts for bulk purchases. A *fixed-order quantity system* may be used for such items. 'B' items are usually placed under statistical control and attract periodic control of the management. (*s, S*) *inventory control system* might be used for these items.

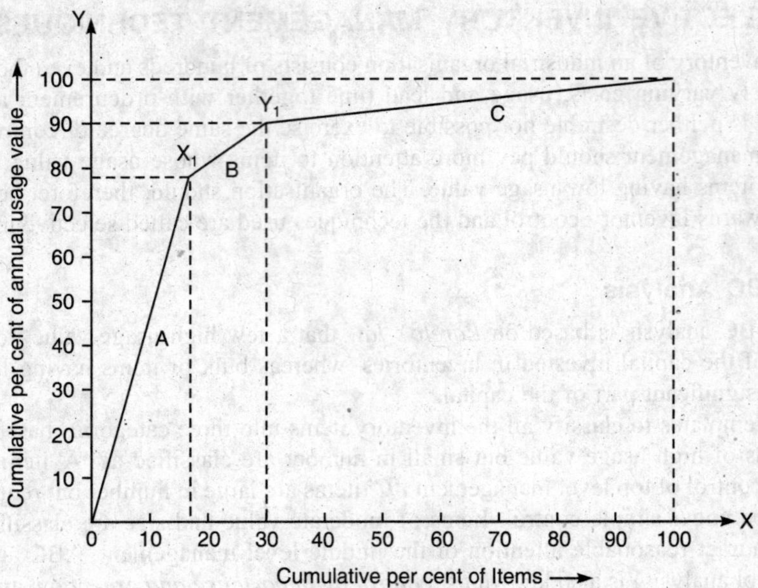

Fig. 12.14. ABC classification of items.

Computational procedure is illustrated in table 12.6.

TABLE 12.6

Item no.	*Annual usage (₹)*	*Cumulative annual usage (₹)*	*% of cumulative annual usage*	*% of total number of items*
1	10,000	10,000	10.00	0.2
2	9,000	19,000	19.00	0.4
3	9,000	28,000	28.00	0.6
⋮	⋮	⋮	⋮	⋮
40	8,000	60,000	60.00	8.0
41	8,000	68,000	68.00	8.2
42	7,000	75,000	75.00	8.4
⋮	⋮	⋮	⋮	⋮
160	400	90,000	90.00	32.0
161	300	90,300	90.30	32.2
162	200	90,500	90.50	32.4
⋮	⋮	⋮	⋮	⋮
498	100	99,860	99.86	99.6
499	80	99,940	99.94	99.8
500	60	1,00,000	100.00	100.0

Important Points for ABC Analysis

1. Whenever items can be substituted for each other, they should be considered as one item.
2. All items consumed by the organisation such as spares, raw materials, semi-finished and finished products must be considered together and then classified into the three categories A, B or C.
3. If required, there may be more than three categories and period of consumption may not be a year.

Advantages of ABC Analysis

1. ABC analysis is a dynamic procedure and must be repeated at least when the product mix changes.
2. It helps in exercising selective control over the items by concentrating efforts in areas where it is needed most. For instance, control over 'C' items may be relaxed even to the extent of dispensing with inventory records. For 'A' items the buffer stocks must be kept the absolute minimum and very careful attention is paid to their demand estimates, scheduling of deliveries, prompt receipt, immediate inspection and rapid flow through the factory.
3. It provides a more sound cost perspective to the management and enables them to assign priorities in cost reduction programme.
4. It avoids wastage of time and energy in making improvements in areas that yield only marginal benefits (class 'C' items).
5. It is used to control raw material, components and work-in-progress inventories.

Limitations of ABC Analysis

1. It ignores all aspects other than the annual usage value. For instance, factors such as market conditions, competitors, possible scarcities, lead time variations, seasonal variations, criticality of the item, etc., are not taken into consideration in carrying out the analysis.
2. If ABC analysis is not updated periodically, the real purpose of control may be defeated. For example, 'C' item like diesel oil in a firm, will become most high value item during power crisis.
3. Large stocks of 'C' items may cause problems of storage space limitations and higher losses due to deterioration, obsolescence and pilferage.
4. When large number and varieties of inventories are involved, it becomes very difficult to categorise them into just three categories.

EXAMPLE 12.12-1

The following information is known about a group of items. Classify the items as A, B and C.

TABLE 12.7

Item No.	*Annual consumption in pieces*	*Unit price in paise*
501	*30,000*	*10*
502	*2,80,000*	*15*
503	*3,000*	*10*
504	*1,10,000*	*5*
505	*4,000*	*5*
506	*2,20,000*	*10*
507	*15,000*	*5*
508	*80,000*	*5*
509	*60,000*	*15*
510	*8,000*	*10*

[*CA. (Final) May, 1980*]

Solution

The fIrst step is to compute the annual usage value for each item by multiplying the per unit price by the annual use and to rank them in the descending order of their annual usage values.

TABLE 12.8

Item no.	*Annual consumption in pieces*	*Unit price in paise*	*Annual usage value in ₹*	*Ranking*
501	30,000	10	3,000	6
502	2,80,000	15	42,000	1
503	3,000	10	300	9
504	1,10,000	5	5,500	4
505	4,000	5	200	10
506	2,20,000	10	22,000	2
507	15,000	5	750	8
508	80,000	5	4,000	5
509	60,000	15	9,000	3
510	8,000	10	800	7

The next step is to accumulate the total number of items and their usage values and then to convert the accumulated values into the percentages of the grand totals. This is done in table 12.9.

TABLE 12.9

Item no.	*Category*	*Annual usage (₹)*	*Cumulative annual usage (₹)*	*Cumulative usage percentage*	*Cumulative percentage of items*
502		42,000	42,000	48	10
506	A	22,000	64,000	73	20
509		9,000	73,000	83	30
504	B	5,500	78,500	90	40
508		4,000	82,500	94	50
501		3,000	85,500	98	60
510		800	86,300	98.6	70
507	C	750	87,050	99.4	80
503		300	87,350	99.8	90
505		200	87,550	100.0	100

The cumulative percentages of usage values and number of items are plotted in Fig. 12.15.

Mark the cut-off points X_1 and Y_1 where the curve changes its shape. This divides the curve into three segments A, B and C. It may also be noted from table 12.9 that the first two items have a large annual value, the next four, a moderate annual value and the remaining four, a small annual value. These may be categorised as 'A', 'B' and 'C' items respectively.

From Fig. 12.15 as well as table 12.9 it is clear that it is necessary to tightly control only 20% of the inventory items (the 'A' class) to achieve tight control over 73% of the total annual value of inventories. On the other hand, 40% of the items (the 'C' class) can be virtually ignored and still there will be loss of control over only less than 2% of the total annual value.

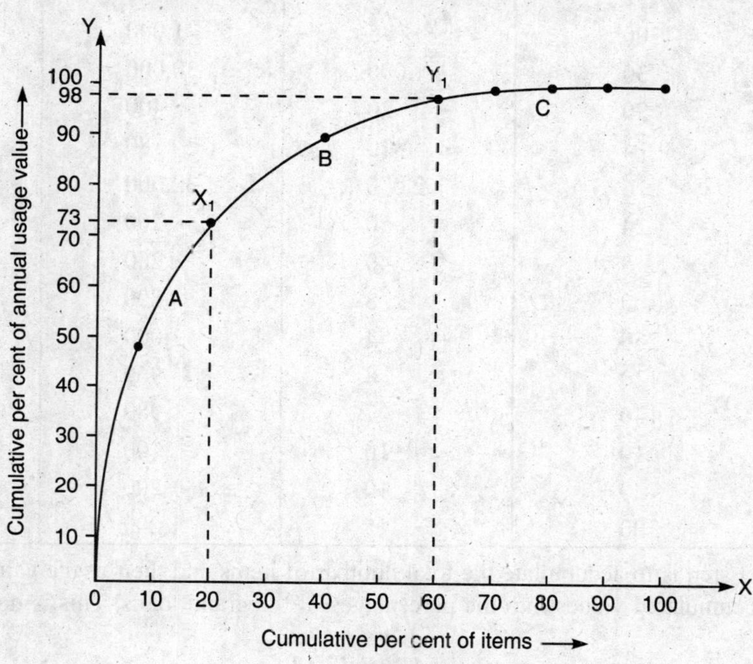

Fig. 12.15

EXAMPLE 12.12-2

Draw the ABC curve for the data given below:

TABLE 12.10

Item no.	*Quantity consumed in a year*	*Cost per unit (₹)*	*Item no.*	*Quantity consumed in a year*	*Cost per unit (₹)*
1	*2*	*40*	*9*	*100*	*8*
2	*200*	*5*	*10*	*250*	*4*
3	*30*	*1,000*	*11*	*120*	*8*
4	*20*	*20*	*12*	*140*	*7*
5	*4*	*20*	*13*	*10*	*10*
6	*16*	*2,000*	*14*	*20*	*10*
7	*24*	*50*	*15*	*200*	*5*
8	*5*	*40*			

[*ICWA (Final) Dec., 1991*]

Solution

The first step is to compute the annual usage value of each item and to rank them in the descending order of their annual usage values.

TABLE 12.11

Item No.	*Quantity consumed in a year*	*Cost per unit (₹)*	*Annual usage value (₹)*	*Ranking*
1	2	40	80	14
2	200	5	1,000	4
3	30	1,000	30,000	2
4	20	20	400	10
5	4	20	80	15
6	16	2,000	32,000	1
7	24	50	1,200	3
8	5	40	200	11
9	100	8	800	9
10	250	4	1,000	5
11	120	8	960	8
12	140	7	980	7
13	10	10	100	13
14	20	10	200	12
15	200	5	1,000	6

The next step is to accumulate the total number of items and their usage values and then to convert the accumulated values into the percentages of the grand totals. This is done in the table below :

TABLE 12.12

Item No.	*Annual usage (₹)*	*Cumulative annual usage (₹)*	*Cumulative usage %*	*Cumulative percentage of items*	*Category*
6	32,000	32,000	45.71	6.67	A
3	30,000	62,000	88.57	13.33	
7	1,200	63,200	90.28	20.00	
2	1,000	64,200	91.71	26.67	
10	1,000	65,200	93.14	33.33	
15	1,000	66,200	94.57	40.00	B
12	980	67,180	95.97	46.67	
11	960	68,140	97.34	53.33	
9	800	68,940	98.49	60.00	
4	400	69,340	99.06	66.67	
8	200	69,540	99.34	73.33	
14	200	69,740	99.63	80.00	C
13	100	69,840	99.77	86.67	
1	80	69,920	99.89	93.33	
5	80	70,000	100.00	100.00	

The cumulative percentages of items and cumulative percentages of their usage values are plotted in Fig. 12.16.

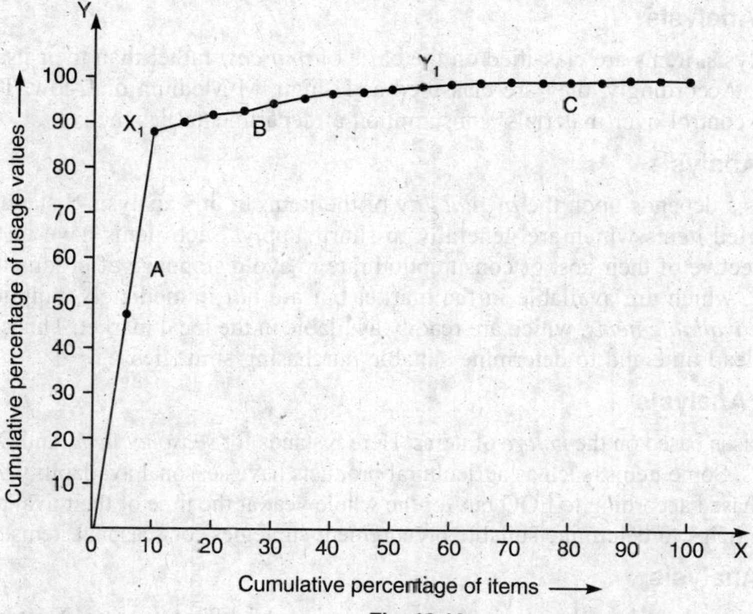

Fig. 12.16

Mark the cut-off points X_1 and Y_1 where the curve changes its shape. This divides the curve into three segments A, B and C.

12.12-2 VED Analysis

This analysis based on experience/judgement, divides items into three categories in the descending order of their *criticality to the production process or other services.* 'V' stands for *vital items* (*e.g.*, clutch wire for a vehicle) and their stock analysis requires more attention since out-of-stock situation would result in stoppage of production. Thus 'V' items should always be sufficiently stocked to ensure smooth operation of the plant. 'E' denotes *essential items* which are necessary for the efficient running of the system but without which the system will not fail. A telephone or an intercom is 'E' item for any organisation. Care should be taken to ensure that they remain always in stock. 'D' represents *desirable items.* They do not immediately affect production but they help to increase efficiency and decrease fatigue. A radio or television will come under this category. As VED analysis categorises the items on the basis of their criticality, it can be used to determine the stock levels of spare parts and special raw materials which are scarce and difficult to procure.

12.12-3 FNSD Analysis

This analysis divides items into four categories in the descending order of their *consumption rate*. 'F' stands for *fast moving items,* stocks for which are consumed over a short span of time. Their stocks must be observed constantly and all steps be taken to replenish their stocks in time to avoid stock-out situations. 'N' denotes *normal moving items,* stocks for which are exhausted over a year or so. 'S' represents *slow moving items,* such items may take 2 years or more to be consumed at the existing consumption rate but they will be consumed anyway. Their stock levels must be carefully reviewed before placement of their replenishment orders to minimise the risks of surplus stock being left when such items become obsolescent or dead. 'D' means *dead stock* and for such items no further demand can be foreseen. Dead stock represents money spent that cannot be realised but it occupies the useful space. Efforts should be made to find alternative uses for such items, failing which they must be disposed of. FNSD analysis, therefore, helps to control obsolescence.

12.12-4 HML Analysis

In this analysis, items are classified on the basis of *unit cost* rather than their usage value as in ABC analysis. Accordingly, they are classified as H-high, M-Medium or L-low. This analysis helps in keeping control over materials' consumption at departmental level.

12.12-5 SDE Analysis

This analysis depends upon the *availability* of the item. In this analysis S stands for *scarce items e.g.*, imported items which are generally in short supply. Such items have to be procured and stored irrespective of their cost or consumption rate to avoid stoppage of production. D refers to *difficult items*, which are available in the market but are not immediately supplied, while E represents *easily available items*, which are readily available in the local market. This classification helps to control lead time and to determine suitable purchasing strategies.

12.12-6 S-OS Analysis

This analysis is based on the *nature* of items. Here S stands for *seasonal items* and OS represents *off-seasonal* items. Some items, such as agricultural products have seasonal availability. Accordingly, they are not purchased according to EOQ but for the whole year at the time of their availability. Thus, this classification helps to determine suitable procurement strategies for seasonal items.

12.12-7 XYZ Analysis

This analysis is based on the *closing inventory values* of different items. X items have high closing inventory values while Z items have low tied-up capital. Y items lie in-between. This analysis helps to reduce the capital investment in high value items.

The various types of analyses discussed are not mutually exclusive. Often, they are used jointly to ensure better inventory control. For instance, ABC and XYZ analyses may be combined to classify and control capital investment, XYZ and FNSD analyses may be combined to control obsolescence and VED analysis coupled with ABC analysis may be used to enhance inventory control efficiency.

12.13 PERIODIC REVIEW SYSTEMS

The foregoing sections dealt with *E.O.Q. system or fixed order quantity system of Inventory control*, wherein an order of *fixed size* q_0 is placed on the vendor, the moment the depleting stock level of an item reaches the R.O.L. level. The order quantity is fixed but the time interval between orders varies to absorb the fluctuations in demand. This system is also known as *perpetual inventory system* or *Q-system* or *two-bin system.* This is called two-bin system because the system is separated into two bins. The first bin contains stock enough to meet customer's demand for the time interval between receipt of goods and the placement of the next order, while the second bin contains stock sufficient to meet the demand during the lead time period. An order is placed as soon as the first bin is exhausted. This system, therefore, is based on three parameters namely, EOQ, ROL and safety stock.

In periodic review systems, the stocks are reviewed periodically (*e.g.,* monthly). There are two commonly used periodic review systems — fixed order cycle system and the sS system which are briefly discussed below.

12.13-1 Fixed Order Cycle System

This system is based on the determination of fixed period at which the inventory is reviewed. Depending upon the type (*e.g.* 'A' class) or demand (*e.g.* fast moving) of items, periodicity of the review may be a week, fortnight, month, quarter or a year. The economic ordering interval t_0 is derived like the E.O.Q. and is equal in days to

$$\frac{365 \times \text{E.O.Q.}}{\text{Annual demand}}.$$

Thus the key issue in this system is the determination of optimal length of review period, t_0.

Usually some items have shorter review period than the others. At each review period, an order is placed for an amount equal to the difference between the maximum predetermined stock level minus the stock level existing at that moment. Thus the order size varies. It would be larger than usual if the demand has been greater than the anticipation and would be smaller than usual if the demand has been smaller than the anticipation. Thus the fluctuations are absorbed by the varying order size since the review period is fixed. This system is also known as *fixed period* or *replenishment system* or *P-system.* The maximum level, *also called target inventory level*, is set equal to the sum of expected demand during the lead time (which is ordinary lead time plus review period) and the safety stock during the period. Fig. 12.17 illustrates the operation of the fixed order cycle system.

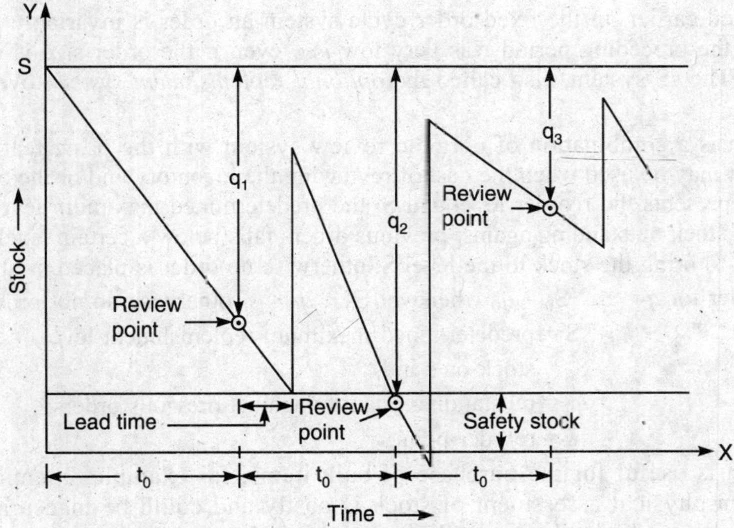

Fig. 12.17. Fixed order cycle system.

A point worth noting about the cycle review system is that an order is invariably placed at the review date (*e.g.,* 7th of month), unless, of course, there has been no demand during the preceding period. Therefore, if the demand during the preceding period has been rather small, an order of small size will have to be placed which will indeed be costly due to the associated ordering cost. Hence, there grew the sS system. The fixed order cycle system is also known as the *topping-up system.* This nomenclature may be well understood by considering the stocking of item like a lubricating oil. The height of the can may represent the maximum level. All that the stock controller has to do is to ensure that at every review date the can is filled upto the brim. Fixed order cycle system is particularly useful when a vendor (supplier) supplies a number of items. Since all the items can be reviewed simultaneously on the review date, joint replenishment orders can be placed. Further, since the supplier has an anticipation about the forthcoming order, he can plan his production better.

The following points about this system are noteworthy :

1. The maximum stock level or target inventory level is obtained by adding the average demand during the review period, the average demand during the (ordinary) lead time and the safety stock, if any. The quantity ordered is then
= Target inventory – stock in hand – previous orders not yet received (if any).
2. This system is comparatively simpler to operate. The person controlling the stock would need to check the stock level, say, every four weeks and just determine the quantity by which the stock on hand is short of the maximum stock level and place order for this quantity.

3. The optimal review period, $t_0 = \frac{q_0}{R} = \sqrt{\frac{2C_3R}{C_1}} \cdot \frac{1}{R} = \sqrt{\frac{2C_3}{RC_1}}$.

4. Safety stock required under this system is larger than the safety stock required under the fixed order quantity system. It is because in the periodic review system, safety stock must be provided as a protection against stockouts during the period prior to the time point when stocks are to be reviewed as well as the stockouts that may occur during the lead time; while in the fixed order quantity system, the safety stock is just enough to protect against stockouts during lead time only.

12.13-2 sS System

As mentioned earlier, in the fixed order cycle system an order is invariably placed even if the demand in the preceding period was very low *i.e.,* even if the order size is small which is uneconomical. The sS system, also called the *optional replenishment system,* overcomes this difficulty.

This system is a combination of periodic review system with the basic feature of fixed quantity system. It may be used when the cost of reviewing the inventory and/or the ordering cost is large. Here s represents the reorder level and S, the predetermined maximum level. When the existing stock and stock outstanding against previous orders falls below a certain level, say s, then an order is placed to bring the stock to the level S, otherwise no order is placed. Mathematically,

place an order for $q = S - S_0 - q_0$ whenever $S_0 + q_0 < s$, otherwise do not order, where

S = predetermined maximum replenishment level,

S_0 = stock on hand,

q_0 = outstanding quantity against previous orders,

and s = reorder point.

This system is useful for the purchase of bulk items, for example, chemicals, scraps and castings when physical assessment of stock is costly and could be inaccurate. In such situations, the stocks can be held, physically, in two bins placed closely. Stock s is placed in bin 1 and the remaining in bin 2. As bin 2 becomes empty, an order is placed so that the total stock becomes S. However, in operating the system, sufficient care should be taken to avoid obsolescence in bin 1.

12.13-3 Comparison Between F.O.Q. System and Periodic Review System

1. In the F.O.Q. system there is continuous watch of the stock level so that the moment the depleting stocks cross the R.O.L., a replenishment order is placed. It is, however, not possible in periodic review system. If there is an important and large-size demand, it is not likely to be filled, particularly towards the end of the review period. The replenishment action is delayed until the review date. However, it may be noted that such large-size demand would occur only seldomly. Thus, in situations where demand is fairly uniform, F.O.Q. system would be unnecessarily costlier.
2. In the F.O.Q. system the safety stock is just sufficient to absorb the demand fluctuations during lead time only, whereas in periodic review system the safety stock must be sufficient enough to meet the fluctuations in demand over the lead time as well as the review period. The latter, therefore, requires a larger safety stock than the former.
3. The F.O.Q. system is more sensitive to fluctuations in demand and promptly responds to any unanticipated demand behaviour. In contrast, once the stocks are computed at the beginning of the period in periodic review system, no changes are made until the next review period, whatever the interim demand fluctuations.
4. The periodic review system is advantageous for joint replenishment orders. For instance, if a vendor is a regular supplier for a dozen items, it will be economical to place a single order for all the 12 items. Apart from savings in paper costs, there would be lower

transportation and receiving costs since the items will be delivered in a single consignment. Joint replenishment also helps advance and proper production planning by the vendor and reduces the production costs.

5. For 'A' class or fast moving items, F.O.Q. system will be better because of its continuous surveillance while periodic review system is more suitable for 'B' and 'C' class or slow moving items.

EXERCISES 12.6

1. (*a*) What is demand forecasting ? Discuss the various techniques of demand forecasting. [*Dayalbagh, Edu. Inst. Agra MBA Dec., 2007; May, 2005; P.U. M.Com., 2002*]
1. (*b*) Describe (*i*) moving average method (*ii*) exponential smoothing method for forecasting. [*Dayalbagh Edu. Inst. Agra M.B.A. Dec., 2007*]
2. Describe a method of forecasting of sale of a product having a seasonal demand. Point out limitations of such type of forecasting. [*Kuru. U. B.Tech. (Mech.) 1992, 91*]
3. Define and explain the terms safety stock and EOQ with the help of ideal inventory model. [*Dayalbagh Edu. Inst. Agra MBA Dec., 2007; May 2005; Pbi. U. MCA, 2001*]
4. Explain the following terms in inventory theory :
(*a*) Lead time (*b*) Reorder level (*c*) Safety stock.
[*Univ. of Madras B.Sc. (Math.) Nov., 2012; J.N.T.U. Hyderabad B.Tech. May, 2011; G.J.U. MBA Nov., 2003; Dayalbagh Edu. Inst. M.B.A. Dec., 2007; G.N.D.U. B.Com., 2005*]
5. (*a*) Write short note on inventory control techniques.
[*J.N.T.U. Hyderabad B.Tech. (C.Sc.) Dec., 2011; IGNOU MBA, Dec., 2006, 2001*]
(*b*) Discuss the relevance and applications of inventory management in business situations. [*Pondicherry MBA August, 2006*]
6. Explain ABC analysis. What are its advantages and disadvantages ?
[*Gujarat Tech. U.B.E. Dec., 2012; P.T.U. BBA, 2011; Dayalbagh Edu. Inst. Agra BBM May, 2005; J.N.T.U. Hyderabad B.Tech. May, 2009; Nagpur U.B.E. (Mech.) 2003*]
7. Explain ABC, VED and FSN analyses. Explain with examples. [*IGNOU MBA, 2003; Dec., 2000*]
8. Discuss the functions and types of inventory control. Also discuss the advantages of ABC analysis to the management. [*Kuru. U. B.Tech. (Indl. Engg.) 1997*]
9. "ABC analysis is a very useful approach for selective inventory control but has some major limitations". Discuss. [*P.T.U. MBA, 2008*]
10. What is periodic review system ? State its advantages and disadvantages. [*ICWA (Final) May, 1993*]
11. Explain and compare fixed order quantity model and fixed order period model and state their applications. [*J.N.T.U. Hyderabad B.Tech. (C.Sc.) Dec., 2011; June, 2009; Dayalbagh Edu. Inst. Agra M.B.A. Dec., 2012; Dec., 2007*]

Section 12.10-2

12. An initial forecast of 39 is given. Using $\alpha = 0.1$, smooth exponentially the following chronological series :
41, 41, 34, 39, 36, 35, 40, 36, 41 and 33.
(*Ans.* 39.2, 39.38, 38.84, 38.85, 38.56, 38.2, 38.4, 38.16, 38.45, 37.9.)
13. An electrical contractor's records during the last five weeks indicate the number of job requests :

Week	:	1	2	3	4	5
Requests	:	20	22	18	21	20

Predict the number of requests for week 6 using the exponential smoothing with exponential smoothing constant of 0.30. [*Dayalbagh Edu. Inst. Agra M.B.A. Dec., 2007*]
(*Ans.* 20.12.)
14. Historical demand for a product is :

Month	:	Jan.	Feb.	March	April	May	June
Demand (*units*)	:	12	11	15	12	16	15

(*i*) Using weighted moving average method with weights of 0.60, 0.30 and 0.10, find the July forecast.
(*ii*) Using simplex exponential smoothing method with $\alpha = 0.2$, find the July forecast.
(*Dayalbagh Edu. Inst. Agra M.Tech. Dec., 2007*]
(*Ans.* (*i*) 13.5 (*ii*) 14.)

15. The following data represents the home mortgage loan interest rates at a local bank over an eight-month period :

Month	*Rate (%)*	*Month*	*Rate (%)*
1	8.7	5	8.6
2	8.7	6	8.4
3	8.6	7	8.8
4	8.6	8	8.8

Using weights of 0.6, 0.3 and 0.1, determine the 3-month weighted moving average forecasts for months 8 and 9. *[Dayalbagh Edu. Inst. Agra MBA May, 2011]*
[**Hint:** Moving average for month 8 = 8.6 × 0.1 + 8.4 × 0.3 + 8.8 × 0.6 = 8.66,
moving average for month 9 = 8.4 × 0.1 + 8.8 × 0.3 + 8.8 × 0.6 = 8.76.]

Section 12.10-3

16. An electronics manufacturer wants to forecast next month's demand for VCRs. Sales to retailer for the past six months are shown below :

Month :	1	2	3	4	5	6
Demand :	829	808	854	874	903	935

Assuming that the forecasted demand for month 1 was 825, calculate the forecasts for months 2 through 6 using the exponential smoothing method with smoothing constants $\alpha = 0.10$ and $\alpha = 0.50$. Which smoothing constant results in smaller MAD ?
[Dayalbagh Edu. Inst. Agra B.Sc. Engg. and M.Tech. Dec., 2011]
(*Ans.* (*i*) 825.4, 823.66, 826.69, 831.42, 838.57.
(*ii*) 827, 817.5, 835.75, 854.87, 878.93. (*iii*) 0.50.)

17. Find the exponential smoothed forecasts with trend correction for the following data:
Initial trend = – 3.00, initial average = 750.00, $\alpha = 0.1$,
monthly sales = 720, 670, 680, 740, 720, 940, 1,020, 1,220, 1,260, 1,300, 1,190 and 1,080.
Also find the forecast error. (*Ans.* Forecast error = 47, 24.6, – 43.79, – 18.75, – 238.28, – 273.71, – 419.68, – 373.71, – 332.75, – 146.23,6.30.)

18. Find the exponential smoothed forecasts with trend correction for the coming month for the data given below. Also find the error.
Initial average = 175.6, initial trend = 0.000, lead time = 2 months, $\alpha = 0.1$,
sales = 169, 180, 135, 213, 181, 148, 204, 228, 225, 198, 200 and 187.
(*Ans.* Error = – 5.8, 40.3, – 45.7, – 4.9, 29.1, – 32.6, – 50.2, – 37.9, – 1.9, – 2.8, 12.1.)

Sections 12.11

19. For a fixed order quantity system find out the various parameters for a problem with the following data:
Annual consumption (R) = 10,000 units,
cost of one unit = ₹ 1.00,
C_3 = ₹ 12.00 per production run,
C_1 = ₹ 0.24 per unit,
past lead times : 15 days, 25 days, 13 days, 14 days, 30 days, 17 days. *[P.U. MBA, 1997]*
(*Ans.* E.O.Q. = 1,000, S.S. = 416.66 ≈ 417, R.O.L. = 834, $q_{average}$ = 917.)

20. A factory uses ₹ 32,000 worth of a new material per year. The ordering cost per order is ₹ 50 and the carrying cost is 20% per year of the average inventory. If the company follows the E.O.Q. purchasing policy, calculate the reorder point, the maximum inventory, the minimum inventory and the average inventory; it being given that the factory works for 360 days a year, the replacement time is 9 days and the safety stock is worth ₹ 300. *[Meerut M.Com., 1975]*
(*Ans.* 1,100, 4,300, 300 and 2,300 units.)

21. Based on the following data, is a lot of 1,000; 3,000; 6,000 or 12,000 units the most economical to manufacture ?

setup cost	:	₹ 3.00,
value	:	₹ 0.04 per unit,
carrying cost	:	20% of value of average inventory,
storage cost	:	₹ 0.03 per unit per year,
consumption	:	12,000 units per year,
minimum safety stock at hand	:	1,000 units.

[Bombay D.I.M., 1975]

22. Data on the distribution of lead time for a pump component are shown below. Management would like to set safety stock levels that will limit the stock-out risk to 10%.

Lead time (weeks)	*Frequency of occurrence*
0 to 1	10
1 to 2	20
2 to 3	70
3 to 4	40
4 to 5	30
5 to 6	10
6 to 7	10
7 to 8	10

How many weeks of safety stock are required to provide the desired service level ? (*Ans.* 2.6 weeks.)

23. A manufacturer of water filters purchases components in E.O.Q.s of 850 units/order. Total demand averages 12,000 components/year and MAD = 32 units/month. If the manufacturer carries a safety stock of 80 units, what service level is provided by him ? (*Ans.* 97.72%.)

24. A cycle brand 'X' has a demand of 9,000 units per year. The cost of one procurement is ₹ 100 and the holding cost/unit is ₹ 2.40 per year. The replacement is instantaneous and no shortages are allowed. Determine
   (*i*) Economic lot size.
   (*ii*) Number of orders per year.
   (*iii*) Time between orders.
   (*iv*) The company operates for 300 days/year. The procurement time is 10 days and the safety stock is maintained at a level of 100 units. Find the reorder point, the maximum inventory and average inventory.
   (*v*) The total cost per year if cost of one cycle is ₹ 300. [*IGNOU MBA, 2001*]

   (*Ans.* (*i*) 866 units (*ii*) 10.4 (*iii*) 29 days (*iv*) 400 units, 966 units, 533 units (*v*) ₹ 27,02,080.)

25. A company uses annually 24,000 units of a raw material which costs ₹ 1.25 per unit. Placing each order costs ₹ 22.50 and the carrying cost is 5.4% per year of average inventory. Find EOQ and total inventory cost (including the cost of material). Should the company accept the offer made by the supplier for a discount of 5% on the cost on a single order of 24,000 units ?

   Suppose the company works for 300 days a year. If the procurement time is 12 days and safety stock is 400 units, find the reorder point, the minimum, maximum and average inventory.

   [*DOEACC, 1996, 95*]

26. The following information is provided :

   Annual demand = 24,000 units, ordering cost = ₹ 120/order,
   carrying cost = 20%, unit cost of item = ₹ 20, lead time = 10 days.

   There are 240 working days a year. Determine the EOQ and number of orders per year. In the past two years, the use rate has gone as high as 140 units a day. For a reordering system based on the inventory level, what safety stock is required to protect against this high use rate ? What should be the reorder point at this safety stock level ? What would be the carrying cost for a year ?

   [*K.U.B. Tech. (Ind. Engg.) 1997*]

27. A company uses annually 50,000 units of an item, each costing ₹ 1.20. Each order costs ₹ 45 and inventory carrying cost is 15% of the average inventory value.
   (*i*) Find the economic order quantity.
   (*ii*) If the company operates 250 days a year and if the procurement time is 10 days and safety stock is 500 units, find the reorder level, maximum, minimum and average inventory. [*P.T.U. MBA June, 2003*]

28. Daily demand for a product is normally distributed with mean 60 units and a standard deviation of 6 units. The lead time is constant at 9 days. The cost of placing an order is ₹ 200 and the annual holding costs are 20% of the unit price of ₹ 50. A 95% service level is desired for the customers, who place orders during the reorder period. Determine the order quantity and the reorder level for the product, assuming that there are 300 working days during a year. [*P.T.U. B.Tech. (Mech.) 2008*]

   (*Ans.* 848.4 units, 547.7 units.)

29. A battery wholesale company purchases batteries for ₹ 140 per unit and it costs ₹ 110 to process an order. The company sells about 12,000 units of a particular type of battery per year at a uniform rate. The company is open 5 days week, for 52 weeks a year. The order lead time is 3 days, and the company wants to have an average of 2 days' sales on hand as safety stock when a new order is scheduled to arrive. The holding cost is estimated to be 24 per cent of the item cost per year. Determine
   (*i*) EOQ
   (*ii*) Expected level of the maximum inventory
   (*iii*) Reorder level
   (*iv*) Average inventory level
   (*v*) Average annual cost to hold inventory. [*IGNOU M.B.A. Dec., 2004*]
   (*Ans.* (*i*) 280.3 units (*ii*) 372.6 units (*iii*) 230.75 units (*iv*) 232.45 units (*v*) ₹ 7,795.)

30. A manufacturing company requires a component at the average annual rate of 1,000 units. Placing an order costs ₹ 480 and has a 5-day lead time. Inventory holding cost is estimated at ₹ 15 per unit per year. The plant operates 250 days/year. It is assumed that the daily demand is normally distributed with an average of 4 units and with a standard deviation of 1.2 units. Suggest an inventory policy to control the inventory of the item based on 95% service level. [*D.U.MBA, 2002; AMIE, 2005*]
   [**Hint** : Here, R = 1,000 units/year = $\frac{1{,}000}{250}$ = 4 units/day, σ_d = 1.2 units/day, LT = 5 days,
   C_1 = ₹ 15/unit/year, C_3 = ₹ 480/order, service level = 95%.
   Service factor Z for service level of 95% from table C-2 = 1.65.
   Now R.O.L. = $M.LT + Z.C_d.\sqrt{LT} = 4 \times 5 + 1.65 \times 1.2\sqrt{5} = 25$ units.
   ∴ S.S. = R.O.L. – average demand during lead time = 25 – 4 × 5 = 5 units.]

31. A company's annual consumption of raw material is 60,000 units. The cost of raw material is ₹ 5 per unit. Placing of one order costs the company ₹ 120 and holding costs are 20% per year of average inventory value. The company works for 320 days in a year and the average procurement time, based on past experience is 16 days. Assume that the safety stock is 800 units to cater for delivery delay. Company follows EOQ system of inventory management. Find out reorder level, maximum and average inventory. [*R.T.M. Nagpur U.B.E. (Mech.) Sept., 2010*]

32. AE Ltd. assembles a component which uses a part bought from an outside supplier at a cost of ₹ 5 per unit. Each month 18,000 components are produced at a steady rate throughout. There is a lead time of one month between ordering and delivery and the current practice is for AE Ltd. to order 72,000 units at a time. This order is placed when the stock level falls to 48,000 units.
   The supplier offers a 10% discount if orders are placed in lot sizes of 2,00,000 units and he is allowed a 2-month delivery period. If AE Ltd. wanted to change to these terms, it would require additional storage which would cost ₹ 24,000 per year and would incur additional handling charges of ₹ 0.05 per unit. The company would maintain the level of protection afforded by the use of safety stock.
   The cost of placing an order is ₹ 200 and the cost of receiving delivery of an order is ₹ 800. The cost of capital normally used for inventory decisions is 12% per annum. You are required
   (*a*) to calculate and state the annual cost following the current practice.
   (*b*) to calculate and state the minimum annual cost if the extra storage space were available so that the discount for larger quantities could be considered.

33. A company uses 1,250 large cans of tomatoes a month, at an average rate of 50 per day for each of the 25 days per month the company is working. Usage can be approximated by a normal distribution with standard deviation of 3 cans per day. Lead time is constant at 5 days. Monthly carrying costs are ₹ 1 per can and ordering costs are ₹ 100 per order.
   (*a*) Determine the economic order quantity.
   (*b*) Find the variable inventory costs per month.
   (*c*) For a service level of 98 per cent, how many cans of tomatoes should the company have on hand when it places the order ? [*Dayalbagh Edu. Inst. Agra BBM May, 2013*]
   (*Ans.* 500 cans, ₹ 500, 263.78 ≃ 264 cans.)

Section 12.12

34. Ten items kept in inventory are listed below. Which items should be classified as 'A', 'B' and 'C' items? What percentage of items is in each class? What percentage of total annual value is in each class?

Item	*Price (₹)*	*Annual use*
1	40.00	200
2	360.00	100
3	0.20	2,000
4	20.00	400
5	0.04	6,000
6	0.80	1,200
7	100.00	120
8	0.70	2,000
9	1.00	1,000
10	400.00	80

(*Ans.*

Class	*Items*	*% of items*	*% of usage value*
A	2, 10	20	68
B	7, 1, 4	30	28
C	8, 9, 6, 3, 5	50	4.)

35. What is selective inventory control ? From the following details draw a plan of ABC selective control.

Item	*Units*	*Unit cost (₹)*
1	7,000	5.00
2	24,000	3.00
3	1,500	10.00
4	600	22.00
5	38,000	1.50
6	40,000	0.50
7	60,000	0.20
8	3,000	3.50
9	300	8.00
10	29,000	0.40
11	11,500	7.10
12	4,100	6.20

[*C.A. (Final) May, 1983*]

(*Ans.*

Class	Items	% of items	% of usage value
A	11, 2, 5	25	59.2
B	1, 12, 6, 3	33.3	26.8
C	4, 7, 10, 8, 9	41.7	14.)

36. XYZ Ltd. does the ABC classification of the various components and parts it uses for assembling its tractors. As an operations manager, you are required to classify the following parts and components into A, B and C categories according to their usage values. Draw the ABC distribution curve. Item no. 8 has a criticality class *i.e.* a shortage of this item may lead to a complete halt in the production process. What special treatment can be given to this item?

Item No.	*Unit price (₹)*	*Annual usage (units)*
1	5	1,00,000
2	35	2,600
3	79	420
4	68	13,600
5	800	210
6	2,300	670
7	450	76
8	6	400
9	92	6,100
10	3	2,50,000

[*P.T.U. MBA, 2012*]

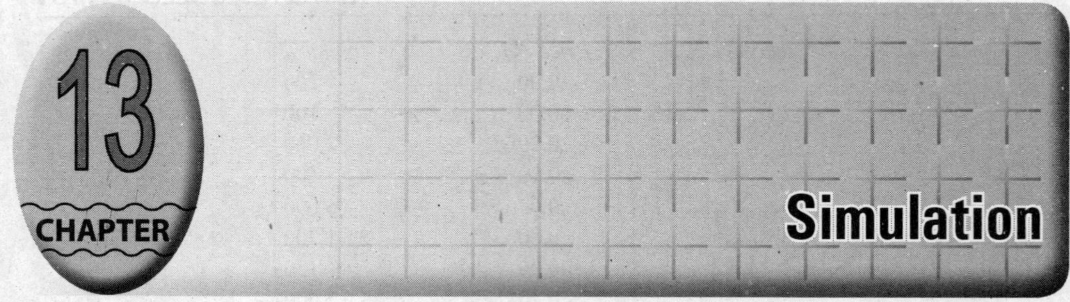

13.1 INTRODUCTION

The technique of simulation has long been used by the designers and analysts in physical sciences and it promises to become an important tool for tackling the complicated problems of managerial decision-making. Scale models of machines have been used to simulate the plant layouts and models of aircrafts have been tested in wind tunnels to determine their aerodynamic characteristics. Simulation, which can appropriately be called management laboratory, determines the effect of a number of alternate policies without disturbing the real system. It helps in selecting the best policy with the prior assurance that its implementation will be beneficial.

Probably the first important application of simulation was made by John Von Neumann and Stanislaw Ulam for studying the tedius behaviour of neutrons in a nuclear shielding problem which was too complex for mathematical analysis. With the remarkable success of the technique on neutron problem, it became popular and found many applications in business and industry. Development of digital computers in early 1950s is further responsible for the rapid progress made by the simulation techniques. The range of simulation application varies from simple queuing models to models of large integrated systems of production.

13.2 WHEN TO USE SIMULATION?

In the foregoing chapters we have discussed a number of operations research tools and techniques for solving various types of managerial decision-making problems. Techniques like linear programming, dynamic programming, queuing theory, network models, etc., are not sufficient to tackle all the important managerial problems requiring data analysis. Each technique has its own limitations.

Linear programming models assume that the data do not alter over the planning horizon. It is one time decision process and assumes average values for the decision variables. If the planning horizon is long, say 10 years, the multiperiod linear programming model may deal with the yearly averaged data, but will not take into account the variations over the months and weeks with the result that month to month and week to week variations are left uncovered. Other important limitation of linear programming is that it assumes the data to be known with certainty. In many real situations the uncertainties about the data are such that they cannot be ignored. In case the uncertainty relates to only a few variables, the sensitivity analysis can be applied to determine its effect on the decision. But, in situations, where uncertainty pervades the entire model, the sensitivity analysis may become too cumbersome and computationly difficult to determine the impact of uncertainty on the recommended plan.

Dynamic programming models, however, can be used to determine optimal strategies, by taking into account the uncertainties and can analyse multiperiod planning problems. In other words, this technique is free from the two main limitations of linear programming. But it has its own shortcomings. Dynamic programming models can be used to tackle very simple situations involving only a few variables. If the number of state variables is a bit larger, the computation task becomes quite complex and involved.

Similar limitations hold good for other mathematical techniques like dynamic stochastic models such as inventory and waiting line situations. Only small scale systems are amenable to these models; moreover, by making a number of assumptions the systems are simplified to such an extent that in many cases the results obtained are only rough approximations.

From the above discussion we conclude that when the characteristics such as uncertainty, complexity, dynamic interaction between the decision and subsequent event, and the need to develop detailed procedures and finely-divided time intervals combine together in one situation, it becomes too complex to be solved by any of the techniques of mathematical programming and probabilistic models. It must be analysed by some other kind of quantitative technique which may give quite accurate and reliable results. Many new techniques are coming up, but, so far, the best available is simulation.

In general, the simulation technique is a dependable tool in situations where mathematical analysis is either too complex or too costly.

13.3 WHAT IS SIMULATION?

Simulation is an imitation of reality. A children cycling park, with various crossings and signals, is a simulated model of the city traffic system. In the laboratories a number of experiments are performed on simulated models to determine the behaviour of the real system in true environments. A simple illustration is the testing of an aircraft model in a wind tunnel from which we determine the performance of the actual aircraft under real operating conditions. Planetarium shows represent a beautiful simulation of the planet system. Environments in a geological garden and in a museum of natural history are other examples of simulation.

In all these examples, it has been tried to imitate the reality to see what might happen under real operating conditions. This imitation of reality which may be in the physical form or in the form of mathematical equations may be called *simulation*.

The simple examples cited above are of simulating the reality in physical form, and are referred to as (*environmental*) *analogue simulation*. For the complex and intricate problems of managerial decision-making, the analogue simulation may not be practicable, and actual experimentation with the system may be uneconomical. Under such circumstances, the complex system is formulated into a mathematical model for which a computer programme is developed, and the problem is solved by using high speed electronic computer, and hence it is named as *computer simulation* or *system simulation*.

With this background it will now be in order to define simulation. According to one definition "*simulation is a representation of reality through the use of a model or other device which will react in the same manner as reality under a given set of conditions.*" Simulation has also been defined as "*the use of a system model that has the designed characteristics of reality in order to produce the essence of actual operation.*" According to Donald G. Malcolm, *a simulated model may be defined as one which depicts the working of a large scale system of men, machines, materials and information operating over a period of time in a simulated environment of the actual real world conditions. According to Shannon simulation is the process of designing a model of the real system by conducting experiments with this model for the purpose of understanding the behaviour of the operation of the system.*

13.4 ADVANTAGES OF THE SIMULATION TECHNIQUE

The simulation technique, when compared with the mathematical programming and standard probability analysis, offers a number of advantages over these techniques; a few important among them can be summarized as follows:

1. Many important managerial decision problems are too intricate to be solved by mathematical programming and experimentation with the actual system, even if possible, is to too costly and risky. Simulation offers the solution by allowing experimentation with model of the

system without interfering with the real system. Simulation is, thus, often a bypass for complex mathematical analysis.

2. Through simulation, management can foresee the difficulties and bottlenecks which may come up due to the introduction of new machines, equipment or process. It, thus, eliminates the need of costly trial and error methods of trying out the new concept on real methods and equipment.
3. Simulation has the advantage of being relatively free from mathematics and, thus, can be easily understood by the operating personnel and non-technical managers. This helps in getting the proposed plans accepted and implemented.
4. Simulation models are comparatively flexible and can be modified to accommodate the changing environments of the real situation.
5. Computer simulation can compress the performance of a system over several years and involving large calculations into a few minutes of computer running time.
6. The simulation technique is easier to use than mathematical models and is considered quite superior to the mathematical analysis.
7. Simulation has advantageously been used for training the operating and managerial staff in the operation of complex plans. It is always advantageous to train people on simulated models before putting into their hands the real system. Simulated exercises have been developed to impart the trainee sufficient exercise and experience. A simulated exercise familiarizes the trainee with the data required and helps in judging what information is really important. Due to his personal involvement into the exercise, the trainee gains sufficient confidence, and moreover becomes familiar with data processing on electronic computer.
8. Once a simulation model has been constructed, it may be used time and again to analyse different situations.
9. It is a valuable and convenient method of breaking down a complicated system into sub-systems and then studying each of these subsystems individually or jointly with others.

13.5 LIMITATIONS OF THE SIMULATION TECHNIQUE

In spite of all the advantages claimed by the simulation technique, many operations research analysts consider it a method of last resort and use it only when all other techniques fail. If a particular type of problem can be well represented by a mathematical model, the analytical approach is considered to be more economical, accurate and reliable. Further, in very large and complex problems simulation may suffer from the same deficiencies as other mathematical models. In brief, the simulation technique suffers from the following limitations:

1. Simulation does not produce optimum results. When the model deals with uncertainties, the results of simulation are only reliable approximations subject to statistical errors.
2. Quantification of the variables is another difficulty. In a number of situations it is not possible to quantify all the variables that affect the behaviour of the system.
3. In very large and complex problems, the large number of variables and the inter-relationships between them make the problem very unwieldy and hard to program. The number of variables may be too large and may exceed the capacity of the available computer.
4. Simulation is, by no means, a cheap method of analysis. In a number of situations, such as corporate planning, simulation is comparatively costlier and time consuming.
5. Other important limitations stem from too much tendency to rely on the simulation models. This results in application of the technique to some simple problems which can more appropriately be handled by other techniques of mathematical programming.

13.6 APPLICATIONS OF SIMULATION

Simulation is quite versatile and commonly applied technique for solving decision problems. It has been applied successfully to a wide range of problems of science and technology as given below:

1. In the field of basic sciences, it has been used to evaluate the area under a curve, to estimate the value of π, in matrix inversion and study of particle diffusion.
2. In industrial problems including the shop floor management, design of computer systems, design of queuing systems, inventory control, communication networks, chemical processes, nuclear reactors and scheduling of production processes.
3. In business and economic problems, including customer behaviour, price determination, economic forecasting, portfolio selection and capital budgeting.
4. In social problems, including population growth, effect of environment on health and group behaviour.
5. In biomedical systems, including fluid balance, distribution of electrolyte in human body and brain activities.
6. In the design of weapon systems, war strategies and tactics.
7. In the study of projects involving risky investments.

13.7 MONTE CARLO SIMULATION

The Monte Carlo method of simulation was developed by the two mathematicians John Von Neumann and Stainslaw Ulam, during World War II to study how far neutrons would travel through different materials. The technique provided an approximate but quite workable solution to the problem. With the remarkable success of this technique on neutron problem, it soon became popular and found many applications in business and industry and at present forms a very important tool of operation researcher's tool kit. 'Monte Carlo' is the code number given to the technique by the above two mathematicians.

The technique employs random numbers and is used to solve problems that involve probability and wherein physical experimentation is impracticable and formulation of mathematical model is impossible. It is a method of simulation by sampling technique. The steps involved in carrying out Monte Carlo simulation are:

1. Select the measure of effectiveness (objective function) of the problem. It is either to be maximized or minimized. For example, it may be idle time of service facility in a queuing problem or number of shortages or the total inventory cost in an inventory control problem.
2. Identify the variables that affect the measure of effectiveness significantly. For example, number of service facilities in a queuing problem or demand, lead time and safety stock in an inventory control problem.
3. Determine the cumulative probability distribution of each variable selected in step 2. Plot these distributions with values of the variables along x-axis and cumulative probability values along the y-axis.
4. Get a set of random numbers from a random number generator.
5. Consider each random number as a decimal value of the cumulative probability distribution. Enter the cumulative distribution plot along the y-axis. Project this point horizontally till it meets the distribution curve. Then project the point of intersection down on the x-axis.
6. Record the value (or values if several variables are being simulated) generated in step 5. Substitute in the formula chosen for measure of effectiveness and find its simulated value.
7. Repeat steps 5 and 6 until sample is large enough to the satisfaction of the decision maker.

Though in any real problem to be solved by simulation, the variables in the problem are probabilistic in nature, we first consider below a problem where they are fixed and constant and see how the simulation technique which involves repetitive experimentation can be used to analyse such a problem. The remaining problems involve variables that are probabilistic in nature.

EXAMPLE 13.7-1 (Event-Type Simulation)

Customers arrive at a service facility to get the required service. The interarrival and service times are constant and are 1.8 minutes and 4 minutes respectively. Simulate the system for 14 minutes. Determine the average waiting time of a customer and idle time of the service facility.

[*Andhra Prod. Council, 1978*]

Solution

The arrival times of customers within 14 minutes period will be :

Customer	:	1	2	3	4	5	6	7	8
Arrival time (minutes)	:	0	1.8	3.6	5.4	7.2	9.0	10.8	12.6

The time at which the service begins and ends within time period of 14 minutes is shown below. Waiting time of customers and idle time of service facility are also calculated.

Customer	*Service* *begins*	*ends*	*Waiting time of customer*	*Idle time of service facility*
1	0	4	0	0
2	4	8	4 – 1.8 = 2.2	0
3	8	12	8 – 3.6 = 4.4	0
4	12	16	12 – 5.4 = 6.6	0

The waiting time of the first four customers is calculated above. For the remaining, it is calculated below:

Customer	:	5	6	7	8
Waiting time (minutes)	:	14 – 7.2 = 6.8	5.0	3.2	1.4

∴ Average waiting time of a customer

$$= \frac{0 + 2.2 + 4.4 + 6.6 + 6.8 + 5 + 3.2 + 1.4}{8} = \frac{29.6}{8} = 3.7 \text{ minutes.}$$

Idle time of facility = nil.

EXAMPLE 13.7-2

Find the value of π experimentally by simulation.

Solution

Draw the coordinate axes OX and OY. With centre O draw an arc PR of unit radius as shown in Fig. 13.1 and complete the square OPQR. Equation of the circle is $x^2 + y^2 = 1$. From random number table C-1 (at the end of the book), select any two random numbers, say 0.2068 and 0.7295 (first two four-digit numbers with decimal from the second column) and let $x = 0.2068$ and $y = 0.7295$. Plot the point P_1 (0.2068, 0.7295). Obviously, if $x^2 + y^2 \le 1$, P_1 will lie inside or on arc of the circle but if $x^2 + y^2 > 1$, the point P_1 will lie outside the arc but within the square.

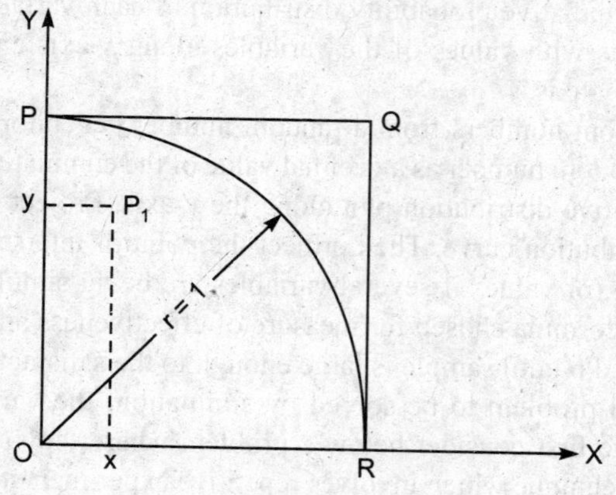

Fig.13.1

In this manner, hundreds or thousands of pairs of random numbers are selected and it is ascertained whether the points representing them lie in/on the arc or beyond the arc but inside the square. Suppose N is the total number of points considered, out of which n lie in/on the arc. Then

$$\frac{n}{N} = \frac{\text{area enclosed by the arc}}{\text{area of the square}}$$

$$= \frac{\frac{\pi}{4}(1)^2}{1} = \frac{\pi}{4} \quad \text{or} \quad \pi = \frac{4n}{N}.$$

The above equation gives the experimental value of π. Obviously, the larger the sample size N, closer will be the obtained value to the true value of π.

EXAMPLE 13.7-3

Three points are chosen at random on the circumference of a circle. Find by Monte Carlo methods the probability that they lie on the same semicircle.

Solution

Draw a circle of circumference unity *i.e.*, of radius $\frac{1}{2\pi}$ as shown in Fig 13.2. Consider a triplet of three random numbers (first three two-digit numbers with decimal from the last column) 0.48, 0.51 and 0.06 from the random number table C-1. These are plotted as points A, B and C in the figure, the distance of a point from O along the circumference anticlockwise being the value of a random number. Since for this triplet, the difference between the maxima (0.51) and minima (0.06) is less than 0.50, the triplet lies obviously on a semicircle.

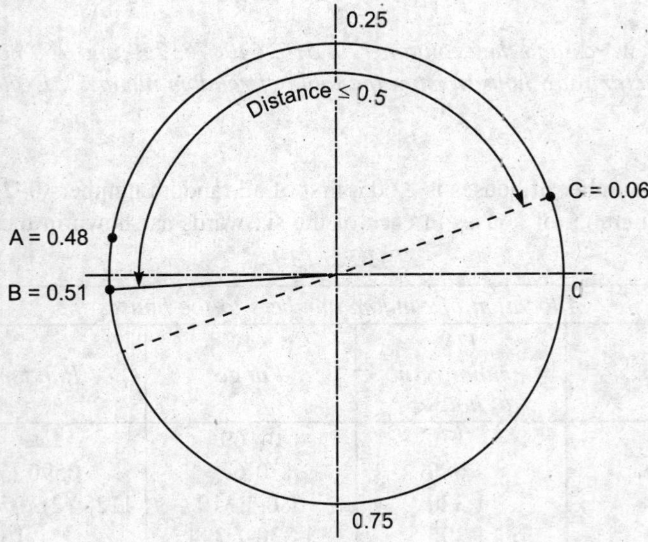

Fig. 13.2

The general rule for ascertaining whether a triplet of random numbers lies on a semicircle or not is as follows:

(*i*) Find the difference between the maxima and minima. If this difference is ≤ 0.50, the triplet lies on a semicircle.

(*ii*) If this difference is > 0.50, add unity to those random number(s) in the triplet which is (are) less than 0.50. Now find the difference between the new maxima and the minima. If this new difference is ≤ 0.50, the triplet lies on a semicircle, otherwise not.

Following the above rule it is ascertained whether each of the following 15 triplets lies (✓) or does not lie (×) on a semicircle.

S.No.	*Triplet*			*Difference between maxima and minima*	*Difference between new maxima and minima*
1	079	0.56	0.06	0.79 – 0.06 = 0.73	1.06 – 0.56 = 0.50 ✓
2	0.91	0.51	0.13	0.91 – 0.13 = 0.78	1.13 – 0.51 = 0.62 ×
3	0.65	0.59	0.51	0.65 – 0.51 = 0.14 ✓	
4	0.50	0.13	0.94	0.94 – 0.13 = 0.81	1.13 – 0.50 = 0.63 ×
5	0.57	0.26	0.78	0.78 – 0.26 = 0.52	1.26 – 0.57 = 0.69 ×
6	0.33	0.60	0.31	0.60 – 0.31 = 0.29 ✓	
7	0.15	0.64	0.89	0.89 – 0.15 = 0.74	1.15 – 0.64 = 0.51 ×
8	0.74	0.99	0.63	0.99 – 0.63 = 0.36 ✓	
9	0.58	0.83	0.44	0.83 – 0.44 = 0.39 ✓	
10	0.64	0.59	0.03	0.64 – 0.03 = 0.61	1.03 – 0.59 = 0.44 ✓
11	0.59	0.30	0.16	0.59 – 0.16 = 0.43 ✓	
12	0.57	0.87	0.21	0.87 – 0.21 = 0.66	1.21 – 0.57 = 0.64 ×
13	0.36	0.60	0.82	0.82 – 0.36 = 0.46 ✓	
14	0.37	0.72	0.33	0.72 – 0.33 = 0.39 ✓	
15	0.90	0.76	0.29	0.90 – 0.29 = 0.61	1.29 – 0.76 = 0.53 ×

Thus out of 15 triplets 9 lie on a semicircle, yielding the required probability $= \frac{9}{15} = 0.6$. However, if a large number of triplets are considered, the probability obtained will be very close to the theoretical value of 0.75.

EXAMPLE 13.7-4

A town has six wards and they contain 170, 510, 640, 75, 250 and 960 houses respectively. Make a random selection of 8 houses using the table of random numbers. Explain the procedure adopted by you. [*C.A. May, 1989*]

Solution

Since the total number of houses is 2,605, first of all random numbers 0–2,604 are allocated in proportion to the number of houses in each of the six wards as shown in the table below:

TABLE 13.1

Allocation of random numbers to the houses

(1) *Ward no.*	(2) *No. of houses*	(3) *Cumulative no. of houses*	(4) *Range*	(5) *Random nos. fitted*
1	170	170	0-169	
2	510	680	170-679	0590 (7), 0354 (8)
3	640	1,320	680-1,319	1128 (2), 0764 (4), 1292 (5)
4	75	1,395	1,320-1,394	1340 (6)
5	250	1,645	1,395-1,644	
6	960	2,605	1,645-2,604	2181 (1), 1749 (3)

The first random number picked up from the random number table is 2181 (first 4-digits of the first random number in table C-1). Since it lies within the interval 1,645-2,604, it is fitted against ward number 6 in column 5. The next random number is 1128, which lies in the interval 680-1,319 and is, therefore, fitted against ward number 3 in column 5. The next random number 7112 is > 2,604 in column 4 and is, therefore, dropped from consideration. In this manner the following random numbers are either fitted in column 5 or dropped; 6557 (D or dropped), 4199 (D), 3545 (D), 1749 (F3), 9103 (D), 0764 (F4), 3493 (D), 1292 (F5), 4397 (D), 3807 (D), 4984

(D), 1340 (F6), 0590 (F7), 9566 (D), 7615 (D), 8508 (D), 6970 (D), 5799 (D), 6343 (D), 4165 (D), 0354 (F5). We stop because 8 houses have been selected. The eight houses selected belong to ward number 6, 3, 6, 3, 3, 4, 2 and 2 respectively.

EXAMPLE 13.7-5

A bakery keeps stock of a popular brand of cake. Daily demand based on past experience is given below:

Daily demand	*0*	*15*	*25*	*35*	*45*	*50*
Probability	*0.01*	*0.15*	*0.20*	*0.50*	*0.12*	*0.02*

Consider the following sequence of random numbers:

48, 78, 09, 51, 56, 77, 15, 14, 68 and 09.

(i) Using the sequence, simulate the demand for the next 10 days.

(ii) Find the stock situation if the owner of the bakery decides to make 35 cakes every day. Also estimate the daily average demand for the cakes on the basis of the simulated data.

[J.N.T.U. Hyderabad MBA Nov., 2012; P.T.U. B.Tech. (Mech.) Nov., 2012; Dec., 2011; B.E., 2001; Nellore MBA, 2001; P.U. BBA, 2001]

Solution

(*i*) The simulated demand for the cakes for the next 10 days can be obtained from the table below.

TABLE 13.2

Allocation of random numbers to demand of cakes				
Demand	*Probability*	*Cumulative probability*	*Random number interval*	*Random numbers fitted*
0	0.01	0.01	00	
15	0.15	0.16	01 – 15	09(3), 15(7), 14(8), 09(10)
25	0.20	0.36	16 – 35	
35	0.50	0.86	36 – 85	48(1), 78(2), 51(4), 56(5), 77(6), 68(9)
45	0.12	0.98	86 – 97	
50	0.02	1.00	98 – 99	

In order to simulate the demand, the number 00 is assigned to zero demand, numbers 01–15 are assigned to demand of 15 cakes, 16 – 35 are assigned to demand of 25 cakes and so on. The given 10 random numbers are fitted in the last column corresponding to the ranges against the demand values. These random numbers give the demand for cakes for next 10 days. Serial no. of these random numbers are shown in the parentheses.

∴ Number of cakes demanded in the next 10 days are :

35, 35, 15, 35, 35, 35, 15, 15, 35 and 15 respectively.

(*ii*) The stock situation for various days if the decision is made to make 35 cakes everyday is given in the table below:

TABLE 13.3

Day	*Demand*	*No. of cakes made*	*Stock*
1	35	35	–
2	35	35	–
3	15	35	20
4	35	35	20
5	35	35	20
6	35	35	20
7	15	35	40
8	15	35	60
9	35	35	60
10	15	35	80

$$\therefore \text{Average daily demand} = \frac{1}{10}[35 + 35 + 15 + 35 + 35 + 35 + 15 + 15 + 35 + 15]$$
$$= \frac{270}{10} = 27 \text{ cakes.}$$

EXAMPLE 13.7-6

A company manufactures around 200 mopeds. Depending upon the availability of raw materials and other conditions, the daily production has been varying from 196 mopeds to 204 mopeds, whose probability distribution is as given below:

Production/day	:	*196*	*197*	*198*	*199*	*200*	*201*	*202*	*203*	*204*
Probability	:	*0.05*	*0.09*	*0.12*	*0.14*	*0.20*	*0.15*	*0.11*	*0.08*	*0.06*

The finished mopeds are transported in a specially designed three-storeyed lorry that can accommodate only 200 mopeds. Using the following 15 random numbers 82, 89, 78, 24, 53, 61, 18, 45, 04, 23, 50, 77, 27, 54 and 10, simulate the process to find out

(i) what will be the average number of mopeds waiting in the factory?

(ii) what will be the number of empty spaces in the lorry?

[*R.U. MBA June, 2011; P.T.U. B.Tech., 2001*]

Solution

The random numbers are established as in the table below:

TABLE 13.4

Production/day	*Probability*	*Cumulative probability*	*Random number interval*
196	0.05	0.05	00 – 04
197	0.09	0.14	05 – 13
198	0.12	0.26	14 – 25
199	0.14	0.40	26 – 39
200	0.20	0.60	40 – 59
201	0.15	0.75	60 – 74
202	0.11	0.86	75 – 85
203	0.08	0.94	86 – 93
204	0.06	1.00	94 – 99

Based on the 15 random numbers given, we simulate the production per day in the table below.

TABLE 13.5

Day no.	*Random number*	*Production per day*	*No. of mopeds waiting*	*Empty spaces in the lorry*
1	82	202	2	–
2	89	203	5	–
3	78	202	7	–
4	24	198	5	–
5	53	200	5	–
6	61	201	6	–
7	18	198	4	–
8	45	200	4	–
9	04	196	–	–
10	23	198	–	2
11	50	200	–	–
12	77	202	2	–
13	27	199	1	–
14	54	200	1	–
15	10	197	–	2

∴ Average number of mopeds waiting in the factory

$$= \frac{1}{15}[2+5+7-5+5+6+4+4+2+1+1] = 2.8.$$

Average number of empty spaces in the lorry = $\frac{4}{15}$ = 0.27.

EXAMPLE 13.7-7 (Queuing Problem)

Two persons X and Y work on a two-station assembly line. The distributions of activity times at their stations are

TABLE 13.6

Time in seconds	*Time frequency for X*	*Time frequency for Y*
10	4	2
20	7	3
30	10	6
40	15	8
50	35	12
60	18	9
70	8	7
80	3	3

(a) Simulate operation of the line for eight items.

(b) Assuming Y must wait until X completes the first item before starting work, will he have to wait to process any of the other seven items ? What is the average waiting time of items for Y. Use the following random numbers:

For X : 83, 70, 02, 12, 59, 46, 54 and 03.

For Y : 51, 99, 84, 81, 15, 36, 12 and 54.

(c) Determine the inventory of items between the two stations.

(d) What is the average production rate?

[R.T.M. Nagpur U. B.Tech. June, 2006; Kuru. U. B.E. (Mech.) June, 2012]

Solution

(*a*) Table below shows the cumulative frequency distribution for X. Eight random numbers given for person X are also fitted. The serial numbers of random numbers are shown in the parentheses.

TABLE 13.7

Time in seconds	*Time frequency for X*	*Cumulative frequency*	*Range*	*Random numbers fitted*
10	4	4	00 - 03	02(3), 03(8)
20	7	11	04 - 10	
30	10	21	11 - 20	12(4)
40	15	36	21 - 35	
50	35	71	36 - 70	70(2), 59(5), 46(6), 54(7)
60	18	89	71 - 88	83(1)
70	8	97	89 - 96	
80	3	100	97 - 99	

Thus the eight times for X are 60, 50, 10, 30, 50, 50, 50 and 10 seconds respectively. Likewise, the eight times for Y are derived from his cumulative distribution below.

TABLE 13.8

Time in seconds	Time frequency for Y	Cumulative frequency (i)	(ii)=2×(i)	Range	Random numbers fitted
10	2	2	4	00-03	
20	3	5	10	04-09	
30	6	11	22	10-21	15(5), 12(7)
40	8	19	38	22-37	36(6)
50	12	31	62	38-61	51(1), 54(8)
60	9	40	80	62-79	
70	7	47	94	80-93	84(3), 81(4)
80	3	50	100	94-99	99(2)

Thus the eight times for Y are 50, 80, 70, 70, 30, 40, 30 and 50 seconds respectively. Note that the cumulative frequency has been multiplied by 2 to make it 100.

(*b*) The above times for persons X and Y are used to calculate the waiting time, if any.

TABLE 13.9

Item no.	Person X		Person Y		Waiting time on the part of Y	Waiting time on the part of item
	Time in	Time out	Time in	Time out		
1	0	60	60	110	60	—
2	60	110	110	190	—	—
3	110	120	190	260	—	70
4	120	150	260	330	—	110
5	150	200	330	360	—	130
6	200	250	360	400	—	110
7	250	300	400	430	—	100
8	300	310	430	480		120

Thus person Y will not have to wait for the remaining seven items.

$$\text{Average waiting time of items} = \frac{0+0+70+110+130+110+100+120}{8} = \frac{640}{8} = 80 \text{ secs.}$$

(*c*) In all there are 6 items waiting between the two stations.

(*d*) Total time taken to process 8 items = 480 secs = 8 minutes.

$$\therefore \text{ Average production rate} = \frac{8}{8} = 1 \text{ item/minute.}$$

EXAMPLE 13.7-8 (Queuing Problem)

A dentist schedules all her patients for 30 minutes appointments. Some of the patients take more or less than 30 minutes depending on the type of dental work to be done. The following summary shows the various categories of work, their probabilities and the time needed to complete the work.

TABLE 13.10

Category	*Time required (minutes)*	*Probability of category*
Filling	45	0.40
Crown	60	0.15
Cleaning	15	0.15
Extraction	45	0.10
Checkup	15	0.20

Simulate the dentist's clinic for four hours and determine the average waiting time for the patients as well as the idleness of the doctor. Assume that all the patients show up at the clinic at exactly their scheduled arrival times, starting at 8 A.M. Use the following random numbers for handling the above problem: 40, 82, 11, 34, 25, 66, 17 and 79. [P.T.U. B.Tech. April, 2012; R.T.M. Nagpur U. B.E. (Mech.) 2011; I.T., 2009; June, 2005]

Solution

The time taken by the dentist to treat the eight patients arriving in four hours at the clinic is calculated in the table below.

TABLE 13.11

Category	*Time (minutes)*	*Probability*	*Cumulative probability*	*Random no. interval*	*Random no. fitted*
Filling	45	0.40	0.40	00-39	11(3), 34(4), 25(5), 17(7)
Crown	60	0.15	0.55	40-54	40(1)
Cleaning	15	0.15	0.70	55-69	66(6)
Extraction	45	0.10	0.80	70-79	79(8)
Checkup	15	0.20	1.00	80-99	82(2)

Thus the times taken by the dentist to treat the eight patients are 60, 15, 45, 45, 45, 15, 45 and 45 minutes respectively.

Let us simulate the dentist's clinic (for eight patients) starting at 8 A.M.

TABLE 13.12

Patient no.	*Arrival time*	*Dentist's treatment Starts*	*Ends*	*Waiting time on the part of the patient*	*Idle time for the dentist*
1	8.00	8.00	9.00	–	–
2	8.30	9.00	9.15	30	–
3	9.00	9.15	10.00	15	–
4	9.30	10.00	10.45	30	–
5	10.00	10.45	11.30	45	–
6	10.30	11.30	11.45	60	–
7	11.00	11.45	12.30	45	–
8	11.30	12.30	13.15	60	–

$$\therefore \text{ Average waiting time for the patients} = \frac{1}{8}[30 + 15 + 30 + 45 + 60 + 45 + 60]$$

$$= \frac{285}{8} = 35.625 \text{ minutes.}$$

Average idleness of the dentist = Nil.

EXAMPLE 13.7-9

A company manufactures 30 items per day. The sale of these items depends upon demand which has the following distribution:

Sales (units)	*Probability*
27	0.10
28	0.15
29	0.20
30	0.35
31	0.15
32	0.05

The production cost and sale price of each unit are ₹ 40 and ₹ 50 respectively. Any unsold product is to be disposed of at a loss of ₹ 15 per unit. There is a penalty of ₹ 5 per unit if the demand is not met. Using the following random numbers estimate total profit/loss for the company for the next 10 days : 10, 99, 65, 99, 95, 01, 79, 11, 16, 20.

If the company decides to produce 29 items per day, what is the advantage or disadvantage to the company ? *[P.T.U. B.Tech. (Prod.) Nov., 2012; April, 2012; R.U. MBA Dec., 2011; M.D.U. Rohtak B.E. (Mech.) Dec., 2006]*

Solution

First of all, random numbers 00-99 are allocated in proportion to the probabilities associated with the sale of the items as given below:

TABLE 13.13

Sales (units)	*Probability*	*Cumulative probability*	*Random number interval*
27	0.10	0.10	00-09
28	0.15	0.25	10-24
29	0.20	0.45	25-44
30	0.35	0.80	45-79
31	0.15	0.95	80-94
32	0.05	1.00	95-99

Let us now simulate the demand for next 10 days using the given numbers in order to estimate the total profit/loss for the company. Since the production cost of each item is ₹ 40 and sale price is ₹ 50, therefore the profit per unit of the sold item will be ₹ 10. There is a loss of ₹ 15 per unit associated with each unsold unit and a penalty of ₹ 5 per unit if the demand is not met. Accordingly, the profit/loss for next ten days are calculated in column (*iv*) of the table below if the company manufactures 30 items per day.

TABLE 13.14

(i) Day	*(ii)* Random number	*(iii)* Estimated sale	*(iv)* Profit/loss per day when Production = 30 items per day	*(v)* Profit/loss per day when Production = 29 items per day
1	10	28	28 × ₹ 10–2 × ₹ 15 = 250	28 × ₹ 10–1 × ₹ 15 = 265
2	99	32	30 × ₹ 10–2 × ₹ 5 = 290	29 × ₹ 10–3 × ₹ 5 = 275
3	65	30	30 × ₹ 10 = 300	29 × ₹ 10–1 × ₹ 5 = 285
4	99	32	30 × ₹ 10–2 × ₹ 5 = 290	29 × ₹ 10–3 × ₹ 5 = 275
5	95	32	30 × ₹ 10–2 × ₹ 5 = 290	29 × ₹ 10–3 × ₹ 5 = 275
6	01	27	27 × ₹ 10–3 × ₹ 15 = 225	27 × ₹ 10–2 × ₹ 15 = 240
7	79	30	30 × ₹ 10 = 300	29 × ₹ 10–1 × ₹ 5 = 285
8	11	28	28 × ₹ 10–2 × ₹ 15 = 250	28 × ₹ 10–1 × ₹ 15 = 265
9	16	28	28 × ₹ 10–2 × ₹ 15 = 250	28 × ₹ 10–1 × ₹ 15 = 265
10	20	28	28 × ₹ 10–2 × ₹ 15 = 250	28 × ₹ 10–1 × ₹ 15 = 265
Total profit			₹ 2,695	₹ 2,695

The total profit for next 10 days will be ₹ 2,695 if the company manufactures 30 items per day. In case, the company decides to produce 29 items per day, then the profit of the company for next 10 days is calculated in column (v) of the above table. It is evident from this table that there is no additional profit or loss if the production is reduced to 29 items per day since the total profit remains unchanged *i.e.*, ₹ 2,695.

EXAMPLE 13.7-10 (Investment and Budgeting Problem)

An Investment Corporation wants to study the investment projects based on three factors: market demand in units, price per unit minus cost per unit, and the investment required. These factors are felt to be independent of each other. In analyzing a new consumer product, the corporation estimates the following probability distributions:

TABLE 13.15

Annual demand	*Probability*	*(Price–Cost) per unit (₹)*	*Probability*	*Investment required (₹)*	*Probability*
25,000	0.05	3.00	0.10	27,50,000	0.25
30,000	0.10	5.00	0.20	30,00,000	0.50
35,000	0.20	7.00	0.40	35,00,000	0.25
40,000	0.30	9.00	0.20		
45,000	0.20	10.00	0.10		
50,000	0.10				
55,000	0.05				

Using simulation process, repeat the trial 10 times. Compute the return on investment for each trial, taking these factors into account. Approximately, what is the highest likely return? Use the following random numbers for annual demand, (price–cost) and the investment required:

28, 57, 60, 17, 64, 20, 27, 58, 61, 30; 19, 07, 90, 02, 57,
28, 29, 83, 58, 41; 18, 67, 16, 71, 43, 68, 47, 24, 19, 97.

Solution

First of all, random numbers 00-99 are assigned in proportion to the probabilities associated with the annual demand, (price–cost) and investment as given below :

TABLE 13.16

Annual demand (000's)	*Prob.*	*Cum. prob.*	*R. No. interval*	*(Price–cost) per unit*	*Prob.*	*Cum. prob.*	*R. No. interval*	*Invest. (000's) (₹)*	*Prob.*	*Cum. prob.*	*R. No. interval*
25	0.05	0.05	00-04	3.00	0.10	0.10	00-09	2,750	0.25	0.25	00-24
30	0.10	0.15	05-14	5.00	0.20	0.30	10-29	3,000	0.50	0.75	25-74
35	0.20	0.35	15-34	7.00	0.40	0.70	30-69	3,500	0.25	1.00	75-99
40	0.30	0.65	35-64	9.00	0.20	0.90	70-89				
45	0.20	0.85	65-84	10.00	0.10	1.00	90-99				
50	0.10	0.95	85-94								
55	0.05	1.00	95-99								

The yearly return can be determined by the formula:

$$\text{Return (R)} = \frac{(\text{Price} - \text{Cost}) \times \text{Number of units demanded}}{\text{Investment}} \times 100.$$

The results of the simulation are shown in the table given below:

TABLE 13.17

Trials	*Random number for demand*	*Simulated demand (000's)*	*Random number for profit (price–cost) per unit*	*Simulated profit (₹)*	*Random number for investment*	*Simulated investment (000's) (₹)*	*Simulated return (%)* $= \frac{\text{Demand} \times \text{Profit}}{\text{Investment}} \times 100$
1	28	35	19	5.00	18	2,750	6.36
2	57	40	07	3.00	67	3,000	4.00
3	60	40	90	10.00	16	2,750	14.55
4	17	35	02	3.00	71	3,000	3.50
5	64	40	57	7.00	43	3,000	9.33
6	20	35	28	5.00	68	3,000	5.83
7	27	35	29	5.00	47	3,000	5.83
8	58	40	83	9.00	24	2,750	13.10
9	61	40	58	7.00	19	2,750	10.18
10	30	35	41	7.00	97	3,500	7.00

Above table shows that the highest likely return is 14.55% which is corresponding to the annual demand of 40,000 units resulting a profit of ₹ 10 per unit and the required investment will be ₹ 27,50,000.

EXAMPLE 13.7-11

The occurrence of rain in a city on a day is dependent upon whether or not it trained on the previous day. If it rained on the previous day, the rain distribution is given by:

Event	*Probability*
No rain	*0.50*
1 cm rain	*0.25*
2 cm rain	*0.15*
3 cm rain	*0.05*
4 cm rain	*0.03*
5 cm rain	*0.02*

If it did not rain the previous day, the rain distribution is given by:

Event	*Probability*
No rain	*0.75*
1 cm rain	*0.15*
2 cm rain	*0.06*
3 cm rain	*0.04*

Simulate the city's weather for 10 days and determine by simulation the total days without rain as well as the total rainfall during the period. Use the following random numbers:

67 63 39 55 29 78 70 06 78 76

for simulation. Assume that for the first day of the simulation it had not rained the day before.

[*R.U. MBA June, 2011*]

Solution

The numbers 00-99 are allocated in proportion to the probabilities associated with each event. If it rained on the previous day, the rain distribution and the random number allocation are given below:

TABLE 13.18

Event	*Probability*	*Cumulative probability*	*Random number interval*
No rain	0.50	0.50	00 – 49
1 cm rain	0.25	0.75	50 – 74
2 cm rain	0.15	0.90	75 – 89
3 cm rain	0.05	0.95	90 – 94
4 cm rain	0.03	0.98	95 – 97
5 cm rain	0.02	1.00	98 – 99

Similarly, if it did not rain the previous day, the necessary distribution and the random number allocation is given below:

TABLE 13.19

Event	*Probability*	*Cumulative probability*	*Random number interval*
No rain	0.75	0.75	00-74
1 cm rain	0.15	0.90	75-89
2 cm rain	0.06	0.96	90-95
3 cm rain	0.04	1.00	96-99

Let us now simulate the rainfall for 10 days using the given random numbers. For the first day it is given that it had not rained the day before :

TABLE 13.20

Day	*Random numbers*	*Event*	*Remarks*
1	67	No rain	(from table 2)
2	63	No rain	(from table 2)
3	39	No rain	(from table 2)
4	55	No rain	(from table 2)
5	29	No rain	(from table 2)
6	78	1 cm rain	(from table 2)
7	70	1 cm rain	(from table 1)
8	06	No rain	(from table 1)
9	78	1 cm rain	(from table 2)
10	76	2 cm rain	(from table 1)

Hence, during the simulated period, it did not rain on 6 days out of 10. The total rainfall during the period was 5 cm.

EXAMPLE 13.7-12 (Quality Control Problem)

The output of a production line is checked by an inspector for one or more of three different types of defects, called defects A, B and C. If defect A occurs, the item is scrapped. If defect B or C occurs, the item must be reworked. The time required to rework a B defect is 15 minutes and the time required to rework a C defect is 30 minutes. The probabilities of an A, B and C defects are 0.15, 0.20 and 0.10 respectively. For ten items coming off the assembly line, determine the number of items without any defects, the number scrapped and the total minutes of rework time. Use the following random numbers:

RN for defect A	:	48	55	91	40	93	01	83	63	47	52
RN for defect B	:	47	36	57	04	79	55	10	13	57	09
RN for defect C	:	82	95	18	96	20	84	56	11	52	03

Solution

The probabilities of occurrence of A, B ad C defects are 0.15, 0.20 and 0.10 respectively. So, the numbers 00-99 are allocated in proportion to the probabilities associated with each of the three defects.

TABLE 13.21

Defect A		*Defect B*		*Defect C*	
Exists?	*Random numbers assigned*	*Exists?*	*Random numbers assigned*	*Exists?*	*Random numbers assigned*
Yes	00-14	Yes	00-19	Yes	00-09
No	15-99	No	20-99	No	10-99

Let us now simulate the output of the assembly line for 10 items using the given random numbers in order to determine the number of items without any defect, the number of items scrapped and the total minutes of rework time required:

TABLE 13.22

Item No.	*RN for defect A*	*RN for defect B*	*RN for defect C*	*Whether any defect exists*	*Rework time in minutes*	*Remarks*
1	48	47	82	None	-	-
2	55	36	95	None	-	-
3	91	57	18	None	-	-
4	40	04	96	B	15	-
5	93	79	20	None	-	-
6	01	55	84	A	-	Scrap
7	83	10	56	B	15	-
8	63	13	11	B	15	-
9	47	57	52	None	-	-
10	52	09	03	B,C	15 + 30 = 45	-

During the simulated period, 5 out of the ten items had no defects, one item was scrapped and 90 minutes of total rework time was required by 4 items.

EXAMPLE 13.7-13 (Investment and Budgeting Problem)

The management of ABC company is considering the question of marketing a new product. The fixed cost required in the project is ₹ 4,000. Three factors are uncertain viz. the selling price, variable cost and the annual sales volume. The product has a life of only one year. The management has the data on these three factors as under:

TABLE 13.23

Selling price (₹)	*Probability*	*Variable cost (₹)*	*Probability*	*Sales volume (units)*	*Probability*
3	0.2	1	0.3	2,000	0.3
4	0.5	2	0.6	3,000	0.3
5	0.3	3	0.1	5,000	0.4

Consider the following sequence of thirty random numbers:

81 32 60 ; 04 46 31 ; 67 25 24 ; 10 40 02 ; 39 68 08 ;
59 66 90 ; 12 64 79 ; 31 86 68 ; 82 89 25 ; 11 98 16.

Using the sequence (First 3 random numbers for the first trial, etc.) simulate the average profit for the above project on the basis of 10 trials. [P.T.U. B.Tech. (Prod.) Nov., 2012]

Solution

First of all, random numbers 00-99 are allocated in proportion to the probabilities associated with each of the three variables as given under:

TABLE 13.24

Selling price (₹)	*Probabilities*	*Cumulative probabilities*	*Random numbers assigned*
3	0.2	0.2	00-19
4	0.5	0.7	20-69
5	0.3	1.0	70-99
Variable cost (₹)			
1	0.3	0.3	00-29
2	0.6	0.9	30-89
3	0.1	1.0	90-99
Sales volume (units)			
2,000	0.3	0.3	00-29
3,000	0.3	0.6	30-59
5,000	0.4	1.0	60-99

Let us now simulate the output of ten trials using the given random numbers in order to find the average profit for the project:

TABLE 13.25

S. No.	*Random No.*	*Selling price (₹)*	*Random No.*	*Variable cost (₹)*	*Random No.*	*Sales volume ('000 units')*
1	81	5	32	2	60	5
2	04	3	46	2	31	3
3	67	4	25	1	24	2
4	10	3	40	2	02	2
5	39	4	68	2	08	2
6	59	4	66	2	90	5
7	12	3	64	2	79	5
8	31	4	86	2	68	5
9	82	5	89	2	25	2
10	11	3	98	3	16	2

Profit = (Selling price – Variable cost) × Sales volume – Fixed cost.

Simulated profit in ten trials would be as follows:

TABLE 13.26

S. No.	*Profit*		
1	(₹ 5 – ₹ 2) × 5,000 units – ₹ 4,000	=	₹ 11,000
2	(₹ 3 – ₹ 2) × 3,000 units – ₹ 4,000	=	– ₹1,000
3	(₹ 4 – ₹ 1) × 2,000 units – ₹ 4,000	=	₹ 2,000
4	(₹ 3 – ₹ 2) × 2,000 units – ₹ 4,000	=	– ₹ 2,000
5	(₹ 4 – ₹ 2) × 2,000 units – ₹ 4,000	=	0
6	(₹ 4 – ₹ 2) × 5,000 units – ₹ 4,000	=	₹ 6,000
7	(₹ 3 – ₹ 2) × 5,000 units – ₹ 4,000	=	₹ 1,000
8	(₹ 4 – ₹ 2) × 5,000 units – ₹ 4,000	=	₹ 6,000
9	(₹ 5 – ₹ 2) × 2,000 units – ₹ 4,000	=	₹ 2,000
10	(₹ 3 – ₹ 3) × 2,000 units – ₹ 4,000	=	– ₹ 4,000
			Total ₹ 21,000

Therefore, average profit per trial = $\frac{₹\,21,000}{10}$ = ₹ 2,100.

EXAMPLE 13.7-14

The director of finance for a farm cooperative is concerned about the yield per acre she can expect from this year's corn crop. The probability distribution of the yields for the current weather conditions is given below:

Yield in kg per acre	*Probability*
120	*0.18*
140	*0.26*
160	*0.44*
180	*0.12*

She would like to see a simulation of the yield she might expect over the next 10 years for weather conditions similar to those she is now experiencing.

(i) Simulate the average yield she might expect per acre using the following random numbers: 20, 72, 34, 54, 30, 22, 48, 74, 76, 02.

She is also interested in the effect of market price fluctuations on the cooperative's farm revenue. She makes this estimate of per kg prices for corn:

Price per kg (₹)	*Probability*
2.00	*0.05*
2.10	*0.15*
2.20	*0.30*
2.30	*0.25*
2.40	*0.15*
2.50	*0.10*

(ii) Simulate the price she might expect to observe over the next 10 years using the following random numbers:

82, 95, 18, 96, 20, 84, 56, 11, 52, 03.

(iii) Assuming that prices are independent of yields, combine these two into the revenue per acre and also find out the average revenue per acre she might expect every year.

[*C.A. (Final) May, 1991*]

Solution

(*i*) Simulation for 10 years is carried out in the table below:

TABLE 13.27

Yield in kg/acre	*Probability*	*Cumulative probability*	*Range*	*Random numbers fitted*
120	0.18	00.18	0–17	02(10)
140	0.26	0.44	18–43	20(1), 34(3), 30(5), 22(6)
160	0.44	0.88	44–87	72(2), 54(4), 48(7), 74(8), 76(9)
180	0.12	1.00	88–99	

∴ Yields over the next ten years are 140, 160, 140, 160, 140, 140, 160, 160, 160 and 120 kg respectively.

(*ii*) Price/kg of the corn crop over the next 10 years is simulated in the table below:

TABLE 13.28

Price/kg (₹)	*Probability*	*Cumulative probability*	*Range*	*Random numbers fitted*
2.00	0.05	0.05	00–04	03(10)
2.10	0.15	0.20	05–19	18(3), 11(8)
2.20	0.30	0.50	20–49	20(5)
2.30	0.25	0.75	50–74	56(7), 52(9)
2.40	0.15	0.90	75–89	82(1), 84(6)
2.50	0.10	1.00	90–99	95(2), 96 (4)

∴ Price/kg over the next 10 years is ₹ 2.40, 2.50, 2.10, 2.50, 2.20, 2.40, 2.30, 2.10, 2.30 and 2.00 respectively.

(*iii*) Revenue/acre = Yield in kg/acre × price in ₹/kg.

∴ Revenue/acre over the next 10 years is ₹ 336, 400, 294, 400, 308, 336, 368, 336, 368 and 240 respectively.

Expected yield/acre = 120 × 0.18 +140 × 0.26 + 160 × 0.44 + 180 × 0.12
= (21.6 + 36.4 + 70.4 + 21.6) kg = 150 kg.

Expected price/kg = ₹ (2 × 0.05 + 2.10 × 0.15 + 2.20 × 0.30 + 2.30 × 0.25
+ 2.40 × 0.15 + 2.50 × 0.10)
= ₹ (0.10 + 0.315 + 0.66 + 0.575 + 0.36 + 0.25) = ₹ 2.26.

∴ Average revenue/acre = ₹ 150 × 2.26 = ₹ 339.

EXAMPLE 13.7-15

Popa Ltd. trade in a perishable commodity. Each day Popa Ltd. receives supplies of the goods from a wholesaler but the quantity supplied is a random variable, as is the subsequent retail customer demand for the commodity. Both supply and demand are expressed in batches of 50 units and over the past working year (300 days), Popa Ltd. has kept records of supplies and demands. The results are in the table below:

TABLE 13.29

Wholesaler supplies	*No. of days occurring*	*Customer's demand*	*No. of days occurring*
50	*60*	*50*	*60*
100	*90*	*100*	*60*
150	*90*	*150*	*150*
200	*60*	*200*	*30*

Popa Ltd. buys the commodity at ₹ 6/unit and sells at ₹ 10/unit. At present unsold units at the end of the day are worthless and there are no storage facilities. Popa Ltd. estimates that each unit of unsatisfied demand on any day costs them ₹ 2. Using the following random numbers:

8, 4, 8, 0, 3, 3; 4, 7, 9, 6, 1 and 5,

(i) simulate six days' trading and estimate the annual profit.

(ii) repeat the exercise to estimate the value of storage facilities. [*ICWA (Final) 2000*]

Solution

Wholesaler's supplies are simulated for 6 days in the table below:

TABLE 13.30

Supplies	*No. of days*	*Total no. of days*	*No. of days out of 10*	*Random no. range*	*Random no. fitted*
50	60	60	2	00–01	0(4)
100	90	150	5	02–04	4(2), 3(5), 3(6)
150	90	240	8	05–07	
200	60	300	10	08–09	8(1), 8 (3)

∴ Wholesaler's supplies in the next 6 days are 200, 100, 200, 50, 100 and 100 units respectively.

Similarly, customer's demand over the next 6 days is simulated in the table below:

TABLE 13.31

Demand	*No. of days occurring*	*Total no. of days*	*No. of days out of 10*	*Random no. range*	*Random no. fitted*
50	60	60	2	00–01	1(5)
100	60	120	4	02–03	4(1), 7(2), 6(4), 5(6)
200	30	300	10	09	9(9)

∴ Customer's demand in the next 6 days is 150, 150, 200, 150, 50 and 150 units respectively.

The shortage and net profit or loss in the 6 days is now calculated as shown in the table below:

TABLE 13.32

Day	*Supply*		*Demand*		*Shortage*		*Net profit*
no.	*units*	*cost (₹)*	*units*	*sales (₹)*	*units*	*cost (₹)*	*or loss (₹)*
1	200	1,200	150	1,500	—	—	1,500 – 1,200 = 300
2	100	600	150	1,500	50	100	1,500 – 600 – 100 = 800
3	200	1,200	200	2,000	—	—	2,000 – 1,200 = 800
4	50	300	150	1,500	100	200	1,500 – 300 – 200 = 1,000
5	100	600	50	500	—	—	500 – 600 = – 100
6	100	600	150	1,500	50	100	1,500 – 600 – 100 = 800

(*i*) Net profit from table 13.32 for 6 days = ₹ 3,600.

$$\therefore \text{ Annual profit} = ₹\ \frac{3,600 \times 300}{6} = ₹\ 1,80,000.$$

(*ii*) To determine the value of storage facilities we, first, construct table 13.33.

TABLE 13.33

Day no.	*Supply*	*Demand*	*Storage*	*Remarks*
1	200	150	50	
2	100	150	Nil	Shortage cost of ₹ 100 for 50 units could be avoided.
3	200	200	Nil	
4	50	150	Nil	
5	100	50	50	
6	100	150	Nil	Shortage cost of ₹ 100 for 50 units could be avoided.

If the storage facilities are provided, as mentioned in the remarks column, ₹ 200 of shortage cost could be avoided by storing 50 + 50 = 100 units. These 100 units could be then sold, yielding a profit of ₹ 4 × 100 = ₹ 400.

∴ The value of storage facilities = ₹ (200 + 400) = ₹ 600.

EXAMPLE 13.7-16 (Job Sequencing Problem)

Phillips India is engaged in manufacturing different types of equipment for various consumers. The company has two assembly lines to produce its product. The processing time for each of the assembly lines is regarded as a random variable and is described by the following distributions:

TABLE 13.34

Processing time (min)	*Assembly X*	*Assembly Y*
40	0.10	0.20
42	0.15	0.40
44	0.40	0.20
46	0.10	0.15
48	0.25	0.05

Using the following random numbers, generate data on the processing times for 10 units of the product and compute the expected processing time for the product:

4236, 7573, 4943, 1283, 2014, 3604, 9344, 5316, 7606, 0089.

For the purpose, read the numbers horizontally, taking the first two digits for the processing time on assembly X and the last two digits for processing time on assembly Y.

[P.T.U. B.Tech. April, 2012]

Solution

First of all we allocate random number intervals for various processing times.

TABLE 13.35

Processing times (min)	*Assembly X*			*Assembly Y*		
	Prob.	*Cum. prob.*	*R.N. interval*	*Prob.*	*Cum. prob.*	*R.N. interval*
40	0.10	0.10	00 – 09	0.20	0.20	00 – 19
42	0.15	0.25	10 – 24	0.40	0.60	20 – 59
44	0.40	0.65	25 – 64	0.20	0.80	60 – 79
46	0.10	0.75	65 – 74	0.15	0.95	80 – 94
48	0.25	1.00	75 – 99	0.05	1.00	95 – 99

Random numbers for the first unit are 42 and 36 respectively for assemblies *X* and *Y*. We observe that the processing times corresponding to these are 44 and 42 minutes respectively. Similarly, processing times for various units are computed in the table given below.

TABLE 13.36

S. No.	*Assembly X*		*Assembly Y*		*Total time (min.)*
	R. No.	*Time (min)*	*R. No.*	*Time (min)*	
1	42	44	36	42	86
2	75	48	73	44	92
3	49	44	43	42	86
4	12	42	83	46	88
5	20	42	14	40	82
6	36	44	04	40	84
7	93	48	44	42	90
8	53	44	16	40	84
9	76	48	06	40	88
10	00	40	89	46	86

∴ Total time for 10 units = 866 minutes.

$$\therefore \text{ Expected time for the product} = \frac{866}{10} = 86.6 \text{ minutes.}$$

EXAMPLE 13.7-17 (Queuing Problem)

At a small store of ready made garments, there is one clerk at the counter who is to check the bills, receive payments and place the packed garments into fancy bags, etc. The customers' arrival at the check counter is a random phenomenon and the time between the arrivals varies from one minute to five minutes, the frequency distribution for which is given in table 13.37. The service time (time taken by the counter clerk) varies from one minute to three minutes. The manager of the store feels that the counter clerk is not sufficiently loaded with work and wants to assign to him some additional work. But before taking the decision he likes to know precisely by what percentage of time the counter clerk is idle.

TABLE 13.37

Frequency distribution of interarrival times			
Time between arrivals (minutes)	*Frequency %*	*Cumulative frequency (%)*	*Random no. range*
1	35	35	00 – 34
2	25	60	35 – 59
3	20	80	60 – 79
4	12	92	80 – 91
5	8	100	92 – 99

TABLE 13.38

Frequency distribution of service times			
Service time (minutes)	*Frequency %*	*Cumulative frequency (%)*	*Random no. range*
1.0	20	20	00 – 19
1.5	35	55	20 – 54
2.0	25	80	55 – 79
2.5	15	95	80 – 94
3.0	5	100	95 – 99

Solution

As the random numbers are not provided in the problem, we select them from the random number table C-1 as indicated in table 13.39. The process of arrivals and service is simulated for 20 customers.

TABLE 13.39

Arrivals (1)	*Random number (First two digits of last col. in table C-1) (2)*	*Interarrival time (minutes) (3)*	*Random no.(Last two digits of last col. in table C-1) (4)*	*Service time (minutes) (5)*
1	48	2	22	1.5
2	51	2	62	2
3	06	1	25	1.5
4	22	1	31	1.5
5	79	3	23	1.5
6	56	2	07	1
7	06	1	93	2.5
8	91	4	44	1.5
9	51	2	12	1
10	13	1	26	1.5
11	65	3	93	2.5

12	59	2	01	1
13	51	2	17	1
14	50	2	49	1.5
15	13	1	58	2
16	94	5	98	3
17	57	2	61	2
18	26	1	41	1.5
19	78	3	13	1
20	33	1	59	2

The computations carried for 20 customer arrivals are shown in table 13.40. When the first customer arrives, counter clerk is free and service immediately begins. Service time required is 1.5 minutes (table 13.39). Time between the first and second arrivals is 2 minutes (table 13.39) and thus the clerk is idle for 0.5 minute before the next arrival occurs. When the second customer arrives, service immediately starts, required service time for 2nd arrival is 2 minutes and the time between the 2nd and 3rd arrivals is also 2 minutes. Therefore, there is no idle time for the counter clerk between the second and third arrivals. For the third arrival, service time is 1.5 minutes and the inter-arrival time between 3rd and 4th arrivals is only one minute and obviously 4th customer will have to wait for 0.5 minute before the service can begin. This way the computations are continued (table 13.40). For 20 customer arrivals the counter clerk is idle for 10.5 minutes, while the customers have to wait for 7.5 minutes. The total time taken by 20 arrivals is 41 minutes (summing up the interarrival times). Therefore, the counter clerk is idle for about $\frac{10.5 \times 100}{41} = 25.6\%$ of the time. Based on this specific information, the manager can take the decision of assigning some additional work to the counter clerk.

TABLE 13.40

Interarrival time (min)	*Actual arrival time (min)*	*Service time (min)*	*Service starts (min)*	*Service ends (min)*	*Counter clerk's idle time (min)*	*Customer's waiting time (min)*
2	2	1.5	2	3.5	2	-
2	4	2	4	6	0.5	-
1	5	1.5	6	7.5	-	1
1	6	1.5	7.5	9	-	1.5
3	9	1.5	9	10.5	-	-
2	11	1	11	12	0.5	-
1	12	2.5	12	14.5	-	-
4	16	1.5	16	17.5	1.5	-
2	18	1	18	19	0.5	-
1	19	1.5	19	20.5	-	-
3	22	2.5	22	24.5	1.5	-
2	24	1	24.5	25.5	-	0.5
2	26	1	26	27	0.5	-
2	28	1.5	28	29.5	1	-
1	29	2	29.5	31.5	-	0.5
5	34	3	34	37	2.5	-
2	36	2	37	39	-	1
1	37	1.5	39	40.5	-	2
3	40	1	40.5	41.5	-	0.5
1	41	2	41.5	43.5	-	0.5
					10.5	7.5

EXAMPLE 13.7-18 (Queuing Problem)

A small scale factory has a machinist to process the jobs. The interarrival time for the jobs is not fixed. The processing time on the jobs also varies. These times are described by frequency distributions given below:

TABLE 13.41

Interarrival time distribution		*Processing time distribution*	
Interarrival time (min)	*Frequency*	*Processing time (min)*	*Frequency*
4	*10*	*3*	*5*
5	*20*	*4*	*30*
6	*40*	*5*	*30*
7	*20*	*6*	*30*
8	*10*	*7*	*5*
	100		*100*

Determine the idle time of the machinist and the waiting time of jobs in a period of 2 hours.

If the machinist's wages are ₹ 20 per hour and the job's waiting time costs ₹ 30 per hour, would it be economical to engage a second attendant ? [*P.T.U. B.Tech. April, 2012*]

Solution

Table below shows the cumulative frequency distribution for interarrival times. Twenty five random nos. picked from random no. table are also plotted. The serial numbers of the random nos. are shown in the parentheses.

TABLE 13.42

Interarrival time (min)	*Frequency*	*Cumulative frequency*	*Range*	*Random nos. fitted*
4	10	10	00-09	03(5), 09(17), 02(23)
5	20	30	10-29	22(1), 19(2), 16 (3), 23(8), 15(9), 18(15), 12(18)
6	40	70	30-69	58(10), 57(11), 48(12), 61(13), 36(14), 38(20), 53(21), 40(22)
7	20	90	70-89	78(4), 78(7), 88(16), 85(19), 85(25)
8	10	100	90-99	93(6), 95(24)

Thus the interarrival times of the jobs are 5, 5, 5, 7, 4, 8, 7, 5, 5, 6, 6, 6, 6, 6, 5, 7, 4, 5, 7, 6, 6, 6, 4, 8, and 7 minutes respectively.

Likewise, the twenty five jobs will have the processing times derived from the following table:

TABLE 13.43

Processing time (min)	*Frequency*	*Cumulative frequency*	*Range*	*Random nos. fitted*
3	5	5	00-04	
4	30	35	05-34	13(2), 09(3), 20(4), 18(10), 24(11), 22(12), 07(13), 29 (14), 33(16), 12(23), 31(24)
5	30	65	35-64	57(15), 49(17), 64(18), 57(22)
6	30	95	65-94	68(1), 73(5), 87(6), 92(7), 93(9), 92(19)
7	5	100	95-99	99(8), 98(20), 99(21), 96(25)

Thus the processing times for the jobs are 6, 4, 4, 4, 6, 6, 6, 7, 6, 4, 4, 4, 4, 4, 5, 4, 5, 5, 6, 7, 7, 5, 4, 4 and 7 minutes respectively.

Table 13.37 can now be prepared by linking the interarrival times and processing times of the jobs.

TABLE 13.44

Interarrival time (min)	*Actual arrival time (min)*	*Processing time (min)*	*Processing starts (min)*	*Processing ends (min)*	*Machinist idle time (min)*	*Job's waiting time (min)*
5	5	6	5	11	5	-
5	10	4	11	15	-	1
5	15	4	15	19	-	-
7	22	4	22	26	3	-
4	26	6	26	32	-	-
8	34	6	34	40	2	-
7	41	6	41	47	1	-
5	46	7	47	54	-	1
5	51	6	54	60	-	3
6	57	4	60	64	-	3
6	63	4	64	68	-	1
6	69	4	69	73	1	-
6	75	4	75	79	2	-
6	81	4	81	85	2	-
5	86	5	86	91	1	-
7	93	4	93	97	2	-
4	97	5	97	102	-	-
5	102	5	102	107	-	-
7	109	6	109	115	2	-
6	115	7	115	122	-	-

From table 13.44,

total idle time for the machinist in 2-hour period = 21 minutes,

total waiting time for the jobs in 2-hour period = 9 minutes.

∴ Average idle time for the machinist / hour $= \frac{21}{2} = 10.5$ minutes, and idle-time cost of the machinist / hour $\frac{10.5}{60} \times 20 = ₹\, 3.50$.

Average waiting time for the jobs / hour $= \frac{9}{2} = 4.5$ minutes, and waiting-time cost of the jobs/ hour $= \frac{4.5}{60} \times 30 = ₹\, 2.25$.

Since the idle-time cost of the machinist/hour is more than the waiting-time cost of the jobs/ hour, it is not economical to engage the second attendant.

EXAMPLES 13.7-19 (Queuing Problem)

In a workshop, fitters report at the tool crib after 8 A.M. to get the tools where the tool room attendant is present to issue them. The arrival and service time distributions are shown below:

TABLE 13.45

Arrival distribution		*Service distribution*	
Interarrival time (min)	*Frequency*	*Service time (min)*	*Frequency*
3.5 – 4.5	0.05	3.5-4.5	0.10
4.5 – 5.5	0.20	4.5-5.5	0.20
5.5 – 6.5	0.35	5.5-6.5	0.40
6.5 – 7.5	0.25	6.5-7.5	0.20
7.5 – 8.5	0.10	7.5-8.5	0.10
8.5 – 9.5	0.05		

Determine the average waiting time of a fitter in the queue. What is the average time he spends in the system? Simulate the queuing phenomenon for a period of 2 hours. Also find average waiting time in non-empty queue and per cent time the tool room attendant remains busy in this period.

Solution

First, mean values of interarrival times and service times are computed. Then cumulative frequency distributions for interarrival times are calculated. Random numbers are also plotted; their serial nos. are shown in parentheses.

TABLE 13.46

Mean interarrival time (min)	*Frequency (%)*	*Cumulative frequency*	*Range*	*Random numbers fitted*
4	5	5	00-04	01 (15)
5	20	25	05-24	15 (1), 09 (2), 20 (12)
6	35	60	25-59	41 (3), 55 (7), 35 (9), 41 (10), 45 (13), 38 (14), 39 (18), 55 (19)
7	25	85	60-84	74 (4), 72 (5), 67 (6), 71 (8), 67 (16), 63 (17)
8	10	95	85-94	
9	5	100	95-99	96 (11)

Thus the interarrival times of the fitters are 5, 5, 6, 7, 7, 7, 6, 7, 6, 6, 9, 5, 6, 6, 4, 7, 7, 6 and 6 minutes respectively.

Likewise, the service times for the 19 fitters can be obtained from the following table:

TABLE 13.47

Mean service time (minutes)	*Frequency (%)*	*Cumulative frequency*	*Range*	*Random numbers fitted*
4	10	10	00-09	02 (11), 07 (12)
5	20	30	10-29	20 (1), 22 (7), 23 (15)
6	40	70	30-69	34 (3), 54 (4), 40 (5), 31 (6), 48 (8), 64 (13), 48 (17), 55 (18)
7	20	90	70-89	72 (2), 74 (9), 76 (10)
8	10	100	90-99	95 (14), 91 (16), 91 (19)

Thus the service times for the fitters are 5, 7, 6, 6, 6, 6, 5, 6, 7, 7, 4, 4, 6, 8, 5, 8, 6, 6 and 8 minutes respectively.

Table 13.48 can now be prepared by linking the interarrival and service times of the fitters.

TABLE 13.48

S. No.	*Interarrival time (min)*	*Actual arrival time (min)*	*Service time (min)*	*Service starts (min)*	*Service ends (min)*	*Fitter's waiting time (min)*	*Attendant's idle time (min)*
1	5	8.05	5	8.05	8.10	-	5
2	5	8.10	7	8.10	8.17	-	-
3	6	8.16	6	8.17	8.23	1	-
4	7	8.23	6	8.23	8.29	-	-
5	7	8.30	6	8.30	8.36	-	1
6	7	8.37	6	8.37	8.43	-	1
7	6	8.43	5	8.43	8.48	-	-
8	7	8.50	6	8.50	8.56	-	2
9	6	8.56	7	8.56	9.03	-	-
10	6	9.02	7	9.03	9.10	1	-
11	9	9.11	4	9.11	9.15	-	1
12	5	9.16	4	9.16	9.20	-	1
13	6	9.22	6	9.22	9.28	-	2
14	6	9.28	8	9.28	9.36	-	-
15	4	9.32	5	9.36	9.41	4	-
16	7	9.39	8	9.41	9.49	2	-
17	7	9.46	6	9.49	9.55	3	-
18	6	9.52	6	9.55	10.01	3	-
19	6	9.58					
			108			14	13

From table 13.48,
total waiting time on the part of all the 18 fitters = 14 minutes.

$\therefore$ Average waiting time of a fitter in the queue $= \frac{14}{18} = \frac{7}{9}$ minute.

Average time a fitter spends in the system $= \frac{7}{9} + \frac{108}{18} = 6\frac{7}{9}$ minutes.

Average waiting time of a fitter in non-empty queue

$$= \frac{\text{total waiting time}}{\text{no. of cases when fitter has to wait}}$$

$$= \frac{14}{6} = 2\frac{1}{3} \text{ minutes.}$$

Total tool room attendants' time for 18 fitters = Service time + Idle time = 108 + 13 = 121 minutes.
Percentage time the tool room attendant remains busy

$$= \frac{108}{121} \times 100 = 89.26\%.$$

EXAMPLE 13.7-20 (Maintenance Problem)

Determine the optimum number of mechanics for 100 semi-automatic machine tools. The operation of the machine tools is automatic and warrants attention of the mechanics only when there is breakdown. The breakdowns have been seen to occur at the following times:

Breakdown	:	*1*	*2*	*3*	*4*	*5*	*6*	*7*	*8*	*9*
Time (hour)	:	*0*	*1.2*	*2.1*	*2.4*	*2.6*	*3.8*	*4.3*	*5.1*	*6.0*

The repair times for the machine tools have been observed to be according to the following distribution :

Time of repair (hour)	:	1.2	1.3	1.4	1.5	1.6	1.7	1.8	1.9	2.0
Frequency	:	50	110	210	350	105	70	50	45	10

The wage of a mechanic is ₹ 18 per hour. Downtime cost of the machine is ₹ 5 per hour. Calculate whether two or three mechanics should be employed. Use random numbers: 105, 159, 885, 989, 657, 888, 729, 285 and 530.

Solution

Since frequency distribution is given for the repair times only, they are calculated from the table below:

TABLE 13.49

Repair time	*Frequency*	*Cumulative frequency*	*R.N. Range*	*Random numbers fitted*
1.2	50	50	000-049	
1.3	110	160	050-159	105 (1), 159 (2)
1.4	210	370	160-369	285 (8)
1.5	350	720	370-719	657 (5), 530 (9)
1.6	105	825	720-824	729 (7)
1.7	70	895	825-894	885 (3), 888 (6)
1.8	50	945	895-944	
1.9	45	990	945-989	989 (4)
2.0	10	1,000	990-999	

Thus the repair times for the nine break downs are 1.3, 1.3, 1.7, 1.9, 1.5, 1.7, 1.6, 1.4 and 1.5 hours respectively. Table 13.50 is now prepared by linking the machine tool breakdown times with the repair times when two mechanics are employed.

It may be noted that the breakdown time is clock time and not the interbreak down time. Accordingly, breakdown times are not added in this table whereas we added them in the previous examples.

TABLE 13.50

M/c tool breakdown time (hr)	*Repair time (hr)*	*Mechanic engaged*	*Repair starts (hr)*	*Repair ends (hr)*	*Waiting time of the m/c tool (hr)*	*Idle time of the mechanic (hr)*
0	1.3	1st	0	1.3	-	-
1.2	1.3	2nd	1.2	2.5	-	1.2
2.1	1.7	1st	2.1	3.8	-	0.8
2.4	1.9	2nd	2.5	4.4	0.1	-
2.6	1.5	1st	3.8	5.3	1.2	-
3.8	1.7	2nd	4.4	6.1	0.6	-
4.3	1.6	1st	5.3	6.9	1.0	-
5.1	1.4	2nd	6.1	7.5	1.0	-
6.0	1.5	1st	6.9	8.4	0.9	-
					Total: 4.8	Total: 2.0

Next, table 13.51 is prepared if three persons are employed.

TABLE 13.51

M/c tool breakdown time (hr)	*Repair time (hr)*	*Mechanic engaged*	*Repair starts (hr)*	*Repair ends (hr)*	*Waiting time of the m/c tool (hr)*	*Idle time of the mechanic (hr)*
0	1.3	1st	0	1.3	-	-
1.2	1.3	2nd	1.2	2.5	-	1.2
2.1	1.7	3rd	2.1	3.8	-	2.1
2.4	1.9	1st	2.4	4.3	-	1.1
2.6	1.5	2nd	2.6	4.1	-	0.1
3.8	1.7	3rd	3.8	5.5	-	-
4.3	1.6	2nd	4.3	5.9	-	0.2
5.1	1.4	1st	5.1	6.4	-	0.8
6.0	1.5	3rd	6.0	7.5	-	0.5
					Total: Nil	Total: 6.0

Cost analysis

1. *For 2-mechanic system*
   Wages to be paid/hr = ₹ 2 × 18 = ₹ 36,
   downtime cost of the machine tools = ₹ 5 × 4.8 = ₹ 24.
   ∴ Total cost/hr = ₹ (35+24) = ₹ 60.
2. *For 3-mechanic system*
   Wages to be paid/hr = ₹ 3 × 18 = ₹ 54,
   downtime cost of the machine tools = ₹ 5 × 0 = ₹ 0.
   ∴ Total cost/hr = ₹ (54 + 0) = ₹ 54.

Thus engaging three mechanics is more economical as it reduces the total cost/hour by ₹6.

EXAMPLE 13.7-21 (Simulation in Inventory Control)

A company trading in motor vehicle spares wishes to determine the level of stock it should carry for the items in its range. Demand is not certain and there is a lead time for stock replenishment. For one item X, the following information is obtained:

Demand (units/day)	:	3	4	5	6	7
Probability	:	0.1	0.2	0.3	0.3	0.1

Carrying cost per unit per day = *20 paise,*
ordering cost per order = *₹ 5,*
lead time for replenishment = *3 days.*

Stock in hand at the beginning of the simulation exercise was 20 units. You are required to carry out a simulation run over a period of 10 days with the objective of evaluating the following inventory rule:

Order 15 units when present inventory plus any outstanding order falls below 15 units.

The sequence of random nos. used is 0, 9, 1, 1, 5, 1, 8, 6, 3, 5, 7, 1, 2, 9 using the first number for day one. Your calculation should include the total cost of operating this inventory rule for 10 days. [*P.T.U. B.Tech. (Prod.) May, 2011*]

Solution

First, the demand in each of the 10 days is determined.

TABLE 13.52

Probability distribution of demand				
Demand	*Probability*	*Cumulative probability*	*Range*	*Random nos. fitted*
3	0.1	0.1 × 10 = 1	0	0 (1)
4	0.2	0.3 × 10 = 3	1-2	1 (3), 1 (4), 1 (6)
5	0.3	0.6 × 10 = 6	3-5	5 (5), 3 (9), 5 (10)
6	0.3	0.9 × 10 = 9	6-8	8 (7), 6 (8)
7	0.1	1.0 × 10 = 10	9	9 (2)

Thus the demand for item X on the ten days is 3, 7, 4, 4, 5, 4, 6, 6, 5 and 5 units respectively. Out of the random numbers given, the first ten numbers have been used to simulate the demand for 10 days.

The inventory carrying costs and ordering costs are computed in the table below:

TABLE 13.53

Simulation of demand, delivery and costs							
Day	*Demand (units)*	*Units ordered*	*Lead time (days)*	*Units received*	*Inventory*	*Inventory carrying cost (₹)*	*Ordering cost (₹)*
0	-				20	4.00	
1	3				17	3.40	
2	7	15	3		10	2.00	5.00
3	4				6	1.20	
4	4				2	0.40	
5	5	15	3	15	12	2.40	5.00
6	4				8	1.60	
7	6				2	0.40	
8	6	15	3	15	11	2.20	5.00
9	5				6	1.20	
10	5				1	0.20	
						19.00	15.00

Total cost of operating inventory for 10 days = ₹ (19 + 15) = ₹ 34.

EXAMPLE 13.7-22 (Simulation in Inventory Control)

Consider an inventory control problem in which demand during lead time as well as lead time distributions are given in table 13.54. The reorder point is 6 units and reorder quantity is 12 units. If the ordering cost is ₹ 100/order, inventory carrying cost is ₹ 4/unit/week and the shortage cost is ₹ 60/unit/week, find the total inventory cost for 15 weeks. Assume an initial inventory of 10 units.

TABLE 13.54

Demand	*Probability*	*Lead time (weeks)*	*Probability*
0	0.10	2	0.20
1	0.45	3	0.65
2	0.30	4	0.15
3	0.15		

Assume the following random numbers for the demand: 49, 67, 06, 30, 95, 01, 10, 70, 80, 66, 69, 76, 86, 56 and 84. Also assume the following random numbers for the lead time: 84, 79, 15, 03.

[P.U. B.E. (E. & Ec.) April, 2008]

Solution

First of all probability distribution of demand as well as that of lead time are determined.

TABLE 13.55

Probability distribution of demand during lead time			
Demand	*Probability*	*Cumulative probability*	*Random no. range*
0	0.10	0.10	00-09
1	0.45	0.55	10-54
2	0.30	0.85	55-84
3	0.15	1.00	85-99

TABLE 13.56

Probability distribution of lead time			
Lead time	*Probability*	*Cumulative probability*	*Random no. range*
2	0.20	0.20	00-19
3	0.65	0.85	20-84
4	0.15	1.00	85-99

It is assumed that all orders are placed at the beginning of the week and deliveries against these orders are also received at the beginning of the corresponding week.

Simulation of demand and lead time for 15 weeks are shown in table 13.57.

TABLE 13.57

Week	*Stock on hand at the beginning of the week*	*Demand*		*Quantity received*	*Stock on hand at the end of the week*	*Short-age*	*Lead time*	
		Random number	*Quantity demanded*				*Random number*	*Period*
(1)	(2)	(3)	(4)	(5)	(6)	(7)	(8)	(9)
1	10	49	1	-	9	-	-	-
2	9	67	2	-	7	-	-	-
3	7	06	0	-	7	-	-	-
4	7	30	1	-	6	-	-	-
5	6	95	3	-	3	-	84	3
6	3	01	0	-	3	-	-	-
7	3	10	1	-	2	-	-	-
8	2	70	2	12	12	-	-	-
9	12	80	2	-	10	-	-	-
10	10	66	2	-	8	-	-	-
11	8	69	2	-	6	-	-	-
12	6	76	2	-	4	-	79	3
13	4	86	3	-	1	-	-	-
14	1	56	2	-	0	1	-	-
15	0	84	2	12	10	-	-	-
	88				88	1		

In the first week, simulated demand of 1 unit as obtained from table 13.55 against random number 49, is filled in column (4) of table 13.57. Closing inventory of 9 units is entered in column (6) of this table. Closing inventory for the remaining weeks is calculated the same way. At the end of week 4, the closing inventory is 6 units. So, an order is placed in the beginning of week 5 for order quantity of 12 units.

Simulated lead time as obtained from table 13.56 against random number 84 is 3 weeks. The ordered quantity of 12 units is, therefore, received at the beginning of week 8. This is entered in column (5) of table 13.57. From this table we notice that another order (of 12 units) is placed at the beginning of week 12, since the stock on hand at the end of week 11 reduces to 6 units. Again, simulated lead time is 3 weeks and the 12 units are received at the beginning of week 15. In the beginning of week 14, the stock on hand is 1 unit whereas the demand is 2 units. This results in shortage of 1 unit.

$$\text{Total average inventory in 15 weeks} = \frac{88 + 88}{2} = 88 \text{ units.}$$

$\therefore$ Inventory carrying cost = ₹ 88 × 4 = ₹ 352.

Ordering cost = ₹ 100 × 2 = ₹ 200.

Shortage cost = ₹ 60 × 1 = ₹ 60.

$\therefore$ Total inventory cost in 15 weeks = ₹ (352 + 200 + 60) = ₹ 612.

Note: By changing the values of the two parameters (the order quantity and reorder level), the management can find out the effect of such a policy on the inventory cost (say annual). Therefore, simulation permits the management to compare the alternate ordering policies so as to select the most economical one. Also if there is a change in the inventory carrying, ordering or stock-out costs, their effect on the (annual) inventory costs can be determined by simulation.

EXAMPLE 13.7-23 (Simulation of Networks)

Fig. 13.3 represents the network of a small project. The durations of the activities along with their associated probabilities are given in table 13.58. Simulate the duration of the project ten times and estimate the chances of various paths to be critical. Also determine the average duration of the project.

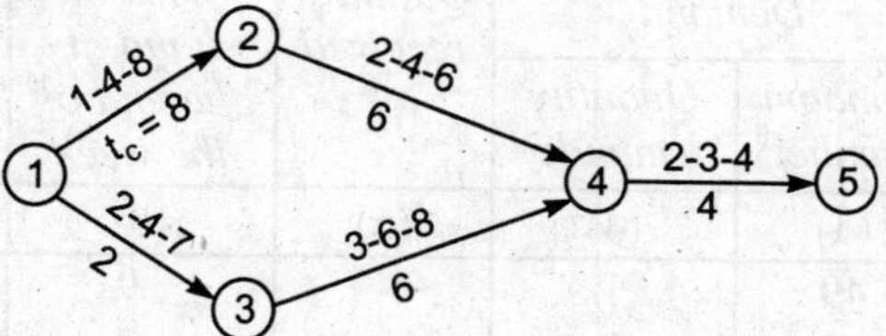

Fig. 13.3

TABLE 13.58

Activity	*Duration (days)*	*Probability*	*Cumulative probability*	*Random no. range*
	1	0.2	0.2	0-1
1-2	4	0.5	0.7	2-6
	8	0.3	1.0	7-9
1-3	2	0.3	0.3	0-2
	4	0.5	0.8	3-7
	7	0.2	1.0	8-9
2-4	2	0.3	0.3	0-2
	4	0.3	0.6	3-5
	6	0.4	1.0	6-9
3-4	3	0.3	0.3	0-2
	6	0.4	0.7	3-6
	8	0.3	1.0	7-9
4-5	2	0.2	0.2	0-1
	3	0.2	0.4	2-3
	4	0.6	1.0	4-9

Solution

As observed from Fig. 13.3, there are two paths, namely 1–2–4–5 and 1–3–4–5 connecting the first to the last event. In trial 1, random numbers 8, 1, 8, 3 and 6 are selected for activities 1-2, 1–3, 2–4, 3–4 and 4–5 for which durations of 8, 2, 6, 6 and 4 days respectively are obtained. These durations are entered in Fig. 13.3. The critical path is 1–2–4–5 with duration of 8 + 6 + 4 = 18 days. These data form row 1 of table 13.59. The remaining rows represent the data for trial 2, 3, ..., 10 respectively.

TABLE 13.59

Trial no.	*Activity 1-2*		*Activity 1-3*		*Activity 2-4*		*Activity 3-4*		*Activity 4-5*		*Project duration*	*Critical path*
	R.N.	*Duration*	*R.N.*	*Duration*	*R.N.*	*Duration*	*R.N.*	*Duration*	*R.N.*	*Duration*		
1	8	8	1	2	8	6	3	6	6	4	18	1–2–4–5
2	5	4	5	4	8	6	1	3	7	4	14	1–2–4–5
3	5	4	6	4	7	6	4	6	7	4	14	1–2–4–5 1–3–4–5
4	7	8	5	4	1	2	9	8	5	4	16	1–3–4–5
5	0	1	6	4	8	6	1	3	8	4	11	1–2–4–5 1–3–4–5
6	8	8	3	4	0	2	4	6	3	3	13	1–2–4–5 1–3–4–5
7	4	4	7	4	4	4	0	3	3	3	11	1–2–4–5
8	5	4	8	7	2	2	6	6	6	4	17	1–3–4–5
9	2	4	5	4	9	6	0	3	3	3	13	1–2–4–5
10	6	4	1	2	3	4	7	8	0	2	12	1–3–4–5

From table 13.59 it is observed that there is 70 per cent chance of path 1-2-4-5 to be critical, while there is 60 per cent chance that path 1-3-4-5 is critical.

Average duration of the project

$$= \frac{1}{10}[18 + 14 + 14 + 16 + 11 + 13 + 11 + 17 + 13 + 12]$$

$$= \frac{139}{10} = 13.9 \text{ days.}$$

13.8 GENERATION OF RANDOM NUMBERS

In the illustrative examples 13.7.2 through 13.7.23 random numbers were either given in the problem or taken from random number table for carrying out hand computations. However, in computer simulation, the random numbers can be obtained by the following methods:

1. Random numbers may be drawn from random number table stored in the memory of the computer. This process, however, is neither practicable nor economical. It is a very slow process and moreover, the random numbers occupy a large portion of the computer memory. Even on methodological grounds it is objectionable to use the same set of random numbers again and again. Therefore, several methods of generating the random numbers internally by the computer have been evolved. The necessary formulae occupy relatively little space.
2. An *electronic device* may be constructed as part of the digital computer to generate true random numbers. The method, however, is considered to be very expensive.
3. *Mid-square method of generating pseudo-random numbers*

A four-digit number is taken. By squaring it a high digit figure is obtained, from which the middle four digits are picked up. This yields the second random number and the process is repeated and a sequence of pseudo-random numbers is obtained. For instance,

if $x_1 = 2421$,

then $x_1^2 = 05861241$.

$\therefore$ $x_2 = 8612$.

$x_2^2 = 74166544$.

$\therefore$ $x_3 = 1665$.

$x_3^2 = 02772225$.

$\therefore$ $x_4 = 7722$ and so on.

However, one may come across the following situations:

(*i*) The series may vanish because a random number obtained is 0000.

(*ii*) A random number reproduces itself, *e.g.*, $x_7 = 7600$, $x_8 = 7600$, $x_9 = 7600$.

(*iii*) A loop occurs, *e.g.*, $x_{11} = 6100$, $x_{12} = 2100$, $x_{13} = 4100$, $x_{14} = 8100$, $x_{15} = 6100$ and the process continues in this circle.

4. Pseudo-random numbers may also be generated by some *arithmetic operations*. A number of recursive procedures are given in the literature but the one most commonly used is the *congruence method or the residue method*, which is described by the expression:

$$r_{i+1} = (ar_i + b) \text{ (modulo } m), \qquad ...(13.1)$$

where a, b and m are constants and r_i, r_{i+1} are the ith and $(i + 1)$th random numbers.

The expression implies multiplying of a by r_i, addition of b and then dividing by m. Then r_{i+1} is the remainder or residue. To begin the process of random number generation, in addition to a, b and m, the value of r_0 is also required. It may be any random number and is called *seed.*

The congruence random number generator may be of the *additive, multiplicative or mixed* type. Equation (13.1) gives the mixed type.

If $a = 1$, the expression (13.1) reduces to the additive type as in expression (13.2).

$$r_{i+1} = (r_i + b) \text{ (modulo } m). \qquad ...(13.2)$$

If $b = 0$, the congruence method is called the multiplicative type, as in equation (13.3).

$$r_{i+1} = ar_i \text{ (modulo } m). \qquad ...(13.3)$$

The multiplicative methods are considered better than the additive methods and as good as the mixed methods. The generation of random numbers by these congruence methods is demonstrated in example 13.8-1.

The selection of the values for the constants a, b and m is very important, because on them depends the length of the sequence of random numbers, after which the sequence repeats. It is not possible to generate a non-repeating sequence of numbers with these methods. However, a sufficiently long string of random numbers can be obtained by making a suitable selection of constants. Since the number r_{i+1} can be predicted from r_i and the whole string of random numbers is reproducible, the numbers obtained are not truly random. They are called pseudo-random numbers, and the method is termed as the pseudo-random number generator.

The validation of a pseudo-random number generator is very essential, before putting it to use. A number of tests have been proposed in the literature for testing the randomness of a sequence. A sequence of random numbers is considered to be adequately random, if its uniformity is assured, and the successive numbers in the sequence are independent.

The *chi-square test* of goodness of fit is employed to check that the sequence of numbers is generated from a (0, 1) uniform distribution. The randomness or *independence test* is used to check that the successive numbers are not correlated. One of the most effective methods for this purpose is the *poker test.*

Most of the computer systems have a subroutine available for generating random numbers. In DEC-20 computer system, a random number (say Y) is generated by using the following statement.

$$Y = \text{RAN}\ (x),$$

where x may be any number of alphabet.

EXAMPLE 13.8-1

The procedure of random number generation can be illustrated by taking some values for the constants a, b and m in equations (13.1) to (13.3).

Let a = 16, b = 18 and m = 23.

(*a*) *Mixed Congruence Method*

$$r_{i+1} = (ar_i + b)\ (\text{modulo } m).$$

Taking

$$r_0 = 1,$$

$$r_1 = \frac{16 \times 1 + 18}{23} = \frac{34}{23} = 1 + \text{remainder } 11,$$

$$r_2 = \frac{16 \times 11 + 18}{23} = \frac{194}{23} = 8 + \text{remainder } 10,$$

$$r_3 = \frac{16 \times 10 + 18}{23} = \frac{178}{23} = 7 + \text{remainder } 17,$$

$$r_4 = \frac{16 \times 17 + 18}{23} = \frac{290}{23} = 12 + \text{remainder } 14,$$

$$r_5 = \frac{16 \times 14 + 18}{23} = \frac{242}{23} = 10 + \text{remainder } 12,$$

$$r_6 = \frac{16 \times 12 + 18}{23} = \frac{210}{23} = 9 + \text{remainder } 3,$$

$$r_7 = \frac{16 \times 3 + 18}{23} = \frac{66}{23} = 2 + \text{remainder } 20,$$

$$r_8 = \frac{16 \times 20 + 18}{23} = \frac{338}{23} = 14 - \text{remainder } 16,$$

$$r_9 = \frac{16 \times 16 + 18}{23} = \frac{274}{23} = 11 + \text{remainder } 21,$$

$$r_{10} = \frac{16 \times 21 + 18}{23} = \frac{354}{23} = 15 + \text{remainder } 9,$$

$$r_{11} = \frac{16 \times 9 + 18}{23} = \frac{162}{23} = 7 + \text{remainder } 1.$$

The string of random numbers obtained is 1, 11, 10, 17, 14, 12, 3, 20, 16, 21, 9, after which the sequence starts repeating.

(*b*) *Multiplicative Congruential Method*

$$r_{i+1} = 16 r_i\ (\text{modulo } 23).$$

Taking

$$r_0 = 1,$$

$$r_1 = \frac{16 \times 1}{23} = 0 + \text{remainder } 16,$$

$$r_2 = \frac{16 \times 16}{23} = 11 + \text{remainder } 3,$$

$$r_3 = \frac{16 \times 3}{23} = 2 + \text{remainder } 2, \text{ and so on.}$$

This way the following sequence of random numbers can be generated :

1, 16, 3, 2, 9, 6, 4, 18, 12, 8, 13, 1.

(*c*) *Additive Congruential Method*

$$r_{i+1} = (r_i + 18) \text{ (modulo 23).}$$

Taking $r_0 = 1$,

$$r_1 = \frac{1+18}{23} = 0 + \text{remainder } 19,$$

$$r_2 = \frac{19+18}{23} = 1 + \text{remainder } 14,$$

$$r_3 = \frac{14+18}{23} = 1 + \text{remainder } 9,$$

$$r_4 = \frac{9+18}{23} = 1 + \text{remainder } 4, \text{ and so on.}$$

This method results in the following string of 23 random numbers:
1, 19, 14, 9, 4, 22, 17, 12, 7, 2, 20, 15, 10, 5, 0, 18, 13, 8, 3, 21, 16, 11, 6, 1.

13.9 SIMULATION LANGUAGES

The efficiency of programming and execution of a simulation project depends upon the programming language used. In addition to the general purpose languages such as FORTRAN and PL1, a large number of specialised computer languages are used to write the simulation programmes. The FORTRAN, being highly general in nature, can be used for any simulation project. Being well-known and commonly available on computer systems, FORTRAN is quite often used to write the simulation programmes. It is generally considered to be more efficient in computer time and storage requirements. However, programming in FORTRAN is more difficult and time consuming, as compared to the special simulation languages. When the complexities of the simulation project increase, the bookkeeping of the intricate details of the simulation becomes difficult and this makes the programming in FORTRAN harder. Thus for realistic situations, simulation programs should be written in specialised simulation languages, which are designed to meet the following objectives:

— to conveniently describe the elements which commonly appear in simulation, such as the generation of random variates for most of the statistical distributions.

— flexibility of changing the design configuration of the system so as to consider alternate configurations.

— internal timing and control mechanism for bookkeeping of the vital information during the simulation run.

— to obtain conveniently the data and statistics about the behaviour of the system.

— to provide simple operational procedures, such as altering the initial state of the system, and kind of output data to be generated, etc.

GASP and SIMSCRIPT are two widely used general simulation languages, which can easily do the job of FORTRAN or PL 1. These are FORTRAN based languages and hence the knowledge of FORTRAN is a prerequisite for learning GASP and SIMSCRIPT.

The most commonly used simulation language is GPSS (General purpose simulation system), which was developed by IBM. It is easy to learn and incorporates all the features which are unique to simulation. GPSS is a problem-oriented language, but has a wide range of applications. It employs the next event incrementing time-flow mechanism and uses integral time units. The calculations in integer arithmetic help to keep the round-off errors to minimum. In GPSS, the system to be simulated is flow charted in the form of block diagrams, and the blocks are then written in GPSS statements.

SIMSCRIPT was developed in early 1960s by RAND corporation of USA. This language depends neither on any predefined coding forms nor on any intermediate language.

The simulation programming languages are very economical in respect of the users' programming time, though they take a slightly larger CPU time in execution of the programme. Some of the many simulation languages are, DYNAMO, SIMPAC, SIMULATE, SIMULA, CSMP, GSP, ESP and CSL.

EXERCISES

1. What is simulation? Describe its advantages in solving the problems. Give its main limitations with suitable examples. *[JNTU Hyderabad B.Tech. (Mech.) May, 2012; May, 2011; April, 2010; Nov., 2010; R.U. MBA June, 2011; Gujarat Tech. U. MBA Jan., 2011; R.T.M. Nagpur B.E. (Mech.) Dec., 2008, 2006; IGNOU MBA June, 2007; Dec., 2006; P.T.U. B.Tech. (Mech.) 2011, 2010, (C.Sc.) 2010, (Mech.) Dec., 2006; M.D.U. Rohtak B.E. (Mech.) Dec., 2006; P.U. B.E. (E.& Ec.) 2002, 2000]*

2. What is simulation? Describe the simulation process. What are the reasons for using simulation? *[Gujarat Tech. U.B.E. Dec., 2012; J.N.T.U. Hyderabad B.Tech. (Mech.) May, 2012; May, 2011; April, 2011; P.T.U. B.Tech. (Mech.) Dec., 2011; R.U. MBA, June, 2011; Gujarat Tech. U. MBA, 2010; M.D.U. Rohtak B.E. (Mech.) Dec., 2006; P.U.BBA, 2001]*

3. List (*a*) the advantages (*b*) the applications (*c*) the limitations and (*d*) the methodology of simulation. *[Gujarat Tech, U.B.E. Dec. 2012; J.N.T.U. Hyderabad B.Tech. May, 2011; April, 2011; Nov., 2010; Chennai U.B.C.A. Nov., 2010; P.U.B.E. (Mech.) Dec., 2004; Nellore MBA, 2001]*

4. Define simulation. "When it becomes difficult to use an optimization technique for solving a problem, one has to resort to simulation." Discuss. *[R.U. MBA June, 2011; J.N.T.U. Hyderabad B.Tech. 2012, 2011; M.D.U. Rohtak B.E. (Mech.) Dec., 2006; P.U. BBA, 2001]*

5. What is the need of simulation? How can you use Monte Carlo simulation for industrial problems? Give examples. *[P.U.B.E. (E. & Ec.) April, 2006]*

6. Explain how do you apply Monte Carlo simulation technique for (*a*) queuing problem (*b*) PERT-networks. Illustrate with examples. *[Karn. U.B.E.(Mech.) 1998]*

7. (*a*) Explain Monte Carlo method and give the situations where these methods are useful. *[P.T.U. B.Tech. (Mech.) May, 2012; J.N.T.U. Hyderabad MBA, Nov., 2012; B.Tech. May, 2011; Gujarat Tech. U.MBA Dec , 2010; P.T.U. MCA, 2010]*

(*b*) Explain in brief the advantages and disadvantages of Monte Carlo methods.

(*c*) Explain the different mathematical steps in a Monte Carlo method. *[R.U. MBA June, 2011; Dec., 2011; P.T.U. B.Tech. (C.Sc.) 2010, 2009]*

(*d*) Give at least five illustrations showing the applications of Monte Carlo method. *[R.U. MBA Dec., 2011]*

8. (*a*) Explain the application of simulation technique to the inventory problems. *[J.N.T.U. Hyderabad B.Tech. (Mech.) May, 2012; April, 2011; Nov., 2011]*

(*b*) Explain how do you simulate a PERT-network with an example. *[J.N.T.U. Hyderabad B.Tech. May 2011; P.T.U. B.Tech. (C.Sc.) 2010]*

9. Explain with suitable examples the Monte Carlo method for solving the theoretical problems. *[JNTU Hyderabad,B.Tech. May, 2011; MBA, 2012; P.T.U.B. Tech. (Mech.) May, 2007; K.U. M.Sc., 2001; B. Tech. (Mech.) 1989; P.U.B.E. (E. & Ec.) 2001; M. Com. Sept., 2004]*

10. List the applications of Monte Carlo simulation in inventory control and capital budgeting. *[P.U. MCA, 2001; P.U. MBA. 1996; ICWA (Final), 1996]*

11. Describe a method for generation of random numbers. Generate 10 random numbers by using the method suggested. *[P.U.M.E. (Mech.) May, 1995]*

12. With the help of an example, explain the mixed type of congruence random number generator. *[P.T.U. B.Tech. (Prod.) May, 2011; Chennai U., 2002]*

13. (*a*) Describe one method of simulation. *[ICWA (Final) June, 1991]*

(*b*) Generate a sequence of 5 three-digit random numbers such that $r_{i+1} = (301\ r_i + 503)$ (Modulo 1,000) and $r_0 = 500$.

(*c*) In a mixed congruential recursive equation: $x_{n+1} = (ax_n + b)$ (modulo m), what should be the value of m so that the random numbers generated are between 0 and 40? Generate a string of 5 such numbers. *[P.U.B.E. (Prod.) 2001]*

14. Ten villages contain 500, 420, 690, 810, 230, 140, 1064, 290, 385 and 680 fields respectively. Make a random selection of six fields using the random number table.

15. The management of a bank is thinking of opening a drive-in facility for its branch office in a commercial area. The interarrival times of the customers at the branch are as follows:

Interarrival time (minutes)	*Probability*
3	0.17
4	0.25
5	0.25
6	0.20
7	0.13

It is planned to have one cashier who can serve the customers at the following rate:

Service time (minutes)	*Probability*
3	0.10
4	0.30
5	0.40
6	0.15
7	0.05

Determine the number of spaces to be planned for the waiting cars. Simulate the operation of the facility for arriving sample of 25 cars. If the location has space for not more than two waiting cars, how many customers would be turned away due to lack of space? What is the average waiting time of a customer?

16. The demand for a particular item has the probability distribution shown below:

Daily demand (units)	:	4	5	6	7	8	9	10	11	12
Probability	:	0.06	0.14	0.18	0.17	0.16	0.12	0.08	0.06	0.03

If the lead time is 5 days, using simulation study the implications of inventory policy of ordering 50 units whenever the inventory at the end of the day is 40 units. Assume the initial stock level of 75 units and run the simulation for 25 days.

17. Six truck loads of material are delivered every day at a factory at regular intervals of 45 minutes. The trucks carry 2, 4, 2, 4, 3, 3 tons of material respectively. Unloading has to be carried out by teams of two men, each team capable of handling 800 kg/hr, upto a maximum of 6 items simultaneously. Assuming that penalty for detaining a lorry for more than 45 minutes (including unloading time) is ₹ 10 per hour and the cost of each labourer is ₹ 8 per day, determine the least costly number of teams. (*Ans.* 5.)

18. Hundred unemployed persons were found to arrive at a one-person state employment office to obtain their unemployment compensation cheques according to the following frequency distribution :

TABLE 13.60

Interarrival time (minutes)	*Frequency*	*Service time (minutes)*	*Frequency*
2	10	2	10
3	20	3	20
4	40	4	40
5	20	5	20
6	10	6	10

The Govt. is interested in predicting the operating characteristics of this office during a typical day from 10 A.M. to 11 A.M. Use simulation to determine the average waiting time, the total time in the system and the maximum queue length.

19. A sample of 100 arrivals of customers at a retail sales depot is according to the following distribution:

Time between arrivals (minutes)	:	0.5	1	1.5	2	2.5	3	3.5	4	4.5	5
Frequency	:	2	6	10	25	20	14	10	7	4	2

A study of the time required to service customers by adding up the bills, receiving payments, placing packages, etc. yields the following distribution:

Service time (minutes)	:	0.5	1	1.5	2	2.5	3
Frequency	:	12	21	36	19	7	5

Estimate the average percentage customer waiting time and average percentage idle time of the server by simulation for the next 10 arrivals. [*B.U.(D.C.M.) 1972*]

20. The number of customers arriving in a barber shop follows distribution as given below :

No. of customers	*Probability of arrival*
0	0
1	0.10
2	0.15
3	0.15
4	0.20
5	0.40

Using Monte Carlo simulation method :

(i) Find the probability that customers cannot be entertained because of short of service assuming that there are only three barbers in the shop.

(ii) Also find the probability that the customer entering the shop is admitted for service immediately. [*R.T.M. Nagpur U. B.Tech. Dec., 2005*]

21. (*a*) Philips India is engaged in manufacturing different types of equipments for various consumers. The company has two assembly lines to produce its product. The processing time for each of the assembly line is regarded as a random variable and is described by the following distributions:

TABLE 13.61

Processing time (minutes)	*Assembly X*	*Assembly Y*
40	0.10	0.20
42	0.15	0.40
44	0.40	0.20
46	0.10	0.15
48	0.25	0.05

Using the following random numbers, generate data on the process times for 10 units of the items and compute the expected process time for the product:

4236 7573 4973 1283 2014 3604 9344 5316 7606 0089

For the purpose, read the numbers horizontally, taking first two digits for the assembly X and last two digits for the assembly Y.

(*b*) Briefly explain the Monte Carlo simulation with suitable example.

[*R.T.M. Nagpur U. B.Tech. Dec., 2004*]

22. A sample of 100 arrivals of customers at a retail-sale shop and time required to give service to the customers is distributed in following manner. Simulate 20 samples.

TABLE 13.62

Arrival distribution		*Service distribution*	
Interarrival time	*Frequency*	*Service time*	*Frequency*
1.0	10	1.0	20
1.5	15	1.5	30
2.0	30	2.0	30
2.5	25	2.5	10
3.0	15	3.0	10
3.5	5		

Calculate waiting time, if any, for the customers. [*R.T.M. Nagpur U. B.Tech. Dec., 2004*]

23. A plant has a large number of similar machines. The machine breakdowns or failures are random and independent. The shift in-charge of a plant collected the data about the various times, between successive machine breakdowns and the repair time required on hourly basis and the data are tabulated as follows:

TABLE 13.63

Time between successive machine breakdowns (hours)	*Probability*
0.5	0.05
1	0.06
1.5	0.16
2	0.33
2.5	0.21
3	0.19

TABLE 13.64

Repair time required (hours)	*Probability*
1	0.28
2	0.52
3	0.20

For each hour that a machine is down due to being repaired or waiting to be repaired, the plant loses ₹ 70 by way of lost production. A repairman is paid ₹ 20 per hour.

(*i*) Simulate this maintenance system for 15 breakdowns.

(*ii*) How many repairmen should the plant hire for repair work?

[R.T.M. Nagpur U. B.Tech. Dec., 2003]

24. An army maintenance organisation is responsible for the maintenance of vehicles of operational units. Higher authorities ordered a study to find out present efficiency of the maintenance organisation. Data collected for 30 days are presented below:

TABLE 13.65

Arrival of vehicles

No. of arrivals	*Frequency*	*Probability*
0	1	0.03
1	5	0.05
2	10	0.5
3	6	0.3
4	2	0.1
5	2	0.02

TABLE 13.66

Servicing of vehicles

No. serviced	*Frequency*	*Probability*
0	2	0.1
1	6	0.3
2	12	0.5
3	4	0.05
4	2	0.03
5	2	0.02

Simulate arrival and service patterns over 10- day period. Comment on the efficiency of the organisation and suggest measures for improvement. *[R.T.M. Nagpur U. B.E.(Mech.) Sept., 2010]*

25. An Automatic machinery company receives different numbers of orders each day and the orders vary in the time required to process them. The firm is interested in determining how many machines it should have in the departments to minimize the combined cost of machine-idle time and order waiting time. The firm knows from the past experience the average number of orders per day and the average number of hours per order, which are as follows:

TABLE 13.67

Number of orders/day	*Probability*	*Hours / order*	*Probability*
0	0.10	5	0.05
1	0.15	10	0.05
2	0.25	15	0.10
3	0.30	20	0.10
4	0.15	25	0.20
5	0.05	30	0.25
		35	0.15
		40	0.10

Cost / hour of idle-machine time = ₹ 4.00,
cost / hour for orders waiting = ₹ 6.00.

Assuming 24-hour working in three shifts, solve the problem using simulation.

[*R.T.M. Nagpur B.E. (Mech.) Dec., 2008*]

26. The materials manager of a firm wishes to determine the expected (mean) demand for a particular item in stock during the reorder lead time. This information is needed to determine how far in advance to reorder, before the stock leve is reduced to zero. However, both the lead time (in days) and the demand per day for the item are random variables, described by the probability distribution given below :

TABLE 13.68

Lead time (days)	*Prob. of occurrence*	*Demand/day (units)*	*Prob.*
1	0.50	1	0.10
2	0.30	2	0.30
3	0.20	3	0.40
		4	0.20

Manually simulate the problem for 20 reorders to estimate the demand during the lead time.

[*R.T.M. Nagpur B.Tech. (Mech) June, 2007; Dec., 2006*]

27. A firm has a single-channel service station with the following arrival and service time probability distributions :

TABLE 13.69

Interarrival time (min)	*Probability*	*Service time (min)*	*Probability*
10	0.10	5	0.08
15	0.25	10	0.14
20	0.30	15	0.18
25	0.25	20	0.24
30	0.10	25	0.22
		30	0.14

Customers arrive in random fashion and are served on first-in first-out basis. The process begins at 10:00 a.m. and continues for nearly 8 hours. Every customer is ready to wait.

If the attendant's wages are ₹ 10 per hour and the customer's waiting time costs ₹ 15 per hour, would it be an economical proposition to engage a second attendant ? Use Monte Carlo simulation method.

[*R.T.M. Nagpur U. B.Tech. June, 2013*]

28. A bread vendor buys every morning loaves of bread at ₹ 0.45 each by placing his order one day in advance (at the time of receiving his previous order) and sells them at ₹ 0.70 each. Unsold bread can be sold the next day at ₹ 0.20 per loaf and discarded thereafter. The pattern of demand for bread is given below:

Daily sales (Fresh bread) :	50	51	52	53	54	55	56	57	58	59	60
Probability of demand :	0.01	0.03	0.04	0.07	0.09	0.11	0.15	0.21	0.18	0.09	0.02
Daily sales (One day old bread) :	0	1	2	3							
Probability of demand :	0.70	0.20	0.08	0.02							

The vendor adopts the following order rule : If there is no stock with him at the end of the previous day, he orders 60 units. Otherwise, he orders 50 or 55 whichever is nearest the actual fresh bread sale on the previous day. Starting with zero stock and a pending order for 55 loaves, simulate for 10 days and calculate the vendor's profits. *[B.U. (D.C.M.) 1993]*

29. The following table gives the arrival pattern at a coffee counter for 'one minute' intervals. The service is taken as 2 persons in one minute in one counter.

No. of persons arriving :	0	1	2	3	4	5	6	7
Probability percentage :	5	10	15	30	20	10	5	5

Using Monte Carlo simulation technique and the following random numbers, generate the pattern of arrivals and the queue formed when the following 20 random numbers are given:

5, 25, 16, 80, 35, 48, 67, 79, 90, 92, 9, 14, 1, 55, 20, 71, 30, 42, 60 and 85.

Find the queue length if two counters are used *i.e.*, 4 persons in one minute.

[P.U. B.E. (Prod.) 1997]

30. A production shop has a group of 20 automatic machines being maintained by a crew of five mechanics. It is observed that quite often the machines have to wait for repairs for long spells of time, resulting in loss of production. To save the downtime of the machines the management is interested in employing additional repairmen. The problem is of determining the proper crew size. Fringe benefits of servicemen and the cost of machine time lost in waiting is ₹ 15 per hour.

From a thorough scrutiny of the previous records of machine break downs, it is estimated that for a group of 20 similar machines working under similar conditions, the breakdowns and service time follow the frequency distribution shown below.

Breakdown/hr :	≤ 7	8	9	10	11	≥ 12
Frequency :	5	12	25	30	20	8
Service time (minutes) :	10	20	30	40	50	
Frequency :	5	25	40	25	5	

31. A newspaper vendor purchases newspapers for ₹ 0.80 each and sells them for ₹ 1 each. The daily demand of newspapers is distributed normally with a mean of 30 and standard deviation of 1. If the vendor cannot return unsold papers, how many papers should he purchase daily? Use Monte Carlo simulation technique and simulate 10 samples. *[Nagpur U.B.E. (I.T.) 2003]*

32. A barber shop has 2 barbers to serve the customers. The customers arrive at the shop in Poisson fashion with a mean arrival rate of 5 per hour. If service time is distributed normally with a mean of 15 minutes and standard deviation of 2 minutes, find out the probability that a customer has to wait for more than 10 minutes. Use Monte Carlo simulation technique and take 10 samples only.

[Nagpur U.B.E. (I.T.) 2003]

33. A company trading motor car spares wishes to determine the level of stock it should carry for the items in its range. Demand is not certain and there is lead time for stock replenishment. For one item, the following information is obtained:

Demand (units/day) :	3	4	5	6	7
Probability :	0.1	0.2	0.3	0.3	0.1

Carrying cost/unit/day = 20 paise,
ordering cost/order = ₹ 5,
lead time = 3 days.

Stock in hand at the beginning of the simulation process is 20 units. You are required to carry out a simulation run over a period of 10 days if the ordering policy is to order 15 units when the stock in hand falls to 15 units.

Calculate the total cost of operating this inventory for 10 days using the following sequence of random numbers:

00, 90, 10, 10, 50, 10, 80, 60, 30, 50, 70, 10, 20 and 90. (*Ans.* ₹ 32.70.)

34. Western Travel agents have a touring van that requires a special grade of fuel. During the past few months the van's use has varied so much that the amount of fuel necessary for keeping the van operating has varied considerably. A study of the past 200 days reveals that demand for the car has fluctuated between 0 to 5 trips/ week.

Trips/week	:	0	1	2	3	4	5
Frequency	:	16	24	30	60	40	30

Using the following random numbers, simulate the demand for a ten-week period:

25, 84, 21, 38, 36, 73, 16, 81, 59, 83.

[*Karn. U. B.E. (Mech.) 1998*]

35. The proprietor of a coffee house has employed three bearers for offering service. He wishes to find out if some more bearers should be recruited by conducting simulation based on the following data:

Interarrival time (min)	:	0	0.5	1	1.5	2	2.5	3
Frequency (%)	:	5	35	25	15	10	7	3
Service time (min)	:	1	2	3	4	5		
Frequency (%)	:	5	25	35	20	15		

Simulate the system for 10 arrivals and find out the average waiting time of customers and average idle time of the bearers. Use the random numbers in the order given below:

21, 81, 92, 23, 96, 20, 68, 57, 79, 84; 82, 62, 13, 08, 92, 83, 74, 85, 60, 49.

[*Karn. U. B.E. (Mech.) 1997*]

36. The owner of a small grocery store wishes to evaluate his daily ordering policy for bread. His current rule is: order the amount demanded the previous day and he never runs out-of-stock. He purchases bread at the rate of ₹ 1.50 per bread and sells it for ₹ 1.75. The breads are ordered at the end of each day and are received the following morning. From historical data the following probability distribution of demand for any day has been estimated:

Daily demand	:	10	20	30
Probability	:	0.25	0.50	0.25

The shop owner is considering the following two ordering policies :

Policy 1 : Order the amount of bread that was demanded on the previous day.

Policy 2 : Average of previous two days' demands should be ordered each day.

Simulate for 10 days to determine the best policy for maximum profit. Use random numbers: 40, 19, 87, 83, 73, 84, 29, 09, 02 and 20. [*G.J.U.B.E. (Mech.) 1996*]

37. Arrivals at a service station have been found to follow a Poisson process. Mean arrival rate $\lambda = 6$ units/ hour. Simulate five hours of arrivals at the service station. [*P.T.U. B.Tech. (Mech.) 2009*]

38. Suppose we are studying the inventory situation of a plant and are interested in generating possible sales for 30 days. Assuming that the number of sales per day is Poisson with mean 5, generate 30 days of sales by Monte Carlo methods. [*P.T.U. B.Tech. (C.Sc.) 2009*]

39. The daily demand for a product is normally distributed with a mean of 120 and a standard deviation of 10. Describe any method to simulate the demand. [*P.U. M.E. (Mech.) May, 1995*]

40. The arrival of customers and service times of customers are having the following distributions. Simulate this queuing system for 10 periods by using the following random numbers and calculate mean waiting time and mean queue length.

Interarrival time (minutes)	*Probability*	*Service time (minutes)*	*Probability*
5	0.15	7	0.10
6	0.35	8	0.35
7	0.40	9	0.45
8	0.10	10	0.10

Random numbers for arrivals : 36, 60, 82, 14, 14, 62, 62, 10, 55, 14.

Random numbers for services : 34, 35, 31, 62, 48, 73, 88, 70, 19, 40.

41. The output of a production line is subjected to a rigorous quality inspection. The defects are classified into three categories namely, A, B and C. If a C grade defect is noticed, the product is scrapped. The other two types of defects can be rectified and passed. The rectification time is 25 minutes for A grade defects and 45 minutes for B grade defects. The probabilities of A, B and C grade defects occurring are 0.10, 0.20 and 0.15 respectively. Taking the following random numbers, simulate the quality inspection test for 10 units of production and give your findings on the following:

(*i*) Number of units which passed inspection without any defect.

(*ii*) Number of units scrapped.

(*iii*) Number of units subjected to rework.

(*iv*) Total time spent on rework of defective units. Random numbers are:

Defect A :	82,	95,	18,	96,	20,	84,	56,	11,	52,	03;
Defect B :	47,	36,	57,	04,	79,	55,	10,	13,	57,	09;
Defect C :	48,	55,	91,	40,	93,	01,	83,	63,	47,	52.

[*C.A. (Final) June, 2003*]

42. The distribution of interarrival times in a single-server model is

t	:	1	2	3
$f(t)$	:	1/4	1/2	1/4

and the distribution of service times is

s	:	1	2	3
$f(s)$	:	1/2	1/4	1/4

Compute the following table, using the two-digit random numbers 11, 20, 47, 68, 90, 62 and 35 to generate arrivals and 15, 86, 20, 42, 11, 36 and 48 to generate the corresponding service times.

TABLE 13.70

Arrivals	*Arrival time*	*Time service begins*	*Time service ends*	*Waiting time in queue*
1				
2				
:				
:				
7				

[*G.J.U. Hisar B.E., 1996*]

43. A manufacturing firm has 25 semi-automatic machines in one section. Machines work for eight hours a day and a repair squad of 5 mechanics attends to their maintenance. The machines are such that only one mechanic can work on a machine at one time. It has been determined from the past breakdown history that there are ten percent chances that a machine will breakdown in any given hour. The times required for repairs and their probability distribution is given in the table below.

TABLE 13.71

Time required to repair each machine (minutes)	*Probability (%)*
15	5
20	10
25	20
30	35
35	22
40	8

The management of the firm is interested in knowing whether this strength of repair squad is optimum and if, not, what is the optimum number. The cost of idle-machine time to the company is ₹ 10 per hour, while the wages paid to a repairman are ₹ 5 per hour. Company allows 10 minutes per hour as each repairman's personal time.

44. In the child welfare section of a hospital, two specialists attend to the outdoor patients daily from 2 P.M. to 5 P.M. There is a general complaint from the public that they have to wait too long. The duty doctors also complain that due to excess of patients they have to sit beyond 5 P.M. on many of the days. From the data collected over the past months, the following distributions of patients' arrivals and the check-up times are determined:

TABLE 13.72

Number of patients per day	*Frequency (%)*	*Check-up time per patient (minutes)*	*Frequency (%)*
20	40	8	20
25	30	12	40
30	20	15	35
40	10	20	5

What should be the number of doctors on duty so that their average busy time does not exceed 3 hours/day ?

45. A printing press receives a different number of orders each day. The time required for composing and printing varies from order to order. There is sufficient number of printing machines and the orders usually do not have to wait for printing. The critical time is that of composing. The manager of the press is interested in knowing the number of composers he should have so that the sum of the cost of composer-idle time and the cost of orders is minimized. The following data regarding the number of orders per day and the composing times are available:

TABLE 13.73

No. of orders per day	*Frequency (%)*	*Composing time per order (hours)*	*Frequency (%)*
3	10	2	10
5	20	3	25
8	35	4	30
10	25	5	25
12	10	6	10

The press works for eight hours per day, but a composer can work effectively for only seven hours a day. An order is accepted only if it can be processed within two days. The wages of the composer are ₹ 3 per hour, while the cost of orders back-ordered comes to ₹ 5 per hour.

46. At a toll office, a sample of 100 arrivals of vehicles gives the following frequency distribution of the interarrival and service times:

TABLE 13.74

Interarrival time (minutes)	*Frequency (%)*	*Service time (minutes)*	*Frequency (%)*
1.0	2	1.5	10
1.5	5	-	-
2.0	9	2.0	22
2.5	25	-	-
3.0	27	2.5	40
3.5	11	-	-
4.0	10	3.0	20
4.5	6	-	-
5.0	3	3.5	8
5.5	2	-	-

There is one clerk at the toll office. Simulate the process for 25 arrivals and estimate the average per cent vehicle waiting time and the average per cent idle time of the clerk. [*PTU B.Tech., 2000*]

47. A coffee house in the busy market of a city operates counter service. The proprietor of the coffee house has approached you with the problem of determining the number of bearers he should employ at the counter. He wants that the average waiting time of the customer should not exceed 2 minutes. After recording the data for a number of days, the following frequency distribution of interarrival time of customers and the service time at the counter are established.

TABLE 13.75

Interarrival time (minutes)	*Frequency (%)*	*Service time (minutes)*	*Frequency (%)*
0	5	1.0	5
0.5	35	2.0	25
1.0	25	3.0	35
1.5	15	4.0	20
2.0	10	5.0	15
2.5	7		
3.0	3		

Simulate the system for 30 arrivals for various alternate numbers of bearers.

[*Karn.U. B.E.(Mech.) 1995*]

48. A bookstore wishes to keep 'Ramayana' in stock. Demand is probabilistic and replenishment of stock takes 2 days (*i.e.*, if an order is placed on March 1, it will be delivered at the end of the day on March 3). The probabilities of demand are given below :

Demand (daily)	:	0	1	2	3	4
Probability	:	0.05	0.10	0.30	0.45	0.10

Each time an order is placed, the store incurs an ordering cost of ₹ 10. The store incurs a carrying cost of ₹ 0.50 per book per day. The inventory carrying cost is calculated on the basis of stock at the end of each day. The manager of the bookstore wishes to compare two options for his inventory decision:

Option A : Order 5 books when the inventory at the beginning of the day plus orders outstanding is less than 8 books.

Option B : Order 8 books when the inventory at the beginning of the day plus orders outstanding is less than 8 books.

Currently (beginning of 1st day) the store has a stock of 8 books plus 6 books ordered a day before and expected to arrive next day. Using Monte Carlo simulation for 10 cycles, recommend which option the manager should choose. The two-digit random numbers are given as 89, 34, 78, 63, 61, 81, 39, 16, 13 and 73.

[*I.C.W.A. June, 1988*]

(*Ans.* A : Total cost = ₹ 59.50; B : Total cost = ₹ 52.50; Option B.)

49. The common maintenance problem with a heavily-loaded machine is the failure of its bearings. There are three bearings which cause the trouble and keep the machine down for a considerable part of time. It looks that the present practice of replacing a bearing as and when it fails is not a good policy. It is decided to evaluate the following three alternate policies: 1. The present policy of replacing a bearing as and when it fails. 2. Replace all the three bearings when any of them fails. 3. Replace all the bearings which have been in use for 1,000 hours or more when a bearing fails.

It has been observed that it takes 7 hours on the part of one mechanic to replace one bearing. If two bearings are replaced, maintenance time is 9 hours and it takes 11 hours to replace all the three bearings.

The wages of a maintenance mechanic are ₹ 5 per hour, while machine downtime cost is ₹ 4 per hour. The cost of each bearing is ₹10.

From the past performance the following frequency distribution of the actual working lives of bearings is available:

TABLE 13.76

Bearing life (hours)	*Frequency %*
600	2
700	6
800	8
900	14
1,000	17
1,100	20
1,200	15
1,300	10
1,400	7
1,500	1

Determine the best policy of replacing the bearings by simulating approximately 10^6 hours of service time for each of the three policies.

50. Consider a single-chair barber shop having uniformly distributed inter-arrival time between 10 and 20 minutes. Service time is normally distributed with mean 15 and variance 4. The maximum queue length allowed is 3. Develop a computer simulation model of the system, employing the next event incrementing method. Run the programme to simulate the operation of the shop for 1,000 hours. Compute the following:

(*a*) Average waiting time of a customer.

(*b*) Percentage idle time of the barber.

(*c*) Number of customers lost as percentage of arrivals.

51. Use the mixed congruential method to generate the following sequences of random numbers:

(*a*) A sequence of five two-digit numbers, such that

$r_{i+1} = (21\,r_i + 53)$ (modulo 100), take $r_0 = 46$. [*P.T.U. B.Tech. (Mech.) 2010*]

(*b*) A sequence of five random numbers between 0 and 31, such that $r_{n+1} = (9\,r_n + 15)$ (modulo 32), take $r_0 = 12$.

52. Solve problem 51, when mixed congruential method is reduced to multiplicative method.

53. In a mixed congruence method of generation of random numbers, a random number $r + 1$ is given by $r_{i+1} = (ar_i + b)$ (modulo m),

where a, b and m are constants. Generate 20 random numbers taking $r_0 = 24$, $a = 51$, $b = 59$ and $m = 93$.

The weekly demand for a product has the following distribution:

Demand	:	10	15	20	25	30
Probability	:	0.12	0.22	0.28	0.25	0.13

Using the random numbers generated above, simulate the demand for the coming 20 days.

[*P.U. M.E. (Mech.) 1996*]

CHAPTER 14 Network Analysis in Project Planning (PERT and CPM)

14.1 PROJECT

The term project has been defined by many authors, and each one has defined it from his own point of view and in the perspective of his own field of activity. *Most often a project is defined as a combination of interrelated activities which must be executed in a certain order before the entire task is completed.* The salient characteristics of a project are

1. A project has identifiable beginning and end points; it is an entity by itself.
2. It is not a permanent entity, it is usually a non-repetitive task.
3. It can be broken down into identifiable activities which require time and resources for their execution.
4. It is scheduled to be completed by a target date.
5. The objectives are clear and output or end product definite.
6. It is usually large and complex with time horizon of 2 to 3 years. However, some projects have taken more than 10 years while others have lasted for less than 6 months.
7. It usually involves heavy investment.
8. Execution of project activities and hence completion of the project is always subject to some uncertainties and risks.

Each project, whether big or small, has three basic requirements:

(*i*) It should be completed without any delay.

(*ii*) It should use as small man power and other resources as possible.

(*iii*) It should involve as small investment as possible.

The project management helps to fulfill the above requirements.

The project management involves the following three phases:

(*i*) Project planning

(*ii*) Project scheduling

(*iii*) Project controlling

Out of these three phases, the first two are accomplished before the start of the actual project. The third phase comes into operation during the execution of the project. It highlights the bottlenecks during execution of the project and spells out measures to remove bottlenecks & complete the project in time. *The network techniques of PERT and CPM are valuable during all the three phases of project management.*

14.2 PROJECT PLANNING

Project planning is an important phase during which are set the plans and strategies of project execution, keeping in mind the policies, procedures and rules of the organisation. It has two important aspects—identification of the activities (jobs or tasks) to be performed and estimation of the required resources. Resources are of many kinds and are classified as:

1. Manpower resources
2. Equipment (machinery) resources

3. Financial resources
4. Material resources
5. Time & space resources

The manpower resources, say, in a construction project, consist of skilled workers (such as carpenters, turners, plumbers, fitters, etc.), unskilled labour, supervisory staff and top management. The equipment resources include plant and machinery such as dragline, power shovel, concrete mixing plant, etc. The financial resources comprise the money required for the project. The material resources include all the materials such as cement, sand, concrete, gravel, bricks, steel, etc. to be used. Space resources include the total space available for the project. It may be limited, thus causing constraints on the activities of the project. Time resources involve the total time available, which may also be limited in some projects.

Since resources are the starting points of projects, their proper planning and estimation helps to estimate the time and cost of the various activities and hence of the entire project.

Project planning involves the following steps:

1. Setting the objectives of the project and the assumptions to be made.
2. Developing the W.B.S. (*Work Breakdown Structure*). Depending upon the objectives of the management, the extent of control desired and the availability of computational aids, the project is brokendown into clearly definable activities.
3. Determination of time estimates of these activities.
4. Estimation of resources–financial, managerial and operational.
5. Study of alternative ways of attaining the goals.
6. Establishment of interdependence relationship between the activities *i.e.*, the sequence of performing the activities.

14.3 PROJECT SCHEDULING

Scheduling is the laying out of the project activities along a time sequence in which they are to be performed so as to assign the starting and finishing dates to various activities and to allocate resources to them. In other words, scheduling is the preparation of time table of the implementation of the activities and computation of resources required at different stages of time. It also includes identifying the tasks that are critical & the resources that are limited so that the entire project proceeds in a logical, orderly and systematic manner. In short, the scheduling phase consists of determining:

1. Start and finish times of each activity and the earliest and latest times at which events can occur.
2. Critical activities that require special attention.
3. Allocating resources—men, machines, materials, etc. to each activity.
4. Slacks and floats for noncritical activities.
5. Various constraints due to limitation of resources.

14.4 PROJECT CONTROLLING

Controlling phase is the follow-up of the planning and scheduling phases. While planning and scheduling are undertaken before the actual project starts, the controlling phase is undertaken during the actual execution of the project. The project is monitored to find deviations in actual progress from the scheduled plan and to apply the corrective measure, so as to achieve the targets. Project controlling usually involves the following steps:

1. Setting standards and targets with regard to time and cost of the project.
2. Reviewing the progress by comparing the work accomplished to the work scheduled at different stages of time and finding the deviations.
3. Evaluating the effect of deviations on the project plan.
4. Updating the project schedule.

5. The corrective measures to rectify the deviations from the plan should be suggested. This requires decision-making with regard to scheduling of resources, scheduling of jobs, crashing of projects, etc.

14.5 WORK BREAKDOWN STRUCTURE (W.B.S.)

A Project is a combination of interrelated activities which must be performed in a certain order for its completion. The process of dividing the project into these activities is called Work Breakdown Structure (W.B.S.). The *activity* or *unit of work* or *work content* is a clearly identifiable and manageable work unit. The number of activities or the size of each activity will depend upon the level of detail desired.

14.6 BASIC TOOLS AND TECHNIQUES OF PROJECT MANAGEMENT

The various tools and techniques of project management are grouped into the following two heads:

1. Bar charts, milestone charts and velocity diagrams.
2. Network techniques.

14.6-1 Bar charts, Milestone charts and Velocity diagrams

Bar charts are the two-dimensional pictorial representation of a project. In a bar chart, the activities of the project are shown on one axis and their durations are represented on the other axis. A bar chart helps to review the project progress, allows for rescheduling the project and highlights the critical activities and other bottlenecks in the completion of the project. A bar chart, however, is normally suited to small projects. It cannot take into account the uncertainties in activity duration nor represent the interrelationships between the various activities of the project.

Milestone charts are the modified and improved versions of bar charts. However, whereas bar charts represent activities, milestone charts represent the events which mark either the beginning or the end of the activities. Though milestone charts are more detailed and offer better control than bar charts, they possess most of the drawbacks inhert in bar charts.

Velocity diagrams are useful for representing the activities which require a series of crews working in a given sequence.

14.6-2 Network Techniques

A *network* (also called *network diagram or network technique*) is a symbolic representation of the essential characteristics of a project. PERT and CPM are the two most widely applied techniques.

(*a*) Programme Evaluation and Review Technique (PERT)

It uses event oriented network in which successive events are joined by arrows. It is preferred for projects that are non-repetitive and in which time for various activities cannot be precisely predetermined. There is no significant past experience to guide; they are once-through projects. Launching a new product in the market by a company, research and development of a new war weapon, launching of a satellite, sending space craft to Mars are PERT projects. Three time estimates — the optimistic time estimate, the pessimistic time estimate and the most likely time estimate are associated with each and every activity to take into account the uncertainty in their times.

(*b*) Critical Path Method (CPM)

It uses activity oriented network which consists of a number of well recognised jobs, tasks or activities. Each activity is represented by arrow and the activities are joined together by events. CPM is generally used for simple, repetitive types of projects for which the activity times and costs are certainly and precisely known. Projects like construction of a building, road, bridge, physical verification of store, yearly closing of accounts by a company can be handled by CPM. Thus it is deterministic rather than probabilistic model.

14.7 ROLE OF NETWORK TECHNIQUES IN PROJECT MANAGEMENT

The complexities of the present-day management problems and the business competitions have added to the pressure on the brains of decision-makers. In a large and complex project involving a number of interrelated activities, requiring a number of men, machines and materials, it is not possible for the management to make and execute an optimum schedule just by intuition based on the organisational capabilities and work experience. Managements are, thus, always on the look out for some methods and techniques which may help in planning, scheduling and controlling the project. The aim of planning is to develop a sequence of activities of the project, so that the project completion time and cost are properly balanced and the excessive demand of key resources is avoided. To meet the object of systematic planning, the managements have evolved a number of techniques applying network strategy. As already explained, PERT and CPM are two such widely applied techniques used for planning, scheduling and controlling of large and complex projects. With slight modifications both have given rise to several other network techniques, such as PEP (Programme Evaluation Procedure), RAMPS (Resource Allocation for Multi-Project Scheduling), LESS (Least Cost Estimating and Scheduling) and SCANS (Scheduling and Control by Automated Network System), etc.

14.8 NETWORK LOGIC (NETWORK OR ARROW DIAGRAM)

Some of the terms commonly used in networks are defined below.

Activity

It is physically identifiable part of a project which requires time and resources for its execution. An activity is represented by an arrow, the tail of which represents the start and the head, the finish of the activity. The length, shape and direction of the arrow has no relation to the size of the activity.

Event

The beginning and end points of an activity are called events or nodes. Event is a point in time and does not consume any resources. It is represented by a circle. The head event, called the *j*th event, has always a number higher than the tail event, called the *i*th event *i.e.*, $j > i$. For example

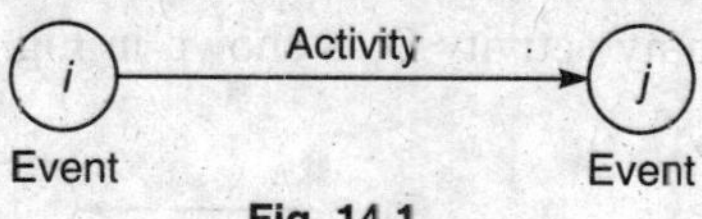

Fig. 14.1

'Making the pattern of impeller' is an activity.

'Start making the pattern of impeller' is an event.

'Pattern making completed' is an event.

An event in which more than activity comes in is called *merge event* and an event from which more than one activity leaves is called *burst event*. An even can simultaneously be merge as well as burst event. Such an event will have more than one activity coming into it as well as more than one activity leaving it. Event F in Fig. 14.7 is such an event.

Path

An unbroken chain of activity arrows connecting the initial event to some other event is called a path.

Network

It is the graphical representation of logically and sequentially connected arrows and nodes representing activities and events of a project. Networks are also called *arrow diagrams*.

Network Construction

Firstly the project is split into activities. Start and finish events of the project are then decided. After deciding the precedence order, the activities are put in a logical sequence by using the graphical notations. While constructing the network, in order to ensure that the activities fall in a logical sequence, following questions are checked:

(*i*) What activities must be completed before a particular activity starts ?
(*ii*) What activities follow this ?
(*iii*) What activities must be performed concurrently with this ?

Activities which must be completed before a particular activity starts are called the *predecessor activities* and those which must follow a particular activity are called *successor activities*.

While drawing the network following points should be kept in mind:

1. Each activity is represented by one and only one arrow. But in some situations where an activity is further subdivided into segments, each segment will be represented by a separate arrow.
2. Time flows from left to right. Arrows pointing in opposite direction are to be avoided.
3. Arrows should be kept straight and not curved.
4. Angles between the arrows should be as large as possible.
5. Arrows should not cross each other. Where crossing cannot be avoided, bridging should be done as shown in Fig. 14.6.
6. Each activity must have a tail and a head event. No two or more activities can have the same tail and head events.
7. An event is not complete until all the activities flowing into it are completed.
8. No subsequent activity can begin until its tail event is completed.
9. In a network diagram there should be only one initial event and one end event.

Dummy

An activity which only determines the dependency of one activity on the other, but does not consume any time is called a dummy activity. Dummies are usually represented by dotted line arrows.

To illustrate the use of dummy, refer to Fig. 14.2 (*a*) and assume that the start of activity C depends upon the completion of activities A and B and that the start of activity E depends only on the completion of activity B. For this situation, figure 14.2 (*a*) is a faulty representation. This is corrected by introducing a dummy activity D as shown in Fig. 14.2 (*b*).

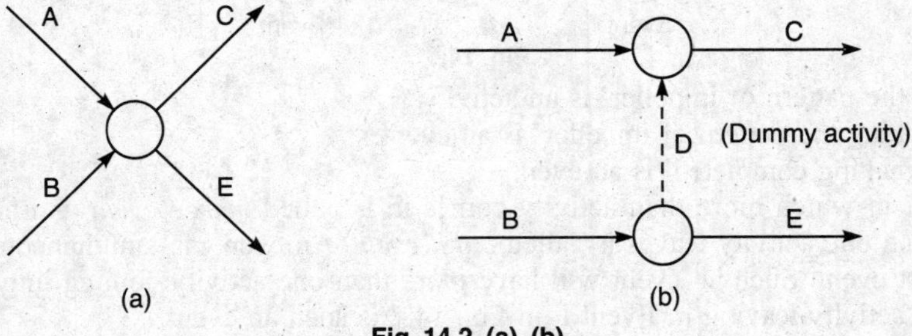

Fig. 14.2. (a), (b)

A dummy activity is introduced in the network for two basic reasons:

1. To maintain the precise logic of the precedence of activities. Such a dummy is called '*logical dummy*'. It is shown in Fig. 14.2 (*b*).
2. To comply with the rule that no two or more activities can have the same pair of tail and head events. Such a dummy is called '*grammatical dummy*'. In Fig. 14.2 (*c*), both activities A and B have the same tail event 10 and same head event 20, which is incorrect since no two activities can have the same pair of tail and head events. Such activities are called duplicate activities. This difficulty is resolved by the introduction of a dummy activity in any of the four ways represented in Fig. 14.2 (*d*), (*e*), (*f*) or (*g*).

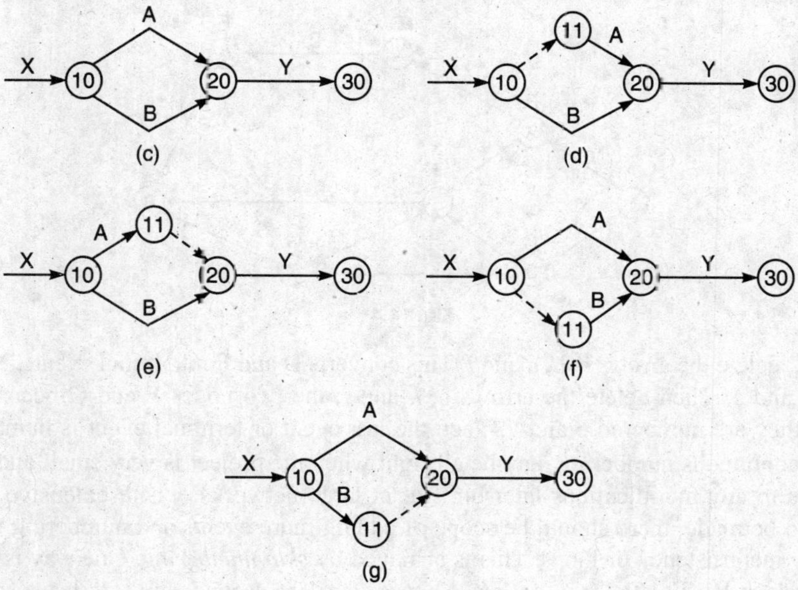

Fig. 14.2. (c) to (g)

Looping (Cycling)

Sometimes due to faulty network sequence a condition illustrated in figure 14.3, arises. Here the activities D, E and F form a loop (cycle). Activity D cannot start until F is completed, which, in turn, depends upon the completion of E. But E is dependent upon the completion of D. Thus the network cannot proceed. This situation can be avoided by checking the precedence relationship of the activities and by numbering them in a logical sequence.

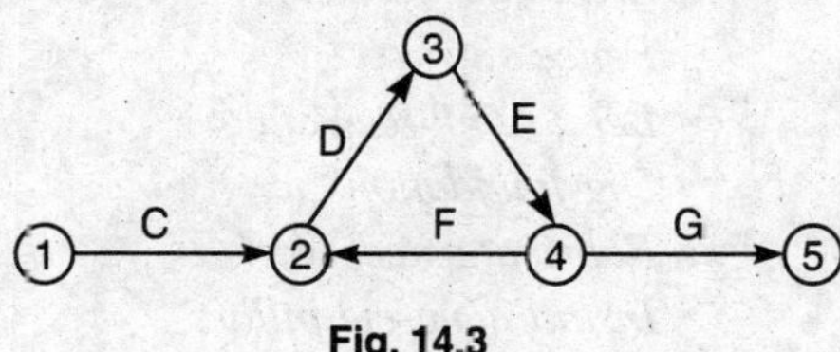

Fig. 14.3

14.9 NUMBERING THE EVENTS (FULKERSON'S RULE)

After the network is drawn in a logical sequence, every event is assigned a number which is placed inside the node circle. The number sequence should be such as to reflect the flow of the network. The rule devised by D.R. Fulkerson is used for the purpose of numbering. It involves the following steps:

1. The initial event which has all outgoing arrows with no incoming arrow is numbered '1'.
2. Delete all the arrows coming out from node '1'. This will convert some more nodes (at least one) into initial events. Number these events 2, 3,...
3. Delete all the arrows going out from these numbered events to create more initial events. Assign the next numbers to these events.
4. Continue until the final or terminal node, which has all arrows coming in with no arrow going out, is numbered.

To illustrate the numbering technique let us consider the network shown in figure. 14.4.

Event A is initial event and is numbered 1. Delete the arrows *a* and *b*. This will create two more (B & C) initial events. Number these 2 & 3. Now delete the arrows coming out from nodes

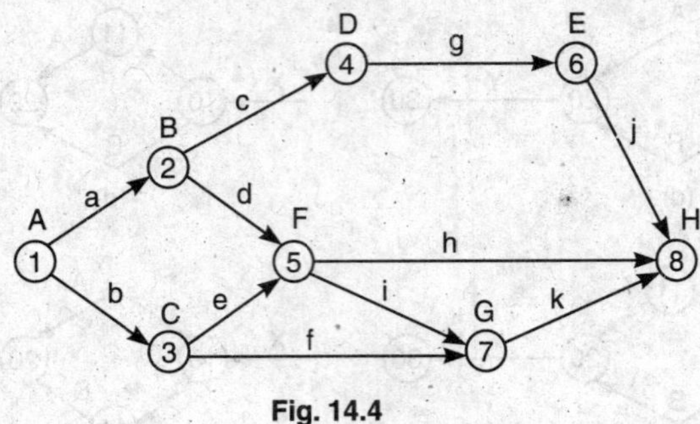

Fig. 14.4

2 and 3, *i.e.*, delete the arrows *c*, *d*, *e* and *f*. This converts D and F into initial events. Number these nodes as 4 and 5. Then delete the arrows *g*, *h* and *i*; the two nodes E and G become the initial nodes and they are numbered 6 and 7. Then the last event or terminal event is numbered as 8.

This continuous numbering may be all right when the project is very small and the network is not liable to any modifications later on. But in large networks, where extensive modification may have to be made, there should be scope of adding more events and numbering them without causing any inconsistency or loops. This is achieved by *skip numbering*. One way is to assign the numbers such as 10, 20, 30, 40,..., or 4, 8, 12,16,..., etc. The second way is to leave some numbers such as 7, 8, 9; 17, 18, 19; 27, 28, 29;... and allot them to the events added afterwards. There can be still more ways of doing skip numbering.

EXAMPLE 14.8-1

Draw a network for the simple project of erection of steel works for a shed. The various activities of the project are as under:

Activity	*Description*	*Preceded by*
A	*Erect site workshop*	—
B	*Fence site*	—
C	*Bend reinforcement*	*A*
D	*Dig foundation*	*B*
E	*Fabricate steel work*	*A*
F	*Install concrete pillars*	*B*
G	*Place reinforcement*	*C, D*
H	*Concrete foundation*	*G, F*
I	*Erect steel work*	*E*
J	*Paint steel work*	*H, I*
K	*Give finishing touch*	*J*

Solution

(*i*) Activities A and B have no preceding activities and can commence immediately [Fig. 14.5 (*a*)].

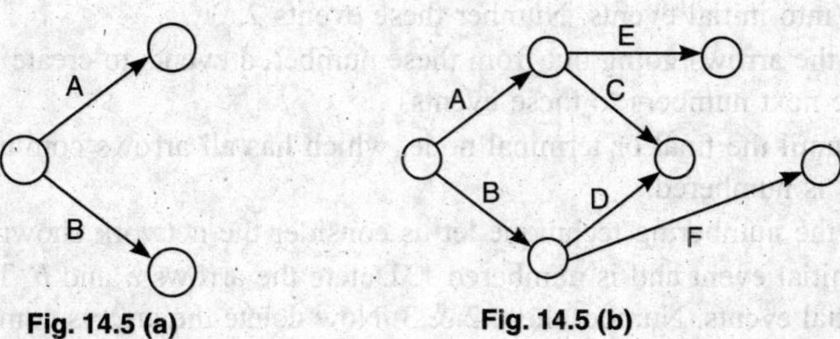

Fig. 14.5 (a) Fig. 14.5 (b)

(*ii*) Activities C and E can start once A has finished, while D and F can start once B has finished. Note that activity D has been given the same head event as activity C in Fig. 14.5 (*b*).

(*iii*) The remaining network is completed as follows : Activity G follows C and D. Since H is preceded by G and F, the two have the same head event, which becomes the tail event for H. Similarly, I and H have been shown to be preceding J. Activity K follows J [Fig. 14.5 (*c*)].

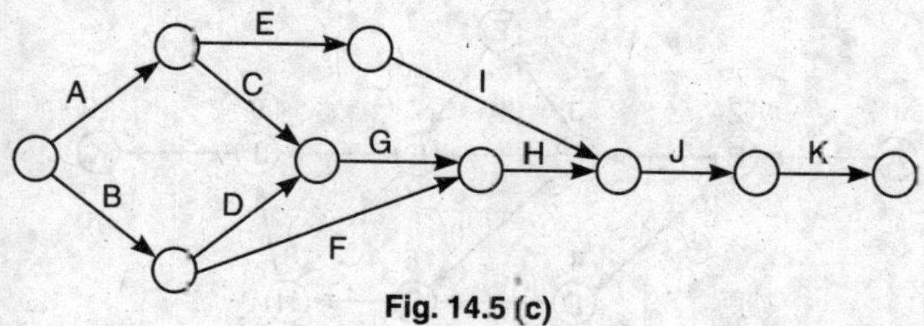

Fig. 14.5 (c)

EXAMPLE 14.8-2

A project consists of a series of tasks labelled A, B, ..., H, I with the following relationships (W < X, Y means X and Y cannot start until W is completed; X, Y < W means W cannot start until both X and Y are completed). With this notation construct the network diagram having the following constraints:

A < D, E; B, D < F; C < G; B < H; F, G < I.

[*G.N.D.U. B.Com. April, 2006; P.U.B.Com. Sept., 2005*]

Solution

For the given precedence relationships, the project network shown in Fig. 14.6 is obtained. Since H is preceded by B while F is preceded by B and D, a dummy activity must be incorporated to draw the network. As explained in article 14.8, this dummy is a logical dummy. The last three activities E, H and I are made to join at the last event as a network can have only one start and only one end event.

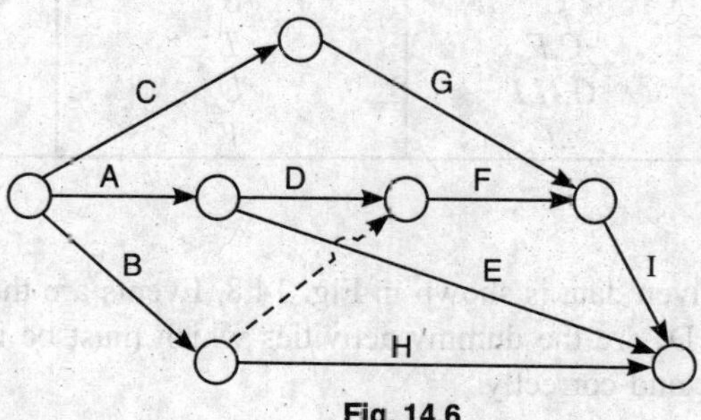

Fig. 14.6

EXAMPLE 14.8-3

Draw a network for the following project and number the events according to Fulkerson's rule:

A is the start event and K is the end event,
A precedes event B,
J is the successor event to F,
C and D are successor events to B,
D is the preceding event to G,
E and F occur after event C,
E precedes F,
C restraints the occurrence of G and G precedes H,
H precedes J and K succeeds J,
F restraints the occurrence of H.

[*Bombay B.Sc. (Stat.) 1974*]

Solution

In this problem, the events A, B, C, D, E, F, G, H, J, and K constitute the network. The network is shown in Fig. 14.7. Along the nodes are given their numbers as obtained by Fulkerson's rule.

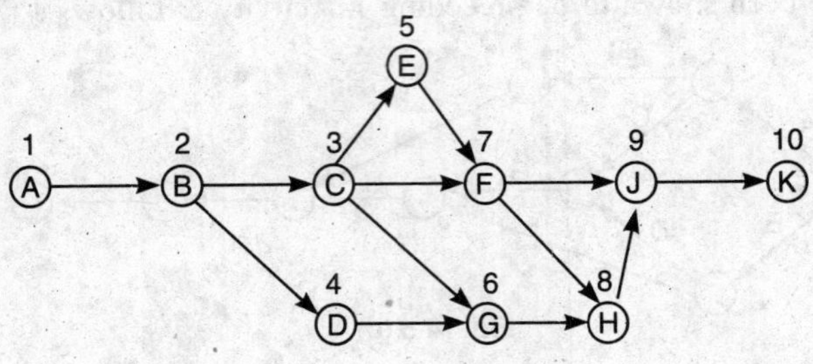

Fig. 14.7

EXAMPLE 14.8-4

Draw the network diagram for the following list of activities:

Activity	*Immediate predecessor*	*Activity*	*Immediate predecessor*
A	-	*L*	*K*
B	*A*	*M*	*K*
C	*B*	*N*	*K*
D	*C*	*O*	*D*
E	*D*	*P*	*O*
F	*E*	*Q*	*B*
G	*E*	*R*	*N*
H	*C*	*S*	*L,M*
I	*C,F*	*T*	*S*
J	*G,H,I*	*U*	*P,Q*
K	*J*	*V*	*U*

[*C.A. Nov., 1982*]

Solution

The network for the given data is shown in Fig. 14.8. Events are then numbered according to Fulkerson's rule. D_1 and D_2 are the dummy activities which must be incorporated to connect the given activities logically and correctly.

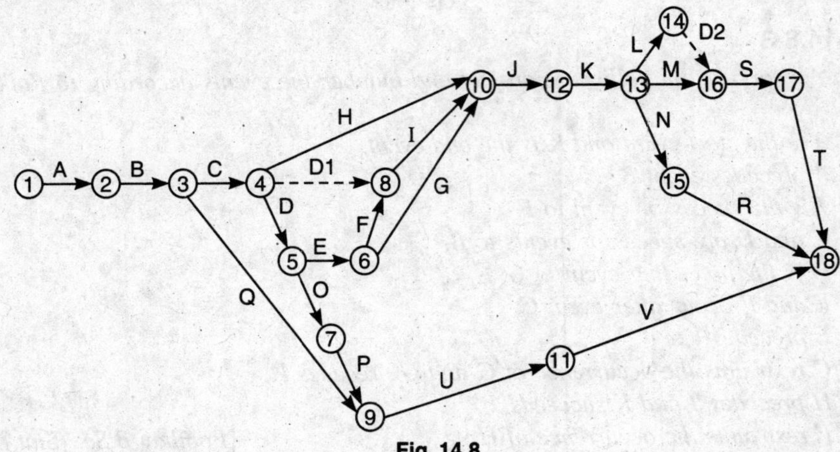

Fig. 14.8

EXAMPLE 14.8-5

Depict the following dependency relationships by means of network diagrams. The alphabets stand for activities.

(i) *A and B control F; B and C control G.*

(ii) *A and B control F; B controls G while C controls G and H.*

(iii) *A controls F and G; B controls G while C controls G and H.*

(iv) *F and G are controlled by A; G and H are controlled by B with H controlled by B and C.*

(v) *A controls F, G and H: B controls G and H with H controlled by C.*

Solution

The dependency relationships are depicted by Fig. 14.9 (i) through (v). The use of dummy activities is to be noted.

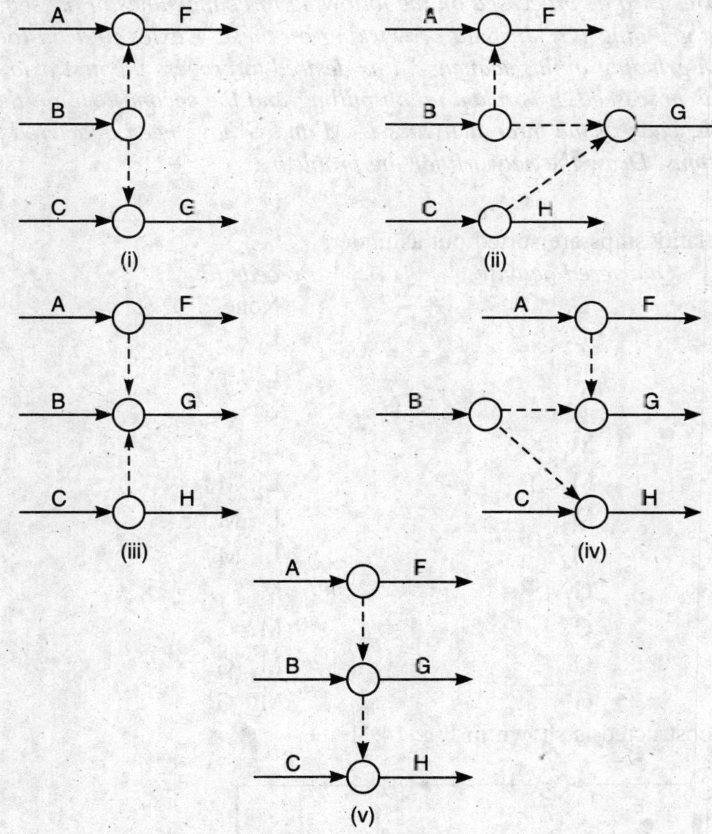

Fig. 14.9 (i) to (v)

EXAMPLE 14.8-6

Construct a network diagram for a project comprising of activities B, C, E, F, G, H, I, J, L, M, N, P and Q such that the following precedence relationships are satisfied:

B < E, F; C, F < G; C < L; E, G < H; H, L < I; H < J; L < M; H, M < N; I, J < P; N < Q. [*J.U. B.E.(Mech.) 2004*]

Solution

The network is shown in Fig. 14.10. Four dummy activities have been used. Since activity L depends upon C, and G depends upon both F and C, dummy D_1 is required. Dummies D_2 and

D_3 establish that I depends on both H and L, while J depends only on H. Activity N depends on H and M both, while J depends on H. These precedence orders are established by employing D_4. The nodes of the network have been numbered using the Fulkerson's rule.

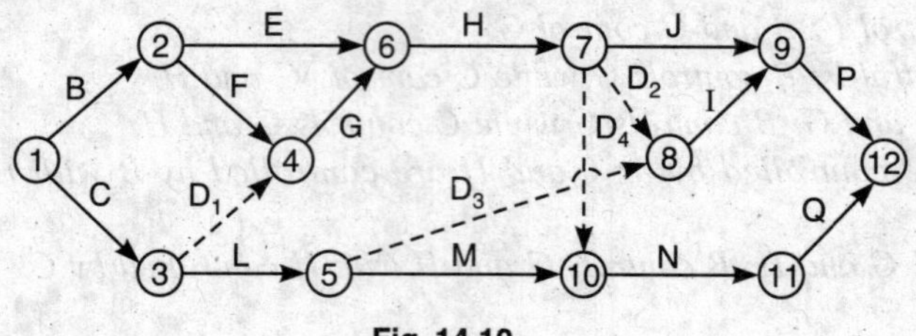

Fig. 14.10

EXAMPLE 14.8-7

A batch of 4 axles is to be processed on the following three machines in the sequence: lathe (L), milling (M) and grinding (G). Instead of working on these 4 axles first on lathe, then on milling and finally on grinding in this sequence, it is desired to process the first axle on the lathe and as and when it is processed, it is taken up on milling and the second axle on the lathe, and so on. In other words, each of the three activities L, M and G have been quartered for the sake of concurrent operations. Draw the network for the problem.

Solution

Dependency relationships are sorted out as under:

Quartered activity	*Preceded by*
L_1	None
L_2	L_1
L_3	L_2
L_4	L_3
M_1	L_1
M_2	L_2, M_1
M_3	L_3, M_2
M_4	L_4, M_3
G_1	M_1
G_2	M_2, G_1
G_3	M_3, G_2
G_4	M_4, G_3

The network constructed is shown in Fig. 14.11

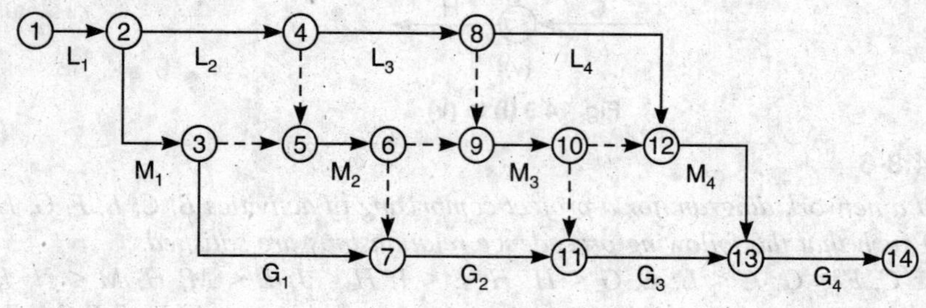

Fig. 14.11

EXAMPLE 14.8-8

The activities along with their dependency relationships are given below. Draw an arrow diagram.

Activity	*A*	*B*	*C*	*D*	*E*	*F*	*G*	*H*	*I*
Immediate predecessor	—	—	—	*C*	*A,B*	*C*	*E,F*	*D*	*F,H*

Solution

Activities A, B and C do not have any predecessors, so they can start from the same initial event. D has to follow C. Activity E follows A and B. Since E is to start from one event, a dummy is required. Activity F follows C and H follows D. Next, activity G depends upon E and F. Both E and F could be made to merge in one event. But E also controls I. I is controlled by H as well as E. Thus two more dummies are required to complete the project as shown in Fig. 14.12. Activities G and I are made to meet at the last event.

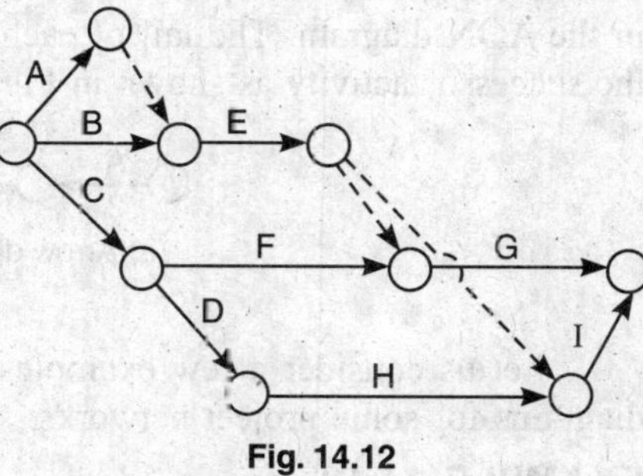

Fig. 14.12

EXAMPLE 14.8-9

The activities along with their dependency relationships are given below. Draw the arrow diagram.

Activity	*Immediate predecessor*	*Activity*	*Immediate predecessor*
A	—	*G*	*B,C*
B	—	*H*	*C*
C	—	*I*	*E, F*
E	*A*	*J*	*G, H*
F	*A,B*	*K*	*H*

Solution

The activity on arrow diagram for this data is shown in Fig. 14.13. It can be observed that there are five dummy activities D_1, D_2, D_3, D_4 and D_5 in the network, while there are ten real activities.

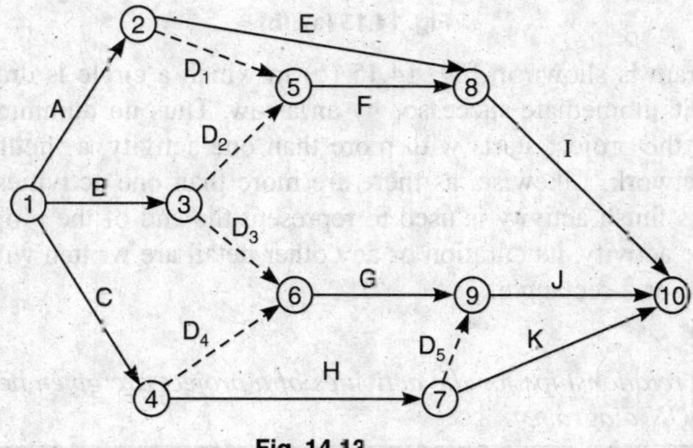

Fig. 14.13

14.10 ACTIVITY ON NODE DIAGRAM

It is observed from the above diagrams that while constructing the arrow diagram (conventional network), many a times dummy activities have to be included to represent the precedence relationship between the activities correctly *i.e.*, to maintain the logic. This results in increased number of activities, lengthy and cumbersome networks and more time and effort for analysis.

The activity on node (AON) diagram, as the name suggests, represents the activities by nodes or circles with the arrows connecting them representing the precedence relationship between them. Though all the arrows in AON diagram are like dummies, since they do not require any time or resources and represent only the dependency relationships, yet no dummies are required in the AON diagram. The tail of each arrow is on the predecessor activity, while the head is on the successor activity as shown in Fig. 14.14 (*b*) in which activity A precedes B.

A B
3 5
(a) Arrow diagram

A,3 B,5
(b) AON diagram

Fig. 14.14

Let us consider a few examples and compare the conventional arrow diagrams and AON diagrams for some project networks.

EXAMPLE 14.10

The dependency relationships between the activities of a project are shown below. Draw the arrow and AON diagrams.

Activity	:	*A*	*B*	*C*	*D*	*E*	*F*
Immediate predecessor	:	-	-	-	*A,B*	*B*	*B,C*

Solution

The arrow diagram for these dependency relationships is shown in Fig. 14.15 (a). It may be observed that two dummy activities D_1 and D_2 have to be included since activities D and F have, in addition to A and C, activity B as a common immediate predecessor.

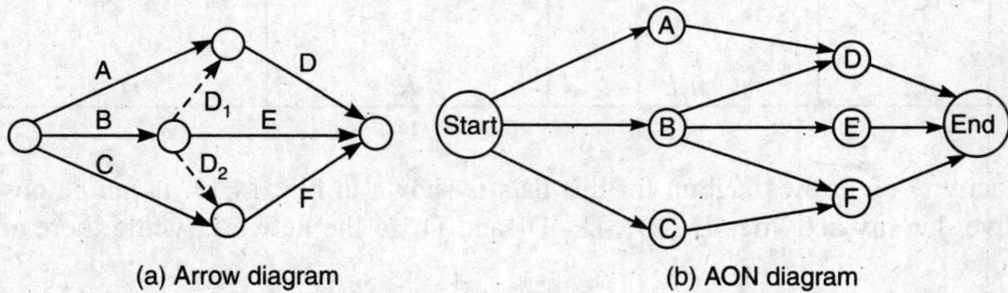

Fig. 14.15 (a), (b)

The AON diagram is shown in Fig. 14.15 (*b*) in which a circle is drawn for each activity and it is joined with its immediate successor by an arrow. Thus no dummies are required in the AON diagram. Since the project starts with more than one activity, a 'fictitious' start activity is used to initiate the network. Likewise, as there are more than one activities marking the end of the project, a fictitious finish activity is used to represent the end of the project.

The name of the activity, its duration or any other detail are written within the activity node which may be a circle or a rectangle.

EXAMPLE 14.10-2

The precedence relationships for the activities of a project are given below. Draw the arrow diagram as well as AON diagram.

Activity	*Immediate predecessor*	*Activity*	*Immediate predecessor*
A	-	*G*	*B,C*
B	-	*H*	*C*
C	-	*I*	*E, F*
E	*A*	*J*	*G, H*
F	*A, B*	*K*	*H*

Solution

The activity on arrow diagram for this project is drawn in Fig. 14.16 (a). It can be observed that there are five dummy activities D_1, D_2, D_3, D_4 and D_5 and ten real activities. Fig. 14.16 (b) shows the AON diagram which is free from dummy activities.

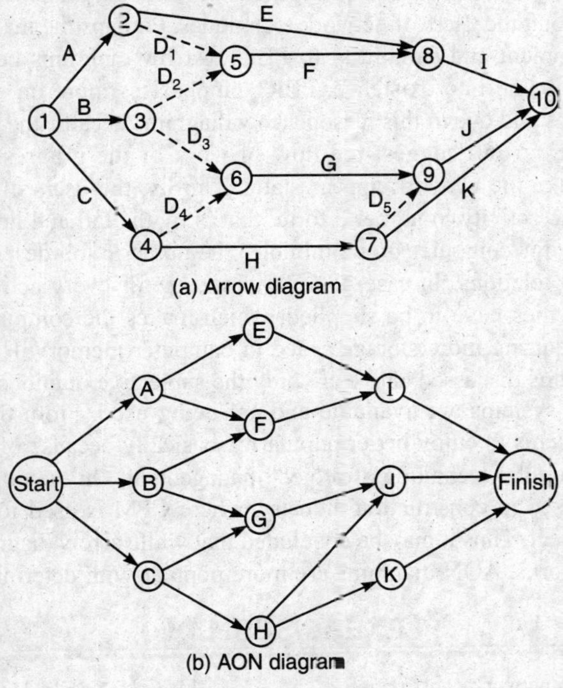

Fig. 14.16 (a), (b)

EXAMPLE 14.10-3

Draw the AON diagram for the following data

Activity	*Immediate predecessor*	*Duration (weeks)*
A	—	5
B	*A*	4
C	*A*	7
D	*B*	6
E	*B, C*	6
F	*C*	5
G	*D, E, F*	7

Solution

The AON diagram is drawn in Fig. 14.17. The rectangles for activity nodes are drawn first and they are then joined by arrows to represent the given precedence relationships.

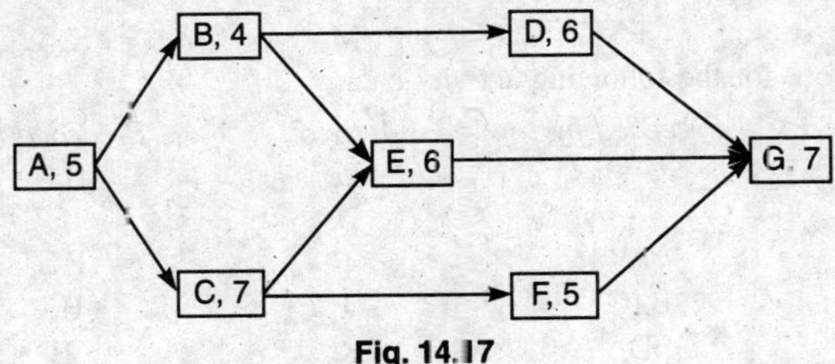

Fig. 14.17

14.11 MERITS AND DEMERITS OF AON DIAGRAMS

The greatest merit of AON diagram is its simplicity. It is easier to draw, interpret, review and revise. Absence of dummies makes it more readily understood by non-technical users.

However, in spite of simplicity and other merits of AON diagrams, arrow diagrams continue to enjoy popularity among the users of network techniques. Perhaps the main reasons of popularity are their early development and suitability to PERT. Arrow diagrams became well established before AON diagrams came into existence. PERT emphasises more on events, which form the nodes of arrow diagrams and due to this reason arrow diagrams became the basis of PERT analysis. Secondly, activities on arrows suggest the flow of work or the progress of the project, while activities on nodes make the network appear static. Thirdly, the users of arrow diagrams argue that identification of the activity in numeric form, that is by the tail and head event numbers (i, j) makes it more suitable for computer programming. The numeric job description, supplies all the connected dependency relations. In case of AON diagram, for every activity, its predecessor as well as successor activities have to be supplied, which makes the computer programming more involved as well as requiring more storage space in computer memory. However, the merits and demerits of both diagrams discussed above are only the subjective opinions of its users. Computer programs for both the systems are available and are being used. From the application point of view, arrow diagram seems to enjoy better popularity, basically because of its better suitability to PERT, which is very popular technique of project management. On the other hand AON diagram is being increasingly used in construction industry, where CPM is used for planning, scheduling and controlling the project. Thus it may be concluded that while arrow diagrams are more common with probabilistic networks, AON diagrams are more popular with deterministic networks.

EXERCISES 14.1

1. Explain the rules of network construction. *[M.G.U. Kerala M.Com., June, 2012; P.T.U. B.Tech., 2010; Chennai U.B.B.A. Nov., 2010]*
2. Define event, activity, looping, dangling, network and project. *[Mumbai U.B.Com. April, 2013; R.U. MBA Dec., 2011; Chennai U.B.C.A. Nov., 2010; P.T.U. B.Tech. (C.Sc.) 2010; (Mech.)* 2011, 2010; *P.U. B.Com. Jan., 2005; R.T.M. Nagpur U. B.Tech. Dec., 2003]*
3. Explain the rules devised by Fulkerson. *[H.P.U.B. Tech. (Mech.) Sept., 2013; P.T.U. B.Tech. (C.Sc.) 2010; P.U. B.Com. Jan., 2005; Sept., 2005]*
4. What are the different phases of project management ? What do you understand by event, path, dummy and looping ? *[P.T.U. B.Tech. (Mech.) April, 2013; P.U. B.E. (T.I.T.) Dec., 2006; B.E. (Mech.) 2006]*
5. Construct the network for the following activity data:

Activity	*Preceded by*	*Activity*	*Preceded by*
A	—		
B	—	H	F
C	B	I	H
D	A	J	I
E	C	K	D, E, G, J
F	C	L	I
G	F	M	K, L

6. Construct the network for the following activity data:

Activity	*Preceded by*	*Activity*	*Preceded by*
A	—	G	B,C
B	—	H	F
C	A	I	F,G
D	B, C	J	H,I
E	D	K	B
F	E	L	F,G,K

7. Draw the network for the following activities:

Activity	*Preceded by*	*Activity*	*Preceded by*
A		K	I
B	A	L	I,J
C	A	M	L
D	C	N	K,M
E	C	O	N
F	B,D	P	N
G	E	Q	N
H	F,G	R	N
I	H	S	N
J	H	T	N

8. A new type of conveyor is to be designed. The following list represents the major activities together with the precedence relationship. Construct the network diagram.

Activity no. :	1	2	3	4	5	6	7	8	9	10	11
Preceding activity :	—	1	1	3	2,3	4,5	5	7	6	9,8	10

9. Construct a PERT network for the following activity data:

Activity no. :	A	B	C	D	E	F	G	H	I	J	K	L
Immediate predecessor :	None	None	A	B	C	E	F	F	H	G,I	D,G	K

10. Assume that you are letting a contract for widening a street. Draw a network for the activities from the start of preparation of specifications until contractor goes ahead.

Task :	A	B	C	D	E	F	G	H	I	J	K	L
Immediate predecessor :	—	A	A	B	C	C	E	F	G, H	G, H	I	J

11. Construct the network for the following information:

Activity no. :	A	B	C	D	E	F	G	H	I	J	K	L	M	N
Immediate predecessor :	—	—	—	C	A, D	E	B	F	H	I	G, J	G, J	K	L, M

12. Construct the network for the following set of activities:

Activity no. :	A	B	C	D	E	F	G	H	I	J	K	L
Predecessor :	—	—	—	A	B	C	B, D	C, E	F	F	E, G, I	H, J

13. Construct the network for a project in which activities have the following precedence relationships: A,C,D can start immediately. E > B, C ; F, G > D ; H, I > E, F ; J > I, G; K > H ; B > A.

[*P.U. E.E. (Mech.) April, 1976*]

14. Construct the network for the following set of activities:

Activity :	A	B	C	D	E	F	G	H	I	J
Immediate predecessor :	—	—	B	A, B	A, B	B	E, D, F	D, E	E, F	H, G,I,C

[**Hint.** The network is drawn below.]

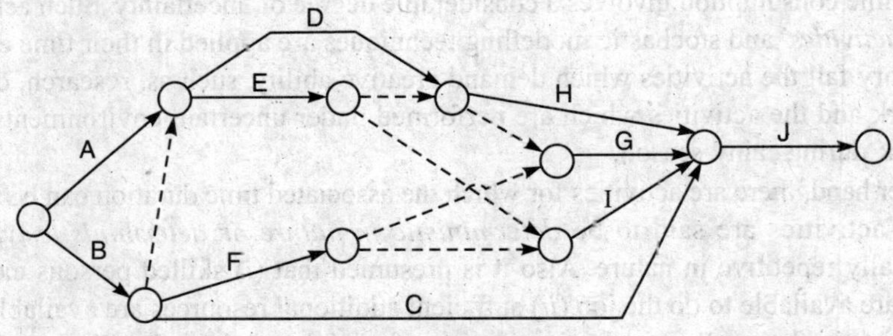

Fig. 14.18

15. The Rubik's cube is manufactured in six steps, labelled A through F. Because of its size and complexity, the cube is produced one at a time. The production control manager thinks that network scheduling techniques might be useful in planning future production. He recorded the following information:

(*i*) A is the initial step and precedes B and C
(*ii*) C precedes D & E
(*iii*) B succeeds D and precedes E
(*iv*) F succeeds E and
(*v*) D precedes F.

Simplify the diagram by removing the redundant activities. Draw the AON diagram. After rechecking the network it was concluded that B is really a predecessor of D rather than vice versa.

16. A project consists of activities from A to L. The order in which the activities fall is as follows: A comes first and precedes B, C, D. Both B and C must be completed before E starts. C and D must come before F but G and H can start as soon as D is completed. Activity I succeeds D, E, F and G. Activities J and K succeed G, H, I but precede L.

Eliminate the redundant activities and drew AON diagram.

17. The dependency relationships of the activities of a project are given below:

Activity A is followed by B; B is followed by C; D depends on C and G; G depends on A and B; E depends on B, C, D; J and H follow activity G; I follows G, D, H; K depends on D, H; F depends on E, H, I. L depends on D, J & K. Draw the AON diagram.

18. A list of activities and their precedence relationships are given below:

Activity :	A	B	C	D	E	F	G	H	I	J	K
Predecessor activity :	—	A	B	A, C	D	E	C	D, E, G, I	C	G, H	F, H, J

Draw an activity on node network diagram. [*IGNOU MBA, 2002*]

[**Hint :** The AON diagram is shown in Fig. 14.19.]

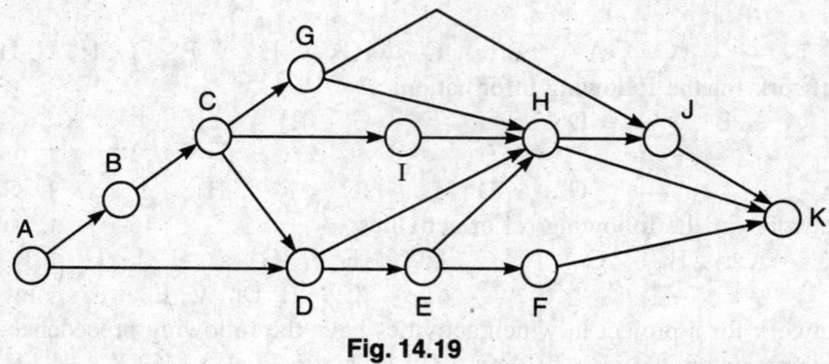

Fig. 14.19

14.12 CRITICAL PATH METHOD

Measure of Activity

Each task or activity takes some time for its completion. This time duration depends upon the nature of the activity. Some activities are rarely performed and no data exists for their time durations. Their time consumption involves a considerable degree of uncertainty. Such activities are called '*variable activities*' and stochastic modelling techniques are applied in their time estimation. Under this category fall the activities which demand creative ability, such as, research, design and development work and the activities which are performed under uncertain environments, such as, construction work during rainy season.

On the other hand, there are activities for which the associated time duration can be accurately estimated. Such activities are said to be *deterministic in nature or deterministic type*. These activities are usually repetitive in nature. Also it is presumed that (*i*) skilled persons experienced in method study are available to do the job (*ii*) sufficient additional resources are available to allow uninterrupted activity. Above all, it is the assumption of confidence that all will go well. Figures 14.20 (*a*) and (*b*) show frequency distribution curves for the two types of activities. In Figure 14.20 (*a*), the dispersion of the curve is more and hence more is the uncertainty. In Fig. 14.20 (*b*), for deterministic type activity, the dispersion is less and the system tends to be more deterministic.

The projects which comprise of the variable type activities associated with probabilistic time estimates, employ PERT version of the networks and the projects comprising of deterministic type of activities are handled by CPM version of networks.

This is the main difference between the two techniques. The other difference between the two is that PERT is event-oriented while the CPM is activity-oriented. In Fig. 14.20 (*a*) and (*b*),

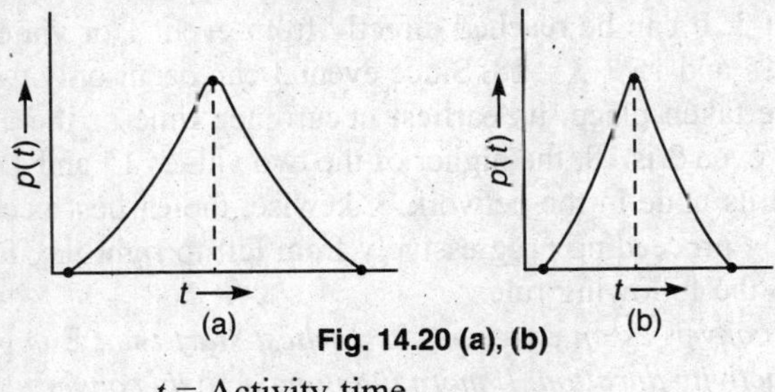

Fig. 14.20 (a), (b)

t = Activity time,

$p\ (t)$ = relative frequency of occurrence.

Time Units

Any convenient time unit can be used, but it must be consistent throughout the network. Depending upon the project length and level of detail, time unit may be working days, shifts or weeks. Full time units are usually used, for instance activity estimated at 3 days and 6 hours will be assigned 4 days.

Critical Path Analysis

The Critical path of a network gives the shortest time in which the whole project can be completed. It is the chain of activities with the longest time durations. These activities are called *critical activities*. They are critical in the sense that delay in any of them results in the delay of the completion of the project. There may be more than one critical path in a network and it is possible for the critical path to run through a dummy. The critical path analysis consists of the following steps:

1. *Calculate the time schedule for each activity* : It involves the determination of the time by which an activity must begin and the time before which it must be completed. The time schedule data for each activity include the calculation of the earliest start, the earliest finish, the latest start, the latest finish times and the float.
2. *Calculate the time schedule for the completion of the entire project* : It involves the calculation of project completion time.
3. *Identify the critical activities and find the critical path* : Critical activities are the ones which must be started and completed on schedule or else the project may get delayed. The path containing these activities is the critical path and is the longest path in terms of duration.

Consider the network shown in Fig. 14.21 which consists of the following activities:

Activity :	1-2	1-3	2-3	2-5	3-4	3-6	4-5	4-6	5-6	6-7
Duration (weeks) :	15	15	3	5	8	12	1	14	3	14

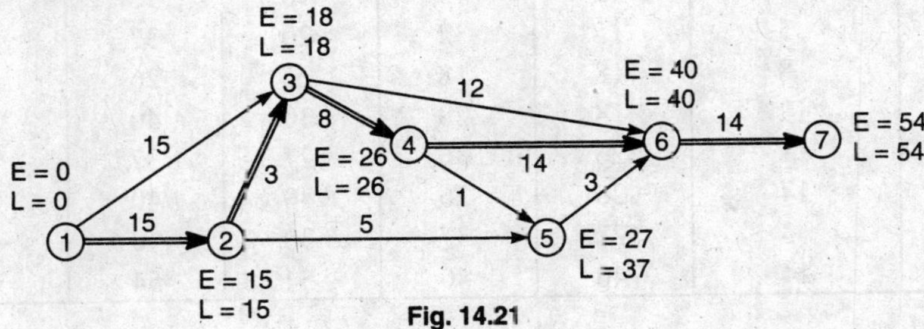

Fig. 14.21

The *earliest start time* (E) for an activity represents the time at which an activity can begin at the earliest. It assumes that all the preceding activities start and finish at their earliest times. For instance earliest start times of activities 1-2 and 1-3 are zero each or the earliest occurrence time of event 1 is zero. Earliest start times of activities 2-3 and 2-5 or the earliest occurrence time of event 2 is obtained by adding activity time t_{12} to earliest occurrence time of event 1 *i.e.*, it is 0 + 15 = 15.

Next consider event 3. It can be reached directly from event 1 or via event 2, the times for the two sequences being 15 and 15 + 3 = 18. Since event 3 can occur only when all the preceding activities and events have taken place, its earliest occurrence time or the earliest start times of activities emanating from even 3 is 18, the higher of the two values 15 and 18. This is represented by putting E = 18 around its node in the network. Likewise, the earliest occurrence time of each event can be determined by proceeding progressively from left to right *i.e.*, following the *forward pass method* according to the following rule:

If only one activity converges on an event, its earliest start time E is given by E of the tail event of the activity plus activity duration. If more than one activity converges on an event, E's via all the paths would be computed and the highest value chosen and put around the node.

The E's calculated for the problem at hand are shown in the network diagram.

The *latest finish time* (L) for an activity represents the latest by which an activity must be completed in order that the project may not be delayed beyond its targeted completion time. This is calculated by proceeding progressively from the end event to the start event. The L for the last event is assumed to be equal to its E and the L's for the other events are computed by the following rule (using *backword pass method*):

If only one activity emanates from an event, compute L by subtracting activity duration from L of its head event. If more than one activity emanates from an event, compute L's via all the paths and choose the smallest and put it around the event at hand.

The L's calculated for the problem at hand are shown in the network diagram.

Next, the *earliest finish time* (T_{EF}) and the *latest start time* (T_{LS}) for an activity are computed:

$$T_{EF} = E + t_{ij},$$
$$T_{LS} = L - t_{ij},$$

where t_{ij} is the duration for activity $i - j$. Float (also called *total float*) for an activity is then calculated:

$$F = L - T_{EF} \text{ or } F = T_{LS} - E.$$

Float is, thus, the positive difference between the finish times or the positive difference between the start times. The following network analysis table is then compiled:

TABLE 14.1

Activity (i – j)	Duration (D)	Start time		Finish time		Total Float
		Earliest	Latest	Earliest	Latest	
(1)	(2)	(3)	(4)	(5)	(6)	(7)
1-2	15	0	0	15	15	0
1-3	15	0	3	15	18	3
2-3	3	15	15	18	18	0
2-5	5	15	32	20	37	17
3-4	8	18	18	26	26	0
3-6	12	18	28	30	40	10
4-5	1	26	36	27	37	10
4-6	14	26	26	40	40	0
5-6	3	27	37	30	40	10
6-7	14	40	40	54	54	0

Columns 1 and 2 contain the activities and their durations is weeks. Under column 3 are noted the E's for the tail events of the activities and under column 6 are noted the L's of the head events of the activities. Other columns are then computed as follows:

column 4 = column 6 – column 2,
column 5 = column 3 + column 2,
and column 7 = column 6 – column 5,
= column 4 – column 3.

As an example, consider activity 1–2. Its tail event 1 has E = 0. Put 0 against this activity under column 3. Its head event 2 has L = 15. Put 15 against it under column 6. Under column 4 write the value in column 6 minus activity duration *i.e.*, 15 – 15 = 0. Under column 5 note the value in column 3 plus activity duration *i.e.*, 0 + 15 = 15. Compute total float by subtracting column 5 from 6 or column 3 from 4. Total float for activity 1-2 is 0. Similarly, calculate total float for other activities. Critical path is the path containing activities with zero float. These activities demand above normal attention with no freedom of action. For the problem at hand it is 1-2-3-4-6-7 and is shown by double arrows in Fig. 14.21. The project duration is 54 weeks. Sometimes, there may be more than one critical path *i.e.*, two or more paths with the same maximum completion time. Non-critical activities have positive float (slack or leeway) so that we may slacken while executing them and concentrate on the critical activities. While delay in any critical activity will delay the project completion, this may not be so with the noncritical activities.

The Four Floats

Total float : It is the difference between the maximum time available to perform the activity and the activity duration. The maximum time available for any activity is from the earliest start time to the latest completion time. Thus for an activity i - j having duration t_{ij},

Maximum time available = L – E.

$$\therefore \quad \text{Total Float} = L - E - t_{ij}$$
$$= (L - t_{ij}) - E \text{ or } L - (E + t_{ij})$$
$$= T_{LS} - E \text{ or } L - T_{EF}.$$

Thus the total float of an activity is the difference of its latest start and earliest start times or the difference of its latest finish and earliest finish times. Total float represents the maximum time within which an activity can be delayed without affecting the project completion time.

Free Float : It is that portion of the total float within which an activity can be manipulated without affecting the floats of subsequent activities, It is computed by subtracting the head event slack from the total float. The head event slack is (L – E) of that event.

∴ Free float of activity

$$i - j = \text{T.F.} - (L - E) \text{ of event } j.$$

Thus free float is the time by which completion of an activity can be delayed without delaying its immediate successor activities.

Independent Float : It is that portion of the total float within which an activity can be delayed for start without affecting the floats of preceding activities. It is computed by subtracting the tail event slack from the free float. If the result is negative, it is taken as zero.

∴ Independent float of activity

$$i - j = \text{F.F.} - (L - E) \text{ of tail event } i.$$

Apart from the above three floats, there is another float, namely the interfering float for the activities.

Interfering Float : Utilization of the float of an activity can affect the floats of the subsequent activities in the network. Thus, interfering float can be defined as that part of the total float which causes a reduction in the floats of the succeeding activities. In other words *it can be defined as the difference between the latest finish time of the activity under consideration and the earliest start time of the following activity, or zero, whichever is larger*. Thus, interfering float refers to that portion of the activity float which cannot be consumed without adversely affecting the floats of the subsequent activities.

It is numerically equal to the difference between the total float and the free float of the activity. It is also equal to the head event slack of the activity.

Thus interfering float of an activity = T.F. – F.F. = (L – E) of the head event of the activity.

Subcritical Activity : Activity having next higher float than the critical activity is called the subcritical activity and demands normal attention but allows some freedom of action. The path connecting such activities is named as the *subcritical path*. A network may have more than one subcritical path.

Supercritical Activity : An activity having negative float is called supercritical activity. Such an activity demands very special attention and action. It results when activity duration is more than the time available. Such negative float, though possible, indicates an abnormal situation requiring a decision as to how to compress the activity. It can be done by employing more resources so as to make the total float zero or positive. Compression of the network, however, involves an extra cost.

Slack : It is the time by which occurrence of an event can be delayed. It is denoted by S and is the difference between the latest occurrence time and earliest occurrence time of the event.

i.e., S = L – E of the event.

In the above discussion, the term float has been used in connection with the activities and slack for the events. However, the two terms are being used interchangeably *i.e.*, slack for the activities and float for the events by some of the writers.

EXAMPLE 14.12-1

Tasks A, B, C,..., H, I constitute a project. The precedence relationships are

$$A < D;\ A < E;\ B < F;\ D < F;\ C < G;\ C < H;\ F < I;\ G < I.$$

Draw a network to represent the project and find the minimum time of completion of the project when time, in days, of each task is as follows:

Task	*A*	*B*	*C*	*D*	*E*	*F*	*G*	*H*	*I*
Time	*8*	*10*	*8*	*10*	*16*	*17*	*18*	*14*	*9*

Also identify the critical path. [*Dayalbagh Edu. Inst. Agra MBA May, 2014; P.T.U. B.Tech. April, 2012; P.U. B.Com. Sept., 2005*]

Solution

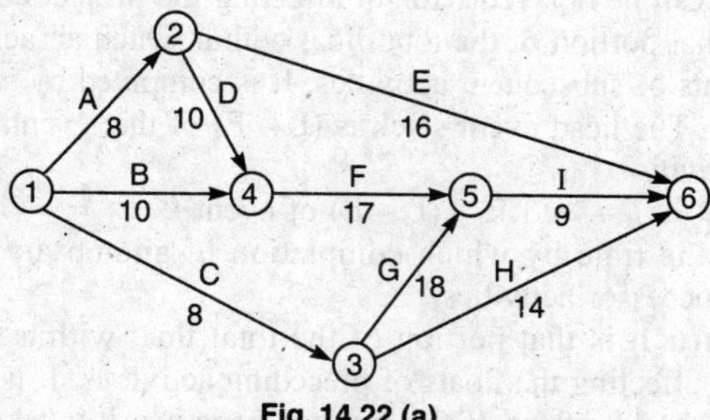

Fig. 14.22 (a)

The given precedence order reveals that there are no predecessors to activities A, B, and C and hence they all start from the initial node. Similarly, there are no successor activities to activities E, H and I and hence, they all merge into the end node of the project. The network obtained is shown in Fig. 14.22 (*a*).

The nodes of the network have been numbered by using the Fulkerson's rule. The activity descriptions and times are written along the activity arrows. To determine the minimum project completion time, let event 1 occur at zero time. The earliest occurrence time (E) and the latest occurrence time (L) of each event is then computed.

$$E_1 = 0,$$
$$E_2 = E_1 + t_{12} = 0 + 8 = 8,$$
$$E_3 = E_1 + t_{13} = 0 + 8 = 8,$$

$E_4 = \text{Max.}\ [0 + 10, 8 + 10] = 18,$
$E_5 = \text{Max.}\ [18 + 17, 8 + 18] = 35,$
$E_6 = \text{Max.}\ [8 + 16, 35 + 9, 8 + 14] = 44.$

Similarly,

$L_6 = E_6 = 44,$
$L_5 = L_6 - t_{56} = 44 - 9 = 35,$
$L_4 = L_5 - t_{45} = 35 - 17 = 18,$
$L_3 = \text{Min.}\ [44 - 14, 35 - 18\ ] = 17,$
$L_2 = \text{Min.}\ [44 - 16, 18 - 10] = 8,$
$L_1 = \text{Min.}\ [8 - 8, 17 - 8, 18 - 10] = 0.$

The E and L values for each event have been written along the nodes in Fig. 14.22 (*b*).

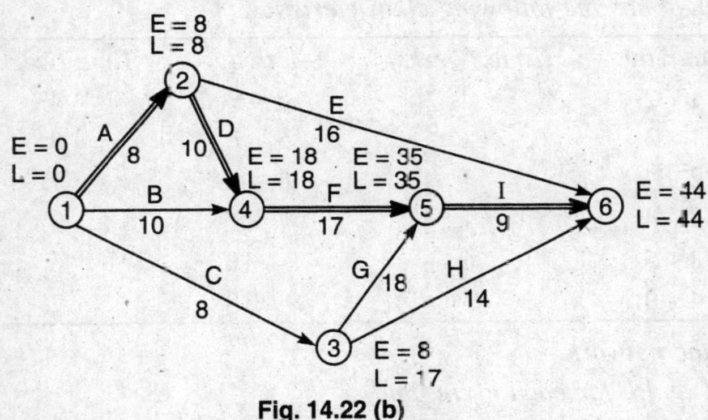

Fig. 14.22 (b)

The critical path is now determined by any of the following methods:

Method 1. The network analysis table is compiled as below.

TABLE 14.2

Activity	*Duration*	*Start time* *Earliest*	*Start time* *Latest*	*Finish time* *Earliest*	*Finish time* *Latest*	*Total Float*
1-2	8	0	0	8	8	0
1-3	8	0	9	8	17	9
1-4	10	0	8	10	18	8
2-4	10	8	8	18	18	0
2-6	16	8	28	24	44	20
3-5	18	8	17	26	35	9
3-6	14	8	30	22	44	22
4-5	17	18	18	35	35	0
5-6	9	35	35	44	44	0

Activities 1-2, 2-4, 4-5 and 5-6 having zero float are the critical activities and 1-2-4-5-6 is the critical path.

Method 2. For identifying the critical path, the following conditions are checked. If an activity satisfies all the three conditions, it is critical.

(*i*) E = L for the tail event.

(*ii*) E = L for the head event.

(*iii*) $E_j - E_i = L_j - L_i = t_{ij}$.

Activities 1-2, 2-4, 4-5 and 5-6 satisfy these conditions. Other activities do not fulfil all the three conditions. The critical path is, therefore, 1-2-4-5-6.

Method 3. The various paths and their durations are:

Path	*Duration (days)*
1–2–6	8 + 16 = 24
1–2–4–5–6	8 + 10 + 17 + 9 = 44
1–4–5–6	10 + 17 + 9 = 36
1–3–5–6	8 + 18 + 9 = 35
1–3–6	8 + 14 = 22

Path 1-2-4-5-6, the longest in time involving 44 days, is the critical path. It represented by bold lines in Fig. 14.22 (*b*).

EXAMPLE 14.12-2

A project schedule has the following characteristics:

Activity	*Time (weeks)*	*Activity*	*Time (weeks)*
1 - 2	4	5 - 6	4
1 - 3	1	5 - 7	8
2 - 4	1	6 - 8	1
3 - 4	1	7 - 8	2
3 - 5	6	8 - 10	5
4 - 9	5	9 - 10	7

(*i*) *Construct the network.*

(*ii*) *Compute E and L for each event, and*

(*iii*) *Find the critical path.*

[*P.T.U. B.Tech. April, 2012; P.U.B.E. (Mech.) 2012; Kuru. U. B.E. (Mech.) June, 2012; J.N.T.U. Hyderabad B.Tech. Sept., 2011; G.N.D.U. B.Com. April, 2009; P.U.B. Com. April, 2006, 2000; P.T.U. B.E. (Mech.) May, 2006*]

Solution

The given data results in a network shown in Fig. 14.23. The figures along the arrows represent the activity times.

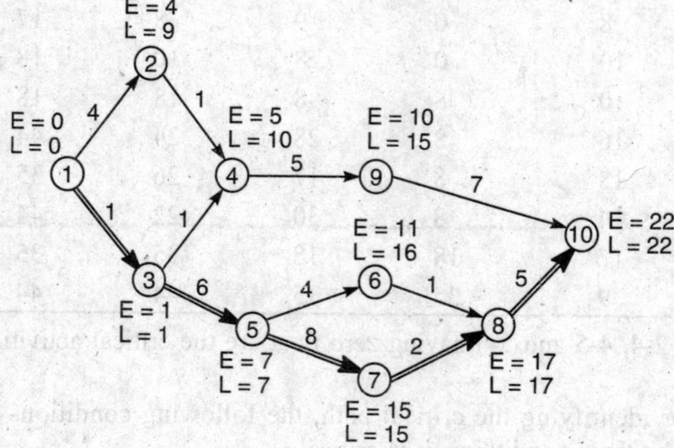

Fig. 14.23

The earliest occurrence time (E) and the latest occurrence time (L) of each event are now computed by employing forward and backward pass calculations.

In forward pass computations,

$$E_1 = 0,$$
$$E_2 = E_1 + t_{12} = 0 + 4 = 4,$$
$$E_3 = E_1 + t_{13} = 0 + 1 = 1,$$
$$E_4 = \underset{i=2,3}{\text{Max}} \; [E_i + t_{i4}] = \text{Max. } [4 + 1, 1 + 1] = 5,$$
$$E_5 = E_3 + t_{35} = 1 + 6 = 7,$$
$$E_6 = E_5 + t_{56} = 7 + 4 = 11,$$
$$E_7 = E_5 + t_{57} = 7 + 8 = 15,$$
$$E_8 = \underset{i=6,7}{\text{Max}} \; [E_i + t_{i8}] = \text{Max. } [11 + 1, 15 + 2] = 17,$$
$$E_9 = E_4 + t_{49} = 5 + 5 = 10, \text{ and}$$
$$E_{10} = \underset{i=8,9}{\text{Max}} \; [E_i + T_{i10}] = \text{Max. } [17 + 5, 10 + 7] = 22.$$

E values are represented in Fig. 14.23.

In backward pass computations,

$$L_{10} = E_{10} = 22,$$
$$L_9 = L_{10} - t_{9,\,10} = 22 - 7 = 15,$$
$$L_8 = L_{10} - t_{8,\,10} = 22 - 5 = 17,$$
$$L_7 = L_8 - t_{78} = 17 - 2 = 15,$$
$$L_6 = L_8 - t_{68} = 17 - 1 = 16,$$
$$L_5 = \underset{j=6,7}{\text{Min}} \; [L_j - t_{5j}] = \text{Min. } [16 - 4, 15 - 8] = 7,$$
$$L_4 = L_9 - t_{49} = 15 - 5 = 10,$$
$$L_3 = \underset{j=4,5}{\text{Min}} \; [L_j - t_{3j}] = \text{Min. } [10 - 1, 7 - 6] = 1,$$
$$L_2 = L_4 - t_{24} = 10 - 1 = 9,$$
$$L_1 = \underset{j=2,3}{\text{Min}} \; [L_j - t_{1j}] = \text{Min. } [9 - 4, 1 - 1] = 0.$$

L values are also represented in Fig. 14.23. Network analysis table is given below.

TABLE 14.3

Activity	*Duration (weeks)*	*Start time*		*Finish time*		*Total Float*
		Earliest	*Latest*	*Earliest*	*Latest*	
1 - 2	4	0	5	4	9	5
1 - 3	1	0	0	1	1	0
2 - 4	1	4	9	5	10	5
3 - 4	1	1	9	2	10	8
3 - 5	6	1	1	7	7	0
4 - 9	5	5	10	10	15	5
5 - 6	4	7	12	11	16	5
5 - 7	8	7	7	15	15	0
6 - 8	1	11	16	12	17	5
7 - 8	2	15	15	17	17	0
8 - 10	5	17	17	22	22	0
9 - 10	7	10	15	17	22	5

Path 1-3-5-7-8-10 with project duration of 22 weeks is the critical path.

EXAMPLE 14.12-3

The utility data for a network are given below. Determine the total, free, independent and interfering floats and identify the critical path.

Activity :	*0-1*	*1-2*	*1-3*	*2-4*	*2-5*	*3-4*	*3-6*	*4-7*	*5-7*	*6-7*
Duration :	*2*	*8*	*10*	*6*	*3*	*3*	*7*	*5*	*2*	*8*

[G.N.D.U. B.Com April, 2012; Univ of Madras B.Sc. (Math.) Nov., 2012; P.T.U. B. Tech. (Mech.) 2010; H.P.U.B. Tech. (Mech.) Nov., 2006; P.U.B. Com. Sept., 2004]

Solution

The network diagram for the given project data is shown in Fig. 14.24. Activity durations are written along the activity arrows.

The earliest start and latest finish times of the activities are computed by employing the forward pass and backward pass calculations as explained in example 14.12-2. These times are represented in the network around the respective nodes.

The network analysis table is now constructed.

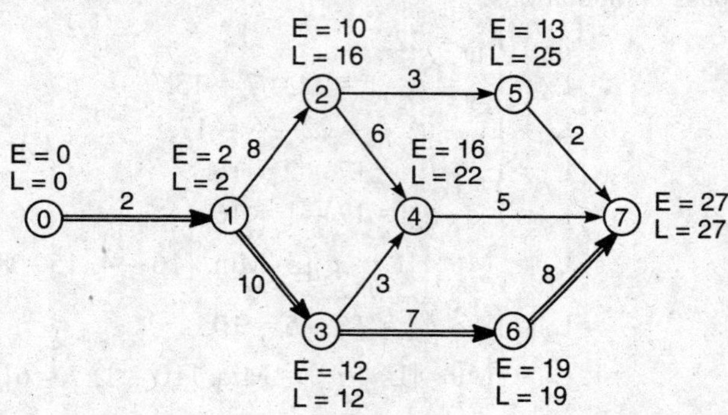

Fig. 14.24

TABLE 14.4

Activity	*Duration*	*Start time*		*Finish time*		*Float*			
		Earliest	*Latest*	*Earliest*	*Latest*	*Total*	*Free*	*Independent*	*Interfering*
1	2	3	4	5	6	7	8	9	10
0 - 1	2	0	0	2	2	0	0	0	0
1 - 2	8	2	8	10	16	6	0	0	6
1 - 3	10	2	2	12	12	0	0	0	0
2 - 4	6	10	16	16	22	6	0	$-6 \approx 0$	6
2 - 5	3	10	22	13	25	12	0	$-6 \approx 0$	12
3 - 4	3	12	19	15	22	7	1	1	6
3 - 6	7	12	12	19	19	0	0	0	0
4 - 7	5	16	22	21	27	6	6	0	0
5 - 7	2	13	25	15	27	12	12	0	0
6 - 7	8	19	19	27	27	0	0	0	0

Total float is the positive, difference between latest and earliest finish times or latest and earliest start times. For activity, say, 1-2,

$$\text{total float (T.F.)} = 16 - 10 = 8 - 2 = 6.$$

Similarly, for activity, say 2-5,

$$\text{total float} = 25 - 13 = 22 - 10 = 12 \text{ and so on.}$$

Total float calculations are depicted in column 7 of table 14.4.

Free float of activity i - j = T.F. – head event slack
= T.F. – (L – E) of event *j*.

Thus free float of activity 0 - 1
= 0 – (L – E) of event 1,
= 0 – (2 – 2) = 0,

free float of activity 1 - 2 = 6 – (16 – 10) = 6 – 6 = 0 etc.

Free floats of various activities are calculated in column 8 of the network analysis table.

Independent float of activity *i - j* = F.F. – tail event slack
= F.F. – (L – E) of event *i*.

Thus independent float of activity 0 - 1 = 0 – (0 – 0) = 0,
independent float of activity 1 - 2= 0 – (2 – 2) = 0,
independent float of activity 2 - 4= 0 – (16 – 10) = – 6 ≈ 0 and so on.

Independent floats of various activities are calculated in column 9 of the table. If independent float of an activity is negative, it is taken as zero.

Interfering float of activity *i - j* = Max. [L.F. time of *i - j* – E.S. time of *j - k*, 0]

Thus interfering float of activity 0 - 1
= Max.[L.F. time of 0 - 1 – E.S.time of 1 - 2 or 1 - 3, 0]
= Max. [2–2, 0] = 0,

interfering float of activity 1 - 2 = Max. [L.F. time of 1 - 2 – E.S. time of 2 - 4 or 2 - 5, 0]
= Max. [16 – 10, 0] = 6, etc.

More conveniently, interfering float of an activity = T.F. – F.F.

Thus, interfering float of activity 2 - 5 = 12 – 0 = 12, etc.

Alternatively, interfering float of an activity = Head event slack.

Thus, interfering float of activity 2 - 5 = 25 – 13 = 12, etc.

Interfering floats of various activities are calculated in column 10 of the table 14.4.

EXAMPLE 14.12-4

For the network given in Fig. 14.25, determine the total, free, independent and interfering floats for each activity. Times for activities are in months.

[P.T.U. B.Tech. (Mech.) May, 2011; H.P.U.B.Tech. (Mech.) Nov., 2010; G.N.D.U. B.Com. Sept., 2008; P.U.B.E. (T.I.T.) Nov., 2006; B.Com. April, 2007]

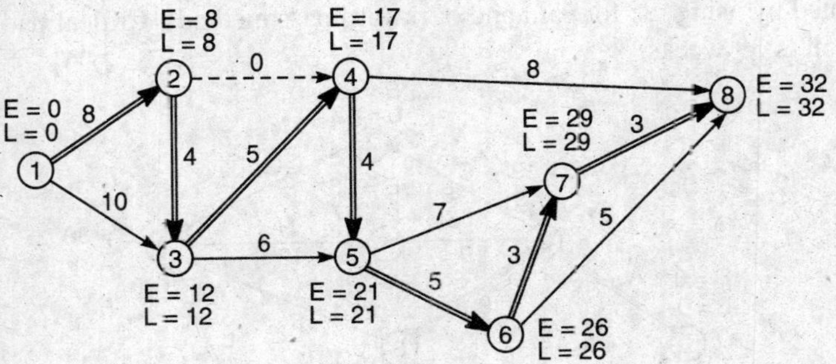

Fig. 14.25

Solution

The computations of earliest start, earliest finish, latest start and latest finish times along with floats are given in table 14.5.

TABLE 14.5

Activity	*Duration (months)*	*Start time*		*Finish time*		*Float*			
		Earliest	*Latest*	*Earliest*	*Latest*	*Total*	*Free*	*Independent*	*Interfering*
1-2	8	0	0	8	8	0	0	0	0
1-3	10	0	2	10	12	2	2	2	0
2-3	4	8	8	12	12	0	0	0	0
2-4	0	8	17	8	17	9	9	9	0
3-4	5	12	12	17	17	0	0	0	0
3-5	6	12	15	18	21	3	3	3	0
4-5	4	17	17	21	21	0	0	0	0
4-8	8	17	24	25	32	7	7	7	0
5-6	5	21	21	26	26	0	0	0	0
5-7	7	21	22	28	29	1	1	1	0
6-7	3	26	26	29	29	0	0	0	0
6-8	5	26	27	31	32	1	1	1	0
7-8	3	29	29	32	32	0	0	0	0

Activities 1-2, 2-3, 3-4, 4-5, 5-6, 6-7 and 7-8 have zero float and hence are critical. The path 1-2-3-4-5-6-7-8 is the critical path with the project duration of 32 months. Total, free, independent and interfering floats are calculated as explained in example 14.12.3 and are represented in the last four columns of the table.

EXAMPLE 14.12-5

Estimated times for the jobs of a project are given below:

Job	:	*A*	*B*	*C*	*D*	*E*	*F*	*G*	*H*	*I*	*J*	*K*	*L*
Time (weeks)	:	*13*	*5*	*8*	*10*	*9*	*7*	*7*	*12*	*8*	*9*	*4*	*17*

The constraints governing the jobs are as follows:

A and B are start jobs; A controls C, D and E; B controls F and J; G depends upon C; H depends on D; E and F control I and L; K follows J ; L is also controlled by K; G, H, I and L are the last jobs. Draw the network, determine the project duration and the critical path.

[*H.P.U.B.Tech. (Mech.) June, 2010; P.T.U. B.Tech. (C.Sc.) 2010; P.U.B. Com. April, 2006*]

Solution

The network obtained by using the given precedence relationship is shown in Fig. 14.26. Events have been numbered using the Fulkerson's rule. Note that a dummy activity 6-8 has been included to draw the network. The earliest start times and latest completion times of the activities can be computed by using the forward and backward pass methods. Critical path is 1-2-6-8-9 and project duration is 39 weeks.

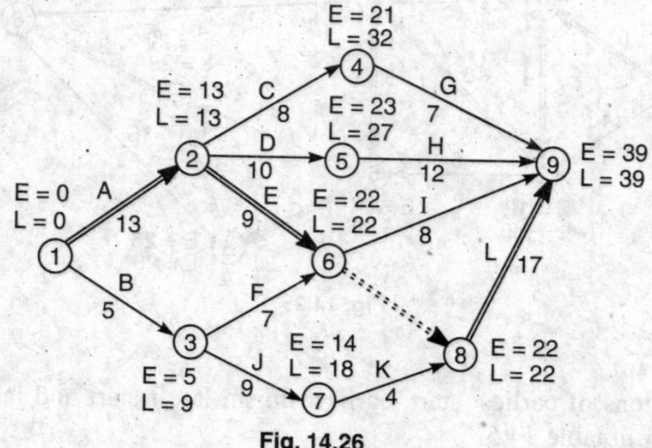

Fig. 14.26

EXERCISES 14.2

1. Define float. Explain its different types and their importance.
[*G.N.D.U. B.Com. Nov., 2014; P.U.MBA Feb, 2009; B.E. (Mech.) Nov., 2002; R.T.M. Nagpur U.B. Tech. June 2003; P.U. B.Com., Jan., 2005; MBA, 2000*]
2. What do you mean by slack ? Define critical path in the light of the definition of slack.
[*H.P.U.B. Tech. (Mech.) Sept., 2013; P.U. B.E. (Ec. & Comm.) Nov. 2011; Mumbai U.MBA, 2010; Osmania U. MBA July, 2010; Chennai U.B.B.A. Nov., 2010; MBA Feb., 2009; P.T.U. MBA, May, 2014; 2005; P.U. B.E., 2001; K.U. M.Sc., 2001; P.U. B.E. (Mech.) 2000*]
3. Discuss all the four types of floats. Discuss their importance.
[*Gujarat Tech. U.B.E. Dec., 2012; Mumbai U.MBA, 2010; Osmania U. MBA July, 2010; P.T.U. B.Tech. (Mech.) May, 2011, 2008*]
4. What does a critical path actually signify ? In what ways does it differ from any other path and in what ways all its activities are particularly important ? [*G.N.D.U. April, 2013; Sept., 2012*]
5. Mention any two limitations of critical path. [*Chennai U. BBA Nov., 2010*]
6. Explain forward and backward planning. [*P.U. B.E. (Mech.) Nov., 1996*]
7. A project consists of a series of tasks labelled A, B, ..., I with the following relationships. Draw the network diagram.

$$A < D, E \; ; \; B, D < F \; ; \; C < G \; ; \; B < H \; ; \; F, G < I.$$

Also find the minimum time of completion of the project, when the time in days of completion of each task is as follows:

Task :	A	B	C	D	E	F	G	H	I
Time :	23	8	29	16	24	18	19	4	10

[*P.U. MBA Feb., 2009*]

8. For the following activity data draw the network, find the critical path and the three floats for each activity:

Activity :	1-2	1-4	2-3	3-5	3-8	4-8	5-6	5-8	6-7	7-8	7-9	8-9	9-10
Duration (days) :	4	36	2	15	10	2	4	9	9	9	8	20	20

[*P.T.U. B.Tech. April, 2012; P.U. B.Com,. April, 2008*]
(*Ans.* 83 days.)

9. The following tasks are to be completed on vehicles at a service station:

Task	*Description*	*Preceding tasks*	*Time (sec)*
A	Driver arrives and stops	—	20
B	Driver selects brands of oil and petrol	A	10
C	Fill petrol tank	B	100
D	Prepare bill	C and L	50
E	Receive payment	D	50
F	Wash wind-screen	A	20
G	Polish wind-screen	F	20
H	Check tyre pressure	A	100
J	Inflate tyre	H	90
K	Open bonnet	A	20
L	Check oil requirement	K	80
M	Fill oil	B and L	20
N	Add distilled water to battery	K	30
O	Fill radiator	K	30
P	Close bonnet	M, N, P	10
R	Driver departs from forecourt	E, G, J, Q	20

Draw the CPM network and find the total float, independent float and free float for each activity.

10. The activity durations for a project are given below. Draw the network and identify the critical path. Compute the earliest and latest occurrence times of the events and slack on each event. Perform the forward and backward computations in the tabular form. Durations of the activities are in days.

Activity	*Duration*	*Activity*	*Duration*
10-20	7	30-60	10
10-30	10	40-60	7
20-30	4	50-70	10
20-40	5	60-70	8
30-40	6	60-80	12
30-50	11	70-80	10

11. Draw a network diagram corresponding to the following information. Obtain the early and late start and completion times. Also determine the critical path and duration of the project.

Activity :	1-2	1-3	2-6	3-4	3-5	4-6	5-6	5-7	6-7
Duration (days) :	4	6	8	7	4	6	5	19	10

[*P.T.U. B.Tech. April, 2012; Osmania U. MBA July, 2010*]

12. A project schedule has the following characteristics :

Activity :	1-2	1-3	2-4	3-4	3-5	4-9	5-6	5-7	6-8	7-8	8-9	8-10	9-10
Time (days) :	4	1	1	1	6	5	4	8	1	2	1	8	7

(*i*) Construct the network diagram.
(*ii*) Find the critical path and total project duration.
(*iii*) Calculate free float and independent float of each activity.

[*U.P. Technological U. MBA, 2009; G.N.D.U. B.Com., 2009*]
(*Ans.* (*ii*) 1-3-5-7-8-10 and 1-3-5-7-8-9-10; 25 days.)

13. For the network of example 14.8-2, find the minimum time of completion of the project when the time in days of completion of each task is as follows :

Task :	A	B	C	D	E	F	G	H	I
Time :	27	9	22	18	22	19	20	6	12

[*G.N.D.U. B.Com. April, 2006*]
(*Ans.* A → D → F → I; 76 days.)

14. The following table lists all the activities which together constitute a small engineering project :

Activity :	A	B	C	D	E	F	G	H	I	J
Immediate predecessor :	—	A	A	A	B	C, D	D	B	E, P, G	G
Duration (days) :	2	3	4	5	6	4	7	2	3	3

(*a*) Construct an activity network.
(*b*) Draw the critical path.
(*c*) Compute total float for each activity.
(*d*) Find the effect on the project if activity F were to take 6 days.
(*e*) Determine project completion time. [*G.N.D.U. B.Com. April, 2005*]
(*Ans.* A-D-G-J or A-D-G-I; 17 days.)

15. Draw the network diagram on the basis of the following data :

Activity :	1-2	1-4	1-7	2-3	3-6	4-5	4-8	5-6	6-9	7-8	8-9	9-10
Time (days) :	2	2	1	4	1	5	8	4	3	3	5	2

Find the critical path, total duration and activity slacks.

[*P.T.U. B.Tech. (Prod.) Nov., 2012; R.U. M.Sc. (Math.) 2011*]
(*Ans.* 1-4-8-9-10; 17 days.)

16. Determine the critical path for the activity data given below :

Initial node	1	1	2	2	3	3	4	4	5
Final node	2	3	3	4	5	6	5	6	6
Duration (days)	5	6	3	8	2	11	0	1	12

Calculate EST, EFT, LST, LFT, TF and FF for each activity. [*V.T.U. Karnataka B.E. Dec., 2011*]

17. A project consists of the following activities with their precedence relationship and duration in days:
(*i*) Draw the network of the project.
(*ii*) Identify the critical path and project duration.
(*iii*) Calculate EST, EFT, LST, LFT, TF, FF and IF for each activity.

Activity	A	B	C	D	E	F	G	H
Precedence	–	A	A	B	B	B, C	B, C	D, F
Duration (days)	10	8	7	9	6	10	4	12

[*V.T.U. Karnataka B.E. June, 2012*]

18. A small project consists of six activities. The duration (in days) of each activity and their immediate predecessors are shown below :

Activity	A	B	C	D	E	F
Immediate predecessor	–	–	–	A, B	B	B, C
Duration (days)	5	3	7	8	4	5

(*i*) Draw the network.
(*ii*) Find the critical path.
(*iii*) Verify the critical path by earliest time and latest time values. [*V.T.U. Karnataka B.E. Dec., 2011*]

19. (*a*) Define : (*i*) Critical path (*ii*) Total slack (*iii*) Free slack.
(*b*) Draw the network for the following project. Identify the critical path and calculate the total slack and free slack.

Activity	A	B	C	D	E	F	G	H	I	J
Precedence	–	–	A	A	B, C	B, C	E	E	D, G	F, H, I
Time (weeks)	15	15	3	5	8	12	1	14	3	14

[*V.T.U. Karnataka B.E. Dec., 2010*]

20. (*a*) Construct the network and calculate project duration and critical path and find out TF, FF and IF for noncritical activities:

Activity	*Depends on*	*Duration in days*
A	I	05
B	H, F	10
C	D	03
D	I	12
E	C, G	08
F	A, D	10
G	A, D	05
H	A	11
I	—	05

[*R.T.M. Nagpur U. B.E. (I.T.) 2009*]

(*b*) Explain the following terms in PERT/CPM :
(*i*) Earliest time (*ii*) Latest time (*iii*) Total float for each activity
(*iv*) Event slack, and (*v*) Critical path. [*Kuru U. B.E. (Mech.) June, 2012*]

21. (*a*) Explain the following in the context of project management :
(*i*) Activity variance (*ii*) Project variance.
(*b*) For a small project of 12 activities, the details are given below :

Activity	*Precedence*	*Duration (in hours)*
A	—	14
B	A	22
C	B	10
D	B	16
E	B	12
F	C	10
G	C	6
H	F, G	8
I	D, E, H	24
J	I	16

(*i*) Draw an arrow diagram for this project.
(*ii*) Identify the critical path. What is its length ?
(*iii*) Find the total float and free float for each task. [*R.T.M. Nagpur B.E. (Mech.) Dec., 2008*]

22. The network for a project is given in Fig. 14.27. The contractual obligation time for the project is 50 weeks. Compute the slack for each event and identify the critical path. If the activity of 12 weeks duration is constrained to start after 15 weeks, what would be the earliest completion time of the project ? Find the critical path for this situation.

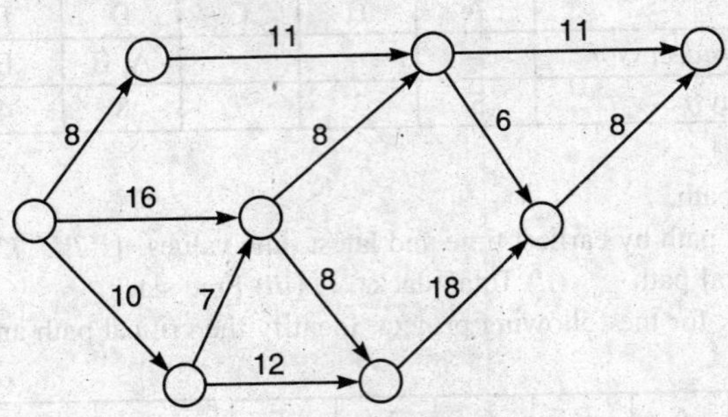

Fig. 14.27

23. Consider a project comprising of 12 activities with following precedence relationships and durations:

Activity :	A	B	C	D	E	F	G	H	I	J	K	L
Immediate predecessor :	-	-	A	A	A	D	C	D	E,F	B,I	G,H	J,K
Duration (weeks) :	4	8	2	4	9	1	7	3	2	2	5	4

(*i*) Draw the network and find the critical path.
(*ii*) List the total float, free float and independent float for all the activities.

[*P.U.B.E. (T.I.T.) Dec., 2008*]

24. A project has the following characteristics:

Activity	*Preceding activity*	*Duration* (*weeks*)
A	-	5
B	A	2
C	A	6
D	B	12
E	D	10
F	D	9
G	D	5
H	B	9
I	C, E	1
J	G	2
K	F, I, J	3
L	K	9
M	H, G	7
N	M	8

(*a*) Draw network for this project.
(*b*) Find the various paths, the critical path and the project completion time.
(*c*) Prepare an activity schedule showing the ES, EF, LS, LF and float for each activity.
(*d*) Will the critical path change if activity G takes 10 weeks instead of 5 weeks ? If so, what will be the new critical path ? [*P.U. B.Com. April, 2008; Dayalbagh Edu. Inst. Agra MBA May, 2005*]

(*Ans.* (*b*) 1-2-3-4-5-8-10-11; 1-2-3-4-6-9-10-11; 42 weeks. (*d*) 1-2--3-4-6-7-9-11; 44 weeks.)

25. A person P has been commissioned by the food manufacturer XYZ to carry out market research in a new product development project prior to a test match launch. The table below lists required activities and their durations in weeks.

Activity	*Immediate predecessor*	*Duration*
A	-	6
B	-	40
C	A	20
D	B	12
E	B	11
F	C	5
G	C, D, E	4
H	E	30
I	G	8
J	G	10
K	F, I	7
L	H, J, K	6
M	H, J, K	4
N	L	10
P	M, N	3

(*a*) Draw the product development network; state and explain the critical path and its duration.

(*b*) Prepare a table of the earliest start and finish times, the latest start and finish times and the total and free float. Explain the importance of the 'float' for management.

(*Ans.* (*a*) A-C-R-G-I-K-L-N-P & B-E-H-L-N-P; 64 weeks.)

26. A project which is about to start consists of the activities listed below:

Activity	*Immediate predecessor*	*Duration*
A	None	4
B	A	13
C	A	5
D	C	11
E	C	3
F	D, E	4
G	None	3
H	A, G	5
I	G	4
J	H	17
K	H	2
L	J, K	3
M	F, L	3
N	B, M	3
O	L, M	2
P	O	3
Q	N, P	4

The project should be completed by the end of week 38. If the project is delayed beyond this date, it is estimated that it will cost the firm ₹ 30,000 a week.

(*a*) Draw a network to represent the project and determine the critical path. What is the earliest time at which the project can be completed and what penalty cost, if any, will be incurred ?

(*b*) Activity K is a two-week course to train new salesmen. The hotel which will be used for the course has been booked for weeks 12 and 13. In the light of your analysis, should this booking be changed ?

(*Ans.* (*a*) A-H-J-L-M-O-P-Q, 41 weeks, ₹ 90,000 (*b*) No.)

27. A project has the following activities with their durations:

Activity	:	A	B	C	D	E	F	G	H
Time (days)	:	1	2	2	2	4	1	4	8
Preceding activity	:	–	–	–	A, B	B, C	C	D	E, F, G

(*a*) Draw the project network and indicate the critical path.

(*b*) What is the minimum project completion time?

(c) During the second day of the work it is discovered that activity F will take 4 days instead of 1. Will this delay the project? If this activity takes 6 days, will the project be delayed?

(*d*) The company has limited number of men available to work on the project. Only two activities can be under way at the same time. Will this delay the project over what the time would have been with unlimited resources? Activity F takes 6 days to complete.

(*Ans.* (*a*) B-D-G-H (*b*) 16 days (*c*) No (*d*) Yes.)

28. Construct a network representing the following project consisting of activities A, B, C, D, E, F, G, H, I and J whose durations of completion are 6, 11, 6, 3, 2, 6, 10, 10, 7 and 8 weeks respectively.

(*a*) Activities A, B and C are first to start simultaneously.

(*b*) E and D follow A, and F and G follow B and D.

(*c*) H follows C and F.

(*d*) I follows E.

(*e*) J follows I and G.

(*f*) J and H are terminal activities.

Use CPM method to compute critical path and minimum duration of completion of the project. Do the numbering of the nodes by Fulkerson's method. Find C.P. using EST and LCT. [*BITS Pilani, 2000*]

29. A small project consists of seven activities for which the relevant data is given below :

Activity	*Preceding activities*	*Duration (days)*
A	–	4
B	–	7
C	–	6
D	A, B	5
E	A, B	7
F	C, D, E	6
G	C, D, E	5

(*i*) Draw the network and find the project completion time.

(*ii*) Calculate the three floats for each activity.

[*P.U. UIAMS MBA May, 2015; R.U. M.Sc. (Math.) 2011; H.P.U.B. Tech. (Mech.) Nov., 2007; G.N.D.U. B.Com. April, 2003; P.U. M.Com., 2001*]

(*Ans.* (*i*) 20 days, C.P. : B-E-F (1-3-5-6-7.)

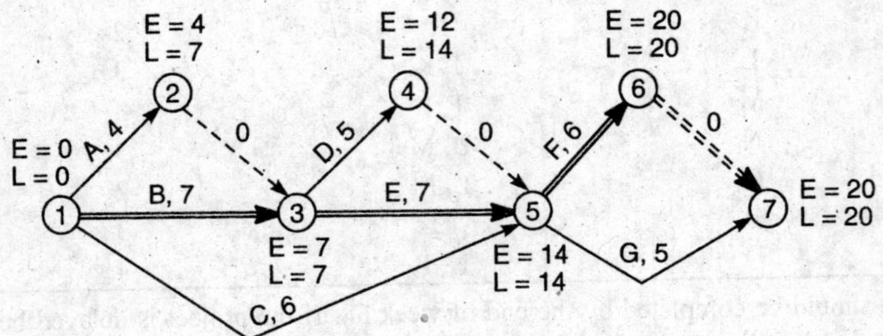

Fig. 14.28

(*ii*) *Activity*	:1-2	1-3	1-5	2-3	3-4	3-5	4-5	5-6	5-7	6-7
T.F.	: 3	0	8	3	2	0	2	0	1	0
F.F.	: 0	0	8	0	0	0	2	0	1	0
I.F.	: 0	0	8	0	0	0	0	0	1	0

30. The following data for the activities of a project are available :

Activity	*Dependence*	*Duration (days)*
A	–	6
B	–	4
C	–	7
D	A, B, C	5
E	A, B, C	6
F	D	9
G	E	4
H	F, G	8
I	F, G	6
J	H	7

(*i*) Draw the network, number the nodes, find the project completion time and calculate total, free and independent floats for the activities.

(*ii*) When the activity duration of G is doubled, identify the critical path. [*ICWA, 1996*]

31. The following table gives the activities of a project, their times and precedence relationships. Draw the project network, find the critical path and the three floats of each activity.

Activity	:	A	B	C	D	E	F	G	H	I	J	K	L
Immediate predecessor	:	–	–	A	A	A	D	C	B, F	F	E, I, G, H	J	K
Activity time (days)	:	6	20	4	6	11	3	9	5	4	4	7	6

[*H.P.U. B.Tech. (Mech.) Nov., 2010*]

32. A list of activities, their precedence relations and activity completion times is given in the following table:

Activity	:	A	B	C	D	E	F	G	H	I	J	K
Predecessor activities	:	–	A	B	A, C	D	E	C	D, E G, I	C	G, H	F, H, J
Time (days)	:	5	4	2	6	8	5	4	13	2	1	6

(*i*) Draw an activity on node network diagram.

(*ii*) Compute the early start (ES), late start (LS), early finish (EF) and late finish (LF) and slack times for each activity in the network.

(*iii*) What is the critical path and expected completion time for the project?

[*Dayalbagh Edu. Inst. Agra MBA May, 2011*]

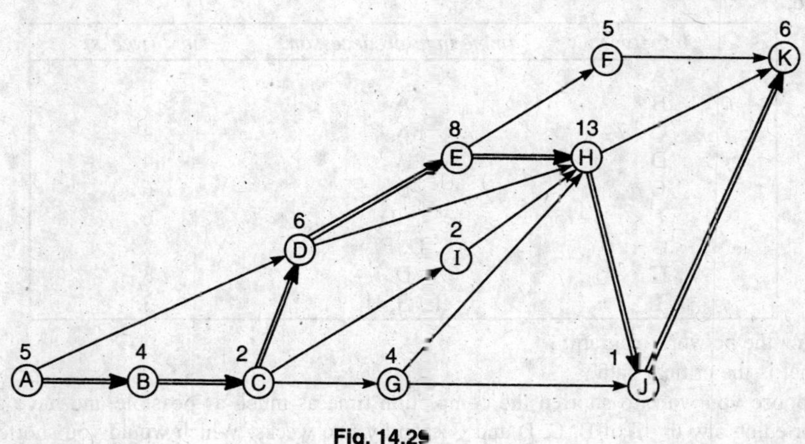

Fig. 14.29

(*Ans.* A-B-C-D-E-H-J-K; 45 days.)

33. A small maintenance project consists of the following 10 jobs whose precedence relationships are identified by their node numbers:

Job	:	*a*	*b*	*c*	*d*	*e*	*f*	*g*	*h*	*i*	*j*
(i - j)	:	1-2	2-3	2-4	3-5	3-6	4-6	4-7	5-8	6-8	7-8
Duration (days)	:	2	3	5	4	1	6	2	8	7	4

(*a*) Draw the arrow diagram representing the project.

(*b*) Calculate early and late start and finish time for each job.

(*c*) How much slack does job 3-5 have? Job-4-6? Job 7-8?

(*d*) Which jobs are critical ?

(*e*) If job 2-3 were to take 6 days instead of 3, how would the project finish date be affected ?

(*f*) Do any jobs have free slack ? If so, which ones and how much ? [*P.U. B.E.(E. & Ec.) Dec., 1996*]

34. Given below are the different activities associated with a project consisting of 12 tasks (A,B,...,L) in which the following precedence relationship must hold:

A < C, A < B, B < D; B < G, B < K, C < D, C < G, D < E, E < F, F < H, F < I, F < L, G < I, G < L, H < J, I < J and K < L.

The times for the various activities are:

Activity	:	A	B	C	D	E	F	G	H	I	J	K	L
Time(days)	:	30	7	10	14	10	7	21	7	12	15	30	15

Draw the network diagram, determine the critical path and the project duration.

[*P.U.B.Com. April, 2001*]

35. The data regarding the activities of a project are given below :

Activity	*Precedes*	*Duration (days)*
start	a,b,c	–
a	d	5
d	f	6
f	g	2
b	e	5
e	f	9
c	h	4
h	g, i	6
g	end	3
i	end	1

Draw the A-O-A network diagram. Identify the critical path. Determine the project duration and slack period for each activity. [*Dayalbagh Edu. Inst. Agra MBA May, 2010*]

36. The R and D department is planning to bid on a large project for the development of a new communication system for commercial planes. The accompanying table shows the activities, times and sequences required.

Activity	*Immediate predecessor*	*Time (weeks)*
A	–	3
B	A	2
C	A	4
D	A	4
E	B	6
F	C, D	6
G	D, F	2
H	D	3
I	E, G, H	3

(*a*) Draw the network diagram.

(*b*) What is the critical path?

(*c*) Suppose you want to shorten the completion time as much as possible and have the option of shortening any or all of B, C, D and G each by two weeks. Which would you shorten?

(*d*) What is the new critical path and earliest completion time?

[*P.T.U. B.Tech. Dec., 2011; IGNOU MBA June, 2004*]

(*Ans.* (*b*) A-C-F-G-I and A-D-F-G-I. (*c*) C, D, G each by 2 weeks.
(*d*) A-B-E-I, A-C-F-G-I, A-D-F-G-I, 14 weeks.)

37. Given below is the information regarding a project:

Activity	:	A	B	C	D	E	F	G	H	I	J	K	L
Preceding activity	:	–	–	–	A, B	B	B	F, C	B	E, H	E, H	C, D, F, J	K
Duration (days)	:	3	4	2	5	1	3	6	4	4	2	1	5

Draw the network and find the project critical path.

[*P.T.U. B.Tech. (Mech.) Nov., 2012; P.U. M.Com. Sept., 2004*]

(*Ans.* B-H-J-K-L; 16 days.)

38. An architect has been awarded a contract to prepare a plan for an urban renewal project. The job consists of the following activities and their estimated times:

Activity	:	A	B	C	D	E	F	G
Immediate predecessor	:	-	-	A	A,B	C,D	B,D	E,F
Time (days)	:	2	1	3	2	1	3	1

(*i*) Draw an arrow diagram for this project.

(*ii*) Indicate the critical path. Find the total float and free float for each activity.

[*SVSM PGDM, 2009; P.T.U. MBA June, 2003*]

39. Draw the network for the following project:

Activity	:	A	B	C	D	E	F	G	H	I	J	K	L
Preceded by	:	–	A	A	B	B	C	C	F	D	G, H	E	I
Time (weeks)	:	10	9	7	6	12	6	8	8	4	11	5	7

Find the critical path, event slacks, total, free and independent floats. [*P.U .B.Com. April, 2004*]

40. The details of a project are as follows:

Activity	*Immediate predecessor*	*Duration (weeks)*
A	—	4
B	—	3
C	—	2
D	A, B, C	5
E	A, B, C	6
F	D	7
G	D, E	6
H	D, E	9
I	F	4
J	G	6
K	H	8

Find the critical path and the corresponding project completion time. [*Chennai U.B.C.A. Nov., 2010*]

(*Ans.* A-D-Dm-H-K; 27 weeks.)

41. A construction project is broken down into the following 10 activities:

Activity	:	1	2	3	4	5	6	7	8	9	10
Immediate predecessor	:	–	1	1	1	2, 3	3	4	5	6, 7	8, 9
Time (weeks)	:	4	2	4	3	5	6	2	3	5	7

(*i*) Draw the network diagram.

(*ii*) Find the critical path.

(*iii*) If activities 1 and 10 cannot be shortened, but activities 2 through 9 can be shortened to a minimum of one week at a cost of ₹ 50,000 per week, which activities would you shorten to cut the project by 4 weeks? [*IGNOU M.B.A. Dec., 2004*]

(*Ans.* (*ii*) 1-3-6-9-10 (*iii*) 3, 6 and 9.)

42. Describe the following by network:

A→B	A→C	B→C	B→D	C→F	D→E	E→G	E→H	F→H	G→H
2	3	4	3	3	12	3	5	8	0

The times are in days. There is a constraint that activity F→H cannot start till the activity D→E is completed. Determine the critical path and tabulate the earliest start time, earliest finish time, latest start time, latest finish time, total float and free float for the activities. [*P.U. M.B.A., 2000*]

43. Activities in the following table describe the construction of a new house. Construct the associated project network and find the critical path.

Activity	*Description*	*Predecessor*	*Duration (days)*
A	Clear site	–	1
B	Bring utilities to site	–	2
C	Excavate	A	1
D	Pour foundation	C	2
E	Outside plumbing	B, C	6
F	Frame house	D	10
G	Do electric wiring	F	3
H	Lay floor	G	1
I	Lay roof	F	1
J	Inside plumbing	E, H	5
K	Shingling	I	2
L	Outside sheathing insulation	F, J	1
M	Install windows & outside doors	F	2
N	Do brick work	L, M	4
O	Insulate walls & ceilings	G, J	2
P	Cover walls & ceilings	O	2
Q	Insulate roof	I, P	1
R	Finish interior	P	7
S	Finish exterior	I, N	7
T	Landscape	S	3

[*P.T.U. B.Tech., 2000*]

14.13 PROGRAMME EVALUATION AND REVIEW TECHNIQUE (PERT)

Time Estimates

The CPM system of networks omits the probabilistic considerations and is based on a *Single Time Estimate* of the average time required to execute the activity.

In PERT analysis, time duration of each activity is no longer a single time estimate, but is a random variable characterised by some probability distribution – usually a β-distribution. To estimate the parameters of the β-distribution (the mean and variance), the PERT system is based on *Three Time Estimates* of the performance time of an activity. They are

(*i*) *The Optimistic Time Estimate (t_o or a)* : The shortest possible time required for the completion of an activity, if all goes extremely well. No provisions are made for delays or setbacks while estimating this time.

(*ii*) *The Pessimistic Time Estimate (t_p or b)* : The maximum possible time the activity will take if everything goes bad. However, major catastrophes such as earthquakes, floods, storms and labour troubles are not taken into account while estimating this time.

(*iii*) *The Most Likely Time Estimate (t_m or m)* : The time an activity will take if executed under normal conditions. It is the modal value. It is assumed that the situation is normal with usual setbacks or lapses.

For determining the single time estimates used in CPM, some historical data may be available, but the best way of predicting the three time estimates is by intelligent guessing. The experienced person who may be an engineer, foreman or worker having sufficient experience and technical competence is asked to guess the various time estimates. For estimation the activity should be taken randomly, so that the guess of the assessor is not prejudiced by the predecessor and the successor activities.

Frequency Distribution Curve for PERT

We have three time estimates for a PERT activity, the optimistic (t_0), pessimistic (t_p) and the most likely time (t_m). In the range from optimistic to pessimistic, there can be a number of time estimates for the activity. If a frequency distribution curve for the activity times is plotted, it will look like the one shown in figure 14.30. It is assumed to be a β-distribution curve with a unimodal point occurring at t_m and its end points occurring at t_0 and t_p. The most likely time need not be the midpoint of t_0 and t_p and hence the frequency distribution curve may be skewed to the left, skewed to the right or symmetric. The assumption of β-distribution, however, is not flawless and the calculations made on this assumption may, sometimes, be in error to the tune of 30%.

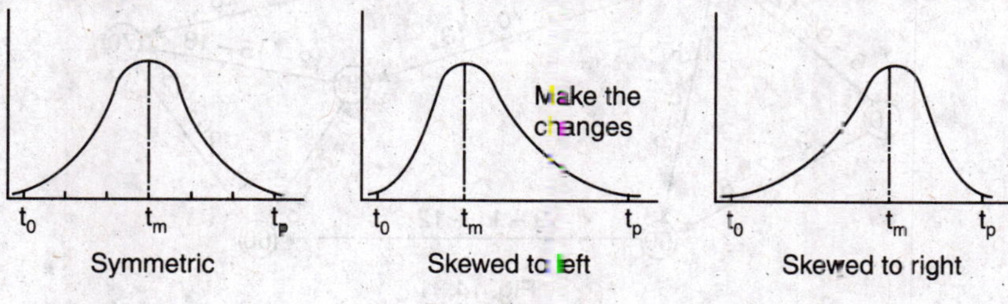

Fig. 14.30

Though the curve is not fully described by the mean (μ) and the standard deviation (σ), yet in PERT the following relations are approximated for μ and σ:

Variance $$V = \sigma^2 = \left(\frac{t_p - t_0}{6}\right)^2$$

or $$\sigma = \frac{t_p - t_o}{6},$$

and $$\mu = \frac{t_0 + 4t_m + t_p}{6}.$$

Expected time or *average time* of an activity is taken equal to mean. This is the time that the activity is expected to consume while executed. Thus

$$t_e = \mu = \frac{t_0 + 4t_m + t_p}{6}.$$

The expected time is then used as the activity duration and the critical path is obtained by the analytical method explained earlier.

The variance or standard deviation is used to find the probability of completing the whole project by a given date. The underlying procedure is as follow:

Compute the variance of all the activity durations of the critical path. Add them up and take the square root to find the standard deviation of the total project duration and denote it by σ. Now, while a β -distribution curve approximately represents the activity-time frequency distribution, the project expected time follows approximately a normal distribution curve. The standard normal distribution curve has an area equal to unity and a standard deviation of one and is symmetrical about the mean value as shown in Fig. 8.8. ±3 σ give the limits of the total possible duration with 99 per cent confidence *i.e.*, 99 per cent of the area under normal distribution curve is within ±3 σ from the mean. In other words, to find the probability of completing the project in time T, we calculate the *standard normal variate*,

$$Z = \frac{T - T_{cp}}{\sigma},$$

where Z is the number of standard deviations the scheduled time or target date lies away from the mean or expected date. Here, T is called *the desired time or due time or contractual obligation time* and T_{cp} is the expected time to complete the project *i.e., duration of the critical path.*

The probability is then read from the standard normal probability distribution table (table C-2 at the end of the book) for the value of Z calculated above.

EXAMPLE 14.13-1

Consider the network shown Fig. 14.31. For each activity, the three time estimates t_0, t_m and t_p are given along the arrows in the $t_0 - t_m - t_p$ order. Determine variance and expected time for each activity.

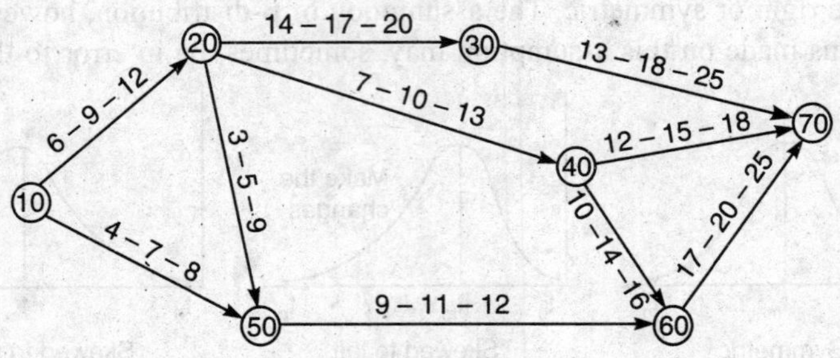

Fig. 14.31

Solution

We put the events in a tabular form and calculate the variance and expected times. These calculations can be carried on the network also.

TABLE 14.6

Activity i-j						
Predecessor event i	*Successor event j*	t_o	t_m	t_p	$\sigma^2 = V = \left(\frac{t_p - t_0}{6}\right)^2$	$t_e = \frac{t_0 + 4t_m + t_p}{6}$
10	20	6	9	12	1.00	9.0
10	50	4	7	8	0.44	6.7
20	30	14	17	20	1.00	17.0
20	40	7	10	13	1.00	10.0
20	50	3	5	9	1.00	5.33
30	70	13	18	25	4.00	18.33
40	60	10	14	16	1.00	13.67
40	70	12	15	18	1.00	15.00
50	60	9	11	12	0.25	10.83
60	70	17	20	25	1.78	20.33

The entry in the tabular form starts with the initial event, by entering first number (10 in this case) in the first row under the column 'predecessor event *i*.' Then the activities emerging out from the initial event (here 10-20 and 10-50) are entered in the ascending order. Then, we go to the next higher number (here 20) in the predecessor event column and enter all the activities emerging out from this event *i.e.*, 20-30, 20-40 and 20-50. This procedure is repeated until all the events are entered.

The variance $v = \sigma^2$ and the expected activity time t_e are then computed by employing the relations:

$$v = \sigma^2 = \left(\frac{t_p - t_0}{6}\right)^2,$$

and
$$t_e = \frac{t_o + 4t_m + t_p}{6}.$$

EXAMPLE 14.13-2

Consider the network shown in Fig. 14.32. The three time estimates for the activities are given along the arrows. Determine the critical path. What is the probability that the project will be completed in 20 days?

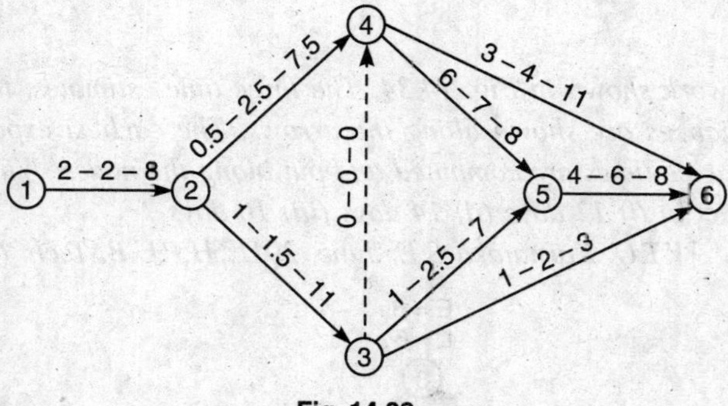

Fig. 14.32

[P.U.B. Com. April, 2006]

Solution

First step is to number the events. In this network the events are already numbered. The calculations can be performed on the network itself or in the tabular form. After calculating the expected times and the variances of the activities they are put along the arrows as shown in Fig. 14.33. By carrying the forward pass and backward pass computations E and L values are determined for all the events. By applying the conditions of critical activities (method 3 of example 14.12-1), it is determined that 1-2-3-4-5-6 and 1-2-4-5-6 are the two critical paths.

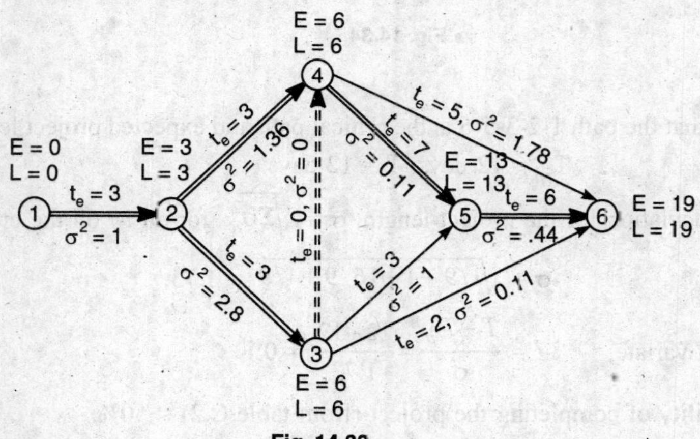

Fig. 14.33

Expected duration of the project, T_{cp} = 19 days.

Contractual obligation time, T = 20 days. Variance $\sigma^2 = \left(\dfrac{t_p - t_o}{6}\right)^2$ and $t_e = \dfrac{t_o + 4t_m + t_p}{6}$.

Standard deviation of the project,

$$\sigma = \sqrt{\Sigma\sigma_{ij}^2} \text{ for all } i\text{-}j \text{ on the critical path.}$$

$\therefore$ σ for path 1-2-4-5-6 $= \sqrt{1+1.36+0.11+0.44} = 1.70$,

σ for path 1-2-3-4-5-6 $= \sqrt{1+2.8+0+0.11+0.44} = 2.08$.

$\therefore$ $\sigma = 2.08$ is chosen as it is higher of the two values.

$\therefore$ Normal variate, $Z = \dfrac{T - T_{cp}}{\sigma} = \dfrac{20-19}{2.08} = 0.48$.

From table C-2, probability = 68.44%.

EXAMPLE 14.13-3

Consider the network shown in Fig. 14.34. The three time estimates, the expected activity durations and the variances are shown along the arrows. The earliest expected times and the latest allowable occurrence times are computed and put along the nodes. What is the probability of completing the project in (i) 12 days (ii) 14 days (iii) 10 days ?

[*V.T.U. Karnataka B.E. June, 2011; H.P.U.B. Tech. (Mech.) Nov., 2010*]

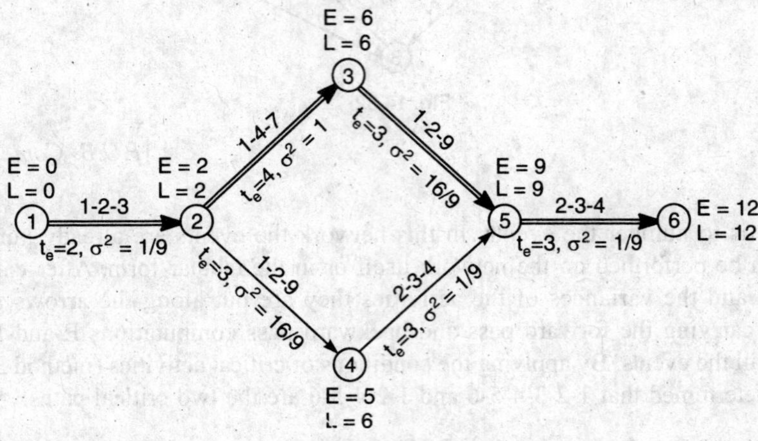

Fig. 14.34

Solution

We identify that the path 1-2-3-5-6 is the critical path and expected project length is 12 days.

(*i*) Here, T_{cp} = 12 days, T = 12 days.

Standard deviation for the project length, $\sigma = \sqrt{\Sigma\sigma_{ij}^2}$ for all *i-j* on the critical path.

$$\therefore \quad \sigma = \sqrt{1/9+1+16/9+1/9} = 1.73.$$

$$\therefore \text{ Normal variate,} \quad Z = \frac{T-T_{cp}}{\sigma} = \frac{12-12}{1.73} = 0.$$

∴ Probability of completing the project (from table C.2) = 50%.

(*ii*) Here, T = 14 days.

$$\therefore \quad Z = \frac{14-12}{1.73} = 1.16.$$

∴ Corresponding probability = 87.7%.

(*iii*) Here, T = 10 days.

$$\therefore \quad Z = \frac{10-12}{1.73} = -1.16.$$

∴ Corresponding probability = 1 – 0.877 = 0.123 = 12.3%.

EXAMPLE 14.13-4

Consider the PERT network given in Fig. 14.35. Determine the float of each activity and identify the critical path if the scheduled completion time for the project is 20 weeks. Also identify the subcritical path and slacks for events.

[*Kuru.U. B.E.(Mech.) June, 2012; H.P.U.B.Tech. (Mech.) Sept., 2009; P.T.U. B.E., 2001*]

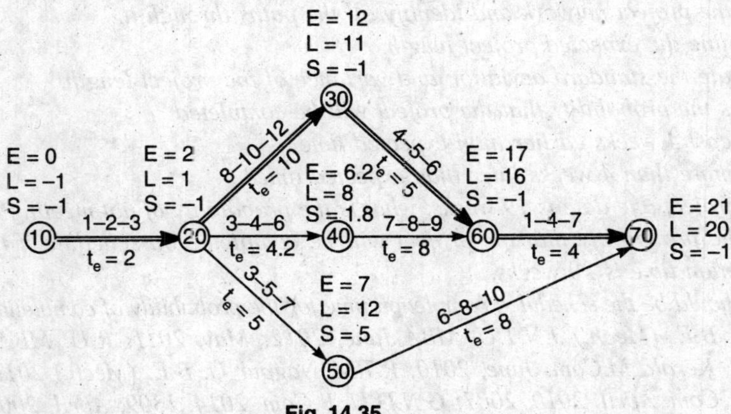

Fig. 14.35

Solution

First the expected activity times and then the earliest expected times of the events are calculated. For the end event, E = 21. The scheduled completion time is 20 weeks. Taking L = T = 20 for the end event, the latest occurrence times of events are calculated by the backward pass method. Slack for an event is (L–E) for that event. The usual network analysis table follows.

TABLE 14.7

Activity	t_0	t_m	t_p	$t_e = \dfrac{t_0 + 4t_m + t_p}{6}$	*Start*		*Finish*		*Total float*
					Earliest	*Latest*	*Earliest*	*Latest*	
10-20	1	2	3	2	0	–1	2	1	–1
20-30	8	10	12	10	2	1	12	11	–1
20-40	3	4	6	4.2	2	3.8	6.2	8	1.8
20-50	3	5	7	5	2	7	7	12	5
30-60	4	5	6	5	12	11	17	16	–1
40-60	7	8	9	8	6.2	8	14.2	16	1.8
50-70	6	8	10	8	7	12	15	20	5
60-70	1	4	7	4	17	16	21	20	–1

The most negative slack is – 1 and it is for events 10, 20, 30, 60 and 70. The path joining these events 10-20-30-60-70 is the critical path.

Subcritical path. The path with the next least floats is the subcritical path. As activities 20-40 and 40-60 have floats of 1.8 each, path 20-40-60 is the subcritical path.

EXAMPLE 14.13-5

The time estimates (in weeks) for the activities of a PERT network are given below.

Activity	t_0	t_m	t_p
1-2	*1*	*1*	*7*
1-3	*1*	*4*	*7*
1-4	*2*	*2*	*8*
2-5	*1*	*1*	*1*
3-5	*2*	*5*	*14*
4-6	*2*	*5*	*8*
5-6	*3*	*6*	*15*

(a) *Draw the project network and identify all the paths through it.*
(b) *Determine the expected project length.*
(c) *Calculate the standard deviation and variance of the project length.*
(d) *What is the probability that the project will be completed*
  (i) *at least 4 weeks earlier than expected time?*
  (ii) *no more than 4 weeks later than expected time?*
(e) *If the project due date is 19 weeks, what is the probability of not meeting the due date?*
(f) *Find the probability that the project will be completed on schedule if the scheduled completion time is 20 weeks.*
(g) *What should be the scheduled completion time for the probability of completion to be 90%?*
[P.T.U. B.E. (Mech.) J.N.T.U. MBA June, 2012; May, 2011; R.U. MBA Dec., 2011; M.G.U. Kerala M.Com. June, 2010; R.T.M. Nagpur U. B.E. (Mech.) 2011, 08, 06, 05; P.U. B. Com. April, 2010, 2007; G.N.D.U. B.Com. 2014, 1309; April, 2004; Jammu U. B.E. (Mech.) 2004]

Solution

(*a*) The network for the given data is drawn in Fig. 14.36. The various paths through the network are 1-2-5-6, 1-3-5-6, and 1-4-6.

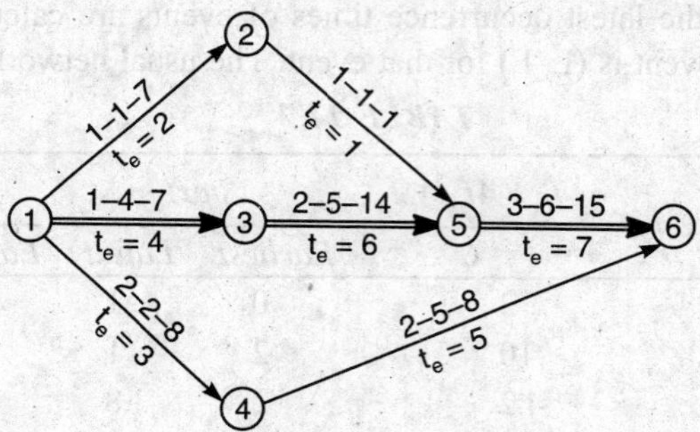

Fig. 14.36

(*b*) For determining the expected project length, the expected activity times need to be calculated. The same, along with the variances, are computed below.

Activity	t_0	t_m	t_p	$t_e = \dfrac{t_o + 4t_m + t_p}{6}$	$\sigma^2 = \left(\dfrac{t_p - t_o}{6}\right)^2$
1-2	1	1	7	2	1
1-3	1	4	7	4	1
1-4	2	2	8	3	1
2-5	1	1	1	1	0
3-5	2	5	14	6	4
4-6	2	5	8	5	1
5-6	3	6	15	7	4

Length of path 1-2-5-6 $= 2 + 1 + 7 = 10$,
length of path 1-3-5-6 $= 4 + 6 + 7 = 17$, and
length of path 1-4-6 $= 3 + 5 = 8$.

Since 1-3-5-6 has the longest duration, it is the critical path of the network.

$\therefore$ The expected project length = 17 weeks.

(*c*) Variance of the project length is the sum of the variances of the activities on the critical path.

$$V_{cp} = V_{1\text{-}3} + V_{3\text{-}5} + V_{5\text{-}6} = 1 + 4 + 4 = 9.$$

$$\therefore \qquad \sigma = 3 \text{ weeks.}$$

(*d*) (*i*) Probability that the project will be completed at least 4 weeks earlier than expected time:

Expected time = 17 weeks,

and scheduled time = 17 – 4 = 13 weeks.

∴ The standard normal variate,

$$Z = \frac{13-17}{3} = -1.33.$$

For Z = –1.33, probability is 1 – 0.9082 = 0.0918 or the probability of completing the project at least 4 weeks earlier than expected time *i.e.*, within 13 weeks is ≤ 9.18%.

(*ii*) Probability that the project will be completed no more than 4 weeks later than expected time:

Expected time = 17 weeks.

∴ Scheduled time = 17 + 4 = 21 weeks.

$$\therefore \quad Z = \frac{21-17}{3} = 1.33$$

$$\therefore \quad p = 0.9082.$$

Therefore, the probability of completing the project in not more that 21 weeks is ≤ 90.82%.

(*e*) When the project due date is 19 weeks:

$$Z = \frac{19-17}{3} = 0.667 \approx 0.67,$$

for which, $p = 0.7486$ or 74.86%.

∵ The probability of meeting the due date is 74.86% and the probability of not meeting the due date is 25.14%.

(*f*) Scheduled time = 20 weeks.

$$\therefore \quad Z = \frac{20-17}{3} = 1, \text{ for which } p = 84.13\%.$$

(*g*) Value of Z for $p = 0.9$ is = 1.28.

$$\therefore \quad 1.28 = \frac{T-17}{3} \text{ or T} = 17 + 3.84 = 20.84 \text{ weeks.}$$

EXAMPLE 14.13-6

A PERT network is shown in Fig. 14.37. The activity times in days are given along the arrows. The scheduled times for some important events are given along the nodes. Determine the critical path and probabilities of meeting the scheduled dates for the specified events. Tabulate the results and determine slack for each event.

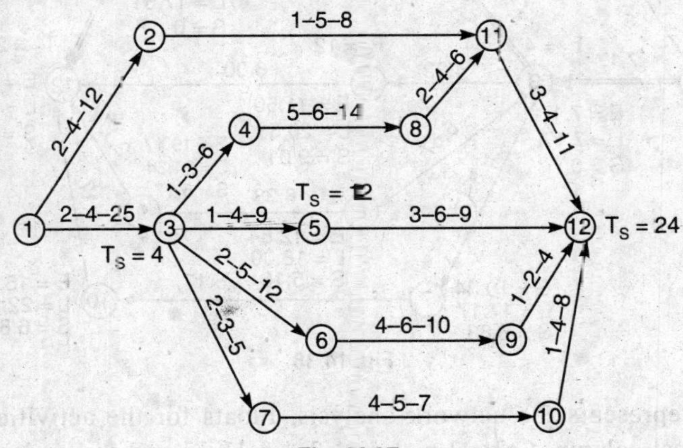

Fig. 14.37

[*H.P.U. B. Tech. (Mech.) June, 2007*]

Solution

The expected activity times and variances are computed below.

Activity	t_o	t_m	t_p	t_e	σ^2
1 - 2	2	4	12	5.00	2.78
1 - 3	2	4	25	7.17	14.69
2 - 11	1	5	8	4.83	1.36
3 - 4	1	3	6	3.17	0.69
3 - 5	1	4	9	4.33	1.78
3 - 6	2	5	12	5.67	2.78
3 - 7	2	3	5	3.17	0.25
4 - 8	5	6	14	7.17	2.25
5 - 12	3	6	9	6.00	1.00
6 - 9	4	6	10	6.33	1.00
7 - 10	4	5	7	5.17	0.25
8 - 11	2	4	6	4.00	0.44
9 - 12	1	2	4	2.17	0.25
10 - 12	1	4	8	4.17	1.36
11 - 12	3	4	11	5.00	1.78

The arrow diagram for the given data is shown in Fig. 14.38. The expected activity times are shown along the arrows. The earliest and latest occurrence times as well as the slacks of the events are also written along the nodes.

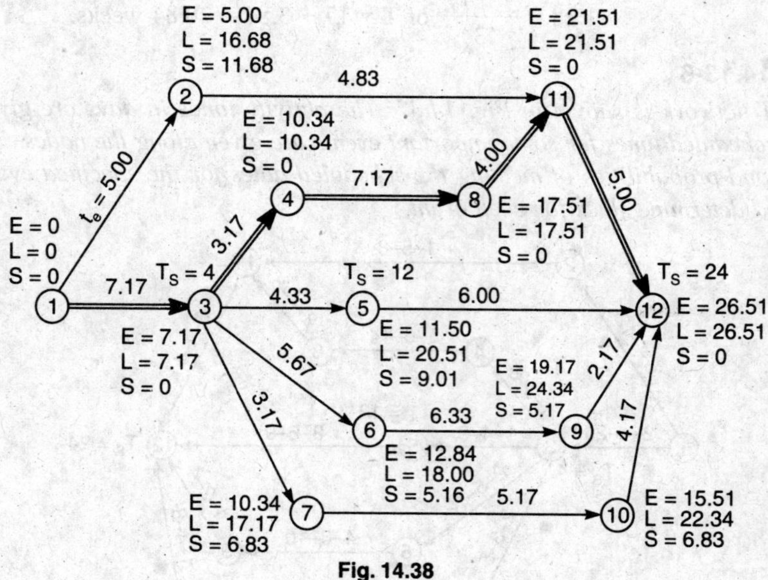

Fig. 14.38

Table 14.8 represents the network analysis. Floats for the activities in question are calculated in the last column. Critical path is 1-3-4-8-11-12 and the project completion time is 26.51 days.

TABLE 14.8

Activity	*Expected duration*	*Start time*		*Finish time*		*Total float*
		Earliest	*Latest*	*Earliest*	*Latest*	
1 - 2	5.00	0	11.68	5.00	16.68	11.68
1 - 3	7.17	0	0	7.17	7.17	0
2 - 11	4.83	5.00	16.68	9.83	21.51	11.68
3 - 4	3.17	7.17	7.17	10.34	10.34	0
3 - 5	4.33	7.17	16.18	11.50	20.51	9.01
3 - 6	5.67	7.17	12.33	12.84	18.00	5.16
3 - 7	3.17	7.17	14.00	10.34	17.17	6.83
4 - 8	7.17	10.34	10.34	17.51	17.51	0
5 - 12	6.00	11.50	20.51	17.50	26.51	9.01
6 - 9	6.33	12.84	18.01	19.17	24.34	5.17
7 - 10	5.17	10.34	17.17	15.51	22.34	6.83
8 - 11	4.00	17.51	17.51	21.51	21.51	0
9 - 12	2.17	19.17	24.34	21.34	26.51	5.17
10 - 12	4.17	15.51	22.34	19.68	26.51	6.83
11 - 12	5.00	21.51	21.51	26.51	26.51	0

Probability of completing the project in the scheduled completion time of 24 days (since T_s (12) = 24):

$$Z = \frac{24 - 26.51}{\sqrt{14.69 + 0.69 + 2.25 + 0.44 + 1.78}} = \frac{-2.51}{\sqrt{19.85}} = -0.5634.$$

$\therefore$ $p(T_s \le 24) = 1 -$ value of probability for Z value of $0.5634 = 1 - 0.7146 = 29.54\%$.

Probability that event 3 will occur on the scheduled date:

$$T_s(3) = 4, \; E = L = 7.17.$$

$$\therefore \quad Z = \frac{4 - 7.17}{\sqrt{14.69}} = -0.8271.$$

$\therefore$ $p = 1 -$ value of probability for Z value of $0.8271 = 1 - 0.7956 = 20.44\%$.

Probability of meeting the scheduled date for event 5:

The earliest occurrence time of event 5 is 11.50, while the scheduled time is 12. Event 5 is not on critical path and hence its occurrence can be delayed by 9 days.

Variance of path 1-3-5 = 14.69 + 1.78 = 16.47.

$T_s = 12$, $E = 11.50$.

$$\therefore \quad Z = \frac{12 - 11.50}{\sqrt{16.47}} = 0.123.$$

$\therefore$ Probability = 54.89%.

$T_s = 12$, $L = 20.51$.

$$\therefore \quad Z = \frac{12 - 20.51}{\sqrt{16.47}} = -2.1.$$

$\therefore$ Probability = 1–0.982 = 0.018 = 1.8%.

Thus the probability of meeting the scheduled date in case of event 5 is less than or equal 54.89% with minimum of 1.8% *i.e.*, it lies between 1.8% and 54.89%.

EXAMPLE 14.13-7

In the PERT network shown in Fig. 14.39, the activity time estimates (in weeks) are given along the arrows. If the scheduled completion time is 23 weeks, calculate the latest possible occurrence times of the events. Calculate the slack for each event and identify the critical path. What is the probability that the project will be completed on the scheduled date ?

[*P.TU. B.Tech. (Mech.) Nov., 2012; H.P.U.B. Tech. (Mech.) Nov., 2007*]

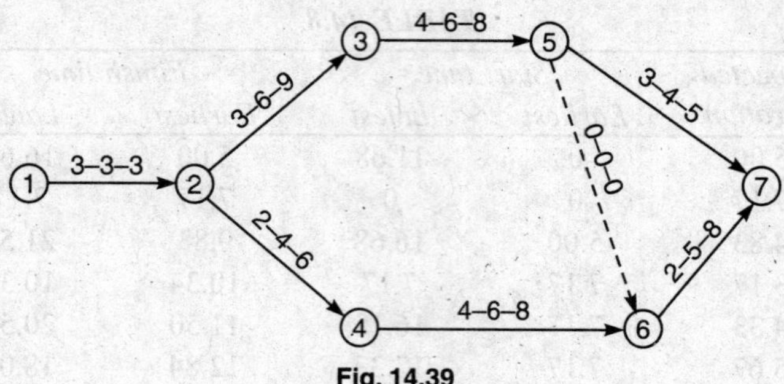

Fig. 14.39

Solution

The expected time of the activities and their variances are computed below.

Activity	t_o	t_m	t_p	t_e	σ^2
1-2	3	3	3	3	0
2-3	3	6	9	6	1
2-4	2	4	6	4	4/9
3-5	4	6	8	6	4/9
4-6	4	6	8	6	4/9
5-6	0	0	0	0	0
5-7	3	4	5	4	1/9
6-7	2	5	8	5	1

The earliest occurrence times of the events have been computed on the network of Fig. 14.40, taking the earliest time of event 1 as zero. The earliest occurrence time of event 7 is 20. But the scheduled completion time of the project is 23 weeks and hence the latest occurrence times of the events have been computed taking L(7) = 23. Slacks for the events have been shown along the nodes. Path 1-2-3-5-6-7 is the critical path.

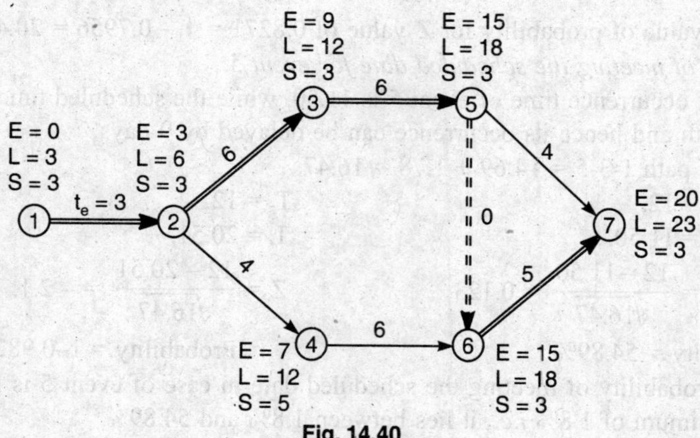

Fig. 14.40

Probability of completing the project on scheduled date:

T = 23 weeks, E = 20 weeks.

Variance of the critical path = 0 + 1 + 4/9 + 0 + 1 = 22/9 = 2.444.

$$\therefore \qquad Z = \frac{23 - 20}{\sqrt{2.444}} = 1.92.$$

$$\therefore \qquad \text{Probability} = 97.26\%.$$

EXAMPLE 14.13-8

The optimistic, most likely and pessimistic times of the activities of a project are given below. Activity 40-50 must not start before 22 days, while activity 70-90 must end by 35 days. The scheduled completion time of the project is 46 days. Draw the network and determine the critical path. What is the probability of completing the project in scheduled time?

Activity	$t_0 - t_m - t_p$	*Activity*	$t_0 - t_m - t_p$
10-20	*4–8–12*	*50-70*	*3–6–9*
20-30	*1–4–7*	*50-80*	*4–6–8*
20-40	*8–12–16*	*60-100*	*4–6–8*
30-50	*3–5–7*	*70-90*	*4–8–12*
40-50	*0–0–0*	*80-90*	*2–5–8*
40-60	*3–6–9*	*90-100*	*4–10–16*

[*P.U.B.E. (Ec. & Comm.) Nov., 2011; H.P.U. B.Tech. (Mech.) Dec., 2009*]

Solution

The expected times and variances of the activities are given below, while network for the given data is shown in Fig. 14.41. The expected activity times are written along the activity arrows.

Activity	t_e	σ^2	*Activity*	t_e	σ^2
10-20	8	1.77	50-70	6	1.00
20-30	4	1.00	50-80	6	0.44
20-40	12	1.77	60-100	6	0.44
30-50	5	0.44	70-90	8	1.77
40-50	0	0.00	80-90	5	1.00
40-60	6	1.00	90-100	10	4.00

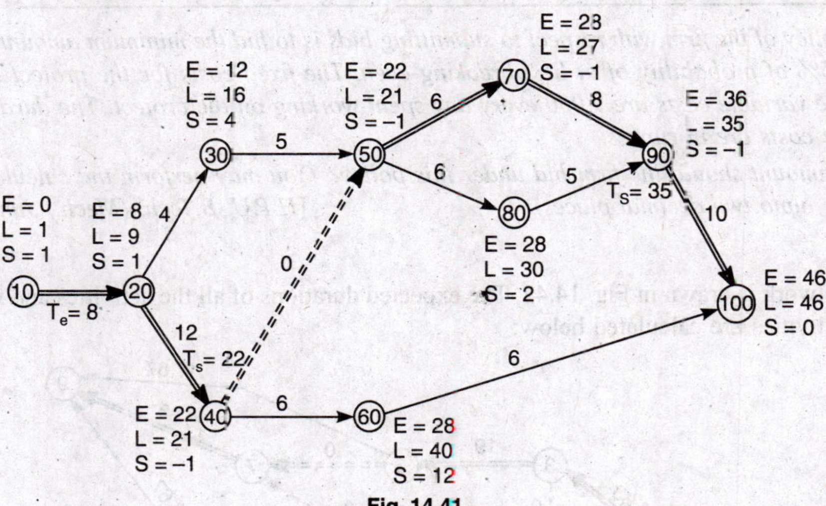

Fig. 14.41

In this problem the earliest start time of 40–50, which is dummy activity, is 22 days. In other words the earliest occurrence time of event 40 is 22. The latest completion time of activity 70–90 is given as 35 days. Or, the latest occurrence time of event 90 is 35. These two intermediate schedule times are also shown in Fig. 14.41. Thus E (40) = 22 and L (90) = 35 have been fixed.

The computations of earliest and latest times are carried by the forward and backward pass computations. The E and L values for different events along with slacks are shown along the nodes. Events 40, 50, 70 and 90 have slack of –1 day, activities 40-50, 50-70 and 70-90 are thus the most critical. Event 100 has zero slack, while events 10 and 20 have a positive slack of 1 day each. Thus the path 10-20-40-50-70-90-100 is the critical path of this network.

Since the scheduled completion time of the project is the same as the expected completion time, probability of completion in scheduled time is 50%.

EXAMPLE 14.13-9

A civil engineering firm has to bid for the construction of a dam. The activities and their time estimates are given below:

Activity	*Optimistic*	*Most likely*	*Pessimistic*
1-2	*14*	*17*	*25*
2-3	*14*	*18*	*21*
2-4	*13*	*15*	*18*
2-8	*16*	*19*	*28*
3-4 (dummy)	*0*	*0*	*0*
3-5	*15*	*18*	*27*
4-6	*13*	*17*	*21*
5-7 (dummy)	*0*	*0*	*0*
5-9	*14*	*18*	*20*
6-7 (dummy)	*0*	*0*	*0*
6-8 (dummy)	*0*	*0*	*0*
7-9	*16*	*20*	*41*
8-9	*14*	*16*	*22*

The policy of the firm with respect to submitting bids is to bid the minimum amount that will provide a 95% of probability of at best breaking-even. The fixed costs for the project are eight lakhs and the variable costs are 9,000 every day spent working on the project. The duration is in days and the costs are in rupees.

What amount should the firm bid under this policy? (You may perform the calculations on duration etc., upto two decimal places). [H.P.U. B.Tech. (Mech.) June, 2010]

Solution

The network is drawn in Fig. 14.42. The expected durations of all the activities and variances of critical activities are calculated below:

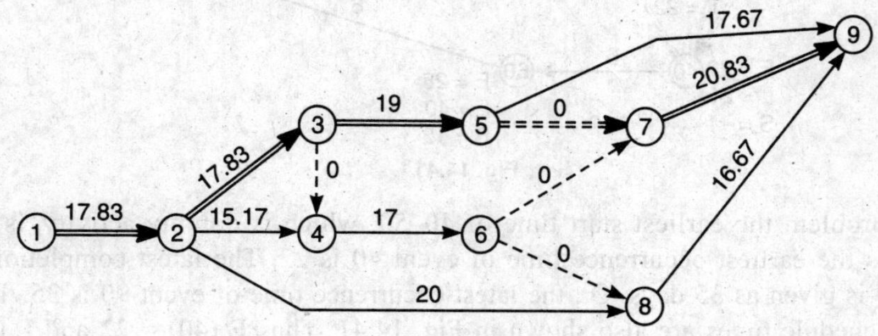

Fig. 14.42

Activity	*Duration*			$t_e = \frac{t_o - t_p + 4t_m}{6}$	$V = \left(\frac{t_p - t_o}{6}\right)^2$
	Optimistic (t_0)	*Pessimistic* (t_p)	*Most likely* (t_m)		
1-2	14	25	17	17.83	3.36
2-3	14	21	18	17.83	1.36
2-4	13	18	15	15.17	
2-8	16	28	19	20	
3-4	0	0	0	0	
3-5	15	27	18	19	4
4-6	13	21	17	17	
5-7	0	0	0	0	
5-9	14	20	18	17.67	
6-7	0	0	0	0	
6-8	0	0	0	0	
7-9	16	41	20	22.83	17.36
8-9	14	22	16	16.67	

Various paths are

1-2-3-5-7-9 : 77.49 days,
1-2-3-5-9 : 72.33 days,
1-2-3-4-6-7-9 : 75.49 days,
1-2-3-4-6-8-9 : 69.33 days,
1-2-8-9 : 54.5 days,
1-2-4-6-8-9 : 66.67 days,
1-2-4-6-7-9 : 72.83 days.

Hence 1-2-3-5-7-9 is the critical path with project duration of 77.49 days. Variances of the critical activities have been calculated.

Variance of the critical path, V = 26.08.

∴ S.D. of the critical path, $\sigma = \sqrt{26.08} = 5.106$ days.

Now we are to determine the time within which the project should be completed so as to provide 95% probability of break-even.

Now $p = 0.95$.

∴ Normal variate, Z = 1.65.

∴ $$1.65 = \frac{T - 77.49}{5.106}$$

or T = 85.91 days ~ 86 days.

The fixed cost of the project is ₹ 8 lakhs and the variable cost is ₹ 9,000 per day.

∴ The amount to bid = ₹ (8,00,000 + 9,000 × 86) = ₹ 15,74,000.

EXAMPLE 14.13-10

(a) A mother notes that when her teenage son uses the telephone, he takes no less than 10 minutes for a call and sometimes as much as one hour. Twenty-minute calls are more frequent than calls of any other duration. If son's phone call were an activity in a PERT project:

(i) What would be the phone call's expected duration?

(ii) What would be its variance?

(iii) In scheduling the project, how much time would be allocated for the phone call?

(b) For the project network shown in Fig. 14.43,

(i) Calculate for each activity its earliest start, earliest finish, late start, late finish, total float and free float for each activity.

(ii) Identify the critical path.

(iii) If the project manager finds that either of the activities 2-6 or 4-5 can each be speeded up by two days at the same cost, which of the two activities should be speeded up? Explain.

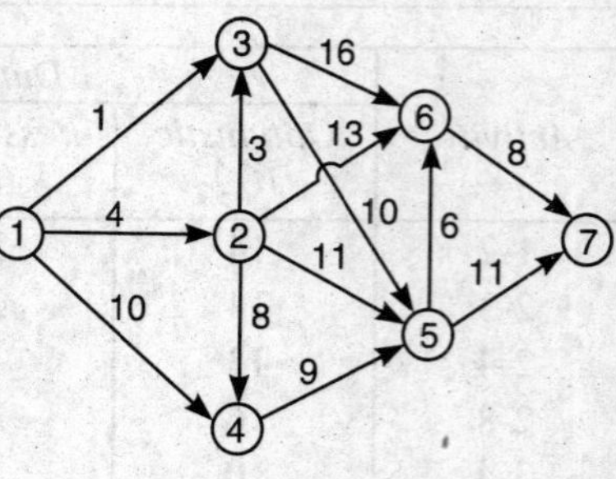

Fig. 14.43

(c) Assuming that the time estimates in days indicated in the above network represent the expected duration based on three time estimates and suppose the variance along the critical path is 81 days, what is the probability that the project will be completed within 33 days? Within 44 days?

[C.A.(Final) Nov., 1990]

Solution

(*a*) (*i*) $t_0 = 10$ minutes, $t_p = 60$ minutes and $t_m = 20$ minutes.

$$\therefore \quad t_e = \frac{t_o + t_p + 4t_m}{6} = \frac{10 + 60 + 20 \times 4}{6} = \frac{150}{6} = 25 \text{ minutes.}$$

(*ii*)
$$\text{Variance} = \left(\frac{t_p - t_o}{6}\right)^2 = \left(\frac{60 - 10}{6}\right)^2 = \left(\frac{25}{3}\right)^2 = \frac{625}{9} = 69.45.$$

(*iii*) For scheduling the project, obviously one should allocate expected duration for the phone call *i.e.*, 25 minutes.

(*b*) (*i*) The earliest and latest occurrence times for each event are calculated in Fig. 14.44.

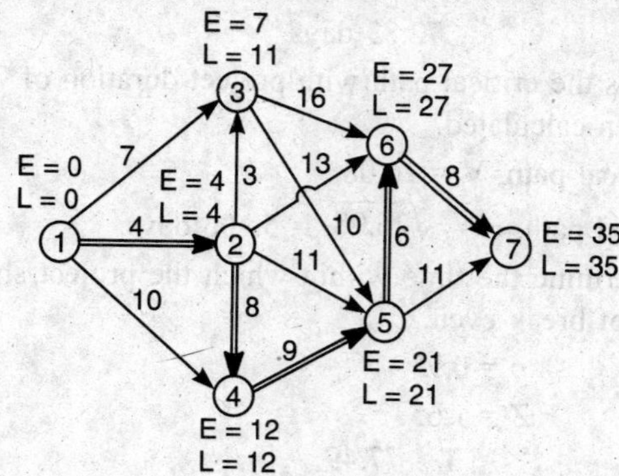

Fig. 14.44

The various values are calculated in the table below.

TABLE 14.9

Activity	*Duration (days)*	*ES*	*LS*	*EF*	*LF*	*Total float*	*Free float*
1-2	4	0	0	4	4	0	0
1-3	7	0	4	7	11	4	0
1-4	10	0	2	10	12	2	2
2-3	3	4	8	7	11	4	0
2-4	8	4	4	12	12	0	0
2-5	11	4	10	15	21	6	6

2-6	13	4	9	22	27	5	5
3-5	10	7	11	17	21	4	4
3-6	16	7	11	23	27	4	4
4-5	9	12	12	21	21	0	0
5-6	6	21	21	27	27	0	0
5-7	11	21	24	32	35	3	3
6-7	8	27	27	35	35	0	0

(*ii*) The critical path is 1-2-4-5-6-7 with project duration of 35 days.

(*iii*) Activity 4-5 should be speeded up since it is a critical activity and speeding it up will reduce the project duration.

(*c*) (*i*) $T = 33$ days,

$T_{cp} = 35$ days,

$\text{S.D.} = \sqrt{V} = \sqrt{81} = 9$ days.

∴ Normal variate, $Z = \dfrac{T - T_{cp}}{\text{S.D}} = \dfrac{33-35}{9} = -0.222.$

From table C.1, $p = 1 - 0.5871 = 0.4129 = 41.29\%$.

(*ii*) $T = 44$ days.

∴ $Z = \dfrac{44-35}{9} = 1.$

∴ $p = 0.8413 = 84.13\%$.

EXERCISES 14.3

1. Explain the term PERT. [*Chennai Univ. B.B.A. Nov., 2010*]

2. Explain the terms: (*i*) optimistic time (*ii*) pessimistic time (*iii*) most likely time and (*iv*) expected time in PERT networks. [*R.U. MBA Dec., 2011; Univ. of Madras B.Sc. (Math.) Nov. 2012; P.T.U. MBA, 2009; C.A.(Final) Dec. 1990; G.N.D.U. B.Com. Sept., 2012; April, 2004*]

3. How will you make use of PERT in installation of a distribution transformer in a new locality? [*P.U. B.E. (Elect.) 1998*]

4. What does the critical path actually signify ? In what ways does it differ from other paths and in what ways are its activities particularly important ? [*G.N.D.U. B.Com. 2004, 2007*]

5. How will you find the probability of completing a PERT project by a particular due date? [*J.N.T.U. Hyderabad MBA April, 2012; P.U. B.Com. Jan., 2005*]

6. The following table lists the jobs of a network along with their time estimates:

Job (i - j)	*Duration (days)*			*Job (i - j)*	*Duration (days)*		
	t_0	t_m	t_p		t_0	t_m	t_p
1-2	3	6	15	3-5	5	11	17
1-6	2	5	14	4-5	3	6	15
2-3	6	12	30	5-8	1	4	7
2-4	2	5	8	6-7	3	9	27
				7-8	4	19	28

(*a*) Draw the project network.

(*b*) Calculate the length and variance of the critical path. [*Univ. of Madras BBA April, 2012*]

(*c*) What is the probability that the jobs on the critical path will be completed in 41 days?

(*d*) What is the probability that the jobs on the next most critical path will be completed by the due date of 41 days? [*G.N.D.U. B Com. April, 2011; V.T.U. Karnataka B.E. June, 2010; R.T.M. Nagpur U.B. Tech. Dec., 2004; Pondicherry U.M.B.A. June, 2007*]

[*Ans.* (*b*) 36 days, 25 (*c*) 0.8413 (*d*) 0.8508.]

7. Project schedule has the following characteristics:

Activity	t_o	t_m	t_p	*Activity*	t_o	t_m	t_p
1-2	1	2	3	5-7	4	5	6
2-3	1	2	3	6-7	6	7	8
2-4	1	3	5	7-8	2	4	6
3-5	3	4	5	7-9	4	6	8
4-5	2	3	4	8-10	1	2	3
4-6	3	5	7	9-10	3	5	7

(*a*) Construct the project network.
(*b*) Find expected duration and variance for each activity.
(*c*) Find the critical path and expected project length.
(*d*) What is the probability of completing the project in 30 days? [*Ans.* (*c*) 28 (*d*) 92%.]

8. Consider a project for which the following activities and time estimates in weeks apply:

Activity	t_o	t_m	t_p	*Activity*	t_o	t_m	t_p
1-2	3	5	8	3-4	1	3	6
1-3	2	3	5	3-5	2	4	6
1-5	2	3	4	4-5	1	2	4
2-3	1	2	5	5-6	1	2	3
2-6	7	8	9				

(*a*) Draw the project network.
(*b*) Compute expected time and variance for each activity.
(*c*) Compute slack for each event and find the critical path.
(*d*) Find the length of the critical path and the project duration.
(*e*) Approximate the probability that activity 3-4 wil have positive slack. What is the managerial implication of that probability?

9. (*a*) Construct a PERT network from the following information and determine the critical path:

Activity	*Immediate predecessor*	t_o	t_m	t_p
A	–	1	2	3
B	A	2	4	6
C	A	2	6	10
D	B	6	8	10
E	C	4	6	8
F	C	6	10	14
G	E	8	10	12
H	F	12	14	16
I	G, H	4	8	12
J	G, H	10	12	14
K	I	2	4	6
L	J	6	10	14

(*b*) Assuming that the schedule allows 40 days to complete the whole project, calculate the probability of completion by the scheduled date.
(*c*) The contractor wants a scheduled completion date that will give him 98% chance of attaining, how many days should be allowed in his schedule? [*H.P.U.B.E. (Mech.) 2008*]

(*Ans.* (*a*) A-C-F-H-J-L, 54 days (*b*) *88.3%* (*c*) 59.2 days.)

10. The activity data for a project are given below:

Activity	:	A	B	C	D	E	F	G	H	I
		(1-2)	(1-3)	(1-4)	(2-5)	(2-6)	(3-6)	(4-7)	(5-7)	(6-7)
Least time	:	5	18	26	16	15	6	7	7	3
Greatest time	:	10	22	40	20	25	12	12	9	5
Most likely time	:	8	20	33	18	20	9	10	8	4

Determine the following:
(*a*) expected task times and variances.
(*b*) the earliest and latest expected times to reach each node.
(*c*) the critical path, and
(*d*) the probability of node occurring at the proposed completion date if the original contract time of completing the project is 41.5 weeks. [*P.T.U. B.Tech. (Mech.) Dec., 2011; R.T.M. Nagpur U. B.Tech., June 2005*]

(*Ans.* (*c*) CG (1-4-7), 42.8 weeks (*d*) 30%.)

11. Consider the network consisting of the following activities:

Activity	t_0	t_m	t_p	*Activity*	t_0	t_m	t_p
1-2	1	2	9	4-5	4	6	8
2-3	1	4	7	4-6	3	5	7
2-4	2	4	12	5-6	1/2	1	3/2
3-4	0	0	0	5-7	5	7	15
3-5	2	3	4	6-7	3	5	13
3-7	6	8	16				

Find the probability of completing the project in 25 days. (*Ans.* 86%.)

12. For the following project, find the critical path by constructing a network.

Activity	*Times (days)*	*Activity*	*Times (days)*
10 - 20	4, 8, 12	20 - 30	1, 4, 7
20 - 40	8, 12, 16	30 - 50	3, 5, 7
40 - 50	0, 0, 0	40 - 60	3, 6, 9
50 - 70	3, 6, 9	50 - 80	4, 6, 8
60 - 100	4, 6, 8	70 - 90	4, 8, 12
80 - 90	2, 5, 8	90 - 100	4, 10, 16

The scheduled completion time for the project is 48 days. Calculate the probability of finishing the project within this time, given that 89.5% probability corresponds to a normal deviation of + 1.25.

[*PTU Dec., 1998*]

(*Ans.* 0.894.)

13. Following table lists the data for a PERT network:

Activity (*i - j*)	:	1-2	1-3	1-4	2-3	2-5	3-4	3-6	4-6	5-6
a (days)	:	2	6	6	2	11	15	3	9	4
m (days)	:	4	6	12	5	14	24	6	15	10
b (days)	:	6	6	24	8	28	45	9	27	16

(*i*) Draw the network, estimate the earliest and latest event times for all nodes and hence derive critical path.
(*ii*) Estimate the expected duration of the project and the corresponding variance.
(*iii*) What is the probability that the project duration will exceed 60 days?

[*R.U. MBA June, 2011; Osmaina U.MBA July, 2010; H.P.U.B. Tech. (Mech.) Nov., 2014; Nov., 2010; P.U. M.Com., 2001*]

14. The following table gives the data for the activities of a small project:

Job (i - j)	:	1-2	1-3	2-4	2-6	3-4	3-5	4-5	5-6
Optimistic time (days)	:	1	5	3	1	8	2	5	2
Most likely time (days)	:	4	10	3	4	15	4	5	5
Pessimistic time (days)	:	7	17	3	7	26	8	5	8

(*i*) Draw the network and find the expected project completion time.
(*ii*) What is the probability that it would take 5 days more than the expected duration?
(*iii*) Find the project completion time which will have 95% confidence.

[*P.U. B.Com. April, 2009; H.P.U. B.Tech. (Mech.) June, 2010*]

(*Ans.* (*i*) 36 days (*ii*) 90.9% (*iii*) 42.16 days.)

15. A project has the following characteristics:

Activity	:	1-2	2-3	2-4	3-5	4-5	4-6	5-7	6-7	7-8	7-9	8-10	9-10
t_0 *(weeks)*	:	1	1	1	3	2	3	4	6	2	5	1	3
t_p *(weeks)*	:	5	3	5	5	4	7	6	8	6	8	3	7
t_m *(weeks)*	:	1.5	2	3	4	3	5	5	7	4	6	2	3

Construct a PERT network. Find the critical path and variance for each event. Find the project duration at 95% probability.

[*G.N.D.U. B.Com. Sept., 2011; P.U. (Ec. & Comm.) Nov., 2011; B.Com., 2002; M.B.A., 2003*]

(*Ans.* (*i*) 1-2-4-6-7-9-10.
(*ii*) 0, 4/9, 5/9, 8/9, 1, 12/9, 13/9, 17/9, 61/36, 19/9. (*iii*) 30.64 weeks.)

16. The expected times and variances for the activities of a PERT network are given below. Determine the slack time for each event and the critical path. If the scheduled completion time is 32 months, find the probability of completion on schedule.

Activity	:	1-2	1-3	2-4	2-5	3-4	3-6	4-5	4-6	5-7	6-7
Expected time (months)	:	4	5	2	12	3	8	10	6	8	10
Variance	:	8	3	1	5	2	4	4	2	1	8

[*Chennai Univ., 2002*]

17. A project is composed of the following 7 activities:

1-2, 1-3, 1-4, 2-5, 3-5, 4-6, and 5-6.

The time estimates in days for the activities are as follows:

Activity	:	1-2	1-3	1-4	2-5	3-5	4-6	5-6
t_0	:	12	3	12	1	2	4	5
t_m	:	15	4	22	1	5	5	6
t_p	:	17	7	28	1	14	8	10

(*i*) Draw the network.
(*ii*) Identify all the paths through it.
(*iii*) Identify critical path through it.
(*iv*) Find the expected project length.

[*P.U. B.E. (Mech.) 1998*]

(*Ans.* (*ii*) 1-2-5-6, 1-3-5-6, 1-4-6 (*iii*) 1-2-5-6 (*iv*) 22.33 days.)

18. Given the following network and activity time estimates, determine the expected project completion time and variance.

Activity	*Time estimates (days)*		
	t_o	t_m	t_p
1 - 2	5	8	17
1 - 3	7	10	13
2 - 3	3	5	7
2 - 4	1	3	5
3 - 4	4	6	8
3 - 5	3	3	3
4 - 5	3	4	5

[*U.P. Tech.U. MBA, 2010*]

19. A project is composed of 7 jobs whose time estimations in days are given below :

Activity	1-2	1-3	1-4	2-5	3-5	4-6	5-6
Most likely time	7	16	7	9	20	14	2
Optimistic time	8	18	9	10	24	16	3
Pessimistic time	9	20	11	11	28	18	4

(*i*) Draw the network and calculate the length and variance along the critical path.
(*ii*) Find the probability of completing the project one day earlier and 2 days later.

[*H.P.U. B.Tech. (Mech.) June, 2015; V.T.U. Karnataka B.E. June, 2012*]

20. Time estimates for a particular activity are provided by two engineers A and B as follows :

Engineer	*Optimistic time*	*Most likely time*	*Pessimistic time*
A	3	6	7
B	4	5	9

State who is more certain about his estimation.

21. A project is expected to take 12 months with a standard deviation of 4 months. What is the probability of completing the project within (*i*) 10 months (*ii*) 15 months ? [*V.T.U. Karnataka B.E. Jan., 2010*]

22. Assuming that the expected times are normally distributed, find the probability of meeting the scheduled date as given for the network :

Activity (i - j)	*Days*		
	Optimistic	*Most likely*	*Pessimistic*
1 - 2	2	5	14
1 - 3	9	12	15
2 - 4	5	14	17
3 - 4	2	5	8
4 - 5	6	6	12
3 - 5	8	17	20

Scheduled project completion date is 30 days. Also find the data on which the project manager can complete the project with a probability of 0.90. [*R.T.M. Nagpur U. B.Tech. Dec., 2006*]

23. Table below gives list of activities along with predecessors and three time estimates in weeks.

Activity	*Predecessor activity*	*Optimistic time*	*Most likely time*	*Pessimistic time*
A	–	1	2	9
B	A	2	3	4
C	A	2	4	6
D	A	3	5	7
E	C	5	7	9
F	D	1	3	5
G	B	1	4	7
H	G	2	6	10
I	E, H	4	8	6
J	F	2	6	10

(*a*) Draw the project network. (*b*) Find the critical path.
(*c*) Find the probability of completion in 21 weeks and 25 weeks.

[*R.T.M. Nagpur B.E. (Mech.) Sept., 2010*]

24. Draw the network and indicate the critical path in the network :

Activity	*Depends on*	*Activity duration in hours*		
		t_o	t_p	t_m
A	–	80	150	100
B	F	10	30	20
C	–	10	30	20
D	G	10	40	20
E	G, D, F	40	60	50
F	G, C	20	40	30
G	–	20	50	30

[*R.T.M. Nagpur B.Tech. Dec., 2004*]

25. (*a*) A small project consists of seven activities, the details of which are given below :

Activity	*Duration (in days)*			*Immediate predecessor*
	Most likely	*Optimistic*	*Pessimistic*	
A	3	1	7	–
B	6	2	14	A

C	3	3	3	A
D	10	4	22	B, C
E	7	3	15	B
F	5	2	14	D, E
G	4	4	4	D

(*i*) Draw the network, number the nodes, find the critical path, the expected project completion time and the next most critical path.

(*ii*) What project duration will have 95% confidence of completion?

(*a*) What is float ? What are the different types of floats ? Discuss total float and free float; explain their uses in networks. [*R.T.M. Nagpur U.B. Tech. Dec., 2003*]

26. A small project consists of the following activities :

Activity	*Immediate predecessor*	*Time (days)*		
		Optimistic	*Most likely*	*Pessimistic*
A	–	4	6	8
B	A	5	7	15
C	A	4	8	12
D	B	15	20	25
E	B	10	18	26
F	C	8	9	16
G	E	4	8	12
H	D, F	1	2	3
I	G, H	6	7	8

(*i*) Construct an arrow diagram for this problem.

(*ii*) Determine the critical path and compute the expected completion time.

(*iii*) Determine the probability of completing the project within 52 days.

(*iv*) What project duration will have 40% confidence of completion of project ?

[*R.T.M. Nagpur U. B.Tech. June, 2003*]

27. The table below shows the expected time and variance for each activity involved in a process:

Predecessor event i	*Successor event j*	t_e *(days)*	σ^2
10	20	2	1/9
10	30	3	1/8
20	40	3	1
30	40	4	1/16
30	50	4	1/8
40	50	3	16/9
50	60	2	1/9

(*i*) Find out which of the activities involved in the process should be completed in time so that the project is completed in minimum time.

(*ii*) Find the critical path.

(*iii*) For a similar process the time estimates are same but the standard deviation for the network is 1.9. For which case the uncertainty involved in completion of the project will be more?

28. Consider a task of obtaining ISO-9000 quality system certification for an organisation. The activities involved, dependence and estimated durations are given below:

Activity	*Dependence*	*Estimated duration (weeks)*		
		t_p	t_m	t_0
A	–	7	4	1
B	–	9	6	3
C	A	14	5	2
D	C	3	2	1

E	A, B	18	9	6
F	D	27	18	9
G	D, E	40	20	10
H	F, G	18	9	6
I	D, E	28	10	4
J	A, B	5	5	5

(*i*) Draw the network and find the expected duration of the task which will have 95% confidence of completion.
[given p (Z <1.645) = 0.95.]

(*ii*) What is the minimum duration of completing the task? Compute its probability.
[given p (Z > 3) = 1.] *[H.P.U. B.Tech. (Mech.) June, 2007]*

(*Ans.* (*i*) 47.7 weeks, 57.2 weeks; (*ii*) 25 weeks, p = 0.5.)

29. Draw a PERT network for the following events and number the events.
A is the start event and L the last event.
B and D are successor events to A.
D precedes E and F.
C succeeds B.
E restricts the occurrence of C.
E and F precede G.
H is a successor event to C and E.
G restricts the occurrence of H.
J succeeds I and I succeeds H.
I & J precede K.
L is a successor event to K.
For the above network if three time estimates (days) for the activities are as under, find
(*i*) Earliest expected time and latest allowable occurrence time of each event.
(*ii*) Earliest expected time for the project.
(*iii*) Critical path.

Activity	t_o	t_m	t_p
A - B	2	4	6
B - C	6	8	12
C - H	4	8	12
H - I	3	6	9
I - K	1	2	3
K - L	6	8	10
A - D	3	6	9
D - E	8	10	12
E - H	6	8	10
E - G	14	16	18
D - F	7	9	11
F - G	6	9	12
G - J	3	4	5
J - K	1	3	5

[P.U. B.E. (E. & Ec.) June, 1993]

[**Hint.** The network for the problem is drawn below.]

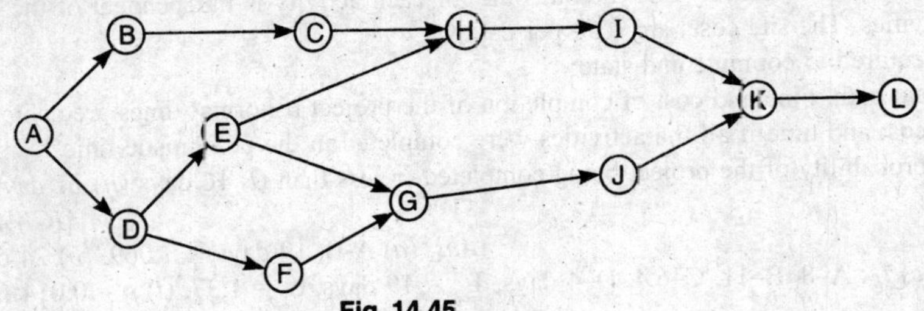

Fig. 14.45

30. Consider the following table:

Activity	Predecessor activity	Time in weeks t_o	t_m	t_p
A	–	2	3	10
B	–	2	3	4
C	A	1	2	3
D	A	4	6	14
E	B	4	5	12
F	C	3	4	5
G	D, E	1	1	7

(*i*) Draw the network diagram.
(*ii*) Find the critical path and variance of each event.
(*iii*) What is the probability that the project will be completed in 16 weeks?

[*H.P.U. B.Tech. (Mech.) 2012; G.N.D.U. B.Com. Sept., 2010; P.U. B.Com. April, 2003*]

31. A project has the following activities and other characteristics:

Activity	Preceding activity	Time in weeks t_o	t_m	t_p
A	–	4	7	16
B	–	1	5	15
C	A	6	12	30
D	A	2	5	8
E	C	5	11	17
F	D	3	6	15
G	B	3	9	27
H	E, F	1	4	7
I	G	4	19	28

(*i*) Draw the PERT network.
(*ii*) Identify the critical path.
(*iii*) Determine the mean project completion time.
(*iv*) Find the probability that the project is completed in 36 weeks.
(*v*) If the project manager wishes to be 99% sure that the project is completed on June 30, 2016, when should he start the project work?

(*Ans.* (*ii*) A-C-E-H (*iii*) 37 weeks (*iv*) 0.4207
(*v*) 48.65 weeks before June 30, 2016; *i.e*, around 26th July, 2015.)

32. Swaraj Ltd. is planning a project to introduce a new product and has listed the following activities, their normal, optimistic and pessimistic times and costs:

Activity	Preceding activity	Normal Days	Normal ₹	Optimistic Days	Optimistic ₹	Pessimistic Days	Pessimistic ₹
A	–	8	32	7	28	9	36
B	A	11	33	7	21	15	45
C	A	6	30	7	25	7	35
D	C	4	24	3	18	5	30

The probabilities associated with normal, optimistic and pessimistic times are 0.6, 0.2 and 0.2 respectively for each activity and the outcome for each activity is independent of the outcome of the other activities. The site costs are ₹ 50 per day.

You are required to compute and state:

(*a*) Critical path, time and cost of completion of the project if normal times are achieved.
(*b*) The cost and time if all the activities were completed in the pessimistic times.
(*c*) The probability of the project being completed in less than (*i*) 16 days (*ii*) 21 days.

[*ICWA (Final) 2000*]

(*Ans.* (*a*) A-B, 19 days, ₹ 1,069. (*b*) 24 days, ₹ 1, 346.
(*c*) t_e : A–8, B–11, C–6.4, D–4 days, T_{cp} = 19 days, σ_{cp} = 1.37, (*i*) p = 0.014 (*ii*) p = 0.928.)

33. Three time estimates (in months) of all the activities of a project are given below.

Activity	t_o	t_m	t_p
1 - 2	3	4	5
2 - 3	6	8	10
2 - 4	2	3	4
3 - 4	4	5	12
4 - 5	5	7	9
5 - 6	9	16	17

(*a*) Find the expected duration and standard deviation of each activity.
(*b*) Construct the project network.
(*c*) Determine the critical path, expected project length and variance of the project.

[*H.P.U. B.Tech. June, 2015; Sept., 2013; P.T.U. MBA, 2008*]

(*Ans.* (*a*) (*i*) 4, 8, 3, 6, 7, 15 months. (*ii*) $\frac{1}{3}, \frac{2}{3}, \frac{1}{3}, \frac{4}{3}, \frac{2}{3}, \frac{4}{3}$ months.
(*c*) 1-2-3-4-5-6; 40 months; $\frac{41}{9}$)

34. A project comprising of eight tasks (A to H) has the following characteristics :

Task	*Predecessor*	Duration (weeks)		
		Optimistic	*Most likely*	*Pessimistic*
A	–	2	4	12
B	–	10	12	26
C	A	8	9	10
D	A	10	15	20
E	A	7	7.5	11
F	B, C	9	9	9
G	D	3	3.5	7
H	E, F, G	5	5	5

(*a*) Calculate the duration of each activity and the variance.
(*b*) Draw the network diagram, determine the critical path and mark it in the network. What is the total project duration ?
(*c*) What is the probability of achieving the project completion with the deadline of 30 weeks ?

[*H.P.U. B.Tech. Nov., 2015; G.N.D.U. B.Com.April, 2007; P.T.U. MBA, 2005*]

(*Ans.* (*a*) (*i*) 5, 14, 9, 15, 8, 9, 4, 5 weeks. (*ii*) $\frac{25}{9}, \frac{64}{9}, \frac{1}{9}, \frac{25}{9}, \frac{4}{9}, 0, \frac{4}{9}$ 0..
(*b*) A–D–G–H; 29 weeks. (c) 65.6%.)

35. For the data given below, find the following:
(*i*) The expected task times and their variances.
(*ii*) The earliest expected and latest allowable occurrence times of each event.
(*iii*) The critical path.
(*iv*) The probability that each task will be completed on schedule.

Task	:	A	B	C	D	E	F	G	H	I	J	K	L
Least time (days)	:	3	1	2	6	8	0	5	6	1	3	8	2
Most likely time (days)	:	5	2	4	8	12	0	7	9	2	6	15	4
Greatest time (days)	:	6	3	6	12	17	0	9	12	3	8	20	6

Precedence relationship:
A and B can start immediately; C, D > A ; E > B, C; F, H > E ; G > D, F ; J > G; I, K > H; L > J, I.

(*Ans.* Critical path = A-C-E-H-K.)

36. In the PERT network shown in Fig. 14.46, the activity time estimates (in weeks) are given along the arrows. If the scheduled completion time of the project is 23 weeks, calculate the latest possible occurrence times on the basis of the scheduled date of final event. Calculate the slack for each event and identify the critical path. What is the probability that the project will be completed on the scheduled date ?

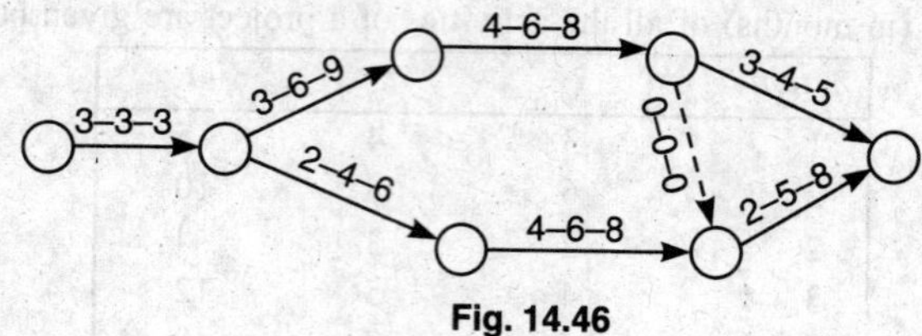

Fig. 14.46

[*Ans.* 97.26 %.]

37. A PERT network is shown in Fig. 14.47. The activity times (in hours) are given along the arrows. The scheduled times for some important events are given along the nodes. Determine the critical path and the probabilities of meeting the scheduled dates for the specified events. Tabulate the results and determine the slacks. [*Kuru. U. B.Tech. Dec., 1988*]

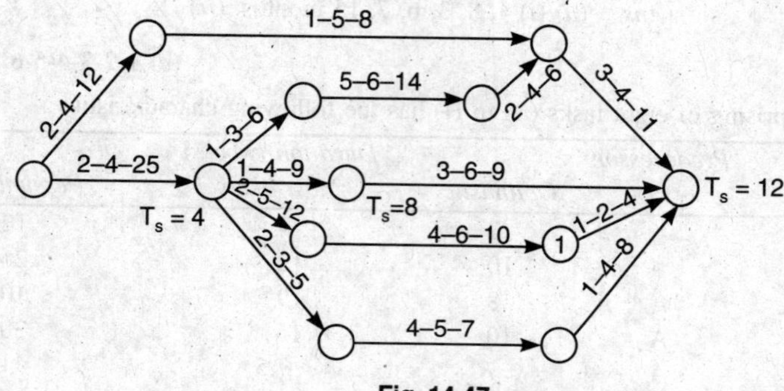

Fig. 14.47

(*Ans.* 20.3%, 19.5%, 0.07%.)

38. PERT calculations yield a project length of 60 weeks with variance of 9. Within how many weeks would you expect the project to be completed with probability of 0.99? (*Ans.* 69 weeks.)

14.14 COST ANALYSIS AND CRASHING THE NETWORK

14.14-1 Project Cost

Each activity of the project consumes some resources and hence has cost associated with it. In most of the cases cost of an activity will vary to some extent with the amount of time consumed by the activity. The cost of total project, which is the aggregate of the activity costs will also depend upon the project duration. Thus by increasing the costs, the project duration can be cut down to some extent. The aim is always to strike a balance between the costs and time, and to obtain an optimum project schedule. An optimum project schedule implies lowest possible cost and the associated time for the project. The total cost of any project consists of the direct and indirect costs involved in its execution.

Direct Cost

This cost is directly dependent upon the amount of resources involved in the execution of the individual activities. This is the cost of the materials, equipment and labour required to perform the activity. If the activity is performed by a subcontractor, the price of the subcontract will be the activity direct cost. It can be seen from the direct cost-time relationship shown in Fig. 14.48 that the activity duration can be varied by varying the cost. Point N, referred to as the '*normal point*' corresponds to the normal activity time. If the duration is further increased, the decrease in cost is insignificant. As the activity is compressed, the direct cost goes on increasing. If it is compressed beyond C, the cost increases very rapidly for insignificant change in the activity duration. This point is called '*crash point*'. Crash time is thus the minimum activity duration to which an activity can be compressed by increasing the resources and hence by increasing the direct cost.

To make the calculations simple, the direct cost-time curve is approximated to either a single straight line or multi-straight lines (segments), as shown in Fig. 14.49(*a*) and 14.49(*b*) respectively. The slope of the line (or a segment of line) gives the increase in direct cost per unit time for expediting the activity. This is called *cost slope*.

For the straight line approximation in figure 14.49 (*a*),

$$\text{cost slope} = \frac{C_C - C_n}{T_n - T_C} = \frac{\Delta C}{\Delta T}.$$

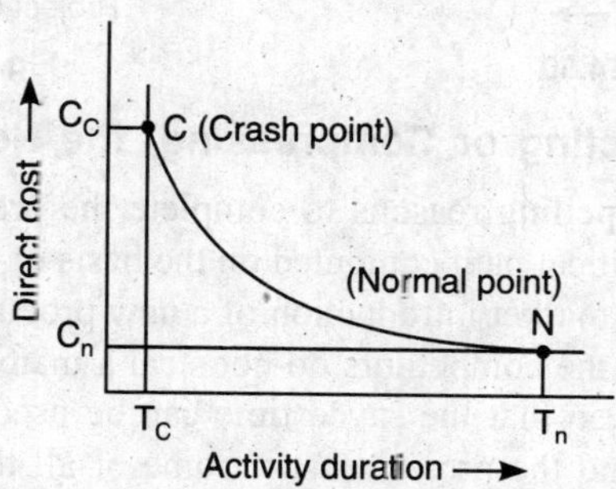

Fig. 14.48

The choice between the single straight line and segmented approximation depends upon the non-linearity of the cost curve. Also the segmented approximation is adopted only when the activity can be broken down into subactivities. Above all, it is the judgment of the executive whether to approximate the curve by segments and go through involved calculations or to use a little rough single slope approximation and save calculation work.

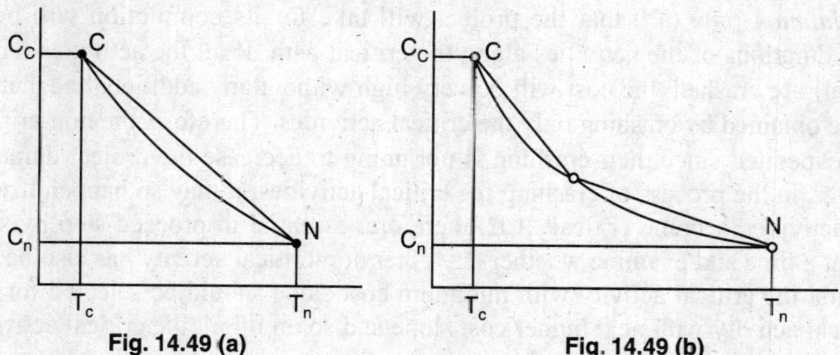

Fig. 14.49 (a) Fig. 14.49 (b)

Indirect Cost

Project indirect cost can further be subdivided into two parts: fixed indirect cost and variable indirect cost. The fixed indirect cost is due to the general and administrative expenses, licence fee, insurance cost and taxes and does not depend upon the progress of the project. The variable indirect cost depends upon the time consumed by the project and consists of overhead expenditure, supervision, interest on capital and depreciation, penalty for delays (if any), etc. It is assumed that the indirect cost increases linearly with time as shown in figure 14.50.

The sum of the direct and indirect cost gives the *project total cost*. As the direct cost decreases with time and indirect cost increases with time, the project total cost curve will have a point where the total cost will be minimum (Fig. 14.51). The time corresponding to this point is called the *optimum duration* and the cost, the *optimum cost*.

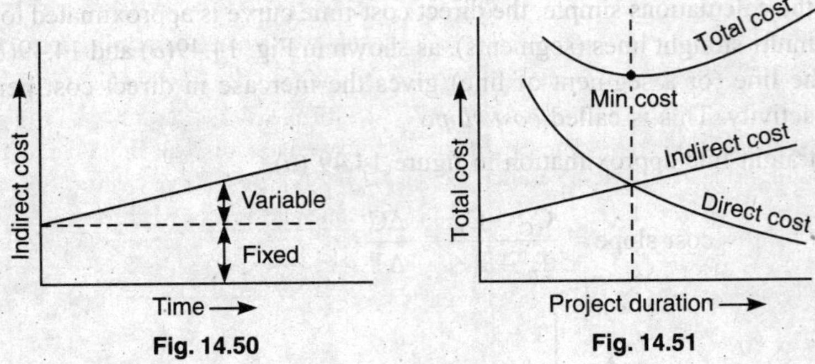

Fig. 14.50

Fig. 14.51

14.14-2 Crashing (Contracting or Compressing) the Network

Often there may be compelling reasons to complete the project earlier than would be the case with the duration of the critical path computed on the basis of normal expected activity times. Examples are war situations or market introduction of a new product. The motive in hastening the project might be to ensure that the competitors do not steal a march. Also the managements often want to reduce the target time so that the saved time can be used for some extra work. In such situations, our concern is to find the project cost if some or all the activities are crashed. From the knowledge of the normal direct cost and crashed direct cost, the cost slope for each activity can be determined. If the indirect cost per unit time is known, the total cost of the project can be found by adding the direct and indirect costs.

The *normal time* (T_n) for the completion of the project will be the sum of the normal time durations of the critical activities and the *normal direct cost* (C_n) of the project will be the sum of the normal cost of all the activities since each and every activity has to be executed to complete the project.

The *minimum time* (T_c) that the project will take for its completion will be sum of the crashed time durations of the activities along the critical path. If all the activities (critical as well as non-critical) are crashed, the cost will be very high without any additional advantage over and above the one obtained by crashing only the critical activities. Therefore, the non-critical activities need not be expedited since their crashing is not going to decrease the project duration further.

However, in the process of crashing the critical activities, it may so happen that some of the non-critical activities become critical. It is, therefore, essential to proceed step by step, crashing one activity at a time and examine whether any other non-critical activity has also become critical. Obviously, first the critical activity with minimum cost slope should be selected for crashing and then the critical activity with next higher cost slope and so on till all the critical activities are fully crashed or no further crashing is possible.

The time-cost trade-off method consists of systematic analysis of the project time and cost. At each step of crashing, the direct cost is calculated; it would naturally be higher than the normal direct cost as it includes the additional cost of crashing too. However, the indirect cost will reduce as the project duration has been reduced. The total cost is then found at each step. A table or a curve may be constructed between the total cost and time. It is found that as the project duration is decreased, the total cost may also decrease, reaching the minimum value, beyond which it may increase. This minimum cost is called the *optimum project cost* and the corresponding time, the *optimum project time*. In emergencies and during sudden rush of orders from the customers, the crashing may be further continued to get the *minimum* or *crash project time* and the corresponding *crash cost*.

14.14-3 Time-Cost Trade-Off Procedure

It consists of the following steps :

1. Draw the project network, identify the critical path and calculate the normal cost of the project.

2. Determine the cost slope for each activity.

$$\text{Cost slope} = \frac{\text{Crash cost} - \text{Normal direct cost}}{\text{Normal time} - \text{Crash time}}.$$

The cost slope represents the additional cost incurred per unit time (saved) in reducing the duration of the activity.

3. Crash the critical activity with minimum cost slope. Calculate the new direct cost by adding the additional cost of crashing to the normal cost.
4. As the crashing is done, it is possible some non-critical activities also become critical. Thus we may have multiple or parallel critical paths. If so, choose an activity from each such path for crashing.
5. Of the various available combinations, select the one with least cost.
6. Revise the network by adjusting the time and cost of the crashed activity/activities. Identify the critical path (s) again.
7. Continue the process till no more crashing is possible. This gives the crash time. Calculate the associated total cost (by adding the normal direct cost, additional crash cost and indirect cost). This is the corresponding crash cost.
8. Prepare the total cost table corresponding to different project durations.
9. The minimal total cost is called the optimum cost and the associated time is called the optimum time.

EXAMPLE 14.14-1

List of activities for erecting a canteen in a factory is given below with other relevant details. Job A must precede all others, while job E must follow others. Apart from this, jobs can run concurrently.

Code	*Job description*	*Normal*		*Crash*	
		Duration (days)	*Cost (₹)*	*Duration (days)*	*Cost (₹)*
A	*Lay foundation and build walls*	5	3,000	4	4,000
B	*Tile roofing*	6	1,200	2	2,000
C	*Instal electricity*	4	1,000	3	1,800
D	*Instal plumbing*	5	1,200	3	2,000
E	*Connect services to finish*	3	1,600	3	1,600
			8,000		

(i) Draw the network and identify the critical path.
(ii) Crash the network fully to find out minimum duration.
(iii) If indirect costs are ₹ 300 per day, determine time-cost trade off for the project.

[*Dayalbagh Edu. Inst. Agra MBA May, 2013*]

Solution

First, the cost slope for each activity and the normal direct cost of the project is calculated. This is shown in the table below.

Job	:	A (1-2)	B (2-3)	C (2-5)	D (2-4)	E (5-6)
Cost slope (₹/day)	:	1,000	200	800	400	—

Normal direct cost from the given table = ₹ 8,000.

Next, the network is drawn and the critical path is determined. An activity $(i - j)$ is critical only if E = L for its tail event, E = L for its head event and $E_j - E_i = L_j - L_i = t_{ij}$. Critical path is shown in Fig. 14.52.

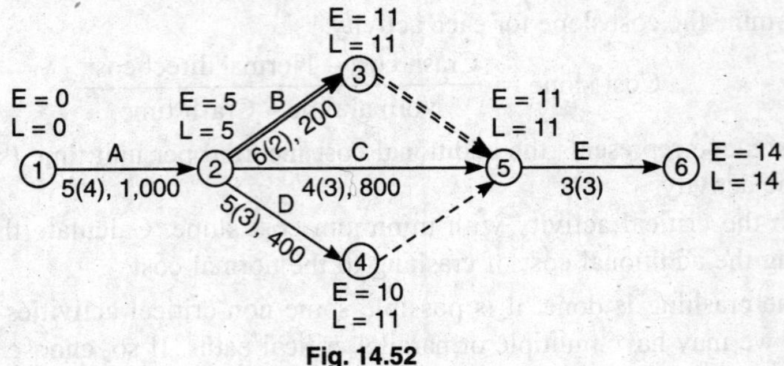

Fig. 14.52

(*i*) Critical path is 1-2-3-5-6.

Normal duration = 14 days.

Normal cost = ₹ (8,000 + 300 × 14) = ₹ 12,200.

(*ii*) Represent the network on time-scaled diagram. This is shown in Fig. 14.53 Activities along the critical path are arranged along the horizontal line 1-2-3-5-6.

Early start times for the activities have been assumed. Dotted lines show the floats for the non-critical activities.

Project length can be reduced by crashing the critical activities. This will involve extra direct-cost. While crashing a critical activity, it is possible that some associated non-critical activity (or activities) may also have to be crashed. If float is available no extra cost for such activity (or activities) will be involved; if not, the cost of crashing such activity (activities) will also be considered and the total cost will be calculated. Then the critical activity involving the least associated cost will be selected for crashing.

While crashing a critical activity, only those non-critical activities will require crashing which start from the tail event of the critical activity under consideration or earlier and finish at the head event of the critical activity or later than that. This rule may be kept in mind while crashing the activities.

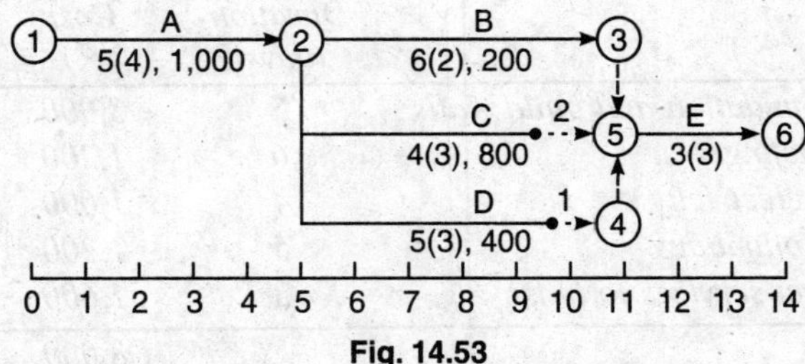

Fig. 14.53

Crash activity B (2–3), C (2–5) and D (2–4) by one day each.

The various alternative critical activities and their crash costs are given below.

Activity	*Cost (₹)*	*Activity*	*Cost (₹)*
A (1-2)	1,000	B (2-3)	200
		D (2-4)	Nil
		C (2-5)	Nil
			200

Since activity 2-3 has the lower associated crash cost of ₹ 200 per day, it is crashed by one day. With this activity, activities 2-4 and 2-5 will also have to be crashed. Since these activities have floats, crash cost for one day of crashing will be nil for either of them. This is shown in the table above.

∴ Additional crash cost = ₹ 200,

project duration = 13 days.

The network is shown in Fig. 14.54.

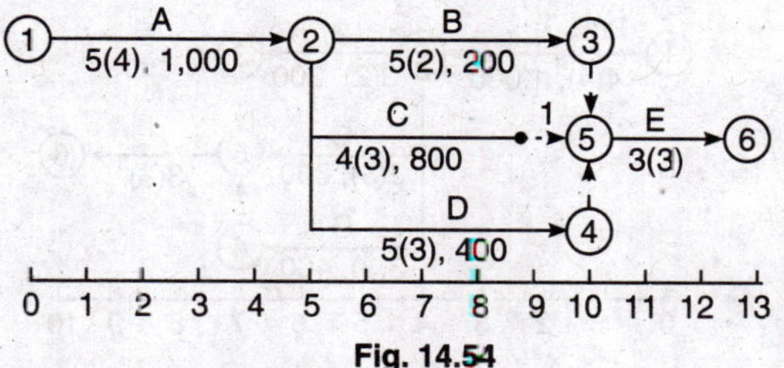

Fig. 14.54

Crash activities B, C and D by one day each.

The various activities and their crash costs are given below.

Activity	*Cost (₹)*	*Activity*	*Cost (₹)*
A (1-2)	1,000	B (2-3)	200
		D (2-4)	400
		C (2-5)	Nil
			600

∴ Total additional crash cost=₹ (200 + 600) = ₹ 800,

project duration = 12 days.

The network is shown in Fig. 14.55.

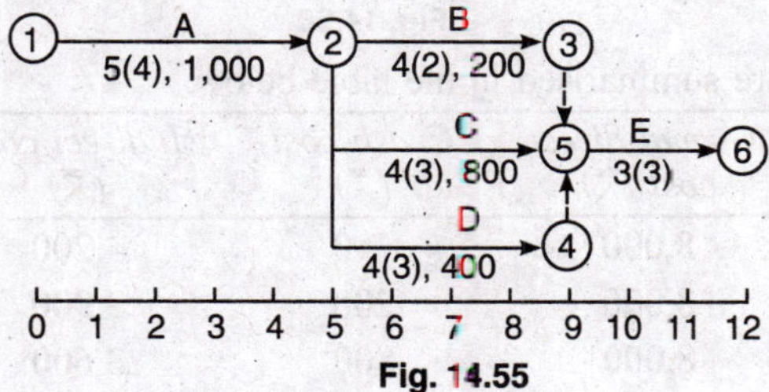

Fig. 14.55

Crash activity A (1-2) by one day.

The various activities and their crash costs are given below.

Activity	*Cost (₹)*	*Activity*	*Cost (₹)*
A (1-2)	1,000	B (2-3)	200
		D (2-4)	400
		C (2-5)	800
			1,400

∴ Total additional crash cost=₹ (1,000 + 800) = ₹ 1,800,

project duration = 11 days.

The network is shown in Fig. 14.56

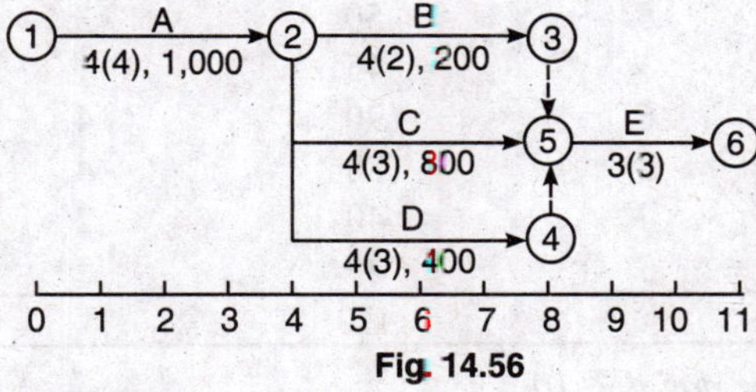

Fig. 14.56

Crash activities B, c and D by one day each.

∴ Total additional crash cost=₹ (1,400 + 1,800) = ₹ 3,200,

project duration = 10 days.

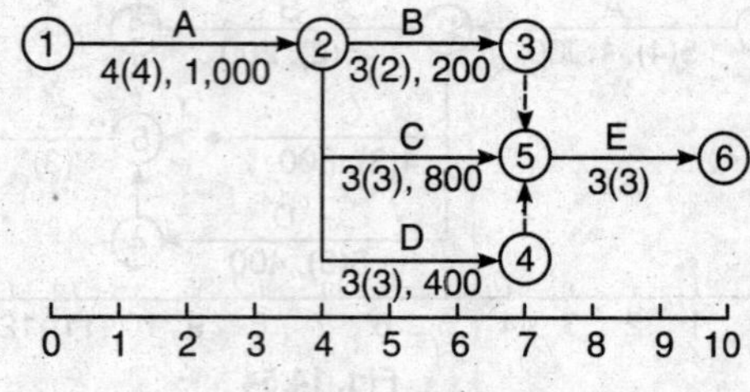

Fig. 14.57

The network is shown in Fig. 14.57. All activities are fully crashed. Thus minimum project duration is 10 days. The complete crashing of the network from 14 days to 10 days can be shown in a single diagram (Fig. 14.58) to save time.

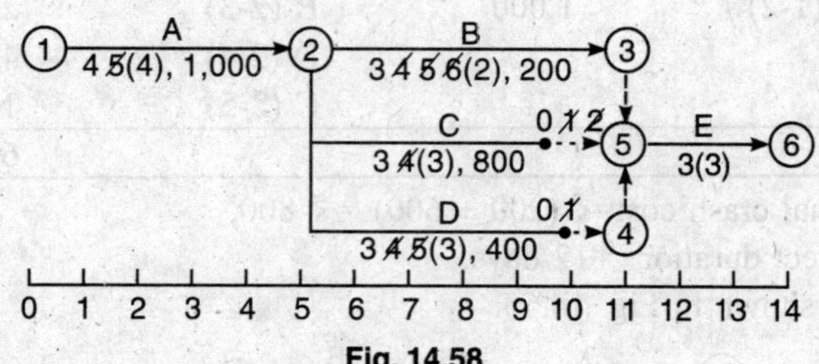

Fig. 14.58

The above results are summarised in the table below.

Duration (days)	*Normal direct cost (₹)*	*Crash cost (₹)*	*Indirect cost (₹)*	*Total cost (₹)*
14	8,000	0	4,200	12,200
13	8,000	200	3,900	12,100
12	8,000	800	3,600	12,400
11	8,000	1,800	3,300	13,100
10	8,000	3,200	3,000	14,200

(*iii*) Thus time-cost trade off exists at 13 days when B is crashed by 1 day and the total minimum cost is ₹ 12,100.

EXAMPLE 14.14-2

The following table gives data on normal time and cost and crash time and cost for a project:

Activity	*Normal*		*Crash*	
	Time (days)	*Cost (₹)*	*Time (days)*	*Cost (₹)*
1-2	6	60	4	100
1-3	4	60	2	200
2-4	5	50	3	150
2-5	3	45	1	65
3-4	6	90	4	200
4-6	8	80	4	300
5-6	4	40	2	100
6-7	3	45	2	80
		470		

The indirect cost per day is ₹ 10.

(*i*) *Draw the network for the project.*

(*ii*) *Find the critical path.*

(*iii*) *Determine minimum total time and corresponding cost.*

[*H.P.U.B. Tech. (Mech.) Nov., 2014; Nov., 2006; M.D.U. Rohtak B.E. (Mech.) Dec., 2006*]

Solution

First, the cost slope for each activity and the normal direct cost of the project is calculated. This is shown in the table below. Normal direct cost of the project is ₹ 470.

Activity	:	1-2	1-3	2-4	2-5	3-4	4-6	5-6	6-7
Cost slope (₹/day)	:	20	70	50	10	55	55	30	35

(*i*) Next, the network is drawn and the critical path is determined. This is shown in Fig. 14.59.

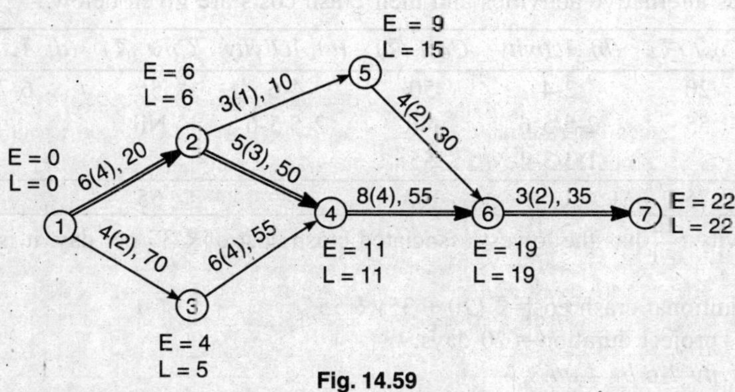

Fig. 14.59

(*ii*) The critical path is 1-2-4-6-7.

(*iii*) Normal duration = 22 days.

Normal cost = ₹ (470 + 22 × 10) = ₹ 690.

Now represent the network on time-scaled diagram. This is shown in Fig. 14.60.

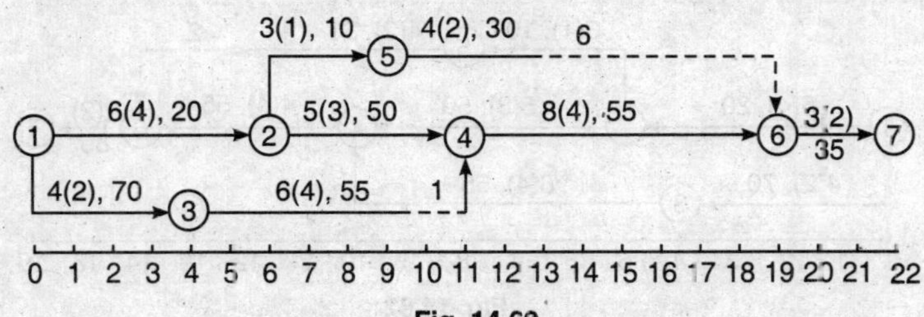

Fig. 14.60

Crash activity 1-2 by 1 day.

The various alternative activities and their crash costs are given below.

(a) Activity	*Cost (₹)*	*(b) Activity*	*Cost (₹)*	*(c) Activity*	*Cost (₹)*	*(d) Activity*	Cost (₹)
1-2	20	2-4	50	4-6	55	6-7	35
1-3/3-4	Nil	2-5/5-6	Nil	2-5/5-6	Nil		
		1-3/3-4	Nil				
	20		50		55		35

Since activity 1-2 has the lowest associated crash cost of ₹ 20 per day, it is crashed by one day.

∴ Additional crash cost = ₹ 20,

project duration = 21 days.

The network is shown in Fig. 14.61

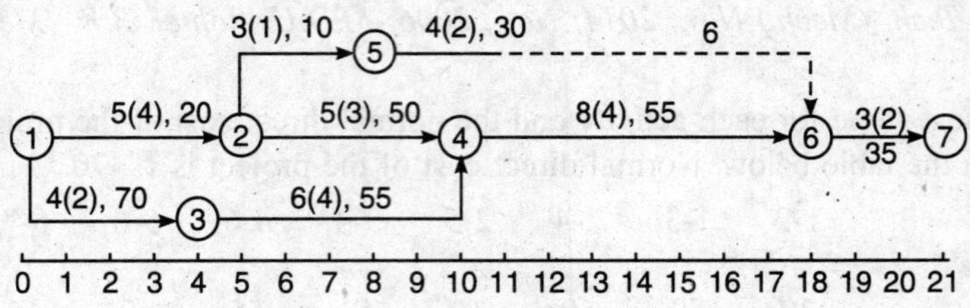

Fig. 14.61

Crash activity 6-7 by 1 day.

The various alternative activities and their crash costs are given below.

(a) Activity	Cost (₹)	(b) Activity	Cost (₹)	(c) Activity	Cost (₹)	(d) Activity	Cost (₹)
1-2	20	2-4	50	4-6	55	6-7	35
1-3/3-4	55	2-5/5-6	Nil	2-5/5-6	Nil		
		1-3/3-4	55				
	75		105		55		35

Since activity 6-7 has the lowest associated crash cost of ₹ 35 per day, it is crashed by one day.

∴ Total additional crash cost=₹ (20 + 35) ₹ 55,

project duration = 20 days.

Crash activity 4-6 by 4 days.

As evident from the above table, next activity 4-6 has the lowest associated crash cost of ₹ 55 per day and as seen from Fig. 14.61 it can be crashed by 4 days.

∴ Total additional crash cost=₹ (55 + 4 × 55) = ₹ 275,

project duration = 16 days.

The network is shown in Fig. 14.62.

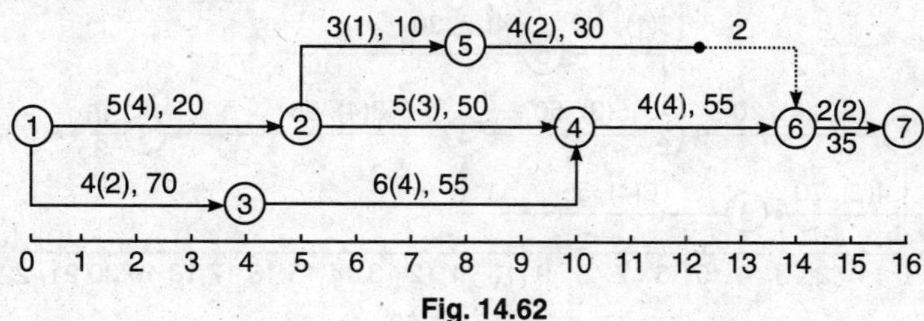

Fig. 14.62

Crash activity 1-2 by 1 day.

Next, activity 1-2 is crashed by 1 day at a cost of ₹ 75 per day.

∴ Total additional crash cost=₹ (275 + 75) = ₹ 350,

project duration = 15 days.

The network is shown in Fig. 14.63.

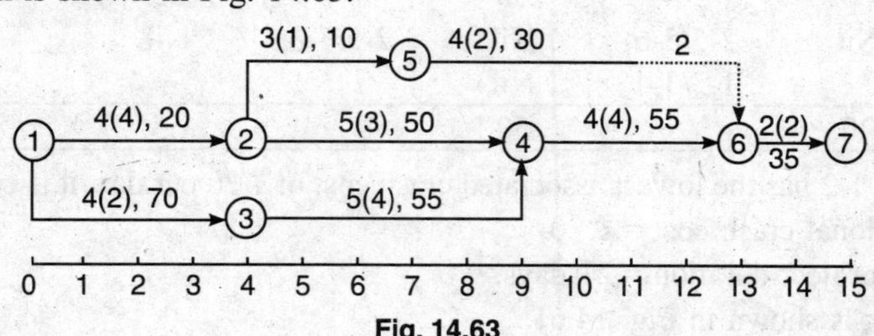

Fig. 14.63

Crash activity 2-4 by 1 day.

Now activity 2-4 is crashed by 1 day at a cost of ₹ 105 per day.

∴ Total additional crash cost= ₹ (350 + 105) = ₹ 455,

project duration = 14 days.

The network is shown in Fig. 14.64. No further crashing is possible.

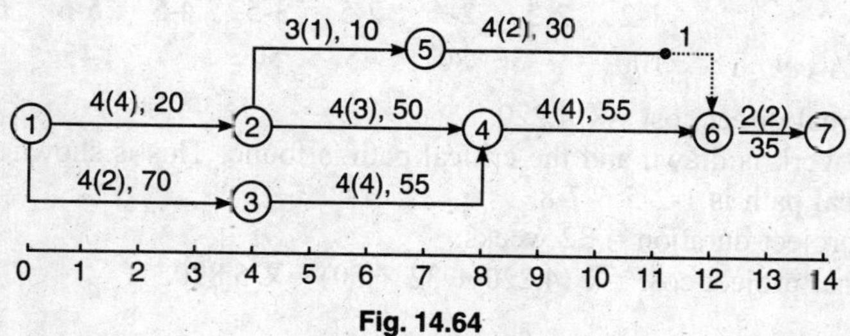

Fig. 14.64

The complete crashing of the network from 22 days to 14 days can be represented in a single diagram (Fig. 14.65).

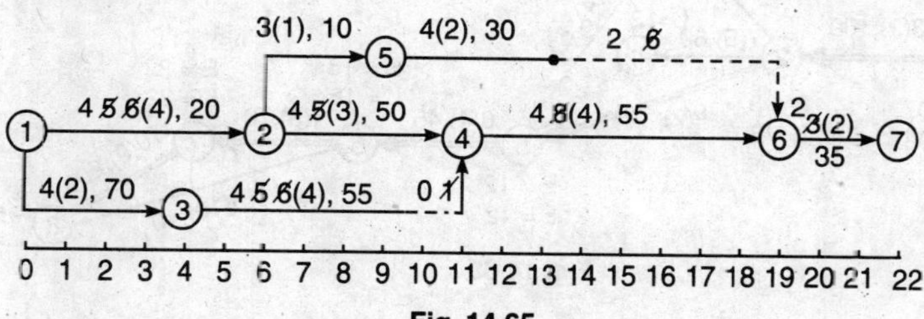

Fig. 14.65

∴ Minimum total time = 14 days,

corresponding cost = ₹ (470 + 14 × 10 + 455) = ₹ 1,065.

EXAMPLE 14.14-3

The following table gives data on normal time and cost and crash time and cost for a project.

(a) Draw the network and identify the critical path.

(b) What is the normal project duration and associated cost?

(c) Find out total float for each activity.

(d) Crash the relevant activities systematically and determine the optimum project time ana cost.

Activity	*Normal*		*Crash*	
	Time (weeks)	*Cost (₹)*	*Time (weeks)*	*Cost (₹)*
1-2	*3*	*300*	*2*	*400*
2-3	*3*	*30*	*3*	*30*
2-4	*7*	*420*	*5*	*580*
2-5	*9*	*720*	*7*	*810*
3-5	*5*	*250*	*4*	*300*
4-5	*0*	*0*	*0*	*0*
5-6	*6*	*320*	*4*	*410*
6-7	*4*	*400*	*3*	*470*
6-8	*13*	*780*	*10*	*900*
7-8	*10*	*1,000*	*9*	*1,200*
		4,220		

Indirect costs are ₹ 50 per week. [*Univ. of Madras MBA April, 2012; R.T.M. Nagpur U. B.E. (Mech.) 2011, 05; Dec., 2003*]

Solution

First, the cost slope for each activity and the normal direct cost of the project are calculated. This is shown in the table below.

Activity	:	1-2	2-3	2-4	2-5	3-5	4-5	5-6	6-7	6-8	7-8
Cost slope (₹/week)	:	100	–	80	45	50	–	45	70	40	200

Normal direct cost = ₹ 4,220.

Next, the network is drawn and the critical path is found. This is shown in Fig. 14.66.

(*a*) The critical path is 1-2-5-6-7-8.

(*b*) Normal project duration = 32 weeks,

normal project cost = ₹ (4,220 + 32 × 50) = ₹ 5,820.

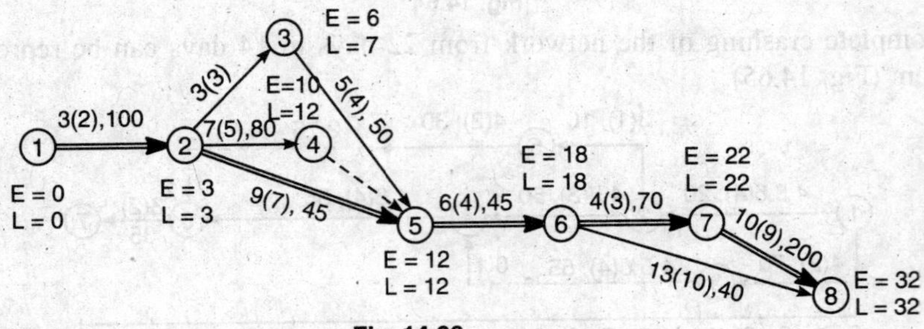

Fig. 14.66

(*c*) Total float for each activity is found in the table below.

Activity	*Duration*	*Start* *Earliest*	*Start* *Latest*	*Finish* *Earliest*	*Finish* *Latest*	*Total float*
1-2	3	0	0	3	3	0
2-3	3	3	4	6	7	1
2-4	7	3	5	10	12	2
2-5	9	3	3	12	12	0
3-5	5	6	7	11	12	1
4-5	0	10	12	10	12	2
5-6	6	12	12	18	18	0
6-7	4	18	18	22	22	0
6-8	13	18	19	31	32	1
7-8	10	22	22	32	32	0

(*d*) Since the indirect cost is ₹ 50/ week and the network is to be crashed only upto optimum time and cost, only those activities need to be crashed for which the total cost slope is ≤ ₹ 50/ week. The time-scaled diagram of the network is shown in Fig.14.67.

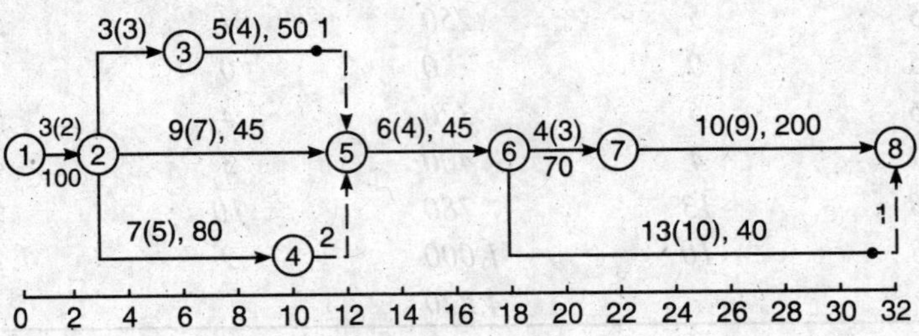

Fig. 14.67

Crash activity 5-6 by 2 days at a crash cost of ₹ *45/week.*

Additional crash cost = ₹ (2 × 45) = ₹ 90,

project duration = 30 weeks.

Crash activity 2-5 by 1 day at a crash cost of ₹ *45/week.*

Total additional crash cost = ₹ (90 + 45) = ₹ 135,

project duration = 29 weeks.

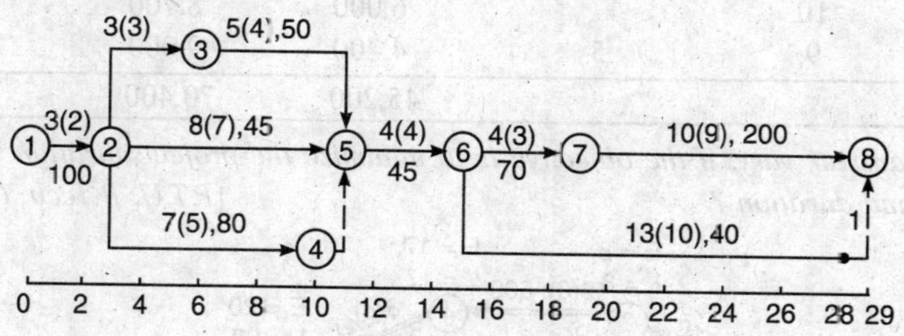

Fig. 14.68

If the activities are crashed further, the crash cost/week will be more than ₹ 50 and hence further crashing is not done. The project is shown in Fig. 14.68.

The crashing of the network from 32 weeks to 29 weeks can be represented in a single diagram (Fig. 14.69).

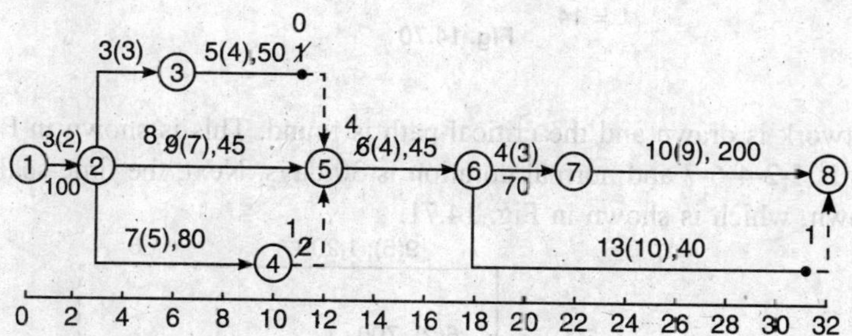

Fig. 14.69

The above results are summarised in the table below :

Duration (weeks)	*Normal direct cost* (₹)	*Crash cost* (₹)	*Indirect cost* (₹)	*Total cost* (₹)
32	4,220	–	1,600	5,820
31	4,220	45	1,550	5,815
30	4,220	90	1,500	5,810
29	4,220	135	1,450	5,805

∴ Optimum project duration = 29 weeks,

optimum total project cost = ₹ 5,805.

EXAMPLE 14.14-4

The following table gives the various activities, their durations and direct costs. The indirect cost is ₹*2,000 per week. Find the optimum cost schedule using CPM technique.*

Activity	*Time in weeks*		*Cost in* ₹		*Cost in* ₹ *to expedite per week*
	Normal	*Crash*	*Normal*	*Crash*	
1-2	8	4	3,000	6,000	750
1-3	5	3	4,000	8,000	2,000

2-4	9	6	4,000	5,500	500
3-5	7	5	2,000	3,200	600
2-5	5	1	8,000	12,000	1,000
4-6	3	2½	10,000	11,200	2,400
5-6	6	2	4,000	6,800	700
6-7	10	7	6,000	8,700	900
5-7	9	5	4,200	9,000	1,200
			45,200	70,400	

Does your answer vary, if the objective is to minimize the project duration ? In that case what is the cost and duration ? [*P.T.U. B.Tech. (Mech.) 2008*]

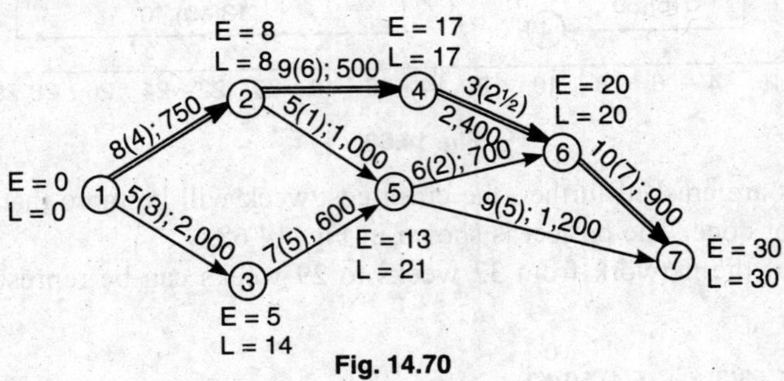

Fig. 14.70

Solution

First, the network is drawn and the critical path is found. This is shown in Fig. 14.70.

Critical path is 1-2-4-6-7 and normal duration is 30 days. Next, the time-scaled diagram of the network is drawn, which is shown in Fig. 14.71.

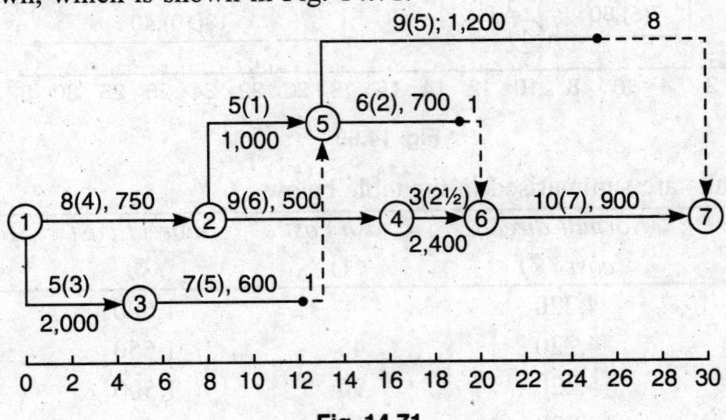

Fig. 14.71

Crash activity 2–4 by one week.

The various alternative activities and their crash costs are given below :

Activity	*Cost (₹)*	*Activity*	*Cost (₹)*	*Activity*	*Cost (₹)*	*Activity*	*Cost (₹)*
1-2	750	2-4	500	4-6	2,400	6-7	900
3-5	Nil	5-6	Nil	5-6	Nil	5-7	Nil
		5-7	Nil	5-7	Nil		
	750		500		2,400		900

Since activity 2-4 has the lowest associated cost of ₹ 500/week, it is crashed by one week.

∴ Additional crash cost = ₹ 500,

project duration = 29 weeks.

The crashed network is shown in Fig. 14.72.

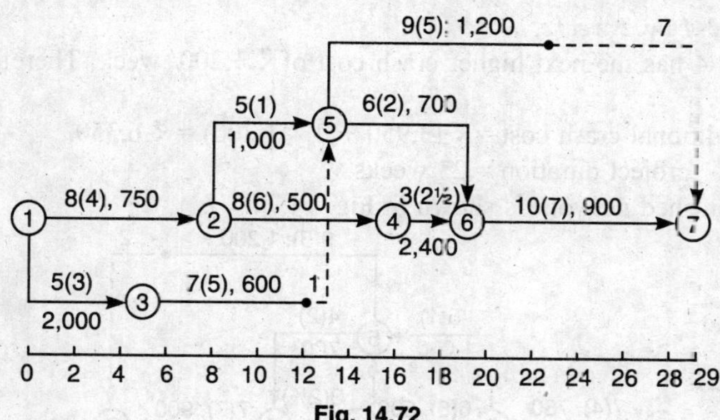

Fig. 14.72

Crash activity 1-2 by one week.

The various alternative activities and their crash costs are given below :

Activity	*Cost (₹)*	*Activity*	*Cost (₹)*	*Activity*	*Cost (₹)*	*Activity*	*Cost (₹)*
1-2	750	2-4	500	4-6	2,400	6-7	900
3-5	Nil	5-6	700	5-6	700	5-7	Nil
		5-7	Nil	5-7	Nil		
	750		1,200		3,100		900

Since activity 1-2 has the lowest associated cost of ₹ 750/ week, it is crashed by one week.

∴ Total additional crash cost = ₹ (500 + 750)
= ₹ 1,250,
project duration = 28 weeks.

The crashed network is shown in Fig. 14.73.

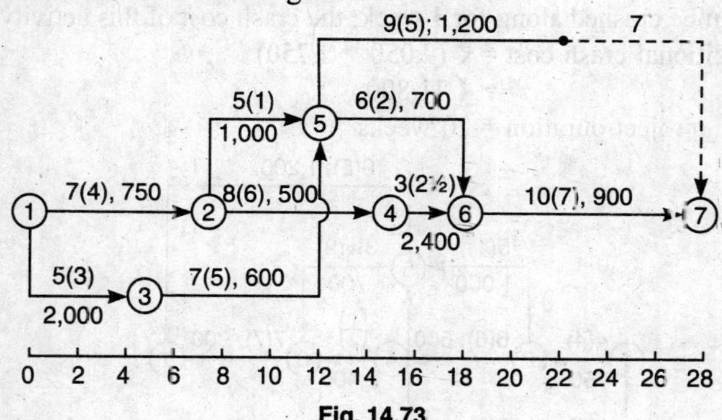

Fig. 14.73

Crash activity 6-7 by 3 weeks.

The various alternative activities and their crash costs are given below :

Activity	*Cost (₹)*	*Activity*	*Cost (₹)*	*Activity*	*Cost (₹)*	*Activity*	*Cost (₹)*
1-2	750	2-4	500	4-6	2,400	6-7	900
3-5	600	5-6	700	5-6	700	5-7	Nil
		5-7	Nil	5-7	Nil		
	1,350		1,200		3,100		900

Since activity 6-7 has the lowest crash cost of ₹ 900/ week, it is crashed by 3 weeks.

∴ Total additional crash cost = ₹ (1,250 + 900 × 3)
= ₹ 3,950,
project duration = 25 weeks.

Crash activity 2-4 by 2 weeks.

Now activity 2-4 has the next higher crash cost of ₹ 1,200/ week. Therefore, it is crashed by 2 weeks.

∴ Total additional crash cost = ₹ (3,950 + 2 × 1,200) = ₹ 6,350,

project duration = 23 weeks.

The resulting crashed network is shown in Fig. 14.74.

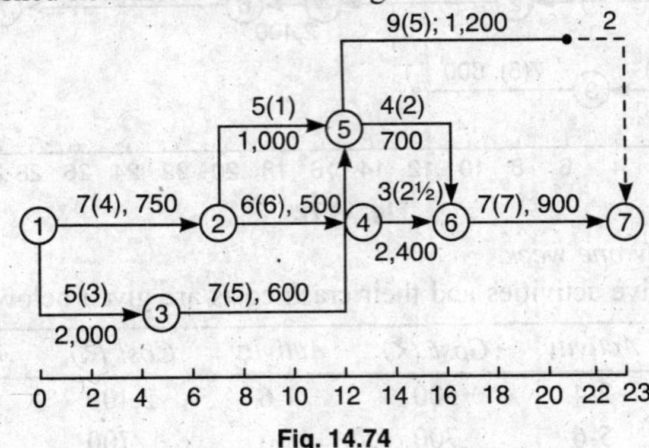

Fig. 14.74

Crash activity 1-2 by 2 weeks.

Next, activity 1-2 can be crashed by 2 weeks at an extra crash cost of ₹ 1,350 per week.

∴ Total additional crash cost = ₹ (6,350 + 2 × 1,350)

= ₹ 9,050,

project duration = 21 weeks.

Crash activity 1-2 by 1 week.

Activity 1-2 can be further crashed by 1 week. Since activity 3-5 has been fully crashed to 5 weeks, activity 1-3 can be crashed along for 1 week; the crash cost of this activity is ₹ 2,000/week.

∴ Total additional crash cost = ₹ (9,050 + 2,750)

= ₹ 11,800,

project duration = 20 weeks.

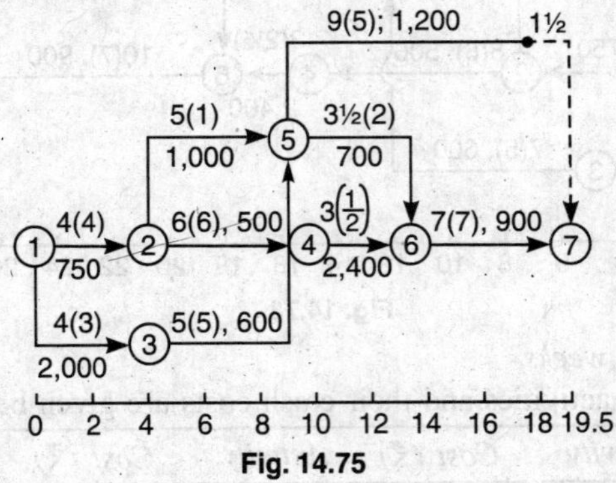

Fig. 14.75

Crash activity 4-6 by ½ week.

Next, activity 4-6 can be crashed for 1/2 week. The cost slope of this activity is ₹ (2,400 + 700) = ₹ 3,100/week. The resulting crashed network is shown in Fig. 14.75.

$$\text{Total additional crash cost} = ₹ \left(11,800 + \frac{3,100}{2}\right)$$

= ₹ 13,350,

$$\text{project duration} = 19\ \frac{1}{2}\ \text{weeks.}$$

The project cannot be crashed further.

The complete crashing of the network from 30 days to 19.5 days can be shown in a single diagram (Fig. 14.76) also.

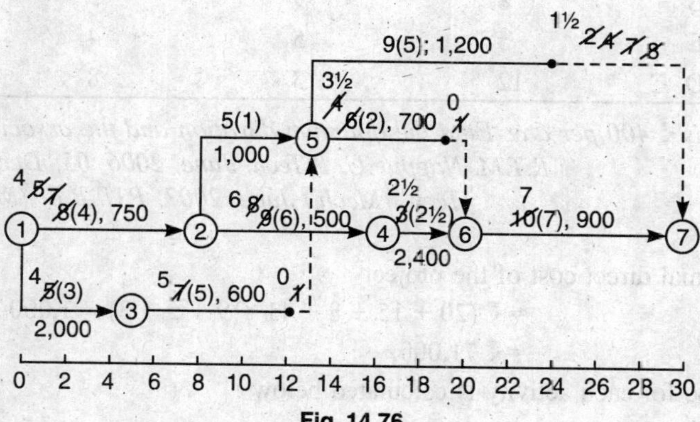

Fig. 14.76

The following table representing the total cost for different durations of the project is now constructed:

Week	*Direct cost (₹)*	*Indirect cost (₹)*	*Crash cost (₹)*	*Total cost (₹)*
30	45,200	60,000	0	1,05,200
29	45,200	58,000	500	1,03,700
28	45,200	56,000	1,250	1,02,950
27	45,200	54,000	2,150	1,01,350
26	45,200	52,000	3,050	1,00,250
25	45,200	50,000	3,950	99,150
24	45,200	48,000	5,150	98,350
23	45,200	46,000	6,350	97,550
22	45,200	44,000	7,700	96,900
21	45,200	42,000	9,050	96,250
20	45,200	40,000	11,800	97,000
$19\frac{1}{2}$	45,200	39,000	13,350	97,550

From the above table, minimum cost = ₹ 96,250,

minimum cost schedule = 21 days.

Minimum project duration = $19\frac{1}{2}$ days,

corresponding total cost = ₹ 97,550.

EXAMPLE 14.14-5

The following is a table showing details of a project :

Task	*Immediate predecessor*	*Normal Time (weeks)*	*Normal Cost (₹'000)*	*Crash Time (weeks)*	*Crash Cost (₹'000)*
A	–	10	20	7	30
B	–	8	15	6	20

C	B	5	8	4	14
D	B	6	11	4	15
E	B	8	9	5	15
F	E	5	5	4	8
G	A, D, C	12	3	8	4

Indirect cost is ₹ 400 per day. Find the optimum duration and the associated minimum project cost. [*R.T.M. Nagpur U. B.Tech. June, 2006, 05; Dec., 2004; H.P.U.B. Tech. (Mech.) June, 2007; P.U. B.E. (Mech.) Nov., 2006*]

Solution

The total normal direct cost of the project

$$= ₹ (20 + 15 + 8 + 11 + 9 + 5 + 3) \times 1{,}000$$
$$= ₹ 71{,}000.$$

The cost slope for each activity is calculated below :

Activity	:	A	B	C	D	E	F	G
Cost slope	:	10/3	2.5	6	2	2	3	0.25
(₹ '000/week)								

Next, the network is drawn and the critical path is found. This is shown in Fig. 14.77. Project duration is 26 weeks and 1-2-3-4-6 is the critical path.

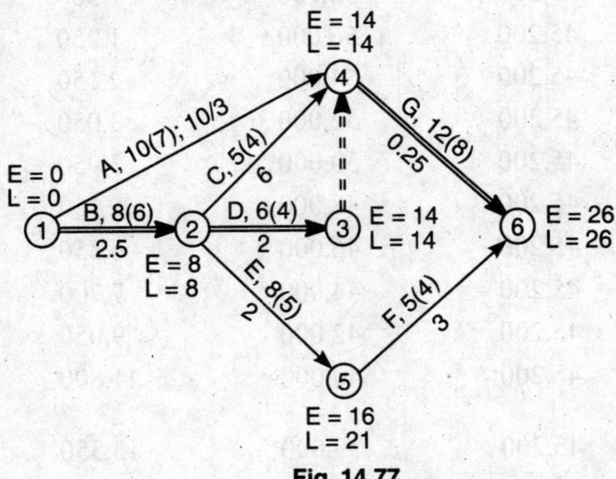

Fig. 14.77

To crash the network, time-scaled diagram is drawn first. This is shown in Fig. 14.78.

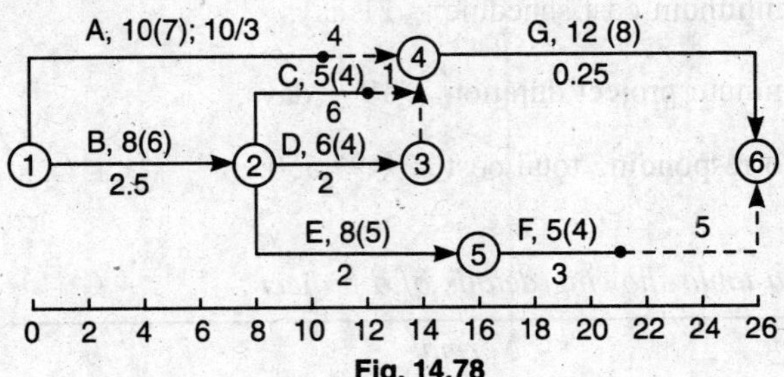

Fig. 14.78

Since the network is to be crashed to find the optimum duration and the indirect cost is ₹ 400/day or ₹ 2,800/week, the critical activities will be crashed so long as the cost of crashing them/week does not exceed ₹ 2,800.

Crash activity 4-6 by four weeks.

The various alternative activities and their crash costs are given below:

Activity	*Cost* (₹)	*Activity*	*Cost* (₹)	*Activity*	*Cost* (₹)
1-2	2,500	2-3	2,000	4-6	250
1-4	Nil	2-4	Nil	5-6	Nil
		1-4	Nil		
		2-5/5-6	Nil		
	2,500		2,000		250

Since activity 4-6 has the lowest associated cost of ₹ 250/week, it is crashed by 4 weeks.

∴ Project duration = 22 weeks.

Additional crash cost = ₹ (4 × 250) = ₹ 1,000.

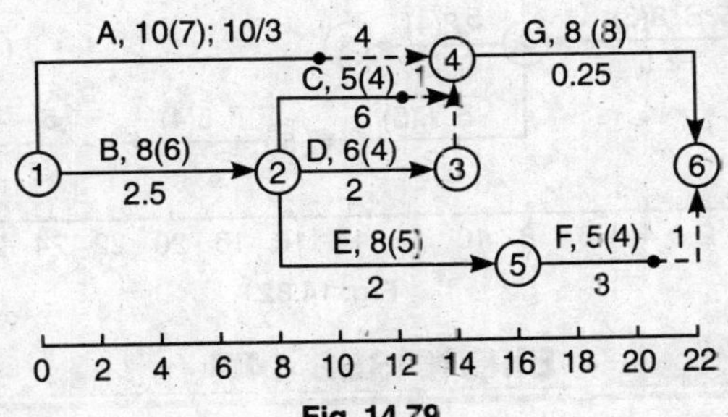

Fig. 14.79

The crashed network is shown in Fig. 14.79.

Crash activity 2-3 by one week.

As seen earlier, activity 2-3 can be crashed by one week at an additional crash cost of ₹ 2,000 per week.

∴ Project duration = 21 weeks,

total additional crash cost = ₹ (1,000 + 2,000) = ₹ 3,000.

The crashed network is shown in Fig. 14.80.

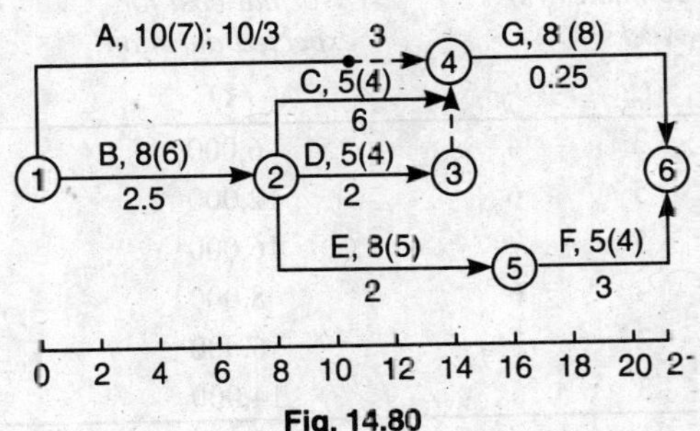

Fig. 14.80

Crash activity 1-2 by 2 weeks.

As indicated earlier, activity 1-2 can be crashed by 2 weeks at an additional crash cost of ₹ 2,500 per week.

∴ Project duration = 19 weeks,

total additional crash cost = ₹ (3,000 + 2,500 × 2)

= ₹ 8,000.

The crashed network is shown in Fig. 14.81.

Activity 2-3 can be crashed further by one week but the crash cost will be more than the indirect cost of ₹ 2,800 per week. Therefore, it is not crashed.

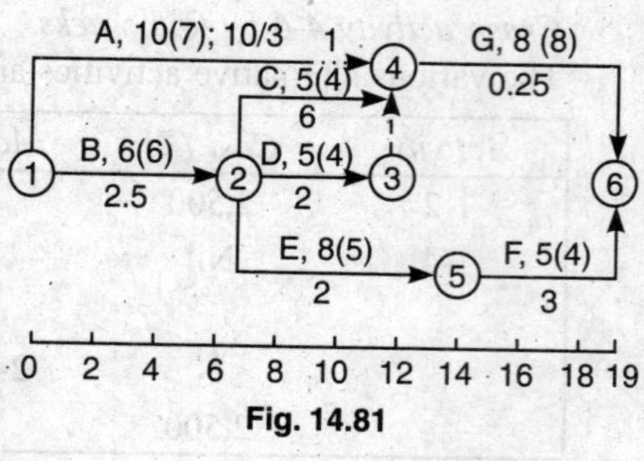

Fig. 14.81

∴ Minimum cost project duration

= 19 weeks,

optimum project cost

= Normal direct cost + total additional crash cost + indirect cost of 19 weeks

= ₹ [71,000 + 8,000 + 2,800 × 19]

= ₹ 1,32,200.

The complete crashing of the network from 26 weeks to 19 weeks is represented in a single diagram (Fig. 14.82).

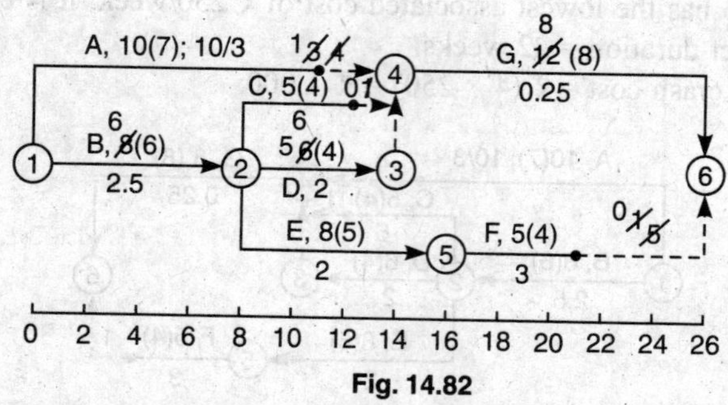

Fig. 14.82

EXERCISES 14.4

1. Explain crashing of project networks.
   [*P.T.U. MBA May, 2015; G.N.D.U. B.Com Sept., 2014; April, 2013; Sept., 2011; April, 2009; V.T.U. Karnataka B.Tech. (Mech.) 2012; J.N.T.U. MBA April, 2012; G.N.D.U. B.Com. April, 2006; Sept., 2000*]
2. Explain project time-project cost trade off.
   [*V.T.U. Karnataka B.Tech. (Mech.) 2012; Osmania U.MBA, 2010; Nagpur U. B.E. (Mech.) 2003*]
3. As the project manager of Quick Construction Company, you are involved in drawing a PERT network for laying the foundation of a new art museum. The relevant information for all the activities of this project is given in the table below:

Activity	*Time estimates (in weeks)*			*Normal cost for expected duration*	*Crash cost*	*Immediate predecessors*
	t_0	t_m	t_p	(₹)	(₹)	
A	2	3	4	6,000	8,000	—
B	4	5	6	12,000	13,500	A
C	3	5	7	16,000	22,000	A
D	2	4	6	8,000	10,000	A
E	1	2	3	6,000	7,500	C, D
F	1	3	5	14,000	20,000	B, E
				62,000		

(*i*) Construct the PERT network for the project and determine the critical path and the expected duration of the project.

(*ii*) The Director of the company is not impressed by your PERT analysis. He draws your attention that the project must be completed by seven weeks and refers to the penalty clause in the agreement which provides for payment of penalty at the rate of ₹ 2,500 for every week or part there of exceeding seven weeks. Your Director also strongly believes that the time duration of various activities of the project can be crashed to their optimistic time estimates with the crashing costs mentioned in the above table. Determine the optimum duration of the project if your objective is to minimize the sum of the project execution cost and the penalty cost. [*P.T.U. June, 1999*]

(*Ans.* (*i*) 1–2–4–5–6, 13 weeks (*ii*) 11 weeks, ₹ 75,500.)

4. The activity data for a project are given in the table below :

Task	*Predecessor*	*Normal time (weeks)*	*Minimum time (weeks)*	*Crash cost per week* (₹)
A	–	8	7	1,000
B	A	3	2	500
C	A	5	4	1,200
D	B, C	6	5	1,500
E	D	3	2	800
F	D	5	4	900
G	E, F	6	5	3,000

(*a*) What is the minimum possible project duration attainable ?

(*b*) If the project is to be shortened by two weeks, which tasks should be crashed and how much while minimizing direct costs ? [*H.P.U. B.Tech. (Mech.) 2012; U.P. Tech. U. MBA, 2009*]

5. The following table gives the activities of the project along with their normal durations and costs as well as crash durations and costs :

Activity (i – j)	*Normal*		*Crash*	
	Duration (days)	*Cost* (₹)	*Duration (days)*	*Cost* (₹)
1 - 2	5	560	4	600
2 - 3	8	1,640	6	1,820
2 - 4	11	2,360	7	2,580
2 - 5	9	1,320	7	1,800
3 - 5	10	600	8	1,000
4 - 5	7	1,800	5	1,970
5 - 6	5	680	4	960

The indirect cost is ₹ 160 per day.

(*a*) Draw the project network and determine the critical path based on normal durations of the activities.

(*b*) What is the total normal cost of the project ?

(*c*) Suitably crashing the activities, obtain the optimum duration and the corresponding cost.

[*H.P.U. B.Tech. (Mech.) June, 2015; Mumbai U. MBA, 2010*]

6. Relevant information about the project undertaken by Best Construction Company is given in the following table :

Activity	*Immediate predecessor*	*Time in weeks*		*Cost in ₹*	
		Normal	*Crash*	*Normal*	*Crash*
A	–	3	2	6,000	8,000
B	A	5	4	12,000	13,500
C	A	5	3	16,000	22,000
D	A	4	2	8,000	10,000
E	C, D	2	1	6,000	7,500
F	B, E	3	1	14,000	20,000

(*a*) Construct the network and determine the critical path.

(*b*) Find the duration of the project.

(*c*) The Director of the company wants the project to be completed within 7 weeks and refers to the penalty clause in the agreement that provides for payment of penalty at the rate of ₹ 25,000 for every week exceeding 7 weeks. Determine the optimal duration of the project so as to minimize the sum of the project execution cost and the penalty cost.

[*H.P.U. B.Tech. Nov., 2015; Mumbai U. MBA, 2010*]

7. The following table contains details of activities in a construction project and other relevant information:

Activities	Normal		Crash	
	Time (days)	Cost (₹)	Time (days)	Cost (₹)
1 - 2	20	600	17	720
1 - 3	25	200	25	200
2 - 3	10	300	8	440
2 - 4	12	400	6	700
3 - 4	5	300	2	420
4 - 5	10	300	5	600
4 - 6	5	600	3	900
5 - 7	10	500	5	800
6 - 7	8	400	3	700

(*a*) Draw network diagram for the project.

(*b*) Crash the activities step by step until all the paths are critical.

[*H.P.U. B.Tech. (Mech.) Sept., 2013; G.N.D.U. B.Com. April. 2010; R.T.M. Nagpur U. B.Tech. Dec., 2006*]

[**Ans.** 37 days; ₹ 4,860;]

8. The following table gives the activities and other relevant data for a project :

Activity	Normal time (days)	Crash time (days)	Normal cost (₹)	Crash cost (₹)
1 - 2	4	3	600	800
1 - 3	2	2	400	400
1 - 4	5	4	750	900
2 - 3	7	5	400	600
2 - 5	7	6	800	1,000
3 - 5	2	1	500	650
4 - 5	5	4	600	850

Indirect cost per day for the project is ₹ 200.

(*a*) Draw the project network.

(*b*) Find the normal duration and cost of the project.

(*c*) Find the optimum duration and cost of the project.

[*H.P.U. B.Tech. June, 2015; P.T.U. MBA Dec., 2013; G.N.D.U. B.Com. April, 2008*]

9. The following table shows for each activity, the normal time, the shortest time and the cost per day for reducing the time. The contract includes a penalty clause of ₹ 100 per day over 17 days. The overhead cost per day is ₹ 160.

Activity	Normal time (days)	Shortest time (days)	Cost of reduction per day (₹)
1 - 2	6	4	80
1 - 3	8	4	90
1 - 4	5	3	30
2 - 4	3	3	–
2 - 5	5	3	40
3 - 6	12	8	200
4 - 6	8	5	50
5 - 6	6	6	–

The cost of completing the eight activities in normal time is ₹ 6,500. Calculate the normal duration, its cost and the critical path. Also calculate the cost per time function for the project and state the lowest cost and associated time.

[*G.N.D.U. B.Com. Sept., 2008*]

10. The relevant data for a project are given below :

Activitiy	*Time in days*		*Direct cost in ₹*	
	Normal	*Crash*	*Normal*	*Crash*
1 - 2	16	13	12,000	19,500
1 - 3	18	15	9,000	13,500
2 - 3	14	11	11,000	14,000
2 - 4	15	13	13,000	20,000
3 - 4	15	15	10,000	10,000

Indirect cost is ₹ 8,000 per week. Determine

(*a*) Normal duration and normal cost.

(*b*) Optimum duration and cost.

(*c*) Minimum duration and associated cost. [*G.D.N.U. B.Com. Sept., 2002*]

11. The data for a project are given in the table below :

Activitiy	*Time in days*		*Direct cost in ₹*	
	Normal	*Crash*	*Normal*	*Crash*
1 - 2	4	3	60	90
1 - 3	2	1	38	60
1 - 4	6	4	150	250
2 - 4	5	3	150	250
2 - 5	7	5	115	175
3 - 4	2	2	100	100
4 - 5	4	2	100	240

Indirect cost also varies as follows :

Days	:	15	14	13	12	11	10	9	8	7	6
Cost (₹)	:	600	500	400	250	175	100	75	50	35	25

Draw the network. Find the optimal cost and duration. Also find the minimum duration and the associated cost. [*R.T.M. Nagpur U. B.Tech. (Mech.) June, 2007; G.N.D.U. B.Com. Sept., 2000; P.U. M.Com., 2001*]

(*Ans.* ₹ 943, 10 days ; ₹ 1,093, 8 days.)

12. The utility data for a network are given below :

Activities	*Normal*		*Crash*	
	Time (days)	*Cost (₹)*	*Time (days)*	*Cost (₹)*
1 - 2	8	100	6	200
1 - 3	4	150	2	350
2 - 4	2	50	1	90
3 - 4	5	100	1	200

Indirect cost is ₹ 100 per day. Crash systematically and determine the optimum project duration and cost. [*V.T.U. Karntaka B.E. Jan., 2010*]

13. Normal and crash durations with costs for various activities involved in a repair work are given in the table below. The indirect cost per day is ₹ 2,000.

Activities	*Time (days)*		*Cost (₹)*	
	Normal	*Crash*	*Normal*	*Crash*
1 - 2	6	2	4,000	12,000
1 - 3	8	3	3,000	6,000
2 - 4	7	4	2,800	4,000
3 - 4	12	8	9,000	11,000
4 - 6	3	1	10,000	13,000
5 - 6	5	2	4,900	7,000

3 - 5	7	3	1,800	5,000
5 - 7	11	5	6,600	12,000
6 - 7	10	6	4,000	8,400

(*a*) Draw network diagram for these activities indicating earliest and latest start and finishing times.

(*c*) What is the optimum time and cost ?

(*d*) What is the minimum time and cost ? [*R.T.M. Nagpur B.E. (Mech.) Sept., 2010*]

14. Find optimum schedule for a project for which data are given below :

Activity	*Normal*		*Crash*	
	Time (hr)	*Cost (₹)*	*Time (hr)*	*Cost (₹)*
1 - 2	80	1,000	60	2,000
1 - 3	40	1,500	20	350
2 - 4	20	500	10	900
2 - 5	100	1,000	50	4,000
3 - 4	50	1,000	10	2,000
4 - 5	30	800	10	1,000

Find and indicate cost slopes. [*R.T.M. Nagpur U. B.Tech. Dec., 2004*]

15. The required data for a small project consisting of different activities are given below :

Activity	*Dependence*	*Normal duration (days)*	*Normal cost (₹)*	*Crash duration (days)*	*Crash cost (₹)*
A	—	6	300	5	400
B	—	8	400	6	600
C	A	7	400	5	600
D	B	12	1,000	4	1,400
E	C	8	800	8	800
F	B	7	400	6	500
G	D, E	5	1,000	3	1,400
H	F	8	500	5	700

(*i*) Draw the network and find out the normal project length and minimum project length.

(*ii*) If the project is to be completed in 21 days with minimum crash cost which activities should be crashed and by how many days ? [*R.T.M. Nagpur U. B.Tech. Dec., 2003*]

16. The table below provides cost and time estimates of the seven activities of a project.

Activity (i-j)	*Time estimates (weeks)*		*Direct cost estimates (₹ in thousands)*	
	Normal	*Crash*	*Normal*	*Crash*
1-2	2	1	10	15
1-3	8	5	15	21
2-4	4	3	20	24
3-4	1	1	7	7
3-5	2	1	8	15
4-6	5	3	10	16
5-6	6	2	12	36

(*i*) Draw the project network corresponding to the normal times.

(*ii*) Determine the critical path and the normal duration and normal cost of the project.

(*iii*) Crash the activities so that the project completion time reduces to 9 weeks, with minimum additional cost. [*P.T.U. B.Tech. (C.Sc.) 2000; Jammu U. B.E. (Mech.) 2004*]

17. Table below shows jobs, their normal time and cost and crash time and cost estimates for a project.

Job	*Normal time (days)*	*Cost (₹)*	*Crash time (days)*	*Cost (₹)*
1-2	6	1,400	4	1,900
1-3	8	2,000	5	2,800
2-3	4	1,100	2	1,500
2-4	3	800	2	1,400
3-4	Dummy	—	—	—
3-5	6	900	3	1,600
4-6	10	2,500	6	3,500
5-6	3	500	2	800
		9,200		

Indirect cost for the project is ₹ 300 per day.

(*i*) Draw the network of the project.

(*ii*) What is the normal duration and cost of the project ?

(*iii*) If all activities are crashed, what will be the minimum project duration and corresponding cost ?

(*iv*) Find the optimal duration & minimum project cost.

[*R.T.M. Nagpur U. B.E. (I.T.) 2009 ; IGNOU MBA, 2000*]

(*Ans.* (*ii*) 20 days; ₹ 15,200 (*iii*) 12 days; ₹ 16,534.34
(*iv*) 17 days ; ₹ 15,000.)

18. The following time-cost table (time in weeks, cost in rupees) applies to a project. Use it to arrive at the network associated with completing the project in minimum time at minimum cost.

	Normal		*Crash*	
Activity	*Time*	*Cost*	*Time*	*Cost*
1-2	2	800	1	1,400
1-3	5	1,000	2	2,000
1-4	5	1,000	3	1,800
2-4	1	500	1	500
2-5	5	1,500	3	2,100
3-4	4	2,000	3	3,000
3-5	6	1,200	4	1,600
4-5	3	900	2	1,600

(*Ans.* Crash activity 1-3 by 3 weeks, 4-5 by 1 week and 3-4 by 1 week, giving an optimal 7-weeks duration project at a cost of ₹ 11,800.)

19. The utility data for a network are given below. Crash the network to minimum project duration and determine the project cost for that duration.

	Normal		*Crash*	
Activity	*Time (weeks)*	*Cost (₹)*	*Time (weeks)*	*Cost (₹)*
0-1	1	5,000	1	5,000
1-2	3	5,000	2	12,000
1-3	7	11,000	4	17,000
2-3	5	10,000	3	12,000
2-4	8	8,500	6	12,500
3-4	4	8,500	2	16,500
4-5	1	5,000	1	5,000

[*Jammu U. B.E. (Mech.) 2004*]

(*Ans.* 10 days; ₹ 74,000.)

20. Consider a network problem for which the utility data are given in the table. Crash systematically the activities and determine the optimum project duration and cost.

Activity	*Normal*		*Crash*		ΔT	ΔC	$\frac{\Delta D}{\Delta T}$
	Time (days)	*Cost (₹)*	*Time (days)*	*Cost (₹)*			
1-2	8	100	6	200	2	100	50
1-3	4	150	2	350	2	200	100
2-4	2	50	1	90	1	40	40
2-5	10	100	5	400	5	300	60
3-4	5	100	1	200	4	100	25
4-5	3	80	1	100	2	20	10
	Total	580					

Indirect cost = ₹ 70 per day. (*Ans.* 11 days; ₹ 1,760.)

21. The utility data for a network are given in the table. Crash the network to minimum possible duration. and find the corresponding optimal project cost. The total normal cost of the project is ₹ 9,00,000.

Activity	*Duration (weeks)*		*Cost slope (thousands of ₹)*
	Normal	*Crash*	
1-2	4	2	7
1-3	7	4	4
2-3	7	4	3
2-4	5	3	12
3-5	6	3	6
4-5	4	1	8
4-6	10	6	10
5-6	6	6	—
5-7	8	6	10
6-8	6	4	12
7-8	5	2	7

22. The activity data for a project are given in the table. Find the
(*a*) normal duration and the normal cost.
(*b*) optimal duration and the minimum total cost.
(*c*) minimum duration and the associated project cost.

Activity	*Normal*		*Crash*		ΔT	ΔC	$\frac{\Delta C}{\Delta T}$
	Time (weeks)	*Cost (₹)*	*Time (weeks)*	*Cost (₹)*			
1-2	8	7,000	3	10,000	5	3,000	600
1-3	4	6,000	2	8,000	2	2,000	1,000
2-3	0	0	0	0	0	0	0
2-5	6	9,000	1	11,500	5	2,500	500
3-4	7	2,500	5	3,000	2	500	250
4-6	12	10,000	8	16,000	4	6,000	1,500
5-6	15	12,000	10	16,000	5	4,000	800
5-7	7	12,000	6	14,000	1	2,000	2,000
6-8	5	10,000	5	10,000	0	0	—
7-8	14	6,000	7	7,400	7	1,400	200
7-9	8	6,000	5	12,000	3	6,000	2,000
8-9	6	6,000	4	7,800	2	1,800	900
	Total	86,500		1,15,700			

Indirect cost = ₹ 1,000 per week. [P.U. MBA, 2000]

(*Ans.* (*a*) 41 days; ₹ 1,27,500 (*b*) 30 days; ₹ 1,25,700 (*c*) 25 days; ₹ 1,32,700.)

23. (*a*) The following data pertain to a CPM network. It is desired to compress the project to the least possible duration day by day and estimate the extra cost.

i-j	T_n	T_C	*Cost slope*
1-2	3	2	700
1-3	7	4	200
2-3	5	3	100
2-4	8	6	200
3-4	4	2	400

(*b*) If there is an indirect cost of ₹ 800 per day, what will be the least project duration and the associated cost ?

(*Ans.* (*a*) 8 days, ₹ 2,100;
(*b*) 9 days, ₹ 8,400.)

24. A small maintenance project consists of jobs in the table below. With each job is listed its normal time and minimum or crash time in days. The cost in ₹ per day of each job is also given.

Job i-j	*Normal duration*	*Minimum (crash) duration*	*Cost/day (₹)*
1-2	9	6	20
1-3	9	5	25
1-4	15	10	30
2-4	5	3	10
3-4	10	6	15
4-5	2	1	40

(*a*) What is the normal project length and the minimum project length ?

(*b*) Determine the minimum crashing cost of schedules ranging from normal length down to, and including, the minimum length schedule. That is, if L = length of the schedule, find the costs of schedules which are L, L – 1, L – 2 and so on.

(*c*) Overhead costs total ₹ 60 per day. What is the optimum length schedule in terms of both crashing and overhead cost? List the scheduled duration of each job for your solution.

[*P.U. B.E. (Elect.) 1999, 1998; IGNOU MBA, 1999*]

(*Ans.* (*a*) 20 days, 12 days;
(*b*) 12 days, C_c = ₹ 335, C_T = ₹ 1,055
(*c*) 15 days.)

25. The utility data for a network are given below. The activity durations are in days and the cost in rupees. The indirect cost per day is ₹ 250. Determine the optimum project schedule.

Activity	*Normal*		*Crash*	
	Time (days)	*Direct cost (₹)*	*Time (days)*	*Direct cost (₹)*
1–2	4	600	2	800
1–3	2	500	1	900
2–4	6	1,000	3	1,750
2–5	4	1,200	4	1,200
3–5	5	1,000	3	1,200
3–7	10	2,500	5	3,500
4–5	5	1,300	5	1,300
5–6	8	2,000	6	2,100
5–7	0	0	0	0
6–8	7	2,000	7	2,000
7–8	8	1,600	5	1,780

[*Kuru. U. B.Tech. (Mech.) 1992*]

(*Ans.* Crash 1-2 by 2 days, 2-4 by 1 day, 5-6 by 2 days;
₹ 13,000, 25 days.)

26. Table below gives the data for a network of a product development project. The marketing department realises that if the project is introduced in the market ahead of its completion date, additional profits are available. What would be the additional cost to crash the project by 6 weeks?

Activity	Time		Cost	
	Normal (weeks)	Crash (weeks)	Normal (₹)	Crash (₹)
10-20	3	2	2,000	4,500
10-30	6	5	2,000	5,000
—		4		9,000
20-40	6	5	4,000	9,000
20-50	10	8	9,500	12,000
		7		15,000
30-70	9	8	7,000	8,000
		7		10,500
30-80	10	8	9,500	12,000
		7		15,000
40-60	6	5	3,500	4,000
40-90	6	4	2,000	4,000
		3		7,000
60-110	7	6	3,000	4,000
		5		8,000
70-100		Dummy		
80-100	5	4	3,500	4,000
		2		8,000
90-110		Dummy		
100-120	6	3	6,000	9,900
110-120	5	4	2,000	4,000
120-130	2	1	2,500	4,000

(*Ans.* ₹ 17,100.)

27. The following table gives the activities in a construction project and other relevant information:

Activity	Predecessor	Time (days)		Direct cost (₹)	
		Normal	Crash	Normal	Crash
A	—	4	3	60	90
B	—	6	4	150	250
C	—	2	1	38	60
D	A	5	3	150	250
E	C	2	2	100	100
F	A	7	5	115	175
G	D, B, E	4	2	100	240

Indirect costs vary as follows :

Days	:	15	14	13	12	11	10	9	8	7	6
Cost (₹)	:	600	500	400	250	175	100	75	50	35	25

(*a*) Draw an arrow diagram for the project.

(*b*) Determine the project duration which will return in minimum total project cost.

[*Ans.* 10 days; ₹ 5346]

28. A Project has 7 activities. The relevant data are given below.

[*P.T.U. MBA May, 2015; HPU B.Tech. (Mech.) Dec., 2007 P.U. M.Com., 2001*]

Activity	Dependence	Normal duration (days)	Crash duration (days)	Normal cost (₹)	Crash cost (₹)
A	–	7	5	500	900
B	A	4	2	400	600
C	A	5	5	500	500
D	A	6	4	800	1,000
E	B, C	7	4	700	1,000
F	C, D	5	2	800	1,400
G	E, F	6	4	800	1,600

The project manager wishes to complete the project in the minimum possible time. However, he is not authorised to spend more than ₹ 5,000 on crashing. Suggest the least cost schedule. Assume that there is no indirect or utility cost

[*H.P.U.B. Tech. (Mech.) Dec., 2009*]

(*Ans*. 14 weeks; cost: ₹ 4,600.)

29. The time and cost estimates of different activities of a project and their precedence relationships are given below.

Activity	*Preceding*	*Time (weeks)*		*Cost (₹)*	
		Normal	*Crash*	*Normal*	*Crash*
A	–	6	4	10,000	14,000
B	–	4	3	5,000	8,000
C	A	3	2	4,000	5,000
D	B	8	3	1,000	6,000
E	B	14	6	9,000	13,000
F	C, D	8	4	7,000	8,000

Overhead costs amount to ₹ 1,000 per week.

(*i*) Draw the network and show the critical path.

(*ii*) Crash the network to the minimum possible duration. What will be the critical activities after such crashing? [*H.P.U.B.E. (Mech.) 2008; IGNOU MBA, 2003*]

(*Ans.* (*i*) B-D-F (*ii*) 10 weeks; A-C-F, B-D-F.)

30. The basic cost-time data for jobs in a project are given below.

Job	*Normal*		*Crash*		*Crashing cost per*
	Time (days)	*Cost (₹)*	*Time (days)*	*Cost (₹)*	*day (₹/day)*
A	3	140	2	210	70
B	6	215	5	275	60
C	2	160	1	240	80
D	4	130	3	180	50
E	2	170	1	250	80
F	7	165	4	285	40
G	4	210	3	290	80
H	3	110	2	160	50

The activities, dependencies are as below:

(*i*) A, B, C are starting activities, (*ii*) Activities D, E and F can start when A is completed, (*iii*) C can start after B and D are completed, (*iv*) H can start after C and E are completed, (*v*) G, H and F are final activities. Draw the network and indicate the critical path and the total time of completing the project. If the project is to be completed in 8 days, what is the minimum cost to be incurred? Indicate the cheapest schedule.

[*P.U. B.B.A., 2002; M.B.A., 2001*]

31. A list of activities along with their precedence requirement, normal time and cost and crash time and cost is given in the table below.

Activity	*Immediate predecessor*	*Normal*		*Crash*	
		Time (days)	*Cost (₹)*	*Time (days)*	*Cost (₹)*
A	–	4	300	2	450
B	A	9	600	5	960
C	A	6	620	4	780
D	B	4	320	3	395
E	B, D	6	1,440	3	1,980
F	C, D	4	350	2	470
G	E, F	3	270	2	335

(*a*) Draw the network.

(*b*) What are the normal and crash costs and durations of the project ? How many days will be saved and what will be the project cost if all the activities are crashed to the maximum possible extent ?

It is expected that earlier completion of the project will result in additional profit of ₹ 50 per day. The indirect cost is ₹ 80 per day.

(*c*) Analyse the project for optimum duration cost. [*Karn. U. B.E. (Mech.) 1994*]

32. A maintenance foreman has given the following estimate of times and costs for jobs in a motor overhaul project:

Job	Description	Preceding job	*Normal* Duration (hours)	*Normal* Cost (₹)	*Minimum* Duration (hours)	*Minimum* Cost (₹)
A	Remove and disassemble motor	–	8	80	6	100
B	Clean and paint frame	A	7	40	4	94
C	Rewind armature	A	12	100	5	184
D	Replace bearings	A	9	70	5	102
E	Assemble and instal motor	B, C, D	6	50	6	50

(*a*) Assume that the jobs can be done at either normal or fast pace, but not any pace in-between. Plot the relationship between project completion time and minimum total project cost.

(*b*) Assume that a linear cost relationship exists between job duration and job cost and that job may be scheduled not only at the normal and minimum durations but at any integer duration in-between. With overhead cost of ₹ 25 per hour plot the cost-time relationship.

[*P.U. B.E.(Elect.) 1997*]

33. The following data refer to the various activities of a project. Determine the least time schedule.

Activity	*Preceding activity*	*Following activity*	*Normal* Time (days)	*Normal* Cost (₹)	*Crash* Time (days)	*Crash* Cost (₹)
A	–	D, F	4	1,000	3	2,000
B	–	G	7	2,800	5	5,200
C	–	E, H	3	500	2	1,000
D	A	G	5	2,000	3	3,600
E	C	G	2	1,600	2	1,600
F	A	–	10	2,300	8	3,500
G	B, D, E	–	7	2,000	5	4,800
H	C	–	2	1,000	1	2,000

34. The following is the table showing details of a project :

Task	*Immediate predecessor*	*Normal* Time (days)	*Normal* Cost (₹)	*Crash* Time (days)	*Crash* Cost (₹)
A	–	10	2,000	7	3,000
B	–	8	1,500	6	2,000
C	B	5	800	4	1,400
D	B	6	1,100	4	1,500
E	B	8	900	5	1,500
F	E	5	500	4	800
G	A, D, C	12	300	8	400

Indirect cost is ₹ 40 per day. Find the optimum duration as well as the least duration and the corresponding costs. [*H.P.U. B.Tech. (Mech.) June, 2010*]

(*Ans.* T_0 = 22 days, C_o = ₹ 8,080; T_i = 18 days, C_c = ₹ 9,620.)

35. The activities of a project are tabulated below with immediate predecessors, normal and crash time as well as cost.

Activity	*Immediate predecessor*	*Normal* Cost (₹)	*Normal* Time (days)	*Crash* Cost (₹)	*Crash* Time (days)
A	–	200	3	400	2
B	–	250	8	700	5
C	–	320	5	380	4
D	A	410	6	800	4
E	C	600	2	670	1
F	B, E	400	6	950	1
G	D	300	11	400	9
H	B, E	550	12	1,000	6

(*a*) Draw the network corresponding to normal times

(*b*) Determine the critical path and normal duration and cost of the project.

(*c*) If the activities are fully crashed, what is the least project time and the corresponding cost ?

[*R.T.M. Nagpur U. B.Tech. June, 2005, P.T.U. B.Tech. (Mech.) 2009*]

14.15 RESOURCE SCHEDULING

During the development of PERT and CPM networks we have generally assumed that sufficient resources are available to perform the various activities. At a certain time the demand on a particular resource is the cumulative demand of that resource on all the activities being performed at that time. Going according to the developed plan, the demand on a certain type of resource may fluctuate from very high at one time to a very low at another. If it is a material or unskilled labour which has to be procured from time to time, the fluctuation in demand will not much affect the cost of the project. But if it is some personnel who cannot be hired and fired during the project or machines which are to be hired for the total project duration, the fluctuation in their demand will affect the total project cost due to high idle times. To reduce the idle period, the activities on non-critical paths are shifted by making use of the floats, so as to make the demand of resources as uniform as possible.

Further, in some situations we may be faced with a demand for some critical resource which may be limited in supply. For example, the only bulldozer available may be needed for two activities at two places at a time. This makes the schedule infeasible and calls for a re-examination with the object of generating an alternate plan with feasible scheduling of the limited resource.

Thus the object of resource scheduling is two-fold: it aims at bringing down the costs and at the same time reduces pressure on the limited resources in conflicting demands.

Depending upon the type of constraint the resource scheduling situation may be of two types:

(*a*) The constraint may be the total project duration. In this case the resource scheduling only smoothens the demand on resources in order that the demand of any resource is as uniform as possible.

During the smoothing process, the start times of the activities on the non-critical paths are shifted, while the project duration remains unchanged. In this case the resource scheduling is called '*Resource Smoothing*'.

(*b*) The second type of constraint may be on the availability of certain resources. Here the project duration may be extended but the demand on certain specified resources should not go beyond the specified level. This operation of resource scheduling is called '*Resource Levelling*'.

14.15-1 Resource Smoothing

The first step in resource smoothing is to determine the maximum requirement. One way is to draw the time-scaled version of the network and assign resource requirements to activities. Then, below the time-scaled network, the cumulative resource requirements for each time unit are plotted. The result is a '*Load Histogram*'. The load histogram which is also known as '*force curve*' may be plotted on the basis of early start times or the late start times of the activities. These load histograms establish the framework within which smoothing must occur. Lastly, the start times of non-critical activities first having largest float are shifted to smoothen the requirement of resources.

EXAMPLE 14.15-1.1

A network with the following activity durations and manpower requirement is given. Analyse the project from point of view of resources to bring out the necessary steps involved in the analysis and smoothing of resources.

Activity	:	1-2	2-3	2-4	3-5	4-6	4-7	5-8	6-8	7-9	8-10	9-10
Duration (weeks)	:	2	3	4	2	4	3	6	6	5	4	4
No. of men required	:	4	3	3	5	3	4	3	6	2	2	9

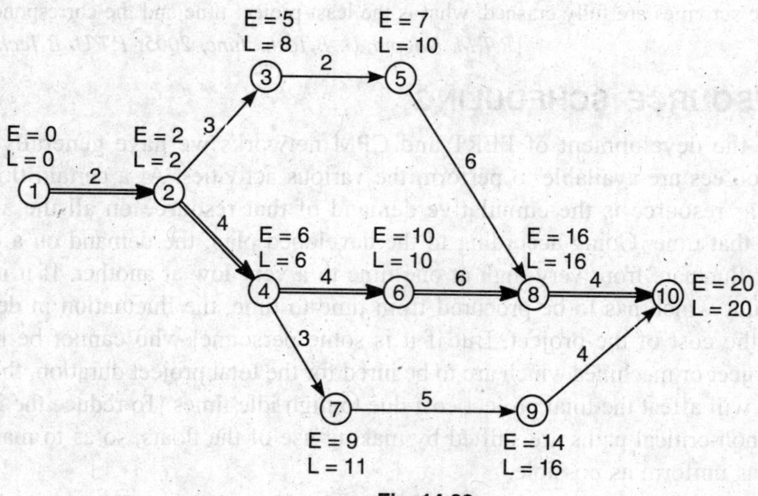

Fig. 14.83

Solution

The earliest and latest occurrence times of events have been calculated and are indicated along the nodes in Fig. 14.83. The critical path is identified as 1-2-4-6-8-10, with the total project duration of 20 weeks. In the time-scaled version of the network which is also called *squared network,* first of all the critical path is drawn along a straight line.

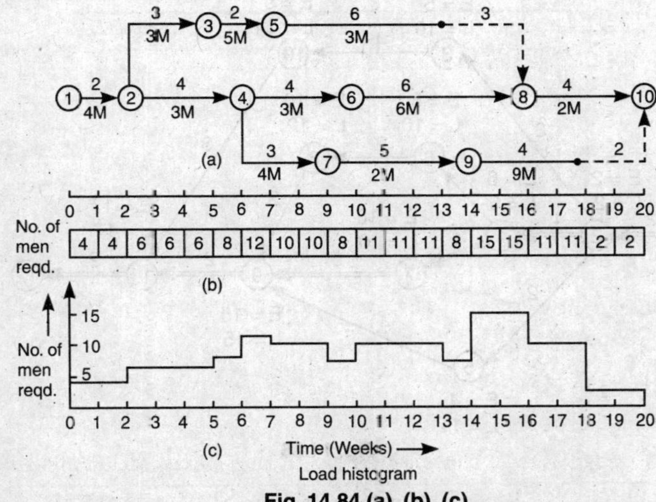

Fig. 14.84 (a), (b), (c)

Then the non-critical paths are added as shown in Fig. 14.84 (*a*). The resource requirements are indicated along the arrows. Below the squared network are shown the loading chart [Fig. 14.84 (*b*)] and the load histogram [Fig. 14.84 (*c*)]. This is based on the earliest start times, and is obtained by vertically summing up the manpower requirements for each week. We observe that the maximum demand of 15 men occurs in the 15th and 16th weeks.

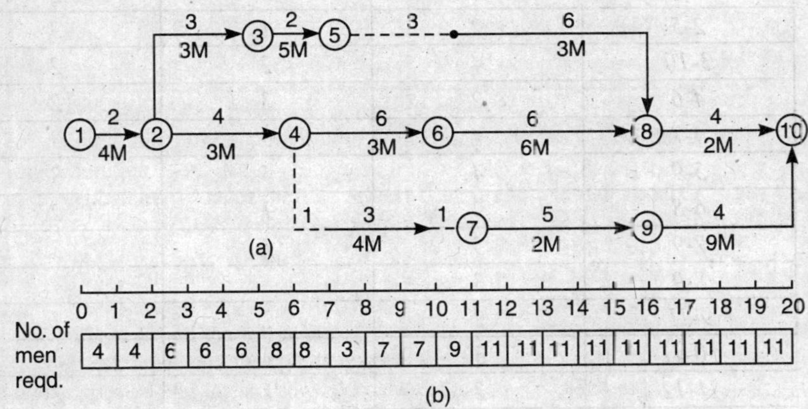

Fig. 14.85. (a), (b)

To smoothen the load, the activities will have to be shifted depending upon the floats. Path 4-7-9-10 has a float of two weeks, and the activities 7-9 and 9-10 are shifted to the right so that the start of each is delayed by two weeks. Similarly, activity 5-8 can be shifted to the right so that it starts on 11th day instead of starting on 8th day. After making the necessary shifting, the network is drawn as shown in Fig. 14-85 (*a*). The loading chart for this network drawn in Fig. 14.85 (*b*) indicates that the maximum manpower required is 11 men. Thus with the new schedule, the same project can be accomplished in the same duration of 20 weeks by 11 men as compared to 15 for the previous schedule.

EXAMPLE 14.15-1.2

Consider the network shown in Fig.14.86, having 14 activities. Durations of the activities are marked along their arrows. Table 14.10 shows the requirement of masons (M) and labourers (L) for each activity. Analyse the project and smoothen the requirement of the resources.

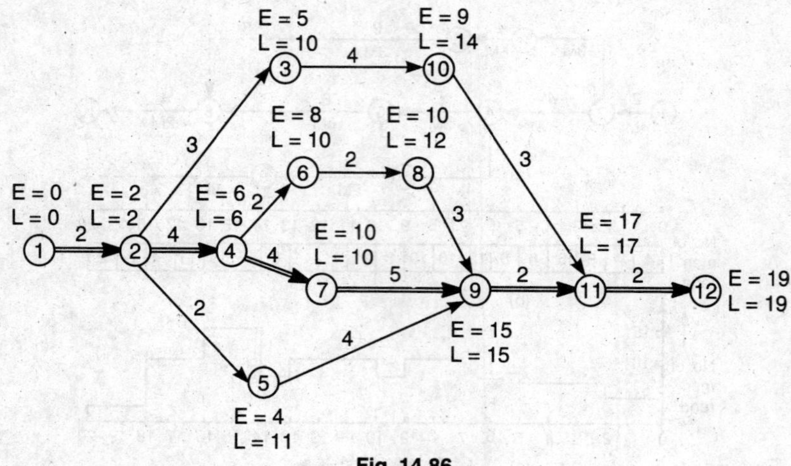

Fig. 14.86

TABLE 14.10

Activity	*Duration (weeks)*	*Masons (M)*	*Labourers (L)*
1-2	*2*	*1*	*2*
2-3	*3*	*2*	*2*
2-4	*4*	*3*	*2*
2-5	*2*	*1*	*3*
3-10	*4*	*2*	*2*
4-6	*2*	*3*	*2*
4-7	*4*	*3*	*3*
5-9	*4*	*5*	*3*
6-8	*2*	*1*	*2*
7-9	*5*	*1*	*3*
8-9	*3*	–	*4*
9-11	*2*	*1*	*1*
10-11	*3*	*1*	*2*
11-12	*2*	*1*	*2*

Solution

The earliest and latest occurrence times for the events are marked along their nodes. Critical path is 1-2-4-7-9-11-12 and the project duration is 19 weeks.

Fig.14.87 (*a*) represents the time-scaled version of the network, assuming early start times for the activities. The activities along the critical path are arranged along the horizontal line. The non-critical paths are then added as shown in Fig. 14.87 (a). The dotted lines show the total float of each activity. Durations and requirements of masons (M) and labourers (L) for each activity are marked along the activity arrows. The loading chart below the time-scaled diagram shows the total numbers of masons as well as labourers required each day. It is seen that the requirement of these resources is not uniform; for masons it is as high as 13 on 7th and 8th day, 10 on 5th and 6th day and as low as 1 from 13th to 19th day. By inspection we find that activities 2-5 and 5-9 have a total float of 7 days. The start time of activity 5-9 can be shifted by 7 days so that it starts on 12th day instead of 5th day. Fig. 14.88 represents the modified network along with the loading chart.

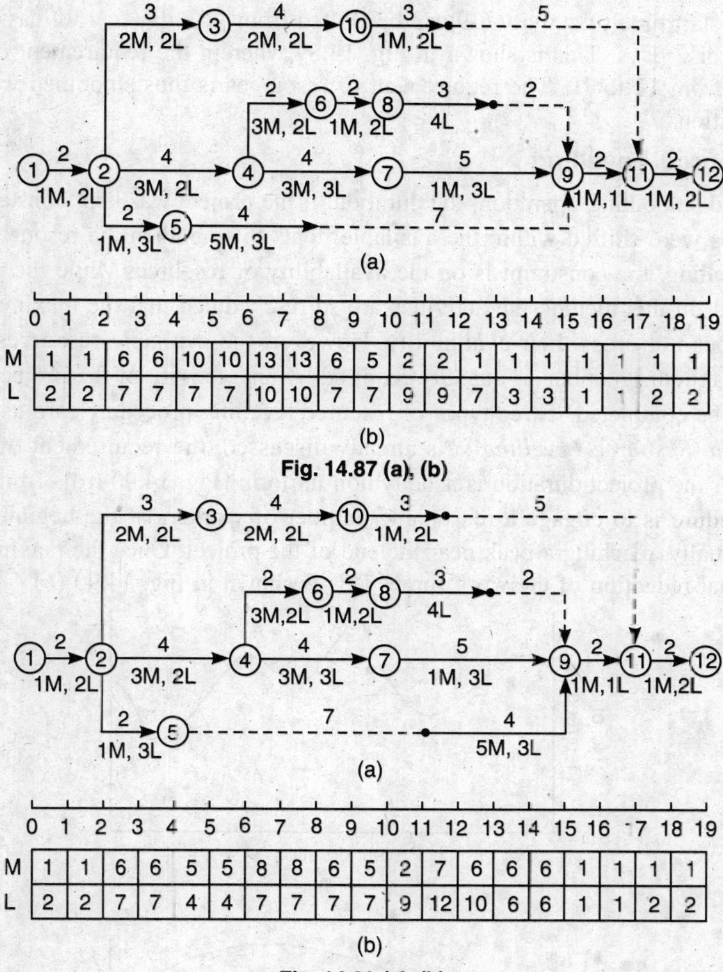

	0–1	1–2	2–3	3–4	4–5	5–6	6–7	7–8	8–9	9–10	10–11	11–12	12–13	13–14	14–15	15–16	16–17	17–18	18–19
M	1	1	6	6	10	10	13	13	6	5	2	2	1	1	1	1	1	1	1
L	2	2	7	7	7	7	10	10	7	7	9	9	7	3	3	1	1	2	2

Fig. 14.87 (a), (b)

	0–1	1–2	2–3	3–4	4–5	5–6	6–7	7–8	8–9	9–10	10–11	11–12	12–13	13–14	14–15	15–16	16–17	17–18	18–19
M	1	1	6	6	5	5	8	8	6	5	2	7	6	6	6	1	1	1	1
L	2	2	7	7	4	4	7	7	7	7	9	12	10	6	6	1	1	2	2

Fig. 14.88 (a), (b)

From Fig. 14.88 we find that the demand for masons has decreased from 13 to 8 on the 7th and 8th days. However, the demand of labourers has increased from 9 to 12 on the 12th day.

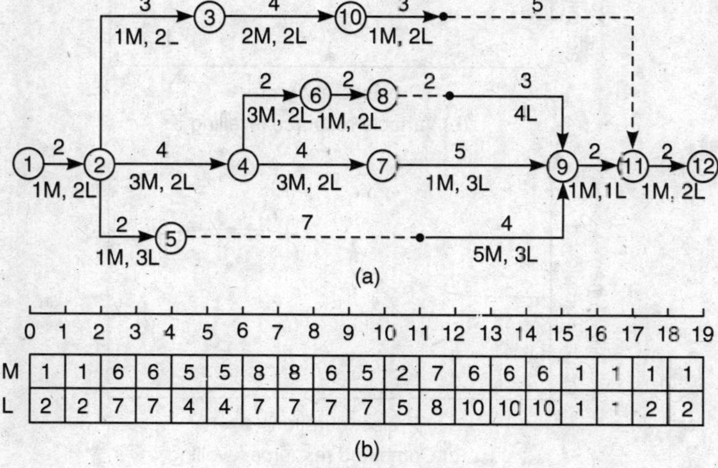

	0–1	1–2	2–3	3–4	4–5	5–6	6–7	7–8	8–9	9–10	10–11	11–12	12–13	13–14	14–15	15–16	16–17	17–18	18–19
M	1	1	6	6	5	5	8	8	6	5	2	7	6	6	6	1	1	1	1
L	2	2	7	7	4	4	7	7	7	7	5	8	10	10	10	1	1	2	2

Fig. 14.89 (a), (b)

Next, the start time of activity 8-9 can be shifted from 11th day to 13th day by utilising the float available for 2 days. This is shown in Fig. 14.89 wherein the requirement of labourers has also decreased from 12 to 10. The requirement of resources is thus smoothed without affecting the project duration.

14.15-2 Resource Levelling

In the load smoothing operation, the duration of the project was kept constant and the non-critical activities were shifted within the available floats to smoothen the resource requirements. In resource levelling, the constraint is on the availability of resources while the project duration can be extended. In this method the activities are so rescheduled that the maximum requirement of resources does not cross their availability. However, the available resources should not be less than the maximum number or quantity required by any activity of the project otherwise that activity cannot be completed. Three types of resource levelling procedures are usually followed.

1. *Variable Resource Levelling* : As already discussed, the requirement of resources (say manpower) over the project duration is usually non-uniform [Fig. 14.90 (*a*)]. To make it uniform, the usual procedure is to engage a reasonable number of workers at the beginning and then to increase it gradually, reaching a peak near the end of the project. Once the maximum is reached, there is a gradual reduction of the work force. This is shown in Fig. 14.90 (*b*).

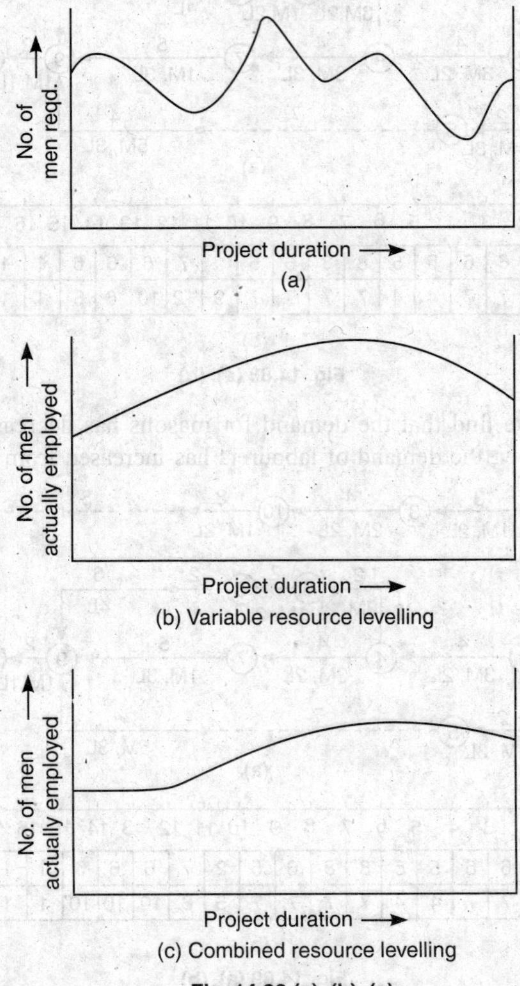

Fig. 14.90 (a), (b), (c)

2. *Fixed Resource Levelling* : Here, the number of workers remains constant throughout the project duration. As the requirement is highly fluctuating, there can be both excessive overtime as well as idle work force at different times. The aim, here, is to select the optimum number of workmen so that both overtime as well as unproductive standby persons are minimised.

3. *Combined Resource Levelling* : Here, fixed no. of persons are initially engaged and to satisfy the increasing needs, the number is increased in accordance with the pattern of variable resource levelling. This is represented in Fig. 14.90(c).

Thus in resource levelling process, whenever the resources available are less than their maximum requirement, the only recourse is to delay the activity which has the largest float. If two or more activities require the same resources, then the activity with minimum duration is chosen for resource allocation. Whenever there is a surplus resource, it should be shifted elsewhere in such a manner as to maximize its utilisation.

14.15-3 Analogy of Queuing Phenomenon to Resource Allocation Problem

The resource allocation problem can be assumed to be analogous to the queuing problem. In a queuing problem there is a service station; customers arrive and form a queue at the service station and are selected for service according to a specific service discipline or rule, *e.g.*, first come, first served. In the resource allocation problem, the resources *e.g.*, men, machines, etc., constitute the service station. Activities 'arrive' and form queue, waiting to be taken up for execution. Float provides the rule by which they are to be selected for execution; activity with the least float to be given top priority, activities with higher floats to be given lesser priorities.

There may be time when the resources are idle but there is no activity in the queue. At other times, there may be too many activities in the queue and all may not be taken at the same time. Therefore, some of them have to be delayed. If the delay is within the free float, it would not affect the subsequent activities; if it is more than the free float, it would cause repercussions on the subsequent activities.

At each time period, therefore, it is to be ascertained if there are activities in the queue and resources are also available. If yes, the activities will be allocated to the resources. If either no activity is to be taken up or no resource is idle, we may simply skip to the next period. A heuristic programme based on the above discussion can be developed to solve resource allocation problems.

EXAMPLE 14.15-3.1

The activities in a project along with their durations are given below. Each activity requires one labourer. Analyse the network from the point of view of levelling of resources so that the project is completed in the shortest possible time.

Activity (i-j)	:	*1-2*	*1-3*	*1-5*	*2-3*	*2-6*	*3-4*	*4-7*	*5-6*	*6-7*
Duration (days)	:	*10*	*6*	*4*	*0*	*8*	*10*	*10*	*6*	*6*

[*M.D.U. Rohtak B.E. (Mech.) Dec., 2006*]

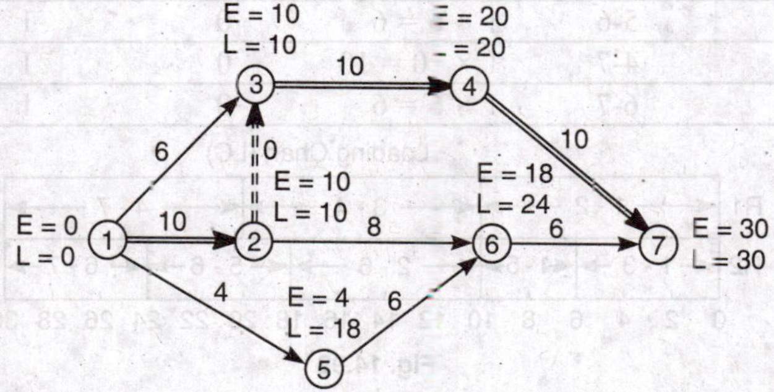

Fig. 14.91

Solution

The heuristic programme to be used for solving the problem consists of the following steps:

Step 1 : Draw the project network and identify the critical path. This is shown in Fig. 14.91. The critical path is 1-2-3-4-7.

Step 2 : Construct the network analysis table (Table 14.11). The labourers required for each activity are shown under the M-column. Man-days required by each activity are noted under the M × D-column.

TABLE 14.11

Network Analysis Table (NAT)

Activity (i-j)	Duration (D)	Men (M)	Man-days (M×D)	Start E	Start L	Finish E	Finish L	Float
1-2*	10	1	1 × 10 = 10	0	0	10	10	0
1-3*	6	1	1 × 6 = 6	0	4	6	10	4
1-5*	4	1	1 × 4 = 4	0/6	14	4/10	18	14/8
2-3*	0	0	0 × 0 = 0	10	10	10	10	0
2-6*	8	1	1 × 8 = 8	10	16	18	24	6
3-4*	10	1	1 × 10 = 10	10	10	20	20	0
4-7*	10	1	1 × 10 = 10	20	20	30	30	0
5-6*	6	1	1 × 6 = 6	4/10/18	18	10/16/24	24	14/8/0
6-7*	6	1	1 × 6 = 6	18/24	24	24/30	30	6/0

The total man-days requirement is 60 and since project duration is 30, the no. of men required to complete the project are 60/30 = 2.

Step 3 : Construct resource allocation table and loading chart : Table 14.12 shows the resource allocation table followed by the loading chart. Their explanation is given below.

TABLE 14.12

Resource Allocation Table (RAT)

Halting time	Available resource	Activities in the queue i-j	M × D	Float	Priority	Allocated to resource
0	R1, R2	1-2	1 × 10 = 10	0	I	R1
		1-3	1 × 6 = 6	4	II	R2
		1-5	1 × 4 = 4	14	III	
6	R2	1-5	1 × 4 = 4	8	I	R2
10	R1, R2	2-6	1 × 8 = 8	6	II	R2
		3-4	1 × 10 = 10	0	I	R1
		5-6	1 × 6 = 6	8	III	
18	R2	5-6	1 × 6 = 6	0	1	R2
20	R1	4-7	1 × 10 = 10	0	I	R1
24	R2	6-7	1 × 6 = 6	0	I	R2

Loading Chart (LC)

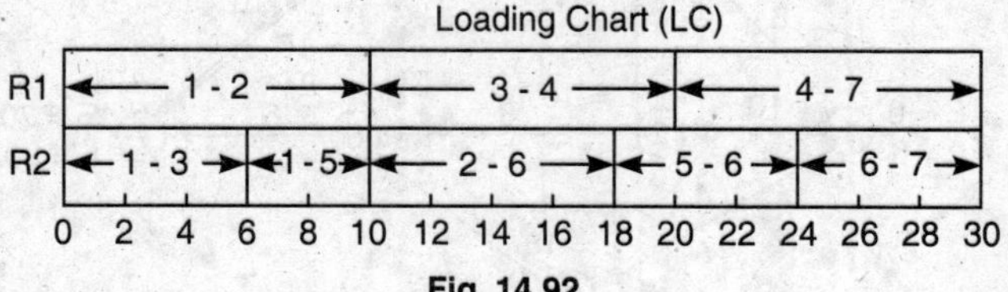

Fig. 14.92

Halting time 0 : Halt at a time when there are both available resources and queuing activities. At time 0, both the labourers denoted by resources R1 and R2 are available. Activities 1-2, 1-3 and 1-5 each have zero earliest start times. As their floats are 0,4 and 14, the priorities assigned to them for execution are I, II and III respectively. Resource R1 is, accordingly, allotted activity 1-2, which he will perform in 10 days. This is shown in the loading chart (Fig.14.92). Activity 1-3 is allocated to resource R2, which he will perform in 6 days; this is shown in the loading chart. ctivity 1-5 cannot be taken at time zero and has to be delayed or floated out. The earliest it can possibly be taken is time 6 when resource R2 will become free, as seen from the loading chart. Activities 1-2 and 1-3 have been allotted and are marked (*) in the network analysis table. Activity 1-5 is floated out in that table by changing its earliest start time from 0 to 6, its earliest finish time from 4 to 10 and its float from 14 to 8. Delaying activity 1-5 for start by 6 days may have repercussions on the following activities 5-6 and 6-7 and it has to be seen whether they also need to be floated out. Since activity 1-5 now finishes at time 10, activity 5-6, cannot start at time 4 and, therefore, its earliest start time is changed to 10. Consequently, its earliest finish time is changed to 16 and float decreased to 8 in the NAT. As the earliest start time of the successor activity 6-7 is 18, there are no repercussions on this activity. As seen from the loading chart, next halting time is 6.

Halting time 6 : Resource available is R2, activity due to be taken up is 1-5 and is allotted to this resource for 4 days. This is shown in the loading chart. Activity 1-5 is marked (*) in NAT.

Halting time 10 : Resources R1 and R2 are available. Activities having earliest start time 10 are 2-3, 2-6, 3-4 and 5-6. However, activity 2-3 is dummy; requires no resources and need not be considered and is marked (*) in NAT. The remaining activities have floats of 6, 0 and 8 respectively and are, therefore, assigned priorities II, I and III in the resource allocation table (RAT) 14.12. Accordingly, activity 3-4 having duration 10 days is allocated to resource R 1 and activity 2-6 requiring 8 days for completion is allotted to resource R2. This is shown in RAT as well as loading chart (LC).

The next halting time is 18. Activities 2-6 and 3-4 are marked (*) in NAT and activity 5-6 is floated out to earliest start time 18. The earliest finish time of this activity is changed to 24 and float to 0. Floating out of activity 5-6 has repercussions on the succeeding activity 6-7. Its earliest start time is increased to 24, its earliest finish time to 30 and float is decreased to zero.

Halting time 18 : Resource available is R2, activity due to be taken up this time is 5-6 and is loaded on resource R2 for 6 days. This is shown in RAT as well as LC. Activity 5-6 is marked (*) in NAT.

Halting time 20 : Resource available is R1, activity 4-7 can be taken up at this time. Its man-days are 10 and is allocated to resource R1 for 10 days. This is shown in RAT as well as LC. This activity is then marked (*) in the NAT. Next halting time is 24.

Halting time 24 : Resource available is R2. Activity due to be started at time 24 is 6-7. Its duration is 6 days. Resource R2 is, therefore, allotted activity 6-7 for 6 days. This completes the resource allocation within 30 days. There is no delay in the project The project can, thus, be completed in 30 days with limited resources (2 labourers) if the activities are allocated as shown in the LC.

Note. The following points are worth noting for developing the algorithm for resource allocation :

1. Halt when both resources and activities are available.
2. Prior to allocation at a halt, update the E.S., E.F. and float of the activities not allocated at earlier halt time and their succeeding activities. The repercussions may have to be traced right upto the last event.
3. (*a*) Priorities are assigned on the basis of floats *e.g.,* 1st priority to activity with least float, 2nd to the activity with the next higher float and so on.
   (*b*) In case of tie in floats, assign priorities on the basis of man-days of the activities *e.g.,* 1st priority to the activity with highest M × D.
   (*c*) In case of tie in man-days even, assign 1st priority to the activity with highest M (gang size).
   (*d*) In case of tie in M's even, assign Ist priority to the activity with lower *i,* where *i* is the tail event number of the activity.

4. When an activity requires more than one man, it may so happen during allocation that the activity requires more number of persons than that available at the halt time under consideration. In such cases, the resources are allocated to the job with next priority for which they are sufficient.
5. During the floating out of activities, the float of an activity may go negative which means that the project duration is going to be extended beyond the critical path. Once the float of an activity becomes negative, therefrom the float criterion for ascertaining priorities is invalidated. The priorities are then fixed on the basis of M × D, gang size and lower *i* criteria respectively.

These points are made clear in the next examples.

EXAMPLE 14.15-3.2

Activities, their durations and crew sizes required to implement them are given below:

Activity (i-j)	:	1-2	1-3	1-5	2-3	2-6	3-4	4-7	5-6	6-7
Duration (days)	:	10	6	5	0	8	10	10	7	5
Crew size (M)	:	1	2	3	0	1	2	3	1	2

Schedule the project when only 3 men are available for executing it.

Solution

It consists of the following steps:

Step 1 : Draw the project network and identify the critical path. This is shown in Fig. 14.93. Critical path is 1-2-3-4-7.

Step 2 : Construct the network analysis table. This is done in table 14.13.

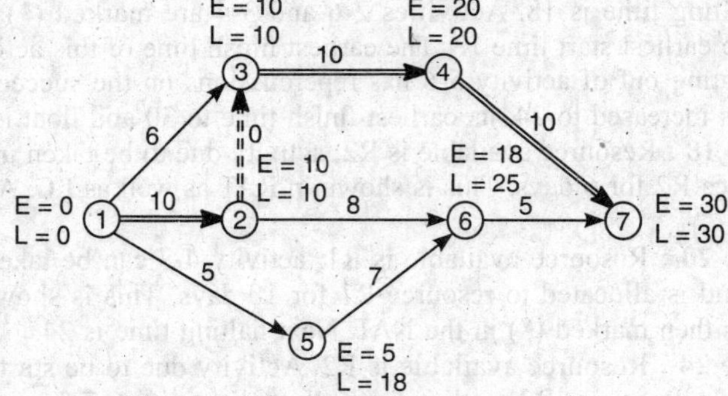

Fig. 14.93

TABLE 14.13

Network Analysis Table

Activity	*Duration*	*Men*	*Man-days*	*Start*		*Finish*		*Float*
(i-j)	*(D)*	*(M)*	*(M × D)*	*E*	*L*	*E*	*L*	
1-2*	10	1	1 × 10 = 10	0	0	10	10	0
1-3*	6	2	2 × 6 = 12	0	4	6	10	4
1-5*	5	3	3 × 5 = 15	0/6/10/18/20/30	13	5/11/15/23/25/35	18	13/7/3/–5
2-3*	0	0	0 × 0 = 0	10	10	10	10	0
2-6*	8	1	1 × 8 = 8	10	17	18	25	7
3-4*	10	2	2 × 10 = 20	10	10	20	20	0
4-7*	10	3	3 × 10 = 30	20	20	30	30	0
5-6*	7	1	1 × 7 = 7	5/11/15/23/25/35	18	12/18/22/30/32/42	25	13/7/3/–5
6-7*	5	2	2 × 5 = 10	18/22/30/32/42	25	23/27/35/37/47	30	7/3/–5

Step 3 : *Construct resource allocation table and loading chart.*

Table 14.14 represents the resource allocation table and Fig. 14.94 shows the loading chart. The procedure to draw them is explained in example 14.15-3.1.

TABLE 14.14

Resource Allocation Table (RAT) with 3 Men

Halting time	*Available resource*	*Activities in the queue* *i-j*	*M × D*	*Float*	*Priority*	*Allocated to resource*
0	R1, R2, R3	1-2	1 × 10 = 10	0	I	R1
		1-3	2 × 6 = 12	4	II	R2, R3
		1-5	3 × 5 = 15	13	III	
6	R2, R3	1-5	3 × 5 = 15	7	I	–
10	R1, R2, R3	1-5	3 × 5 = 15	3	II	–
		2-6	1 × 8 = 8	7	III	R3
		3-4	2 × 10 = 20	0	I	R1, R2
18	R3	1-5	3 × 5 = 15	–	I	–
20	R1, R2, R3	1-5	3 × 5 = 15	–	II	
		4-7	3 × 10 = 30	–	I	R1, R2, R3
30	R1, R2, R3	1-5	3 × 5 = 15	–	I	R1, R2, R3
35	R1, R2, R3	5-6	1 × 7 = 7	–	I	R2
42	R1, R2	6-7	2 × 5 = 10	–	I	R1, R2

Since after time 35 days, three persons are not required to complete activities 5–6 and 6–7, one crew, say R3 can be relieved from the job. The project is delayed from 30 days to 47 days if 3 crews only are available. The activities should be allocated to the crew as per the schedule of Fig. 14.94. Shaded portions show the rest periods of the crew.

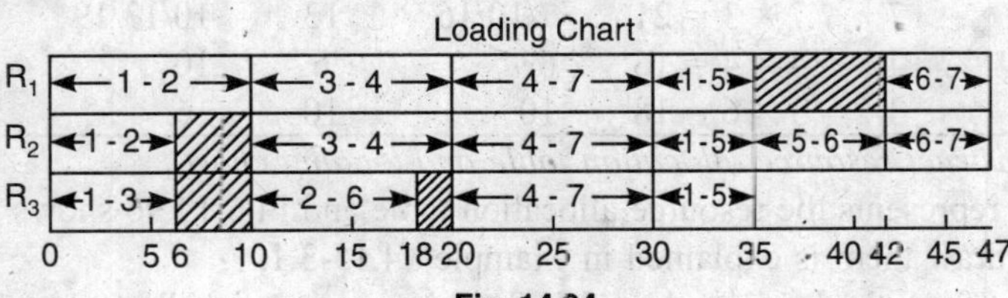

Fig. 14.94

EXAMPLE 14.15-3.3

A project with the following activities, durations and manpower requirements is given:

Activity	:	1-2	1-3	1-4	2-5	2-6	3-7	4-8	5-9	6-9	7-8	8-9
Duration (days)	:	2	2	0	2	5	4	5	6	3	4	6
Manpower requirement	:	5	4	0	2	3	6	2	8	7	4	3

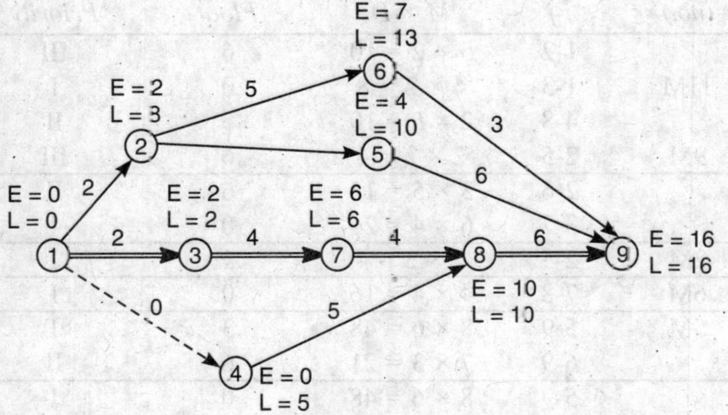

Fig. 14.95

(a) *Draw the network diagram of the project indicating the earliest start, earliest finish, latest start, latest finish and float of each activity.*

(b) There are 11 persons who can be employed for this project. Carry out the appropriate manpower levelling so that the fluctuation of work force requirement from day to day is as small as possible. [*I.C.W.A. June, 1979*]

Solution

It consists of the following steps:

Step 1 : *Draw the project network and identify the critical path.*
Project network is drawn in Fig. 14.95. Critical path is 1-3-7-8-9.

Step 2 : *Construct the network analysis table.* This is done in table 14.15.

TABLE 14.15

Network Analysis Table

Activity (i-j)	*Duration (D)*	*Men (M)*	*Man-days (M × D)*	Start E	Start L	*Finish* E	*Finish* L	*Float*
1-2*	2	5	5 × 2 = 10	0	6	2	8	6
1-3*	2	4	4 × 2 = 8	0	0	2	2	0
1-4*	0	0	0 × 0 = 0	0	5	0	5	5
2-5*	2	2	2 × 2 = 4	2/5	8	4/7	10	6/3
2-6*	5	3	3 × 5 = 15	2	8	7	13	6
3-7*	4	6	6 × 4 = 24	2	2	6	6	0
4-8*	5	2	2 × 5 = 10	0	5	5	10	5
5-9*	6	8	8 × 6 = 48	4/7/10	10	10/13/16	16	6/3/0
6-9*	3	7	7 × 3 = 21	7/10/16	13	10/13/19	16	6/3/–3
7-8*	4	4	4 × 4 = 16	6	6	10	10	0
8-9*	6	3	3 × 6 = 18	10	10	16	16	0

Step 3 : *Construct resource allocation table and loading chart.*

Table 14.16 represents the resource allocation table and Fig. 14.96 shows the loading chart. The procedure to draw them is explained in example 14.15-3.1.

It is apparent from the loading chart that five persons remain idle from 8th to 10th day and four persons remain idle from 17th to 19th day. The Project cannot be completed in the normal time duration of 16 days and has to be delayed by 3 days if 11 persons only are to be employed.

TABLE 14.16

Resource Allocation Table

Halting time	*Available resource (no.)*	*Activities in the queue* i-j	*M × D*	*Float*	*Priority*	*Allocated to resource*
		1-2	5 × 2 = 10	6	III	5M
0	11M	1-3	4 × 2 = 8	0	I	4M
		4-8	2 × 5 = 10	5	II	2M
2	9M	2-5	2 × 2 = 4	6	III	–
		2-6	3 × 5 = 15	6	II	3M
		3-7	6 × 4 = 24	0	I	6M
5	2M	2-5	2 × 2 = 4	3	I	2M
6	6M	7-8	4 × 4 = 16	0	I	4M
7	5M	5-9	8 × 6 = 48	3	I	–
		6-9	7 × 3 = 21	6	II	–
		5-9	8 × 6 = 48	0	1	8M
10	11M	6-9	7 × 3 = 21	3	III	–
		8-9	3 × 6 = 18	0	II	3M
16	11M	6-9	7 × 3 = 21	–	I	7M

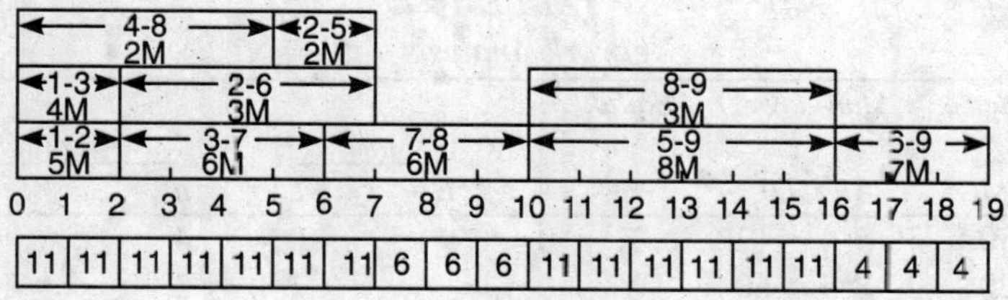

Fig. 14.96. Loading chart

EXAMPLE 14.15-3.4

For a project consisting of several activities, the durations and required resources for carrying out each of the activities and their availabilities are given below.

(a) Draw the network, identify critical path and compute the total float for each of the activities.

(b) Find the project completion time under the given resource constraints.

Resources required

Activity	*Equipment*	*Operators*	*Duration (days)*
1-2	*X*	*30*	*4*
1-3	*Y*	*20*	*3*
1-4	*Z*	*20*	*6*
2-4	*X*	*30*	*4*
2-5	*Z*	*20*	*8*
3-4	*Y*	*20*	*4*
3-5	*Y*	*20*	*4*
4-5	*X*	*30*	*6*

Resources availability :

No. of operators = 50,

equipment X = 1,

equipment Y = 1,

equipment Z = 1. [*C.A. (Final) Nov., 1985*]

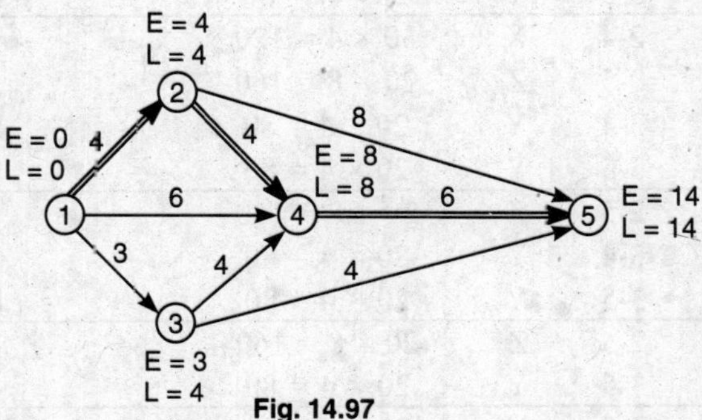

Fig. 14.97

Solution

It consists of the following steps :

Step 1 : Draw the project network and identify the critical path.

Project network is drawn in Fig. 14.97. Critical path is 1-2-4-5.

Step 2 : Construct the network analysis table.

This is done in table 14.17.

TABLE 14.17

Network Analysis Table

Activity (i-j)	*Duration (D)*	*Men (M)*	*Man-days (M × D)*	*Equip.*	*Start E*	*Start L*	*Finish E*	*Finish L*	*Float*
1-2	4	30	30 × 4 = 120	X	0	0	4	4	0
1-3	3	20	20 × 3 = 60	Y	0	1	3	4	1
1-4	6	20	20 × 6 = 120	Z	0/3	2	6/9	8	2/-1
2-4	4	30	30 × 4 = 120	X	4	4	8	8	0
2-5	8	20	20 × 8 = 160	Z	4/8/9	6	12/16/17	14	2
3-4	4	20	20 × 4 = 80	Y	3/4/8	4	7/8/12	8	1
3-5	4	20	20 × 4 = 80	Y	3/4/8/9/12/17	10	7/8/12/13/16/21	14	7
4-5	6	30	30 × 6 = 180	X	8/9/12	8	14/15/18	14	0/-1

Step 3 : Construct resource allocation table and loading chart.

Table 14.18 represents the resource allocation table and loading chart is drawn in Fig. 14.98. The procedure is explained in example 14.15-3.1.

Activities 1-2, 1-3 are taken up at time 0 while 1-4 is delayed to start at time 3. Float of activity 1-4 becomes negative and therefore float will not be the criterion for finding priorities henceforth. At time 3, activities 3-4 and 3-5 have the same man-days, gang size and activity sequence. Therefore, activity 3-4 is arbitrarily assigned priority II and activity 3-5, priority III.

TABLE 14.18

Resource Allocation Table

Halting time	*Available resources*	*Activities in the queue (i-j)*	*Equip.*	*M × D*	*Float*	*Priority*	*Allocated to resources*
0	50M; X, Y, Z	1-2	X	30 × 4 = 120	0	I	30M, X
		1-3	Y	20 × 3 = 60	I	II	20M, Y
		1-4	Z	20 × 6 = 120	2	III	
3	20M; Y, Z	1-4	Z	20 × 6 = 120	–	I	20M, Z
		3-4	Y	20 × 4 = 80	–	II	
		3-5	Y	20 × 4 = 80	–	III	
4	30M; X, Y	2-4	X	30 × 4 = 120	–	II	30M, X
		2-5	Z	20 × 8 = 160	–	I	–
		3-4	Y	20 × 4 = 80	–	III	
		3-5	Y	20 × 4 = 80	–	IV	
8	30M; X, Y	2-5	Z	20 × 8 = 160	–	I	–
		3-4	Y	20 × 4 = 80	–	II	20M, Y
		3-5	Y	20 × 4 = 80	–	III	
9	30M; X, Z	2-5	Z	20 × 8 = 160	–	I	20M, Z
		3-5	Y	20 × 4 = 80	–	II	
12	30M; X, Y	3-5	Y	20 × 4 = 80	–	II	
		4-5	X	30 × 6 = 180	–	I	30M, X
17	20M; Y, Z	3-5	Y	20 × 4 = 80	–	I	20M, Y

At time 4, available resources are 30M, X and Y. Activity 2-5 has the highest man-days and is assigned priority I. However, since it requires equipment Z, it cannot be taken up and, instead, activity 2-4 with priority II is selected for execution. From Fig. 14.98 it can be seen that the project requires 21 days for completion and is, therefore, delayed by 7 days beyond normal completion time. The idle man-days are shown shaded. It may be observed that during 19th, 20th & 21st days only 20 persons are required. The remaining 30 persons can be relieved/shifted to other project after 18 days. Day-by-day requirement of operators and equipment is also shown on the loading chart.

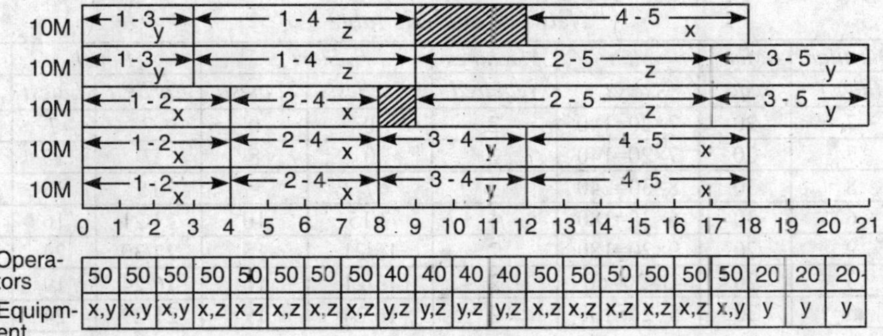

Operators	50	50	50	50	50	50	50	50	40	40	40	40	50	50	50	50	50	50	20	20	20
Equipment	x,y	x,y	x,y	x,z	x z	x,z	x,z	x,z	y,z	y,z	y,z	y,z	x,z	x,z	x,z	x,z	x,z	x,y	y	y	y

Fig. 14.98. Loading chart

EXAMPLE 14.15-3.5

The following table gives for each activity of a project its duration and corresponding resource requirements as well as total availability of each type of resource :

Activity	*Duration (days)*	*Resources required*	
		Machines	*Men*
1-2	7	2	20
1-3	7	2	20
2-3	8	3	30
2-4	6	4	30
3-6	9	2	20
4-5	3	2	20
5-6	5	2	20
		Machines	*Men*
Minimum available resources :		4	40

(i) Draw the network, compute earliest occurrence time and latest occurrence time for each event, the total float for each activity and identify the critical path assuming that there are no resource constraints.

(ii) Under the given resource constraints find out the minimum duration to complete the project and compare the utilisation of resources for that duration.

Solution

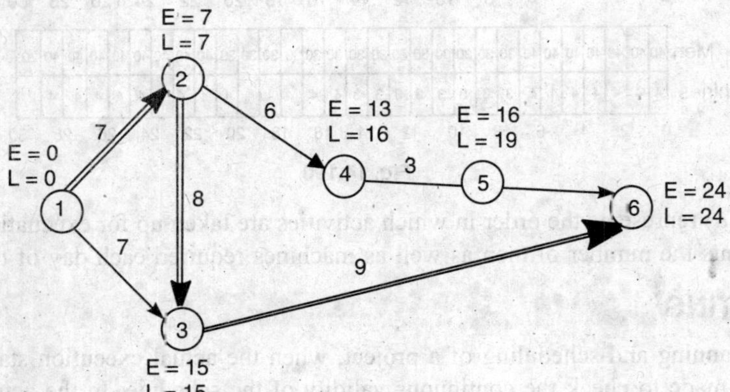

Fig. 14.99

(*i*) The network is drawn in Fig 14.99. Earliest occurrence time and latest occurrence time for each event are shown on the network.

Total float for each activity is calculated in the network analysis table (NAT) below.

Network analysis table

Activity	*Duration (days)*	*Men reqd.*	*Man-days*	*Machines required*	*Start*		*Finish*		*Total float*
					Earliest	*Latest*	*Earliest*	*Latest*	
1–2	7	20	7×20=140	2	0	0	7	7	0
1–3	7	20	7×20=140	2	0	8	7	15	8
2–3	8	30	8×30=240	3	7	7	15	15	0
2–4	6	30	6×30=180	4	7/15	10	13/21	16	3/-5
3–6	9	20	9×20=180	2	15/21	15	24/30	24	0
4–5	3	20	3×20=60	2	13/21	16	16/24	19	3/-5
5–6	5	20	5×20=100	2	16/24	19	21/29	24	3/-5

Critical path under conditions of no resource constraints is 1–2–3–6.

(ii) Resource allocation table is constructed below.

Resource allocation table

Halting time	*Resources available*	*Activities in the queue*					*Allocated to resource*
		Activity	*Man-days*	*Machines*	*Float*	*Priority*	
0	4 Ma, 40 M	1–2	7×20=140	2	0	I	2Ma, 20M
		1–3	7×20=140	2	8	II	2Ma, 20.M
7	4Ma, 40 M	2–3	8×30=240	3	0	I	3Ma, 30M
		2–4	6×30=180	4	3	II	
15	4Ma, 40 M	2–4	6×30=180	4	–	I	4Ma, 30M
		3–6	9×20=180	2	–	II	
21	4Ma, 40 M	3–6	9×20=180	2	–	I	2Ma, 20M
		4–5	3×20=60	2	–	II	2Ma, 20M
24	2Ma, 20 M	5–6	5×20=100	2	–	I	2Ma,20M

Loading chart is drawn in Fig. 14.100. Due to constraint of resources, the project gets delayed to 30 days.

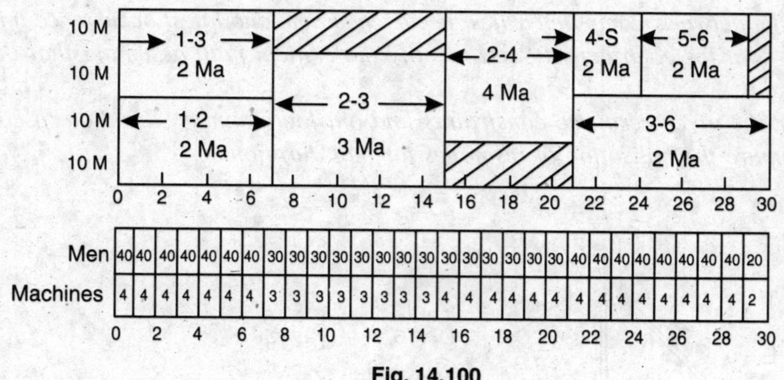

Fig. 14.100

Fig. 14.100(*a*) represents the order in which activities are taken up for execuation while Fig. 14.100(*b*) represents the number of men as well as machines required each day of the project.

14.16 UPDATING

After the planning and scheduling of a project, when the actual execution starts, a regular review should be made to check the continuous validity of the schedule. In the actual execution it generally happens that the time schedule developed for the project is not exactly followed.

Some of the jobs take more time than estimated and some others are completed in period lesser than estimated. There may be a number of reasons for this, such as the non-availability of the resources, break down of machinery, labour strikes, wrong estimations of the planner and natural calamities, etc. All these will delay the jobs. On the other hand, jobs may be expedited due to the commissioning of a new machine, development of a better process and wrong estimations of the planner, etc. The review of the situation presents a clear picture of the progress and helps in making the necessary changes in the schedule thus adding dynamism to the nature of the network. This process of making review and adding necessary clarifications to the network is called *updating*.

How often the updating should be done? There is no special rule to decide about the frequency of updating. This depends upon the nature and the size of the project and upon the attitude of the management. Updating may be done every fortnight or every month or every three months and so on. However, a general observation can be made that frequency of updating may be less at the initial stages but should be more frequent near the completion of the project. Some slippages at the beginning can be absorbed, but a slip near completion will delay the project. In small projects, as the time for absorbing the slippages is less, more frequent updating is called for.

Updating can be done in two ways. The first is to use the revised time estimates and compute from the initial starting event the earliest and latest completion time of each event in the usual manner to determine the project completion time. The second method, which is more convenient, is to change the completed work to zero duration and bunch all the jobs already performed into one arrow called the *elapsed time arrow.* The nodes in the new network are numbered in a different fashion. The time durations assigned to the activities are the revised times.

Both these methods are explained with the help of examples.

EXAMPLE 14.16-1

After 15 days of working the following progress is noted for the network of an erection job:

(a) Activities 1-2, 1-3 and 1-4 completed as per original schedule.

(b) Activity 2-4 is in progress and will be completed in 3 more days.

(c) Activity 3-6 is in progress and will need 18 days more for completion.

(d) Activity 6-7 appears to present some problem and its new estimated time of completion is 12 days.

(e) Activity 6-8 can be completed in 5 days instead of originally planned for 7 days.

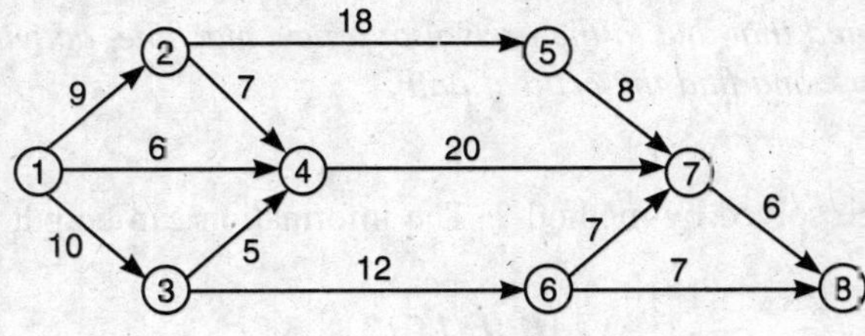

Fig. 14.101

Update the above network after 15 days of start of work. Find the critical path and project duration of the updated network. [P.U.BBA, 2001]

Solution

This problem will be solved by method 1. Activities 1-2, 1-3, 1-4 have already been completed and nothing needs to be done about them. Activities 2-4 and 3-6 are in progress; their revised durations will be calculated.

Revised duration of activity 2-4 = (15 + 3) – 9 = 9 days, and revised duration of activity 3-6 = (15 + 18) – 10 = 23 days.

Activities 6-7 and 6-8 have not started on 16th day; they are assigned the new estimated times of 12 days and 5 days respectively in the updated network. The durations of the remaining activities are kept unchanged in the updated network (Fig. 14.102).

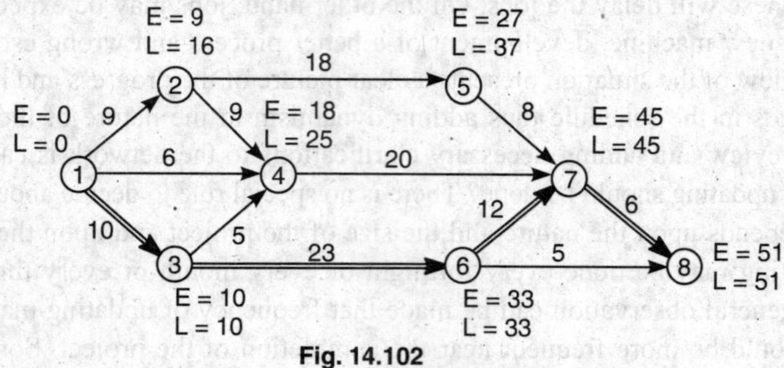

Fig. 14.102

The project duration is 51 days. Critical path is 1-3-6-7-8.

Example 14.16-2

The network for a project is shown in Fig. 14.103. A review of the project after 10 days reveals that

(i) activities 0-1, 0-2 and 1-3 are completed.

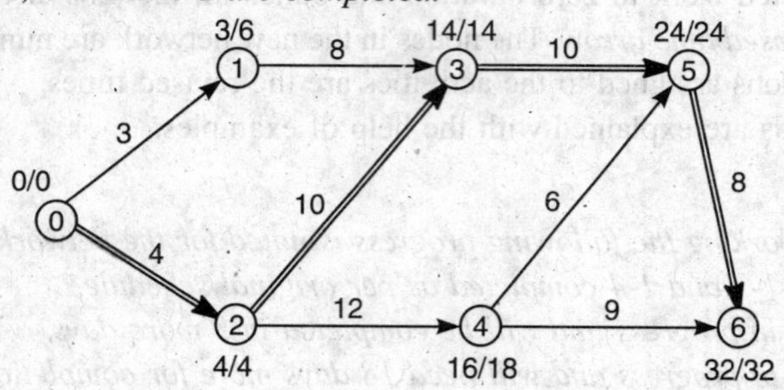

Fig. 14.103

(ii) activity 2-3 is in progress and will take 6 days more,

(iii) activity 2-4 is in progress and will take 7 days more,

(iv) also it is estimated that due to the arrival of a new machine, activity 3-5 will take only 6 days. Update the network and find the critical path.

Solution

This problem will be solved by method 2. The information can be put into a tabular form, as shown in table 14.19.

TABLE 14.19

Review time after 10 days

Activity	*More time required (days)*	*Situation*
0-1	0	Completed
0-2	0	Completed
1-3	0	Completed
2-3	6	In progress
2-4	7	In progress
3-5	6	Not started
4-5	6	Not started
4-6	9	Not started
5-6	8	Not started

This table represents the situation of the project after 10 days. The time durations assigned to the activities are revised times. In the new network shown in Fig. 14.104, activity 10-20 shows the elapsed time of 10 days. Activities 20-30 and 20-40 are assigned the times they need for their completion. Along other activities are put their new time estimates.

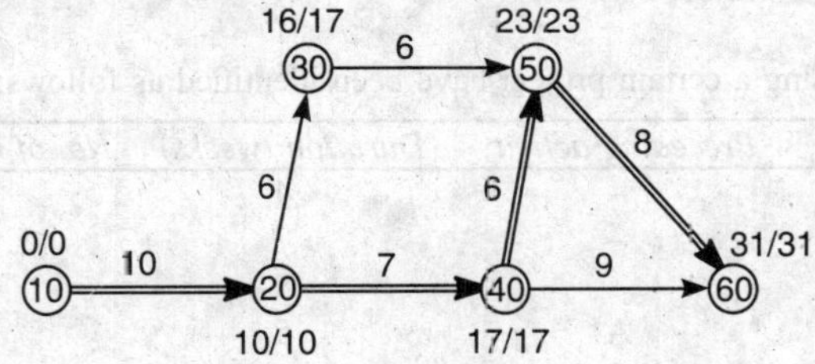

Fig. 14.104

After computing the earliest occurrence times and the latest occurrence times for events, we find that the critical path has changed to 20-40-50-60. The total duration has also come down by one day.

EXAMPLE 14.16-3

The network for a project is given in Fig. 14.105. A review of the project after 15 days reveals that

(a) Activities 1-2, 1-3, 2-3, 2-4 and 3-4 are completed.

(b) Activities 3-5 and 4-6 are in progress and need 2 and 4 days but 7-9 will need 10 days. Formulate a new network after updating the project and determine the new critical path.

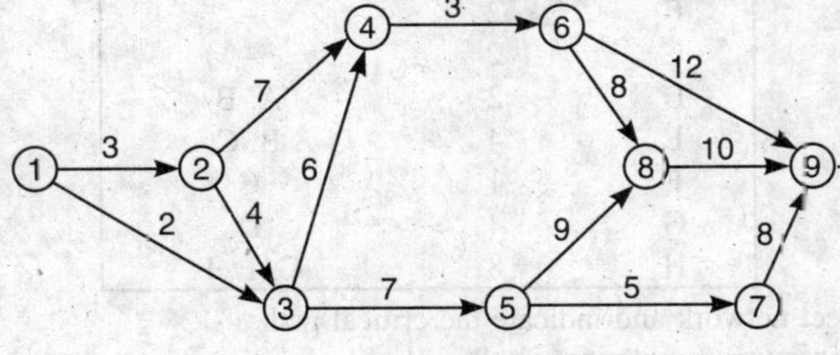

Fig. 14.105

Solution

The activities completed upto 15th day *viz.* 1-2, 1-3, 2-3, 2-4 and 3-4 are combined into one activity called the elapsed time activity. The same is represented in the updated network of Fig. 14.106 by the arrow 10-20. The activities in progress are taken to emanate from the head of elapsed time activity. Activities 3-5 and 4-6 which need 2 and 4 days more respectively are represented by the arrows 20-5 and 20-6 in the updated network. The remaining network is drawn for the changed

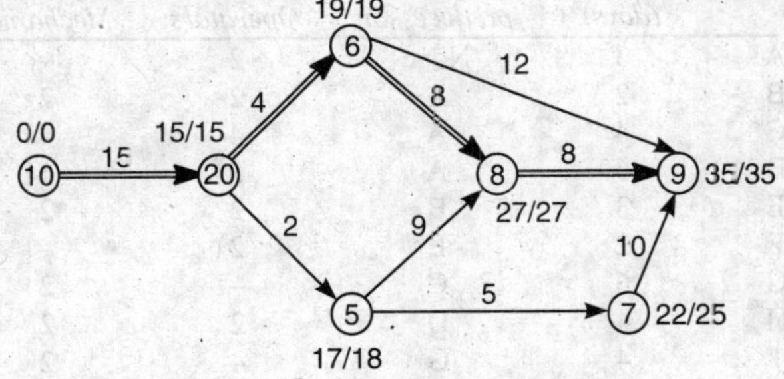

Fig. 14.106

activity durations. The earliest and latest event times are given along the nodes. The critical path of the updated network is 10-20-6-8-9 and the project duration is 35 days.

EXERCISES 14.5

1. Write notes on resource levelling and resource smoothing.

[*R.T.M. Nagpur U. B.Tech. Dec., 2005; P.T.U. MBA, 2005*]

2. Explain updating of the project networks.

[*P.T.U. MCA, 2010*]

3. The activities comprising a certain project have been identified as follows:

Activity	*Preceding activity*	*Duration (weeks)*	*No. of men required*
A	–	4	1
B	–	7	1
C	–	8	2
D	A	5	3
E	C	4	1
F	B, E	4	2
G	C	11	2
H	G, F	4	1

(*a*) For the above project, draw the network. Determine the critical path and its duration.

(*b*) If there were only three men available at anyone time, how long would the project take and how would you allocate the men to the activities?

(*c*) If there were no restrictions on the amount of labour available, explain how you might schedule the activities. (*Ans.* (*a*) C-G-H, 23 weeks. (*b*) Project duration increases to 32 weeks.)

4. A project has the following activities and their durations:

Activity	*Time (days)*	*Preceding activity*
A	1	–
B	2	–
C	2	–
D	2	A, B
E	4	B, C
F	1	C
G	4	D
H	8	G, E, F

(*i*) Draw the project network and indicate the critical path.

(*ii*) What is the minimum completion time?

(*iii*) During the second day of work it is discovered that activity F will take 4 days instead of 1. Will this delay the project? If this activity takes 6 days, will the project be delayed?

(*iv*) The company has limited number of men available to work on the project. Only two activities can be under way at the same time. Will this delay the project over what the time would have been with unlimited resources? (Activity F takes 6 days to complete).

(*Ans.* (*i*) B-D-G-H (*ii*) 16 days (*iii*) No (*iv*) Yes.)

5. The following table gives the activities in a small project and other relevant information:

Activity	*Duration (days)*	*Immediate predecessor*	*Resources required*	
			Operators	*Mechanics*
A	3	None	2	–
B	2	A	2	2
C	4	A	4	4
D	6	A	5	5
E	3	B	2	2
F	2	E	2	–
G	6	C	–	2
H	4	D	2	2
I	4	G	4	2
J	2	D	2	–
K	2	J	2	2
L	4	F, H, I	4	4

(*a*) Draw the network, compute earliest start time and latest finish time for each of the activities and find out the project completion time and identify the critical path.

(*b*) Draw the time-scaled diagram with resource accumulation table. Comment on demand for the operators and mechanics for the entire project duration and suggest the method of smoothing the resources. [*C.A. (Final) May, 1988*]

(*Ans* (*a*) 21 days, A-C-G-I-L.)

6. Duration and requirement of work force for each activity is tabulated below for a network.

Activity	*Duration*	*No. of men*
1-2	3	5
2-4	2	3
2-3	3	7
3-4	0	0
3-5	3	2
4-5	7	2
3-6	2	1
5-6	6	6
4-6	5	5

(*a*) Draw the network and comment on the scheduling of activities to smoothen the deployment of the work force.

(*b*) Indicate the maximum crew size in each case.

(*c*) Reschedule the activities for smooth development. [*I.C.W.A. (Final) June, 1977*]

7. Following are the manpower requirements for each activity in a project:

Activity	*Normal time (days)*	*Manpower required per day*
1-2	10	2
1-3	11	3
2-4	13	4
2-6	14	3
3-4	10	1
4-5	7	3
4-6	17	5
5-7	13	3
6-7	9	8
7-8	1	11

(*i*) Draw the network and find out total float and free float for each activity.

(*ii*) The contractor stipulates that during the first 26 days only 4 to 5 men and during remaining days 8 to 11 men only can be made available. Rearrange the activities suitably for levelling the man power resource satisfying the above conditions. [*Nagpur U. MBA, 1998*]

8. Consider the project whose details are given below:

Activity	:	1-2	2-3	2-4	3-4	3-5	3-6	4-5	4-6	5-6
Duration (days)	:	3	3	2	0	3	2	7	5	6
Resources	:	5	7	3	0	2	1	2	5	6

(*a*) Find the duration of the project.

(*b*) Find the resource level of the project.

(*c*) Find the resource allocation using 7 resources by series method *i.e.*, make the complete allocation table. [*BITS Pilani, 2000*]

9. A project schedule has the following characteristics:

Activity	*Time*	*Activity*	*Time*
1-2	2	4-5	5
1-4	2	4-8	8
1-7	1	5-6	4
2-3	4	6-9	3
3-6	1	7-8	3
		8-9	5

(*a*) Construct network and find critical path and time duration of the project.

(*b*) Activities 2–3, 4–5 and 6–9 each require one unit of the same key equipment to complete it. Do you think availability of one unit of the equipment in the organisation is sufficient for completing the project without delaying it? If so, what is the schedule of these activities?

[*G.N.D.U. B.Com. April., 2006; P.T.U. MBA Dec., 2004*]

(*Ans.* (*a*) Critical path is 1-4-8-9, 15 time units; (*b*) 4-5, 2-3, 6-9 in this order.)

simple project has the following time and resource data:

Activity	*Preceding activity*	*Duration (days)*	*Labour requirement*
A	–	1	2
B	–	2	1
C	A	1	I
D	–	5	1
E	B	1	1
F	C	1	1

(*a*) Determine the minimum project schedule.

(*b*) Find the project schedule if only 2 men are available.

(*c*) Determine the number of men required if the project duration in (*a*) cannot be extended.

(*Ans.* (*a*) 5 days; (*b*) 6 days; (*c*) 3 men from day 2 to day 4.)

11. A project has the following activities and their durations:

Activity	:	12	13	14	24	25	34	36	47	57	67	68	78
Duration (days)	:	13	15	9	10	27	7	18	30	12	10	10	9

(*a*) Draw the network of the project and find its duration.

(*b*) At the end of 25 days it is observed that

(*i*) activities 12, 13, 14 have been completed,

(*ii*) activity 24 is being done and will be completed in 5 more days,

(*iii*) activity 36 is in progress and will need 20 more days for completion,

(*iv*) activity 67 is presenting some problem and will take 15 days.

Draw the updated network and find out its revised duration, 12 denotes activity 1-2 and same is true for other activities. [*V.T.U. Karnataka B.Tech. (Mech.) 2012*]

12. The network for a project is given in Fig. 14.107.

Suppose the progress of work is checked after 15 days, that is at the end of 15th day, and it is observed that

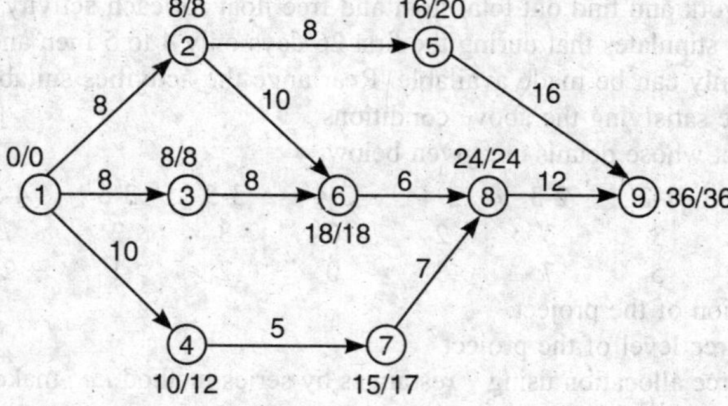

Fig. 14.107

– activities 1-2, 1-3, 1-4 and 2-5 are completed,

– activity 2-6 is in progress and needs 2 days more,

– activity 3-6 is in progress and needs 5 days more,

– activity 4-7 is in progress and needs 1 day more, and

– activity 5-9 is in progress and needs 14 days more.

Also, it is estimated that due to the non-availability of fast setting cement, activity 7-8 will take 12 days while due to the arrival of a new crane, activity 8-9 will now require only 10 days.

Formulate the new network after updating the project and determine the new critical path.

(*Ans.* Critical path: 10-20-70-80-90, project duration : 38 days.)

13. For the network shown in Fig. 14.108, a review of the project after 15 days reveals the following situation:

(*a*) Activities 1-2, 1-3, 2-3, 2-4 and 3-4 are completed.

(*b*) Activities 3-5 and 4-6 are in progress and need 2 and 4 days more respectively.

(*c*) The revised estimate shows that activity 8-9 will take only 8 days, but activity 7-9 will need 10 days.

Formulate a new network after updating and determine the new critical path. Show the progress of the project on a bar chart and indicate the modification based on updating.

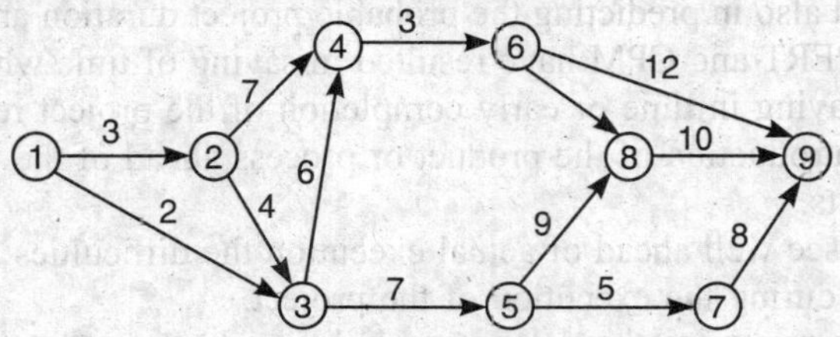

Fig. 14.108

(*Ans.* Critical path remains unchanged.)

14. The estimated cost for work packages and the activity duration in each work package pertaining to a certain project are shown below:

Work package	*Activities in work package*	*Duration (weeks)*
Engineering design	1-2, 2-3, 3-4, 3-7, 7-8	4, 3, 2, 6, 2
Steel and other materials	4-5, 5-6, 6-11, 9-12, 12-13, 13-14	1, 1, 24, 1, 1, 16
Fabrication	8-9, 9-10, 10-11, 11-14, 14-15, 15-16, 16-17, 17-18	2, 4, 1, 3, 5, 1, 1, 1

(*a*) Draw the network diagram indicating earliest occurrence times and latest occurrence times of the events. Find the critical path and project duration.

(*b*) The physical progress of activities at the end of 16 weeks reported is as under:

Completed activities	:	1-2	2-3	3-4	3-7	4-5	5-6	7-8
Actual duration	:	3	4	2	7	1	2	2

Activities in progress are:

8–9 : Estimated to complete in 2 weeks from now.

6–11 : Estimated to complete in 18 weeks from now.

Draw the original as well as updated networks and find their critical paths.

14.17 OBJECTIVES OF NETWORK ANALYSIS

Some of the main objectives of network analysis are:

(*i*) to complete the project within the stipulated period.

(*ii*) optimum utilization of the available resources.

(*iii*) minimization of cost and time required for the completion of the project.

(*iv*) minimization of idle resources and investments in inventory.

(*v*) to identify the bottlenecks, if any, and to focus attention on critical activities.

(*iv*) to reduce the set-up and changeover costs.

14.18 ADVANTAGES OF NETWORK TECHNIQUES

1. They are most valuable and powerful for planning, scheduling and control of operations in large and complex projects.

2. They are useful tools to evaluate the level of performance by comparing actual performance against the planned targets.
3. They help to determine the interdependence of various activities for proper integration and coordination of various operations.
4. They help to evaluate the time-cost trade off and determine the optimum schedule.
5. These techniques are simple and can be easily oriented towards computers.
6. The networks clearly designate the responsibilities of different supervisors. Supervisor of an activity knows his time schedule precisely and also the supervisors of other activities with whom he has to coordinate.
7. These techniques help the management in achieving the objective with minimum of time and least cost and also in predicting the probable project duration and the associated cost.
8. Applications of PERT and CPM have resulted in saving of time which directly results in saving of cost. Saving in time or early completion of the project results in earlier return of revenue and introduction of the product or process ahead of the competitors, resulting in increased profits.
9. They help to foresee well ahead of actual execution the difficulties and problems that are likely to crop up during the execution of the project.
10. They also help to minimize the delays and holdups during execution. Corrective action can also be taken well in time.
11. Application of network techniques has resulted in better managerial control, improved utilisation of resources, improved communication and progress reporting and better decision-making.

14.19 LIMITATIONS OF NETWORKS

1. Construction of networks for complex projects is complicated and time consuming due to trial and error approach.
2. Estimation of reliable and accurate durations of various activities is a difficult exercise.
3. With too many resource constraints the analysis becomes very difficult.
4. Time-cost trade off procedure, in many situations, is complicated.

14.20 DIFFICULTIES IN USING NETWORK METHODS

Following are some of the problems faced in the managerial use of network methods :

1. Difficulty in securing the realistic time estimates. In the case of new and non-repetitive type projects, the time estimates are often mere guesses.
2. The natural tendency to oppose changes results in the difficulty of persuading the management to accept these techniques.
3. The planning and implementation of networks require personnel trained in the network methodology. Managements are reluctant to spare the existing staff to learn these techniques or to recruit trained personnel.
4. Developing a clear logical network is also troublesome. This depends upon the data input and thus the plan can be no better than the personnel who provides the data.
5. Determination of the level of network detail is another troublesome area. The level of detail varies from planner to planner and depends upon the judgement and experience.

14.21 COMMENTS ON THE ASSUMPTIONS OF PERT/CPM

1. In PERT analysis β-distribution curve is assumed for expected times of all the activities. However, actually β-distribution curve may not be applicable to each and every activity.
2. The formulae for the expected duration and standard deviation are simplified. In certain cases the errors, due to these simplifications, may even be of the order of 33%.
3. PERT analysis assumes independence of activities. Limitation of resources may invalidate the independence of activities.

4. It is not always possible to sort out completely identifiable activities and their start and finish times.
5. Time estimates have an element of subjectiveness in them. The whole analysis, being based on them is, therefore, weak. The analysis can, at best, be as good as the time estimates.
6. The CPM model has an assumption that *the duration of an activity is linearly and inversely related to the cost of resources consumed for the activity.* Cost-time trade off relationships are difficult to obtain in many cases either because data are not available or because their estimation is too complex and expensive. A great deal of effort and expertise is required to estimate them.

14.22 APPLICATIONS OF NETWORK TECHNIQUES

Networks provide a comprehensive study of the entire project in terms of precedence and succession of various activities as well as resources available to perform them to evolve some better and quicker plan to complete the project. They can be used for complicated large scale projects involving financial and administrative problems.

The list containing PERT and CPM applications is very large and the applications are expanding to many new areas. Following are a few typical areas in which these techniques are widely accepted:

1. *Construction Industry :* It is one of the largest areas in which the network techniques of project management have found application. These techniques are used in the construction of buildings, roads, highways, bridges, dams and irrigation projects.
2. *Manufacturing :* The design, development and testing of new machines, installing machines and plant layouts are a few examples of how it can be applied to the manu-facturing function of a firm. It has been used in manufacturing of ships, aeroplanes, etc.
3. *Maintenance planning :* R and D has been the most extensive area where PERT has been used for development of new products, processes and systems. It has been used in missile development, space programmes, strategic and tactical military operations, etc.
4. *Administration :* Networks have been used by the administration for streamlining paperwork system, for making major administrative system revisions, for long range planning and developing staffing plans, etc.
5. *Marketing :* Networks have been used for advertising programmes, for development and launching of new products and for planning their distribution.
6. *Inventory planning :* Installation of production and inventory control, acquisition of spare parts, etc. have been greatly helped by network techniques.
7. *Other areas of application* are preparation of budget and auditing, installation of computers and large machinery, best traffic flow patterns, organisation of big conferences and public works, advertising and sales promotion strategies, etc.

14.23 DISTINCTIONS BETWEEN PERT AND CPM

The PERT and CPM techniques are similar in terms of their basic structure, rationale and mode of analysis. However, there are certain distinctions between PERT and CPM networks which are described below:

1. CPM is activity oriented *i.e,* CPM network is built on the basis of activities. Also results of various calculations are considered in terms of activities of the project. On the other hand, PERT is event oriented. Here, emphasis is on the completion of a task rather than the activities required to be performed to reach a particular event or task.
2. CPM is a deterministic model. It does not take into account the uncertainties involved in the estimation of time for the execution of an activity. Each activity is assigned a single time based on past experience. PERT, however, is a probabilistic model. It uses three estimates of the activity time, namely, optimistic, pessimistic and most likely, with a

view to take into account uncertainty in time. Thus expected duration of each activity is probabilistic and expected duration indicates that there is 50% chance of completing the activity within that time.

3. CPM places dual emphasis on project time as well as cost and finds the trade-off between project time and project cost. By employing additional resources, it helps to manipulate project duration within certain limits so that it can be reduced at optimum cost. On the other hand, PERT is primarily concerned with time only. It helps to schedule and coordinate various activities so that project can be completed in scheduled time.
4. CPM is primarily used for projects which are repetitive in nature and comparatively small in size. PERT is generally used for projects where time required to complete the activities is not known a priori. Thus PERT is used for large, one-time research and development type of projects.

These distinctions, however, have become less important over time because cost considerations have also been brought in PERT analysis. Differences are insignificant and of academic interest only and both PERT and CPM are treated to be synonymous for the purpose of analysis.

14.24 LINEAR PROGRAMMING FORMULATION

A project, as discussed earlier, consists of a large number of activities resulting in a number of constraints. It may, therefore, be desirable to formulate the problem in linear programming format. Problems may involve either of the following situations:

1. Given a project involving n activities with their normal durations, crash durations and cost slopes, determine the duration of each activity so that the total cost is minimum.
2. Given a project involving n activities with their normal durations, crash durations, cost slopes and indirect cost, determine the project duration so that the total cost is minimum.

If $x_1, x_2, ..., x_n$ denote the durations of the n activities and $c_1, c_2, ..., c_n$ are their associated costs per unit time, the L.P. formulation of the problem is

$$\text{minimize } Z = c_1 x_1 + c_2 x_2 + ... + c_n x_n,$$

subject to constraints

$$x_1 + x_2 + ... + x_n \leq \text{normal time},$$
$$x_1 + x_2 + ... + x_n \geq \text{crash time},$$

where $x_1, x_2, ..., x_n \geq 0$.

EXERCISES 14.6

1. Discuss the similarities and differences of CPM and PERT.
[P.T.U. MBA Dec., 2004; May, 2014; P.U.B.Com Nov., 2014; G.N.D.U. Sept., 2014; Mumbai U. B.Com. April, 2013; R.U. MBA June, 2011; H.P.U. B.Tech.(Mech.) 2012; V.T.U. Karnataka B.Tec. (Mech.) 2012; Chennai U. B.C.A. Nov., 2010; P.T.U.B.E. (Mech.) 2011; 2008; May, 2006; P.U. B.Com. April, 2007; B.E. (T. & I.T.) Nov., 2005; Nov., 2004; B.E. (Mech.) 2002; M.Com. Sept., 2004; Univ. of Madras MBA Nov., 2012; Univ. of Mumbai PGDM, 2012; V.T.U. Karanatka B.E. June, 2010; R.T.M. Nagpur U.B.E. (I.T.) 2009,05; Dec., 2004; Dec., 2003]

2. Discuss applications of PERT/CPM in project planning and explain the difference between them.
[P.T.U. MBA, 2008; P.U. M.Com., 2002; B.E. (Elect.) 2001; (Mech.) 2012; B.Com., 2000; MBA, 2000]

3. State the requirements for the application of PERT technique and practical limitations of using PERT. How does PERT differ from CPM? *[G.N.D.U. B.Com. April, 2008; R.C.C. CHD., 2002]*

4. Write a detailed note on the applications of network techniques.
[G.N.D.U. B.Com. Sept., 2010; R.T.M. Nagpur U.B.Tech. Dec., 2004; P.U.B.E. (T.I.T.) Nov., 2006; M.Com., 2001]

5. Answer the following :

(*i*) Advantages of network models
[P.U. UIAMS MBA May, 2015; G.N.D.U. Nov., 2014; P.T.U. MBA, 2009]

(*ii*) Difficulties in using network models *[P.U. UIAMS MBA May, 2015; B.E. (TIT) Dec., 2008]* (*iii*) Applications of network techniques [*M.D.U. Rohtak B.E. (Mech.) Dec., 2006*]

(*iv*) Compare and contrast CPM and PERT models.

[*P.U. UIAMS MBA May 2015; R.U. MBA June 2011; Dec., 2011; Univ. of Madras MBA, 2012; Univ. of Mumbai MBA, 2012; P.T.U. MBA, 2009; Nellore MBA, 2002*]

6. Write short note on assumptions in PERT technique.

[*H.P.U. B.Tech. (Mech.) 2012; M.G.U. Karnataka M.Com. June, 2012; June, 2010; P.T.U. MBA, 2009*]

7. What is PERT/CPM? What does each involve ? How are they similar ? Different ? What particular advantages does PERT have over CPM ? State the situations where CPM is better technique than PERT.

[*G.N.D.U. B.Com. April, 2010; April, 2007; P.U. M.B.A., 2003*]

8. Describe the role of network models of operations research for managerial decision-making.

9. Which model (PERT or CPM) do you advocate for execution of ultra mega power projects in India ?

[*P.T.U. MBA, 2009*]

(*Ans.* PERT.)

10. State the circumstances where CPM is a better technique of project management than PERT.

[*G.N.D.U. B.Com. Sept. 2009; Kuru.U. B.E. (Mech.) June, 2012*]

11. Describe the evolution of PERT and CPM. Compare them.

[*P.T.U. MBA Nov., 2012*]

Chapter 15 Statistical Quality Control

15.1 DEFINITION

The quality of a product is the 'degree of perfection'. Every product has to be manufactured according to certain specifications *e.g.*, dimensions, strength, appearance, surface finish, hardness, etc. The quality of the product depends upon a number of factors such as its design and specifications, production process, quality of raw materials, quality of machines and equipments, manpower expertise and skill and the inspection. To control the quality of the product, these factors responsible for its quality must be controlled properly.

According to Alford and Beatly, "Quality control is defined as an industrial management technique by means of which products of uniform acceptable quality are manufactured. It is concerned mainly with making things right rather than discovering and rejecting those made wrong." Quality control determines what, when and how much to inspect and what measures to take so that defective items are not produced. It is preventive rather than a corrective measure. The corrective action rests with the personnel.

One simple way to control the quality is to conduct 100% inspection. However, it will be very costly and time consuming. Nowadays statistics is used for quality control and this method is known as Statistical Quality Control (S.Q.C.). Statistical quality control is defined as the technique of applying statistical methods based on theory of probability to establish quality standards and to maintain it in the most economical manner.

15.2 OBJECTIVES OF QUALITY CONTROL

1. To set up standards of quality acceptable to the customer and economical to achieve and maintain.
2. To locate and identify the process faults in order to control the defectives, scrap and waste.
3. To take necessary corrective measures to maintain the quality of the products.
4. To ensure that sub-standard products do not reach the customers.
5. To achieve better utilization of raw materials and equipments.

15.3 STEPS IN QUALITY CONTROL PROGRAMME

1. Formulation of quality control policy.
2. Determination of producer's requirements and the specifications on the basis of customer's preference, manufacturing cost and profits.
3. Selection of appropriate inspection plan for checking the quality of the products.
4. Determination of deviation from the desired specifications and standards.
5. Suggestion of the appropriate corrective action.

15.4 ADVANTAGES OF STATISTICAL QUALITY CONTROL

1. When the quality of a product is tested by destructive testing, then 100% testing will spoil all the products. Under statistical quality control very few products will be destroyed in testing.

2. It ensures control, maintenance and improvement in the quality standards.
3. It provides better quality assurance at lower inspection cost.
4. It reduces the wastage of time and material to the minimum. It reduces the inspection and manufacturing cost and enhances profits.
5. The very presence of a SQC policy in an organisation improves and alerts the personnel and makes them 'quality conscious'.

15.5 CAUSES OF VARIATION IN QUALITY

Variation in quality of the product can be due to chance causes or assignable causes.

Chance causes: These causes vary at random independent of each other and it is difficult as well as uneconomical to detect and eliminate them. These causes are natural to any manufacturing process and are beyond human control. For instance, slight variation in temperature , pressure and humidity, etc. interact randomly to produce slight variation in the quality of the product. This variation is known as *natural, permissible* or *allowable variation*. When the variation in the production process is confined to chance causes alone, the process is said to be in a state of statistical control.

Assignable Causes: These are non-random causes that can be identified. The assignable cause may creep in at any stage of the process, right from the arrival of the raw material to the despatch of the finished product. Some of the assignable causes of variation are defective raw materials, improper machine setups, worn equipments, unskilled and fatigued workers and so on. This variation can be detected and eliminated and is, therefore, called *controllable* or *preventable variation*. A process is said to be out of statistical control, whenever it indicates the presence of some assignable variation . The objective of the SQC is to devise statistical methods that isolate assignable variation from random variation and enable us to detect, identify and eliminate the assignable causes of variation.

15.6 TECHNIQUES OF SQC

There are two broad ways of controlling the quality of the product

1. *Process control*: It is concerned with controlling the quality of the product during the production process. It ensures that a product of only requisite standard is produced and makes use of the 'control charts'.
2. *Product control*: It is concerned with controlling the quality of the product by critical examination at strategic points. It is concerned with inspection of goods already produced to ascertain whether they are fit to be despatched or not. It makes use of sampling inspection plans to achieve the objective.

15.7 CONTROL CHARTS

A control chart is an important statistical tool used for the study and control of repetitive processes. This has been devised by W.A. Shewhart and is based on the fact that variability does exist in all repetitive processes. The differences in dimensions or any other quality of the products are bound to happen if (*i*) different machine tools are used (*ii*) different cutting tools are used (*iii*) materials of different properties are used (*iv*) working conditions are different (*v*) workers of different skills manufacture the products and (*vi*) improper jigs, tools and fixtures are used.

However, variability in size is observed even if the products are manufactured on the same machine tool, using the same cutting tool by the same worker on the same material using proper jigs, tools and fixtures.

As already mentioned this variability is due to chance causes as well as assignable causes. A control chart accepts the normal variation due to chance causes but eliminates entirely the errors due to assignable causes.

Chance (usual) variations are normally of a lesser magnitude than assignable (unusual) variations, occur randomly and can be described by the normal probability distribution curves. Control limits are defined within which variations are acceptable and beyond which they are unacceptable. For a normal probability distribution, 99.73 per cent of all chance variations are expected to occur within limits of three standard deviations larger or smaller than the mean value of a variable. Any variation beyond these limits, therefore, can be expected to be caused by unusual or assignable causes which need to be investigated and then controlled. A process is said to be 'in control' if it produces items whose attributes or variables fall within the acceptable range and is said to be 'out of control' if it produces items whose attributes or variables are beyond the acceptable range .

A control chart consists of

(*i*) *a control or centre line* (CL) that indicates the desired control level of the process,

(*ii*) *an upper control limit* (UCL) that indicates the upper tolerance limit,

(*iii*) *a lower control limit* (LCL) that indicates the lower tolerance limit.

The control chart has a horizontal scale that represents the consecutive sample number and a vertical scale representing the characteristic quality of each sample. This is shown in Fig. 15.1

The data are collected on a series of samples taken during a production process at different time intervals and are plotted on the graph. As long as the points fall within the control limits, the variations are due to chance causes only, the process is under statistical control and we do not question the quality of the product. However, if a plotted point falls outside the control limits, this alerts the production manager to the possibility that the quality of the product is unacceptable and that the process is not under statistical control. If points lie predominantly on one side of the centre line, then it is not safe to derive any conclusion about the process control.

If the control chart indicates that the observed variation is due to chance causes alone, the process is said to be 'in control'. If on the other hand, the control chart indicates that the observed variation is not likely to be due to chance, it can be said that the manufacturing process is 'out of control'. In that event, the process is halted and effort is made to seek and correct the possible cause.

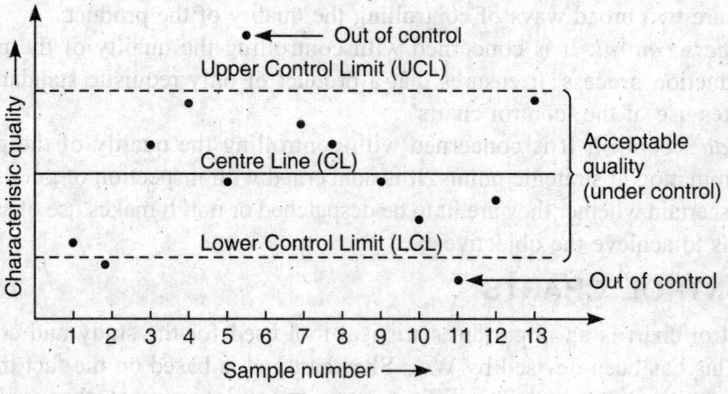

Fig. 15.1

Two types of control charts are usually used:

(*i*) *Control charts for variables*: They are used to achieve and maintain an acceptable quality level for a process whose product can be subjected to quantitative measurements such as diameter of a hole , length of a bolt, thickness of a pipe, specific resistance of a wire and strength of a yarn, etc. Such characteristics usually follow normal distribution.

(*ii*) *Control charts for attributes*: They are used to achieve and maintain an acceptable quality level for a process whose product can not be subjected to quantitative measurement but can be classified as 'good' or 'bad', as 'acceptable' or 'not acceptable', as 'defective' or 'not defective'. For instance surface finish of a table, colour or brightness of an article is either acceptable or not acceptable. Such characteristics usually follow binomial or Poisson distribution.

15.8 CONTROL CHARTS FOR VARIABLES

They are used for measurable quality characteristics. They are two kinds:

1. Control charts for sample means ($\overline{x}$ -charts)
2. Control charts for sample ranges (R-charts)

These charts are constructed as follows:

Step 1 : A random sample of size n (n is usually 4 or 5 units) is taken during a manufacturing process over a period of time and the quality measurements $x_1, x_2, \ldots, x_n$ are noted.

Step 2 : The sample mean $\overline{x}$ and the sample range R are calculated using

$$\overline{x} = \frac{x_1 + x_2 + \ldots + x_n}{n} = \frac{\sum_{i=1}^{n} x_i}{n} = \frac{1}{n}\sum_{i=1}^{n} x_i$$

and $$R = x_{max} - x_{min},$$

where x_{max} and x_{min} are the largest and smallest values respectively of measurements $x_1, x_2, \ldots, x_n$.

Step 3 : If the process is found to be stable, k successive samples (k usually varies between 20 to 30) are selected and for each sample, mean $\overline{x}$ and Range R are calculated. Then $\overline{\overline{x}}$ and $\overline{R}$ are computed using

$$\overline{\overline{x}} = \frac{\overline{x}_1 + \overline{x}_2 + \ldots + \overline{x}_k}{k} = \frac{1}{k}\sum_{i=1}^{k} \overline{x}_i,$$

and $$\overline{R} = \frac{R_1 + R_2 + \ldots + R_k}{k} = \frac{1}{k}\sum_{i=1}^{k} R_i.$$

$\overline{x}$ -Chart

Case 1. When mean μ and standard deviation σ are given

If μ and σ are the standard values of mean and standard deviation and if each sample is of size n, then the control limits are given by

$$UCL = \mu + 3\frac{\sigma}{\sqrt{n}},$$

$$CL = \mu,$$

$$LCL = \mu - \frac{3\sigma}{\sqrt{n}}.$$

Case 2. When μ is unknown but σ is known

$$\text{Here, mean} = \overline{\overline{x}} = \frac{\overline{x}_1 + \overline{x}_2 + \ldots.. + \overline{x}_k}{k}.$$

$$\therefore \quad UCL = \overline{\overline{x}} + \frac{3\sigma}{\sqrt{n}},$$

$$CL = \overline{\overline{x}},$$

$$LCL = \overline{\overline{x}} - 3\frac{\sigma}{\sqrt{n}}.$$

Case 3. When μ is known but σ is unknown

In such cases, range is used as a measure of dispersion. It is easy to calculate and is closely related to standard deviation. The average value of range, $\overline{R} = \frac{R_1 + R_2 + \ldots. + R_k}{k}$. Then

$$UCL = \mu + A_2\overline{R},$$

$$CL = \mu,$$

$$\text{LCL} = \mu - A_2\bar{R},$$

where A_2 is found from table 15.1 and depends on the sample size n.

Case 4. When both μ and σ are unknown

In such cases mean is $\bar{\bar{x}}$ and standard deviation is represented by $\bar{R}$. Then

$$\text{UCL} = \bar{\bar{x}} + A_2\,\bar{\text{R}},$$
$$\text{CL} = \bar{\bar{x}},$$
$$\text{LCL} = \bar{\bar{x}} - A_2\,\bar{\text{R}}.$$

Case 5. When specification limits are given

Let LSL and USL be the lower and upper specification limits given. Then

$$\text{mean} = \bar{\bar{x}} = \frac{\text{LSL} + \text{USL}}{2}.$$

$$\therefore \quad \text{UCL} = \bar{\bar{x}} + A_2\,\bar{\text{R}},$$
$$\text{CL} = \bar{\bar{x}},$$
$$\text{LCL} = \bar{\bar{x}} - A_2\,\bar{\text{R}}.$$

R-Chart

(*a*) Centre line = $\bar{\text{R}}$.

(*b*) The upper and lower control limits for R-chart are set using

$$\text{UCL} = \text{D}_4\,\bar{\text{R}} \text{ and } \text{LCL} = \text{D}_3\,\bar{\text{R}},$$

where D_3 and D_4 are also found from table 15.1 and depend on the sample size n.

Remark 1 : The upper and lower process tolerance limits (also called natural tolerance limits) for individual values of x are computed by using

$$\text{UTL}_x = \bar{\bar{x}} + \frac{3\bar{\text{R}}}{d_2} \text{ and } \text{LTL}_x = \bar{\bar{x}} - \frac{3\bar{\text{R}}}{d_2},$$

where d_2 is also found from table 15.1 and depends upon the sample size . If these natural tolerance limits fall within the customer's specifications, the process is said to be capable of meeting the customer specifications. The process capability

$$= 6\sigma = \frac{6\bar{\text{R}}}{d_2}.$$

Remark 2 : The basic assumption for the use and validity of $\bar{x}$ -chart is that the variability in the process with regard to the quantity characteristic being studied is under control. Thus unless specifically given, it is better to ascertain whether the variability is under control or not. This is done with the help of R-chart. If variability is found out of control, then it is of no use to draw the $\bar{x}$ -chart.

TABLE 15.1

Factors used in the $\bar{x}$ and R Quality Control Charts

No. of units in a sample (n)	*Factor for $\bar{x}$ -chart (A_2)*	*Factors for R-chart*		*Factor for estimating σ from $\bar{R}$ (d_2)*
		Lower control limit (D_3)	*Upper control limit (D_4)*	
2	1.88	0	3.27	1.13
3	1.02	0	2.57	1.69
4	0.73	0	2.28	2.06
5	0.58	0	2.11	2.33
6	0.48	0	2.00	2.53

7	0.42	0.08	1.92	2.70
8	0.37	0.14	1.86	2.85
9	0.34	0.18	1.82	2.97
10	0.31	0.22	1.78	3.08
11	0.29	0.26	1.74	3.17
12	0.27	0.28	1.72	3.26
13	0.25	0.31	1.69	3.34
14	0.24	0.33	1.67	3.41
15	0.22	0.35	1.65	3.47
16	0.21	0.36	1.64	3.53
17	0.20	0.38	1.62	3.59
18	0.19	0.39	1.61	3.64
19	0.19	0.40	1.61	3.69
20	0.18	0.41	1.59	3.74

EXAMPLE 15.8-1

The normal diameter of a shaft was considered to be 3.8 cm with a standard deviation of 0.05 cm. If the sample size is 10, determine the control limits.

Solution

Here, $\mu = 3.8$ cm, $\sigma = 0.05$ cm.

$\therefore$ CL $= \mu = 3.8$,

$$\text{UCL} = \mu + \frac{\sigma}{\sqrt{n}} = 3.8 + \frac{0.05}{\sqrt{10}} = 3.8 + 0.016 = 3.816,$$

$$\text{LCL} = \mu - \frac{\sigma}{\sqrt{n}} = 3.8 - \frac{0.05}{\sqrt{10}} = 3.8 - 0.016 = 3.784.$$

EXAMPLE 15.8-2

Samples of size 100 were taken from mass production of a product and the average of sample means was found to be 40 cm. It is known from past experience that it is reasonable to take 13 cm as the population standard deviation. Determine the control limits.

Solution

Here, mean $= \bar{\bar{x}} = 40$ cm, $\sigma = 13$ cm, $n = 100$.

$\therefore$ CL $= \bar{\bar{x}} = 40$,

$$\text{UCL} = \bar{\bar{x}} + \frac{\sigma}{\sqrt{x}} = 40 + \frac{13}{\sqrt{100}} = 40 + 1.3 = 41.3,$$

$$\text{LCL} = \bar{\bar{x}} - \frac{\sigma}{\sqrt{x}} = 40 - \frac{13}{\sqrt{100}} = 40 - 1.3 = 38.7.$$

EXAMPLE 15.8-3

In a factory 20 samples of 5 units each were taken. The population mean was found to be 25 cm and the sum of the ranges for 20 samples is 130 cm. Find the control limits. A_2 for $n = 5$ is 0.58.

Solution

Here, $\mu = 25$ cm, $n = 5$, $k = 20$, $\bar{R} = \frac{130}{20} = 6.5$ cm, $A_2 = 0.58$.

$\therefore$ CL $= \mu = 25$,

$$\text{UCL} = \mu + A_2\bar{R} = 25 + 0.58 \times 6.5 = 25 + 3.77 = 28.77,$$

$$\text{LCL} = \mu - A_2\bar{R} = 25 - 0.58 \times 6.5 = 25 - 3.77 = 21.23.$$

EXAMPLE 15.8-4

In a factory 20 samples of 4 units each were taken and the critical dimension was measured giving $\Sigma x_i = 400$ cm and $\Sigma R_i = 120$ cm. Determine the control limits. A_2 for $n = 4$ is 0.73.

Solution

Here, $\bar{\bar{x}} = \dfrac{\Sigma x_i}{k} = \dfrac{400}{20} = 20$ cm, $\bar{R} = \dfrac{\Sigma R_i}{k} = \dfrac{120}{20} = 6$ cm.

$\therefore$ CL $= \bar{\bar{x}} = 20$,

UCL $= \bar{\bar{x}} + A_2\bar{R} = 20 + 0.73 \times 6 = 20 + 4.38 = 24.38$,

LCL $= \bar{\bar{x}} - A_2\bar{R} = 20 - 0.73 \times 6 = 20 - 4.38 = 15.62$.

EXAMPLE 15.8-5

A company manufactures screws to a nominal diameter 0.500 ± 0.030 cm. Five samples were taken randomly from the manufactured lot and 3 measurements were taken on each sample at different lengths. The readings are shown in the table below

TABLE 15.2

Sample no.	*Measurements per sample (cm) x*		
	1	*2*	*3*
1	*0.488*	*0.489*	*0.505*
2	*0.494*	*0.495*	*0.499*
3	*0.498*	*0.515*	*0.487*
4	*0.492*	*0.509*	*0.514*
5	*0.490*	*0.508*	*0.499*

Calculate the control limits on $\bar{x}$ and R-charts and draw the charts.

[Dayalbagh Edu. Institute Agra B.B.M. May, 2010]

Solution

Calculation of mean

For sample 1, $\bar{x}_1 = \dfrac{0.488 + 0.489 + 0.505}{3} = 0.494$.

For sample 2, $\bar{x}_2 = \dfrac{0.494 + 0.495 + 0.499}{3} = 0.496$.

Similarly, $\bar{x}_3 = 0.500, \bar{x}_4 = 0.505, \bar{x}_5 = 0.499$.

$\therefore$ $\bar{\bar{x}} = \dfrac{\bar{x}_1 + \bar{x}_2 + \bar{x}_3 + \bar{x}_4 + \bar{x}_5}{5} = 0.499$.

Calculation of range

For sample 1, $R_1 = (X_{max} - X_{min})$ for sample 1

$= 0.505 - 0.488 = 0.017$.

Similarly, $R_2 = 0.499 - 0.494 = 0.005$,

$R_3 = 0.515 - 0.487 = 0.028$,

$R_4 = 0.514 - 0.492 = 0.022$,

and $R_5 = 0.508 - 0.490 = 0.018$.

$\therefore$ $\bar{R} = \dfrac{R_1 + R_2 + R_3 + R_4 + R_5}{5} = 0.018$.

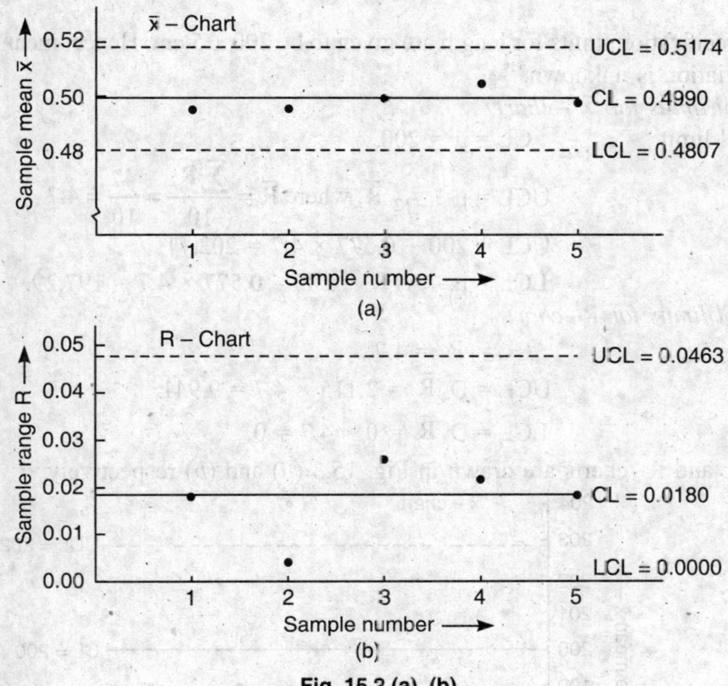

Fig. 15.2 (a), (b)

Trial control limits

Control limits for $\bar{x}$ –chart

$A_2 = 1.02$ for $n = 3$ from table 15.1.

$$\therefore \quad CL = \bar{\bar{x}} = 0.499,$$

$$UCL = \bar{\bar{x}} + A_2\bar{R} = 0.499 + 1.02 \times 0.018 = 0.5174,$$

$$LCL = \bar{\bar{x}} - A_2\bar{R} = 0.499 - 1.02 \times 0.018 = 0.4807.$$

These control limits lie within the manufacturer's assigned limits of $0.50 + 0.03 = 0.53$ and $0.50 - 0.03 = 0.47$.

Control limits for R–chart

$$CL = \bar{R} = 0.018,$$

$$UCL = D_4\bar{R} = 2.57 \times 0.018 = 0.0463, \text{ (From table 15.1 for } n = 3)$$

$$LCL = D_3\bar{R} = 0 \times 0.018 = 0.00.$$

The $\bar{x}$ -chart and R-chart are shown plotted in Fig. 15.2 (*a*) and (*b*) respectively.

It can be seen from the figures that no value of $\bar{x}$ or R is out of the control limits. Therefore, the trial control limits are the actual control limits. The process is in statistical control *i.e.*, it is operating free from assignable causes of variations and is only under the influence of chance causes of variations.

Example 15.8-6

The following are the mean lengths and ranges of lengths of a finished product from 10 samples each of size 5. The specification limits for length are 200 ±5 cm. Construct $\bar{x}$ and R charts and examine whether the process is under control and state your recommendations.

Sample no.	:	*1*	*2*	*3*	*4*	*5*	*6*	*7*	*8*	*9*	*10*
Mean $\bar{x}$	:	*201*	*198*	*202*	*200*	*203*	*204*	*199*	*196*	*199*	*201*
Range R	:	*5*	*0*	*7*	*3*	*4*	*7*	*2*	*8*	*5*	*6*

Assume for $n = 5$, $A_2 = 0.577$, $D_3 = 0$, $D_4 = 2.115$.

[*Dayalbagh Edu. Institute Agra M.Com. Dec., 2008*]

Solution

The specification limits for length are given to be 200 ± 5 cm. Hence, mean is known whereas standard deviation is unknown.

Control limits for $\overline{x}$ –chart

Central limit, $\quad CL = \mu = 200,$

$$UCL = \mu + A_2\ \overline{R}, \text{ where } \overline{R} = \frac{\sum R_i}{10} = \frac{47}{10} = 4.7\,.$$

$$\therefore \quad UCL = 200 + 0.577 \times 4.7 = 202.71,$$

$$LCL = \mu - A_2\overline{R} = 200 - 0.577 \times 4.7 = 197.29.$$

Control limits for R–chart

$$CL = \overline{R} = 4.7,$$

$$UCL = D_4\overline{R} = 2.115 \times 4.7 = 9.941,$$

$$LCL = D_3\overline{R} = 0 \times 4.7 = 0.$$

The $\overline{x}$ and R–charts are drawn in Fig. 15.3 (*a*) and (*b*) respectively.

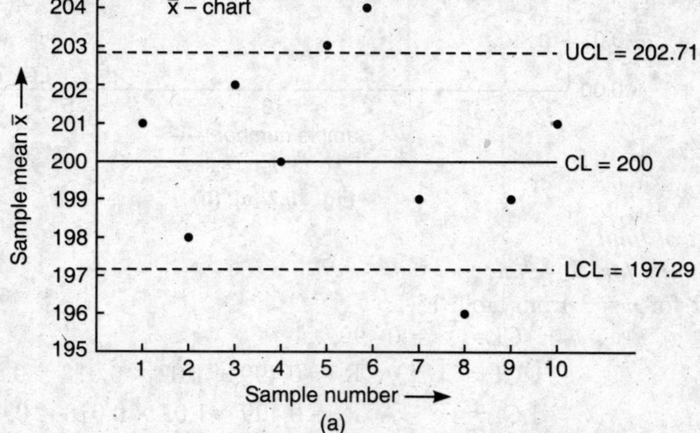

(a)

It can be seen that all points lie within the control limits of R–chart. The process variability is, therefore, under control. However, three points corresponding to sample no. 5,6 and 8 lie outside the control limits of $\overline{x}$ –chart. The process is, therefore, not in statistical control. The process, therefore, should be halted to check whether there are any assignable causes. If they are found, the process should be readjusted to remove them, otherwise fluctuations are going to be there.

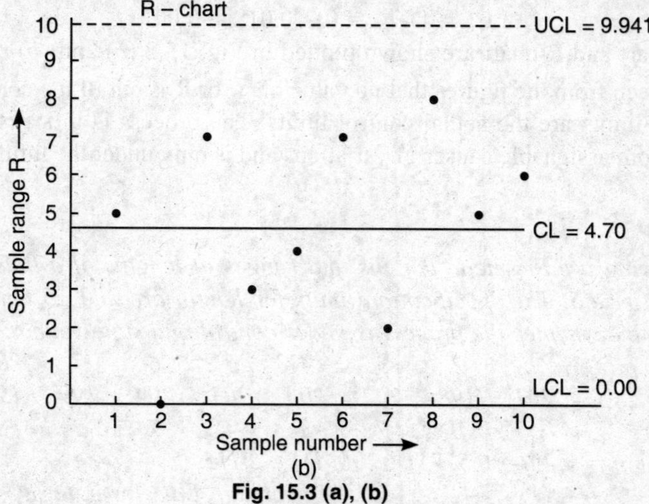

(b)

Fig. 15.3 (a), (b)

EXAMPLE 15.8-7

Consider a cropping press on which bars are to be cut continually to a length of 12 cm. A random sample of 5 bars is taken from each hour's production and for each sample, the mean and range are calculated as shown in table 15.3. Construct $\overline{x}$ and R–charts and examine whether the process is under control and state your recommendations.

TABLE 15.3

Sample (Size n = 5)	Mean $\overline{x}_i$	Range R_i
9 AM	12.004	0.008
10 AM	12.002	0.007
11 AM	11.992	0.010
12 AM	11.993	0.004
1 PM	12.009	0.005
2 PM	12.003	0.015
3 PM	11.995	0.012
4 PM	12.003	0.007
5 PM	12.003	0.009
6 PM	12.000	0.010
7 PM	11.998	0.005
8 PM	11.996	0.014
9 PM	12.001	0.010
10 PM	12.000	0.011

Solution

$$\overline{\overline{x}} = \frac{\sum x_i}{k} = \frac{12.004 + 12.002 + ... + 12.000}{14} = \frac{167.991}{14} = 11.9994,$$

$$\overline{R} = \frac{\sum R_i}{k} = \frac{0.008 + 0.007 + ... + 0.011}{14} = \frac{0.127}{14} = 0.0091.$$

Control limits for $\overline{x}$ –chart

Central limit, CL = $\overline{\overline{x}}$ = 11.9994, upper control limit, UCL = $\overline{\overline{x}} + A_2\overline{R}$,

where A_2 for $n = 5$ from table 15.1 is 0.58.

∴ UCL = 11.9994 + 0.58 × 0.0091 = 12.0047,

LCL = 11.9994 – 0.58 × 0.0091 = 11.994.

Control limits for R –chart

CL = $\overline{R}$ = 0.0091,

UCL = $D_4\overline{R}$ = 2.11 × 0.0091 = 0.0192,

LCL = $D_3\overline{R}$ = 0 × 0.0091 = 0.00.

The $\overline{x}$ –chart and R–chart are shown plotted in Fig. 15.4 (*a*) and (*b*) respectively.

Charts indicate that the process is coming under statistical control and it is beginning to settle down. The mean lengths from earlier samples were probably unacceptable (sample no. 3 and 4) but towards the end of the day the process was under better control.

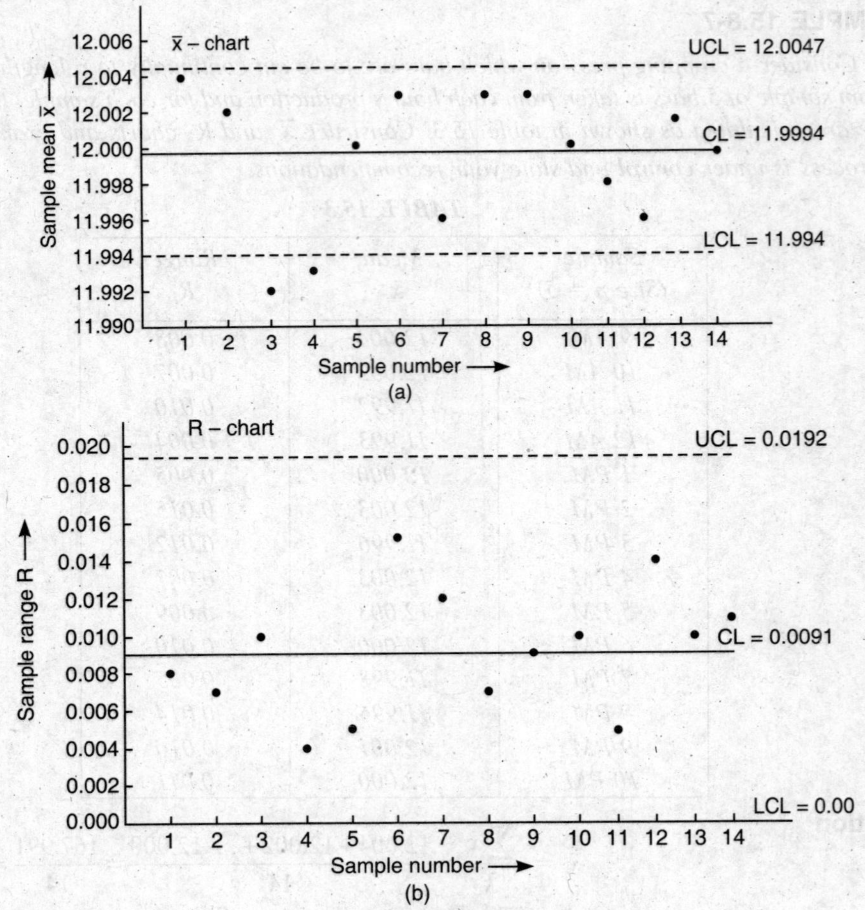

Fig. 15.4 (a) and (b)

EXAMPLE 15.8-8

Construct a control chart for mean and the range for the following data on the basis of fuses, samples of 5 being taken every hour (each set of 5 has been arranged in ascending order of magnitude).

42	*42*	*19*	*36*	*42*	*51*	*60*	*18*	*15*	*69*	*64*	*61*
65	*45*	*24*	*54*	*51*	*74*	*60*	*20*	*30*	*109*	*90*	*78*
75	*68*	*80*	*89*	*57*	*75*	*72*	*27*	*39*	*113*	*93*	*94*
78	*72*	*81*	*77*	*59*	*78*	*95*	*42*	*62*	*118*	*109*	*109*
87	*90*	*81*	*84*	*78*	*132*	*138*	*60*	*84*	*153*	*112*	*136*

Comment on whether the production process seems to be under control.

[*Gujrat Univ. M.B.A., 1983*]

Solution

The sample mean $\overline{x}$ and sample range R are calculated in table 15.4.

TABLE 15.4

Sample no. (1)	*Sample observation, x (2)*					Σx	*Sample mean* $\overline{x} = \Sigma x/5$	*Sample range R*
1	42	65	75	78	87	347	69.4	45
2	42	45	68	72	90	317	63.4	48

3	19	24	80	81	81	285	57.0	62
4	36	54	89	77	84	340	68.0	53
5	42	51	57	59	78	287	57.4	36
6	51	74	75	78	132	410	82.0	81
7	60	60	72	95	138	425	85.0	78
8	18	20	27	42	60	167	33.4	42
9	15	30	39	62	84	230	46.0	69
10	69	109	113	118	153	562	112.4	84
11	64	90	93	109	112	468	93.6	48
12	61	78	94	109	136	478	95.6	75
						Total:	863.2	721

$$\therefore \qquad \bar{\bar{x}} = \frac{863.2}{12} = 71.92, \quad \bar{R} = \frac{721}{12} = 60.08.$$

From taole 15.1 , for $n = 5$, $A_2 = 0.58$, $D_4 = 2.11$, $D_3 = 0$.

Control limits for $\bar{x}$ *– chart*

$$CL = \bar{\bar{x}} = 71.92,$$

$$UCL = \bar{\bar{x}} + A_2\bar{R} = 71.92 + 0.58 \times 60.08 = 106.77,$$

$$LCL = \bar{\bar{x}} - A_2\bar{R} = 71.92 - 0.58 \times 60.08 = 37.07.$$

Control limits for R – chart

$$CL = \bar{R} = 60.08,$$

$$UCL = D_4\bar{R} = 2.11 \times 60.08 = 126.77,$$

$$LCL = D_3\bar{R} = 0 \times 60.08 = 0.00.$$

The $\bar{x}$ – chart and R – chart are shown plotted in Fig. 15.5 (*a*) and (*b*) respectively.

Since sample mean corresponding to sample number 8 and 10 is outside the control limits, the $\bar{x}$ – chart indicates the presence of some assignable causes of variations which should be detected and corrected. The R – chart shows that the process variability is under control since all the sample range points are within the control limits.

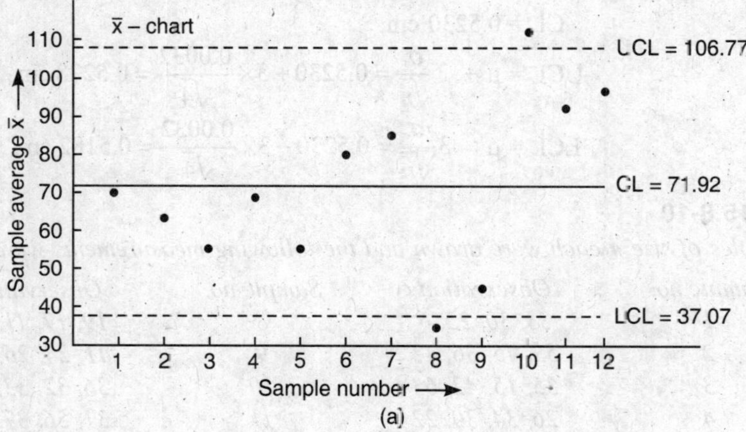

(a)

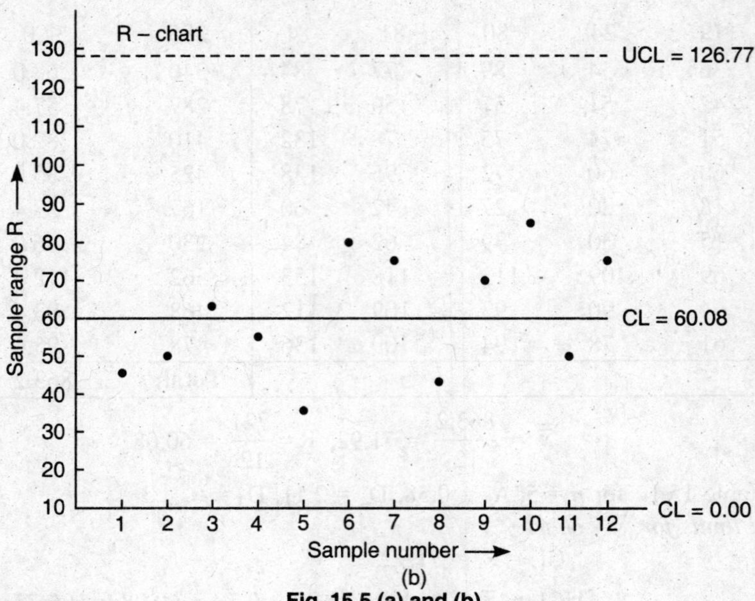

(b)

Fig. 15.5 (a) and (b)

EXAMPLE 15.8-9

A drilling machine bores holes with a mean diameter of 0.5230 cm and a standard deviation of 0.0032 cm. Calculate the 2-sigma and 3-sigma upper and lower control limits for means of sample of 4.

Solution

Here $\mu = 0.5230$ cm, $\sigma = 0.0032$ cm, and $n = 4$.

2-sigma limits for means

$$\text{CL} = 0.5230 \text{ cm},$$

$$\text{UCL} = \mu + 2\frac{\sigma}{\sqrt{n}} = 0.5230 + 2\times\frac{0.0032}{\sqrt{4}} = 0.5262 \text{ cm},$$

$$\text{LCL} = \mu - 2\frac{\sigma}{\sqrt{n}} = 0.5230 - 2\times\frac{0.0032}{\sqrt{4}} = 0.5198 \text{ cm}.$$

3-sigma limits for means

$$\text{CL} = 0.5230 \text{ cm},$$

$$\text{UCL} = \mu + 3\frac{\sigma}{\sqrt{n}} = 0.5230 + 3\times\frac{0.0032}{\sqrt{4}} = 0.5278 \text{ cm},$$

$$\text{LCL} = \mu - 3\frac{\sigma}{\sqrt{n}} = 0.5230 - 3\times\frac{0.0032}{\sqrt{4}} = 0.5182 \text{ cm}.$$

EXAMPLE 15.8-10

15 samples of size 4 each were drawn and the following measurements were made:

Sample no.	*Observation*	*Sample no.*	*Observation*
1	*33, 30, 22, 6*	*8*	*19, 17, 11, 21*
2	*52, 45, 36, 47*	*9*	*11, 24, 26, 31*
3	*35, 15, 42, 63*	*10*	*36, 32, 33, 36*
4	*26, 34, 30, 22*	*11*	*31, 56, 37, 29*
5	*31, 27, 30, 29*	*12*	*40, 27, 47, 53*
6	*29, 34, 27, 16*	*13*	*34, 16, 37, 33*
7	*28, 34, 33, 32*	*14*	*27, 34, 24, 37*
		15	*12, 10, 15, 28*

Determine the control limits for $\overline{x}$ -chart and R-chart and draw these charts. Take $A_2 = 0.729$, $D_3 = 0$ and $D_4 = 2.282$ for $n = 4$.

Solution

The sample mean $\overline{x}$ and variance R are calculated in table 15.5.

TABLE 15.5

Sample no. (1)	*Sample observation, x (2)*				Σx	*Sample mean* $\overline{x} = \Sigma x/4$	*Sample range* $R = x_{max} - x_{min}$
1	33	30	22	6	91	22.75	27
2	52	45	36	47	180	45.00	16
3	35	15	42	63	155	38.75	48
4	26	34	30	22	112	28.00	12
5	31	27	30	29	117	29.25	4
6	29	34	27	16	106	26.50	18
7	28	34	33	32	127	31.75	6
8	19	17	11	21	68	17.00	10
9	11	24	26	31	92	23.00	20
10	36	32	33	26	127	31.75	10
11	31	16	37	29	113	28.25	21
12	40	27	47	53	167	41.75	26
13	34	16	37	33	120	30.00	21
14	27	34	24	37	122	30.50	13
15	12	10	15	28	65	16.25	18
					Total:	440.50	270

$\therefore \quad \overline{\overline{x}} = \dfrac{440.50}{15} = 29.37, \qquad \overline{R} = \dfrac{270}{15} = 18.$

Control limits for $\overline{x}$ -chart

$$CL = \overline{\overline{x}} = 29.37,$$

$$UCL = \overline{\overline{x}} + A_2\overline{R} = 29.37 + 0.729 \times 18 = 29.37 + 13.122 = 42.492,$$

$$LCL = \overline{\overline{x}} - A_2\overline{R} = 29.37 - 0.729 \times 18 = 29.37 - 13.122 = 16.248.$$

Control limits for R-chart

$$CL = \overline{R} = 18,$$

$$UCL = D_4\overline{R} = 2.282 \times 18 = 41.076,$$

$$LCL = D_3\overline{R} = 0 \times 18 = 0.$$

The $\overline{x}$ -chart and R-chart are shown plotted in Fig. 15.6(*a*) and (*b*) respectively.

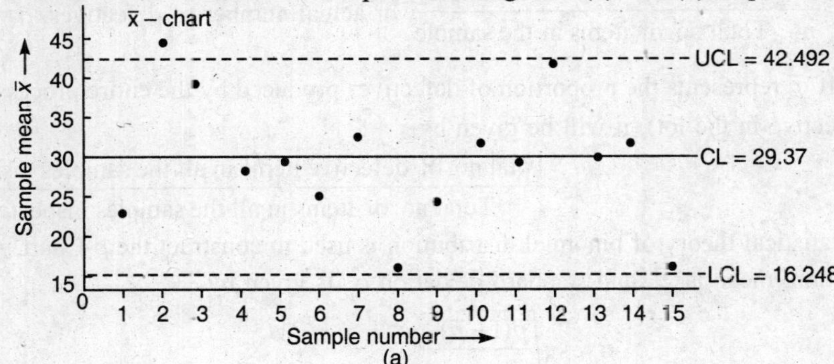

(a)

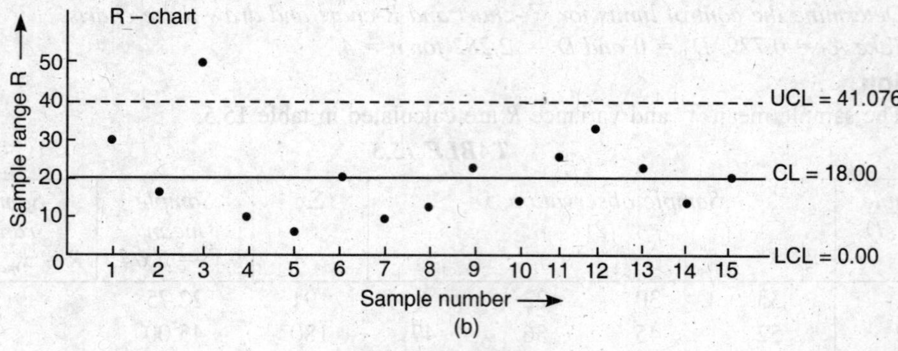

Fig. 15.6 (a) and (b)

Since sample range corresponding to sample no. 3 is outside the control limits, the process is out of control with respect to variability and there is no significance of drawing $\overline{x}$ -chart. However, $\overline{x}$ -chart is also drawn in Fig. 15.6(*a*) to just illustrate the procedure for plotting the points. Even in this chart, sample mean corresponding to sample no. 2 is out of the upper control limit. The process is clearly out of control.

15.9 CONTROL CHARTS FOR ATTRIBUTES

In inspection by variables, actual measurement of the dimensions is done. However, this is sometimes difficult as well as uneconomical.

Inspection by attributes is just the other way of inspection. In this method actual measurements are not done, instead the number of defectives are counted. The size of defect and its location is not important. The products are inspected the same way as by 'GO' and 'NOT GO' gauges and are either accepted or rejected. Some examples of control by attributes are

(*i*) Number of defectives in a lot
(*ii*) Number of mistakes on the part of a typist
(*iii*) Number of spots in a distempered wall
(*iv*) Number of absentees in a department
(*v*) Number of complaints on a product per month, etc.

The three most commonly used control charts for attributes are

1. Control chart for fraction defective (*p*-chart)
2. Control chart for number of defectives (*np*-chart)
3. Control chart for number of defects (C-chart).

Control Chart for Fraction Defective (p-Chart)

Let samples (10 to 20) of size *n* be taken from the production process randomly at different time intervals. If *d* is the number of the defectives in a sample, then the fraction defective in the sample, $p = \frac{d}{n} = \frac{\text{No. of defectives in a sample}}{\text{Total no. of items in the sample}}$ or actual number of defectives, $d = np$.

Then if $\overline{p}$ represents the proportion of defectives produced by the entire process (also called fraction defective in the lot), it will be given by

$$\overline{p} = \frac{\text{Total no. of defective items in all the samples inspected}}{\text{Total no. of items in all the samples inspected}}.$$

The statistical theory of binomial distribution is used to construct the *p*-Chart. According to this distribution, mean is $\overline{p}$ and standard deviation σ_p is given by

$$\sigma_p = \sqrt{\frac{\overline{p}(1-\overline{p})}{n}}.$$

Like other distributions, binomial samples can be assumed to follow a normal distribution. Thus the control limits for the *p*-chart are

$$\text{CL} = \bar{p},$$

$$\text{UCL} = \bar{p} + 3\sigma_p = \bar{p} + 3\sqrt{\frac{\bar{p}(1-\bar{p})}{n}},$$

$$\text{LCL} = \bar{p} - 3\sigma_p = \bar{p} - 3\sqrt{\frac{\bar{p}(1-\bar{p})}{n}}.$$

Since number of defectives cannot be negative, if LCL sometimes comes out to be negative, it is taken as zero. *p*-chart is normally used to plot and control fraction defectives when the sample size does not remain uniform or it varies. However, it may also be used when the sample size remains constant or uniform.

Control Chart for Number of Defectives (*np*-Chart)

Let samples of size n be taken from the production process randomly at different intervals of time. If d is the number of defectives in the sample and p is the fraction defective in the sample, then $d = np$.

Now if $n\bar{p}$ represents the number of defectives per sample of a constant size, then

$$n\bar{p} = \frac{\text{Total no. of defectives of all samples}}{\text{Number of samples inspected}}.$$

Standard deviation σ_{np} of the *np*-chart is given by

$$\sigma_{np} = n\sqrt{\frac{\bar{p}(1-\bar{p})}{n}} = \sqrt{n\bar{p}(1-\bar{p})}.$$

Thus the control limits for the *np*-chart are

$$\text{CL} = n\bar{p},$$

$$\text{UCL} = n\bar{p} + 3\sigma_{np} = n\bar{p} + 3\sqrt{n\bar{p}(1-\bar{p})},$$

$$\text{LCL} = n\bar{p} - 3\sigma_{np} = n\bar{p} - 3\sqrt{n\bar{p}(1-\bar{p})}.$$

If LCL comes out to be negative, it should be taken as zero. *np*-chart is used to plot and control the number of defectives when the sample size remains constant.

Remarks: 1. The control limit found initially may be revised for out of control points provided the assignable causes are located and one can hope that they remain suppressed in future also.

2. The control charts may be reviewed periodically. A sustained evidence of reduction in fraction defectives should be viewed as an improvement in the production process rather than relaxation in inspection.

3. If a process is statistically in control as per *p*-chart but number of fraction defectives is too high, it means the situation can be improved only by some fundamental change.

4. *p* and *np*-charts are not as sensitive as the control charts for variables as they require much larger sample size.

Control Chart for Number of Defects (C-Chart)

It is a type of control chart used to monitor 'count' type of data. When the production process involves complex assembly of a large number of components, such as in the manufacture of an aircraft, an automobile, a T.V., a computer , cloth, etc. a knowledge of the number of defects per unit is useful in maintaining a satisfactory level of quality. Other examples that fall within this category are number of mistakes in a paragraph, number of complaints received per day by an organisation and number of phone calls received per unit of time. In such cases we can base control limits on the assumption that the Poisson distribution is applicable. Since the mean and variance of a Poisson distribution are equal, the standard deviation is given by

$$\sigma_c = \sqrt{\bar{C}},$$

where $\bar{C}$ denotes the average number of defects in a sample and is given by

$$\bar{C} = \frac{\text{Total no. of defects in all the samples}}{\text{Total no. of samples inspected}}.$$

Thus the control limits for the C-chart are

$$\text{CL} = \bar{C},$$

$$\text{UCL} = \bar{C} + 3\sigma_c = \bar{C} + 3\sqrt{\bar{C}},$$

$$\text{LCL} = \bar{C} - 3\sigma_c = \bar{C} - 3\sqrt{\bar{C}}.$$

The C-chart relates to samples of constant size. In case the sample size varies, the control chart for number of defects per unit, $u = \dfrac{C}{n}$ is used. The average number of defects per unit, $\bar{u} = \dfrac{\Sigma C}{\Sigma n}$ and the control limits are given by

$$\text{CL} = \bar{u},$$

$$\text{UCL} = \bar{u} + 3\sqrt{\frac{\bar{u}}{n}},$$

$$\text{LCL} = \bar{u} - 3\sqrt{\frac{\bar{u}}{n}}.$$

Remarks: 1. The defects need not be just of one kind only.

2. Quite often, all the defects have to be removed by 100% inspection, especially in case of large assemblies and subassemblies.

3. C-chart can also be applied for acceptance sampling.

4. All defects may not be of the same nature. Some may be more serious than others. In such situations, the defects may be classified into different categories A, B, C etc., appropriate weightage may be assigned to each category by the experts and the number of *demerits* rather than defects may be computed. For instance, an item may have two types of defects, say A and B. If there are two type A defects and three type B defects and the weights attached to the two types of defects are 3 and 4, then the demerit level of the item = (2 × 3 + 3 × 4) = 18. The control chart may then be based on demerits, rather than defects.

EXAPMLE 15.9-1

In a blade manufacturing factory 1,000 blades are examined daily. Following information shows number of defective blades obtained thereto. Draw the np-chart and give your findings.

Day (i)	:	*1*	*2*	*3*	*4*	*5*	*6*	*7*	*8*	*9*	*10*	*11*	*12*	*13*	*14*	*15*
No. of defective blades (p_i)	:	*9*	*10*	*12*	*8*	*7*	*15*	*10*	*12*	*10*	*8*	*7*	*13*	*14*	*15*	*16*

[Dayalbagh Edu. Inst. Agra BBM May, 2001]

Solution

Here, n = 1,000 and k = 15. If $\bar{p}$ denotes the fraction of defectives produced by the entire process, then

$$\bar{p} = \frac{\Sigma p_i}{15 \times 1{,}000} = \frac{166}{15{,}000} = 0.011.$$

$$\therefore \quad n\bar{p} = 0.011 \times 1{,}000 = 11.$$

$$\therefore \quad \text{CL} = n\bar{p} = 11,$$

$$\text{UCL} = n\bar{p} + 3\sqrt{n\bar{p}\,(1-\bar{p})} = 11 + 3\sqrt{11\,(1-0.011)}$$

$$= 11 + 3 \times 3.298 = 20.89,$$

$$LCL = n\overline{p} - 3\sqrt{n\overline{p}\,(1-\overline{p})} = 11 - 3\sqrt{11\,(1-0.011)}$$
$$= 11 - 3 \times 3.298 = 1.105.$$

The *np*-chart is drawn in Fig. 15.7.

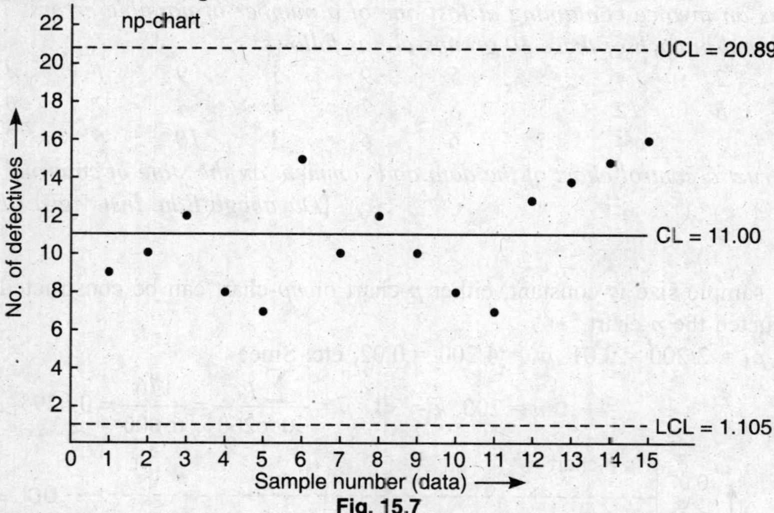

Fig. 15.7

Since, all the 15 points lie within the control limits, the process is under control.

EXAMPLE 15.9-2

The average percentage of defectives in 27 samples of size 1,500 each was found to be 13.7%. Construct a suitable control chart for this situation. Explain how the control chart can be used to control quality. [*C.A. (Final) 1989*]

Solution

For this problem both *np*-chart and *p*-chart can be constructed as sample size is constant. However, we shall construct *p*-chart only.

Here, $k = 27$, $n = 1{,}500$ and $\overline{p} = 0.137$.

$$\therefore \quad CL = \overline{p} = 0.137,$$

$$UCL = \overline{p} + 3\sqrt{\frac{\overline{p}\,(1-\overline{p})}{n}} = 0.137 + 3\sqrt{\frac{0.137\,(1-0.137)}{1{,}500}}$$
$$= 0.137 + 3 \times 8.878 \times 10^{-3} = 0.137 + 0.027 = 0.164,$$

$$LCL = \overline{p} - 3\sqrt{\frac{\overline{p}\,(1-\overline{p})}{n}} = 0.137 - 0.027 = 0.110$$

The *p*-chart is drawn in Fig. 15.8. This chart can be used for quality control. If all the defectives (to be plotted as points in the chart) lie within the control limits, the process is under control. If some defectives fall outside these limits, one should look for assignable cause.

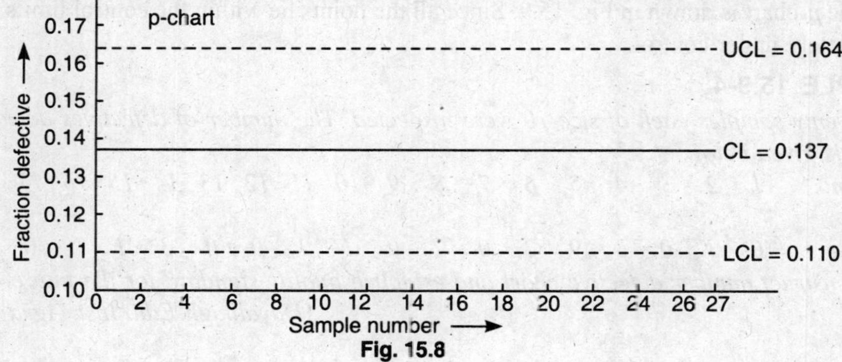

Fig. 15.8

EXAMPLE 15.9-3

A nationwide mail order house desires to verify the accuracy of its clerical work in completing invoices. Subgroups of 200 are taken each day for 30 consecutive days for inspection. A defective is defined as an invoice containing at last one of a number of possible errors. The numbers of defectives found in each of these 30 groups are as follows:

2	4	3	5	9	5	9	1	4	8
8	12	5	8	7	4	4	7	9	9
5	4	5	6	6	3	10	6	2	6

Construct a control chart of the data and comment on the state of control.

[*Dayabagh Edu. Inst. Agra BBM May, 2008*]

Solution

Since sample size is constant, either *p*-chart or *np*-chart can be constructed. However, we shall constructed the *p*-chart.

Here, $p_1 = 2/200 = 0.01$, $p_2 = 4/200 = 0.02$, etc. Since

$$n = 200,\ k = 30,\ \overline{p} = \frac{\sum p_i}{30 \times 200} = \frac{176}{6{,}000} = 0.0293.$$

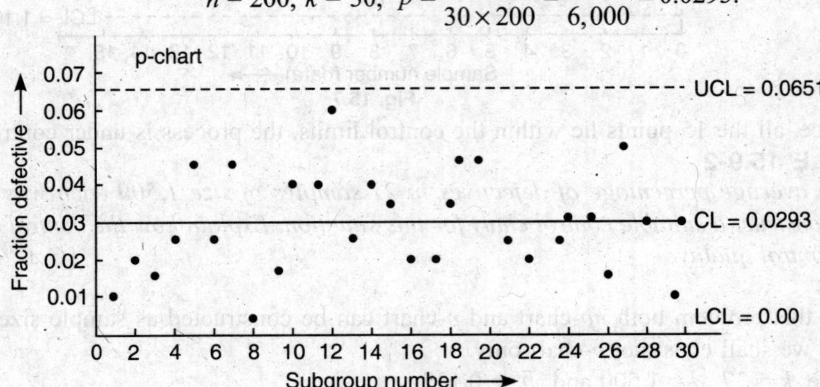

Fig. 15.9

∴ Control limits for the *p*-chart are

$$\text{CL} = \overline{p} = 0.0293,$$

$$\text{UCL} = \overline{p} + 3\sqrt{\frac{\overline{p}(1-\overline{p})}{n}} = 0.0293 + 3\sqrt{\frac{0.0293\,(1-0.0293)}{200}}$$

$$= 0.0293 + 3 \times 0.0119 = 0.0651,$$

$$\text{LCL} = \overline{p} - 3\sqrt{\frac{\overline{p}(1-\overline{p})}{n}} = 0.0293 - 3 \times 0.0119 = -0.0064 \simeq 0\cdot$$

The *p*-chart is drawn in Fig. 15.9. Since all the points lie within the control limits, the process is completely under control.

EXAMPLE 15.9-4

Twenty samples each of size 10 were inspected. The number of defectives detected in each of them is given below.

Sample no. :	*1*	*2*	*3*	*4*	*5*	*6*	*7*	*8*	*9*	*10*	*11*	*12*	*13*	*14*	*15*	*16*	*17*	*18*	*19*	*20*
No. of defectives :	*0*	*1*	*0*	*3*	*9*	*2*	*0*	*7*	*0*	*1*	*1*	*0*	*0*	*3*	*1*	*0*	*0*	*2*	*0*	*0*

Construct number defective chart and establish quality standard for the future.

[*Dayalbagh Edu. Inst. Agra Dec., 2006*]

Solution

Here, $n = 10$, $k = 20$.

$$\therefore \qquad \bar{p} = \frac{\sum p_i}{20 \times 10} = \frac{30}{200} = 0.15$$

and $\qquad n\bar{p} = 0.15 \times 10 = 1.5.$

Control limits for *np*-chart are

$$\text{CL} = 1.5,$$

$$\text{UCL} = n\bar{p} + 3\sqrt{n\bar{p}(1-\bar{p})} = 1.5 + 3\sqrt{1.5\,(1-0.15)} = 4.89,$$

$$\text{LCL} = n\bar{p} - 3\sqrt{n\bar{p}(1-\bar{p})} = 1.5 - 3\sqrt{1.5\,(1-0.15)} = -1.89 \simeq 0.$$

np-chart is shown in Fig. 15.10.

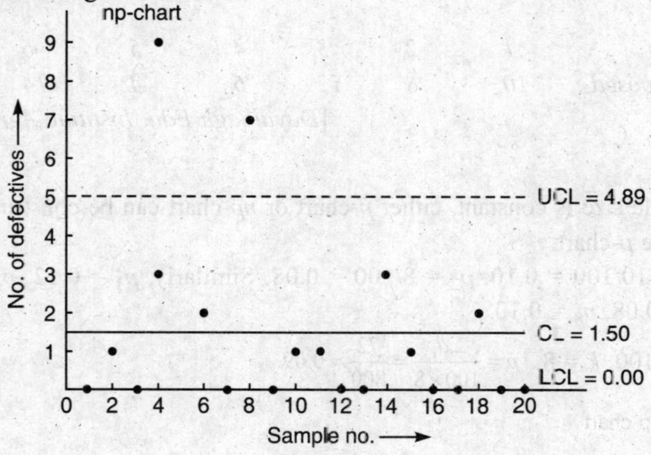

Fig. 15.10

Since two points (corresponding to sample nos. 5 and 8) lie outside the control limits, the process is out of control. To establish quality control *for the future*, we homogenise the data. Deleting sample number 5 and 8, we compute again new values of the limits.

$$\therefore \qquad \bar{p}_1 = \frac{30-(9+7)}{200-(10+10)} = \frac{14}{180} = 0.078,$$

$$n\bar{p}_1 = 0.078 \times 10 = 0.78.$$

New control limits for *np*-chart are

$$\text{CL}_1 = n\bar{p}_1 = 0.78,$$

$$\text{UCL}_1 = n\bar{p}_1 + 3\sqrt{n\bar{p}_1(1-\bar{p}_1)} = 0.78 + 3\sqrt{0.78\,(1-0.078)}$$

$$= 0.78 + 3 \times 0.848 = 3.324,$$

$$\text{LCL}_1 = 0.78 - 3 \times 0.848 = -1.764 \simeq 0.$$

The *np*-chart is shown in Fig. 15.11.

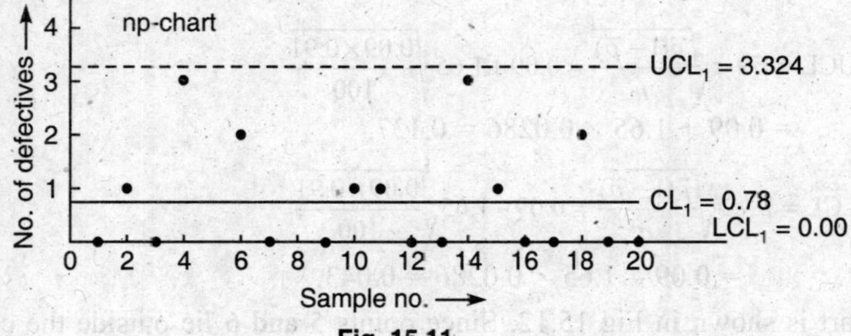

Fig. 15.11

Since in Fig. 15.11, all the points (except the two which have been deleted) lie within the control limits, we take these new limits, along with the new centre line as standards for controlling production *in the future.*

EXAMPLE 15.9-5

A town's department of Public Works is concerned about adverse public reaction to a sewer project that is currently in progress. Because of this, the commissioner of Public Works has authorised a weekly survey to be conducted of the residents. Each week, a sample of 100 residents is questioned on their feelings towards the project. The results todate are shown below. Analyse this data using an appropriate control chart with 5% risk of Type 1 error. Is the community sentiment stable ?

Week :	*1*	*2*	*3*	*4*	*5*	*6*	*7*	*8*
Number opposed :	*10*	*8*	*12*	*6*	*4*	*14*	*8*	*10*

[*Dayalbagh Edu. Institute Agra MBA, May, 2010*]

Solution

Since sample size is constant, either *p*-chart or *np*-chart can be constructed. However, we shall construct the *p*-chart.

Here, $p_1 = 10/100 = 0.10$, $p_2 = 8/100 = 0.08$. Similarly, $p_3 = 0.12$, $p_4 = 0.06$, $p_5 = 0.04$, $p_6 = 0.14$, $p_7 = 0.08$, $p_8 = 0.10$.

Since, $n = 100$, $k = 8$, $\overline{p} = \dfrac{\Sigma d_i}{100 \times 8} = \dfrac{72}{800} = 0.09.$

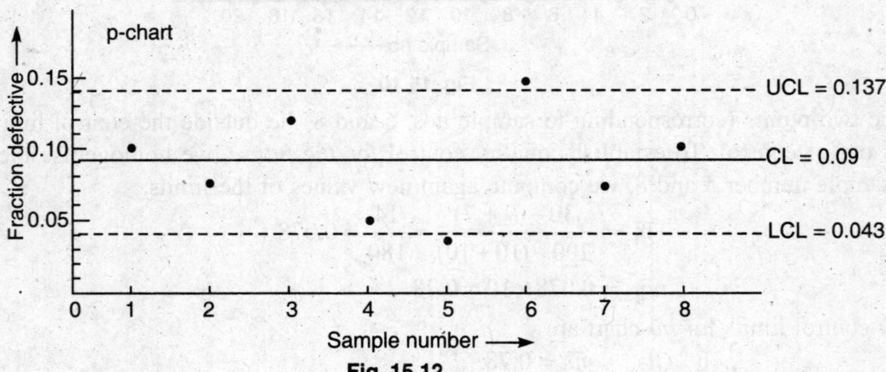

Fig. 15.12

A control chart with 5% risk of type 1 error means a chart for probability of confidence of 0.95. Value of *z* for this probability, as seen from table C-2, is 1.65.

∴ Control limits for the *p*-chart are

$$CL = \overline{p} = 0.09,$$

$$UCL = \overline{p} + z\sqrt{\frac{\overline{p}(1-\overline{p})}{n}} = 0.09 + 1.65\sqrt{\frac{0.09 \times 0.91}{100}}$$

$$= 0.09 + 1.65 \times 0.0286 = 0.137.$$

$$LCL = \overline{p} - z\sqrt{\frac{\overline{p}(1-\overline{p})}{n}} = 0.09 - 1.65\sqrt{\frac{0.09 \times 0.91}{100}}$$

$$= 0.09 - 1.65 \times 0.0286 = 0.043.$$

The *p*-chart is shown in Fig 15.12. Since points 5 and 6 lie outside the control limits, the community sentiment is not stable.

EXAMPLE 15.9-6

In the production of tyres, the output of a given size was inspected everyday prior to the tyres being given to the finished goods stores. The number of defectives found every day was summarized in column (3) of the following table, from which the mean defective $\overline{p}$ *and the control limits were calculated. Draw the control chart for fraction defective.*

TABLE 15.6

(1) Date	(2) Number inspected (n)	(3) Defectives (np)	(4) Fraction defective (p_i)	(5) $3\sigma_p = \frac{0.989}{\sqrt{n}}$	(6) UCL $\overline{p} + 3\sigma_p$	(7) LCL $= \overline{p} - 3\sigma_p$
1	600	77	0.128	0.040	0.164	0.084
2	500	78	0.156	0.044	0.168	0.080
3	540	64	0.119	0.042	0.166	0.082
4	610	90	0.147	0.040	0.164	0.084
5	670	96	0.143	0.038	0.162	0.086
6	660	110	0.167	0.038	0.162	0.086
7	650	78	0.120	0.039	0.163	0.085
8	730	88	0.121	0.037	0.161	0.087
9	750	80	0.107	0.036	0.160	0.088
10	720	90	0.125	0.037	0.161	0.087
11	670	71	0.106	0.038	0.162	0.086
12	660	75	0.114	0.038	0.162	0.086
13	650	85	0.131	0.039	0.163	0.085
14	510	70	0.137	0.044	0.168	0.080
15	550	58	0.106	0.042	0.166	0.082
16	590	61	0.103	0.041	0.165	0.083
17	630	65	0.103	0.039	0.163	0.085
18	650	115	0.177	0.039	0.163	0.085
19	700	82	0.117	0.037	0.161	0.087
20	740	55	0.074	0.036	0.160	0.088
Total	12,780	1,588				

Solution

Since the sample size varies, the control limits for constructing the *p*-chart are computed as below:

(*i*) Fraction defective p_i for each sample is calculated. For instance, for sample 1 its value will be = 77/600 = 0.128. These are shown in column (4) of table 15.6.

(*ii*) The average fraction defective is now calculated. It is given by

$$\overline{p} = \frac{\sum np}{\sum n} = \frac{1{,}588}{12{,}780} = 0.124\cdot$$

(*iii*) The value of 3-sigma is different for each sample as the sample size *n* is different. Now

$$3\sigma_p = 3\sqrt{\frac{\bar{p}(1-\bar{p})}{n}} = 3\sqrt{\frac{0.124\,(1-0.124)}{n}} = \frac{0.989}{\sqrt{n}}.$$

The values of $3\sigma_p$ for each sample are computed in column (5) of the table. For sample 1, the value is $0.989/\sqrt{600} = 0.040$.

(*iv*) The upper and lower control limits for each sample are calculated in column (6) and (7) respectively. For sample 1, these values are

$$\text{CL} = \bar{p} = 0.124,$$
$$\text{UCL}_1 = \bar{p} + 3\sigma_p = 0.124 + 0.040 = 0.164,$$
$$\text{LCL}_1 = \bar{p} - 3\sigma_p = 0.124 - 0.040 = 0.084.$$

The control limits CL, UCL and LCL along with variations of p_i for each sample (date) are plotted in Fig. 15.13.

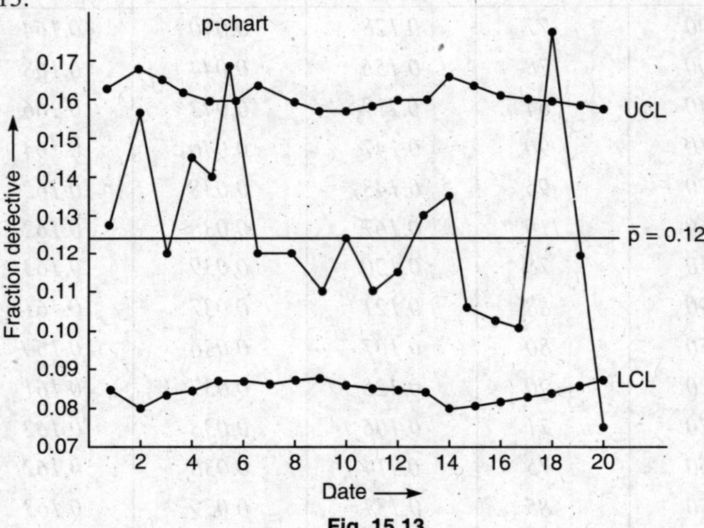

Fig. 15.13

EXAMPLE 15.9-7

Twenty samples each of size 100 were inspected and the results are given below:

Sample no. :	*1*	*2*	*3*	*4*	*5*	*6*	*7*	*8*	*9*	*10*
No. of defectives :	*2*	*1*	*3*	*0*	*2*	*3*	*1*	*2*	*0*	*4*
Sample no. :	*11*	*12*	*13*	*14*	*15*	*16*	*17*	*18*	*19*	*20*
No. of defectives :	*3*	*2*	*0*	*4*	*1*	*7*	*0*	*1*	*3*	*1*

Draw *p*-chart taking 3σ limits and *np*-chart with 1σ limits.

Solution

Here, $n = 100$, $k = 20$.

$$\therefore\ \bar{p} = \frac{\Sigma p_i}{20 \times 100} = \frac{40}{2{,}000} = 0.02,$$

and $n\bar{p} = 0.02 \times 100 = 2.$

***p*-chart**

Control limits for *p*-chart for 3σ limits are

$$\text{CL} = \bar{p} = 0.02,$$
$$\text{UCL} = \bar{p} + 3\sqrt{\frac{\bar{p}(1-\bar{p})}{n}} = 0.02 + 3.\sqrt{\frac{0.02 \times 0.98}{100}} = 0.02 + 0.042 = 0.062,$$
$$\text{LCL} = 0.02 - 0.042 = -0.022 \simeq 0.$$

- ***np*-chart**

Control limits for *np*-chart for 1σ limits are

$$CL = n\overline{p} = 2,$$

$$UCL = n\overline{p} + \sqrt{n\overline{p}\,(1-\overline{p})} = 2 + \sqrt{2(1-0.02)} = 2 + \sqrt{2 \times 0.98} = 2 + 1.4 = 3.4,$$

$$LCL = n\overline{p} - \sqrt{n\overline{p}\,(1-\overline{p})} = 2 - 1.4 = 0.6.$$

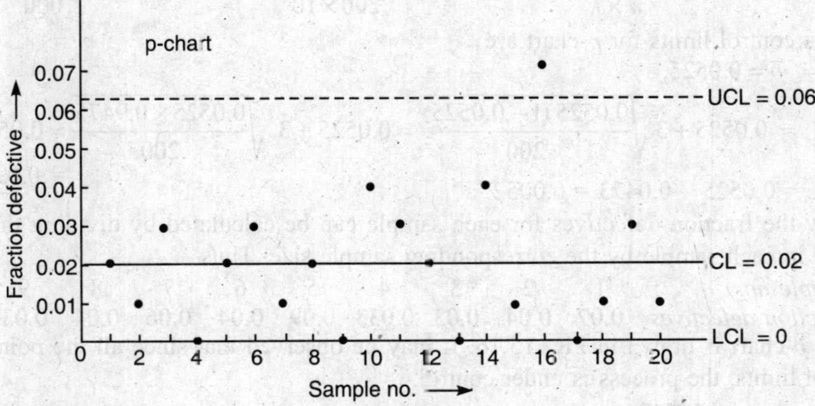

Fig. 15.14

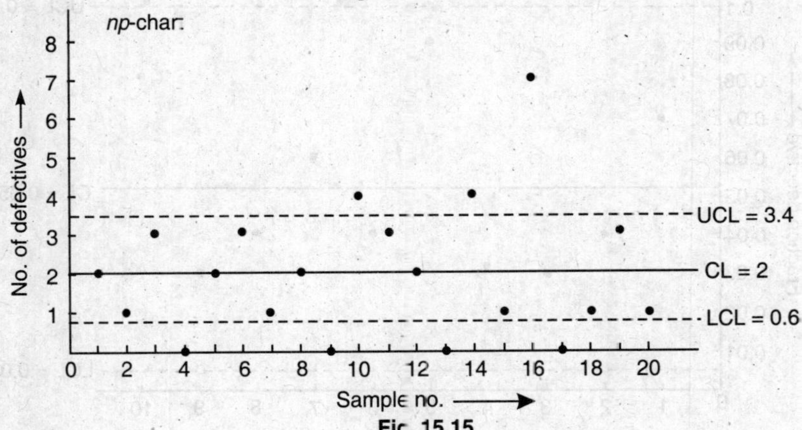

Fig. 15.15

p-chart for 3σ limits is drawn in Fig. 15.14. It can be observed that the point corresponding to sample number 16 lies outside the upper control limit.

np-chart is drawn in Fig. 15.15. It can be seen that as many as 7 points lie outside the control limits. The reason is that the control limits have been drawn for μ ± 1σ limits rather than μ ± 3σ limits.

EXAMPLE 15.9-8

Ten samples of different sizes were taken and the number of defectives in each sample are noted below:

Sample no.	:	*1*	*2*	*3*	*4*	*5*	*6*	*7*	*8*	*9*	*10*
Sample size	:	*100*	*300*	*200*	*150*	*200*	*250*	*300*	*150*	*100*	*250*
No. of defectives	:	*7*	*12*	*6*	*5*	*18*	*10*	*18*	*6*	*3*	*20*

Draw a control chart for fraction defectives taking ± 3σ control limits.

[*Dayalbagh Edu. Inst. Agra MBA May, 2014*]

Solution

Since sample size is different for the various samples, it is required to find the average sample size, $\overline{n}$.

$$\bar{n} = \frac{\text{Sum of size of each sample}}{\text{Total number of samples}}$$

$$= \frac{100 + 300 + 200 + 150 + 200 + 250 + 300 + 150 + 100 + 250}{10} = 200.$$

Now, $\bar{p} = \frac{\Sigma p_i}{\bar{n} \times k} = \frac{7 + 12 + 6 + 5 + 18 + 10 + 18 + 6 + 3 + 20}{200 \times 10} = \frac{105}{2,000} = 0.0525.$

Thus control limits for *p*-chart are

CL = $\bar{p} = 0.0525$,

UCL = $0.0525 + 3.\sqrt{\frac{0.0525\,(1 - 0.0525)}{200}} = 0.0525 + 3.\sqrt{\frac{0.0525 \times 0.9475}{200}} = 0.0525 + 0.0473$
$= 0.0998,$

LCL = 0.0525 – 0.0473 = 0.0052.

Now the fraction defectives for each sample can be calculated by dividing the number of defectives in each sample by the corresponding sample size. Thus

Sample no. :	1	2	3	4	5	6	7	8	9	10
Fraction defectives :	0.07	0.04	0.03	0.033	0.09	0.04	0.06	0.04	0.03	0.08

The *p*-chart is drawn in Fig. 15.16. It may be observed that since all the points lie within the control limits, the process is under control.

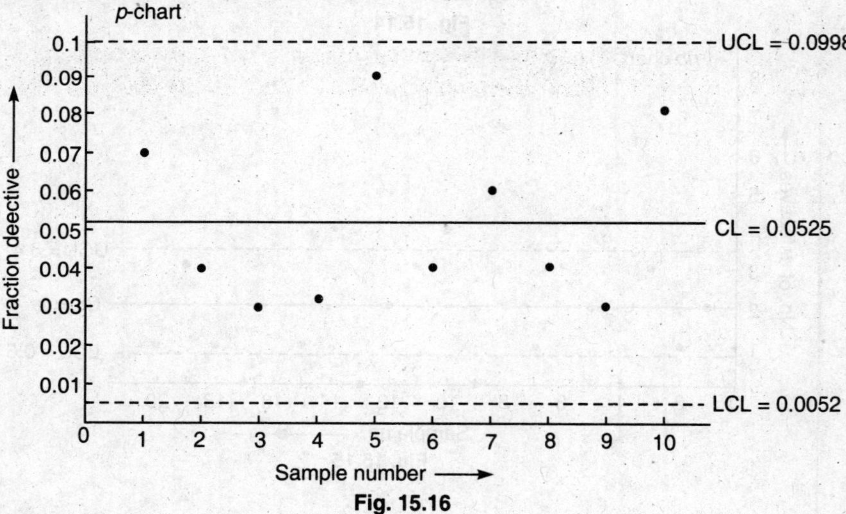

Fig. 15.16

EXAMPLE 15.9-9

The cloth of a particular manufacturer was inspected. 100 sq. meters is considered as a unit. The defects in each unit were recorded and are given below. Is the production process under statistical control ?

100 sq. m. cloth length no. :	*1*	*2*	*3*	*4*	*5*	*6*	*7*	*8*	*9*	*10*
No. of defects in each sample :	*2*	*3*	*1*	*4*	*4*	*0*	*2*	*1*	*4*	*2*

Solution

Here, no. of samples = 10, total number of defects = 23.

$\therefore$ Average number of defects in a sample, $\bar{C}$ = 23/10 = 2.3,

standard deviation, $\sigma_c = \sqrt{\bar{C}} = \sqrt{2.3} = 1.517.$

$\therefore$ CL = $\bar{C}$ = 2.3,

$$\text{UCL} = \overline{\text{C}} + 3\sqrt{\overline{\text{C}}} = 2.3 + 3 \times 1.517 = 6.85,$$

$$\text{LCL} = \overline{\text{C}} - 3\sqrt{\overline{\text{C}}} = 2.3 - 3 \times 1.517 = -2.251 \simeq 0\cdot$$

Since the no. of defects for each sample lie within the control limits, the process is in control.

EXAMPLE 15.9-10

The number of customer complaints received daily by an organisation is given below.

Day	:	*1*	*2*	*3*	*4*	*5*	*6*	*7*	*8*	*9*	*10*	*11*	*12*	*13*	*14*	*15*
Complaints	:	*2*	*3*	*0*	*1*	*9*	*2*	*0*	*0*	*4*	*2*	*0*	*7*	*0*	*2*	*4*

Does it mean that the number of complaints is under statistical control ? Establish a control scheme for the future. [*Dayalbagh Edu. Inst. Agra May, 2013, 2006*]

Solution Average number of complaints/day, $\overline{\text{C}} = \dfrac{\sum C_i}{15} = \dfrac{36}{15} = 2.4.$

$\therefore$ $\text{CL} = 2.4,$

$$\text{UCL} = \overline{\text{C}} + 3\sqrt{\overline{\text{C}}} = 2.4 + 3\sqrt{2.4} = 7.05,$$

$$\text{LCL} = \overline{\text{C}} - 3\sqrt{\overline{\text{C}}} = 2.4 - 3\sqrt{2.4} = -2.25 \simeq 0.$$

On inspection of the data it is found that the process is not under control since observation of day 5 lies outside the upper control limit.

In order to establish a control scheme for the future, it is necessary to homogenise the data by deleting the 5th observation.

$\therefore$ New value of $\overline{\text{C}} = \dfrac{36-9}{15-1} = \dfrac{27}{14} = 1.93.$

$\therefore$ $\text{CL} = 1.93,$

$$\text{UCL} = 1.93 + 3\sqrt{1.93} = 6.10,$$

$$\text{LCL} = 1.93 - 3\sqrt{1.93} = -2.24 \simeq 0.$$

We find that the process is still not under control since observation no. 12 is still outside the new UCL. It is, therefore , necessary to again homogenise the data by deleting the 12th observation.

$\therefore$ $\overline{\text{C}} = \dfrac{27-7}{14-1} = \dfrac{20}{13} = 1.54.$

$\therefore$ $\text{CL} = 1.54,$

$$\text{UCL} = 1.54 + 3\sqrt{1.54} = 5.26,$$

$$\text{LCL} = 1.54 - 3\sqrt{1.54} = -2.18 \simeq 0.$$

The corresponding C-chart is drawn in Fig. 15 17. Now all the thirteen observations lie within the control limits. Thus the control scheme for the future is to operate this C-chart.

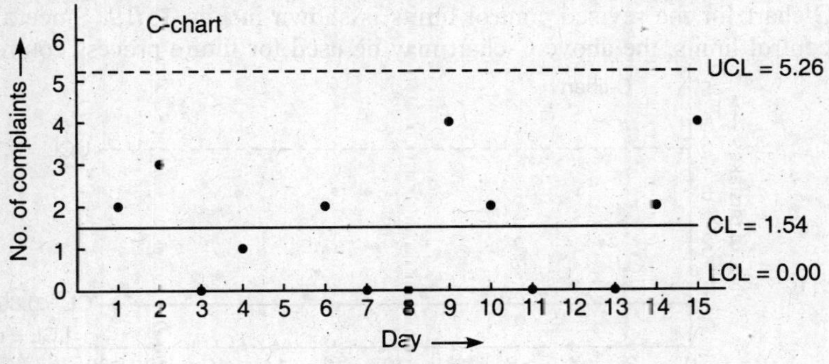

Fig. 15.17

EXAMPLE 15.9-11

The number of mistakes made by an accounts clerk is given below.

Week no.	:	*1*	*2*	*3*	*4*	*5*	*6*	*7*	*8*	*9*	*10*
Number of mistakes	:	*1*	*0*	*2*	*0*	*1*	*0*	*1*	*0*	*1*	*2*
Week No.	:	*11*	*12*	*13*	*14*	*15*	*16*	*17*	*18*	*19*	*20*
Number of mistakes	:	*3*	*3*	*1*	*0*	*0*	*7*	*1*	*0*	*1*	*0*

Establish a suitable control chart and state how it should be used in future in order to control the mistakes of the clerk.

Solution The control chart to be used for the given problem is the number of defects chart *i.e.*, C-chart.

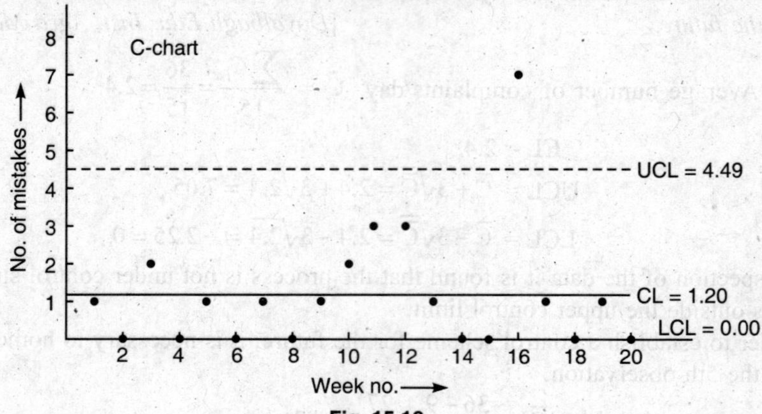

Fig. 15.18

Average no. of mistakes, $\bar{C} = \dfrac{\sum C_i}{20} = \dfrac{24}{20} = 1.2.$

$$\therefore \quad CL = 1.2,$$

$$UCL = \bar{C} + 3\sqrt{\bar{C}} = 1.2 + 3\sqrt{1.2} = 4.49,$$

$$LCL = 1.2 - 3\sqrt{1.2} = -2.09 \simeq 0 .$$

The control chart for the above limits is drawn in Fig. 15.18. Since the number of mistakes during the 16th week lies outside the upper control limit, the process is not under statistical control.

To establish a suitable control chart for future, we homogenise the data for future control by eliminating the data corresponding to the 16th week. The revised control limits are given below:

$$CL = \bar{C} = \frac{17}{19} = 0.895,$$

$$UCL = \bar{C} + 3\sqrt{\bar{C}} = 0.895 + 3\sqrt{0.895} = 3.73,$$

$$LCL = \bar{C} - 3\sqrt{\bar{C}} = 0.895 - 3\sqrt{0.895} = -1.94 \simeq 0.$$

The C-chart for the revised control limits is shown in Fig. 15.19. Since all the points lie within the control limits, the above C-chart may be used for future process control.

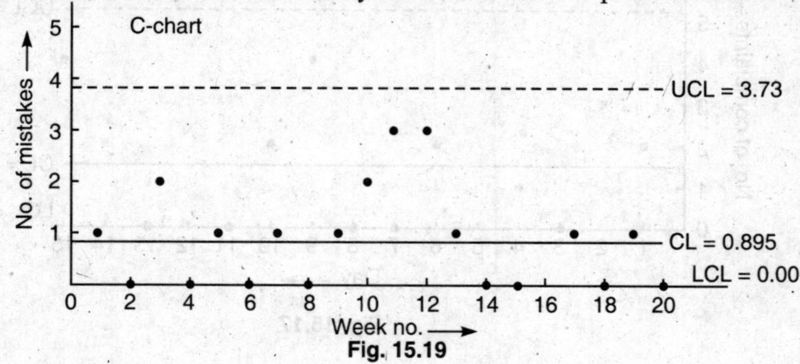

Fig. 15.19

EXAMPLE 15.9-12

The number of defects inspected in rational subgroups of size 5 and for a sample of size 10 are as follows:

Sample no.	*Number of defects*					c_i	u_i
1	2	1	0	1	2	6	6/5
2	1	1	0	0	1	3	3/5
3	2	2	2	1	0	7	7/5
4	1	0	0	0	1	2	2/5
5	3	1	2	1	1	8	8/5
6	3	1	2	0	2	8	8/5
7	1	1	0	0	1	3	3/5
8	2	2	1	1	2	8	8/5
9	2	1	1	0	1	5	1
10	3	2	3	1	0	9	9/5

Set up appropriate control chart and give your comments. [Calicut M.Com., 1983]

Solution

Here, we shall construct a *u*-chart. If c_i is the total number of defects in the *i*th rational subgroup of 5, then the number of defects per unit in the *i*th sample is $u = c_i/5$.

The process average number of defects per unit is given by

$$\bar{u} = \frac{\sum u_i}{10} = \frac{59}{5 \times 10} = 1.18.$$

∴ The control limits are

$$\text{CL} = \bar{u} = 1.18,$$

$$\text{UCL} = \bar{u} + 3\sqrt{\frac{\bar{u}}{5}} = 1.18 + 3\sqrt{\frac{1.18}{5}} = 2.64,$$

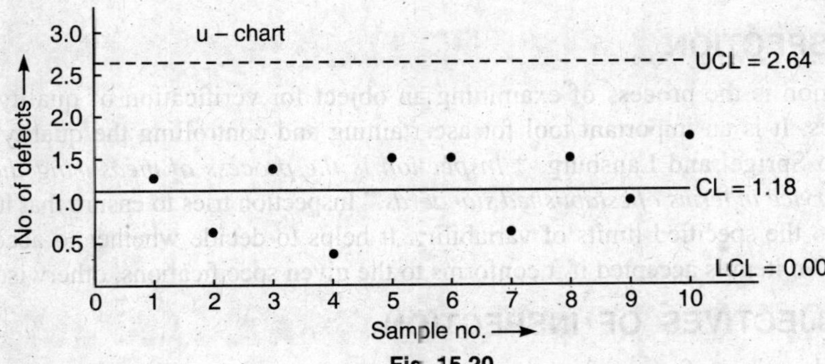

Fig. 15.20

$$\text{LCL} = \bar{u} - 3\sqrt{\frac{\bar{u}}{5}} = 1.18 - 3\sqrt{\frac{1.18}{5}} = -0.28 \simeq 0.$$

The control chart is shown in Fig. 15.20.

As all the points lie within the control limits, the process is under statistical control.

EXAMPLE 15.9-13

The observations of inspection of television sets on different dates are given below. Calculate the control limits.

Day	:	*1*	*2*	*3*	*4*	*5*	*6*	*7*	*8*	*9*	*10*
No. inspected	:	*5*	*5*	*6*	*2*	*4*	*6*	*2*	*5*	*6*	*3*
Defects per sample	:	*15*	*15*	*24*	*6*	*12*	*18*	*9*	*14*	*19*	*7*

Solution

Since the sample size varies , the control chart for number of defects per unit, $u = c/n$ is used. Separate limits for each subgruop are calculated. The calculations are shown in table 15.7.

TABLE 15.7

Day	*Number inspected* n	*Total defects* c	*Defects per unit* c/n	*UCL* = $\bar{u}+3\sqrt{\bar{u}/n}$ $= 3.16+5.33/\sqrt{n}$	*LCL* = $\bar{u}-3\sqrt{\bar{u}/n} =$ $3.16 - 5.33/\sqrt{n}$
1	5	15	3	5.54	0.78
2	5	15	3	5.54	0.78
3	6	24	4	5.34	0.98
4	2	6	3	6.93	–0.61
5	4	12	3	5.83	0.50
6	6	18	3	5.34	0.98
7	2	9	4.5	6.93	–0.61
8	5	14	2.8	5.54	0.78
9	6	19	3.2	5.34	0.98
10	3	7	2.3	6.24	0.08
Total:	44	139			

Now $$\bar{u} = \frac{\sum c}{\sum n} = \frac{139}{44} = 3.16.$$

Since the defects per unit lie within the control limits, these control limits are the actual control limits.

15.10 INSPECTION

Inspection is the process of examining an object for verification of quality in any of its characteristics. It is an important tool for ascertaining and controlling the quality of a product. According to Sprigel and Lansburg, " *Inspection is the process of measuring the quality of a product or service in terms of established standards*." Inspection tries to ensure that items produced remain within the specified limits of variability. It helps to decide whether to accept or reject a certain item. An item is accepted if it conforms to the given specifications, otherwise it is rejected.

15.11 OBJECTIVES OF INSPECTION

Basic objectives of inspection are :

1. It ensures the quality of the finished product by comparing raw materials, production process and the final product with specified standards.
2. It prevents further processing of semi-finished products that are detected as spoiled.
3. It tries to detect the defective items and the reasons behind so that corrective action may be initiated. This helps to enhance the confidence and prestige of the organisation in the eyes of the consumer.
4. Corrective actions initiated as a result of inspection, reduce the final rejections and hence reduce the production cost.

15.12 TYPES OF INSPECTION

The basic purpose of inspection is to locate the defects as soon as they occur and to ensure that they are not repeated in future operations. For this, following types of inspection may be carried out:

1. Purchaser or Vendor Place Inspection

This type of inspection is carried out mainly to ascertain the quality of raw materials. In general, the quality of the finished product depends upon the quality of the raw material and proper inspection at this stage would minimize the rejections at the later stage. This type of inspection can be done either at the vendor's place or at the purchaser's place. For heavy and large size items, it is always more convenient to inspect them at the vendor's place by the inspectors of the purchaser. This reduces the costs of material handling and transportion. Also, the defective parts, if any, can be replaced immediately.

2. In-Process Inspection

In-process inspection is done to locate the defective items as quickly as possible so that timely remedial measures may be adopted to avoid future rejections. In-process inspection is of the following types:

(*a*) **Trial run inspection :** Here, the machine tool is checked against the specifications before the production starts. Then a trial is made on a single piece. If the piece conforms to the specifications, the production is allowed to be carried out, otherwise remedial measures are taken.

(*b*) **First-off inspection:** The items produced in the first production run are examined thoroughly with respect to specifications. The reasons for discrepancy, if any, are located and corrected. This reduces the chances of scrap later when the production is in full swings.

(*c*) **Inspection by self control:** This type of inspection is done by the operators controlling the operations at different levels of the production process. The remedial action can be taken immediately and it reduces the chances of scrap.

(*d*) **Decentralised floor inspection:** Here, the semi-finished items are inspected either on the machine or in the production line. It reduces the necessity of product handling and transportation. Also, the defects, if any, are located immediately.

(*e*) **Centralised inspection:** The basic idea in centralised inspection is to separate the inspection from production.

There may be a single inspection unit for the whole plant or each production unit may have a separate inspection unit to inspect the items produced by it. The items are shifted to the inspection unit for the necessary inspection. The inspection staff is likely to be more skilled and expert in its work. Better, sophisticated, sensitive and reliable instruments are available to ascertain the quality. However, chances of goods handling and transportation are also more, resulting in increased inspection cost.

3. Finished Products' Inspection

The finished products are inspected and tested to ascertain their quality standards. The items found to be defective are not marketed. Thus only items of desired specifications go into the hands of the consumer. However, this type of inspection increases the scrap as the rejected items cannot be corrected at this stage.

4. Post-Sales Quality Evaluation

It is possible that an item, though approved as per the quality standards, may not provide satisfactory and reliable service to the customer. Therefore, the customer may have complaints about the item. Accordingly, the item must be thoroughly inspected, faults must be located and the necessary improvements must be incorporated. This can be done by providing after-sales service to the customer.

15.13 PRODUCT CONTROL

Product control is concerned with classification of raw materials, semi-finished goods or finished goods into acceptable or rejectable items. It is concerned with the inspection of goods already produced to judge whether these are fit to be used or dispatched. Acceptance sampling is normally used for product control which indicates whether the lot should be accepted without further inspection or another sample be taken for deciding about the quality of the lot.

15.14 ACCEPTANCE SAMPLING

One simple way to control the quality of a product is to conduct 100% inspection so that no defective item would pass unnoticed. However, 100% inspection may be uneconomical or even impossible due to the following reasons:

1. When the quality of a product is tested by destructive testing (*e.g.*, testing of electrical fuses), then 100% testing will spoil all the products.
2. 100% inspection causes enormous fatigue which affects the accuracy and judgement of the inspectors.
3. Handling of the product may induce defects or result in its deterioration.
4. Cost of inspection may be very high due to unpacking or dismantling of the product if it so requires and due to the use of special machines.
5. Inspection may be hazardous or even dangerous (*e.g.* testing of pressure vessels).

For these reasons, some form of acceptance sampling or sampling inspection is often required. In acceptance sampling, the decisions about the quality of batches are made on the inspection of only a portion of the total number of items. If the sample of items conforms to the desired quality level, then the whole batch is accepted. if it does not, the whole batch is rejected or subjected to further inspection. Acceptance sampling is, therefore, a quick, easy and economical method to take decisions about the quality levels of the products. However, the method involves a certain amount of risk since the decisions of acceptance or rejection are based only on the sample which may not conform to the quality of the remaining batch.

Two types of risks viz. producer's risk and consumer's risk (also called type I and type II errors respectively) are involved in acceptance sampling. On the basis of sample inspection under a sampling plan, there remains a possibility of accepting a lot which otherwise would have been rejected *i.e.*, the whole lot in reality does not conform to specifications, but in spite of this fact, the lot is accepted. This is known as *consumer's or buyer's risk*. It is the probability of defective lots being accepted which, otherwise, would have been rejected. Similarly, there may be a possibility of rejecting a lot, on the basis of sampling inspection, which otherwise should have been accepted *i.e.*, the lot in reality has a lower percentage of reject items than specified but still the same is rejected. This will result in a loss to the producer and is known as *producer's risk or seller's risk*. It is the probability of rejecting a good lot which, otherwise, would have been accepted. Acceptance sampling is used to help both the buyer and the seller by providing the requisite degrees of protection from the risks to which they are exposed.

The two terms AQL (*Acceptable Quality Level*) and RQL (*Reject Quality Level*), or LTPD (*Lot Tolerance Per cent Defective*) are also used while developing an acceptance sampling plan. AQL refers to the maximum percentage of defectives in the sample so that the lot is acceptable whereas RQL refers to the percentage of defectives in the sample beyond which the lot is rejected.

All these parameters *viz.* AQL, RQL, consumer's risk and producer's risk should be settled at the time of contract between the producer on one side and the consumer on the other side. Once values for these parameters are specified, a sampling plan is designed by applying appropriate techniques. In its simplest form, acceptance sampling requires selecting a random sample of size

'n' from a lot of size 'N', determining the number of defectives in the sample and comparing this number with a predetermined value 'c', the critical value or the *acceptance number*. If the number of defectives is less than or equal to 'c', the lot is accepted, otherwise it is rejected.

Acceptance sampling is classified in two ways:

1. Acceptance sampling by attributes.
2. Acceptance sampling by variables.

In acceptance sampling by attributes, the products are inspected on the basis of 'GO' and 'NOT GO' gauges. So the actual measurement is not done. If the product conforms to the given specification it is accepted, otherwise rejected, however small may be the error. Thus dimension of the error is not important. For instance, the pipes without cracks are accepted, those with cracks are rejected, and size and shape of the crack is not measured.

In acceptance sampling by variables, actual measurement of dimensions or physical and chemical properties are done.

Sampling inspection procedure consists of the following steps:

(*i*) Make inspection batches of the total quantity.
(*ii*) Draw random samples from each batch.
(*iii*) Carry out proper inspection to ascertain the quality of the random sample.
(*iv*) Select a sampling plan and establish an acceptable per cent defective.

Three types of sampling inspection plans commonly used are:

(*i*) Single sampling plan
(*ii*) Double sampling plan
(*iii*) Multiple (sequential) sampling plan

The followings symbols will be used in all the sampling plans:

N : number of items in a given batch,
n : number of items in the sample drawn from the batch of N,
c : acceptance number *i.e.*, maximum number of defectives allowed in a sample of size n.

15.15 SINGLE SAMPLING PLAN

The procedure of single sampling plan consists of the following steps:

1. Draw a sample of size n from a batch of N and inspect all the n items.
2. If the number of defectives in the sample of size n are $\leq c$, accept the batch of N after replacing the defective items.
3. If the number of defectives in $n > c$, inspect all the remaining $(N - n)$ products.
4. Correct or replace all the defective items found.

For instance, assume N = 400, n = 20 and c = 2. According to this plan, a sample of size 20 would be chosen at random out of 400 and inspected. If number of defectives is 2 or less, the whole batch of 400 will be accepted. If the number of defectives is more than 2, then all the remaining 380 items would be inspected and all the defectives in them would either be rectified or replaced by good ones and only then the batch of 400 would be accepted.

15.16 OPERATING CHARACTERISTIC CURVE (O.C.C.)

The graphical relationship between percentage defectives in the lots being submitted for inspection and the probability of acceptance is termed as *operating characteristics* of a particular sampling plan. An *operating characteristic curve* for a particular combination of n and c shows how well the given sampling plan discriminates between good and bad lots. Fig. 15.21 shows a typical O.C.C . for a sampling plan with n = 50 and c =1. It gives a clear picture about the probability of acceptance of a lot for various values of per cent defectives in the lot. The probability of acceptance of a lot is high for low values of actual percentage defectives and it is low for high values of actual percentage defectives. For example, if the actual per cent defectives in a lot are 1, then the probability of its getting accepted is about 94%, and that of its getting rejected is about 6%. On the other hand , if the actual per cent defectives in a lot are 7, then the probability of its

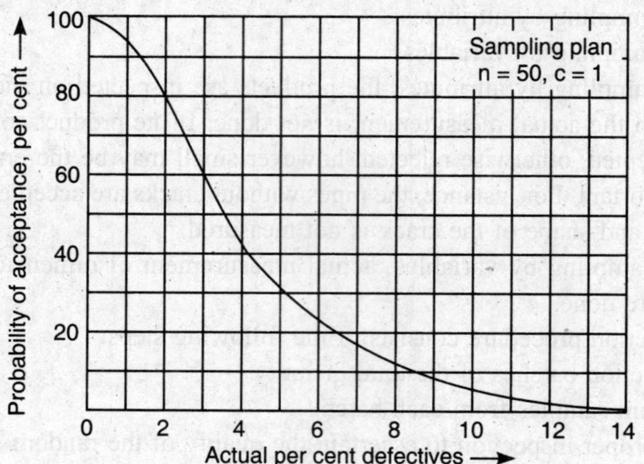

Fig. 15.21. O.C. curve for sampling plan if n = 50, c = 1.

getting accepted is about 17% (quite low). This is the desirable feature of a sampling plan. That is, if the actual quality of a lot is good, there should be high probability of its acceptance, but, if the actual quality is poor, it is desired that the probability of its acceptance must be low.

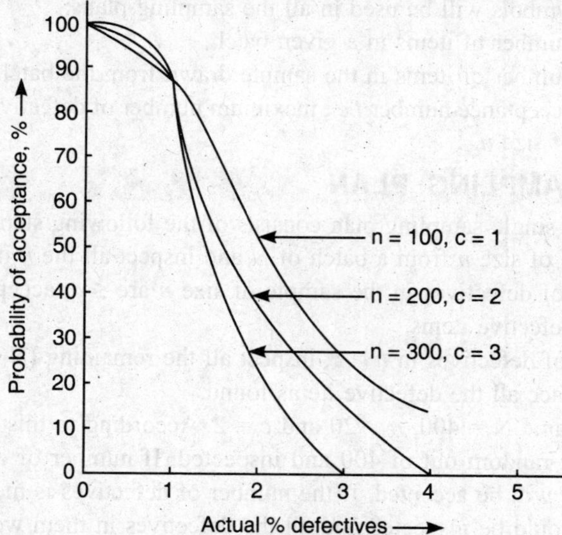

Fig. 15.22. Typical O.C. Curvs for Different Sample Sizes (n).

The discriminating power of a sampling plan is greatly dependent upon the sample size. Fig. 15.22. shows typical O.C. curves for sample sizes (n) of 100, 200 and 300 with the acceptance numbers (c) proportional to sample size. It is clear that the as the sample size increases, the curve becomes steeper, that is, more discriminating. Fig. 15.23 shows O.C. curves with same sample size (n) but different values of acceptance number, (c). It is clear that as the acceptance number decreases the sampling plan becomes tighter, that is, more discriminating.

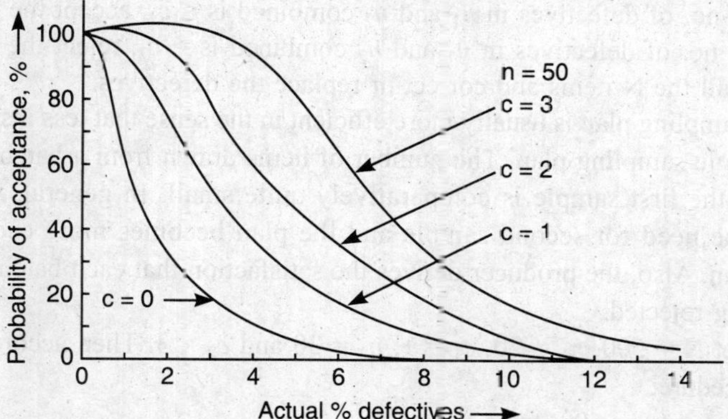

Fig. 15.23. Typical O.C. Curves for n = 50, but c increasing 0 to 3.

Construction of O.C. Curve. To develop a sampling plan for acceptance sampling, an appropriate O.C. curve must be selected. To construct an O.C. curve, an agreement has to be reached between the producer and the consumer on the following four points:

1. **Acceptable Quality Level (AQL).** This is the maximum proportion of defectives that will make the lot definitely acceptable.
2. **Lot Tolerance Percentage Defective (LTPD):** This is the maximum proportion of defectives that will make the lot definitely unacceptable.
3. **Producer's Risk (α).** This is the risk, the producer is willing to take that lots of the quality level AQL will be rejected, even though, they are acceptable. Usually $\alpha = 5\%$.
4. **Consumer's Risk (β).** This is the risk, the consumer is willing to take that lots of the quality level LTPD will be accepted, even though, they are actually unacceptable. Usually, $\beta = 10\%$.

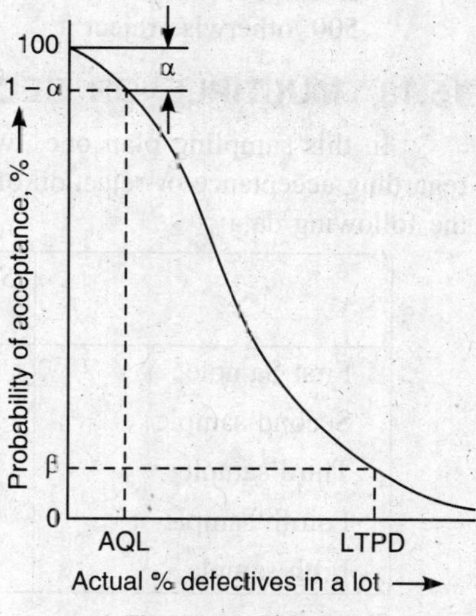

Fig. 15.24. O.C. Curve

With the above four items known, O.C.C. for a sampling plan can be constructed, as shown in Fig. 15.24. An O.C.C. can also be plotted, by determining the various values of probability of lots being accepted, for various values (by Poisson or binomial distribution) of per cent defectives.

15.17 DOUBLE SAMPLING PLAN

Let N = no. of items in a given batch,
n_1 = no. of items in the first random sample,
c_1 = acceptance number for the first sample,
n_2 = no. of products in the second random sample,
c_2 = acceptance number for both the samples combined.

The procedure for double sampling plan consists of the following steps:

1. Draw a sample containing n_1 items randomly from N and inspect all the n_1 items.
2. If the no. of defectives is $\le c_1$, accept the whole batch of N without any further inspection, after replacing the defective items.
3. If the no. of defectives in $n_1 > c_2$, reject the whole batch of N.
4. If the no. of defectives in n_1 is more than c_1 but less than c_2, then choose a second sample of size n_2 and inspect all the n_2 items.

5. If the total no. of defectives in n_1 and n_2 combined is $\leq c_2$, accept the batch of N.
6. If the total no. of defectives in n_1 and n_2 combined is $> c_2$, reject the whole batch of N or inspect all the N items and correct or replace the defectives.

The double sampling plan is usually more efficient in the sense that less inspection is required as compared to single sampling plan. The number of items drawn from a batch in case of double sampling plan for the first sample is comparatively quite small. In general, when the batch is good, seldom is the need for second sample and the plan becomes more economical than the single sampling plan. Also, the producer derives the satisfaction that each batch is given a second chance before being rejected.

Example: Let N = 500, $n_1 = 20$, $c_1 = 1$, $n_2 = 30$ and $c_2 = 3$. Then according to the double sampling plan procedure:

1. Each batch contains 500 items.
2. Pick up a sample of 20 items at random from 500 and inspect the 20 items.
3. If the no. of defectives is ≤ 1, accept the batch of 500 without further inspection.
4. If the no. of defectives is > 3, reject the whole batch of 500.
5. If the no. of defectives in 20 is more than 1 but ≤ 3, then take a second sample of 30 items from the batch of remaining 500 – 20 = 480 items and inspect them.
6. If the total number of defectives in 20 + 30 = 50 items is ≤ 3, then accept the batch of 500, otherwise reject it.

15.18 MULTIPLE OR SEQUENTIAL SAMPLING PLAN

In this sampling plan one, two, three or more samples may be taken to reach a decision regarding acceptance or rejection of a batch. To explain the procedure of this plan, let us assume the following data:

	Sample size	*Combined sample size*	*Acceptance number c*	*Rejection number*
First Sample	50	50	≤ 0	≥ 3
Second sample	25	75	1	4
Third sample	25	100	2	5
Fourth sample	25	125	3	5
Fifth sample	25	150	4	5

Procedure:

1. Pick up a sample of 50 items from the batch of N and inspect all the items.
2. If there is no defective item, accept the whole batch of N without further inspection.
3. If it contains ≥ 3 defectives, reject the batch of N.
4. If it contains ≤ 2 defectives, take a second sample of 25 items at random and inspect them.
5. If the total number of defectives from the first and the second samples is 1, accept the batch of N.
6. If the total defectives from first and second samples is ≥ 4, reject the batch of N.
7. If the total defectives is less than 4 and great than 1, take third sample of 25 items and inspect them.
8. If the total defectives in 50 + 25 + 25 = 100 items is ≤ 2, accept the batch of N.
9. If the total defectives is ≥ 5, reject the batch of N.
10. If the total defectives is more than 2 but less than 5, take another sample of 25 items and inspect them. In this way the sampling is carried out.

EXERCISES

1. Explain the term 'Statistical Quality Control'. How is the process control achieved with the help of control charts? What are the fundamentals underlying the construction of a quality control chart? [*P.T.U. B.Tech. (M.E.) April, 2013; BBA, 2011; Dayalbagh Edu. Inst. Agra M.Com. Dec., 2007*]

2. Explain the working of $\overline{x}$ and R-charts. Derive their control limits. How will you take your decision about the quality of the lot on the basis of $\overline{x}$ and R-charts jointly? [*Sourashtra M.Com., 1983*]

3. Distinguish between process control and product control. Define producer's risk. [*I.C.W.A. June, 1979*]

4. What do you understand by sampling inspection plans? How are they used in controlling the quality of a manufactured product? State the different types of acceptance sampling plans. [*Dayabagh Edu. Inst. Agra BBM May, 2005; Maharishi Dayanand M.Com., 1982*]

5. Explain the following terms used in acceptance sampling: (*i*) Single sampling (*ii*) Double sampling (*iii*) Consumer's risk (*iv*) AOQL (*v*) LTPD. [*M.S.Baroda B.E. (Mech.) 1977*]

6. What is meant by statistical quality control? State clearly the assumptions behind the control chart technique. [*ICWA (Final) Dec., 1976*]

7. (*a*) Why both $\overline{x}$ and R-charts are drawn for one job? Also list the applications of p-chart and c-chart.
(*b*) What are the functions of O.C. curve? [*P.T.U. B Tech. (M.E.) April, 2013*]

8. Discuss the various sampling plans. [*IGNOU MBA June, 2000; Dayalbagh Edu. Inst. Agra BBM May, 2005*]

9. (*a*) What is inspection? Discuss the important activities assigned to a quality control department in an industry. Discuss under what conditions 'statistical quality control' would be preferred to 100% inspection? [*Kuru. U.B. Tech. (Mech.) 1997*]
(*b*) What are the basic issues in inspection ? What amount of inspection is optimal ? Distinguish between random variation and assignable variation. [*Dayalbagh Edu. Inst. Agra B.B.M. May, 2007*]

10. Discuss the importance of statistical quality control in business with suitable examples. [*Osmania U. Hyderabad MBA July, 2010*]

11. Explain the benefits to be expected from the use of quality control programme. State various factors affecting the quality of a product. [*Kuru. U.B. Tech. (Mech.) 1997*]

12. Briefly explain and discuss the meanings of $\overline{x} \pm \sigma$, $\overline{x} \pm 2\sigma$ and $\overline{x} \pm 3\sigma$ being most commonly quoted units with normal curves. [*Kuru. U. B. Tech. (Mech.) 1997*]

13. Draw an O.C. Curve. Show its different regions. Discuss its characteristics. [*IGNOU MBA June, 2001; Dec., 2000; June, 2000*]

14. Discuss the practical limitations of control charts for variables. [*Kuru U. B.Tech. (Mech.) 1991*]

15. Write note on acceptance sampling. [*IGNOU MBA June, 2000*]

16. (*a*) Discuss the interest of the consumer and the producer in the selection of sampling plans.
(*b*) State and explain the advantages and limitations of acceptance sampling over 100% inspection. [*Kuru. U. B.Tech. May, 1990*]

17. Mention the advantages of double sampling plan over single sampling plan. [*Dayalbagh Edu. Inst. Agra BBM May, 2005*]

18. Give the comparison of $\overline{x}$ and R-charts with p-chart. [*Kuru. U. B.Tech. (Mech.) May, 1990*]

19. Discuss the fundamental difference between use of acceptance sampling plans and process control charts. [*IGNOU MBA Dec., 1999*]

20. Write short note on statistical quality control. [*IGNOU MBA June, 1998*]

21. The following data shows the values of sample mean $\overline{x}$ and the range R for 10 samples of size 5 each. Calculate the values for centre line and control limits for mean chart and range chart and determine whether the process is under control.

Sample no.	:	1	2	3	4	5	6	7	8	9	10
$\overline{x}$	:	11.2	11.8	10.8	11.6	11.0	9.6	10.4	9.6	10.6	10.0
R	:	7	4	8	5	7	4	8	4	7	9

(Conversion factors for $n = 5$ are $A_2 = 0.577$, $D_3 = 0$, $D_4 = 2.115$.) [*I.C.W.A.(Final) Dec., 1976*]

(*Ans.* $CL_{\overline{x}} = 10.66$, $UCL_{\overline{x}} = 14.295$, $LCL_{\overline{x}} = 7.025$; $CL_R = 0.3$, $UCL_R = 13.32$, $LCL_R = 0$.)

22. Conrol charts for $\overline{x}$ and R are maintained on certain dimension of a manufactured part. The subgroup size is 4. The values of $\overline{x}$ and R are computed for each subgroup. After 20 subgroups, $\sum \overline{x} = 41.340$ and $\sum R = 0.320$. Compute the values of 3σ limits for $\overline{x}$ and R-charts and estimate the values of σ_1 on the assumption that the process is under statistical control. If the specifications are 2.050 ± 0.02 and its dimension falls above *u*, rework is required; if below L, the part must be scrapped. What can you conclude regarding process ability to meet specifications? Can you make any suggestions for improvement ? [*Kuru. U.B.E.(Mech.)1997*]

23. The surface hardness of crank pins was measured along their length. On each, three measurements were taken. In all six pins were randomly selected from a lot and measurements were taken. Find the control limits for $\overline{x}$ and R-charts.

Sample	*Measurement over the length*		
	1	2	3
1	100	102	101
2	102	101	101.5
3	104	101	101.5
4	99	102	101
5	94	100	104
6	97	99	100

[*Kuru. U. B.Tech.(Mech.) May, 1990*]

24. Four samples of three observations each have been taken, with actual measurements in cm shown below. Construct 3σ mean and range charts and determine whether the production process is under statistical control.

Sample			
1	2	3	4
12.5	11.8	12.2	12.0
12.2	12.0	12.2	11.8
12.3	12.3	11.9	11.8

[*Dayalbagh Edu. Inst. Agra B.B.M. May, 2007*]

(*Ans.* $\overline{x}$ – chart : 12.08, 12.4115, 11.7485; R – chart: 0.325, 0.835, 0.)

25. A machine is set to deliver packets of a given weight. Ten samples of size five each were examined and the following results were obtained:

Sample	:	1	2	3	4	5	6	7	8	9	10
Mean	:	15	17	15	18	17	14	18	15	17	5
Range	:	7	7	4	9	8	7	12	4	11	5

Calculate the values for the central line and the control limits for the mean ($\overline{x}$) chart and range chart. Comment on the state of control.

[*Dayalbagh Edu. Inst. Agra B.B.M. May, 2014; IGNOU MBA June, 2000*]

(*Ans.* $\overline{x}$ -chart : 15.1, 20.3, 9.9; R-chart: 7.4, 15.65, 0; one sample mean lies outside the control limits.)

26. A task performer takes 10 rational subgroups, each of size 4 at regular interval of 30 minutes. He has to control the diameter of the component for which specification limits are 5.00 ± 0.05. The mean and range for each of the subgroups are given below:

Subgroup no. (i)	:	1	2	3	4	5	6	7	8	9	10
Mean x_i	:	4.98	5.01	5.02	4.99	5.00	5.01	4.99	4.99	5.02	5.00
Range R_i	:	0.06	0.04	0.02	0.06	0.00	0.02	0.03	0.05	0.00	0.02

Test whether the process is under statistical control using the suitable control charts and compute the process capability. Prepare the control chart for the future.

(For $n = 4$, $A_2 = 0.729$, $D_3 = 0$, $D_4 = 2.282$, $d_2 = 2.059$.) [*CA (Final) Nov., 1991*]

(*Ans.* $CL_{\overline{x}} = 5.00$, $UCL_{\overline{x}} = 5.02187$, $LCL_{\overline{x}} = 4.97813$; $CL_R = 0.03$, $UCL_R = 0.06846$, $LCL_R = 0$.)

27. Construct a control chart for the thickness of sheets of plywood for ±3 standard errors based on the data below.

Sample no.	*Thickness in cm*				
1	2.111	2.101	2.115	2.015	2.213
2	2.011	2.059	2.143	2.114	2.221
3	2.125	2.215	2.114	2.141	2.321
4	2.055	2.043	2.100	2.097	2.189
5	2.210	2.120	2.012	2.099	2.177
6	2.178	2.213	2.014	2.019	2.191
7	2.189	2.187	2.217	2.143	2.154
8	2.212	2.125	2.200	2.099	2.117
9	2.194	2.087	2.094	2.049	2.196
10	2.287	2.097	2.189	2.205	2.111

(*Ans.* UCL = 2.234 cm, CL = 2.138 cm, LCL = 2.042 cm.)

28. Based on 15 subgroups each of size 200 taken at intervals of 45 minutes from a manufacturing process, the average fraction defective was found to be 0.0[illegible]8. Calculate the values of the centre line and the control limits for a p-chart.

29. In a manufacturing concern producing radio transistors, lots of 250 items are inspected at a time. Considering the number of defectives in 20 lots shown in the table below, draw suitable control chart and write a brief report based on the evidence of the chart.

Lot no.	:	1	2	3	4	5	6	7	8	9	10
No. of defectives	:	25	47	23	36	24	34	39	32	35	22
Lot no.	:	11	12	13	14	15	16	17	18	19	20
No. of defectives	:	45	40	32	35	21	40	15	28	23	42

[*Chennai Univ. M.B.A., 1983*]

(*Ans.* Control limits are 32± 15.84.)

30. If the average fraction defective of a large sample of a product is 0.1537, calculate the control limits, given that subgroup size is 2,000. What modifications do you need if the subgroup size is not constant? [*I.C.W.A. (Final) June, 1979*]

(*Ans.* UCL_p = 0.1779, LCL_p = 0.1295.)

31. During an examination of equal length of cloth, the following are the number of defects observed: 2, 3, 4, 0, 5, 6, 7, 4, 3, 2. Draw a control chart for the number of defects and comment whether the process is under control or not. [*I.C.W.A.(Final) June, 1980*]

(*Ans.* CL_c = 3.6, UCL_c = 9.2922, LCL_c = –2.0902 ~ 0.)

32. The following table shows the number of missing rivets observed at the time of inspection of 12 aircrafts. Find the control limits for the number of defects chart and comment on the state of control.

Aircraft no.	:	1	2	3	4	5	6	7	8	9	10	11	12
No. of missing rivets	:	7	15	13	18	10	14	13	10	20	4	22	15

[*I.C.W.A.(Final) Dec., 1978*]

(*Ans.* UCL_c = 25.23, LCL_c = 2.77; Process is in control.)

33. Switches manufactured by a small manufacturing company are tested in batches of 50. Historically, 3 per cent of the switches have failed to pass the test. Construct a control chart for testing the switches.

(*Ans.* UCL = 0 102, CL = 0.03, LCL = 0.)

34. State the importance of control limits on p-charts. Haryana State Electricity Board purchases bolts in cartons that usually contain several thousand bolts. Each shipment consists of a number of cartons. As a part of acceptance procedure for these bolts, 400 bolts are selected at random from each carton and are subjected to usual inspection for certain non-conformities. In a shipment of 10 cartons, the respective percentages of rejected bolts from each carton are 0, 0, 0.5, 0.75, 0, 2.0, 0.25, 0, 0.25 and 1.25. Does this shipment of bolts appear to exhibit statistical quality control with respect to the quality characteristic examined in this inspection? [*Kuru. U.B. Tech.(Mech.) 1997*]

35. The table below represents a listing of the number of mechanical defects observed on lots of 10 miniature worm-gear drives drawn daily from the line. This is a pilot production run lasting 20 days. Construct a control chart and plot the points.
Suppose the reasons for out-of-control situation (lot no. 10) are known, what is your decision regarding the control limits *for future use*?

Lot no.	:	1	2	3	4	5	6	7	8	9	10
No. of defects	:	13	15	19	8	6	17	7	9	3	23
Lot no.	:	11	12	13	14	15	16	17	18	19	20
No. of defects	:	17	11	7	11	14	6	16	10	2	6

[*I.C.W.A. May, 1993*]

36. In a manufacturing process the number of defectives found in the inspection of 15 lots of 400 items each are given below:
2, 5, 0, 14, 3, 0, 1, 0, 18, 8, 6, 0, 3, 0, and 6.
(*i*) Determine the trial control limits and state whether the process is in control.
(*ii*) What will be the corresponding control limits if some obvious points outside the control limits are eliminated? Examine whether the process is still in control or not.

[*Kuru. U.B. Tech.(Mech.) 1992*]

37. The following table gives the number of defectives found in an aircraft assembly. The lot size consists of 200 units. Determine the UCL and LCL for an *np*-chart and show whether the process exhibits statistical control or not.

Production order number	:	1	2	3	4	5	6	7	8	9	10	11	12
No. of defectives (np)	:	23	15	17	15	41	0	25	31	29	0	8	16

[*Kuru. U.B. Tech.(Mech.) 1991*]

38. A single sampling plan has $n = 110$ and $c = 3$. The lot size is large as compared to sample size. Plot the O.C. curve and find the values of lot tolerance per cent defective for which the probabilities of acceptance are 0.95, 0.50 and 0.10 respectively. If AQL = 1% and LTPD = 4%, determine the producer's risk and consumer's risk. Here n = sample size and c = acceptance number.

[*Kuru. U.B. Tech.(Mech.) May, 1990*]

39. In a double sampling plan, lot size is 5,000.
I. sample size $n_1 = 100$, $c_1 = 0$;
II. sample size $n_2 = 100$, $c_2 = 1$.
(*i*) Compute the probability of acceptance of 1% defective lot.
(*ii*) If the rejected lot is 100% inspected, what is AOQ? [*Kuru. U.B. Tech.(Mech.) May, 1990*]

40. The data given below pertains to the production of 100 days:

Lot no.	:	1	2	3	4	5	6	7	8	9	10
Number inspected	:	500	600	600	300	300	600	200	500	200	200
Number defective	:	6	9	4	9	3	3	1	2	1	2

Plot a control chart based on average number of pieces in a lot. Also show variable control limits for all the batches. Suppose the reasons of abnormality for the 4th lot are known and remedied, establish the *p*-value for future production. [*Kuru. U.B. Tech.(Mech.) May, 1990*]

41. In the following table are given the number of defectives found on 24 consecutive production days in daily samples of 200 items. Draw *np*-chart and *p*-chart.

Production day	:	1	2	3	4	5	6	7	8	9	10	11	12
No. of defectives	:	10	5	10	12	11	9	19	4	12	27	25	9
Production day	:	13	14	15	16	17	18	19	20	21	22	23	24
No. of defectives	:	12	15	8	14	10	4	11	11	26	3	10	11

[*Kuru. U.B.E. Tech.(Mech.) 1997*]

42. (*a*) Explain the following:
(*i*) Operating characteristic curve in single sampling fraction defective plans.
(*ii*) Acceptable quality level.
(*iii*) Lot tolerance fraction defective.
(*b*) The dispatcher of an office should stamp the envelopes containing letters before dispatching. Due to his inefficiency certain envelopes miss the stamping. A sample of 64 envelopes was selected on each of the past 10 days and inspected for stamping. It was found that the number of envelopes that

were not stamped in the samples were 11, 20, 5, 32, 10, 16, 2, 8, 13 and 19 respectively. Evaluate his performance by means of a control chart. Suggest modifications, if any, in the process.

[*CA(Final) May, 1990*]

(*Ans. np*-chart; CL = 13.6, UCL = 23.42, LCL = 3.78; process not in statistical control.)

43. The number of mistakes made by an accounts clerk per week were recorded for 15 weeks and the data are given below:

Week no.	:	1	2	3	4	5	6	7	8	9	10	11	12	13	14	15
No. of mistakes	:	2	3	0	1	9	2	0	0	4	2	0	7	0	2	4

(*i*) Does it mean that the number of mistakes is under statistical control?

(*ii*) Establish a control scheme for the future.

[*Dayalbagh Edu. Inst. Agra M.Com. Dec., 2007*]

(*Ans.* CL = 1.54, UCL = 6.15, LCL = 0; in control for future.)

44. A company manufactures bushings. After every one hour a sample of 125 finished bushings is drawn from the output. The data on 10 consecutive samples is given below :

Sample no. :	1	2	3	4	5	6	7	8	9	10
Defectives :	15	13	16	11	13	14	20	25	30	45

Use a proper control chart to ascertain whether the system is under control. Find control limits for future.

[*Dayalbagh Edu. Inst. Agra M.B.A. Dec., 2007*]

[*Ans.* CL_1 = 20.2, UCL_1 = 32.545, LCL_1 = 7.855; CL_2 = 17.44, UCL_2 = 29.09, LCL_2 = 5.79.]

45. There were 60 observations and 22 runs. What can the analyst conclude from this information ? Construct the appropriate control chart for the sample observations listed below and determine if the process is in control using 2σ limits.

Observation :	1	2	3	4	5	6	7	8	9	10	11
No of defects/unit :	9	4	3	5	6	3	4	2	3	2	3

[*Dayalbagh Edu. Inst. Agra MBA May, 2011*]

[*Ans.* CL = 4, UCL = 8, LCL = 0; not under statistical control]

46. Construct the appropriate control chart for the following data. 12 samples of five cookies each during two weeks were considered.

Sample no.	*Chips per cookie*				
1	2	3	3	4	3
2	5	3	6	2	1
3	4	3	3	2	2
4	6	1	5	3	3
5	2	4	1	4	4
6	5	1	3	3	3
7	2	3	3	2	1
8	1	1	3	1	2
9	6	3	3	3	3
10	6	7	5	5	6
11	6	1	1	3	2
12	5	5	3	1	3

[*Osmania U.MBA July, 2010*]

[*Hint.* Construct C-chart.]

Non-Linear Programming

16.1 INTRODUCTION

In linear programming models, the characteristic assumption is the linearity of the objective and constraint functions. Although this assumption holds in numerous practical situations, yet we come across many situations where the objective function and/or some or all of the constraints are non-linear functions. For instance in transportation problem, there may be bulk transportation rates which are cheaper than the normal transportation rates. These rates are applicable if the quantity transported is more than a certain size. Likewise, in a manufacturing problem, production cost decreases as the production level increases. The objective function in such situations becomes non-linear. In some cases, it is possible to formulate a non-linear programming problem into a linear programming model, but generally, specific algorithms are employed for tackling the non-linearity.

A linear programming problem is expressed as

$$\begin{aligned} &\text{maximize or minimize} && Z = f(x_1, x_2, \ldots, x_n), \\ &\text{subject to the constraints} && g^1(x_1, x_2, \ldots, x_n) \leq, =, \geq b_1, \\ &&& g^2(x_1, x_2, \ldots, x_n) \leq, =, \geq b_2, \\ &&& \vdots \qquad\qquad\qquad\qquad \vdots \\ &&& g^m(x_1, x_2, \ldots, x_n) \leq, =, \geq b_m, \\ &&& x_j \geq 0, j = 1, 2, \ldots, n. \end{aligned}$$

If either the objective function and/or one or more of the constraints are non-linear in X $(x_1, x_2, \ldots, x_n)$, the problem is called a non-linear programming problem. In other words, the general non-linear programming problem (NLPP) is to determine the n-tuple $X = (x_1, x_2, \ldots, x_n)$, so as to

$$\begin{aligned} &\text{maximize or minimize} && Z = f(X), \\ &\text{subject to} && g^i(X) \leq, =, \geq b_i, \; i = 1, 2, \ldots, m, \\ &&& X \geq 0, \end{aligned}$$

where $f(X)$ or some $g^i(X)$ or both are non-linear.

The method of solving an L.P. problem is based on the property that the optimal solution lies at one or more extreme points of the feasible region. This limits our search to corner points only and the optimal solution is obtained after a finite number of iterations as in simplex method. Unfortunately, the same is not true for non-linear programming problems. In such problems the optimal solution can be located at any point along the boundaries of the feasible region or even within the region.

Secondly, due to non-linearity of the objective function and constraints, it becomes difficult to distinguish between the *local* and *global* solution.

Thirdly, it is sometimes difficult to test the optimality of the non-linear programming problems, especially when the feasible region is not convex.

Therefore, the non-linearity of the functions makes the solution of the problem much more involved as compared to linear programming problems and there is no single algorithm like the simplex method, which can be employed to solve efficiently all non-linear programming problems.

An algorithm that performs well on one type of problem may perform poorly on problem with a different structure. A number of algorithms have been developed by the researchers, each applicable to a specific type of NLPP only. However, an efficient method for the solution of general non-linear programming problem is still a subject of research.

16.2 ILLUSTRATIVE EXAMPLES

The number of applications of non-linear programming are very large and it is not possible to give a comprehensive survey of all of them. However, some examples illustrating a few of the many situations, where non-linear programming can be applied, are given below.

16.2-1 The Product mix problem

In the product mix problems discussed in chapter 2 on linear programming, the objective was to determine the product mix, so as to maximize the profits, subject to the constraints on the availability of resources. The objective function was linear as we assumed that there was fixed unit profit associated with each product. This, however, is not always true. In case of large manufacturers, the price of a product is dependent on the quantity demanded. More the volume of sales, lesser the per unit price, which is called *advantage of scale.* In other words, there is *price elasticity*. The price-demand curve is not linear, but may look like the one shown in Fig. 16.1, where the price $p(x)$ is very high when x is very small and the price drops rapidly as x increases and then tends to stabilise.

If we assume that unit production and distribution cost of the product is fixed at C, then the profit from x units is given by

$$P(x) = x\,[p(x) - c] = xp(x) - cx, \text{ which is a non-linear function.}$$

If the manufacturing firm produces n products x_j ($j = 1, 2, ..., n$) with identical profit functions $P_j\,(x_j)$, then the overall objective function is the sum of n non-linear functions.

$$f(X) = \sum_{j=1}^{n} P_j\,(x_j); \qquad j = 1, 2, ..., n.$$

In addition to price elasticity, there can be a number of other reasons for the objective function to be non-linear. The unit production cost may decrease with increase in volume of production because of the *learning curve effect* or it may increase if some special steps are required to be taken to increase the production level.

The constraint functions $g^i(X)$ can also be non-linear, when the use of resources is not strictly proportional to the production levels of respective products.

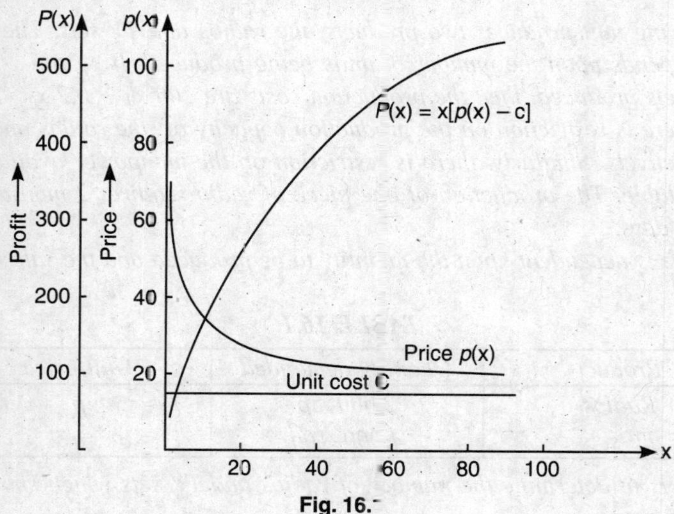

Fig. 16.1

16.2-2 Transportation problem

In the transportation problems discussed in chapter 3, it was assumed that the per unit transportation cost from a given source to a given distribution centre was fixed, irrespective of the quantity transported. But in actual practice volume or *quantity discounts* are generally available. With the increase in volume, the unit transportation cost decreases, as shown in Fig. 16.2 (*a*). The resulting total cost C(x) of transporting x units will be as shown in Fig. 16.2 (*b*), which is non-linear. This curve is a piece-wise linear function with slope at a point giving the marginal cost at that point. Thus, if each combination of m sources and n destinations has a similar cost function, that is, the cost of transporting x_{ij} units from source i to destination j is given by a non-linear function $C_{ij}(x_{ij})$, then the overall objective function is

$$\text{maximize } f(x) = \sum_{i=1}^{m} \sum_{j=1}^{n} C_{ij}(x_{ij}),$$

where $i = 1, 2, \ldots, m,$

$j = 1, 2, \ldots, n.$

The constraints due to the availability at the sources and requirements at the destinations, may remain linear functions.

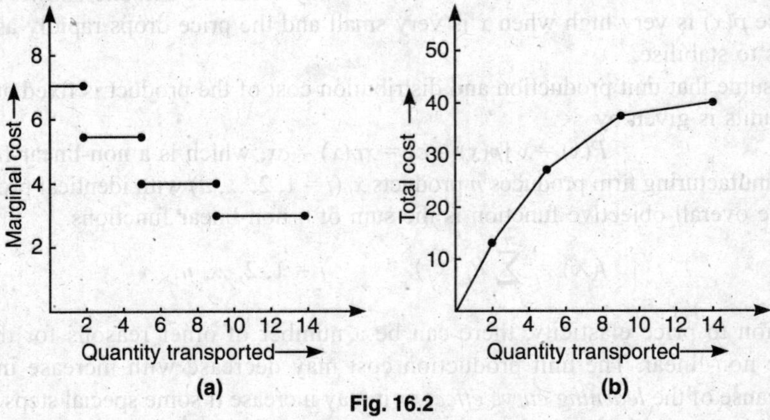

Fig. 16.2

16.3 PROBLEM FORMULATION EXAMPLES

EXAMPLE 16.3-1

A manufacturing unit produces two products, the radios and TV sets. The production cost of each product depends upon the number of units being produced. If x_1 *and* x_2 *are the number of radios and TV sets produced, then the production costs are* $200\,x_1 + 0.2\,x_1^2$ *and* $300\,x_2 + 0.2\,x_2^2$ *respectively. There is restriction on the production capacity of the radios and TV sets to 100 and 80 units respectively. Similarly, there is restriction on the manpower available. A total 520 man-days are available. The production of one piece of radio requires 2 man-days and one TV set requires 3 man-days.*

The sale price is dependent upon the quantity to be produced and the sale relationships are given in Table 16.1.

TABLE 16.1

Product	*Quantity demanded*	*Unit price*
Radios	*2,000–5p*	*p*
TV sets	*4,000–10q*	*q*

The problem is to determine the number of radios and TV sets which should be produced to maximize the profits.

Formulation of Mathematical Model

Since x_1 and x_2 are the quantities of radios and TV sets to be produced by the firm,

$$x_1 = 2{,}000 - 5p \quad \text{or} \quad p = 400 - 0.2\,x_1,$$

and

$$x_2 = 4{,}000 - 10q \quad \text{or} \quad q = 400 - 0.1\,x_2.$$

If the total production cost of x_1 unit of radios and x_2 units of TV sets is denoted by C_1 and C_2 respectively, then it is also given that

$$C_1 = 200\,x_1 + 0.2\,x_1^2$$

$$C_2 = 300\,x_2 + 0.2\,x_2^2.$$

The total revenue = Revenue of radios + Revenue of TV sets.

i.e.,

$$R = px_1 + qx_2$$

$$= (400 - 0.2x_1)\,x_1 + (400 - 0.1x_2)\,x_2$$

$$= 400x_1 - 0.2\,x_1^2 + 400\,x_2 - 0.1\,x_2^2.$$

∴ Total profit P is,

$$P = R - (C_1 + C_2)$$

$$= 400\,x_1 - 0.2\,x_1^2 + 400\,x_2 - 0.1\,x_2^2 - 200\,x_1 - 0.2\,x_1^2 - 300\,x_2 - 0.2\,x_2^2$$

$$= 200\,x_1 - 0.4\,x_1^2 + 100\,x_2 - 0.3\,x_2^2.$$

There are constraints on the production capacity:

$$x_1 \le 100,$$

$$x_2 \le 80.$$

Similarly, man-days available are also limited to 520. Since one unit of radio requires 2 man-days and one unit of TV requires 3 man-days,

$$2\,x_1 + 3\,x_2 \le 520.$$

Since x_1 and x_2 cannot take negative values,

$$x_1, x_2 \ge 0.$$

Thus the model is

$$\text{Maximize} \quad f(x_1, x_2) = 200\,x_1 - 0.4\,x_1^2 + 100\,x_2 - 0.3\,x_2^2,$$

subject to the constraints

$$2\,x_1 + 3\,x_2 \le 520,$$

$$x_1 \le 100,$$

$$x_2 \le 80,$$

$$x_1, x_2 \ge 0.$$

Since the objective function is non-linear, it is a non-linear programming problem.

EXAMPLE 16.3-2

60 m^3 of a granular product are to be transported across a river in a ferry. The transportation cost across the river is ₹ 100 per trip, irrespective of the amount transported, but there is restriction on the number of trips, which should not be more than 40. The cost of the container depends upon its dimensions as given below:

Cost of bottom = ₹ 10 per square metre,

cost of front and back sides = ₹ 10 per square metre,

and cost of the ends = ₹ 20 per square metre.

Thus if a small container is used, cost of container will be less, but the number of trips will be more, and if a large container is used, cost of container will be more, but number of trips will be less. Find the dimensions of the container so that the sum of the container cost and transportation cost is minimized.

Formulation of Mathematical model

Let x_1, x_2 and x_3 be the length, width and depth of the container as shown in Fig. 16.3.

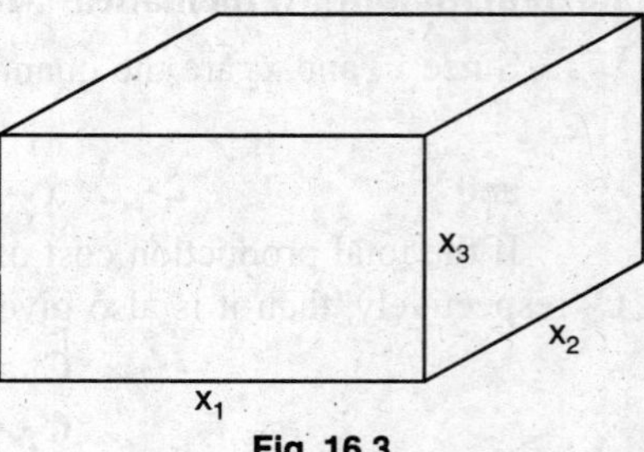

Fig. 16.3

Volume of the container = $x_1\, x_2\, x_3$.

$$\text{Number of trips} = \frac{60}{x_1\, x_2\, x_3}.$$

$$\therefore \quad \text{Transportation cost} = \frac{60 \times 100}{x_1\, x_2\, x_3}.$$

Cost of container = Cost of bottom + cost of front and back + cost of two sides

$$= x_1\, x_2 \times 10 + 2\, x_1\, x_3 \times 10 + 2\, x_2\, x_3 \times 20.$$

$$\therefore \quad \text{Total cost} = \frac{6000}{x_1\, x_2\, x_3} + 10\, x_1\, x_2 + 20\, x_1\, x_3 + 40\, x_2\, x_3.$$

Constraint is on the number of trips, which should not be more than 40.

$$\text{Or} \quad \frac{60}{x_1\, x_2\, x_3} \leq 40.$$

Since x_1, x_2 and x_3 cannot take negative values,

$$x_1, x_2, x_3 \geq 0.$$

∴ The problem can be put as,

$$\text{minimize } f(x_1, x_2, x_3) = \frac{6,000}{x_1 x_2 x_3} + 10\, x_1\, x_2 + 20\, x_1\, x_3 + 40\, x_2\, x_3,$$

$$\text{subject to } g(x_1, x_2, x_3) = \frac{60}{x_1 x_2 x_3} \leq 40,$$

$$x_1, x_2, x_3 \geq 0.$$

Here both the objective function and constraint are non-linear functions of the variables.

EXAMPLE 16.3-3

A company manufactures two products A and B. It takes 30 minutes to process one unit of product A and 15 minutes for one unit of product B. The maximum machine time available is 35 hours per week. One unit of product A requires 2 kg of raw material, while product B requires 3 kg of raw material per unit. The available raw material is limited to 180 kg per week.

The products A and B have unlimited market potential and sell for ₹ 200 and ₹ 500 per unit respectively. If the manufacturing costs for products A and B are $2x^2$ and $3y^2$ respectively, find how much of each product should be produced per week, where x any y are respectively the quantities of A and B to be produced.

Formulation of Mathematical Model

Here x and y are the quantities of products A and B respectively, which are to be manufactured per week. The selling price of products A and B is ₹ 200 and ₹ 500 per unit respectively.

∴ Total revenue per week = $200\,x + 500y$.

The manufacturing cost of A is $2x^2$ and of B is $3y^2$ per unit.

Thus total manufacturing cost per week = $2x^2 + 3y^2$.

$$\therefore \quad \text{Profit per week} = 200x + 500y - 2x^2 - 3y^2.$$

The machining of product A requires 30 minutes per unit, while product B requires 15 minutes per unit. Since a maximum of 35 hours of machining time are available,

$$30x + 15y \leq 35 \times 60$$

$$\text{or} \quad 2x + y \leq 140.$$

Constraint on the availability of raw material is expressed as

$$2x + 3y \leq 180.$$

Since x and y cannot take negative values,

$$x, y \geq 0.$$

Thus the problem can be expressed as,

maximize $\quad f(x, y) = 200x + 500y - 2x^2 - 3y^2,$

subject to

$$2x + y \leq 140,$$
$$2x + 3y \leq 180,$$
$$x, y \geq 0.$$

Here the objective function is non-linear, while constraints are linear.

16.4 LOCAL AND GLOBAL OPTIMUM

In non-linear programming, a function may have more than one *maxima* or *minima* values. That is, when the function is plotted, it has more than one peak and more than one valley. Each of these is a local maximum or local minimum. A *local* or *relative maximum* need not be a global maximum. A *global* or *absolute maximum* of a function is a value which is higher than all the values of the function. Similarly a *global minimum* of a function is a value which is the lowest of all the values of the function.

Consider the single variable function plotted in Fig. 16.4. Over the interval $x = a$ and $x = b$, this function has three local maxima at x_1, x_3 and x_6. The global maxima is at x_6.

$$\therefore \quad f(x)_{max} = \max \{f(x_1), f(x_3), f(x_6)\} = f(x_6).$$

Similarly, there are three local minima at x_2, x_4 and x_7. The global minima is $f(x_7)$ at $x = x_7$.

Point corresponding to $f(x_5)$, which has zero slope is called *point of inflection*. If a point with zero slope is not a maximum or a minimum then it must automatically be an inflection point or a *saddle point*.

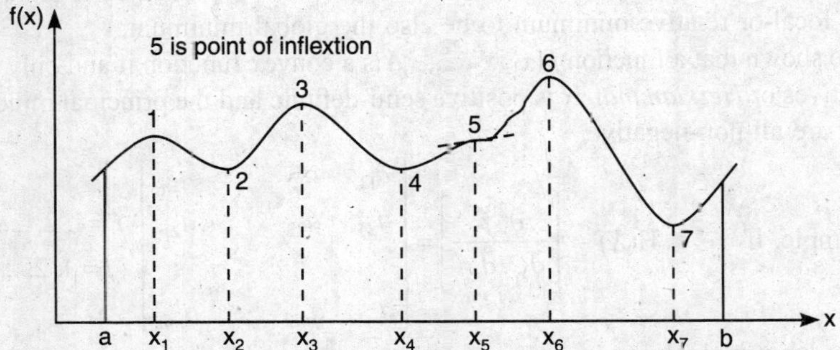

Fig. 16.4. A function with several local maxima and several local minima.

16.5 CONCAVE AND CONVEX FUNCTIONS

A single variable function, which when plotted, results in a curve, always curving downwards or not curving at all, is called a *concave function*. Fig 16.5 shows a single variable concave function. The shape of this function is such that for any two points on the curve, in the feasible region S, the line joining the points is always below the function. It is clear from the figure that there is always a unique global maximum of such a function.

It can be shown for a concave function of several variables, that if it has a local maximum, the same is also its global maximum. A concave function can also be defined as: A function $f(x)$ is said to be concave over a region S, if for any two points x and y in S,

$f[\lambda x + (1 - \lambda) y] \geq \lambda f(x) + (1 - \lambda) f(y)$, where $0 \leq \lambda \leq 1$.

A function, which when plotted, results in a curve always curving upwards or not curving at all is called a *convex function*. Fig. 16.6 shows a single variable convex function. A line joining any two points on the curve, in the feasible region S, is always above the function. There is always a unique global minimum of such a function.

For a convex function of several variables, if there exists a local minimum, it can be proved, that the same is also the global minimum.

In mathematical form,

A function $f(x)$ is a convex function over a convex set S, if for any two points x and y is S, $f[\lambda x + (1 - \lambda)y] \leq \lambda f(x) + (! - \lambda) f(y)$, where $0 \leq \lambda \leq 1$.

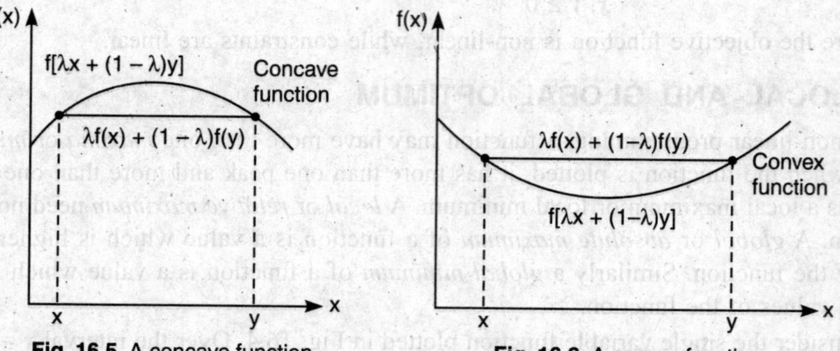

Fig. 16.5. A concave function.

Fig. 16.6. A convex function.

It may be recalled from calculus that when an ordinary doubly differentiable function of a single variable $f(x)$, without any constraints is maximized, then for the local or relative maximum to be also the global maximum,

$$\frac{d^2 f}{dx^2} \leq 0, \text{ for all } x.$$

Such a function is concave function. Similarly, if ≤ is replaced by ≥ sign, it is a convex function with local or relative minimum to be also the global minimum.

It can be shown that a function $f(x_1, x_2, ..., x_n)$ is a convex function if and only if the matrix of second derivatives or *Hessian matrix* is positive semi-definite and the principal minor determinants of this matrix are all non-negative.

For example, if $$H(X) = \left[\frac{\partial^2 f}{\partial_{x_i} . \partial_{x_j}}\right] = \begin{bmatrix} a_{11} & a_{12} & \cdots & a_{1n} \\ a_{21} & a_{22} & \cdots & a_{2n} \\ \vdots & \vdots & & \vdots \\ a_{m1} & a_{m2} & \cdots & a_{mn} \end{bmatrix}, \quad i = 1, 2, ..., m; \; j = 1, 2, ..., n.$$

Then the kth principal minor determinant is

$$\begin{vmatrix} a_{11} & a_{12} & \cdots & a_{1k} \\ a_{21} & a_{22} & \cdots & a_{2k} \\ \vdots & \vdots & & \\ a_{k1} & a_{k2} & \cdots & a_{kk} \end{vmatrix}, \text{ where } k \leq m \leq n.$$

The function $f(x_1, x_2, ..., x_n)$ is a concave function if and only if H(X) is negative semi-definite

i.e., $$H(X) = \left[\frac{\partial^2 f}{\partial x_i \, \partial x_j}\right] \leq 0 \text{ for all } x \neq 0,$$

and the principal minors have sign of $(-1)^k$ for $k = 1, 2, 3, ...$

EXAMPLE 16.5-1

For each of the following functions show whether it is convex, concave or neither:

(a) $f(x) = 10 - x^2$
(b) $f(x) = x^4 + 6x^2 + 12x$
(c) $f(x) = 2x^3 - 3x^2$
(d) $f(x) = x^4 + x^2$
(e) $f(x) = x^3 + x^4$.

Solution

(*a*) $f(x) = 10 - x^2$.

$$\therefore \quad \frac{df}{dx} = 0 - 2x \text{ and } \frac{d^2 f}{dx^2} = -2.$$

Since $\frac{d^2 f}{dx^2}$ is always < 0 for all values of x, the function is concave.

(*b*) $f(x) = x^4 + 6x^2 + 12x$.

$$\therefore \quad \frac{df}{dx} = 4x^3 + 12x + 12 \text{ and } \frac{d^2 f}{dx^2} = 12x^2 + 12.$$

Since $\frac{d^2 f}{dx^2}$ is always > 0 for all values of x, the function is convex.

(*c*) $f(x) = 2x^3 - 3x^2$.

$$\therefore \quad \frac{df}{dx} = 6x^2 - 6x \text{ and } \frac{d^2 f}{dx^2} = 12x - 6.$$

At $x = 0$, $\frac{d^2 f}{dx^2}$ is negative; at $x = \frac{1}{2}$, $\frac{d^2 f}{dx^2} = 0$, while for all values of x greater than $\frac{1}{2}$, $\frac{d^2 f}{dx^2}$ is positive. Hence the function is convex for $x \geq \frac{1}{2}$.

(*d*) $f(x) = x^4 + x^2$.

$$\therefore \quad \frac{df}{dx} = 4x^3 + 2x \text{ and } \frac{d^2 f}{dx^2} = 12x^2 + 2.$$

Since $\frac{d^2 f}{dx^2}$ is > 0 for all values of x, the function is convex.

(*e*) $f(x) = x^3 + x^4$.

$$\therefore \quad \frac{df}{dx} = 3x^2 + 4x^3 \text{ and } \frac{d^2 f}{dx^2} = 6x + 12x^2,$$

which is positive *i.e.*, ≥ 0 for all value of $x \geq -0.5$. Thus the function is convex when x is ≥ -0.5.

EXAMPLE 16.5-2

For each of the following functions determine whether it is convex, concave or neither.

(*a*) $f(X) = x_1 x_2 - x_1^2 - x_2^2$
(*b*) $f(X) = 3x_1 + 2x_1^2 + 4x_2 + x_2^2 - 2x_1x_2$
(*c*) $f(X) = x_1^2 + 3x_1x_2 + 2x_2^2$
(*d*) $f(X) = x_1^2 + x_2^2 - 2x_1 x_2$
(*e*) $f(X) = 20x_1 + 10x_2$
(*f*) $f(X) = x_1 x_2$.

Solution

In this problem, all the functions are two-variable functions. For the two-variable functions, the convexity test is as given in table 16.2.

TABLE 16.2

Quantity	*Convex*	*Strictly convex*	*Concave*	*Strictly concave*
$\frac{\partial^2 f}{\partial x_1^2} \cdot \frac{\partial^2 f}{\partial x_2^2} - \left[\frac{\partial^2 f}{\partial x_1 \partial x_2}\right]^2$	≥ 0	> 0	≥ 0	> 0
$\frac{\partial^2 f}{\partial x_1^2}$	≥ 0	> 0	≤ 0	< 0
$\frac{\partial^2 f}{\partial x_1^2}$	≥ 0	> 0	≤ 0	< 0

For each of the given functions, the above three conditions are to be checked :

(*a*) $$f(X) = x_1 x_2 - x_1^2 - x_2{}^2.$$

$$\therefore \quad \frac{\partial f}{\partial x_1} = x_2 - 2x_1 \text{ and } \frac{\partial^2 f}{\partial x_1^2} = -2, \text{ which is} < 0,$$

$$\frac{\partial f}{\partial x_2} = x_1 - 2x_2 \text{ and } \frac{\partial^2 f}{\partial x_2^2} = -2, \text{ which is} < 0,$$

$$\frac{\partial^2 f}{\partial x_1 \partial x_2} = 1.$$

$$\therefore \quad \frac{\partial^2 f}{\partial x_1^2} \cdot \frac{\partial^2 f}{\partial x_2^2} - \left[\frac{\partial^2 f}{\partial x_1 \partial x_2}\right]^2 = (-2)(-2) - (1)^2 = 3, \text{ which is} > 0.$$

∴ The given function is strictly concave.

(*b*) $$f(X) = 3x_1 + 2x_1{}^2 + 4x_2 + x_2^2 - 2x_1x_2.$$

$$\therefore \quad \frac{\partial f}{\partial x_1} = 3 + 4x_1 - 2x_2\,; \quad \frac{\partial^2 f}{\partial x_1^2} = 4, \text{ which is} > 0\,,$$

$$\frac{\partial f}{\partial x_2} = 4 + 2x_2 - 2x_1\,; \quad \frac{\partial^2 f}{\partial x_2^2} = 2 \text{ which is} > 0\,,$$

$$\frac{\partial^2 f}{\partial x_1 \partial x_2} = -2.$$

$$\therefore \quad \frac{\partial^2 f}{\partial x_1^2} \cdot \frac{\partial^2 f}{\partial x_2^2} - \left[\frac{\partial^2 f}{\partial x_1 \partial x_2}\right]^2 = 4 \times 2 - (-2)^2 = 4 > 0.$$

∴ Function is strictly convex.

(*c*) $$f(X) = x_1^2 + 3x_1x_2 + 2x_2^2.$$

$$\therefore \quad \frac{\partial f}{\partial x_1} = 2x_1 + 3x_2\,; \quad \frac{\partial^2 f}{\partial x_1^2} = 2, \text{ which is} > 0,$$

$$\frac{\partial f}{\partial x_2} = 3x_1 + 4x_2\,; \quad \frac{\partial^2 f}{\partial x_2^2} = 4, \text{ which is} > 0\,,$$

$$\frac{\partial^2 f}{\partial x_1 \partial x_2} = 3.$$

$$\therefore \quad \frac{\partial^2 f}{\partial x_1^2} \cdot \frac{\partial^2 f}{\partial x_2^2} - \left[\frac{\partial^2 f}{\partial x_1\, \partial x_2}\right]^2 = 2 \times 4 - (3)^2 = -1, \text{ which is } < 0.$$

$\therefore$ The function is neither convex nor concave.

(*d*) $$f(X) = x_1^2 + x_2^2 - 2x_1x_2.$$

$$\therefore \quad \frac{\partial f}{\partial x_1} = 2x_1 - 2x_2 \; ; \; \frac{\partial^2 f}{\partial x_1^2} = 2, \text{ which is } > 0 \, ,$$

$$\frac{\partial f}{\partial x_2} = 2x_2 - 2x_1 \; ; \; \frac{\partial^2 f}{\partial x_2^2} = 2, \text{ which is } > 0,$$

$$\frac{\partial^2 f}{\partial x_1 \partial x_2} = -2.$$

$$\therefore \quad \frac{\partial^2 f}{\partial x_1^2} \cdot \frac{\partial^2 f}{\partial x_2^2} - \left[\frac{\partial^2 f}{\partial x_1 \partial x_2}\right]^2 = 2 \times 2 - (-2)^2 = 0, \text{ which is } \geq 0.$$

$\therefore$ Function is convex but not strictly convex.

(*e*) $$f(X) = 20x_1 + 10x_2.$$

$$\therefore \quad \frac{\partial f}{\partial x_1} = 20 \; ; \; \frac{\partial^2 f}{\partial x_1^2} = 0.$$

$$\frac{\partial f}{\partial x_2} = 10 \; ; \; \frac{\partial^2 f}{\partial x_2^2} = 0,$$

$$\frac{\partial^2 f}{\partial x_1 \partial x_2} = 0.$$

Since, all the three conditions result into zeroes, the function is both convex and concave.

(*f*) $$f(X) = x_1x_2.$$

$$\therefore \quad \frac{\partial f}{\partial x_1} = x_2 \; ; \; \frac{\partial^2 f}{\partial x_1^2} = 0.$$

$$\frac{\partial f}{\partial x_2} = x_1 \; ; \; \frac{\partial^2 f}{\partial x_2^2} = 0.$$

$$\frac{\partial^2 f}{\partial x_1 \partial x_2} = 1.$$

$$\therefore \quad \frac{\partial^2 f}{\partial x_1^2} \cdot \frac{\partial^2 f}{\partial x_2^2} - \left[\frac{\partial^2 f}{\partial x_1 \partial x_2}\right]^2 = 0 - 1 = -1, \text{ which is } < 0.$$

$\therefore$ The function is both convex and concave.

EXAMPLE 16.5-3

Consider the following function:

$$f(X) = 5x_1 + 2x_2^2 + x_3^2 - 3x_3x_4 + 4x_4^2 + 2x_5^4 + x_5^2 - 3x_5x_6 + 6x_6^2 + 3x_6x_7 + x_7^2.$$

Show that f (X) is convex by expressing it as a sum of functions of one or two variables and then proving that all the functions are convex.

Solution

The given function $f(X)$ can be split into a number of functions of one or two variables, as under:

$$f_1(X) = 5x_1 + 2x_2^2,$$
$$f_2(X) = x_3^2 - 3x_3x_4 + 4x_4^2,$$
$$f_3(X) = 2x_5^4 + x_5^2 + 3x_5x_6 + 3x_6^2,$$
$$f_4(X) = 3x_6^2 + 3x_6x_7 + x_7^2.$$

Taking $f_1(X) = 5x_1 + 2x_2^2$.

$$\frac{\partial f}{\partial x_1} = 5 \; ; \; \frac{\partial^2 f}{\partial x_1^2} = 0,$$

$$\frac{\partial f}{\partial x_2} = 4x_2 \; ; \; \frac{\partial^2 f}{\partial x_2^2} = 4, \text{ which is} > 0 \,,$$

$$\frac{\partial^2 f}{\partial x_1 \partial x_2} = 0.$$

$$\therefore \quad \frac{\partial^2 f}{\partial x_1^2} \cdot \frac{\partial^2 f}{\partial x_2^2} - \left[\frac{\partial^2 f}{\partial x_1 \partial x_2}\right]^2 = 0 \times 4 - 0 = 0.$$

∴ The function is convex.

Taking $f_2(X) = x_3^2 - 3x_3x_4 + 4x_4^2$.

$$\frac{\partial f}{\partial x_3} = 2x_3 - 3x_4 \; ; \; \frac{\partial^2 f}{\partial x_3^2} = 2, \text{ which is} > 0 \,,$$

$$\frac{\partial f}{\partial x_4} = -3x_3 + 8x_4 \; ; \; \frac{\partial^2 f}{\partial x_4^2} = 8, \text{ which is} > 0,$$

$$\frac{\partial^2 f}{\partial x_3 \, \partial x_4} = -3.$$

$$\therefore \quad \frac{\partial^2 f}{\partial x_3^2} \cdot \frac{\partial^2 f}{\partial x_4^2} - \left[\frac{\partial^2 f}{\partial x_3 \partial x_4}\right]^2 = 2 \times 8 - (-3)^2 = 7, \text{ which is} > 0.$$

∴ The function in convex.

Taking $f_3(X) = 2x_5^4 + x_5^2 + 3x_5x_6 + 3x_6^2$.

$$\frac{\partial f}{\partial x_5} = 8x_5^3 + 2x_5 + 3x_6 \; ; \; \frac{\partial^2 f}{\partial x_5^2} = 24x_5^2 + 2,$$

which is > 0 for all values of x_5.

$$\frac{\partial f}{\partial x_6} = 3x_5 + 6x_6 \; ; \; \frac{\partial^2 f}{\partial x_6^2} = 6, \text{ which is} > 0,$$

$$\frac{\partial^2 f}{\partial x_5 \partial x_6} = 3.$$

$$\therefore \quad \frac{\partial^2 f}{\partial x_5^2} \cdot \frac{\partial^2 f}{\partial x_6^2} - \left[\frac{\partial^2 f}{\partial x_5 \partial x_6}\right]^2 = (24x_5^2 + 2)\, 6 - (3)^2$$

$$= 144x_5^2 + 12 - 9 = 144x_5^2 + 3,$$

which is > 0 for all values of x_5.

Thus, the function is convex.

Taking $f_4(X) = 3x_6^2 + 3x_6x_7 + x_7^2$

$$\frac{\partial f}{\partial x_6} = 6x_6 + 3x_7 \; ; \; \frac{\partial^2 f}{\partial x_6^2} = 6,$$

$$\frac{\partial f}{\partial x_7} = 3x_6 + 2x_7 \; ; \; \frac{\partial^2 f}{\partial x_7^2} = 2,$$

$$\frac{\partial^2 f}{\partial x_6 \partial x_7} = 3.$$

$$\therefore \quad \frac{\partial^2 f}{\partial x_6^2} \cdot \frac{\partial^2 f}{\partial x_7^2} - \left[\frac{\partial^2 f}{\partial x_6 \partial x_7}\right]^2 = 6 \times 2 - (3)^2 = 3, \text{ which is } > 0.$$

$\therefore$ The function is convex.

Since all the component functions $f_1(X), f_2(X), f_3(X)$ and $f_4(X)$ are convex, the given function, which is the sum of these four functions, is also convex.

EXAMPLE 16.5-4

Consider the following N.L.P.P.:

Minimize $\quad Z = 2x_1^2 - 24x_1 + 2x_2^2 - 8x_2 + 2x_3^2 - 12x_3 + 200.$

By separating this function into three one-variable functions, show that the function is convex. Solve the problem by solving each one-variable function by calculus.

Solution

The given function can be separated into three functions $f(x_1), f(x_2)$ and $f(x_3)$, such that

$$f(X) = f(x_1) + f(x_2) + f(x_3).$$
$$f(x_1) = 2x_1^2 - 24x_1,$$
$$f(x_2) = 2x_2^2 - 8x_2,$$
$$f(x_3) = 2x_3^2 - 12x_3 + 200.$$

Now $\quad \dfrac{df}{dx_1} = 4x_1 - 24 \; ; \; \dfrac{d^2 f}{dx_1^2} = 4 > 0.$

$\therefore$ Function $f(x_1)$ is convex.

$$\frac{df}{dx_2} = 4x_2 - 8 \; ; \; \frac{d^2 f}{dx_2^2} = 4 > 0.$$

$\therefore$ Function $f(x_2)$ is convex.

$$\frac{df}{dx_3} = 4x_3 - 12 \; ; \; \frac{d^2 f}{dx_3^2} = 4 > 0.$$

$\therefore$ Function $f(x_3)$ is convex.

Since the three component functions are convex, the given function, which is the sum of these convex functions is also convex.

Now $\quad \dfrac{df}{dx_1} = 4x_1 - 24 = 0 \quad$ gives $x_1 = 6,$

$$\frac{df}{dx_2} = 4x_2 - 8 = 0 \quad \text{gives } x_2 = 2,$$

$$\frac{df}{dx_3} = 4x_3 - 12 = 0 \qquad \text{gives } x_3 = 3.$$

Thus the optimal solution is $x_1^* = 6$, $x_2^* = 2$ and $x_3^* = 3$;

$$Z_{min} = 72 - 144 + 8 - 16 + 18 - 36 + 200 = 102.$$

EXAMPLE 16.5-5

Determine the relative maximum and minimum (if any) of the following function:

$$f(X) = x_1 + 2x_3 + x_2x_3 - x_1^2 - x_2^2 - x_3^2.$$

Solution

The function will have maximum if it is concave, and minimum if it is convex. The necessary conditions for the function to be maximum or minimum are, $\frac{\partial(X)}{\partial x_i} = 0$ for $i = 1, 2, ..., n$. The sufficient conditions are determined from the Hessian matrix,

$$H(X) = \left[\frac{\partial^2 f}{\partial x_i \, \partial x_j}\right].$$

If H(*X*) is positive definite or positive semi-definite, the function $f(X)$ is convex function. If it is negative definite or negative semi-definite, the function is concave. In case of convex function, the principal minor determinants are all positive (non-negative), while in case of concave function, the principal minors are of the sign $(-1)^k$, $k = 1, 2, 3, ...$.

Now the *necessary conditions* are

$$\frac{\partial f}{\partial x_1} = 1 - 2x_1 = 0,$$

$$\frac{\partial f}{\partial x_2} = x_3 - 2x_2 = 0,$$

$$\frac{\partial f}{\partial x_3} = 2 + x_2 - 2x_3 = 0.$$

These result into the solution $x_1 = \frac{1}{2}$, $x_2 = \frac{2}{3}$ and $x_3 = \frac{4}{3}$.

For the *sufficient conditions*, we have to write the Hessian matrix.

Now
$$\frac{\partial^2 f}{\partial x_1^2} = -2\,; \quad \frac{\partial^2 f}{\partial x_1 \partial x_2} = 0\,; \quad \frac{\partial^2 f}{\partial x_1 \partial x_3} = 0;$$

$$\frac{\partial^2 f}{\partial x_2 \partial x_1} = 0\,; \quad \frac{\partial^2 f}{\partial x_2^2} = -2\,; \quad \frac{\partial^2 f}{\partial x_2 \partial x_3} = 1;$$

$$\frac{\partial^2 f}{\partial x_3 \partial x_1} = 0\,; \quad \frac{\partial^2 f}{\partial x_3 \partial x_2} = 1\,; \quad \frac{\partial^2 f}{\partial x_3^2} = -2.$$

$$\therefore \qquad H(X) = \begin{bmatrix} \frac{\partial^2 f}{\partial x_1^2} & \frac{\partial^2 f}{\partial x_1 \partial x_2} & \frac{\partial^2 f}{\partial x_1 \partial x_3} \\ \frac{\partial^2 f}{\partial x_2 \partial x_1} & \frac{\partial^2 f}{\partial x_2^2} & \frac{\partial^2 f}{\partial x_2 \partial x_3} \\ \frac{\partial^2 f}{\partial x_3 \partial x_1} & \frac{\partial^2 f}{\partial x_3 \partial x_2} & \frac{\partial^2 f}{\partial x_3^2} \end{bmatrix} = \begin{bmatrix} -2 & 0 & 0 \\ 0 & -2 & 1 \\ 0 & 1 & -2 \end{bmatrix}.$$

Now the principal minors of H(X) are

$$a_{11} = -2\ ; \quad \begin{vmatrix} a_{11} & a_{12} \\ a_{21} & a_{22} \end{vmatrix} = \begin{vmatrix} -2 & 0 \\ 0 & -2 \end{vmatrix} = 4\ ;$$

$$\begin{vmatrix} a_{11} & a_{12} & a_{13} \\ a_{21} & a_{22} & a_{23} \\ a_{31} & a_{32} & a_{33} \end{vmatrix} = \begin{vmatrix} -2 & 0 & 0 \\ 0 & -2 & 1 \\ 0 & 1 & -2 \end{vmatrix} = -2\,[4-1] - 0\,[0-0] + 0\,[0-0] = -6.$$

The signs of principal minors are –, +, – that is $(-1)^k$, for k = 1, 2 and 3.

∴ The Hessian matrix is negative definite and, hence, the function is concave and the solution point $\frac{1}{2}, \frac{2}{3}, \frac{4}{3}$ is local maximum.

$$f(X)_{\max} = \frac{1}{2} + 2 \times \frac{4}{3} + \frac{2}{3} \times \frac{4}{3} - \left(\frac{1}{2}\right)^2 - \left(\frac{2}{3}\right)^2 - \left(\frac{4}{3}\right)^2 = \frac{57}{36}.$$

EXAMPLE 16.5-6

Verify whether the following function is convex or concave and find the maximum or minimum solution point:

$$f(X) = 4x_1^2 + 3x_2^2 + x_3^2 - 6x_1x_2 + x_1x_3 - \frac{x_1}{2} - 2x_2 + 15.$$

Solution

The necessary conditions are

$$\frac{\partial f}{\partial x_1} = 8x_1 - 6x_2 + x_3 - \frac{1}{2} = 0,$$

$$\frac{\partial f}{\partial x_2} = 6x_2 - 6x_1 - 2 = 0,$$

$$\frac{\partial f}{\partial x_3} = 2x_3 + x_1 = 0.$$

The solution of these equations gives $x_1 = \frac{5}{3}$, $x_2 = 2$, $x_3 = \frac{-5}{6}$.

$$H(X) = \begin{bmatrix} \frac{\partial^2 f}{\partial x_1^2} & \frac{\partial^2 f}{\partial x_1\,\partial x_2} & \frac{\partial^2 f}{\partial x_1\,\partial x_3} \\ \frac{\partial^2 f}{\partial x_2\,\partial x_1} & \frac{\partial^2 f}{\partial x_2^2} & \frac{\partial^2 f}{\partial x_2\,\partial x_3} \\ \frac{\partial^2 f}{\partial x_3\,\partial x_1} & \frac{\partial^2 f}{\partial x_3\,\partial x_2} & \frac{\partial^2 f}{\partial x_3^2} \end{bmatrix} = \begin{bmatrix} 8 & -6 & 1 \\ -6 & 6 & 0 \\ 1 & 0 & 2 \end{bmatrix}.$$

The principal minor determinants are $|8|$, $\begin{vmatrix} 8 & -6 \\ -6 & 6 \end{vmatrix} = 12$, $\begin{vmatrix} 8 & -6 & 1 \\ -6 & 6 & 0 \\ 1 & 0 & 2 \end{vmatrix}$

$$= 8\,(12-0) - (-6)\,[-12-0] + 1\,(0-6)$$

$$= 96 - 72 - 6 = 18.$$

Since all the principal minor determinants are non-negative, the function is convex. The function has local minimum at $x_1 = \frac{5}{3}$, $x_2 = 2$ and $x_3 = \frac{-5}{6}$.

$$f(x)_{\min} = 12.59.$$

Note : The Hessian matrix,

$$H(X) = \begin{bmatrix} \frac{\partial^2 f}{\partial x_1^2} & \frac{\partial^2 f}{\partial x_1 \cdot \partial x_2} & \frac{\partial^2 f}{\partial x_1 \cdot \partial x_3} \\ \frac{\partial^2 f}{\partial x_2 \cdot \partial x_1} & \frac{\partial^2 f}{\partial x_2^2} & \frac{\partial^2 f}{\partial x_2 \cdot \partial x_3} \\ \frac{\partial^2 f}{\partial x_3 \cdot \partial x_1} & \frac{\partial^2 f}{\partial x_3 \cdot \partial x_2} & \frac{\partial^2 f}{\partial x_3^2} \end{bmatrix} \text{ is}$$

(*a*) positive definite if

$$D_1 = \frac{\partial^2 f}{\partial x_1^2} > 0, \quad D_2 = \begin{vmatrix} \frac{\partial^2 f}{\partial x_1^2} & \frac{\partial^2 f}{\partial x_1 \cdot \partial x_2} \\ \frac{\partial^2 f}{\partial x_2 \cdot \partial x_1} & \frac{\partial^2 f}{\partial x_2^2} \end{vmatrix} > 0,$$

$$D_3 = \begin{bmatrix} \frac{\partial^2 f}{\partial x_1^2} & \frac{\partial^2 f}{\partial x_1 \cdot \partial x_2} & \frac{\partial^2 f}{\partial x_1 \cdot \partial x_3} \\ \frac{\partial^2 f}{\partial x_2 \cdot \partial x_1} & \frac{\partial^2 f}{\partial x_2^2} & \frac{\partial^2 f}{\partial x_2 \cdot \partial x_3} \\ \frac{\partial^2 f}{\partial x_3 \cdot \partial x_1} & \frac{\partial^2 f}{\partial x_3 \cdot \partial x_2} & \frac{\partial^2 f}{\partial x_3^2} \end{bmatrix} > 0, \ldots, D_n > 0,$$

i.e., all the principal minor determinants are positive.

(*b*) negative definite if
$D_1 < 0, D_2 > 0, D_3 < 0, \ldots, (-1)^n D_n > 0.$

(*c*) positive semi-definite if the variables can be ordered so that
$D_1 > 0$ and $D_2 \geq 0, i = 2, 3, \ldots, n.$

(*d*) negative semi-definite if the variables can be ordered so that
$D_1 < 0, D_2 \geq 0, D_3 \leq 0, \ldots, (-1)^n D_n \geq 0.$

(*e*) indefinite if none of the above cases occur.
For example, if

$$f(X) = -7x_1^2 - 10x_2^2 - x_3^2 + 4x_1x_2 - 2x_1x_3 + 4x_2x_3,$$

$$H = \begin{bmatrix} -14 & 4 & -2 \\ 4 & -20 & 4 \\ -2 & 4 & -2 \end{bmatrix},$$

$$D_1 = -14 < 0, D_2 = \begin{vmatrix} -14 & 4 \\ 4 & -20 \end{vmatrix} = 280 - 16 = 264 > 0,$$

and
$$D_3 = \begin{bmatrix} -14 & 4 & -2 \\ 4 & -20 & 4 \\ -2 & 4 & -2 \end{bmatrix} = -14(40-16) - 4(-8+8) - 2(16-40)$$

$$= -336 - 0 + 48 = -288 < 0.$$

∴ H is negative definite.

EXAMPLE 16.5-7

Show that (0, 0) is the saddle point to the function
$f(x_1, x_2) = 18x_1x_2 + 5x_2^2$.

Solution

Applying the necessary conditions for the function to be maximum or minimum,

$$\frac{\partial f}{\partial x_1} = 18x_2 = 0 \quad \text{or} \quad x_2 = 0,$$

$$\frac{\partial f}{\partial x_2} = 18x_1 + 10x_2 = 0 \quad \text{or} \quad 18x_1 = 0 \text{ or } x_1 = 0.$$

Thus (0, 0) is the only point that satisfies the necessary conditions. To establish sufficient conditions, the Hessian matrix is written as

$$H(X) = \begin{vmatrix} \frac{\partial^2 f}{\partial x_1^2} & \frac{\partial^2 f}{\partial x_1 \cdot \partial x_2} \\ \frac{\partial^2 f}{\partial x_2 \cdot \partial x_1} & \frac{\partial^2 f}{\partial x_2^2} \end{vmatrix} = \begin{bmatrix} 0 & 18 \\ 18 & 10 \end{bmatrix}.$$

The principal minor determinants of H(X) have values 0 and –324 respectively.

Hence H(X) is indefinite and (0, 0) is the saddle point.

16.6 TYPES OF NON-LINEAR PROGRAMMING PROBLEMS

There is a wide variety of non-linear programming problems. Some of the most important types are briefly introduced here. Unlike the linear programming, no standard algorithm like the simplex method can be employed to solve the non-linear programming problems. Many different algorithms have been developed to solve the different class of problems. It is beyond the scope of this book to cover all the types of N.L.P.P. and their solutions.

16.6-1 Unconstrained Optimization

In case of unconstrained optimization problems, there are no constraints, but only the objective function. The problem is simply to

$$\text{Maximize / minimize } f(X)$$

over all values of $X = (x_1, x_2, ..., x_n)$. The necessary condition for a particular solution to be optimal is

$$\frac{\partial f}{\partial x_j} = 0 \text{ at } x = X^* \text{ for } j = 1, 2, ..., n,$$

where $f(X)$ is differentiable. This condition is also sufficient condition for maximization when $f(X)$ is a concave function and for minimization when $f(X)$ is a convex function. Thus the solution can be obtained by solving n equations obtained by setting the n partial derivatives equal to zero. Examples 16.5-4 through 16.5-7 are on unconstrained optimization. However, it is not that simple. For a non-linear function, these equations are often non-linear, and it becomes impossible to solve these equations analytically. Some search procedures have been developed by researchers to solve such problems.

16.6-2 Linearly Constrained Optimization

As the name indicates, in this type of NLPP, all the constraints $g^i(X)$ are of linear type, while the objective function $f(X)$ is non-linear. Since only one non-linear function is to be handled, the problem becomes comparatively simple to solve. A number of special algorithms have been developed, by extending the simplex method, to handle the non-linear objective function.

16.6-3 Quadratic Programming

This again is a linearly constrained problem, but the objective function $f(X)$ is quadratic. In other words, the objective function contains the terms which are either square of a variable or product of two variables. The general structure of a quadratic programming problem is as follows:

$$\text{Optimize (Max or Min)} \quad Z = \left\{ \sum_{j=1}^{n} c_j x_j + \frac{1}{2} \sum_{j=1}^{n} \sum_{k=1}^{n} x_j \, d_{jk} \, x_k \right\},$$

$$\text{subject to} \quad \sum_{j=1}^{n} a_{ij} \; x_j \leq b_i, \; i = 1, 2, ..., n,$$

$$\text{and} \qquad x_j \geq 0, j = 1, 2, ..., n.$$

Since, such problems arise very frequently in practical situations, quadratic programming is an important class of NLPP. Many algorithms are available to solve quadratic programming problems.

16.6-4 Convex Programming

Convex programming covers special cases of various types of NLPP, where the objective function $f(X)$ is a concave function and each of the constraints $g^i(X)$ is a convex function. These assumptions ensure that a local maximum is also a global maximum.

16.6-5 Separable Programming

Separable programming is a special case of convex programming. One additional assumption made here is that all the $f(X)$ and $g^i(X)$ are separable functions.

A function is called separable, when it can be expressed as a sum of subfunctions where each subfunction is a function of one variable only. For example, if $f(X)$ is a separable function, it can be expressed as

$$f(X) = \sum_{i=1}^{n} f_i(x_i),$$

where each $f_i(x_i)$ is a function comprising of terms involving only x_i. Consider the two-variable objective function

$$f(x_1, x_2) = 4x_1 + 9x_2 - x_1^2 - x_2^2,$$

which can be expressed as

$$f(x_1, x_2) = (4x_1 - x_1^2) + (9x_2 - x_2^2)$$

$$= f(x_1) + f(x_2),$$

where $\quad f(x_1) = 4x_1 - x_1^2,$

and $\quad f(x_2) = 9x_2 - x_2^2.$

The separable programming problems are solved by methods which are extensions of the simplex method. They are applicable only if the objective function as well as all the constraints are separable.

16.6-6 Non-convex Programming

All NLPP that do not satisfy the assumptions of convex programming, fall in this category of non-convex programming. There is no algorithm that can result into global optimal solution of such problems. Some algorithms attempt to find the local minima in case the problem does not deviate much from the assumptions of convex programming.

Some specific types of non-convex programming problems can be solved by employing specific methods. Two important types of NLPP under this category are Geometric programming and Fractional Programming.

16.7 CONSTRAINED EXTREMAL PROBLEMS

The optimization problems having continuous objective function and equality or inequality type constraints are called constrained extremal problems. The solution of such problems, having differentiable objective function and equality type constraints can be obtained by a number of methods, but the most common is the *Lagrange multipliers method.*

16.7-1 Problem with one Equality Constraint

The use of Lagrange function can best be understood with the help of an example. Let us consider a simple two-variable problem having a single equality type constraint.

Maximize or minimize $Z = f(x_1, x_2)$,

subject to $g(x_1, x_2) = b$,

$x_1, x_2 \geq 0$,

where the objective function as well as the constraint are differentiable w.r.t. x_1 and x_2 and $f(x_1, x_2)$ or $g(x_1, x_2)$ or both are non-linear. The constraint function can be replaced by another differentiable function $h(x_1, x_2)$ such that

$$h(x_1, x_2) = g(x_1, x_2) - b = 0.$$

The problem, then, reduces to

maximize or minimize $z = f(x_1, x_2)$,

subject to $h(x_1, x_2) = 0$,

$x_1, x_2 \geq 0$.

The Lagrangean function can now be formulated as

$$L(x_1, x_2, \lambda) = f(x_1, x_2) - \lambda\, h(x_1, x_2),$$

where λ is the *Lagrange multiplier.*

The necessary conditions for the maximum or minimum of $f(x_1, x_2)$, subject to the constraint $h(x_1, x_2) = 0$, can be obtained as

$$\frac{\partial L}{\partial x_1} = 0,$$

$$\frac{\partial L}{\partial x_2} = 0,$$

and $$\frac{\partial L}{\partial \lambda} = 0,$$

where $L = L(x_1, x_2, \lambda)$.

If $f = f(x_1, x_2)$ and $h = h(x_1, x_2)$, the above three necessary conditions for optimization are given by

$$\frac{\partial L}{\partial x_1} = \frac{\partial f}{\partial x_1} - \lambda \frac{\partial h}{\partial x_1} = 0 \quad \text{or} \quad \frac{\partial f}{\partial x_1} = \lambda \frac{\partial h}{\partial x_1},$$

$$\frac{\partial L}{\partial x_2} = \frac{\partial f}{\partial x_2} - \lambda \frac{\partial h}{\partial x_2} = 0 \quad \text{or} \quad \frac{\partial f}{\partial x_2} = \lambda \frac{\partial h}{\partial x_2},$$

and $$\frac{\partial L}{\partial \lambda} = 0 - h = 0 \quad \text{or} \quad -h = 0.$$

The necessary conditions for optima of $f(x_1, x_2)$, subject to $h(x_1, x_2) = 0$, are thus given by

$$f_1 = \lambda h_1,$$

$$f_2 = \lambda h_2,$$

and $$-h = 0.$$

These necessary conditions are also the sufficient conditions for a maximum if the objective function is concave and for a minimum if the objective function is convex.

16.7-2 Necessary and Sufficient Conditions for a General NLPP

A general NLPP having n variables and m constraints ($n \geq m$), can be expressed as

maximize or minimize $\quad Z = f(X),\ X = (x_1, x_2, ..., x_n),$

subject to $\quad g^i(X) = b_i, \quad i = 1, 2, ..., m,$

$X \geq 0.$

The constraint can also be written as

$$h^i(X) = g^i(X) - b_i = 0,\ i = 1, 2, ..., m.$$

By introducing the Lagrange multipliers, $\lambda = (\lambda_1, \lambda_2, ..., \lambda_m)$, the Lagrange function is formed as

$$L(X, \lambda) = f(X) - \sum_{i=1}^{m} \lambda_i h^i(X).$$

Assuming that all the functions L, f and h^i are differentiable partially w.r.t. $x_1, x_2, ..., x_n$ and $\lambda_1, \lambda_2, ..., \lambda_m$, the necessary conditions for the objective function to be a maximum or a minimum are

$$\frac{\partial L}{\partial x_j} = \frac{\partial f}{\partial x_j} - \sum_{i=1}^{m} \lambda_i \frac{\partial h^i}{\partial x_j} = 0 \quad \text{or} \quad \frac{\partial f}{\partial x_j} = \sum_{i=1}^{m} \lambda_i \frac{\partial h^i}{\partial x_j},$$

and $$\frac{\partial L}{\partial \lambda_i} = 0 - h^i = 0 \quad \text{or} \quad -h^i = 0,\ i = 1, 2, ..., m;\ j = 1, 2, ..., n.$$

These $(m + n)$ necessary conditions also become the sufficient conditions for a maximum if the objective function is concave and for a minimum if the objective function is convex.

16.7-3 When concavity (convexity) is not known

As discussed in section 16.7-2, for an n-variable non-linear programming problem having one equality type constraint, the necessary conditions for a stationary point to be a maximum or minimum are

$$\frac{\partial L}{\partial x_j} = \frac{\partial f}{\partial x_j} - \lambda \frac{\partial h}{\partial x_j} = 0, \qquad j = 1, 2, ..., n,$$

and $$\frac{\partial L}{\partial \lambda} = -h(X) = 0.$$

From the first condition, $\lambda = \dfrac{\partial f}{\partial x_j} \Big/ \dfrac{\partial h}{\partial x_j}$, for $j = 1, 2, ..., n.$

These necessary conditions provide an optimal solution to the problem. The sufficient conditions for determining whether the solution results in maximization or minimization of the objective function involve the solution of $(n - 1)$ principal minors of the following determinant:

$$\Delta_{n+1} = \begin{vmatrix} 0 & \dfrac{\partial h}{\partial x_1} & \dfrac{\partial h}{\partial x_2} & \cdots & \dfrac{\partial h}{\partial x_n} \\ \dfrac{\partial h}{\partial x_1} & \dfrac{\partial^2 f}{\partial x_1^2} - \lambda \dfrac{\partial^2 h}{\partial x_1^2} & \dfrac{\partial^2 f}{\partial x_1 \partial x_2} - \lambda \dfrac{\partial^2 h}{\partial x_1 \partial x_2} & \cdots & \dfrac{\partial^2 f}{\partial x_1 \partial x_n} - \lambda \dfrac{\partial^2 h}{\partial x_1 \partial x_n} \\ \dfrac{\partial h}{\partial x_2} & \dfrac{\partial^2 f}{\partial x_2 \partial x_1} - \lambda \dfrac{\partial^2 h}{\partial x_2 \partial x_1} & \dfrac{\partial^2 f}{\partial x_2^2} - \lambda \dfrac{\partial^2 h}{\partial x_2^2} & \cdots & \dfrac{\partial^2 f}{\partial x_2 \partial x_n} - \lambda \dfrac{\partial^2 h}{\partial x_2 \partial x_n} \\ \vdots & & & & \\ \dfrac{\partial h}{\partial x_n} & \dfrac{\partial^2 f}{\partial x_n \partial x_1} - \lambda \dfrac{\partial^2 h}{\partial x_n \partial x_1} & \dfrac{\partial^2 f}{\partial x_n \partial x_2} - \lambda \dfrac{\partial^2 h}{\partial x_n \partial x_2} & \cdots & \dfrac{\partial^2 f}{\partial x_n^2} - \lambda \dfrac{\partial^2 h}{\partial x_n^2} \end{vmatrix}$$

If the signs of minors Δ_3, Δ_4, Δ_5, etc. are alternatively +ve and –ve, the stationary point is a local maximum, and if all the minors are negative, the local stationary point is a minimum.

EXAMPLE 16.7-1

Solve the NLPP:

Maximize $Z = 4x_1 - x_1^2 + 8x_2 - x_2^2$,

subject to $x_1 + x_2 = 2$,

$x_1, x_2 \geq 0$.

Solution

The objective function as well as the constraint are differentiable w.r.t. x_1 and x_2. The constraint can be replaced by another differentiable function such as

$$x_1 + x_2 - 2 = 0.$$

The Lagrangean function can be written as

$$L(x_1, x_2, \lambda) = 4x_1 - x_1^2 + 8x_2 - x_2^2 - \lambda(x_1 + x_2 - 2).$$

The necessary conditions for a maxima or minima of the objective function are

$$\frac{\partial L}{\partial x_1} = 4 - 2x_1 - \lambda = 0, \quad ...(i)$$

$$\frac{\partial L}{\partial x_2} = 8 - 2x_2 - \lambda = 0, \quad ...(ii)$$

and $$\frac{\partial L}{\partial \lambda} = -(x_1 + x_2 - 2) = 0. \quad ...(iii)$$

From (*i*) and (*ii*), $4 - 2x_1 = 8 - 2x_2$

or $x_2 - x_1 = 2$,

and from (*iii*), $x_2 + x_1 = 2$,

which give $x_1 = 0$, $x_2 = 2$ and $\lambda = 4$.

The sufficient conditions for determining whether the above solution results in maximization or minimization of the objective function involve the solution of $(n - 1) = 2 - 1 = 1$ principal minor of the following determinant of order 3:

$$D_3 = \begin{vmatrix} 0 & 1 & 1 \\ 1 & -2 & 0 \\ 1 & 0 & -2 \end{vmatrix} = -1(-2) + 1(2) = 2 + 2 = 4.$$

Since D_3 is positive, the solution $x_1 = 0$, $x_2 = 2$ maximizes the objective function and

$$Z_{max} = 0 - 0 + 16 - 4 = 12.$$

EXAMPLE 16.7-2

Solve the following NLPP :

Maximize $Z = 4x_1 + 6x_2 - 2x_1^2 - 2x_1x_2 - 2x_2^2$,

subject to $x_1 + 2x_2 = 2$,

$x_1, x_2 \geq 0$. *[P.U. M.E. (Mech.) 1987]*

Solution

The objective function as well as the constraint are differentiable w.r.t. x_1 and x_2. The constraint can be replaced by another differentiable function such as,

$$x_1 + 2x_2 - 2 = 0.$$

The Lagrangean function can be written as

$$L(x_1, x_2, \lambda) = 4x_1 + 6x_2 - 2x_1^2 - 2x_1x_2 - 2x_2^2 - \lambda(x_1 + 2x_2 - 2).$$

The necessary conditions for a maxima or minima of the objective function are

$$\frac{\partial L}{\partial x_1} = 0,$$

$$\frac{\partial L}{\partial x_2} = 0,$$

and $$\frac{\partial L}{\partial \lambda} = 0,$$

or $4 - 4x_1 - 2x_2 - \lambda = 0,$ ...(*i*)

$6 - 2x_1 - 4x_2 - 2\lambda = 0,$ ...(*ii*)

and $-(x_1 + 2x_2 - 2) = 0.$ ...(*iii*)

Solving (*i*) and (*ii*), we get $x_1 = 1/3$ which when substituted in (*iii*) gives $x_2 = 5/6$ and for this solution $\lambda = 1$.

The sufficient conditions for determining whether this solution results in maximization or minimization of the objective function involve the solution of $(n - 1) = 2 - 1 = 1$ principal minor of the following determinant of order 3 :

$$D_3 = \begin{vmatrix} 0 & 1 & 2 \\ 1 & -4 & -2 \\ 2 & -2 & -4 \end{vmatrix} = -1\,(-4+4) + 2\,(-2+8) = 12.$$

Since D_3 is positive, the solution $x_1 = 1/3$ and $x_2 = 5/6$ maximizes the objective function.

$$\therefore \quad Z_{max} = 4 \times \frac{1}{3} + 6 \times \frac{5}{6} - 2\left(\frac{1}{3}\right)^2 - 2 \times \frac{1}{3} \times \frac{5}{6} - 2\left(\frac{5}{6}\right)^2$$

$$= \frac{150}{36} = 4.166.$$

EXAMPLE 16.7-3

Solve the following N.L.P.P.:

Maximize $Z = 5x_1 + x_2 - (x_1 - x_2)^2,$

subject to $x_1 + x_2 = 4,$

$x_1, x_2 \geq 0$

Solution

The Lagrangean function for the above problem can be formed as

$$L\,(X, \lambda) = 5x_1 + x_2 - (x_1 - x_2)^2 - \lambda\,(x_1 + x_2 - 4).$$

THe necessary conditions for the objective function to be maximum or minimum are

$$\frac{\partial L}{\partial x_1} = 5 - 2\,(x_1 - x_2) - \lambda = 0, \quad ...(i)$$

$$\frac{\partial L}{\partial x_2} = 1 + 2\,(x_1 - x_2) - \lambda = 0, \quad ...(ii)$$

and $$\frac{\partial L}{\partial \lambda} = -(x_1 + x_2 - 4) = 0. \quad ...(iii)$$

The solution of these equations yields

$$x_1 = \frac{5}{2},\ x_2 = \frac{3}{2} \text{ and } \lambda = 3.$$

Now $$D_3 = \begin{vmatrix} 0 & 1 & 1 \\ 1 & -2 & 2 \\ 1 & 2 & -2 \end{vmatrix} = -1\,(-2-2) + 1(2+2) = 4 + 4 = 8.$$

Since D_3 is positive, the solution $x_1 = 5/2$ and $x_2 = 3/2$ maximizes the objective function and

$$Z_{\max} = 5\left(\frac{5}{2}\right) + \frac{3}{2} - \left(\frac{5}{2} - \frac{3}{2}\right)^2 = \frac{25}{2} + \frac{3}{2} - 1 = 13.$$

EXAMPLE 16.7-4

Solve the following N.L.P.P. by using Lagrangean multipliers method:

Minimize $Z = x_1^2 + x_2^2 + x_3^2,$

subject to $4x_1 + x_2^2 + 2x_3 = 14,$

$x_1, x_2 \geq 0.$ *[B.P.U.T. 6th. Sem., 2011]*

Solution

The Lagrangean function for the given problem can be written as

$$L(x_1, x_2, x_3, \lambda) = x_1^2 + x_2^2 + x_3^2 - \lambda(4x_1 + x_2^2 + 2x_3 - 14).$$

The necessary conditions for the above convex function to be minimum are

$$\frac{\partial L}{\partial x_1} = 2x_1 - 4\lambda = 0, \quad \text{...}(i)$$

$$\frac{\partial L}{\partial x_2} = 2x_2 - 2\lambda x_2 = 0, \quad \text{...}(ii)$$

$$\frac{\partial L}{\partial x_3} = 2x_3 - 2\lambda = 0, \quad \text{...}(iii)$$

$$\frac{\partial L}{\partial \lambda} = -(4x_1 + x_2^2 + 2x_3 - 14) = 0. \quad \text{...}(iv)$$

From (*i*) $\lambda = \frac{x_1}{2}$ and from (*iii*) $\lambda = x_3$.

From (*ii*) $x_2(1 - \lambda) = 0$ *i.e.*, either $x_2 = 0$ or $\lambda = 1$.

When $x_2 = 0,$

from (*iv*) $4(2\lambda) + 0 + 2\lambda = 14$ or $\lambda = 1.4$.

This gives the solution $x_1 = 2.8, x_2 = 0, x_3 = 1.4,$

with $Z_{\min} = 9.8.$

When $\lambda = 1,$

from (*i*) $x_1 = 2,$

from (*iii*) $x_3 = 1,$

and from (*iv*) $8 + x_2^2 + 2 = 14$ or $x_2^2 = 4$

or $x_2 = \pm 2.$

Since $x_2 \geq 0, x_2 = -2$ is discarded.

$\therefore$ The second solution is $x_1 = 2, x_2 = 2, x_3 = 1$, giving $Z_{\min} = 9.$

Since $(x_1, x_2, x_3) = (2, 2, 1)$ gives the smaller value of $Z_{\min}$, it is the optional solution.

EXAMPLE 16.7-5

Obtain the necessary and sufficient conditions for the optimal solution of the following problem. What is the optimal solution?

Minimize $Z = 2e^{3x_1+1} + e^{2x_2+3},$

subject to the constraint

$x_1 + x_2 = 5,$

$x_1, x_2 \geq 0.$ *[Marathwada M.Sc. (Appl. Math.) 1982]*

Solution

The objective function as well as the constraint are differentiable with respect to x_1 and x_2 and the Lagrangean function for the above problem can be formed as

$$L(X, \lambda) = 2e^{3x_1+1} + e^{2x_2+3} - \lambda(x_1 + x_2 - 5).$$

The necessary and sufficient conditions for maximization or minimization of $Z = f(x_1, x_2)$ can be obtained as

$$\frac{\partial L}{\partial x_1} = 6e^{3x_1+1} - \lambda = 0, \quad ...(i)$$

$$\frac{\partial L}{\partial x_2} = 2e^{2x_2+3} - \lambda = 0, \quad ...(ii)$$

and $$\frac{\partial L}{\partial \lambda} = -(x_1 + x_2 - 5) = 0. \quad ...(iii)$$

From (*i*) and (*ii*), $6e^{3x_1+1} = 2e^{2x_2+3}$ and from (*iii*) $x_1 + x_2 = 5$.

$\therefore \quad 6e^{3x_1+1} = 2e^{2(5-x_1)+3} = 2e^{13-2x_1}$

or $\quad 3e^{3x_1+1} = e^{13-2x_1}$

or $\quad \log_e 3 + 3x_1 + 1 = 13 - 2x_1$

or $\quad x_1 = \frac{1}{5}(12 - \log_e 3),$

and $\quad x_2 = 5 - \frac{1}{5}(12 - \log_e 3) = \frac{1}{5}(13 + \log_e 3).$

Now
$$D_3 = \begin{vmatrix} 0 & 1 & 1 \\ 1 & 18e^{3x_1+1} & 0 \\ 1 & 0 & 4e^{2x_2+3} \end{vmatrix}$$

$$= -1(4e^{2x_2+3}) + 1(-18e^{3x_1+1})$$

$$= -2(9e^{2x_1+3} + 2e^{2x_2+3})$$

$$= -ve.$$

[Since the expression within parenthesis is positive for all values of x_1 and x_2.]

Since D_3 is negative, the above solution minimizes the objective function and

$$Z_{min} = 2e^{3\left\{\frac{1}{5}(12-\log_e 3)\right\}+1} + e^{2\left\{\frac{1}{5}(13-\log_e 3)\right\}+3}$$

$$= 2e^{\frac{1}{5}(41-3\log_e 3)} + e^{\frac{1}{5}(41+2\log_e 3)}.$$

EXAMPLE 16.7-6

Determine the optimal solution for the following NLPP and check whether it maximizes or minimizes the objective function:

Optimize $\quad Z = x_1^2 - 10x_1 + x_2^2 - 6x_2 + x_3^2 - 4x_3,$

subject to $\quad x_1 + x_2 + x_2 = 7,$

$\quad x_1, x_2, x_3 \geq 0.$

Solution

The objective function as well as the constraint are differentiable with respect to x_1, x_2 and x_3 and the Lagrangean function can be formed as

$$L(X, \lambda) = x_1^2 - 10x_1 + x_2^2 - 6x_2 + x_3^2 - 4x_3 - \lambda(x_1 + x_2 + x_3 - 7).$$

The necessary conditions for Z to be maximum or minimum are

$$\frac{\partial L}{\partial x_1} = 2x_1 - 10 - \lambda = 0,$$

$$\frac{\partial L}{\partial x_2} = 2x_2 - 6 - \lambda = 0,$$

$$\frac{\partial L}{\partial x_3} = 2x_3 - 4 - \lambda = 0,$$

and
$$\frac{\partial L}{\partial \lambda} = -(x_1 + x_2 + x_3 - 7) = 0.$$

The resulting solution is $x_1 = 4$, $x_2 = 2$, $x_3 = 1$ and $\lambda = -2$.

To determine whether this solution results in maximization or minimization, $(n-1) = 3 - 1 = 2$ principal minors D_3 and D_4 of the determinants of order 3 and 4 are solved.

$$D_3 = \begin{pmatrix} 0 & \dfrac{\partial h}{\partial x_1} & \dfrac{\partial h}{\partial x_2} \\ \dfrac{\partial h}{\partial x_1} & \dfrac{\partial^2 f}{\partial x_1^2} - \lambda \dfrac{\partial^2 h}{\partial x_1^2} & \dfrac{\partial^2 f}{\partial x_1 \partial x_2} - \lambda \dfrac{\partial^2 h}{\partial x_1 \partial x_2} \\ \dfrac{\partial h}{\partial x_2} & \dfrac{\partial^2 f}{\partial x_2 \partial x_1} - \lambda \dfrac{\partial^2 h}{\partial x_2 \partial x_1} & \dfrac{\partial^2 f}{\partial x_2^2} - \lambda \dfrac{\partial^2 h}{\partial x_2^2} \end{pmatrix} = \begin{pmatrix} 0 & 1 & 1 \\ 1 & 2 & 0 \\ 1 & 0 & 2 \end{pmatrix} = -1\,(2) + 1\,(-2) - 4,$$

$$D_4 = \begin{pmatrix} 0 & 1 & 1 & 1 \\ 1 & 2 & 0 & 0 \\ 1 & 0 & 2 & 0 \\ 1 & 0 & 0 & 2 \end{pmatrix} = -1 \begin{vmatrix} 1 & 0 & 0 \\ 1 & 2 & 0 \\ 1 & 0 & 2 \end{vmatrix} + 1 \begin{vmatrix} 1 & 2 & 0 \\ 1 & 0 & 0 \\ 1 & 0 & 2 \end{vmatrix} - 1 \begin{vmatrix} 1 & 2 & 0 \\ 1 & 0 & 2 \\ 1 & 0 & 0 \end{vmatrix}$$

$$= -1\,\{1\,(4)\} + 1\,\{1\,(0) - 2\,(2)\} - 1\,\{1\,(0) - 2\,(-2)\} = -4 - 4 - 4 = -12.$$

Since the principal minors D_3 and D_4 are negative, the solution $x_1 = 4$, $x_2 = 2$, $x_3 = 1$ minimizes the objective function, and

$$Z_{min} = 16 - 40 + 4 - 12 + 1 - 4 = -35.$$

EXAMPLE 16.7-7

Use the method of Lagrangean multipliers to solve the following NLPP. Does the solution maximize or minimize the objective function ?

Optimize $\quad Z = 2x_1^2 + x_2^2 + 3x_3^2 + 10x_1 + 8x_2 + 6x_3 - 100,$

subject to $\quad x_1 + x_2 + x_3 = 20,$

$\quad x_1, x_2, x_3 \geq 0.$

[*K.U. M. Tech. (Mech.) May, 1994; Chennai B.E. (Mech.) 1981*]

Solution

The objective function and the constraint are differentiable w.r.t. x_1, x_2 and x_3, and the Lagrangean function can be written as

$$L(X, \lambda) = 2x_1^2 + x_2^2 + 3x_3^2 + 10x_1 + 8x_2 + 6x_3 - 100 - \lambda\,(x_1 + x_2 + x_3 - 20).$$

The necessary conditions for the maxima or minima of the objective function are

$$\frac{\partial L}{\partial x_1} = 4x_1 + 10 - \lambda = 0, \quad ...(i)$$

$$\frac{\partial L}{\partial x_2} = 2x_2 + 8 - \lambda = 0, \quad ...(ii)$$

$$\frac{\partial L}{\partial x_3} = 6x_3 + 6 - \lambda = 0, \quad \text{...}(iii)$$

and $$\frac{\partial L}{\partial \lambda} = -(x_1 + x_2 + x_3 - 20) = 0. \quad \text{...}(iv)$$

From (i) $$x_1 = \frac{\lambda - 10}{4},$$

from (ii) $$x_2 = \frac{\lambda - 8}{2},$$

and from (iii) $$x_3 = \frac{\lambda - 6}{6}.$$

$$\therefore \quad \frac{\lambda - 10}{4} + \frac{\lambda - 8}{2} + \frac{\lambda - 6}{6} = 20, \text{ which gives } \lambda = 30,$$

and $x_1 = 5$, $x_2 = 11$ and $x_3 = 4$.

Thus the stationary point is $(x_1, x_2, x_3) = (5, 11, 4)$.

To determine whether the stationary point results in maximization or minimization of the objective function, $(n - 1) = 3 - 1 = 2$ principal minor determinants D_3 and D_4 are solved.

$$D_4 = \begin{vmatrix} 0 & 1 & 1 & 1 \\ 1 & 4 & 0 & 0 \\ 1 & 0 & 2 & 0 \\ 1 & 0 & 0 & 6 \end{vmatrix} = -1\begin{vmatrix} 1 & 0 & 0 \\ 1 & 2 & 0 \\ 1 & 0 & 6 \end{vmatrix} + 1\begin{vmatrix} 1 & 4 & 0 \\ 1 & 0 & 0 \\ 1 & 0 & 6 \end{vmatrix} - 1\begin{vmatrix} 1 & 4 & 0 \\ 1 & 0 & 2 \\ 1 & 0 & 0 \end{vmatrix}$$

$$= \{1(12)\} + 1\{1(0) - 4(6)\} - 1\{1(0) - 4(-2)\}$$

$$= -12 - 24 - 8 = -44,$$

and $$D_3 = \begin{vmatrix} 0 & 1 & 1 \\ 1 & 4 & 0 \\ 1 & 0 & 2 \end{vmatrix} = -1\{2\} + 1\{-4\} = -6.$$

Since both D_3 and D_4 are negative, the stationary point is the minima.

Thus $$Z_{min} = 2 \times 25 + 121 + 3 \times 16 + 50 + 88 + 24 - 100$$
$$= 381 - 100 = 281.$$

EXAMPLE 16.7-8

A positive quantity b is to be divided into n parts in such a way that the product of n parts is to be a maximum. Use Lagrange multipliers method to obtain the optimal subdivision.

Solution

Let $x_1, x_2, ..., x_n$ be the n parts into which b is divided. Then our problem becomes:

Maximize $$Z = x_1.x_2.x_3 \ldots x_n,$$
subject to $$x_1 + x_2 + x_3 + \ldots + x_n = b,$$
$$x_j \geq 0, j = 1, 2, ..., n.$$

The Lagrangean function L can be formed as

$$L(X, \lambda) = x_1.x_2.x_3 \ldots x_n - \lambda(x_1 + x_2 + \ldots + x_n - b).$$

The necessary conditions for a maxima or minima of the objective function are

$$\frac{\partial L}{\partial x_1} = x_2 \,.\, x_3 \,.\, \ldots x_n - \lambda = 0,$$

$$\frac{\partial L}{\partial x_2} = x_1 \cdot x_3 \ldots x_n - \lambda = 0,$$

$$\vdots$$

$$\frac{\partial L}{\partial x_n} = x_1 \cdot x_2 \cdot \ldots x_{n-1} - \lambda = 0,$$

and
$$\frac{\partial L}{\partial \lambda} = -(x_1 + x_2 + \ldots - x_n - b) = 0.$$

Multiplying the first n of the above equations by $x_1, x_2, \ldots, x_n$ respectively and adding, we get

$$n (x_1 \cdot x_2 \cdot \ldots x_n) - \lambda (x_1 - x_2 + \ldots + x_n) = 0,$$

and the last equation gives $x_1 + x_2 + \ldots + x_n = b$.

$\therefore$
$$n (x_1 \cdot x_2 \cdot \ldots x_n) - \lambda b = 0$$

or
$$\lambda = \frac{n (x_1 \cdot x_2 \cdot \ldots x_n)}{b}.$$

Substituting this value of λ in each of the $\partial L / \partial x_j$ equations, we get

$$x_1 = x_2 = x_3 \ldots = x_n = \frac{b}{n}.$$

$\therefore$
$$Z = \frac{b}{n} \cdot \frac{b}{n} \cdot \frac{b}{n} \cdot \ldots n \text{ times} = \left(\frac{b}{n}\right)^n.$$

Since these values of x_j ($j = 1, 2, \ldots, n$) satisfy the constraint and give a value of Z larger than the value when any of $x_1, x_2, \ldots, x_n$ is zero; $x_1 = x_2 = \ldots = x_n = b/n$ yield the optimal subdivision of b.

16.8 CONSTRAINED EXTREMAL PROBLEM WITH MORE THAN ONE EQUALITY CONSTRAINT

The non-linear programming problem having n variables and m equality constraints ($m < n$), can be expressed in the general form as

maximize (or minimize) $Z = f(X)$,

subject to $h^i(X) = 0,\ i = 1, 2, \ldots, m$,

$X \geq 0$.

The Lagrangean function can be formed as

$$L(X, \lambda) = f(X) - \sum_{i=1}^{m} \lambda_i h^i(X),$$

where λ_i, ($i = 1, 2, \ldots, m$) are the Lagrangean multipliers. As in the previous cases, here again it is assumed that the functions $L(X, \lambda)$, $f(X)$ and $h^i(X)$ are partially differentiable w.r.t. X and λ.

The necessary conditions for the optimum solution are

$$\frac{\partial L}{\partial x_j} = 0,\ j = 1, 2, \ldots, n,$$

and
$$\frac{\partial L}{\partial \lambda_i} = 0,\ i = 1, 2, \ldots, m.$$

The sufficient conditions for the stationary point to be a maxima or minima are obtained by solving the principal minors of the *bordered Hessian* matrix,

$$H^B = \left(\begin{array}{c|c} O & P \\ \hline P^T & Q \end{array}\right)_{(m+n)\times(m+n)},$$

where O is an $m \times m$ null matrix,

$$P = \begin{pmatrix} \frac{\partial h_1}{\partial x_1} & \frac{\partial h_1}{\partial x_2} & \frac{\partial h_1}{\partial x_3} & \cdots & \frac{\partial h_1}{\partial x_n} \\ \frac{\partial h_2}{\partial x_1} & \frac{\partial h_2}{\partial x_2} & \frac{\partial h_2}{\partial x_3} & \cdots & \frac{\partial h_2}{\partial x_n} \\ \vdots & & & & \\ \frac{\partial h_m}{\partial x_1} & \frac{\partial h_m}{\partial x_2} & \frac{\partial h_m}{\partial x_3} & \cdots & \frac{\partial h_m}{\partial x_n} \end{pmatrix}_{(m \times n)}$$

P^T = Transpose of P,

and

$$Q = \begin{pmatrix} \frac{\partial^2 L}{\partial x_1^2} & \frac{\partial^2 L}{\partial x_1 \partial x_2} & \cdots & \frac{\partial^2 L}{\partial x_1 \partial x_n} \\ \frac{\partial^2 L}{\partial x_2 \partial x_1} & \frac{\partial^2 L}{\partial x_2^2} & \cdots & \frac{\partial^2 L}{\partial x_2 \partial x_n} \\ \vdots & & & \\ \frac{\partial^2 L}{\partial x_n \partial x_1} & \frac{\partial^2 L}{\partial x_n \partial x_2} & \cdots & \frac{\partial^2 L}{\partial x_n^2} \end{pmatrix}.$$

If (X^*, λ^*) is the stationary point for the function $L(X, \lambda)$ and H^{B^*} is the corresponding bordered Hessian matrix, the sufficient but not necessary condition for the maxima and minima is determined by the signs of the last $(n - m)$ principal minors of H^{B^*}, starting with the principal minor of the order $(2m + 1)$

X^* maximizes the function if the signs alternate, starting with $(-1)^{m+n}$ and X^* minimizes the function if all the signs are same and of the $(-1)^m$ type.

EXAMPLE 16.8-1

Solve the non-linear programming problem given below:

Optimize $\quad Z = x_1^2 + x_2^2 + x_3^2,$

subject to $\quad x_1 + x_2 + 3x_3 = 2,$

$5x_1 + 2x_2 + x_3 = 5,$

$x_1, x_2, x_3 \geq 0.$ *[B.P.U.T. 6th Sem., 2011]*

Solution

The objective function as well as constraints are differentiable with respect of x_1, x_2 and x_3 and the Lagrangean function is formed as

$$L(X, \lambda) = x_1^2 + x_2^2 + x_3^2 - \lambda_1 (x_1 + x_2 + 3x_3 - 2) - \lambda_2 (5x_1 + 2x_2 + x_3 - 5).$$

The necessary conditions for the maxima or minima of the objective function are obtained as

$$\frac{\partial L}{\partial x_1} = 2x_1 - \lambda_1 - 5\lambda_2 = 0, \quad \ldots (i)$$

$$\frac{\partial L}{\partial x_2} = 2x_2 - \lambda_1 - 2\lambda_2 = 0, \quad \ldots (ii)$$

$$\frac{\partial L}{\partial x_3} = 2x_3 - 3\lambda_1 - \lambda_2 = 0, \quad \ldots (iii)$$

$$\frac{\partial L}{\partial \lambda_1} = -(x_1 + x_2 + 3x_3 - 2) = 0, \qquad \text{... (iv)}$$

and

$$\frac{\partial L}{\partial \lambda_2} = -(5x_1 + 2x_2 + x_3 - 5) = 0. \qquad \text{... (v)}$$

Substituting the values of x_1, x_2, x_3 from (*i*), (*ii*) and (*iii*) in (*iv*) and (*v*), we get

$$\frac{\lambda_1 + 5\lambda_2}{2} + \frac{\lambda_1 + 2\lambda_2}{2} + 3\left(\frac{3\lambda_1 + \lambda_2}{2}\right) - 2 = 0 \quad \text{or} \quad 11\lambda_1 + 10\lambda_2 = 4, \qquad \text{...(vi)}$$

and

$$\frac{5\cdot(\lambda_1 + 5\lambda_2)}{2} + \frac{2(\lambda_1 + 2\lambda_2)}{2} + \frac{3\lambda_1 + \lambda_2}{2} - 5 = 0$$

or $\quad 10\lambda_1 + 30\lambda_2 = 10 \quad$ or $\quad \lambda_1 + 3\lambda_2 = 1. \qquad$ ...(*vii*)

Solving eqns (*vi*) and (*vii*), $\lambda_1 = 0.087$ and $\lambda_2 = 0.304$.

Equations (*i*), (*ii*) and (*iii*) yield $x_1 = 0.804$, $x_2 = 0.348$ and $x_3 = 0.283$ as the solution.

To determine whether this solution point is a maxima or minima, the following bordered Hessian matrix is constructed:

$$H^B = \left[\begin{array}{c|c} O & P \\ \hline P^T & Q \end{array}\right]_{(m+n)\times(m+n)},$$

where

$$O = \begin{bmatrix} 0 & 0 \\ 0 & 0 \end{bmatrix},$$

$$P = \begin{bmatrix} 1 & 1 & 3 \\ 5 & 2 & 1 \end{bmatrix},$$

$$P^T = \begin{bmatrix} 1 & 5 \\ 1 & 2 \\ 3 & 1 \end{bmatrix},$$

and

$$Q = \begin{bmatrix} 2 & 0 & 0 \\ 0 & 2 & 0 \\ 0 & 0 & 2 \end{bmatrix}.$$

$$\therefore \quad H^B = \left[\begin{array}{cc|ccc} 0 & 0 & 1 & 1 & 3 \\ 0 & 0 & 5 & 2 & 1 \\ \hline 1 & 5 & 2 & 0 & 0 \\ 1 & 2 & 0 & 2 & 0 \\ 3 & 1 & 0 & 0 & 2 \end{array}\right]$$

Since $n = 3$, $m = 2$; $n - m = 1$ and $2m + 1 = 5$. This means that only one principal minor of H^B of order 5 needs to be solved. For maximization, the sign should be $(-1)^{m+n} = (-1)^5 = -$ve and for minimization, the sign should be $(-1)^m = (-1)^2 = +$ ve. Now the determinant of H^B of order 5 is

$$\begin{vmatrix} 0 & 0 & 1 & 1 & 3 \\ 0 & 0 & 5 & 2 & 1 \\ 1 & 5 & 2 & 0 & 0 \\ 1 & 2 & 0 & 2 & 0 \\ 3 & 1 & 0 & 0 & 2 \end{vmatrix} = 1\begin{vmatrix} 0 & 0 & 2 & 1 \\ 1 & 5 & 0 & 0 \\ 1 & 2 & 2 & 0 \\ 3 & 1 & 0 & 2 \end{vmatrix} - 1\begin{vmatrix} 0 & 0 & 5 & 1 \\ 1 & 5 & 2 & 0 \\ 1 & 2 & 0 & 0 \\ 3 & 1 & 0 & 2 \end{vmatrix} + 3\begin{vmatrix} 0 & 0 & 5 & 2 \\ 1 & 5 & 2 & 0 \\ 1 & 2 & 0 & 2 \\ 3 & 1 & 0 & 0 \end{vmatrix}$$

$$= 1\left[2\begin{vmatrix}1&5&0\\1&2&0\\3&1&2\end{vmatrix}-1\begin{vmatrix}1&5&0\\1&2&2\\3&1&0\end{vmatrix}\right]-1\left[5\begin{vmatrix}1&5&0\\1&2&0\\3&1&2\end{vmatrix}-1\begin{vmatrix}1&5&2\\1&2&0\\3&1&0\end{vmatrix}\right]$$

$$+3\left[5\begin{vmatrix}1&5&0\\1&2&2\\3&1&0\end{vmatrix}-2\begin{vmatrix}1&5&2\\1&2&0\\3&1&0\end{vmatrix}\right]$$

$$= 1\left[2\{1(4-0)-5(2-0)\}-1\{1(0-2)-5(0-6)\}\right]$$

$$-1\left[5\{1(4-0)-5(2-0)\}-1\{1(0-0)-5(0-0)+2(1-6)\}\right]$$

$$+3\left[5\{1(0-2)-5(0-6)\}-2\{1(0-0)-5(0-0)+2(1-6)\}\right]$$

$$= 1[2(4-10)-1(-2+30)]-1[5(4-10)-1(0-0-10)]$$

$$+3[5(-2+30)-2(0-0-10)]$$

$$= 1[-12-28]-1[-30+10]+3[140+20] = -40+20+480 = 460.$$

Since the value is +ve, the above solution minimizes the objective function and

$$Z_{\min} = (0.804)^2 + (0.348)^2 + (0.283)^2 = 0.847.$$

EXAMPLE 16.8-2

Solve the following non-linear programming problem, using the Lagrangean multipliers :

Optimize $Z = 4x_1^2 + 2x_2^2 + x_3^2 - 4x_1x_2,$

subject to $x_1 + x_2 + x_3 = 15,$

$2x_1 - x_2 + 2x_3 = 20,$

$x_1, x_2, x_3 \geq 0.$

[*B.P.U.T. 6th. Sem., 2011*]

Solution

The Lagrangean function can be constructed as

$$L(X, \lambda) = 4x_1^2 + 2x_2^2 + x_3^2 - 4x_1x_2 - \lambda_1 (x_1 + x_2 + x_3 - 15) - \lambda_2 (2x_1 - x_2 + 2x_3 - 20).$$

The necessary conditions for the maxima or minima of the objective function are

$$\frac{\partial L}{\partial x_1} = 8x_1 - 4x_2 - \lambda_1 - 2\lambda_2 = 0,$$

$$\frac{\partial L}{\partial x_2} = 4x_2 - 4x_1 - \lambda_1 + \lambda_2 = 0,$$

$$\frac{\partial L}{\partial x_3} = 2x_3 - \lambda_1 - 2\lambda_2 = 0,$$

$$\frac{\partial L}{\partial \lambda_1} = -(x_1 + x_2 + x_3 - 15) = 0,$$

and
$$\frac{\partial L}{\partial \lambda_2} = -(2x_1 - x_2 + 2x_3 - 20) = 0.$$

The solution of these simultaneous equations is given by

$$x_1 = \frac{11}{3},\ x_2 = \frac{10}{3},\ x_3 = 8,\ \lambda_1 = \frac{40}{9} \text{ and } \lambda_2 = \frac{52}{9}.$$

Next, to determine whether the stationary point is a maxima or a minima, the following bordered Hessian matrix is constructed :

$$H^B = \left[\begin{array}{c|c} O & P \\ \hline P^T & Q \end{array}\right]_{(m+n)(m+n)} = \left(\begin{array}{cc|ccc} 0 & 0 & 1 & 1 & 1 \\ 0 & 0 & 2 & -1 & 2 \\ \hline 1 & 2 & 8 & -4 & 0 \\ 1 & -1 & -4 & 4 & 0 \\ 1 & 2 & 0 & 0 & 2 \end{array}\right) = 72 > 0.$$

Since $n = 3$ and $m = 2$, $n - m = 1$ and $2m + 1 = 5$. This means that only one principal minor of H_B of the order 5 needs to be solved. For maximization, the sign should be $(-1)^{m+r} = (-1)^5$ = – ve and for minimization, the sign should be $(-1)^m = (-1)^2$ = + ve. In the present case, H^B = 72 is +ve, hence X_0 is a minimum point.

Thus the solution $X_0 = (x_1, x_2, x_3) = (11/3, 10/3, 8)$ minimizes the objective function, and

$$Z_{min} = 4\left(\frac{11}{3}\right)^2 + 2\left(\frac{10}{3}\right)^2 + (8)^2 - 4 \times \frac{11}{3} \times \frac{10}{3} = \frac{820}{9}.$$

EXAMPLE 16.8-3

Solve the following non-linear programming problem:

Optimize $\quad Z = 4x_1 + 9x_2 - x_1^2 - x_2^2,$

subject to $\quad 4x_1 + 3x_2 = 15,$

$\quad 3x_1 + 5x_2 = 14,$

$\quad x_1, x_2 \geq 0.$

Solution

Construct the Lagrangean function as

$$L(X, \lambda) = 4x_1 + 9x_2 - x_1^2 - x_2^2 - \lambda_1 (4x_1 + 3x_2 - 15) - \lambda_2 (3x_1 + 5x_2 - 14).$$

The necessary conditions for a stationary point are

$$\frac{\partial L}{\partial x_1} = 4 - 2x_1 - 4\lambda_1 - 3\lambda_2 = 0,$$

$$\frac{\partial L}{\partial x_2} = 9 - 2x_2 - 3\lambda_1 - 5\lambda_2 = 0,$$

$$\frac{\partial L}{\partial \lambda_1} = -(4x_1 + 3x_2 - 15) = 0,$$

and $$\frac{\partial L}{\partial \lambda_2} = -(3x_1 + 5x_2 - 14) = 0.$$

The solution to these simultaneous equations yields $x_1 = 3$ and $x_2 = 1$. The bordered Hessian matrix at this solution is given by

$$H^B = \left(\begin{array}{cc|cc} 0 & 0 & 4 & 3 \\ 0 & 0 & 3 & 5 \\ \hline 4 & 3 & -2 & 0 \\ 3 & 5 & 0 & -2 \end{array}\right) = 121 > 0.$$

The stationary point $X_0 = (x_1, x_2) = (3, 1)$ is a minima and hence minimizes the objective function and $Z_{min} = 4 \times 3 + 9 \times 1 - (3)^2 - 1 = 11.$

16.9 NON-LINEAR PROGRAMMING PROBLEM WITH ONE INEQUALITY CONSTRAINT

Consider a general non-linear programming problem having one inequality constraint of the type

Maximize $Z = f(X)$,

subject to $g(X) \leq b$,

$X \geq 0$, $X = x_1, x_2, ..., x_n$.

Introducing a slack variable S in the form of S^2 so as to ensure that it is always non-negative, the constraint equation can be modified to

$$h(X) + S^2 = 0,$$

where $h(X) = g(X) - b \leq 0$.

The problem can now be expressed as

maximize $Z = f(X)$,

subject to $h(X) + S^2 = 0$,

$X \geq 0$,

which is an $(n + 1)$ variable, single equality constraint problem of constrained optimization and can be solved by the method of Lagrangean multipliers.

The Lagrangean function can be constructed as

$$L(X, S, \lambda) = f(X) - \lambda[h(X) + S^2].$$

The necessary conditions for the stationary point are

$$\frac{\partial L}{\partial x_j} = \frac{\partial f}{\partial x_j} - \lambda \frac{\partial h}{\partial x_j} = 0, j = 1, 2, ..., n,$$

$$\frac{\partial L}{\partial \lambda} = -[h(X) + S^2] = 0,$$

and $$\frac{\partial L}{\partial S} = -2S\lambda = 0.$$

The condition $\frac{\partial L}{\partial S} = 0$ implies that either $S = 0$ or $\lambda = 0$. If $S = 0$, then condition $\frac{\partial L}{\partial \lambda} = 0$ gives $h(X) = 0$. Thus either λ or $h(X) = 0$.

i.e., $\lambda . h . (X) = 0$.

Since S^2 has been taken to be a non-negative slack variable, $h(X) \leq 0$.

This implies that when $h(X) < 0$, $\lambda = 0$;

and when $\lambda > 0$, $h(X) = 0$.

The necessary conditions for maximization problem can thus be summarized as

$$\frac{\partial f}{\partial x_j} - \lambda \frac{\partial h}{\partial x_j} = 0,$$

$$\lambda h(X) = 0,$$

$$h(X) \leq 0,$$

$$\lambda \geq 0.$$

These necessary conditions are also called *Kuhn-Tucker conditions*.

A similar argument holds for the minimization non-linear programming problem :

Minimize $Z = f(X)$,

subject to $g(X) \geq b$,

$X \geq 0$.

Introduction of $h(X) = g(X) - b$, reduces the constraint to $h(X) \geq 0$. The surplus variable S^2 can be introduced so that the constraint becomes $h(X) - S^2 = 0$. The appropriate Lagrangean functions is

$L(X, S, \lambda) = f(X) - \lambda[h(X) - S^2]$.

Following an analysis similar to the one for maximization problem, the *Kuhn-Tucker conditions* for the minimization non-linear programming problem can be obtained as:

$$\frac{\partial f}{\partial x_j} - \lambda \frac{\partial h}{\partial x_j} = 0,$$

$$\lambda h(X) = 0,$$

$$h(X) \geq 0,$$

$$\lambda \leq 0.$$

For a single constraint non-linear programming problem, the necessary Kuhn-Tucker conditions are also the sufficient conditions for

– the maximization problem, when $f(X)$ is concave and $h(X)$ is convex.

– the minimization problem, when both $f(X)$ and $h(X)$ are convex.

EXAMPLE 16.9-1

Solve the NLPP:

Maximize $Z = 4x_1 - x_1^3 + 2x_2$,

subject to $x_1 + x_2 \leq 1$,

$x_1, x_2 \geq 0$.

Solution

The problem can be put as

$$f(X) = 4x_1 - x_1^3 + 2x_2,$$

$$h(X) = x_1 + x_2 - 1.$$

The problem is of maximization, and Kuhn-Tucker conditions are

$$\frac{\partial f(X)}{\partial x_j} - \lambda \frac{\partial h(X)}{\partial x_j} = 0,$$

$$\lambda h(X) = 0,$$

$$h(X) \leq 0,$$

$$\lambda \geq 0.$$

Applying these conditions, we get

$$4 - 3x_1^2 - \lambda = 0, \quad \text{... (i)}$$

$$2 - \lambda = 0, \quad \text{...(ii)}$$

$$\lambda(x_1 + x_2 - 1) = 0, \quad \text{...(iii)}$$

$$x_1 + x_2 - 1 \leq 0, \quad \text{...(iv)}$$

$$\lambda \geq 0. \quad \text{...(v)}$$

From (*ii*) $\lambda = 2$, therefore from (*iii*) $x_1 + x_2 - 1 = 0$. These results satisfy the conditions (*iv*) and (*v*). Solution of (*i*), (*ii*) and (*iii*) yields

$$x_1 = \sqrt{\frac{2}{3}} = 0.8165,$$

and

$$x_2 = 1 - \sqrt{\frac{2}{3}} = 0.1835.$$

It can be easily observed that $f(X)$ is concave in X, while $h(X)$ is a convex function. Hence the solution $X^* = (0.8165, 0.1835)$ maximizes the objective function which comes to $Z_{max} = 3.0887$.

EXAMPLE 16.9-2

Maximize $Z = 10x_1 + 4x_2 - 2x_1^2 - x_2^2,$

subject to $2x_1 + x_2 \leq 5,$

$x_1, x_2 \geq 0.$

Solution

We have, $f(X) = 10x_1 + 4x_2 - 2x_1^2 - x_2^2,$

$h(X) = 2x_1 + x_2 - 5.$

The Kuhn-Tucker conditions for the maximization problem are

$$\frac{\partial f(X)}{\partial x_j} - \lambda \frac{\partial h(X)}{\partial x_j} = 0,$$

$$\lambda h(X) = 0,$$

$$h(X) \leq 0,$$

$$\lambda \geq 0.$$

Applying these conditions, we get

$$10 - 4x_1 - 2\lambda = 0, \quad ...(i)$$

$$4 - 2x_2 - \lambda = 0, \quad ...(ii)$$

$$\lambda(2x_1 + x_2 - 5) = 0, \quad ...(iv)$$

$$2x_1 + x_2 - 5 \leq 0. \quad ...(iv)$$

$$\lambda \geq 0. \quad ...(v)$$

From (*iii*) either $\lambda = 0$ or $2x_1 + x_2 - 5 = 0$.

When $\lambda = 0$, the solution of (*i*) and (*ii*) gives $x_1 = 2.5$ and $x_2 = 2.0$, which does not satisfy the equation (*iv*). Hence $\lambda = 0$ does not yield a feasible solution.

When $2x_1 + x_2 - 5 = 0$ and $\lambda \neq 0$, the solution of (*i*), (*ii*) and (*iii*) yields, $x_1 = \frac{11}{6}$, $x_2 = \frac{4}{3}$, $\lambda = \frac{4}{3}$, which satisfies all the necessary conditions.

It can be verified that the objective function is concave in X, while the constraint is convex in X. Thus these necessary conditions are also the sufficient conditions of maximization of $f(X)$.

$\therefore$ The optimal solution is $x_1^* = \frac{11}{6}$, $x_2^* = \frac{4}{3}$, which gives $Z_{max} = \frac{91}{6}$.

EXAMPLE 16.9-3

Solve the following NLPP using the Kuhn-Tucker conditions:

Maximize $Z = 2x_1^2 - 7x_2^2 + 12x_1x_2,$

subject to $2x_1 + 5x_2 \leq 98,$

$x_1, x_2 \geq 0.$

Solution

The given problem can be put as

$$f(X) = 2x_1^2 - 7x_2^2 + 12x_1x_2,$$

$$h(X) = 2x_1 + 5x_2 - 98.$$

The Kuhn-Tucker conditions are

$$\frac{\partial f}{\partial x_1} - \lambda \frac{\partial h}{\partial x_1} = 0,$$

$$\frac{\partial f}{\partial x_2} - \lambda \frac{\partial h}{\partial x_2} = 0,$$

$$\lambda h(X) = 0,$$

$$h(X) \le 0,$$
$$\lambda \ge 0.$$

Applying these conditions, we get

$$4x_1 + 12x_2 - 2\lambda = 0, \qquad ...(i)$$
$$12x_1 - 14x_2 - 5\lambda = 0, \qquad ...(ii)$$
$$\lambda\,(2x_1 + 5x_2 - 98) = 0, \qquad ...(iii)$$
$$2x_1 + 5x_2 - 98 \le 0, \qquad ...(iv)$$
$$\lambda \ge 0. \qquad ...(v)$$

From equation (*iii*) either $\lambda = 0$ or $2x_1 + 5x_2 - 98 = 0$.

When $\lambda = 0$, equations (*i*) and (*ii*) give $x_1 = x_2 = 0$, which does not satisfy condition (*iv*). Thus a feasible solution cannot be obtained for $\lambda = 0$.

When $2x_1 + 5x_2 - 98 = 0$, this equation along with (*i*) and (*ii*) gives the solution, $x_1 = 44$ and $x_2 = 2$ with $\lambda = 100$ and $Z_{max} = 4,900$.

16.10 NLPP WITH MORE THAN ONE INEQUALITY CONSTRAINT

Let us consider a general non-linear programming problem of the maximization type.

Maximize $\quad Z = f(X)$,

subject to $\quad g^i(X) \le b_i$,

$$X \ge 0\ ;\ i = 1, 2, ..., m.$$

The constraint equation can be written in the form

$$h^i(X) = g^i(X) - b_i \le 0,$$

which can be further modified to equality constraint by introducing slack variables.

$$\therefore \qquad h^i(X) + S_i^2 = 0, \qquad i = 1, 2, ..., m.$$

The Lagrangian function is constructed as

$$L\,(X, S, \lambda) = f\,(X) - \sum_{i=1}^{m} \lambda_i\,[h^i(X) + S_i^2].$$

The necessary conditions for maximization are

$$\frac{\partial L}{\partial x_j} = \frac{\partial f(X)}{\partial x_j} - \sum_{i=1}^{m} \lambda_i \frac{\partial h^i X}{\partial x_j} = 0, \qquad ...(i)$$

$$\frac{\partial L}{\partial \lambda_i} = -\,[h^i(X) + S_i^2] = 0, \qquad ...(ii)$$

$$\frac{\partial L}{\partial S_i} = -\,2\,S_i\,\lambda_i = 0, \qquad ...(iii)$$

$$i = 1, 2, ..., m,$$
$$j = 1, 2, ..., n.$$

The conditions (*ii*) and (*iii*) can be replaced by the following set of conditions, by carrying out analysis similar to the one done in case of single inequality constraint.

$$\lambda_i\,h^i(X) = 0, \qquad ...(iv)$$
$$h^i(X) \le 0, \qquad ...(v)$$
$$\lambda_i \ge 0. \qquad ...(vi)$$

Thus the Kuhn-Tucker conditions for a non-linear programming problem of maximizing $f(X)$ subject to the constraints $h^i(X) \le 0$, can be summarized as

$$f_j(X) - \sum_{i=1}^{m} \lambda_i\ h_j^i\,(X) = 0,$$

$$\lambda_i\,h^i(X) = 0,$$

$$h^i(\text{X}) \le 0,$$
$$\lambda_i \ge 0,$$
$$i = 1, 2, ..., m,$$
$$j = 1, 2, ..., n.$$

It can be shown that the Kuhn-Tucker conditions for a minimization non-linear programming problem are

$$f_j(\text{X}) - \sum_{i=1}^{m} \lambda_i \, h_j^i \, (\text{X}) = 0,$$
$$\lambda_i \, h^i(\text{X}) = 0,$$
$$h^i(\text{X}) \ge 0,$$
$$\lambda_i \ge 0,$$

The Kuhn-Tucker conditions are also the sufficient conditions.

– for a maximum, if f (X) is concave and all h^i(X) are convex in X.

– for a minimum, if f (X) is convex and all h^i(X) are concave in X.

In both the maximization and minimization problems, the Lagrange's multipliers corresponding to the equality constraints must be unrestricted in sign. In maximization problems all constraints should be of ≤ type, while in minimization, the constraints should be of ≥ type. These conditions can be obtained by performing the necessary transformations as discussed in linear programming.

EXAMPLE 16.10-1

Solve the following NLPP:

Maximize $Z = 7x_1^2 + 6x_1 + 5x_2^2,$

subject to $x_1 + 2x_2 \le 10,$

$x_1 - 3x_2 \le 9,$

$x_1, x_2 \ge 0.$

Solution

We have

$$f(\text{X}) = 7x_1^{\,2} + 6x_1 + 5x_2^{\,2},$$
$$h^1(\text{X}) = x_1 + 2x_2 - 10,$$
$$h^2(\text{X}) = x_1 - 3x_2 - 9.$$

The Kuhn-Tucker conditions for a maximization problem are

$$f_j(\text{X}) - \sum_{i=1}^{m} \lambda_i \, h_j^i \, (\text{X}) = 0,$$
$$\lambda_i \, h^i(\text{X}) = 0,$$
$$h^i(\text{X}) \le 0,$$
$$\lambda_i \ge 0.$$

Applying these conditions, we get

$$14x_1 + 6 - \lambda_1 - \lambda_2 = 0, \quad ...(i)$$
$$10x_2 - 2\lambda_1 - 3\lambda_2 = 0, \quad ...(ii)$$
$$\lambda_1 \, (x_1 + 2x_2 - 10) = 0, \quad ...(iii)$$
$$\lambda_2 \, (x_1 - 3x_2 - 9) = 0, \quad ...(iv)$$
$$x_1 + 2x_2 - 10 \le 0,$$
$$x_1 - 3x_2 - 9 \le 0,$$
$$\lambda_1, \lambda_2 \ge 0.$$

Here we have two Langrange's multipliers λ_1 and λ_2 which can take zero or non-zero positive values. Thus four solutions corresponding to the following four combinations of λ_i (i = 1, 2) values can be obtained:

(i) $\lambda_1 = 0, \quad \lambda_2 = 0;$
(ii) $\lambda_1 = 0, \quad \lambda_2 \neq 0;$
(iii) $\lambda_1 \neq 0, \quad \lambda_2 = 0;$
(iv) $\lambda_1 \neq 0, \quad \lambda_2 \neq 0;$

Solution 1: $\lambda_1 = 0$ and $\lambda_2 = 0$ result in $x_1 = -\frac{6}{14}$ and $x_2 = 0$, which is an infeasible solution.

Solution 2: $\lambda_1 = 0, \lambda_2 \neq 0$.

Since $\lambda_2 \neq 0$, from (iv) $x_1 - 3x_2 - 9 = 0$,
from (i) and (ii), $14x_1 + 6 - \lambda_2 = 0$,
and $10x_2 + 3\lambda_2 = 0$

Solution of these equations yields

$$x_1 = \frac{19}{119},\ x_2 = -\frac{1{,}052}{357},\ \lambda_1 = 0,\ \lambda_2 = \frac{980}{119}.$$

This again is an infeasible solution.

Solution 3: $\lambda_1 \neq 0,\ \lambda_2 = 0$.

From (i), (ii) and (iii) we have

$$14x_1 + 6 - \lambda_1 = 0,$$
$$10x_2 - 2\lambda_1 = 0,$$
and $$x_1 + 2x_2 - 10 = 0.$$

The solution of these equations yields

$$x_1 = \frac{38}{33},\ x_2 = \frac{146}{33},\ \lambda_1 = \frac{730}{33},\ \lambda_2 = 0.$$

This is a feasible solution giving Z = 114.061.

Solution 4: $\lambda_1 \neq 0, \lambda_2 \neq 0$.

From (i), (ii), (iii) and (iv), we have

$$14x_1 + 6 - \lambda_1 - \lambda_2 = 0,$$
$$10x_2 - 2\lambda_1 + 3\lambda_2 = 0,$$
$$x_1 + 2x_2 - 10 = 0,$$
and $$x_1 - 3x_2 - 9 = 0.$$

The solution of these four equations yields

$$x_1 = \frac{48}{5},\ x_2 = \frac{1}{5},\ \lambda_1 = \frac{2{,}116}{25},\ \lambda_2 = \frac{1{,}394}{25}.$$

This also is a feasible solution giving Z = 702.92. Since the maximum value of Z is obtained for solution 4, where $\lambda_1 \neq 0$ and $\lambda_2 \neq 0$, the optimal solution is

$$x_1^* = \frac{48}{5},\ x_2^* = \frac{1}{5} \text{ and } Z_{max} = 702.92.$$

EXAMPLE 16.10-2

Optimize $Z = 2x_1 + 3x_2 - (x_1^2 + x_2^2 + x_3^2),$
subject to $x_1 + x_2 \leq 1,$
$2x_1 + 3x_2 \leq 6,$
$x_1, x_2 \geq 0.$

Solution

We have $f(X) = 2x_1 + 3x_2 - x_1^2 - x_2^2 - x_3^2,$
$h^1(X) = x_1 + x_2 - 1,$
and $h^2(X) = 2x_1 + 3x_2 - 6.$

Before applying the Kuhn-Tucker conditions, it is essential to determine whether the problem is of maximization or of minimization type. For that, we construct the bordered Hessian matrix.

$$H^B = \left(\begin{array}{c|c} O & P \\ \hline P^T & Q \end{array}\right)_{(m+n)(m+n)}$$

$$= \left(\begin{array}{cc|ccc} 0 & 0 & 1 & 1 & 0 \\ 0 & 0 & 2 & 3 & 0 \\ \hline 1 & 2 & -2 & 0 & 0 \\ 1 & 3 & 0 & -2 & 0 \\ 0 & 0 & 0 & 0 & -2 \end{array}\right) = -10. \qquad \begin{array}{r} n = 3, \\ m = 2, \\ n - m = 1, \\ 2m + 1 = 5. \end{array}$$

For maximization, the sign of H^B should be $(-1)^{m+1}$ *i.e.*, –ve, while for minimization it should be $(-1)^m$ *i.e.*, +ve. Since $H^B < 0$, the solution point should maximize the objective function.

The Kuhn-Tucker conditions for this case are

$$f_j(X) - \sum_{i=1}^{m} \lambda_i \, h_j^i (X) = 0,$$
$$\lambda_i \, h^i (X) = 0,$$
$$h^i (X) \le 0,$$
$$\lambda_i \ge 0.$$

Therefore , we have

$$2 - 2x_1 - \lambda_1 - 2\lambda_2 = 0, \qquad ...(i)$$
$$3 - 2x_2 - \lambda_1 - 3\lambda_2 = 0, \qquad ...(ii)$$
$$-2x_3 = 0, \qquad ...(iii)$$
$$\lambda_1(x_1 + x_2 - 1) = 0, \qquad ...(iv)$$
$$\lambda_2 (2x_1 + 3x_2 - 6) = 0, \qquad ...(v)$$
$$x_1 + x_2 - 1 \le 0, \qquad ...(vi)$$
$$2x_1 + 3x_2 - 6 \le 0, \qquad ...(vii)$$
$$\lambda_1, \lambda_2 \ge 0. \qquad ...(viii)$$

Four solutions corresponding to the following values of λ_1 and λ_2 can be obtained:

(*i*) $\lambda_1 = 0$, $\lambda_2 = 0$,
(*ii*) $\lambda_1 = 0$, $\lambda_2 \neq 0$,
(*iii*) $\lambda_1 \neq 0$, $\lambda_2 = 0$,
(*iv*) $\lambda_1 \neq 0$, $\lambda_2 \neq 0$.

Solution 1: $\lambda_1 = 0$, $\lambda_2 = 0$.

Equations (*i*), (*ii*) and (*iii*) give $x_1 = 1, x_2 = 3/2, x_3 = 0$. This solution does not satisfy equation (*vi*) and is, therefore, discarded.

Solution 2: $\lambda_1 = 0$, $\lambda_2 \neq 0$.

The solution of equations (*i*), (*ii*), (*iii*) and (*v*) gives

$$x_1 = \frac{12}{13},\ x_2 = \frac{18}{13},\ x_3 = 0,\ \lambda_2 = \frac{1}{13}.$$

This solution, again, does not satisfy equation (*vi*) and is, therefore, discarded.

Solution 3: $\lambda_1 \neq 0$, $\lambda_2 = 0$.

The solution of equations (*i*), (*ii*), (*iii*) and (*iv*) yields

$$x_1 = \frac{1}{4},\ x_2 = \frac{3}{4},\ x_3 = 0,\ \lambda_1 = \frac{3}{2}.$$

This solution satisfies all the conditions, and gives

$$Z = \frac{17}{8}.$$

Solution 4: $\lambda_1 \neq 0,\ \lambda_2 \neq 0.$

The solution of equations (*i*), (*ii*), (*iii*), (*iv*) and (*v*) gives

$$x_1 = -3,\ x_2 = 4,\ x_3 = 0,\ \lambda_1 = -34,\ \lambda_2 = 13.$$

This solution violates condition (*viii*) and is thus infeasible and is, therefore, discarded.

Since only one solution satisfies all the conditions, the same is the optimal solution.

$$\therefore \qquad x_1^* = \frac{1}{4},\ x_2^* = \frac{3}{4},\ x_3^* = 0,$$

$$\text{and} \qquad Z_{max} = \frac{1}{78}.$$

EXAMPLE 16.10-3

Use the Kuhn-Tucker conditions to solve the following non-linear programming problem:

Maximize $Z = 2x_1 - x_1^2 + x_2,$

subject to the constraints

$$2x_1 + 3x_2 \leq 6,$$
$$2x_1 + x_2 \leq 4,$$
$$x_1, x_2 \geq 0.$$

[*Nagpur U. B.E. (Comp. Sc.) 2004*]

Solution

We have $f(X) = 2x_1 - x_1^2 + x_2,$

$$h^1(X) = 2x_1 + 3x_2 - 6,$$

and $h^2(X) = 2x_1 + x_2 - 4.$

The Kuhn-Tucker conditions for a maximization problem are

$$f_j(X) - \sum_{i=1}^{m} \lambda_i h_j^i(X) = 0,$$
$$\lambda_i h^i(X) = 0,$$
$$h^i(X) \leq 0,$$
$$\lambda_i \geq 0.$$

Applying these conditions to the given functions, we get

$$2 - 2x_1 - 2\lambda_1 - 2\lambda_2 = 0, \qquad ...(i)$$
$$1 - 3\lambda_1 - \lambda_2 = 0, \qquad ...(ii)$$
$$\lambda_1 (2x_1 + 3x_2 - 6) = 0, \qquad ...(iii)$$
$$\lambda_2 (2x_1 + x_2 - 4) = 0, \qquad ...(iv)$$
$$2x_1 + 3x_2 - 6 \leq 0, \qquad ...(v)$$
$$2x_1 + x_2 - 4 \leq 0, \qquad ...(vi)$$
$$\lambda_1, \lambda_2 \geq 0. \qquad ...(vii)$$

The following situations can now arise:

Case 1: $\lambda_1 = 0, \quad \lambda_2 = 0;$

Case 2: $\lambda_1 = 0, \quad \lambda_2 \neq 0;$

Case 3: $\lambda_1 \neq 0, \quad \lambda_2 = 0;$

Case 4: $\lambda_1 \neq 0, \quad \lambda_2 \neq 0.$

Case 1: When $\lambda_1 = 0$, $\lambda_2 = 0$, condition (*ii*) is violated and this solution is, therefore, discarded.

Case 2: When $\lambda_1 = 0$, $\lambda_2 \neq 0$, solution of equations (*i*), (*ii*), (*iii*) and (*iv*) gives

$$x_1 = 0\ ,\ x_2 = 4 \text{ and } \lambda_2 = 1.$$

As this solution does not satisfy equation (*v*), it is discarded,.

Case 3: When $\lambda_1 \neq 0$, $\lambda_2 = 0$, solution of equations (*i*), (*ii*), (*iii*), and (*iv*) yields

$$x_1 = \frac{2}{3},\ x_2 = \frac{14}{9},\ \lambda_1 = \frac{1}{3}.$$

This solution satisfies all the constraint equations and is thus feasible solution, giving Z = 22/9.

Case 4: When $\lambda_1 \neq 0$, and $\lambda_2 \neq 0$, the solution of equations (*i*), (*ii*), (*iii*) and (*iv*) gives

$$x_1 = \frac{3}{2},\ x_2 = 1,\ \lambda_1 = \frac{3}{4} \text{ and } \lambda_2 = -\frac{5}{4}.$$

This solution violates condition (*vii*), which is $\lambda_1, \lambda_2 \geq 0$ and hence is infeasible.

Thus the optimal solution is

$$x_1^* = \frac{2}{3},\ x_2^* = \frac{14}{9},\ \text{giving } Z_{max} = \frac{22}{9}.$$

EXAMPLE 16.10-4

Use the Kuhn-Tucker conditions to solve the following non-linear programming problem:

Maximize $Z = 7x_1^2 - 6x_1 + 5x_2^2,$

subject to the constraints $x_1 + 2x_2 \leq 10,$

$x_1 - 3x_2 \leq 9,$

$x_1, x_2 \geq 0.$

Solution:

The Kuhn-Tucker conditions for a maximization problem are

$$f_j(X) - \sum_{i=1}^{m} \lambda_i h_j^i(X) = 0,$$

$$\lambda_i h^i(X) = 0,$$

$$h^i(X) \leq 0,$$

$$\lambda_i \geq 0.$$

Applying these conditions, we get

$$14x_1 - 6 - \lambda_1 - \lambda_2 = 0, \quad \text{...}(i)$$

$$10x_2 - 2\lambda_1 + 3\lambda_2 = 0, \quad \text{...}(ii)$$

$$\lambda_1(x_1 + 2x_2 - 10) = 0, \quad \text{...}(iii)$$

$$\lambda_2(x_1 - 3x_2 - 9) = 0, \quad \text{...}(iv)$$

$$x_1 + 2x_2 - 10 \leq 0, \quad \text{...}(v)$$

$$x_1 - 3x_2 - 9 \leq 0, \quad \text{...}(vi)$$

$$\lambda_1, \lambda_2 \geq 0. \quad \text{...}(vii)$$

Case 1: $\lambda_1 = \lambda_2 = 0$.

Equations (*i*) and (*ii*) give $x_1 = 3/7$ and $x_2 = 0$. This satisfies the constraints (*v*), (*vi*) and (*vii*), and is thus a feasible solution, with Z = –9/7.

Case 2: $\lambda_1 \neq 0$, $\lambda_2 = 0$.

Equations (*i*), (*ii*) and (*iii*) give

$$x_1 = \frac{62}{33},\ x_2 = \frac{134}{33} \text{ and } \lambda_1 = \frac{670}{33}.$$

This solution satisfies the other conditions and gives Z = 95.78.

Case 3: $\lambda_1 = 0$ and $\lambda_2 \neq 0$.

Equations (*i*), (*ii*) and (*iv*) give

$$x_1 = \frac{288}{17} \text{ and } x_2 = \frac{-45}{17}.$$

This is an infeasible solution.

Case 4: $\lambda_1 \neq 0$ and $\lambda_2 \neq 0$.

Equations (*iii*) and (*iv*) give $x_1 = \frac{48}{5}$ and $x_2 = \frac{1}{5}$ and then equations (*i*) and (*ii*) give $\lambda_1 = \frac{1,936}{25}$ and $\lambda_2 = \frac{1,274}{25}$. This solution satisfies all the conditions and gives Z = 587.72.

Hence optimal solution is $x_1^* = \frac{48}{5}$ and $x_2^* = \frac{1}{5}$ with $Z_{max} = 587.72$.

16.11 THE GRAPHICAL METHOD

The graphical method of solving a linear programming problem has been discussed in the chapter on linear programming. In a similar fashion, the graphical method can be employed to solve the two-variable non-linear programming problem also. In linear programming , the solution point is generally a corner point of convex solution space, while in non-linear programming, the solution point is not necessarily a corner or an edge. In other words, the optimal solution is not a corner point feasiable (CPF) solution.

EXAMPLE 16.11-1

Determine the values of x_1 and x_2 so as to

minimize $Z = x_1^2 + x_2^2$,

subject to $x_1 + x_2 \geq 8$,

$x_1 + 2x_2 \geq 10$,

$2x_1 + x_2 \geq 10$,

$x_1, x_2 \geq 0$.

Solution

The constraint equations in this case are all linear and give the solution space bounded by a convex region ABCD as shown in Fig. 16.7.

The objective function in this case is non-linear and represents a circle . If r is the radius of the circle, $Z = r^2 = x_1^2 + x_2^2$, then, the objective is to determine the minimum value of r, so that the circle with center (0, 0) and radius r just touches the solution space. In Fig. 16.7 desired solution point (4, 4) lies on the line $x_1 + x_2 = 8$, and the line is tangent to the circle at this point.

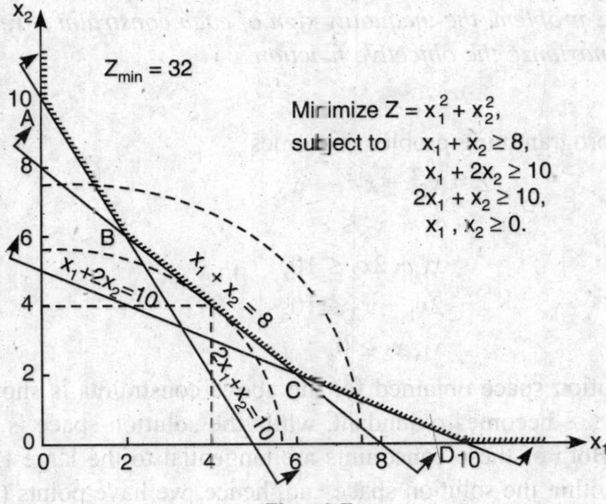

Fig. 16.7

Note: Since the circle will touch one of the sides of the convex region, one of the sides of the convex solution space would be tangential to the circle and thus the solution can also be obtained as follows:

Differentiate the equation of the circle $x_1^2 + x_2^2 = r^2$.

$$\therefore \qquad 2x_1 dx_1 + 2x_2 dx_2 = 0$$

or
$$\frac{dx_2}{dx_1} = -\frac{x_1}{x_2}. \qquad ...(i)$$

Differentiate the constraint equations which form the sides of the convex space.

$$dx_1 + dx_2 = 0 \quad \text{or} \quad \frac{dx_2}{dx_1} = -1, \qquad ...(ii)$$

$$dx_1 + 2dx_2 = 0 \quad \text{or} \quad \frac{dx_2}{dx_1} = -\frac{1}{2}, \qquad ...(iii)$$

and
$$2dx_1 + dx_2 = 0 \quad \text{or} \quad \frac{dx_2}{dx_1} = -2. \qquad ...(iv)$$

Three solutions can be obtained:

Solution 1: Taking equation (*i*) and (*ii*) and constraint $x_1 + x_2 = 8$,

$$\frac{dx_2}{dx_1} = -\frac{x_1}{x_2} = -1 \quad \text{or} \quad x_1 = x_2, \text{ which gives } x_1 = x_2 = 4.$$

This solution satisfies all the constraint equations and is thus feasible.

Solution 2: Taking equations (*i*) and (*iii*) and constraint $x_1 + 2x_2 = 10$,

$$\frac{dx_2}{dx_1} = -\frac{x_1}{x_2} = -\frac{1}{2}, \text{ which gives } x_1 = 2 \text{ and } x_2 = 4.$$

This solution does not satisfy the constraints and is discarded.

Solution 3: Taking (*i*) and (*iv*) and the constraint $2x_1 + x_2 = 10$,

$$\frac{dx_2}{dx_1} = -\frac{x_1}{x_2} = -2 \quad \text{or} \quad x_2 = \frac{x_1}{2}, \text{ which gives } x_1 = 4 \text{ and } x_2 = 2.$$

The solution, again, does not satisfy the constraints and is discarded. Therefore, optimal solution is $x_1^* = 4$, $x_2^* = 4$, giving $Z_{min} = 32$.

EXAMPLE 16.11-2

If in the previous problem, the inequality sign of each constraint is reversed, find the values of x_1 and x_2 so as to maximize the objective function.

Solution:

The non-linear programming problem becomes

$$\text{maximize} \qquad Z = x_1^2 + x_2^2,$$
$$\text{subject to} \qquad x_1 + x_2 \leq 8,$$
$$x_1 + 2x_2 \leq 10,$$
$$2x_1 + x_2 \leq 10,$$
$$x_1, x_2 \geq 0.$$

The convex solution space obtained for the above constraints is shown in Fig. 16.8. Here the constraint $x_1 + x_2 \leq 8$ becomes redundant, while the solution space is bounded by the other two constraints only. Both of these constraints are tangential to the largest circle ($r^2 = x_1^2 + x_2^2$) which can be drawn within the solution space and, hence, we have points (4, 2) and (2, 4) as the alternate optimal solutions, giving $Z_{max} = 20$.

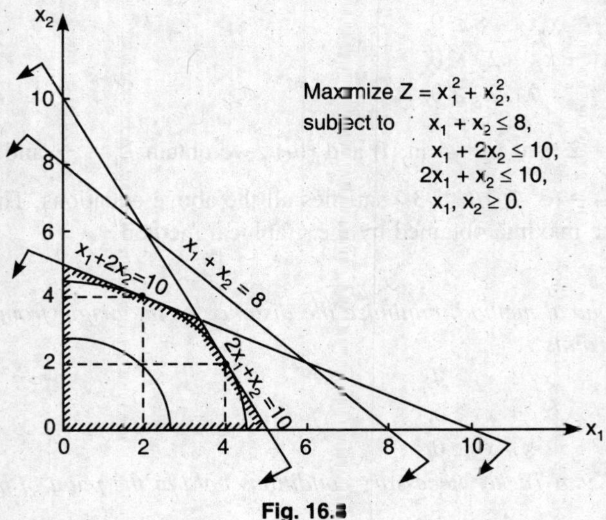

Fig. 16.8

EXAMPLE 16.11-3

Determine graphically the values of x_1 and x_2 so as to

maximize $\quad Z = 2x_1 + 3x_2,$

subject to $\quad x_1 . x_2 \leq 8,$

$$x_1^2 + x_2^2 \leq 20,$$

$$x_1, x_2 \geq 0.$$

Verify that the Kuhn-Tucker conditions hold for the maxima.

[*I.I.Sc. (Dip. Oper. Mgmt.) 1978*]

Solution

In this problem, the constraints are non-linear. The constraint $x_1 . x_2 \leq 8$ represents a rectangular hyperbola, while the constraint $x_1^2 + x_2^2 = 20$ is a circle. Fig. 16.9 shows the two constraints and the resulting solution space. The objective function is linear. The optimal solution is obtained by moving the objective function line away from the origin. This gives the following optimal solution:

$$x_1^* = 2, x_2^* = 4, \text{ which gives } Z_{max} = 16.$$

The Kuhn-Tucker conditions for the non-linear programming problem of the maximization type are

$$f_j(X) - \sum_{i=1}^{m} \lambda_i h_j^i(X) = 0,$$

$$\lambda_i h^i(X) = 0,$$

$$h^i(X) \leq 0,$$

$$\lambda_i \geq 0.$$

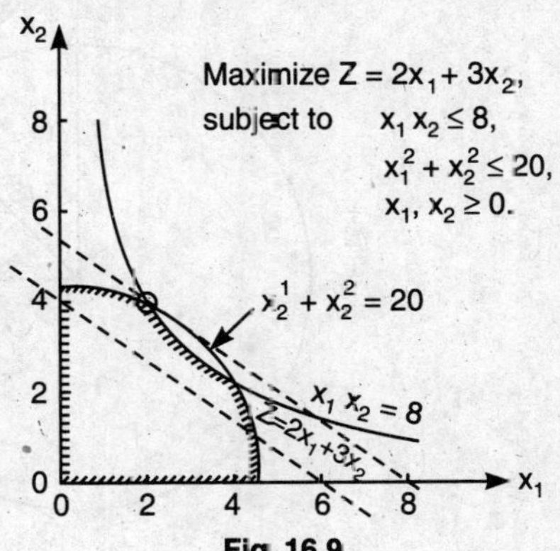

Fig. 16.9

For the given problem we have

$$f(X) = 2x_1 + 3x_2,$$

$$h^1(X) = x_1x_2 - 8,$$

and $\quad h^2(X) = x_1^2 + x_2^2 - 20$

Applying the Kuhn-Tucker conditions,

$$2 - \lambda_1 x_2 - 2\lambda_2 x_1 = 0, \quad ...(i)$$

$$3 - \lambda_1 x_1 - 2\lambda_2 x_2 = 0, \quad ...(ii)$$

$$\lambda_1(x_1 x_2 - 8) = 0, \quad ...(iii)$$

$$\lambda_2 (x_1^2 + x_2^2 - 20) = 0, \quad ...(iv)$$

$$x_1x_2 - 8 \leq 0, \quad \text{...(v)}$$
$$x_1^2 + x_2^2 - 20 \leq 0, \quad \text{....(vi)}$$
$$\lambda_1, \lambda_2 \geq 0. \quad \text{....(vii)}$$

Substituting $x_1 = 2$, and $x_2 = 4$ in (*i*) and (*iii*) , we obtain $\lambda_1 = \dfrac{1}{6}$ and $\lambda_2 = \dfrac{1}{3}$. This set of values of $x_1, x_2, \lambda_1, \lambda_2$ = (2, 4, 1/6, 1/3) satisfies all the above equations. Thus the Kuhn-Tucker conditions hold for the maxima obtained by the graphical method.

EXAMPLE 16.11-4

Employing graphical method, minimize the distance of the origin from the concave region bounded by the constraints :

$$x_1 + x_2 \geq 4,$$
$$2x_1 + x_2 \geq 5,$$
$$x_1, x_2 \geq 0.$$

Verify that the Kuhn-Tucker necessary conditions hold at the point of minimum distance.

Solution

The problem comprises of two linear constraints of ≥ type, which when plotted on graph result in an unbounded space. The problem is of minimization, where the minimum distance of the solution point from the origin is to be determined. This amounts to minimizing the circle with centre at origin, and touching the convex region bounded by the given constraints. Thus the problem becomes

minimize $\quad Z = r^2 = x_1^2 + x_2^2,$

subject to $\quad x_1 + x_2 \geq 4,$

$\quad 2x_1 + x_2 \geq 5,$

$\quad x_1, x_2 \geq 0.$

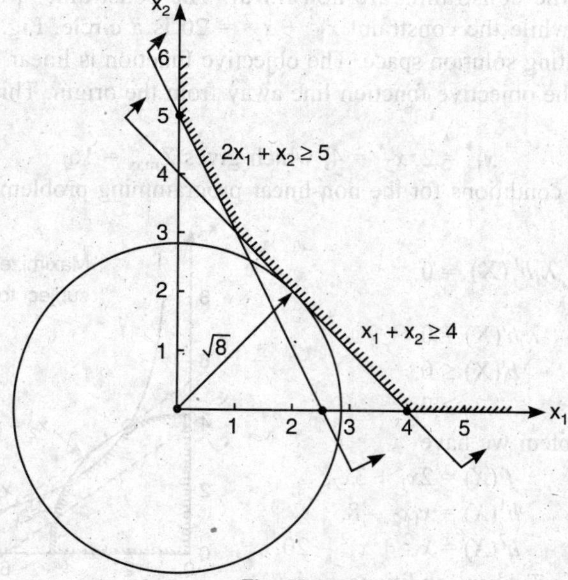

Fig. 16.10

The constraints are linear and are shown plotted in Fig. 16.10. Since the circle, that represents the objective function will touch one of the sides of the convex space, one side of the convex region should be tangent to the circle.

Differentiating the equation of the circle and equating to zero,

$$2x_1 dx_1 + 2x_2 dx_2 = 0$$

or $$\frac{dx_2}{dx_1} = -\frac{x_1}{x_2}. \quad ...(i)$$

Differentiating the constraint equation $2x_1 + x_2 = 5$,

$$\frac{dx_2}{dx_1} = -2, \quad ...(ii)$$

and differentiating the constraint equation $x_1 - x_2 = 4$,

$$\frac{dx_2}{dx_1} = -1. \quad ...(iii)$$

Solving (*i*) and (*ii*) and constraint $2x_1 + x_2 = 5$,

$$-\frac{x}{x_2} = \frac{dx_2}{dx_1} = -2, \quad \text{or} \quad x_1 = 2x_2, \text{ which gives}$$

$$x_1 = 2 \text{ and } x_2 = 1 \text{ as solution point .}$$

Solving (*i*) and (*iii*) with constraints $x_1 + x_2 = 4$,

$$-\frac{x_1}{x_2} = \frac{dx_2}{dx_1} = -1, \quad \text{or} \quad x_1 = x_2 \text{ , which gives}$$

$$x_1 = 2, x_2 = 2 \text{ as solution point.}$$

The solution $(x_1, x_2 = 2, 1)$ does not satisfy the constraint $x_1 + x_2 \geq 4$; hence this solution is not feasible. Point $(x_1, x_2) = (2, 2)$ satisfies the constraints and hence is the optimal solution to the problem.

The minimum distance of solution point from the origin is the radius,

$$r = \sqrt{x_1^2 + x_2^2} = \sqrt{8}.$$

Verification of Kuhn-Tucker conditions:

Rewrite the problem as

Minimize $\quad f(X) = x_1^2 + x_2^2,$

subject to $\quad h^1(X) = x_1 + x_2 - 4,$

$h^2(X) = 2x_1 + x_2 - 5,$

$X \geq 0.$

The Kuhn-Tucker conditions, for the minimization of NLPP are given as

$$f_j(X) - \sum \lambda_i \, h_j^i(X) = 0,$$
$$\lambda_i \cdot h^i(X) = 0,$$
$$h^i(X) \geq 0,$$
$$\lambda_i \geq 0,$$

where $$f_j(X) = \frac{\partial f(X)}{\partial x_j}, \; h_j^i = \frac{\partial h^i(X)}{\partial x_j} \quad (j = 1, 2),$$

and λ_1 and λ_2 are Lagrangian multipiers.

Applying the conditions, we get

$$2x_1 - \lambda_1 - 2\lambda_2 = 0, \quad ...(i)$$
$$2x_2 - \lambda_1 - \lambda_2 = 0, \quad ...(ii)$$
$$\lambda_1 (x_1 + x_2 - 4) = 0, \quad ...(iii)$$
$$\lambda_2 (2x_1 + x_2 - 5) = 0, \quad ...(iv)$$
$$x_1 + x_2 - 4 \geq 0, \quad ...(v)$$
$$2x_1 + x_2 - 5 \geq 0, \quad ...(vi)$$
$$\lambda_1 \geq 0 \, , \lambda_2 \geq 0. \quad ...(vii)$$

The solution obtained by graphical method is $x_1 = 2$, $x_2 = 2$.

Substituting these values in (*i*) and (*ii*),

$$\lambda_1 + 2\lambda_2 = 4,$$
$$\lambda_1 + \lambda_2 = 4,$$

which gives $\lambda_2 = 0$ and $\lambda_1 = 4$.

The solution $x_1 = 2, x_2 = 2$ and $\lambda_1 = 4, \lambda_2 = 0$ satisfies all the equations (*i*) through (*vii*) and hence satisfies the Kuhn-Tucker conditions.

EXAMPLE 16.11-5

Solve the following NLPP graphically:

$$\text{Maximize} \quad Z = 10x_1 - x_1^2 + 10x_2 - x_2^2,$$
$$\text{subject to} \quad x_1 + x_2 \le 12,$$
$$x_1 - x_2 \le 6,$$
$$x_1, x_2 \ge 0.$$

Solution

The objective function in this problem is non-linear, while the constraints are linear. The constraints are plotted by the usual method. The optimal solution point x_1, x_2 must lie somewhere in the solution space. Since the objective function is a circle, the optimal point x_1, x_2 would be a point at which the side of the convex region is tangent to the circle. The graphical solution is shown in Fig. 16.11.

The gradient of the tangent to the circle can be obtained by differentiating the equation of the circle,

$$Z = 10x_1 - x_1^2 + 10x_2 - x_2^2 \text{ w.r.t. } x_1 \text{ and equating to zero.}$$

i.e.,
$$10 - 2x_1 + 10\,\frac{dx_2}{dx_1} - 2x_2\frac{dx_2}{dx_1} = 0$$

or
$$\frac{dx_2}{dx_1} = \frac{2x_1 - 10}{10 - 2x_2}. \qquad ...(i)$$

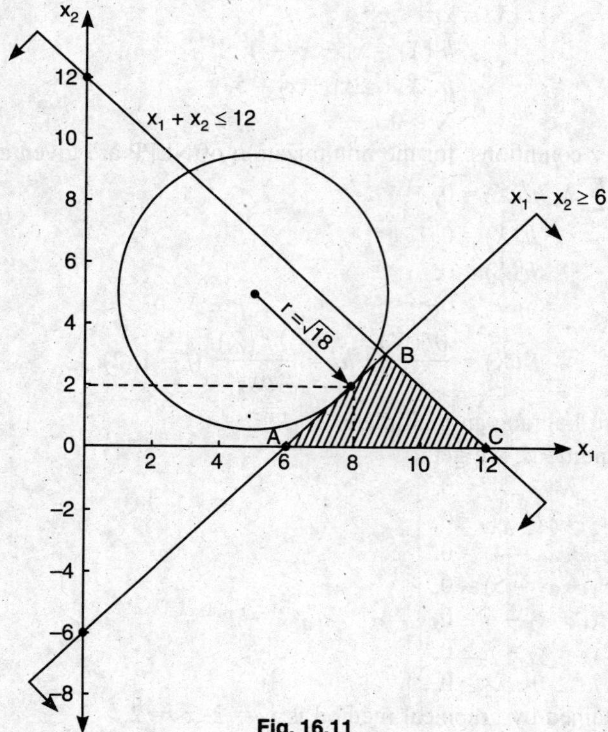

Fig. 16.11

The gradients of the lines representing constraints can be obtained as under:

The gradient of line $x_1 + x_2 = 12$ is

$$1 + \frac{dx_2}{dx_1} = 0 \quad \text{or} \quad \frac{dx_2}{dx_1} = -1. \qquad ...(ii)$$

The gradient of line $x_1 - x_2 = 6$ is

$$1 - \frac{dx_2}{dx_1} = 0 \quad \text{or} \quad \frac{dx_2}{dx_1} = 1. \qquad ...(iii)$$

Now two alternative solutions are possible:

(*i*) Taking (*i*), (*ii*) and constraint $x_1 + x_2 = 12$,

$$\frac{dx_2}{dx_1} = \frac{2x_1 - 10}{10 - 2x_2} = -1 \text{ which gives } x_1 = x_2.$$

Since $x_1 + x_2 = 12$, $x_1 = x_2 = 6$.

This solution does not satisfy the constraint $x - x_2 \geq 6$, and hence is not feasible.

(*ii*) Taking equations (*i*) and (*iii*) and the constraint

$$x_1 - x_2 = 6,$$

$$\frac{dx_2}{dx_1} = \frac{2x_1 - 10}{10 - 2x_2} = 1, \text{ which gives } x_1 + x_2 = 10.$$

Solving $x_1 + x_2 = 10$ and $x_1 - x_2 = 6$, we get $x_1 = 8$, $x_2 = 2$. This solution satisfies all the constraints. Hence, $x_1 = 8$, $x_2 = 2$ is the optimal solution, which gives $Z_{max} = 32$.

EXAMPLE 16.11-6

Solve graphically the followings NLP problem

$$\begin{aligned} &\textit{Maximize} && Z = x_1 + x_2, \\ &\textit{subject to} && x_1x_2 - 2x_2 \geq 3, \\ & && 3x_1 + 2x_2 \leq 24 \\ & && x_1, x_2 \geq 0. \end{aligned}$$

Solution

The objective function, in this problem, is linear, while one of the constraints is non-linear. The constraint $x_1x_2 - 2x_2 \geq 3$ can be plotted by assuming it as an equation $x_1x_2 - 2x_2 = 3$ or $x_2(x_1 - 2) = 3$. For $x_2 \geq 0$, the value of x_1 cannot be less than 2.

Let us take some values of x_1 and find the corresponding values of x_2, which satisfy the equation $x_1x_2 - 2x_2 = 3$ (Table 16.3).

TABLE 16.3

x_1	2.1	2.2	2.4	2.6	3.0	3.5	4.0	5.0	6.0	7.0	8.0	12.0
x_2	30	15	7.5	5.0	3	2	1.5	1.0	0.75	0.6	0.5	0.3

These points are plotted to obtain the graph of $x_1x_2 - 2x_2 = 3$, as shown in Fig 16.12. For plotting constraint $3x_1 + 2x_2 = 24$, we have the end point of the line $x_1 = 0$, $x_2 = 12$ and $x_1 = 8$, $x_2 = 0$. The solution space is obtained by both the constraints. The solution point lies in the shaded area.

The objective function $Z = x_1 + x_2$ is a line inclined at 45°. When this line is moved away from the origin to maximize the value of Z, the farthest point through which it passes is the point A, which gives optimal solution $x_2^* = 8.45$ and $x_1^* = 2.35$.

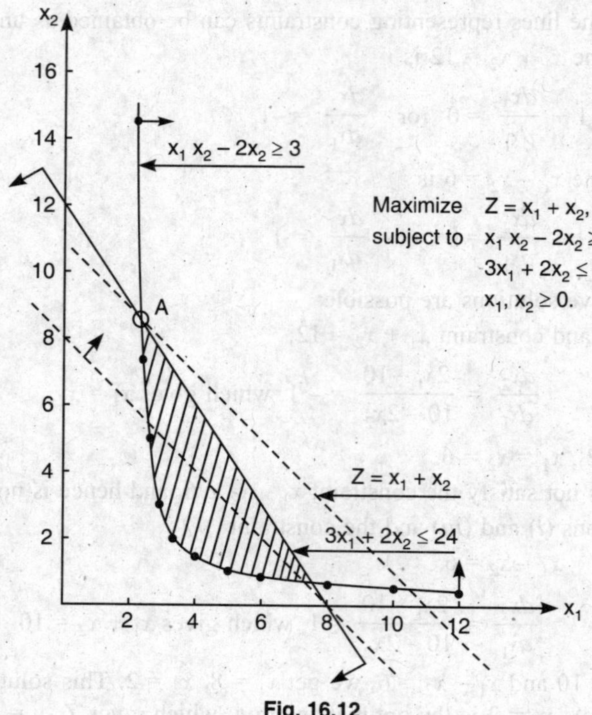

Fig. 16.12

Alternatively, the exact values of x_1^* and x_2^* can be determined by solving the two constraint equations for x_1 and x_2.

From constraint $3x_1 + 2x_2 = 24$, we get $x_1 = \dfrac{24 - 2x_2}{3}$. Substituting this value of x_1 in the other constraint equation,

$$\left(\frac{24 - 2x_2}{3}\right)x_2 - 2x_2 = 3$$

or $\quad 24x_2 - 2x_2^2 - 6x_2 = 9$

or $\quad 2x_2^2 - 18x_2 + 9 = 0$, which gives

$$x_2 = \frac{18 \pm \sqrt{324 - 72}}{4} = 8.4686,\ 0.53125.$$

For $\quad x_2 = 8.4686,\ x_1 = \dfrac{24 - 2 \times 8.486}{3} = 2.3427$, which gives $Z = 10.8113$.

For $\quad x_2 = 0.53125,\ x_1 = \dfrac{24 - 2 \times 0.53125}{3} = 7.6433$, which gives $Z = 8.17455$.

$\therefore \quad Z_{\max} = 10.813,\ x_1^* = 2.3427$ and $x_2^* = 8.4686$.

16.12 ONE-VARIABLE UNCONSTRAINED OPTIMIZATION

Let us consider the simplest case of non-linear programming, when the objective function has only one variable $x (n = 1)$ and there is no constraint. The differentiable function $f(x)$ is to be maximized and is concave. In such a case, the necessary and sufficient condition for a particular solution $x = x^*$ to be optimal, that is global maximum is

$$\frac{df(x)}{dx} = 0 \quad \text{at} \quad x = x^*.$$

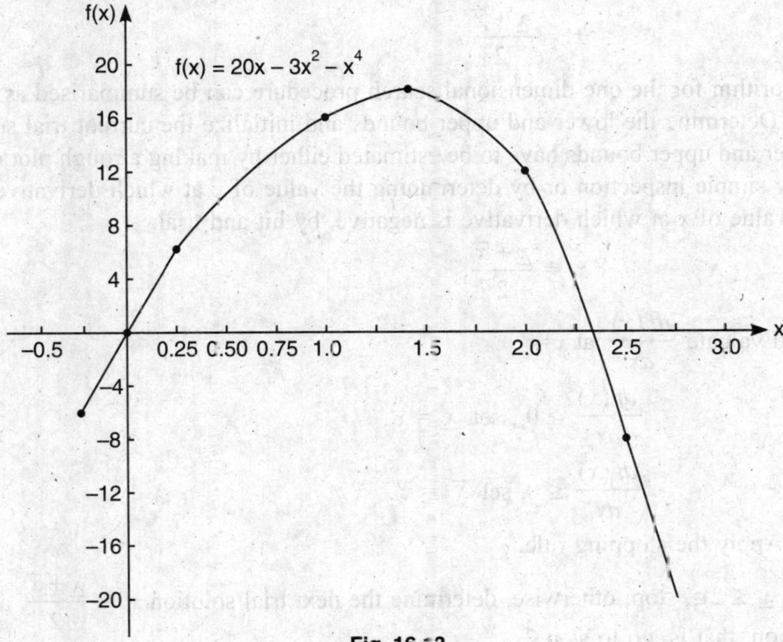

Fig. 16.13

Fig. 16.13 shows a concave function of this type. In simple case, the function may be directly solvable for x^*. But if $f(x)$ is complicated, and its derivative $\dfrac{df(x)}{dx}$ is neither linear nor quadratic equation, it may not be possible to solve the problem analytically. In such a case, the problem is solved numerically by employing the one-dimensional search procedure.

16.13 ONE-DIMENSIONAL SEARCH PROCEDURE

Like any search procedure, the one-dimensional search procedure generates a sequence of trial solutions, that lead towards the optimal solution. To start the search, the *lower* and *upper bounds* on the value of the variable are estimated and first *trial solution* is determined. The function $f(x)$ is differentiated with respect to the variable x. Depending upon whether the derivative is +ve or –ve at the trial solution, the direction of incrementing the variable is determined. If the derivative is +ve, then optimal x *i.e.,* x^* must be larger than the current value of x and hence the current x becomes the lower bound for the next trial solution. If the derivative is negative, the optimal value x^* must be less than the present x, and this x becomes the upper bound for the next trial solution. With each iteration, the distance between the upper and lower bounds decreases and the trial solution converges towards x^*. For the efficient convergence of trails, appropriate rules for selecting the trail solution between the two bounds should be applied. Also stopping rule, which determines the *error tolerance*, must be clearly specified.

The above search procedure can be summarised as under:

Let x' = current trial solution,

$\underline{x}$ = current lower bound on x^*,

$\overline{x}$ = current upper bound on x^*,

$\in$ = error tolerance for x^*.

Bolzeno search plan or *midpoint rule* is commonly employed for selecting the next trial solution between the two bounds. According to this rule, the midpoint of the current lower and upper bounds is selected as the next trial solution, that is

$$x' = \frac{\underline{x} + \overline{x}}{2}.$$

The algorithm for the one-dimensional search procedure can be summarised as under:

Step 1. Determine the lower and upper bounds and initialize the current trial solution. The values of lower and upper bounds have to be estimated either by making a rough plot of the given function or by simple inspection or by determining the value of x at which derivative is positive and then the value of x at which derivative is negative, by hit and trial.

$$x' = \frac{\underline{x} + \overline{x}}{2}.$$

Step 2. Evaluate $\dfrac{df(x)}{dx}$ at $x{=}x'$.

If $\quad \dfrac{df(x)}{dx} \geq 0$, set $\underline{x} = x'$,

if $\quad \dfrac{df(x)}{dx} \leq 0$, set $\overline{x} = x'$.

Step 3. Apply the stopping rule.

If $\overline{x} - \underline{x} \leq 2\in$, stop; otherwise, determine the next trial solution $x' = \dfrac{\underline{x} + \overline{x}}{2}$ and perform the new iteration, that is, go to step 2.

The accuracy of the result will depend upon the value of $\in$, the error tolerance, and the minimum error will be $x^* - x'$.

Solution of any reasonable problem will involve a large amount of computations, which can be carried out only by computers. Though software are available for carrying out the search, the students are advised to develop their own computer programs.

Some simple examples involving reasonable computations have been solved here to illustrate the search procedure.

EXAMPLE 16.13-1

Maximize $f(x) = 20x - 3x^2 - x^4$ by using one-dimensional search procedure.

Solution

This is a one-dimensional *i.e.* one-variable non-linear function. Its first two derivatives are

$$\frac{df(x)}{dx} = 20 - 6x - 4x^3,$$

and $$\frac{d^2 f(x)}{dx^2} = -6 - 12x^2 = -6\,(1 + 2x^2).$$

Since the second derivative is non-positive everywhere, $f(x)$ is convex and hence one-dimensional search procedure can be applied.

Fig. 16.13. depicts a rough plot of the function, which shows that $f(x)$ is negative for $x < 0$, or $x > 2.5$. These values can be taken as the starting lower and upper bounds, *i.e.*, $\underline{x} = 0$ and $\overline{x} = 2.5$, with midpoint $= \dfrac{0 + 2.5}{2} = 1.25$ as the initial trial solution x'. Let the error of tolerance $\in = 0.01$.

The search starts with $\underline{x} = 0$, $\overline{x} = 2.5$, $x' = 1.25$.

Now $\quad f(x) = 20x - 3x^2 - x^4.$

$\therefore \quad \dfrac{df}{dx} = 20 - 6x - 4x^3.$

At $\quad x = 1.25, \ \dfrac{df}{dx} = 4.6875.$

Since the value of derivative at $x' = 1.25$ is positive, x' becomes the lower bound for the next trial solution.

Thus $\quad \underline{x} = 1.25, \ \overline{x} = 2.5,$ and $\overline{x} - \underline{x} \nleq 2\epsilon.$

$\therefore \quad x' = \dfrac{1.25 + 2.5}{2} = 1.875.$

Now $\dfrac{df}{dx}$ at 1.875 = – 17.624219. Since it is negative, this value of x' becomes the upper bound for the next trial solution.

Now $\quad \underline{x} = 1.25, \ \overline{x} = 1.875$ and $\overline{x} - \underline{x} = 0.675 \nleq 2\epsilon.$

$\therefore \quad x' = \dfrac{1.25 + 1.875}{2} = 1.5625.$

The iterations are continued, until $\overline{x} - \underline{x}$ becomes less than or equal to 2ϵ. The sequence of solutions obtained in the search is given in table 16.4. The optimal solution obtained is $x^* = 1.4160157$,

and $\quad f(x^*) = 18.284584.$

TABLE 16.4 **Sequence of solutions in the search.**

Interation	$\underline{x}$	$\overline{x}$	x'	$\overline{x} - \underline{x}$	$\dfrac{df(x')}{dx}$
0	0	2.5	1.25	2.5	4.6875
1	1.25	2.5	1.875	1.25	– 17.624219
2	1.25	1.875	1.5625	0.6257	– 4.633789
3	1.25	1.5625	1.40625	0.31257	0.438842
4	1.40625	1.5625	1.484375	0.15625	– 1.988734
5	1.40625	1.484375	1.4453125	0.078125	– 0.748491
6	1.40625	1.4453125	1.4257813	0.0390625	– 0.148299
7	1.40625	1.4257813	1.4160157	0.0195314	Stop

EXAMPLE 16.13-2

Use the one-dimensional search procedure to solve the following non-linear problem:

Maximize $f(x) = 6x - x^2.$

Take the initial upper and lower bounds as $\overline{x} = 4.8$ *and* $\underline{x} = 0$ *and error tolerance* $\epsilon = 0.04$.

Solution

This is one-variable non-linear function

$$f(x) = 6x - x^2,$$

$$\frac{df(x)}{dx} = 6 - 2x,$$

$$\frac{d^2 f(x)}{dx^2} = -2.$$

Since the second derivative is non-positive, function $f(x)$ is concave everywhere and hence search procedure can be employed.

The starting solution is $\underline{x} = 0, \ \overline{x} = 4.8.$

$$\therefore \qquad x' = \frac{0+4.8}{2} = 2.4.$$

The value of $\frac{df(x)}{dx}$ at $x = 2.4$ is $6 - 4.8 = 1.2$.

Since $\frac{df(x)}{dx}$ is positive, x' becomes lower bound for the next trial solution.

Now $\qquad \underline{x} = 2.4,\ \overline{x} = 4.8,\ \overline{x} - \underline{x} = 2.4 \not\leq 2\epsilon.$

$$\therefore \qquad x' = \frac{2.4+4.8}{2} = 3.6,$$

$\frac{df(x)}{dx}$ at $x' = 3.6$ is $6 - 7.2 = -1.2$.

Since $\frac{df(x)}{dx}$ is negative, x' becomes the upper bound for the next trial solution.

$\therefore \qquad \underline{x} = 2.4,\ \overline{x} = 3.6.\ \therefore\ \overline{x} - \underline{x} = 1.2 \not\leq 2\epsilon.$

$$\therefore \qquad x' = \frac{2.4+3.6}{2} = 3.0.$$

Derivative $\frac{df(x)}{dx}$ at $x = 3.0$ is neither negative nor positive. Thus we reach the exact solution, $x^* = 3.0$.

EXAMPLE 16.13-3

Use the one-dimensional search procedure to interactively solve, approximately, the following equation:

Maximize $f(x) = x^3 + 2x - 2x^2 - 0.25x^4$.

Use an error tolerance $\epsilon = 0.04$ *and the initial bounds as* $\underline{x} = 0,\ \overline{x} = 2.4$.

Solution

The first and second derivatives of the function are

$$\frac{df(x)}{dx} = 3x^2 + 2 - 4x - x^3,$$

$$\frac{d^2 f(x)}{dx^2} = 6x - 4 - 3x^2.$$

The second derivative is negative at $x = 0, x = 1, x = -1, x = 2, x = -2$, ... *i.e.*, at all values of x and hence the function $f(x)$ is concave.

Now the starting trial solution is

$$x' = \frac{\underline{x} + \overline{x}}{2} = \frac{0+2.4}{2} = 1.2,$$

and $\qquad \frac{df(x)}{dx}$ at $x = x' = 1.2$ is $3\,(1.2)^2 + 2 - 4\,(1.2) - (1.2)^3 = -0.208$.

Since the derivative is negative, the current solution $x' = 1.2$ becomes the upper bound for the next trial solution.

Now $\qquad \underline{x} = 0,\ \overline{x} = 1.2,$

$$x' = \frac{0+1.2}{2} = 0.6,$$

and $\qquad \frac{df(x')}{dx} = 3\,(0.6)^2 + 2 - 4\,(0.6) - (0.6)^3 = 0.464.$

Since the derivative at $x' = 0.6$ is positive, it becomes the lower bound for the next trial solution.

Now $\qquad \underline{x} = 0.6,\ \bar{x} = 1.2;\quad \bar{x} - \underline{x} = 0.6 \nleq 2\epsilon,$

$$x' = \frac{0.6 + 1.2}{2} = 0.9$$

and $\qquad \dfrac{df(x')}{dx} = 3\,(0.9)^2 + 2 - 4\,(0.9) - (0.9)^3 = 0.101.$

Since the derivative at $x' = 0.9$ is +ve, it becomes the lower bound for the new trial solution.

Now $\qquad \underline{x} = 0.9,\ \bar{x} = 1.2;\quad \bar{x} - \underline{x} = 0.3 \nleq 2\epsilon,$

$$x' = \frac{0.9 + 1.2}{2} = 1.05,$$

and $\qquad \dfrac{df(x')}{dx} = 3\,(1.05)^2 + 2 - 4\,(1.05) - (1.05)^3 = -0.050125.$

Since the derivative at $x' = 1.05$ is –ve, it becomes the upper bound for the next trial solution.

Now $\qquad \underline{x} = 0.9,\ \bar{x} = 1.05;\quad \bar{x} - \underline{x} = 0.15 \nleq 2\epsilon,$

$$x' = \frac{0.9 + 1.05}{2} = 0.975,$$

and $\qquad \dfrac{df(x')}{dx} = 3\,(0.975)^2 + 2 - 4\,(0.975) - (0.975)^3 = 0.0250156.$

Since $\dfrac{df(x')}{dx}$ is +ve, $x' = 0.975$ becomes the lower bound for the next trial solution.

Now $\qquad \underline{x} = 0.975,\ \bar{x} = 1.05;\quad \bar{x} - \underline{x} = 0.075 < 2\epsilon,$

$$x' = \frac{0.975 + 1.05}{2} = 1.0125.$$

Since the solution $x' = 1.0125$, is within the specified tolerance, the iterations are stopped. The approximate optimal solution is $x^* = 1.0125$.

EXAMPLE 16.13-4

Solve the following convex programming problem with lower and upper bounds as $\underline{x} = 0$, $\bar{x} = 2$, *and an error tolerance* $\epsilon = 0.01$:

Minimize $\qquad Z = x^4 - x^2 - 4x.$

Solution

This is a convex programming problem of the minimization type. The one-dimensional search procedure remains the same, only the conditions for selecting the lower and upper bounds change. If the derivative of the function at a solution point is positive , the solution becomes the upper bound for the next trial solution and if the derivative is negative , the solution becomes the lower bound for the next trial solution.

The convex function is

$$f(x) = x^4 - x^2 - 4x.$$

The first and second derivatives are

$$\frac{df(x)}{dx} = 4x^3 - 2x - 4,$$

$$\frac{d^2 f(x)}{dx^2} = 12x^2 - 2.$$

For every value of $x > 0.45$ the second derivative is positive, hence the function is convex and search procedure can be applied.

The starting solution is given as,

$$\underline{x} = 0 \qquad \overline{x} = 2, \text{ which gives } x' = 1,$$

and $$\frac{df(x)}{dx} \text{ (at } x = x') = 4 - 2 - 4 = -2.$$

Since the derivative is negative, the present solution $x' = 1$, will become the lower bound for the next trial solution.

Now $$\underline{x} = 1, \ \overline{x} = 2, \ \overline{x} - \underline{x} = 1 \not\leq 2\epsilon,$$

$$x' = \frac{1+2}{2} = 1.5,$$

and $$\frac{df(x)}{dx} \text{ (at } x' = 1.5) = 4(1.5)^3 - 2(1.5) - 4 = 5.0.$$

Since the derivative is positive, $x' = 1.5$ becomes the upper bound on the next trial solution, *i.e.*, $\overline{x} = 1.5$. The iterations are continued till the difference between the upper and lower bounds becomes less than or equal to 2ϵ. The computations are given in Table 16.5.

TABLE 16.5

$\underline{x}$	$\overline{x}$	x'	$\overline{x} - \underline{x}$	$\frac{df(x')}{dx}$
0	2	1	2	– 2
1	2	1.5	1	5
1	1.5	1.25	0.5	1.3125
1	1.25	1.125	0.25	– 0.55469
1.125	1.25	1.1875	0.125	0.32324
1.125	1.1875	1.15625	0.0625	– 0.12928
1.15625	1.1875	1.171825	0.03125	0.09355
1.15625	1.171875	1.1640625	0.015625	stop.

The solution point $x' = 1.1640625$ is well within the tolerance error of 0.01 since $\overline{x} - \underline{x} = 0.015625$ is less than 2ϵ *i.e.*, less than 0.02.

$$Z_{min} = (1.1640625)^4 - (1.1640625)^2 - 4(1.1640625)$$
$$= -4.175153.$$

16.14 MULTI-VARIABLE UNCONSTRAINED OPTIMIZATION

In this section we deal with the optimization of problems having objective function comprising of more than one variable and without any constraints. The multivariable function should either be concave or convex function in the specified region or a unimodel function. In case of concave function, the objective is to maximize; while in case of convex function, the objective is to minimize.

Let us consider a multivariable concave function f (X), X = $x_1, x_2, ..., x_n$, without any constraints on the feasible values. The function is to be maximized. One method of solving this problem is by setting the respective partial derivatives equal to zero and solving the equations analytically. But we assume that these equations cannot be solved analytically and numerical search procedure must be employed.

In case of single variable problem, the value of the ordinary derivative was used to determine, whether the value of variable x was to be increased or decreased for the next trial solution. The iterations were carried to reach a point where the value of the derivative was nearly zero. In case of multivariable problem, there are a number of variables, and hence a number of directions in which the solution can move. The goal is to reach a point where all the partial derivatives are nearly zero. The value of each variable at this point is nearly optimal. The extension of the one-variable search procedure requires that the values of the partial derivatives be used to select the directions of different variables in which they should move. But this is a highly cumbersome procedure.

In case of multivariable problem, the objective function $f(X)$ is assumed to be differentiable and hence possesses a gradient. This gradient is used to determine whether the variable is to be increased or decreased.

Let $\nabla f(x)$ be the gradient at point x. At any point X = X′, the gradient is the vector of partial derivatives corresponding to various variables.

$$\nabla f(X') = \left(\frac{\partial f}{\partial x_1}, \frac{\partial f}{\partial x_2}, \ldots, \frac{\partial f}{\partial x_n}\right) \text{ at } X = X'.$$

16.15 THE GRADIENT SEARCH PROCEDURE

Since, the objective is to maximize $f(X)$, the search should move in the direction of gradient $\nabla f(X)$ as fast as possible, and keep moving until it reaches the optimal solution. The rate at which the function $f(X)$ increases is maximized, if the infinitesimal changes in X are in the direction of the gradient $\nabla f(X)$. Changing X continuously in the direction of the $\nabla f(X)$ may not be possible, because it would require continuously re-evaluating the partial derivatives $\frac{\partial f}{\partial x_j}$ for $j = 1, 2, \ldots, n$, and changing the direction of the path. A better approach is to keep moving in a fixed direction and stop only when $f(X)$ stops increasing . At this point, again determine the direction in which $f(X)$ increases, and continue moving in that direction so long as the value of $f(X)$ increases. This is like climbing up a hill, the top of which is not visible to you. From the point you start , move in the direction having highest upward slope. Keep moving up until the slope becomes zero. Here again determine the direction in which the slope upward is maximum. This way you will reach the top of the hill. Climbing up the hill is a two-variable problem, where (x_1, x_2) represent the co-ordinates of the current location. The function $f(x_1, x_2)$ gives the height of the hill at point (x_1, x_2). The search traces a zig-zag path up the hill. Each corner is the trial solution which is modified in successive iterations. In a multivariable problem, the number of variables is more than two. Each iteration involves changing the current value of each variable of X′. That is, at each iteration,

$$\text{reset } X' = X' + t^* \nabla f(X'),$$

where t^* is the positive value of t which maximizes $f(X' + t\nabla f(X'))$; that is

$$f(X' + t^* \nabla f(X)) = \max_{t \geq 0} f(X' + t\nabla f(X')).$$

It may be noted that $f(X' + t\nabla f(X'))$ is simply $f(X)$,

$$\text{where } x_j = x_j' + t\left(\frac{\partial f}{\partial x_j}\right)_{X=X'} \quad \text{for } j = 1, 2, \ldots n.$$

The search procedure is continued, until the value of $\nabla f(X)$ is within the specified error tolerance, that is $\left|\frac{\partial f}{\partial x_j}\right| \leq \epsilon$ for $j = 1, 2, \ldots, n$.

The search procedure can be summarised as under:

Step 1. Estimate the initial trial solution.

Step 2. Evaluate the gradient $\nabla f(X')$ and set $x_j = x_j' + t\left(\frac{\partial f}{\partial x_j}\right)$ for $j = 1, 2, ..., n$.

Substitute these expressions into $f(X)$ to obtain $f(X' + t\,\nabla f(X'))$ as a function of t.

Step 3. By differentiating the above function with respect to t, find the value of t^* that maximizes

$$f(X' + t\,\nabla f(X')) \text{ over } t \geq 0.$$

The t^* can also be determined by one-dimensional search procedure.

Step 4. Find the next trial solution $X' = X' + t^*\,\nabla f(X')$.

Step 5. Apply the stopping rule. For that, evaluate $\nabla f(X')$ at $X = X'$ and check if $\left|\frac{\partial f}{\partial x_j}\right| \leq \epsilon$ for all $j = 1, 2, ..., n$.

If it is so, stop the iteration. The current trial solution is the desired near optimal solution. If not, go to step 2 for the next iteration.

EXAMPLE 16.15-1

Solve the following two-variable unconstrained non-linear problem using search procedure:

Maximize $f(X) = 2x_1x_2 + x_2 - x_1^2 - 2x_2^2$. [*R.U. M.Sc. (Math.) 2011*]

Solution

The partial derivatives of $f(X)$ w.r.t. x_1 and x_2 are

$$\frac{\partial f}{\partial x_1} = 2x_2 - 2x_1,$$

$$\frac{\partial f}{\partial x_2} = 2x_1 + 1 - 4x_2.$$

To begin with the gradient search procedure, let us take $x_1 = 0$, $x_2 = 0$ as the initial trial solution.

For the current trial solution $X = (0, 0)$,

$$\frac{\partial f}{\partial x_1} = 0 \text{ and } \frac{\partial f}{\partial x_2} = 1 \text{ or } \nabla f(0, 0) = (0, 1).$$

Therefore, to begin the first interation, set

$$x_1 = x_1 + t\left(\frac{\partial f}{\partial x_1}\right) = 0 + t\,(0) = 0,$$

$$x_2 = x_2 + t\left(\frac{\partial f}{\partial x_2}\right) = 0 + t\,(1) = t.$$

Now substitute these expressions into $f(X)$ to obtain

$$\begin{aligned} f(X' + t\,\nabla f(X')) &= f(0, t) \\ &= 2\,(0)\,(t) + t - (0)^2 - 2t^2 \\ &= t - 2t^2. \end{aligned}$$

Now, since $f(0, t^*) = \max\limits_{t\geq 0} f(0, t) = \max\limits_{t\geq 0} (t - 2t^2)$,

$$\frac{d}{dt}(t - 2t^2) = 1 - 4t = 0 \quad \text{or} \quad t^* = 1/4.$$

Hence, reset $\quad X' = (0, 0) + \frac{1}{4}(0, 1) = (0, \frac{1}{4})$ *i.e.*, $x_1 = 0, x_2 = \frac{1}{4}$.

For this new trial solution,

$$\frac{\partial f}{\partial x_1} = 2 \times \frac{1}{4} - 0 = \frac{1}{2}$$

$$\frac{\partial f}{\partial x_2} = 0 + 1 - 4 \times \frac{1}{4} = 0,$$

or $\quad \nabla f\left(0, \frac{1}{4}\right) = \left(\frac{1}{2}, 0\right).$

For the second iteration, set

$$X = \left(0, \frac{1}{4}\right) + t\left(\frac{1}{2}, 0\right) = \left(\frac{t}{2}, \frac{1}{4}\right).$$

So $\quad f(X' + t\,\nabla f(X')) = f\left(0 + \frac{t}{2}, \frac{1}{4}\right) = f\left(\frac{t}{2}, \frac{1}{4}\right)$

$$= 2 \times \frac{t}{2} \times \frac{1}{4} + \frac{1}{4} - \frac{t^2}{4} - 2 \times \frac{1}{16} = \frac{1}{8}(2t + 2 - 2t^2 - 1)$$

$$= \frac{1}{8}(2t - 2t^2 + 1).$$

Now $\quad \frac{d}{dt}\left(\frac{1}{8}(2t - 2t^2 + 1)\right) = 0,$

or $\quad \frac{d}{dt}(2t - 2t^2 + 1) = 0 \quad$ or $\quad 2 - 4t = 0$ or $t^* = \frac{1}{2}$.

Again, set $\quad X' = X' + t^*\,\nabla f(X')$

$$= \left(0, \frac{1}{4}\right) + \frac{1}{2}\left(\frac{1}{2}, 0\right) = \left(\frac{1}{4}, \frac{1}{4}\right).$$

For this new trial solution, $X' = \left(\frac{1}{4}, \frac{1}{4}\right)$,

$$\frac{\partial f}{\partial x_1} = 2 \times \frac{1}{4} - 2 \times \frac{1}{4} = 0 \text{ and } \frac{\partial f}{\partial x_2} = 2 \times \frac{1}{4} + 1 - 4 \times \frac{1}{4} = \frac{1}{2},$$

or $\quad \nabla f\left(\frac{1}{4}, \frac{1}{4}\right) = \left(0, \frac{1}{2}\right).$

Set $\quad X = \left(\frac{1}{4}, \frac{1}{4}\right) + t\left(0, \frac{1}{2}\right)$

$$= \left(\frac{1}{4}, \frac{1}{4} + \frac{t}{2}\right) = \left(\frac{1}{4}, \frac{1 + 2t}{4}\right).$$

Substituting these values in $f(X)$,

$$f(X' + \nabla f(X')) = 2 \times \frac{1}{4} \times \left(\frac{1 - 2t}{4}\right) + \frac{1 + 2t}{4} - \frac{1}{16} - 2\left(\frac{1 + 2t}{4}\right)^2$$

$$= \frac{1}{16}(3 + 4t - 8t^2).$$

Now $\quad \frac{d}{dt}(3 + 4t - 8t^2) = 0,$

or $\quad 4 - 16t = 0 \quad$ or $\quad t^* = \dfrac{1}{4}.$

Hence, set
$$X' = X' + t^* \nabla f(X')$$
$$= \left(\frac{1}{4}, \frac{1}{4}\right) + \frac{1}{4}\left(0, \frac{1}{2}\right) = \left(\frac{1}{4}, \frac{3}{8}\right).$$

For this new trial solution,
$$\frac{\partial f}{\partial x_1} = 2 \times \frac{3}{8} - 2 \times \frac{1}{4} = \frac{1}{4},$$

and
$$\frac{\partial f}{\partial x_2} = \frac{2}{4} + 1 - 4 \times \frac{3}{8} = 0,$$
$$\nabla f\left(\frac{1}{4}, \frac{3}{8}\right) = \left(\frac{1}{4}, 0\right).$$

Set
$$X = \left(\frac{1}{4}, \frac{3}{8}\right) + t\left(\frac{1}{4}, 0\right) = \left(\frac{1+t}{4}, \frac{3}{8}\right).$$

Substituting these values in function $f(X)$,
$$f(X' + t\nabla f(X')) = 2\left(\frac{1+t}{4}\right) \times \frac{3}{8} + \frac{3}{8} - \left(\frac{1+t}{4}\right)^2 - 2\left(\frac{3}{8}\right)^2$$
$$= \frac{1}{32}(7 + 2t - 2t^2).$$

Now
$$\frac{d}{dt} f(X) = 0.$$

$$\therefore \quad \frac{d}{dt}(7 + 2t - 2t^2) = 0 \quad \text{or} \quad 2 - 4t = 0 \quad \text{or} \quad t^* = \frac{1}{2}.$$

Now reset
$$X' = \left(\frac{1}{4}, \frac{3}{8}\right) + \frac{1}{2}\left(\frac{1}{4}, 0\right) = \left(\frac{3}{8}, \frac{3}{8}\right).$$

For this new trial solution,
$$\frac{\partial f}{\partial x_1} = \frac{3}{4} - \frac{3}{4} = 0, \quad \frac{\partial f}{\partial x_2} = \frac{3}{4} + 1 - \frac{3}{2} = \frac{1}{4},$$

or
$$\nabla f\left(\frac{3}{8}, \frac{3}{8}\right) = \left(0, \frac{1}{4}\right).$$

Now
$$X = \left(\frac{3}{8}, \frac{3}{8}\right) + t\left(0, \frac{1}{4}\right) = \left(\frac{3}{8}, \frac{3+2t}{8}\right).$$

Substituting in $f(X)$,
$$f(X') + t\nabla f(X')) = 2 \times \frac{3}{8} \times \frac{3+2t}{8} + \frac{3+2t}{8} - \frac{9}{64} - 2\left(\frac{3+2t}{8}\right)^2$$
$$= \frac{1}{64}(15 + 4t - 8t^2).$$

$$\therefore \quad \frac{d}{dt}(15 + 4t - 8t^2) = 0 \quad \text{or} \quad 4 - 16t = 0 \quad \therefore t^* = \frac{1}{4}.$$

Next trial solution
$$X' = \left(\frac{3}{8}, \frac{3}{8}\right) + \frac{1}{4}\left(0, \frac{1}{4}\right) = \left(\frac{3}{8} + \frac{7}{16}\right).$$

The computations carried till now can be summarised in a tabular form as in Table 16.6.

TABLE 16.6 Sequence of solutions in multivariable search

Interation	X'	$\nabla f(X')$	$X' + t\nabla f(X')$	$f(X' + t\nabla f(X'))$	t^*	$X' + t^*\nabla f(X')$
1	(0, 0)	(0, 1)	(0, t)	$t - 2t^2$	$\frac{1}{4}$	$\left(0, \frac{1}{4}\right)$
2	$\left(0, \frac{1}{4}\right)$	$\left(\frac{1}{2}, 0\right)$	$\left(\frac{t}{2}, \frac{1}{4}\right)$	$\frac{1}{8}(2t - 2t^2 + 1)$	$\frac{1}{2}$	$\left(\frac{1}{4}, \frac{1}{4}\right)$
3	$\left(\frac{1}{4}, \frac{1}{4}\right)$	$\left(0, \frac{1}{2}\right)$	$\left(\frac{1}{4}, \frac{1+2t}{4}\right)$	$\frac{1}{16}(3 + 4t - 8t^2)$	$\frac{1}{4}$	$\left(\frac{1}{4}, \frac{3}{8}\right)$
4	$\left(\frac{1}{4}, \frac{3}{8}\right)$	$\left(\frac{1}{4}, 0\right)$	$\left(\frac{1+t}{4}, \frac{3}{8}\right)$	$\frac{1}{32}(7 + 2t - 2t^2)$	$\frac{1}{2}$	$\left(\frac{3}{8}, \frac{3}{8}\right)$
5	$\left(\frac{3}{8}, \frac{3}{8}\right)$	$\left(0, \frac{1}{4}\right)$	$\left(\frac{3}{8}, \frac{3+2t}{8}\right)$	$\frac{1}{64}(15 + 4t - 8t^2)$	$\frac{1}{4}$	$\left(\frac{3}{8}, \frac{7}{16}\right)$

The progress of search from X′ = (0, 0) towards the optimal point is illustrated in Fig. 16.14. With each iteration the increment step goes on decreasing. The convergence sequence of trial solutions may never reach the optimal point. The procedure of search has to be stopped close to the optimal point, according to the specified tolerance error ∈. The optimal solution of this problem could easily be determined by solving the equations obtained from the first partial derivatives, which comes to $X^* = \left(\frac{1}{2}, \frac{1}{2}\right)$. The search also tends towards this optimal solution.

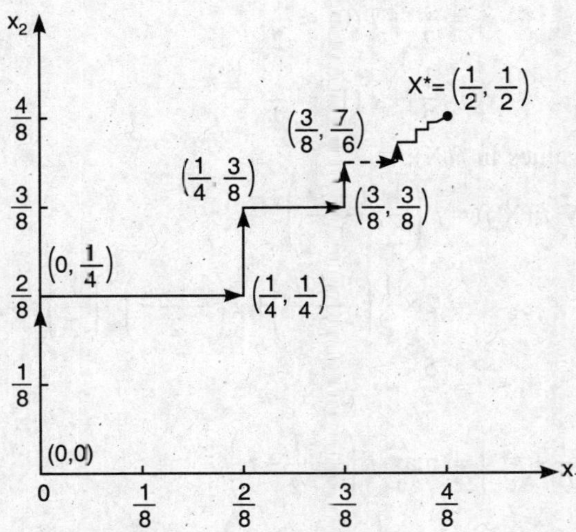

Fig. 16.14. Two variable gradient search for $f(x) = 2x_1x_2 + x_2 - x_1^2 - 2x_2^2$.

The problem solved above was a maximization problem with f(X) being a concave function. If the problem is of minimization with f (X) being a convex function, the rule for obtaining the next trial solution would be,

$$X' = X' - t^* \nabla f(X'),$$

and t^* would now be non-negative value of t that minimizes $f(X' - t\nabla f(X'))$; that is

$$f(X' - t^* \nabla f(X')) = \min_{t \geq 0} f(X' - t \nabla f(X')).$$

EXAMPLE 16.15-2

Show three iterations of the solution of the following two-variable problem by the gradient search procedure. The function f(X) is concave.

$$\text{Maximize } f(X) = 2x_1x_2 + 2x_2 - x_1^2 - 2x_2^2.$$

$X = \left(\frac{1}{2}, \frac{1}{2}\right)$ *may be taken as the starting trial solution. Draw the path of the trial solutions by solving the systems of linear equations by setting* $\nabla f(X) = 0$.

Solution

The partial derivatives of function $f(X)$ with respect to x_1 and x_2 are

$$\frac{\partial f}{\partial x_1} = 2x_2 - 2x_1,$$

$$\frac{\partial f}{\partial x_2} = 2x_1 + 2 - 4x_2.$$

The starting solution is $X = \left(\frac{1}{2}, \frac{1}{2}\right)$, for which

$$\frac{\partial f}{\partial x_1} = 2 \times \frac{1}{2} - 2 \times \frac{1}{2} = 0 \text{ and } \frac{\partial f}{\partial x_2} = 2 \times \frac{1}{2} + 2 - 4 \times \frac{1}{2} = 1.$$

Thus the gradient is $\nabla f\left(\frac{1}{2}, \frac{1}{2}\right) = (0, 1)$.

Now set $\quad x_j = x_j^i + t\left(\frac{\partial f}{\partial x_j}\right)$, for $j = 1, 2$.

$$\therefore \quad x_1 = \frac{1}{2} + t\,(0) = \frac{1}{2},$$

$$x_2 = \frac{1}{2} + t\,(1) = \frac{1}{2} + t.$$

Substituting these values in $f(X)$,

$$f(X' + t\,\nabla f(X')) = f\left(\frac{1}{2}, \frac{1+2t}{2}\right)$$

$$= 2\times\frac{1}{2}\left(\frac{1+2t}{2}\right) + 2\left(\frac{1+2t}{2}\right) - \left(\frac{1}{2}\right)^2 - 2\left(\frac{1+2t}{2}\right)^2$$

$$= \frac{5}{4} + t - 2t^2.$$

Because $\quad f\left(\frac{1}{2}, \frac{1}{2} + t^*\right) = \max_{t \ge 0} f\left(\frac{1}{2}, \frac{1}{2} + t\right)$

$$= \max_{t \ge 0}\left(\frac{5}{4} + t - 2t^2\right),$$

$$\frac{d}{dt}\left(\frac{5}{4} + t - 2\,t^2\right) = 0$$

or, $\quad 1 - 4t = 0 \quad$ or $\quad t^* = \frac{1}{4}.$

Now reset the value of trial solution

$$X' = \left(\frac{1}{2}, \frac{1}{2}\right) + t\,(0, 1) = \left(\frac{1}{2}, \frac{1}{2}\right) + \frac{1}{4}(0, 1) = \frac{1}{2}, \frac{3}{4}.$$

For the new trial solution, the gradients

$$\frac{\partial f}{\partial x_1} = 2 \times \frac{3}{4} - 2 \times \frac{1}{2} = \frac{1}{2},$$

$$\frac{\partial f}{\partial x_2} = 2 \times \frac{1}{2} + 2 - 4 \times \frac{3}{4} = 0,$$

and $$\nabla f\left(\frac{1}{2}, \frac{3}{4}\right) = \left(\frac{1}{2}, 0\right).$$

Now set $$x_j = x_j' + t\left(\frac{\partial f}{\partial x_j}\right) \text{ for } j = 1, 2.$$

$$\therefore \quad x_1 = \frac{1}{2} + t\left(\frac{1}{2}\right) = \frac{1+t}{2},$$

$$x_2 = \frac{3}{4} + 0 = \frac{3}{4}.$$

Substituting these values,

$$f(X') = 2 \times \left(\frac{1+t}{2}\right) \times \frac{3}{4} + 2\left(\frac{3}{4}\right) - \left(\frac{1+t}{2}\right)^2 - 2\left(\frac{3}{4}\right)^2$$

$$= \frac{1}{8}\,(1 + 2t - 2t^2).$$

$$\therefore \quad \frac{d}{dt}\,(1 + 2t - 2t^2) = 0$$

or $$2 - 4t = 0 \quad \text{or} \quad t^* = \frac{1}{2}.$$

Reset the value of trial solution

$$x' = \left(\frac{1}{2}, \frac{3}{4}\right) + \frac{1}{2}\left(\frac{1}{2}\;\; 0\right) = \left(\frac{3}{4}, \frac{3}{4}\right).$$

For this new trial solution, the gradient

$$\nabla f\left(\frac{3}{4}, \frac{3}{4}\right) = \left(0, \frac{5}{2}\right).$$

Now $$x_1 = \frac{3}{4} + t\,(0) = \frac{3}{4}, \quad x_2 = \frac{3}{4} + t\left(\frac{5}{2}\right) = \frac{3}{4} + \frac{5t}{2}.$$

Substituting these values,

$$f(X') = 2 \times \frac{3}{4} \times \left(\frac{3}{4} + \frac{5t}{2}\right) + 2\left(\frac{3}{4} + \frac{5t}{2}\right) - \left(\frac{3}{4}\right)^2 - 2\left(\frac{3}{4} + \frac{5t}{2}\right)^2$$

$$= \frac{15}{16} + \frac{5}{4}t - \frac{25t^2}{2}.$$

$$\therefore \quad \frac{d}{dt}\left(\frac{15}{16} + \frac{5}{4}t - \frac{25}{2}t^2\right) = 0$$

or $$0 + \frac{5}{4} - 25t = 0 \quad \text{or} \quad t^* = \frac{1}{20}.$$

Next trial solution is thus,

$$X' = \left(\frac{3}{4}, \frac{3}{4}\right) + \frac{1}{20}\left(0, \frac{5}{2}\right) = \left(\frac{3}{4}, \frac{7}{8}\right).$$

The computations carried till now are summarised in table 16.7.

TABLE 16.7

Progress of search procedure for 3 iterations.

Interation	X'	$\nabla f(X')$	$X' + t\nabla f(X')$	t^*	$X' + t^*\nabla f(X')$
1	$\left(\frac{1}{2}, \frac{1}{2}\right)$	(0, 1)	$\frac{5}{4} + t - 2t^2$	$\frac{1}{4}$	$\left(\frac{1}{2}, \frac{3}{4}\right)$
2	$\left(\frac{1}{2}, \frac{3}{4}\right)$	$\left(\frac{1}{2}, \frac{3}{4}\right)$	$\frac{1}{8} + \frac{t}{4} - \frac{t^2}{4}$	$\frac{1}{2}$	$\left(\frac{3}{4}, \frac{3}{4}\right)$
3	$\left(\frac{3}{4}, \frac{3}{4}\right)$	$\left(0, \frac{5}{2}\right)$	$\frac{15}{16} + \frac{5t}{4} - \frac{25t^2}{2}$	$\frac{1}{20}$	$\left(\frac{3}{4}, \frac{7}{8}\right)$

In the three iterations carried out above, the solution moves from $\left(\frac{1}{2}, \frac{1}{2}\right)$ to $\left(\frac{3}{4}, \frac{7}{8}\right)$. The solution is gradually moving towards the exact solution (1, 1), which can be determined by setting

$$\nabla f(X) = 0.$$

$$\therefore \quad \frac{\partial f}{\partial x_1} = 2x_2 - 2x_1 = 0,$$

$$\frac{\partial f}{\partial x_2} = 2x_1 + 2 - 4x_2 = 0,$$

which gives $\quad x_1 = x_2 = 1.$

In the trial solution, the increment has gradually decreased. It can be estimated that the next iterations will result into $\left(\frac{7}{8}, \frac{7}{8}\right), \left(\frac{7}{8}, \frac{15}{16}\right), \left(\frac{15}{16}, \frac{15}{16}\right)$, and $\left(\frac{15}{16}, \frac{31}{32}\right)$, etc. converging to (1, 1). The desired optimal solution will depend upon the tolerance error.

The zig-zag path of the trial solutions is shown in Fig. 16.15.

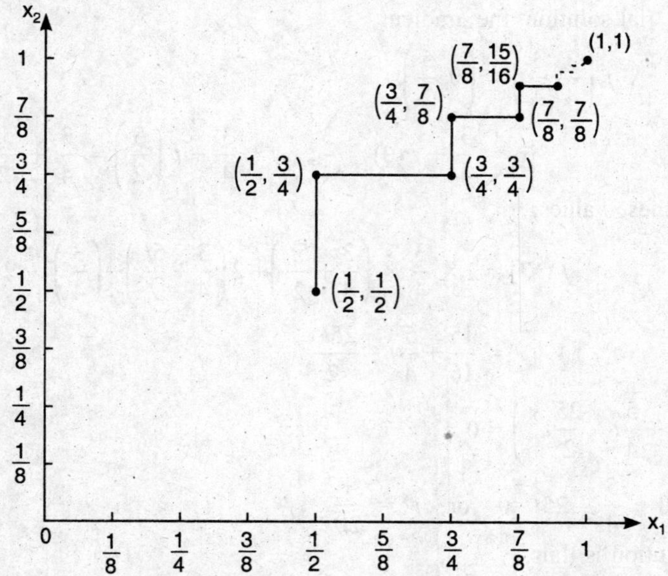

Fig. 16.15. Gradient search procedure for $f(x) = 2x_1 x_2 + 2x_2 - x_1^2 - 2x_2^2$.

EXAMPLE 16.15-3

Starting from the initial trial solution $(x_1, x_2) = (0, 0)$, interactively apply two iterations of the gradient search procedure to the following two-variable unconstrained problem. Also determine the exact solution by solving $\nabla f(X) = 0$.

$$\text{Miximize } f(X) = 8x_1 - x_1^2 - 12x_2 - 2x_2^2 + 2x_1x_2.$$

Solution

The partial derivatives of the function are

$$\frac{\partial f}{\partial x_1} = 8 - 2x_1 + 2x_2,$$

and
$$\frac{\partial f}{\partial x_2} = -12 - 4x_2 + 2x_1.$$

Initial trial solution is $(x_1, x_2) = (0, 0)$, for which,

$$\frac{\partial f}{\partial x_1} = 8, \quad \frac{\partial f}{\partial x_2} = -12, \quad \text{or} \quad \nabla f(0, 0) = (8, -12).$$

Now for first iteration, set

$$x_1 = 0 + t(8) = 8t$$

and
$$x_2 = 0 + t(-12) = -12t.$$

Substituting these values in $f(X)$,

$$f(X) = 64t - 64t^2 + 144t - 288t^2 - 192t^2 = 208t - 544t^2.$$

Now put $\frac{d}{dt}(208 - 544t^2) = 0$

or
$$208 - 1088t = 0 \quad \text{or} \quad t^* = \frac{13}{68}.$$

$\therefore$
$$x_1 = 8t = \frac{26}{17} \quad \text{and} \quad x_2 = -12t = -\frac{39}{17}.$$

(or $x_1 = 1.5295$ and $x_2 = -2.2942$).

Now
$$\frac{\partial f}{\partial x_1} = 8 - 2 \times \frac{26}{17} - 2 \times \frac{39}{17} = \frac{35}{17},$$

$$\frac{\partial f}{\partial x_2} = -12 + 4 \times \frac{39}{17} + \frac{52}{17} = \frac{4}{17}.$$

$\therefore$
$$\nabla f\left(\frac{26}{17}, \frac{-39}{17}\right) = \left(\frac{35}{17}, \frac{4}{17}\right).$$

For the second iteration,

$$x_1 = \frac{26}{17} + \frac{35}{17}t = \frac{1}{17}(26 + 35t),$$

and
$$x_2 = -\frac{39}{17} + \frac{4}{17}t = \frac{1}{17}(4t - 39).$$

Substituting these values in $f(X)$,

$$f(X) = \frac{8}{17}(26 + 35t) - \frac{1}{17} \times \frac{1}{17}(676 + 1225t^2 + 1820t) - \frac{12}{17}(4t - 39)$$

$$- 2 \times \frac{1}{17} \times \frac{1}{17}(4t^2 + 1521 - 312t) + 2 \times \frac{1}{17} \times \frac{1}{17}(26 + 35t)(4t - 39)$$

$$= 460.35 + 0.752t - 3.29t^2.$$

Now put $\frac{d}{dt}(460.35 + 0.752t - 3.295t^2) = 0$

or $0.752 - 6.59t = 0$ or $t^* = 0.115$.

$\therefore$ $$x_1 = \frac{1}{17}(26 + 35 \times 0.115) = 1.767,$$

and $$x_2 = \frac{1}{17}(4 \times 0.115 - 39) = -2.267.$$

Thus in these two iterations, solution moves from (0, 0) to (1.5295, – 2.2942) to (1.767, – 2.267). If the search procedure is continued, we will reach a nearly optimal solution after some iterations.

The exact solution is obtained by setting $\nabla f(X) = 0$.

Or $$\frac{\partial f}{\partial x_1} = 8 - 2x_1 + 2x_2 = 0 \quad \text{or} \quad 2x_1 - 2x_2 = 8,$$

and $$\frac{\partial f}{\partial x_2} = -12 - 4x_2 + 2x_1 = 0 \quad \text{or} \quad 2x_1 - 4x_2 = 12.$$

The solution of these equations gives
$$x_1 = 2 \text{ and } x_2 = -2.$$

EXAMPLE 16.15-4

Consider the following linearly constrained convex programming problem:

$$\text{Maximize} \quad f(X) = 32x_1 + 50x_2 - 10x_2^2 + x_2^3 - x_1^4 - x_2^4,$$
$$\text{subject to} \quad 3x_1 + x_2 \le 11,$$
$$2x_1 + 5x_2 \le 16,$$
$$x_1, x_2 \ge 0.$$

Ignore the constraints and solve the resulting two one-variable unconstrained optimization problems. Use calculus to solve the problem involving x_1 and use the one-dimensional search procedure with $\in = 0.005$ and initial bounds 0 and 4 to solve the problem involving x_2. Show that the resulting solution satisfies the constraints.

Solution

The given function can be put as the sum of two one-variable functions $f(x_1)$ and $f(x_2)$, where

$$f(x_1) = 32x_1 - x_1^4,$$
$$f(x_2) = 50x_2 - 10x_2^2 + x_2^3 - x_2^4.$$

The function $f(x_1)$ can be solved by simple calculus.

$$\frac{df(x_1)}{dx_1} = 32 - 4x_1^3 = 0 \quad \text{or} \quad x_1^* = 2.$$

Now the function $f(x_2)$ is to be solved by the one-dimensional search procedure.

$$f(x_2) = 50x_2 - 10x_2^2 + x_2^3 - x_2^4.$$

Initial trial solution is determined from the given upper and lower bounds.

$$\underline{x}_2 = 0 \text{ and } \overline{x}_2 = 4,$$

$\therefore$ $$x_2' = \frac{0+4}{2} = 2,$$

and $$\frac{df(x_2)}{dx_2} = 50 - 20x_2 + 3x_2^2 - 4x_2^3.$$

At $$x_2' = 2, \quad \frac{df(x_2)}{dx_2} = 50 - 40 + 12 - 32 = -10.$$

Since $\dfrac{df(x_2)}{dx_2} \le 0$, and problem is of maximization, the current solution becomes the upper bound for the next trial solution.

$$\bar{x}_2 = 2,$$

$$x_2' = \frac{0+2}{2} = 1,$$

$$\frac{df(x_2)}{dx_2} = 50 - 20 + 3 - 4 = 29.$$

Since $\dfrac{df(x_2)}{dx_2}$ is positive, x_2' becomes the lower bound for the next trial solution.

$$\underline{x}_2 = 1, \ \bar{x}_2 = 2,$$

$$x_2' = \frac{1+2}{2} = 1.5 \text{ or } \frac{3}{2},$$

$$\frac{df(x_2)}{dx_2} = 50 - 30 + \frac{27}{4} - \frac{27}{2} = \frac{53}{4}.$$

x_1' becomes the lower bound for the next trial solution.

$$\underline{x}_2 = 1.5, \ \bar{x}_2 = 2,$$

$$x_2' = 1.75 \text{ or } \frac{7}{4},$$

$$\frac{df(x_2)}{dx_2} = 50 - 20 \times \frac{7}{4} + 3\left(\frac{7}{4}\right)^2 - 4\left(\frac{7}{4}\right)^3 = \frac{11}{4} = 2.75.$$

Since $\dfrac{df(x_2)}{dx_2} \ge 0$, x_2' becomes lower bound.

$$\underline{x}_2 = 1.75, \quad \bar{x}_2 = 2,$$

$$x_2' = \frac{1.75+2}{2} = 1.875,$$

$$\frac{df(x_2)}{dx_2} = 50 - 20 \times 1.875 + 3\,(1.875)^2 - 4\,(1.875)^3 = -\,3.3203.$$

Since $\dfrac{df(x_2)}{dx_2} \le 0$, x_2' becomes upper bound.

$$\underline{x}_2 = 1.75, \ \bar{x}_2 = 1.875,$$

$$x_2' = \frac{1.75+1.875}{2} = 1.8125,$$

$$\frac{df(x_2)}{dx_2} = 50 - 20\,(1.8125) + 3\,(1.8125)^2 - 4\,(1.8125)^3 = -\,0.2119.$$

$\therefore$ x_2' becomes the upper bound for the next trial solution.

$$\underline{x}_2 = 1.75, \ \bar{x}_2 = 1.8125,$$

$$x_2' = \frac{1.75+1.8125}{2} = 1.7813,$$

$$\frac{df(x_2)}{dx_2} = 50 - 20\,(1.7813) + 3\,(1.7813)^2 - 4\,(1.7813)^3 = 1.2846.$$

$\therefore$ x_2' becomes the lower bound for the next trial solution.

$$\underline{x}_2 = 1.7813,\ \overline{x}_2 = 1.8125\ ;\ \overline{x}_2 - \underline{x}_2 = 0.0312.$$

The value of $\overline{x}_2 - \underline{x}_2$ is greater than $2\in$, hence search is to be continued.

$$x_2' = \frac{1.7813 + 1.8125}{2} = 1.7969,$$

$$\frac{df(x_2)}{dx_2} = 50 - 20\ (1.7969) + 3\ (1.7969)^2 - 4\ (1.7969)^3 = 0.5409.$$

$\therefore$ x_2' becomes the lower bound .

$$\underline{x}_2 = 1.7969,\ \overline{x}_2 = 1.8125,\ \overline{x}_2 - \underline{x}_2 = 0.0156 \not\leq 2\in,$$

$$x_2' = \frac{1}{2}\ (1.7969 + 1.8125) = 1.8047,$$

$$\frac{df(x_2)}{dx_2} = 50 - 20\ (1.8047) + 3\ (1.8047)^2 - 4\ (1.8047)^3 = 0.1856.$$

x_2' again becomes the lower bound.

$$\underline{x}_2 = 1.8047,\ \overline{x}_2 = 1.8125,\ \overline{x}_2 - \underline{x}_2 = 0.0078.$$

Here the value of $\overline{x}_2 - \underline{x}_2 = 0.0078$ is less than $2\in$ *i.e.*, .01. Hence the solution is within the specified error tolerance $\in = 0.005$.

$\therefore$ $$x_2' = \frac{1}{2}\ (1.8047 + 1.8125) = 1.8086$$

or $$x_2^* = 1.8086.$$

We have already determined that $x_1^* = 2$.

By substituting these values, it can be verified as shown below that all the constraints are satisfied.

$$3x_1 + x_2 = 6 + 1.8086 = 7.8086 \leq 11,$$

$$2x_1 + 5x_2 = 4 + 9.0430 = 13.0430 \leq 16,$$

$$x_1 \geq 0,\ x_2 \geq 0.$$

$$F(X)_{max} = 64 - 16 + 50\ (1.8086) - 10\ (1.8086)^2 + (1.8086)^3 - (1.8086)^4 = 100.9369.$$

16.16 QUADRATIC PROGRAMMING PROBLEM

The quadratic programming problem is expressed as

$$\text{maximize } f(X) = \sum_{j=1}^{n} c_j x_j + \frac{1}{2} \sum_{j=1}^{n} \sum_{k=1}^{n} x_j d_{jk} x_k, \qquad ...(i)$$

$$\text{subject to } \sum_{j=1}^{n} a_{ij} x_j \leq b_i, \qquad ...(ii)$$

and $$x_j \geq 0, \qquad ...(iii)$$

where $$i = 1, 2, ..., m,$$

and $$j = 1, 2, ..., n.$$

16.16-1 Kuhn-Tucker Conditions

The necessary and sufficient conditions for an optimal solution of quadratic programming problem with objective function of maximization type and linear constraints, can be obtained as under:

Introduce slack variables s_i^2 and r_j^2 in constraints (*ii*) and (*iii*). The problem modifies to

$$\text{maximize } f(X) = \sum_{j=1}^{n} c_j\, x_j + \frac{1}{2}\sum_{j=1}^{n}\sum_{k=1}^{n} x_j\, d_{jk}\, x_k,$$

$$\text{subject to } \sum_{j=1}^{n} a_{ij} x_j + s_i^2 = b_i\ ;\ i = 1, 2, ..., m,$$

$$-x_j + r_j^2 = 0\ ;\ j = 1, 2, ...\ n.$$

Now the Lagrange function can be written as

$$L\,(X, s, r, \lambda, \mu) = f(X) - \sum_{j=1}^{n} \lambda_i (a_j x_j + s_i^2 - b_i) - \sum_{j=1}^{n} \mu_j (-x_j + r_j^2)$$

$$= \sum_{j=1}^{n} c_j x_j + \frac{1}{2}\sum_{j=1}^{n}\sum_{k=1}^{n} x_j d_{jk} x_k - \sum_{j=1}^{n} \lambda_i (a_{ij} x_j + s_i^2 - b_i) - \sum_{j=1}^{n} \mu_j (-x_j + r_j^2).$$

To derive the Kuhn-Tucker necessary conditions, differentiate the Lagrange function partially with respect to its constraint variables and equate each partial derivative to zero.

Differentiating L (X, s, r, λ, μ) partially w.r.t. $X = (x_1, x_2, ..., x_n)$,

$$c_j - \sum_{k=1}^{n} x_k d_{jk} - \sum_{i=1}^{m} \lambda_i a_{ij} + \mu_j = 0\ ;\ \ j = 1, 2, ..., n. \qquad ...(i)$$

Differentiating with respect to s,

$$-2\lambda s = 0 \text{ or } \lambda_i s_i = 0 \text{ or } \lambda_i s_i^2 = 0, \qquad ....(ii)$$

or $\quad \lambda_i \left\{\Sigma a_{ij}\, x_j - b_i\right\} = 0.$

Differentiating w.r.t. r,

$$-2\,\mu\, r = 0 \text{ or } \mu_j r_j = 0,$$

or $\quad \mu_j x_j = 0, j = 1, 2, ..., n. \qquad ...(iii)$

Differentiating w.r.t. λ,

$$\sum_{j=1}^{n} a_{ij} x_j + s^2 - b_i = 0 \text{ or } \sum_{j=1}^{n} a_{ij} x_j \le b_i, i = 1, 2..., m. \qquad ...(iv)$$

Differentiating w.r.t. μ,

$$-x_j + r_j^2 = 0,$$

or $\quad x_j \ge 0, j = 1, 2,..., n. \qquad ....(v)$

And all the variables are non-negative,

$$x_j,\ s_i,\ r_j,\ \lambda_i,\ \mu_j \ge 0. \qquad ...(vi)$$

The conditions number (*ii*) $\lambda_i s_i = 0$ and (*iii*) $\mu_j\, x_j = 0$ are called *complementary slackness conditions*. $\lambda_i s_i = \mu_j\, x_j = 0$ implies that the variables x_j, μ_j and s_i cannot become basic variables simultaneously. Other conditions (*i*), (*iv*), (*v*) and (*vi*) are nothing but linear programming constraints in 2 $(n + m)$ variables.

16.17 WOLF'S MODIFIED SIMPLEX METHOD

Wolf's method is an extension of the simplex method, where the two phase simplex method has been modified to solve the non-linear programming problem. The method comprises of following iterative steps:

Step 1: Convert the inequality constraints to equations by introducing slack variables s_i^2 and r_i^2 into constraints as discussed earlier.

Step 2: Form the Lagrange function and derive the Kuhn-Tucker conditions.

Step 3: Introduce the artificial variables A_j, $j = 1, 2, ..., n$ in the Kuhn-Tucker conditions and construct an objective function of the type, minimize $Z = \sum_{j=1}^{n} A_j$.

Step 4: Obtain an initial basic fessible solution to the problem

$$\text{minimize } Z = \sum_{j=1}^{n} A_j,$$

subject to the constraints

$$\sum_{k=1}^{n} x_k d_{jk} + \sum_{i=1}^{n} \lambda_i a_{ij} - \mu_j + A_j = C_j \, ; \, j = 1, 2, ..., n,$$

$$\sum_{i=1}^{n} a_{ij} x_j + s_i^2 = b_i \, ; \, i = 1, 2, ..., m,$$

$$\lambda_i, x_j, \mu_j, s_i, A_j \geq 0 \text{ for all } i \text{ and } j,$$

$$\left.\begin{array}{l} \lambda_i \, s_i = 0, \\ \mu_j \, x_j = 0. \end{array}\right\} \text{ complementary slackness conditions.}$$

Step 5: Apply *two-phase simplex method* to obtain the optimal solution to the above problem. This optimal solution is also the optimal solution to the given quadratic programming problem.

EXAMPLE 16.17-1

Use Wolf's method to solve the following quadratic programming problem:

$$\begin{array}{ll} \textit{Maximize} & Z = 2x_1 + x_2 - x_1^2, \\ \textit{subject to} & 2x_1 + 3x_2 \leq 6, \\ & 2x_1 + x_2 \leq 4, \\ & x_1, x_2 \geq 0. \end{array}$$

[Utkal M.Sc. (Math.) 1984]

Solution

Introducing slack variables, the problem takes the form:

$$\begin{array}{ll} \text{Maximize} & Z = 2x_1 + x_2 - x_1^2, \\ \text{subject to} & 2x_1 + 3x_2 + s_1^2 = 6, \\ & 2x_1 + x_2 + s_2^2 = 4, \\ & -x_1 + r_1^2 = 0, \\ & -x_2 + r_2^2 = 0. \end{array}$$

Now construct the Lagrange function:

$$L(x_1, x_2, s_1, s_2, r_1, r_2, \lambda_1, \lambda_2, \mu_1, \mu_2) = (2x_1 + x_2 - x_1^2)$$
$$- \lambda_1 (2x_1 + 3x_2 + s_1^2 - 6) - \lambda_2 (2x_1 + x_2 + s_2^2 - 4) - \mu_1 (-x_1 + r_1^2) - \mu_2(-x_2 + r_2^2).$$

The necessary and sufficient conditions for the maximization of L and hence of the objective function Z are as under:

$$\frac{\partial L}{\partial x_1} = 2 - 2x_1 - 2\lambda_1 - 2\lambda_2 + \mu_1 = 0, \quad ...(i)$$

$$\frac{\partial L}{\partial x_2} = 1 - 3\lambda_1 - \lambda_2 + \mu_2 = 0, \quad ...(ii)$$

$$\frac{\partial L}{\partial s_1} = -2\,\lambda_1 s_1 = 0, \quad ...(iii)$$

$$\frac{\partial L}{\partial s_2} = -2\,\lambda_2 s_2 = 0, \quad ...(iv)$$

$$\frac{\partial L}{\partial r_1} = -2\mu_1 r_1 = 0, \qquad \text{...}(v)$$

$$\frac{\partial L}{\partial r_2} = -2\mu_2 r_2 = 0, \qquad \text{...}(vi)$$

$$\frac{\partial L}{\partial \lambda_1} = 2x_1 + 3x_2 + s_1^2 - 6 = 0, \qquad \text{...}(vii)$$

$$\frac{\partial L}{\partial \lambda_2} = 2x_1 + x_2 + s_2^2 - 4 = 0, \qquad \text{...}(viii)$$

$$\frac{\partial L}{\partial \mu_1} = -x_1 + r_1^2 = 0, \qquad \text{...}(ix)$$

$$\frac{\partial L}{\partial \mu_2} = -x_2 + r_2^2 = 0. \qquad \text{...}(x)$$

On simplification, conditions (*i*), (*ii*), (*vi*) and (*vii*) result into the following equations:

$$\begin{aligned} 2x_1 + 2\lambda_1 + 2\lambda_2 - \mu_1 &= 2, \\ 3\lambda_1 + \lambda_2 - \mu_2 &= 1, \\ 2x_1 + 3x_2 + s_1^2 &= 6, \\ 2x_1 + x_2 + s_2^2 &= 4. \end{aligned}$$

On simplification of conditions (*iii*), (*iv*), (*v*), (*vi*) along with (*ix*) and (*x*), we get

$$\begin{aligned} \lambda_1 s_1 &= 0, \\ \lambda_2 s_2 &= 0, \\ \mu_1 r_1 &= 0 \text{ or } \mu_1 r_1^2 = 0. \end{aligned}$$

Since $\quad -x_1 + r_1^2 = 0$, hence $\mu_1 x_1 = 0$.

Similarly $\quad \mu_2 r_2 = 0$ or $\mu_2 x_2 = 0$.

or $$\left.\begin{aligned} \lambda_1 s_1 &= \lambda_2 s_2 = 0, \\ \mu_1 x_1 &= \mu_2 x_2 = 0. \end{aligned}\right\} \text{ complementary slackness conditions.}$$

And the non-negativity constraints can be expressed as

$$x_1, x_2, s_1^2, s_2^2, r_1^2, r_2^2, \lambda_1, \lambda_2, \mu_1, \mu_2 \geq 0.$$

The necessary and sufficient conditions, also called the Kuhn-Tucker conditions can be rewritten as

$$\begin{aligned} 2x_1 + 2\lambda_1 + 2\lambda_2 - \mu_1 &= 2, \\ 3\lambda_1 + \lambda_2 - \mu_2 &= 1, \\ 2x_1 + 3x_2 + s_1^2 &= 6, \\ 2x_1 + x_2 + s_2^2 &= 4, \\ \lambda_1 s_1 = \lambda_2 s_2 &= 0, \\ \mu_1 r_1 = \mu_2 r_2 &= 0, \end{aligned}$$

$$x_1, x_2, s_1^2, s_2^2, r_1^2, r_2^2, \lambda_1, \lambda_2, \mu_1, \mu_2 \geq 0.$$

Now we introduce artificial variables A_1 and A_2 in the first two constraints and replace s_1^2 and s_2^2 by s_1 and s_2 in the third and fourth constraints and construct the dummy objective function $Z = A_1 + A_2$. The problem, thus, reduces to the Linear Programming Problem:

Minimize $\quad Z = A_1 + A_2,$

subject to $\quad 2x_1 + 2\lambda_1 + 2\lambda_2 - \mu_1 + A_1 = 2,$

$\quad 3\lambda_1 + \lambda_2 - \mu_2 + A_2 = 1,$

$$2x_1 + 3x_2 + s_1 = 6,$$
$$2x_1 + x_2 + s_2 = 4,$$
$$x_1, x_2, s_1, s_2, \lambda_1, \lambda_2, \mu_1, \mu_2, A_1, A_2 \geq 0.$$

Substituting $x_1 = x_2 = \lambda_1 = \lambda_2 = \mu_1 = \mu_2 = 0$, the starting solution is $A_1 = 2, A_2 = 1, s_1 = 6$ and $s_2 = 4$.

The problem is now put in the form of a simplex table (Table 16.8).

TABLE 16.8

	C_j	0	0	0	0	0	0	0	0	1	1			
C_B	Basis	x_1	x_2	s_1	s_2	λ_1	λ_2	μ_1	μ_2	A_1	A_2	b	θ	
1	A_1	**(2)**	0	0	0	2	2	−1	0	1	0	2	1	→
1	A_2	0	0	0	0	3	1	0	−1	0	1	1	–	
0	s_1	2	3	1	0	0	0	0	0	0	0	6	3	
0	s_2	2	1	0	1	0	0	0	0	0	0	4	2	
$Z_j = \sum C_B a_{ij}$		2	0	0	0	5	3	−1	−1	1	1			
$C_j - Z_j$		−2	0	0	0	−5	−3	1	1	0	0			
		↑												

Here λ_1 has the largest negative $C_j - Z_j$ value and λ_2 has the second largest negative value, but none of these can be selected as the entering variable because of the complementary slackness conditions $\lambda_1 s_1$ and $\lambda_2 s_2 = 0$ and because s_1 and s_2 are in the current basic solution. Therefore, x_1 is selected as the entering variable.

To determine the leaving variable, elements in column b are divided by the corresponding co-efficients in the key column. The row containing the smallest positive quotient is called the key row and the corresponding basic variable becomes the leaving variable. Hence, A_1 in the leaving variable.

Replace A_1 by x_1 and perform the necessary tranformations to obtain the next table 16.9.

TABLE 16.9

	C_j	0	0	0	0	0	0	0	0	1			
C_B	Basis	x_1	x_2	s_1	s_2	λ_1	λ_2	μ_1	μ_2	A_2	b	θ	
0	x_1	1	0	0	0	1	1	$-\frac{1}{2}$	0	0	1	–	
1	A_2	0	0	0	0	3	1	0	−1	1	1	–	
0	s_1	0	**(3)**	1	0	−2	−2	1	0	0	4	$\frac{4}{3}$	→
0	s_2	0	1	0	1	−2	−2	1	0	0	2	2	
$Z_j = \sum C_B a_{ij}$		0	0	0	0	3	1	0	−1	1			
$C_j - Z_j$		0	0	0	0	−3	−1	0	1	0			
			↑										

Here again λ_1 or λ_2 cannot be selected as the entering variable because of the complementary conditions. Hence x_2 enters the basis. s_1 is the leaving variable.

Now replace s_1 by x_2 in the current basic solution and perform the necessary transformations to obtain the next table (Table 16.10).

TABLE 16.10

C_B	Basis	C_j: 0 x_1	0 x_2	0 s_1	0 s_2	0 λ_1	0 λ_2	0 μ_1	0 μ_2	1 A_2	b	θ	
0	x_1	1	0	0	0	1	1	$\frac{-1}{2}$	0	0	1	1	
1	A_2	0	0	0	0	(3)	1	0	–1	1	1	$\frac{1}{3}$	→
0	x_2	0	1	$\frac{1}{3}$	0	$-\frac{2}{3}$	$-\frac{2}{3}$	$\frac{1}{3}$	0	0	$\frac{4}{3}$	–2	
0	s_2	0	0	$-\frac{1}{3}$	1	$-\frac{4}{3}$	$-\frac{4}{3}$	$\frac{2}{3}$	0	0	$\frac{2}{3}$	$-\frac{1}{2}$	
	Z_j	0	0	0	0	3	1	0	–1	1			
	$C_j - Z_j$	0	0	0	0	–3	–1	0	1	0			
						↑							

Here λ_1 has the largest negative $C_j - Z_j$ value and since s_1 is not in the basis, λ_1 can be selected as the entering variable. Since smallest positive value of θ corresponds to A_2, variable A_2 becomes the leaving variable.

Replace A_2 by λ_1 in the current basic solution and perform the necessary transformations to obtain the next table (Table 16.11).

As all $Cj - Zj$ values are either positive or zero, the solution obtained in table 16.11. is optimal.

$$\therefore \quad x_1^* = \frac{2}{3},\ x_2^* = \frac{14}{9}, \quad \text{and} \quad Z_{max} = 2x_1 + x_2 - x_1^2$$

$$= 2 \times \frac{2}{3} + \frac{14}{9} - \frac{4}{9} = \frac{22}{9}.$$

TABLE 16.11

C_B	Basis	C_j: 0 x_1	0 x_2	0 s_1	0 s_2	0 λ_1	0 λ_2	0 μ_1	0 μ_2	1 A_2	b	θ
0	x_1	1	0	0	0	0	$\frac{2}{3}$	$-\frac{1}{2}$	$\frac{1}{3}$	$-\frac{1}{3}$	$\frac{2}{3}$	
0	λ_1	0	0	0	0	1	$\frac{1}{3}$	0	$-\frac{1}{3}$	$\frac{1}{3}$	$\frac{1}{3}$	
0	x_2	0	1	$\frac{1}{3}$	0	0	$-\frac{4}{9}$	$\frac{1}{3}$	$-\frac{2}{9}$	$\frac{2}{9}$	$\frac{14}{9}$	
0	s_2	0	0	$-\frac{1}{3}$	1	0	$-\frac{8}{9}$	$\frac{2}{3}$	$-\frac{4}{3}$	$\frac{4}{9}$	$\frac{10}{9}$	
	Z_j	0	0	0	0	0	0	0	0	0		
	$C_j – Z_j$	0	0	0	0	0	0	0	0	1		

EXAMPLE 16.17-2

Solve the following Q.P.P. using Wolf's method:

Maximize $\quad Z = 15x_1 + 30x_2 + 4x_1x_2 - 2x_1^2 - 4x_2^2,$

subject to $\quad x_1 + 2x_2 \leq 30,$

$\quad x_1, x_2 \geq 0.$

Solution

Consider non-negativity constraints x_1, $x_2 \geq 0$ as inequality constraints, and add slack variables to all the inequality constraints. The problem becomes

$$\begin{aligned} \text{maximize} \quad & Z = 15x_1 + 30x_2 + 4x_1x_2 - 2x_1^2 - 4x_2^2, \\ \text{subject to} \quad & x_1 + 2x_2 + s_1{}^2 = 30, \\ & -x_1 + r_1{}^2 = 0, \\ & -x_2 + r_2{}^2 = 0, \\ & x_1, x_2, s_1, r_1, r_2, \geq 0. \end{aligned}$$

Now construct the Lagrange function

$$\begin{aligned} L(x_1, x_2, s_1, \lambda_1, \mu_1, \mu_2, r_1, r_2) = {} & (15x_1 + 30x_2 + 4x_1x_2 - 2x_1^2 - 4x_2{}^2) \\ & - \lambda_1(x_1 + 2x_2 + s_1^2 - 30) - \mu_1(-x_1 + r_1^2) - \mu_2(-x_2 + r_2^2). \end{aligned}$$

The necessary and sufficient conditions for the maximization of L and hence of Z are:

$$\frac{\partial L}{\partial x_1} = 15 + 4x_2 - 4x_1 - \lambda_1 + \mu_1 = 0,$$

$$\frac{\partial L}{\partial x_2} = 30 + 4x_1 - 8x_2 - 2\lambda_1 + \mu_2 = 0,$$

$$\frac{\partial L}{\partial \lambda_1} = x_1 + 2x_2 + s_1^2 - 30 = 0,$$

$$\frac{\partial L}{\partial s_1} = 2\lambda_1 s_1 = 0,$$

$$\frac{\partial L}{\partial \mu_1} = -x_1 + r_1^2 = 0\,; \frac{\partial L}{\partial \mu_2} = -x_2 + r_2^2 = 0,$$

$$\frac{\partial L}{\partial r_1} = 2\mu_1 r_1 = 0\,; \frac{\partial L}{\partial r_2} = 2\mu_2 r_2 = 0.$$

After simplification of these equations, we get

$$\begin{aligned} & 4x_1 - 4x_2 + \lambda_1 - \mu_1 = 15, \\ & -4x_1 + 8x_2 + 2\lambda_1 - \mu_2 = 30, \\ & x_1 + 2x_2 + s_1^2 = 30, \\ & \left.\begin{aligned} & \lambda_1 s_1 = 0, \\ & \mu_1 x_1 = \mu_2 x_2 = 0, \end{aligned}\right\} \text{ complementary slackness conditions.} \\ & x_1, x_2, \lambda_1, \mu_1, \mu_2, s_1 \geq 0. \end{aligned}$$

Now introduce artificial variables A_1 and A_2 in the first two constraint equations and replace s_1^2 by S_1 in the third constraint equation. The modified LPP becomes

$$\text{minimize} \quad Z = A_1 + A_2,$$

subject to the constraints

$$\begin{aligned} & 4x_1 - 4x_2 + \lambda_1 - \mu_1 + A_1 = 15, \\ & -4x_1 + 8x_2 + 2\lambda_1 - \mu_2 + A_2 = 30, \\ & x_1 + 2x_2 + S_1 = 30, \\ & x_1, x_2, \lambda_1, \mu_1, \mu_2, A_1, A_2, S_1 \geq 0. \end{aligned}$$

The artificial variables A_1, A_2 and the slack variable S_1 can be taken as the initial basic feasible solution with $x_1 = x_2 = \lambda_1 = \lambda_2 = \mu_1 = \mu_2 = 0$, $A_1 = 15$, $A_2 = 30$ and $S_1 = 30$. The initial basic solution is now put in the tabular form (Table 16.12).

TABLE 16.12

C_B	Basis \ C_j	x_1 (0)	x_2 (0)	λ_1 (0)	μ_1 (0)	μ_2 (0)	S_1 (0)	A_1 (0)	A_2 (1)	b	θ	
1	A_1	4	–4	1	–1	0	0	1	0	15	–	
1	A_2	–4	(8)	2	0	–1	0	0	1	30	$\frac{15}{4}$	→
0	S_1	1	2	0	0	0	1	0	0	30	$\frac{15}{2}$	
	$Z_j = \sum C_B a_{ij}$	0	4	3	–1	–1	0	1	1			
	$C_j - Z_j$	0	–4 ↑	–3	1	1	0	0	0			

From above table x_2 in the entering variable and A_2 is the leaving variable. Hence replace A_2 by x_2 in the basis and perform the necessary transformations to obtain table 16.13.

TABLE 16.13

C_B	Basis \ C_j	x_1 (0)	x_2 (0)	λ_1 (0)	μ_1 (0)	μ_2 (0)	S_1 (0)	A_1 (1)	b	θ	
1	A_1	2	0	2	–1	$-\frac{1}{2}$	0	1	30	15	
0	x_2	$-\frac{1}{2}$	1	$\frac{1}{4}$	0	$-\frac{1}{8}$	0	0	$\frac{30}{8}$	–	
0	S_1	(2)	0	$-\frac{1}{2}$	0	$\frac{1}{4}$	1	0	$\frac{45}{2}$	$\frac{45}{4}$	→
	Zj	2	0	2	–1	$-\frac{1}{2}$	0	1			
	$C_j - Z_j$	–2 ↑	0	–2	1	$\frac{1}{2}$	0	0			

Replace the leaving variable S_1 by entering variable x_1 in the current basic solution and write the new table 16.14.

TABLE 16.14

C_B	Basis \ C_j	x_1 (0)	x_2 (0)	λ_1 (0)	μ_1 (0)	μ_2 (0)	S_1 (0)	A_1 (1)	b	θ	
1	A_1	0	0	$(\frac{5}{2})$	–1	$\frac{3}{4}$	–1	1	$\frac{15}{2}$	3	→
0	x_2	0	1	$\frac{1}{8}$	0	$\frac{3}{16}$	$\frac{1}{4}$	0	$\frac{75}{8}$	75	
0	x_1	1	0	$-\frac{1}{4}$	0	$\frac{1}{8}$	$\frac{1}{2}$	0	$\frac{45}{4}$	–	
	Z_j	0	0	$\frac{5}{2}$	–1	$\frac{3}{4}$	–1	1			
	$C_j - Z_j$	0	0	$-\frac{5}{2}$ ↑	1	$\frac{3}{4}$	1	0			

Replace A_1 by λ_1 in the basis and obtain table 16.15.

TABLE 16.15

C_B	Basis \ C_j	0 x_1	0 x_2	0 λ_1	0 μ_1	0 μ_2	0 S_1	b
0	λ_1	0	0	1	$-\frac{2}{5}$	$-\frac{3}{10}$	$-\frac{2}{5}$	3
0	x_2	0	1	0	$\frac{1}{20}$	$-\frac{3}{20}$	$-\frac{1}{5}$	9
0	x_1	1	0	0	$-\frac{1}{10}$	$\frac{1}{20}$	$-\frac{1}{20}$	12
	Z_j	0	0	0	0	0	0	
	$C_j - Z_j$	0	0	0	0	0	0	

Since all $C_j - Z_j$ values are zero, the solution obtained above is obtimal.

$\therefore \qquad x_1^* = 12,\ x_2^* = 9,$

and
$$Z_{max} = 15x_1 + 30x_2 + 4x_1x_2 - 2x_1^2 - 4x_2^2$$
$$= 180 + 270 + 432 - 288 - 324 = 270.$$

EXERCISES

1. Explain the following :
   (*i*) Meaning of local optimal point
   (*ii*) Significance of inflection point
   (*iii*) Common characteristics of gradient based methods
   (*iv*) Kuhn-Tucker conditions. [*P.T.U. B.Tech. (CH.) 2010, 2009*]
2. Differentiate between constrained and unconstrained problem with the help of an example. [*Bharathiar U. Coimbatore B.Sc. April, 2011; P.T.U. B.Tech. (CH.) 2009*]
3. Explain the Lagrange multiplier method of solving an NLPP with equality constraints. [*Bharathiar U. Coimbatore B.Sc. April, 2011*]
4. What is convex programming problem and what is its significance ? [*P.T.U. B.Tech. (CH.) 2009*]
5. Give the classification of optimization problems. [*P.T.U. B.Tech. (CH.) 2009*]
6. (*a*) Write short note on non-linear programming. [*IGNOU MBA June, 2007; Dec., 2006*]
   (*b*) M/s Gill Fabricators manufacture two products A and B. The manufacturing and raw mateiral costs of each of the products are proportional to square of the quantities produced. If x and y are the number of units produced of products A and B respectively, then the manufacturing and material costs are $2x^2$ and $3y^2$ respectively. It takes 40 minutes to machine product A and 30 minutes to machine product B, and the machining capacity available is 40 hours a week. One unit of product A requires 3 kg of raw material, while a unit of product B requires 5 kg of raw material and the raw material supply is limited to 300 kg per week. The unit selling price of products A and B is ₹ 250 and ₹ 650 respectively. Find how much of each product should be produced.
   Formulate the problem as a non-linear programming problem.
7. A manufacturing company makes two products P and Q. The demand of these products is related to their selling price. If p and q are the respective selling prices of products P and Q, then their demand is $(1{,}500 - 5p)$ and $(3{,}800 - 10q)$ units respectively. The production cost of the products is a function of their quantities produced. If x and y are the quantities of products P and Q produced each day, then their total production costs are $(200x + 0.1x^2)$ and $(300y + 0.1y^2)$ respectively. Because of the limitations on the processing capacity, the daily production of P cannot be more than 80 units and that of Q cannot be more than 60 units. The production of one unit of P requires 2 man-days while that of Q requires 3 man-days, and total man-days available are 250 per day. It is required to determine the number of units of P and Q which should be produced in order to maximize the total profit. Formulate the problem as a non-linear programming problem.

8. An engineering company has received an order for two product A and B, which are to be produced and supplied within one month. The total profit from these products is a non-linear function of the number of units of each product, which are supplied within the stipulated period.

$$\text{Total profit} = 10x_1 + 12x_2 - x_1^2 - x_2^2 + 80,$$

where x_1 and x_2 are the number of units of products A and B respectively.
Because of other commitments, the company has available only 300 hours for manufacturing these products. It is entimated that each unit of product A will require 30 hours, while each unit of product B will require 20 hours. The company management wants to know the number of units of each product which it should produce in order to maximize the profit.
Formulate this problem as an NLPP model.

9. M/s Sohan Lal and Sons sell two types of items, A and B. On item A, there is no quantity discount and it is sold at fixed price of ₹ 250 per unit. There is quantity discount on item B. Its price decreases as the number of units ordered increases. The sale revenue is a non-linear function of the number of units sold.
Sales revenue of product B = $(40 - 0.40\, x_2)\, x_2$, where x_2 is the number of units sold.
The marketing department has only 1,500 hours available for selling these items in the next year. Further, the company estimates the sales time function as,

$$\text{sales time} = x_1 + 0.3x_1^2 + 3x_2 + 0.5x_2^2.$$

The company can procure a maximum of 6,000 units of the two products combined. How many units of each item should the company procure in order to maximize its revenue ?
Formulate the mathematical model of the problem.

10. For each of the following functions, verify whether it is convex, concave or neither:
(*i*) $f(x) = 6 - x^2$
(*ii*) $f(x) = x^4 + 2x^2 - 2x$
(*iii*) $f(x) = 4x^3 - 3x^2$
(*iv*) $f(x) = 2x^3 + x^2$
(*v*) $f(x) = 2x^3 - x^2$.

11. For each of the following functions, show whether it is convex, concave or neither:
(*i*) $f(X) = 2x_1x_2 - 2x_1^2 - x_2^2$
(*ii*) $f(X) = x_1^2 + 3x_1x_2 + 3x_2^2$
(*iii*) $f(X) = 10x_1 - 15x_2$
(*iv*) $f(X) = 2x_1 + 3x_1^2 + 4x_2 + 2x_2^2 - 4x_1x_2$
(*v*) $f(X) = 2x_1x_2$.

12. Verify whether the following functions are convex or concave:
(*a*) $f(X) = 7x_1^2 + 10x_2^2 + 7x_3^2 - 4x_1x_2 + 2x_1x_3 - 4x_2x_3$
(*b*) $f(X) = 7x_1^2 + 4x_2 + x_1x_2 - x_1^2 - x_2^2$
(*c*) $f(X) = 2x_1^3 - 6x_2^2$
(*d*) $f(X) = 2x_1^2 + 2x_1x_2 + 1.5x_2^2 + 7x_1 + 8x_2 + 24.$ [*P.T.U. B.Tech. (CH.) 2009*]

13. Determine the relative maximum or minimum value (if any) of the function:

$$f(X) = 12x^5 - 45x^4 + 40x^3 + 5.$$

14. Consider the function

$$f(X) = 6x_1^2 + x_2^3 + 6x_1x_2 + 3x_2^2.$$

Find the stationary points and classify them using the Hessian matrix. [*P.T.U. B.Tech. (CH.) 2009*]

15. Determine the relative maximum or minimum value (if any) of the following function:

$$f(X) = x_1 + 2x_2 + x_1x_2 - x_1^2 - x_2^2.$$

16. Consider the following function:

$$f(X) = 48x - 60x^2 + x^3.$$

Determine the relative maxima and minima and show that this function has neither a global maximum nor a global minimum.

17. Find the relative maximum, minimum or saddle point (if any) for the function,

$$f(x_1, x_2, x_3) = x_1^3 + x_2^3 - 3x_1 - 12x_2 + 25.$$ [*Madurai B.E. (Elect.) 1990*]

18. Determine the maximum or minimum (if any) of the following functions:

(*a*) $f(X) = x_1^2 + 2x_2^2 + x_3^2 + x_1x_2 - 2x_2 - 7x_1 + 12$ (*Ans.* Relative minimum at $(x_1, x_2, x_3) = (4, -1, 1.)$)

(*b*) $f(X) = -x_1^2 - 2x_2 - x_2^2 - 2x_1x_2$ (*Ans.* Relative maximum at $x_1 = x_2 = x_3 = 0.$)

(*c*) $f(X) = x_1x_2 + 10x_1 - x_1^2 - x_2^2 - x_3^2$.

19. Solve the following NLPP by using the Lagrangian multipliers method:

(*a*) Maximize $Z = 10x_1 + 4x_2 - x_1^2 + 4x_1x_2 - 5x_2^2$,

subject to $x_1 + x_2 = 0$,

$x_1, x_2 \geq 0$. $\left(Ans.\ x_1 = \frac{9}{2}, x_2 = \frac{3}{2}.\right)$

(*b*) Maximize $Z = 6x_1x_2$,

subject to $2x_1 + x_2 = 10$,

$x_1, x_2 \geq 0$. (*Ans.* $x_1 = 2.5, x_2 = 5.$)

(*c*) Minimize $Z = 2x_1^2 - 24x_1 + 2x_2^2 - 8x_2 + 2x_3^2 - 12x_3$,

subject to $x_1 + x_2 + x_3 = 1$,

$x_1, x_2, x_3 \geq 0$.

20. Minimize $Z = 3x_1^2 + x_2^2 + x_3^2$,

subject to $x_1 + x_2 + x_3 = 2$,

$x_1, x_2, x_3 \geq 0$. [*Bharathiar U. Coimbatore B.Sc. April, 2011*]

21. Solve the following NLPP. Is the solution a maxima or a minima ?

(*a*) Optimize $Z = 6x_1x_2 - 10x_3$,

subject to $2x_1 + x_2 + 3x_3 = 10$,

$x_1, x_2, x_3 \geq 0$.

(*b*) Optimize $Z = x_1^2 - 10x_1 + x_2^2 - 6x_2 + x_3^2 - 4x_3$,

subject to $x_1 + x_2 + x_3 = 7$,

$x_1, x_2, x_3 \geq 0$. (*Ans.* $(x_1, x_2, x_3) = (4, 2, 1)$, $Z_{min} = -35.$)

(*c*) Optimize $Z = 4x_1 + 9x_2 - x_1^2 - x_2^2$,

subject to $4x_1 + 3x_2 = 15$,

$3x_1 + 5x_2 = 14$,

$x_1, x_2 \geq 0$. (*Ans.* $x_1 = 3, x_2 = 1.$)

(*d*) Optimize $Z = 4x_1 + 2x_2^2 + x_3^2 - 4x_1x_2$,

subject to $x_1 + x_2 + x_3 = 15$,

$2x_1 - x_2 + 2x_3 = 20$,

$x_1, x_2, x_3 \geq 0$.

(*Ans.* $x_1 = \frac{11}{3}$, $x_2 = \frac{10}{3}$, $x_3 = 8$, $Z_{min} = 52.$)

22. Solve the following NLPP, showing the necessary and sufficient conditions:

Minimize $Z = 3x_1^2 + x_2^2 + 2x_1x_2 + 6x_1 + 2x_2$,

subject to $2x_2 - x_2 = 4$,

$x_1, x_2 > 0$. (*Ans.* $x_1 = 1, x_2 = -2$, $Z_{min} = 5.$)

23. Maximize $f(x_1, x_2) = 3x_1^2 + x_2^2 + 2x_1x_2 + 6x_1 + 2x_2$,

subject to the constraints $2x_1 - x_2 = 4$,

$x_1, x_2 \geq 0$.

Use the Lagrangian multiplier method. (*Ans.* $(x_1, x_2) = (1, 2)$; Max $f(x_1, x_2) = 5.$)

24. Maximize $Z = 3.6x_1 - 0.4x_1^2 + 1.6x_2 - 0.2x_2^2$,

subject to $2x_1 + x_2 = 0$,

$x_1, x_2 \geq 0$. [*Dibrugarh M.Sc (Math.) 1991*]

(*Ans.* $x_1 = 3.5, x_2 = 3.$)

25. Solve the following NLPP by the method of Lagrange multiplier:

Minimize $Z = x_1^2 + (x_2 + 1)^2 + (x_3 - 1)^2$,

subject to $x_1 + 5x_2 - 3x_3 = 6$,

$x_1, x_2 \geq 0$.

Show the necessary and sufficient conditions for the solution to be a minima.

$$\left(Ans. (x_1, x_2, x_3) = \left(\frac{2}{5}, 1, -\frac{1}{5}\right), Z_{min} = \frac{28}{5}.\right)$$

26. Solve the following NLPP, clearly showing the necessary and sufficient conditions:

Maximize $Z = 8x_1 + 10x_2 - x_1^2 - x_2^2$,

subject to $3x_1 + 2x_2 \leq 6$,

$x_1, x_2 \geq 0$.

27. Solve the following NLPP and show the necessary and sufficient conditions:

Maximize $Z = 7x_1^2 + 6x_1 + 5x_2^2$,

subject to $x_1 + 2x_2 \leq 10$,

$x_1 - 3x_2 \leq 9$,

$x_1, x_2 \geq 0$.

28. Find the values of x_1 and x_2 for (*a*) maximization of Z (*b*) minimization of Z, when

$Z = (x_1 - 2)^2 + (x_2 - 1)^2$,

subject to $x_1 \leq 2$ and $x_2 \leq 1$,

$x_1, x_2 \geq 0$.

29. Obtain the necessary and sufficient conditions for the optimum solution of the following NLPP:

Minimize $Z = f(x_1, x_2) = 3e^{2x_1+1} + 2e^{x_2+5}$,

subject to $x_1 + x_2 = 7$,

$x_1, x_2 \geq 0$.

$$\left(Ans.\ x_1 = \frac{1}{3}(11 - \log 3);\ x_2 = \frac{1}{3}(10 + \log 3).\right)$$

30. Find the solution of the following problem:

Minimize $f(x, y) = k\,x^{-1}\,y^{-2}$,

subject to $x^2 + y^2 = a^2$,

$x, y \geq 0$.

$$\left(Ans.\ x = \frac{1}{\sqrt{3}}a,\ y = \frac{\sqrt{2}}{\sqrt{3}}a.\right)$$

31. Obtain the set of necessary conditions for the following non-linear programming problem:

$Z = x_1^2 + 3x_2^2 + 5x_3^2$,

subject to $x_1 + x_2 + 3x_3 = 0$,

$5x_1 + 2x_2 + x_3 = 5$,

$x_1, x_2, x_3 \geq 0$

[*Delhi M.sc. (Math.) 1973*]

32. Use the method of Lagrangian multipliers to solve the following:

(*a*) Minimize $Z = 2x_1^2 + x_2 + 3x_3^2 + 10x_1 + 8x_2 + 6x_3 - 100$,

subject to $x_1 + x_2 + x_3 = 20$,

$x_1, x_2, x_3 \geq 0$.

[*Chennai B.Sc. (Math.) 1981*]

$$(Ans. (x_1, x_2, x_3) = (5, 11, 4); Z_{min} = 281.)$$

(*b*) Maximize $Z = 6x_1 + 8x_2 - x_1^2 - x_2^2$,

subject to $4x_1 + 3x_2 = 16$,

$3x_1 + 5x_2 = 15$,

$x_1, x_2 \geq 0$.

$$\left(Ans. (x_1, x_2) = \left(\frac{35}{11}, \frac{12}{11}\right)\right)$$

(*c*) Maximize $Z = -x_1^2 - x_2^2 - x_3^2 + 4x_1 + 6x_2$,

subject to $x_1 + x_2 \leq 2$,

$2x_1 + 3x_2 \leq 12$,

$x_1, x_2 \geq 0$.

[*Karnatka B.E (Mech.) 1984; IAS, 1992*]

$$\left(Ans.\ x_1 = \frac{1}{2}, x_2 = \frac{3}{2}, x_3 = 0; Z_{max} = 8.5.\right)$$

33. Maximize $Z = 12x_1 + 21x_2 + 2x_1x_2 - 2x_1^2 - 2x_2^2,$
subject to $x_2 \leq 8,$
$x_1 + x_2 \leq 10,$
$x_1, x_2 \geq 0.$ *[Bharathiar U. Coimbatore B.Sc. April, 2011]*

34. Write the Kuhn-Tucker conditions for the following problems and obtain the optimal solution.

(*a*) Minimize $Z = 2x_1 + 3x_2 - x_1^2 - 2x_2^2,$
subject to $x_1 + 3x_2 \leq 6,$
$5x_1 + 2x_2 \leq 10,$
$x_1, x_2 \geq 0.$ *[R.U.M.Sc. (Math.) 2011; B.P.U.T. 2011]*

$$\left(\textit{Ans. } x_1 = \frac{2}{3}, x_2 = \frac{14}{9}; Z_{\min} = \frac{22}{9}.\right)$$

(*b*) Minimize $Z = x_1^2 + x_2^2,$
subject to $x_1 + x_2 \geq 4,$
$2x_1 + x_2 \geq 5,$
$x_1, x_2 \geq 0.$

35. Solve the following NLPP graphically:

(*i*) Maximize $Z = x_1,$
subject to $(3 - x_1)^2 - (x_2 - 2) \geq 0,$
$(3 - x_1)^2 + (x_2 - 2) \geq 0,$
$x_1 x_2 \geq 0.$

(*ii*) Maximize $Z = x_1,$
subject to $(1 - x_1)^2 - x_2 \geq 0,$
$x_1, x_2 \geq 0.$

Also show that Kuhn–Tucker conditions for maxima do not hold. What do you conclude ?

36. Solve the following NLPP graphically:

(*i*) Maximize $Z = 100x_1 - x_1^2 + 100x_2 - x_2^2,$
subject to $x_1 + x_2 \geq 80,$
$x_1 + x_2 \leq 100,$
$x_1, x_2 \geq 0.$

(*ii*) Maximize $Z = x_1 + 2x_2^2,$
subject to $x_1^2 + x_2^2 \leq 1,$
$2x_1 + x_2 \leq 2,$
$x_1, x_2 \geq 0.$

(*iii*) Minimize $Z = (x_1 - 2)^2 + (x_2 - 1)^2,$
subject to $-x_1 + x_2 \geq 0,$
$x_1 + x_2 \leq 2,$
$x_1, x_2 \geq 0.$

37. Solve the following non-linear programming problem graphically:

Maximize $f(X) = 3x_1 + 5x_2,$
subject to $x_1 \leq 4,$
$9x_1^2 + 5x_2^2 \leq 216,$
$x_1, x_2 \geq 0.$

38. Solve graphically the following NLPP:

Maximize $Z = 8x_1 - x_1^2 + 8x_2 - x_2^2,$
subject to $x_1 + x_2 \leq 12,$
$x_1 - x_2 = 4,$
$x_1, x_2 \geq 0.$

39. Solve the following NLPP graphically:

(*i*) Maximize $Z = 126x_1 - 9x_1^2 + 182x_2 - 13x_2^2$,

subject to the constraints $x_1 \le 4$,

$2x_2 \le 12$,

$3x_1 + 2x_2 \le 8$,

$x_1, x_2 \ge 0$.

(*ii*) Solve the above problem when the objective function is replaced by

Maximize $Z = 54x_1 - 9x_1^2 + 78x_2 - 13x_2^2$.

What is the difference between the two problems ?

40. Use the one-dimensional search procedure to interactively solve (approximately) the following problem:

Maximize $f(x) = 12x - 3x^4 - 2x^6$.

The initial bounds may be taken as $\underline{x} = 0$ and $\overline{x} = 2$ and the error to tolerance $\in = 0.02$.

41. Use the one-dimensional search procedure to interactively solve (approximately) the following problem:

Minimize $f(x) = 6x + 7x^2 + 4x^3 + x^4$.

Take the initial bounds $\underline{x} = -4$ and $\overline{x} = 1$ and $\in = 0.05$.

42. Taking the initial bound as $\underline{x} = -1$ and $\overline{x} = 4$ and the error tolerance $\in = 0.08$, solve the following NLPP using the one-dimensional search procedure:

Maximize $Z = 48x^5 + 42x^3 + 3.5x - 16x^6 - 61x^4 - 16.5x^2$.

43. Perform four iterations of the one-dimensional search procedure for solving the following problem:

$$f(x) = x^3 + 30x - x^6 - 2x^4 - 3x^2.$$

Find the initial bounds by inspection of the function.

44. Solve the following problem using the gradient search procedure:

Maximize $f(X) = 4x_1x_2 - 2x_1^2 - 3x_2^2$.

Take the initial trial solution $(x_1, x_2) = (1, 1)$ and the tolerance error $\in = 0.02$.

45. Solve the following two-variable NLPP using the gradient search procedure. The starting solution may be taken as $(x_1, x_2) = (0, 0)$ and error of tolerance $\in = 0.05$.

$$f(X) = 4x_1 - x_1^2 - 5x_2 - x_2^2 + x_1x_2.$$

Also obtain the exact solution by solving $\nabla f(X) = 0$.

46. Solve the following NLPP by employing the gradient search procedure. Taking initial solution $(x_1, x_2) = (0, 0)$, show three iterations. Also obtain the exact solution by solving $\nabla f(X) = 0$.

$$f(X) = 6x_1 + 2x_1x_2 - 2x_2 - x_1^2 - x_2^2.$$

47. Solve the following NLPP by the gradient search procedure, taking the initial trial solution $(x_1, x_2) = (0, 0)$ and error tolerance $\in = 1$.

$$f(X) = x_1^2 x_2^2 + 2x_1^2 + 2x_2^2 - 4x_1 + 4x_2.$$

48. Consider the following quadratic programming problem:

Maximize $f(X) = 8x_1 - x_1^2 + 4x_2 - x_2^2$,

subject to $x_1 + x_2 \le 2$ and $x_1, x_2 \ge 0$.

(*a*) Use the Kuhn-Tucker conditions to determine the optimal solution.

(*b*) Use Wolf's modified simplex method to solve the problem.

49. Use Wolf's method for solving the following quadratic programming problems:

(*a*) Maximize $f(x_1, x_2) = 2x_1 + 3x_2 - 2x_1^2$,

subject to $x_1 + 4x_2 \le 4$,

$x_1 + x_2 \le 2$

$x_1, x_2 \ge 0$.

[*Kuru U. B.E. (Mech.) June, 2012*]

$\left(Ans.\ x_1 = \dfrac{5}{16}, x_2 = \dfrac{59}{64};\ \text{max } Z = 3.19. \right)$

(*b*) Maximize $Z = 6 - 6x_1 + 2x_1^2 - 2x_1x_2 + 2x_2^2,$
subject to $x_1 + x_2 \leq 2,$
$x_1, x_2 \geq 0.$ [*R.U. M.Sc. (Math.) 2011*]

$$\left(Ans.\ x_1 = \frac{3}{2},\ x_2 = \frac{1}{2};\ \max Z = \frac{1}{2}.\right)$$

(*c*) Maximize $Z = 4x_1 + 6x_2 - 2x_1^2 - 2x_1x_2 - 2x_2^2,$
subject to $x_1 + 2x_2 \leq 2,$
$x_1, x_2 \geq 0.$ [*I.A.S 1994, Anna. U. B.E. (Prod.) 1982*]

$$\left(Ans.\ x_1 = \frac{1}{3},\ x_2 = \frac{5}{6};\ Z_{\max} = \frac{25}{6}.\right)$$

(*d*) Maximize $Z = 1.8x_1 + 3x_2 - 0.001x_1^2 - 0.005x_2^2 - 100,$
subject to $2x_1 + 3x_2 \leq 2500,$
$x_1 + 2x_2 \leq 1500,$
$x_1, x_2 \geq 0.$ [*Bharthiar M.E.(Elect.) 1981*]

($Ans.\ x_1 = 500,\ x_2 = 500;\ Z_{max} = 800.$)

50. Consider the following convex programming problem:
Maximize $f(X) = 10x_1 - 2x_1^2 - x_1^3 + 8x_2 - x_2^2,$
subject to $x_1 + x_2 \leq 2,$
$x_1, x_2 \geq 0.$

Use the Kuhn-Tucker conditions to demonstrate that $(x_1, x_2) = (1, 1)$ is not an optimal solution. Use the Kuhn-Tucker conditions to determine the optimal solution.

51. Solve the following quadratic programming problem by Wolf's modified simplex method:
Maximize $f(X) = 20x_1 - 20x_1^2 + 50x_2 - 5x_2^2 + 18x_1x_2,$
subject to $x_1 + x_2 \leq 6,$
$x_1 + 4x_2 \leq 18,$
$x_1, x_2 \geq 0.$

52. Consider the following quadratic programming problem:
Maximize $Z = 2x_1 + 3x_2 - x_1^2 - x_2^2,$
subject to $x_1 + x_2 \leq 2,$
$x_1, x_2 \geq 0.$

(*a*) Use the Kuhn-Tucker conditions to derive an optimal solution.
(*b*) Solve the problem by Wolf's modified simplex method.

53. Find the dimensions of a cylindrical tin (with top and bottom) made up of sheet to maximize its volume, such that the total surface area is equal to $A_0 = 24\pi$. [*M.E. Anna.U., 2004*]

54. The relationship between sales S and the amounts *x* and *y* spent on two advertising media is given by

$$S = \frac{200x}{(5+x)} + \frac{100y}{(10+y)}.$$

The net profit is $\frac{1}{5}$ of the sales minus the cost of advertising. The advertising budget has a maximum of 20 monetary units. Determine how it should be allocated between the two media to maximize the net profit, using Kuhn-Tucker conditions. [*M.E. (S.E.) Anna. U., 2004*]

APPENDICES

REVIEW OF VECTORS AND MATRICES

A-1 VECTORS

A.1-1 Definition

A vector is an ordered set of real numbers. Let $a_1, a_2, ..., a_n$ be any n real numbers called *elements* or *components*, then

$$\mathbf{a} = (a_1, a_2, ..., a_n),$$

where **a** is called an n-vector (or simply a vector). Generally, a *row* vector is written as $(a_1, a_2, .., a_n)$, while a column vector is written as

$$\begin{pmatrix} a_1 \\ a_2 \\ \vdots \\ a_n \end{pmatrix}.$$

The vector $\mathbf{0} = (0, 0, ..., 0)$ is called the *null* vector.

A.1-2 Addition (Subtraction) of Vectors

Let $\mathbf{a} = (a_1, a_2, ..., a_n)$ and $\mathbf{b} = (b_1, b_2, ..., b_n)$ be two vectors in the n-dimensional space. Then

$$\left.\begin{array}{l}\mathbf{a} + \mathbf{b} = \mathbf{c} = (a_1 + b_1, a_2 + b_2, ..., a_n + b_n), \\ \mathbf{a} - \mathbf{b} = \mathbf{d} = (a_1 - b_1, a_2 - b_2, ..., a_n - b_n),\end{array}\right] \quad \text{(commutative law)}$$

$$(\mathbf{a} + \mathbf{b}) + \mathbf{e} = \mathbf{a} + (\mathbf{b} + \mathbf{e}), \quad \text{(associative law)}$$

$$\mathbf{a} + (-\mathbf{a}) = \mathbf{0}. \quad \text{(zero or null vector)}$$

A.1-3 Multiplication of Vectors by Scalars

Given an n-vector **a** and a scalar (constant) quantity α, the new vector

$$f = \alpha\mathbf{a} = \alpha\ (a_1, a_2, ..., a_n)$$
$$= (\alpha\ a_1, \alpha\ a_2, ..., \alpha\ a_n)$$

is called the *scalar product* of **a** and α.

In general, given the n-vectors **a** and **b** and the scalars α and β,

$$\alpha\ (\mathbf{a} + \mathbf{b}) = \alpha\mathbf{a} + \alpha\mathbf{b}, \quad \text{(distributive law)}$$
$$\alpha\ (\beta\mathbf{a}) = (\alpha\beta)\ \mathbf{a}. \quad \text{(associative law)}$$

A.1-4 Inner Product of Vectors

The inner product of two n-vectors **a** and **b** is the scalar (number) written as **a.b** or simply **ab** and is given by

$$a_1 b_1 + a_2 b_2 + ... + a_n\ b_n.$$

For example, if $\mathbf{a} = (2, 3, 4)$ and

$$\mathbf{b} = \begin{pmatrix} 1 \\ 5 \\ 6 \end{pmatrix}, \text{ then } \mathbf{a} \cdot \mathbf{b} = 2 + 15 + 24 = 41.$$

A.1-5 Linearly Dependent and Independent Vectors

A set of vectors $\mathbf{a}_1, \mathbf{a}_2, ..., \mathbf{a}_n$, is *linearly dependent* if there exist scalars $\alpha_1, \alpha_2, ..., \alpha_n$, not all zero, such that

$$\sum_{i=1}^{n} \alpha_i \mathbf{a}_i = 0$$

or $$\alpha_1 \mathbf{a}_1 + \alpha_2 \mathbf{a}_2 + ... + \alpha_n \mathbf{a}_n = 0.$$

In this case, at least one vector can be written as a *linear combination* of the others. For example,

$$\mathbf{a}_1 = k_2\mathbf{a}_2 + k_3\mathbf{a}_3 + ... + k_n\mathbf{a}_n.$$

If $$\sum_{i=1}^{n} \alpha_i \mathbf{a}_i = 0$$

only if all $\alpha_i = 0$, then the given set of vectors $\mathbf{a}_1, \mathbf{a}_2, ..., \mathbf{a}_n$ is said to be *linearly independent.*

For example, the vectors

$$\mathbf{a}_1 = (2, 3, 4) \text{ and } \mathbf{a}_2 = (6, 9, 12)$$

are linearly dependent since there exist $\alpha_1 = 3$ and $\alpha_2 = -1$ for which

$$\alpha_1\mathbf{a}_1 + \alpha_2 \mathbf{a}_2 = 0.$$

If a set of vectors is linearly independent, any subset of it is also linearly independent. For a linearly dependent set of vectors, its super set is also linearly dependent.

A.1-6 Equality (Inequality) of Vectors

Let $\mathbf{a} = (a_1, a_2, ..., a_n)$ and $\mathbf{b} = (b_1, b_2, ..., b_n)$ be the two n-vectors. Then

$\mathbf{a} = \mathbf{b}$ if $a_i = b_i$, for all $i = 1, 2, ..., n$,

$\mathbf{a} > \mathbf{b}$ if $a_i > b_i$, for all $i = 1, 2, ..., n$,

$\mathbf{a} < \mathbf{b}$ if $a_i < b_i$, for all $i = 1, 2, ..., n$,

$\mathbf{a} \geq 0$ implies that $a_i \geq 0$, for all $i = 1, 2, ..., n$ *i.e.*, each component of vector **a** is non-negative.

A.1-7 Identity (Unit) Vector

An identity vector $\mathbf{e}_i$ is a vector with its ith component unity and all other components zero. For example,

$$\mathbf{e}_1 = (1, 0, 0, ..., 0),$$
$$\mathbf{e}_2 = (0, 1, 0, ..., 0),$$
$$\mathbf{e}_i = (0, 0, ..., 1, ..., 0),$$
$$\mathbf{e}_n = (0, 0, ..., 1).$$

A.1-8 Euclidean Space

Euclidean n-space, also called *vector space* is the set (collection) of all n-vectors and is denoted by **v**.

A.1-9 Basis Set

A set of vectors is said to *span* a vector space **v** if every vector of **v** can be expressed as a linear combination of the vectors in the set. A *basis set* for the vector space **v** is a set of linearly independent vectors that spans **v**.

A-2 MATRICES

A.2-1 Definition

A *matrix* **A** of size $(m \times n)$ is a rectangular array (table) of numbers arranged in m rows and n columns. Thus

$$\mathbf{A} = \begin{pmatrix} a_{11} & a_{12} & \dots & a_{1n} \\ a_{21} & a_{22} & \dots & a_{2n} \\ \vdots & \vdots & & \vdots \\ a_{m1} & a_{m2} & \dots & a_{mn} \end{pmatrix}$$

The (i, j)th element of **A**, denoted by a_{ij}, is the element in the ith row and jth column of **A**. A matrix of size or order $(m \times n)$ is written as

$$\mathbf{A}_{(m \times n)} \text{ or } [a_{ij}]_{m \times n} \text{ or simply } [a_{ij}].$$

The elements a_{ij}, for $i = j$ are called *diagonal* elements, while the a_{ij} for $i \neq j$ are called *off-diagonal* elements.

A.2-2 Types of Matrices

Square matrix : is a matrix in which $m = n$.

Diagonal matrix : is a square matrix in which $a_{ij} = 0$ for $i \neq j$ *i.e.*, in which off-diagonal elements are all zero.

Identity (*Unit*) *matrix* : is a square matrix in which diagonal elements are all unity and off-diagonal elements are all zero; that is,

$$a_{ij} = 1, \text{ for } i = j,$$
$$a_{ij} = 0, \text{ for } i \neq j.$$

An identity matrix of order n is denoted by $\mathbf{I}_n$ or simply **I**. For example, for $n = 3$, we have

$$\mathbf{I}_3 = \begin{pmatrix} 1 & 0 & 0 \\ 0 & 1 & 0 \\ 0 & 0 & 1 \end{pmatrix}.$$

Row vector : Elements of each row of a matrix define a vector called a *row vector*. Thus a row vector is a matrix with one row and n columns $(1 \times n$ matrix).

Column vector : Elements of each column of a matrix define a vector called a *column vector*. Thus a column vector is a matrix with m rows and one column $(m \times 1$ matrix).

Null matrix : is a matrix whose elements are all zero.

Transpose of matrix : The transpose of matrix $\mathbf{A} = [a_{ij}]$, denoted by $\mathbf{A}'$ or $\mathbf{A}^T$ is a matrix obtained by interchanging the rows and columns of **A**. In other words, the element a_{ij} in **A** is equal to the element a_{ji} in $\mathbf{A}^T$ for all i and j.

For example, if

$$\mathbf{A} = \begin{pmatrix} 1 & 2 & 3 \\ 4 & 5 & 6 \end{pmatrix}, \text{ then } \mathbf{A}^T = \begin{pmatrix} 1 & 4 \\ 2 & 5 \\ 3 & 6 \end{pmatrix}.$$

Thus if **A** is of order $(m \times n)$, $\mathbf{A}^T$ will be of order $(n \times m)$.

Symmetric matrix : The matrix **A** is said to be symmetric if $\mathbf{A}^T = \mathbf{A}$ *i.e.*, if $a_{ij} = a_{ji}$ for all i and j.

Equal matrices : Two matrices $\mathbf{A} = [a_{ij}]$ and $\mathbf{B} = [b_{ij}]$ are said to be equal matrices if they have the same order and each $a_{ij} = b_{ij}$ for all i and j.

Orthogonal matrix : A square matrix **A** is said to be *orthogonal* if

$$\mathbf{A}\mathbf{A}^T = \mathbf{A}^T\mathbf{A} = \mathbf{I}.$$

A.2-3 Addition (Subtraction) of Matrices

The *sum* or *difference* of two matrices **A** and **B** of the same order is matrix **C** (written as **C** = **A** ± **B**) where the elements of **C** are given by

$$c_{ij} = a_{ij} \pm b_{ij}.$$

The following are the examples of matrix addition and subtraction :

Addition

Matrix **A** + Matrix **B** = Matrix **C**

$$\begin{pmatrix} 1 & 2 & 3 \\ 4 & 5 & 6 \end{pmatrix} + \begin{pmatrix} 7 & 8 & 9 \\ 10 & 11 & 12 \end{pmatrix} = \begin{pmatrix} 8 & 10 & 12 \\ 14 & 16 & 18 \end{pmatrix},$$

$$\begin{pmatrix} 2 & 5 & -3 \\ 1 & -6 & 4 \end{pmatrix} + \begin{pmatrix} 1 & 3 & -7 \\ 2 & 9 & -3 \end{pmatrix} = \begin{pmatrix} 3 & 8 & -10 \\ 3 & 3 & 1 \end{pmatrix}.$$

Subtraction

Matrix **A** − Matrix **B** = Matrix **C**

$$\begin{pmatrix} 6 & 5 & 7 \\ 2 & 1 & 8 \end{pmatrix} + \begin{pmatrix} 2 & 5 & 9 \\ 1 & 4 & 6 \end{pmatrix} = \begin{pmatrix} 4 & 0 & -2 \\ 1 & -3 & 2 \end{pmatrix},$$

$$\begin{pmatrix} 1 & -4 & 10 \\ 2 & -3 & -7 \end{pmatrix} - \begin{pmatrix} -1 & 5 & 9 \\ -1 & -2 & 4 \end{pmatrix} = \begin{pmatrix} 2 & -9 & 1 \\ 3 & -1 & -11 \end{pmatrix}.$$

If matrices **A**, **B** and **C** are of the same order, then

$$\mathbf{A} + \mathbf{B} = \mathbf{B} + \mathbf{A}, \qquad \text{(commutative law)}$$

$$\mathbf{A} \pm (\mathbf{B} \pm \mathbf{C}) = (\mathbf{A} \pm \mathbf{B}) \pm \mathbf{C}, \qquad \text{(associative law)}$$

$$\mathbf{A} + (-\mathbf{A}) = 0 = (-\mathbf{A}) + \mathbf{A},$$

$$\alpha\,(\mathbf{A} \pm \mathbf{B}) = \alpha\,\mathbf{A} \pm \alpha\,\mathbf{B},$$

$$\alpha\,(\beta\,\mathbf{A}) = \beta\,(\alpha\,\mathbf{A}) = (\alpha\,\beta)\,\mathbf{A}.$$

A. 2-4 Product of Matrices

For two matrices **A** and **B**, the product **AB** is defined if and only if the number of columns of **A** is equal to the number of rows of **B**. If **A** is $(m \times r)$ matrix and **B** is $(r \times n)$ matrix, then **C** = **AB** is defined and is of size $(m \times n)$. The (i, j)th element of **C** is given by

$$c_{ij} = \sum_{k=1}^{r} a_{ik}\, b_{kj}, \text{ for all } i \text{ and } j.$$

EXAMPLE A. 2-4.1

Let $\mathbf{A} = \begin{pmatrix} 1 & 2 \\ 3 & 4 \end{pmatrix}$ and $\mathbf{B} = \begin{pmatrix} 5 & 6 & 7 \\ 8 & 9 & 10 \end{pmatrix}$,

then
$$\mathbf{C} = \mathbf{AB} = \begin{pmatrix} 1 & 2 \\ 3 & 4 \end{pmatrix}\begin{pmatrix} 5 & 6 & 7 \\ 8 & 9 & 10 \end{pmatrix}$$

$$= \begin{bmatrix} (1\times5+2\times8) & (1\times6+2\times9) & (1\times7+2\times20) \\ (3\times5+4\times8) & (3\times6+4\times9) & (3\times7+4\times10) \end{bmatrix} = \begin{bmatrix} 21 & 24 & 47 \\ 47 & 54 & 61 \end{bmatrix}.$$

EXAMPLE A. 2-4.2

Let $\mathbf{A} = \begin{bmatrix} 1 & 3 & 5 \\ 2 & 4 & 6 \end{bmatrix}$ and $\mathbf{X} = \begin{bmatrix} 1 \\ 2 \\ 3 \end{bmatrix}$,

then
$$\mathbf{AX} = \begin{bmatrix} 1 & 3 & 5 \\ 2 & 4 & 6 \end{bmatrix}\begin{bmatrix} 1 \\ 2 \\ 3 \end{bmatrix} = \begin{bmatrix} 1\times1+3\times2+5\times3 \\ 2\times1+4\times2+6\times3 \end{bmatrix} = \begin{bmatrix} 22 \\ 28 \end{bmatrix}.$$

EXAMPLE A. 2-4.3

Let $\mathbf{A} = \begin{bmatrix} 1 & 2 & 3 \\ 4 & 5 & 6 \end{bmatrix}$ and $\mathbf{Y} = [2, 3]$,

then $\mathbf{YA} = [2, 3] \begin{bmatrix} 1 & 2 & 3 \\ 4 & 5 & 6 \end{bmatrix}$

$$= [(2 \times 1 + 3 \times 4) \quad (2 \times 2 + 3 \times 5) \quad (2 \times 3 + 3 \times 6)] = [14 \quad 19 \quad 24].$$

Matrix multiplication satisfies the following properties:

$$(\mathbf{AB})\,\mathbf{C} = \mathbf{A}\,(\mathbf{BC}),$$
$$(\mathbf{A} + \mathbf{B})\,\mathbf{C} = \mathbf{AC} + \mathbf{BC},$$
$$\mathbf{C}\,(\mathbf{A} + \mathbf{B}) = \mathbf{CA} + \mathbf{CB},$$
$$\mathbf{IA} = \mathbf{AI} = \mathbf{A},$$
$$\alpha\,(\mathbf{AB}) = (\alpha\mathbf{A})\mathbf{B} = \mathbf{A}\,(\alpha\mathbf{B}),\ \alpha \text{ is a scalar, } \mathbf{AB} \neq \mathbf{BA} \text{ in general.}$$

If **AB** is defined, **BA** is not necessarily defined.

If **AB** = 0, it is not necessary that either **A** or **B** must be zero.

A.2-5 Determinant of a Square Matrix

A *determinant* of a square matrix **A**, denoted by |**A**|, is a number obtained by performing certain operations of the elements of **A**.

If **A** is (2 × 2) matrix, then

$$|\mathbf{A}| = \begin{vmatrix} a_{11} & a_{12} \\ a_{21} & a_{22} \end{vmatrix} = a_{11}a_{22} - a_{12}a_{21}.$$

If **A** is (3 × 3) matrix, then

$$|\mathbf{A}| = \begin{vmatrix} a_{11} & a_{12} & a_{13} \\ a_{21} & a_{22} & a_{23} \\ a_{31} & a_{32} & a_{33} \end{vmatrix} = a_{11} \begin{vmatrix} a_{22} & a_{23} \\ a_{32} & a_{33} \end{vmatrix} - a_{12} \begin{vmatrix} a_{21} & a_{23} \\ a_{31} & a_{33} \end{vmatrix} + a_{13} \begin{vmatrix} a_{21} & a_{22} \\ a_{31} & a_{32} \end{vmatrix}$$

$$= a_{11}\,a_{22}\,a_{33} - a_{11}a_{23}a_{32} - a_{12}a_{21}a_{33} + a_{12}a_{23}a_{31} + a_{13}a_{21}a_{32} - a_{13}a_{22}a_{31}.$$

If **A** is an $(n \times n)$ matrix, then

$$|\mathbf{A}| = \sum_{i=1}^{n} a_{i1}(-1)^{i+1}\,|\mathbf{M}_{i1}|,$$

where |**M**| is a submatrix obtained by deleting row *i* and column 1 of |**A**|. For example,

if $\mathbf{A} = \begin{bmatrix} 1 & 4 & 7 \\ 2 & 5 & 8 \\ 3 & 6 & 9 \end{bmatrix}$,

then $|\mathbf{A}| = 1 \begin{vmatrix} 5 & 8 \\ 6 & 9 \end{vmatrix} - 4 \begin{vmatrix} 2 & 8 \\ 3 & 9 \end{vmatrix} + 7 \begin{vmatrix} 2 & 5 \\ 3 & 6 \end{vmatrix}$

$$= (45 - 48) - 4\,(18 - 24) + 7(12 - 15) = -3 + 24 - 21 = 0.$$

A matrix **A** is said to be *singular* if |**A**| = 0. If |**A**| ≠ 0, the matrix **A** is called *nonsingular*.

Some of the major properties of determinants are given below.

1. If every element of a column or a row is zero, then the value of the determinant is zero.
   i.e., $|\mathbf{0}| = 0.$
2. The value of the determinant does not change if its rows and columns are interchanged.
   i.e., $|\mathbf{A}^{\mathbf{T}}| = |\mathbf{A}|.$

3. If $|\mathbf{B}|$ is obtained by interchanging any two rows (columns) of $|\mathbf{A}|$, then
$$|\mathbf{B}| = -|\mathbf{A}|.$$
4. If two rows (columns) of matrix **A** are identical, then
$$|\mathbf{A}| = 0.$$
5. If **B** is obtained from **A** by adding to its ith row (column), scalar α times its jth row (column), then
$$|\mathbf{B}| = |\mathbf{A}|.$$
6. If every element of a row (column), of a determinant is multiplied by a scalar α, the value of determinant is multiplied by α.
7. If **A** and **B** are two square matrices of the same order, then
$$|\mathbf{AB}| = |\mathbf{A}|\ |\mathbf{B}|.$$

A.2-6 Inverse of a Matrix

If **A** is non-singular square matrix and if there exists a non-singular square matrix **B** such that
$$\mathbf{AB} = \mathbf{I} = \mathbf{BA},$$
then **B** is called an *inverse* of **A** and is denoted by $\mathbf{A}^{-1}$.

The inverse matrix $\mathbf{A}^{-1}$ can be obtained by performing the following two row operations on the original matrix **A** :

1. Multiply or divide any row by a number.
2. Multiply any row by a number and add it to another row.

EXAMPLE A. 2-6.1

If $\mathbf{A} = \begin{bmatrix} 1 & 2 \\ 1 & -1 \end{bmatrix}$, find $\mathbf{A}^{-1}$.

Solution

Since $|\mathbf{A}| = -1 - 2 = -3$, **A** is non-singular and hence $\mathbf{A}^{-1}$ exists. To find $\mathbf{A}^{-1}$ we start with the following matrix:
$$\mathbf{AI} = \begin{bmatrix} 1 & 2 & : & 1 & 0 \\ 1 & -1 & : & 0 & 1 \end{bmatrix},$$

Subtract row 1 from row 2 :
$$\begin{bmatrix} 1 & 2 & : & 1 & 0 \\ & & : & & \\ 0 & -3 & : & -1 & 1 \end{bmatrix}$$

Divide row 2 by – 3 :
$$\begin{bmatrix} 1 & 2 & : & 1 & 0 \\ & & : & & \\ 0 & 1 & : & \frac{1}{3} & -\frac{1}{3} \end{bmatrix}.$$

Subtract twice of row 2 from row 1:
$$\begin{bmatrix} 1 & 0 & : & \frac{1}{3} & \frac{2}{3} \\ & & : & & \\ 0 & 1 & : & \frac{1}{3} & -\frac{1}{3} \end{bmatrix}.$$

Thus $$\mathbf{A}^{-1} = \begin{bmatrix} \frac{1}{3} & \frac{2}{3} \\ \frac{1}{3} & -\frac{1}{3} \end{bmatrix}.$$

The concept of matrix inversion can be used in solving n linearly independent equations. Consider a system of n linear independent equations in n unknowns:

$$\begin{aligned} a_{11} x_1 + a_{12} x_2 + \ldots + a_{1n} x_n &= b_1, \\ a_{21} x_1 + a_{22} x_2 + \ldots + a_{2n} x_n &= b_2, \\ \vdots \qquad & \quad \vdots \\ a_{n1} x_1 + a_{n2} x_2 + \ldots + a_{nn} x_n &= b_n. \end{aligned}$$

This system of equations can be written as

$$\mathbf{AX} = \mathbf{b},$$

where $$\mathbf{A} = \begin{bmatrix} a_{11} & a_{12} & \cdots & a_{1n} \\ a_{21} & a_{22} & \cdots & a_{2n} \\ \vdots & \vdots & \vdots & \vdots \\ a_{n1} & a_{n2} & \cdots & a_{nn} \end{bmatrix},$$

$$\mathbf{X} = \begin{bmatrix} x_1 \\ x_2 \\ \vdots \\ x_n \end{bmatrix},$$

and $$\mathbf{b} = \begin{bmatrix} b_1 \\ b_2 \\ \vdots \\ b_n \end{bmatrix}.$$

Since the equations are independent, **A** is non-singular. Thus

$$\mathbf{A}^{-1}\,\mathbf{AX} = \mathbf{A}^{-1}\mathbf{b} \text{ or } \mathbf{X} = \mathbf{A}^{-1}\mathbf{b},$$

gives the solution of n unknowns.

APPENDICES

B.1 DERIVATION OF POISSON DISTRIBUTION

Here, we need to determine the probability of n arrivals in time interval of length t *i.e.*, $p_n(t)$.

Case I. when $n > 0$ or $n \geq 1$:

First we shall find $p_n(t + dt)$. This event can happen in two mutually exclusive and exhaustive ways:

Event no.	*No. of units at time t*	*No. of arrivals in time dt*	*No. of units at time t + dt*
1	n	0	n
2	$n - 1$	1	n

Probability of occurrence of event 1 $= p_n(t) \,.\, (1 - \lambda \,.dt)$,

probability of occurrence of event 2 $= p_{n-1}(t) .\ \lambda\, dt$.

$$\therefore\ p_n(t + dt) = p_n(t)\,[1 - \lambda\, dt] + p_{n-1}(t)\,.\,\lambda dt$$

$$= p_n(t) + \lambda\, dt\,[p_{n-1}(t) - p_n(t)]$$

or $$\frac{p_n(t+dt) - p_n(t)}{dt} = \lambda\,[p_{n-1}(t) - p_n(t)]$$

or $$\frac{d}{dt} p_n(t) = \lambda\,[p_{n-1}(t) - p_n(t)]$$

or $$p_n'(t) = \lambda[p_{n-1}(t) - p_n(t)],\ n > 0. \qquad ...(1)$$

Case II. When $n = 0$:

Here, we shall find $p_0(t + dt)$. This event can happen only in one way:

Event no.	*No. of units at time t*	*No. of arrivals in time dt*	*No. of units at time t + dt*
1	0	0	0

Probability of this event no. 1 $= p_0(t).(1 - \lambda\, dt)$.

$$\therefore \qquad p_0(t + dt) = p_0(t)\,.\,(1 - \lambda\, dt).$$

or $$\frac{p_0(t+dt) - p_0(t)}{dt} = -\lambda p_0(t)$$

or $$\frac{d}{dt}\,[p_0(t)] = -\lambda\,.\,p_0(t)$$

or $$p_0'(t) = -\lambda\, p_0(t),\ n = 0. \qquad ...(2)$$

To solve equations (1) and (2) by iterative method

Equation (2) may be written as

$$\frac{p_0'(t)}{p_0(t)} = -\lambda \text{ or } \frac{d}{dt}\,[\log\{p_0(t)\}] = -\lambda.$$

Integrating both sides w.r.t.'t',

$$\log\{p_0(t)\} = -\lambda t + C_1. \qquad ...(3)$$

Now at time $t = 0$, $p_n(t) = p_n(0)$, which is the probability of n customers just at the beginning.

Now $$p_n(0) = \begin{cases} 1, \text{ when } n = 0, \\ 0, \text{ when } n > 0. \end{cases} \qquad ...(A)$$

Substituting $t = 0$ in equation (3),

$$\log[p_0(0)] = -0 + C_1 \text{ or } \log 1 = C_1 \text{ or } C_1 = 0.$$

$$\therefore \quad \log[p_0(t)] = -\lambda t. \therefore p_0(t) = e^{-\lambda t}. \qquad ...(4)$$

Substituting $n = 1$ in equation (1),

$$p_1'(t) = \lambda [p_0(t) - p_1(t)].$$

$$\therefore \quad p_1'(t) + \lambda p_1(t) = \lambda p_0(t) = \lambda \,.\, e^{-\lambda t}.$$

Multiplying both sides by $e^{\lambda t}$,

$$e^{\lambda t} [p_1'(t) + \lambda p_1(t)] = \lambda$$

or $$\frac{d}{dt}[e^{\lambda t}. p_1(t)] = \lambda.$$

Integrating both sides of the equation w.r.t. 't'

$$e^{\lambda t}. p_1(t) = \lambda t + C_2.$$

To find constant C_2, put $t = 0$ in the above equation.

$$\therefore \quad p_1(0) = C_2. \quad \text{But } p_1(0) = 0 \text{ from (A).}$$

$$\therefore \quad C_2 = 0.$$

$$e^{\lambda t}. p_1(t) = \lambda t$$

or $$p_1(t) = \lambda t e^{-\lambda t} = \lambda t \frac{e^{-\lambda t}}{1!}. \qquad ...(5)$$

Similarly, substituting $n = 2$ in equation (1),

$$p_2'(t) = \lambda[p_1(t) - p_2(t)]$$

or $$p_2'(t) + \lambda p_2(t) = \lambda p_1(t)$$

or $$p_2'(t) + \lambda p_2(t) = \lambda \quad \frac{\lambda t. e^{-\lambda t}}{1!} = \frac{\lambda^2 t. e^{-\lambda t}}{1!}.$$

Multiplying both sides by $e^{\lambda t}$,

$$e^{\lambda t} [p_2'(t) + \lambda p_2(t)] = \frac{\lambda^2 t}{1!}$$

or $$\frac{d}{dt}[e^{\lambda t} \cdot P_2(t)] = \frac{\lambda^2 t}{1!}.$$

Integrating both sides w.r.t. 't'

$$e^{\lambda t}. p_2(t) = \frac{\lambda^2. t^2}{2.1!} + C_3.$$

To find constant C_3, put $t = 0$ in the above equation.

$$\therefore \quad p_2(0) = C_3, \text{ but } p_2(0) = 0 \text{ from } \mathbf{A}.$$

$$\therefore \quad C_3 = 0.$$

$$\therefore \quad e^{\lambda t}. p_2(t) = \frac{(\lambda t)^2}{2!}.$$

$$\therefore \quad p_2(t) = \frac{(\lambda t)^2. e^{-\lambda t}}{2!}.$$

From (4), (5) and (6) it follows that

when $n = 3$, $\quad p_3(t) = \dfrac{(\lambda t)^3 . e^{-\lambda t}}{3!}$,

$\vdots$

when $n = n$, $\quad p_n(t) = \dfrac{(\lambda t)^n . e^{-\lambda t}}{n!}$.

B-2 PROPERTIES OF A POISSON PROCESS

During a Poisson process,

$$p_n(t) = \frac{(\lambda t)^n . e^{-\lambda t}}{n!}.$$

Now mean is given by $\bar{x} = \sum_{i=0}^{\infty} x_i p(x_i) = \sum_{n=0}^{\infty} n . p_n(t)$.

$$\therefore \quad \bar{x} = 0 \cdot p_0(t) + 1 \cdot p_1(t) + 2 \cdot p_2(t) + 3 \cdot p_3(t) + \ldots \infty$$

$$= 0 + 1 \cdot \frac{(\lambda t)^1 . e^{-\lambda t}}{1!} + 2 . \frac{(\lambda t)^2 . e^{-\lambda t}}{2!} + 3 . \frac{(\lambda t)^3 . e^{-\lambda t}}{3!} + \ldots \infty$$

$$= 0 + \lambda t \, e^{-\lambda t} + \frac{(\lambda t)^2 . e^{-\lambda t}}{1!} + \frac{(\lambda t)^3 . e^{-\lambda t}}{2!} + \ldots \infty$$

$$= \lambda t e^{-\lambda t} \left[1 + \lambda t + \frac{(\lambda t)^2}{2!} + \ldots \infty \right]$$

$$= \lambda t e^{-\lambda t} . e^{\lambda t} = \lambda t.$$

$$\therefore \text{ Mean arrival rate} = \frac{\text{Average no. of customers arriving in time } t}{t} = \lambda.$$

TABLE C-1

Random Numbers Table

2181922396	2068577984	8262130392	8374856049	4837657422
1128105582	7295088579	9586111552	7055508767	5172382962
7112077556	3440672486	1882412963	0684012006	0633147925
6557477468	5435810788	9670852913	1291265730	2290031331
4199520858	3090908872	2039593181	5973470495	7976135523
3545174840	2275698645	8416579348	4676463101	5629367907
1749420382	4832630032	5670984959	5432114610	0666095693
9103161011	7413686599	1198757695	0414294470	9140121544
0764238934	7666127259	5263097712	5133648980	5111965912
3493969525	0272759769	0385998136	9999089966	1344056826
1292054466	0700014629	5169439659	8408705169	6574373193
4397426117	6488838550	4031652526	8123543276	5927534501
3807950579	9564258448	3457416988	1531027886	5116633717
4984768758	2389278610	3859431781	3643768456	5041314549
1340145867	9120831830	7228567652	1267173884	1320651658
0590453442	4800088084	1165628554	5407921254	9468932498
9566554338	5585265145	5089052204	9780623691	5795448061
7615116284	9172824179	5544814334	0016943666	2628538741
8508771938	4035554324	0840126299	4942059208	7875623913
6970024586	9324732696	1186263397	4425143189	3316653259
5799997185	0135968939	7678931194	1351031403	6002561840
6364375912	8383232768	1892850701	2323673751	3188881718
4165492027	6359104233	3382569662	4579426926	1513082455
0354683246	4765104877	8149224168	5468631609	6474393896
9130555058	5255147182	3519287786	2481675649	8907598697
5826984369	4725370390	9641916289	5049082870	7463807244
6285048453	3646121751	8436077768	2928794356	9956043516
7527791048	5765558107	8762562043	6185670830	6363845920
8976470693	0441608934	8749472723	2202271078	5897002653
2327991661	7936797054	9527542791	4711871173	8300978148
2182095589	5535798279	4764439855	6279247618	4446895088
3659397698	1057981450	8416605706	8234013222	6426813469
5924779358	1333750468	9434074212	5273692238	5902177065
3941092295	5726289716	3420847871	1820481234	0318831723
1955104281	0903099163	6827821899	6383872737	5901682626
2117595534	1634107293	8521057472	1471300754	3044151557
7471564123	7344613447	1128117244	3208461091	1699403490
8674262892	2809456764	5806554509	8224980942	5738031833
9061122874	0746980892	9285305274	6331989649	8764464686
6438538678	3049068967	6955157269	5482964330	2161984904
1834182305	6203476893	5937802079	3445280195	3694915658
1884227732	2923727501	8044389132	4611203081	6072112445
6791857341	6696243386	2219599137	3193884246	8224729918

TABLE C-2

Proportion of total area under the normal curve from $-\infty$ to z.

where $z = \dfrac{x-\mu}{\sigma}$.

z	$\psi(z)$	z	$\psi(z)$	z	$\psi(z)$	z	$\psi(z)$
0.00	0.5000	0.65	0.7422	1.30	0.9032	1.95	0.9744
0.01	0.5040	0.66	0.7454	1.31	0.9049	1.96	0.9750
0.02	0.5080	0.67	0.7486	1.32	0.9066	1.97	0.9756
0.03	0.5120	0.68	0.7517	1.33	0.9082	1.98	0.9761
0.04	0.5160	0.69	0.7549	1.34	0.9099	1.99	0.9767
0.05	0.5199	0.70	0.7580	1.35	0.9115	2.00	0.9772
0.06	0.5239	0.71	0.7611	1.36	0.9131	2.02	0.9783
0.07	0.5279	0.72	0.7642	1.37	0.9147	2.04	0.9793
0.08	0.5319	0.73	0.7673	1.38	0.9162	2.06	0.9803
0.09	0.5359	0.74	0.7703	1.39	0.9177	2.08	0.9812
0.10	0.5398	0.75	0.7734	1.40	0.9192	2.10	0.9821
0.11	0.5438	0.76	0.7764	1.41	0.9207	2.12	0.9830
0.12	0.5478	0.77	0.7794	1.42	0.9222	2.14	0.9838
0.13	0.5517	0.78	0.7823	1.43	0.9236	2.16	0.9846
0.14	0.5557	0.79	0.7852	1.44	0.9251	2.18	0.9854
0.15	0.5596	0.80	0.7881	1.45	0.9265	2.20	0.9861
0.16	0.5636	0.81	0.7910	1.46	0.9279	2.22	0.9868
0.17	0.5675	0.82	0.7939	1.47	0.9292	2.24	0.9875
0.18	0.5714	0.83	0.7967	1.48	0.9306	2.26	0.9881
0.19	0.5753	0.84	0.7995	1.49	0.9319	2.28	0.9887
0.20	0.5793	0.85	0.8023	1.50	0.9332	2.30	0.9893
0.21	0.5832	0.86	0.8051	1.51	0.9345	2.32	0.9898
0.22	0.5871	0.87	0.8078	1.52	0.9357	2.34	0.9904
0.23	0.5910	0.88	0.8106	1.53	0.9370	2.36	0.9909
0.24	0.5948	0.89	0.8133	1.54	0.9382	2.38	0.9913
0.25	0.5987	0.90	0.8159	1.55	0.9394	2.40	0.9918
0.26	0.6026	0.91	0.8186	1.56	0.9406	2.42	0.9922
0.27	0.6064	0.92	0.8212	1.57	0.9418	2.44	0.9927
0.28	0.6103	0.93	0.8238	1.58	0.9429	2.46	0.9931
0.29	0.6141	0.94	0.8264	1.59	0.9441	2.48	0.9934
0.30	0.6179	0.95	0.8289	1.60	0.9452	2.50	0.9938
0.31	0.6217	0.96	0.8315	1.61	0.9463	2.52	0.9941
0.32	0.6255	0.97	0.8340	1.62	0.9474	2.54	0.9945
0.33	0.6293	0.98	0.8365	1.63	0.9484	2.56	0.9948
0.34	0.6331	1.99	0.8389	1.64	0.9495	2.58	0.9951
0.35	0.6368	1.00	0.8413	1.65	0.9505	2.60	0.9953
0.36	0.6406	1.01	0.8438	1.66	0.9515	2.62	0.9956
0.37	0.6443	1.02	0.8461	1.67	0.9525	2.64	0.9959
0.38	0.6480	1.03	0.8485	1.68	0.9535	2.66	0.9961
0.39	0.6517	1.04	0.8508	1.69	0.9545	2.68	0.9963
0.40	0.6554	1.05	0.8531	1.70	0.9554	2.70	0.9965

0.41	0.6591	1.06	0.8554	1.71	0.9564	2.72	0.9967
0.42	0.6628	1.07	0.8577	1.72	0.9573	2.74	0.9969
0.43	0.6664	1.08	0.8599	1.73	0.9582	2.76	0.9971
0.44	0.6700	1.09	0.8621	1.74	0.9591	2.78	0.9973
0.45	0.6736	1.10	0.8643	1.75	0.9599	2.80	0.9974
0.46	0.6772	1.11	0.8665	1.76	0.9608	2.82	0.9976
0.47	0.6808	1.12	0.8686	1.77	0.9616	2.84	0.9977
0.48	0.6844	1.13	0.8708	1.78	0.9625	2.86	0.9979
0.49	0.6879	1.14	0.8729	1.79	0.9633	2.88	0.9980
0.50	0.6915	1.15	0.8749	1.80	0.9641	2.90	0.9981
0.51	0.6950	1.16	0.8770	1.81	0.9649	2.92	0.9982
0.52	0.6985	1.17	0.8790	1.82	0.9656	2.94	0.9984
0.53	0.7019	1.18	0.8810	1.83	0.9664	2.96	0.9985
0.54	0.7054	1.19	0.8830	1.84	0.9671	2.98	0.9986
0.55	0.7088	1.20	0.8849	1.85	0.9678	3.00	0.99865
0.56	0.7123	1.21	0.8869	1.86	0.9686	3.20	0.99931
0.57	0.7157	1.22	0.8888	1.87	0.9693	3.40	0.99966
0.58	0.7190	1.23	0.8907	1.88	0.9699	3.60	0.999841
0.59	0.7224	1.24	0.8925	1.89	0.9706	3.80	0.999928
0.60	0.7257	1.25	0.8944	1.90	0.9713	4.00	0.999968
0.61	0.7291	1.26	0.8962	1.91	0.9719	4.50	0.999997
0.62	0.7324	1.27	0.8980	1.92	0.9726	5.00	0.999997
0.63	0.7357	1.28	0.8997	1.93	0.9732		
0.64	0.7389	1.29	0.9015	1.94	0.9738		

BIBLIOGRAPHY

1. ABE Shuchman, *Scientific Decision Making in Business*, Hold, Rinehart and Winston, Inc., 1963.
2. Ackoff, R. and Sasieni, M., *Fundamentals of Operations Research*, John Wiley and Sons, Inc., New York, 1991.
3. Akers, S.B. Jr. and Friedman, J., *A Non-numerical Approach to Production Scheduling Problems*, J. Opns. Res. Soc. A. No. 4, 429-442, Nov., 1955.
4. Askhedkar, R.D. and Kulkarni, R.V., *Operations Research*, Dhanpat Rai and co. (Pvt.) Ltd., Delhi, 1998.
5. Basu, S.K.; Pal, D.K. and Bagchi, H., *Operations Research for Engineers*, Oxford and IBH Publishing Co. Pvt. Ltd., New Delhi, 1989.
6. Batlersky, A., *Network Analysis for Planning and Scheduling*, Macmillan and Co., London.
7. Bhattacharya, A., *Management by Network Analysis*, The Institution of Engineers(India), Kolkata, 1973.
8. Bock, F., *Mathematical Programming : Solution of Travelling Salesman Examples*, Recent Advances in Mathematical Programming, R.L. Graves and P. Wolfe (eds.), McGraw-Hill Book Co., New York, 1963.
9. Brein, O., *CPM in Construction Management*, McGraw-Hill Book Co., New York, 1965.
10. Brein, O., *Scheduling Hand Book*, McGraw-Hill Book Co., New York, 1969.
11. Breunan, J., *Applications of Critical Path Techniques*, The English Universities Press Ltd., St. Paul's House, Warwick Lane, London, 1967.
12. Buffa, E.S., *Operations Management : Problems and Models*, Wiley International Edition, 1972.
13. Calson, J.G. and Misshauk, M.J., *Introduction to Gaming : Management Decision Simulations*, John Wiley and Sons, Inc., New York, 1972.
14. Charnes, A. and Cooper, W.W., *Management Models and Industrial Applications of Linear Programming*, John Wiley and Sons, New York, 1961.
15. Churchman, C.W.; Ackoff, R.L. and Arnoff, E.L., *Introduction to Operations Research*, John Wiley and Sons, Inc., New York, 1957.
16. Cooper, L. and Steinberg, D., *Methods and Applications of Linear Programming*, Philadelphia : W.B. Saunders, 1974.
17. Cooper, R.B., *Introduction to Queuing Theory*, The Macmillan Company, New York, 1972.
18. Cox, D.R. and Smith, W.L., *Queues*, John Wiley and Sons, Inc., New York, 1961.
19. Dantzig, G. B., *Linear Programming and Extensions*, Princeton University Press, Princeton, New Jersey, 1963.
20. Deo Narsingh, *System Analysis with Digital Computer*, Prentice Hall of India, New Delhi, 1979.

21. Enrick, N.L., *Management Operations Research*, Amerind Publishing Co. Pvt. Ltd., New Delhi, 1979.

22. Fabrycky, W. and Torgerson, P., *Operations Economy*, Prentice-Hall, Inc., Englewood Cliffs, New Jersey, 1966.

23. Feller, W., *An Introduction to Probability Theory and its Applications*, Vol. I, John Wiley and Sons, Inc., New York, 1972.

24. Ferguson, R. and Sargent, L., *Linear Programming-Fundamentals and Applications*, McGraw-Hill Book Co., New York, 1958.

25. Ford, L.R. and Fulkerson, D.R., *Flows in Networks*, Princeton Univ. Press, Princeton, N.J., 1962

26. Gale, D., *The Theory of Linear Economic Models*, McGraw-Hill Book Co., New York, 1960.

27. Garvin, W.W., *Introduction to Linear Programming*, McGraw-Hill Book Co., New York, 1960.

28. Gass, S.I., *Linear Programming*, 3rd. Ed., McGraw-Hill Book Co., New York, 1969.

29. Ghosal, A., *Elements of Operations Research*, Hindustan Publishing Corporation, New Delhi, 1969.

30. Gillet, B.E., *Introduction to Operations Research — A Computer Oriented Algorithmic Approach*, Tata McGraw-Hill, New Delhi, 1979.

31. Gordon, G., *System Simulation*, Prentice-Hall of India, New Delhi, 1980.

32. Gue, R.L. and Thomas, M.E., *Mathematical Methods in Operations Research,* The Macmillan Co., New York, 1968.

33. Gupta, P.K. and Hira, D.S., *Problems in Operations Research: Principles and Solutions*, S. Chand and Co. Ltd., New Delhi, 2006.

34. Gupta, P.K., *Linear Programming and Theory of Games*, Khanna Publishers, Delhi, 1987.

35. Hadley, G., *Linear Programming*, Addison-Wesley Publishing Co., Inc., Reading, Massachusetts, 1962.

36. Hadley, G., *Nonlinear and Dynamic Programming*, Addison-Wesley Publishing Co., Inc., Reading, Massachusetts, 1964.

37. Hein, L. W., *The Quantitative Approach to Managerial Decisions*, Englewood Cliffs, Prentice-Hall, N.J., 1967.

38. Hillier, F.S. and Lieberman, G.J., *Introduction to Operations Research*, Houlden-Day, Inc., San Francisco, California, 1974.

39. Hira, D.S., *Analysis and Optimisation of Flow Line Production Systems*, Ph.D. Thesis, Univ. of Roorkee, 1983.

40. Hira, D.S., *Project Management with PERT and CPM*, S.K.Kataria and Sons, Ludhiana, India, 1990.

41. Houlden, B.T. (ed.), *Some Techniques of Operations Research*, Ed. 4, The English Universities Press Ltd., London, 1968.

42. House, W. (ed.), *Operations Research-An Introduction to Modern Applications*, Auerback Publishers, Princeton, 1972.

43. Jhonson, L. and Montogomery, D., *Inventroy Control*, John Wiley and Sons, New York, 1974.

44. Kapoor, V.K., *Operations Research Techniques for Management*, Sultan Chand and Sons, New Delhi, 2001.

45. Kaufman, A., *Methods and Models of Operations Research*, Prentice-Hall, Englewood Cliffs, N.J., 1963.
46. Kuhn, H.W. and Tucker (Eds.), *Contributions to the Theory of Games*, Princeton Univ. Press, Princeton, 1953.
47. Kulshresta, P.K., *Probability and Mathematical Statistics*, S. Chand and Co. Ltd., New Delhi, 1961.
48. Lee, S.M., *Goal Programming for Decision Analysis*, Auerback Publishers, Inc., Philadelphia, Pa., 1972.
49. Levin, R.I. and Kirkpatrick, C.A., *Quantitative Approaches to Management*, 2nd ed., McGraw-Hill Book Co., New York, 1971.
50. Loomba, N.P., *Linear Programming*, McGraw-Hill Book Co., New York, 1964.
51. Martin, M.J.C. and Denison, R.A. (eds.), *Case Exercises in Operations Research*, Interscience Publishers, John Wiley and Sons, Inc., New York, 1971.
52. McCloskey, J. and Trefethen, F. (ed.), *Operations Research for Management*, Johns Hopkins Univ. Press, Baltimore, 1954.
53. McMillan, c. and Gonzalez, R.F., *Systems Analysis, A Computer Approach to Decision Models*, 3rd ed., Richard D. Irwin. Inc., Homewood, Illinois, 1972.
54. Metzer, R., *Elementary Mathematical Programming*, John Wiley and sons, Inc., New York, 1958.
55. Miller, D.W. and Starr, M.K., *Executive Decisions and Operations Research*, 2nd ed., Prentice-Hall, Inc., Englewood Cliffs, N.J., 1973.
56. Moder, J.J. and Phillips, C.R., *Project Management with CPM and PERT*, 2nd ed., Reinhold Publishing Corporation, New York, 1971.
57. Morse, P.M., *Queues, Inventories and Maintenance*, John Wiley and Sons, New York, 1958.
58. Murthy, R.M., *Linear and Non-Linear Programming*, S.Chand and Co. Ltd., New Delhi, 1999.
59. Mustafi, O.K., *Operations Research-Methods and Practice*, Wiley Eastern Ltd., New Delhi, 1988.
60. Naylor, T.H., Blaintfy, J.L., Burdick, D.S. and Chu, K., *Computer Simulation Techniques*, John Wiley and Sons, Inc., New York, 1968.
61. Nemhanser, G.L., *Introduction to Dynamic Programming*, John Wiley and Sons, Inc., New York, 1966.
62. Phillips, Don T., Ravindran A. and Soldberg, J.J., *Operations Research-Principles and Practice*, John Wiley and Sons, Inc., New York, 1976.
63. Plane, D.R. and Kochenberger, G.A., *Operations Reseach for Managerial Decisions*, Richard D. Irwin, Inc., Homewood, Ill., 1972.
64. Raiffa, R.D., *Games and Decisions*, John Wiley and Sons, Inc., New York, 1958.
65. Rao, S.S., *Optimisation-Theory and Practice*, Wiley Eastern Ltd., New Delhi, 1978.
66. Riggs, J.L., *Economic Decision Moels for Engineers and Managers*, McGraw-Hill Book Co., New York, 1968.
67. Riggs, J.L. and Inoue, M.S., *Introduction to Operations Research and Management Science* : A General Systems Approach, McGraw-Hill Kogakusha Ltd., New Delhi, 1975.
68. Saaty, T.L., *Mathematical Methods of Operations Research*, McGraw-Hill Book Co., New York, 1959.

69. Sadowski, W., *The Theory of Decision-Making*, Pergamon Press, London, 1965.
70. Sasieni, M., Yaspan, A. and Friedman, L., *Operations Research-Methods and Problems*, John Wiley and Sons, Inc., New York, 1959.
71. Bronson, R. and Naadimuthu, G., Schaum's *Outlines-Operations Research*, Tata McGraw-Hill Publishing Co. Ltd., New Delhi, 1997
72. Sharma, S.D., *Operations Research,* Kedar Nath Ram Nath and Co., Meerut, 2002.
73. Shamblin, J. E. and Stevens, G. T., Jr., *Operations Research: A Fundamental Approach*, McGraw-Hill Book Co., New York, 1974.
74. Shenoy, G.V., Srivastava, U.K. and Sharma S.C., *Operations Research for Management*, 2nd Ed., New Age International (P) Ltd. Publishers, N. Delhi, 1998.
75. Simmonard, M., *Linear Programming*, Prentice-Hall, Inc., Englewood Cliffs, N.J., 1966.
76. Simmons, D.D., *Linear Programming for Operations Research*, Holden Day, Inc., San Francisco, 1972.
77. Spiegel, R., *Theory and Problems of Statistics*, Schaum's Outline Series, McGraw-Hill Book Co., New York, 1961.
78. Srinath, L.S., PERT and CPM: *Principles and Applications*, Affiliated East West Press Pvt. Ltd., New Delhi, 1975.
79. Srinath, L.S., *Linear Programming : Principles and Cases*, Affiliated East West Press Pvt. Ltd., New Delhi, 1975.
80. Swarup Kanti, Gupta, P.K. and Man Mohan, *Operations Research*, Sultan Chand and Sons, New Delhi, 2005.
81. Taha, H.A., *Operations Research : An Introduction*, 6th ed., Macmillan Publishing Co., New York, 2001.
82. Thierauf, R.J. and Klekamp, R.C., *Decision Making Through Operations Research*, John Wiley and Sons, Inc., New York, 1975.
83. Vajda, S., *Theory of Linear and Non-linear Programming*, Longmans Green and Co., London, 1974.
84. Vohra, N.D., *Quantitative Techniques in Management*, Tata McGraw-Hill Publishing Co. Ltd., New Delhi, 2004.
85. Von Neuman, J. and Morgenstern, O., *Theory of Games and Economic Behaviour*, Princeton Univ. Press, Princeton, N.J., 1947.
86. Wagner, H.M., *Principles of Operations Research*, Prentice-Hall of India, New Delhi, 1973.
87. Whitehouse, J.E. and Wechsler. B.L., *Applied Operations Research : A survey*, John Wiley and Sons, Inc., New York, 1976.
88. Wiest, J.D. and Levy. F.K., *A Management Guide to PERT/CPM*, Prentice Hall of India Pvt. Ltd., New Delhi, 1972.
89. Wilde, D.J. and Beightler, *Foundations of Optimization*, Prentice-Hall, Inc., Englewood Cliffs, N.J., 1967.

INDEX

K

L

M

N

O

P

Q

R

S

T

U

V

W

Z